AA



# Hotel Guide 2002

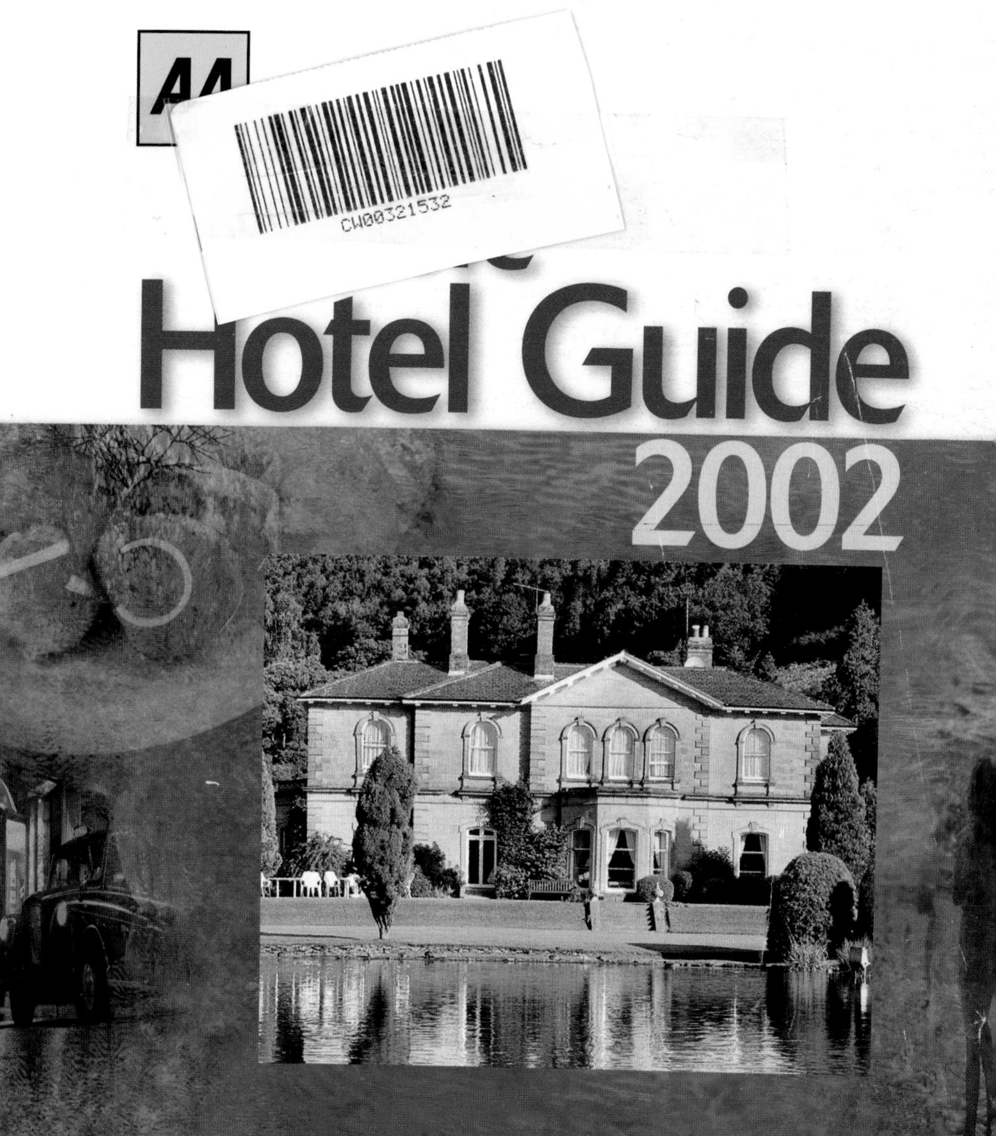

AA Lifestyle Guides

35th edition September 2001

First published by the Automobile Association as the Hotel and Restaurant Guide, 1967



Mapping produced by the Cartographic Department of The Automobile Association.

Cover design by Sue Climpson, Whitchurch, England
Design by Nautilus Design UK Ltd, Basingstoke, Hampshire

The main cover photograph shows Hackness Grange Country House Hotel, Hackness, North Yorkshire. Image courtesy of English Rose Hotels.

Typesetting and colour repro by Microset Graphics Ltd, Basingstoke, England

Printed and bound in Italy by Rotolito Lombarda SpA

Directory compiled by the AA Hotel Services Department and generated from the AA establishment database.
www.theAA.com/getaway

To contact us:
Advertising Sales Department: advertisingsales@theAA.com
Editorial Department: lifestyleguides@theAA.com



A CIP catalogue record for this book is available from the British Library
ISBN 0 7495 3108 8

Published by AA Publishing, a trading name of Automobile Association Developments Limited, whose registered office is Millstream, Maidenhead Road, Windsor, Berkshire SL4 5GD.
Registered number 1878835
Published in USA by AAA.

AA
★★★★★
Hotel

# Contents

# How to Use this Guide

1 ANYTOWN, Anyshire Map 4 SU46

2 ★★★★71% The Example Hotel
Any Road XX1 XX11.
☎ 0022 001122 Fax 0022 001122
e-mail: sendto@isp.co.uk
3 *Dir:* *2m north of Any Town - Any Road signed turn left at Business Park.*
A purpose-built modern complex with a well equipped leisure and conference centre in a separate, linked building. Bedrooms are generously planned to give working space and adequate power points and lighting. Reception rooms consist of a bar lounge and carvery-style dining room.
4 **ROOMS:** 50 en suite (6 fmly) s fr £68; d fr £125 (incl. bkfst) * **LB**
5 **FACILITIES:** Spa STV air con. Indoor swimming(H) Squash Snooker Gym Sauna **CONF:** Thtr 80 Class 30 Board 40 **PARKING:** 30 **NOTES:** No dogs No children 14 yrs No smoking in restaurant Civ Wed 80
8 **CARDS:** 6 7 *Sample Entry*

## Explanation of entries and notes on abbreviations

(see also the key opposite)

1 **Towns** are listed alphabetically within each country section: England, Channel Islands, Isle of Man, Scotland, Wales, Ireland. The administrative county or region follows the town name. Towns on islands are listed under the island (e.g. Wight, Isle of). The map reference gives the map page number, then the National Grid Reference. Read the first figure across and the second figure vertically within the lettered square.

2 The **hotel name** is preceded by the star rating, Quality Percentage Score (see page 9) and Rosette Award, followed by the address, phone/fax numbers and e-mail address where applicable. Please note that e-mail addresses are believed correct at the time of printing but may change during the currency of the guide. Hotels are listed in star and Quality Percentage Score order within each

location. If the hotel name is in *italic* type the information that follows has not been confirmed by the hotel management. A company or consortium name or logo may appear (hotel groups are listed on pages 29-35); for those with a central reservation number, specify the name and location of the hotel when booking.

3 **Dir:** Directions to the hotel.

4 ROOMS The first figure shows the number of en suite letting bedrooms, or total number of bedrooms, then the number with en suite or family facilities. Bedrooms in an annexe or extension are only noted if they are at least equivalent to those in the main building, but facilities and prices may differ. In some hotels all bedrooms are in an annexe/extension. **Prices** (per room per night) are provided by hoteliers in good faith and are indications not firm quotations. Some hotels only accept cheques if notice is given and a cheque card produced. Not all hotels take travellers cheques. LB indicates that the hotel offers special leisure breaks; these may be activity-based breaks or 'two nights for the price of one' type offers. Spa is highlighted in blue in this edition.

5 FACILITIES **Colour TV** is provided in all bedrooms unless otherwise indicated. Where **entertainment** appears, weekly live entertainment should be available at least once a week all year. Some other hotels provide entertainment only in summer or on special occasions; check when booking. **Leisure facilities** are as stated. **Child facilities** may include: baby intercom, babysitting service, playroom, playground, laundry, drying/ironing facilities, cots, high chairs, special meals. In some hotels children can sleep in parents' rooms at no extra cost; check all details when booking.

6 PARKING Shows number of spaces available for guests' use. May include covered, charged spaces.

7 NOTES **No dogs** Although many hotels allow dogs, some breeds may be forbidden and dogs may be excluded from areas of the hotel, especially the dining room. It is essential to check when booking. **No children** A minimum age may be given, e.g. 'No children 4 years'. If neither **'ch fac'** (see FACILITIES) or **'no children'** appears, the hotel accepts children but may not offer special facilities such as high chairs; check before booking if you have very young children. **RS** Some hotels have a restricted service during quieter months, when some of the listed facilities are not available; ask when booking. **Civ Wed 50** indicates that the hotel is licensed for civil weddings and can accommodate up to 50 guests for the ceremony N.B. All hotels in Scotland are licensed for civil weddings; check details with the hotel.

8 CARDS Credit cards may be subject to a surcharge; check when booking if this is how you intend to pay.

# Symbols and Abbreviations

## AA RATINGS & AWARDS

| | |
|---|---|
| ★ | Star Classification (see page 7) |
| % | Quality Percentage Score (see page 9) |
| ★ | Red Stars indicate the AA's highest quality award (see pages 9 and 21-27) |
| ❀ | Rosette Award for quality of food (see page 19) |
| 🌲 | Country House Hotel |
| ○ | Hotel due to open during the currency of the guide, or star rating not yet confirmed (see page 11) |
| * | 2001 prices |

Different accommodation categories

| | |
|---|---|
| 🏘 | Town House Accommodation |
| ⇧ | Travel Accommodation |

(see page 11 for explanation)

## ROOMS

| | |
|---|---|
| fmly | Family rooms (and number) |
| s | Single room |
| d | Double room |
| bkfst incl. | Breakfast included |
| LB | Special leisure breaks available |

Bedroom restrictions are stated, e.g. no smoking in 15 bedrooms

## FACILITIES

| | |
|---|---|
| STV | Satellite television |
| air con | Air conditioning |
| Indoor swimming (H) | Heated indoor swimming pool |
| Outdoor swimming (H) | Heated outdoor swimming pool |
| ch fac | Special facilities for children |
| Xmas | Special programme for Christmas/ New Year |

Leisure facilities are as stated, e.g. Squash, Snooker, Spa

| | |
|---|---|
| CONF | Conference facilities available |
| Thtr | Seats theatre style (and number) |
| Class | Seats classroom style (and number) |
| Board | Seats boardroom style (and number) |
| Del | Typical overnight delegate rate |

## NOTES

| | |
|---|---|
| No dogs | No dogs allowed in bedrooms (guide dogs for the blind may be accepted) |
| No children | Indicates that children cannot be accommodated |
| RS | Restricted opening, e.g. RS Jan-Mar, Closed Xmas/New Year |
| Civ Wed | Licensed for civil weddings (and maximum number of guests for ceremony) |

Other restrictions as stated, e.g. No smoking in restaurant

## CARDS

Cards accepted where symbols are shown

MasterCard
AMERICAN EXPRESS

VISA

DELTA

SWITCH

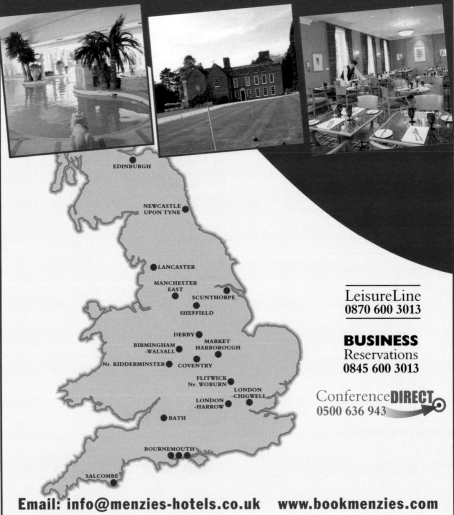

# AA Star Classification

## Quality standards you can expect from an AA recognised hotel

All hotels recognised by the AA should have the highest standards of cleanliness, proper records of booking, give prompt and professional service to guests, assist with luggage on request, accept and deliver messages, provide a designated area for breakfast and dinner with drinks available in a bar or lounge, provide an early morning call on request, good quality furniture and fittings, adequate heating and lighting and proper maintenance. A guide to some of the general expectations for each star classification is as follows:

### What you can expect from a one star hotel

Polite, courteous staff providing a relatively informal yet competent style of service, available during the day and evening to receive guests. At least one designated eating area open to residents for breakfast and dinner. Last orders for dinner no earlier than 6.30pm, a reasonable choice of hot and cold dishes and a short range of wines available. Television in lounge or bedroom. Majority of rooms en suite, bath or shower room available at all times.

### What you can expect from a two star hotel

★★

Smartly and professionally presented management and staff providing competent, often informal service, available throughout the day and evening to greet guests. At least one restaurant or dining room open to residents for breakfast and dinner. Last orders for dinner no earlier than 7pm, a choice of substantial hot and cold dishes and a short range of wines available. Television in bedrooms. En suite or private bath or shower and WC.

### What you can expect from a three star hotel

Management and staff smartly and professionally presented and usually uniformed. Technical and social skills of a good standard in responding to requests. A dedicated receptionist on duty, clear direction to rooms and some explanation of hotel facilities. At least one restaurant or dining room open to residents and non-residents for breakfast and dinner whenever the hotel is open. A wide selection of drinks served in a bar or lounge, available to residents and their guests throughout the day and evening. Last orders for dinner no earlier than 8pm, full dinner service provided. Remote-control television, direct-dial telephone. En suite bath or shower and WC.

### What you can expect from a four star hotel

★★★★

A formal, professional staffing structure with smartly presented, uniformed staff, anticipating and responding to your needs or requests. Usually spacious, well-appointed public areas. Bedrooms offering superior quality and comfort than at three star. A strong emphasis on food and beverages and a serious approach to cuisine. Reception staffed 24 hours per day by well-trained staff. Express checkout facilities where appropriate. Porterage available on request and readily provided by uniformed staff. Night porter available. Newspapers can be ordered and delivered to your room, additional services and concierge as appropriate to the style and location of the hotel. At least one restaurant open to residents and non-residents for all meals seven days per week. Drinks available to residents and their guests throughout the day and evening, table service available. Last orders for dinner no earlier than 9pm, an extensive choice of hot and cold dishes and comprehensive list of wines. Remote-control television, direct-dial telephone, a range of high-quality toiletries. En suite bath with fixed overhead shower, WC.

### What you can expect from a five star hotel

★★★★★

Flawless guest services, professional, attentive staff, technical and social skills of the highest order. Spacious and luxurious accommodation and public areas with a range of extra facilities. As a minimum, first-time guests shown to their bedroom. Multilingual service consistent with the needs of the hotel's normal clientele. Guest accounts well explained and presented. Porterage offered and provided by uniformed staff. Luggage handling on arrival and departure. Doorman or means of greeting guests at the hotel entrance, full concierge service.

At least one restaurant open to residents and non-residents for all meals seven days per week. Staff showing knowledge of food and wine. A wide selection of drinks, including cocktails, available in a bar or lounge, table service provided. Last orders for dinner no earlier than 10pm. High-quality menu and wine list properly reflecting and complementing the style of cooking and providing exceptional quality. Evening turn-down service. Remote-control television, direct-dial telephone at bedside and desk, a range of luxury toiletries, bath sheets and robes. En suite bath with fixed overhead shower, WC.

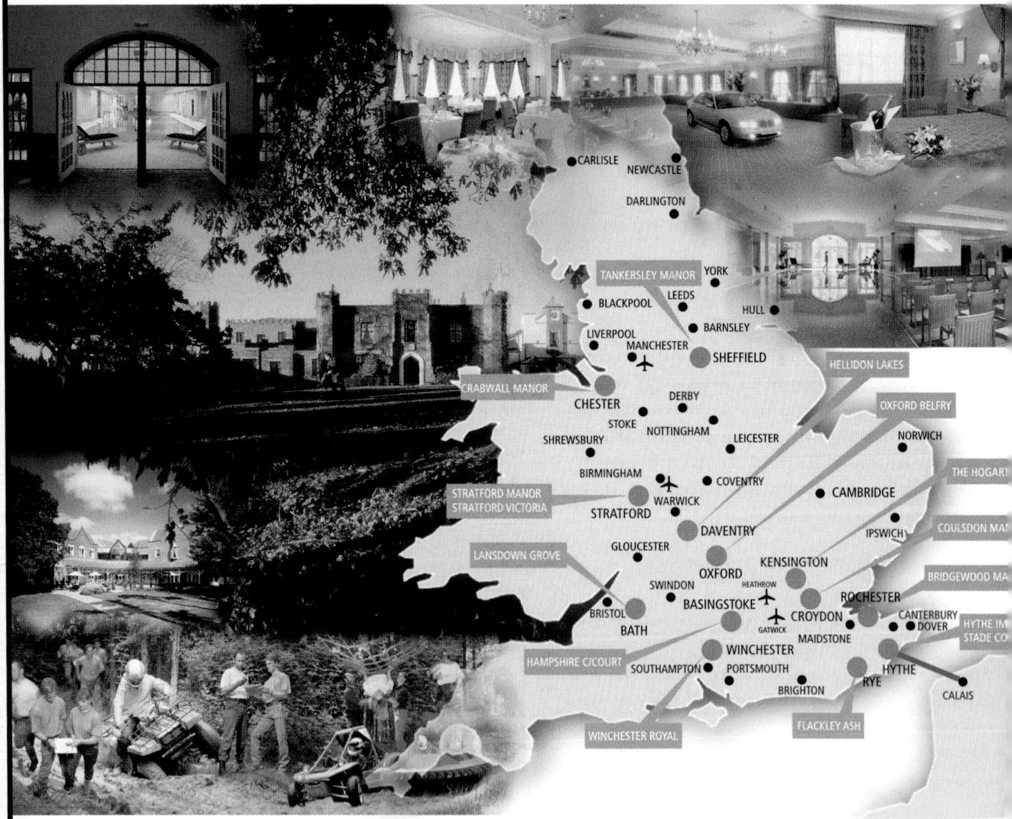

# How Does the AA *Assess a Hotel?*

Hotels applying for AA recognition are visited on a 'mystery guest' basis by one of the AA's team of qualified hotel and restaurant inspectors. The inspector stays overnight to make a thorough test of the accommodation, food and hospitality offered and as many of the hotel's facilities as possible. After settling the bill the following morning they declare their identity and ask to be shown round the entire premises. The inspector completes a full report, making a recommendation for the appropriate star classification and Quality Percentage Score.

After the first inspection, the hotel receives an annual unannounced visit to check that standards are maintained. If the hotel changes hands, the new owners must reapply for classification as AA recognition is not transferable.

Hotels featured pay an annual fee for AA inspection, recognition and rating. One of the benefits of such recognition is a basic text entry in the AA Hotel Guide. The annual fee varies according to the star classification and the number of rooms. AA inspectors pay as a guest for their inspection visit. In addition to the text entry in the guide, hotels may purchase additional advertising such as a photograph or display advertisement.

## Further AA Quality Assessments

In addition to the star classification, the AA makes a further quality assessment to help guests in their choice of hotel, the Quality Percentage Score. The highest achievers in this assessment are awarded Red Stars and can be easily identified in the guide, appearing first in their location with a highlighted entry entitled Premier Collection. The Quality Percentage Score and Red Star awards are assessed as follows:

## Quality Percentage Score –
### making hotel choice easier

AA inspectors supplement their general report with an additional quality assessment of everything the hotel offers, including hospitality, based on what they experience as the 'mystery guest'. This enables them to award an overall Quality Percentage Score.

The Quality Percentage Score offers a comparison of quality within the star classification, so a one star hotel may receive as high a Quality Percentage Score within its classification as a four or five star hotel.

When using the guide, guests can see at a glance, for example, that a two star hotel with a percentage score of 69 offers a higher quality experience within its star classification than a two star hotel with a percentage score of 59.

To gain AA recognition in the first place, a hotel must achieve a minimum quality score of 50 per cent. The Quality Percentage Score for ordinary star classification effectively runs between 50 and 80 per cent.

## Red Star Awards –
### 'Best Hotels in Britain and Ireland'

At each of the five classification levels, the AA recognises exceptional quality of accommodation and hospitality by awarding Red Stars for excellence. A hotel with Red Stars is judged to be the best in its star classification and this award recognises that the hotel offers outstanding levels of comfort, hospitality and customer care. As a general rule, Red Star hotels achieve a Quality Percentage Score between 81 and 100 per cent; the actual percentage score is not shown in the guide.

# Booking Your Stay

Book as early as possible, particularly for the peak holiday period from the beginning of June to the end of September, and bear in mind that Easter and other public holidays may be busy too. In some parts of Scotland, the ski season is a peak holiday period. Some hotels will ask for a deposit or full payment in advance, especially for one-night bookings. Not all hotels will take advance bookings for bed and breakfast, overnight or short stays. Some will not make reservations from mid week. Some hotels charge half-board (bed, breakfast and dinner) whether you eat the meals or not. Some hotels only accept full-board bookings.

Bookings can also be made online at www.theAA.com. You can search by location, select a hotel, check availability and current prices, then complete your booking online and receive an instant confirmation.

## Cancellation

Once a booking is confirmed, let the hotel know at once if you are unable to keep your reservation. If the hotel cannot re-let your room you may be liable to pay about two-thirds of the room price (a deposit will count towards this payment). In Britain a legally binding contract is made when you accept an offer of accommodation, either in writing or by telephone. Illness is not accepted as a release from this contract. You are advised to take out insurance against possible cancellation, for example AA Single Trip Insurance (telephone 0870 606 1612 or consult the AA website www.theAA.com for details).

## Complaints

If you have a complaint about hotel food, services or facilities, we strongly advise you to take it up with the management there and then, in order to give the hotelier a chance to put things right straight away. If this personal approach fails, you can write to AA Hotel Services, Fanum House, Basing View, Basingstoke, Hampshire RG21 4EA. The AA does not undertake to obtain compensation for complaints, or to enter into any correspondence.

# Other Categories of Accommodation

## Country House Hotels

Country house hotels offer a relaxed, informal atmosphere, with an emphasis on personal welcome. They are usually, but not always, in a secluded or rural setting and should offer peace and quiet regardless of location.

## Town House Accommodation

These small, individual, town-centre hotels provide a high degree of privacy. They concentrate on luxuriously furnished bedrooms and suites with high-quality room service, rather than the public rooms or formal dining rooms usually associated with hotels. Town house hotels are usually in areas well served by restaurants. All fall broadly within the four or five star classification, though no Quality Percentage Score is shown in the guide. Town house hotels have a special highlighted entry.

## Travel Accommodation

This classification indicates budget or lodge accommodation suitable for an overnight stay, usually in purpose-built units close to main roads and motorways, often forming part of motorway service areas. They provide consistent levels of accommodation and service, matching today's expectations.

## ○ Hotels with no star classification

A small number of hotels in the guide have a ○ symbol instead of a star rating. These are either due to open during the year or have not had their star classification confirmed at the time of going to print. Check the AA website www.theAA.com for current information.

# Useful Information

## BRITAIN

**The Fire Precautions Act** does not apply to the Channel Islands, Republic of Ireland, or the Isle of Man, which have their own rules. As far as we are aware, all hotels listed in Great Britain have applied for and not been refused a fire certificate.

**Licensing laws** differ in England, Wales, Scotland, the Republic of Ireland, the Isle of Man, the Isles of Scilly and the Channel Islands. Public houses are generally open from mid morning to early afternoon, and from about 6 or 7pm until 11pm, although closing times may be earlier or later and some pubs are open all afternoon. Unless otherwise stated, establishments listed are licensed. Hotel residents can obtain alcoholic drinks at all times, if the licensee is prepared to serve them. Non-residents eating at the hotel restaurant can have drinks with meals. Children under 14 (or 18 in Scotland) may be excluded from bars where no food is served. Those under 18 may not purchase or consume alcoholic drinks. Club licence means that drinks are served to club members only, 48 hours must elapse between joining and ordering. Please note that at the time of going to press licensing laws were under review and may well change during the currency of the guide.

**Prices** The AA encourages the use of the Hotel Industry Voluntary Code of Booking Practice, which aims to ensure that guests know how much they will have to pay and what services and facilities that includes, before entering a financially binding agreement. If the price has not previously been confirmed in writing, guests should be given a card stipulating the total obligatory charge when they register at reception.

**The Tourism** (Sleeping Accommodation Price Display) Order of 1977 compels hotels, travel accommodation, guest houses, farmhouses, inns and self-catering accommodation with four or more letting bedrooms, to display in entrance halls the minimum and maximum prices charged for each category of room. Tariffs shown are the minimum and maximum for one or two persons but they may vary without warning.

## NORTHERN IRELAND & REPUBLIC OF IRELAND

**The Euro** On 1 January 2002, Euro banknotes and coins will come into circulation throughout the Republic of Ireland. There will be a dual circulation period, during which Irish pound notes and coins will begin to be withdrawn. As we went to press, this dual circulation period was expected to end on 9 February 2002, and certainly before 30 June 2002, after which Irish notes and coins will no longer be legal tender. Prices in the guide are shown in Irish Punts (IEP) as prices in Euros were not available at the time of publication (IEP1 = 1.27 Euros; £1 = 1.68 Euros, at time of going to press).

**The Fire Services (NI) Order 1984** covers establishments accommodating more than six people, which must have a certificate from the Northern Ireland Fire Authority. Places accommodating fewer than six persons need adequate exits. AA officials inspect emergency notices, fire-fighting equipment and fire exits here. Republic of Ireland safety regulations are a matter for local authority regulations. For your own and others' safety, read the emergency notices and be sure you understand them.

### Licensing Regulations

**Northern Ireland:** public houses open Mon-Sat 11.30-23.00 and Sun 12.30-14.30 and 19.00-22.00. Hotels can serve residents without restriction. Non-residents can be served from 12.30-22.00 on Christmas Day. Children under 18 are not allowed in the bar area and may not buy or consume liquor in hotels. **Republic of Ireland:** General licensing hours are Mon-Sat 10.30-23.00 (23.30 in summer). Sun and St Patrick's Day (17 March), 12.30-14.00 and 16.00-23.00. Hotels can serve residents without restriction. There is no service on Christmas Day (except for hotel residents) or Good Friday.

**Telephone numbers** Area codes for numbers in the Republic of Ireland apply only within the Republic. If dialling from outside check the telephone directory. Area codes for numbers in Britain and Northern Ireland cannot be used directly from the Republic.
For the latest travel information on Ireland see AA Ireland's website www.aaireland.ie.

# AA Awards 2001-2002

## Hotel of the Year Award

Hotel of the Year is the AA's most prestigious award. Winning hotels receive a specially commissioned, framed watercolour of the hotel by artist Duncan Palmar. National awards are made for England, Scotland, Wales and Ireland; a photograph of the winning hotel appears at the beginning of the relevant country section in the guide. Awards for 2001–2002 are as follows:

### Hotel of the Year, England

★★★★★ ◎◎◎ 72%

PENNYHILL PARK HOTEL & COUNTRY CLUB

Bagshot, Surrey
Proprietor: Mr D. Pecorelli

### Hotel of the Year, Scotland

★★★ ◎ 75%

POOL HOUSE HOTEL

Poolewe, Highland
Proprietors: Mr & Mrs P. Harrison

### Hotel of the Year, Wales

★★★ ◎◎◎

YNYSHIR HALL

Eglwysfach, Ceredigion
Proprietors: Mr & Mrs R. J. Reen

### Hotel of the Year, Ireland

★★★★ ◎◎◎ 79%

AGHADOE HEIGHTS HOTEL

Killarney, Co Kerry
Proprietor: Mr P. Curran

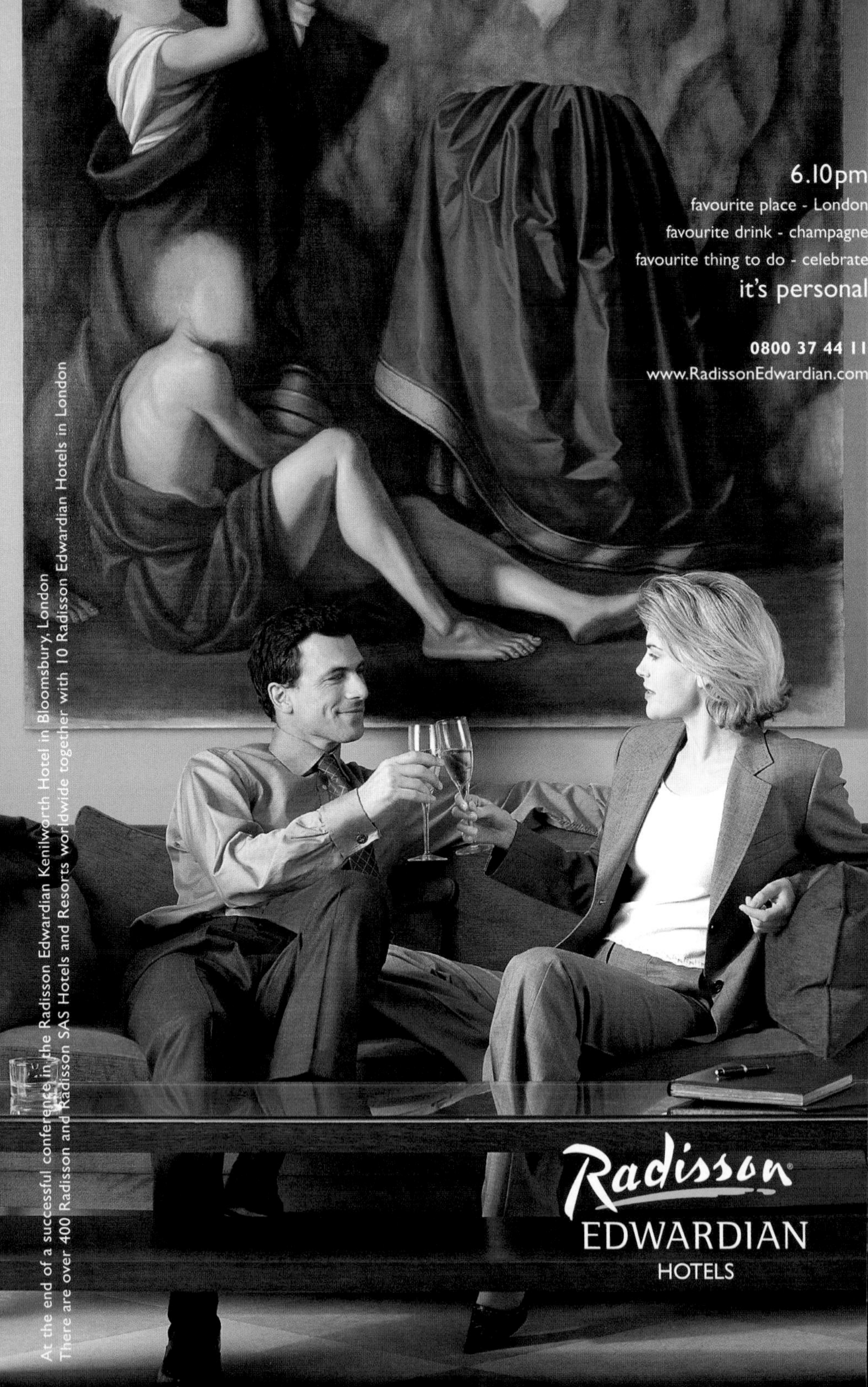
6.10pm
favourite place - London
favourite drink - champagne
favourite thing to do - celebrate
it's personal
0800 37 44 11
www.RadissonEdwardian.com
At the end of a successful conference in the Radisson Edwardian Kenilworth Hotel in Bloomsbury, London
There are over 400 Radisson and Radisson SAS Hotels and Resorts worldwide together with 10 Radisson Edwardian Hotels in London
Radisson
EDWARDIAN
HOTELS

# AA Awards 2001-2002

## Courtesy and Care Award

This award is made to hotels where staff offer exceptionally high standards of courtesy and care. National awards are made for England, Scotland, Wales and Ireland. Members of staff receive a specially designed lapel badge to wear on duty. In addition, a large framed certificate is commissioned for display by the hotels and they have a highlighted entry with photograph in the guide. Awards for 2001–2002 are as follows:

### Courtesy and Care Award, England

★★★ 79%

**Riverside House Hotel**

Ashford-in-the-Water, Derbyshire
Proprietor: Mr J. Lamb

### Courtesy and Care Award, Scotland

★★★ 80%

**Inver Lodge Hotel**

Lochinver, Highland
Proprietors: Edmund & Ann Vestey

### Courtesy and Care Award, Wales

★★★ 75%

**Conrah Hotel**

Aberystwyth, Ceredigion
Proprietors: Mr F. J. & Mrs P. Heading

### Courtesy and Care Award, Ireland

★★★ 76%

**Abbeyglen Castle**

Clifden, Galway
Proprietor: Mr P. Hughes

# AA Rosette Awards

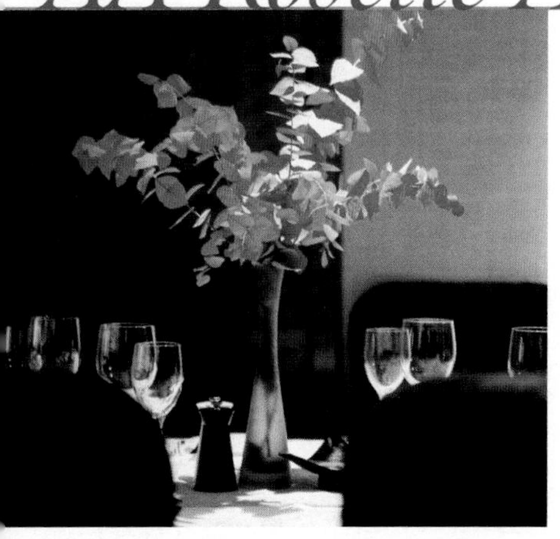

## How the AA assesses restaurants for Rosette Awards

The AA's rosette award scheme was the first nationwide scheme for assessing the quality of food served by restaurants and hotels. The rosette scheme is an award scheme, not a classification scheme and although there is necessarily an element of subjectivity when it comes to assessing taste, we aim for a consistent approach to our awards throughout the UK. It is important, however, to remember that many places serve enjoyable food but do not qualify for an AA award.

Our awards are made solely on the basis of a meal visit or visits by one or more of our hotel and restaurant inspectors who have an unrivalled breadth and depth of experience in assessing quality. They award rosettes annually on a rising scale of one to five.

## So what makes a restaurant worthy of a Rosette Award?

For our inspectors the top and bottom line is the food. The taste of the food is what counts for them, and whether the dish successfully delivers to the diner what the menu promises. A restaurant is only as good as its worst meal. Although presentation and competent service should be appropriate to the style of the restaurant and the quality of the food, they cannot affect the rosette assessment as such, either up or down.

The following summaries attempt to explain what our inspectors look for, but are intended only as guidelines. The AA is constantly reviewing its award criteria and competition usually results in an all-round improvement in standards, so it becomes increasingly difficult for restaurants to reach award level.

### One rosette 

At the simplest level, one rosette, the chef should display a mastery of basic techniques and be able to produce dishes of sound quality and clarity of flavours, using good, fresh ingredients

### Two rosettes 

To gain two rosettes, the chef must show greater technical skill, more consistency and judgement in combining and balancing ingredients and a clear ambition to achieve high standards. Inspectors will look for evidence of innovation to test the dedication of the kitchen brigade, and the use of seasonal ingredients sourced from quality suppliers.

### Three rosettes  

This award takes a restaurant into the big league, and, in a typical year, fewer than 10 per cent of restaurants in our scheme achieve this distinction. Expectations of the kitchen are high, and inspectors find little room for inconsistencies. Exact technique, flair and imagination will come through in every dish, and balance and depth of flavour are all-important.

### Four rosettes  

This is an exciting award because, at this level, not only should all technical skills be exemplary, but there should also be daring ideas, and they must work. There is no room for disappointment. Flavours should be accurate and vibrant.

### Five rosettes  

This award is the ultimate awarded only when the cooking is at the pinnacle of achievement. Technique should be of such perfection that flavours, combinations and textures show a faultless sense of balance, giving each dish an extra dimension. The sort of cooking that never falters and always strives to give diners a truly memorable taste experience.

Further details of all restaurants with AA rosette awards can be found in The Restaurant Guide published annually by the AA and available from bookshops.

AA
The Restaurant Guide 2002
"The guide I would recommend"
Marco Pierre White

AA

# Red Star Awards 2001-2002

G
Hotel
Goring Hotel, London SW1

# Best Hotels in Britain and Ireland

**AA Red Star Awards for hotels are made annually in recognition of excellence within each star rating.**

**The Red Star Award demands consistently outstanding levels of hospitality, service, food and comfort.**

# Red Star Hotels Map

Central London
Regent's Park
BLOOMSBURY
MARYLEBONE
STRAND
MAYFAIR
Hyde Park
KNIGHTS-BRIDGE
WESTMINSTER
LAMBETH
Thames
Inverness
Aberdeen
Fort William
Perth
Glasgow
Edinburgh
Stranraer
Belfast
Newcastle
Carlisle
Kendal
Middlesbrough
York
Leeds
Hull
Dublin
Galway
Liverpool
Manchester
Sheffield
Holyhead
Lincoln
Limerick
Nottingham
Rosslare
Norwich
Birmingham
Aberystwyth
Cork
Cambridge
Carmarthen
Gloucester
Oxford
Colchester
Cardiff
Bristol
LONDON
Maidstone
Guildford
Barnstaple
Dover
Southampton
Exeter
Brighton
Dorchester
Plymouth
Penzance
Isles of Scilly
The Channel Islands

# Red Star Hotels
## *Regional Index*

The number shown against each hotel in the index corresponds with the number given on the Red Star Hotels Map. Hotels are listed in Country and County order, showing their star classification, rosettes and telephone number.

*Buckland Manor, Buckland*

## ENGLAND

| No. | Stars | Rosettes | Town | Hotel | Telephone |
|---|---|---|---|---|---|
| **BERKSHIRE** | | | | | |
| 1 | ★★★★ | ❀❀❀ | MAIDENHEAD | Fredrick's Hotel | ☎ 01628 581000 |
| **BUCKINGHAMSHIRE** | | | | | |
| 2 | ★★★★ | ❀❀❀ | AYLESBURY | Hartwell House | ☎ 01296 747444 |
| 3 | ★★★★★ | ❀❀❀ | TAPLOW | Cliveden | ☎ 01628 668561 |
| **CHESHIRE** | | | | | |
| 4 | ★★★ | ❀❀ | SANDIWAY | Nunsmere Hall Country House Hotel | ☎ 01606 889100 |
| **CORNWALL & ISLES OF SCILLY** | | | | | |
| 5 | ★★ | ❀❀❀ | LISKEARD | Well House Hotel | ☎ 01579 342001 |
| 6 | ★★★ | ❀❀ | PORTSCATHO | Rosevine Hotel | ☎ 01872 580206 |
| 7 | ★★★ | ❀❀❀ | ST MARTIN'S | St Martin's on the Isle | ☎ 01720 422090 |
| **CUMBRIA** | | | | | |
| 8 | ★★★ | ❀❀ | BRAMPTON | Farlam Hall Hotel | 016977 46234 |
| 9 | ★★★ | ❀❀❀❀ | GRASMERE | Michael's Nook Country House Hotel & Restaurant | ☎ 015394 35496 |
| 10 | ★ | ❀ | GRASMERE | White Moss House | ☎ 015394 35295 |
| 11 | ★★★ | ❀❀❀ | HOWTOWN | Sharrow Bay Country House Hotel | ☎ 017684 86301 |
| 12 | ★ | ❀ | KIRKBY LONSDALE | Hipping Hall | ☎ 015242 71187 |
| 13 | ★ | ❀ | WATERMILLOCK | Old Church Hotel | ☎ 017684 86204 |
| 14 | ★★★ | ❀❀❀ | WINDERMERE | Gilpin Lodge Country House Hotel & Restaurant | ☎ 015394 88818 |
| 15 | ★★★ | ❀❀❀ | WINDERMERE | Holbeck Ghyll Country House Hotel | ☎ 015394 32375 |
| 16 | ★★★ | ❀❀ | WINDERMERE | Linthwaite House Hotel & Restaurant | ☎ 015394 88600 |
| 17 | ★★ | ❀❀ | WINDERMERE | Miller Howe Hotel | ☎ 015394 42536 |
| **DERBYSHIRE** | | | | | |
| 18 | ★★ | ❀❀❀ | BASLOW | Fischer's Baslow Hall | ☎ 01246 583259 |
| **DEVON** | | | | | |
| 19 | ★★ | ❀❀ | BARNSTAPLE | Halmpstone Manor | ☎ 01271 830321 |
| 20 | ★★★ | ❀❀ | BURRINGTON | Northcote Manor | ☎ 01769 560501 |
| 21 | ★★★ | ❀❀❀❀❀ | CHAGFORD | Gidleigh Park | ☎ 01647 432367 |
| 22 | ★★★ | ❀❀ | LEWDOWN | Lewtrenchard Manor | ☎ 01566 783256 & 783222 |
| 23 | ★★★ | ❀❀ | SALCOMBE | Soar Mill Cove | ☎ 01548 561566 |
| **DORSET** | | | | | |
| 24 | ★★★ | ❀❀❀ | EVERSHOT | Summer Lodge | ☎ 01935 83424 |
| 25 | ★★★ | ❀❀ | WAREHAM | Priory Hotel | ☎ 01929 551666 |
| **ESSEX** | | | | | |
| 26 | ★★★ | ❀❀ | DEDHAM | Maison Talbooth | ☎ 01206 322367 |
| **GLOUCESTERSHIRE** | | | | | |
| 27 | ★★★ | ❀❀❀ | BUCKLAND | Buckland Manor | ☎ 01386 852626 |
| 28 | ★★★ | ❀❀❀ | CHELTENHAM | Hotel on the Park | ☎ 01242 518898 |
| 29 | ★★★ | ❀❀❀ | CHELTENHAM | The Greenway | ☎ 01242 862352 |
| 30 | ★★★ | ❀❀ | CHIPPING CAMPDEN | Cotswold House | ☎ 01386 840330 |
| 31 | ★★ | ❀❀ | COLN ST-ALDWYNS | The New Inn At Coln | ☎ 01285 750651 |

| No. | Rating | Location | Hotel | Telephone |
|---|---|---|---|---|
| 32 | ★★★ ❁❁❁ | LOWER SLAUGHTER | Lower Slaughter Manor | ☎ 01451 820456 |
| 33 | ★★★ ❁❁ | TETBURY | Calcot Manor | ☎ 01666 890391 |
| 34 | ★★★ ❁❁ | THORNBURY | Thornbury Castle | ☎ 01454 281182 |
| 35 | ★★★ ❁❁❁❁ | UPPER SLAUGHTER | Lords of the Manor | ☎ 01451 820243 |
| **HAMPSHIRE** | | | | |
| 36 | ★★★★★ ❁❁❁ | NEW MILTON | Chewton Glen Hotel | ☎ 01425 275341 |
| 37 | ★★★★ ❁❁ | ROTHERWICK | Tylney Hall Hotel | ☎ 01256 764881 |
| **HEREFORDSHIRE** | | | | |
| 38 | ★★★ ❁❁❁❁ | HEREFORD | Castle House | ☎ 01432 356321 |
| **ISLE OF WIGHT** | | | | |
| 39 | ★★★ ❁❁❁ | YARMOUTH | George Hotel | ☎ 01983 760331 |
| **KENT** | | | | |
| 40 | ★★ ❁❁ | CRANBROOK | Kennel Holt Hotel | ☎ 01580 712032 |
| **LEICESTERSHIRE** | | | | |
| 41 | ★★★★ ❁❁ | MELTON MOWBRAY | Stapleford Park | ☎ 01572 787522 |
| **LINCOLNSHIRE** | | | | |
| 42 | ★★ ❁❁❁❁ | WINTERINGHAM | Winteringham Fields | ☎ 01724 733096 |
| **CENTRAL LONDON** | | | | |
| 43 | ★★★★★ ❁❁❁❁ | LONDON NW1 | Landmark Hotel | ☎ 020 7631 8000 |
| 44 | ★★★★ ❁❁ | LONDON SW1 | Goring Hotel | ☎ 020 7396 9000 |
| 45 | ★★★★★ ❁❁❁❁ | LONDON SW1 | Mandarin Oriental Hyde Park | ☎ 020 7235 2000 |
| 46 | ★★★★★ ⌂ | LONDON SW1 | No 41 | ☎ 020 7300 0041 |
| 47 | ★★★★★ ❁❁❁ | LONDON SW1 | The Berkeley | ☎ 020 7235 6000 |
| 48 | ★★★★ ❁❁❁ | LONDON SW1 | The Halkin Hotel | ☎ 020 7333 1000 |
| 49 | ★★★★★ ❁❁ | LONDON SW1 | The Lanesborough | ☎ 020 7259 5599 |
| 50 | ★★★★ ❁❁ | LONDON SW1 | The Stafford | ☎ 020 7493 0111 |
| 51 | ★★★★ ❁❁❁ | LONDON SW3 | The Capital | ☎ 020 7589 5171 |
| 52 | ★★★★ ❁ | LONDON W1 | Athenaeum Hotel & Apartments | ☎ 020 7499 3464 |
| 53 | ★★★★★ ❁❁ | LONDON W1 | Claridge's | ☎ 020 7629 8860 |
| 54 | ★★★★★ ❁❁ | LONDON W1 | Four Seasons Hotel | ☎ 020 7499 0888 |
| 55 | ★★★★★ ❁❁ | LONDON W1 | The Connaught | ☎ 020 7499 7070 |
| 56 | ★★★★★ ❁❁❁ | LONDON W1 | The Dorchester | ☎ 020 7629 8888 |
| 57 | ★★★★★ ⌂ | LONDON W8 | Milestone Hotel & Apartments | ☎ 020 7917 1000 |
| 58 | ★★★★★ ❁❁❁ | LONDON WC2 | The Savoy | 020 7836 4343 |
| **NORFOLK** | | | | |
| 59 | ★★ ❁❁❁ | BLAKENEY | Morston Hall | ☎ 01263 741041 |
| 60 | ★★★ ❁❁ | GRIMSTON | Congham Hall Country House Hotel | ☎ 01485 600250 |
| **OXFORDSHIRE** | | | | |
| 61 | ★★★★ ❁❁❁❁❁ | GREAT MILTON | Le Manoir Aux Quat' Saisons | ☎ 01844 278881 |
| **RUTLAND** | | | | |
| 62 | ★★★ ❁❁❁❁ | OAKHAM | Hambleton Hall | ☎ 01572 756991 |
| **SHROPSHIRE** | | | | |
| 63 | ★★★ ❁❁❁ | WORFIELD | Old Vicarage Hotel | ☎ 01746 716497 |
| **SOMERSET** | | | | |
| 64 | ★★★ ❁❁ | BATH | The Queensberry Hotel | ☎ 01225 447928 |
| 65 | ★★ ❁ | DULVERTON | Ashwick House Hotel | ☎ 01398 323868 |
| 66 | ★★★ ❁❁❁ | HINTON CHARTERHOUSE | Homewood Park Hotel | ☎ 01225 723731 |
| 67 | ★★ ❁ | PORLOCK | The Oaks Hotel | ☎ 01643 862265 |
| 68 | ★★★ ❁❁❁ | SHEPTON MALLET | Charlton House | ☎ 01749 342008 |
| 69 | ★★★★ ❁❁ | STON EASTON | Ston Easton Park | ☎ 01761 241631 |
| 70 | ★★★ ❁❁❁ | TAUNTON | Castle Hotel | ☎ 01823 272671 |

*Calcot Manor, Tetbury*

| No. | Stars | Rosettes | Location | Hotel | Telephone |
|---|---|---|---|---|---|
| 71 | ★★★ | ❀❀ | WELLINGTON | Bindon Country House Hotel & Restaurant | ☎ 01823 400070 |
| 72 | ★★ | ❀❀ | WIVELISCOMBE | Langley House Hotel & Restaurant | ☎ 01984 623318 |
| 73 | ★ | ❀❀❀ | YEOVIL | Little Barwick House | ☎ 01935 423902 |
| | **STAFFORDSHIRE** | | | | |
| 74 | ★★ | ❀❀❀ | WATERHOUSES | Old Beams Restaurant with Rooms | ☎ 01538 308254 |
| | **SUFFOLK** | | | | |
| 75 | ★★★★ | ❀❀❀ | HINTLESHAM | Hintlesham Hall Hotel | ☎ 01473 652334 |
| | **SUSSEX EAST** | | | | |
| 76 | ★★★★ | ❀❀ | FOREST ROW | Ashdown Park Hotel and Country Club | ☎ 01342 824988 |
| | **SUSSEX WEST** | | | | |
| 77 | ★★★ | ❀❀ | AMBERLEY | Amberley Castle | ☎ 01798 831992 |
| 78 | ★★★ | ❀❀❀ | EAST GRINSTEAD | Gravetye Manor Hotel | ☎ 01342 810567 |
| 79 | ★★★★ | ❀❀❀ | LOWER BEEDING | South Lodge Hotel | ☎ 01403 891711 |
| 80 | ★★★ | ❀❀❀ | TURNERS HILL | Alexander House Hotel | ☎ 01342 714914 |
| | **WARWICKSHIRE** | | | | |
| 81 | ★★★ | ❀❀❀ | ROYAL LEAMINGTON SPA | Mallory Court Hotel | ☎ 01926 330214 |
| | **WEST MIDLANDS** | | | | |
| 82 | ★★★ | ❀❀ | HOCKLEY HEATH | Nuthurst Grange Country House Hotel | ☎ 01564 783972 |
| 83 | ★★★★ | ❀❀ | SUTTON COLDFIELD | New Hall | ☎ 0121 378 2442 |
| | **WILTSHIRE** | | | | |
| 84 | ★★★★ | ❀❀❀ | CASTLE COMBE | Manor House Hotel | ☎ 01249 782206 |
| 85 | ★★★★ | ❀❀ | COLERNE | Lucknam Park | ☎ 01225 742777 |
| 86 | ★★ | ❀❀❀ | SALISBURY | Howard's House Hotel | ☎ 01722 716392 |
| | **WORCESTERSHIRE** | | | | |
| 87 | ★★★★ | ❀❀ | BROADWAY | The Lygon Arms | ☎ 01386 852255 |
| 88 | ★★★ | ❀❀ | CHADDESLEY CORBETT | Brockencote Hall Country House Hotel | ☎ 01562 777876 |
| | **YORKSHIRE NORTH** | | | | |
| 89 | ★★★ | ❀❀ | BOLTON ABBEY | The Devonshire Arms Country House Hotel | ☎ 01756 710441 |
| 90 | ★★★ | ❀❀❀ | YORK | Middlethorpe Hall Hotel | ☎ 01904 641241 |
| 91 | ★★★ | ❀❀ | YORK | The Grange Hotel | ☎ 01904 644744 |

*Greywalls Hotel, Gullane*

## CHANNEL ISLANDS

| No. | Stars | Rosettes | Location | Hotel | Telephone |
|---|---|---|---|---|---|
| | **JERSEY** | | | | |
| 92 | ★★★ | ❀❀ | ROZEL BAY | Château La Chaire | ☎ 01534 863354 |
| 93 | ★★★★ | ❀❀❀ | ST SAVIOUR | Longueville Manor Hotel | ☎ 01534 725501 |

## SCOTLAND

| No. | Stars | Rosettes | Location | Hotel | Telephone |
|---|---|---|---|---|---|
| | **ABERDEENSHIRE** | | | | |
| 94 | ★★ | ❀ | BALLATER | Balgonie Country House Hotel | ☎ 013397 55482 |
| | **ARGYLL & BUTE** | | | | |
| 95 | ★★★★ | ❀❀❀ | ERISKA | Isle of Eriska | ☎ 01631 720371 |
| 96 | ★★★ | ❀❀❀ | PORT APPIN | Airds Hotel | ☎ 01631 730236 |
| | **CITY OF EDINBURGH** | | | | |
| 97 | ★★★★ | ⌂ | EDINBURGH | The Howard | ☎ 0131 315 2220 |
| | **DUMFRIES & GALLOWAY** | | | | |
| 98 | ★ | ❀❀ | MOFFAT | Well View Hotel | ☎ 01683 220184 |
| 99 | ★★★ | ❀❀❀ | NEWTON STEWART | Kirroughtree House | ☎ 01671 402141 |
| | **EAST LOTHIAN** | | | | |
| 100 | ★★★ | ❀❀ | GULLANE | Greywalls Hotel | ☎ 01620 842144 |
| | **FIFE** | | | | |
| 101 | ★★★★ | ❀ | MARKINCH | Balbirnie House | ☎ 01592 610066 |
| 102 | ★★ | ❀❀❀ | PEAT INN | The Peat Inn | ☎ 01334 840206 |
| 103 | ★★★ | ❀❀ | ST ANDREWS | Rufflets Country House & Garden Restaurant | ☎ 01334 472594 |

| No. | Stars | Rosettes | Location | Hotel | Telephone |
|---|---|---|---|---|---|
| **HIGHLAND** | | | | | |
| 104 | ★★★ | ✿✿✿ | ARISAIG | Arisaig House | ☎ 01687 450622 |
| 105 | ★★ | ✿✿✿ | COLBOST | The Three Chimneys & House Over-By | ☎ 01470 511258 |
| 106 | ★★★★ | ✿✿✿ | FORT WILLIAM | Inverlochy Castle Hotel | ☎ 01397 702177 |
| 107 | ★★ | ✿✿✿ | KINGUSSIE | The Cross | ☎ 01540 661166 |
| 108 | ★ | ✿✿ | MUIR OF ORD | The Dower House | ☎ 01463 870090 |
| 109 | ★★ | ✿✿✿ | NAIRN | Boath House | ☎ 01667 454896 |
| 110 | ★★★ | ✿✿ | TORRIDON | Loch Torridon Country House Hotel | ☎ 01445 791242 |
| **NORTH AYRSHIRE** | | | | | |
| 111 | ★★ | ✿ | BRODICK | Kilmichael Country House Hotel | ☎ 01770 302219 |
| **PERTH & KINROSS** | | | | | |
| 112 | ★★★★★ | ✿✿ | AUCHTERARDER | The Gleneagles Hotel | ☎ 01764 662231 |
| 113 | ★★★ | ✿✿✿ | BLAIRGOWRIE | Kinloch House Hotel | ☎ 01250 884237 |
| 114 | ★★★ | ✿✿✿ | DUNKELD | Kinnaird | ☎ 01796 482440 |
| **SOUTH AYRSHIRE** | | | | | |
| 115 | ★★★ | ✿✿ | BALLANTRAE | Glenapp Castle | ☎ 01465 831212 |
| 116 | ★★ | ✿ | MAYBOLE | Ladyburn | ☎ 01655 740585 |
| 117 | ★★★ | ✿✿✿ | TROON | Lochgreen House | ☎ 01292 313343 |
| **STIRLING** | | | | | |
| 118 | ★★★ | ✿✿ | DUNBLANE | Cromlix House Hotel | ☎ 01786 822125 |
| 119 | ★ | ✿✿ | STRATHYRE | Creagan House | ☎ 01877 384638 |
| **WALES** | | | | | |
| **CEREDIGION** | | | | | |
| 120 | ★★★ | ✿✿✿ | EGLWYSFACH | Ynyshir Hall | ☎ 01654 781209 |
| **CONWY** | | | | | |
| 121 | ★★ | ✿✿✿ | BETWS-Y-COED | Tan-y-Foel Country House | ☎ 01690 710507 |
| 122 | ★★ | ✿✿✿ | CONWY | The Old Rectory Country House | ☎ 01492 580611 |
| 123 | ★★★★ | ✿✿ | LLANDUDNO | Bodysgallen Hall Hotel | ☎ 01492 584466 |
| 124 | ★★ | ✿✿✿ | LLANDUDNO | St Tudno Hotel and Restaurant | ☎ 01492 874411 |
| **DENBIGHSHIRE** | | | | | |
| 125 | ★★ | ✿✿ | LLANDRILLO | Tyddyn Llan Country Hotel & Restaurant | ☎ 01490 440264 |
| **GWYNEDD** | | | | | |
| 126 | ★★ | ✿✿✿ | TALSARNAU | Hotel Maes y Neuadd | ☎ 01766 780200 |
| **POWYS** | | | | | |
| 127 | ★★★ | ✿✿ | LLANGAMMARCH WELLS | Lake Country House Hotel | ☎ 01591 620202 |
| 128 | ★★★★ | ✿✿ | LLYSWEN | Llangoed Hall | ☎ 01874 754525 |
| **SWANSEA** | | | | | |
| 129 | ★★ | ✿✿✿ | REYNOLDSTON | Fairyhill | ☎ 01792 390139 |
| **IRELAND** | | | | | |
| **CLARE** | | | | | |
| 130 | ★★★ | ✿✿ | BALLYVAUGHAN | Gregans Castle | ☎ 065 7077 005 |
| **CORK** | | | | | |
| 131 | ★★★★ | ✿✿ | CORK | Hayfield Manor | ☎ 021 315600 |
| 132 | ★★★ | ✿✿✿ | MALLOW | Longueville House Hotel | ☎ 022 47156 |
| **DUBLIN** | | | | | |
| 133 | ★★★★ | ✿✿ | DUBLIN | The Clarence | ☎ 01 4070800 |
| **GALWAY** | | | | | |
| 134 | ★★★ | ✿✿ | CASHEL | Cashel House Hotel | ☎ 095 31001 |
| 135 | ★★★★ | ✿✿ | GALWAY | Glenlo Abbey Hotel | ☎ 091 526666 |
| **KERRY** | | | | | |
| 136 | ★★★★ | ✿✿✿ | KENMARE | Park Hotel Kenmare | ☎ 064 41200 |
| 137 | ★★★★ | ✿✿ | KENMARE | Sheen Falls Lodge | ☎ 064 41600 |
| 138 | ★★★★ | ✿✿ | KILLARNEY | Killarney Park Hotel | ☎ 064 35555 |
| **KILDARE** | | | | | |
| 139 | ★★★★★ | ✿✿✿ | STRAFFAN | The Kildare Hotel & Golf Club | ☎ 01 6017200 |
| **KILKENNY** | | | | | |
| 140 | ★★★★ | ✿✿ | THOMASTOWN | Mount Juliet Hotel | ☎ 056 73000 |
| **WEXFORD** | | | | | |
| 141 | ★★★ | ✿✿ | ARTHURSTOWN | Dunbrody Country House & Restaurant | ☎ 051 389600 |
| 142 | ★★★ | ✿✿ | GOREY | Marlfield House Hotel | ☎ 055 21124 |
| **WICKLOW** | | | | | |
| 143 | ★★★ | ✿✿ | RATHNEW | Tinakilly Country House & Restaurant | ☎ 0404 69274 |

Red Star Hotels are listed here in star order, from five stars to one star. The number corresponds with the Red Star Hotels Map and Regional Index.

## ★★★★★

43 Landmark Hotel
45 Mandarin Oriental Hyde Park
36 Chewton Glen Hotel
3 Cliveden
47 The Berkeley
56 The Dorchester
139 The Kildare Hotel & Golf Club
58 The Savoy
53 Claridge's
54 Four Seasons Hotel
55 The Connaught
112 The Gleneagles Hotel
49 The Lanesborough
57 Milestone Hotel & Apartments
46 No 41

## ★★★★

61 Le Manoir Aux Quat' Saisons
1 Fredrick's Hotel
2 Hartwell House
75 Hintlesham Hall Hotel
106 Inverlochy Castle
95 Isle of Eriska
93 Longueville Manor Hotel
84 Manor House Hotel
136 Park Hotel Kenmare
79 South Lodge Hotel
51 The Capital
48 The Halkin Hotel
76 Ashdown Park Hotel & Country Club
123 Bodysgallen Hall Hotel
135 Glenlo Abbey Hotel
44 Goring Hotel
131 Hayfield Manor
138 Killarney Park Hotel
128 Llangoed Hall
85 Lucknam Park
140 Mount Juliet Hotel
83 New Hall
137 Sheen Falls Lodge
41 Stapleford Park
69 Ston Easton Park
133 The Clarence
87 The Lygon Arms
50 The Stafford
37 Tylney Hall Hotel
52 Athenaeum Hotel & Apartments
101 Balbirnie House
97 The Howard

## ★★★

21 Gidleigh Park
38 Castle House
62 Hambleton Hall
35 Lords of the Manor
9 Michael's Nook Country House
96 Airds Hotel
80 Alexander House Hotel
104 Arisaig House
27 Buckland Manor
70 Castle Hotel
68 Charlton House
39 George Hotel
14 Gilpin Lodge Country House
78 Gravetye Manor Hotel
15 Holbeck Ghyll Country House Hotel
66 Homewood Park Hotel
28 Hotel on the Park
113 Kinloch House Hotel
114 Kinnaird
99 Kirroughtree House
117 Lochgreen House
132 Longueville House Hotel
32 Lower Slaughter Manor
81 Mallory Court Hotel
90 Middlethorpe Hall Hotel
63 Old Vicarage Hotel
11 Sharrow Bay Country House Hotel
7 St Martin's on the Isle
24 Summer Lodge
29 The Greenway
120 Ynyshir Hall
77 Amberley Castle
71 Bindon Country House Hotel
88 Brockencote Hall Country House Hotel
33 Calcot Manor
134 Cashel House Hotel
92 Château La Chaire
60 Congham Hall Country House Hotel
30 Cotswold House
118 Cromlix House Hotel
141 Dunbrody Country House
8 Farlam Hall Hotel
115 Glenapp Castle
130 Gregans Castle
100 Greywalls Hotel
127 Lake Country House Hotel
22 Lewtrenchard Manor
16 Linthwaite House Hotel
110 Loch Torridon Country House Hotel
26 Maison Talbooth
142 Marlfield House Hotel
20 Northcote Manor
4 Nunsmere Hall Country House Hotel
82 Nuthurst Grange Country House Hotel
25 Priory Hotel
6 Rosevine Hotel
103 Rufflets Country House
23 Soar Mill Cove
89 The Devonshire Arms Country House
91 The Grange Hotel
64 The Queensberry Hotel
34 Thornbury Castle
143 Tinakilly Country House & Restaurant

## ★★

42 Winteringham Fields
109 Boath House
129 Fairyhill
18 Fischer's Baslow Hall
126 Hotel Maes y Neuadd
86 Howard's House Hotel
59 Morston Hall
74 Old Beams Restaurant with Rooms
124 St Tudno Hotel
121 Tan-y-Foel Country House
107 The Cross
122 The Old Rectory Country House
102 The Peat Inn
105 The Three Chimneys & House Over-By
5 Well House Hotel
19 Halmpstone Manor
40 Kennel Holt Hotel
72 Langley House Hotel
17 Miller Howe Hotel
31 The New Inn At Coln
125 Tyddyn Llan Country Hotel
65 Ashwick House Hotel
94 Balgonie Country House Hotel
111 Kilmichael Country House Hotel
116 Ladyburn
67 The Oaks Hotel

## ★

73 Little Barwick House
119 Creagan House
108 The Dower House
98 Well View Hotel
10 White Moss House
12 Hipping Hall
13 Old Church Hotel

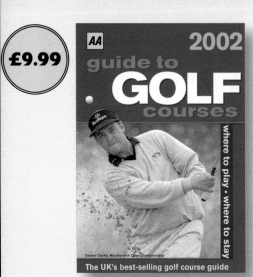

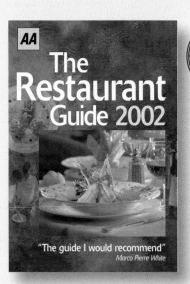

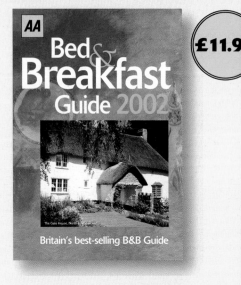

# Hotel Groups Information

The following hotel groups have at least 5 hotels and 400 rooms or are part of an internationally significant brand with a central reservations number.

| Brand Logo | Company Statement | Central Reservations/Contact Number |
|---|---|---|
|  ARCADIAN HOTELS Distinctly Different | A group of three and four star hotels, many are rurally based, with a real emphasis on quality food | 0800 9 177 877 |
|  Best Western | Great Britain's largest group has around 400 independently owned hotels, modern and traditional, mainly in the three and four star markets. Many have leisure facilities and many have rosette awards | 08457 73 73 73 |
|  PRB Brend Hotels | A privately owned group of eleven three and four star hotels in Devon and Cornwall | 01271 34 44 9 |
|  HOTEL & RESTAURANT Campanile | Campanile offers modern accommodation for the budget market | 020 8569 6969 |
|  Sleep Comfort Quality Clarion CHOICE HOTELS EUROPE | Choice offers mainly two brands in the UK: Quality Hotels in the three star market, and Comfort Inns at two star | 0800 44 44 44 |
|  corus | A growing brand of three star hotels, representing the best of Regal Hotel Group | 08457 33 44 00 |
|  COURTYARD | There are eleven hotels in the UK, part of the international brand of modern three star hotels | 0800 221 222 |
|  CROWNE PLAZA HOTELS · RESORTS | These modern hotels offer four star level accommodation around the country. They often have leisure facilities | 0800 897121 |
|  DAYS INN | A new brand of good quality modern budget accommodation at motorway services | 0800 02 80 400 |
|  DE VERE HOTELS Hotels of character, run with pride. | De Vere comprises around sixteen four and five star hotels, which specialise in leisure, golf and conferences | 01925 639499 |
|  Express by Holiday Inn | Holiday Inn's most recent development in the UK, which reaches the superior budget marketplace | 0800 89 71 21 |
|  Forestdale Hotels | A privately owned group of about a dozen three star hotels across the south of England | 0500 276440 |
|  FOUR PILLARS HOTELS | Half a dozen three and four star hotels based in the Oxfordshire area | 01993 700100 |

| | | |
|---|---|---|
| GRESHAM HOTELS | A collection of four star properties, conveniently located in city centre locations in the Republic of Ireland | 00 353 1 878 7966 (Head Office) |
| HANOVER INTERNATIONAL HOTELS & CLUBS | A small group of three and four star hotels located mainly in the central counties of England | 08457 444 123 |
| HERITAGE HOTELS | A group of provincial hotels across the UK, mainly three star, including many well known former coaching inns | 0800 40 40 40 |
| ibis ACCOR hotels | Ibis is a chain of modern travel accommodation | 020 8283 4550 |
| THE INDEPENDENTS | A consortium of independently owned mainly two and three star hotels across Britain | 0800 88 55 44 |
| Innkeeper's Lodge | A new concept in travel accommodation from Bass Leisure Retail, featuring comfortable rooms and complimentary breakfast | 0870 243 0500 |
| INTER·CONTINENTAL HOTELS AND RESORTS | This internationally known group is primarily represented in the UK with three five star hotels in central London | 0800 0289 387 |
| IRELAND'S BLUE BOOK | An association of owner-managed establishments across Ireland | 00 353 1 0462 3416 |
| JURYS DOYLE HOTELS | This Irish company has a range of three and four star hotels in the UK and the Republic of Ireland | 00 353 1 0607 5000 |
| Leisureplex | A group of 14 two star hotels located in the 'Best of British' seaside resorts | 01772 621700 (Head Office) |
| MACDONALD HOTELS | A large number of hotels in the three and four star markets, traditional and modern | 01506 815215 |
| Malmaison | A growing brand of three star city centre hotels, all rated over 70% | 0141 221 1052 (Head Office) |
| MANOR HOUSE HOTELS | Manor House Hotels of Ireland are country house hotels; they include castles, stately homes and Georgian manors | 08705 300 200<br>00 353 1 295 8900 |
| Marriott HOTELS · RESORTS · SUITES | This international brand operates four star hotels in primary locations; most are modern and have leisure facilities. Some have a focus on golf | 0800 221 222 |
| MARSTON HOTELS | A quality independent group of mainly four star hotels with leisure facilities in primary locations across England | 0845 1300 700 |

| | | |
|---|---|---|
|   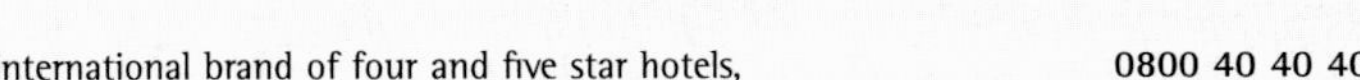 | A group of three and four star hotels across Britain | 0870 600 3013 |
|  | An international brand of four and five star hotels, represented mainly in and around London | 0800 40 40 40 |
| | Modern four star hotels in primary provincial locations and central London | 0845 30 20 001 |
|  | A consortium of independently owned mainly two and three star hotels across Britain | 01253 292000 |
|  | Part of French group Accor, Novotel provides modern three star hotels | 020 8283 4500 |
|  | A large collection of former coaching inns, mainly in the two and three star markets | 0800 917 3085 |
|  | Over 16 mainly four and five star hotels across the UK | 0500 342 543 |
|  | A group of mainly three star hotels located across the UK | 0845 601 7335 |
|  | Over 80 modern three star hotels, recently acquired by Holiday Inn Hotels & Resorts. Many have leisure facilities | 0800 40 40 40 |
|  | A new brand of modern travel accommodation across the UK. Every lodge features an adjacent licensed popular restaurant, such as Millers Kitchen, Outside Inn, Chef & Brewer | 08702 01 02 03 |
|  | A consortium of privately owned British hotels, often in the country house style | 01264 324400 (Head Office) |
|  | A small group of three and four star hotels in various locations across the country | 0800 454 454 |
|  | There are ten hotels at three, four and five star levels, almost entirely in central London. | 0800 37 44 11 |
|  | A unique collection of prestigious four and five star central London hotels, providing luxurious surroundings and a commitment to outstanding personal service | 020 7514 5633 (Head Office) |
|  | A large national hotel company with almost 100 three star hotels in both town centre and country locations | 08457 33 44 00 |
|  | An international consortium of rural privately owned hotels, mainly in the country house style | 00 33 1 457 296 50 |

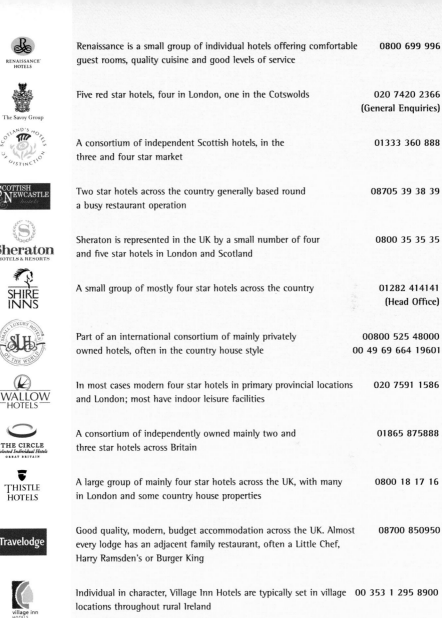

|  |  |  |
|---|---|---|
| RENAISSANCE HOTELS | Renaissance is a small group of individual hotels offering comfortable guest rooms, quality cuisine and good levels of service | **0800 699 996** |
| The Savoy Group | Five red star hotels, four in London, one in the Cotswolds | **020 7420 2366 (General Enquiries)** |
| Scotland's Hotels of Distinction | A consortium of independent Scottish hotels, in the three and four star market | **01333 360 888** |
| Scottish Newcastle hotels | Two star hotels across the country generally based round a busy restaurant operation | **08705 39 38 39** |
| Sheraton HOTELS & RESORTS | Sheraton is represented in the UK by a small number of four and five star hotels in London and Scotland | **0800 35 35 35** |
| SHIRE INNS | A small group of mostly four star hotels across the country | **01282 414141 (Head Office)** |
| Small Luxury Hotels of the World | Part of an international consortium of mainly privately owned hotels, often in the country house style | **00800 525 48000**<br>**00 49 69 664 19601** |
| SWALLOW HOTELS | In most cases modern four star hotels in primary provincial locations and London; most have indoor leisure facilities | **020 7591 1586** |
| THE CIRCLE Selected Individual Hotels GREAT BRITAIN | A consortium of independently owned mainly two and three star hotels across Britain | **01865 875888** |
| THISTLE HOTELS | A large group of mainly four star hotels across the UK, with many in London and some country house properties | **0800 18 17 16** |
| Travelodge | Good quality, modern, budget accommodation across the UK. Almost every lodge has an adjacent family restaurant, often a Little Chef, Harry Ramsden's or Burger King | **08700 850950** |
| village inn HOTELS | Individual in character, Village Inn Hotels are typically set in village locations throughout rural Ireland | **00 353 1 295 8900** |
|  | Von Essen, a small, privately owned group of country house hotels, all individual in style and based in the south of England | **01761 241023** |
| Welcome Break | Lodge accommodation at motorway services | **0800 731 4466** |
| ZOFFANY HOTELS | A small group of three star hotels, mainly in the southern half of England | **01635 35494 (Head Office)** |

The Celtic Manor Resort, Newport

# *Taking the Waters*

***Pre-wedding pamper, hen weekend, a well-earned break with a friend, or time out from a business trip – there are many reasons to visit a spa, whether you're looking for top-to-toe treatments or to recharge your batteries in peaceful surroundings. Over 250 AA-rated hotels have spa facilities; look out for 'Spa' highlighted in their gazetteer entry, or consult the handy index at the back of the guide. We've picked out just a few here to give you an idea of the variety of locations and treatments available, and arranged a series of special offers for Hotel Guide readers***

## *Chewton Glen, New Milton, Hampshire*

Surrounded by *trompe l'oeil* frescoes, pillars and plants, and with views over 130 acres of grounds, Chewton Glen's award-winning Romanesque swimming pool makes a stunning centrepiece for the hotel's health club. But it's not just the surroundings that set this pool apart. The water is ozone treated to ensure it remains crystal clear and to reduce chlorine irritation, while the special air treatment reduces humidity. It's this level of attention to detail that is synonymous with Chewton Glen – even the steam room is scented with eucalyptus. If swimming or a session in the well-equipped gym seems too energetic, a full range of body and beauty treatments is available, including complementary therapies such as iridology, reiki and Indian head massage. Mums-to-be should try the special maternity massage from the comfort of a specially designed couch.

*For an exclusive offer for AA guide readers call 01425 275341 or e-mail spa@chewtonglen.com, quoting the AA Hotel Guide.*

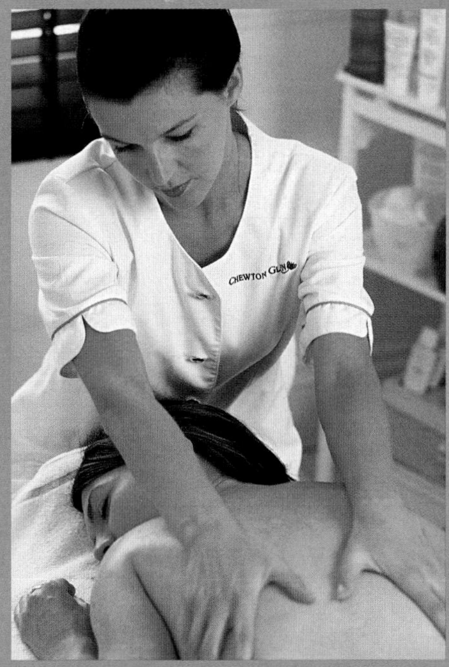
CHEWTON GLEN
Chewton Glen, New Milton

Cliveden, Taplow

## Cliveden, Taplow, Buckinghamshire

Commissioned by Lady Astor's husband to discourage her from bathing in the Thames, the outdoor pool at Cliveden is well known as the setting for John Profumo's first encounter with Christine Keeler. An ozone-treated indoor pool, marble-lined changing rooms, saunas, steam and treatment rooms have since been added to create the luxurious Pavilion Spa, where the ultra-modern facilities are in direct contrast with the 17th-century grandeur of the house. Choose from a variety of massage, health and beauty therapies, such as the detoxifying seaweed wrap, which reduces the levels of toxins in the body, or the evening primrose oil bath to soothe and soften sensitive skin. Children are welcome at the Pavilion Spa at certain times; phone the number below for details.

*Call 01628 668561 or e-mail reservations@ clivedenhouse.co.uk, quoting the AA Hotel Guide, for details of an exclusive offer for guide readers.*

## Crieff Hydro, Crieff, Perth & Kinross

This is the perfect spa destination for those with children in tow. For eleven hours during the day, you can leave your little treasures under the professional supervision of the Children's Club while you unwind in the Lagoon complex. Facilities include a swimming pool, sauna, steam room and spa bath, a gym and a multi-purpose sports hall offering a variety of fitness classes. The Beauty Salon provides aromatherapy and body massages as well as various skincare treatments. If you're looking to spend some quality time with the kids, there is a huge number of family-friendly activities to choose from on Crieff Hydro's 900-acre estate.

*For more information on Crieff Hydro's exclusive offer for guide readers call 01764 655555 or e-mail enquiries@crieffhydro.com, quoting the AA Hotel Guide.*

## The Westin Turnberry Resort Hotel, Turnberry, South Ayrshire

Situated on Scotland's beautiful west coast, overlooking the Isles of Arran and Ailsa Craig, Turnberry's dramatic location makes it ideal for a relaxing break 'away from it all'. The spa boasts the latest in health and fitness equipment, including a 20-metre swimming pool with underwater lighting and music. You can unwind in a variety of plunge pools, saunas and steam rooms, under a jet blitz shower, or allow one of the professionally trained staff to pamper you with an aromatherapy or hydrotherapy treatment. The spa's philosophy is holistic in approach, its aim being 'to promote well-being through harmony between body and mind'. Products use only the highest quality wild or organically grown plants.

*Call 01655 331000 or e-mail turnberry@westin.com for more information.*

## The St David's Hotel & Spa, Cardiff

With its imposing waterfront location and hydrotherapy spa overlooking Cardiff Bay, The St David's Hotel & Spa is a

paradise for water babies. In addition to the 15-metre exercise pool, there are two saltwater hydropools with energising underwater jets, swan neck fountains and underwater recliners, and a jet blitz shower to increase circulation and stimulate the metabolism. Numerous body and beauty treatments are available but the Spa's real speciality is hydrotherapy, whereby saltwater is heated to body temperature to enable the salts within the water to draw out impurities as the body absorbs salts and trace minerals. 'Spa cuisine', a range of specially adapted lighter dishes, is served in the spa dining lounge.

*Call 029 2031 3084/83 or e-mail spa@thestdavidshotel.com, quoting the AA Hotel Guide, for information on an exclusive reader offer.*

## The Celtic Manor Resort, Newport

The Forum Health Club & Spa at The Celtic Manor Resort offers a huge range of treatments and therapies from all over the world, some of which are unique to the Spa. The Rasul Mud Ceremony combines the benefits of a mud pack with a steam bath to cleanse and exfoliate the skin. Guests apply medicinal earths to selected parts of the body and sit in a heated chamber while shots of steam blow through dried herbs. A tropical rain shower helps to remove the mud before nourishing oils are applied to the skin. The Rasul Mud Ceremony forms part of some of the specially designed day programmes available at Celtic Manor, the price of which includes full use of the high-tech gym, Romanesque swimming pool, sauna, steam room and 50-seater spa pool. The Hideaway Club will entertain the kids while you relax and unwind.

*The Celtic Manor Resort, Newport*

*Call 01633 413 000 or e-mail postbox@celtic-manor.com for more information.*

*Lodge & Spa at Inchydoney Island*

## Lodge & Spa at Inchydoney Island, Clonakilty, Co Cork

Linked to the mainland via a causeway, The Lodge & Spa at Inchydoney Island is situated on a headland above two of the finest EU Blue Flag beaches in Ireland. Its state-of-the art Thalassotherapy Centre uses seawater pumped from the ocean to treat conditions such as arthritis, obesity, stress and fatigue. The centre, which is made up of private rooms, offers up-to-the-minute therapies such as pressotherapy to encourage lymphatic drainage and improve circulation, and marine brumisation, where a negative ionised mist of seawater is pumped into a treatment room, aiding breathing and promoting relaxation. The centre's own medical consultant, Dr Christian Jost, can create a personalised programme to suit your needs. However, you may just wish to lounge in the therapeutic seawater pool, with its underwater massage seats and jets, neck showers, microbubble seats, waterfall, geyser spa and air spa.

*For details of the Lodge & Spa's exclusive offer for guide readers call 00 353 23 33143 or e-mail reservations@inchydoneyisland.com, quoting the AA Hotel Guide.*

The Merrion Hotel, Dublin

## *The Merrion Hotel, Dublin*

The focal point of the luxurious Tethra Spa at The Merrion Hotel is an 18-metre 'infinity' swimming pool, so called because of its magnificent *trompe l'oeil* landscape mural which creates an impression of space. The atmosphere throughout the spa is one of relaxed tranquillity, enhanced by the sumptuous surroundings of the Italian marble steam room and the stylish changing rooms with underfloor heating. If a workout in the state-of-the-art gym leaves you with aching limbs, try the aromatherapy sport and fitness massage. Ideal for sporting guests or those with physically demanding jobs, this treatment uses lavender, clove and rosemary oils to boost circulation and warm muscles. Frequent air travellers will benefit from the flight reviver, an aromatherapy massage incorporating a scalp treatment to diminish stress and tension.

*Call 00 353 1 603 0600 or e-mail info@merrionhotel.com for details of The Merrion Hotel's exclusive reader offer. Please quote the AA Hotel Guide.*

There are a number of hotel groups which are particularly well known for their excellent spa and leisure facilities, for example, De Vere and Marriott. A full list of these and other hotels with spas can be found in the index at the back of the guide.

# Hotel of the Year, England

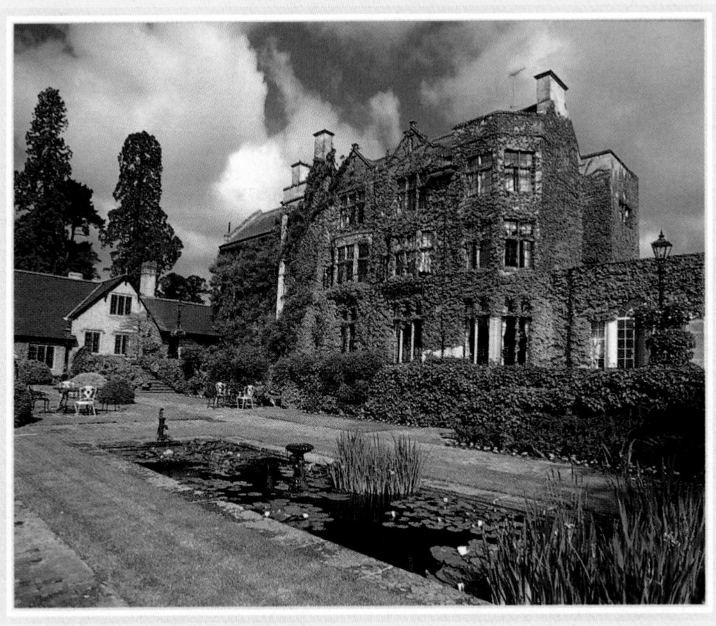

## Pennyhill Park Hotel & Country Club,

### Bagshot

ABBERLEY, Worcestershire

○ **The Elms**
Stockton Rd WR6 6AT
☎ 01299 896666 🖷 01299 896804
***Dir:*** *on A443 between Worcester and Tenbury Wells 2m beyond Great Witley*
At the time of going to press, the star classification for this hotel was not confirmed. Please refer to the AA internet site www.theAA.com for current information.
**ROOMS:** 16 en suite **FACILITIES:** Tennis (hard) Croquet lawn **CONF:** Thtr 60 Class 30 Board 24 **PARKING:** 61 **NOTES:** No dogs (ex guide dogs) No smoking in restaurant **CARDS:**

ABBOT'S SALFORD, Warwickshire Map 04 SP05

★★★75% **Salford Hall**
WR11 5UT
☎ 01386 871300 🖷 01386 871301
e-mail: reception@salfordhall.co.uk
***Dir:*** *from A46 take road signed Salford Priors, Abbot's Salford & Harvington. Hotel 1.5m on left*

Salford Hall is a beautifully restored 15th-century manor house which retains many of its period features. Public rooms include a cosy bar, a conservatory courtyard and an oak-panelled restaurant. Bedrooms are superbly equipped and feature a wealth of thoughtful extras. The outdoor tennis courts overlook a pretty country garden, and there is also a snooker room, solarium and sauna.
**ROOMS:** 14 en suite 19 annexe en suite s £75-£140; d £118-£150 (incl. bkfst) * **LB** **FACILITIES:** Tennis (hard) Snooker Sauna Solarium **CONF:** Thtr 50 Class 35 Board 25 Del from £130 * **PARKING:** 51 **NOTES:** No dogs (ex guide dogs) No smoking in restaurant Closed 24-30 Dec Civ Wed 50 **CARDS:**

*See advert under STRATFORD-UPON-AVON*

ABINGDON, Oxfordshire Map 04 SU49

★★★66% **Upper Reaches**
Thames St OX14 3JA
☎ 0870 400 8101 🖷 01235 555182
e-mail: heritagehotels_abingdon.upper_reaches@forte.hotels.com
***Dir:*** *on A415 in Abingdon follow signs for Dorchester and turn left just before the bridge over the Thames*
Dating back to the 17th century this hotel was once a water mill. Ideally set on the banks of the Thames with moorings for boats, it is within walking distance of the town. The spacious bedrooms offer a high standard of comfort.
**ROOMS:** 31 en suite (4 fmly) No smoking in 15 bedrooms s £105-£115; d £115-£135 * **LB** **FACILITIES:** STV Fishing free use of leisure centre across road Xmas **CONF:** Thtr 25 Class 15 Board 18 Del £125 * **PARKING:** 60 **NOTES:** No smoking in restaurant **CARDS:**

★★★64% **Abingdon Four Pillars Hotel**
Marcham Rd OX14 1TZ
☎ 01235 553456 🖷 01235 554117
e-mail: enquiries@four-pillars.co.uk
***Dir:*** *turn off A34 at junct with A415, on entry into Abingdon, turn right at rdbt, hotel on right*
This busy hotel, close to major road links, offers a good base for business or conference guests. It has well-equipped, comfortable bedrooms with satellite TV and trouser presses. The Conservatory offers good food in an attractive garden setting.
**ROOMS:** 62 en suite (7 fmly) No smoking in 40 bedrooms s £79-£89; d £89-£99 * **LB** **FACILITIES:** STV entertainment Xmas **CONF:** Thtr 140 Class 80 Board 48 Del from £115 * **PARKING:** 85 **NOTES:** No smoking in restaurant Civ Wed 100 **CARDS:**

ACCRINGTON, Lancashire Map 07 SD72

★★★★65% **Dunkenhalgh**
Blackburn Rd, Clayton-le-Moors BB5 5JP
☎ 01254 398021 🖷 01254 872230
e-mail: info@dunkenhalgh.macdonald-hotels.co.uk
***Dir:*** *adj to M65 junct 7*

MACDONALD
HOTELS

This historic country house, set back from the road in attractive grounds, has been considerably extended. It boasts a new wing of executive club rooms, all providing a high standard of comfort and facilities. Excellent conferencing and leisure facilities are also available.
**ROOMS:** 53 en suite 69 annexe en suite (33 fmly) No smoking in 56 bedrooms s £55-£95; d £65-£105 * **LB** **FACILITIES:** STV

★★★61% **Sparth House Hotel**
Whalley Rd, Clayton Le Moors BB5 5RP
☎ 01254 872263 🖷 01254 872263
***Dir:*** *take A6185 to Clitheroe along Dunkenhalgh Way, right at lights onto A678, left at next lights - A680 to Whalley. Hotel on left after 2 lights*

This 18th-century listed building is set in three acres of well-tended gardens. Bedrooms are individually styled and those in the

*continued*

original house are particularly spacious, including one with original furnishings from one of the great liners. The panelled restaurant is a peaceful setting in which to enjoy a wide range of dishes.
**ROOMS:** 16 en suite (3 fmly) **CONF:** Thtr 160 Class 50 Board 40 Del from £85 * **PARKING:** 50 **NOTES:** No smoking in restaurant Civ Wed 100 **CARDS:**

## ACLE, Norfolk — Map 05 TG41

### Travelodge
NR13 3BE
☎ 01493 751970 01493 751970
***Dir:*** *junc A47 & Acle Bypass*
Travelodge offers good quality, good value, modern accommodation. Ideal for families, the spacious, en suite bedrooms include remote-control TV, tea and coffee-making facilities, luxury beds and free morning newspaper. Meals can be taken at the nearby family restaurant. For further details and the Travelodge phone number, consult the Hotel Groups page.

**ROOMS:** 40 en suite

## ALBRIGHTON, Shropshire — Map 07 SJ80

### ★★★63% Lea Manor Hotel
Holyhead Rd WV7 3BX
☎ 01902 373266 01902 372853
e-mail: hotel@leamanor.co.uk
***Dir:*** *junct 3 of M54, follow A41 towards Wolverhampton then A464 towards Shifnal for approx 2m, hotel on the left*

LEA MANOR

This hotel offers well equipped bedrooms including ironing facilities. Greatly extended, half of the bedrooms are in the original building and half are on the ground floor of a nearby modern building. The restaurant and lounge bar serve a good range of popular dishes. There is also a large function room and three conference rooms.
**ROOMS:** 8 en suite 8 annexe en suite No smoking in 10 bedrooms s £50-£65; d £60-£75 (incl. bkfst) * **LB** **CONF:** Thtr 200 Class 50 Board 50 Del from £90 * **PARKING:** 200 **NOTES:** No dogs (ex guide dogs) No smoking in restaurant Civ Wed 100
**CARDS:**

## ALCESTER, Warwickshire — Map 04 SP05

### ★★★67% Kings Court
Kings Coughton B49 5QQ
☎ 01789 763111 01789 400242
e-mail: info@kingscourthotel.co.uk
***Dir:*** *1m N on A435*
This privately owned hotel partly dates back to Tudor times. Many of the well-equipped bedrooms are in a modern wing, some on the ground floor and some suitable for disabled guests. Bedrooms in the original house boast oak beams and rustic appeal. A choice of menus is served in the smart restaurant and quaint bar.
**ROOMS:** 4 en suite 38 annexe en suite (3 fmly) No smoking in 15 bedrooms s fr £59; d fr £86 (incl. bkfst) * **LB** **CONF:** Thtr 120 Class 40 Board 30 **PARKING:** 120 **NOTES:** Closed 24-30 Dec
**CARDS:**

### Travelodge
A435 Birmingham Rd, Oversley Mill Roundabout
B49 6AA
☎ 08700 850950
***Dir:*** *at junc A46/A435*
Travelodge offers good quality, good value, modern accommodation. Ideal for families, the spacious, en suite bedrooms include remote-control TV, tea and coffee-making facilities, luxury beds and free morning newspaper. Meals can be taken at the nearby family restaurant. For further details and the Travelodge phone number, consult the Hotel Groups page.

**ROOMS:** 40 en suite

## ALDEBURGH, Suffolk — Map 05 TM45

### ★★★74% Wentworth
Wentworth Rd IP15 5BD
☎ 01728 452312 01728 454343
e-mail: wentworth.hotel@anglianet.co.uk
***Dir:*** *turn off A12 onto A1094, 6m to Aldeburgh, leave church on left and turn left at bottom of hill*
This charming hotel, which is situated near the seafront, has a loyal following. Public areas feature log fires, and are welcoming, spacious and comfortably furnished. Bedrooms are well-equipped and attractively decorated. Some very spacious Mediterranean-style bedrooms are located in Darfield House across the road.
**ROOMS:** 30 rms (28 en suite) 7 annexe en suite No smoking in all bedrooms s £69-£89; d £100-£130 (incl. bkfst) * **LB** **FACILITIES:** STV Xmas **CONF:** Thtr 15 Class 12 Board 14 Del from £99 * **PARKING:** 30 **NOTES:** No smoking in restaurant Closed 28 Dec-4 Jan
**CARDS:**

*See advert on page 47*

### ★★★74% White Lion
Market Cross Place IP15 5BJ
☎ 01728 452720 01728 452986
e-mail: whitelionaldeburgh@btinternet.com
***Dir:*** *from A12 at Saxmundham take A1094 approx 5m, on seafront*

This popular hotel is situated at the quiet end of town overlooking the sea. Fresh shellfish and seafood are the speciality of the beamed restaurant in the evenings and there is a modern

*continued on p46*

A

ALDEBURGH, continued

brasserie for lunch. Comfortable public areas include a smart air-conditioned conference room and two lounges with open fires.
**ROOMS:** 38 en suite (1 fmly) No smoking in 15 bedrooms s £70-£87.50; d £108-£140 (incl. bkfst) * **LB** **FACILITIES:** STV Xmas **CONF:** Thtr 120 Class 50 Board 50 Del from £85 * **PARKING:** 15 **NOTES:** No smoking in restaurant **CARDS:**

★★★68% **The Brudenell**
The Parade IP15 5BU
☎ 01728 452071 01728 454082
e-mail: info@brudenellhotel.co.uk
***Dir:*** *on seafront, adjoining Fort Green car park*

Situated at the far end of the town centre overlooking the beach and sea beyond. The spacious bedrooms are pleasantly decorated and thoughtfully equipped, many rooms have superb sea views. Public rooms feature a newly refurbished lounge bar and a smart restaurant serving a variety of dishes, including locally caught fish.
**ROOMS:** 47 en suite (1 fmly) No smoking in 11 bedrooms s £63-£84; d £101-£113 (incl. bkfst) * **LB** **FACILITIES:** Xmas **CONF:** Thtr 50 Class 25 Board 28 Del from £90 * **SERVICES:** Lift **PARKING:** 22
**NOTES:** No smoking in restaurant **CARDS:**

★★70% ***Uplands***
Victoria Rd IP15 5DX
☎ 01728 452420 01728 454872
***Dir:*** *turn off A12 onto A1094, Aldeburgh 6m, Parish Church on left, hotel is opposite*

Friendly, family run hotel situated on the edge of town beside the church. The spacious public areas include an airy conservatory, two lounges with open fires, an elegant dining room, an intimate bar and an attractive walled garden. Bedrooms vary in size and style, with period furnishings in the main house and a contemporary look in the newly refurbished chalet-style garden cottages.
**ROOMS:** 10 en suite 7 annexe en suite (4 fmly) **PARKING:** 22
**NOTES:** No smoking in restaurant Closed 23 Dec-3 Jan
**CARDS:**

ALDERLEY EDGE, Cheshire Map 07 SJ87

★★★73% ⊛⊛ **Alderley Edge**
Macclesfield Rd SK9 7BJ
☎ 01625 583033 01625 586343
e-mail: sales@alderley-edge-hotel.co.uk
***Dir:*** *turn off A34 in Alderley Edge onto B5087 towards Macclesfield. Hotel 200yds on right*
This well furnished hotel with its charming grounds was originally a country house built for one of the region's cotton kings. The bedrooms and suites are attractively furnished, offering excellent quality and comfort. The welcoming bar and adjacent lounge lead into the split-level conservatory restaurant, which offers well cooked and very imaginative dishes. Service is very attentive from a dedicated team.
**ROOMS:** 46 en suite s £109-£400; d £130-£400 * **LB** **FACILITIES:** STV entertainment Xmas **CONF:** Thtr 120 Class 80 Board 40 Del £145 *
**SERVICES:** Lift **PARKING:** 90 **NOTES:** No dogs (ex guide dogs) Civ Wed 100 **CARDS:**

***Premier Lodge (Wilmslow South)***
London Rd, Alderley Edge SK9 7AA
☎ 0870 700 1576 0870 700 1577
Premier Lodge offers modern, well-equipped, en suite accommodation suitable for both business and leisure travellers. Meals can be taken at the adjacent popular restaurant and bar, which is fully licensed. For further details, consult the Hotel Groups page.
**ROOMS:** 37 en suite

○ **Innkeeper's Lodge Alderley Edge**
5-9 Wilmslow Rd SK9 7QN
A new concept in the travel accommodation market. Smart rooms meet essential business requirements but also have home comforts. Dining options include all-day menus plus the added advantage of breakfast, which is included in the room price. Reservations can be made seven days a week through the room reservations number: 0870 243 0500. For further details, consult the Hotel Groups page.
**ROOMS:** 10 en suite **NOTES:** Open now

ALDERMINSTER, Warwickshire Map 04 SP24

★★★★75% ⊛⊛ ***Ettington Park***
CV37 8BU
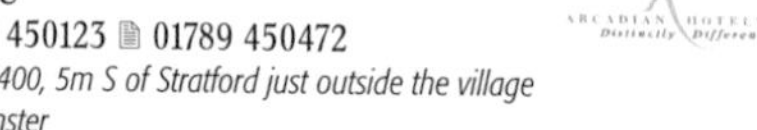
☎ 01789 450123 01789 450472
***Dir:*** *off A3400, 5m S of Stratford just outside the village of Alderminster*

A magnificent Grade I listed Victorian mansion with superb architectural features, set in 40 acres of attractive parkland on the banks of the Stour. Bedrooms are elegantly furnished and have

continued

tylish bathrooms; many rooms have views of the gardens and the 2th-century chapel. Service is friendly and attentive yet discreet.
**OOMS:** 48 en suite (5 fmly) **FACILITIES:** STV Indoor swimming (H) ennis (hard) Fishing Riding Sauna Solarium Croquet lawn Jacuzzi Clay igeon shooting Archery Hot Air Ballooning Health & Beauty salon ntertainment **CONF:** Thtr 75 Class 40 Board 48 **SERVICES:** Lift **ARKING:** 150 **NOTES:** No smoking in restaurant
**ARDS:**

*See advert under STRATFORD-UPON-AVON*

## LDERSHOT, Hampshire
Map 04 SU85

### ★★★69% *Potters International*
Fleet Rd GU11 2ET
☎ 01252 344000 01252 311611
**Dir:** *access via A325 and A321 towards Fleet*

This modern hotel and leisure complex is located within easy reach of Aldershot and the surrounding areas. Bedrooms are spacious, well-equipped and have been attractively decorated and urnished. Extensive air-conditioned public areas include a pub and a more formal restaurant; there are also conference rooms and a very good leisure club.
**ROOMS:** 97 en suite (6 fmly) No smoking in 10 bedrooms **FACILITIES:** STV Indoor swimming (H) Sauna Solarium Gym Jacuzzi **CONF:** Thtr 400 Class 150 Board 40 **SERVICES:** Lift **PARKING:** 120 **NOTES:** No dogs (ex guide dogs) No smoking in restaurant
**CARDS:**

## ALDWARK, North Yorkshire
Map 08 SE46

### ★★★71% Aldwark Manor Hotel, Golf & Country Club
YO61 1UF
☎ 01347 838146 & 838251 01347 838867
e-mail: reception@aldwarkmanor.co.uk
**Dir:** *from A1, A59 towards Green Hammerton, B6265 Little Ouseburn & follow signs Aldwark Bridge/Manor. A19 through Linton on Ouse*

Surrounded by a well designed golf course, this 19th-century manor house offers spacious bedrooms and public rooms furnished in period style. There is a members bar and a Brasserie serving a range of light meals and snacks. The restaurant offers

*continued on p48*

A

ALDWARK, continued

skilfully prepared dishes in a formal setting, and in an adjacent building there are extensive leisure facilities.
**ROOMS:** 25 en suite 3 annexe rms (2 en suite) (2 fmly) s £65-£75; d £120-£150 (incl. bkfst) * **LB FACILITIES:** Spa STV Indoor swimming (H) Golf 18 Fishing Sauna Solarium Gym Putting green Jacuzzi Coarse fishing,Health & beauty Xmas **CONF:** Thtr 80 Class 40 Board 30 **PARKING:** 150 **NOTES:** No smoking in restaurant Civ Wed 100 **CARDS:**

*See advert under YORK*

## ALFRETON, Derbyshire — Map 08 SK45

### *Travelodge*
Old Swanwick Colliery Rd DE55 1HJ
☎ 01773 520040 🖷 01773 520040
***Dir:** 3m from junc 28 M1 where the A38 joins the A61*

Travelodge

Travelodge offers good quality, good value, modern accommodation. Ideal for families, the spacious, en suite bedrooms include remote-control TV, tea and coffee-making facilities, luxury beds and free morning newspaper. Meals can be taken at the nearby family restaurant. For further details and the Travelodge phone number, consult the Hotel Groups page.

**ROOMS:** 60 en suite

## ALFRISTON, East Sussex — Map 05 TQ50

### ★★★68% White Lodge Country House
Sloe Ln BN26 5UR
☎ 01323 870265 🖷 01323 870284
e-mail: sales@whitelodge-hotel.com
***Dir:** on B2108 between A27 & A259*
An ideal retreat in peaceful surroundings, with views over the Cuckmere River Valley. Bedrooms are individually decorated with refurbishment on-going. Weekend breaks are well-planned and special events are very popular. Public areas include a choice of elegant lounges and two restaurants.
**ROOMS:** 19 en suite (1 fmly) No smoking in 1 bedroom s £45-£90; d £90-£180 (incl. bkfst) * **FACILITIES:** STV **CONF:** Thtr 30 Class 20 Board 15 Del from £65 * **SERVICES:** Lift **PARKING:** 20 **CARDS:**

*See advert on opposite page*

### ★★★67% Deans Place
Seaford Rd BN26 5TW
☎ 01323 870248 🖷 01323 870918
e-mail: mail@deansplacehotel.co.uk
***Dir:** turn off A27 signposted Alfriston & Drusillas Zoo Park. Pass through village towards south side*

Best Western

This hotel is set in its own attractive gardens on the southern fringes of the village. Bedrooms vary in size and are well-appointed with good facilities. A wide range of food is offered including an extensive bar menu to suit the needs of all guests.
**ROOMS:** 36 en suite (2 fmly) No smoking in 11 bedrooms s £95; d £120 (incl. bkfst) **LB FACILITIES:** STV Outdoor swimming (H) Croquet lawn Putting green ch fac Xmas **CONF:** Thtr 200 Class 70 Board 45 Del £130 * **PARKING:** 100 **NOTES:** No smoking in restaurant Civ Wed 150 **CARDS:**

### ★★★67% The Star Inn
BN26 5TA
☎ 0870 400 8102 🖷 01323 870922
***Dir:** 2m off A27 at Drusillas roundabout*
This 14th-century hotel combines modern comforts with original character. Bedrooms are divided between the main building and the newer extension, all are well-equipped and traditionally furnished. There are two beamed lounges with open fires and a bar with a flagstone floor.

**ROOMS:** 37 en suite (1 fmly) No smoking in 10 bedrooms s £70-£90; d £140-£170 (incl. bkfst) * **LB FACILITIES:** Xmas **CONF:** Thtr 30 Class 15 Board 25 Del from £99 * **PARKING:** 27 **NOTES:** No smoking in restaurant **CARDS:**

## ALNWICK, Northumberland — Map 12 NU11
see also Embleton

### ★★★60% White Swan
Bondgate Within NE66 1TD
☎ 01665 602109 🖷 01665 510400
***Dir:** from A1 follow town centre. Through Bondgate Tower archway on right*

HOTEL

This 300 year old coaching inn has a prime location in the heart of Alnwick and is particularly popular with tours. Bedrooms vary in size and style, but newer rooms are attractively furnished and thoughtfully equipped. Public areas include the Olympic Suite, featuring hand-carved panelling from the SS Olympic, sister ship to the ill-fated Titanic.
**ROOMS:** 58 en suite (4 fmly) No smoking in 15 bedrooms s £69; d £84 (incl. bkfst) * **LB FACILITIES:** Xmas **CONF:** Thtr 200 Class 80 Board 15 Del from £79.50 * **PARKING:** 30 **NOTES:** No smoking in restaurant Civ Wed 120 **CARDS:**

## ALRESFORD, Hampshire — Map 04 SU53

### ★★63% Swan
11 West St SO24 9AD
☎ 01962 732302 & 734427 🖷 01962 735274
e-mail: swanhotel@btinternet.com
***Dir:** turn off A31 onto B3047*
Located in the centre of this pretty town, there has been an inn on this site for 300 years. Bedrooms are in the old main building and

*continued*

the more modern wing. The lounge bar is open all day. There is also a separate restaurant.
**ROOMS:** 11 rms (10 en suite) 12 annexe en suite (3 fmly) s £30-£60; d £55-£95 (incl. bkfst & dinner) * **CONF:** Thtr 90 Class 60 Board 40 Del from £55 * **PARKING:** 75 **NOTES:** No dogs (ex guide dogs) No smoking in restaurant RS 25-26 Dec **CARDS:**

*See advert on this page*

## ALREWAS, Staffordshire

Map 07 SK11

### ★★62% *Claymar Hotel*

118A Main St DE13 7AE
☎ 01283 790202 📠 01283 791465
This hotel sits in the centre of the village, just off the A38. Personal and friendly service ensures a welcoming environment. There is a lounge bar and restaurant with carte, vegetarian and special diet meals available. Bedrooms are well equipped.
**ROOMS:** 20 en suite **PARKING:** 35 **CARDS:**

## ALSAGER, Cheshire

Map 07 SJ75

### ★★★71% ®® Manor House

Best Western

Audley Rd ST7 2QQ
☎ 01270 884000 📠 01270 882483
e-mail: manres@compasshotels.co.uk
***Dir:*** *from M6 junct 16 take A500 toward Stoke. In approx 0.5m take 1st slip road, Alsager, turn left at top & continue, hotel on left approaching village*
This modern hotel has been developed around an old farmhouse, the original oak beams of which are still a feature in the restaurant and bars. The bedrooms are well-equipped and include ground floor rooms and family accommodation. A pleasant patio garden and indoor swimming pool are available. The cuisine served in the restaurant is imaginative and very satisfying.
**ROOMS:** 57 en suite (4 fmly) No smoking in 12 bedrooms s £72-£89; d £99-£109 (incl. bkfst) * **LB** **FACILITIES:** STV Indoor swimming (H) Jacuzzi Xmas **CONF:** Thtr 200 Class 108 Board 82 Del from £105 * **PARKING:** 150 **NOTES:** No dogs (ex guide dogs) No smoking in restaurant Civ Wed 50 **CARDS:**

*See advert under STOKE-ON-TRENT*

## ALSTON, Cumbria

Map 12 NY74

### ★★74% ® *Lovelady Shield Country House*

CA9 3LF
☎ 01434 381203 & 381305 📠 01434 381515
e-mail: enquiries@lovelady.co.uk
***Dir:*** *2m E, signposted off A689 where it joins the B6294*

This charming small country house hotel is peacefully set in three acres of gardens, high in the Pennines. Bedrooms are generally spacious and are thoughtfully equipped. Public areas include a

*continued on p50*

ALSTON, continued

choice of attractive, inviting lounges and an elegant dining room where carefully prepared meals are served.
**ROOMS:** 10 en suite (1 fmly) **CONF:** Class 12 Board 12 **PARKING:** 20 **NOTES:** No smoking in restaurant Civ Wed 100
**CARDS:**

*See advert on opposite page*

### ★★68% *Lowbyer Manor Country House*
CA9 3JX
☎ 01434 381230 01434 382937
***Dir:*** *on the edge of town on A686 towards Newcastle*
A 17th-century manor house situated in mature, well-tended gardens on the edge of town, this friendly hotel offers comfortable accommodation and a warm and relaxing atmosphere. Home cooked dishes feature on the dinner menu which includes a vegetarian section.
**ROOMS:** 8 en suite 4 annexe en suite **CONF:** Thtr 40 Class 14 Board 10 **PARKING:** 14 **CARDS:**

### ★★68% Nent Hall Country House Hotel
CA9 3LQ
☎ 01434 381584 01434 382668
e-mail: info@nenthallhotel.com
***Dir:*** *2m SE of Alston, on the A689 heading towards Nenthend, Stanhope & Durham*
A smartly presented hotel, nestling in delightful gardens, south-east of Alston. The bedrooms are well-equipped, stylish and modern. Public areas have a relaxed country house atmosphere and enjoyable dinners are served in the spacious dining room.
**ROOMS:** 8 en suite 9 annexe en suite (2 fmly) No smoking in all bedrooms s £42; d £62 (incl. bkfst) * **LB** **CONF:** Thtr 25 Class 25 Board 50 **PARKING:** 37 **NOTES:** No smoking in restaurant Closed 24-26 Dec **CARDS:**

## ALTARNUN, Cornwall & Isles of Scilly — Map 02 SX28

### ★★75% *Penhallow Manor Country House*
PL15 7SJ
☎ 01566 86206 01566 86179
e-mail: penhallow@ukonline.co.uk
***Dir:*** *8m W of Launceston towards Bodmin village, 1m N of A30. Hotel is next to church*

Located on the edge of Bodmin Moor, this Grade II listed building is situated beside the village church. Bedrooms are individually decorated, well-equipped and include many thoughtful extras, three rooms are available in an adjacent coach house. The menu offers a wide choice of dishes, featuring local produce and a

*continued*

carefully selected wine list. Breakfast is served in the conservatory, overlooking the pretty garden.
**ROOMS:** 6 en suite No smoking in all bedrooms **FACILITIES:** Croquet lawn Art courses Hawking Bird Watching **CONF:** Thtr 30 Class 16 Board 12 **PARKING:** 10 **NOTES:** No children 12yrs No smoking in restaurant Closed 3 Jan-14 Feb **CARDS:**

## ALTON, Hampshire — Map 04 SU73

### ★★★66% Alton Grange
London Rd GU34 4EG
☎ 01420 86565 01420 541346
e-mail: info@altongrange.co.uk
***Dir:*** *from A31 take first right at rdbt signed Alton/Holybourne/Bordon B3004, hotel will be found 300yds on left*
This friendly hotel, on the edge of the town, provides well equipped accommodation. Bedrooms, including some on the ground floor, are spacious and individually decorated. Guests can dine in Truffles Restaurant or more informally at the bar. The beautiful two acre garden is designed in an Oriental style.
**ROOMS:** 26 en suite 4 annexe en suite (4 fmly) No smoking in 4 bedrooms s £76-£92.50; d £92.50-£110 (incl. bkfst) * **FACILITIES:** STV Hot air ballooning **CONF:** Thtr 80 Class 30 Board 40 **PARKING:** 48 **NOTES:** No children 3yrs No smoking in restaurant Closed 24 Dec-2 Jan Civ Wed 100 **CARDS:**

### ★★★65% *Alton House*
Normandy St GU34 1LD
☎ 01420 80033 01420 89222
e-mail: mail@altonhouse.com
***Dir:*** *turn off A31, close to railway station*
Conveniently located on the edge of the town, this popular hotel offers comfortably furnished and well-equipped bedrooms. The restaurant serves carte and daily set menus. There is also an attractive garden with outdoor pool.
**ROOMS:** 39 en suite (3 fmly) No smoking in 2 bedrooms **FACILITIES:** STV Outdoor swimming (H) Tennis (hard) Snooker Croquet lawn **CONF:** Thtr 150 Class 80 Board 50 Del from £100 * **PARKING:** 94 **NOTES:** No dogs (ex guide dogs) Closed 25-26 Dec RS 27-29 Dec Civ Wed 70 **CARDS:**

*See advert on opposite page*

## ALTRINCHAM, Greater Manchester — Map 07 SJ78

### ★★★73% Woodland Park
Wellington Rd, Timperley WA15 7RG
☎ 0161 928 8631 0161 941 2821
e-mail: info@woodlandpark.co.uk
***Dir:*** *off the A560*
This friendly hotel is situated in a quiet residential area, yet near to the motorways. Bedrooms are individually furnished and the lounges are elegant. Carefully prepared meals are served in the Terrace Restaurant. Air-conditioned function rooms are available.
**ROOMS:** 46 en suite (2 fmly) No smoking in 20 bedrooms s £55-£77.50; d £80-£120 (incl. bkfst) * **LB** **FACILITIES:** STV **CONF:** Thtr 150 Class 100 Board 50 Del from £100 * **PARKING:** 151 **NOTES:** No dogs (ex guide dogs) No smoking in restaurant Civ Wed 80
**CARDS:**

### ★★★67% Cresta Court
Church St WA14 4DP
☎ 0161 927 7272 0161 926 9194
e-mail: info@cresta-court.co.uk
***Dir:*** *on the A56 town centre Altrincham. Courtesy Transport available from Manchester Airport*
Accommodation at this large, town centre hotel has been refurbished and now includes a number of four-poster suites with

*continued*

spa baths. Meals are available all day in the popular bar and there is also a restaurant.
**ROOMS:** 137 en suite (5 fmly) No smoking in 40 bedrooms s £78.50; d £78.50 * **LB FACILITIES:** STV Gym Beauty Salon Xmas **CONF:** Thtr 320 Class 140 Board 50 Del from £100 * **SERVICES:** Lift
**PARKING:** 200 **NOTES:** No smoking in restaurant Civ Wed 300
**CARDS:**

### ★★★67% Quality Hotel Altrincham

Langham Rd, Bowdon WA14 2HT
☎ 0161 928 7121 Fax 0161 927 7560
e-mail: admin@gb064.u-net.com
***Dir:*** *M6 leave junct 19 to airport, join A556, cross M56 rdbt onto A56, right at lights onto B5161, hotel 1m on right*
Located within easy reach of the motorways and airport, this popular hotel provides comfortable and well-equipped bedrooms. There are two styles of eating options, the modern Cafe Continental which serves light snacks, or the main restaurant offering more formal dining.
**ROOMS:** 89 en suite (4 fmly) No smoking in 19 bedrooms s £45-£85; d £70-£99 * **LB FACILITIES:** STV Indoor swimming (H) Sauna Solarium Gym Jacuzzi Beauty treatments ch fac Xmas **CONF:** Thtr 165 Class 60 Board 48 Del from £92.50 * **PARKING:** 160
**NOTES:** Civ Wed 165 **CARDS:**

### *Premier Lodge (Altrincham North)*

Manchester Rd, West Timperley WA14 5NH
☎ 0870 700 1308 Fax 0870 700 1309
Premier Lodge offers modern, well-equipped, en suite accommodation suitable for both business and leisure travellers. Meals can be taken at the adjacent popular restaurant and bar, which is fully licensed. For further details, consult the Hotel Groups page.
**ROOMS:** 48 en suite

### *Premier Lodge (Altrincham South)*

PREMIER LODGE

Manchester Rd WA14 4PH
☎ 0870 700 1306 Fax 0870 700 1307
Premier Lodge offers modern, well-equipped, en suite accommodation suitable for both business and leisure travellers. Meals can be taken at the adjacent popular restaurant and bar, which is fully licensed. For further details, consult the Hotel Groups page.
**ROOMS:** 46 en suite

## ALVELEY, Shropshire — Map 07 SO78

### ★★★★66% Mill Hotel & Restaurant

WV15 6HL
☎ 01746 780437 Fax 01746 780850
***Dir:*** *Midway between Kidderminster/Bridgnorth, turn off A442 signposted Enville/Turley Green*
Built around a 17th century flour mill, with the original water wheel still on display, this modern hotel is set in eight acres of landscaped grounds. Bedrooms are pleasant and include some superior rooms, which have sitting areas, and some rooms with four-poster beds. The restaurant provides carefully prepared dishes.
**ROOMS:** 21 en suite (3 fmly) No smoking in 18 bedrooms s £68-£90; d £82-£116 (incl. cont bkfst) * **LB FACILITIES:** STV Gym
**CONF:** Thtr 220 Class 150 Board 80 Del from £110 * **SERVICES:** Lift
**PARKING:** 200 **NOTES:** No dogs No smoking in restaurant Civ Wed 200
**CARDS:**

ALVESTON, Gloucestershire Map 03 ST68

**★★★75% Alveston House**
Davids Ln BS35 2LA
☎ 01454 415050 🖷 01454 415425
e-mail: info@alvestonhousehotel.co.uk
***Dir:*** *near A38, between juncts 14 & 16 of M5*
This popular hotel is particularly well suited to the business traveller, being conveniently yet quietly located just a short drive from both the M4 and the M5. The modern bedrooms are well-maintained and have many useful extras. The open-plan restaurant and bar extend into a conservatory. Menus offer a good choice and service is very efficient.
**ROOMS:** 30 en suite (1 fmly) No smoking in 18 bedrooms s £89.50-£94.50; d £94.50-£104.50 (incl. bkfst) * LB **FACILITIES:** STV **CONF:** Thtr 85 Class 48 Board 50 Del from £135 * **PARKING:** 75 **NOTES:** No smoking in restaurant Civ Wed 75
**CARDS:**
*See advert under BRISTOL and on opposite page*

**Premier Lodge (Bristol North)**
Thornbury Rd BS35 3LL
PREMIER LODGE THE BEST. BEST ASSURED.
☎ 0870 700 1338 🖷 0870 7001339
***Dir:*** *on the main A38 on the outskirts of Thornbury, approx 10 miles N of Bristol*
Premier Lodge offers modern, well-equipped, en suite accommodation suitable for both business and leisure travellers. Meals can be taken at the adjacent popular restaurant and bar, which is fully licensed. For further details, consult the Hotel Groups page.
**ROOMS:** 74 en suite s £49.95; d £49.95 * **CONF:** Thtr 70 Class 40 Board 40 Del from £110 *

AMBERLEY, West Sussex Map 04 TQ01

*Premier Collection*

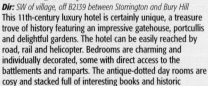

**★★★ Amberley Castle**
BN18 9ND
PRIDE OF BRITAIN MEMBER
☎ 01798 831992 🖷 01798 831998
e-mail: info@amberleycastle.co.uk
***Dir:*** *SW of village, off B2139 between Storrington and Bury Hill*
This 11th-century luxury hotel is certainly unique, a treasure trove of history featuring an impressive gatehouse, portcullis and delightful gardens. The hotel can be easily reached by road, rail and helicopter. Bedrooms are charming and individually decorated, some with direct access to the battlements and ramparts. The antique-dotted day rooms are cosy and stacked full of interesting books and historic ornaments; guests can enjoy morning coffee in these areas. The Queens Room restaurant offers accomplished cooking.
**ROOMS:** 14 en suite 5 annexe en suite s £145-£325; d £145-£325 * LB **FACILITIES:** Tennis (hard) Croquet lawn Putting green Jacuzzi Xmas **CONF:** Thtr 50 Board 24 Del from £250 * **PARKING:** 50 **NOTES:** No dogs No children 12yrs No smoking in restaurant Civ Wed 48 **CARDS:**

AMBLESIDE, Cumbria Map 07 NY30
see also Elterwater

**★★★76% Rothay Manor**
Rothay Bridge LA22 0EH
☎ 015394 33605 🖷 015394 33607
e-mail: hotel@rothaymanor.co.uk
***Dir:*** *in Ambleside follow signs for Coniston. Hotel is 0.25m SW on the road to Coniston opposite rugby pitch*

A Regency-style hotel in landscaped gardens, within walking distance of the town centre. Public rooms are relaxing and the bedrooms, all with personal touches such as fruit and flowers, are spacious and stylish. Some family rooms and rooms with balconies are available.
**ROOMS:** 15 en suite 3 annexe en suite (7 fmly) s £70-£80; d £120-£140 (incl. bkfst) * LB **FACILITIES:** Nearby leisure centre free to guests Xmas **CONF:** Thtr 22 Board 18 Del £125 * **PARKING:** 45 **NOTES:** No dogs (ex guide dogs) No smoking in restaurant Closed 3 Jan-9 Feb
**CARDS:**
*See advert on opposite page*

**★★★75% *Nanny Brow Country House***
Clappersgate LA22 9NF
☎ 015394 32036 🖷 015394 32450
e-mail: reservations@nannybrowhotel.demon.co.uk
***Dir:*** *on A593, 1.5m from Ambleside*
Sitting in five acres of gardens and woodlands, this beautiful country house hotel dates back to 1902. Bedrooms vary in style and include four-poster rooms and family garden suites. There is a cosy bar, a comfortable drawing room and an elegant restaurant where carefully prepared dishes are served.
**ROOMS:** 17 en suite (3 fmly) No smoking in all bedrooms **FACILITIES:** STV Fishing Solarium Croquet lawn Putting green Jacuzzi Free use of private leisure club **CONF:** Thtr 30 Class 30 Board 20 **PARKING:** 20 **NOTES:** No smoking in restaurant
**CARDS:**

**★★★74% Regent**
Waterhead Bay LA22 0ES
☎ 015394 32254 🖷 015394 31474
e-mail: info@regentlakes.co.uk
***Dir:*** *1m S A591*
This attractive holiday hotel, situated close to Waterhead Bay, offers a warm welcome. Bedrooms are comfortably furnished,
*continued*

including three suites and five bedrooms in the Garden wing. There is a choice of relaxing lounges, one of which contains a bar, and the elegant restaurant offers a fine dining experience using quality fresh ingredients.

**ROOMS:** 30 en suite (7 fmly) No smoking in 4 bedrooms s £56-£65 (incl. bkfst) * **LB** **FACILITIES:** membership to local leisure club entertainment Xmas **PARKING:** 38 **NOTES:** No smoking in restaurant **CARDS:**

### ★★★71% Ambleside Salutation Hotel

Lake Rd LA22 9BX
☎ 015394 32244 015394 34157
e-mail: enquiries@hotelambleside.uk.com
***Dir:*** *take A591 to Ambleside and follow one way system down Wansfell Road into Compston Road. At traffic lights take right hand lane back into village*

This former coaching inn has been tastefully transformed into a comfortable, stylish hotel. The well-equipped bedrooms vary in

*continued on p54*

AMBLESIDE, continued

size, with many enjoying open patios and delightful views. There is a spacious air-conditioned lounge and a restaurant offering an ambitious menu. A range of snacks is also available in the bar.
**ROOMS:** 38 en suite 4 annexe en suite (4 fmly) No smoking in 9 bedrooms s £46-£54; d £92-£108 (incl. bkfst) * **LB** **FACILITIES:** STV Sauna Gym Jacuzzi Free membership of nearby leisure club Xmas **CONF:** Thtr 150 Class 40 Board 16 Del from £78 * **PARKING:** 41 **NOTES:** No smoking in restaurant **CARDS:**

*See advert on page 53*

### ★★72% Fisherbeck

Lake Rd LA22 0DH
☎ 015394 33215 015394 33600
***Dir:*** *S of Ambleside on A591*

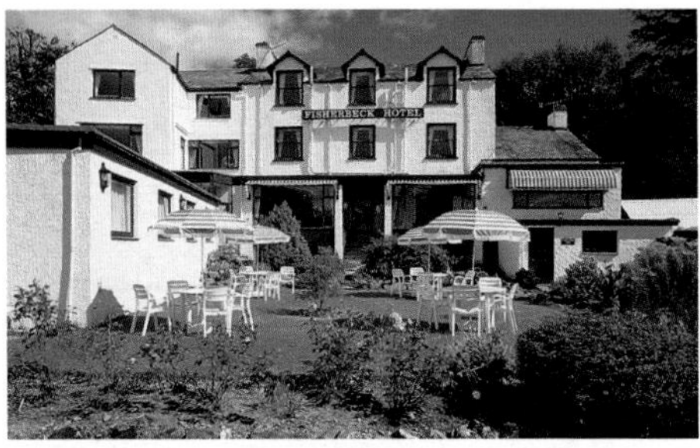
FISHERBECK HOTEL

A welcoming, family-run hotel offering friendly and attentive service. Bedrooms vary in style and include several on the ground floor and some smart rooms with balconies. There is a split-level restaurant and lounge bar, both serving creative dishes.
**ROOMS:** 18 en suite (2 fmly) No smoking in 6 bedrooms s £39-£45; d £70-£90 (incl. bkfst) * **LB** **FACILITIES:** Free use of nearby Leisure Complex Xmas **CONF:** Del from £75 * **PARKING:** 24 **NOTES:** No dogs No smoking in restaurant Closed 26 Dec-15 Jan
**CARDS:**

### ★★71% Skelwith Bridge

Skelwith Bridge LA22 9NJ
☎ 015394 32115 015394 34254
e-mail: skelwithbr@aol.com
***Dir:*** *2.5m W on the A593 at junction of B5343 to Langdale*

Lying at the heart of the Lake District National Park, this is a welcoming family-run hotel. There is a good choice of lounges and contrasting bars, and the restaurant offers carefully prepared fare. Bedrooms are comfortable and modern in style.
**ROOMS:** 23 en suite 6 annexe en suite (3 fmly) s £50-£69; d £94-£128 (incl. bkfst & dinner) * **LB** **FACILITIES:** **Spa** Fishing pool table during winter months Xmas **CONF:** Thtr 45 Class 25 Board 25 Del from £52 * **PARKING:** 60 **NOTES:** No smoking in restaurant Closed 15-24 Dec
**CARDS:**

*See advert on opposite page*

### ★★65% Waterhead

Lake Rd LA22 0ER
☎ 015394 32566 015394 31255
e-mail: waterhead@elhmail.co.uk
***Dir:*** *A591 into Ambleside, hotel is opposite Waterhead Pier*
Situated opposite the bay, this holiday hotel boasts views of the lakeside and gardens where guests can sit and enjoy the surroundings. In addition to the main restaurant there is also a Mediterranean style café bar and an Irish theme bar. Bedrooms, all well-equipped, vary in style.
**ROOMS:** 28 en suite (3 fmly) No smoking in 14 bedrooms s £44; d £88 (incl. bkfst) * **LB** **FACILITIES:** STV Use of sister hotel's leisure facilities entertainment Xmas **CONF:** Thtr 40 Class 30 Board 25 Del from £88.12 * **PARKING:** 50 **NOTES:** No smoking in restaurant
**CARDS:**

## AMERSHAM, Buckinghamshire — Map 04 SU99

### ★★★68% The Crown

High St HP7 0DH
☎ 0870 400 8103 01494 431283
e-mail: heritagehotelsamersham.crown@forte-hotels.com
***Dir:*** *access to car park immediately next to Nags Head pub*
A convenient base for antique shopping and walks in the Chilterns, this 16th-century coaching inn combines the charm of the period with modern comforts. The attractive bedrooms vary in style, some featuring original hand painted murals; newly added rooms cleverly combine comfort and design, many with CD players and mini bars. The hotel was featured in the hit film, *Four Weddings and a Funeral.*
**ROOMS:** 19 en suite 18 annexe en suite No smoking in 7 bedrooms s £70-£130; d £110-£170 * **LB** **FACILITIES:** Croquet lawn Xmas **CONF:** Board 15 Del £180 * **PARKING:** 60 **NOTES:** No smoking in restaurant **CARDS:**

## AMESBURY, Wiltshire — Map 04 SU14

### ★★60% *Antrobus Arms*

MINOTEL
Great Britain

15 Church St SP4 7EU
☎ 01980 623163 01980 622112
e-mail: reception@antrobushotel.co.uk
***Dir:*** *from rdbt on A303 proceed through town on one way system to T junct, turn left, hotel on left*
The Antrobus Arms, advertised as the nearest hotel to Stonehenge, offers individually furnished bedrooms, some overlooking the

*continued*

walled Victorian garden. Bar meals are available as an alternative to the main restaurant.

**ROOMS:** 16 en suite (2 fmly) **FACILITIES:** STV Tennis (hard) **CONF:** Thtr 40 Class 40 Board 20 **PARKING:** 15 **NOTES:** No smoking in restaurant **CARDS:**

### ⌂ *Travelodge*

Countess Services SP4 7AS
☎ 01980 624966 📠 01980 624966
***Dir:*** *junc A345 & A303 eastbound*

Travelodge

Travelodge offers good quality, good value, modern accommodation. Ideal for families, the spacious, en suite bedrooms include remote-control TV, tea and coffee-making facilities, luxury beds and free morning newspaper. Meals can be taken at the nearby family restaurant. For further details and the Travelodge phone number, consult the Hotel Groups page.

**ROOMS:** 32 en suite

## ANDOVER, Hampshire — Map 04 SU34

### ★★★73% ❀❀ Esseborne Manor

Hurstbourne Tarrant SP11 0ER
☎ 01264 736444 📠 01264 736725
e-mail: esseborne@cs.com
***Dir:*** *halfway between Andover & Newbury on A343, just N of Hurstbourne Tarrant*

An attractive manor house, set in two acres of well-tended gardens, surrounded by open countryside. The individually furnished, spacious bedrooms, including many thoughtful extras, are split between the main house, adjoining courtyard and a separate garden cottage. There are also comfortable public rooms.
**ROOMS:** 6 en suite 8 annexe en suite s £95-£105; d £100-£150 (incl. bkfst) * **LB** **FACILITIES:** STV Tennis (hard) Croquet lawn Putting green Jacuzzi **CONF:** Thtr 40 Class 35 Board 30 Del £140 * **PARKING:** 50 **NOTES:** No dogs (ex guide dogs) No smoking in restaurant Civ Wed 120 **CARDS:**

*See advert on this page*

ANDOVER, continued

### ★★★62% Quality Hotel Andover
Micheldever Rd SP11 6LA
☎ 01264 369111 🖷 01264 369000
e-mail: andover@quality-hotels.co.uk
*Dir: turn off A303 at A3091. 1st rdbt take 1st exit, 2nd rdbt take 1st exit.*

*Turn left immediately before BP petrol station, then left*

This peaceful hotel is set in grounds on the outskirts of the town. Bedrooms are comfortable and well-equipped, with extras such as modem points and satellite TV. The range of conference and meeting rooms makes this hotel a popular venue for functions and weddings.

**ROOMS:** 13 en suite 36 annexe en suite No smoking in 21 bedrooms s £55-£79; d £65-£94 * **LB** **FACILITIES:** STV **CONF:** Thtr 180 Class 40 Board 60 Del from £99 * **PARKING:** 100 **NOTES:** No dogs (ex guide dogs) No smoking in restaurant Civ Wed 85
**CARDS:**

ANSTY, Warwickshire

### ○ *Ansty Hall*
CV7 9HZ
☎ 01203 612222 🖷 01203 602155
*Dir: turn off M6 at junct 2 onto B4506 signed 'Ansty'. Hotel 1.5m on left*

MACDONALD HOTELS ★★★★

At the time of going to press, the star classification for this hotel was not confirmed. Please refer to the AA internet site www.theAA.com for current information.

**ROOMS:** 25 en suite 5 annexe en suite (3 fmly) No smoking in 6 bedrooms **FACILITIES:** STV Croquet lawn **CONF:** Thtr 200 Class 50 Board 45 **PARKING:** 50 **NOTES:** No smoking in restaurant
**CARDS:**

APPLEBY-IN-WESTMORLAND, Cumbria Map 12 NY62

### ★★★77% ◎ Appleby Manor Country House
Roman Rd CA16 6JB
☎ 017683 51571 🖷 017683 52888
e-mail: reception@applebymanor.co.uk
*Dir: from M6 junct 40, take A66 towards Brough. Take Appleby turn off, then immediately right and continue for 0.5m*

This family run, former Victorian mansion offers friendly, attentive service. Rooms vary in style and include garden rooms, coach-house rooms, and period style rooms located in the main house. Public areas are spacious and a well-stocked bar offers a large selection of malt whiskies. Meals can be enjoyed in the restaurant which offers views over the Cumbrian fells.

**ROOMS:** 23 en suite 7 annexe en suite (9 fmly) No smoking in 6 bedrooms s £79-£94; d £120-£150 (incl. bkfst) * **LB** **FACILITIES:** STV Indoor swimming (H) Sauna Solarium Putting green Jacuzzi Steam room Table tennis **CONF:** Thtr 38 Class 25 Board 28 Del £119 * **PARKING:** 53 **NOTES:** No smoking in restaurant Closed 24-26 Dec
**CARDS:**

*See advert on opposite page*

### ★★★70% ◎ Tufton Arms
Market Square CA16 6XA
☎ 017683 51593 🖷 017683 52761
e-mail: info@tuftonarmshotel.co.uk
*Dir: in the centre of Appleby, by-passed by the A66, on B6260*

Situated in the centre of this popular market town, this hotel is stylishly furnished to reflect its Victorian character. Bedrooms include some fine period suites, studio rooms and mews rooms. The smart conservatory restaurant serves dishes which combine classical and modern cooking to appeal to all tastes.

**ROOMS:** 21 en suite (4 fmly) s £55-£95; d £90-£145 (incl. bkfst) * **LB** **FACILITIES:** STV Fishing Shooting Xmas **CONF:** Thtr 100 Class 60 Board 50 Del from £99 * **PARKING:** 17 **NOTES:** Civ Wed 100
**CARDS:**

### ★★69% *Royal Oak Inn*
Bongate CA16 6UN
☎ 017683 51463 🖷 017683 52300
e-mail: m.m.royaloak@btinternet.com
*Dir: from M6 junct 38 follow B6260, hotel is 0.5m from Appleby centre on old A66 in direction of Scotch Corner*

An inn of character, providing smart well-equipped accommodation. The traditional bars are packed full of history and include beamed ceilings, open fires and real ales. A commendable range of food is served in hearty portions from imaginative menus.

**ROOMS:** 9 rms (7 en suite) (1 fmly) **CONF:** Class 20 Board 15 **PARKING:** 13 **CARDS:**

APPLETON-LE-MOORS, North Yorkshire Map 08 SE78

### ★★68% Appleton Hall Country House Hotel
YO62 6TF
☎ 01751 417227 🖷 01751 417540
*Dir: 1.5m off A170 between Helmsley & Pickering*

Set in extensive gardens, this well maintained gracious Victorian country house offers a comfortable lounge with a real fire in a marble fireplace, a cosy residents' bar and an elegant dining room, where interesting traditional cooking is served. Bedrooms are all individually and attractively decorated, well-equipped, and two have their own lounges.

**ROOMS:** 9 en suite No smoking in all bedrooms s £64-£74; d £128-£166 (incl. bkfst & dinner) * **FACILITIES:** Croquet lawn **SERVICES:** Lift **PARKING:** 12 **NOTES:** No dogs (ex guide dogs) No children 14yrs No smoking in restaurant **CARDS:**

ARNCLIFFE, North Yorkshire Map 07 SD97

### ★★76% ◎◎ *Amerdale House*
BD23 5QE
☎ 01756 770250 🖷 01756 770266
*Dir: fork left off Threshfield-Kettlewell road 0.5m past Kilnsey Crag*

There are fine views of the dale and fells from every bedroom in this delightful former manor house. The welcoming lounges have roaring fires in cold weather, and the comfortable bedrooms are

*continued*

decorated with style and elegance. In the dining room a hand-written dinner menu offers skilfully prepared dishes utilising local ingredients.

**ROOMS:** 10 en suite 1 annexe en suite (3 fmly) **PARKING:** 30 **NOTES:** No dogs (ex guide dogs) No smoking in restaurant Closed mid Nov-mid Mar **CARDS:**

ARUNDEL, West Sussex Map 04 TQ00

### ★★★71% Burpham Country House & Restaurant

Old Down, Burpham BN18 9RJ
☎ 01903 882160 01903 884627
***Dir:*** *3m NE off A27 turning by Arundel Railway Station clearly signed to hotel, Warningcamp & Burpham, continue for 2.5m along lane, hotel on right*

Dating back to the 18th century, this hotel has an interesting history. Nowadays this small country house hotel offers a warm welcome and attractive accommodation, which so many regulars enjoy. The cosy public areas include a bar and lounge. The smart restaurant, which is part conservatory, serves good quality meals. **ROOMS:** 10 en suite No smoking in all bedrooms s £45-£65; d £90-£110 * **LB FACILITIES:** Croquet lawn **CONF:** Board 12 **PARKING:** 12 **NOTES:** No dogs No children 10yrs No smoking in restaurant RS Mon **CARDS:**

### ★★★66% Norfolk Arms

Forestdale Hotels

High St BN18 9AD
☎ 01903 882101 01903 884275
e-mail: norfolk.arms@forestdale.com
***Dir:*** *in centre of High Street*

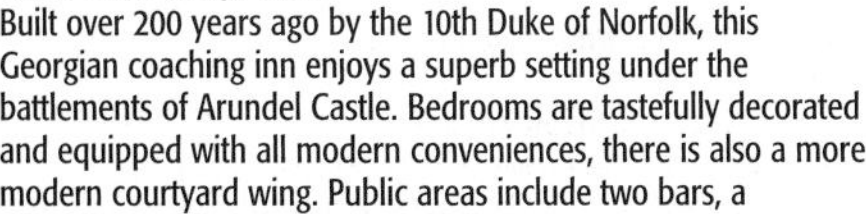

Built over 200 years ago by the 10th Duke of Norfolk, this Georgian coaching inn enjoys a superb setting under the battlements of Arundel Castle. Bedrooms are tastefully decorated and equipped with all modern conveniences, there is also a more modern courtyard wing. Public areas include two bars, a

*continued on p58*

ARUNDEL, continued

comfortable lounge, a traditional English restaurant and a range of meeting rooms.
**ROOMS:** 21 en suite 13 annexe en suite (4 fmly) No smoking in 3 bedrooms s £62-£67; d £124-£134 (incl. bkfst & dinner) * **LB** **FACILITIES:** Xmas **CONF:** Thtr 100 Class 40 Board 40 Del £100 * **PARKING:** 34 **NOTES:** Civ Wed **CARDS:**

### ★★68% Comfort Inn

Junction A27/A284, Crossbush BN17 7QQ
☎ 01903 840840 🖹 01903 849849
e-mail: admin@gb642.u-net.com
***Dir:*** *from Worthing on the A27 towards Arundel, turn left on the A284 towards Littlehampton and straight right, hotel next to McDonalds restaurant*
This modern, purpose-built hotel provides a good base for exploring the nearby historic town of Arundel and the ancient walled city of Chichester. Good access to local road networks and a range of meeting rooms also make this an ideal venue for business guests. Bedrooms are spacious, smartly decorated and very well-equipped.
**ROOMS:** 53 en suite (4 fmly) No smoking in 39 bedrooms s £65; d £44-£75 * **LB** **FACILITIES:** STV Xmas **CONF:** Thtr 30 Class 12 Board 24 Del from £49.50 * **PARKING:** 50 **NOTES:** No smoking in restaurant **CARDS:**

## ASCOT, Berkshire — Map 04 SU96

### ★★★★68% The Royal Berkshire

London Rd, Sunninghill SL5 0PP
☎ 01344 623322 🖹 01344 627100
e-mail: royalberkshireRS@jarvis.co.uk
***Dir:*** *from A30, toward Bagshot turn right opposite Wentworth Club onto A329, continue for 2m hotel entrance on right*

Originally built for the Churchill family, the Royal Berkshire Hotel enjoys a peaceful location, set in 14 acres of grounds and gardens. Bedrooms are generally spacious and well-equipped. There is also an elegant lounge and a smart restaurant.
**ROOMS:** 63 en suite (1 fmly) No smoking in 34 bedrooms s £195; d £220 (incl. bkfst) * **LB** **FACILITIES:** STV Indoor swimming (H) Tennis (hard) Sauna Gym Croquet lawn Putting green Jacuzzi **CONF:** Thtr 80 Class 60 Board 35 Del from £175 * **PARKING:** 250 **NOTES:** No smoking in restaurant Civ Wed 40
**CARDS:**

> Late for dinner? Quality Standards star rating means that last orders for dinner should be no earlier than:
> ★ 6.30pm ★★ 7.00pm ★★★ 8.00pm
> ★★★★ 9.00pm ★★★★★ 10.00pm

### ★★★★64% The Berystede

Bagshot Rd, Sunninghill SL5 9JH
☎ 0870 400 8111 🖹 01344 872301
e-mail: brianshanahan@forte-hotels.com
***Dir:*** *turn off A30 onto B3020 (Windmill Pub). Continue for approx. 1.25m to hotel on left just before junct with A330*
This impressive Victorian mansion, close to Ascot Racecourse, is set in nine acres of wooded grounds. Spacious bedrooms have comfortable armchairs and Internet facilities for guest use. There is a cosy bar and a restaurant which overlooks the heated outdoor swimming pool and gardens.
**ROOMS:** 90 en suite (6 fmly) No smoking in 36 bedrooms s fr £166; d fr £198 (incl. bkfst) * **LB** **FACILITIES:** STV Outdoor swimming (H) Croquet lawn Putting green Xmas **CONF:** Thtr 120 Class 55 Board 50 Del from £105 * **SERVICES:** Lift **PARKING:** 240 **NOTES:** No smoking in restaurant Civ Wed 60 **CARDS:**

### ★★74% *Highclere*

19 Kings Rd, Sunninghill SL5 9AD
☎ 01344 625220 🖹 01344 872528
***Dir:*** *opposite Sunninghill Post Office*
This privately owned and run hotel is quietly situated in a residential area of the town. Bedrooms are attractively furnished, whilst good home cooked meals are served in the restaurant. The cosy bar is complemented by a conservatory lounge and service is both attentive and friendly.
**ROOMS:** 11 en suite (1 fmly) No smoking in 3 bedrooms **FACILITIES:** STV **PARKING:** 11 **NOTES:** No dogs (ex guide dogs) No smoking in restaurant **CARDS:**

### ★★66% Brockenhurst

Brockenhurst Rd SL5 9HA
☎ 01344 621912 🖹 01344 873252
***Dir:*** *on A330*
This attractive Edwardian house is situated south of the town and offers easy access to the race course, the historic town of Windsor and several local golf courses. Bedrooms are spacious and feature a range of thoughtful extras.
**ROOMS:** 11 en suite 5 annexe en suite (2 fmly) s £100; d £89-£150 (incl. cont bkfst) * **FACILITIES:** STV ch fac Xmas **CONF:** Thtr 50 Class 25 Board 30 Del from £135 * **PARKING:** 32 **NOTES:** No dogs (ex guide dogs) **CARDS:**

### ○ Innkeeper's Lodge Ascot

London Rd SL5 7SB
A new concept in the travel accommodation market. Smart rooms meet essential business requirements but also have home comforts. Dining options include all-day menus plus the added advantage of breakfast, which is included in the room price. Reservations can be made seven days a week through the room reservations number: 0870 243 0500. For further details, consult the Hotel Groups page.
**ROOMS:** 10 en suite **NOTES:** Open now

## ASHBOURNE, Derbyshire — Map 07 SK14

### ★★★73% Callow Hall

Mappleton Rd DE6 2AA
☎ 01335 300900 🖹 01335 300512
e-mail: reservations@callowhall.demon.co.uk
***Dir:*** *take A515 through Ashbourne toward Buxton, turn left at Bowling Green pub on left, then first right*
This delightful, creeper-clad, early Victorian house, set in a 44 acre estate, enjoys views over Bentley Brook and the Dove Valley. The atmosphere is relaxed and welcoming and some spacious main house bedrooms have comfortable sitting areas. Public rooms

*continued*

feature high ceilings, ornate plasterwork and antique furniture. There is a good range of dishes available from the fixed price and carte menus.

**ROOMS:** 16 en suite (2 fmly) No smoking in 8 bedrooms s £85-£110; d £130-£165 (incl. bkfst) * **LB** **FACILITIES:** Fishing **CONF:** Thtr 30 Board 16 Del from £136.50 * **PARKING:** 21 **NOTES:** No dogs (ex guide dogs) No smoking in restaurant Closed 25-26 Dec
**CARDS:**

*See advert on this page*

**★★★66% Hanover International Hotel & Club**
Derby Rd DE6 1XH
☎ 01335 346666 01335 346549
e-mail: hanoversales@ashbourneh.freeserve.co.uk
***Dir:*** *on A52 to Ashbourne at rdbt take right turn to Airfield Ind Est, hotel is 400yds on right*

Just a short drive from the town, this modern, purpose-built hotel offers comfortable, well-equipped bedrooms, some especially designed for visitors with disabilities. The attractive Brasserie 209 offers a good choice of dishes.
**ROOMS:** 50 en suite (5 fmly) No smoking in 10 bedrooms s £85-£95; d £100-£110 (incl. bkfst) * **LB** **FACILITIES:** STV Indoor swimming (H) Sauna Gym Steam room Fitness room **CONF:** Thtr 200 Class 100 Board 80 Del £110 * **SERVICES:** Lift **PARKING:** 130 **NOTES:** No dogs (ex guide dogs) No smoking in restaurant Civ Wed 200
**CARDS:**

**★★61% *The Dog & Partridge***
Swinscoe DE6 2HS
☎ 01335 343183
***Dir:*** *from Ashbourne take A52 towards Leek, hotel after 4m on left*
This 17th-century inn sits in the hamlet of Swinscoe, within easy reach of Alton Towers. Accommodation styles vary, most are separate weather boarded rooms within the grounds. Well-

*continued on p60*

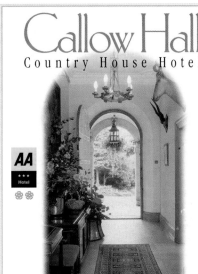

ASHBOURNE, continued

A

presented self-catering units are sometimes used during quieter periods. Meals are available every evening until late.
**ROOMS:** 25 en suite **PARKING:** 90
**CARDS:**

## ASHBURTON, Devon Map 03 SX77

### ★★★74% Holne Chase
Two Bridges Rd TQ13 7NS
☎ 01364 631471 01364 631453
e-mail: info@holne-chase.co.uk
***Dir:*** *3m N on Two Bridges/Tavistock road (unclass)*
This former hunting lodge is peacefully situated in a secluded position with sweeping lawns leading down to the river. Bedrooms, attractively and individually furnished, are split between the main house and a converted stable block, and a number of split-level suites are available. Good quality local produce features on the daily changing menu. At our press date Rosettes for food were not yet confirmed. Please check the AA website for current information.
**ROOMS:** 11 en suite 6 annexe en suite (8 fmly) s £95-£105; d £130-£170 (incl. bkfst) * **LB** **FACILITIES:** Fishing Croquet lawn Putting green Fly fishing ch fac Xmas **CONF:** Thtr 30 Class 20 Board 20 Del from £150 * **PARKING:** 40 **NOTES:** No smoking in restaurant
**CARDS:**

*See advert on page 59*

### ★★67% *The Lavender House*
Knowle Hill TQ13 7QY
☎ 01364 652697 01364 654325
e-mail: leonroberts@btconnect.com
***Dir:*** *turn off A38 at Peartree, go uphill & after approx 400yds look for hotel sign on right, hotel within 100yds*
Much renovation has taken place here over the last few years to create a hotel with pretty, stylish, individual bedrooms, a very comfortable lounge, welcoming bar and more intimate restaurant. Set in approximately three acres, views are lovely and peace and quiet prevail.
**ROOMS:** 10 en suite (2 fmly) **CONF:** Thtr 60 Class 50 Board 16
**PARKING:** 100 **NOTES:** No smoking in restaurant Civ Wed
**CARDS:**

## ASHFORD, Kent Map 05 TR04

### ★★★★75% Eastwell Manor
Eastwell Park, Boughton Lees TN25 4HR
☎ 01233 213000 01233 635530
e-mail: eastwell@btinternet.com
***Dir:*** *on A251, 200 yds on left when entering Boughton Aluph*

PRIDE OF BRITAIN MEMBER

A fine hotel set in 62 acres of beautiful grounds and gardens.

*continued*

Original features such as open fires and wood panelling create impressive public areas. Spacious, individually decorated bedrooms include many thoughtful extras. A high standard of cuisine is served in the traditional dining room. The recently built spa complex is superb.
**ROOMS:** 23 en suite 39 annexe en suite (2 fmly) No smoking in 4 bedrooms s £170-£325; d £200-£355 (incl. bkfst) * **LB**
**FACILITIES:** Spa STV Indoor swimming (H) Outdoor swimming (H) Tennis (hard) Sauna Solarium Gym Croquet lawn Putting green Jacuzzi Boule, Hairdressing salon & Beauty spa entertainment Xmas **CONF:** Thtr 200 Class 60 Board 48 Del £195 * **SERVICES:** Lift **PARKING:** 80
**NOTES:** No smoking in restaurant Civ Wed 250
**CARDS:**

### ★★★★64% Ashford International
Simone Weil Av TN24 8UX
☎ 01233 219988 01233 647743
e-mail: info@ashfordinthotel.co.uk
***Dir:*** *off junct 9, M20*
A modern, purpose-built hotel, within easy reach of the M20. As a central feature it boasts a long mall containing boutiques and several places to eat, including a popular brasserie and The Alhambra, a more formal restaurant. Bedrooms are spacious and well-equipped.
**ROOMS:** 200 en suite (4 fmly) No smoking in 57 bedrooms s £99; d £99 * **LB** **FACILITIES:** Indoor swimming (H) Sauna Solarium Gym Jacuzzi Xmas **CONF:** Thtr 400 **SERVICES:** Lift **PARKING:** 400
**NOTES:** No smoking in restaurant Civ Wed
**CARDS:**

### ★★★64% *Posthouse Ashford*
Canterbury Rd TN24 8QQ

Posthouse

☎ 0870 400 9001 01233 643176
***Dir:*** *off A28*
Suitable for both the business and leisure traveller, this bright hotel provides modern accommodation in well-equipped bedrooms. The bar and restaurant are full of character and old world charm.
**ROOMS:** 103 en suite (45 fmly) No smoking in 60 bedrooms
**FACILITIES:** ch fac **CONF:** Thtr 120 Class 65 Board 40 **PARKING:** 130
**CARDS:**

### ★★68% Pilgrims Rest
Canterbury Rd, Kennington TN24 9QR

Best Western

☎ 01233 636863 01233 610119
e-mail: pilgrimsrest@fullers.demon.co.uk
***Dir:*** *on A28 1m N of town centre, and 1m from junct 9/10 on M20*
Set in five acres of mature grounds, this hotel overlooks the North Downs. Bedrooms are comfortably appointed and well-equipped with modern amenities. The focal point is the informal, open plan bar and restaurant which has been extensively refurbished.
**ROOMS:** 34 en suite (1 fmly) No smoking in 12 bedrooms s £49-£55; d £49-£55 * **LB** **FACILITIES:** STV **CONF:** Thtr 75 Class 40 Board 40 Del from £85 * **PARKING:** 60 **CARDS:**

Read all about it! Newspapers delivered to bedrooms in four and five star hotels.

Popped the question? Hotels with Civ Wed in their entry are licensed for civil wedding ceremonies. Maximum numbers for the ceremony only are shown, e.g. Civ Wed 120

**Travelodge**
Eureka Leisure Park TN25 4BN
☎ 08700 850 950

Travelodge

Travelodge offers good quality, good value, modern accommodation. Ideal for families, the spacious, en suite bedrooms include remote-control TV, tea and coffee-making facilities, luxury beds and free morning newspaper. Meals can be taken at the nearby family restaurant. For further details and the Travelodge phone number, consult the Hotel Groups page.

## ASHFORD-IN-THE-WATER, Derbyshire Map 07 SK17

*Courtesy & Care Award*

★★★79% Riverside House
Fennel St DE45 1QF
☎ 01629 814275 01629 812873
e-mail: riversidehouse@enta.net
***Dir:*** *turn right off A6 Bakewell/Buxton road 2m from Bakewell village, hotel at end of main street*
Partly dating back to 1630, this delightful hotel in the centre of the village is surrounded by gardens beside the River Wye. It offers individually decorated bedrooms, and public rooms include a conservatory, an oak-panelled lounge with inglenook fireplace, a drawing room and two dining rooms. Good quality cuisine is served and service is attentive. Riverside House has been awarded the AA Courtesy & Care Award for England 2001-2002.
**ROOMS:** 15 en suite No smoking in all bedrooms s £95-£135; d £115-£155 (incl. bkfst) * **LB** **FACILITIES:** STV Croquet lawn Xmas **CONF:** Thtr 15 Class 15 Board 15 Del £170 * **PARKING:** 40 **NOTES:** No dogs (ex guide dogs) No children 10yrs No smoking in restaurant Civ Wed 30 **CARDS:**

*See advert on this page*



## ASHTON-UNDER-LYNE, Greater Manchester Map 07 SJ99

★★71% **York House**
York Place, Richmond St OL6 7TT
☎ 0161 330 9000 0161 343 1613
e-mail: enquiries@yorkhouse-hotel.co.uk
***Dir:*** *close to junct A635/A6017*
This elegant Victorian style hotel, offering friendly and attentive service, is conveniently located for Manchester Airport and the city centre. Set around a central courtyard, bedrooms - some housed in cottages - are comfortable and thoughtfully equipped. Seasons Restaurant offers a classical carte menu as well as seasonal changing dishes.
**ROOMS:** 24 en suite 10 annexe en suite (2 fmly) s £52-£65; d £80-£83 (incl. bkfst) * **LB** **FACILITIES:** STV Reduced cost at local gym/pool **CONF:** Thtr 50 Class 20 Board 20 Del £88 * **PARKING:** 34 **NOTES:** Closed 26 Dec RS Sun Civ Wed 60
**CARDS:**

## ASPLEY GUISE, Bedfordshire Map 04 SP93

★★★68% **Moore Place**
The Square MK17 8DW
☎ 01908 282000 01908 281888
e-mail: info@mooreplace.co.uk
***Dir:*** *from M1 junct 13, take A507, follow signs for Aspley Guise and Woburn Sands. Hotel is on left hand side of village square*
This impressive Georgian house, set in delightful gardens in the centre of the village, is very conveniently located for access to the M1. Public rooms include a foyer lounge, a cosy bar and a smart conservatory restaurant, all overlooking the pretty gardens. The bedrooms do vary in size, but consideration has been given to

*continued on p62*

ASPLEY GUISE, continued

guest comfort, with many thoughtful extras provided. The range of meeting rooms and private dining options are considerable.

*Moore Place, Aspley Guise*

**ROOMS:** 39 en suite 15 annexe en suite s £90-£190; d £100-£200 (incl. bkfst) * **LB FACILITIES:** STV Xmas **CONF:** Thtr 40 Class 24 Board 20 Del £155 * **PARKING:** 70 **NOTES:** No smoking in restaurant Civ Wed 80 **CARDS:**

## ASTON CLINTON, Buckinghamshire

### ○ Innkeeper's Lodge Aylesbury

London Rd HP22 5HP

A new concept in the travel accommodation market. Smart rooms meet essential business requirements but also have home comforts. Dining options include all-day menus plus the added advantage of breakfast, which is included in the room price. Reservations can be made seven days a week through the room reservations number: 0870 243 0500. For further details, consult the Hotel Groups page.

**ROOMS:** 10 en suite **NOTES:** Opening Autumn 2001

## ATHERSTONE, Warwickshire — Map 04 SP39

### ★★75% Chapel House

Friar's Gate CV9 1EY

☎ 01827 718949 Fax 01827 717702

***Dir:*** *next to St Marys Church in Market Square*

Beside the church, this hotel is an oasis of hospitality and good cooking. The house offers well appointed and appealing dining rooms and a comfortable conservatory lounge overlooking the attractive walled garden; service is both attentive and friendly. Bedrooms are all individual in size and specification. The kitchen produces an interesting variety of dishes.

**ROOMS:** 14 en suite s £52.50-£60 (incl. bkfst) * **LB CONF:** Thtr 15 Board 20 Del from £82.50 * **NOTES:** No dogs (ex guide dogs) No smoking in restaurant Closed 24-26 Dec RS BH

**CARDS:**

*See advert on opposite page*

## AXMINSTER, Devon — Map 03 SY29

### ★★★74% Fairwater Head

Hawkchurch EX13 5TX

☎ 01297 678349 Fax 01297 678459

e-mail: reception@fairwater.demon.co.uk

***Dir:*** *turn off B3165 (Crewkerne to Lyme Regis Road) hotel signposted to Hawkchurch*

A delightful Edwardian house, set in landscaped gardens and rolling countryside. Bedrooms are attractively decorated and furnished, several are in a separate modern house in the grounds. Public areas include comfortable sitting rooms and a spacious dining room, where freshly prepared meals using local produce are served.

**ROOMS:** 14 en suite 7 annexe en suite s £84-£89; d £148-£158 (incl. bkfst) * **LB FACILITIES:** Croquet lawn entertainment ch fac Xmas **CONF:** Thtr 12 Class 12 Board 12 **PARKING:** 30 **NOTES:** No smoking in restaurant Closed mid Dec- Feb (ex Xmas pakages)

**CARDS:**

### ★★79% Lea Hill

Membury EX13 7AQ

☎ 01404 881881 & 881388 Fax 01404 881890

e-mail: reception@leahillhotel.co.uk

***Dir:*** *from George Hotel in Axminster take Membury road and cross level crossing. In Membury continue through village past Trout Farm. Hotel 0.5m on right*

A delightful thatched Devon longhouse, partly dating back to the 1300s, set in unspoilt countryside. Bedrooms are mostly situated in thatched cottages and converted barns around the main house. Rooms are decorated to enhance their cottage style and there is a lounge bar, a study and a meeting room. The flagstone, beamed restaurant serves an imaginative fixed-price menu, prepared from fresh produce, often featuring local fish.

**ROOMS:** 2 en suite 9 annexe en suite No smoking in all bedrooms s £81-£89; d £142-£158 (incl. bkfst & dinner) * **LB FACILITIES:** Golf 9 Croquet lawn Jacuzzi Par 3 9-hole golf course Xmas **CONF:** Del £95 * **PARKING:** 25 **NOTES:** No children 16yrs No smoking in restaurant Closed 3 Jan-1st wk Mar **CARDS:**

## AYLESBURY, Buckinghamshire — Map 04 SP81

**Premier Collection**

### ★★★★ Hartwell House

Oxford Rd HP17 8NL

☎ 01296 747444 Fax 01296 747450

e-mail: info@hartwell-house.com

***Dir:*** *signposted 2m SW on A418 towards Oxford*

This comfortable, welcoming hotel is set in 90 acres of unspoilt parkland. The beautiful historic house has public rooms which are both magnificent and grand. Many fine pieces of art are displayed throughout, whilst the bedrooms are spacious and high in comfort with many thoughtful extras. The restaurant is very elegant with a high standard of service. It serves an imaginative selection of excellent dishes that are created from quality local produce.

**ROOMS:** 30 en suite 16 annexe en suite No smoking in 12 bedrooms s £140-£145; d £225-£235 * **LB FACILITIES:** Indoor swimming (H) Tennis (hard) Fishing Sauna Solarium Gym Croquet lawn Jacuzzi Treatment rooms & Steam rooms entertainment Xmas **CONF:** Thtr 100 Class 40 Board 40 Del from £245 * **SERVICES:** Lift **PARKING:** 91 **NOTES:** No children 8yrs No smoking in restaurant **CARDS:**

**★★★69% Posthouse Aylesbury**
Aston Clinton Rd HP22 5AA
☎ 0870 400 9002 🖹 01296 392211

Posthouse

***Dir:*** *From M25 take junct 20 and follow A41.Posthouse on left as you enter Aylesbury*

This hotel enjoys a prominent position on the south side of the town. It provides a super range of modern meeting rooms within the Academy, and spacious public areas designed to offer superior comfort and flexibility. Bedrooms offer useful facilities for business guests, yet also offer much to guests wishing to while away the afternoon in the leisure centre or bar.

**ROOMS:** 140 en suite (46 fmly) No smoking in 46 bedrooms d £89-£99 * **LB** **FACILITIES:** Indoor swimming (H) Sauna Solarium Gym Jacuzzi ch fac Xmas **CONF:** Thtr 110 Class 80 Board 40 **PARKING:** 164
**CARDS:**

BABBACOMBE See Torquay

## BADMINTON, Gloucestershire

Map 03 ST88

**★★66% Bodkin House**
Petty France GL9 1AF
☎ 01454 238310 🖹 01454 238422
e-mail: info@bodkin-house-hotel.co.uk
***Dir:*** *5.5m N of M4 J18 on A46*

THE CIRCLE
Selected Individual Hotels
GREAT BRITAIN

This charming 17th-century inn is full of historic character, featuring open fires, flagstone floors and oak panelling. Comfortable bedrooms combine traditional style with modern facilities. The restaurant and lounge are attractively decorated and meals can also be taken in the bar.

**ROOMS:** 9 en suite (2 fmly) No smoking in 4 bedrooms
**FACILITIES:** Children's play area **CONF:** Board 20 Del from £80 *
**PARKING:** 40 **NOTES:** No smoking in restaurant
**CARDS:**

*See advert on this page*

## BAGINTON, Warwickshire

Map 04 SP37

**★★70% *Old Mill***
Mill Hill CV8 3AH
☎ 024 76302241 🖹 024 76307070

SCOTTISH NEWCASTLE hotels

***Dir:*** *in village 0.25m from junction A45 & A46*

Enjoying a peaceful riverside location yet within easy access of the motorway networks, the Old Mill has been completely refurbished to a high standard. Spacious bedrooms are smartly appointed and well-equipped. Public areas include the popular Chef & Brewer bar and restaurant.

**ROOMS:** 28 en suite (6 fmly) **CONF:** Class 16 Board 20 **PARKING:** 200
**NOTES:** No dogs (ex guide dogs) No smoking in restaurant
**CARDS:**

BAGSHOT, Surrey Map 04 SU96

## Hotel of the Year

**★★★★★72% Pennyhill Park**
London Rd GU19 5EU
☎ 01276 471774 01276 473217
e-mail: pennyhillpark@msn.com
***Dir:*** *on A30 between Bagshot and Camberley opposite Texaco garage*
This delightful Victorian country house hotel, set in 120 acres of grounds, enjoys the character of the period combined with modern comforts and facilities. Public rooms include a stylish bar and a choice of eating options, one of which serves food with a strong French influence. Individually decorated bedrooms are particularly impressive for their sumptuous furnishings, most of which are antique. Pennyhill Park has been chosen as the AA's Hotel of the Year for England 2001-2002.
**ROOMS:** 26 en suite 97 annexe en suite (6 fmly) No smoking in 20 bedrooms s £193.87-£205.62; d £205.62-£587.50 * **LB**
**FACILITIES:** Outdoor swimming (H) Golf 9 Tennis (hard) Fishing Gym Croquet lawn Archery Clay pigeon shooting Volleyball entertainment ch fac Xmas **CONF:** Thtr 160 Class 80 Board 60 Del from £305.50 * **SERVICES:** Lift **PARKING:** 500 **NOTES:** No smoking in restaurant Civ Wed 160 **CARDS:**

*See advert on opposite page*

BAINBRIDGE, North Yorkshire Map 07 SD99

**★★62% Rose & Crown**
DL8 3EE
☎ 01969 650225 01969 650735
e-mail: stay@rose-and-crown.freeserve.co.uk
***Dir:*** *on A684 between Hawes and Leyburn*

For almost 700 years this appealing coaching inn has warmly welcomed guests crossing the Pennines. There is a strong sense of heritage and character in the bars, featuring roaring open fires.
*continued*
Bedrooms, modern in style, are well-equipped. A wide range of food is served in the bars or in the spacious restaurant.
**ROOMS:** 12 rms (11 en suite) (1 fmly) No smoking in 2 bedrooms s £26-£32; d £52-£64 (incl. bkfst) * **LB** **CONF:** Class 30 Board 30
**PARKING:** 65 **NOTES:** No smoking in restaurant
**CARDS:**

BAKEWELL, Derbyshire Map 08 SK26

**★★★73% Hassop Hall**
Hassop DE45 1NS
☎ 01629 640488 01629 640577
e-mail: hassophallhotel@btinternet.com
***Dir:*** *take B6001 from Bakewell for approx. 2m into Hassop, hotel opposite church*
This magnificent stately home has a history that dates back 900 years to the Domesday Book. It has been lovingly restored whilst retaining all of its charm and character to provide comfortable, thoughtfully equipped accommodation. Public areas are spacious, furnished with antique and period pieces and afford wonderful views over the beautifully tended grounds and gardens.
**ROOMS:** 13 en suite (2 fmly) d £79-£149 * **LB** **FACILITIES:** Tennis (hard) entertainment ch fac **CONF:** Del from £149 * **SERVICES:** Lift
**PARKING:** 80 **NOTES:** Closed 24-25 Dec RS 26 Dec Civ Wed 120
**CARDS:**

**★★★69% Rutland Arms**
The Square DE45 1BT
☎ 01629 812812 01629 812309
e-mail: rutland@bakewell.demon.co.uk
***Dir:*** *on main A6 between Matlock/Manchester. In main square opposite War Memorial*

This historic hotel lies at the very centre of Bakewell. There is a wide range of quality accommodation. The friendly staff are attentive and welcoming, both in the adjacent Tavern bar and in the main hotel. The Four Seasons restaurant offers an interesting menu and fine dining.
**ROOMS:** 18 en suite 17 annexe en suite (1 fmly) No smoking in 10 bedrooms s £47-£52; d £79-£84 (incl. bkfst) * **LB** **FACILITIES:** STV Xmas **CONF:** Thtr 100 Class 60 Board 40 **PARKING:** 25 **NOTES:** No smoking in restaurant **CARDS:**

**★★73% Croft Country House**
Great Longstone DE45 1TF
☎ 01629 640278 01629 640369
e-mail: jthursby@ukonline.co.uk
***Dir:*** *3m N of Bakewell via A619 or A6 and A6020*
Hidden away in mature gardens and grounds, this delightful Victorian house exudes charm. Public rooms leading off from the central galleried lounge include a cosy bar and a restaurant. Meals are served from an interesting four-course set menu. Bedrooms have modern comforts and some fine period pieces. The

*continued on p66*

# ★★ THE CROFT COUNTRY HOUSE HOTEL

The Croft stands in three acres of secluded grounds and was converted to a Country House Hotel in 1984. Consequently, all modern facilities are provided, with the décor and furnishing reflecting the Victorian period from which the house dates.
A spectacular feature of the house is the Main Hall with its lantern ceiling and galleried landing. From the landing lead nine en-suite bedrooms, all with colour TV, tea and coffee making facilities. There is a lift, and one bedroom suitable for wheelchair access.
The restaurant offers a table d'hôte menu, which is changed daily with imaginative dishes based on local produce. To accompany your meal, you can select from the extensive wine list and if you pick a Saturday night for your soiree Magic! is always on the menu with tea, coffee and drinks in the Main Hall or Sitting Room.

**Great Longstone, Bakewell, Derbyshire DE45 1TF**
**Telephone: 01629 640278 Fax: 01629 640369**
**Email: jthursby@ukonline.co.uk**
**Website: www.croftcountryhouse.co.uk**

# EAST LODGE

## COUNTRY HOUSE HOTEL & RESTAURANT

East Lodge, a haven of peace and tranquillity, set in 10 acres of picturesque Derbyshire countryside has a reputation for service, comfort and style with a delightfully warm and friendly ambience.

All the fully en-suite bedrooms are charmingly individual, and equipped with all the facilities required for you comfort, convenience and enjoyment. With the elegant public rooms, and fully licensed bar it adds up to a convivial and convenient location for exploring the many delights of the Peak District.

The newly refurbished, air conditioned award wining restaurant at East Lodge is open for lunch & dinner every day.

*For reservations, brochures and other details.*
**Telephone: 01629 734474 Fax: 01629 733949**
★★★ **Email: info@eastlodge.com**
AA Rowsley, Matlock, Derbyshire

# EXCLUSIVE
## HOTELS & GOLF CLUBS

★★★★★

Pennyhill Park
HOTEL & COUNTRY CLUB

AA *Hotel of the Year, England*

"Having never stayed in a five star hotel before we can see how you achieve such a status...The staff go above and beyond to make you feel at home"

*Mark Startin*

"We have been going to Pennyhill since it opened as a hotel... it just gets better and better"

*Alex Watters*

*London Road, Bagshot, Surrey GU19 5EU*
*Telephone:* ***01276 471774***
*Reservations Fax: 01276 473217*
*Email: enquiries@pennyhillpark.co.uk*

www.exclusivehotels.co.uk

*Pennyhill Park Hotel & Country Club • South Lodge Hotel • Mannings Heath Golf Club • Lainston House Hotel*
*The Manor House Hotel at Castle Combe • The Manor House Golf Club at Castle Combe*

BAKEWELL, continued

proprietor is an accomplished magician and there is usually an after-dinner performance on a Saturday night.

*Croft Country House, Bakewell*

**ROOMS:** 9 en suite No smoking in all bedrooms s fr £63; d fr £104 (incl. bkfst) * LB **FACILITIES:** Xmas **SERVICES:** Lift **PARKING:** 30 **NOTES:** No dogs (ex guide dogs) No children 10yrs No smoking in restaurant Closed Jan-2nd wk Feb **CARDS:**

*See advert on page 65*

### ★★68% Monsal Head Hotel

Monsal Head DE45 1NL
☎ 01629 640250 ▤ 01629 640815
e-mail: christine@monsalhead.com
***Dir:*** *Take A6 from Bakewell to Buxton in 2m turn into Ashford in the Water, take B6465 for 1m*

Popular with walkers, this friendly hotel overlooks the Monsal Dale in the centre of the Peak District National Park. Bedrooms are well-equipped, and four have superb views along the valley. There is a comfortable lounge with an open fire and a good selection of games. The hotel specialises in local food, real ales and fine wines. **ROOMS:** 8 en suite (1 fmly) s £38-£45; d £46-£60 (incl. bkfst) * LB **FACILITIES:** entertainment **CONF:** Thtr 80 Class 30 Board 30 **PARKING:** 20 **NOTES:** No smoking in restaurant Closed 25 Dec **CARDS:**

## BALDOCK, Hertfordshire — Map 04 TL23

### Travelodge

Travelodge

Great North Rd, Hinxworth SG7 5EX
☎ 01462 835329 ▤ 01462 835329
***Dir:*** *on A1, southbound*

Travelodge offers good quality, good value, modern accommodation. Ideal for families, the spacious, en suite bedrooms include remote-control TV, tea and coffee-making facilities, luxury beds and free morning newspaper. Meals can be taken at the nearby family restaurant. For further details and the Travelodge phone number, consult the Hotel Groups page.

**ROOMS:** 40 en suite

## BALSALL COMMON, West Midlands — Map 04 SP27

### ★★★★67% Nailcote Hall

Nailcote Ln, Berkswell CV7 7DE
☎ 024 7646 6174 ▤ 024 7647 0720
e-mail: info@nailcotehall.co.uk
***Dir:*** *on B4101*

Steeped in history, this charming Elizabethan manor house remains largely unspoilt. The intimate restaurant offers exciting menus and fine dining, and more informal options are offered within Rick's leisure and conference complex. The modern bedroom wing provides a contrast of styles, while the more traditional bedrooms are in the main house.

**ROOMS:** 21 en suite 17 annexe en suite (2 fmly) s £145; d £155 (incl. bkfst) * LB **FACILITIES:** Indoor swimming (H) Golf 9 Tennis (hard) Snooker Solarium Gym Croquet lawn Putting green Jacuzzi entertainment Xmas **CONF:** Thtr 100 Class 80 Board 45 **SERVICES:** Lift **PARKING:** 200 **NOTES:** No dogs (ex guide dogs) No smoking in restaurant Civ Wed 120 **CARDS:**

*See advert under SOLIHULL*

### ★★76% Haigs

Kenilworth Rd CV7 7EL
☎ 01676 533004 ▤ 01676 535132
***Dir:*** *on A452 4m N of Kenilworth and 6m S of M6 junct 4. 5m S of M42 junct 6. 8m N of M40 junct 15*

Set in residential surroundings, this charming, stylish hotel offers a warm welcome and attentive service. The newer bedrooms are particularly attractive and comfortable. Public areas include the lounge bar, a meeting room and The Poppies restaurant, where an interesting and varied range of carefully prepared dishes is offered.
**ROOMS:** 23 en suite No smoking in 8 bedrooms s £60-£66; d £85-£90 (incl. bkfst) * **CONF:** Thtr 35 Class 20 Board 20 Del from £120 * **PARKING:** 22 **NOTES:** No dogs (ex guide dogs) No smoking in restaurant Closed 26 Dec-3 Jan & Etr **CARDS:**

## BAMBURGH, Northumberland — Map 12 NU13

### ★★★68% Waren House

Waren Mill NE70 7EE
☎ 01668 214581 ▤ 01668 214484
e-mail: enquiries@warenhousehotel.co.uk
***Dir:*** *2m E of A1 turn off on B1342 to Waren Mill, at T-junct turn right, hotel 100yds on right*

Set in six acres of mature woodlands and formal gardens, this delightful Georgian country house hotel offers guests a peaceful haven. Beautiful bedrooms and suites are themed in differing

*continued*

styles and all provide good levels of comfort. Public rooms are attractively furnished and include an elegant dining room, comfortable drawing room and adjoining library.
**ROOMS:** 10 en suite No smoking in 9 bedrooms s fr £90; d £120-£190 (incl. bkfst) * **LB** **FACILITIES:** Croquet lawn Xmas **CONF:** Class 24 Board 24 Del from £98 * **PARKING:** 20 **NOTES:** No children 14yrs No smoking in restaurant **CARDS:**

### ★★73% Victoria
Front St NE69 7BP
☎ 01668 214431 01668 214404
e-mail: enquiries@victoriahotel.net
***Dir:*** *turn off the A1 north of Alnwick onto the B1342, near Belford & follow signs to Bamburgh. Hotel in centre of Bamburgh opposite the village green.*

Friendly and attentive service is just one feature of this hotel, which has been stylishly refurbished. The ground floor areas include a light modern Brasserie with conservatory roof, a popular bar with open fire, and an indoor children's play den. Bedrooms are cheerful and well equipped.
**ROOMS:** 29 en suite (2 fmly) No smoking in 18 bedrooms s £47-£50; d £84-£130 (incl. bkfst) * **LB** **FACILITIES:** Gamesroom Childrens play den entertainment ch fac Xmas **CONF:** Thtr 50 Class 30 Board 20 **PARKING:** 12 **NOTES:** No smoking in restaurant
**CARDS:**

### ★★66% Lord Crewe Arms
Front St NE69 7BL
☎ 01668 214243 01668 214273
e-mail: lca@tinyonline.co.uk
***Dir:*** *just below the castle*
Developed from an old country inn, this inviting hotel lies in the centre of the village, where the impressive Bamburgh Castle dominates the skyline. There is a choice of lounges, and food is served in both of the bar lounges and the cosy cottage-style restaurant.
**ROOMS:** 18 rms (17 en suite) s £40-£60; d £65-£99 (incl. bkfst) * **PARKING:** 20 **NOTES:** No dogs (ex guide dogs) No children 5yrs No smoking in restaurant Closed Dec-Feb **CARDS:**

### ★★65% *The Mizen Head*
Lucker Rd NE69 7BS
☎ 01668 214254 01668 214104
***Dir:*** *turn off the A1 onto the B1341 for Bamburgh, the hotel is the first building on the left as you enter the village*
Set in gardens, on the western edge of the village, this family-run hotel offers a relaxed and friendly atmosphere. Ample car-parking, an excellent base for touring Northumberland, and a wide range of good value meals are the hallmarks of this hotel.

**ROOMS:** 13 rms (12 en suite) (2 fmly) **FACILITIES:** Darts ch fac **CONF:** Class 45 **PARKING:** 30 **NOTES:** No smoking in restaurant **CARDS:**

## BAMFORD, Derbyshire — Map 08 SK28

### ★★70% Yorkshire Bridge Inn
Ashopton Rd, Hope Valley S33 0AZ
☎ 01433 651361 01433 651361
e-mail: mr@ybridge.force9.co.uk
***Dir:*** *A57 Sheffield/Glossop Road, at Ladybower Reservoir take A6013 Bamford Road, Yorkshire Bridge Inn is on the right hand side in 1m*
A well-established country inn, ideally located within reach of the Peak District's many attractions and beauty spots. The hotel offers a wide range of excellent dishes in both the bar and dining area, along with a good selection of real ales. Bedrooms are attractively furnished, comfortable and well-equipped.
**ROOMS:** 14 en suite (3 fmly) No smoking in 10 bedrooms s £43; d £58-£64 (incl. bkfst) * **LB** **FACILITIES:** Xmas **CONF:** Class 12 **PARKING:** 40 **CARDS:**

## BANBURY, Oxfordshire — Map 04 SP44

### ★★★70% Banbury House
Best Western
Oxford Rd OX16 9AH
☎ 01295 259361 01295 270954
e-mail: banburyhouse@compuserve.com
***Dir:*** *approx 200yds from Banbury Cross on the A423 towards Oxford*
An attractive Georgian property, Banbury House is smart and comfortable with modern facilities. Friendly and attentive staff help to create a welcoming atmosphere. Public areas include a lounge, cellar bar and a restaurant. A bar menu is available.
**ROOMS:** 63 en suite (4 fmly) No smoking in 24 bedrooms s £87; d £97 * **LB** **FACILITIES:** STV **CONF:** Thtr 70 Class 35 Board 28 Del from £125 * **PARKING:** 60 **NOTES:** No dogs (ex guide dogs) Closed 24 Dec-1 Jan **CARDS:**

### ★★★70% Wroxton House
Best Western
Wroxton St Mary OX15 6QB
☎ 01295 730777 01295 730800
e-mail: wroxtonhse@aol.com
***Dir:*** *follow A422 from Banbury, 2.5m to Wroxton, hotel on right on entering village*
Converted from three 17th-century cottages, this charming hotel is situated just two miles west of Banbury. Guests will find this a pleasant retreat. Bedrooms are well-equipped and vary in style from the more traditionally furnished in the older wing to modern

*continued on p68*

BANBURY, continued

rooms. The elegant restaurant offers a range of dishes, making good use of local produce.
**ROOMS:** 29 en suite 3 annexe en suite (1 fmly) No smoking in 14 bedrooms s £80-£95; d £95-£105 * **LB** **FACILITIES:** STV Xmas **CONF:** Thtr 45 Class 20 Board 28 **PARKING:** 50 **NOTES:** No dogs (ex guide dogs) No smoking in restaurant Closed 28-30 Dec RS 31 Dec & 1 Jan Civ Wed 60 **CARDS:**

### ★★★68% Whately Hall

Banbury Cross OX16 0AN
☎ 0870 400 8104 🖷 01295 271736
e-mail: whately_hall@forte-hotels.com
***Dir:*** *from M40 junct 11. Straight over 2 rdbts, turn left at 3rd, carry on to Banbury Cross about 1/4m & hotel on right*
This hotel, originally a 17th-century coaching inn, is close to Banbury Cross. The bedrooms, varying in size and style, are well-equipped. Spacious and very comfortable public areas include cosy lounges and an informal bar. Some of the original oak panelling and the black beams are still intact and service is attentive and friendly.
**ROOMS:** 72 en suite (1 fmly) No smoking in 24 bedrooms s £85-£118; d £95-£128 (incl. bkfst) * **LB** **FACILITIES:** Croquet lawn Xmas **CONF:** Thtr 150 Class 80 Board 40 **SERVICES:** Lift **PARKING:** 80 **NOTES:** Civ Wed 100 **CARDS:**

### ★★63% *Cromwell Lodge Hotel*

North Bar OX16 0TB
☎ 01295 259781 🖷 01295 276619
Conveniently located in the north of the town, the building dates back to the 17th century. The walled garden with enormous beech trees is a great attraction in summer months. Bedrooms are modern and well-equipped, some opening directly into the garden. Both more formal restaurant style dining and bar meals are available.
**ROOMS:** 32 en suite (1 fmly) **FACILITIES:** ch fac **PARKING:** 25 **NOTES:** Closed 1 wk Xmas & New Year **CARDS:**

### 🏠 *Premier Lodge*

PREMIER LODGE

Warwick Rd, Warmington OX17 1JJ
☎ 0870 700 1310 🖷 0870 7001311
Premier Lodge offers modern, well-equipped, en suite accommodation suitable for both business and leisure travellers. Meals can be taken at the adjacent popular restaurant and bar, which is fully licensed. For further details, consult the Hotel Groups page.
**ROOMS:** 15 en suite

## BARFORD, Warwickshire — Map 04 SP26

### ★★★69% The Glebe at Barford

Church St CV35 8BS
☎ 01926 624218 🖷 01926 624625
e-mail: sales@glebehotel.co.uk
***Dir:*** *leave M40 junct 15, take exit A429 Barford/Wellesbourne, at mini island turn left, hotel 500mtrs on right*
The giant Lebanese cedar tree in front of this hotel was ancient even in 1820 when the original rectory was first built. Today, bedrooms have been individually decorated in soft pastel fabrics, with coronet, tented ceiling or four-poster style beds. Public rooms include the Cedars Conservatory Restaurant, a small, well-equipped leisure facility and lounge bar with marbled floor.
**ROOMS:** 39 en suite (3 fmly) s £98; d £118 (incl. bkfst) * **FACILITIES:** STV Indoor swimming (H) Sauna Solarium Gym Croquet lawn Jacuzzi Beauty salon Xmas **CONF:** Thtr 120 Class 60 Board 60 Del £149 * **SERVICES:** Lift **PARKING:** 60 **CARDS:**

## BARKING, Greater London — Map 05 TQ48

### 🏠 Hotel Ibis

Highbridge Rd IG11 7BA
☎ 020 8477 4100 🖷 020 8477 4101
e-mail: H2042@accor-hotels.com
***Dir:*** *exit Barking on A406*
Modern, budget hotel offering comfortable accommodation in bright and practical bedrooms. Breakfast is self-service and dinner is available in the restaurant. For further details, consult the Hotel Groups page.
**ROOMS:** 86 en suite s fr £58; d fr £62 *

## BARLBOROUGH, Derbyshire — Map 08 SK47

### 🏠 Hotel Ibis

Tally's End, Chesterfield Rd S43 4TX
☎ 01246 813222 🖷 01246 813444
***Dir:*** *leave M1 junct 30. Head towards A619. Right at rdbt towards Chesterfield. Hotel is immediately left*
Modern, budget hotel offering comfortable accommodation in bright and practical bedrooms. Breakfast is self-service and dinner is available in the restaurant. For further details, consult the Hotel Groups page.
**ROOMS:** 86 en suite s £32-£42; d £32-£42 * **CONF:** Thtr 35 Board 20 Del £79 *

## BARNARD CASTLE, Co Durham — Map 12 NZ01

### ★★★67% Morritt Arms Hotel & Restaurant

Greta Bridge DL12 9SE
☎ 01833 627232 🖷 01833 627392
e-mail: relax@themorritt.co.uk
***Dir:*** *A1 Scotch Corner, turn onto A66 in direction of Penrith and after 9m turn off at Greta Bridge. Hotel just over the bridge on left*
This delightful 17th century coaching house offers comfortable public rooms, including an open-plan lounge and a bar with an interesting Dickensian mural. The well-equipped bedrooms come in a variety of shapes and sizes and the wood-panelled dining room serves a selection of appetising meals. Service is friendly and professional.
**ROOMS:** 23 en suite No smoking in 16 bedrooms s £59.50-£75; d £83.50-£101.50 (incl. bkfst) * **LB** **FACILITIES:** Membership of nearby leisure facility Xmas **CONF:** Thtr 200 Class 100 Board 125 Del £85.50 * **PARKING:** 100 **NOTES:** No smoking in restaurant Civ Wed 200 **CARDS:**

## BARNHAM BROOM, Norfolk — Map 05 TG00

### ★★★74% Barnham Broom Hotel & Country Club

NR9 4DD
☎ 01603 759393 🖷 01603 758224
e-mail: enquiry@barnhambroomhotel.co.uk
***Dir:*** *signposted from A11 and A47, follow brown tourist signs with Barnham Broom and golf flag*
This hotel, set in a rural location, is about 15 miles from Norwich city centre. Extensive public areas include the Sports bar, where a range of meals is available all day, and the smart, more formal restaurant serving carte and set choice menus. Bedrooms are modern, attractive and well-equipped. There is also a golf simulator and two 18-hole courses.
**ROOMS:** 52 en suite (8 fmly) s £85-£150; d £105-£175 (incl. bkfst) * **LB** **FACILITIES:** Spa Indoor swimming (H) Golf 36 Tennis (hard) Squash Sauna Solarium Gym Putting green Hairdressing salon Beautician Xmas **CONF:** Thtr 150 Class 90 Board 70 Del from £82 * **PARKING:** 200 **NOTES:** No dogs (ex guide dogs) No smoking in restaurant Civ Wed 120 **CARDS:**

BARNSDALE BAR SERVICE AREA, North Yorkshire — Map 08 SE51

### ⌂ *Travelodge*

Travelodge

Wentbridge WF8 3JB
☎ 01977 620711 🖹 01977 620711
***Dir:*** *on A1, southbound*

Travelodge offers good quality, good value, modern accommodation. Ideal for families, the spacious, en suite bedrooms include remote-control TV, tea and coffee-making facilities, luxury beds and free morning newspaper. Meals can be taken at the nearby family restaurant. For further details and the Travelodge phone number, consult the Hotel Groups page.

**ROOMS:** 56 en suite

BARNSLEY, South Yorkshire — Map 08 SE30
see also Tankersley

### ★★★72% Ardsley House

Forestdale
Hotels

Doncaster Rd, Ardsley S71 5EH
☎ 01226 309955 🖹 01226 205374
e-mail: sales@ardsley-house.co.uk
***Dir:*** *on A635, 0.75m from Stainfoot Rdbt*

Quietly situated two miles east of Barnsley, this extended Georgian house offers modern, well-equipped bedrooms. Public rooms include a choice of bars and a pleasant restaurant, where diners can choose from a good range of carefully prepared dishes.

*continued on p70*

BARNSLEY, continued

A useful range of meeting rooms and function suites are also available.
**ROOMS:** 74 en suite (12 fmly) No smoking in 35 bedrooms s fr £79; d fr £94 * **LB** **FACILITIES:** **Spa** STV Indoor swimming (H) Sauna Solarium Gym Jacuzzi entertainment Xmas **CONF:** Thtr 350 Class 250 Board 40 **PARKING:** 200 **CARDS:**

*See advert on page 69*

### ★★★69% Tankersley Manor

Church Ln S75 3DQ
☎ 01226 744700 🖷 01226 745405
e-mail: info@tankersleymanor.co.uk
(For full entry see Tankersley)

### ⌂ *Travelodge*

520 Doncaster Rd S70 3PE
☎ 01226 298799 🖷 01226 298799
***Dir:*** *at Stairfoot roundabout A633/A635*
Travelodge offers good quality, good value, modern accommodation. Ideal for families, the spacious, en suite bedrooms include remote-control TV, tea and coffee-making facilities, luxury beds and free morning newspaper. Meals can be taken at the nearby family restaurant. For further details and the Travelodge phone number, consult the Hotel Groups page.

**ROOMS:** 32 en suite

BARNSTAPLE, Devon Map 02 SS53

### ★★★★70% The Imperial

Taw Vale Pde EX32 8NB
☎ 01271 345861 🖷 01271 324448
e-mail: info@brend-imperial.co.uk
***Dir:*** *from M5 junct 27, A361 Barnstaple. Follow signs for town centre, passing Tescos. Straight ahead at next 2 rdbts. Hotel is on the right*

Overlooking the river and an easy stroll away from the town centre, this hotel offers the warm hospitality associated with the Brend group of hotels. Bedrooms are richly decorated and the sumptuously furnished reception rooms have a peaceful, relaxing atmosphere.
**ROOMS:** 63 en suite (7 fmly) s £64-£110; d £70-£110 * **LB** **FACILITIES:** STV entertainment ch fac Xmas **SERVICES:** Lift **PARKING:** 80 **NOTES:** No dogs (ex guide dogs) No smoking in restaurant **CARDS:**

*See advert on opposite page*

> Early start? Hotels at all star levels should provide in-room alarm clocks and/or alarm calls.

### ★★★71% ⊛ Royal & Fortescue

Boutport St EX31 1HG
☎ 01271 342289 🖷 01271 340102
e-mail: sales@royalfortescue.co.uk
***Dir:*** *follow A361 along Barbican Rd signposted town centre, turn right into Queen St & left (oneway) Boutport St, hotel on left*
Originally a coaching inn this hotel, situated in the centre of this delightful market town, offers a friendly atmosphere. Bedrooms vary in size, all are decorated and furnished to a high standard. In addition to the formal restaurant, guests can take snacks in the coffee shop or dine more informally in The Bank, a bistro and cafe bar.
**ROOMS:** 50 en suite (5 fmly) s £45-£69; d £45-£69 * **LB** **FACILITIES:** STV entertainment Xmas **CONF:** Thtr 50 Class 50 Board 50 **SERVICES:** Lift **PARKING:** 40
**CARDS:**

### ★★★70% Barnstaple Hotel

Braunton Rd EX31 1LE
☎ 01271 376221 🖷 01271 324101
e-mail: info@barnstaplehotel.co.uk
***Dir:*** *on the outskirts of Barnstaple on A361*
Situated on the edge of the town, this purpose-built hotel offers an excellent range of facilities. The restaurant serves a wide range of dishes, whilst an extensive snack menu is available in the lounge bar. There is also a pool-side cafe. Bedrooms are set around the outdoor pool and sun terrace, many with direct access. Meeting rooms and an impressive function suite are also available.
**ROOMS:** 60 en suite (3 fmly) s £50-£75; d £60-£85 * **LB** **FACILITIES:** **Spa** STV Indoor swimming (H) Outdoor swimming (H) Snooker Sauna Solarium Gym ch fac Xmas **CONF:** Thtr 250 Class 250 Board 250 **PARKING:** 250 **NOTES:** No dogs (ex guide dogs) Civ Wed
**CARDS:**

### ★★★66% Park

Taw Vale EX32 9AE
☎ 01271 372166 🖷 01271 323157
e-mail: info@parkhotel.co.uk
***Dir:*** *opposite Rock Park, 0.5m from town centre*
Situated opposite the park, within easy walking distance of the town centre, this modern hotel has bedrooms in both the main building and the Garden Court, which is just across the car park. Public rooms are open-plan in style and the friendly staff offer attentive service in a relaxed atmosphere.
**ROOMS:** 25 en suite 17 annexe en suite (7 fmly) s £45-£69; d £45-£69 * **LB** **FACILITIES:** STV entertainment Xmas **CONF:** Thtr 150 Class 150 Board 150 **PARKING:** 80 **NOTES:** Civ Wed 100
**CARDS:**

## *Premier Collection*

### ★★ ⊛⊛ Halmpstone Manor

Bishop's Tawton EX32 0EA
☎ 01271 830321 🖷 01271 830826
e-mail: jane@halmpstonemanor.co.uk
***Dir:*** *5m S of Barnstaple, leave A377 at Bishop's Tawton opposite petrol station and follow unclassified road 2m then right at Halmpstone Manor sign*
This small Queen Anne manor house, family home and working farm, has fine views across Dartmoor. Bedrooms, including two with four poster beds, have many useful extras and thoughtful touches. Public rooms have special character - the comfortable, spacious and relaxing lounge with log fire, and a pine-panelled dining room. The proprietors provide

*continued*

warm and attentive service at the front, and delicious meals using quality local produce. This proves to be a perfect combination.

**ROOMS:** 5 en suite No smoking in 1 bedroom s £70; d £100-£140 (incl. bkfst) * **CONF:** Thtr 12 Class 12 Board 12 Del from £115 * **PARKING:** 12 **NOTES:** No children 12yrs No smoking in restaurant Closed Feb & part Nov/Oct **CARDS:**

## BARROW-IN-FURNESS, Cumbria — Map 07 SD16

### ★★★69% *Clarke's Hotel & Brasserie*

Rampside LA13 0PX
☎ 01229 820303 🖷 01229 430594
***Dir:*** *M6 J36 then A590 at Ulverston turn left after 1st pedestrian lights signed A5087. Take coastal route for 8 miles turn left at rdbt into Rampside*

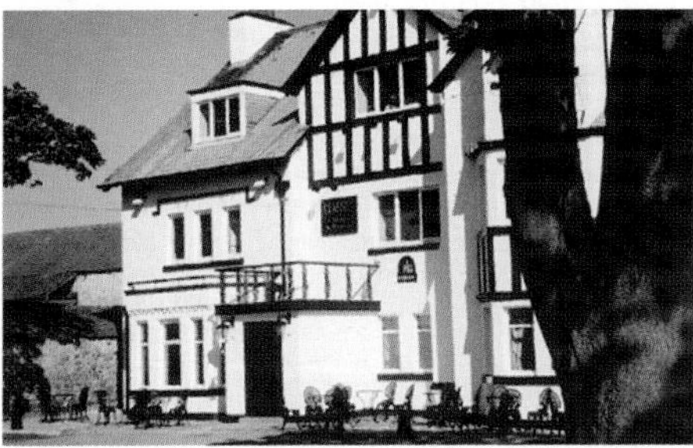

Situated on the south Cumbrian coastline, overlooking Morecambe bay, this friendly hotel offers smart, well-equipped accommodation. An attractive open-plan brasserie and bar serves freshly prepared food throughout the day. At the time of our last inspection, major extension work, to include a second restaurant and further bedrooms, was underway.
**ROOMS:** 14 en suite (1 fmly) No smoking in 3 bedrooms
**FACILITIES:** STV entertainment **PARKING:** 50
**CARDS:**

### ★★60% *Lisdoonie*

307/309 Abbey Rd LA14 5LF
☎ 01229 827312 🖷 01229 820944
***Dir:*** *on A590, first set of traffic lights in town (Strawberry pub on left), continue for 100yds, hotel on right. Car park right in Furness Park Rd*
This popular and friendly hotel, conveniently located close to the centre of the town, features two lounges, one of which has a bar. There is also a traditionally-styled dining room and comfortable bedrooms which vary in size and style.
**ROOMS:** 12 en suite (2 fmly) **CONF:** Class 255 **PARKING:** 30
**NOTES:** Closed Xmas & New Year **CARDS:**

B

## BARTON, Lancashire
Map 07 SD53

### ★★★70% Barton Grange
Best Western

Garstang Rd PR3 5AA
☎ 01772 862551 📠 01772 861267
e-mail: stay@bartongrangehotel.com
***Dir:*** *from M6 junct 32 follow A6, signed Garstang , for 2.5m, hotel on the right*

The extensive public areas at this hotel feature a renowned garden centre, leisure facilities and a hair and beauty salon. Bedrooms are well-appointed and include a four-poster and family rooms; some are in an adjacent cottage. Food and refreshments are served all day in the unique Walled Garden restaurant.
**ROOMS:** 42 en suite 8 annexe en suite (4 fmly) s £79; d £89 (incl. bkfst) * **LB** **FACILITIES:** STV Indoor swimming (H) Sauna Gym Jacuzzi Garden Centre Beauty salon Xmas **CONF:** Thtr 300 Class 100 Board 80 Del from £110 * **SERVICES:** Lift **PARKING:** 250 **NOTES:** No dogs (ex guide dogs) No smoking in restaurant Civ Wed 120
**CARDS:**

## BARTON MILLS, Suffolk
Map 05 TL77

### ⌂ *Travelodge*
Travelodge

IP28 6AE
☎ 01638 717675 📠 01638 717675
***Dir:*** *on A11*
Travelodge offers good quality, good value, modern accommodation. Ideal for families, the spacious, en suite bedrooms include remote-control TV, tea and coffee-making facilities, luxury beds and free morning newspaper. Meals can be taken at the nearby family restaurant. For further details and the Travelodge phone number, consult the Hotel Groups page.

**ROOMS:** 40 en suite

## BARTON-ON-SEA, Hampshire
Map 04 SZ29

### ★★73% The Cliff House
Marine Dr West BH25 7QL
☎ 01425 619333 📠 01425 612462
***Dir:*** *turn off A337 on to Sea Road at Barton-on-Sea. Hotel at end of road on cliff top*
In a stunning clifftop location looking out to sea with the Isle of Wight in the distance, this charming family-run hotel has a warm and welcoming atmosphere. Many of the comfortable bedrooms benefit from fine views. Serving a range of menus, the restaurant is popular with locals and visitors alike; booking is essential for Sunday lunch.
**ROOMS:** 9 en suite No smoking in all bedrooms s £39-£55; d £80-£100 (incl. bkfst) * **LB** **FACILITIES:** STV **PARKING:** 50 **NOTES:** No dogs (ex guide dogs) No children 10yrs No smoking in restaurant
**CARDS:**

## BARTON STACEY, Hampshire
Map 04 SU44

### ⌂ *Travelodge*
Travelodge

SP21 3NP
☎ 01264 720260 📠 01264 720260
***Dir:*** *on A303*
Travelodge offers good quality, good value, modern accommodation. Ideal for families, the spacious, en suite bedrooms include remote-control TV, tea and coffee-making facilities, luxury beds and free morning newspaper. Meals can be taken at the nearby family restaurant. For further details and the Travelodge phone number, consult the Hotel Groups page.

**ROOMS:** 20 en suite

## BARTON-UNDER-NEEDWOOD, Staffordshire
Map 07 SK11

### ⌂ *Travelodge (Northbound)*
Travelodge

DE13 8ED
☎ 01283 716343 📠 01283 716343
***Dir:*** *on A38,northbound*
Travelodge offers good quality, good value, modern accommodation. Ideal for families, the spacious, en suite bedrooms include remote-control TV, tea and coffee-making facilities, luxury beds and free morning newspaper. Meals can be taken at the nearby family restaurant. For further details and the Travelodge phone number, consult the Hotel Groups page.

**ROOMS:** 20 en suite

### ⌂ *Travelodge (Southbound)*
Travelodge

Rykneld St DE13 8EH
☎ 01283 716784 📠 01283 716784
***Dir:*** *on A38, southbound*
Travelodge offers good quality, good value, modern accommodation. Ideal for families, the spacious, en suite bedrooms include remote-control TV, tea and coffee-making facilities, luxury beds and free morning newspaper. Meals can be taken at the nearby family restaurant. For further details and the Travelodge phone number, consult the Hotel Groups page.

**ROOMS:** 40 en suite

## BARTON-UPON-HUMBER, Lincolnshire
Map 08 TA02

### ★★★70% Reeds Hotel
Westfield Lakes, Far Ings Rd DN18 5RG
☎ 01652 632313 📠 01652 636361
e-mail: info@reedshotel.co.uk
***Dir:*** *at A15 rdbt take 2nd exit (sign posted Humber bridge).Leave A15 at Barton-Upon-Humber.Left at rdbt, 200 yds turn right at sign for Reeds hotel, down hill, Reeds hotel at junct.*

Situated beside the Humber, between a couple of freshwater

*continued*

lakes, this hotel enjoys splendid views of the Humber Bridge. Public rooms include an attractive restaurant, foyer lounge and 'Clippers Tea Room' with panoramic views. Bedrooms vary in size, all are well equipped and nicely presented.
**ROOMS:** 6 en suite (1 fmly) No smoking in all bedrooms s £75; d £98-£125 (incl. bkfst) **LB** **FACILITIES:** Alternative therapy centre ch fac **CONF:** Thtr 300 Class 200 Board 70 **PARKING:** 55 **NOTES:** No dogs (ex guide dogs) No smoking in restaurant Civ Wed 100
**CARDS:**

## BASILDON, Essex — Map 05 TQ78

### ★★★69% Chichester
Old London Rd, Wickford SS11 8UE
☎ 01268 560555 📠 01268 560580
***Dir:*** *off A129*
Situated just off the A130 amidst its own landscaped grounds this friendly, family-run hotel is surrounded by open farmland. The spacious, comfortable bedrooms are located around an attractive courtyard. The restaurant offers both carte and set menus, and more informal meals are served in the bar area.
**ROOMS:** 2 en suite 32 annexe en suite s £59.75-£72; d £69.75-£72 * **LB** **PARKING:** 150 **NOTES:** No dogs (ex guide dogs) No children 5yrs No smoking in restaurant **CARDS:**

### ★★★65% *Posthouse Basildon*
Posthouse
Cranes Farm Rd SS14 3DG
☎ 0870 400 9003 📠 01268 530119
***Dir:*** *off A1235, via A127*
Conveniently located for the town centre, this modern hotel is popular with both business and leisure guests. Bedrooms are bright and contemporary in style and a good range of in-room facilities is provided. Meals can be taken in the upstairs Junction Restaurant.
**ROOMS:** 149 en suite (30 fmly) No smoking in 70 bedrooms **FACILITIES:** Use of nearby Leisure Club (David Lloyd) **CONF:** Thtr 300 Class 80 Board 80 **SERVICES:** Lift **PARKING:** 200
**CARDS:**

### ⇧ Premier Lodge

PREMIER LODGE
THE BEST. REST ASSURED.
Pipps Hill Rd South, Festival Leisure Park SS14 3WB
☎ 0870 700 1376 📠 0870 700 1377
***Dir:*** *From M25 junct 29 take A127 towards Basildon then follow East*
Premier Lodge offers modern, well-equipped, en suite accommodation suitable for both business and leisure travellers. Meals can be taken at the adjacent popular restaurant and bar, which is fully licensed. For further details, consult the Hotel Groups page.
**ROOMS:** 64 en suite d £49.95 * **CONF:** Thtr 20 Class 20 Board 12

### ⇧ Campanile

Campanile
Pipps Hill, Southend Arterial Rd SS14 3AE
☎ 01268 530810 📠 01268 286710
***Dir:*** *M25 junct29 exit in direction of Basildon take first exit to Basildon, go back under A127 then at roundabout go left*
This modern building offers accommodation in smart, well-equipped bedrooms, all with en suite bathrooms. Refreshments
continued
may be taken at the informal Bistro. For further details and the Campanile phone number, consult the Hotel Groups page.

**ROOMS:** 98 annexe en suite d £41.95 * **CONF:** Thtr 35 Class 18 Board 20 Del £68 *

### ○ *Travelodge Basildon*
Travelodge
Festival Leisure Park, Festival Way SS14 3WB
☎ 01268 284887
**NOTES:** Opening Winter 2001

## BASINGSTOKE, Hampshire — Map 04 SU65
see also North Waltham, Odiham & Stratfield Turgis

### ★★★★ 🏵🏵 Tylney Hall Hotel
RG27 9AZ
☎ 01256 764881 📠 01256 768141
e-mail: sales@tylneyhall.com
(For full entry see Rotherwick)

### ★★★★68% 🏵 *Audleys Wood*
THISTLE HOTELS
Alton Rd RG25 2JT
☎ 01256 817555 📠 01256 817500
e-mail: audleys.wood@thistle.co.uk
***Dir:*** *1.5m S of Basingstoke on A339*
This Gothic Renaissance style residence is set in seven acres of woodland. It offers contemporary style spacious bedrooms with bathrooms fitted in marble. The bar and lounges retain much of their original character.
**ROOMS:** 71 en suite (6 fmly) No smoking in 35 bedrooms **FACILITIES:** STV Croquet lawn Putting green Archery Bicycles **CONF:** Thtr 50 Class 20 Board 26 **PARKING:** 100 **NOTES:** No smoking in restaurant **CARDS:**

### ★★★74% 🏵 Romans
Best Western
Little London Rd RG7 2PN
☎ 0118 970 0421 📠 0118 970 0691
e-mail: romanhotel@hotmail.com
(For full entry see Silchester and advert on page 75)

### ★★★71% The Hampshire Centrecourt Hotel
MARSTON HOTELS
Centre Dr, Chineham RG24 8FY
☎ 01256 816664 📠 01256 816727
e-mail: hampshire@marstonhotels.com
***Dir:*** *off A33 Reading Road behind the Chineham Shopping Centre via Great Binfields Road*
This modern single storey hotel, with an established leisure and tennis club, has easy access to the M3, M4 and business areas. Weekend breaks include coaching and lessons. Bedrooms are
continued on p74

BASINGSTOKE, continued

spacious and well-equipped, some with balconies overlooking the tennis courts. Public areas have a relaxed and friendly atmosphere.
**ROOMS:** 50 en suite (6 fmly) No smoking in 25 bedrooms s £109-£119; d £120-£140 * **LB** **FACILITIES:** STV Indoor swimming (H) Tennis (hard) Sauna Solarium Gym Jacuzzi Steam room Beauty salon **CONF:** Thtr 100 Class 40 Board 40 Del from £115 * **SERVICES:** Lift **PARKING:** 120 **NOTES:** No dogs (ex guide dogs) No smoking in restaurant Closed 24 Dec-31 Jan **CARDS:**

### ★★★70% Hanover International Hotel & Club

Scures Hill, Nately Scures, Hook RG27 9JS
☎ 01256 764161 01256 768341
e-mail: maxine.butler@hotels.com
***Dir:*** *leave M3 junct 5 take turning on roundabout to Newnham/Basingstoke, proceed 0.5m until reaching T junct, turn left onto A30, hotel is 200yds on right*

Hanover International Hotels & Clubs

This extensive hotel is very popular with the business community who appreciate the well-designed rooms. Bedrooms are spacious and very well-equipped. Good conference and meetings facilities can cater for a variety of functions. The Winchester restaurant offers contemporary dishes served in comfortable surroundings.
**ROOMS:** 100 en suite (8 fmly) No smoking in 35 bedrooms s £130-£160; d £140-£200 * **LB** **FACILITIES:** Spa STV Indoor swimming (H) Sauna Solarium Gym Jacuzzi Beauty salon Dance studio **CONF:** Thtr 200 Class 95 Board 80 Del from £150 * **SERVICES:** Lift **PARKING:** 164 **NOTES:** Civ Wed 200 **CARDS:**

### ★★★65% Apollo

Aldermaston Roundabout RG24 9NU
☎ 01256 796700 01256 796701
e-mail: apollohotel@aol.com
***Dir:*** *situated off M3 junct 6. Follow ringroad N to exit A340 (Aldermaston), hotel on rdbt take 5th exit into Popley Way for access*

The Apollo is conveniently located for access to major routes and remains a popular venue for both business and leisure guests.

*continued*

Bedrooms are modern and pay great attention to comfort and quality.
**ROOMS:** 125 en suite No smoking in 100 bedrooms s £110-£130; d £140-£195 * **LB** **FACILITIES:** Spa STV Indoor swimming (H) Sauna Solarium Gym Xmas **CONF:** Thtr 255 Class 196 Board 30 Del from £154 * **SERVICES:** Lift **PARKING:** 200 **NOTES:** No dogs (ex guide dogs) Civ Wed 180 **CARDS:**

*See advert on this page*

### ★★★65% *Posthouse Basingstoke*

Posthouse

Grove Rd RG21 3EE
☎ 0870 400 9004 01256 840081
***Dir:*** *on A339 Alton road S of Basingstoke*

This modern, purpose-built hotel, situated on the outskirts of Basingstoke, is ideally located for easy access to the M3. It offers a good standard of accommodation; all rooms are well-equipped. There is also a popular restaurant and 'Academy' function rooms available.
**ROOMS:** 84 en suite (3 fmly) No smoking in 42 bedrooms **FACILITIES:** Childrens indoor/outdoor play areas ch fac **CONF:** Thtr 150 Class 80 Board 80 **PARKING:** 150 **CARDS:**

### ★★★63% Red Lion

ZOFFANY HOTELS

24 London St RG21 7NY
☎ 01256 328525 01256 844056
e-mail: redlion@zoffanyhotels.co.uk

Central to Basingstoke town, the Red Lion is an ideal choice for business guests. Bedrooms, mostly spacious, are pleasantly appointed. Public areas include an attractive lounge and restaurant, and a popular bar.
**ROOMS:** 59 en suite (2 fmly) No smoking in 6 bedrooms s £105; d £117 (incl. bkfst) * **LB** **FACILITIES:** STV Xmas **CONF:** Thtr 40 Class 40 Board 20 Del from £117 * **SERVICES:** Lift **PARKING:** 62 **NOTES:** No smoking in restaurant **CARDS:**

*See advert on opposite page*

B

BASINGSTOKE, continued

### *Travelodge*

Travelodge

Stag and Hounds, Winchester Rd RG22 5HN
☎ 01256 843566 01256 843566
***Dir:*** *off A30*

Travelodge offers good quality, good value, modern accommodation. Ideal for families, the spacious, en suite bedrooms include remote-control TV, tea and coffee-making facilities, luxury beds and free morning newspaper. Meals can be taken at the nearby family restaurant. For further details and the Travelodge phone number, consult the Hotel Groups page.

**ROOMS:** 32 en suite

BASLOW, Derbyshire Map 08 SK27

### ★★★76% Cavendish

DE45 1SP
☎ 01246 582311 01246 582312
e-mail: info@cavendish-hotel.net
***Dir:*** *from M1 junct 29, take A617 west to Chesterfield. A619 to Baslow, hotel situated in centre of village, off main road*

This country house hotel is situated on the edge of the Chatsworth estate, and dates back to the 18th century. Bedrooms are elegantly appointed and offer every thoughtful convenience, whilst comfortable public areas are furnished with period pieces and paintings. Guests have the choice of informal dining in the conservatory Garden Room or the contemporary elegance of The Gallery Restaurant. The public rooms and the elegant bedrooms all afford wonderful views over the estate.
**ROOMS:** 24 en suite (3 fmly) No smoking in 2 bedrooms s £95-£115; d £125-£145 * **LB** **FACILITIES:** STV Fishing Putting green ch fac Xmas **CONF:** Thtr 25 Board 18 Del from £174 * **PARKING:** 50 **NOTES:** No dogs (ex guide dogs) No smoking in restaurant
**CARDS:**

## *Premier Collection*

### ★★ Fischer's Baslow Hall

Calver Rd DE45 1RR
☎ 01246 583259 01246 583818
***Dir:*** *on the A623 between Baslow & Calver*

On the edge of the Chatsworth estate stands this beautiful Derbyshire manor house offering sumptuous accommodation and facilities. All of the staff offer friendly, personal, attentive hospitality and service. Two styles of bedrooms include traditional, individually themed rooms in the main house and spacious, more contemporary styled rooms with Italian marbled bathrooms in the Garden House. The cuisine is extremely memorable and a highlight of any stay.
**ROOMS:** 6 en suite 5 annexe en suite No smoking in all bedrooms s £80-£100; d £150 (incl. cont bkfst) * **LB** **CONF:** Thtr 40 Board 18 Del from £130 * **PARKING:** 40 **NOTES:** No dogs (ex guide dogs) No smoking in restaurant Closed 25-26 Dec Civ Wed 40
**CARDS:**

BASSENTHWAITE, Cumbria Map 11 NY23

### ★★★★73% Armathwaite Hall

CA12 4RE
☎ 017687 76551 017687 76220
e-mail: reservations@armathwaite-hall.com
***Dir:*** *M6 junct40, A66 to Keswick roundabout then A591 signposted Carlisle. 8m to Castle Inn junction, turn left hotel 300yds ahead*

Dating from the 17th century, this impressive mansion house is beautifully set amid 400 acres of deerpark and woodland, under the shadow of Skiddaw with views of Bassenthwaite Lake. Many of the fine original features have been sympathetically retained in the charming reception rooms, with lovely panelling, ornate ceilings, and splendid fireplaces. Bedrooms have pleasing colour schemes and are comfortably furnished and well-equipped. Staff are friendly and provide good levels of guest care.
**ROOMS:** 43 en suite (4 fmly) s £62-£125; d £124-£250 (incl. bkfst) * **LB** **FACILITIES:** STV Indoor swimming (H) Tennis (hard) Fishing Riding Snooker Sauna Solarium Gym Croquet lawn Putting green Jacuzzi Archery Beauty salon Clayshooting Quad bikes Falconry ch fac Xmas **CONF:** Thtr 120 Class 50 Board 60 Del from £115 * **SERVICES:** Lift **PARKING:** 100 **NOTES:** No smoking in restaurant Civ Wed 100
**CARDS:**

*See advert under KESWICK*

### ★★★65% Castle Inn

REGAL

CA12 4RG
☎ 017687 76401 017687 76604
***Dir:*** *leave A66 at Keswick and take A591 towards Carlisle, pass Bassenthwaite village on right and hotel is 6m on the left*

Located to the north of the lake and enjoying distant mountain views, this hotel attracts leisure guests and small conferences.

*continued*

Bedrooms are well-equipped and come in contrasting styles and sizes. Public areas are comfortable and relaxing.

**ROOMS:** 48 en suite (6 fmly) No smoking in 14 bedrooms s £46-£49; d £92-£98 (incl. bkfst) * **LB** **FACILITIES:** STV Indoor swimming (H) Tennis (grass) Snooker Sauna Solarium Gym Putting green Jacuzzi Badminton Table tennis Health/Beauty spa Xmas **CONF:** Thtr 120 Class 35 Board 40 Del £105 * **PARKING:** 100 **NOTES:** No smoking in restaurant Civ Wed 120 **CARDS:**

### ★★70% Ravenstone

CA12 4QG
☎ 017687 76240 017687 76733
e-mail: info@ravenstone-hotel.co.uk
***Dir:*** *4.5m N of Keswick on Carlisle road A591*

Set in terraced gardens and enjoying fine panoramic views across the valley, this delightful country house retains its original character, with oak panelling and artefacts featuring. Far from being stuffy however, this is a relaxing and friendly hotel run by a young family who make families welcome. The set menu features good freshly prepared dishes.

**ROOMS:** 20 en suite (2 fmly) No smoking in all bedrooms s £40; d £80 (incl. bkfst) * **LB** **FACILITIES:** Snooker Table tennis Xmas **PARKING:** 25 **NOTES:** No dogs No smoking in restaurant **CARDS:**

## BATH, Somerset

Map 03 ST76

see also Chelwood, Colerne & Hinton Charterhouse

### ★★★★★72% The Royal Crescent

16 Royal Crescent BA1 2LS
☎ 01225 823333 01225 339401
e-mail: reservations@royalcrescent.co.uk
***Dir:*** *cont along A4. R at traffic lights. 2nd L onto Bennett St. Cont into the Circus, 2nd exit onto Brock St, proceed ahead to cobbled street & No.16.*

In the centre of the world famous Royal Crescent, John Wood's masterpiece of fine Georgian architecture offers exemplary service and cuisine and hospitality of the highest standard. All rooms have fax machines and videos and all are individually designed and furnished with antiques. The Bath House offers complementary therapies and treatments. Staff throughout the hotel are friendly and courteous and very attentive, providing an excellent level of professional service.

**ROOMS:** 45 en suite (8 fmly) No smoking in 8 bedrooms s £220-£800; d £220-£800 * **FACILITIES:** Indoor swimming (H) Sauna Croquet lawn Hot air ballooning, 1920s river launch, Outdoor heated plunge pool entertainment Xmas **CONF:** Thtr 30 Class 30 Del £275 * **SERVICES:** Lift air con **PARKING:** 27 **NOTES:** No smoking in restaurant Civ Wed 40 **CARDS:**

### ★★★★★65% The Bath Spa

Sydney Rd BA2 6JF
☎ 0870 400 8222 01225 444006
e-mail: fivestar@bathspa.u-net.com
***Dir:*** *M4 junct 18 to A46 for Bath. Right at rdbt for A4 city centre. Left for A36 at first lights. Right at mini rdbt then left into Sydney Place*

This Georgian mansion is situated close to the city centre, yet with its seven acres of grounds including formal gardens, fountains and ponds, this is a perfect retreat from the hustle and bustle of the city. A recent refurbishment programme has resulted in bedrooms of contemporary style, with an enhanced range of features and facilities. Public rooms have also benefited from a lift and include a busy leisure club, two restaurants and a range of meeting rooms.

**ROOMS:** 102 en suite No smoking in 31 bedrooms **FACILITIES:** **Spa** STV Indoor swimming (H) Tennis (hard) Sauna Gym Croquet lawn Jacuzzi Beauty treatment Hair salon entertainment **CONF:** Thtr 120 Class 100 Board 50 Del from £229 * **SERVICES:** Lift **PARKING:** 156 **NOTES:** No smoking in restaurant Civ Wed 120 **CARDS:**

### ★★★★78% *Bath Priory*

Weston Rd BA1 2XT
☎ 01225 331922 01225 448276
e-mail: 106076.1265@compuserve.com

This delightful Georgian house contains a smart leisure centre themed on the Roman Baths. The individually styled bedrooms display unique charm and are furnished with antiques. There are two elegant sitting rooms and a dining room overlooking beautiful gardens. Accomplished cuisine, using the finest fresh ingredients, is served in the restaurant.

**ROOMS:** 28 en suite (6 fmly) **FACILITIES:** STV Indoor swimming (H) Outdoor swimming (H) Sauna Solarium Gym Croquet lawn Jacuzzi **CONF:** Thtr 60 Class 30 Board 24 **PARKING:** 28 **NOTES:** No dogs (ex guide dogs) No smoking in restaurant **CARDS:**

Bad hair day? Hairdryers in all rooms three stars and above.

BATH, continued

**★★★★62% Combe Grove Manor Hotel & Country Club**
Brassknocker Hill, Monkton Combe BA2 7HS
☎ 01225 834644 01225 834961
e-mail: james.parker@combegrovemanor.com
**Dir:** *exit at junct 18 of the M4, follow A46 to City Centre. Next follow signs for University and American Museum, hotel is 2m past University on left*
Set in over eighty acres of gardens and meadows and based around a Georgian manor house, this hotel commands stunning views over the Limpley Stoke valley. Stylishly furnished, the main house offers a choice of two restaurants. Most bedrooms are in the Garden Lodge and include balconies with garden furniture. There is also a superb range of indoor and outdoor leisure facilities including a beauty clinic with holistic therapies.
**ROOMS:** 9 en suite 31 annexe en suite (11 fmly) s £99-£320; d £99-£320 (incl. bkfst) * LB **FACILITIES:** STV Indoor swimming (H) Outdoor swimming (H) Golf 5 Tennis (hard) Sauna Solarium Gym Croquet lawn Putting green Jacuzzi Aerobics Beauty salon Xmas **CONF:** Thtr 80 Class 32 Board 36 Del £60 * **PARKING:** 150 **NOTES:** No dogs No smoking in restaurant Civ Wed 50 **CARDS:**

## Premier Collection

**★★★ Queensberry**
Russel St BA1 2QF
☎ 01225 447928 01225 446065
e-mail: queensberry@dial.pipex.com
**Dir:** *100mtrs from the Assembly Rooms*
The Queensberry Hotel is a privately owned town house hotel nestling in a quiet residential street. This carefully restored Bath-stone house is conveniently located within walking distance of the city centre and tourist attractions. Bedrooms are individually decorated and tastefully furnished with sofas, fresh flowers and marble bathrooms adding to their appeal. The comfortable bar/lounge opens onto a courtyard garden. The Olive Tree Restaurant enjoys a popular local reputation and offers freshly cooked cuisine with a Mediterranean influence.
**ROOMS:** 29 en suite s £90-£145; d £120-£210 (incl. cont bkfst) * LB **CONF:** Thtr 35 Board 25 Del £145 * **SERVICES:** Lift **PARKING:** 6 **NOTES:** No dogs (ex guide dogs) No smoking in restaurant Closed 24-28 Dec RS Sun **CARDS:**

**★★★76% Dukes' Hotel & Fitzroys**

THE CIRCLE
Selected Individual Hotels
GREAT BRITAIN

Great Pulteney St BA2 4DN
☎ 01225 787960 01225 488738
e-mail: info@dukesbath.co.uk
This magnificent Palladian mansion has recently been restored to its original Georgian splendour. Located on Great Pulteney Street, the centre of the city is a short walk away, making an ideal base to explore Bath. A unique tie-up with Martin Blunos, local award-winning chef, ensures that menus offer something for everyone and that only the best of fresh produce is used.

**ROOMS:** 18 en suite (1 fmly) **FACILITIES:** STV Xmas **CONF:** Thtr 20 Class 10 Board 14 **NOTES:** No smoking in restaurant
**CARDS:**

See advert on opposite page

**★★★73% Cliffe**
Best Western
Crowe Hill, Limpley Stoke BA2 7FY
☎ 01225 723226 01225 723871
e-mail: cliffe@bestwestern.co.uk
**Dir:** *A36 S from Bath,in approx 3m at traffic lights take B3108 to Lower Limpley Stoke. At sharp left hand bend take minor road to village*

With stunning views over the surrounding countryside, this attractive country house is just a short drive from the city. Bedrooms vary in size and style, all are well-equipped, several are particularly spacious and a number of rooms are situated on the ground floor. The restaurant overlooks the outdoor pool and the well-tended garden.
**ROOMS:** 11 en suite (4 fmly) s £75-£95; d £95-£125 (incl. bkfst) * LB **FACILITIES:** STV Outdoor swimming (H) ch fac Xmas **CONF:** Thtr 20 Board 10 Del from £110 * **PARKING:** 40 **NOTES:** No smoking in restaurant Civ Wed 50 **CARDS:**

See advert on opposite page

**★★★72% Lansdown Grove Hotel**
MARSTON HOTELS
Lansdown Rd BA1 5EH
☎ 01225 483888 01225 483838
e-mail: lansdown@marstonhotels.com
**Dir:** *follow signs to Lansdown Park & Ride and continue towards town centre. Hotel on left*
A well-established hotel, an uphill walk from the city centre, offering a relaxed atmosphere and comfortable accommodation. The well-equipped, tastefully decorated bedrooms, some with access to an ornate veranda, vary in size. There is a reception

continued

lounge, bar and peaceful drawing room. Innovative dishes are served in the elegant dining room.
**ROOMS:** 50 en suite (3 fmly) No smoking in 9 bedrooms s £89-£99; d £105-£125 * **LB** **FACILITIES:** Gym Xmas **CONF:** Thtr 100 Class 45 Board 40 Del from £94 * **SERVICES:** Lift **PARKING:** 44 **NOTES:** No dogs (ex guide dogs) **CARDS:**

**★★★70% The Francis**
Queen Square BA1 2HH
☎ 0870 400 8223 📠 01225 319715
e-mail: heritagehotels_bath.francis@forte-hotels.com
***Dir:*** *M4 junct 18, follow A46 until Bath junct. 3rd exit onto A4. Right fork into George St, sharp left into Gay St onto Queen Sq and hotel on left*
Overlooking Queen Square in the centre of the city, The Francis is a long established hotel. Various eating options include a traditional lounge, a café-bar and a more formal restaurant. Bedrooms, which are on three floors, are comfortable and attractively decorated.
**ROOMS:** 94 en suite (1 fmly) No smoking in 38 bedrooms s £104-£109; d £108-£140 (incl. bkfst) * **LB** **FACILITIES:** use of facilities at bath spa Xmas **CONF:** Thtr 80 Class 40 Board 30 Del from £125 * **SERVICES:** Lift **PARKING:** 42 **NOTES:** No smoking in restaurant **CARDS:**

**★★★68% Pratts**
South Pde BA2 4AB
☎ 01225 460441 📠 01225 448807
e-mail: pratts@forestdale.com
***Dir:*** *take A46 into Bath City Centre*
Part of an attractive Georgian terrace, this long established and popular hotel stands at the heart of the city centre. Public rooms

*continued on p80*

BATH, continued

retain a traditional atmosphere, with an intimate writing room, two lounges and a modern bar. Bedrooms vary in size and are all well-equipped; some rooms are cosy with low ceilings and small windows.
**ROOMS:** 46 en suite (2 fmly) No smoking in 2 bedrooms s £63-£73; d £126-£146 (incl. bkfst & dinner) * **LB** **FACILITIES:** Xmas **CONF:** Thtr 50 Class 12 Board 30 Del £110 * **SERVICES:** Lift **NOTES:** No smoking in restaurant **CARDS:**

### ★★★67% The Abbey Hotel

Best Western

North Pde BA1 1LF
☎ 01225 461603 📠 01225 447758
e-mail: ahres@compasshotels.co.uk
***Dir:*** *close to the Abbey in city centre*
Originally built for a wealthy merchant in the 1740s and forming part of a handsome Georgian terrace, this welcoming hotel is situated in the heart of the city. The thoughtfully equipped bedrooms vary in size and style. Public areas include a smart lounge bar and a formal restaurant.

THE ABBEY HOTEL

**ROOMS:** 60 en suite (4 fmly) No smoking in 22 bedrooms s £75-£90; d £120-£135 (incl. bkfst) * **LB** **FACILITIES:** STV Xmas **SERVICES:** Lift **NOTES:** No smoking in restaurant **CARDS:**
*See advert on page 79*

### ★★74% Haringtons

8/10 Queen St BA1 1HE
☎ 01225 461728 📠 01225 444804
e-mail: post@haringtonshotel.co.uk
***Dir:*** *from A4 go to George St and turn into Milsom St. 1st right into Quiet St and 1st left into Queen St*
Dating back to the 18th century, this hotel has been completely refurbished to accommodate all modern facilities and comforts. The cafe-bar is open throughout the day for light meals and refreshments. A warm welcome is assured from the proprietors and their staff who have created a delightful place to stay right in the centre of the city.
**ROOMS:** 13 en suite (3 fmly) No smoking in all bedrooms s £65-£88; d £88-£118 (incl. bkfst) * **LB** **FACILITIES:** STV **NOTES:** No dogs (ex guide dogs) No smoking in restaurant Closed 24-26 Dec
**CARDS:**

### ★★68% Avondale Hotel & Waterside Restaurant

London Rd East, Bathford BA1 7RB
☎ 01225 859847 & 852207 📠 01225 859847
***Dir:*** *from A46/A4 junct follow signs Chippenham/Batheaston/Bathford. Continue through Batheaston towards large rdbt & hotel on right just before rdbt*
In a pleasant riverside location, this hotel offers a good standard of accommodation. The restaurant serves an imaginative range of dishes, together with a selection of real ales and malt whiskies.
*continued*

Staff work hard to create a relaxed atmosphere so guests can enjoy the peaceful surroundings.
**ROOMS:** 15 rms (13 en suite) (3 fmly) s £49-£69; d £69-£115 (incl. bkfst) * **LB** **FACILITIES:** Fishing Boating ch fac **CONF:** Thtr 20 **PARKING:** 40 **NOTES:** No dogs (ex guide dogs)
**CARDS:**

### ★★68% The Old Mill

Tollbridge Rd, Batheaston BA1 7DE
☎ 01225 858476 📠 01225 852600
e-mail: info@oldmillbath.co.uk
***Dir:*** *take A46 for 8m, turn left for Bath at large rdbt turn left towards Batheaston in 0.5m turn right after Waggon & Horses to Bathampton Toll Bridge*
This attractive, creeper-clad hotel was formerly a flourmill. The original waterwheel can be seen from the restaurant, which overlooks the gardens. Bedrooms vary in size, all offering good levels of decor and comfort. The varied menus offer something for everyone. All bedrooms have computer modem points and golf can be arranged for guests.
**ROOMS:** 17 en suite 10 annexe en suite (5 fmly) **FACILITIES:** STV Fishing **CONF:** Thtr 100 Class 40 Board 36 Del from £85 * **PARKING:** 50 **NOTES:** No dogs (ex guide dogs) No smoking in restaurant Civ Wed 70 **CARDS:**

### ★★67% Wentworth House Hotel

106 Bloomfield Rd BA2 2AP
☎ 01225 339193 📠 01225 310460
e-mail: stay@wentworthhouse.co.uk
***Dir:*** *A367 Radstock/Shepton Mallet signs follow road to small shopping area, pub on right 'The Bear'. Bloomfield Rd 2nd turning past pub. Hotel on right*

An imposing Victorian mansion built in 1887, enjoying a peaceful location overlooking the city of Bath, yet only a fifteen minute walk to the centre. Bedrooms are individually furnished and include many thoughtful extras. Enjoyable home-cooked dinners and hearty breakfasts are served in the conservatory restaurant.
**ROOMS:** 18 en suite (2 fmly) No smoking in 5 bedrooms s £50-£75; d £60-£105 (incl. bkfst) * **LB** **FACILITIES:** Outdoor swimming (H) **PARKING:** 18 **NOTES:** No dogs No children 5yrs No smoking in restaurant Closed Xmas & New Year weeks
**CARDS:**
*See advert on opposite page*

### ★★66% Old Malt House

MINOTEL Great Britain

Radford, Timsbury BA2 0QF
☎ 01761 470106 📠 01761 472726
e-mail: hotel@oldmalthouse.co.uk
***Dir:*** *from Bath take A367 south for 1.5m then right onto B3115 towards Timsbury. Continue down hill to Camerton Inn then second left and second left again*
This former brewery malt house is peacefully located just outside
*continued*

Bath and provides a good base from which to explore the local area. Bedrooms, including several on the ground floor, are well equipped and include thoughtful extras. There is a wood-burning stove in the bar and a varied choice of home-cooked meals is served in the pleasant restaurant.
**ROOMS:** 12 en suite (2 fmly) s £40-£48; d £80 (incl. bkfst) **LB**
**PARKING:** 25 **NOTES:** No smoking in restaurant Closed 24-27 Dec
**CARDS:**

## *Town House*

### ★★★★ The Windsor Hotel

69 Great Pulteney St BA2 4DL
☎ 01225 422100 01225 422550
e-mail: sales@bathwindsorhotel.com
This delightful Georgian town house, situated in handsome Great Pulteney Street, is a short level walk from the centre of town. The Grade I listed terraced house has been refurbished to the highest standard and sumptuously furnished with antique pieces. The restaurant, Sakura, with its traditional Japanese décor overlooks a small Japanese garden, and offers a choice of either sukiyaki or shabu shabu; fresh ingredients are cooked at the table by Japanese waiting staff. The Windsor is a non-smoking establishment.
**ROOMS:** 14 en suite (3 fmly) No smoking in all bedrooms s £85-£135; d £135-£240 (incl. bkfst) * **LB** **FACILITIES:** STV **CONF:** Thtr 15 Board 15 Del £190 * **PARKING:** 11 **NOTES:** No dogs No children 12yrs No smoking in restaurant
**CARDS:**

BATH, continued

### ⇧ *Travelodge*

York Buildings, George St BA1 3EB
☎ 01225 448999

Travelodge offers good quality, good value, modern accommodation. Ideal for families, the spacious, en suite bedrooms include remote-control TV, tea and coffee-making facilities, luxury beds and free morning newspaper. Meals can be taken at the nearby family restaurant. For further details and the Travelodge phone number, consult the Hotel Groups page.

### ○ Menzies Waterside Hotel

Widcombe Basin BA2 4JP
☎ 01225 338855 🖷 01225 428941
***Dir:*** *on A36, 1m from junct with A4*

This hotel was acquired by Menzies as the guide went to press. Public areas are being upgraded and the company's brasserie restaurant concept is being introduced. Please refer to the AA internet site www.theAA.com for current information.
**ROOMS:** 113 rms **CONF:** Thtr 80 Class 40 Board 40

### ○ Express by Holiday Inn

☎ 0800 897121
A modern budget hotel offering comfortable accommodation in refreshing, spacious and comprehensively equipped bedrooms, en suite bathrooms with power showers and continental buffet breakfast included in the room rate. Suitable for business travellers or families. For further details and the Express by Holiday Inn phone number, consult the Hotel Groups page.
**ROOMS:** 86 en suite **NOTES:** Opening February 2002

BATLEY, West Yorkshire Map 08 SE22

### ★★70% Alder House

Towngate Rd, Healey Ln WF17 7HR
☎ 01924 444777 🖷 01924 442644
e-mail: info@alderhousehotel.co.uk
***Dir:*** *M62 junct 27, take A62. After 2m, turn left into Whitelee Rd and left at next junct. Next left into Healey Ln, after 0.25m, hotel on left down Towngate Rd*
An attractive Georgian house tucked away in leafy grounds. Bedrooms are pleasantly furnished and extremely well-equipped. There is a cosy dining room offering a selection of interesting dishes. There is also a bar and a separate lounge area.
**ROOMS:** 20 en suite (1 fmly) s £49.50-£58; d £62-£100 (incl. bkfst) * **LB** **FACILITIES:** STV **CONF:** Thtr 80 Class 40 Board 35 Del from £70 * **PARKING:** 52 **NOTES:** No smoking in restaurant Civ Wed 100 **CARDS:**

BATTLE, East Sussex Map 05 TQ71

### ★★★70% Powder Mills

Powdermill Ln TN33 0SP
☎ 01424 775511 🖷 01424 774540
e-mail: powdc@aol.com
***Dir:*** *through town in direction of Hastings, past abbey on A2100, 1st turning on right and hotel on right after a mile*
An 18th-century mansion set in 150 acres of grounds with lakes and woodlands. The bedrooms in the main building have character and are individually furnished, newer rooms in a separate building are also well-equipped. Extensive day rooms are filled with antiques and provide a relaxing setting.
**ROOMS:** 25 en suite 10 annexe en suite s £75; d £99 (incl. bkfst) * **LB** **FACILITIES:** STV Outdoor swimming Fishing Xmas **CONF:** Thtr 250 Class 50 Board 16 Del £135 * **PARKING:** 101 **NOTES:** No smoking in restaurant Civ Wed 100 **CARDS:**

*See advert on opposite page*

### ★★64% Leeford Place Hotel

Mill Ln, Whatlington TN33 0ND
☎ 01424 772863 🖷 01424 776707
e-mail: info@leefordplace.co.uk
***Dir:*** *A21 towards Hastings turn right at Whatlington Road by the Royal Oak, Leeford Place is 0.5m further on the right*
A pleasant hotel in a peaceful location a short drive from the centre of Battle. Bedrooms are individually decorated and comfortably furnished, many rooms overlook the pretty gardens. Public areas include an attractive lounge bar, a cosy restaurant and banqueting suite.
**ROOMS:** 17 en suite (3 fmly) s £35-£42.50; d £55-£110 (incl. bkfst) * **LB** **FACILITIES:** Fishing **CONF:** Thtr 200 Class 150 Board 40 Del from £95 * **PARKING:** 60 **NOTES:** No smoking in restaurant Civ Wed 70 **CARDS:**

BAWTRY, South Yorkshire Map 08 SK69

### ★★★63% The Crown

REGAL

High St DN10 6JW
☎ 01302 710341 🖷 01302 711798
***Dir:*** *leave A1 at Blyth Service Station, taking A614 to Bawtry. The Crown is on the left hand side in the town centre*
Situated in the centre of the town, this 17th-century coaching inn retains much of its original charm. Public areas include an oak-panelled bar and a cosy restaurant. Well-equipped bedrooms

*continued*

come in a variety of styles and sizes and some have been refurbished to the new 'Corus' brand standard.

CROWN HOTEL
POSTING HOUSE

**ROOMS:** 57 en suite (4 fmly) No smoking in 18 bedrooms s £65; d £50-£75 * **LB** **CONF:** Thtr 150 Class 80 Board 60 Del from £95 * **PARKING:** 50 **NOTES:** No smoking in restaurant Civ Wed 100 **CARDS:**

## BEACONSFIELD, Buckinghamshire — Map 04 SU99

### ★★★★69% Bellhouse

Oxford Rd HP9 2XE
☎ 01753 887211 🖷 01753 888231
e-mail: bellhouse@devere-hotels.com
***Dir:*** *leave M40 at junct 2, exit signed Gerrards Cross/Beaconsfield. At rdbt take A40 to Gerrards Cross. Hotel is 1m on right hand side*

This smart Mediterranean-style hotel is conveniently located close to the M40 and M25. The bedrooms are compact though all offer great comfort and are well-equipped. There is a relaxed brasserie and also a more formal restaurant, with an interesting menu. A range of conference and leisure facilities is available.

**ROOMS:** 136 en suite (11 fmly) No smoking in 86 bedrooms s fr £155; d fr £175 (incl. bkfst) * **LB** **FACILITIES:** STV Indoor swimming (H) Squash Snooker Sauna Solarium Gym Jacuzzi Beauty therapy room Xmas **CONF:** Thtr 400 Class 200 Board 40 **SERVICES:** Lift **PARKING:** 405 **NOTES:** No smoking in restaurant Civ Wed 200 **CARDS:**

### ○ Innkeeper's Lodge Beaconsfield

Aylesbury End HP9 1LW

A new concept in the travel accommodation market. Smart rooms meet essential business requirements but also have home comforts. Dining options include all-day menus plus the added advantage of breakfast, which is included in the room price. Reservations can be made seven days a week through the room reservations number: 0870 243 0500. For further details, consult the Hotel Groups page.

**ROOMS:** 32 en suite **NOTES:** Open now

## BEAMINSTER, Dorset — Map 03 ST40

### ★★★71% ❀ Bridge House

3 Prout Bridge DT8 3AY
☎ 01308 862200 🖷 01308 863700
e-mail: enquiries@bridge-house.co.uk
***Dir:*** *off A3066, 100yds from Town Square*

This family-owned, 13th-century property offers friendly and attentive service. The tastefully decorated bedrooms are divided between the main house and the adjacent coach house. Smart

*continued*

public areas include the Georgian dining room and a breakfast room overlooking the attractive garden.

**ROOMS:** 9 en suite 5 annexe en suite (1 fmly) No smoking in all bedrooms s £51.50-£94; d £114-£119 (incl. bkfst) * **LB** **FACILITIES:** Tennis (hard) Xmas **CONF:** Thtr 20 Class 16 Board 16 Del from £120 * **PARKING:** 22 **NOTES:** No smoking in restaurant Closed 27-31 Dec **CARDS:**

## BEAMISH, Co Durham — Map 12 NZ25

### ★★★69% ❀❀ Beamish Park

Beamish Burn Rd NE16 5EG
☎ 01207 230666 🖷 01207 281260
e-mail: reception@beamish-park-hotel.co.uk
***Dir:*** *from A1(M) take A692 towards Consett, then A6076 towards Stanley. Hotel on left behind Causey Arch Inn*

This stylish, modern hotel is within easy reach of the main north-east commercial and heritage centres and offers bedrooms that come in a variety of styles; downstairs rooms boast patios. Public areas include a lounge bar and conservatory bistro, where cutting edge, carefully prepared food is served. There is also an outside pub, a golf driving range and a nine-hole golf course.

**ROOMS:** 47 en suite (7 fmly) No smoking in 20 bedrooms s £39.50-£44.50; d £49-£65.50 * **LB** **FACILITIES:** STV Golf 9 Putting green 20 bay floodlit golf driving range. Golf tuition by PGA professional ch fac **CONF:** Thtr 50 Class 20 Board 30 Del from £74 * **PARKING:** 100 **CARDS:**

B

## BEAULIEU, Hampshire

Map 04 SU30

### ★★★76% Master Builders House Hotel

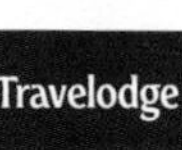
Best Western

SO42 7XB
☎ 01590 616253 01590 616297
e-mail: res@themasterbuilders.co.uk
***Dir:*** *turn off M27, junct2, follow signs Beaulieu, at T junct left onto B3056 1st left to Bucklers Hard, hotel is 2m on left just before village entrance*

The name of the hotel is a testament to the master shipbuilder Henry Adams whose house this once was. A full list of the famous ships built within the village may be found in the Yachtsman's Bar. The Riverside Restaurant and many of the individually styled bedrooms enjoy views over the Beaulieu River. For those guests wishing to travel to the Isle of Wight, the hotel also has its own boat.

**ROOMS:** 8 en suite 17 annexe en suite (2 fmly) No smoking in 12 bedrooms s £115; d £155-£205 (incl. bkfst) * **LB** **FACILITIES:** STV Fishing can sail from hotel on Beaulieu river Xmas **CONF:** Thtr 50 Class 50 Board 25 Del £175 * **PARKING:** 70 **NOTES:** No dogs (ex guide dogs) No smoking in restaurant Civ Wed 60 **CARDS:**

### ★★★70% Montagu Arms

Palace Ln SO42 7ZL
☎ 01590 612324 01590 612188
e-mail: enquires@montagu-arms.co.uk
***Dir:*** *leave M27 at junct 2, turn left at rdbt, then follow tourist signs for Beaulieu, continue to Dibden Purlieu, then right at rdbt, hotel is on left*

This attractive, creeper-clad hotel stands in the centre of picturesque Beaulieu. Bedrooms are tastefully decorated and thoughtfully equipped. Public rooms include a cosy bar, an elegant lounge and adjoining conservatory, which overlooks the pretty walled garden. Guests can dine in either the restaurant or the more informal Monty's.

**ROOMS:** 24 en suite s £80; d £130-£200 (incl. bkfst) * **LB** **FACILITIES:** Use of health club in Brockenhurst Xmas **CONF:** Thtr 50 Class 16 Board 26 Del £135 * **PARKING:** 86 **NOTES:** Civ Wed 50 **CARDS:**

*See advert on opposite page*

### ★★★65% Beaulieu

Beaulieu Rd SO42 7YQ
☎ 023 8029 3344 023 8029 2729
e-mail: reservations@carehotels.co.uk
***Dir:*** *M27 junct 1 follow signs onto A337 towards Lyndhurst. Left at traffic lights in Lyndhurst through village turn right onto B3056 & continue for 3m*

Conveniently located in the heart of the New Forest and close to Beaulieu Road railway station, this popular, small hotel provides an ideal base for exploring the surrounding area. Facilities include an indoor swimming pool, an outdoor children's play area and an

*continued*

adjoining pub. A daily changing menu is offered in the restaurant, which has excellent views.

**ROOMS:** 15 en suite 3 annexe en suite (2 fmly) s £65-£80; d £120-£140 (incl. bkfst) * **LB** **FACILITIES:** Indoor swimming (H) Steam room ch fac Xmas **CONF:** Thtr 60 Class 40 Board 30 Del from £90 * **PARKING:** 60 **NOTES:** No smoking in restaurant Civ Wed 80 **CARDS:**

## BEBINGTON, Merseyside

Map 07 SJ38

### ⌂ *Travelodge*

Travelodge

New Chester Rd L62 9AQ
☎ 0151 327 2489 0151 327 2489
***Dir:*** *on A41, northbound off, junct 5 on M53*

Travelodge offers good quality, good value, modern accommodation. Ideal for families, the spacious, en suite bedrooms include remote-control TV, tea and coffee-making facilities, luxury beds and free morning newspaper. Meals can be taken at the nearby family restaurant. For further details and the Travelodge phone number, consult the Hotel Groups page.

**ROOMS:** 31 en suite

## BECKENHAM, Kent

### ○ Innkeeper's Lodge Beckenham

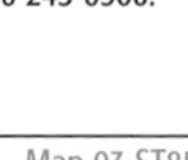
Innkeeper's Lodge

422 Upper Elmers End Rd BR3 3HQ

A new concept in the travel accommodation market. Smart rooms meet essential business requirements but also have home comforts. Dining options include all-day menus plus the added advantage of breakfast, which is included in the room price. Reservations can be made seven days a week through the room reservations number: 0870 243 0500. For further details, consult the Hotel Groups page.

**ROOMS:** 24 en suite

## BECKINGTON, Somerset

Map 03 ST85

### ★★69% *Woolpack Inn*

BA3 6SP
☎ 01373 831244 01373 831223
***Dir:*** *on A36*

This charming coaching inn dates back to the 16th century and retains many original features including flagstone floors, open fireplaces and exposed beams. There is a cosy lounge and a choice of places to eat: the bar for light snacks and for more substantial meals the Oak Room or the Garden Room, which leads onto a pleasant inner courtyard.

**ROOMS:** 12 en suite No smoking in 1 bedroom **FACILITIES:** STV **CONF:** Thtr 30 Class 20 Board 20 **PARKING:** 16 **NOTES:** No children 5yrs **CARDS:**

### ⌂ *Travelodge*

Travelodge

BA3 6SF
☎ 01373 830251 01373 830251
***Dir:*** *on A36*

Travelodge offers good quality, good value, modern accommodation. Ideal for families, the spacious, en suite bedrooms include remote-control TV, tea and coffee-making facilities, luxury beds and free morning newspaper. Meals can be taken at the nearby family restaurant. For further details and the Travelodge phone number, consult the Hotel Groups page.

**ROOMS:** 40 en suite

## BEDFORD, Bedfordshire    Map 04 TL04

### ★★★74% Woodlands Manor
Green Ln, Clapham MK41 6EP
☎ 01234 363281 📠 01234 272390
e-mail: woodlands.manor@pageant.co.uk
***Dir:*** *A6 from Bedford, towards Kettering. Clapham is 1st village N of town centre, on entering village first right into Green Lane, Manor 200mtrs on right*

A country house hotel set in wooded grounds on the outskirts of the village. The drawing room, with its rich colour scheme, wood panelled walls and large sofas, is very comfortable. Bedrooms are pleasantly decorated with cherry wood furniture and co-ordinated colour schemes. The elegant restaurant offers imaginative cooking.
**ROOMS:** 30 en suite 3 annexe en suite (4 fmly) No smoking in 6 bedrooms s £59.50-£80; d £80-£150 (incl. bkfst) * **LB** **FACILITIES:** STV Full facilities nearby at no extra cost. Xmas **CONF:** Thtr 80 Class 28 Board 40 Del from £105 * **PARKING:** 100 **NOTES:** No smoking in restaurant Civ Wed 50 **CARDS:**

### ★★★70% The Barns
Cardington Rd MK44 3SA
☎ 01234 270044 📠 01234 273102
***Dir:*** *take A421 from M1 and turn off at A603 Sandy, turn left to Bedford on A603*

This stylish hotel enjoys a tranquil riverside location. The well-equipped bedrooms reflect a modern, comfortable approach with many rooms providing extra space. Equally pleasing are the cosy day rooms, which include two informal bars and a recently refurbished restaurant.
**ROOMS:** 48 en suite No smoking in 16 bedrooms s £95; d £105 * **LB** **FACILITIES:** STV Free use of local leisure centre (1mile) Xmas **CONF:** Thtr 120 Class 40 Board 40 Del from £99 * **PARKING:** 90 **NOTES:** No smoking in restaurant Civ Wed 100 **CARDS:**

### ⌂ *Travelodge Bedford East*
Black Cat Roundabout MK44 3QT
☎ 08700 850 950
Travelodge offers good quality, good value, modern accommodation. Ideal for families, the spacious, en suite bedrooms include remote-control TV, tea and coffee-making facilities, luxury beds and free morning newspaper. Meals can be taken at the nearby family restaurant. For further details and the Travelodge phone number, consult the Hotel Groups page.

### ○ Innkeeper's Lodge Bedford
403 Goldington Rd MK41 0DS
☎ 0870 243 0500
A new concept in the travel accommodation market. Smart rooms meet essential business requirements but also have home comforts. Dining options include all-day menus plus the added advantage of breakfast, which is included in the room price. Reservations can be made seven days a week through the room reservations number: 0870 243 0500. For further details, consult the Hotel Groups page.
**ROOMS:** 47 en suite

## BELFORD, Northumberland    Map 12 NU13

### ★★★69% *Blue Bell*
Market Place NE70 7NE
☎ 01668 213543 📠 01668 213787
e-mail: bluebel@globalnet.co.uk
***Dir:*** *centre of village on left of St Mary's church*
This long-established and popular former coaching inn lies in the Village Square. Guests are well looked after by friendly and

*continued on p86*

BELFORD, continued

attentive staff. There is a choice of superior or standard bedrooms, all well-equipped. A variety of menus provide an extensive choice of food in the bar, bistro and main restaurant.
**ROOMS:** 17 en suite (1 fmly) No smoking in 4 bedrooms **CONF:** Thtr 140 Class 120 Board 30 **PARKING:** 17 **NOTES:** No smoking in restaurant **CARDS:**

### ⌂ Purdy Lodge

Adderstone Services NE70 7JU
☎ 01668 213000 ▤ 01668 213131
e-mail: james@purdylodge.co.uk
***Dir:*** *between Alnwick & Berwick turn off A1 to B1341*
Conveniently situated on the A1, this family-owned lodge provides practical accommodation. All the bedrooms look out over fields to the rear and are insulated from road noise. As well as a 24-hour café there is a restaurant open for dinners and a cosy lounge bar, also serving food.
**ROOMS:** 20 en suite s £39.35-£42; d £39.95-£42 * **CONF:** Thtr 40 Class 30 Board 20

## BELLINGHAM, Northumberland — Map 12 NY88

### ★★67% Riverdale Hall

NE48 2JT
☎ 01434 220254 ▤ 01434 220457
e-mail: iben@riverdalehall.demon.co.uk
***Dir:*** *turn off B6320, after bridge, hotel on left*

Standing in grounds overlooking its own cricket pitch and the North Tyne, this hotel offers well-equipped bedrooms, some with south facing balconies. Menus are imaginative, featuring much of the local produce, and vegetarians are well catered for. Australian wines feature strongly on the wine list.
**ROOMS:** 20 en suite (11 fmly) s £39-£48; d £69-£84 (incl. bkfst) * **LB** **FACILITIES:** Indoor swimming (H) Fishing Sauna Croquet lawn Putting green Cricket field Petanque ch fac Xmas **CONF:** Thtr 40 Class 40 Board 20 Del from £69 * **PARKING:** 60 **CARDS:**

## BELPER, Derbyshire — Map 08 SK34

### ★★★73% Makeney Hall Country House

corus

Makeney, Milford DE56 0RS
☎ 01332 842999 ▤ 01332 842777
e-mail: reservations@corushotels.com
***Dir:*** *turn off A6 between Belper and Duffield at Milford, signposted Makeney. Hotel is 0.25m further along on left*
A beautifully restored Victorian mansion standing in six acres of delightful gardens and grounds above the River Derwent. Bedrooms vary in style and size and are divided between the main house rooms and the ground floor courtyard rooms; two bedrooms have been specifically designed for disabled access. Public rooms include Lavinia's restaurant where diners are offered a range of interesting dishes.

**ROOMS:** 27 en suite 18 annexe en suite (3 fmly) No smoking in 6 bedrooms s fr £85; d fr £95 * **LB** **FACILITIES:** STV Xmas **CONF:** Thtr 180 Class 80 Board 50 Del from £130 * **SERVICES:** Lift **PARKING:** 150 **NOTES:** No smoking in restaurant Civ Wed 150
**CARDS:**

### ★★68% *The Lion Hotel & Restaurant*

Bridge St DE56 1AX
☎ 01773 824033 ▤ 01773 828393
e-mail: enquiries@lionhotel.uk.com
***Dir:*** *Belper is 8m NW of Derby, hotel is on the A6*

THE
LION
HOTEL

On the border of the Peak District, yet convenient distance for the M1, this 18th-century hotel provides an ideal base for exploring local attractions. The tasteful bedrooms are well-equipped and the public rooms include an attractive restaurant and two cosy bars; a modern function suite also proves popular.
**ROOMS:** 20 rms (14 en suite) (2 fmly) **FACILITIES:** STV **CONF:** Thtr 130 Class 60 Board 50 **PARKING:** 30 **NOTES:** No smoking in restaurant
**CARDS:**

## BELTON, Lincolnshire — Map 08 SK93

### ★★★★77% Belton Woods

De Vere Hotels

NG32 2LN
☎ 01476 593200 ▤ 01476 574547
e-mail: devere.belton@airtime.co.uk
***Dir:*** *from A1 turn onto B1174, follow signs to Belton House. Turn left towards Great Gonerby. Then left onto A607. Hotel 0.5m on left*
A destination venue for golf and sports lovers as well as a relaxing executive retreat for seminars, Belton Woods benefits both from easy access to major routes and from an idyllic parkland location. Attractive public areas include a choice of restaurants and bars.

*continued*

The smartly appointed bedrooms, many of which overlook the golf courses, are both spacious and well-equipped.
**ROOMS:** 136 en suite No smoking in 48 bedrooms s £129; d £149 * **LB FACILITIES:** STV Indoor swimming (H) Golf 45 Tennis (hard) Squash Snooker Sauna Solarium Gym Croquet lawn Putting green Jacuzzi Hair & beauty salon Steamroom Xmas **CONF:** Thtr 245 Class 130 Board 80 Del from £175.07 * **SERVICES:** Lift **PARKING:** 500 **NOTES:** No smoking in restaurant Civ Wed 60
**CARDS:**

## BEMBRIDGE See Wight, Isle of

## BERKELEY, Gloucestershire Map 03 ST69

### ★★76% The Old Schoolhouse

34 Canonbury St GL13 9BG
☎ 01453 811711 01453 511761
e-mail: oldschoolhouse@btinternet.com
***Dir:*** *0.5m off A38 next to Berkeley Castle. Follow brown tourist signs*
Situated next to Berkeley Castle, this fine old building was formerly a school. Bedrooms, all of a generous size, have extensive modern facilities. Cooking is of a high standard and a varied menu is served. The owners are renowned for their excellent hospitality.
**ROOMS:** 8 en suite (1 fmly) No smoking in all bedrooms s £55; d £66 (incl. bkfst) * **LB FACILITIES:** ch fac Xmas **CONF:** Del £75 * **PARKING:** 20 **NOTES:** No smoking in restaurant
**CARDS:**

Fancy a Singapore Sling? Bar staff in five star hotels should be skilled cocktail mixers.

## BERKELEY ROAD, Gloucestershire Map 03 ST79

### ★★★66% Prince of Wales

Berkeley Rd GL13 9HD
☎ 01453 810474 01453 511370
e-mail: PrinceofWaleshotel@Berkeleyglos.fsnet.co.uk
***Dir:*** *on A38, 6m S of M5 junc 13 and 6m N of junc 14*
This smartly presented hotel enjoys a peaceful location and provides well-equipped accommodation. There is an informal bar, a restaurant that serves food with an Italian influence, meeting rooms and a spacious car park.
**ROOMS:** 43 en suite (2 fmly) No smoking in 10 bedrooms
**FACILITIES:** Spa STV ch fac **CONF:** Thtr 200 Class 60 Board 60 Del from £85 * **PARKING:** 150 **CARDS:**

## BERWICK-UPON-TWEED, Northumberland Map 12 NT95

### ★★★66% Marshall Meadows Country House

TD15 1UT
☎ 01289 331133 01289 331438
e-mail: stay@marshallmeadows.co.uk
***Dir:*** *signposted directly off A1, 200 yds from Scottish Border*
This stylish Georgian mansion, set in wooded grounds flanked by farmland, is a popular venue for weddings and conferences. Bedrooms are comfortable and well-equipped. Public rooms include a cosy bar, an inviting lounge and a two-tier restaurant, serving imaginative dishes.
**ROOMS:** 19 en suite (2 fmly) No smoking in 10 bedrooms s £75; d £85-£100 (incl. bkfst) * **LB FACILITIES:** Croquet lawn Petanque Xmas **CONF:** Thtr 120 Class 180 Board 60 Del from £95 * **PARKING:** 87 **NOTES:** No smoking in restaurant Civ Wed
**CARDS:**

*See advert on this page*

BERWICK-UPON-TWEED, continued

### ★63% Queens Head
Sandgate TD15 1EP
☎ 01289 307852 🖹 01289 307858
***Dir:*** *into town centre from A1, head towards Town Hall down High St, right at bottom to Hide Hill,located next to cinema*
Set in the centre, close to the old walls of this garrison town, the Queens Head Hotel provides mainly spacious bedrooms. Good value meals are served in either the lounge area or the dining room.
**ROOMS:** 6 en suite (5 fmly) No smoking in all bedrooms s £35; d £55 (incl. bkfst) * **LB** **NOTES:** No smoking in restaurant
**CARDS:**

## BEVERLEY, East Riding of Yorkshire — Map 08 TA03

### ★★★67% Beverley Arms
REGAL
North Bar Within HU17 8DD
☎ 01482 869241 🖹 01482 870907
e-mail: 113566,1542@compuserve.com
***Dir:*** *opposite St Marys Church, just before North Bar*

History links this hotel to the highwayman Dick Turpin. Today a feature of the establishment is the spacious, flagstoned, Shires Lounge. There are also two bars and an attractively appointed restaurant. Bedrooms, in the older part of the building, are particularly charming. All rooms are equipped with modern comforts. Staff are friendly and helpful.
**ROOMS:** 56 en suite (4 fmly) No smoking in 30 bedrooms s £90; d £100-£110 * **LB** **FACILITIES:** Xmas **CONF:** Thtr 60 Class 40 Board 30 Del from £105 * **SERVICES:** Lift **PARKING:** 50 **NOTES:** No smoking in restaurant **CARDS:**

### ★★★67% Tickton Grange
Tickton HU17 9SH
☎ 01964 543666 🖹 01964 542556
e-mail: maggy@tickton-grange.demon.co.uk
***Dir:*** *3m NE on A1035*
A charming Georgian country house situated in four acres of grounds and attractive gardens. Bedrooms are characterful, and individually furnished and decorated. A pre-dinner drink can be taken in the comfortable lounge bar prior to enjoying fine modern British cooking in the restaurant. The hotel is a popular venue for weddings and business conferences.
**ROOMS:** 17 en suite (2 fmly) s £65; d £75 * **LB** **FACILITIES:** STV **CONF:** Thtr 200 Class 100 Board 80 **PARKING:** 65 **NOTES:** No dogs (ex guide dogs) No smoking in restaurant RS 25-29 Dec Civ Wed 150
**CARDS:**

Need to unwind? Look out for hotels with Spa in their entry.

### ★★★66% Lairgate Hotel
30 Lairgate Rd HU17 8EP
☎ 01482 882141 🖹 01482 861067
Fully refurbished, this Georgian hotel is just off the market square. It offers modern, comfortable facilities in its bedrooms, a comfortable lounge and restaurant, and a popular sun terrace and car park at the rear.
**ROOMS:** 16 en suite No smoking in 12 bedrooms s £70-£80; d £85-£95 (incl. bkfst) * **CONF:** Board 20 **NOTES:** No dogs (ex guide dogs) No smoking in restaurant **CARDS:**

### ★★73% The Manor House
Northlands, Walkington HU17 8RT
☎ 01482 881645 🖹 01482 866501
e-mail: the-manor-house@fsbusiness.co.uk
***Dir:*** *4m SW off B1230. Follow brown 'Walkington' signs from junct 38 on M62*
This delightful country house hotel is set in beautiful, well-tended gardens. The spacious bedrooms have been attractively decorated and thoughtfully equipped. Public rooms include a conservatory restaurant and an inviting lounge. A good range of dishes is available from two menus, with an emphasis on local produce.
**ROOMS:** 6 en suite 1 annexe en suite (1 fmly) s £70-£80; d £80-£110 * **LB** **CONF:** Thtr 20 Class 20 Board 20 **PARKING:** 40 **NOTES:** No smoking in restaurant Civ Wed 70 **CARDS:**

## BEWDLEY, Worcestershire — Map 07 SO77

### ★★63% The George
Load St DY12 2AW
☎ 01299 402117 🖹 01299 401269
e-mail: enquiries@georgehotelbewdley.co.uk
***Dir:*** *in town centre opposite town hall*
Situated in the heart of Bewdley, this friendly 16th-century inn features large oak beams, panelling, slate tiles and traditional fireplaces. Bedrooms are individually decorated and furnished to a good standard. Public areas include a coffee shop, function rooms, bars and a restaurant serving a wide-ranging menu.
**ROOMS:** 11 en suite s £45-£55; d £65-£85 (incl. bkfst) * **LB** **CONF:** Thtr 50 Class 50 Board 40 Del from £70 * **PARKING:** 50 **NOTES:** No dogs (ex guide dogs) No smoking in restaurant
**CARDS:**

### ★★60% Black Boy
Kidderminster Rd DY12 1AG
☎ 01299 402119 🖹 01299 403250
e-mail: rc@midnet.co.uk
This 18th-century inn stands on the A456 close to both the River Severn and the centre of this lovely old town. The bedrooms are simple but comfortable. There are pleasant bar facilities and a small, cosy restaurant.
**ROOMS:** 6 en suite (2 fmly) s fr £42; d £55-£75 (incl. bkfst) * **LB** **PARKING:** 28 **NOTES:** No dogs (ex guide dogs) No smoking in restaurant **CARDS:**

## BEXLEY, Greater London — Map 05 TQ47

### ★★★★71% Bexleyheath Marriott Hotel
Marriott HOTELS · RESORTS · SUITES
1 Broadway DA6 7JZ
☎ 020 8298 1000 🖹 020 8298 1234
e-mail: bexleyheath@marriotthotels.co.uk
***Dir:*** *take A2 (London Bound) from junct 2 of M25 exit Black Prince interchange onto A220, follow signs Bexleyheath, left at 2nd set of traffic lights in to hotel*
Situated on the edge of town, this extremely modern hotel is linked to a covered municipal car park. The spacious bedrooms are smartly appointed, comfortable and well laid out. There are

continued

wo restaurants, as well as full room service. The hotel also offers conference facilities and has a well-equipped leisure club.

**ROOMS:** 138 en suite (16 fmly) No smoking in 53 bedrooms d £105 * **LB FACILITIES:** Spa STV Indoor swimming (H) Solarium Gym Steam room entertainment Xmas **CONF:** Thtr 250 Class 120 Board 34 Del £150 * **SERVICES:** Lift air con **PARKING:** 100 **NOTES:** Civ Wed 40 **CARDS:**

★★★64% **Posthouse Bexley** **Posthouse**
Black Prince Interchange, Southwold Rd
DA5 1ND
☎ 0870 400 9006 🖹 01322 526113
***Dir:*** *follow A2 to exit signposted A220/A223 Black Prince interchange Bexley, Bexleyheath & Crayford*

A purpose built hotel with well-equipped bedrooms, all smartly appointed in a modern style. Public areas include a choice of bars and the restaurant, offering a range of popular dishes. The hotel offers meeting rooms and a business centre.

**ROOMS:** 105 en suite (10 fmly) No smoking in 50 bedrooms d £89-£99 * **LB FACILITIES:** Xmas **CONF:** Thtr 70 Class 30 Board 30 **SERVICES:** Lift **PARKING:** 200 **CARDS:**

## BIBURY, Gloucestershire Map 04 SP10

★★★79% ❀❀ **Swan**
GL7 5NW
☎ 01285 740695 🖹 01285 740473
e-mail: swanhot1@swanhotel-cotswolds.co.uk
***Dir:*** *off B4425, by bridge over the River Coln*

The Swan hotel, originally built as a 17th-century coaching inn, is set in peaceful, picturesque and beautiful surroundings. It now provides well-equipped and smartly presented accommodation, and public areas that are comfortable and elegant. There is a choice of dining options to suit all tastes.

**ROOMS:** 18 en suite (1 fmly) s £99-£125; d £180-£260 (incl. bkfst) * **LB FACILITIES:** Fishing Jacuzzi Xmas **CONF:** Thtr 80 Board 30 **SERVICES:** Lift **PARKING:** 16 **NOTES:** No dogs (ex guide dogs) No smoking in restaurant Civ Wed **CARDS:**

*See advert on this page*

BIBURY, continued

**★★★72% ◎◎ Bibury Court**
GL7 5NT
☎ 01285 740337 📠 01285 740660
e-mail: info@biburycourt.co.uk
***Dir:*** *on B4425 beside the River Coln, behind St Marys Church*
Located in extensive grounds beside the River Coln, this elegant manor house dates back to Tudor times. Spacious public areas offer charm and character, the bedrooms are furnished in keeping with the style of the building and enjoyable food is served in the restaurants.
**ROOMS:** 18 en suite (3 fmly) s £100; d £115-£180 (incl. cont bkfst) * **LB** **FACILITIES:** Fishing Croquet lawn **CONF:** Board 12 Del £170 * **PARKING:** 100 **NOTES:** No smoking in restaurant
**CARDS:**

*See advert on page 89*

BICESTER, Oxfordshire Map 04 SP52

**★★76% ◎ Bignell Park Hotel & Restaurant**
Chesterton OX26 1UE
☎ 01869 241444 & 241192 📠 01869 241444
***Dir:*** *on A4095 Witney road*

This charming hotel near Bicester features a dramatic galleried restaurant with fine artwork, a fireplace and exposed beams. The cuisine is imaginative and many of the dishes use fresh local produce. Bedrooms are stylish and comfortably furnished with some unusual pieces of furniture, the newer rooms are particularly spacious.
**ROOMS:** 23 en suite s £85-£95; d £90-£100 (incl. bkfst) * **FACILITIES:** STV **CONF:** Thtr 25 Class 25 Board 14 **PARKING:** 40 **NOTES:** No dogs (ex guide dogs) No children 6yrs No smoking in restaurant RS Sun **CARDS:**

**⇧ *Travelodge***
Northampton Rd, Ardley OX6 9RD
☎ 01869 346060 📠 01869 345030
***Dir:*** *M40 junct 10*
Travelodge offers good quality, good value, modern accommodation. Ideal for families, the spacious, en suite bedrooms include remote-control TV, tea and coffee-making facilities, luxury beds and free morning newspaper. Meals can be taken at the nearby family restaurant. For further details and the Travelodge phone number, consult the Hotel Groups page.

**ROOMS:** 98 en suite **CONF:** Thtr 40 Class 20 Board 20

Packed in a hurry? Ironing facilities should be available at all star levels, either in rooms or on request.

BIDEFORD, Devon Map 02 SS4

**★★★67% Royal**
Barnstaple St EX39 4AE
☎ 01237 472005 📠 01237 478957
e-mail: info@royalbideford.co.uk
***Dir:*** *at eastern end of Bideford Bridge*
Attractive and well-equipped bedrooms are offered at this late 16th-century hotel, conveniently situated near the town centre and the quay. Freshly prepared meals are served in the spacious restaurant, while in the bar, a range of lighter meals is available. The wood panelled Kingsley suite is ideal for functions or meetings. Service is friendly and attentive.
**ROOMS:** 31 en suite (3 fmly) s £45-£69; d £45-£69 * **LB** **FACILITIES:** STV entertainment Xmas **CONF:** Thtr 100 Class 100 Board 100 **SERVICES:** Lift **PARKING:** 70 **NOTES:** Civ Wed 100
**CARDS:**

**★★75% ◎ Yeoldon Country House**
Durrant Ln, Northam EX39 2RL
☎ 01237 474400 📠 01237 476618
e-mail: yeoldonhouse@aol.com
***Dir:*** *from Barnstaple follow A39 over River Torridge Bridge, at rdbt turn right onto A386 towards Northam then 3rd right into Durrant Ln*
This charming Victorian country house hotel boasts a superb location, peacefully situated overlooking the River Torridge. Individually decorated bedrooms have bags of character, allied with useful additional facilities. The attractive dining room is the venue for imaginative menus, making optimum usage of fresh local produce. There is a comfortable lounge bar, and a relaxing lounge.
**ROOMS:** 10 en suite No smoking in all bedrooms s £50-£60; d £80-£95 (incl. bkfst) * **LB** **FACILITIES:** ch fac **PARKING:** 15 **NOTES:** No smoking in restaurant Closed 24-27 Dec
**CARDS:**

*See advert on opposite page*

BIGBURY-ON-SEA, Devon Map 03 SX64

**★★69% Henley**
TQ7 4AR
☎ 01548 810240 📠 01548 810240
***Dir:*** *through Bigbury village, pass Golf Centre into Bigbury-on-Sea. Hotel on left as road slopes towards the shore*
This delightfully different small hotel boasts spectacular views, embracing the Avon estuary, Bigbury Bay and beyond. Originally built during Edwardian times, there is a wonderfully unhurried atmosphere here, combined with understated style; all the elements required for an utterly relaxing break! The menu offers dishes cooked with care and imagination, utilising excellent local produce. A sandy beach can be reached by a private cliff path descending through the hotel's pretty gardens.
**ROOMS:** 6 en suite (1 fmly) No smoking in all bedrooms s £45-£50; d £70-£80 (incl. bkfst) * **LB** **PARKING:** 9 **NOTES:** No smoking in restaurant Closed Dec-Feb **CARDS:**

BIGGLESWADE, Bedfordshire Map 04 TL14

**★★67% *Stratton House Hotel***
London Rd SG18 8ED
☎ 01767 312442 📠 01767 600416
e-mail: reception@strattonhouse.demon.co.uk
***Dir:*** *Nthbound; A1 1st turning to Biggleswade, hotel before town centre. Sthbound; A1 leave at Sainsburys rdbt through town on right opposite Red Lion PH*
Ideally situated just a few minutes from the A1, this small hotel

*continued*

offers comfortable accommodation. Bedrooms are well presented and public areas include a cosy lounge, with a fire and a popular bar; service is both efficient and friendly.
**ROOMS:** 31 en suite (1 fmly) No smoking in 6 bedrooms **CONF:** Thtr 50 Class 30 Board 28 **PARKING:** 40 **CARDS:**

## BILBROUGH, North Yorkshire — Map 08 SE54

### Travelodge

Tadcaster LS24 8EG
☎ 01937 531823 Fax 01937 531823
***Dir:*** *A64 eastbound*

Travelodge

Travelodge offers good quality, good value, modern accommodation. Ideal for families, the spacious, en suite bedrooms include remote-control TV, tea and coffee-making facilities, luxury beds and free morning newspaper. Meals can be taken at the nearby family restaurant. For further details and the Travelodge phone number, consult the Hotel Groups page.

**ROOMS:** 62 en suite

## BILLINGHAM See Stockton-on-Tees

## BINFIELD, Berkshire — Map 04 SU87

### Travelodge

London Rd RG42 4AA
☎ 01344 485940
***Dir:*** *exit junct 10 on M4(Bracknell) take 1st exit towards Binfield*

Travelodge

Travelodge offers good quality, good value, modern accommodation. Ideal for families, the spacious, en suite bedrooms include remote-control TV, tea and coffee-making facilities, luxury beds and free morning newspaper. Meals can be taken at the nearby family restaurant. For further details and the Travelodge phone number, consult the Hotel Groups page.

**ROOMS:** 35 en suite

## BIRCH MOTORWAY SERVICE AREA (M62), Greater Manchester — Map 07 SD80

### Travelodge (East)

M62 Service Area East Bound OL10 2HQ
☎ 08700 850950

Travelodge

Travelodge offers good quality, good value, modern accommodation. Ideal for families, the spacious, en suite bedrooms include remote-control TV, tea and coffee-making facilities, luxury beds and free morning newspaper. Meals can be taken at the nearby family restaurant. For further details and the Travelodge phone number, consult the Hotel Groups page.

**ROOMS:** 55 en suite

### Travelodge (West)

M62 Service Area West Bound OL10 2HQ
☎ 08700 850950

Travelodge

Travelodge offers good quality, good value, modern accommodation. Ideal for families, the spacious, en suite bedrooms include remote-control TV, tea and coffee-making facilities, luxury beds and free morning newspaper. Meals can be taken at the nearby family restaurant. For further details and the Travelodge phone number, consult the Hotel Groups page.

## BIRKENHEAD, Merseyside — Map 07 SJ38

### ★★★69% Bowler Hat

2 Talbot Rd, Prenton CH43 2HH
☎ 0151 652 4931 Fax 0151 653 8127
e-mail: bowlerhathotel@corushotelsoa.com
***Dir:*** *1m from junct 3 of M53*

corus

This friendly hotel is situated in a quiet, leafy area on the edge of town. Extensive function facilities are provided and the hotel is popular for wedding receptions. Bedrooms are well-equipped with modern facilities. There is a popular restaurant and a selection of lighter meals is available in the bar.
**ROOMS:** 32 en suite No smoking in 18 bedrooms s £45-£75; d £65-£90 (incl. cont bkfst) * **LB** **FACILITIES:** STV Xmas **CONF:** Thtr 150 Class 80 Board 40 Del £100 * **PARKING:** 85 **NOTES:** No smoking in restaurant RS Saturdays Civ Wed 90 **CARDS:**

BIRKENHEAD, continued

**★★★67% Riverhill**
Talbot Rd, Prenton CH43 2HJ
☎ 0151 653 3773 Fax 0151 653 7162
e-mail: riverhill@tinyonline.co.uk
***Dir:*** *1m from M53 junct 3, along the A552 turn left onto B5151 at traffic lights hotel 0.5m on right*
Pretty lawns and gardens provide the setting for this friendly hotel, conveniently situated about a mile from the M53. Attractively furnished, well-equipped bedrooms include ground floor, family, and four-poster rooms. Business meetings and weddings can be catered for. A wide choice of dishes is available in the restaurant, overlooking the garden.
**ROOMS:** 14 en suite (1 fmly) s £49.50; d £49.50 * **LB**
**FACILITIES:** STV Free use of local leisure facilities **CONF:** Thtr 50 Class 30 Board 52 Del £95 * **PARKING:** 32 **NOTES:** No dogs (ex guide dogs) No smoking in restaurant Civ Wed 40
**CARDS:**

**Premier Lodge (Wirral)**
Greasby Rd CH49 2PP
☎ 0870 700 1582 Fax 0870 700 1583
***Dir:*** *Situated 9m from Liverpool city centre.& 2m from junct 2 M53 just off B5139*
Premier Lodge offers modern, well-equipped, en suite accommodation suitable for both business and leisure travellers. Meals can be taken at the adjacent popular restaurant and bar, which is fully licensed. For further details, consult the Hotel Groups page.
**ROOMS:** 30 en suite d £42 *

BIRMINGHAM, West Midlands Map 07 SP08
see also Bromsgrove, Lea Marston, Oldbury & Sutton Coldfield

**★★★★★67% Birmingham Marriott Hotel**

Marriott
HOTELS · RESORTS · SUITES
12 Hagley Rd, Five Ways B16 8SJ
☎ 0121 452 1144 Fax 0121 456 3442
e-mail: claire.lawson@whitbread.com

Set in the Birmingham suburb of Edgbaston, this Edwardian hotel is a building of great charm and character. The smart, air-conditioned bedrooms are spacious and equipped with a comprehensive range of facilities. Guests have the choice of two dining options, Langtry's Brasserie with its Edwardian conservatory theme and the Sir Edward Elgar Restaurant for fine dining.
**ROOMS:** 98 en suite No smoking in 54 bedrooms d £119-£199 * **LB**
**FACILITIES:** STV Indoor swimming (H) Solarium Gym Jacuzzi Beauty salon Steam room entertainment Xmas **CONF:** Thtr 30 Board 20 Del from £175 * **SERVICES:** Lift air con **PARKING:** 70
**CARDS:**

**★★★★70% The Burlington**
Burlington Arcade, 126 New St B2 4JQ
☎ 0121 643 9191 Fax 0121 628 5005
e-mail: mail@burlingtonhotel.com
***Dir:*** *M6 junct 6 and follow signs for City Centre, then onto A38*

BURLINGTON
HOTEL

The Burlington's original Victorian design, much of it still in evidence, has been blended together with modern facilities. Bedrooms are furnished and equipped to a good standard. Carefully prepared meals are served in the Berlioz Restaurant.
**ROOMS:** 112 en suite (6 fmly) No smoking in 49 bedrooms s £130-£175, d £140-£175 (incl. bkfst) * **LB** **FACILITIES:** STV Sauna Solarium Gym Jacuzzi Xmas **CONF:** Thtr 400 Class 175 **SERVICES:** Lift
**NOTES:** Civ Wed 200 **CARDS:**

**★★★★69% Crowne Plaza Birmingham**
Central Square B1 1HH
☎ 0121 631 2000 Fax 0121 643 9018
***Dir:*** *from A38, follow City Centre signs, go over flyover & through 2 tunnels. After 2nd tunnel-Suffolk Queensway-join left slip road*
Located in the city centre, this smart hotel offers spacious, very well-equipped bedrooms with air-conditioning. Additional facilities include a good range of conference and meeting rooms and a leisure club. Service is both professional and friendly.
**ROOMS:** 284 en suite (188 fmly) No smoking in 159 bedrooms s £125-£139; d £125-£149 * **LB** **FACILITIES:** Spa STV Indoor swimming (H) Sauna Solarium Gym Jacuzzi Children's pool, steam room. Xmas
**CONF:** Thtr 150 Class 75 Board 50 Del from £155 * **SERVICES:** Lift air con **NOTES:** No smoking in restaurant
**CARDS:**

**★★★66% Copthorne Hotel Birmingham**
Paradise Circus B3 3HJ
☎ 0121 200 2727 Fax 0121 200 1197
e-mail: sales.birmingham@mill-cop.com
***Dir:*** *follow signs to 'International Convention Centre, then bear right for hotel entrance*
One of the few city centre hotels with its own parking facility. Bedrooms are spacious with a choice of styles and all with excellent facilities. Guests can enjoy a variety of dining options, Goldies Brasserie having a contemporary menu. Additional features include a wide range of function rooms, a business centre, and a leisure complex.
**ROOMS:** 212 en suite No smoking in 108 bedrooms s £79-£145; d £79-£165 * **LB** **FACILITIES:** STV Indoor swimming (H) Sauna Gym Jacuzzi
**CONF:** Thtr 200 Class 120 Board 30 **SERVICES:** Lift **PARKING:** 88
**NOTES:** No dogs (ex guide dogs) **CARDS:**

Weekend away? Hotels with LB in their entry offer leisure breaks.

★★★71% **The Westley**

Best Western

30-90 Westley Rd, Acocks Green B27 7UJ
☎ 0121 706 4312 🖷 0121 706 2824
e-mail: reservations@westeyhotel.co.uk
***Dir:*** *take A41 signed Birmingham on Solihull By-Pass and continue to Acocks Green. At rdbt, 2nd exit B4146 Westley Rd, hotel 200 yds on left*
Set in the city suburbs and conveniently located for the N.E.C and airport, this friendly hotel provides well-equipped, smartly presented bedrooms. In addition to the main restaurant, there is also a lively bar and brasserie together with a large function room.
**ROOMS:** 27 en suite 11 annexe en suite (1 fmly) No smoking in 10 bedrooms s £59.95-£80; d £95 * **LB** **FACILITIES:** STV **CONF:** Thtr 200 Class 80 Board 50 Del from £110 * **PARKING:** 150 **NOTES:** Civ Wed 70
**CARDS:**

★★★67% ***Posthouse Birmingham Great Barr***

Posthouse

Chapel Ln, Great Barr B43 7BG
☎ 0870 400 9009 🖷 0121 357 7503
***Dir:*** *take Jct7 M6. Turn onto A34 signposted Walsall. Hotel located 200yds on the right hand side across the carriage-way in Chapel Lane*
Situated in pleasant surroundings, this modern hotel offers well-equipped and comfortable bedrooms. In addition to the popular Traders restaurant there is an all-day lounge menu and 24-hour room service. There is also a courtyard patio and garden, with a children's play area.
**ROOMS:** 192 en suite (36 fmly) No smoking in 108 bedrooms **FACILITIES:** Indoor swimming (H) Sauna Solarium Gym Jacuzzi Aerobics studio Beauty treatments **CONF:** Thtr 120 Class 70 Board 50 **PARKING:** 400 **CARDS:**

★★★66% **Westmead**

corus

Redditch Rd, Hopwood B48 7AL
☎ 0121 445 1202 🖷 0121 445 6163
***Dir:*** *M42 junct 2 head towards Birmingham on A441 upto rdbt and turn right, follow A441 for 1m and hotel is on right hand side*
This hotel is in a rural location on the edge of the city. All bedrooms are attractive, spacious and well-equipped. There are plenty of meeting rooms and a function suite, which hosts regular cabaret evenings.
**ROOMS:** 58 en suite (2 fmly) No smoking in 28 bedrooms s fr £98; d fr £108 * **LB** **FACILITIES:** STV Sauna Solarium **CONF:** Thtr 220 Class 120 Board 80 Del from £120 * **PARKING:** 155 **NOTES:** No dogs (ex guide dogs) No smoking in restaurant Civ Wed 120
**CARDS:**

★★★65% **Novotel Birmingham City Centre**

NOVOTEL

70 Broad St B1 2HT
☎ 0121 643 2000 🖷 0121 643 9796
e-mail: h1077@accor-hotels.com
***Dir:*** *2mins from the International Conference Centre*
This large, modern, purpose built hotel benefits from an excellent city centre location, with the bonus of secure car parking. Bedrooms are spacious, modern in style and well-equipped for business users. Four rooms have facilities for disabled guests. Public areas include the Garden Brasserie, a range of function rooms and a fitness room.
**ROOMS:** 148 en suite (148 fmly) No smoking in 98 bedrooms s £95; d £95 * **LB** **FACILITIES:** STV Sauna Gym Jacuzzi **CONF:** Thtr 300 Class 120 Board 90 Del £135 * **SERVICES:** Lift air con **PARKING:** 50
**CARDS:**

*See entry under Sutton Coldfield*

★★★64% **Portland**
313 Hagley Rd B16 9LQ
☎ 0121 455 0535 🖷 0121 456 1841
e-mail: sales@portland-hotel.demon.co.uk
***Dir:*** *2m from city centre on A456*
A large, purpose-built, privately owned hotel just west of the city centre. It provides well-equipped, modern accommodation including some ground floor rooms. There is an attractive restaurant, a pleasant lounge bar and a choice of function suites and meeting rooms.
**ROOMS:** 63 en suite No smoking in 7 bedrooms s £39.95-£59.95; d £54.50-£79.95 (incl. bkfst) * **LB** **FACILITIES:** STV **CONF:** Thtr 80 Class 40 Board 40 Del from £79.95 * **SERVICES:** Lift **PARKING:** 80 **NOTES:** No dogs (ex guide dogs) **CARDS:**

★★★64% **Posthouse Birmingham City**

Posthouse

Smallbrook Queensway B5 4EW
☎ 0870 400 9008 🖷 0121 631 2528
e-mail: gm1841@forte-hotels.com
***Dir:*** *from M6 junct 6 follow signs on A38 for 'City Centre' through two tunnels. Take second slip road off, then 1st left to hotel in 100yds*
A large, modern hotel in the city centre. Bedrooms are comfortable and well-designed. Facilities include extensive meeting rooms, and a business centre. There is a lounge bar with a roof terrace and a well prepared carvery menu in the restaurant. 24-hour room service is also available.
**ROOMS:** 280 en suite (3 fmly) No smoking in 205 bedrooms s £149; d £89-£169 * **LB** **FACILITIES:** Xmas **CONF:** Thtr 630 Class 380 Board 50 **SERVICES:** Lift **CARDS:**

B

BIRMINGHAM, continued

### ★★★63% Plough & Harrow

REGAL

135 Hagley Rd B16 8LS
☎ 0121 454 4111 ⎙ 0121 454 1868
e-mail: reservations@plough.co.uk
***Dir:*** *from the city travel along the A456 (Hagley Road), the hotel is on the right hand side after 5 ways roundabout*

HOTEL

A well established hotel, approximately a mile west of the city centre, with a relaxed and friendly atmosphere. Bedrooms come in a variety of styles and sizes, although all are well-equipped and comfortable. The attractive garden restaurant offers a good selection of freshly prepared dishes.
**ROOMS:** 44 en suite No smoking in 11 bedrooms s £110; d £40-£125 * **LB** **FACILITIES:** STV Xmas **CONF:** Thtr 100 Class 60 Board 50 Del from £95 * **SERVICES:** Lift **PARKING:** 80 **NOTES:** No smoking in restaurant **CARDS:**

### ★★★62% Quality Inn & Suites

Quality Hotel

257/267 Hagley Rd, Edgbaston B16 9NA
☎ 0121 454 8071 ⎙ 0121 455 6149
e-mail: admin@gb606.u-net.com
***Dir:*** *M6-A38 onto ringroad towards Kidderminster, after 4m right at rdbt, hotel on right*
Close to the city centre, this large hotel is particularly popular with business travellers. Bedrooms vary in size and style. Guests have the benefit of using the leisure facilities at a nearby sister hotel.
**ROOMS:** 166 en suite No smoking in 40 bedrooms d £50-£60 * **LB** **FACILITIES:** STV **CONF:** Thtr 100 Class 40 Board 30 **SERVICES:** Lift **PARKING:** 120 **NOTES:** No smoking in restaurant Civ Wed 40 **CARDS:**

### ★★★61% Great Barr Hotel & Conference Centre

Pear Tree Dr, Newton Rd, Great Barr B43 6HS
☎ 0121 357 1141 ⎙ 0121 357 7557
e-mail: sales@thegreatbarrhotel.co.uk
***Dir:*** *M6 junct 7, at Scott Arms x-rds right towards Bromwich (A4010) Newton Rd. Hotel 1 mile from Scotts Arms, right hand side in Pear Tree Drive (just past Malt Shovel Inn)*
This busy hotel, situated in a residential area, is particularly popular with conference delegates and business people. Bedrooms are well equipped and modern in style, with some executive rooms. There is a wide range of meeting and function rooms, and a cosy bar and more formal restaurant.
**ROOMS:** 105 en suite (1 fmly) s £69-£75; d £85-£111 (incl. bkfst) * **LB** **FACILITIES:** STV Xmas **CONF:** Thtr 200 Class 90 Board 60 Del from £69.50 * **PARKING:** 200 **NOTES:** No dogs (ex guide dogs) RS BH (restaurant may be closed) **CARDS:**

### ★★70% Copperfield House

60 Upland Rd, Selly Park B29 7JS
☎ 0121 472 8344 ⎙ 0121 415 5655
e-mail: info@copperfieldhousehotel.fsnet.co.uk
***Dir:*** *M6 junct 6, take A38 N through city centre, at 2nd set of traffic lights turn left, at next traffic lights turn right (A441), third right*
Copperfield House is a delightful Victorian hotel, built in 1868. It is situated within easy reach of the centre of Birmingham and close to the BBC's Pebble Mill Studios. The hotel provides smartly presented and well-equipped accommodation; the executive rooms are particular spacious. Carefully prepared, interesting dishes are served in the restaurant.
**ROOMS:** 17 en suite (1 fmly) s £59.50-£69.50; d £69.50-£79.50 (incl. bkfst) * **LB** **PARKING:** 11 **NOTES:** No dogs (ex guide dogs) No smoking in restaurant **CARDS:**

### ★★68% Norwood

87-89 Bunbury Rd, Northfield B31 2ET
☎ 0121 411 2202 ⎙ 0121 477 7447
e-mail: norwoodhotel@aol.com
***Dir:*** *turn left on A38 at Grosvenor shopping centre, 5m S of city centre*
This comfortable, tastefully appointed hotel provides well-equipped accommodation with several executive rooms. Pleasant public rooms, including the conservatory, enjoy an outlook over the pretty garden. Carefully prepared home cooking is served in the attractive dining room and the service is both friendly and attentive.
**ROOMS:** 18 en suite s £45-£75; d £60-£80 (incl. bkfst) * **LB** **FACILITIES:** STV **CONF:** Thtr 40 Class 24 Board 20 **PARKING:** 11 **NOTES:** Closed 23 Dec-2 Jan **CARDS:**

### ★★68% Oxford Hotel

Best Western

21 Oxford Rd B13 9EH
☎ 0121 449 3298 ⎙ 0121 442 4212
e-mail: oxford@bestwestern.co.uk
***Dir:*** *3m S of Birmingham A435, on entering Moseley village turn R at traffic lights, then R again at Ford Garage. Hotel is situated 50yds on the L.*
Situated three miles south of Birmingham, this privately-owned hotel offers a comfortable and relaxed atmosphere. Bedrooms are spacious, attractively decorated and well equipped. Additional features include a dining room, a cosy lounge and a bar. Meeting rooms are also available.
**ROOMS:** 15 en suite No smoking in 7 bedrooms s £69-£79; d £79-£89 (incl. bkfst) * **FACILITIES:** STV Snooker **CONF:** Thtr 60 Class 30 Board 30 Del from £119.95 * **SERVICES:** air con **PARKING:** 60 **NOTES:** No dogs (ex guide dogs) No smoking in restaurant RS Bank holidays **CARDS:**

### ★★66% Fountain Court

339-343 Fountain Court Hotel B17 8NH
☎ 0121 429 1754 ⎙ 0121 429 1209
e-mail: fountain-court@excite.co.uk
***Dir:*** *on A456, towards Birmingham*
This family-owned hotel is on the A456, near to the M5 and Birmingham. Bedrooms include a family suite and some rooms on the ground floor. There is a brightly decorated dining room, a choice of sitting areas and a bar.
**ROOMS:** 23 en suite (4 fmly) s £39.50-£48.50; d £55-£65 (incl. bkfst) * **PARKING:** 20 **CARDS:**

B

★65% **Sheriden House**
2 Handsworth Wood Rd, Handsworth Wood B20 2PL
☎ 0121 554 2185 & 0121 523 5960 📠 0121 551 4761
e-mail: sheridenhotel@lineone.net
*Dir: at junct 7 of M6 turn onto A34, through traffic lights at A4041 next right filter onto B4124, straight through to hotel approx 1.5m on left*
This privately owned and personally-run hotel provides well-equipped comfortable accommodation. The pleasant bar and a cosy lounge overlook pretty gardens and a patio area. The restaurant provides the ideal setting for a wholesome breakfast or evening meal.
**ROOMS:** 11 en suite No smoking in 3 bedrooms s £34-£39; d £46-£56 (incl. bkfst) * **LB CONF:** Thtr 50 Class 30 Board 20 Del from £47.50 * **PARKING:** 30 **NOTES:** No dogs (ex guide dogs) No smoking in restaurant **CARDS:**

*See advert on this page*

★★61% **Astoria**
311 Hagley Rd B16 9LQ
☎ 0121 454 0795 📠 0121 456 3537
e-mail: anne@astoriahotel.uk.com
*Dir: on A456 2m from city centre*
This Victorian property stands between the city centre and the M5 motorway. Personally run, it provides modern accommodation which includes some family and ground floor rooms. There is a choice of lounges and a homely bar. The traditionally furnished dining room serves a selection of grill-type dishes.
**ROOMS:** 26 en suite (6 fmly) No smoking in 2 bedrooms s £40-£49; d £50-£63 (incl. bkfst) * **FACILITIES:** STV **PARKING:** 27 **NOTES:** No dogs (ex guide dogs) No smoking in restaurant
**CARDS:**

## *Town House*

★★★★ **Hotel Du Vin**
25 Church St B3 2NR
☎ 0121 236 0559 📠 0121 236 0889
e-mail: info@birmingham.hotelduvin.com
***Dir:** M6 junct 6 follow A38(M) to city centre, go over flyover, keep left exit St Chads Circus signposted Jewellery Quarter, at lights & rdbt 1st exit follow signs for Colmore Row, opposite St Philips Cathedral right into Church St, across Berwick St hotel right.*
The former Birmingham Eye Hospital has undergone a remarkable transformation, the Victorian architecture lending itself perfectly to the conversion. Public areas include The Bistro, now a popular theme in these hotels with its relaxed atmosphere, the Bubble Lounge, inspired by Café Florin in Venice, and a cellar bar. Facilities include an impressive health club, extensive private dining and a cigar and wine shop. Accommodation is stylish and comfortable with some stunning feature bathrooms.
**ROOMS:** 66 en suite s £110-£175; d £110-£175 * **FACILITIES:** STV Snooker Sauna Solarium Gym Pool table Xmas **CONF:** Thtr 80 Class 40 Board 40 Del £175 * **SERVICES:** Lift **NOTES:** No dogs (ex guide dogs) **CARDS:**

Late for dinner? Quality Standards star rating means that last orders for dinner should be no earlier than:
★ 6.30pm ★★ 7.00pm ★★★ 8.00pm
★★★★ 9.00pm ★★★★★ 10.00pm

BIRMINGHAM, continued

### Hotel Ibis

Arcadian Centre, Ladywell Walk B5 4ST
☎ 0121 622 6010 🖷 0121 622 6020
e-mail: h1459@accor-hotels.com
***Dir:*** *M6 junct 7 take A34 to city centre & follow signs to Market areas. M5 junct 3 take A456 to centre then Market areas*
Modern, budget hotel offering comfortable accommodation in bright and practical bedrooms. Breakfast is self-service and dinner is available in the restaurant. For further details, consult the Hotel Groups page.
**ROOMS:** 159 en suite s £42; d £42 * **CONF:** Thtr 100 Class 60 Board 40

### Hotel Ibis

55 Irving St B1 1DH
☎ 0121 622 4925 🖷 0121 622 4195
e-mail: h2092@accor-hotels.com

***Dir:*** *150yds from Dome Night Club, just off Bristol Street*
Modern, budget hotel offering comfortable accommodation in bright and practical bedrooms. Breakfast is self-service and dinner is available in the restaurant. For further details, consult the Hotel Groups page.
**ROOMS:** 51 en suite s £39.95; d £39.95 * **CONF:** Thtr 35 Class 18 Board 20

### Campanile

Aston Locks, Chester St B6 4BE
☎ 0121 359 3330 🖷 0121 359 1223
***Dir:*** *next to rdbt at junct of A4540/A38*

This modern building offers accommodation in smart, well-equipped bedrooms, all with en suite bathrooms. Refreshments may be taken at the informal Bistro. For further details and the Campanile phone number, consult the Hotel Groups page.
**ROOMS:** 111 en suite d £41 * **CONF:** Thtr 245 Class 105 Board 122 Del from £65 *

### Express by Holiday Inn Birmingham North

Birmingham Rd, Great Barr B43 7AG
☎ 0121 3584044 🖷 0121 358 4644
e-mail: exhi@birminghamnorth.fs.business.co.uk
***Dir:*** *M6 junct7 onto A34 towards Walsall*
A modern budget hotel offering comfortable accommodation in refreshing, spacious and comprehensively equipped bedrooms, en suite bathrooms with power showers and continental buffet breakfast included in the room rate. Suitable for business travellers or families. For further details and the Express by Holiday Inn phone number, consult the Hotel Groups page.

**ROOMS:** 32 en suite (incl. cont bkfst) s £52.50; d £52.50 * **CONF:** Th 25 Class 20 Board 16

### Express by Holiday Inn Castle Bromwich

1200 Chester Rd, Castle Bromwich B35 7AF
☎ 0121 747 6633 🖷 0121 747 6644
e-mail: castlebromwich@premierhotels.co.uk
***Dir:*** *travelling N, off at jct5. Follow Fort Shopping Park signs. Travelling S, off at jct6. Take A38 for Tyburn, right into Chester Rd, follow Park signs*

A modern budget hotel offering comfortable accommodation in refreshing, spacious and comprehensively equipped bedrooms, e suite bathrooms with power showers and continental buffet breakfast included in the room rate. Suitable for business travellers or families. For further details and the Express by Holiday Inn phone number, consult the Hotel Groups page.
**ROOMS:** 110 en suite (incl. cont bkfst) s £63.95-£105; d £63.95-£105 * **CONF:** Thtr 25 Class 10 Board 15 Del from £90 *

### Hotel Ibis Birmingham Bordesley

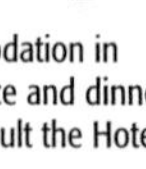

1 Bordesley Park Rd, Bordesley B10 0PD
☎ 0121 506 2600 🖷 0121 506 2610
e-mail: H2178@accor-hotels.com
Modern, budget hotel offering comfortable accommodation in bright and practical bedrooms. Breakfast is self-service and dinner is available in the restaurant. For further details, consult the Hotel Groups page.
**ROOMS:** 87 en suite s £39.95-£42; d £39.95-£42 *

### *Premier Lodge (Birmingham City Centre)*

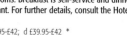

80 Broad St B15 1LY
☎ 0870 700 1316 🖷 0870 7001317
Premier Lodge offers modern, well-equipped, en suite accommodation suitable for both business and leisure travellers. Meals can be taken at the adjacent popular restaurant and bar,

continued

which is fully licensed. For further details, consult the Hotel Groups page.
**ROOMS:** 60 en suite

### ⇧ Premier Lodge (Birmingham South)

Birmingham Great Park, Bristol Rd South, Rubery B45 9PA
☎ 0870 700 1324 ⎙ 0870 700 1325
***Dir:*** *Take Junct 4 off M5, then proceed onto A38. Follow for 0.5m. Lodge directly behind Safeway on left hand side*
Premier Lodge offers modern, well-equipped, en suite accommodation suitable for both business and leisure travellers. Meals can be taken at the adjacent popular restaurant and bar, which is fully licensed. For further details, consult the Hotel Groups page.
**ROOMS:** 62 en suite d £42 *

### ⇧ *Travelodge (Birmingham Central)*

230 Broad St B15 1AY
☎ 0121 644 5266
Travelodge offers good quality, good value, modern accommodation. Ideal for families, the spacious, en suite bedrooms include remote-control TV, tea and coffee-making facilities, luxury beds and free morning newspaper. Meals can be taken at the nearby family restaurant. For further details and the Travelodge phone number, consult the Hotel Groups page.

**ROOMS:** 136 en suite

### ⇧ *Travelodge (Birmingham East)*

A45 Coventry Rd, Acocks Green B26 1DS
☎ 08700 850950
Travelodge offers good quality, good value, modern accommodation. Ideal for families, the spacious, en suite bedrooms include remote-control TV, tea and coffee-making facilities, luxury beds and free morning newspaper. Meals can be taken at the nearby family restaurant. For further details and the Travelodge phone number, consult the Hotel Groups page.

**ROOMS:** 40 en suite

### ○ Crowne Plaza Birmingham - The NEC

Pendigo Way B40 1SP
☎ 0121 224 5058
At the time of going to press, the star classification for this hotel was not confirmed. Please refer to the AA internet site www.theAA.com for current information.
**ROOMS:** 241 rms **NOTES:** Due to open Spring 2002

### ○ Innkeeper's Lodge Birmingham East

Chester Rd, Streetley B73 6SP
A new concept in the travel accommodation market. Smart rooms meet essential business requirements but also have home comforts. Dining options include all-day menus plus the added advantage of breakfast, which is included in the room price. Reservations can be made seven days a week through the room reservations number: 0870 243 0500. For further details, consult the Hotel Groups page.
**ROOMS:** 66 en suite

### ○ Jury's Inn Birmingham

245 Broad St B1 2HQ
☎ 0121 626 0626
At the time of going to press, the star classification for this hotel was not confirmed. Please refer to the AA internet site www.theAA.com for current information.
**ROOMS:** 445 rms **NOTES:** Open now

### ○ Malmaison Birmingham

At the time of going to press, the star classification for this hotel was not confirmed. Please refer to the AA internet site www.theAA.com for current information.
**ROOMS:** 184 rms **NOTES:** Due to open July 2002

### ○ Innkeeper's Lodge Birmingham West

563 Hagley Rd West, Quinton B32 1HP
☎ 0870 243 0500
A new concept in the travel accommodation market. Smart rooms meet essential business requirements but also have home comforts. Dining options include all-day menus plus the added advantage of breakfast, which is included in the room price. Reservations can be made seven days a week through the room reservations number: 0870 243 0500. For further details, consult the Hotel Groups page.
**ROOMS:** 24 en suite

## BIRMINGHAM AIRPORT, West Midlands — Map 07 SP18

### ★★★66% Novotel Birmingham Airport

B26 3QL
☎ 0121 782 7000 ⎙ 0121 782 0445
e-mail: H1158@accor-hotels.com
***Dir:*** *M42 junct 6, A45 direction Birmingham, follow signs to airport, hotel opposite main terminal*
This purpose built hotel is located directly opposite the main passenger terminal and benefits from a monorail link to the railway station and to the NEC. Bedrooms are spacious, modern in style and well-equipped for the business traveller. Two rooms have facilities for disabled guests. Food service in the hotel is very flexible with The Garden Brasserie restaurant open from very early morning to late at night.
**ROOMS:** 195 en suite (20 fmly) No smoking in 150 bedrooms s £69-£135; d £79-£144 (incl. bkfst) * **FACILITIES:** STV **CONF:** Thtr 35 Class 20 Board 22 Del from £109 * **SERVICES:** Lift air con
**CARDS:**

### ★★★65% *Posthouse Birmingham Airport*

Coventry Rd B26 3QW
☎ 0870 400 9007 ⎙ 0121 782 2476
***Dir:*** *from junct 6 of M42 take A45 towards Birmingham for 1.5m*
This hotel, close to the NEC and Birmingham Airport, offers a range of well-equipped, comfortable bedrooms. Guests may enjoy a snack in the bar or a more substantial meal in the restaurant. It has a range of function and meeting rooms providing great flexibility to the corporate guest.
**ROOMS:** 141 en suite (3 fmly) No smoking in 84 bedrooms **CONF:** Thtr 130 Class 100 Board 70 **PARKING:** 250
**CARDS:**

## BIRMINGHAM (NATIONAL EXHIBITION CENTRE), West Midlands — Map 07 SP18

see also Sutton Coldfield

### ★★★★67% ❀❀ Nailcote Hall

Nailcote Ln, Berkswell CV7 7DE
☎ 024 7646 6174 ⎙ 024 7647 0720
e-mail: info@nailcotehall.co.uk
(For full entry see Balsall Common and advert under Solihull)

> Read all about it! Newspapers delivered to bedrooms in four and five star hotels.

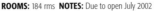

BIRMINGHAM (NATIONAL EXHIBITION CENTRE), continued

**★★★74% Moor Hall**
Moor Hall Dr, Four Oaks B75 6LN
☎ 0121 308 3751 ⎙ 0121 308 8974
e-mail: mail@moorhallhotel.co.uk
(For full entry see Sutton Coldfiled and advert under Birmingham)

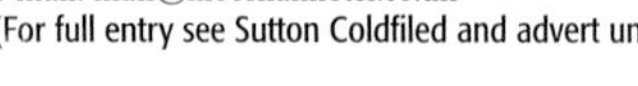

**★★★65% Arden Hotel & Leisure Club**
Coventry Rd, Bickenhill B92 0EH
☎ 01675 443221 ⎙ 01675 445604
e-mail: enquiries@ardenhotel.co.uk
***Dir:*** *from junc 6 of M42 take A45 towards Birmingham, hotel 0.25m on right hand side, just off B'ham International railway Island*

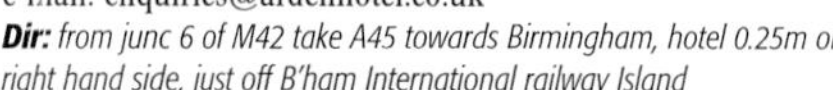

This successful, family-run hotel thrives from the business created by the adjacent N.E.C. All the bedrooms are modern and well-equipped. Facilities here include a coffee shop overlooking the leisure facilities, a formal restaurant and terraced water gardens.
**ROOMS:** 216 en suite (6 fmly) s £95; d £105-£125 * **FACILITIES:** STV Indoor swimming (H) Snooker Sauna Solarium Gym Jacuzzi Steamroom entertainment Xmas **CONF:** Thtr 200 Class 40 Board 60 Del from £137 * **SERVICES:** Lift **PARKING:** 300 **NOTES:** Civ Wed 120
**CARDS:**

*See advert under SOLIHULL*

**★★★63% Quality Hotel Sutton Court**
60-66 Lichfield Rd B74 2NA
☎ 0121 354 4991 ⎙ 0121 355 0083
e-mail: reservations@sutton-court-hotel.co.uk
(For full entry see Sutton Coldfield and advert under Birmingham)

**★★76% ✪✪ Haigs**
Kenilworth Rd CV7 7EL
☎ 01676 533004 ⎙ 01676 535132
(For full entry see Balsall Common)

**★★67% Heath Lodge**
117 Coleshill Rd, Marston Green B37 7HT
☎ 0121 779 2218 ⎙ 0121 779 2218
e-mail: reception@heathlodgehotel.freeserve.co.uk
***Dir:*** *join A446 from M6 J4 travelling north to Coleshill, after 0.5m turn left into Coleshill Heath Rd, signposted to Marston Green. Hotel on right*

HEATH
LODGE
HOTEL

This privately-owned and personally-run hotel is within easy reach of the NEC and Birmingham Airport. The bedrooms have all benefited from refurbishment, and are well-equipped and comfortable. Public areas consist of a small bar, a lounge and a dining room overlooking the garden.
**ROOMS:** 17 rms (16 en suite) (1 fmly) s £49-£54; d £59-£69 (incl. bkfst) * **CONF:** Thtr 20 Class 16 Board 14 **PARKING:** 22 **NOTES:** No smoking in restaurant **CARDS:**

**⌂ Express by Holiday Inn**
Bickenhill Parkway B40 1QA
☎ 0121 782 3222 ⎙ 0121 780 4224
e-mail: sales_nec@ingramhotels.co.uk
***Dir:*** *follow signs for National Exhibition Centre (NEC) from M42 junct 6*

A modern budget hotel offering comfortable accommodation in refreshing, spacious and comprehensively equipped bedrooms, en suite bathrooms with power showers and continental buffet breakfast included in the room rate. Suitable for business travellers or families. For further details and the Express by Holiday Inn phone number, consult the Hotel Groups page.
**ROOMS:** 179 en suite **CONF:** Thtr 100

BISHOP'S STORTFORD, Hertfordshire Map 05 TL42

**★★★★69% ✪✪ Down Hall Country House**
Hatfield Heath CM22 7AS
☎ 01279 731441 ⎙ 01279 730416
e-mail: reservations@downhall.co.uk
***Dir:*** *follow A1060, at Hatfield Heath keep left, turn right into lane opposite Hunters Meet restaurant & left at the end following signpost*

An impressive Victorian country house hotel set in 100 acres of mature grounds and within easy driving distance of Stanstead Airport. Bedrooms are situated in the main building and the newer west wing. The Downham and Ibbetsons restaurants offer a choice of dining, alternatively snacks are available in the bar or lounge.
**ROOMS:** 99 en suite s £120-£235; d £175-£275 * **LB** **FACILITIES:** STV Indoor swimming (H) Tennis (hard) Snooker Sauna Gym Croquet lawn Putting green Jacuzzi Petanque Giant chess Whirlpool Xmas **CONF:** Thtr 200 Class 140 Board 70 Del from £190 * **SERVICES:** Lift **PARKING:** 150 **NOTES:** Civ Wed
**CARDS:**

Early start? Hotels at all star levels should provide in-room alarm clocks and/or alarm calls.

## BISHOPSTEIGNTON, Devon Map 03 SX97

### ★★65% Cockhaven Manor Hotel

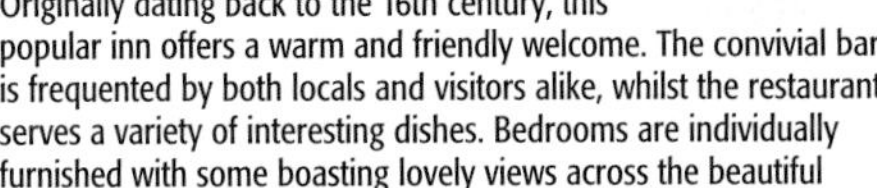

Cockhaven Rd TQ14 9RF
☎ 01626 775252 🖷 01626 775572
Originally dating back to the 16th century, this popular inn offers a warm and friendly welcome. The convivial bar is frequented by both locals and visitors alike, whilst the restaurant serves a variety of interesting dishes. Bedrooms are individually furnished with some boasting lovely views across the beautiful Teign estuary.
**ROOMS:** 12 en suite (2 fmly) No smoking in 10 bedrooms s £30; d £50-£60 (incl. bkfst) * **LB** **FACILITIES:** Petanque Xmas **CONF:** Thtr 50 Class 50 Board 30 Del from £50 * **PARKING:** 50 **NOTES:** No smoking in restaurant **CARDS:**

## BLACKBURN, Lancashire Map 07 SD62

see also Langho

### ★★★★58% Clarion Hotel & Suites Foxfields

Whalley Rd, Billington BB7 9HY
☎ 01254 822556 🖷 01254 824613
e-mail: admin@gb065.u-net.com
***Dir:*** *turn off A59 at signpost for Billington/Whalley & hotel after 0.5m on right*
This modern hotel has a beautiful rural setting, just off the A59 close to Whalley in the Ribble Valley. Smart bedrooms are spacious, well-equipped and all have either separate sitting or dressing rooms, some with beautiful views of the countryside. Pre-dinner drinks can be enjoyed in the cocktail bar adjacent to the elegant restaurant. A smart leisure club is also available to guests.
**ROOMS:** 44 en suite (27 fmly) No smoking in 17 bedrooms s £92-£107; d £107-£123 * **LB** **FACILITIES:** STV Indoor swimming (H) Sauna Gym Steam room entertainment Xmas **CONF:** Thtr 180 Class 60 Board 60 Del from £85 * **PARKING:** 170 **NOTES:** No dogs (ex guide dogs) No smoking in restaurant Civ Wed 100
**CARDS:**

### ★★★63% County Hotel Blackburn

Yew Tree Dr, Preston New Rd BB2 7BE
☎ 01254 899988 🖷 01254 682435
e-mail: countyblackburn@corushotels.com
***Dir:*** *on A667/A6119 junct W of town*
This modern, purpose built hotel offers a friendly and willing service. All of the bedrooms are well-appointed and bright, whilst the public areas are stylish. Meeting, conference and banqueting facilities are also available.
**ROOMS:** 101 en suite (1 fmly) No smoking in 70 bedrooms d £50 * **LB** **FACILITIES:** Pool Table Xmas **CONF:** Thtr 350 Class 150 Board 100 Del from £85 * **SERVICES:** Lift **PARKING:** 200 **NOTES:** No smoking in restaurant **CARDS:**

### ★★74% ◉ Millstone

Church Ln, Mellor BB2 7JR
☎ 01254 813333 🖷 01254 812628
e-mail: millstone@shireinns.co.uk
***Dir:*** *3m NW off A59*
This inviting stone-built former coaching inn provides a very high standard of accommodation, professional and friendly service and food of a good quality. Bedrooms, some in an adjacent house, have been tastefully furnished. All are very well-equipped. Rooms on the ground floor and a room for disabled guests are also available. There is a choice of charming bars.
**ROOMS:** 18 en suite 6 annexe en suite (1 fmly) No smoking in 4 bedrooms s £93; d £113 (incl. bkfst) * **LB** **FACILITIES:** STV Xmas **CONF:** Thtr 25 Class 15 Board 16 **PARKING:** 40 **NOTES:** No smoking in restaurant Civ Wed **CARDS:**

### ⌂ *Premier Lodge*

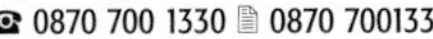

Myerscough Rd, Balderstone BB2 7LE
☎ 0870 700 1330 🖷 0870 7001331
Premier Lodge offers modern, well-equipped, en suite accommodation suitable for both business and leisure travellers. Meals can be taken at the adjacent popular restaurant and bar, which is fully licensed. For further details, consult the Hotel Groups page.
**ROOMS:** 20 en suite

## BLACKPOOL, Lancashire Map 07 SD33

### ★★★★64% De Vere

East Park Dr FY3 8LL
☎ 01253 838866 🖷 01253 798800
***Dir:*** *M6 junct 32/M55 junct 4, A583, at 4th set of traffic lights turn right into South Park Drive & follow signs for zoo. Hotel on right*
This popular, modern hotel, conveniently located on the quieter edge of town, offers excellent indoor and outdoor leisure facilities, including a championship golf course. There is a choice of smart bars and dining options. Many of the bedrooms enjoy views over the golf course.
**ROOMS:** 164 en suite No smoking in 70 bedrooms s £135; d £145 (incl. bkfst) * **LB** **FACILITIES:** **Spa** STV Indoor swimming (H) Golf 18 Tennis (hard) Squash Snooker Sauna Solarium Gym Putting green Jacuzzi Aerobic studio Beauty room Spinning Studio Xmas **CONF:** Thtr 600 Class 310 Board 30 Del from £130 * **SERVICES:** Lift **PARKING:** 500 **NOTES:** No dogs (ex guide dogs) No smoking in restaurant Civ Wed 600
**CARDS:**

### ★★★★63% Imperial

North Promenade FY1 2HB
☎ 01253 623971 🖷 01253 751784
e-mail: imperialblackpool@paramount-hotels.co.uk
***Dir:*** *Off town centre on the North Promenade*
This large seafront hotel situated on the North Promenade retains much of its Victorian grandeur and character. Bedrooms are of varying shape and style, comfortably appointed and fully equipped with modern amenities. Spacious public areas include the No.10 bar, Palm Court restaurant, basement leisure centre and a notable selection of conference rooms.
**ROOMS:** 181 en suite (6 fmly) No smoking in 80 bedrooms s £115; d £166 (incl. bkfst) * **LB** **FACILITIES:** STV Indoor swimming (H) Sauna Solarium Gym Jacuzzi **CONF:** Thtr 550 Class 240 Board 128 Del from £129 * **SERVICES:** Lift **PARKING:** 150 **NOTES:** No smoking in restaurant Civ Wed 336 **CARDS:**

### ★★★60% Savoy

Queens Promenade, North Shore FY2 9SJ
☎ 01253 352561 🖷 01253 595549
***Dir:*** *located along the seafront at Queens Promenade, 0.75m N of Blackpool Tower*
In a prime seafront location on North Promenade, this imposing hotel offers various styles of accommodation. Newer bedrooms are attractively decorated and have chic, fully-tiled bathrooms; older rooms are more traditional in style. There is a pleasant, open-plan lounge and a smart, split-level restaurant.
**ROOMS:** 131 en suite (14 fmly) No smoking in 58 bedrooms s £45-£55; d £90-£130 (incl. bkfst) * **LB** **FACILITIES:** Xmas **CONF:** Thtr 400 Class 250 Board 50 Del from £75 * **SERVICES:** Lift **PARKING:** 40
**NOTES:** No dogs (ex guide dogs) No smoking in restaurant Civ Wed 200
**CARDS:**

B

BLACKPOOL, continued

**★★68% Hotel Sheraton**
54-62 Queens Promenade FY2 9RP
☎ 01253 352723 01253 595499
e-mail: hotelsheraton@aol.com
***Dir:*** *1m N from Blackpool Tower on promenade towards Fleetwood*
This family owned hotel is located at the quieter northern end of the Promenade. Public areas are spacious with a choice of lounges and a large function suite where dancing and cabaret evenings are a regular occurrence. There is also a heated indoor swimming pool. Bedrooms vary in size and style, but the corner bay rooms and the smart newly refurbished rooms are particularly spacious and comfortable.
**ROOMS:** 104 en suite (44 fmly) s £42-£64; d £84-£108 (incl. bkfst & dinner) * **LB** **FACILITIES:** Indoor swimming (H) Sauna Table tennis Darts entertainment Xmas **CONF:** Thtr 200 Class 100 Board 150 Del from £35 * **SERVICES:** Lift **PARKING:** 20 **NOTES:** No dogs (ex guide dogs) **CARDS:**

*See advert on opposite page*

**★★67% Brabyns**
1-3 Shaftesbury Av, North Shore FY2 9QQ
☎ 01253 354263 352163 01253 352915
e-mail: brabynshotel@netscapeonline.co.uk
MINOTEL Great Britain
In a residential area close to the seafront, this privately owned hotel is a popular venue. Freshly decorated bedrooms are comfortable and thoughtfully equipped. There is a cosy lounge bar and an attractive, wood-panelled dining room. Service is friendly and hospitable.
**ROOMS:** 22 en suite 3 annexe en suite s £25-£40; d £50-£70 (incl. bkfst) * **LB** **FACILITIES:** STV Xmas **PARKING:** 12 **NOTES:** No children No smoking in restaurant **CARDS:**

**★★64% Belgrave**
270-274 Queens Promenade FY2 9HD
☎ 01253 351570 01253 500698
This friendly, family-run hotel is situated on the North Shore seafront at the quieter end of town. Bedrooms vary in size, all are thoughtfully equipped and one has a four-poster bed. There is often live entertainment in the spacious lounge bar. Both the bright restaurant and the television lounge have views across the promenade to the sea.
**ROOMS:** 33 en suite (7 fmly) s £22-£32; d £40-£60 (incl. bkfst) * **LB** **FACILITIES:** STV Xmas **SERVICES:** Lift **PARKING:** 32 **NOTES:** No dogs No smoking in restaurant **CARDS:**

**★★62% Warwick**
603-609 New South Promenade FY4 1NG
☎ 01253 342192 01253 405776
***Dir:*** *from M55 junct 4 take A5230 for South Shore then rt on A584, Promenade South*
Standing on the south shore, close to the famous Pleasure Beach, this popular hotel offers comfortable accommodation that is suitable for families. Larger rooms are situated at the front of the hotel on the first floor, overlooking the sea. Public areas include an indoor swimming pool, an attractive bar and a restaurant.
**ROOMS:** 50 en suite (11 fmly) s £23-£35; d £46-£70 (incl. bkfst & dinner) * **LB** **FACILITIES:** Indoor swimming (H) Solarium Table tennis, pool, darts entertainment Xmas **CONF:** Thtr 50 Class 24 Board 30 **SERVICES:** Lift **PARKING:** 32 **NOTES:** No smoking in restaurant Closed Jan **CARDS:**

Bad hair day? Hairdryers in all rooms three stars and above.

**★★60% Revill's**
190-194 North Promenade FY1 1RJ
☎ 01253 625768 01253 624736
e-mail: revills.hotel@blackpool.net
***Dir:*** *just N of Blackpool Tower, almost opposite the North Pier*
With a seafront location, close to North Pier, this well-established family run hotel offers well-equipped accommodation. Bedrooms vary in style and some are suitable for families. Public areas include spacious lounges and a choice of bars, enjoying views across the famous promenade.
**ROOMS:** 47 en suite (10 fmly) s £20-£31; d £40-£57 (incl. bkfst) * **LB** **FACILITIES:** Xmas **SERVICES:** Lift **PARKING:** 23 **NOTES:** No dogs No smoking in restaurant **CARDS:**

**○ Carlton**
North Promenade FY1 2EZ
☎ 01253 628966
At the time of going to press, the star classification for this hotel was not confirmed. Please refer to the AA internet site www.theAA.com for current information.
**ROOMS:** 58 rms **NOTES:** Opening July 2001

BLAKENEY, Norfolk — Map 09 TG04

**★★★74% The Blakeney**
The Quay NR25 7NE
☎ 01263 740797 01263 740795
e-mail: reception@blakeney-hotel.co.uk
***Dir:*** *off A149*
Delightful hotel situated on the quayside with superb views across the estuary and the salt marshes to Blakeney Point. Public rooms include an elegant restaurant, a relaxing first floor sun lounge overlooking the harbour, a bar and a further ground floor lounge. Although the bedrooms vary in size and style they are all attractively decorated and well-equipped.
**ROOMS:** 49 en suite 10 annexe en suite (11 fmly) s £67-£116; d £134-£232 (incl. bkfst & dinner) * **LB** **FACILITIES:** Indoor swimming (H) Snooker Sauna Gym Jacuzzi Table tennis Xmas **CONF:** Thtr 70 Class 40 Board 32 Del from £89 * **SERVICES:** Lift **PARKING:** 60 **NOTES:** No smoking in restaurant **CARDS:**

## Premier Collection

**★★ ®®® Morston Hall**
Morston, Holt NR25 7AA
☎ 01263 741041 01263 740419
e-mail: reception@morstonhall.com
***Dir:*** *1m W of Blakeney on A149 Kings Lynn/Cromer Rd coastal road*
Located two miles from Blakeney on the north coast of Norfolk, Morston Hall is a small, intimate country house hotel with its origins in the 17th century. In a tranquil setting

*continued*

overlooking well-kept gardens and enjoying lovely views, the hotel offers public rooms with a choice of attractive lounges and a sunny conservatory. The elegant dining room is an ideal place to relax and enjoy the award winning cuisine. Bedrooms are spacious and individually decorated.
**ROOMS:** 6 en suite s £100-£140; d £200-£210 (incl. bkfst & dinner) * LB **FACILITIES:** ch fac **CONF:** Del from £130 * **PARKING:** 40 **NOTES:** No smoking in restaurant Closed 25-26 Dec
**CARDS:**

★★73% **The Pheasant**
Coast Rd, Kelling NR25 7EG
☎ 01263 588382 01263 588101
e-mail: enquiries@pheasanthotelnorfolk.co.uk
***Dir:*** *on A419 coast road, mid-way between Sheringham & Blakeney*
Set well back from the coast road amidst landscaped grounds, this popular hotel offers traditional-style bedrooms in the main house and more modern and spacious rooms in a newer wing. The restaurant serves a wide ranging selection of appetising dishes and guests also have the use of a lounge and bar area.
**ROOMS:** 30 rms (27 en suite) No smoking in all bedrooms s fr £49; d fr £78 (incl. bkfst) * **LB** **FACILITIES:** Xmas **CONF:** Thtr 80 Class 50 Board 50 **PARKING:** 80 **NOTES:** No smoking in restaurant
**CARDS:**

★★66% **Manor**
Blakeney NR25 7ND
☎ 01263 740376 01263 741116
e-mail: reception@blakeneymanor.co.uk
***Dir:*** *turn off A149 at St Mary's church*
This popular hotel is situated just a short walk from the quayside and overlooks the marsh. The bedrooms, located in courtyards adjacent to the main building, were converted from flint face barns and come in a variety of styles. The spacious public rooms offer guests a choice of dining options, informal bar fare or imaginative restaurant cuisine.
**ROOMS:** 8 en suite 30 annexe en suite s £40-£74; d £70-£98 (incl. bkfst) * **LB** **FACILITIES:** Xmas **PARKING:** 40 **NOTES:** No children 14yrs No smoking in restaurant Closed 6 Jan-28 Jan
**CARDS:**

## BLANCHLAND, Northumberland — Map 12 NY95

★★69% ***Lord Crewe Arms***
DH8 9SP
☎ 01434 675251 01434 675337
e-mail: lord@crewearms.freeserve.co.uk
***Dir:*** *10m S of Hexham via B6306*
Many rooms in this historic, monastic hotel date from medieval times. Public areas feature flagstone floors, vaulted ceilings and original inglenook with priesthole. Bedrooms are split between the main hotel and a former estate building just across the road. All are well-equipped, and retain a period style. Bar meals are popular and there is an elegant restaurant.
**ROOMS:** 9 en suite 10 annexe en suite (2 fmly) **CONF:** Thtr 20 Class 20 Board 16 **NOTES:** Civ Wed 65 **CARDS:**

## BLANDFORD FORUM, Dorset — Map 03 ST80

★★★67% **Crown**
West St DT11 7AJ
☎ 01258 456626 01258 451084
***Dir:*** *100mtrs from town bridge*

Best Western

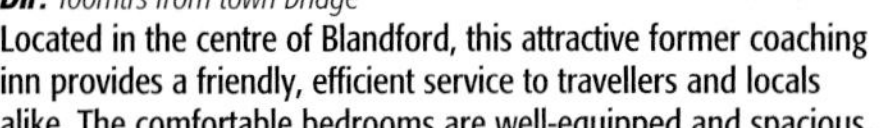

Located in the centre of Blandford, this attractive former coaching inn provides a friendly, efficient service to travellers and locals alike. The comfortable bedrooms are well-equipped and spacious.
*continued on p102*

B

## BLANDFORD FORUM, continued

In the wood panelled dining room a choice of menus is available, while in the bar an extensive range of snacks and lighter options is served.

*Crown, Blandford Forum*

**ROOMS:** 32 en suite (2 fmly) No smoking in 11 bedrooms s £60-£70; d £80 (incl. bkfst) * **LB** **FACILITIES:** STV Fishing ch fac **CONF:** Thtr 250 Class 200 Board 60 **SERVICES:** Lift **PARKING:** 144 **NOTES:** Closed 25-28 Dec Civ Wed 140 **CARDS:**

*See advert on page 101*

## BLYTH, Nottinghamshire — Map 08 SK68

### ★★★69% Charnwood

Best Western

Sheffield Rd S81 8HF
☎ 01909 591610 01909 591429
e-mail: info@charnwoodhotel.com
***Dir:*** *A614 into Blyth village, turn right past church onto A634 Sheffield road. Hotel 0.5m on right past humpback bridge*

This hotel enjoys a rural setting, surrounded by attractive gardens complete with pond. Bedrooms are comfortably furnished and attractively decorated. A range of carefully prepared meals and snacks is offered in the restaurant, or in the modern restyled lounge bar overlooking the gardens. Service is both friendly and attentive.

**ROOMS:** 34 en suite (1 fmly) No smoking in 6 bedrooms s £50-£65; d £60-£90 (incl. bkfst) * **LB** **FACILITIES:** STV Mini-gym ch fac **CONF:** Thtr 135 Class 60 Board 45 Del from £95 * **PARKING:** 70 **NOTES:** No dogs (ex guide dogs) No smoking in restaurant Civ Wed 120 **CARDS:**

### ⇧ *Travelodge*

Travelodge

Hilltop Roundabout S81 8HG
☎ 01909 591841
***Dir:*** *at junct of A1M/A614*

Travelodge offers good quality, good value, modern accommodation. Ideal for families, the spacious, en suite bedrooms include remote-control TV, tea and coffee-making facilities, luxury beds and free morning newspaper. Meals can be taken at the nearby family restaurant. For further details and the Travelodge phone number, consult the Hotel Groups page.

**ROOMS:** 39 en suite

## BODMIN, Cornwall & Isles of Scilly — Map 02 SX06

### ★★74% Trehellas House

Washaway PL30 3AD
☎ 01208 72700 01208 73336
***Dir:*** *3.5m N of Bodmin on A389. On right opposite a Celtic Cross*

This early 18th-century former posting inn retains many original features, cleverly interwoven with contemporary additions, to create appealing accommodation. Bedrooms are located in the main house and adjacent coach house; all have been refurbished to the same high standard. Authentic Malaysian cuisine is served in the slate-floored Memories of Malaya Restaurant.

**ROOMS:** 5 en suite 7 annexe en suite No smoking in all bedrooms s £35-£40; d £70-£100 (incl. bkfst) * **FACILITIES:** Outdoor swimming (H) **PARKING:** 30 **NOTES:** No dogs No smoking in restaurant Closed Jan **CARDS:**

### ★66% Westberry

Rhind St PL31 2EL
☎ 01208 72772 01208 72212
***Dir:*** *on ring road directly off A30 & A38*

This popular hotel is convenient for Bodmin town centre and the A30. Bedrooms are comfortably furnished and equipped with a range of facilities. A spacious bar-lounge is provided, plus a billiard room. The restaurant serves both fixed-price and carte menus, and an extensive bar menu is available for lunch.

**ROOMS:** 10 en suite 8 annexe en suite (1 fmly) **FACILITIES:** STV Snooker Gym **CONF:** Thtr 60 Class 20 Board 30 **PARKING:** 30 **NOTES:** Closed 5 days Xmas/New Year **CARDS:**

## BOGNOR REGIS, West Sussex — Map 04 SZ99

### ★★★61% *The Inglenook*

255 Pagham Rd, Nyetimber PO21 3QB
☎ 01243 262495 & 265411 01243 262668
e-mail: inglenook@btinternet.com

This charming 16th-century inn retains much of its original character with exposed beams throughout. Bedrooms, which vary in shape and size, are all individually decorated and well-equipped. Public areas include a cosy lounge, and the bar offers a popular evening menu and a good atmosphere. The restaurant overlooks the garden and serves enjoyable cuisine.

**ROOMS:** 18 en suite (1 fmly) No smoking in all bedrooms **CONF:** Thtr 100 Class 50 Board 50 **PARKING:** 35 **NOTES:** Civ Wed 120 **CARDS:**

### ★★71% Beachcroft

Clyde Rd, Felpham Village PO22 7AH
☎ 01243 827142 01243 827142
e-mail: reservations@beachcroft-hotel.co.uk
***Dir:*** *turn off A259 at Butlins rdbt into Felpham Village, in 800mtrs turn right into Sea Rd then 2nd left into Clyde Rd*

This family-run hotel overlooks a secluded part of the sea front. Bedrooms are bright and spacious with good facilities. Cuisine provides good choice with the traditional restaurant menus or the

*continued*

more informal cosy bar. There is a heated indoor swimming pool and some car parking.

**ROOMS:** 32 en suite (4 fmly) No smoking in 6 bedrooms s £41-£55; d £73-£90 (incl. bkfst) **LB** **FACILITIES:** STV Indoor swimming (H) **CONF:** Thtr 50 Class 30 Board 30 Del from £67 * **PARKING:** 27 **NOTES:** No dogs Closed 24 Dec-10 Jan **CARDS:**

### ★★69% Aldwick Hotel

Aldwick Rd, Aldwick PO21 2QU
☎ 01243 821945 📠 01243 821316
e-mail: tim@aldwickhotel.co.uk
***Dir:*** *at rbt junct with A259/A29 take Victoria Drive, signed Aldwick. At traffic lights turn rt into Aldwick Road. Hotel 250yds on left-1km W of Pier*

This friendly, refurbished hotel has the benefit of a quiet residential location, close to Marine Park Gardens and the beach. All the bedrooms are freshly decorated and well-equipped. Public areas include a spacious dining room, smart bar and lounges.

**ROOMS:** 20 en suite No smoking in all bedrooms s fr £37; d fr £74 (incl. bkfst) * **LB** **FACILITIES:** Xmas **CONF:** Thtr 50 Class 20 Board 24 **SERVICES:** Lift **PARKING:** 10 **NOTES:** No dogs No smoking in restaurant **CARDS:**

### ⌂ Premier Lodge

PREMIER LODGE

Main Rd, Shripney PO22 9PA
☎ 0870 700 1332 📠 0870 7001333
***Dir:*** *on A29*

Premier Lodge offers modern, well-equipped, en suite accommodation suitable for both business and leisure travellers. Meals can be taken at the adjacent popular restaurant and bar, which is fully licensed. For further details, consult the Hotel Groups page.

**ROOMS:** 24 en suite d £42 * **CONF:** Thtr 80 Class 40 Board 30

## BOLTON, Greater Manchester — Map 07 SD70

### ★★★★65% *Last Drop Hotel*

MACDONALD
HOTELS
★★★★

The Last Drop Village & Hotel, Bromley Cross BL7 9PZ
☎ 01204 591131 📠 01204 304122
e-mail: info@lastdrop.macdonald-hotels.co.uk
***Dir:*** *3m N of Bolton off B5472*

Little remains of the agricultural origins of this stylish hotel although photos are found throughout detailing the remarkable transformation from farm to hotel. The hotel enjoys panoramic views across the valley and surrounding countryside. Bedrooms are spacious and well-equipped and staff are friendly and happy

*continued*

to chat. The hotel is a popular conference venue, with an extensive range of function rooms and a fully equipped leisure complex.

**ROOMS:** 118 en suite 10 annexe en suite (72 fmly) No smoking in 60 bedrooms **FACILITIES:** STV Indoor swimming (H) Squash Snooker Sauna Solarium Gym Jacuzzi Craft shops entertainment **CONF:** Thtr 700 Class 300 Board 95 **SERVICES:** Lift **PARKING:** 400 **NOTES:** No smoking in restaurant **CARDS:**

### ★★★60% *Posthouse Bolton*

Posthouse

Beaumont Rd BL3 4TA
☎ 0870 400 9011 📠 01204 61064
***Dir:*** *on A58 W of town*

A modern hotel situated close to the M61. Bedrooms are comfortable and modern. Public areas include 'Seasons' restaurant and bar, a banqueting suite and conference facilities. Staff are friendly and helpful and there is an all-day lounge menu and 24-hour room service.

**ROOMS:** 101 en suite No smoking in 50 bedrooms **FACILITIES:** ch fac **CONF:** Thtr 130 Class 100 Board 50 **PARKING:** 150 **CARDS:**

### ★★★58% Pack Horse Hotel

Nelson Square, Bradshawgate BL1 1DP
☎ 01204 527261
***Dir:*** *from M61 to A666 exit for Bolton centre to traffic lights,straight through next set of lights, continue up hill, after pedestrian crossing right to Nelson Square*

A large late Georgian property, the Pack Horse is located in the town centre, close to an NCP car park which guests can use free of charge. A full lunch menu is now available; facilities include a choice of bars and several function rooms. Well-equipped bedrooms come in a range of sizes and styles.

**ROOMS:** 74 en suite (7 fmly) No smoking in 26 bedrooms s £50-£65; d £50-£75 * **LB** **FACILITIES:** STV Xmas **CONF:** Thtr 275 Class 100 Board 60 Del from £95 * **SERVICES:** Lift **CARDS:**

### ⌂ *Comfort Inn Bolton*

Comfort
Inn

Bolton West Service Area, Horwich BL6 5UZ
☎ 01204 468641 📠 01204 668585
**ROOMS:** 32 en suite **CONF:** Thtr 60 Class 60 Board 30

### ⌂ Express by Holiday Inn Bolton

Arena Approach 3, Horwich BL6 6LB
☎ 01204 469111 📠 469222
***Dir:*** *turn off M61 junct6 onto slip road, turn right at rdbt & left at 2nd*

A modern budget hotel offering comfortable accommodation in refreshing, spacious and comprehensively equipped bedrooms, en suite bathrooms with power showers and continental buffet breakfast included in the room rate. Suitable for business

*continued on p104*

B

BOLTON, continued

travellers or families. For further details and the Express by Holiday Inn phone number, consult the Hotel Groups page.

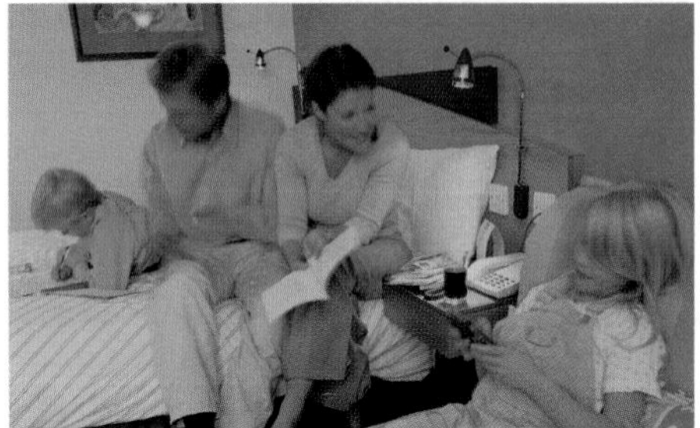

*Express by Holiday Inn, Bolton*

**ROOMS:** 74 en suite (incl. cont bkfst) s £35-£80; d £35-£80 *
**CONF:** Thtr 30 Class 20 Board 20

### ○ Egerton House

MACDONALD HOTELS ★★★★

Blackburn Rd, Egerton BL7 9PL
☎ 01204 307171 🖷 01204 593030
***Dir:*** *3m N of Bolton off A666*
At the time of going to press, the star classification for this hotel was not confirmed. Please refer to the AA internet site www.theAA.com for current information.
**ROOMS:** 32 en suite **CONF:** Thtr 150 Class 90 Board 60

BOLTON ABBEY, North Yorkshire — Map 07 SE05

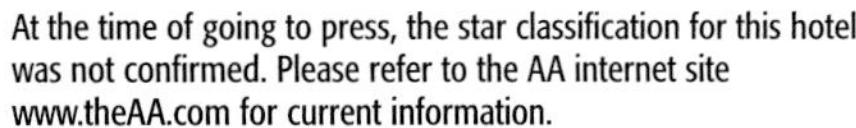
Premier Collection

### ★★★ ⊛⊛ *The Devonshire Arms Country House*

BD23 6AJ
☎ 01756 710441 🖷 01756 710564
e-mail: dev.arms@legend.co.uk
***Dir:*** *on B6160, 250yds N of junct with A59*
With stunning views of the Wharfedale countryside, this beautiful hotel, owned by the Duke & Duchess of Devonshire, dates back to the 17th century. Bedrooms are all elegantly furnished and those in the old part of the house are particularly spacious, complete with four-poster beds and fine antique pieces. Public areas include the elegant Burlington Restaurant offering traditional cooking and the Brasserie, *continued* which is more modern and less formal. There is a well-equipped leisure club.
**ROOMS:** 41 en suite No smoking in 12 bedrooms
**FACILITIES:** Indoor swimming (H) Tennis (hard) Fishing Sauna Solarium Gym Croquet lawn Putting green Jacuzzi Laser pigeon shooting Falconry **CONF:** Thtr 120 Class 80 Board 40
**PARKING:** 150 **NOTES:** No smoking in restaurant
**CARDS:**

BONCHURCH See Wight, Isle of

BOREHAMWOOD, Hertfordshire

### ○ Innkeeper's Lodge Borehamwood

Innkeeper's Lodge

Studio Way WD6 5JY
A new concept in the travel accommodation market. Smart rooms meet essential business requirements but also have home comforts. Dining options include all-day menus plus the added advantage of breakfast, which is included in the room price. Reservations can be made seven days a week through the room reservations number: 0870 243 0500. For further details, consult the Hotel Groups page.
**ROOMS:** 39 en suite

BOROUGHBRIDGE, North Yorkshire — Map 08 SE36

### ★★★70% Crown

Best Western

Horsefair YO51 9LB
☎ 01423 322328 🖷 01423 324512
e-mail: emmalee.crown@barclays.net
***Dir:*** *A1(M) junct 48, hotel 1m towards town centre at T-junct*
Situated just off the A1, The Crown provides well appointed bedrooms and a range of comfortable public rooms, including a delightful restaurant which serves a wide range of well-prepared food; service is relaxed and friendly. Several modern conference rooms are available, as well as a leisure complex.
**ROOMS:** 37 en suite (3 fmly) No smoking in all bedrooms s £65-£82.50; d £80-£95 (incl. bkfst) * **LB** **FACILITIES:** STV Indoor swimming (H) Sauna Gym Jacuzzi Beauty therapist Xmas **CONF:** Thtr 150 Class 80 Board 80 Del £105 * **SERVICES:** Lift **PARKING:** 60 **NOTES:** No dogs (ex guide dogs) No smoking in restaurant Civ Wed 70
**CARDS:**

### ★★★69% Rose Manor

Horsefair YO51 9LL
☎ 01423 322245 🖷 01423 324920
e-mail: rosemanorhotel@ukf.net
***Dir:*** *turn off A1(M) at exit 48 onto B6265, hotel within 1m*
Rose Manor is a comfortable country mansion, lying on the south side of Boroughbridge, with a friendly and relaxing atmosphere. It has an inviting lounge and a split-level dining room. Bedrooms are well-decorated and equipped with modern facilities (including modem sockets). The large self-contained conference and banqueting suite is particularly popular.
**ROOMS:** 19 en suite 2 annexe en suite (1 fmly) No smoking in 11 bedrooms s fr £80; d £110-£116 (incl. bkfst) * **LB** **FACILITIES:** STV **CONF:** Thtr 250 Class 250 Board 25 Del from £99.50 * **PARKING:** 100 **NOTES:** No dogs **CARDS:**

Need to unwind? Look out for hotels with Spa in their entry.

## BORROWDALE, Cumbria
Map 11 NY21

see also Keswick & Rosthwaite

### ★★★77% **Borrowdale Gates Country House**
CA12 5UQ
☎ 017687 77204 017687 77254
e-mail: hotel@borrowdale-gates.com
***Dir:*** *from Keswick follow Borrowdale signs on B5289, after approx 4m turn right at sign for Grange, hotel is on right approx 0.25m through village*

In a sedate woodland setting, this family-run hotel commands stunning views of the Borrowdale valley. Inviting public rooms include lounges, a cosy bar and an attractive restaurant. The recently completed wing of bedrooms provides a high standard of facilities.
**ROOMS:** 31 en suite (1 fmly) s £71.25-£85; d £142.50-£180 (incl. bkfst & dinner) * **LB** **FACILITIES:** STV ch fac Xmas **PARKING:** 40 **NOTES:** No dogs (ex guide dogs) No smoking in restaurant Closed Jan **CARDS:**

*See advert under KESWICK*

### ★★★70% **Borrowdale**
CA12 5UY
☎ 017687 77224 017687 77338
e-mail: theborrowdalehotel@yahoo.com
***Dir:*** *on B5289 at south end of Lake Derwentwater*
A traditional holiday hotel in the beautiful Borrowdale Valley overlooking Derwentwater and 15 minutes' drive from Keswick. Extensive public areas include a choice of lounges, a stylish dining room, and a lounge bar and conservatory serving hearty bar meals. There is a wide choice of bedroom sizes, the larger rooms being best.
**ROOMS:** 33 en suite (9 fmly) **FACILITIES:** Free use of nearby Health Club **CONF:** Class 30 **PARKING:** 100 **NOTES:** No smoking in restaurant **CARDS:**

### ★69% **Royal Oak**
CA12 5XB
☎ 017687 77214 017687 77214
e-mail: royaloak@ukgateway.net
Set in a village in one of Lakeland's most picturesque valleys, this family-run hotel offers friendly and obliging service. A variety of accommodation styles are available, with particularly impressive rooms located in a converted barn across the courtyard. There is a choice of lounges and a cosy bar. A set home-cooked dinner is served at 7pm.
**ROOMS:** 11 rms (8 en suite) 4 annexe en suite (6 fmly) s £38-£51; d £58-£92 (incl. bkfst & dinner) * **LB** **FACILITIES:** no TV in bdrms **PARKING:** 15 **NOTES:** No smoking in restaurant Closed 7-18 Jan & 2-27 Dec **CARDS:**

## BOSCASTLE, Cornwall & Isles of Scilly
Map 02 SX09

### ★★65% **The Wellington Hotel**
THE CIRCLE Selected Individual Hotels GREAT BRITAIN

Old Rd PL35 0AQ
☎ 01840 250202 01840 250621
e-mail: vtobutt@enterprise.net
***Dir:*** *from A30 Launceston turn onto A395, right at Davidstow and follow signs to Boscastle*
Dating back some 400 years, 'The Welly', as it's affectionately known locally, boasts connections with both Thomas Hardy and, more recently, Guy Gibson of 'Dambusters' fame. Built of stone, with a castellated tower on one corner, the hotel offers a choice of comfortable lounges and a cheery beamed bar. An appetising menu of home-cooked dishes with a strong French influence is served each evening in the dining room.
**ROOMS:** 16 en suite s £37-£40; d £66-£72 (incl. bkfst) * **LB** **FACILITIES:** Games room entertainment Xmas **CONF:** Class 12 Board 12 Del from £50 * **PARKING:** 20 **NOTES:** No children 7yrs RS 29 Nov-16 Dec & 10 Jan-10 Feb **CARDS:**

## BOSHAM, West Sussex
Map 04 SU80

### ★★★74% **The Millstream**
Bosham Ln PO18 8HL
☎ 01243 573234 01243 573459
e-mail: info@millstream-hotel.co.uk
***Dir:*** *4m W of Chichester on A259, turn left at Bosham roundabout, 1m turn right at T junct follow signs to church & quay hotel 0.5m on right*

Millstream
Hotel
Restaurant

Lying in the idyllic village of Bosham, this attractive hotel provides comfortable and tastefully decorated bedrooms, each with an individual theme. Public rooms include a cocktail bar, which opens out onto the garden, a lounge and a well-appointed restaurant.
**ROOMS:** 33 en suite 2 annexe en suite (2 fmly) No smoking in 20 bedrooms s £75-£85; d £120 (incl. bkfst) * **LB** **FACILITIES:** Sailing breaks Bridge breaks entertainment ch fac Xmas **CONF:** Thtr 45 Class 20 Board 20 Del from £99 * **PARKING:** 44 **NOTES:** No smoking in restaurant Civ Wed 90 **CARDS:**

*See advert under CHICHESTER*

## BOSTON, Lincolnshire
Map 08 TF34

### ★★★62% ***New England***
49 Wide Bargate PE21 6SH
☎ 01205 365255 01205 310597
***Dir:*** *In town keep on A52 which becomes John Adams Way. Continue over rdbt & through 4 sets of lights. Hotel located on far side of car park at large rdbt*
This popular hotel, situated in the town centre, continues to improve. Morning coffee and afternoon tea are served in its open-

*continued on p106*

BOSTON, continued

plan public areas, and the restaurant serves a good range of dishes.

NEW ENGLAND HOTEL

*New England, Boston*

**ROOMS:** 25 en suite (1 fmly) No smoking in 6 bedrooms **FACILITIES:** STV **CONF:** Thtr 90 Class 50 Board 40 **PARKING:** 25 **NOTES:** No smoking in restaurant **CARDS:**

### ★★63% Comfort Friendly Inn

Donnington Rd, Bicker Bar Roundabout
PE20 3AN
☎ 01205 820118 🖷 01205 820228
e-mail: admin@gb607.u-net.com
***Dir:*** *head towards A16 Spaking, situated on A17/A52 rdbt, 11 miles from Boston town centre*

This purpose-built hotel has well-equipped bedrooms offering good levels of comfort and value for money. Facilities include two meeting rooms, a small open-plan lounge bar with TV and adjacent restaurant. Reasonably priced meals are available all day.
**ROOMS:** 55 en suite (15 fmly) No smoking in 25 bedrooms d fr £58 (incl. bkfst) * **FACILITIES:** STV Xmas **CONF:** Thtr 70 Class 30 Board 35 Del from £72.50 * **PARKING:** 60 **NOTES:** No smoking in restaurant
**CARDS:**

## BOTLEY, Hampshire — Map 04 SU51

### ★★★★69% *Botley Park Hotel Golf & Country Club*

Winchester Rd, Boorley Green SO32 2UA
☎ 01489 780888 🖷 01489 789242
***Dir:*** *on B3354, approx 2m from village*

Set in 176 acres of landscaped park and golf course, Botley Park boasts extensive sports and leisure facilities. These include squash courts, dance studio, fitness centre and pool with steam room. Bedrooms are spacious and quiet. Guests have a choice of dining options; in the restaurant or more casually in the Swing and Divot bar.
**ROOMS:** 100 en suite No smoking in 52 bedrooms **FACILITIES:** STV Indoor swimming (H) Golf 18 Tennis (hard) Squash Snooker Sauna Solarium Gym Croquet lawn Jacuzzi Aerobics studio Beauty salon entertainment **CONF:** Thtr 240 Class 100 Board 60 **PARKING:** 250 **NOTES:** No smoking in restaurant **CARDS:**

*See advert under SOUTHAMPTON*

## BOUGHTON STREET, Kent — Map 05 TR05

### ★★★69% *The Garden Hotel & Restaurant*

167-169 The Street, Boughton ME13 9BH
☎ 01227 751411 🖷 01227 751801
e-mail: gardenhotel@lineone.net
***Dir:*** *from M2 junct 7 follow signs Canterbury/Dove (A2). Take first left signposted Boughton/Dunkirk*

This welcoming family-run hotel is just off the Canterbury road in the pretty village of Boughton. Bedrooms are fresh, modern and thoughtfully equipped. The airy conservatory restaurant looks out over the attractive garden and serves carefully prepared dishes in a modern style.
**ROOMS:** 10 en suite (1 fmly) **CONF:** Thtr 30 Board 18 **PARKING:** 50 **NOTES:** No smoking in restaurant RS Rest closed Sun evening
**CARDS:**

## BOURNEMOUTH, Dorset — Map 04 SZ09

see also Christchurch

### ★★★★74% Bournemouth Highcliff Marriott

St Michaels Rd, West Cliff BH2 5DU
☎ 01202 557702 🖷 01202 292734
e-mail: reservations.bournemouth@marriotthotels.co.uk
***Dir:*** *take A338 dual carriageway through Bournemouth. Follow signs for Bournemouth International Centre to West Cliff Rd, take 2nd turning right,into St Michaels road. Hotel at end of road on left*

Following substantial refurbishment, this hotel has further raised the standards of its bedrooms and public rooms to truly impressive levels. Many of the bedrooms benefit from panoramic sea views, all are impeccably maintained and offer an excellent range of facilities. The hotel has both indoor and outdoor leisure facilities and also boasts extensive conference, banqueting and private dining rooms.
**ROOMS:** 138 en suite 14 annexe en suite (26 fmly) No smoking in 65 bedrooms d £79-£102 * **LB** **FACILITIES:** STV Indoor swimming (H) Outdoor swimming (H) Tennis (hard) Sauna Solarium Gym Croquet lawn Putting green Jacuzzi Beautician Volleyball Childs play area Xmas **CONF:** Thtr 350 Class 180 Board 90 Del from £105 * **SERVICES:** Lift **PARKING:** 100 **NOTES:** No smoking in restaurant Civ Wed 100
**CARDS:**

*continued*

**★★★★71% Menzies East Cliff Court**
East Overcliff Dr BH1 3AN

☎ 0870 6003013 ▤ 01332 511144
e-mail: info@menzies-hotels.co.uk
***Dir:*** *from A338 follow signs to East Cliff*
Enjoying panoramic views across the bay, this popular hotel offers accommodation of high quality, with many rooms benefiting from balconies and sea views. Stylish public areas provide both comfort and tasteful vibrancy with a choice of lounges available. Additional facilities include south-facing terraces leading down to a heated swimming pool.
**ROOMS:** 70 en suite (10 fmly) s £85; d £105 * **LB** **FACILITIES:** STV Outdoor swimming (H) Leisure facilities at nearby hotel Xmas **CONF:** Thtr 150 Class 40 Board 45 Del from £115 * **SERVICES:** Lift **PARKING:** 70 **NOTES:** No smoking in restaurant Civ Wed 100
**CARDS:**

**★★★★68% Menzies Carlton**
East Overcliff BH1 3DN
☎ 0870 6003013 ▤ 01332 511144
e-mail: info@menzies-hotels.co.uk
***Dir:*** *take A338 to the East Cliff*
Enjoying a prime location on the East Cliff, and with views of the Isle of Wight and Dorset coastline, the Carlton is set in attractive gardens and offers good leisure and meeting facilities. Most of the spacious bedrooms enjoy sea views and all are well-equipped.
*continued*
Guests can enjoy an interesting range of carefully prepared dishes in Fredericks restaurant.
**ROOMS:** 74 en suite No smoking in 20 bedrooms s £120; d £120 * **LB** **FACILITIES:** STV Indoor swimming (H) Outdoor swimming (H) Sauna Solarium Gym Jacuzzi Xmas **CONF:** Thtr 140 Class 90 Board 45 Del from £130 * **SERVICES:** Lift **PARKING:** 70 **NOTES:** No smoking in restaurant Civ Wed 80 **CARDS:**

**★★★★68% Royal Bath**
Bath Rd BH1 2EW
☎ 01202 555555 ▤ 01202 554158
e-mail: royalbath@devere-hotels.com
***Dir:*** *from A338 follow tourist signs for Pier and Beaches. The hotel is on Bath Rd just before Lansdowne rdbt and the Pier*
This longstanding and very popular hotel, surrounded by well-tended gardens, enjoys an enviable position overlooking Bournemouth Bay. Significant investment has been made in the public rooms, which include spacious lounges, a choice of restaurants and state of the art leisure facilities. Valet parking is provided for a small charge.
**ROOMS:** 140 en suite s £130; d £160 (incl. bkfst) * **LB** **FACILITIES:** STV Indoor swimming (H) Sauna Solarium Gym Jacuzzi Beauty salon Hairdressing entertainment Xmas **CONF:** Thtr 400 Class 220 Board 100 Del from £120 * **SERVICES:** Lift **PARKING:** 70 **NOTES:** No dogs (ex guide dogs) Civ Wed 200
**CARDS:**

B

BOURNEMOUTH, continued

### ★★★75% Chine

Boscombe Spa Rd BH5 1AX
☎ 01202 396234 01202 391737
e-mail: reservations@chinehotel.co.uk

Set in delightful gardens with private access to the seafront and beach, this Victorian hotel benefits from superb views. An excellent range of facilities is provided, including both an indoor and outdoor pool. Attractively decorated and thoughtfully equipped bedrooms are comfortable, some have balconies. Staff are friendly and unfailingly helpful.

**ROOMS:** 69 en suite 23 annexe en suite (13 fmly) No smoking in 14 bedrooms **FACILITIES:** STV Indoor swimming (H) Outdoor swimming (H) Sauna Solarium Croquet lawn Putting green Games room Outdoor & indoor childrens play area **CONF:** Thtr 140 Class 70 Board 30 **SERVICES:** Lift **PARKING:** 50 **NOTES:** No dogs (ex guide dogs) No smoking in restaurant **CARDS:**

*See advert on page 107*

### ★★★74% Elstead

Knyveton Rd BH1 3QP
☎ 01202 293071 01202 293827
e-mail: info@the-elstead.co.uk

Guests are assured of a friendly welcome and comfortable, well-equipped accommodation at this peacefully located hotel. Within a short stroll of the heart of the town, it is conveniently situated for all the major transport networks. The hotel also has a bar, restaurant and excellent leisure facilities, as well as convenient parking.

**ROOMS:** 50 en suite (15 fmly) No smoking in 15 bedrooms s £54-£69; d £87-£119 (incl. bkfst) * **LB** **FACILITIES:** **Spa** STV Indoor swimming (H) Snooker Sauna Gym Jacuzzi Steam room **CONF:** Thtr 80 Class 60 Board 40 Del from £85 * **SERVICES:** Lift **PARKING:** 40 **NOTES:** No smoking in restaurant **CARDS:**

*See advert on opposite page*

### ★★★73% Langtry Manor

Derby Rd, East Cliff BH1 3QB
☎ 01202 553887 01202 290115
e-mail: lillie@langtrymanor.com
***Dir:*** *from A31 onto A338 at 1st rdbt by rail station turn left over next rdbt 1st left into Knyveton Rd, hotel on opposite corner of small rdbt*

Langtry Manor Hotel

Built in 1877 by Edward VII as a rendezvous for he and his mistress Lillie Langtry, the house retains a stately atmosphere. The stylish bedrooms are individually furnished and several boast four-poster beds. The magnificent dining hall includes several large Tudor tapestries in addition to providing thoroughly enjoyable cuisine. Saturday night is Edwardian Banquet night.

**ROOMS:** 14 en suite 13 annexe en suite (2 fmly) No smoking in 2 bedrooms s £75-£105; d fr £120 (incl. bkfst) * **LB** **FACILITIES:** STV Free use of local health club entertainment Xmas **CONF:** Thtr 100 Class 60 Board 40 Del from £100 * **PARKING:** 30 **NOTES:** No smoking in restaurant Civ Wed 100 **CARDS:**

### ★★★71% Durley Hall

Durley Chine Rd, West Cliff BH2 5JS
☎ 01202 751000 01202 757585
e-mail: Sales@durleyhall.co.uk
***Dir:*** *from A338 follow signs to the West Cliff & Bournemouth International Centre*

Equally suitable for leisure and business guests, this smartly presented hotel is well situated on the West Cliff. Bedrooms are very well decorated and furnished. There are several executive and honeymoon rooms, some with feature beds and baths. As well as the Starlight restaurant there is a café overlooking the outdoor pool. In addition, the range of leisure facilities is particularly impressive and the hotel has extensive conference facilities.

**ROOMS:** 70 en suite 11 annexe en suite (27 fmly) s £50-£66; d £100-£132 (incl. bkfst) * **LB** **FACILITIES:** STV Indoor swimming (H) Outdoor swimming (H) Sauna Solarium Gym Jacuzzi Beauty therapist Table tennis entertainment ch fac Xmas **CONF:** Thtr 200 Class 80 Board 35 Del from £72 * **SERVICES:** Lift **PARKING:** 150 **NOTES:** No dogs (ex guide dogs) No smoking in restaurant Civ Wed 85

**CARDS:**

Packed in a hurry? Ironing facilities should be available at all star levels, either in rooms or on request.

Arriving late? Four and five star hotels have night porters to assist with your luggage, and 24-hour room service.

### ★★★70% *Hermitage*
Exeter Rd BH2 5AH
☎ 01202 557363 📠 01202 559173
e-mail: info@hermitage-hotel.co.uk
***Dir:*** *follow signs for Bournemouth International Centre or pier, hotel opposite both*

Situated in the heart of Bournemouth's town centre, the Hermitage has direct access to the shops, beaches and Pavilion gardens. Bedrooms and bathrooms are all very smart, well coordinated with good quality furnishing and many useful extra facilities. Public areas are attractive and very comfortable.
**ROOMS:** 63 en suite 12 annexe en suite (10 fmly) No smoking in 52 bedrooms **FACILITIES:** Free swimming at Bournemouth International Centre **CONF:** Thtr 180 Class 60 Board 60 **SERVICES:** Lift **PARKING:** 58 **NOTES:** No dogs (ex guide dogs) No smoking in restaurant **CARDS:**

### ★★★70% *Hotel Miramar*
East Overcliff Dr, East Cliff BH1 3AL
☎ 01202 556581 📠 01202 291242
e-mail: sales@miramar-bournemouth.com

On the East Cliff, close to the town centre, this smart hotel sits in landscaped gardens with super views of the sea. All public areas and bedrooms offer a high standard of decoration, quality and comfort in addition to a number of thoughtful extras. A number of superior rooms include the benefit of a relaxing, sea view balcony.
**ROOMS:** 45 en suite (6 fmly) No smoking in 10 bedrooms **FACILITIES:** STV Croquet lawn entertainment **CONF:** Thtr 200 Class 50 Board 50 **SERVICES:** Lift **PARKING:** 80 **NOTES:** No smoking in restaurant Civ Wed 130 **CARDS:**

### ★★★70% Piccadilly
Bath Rd BH1 2NN
☎ 01202 552559 📠 01202 298235
***Dir:*** *follow signs for 'Lansdowne'*

Personally run by the proprietors and a welcoming team of staff, this hotel prides itself on its friendly atmosphere and superb ballroom. Bedrooms are comfortably furnished, pleasantly

*continued*

decorated and well-equipped. There is a spacious open-plan lounge and bar and an attractive dining room where the table d'hôte including carvery is very popular at dinner.
**ROOMS:** 45 en suite (2 fmly) s £65; d £95 (incl. bkfst) * **LB** **FACILITIES:** STV Ballroom dancing Xmas **CONF:** Thtr 100 Class 50 Board 40 **SERVICES:** Lift **PARKING:** 30 **NOTES:** No dogs (ex guide dogs) No smoking in restaurant **CARDS:**

### ★★★70% ❀ Queens
Meyrick Rd, East Cliff BH1 3DL
☎ 01202 554415 📠 01202 294810
e-mail: hotels@arthuryoung.co.uk

Only yards from the seafront, this hotel enjoys a good location and is popular for conferences and functions. The public areas include a bar, lounge and a stunning restaurant. The Queensbury Leisure Club has much to offer guests. Bedrooms do vary in size and style, although all are well-equipped and comfortable.
**ROOMS:** 109 en suite (15 fmly) s £51.50-£62.50; d £90-£125 (incl. bkfst) * **LB** **FACILITIES:** **Spa** Indoor swimming (H) Snooker Sauna Solarium Gym Jacuzzi Beauty salon, Games Room entertainment ch fac Xmas **CONF:** Thtr 220 Class 120 Board 50 Del from £77.50 * **SERVICES:** Lift **PARKING:** 80 **NOTES:** No smoking in restaurant **CARDS:**

*See advert on page 111*

### ★★★69% Cumberland
East Overcliff Dr BH1 3AF
☎ 01202 290722 📠 01202 311394
e-mail: reservations@cumberlandhotel.uk.com

Many of the well-equipped and attractively decorated bedrooms benefit from sea views and balconies here. The public areas are spacious and comfortable. The restaurant offers a daily changing

*continued on p110*

BOURNEMOUTH, continued

fixed price menu. Guests have use of the leisure club at the sister hotel, The Queens.
**ROOMS:** 102 en suite (12 fmly) s £47-£62.50; d £94-£125 (incl. bkfst) * LB **FACILITIES:** Outdoor swimming (H) Free membership of nearby Leisure Club entertainment Xmas **CONF:** Thtr 120 Class 70 Board 45 Del from £69.50 * **SERVICES:** Lift **PARKING:** 51 **NOTES:** No smoking in restaurant **CARDS:**

### ★★★69% East Anglia

Best Western

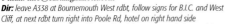

6 Poole Rd BH2 5QX
☎ 01202 765163 📠 01202 752949
e-mail: info@eastangliahotel.com
***Dir:*** *leave A338 at Bournemouth West rdbt, follow signs for B.I.C. and West Cliff, at next rdbt turn right into Poole Rd, hotel on right hand side*
Attractive bedrooms provide comfortable accommodation at this well-managed hotel. This is enhanced by the friendly team of staff, who ensure a warm welcome and pleasant service throughout. Public areas include a number of function/conference rooms, ample lounges and an air-conditioned restaurant.
**ROOMS:** 45 en suite 25 annexe en suite (18 fmly) No smoking in 2 bedrooms s fr £59; d fr £110 (incl. bkfst & dinner) * LB **FACILITIES:** Spa STV Outdoor swimming (H) Sauna Xmas **CONF:** Thtr 150 Class 75 Board 60 **SERVICES:** Lift **PARKING:** 70 **NOTES:** No dogs (ex guide dogs) No smoking in restaurant Closed 2-8 Jan
**CARDS:**

### ★★★69% Trouville

Priory Rd BH2 5DH
☎ 01202 552262 📠 01202 293324
e-mail: hotels@arthuryoung.co.uk
***Dir:*** *close to International Centre*
Close to Bournemouth's International Centre and the seafront, this large privately-owned hotel is situated on the West Cliff. The bedrooms are attractively decorated and well co-ordinated. In addition to a smart leisure suite, there is a comfortable bar and separate lounge.
**ROOMS:** 77 en suite (21 fmly) s £51-£64; d £102-£128 (incl. bkfst) * LB **FACILITIES:** Indoor swimming (H) Sauna Solarium Gym Jacuzzi entertainment Xmas **CONF:** Thtr 100 Class 45 Board 50 Del from £75 * **SERVICES:** Lift **PARKING:** 60 **NOTES:** No smoking in restaurant
**CARDS:**

### ★★★69% Wessex

Forestdale Hotels

West Cliff Rd BH2 5EU
☎ 01202 551911 📠 01202 297354
e-mail: wessex@forestdale.com
***Dir:*** *via M27/A35 through New Forest. A338 from Dorchester and A347 to the North. Hotel on West Cliff side of the town*
Centrally located for the town centre and beach, the Wessex is a popular, relaxing hotel. Bedrooms vary in size and include 25 premier rooms; all are comfortable, and equipped with a range of modern amenities. There are excellent leisure facilities, ample function rooms and an open-plan bar and lounge.
**ROOMS:** 109 en suite (22 fmly) No smoking in 3 bedrooms s £68-£78; d £136-£156 (incl. bkfst & dinner) * LB **FACILITIES:** STV Indoor swimming (H) Outdoor swimming (H) Snooker Sauna Solarium Gym Table tennis Xmas **CONF:** Thtr 400 Class 160 Board 160 **SERVICES:** Lift **PARKING:** 250 **NOTES:** No smoking in restaurant Civ Wed
**CARDS:**

> Bad hair day? Hairdryers in all rooms three stars and above.

### ★★★68% Cliffeside

East Overcliff Dr BH1 3AQ
☎ 01202 555724 📠 01202 314534
e-mail: hotels@arthuryoung.co.uk
***Dir:*** *from M27 to Ringwood A338. From Ringwood approximately 7m, then first rdbt left into East Cliff*
Many of the public areas and bedrooms benefit from bay views at this popular hotel. The friendly staff create a good rapport with guests and a relaxed atmosphere prevails. The bedrooms are attractively decorated. A set price menu is offered in the restaurant.
**ROOMS:** 62 en suite (10 fmly) s £69.50; d £139 (incl. bkfst & dinner) * LB **FACILITIES:** Outdoor swimming (H) Table tennis Xmas **CONF:** Thtr 180 Class 140 Board 60 **SERVICES:** Lift **PARKING:** 45
**CARDS:**

*See advert on opposite page*

### ★★★68% The Connaught

Best Western

West Hill Rd, West Cliff BH2 5PH
☎ 01202 298020 📠 01202 298028
e-mail: sales@theconnaught.co.uk
***Dir:*** *follow signs 'Town Centre West & BIC'*
An attractive hotel on Bournemouth's West Cliff. Bedrooms are neatly decorated and equipped with modern facilities. There is a choice of lounges and a smart leisure centre. Extensive meeting facilities are available. Professional staff are attentive and friendly.
**ROOMS:** 60 en suite (15 fmly) No smoking in 4 bedrooms s fr £70; d fr £120 (incl. bkfst) * LB **FACILITIES:** STV Indoor swimming (H) Snooker Sauna Solarium Gym Jacuzzi Cardio-vascular,Table tennis,Pool entertainment Xmas **CONF:** Thtr 200 Class 70 Board 70 Del from £85 * **SERVICES:** Lift **PARKING:** 45 **NOTES:** No smoking in restaurant
**CARDS:**

### ★★★68% Hinton Firs

Manor Rd, East Cliff BH1 3HB
☎ 01202 555409 📠 01202 299607
e-mail: hintonfirs@bournemouth.co.uk
***Dir:*** *from A338 turn west at St Paul's Rdbt across next 2 rdbts then immediately fork left to side of church, hotel on next corner*

A friendly team of staff welcome guests old and new to this hotel, conveniently situated on the East Cliff. Bedrooms, six of which are in a separate wing, are pleasantly decorated and comfortable. Included in the facilities are indoor and outdoor pools, a games room, bar and lounges. Dinner offers a good choice of well-cooked dishes.
**ROOMS:** 46 en suite 6 annexe en suite (12 fmly) s £40-£65; d £75-£110 (incl. bkfst & dinner) * LB **FACILITIES:** Indoor swimming (H) Outdoor swimming (H) Sauna Jacuzzi Games room entertainment ch fac Xmas **CONF:** Thtr 60 Class 40 Board 30 Del from £70 * **SERVICES:** Lift **PARKING:** 40 **NOTES:** No dogs No smoking in restaurant
**CARDS:**

### ★★★68% Menzies Anglo-Swiss

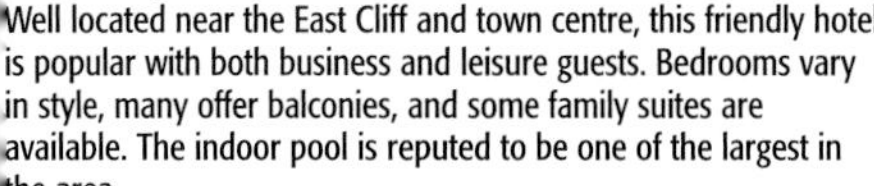
MENZIES HOTELS

16 Gervis Rd, East Cliff BH1 3EQ
☎ 0870 6003013 🖷 01332 511144
e-mail: info@menzies-hotels.co.uk
**Dir:** *follow signs to East Cliff from A338*

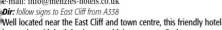

Well located near the East Cliff and town centre, this friendly hotel is popular with both business and leisure guests. Bedrooms vary in style, many offer balconies, and some family suites are available. The indoor pool is reputed to be one of the largest in the area.

**ROOMS:** 57 en suite 8 annexe en suite (16 fmly) No smoking in 16 bedrooms s £70; d £90 * **LB** **FACILITIES:** STV Indoor swimming (H) Sauna Solarium Gym Jacuzzi Xmas **CONF:** Thtr 75 Class 30 Board 30 Del from £95 * **SERVICES:** Lift **PARKING:** 70 **NOTES:** No smoking in restaurant Civ Wed 150 **CARDS:**

### ★★★66% Bay View Court

35 East Overcliff Dr BH1 3AH
☎ 01202 294449 🖷 01202 292883
e-mail: enquiry@bayviewcourt.co.uk
**Dir:** *on A338 left at St Pauls roundabout. Go straight over St Swithuns roundabout. Left down Manor Rd, bear left onto Manor Rd, 1st right, next right*

This friendly family-run hotel enjoys splendid views across the bay. Bedrooms vary in size but all are attractively furnished. The lounges are comfortable and south-facing, and leisure facilities are appealing.

**ROOMS:** 64 en suite (11 fmly) s £52-£54; d £104-£108 (incl. bkfst & dinner) * **LB** **FACILITIES:** **Spa** STV Indoor swimming (H) Snooker Gym Steam room entertainment Xmas **CONF:** Thtr 170 Class 85 Board 50 Del from £58 * **SERVICES:** Lift **PARKING:** 58 **NOTES:** No smoking in restaurant **CARDS:**

B

BOURNEMOUTH, continued

**★★★66% Carrington House**
31 Knyveton Rd BH1 3QQ
ZOFFANY HOTELS
☎ 01202 369988 01202 292221
e-mail: carrington@zoffanyhotels.co.uk
***Dir:*** *Turn off A338 at St Paul's rdbt, continue for 200 mtrs & turn left into Knyveton Rd. Hotel approx 400 mtrs on right*
This hotel, situated in a quiet tree-lined avenue, within easy reach of local amenities, offers excellent conference rooms and award-winning facilities for disabled guests. Children are especially well-catered for, with their own play rooms and menu.
**ROOMS:** 145 en suite (42 fmly) No smoking in 40 bedrooms s £85; d £105 (incl. bkfst) * **FACILITIES:** STV Indoor swimming (H) Snooker Gym Purpose built children's play area ch fac Xmas **CONF:** Thtr 500 Class 260 Board 80 Del from £75 * **SERVICES:** Lift **PARKING:** 100 **NOTES:** No smoking in restaurant Civ Wed 250
**CARDS:**

**★★★66% Heathlands Hotel**
12 Grove Rd, East Cliff BH1 3AY
☎ 01202 553336 01202 555937
e-mail: info@heathlandshotel.com
***Dir:*** *from A338 St Pauls rdbt take 3rd exit to Holdenhurst Road, then take 2nd exit off Lansdowne rdbt, into Meyrick Rd. Left into Gervis Rd. Hotel on Right*
A large hotel on the East Cliff, Bournemouth Heathlands is popular with groups and conferences. Public areas are bright and spacious. The coffee shop is open all day and there is regular live entertainment.
**ROOMS:** 115 en suite (13 fmly) No smoking in 15 bedrooms s £37-£79; d £74-£158 (incl. bkfst) * **LB** **FACILITIES:** STV Outdoor swimming (H) Sauna Gym Jacuzzi Health suite entertainment ch fac Xmas **CONF:** Thtr 270 Class 102 Board 54 Del from £65 * **SERVICES:** Lift **PARKING:** 100 **NOTES:** No smoking in restaurant Civ Wed 150
**CARDS:**

*See advert on opposite page*

**★★★66% Marsham Court**
Russell Cotes Rd, East Cliff BH1 3AB
☎ 01202 552111 01202 294744
e-mail: reservations@marshamcourt.co.uk
***Dir:*** *From Wessex Way turn towards Bournemouth East at St Pauls rdbt, straight across station rdbt follow ringroad, across St Swithuns rdbt, bear left with church on left across Meyrick rdbt, left at St Peters rdbt hotel left*
With splendid views over the sea and town, this hotel is conveniently located on the East Cliff, only a short walk from the town centre. Public areas include a comfortable bar and lounge, a range of conference/function rooms, and a spacious restaurant. The bedrooms vary in size and style, the front facing rooms always proving popular.
**ROOMS:** 86 en suite (15 fmly) s £60; d £100 (incl. bkfst) * **LB** **FACILITIES:** STV Outdoor swimming (H) Free swimming at BIC,Pool room Xmas **CONF:** Thtr 200 Class 100 Board 80 Del from £70 * **SERVICES:** Lift **PARKING:** 100 **NOTES:** No dogs (ex guide dogs) Civ Wed 200 **CARDS:**

**★★★66% Pavilion**
22 Bath Rd BH1 2NS
☎ 01202 291266 01202 559264
Guests are assured of a warm welcome at this friendly hotel, located close to the town centre and with easy access to the seafront and attractions. Equally suited to both leisure and business guests, the hotel offers well-equipped bedrooms which vary in size, spacious and comfortable public areas and good conference facilities.
**ROOMS:** 44 en suite (6 fmly) s £37-£45; d £74-£90 (incl. bkfst & dinner) * **LB** **FACILITIES:** Special rates for International Centre entertainment Xmas **CONF:** Thtr 100 Class 50 Board 50 Del £57.50 * **SERVICES:** Lift **PARKING:** 40 **NOTES:** No smoking in restaurant
**CARDS:**

**★★★66% *Quality Hotel Bournemouth***
8 Poole Rd BH2 5QU
☎ 01202 757758
e-mail: admin@gb641.u-net.com
***Dir:*** *0.5m from A338 road and by-pass. Follow signs B.I.C. from by-pass then right at rbt into Poole Road*
A popular modern hotel on the West Cliff, this is a good base for visiting the attractions and beach. Bedrooms are attractively decorated and well-equipped. Public areas, although not extensive, are bright and comfortable with a relaxed, friendly atmosphere.
**ROOMS:** 54 en suite (3 fmly) No smoking in 17 bedrooms
**FACILITIES:** STV **CONF:** Thtr 70 Class 36 Board 32 **SERVICES:** Lift **PARKING:** 55 **NOTES:** No smoking in restaurant
**CARDS:**

**★★★65% Belvedere**
Bath Rd BH1 2EU
☎ 01202 297556 & 293336 01202 294699
e-mail: belvedere_hotel@msn.com
***Dir:*** *from A338 keep railway station & ASDA on left at rdbt take 1st left then 3rd exit at next 2 rdbts. Hotel on Bath Hill just after 4th rdbt*
Close to the town centre and the seafront, this friendly, family-run hotel offers spacious public areas and comfortable bedrooms. In addition to the lively bar and attractive restaurant, popular with locals, the meeting rooms provide an ideal location for both conferences and functions.
**ROOMS:** 61 en suite (12 fmly) s £39-£59; d £58-£98 (incl. bkfst) * **LB** **FACILITIES:** STV entertainment Xmas **CONF:** Thtr 80 Class 30 Board 30 **SERVICES:** Lift **PARKING:** 55 **NOTES:** No dogs (ex guide dogs) No smoking in restaurant **CARDS:**

**★★★65% Durlston Court**
47 Gervis Rd, East Cliff BH1 3DD
☎ 01202 316316 01202 316999
e-mail: dch@seaviews.co.uk
***Dir:*** *on A338 10m from M27/A338 junct left large rdbt, right next rdbt, 3rd junct next rdbt (Meyrick Rd) next rdbt right into Gervis Rd. Hotel on left*

This hotel, located on the East Cliff, is close to the town's attractions and beaches. Comfortable bedrooms vary in size with one room specifically for disabled guests. The bright and airy bar

*continued*

and lounge overlook the sheltered pool and terrace. A fixed price menu is available in the spacious restaurant.
**ROOMS:** 57 en suite (11 fmly) No smoking in 8 bedrooms
**FACILITIES:** STV Indoor swimming (H) Sauna Gym Jacuzzi Pool table entertainment **CONF:** Thtr 120 Class 60 Board 35 Del £65 *
**SERVICES:** Lift **PARKING:** 36 **NOTES:** No dogs (ex guide dogs)
**CARDS:**

### ★★★65% Grosvenor
Bath Rd, East Cliff BH1 2EX
☎ 01202 558858 🖹 01202 298332
e-mail: enquiries@grosvenor-bournemouth.co.uk
Within a short walk of the seafront and conveniently close to the shops, this hotel offers a range of comfortable bedrooms. Guests can relax in the well-furnished lounge bar and a separate sitting room is available. There is a popular indoor leisure suite. The restaurant provides tasty, well-prepared dishes.
**ROOMS:** 40 en suite (12 fmly) s £42.50-£52.50; d £65-£100 (incl. bkfst) * **LB** **FACILITIES:** STV Indoor swimming (H) Sauna Gym Jacuzzi entertainment Xmas **CONF:** Thtr 30 Class 50 Board 20 Del from £45 *
**SERVICES:** Lift **PARKING:** 40 **NOTES:** No dogs (ex guide dogs) No smoking in restaurant **CARDS:**

### ★★★65% Montague
Durley Rd South, West Cliff BH2 5JH
☎ 01202 551074 🖹 01202 553948
e-mail: enquiries@montaguehotel.co.uk
***Dir:*** *from A31/A338 to Bournemouth. At Bournemouth West roundabout take 1st left into Cambridge Rd, 2nd exit at roundabout into Durley Chine Rd. Proceed to the next roundabout and take 2nd exit, hotel on right.*
Ideally located for both the beach and the BIC, this welcoming hotel providing attentive hospitality and service has recently undergone a total refurbishment. Bedrooms and bathrooms vary in size, but all offer high quality furnishings. Relaxing public areas include a stylish bar/lounge and a restaurant offering enjoyable home cooking style dinners.
**ROOMS:** 37 rms (34 en suite) (9 fmly) No smoking in 6 bedrooms s £26-£44; d £50-£80 (incl. bkfst) * **LB** **FACILITIES:** Outdoor swimming (H) Xmas **CONF:** Thtr 20 Class 12 Board 12 Del from £50 *
**SERVICES:** Lift **PARKING:** 50 **NOTES:** No smoking in restaurant
**CARDS:**

### ★★★65% New Durley Dean
West Cliff Rd BH2 5HE
☎ 01202 557711 🖹 01202 292815
e-mail: new-durley-dean@durley.fsbusiness.co.uk
***Dir:*** *off A338*
This impressive period building in West Cliff, has undergone major refurbishment. Its spacious rooms offer comfortable, well-equipped accommodation. The leisure centre and night-club provide ideal locations for guests to relax after a meal in the restaurant or a drink in the bar.
**ROOMS:** 123 en suite (27 fmly) s £25-£61; d £50-£122 (incl. bkfst) * **LB** **FACILITIES:** STV Indoor swimming (H) Sauna Solarium Gym Jacuzzi Table tennis Steam room entertainment Xmas **CONF:** Thtr 120 Class 30 Board 30 Del from £60 * **SERVICES:** Lift **PARKING:** 35
**NOTES:** No smoking in restaurant **CARDS:**

### ★★★65% Suncliff
29 East Overcliff Dr BH1 3AG
☎ 01202 291711 🖹 01202 293788
e-mail: reservations@suncliffhotel.com
***Dir:*** *A338 to Bournemouth. 1st left at rdbt into St Pauls Rd, follow signs for East Cliff*
A large privately owned hotel on the East Cliff with glorious views from the public rooms and many bedrooms. Rooms are equipped

*continued on p114*

BOURNEMOUTH, continued

with modern facilities, and are spacious and comfortably furnished. Public rooms include a pleasant conservatory, lounge and restaurant.
**ROOMS:** 94 en suite (29 fmly) s £33-£47; d £66-£94 (incl. bkfst) * **LB** **FACILITIES:** **Spa** Indoor swimming (H) Squash Sauna Solarium Gym Jacuzzi Table tennis pool entertainment ch fac Xmas **CONF:** Thtr 100 Class 70 Board 60 Del from £62 * **SERVICES:** Lift **PARKING:** 60 **NOTES:** No smoking in restaurant **CARDS:**

### ★★★64% Burley Court

Bath Rd BH1 2NP
☎ 01202 552824 & 556704 01202 298514
e-mail: burleycourt@btclick.com
***Dir:*** *leave A338 at St Pauls rdbt, take 3rd exit at next rdbt (Holdenhurst Rd), 3rd exit at next rdbt (Bath Rd), overcrossing, 1st left*
This personally owned and managed hotel is within easy walking distance of the town centre, attracting many loyal guests. Bedrooms vary in style and standard. Public areas are spacious and comfortable. A daily changing table d'hote menu is served in the dining room.
**ROOMS:** 38 en suite (8 fmly) No smoking in 19 bedrooms s £31-£43; d £62-£84 (incl. bkfst) * **LB** **FACILITIES:** Outdoor swimming (H) Solarium Free use of local indoor leisure pool Xmas **CONF:** Thtr 30 Class 15 Board 15 **SERVICES:** Lift **PARKING:** 35 **NOTES:** No smoking in restaurant Closed 30 Dec-14 Jan **CARDS:**

### ★★★64% Hotel Courtlands

Best Western

16 Boscombe Spa Rd, East Cliff BH5 1BB
☎ 01202 302442 01202 309880
***Dir:*** *from A338 towards Bournemouth, then East Cliff, then Boscombe. Turn left over 1st rdbt left at 2nd & next right after Boscombe Gdns*
This busy hotel close to Boscombe Pier caters well for both corporate and leisure guests. It offers comfortable, well-equipped bedrooms. The outdoor swimming pool, crazy golf and games room are all popular. The Courtlands boasts extensive function and meeting rooms as well as lounges to relax in and a restaurant in which to dine.
**ROOMS:** 58 en suite (8 fmly) s £42-£49; d £80-£95 (incl. bkfst) * **LB** **FACILITIES:** **Spa** STV Outdoor swimming (H) Sauna Solarium Jacuzzi Free use of nearby Health Club Xmas **CONF:** Thtr 120 Class 85 Board 20 Del from £62 * **SERVICES:** Lift **PARKING:** 50 **NOTES:** No smoking in restaurant **CARDS:**

### ★★★63% Chesterwood

East Overcliff Dr BH1 3AR
☎ 01202 558057 01202 556285
e-mail: enquiry@chesterwoodhotel.co.uk
All of the public rooms enjoy splendid sea views from this hotel on the East Cliff. In the spacious restaurant a fixed price menu is available each evening and Sunday lunches are provided. A comfortable bar lounge offers an informal seating alternative to the drawing room. The bedrooms are pleasing and well-equipped.
**ROOMS:** 50 en suite (13 fmly) s £42-£54; d £84-£108 (incl. bkfst & dinner) * **LB** **FACILITIES:** Outdoor swimming (H) entertainment ch fac Xmas **CONF:** Thtr 150 Class 100 Board 30 Del from £55 * **SERVICES:** Lift **PARKING:** 39 **NOTES:** No smoking in restaurant **CARDS:**

*See advert on page 113*

### ★★72% Sun Court

West Hill Rd, West Cliff BH2 5PH
☎ 01202 551343 01202 316747
e-mail: info@suncourthotel.com
***Dir:*** *From A338 into Bournemouth at 2nd rdbt turn left, next rdbt turn left into Poole Rd. West Hill Rd 1st on right*
Standing on the West Cliff, this hotel is family-owned and run by particularly friendly and helpful staff. Bedrooms vary in size and style, but all are well-equipped, and several have lounge areas. Public areas include the Palm Court Bar and a spacious dining room. All guests are offered temporary membership of a nearby leisure club owned by a sister hotel.
**ROOMS:** 33 en suite (7 fmly) s £31-£45; d £60-£90 (incl. bkfst) * **LB** **FACILITIES:** Outdoor swimming (H) Facilities available next door **SERVICES:** Lift **PARKING:** 50 **CARDS:**

### ★★70% Arlington

Exeter Park Rd BH2 5BD
☎ 01202 552879 & 553012 01202 298317
e-mail: enquiries@arlingtonbournemouth.co.uk
***Dir:*** *follow signs to Bournemouth International Centre through Priory Rd, onto rdbt and exit at Royal Exeter Hotel sign. Hotel is along Exeter Park Rd*
The Arlington has a relaxed, friendly atmosphere and a superb location midway between the Square and Bournemouth Pier. The attractive bar/lounge overlooks the main Bournemouth Flower Gardens and bandstand. Well-equipped bedrooms are decorated to a good standard and downstairs home cooked dishes are served in Impressions Restaurant.
**ROOMS:** 27 en suite 1 annexe en suite (6 fmly) s £38.50-£46.50; d £77-£93 (incl. bkfst & dinner) * **LB** **FACILITIES:** STV Xmas **SERVICES:** Lift **PARKING:** 21 **NOTES:** No dogs No children 2yrs Closed 4-15 Jan **CARDS:**

### ★★70% *Whitehall*

Exeter Park Rd BH2 5AX
☎ 01202 554682 01202 554682
e-mail: whitehallhotel@lineone.net
***Dir:*** *follow signs B.I.C. then turn into Exeter Park Road off Exeter Road*
The warmest of welcomes awaits guests at this comfortable hotel. Bedrooms are bright and attractively decorated in co-ordinating fabrics. Enjoyable home-cooked meals are served in the large dining room, before which guests are invited to enjoy a drink in the small, well-stocked bar. Two attractive lounges are also provided.
**ROOMS:** 47 rms (44 en suite) (5 fmly) **SERVICES:** Lift **PARKING:** 25 **NOTES:** No smoking in restaurant Closed Nov-Feb **CARDS:**

### ★★69% Chinehurst

Alum Chine, 18-20 Studland Rd, Westbourne BH4 8JA
☎ 01202 764583 01202 762854
***Dir:*** *turn off A338, second junct off Frizzel rndbt, follow signs for Alum Chine*
A warm welcome is assured at this family run hotel, peacefully situated on the west side of town. Bedrooms are bright and attractive, some with sea views, including the honeymoon suite which has a super outlook. There is a path leading to the beach and regular buses run to the town centre if required.
**ROOMS:** 30 en suite (4 fmly) No smoking in 4 bedrooms s £30-£50; d £60-£80 (incl. bkfst) * **LB** **FACILITIES:** **Spa** Games room entertainment Xmas **CONF:** Thtr 60 Class 40 Board 40 **PARKING:** 14 **NOTES:** No children 3yrs No smoking in restaurant **CARDS:**

### ★★68% *Hotel Collingwood*
11 Priory Rd, West Cliff BH2 5DF
☎ 01202 557575 📠 01202 293219
***Dir:*** *from A338 left at West Cliff sign across 1st rdbt left at 2nd rdbt, hotel 500yds on left in Priory Rd*
Privately owned and well managed, this hotel is ideally located for the BIC, the town centre and the seafront, and offers good leisure facilities. Bedrooms are airy, with the accent on comfort. Public areas are spacious and each evening in Pinks Restaurant, a fixed-price menu is available.

**ROOMS:** 53 en suite (16 fmly) **FACILITIES:** STV Indoor swimming (H) Snooker Sauna Solarium Jacuzzi Mini gym Steam room Games room Pool table entertainment **SERVICES:** Lift **PARKING:** 55 **NOTES:** No smoking in restaurant **CARDS:**

*See advert on this page*

### ★★68% Durley Grange
6 Durley Rd, West Cliff BH2 5JL
☎ 01202 554473 & 290743 📠 01202 293774
***Dir:*** *turn left off Wessex Way-A338 on St Michaels rdbt, through next rdbt, 1st left into Sommerville Rd, turn right into Durley Rd*
This friendly hotel is located in a quiet area, within easy walking distance of the pier and town centre. Bedrooms are simply decorated, comfortable and well equipped. Home-cooked meals are served in the dining room and there is a relaxing lounge bar, and a swimming pool available for guests' use.
**ROOMS:** 51 en suite (4 fmly) No smoking in 2 bedrooms s £38-£48; d £76-£96 (incl. bkfst & dinner) * **LB** **FACILITIES:** STV Indoor swimming (H) Sauna Solarium Jacuzzi entertainment Xmas **SERVICES:** Lift **PARKING:** 35 **NOTES:** No children 5yrs No smoking in restaurant Closed 2 Jan-1 Feb **CARDS:**

### ★★68% *Mansfield*
West Cliff Gardens BH2 5HL
☎ 01202 552659
***Dir:*** *from A338 follow signs for West Cliff, straight on at two rdbts via Cambridge & Durley Chine Rd*
Located in a quiet crescent on the West Cliff, the Mansfield Hotel is convenient for access to the seafront and town centre. Bedrooms are comfortably furnished, and staff make every effort to ensure that guests have an enjoyable stay.
**ROOMS:** 30 en suite (7 fmly) **PARKING:** 12 **NOTES:** No dogs No smoking in restaurant Closed 29 Dec-17 Jan **CARDS:**

### ★★67% *Croham Hurst*
9 Durley Rd South, West Cliff BH2 5JH
☎ 01202 552353 📠 01202 311484
***Dir:*** *off A35 at Cambridge Rd roundabout, follow signs to BIC, hotel on the right just before Durley roundabout*
Enjoying high levels of repeat business from loyal customers, this popular family-run hotel is convenient for both the beach and town centre. Bedrooms offer a mixture of traditional and modern

*continued*



styles but all are spacious and well-equipped. The lounge doubles as an entertainment venue and the spacious restaurant offers traditional home-cooked dishes.

croham hurst
hotel

**ROOMS:** 40 en suite (10 fmly) **FACILITIES:** STV entertainment **SERVICES:** Lift **PARKING:** 30 **NOTES:** No dogs (ex guide dogs) No smoking in restaurant Closed 2 Jan-10 Feb **CARDS:**

### ★★66% Ullswater
West Cliff Gardens BH2 5HW
☎ 01202 555181 📠 01202 317896
e-mail: enq@ullswater.uk.com
***Dir:*** *on entering Bournemouth follow signs to Westcliff, hotel just off Westcliff Road*
Situated on the West Cliff, this hotel attracts a loyal following. Bedrooms vary in size but all are decorated in fresh colours and furnished to a good standard. Downstairs there is a spacious and

*continued on p116*

BOURNEMOUTH, continued

comfortable lounge bar and a very attractive dining room, where a good choice of dishes are on offer.
**ROOMS:** 42 en suite (7 fmly) s £26-£32; d £52-£64 (incl. bkfst) * **LB** **FACILITIES:** Snooker Table tennis entertainment Xmas **CONF:** Thtr 40 Class 30 Board 24 Del from £45 * **SERVICES:** Lift **PARKING:** 10 **NOTES:** No smoking in restaurant **CARDS:**

### ★★65% Cliff Court
15 Westcliff Rd BH2 5EX
☎ 01202 555994 01202 780954
e-mail: info@cliffcourthotel.com
***Dir:*** *A338 (Wessex Way) into Cambridge Road, follow Durley Chine Road into West Cliff Road*
This hotel is located on the West Cliff within easy reach of the town centre, beach and the many attractions of the area. In addition to the spacious dining room, the public rooms include a bar and small lounge. In the comfortable bedrooms, the best use has been made of the available space.
**ROOMS:** 40 en suite (4 fmly) No smoking in 5 bedrooms s £26-£40; d £52-£80 (incl. bkfst) * **LB** **FACILITIES:** STV entertainment Xmas **SERVICES:** Lift **PARKING:** 39 **NOTES:** No smoking in restaurant **CARDS:**

### ★★65% *Diplomat Hotel*
6/8 Durley Chine Rd, West Cliff BH2 5JY
☎ 01202 555025 01202 559019
***Dir:*** *in Bournemouth follow Town Centre/West Cliff sign. Cross St Michaels rdbt and hotel on left*

The Diplomat is ideally placed to benefit from all of the town's attractions. Bedrooms have all the expected amenities and are decorated in warm colours. The recently refurbished bar area now provides guests with a range of dining options in addition to the main restaurant menu.
**ROOMS:** 58 en suite (10 fmly) **FACILITIES:** STV entertainment **SERVICES:** Lift **PARKING:** 40 **NOTES:** No smoking in restaurant **CARDS:**

### ★★65% Fircroft
4 Owls Rd BH5 1AE
☎ 01202 309771 01202 395644
***Dir:*** *off A338 signposted Boscombe Pier, hotel is 400yds from pier close to Christchurch Road*
Guests will find a warm welcome at this hotel, which is popular with tour groups, and well-situated close to Boscombe Pier. Bedrooms are well-equipped and comfortable. In addition to a separate cocktail bar, there are a number of lounge areas for guests' use.
**ROOMS:** 51 en suite (20 fmly) s £25-£31; d £50-£62 (incl. bkfst) * **LB** **FACILITIES:** **Spa** Indoor swimming (H) Squash Sauna Solarium Gym Jacuzzi Sports at health club owned by hotel Xmas **CONF:** Thtr 200 Class 100 Board 40 Del £50 * **SERVICES:** Lift **PARKING:** 50 **NOTES:** No smoking in restaurant **CARDS:**

### ★★65% *New Westcliff*
29 Chine Crescent, West Cliff BH2 5LB
☎ 01202 551926 01202 310671
***Dir:*** *follow signs for Bournemouth International Centre, West Cliff and Town Centre pass Durley Hall Hotel on right, New Westcliff hotel is 50yds on right*
Ideally located for town and beach, a warm welcome awaits guests at this family run hotel. While varied in size, the bedrooms are attractively decorated and well-equipped. There is a lovely garden and three lounges. All-weather leisure facilities, including a small cinema, are a definite plus.
**ROOMS:** 23 en suite 17 annexe en suite (7 fmly) **PARKING:** 40 **NOTES:** No smoking in restaurant Closed 2-16 Jan
**CARDS:**

### ★★62% Devon Towers
58-62 St Michael's Rd, West Cliff BH2 5ED
☎ 01202 553863 01202 315265
Leisureplex
Quietly located hotel yet within easy walking distance of the sea front and Town Centre. Bedrooms are generally spacious while the extensive public areas have been recently refurbished and include a comfortable lounge/bar. Regular entertainment is provided during the season.
**ROOMS:** 54 en suite s £27-£33; d £46-£58 (incl. bkfst) * **LB** **FACILITIES:** entertainment Xmas **SERVICES:** Lift **PARKING:** 6 **NOTES:** No dogs (ex guide dogs) No smoking in restaurant Closed Jan-mid Feb RS Nov-mid Mar (open Mon-Fri only) **CARDS:**

### ★★61% Bourne Hall Hotel
14 Priory Rd, West Cliff BH2 5DN
☎ 01202 299715 01202 552669
e-mail: info@bournehall.co.uk
***Dir:*** *A31 & M27 from Ringwood into Bournemouth on A338 (Wessex Way) - pick up signs to B.I.C. onto West Cliff - Hotel on right*

This spacious hotel is a short stroll from the town centre, seafront and theatres. The well-equipped bedrooms are furnished for comfort. Downstairs there is a large lounge bar and the lower bar can also provide a useful area for meetings. The atmosphere throughout is relaxed and welcoming.
**ROOMS:** 48 en suite (9 fmly) No smoking in 12 bedrooms s £30-£45; d £55-£78 (incl. bkfst) * **LB** **FACILITIES:** STV Xmas **CONF:** Thtr 70 Class 70 Board 40 Del from £60 * **SERVICES:** Lift **PARKING:** 35 **NOTES:** No smoking in restaurant **CARDS:**

**★★61% *Lynden Court***
8 Durley Rd, West Cliff BH2 5JL
☎ 01202 553894 📠 01202 317711
***Dir:*** *A338 from Ringwood, left at Town Centre West rdbt to St Michaels rdbt, straight across and second left, hotel facing*
This hotel is well situated on the West Cliff. Bedrooms vary in size; some are suited for family occupation and some conveniently located on the ground floor. The public areas include a comfortable lounge and bar, and an attractive restaurant. A choice from the English menu is offered at dinner and breakfast.
**ROOMS:** 32 en suite (10 fmly) **FACILITIES:** STV entertainment **SERVICES:** Lift **PARKING:** 20 **CARDS:**

**★★56% Russell Court**
Bath Rd BH1 2EP
☎ 01202 295819 📠 01202 293457
e-mail: russellcrt@aol.com
Bright, well-maintained bedrooms are provided at this popular coaching hotel, several benefiting from sea views. Live entertainment features on some evenings in the spacious and comfortable public rooms. Informal and friendly service is provided by the young staff.
**ROOMS:** 62 rms (58 en suite) (6 fmly) s £49.50-£69.50; d £89-£119 (incl. bkfst & dinner) * **LB** **FACILITIES:** entertainment Xmas **CONF:** Thtr 20 **SERVICES:** Lift **PARKING:** 60 **NOTES:** No dogs (ex guide dogs) No smoking in restaurant **CARDS:**

**○ East Cliff Manor**
30 Manor Rd BH1 3JD
☎ 01202 556456
At the time of going to press, the star classification for this hotel was not confirmed. Please refer to the AA internet site www.theAA.com for current information.

**○ Lodge at Meyrick Park**
Central Dr BH2 6LH
☎ 01202 786000
At the time of going to press, the star classification for this hotel was not confirmed. Please refer to the AA internet site www.theAA.com for current information.

**○ Innkeeper's Lodge Bournemouth**
Cooper Dean Roundabout, Castle Ln East BH6 9UQ
☎ 0870 243 0500

Innkeeper's
Lodge

A new concept in the travel accommodation market. Smart rooms meet essential business requirements but also have home comforts. Dining options include all-day menus plus the added advantage of breakfast, which is included in the room price. Reservations can be made seven days a week through the room reservations number: 0870 243 0500. For further details, consult the Hotel Groups page.
**ROOMS:** 28 en suite

## BOURTON-ON-THE-WATER, Gloucestershire Map 04 SP12

**★★74% ❀❀ Dial House**
The Chestnuts, High St GL54 2AN
☎ 01451 822244 📠 01451 810126
e-mail: info@dialhousehotel.com
***Dir:*** *off A429, 0.5m to village centre*
This charming hotel built of mellow Cotswold stone dates back to 1698. Public rooms are tastefully appointed and include a cosy bar and adjoining lounge and two small dining rooms. Bedrooms vary in size and style, all are comfortably furnished and well-equipped. Guests appreciate the high standard of cooking.

**ROOMS:** 14 en suite No smoking in 3 bedrooms s £45-£57; d £90-£114 (incl. bkfst) * **LB** **FACILITIES:** Croquet lawn Putting green Xmas **CONF:** Del £150 * **PARKING:** 20 **NOTES:** No dogs (ex guide dogs) No children 10yrs No smoking in restaurant **CARDS:**

*See advert on this page*



Need to unwind? Look out for hotels with Spa in their entry.

B

BOURTON-ON-THE-WATER, continued

### ★★68% *Old New Inn*
High St GL54 2AF
☎ 01451 820467 📠 01451 810236
e-mail: 106206.2571@compuserve.com
***Dir:*** *off A429*

Situated near the famous model village, the inn offers a variety of styles of bedroom, some in a nearby cottage. Public areas are full of character and staff offer a warm and friendly welcome.
**ROOMS:** 16 rms (8 en suite) 4 annexe rms **PARKING:** 31 **NOTES:** No smoking in restaurant Closed 25 Dec **CARDS:**

### ★★67% *Chester House Hotel & Motel*
MINOTEL Great Britain
Victoria St GL54 2BU
☎ 01451 820286 📠 01451 820471
e-mail: juliand@chesterhouse.u-net.com
Chester House occupies a secluded but central location in this delightful Cotswold village. Rooms are comfortable and thoughtfully equipped. Public areas include an attractive restaurant and separate breakfast room. The family and ground floor rooms and 'pets welcome' philosophy appeal to many visitors. The car park is also a bonus.
**ROOMS:** 13 en suite 10 annexe en suite (8 fmly) **CONF:** Board 121 **PARKING:** 20 **NOTES:** Closed mid Dec-Jan
**CARDS:**

## BOVEY TRACEY, Devon
Map 03 SX87

### ★★★73% ®® Edgemoor
Haytor Rd, Lowerdown Cross TQ13 9LE
☎ 01626 832466 📠 01626 834760
e-mail: edgemoor@btinternet.com
***Dir:*** *from A382 follow signs for Haytor and Widecombe*
This peaceful country house hotel is situated in two acres of gardens and grounds. The well-equipped bedrooms are individually furnished and decorated. A tempting selection of award-winning cooking is served in the elegant dining room, while there are bar meals available. Guests enjoy relaxing in the comfortable, spacious lounge, with its log fire burning during cooler months.
**ROOMS:** 11 en suite 5 annexe en suite s £57-£73; d £90-£100 (incl. bkfst) * **LB** **FACILITIES:** STV Xmas **CONF:** Thtr 60 Class 35 Board 20 Del from £75 * **PARKING:** 45 **NOTES:** No children 10yrs No smoking in restaurant **CARDS:**

*See advert on opposite page*

### ★★67% Coombe Cross

THE CIRCLE
Selected Individual Hotels
GREAT BRITAIN
Coombe Cross TQ13 9EY
☎ 01626 832476 📠 01626 835298
e-mail: info@coombecross.co.uk
***Dir:*** *from A38 follow signs for Bovey Tracey and town centre, along High St & up the hill 400yds beyond the Parish Church, hotel on the left*
Set in its own pretty gardens, with delightful views over the surrounding countryside, Coombe Cross is only a short walk from the town centre. The new proprietors are keen to ensure guests a warm, friendly stay with enjoyable food. Decor throughout is smart and bedrooms offer a good level of comfort and some useful extras. There is an elegant dining room, two lounges, a small bar and some lovely leisure facilities.
**ROOMS:** 24 en suite (2 fmly) No smoking in all bedrooms s £39-£45; d £60-£70 (incl. bkfst) * **LB** **FACILITIES:** **Spa** Indoor swimming (H) Sauna Solarium Gym Table tennis ch fac **CONF:** Thtr 80 Class 30 Board 30 Del from £66.45 * **PARKING:** 26 **NOTES:** No smoking in restaurant **CARDS:**

## BOWNESS ON WINDERMERE See Windermere

## BRACKNELL, Berkshire
Map 04 SU86
see also Wokingham

### ★★★★76% ®® Coppid Beech
John Nike Way RG12 8TF
☎ 01344 303333 📠 01344 301200
e-mail: welcome@coppid-beech-hotel.co.uk
***Dir:*** *from junct 10 on M4 take Wokingham/Bracknell option on to A329, in 2 miles at roundabout take B3408 to Binfield, hotel 200yds on the right hand side*
Facilities at the chalet-style Coppid Beech complex include a health club, ski slope, ice rink, night club and bierkeller. Bedrooms are spacious and all beds have feather duvets. Rowan's restaurant serves awardwinning cuisine.
**ROOMS:** 205 en suite (6 fmly) No smoking in 138 bedrooms s £155-£165; d £175-£185 (incl. bkfst) **LB** **FACILITIES:** **Spa** STV Indoor swimming (H) Sauna Solarium Gym Jacuzzi Dry ski slope,ice rink,Toboggan run entertainment Xmas **CONF:** Thtr 400 Class 240 Board 24 Del from £225 * **SERVICES:** Lift air con **PARKING:** 350 **NOTES:** Civ Wed 150 **CARDS:**

*See advert on opposite page*

### ★★★72% ® Stirrups Country House
Maidens Green RG42 6LD
☎ 01344 882284 📠 01344 882300
e-mail: reception@stirrupshotel.co.uk
***Dir:*** *3m N on B3022 towards Windsor*
Situated in a peaceful location between Maidenhead, Bracknell and Windsor, this hotel has high standards of comfort in the bedrooms, with newer rooms boasting a small sitting room area. Bathrooms all have power showers. There is a popular bar and refurbished restaurant.
**ROOMS:** 29 en suite (4 fmly) No smoking in 16 bedrooms s £105-£135; d £110-£140 * **LB** **FACILITIES:** STV **CONF:** Thtr 100 Class 50 Board 40 Del from £135 * **SERVICES:** Lift **PARKING:** 100 **NOTES:** No dogs (ex guide dogs) No smoking in restaurant Civ Wed 50
**CARDS:**

### ○ Grange Bracknell
Charles Square RG12 1OF
☎ 01344 474000
At the time of going to press, the star classification for this hotel was not confirmed. Please refer to the AA internet site www.theAA.com for current information.
**ROOMS:** 120 **NOTES:** Open now

BRADFORD, West Yorkshire Map 07 SE13
see also Gomersal & Shipley

**★★★★63% Cedar Court Hotel Bradford**
Mayo Av, Off Rooley Ln BD5 8HZ
☎ 01274 406606 & 406601 🖹 01274 406600
e-mail: sales@cedar-court.com
***Dir:*** *leave M62 junct 26, then follow M606. At the end take 3rd exit off rdbt onto A6177 toward Bradford, take 1st sharp right at lights*
This large, modern hotel offers attractively furnished bedrooms and a wide range of facilities. There is a well-equipped leisure centre, a choice of meeting and function suites, as well as the elegant Four Seasons restaurant.
**ROOMS:** 131 en suite (7 fmly) No smoking in 75 bedrooms s £89-£99; d £89-£99 * **LB** **FACILITIES:** **Spa** Indoor swimming (H) Sauna Solarium Gym Jacuzzi Beauty treatments,Pool table Xmas **CONF:** Thtr 800 Class 300 Board 100 Del from £70 * **SERVICES:** Lift **PARKING:** 350 **NOTES:** RS Xmas & New Year Civ Wed 600
**CARDS:**

**★★★68% *Courtyard by Marriott Leeds/Bradford***
The Pastures, Tong Ln BD4 0RP
☎ 0113 285 4646 🖹 0113 285 3661
***Dir:*** *from junct 27 M62, take A650 towards Bradford. 3rd rdbt, take 3rd exit 'Tong Village & Pudsey'. Turn left Tong Lane. Hotel 0.5m on right*
Built onto an elegant, 19th-century former vicarage, this modern hotel has been sympathetically designed to combine with its Victorian surroundings. The hotel is particularly well-located for both Leeds and Bradford as well as local motorway networks.

continued on p120

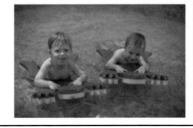

BRADFORD, continued

Bedrooms are furnished and decorated to a high standard and provide a superb range of facilities.

*Courtyard by Marriott Leeds/Bradford, Bradford*

**ROOMS:** 53 en suite (5 fmly) No smoking in 28 bedrooms **FACILITIES:** STV Gym **CONF:** Thtr 300 Class 150 Board 100 **SERVICES:** Lift **PARKING:** 300 **NOTES:** No dogs (ex guide dogs) Civ Wed **CARDS:**

### ★★★68% Quality Hotel Bradford

Bridge St BD1 1JX
☎ 01274 728706 🖷 01274 736358
e-mail: admin@gb654.u-net.com
***Dir:*** *behind Bradford Interchange Station, next to St Georges Concert Hall*

This Victorian hotel is situated right in the city centre, adjacent to the railway station. It benefits from its own secure car park, leisure facilities and a choice of eating and drinking options in the form of a brasserie and a lively bar. Modern bedrooms and suites are thoughtfully equipped.

**ROOMS:** 60 en suite (4 fmly) No smoking in 40 bedrooms s fr £75; d fr £90 * **LB** **FACILITIES:** STV Sauna Gym Xmas **CONF:** Thtr 150 Class 90 Board 60 Del from £75 * **SERVICES:** Lift **PARKING:** 69 **NOTES:** No smoking in restaurant **CARDS:**

### ★★★67% Apperley Manor

Apperley Ln, Apperley Bridge BD10 0PQ
☎ 0113 250 5626 🖷 0113 250 0075
e-mail: janette@apperleymanor.co.uk
***Dir:*** *on A658 Bradford to Harrogate road, 2m from Leeds/Bradford Int Airport*

Set in its own grounds, this welcoming hotel has easy access to the airport. Spacious bedrooms are comfortably furnished and equipped with modern facilities. A choice of dining options is available, the main restaurant or the more informal atmosphere of the brasserie.

**ROOMS:** 13 en suite (2 fmly) s £59.50-£65; d £69.50-£80 * **FACILITIES:** Jacuzzi in 2 bedrooms ch fac **CONF:** Thtr 80 Class 40 Board 30 Del £97 * **SERVICES:** Lift **PARKING:** 100 **NOTES:** No dogs (ex guide dogs) **CARDS:**

### ★★★67% Midland Hotel

PEEL HOTELS

Forster Square BD1 4HU
☎ 01274 735735 🖷 01274 720003
e-mail: info@midland-hotel-bradford.com
***Dir:*** *from A6177 onto A641 then onto A6181. Follow past St Georges Hall to Eastbrook Well rdbt take 1st exit along Petergate to Forster square, left to Cheapside. Hotel is on right*

Located in the centre of the city, this grand Victorian hotel provides modern, well-equipped accommodation, comfortable, spacious day rooms, and friendly staff. Ample, secure parking is available in what used to be the city's railway station, and a preserved Victorian passage linking the hotel to the old platform can still be used today.

**ROOMS:** 90 en suite (4 fmly) No smoking in 8 bedrooms s £59-£79; d £69-£89 (incl. bkfst) * **FACILITIES:** STV Free use of local health club entertainment Xmas **CONF:** Thtr 450 Class 150 Board 100 Del from £95 * **SERVICES:** Lift **PARKING:** 50 **NOTES:** No dogs (ex guide dogs) **CARDS:**

### ★★★65% Guide Post Hotel

Common Rd, Low Moor BD12 0ST
☎ 01274 607866 🖷 01274 671085
e-mail: bookings@guideposthotel.net
***Dir:*** *follow A638 towards Oakenshaw/Low Moor, pass large factory (CIBA), pass petrol station on left, take 2nd left into Common Road*

Conveniently situated for the motorway network and city centre, this hotel offers attractively furnished, comfortable bedrooms. The restaurant offers an extensive range of food utilising fresh, local produce; lighter snack meals are served in the bar. There is a choice of well-equipped meeting and function rooms.

**ROOMS:** 43 en suite (3 fmly) No smoking in 7 bedrooms s fr £68; d fr £78 (incl. bkfst) * **LB** **FACILITIES:** STV **CONF:** Thtr 120 Class 80 Board 60 Del from £87.50 * **PARKING:** 100 **NOTES:** No dogs (ex guide dogs) Civ Wed **CARDS:**

*See advert on opposite page*

### ★★★62% Novotel Bradford

NOVOTEL

6 Roydsdale Way, Euroway Estate BD4 6SA
☎ 01274 683683 🖷 01274 651342
e-mail: h0510@accor-hotels.com
***Dir:*** *adjacent to M606 junct 2, 3m from city centre*

Situated just off the motorway, this was one of the first Novotels built in this country. The bedrooms are spacious and have just benefited from refurbishment. Public areas include a stylish bar, and a lounge that leads into the Garden Brasserie. Two rooms have facilities for visitors with disabilities. Several function rooms are also available.

**ROOMS:** 127 en suite (127 fmly) No smoking in 74 bedrooms s £58; d £58 * **FACILITIES:** STV Outdoor swimming (H) **CONF:** Thtr 300 Class 280 Board 200 Del from £85 **SERVICES:** Lift **PARKING:** 180 **NOTES:** Civ Wed 150 **CARDS:**

### ★★68% Park Drive

THE INDEPENDENTS

12 Park Dr BD9 4DR
☎ 01274 480194 🖷 01274 484869
e-mail: sales@parkdrivehotel.co.uk
***Dir:*** *turn off A650 Keighley Road into Emm Lane, at Lister Park, then turn 2nd right*

This hotel stands in a quiet residential area overlooking open country, close to Lister Park. The bedrooms vary in size and style

*continued*

with some recently refurbished rooms. Wholesome home cooking is a feature of the neatly presented dining room.

**ROOMS:** 11 en suite (1 fmly) s £49-£54; d £59-£64 (incl. bkfst) * **LB**
**CONF:** Thtr 20 Class 8 Board 12 Del from £74 * **PARKING:** 10
**NOTES:** No smoking in restaurant **CARDS:**

*See advert on this page*

### ★★67% Park Grove

MINOTEL Great Britain

28 Park Grove, Frizinghall BD9 4JY
☎ 01274 543444 Fax 01274 495619
e-mail: enquiry@parkgrovehotel.co.uk
***Dir:*** *off A650 Keighley road, turn right after the Park Pub*
This welcoming, family-run hotel offers spacious, comfortable bedrooms which contain a wide range of facilities. There is a small lounge and bar next to the attractive restaurant, where a choice of freshly cooked Punjabi or English cuisine is offered.
**ROOMS:** 15 en suite (3 fmly) s £40-£47; d £50-£62 (incl. bkfst) * **LB**
**FACILITIES:** STV **PARKING:** 8 **NOTES:** No dogs
**CARDS:**

B

## BRADFORD-ON-AVON, Wiltshire Map 03 ST86

### ★★★74% Woolley Grange

Woolley Green BA15 1TX
☎ 01225 864705 01225 864059
e-mail: info@woolleygrange.com
***Dir:*** *on B3105, 0.5m NE at Woolley Green*

A splendid Cotswold manor house set in beautiful countryside. Children are made welcome; there is a trained nanny on duty in the nursery. Bedrooms and public areas are charmingly furnished and decorated in true country house style with many thoughtful touches and luxurious extras. The hotel offers a varied and well-balanced menu selection, which continues to gain praise.
**ROOMS:** 14 en suite 9 annexe en suite (8 fmly) s £90-£130; d £125-£260 (incl. bkfst) * **LB** **FACILITIES:** STV Outdoor swimming (H) Tennis (grass) Croquet lawn Putting green Badminton Games room ch fac Xmas **CONF:** Thtr 35 Class 12 Board 22 Del from £150 *
**PARKING:** 40 **NOTES:** No smoking in restaurant
**CARDS:**

*See advert on opposite page*

### ★★★65% *Leigh Park Hotel*

Best Western

Leigh Park West BA15 2RA
☎ 01225 864885 01225 862315
***Dir:*** *A363 Bath/Frome road, take B3105 (signed Holt/Woolley Green) hotel 0.25m on right on crossroads of B3105/B3109, N side of Bradford-on-Avon*
Set in five acres of well tended grounds, complete with a vineyard, this relaxing Georgian hotel enjoys splendid views and combines charm and character with modern facilities. The restaurant serves dishes cooked to order, using home-grown fruit and vegetables, and wine from the vineyard.
**ROOMS:** 21 en suite (4 fmly) No smoking in 7 bedrooms
**FACILITIES:** Tennis (hard) Snooker **CONF:** Thtr 120 Class 60 Board 60
**PARKING:** 80 **NOTES:** No smoking in restaurant
**CARDS:**

## BRAINTREE, Essex Map 05 TL72

### ★★★63% *White Hart*

Old English Inns

Bocking End CM7 9AB
☎ 01376 321401 01376 552628
e-mail: reservations@thewhiteharthotel.freeserve.co.uk
***Dir:*** *turn off A120. Head into Town Centre. Hotel at junct B1256 & Bocking Causeway*
It is thought an inn may have stood on this site since Roman times. The present inn is rather more recent, with parts dating back to the 18th century, lending the building its character and a degree of old world charm. Bedrooms vary with some feature rooms in the old part of the hotel and more modern accommodation in the extension.
**ROOMS:** 31 en suite (8 fmly) No smoking in 9 bedrooms
**FACILITIES:** STV Sauna Solarium Gym **CONF:** Thtr 40 Class 16 Board 24 **PARKING:** 52 **NOTES:** No dogs (ex guide dogs) Civ Wed 60
**CARDS:**

### Express by Holiday Inn Braintree

Express by Holiday Inn

Galley's Corner, Cressing Rd CM7 8DJ
☎ 01376 551141 01376 551142
***Dir:*** *turn off A120 onto B1018 at Galley's Corner. Hotel is situated next door to Wyevale Garden Centre*

RECEPTION

A modern budget hotel offering comfortable accommodation in refreshing, spacious and comprehensively equipped bedrooms, en suite bathrooms with power showers and continental buffet breakfast included in the room rate. Suitable for business travellers or families. For further details and the Express by Holiday Inn phone number, consult the Hotel Groups page.
**ROOMS:** 47 en suite (incl. cont bkfst) s fr £52.50; d fr £52.50 *
**CONF:** Thtr 30 Class 20 Board 20

## BRAITHWAITE, Cumbria Map 11 NY22

### ★★68% Ivy House

CA12 5SY
☎ 017687 78338 017687 78113
e-mail: info@ivy-house.co.uk
***Dir:*** *in the middle of the village turn left immediately after the Royal Oak pub*
This attractive house dates from the 17th century and its ancient timbers can be seen in the cosy lounge where open fires burn in winter. The galleried restaurant, candlelit by night, serves a skilfully prepared daily-changing menu.
**ROOMS:** 12 en suite s £31-£37; d £62-£74 (incl. bkfst) * **PARKING:** 17
**NOTES:** No children 6yrs No smoking in restaurant Closed 21 Dec-End Jan **CARDS:**

## BRAMHALL, Greater Manchester Map 07 SJ88

### ★★★65% County Hotel Bramhall

REGAL

Bramhall Ln South SK7 2EB
☎ 0161 455 9988 0161 440 8071
***Dir:*** *M56 junct6 to Wilmslow A34 bypass towards Manchester, A5102 to Bramhall. From M60 junct3, A34 bypass to Congleton - A5102 to Bramhall*
This modern hotel is set in a pleasant residential area and is very convenient for Manchester airport. The bedrooms are modern and

*continued*

B

well-equipped while public rooms are comfortable. There are extensive meeting facilities.

COUNTY HOTEL

**ROOMS:** 65 en suite (3 fmly) No smoking in 20 bedrooms s £85-£105; d £95-£115 * **LB** **FACILITIES:** Xmas **CONF:** Thtr 200 Class 80 Board 60 Del from £90 * **PARKING:** 120 **NOTES:** No smoking in restaurant Civ Wed 140 **CARDS:**

BRAMHOPE, West Yorkshire Map 08 SE24

### ★★★70% *Posthouse Bramhope*

Posthouse

Leeds Rd LS16 9JJ
☎ 0113 284 2911 📠 0113 284 3451
***Dir:*** *on A660 6m N of Leeds city centre. Follow signs 'Leeds/Bradford Airport'*

This modern hotel nestles peacefully within 16 acres of well-tended grounds. Bedrooms offer a good range of facilities and are comfortably appointed. Public areas are smartly presented and include a stylish restaurant, various conference rooms and a training centre. A modern leisure club comprises of an indoor pool and fitness gym.

**ROOMS:** 124 en suite No smoking in 40 bedrooms **FACILITIES:** STV Indoor swimming (H) Sauna Solarium Gym Jacuzzi **CONF:** Thtr 160 Class 80 Board 40 **SERVICES:** Lift air con **PARKING:** 126 **NOTES:** No smoking in restaurant **CARDS:**

BRAMPTON, Cumbria Map 12 NY56

**Premier Collection**

### ★★★ ❀❀ Farlam Hall

Hallbankgate CA8 2NG
☎ 016977 46234 📠 016977 46683
e-mail: farlamhall@dial.pipex.com
***Dir:*** *from A69 take A689 to Alston, the hotel is approx 2m on the left, not in Farlam village*

RELAIS & CHATEAUX.

This delightful family-run country house dates back to 1428. Steeped in history and set in beautifully landscaped Victorian gardens, this house is complete with an ornamental lake and stream, and has been lovingly restored to provide the highest standard of comfort and quality. Both bedrooms and the public areas are spacious and beautifully furnished. Carefully prepared English country house cooking can be enjoyed in the elegant dining room that overlooks the fantastic gardens.

**ROOMS:** 11 en suite 1 annexe en suite s £125-£140; d £230-£260 (incl. bkfst & dinner) * **LB** **FACILITIES:** Croquet lawn **CONF:** Thtr 12 Class 12 Board 12 Del from £150 * **PARKING:** 35 **NOTES:** No children 5yrs Closed 25-30 Dec **CARDS:**



### ★★65% Tarn End House

Talkin Tarn CA8 1LS
☎ 016977 72340 📠 016977 2089
***Dir:*** *from A69 take B6413 for 2m and turn off towards Talkin Village*

TARN
END
HOUSE
HOTEL

A relaxed and informal atmosphere prevails at this comfortable family-run hotel, a former estate farmhouse overlooking Talkin

continued on p124

BRAMPTON, continued

Tarn. Pretty co-ordinated fabrics have been used to good effect in the comfortably furnished bedrooms. Public areas include a cosy well stocked bar, relaxing lounge, and a tastefully appointed restaurant.
**ROOMS:** 7 en suite (1 fmly) No smoking in 3 bedrooms s £39-£58; d £60-£85 (incl. bkfst) * **LB** **FACILITIES:** Xmas **CONF:** Board 20 Del from £60 * **PARKING:** 40 **NOTES:** No smoking in restaurant Closed 27-29 Dec & 3-25 Jan **CARDS:**

*See advert under CARLISLE*

## BRANCASTER, Norfolk — Map 09 TF74

### ★★73% White Horse
Brancaster Staithe PE31 8BW
☎ 01485 210262 01485 210930
e-mail: reception@whitehorsebrancaster.co.uk
***Dir:*** *2km E of Brancaster at Brancaster Staithe. From King's Lynn follow A149 coast road. From Norwich take A1067 to Fakenham, then B1355.*
This hotel is situated on the North Norfolk coastline with stunning views over the tidal marsh to Scolt Head Island. The cobbled bedrooms are an interesting feature and are situated in a wing adjacent to the building. Each room is tastefully decorated, thoughtfully equipped and has a lovely terrace. Public rooms include a large bar and a lounge area leading through to the conservatory restaurant.
**ROOMS:** 8 en suite (3 fmly) s £50-£65; d £60-£90 (incl. bkfst) * **LB** **FACILITIES:** Pool table **PARKING:** 60 **NOTES:** No smoking in restaurant **CARDS:**

## BRANDESBURTON, East Riding of Yorkshire — Map 08 TA14

### ★★68% Burton Lodge
YO25 8RU
☎ 01964 542847 01964 544771
e-mail: email@burtonlodge.fsnet.co.uk
***Dir:*** *7m from Beverley off A165, adjoining Hainsworth Park Golf Club*
Extensive gardens containing sports play areas surround this friendly, modern hotel, which is inset into a golf course. The hotel offers pleasant accommodation, an open fire is a welcoming feature in the lounge, and good home cooking is served in the attractive dining room.
**ROOMS:** 7 en suite 2 annexe en suite (2 fmly) s £34-£36; d £48-£52 (incl. bkfst) * **LB** **FACILITIES:** Golf 18 Tennis (grass) Putting green Pitch and putt **PARKING:** 14 **NOTES:** No smoking in restaurant **CARDS:**

## BRANDON, Suffolk — Map 05 TL78

### ★★70% Brandon House
High St IP27 0AX
☎ 01842 810171 01842 814859
e-mail: reservations@brandonhouse.co.uk
***Dir:*** *In town centre take left at traffic lights into High Street. Hotel 400yds on right just beyond small bridge over the Ouse*
This striking redbrick 18th-century manor house is within easy walking distance of the town centre. The bedrooms vary in size and style but all are pleasantly decorated and well equipped. The spacious public rooms include the traditional Conifers English Restaurant for serious dining as well as a more informal bistro and a large lounge bar.
**ROOMS:** 15 en suite (3 fmly) s £55; d £75 (incl. bkfst) * **LB** **FACILITIES:** STV **CONF:** Thtr 70 Class 25 Board 20 **PARKING:** 40 **NOTES:** No smoking in restaurant Closed 25-26 Dec & 1 Jan **CARDS:**

MINOTEL Great Britain

## BRANDON, Warwickshire — Map 04 SP47

### ★★★64% The Brandon Hall
Main St CV8 3FW
☎ 0870 400 8105 024 7654 4909
***Dir:*** *off A428 to Rugby*
Peacefully located in 17 acres of lawns and woodland, this former shooting lodge is found by following signs for the village centre of Brandon. Many bedrooms have been refurbished to a very high standard, providing a good range of modern facilities and very smart bathrooms.
**ROOMS:** 60 en suite No smoking in 29 bedrooms d £110-£130 * **LB** **FACILITIES:** STV Squash Croquet lawn Putting green Xmas **CONF:** Thtr 90 Class 40 Board 40 Del £145 * **PARKING:** 250 **NOTES:** No smoking in restaurant Civ Wed 90 **CARDS:**

## BRANDS HATCH, Kent — Map 05 TQ56

### ★★★67% Brandshatch Place
Brandshatch Rd, Fawkham DA3 8NQ
☎ 01474 872239 01474 879652
e-mail: brandshatch@arcadianhotels.co.uk
***Dir:*** *M25 junct 3, take A20 West Kingsdown, left at sign for paddock entrance/Fawkham Green. 3rd left signed Fawkham road hotel 500 meters right*

ARCADIAN HOTELS Distinctly Different

Charming 18th century Georgian country house set amidst 12 acres of parkland in the Kent countryside close to the famous racing circuit. Public rooms feature an attractive lounge and the elegant Hatchwood restaurant. The spacious bedrooms are pleasantly decorated and equipped with many useful extras. In addition the hotel has excellent leisure facilities and a range of meeting rooms.
**ROOMS:** 29 en suite 12 annexe en suite (2 fmly) s fr £75; d fr £85 * **LB** **FACILITIES:** **Spa** STV Indoor swimming (H) Tennis (hard) Squash Snooker Sauna Solarium Gym Jacuzzi Dance studio, Hair salon, treatment rooms ch fac Xmas **CONF:** Thtr 100 Class 60 Board 40 Del from £135 * **PARKING:** 100 **NOTES:** No smoking in restaurant Civ Wed 80 **CARDS:**

## BRANKSOME See Poole

## BRANSCOMBE, Devon — Map 03 SY18

### ★★67% The Masons Arms
EX12 3DJ
☎ 01297 680300 01297 680500
e-mail: reception@yeoldemasonsarms.freeserve.co.uk
***Dir:*** *turn off A3052 towards Branscombe, head down hill, hotel in the valley at the bottom of the hill*
This charming 14th-century inn is only half a mile from the sea in the picturesque village of Branscombe. There is a choice of bedrooms offering cottage rooms or comfortable berths in the

*continued*

main house. There is a cosy first floor lounge, and the bar is built around a central fireplace, serving fine ales and food. Oak beams feature in the restaurant.

**ROOMS:** 6 rms (4 en suite) 16 annexe rms (15 en suite) (2 fmly) s £24-£105; d £44-£150 (incl. bkfst) * **LB** **FACILITIES:** Xmas **CONF:** Thtr 60 Class 20 Board 20 Del from £95 * **PARKING:** 43 **NOTES:** No smoking in restaurant **CARDS:**

*See advert on this page*



## BRANSTON, Lincolnshire — Map 08 TF06

### ★★★67% Branston Hall

Branston Park LN4 1PD
☎ 01522 793305 01522 790549
e-mail: brahal@enterprise.net
***Dir:*** *3m from Lincoln city centre along B1188 towards Woodhall Spa. On entering Branston village, hotel is located directly opposite the village hall*

Set in picturesque parkland with a lake in its grounds, this imposing house still has many of its original architectural features. The well-equipped bedrooms come in a variety of sizes and styles. In the restaurant an ambitious menu covers most tastes with cooking showing flair and imagination. There is also a bar, lounge, conference rooms and leisure centre with a pool.

**ROOMS:** 38 en suite 7 annexe en suite (3 fmly) s fr £59.50; d £79.50-£129.50 (incl. bkfst) * **LB** **FACILITIES:** Indoor swimming (H) Sauna Gym Croquet lawn Jacuzzi Jogging circuit Xmas **CONF:** Thtr 200 Class 70 Board 60 Del £90 * **SERVICES:** Lift **PARKING:** 150 **NOTES:** No smoking in restaurant Civ Wed 120
**CARDS:**

### ★★70% Moor Lodge

Best Western

Sleaford Rd LN4 1HU
☎ 01522 791366 01522 794389
e-mail: moorlodge@bestwestern.co.uk
***Dir:*** *3m S of Lincoln on B1188*

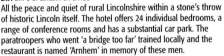

All the peace and quiet of rural Lincolnshire within a stone's throw of historic Lincoln itself. The hotel offers 24 individual bedrooms, a range of conference rooms and has a substantial car park. The paratroopers who went 'a bridge too far' trained locally and the restaurant is named 'Arnhem' in memory of these men.

**ROOMS:** 24 en suite (2 fmly) No smoking in 8 bedrooms s £48-£52.50; d fr £60 (incl. bkfst) * **LB** **CONF:** Thtr 200 Class 80 Board 60 Del from £75 * **PARKING:** 150 **NOTES:** No smoking in restaurant
**CARDS:**

TV dinner? Room service at three stars and above.

## BRAY, Berkshire — Map 04 SU97

### ★★★★66% Monkey Island

Old Mill Ln SL6 2EE
☎ 01628 623400 01628 784732
e-mail: monkeyisland@btconnect.com
***Dir:*** *M4 J8/9 and take A308 signposted Windsor, take 1st left into Bray then 1st right into Old Mill Lane, which is opposite the Crown pub*

A charming feature of this riverside hotel is its island setting. Access is by footbridge or boat but there is a large carpark nearby. The hotel comprises two buildings, one for accommodation and the other for dining and drinking. Ample grounds provide a peaceful haven for wildlife.

**ROOMS:** 26 en suite s £130-£170; d £145-£190 (incl. bkfst) * **FACILITIES:** STV Fishing Gym Croquet lawn Boating Xmas **CONF:** Thtr 120 Class 70 Board 50 Del £230 * **PARKING:** 100 **NOTES:** No dogs (ex guide dogs) No smoking in restaurant Civ Wed 120
**CARDS:**

*See advert under MAIDENHEAD*

### ★★★68% Chauntry House Hotel & Restaurant

SL6 2AB
☎ 01628 673991 01628 773089
e-mail: res@chauntryhouse.com
***Dir:*** *from M4 junct 8/9 take A308(M) towards Windsor then B3028 to Bray village. Hotel on left*

Located in an attractive Berkshire village, this smart, traditional country house hotel features spacious and stylish bedrooms, each individually appointed and decorated. The lounge bar and

*continued on p126*

BRAY, continued

restaurant provide a tranquil environment for guests to relax and the standard of cuisine is high.

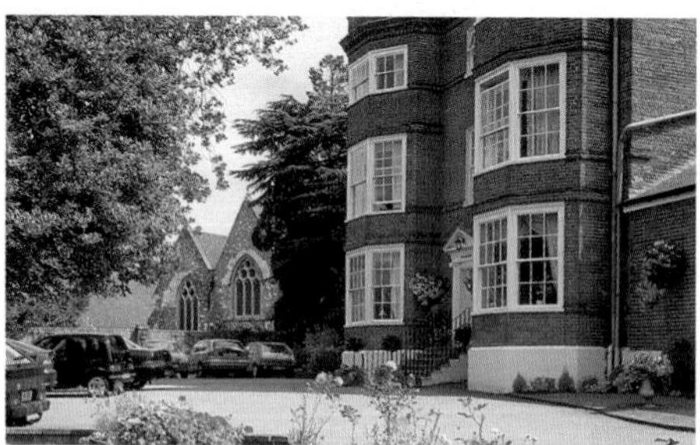

*Chauntry House Hotel & Restaurant, Bray*

**ROOMS:** 11 en suite 4 annexe en suite No smoking in 4 bedrooms s fr £115; d £150-£175 (incl. bkfst) * **FACILITIES:** STV **CONF:** Thtr 30 Board 22 Del from £145 * **PARKING:** 35 **NOTES:** No smoking in restaurant Closed 24 Dec-2 Jan Civ Wed 55
**CARDS:**

## BREADSALL, Derbyshire

Map 08 SK33

### ★★★★64% Marriott Breadsall Priory Hotel & Country Club

Marriott HOTELS · RESORTS · SUITES

Moor Rd DE7 6DL
☎ 01332 832235 🖹 01332 833509
***Dir:*** *take A52 to Derby, then signs to Chesterfield. Right at 1st rndbt, left at next following A608 to Heanor road, after 3m left then left again*

This extended mansion house is set in 400 acres of parkland. The smart bedrooms are mostly contained in the modern wing. There is a vibrant café-bar, a more formal restaurant and a large room service selection. The extensive leisure facilities, golf course and swimming pool are an asset.
**ROOMS:** 12 en suite 100 annexe en suite (35 fmly) No smoking in 69 bedrooms d £110-£130 * **LB** **FACILITIES:** STV Indoor swimming (H) Golf 36 Tennis (hard) Sauna Solarium Gym Croquet lawn Putting green Jacuzzi Health/beauty/hair salon Dance studio Xmas **CONF:** Thtr 120 Class 50 Board 36 **SERVICES:** Lift **PARKING:** 300 **NOTES:** No dogs (ex guide dogs) No smoking in restaurant Civ Wed 100
**CARDS:**

## BRENT KNOLL, Somerset

Map 03 ST35

### ★★70% Woodlands Country House

Hill Ln TA9 4DF
☎ 01278 760232 🖹 01278 769090
e-mail: info@woodlands-hotel.co.uk
***Dir:*** *from A38 take first left into village, then fifth right and first left*
With glorious views over the surrounding countryside to the Quantocks in the distance, this family-run hotel is set in four acres of gardens and grounds. The attractively co-ordinated bedrooms are comfortable and well-equipped. An imaginative dinner menu is served in elegant surroundings, and on cooler evenings, guests can enjoy a log fire in the lounge-bar.
**ROOMS:** 8 en suite No smoking in all bedrooms s £45-£80; d £60-£115 (incl. bkfst) * **LB** **FACILITIES:** Outdoor swimming Xmas **CONF:** Thtr 70 Class 30 Board 30 **PARKING:** 12 **NOTES:** No smoking in restaurant
**CARDS:**

*See advert under WESTON-SUPER-MARE*

### ★★66% *Battleborough Grange Hotel*

Bristol Rd TA9 4HJ
☎ 01278 760208 🖹 01278 760208
e-mail: battleborough@hotel1999.freeserve.co.uk
***Dir:*** *on A38 Weston-Super-Mare Rd, opposite the Goat House*

Surrounded by mellow Somerset countryside, this popular hotel is conveniently located with easy access to the M5. Some bedrooms have superb views of the historic Iron Age fort of Brent Knoll; all rooms are well-equipped. A convivial bar and conservatory restaurant are available; extensive function facilities are also provided.
**ROOMS:** 16 rms (14 en suite) **FACILITIES:** Jacuzzi **CONF:** Thtr 80 Class 40 Board 40 **PARKING:** 50 **NOTES:** No dogs (ex guide dogs) No smoking in restaurant Civ Wed 80
**CARDS:**

## BRENTWOOD, Essex

Map 05 TQ59

### ★★★★72% ❀ Marygreen Manor

London Rd CM14 4NR
☎ 01277 225252 🖹 01277 262809
***Dir:*** *on A1023*
Impressive 16th-century house, a few minutes drive from the M25, with direct motorway links to the Channel Tunnel and major airports. In 1535, Robert Wright named the house his 'Manor of Mary Green' after his young bride. The public rooms feature beamed ceilings and carved panelling, and the baronial restaurant

*continued*

B

is particularly striking. Generously proportioned, well-equipped bedrooms are housed in courtyard style buildings.

**ROOMS:** 3 en suite 40 annexe en suite No smoking in 8 bedrooms s £119.50-£176; d £132-£211 * **FACILITIES:** STV **CONF:** Thtr 60 Class 20 Board 25 Del from £195 * **PARKING:** 100 **NOTES:** No dogs (ex guide dogs) No smoking in restaurant Civ Wed 60
**CARDS:**

*See advert on this page*

### ★★★69% *Posthouse Brentwood*

Brook St CM14 5NF **Posthouse**
☎ 0870 400 9012 🖷 01277 264264
***Dir:*** *close to M25/A12 interchange*
This hotel is conveniently located and features a well-appointed health club and a range of meeting rooms. Bedrooms are smartly decorated and offer a wide range of modern facilities. Guests have a wide choice of areas in which to relax and dining options include the Traders restaurant, Café Express and Atrio Restaurant.
**ROOMS:** 145 en suite (30 fmly) No smoking in 80 bedrooms **FACILITIES:** Indoor swimming (H) Sauna Solarium Gym Health & fitness club **CONF:** Thtr 120 Class 60 Board 50 **SERVICES:** Lift **PARKING:** 190
**CARDS:**

## BRIDGNORTH, Shropshire Map 07 SO79

see also Alveley

### ★★★★66% Mill Hotel & Restaurant

WV15 6HL
☎ 01746 780437 🖷 01746 780850
(For full entry see Alveley)

### ★★★ ⊛⊛⊛ Old Vicarage Hotel

PRIDE OF BRITAIN
MEMBER

WV15 5JZ
☎ 01746 716497 & 0800 0968010
🖷 01746 716552
e-mail: admin@the-old-vicarage.demon.co.uk
(For full entry see Worfield)

### ★★65% Parlors Hall

Mill St WV15 5AL
☎ 01746 761931 🖷 01746 767058
***Dir:*** *turn left off A454 then right and right again for 200yds*
Parlors Hall has been a hotel since 1929 and retains many original features, such as oak panelling and magnificent fireplaces. Named after the family who lived here between 1419 and 1539, the property now features well-equipped bedrooms, some with four-poster beds, restaurant and charming bar.
**ROOMS:** 15 en suite (2 fmly) s £42; d £54-£60 (incl. bkfst) * **FACILITIES:** Xmas **CONF:** Thtr 50 Class 25 Board 25 **PARKING:** 24 **NOTES:** No dogs (ex guide dogs) **CARDS:**

*See advert on this page*

BRIDGNORTH, continued

### ★★63% Falcon Hotel

Saint John St, Lowtown WV15 6AG
☎ 01746 763134 01746 765401
e-mail: enquiries@thefalconhotel.co.uk
***Dir:*** *from A442 Telford-Kidderminster follow Bridgnorth town centre signs. Hotel 100yds on left before bridge over the River Severn*

Falcon

This 17th-century former coaching inn stands near the River Severn in the Lowtown area of Bridgnorth. Bedrooms are equipped to modern standards, and a good selection of dishes is served in the open-plan bar with its beamed restaurant.
**ROOMS:** 12 en suite (4 fmly) No smoking in 5 bedrooms s £39-£45; d £49-£55 (incl. bkfst) * **LB** **CONF:** Thtr 40 Class 20 Board 25 Del from £70 * **PARKING:** 100 **CARDS:**

## BRIDGWATER, Somerset — Map 03 ST33

see also Holford

### ★★★73% Walnut Tree Hotel

North Petherton TA6 6QA
☎ 01278 662255 01278 663946
e-mail: sales@walnut-tree-hotel.co.uk
***Dir:*** *on A38, 1m S of exit 24 on M5*

Conveniently located, with easy access to the M5, this 18th-century former coaching inn remains a popular choice. The majority of bedrooms are furnished and decorated to an executive standard, all are equipped with an extensive range of facilities. In addition to the formal Dukes Restaurant with its interesting carte, Dukes Bistro serves a range of meals and snacks in informal surroundings.
**ROOMS:** 32 en suite (5 fmly) No smoking in 7 bedrooms s £59-£95; d £74-£105 * **LB** **FACILITIES:** STV ch fac Xmas **CONF:** Thtr 120 Class 76 Board 70 Del from £86 * **PARKING:** 70 **NOTES:** Civ Wed 72
**CARDS:**

### ★★66% Friarn Court

37 St Mary St TA6 3LX
☎ 01278 452859 01278 452988
***Dir:*** *at junct of A38 & A39 turn into St Mary St*

Centrally located, service at this popular hotel is friendly and relaxed. Bedrooms are comfortably furnished and tastefully appointed, guests have a choice of either executive or standard. In the spacious restaurant at the rear of the property, a full carte menu is served; in addition, there is also a cosy bar and separate lounge.
**ROOMS:** 16 en suite (3 fmly) No smoking in 4 bedrooms s £39.90-£59.90; d £59.90-£69.90 (incl. bkfst) * **LB** **CONF:** Thtr 60 Class 40 Board 30 Del from £73.50 * **PARKING:** 14
**CARDS:**

## BRIDLINGTON, East Riding of Yorkshire — Map 08 TA16

### ★★★69% Revelstoke

1-3 Flamborough Rd YO15 2HU
☎ 01262 672362 01262 672362
e-mail: info@revelstokehotel.co.uk
***Dir:*** *take B1255 Flamborough Head rd & in 0.5m turn right at mini rdbt to junct of the Promenade & Flamborough Rd. Hotel across from Holy Trinity*

Family owned and run, this friendly hotel is near to both the town centre and seafront. A popular place to stay, the bedrooms are well equipped, and very comfortable. Lounges are well-furnished and the restaurant serves a wide range of well-produced dishes.
**ROOMS:** 25 en suite (5 fmly) **FACILITIES:** STV entertainment
**CONF:** Thtr 250 Class 200 Board 100 **PARKING:** 14 **NOTES:** No dogs (ex guide dogs) Civ Wed 200 **CARDS:**

*See advert on opposite page*

### ★★★67% Expanse

North Marine Dr YO15 2LS
☎ 01262 675347 01262 604928
e-mail: expanse@brid.demon.co.uk
***Dir:*** *follow signs North Beach, pass under railway arch for North Marine Drive. Hotel at bottom of hill*

This traditional seaside hotel overlooks the bay and has been in the same family's ownership for many years. The service at Expanse Hotel is relaxed and friendly. Comfortable public areas

*continued on p130*

THE
# EXPANSE
HOTEL

*A haven of peace and comfort overlooking the Beach and Flamborough Head Heritage Coast, where the beach and cliff walks beckon. The Expanse is a place to relax, with a feel all of its own – built to capture those unique views, where friendly old world courtesy and modern facilities combine for a special break.*

North Marine Drive
Bridlington · YO15 2LS
Tel 01262 675347
Fax 01262 604928

# Shapwick House Hotel

***Shapwick, Somerset TA7 9NL***
*Tel: (01458) 210321  Fax: (01458) 210729*

SHAPWICK HOUSE – a magnificent Medieval manor house dating to 1489, set amidst the rolling countryside of Somerset. The well proportioned public rooms are furnished with antiques and retain impressive original features and open fireplaces. All the en-suite bedrooms are equally well appointed and enjoy magnificent views.
The cuisine (1 rosette) is imaginative and expertly prepared, its accent on traditional English dishes.

# The Revelstoke Hotel

**1-3 Flamborough Road**
**Bridlington**
**East Yorkshire YO15 2HU**

Telephone: (01262) 672362 · Fax: (01262) 672362
E-mail: info@revelstokehotel.co.uk · Website: revelstokehotel.co.uk

**The Revelstoke Hotel is one of the finest hotels in the Bridlington area.**

Ideally located on north side of the town and only two minutes walk away from the sea-front and the town centre.
Our English and Continental restaurant is renowned for its high standards.
Function and conference facilities are available to accommodate up to 250 covers.
Our fully licensed lounge and public bar offer a host of popular beers and lager.
We specialise in short Golf Breaks.
Sky Digital TV installed in all our rooms.
A comprehensive wine list is available with reasonable prices.
*For more information about our hotel, visit our website, e-mail or telephone for one of our brochures or information packs.*

BRIDLINGTON, continued

include a conference suite, a large bar and an inviting lounge. Guests can expect to find their modern bedrooms well-equipped.

*Expanse, Bridlington*

**ROOMS:** 48 en suite (4 fmly) s £33-£46; d £62-£84 (incl. bkfst) * **LB** **FACILITIES:** entertainment Xmas **SERVICES:** Lift **PARKING:** 23 **NOTES:** No dogs (ex guide dogs) Civ Wed 75 **CARDS:**

*See advert on page 129*

BRIDPORT, Dorset Map 03 SY49

### ★★★62% Haddon House

West Bay DT6 4EL
☎ 01308 423626 & 425323 🖹 01308 427348
***Dir:*** *0.5m off the A35 Crown Inn rdbt signposted to West Bay*

Within a few minutes walk of the sea-front and quay, this attractive hotel offers good standards of accommodation. In addition to the extensive range of dishes served in the popular bar, a selection of carefully prepared dishes is served in the restaurant. There is a comfortable lounge and small meeting room.

**ROOMS:** 12 en suite (2 fmly) **FACILITIES:** STV Solarium **CONF:** Thtr 50 Class 30 Board 20 **PARKING:** 74 **NOTES:** No dogs (ex guide dogs) No smoking in restaurant **CARDS:**

### ★★70% Roundham House

Roundham Gardens, West Bay Rd DT6 4BD
☎ 01308 422753 🖹 01308 421500
e-mail: cyprencom@compuserve.com
***Dir:*** *Take A35 Bridport road, do not take left turn to Bridport follow A35 to rdbt Crown Inn, follow signs for West Bay along West Bay Rd hotel signed*

This welcoming and friendly hotel is located on the edge of the town and benefits from wonderful views across the Dorset countryside. Considerable refurbishment has now been completed throughout the hotel and bedrooms in particular offer good levels of comfort and equipment. Enjoyable homecooked dinners are served in the relaxing restaurant.

**ROOMS:** 8 en suite (2 fmly) No smoking in all bedrooms s £35-£40; d £60-£80 (incl. bkfst) * **LB** **FACILITIES:** Xmas **CONF:** Thtr 20 Class 20 Board 15 **PARKING:** 12 **NOTES:** No smoking in restaurant Closed 3 Jan-Feb **CARDS:**

### ★64% Bridge House

115 East St DT6 3LB
☎ 01308 423371 🖹 01308 423371
***Dir:*** *turn off at rdbt with A35 & A3066, hotel 150yds on right next to River Asker bridge*

This 18th-century hotel is a short stroll from the town centre. The well-equipped bedrooms vary in size. In addition to the main lounge, there is a small bar-lounge and a separate breakfast room. Good home-cooked meals that use top quality produce are provided in the lower ground floor restaurant.

**ROOMS:** 10 en suite (2 fmly) s £38; d £54 (incl. bkfst) * **LB** **CONF:** Thtr 20 Board 12 Del £65 * **PARKING:** 12 **NOTES:** No dogs (ex guide dogs) **CARDS:**

BRIGG, Lincolnshire Map 08 TA00

### ★★63% The Red Lion Hotel

Main Rd, Redbourne DN21 4QR
☎ 01652 648302 🖹 01652 648302
e-mail: enquiries@redlion.org
***Dir:*** *Take A15 south from M180 junct 4, after 5m follow signs left to Redbourne. Hotel first building on left in village*

Dating back to the 17th century, this coaching inn overlooks the village green. It offers pleasantly furnished bedrooms while a good range of food is available either in the bar or dining room. Staff are friendly and helpful.

**ROOMS:** 8 rms (7 en suite) (1 fmly) s £40; d £50 (incl. bkfst) * **LB** **FACILITIES:** entertainment **CONF:** Thtr 35 Class 35 Board 35 Del from £60 * **PARKING:** 60 **NOTES:** No smoking in restaurant **CARDS:**

BRIGHOUSE, West Yorkshire Map 07 SE12

### ★★★68% Posthouse Brighouse

**Posthouse**

Clifton Village HD6 4HW
☎ 0870 400 9013 🖹 01484 400068
e-mail: gm1736@forte-hotels.com
***Dir:*** *take junct 25 off M62 follow the A644 Spur road for Brighouse. Hotel on right*

Bedrooms at this modern hotel are spacious and comfortably furnished. Public areas are also a key feature and include an attractively appointed Junction restaurant, several versatile conference and meeting rooms and a fully equipped leisure club.

*continued*

Service includes the provision of an all-day lounge menu and 24 hour room service.
**ROOMS:** 94 en suite (12 fmly) No smoking in 59 bedrooms d £89-£99 (incl. bkfst) * **LB FACILITIES:** Indoor swimming (H) Sauna Gym Croquet lawn Jacuzzi steam room ch fac Xmas **CONF:** Thtr 200 Class 120 Board 60 Del from £105 * **PARKING:** 210 **NOTES:** Civ Wed 120 **CARDS:**

## BRIGHTON & HOVE, East Sussex Map 04 TQ30

### ★★★★★66% Grand

De Vere Hotels

King's Rd BN1 2FW
☎ 01273 224300 🖷 01273 224321
e-mail: reservations@grandbrighton.co.uk
***Dir:** next to Brighton Centre facing Brighton Pier & seafront, turn right along Grand Junction Rd into King's Rd.*
This landmark hotel has graced the Brighton seafront since 1864 and continues to be a popular choice with both leisure and business guests. Bedrooms, many of which enjoy sea views, are smart and equipped to a very high standard. Features include a bar with adjoining conservatory, an attractive restaurant, a leisure club, and extensive conference facilities.
**ROOMS:** 200 en suite (70 fmly) s £155-£315; d £220-£315 (incl. bkfst) * **LB FACILITIES:** Spa STV Indoor swimming (H) Sauna Solarium Gym Jacuzzi Hairdresser,Beauty & fitness, masseur, Steam Room, Fitness studio, Tropicorium, entertainment Xmas **CONF:** Thtr 800 Class 420 **SERVICES:** Lift **PARKING:** 65 **NOTES:** Civ Wed 400 **CARDS:**

### ★★★★65% Old Ship

PARAMOUNT GROUP OF HOTELS

King's Rd BN1 1NR
☎ 01273 329001 🖷 01273 820718
e-mail: oldship@paramount-hotels.co.uk
***Dir:** follow A23 to seafront, turn right at roundabout along Kings Rd. Hotel located 200yds on right*
The Old Ship enjoys a stunning seafront location and since refurbishment offers guests elegant surroundings in which to relax. Bedrooms are well-designed with modern facilities ensuring guest comfort. Many original features have been retained, including the oak-panelled bar. Facilities include a variety of conference rooms and a hotel car park.
**ROOMS:** 152 en suite (10 fmly) No smoking in 49 bedrooms s fr £65; d fr £130 (incl. bkfst) * **LB FACILITIES:** STV entertainment Xmas **CONF:** Thtr 300 Class 100 Board 60 Del £135 * **SERVICES:** Lift **PARKING:** 40 **NOTES:** No dogs (ex guide dogs) Civ Wed 70 **CARDS:**

### ★★★68% Queens Hotel

1 King's Rd BN1 1NS
☎ 01273 321222 🖷 01273 203059
e-mail: reservations@queenshotelbrighton.co.uk
***Dir:** From M23/A23 follow signs to the seafront, at the seafront turn right, the hotel is approx 400yds on right*
This hotel with a seafront location has recently been refurbished to a high standard. All the bedrooms are richly decorated with warm colours, offer good facilities and many have wonderful sea views. A modern leisure suite and Atrium bar allow guests to relax; there are also several meeting rooms available.
**ROOMS:** 94 en suite (8 fmly) No smoking in 30 bedrooms s £60-£140; d £60-£140 (incl. bkfst) * **LB FACILITIES:** STV Indoor swimming (H) Sauna Solarium Gym Jacuzzi **CONF:** Thtr 75 Class 50 Board 34 Del from £105 * **SERVICES:** Lift **NOTES:** No dogs (ex guide dogs) No smoking in restaurant Civ Wed **CARDS:**

### ★★★66% Imperial

First Av BN3 2GU
☎ 01273 777320 🖷 01273 777310
e-mail: info@imperial-hove.com
***Dir:** M23 to Brighton seafront, right at roundabout to Hove, 1.5 miles to First Avenue turn right*

Located within minutes of the sea front, this Regency hotel is being constantly improved and upgraded. Bedrooms are generally spacious, well appointed and with a good range of facilities. Public areas include a lounge, a smart bar area and an attractive restaurant. Substantial conferencing is available.
**ROOMS:** 76 en suite (4 fmly) No smoking in 10 bedrooms s £45-£78; d £75-£105 (incl. bkfst) * **LB FACILITIES:** Xmas **CONF:** Thtr 110 Class 30 Board 34 Del from £85 * **SERVICES:** Lift **NOTES:** No dogs (ex guide dogs) **CARDS:**

*See advert on this page*

BRIGHTON & HOVE, continued

### ★★★66% Princes Marine

153 Kingsway BN3 4GR
☎ 01273 207660 🖷 01273 325913
e-mail: princesmarine@bestwestern.co.uk
***Dir:*** *turn right at Palace Pier and follow seafront for approx 2m, hotel is approx 200yds from King Alfred sports & leisure centre*

Enjoying a seafront location to the west of town, this friendly hotel offers spacious, comfortable bedrooms equipped with a good range of facilities. There is a cosy restaurant, bar and a useful meeting room.
**ROOMS:** 48 en suite (4 fmly) No smoking in 6 bedrooms s £40-£60; d £70-£90 (incl. bkfst) * **LB** **FACILITIES:** Xmas **CONF:** Thtr 80 Class 40 Board 40 Del from £80 * **SERVICES:** Lift **PARKING:** 30
**CARDS:**

### ★★★64% Brighton Hotel

143/145 King's Rd BN1 2PQ
☎ 01273 820555 🖷 01273 821555
e-mail: bthotel@pavilion.co.uk
***Dir:*** *follow signs to Palace Pier, turn right and hotel is 100yds past West Pier*
Enjoying a prime seafront location close to the historic West Pier, this friendly family-run hotel is well placed. All rooms are bright, comfortably appointed and well-equipped. The limited car parking facilities are a real bonus in Brighton.
**ROOMS:** 52 en suite s £55-£63; d £80-£84 (incl. bkfst) * **LB** **FACILITIES:** STV Xmas **CONF:** Thtr 130 Class 35 Board 35 **SERVICES:** Lift **PARKING:** 18 **NOTES:** Civ Wed 120
**CARDS:**

### ★★★64% Courtlands

15-27 The Drive BN3 3JE
☎ 01273 731055 🖷 01273 328295
e-mail: courtlands@pavilion.co.uk
***Dir:*** *A23 junct A27 Worthing-take 1st exit to Hove, 2nd exit at rdbt, then right at 1st junct and turn left at shops. Straight on at junct, hotel on left*
This hotel is within walking distance of the seafront and has its own small carpark. The bedrooms are newly decorated and have smart bathrooms. Guests have the use of a comfortable lounge, a light and spacious restaurant and a covered swimming pool.
**ROOMS:** 60 en suite 7 annexe en suite (8 fmly) No smoking in 20 bedrooms s £65; d £85-£130 (incl. bkfst) * **LB** **FACILITIES:** Indoor swimming (H) Solarium Xmas **CONF:** Thtr 60 Class 20 Board 30 Del from £80 * **SERVICES:** Lift **PARKING:** 24
**CARDS:**

### ★★★64% Quality Hotel Brighton

Quality
Hotel

West St BN1 2RQ
☎ 01273 220033 🖷 01273 778000
e-mail: admin@gb057.u-net.com
***Dir:*** *follow A23 into Brighton. Follow signs for Town Centre & seafront. Take A259 to Hove & Worthing. Hotel situated next door to Brighton Centre*
Conveniently located for the seafront and close to the town centre, this purpose built hotel offers modern and well-equipped bedrooms. Public areas include a spacious, open plan lobby area, a feature staircase, smoking and non smoking areas in the lounge/bar and Spinnakers restaurant which serves a range of international dishes.
**ROOMS:** 138 en suite No smoking in 60 bedrooms s £88-£115; d £99-£125 * **LB** **FACILITIES:** STV **CONF:** Thtr 200 Class 80 Board 60 Del from £75 * **SERVICES:** Lift **NOTES:** No dogs (ex guide dogs) No smoking in restaurant **CARDS:**

### ★★★63% The Granville

124 King's Rd BN1 2FA
☎ 01273 326302 🖷 01273 728294
e-mail: granville@brighton.co.uk
***Dir:*** *On seafront opposite West Pier*
This stylish hotel is located on Brighton's busy seafront. Bedrooms are carefully furnished and decorated with great style. A casual informal service and atmosphere is provided in Trogs vegetarian restaurant and the adjoining bar; great care is taken to source quality organic foods. Tasty traditional breakfasts are a concession to the carnivorous guest in the morning.
**ROOMS:** 24 en suite (1 fmly) No smoking in all bedrooms s £50-£85; d £85-£155 (incl. bkfst) * **LB** **FACILITIES:** Jacuzzi **CONF:** Thtr 40 Class 20 Del from £120 * **SERVICES:** Lift **PARKING:** 3 **NOTES:** No smoking in restaurant **CARDS:**

### ★★★62% The Dudley

Lansdowne Place BN3 1HQ
☎ 01273 736266 🖷 01273 729802
e-mail: admin@thedudleyhotel.co.uk
***Dir:*** *Enter Brighton by M23 & A23, right at seafront heading W, in Hove Lansdowne Place is 1st turning after Brunswick Sq.*

This Regency fronted hotel is located just a few metres from the seafront. The Dudley offers well-appointed public areas and an extensive range of function rooms. Bedroom refurbishment is ongoing to restore the hotel to its former glory.
**ROOMS:** 71 en suite (3 fmly) No smoking in 40 bedrooms s fr £50; d fr £100 (incl. bkfst) * **LB** **FACILITIES:** Xmas **CONF:** Thtr 150 Class 100 Board 90 Del from £70 * **SERVICES:** Lift **PARKING:** 20 **NOTES:** No dogs (ex guide dogs) No smoking in restaurant
**CARDS:**

*See advert on opposite page*

B

★★63% **St Catherines Lodge**
Seafront, Kingsway BN3 2RZ
☎ 01273 778181 📠 01273 774949
**Dir:** *opposite King Alfred Leisure Centre on main A259*

**Privately owned and family-run, this hotel is located by the seafront at Hove. Bedrooms are neatly decorated and comfortably appointed. Public areas retain many original features including Adam-style ceilings and antique Delft tiling in the restaurant.**
**ROOMS:** 40 en suite (4 fmly) s £55-£65; d £75-£85 (incl. bkfst)
**FACILITIES:** Games room Xmas **CONF:** Thtr 35 Class 24 Board 24 Del from £75 * **SERVICES:** Lift **PARKING:** 5 **NOTES:** No dogs (ex guide dogs) **CARDS:**

*See advert on this page*

**Arriving late? Four and five star hotels have night porters to assist with your luggage, and 24-hour room service.**

BRIGHTON & HOVE, continued

### ⌂ *Premier Lodge*

144 North St BN1 1DN

☎ 0870 700 1334 📠 0870 700 1335

Premier Lodge offers modern, well-equipped, en suite accommodation suitable for both business and leisure travellers. Meals can be taken at the adjacent popular restaurant and bar, which is fully licensed. For further details, consult the Hotel Groups page.

**ROOMS:** 160 en suite

### ⌂ *Travelodge*

Preston Rd BN1 6AN

☎ 01273 55024

Travelodge offers good quality, good value, modern accommodation. Ideal for families, the spacious, en suite bedrooms include remote-control TV, tea and coffee-making facilities, luxury beds and free morning newspaper. Meals can be taken at the nearby family restaurant. For further details and the Travelodge phone number, consult the Hotel Groups page.

## BRISTOL, Bristol

Map 03 ST57

### ★★★★75% Bristol Marriott Royal Hotel

College Green BS1 5TA

☎ 0117 925 5100 📠 0117 925 1515

e-mail: bristol.royal@marriotthotels.co.uk

***Dir:*** *in the city centre next to the cathedral*

A truly stunning hotel, located in the centre of the city, next to the cathedral. Public areas are particularly impressive with luxurious lounges and an impressive leisure club. Dining options include the more informal terrace restaurant and the very impressive Palm Court. Charming bedrooms have good quality furnishings, comfortable armchairs, luxurious marbled bathrooms and air conditioning.

**ROOMS:** 242 en suite (14 fmly) No smoking in 163 bedrooms d £115-£145 * **LB FACILITIES: Spa** STV Indoor swimming (H) Sauna Solarium Gym Xmas **CONF:** Thtr 300 Class 140 Board 30 Del from £165 * **SERVICES:** Lift air con **PARKING:** 200 **NOTES:** No dogs (ex guide dogs) Civ Wed 220 **CARDS:**

### ★★★★70% Aztec

Aztec West Business Park, Almondsbury BS32 4TS

☎ 01454 201090 📠 01454 201593

e-mail: aztec@shireinns.co.uk

***Dir:*** *access via M5 (junct 16) & M4*

This hotel is well situated close to Cribbs Causeway shopping centre and the M4 and M5. Built with leanings towards Nordic styling, public rooms boast log fires and vaulted ceilings. Leisure facilities include a very well-equipped gym and a large pool. The new-look Danbys bar offers all-day food and drink.

**ROOMS:** 128 en suite (13 fmly) No smoking in 55 bedrooms s £149 (incl. bkfst) * **LB FACILITIES: Spa** STV Indoor swimming (H) Squash Sauna Solarium Gym Jacuzzi Steam room Health & beauty Childrens splash pool Xmas **CONF:** Thtr 250 Class 120 Board 48 Del £170 * **SERVICES:** Lift air con **PARKING:** 240 **NOTES:** No smoking in restaurant Civ Wed 250 **CARDS:**

### ★★★★67% Bristol Marriott Hotel, City Centre

Lower Castle St BS1 3AD

☎ 0117 929 4281 📠 0117 927 6377

***Dir:*** *from M32 follow signs to Broadmead, taking slip road to large rdbt. Take 3rd exit. Hotel located on right hand side*

BUS

Situated at the foot of the picturesque Castle Park, the hotel is well located for the city centre with its many historical attractions and shops. Free parking is available for residents along with complimentary membership of the hotel's leisure club. Guests have the choice of two dining options, an informal Brasserie and Le Chateau Restaurant.

**ROOMS:** 289 en suite (136 fmly) No smoking in 221 bedrooms d £110-£115 * **LB FACILITIES:** STV Indoor swimming (H) Sauna Solarium Gym Jacuzzi Steam room **CONF:** Thtr 600 Class 280 Board 40 Del £165 * **SERVICES:** Lift air con **NOTES:** No dogs (ex guide dogs) Civ Wed 500 **CARDS:**

### ★★★★64% Jurys Bristol Hotel

Prince St BS1 4QF

☎ 0117 923 0333 📠 0117 923 0300

e-mail: bristol_hotel@jurysdoyle.com

***Dir:*** *from Temple Meads turn right at 1st rdbt into Victoria St. At Bristol Bridge traffic lights left Baldwil St, 2nd left Marsh St, right at rdbt*

This popular hotel is centrally located on the waterside, close to Bristol's Millennium development. Bedrooms are spacious and well-equipped with modern amenities. Public rooms include a

continued

ange of eating options including a Quayside pub. The hotel also ffers extensive conference facilities.
**OOMS:** 191 en suite (22 fmly) No smoking in 53 bedrooms s £135; £135 * **LB** **FACILITIES:** STV 50% Discount at local Gym ntertainment Xmas **CONF:** Thtr 350 Class 140 Board 80 Del from £140 * **SERVICES:** Lift **NOTES:** No dogs (ex guide dogs)
**ARDS:**

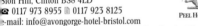

*See advert on this page*

### ★★★69% Berkeley Square

5 Berkeley Square, Clifton BS8 1HB
0117 925 4000 0117 925 2970
-mail: berkeleysquare@bestwestern.co.uk
**Dir:** *from M32 follow signs for Clifton, take first turn left at traffic lights by Villis Memorial Tower (University) into Berkeley Sq*

Best Western

et in a peaceful square close to the university, art gallery and lifton village, this smart, elegant Georgian hotel has tastefully lecorated bedrooms. There is a busy bar in the basement, and the estaurant features interesting dishes from a choice of menus.
**ROOMS:** 42 en suite No smoking in 12 bedrooms s £49-£101; d £80-122 (incl. bkfst) * **LB** **FACILITIES:** STV **CONF:** Thtr 15 Class 12 Board 2 Del £120 * **SERVICES:** Lift **PARKING:** 20
**ARDS:**

### ★★★69% Posthouse Bristol

ilton Rd, Hambrook BS16 1QX
0870 400 9014 0117 956 9735
**Dir:** *M4 junct 19 onto M32. Take junct 1 off M32 onto 4174 towards Filton, Bristol and Parkway Station. Hotel 800yds on the left*

Posthouse

Adjacent to the Frenchay Campus of UWE, this modern hotel ttracts conferences with its range of meeting rooms and business acilities. The restyled bedrooms offer many welcome extras. Meals are served in the Junction brasserie and in the new Eastern-style restaurant. Lighter snacks are available in the lounge, which s particularly popular for informal business meetings.
**ROOMS:** 198 en suite (36 fmly) No smoking in 131 bedrooms s £69-139; d £69-£139 * **LB** **FACILITIES:** STV Indoor swimming (H) Fishing auna Solarium Gym Outdoor badminton Xmas **CONF:** Thtr 250 Class 30 Board 60 Del £165 * **SERVICES:** Lift **PARKING:** 400
**NOTES:** Civ Wed 70 **CARDS:**

### ★★★67% The Avon Gorge

Sion Hill, Clifton BS8 4LD
0117 973 8955 0117 923 8125
-mail: info@avongorge-hotel-bristol.com

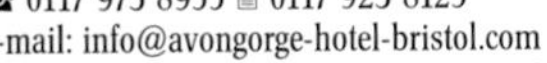

PEEL HOTELS

**Dir:** *From M4 junct19 onto M32 to city centre, follow signs for Clifton to T unct. Turn right then left into Princess Victoria street down to the end*

Overlooking Avon Gorge and Brunel's famous suspension bridge, this popular hotel offers rooms with some glorious views. Facilities nclude additional telephone points and ceiling fans. The hotel offers a choice of bars (one with a popular terrace) and an attractive restaurant.
**ROOMS:** 76 en suite (6 fmly) No smoking in 30 bedrooms s £99-£104; d £104-£109 (incl. bkfst) * **LB** **FACILITIES:** STV Childrens activity play area entertainment Xmas **CONF:** Thtr 100 Class 50 Board 26 Del from £85 * **SERVICES:** Lift **PARKING:** 23 **NOTES:** No smoking in restaurant Civ Wed 100 **CARDS:**

### ★★★66% Redwood Lodge Hotel

Beggar Bush Ln, Failand BS8 3TG
01275 393901 01275 392104
-mail: redwood.lodge@virgin.net
**Dir:** *M5 junct 19, A369 for 3m then right at lights, hotel is 1m on left*

REGAL

Situated just outside the city this popular hotel offers guests a calm location combined with excellent leisure facilities. The gym, squash, badminton and tennis facilities, plus indoor and outdoor

*continued on p136*

BRISTOL, continued

pools, are a great attraction. Bedrooms have plenty of amenities suited to the business visitor.

*Redwood Lodge Hotel, Bristol*

**ROOMS:** 112 en suite (4 fmly) No smoking in 81 bedrooms d fr £110 * **LB** **FACILITIES:** STV Indoor swimming (H) Outdoor swimming Tennis (hard) Squash Sauna Solarium Gym 175 seater Cinema Aerobics/Dance studios Xmas **CONF:** Thtr 175 Class 80 Board 30 Del from £115 * **PARKING:** 1000 **NOTES:** No dogs (ex guide dogs) No smoking in restaurant **CARDS:**

### ★★★65% Henbury Lodge

Station Rd, Henbury BS10 7QQ
☎ 0117 950 2615 ▯ 0117 950 9532
e-mail: enquiries@henburylodge.com
***Dir:*** *4.5m NW of city centre off A4018, 1m from M5 junct 17*

This comfortable former country house, built in 1760, is conveniently situated in a quiet suburb within easy access of the M5. Bedrooms are available both within the main house and in the adjoining stable conversion; all are attractively decorated and well-equipped. The dining room offers a range of simple, freshly cooked dishes.

**ROOMS:** 12 en suite 9 annexe en suite (4 fmly) No smoking in 6 bedrooms s £53-£103; d £86-£113 (incl. bkfst) * **LB** **FACILITIES:** STV Sauna Solarium Gym Xmas **CONF:** Thtr 32 Class 20 Board 20 Del from £120 * **PARKING:** 24 **NOTES:** No smoking in restaurant
**CARDS:**

### ★★70% *Clifton*

St Pauls Rd, Clifton BS8 1LX
☎ 0117 973 6882 ▯ 0117 974 1082
***Dir:*** *take M32 into Bristol & follow signs for Clifton. Go up Park St (very steep hill) follow road ahead & turn left at traffic lights into St Pauls Rd*

This popular hotel offers very well-equipped bedrooms. There is a smart lounge at reception and during summer months drinks can be taken on the terrace. Racks Bar and Restaurant offers an interesting selection of modern dishes from an imaginative menu. Some street parking is possible although for a small charge, secure garage parking is available.

**ROOMS:** 60 rms (48 en suite) (2 fmly) No smoking in 15 bedrooms **FACILITIES:** STV **SERVICES:** Lift **PARKING:** 20 **NOTES:** Closed 23-29 Dec **CARDS:**

### ★★70% Seeley's

17-27 St Paul's Rd, Clifton BS8 1LX
☎ 0117 973 8544 ▯ 0117 973 2406
e-mail: admin@seeleys.demon.co.uk
***Dir:*** *M5 junct 17, follow A4018 for 4.5 m to BBC studios, turn right at lights and hotel is on the left*

A privately owned, efficiently run hotel with easy access to Clifton Village, the university and city centre. Comfortable public areas are spacious. A wide selection of dishes is offered in Le Chasseur Restaurant, lighter meals and snacks are served in the bar. The bedrooms, some in adjacent properties, are all pleasing and particularly well-equipped.

**ROOMS:** 37 en suite 18 annexe en suite (10 fmly) s £65-£80; d £80-£9 (incl. bkfst) * **LB** **FACILITIES:** STV Sauna Solarium Gym Fitness Cent **CONF:** Thtr 70 Class 30 Board 25 Del from £92.50 * **PARKING:** 25 **NOTES:** No dogs (ex guide dogs) Closed 24 Dec-2 Jan
**CARDS:**

### ★★66% The Bowl Inn

16 Church Rd, Lower Almondsbury BS32 4DT
☎ 01454 612757 ▯ 01454 619910
e-mail: thebowl@3wa.co.uk
***Dir:*** *from M5 junct 6 on Gloucester road turn left Over Lane by Almondsbury Garden Centre. Hotel next to St Mary's Church on right*

Situated less than two miles from M5 and M4 motorway junction this village inn offers all the comforts of modern life housed withi the character and architecture of a 16th-century hostelry. Each bedroom has been individually furnished to complement the many original features. Huge ceiling beams, stonework niches an fireplaces abound. Dining options include an extensive bar menu with cask ales, or a more intimate restaurant.

**ROOMS:** 11 en suite 2 annexe en suite No smoking in 5 bedrooms s £40-£88; d £64-£108 (incl. bkfst) * **LB** **FACILITIES:** STV **CONF:** Thtr 30 Class 20 Board 20 **PARKING:** 30 **NOTES:** No dogs (ex guide dogs) RS 25 Dec 11am-1pm **CARDS:**

### ★★65% Best Western Glenroy

Victoria Square, Clifton BS8 4EW
☎ 0117 973 9058 ▯ 0117 973 9058
e-mail: admin@glenroyhotel.demon.co.uk
***Dir:*** *junct 19 of M5, follow signs for Clifton come over suspension bridge and turn left after the bakery, hotel around corner on right*

Predominantly used by short stay guests on business, this hotel is conveniently close to the university and city centre. Bedrooms, in the main house and an adjacent property, are considerably variec in size and all well-equipped. Facilities include a congenial open-plan bar, carvery restaurant, and the Victoria and Albert conference rooms.

**ROOMS:** 25 en suite 19 annexe en suite (9 fmly) s £62-£82; d £82-£92 (incl. bkfst) * **FACILITIES:** STV **CONF:** Thtr 45 Class 25 Board 25 Del from £95 * **PARKING:** 16 **NOTES:** Closed 24-31 Dec Civ Wed
**CARDS:**

### ★★64% *Rodney Hotel*

4 Rodney Place, Clifton BS8 4HY
☎ 0117 973 5422 ▯ 0117 946 7092
***Dir:*** *off Clifton Down Road*

With easy access from the M5, this attractive, listed building in Clifton is conveniently close to the city centre. The individually

*continue*

ecorated bedrooms provide a useful range of extra facilities for e business traveller. Snacks are served in the bar-lounge or by ay of room service and the more formal restaurant offers an ppealing selection of dishes.
**OOMS:** 31 en suite No smoking in 9 bedrooms **FACILITIES:** STV
**ONF:** Thtr 30 Class 20 Board 15 **NOTES:** Closed 22 Dec-3 Jan RS Sun
**ARDS:**

## *Town House*

### ★★★★ Hotel du Vin & Bistro
The Sugar House, Narrow Lewins Mead BS1 2NU
☎ 0117 925 5577 0117 925 1199
e-mail: info@bristol.hotelduvin.com
***Dir:*** *From A4 follow signs for city centre. After 400 yds pass Rupert street NCP on right. Hotel situated on the opposite side of carriageway*
The third property in one of Britain's most exciting and innovative hotel groups maintains and extends the high standards the chain is renowned for. The hotel is housed in a Grade II listed, converted 18th-century sugar refinery. Bedrooms are exceptionally well-designed. Great facilities are provided and the modern minimalist feel is a welcome change from chintz. The bistro offers an excellent menu of simply constructed dishes.
**ROOMS:** 40 en suite d £109-£225 * **FACILITIES:** STV Snooker Xmas **CONF:** Thtr 50 Class 25 Board 26 Del £190 *
**SERVICES:** Lift **PARKING:** 33 **NOTES:** No dogs (ex guide dogs)
**CARDS:**

### *Travelodge*
ribbs Causeway BS10 7TL
☎ 0117 950 1530 0117 950 1530
***Dir:*** *A4018, just off junc17 M5*
ravelodge offers good quality, good value, modern ccommodation. Ideal for families, the spacious, en suite edrooms include remote-control TV, tea and coffee-making acilities, luxury beds and free morning newspaper. Meals can be aken at the nearby family restaurant. For further details and the ravelodge phone number, consult the Hotel Groups page.

**OOMS:** 56 en suite

### *Express by Holiday Inn Bristol*
emple Gate BS1 6PL
☎ 0117 9304800 0117 9304900
***ir:*** *M4 junct 19 leads to M32 into Bristol. Keep left & ollow signs to Temple Meads Train Station. Hotel directly opposite on emple Gate*

A modern budget hotel offering comfortable accommodation in efreshing, spacious and comprehensively equipped bedrooms, en suite bathrooms with power showers and continental buffet breakfast included in the room rate. Suitable for business travellers or families. For further details and the Express by Holiday Inn phone number, consult the Hotel Groups page.
**ROOMS:** 94 en suite **CONF:** Thtr 35 Class 16 Board 20

### Premier Lodge (Bristol City East)

Shield Retail Park, Gloucester Rd North, Filton BS35 4BH
☎ 0870 700 1336 0870 7001337
Premier Lodge offers modern, well-equipped, en suite accommodation suitable for both business and leisure travellers. Meals can be taken at the adjacent popular restaurant and bar, which is fully licensed. For further details, consult the Hotel Groups page.
**ROOMS:** 60 en suite d £50 * **CONF:** Del from £455.65 *

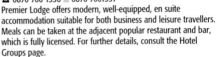

### *Travelodge (Bristol Central)*
Anchor Rd, Harbourside BS1
☎ 08700 850950
Travelodge offers good quality, good value, modern accommodation. Ideal for families, the spacious, en suite bedrooms include remote-control TV, tea and coffee-making facilities, luxury beds and free morning newspaper. Meals can be taken at the nearby family restaurant. For further details and the Travelodge phone number, consult the Hotel Groups page.

## BRIXHAM, Devon — Map 03 SX95

### ★★★68% Quayside
41-49 King St TQ5 9TJ
☎ 01803 855751 01803 882733
e-mail: quayside.hotel@virgin.net
***Dir:*** *from Exeter follow signs for Torquay on A380, at the 2nd rdbt at Kinkerswell follow signs for Brixham on A3022, hotel overlooks the harbour*

Created from six cottages and enjoying panoramic views over the harbour and bay, the Quayside Hotel offers friendly and attentive service. The public rooms include a cosy lounge, residents' bar and Ernie Lister's public bar. An extensive range of enjoyable dishes is available in the intimate restaurant, including freshly landed fish. Bedrooms are modern and well-equipped.
**ROOMS:** 29 en suite (2 fmly) No smoking in 6 bedrooms s £48-£65; d £66-£94 (incl. bkfst) * **LB** **FACILITIES:** entertainment Xmas
**CONF:** Thtr 25 Class 18 Board 18 **PARKING:** 30 **NOTES:** No smoking in restaurant **CARDS:**

Early start? Hotels at all star levels should provide in-room alarm clocks and/or alarm calls.

B

BRIXHAM, continued

**★★★66% Berryhead**
Berryhead Rd TQ5 9AJ
☎ 01803 853225 Fax 01803 882084
e-mail: berryhd@aol.com
***Dir:*** *to Brixham Harbour turn right past statue & then left to Marina; straight on another quarter of a mile past Marina*
Enjoying spectacular views from its stunning clifftop location, this imposing property dates back to 1809 and was the former residence of Rev. Henry Lyte, composer of many hymns including 'Abide with Me'. The hotel offers a range of bedrooms and its public areas include an outdoor terrace, popular bars and a swimming pool.
**ROOMS:** 32 en suite (7 fmly) s £52-£68; d £104-£136 (incl. bkfst) * **LB** **FACILITIES:** Indoor swimming (H) Croquet lawn Jacuzzi Petanque Sailing Deep sea fishing entertainment Xmas **CONF:** Thtr 300 Class 250 Board 40 Del from £65 * **PARKING:** 200 **NOTES:** No smoking in restaurant Civ Wed 200 **CARDS:**

*See advert on opposite page*

**★★73% Maypool Park**
Maypool, Galmpton TQ5 0ET
☎ 01803 842442 Fax 01803 845782
e-mail: peacock@maypoolpark.co.uk
***Dir:*** *at Churston (A3022) turn SW signed Maypool/Passenger ferry/Greenway Quay to Manor Vale Rd. Follow signs through village to hotel*

Bordering onto the estate of the late Agatha Christie, Maypool Park benefits from stunning views over a wooded valley. The delightful bedrooms provide every modern comfort. Guests are assured of a warm welcome and some imaginative dishes from the daily changing menu. A choice of lounges and a cosy bar are available.
**ROOMS:** 10 en suite No smoking in all bedrooms s £48-£66; d £74-£104 (incl. bkfst) * **LB** **FACILITIES:** Xmas **CONF:** Thtr 30 Class 20 Board 20 **PARKING:** 15 **NOTES:** No dogs (ex guide dogs) No children 10yrs No smoking in restaurant **CARDS:**

**★58% Smuggler's Haunt**
Church Hill East TQ5 8HH
☎ 01803 853050 & 859416 Fax 01803 858738
e-mail: enquires@smugglershaunt-hotel-devon.co.uk
***Dir:*** *at the end of A3022 turn left and hotel 200yds straight ahead*
Located in the centre of this historic fishing village, this 300-year-old hotel offers straightforward accommodation. A wide range of carefully cooked dishes is available in both the restaurant and bar.
**ROOMS:** 14 en suite (4 fmly) s £29-£33; d £48-£54 (incl. bkfst) * **LB** **FACILITIES:** Xmas **CARDS:**

BROADSTAIRS, Kent Map 05 TR3

**★★★64% Royal Albion**
Albion St CT10 1AN
☎ 01843 868071 Fax 01843 861509
e-mail: enquiries@albion-bstairs.demon.co.uk
***Dir:*** *on entering the town follow signs for seafront & town centre*
A traditional seafront hotel with delightful views from bedrooms, and the newly refurbished bar and lounge. The restaurant is two doors down the street in Marchesi's. Staff are friendly and the atmosphere is relaxed and informal.
**ROOMS:** 19 en suite (3 fmly) No smoking in 4 bedrooms s £49-£65; d £59-£84 * **LB** **FACILITIES:** STV entertainment Xmas **CONF:** Thtr 30 Class 20 Board 20 Del from £60 * **PARKING:** 21 **NOTES:** No dogs (ex guide dogs) RS Sun **CARDS:**

BROADWAY, Worcestershire Map 04 SP0
see also Buckland

**Premier Collection**

**★★★★ The Lygon Arms**
High St WR12 7DU
☎ 01386 852255 Fax 01386 858611
e-mail: info@the-lygon-arms.co.uk
The Savoy Group
***Dir:*** *in centre of village*
This hotel features a wealth of historical charm and character. Situated in the heart of Broadway, the Lygon Arms is steeped in history dating back to the 16th century. The bedrooms vary in style and layout, offering comfort, modern facilities and some fine antique furniture. Public rooms include a variety of lounge areas, some of which have open fires, and a choice of dining options – the Great Hall or the more informal Oliver's Brasserie.
**ROOMS:** 69 rms (66 en suite) (3 fmly) s £135-£147; d £182-£645 * **LB** **FACILITIES:** Spa STV Indoor swimming (H) Tennis (hard) Snooker Sauna Gym Croquet lawn Jacuzzi Beauty treatments Steam Room Bike Hire Xmas **CONF:** Thtr 80 Class 48 Board 30 Del from £215 * **PARKING:** 152 **NOTES:** No smoking in restaurant Civ Wed 80 **CARDS:**

**★★★76% Dormy House**
Willersey Hill WR12 7LF
☎ 01386 852711 Fax 01386 858636
e-mail: reservations@dormyhouse.co.uk.
***Dir:*** *2m E off A44, at top of Fish Hill 1.5m from Broadway village, take turn signposted Saintbury/Picnic area. After 0.5m fork left Dormy House on left*
A large hotel, developed from a 17th-century farmhouse, and surrounded by extensive grounds. Situated high above Broadway, with lovely views, it offers tastefully appointed accommodation, traditionally furnished and well-equipped; some rooms have four-

*continued*

poster beds. Charming public rooms include comfortable lounge areas, a pleasant bar and a very attractive restaurant, where guests can enjoy imaginative culinary skills. The 'Barn Owl' pub offers a less formal eating option.
**ROOMS:** 25 en suite 23 annexe en suite (3 fmly) s £105-£109; d £150-£179 (incl. bkfst) * **LB** **FACILITIES:** Sauna Gym Croquet lawn Putting green Games room Nature/jogging trail **CONF:** Thtr 200 Class 100 Board 25 Del from £185 * **PARKING:** 80 **NOTES:** Closed 25 & 26 Dec Civ Wed 170 **CARDS:**

*See advert on this page*

### ★★★68% Broadway

The Green, High St WR12 7AA
☎ 01386 852401 📠 01386 853879
e-mail: bookings@cotswold-inns-hotels.co.uk
***Dir:** set back from the High Street, behind the village green*
The Broadway Hotel is a 15th-century property built as a retreat for the Abbots of Pershore. Following refurbishment the hotel now combines modern and attractive decor with original charm and character. Bedrooms are tastefully furnished, well-equipped and public rooms include a relaxing lounge, cosy bar and charming restaurant.
**ROOMS:** 20 en suite (1 fmly) No smoking in 4 bedrooms d £115-£135 (incl. bkfst) * **LB** **FACILITIES:** Xmas **CONF:** Thtr 20 Board 16 **PARKING:** 20 **NOTES:** No smoking in restaurant Civ Wed 50 **CARDS:**

## BROCKENHURST, Hampshire — Map 04 SU30

### ★★★76% Rhinefield House

Rhinefield Rd SO42 7QB
☎ 01590 622922 📠 01590 622800
e-mail: Rhinefield-house@arcadianhotels.co.uk
***Dir:** take A35 towards Chistchurch. 3m from Lyndhurst turn left to Rhinefield, 1.5m to hotel*
This splendid 19th-century, mock-Elizabethan mansion is set in 40 acres of beautifully landscaped gardens. Bedrooms are spacious with great consideration given to guest comfort. The open-plan lounge and bar overlook an ornamental pond and the elegant restaurant is impressive, with antique features such as carved panelled walls.
**ROOMS:** 34 en suite No smoking in 12 bedrooms s £110-£120; d £135-£160 (incl. bkfst) * **LB** **FACILITIES:** STV Indoor swimming (H) Outdoor swimming (H) Tennis (hard) Sauna Gym Croquet lawn Putting green Jacuzzi Xmas **CONF:** Thtr 150 Class 50 Board 35 Del from £125 * **PARKING:** 100 **NOTES:** No dogs (ex guide dogs) No smoking in restaurant Civ Wed 125 **CARDS:**

### ★★★75% New Park Manor

Lyndhurst Rd SO42 7QH
☎ 01590 623467 Y 📠 01590 622268
e-mail: enquires@newparkmanorhotel.co.uk
***Dir:** on A337 1.5m from Lyndhurst between Brockenhurst and Lyndhust*
Once a favoured hunting lodge of King Charles II, this hotel enjoys a tranquil setting and its own equestrian centre. Fully modernised, it boasts a conference wing and bedrooms refurbished to a high

*continued on p140*

ETC
★★★

DORMY HOUSE
DORMY HOUSE
HOTEL ★★★

BROCKENHURST, continued

standard. The comfortable public areas include the Stag restaurant and Rufus bar, both with log fires and historic features.

*New Park Manor, Brockenhurst*

**ROOMS:** 24 en suite (6 fmly) No smoking in 4 bedrooms s fr £85; d £110-£170 (incl. bkfst) * **FACILITIES:** Outdoor swimming (H) Tennis (hard) Riding Xmas **CONF:** Thtr 120 Class 80 Board 60 Del from £110 * **PARKING:** 50 **NOTES:** No smoking in restaurant Civ Wed 50
**CARDS:**

*See advert on opposite page*

### ★★★74% Careys Manor

New Forest SO42 7RH
☎ 01590 623551 01590 622799
e-mail: careysmanor@btinternet.com
***Dir:*** *follow signs for Lyndhurst & Lymington A337,approaching Brockenhurst, hotel on left after 30mph sign*

Careys Manor was one of the first buildings in the village. Public areas include the large naturally lit lounge with massive log fire. The leisure centre is definitely worth a visit, as it includes a good-sized pool and recently upgraded gym and beauty area. Le Blaireau Cafe provides an informal French style dining option, and the main restaurant enjoys a good local reputation.

**ROOMS:** 15 en suite 64 annexe en suite No smoking in 28 bedrooms s £89-£109; d £129-£199 (incl. bkfst) * **LB** **FACILITIES:** STV Indoor swimming (H) Sauna Gym Croquet lawn Jacuzzi Steam room Beauty therapists Xmas **CONF:** Thtr 120 Class 70 Board 40 **PARKING:** 180 **NOTES:** No smoking in restaurant Civ Wed 100
**CARDS:**

### ★★★74% Whitley Ridge Country House

Beaulieu Rd SO42 7QL
☎ 01590 622354 01590 622856
e-mail: whitleyridge@brockenhurst.co.uk
***Dir:*** *access via B3055 towards Beaulieu*

This charming hotel enjoys a picturesque setting in the heart of the New Forest. Day rooms include two relaxing lounges and large dining room, all with lovely views of the forest. Each bedroom ha an individual style and bathrooms have recently been refurbished to a very high standard.

**ROOMS:** 14 rms (13 en suite) No smoking in all bedrooms s £86-£96; d £132-£142 (incl. bkfst & dinner) * **LB** **FACILITIES:** Tennis (hard) Xma **CONF:** Thtr 40 Class 40 Board 20 Del from £106 * **PARKING:** 32 **NOTES:** No smoking in restaurant **CARDS:**

### ★★★72% Balmer Lawn

Lyndhurst Rd SO42 7ZB
☎ 01590 623116 01590 623864
e-mail: blh@btinternet.com
***Dir:*** *take A337 towards Lymington, hotel on left hand side behind village cricket green*

One of the best locations in the heart of the New Forest, this historic house provides comfortable public rooms and a good range of bedrooms. The terrace is ideal for watching the world go by. A selection of varied and enjoyable dishes are offered in the pleasant restaurant. Extensive function and leisure facilities make this a popular conference venue.

**ROOMS:** 55 en suite (4 fmly) No smoking in 45 bedrooms s fr £60; d fr £120 (incl. bkfst & dinner) * **LB** **FACILITIES:** Indoor swimming (H) Outdoor swimming (H) Tennis (hard) Squash Sauna Gym Jacuzzi Xma **CONF:** Thtr 150 Class 50 Board 50 Del from £105 * **SERVICES:** Lift **PARKING:** 100 **NOTES:** No smoking in restaurant Civ Wed 120
**CARDS:**

*See advert on opposite pag*

### ★★★66% Forest Park



Rhinefield Rd SO42 7ZG
☎ 01590 622844 01590 623948
e-mail: forest.park@forestdale.com
***Dir:*** *from A337 to Brockenhurst turn into Meerut Rd, follow winding road through Waters Green, 0.5m to a T junct, turn right into Rhinefield Road*

A friendly hotel offering good facilities for adults and children. A heated pool, riding, children's meal times and a quiet location in the forest are a few of the advantages here. The well-equipped,

*continue*

B

omfortable bedrooms vary in size and style. A choice of lounge nd bar areas is available.

**OOMS:** 38 en suite (2 fmly) No smoking in 2 bedrooms s £65-£73; £130-£146 (incl. bkfst & dinner) * **LB** **FACILITIES:** Outdoor swimming ) Tennis (hard) Riding Sauna Xmas **CONF:** Thtr 50 Class 20 Board Del £110 * **PARKING:** 80 **NOTES:** Civ Wed

**ARDS:**

★★74% **Cloud**

Ieerut Rd SO42 7TD

☎ 01590 622165 📠 01590 622818

-mail: enquires@cloudhotel.co.uk

*ir: first turning right off A337 approaching Brockenhurst from Lyndhurst. ollow brown tourist signs*

his charming hotel enjoys a peaceful location on the edge of the llage. The bedrooms are bright and comfortable with pine rnishings and smart en suite facilities. Public rooms include a election of cosy lounges, a delightful rear garden with outdoor eating and a restaurant specialising in homecooked wholesome nglish food.

**OOMS:** 18 en suite (3 fmly) s fr £60; d fr £92 (incl. bkfst) * **LB**
**ACILITIES:** Croquet lawn Xmas **CONF:** Thtr 40 Class 12 Board 12
**ARKING:** 20 **NOTES:** No smoking in restaurant Civ Wed 40
**ARDS:**

★★67% **Watersplash**

he Rise SO42 7ZP

☎ 01590 622344 📠 01590 624047

-mail: bookings@watersplash.co.uk

*ir: From M3 exit at junct 13 and follow M27 west. Exit at junct 1& join 337 s/bound through Lyndhurst to Brockenhurst. On passing through rockenhurst The Rise is on left, once reaching hotel on left*

his popular, welcoming Victorian hotel has been in the same amily for 40 years. Upgraded bedrooms have co-ordinated decor nd good facilities. The restaurant overlooks the neatly tended arden. There is also a comfortably furnished lounge, separate bar nd an outdoor pool.

**OOMS:** 23 en suite (6 fmly) s £55-£75; d £76-£106 (incl. bkfst) * **LB**
**ACILITIES:** Outdoor swimming (H) ch fac Xmas **CONF:** Thtr 80 Class ) Board 20 Del from £75 * **PARKING:** 29 **NOTES:** No smoking in estaurant **CARDS:**

ROME, Suffolk — Map 05 TM17

★★★73% Cornwallis Country
**lotel & Restaurant**

P23 8AJ

☎ 01379 870326 📠 01379 870051

-mail: info@thecornwallis.com

*ir: off B1077, 50yds from junct with A140 in direction of Eye*

eatures of this property include a tree-lined drive, walled gardens nd well-tended topiary trees creating an elegant surrounding.

*continued on p142*

BROME, continued

Bedrooms, some of which are in the Coach House, are all spacious and appointed with style and quality. The restaurant serves cuisine to a good standard and the popular bar offers a more informal option.
**ROOMS:** 11 en suite 5 annexe en suite (2 fmly) No smoking in 2 bedrooms s fr £79.50; d £99.50-£135 (incl. bkfst) * **LB**
**FACILITIES:** STV Archery Hot air ballooning ch fac Xmas **CONF:** Thtr 120 Class 60 Board 48 Del £137.95 * **PARKING:** 200 **NOTES:** No smoking in restaurant Civ Wed 120 **CARDS:**

BROMLEY, Greater London
See LONDON SECTION plan 1 G1

### ★★★71% Bromley Court

Bromley Hill BR1 4JD
☎ 020 8461 8600 020 8460 0899
e-mail: bromleyhotel@btinternet.com
***Dir:*** *N, signposted off A21.London Rd opposite Mercedes Benz garage on Bromley Hill*

A grand mansion with modern extensions in three acres of grounds. Bedrooms vary in size, all are exceptionally well-designed. The popular restaurant offers good choices in comfortable surroundings. Extensive facilities include a leisure club and good meeting rooms.
**ROOMS:** 115 en suite (3 fmly) No smoking in 35 bedrooms s £100-£105; d £107-£115 (incl. bkfst) * **FACILITIES:** STV Sauna Gym Putting green Jacuzzi **CONF:** Thtr 150 Class 80 Board 45 Del from £130 * **SERVICES:** Lift **PARKING:** 100 **NOTES:** Civ Wed 50
**CARDS:**

BROMSGROVE, Worcestershire Map 07 SO97

### ★★★★65% Hanover International Hotel & Club

Kidderminster Rd B61 9AB
☎ 01527 576600 01527 878981
e-mail: enquiries.Hanover-international@virgin.net
***Dir:*** *on A448 Bromsgrove to Kidderminster road, 1m W of Bromsgrove town centre*

This hotel is a well-known landmark to all that use the M5. Interiors are themed around Mediterranean styling with plenty of natural light. Bedrooms are in a variety of styles, some are more compact than others. All offer an excellent working environment for the business guest. Good leisure facilities including steam room, pool and gym are an asset.
**ROOMS:** 114 en suite (18 fmly) No smoking in 18 bedrooms s £85-£130; d £100-£150 (incl. bkfst) * **LB** **FACILITIES:** STV Indoor swimming (H) Snooker Sauna Solarium Gym Jacuzzi Childrens play area ch fac Xmas **CONF:** Thtr 200 Class 140 Board 30 Del from £130 * **SERVICES:** Lift **PARKING:** 250 **NOTES:** No smoking in restaurant Civ Wed 200
**CARDS:**

### *Premier Lodge*

Worcester Rd, Upton Warren B61 7ET
☎ 0870 700 1314 0870 700 1315
Premier Lodge offers modern, well-equipped, en suite accommodation suitable for both business and leisure travellers. Meals can be taken at the adjacent popular restaurant and bar, which is fully licensed. For further details, consult the Hotel Groups page.
**ROOMS:** 27 en suite

### ○ Innkeeper's Lodge Bromsgrove

462 Birmingham Rd, Marlbrook B61 0HR
☎ 0870 243 0500
A new concept in the travel accommodation market. Smart rooms meet essential business requirements but also have home comforts. Dining options include all-day menus plus the added advantage of breakfast, which is included in the room price. Reservations can be made seven days a week throug the room reservations number: 0870 243 0500. For further detail consult the Hotel Groups page.
**ROOMS:** 29 en suite

BROOK (NEAR CADNAM), Hampshire Map 04 SU

### ★★★67% Bell Inn

SO43 7HE
☎ 023 8081 2214 023 8081 3958
e-mail: bell@bramshaw.co.uk
***Dir:*** *leave M27 junct 1 onto B3079, hotel a mile and a half on right*

The Inn is part of the Bramshaw Golf Club and has tailored its style to suit this market, but it is also an ideal base from which to visit the New Forest. Bedrooms are comfortable and attractively furnished, and the public areas, particularly the welcoming bar, have a cosy and friendly atmosphere.
**ROOMS:** 25 en suite No smoking in 11 bedrooms s £60-£65; d £80-£8 (incl. bkfst) * **LB** **FACILITIES:** Golf 36 Putting green Xmas **CONF:** Tht 50 Class 20 Board 30 Del from £80 * **PARKING:** 150 **NOTES:** No dogs (ex guide dogs) No smoking in restaurant
**CARDS:**

BROXTON, Cheshire Map 07 SJ4

### ★★★★70% De Vere Carden Park

Carden Park CH3 9DQ
☎ 01829 731000 01829 731032
e-mail: reservation@carden-park.co.uk
***Dir:*** *leave M56 junct 15 for M53 Chester, take A41 for Whitchurch for approx 8m, at Broxton rdbt turn right on to A534 Wrexham, continue 1.5m hotel on left*

This fine modern hotel is located amidst 750 acres of Cheshire estate and offers extensive business, leisure and golf facilities. In addition to the impressive health spa and the superb indoor and

*continued*

ıtdoor leisure facilities, the hotel boasts 45 holes of golf, cluding the challenging Nicklaus course. Accommodation is ·acious, well-equipped and includes a number of rooms located nearby buildings with views over the courses.
**ɔOMS:** 115 en suite 77 annexe en suite (24 fmly) No smoking in 134 drooms s £115; d £130 * **LB** **FACILITIES:** **Spa** STV Indoor ·imming (H) Golf 45 Tennis (hard) Snooker Sauna Solarium Gym oquet lawn Putting green Jacuzzi Archery Quadbikes Jack Nicklaus Golf hool Xmas **CONF:** Thtr 400 Class 240 Board 125 Del from £120 * **:RVICES:** Lift **PARKING:** 500 **NOTES:** No dogs (ex guide dogs) No ıoking in restaurant Civ Wed 100 **CARDS:**

### ·★★64% Broxton Hall Country House
'hitchurch Rd CH3 9JS
☎ 01829 782321 📠 01829 782330
mail: reservations@broxtonhall
*r: on A41 S of Chester at Broxton Rdbt A534, halfway between hitchurch & Chester*
ɜt in its own beautiful grounds, this impressive half-timbered ıdor hall offers public areas elegantly equipped with antique and ɜriod furnishings. Bedrooms are all individually furnished to a gh standard, some with beautiful antique four-poster beds. The ɔpular restaurant overlooks the well-tended gardens.
**OOMS:** 10 en suite s £65-£75; d £75-£85 (incl. bkfst) * **LB**
**ACILITIES:** Croquet lawn ch fac **CONF:** Thtr 23 Board 12
**ARKING:** 30 **NOTES:** No children 12yrs No smoking in restaurant osed 25 Dec & 1 Jan **CARDS:**

### .★73% Frogg Manor
ıllersmoor, Nantwich Rd CH3 9JH
☎ 01829 782629 & 782280 📠 01829 782459
*ir: from Chester take A41 towards Whitchurch, then left on A534 towards antwich. Hotel 0.75m on right*
his delightful Georgian house has been tastefully refurbished to 'eate a small, personally run hotel. Bedrooms are well-equipped nd the eight acres of grounds include a tennis court and beautiful ardens.
**OOMS:** 6 en suite s £50-£100; d £70-£135 * **LB** **FACILITIES:** STV ɜnnis (hard) **CONF:** Thtr 25 Class 15 Board 10 Del from £100 *
**ARKING:** 37 **NOTES:** No children 4yrs No smoking in restaurant RS ɜstaurant must be pre-booked Civ Wed 60
**ARDS:**

## RYHER See Scilly, Isles of

## UCKDEN, North Yorkshire
Map 07 SD97

### ★★67% @@ Buck Inn
·D23 5JA
☎ 01756 760228 & 760416 📠 01756 760227
·mail: thebuckinn@yorks.net
*ir: from A59 take B6265 to Threshfield, then B6160 to Buckden passing rough Kettlewell & Starbotton*
his traditional and welcoming Georgian inn has fine views from ıany of the rooms. Well-equipped bedrooms are smartly resented and there is a cosy lounge area for visitors. A wide ɜnge of interesting snacks and meals is served in the lounge bar 'hilst the Courtyard restaurant provides a more formal menu sing fresh, local, quality produce.
**OOMS:** 14 en suite (2 fmly) **CONF:** Class 30 **PARKING:** 30
**OTES:** No smoking in restaurant Closed 2 wks early Jan
**ARDS:**

Fancy a Singapore Sling? Bar staff in five star hotels should be skilled cocktail mixers.

## BUCKHURST HILL, Essex
Map 05 TQ49

### ★★★63% Roebuck
North End IG9 5QY
☎ 020 8505 4636 📠 020 8504 7826

corus

The pleasant rural appeal of the creeper-clad exterior belies the modern style of the interior here. The new restaurant features a bold colour scheme which also extends to the bar. The modern theme is carried through to the bedrooms which tend to be quite spacious and feature a good range of facilities.
**ROOMS:** 28 en suite No smoking in 10 bedrooms s £95; d £105 * **LB**
**FACILITIES:** STV Xmas **CONF:** Thtr 200 Class 60 Board 14 Del £125 *
**PARKING:** 40 **NOTES:** Civ Wed 120
**CARDS:**

### Express by Holiday Inn
High Rd IG9 5HT
☎ 0800 897121

Express
by Holiday Inn

A modern budget hotel offering comfortable accommodation in refreshing, spacious and comprehensively equipped bedrooms, en suite bathrooms with power showers and continental buffet breakfast included in the room rate. Suitable for business travellers or families. For further details and the Express by Holiday Inn phone number, consult the Hotel Groups page.
**ROOMS:** 49 rms

## BUCKINGHAM, Buckinghamshire
Map 04 SP63

### ★★★72% @@ Villiers
3 Castle St MK18 1BS
☎ 01280 822444 📠 01280 822113
e-mail: villiers@villiers-hotels.demon.co.uk
Built around a cobbled courtyard, this comfortable, welcoming hotel boasts a state-of-the-art conference facility. The roomy bedrooms provide high levels of comfort and are very well-equipped. Split-level suites and new purpose-designed Executive rooms are also available. There are relaxing sitting areas and a

*continued on p144*

BUCKINGHAM, continued

choice of contrasting bars, while Henry's Restaurant offers a fine dining experience.
**ROOMS:** 38 en suite (25 fmly) **FACILITIES:** STV Free membership of nearby leisure club entertainment **CONF:** Thtr 250 Class 100 Board 60 **SERVICES:** Lift **PARKING:** 53 **NOTES:** No dogs (ex guide dogs) **CARDS:**

*See advert on opposite page*

### ★★★65% Buckingham Four Pillars Hotel

Buckingham Ring Rd South MK18 1RY
☎ 01280 822622 🖹 01280 823074
e-mail: buckingham@four-pillars.co.uk
***Dir:*** *on A421 near junct with A413*
A purpose built hotel, designed with the needs of the business traveller in mind, provides extensive conference facilities and large, well-appointed bedrooms with plenty of desk space. The open-plan restaurant and bar offers a good range of dishes including a carvery on selected days. The well equipped leisure suite is popular with guests.
**ROOMS:** 70 en suite (6 fmly) No smoking in 24 bedrooms s £69-£85; d £79-£95 * **LB** **FACILITIES:** STV Indoor swimming (H) Sauna Solarium Gym Jacuzzi Steam room entertainment Xmas **CONF:** Thtr 160 Class 90 Board 50 **PARKING:** 120 **NOTES:** Closed 28/29 Dec Civ Wed 160 **CARDS:**

BUCKLAND (NEAR BROADWAY), Gloucestershire — Map 04 SP03

## Premier Collection

### ★★★ ◎◎◎ Buckland Manor

RELAIS & CHATEAUX.

WR12 7LY
☎ 01386 852626 🖹 01386 853557
e-mail: buckland-manor-uk@msn.com
***Dir:*** *off B4632*
Buckland Manor is a grand 13th-century manor house which stands in extensive grounds with beautiful gardens. Crackling log fires warm the wonderful lounges; indeed, everything here is geared to encourage rest and relaxation. Bedrooms and public areas are furnished with high quality pieces and decorated in keeping with the style of the manor. The cuisine continues to impress, with high quality produce skilfully utilised to produce a blend of traditional favourites with more modern interpretations.
**ROOMS:** 13 en suite (2 fmly) s £200-£345; d £210-£355 (incl. bkfst) * **FACILITIES:** STV Outdoor swimming (H) Tennis (hard) Croquet lawn Putting green Xmas **PARKING:** 30 **NOTES:** No dogs No children 12yrs No smoking in restaurant **CARDS:**

BUCKLOW HILL, Cheshire — Map 07 SJ

### Premier Lodge (Knutsford North)

Bucklow Hill WA16 6RD
☎ 0870 700 1480 🖹 0870 700 1481
***Dir:*** *M56 junct 7, take A556 towards Northwich & M6. Lodge approx 1m at 1st traffic lights on left*
Premier Lodge offers modern, well-equipped, en suite accommodation suitable for both business and leisure travellers. Meals can be taken at the adjacent popular restaurant and bar, which is fully licensed. For further details, consult the Hotel Groups page.
**ROOMS:** 66 en suite d £46 * **CONF:** Thtr 60 Board 30

BUDE, Cornwall & Isles of Scilly — Map 02 SS

### ★★★71% Falcon

Breakwater Rd EX23 8SD
☎ 01288 352005 🖹 01288 356359
e-mail: reception@falconhotel.com
***Dir:*** *turn off A39 into Bude and follow road to Widemouth Bay. Hotel is on right as you cross over canal bridge*

The Falcon Hotel is located on the edge of the town in delightful gardens. An extensive range of menus, including a selection of locally caught fish and a range of vegetarian options, is offered in the elegant restaurant, with a selection of bar meals also available. An impressive function room has recently been added.
**ROOMS:** 27 en suite (5 fmly) s £40-£50; d £80-£84 (incl. bkfst) * **LB** **FACILITIES:** Spa STV Croquet lawn Mini gym **CONF:** Thtr 200 Class 5 Board 50 **PARKING:** 40 **NOTES:** No smoking in restaurant RS Christmas Day Civ Wed 150 **CARDS:**

*See advert on opposite page*

### ★★★70% Hartland

Hartland Ter EX23 8JY
☎ 01288 355661 🖹 01288 355664
e-mail: hartlandhotel@aol.com
***Dir:*** *Turn off A39 to Bude follow signs to town centre, turn left into Hartland terrace. Hotel located opposite Boots chemist*
Conveniently located between the town centre and the beaches, the long-established Hartland Hotel has a loyal following. An interesting fixed-price menu is served in the comfortably furnished restaurant, and entertainment is provided in the ballroom on certain evenings during high season.
**ROOMS:** 28 en suite (2 fmly) No smoking in 8 bedrooms s £41-£52; d £72-£86 (incl. bkfst) * **LB** **FACILITIES:** Outdoor swimming (H) entertainment ch fac Xmas **SERVICES:** Lift **PARKING:** 30 **NOTES:** No smoking in restaurant Closed mid Nov-Etr (ex Xmas & New Year)

TV dinner? Room service at three stars and above.

B

**★★68% Camelot**
Downs View EX23 8RE
☎ 01288 352361 🖷 01288 355470
e-mail: stay@camelot-hotel.co.uk
***Dir:*** *turn off A39 into Bude, right at rdbt, through one-way system keep left, hotel on left overlooking golf course*

Overlooking Bude and Cornwall Golf Club, this Edwardian property has an enviable reputation among the golfing fraternity. Newly refurbished public areas include a well-furnished lounge and bar, the latter featuring golfing ties from around the world. Smart bedrooms are light, airy and furnished in a contemporary style, equally suited to both business and leisure guests.
**ROOMS:** 24 en suite (3 fmly) s £47-£49; d £74-£78 (incl. bkfst) * **LB** **FACILITIES:** Darts Pool table Table tennis **PARKING:** 21 **NOTES:** No dogs (ex guide dogs) No smoking in restaurant
**CARDS:**

**★★66% Atlantic House**
17-18 Summerleaze Crescent EX23 8HJ
☎ 01288 352451 🖷 01288 356666
e-mail: enq@atlantichousehotel.co.uk
***Dir:*** *leave M5 junct 31, follow A30 dual carriageway to bypass Okehampton, follow signs to Bude via Halwill and Holsworthy*

This relaxed and personally run hotel is set in a quiet area overlooking the beach. Bedrooms are comfortable and well maintained; some face the sea and there are some 'teenager rooms'. An imaginative, well-balanced fixed-price menu is served in the restaurant. The hotel is renowned for well-supervised activity holidays.
**ROOMS:** 15 en suite (2 fmly) No smoking in all bedrooms s £31.70-£33.60; d £48.60-£59.20 (incl. bkfst) * **LB** **FACILITIES:** Games room Multi-activity outdoor sports **PARKING:** 10 **NOTES:** No dogs (ex guide dogs) No smoking in restaurant Closed 11 Nov-2 Mar
**CARDS:**

Bad hair day? Hairdryers in all rooms three stars and above.

B

BUDE, continued

**★★66% *Penarvor***
Crooklets Beach EX23 8NE
☎ 01288 352036 📠 01288 355027
e-mail: hotel.penarvor@mcmail.com
***Dir:*** *From A39 towards Bude for 1.5m at 2nd rdbt turn R, pass shops, at top of hill turn L signed Crooklets Beach*
Adjacent to the golf course, within a short walk of the town centre and overlooking Crooklets Beach, this family owned hotel benefits from a relaxed and friendly atmosphere. Bedrooms vary in size but are all equipped to a similar standard. An interesting selection of dishes, using fresh local produce, is available in the restaurant; bar meals are also provided.
**ROOMS:** 16 en suite (6 fmly) No smoking in 4 bedrooms **PARKING:** 20 **NOTES:** No smoking in restaurant **CARDS:**

**★★65% Maer Lodge**
Maer Down Rd, Crooklets Beach EX23 8NG
☎ 01288 353306 📠 01288 354005
e-mail: maerlodgehotel@btinternet.com
***Dir:*** *leave A39 at Stratton to Bude 1m. Go right at mini rdbt into The Strand and up Belle Vue past shops. Bear left at Somerfield to Crooklets Beach, hotel to right*
MINOTEL Great Britain
With views over the Downs and surrounding countryside, this long established, family-run hotel is quietly located. Traditionally furnished public areas are comfortable and include a convivial bar and spacious lounge. In the dining room a choice from a short fixed-price menu is offered. Bedrooms are soundly furnished and appointed, some having the added bonus of lovely views.
**ROOMS:** 19 en suite (4 fmly) No smoking in all bedrooms s £32-£36; d £58-£66 (incl. bkfst) * **LB** **FACILITIES:** STV Putting green Xmas **CONF:** Thtr 60 Class 40 Board 15 Del from £35 * **PARKING:** 15 **NOTES:** No smoking in restaurant **CARDS:**

**★★65% Stamford Hill Hotel**
Stratton EX23 9AY
☎ 01288 352709 📠 01288 352709
e-mail: reception@stamfordhillhotel.co.uk
***Dir:*** *on the edge of the village of Stratton, just off A39, brown tourist signs direct to the hotel*
Built on the site of the Battle of Stamford Hill, this Georgian manor is set in beautiful woodland and gardens, only a mile from Bude's sandy beaches. The hotel offers comfortable, well-equipped bedrooms, many with views over the surrounding countryside. There is a spacious lounge, a relaxing bar and a restaurant serving carefully prepared meals.
**ROOMS:** 14 en suite (5 fmly) No smoking in 1 bedroom s £47-£52; d £75-£84 (incl. bkfst & dinner) * **LB** **FACILITIES:** Outdoor swimming (H) Tennis (grass) Sauna Badminton court Xmas **PARKING:** 20 **NOTES:** No smoking in restaurant Closed 18 Dec-18 Jan **CARDS:**

BURFORD, Oxfordshire Map 04 SP21

**★★★73% ®® The Lamb Inn**
Sheep St OX18 4LR
☎ 01993 823155 📠 01993 822228
***Dir:*** *off Burford High Street*
A wonderful old inn set in a cottage garden in a pretty Cotswold village. Bedrooms retain the character of the building and are well-equipped with tasteful furnishings and fabrics. Flagstone floors and log fires set the tone in the three comfortable lounges, furnished with sumptuous sofas and fireside chairs. Meals are taken in the formal dining room, where guests can savour the fine cuisine.

**ROOMS:** 15 en suite s £70-£85; d £105-£125 (incl. bkfst) * **LB** **PARKING:** 6 **NOTES:** No smoking in restaurant Closed 25-26 Dec **CARDS:**

**★★★72% ® The Bay Tree**
12-14 Sheep St OX18 4LW
☎ 01993 822791 📠 01993 823008
e-mail: bookings@cotswold-inns-hotels.co.uk
***Dir:*** *off A40, down hill onto A361 towards Burford, Sheep St 1st left*
This historic inn retains many original features; the main staircase with its heraldic decor is particularly impressive. The bedrooms are individually decorated with traditional style furnishings, and equipped to a high standard. A number of rooms feature four-poster and half-tester beds, and the cottage rooms overlook an attractive walled garden.
**ROOMS:** 7 en suite 14 annexe en suite (1 fmly) s £99; d £135 (incl. bkfst) * **LB** **FACILITIES:** Croquet lawn Xmas **CONF:** Thtr 40 Class 12 Board 25 Del £145 * **PARKING:** 50 **NOTES:** No smoking in restaurant Civ Wed 70 **CARDS:**

**★★★65% Cotswold Gateway**
Cheltenham Rd OX18 4HX
☎ 01993 822695 📠 01993 823600
e-mail: cotswold.gateway@dial.pipex.com
***Dir:*** *situated at the roundabout on the A40 Oxford/Cheltenham at junct with A361*

Situated on the A40 route to Cheltenham, this friendly hotel is a convenient base from which to explore the Cotswolds. Bedrooms are decorated with pleasant fabrics and attractive furnishings, the two four-poster rooms are particularly good. There is a separate coffee shop and an elegant restaurant where traditional and modern dishes are served.
**ROOMS:** 13 en suite 8 annexe en suite (2 fmly) No smoking in all bedrooms s fr £70; d fr £95 (incl. bkfst) * **LB** **FACILITIES:** Xmas **CONF:** Thtr 40 Class 20 Board 24 Del from £93 * **PARKING:** 60 **NOTES:** No dogs (ex guide dogs) No smoking in restaurant **CARDS:**

★★★60% ❀ **The Inn For All Seasons**
The Barringtons OX18 4TN
☎ 01451 844324 🖷 01451 844375
e-mail: sharp@innforallseasons.com
***Dir:*** *3m W of Burford on A40*
A warm, friendly welcome awaits at this 16th-century, family-run coaching inn. Comfortable rooms are steadily being upgraded with bright, attractive decor. The interior of the hotel, whilst providing modern amenities, retains original fireplaces, oak beams and period furniture. A good selection of bar meals is available at lunchtime, in addition to a full evening restaurant menu.
**ROOMS:** 9 en suite 1 annexe en suite (2 fmly) s £37.50-£49.50; d £70-£85 (incl. bkfst) * **LB** **FACILITIES:** STV Clay pigeon shooting Xmas **CONF:** Thtr 25 Class 30 Board 30 Del £115 * **PARKING:** 62
**CARDS:**

★★63% ***Golden Pheasant***
91 High St OX18 4QA
☎ 01993 823223 🖷 01993 822621
***Dir:*** *leave M40 at junct 8 and follow signs A40 Cheltenham into Burford*
This attractive old inn on Burford's main street has parts that date back to the 16th century. Bedrooms can be a little compact but all are well-furnished; attractive fabrics and period furniture are combined with useful extras. Meals can either be taken in the bar or in the restaurant with its solid-fuel stove.
**ROOMS:** 12 rms (11 en suite) (1 fmly) **PARKING:** 12 **NOTES:** No smoking in restaurant **CARDS:**

⌂ ***Travelodge***
Bury Barn OX18 4JF
☎ 01993 822699 🖷 01993 822699
***Dir:*** *A40*
Travelodge offers good quality, good value, modern accommodation. Ideal for families, the spacious, en suite bedrooms include remote-control TV, tea and coffee-making facilities, luxury beds and free morning newspaper. Meals can be taken at the nearby family restaurant. For further details and the Travelodge phone number, consult the Hotel Groups page.

**ROOMS:** 40 en suite

## BURLEY, Hampshire
Map 04 SU20

★★★69% **Burley Manor**
Ringwood Rd BH24 4BS
☎ 01425 403522 🖷 01425 403227
e-mail: burley.manor@forestdale.com
***Dir:*** *leave A31 at Burley signpost, hotel 3m on left*
Set in extensive grounds, this 18th-century hotel enjoys a relaxed ambience and a peaceful setting. Half of the well equipped, comfortable bedrooms, including several with four-posters, are located in the main house and the remainder, many of which have balconies, in the adjacent converted stable block and new wing. Riding can be arranged. Cosy public rooms are warmed by log fires in winter.
**ROOMS:** 21 en suite 17 annexe en suite (3 fmly) No smoking in 4 bedrooms s £75-£85; d £130-£150 (incl. bkfst & dinner) * **LB** **FACILITIES:** Outdoor swimming (H) Fishing Riding Croquet lawn Xmas **CONF:** Thtr 60 Class 40 Board 40 Del £115 * **PARKING:** 60 **NOTES:** Civ Wed **CARDS:**

★★★63% **Moorhill House**
BH24 4AG
☎ 01425 403285 🖷 01425 403715
e-mail: info@carehotels.co.uk
***Dir:*** *follow A31 for approx 5m pass two shell gardens on either side of the road & sign for Burley, into village. Road opposite Queens Head then 1st left*
Originally built in 1861 as a grand gentleman's residence, this relaxed and friendly hotel is situated in the heart of the New Forest. With over three acres of gardens, this is the ideal place for a peaceful getaway. Bedrooms vary in size and character, whilst facilities include both heated indoor pool and sauna.
**ROOMS:** 24 en suite (7 fmly) s £73-£80; d £115-£130 (incl. bkfst) * **LB** **FACILITIES:** Indoor swimming (H) Sauna Croquet lawn Putting green badminton (Apr-Sep) ch fac Xmas **CONF:** Thtr 22 Class 24 Board 22 Del from £90 * **PARKING:** 30 **NOTES:** No smoking in restaurant
**CARDS:**

## BURNHAM, Buckinghamshire
Map 04 SU98

★★★71% ❀ **Grovefield**
Taplow Common Rd SL1 8LP
☎ 01628 603131 🖷 01628 668078

Grovefield is set in spacious grounds, and is situated conveniently close to Heathrow and Gatwick. Bedrooms are spacious and attractively decorated. The restaurant is a comfortable place to eat rosette worthy cuisine and the bar lounge has been refurbished. Its location near the golf course makes it ideal for weekend breaks.
**ROOMS:** 40 en suite (5 fmly) No smoking in 24 bedrooms s £120-£150; d £130-£160 * **LB** **FACILITIES:** STV Fishing Croquet lawn Putting green Xmas **CONF:** Thtr 250 Class 80 Board 80 Del from £195 * **SERVICES:** Lift **PARKING:** 155 **NOTES:** No smoking in restaurant Civ Wed 200 **CARDS:**

★★★67% ❀ **Burnham Beeches**
Grove Rd SL1 8DP
☎ 01628 429955 🖷 01628 603994
***Dir:*** *follow A355 towards Slough. Straight on at 1st rbt, right at 2nd and right at 3rd then follow signs to hotel*
In its own grounds, this extended Georgian manor house stands on the fringes of woodland convenient for the M4 and M40. Spacious bedrooms are comfortable, quiet and well-equipped.
*continued on p148*

BURNHAM, continued

Facilities include a fitness centre, pool and a cosy lounge bar where all-day snacks are available.

*Burnham Beeches, Burnham*

**ROOMS:** 82 en suite (19 fmly) No smoking in 18 bedrooms s £45-£140; d £90-£150 * LB **FACILITIES:** STV Indoor swimming (H) Tennis (hard) Snooker Sauna Solarium Gym Croquet lawn Jacuzzi Xmas **CONF:** Thtr 180 Class 100 Board 60 Del from £150 * **SERVICES:** Lift **PARKING:** 200 **NOTES:** No dogs (ex guide dogs) Civ Wed 120 **CARDS:**

## BURNHAM MARKET, Norfolk

Map 09 TF84

### ★★74% Hoste Arms

The Green PE31 8HD
☎ 01328 738777 01328 730103
e-mail: 106504.2472@compuserve.com
***Dir:*** *signposted on B1155, 5m W of Wells-Next-the-Sea*

A stylish small hotel, with a relaxed, friendly atmosphere. Attentive service is provided in the air-conditioned dining rooms and traditional pub. Bedroom sizes vary, the most recent additions are really quite palatial, and each room is thoughtfully equipped and tastefully appointed. Future plans include the development of another wing of deluxe bedrooms and additional conservatory lounge areas.

**ROOMS:** (1 fmly) s fr £66; d fr £90 (incl. bkfst) * LB **FACILITIES:** Xmas **CONF:** Thtr 30 Class 22 Board 24 **PARKING:** 60 **CARDS:**

Early start? Hotels at all star levels should provide in-room alarm clocks and/or alarm calls.

## BURNLEY, Lancashire

Map 07 SD83

### ★★★74% Oaks

Colne Rd, Reedley BB10 2LF
☎ 01282 414141 01282 433401
e-mail: oaks@shireinns.co.uk

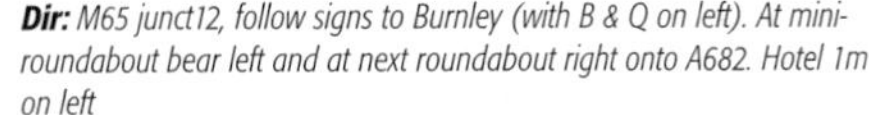
SHIRE
INNS

***Dir:*** *M65 junct12, follow signs to Burnley (with B & Q on left). At mini-roundabout bear left and at next roundabout right onto A682. Hotel 1m on left*

The friendly team here offer great northern hospitality in this former Victorian coffee merchant's house. The hotel offers traditional public areas and modern well-equipped bedrooms. Gym, pool, sauna and steam rooms are all available in the leisure club on site.

**ROOMS:** 50 en suite (10 fmly) No smoking in 20 bedrooms s £96; d £116 (incl. bkfst) * LB **FACILITIES:** STV Indoor swimming (H) Sauna Solarium Gym Jacuzzi Steam room Xmas **CONF:** Thtr 120 Class 48 Board 60 Del £120 * **PARKING:** 110 **NOTES:** Civ Wed 150 **CARDS:**

### ★★★70% Kyriad Sparrow Hawk

Church St BB11 2DN
☎ 01282 421551 01282 456506
***Dir:*** *on Inner Ring Road (A682), opposite St Peters Church*

This friendly Victorian hotel provides comfortable accommodation. Rooms are modern, well-equipped and contain many thoughtful extras. Smart public areas include the bright Mediterranean style Smithies Café Bar and Farriers Restaurant, as well as a traditional real ale bar.

**ROOMS:** 36 en suite (2 fmly) No smoking in 18 bedrooms s £53; d £59.50 (incl. bkfst) * LB **FACILITIES:** STV entertainment Xmas **CONF:** Thtr 80 Class 40 Board 30 Del from £59 * **PARKING:** 24 **NOTES:** No dogs (ex guide dogs) **CARDS:**

### ★★★66% *Rosehill House*

Rosehill Av BB11 2PW
☎ 01282 453931 01282 455628
e-mail: rhhotel@provider.co.uk
***Dir:*** *0.5m S of Burnley town centre, off the A682*

Many original features of this Grade II listed building remain, including some fine ornate ceilings. Public areas include a choice of function rooms, stylish bars, comfortable lounges and a well appointed restaurant and conservatory, where both formal and informal dishes are served by friendly staff. Bedrooms are individually furnished and thoughtfully equipped.

**ROOMS:** 30 en suite (2 fmly) No smoking in 1 bedroom **FACILITIES:** STV Snooker Gym **CONF:** Thtr 50 Class 30 Board 30 **PARKING:** 52 **NOTES:** No dogs (ex guide dogs) Civ Wed 100 **CARDS:**

**★★65% Alexander**
2 Tarleton Av, Todmorden Rd BB11 3ET
☎ 01282 422684 01282 424094
***Dir:*** *leave M65 at junct 10 and follow signs for 'Towneley Hall' to Tarleton Avenue. Hotel 100yds from Towneley Hall main entrance*
Located close to the town centre, this hotel takes pride in its dining facilities, and an extensive range of dishes can be enjoyed in the Gourmet Restaurant or in the more informal surrounds of the attractive café bar. All bedrooms are well-equipped and there are family rooms available.
**ROOMS:** 11 en suite 5 annexe en suite (2 fmly) s £35-£42; d £45-£53 (incl. bkfst) * LB **FACILITIES:** STV Xmas **CONF:** Thtr 120 Class 40 Board 45 **PARKING:** 18 **NOTES:** No dogs (ex guide dogs)
**CARDS:**

**Travelodge**
Cavalry Barracks, Barracks Rd BB11 4AS
☎ 01282 416039 01282 416039
***Dir:*** *junc A671/A679*
Travelodge offers good quality, good value, modern accommodation. Ideal for families, the spacious, en suite bedrooms include remote-control TV, tea and coffee-making facilities, luxury beds and free morning newspaper. Meals can be taken at the nearby family restaurant. For further details and the Travelodge phone number, consult the Hotel Groups page.

**ROOMS:** 32 en suite

## BURNSALL, North Yorkshire — Map 07 SE06

**★★67% Red Lion Hotel**
By the Bridge BD23 6BU
☎ 01756 720204 01756 720292
e-mail: redlion@daelnet.co.uk
***Dir:*** *on B6160 between Grassington and Bolton Abbey*
This charming 16th-century Dales inn stands by a bridge over the River Wharfe - guests are free to fish the hotel's own stretch of water. Attractive bedrooms are comfortable, and the homely lounge is complemented by a traditional bar. The intimate restaurant makes excellent use of fresh local ingredients; breakfast is especially recommended.
**ROOMS:** 7 en suite 4 annexe en suite (2 fmly) s £50-£80; d £100-£160 (incl. bkfst) * LB **FACILITIES:** Fishing Xmas **CONF:** Thtr 30 Class 10 Board 20 **PARKING:** 80 **NOTES:** No dogs No smoking in restaurant Civ Wed 50 **CARDS:**

## BURRINGTON (NEAR PORTSMOUTH ARMS STATION), Devon — Map 03 SS61

### Premier Collection

**★★★ Northcote Manor**
EX37 9LZ
☎ 01769 560501 01769 560770
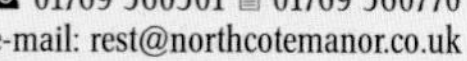
e-mail: rest@northcotemanor.co.uk
***Dir:*** *turn off A377 opposite Portsmouth Arms Pub, into hotel's own drive marked Northcote Manor. Do not enter Burrington village*
Standing in 20 acres of grounds, this beautiful stone-built, gabled house has views over peaceful countryside. Accommodation is extremely comfortable and all modern facilities have been provided without compromising the elegance of the architecture. Award winning cuisine can be enjoyed in the Manor House Restaurant.

**ROOMS:** 11 en suite s £124-£188; d £165-£250 (incl. bkfst) * LB **FACILITIES:** STV Tennis (hard) Croquet lawn Xmas **CONF:** Thtr 20 Class 20 Board 20 Del from £150 * **PARKING:** 20 **NOTES:** No children 12yrs No smoking in restaurant Civ Wed 40
**CARDS:**

## BURTON MOTORWAY SERVICE AREA (M6), Cumbria — Map 07 SD57

**Travelodge**
Burton in Kendal LA6 1JF
☎ 01524 781234
***Dir:*** *between junct35/36 southbound M6*
Travelodge offers good quality, good value, modern accommodation. Ideal for families, the spacious, en suite bedrooms include remote-control TV, tea and coffee-making facilities, luxury beds and free morning newspaper. Meals can be taken at the nearby family restaurant. For further details and the Travelodge phone number, consult the Hotel Groups page.

**ROOMS:** 40 en suite

## BURTON UPON TRENT, Staffordshire — Map 08 SK22

**Express by Holiday Inn**
2nd Av, Centrum 100 DE14 2WF
☎ 01283 504300 504301
e-mail: info@exhiburton.co.uk
***Dir:*** *take A38 Branston exit. Follow signs A5121 Town Centre. At rdbt of McDonalds, turn left into 2nd Avenue. Hotel on left*

A modern budget hotel offering comfortable accommodation in refreshing, spacious and comprehensively equipped bedrooms, en suite bathrooms with power showers and continental buffet breakfast included in the room rate. Suitable for business

continued on p150

## BURTON UPON TRENT, continued

travellers or families. For further details and the Express by Holiday Inn phone number, consult the Hotel Groups page.
**ROOMS:** 82 en suite (incl. cont bkfst) d £49-£59 * **CONF:** Thtr 60 Class 30 Board 30

## BURTONWOOD MOTORWAY SERVICE AREA (M62), Cheshire — Map 07 SJ59

### Welome Lodge

Burtonwood Services (M62), Great Sankey
WA5 3AX
☎ 01925 710376 📠 01925 710378
e-mail: burtonwood.hotel@welcomebreak.co.uk
***Dir:*** *between junc 7 & 9 M62 westbound*
This modern building offers accommodation in smart, spacious and well-equipped bedrooms, suitable for families and business travellers, and all with en suite bathrooms. Refreshments may be taken at the nearby family restaurant. For further details and the Welcome Break phone number, consult the Hotel Groups page.
**ROOMS:** 39 en suite s £39.95-£49.95; d £39.95-£49.95 *
**CONF:** Class 10

## BURWARDSLEY, Cheshire — Map 07 SJ55

### ★★66% Pheasant Inn

Higher Burwardsley CH3 9PF
☎ 01829 770434 📠 01829 771097
e-mail: the pheasantinn@aol.com
***Dir:*** *from A41, left for Tattenhall, once there right at 1st junct & left at 2nd to Higher Burwardsley, as far as post office then left, hotel is signposted*
This 300-year-old inn is set high in the Peckforton Hills, with spectacular views over the Cheshire plain. Well equipped, comfortable bedrooms are housed in an adjacent converted barn. Food is served either in the restaurant or in the traditional beamed bar. Real fires are lit in the winter months.
**ROOMS:** 2 en suite 8 annexe en suite (2 fmly) No smoking in all bedrooms s fr £55; d fr £80 (incl. bkfst) * **PARKING:** 35 **NOTES:** No dogs (ex guide dogs) No smoking in restaurant
**CARDS:**

## BURY, Greater Manchester — Map 07 SD81

### ★★★66% Bolholt Country Park

Walshaw Rd BL8 1PU
☎ 0161 762 4000 📠 0161 762 4100
e-mail: enquiries@bolholt.co.uk
***Dir:*** *M60 junct 17 for Whitefield, A56 (Bury) for 4m, follow signs for A58 (Bolton). Take 3rd lane at car showroom signed Tottington. Left at pub, left*

Situated in pleasant parkland and secluded gardens, this former mill owner's house provides comfortable accommodation, in modern and well-equipped bedrooms. The leisure club includes a fashionable café bar. Conference and banqueting facilities are available and the setting is ideal for weddings.
**ROOMS:** 65 en suite (13 fmly) No smoking in 4 bedrooms
**FACILITIES:** STV Indoor swimming (H) Fishing Squash Sauna Solarium Gym Jacuzzi Fitness & leisure centre entertainment Xmas **CONF:** Thtr 300 Class 120 Board 40 **PARKING:** 300 **NOTES:** No dogs (ex guide dogs) **CARDS:**

Arriving late? Four and five star hotels have night porters to assist with your luggage, and 24-hour room service.

## BURY ST EDMUNDS, Suffolk — Map 05 TL86

### ★★★71% Angel

Angel Hill IP33 1LT
☎ 01284 714000 📠 01284 714001
e-mail: sales@theangel.co.uk
***Dir:*** *from A134 turn left at rdbt into Northgate St, straight on to T junct with traffic lights, right into Mustow St, left onto Angel Hill, on right*

One of the Angel's more notable guests over the last 400 years was Charles Dickens who is reputed to have written part of the *Pickwick Papers* whilst in residence. Today the hotel offers a range of individually designed bedrooms, including a selection of four poster rooms and a suite.
**ROOMS:** 64 en suite (4 fmly) No smoking in 6 bedrooms s £71-£81; d £91-£121 * **LB** **FACILITIES:** STV entertainment Xmas **CONF:** Thtr 80 Class 20 Board 30 **SERVICES:** Lift **PARKING:** 54 **NOTES:** No smoking in restaurant Civ Wed 100 **CARDS:**

*See advert on opposite page*

### ★★★70% The Priory

Tollgate IP32 6EH
☎ 01284 766181 📠 01284 767604
e-mail: reservations@prioryhotel.co.uk
***Dir:*** *off A1101 towards Mildenhall*
This delightful hotel has a country house atmosphere. There are two restaurant areas, a conservatory, dining room and a bustling bar. A range of appetising dishes is available from the carte and fixed-priced menus. Attractively furnished bedrooms are located in the main house and in the garden wings.
**ROOMS:** 9 en suite 30 annexe en suite (1 fmly) No smoking in 15 bedrooms s £75-£83; d £92-£113 (incl. bkfst) * **LB** **FACILITIES:** Xmas **CONF:** Thtr 40 Class 20 Board 20 Del £112 * **PARKING:** 60 **NOTES:** No smoking in restaurant **CARDS:**

### ★★★70% Ravenwood Hall

Rougham IP30 9JA
☎ 01359 270345 📠 01359 270788
e-mail: enquiries@ravenwoodhall.co.uk
***Dir:*** *3m E off A14*
Fifteenth-century building situated amid seven acres of woodland and gardens. The property has many original features including carved timbers and inglenook fireplaces. The generously proportioned bedrooms are attractively decorated, tastefully furnished and equipped with many thoughtful touches. There is an elegant restaurant and a smart lounge bar with an open fire.
**ROOMS:** 7 en suite 7 annexe en suite No smoking in all bedrooms s £71-£95; d £93-£129 (incl. bkfst) * **LB** **FACILITIES:** Outdoor swimming (H) Tennis Riding Croquet lawn Shooting & fishing Xmas **CONF:** Thtr 200 Class 80 Board 40 Del from £106.95 * **PARKING:** 150 **NOTES:** No smoking in restaurant Civ Wed 200
**CARDS:**

### ★★★66% Butterfly

Moreton Hall IP32 7BW
☎ 01284 760884 📠 01284 755476
e-mail: burybutterfly@lineone.net

***Dir:** from A14 take Bury East exit and at rndbt take exit for Moreton Hall. Left at next rndbt*

A modern hotel situated just off the A14 on the edge of town. The comfortable bedrooms are well-suited to business travellers. The hotel offers a variety of rooms that include some on the ground floor, ladies' rooms, studio rooms and those adapted for disabled guests. Walt's Restaurant and Bar offers a comprehensive carte and daily-changing menus, in addition to room and lounge service selections.

**ROOMS:** 65 en suite (2 fmly) No smoking in 10 bedrooms s £63-£88; d £70-£97 (incl. bkfst) * **LB** **CONF:** Thtr 40 Class 21 Board 22 Del £97.50 * **PARKING:** 85 **NOTES:** No dogs (ex guide dogs)
**CARDS:**

## BUTTERMERE, Cumbria — Map 11 NY11

### ★★72% Bridge

CA13 9UZ
☎ 017687 70252 📠 017687 70215
e-mail: enquires@bridge-hotel.com

***Dir:** take A66 around town centre, turn off at Braithwaite & head over the Newlands pass. Follow signs for Buttermere. Hotel in village*

A relaxed and welcoming atmosphere prevails at this long established family-run hotel in the centre of Buttermere. Bedrooms, including some superior and four-poster rooms, are comfortable and the majority enjoy superb views. Televisions are not provided due to poor reception. Inviting public areas include a delightful sitting room, and real ales and a good range of bar meals are served in the informal bar. A five-course set price menu is available in the elegant restaurant.

**ROOMS:** 21 en suite No smoking in 10 bedrooms s £55-£65; d £110-£130 (incl. bkfst & dinner) * **LB** **FACILITIES:** no TV in bdrms ch fac Xmas **PARKING:** 60 **NOTES:** No smoking in restaurant
**CARDS:**

## BUXTON, Derbyshire — Map 07 SK07

### ★★★★64% Palace Hotel

PARAMOUNT
GROUP OF HOTELS

Palace Rd SK17 6AG
☎ 01298 22001 📠 01298 72131
e-mail: palace@paramount-hotels.co.uk

***Dir:** in town centre adjacent to railway station*

There are fine views over the town and surrounding hills from this landmark Victorian hotel. The bedrooms are spacious and

*continued on p152*

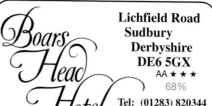

BUXTON, continued

comfortable. Public rooms include a choice of bars, a library lounge and a spacious and elegant restaurant.
**ROOMS:** 122 en suite (12 fmly) No smoking in 33 bedrooms s £84-£105; d £108-£120 (incl. bkfst) * **LB** **FACILITIES:** STV Indoor swimming (H) Sauna Solarium Gym Croquet lawn Putting green Xmas **CONF:** Thtr 350 Class 125 Board 60 Del from £105 * **SERVICES:** Lift **PARKING:** 200 **NOTES:** No smoking in restaurant
**CARDS:**

### ★★★76% Best Western Lee Wood

The Park SK17 6TQ
☎ 01298 23002 01298 23228
e-mail: leewoodhotel@btinternet.com
***Dir:*** *NE on A5004, 300mtrs beyond the Devonshire Royal Hospital*
This elegant Georgian hotel offers high standards of comfort and hospitality. Individually furnished bedrooms are generally spacious, with all the expected modern conveniences. There is a choice of two bars, two comfortable lounges and a conservatory restaurant. Quality cooking is a feature of the hotel, as is good service and fine hospitality.
**ROOMS:** 35 en suite 5 annexe en suite (4 fmly) No smoking in 14 bedrooms s £65-£80; d £95-£110 * **LB** **FACILITIES:** Xmas **CONF:** Thtr 120 Class 65 Board 40 **SERVICES:** Lift **PARKING:** 50
**NOTES:** Civ Wed 160 **CARDS:**

### ★★★65% Buckingham Hotel

1 Burlington Rd SK17 9AS
☎ 01298 70481 01298 72186
e-mail: frontdesk@buckinghamhotel.co.uk
***Dir:*** *follow signs for Pavilion Gardens/Pavilion Gardens Car Park. Hotel opposite car park at junct of St Johns & Burlington Rd*
A welcoming hotel close to the Pavilion Gardens, the Buckingham offers pleasant, modern public areas which include Ramsay's Bar, serving bar meals and real ales, and the popular carvery, serving grills and other dishes. Bedrooms are spacious and comfortable, many overlook the Pavilion Gardens.
**ROOMS:** 36 en suite (13 fmly) No smoking in 27 bedrooms s £50-£65; d £70-£85 (incl. bkfst) * **LB** **FACILITIES:** STV Xmas **CONF:** Thtr 40 Class 20 Board 16 Del from £75 * **SERVICES:** Lift **PARKING:** 36
**NOTES:** No smoking in restaurant Civ Wed 75
**CARDS:**

### ★★64% Portland Hotel & Park Restaurant

32 St John's Rd SK17 6XQ
☎ 01298 71493 22462 01298 27464
e-mail: brian@portland-hotel.freeserve.co.uk
***Dir:*** *on A53 opposite the Pavilion and Gardens*
This popular hotel is situated near the famous Opera House and the Pavilion Gardens. Lounge and a newly refurbished bar provide comfortable and relaxing areas, while the Park Restaurant, housed in the conservatory, specialises in traditional English dishes.
**ROOMS:** 22 en suite (3 fmly) No smoking in 3 bedrooms s £35-£55; d £50-£75 (incl. bkfst) * **LB** **FACILITIES:** STV Xmas **CONF:** Thtr 50 Class 30 Board 25 Del from £65 * **PARKING:** 18 **NOTES:** No smoking in restaurant **CARDS:**

## CADNAM, Hampshire — Map 04 SU21

### ★★★71% *Bartley Lodge*

Lyndhurst Rd SO40 7DU
☎ 023 8081 2248 023 8081 2075
e-mail: info@carehotels.co.uk
***Dir:*** *leave M27 junct 1, at 1st rdbt take 1st exit, at 2nd rdbt take 3rd exit onto A337. On joining this road hotel sign is on left*
This 18th-century former hunting lodge is very quietly situated, yet just minutes from the M27/A35 junction. Rooms vary in size but all are well-equipped. There is a grand entrance hall, cosy bar and an indoor pool with sauna and fitness suite. The Crystal dining room serves very good cuisine.
**ROOMS:** 31 en suite (14 fmly) **FACILITIES:** Indoor swimming (H) Tennis (hard) Sauna Gym Croquet lawn ch fac **CONF:** Thtr 60 Class 40 Board 40 **PARKING:** 60 **NOTES:** No smoking in restaurant Civ Wed 100
**CARDS:**

## CALNE, Wiltshire — Map 03 ST97

### ★★★64% Lansdowne Strand

The Strand SN11 0EH
☎ 01249 812488 01249 815323
e-mail: reservations@lansdownestrand.co.uk
***Dir:*** *on A4*
In the centre of the market town, this former 16th-century coaching inn still retains many period features. Individually decorated bedrooms vary in size. There are two friendly bars, one offers a wide selection of ales and a cosy fireplace. Carriages Restaurant serves a carte and a fixed-price menu.
**ROOMS:** 21 en suite 5 annexe en suite (3 fmly) No smoking in 4 bedrooms s £67-£77; d £78-£88 (incl. bkfst) * **LB** **FACILITIES:** Xmas **CONF:** Thtr 90 Class 28 Board 30 Del from £65 * **PARKING:** 21
**CARDS:**

## CAMBERLEY, Surrey — Map 04 SU86

### ★★★74% Frimley Hall

Lime Av GU15 2BG
☎ 0870 400 8224 01276 691253
e-mail: heritagehotels_camberley.frimley_hall@forte-hotels.com
***Dir:*** *M3 junct 3 follow signs to Bagshot (A321). Through traffic lights, left onto A30 & through Bagshot villiage. Turn left onto A325. Hotel 5th turning on right off A325*
Classic English elegance in the heart of rural Surrey, this ivy-clad Victorian manor house is set in two acres of immaculate grounds. With continued investment in the hotel, both bedrooms and public areas are looking particularly smart and feature a modern yet timeless decorative theme.
**ROOMS:** 86 en suite (17 fmly) No smoking in 33 bedrooms d £170-£220 * **LB** **FACILITIES:** Croquet lawn Putting green **CONF:** Thtr 60 Class 30 Board 40 Del from £160 * **PARKING:** 100 **NOTES:** No smoking in restaurant Civ Wed 110 **CARDS:**

### ★★★64% *Lakeside International*

Wharf Rd, Frimley Green GU16 6JR
☎ 01252 838000 & 838808 01252 837857
***Dir:*** *off A321*
This hotel, geared towards the business market, enjoys a lakeside location with noteworthy views. Bedrooms are modern, comfortable and with a range of facilities. Public areas are spacious and include a residents' lounge, bar and games room, a smart restaurant and an established health and leisure club.
**ROOMS:** 98 en suite (1 fmly) No smoking in 18 bedrooms
**FACILITIES:** STV Indoor swimming (H) Squash Snooker Sauna Solarium Gym Jacuzzi **CONF:** Thtr 100 Class 100 Board 36
**SERVICES:** Lift **PARKING:** 250 **NOTES:** No dogs (ex guide dogs) No smoking in restaurant **CARDS:**

Arriving late? Four and five star hotels have night porters to assist with your luggage, and 24-hour room service.

## CAMBORNE, Cornwall & Isles of Scilly — Map 02 SW64

**★★★62% Tyacks**
27 Commercial St TR14 8LD
☎ 01209 612424 Fax 01209 612435
***Dir:*** *town centre opposite town clock*
This 18th-century former coaching inn has spacious, well furnished public areas which include a smart lounge and bar, a popular public bar and restaurant serving fixed-price and carte menus. The comfortable bedrooms are attractively decorated and well equipped; two have separate sitting areas.
**ROOMS:** 15 en suite (2 fmly) No smoking in 4 bedrooms s fr £45; d fr £65 (incl. bkfst) * **LB** **FACILITIES:** STV entertainment Xmas **PARKING:** 27 **CARDS:**

## CAMBRIDGE, Cambridgeshire — Map 05 TL45

**★★★★62% University Arms**
Regent St CB2 1AD
De Vere Hotels
☎ 01223 351241 Fax 01223 461319
e-mail: dua.sales@devere-hotels.com
***Dir:*** *M11 junct 11, follow signs for city centre for approx 3m turn right at 2nd mini rdbt, continue to set of traffic lights, turn left to Regent Street. Hotel 600yrds on right*
This historic, Victorian style hotel enjoys an enviable position in the heart of the city on the edge of Parker's Piece. Elegant public areas include the central domed lounge, a smart restaurant with its own cocktail bar, a separate bar lounge and extensive conference and banqueting facilities. Bedrooms vary in size but are all well-equipped and stylishly appointed.
**ROOMS:** 115 en suite (5 fmly) No smoking in 38 bedrooms s fr £115; d fr £145 * **LB** **FACILITIES:** STV reduced rate at local fitness centre Xmas **CONF:** Thtr 300 Class 100 Board 60 Del from £140 * **SERVICES:** Lift **PARKING:** 88 **NOTES:** No smoking in restaurant Civ Wed 200 **CARDS:**

**★★★71% Cambridge Quy Mill Hotel**
Newmarket Rd CB5 9AG
Best Western
☎ 01223 293383 Fax 01223 293770
e-mail: cambridgequy@bestwestern.co.uk
***Dir:*** *turn off A14 at junct east of Cambridge onto B1102 for 50yds, hotel entrance opposite church*
Convenient for Cambridge city centre, this 19th-century former watermill is set in water meadows. Well designed public areas include several spacious bar and lounge areas and there are informal and formal eating areas. Bedrooms are smartly appointed and brightly decorated.
**ROOMS:** 24 en suite (2 fmly) s £75-£100; d £90-£150 * **LB** **FACILITIES:** Fishing Clay shting-prior arr.only **CONF:** Thtr 80 Class 24 Board 24 Del from £125 * **PARKING:** 100 **NOTES:** No dogs (ex guide dogs) Closed 26-30 Dec Civ Wed 80
**CARDS:**

**★★★71% Gonville**
Gonville Place CB1 1LY
Best Western
☎ 01223 366611 & 221111 Fax 01223 315470
e-mail: all@gonvillehotel.co.uk

***Dir:*** *leave M11 junct 11, on A1309 follow signs to city centre, at 2nd mini rdbt turn right into Lensfield Road, straight over junct with traffic lights*
Situated on the inner ringroad, this hotel is a leisurely walk across the green to the city centre. Well-established, with regular guests and very experienced staff, the Gonville is popular for its relaxing, informal atmosphere. The air-conditioned public areas are

*continued*

cheerfully furnished, and bedrooms are well-appointed and appealing.
**ROOMS:** 64 en suite (1 fmly) No smoking in 12 bedrooms **FACILITIES:** Arrangement with gym/swimming pool **CONF:** Thtr 200 Class 100 Board 50 Del from £135 * **SERVICES:** Lift **PARKING:** 80 **NOTES:** No smoking in restaurant **CARDS:**

**★★★69% Posthouse Cambridge**
Lakeview, Bridge Rd, Impington CB4 9PH
Posthouse
☎ 0870 400 9015 Fax 01223 233426
***Dir:*** *2.5m N, on N side of rdbt junct A14/B1049*
In a rural location at the junction of the A14 and B1049, this hotel offers spacious, well-appointed bedrooms, which include a good number of superior rooms and facilities for disabled guests. There is a well-equipped health club as well as a secluded courtyard garden with children's play area. The Junction restaurant offers a range of dishes.
**ROOMS:** 165 en suite (14 fmly) No smoking in 105 bedrooms d £99-£139 * **LB** **FACILITIES:** Indoor swimming (H) Sauna Gym Jacuzzi Xmas **CONF:** Thtr 60 Class 30 Board 30 Del from £105 * **PARKING:** 200 **NOTES:** RS 24-27 Dec & 31 Dec **CARDS:**

**★★★68% Royal Cambridge**
Trumpington St CB2 1PY
ZOFFANY
☎ 01223 351631 Fax 01223 352972
e-mail: royalcambridge@zoffanyhotels.co.uk
***Dir:*** *M11 junct 11, follow signs for city centre. At 1st mini rdbt turn left into Fen Causeway, then first right for hotel*
This attractive, friendly Georgian town house offers a wide range of comfortable bedrooms, all of which are well-equipped and pleasingly decorated. Relaxing public rooms are intimate and

*continued on p154*

CAMBRIDGE, continued

include an elegant split-level restaurant serving modern British cuisine. Bar snacks and hot room service meals are also available.

*Royal Cambridge, Cambridge*

**ROOMS:** 49 en suite (8 fmly) No smoking in 28 bedrooms s £90-£107; d £100-£120 * **LB** **FACILITIES:** STV **CONF:** Thtr 120 Class 40 Board 40 Del from £120 * **SERVICES:** Lift **PARKING:** 80 **NOTES:** No smoking in restaurant Civ Wed 100 **CARDS:**

### ★★71% Arundel House

Chesterton Rd CB4 3AN
☎ 01223 367701 📠 01223 367721
e-mail: info@arundelhousehotels.co.uk
***Dir:*** *City centre on A1303, overlooking the River Cam*

Overlooking the Cam and enjoying views over open parkland, this popular hotel was originally a row of Victorian townhouses. The smart public areas feature a conservatory for informal snacks, a spacious bar and an elegant restaurant for serious dining. Bedrooms are attractive and have a special character.
**ROOMS:** 83 rms (80 en suite) 22 annexe en suite (6 fmly) No smoking in all bedrooms s £58-£83; d £73-£105 (incl. cont bkfst) * **LB** **CONF:** Thtr 50 Class 34 Board 32 Del from £92.50 * **PARKING:** 70 **NOTES:** No dogs No smoking in restaurant Closed 25-26 Dec **CARDS:**

Late for dinner? Quality Standards star rating means that last orders for dinner should be no earlier than:
★ 6.30pm ★★ 7.00pm ★★★ 8.00pm
★★★★ 9.00pm ★★★★★ 10.00pm

### ★★69% Centennial

63-71 Hills Rd CB2 1PG
☎ 01223 314652 📠 01223 315443
e-mail: reception@centennialhotel.co.uk
***Dir:*** *from M11 junct 11 take A1309 to Cambridge. Turn right onto Brooklands Ave, at the end of Ave turn left, hotel in 100yds on right*
This friendly hotel is situated close to the railway station and town centre. The public areas include a relaxing bar, a welcoming lounge and a smart restaurant. Bedrooms are generally quite spacious, well-maintained and equipped with a good range of facilities. There are several easy-access rooms on the ground floor.
**ROOMS:** 39 en suite (1 fmly) No smoking in 20 bedrooms s £70-£80; d £88-£96 (incl. bkfst) * **LB** **CONF:** Thtr 25 Class 25 Board 25 **PARKING:** 30 **NOTES:** No dogs No smoking in restaurant Closed 23 Dec-1 Jan **CARDS:**

*See advert on opposite page*

### ★★69% *Sorrento*

190-196 Cherry Hinton Rd CB1 7AN
☎ 01223 243533 📠 01223 213463
e-mail: sorrento-hotel@cb17an.freeserve.co.uk
Situated within easy striking distance of the city centre, this friendly, family-run hotel has an Italian feel in its comfortable public rooms. The bedrooms vary in size and style, all are attractively decorated and equipped with many useful extras.
**ROOMS:** 30 en suite No smoking in 15 bedrooms **FACILITIES:** STV **PARKING:** 25 **CARDS:**

### *Travelodge*

Travelodge

Fourwentways CB1 6AP
☎ 01223 839479
***Dir:*** *adjacent to Little Chef at junct A11/A1307, 5m S of Cambridge*
Travelodge offers good quality, good value, modern accommodation. Ideal for families, the spacious, en suite bedrooms include remote-control TV, tea and coffee-making facilities, luxury beds and free morning newspaper. Meals can be taken at the nearby family restaurant. For further details and the Travelodge phone number, consult the Hotel Groups page.

**ROOMS:** 40 en suite

### ○ Crowne Plaza Cambridge

CROWNE PLAZA

Downing St CB2 3DT
☎ 01223 464466 📠 01223 464440
***Dir:*** *from M11 take A14 and follow signs for City Centre Lion Yard Car Park*
At the time of going to press, the star classification for this hotel was not confirmed. Please refer to the AA internet site www.theAA.com for current information.
**ROOMS:** 196 en suite **CONF:** Thtr 250 Class 120 Board 72

CANNOCK, Staffordshire — Map 07 SJ91

### ★★★62% Roman Way

REGAL

Watling St, Hatherton WS11 1SH
☎ 01543 572121 📠 01543 502749
***Dir:*** *M6 junct 11 towards Cannock (A460), at rdbt take A5 to Telford, hotel 100yds on left. Or M6 junct 12, then A5 towards Cannock, hotel 2m on right*
Named after the Roman road on which it stands, this modern hotel provides a good standard of accommodation. Doric columns

*continued*

and marble floors feature in the reception area and Nero's Restaurant and Gilpin's Lounge provide formal or informal eating.

THE ROMAN WAY HOTEL

**ROOMS:** 56 en suite (17 fmly) No smoking in 23 bedrooms s fr £80; d £99-£120 * **LB** **FACILITIES:** STV Xmas **CONF:** Thtr 150 Class 100 Board 50 **PARKING:** 150 **NOTES:** Civ Wed 150
**CARDS:**

CANTERBURY, Kent Map 05 TR15

**★★★69% County Hotel**
High St CT1 2RX
☎ 01227 766266 📠 01227 451512
e-mail: info@county.macdonald-hotels.co.uk
MACDONALD HOTELS
***Dir:*** *M2, junct 7 follow Canterbury signs onto ringroad, at Wincheap rdbt turn into city. Left into Rosemary Ln continue into Stour St car park*
Located on the pedestrianised High Street, this hotel dates back to the 16th century. The hotel has been recently refurbished to offer high quality accommodation. Public areas include a popular coffee shop, charming first floor lounge and Sully's restaurant.
**ROOMS:** 74 en suite (3 fmly) No smoking in 33 bedrooms s £76-£105; d £76-£105 * **LB** **FACILITIES:** Xmas **CONF:** Thtr 120 Class 80 Board 60 Del from £85 * **SERVICES:** Lift **PARKING:** 62 **NOTES:** No smoking in restaurant Civ Wed 100 **CARDS:**

**★★★68% Falstaff**
8-10 St Dunstans St, Westgate CT2 8AF
☎ 01227 462138 📠 01227 463525
corus
***Dir:*** *from London follow M2 to Canterbury. On entering the city at 1st rdbt turn left into London road. At 2nd mini rdbt turn right into St Dunstans Street. Hotel at the end on left.*

Falstaff Hotel

Located next to the Westgate Tower, the hotel offers easy access to the city centre and motorway network. Many original 16th-century features add to the character of this historic coaching inn. Most bedrooms have been recently refurbished and the rooms in the old building offer individual character.
**ROOMS:** 25 en suite 22 annexe en suite (1 fmly) No smoking in 27 bedrooms s £91; d £100 * **LB** **FACILITIES:** STV **PARKING:** 20 **NOTES:** No smoking in restaurant **CARDS:**

*See advert on this page*

CANTERBURY, continued

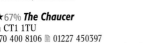

**★★★67% *The Chaucer***
Ivy Ln CT1 1TU
☎ 0870 400 8106 🖹 01227 450397
e-mail: heritagehotels_canterbury.chaucer_hotel@forte-hotels.com
***Dir:*** *approaching city on A2, follow signs for Dover. Turn right at fifth rdbt, then 1st left*
Located just outside the old city walls and within easy walking distance of the city centre and cathedral, this Georgian residence offers comfortably furnished bedrooms. Public areas have been recently refurbished and the restaurant offers an interesting range of carefully prepared dishes.
**ROOMS:** 42 en suite (5 fmly) No smoking in 19 bedrooms **CONF:** Thtr 120 Class 45 Board 45 Del from £125 * **PARKING:** 45 **NOTES:** No smoking in restaurant Civ Wed 100 **CARDS:**

**★★★65% Howfield Manor**
Chartham Hatch CT4 7HQ
☎ 01227 738294 🖹 01227 731535
e-mail: enquiries@howfield.invictanet.co.uk
***Dir:*** *from A2, follow signs for Chartham Hatch after Gate Service Station, continue for 2.25 miles. Hotel is on left at junct with A28*
This charming family run hotel on the outskirts of historic Canterbury sits in several acres of well manicured grounds. Bedrooms are comfortable and traditionally styled. The restaurant, with its feature working well used by former occupants of the house, serves confident modern cuisine.
**ROOMS:** 15 en suite s £75-£80; d £95-£100 (incl. bkfst) * **LB**
**FACILITIES:** Xmas **CONF:** Thtr 100 Class 60 Board 60 Del £109.50 *
**PARKING:** 80 **NOTES:** No dogs (ex guide dogs) No children 10yrs Civ Wed 100 **CARDS:**

**★★75% Ebury**
65/67 New Dover Rd CT1 3DX
☎ 01227 768433 🖹 01227 459187
e-mail: info@ebury-hotel.co.uk
***Dir:*** *follow A2, take Canterbury turn off, then ring road around Canterbury, follow Dover signs at 5th rdbt signs to Dover, in 1m on left is Ebury Hotel*
An appealing family-run hotel in two acres of attractive gardens. Bedrooms are well-furnished with good facilities. Public areas include a spacious restaurant, with an interesting menu of traditional dishes. Room service is available, including continental breakfast.
**ROOMS:** 15 en suite (2 fmly) s £50-£70; d £65-£79 (incl. bkfst) * **LB**
**FACILITIES:** Indoor swimming (H) Jacuzzi ch fac **PARKING:** 30
**NOTES:** No smoking in restaurant Closed 23 Dec-15 Jan
**CARDS:**

**★★69% Bow Window Inn**
50 High St, Littlebourne CT3 1ST
☎ 01227 721264 🖹 01227 721250
e-mail: bow@windowhotel.freeserve.co.uk
A country cottage offering friendly hospitality and comfortable accommodation. Bedrooms are furnished to suit the style of the house and are well-equipped. Public areas are limited but exposed beams provide character. The restaurant offers an interesting menu and serves enjoyable meals.
**ROOMS:** 10 en suite (1 fmly) No smoking in 3 bedrooms s £52; d £58-£68 (incl. bkfst) * **LB** **PARKING:** 16 **NOTES:** No smoking in restaurant
**CARDS:**

Packed in a hurry? Ironing facilities should be available at all star levels, either in rooms or on request.

**★★68% Canterbury**
71 New Dover Rd CT1 3DZ
☎ 01227 450551 🖹 01227 780145
e-mail: canterbury.hotel@btinternet.com
***Dir:*** *on A2, Dover road*
This Georgian-style hotel, close to the city centre, offers two styles of comfortable, well-equipped bedroom accommodation: standard and superior. Public areas are attractively furnished and include a reception bar, and a separate TV lounge which can be used for private meetings. The bright, attractive restaurant has a continental feel, with French staff and a classic French menu.
**ROOMS:** 23 en suite (1 fmly) s £55-£85; d £75-£115 (incl. bkfst) * **LB**
**FACILITIES:** STV **SERVICES:** Lift **PARKING:** 50
**CARDS:**

**★★68% Pointers Hotel**
1 London Rd CT2 8LR
☎ 01227 456846 🖹 01227 452786
e-mail: pointers.hotel@dial.pipex.com
***Dir:*** *Canterbury exit off A2, follow signposts for university. Opposite St Dunstans Church*
The Pointers stands at the end of the high street in historic Canterbury and is an ideal base for visiting the cathedral, or shopping in the town centre. Bedrooms do vary in size, but all are designed with guest comfort in mind. Dinner menus combine local ingredients and skill to produce superb results. There is a secure locked car park on site.
**ROOMS:** 12 en suite (3 fmly) s £50-£60; d £60-£75 (incl. bkfst) **LB**
**PARKING:** 10 **NOTES:** No smoking in restaurant Closed 23 Dec-14 Jan
**CARDS:**

**★★65% Victoria**
59 London Rd CT2 8JY
☎ 01227 459333 🖹 01227 781552
e-mail: manager@vichotel.fsnet.co.uk
***Dir:*** *accessible via main London/Dover M2/A2 onto main A2052, hotel on left off the 1st rdbt*
Just fifteen minutes' walk from the centre of this historic city, the hotel is away from the hustle and bustle of the centre, yet within sight of the cathedral. Bedrooms vary in size and shape, and all are attractively decorated with an excellent range of facilities. Public areas include a busy bar and a carvery restaurant.
**ROOMS:** 34 en suite (12 fmly) No smoking in 4 bedrooms s fr £42; d fr £52 * **LB** **CONF:** Thtr 20 Class 20 Board 20 **PARKING:** 70
**NOTES:** No dogs (ex guide dogs) **CARDS:**

**⌂ *Travelodge***
A2 Gate Services, Dunkirk ME13 9LN
☎ 01227 752781 🖹 01227 752781
***Dir:*** *5m W on A2 northbound*
Travelodge offers good quality, good value, modern accommodation. Ideal for families, the spacious, en suite bedrooms include remote-control TV, tea and coffee-making facilities, luxury beds and free morning newspaper. Meals can be taken at the nearby family restaurant. For further details and the Travelodge phone number, consult the Hotel Groups page.

**ROOMS:** 40 en suite

**⌂ Express by Holiday Inn Canterbury**

Express
by Holiday Inn

Upper Harbledown CT2 9HX
☎ 01227 865000 🖹 01227 865100
e-mail: canterbury@premierhotels.co.uk
***Dir:*** *on A2, 4m from city centre*
A modern budget hotel offering comfortable accommodation in refreshing, spacious and comprehensively equipped bedrooms, en suite bathrooms with power showers and continental buffet

*continued*

breakfast included in the room rate. Suitable for business travellers or families. For further details and the Express by Holiday Inn phone number, consult the Hotel Groups page.

**ROOMS:** 89 en suite (incl. cont bkfst) d £43-£60 * **CONF:** Thtr 35 Class 15 Board 20 Del from £75 *

## CARBIS BAY See St Ives

## CARCROFT, South Yorkshire

Map 08 SE50

### Travelodge

Travelodge

Great North Rd DN6 9LF
☎ 01302 330841 01302 330841
***Dir:*** *on A1 northbound*
Travelodge offers good quality, good value, modern accommodation. Ideal for families, the spacious, en suite bedrooms include remote-control TV, tea and coffee-making facilities, luxury beds and free morning newspaper. Meals can be taken at the nearby family restaurant. For further details and the Travelodge phone number, consult the Hotel Groups page.

**ROOMS:** 40 en suite

## CARLISLE, Cumbria

Map 11 NY45

see also Brampton

### ★★★78% Crosby Lodge Country House

High Crosby, Crosby-on-Eden CA6 4QZ
☎ 01228 573618 01228 573428
e-mail: crosbylodge@crosby-eden.demon.co.uk
***Dir:*** *leave M6 at junc 44, 3.5m from motorway off A689*
Warm hospitality and attentive service await guests at this elegant country house hotel, peacefully situated in its own grounds. Spacious public areas are tastefully furnished with period and antique pieces. Attractive bedrooms are all individually styled and thoughtfully equipped. The elegant restaurant offers a good selection of freshly prepared dishes and an impressive wine list.
**ROOMS:** 9 en suite 2 annexe en suite (3 fmly) s £82-£90; d £115-£150 (incl. bkfst) * **LB** **FACILITIES:** Golf and fishing can be arranged **CONF:** Thtr 25 Board 12 **PARKING:** 40 **NOTES:** No smoking in restaurant Closed 24 Dec-20 Jan RS Sun evening (restaurant-residents only) **CARDS:**

### ★★★69% Crown

Wetheral CA4 8ES
☎ 01228 561888 01228 561637
e-mail: crownhotelwetheral.co.uk
***Dir:*** *from M6 junct 42 take B6263 to Wetheral, turn left at village shop, car park to rear of hotel*
This 19th-century hotel, peacefully situated close to the centre of the village, provides comfortable bedrooms. The conservatory restaurant offers a range of carefully prepared dishes, while more

*continued on p158*

CARLISLE, continued

informal meals are served in the village bar. A well-equipped leisure centre and function rooms complete the package.
**ROOMS:** 49 en suite 2 annexe en suite (3 fmly) No smoking in 10 bedrooms s £75-£102; d £90-£126 (incl. bkfst) * **LB** **FACILITIES:** STV Indoor swimming (H) Squash Sauna Solarium Gym Jacuzzi Children's splash pool Steam room ch fac **CONF:** Thtr 175 Class 90 Board 50 Del from £105 * **PARKING:** 80 **NOTES:** No smoking in restaurant Civ Wed 120 **CARDS:**

### ★★★67% Cumbria Park

32 Scotland Rd, Stanwix CA3 9DG
☎ 01228 522887 🖷 01228 514796
e-mail: enquiries@cumbriaparkhotel.co.uk
***Dir:*** *1.5m N on A7*
Situated to the north of the city within easy access of the M6 and central amenities, this family-run hotel provides a comfortable base for the business person and tourist alike. Public areas are smartly presented, and the tasteful bedrooms offer mixed styles of furnishings along with all the expected facilities.
**ROOMS:** 47 en suite (3 fmly) No smoking in 13 bedrooms s £74-£90; d £95-£125 (incl. bkfst) * **LB** **FACILITIES:** STV Sauna Solarium Gym Jacuzzi Steam room **CONF:** Thtr 200 Class 50 Board 50 Del £105 * **SERVICES:** Lift **PARKING:** 51 **NOTES:** No dogs (ex guide dogs) Closed 25-26 Dec **CARDS:**

### ★★★67% *Posthouse Carlisle*

Posthouse

Parkhouse Rd CA3 0HR
☎ 0870 400 9018 🖷 01228 543178
e-mail: fcmail@fphcarlisle.com
***Dir:*** *junc 44/M6 take A7 signposted Carlisle, hotel on right at first set of traffic lights*
Conveniently located close to the M6, this modern hotel is a popular meeting and conference venue. Bedrooms are well-equipped and vary in style from traditional to stylish Millennium rooms. Spacious family rooms are also available. Both business and leisure facilities are impressive.
**ROOMS:** 127 en suite (34 fmly) No smoking in 85 bedrooms **FACILITIES:** Indoor swimming (H) Sauna Gym Jacuzzi **CONF:** Thtr 120 Class 64 Board 60 **PARKING:** 150
**CARDS:**

### ★★★66% Swallow Hilltop Hotel

London Rd CA1 2PQ
☎ 01228 529255 🖷 01228 525238
e-mail: info@swallowhotels.com
***Dir:*** *from M6 junct 42 take A6 to Carlisle. In 1m hotel on left on hill*

This modern hotel is located within easy reach of both the town centre and the M6. Smart bedrooms are well-appointed and thoughtfully equipped with a host of extra facilities. Public areas include a spacious bar lounge, the Langdale restaurant and a smart, well-equipped leisure suite. Function facilities are also available.
**ROOMS:** 92 en suite (6 fmly) No smoking in 24 bedrooms s £55-£80; d £70-£90 (incl. bkfst) * **LB** **FACILITIES:** STV Indoor swimming (H) Sauna Solarium Gym Jacuzzi Massage Reflexology Steam room entertainment Xmas **CONF:** Thtr 500 Class 250 Board 90 Del from £105 * **SERVICES:** Lift **PARKING:** 350 **NOTES:** Civ Wed 300
**CARDS:**

### ★★★61% The Crown & Mitre

PEEL HOTELS

4 English St CA3 8HZ
☎ 01228 525491 🖷 01228 514553
e-mail: info@crownandmitre-hotel-carlisle.com
***Dir:*** *A6 into city centre, pass station on left then left past Woolworths. Sharp right into Blackfriars St. Hotel car park and rear entrance at end*
Conveniently situated in the centre of town beside the shops, this Edwardian hotel offers public areas that have retained many of the original architectural features. There is a good range of banqueting facilities as well as some leisure facilities. Bedrooms range from comfortable executive rooms to the smaller and more practical standard rooms.
**ROOMS:** 74 en suite 20 annexe en suite (4 fmly) No smoking in 10 bedrooms s fr £84; d fr £109 (incl. bkfst) * **LB** **FACILITIES:** STV Indoor swimming (H) Jacuzzi Xmas **CONF:** Thtr 400 Class 250 Board 50 Del from £95 * **SERVICES:** Lift **PARKING:** 42
**CARDS:**

### ★★★60% *Central Plaza*

Victoria Viaduct CA3 8AL
☎ 01228 520256 🖷 01228 514657
e-mail: info@centralplazahotel.co.uk
***Dir:*** *in city centre, just N of main railway station on A6*
Offering accommodation in a variety of styles, this grand hotel lies in the city centre close to the station. At the time of our last inspection, a refurbishment programme was coming to completion, with all public areas and bedrooms being upgraded to a good standard.
**ROOMS:** 84 en suite (3 fmly) No smoking in 4 bedrooms **FACILITIES:** STV **CONF:** Thtr 100 Class 54 Board 40 **SERVICES:** Lift **PARKING:** 17 **NOTES:** No smoking in restaurant
**CARDS:**

*See advert on page 157*

### ★★64% Pinegrove

MINOTEL Great Britain

262 London Rd CA1 2QS
☎ 01228 524828 🖷 01228 810941
***Dir:*** *on A6*

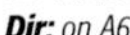

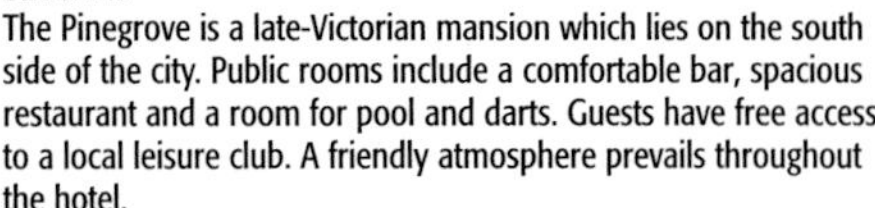

The Pinegrove is a late-Victorian mansion which lies on the south side of the city. Public rooms include a comfortable bar, spacious restaurant and a room for pool and darts. Guests have free access to a local leisure club. A friendly atmosphere prevails throughout the hotel.
**ROOMS:** 27 rms (25 en suite) 4 annexe en suite (8 fmly) s £40-£46; d £50-£58 (incl. bkfst) * **LB** **FACILITIES:** STV Darts,Pool Table **CONF:** Thtr 120 Class 100 Board 100 Del from £70 * **PARKING:** 50 **NOTES:** Closed 25 Dec **CARDS:**

### ⌂ *Premier Lodge*

PREMIER LODGE

Kingstown Rd CA3 0AT
☎ 0870 700 1348 🖷 0870 7001349
Premier Lodge offers modern, well-equipped, en suite accommodation suitable for both business and leisure travellers. Meals can be taken at the adjacent popular restaurant and bar, which is fully licensed. For further details, consult the Hotel Groups page.
**ROOMS:** 49 en suite

### ⌂ *Travelodge (Carlisle North)*

Travelodge

A74 Southbound, Todhills
☎ 0870 850950
Travelodge offers good quality, good value, modern accommodation. Ideal for families, the spacious, en suite bedrooms include remote-control TV, tea and coffee-making facilities, luxury beds and free morning newspaper. Meals can be taken at the nearby family restaurant. For further details and the Travelodge phone number, consult the Hotel Groups page.

## CARNFORTH, Lancashire — Map 07 SD47

### ★★65% *Royal Station*

Market St LA5 9BT
☎ 01524 732033 & 733636 🖷 01524 720267
***Dir:*** *leave M6 junct 35 join A6 signed Carnforth & Morecambe, in 1m at x-rds in centre of Carnforth turn rt into Market St. Hotel opposite railway station*
Adjacent to the railway station, this busy, commercial hotel enjoys a central location. Bedrooms are extremely well equipped and comfortably furnished. Public areas include a lounge bar offering a good range of food, the Sportsman's public bar with pool, darts and a "big screen", as well as an intimate restaurant and good conference facilities.
**ROOMS:** 13 en suite (1 fmly) **CONF:** Thtr 150 Class 100 Board 100
**PARKING:** 8 **NOTES:** No smoking in restaurant Civ Wed 50
**CARDS:**

## CARSHALTON, Greater London — Map 04 TQ26

### ★★★64% Greyhound

2 High St SM5 3PE
☎ 020 8647 1511 🖷 020 8647 4687
e-mail: greyhound@youngs.co.uk
***Dir:*** *Situated on A232 where Carshalton High Street becomes Pound Street*
This recently-refurbished hotel is usefully situated in an accessible location, overlooking a pretty duck pond. The smartly presented bedrooms are spacious, with good facilities. Public areas consist of an informal popular bar with a lounge and dining area.
**ROOMS:** 21 en suite (2 fmly) No smoking in 11 bedrooms
**FACILITIES:** STV **PARKING:** 40 **NOTES:** No dogs (ex guide dogs)
**CARDS:**

## CARTMEL, Cumbria — Map 07 SD37

### ★★76% ® Aynsome Manor

LA11 6HH
☎ 015395 36653 🖷 015395 36016
e-mail: info@aynsomemanorhotel.co.uk
***Dir:*** *from M6 junct 36, follow A590 signed Barrow in Furness. Continue towards Cartmel turn left at end of dual carriageway, hotel just before village*
A lovely old manor house standing peacefully in its own well-tended gardens on the edge of the village, offering wonderful hospitality, good food and a relaxing atmosphere. Inviting public areas include a cosy bar, choice of lounges and an elegant panelled restaurant, where the honest home cooking is carefully prepared and very rewarding.
**ROOMS:** 10 en suite 2 annexe en suite (2 fmly) **PARKING:** 20
**NOTES:** No smoking in restaurant Closed 2-31 Jan
**CARDS:**

Weekend away? Hotels with LB in their entry offer leisure breaks.

## CASTLE ASHBY, Northamptonshire — Map 04 SP85

### ★★71% *Falcon*

NN7 1LF
☎ 01604 696200 🖷 01604 696673
e-mail: falcon@castleashby.co.uk
***Dir:*** *follow signs to Castle Ashby, opposite war memorial*
Set in the heart of a peaceful village, this hotel occupies two separate properties, each with its own character. Bedrooms are all individually decorated and feature a wealth of extras and stylish bold furnishings and decor. Public rooms, in the main house, include a first-floor sitting area, a choice of bars and a cosy restaurant where an interesting selection of dishes is offered.
**ROOMS:** 6 rms (5 en suite) 11 annexe en suite **FACILITIES:** STV
**CONF:** Thtr 30 Class 30 Board 20 **PARKING:** 75 **NOTES:** Civ Wed 60
**CARDS:**

## CASTLE CARY, Somerset — Map 03 ST63

### ★★68% *The George*

Market Place BA7 7AH
☎ 01963 350761 🖷 01963 350035
***Dir:*** *from M5 junct 23 follow A39 to Shepton Mallet then A371 to Castle Cary. From A303 to Wincanton, then A371 to Castle Cary*
A 15th-century coaching inn with a distinctive thatched roof and bay windows. Rooms are generally spacious, offering a good standard of accommodation and comfort. Guests can choose to eat in the formal dining room, with its imaginative range of dishes, or in one of the two cosy bars. An attractive lounge with a real log fire is also available.
**ROOMS:** 14 en suite (1 fmly) No smoking in 4 bedrooms **PARKING:** 10
**NOTES:** No dogs (ex guide dogs) No smoking in restaurant
**CARDS:**

## CASTLE COMBE, Wiltshire — Map 03 ST87

*Premier Collection*

### ★★★★ ®®® Manor House

SN14 7HR
☎ 01249 782206 🖷 01249 782159
e-mail: enquiries@manor-house.co.uk
***Dir:*** *follow Chippenham signs from M4 junct 17, onto A420 signed Bristol, then right onto B4039. Go through village, turn rt after crossing river bridge*
Peacefully set in 26 acres of grounds with a romantic Italian garden and 18-hole golf course, this delightful country house boasts character and charm. Bedrooms, some of which stand in a row of original stone cottages, have been superbly furnished, and named to make the most of their individuality. Public rooms include a number of cosy lounges with roaring

*continued on p160*

CASTLE COMBE, continued

fires. Service is a pleasing blend of professionalism and friendliness, while meals in the hotel restaurant continue to impress.
**ROOMS:** 21 en suite 25 annexe en suite (8 fmly) s £145-£350; d £145-£350 * LB **FACILITIES:** STV Outdoor swimming (H) Golf 18 Tennis (hard) Fishing Snooker Sauna Croquet lawn Jogging track Xmas **CONF:** Thtr 60 Class 36 Board 36 Del from £160 * **PARKING:** 100 **NOTES:** No dogs (ex guide dogs) No smoking in restaurant Civ Wed 90 **CARDS:**

*See advert on opposite page*

### ★★★68% Castle Inn
SN14 7HN
☎ 01249 783030 01249 782315
e-mail: res@castle-inn.co.uk
***Dir:*** *take A420 to Chippenham follow signs for Castle Combe. Hotel is situated in the heart of the village*
This famous 12th-century hostelry is set in the market place of the historic village of Castle Combe. Bedrooms, including many with old beams, are individually decorated, and have plenty of thoughtful extras. Guests can chose from a varied and tempting menu emphasising fresh ingredients, and have the option to dine either in the conservatory style restaurant or the bar.
**ROOMS:** 11 en suite s £69.50-£115; d £95-£165 (incl. bkfst) * LB **FACILITIES:** STV Xmas **CONF:** Thtr 22 Class 19 Board 16 Del from £100 * **NOTES:** No dogs (ex guide dogs) No smoking in restaurant **CARDS:**

CASTLE DONINGTON See East Midlands Airport

CASTLEFORD, West Yorkshire Map 08 SE42

### Premier Lodge
Pioneer Way WF10 5TG
☎ 0870 700 1412 0870 700 1413
PREMIER LODGE
THE BEST. REST ASSURED.
***Dir:*** *Turn off M62 at junct 31 onto A655 to Castleford. At traffic lights turn right on to Commerce park. Lodge 2nd on left.*
Premier Lodge offers modern, well-equipped, en suite accommodation suitable for both business and leisure travellers. Meals can be taken at the adjacent popular restaurant and bar, which is fully licensed. For further details, consult the Hotel Groups page.
**ROOMS:** 62 en suite d £46 * **CONF:** Thtr 20 Class 8 Board 10 Del from £75 *

CATTERICK BRIDGE, North Yorkshire Map 08 SE29

### ★★65% Bridge House
DL10 7PE
☎ 01748 818331 01748 818331
e-mail: bridgehousehotel@hotmail.com
***Dir:*** *4m S of Scotch Corner, on bridge opp Catterick Racecourse*
Formerly a coaching inn, this commercial hotel sits by the River Swale close to the racecourse and has pleasant gardens to the rear. There is a wide choice of bedroom size, and all are well-equipped. A good range of freshly prepared meals is served in the bar and restaurant.
**ROOMS:** 15 en suite (2 fmly) s £40-£50; d £60-£70 (incl. bkfst) * LB **FACILITIES:** STV Fishing **CONF:** Thtr 100 Class 50 Board 40 **PARKING:** 71 **NOTES:** Civ Wed 130 **CARDS:**

CHADDESLEY CORBETT, Worcestershire Map 07 SO87

**Premier Collection**

### ★★★ Brockencote Hall Country House
DY10 4PY
☎ 01562 777876 01562 777872
e-mail: info@brockencotehall.com
***Dir:*** *0.5m W, off A448, opposite St Cassians Church*
Brockencote Hall Country House Hotel is a magnificent, personally run Victorian mansion, set in the heart of scenic Worcestershire countryside. The hotel stands in beautifully maintained grounds, with glorious countryside extending in all directions. Spacious bedrooms are appointed to a high standard, with many thoughtful extras, and enjoy views of the lake or surrounding parkland. There are comfortable lounges and an elegant dining room offering high standards of French cuisine.
**ROOMS:** 17 en suite (2 fmly) s £88-£130; d £108-£170 (incl. bkfst) * LB **FACILITIES:** STV Tennis (hard) Croquet lawn Jacuzzi Reflexology /aromatherapy ch fac Xmas **CONF:** Thtr 30 Class 20 Board 20 Del from £155 * **SERVICES:** Lift **PARKING:** 45 **NOTES:** No dogs (ex guide dogs) No smoking in restaurant **CARDS:**

CHAGFORD, Devon Map 03 SX78

**Premier Collection**

### ★★★ Gidleigh Park
TQ13 8HH
☎ 01647 432367 01647 432574
RELAIS & CHATEAUX.
e-mail: gidleighpark@gidleigh.co.uk
***Dir:*** *approach from Chagford, turn right at Lloyds Bank into Mill St. After 150 yds fork right, follow lane 2m to end*
Gidleigh Park is certainly now a legend in hotel keeping. It is

*continued*

the epitome of relaxed luxury, set in pretty gardens and surrounded by 45 acres of the Dartmoor National Park. Bedrooms vary in size and outlook but all guarantee excellent levels of comfort. Guests are invited to dine in the restaurant where outstanding dishes are produced using quality local ingredients. There is also an attractive selection on the excellent wine list.
**ROOMS:** 12 en suite 3 annexe en suite s £275-£440 (incl. bkfst & dinner) **LB** **FACILITIES:** STV Tennis (hard) Fishing Croquet lawn Putting green Bowls **CONF:** Board 22 Del £300 * **PARKING:** 25
**NOTES:** No smoking in restaurant
**CARDS:**

★★★73%  **Mill End**
Dartmoor National Park, Sandy Park TQ13 8JN
☎ 01647 432282 ▯ 01647 433106
e-mail: millendhotel@talk21.com
***Dir:*** *from A30 at Whiddon Down follow A382 to Moretonhampstead. After 3.5m a hump back bridge at Sandy Park, hotel on right by river*
Peace, quiet and relaxation are the hallmarks of this charming hotel. All bedrooms have countryside views and though they vary in size, they all offer a high standard of decoration and furnishing. The sitting rooms are very comfortable and in the elegant dining

*continued*

room the menu makes optimum use of fresh local produce. Mill End also benefits from six miles of fishing on the Teign.

**ROOMS:** 16 en suite (2 fmly) s £50-£89; d £70-£120 (incl. bkfst) * **LB**
**FACILITIES:** Fishing Croquet lawn ch fac Xmas **CONF:** Thtr 40 Class 20 Board 30 **PARKING:** 21 **NOTES:** No smoking in restaurant
**CARDS:**

★★66% **Three Crowns Hotel**
High St TQ13 8AJ
☎ 01647 433444 ▯ 01647 433117
e-mail: threecrowns@msn.com
***Dir:*** *turn left off A30 at Whiddon Down, in Chagford town centre opposite church*
Located in the heart of the village, the hotel dates back to the 13th century and retains many original architectural features, such as open fires, exposed beams and mullioned windows. Bedrooms vary in size and style, several boasting four-poster beds. Public

*continued on p162*

CHAGFORD, continued

areas include a choice of bars, small lounge and intimate restaurant as well as a function room with separate bar.

*Three Crowns Hotel, Chagford*

**ROOMS:** 17 en suite (1 fmly) No smoking in 4 bedrooms s £32.50-£42.50; d £50-£65 (incl. bkfst) * **LB** **FACILITIES:** STV Xmas **CONF:** Board 90 **PARKING:** 20 **NOTES:** No smoking in restaurant **CARDS:**

CHALE See Wight, Isle of

CHARD, Somerset Map 03 ST30

### ★★★69% Lordleaze

Henderson Dr, Forton Rd TA20 2HW
☎ 01460 61066 📠 01460 66468
e-mail: lordleaze@fsbdial.co.uk
***Dir:*** *from centre of Chard take A358 towards Axminster, pass St Mary's Church on your right then left to Forton & Winsham, 3rd left to hotel*

The Lordleaze is an excellent base from which to explore the West Country. The comfortable bedrooms are well-equipped, with rooms available on the ground floor. A focal point is the relaxed and friendly lounge bar. In addition to the carte served in the restaurant, a tempting selection of bar meals is also available.
**ROOMS:** 16 en suite (1 fmly) No smoking in 4 bedrooms s £52.50-£57.50; d £72.50-£85 (incl. bkfst) * **LB** **FACILITIES:** Xmas **CONF:** Thtr 180 Class 60 Board 40 Del £75 * **PARKING:** 55 **NOTES:** No smoking in restaurant Civ Wed 110 **CARDS:**

*See advert on opposite page*

CHARINGWORTH, Gloucestershire Map 04 SP13

### ★★★74% ® *Charingworth Manor*

GL55 6NS
☎ 01386 593555 📠 01386 593353
e-mail: charingworthmanor@englishrosehotels.co.uk
***Dir:*** *on B4035 3m E of Chipping Campden*
This 14th-century manor house retains many original features including flagstone floors, exposed beams and open fireplaces. The house has a beautiful setting in 50 acres of grounds and has been carefully expanded to provide high quality accommodation. The bedrooms are furnished with period pieces and modern amenities; four-poster rooms and suites are available.
**ROOMS:** 26 en suite **FACILITIES:** STV Indoor swimming (H) Tennis (hard) Sauna Solarium Gym Croquet lawn Steam room **CONF:** Thtr 36 Class 16 Board 30 **PARKING:** 50 **NOTES:** No dogs (ex guide dogs) No smoking in restaurant Civ Wed 50
**CARDS:**

*See advert under CHIPPING CAMPDEN*

CHARMOUTH, Dorset Map 03 SY39

### ★★76% White House

2 Hillside, The Street DT6 6PJ
☎ 01297 560411 📠 01297 560702
e-mail: whitehousehotel@excite.co.uk
***Dir:*** *turn off A35-signed Charmouth, hotel opposite the church*
This friendly hotel offers comfortable accommodation in a charming Regency property. The interesting beach, famous for its fossils and cliff top walks, is nearby. Individually styled bedrooms are equipped with modern facilities. A five course menu is offered at night, cooked using fresh produce.
**ROOMS:** 7 en suite 3 annexe en suite No smoking in all bedrooms s £62-£74; d £104-£118 (incl. bkfst & dinner) * **LB** **PARKING:** 12 **NOTES:** No children 14yrs No smoking in restaurant
**CARDS:**

### ★★67% *Hensleigh Hotel*

Lower Sea Ln DT6 6LW
☎ 01297 560830 📠 01297 560830
This family-run hotel is set midway between the beach and the village. Bedrooms are neatly decorated and furnished. There is a large conservatory leading to a smaller dining room and a cosy lounge bar. For dinner, guests can choose from the menu or specials; breakfast offers a good choice too.
**ROOMS:** 10 en suite (1 fmly) No smoking in all bedrooms **PARKING:** 19 **NOTES:** No smoking in restaurant RS mid-end Feb & 3 Nov-4 Dec **CARDS:**

CHATHAM, Kent Map 05 TQ76

### ★★★★73% ®® Bridgewood Manor Hotel

MARSTON HOTELS

Bridgewood Roundabout, Walderslade Woods ME5 9AX
☎ 01634 201333 📠 01634 201330
e-mail: bridgewoodmanor@marstonhotels.co.uk
***Dir:*** *adjacent to Bridgewood rdbt on A229. Take third exit signed 'Walderslade/Lordswood'. Hotel 50mtrs on left*
This modern hotel is situated on the outskirts of the historic city of Rochester. Bedrooms are furnished and decorated to a high standard with a good range of in-room facilities on offer. There is a comprehensive range of leisure facilities provided, from snooker to the well-equipped health club. Guests can dine in the informal Terrace Bistro or the more formal restaurant.
**ROOMS:** 100 en suite (12 fmly) No smoking in 63 bedrooms s £99-£109; d £120-£140 * **LB** **FACILITIES:** STV Indoor swimming (H) Tennis (hard) Snooker Sauna Solarium Gym Putting green Jacuzzi Hairdressing Beauty treatments Xmas **CONF:** Thtr 200 Class 110 Board 80 **SERVICES:** Lift **PARKING:** 178 **NOTES:** No smoking in restaurant Civ Wed 120 **CARDS:**

TV dinner? Room service at three stars and above.

*continued*

## CHATTERIS, Cambridgeshire

Map 05 TL38

### ★73% Cross Keys

16 Market Hill PE16 6BA
☎ 01354 693036 & 692644 📠 01354 694454
e-mail: thefens@crosskeyshotel.fsnet.co.uk
***Dir:*** *at junct A141/142, opposite parish church*

This charming inn, dating back to Elizabethan times, has been tastefully extended. The spacious restaurant, cosy bar, dining area and residents' lounge are pleasant and relaxing. The bedrooms offer a wide variety of sizes and styles, those in the newer wing are particularly well-equipped and roomy.
**ROOMS:** 12 rms (10 en suite) (1 fmly) No smoking in 5 bedrooms s £21.50; d £32.50 * **LB** **CONF:** Thtr 40 Class 40 Board 20
**PARKING:** 12 **NOTES:** No dogs (ex guide dogs) Closed 26-28 Dec
**CARDS:**

## CHEDDAR See Axbridge

## CHELMSFORD, Essex

Map 05 TL70

### ★★★71% Pontlands Park Country

West Hanningfield Rd, Great Baddow CM2 8HR
☎ 01245 476444 📠 01245 478393
e-mail: sales@pontlandsparkhotel.co.uk
***Dir:*** *leave A12 at junct A130. Take A1116 to Chelmsford. 1st exit at rdbt, 1st slip road on left. Left towards Gt Baddow, 1st left into West Hanningfield road*
Set in a peaceful village within easy driving distance of Chelmsford, this hotel offers spacious, individually decorated and comfortably furnished bedrooms throughout. There is an elegant sitting room and cosy lounge bar, as well as excellent leisure facilities.
**ROOMS:** 36 en suite (4 fmly) s £110-£120; d £130-£170 * **LB**
**FACILITIES:** STV Indoor swimming (H) Outdoor swimming (H) Sauna Solarium Gym Jacuzzi Toning tables **CONF:** Thtr 60 Class 20 Board 4 Del from £149 * **PARKING:** 100 **NOTES:** No dogs (ex guide dogs) Closed 24 Dec-3Jan (ex 31 Dec) Civ Wed 60
**CARDS:**

### ★★★70% County

Rainsford Rd CM1 2PZ
☎ 01245 455700 📠 01245 492762
e-mail: sales@countyhotel-essex.co.uk
***Dir:*** *from town centre continue past railway and bus station to hotel 300yds on left beyond traffic lights*
This hotel is ideally situated close to the railway station and bus depot in the centre of town. It has ample parking and a range of popular meeting rooms. Although the bedrooms vary in size they all offer a range of modern facilities; there are also one or two

*continued*



individually styled feature rooms. Public areas include the Artista Brasserie and the plushly furnished wine bar.
**ROOMS:** 54 en suite 8 annexe en suite No smoking in 28 bedrooms s £79-£130; d £89-£130 (incl. bkfst) * **LB** **FACILITIES:** entertainment
**CONF:** Thtr 200 Class 60 Board 40 Del £120 * **SERVICES:** Lift
**PARKING:** 80 **NOTES:** No dogs (ex guide dogs) Closed 27-30 Dec Civ Wed 80 **CARDS:**

## CHELTENHAM, Gloucestershire

Map 03 SO92

### ★★★★67% Cheltenham Park

PARAMOUNT
GROUP OF HOTELS

Cirencester Rd, Charlton Kings GL53 8EA
☎ 01242 222021 📠 01242 254880
e-mail: cheltenhampark@paramount-hotels.co.uk
***Dir:*** *on the A435, 2m SE of Cheltenham near the Lilley Brook Golf Course*

Conveniently located on the edge of Cheltenham, this is a smart modern hotel set in tranquil gardens. Spacious bedrooms are thoughtfully designed and equipped. The hotel also offers

*continued on p164*

CHELTENHAM, continued

extensive leisure and meeting facilities, including a newly built conference suite.
**ROOMS:** 33 en suite 110 annexe en suite (2 fmly) No smoking in 67 bedrooms s £90-£103; d £120-£131 (incl. bkfst) * **LB FACILITIES:** Spa STV Indoor swimming (H) Sauna Solarium Gym Jacuzzi Beauty treatment rooms Xmas **CONF:** Thtr 350 Class 180 Board 110 Del £157.45 * **SERVICES:** Lift **PARKING:** 170 **NOTES:** No smoking in restaurant Civ Wed 300 **CARDS:**

### ★★★★58% The Queen's

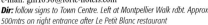

The Promenade GL50 1NN
☎ 0870 400 8107 Fax 01242 224145
e-mail: gm1050@forte-hotels.com
***Dir:*** *follow signs to Town Centre. Left at Montpellier Walk rdbt. Approx 500mtrs on right entrance after Le Petit Blanc restaurant*

The Queen's Hotel is situated in the centre of town and overlooks the Regency Gardens. This elegant and traditional hotel provides well equipped and comfortable accommodation for both leisure and business guests. The attractive lobby and lounge area is a popular place to meet and take refreshments.
**ROOMS:** 79 en suite (8 fmly) No smoking in 20 bedrooms s £110-£125; d £125-£185 * **LB FACILITIES:** STV Xmas **CONF:** Thtr 100 Class 60 Board 40 Del from £140 * **SERVICES:** Lift **PARKING:** 85 **NOTES:** No smoking in restaurant Civ Wed 50
**CARDS:**

## Premier Collection

### ★★★ The Greenway

Shurdington GL51 4UG
☎ 01242 862352 Fax 01242 862780
e-mail: greenway@btconnect.com
***Dir:*** *2.5m SW on A46*

The Greenway is a charming Elizabethan manor house dating back to 1587. The dining room offers a high standard of cuisine that takes full advantage of the fresh local produce. The individually decorated bedrooms are spacious and divided between the main house and the smartly refurbished Georgian coach house. All of the rooms retain many of their original features and present many thoughtful extras.
**ROOMS:** 11 en suite 8 annexe en suite (1 fmly) No smoking in 8 bedrooms s £99-£119; d £165-£230 (incl. bkfst) * **LB**
**FACILITIES:** STV Croquet lawn Clay pigeon shooting, Horse riding, Mountain biking, Guided walks Xmas **CONF:** Thtr 35 Class 25 Board 22 Del from £150 * **PARKING:** 50 **NOTES:** No dogs No children 7yrs No smoking in restaurant Civ Wed 45
**CARDS:**

## Premier Collection

### ★★★ Hotel On the Park

38 Evesham Rd GL52 2AH
☎ 01242 518898 Fax 01242 511526
e-mail: stay@hotelonthepark.co.uk
***Dir:*** *opposite Pittville Park. Join one-way system and turn off A435 towards Evesham*

This 12-bedroom town house hotel is located on the southern tip of the Cotswolds and set conveniently close to the centre of town. The hotel itself is delightful and stylish, whilst bedrooms are individually furnished to a very high standard and feature many thoughtful extras. Elegant public rooms include a Regency style bar and drawing room, and the Bacchanalian restaurant, where the standard of cuisine continues to impress. Service is both attentive and friendly.
**ROOMS:** 12 en suite No smoking in 4 bedrooms s £79.50-£144.50; d £99.50-£159.50 * **LB FACILITIES:** STV **CONF:** Board 18
**PARKING:** 9 **NOTES:** No children 8yrs No smoking in restaurant
**CARDS:**

### ★★★68% Charlton Kings

London Rd, Charlton Kings GL52 6UU
☎ 01242 231061 Fax 01242 241900
***Dir:*** *2.5m SE on A40 1st property on left entering Cheltenham from Oxford on the A40*

On the outskirts of Cheltenham, the Charlton Kings is an attractive and friendly hotel providing comfortable, modern accommodation. Bedrooms are well-equipped and tastefully furnished. The restaurant serves well cooked food from a varied menu based on quality ingredients.
**ROOMS:** 14 en suite (2 fmly) No smoking in 5 bedrooms s £61-£81; d £92-£105 (incl. bkfst) * **LB CONF:** Thtr 20 Class 20 Board 20
**PARKING:** 26 **NOTES:** No smoking in restaurant
**CARDS:**

**★★★67% Carlton**
Parabola Rd GL50 3AQ
☎ 01242 514453 📠 01242 226487
e-mail: enquiries@thecarltonhotel.co.uk
This well presented Regency property is conveniently situated close to the town centre. Family owned and run, it provides spacious and comfortable accommodation. An annexe provides rooms with a more luxurious feel and other features include a choice of bars, lounge and conference facilities.
**ROOMS:** 62 en suite 13 annexe en suite (2 fmly) No smoking in 15 bedrooms s £35-£62.50; d £70-£83.50 (incl. bkfst) * **LB**
**FACILITIES:** STV Xmas **CONF:** Thtr 225 Class 150 Board 100 Del from £79 * **SERVICES:** Lift **PARKING:** 85 **NOTES:** No smoking in restaurant
**CARDS:**

**★★★66% *Royal George***
Birdlip GL4 8JH
☎ 01452 862506 📠 01452 862277
***Dir:*** *on the B4070, off the A417*
Situated in an idyllic village, this mellow stone building has been sympathetically converted and extended into a pleasant hotel. Bedrooms are comfortably furnished with modern facilities. Open-plan public areas are informally designed around the bar and restaurant. A path links the hotel to the Cotswold Way.
**ROOMS:** 34 en suite (4 fmly) No smoking in 6 bedrooms
**FACILITIES:** STV Putting green **CONF:** Thtr 100 Class 50 Board 40
**PARKING:** 120 **NOTES:** No dogs (ex guide dogs)
**CARDS:**

**★★★64% George Hotel**
St Georges Rd GL50 3DZ
☎ 01242 235751 📠 01242 224359
e-mail: hotel@stayatthegeorge.co.uk
***Dir:*** *M5 junct 11 follow signs for town centre, at 1st traffic lights turn left into Gloucester Rd, keep straight on, pass railway station over mini-rdbt, at next lights turn right into St Georges Rd. Hotel 0.75m on left.*

GEORGE HOTEL

The George Hotel is privately owned, and part of a terraced row of Regency properties situated close to the centre of town. Bedrooms are well-equipped and tastefully furnished with additional facilities including a bar, Seasons Restaurant and convenient car park.
**ROOMS:** 38 en suite (2 fmly) No smoking in 20 bedrooms s £70; d £90 (incl. bkfst) * **LB** **FACILITIES:** STV **CONF:** Thtr 40 Class 24 Board 20 Del from £95 * **PARKING:** 30 **NOTES:** No dogs (ex guide dogs) No smoking in restaurant RS possible Xmas
**CARDS:**

Popped the question? Hotels with Civ Wed in their entry are licensed for civil wedding ceremonies. Maximum numbers for the ceremony only are shown, e.g. Civ Wed 120

**★★★64% The Prestbury House Hotel & Restaurant**
The Burgage, Prestbury GL52 3DN
☎ 01242 529533 📠 01242 227076
e-mail: sandjw@freenetname.co.uk
***Dir:*** *1m NE of Cheltenham. From Cheltenham racecourse follow signs for Prestbury, hotel is 2nd on the left 500m from racecouse*

The Prestbury House Hotel retains much of its historical charm and is well-situated for the town centre and racecourse. Well-equipped accommodation is divided between spacious rooms in the main house and those in a converted coach house. The owners also run a management training company, and team-building activities sometimes take place in the hotel grounds.
**ROOMS:** 8 en suite 9 annexe en suite (3 fmly) No smoking in 6 bedrooms s £69-£75; d £88-£98 (incl. bkfst) * **LB** **FACILITIES:** **Spa** STV Riding Croquet lawn Jacuzzi Clay pigeons Archery bike hire riding ch fac Xmas **CONF:** Thtr 70 Class 30 Board 25 Del from £100 * **PARKING:** 50 **NOTES:** No dogs (ex guide dogs) No smoking in restaurant Civ Wed 60 **CARDS:**

CHELTENHAM, continued

**★★★64% White House**
Gloucester Rd GL51 0ST
☎ 01452 713226 📠 01452 857590
e-mail: stay@white-house-hotel.co.uk
***Dir:*** *M5 junct 11 onto A40 to Cheltenham, then left at rdbt hotel 0.5m on left*

C

The White House Hotel is situated on the edge of town, and provides comfortable and modern accommodation. The lounge bar and the restaurant are attractively presented, and staff give guests a warm welcome.
**ROOMS:** 49 en suite (4 fmly) No smoking in 13 bedrooms s £40-£75; d £60-£95 (incl. bkfst) * **LB** **FACILITIES:** STV pool table bar games entertainment **CONF:** Thtr 180 Class 80 Board 45 **PARKING:** 150 **NOTES:** No smoking in restaurant RS 12-16 Mar & 10-12 Nov Civ Wed 180 **CARDS:**

*See advert on page 165*

**★★68% Cotswold Grange**
Pittville Circus Rd GL52 2QH
☎ 01242 515119 📠 01242 241537
e-mail: paul@cotswold-grange.fsnet.co.uk
***Dir:*** *from town centre follow signs 'Prestbury'. Turn right at first rdbt, hotel 200yds on left*
Cotswold Grange is an attractive Georgian property built from mellow Cotswold limestone. Situated conveniently close to the centre of Cheltenham the hotel offers well equipped and comfortable accommodation. Facilities include a busy bar, spacious restaurant, cosy lounge and convenient car park.
**ROOMS:** 25 en suite (4 fmly) s fr £50; d fr £75 (incl. bkfst) * **FACILITIES:** ch fac **CONF:** Thtr 20 Class 15 Board 15 Del from £65 * **PARKING:** 20 **NOTES:** No smoking in restaurant Closed 24 Dec-1 Jan RS Sat & Sun evening (food by arrangement)
**CARDS:**

**★★64% North Hall**
Pittville Circus Rd GL52 2PZ
☎ 01242 520589 📠 01242 261953
e-mail: northhallhotel@btinternet.com
***Dir:*** *head towards Cheltenham Town Centre, following directions for Pittville. At Pittville Circus take 1st left into Pittville Circus Rd. Hotel on right*
This large Victorian house, now a privately owned and personally run hotel, is within easy reach of the town centre. It provides well-equipped accommodation, which is equally suitable for tourists

*continued*

and business people. Facilities include a small bar and a comfortable lounge.

**ROOMS:** 20 en suite (2 fmly) No smoking in 8 bedrooms s £45-£60; d £70-£120 (incl. cont bkfst) * **LB** **FACILITIES:** ch fac Xmas **CONF:** Thtr 40 Class 25 Board 15 Del from £72.50 * **PARKING:** 25 **NOTES:** No smoking in restaurant **CARDS:**

## *Town House*

**★★★★ Kandinsky**
Bayshill Rd, Montpellier GL50 3AS
☎ 01242 527788 📠 01242 226412
e-mail: info@hotelkandinsky.com
***Dir:*** *exit M5 junct 11 follow A40 Town centre. Turn right at 2nd rdbt. At 3rd, take 2nd exit into Bayshill Rd. Hotel on corner of Bayshill/Parabola Rds*
The former Savoy Hotel has been transformed and has reopened under a new name. Bedrooms are stylish and modern in design, all equipped to a high standard with CD and video players. Public areas have a quirky appeal, decorated with an unusual array of trinkets. Cafe Paradiso is bright and buzzy, and hidden in the cellars is U-bahn, a 1950s club.
**ROOMS:** 48 en suite (3 fmly) No smoking in 4 bedrooms s £60-£70; d £65-£85 * **LB** **FACILITIES:** STV entertainment **CONF:** Thtr 20 Class 16 Board 16 Del from £130 * **SERVICES:** Lift **PARKING:** 32 **NOTES:** No dogs (ex guide dogs) No smoking in restaurant **CARDS:**

*See advert on opposite page*

**○ *Travelodge***
Golden Valley Roundabout, Hatherley Ln
☎ 08700 850950
**NOTES:** Opening Winter 2001

Travelodge

CHENIES, Buckinghamshire Map 04 TQ09

**★★★69% Bedford Arms Chenies**

PEEL HOTELS

WD3 6EQ
☎ 01923 283301 📠 01923 284825
***Dir:*** *off A404, signposted*
This attractive, 19th-century country inn enjoys a peaceful rural setting. Attractive bedrooms are decorated in traditional style and feature a range of thoughtful extras. Each room is named after a relation of the Duke of Bedford, whose family has an historic association with the hotel. There are two bars and a popular restaurant.
**ROOMS:** 10 en suite No smoking in 3 bedrooms d £155-£170 * **FACILITIES:** STV **CONF:** Thtr 25 Class 10 Board 15 Del £185 * **PARKING:** 60 **NOTES:** No dogs (ex guide dogs)
**CARDS:**

CHERTSEY, Surrey Map 04 TQ06

**★★★65% The Crown**
7 London St KT16 8AP
☎ 01932 564657 📠 01932 570839
e-mail: crownhotel@youngs.co.uk
***Dir:*** *adjacent to Old Town Hall, located in the Town Centre*
Situated in the centre of historic Chertsey, the Crown offers spacious, comfortable accommodation with good business facilities. The popular public bar and conservatory offer a good selection of house wines by the glass.
**ROOMS:** 30 annexe en suite (4 fmly) No smoking in 13 bedrooms s £105-£130; d £115-£130 (incl. bkfst) * **LB** **FACILITIES:** STV Xmas **CONF:** Thtr 100 Class 40 Board 35 **SERVICES:** air con **PARKING:** 50
**CARDS:**

CHESTER, Cheshire Map 07 SJ46
see also Puddington

**★★★★★79% @@@ The Chester Grosvenor**
Eastgate CH1 1LT
☎ 01244 324024 📠 01244 313246
e-mail: chesgrov@chestergrosvenor.co.uk
***Dir:*** *turn off M56 for M53 Chester, then A56 Chester - follow signs for city centre hotels*
Found within the Roman walls of the city, this popular hotel is the essence of Englishness. The Brasserie is bustling and the Library has a discreet club-like feel. In the Arkle restaurant, guests are offered imaginative cuisine using seasonal ingredients in the modern British style. Suites and bedrooms are designed for guest comfort and are of the highest standard.
**ROOMS:** 85 en suite No smoking in 60 bedrooms s £159-£182; d £229-£276 * **LB** **FACILITIES:** STV Sauna Solarium Gym Membership of Country Club entertainment ch fac **CONF:** Thtr 250 Class 120 Board 48 **SERVICES:** Lift air con **NOTES:** No dogs (ex guide dogs) No smoking in restaurant Closed 25-26 Dec RS 27-30 Dec & 1-23 Jan Civ Wed 150
**CARDS:**

**★★★★77% @@ The Chester Crabwell Manor Hotel**
Parkgate Rd, Mollington CH1 6NE
☎ 01244 851666 📠 01244 851400
e-mail: crabwall@marstonhotels.com
***Dir:*** *NW off A540*
A building on this site was first mentioned in the Domesday Book although the current manor house dates back to the mid 17th century when it was rebuilt. Today the hotel stands in 11 acres of immaculately kept, mature gardens and woodland. Public rooms include a super leisure club, a number of cosy lounges and a stylish conservatory restaurant. The individually designed bedrooms are generally spacious and are traditional in style.
**ROOMS:** 48 en suite No smoking in 2 bedrooms s £118-£218; d £135-£235 * **LB** **FACILITIES:** STV Indoor swimming (H) Snooker Sauna Solarium Gym Croquet lawn Jacuzzi Heli pad Xmas **CONF:** Thtr 100 Class 60 Board 36 Del from £115 * **PARKING:** 120 **NOTES:** No dogs (ex guide dogs) No smoking in restaurant Civ Wed 90
**CARDS:**

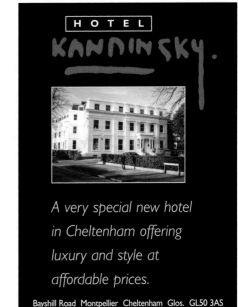



**★★★★70% De Vere Carden Park**
Carden Park CH3 9DQ
☎ 01829 731000 📠 01829 731032
e-mail: reservation@carden-park.co.uk
(For full entry see Broxton)

**★★★★68% Mollington Banastre**
Parkgate Rd CH1 6NN
☎ 01244 851471 📠 01244 851165
***Dir:*** *M56 to junct 16 at next rdbt turn left for Chester A540. Hotel is 2m down the A540 on right*
Set in its own attractive grounds, this hotel caters well for both business and leisure markets. Bedrooms, varying in size, are well-equipped. Stylish public areas include a popular leisure centre, a comfortable bar, the Garden Room restaurant and the less formal Place Apart bistro.
**ROOMS:** 63 en suite (8 fmly) No smoking in 12 bedrooms s £85-£95; d £95-£110 * **LB** **FACILITIES:** STV Indoor swimming (H) Squash Sauna Solarium Gym Croquet lawn Jacuzzi Hairdressing Health & beauty salon entertainment ch fac Xmas **CONF:** Thtr 260 Class 60 Board 50 Del from £105 * **SERVICES:** Lift **PARKING:** 200 **NOTES:** No dogs (ex guide dogs) No smoking in restaurant Civ Wed 150
**CARDS:** 

CHESTER, continued

**★★★★68% Queen**
City Rd CH1 3AH
☎ 01244 305000 🖹 01244 318483
e-mail: reservations.queen@principalhotels.co.uk
***Dir:*** *follow signs for railway station, hotel is opposite*
This former railway hotel has been offering accommodation to visitors to this historic city since the 19th century. The friendly staff and the attentive service lead many guests to return regularly. Bedrooms tend to be spacious and many have views over the garden. Public rooms include an impressive central gallery staircase, two lounges, two bars and a popular restaurant.
**ROOMS:** 128 en suite (6 fmly) No smoking in 24 bedrooms s £85-£119; d £95-£165 (incl. bkfst) * **LB** **FACILITIES:** STV Croquet lawn entertainment Xmas **CONF:** Thtr 280 Class 100 Board 50 Del from £85 * **SERVICES:** Lift **PARKING:** 100 **NOTES:** No smoking in restaurant Civ Wed 250 **CARDS:**

**★★★69% Hoole Hall**
Warrington Rd, Hoole Village CH2 3PD
☎ 01244 408800 🖹 01244 320251
e-mail: hoolehall@corushotels.com
***Dir:*** *from junct 12 on M53 continue 0.5m on A56 towards city centre*

Parts of this hotel date back to the 18th century and it is set in extensive grounds. It is now much extended and modernised, with smart, well-equipped bedrooms. Meetings, banquets and conferences are well catered for and ample car parking space is available.
**ROOMS:** 97 en suite (4 fmly) No smoking in 48 bedrooms s fr £85; d fr £95 * **LB** **FACILITIES:** STV Xmas **CONF:** Thtr 150 Class 40 Board 50 **SERVICES:** Lift **PARKING:** 200 **NOTES:** No smoking in restaurant Civ Wed 140 **CARDS:**

**★★★68% Rowton Hall Country House Hotel**
Whitchurch Rd, Rowton CH3 6AD
☎ 01244 335262 🖹 01244 335464
e-mail: rowtonhall@rowtonhall.co.uk
***Dir:*** *2m SE A41 towards Whitchurch*
This impressive creeper-clad 18th-century country house lies in several acres of mature grounds. Original features include a superb carved staircase and several fireplaces. The modern extensions house a leisure centre and extensive function facilities. The rooms in the manor house are luxuriously spacious and well-equipped. Modern rooms are available in the courtyard.
**ROOMS:** 38 en suite (4 fmly) s £75-£165; d £95-£200 (incl. bkfst) * **LB** **FACILITIES:** STV Indoor swimming (H) Tennis (hard) Sauna Solarium Gym Croquet lawn Jacuzzi Xmas **CONF:** Thtr 200 Class 48 Board 50 Del from £135 * **PARKING:** 120 **NOTES:** No dogs (ex guide dogs) No smoking in restaurant Civ Wed 160 **CARDS:**

**★★★66% Blossoms**
St John St CH1 1HL
☎ 0870 400 8108 🖹 01244 346433
e-mail: heritagehotels-chester.blossoms@forte-hotels.com

***Dir:*** *in city centre, around the corner from the Eastgate Clock*
This well established hotel is ideally situated right in the heart of the city and offers smart, refurbished accommodation. The public areas retain some of their Victorian charm and the atmosphere is enhanced at dinner, on occasions, with live piano music in the lobby. Free parking is available nearby in Newgate Street, close to the hotel.
**ROOMS:** 64 en suite (2 fmly) No smoking in 43 bedrooms s £85; d £105 * **LB** **FACILITIES:** STV Discount at local health club entertainment Xmas **CONF:** Thtr 80 Class 60 Board 60 Del £105 * **SERVICES:** Lift **NOTES:** No smoking in restaurant
**CARDS:**

**★★★66% The Gateway To Wales**
Welsh Rd, Sealand, Deeside CH5 2HX
☎ 01244 830332 🖹 01244 836190
***Dir:*** *4m NW via A548 towards Sealand and Queensferry*
A modern hotel well located for exploring the area, with easy access to Chester. Public areas include The Louis XVI lounge bar, Regency Room restaurant and good leisure facilities. Bedrooms are a good size and well designed.
**ROOMS:** 39 en suite No smoking in 20 bedrooms s £55; d £65 (incl. bkfst) * **LB** **FACILITIES:** STV Indoor swimming (H) Sauna Solarium Gym Jacuzzi Use of Indoor Bowls & Snooker Club Xmas **CONF:** Thtr 150 Class 50 Board 50 **SERVICES:** Lift **PARKING:** 60 **NOTES:** No dogs (ex guide dogs) **CARDS:**

**★★★66% Grosvenor Pulford**
Wrexham Rd, Pulford CH4 9DG
☎ 01244 570560 🖹 01244 570809
e-mail: enquiries@grosvenorpulfordhotel.co.uk
***Dir:*** *exit M53/A55 at junct signposted A483 Chester, Wrexham & North Wales. Turn onto B5445, hotel is 2m on right*
Set in rural surrounds, this hotel features a magnificent leisure club with a large Roman-style swimming pool. A choice of rooms includes several executive suites and others contain spiral staircases leading to the bedroom sections. A Victorian-style, beamed restaurant and bar provide a wide range of imaginative dishes in a relaxed atmosphere.
**ROOMS:** 76 en suite (4 fmly) No smoking in 10 bedrooms s £70-£85; d £85-£110 (incl. bkfst) * **LB** **FACILITIES:** STV Indoor swimming (H) Snooker Sauna Solarium Gym Jacuzzi Hairdressing & Beauty salon ch fac Xmas **CONF:** Thtr 200 Class 100 Board 50 Del from £98 * **SERVICES:** Lift **PARKING:** 160 **NOTES:** Civ Wed 250
**CARDS:**

*See advert on opposite page*

**★★★66% *Posthouse Chester***
Wrexham Rd CH4 9DL
☎ 0870 400 9019 🖹 01244 674100
***Dir:*** *near Wrexham junct on A483, off A55*
This modern, child-friendly hotel has a spacious restaurant, a leisure club and a children's play area. A variety of bedrooms are available, all are well-equipped, particularly the impressive newer Millennium-style and superior rooms. An all-day lounge menu and 24-hour room service are offered.
**ROOMS:** 145 en suite (44 fmly) No smoking in 99 bedrooms
**FACILITIES:** Indoor swimming (H) Sauna Solarium Gym Jacuzzi
**CONF:** Thtr 100 Class 50 Board 40 **PARKING:** 220
**CARDS:**

CHESTER, continued

**★★★64% Broxton Hall Country House**
Whitchurch Rd CH3 9JS
☎ 01829 782321 01829 782330
e-mail: reservations@broxtonhall
(For full entry see Broxton)

**★★68% Dene**
95 Hoole Rd CH2 3ND
☎ 01244 321165 01244 350277
e-mail: denehotel@btconnect.com
***Dir:*** *0.75m E of city centre, from M53 junct 12 take A56 towards Chester, hotel just after Alexander Park*
Conveniently close to the city centre and motorway network, The Dene provides comfortable accommodation. Bedrooms, split between the main house and an adjacent block, vary in size but all are suitably equipped. As well as bar meals an interesting choice of dishes is offered in the welcoming Franc's Brasserie.
**ROOMS:** 44 en suite 8 annexe en suite (5 fmly) No smoking in 16 bedrooms s £46-£49; d £59-£79 (incl. bkfst) * **LB** **FACILITIES:** STV **CONF:** Thtr 30 Class 12 Board 16 Del £70 * **PARKING:** 55 **NOTES:** No smoking in restaurant **CARDS:**

**★★66% *Brookside***
Brook Ln CH2 2AN
☎ 01244 381943 01244 379701
e-mail: info@hotel-chester.com
***Dir:*** *0.5m from city, turn off A5116 into Brook Lane, hotel 300yds on left*
The Brookside is a friendly hotel located just north of the city centre. The attractive public areas consist of a foyer lounge, a small bar and a split-level restaurant. Bedrooms are brightly decorated, and well-equipped.
**ROOMS:** 24 en suite (7 fmly) **FACILITIES:** STV **PARKING:** 20 **NOTES:** No smoking in restaurant **CARDS:**

**★★66% Curzon**
52/54 Hough Green CH4 8JQ
☎ 01244 678581 01244 680866
e-mail: curzon.chester@virgin.net
***Dir:*** *on A5104*

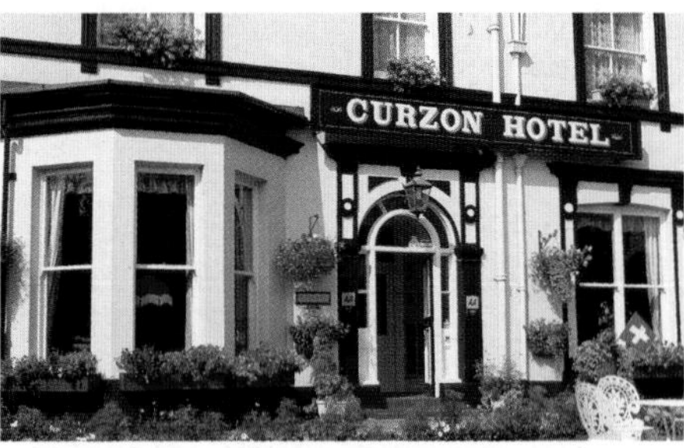
CURZON HOTEL

A detached period property in a predominantly residential suburb close to the racecourse. Bedrooms are large, some have four-poster beds and some are family rooms. The atmosphere is very friendly and the dinner menu offers a good choice.
**ROOMS:** 16 en suite (7 fmly) No smoking in 7 bedrooms s £45-£55; d £60-£75 (incl. bkfst) * **LB** **PARKING:** 20 **NOTES:** No dogs (ex guide dogs) No smoking in restaurant Closed 20-29 Dec
**CARDS:**

*See advert on opposite page*

**★★66% Westminster**
City Rd CH1 3AF
☎ 01244 317341 01244 325369
***Dir:*** *from A56 approx. 3 miles to Chester City Centre, turn left when signposted rail station, hotel directly opposite station*
The Westminster is a long-established hotel which is close to the railway station and city centre. It has an attractive, Tudor-style exterior but bedrooms are brightly decorated with a modern theme. There is a choice of bars and the large dining room serves a good range of dishes.
**ROOMS:** 75 en suite (5 fmly) No smoking in 20 bedrooms **FACILITIES:** STV entertainment Xmas **CONF:** Thtr 150 Class 60 Board 40 Del from £75 * **SERVICES:** Lift **NOTES:** Civ Wed 100
**CARDS:**

**★★65% Chester Court**
48 Hoole Rd CH2 3NL
☎ 01244 320779 or 317809 01244 344795
e-mail: info@chestercourthotel.com
***Dir:*** *M53 junct 12 onto small section of dual carriageway come to large rdbt straight across onto A56. Hotel on right opposite All Saints Church*
Bedrooms are well equipped with modern facilities and many are located at ground level in a peaceful courtyard. Some rooms have four-poster beds, and family accommodation is available. The hotel has a lounge and a bar, and a well-appointed restaurant featuring a pleasing conservatory.
**ROOMS:** 8 en suite 12 annexe en suite (4 fmly) No smoking in 8 bedrooms s £45; d £65-£70 (incl. bkfst) * **LB** **FACILITIES:** STV **CONF:** Thtr 20 Class 9 Board 12 **PARKING:** 30 **NOTES:** No dogs (ex guide dogs) No smoking in restaurant Closed 2 wks Xmas
**CARDS:**

**★★64% Eaton**
29/31 City Rd CH1 3AE
☎ 01244 320840 01244 320850
e-mail: welcome@eatonhotelchester.co.uk
***Dir:*** *400 metres from the station, towards the city centre, adjacent to the canal*
This privately owned hotel is a short walk from the city centre and conveniently placed for the railway station. There is an attractive cane-furnished bar and a wood-panelled dining room with a small daily fixed-price menu. Enclosed car parking is available.
**ROOMS:** 16 en suite (3 fmly) s £45-£55; d £57.50-£75 (incl. bkfst) * **LB** **PARKING:** 10 **CARDS:**

**⇧ *Premier Lodge***
76 Liverpool Rd CH2 1AU
☎ 0870 700 1350 0870 700 1351
Premier Lodge offers modern, well-equipped, en suite accommodation suitable for both business and leisure travellers. Meals can be taken at the adjacent popular restaurant and bar, which is fully licensed. For further details, consult the Hotel Groups page.
**ROOMS:** 31 en suite

**○ Innkeeper's Lodge Chester**
Whitchurch Rd CH3 6AE
A new concept in the travel accommodation market. Smart rooms meet essential business requirements but also have home comforts. Dining options include all-day menus plus the added advantage of breakfast, which is included in the room price. Reservations can be made seven days a week through the room reservations number: 0870 243 0500. For further details, consult the Hotel Groups page.
**ROOMS:** 14 en suite **NOTES:** Open now

### ○ Innkeeper's Lodge Chester Northeast

Warrington Rd, Mickle Trafford CH2 4EX

A new concept in the travel accommodation market. Smart rooms meet essential business requirements but also have home comforts. Dining options include all-day menus plus the added advantage of breakfast, which is included in the room price. Reservations can be made seven days a week through the room reservations number: 0870 243 0500. For further details, consult the Hotel Groups page.

**ROOMS:** 36 en suite

CHESTERFIELD, Derbyshire — Map 08 SK37

### ★★★63% Sandpiper

Sheffield Rd, Sheepbridge S41 9EH

☎ 01246 450550 📠 01246 452805

e-mail: sales.sandpiper@virgin.net

***Dir:*** *leave M1 junct 29 follow A617 to Chesterfield. Follow A61 to Sheffield then at 1st exit take Dronfield Rd. Hotel 0.5m on left*

Conveniently situated for the A61 and M1, just three miles from Chesterfield, this modern hotel offers comfortable and well-furnished bedrooms. Public areas are situated in a separate building across the car park and include a cosy bar and open plan restaurant, serving a range of interesting and popular dishes.

**ROOMS:** 28 annexe en suite (4 fmly) No smoking in 14 bedrooms s £35-£40; d £35-£40 * **LB** **FACILITIES:** STV **CONF:** Thtr 100 Class 35 Board 35 Del from £70 * **PARKING:** 120 **NOTES:** No dogs (ex guide dogs) RS X-mas & New Year Civ Wed 80

**CARDS:**

*See advert on this page*

### ★★69% Abbeydale

Cross St S40 4PD

☎ 01246 277849 📠 01246 558223

e-mail: abbeydale1ef@cs.com

***Dir:*** *M1 junct 29, then A619 towards Buxton, at B&Q island turn by KFC to Flojambe Rd. Over lights into West St, turn right into Cross St*

Situated in a quiet residential area of the town, this friendly hotel offers excellent service and warm hospitality. Bedrooms are bright, fresh and well-equipped. A short selection of very well-prepared dishes is served in the dining room, adjacent to the cosy lounge and bar.

**ROOMS:** 11 en suite (1 fmly) No smoking in 10 bedrooms s £40-£45; d £55-£65 (incl. bkfst) * **LB** **PARKING:** 14 **NOTES:** No smoking in restaurant RS 23-25 & 31 Dec, 1 Jan **CARDS:**

### ⇧ Hotel Ibis

Lordsmill St S41 7RW

☎ 01246 221333 📠 01246 221444

e-mail: H3160@accor-hotels.com

***Dir:*** *M1 junct29, take A617 to Chesterfield. Straight over main rdbt. Hotel is located on the next rdbt*

Modern, budget hotel offering comfortable accommodation in bright and practical bedrooms. Breakfast is self-service and dinner is available in the restaurant. For further details, consult the Hotel Groups page.

**ROOMS:** 86 en suite s fr £42; d fr £42 * **CONF:** Thtr 35 Class 20 Board 22

### ⇧ *Travelodge*

Brimmington Rd, Inner Ring Rd, Wittington Moor S41 9BE

☎ 01246 455411 📠 01246 455411

***Dir:*** *A61, N of town centre*

Travelodge offers good quality, good value, modern accommodation. Ideal for families, the spacious, en suite bedrooms include remote-control TV, tea and coffee-making

*continued on p172*

CHESTERFIELD, continued

facilities, luxury beds and free morning newspaper. Meals can be taken at the nearby family restaurant. For further details and the Travelodge phone number, consult the Hotel Groups page.

**ROOMS:** 20 en suite

C

CHICHESTER, West Sussex Map 04 SU80

**★★★★72% Marriott Goodwood Park Hotel & Country Club**

Marriott
HOTELS · RESORTS · SUITES

PO18 0QB
☎ 01243 775537 01243 520120
(For full entry see Goodwood)

**★★★74% The Millstream**
Bosham Ln PO18 8HL
☎ 01243 573234 01243 573459
e-mail: info@millstream-hotel.co.uk
(For full entry see Bosham and advert on opposite page)

**★★★68% Crouchers Bottom Country Hotel**
Birdham Rd PO20 7EH
☎ 01243 784995 01243 539797
e-mail: crouchers_bottom@btconnect.com
***Dir:*** *turn off A27 to the A286, 1.5m from Chichester centre opposite the Black Horse pub*

Close to the harbour, this family-run hotel provides attractive coach house rooms, all of which are well-equipped. Public areas, including a comfortable lounge and separate bar, have a homely, relaxed atmosphere. There is also a smart, beamed restaurant.
**ROOMS:** 15 en suite (1 fmly) No smoking in 9 bedrooms s £49-£65; d £85-£115 * LB **CONF:** Del from £88 * **PARKING:** 40 **NOTES:** No smoking in restaurant **CARDS:**

**★★★68% Ship**
North St PO19 1NH
☎ 01243 778000 01243 788000
e-mail: bookings@shiphotel.com
***Dir:*** *enter Chichester from A27, go round the inner ring road to Northgate, at large Northgate rdbt turn left into North St, hotel is on left*
This well-presented and friendly Georgian hotel has a prime position at the top of North Street. Popular with non-residents, the bar and restaurant offer a comfortable venue for refreshments and meals. Bedrooms have been refurbished to a high standard,

continued

and all are well-equipped. A subtle nautical theme runs through the hotel, once the home of Admiral George Murray.

**ROOMS:** 36 en suite (4 fmly) s £69-£78; d £95-£118 (incl. bkfst) * LB **FACILITIES:** STV Xmas **CONF:** Thtr 70 Class 35 Board 30 Del from £110 * **SERVICES:** Lift **PARKING:** 38 **NOTES:** No smoking in restaurant
**CARDS:**

*See advert on opposite page*

**★★67% Bedford**
Southgate PO19 1DP
☎ 01243 785766 01243 533175
e-mail: bedford@win-ship.demon.co.uk
***Dir:*** *from A27 (Chichester Bypass) continue N past level crossing at Chichester Station. Hotel 400yds on right*
Close to the centre of Chichester and near the station, this well-presented hotel dates back to the 1700s. Bedrooms are attractively decorated, comfortably furnished and well-equipped. Public areas include a cosy bar, separate lounges (one non smoking) and dining room which overlooks the inviting and shady rear patio. Service is friendly and guests are assured a warm welcome.
**ROOMS:** 19 rms (16 en suite) (2 fmly) No smoking in 11 bedrooms s £60-£65; d £88-£90 (incl. bkfst) * LB **PARKING:** 8 **NOTES:** No dogs (ex guide dogs) No smoking in restaurant Closed 24-30 Dec
**CARDS:**

**★★60% Suffolk House**
3 East Row PO19 1PD
☎ 01243 778899 01243 787282
e-mail: info@suffolkhshotel.co.uk
***Dir:*** *turn right off East St into Little London, follow into East Row, hotel on left*
This Georgian hotel is a few minutes walk from the town centre. Bedrooms vary in shape and size; all are comfortably furnished and feature many thoughtful touches. There is a small bar area, pleasant patio and a restaurant offering an interesting menu. Telephone beforehand about parking.
**ROOMS:** 11 en suite (2 fmly) No smoking in 3 bedrooms s £59; d £89-£125 (incl. bkfst) * LB **CONF:** Thtr 25 Class 12 Board 16 Del £98 * **NOTES:** No dogs (ex guide dogs) **CARDS:**

CHIDEOCK, Dorset Map 03 SY49

**★★71% Chideock House**
Main St DT6 6JN
☎ 01297 489242 01297 489184
e-mail: enquiries@chideockhousehotel.com
***Dir:*** *on A35 between Lyme Regis and Bridport*
This delightful, part-thatched house dates back to the 15th century. It is full of character and retains many original beams and fireplaces. Service here is particularly friendly and welcoming.

continued

Thoughtful touches abound in the varied bedrooms. An interesting and award winning menu is offered in the comfortable restaurant.
**ROOMS:** 9 rms (8 en suite) s £60-£80; d £60-£90 (incl. bkfst) * LB
**FACILITIES:** Xmas **PARKING:** 20 **NOTES:** No smoking in restaurant
Closed 2 Jan-5 Feb **CARDS:**

## CHIPPENHAM, Wiltshire — Map 03 ST97

### ★★★70% Angel Hotel

Best Western

Market Place SN15 3HD
☎ 01249 652615 Fax 01249 443210
e-mail: reception@angelhotelchippenham.co.uk
***Dir:** follow brown tourist signs for Bowood House. Pass under railway arch, then follow signs for 'Borough Parade Parking'. Hotel next to car park*

Dating back many centuries, this impressive building is home to a smart, comfortable hotel. Bedrooms vary from the main house where character is the key, to smart executive style courtyard rooms; both are equipped with modern facilities and are of a good size. There are two popular bars and a lovely panelled dining room.
**ROOMS:** 15 en suite 35 annexe en suite (3 fmly) s £88-£105; d £98-£110 LB **FACILITIES:** STV Indoor swimming (H) Gym **CONF:** Thtr 120 Class 50 Board 50 Del from £120 * **PARKING:** 50 **NOTES:** Civ Wed 25
**CARDS:**

### ★★★68% Stanton Manor Country House Hotel

SN14 6DQ
☎ 01666 837552 Fax 01666 837022
e-mail: reception@stantonmanor.co.uk
(For full entry see Stanton St Quintin)

## CHIPPERFIELD, Hertfordshire — Map 04 TL00

### ★★72% *The Two Brewers*

Scottish Newcastle hotels

The Common WD4 9BS
☎ 01923 265266 Fax 01923 261884
***Dir:** turn left in centre of village, hotel overlooks common*

This 16th-century inn retains much of its old world charm while providing modern comforts and amenities. The spacious bedrooms are tastefully furnished and decorated, offering a comprehensive range of in-room facilities. The focal point of the hotel is the bar which serves an enjoyable pub-style meal and has a loyal local following.
**ROOMS:** 20 en suite No smoking in 10 bedrooms **FACILITIES:** STV
**CONF:** Board 16 **PARKING:** 25 **NOTES:** No dogs (ex guide dogs)
**CARDS:**

## CHIPPING CAMPDEN, Gloucestershire — Map 04 SP13

*Premier Collection*

### ★★★ @@ Cotswold House

The Square GL55 6AN
☎ 01386 840330 Fax 01386 840310
e-mail: reception@cotswoldhouse.com
***Dir:** from A44 take B4081 signposted to Chipping Campden village. Turn right into High St at T junct. Cotswold House is located at the Square*

Located in a prime position in the heart of Chipping Campden, this hotel is the perfect base for a touring holiday or a well-deserved break. It is an elegant 17th-century house that offers a relaxed atmosphere, overlooking the Town Square. The individually decorated bedrooms are comfortable and include many thoughtful extra touches. A choice of eating options is available, from the elegant restaurant overlooking

*continued on p174*

CHIPPING CAMPDEN, continued

the garden, to the stylish and recently completed Hicks' Brasserie and Bar.

COTSWOLD HOUSE

*Cotswold House, Chipping Campden*

**ROOMS:** 15 en suite No smoking in all bedrooms s £75-£80; d £140-£180 (incl. bkfst) * **LB** **FACILITIES:** STV Gym Croquet lawn Access to local Sports Centre entertainment Xmas **CONF:** Thtr 30 Class 20 Board 20 Del from £150 * **PARKING:** 15 **NOTES:** No smoking in restaurant Civ Wed 40
**CARDS:**

### ★★★73% Noel Arms

High St GL55 6AT
☎ 01386 840317 01386 841136
e-mail: bookings@cotswold-inns-hotels.co.uk
***Dir:*** *turn off A44 onto B4081 to Chipping Campden, take 1st right down hill into town. Hotel on right opposite Market Hall.*

Situated right in the heart of the town, this 14th-century hotel retains much of its original character, yet has been extensively refurbished. Bedrooms are well co-ordinated. Public areas include a popular bar, conservatory lounge and bright restaurant offering high standards of cuisine.

**ROOMS:** 26 en suite (1 fmly) **CONF:** Thtr 50 Board 25 **PARKING:** 30 **NOTES:** No smoking in restaurant Civ Wed 70
**CARDS:**

### ★★★73% Seymour House

High St GL55 6AH
☎ 01386 840429 01386 840369
e-mail: enquiry@seymourhousehotel.com
***Dir:*** *Hotel in middle of High St opposite Lloyds Bank*

Centrally located in one of the most idyllic villages in England, this lovely Cotswold property dates back to the early 18th century. Bedrooms vary in size and style, and all offer good levels of comfort. Public rooms, including a drawing room, the Vinery restaurant and separate bar, reflect the house's original charm and character.

**ROOMS:** 11 en suite 4 annexe en suite s fr £72.50; d £95-£180 (incl. bkfst) * **LB** **FACILITIES:** STV ch fac Xmas **CONF:** Thtr 65 Class 26 Board 30 Del from £125 * **PARKING:** 28 **NOTES:** No dogs (ex guide dogs) No smoking in restaurant Civ Wed 65
**CARDS:**

### ★★★73% Three Ways House

Mickleton GL55 6SB
☎ 01386 438429 01386 438118
e-mail: threeways@puddingclub.com
***Dir:*** *situated on B4632 Stratford upon Avon to Broadway Road, hotel in centre of Mickleton Village*

THE CIRCLE
Selected Individual Hotels
GREAT BRITAIN

THREE WAYS HOUSE HOTEL

This charming hotel was built in 1870, and is now the home of the world famous Pudding Club. An extensive refurbishment programme has seen improvements to the now stylish and air-conditioned restaurant and Randalls bar/bistro, along with lounges and meeting rooms. Bedrooms are spacious and attractively furnished with some reflecting the pudding theme.

**ROOMS:** 41 en suite (5 fmly) s £65-£75; d £95-£125 (incl. bkfst) * **LB** **FACILITIES:** entertainment ch fac Xmas **CONF:** Thtr 100 Class 40 Board 35 Del from £125 * **PARKING:** 37 **NOTES:** No smoking in restaurant Civ Wed 80 **CARDS:**

## CHITTLEHAMHOLT, Devon

Map 03 SS62

### ★★★69% Highbullen

EX37 9HD
☎ 01769 540561 01769 540492
e-mail: highbullen@sosi.net
***Dir:*** *leave M5 junct 27 onto A361 to South Molton, then B3226 Crediton Rd after 5.2m turn right up hill to Chittlehamholt, hotel 0.5m beyond village*

Highbullen is a magnificent Victorian gothic mansion, set in parkland with its own 18-hole golf course. An imaginative, fixed-price menu is served in the cellar restaurant, whilst light lunches are served in the bar or courtyard. Breakfast is served in a room with superb views of the valley. There is a wide choice of bedroom type, spread between the mansion and fully converted buildings within the grounds.

**ROOMS:** 12 en suite 25 annexe en suite **FACILITIES:** Indoor swimming (H) Outdoor swimming (H) Golf 18 Tennis (hard) Fishing Squash Snooker Sauna Solarium Gym Croquet lawn Putting green Hairdressing Beauty Massage **CONF:** Board 20 **PARKING:** 60 **NOTES:** No dogs (ex guide dogs) No children 8yrs No smoking in restaurant
**CARDS:**

Packed in a hurry? Ironing facilities should be available at all star levels, either in rooms or on request.

CHOLLERFORD, Northumberland — Map 12 NY97

**★★★73% ⊛ Swallow George Hotel**

SWALLOW
HOTELS

NE46 4EW
☎ 01434 681611 🖷 01434 681727
e-mail: georgehotel@chollerford.fsbusiness.co.uk
***Dir:*** *0.25m W of Hexham turn off A69 onto A6079, follow road NW for 4m until crossroads, turn left onto B6318, hotel 0.25m on right hand side over bridge*

A long-established hotel enjoying a riverside setting in attractive gardens. Comfort and hospitality are strong features. Bedrooms are well-equipped, with several overlooking the river. The elegant restaurant offers a good selection of interesting dishes.
**ROOMS:** 47 en suite (5 fmly) No smoking in 19 bedrooms s £85-£110; d £120-£140 (incl. bkfst) * **LB** **FACILITIES:** STV Indoor swimming (H) Fishing Sauna Solarium Gym Putting green Jacuzzi Jogging track Xmas **CONF:** Thtr 80 Class 30 Board 32 Del from £99 * **PARKING:** 70 **NOTES:** No smoking in restaurant Civ Wed 80
**CARDS:**

CHORLEY, Lancashire — Map 07 SD51

**★★★71% ⊛ Shaw Hill Hotel Golf & Country Club**

Preston Rd, Whittle-le-Woods PR6 7PP
☎ 01257 269221 🖷 01257 261223
e-mail: info@shaw-hill.co.uk
***Dir:*** *off A6, S of junct with B5248 at Whittle-le-Woods. 3m from M6, junct 28; 4m from M55, junct 29; 1m from M61, junct 8*

This impressive Georgian mansion has been lovingly restored whilst still retaining many original features and overlooks its own 18 hole championship golf course. The spacious public areas also offer extensive leisure and conference facilities, as well as numerous lounges and an elegant restaurant. Spacious bedrooms vary in style, but are all thoughtfully equipped and comfortably furnished.
**ROOMS:** 26 en suite 4 annexe en suite (1 fmly) s £73-£100; d £90-£120 (incl. bkfst) * **LB** **FACILITIES:** Spa STV Indoor swimming (H) Golf 18 Snooker Sauna Solarium Gym Putting green Jacuzzi Beauty salon Hairdresser **CONF:** Thtr 350 Class 100 Board 150 Del from £62.50 * **PARKING:** 200 **NOTES:** No dogs (ex guide dogs) Closed 24-27 Dec Civ Wed 200 **CARDS:**

**★★★69% Park Hall**

Park Hall Rd, Charnock Richard PR7 5LP
☎ 01257 452090 455000 🖷 01257 451838
e-mail: conference@parkhall-hotel.co.uk
***Dir:*** *off A49 W of village. Follow brown tourist signs from M6/M61*

Best Western

Situated beside the Camelot Theme Park, the hotel provides a choice of well equipped bedrooms ranging from modern contemporary rooms to themed cottage style accommodation. The Park View Restaurant has light modern decor, or less formal eating

*continued on p176*

CHORLEY, continued

is available in the lounge bar. Packages that include entrance to Camelot Theme Park are available.
**ROOMS:** 54 en suite 84 annexe en suite (59 fmly) No smoking in 11 bedrooms s £89-£119; d £89-£119 * **LB FACILITIES:** Spa STV Indoor swimming (H) Sauna Solarium Gym Jacuzzi Steam room Weights room ch fac Xmas **CONF:** Thtr 700 Class 240 Board 40 Del from £110 * **SERVICES:** Lift **PARKING:** 2600 **NOTES:** No dogs (ex guide dogs) No smoking in restaurant Civ Wed 200
**CARDS:**

### Premier Lodge
Malt House farm, Moss Ln, Whittle le Woods PR6 8AB
☎ 0870 700 1354 📠 0870 700 1355
e-mail: malthousefarm20@hotmail.com
***Dir:*** *M61 junct 8 onto A647 towards Wheelton. Take 1st left turn onto Moss lane sign posted for Whittle-Le-Woods/Whittle springs*
Premier Lodge offers modern, well-equipped, en suite accommodation suitable for both business and leisure travellers. Meals can be taken at the adjacent popular restaurant and bar, which is fully licensed. For further details, consult the Hotel Groups page.
**ROOMS:** 83 en suite d £42 * **CONF:** Thtr 200 Class 80 Board 60 Del £85 *

### *Premier Lodge (Chorley South)*
Bolton Rd PR7 4AB
☎ 0870 700 1352 📠 0870 700 1353
Premier Lodge offers modern, well-equipped, en suite accommodation suitable for both business and leisure travellers. Meals can be taken at the adjacent popular restaurant and bar, which is fully licensed. For further details, consult the Hotel Groups page.
**ROOMS:** 29 en suite

### *Travelodge*
Preston Rd, Clayton-le-Woods PR6 7JB
☎ 01772 311963
***Dir:*** *from M6 junc28 take B5256 for approx 2m, next to Halfway House public house*
Travelodge offers good quality, good value, modern accommodation. Ideal for families, the spacious, en suite bedrooms include remote-control TV, tea and coffee-making facilities, luxury beds and free morning newspaper. Meals can be taken at the nearby family restaurant. For further details and the Travelodge phone number, consult the Hotel Groups page.

**ROOMS:** 40 en suite

### Welcome Lodge
Welcome Break Services PR7 5LR
☎ 01257 791746 📠 01257 793596
e-mail: charnockhotel@welcomebreak.co.uk
***Dir:*** *Located on north-bound side of the Welcome Break service area between junct 27 & 28 of the M6. 500yds from Camelot Theme Park via Mill Lane*
This modern building offers accommodation in smart, spacious and well-equipped bedrooms, suitable for families and business travellers, and all with en suite bathrooms. Refreshments may be taken at the nearby family restaurant. For further details and the Welcome Break phone number, consult the Hotel Groups page.
**ROOMS:** 100 en suite s £35-£50; d £35-£50 * **CONF:** Thtr 12 Class 25 Board 12 Del from £75 *

CHRISTCHURCH, Dorset Map 04 SZ19

### ★★★74% Waterford Lodge
87 Bure Ln, Friars Cliff, Mudeford BH23 4DN
☎ 01425 272948 & 278801 📠 01425 279130
e-mail: Waterford@bestwestern.co.uk
***Dir:*** *from A35 Somerford rdbt 2m E of Christchurch take A337 towards Highcliffe, at next rdbt turn towards Mudeford, hotel on left. Hotel signposted*

Situated within easy reach of Christchurch, the hotel is popular with business guests as well as holiday makers. It offers attractive, spacious bedrooms, a comfortable bar lounge overlooking the gardens and a well-appointed restaurant.
**ROOMS:** 18 en suite (1 fmly) s fr £82; d fr £95 * **LB FACILITIES:** STV ch fac Xmas **CONF:** Thtr 100 Class 48 Board 36 Del from £105.75 * **PARKING:** 38 **NOTES:** No smoking in restaurant Closed 27 Dec-2 Jan
**CARDS:**

### ★★★67% The Avonmouth
95 Mudeford BH23 3NT
☎ 0870 400 8120 📠 01202 479004
e-mail: heritagehotels_mudeford_christchurch.avonmouth@forte-hotels.com
***Dir:*** *approaching Christchurch on A35 from Lyndhurst, left at rdbt on A337 to Highcliffe, right at next rdbt, follow road for approx 1.5m, hotel on left*
In a superb location alongside Mudeford Quay, this friendly hotel offers smart garden rooms with their own small patios. A number of bedrooms in the main house overlook the Quay. Modern facilities and decor enhance overall comfort. Traditional public areas are comfortable and very well-cooked meals are served in the lovely restaurant.
**ROOMS:** 26 en suite 14 annexe en suite No smoking in 14 bedrooms s £74-£104; d £108-£188 (incl. bkfst & dinner) * **LB**
**FACILITIES:** Outdoor swimming (H) Croquet lawn Putting green Boat hire Sailing trips entertainment Xmas **CONF:** Thtr 70 Class 25 Board 24 Del from £90 * **PARKING:** 80 **NOTES:** No smoking in restaurant Civ Wed 70 **CARDS:**

CHURCHILL, Somerset Map 03 ST45

### ★★62% *Winston Manor*
Bristol Rd BS25 5NL
☎ 01934 852348 📠 01934 852033
***Dir:*** *On A38 100yds N of junction with A368 Bath to Weston-Super-Mare*
A friendly small hotel, run in a relaxed manner by the resident proprietors. It is conveniently located for both Bristol International airport and the many local attractions. Bedrooms, including many on the ground floor, are neatly decorated and well-equipped. The

continued

dinner menu includes an interesting selection of fresh home cooking.
**ROOMS:** 14 en suite (1 fmly) No smoking in 4 bedrooms **CONF:** Thtr 40 Class 30 Board 30 **PARKING:** 24 **NOTES:** No smoking in restaurant
**CARDS:**

## CHURCH STRETTON, Shropshire Map 07 SO49

### ★★★66% Stretton Hall Hotel
All Stretton SY6 6HG
☎ 01694 723224 01694 724365
e-mail: aa@strettonhall.co.uk
***Dir:*** *from Shrewsbury, on A49, turn right onto B4370 signed to All Stretton, hotel in 1m on left opposite The Yew Tree PH*

A fine 18th-century country house standing in spacious gardens. Original oak panelling features throughout the lounge bar, lounge and halls. Bedrooms are traditionally furnished yet have modern facilities. Family and four-poster rooms are available and the restaurant has been tastefully refurbished.
**ROOMS:** 12 en suite (1 fmly) s £40-£80; d £60-£110 (incl. bkfst) * **LB** **FACILITIES:** ch fac Xmas **CONF:** Thtr 80 Class 24 Board 18 Del £90 * **PARKING:** 70 **NOTES:** No smoking in restaurant Civ Wed 60
**CARDS:**

### ★★70% Mynd House
Ludlow Rd, Little Stretton SY6 6RB
☎ 01694 722212 01694 724180
e-mail: info@myndhouse.co.uk
***Dir:*** *off A49 onto B4370 and follow signs for Little Stretton, hotel 0.75m on left just beyond Ragleth Inn*
This large Edwardian house is situated in the sleepy hamlet of Little Stretton, and is reached via a steep driveway. The bedrooms have many thoughtful extras and are well-equipped. Public areas include a comfortable lounge, a pleasant bar and a traditional style dining room.
**ROOMS:** 7 en suite (2 fmly) No smoking in all bedrooms s £45-£50; d £60-£120 (incl. bkfst) * **LB** **PARKING:** 8 **NOTES:** No children 10yrs No smoking in restaurant **CARDS:**

## CHURT, Surrey Map 04 SU83

### ★★★70% Frensham Pond Hotel
Best Western
Bacon Ln GU10 2QB
☎ 01252 795161 01252 792631
e-mail: frenshampondhotel@bestwestern.co.uk
***Dir:*** *from A3 turn right onto A287. After 4m turn left at 'Beware Horses' sign to hotel 0.25m along Pond Lane*
This 15th Century house occupies a fantastic location on the edge of Frensham pond. Public areas are light and well-appointed with recent decoration. Bedrooms are generally spacious with some garden suites available. There are conference rooms and leisure, including a squash court.

**ROOMS:** 39 en suite 12 annexe en suite s £80-£95; d £85-£110 (incl. cont bkfst) * **LB** **FACILITIES:** STV Indoor swimming (H) Squash Sauna Gym Jacuzzi Steam room Xmas **CONF:** Thtr 120 Class 45 Board 40 Del from £110 * **PARKING:** 120 **NOTES:** No dogs (ex guide dogs) No smoking in restaurant **CARDS:**

*See advert under FARNHAM*

### ★★70% Pride of the Valley
Jumps Rd GU10 2LE
☎ 01428 605799 01428 605875
***Dir:*** *Turn off A3 at Hindhead traffic lights for Farnham. Follow signs for Tilford, 0.5m turn right Hotel 2m on left hand side.*
This friendly hotel has been totally refurbished in an eclectic style. Bedrooms are all individually decorated with such themes as nautical or Far Eastern. Contrasting in style, the bar and restaurant both offer a good menu and high levels of comfort.
**ROOMS:** 13 en suite 3 annexe en suite (1 fmly) No smoking in all bedrooms s £95; d £125 (incl. bkfst) * **LB** **FACILITIES:** Xmas **CONF:** Thtr 50 Class 30 Board 30 Del from £95 * **PARKING:** 85 **NOTES:** No dogs No smoking in restaurant
**CARDS:**

## CIRENCESTER, Gloucestershire Map 04 SP00

### ★★★69% The Crown of Crucis
Ampney Crucis GL7 5RS
☎ 01285 851806 01285 851735
e-mail: info@thecrownofcrucis.co.uk
***Dir:*** *take A417 to Fairford, hotel is approx 2.5m on left*
This delightful hotel consists of two buildings, one a 16th-century coaching inn, which now houses the bar and restaurant, and a more modern bedroom block which surrounds a courtyard. Rooms are attractively appointed and offer modern facilities, and the restaurant serves good imaginative food.
**ROOMS:** 25 en suite (2 fmly) No smoking in 10 bedrooms s £62; d £88 (incl. bkfst) * **LB** **FACILITIES:** Free membership of local leisure centre **CONF:** Thtr 80 Class 40 Board 25 **PARKING:** 82 **NOTES:** No smoking in restaurant Closed 24-30 Dec **CARDS:**

### ★★★68% Stratton House
Forestdale Hotels
Gloucester Rd GL7 2LE
☎ 01285 651761 01285 640024
e-mail: stratton.house@forestdale.com
***Dir:*** *M4 junct 15, A419 to Cirencester, hotel on left on A417. M5 exit 11 to Cheltenham, follow B4070 to A417, hotel on right*
This attractive 17th-century manor house is quietly situated half a mile or so from the town centre. Bedrooms are well presented, more spacious 'premier' rooms are available in a new wing. The

*continued on p178*

C

CIRENCESTER, continued

comfortable drawing rooms and restaurant have views over well-tended gardens.
**ROOMS:** 41 en suite No smoking in 19 bedrooms s £63-£73; d £126-£146 (incl. bkfst & dinner) * LB **FACILITIES:** Xmas **CONF:** Thtr 150 Class 50 Board 40 Del £145 * **PARKING:** 100 **NOTES:** No smoking in restaurant Civ Wed **CARDS:**

### ★★ The New Inn At Coln
GL7 5AN
☎ 01285 750651 01285 750657
e-mail: stay@new-inn.co.uk
(For full entry see Coln St-Aldwyns)

### ★★69% Corinium Court Hotel
12 Gloucester St GL7 2DG
☎ 01285 659711 01285 885807
e-mail: info@coriniumhotel.co.uk
***Dir:*** *from traffic lights on A417 into Spitalgate Ln, hotel car park 50mtrs on right*
Located just north of the town centre, this personally run hotel is some 400 years old and was once a wool merchant's house. Recent refurbishment has taken place with the accommodation now comfortably furnished throughout. The public areas have a lot of character and include a quaint bar and a large restaurant which is found in what used to be stables.
**ROOMS:** 15 en suite (3 fmly) s £65-£85; d £130-£170 (incl. bkfst) * LB **CONF:** Board 10 **PARKING:** 25 **NOTES:** No smoking in restaurant **CARDS:**

### ○ *Travelodge*
Burford Rd
☎ 08700 850950
**NOTES:** Opening Winter 2001

Travelodge

CLACTON-ON-SEA, Essex — Map 05 TM11

### ★★68% *Esplanade Hotel*
27-29 Marine Pde East CO15 1UU
☎ 01255 220450 01255 221800
***Dir:*** *enter Clacton on Sea on the A133 follow sign to Sea Front (Carnarvon Rd) at sea front turn right, hotel on right in 50yds*
Close to the pier and overlooking the seafront, this hotel is within easy walking distance of the town centre and local attractions. The bedrooms are furnished and decorated to a good standard; many have sea views. There is a comfortable lounge bar, and in Coasters Restaurant guests can choose from the set or carte menus.
**ROOMS:** 29 en suite (2 fmly) **CONF:** Class 50 **PARKING:** 13 **NOTES:** No dogs (ex guide dogs) No smoking in restaurant Civ Wed 70 **CARDS:**

### ★73% Chudleigh
13 Agate Rd, Marine Pde West CO15 1RA
☎ 01255 425407 01255 470280
***Dir:*** *follow signs to Town Centre, Seafront and Pier. Turn right at seafront and then right again into Agate Rd after crossing traffic lights at Pier*
Privately owned, family run hotel situated within easy walking distance of the town centre, pier and seafront. Popular with both business and leisure guests. The spacious bedrooms are attractively decorated and equipped with many thoughtful touches. Public rooms include a cosy lounge and a smart restaurant serving freshly prepared meals.
**ROOMS:** 10 en suite (2 fmly) No smoking in 2 bedrooms s £39; d £55 (incl. bkfst) * **PARKING:** 7 **NOTES:** No smoking in restaurant Closed 22-27 Dec RS Oct-Mar **CARDS:**

CLANFIELD, Oxfordshire — Map 04 SP20

### ★★★71% Plough at Clanfield
Bourton Rd OX18 2RB
☎ 01367 810222 01367 810596
e-mail: ploughatclanfield@hotmail.com
***Dir:*** *on edge of village at junct of A4095/B4020*
An archetypal stone-built Elizabethan manor house retaining many original features. The cosy bar has two log-burning fires and each of the individually styled bedrooms is well-equipped with extra touches such as decanters of sherry and bathrobes. Food is taken seriously and the kitchen brigade cooks with flair. A friendly yet unstuffy professional atmosphere prevails.
**ROOMS:** 12 en suite No smoking in all bedrooms s £82.25-£110; d £95-£125 (incl. bkfst) * LB **FACILITIES:** STV Xmas **CONF:** Board 10 Del £132.50 * **PARKING:** 30 **NOTES:** No dogs (ex guide dogs) No children 12yrs No smoking in restaurant Closed 25-30 Dec
**CARDS:**

CLAVERDON, Warwickshire — Map 04 SP16

### ★★★73% Ardencote Manor Hotel & Country Club
Lye Green Rd CV35 8LS
☎ 01926 843111 01926 842646
e-mail: hotel@ardencote.com
***Dir:*** *follow sign post direction towards Shrewley off A4189 in centre of Claverdon, Hotel 0.5m on right*

The range of public areas and leisure facilities available at Ardencote are unsurpassed in a hotel of this size. Bedrooms are well-equipped and decorated with pretty fabrics and smart furnishings. There is a varied choice of eating options; the Oak Room offers an imaginative modern menu with formal service. Informal snacks and meals are served in the members' bar and at the lakeside sports lodge.
**ROOMS:** 75 en suite (3 fmly) No smoking in 49 bedrooms s £60-£95; d £80-£145 (incl. bkfst) * LB **FACILITIES:** STV Indoor swimming (H) Golf 9 Tennis (hard) Fishing Squash Sauna Solarium Gym Putting green Jacuzzi Xmas **CONF:** Thtr 250 Class 100 Board 50 Del from £100 * **SERVICES:** Lift air con **PARKING:** 150 **NOTES:** No dogs No smoking in restaurant Civ Wed 150 **CARDS:**

*See advert under WARWICK*

CLEARWELL, Gloucestershire — Map 03 SO50

### ★★★67% Wyndham Arms
GL16 8JT
☎ 01594 833666 01594 836450
***Dir:*** *in centre of village on the B4231*
This charming village inn traces its history back over 600 years. Exposed stone walls, original beams and an impressive inglenook fireplace in the bar, add to its character. Most of the bedrooms are in a modern extension close to the main entrance and a new suite

*continued*

has been added to the main house. There are both bar and restaurant menus.
**ROOMS:** 6 en suite 12 annexe en suite (4 fmly) s £60-£66; d £75-£115 (incl. bkfst) * **LB** **FACILITIES:** ch fac **CONF:** Thtr 56 Class 30 Board 22 Del from £57.50 * **PARKING:** 54 **NOTES:** No smoking in restaurant
**CARDS:**

### ★★71% Tudor Farmhouse Hotel & Restaurant
GL16 8JS
☎ 01594 833046 🖷 01594 837093
e-mail: reservations@tudorfarmhse.u-net.com
**Dir:** *Left on A48 at Lydney towards Bream. Through Bream to junct, turn right and then immediate left to Clearwell, pass Castle and Church. At cross turn right and hotel on left*

This idyllic and charming house conceals a host of original characteristics including exposed stonework, oak beams, wall panelling and open inglenook fireplaces. Good quality food is served in the delightful restaurant. Bedrooms are individually styled and thoughtfully equipped, located in the main house and two converted cottages.
**ROOMS:** 6 en suite 15 annexe en suite (6 fmly) No smoking in 13 bedrooms s £50-£65; d £65-£95 (incl. bkfst) * **LB** **FACILITIES:** STV Riding ch fac **CONF:** Thtr 30 Class 20 Board 20 Del £85 *
**PARKING:** 30 **NOTES:** No smoking in restaurant Closed 24-27 Dec
**CARDS:**

## CLEATOR, Cumbria — Map 11 NY01

### ★★★76% Ennerdale Country House

CA23 3DT
☎ 01946 813907 🖷 01946 815260
e-mail: ennerdale@bestwestern.co.uk
**Dir:** *take A5086 towards Egremont after approximately 12m arrive at Cleator Moor. Stay on the A5086 for a further mile until village of Cleator*
Peacefully located in acres of landscaped gardens, this beautiful Grade II listed building houses a delightful, friendly hotel. Bedrooms are stunning and amazingly equipped with complete home entertainment programmes. Four poster rooms are also available. Public areas include an elegant restaurant, comfortable lounge and a themed bar offering bar meals and traditional ales.
**ROOMS:** 30 en suite (4 fmly) No smoking in 4 bedrooms s £99-£115; d £109-£140 (incl. bkfst) * **LB** **FACILITIES:** STV ch fac Xmas
**CONF:** Thtr 150 Class 100 Board 40 Del from £95 * **PARKING:** 65
**NOTES:** No dogs (ex guide dogs) No smoking in restaurant Civ Wed 150
**CARDS:**

Late for dinner? Quality Standards star rating means that last orders for dinner should be no earlier than:
★ 6.30pm ★★ 7.00pm ★★★ 8.00pm
★★★★ 9.00pm ★★★★★ 10.00pm

## CLECKHEATON, West Yorkshire — Map 07 SE12

### ★★★64% The Whitcliffe
Prospect Rd BD19 3HD
☎ 01274 873022 🖷 01274 870376
e-mail: info@thewhitcliffehotel.co.uk
**Dir:** *M62 junct 26, follow A638 towards Dewsbury, through 1st set of lights then right into Mount Street, up to 'T' junction, turn right then 1st left*
This popular commercial hotel offers modern well-equipped accomodation. Spacious day areas offer a variety of amenities, including the Tudor Conference Room, two attractive bars, and a traditionally styled restaurant. Hospitality is a major strength here.
**ROOMS:** 34 en suite 6 annexe en suite (1 fmly) No smoking in 17 bedrooms s £49-£36; d fr £59.50 (incl. bkfst) * **LB** **FACILITIES:** STV Xmas **CONF:** Thtr 100 Class 60 Board 30 Del from £52 *
**PARKING:** 150 **NOTES:** No dogs (ex guide dogs)
**CARDS:**

## CLEETHORPES, Lincolnshire — Map 08 TA30

### ★★★70% Kingsway
Kingsway DN35 0AE
☎ 01472 601122 🖷 01472 601381
**Dir:** *leave A180 at Grimsby, head to Cleethorpes seafront. The hotel is at junct of The Kingsway and Queen Parade (A1098)*
This seafront hotel has been in the same family for four generations and continues to provide traditional comfort and professional friendly service. The lounges are comfortable and good food is served in the pleasant dining room. Most of the

*continued on p180*

CLEETHORPES, continued

bedrooms are of good comfortable proportions, and all are bright and pleasantly furnished.
**ROOMS:** 49 en suite s £49-£75; d £84-£90 (incl. bkfst) * **LB**
**FACILITIES:** STV **CONF:** Thtr 22 Board 18 **SERVICES:** Lift
**PARKING:** 50 **NOTES:** No dogs (ex guide dogs) No children 5yrs Closed 25-26 Dec **CARDS:**

CLEOBURY MORTIMER, Shropshire Map 07 SO67

### ★★66% The Redfern

DY14 8AA
☎ 01299 270395 01299 271011
e-mail: jon@red-fern.demon.co.uk
***Dir:*** *on A4117 midway between Kidderminster & Ludlow*
This privately owned and personally run hotel offers warm and friendly hospitality and has well-equipped accommodation including rooms on the ground and first floors of a purpose-built cottage-style annexe. Other facilities include a restaurant, a pleasant bar and a rooftop conservatory, where breakfast is served and which doubles as a coffee shop.
**ROOMS:** 5 en suite 6 annexe rms (5 en suite) (2 fmly) s £50-£80; d £80-£130 (incl. bkfst) * **LB FACILITIES:** Clay pigeon/Pheasant shooting whirlpools Xmas **CONF:** Thtr 25 Class 12 Board 10 Del from £75 * **PARKING:** 10 **NOTES:** No dogs (ex guide dogs) No smoking in restaurant **CARDS:**

CLEVEDON, Somerset Map 03 ST47

### ★★★65% Walton Park

Wellington Ter BS21 7BL
☎ 01275 874253 01275 343577
e-mail: latona@aol.com
***Dir:*** *M5 junct 20, signs for seafront, stay on coast road, past pier into Wellington Terrace, hotel on left*
Quietly located and enjoying glorious views across the Bristol Channel to Wales, this popular Victorian hotel is friendly and relaxed, with a long-serving team of staff. Bedrooms are well-decorated and equipped, and include many extra facilities. In the comfortable restaurant, a high standard of home-cooked food is served, while in the bar a range of meals is served.
**ROOMS:** 40 en suite (4 fmly) No smoking in 2 bedrooms s £46-£74.50; d £81-£92 (incl. bkfst) * **LB FACILITIES:** STV **CONF:** Thtr 150 Class 80 Board 80 Del from £95 * **SERVICES:** Lift **PARKING:** 50
**NOTES:** Civ Wed 120 **CARDS:**

CLITHEROE, Lancashire Map 07 SD74

### ★★★67% Stirk House

BB7 4LJ
☎ 01200 445581 01200 445744
***Dir:*** *W of village, on A59. Hotel 0.5m on left*
Nestling in secluded grounds, well back from the A59, this historic hotel offers bedrooms in a variety of styles, with delegate rooms providing especially good value. The main house has comfortable lounges and sitting areas. In the restaurant guests will be tempted by the imaginative menu. Staff throughout are friendly and nothing is too much trouble.
**ROOMS:** 40 en suite 10 annexe en suite (2 fmly) No smoking in 25 bedrooms s £60-£70; d £80-£150 (incl. bkfst) * **LB FACILITIES:** STV Indoor swimming (H) Squash Sauna Solarium Gym Jacuzzi entertainment ch fac Xmas **CONF:** Thtr 300 Class 150 Board 50 Del from £85 * **PARKING:** 130 **NOTES:** No dogs (ex guide dogs) No smoking in restaurant Civ Wed 150 **CARDS:**

### ★★68% Shireburn Arms

Whalley Rd, Hurst Green BB7 9QJ
☎ 01254 826518 01254 826208
e-mail: sales@shireburn-hotel.co.uk
***Dir:*** *on B6243 at the entrance to Hurst Green village*
This family owned hotel dates back to the 17th century and enjoys beautiful views over the Ribble Valley. Rooms are individually designed and thoughtfully equipped. The lounge bar offers a selection of real ales, and the spacious restaurant that offers home cooked food, opens onto an attractive patio and garden.
**ROOMS:** 18 en suite (3 fmly) s £45-£65; d £65-£85 (incl. bkfst) * **LB**
**FACILITIES:** ch fac Xmas **CONF:** Thtr 100 Class 50 Board 50 Del £70 *
**PARKING:** 71 **NOTES:** No smoking in restaurant Civ Wed 100
**CARDS:**

CLOVELLY, Devon Map 02 SS32

### ★★71% *New Inn*

High St EX39 5TQ
☎ 01237 431303 01237 431636
e-mail: newinn@clovelly.co.uk
***Dir:*** *at Clovelly Cross, turn off A39 onto B3237. Follow road down hill for 1.5m. Turn right at sign "All vehicles for Clovelly" and park in main car park*
In the heart of this historic fishing village, overlooking the beauty of Barnstaple Bay, the New Inn sits on the cobbled High Street. Carefully renovated and retaining much of its original character, both bedrooms and public areas are smartly presented with quality furnishings. Meals may be taken in the elegant restaurant or the popular Upalongs bar.
**ROOMS:** 8 en suite (2 fmly) **NOTES:** No dogs (ex guide dogs) No smoking in restaurant **CARDS:**

COALVILLE, Leicestershire Map 08 SK41

### ★★65% Charnwood Arms

Beveridge Ln, Bardon Hill LE67 1TB
☎ 01530 813644 01530 815425
e-mail: thecharnwoodarms@work.gb.com
***Dir:*** *1m W of M1 junct 22, on A511*
Conveniently located for access to the M1, this popular inn offers pleasant well-furnished courtyard accommodation. Public areas in the main building include a spacious lounge bar and dining areas in which hearty fare and cask conditioned ales are served.
**ROOMS:** 34 en suite (1 fmly) No smoking in 6 bedrooms s £30-£40; d £30-£40 * **CONF:** Thtr 200 Class 100 Board 60 **PARKING:** 150
**NOTES:** No dogs (ex guide dogs) Civ Wed
**CARDS:**

COBHAM, Surrey Map 04 TQ16

### ⌂ *Premier Lodge*

Portsmouth Rd, Fairmile KT11 1BW
☎ 0870 700 1432 0870 7001433
Premier Lodge offers modern, well-equipped, en suite accommodation suitable for both business and leisure travellers. Meals can be taken at the adjacent popular restaurant and bar, which is fully licensed. For further details, consult the Hotel Groups page.
**ROOMS:** 48 en suite

Popped the question? Hotels with Civ Wed in their entry are licensed for civil wedding ceremonies. Maximum numbers for the ceremony only are shown, e.g. Civ Wed 120

## COCKERMOUTH, Cumbria

Map 11 NY13

**★★★71% The Trout**
Crown St CA13 0EJ
☎ 01900 823591 📠 01900 827514
e-mail: enquirIes@trouthotel.co.uk
***Dir:*** *next to Wordsworth House and Mineral Museum*
Dating back to 1670, this once private residence, next door to Wordsworth's birthplace, has an enviable setting on the banks of the river Derwent. Bedrooms range in style and include superb junior suites and spacious executive rooms. There is a well-stocked bar, a choice of comfortable lounges and an attractive, traditional dinning room offering a good choice of table d'hôte and Carte dishes.
**ROOMS:** 29 en suite (4 fmly) No smoking in 12 bedrooms s £60-£115; d £90-£130 (incl. bkfst) * **LB FACILITIES:** STV Fishing Xmas **CONF:** Thtr 50 Class 30 Board 25 Del from £119.95 * **PARKING:** 60 **NOTES:** No smoking in restaurant Civ Wed 60 **CARDS:**

**★★★65% The Manor House Hotel**
Crown St CA13 0EH
☎ 01900 828663 📠 01900 828679
***Dir:*** *turn off A66 at Cockermouth junct, continue 0.75m to T junct to hotel 700yds on left*
A welcoming atmosphere prevails at this comfortable business and tourist hotel which offers convenient access to central amenities. Co-ordinated fabrics have been used to good effect in the bedrooms, which are comfortably modern in style. Public areas include a relaxing lounge, well-stocked bar, and a separate restaurant.
**ROOMS:** 13 en suite (1 fmly) s fr £55; d £69-£75 (incl. bkfst) * **LB FACILITIES:** Xmas **PARKING:** 20 **CARDS:**

**⌂ Shepherds Hotel**
Lakeland Sheep & Wool Centre, Egremont Rd CA13 0QX
☎ 01900 822673 📠 01900 822673
e-mail: reception@shepherdshotel.co.uk
***Dir:*** *At junc of A66 and A5086 south of Cockermouth,entrance of A5086 200m off roundabout*
This modern hotel on the edge of town offers well-equipped accommodation. There is a restaurant, open all day, serving a selection of bar meals and snacks. The property also houses the Lakeland Sheep and Wool Centre, with live sheep shows from Easter to mid November.
**ROOMS:** 13 en suite (incl. bkfst) s £30-£50; d £39-£50 * **CONF:** Thtr 200 Class 10 Board 10 Del from £50 *

## COGGESHALL, Essex

Map 05 TL82

**★★★68% *White Hart***
Market End CO6 1NH
☎ 01376 561654 📠 01376 561789
e-mail: wharthotel@ndirect.co.uk
***Dir:*** *from A12 follow through Kelvedon & then take B1024 to Coggeshall*
This 15th-century coaching inn in the centre of town offers spacious, comfortable and stylish bedrooms. The bar is the centre point of the hotel and is popular with locals and residents. The restaurant is brimming with character and offers an authentic Italian menu. A wide selection of bar food is also available.
**ROOMS:** 18 en suite (1 fmly) **FACILITIES:** STV **CONF:** Thtr 30 Class 10 Board 22 **PARKING:** 47 **NOTES:** No dogs **CARDS:**

*See advert on this page*



## COLCHESTER, Essex

Map 05 TL92

**★★★ ◎◎ Maison Talbooth**
Stratford Rd CO7 6HN
☎ 01206 322367 📠 01206 322752
e-mail: mtreception@talbooth.co.uk
(For full entry see Dedham)

**★★★73% George**
116 High St CO1 1TD
☎ 01206 578494 📠 01206 761732
***Dir:*** *200yds beyond Town Hall on the High Street*
Appealing 15th-century coaching inn situated in the centre of town. The attractively decorated bedrooms have well-chosen fabrics and furnishings and offer a high degree of comfort. A wide choice of dishes and daily changing specials are served in the smart restaurant whereas bar snacks can be taken in the lounge.
**ROOMS:** 47 en suite No smoking in 32 bedrooms s £55-£95; d £71-£105 * **FACILITIES:** STV **CONF:** Thtr 70 Class 30 Board 30 Del from £107 * **PARKING:** 46 **CARDS:**

**★★★70% *Marks Tey***
London Rd, Marks Tey CO6 1DU
☎ 01206 210001 📠 01206 212167
e-mail: sales@patenhotels.freeserve.co.uk
***Dir:*** *off A12/A120 junction*
A modern, well-kept hotel, situated just off the A12 close to the historic town of Colchester. Bedrooms are comfortable, well-equipped and furnished to a high standard. Wide ranges of

*continued on p182*

COLCHESTER, continued

function rooms are available and the hotel also has an excellent leisure club.
**ROOMS:** 110 en suite (12 fmly) No smoking in 42 bedrooms **FACILITIES:** STV Indoor swimming (H) Tennis (hard) Sauna Solarium Gym Jacuzzi entertainment **CONF:** Thtr 200 Class 100 Board 60 **PARKING:** 200 **NOTES:** No dogs (ex guide dogs) Civ Wed 160 **CARDS:**

C

### ★★★69% Butterfly
Old Ipswich Rd CO7 7QY
☎ 01206 230900 01206 231095
e-mail: colbutterfly@lineone.net
***Dir:*** *A12/A120 Ardleigh Junction*
Situated just off the A12 to London, within easy striking distance of the town centre and the port of Harwich. The spacious, well-equipped bedrooms come in a variety of styles, and public rooms include a smart restaurant, lounge bar and conservatory. A range of conference rooms and a function suite are also available.
**ROOMS:** 50 en suite (2 fmly) No smoking in 30 bedrooms s £55-£75; d £110-£150 * **LB** **FACILITIES:** STV ch fac **CONF:** Thtr 80 Class 40 Board 40 Del £97.50 * **PARKING:** 85 **NOTES:** No dogs (ex guide dogs) **CARDS:**

### ★★★65% *Posthouse Colchester*
Abbotts Ln, Eight Ash Green CO6 3QL
**Posthouse**
☎ 0870 400 9020 01206 766577
***Dir:*** *junct A1124 of A12 signposted to Halstead*
Purpose built hotel situated on the outskirts of town close to the A12. The modern well-equipped bedrooms come in a variety of styles and provide a good degree of comfort. Public rooms include a smart bar, restaurant and a range of meeting rooms. Guests also have the use of the Spa health club.
**ROOMS:** 110 en suite (30 fmly) No smoking in 58 bedrooms **FACILITIES:** Indoor swimming (H) Sauna Solarium Gym Jacuzzi Steam room Treatment rooms **CONF:** Thtr 150 Class 70 Board 60 **PARKING:** 150 **CARDS:**

### ★★★64% The Stoke by Nayland Club Hotel
Keepers Ln, Leavenheath CO6 4PZ
☎ 01206 262836 01206 263356
e-mail: info@golf-club.co.uk
***Dir:*** *turn off A134 onto B1068, hotel 0.75m on right*
Located in the heart of Constable country and within easy reach of local places of interest, this hotel is surrounded by 300 acres of wooded golf courses and lakes. Well-served by road and rail networks, it is also ideal for the business traveller.
**ROOMS:** 30 en suite (4 fmly) No smoking in 15 bedrooms s £69; d £79-£120 (incl. bkfst) * **LB** **FACILITIES:** Spa STV Indoor swimming (H) Golf 18 Fishing Squash Snooker Sauna Solarium Gym Putting green steam room,health & beauty,aerobics Xmas **CONF:** Thtr 500 Class 200 Board 36 Del from £101.50 * **SERVICES:** Lift **PARKING:** 300 **NOTES:** No dogs (ex guide dogs) No smoking in restaurant Civ Wed 500 **CARDS:**

### ★★★63% Quality Hotel
East St CO1 2TS
☎ 01206 865022 01206 792884
e-mail: qhotel@netscapeonline.co.uk
***Dir:*** *Off A137 in the town centre, next to the Siege House pub, just before the bridge over the River Colne*
The hotel is a converted flour mill set alongside the river Colne and within walking distance of the town centre. Much of the original character of the building has been retained. Bedrooms are tastefully decorated and offer all modern conveniences. Public areas include a lounge, residents' bar and the conservatory Quayside restaurant.
**ROOMS:** 58 en suite No smoking in 6 bedrooms s £52-£57; d £69-£99 (incl. bkfst) * **FACILITIES:** Xmas **CONF:** Thtr 80 Class 20 Board 35 Del from £85 * **SERVICES:** Lift **PARKING:** 100 **NOTES:** No smoking in restaurant **CARDS:**

## COLEFORD, Gloucestershire
Map 03 SO5

### ★★★67% The Speech House

GL16 7EL
☎ 01594 822607 01594 823658
e-mail: relax@thespeechhouse.co.uk
***Dir:*** *on B4226 between Cinderford and Coleford*

Dating back to 1676, this former hunting lodge is tucked away in the Forest of Dean. Bedrooms, some with impressive four-poster beds, combine modern amenities with period charm. The beamed restaurant serves good, imaginative food. Additional features include a mini gym, aqua spa and conference facilities.
**ROOMS:** 15 en suite 17 annexe rms (10 en suite) (4 fmly) No smoking in 6 bedrooms s £50-£73; d £82-£140 (incl. bkfst) * **LB** **FACILITIES:** Golf 18 Sauna Solarium Gym Jacuzzi Cricket Bridge Health Spa Xmas **CONF:** Thtr 70 Class 40 Board 40 Del from £105 * **PARKING:** 70 **NOTES:** No smoking in restaurant Civ Wed 60 **CARDS:**

### ★★62% The Angel Hotel
Market Place GL16 8AE
☎ 01594 833113 01594 832413
***Dir:*** *access to hotel via A48 or A40*
This 17th-century coaching inn is centrally located and close to many attractions. Bedrooms are all spacious and well-equipped. Additional features include a bar and restaurant with a traditional feel, and 'Magnums' night club.
**ROOMS:** 9 en suite (1 fmly) s £39-£50; d £55-£75 (incl. bkfst) * **FACILITIES:** STV entertainment **PARKING:** 4 **CARDS:**

## COLERNE, Wiltshire
Map 03 ST8

*Premier Collection*

### ★★★★ Lucknam Park
SN14 8AZ
☎ 01225 742777 01225 743536
e-mail: reservations@lucknampark.co.uk
***Dir:*** *leave M4 at junct 17, A350 to Chippenham, then A420 towards Bristol for 3m. At Ford village, turn left towards Colerne, after 3m right at crossroads*
Lucknam Park is located in a beautiful area of Wiltshire. The building dates back to 1720 and is set in 500 acres of glorious

*continued*

parkland. In this magnificent Palladian mansion, there is evidence of both style and grace. There are elegant day rooms in which guests can relax, and the bedrooms and suites are all individually decorated. There is also a choice of menus, which offer a balanced selection of accomplished cuisine.

**ROOMS:** 23 en suite 18 annexe en suite s £155-£670; d £195-£670 * LB **FACILITIES:** Spa STV Indoor swimming (H) Tennis (hard) Riding Snooker Sauna Solarium Gym Croquet lawn Jacuzzi Whirlpool, Beauty & hair salon, Steam room, Cross country course entertainment Xmas **CONF:** Thtr 64 Class 24 Board 30 **PARKING:** 90 **NOTES:** No dogs (ex guide dogs) No smoking in restaurant Civ Wed 64 **CARDS:**

## COLESHILL, Warwickshire — Map 04 SP28

### ★★★65% Grimstock Country House

Gilson Rd, Gilson B46 1LJ
☎ 01675 462121 & 462161 Fax 01675 467646
e-mail: enquiries@grimstockhotel.co.uk
***Dir:*** *turn off A446 onto B4117 to Gilson, hotel 100yds on right*

This privately owned and friendly hotel stands in its own grounds, convenient for Birmingham International Airport and the NEC. Bedrooms are spacious and well-equipped. Public rooms include a choice of restaurants, an attractive bar, good conference facilities, a car park and a gym.

**ROOMS:** 44 en suite (1 fmly) s £65-£85; d £75-£95 (incl. bkfst) * LB **FACILITIES:** STV Solarium Gym Xmas **CONF:** Thtr 100 Class 60 Board 50 Del from £110 * **PARKING:** 100 **NOTES:** No smoking in restaurant Civ Wed 90 **CARDS:**

## COLN ST-ALDWYNS, Gloucestershire — Map 04 SP10

**Premier Collection**

### ★★ The New Inn At Coln

GL7 5AN
☎ 01285 750651 Fax 01285 750657
e-mail: stay@new-inn.co.uk
***Dir:*** *8m E of Cirencester, between Bibury and Fairford*

This delightful inn is set in the heart of the beautiful Coln Valley, in the southern heart of the Cotswolds. Dating back to the reign of Elizabeth I, this peaceful inn offers genuine hospitality and enchanting bedrooms. All of the facilities are divided between the main building and the Dovecote. Some of the features include flagstone floors, wooden beams and

*continued*

inglenook fireplaces. The popular bar and restaurant serve enjoyable food prepared to a high standard.

**ROOMS:** 8 en suite 6 annexe en suite s £72-£115; d £99-£125 (incl. bkfst) * LB **CONF:** Thtr 20 Board 12 Del from £119.50 * **PARKING:** 22 **NOTES:** No children 10 yrs No smoking in restaurant **CARDS:**

## COLSTERWORTH, Lincolnshire — Map 08 SK92

### Travelodge

NG33 5JR
☎ 01476 861077 Fax 01476 861078
***Dir:*** *on A1/A151 southbound at junct with B151/B676*

Travelodge

Travelodge offers good quality, good value, modern accommodation. Ideal for families, the spacious, en suite bedrooms include remote-control TV, tea and coffee-making facilities, luxury beds and free morning newspaper. Meals can be taken at the nearby family restaurant. For further details and the Travelodge phone number, consult the Hotel Groups page.

**ROOMS:** 31 en suite

### Travelodge

South Witham NG33 5JJ
☎ 01476 861181 Fax 01476 861181
***Dir:*** *at roundabout of junc A1/A151*

Travelodge

Travelodge offers good quality, good value, modern accommodation. Ideal for families, the spacious, en suite bedrooms include remote-control TV, tea and coffee-making facilities, luxury beds and free morning newspaper. Meals can be taken at the nearby family restaurant. For further details and the Travelodge phone number, consult the Hotel Groups page.

**ROOMS:** 32 en suite

## COLTISHALL, Norfolk — Map 09 TG21

### ★★79% Norfolk Mead

Church Loke NR12 7DN
☎ 01603 737531 Fax 01603 737521
e-mail: info@norfolkmead.co.uk
***Dir:*** *from Norwich take B1150. In Coltishall turn right just beyond hump backed bridge. Hotel 600yds on right just before church*

Delightful Georgian manor house, set in a peaceful location amidst 12 acres of gardens leading down to the River Bure. The individually decorated bedrooms are tastefully furnished and have lovely views of the gardens. Dinner is served in the elegant restaurant, which offers a menu featuring local produce.

**ROOMS:** 9 en suite (1 fmly) No smoking in all bedrooms s £70-£90; d £80-£130 (incl. bkfst) * LB **FACILITIES:** Outdoor swimming (H) Fishing Croquet lawn Beauty salon ch fac Xmas **CONF:** Del from £115 * **PARKING:** 50 **CARDS:**

C

## COLYFORD, Devon Map 03 SY29

### ★★77% Swallows Eaves

EX24 6QJ
☎ 01297 553184 01297 553574
***Dir:*** *on A3052, in centre of village, opposite village store*
Many guests return year after year to this delightfully engaging hotel, which has a well-deserved reputation for excellent service, food and hospitality. Bedrooms combine comfort with quality, each individually styled and equipped with thoughtful extras. The restaurant serves a daily menu of carefully prepared dishes, making good use of fresh local ingredients.
**ROOMS:** 8 en suite No smoking in all bedrooms s £45-£55; d £70-£90 (incl. bkfst) * **LB** **FACILITIES:** Free use of nearby Swimming Club Xmas **PARKING:** 10 **NOTES:** No dogs (ex guide dogs) No children 14yrs No smoking in restaurant RS Dec-Jan **CARDS:**

## CONSETT, Co Durham Map 12 NZ15

### ★★★62% The Raven Hotel

Broomhill, Ebchester DH8 6RY
☎ 01207 562562 01207 560262
e-mail: enquiries@ravenhotel.co.uk
***Dir:*** *on B6309, overlooking village*
Spacious bedrooms with magnificent views are a feature of this modern hotel, which stands high on a hillside overlooking the village. Well-prepared meals are served in the attractive conservatory restaurant and a good range of popular bar meals is also available together with a range of hand pulled real ales.
**ROOMS:** 28 en suite 1 annexe en suite (7 fmly) s £55; d £70 (incl. bkfst) * **LB** **FACILITIES:** STV Xmas **CONF:** Thtr 150 Class 80 Board 40 Del from £79.95 * **PARKING:** 75 **NOTES:** No dogs (ex guide dogs) No smoking in restaurant Civ Wed 150
**CARDS:**

## CONSTANTINE, Cornwall & Isles of Scilly Map 02 SW72

### ★★70% Trengilly Wartha Inn

THE CIRCLE
Selected Individual Hotels
GREAT BRITAIN

Nancenoy TR11 5RP
☎ 01326 340332 01326 340332
e-mail: trengilly@compuserve.com
***Dir:*** *take A39 to Falmouth, at rdbt by Asda store in Penryn follow signs to Constantine then direction Gweek, hotel signposted to the left in 1m*
A popular and busy country inn hotel peacefully located in an area of outstanding natural beauty. The smart restaurant and busy bar serve fresh Cornish produce, complemented by a comprehensive wine list. Bedrooms are individual in character. The lounge is the place to relax in front of an open log fire.
**ROOMS:** 6 rms (5 en suite) 2 annexe en suite (2 fmly) No smoking in 2 bedrooms s £48; d £66-£72 (incl. bkfst) * **LB** **FACILITIES:** ch fac **PARKING:** 50 **NOTES:** RS 25 Dec (breakfast only)31Dec no dinner
**CARDS:**

## CONSTANTINE BAY, Cornwall & Isles of Scilly Map 02 SW87

### ★★★77% *Treglos*

PL28 8JH
☎ 01841 520727 01841 521163
e-mail: enquires@treglos-hotel.co.uk
***Dir:*** *turn right at Constantine Bay stores, hotel 50yds on left*
Owned by the same family for over 30 years, this hotel has a tradition of high standards of hospitality. The genuine welcome, a choice of comfortable lounges, an indoor pool and children's play facilities, entices guests back year after year. Bedrooms vary in size; those with sea views are always popular. The restaurant continues to provide imaginative menus incorporating seasonal produce.

**ROOMS:** 44 en suite (12 fmly) **FACILITIES:** Indoor swimming (H) Snooker Croquet lawn Jacuzzi Converted 'boat house' for table tennis ch fac **CONF:** Board 20 **SERVICES:** Lift **PARKING:** 58 **NOTES:** No smoking in restaurant Closed 4 Nov-16 Mar
**CARDS:**

*See advert under PADSTOW*

## COPTHORNE See Gatwick Airport

## CORBRIDGE, Northumberland Map 12 NY96

### ★★68% Angel Inn

Main St NE45 5LA
☎ 01434 632119 01434 633496
e-mail: info@theangelofcorbridge.softnet.co.uk
***Dir:*** *half a mile off A69, signed Corbridge*
Corbridge's oldest inn provides accommodation of modern quality and yet retains much of its original character. Guests can relax in the lounge or enjoy a drink in the snug bar. Diners are offered an excellent choice, whether in the restaurant or the lounge bar, which is set up for meals. Bedrooms vary in size, but all are well-equipped and smart. Staff are willing and efficient.
**ROOMS:** 5 en suite (1 fmly) s fr £49; d fr £74 (incl. bkfst) *
**FACILITIES:** STV Xmas **PARKING:** 20 **NOTES:** No dogs (ex guide dogs)
**CARDS:**

## CORFE CASTLE, Dorset Map 03 SY98

### ★★★73% Mortons House

49 East St BH20 5EE
☎ 01929 480988 01929 480820
e-mail: stay@mortonshouse.co.uk
***Dir:*** *on A351 between Wareham/Swanage) in the Town of Corfe Castle*
A charming hotel, Mortons House continues its sensitive improvements under the careful guidance of the new owners. Hospitality and efficiency here are effortlessly combined. Traditional features include an oak-panelled drawing room and carved wooden friezes. Bedrooms, including several which overlook Corfe Castle, are decorated with style and individuality. An interesting range of enjoyable cuisine is available in the comfortable dining room.
**ROOMS:** 14 en suite 3 annexe en suite (1 fmly) No smoking in all bedrooms s fr £75; d £106-£116 (incl. bkfst) * **LB** **FACILITIES:** Jacuzzi Xmas **CONF:** Thtr 45 Class 45 Board 20 Del from £110 * **PARKING:** 40 **NOTES:** No dogs No smoking in restaurant
**CARDS:**

Read all about it! Newspapers delivered to bedrooms in four and five star hotels.

## CORNHILL-ON-TWEED, Northumberland Map 12 NT83

### ★★★74% Tillmouth Park Country House
TD12 4UU
☎ 01890 882255 01890 882540
e-mail: reception@tillmouthpark.force9.co.uk
**Dir:** *turn off A1(M) at East Ord rdbt at Berwick-upon-Tweed and follow A698 towards Cornhill and Coldstream. Hotel 9m along A698 on left*
Built in 1882, this imposing mansion is set in mature grounds by the banks of the River Till. The house has gracious public rooms including a choice of relaxing lounges. The quietly elegant dining room offers a range of imaginative dishes, and more informal dining is available in the bistro. Bedrooms retain a traditional character and include several magnificent master rooms.
**ROOMS:** 12 en suite 2 annexe en suite (1 fmly) s £65-£115; d £130-£180 (incl. bkfst) * **LB** **FACILITIES:** Croquet lawn Clay pigeon 0.75 snooker table Xmas **CONF:** Thtr 50 Class 20 Board 20 Del from £100 * **PARKING:** 50 **NOTES:** No smoking in restaurant Civ Wed
**CARDS:**

## CORSE LAWN, Gloucestershire Map 03 SO83

### ★★★75% Corse Lawn House
GL19 4LZ
☎ 01452 780479 & 780771 01452 780840
e-mail: hotel@corselawnhouse.u-net.com
**Dir:** *on B4211 5m SW of Tewkesbury*
This Queen Anne country house stands in extensive grounds. There is a bistro and bar in addition to the main restaurant; a drawing room and other seating areas are also provided. The bedrooms are elegantly decorated and feature many extra touches. Cooking is of a high standard with good use made of top-quality ingredients.
**ROOMS:** 19 en suite (2 fmly) s £80; d £125-£160 (incl. bkfst) * **LB** **FACILITIES:** STV Indoor swimming (H) Tennis (hard) Croquet lawn Badminton croquet table tennis **CONF:** Thtr 50 Class 30 Board 25 Del from £130 * **PARKING:** 62 **NOTES:** No smoking in restaurant Closed 24-25 Dec Civ Wed 120 **CARDS:**

*See advert on this page*



## COVENTRY, West Midlands Map 04 SP37
see also Brandon, Meriden & Nuneaton

### ★★★72% Brooklands Grange Hotel & Restaurant
Holyhead Rd CV5 8HX
☎ 024 7660 1601 024 7660 1277
e-mail: enquiries@brooklands-grange.co.uk
**Dir:** *leave A45 at rdbt marked city centre onto A4114 at next rdbt & stay on A4114, hotel 100yds on left*
Behind the Jacobean façade of Brooklands Grange is a modern and comfortable business hotel. The food is worthy of note, with an interesting carte offering carefully presented dishes, and service is both friendly and attentive. Bedrooms are well-equipped and thoughtfully laid out.
**ROOMS:** 30 en suite (1 fmly) No smoking in 15 bedrooms s £90-£110; d £105-£125 (incl. bkfst) * **CONF:** Thtr 20 Class 20 Board 18 **PARKING:** 52 **NOTES:** No dogs (ex guide dogs) No smoking in restaurant Closed 26-28 Dec & 1-2 Jan
**CARDS:**

### ★★★70% *Posthouse Coventry*
Posthouse
Hinckley Rd, Walsgrave CV2 2HP
☎ 0870 400 9021 024 7662 1736
e-mail: gm1412@forte-hotels.com
**Dir:** *on A4600*
This hotel offers bright modern accommodation. Half the bedrooms have been upgraded to an executive standard, and the others are more traditional in style, but equally comfortable and well-equipped. Facilities include the leisure suite, rotisserie, coffee lounge and extensive conference facilities.
**ROOMS:** 160 en suite (15 fmly) No smoking in 112 bedrooms **FACILITIES:** Indoor swimming (H) Sauna Gym Jacuzzi Steam room Childrens play areas entertainment ch fac **CONF:** Thtr 250 Class 150 Board 50 **SERVICES:** Lift **PARKING:** 300 **NOTES:** No smoking in restaurant **CARDS:**

### ★★★69% Hylands
Best Western
Warwick Rd CV3 6AU
☎ 024 7650 1600 024 7650 1027
e-mail: hylands@bestwestern.co.uk
**Dir:** *on A429, 500yds from junct 6 of town centre ring road, opposite Memorial Park*
This hotel is convenient for the station and the city centre, yet overlooks an attractive park. Restaurant 153 offers good standards of food and service. Bedroom styles may vary, yet each room is well-equipped and fully en suite; most recent additions are smart with bold colour schemes.
**ROOMS:** 61 en suite (4 fmly) No smoking in 54 bedrooms s £75-£90; d £90-£100 (incl. bkfst) * **LB** **FACILITIES:** STV **CONF:** Thtr 60 Class 40 Board 30 Del from £90 **PARKING:** 60 **CARDS:**

### ★★★68% Courtyard by Marriott Coventry
COURTYARD
London Rd, Ryton on Dunsmore CV8 3DY
☎ 024 7630 1585 024 7630 1610
**Dir:** *M6 junct 2, take A46 towards Warwick, take turning towards A45 London at Coventry Airport*
This modern hotel is conveniently situated on the outskirts of the

*continued on p186*

COVENTRY, continued

city and provides very comfortable and spacious accommodation. Public areas are particularly well-designed and include a lounge bar, foyer lounge and an informal restaurant. There are versatile meeting and conference facilities.

*Courtyard by Marriott, Coventry*

**ROOMS:** 49 en suite (2 fmly) No smoking in 25 bedrooms s £84-£125; d £90-£131 (incl. bkfst) * **LB** **FACILITIES:** STV Gym Xmas **CONF:** Thtr 300 Class 100 Board 24 Del from £95 * **PARKING:** 120 **NOTES:** No dogs (ex guide dogs) No smoking in restaurant Civ Wed 112
**CARDS:**

### ★★★66% The Chace

London Rd, Toll Bar End CV3 4EQ
☎ 024 7630 3398 🖷 024 7630 1816
e-mail: chacehotel@corushotels.com
***Dir:*** *from S M40, exit junct 15, A46 to Coventry, right onto A45 & follow to 1st rdbt, turn left onto B4110, straight on at next mini rdbt, hotel on left*

This rapidly growing hotel retains many of its original Victorian features. Characterful public rooms have stained glass windows and oak panelling and comprise a large open plan lounge bar and separate restaurant; service is upbeat and friendly. The bedrooms offer modern appointments, a good range of facilities and comfortable furnishings.
**ROOMS:** 66 en suite (23 fmly) No smoking in 34 bedrooms s £90; d £110 **LB** **FACILITIES:** STV Croquet lawn Pool Table Xmas **CONF:** Thtr 65 Class 40 Board 36 Del from £89 * **PARKING:** 120 **NOTES:** No dogs (ex guide dogs) No smoking in restaurant Civ Wed 60
**CARDS:**

### ★★★66% Menzies Leofric

Broadgate CV1 1LZ
☎ 0870 6003013 🖷 01332 511144
e-mail: info@menzies-hotels.co.uk
***Dir:*** *opposite West Orchards Car Park*
Reputedly the first hotel to be built in Britain after the Second World War, the Leofric is situated near the cathedral and the

*continued*

shopping centre. Many of the comfortable, well-equipped bedrooms have benefitted from refurbishment. Open-plan public areas include a choice of bars and a brasserie. The West Orchards car park gives direct access to the hotel.

**ROOMS:** 94 en suite (5 fmly) No smoking in 20 bedrooms s £75; d £8 * **LB** **FACILITIES:** STV Xmas **CONF:** Thtr 500 Class 200 Board 80 Del from £120 * **SERVICES:** Lift **NOTES:** No dogs (ex guide dogs) No smoking in restaurant Civ Wed 500 **CARDS:**

### ★★★63% Allesley

Birmingham Rd, Allesley Village CV5 9GP
☎ 024 7640 3272 🖷 024 7640 5190
e-mail: stay@allesley-hotel.co.uk
***Dir:*** *from A45, exit A4114 Brownshill Green/City Centre. Next rdbt, 4th exit, following rdbt 1st exit Allesley Village. Hotel is 150yds on left*
The Allesley provides well-appointed accommodation that is light and inviting. All rooms are well-equipped for today's corporate guest. Public areas are split over two levels and include a spacious reception foyer, a restaurant and a bar. Extensive conference and function facilities are available and have dedicated audio-visual and secretarial support.
**ROOMS:** 75 en suite 15 annexe en suite (2 fmly) No smoking in 45 bedrooms s £35-£80; d £70-£105 (incl. bkfst) * **LB** **FACILITIES:** entertainment **CONF:** Thtr 450 Class 150 Board 80 Del from £110 * **SERVICES:** Lift **PARKING:** 500 **NOTES:** No smoking in restaurant Civ Wed 350 **CARDS:**

### ★★★62% Novotel Coventry

Wilsons Ln CV6 6HL
☎ 024 7636 5000 🖷 024 7636 2422
e-mail: h0506@accor-hotels.com
***Dir:*** *M6 junct 3, follow signs for B4113 towards Longford, Bedworth. Take 3rd exit on large rdbt*
The first Novotel built in the UK, this modern hotel offers bedrooms which include family as well as two disabled rooms. There is also a useful range of meeting rooms. Guests can dine until midnight in the cheerfully decorated brasserie, or take meals from the extensive room-service menu. The hotel has a children's play area.
**ROOMS:** 98 en suite (98 fmly) No smoking in 60 bedrooms s £67 * **LB** **FACILITIES:** STV Outdoor swimming (H) Petanque **CONF:** Thtr 200 Class 100 Board 40 **SERVICES:** Lift air con **PARKING:** 120
**NOTES:** Civ Wed 8 **CARDS:**

### ⇧ Hotel Ibis Coventry South

Abbey Rd, Whitley CV3 4BJ
☎ 024 7663 9922 🖷 024 7630 6898
e-mail: H2094@accor-hotels.com
***Dir:*** *signposted from A46/A423 roundabout, take A423 towards A45 & London stay in left hand lane. Follow signs for the Racquet Centre*
Modern, budget hotel offering comfortable accommodation in bright and practical bedrooms. Breakfast is self-service and dinner

; available in the restaurant. For further details, consult the Hotel ;roups page.
**ROOMS:** 51 en suite d fr £40 * **CONF:** Thtr 35 Class 18 Board 20

### Hotel Campanile

Campanile

Wigston Rd, Walsgrave CV2 2SD
☎ 024 7662 2311 ▤ 024 7660 2362
*Dir: exit 2 of M6, at 2nd roundabout turn right*

HOTEL
Campanile

This modern building offers accommodation in smart, well-equipped bedrooms, all with en suite bathrooms. Refreshments may be taken at the informal Bistro. For further details and the Campanile phone number, consult the Hotel Groups page.
**ROOMS:** 50 en suite d fr £39.95 * **CONF:** Thtr 35 Class 18 Board 20 Del from £68 *

### Express by Holiday Inn Coventry

Express
by Holiday Inn

Kenpas Highway CV3 6PB
☎ 024 7641 7555 ▤ 024 7641 3388
*Dir: M6 junct 2 onto the A46. Follow the A45 towards Birmingham, the hotel is sitauted just off a roundabout behind the Harvester*

A modern budget hotel offering comfortable accommodation in refreshing, spacious and comprehensively equipped bedrooms, en suite bathrooms with power showers and continental buffet breakfast included in the room rate. Suitable for business travellers or families. For further details and the Express by Holiday Inn phone number, consult the Hotel Groups page.
**ROOMS:** 37 en suite (incl. cont bkfst) d £43-£53 * **CONF:** Thtr 24 Class 16 Board 16

### Hotel Ibis St John Coventry Ringway

Mill Ln, St John's Ringway CV1 2LN
☎ 024 7625 0500 ▤ 024 7655 3548
e-mail: H2793@accer.hotels.com
*Dir: From London, take M1 North. Take exit 17 for M45 towards Coventry & follow signs for City Centre ring road for Birmingham. Take A45 towards Coventry, then A4114 signposted to Jaguar Assembly Plant . At joining Coventry inner ring rd, turn towards ring rd south. Come off at exit 5 for Mill Lane*
Modern, budget hotel offering comfortable accommodation in

continued

bright and practical bedrooms. Breakfast is self-service and dinner is available in the restaurant. For further details, consult the Hotel Groups page.
**ROOMS:** 88 en suite (incl. bkfst) d £40 *

### Premier Lodge

PREMIER LODGE

Combe Fields Rd, Ansty CV7 9JP
☎ 0870 700 1356 ▤ 0870 700 1357
*Dir: Exit M6 junct 2, follow B4065 through Ansty villiage turn right onto B4029. Proceed past golf club & turn right to lodge.*
Premier Lodge offers modern, well-equipped, en suite accommodation suitable for both business and leisure travellers. Meals can be taken at the adjacent popular restaurant and bar, which is fully licensed. For further details, consult the Hotel Groups page.
**ROOMS:** 28 en suite d £42 * **CONF:** Thtr 12 Class 14 Board 14 Del from £80 *

### Innkeeper's Lodge Meriden

Main Rd, Meriden CV7 7NL
A new concept in the travel accommodation market. Smart rooms meet essential business requirements but also have home comforts. Dining options include all-day menus plus the added advantage of breakfast, which is included in the room price. Reservations can be made seven days a week through the room reservations number: 0870 243 0500. For further details, consult the Hotel Groups page.
**ROOMS:** 13 en suite **NOTES:** Open now

TV dinner? Room service at three stars and above.

COWES See Wight, Isle of

CRAMLINGTON, Northumberland

### ○ Innkeeper's Lodge Cramlington

NE23 8AU

A new concept in the travel accommodation market. Smart rooms meet essential business requirements but also have home comforts. Dining options include all-day menus plus the added advantage of breakfast, which is included in the room price. Reservations can be made seven days a week through the room reservations number: 0870 243 0500. For further details, consult the Hotel Groups page.

**ROOMS:** 18 en suite **NOTES:** Open Now

CRANBROOK, Kent Map 05 TQ73

## Premier Collection

### ★★ Kennel Holt

Goudhurst Rd TN17 2PT

☎ 01580 712032 01580 715495

e-mail: hotel@kennelholt.demon.co.uk

***Dir:*** *between Goudhurst and Cranbrook on A262*

This Elizabethan manor house is a charming retreat with immaculately kept gardens, situated in the centre of the Kent and Sussex Weald, an area of outstanding natural beauty. Local attractions include castles and gardens. The relaxing public rooms are full of original features. Individually styled bedrooms, some including four-poster beds, are traditionally comfortable and are furnished in keeping with the style of the property. The food is good and the wine list is a real treat.

**ROOMS:** 10 en suite s £90-£130; d £150-£195 (incl. bkfst) * **LB** **FACILITIES:** Croquet lawn Putting green **CONF:** Board 10 Del from £210 * **PARKING:** 20 **NOTES:** No dogs No children 7yrs No smoking in restaurant Closed 1 wk Jan **CARDS:**

### ★★68% The George Hotel

Stone St TN17 3HE

☎ 01580 713348 01580 715532

e-mail: georgecranbrook@aol.com

***Dir:*** *Turn off A21 to Goudhurst & Cranbrook, continue to large roundabout, then right into Cranbrook*

A town centre inn believed to date to the 13th century, when Edward I reputedly stayed here. The charming bedrooms feature exposed beams, one room has a magnificent four-poster bed. Guests can dine in the informal wine bar or Brooks restaurant.

GEORGE HOTEL

**ROOMS:** 8 en suite No smoking in 7 bedrooms s £60-£90; d £90-£125 (incl. bkfst) * **LB** **FACILITIES:** Xmas **CONF:** Thtr 75 Class 60 Board 50 **PARKING:** 15 **CARDS:**

CRATHORNE, North Yorkshire Map 08 NZ4

### ★★★★78% Crathorne Hall

TS15 0AR

☎ 01642 700398 01642 700814

e-mail: crathorne@arcadianhotels.co.uk

***Dir:*** *off A19, take slip road marked Teesside Airport and Kirklevington, the a right turn signposted Crathorne leads straight to the hotel*

This splendid Edwardian Hall is set in its own beautifully landscaped grounds enjoying fine views of the Leven Valley. Both the impressively equipped bedrooms and the delightful public areas offer a high degree of luxury, comfort and space. Service is friendly and particularly attentive. An imaginative menu offers guests a wide choice of carefully prepared dishes.

**ROOMS:** 37 en suite (4 fmly) No smoking in 15 bedrooms s fr £65; d £70-£149 * **LB** **FACILITIES:** STV Fishing Croquet lawn Jogging track Clay pigeon shooting Xmas **CONF:** Thtr 140 Class 80 Board 60 Del fro £133 * **PARKING:** 120 **NOTES:** No smoking in restaurant Civ Wed 132 **CARDS:**

*See advert on opposite pag*

CRAWLEY See Gatwick Airport

CREWE, Cheshire Map 07 SJ7

### ★★★★68% Crewe Hall

Weston Rd CW1 6UZ

☎ 01270 253333 01270 253322

e-mail: reservations@crewehall.com

***Dir:*** *From M6 junct 16 follow A500 to Crewe. At rdbt take 2nd exit A5020, next rdbt 1st exit to Crewe. Crewe hall approx 150 yds right*

Proudly standing in 500 acres of mature grounds, this historic Hall converted into a very comfortable hotel, dates back to the 17th century. It retains a very elaborate and comfortable interior which is a true reflection of Victorian style. Bedrooms are spacious and offer high levels of comfort. Quality modern cooking is served in the elegant Ranulph restaurant.

**ROOMS:** 25 en suite (4 fmly) No smoking in 10 bedrooms s £120-£250; d £150-£290 (incl. bkfst) * **LB** **FACILITIES:** STV Tennis (hard) Croquet lawn Full size football pitch Xmas **CONF:** Thtr 260 Class 110 Board 100 Del £185 * **SERVICES:** Lift **PARKING:** 140 **NOTES:** No smoking in restaurant Civ Wed 200 **CARDS:**

**★★★66% Hunters Lodge**
Sydney Rd, Sydney CW1 5LU
☎ 01270 583440 🖷 01270 500553
e-mail: info@hunterslodge.co.uk
***Dir:*** *1m from Crewe station, off A534*
Dating back to the 18th century, this family run hotel has been extended and modernised and caters for both the business and leisure markets. Accommodation, mainly located in an adjacent modern bedroom wing, includes family and four-poster rooms. Imaginative dishes are served in the spacious restaurant, and the popular bar also offers a choice of tempting meals.
**ROOMS:** 47 en suite (2 fmly) No smoking in 21 bedrooms s £32-£55; d £58-£85 (incl. bkfst) * **FACILITIES:** Spa STV Sauna Solarium Gym **CONF:** Thtr 160 Class 100 Board 80 Del from £94 * **PARKING:** 240 **NOTES:** No dogs (ex guide dogs) No smoking in restaurant RS Sun Civ Wed 130 **CARDS:**

**★★★66% White Lion**
Weston CW2 5NA
☎ 01270 587011 & 500303 🖷 01270 500303
***Dir:*** *from M6 junct 16 follow A500 signposted 'Crewe, Nantwich, Chester' to 2nd rdbt then right into Weston village. Hotel in centre on left*
Once a Tudor farmhouse, this privately owned hotel provides comfortable, modern accommodation, yet retains much of its old charm. In addition to The White Lion Restaurant and its adjoining cocktail lounge, a selection of bar snacks is also available in the oak beamed Lounge Bar. The hotel holds a licence for civil weddings.
**ROOMS:** 16 en suite (2 fmly) s £58; d £68 (incl. bkfst) * **LB** **FACILITIES:** Crown Green bowling **CONF:** Thtr 50 Class 28 Board 20 Del £90 * **PARKING:** 100 **NOTES:** No smoking in restaurant Closed Xmas & New Year Civ Wed 65 **CARDS:**

**⌂ *Travelodge***
Travelodge
Alsager Rd, Barthomley CW2 5PT
☎ 01270 883157 🖷 01270 883157
***Dir:*** *5m E, at junc 16 M6/A500*
Travelodge offers good quality, good value, modern accommodation. Ideal for families, the spacious, en suite bedrooms include remote-control TV, tea and coffee-making facilities, luxury beds and free morning newspaper. Meals can be taken at the nearby family restaurant. For further details and the Travelodge phone number, consult the Hotel Groups page.

**ROOMS:** 42 en suite

## CRICK, Northamptonshire

Map 04 SP57

**★★★64% *Posthouse Northampton/Rugby***
Posthouse
NN6 7XR
☎ 0870 400 9059 🖷 01788 823955
***Dir:*** *at junct 18 of M1*
A modern hotel whose spacious grounds include a children's play area. Bedrooms, in various styles, include several family rooms; some rooms have pleasant country views. There is a restaurant, a lounge serving refreshments all day, and good leisure facilities and 24-hour room service.
**ROOMS:** 88 en suite (17 fmly) No smoking in 51 bedrooms **FACILITIES:** Indoor swimming (H) Sauna Solarium Gym Jacuzzi ch fac **CONF:** Thtr 200 Class 100 Board 142 **PARKING:** 200 **CARDS:**

Weekend away? Hotels with LB in their entry offer leisure breaks.

## CRICKLADE, Wiltshire

Map 04 SU09

**★★★68% *Cricklade Hotel***
Common Hill SN6 6HA
☎ 01793 750751 🖷 01793 751767
***Dir:*** *turn off A419 onto B4040. Turn left at clock tower. Right at rdbt. Hotel 0.5m up hill on left*

Surrounded by over 30 acres of Wiltshire countryside, the hotel offers a peaceful and tranquil venue for guests. Bedrooms offer high levels of comfort and quality. In addition to the elegant lounge and dining room, a Victorian style conservatory runs the full length of the building, from which wonderful views can be enjoyed.
**ROOMS:** 25 en suite 21 annexe en suite (1 fmly) **FACILITIES:** Indoor swimming (H) Golf 9 Tennis (hard) Snooker Sauna Solarium Gym Croquet lawn Jacuzzi Aromatherapy Beautician entertainment **CONF:** Thtr 130 Class 50 Board 60 **PARKING:** 100 **NOTES:** No dogs (ex guide dogs) No children 14yrs Civ Wed 120
**CARDS:**

## CROMER, Norfolk
Map 09 TG24

### ★★68% *Red Lion*
Brook St NR27 9HD
☎ 01263 514964 01263 512834
***Dir:*** *from town centre take first left after church*
The Red Lion dates from Victorian times and is a focal point for the area. Public rooms are comfortable, and the snooker room is a popular feature. Locals and residents mingle in the bars, which are Edwardian in style. Bedrooms offer a good standard of comfort and come in a variety of attractive styles and sizes.
**ROOMS:** 12 en suite (1 fmly) **FACILITIES:** Snooker Sauna Solarium Discount for local leisure centre **CONF:** Thtr 60 Class 50 Board 40 **PARKING:** 12 **NOTES:** No dogs No smoking in restaurant
**CARDS:**

### ★★64% The Parsons Pleasure Hotel
Church St, Northrepps NR27 0LE
☎ 01263 579691 01263 579691
***Dir:*** *Off A149 follow signs to Northrepps village, hotel just before St Mary's Church*
Ideally located in Northrepps, a small village two miles from Cromer. Traditional Norfolk flint building, formerly a church barn, which has been sympathetically restored. Spacious bedrooms are attractively decorated and equipped with many thoughtful touches, some feature flint walls. There is a smart dining room and a lounge bar with an open log fire.
**ROOMS:** 8 en suite (2 fmly) No smoking in all bedrooms s £33.75-£43.75; d £67.50-£95 (incl. bkfst) * **LB** **PARKING:** 20 **NOTES:** No smoking in restaurant **CARDS:**

### ★★62% Hotel de Paris
Leisureplex
High St NR27 9HG
☎ 01263 513141 01263 515217
***Dir:*** *enter Cromer on A140 (Norwich Rd), turn left at traffic lights on to Mount St. At second set of lights turn right into Prince of Wales Rd. 2nd on right into New St which leads into High St.*
Imposing traditional style resort hotel situated on the sea front overlooking the pier and beach. Bedrooms are pleasantly decorated and well equipped, many rooms have superb sea views. Public rooms include a large lounge bar, a restaurant, games room and a further TV lounge.
**ROOMS:** 56 en suite (5 fmly) s £28-£37; d £42-£66 (incl. bkfst) * **LB** **FACILITIES:** Games room with pool table entertainment Xmas **SERVICES:** Lift **PARKING:** 14 **NOTES:** No dogs (ex guide dogs) No smoking in restaurant Closed Dec-part Feb RS Nov Mar & part Feb (open Mon-Fri only) **CARDS:**

## CROOKLANDS, Cumbria
Map 07 SD58

### ★★★67% Crooklands
Best Western
LA7 7NW
☎ 015395 67432 015395 67525
e-mail: crooklands_hotel@postmaster.co.uk
***Dir:*** *on A65, 1.5m from M6 junct 36*
Situated close to the M6, Lake District and Yorkshire Dales, this is a welcoming family-run hotel. Public areas, which have natural stone walls and heavy beams, include a choice of bars and eating options. Bedrooms, all located in the wing extension, vary in size with mixed styles of furnishings.
**ROOMS:** 30 en suite No smoking in 12 bedrooms s £52.50-£55; d £55-£60 * **LB** **CONF:** Thtr 100 Class 60 Board 50 Del from £95 * **PARKING:** 150 **NOTES:** No dogs Closed 24-26 Dec
**CARDS:**

## CROWTHORNE, Berkshire
Map 04 SU8

### ★★★70% Waterloo
corus
Duke's Ride RG45 6DW
☎ 01344 777711 01344 778913
***Dir:*** *M3 junct 3 towards Bracknell follow A322 then follow signs for Crowthorne, once in village follow sign for Hotel & Conference centre*
Situated in a quiet location between the M3 and M4, this hotel attracts a high proportion of business guests. The modern bedrooms, which include interconnecting pairs of rooms, are attractively appointed and very well- maintained. Public areas include a pleasant brasserie-style restaurant and a choice of bar areas.
**ROOMS:** 58 en suite No smoking in 22 bedrooms s fr £115; d fr £139 * **LB** **FACILITIES:** STV **CONF:** Thtr 50 Class 24 Board 20 Del £148 * **PARKING:** 70 **NOTES:** Civ Wed 40
**CARDS:**

## CROYDE, Devon
Map 02 SS4

### ★★69% Kittiwell House
St Mary's Rd EX33 1PG
☎ 01271 890247 01271 890469
e-mail: kittiwell@aol.com
***Dir:*** *0.5m from village centre in direction of Georgeham*
The comfortable bedrooms in this delightfully cosy, thatched hote are individually decorated and furnished, reflecting the character of the property. Beamed ceilings, open fires and an interesting collection of bric-a-brac create a relaxing environment. Popular locally, the attractive restaurant offers both carte and fixed-price menus.
**ROOMS:** 12 en suite (2 fmly) No smoking in 4 bedrooms s £47-£57; d £74-£82 (incl. bkfst) * **LB** **FACILITIES:** Xmas **PARKING:** 21 **NOTES:** No smoking in restaurant Closed mid Jan-mid Feb
**CARDS:**

## CROYDON, Greater London
Map 04 TQ3

### ★★★★77% Coulsdon Manor
MARSTON HOTELS
Coulsdon Court Rd, Coulsdon CR5 2LL
☎ 020 8668 0414 020 8668 3118
e-mail: coulsdonmanor@marstonhotels.com
***Dir:*** *A23 turn right into Stoats Nest Road. Hotel at top of hill on left*
Set amidst 140 acres of landscaped parkland, which includes a professional 18-hole golf course, this fine Victorian Manor house offers spacious, modern and well-equipped bedrooms. The hotel has gained a deserved reputation for its standards of service and hospitality, not to mention the quality of food served in the restaurant.
**ROOMS:** 35 en suite No smoking in 13 bedrooms s £110; d £142 (incl. bkfst) * **LB** **FACILITIES:** STV Golf 18 Tennis (hard) Squash Sauna Solarium Gym Putting green ch fac Xmas **CONF:** Thtr 180 Class 90 Board 70 Del from £150 * **SERVICES:** Lift **PARKING:** 200 **NOTES:** No dogs (ex guide dogs) No smoking in restaurant Civ Wed 60
**CARDS:**

### ★★★★70% Selsdon Park
PRINCIPAL HOTELS
Addington Rd, Sanderstead CR2 8YA
☎ 020 8657 8811 020 8651 6171
e-mail: selsdonpark@principalhotels.co.uk
***Dir:*** *3m SE off A2022*
The extensive well kept grounds of this imposing Jacobean mansion include a professional 18-hole golf course. Popular for weddings and conferences, guests will find smart bedrooms equipped to a high standard. There is a grand restaurant where

*continued*

teresting food is served. There are also good leisure facilities.
**OOMS:** 204 en suite (12 fmly) s £105-£125; d £140-£160 * **LB**
**ACILITIES:** STV Indoor swimming (H) Outdoor swimming (H) Golf 18
nnis (hard & grass) Squash Sauna Solarium Gym Croquet lawn
itting green Jacuzzi Boules Jogging track entertainment Xmas
**ONF:** Thtr 400 Class 250 Board 60 Del from £199 * **SERVICES:** Lift
**ARKING:** 300 **NOTES:** No dogs (ex guide dogs) No smoking in
staurant Civ Wed 80 **CARDS:**

*See advert on this page*

**★★★65% Posthouse Croydon**

urley Way CR9 4LT

Posthouse

0870 400 9022 020 8681 6438

***ir:** Follow A23 Central London hotel on left next to rport House*

uitable for both the business and leisure traveller, this bright otel provides modern accommodation in well-equipped edrooms with en suite bathrooms.

**OOMS:** 83 en suite No smoking in 40 bedrooms s fr £99; d fr £119 *
**B FACILITIES:** Xmas **CONF:** Thtr 100 Class 50 Board 40
**ARKING:** 70 **NOTES:** Civ Wed 70 **CARDS:**

**★★★64% Dukes Head**

Manor Rd, The Green, Wallington SM6 0AA

020 8401 7410 020 8401 7420

-mail: dukeshead@youngs.co.uk

ocated between Croydon and Sutton, this brewery-owned hotel as spacious bedrooms which are furnished to a high standard ith good facilities. Public areas include a busy traditional bar and brightly appointed restaurant.

**OOMS:** 24 en suite (4 fmly) No smoking in 15 bedrooms s fr £96;
fr £106 (incl. bkfst) * **LB FACILITIES:** STV Xmas **CONF:** Del from
170 * **SERVICES:** air con **PARKING:** 35 **NOTES:** No dogs (ex guide
ogs) **CARDS:**

**★★68% Markington Hotel & Conference Centre**

Haling Park Rd CR2 6NG

020 8681 6494 020 8688 6530

-mail: rooms@markingtonhotel.com

***ir:** travelling N from Purley along A235, Haling Park Rd is 1st on left after us garage. Hotel on left*

his friendly hotel is close to Croydon's centre, but is peaceful and elaxing. Bedrooms are comfortable, smart and well-equipped; ublic areas comprise a smart bar/lounge and attractive dining oom.

**OOMS:** 29 en suite (3 fmly) No smoking in 5 bedrooms s £50-£55;
£71-£87 (incl. bkfst) * **FACILITIES:** STV nearby gym with full facilities
or £1 **CONF:** Thtr 25 Class 20 Board 20 Del from £108 *
**ARKING:** 17 **NOTES:** No dogs (ex guide dogs) No smoking in
estaurant Closed 23 Dec-2 Jan **CARDS:**

**★★67% South Park Hotel**

-5 South Park Hill Rd, South Croydon CR2 7DY

020 8688 5644 020 8760 0861

-mail: RECEPTION@southparkhotel.co.uk

***ir:** from A235 to Croydon town centre, take A212 towards Addington, ontinue for 1.5m to rdbt. Take 3rd exit off onto South Park Hill Rd*

his small privately-owned hotel is ideally located for road and rail inks and there is some off-street parking for guests with cars. edrooms are attractively decorated all with modern pine urniture and offer a good range of in-room facilities. Public areas onsist of a cosy bar, a lounge with large sofas and a delightful ack garden.

**OOMS:** 19 en suite (2 fmly) No smoking in 8 bedrooms s fr £55;
fr £71 (incl. bkfst) * **PARKING:** 15 **NOTES:** No smoking in restaurant
**ARDS:**

***Premier Lodge***

619 Purley Way CR0 4RJ

PREMIER LODGE

0870 700 1434 0870 700 1435

Premier Lodge offers modern, well-equipped, en suite accommodation suitable for both business and leisure travellers. Meals can be taken at the adjacent popular restaurant and bar, which is fully licensed. For further details, consult the Hotel Groups page.

**ROOMS:** 81 en suite

**○ Innkeeper's Lodge Croydon South**

415 Brighton Rd, South Croydon CR2 6EJ

A new concept in the travel accommodation market. Smart rooms meet essential business requirements but also have home comforts. Dining options include all-day menus plus the added advantage of breakfast, which is included in the room price. Reservations can be made seven days a week through the room reservations number: 0870 243 0500. For further details, consult the Hotel Groups page.

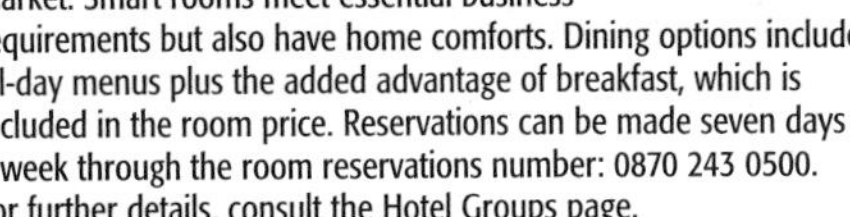

**ROOMS:** 30 en suite

CRUDWELL, Wiltshire Map 03 ST99

**★★★74% The Old Rectory Country House Hotel**

SN16 9EP

01666 577194 01666 577853

***Dir:** 8m from M4 junct 17, follow A429 towards Cirencester, right opposite Plough pub in the middle of Crudwell, hotel next to church*

An attractive 17th-century stone-built rectory, set in three acres of walled Victorian gardens beside the church. A pleasingly friendly informality best describes the style of service provided by the

*continued on p192*

CRUDWELL, continued

owners and their small team of staff. Bedrooms are decorated and furnished to a high standard, and food is a highlight: exciting menus complemented by a selection of interesting wines.
**ROOMS:** 13 en suite No smoking in 5 bedrooms s £65-£95; d £88-£120 (incl. bkfst) * **LB** **FACILITIES:** Croquet lawn Xmas **CONF:** Thtr 40 Class 20 Board 20 Del £115 * **PARKING:** 50 **NOTES:** No smoking in restaurant Civ Wed 42 **CARDS:**

CUCKFIELD, West Sussex Map 04 TQ32

### ★★71% Hilton Park Hotel

Tylers Green RH17 5EG
☎ 01444 454555 01444 457222
e-mail: hiltonpark@janus-systems.com
***Dir:*** *halfway between Cuckfield and Haywards Heath on the A272*
This delightful family-run, Victorian country house set in three acres of landscaped grounds is situated between the lovely village of Cuckfield and Haywards Heath. The bedrooms are tastefully decorated and include an excellent range of extra facilities. Public rooms include an elegant drawing room, a smart dining room and a conservatory bar.
**ROOMS:** 11 en suite (2 fmly) s £75-£80; d £105-£115 (incl. bkfst) * **LB** **FACILITIES:** STV ch fac **CONF:** Thtr 30 Board 12 Del from £125 * **PARKING:** 50 **NOTES:** No dogs (ex guide dogs) No smoking in restaurant **CARDS:**

DARLINGTON, Co Durham Map 08 NZ21
see also Tees-Side Airport

### ★★★73% Hall Garth Golf & Country Club

corus

Coatham Mundeville DL1 3LU
☎ 01325 300400 01325 310083
***Dir:*** *at junct 59 A1(M) take A167 towards Darlington, after 600yds turn left at top of hill, hotel is on right*

Hall Garth enjoys the peace and quiet of a country location yet is close to major routes. Bedrooms in the original house are traditional in style and have every modern facility, rooms in the newer wings are also well-equipped and furnished. Facilities include leisure centre, golf, a pub and a popular restaurant.
**ROOMS:** 30 en suite 11 annexe en suite (4 fmly) No smoking in 21 bedrooms s fr £99; d fr £120 * **LB** **FACILITIES:** STV Indoor swimming (H) Golf 9 Sauna Solarium Gym Putting green Jacuzzi Steam room,Beauty Salon **CONF:** Thtr 300 Class 120 Board 80 Del from £110 * **PARKING:** 150 **NOTES:** No smoking in restaurant Civ Wed 170 **CARDS:**

### ★★★70% Headlam Hall

Headlam, Gainford DL2 3HA
☎ 01325 730238 01325 730790
e-mail: admin@headlamhall.co.uk
***Dir:*** *2m N of A67 between Piercebridge and Gainford*
This impressive Jacobean hall was previously the ancestral home of Lord Brocket and then Lord Gainford. The main house retains many historical features and has a wide range of modern amenities. Bedrooms in the manor house are traditionally styled and those in the converted coach house are more spacious and furnished with pine.
**ROOMS:** 19 en suite 17 annexe en suite (4 fmly) No smoking in 19 bedrooms s £69-£99; d £84-£114 (incl. bkfst) * **LB** **FACILITIES:** STV Indoor swimming (H) Tennis (hard) Fishing Sauna Gym Croquet lawn ch fac **CONF:** Thtr 150 Class 40 Board 40 Del from £110 * **PARKING:** 60 **NOTES:** No dogs (ex guide dogs) No smoking in restaurant Closed 24-25 Dec Civ Wed 150
**CARDS:**

### ★★★67% Blackwell Grange

REGAL

Blackwell Grange DL3 8QH
☎ 01325 509955 01325 380899
***Dir:*** *on A167, 1.5m from central ring road*

This grand 17th-century mansion is set in attractive parkland, surrounded by an 18 hole golf course. Many of the bedrooms are in modern extensions, although more spacious rooms are situated in the original building. The spacious public rooms include a host of meeting rooms, as well as a range of day rooms.
**ROOMS:** 99 en suite 11 annexe en suite (3 fmly) No smoking in 14 bedrooms s £89-£125; d £115-£165 * **LB** **FACILITIES:** STV Indoor swimming (H) Golf 18 Tennis Sauna Solarium Gym Croquet lawn Putting green Jacuzzi Xmas **CONF:** Thtr 300 Class 110 Board 50 **SERVICES:** Lift **PARKING:** 250 **NOTES:** No smoking in restaurant Civ Wed 200 **CARDS:**

### ★★★67% Kings Head

9-12 PriestGate DL1 1NW
☎ 01325 380222 01325 382006
e-mail: lynne@fsbusiness.co.uk
***Dir:*** *A1 northbound follow signs to Darlington. 3rd exit off next rdbt, 2nd off next, 1st exit off next, 1st right then 1st left. Hotel on right*
Adjacent to the Cornmill Shopping Centre, this modern hotel provides a sound standard of accommodation in well-equipped bedrooms. Public areas include the Priestgate foyer lounge, open all day for light snacks, and a traditional restaurant. The hotel has a secure, enclosed car park, and extensive function facilities.
**ROOMS:** 85 en suite (3 fmly) No smoking in 51 bedrooms s £50-£70; d £60-£80 (incl. bkfst) * **LB** **FACILITIES:** free use nearby leisure complex Xmas **CONF:** Thtr 250 Class 100 Board 50 Del from £80 * **SERVICES:** Lift **PARKING:** 28 **CARDS:**

### ★★★66% White Horse Hotel

Harrogate Hill DL1 3AD
☎ 01325 382121 🖹 01325 355953
e-mail: reservations@whitehorsedarlington.co.uk
***Dir:*** *A1(M) junct 59, follow A167 towards Darlington till Harrowgate Village(approx 2 miles) Hotel right after village sign post.*
Situated just outside Darlington, and within very easy reach of the A1, this well-positioned business hotel provides identically equipped bedrooms, including a number of family rooms. Guests can eat informally in one of the smartly presented bars.
**ROOMS:** 40 en suite (3 fmly) No smoking in 20 bedrooms s £45-£57; d £53-£74 (incl. bkfst) * **LB** **CONF:** Thtr 60 Class 10 Board 30 Del from £85 * **SERVICES:** Lift **PARKING:** 120 **NOTES:** No dogs (ex guide dogs) No smoking in restaurant **CARDS:**

### ★★★63% Croft Spa Hotel

Croft-on-Tees DL2 2ST
☎ 01325 720319 🖹 01325 721252
e-mail: information@croftspa.co.uk
***Dir:*** *from Darlington take A167 Northallerton road. Hotel 3m S*
This large hotel stands beside the River Tees and offers mainly spacious and well-equipped bedrooms. The public rooms consist of a large bar lounge together with the pleasant Alice's Restaurant. A fitness centre is also provided, as are good conference facilities.
**ROOMS:** 37 en suite (4 fmly) **FACILITIES:** STV Snooker Sauna Solarium Gym **PARKING:** 200 **NOTES:** No dogs (ex guide dogs) No smoking in restaurant Civ Wed 125 **CARDS:**

### ★★★61% Walworth Castle Hotel

Walworth DL2 2LY
☎ 01325 485470 🖹 01325 462257
e-mail: enquiries@walworthcastle.co.uk
***Dir:*** *A1(M) junct 58 follow signs to Corbridge, left at rdbt, left at The Dog pub, hotel on the left after 1 m*
This 12th-century castle lies in 18 acres amidst farmland. Specialising in weddings and conferences, it is also well-suited to the business market. Accommodation styles vary from compact standard rooms in an adjoining wing, to larger grand rooms in the castle itself. The restaurant and "Farmers Bar" give a choice for formal or informal dining.
**ROOMS:** 20 en suite 14 annexe en suite (4 fmly) No smoking in 6 bedrooms s £45-£55; d £60-£75 (incl. bkfst) * **FACILITIES:** Xmas **CONF:** Thtr 150 Class 100 Board 80 Del from £80 * **PARKING:** 100 **NOTES:** No smoking in restaurant **CARDS:**

### ★★66% Devonport

16-18 The Front, Middleton-one-Row DL2 1AS
☎ 01325 332255 🖹 01325 333242
***Dir:*** *from A67 follow signs to Teeside airport.Head for centre of Middleton St George,turn right after post office.At garage turn left for 1 mile.*
Situated in a former spa village between Darlington and the airport, this historic hotel enjoys fine views across the River Tees and open farmland to the distant hills. Originally a 300-year-old inn, the hotel has been completely refurbished to include a pub and restaurant offering a contemporary bistro-style menu. Bedrooms are well-equipped and comfortable; some are particularly spacious.
**ROOMS:** 16 en suite (1 fmly) No smoking in 5 bedrooms s fr £59; d fr £85 (incl. bkfst) * **LB** **FACILITIES:** Xmas **CONF:** Thtr 50 Class 30 Board 40 **PARKING:** 30 **NOTES:** No dogs (ex guide dogs) **CARDS:**

## DARRINGTON, West Yorkshire — Map 08 SE42

### ★★61% *The Darrington Hotel*

Great North Rd WF8 3BL
☎ 01977 791458 🖹 01977 602286
***Dir:*** *off A1, 2m S of A1/M62 interchange (junct 33). Signposted*
Conveniently close to the A1 and on the edge of the village of Darrington, this popular hotel offers modern and well-equipped bedrooms. There are lively bars and an extensive range of food is available; and service is both friendly and relaxed
**ROOMS:** 27 en suite (1 fmly) **FACILITIES:** STV entertainment **CONF:** Thtr 24 Class 12 Board 12 **PARKING:** 90 **NOTES:** No dogs (ex guide dogs) **CARDS:**

## DARTFORD, Kent — Map 05 TQ57

### ★★★★76% Rowhill Grange Hotel & Spa

DA2 7QH
☎ 01322 615136 🖹 01322 615137
e-mail: admin@rowhillgrange.co.uk
***Dir:*** *From junct 3 M25 take B2173 to Swanley, followed by B258 to Hextable*

Superb country house hotel set amidst nine acres of woodland and pretty gardens. The stylish bedrooms offer a high degree of comfort throughout; they are individually decorated with attractive soft furnishings and have many thoughtful touches. Dinner is available in the Garden restaurant but for those preferring a more relaxed atmosphere try the Topiary Brasserie. Guests also have the use of the hotel's health and leisure spa.
**ROOMS:** 38 en suite (1 fmly) No smoking in 32 bedrooms s £145-£265; d £169-£325 * **LB** **FACILITIES:** Spa STV Indoor swimming (H) Sauna Solarium Gym Croquet lawn Jacuzzi Beauty treatment, Hair salon, Aerobic ,studio ,Therapy pool ch fac Xmas **CONF:** Thtr 160 Class 60 Board 35 Del from £145 * **SERVICES:** Lift **PARKING:** 150 **NOTES:** No dogs (ex guide dogs) No smoking in restaurant Civ Wed 200 **CARDS:**

### ⌂ Campanile

Clipper Boulevard West, Business Park, Crossways DA2 6QN
☎ 01322 278925 🖹 01322 278948
***Dir:*** *follow signs for Ferry Terminal from Dartford Bridge*
This modern building offers accommodation in smart, well-

*continued on p194*

DARTFORD, continued

equipped bedrooms, all with en suite bathrooms. Refreshments may be taken at the informal Bistro. For further details and the Campanile phone number, consult the Hotel Groups page.

RESTAURANT

*Campanile, Dartford*

**ROOMS:** 125 en suite **CONF:** Thtr 50 Class 20 Board 25 Del £68 *

### ⇧ *Express by Holiday Inn Dartford*

University Way DA1 5PA
☎ 01322 290333 📠 290444
e-mail: dartford@premierhotels-7.demon.co.uk
***Dir:*** *follow A206 to Erith. Hotel located off University Way via signposted sliproad*

Express by Holiday Inn

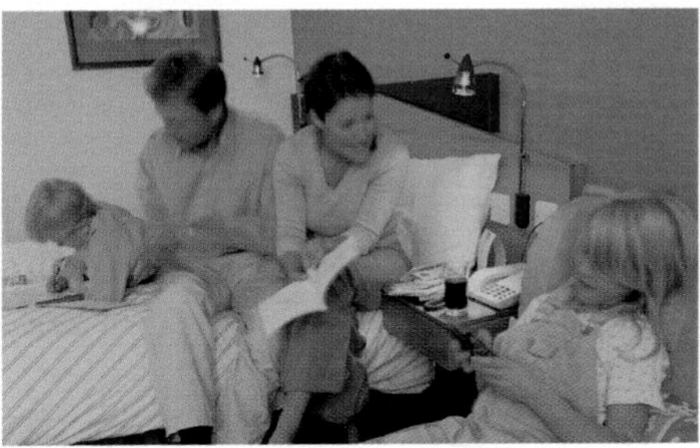

A modern budget hotel offering comfortable accommodation in refreshing, spacious and comprehensively equipped bedrooms, en suite bathrooms with power showers and continental buffet breakfast included in the room rate. Suitable for business travellers or families. For further details and the Express by Holiday Inn phone number, consult the Hotel Groups page.
**ROOMS:** 126 en suite **CONF:** Thtr 35 Board 20

### ○ *Travelodge Dartford*

Charles St, Off Crossway Boulevard DA2 6QQ
☎ 0800 850950
**NOTES:** Open Winter 2001

Travelodge

## DARTMOUTH, Devon

Map 03 SX85

### ★★★73% The Dart Marina

Sandquay TQ6 9PH
☎ 0870 400 8134 📠 01803 835040
e-mail: heritagehotels_dartmouth.dart_marina @forte-hotels.com
***Dir:*** *A3122 from Totnes to Dartmouth, follow road which becomes College Way, just before the Higher Ferry, The Dart Marina is sharp left in Sandquay Rd*

Heritage Hotels

Dartmouth's connections with the sea date back centuries and the hotel itself is an idyllic position by the marina, with direct access to the water. Bedrooms, or cabins as they are referred to, have a nautical theme and are named after famous ships, sailors and shipbuilders.
**ROOMS:** 46 en suite 4 annexe en suite No smoking in 39 bedrooms s £90-£110; d £130-£170 (incl. bkfst & dinner) * **LB** **FACILITIES:** ch fac Xmas **PARKING:** 50 **NOTES:** No smoking in restaurant Civ Wed 70
**CARDS:**

### ★★★71% Royal Castle

11 The Quay TQ6 9PS
☎ 01803 833033 📠 01803 835445
e-mail: enquiry@royalcastle.co.uk
***Dir:*** *in the centre of the town, overlooking Boat float Inner Harbour*

ROYAL
CASTLE
HOTEL

This 17th-century coaching inn stands right on Dartmouth harbour. Its two bars serve traditional ales and a range of locally popular bar meals. Upstairs, there are several quiet lounges and the more formal Adams Restaurant. The attractive, individual bedrooms, several with four-poster beds, offer modern facilities and many personal touches.
**ROOMS:** 25 en suite (4 fmly) s £68-£83; d £104-£150 (incl. bkfst) * **LB** **FACILITIES:** STV entertainment Xmas **CONF:** Thtr 70 Class 40 Board 40 **PARKING:** 17 **NOTES:** No smoking in restaurant Civ Wed 60
**CARDS:**

### ★★★68% Stoke Lodge

Stoke Fleming TQ6 0RA
☎ 01803 770523 📠 01803 770851
e-mail: mail@stokelodge.co.uk
***Dir:*** *2m S A379*

A popular choice, with many guests returning regularly, Stoke Lodge is located in Stoke Fleming, a village not far from Dartmouth. Set in three acres of gardens and grounds, a large range of leisure facilities are available, depending upon the time of year. The restaurant offers an extensive wine list and both carte and fixed-price menus.
**ROOMS:** 25 en suite (5 fmly) s £47.50-£55; d £79-£102 (incl. bkfst) **LB** **FACILITIES:** **Spa** Indoor swimming (H) Outdoor swimming (H) Tennis (hard) Snooker Sauna Putting green Table tennis pool table Xmas **CONF:** Thtr 80 Class 60 Board 30 Del from £60 * **PARKING:** 50 **NOTES:** No smoking in restaurant **CARDS:**

### ★★66% ® *Endsleigh Hotel*

New Rd, Stoke Fleming TQ6 0NR
☎ 01803 770381 📠 01803 770819
***Dir:*** *take Buckfastleigh junct off A38 follow signs to Totnes and then A3122 to Dartmouth. Take A379 coast road to Stoke Fleming, hotel on right in centre of village.*

Located in the picturesque village of Stoke Fleming, this friendly hotel is within easy reach of many superb beaches. Facing south with views across to the sea, a relaxed and informal atmosphere

*continued*

pervades. The stylish restaurant is popular, quality local produce being skilfully prepared. Bedrooms are well-equipped and offer varying levels of comfort.
**ROOMS:** 9 en suite (2 fmly) No smoking in all bedrooms
**FACILITIES:** Croquet lawn **PARKING:** 20 **NOTES:** No dogs (ex guide dogs) No smoking in restaurant **CARDS:**

DARWEN, Lancashire Map 07 SD62

### ★★★70% Whitehall

Springbank, Whitehall BB3 2JU
☎ 01254 701595 01254 773426
e-mail: hotel@thewhitehallhotel.freeserve.co.uk
***Dir:*** *off A666 S of town*
A friendly hotel set in attractive grounds on the edge of town and offering stylish, recently refurbished accommodation. A wide range of dishes is served in the elegant restaurant, and lighter meals are available in the bar and lounge. Leisure facilities include a snooker room and a gymnasium is planned for 2002. Extensive function facilities make this hotel popular for weddings and conferences.
**ROOMS:** 17 en suite (2 fmly) No smoking in 12 bedrooms s £55-£75; d £65-£85 (incl. bkfst) * **FACILITIES:** **Spa** STV Indoor swimming (H) Sauna Solarium Jacuzzi 3/4 size snooker table **CONF:** Thtr 100 Class 50 Board 25 Del from £75 * **PARKING:** 50 **NOTES:** No dogs No smoking in restaurant Civ Wed 120 **CARDS:**

### ★★69% The Old Rosins Inn

Pickup Bank, Hoddlesden BB3 3QD
☎ 01254 771264 01254 873894
***Dir:*** *leave M65 at junct 5, follow signs for Haslingdon then right after 2m signed Egworth, then right after 0.5m and continue 0.5m*
This charming country inn, set in the heart of the Lancashire moors, is only a few minutes drive from the M65. Public areas are full of charm and character and include a cosy bar serving a wide selection of bar meals, an intimate restaurant and a large function room. Modern bedrooms are well equipped and have countryside views.
**ROOMS:** 15 en suite (3 fmly) **FACILITIES:** STV **CONF:** Thtr 30 Class 24 Board 70 **PARKING:** 200 **NOTES:** No dogs (ex guide dogs)
**CARDS:**

DAVENTRY, Northamptonshire Map 04 SP56

### ★★★★74% Fawsley Hall

PRIDE OF BRITAIN MEMBER

Fawsley NN11 3BA
☎ 01327 892000 01327 892001
e-mail: reservation@fawsleyhall.com

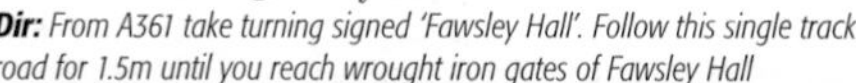

***Dir:*** *From A361 take turning signed 'Fawsley Hall'. Follow this single track road for 1.5m until you reach wrought iron gates of Fawsley Hall*

Dating back to the 15th century in parts, this fine manor house has been sympathetically converted into a comfortable and welcoming hotel. It is set in peaceful open countryside, surrounded by

*continued*

gardens designed by Capability Brown. Bedrooms are comfortably furnished, whilst public areas are set around the courtyard and feature an impressive Great Hall with a vaulted roof. An excellent menu is served in what was once a Tudor kitchen.
**ROOMS:** 30 en suite s £125-£225; d £155-£255 (incl. bkfst) * **LB**
**FACILITIES:** STV Tennis (hard) Croquet lawn Putting green Xmas
**CONF:** Thtr 80 Class 30 Board 33 Del from £175 * **PARKING:** 100
**NOTES:** No smoking in restaurant Civ Wed 80
**CARDS:**

### ★★★★62% Hanover International Hotel & Club

Sedgemoor Way NN11 5SG
☎ 01327 307000 01327 706313
e-mail: reservations@hanoverdaventry.ndo.co.uk
***Dir:*** *N of Daventry on the A361 Ring Road*

This imposing modern hotel overlooking Drayton Water has spacious public areas that include a good range of banqueting, meeting and leisure facilities. The hotel is a popular venue for conferences. The comfortable bedrooms all have double beds.
**ROOMS:** 138 en suite No smoking in 73 bedrooms s fr £40; d £60-£110 * **LB** **FACILITIES:** STV Indoor swimming (H) Sauna Solarium Gym Jacuzzi Steam room Health & beauty salon **CONF:** Thtr 600 Class 200 Board 30 Del from £90 * **SERVICES:** Lift **PARKING:** 350 **NOTES:** No dogs (ex guide dogs) No smoking in restaurant RS 26-30 Dec Civ Wed 200 **CARDS:**

### *Express By Holiday Inn Daventry*

Express
by Holiday Inn

Park Lands, Crick NN6 7EX
☎ 01788 824331 01788 824332
e-mail: crick@premierhotels.co.uk
***Dir:*** *M1 junct18. Take A428 to Daventry. Immediately on right*

A modern budget hotel offering comfortable accommodation in refreshing, spacious and comprehensively equipped bedrooms, en suite bathrooms with power showers and continental buffet breakfast included in the room rate. Suitable for business travellers or families. For further details and the Express by Holiday Inn phone number, consult the Hotel Groups page.
**ROOMS:** 111 en suite **CONF:** Thtr 35 Class 20 Board 20

## DAWLISH, Devon

Map 03 SX97

### ★★★68% Langstone Cliff

Dawlish Warren EX7 0NA
☎ 01626 868000 🖷 01626 868006
e-mail: reception@langstone-hotel.co.uk
***Dir:*** *1.5m NE off A379 Exeter road to Dawllish Warren*

This charming, family owned and run hotel, stands in wooded grounds overlooking the sea and the Exe Estuary. Lounges and bars are spacious and comfortable, with a carvery operation usually offered in the restaurant. Bedrooms vary in size and style, some benefiting from seaward facing balconies. During the winter months, special cabaret weekends attract a regular following.
**ROOMS:** 64 en suite 4 annexe en suite (52 fmly) s £55-£64; d £94-£158 (incl. bkfst) * **LB** **FACILITIES:** STV Indoor swimming (H) Outdoor swimming (H) Tennis (hard) Snooker Gym Table tennis, Golf practice area, Hair and beauty salon entertainment ch fac Xmas **CONF:** Thtr 400 Class 200 Board 80 Del £80 * **SERVICES:** Lift **PARKING:** 200 **NOTES:** Civ Wed 400 **CARDS:**

*See advert on opposite page*

## DEAL, Kent

Map 05 TR35

### ★★★70% Dunkerleys Hotel & Restaurant

19 Beach St CT14 7AH
☎ 01304 375016 🖷 01304 380187
e-mail: dunkerleysofdeal@btinternet.com
***Dir:*** *from M20 or M2 follow signs for A258 Deal. Hotel is situated on the seafront close to Deal Pier.*

Bedrooms are furnished to a high standard with a good range of amenities. The restaurant and bar have views of the Channel and offer interesting meals, well-executed and full flavoured - diners can choose to eat in the restaurant or in the more informal bistro; service throughout is friendly and attentive.
**ROOMS:** 16 en suite (2 fmly) s fr £60; d fr £100 (incl. bkfst) * **LB** **FACILITIES:** STV Jacuzzi Xmas **NOTES:** No dogs (ex guide dogs) No smoking in restaurant RS Mon **CARDS:**

### ★★★67% *Royal Hotel*

Beach St CT14 6JD
☎ 01304 375555 🖷 01304 372270
e-mail: royalhotel@theroyalhotel.com
***Dir:*** *turn off A2 onto the A258. Follow the road for 5m into Deal. Follow the one-way system onto the seafront. The Royal is 100yds from the pier*

The Royal Hotel has provided a focal point for the bustling town of Deal for hundreds of years. The comfortable bedrooms have smart colour schemes, some also have balconies overlooking the sea. The public rooms feature a vibrant brasserie, where an appealing selection of dishes can be enjoyed.
**ROOMS:** 22 en suite (4 fmly) No smoking in 2 bedrooms **FACILITIES:** STV **CONF:** Thtr 50 Class 20 Board 20 **NOTES:** No dogs (ex guide dogs) Civ Wed 30 **CARDS:**

*See advert on opposite page*

## DEDDINGTON, Oxfordshire

Map 04 SP43

### ★★★76% Deddington Arms

Horsefair OX15 0SH
☎ 0800 3287031 🖷 01869 337010
e-mail: deddarms@aol.com
***Dir:*** *From S leave M40 at Junct10 signed Northampton, A43. At 1st rdbt turn left to Aynho where turn left to Deddington. From N Leave M40 at Junct11 to Banbury. Follow signs through Banbury to hospital and Adderbury on A4260, then to Deddington*

There has been an inn on this site for over 400 years and the Deddington Arms retains much of its past character. Accommodation, upgraded and extended, offers smart, modern rooms. In the heart of this historic village the bar has a busy local trade and the delightful restaurant enjoys a good reputation.
**ROOMS:** 27 en suite (4 fmly) s £75-£85; d £80-£110 (incl. bkfst) * **LB** **FACILITIES:** STV Xmas **CONF:** Thtr 40 Class 35 Board 35 Del from £110 * **PARKING:** 36 **CARDS:**

*See advert under BANBURY*

### ★★★71% Holcombe Hotel & Restaurant

Best Western

High St OX15 0SL
☎ 01869 338274 🖷 01869 337167
e-mail: reception@holcombehotel.freeserve.co.uk
***Dir:*** *on the A4260 between Oxford & Banbury, at traffic lights in Deddington*

HOLCOMBE HOTEL

This charming privately owned hotel offers good accommodation and warm hospitality. The bedrooms are attractively decorated, well-maintained and equipped with many useful extras. There is a convivial air in the bar, where informal meals and snacks are available and, for the more serious diner, there is a separate restaurant.
**ROOMS:** 17 en suite (3 fmly) s £68-£79; d £95-£110 (incl. bkfst) * **LB** **FACILITIES:** STV ch fac Xmas **CONF:** Thtr 25 Class 14 Board 18 Del from £120 * **PARKING:** 40 **NOTES:** Closed 2-10 Jan Civ Wed 65 **CARDS:**

*See advert on opposite page*

DEDHAM, Essex Map 05 TM03

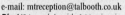

## Premier Collection

★★★ ®® Maison Talbooth

PRIDE OF BRITAIN
MEMBER

Stratford Rd CO7 6HN
☎ 01206 322367 Fax 01206 322752
e-mail: mtreception@talbooth.co.uk

***Dir:*** *A12 towards Ipswich, 1st turning signed Dedham, follow road until nasty left hand bend, take right hand turn, hotel 1m on right*

A warm welcome awaits you at this pretty Georgian hotel which overlooks the tranquil Dedham Vale. Situated in the heart of Constable country, this Victorian house has been operated by the Milsom family since 1952. There is a comfortable drawing room where guests may take afternoon tea or snacks, and excellent breakfasts are served in the

continued on p198

DEDHAM, continued

spacious bedrooms. Residents are chauffeured to the popular Le Talbooth Restaurant just a mile away for dinner.
**ROOMS:** 10 en suite (1 fmly) s £120-£150 (incl. cont bkfst) * LB **FACILITIES:** Croquet lawn Garden chess ch fac Xmas **CONF:** Thtr 30 Class 20 Board 16 **PARKING:** 20 **NOTES:** No dogs (ex guide dogs) Civ Wed 50 **CARDS:**

D

### ★★★70% Milsom's

Stratford Rd, Dedham CO7 6HW
☎ 01206 322795 01206 323689
e-mail: milsoms@talbooth.co.uk
***Dir:*** *6m north of Colchester off the A12*

Attractive detached property situated in a peaceful location on the outskirts of town. The bedrooms are tastefully furnished, thoughtfully equipped and decorated in a contemporary style. Public rooms include a lovely lounge with plush furnishings, a large bar and a split-level restaurant overlooking the garden. There is also a terrace for alfresco dining.
**ROOMS:** 14 en suite (3 fmly) s £80-£120; d £80-£120 * **FACILITIES:** STV **CONF:** Board 14 Del £129.25 * **PARKING:** 70 **NOTES:** No dogs (ex guide dogs) **CARDS:**

## DERBY, Derbyshire — Map 08 SK33

### ★★★★75% Menzies Mickleover Court

Etwall Rd, Mickleover DE3 5XX
☎ 0870 6003013 01332 511144
e-mail: info@menzies-hotels.co.uk
***Dir:*** *take first exit off A516 signposted Mickleover*

MENZIES HOTELS

Enjoying a programme of recent refurbishment, the hotel has much to offer. The circular shape of the building makes a change from the usual, as does the glass lift. Two eating options are available, the new Brasserie and very popular Italian bistro on the top floor. The leisure centre has excellent facilities, which include steam rooms, a gym and a good sized pool. Bedrooms are well-appointed with stylish decor, 19 new bedrooms have just been added.
**ROOMS:** 99 en suite (20 fmly) No smoking in 45 bedrooms d £119 * LB **FACILITIES:** STV Indoor swimming (H) Sauna Solarium Gym Jacuzzi Beauty salon Steam room Xmas **CONF:** Thtr 200 Class 80 Board 40 **SERVICES:** Lift air con **PARKING:** 270 **NOTES:** No dogs (ex guide dogs) No smoking in restaurant Civ Wed 200
**CARDS:**

Early start? Hotels at all star levels should provide in-room alarm clocks and/or alarm calls.

### ★★★★64% Marriott Breadsall Priory Hotel & Country Club

Marriott
HOTELS · RESORTS · SUITES

Moor Rd DE7 6DL
☎ 01332 832235 01332 833509
(For full entry see Breadsall)

### ★★★74% Midland

Best Western

Midland Rd DE1 2SQ
☎ 01332 345894 01332 293522
e-mail: sales@midland-derby.co.uk
***Dir:*** *situated opposite Derby central railway station*

This early Victorian hotel situated opposite Derby Midland Station provides good modern accommodation. The executive rooms are ideal for business travellers, equipped with writing desks, fax/computer points and first class bathrooms. Public rooms have been traditionally decorated and provide a comfortable lounge and a popular restaurant. Service is both professional and friendly. There is also a walled garden and private car parking.
**ROOMS:** 100 en suite No smoking in 41 bedrooms s £80-£98; d £87-£105 * LB **FACILITIES:** entertainment **CONF:** Thtr 150 Class 50 Board 40 Del £128 * **SERVICES:** Lift **PARKING:** 120 **NOTES:** No dogs (ex guide dogs) No smoking in restaurant Closed 24-26 Dec & 1 Jan Civ Wed 100 **CARDS:**

*See advert on opposite page*

### ★★★65% Hotel Ristorante La Gondola

220 Osmaston Rd DE23 8JX
☎ 01332 332895 01332 384512
e-mail: lagondola@rapidial.co.uk
***Dir:*** *on A514 towards Melbourne*

Imaginatively designed and well-equipped bedrooms, including a spacious family suite, are offered at this elegant Georgian house, situated between the inner and outer ring roads. There are two small comfortable lounges and a well-established Italian restaurant. Extensive conference and banqueting rooms are also available.
**ROOMS:** 20 rms (19 en suite) (7 fmly) s £56-£58; d £66-£68 (incl. cont bkfst) * LB **FACILITIES:** STV entertainment Xmas **CONF:** Thtr 80 Class 50 Board 80 Del from £75 * **PARKING:** 70 **NOTES:** No dogs (ex guide dogs) **CARDS:**

### ★★★63% International

288 Burton Rd DE23 6AD
☎ 01332 369321 01332 294430
e-mail: internationalhotel.derby@virgin.net
***Dir:*** *0.5m from city centre on A5250*

Within easy reach of the city centre, this hotel offers comfortable, modern public rooms. An extensive range of dishes is offered in the pleasant restaurant. There is a wide range of bedroom sizes

*continued*

and styles, and each room is very well-equipped; some suites are also available.
**ROOMS:** 41 en suite 21 annexe en suite (4 fmly) No smoking in 5 bedrooms d £51-£75 (incl. bkfst) * **LB** **FACILITIES:** STV entertainment Xmas **CONF:** Thtr 70 Class 40 Board 30 Del from £78 * **SERVICES:** Lift **PARKING:** 100 **NOTES:** Civ Wed 100
**CARDS:**

### European Inn
Midland Rd DE1 2SL
☎ 01332 292000 Fax 01332 293940
e-mail: admin@euro-derby.co.uk
***Dir:*** *200yds from railway station*
Excellent value accommodation is provided at this modern lodge. Bedrooms are well appointed and equipped with modern facilities. Shops form part of the complex and include an Italian pizza restaurant. A good choice of English breakfast is served buffet-style in the breakfast room; takeaway meals can also be eaten here.
**ROOMS:** 88 en suite s £48; d £48 * **CONF:** Thtr 80 Class 30 Board 25 Del £85 *

### *Express by Holiday Inn Derby*
Express by Holiday Inn
Roundhouse Rd, Off Pride Parkway DE24 8HX
☎ 01332 388000 Fax 388038
***Dir:*** *A52 towards Derby, follow for 6m, taking exit signed Pride Park. Straight over 1st three rdbt. Right at 4th, left at next. Take 1st left & hotel on r*

A modern budget hotel offering comfortable accommodation in refreshing, spacious and comprehensively equipped bedrooms, en suite bathrooms with power showers and continental buffet breakfast included in the room rate. Suitable for business travellers or families. For further details and the Express by Holiday Inn phone number, consult the Hotel Groups page.
**ROOMS:** 103 en suite **CONF:** Thtr 28 Class 20 Board 16

### *Premier Lodge*
PREMIER LODGE THE BEST. REST ASSURED.
Foresters Leisure Park, Oamaston Park Rd DE23 8AG
☎ 0870 700 1358 Fax 0870 700 1359
Premier Lodge offers modern, well-equipped, en suite accommodation suitable for both business and leisure travellers. Meals can be taken at the adjacent popular restaurant and bar, which is fully licensed. For further details, consult the Hotel Groups page.
**ROOMS:** 26 en suite

### *Travelodge*
Travelodge
Kingsway, Rowditch DE3 3LY
☎ 08700 850950 Fax 01332 367255
Travelodge offers good quality, good value, modern accommodation. Ideal for families, the spacious, en suite

*continued on p200*

DERBY, continued

bedrooms include remote-control TV, tea and coffee-making facilities, luxury beds and free morning newspaper. Meals can be taken at the nearby family restaurant. For further details and the Travelodge phone number, consult the Hotel Groups page.

### ○ Innkeeper's Lodge Derby

Nottingham Rd, Chaddesdon DE21 6LZ
☎ 0870 243 0500
A new concept in the travel accommodation market. Smart rooms meet essential business requirements but also have home comforts. Dining options include all-day menus plus the added advantage of breakfast, which is included in the room price. Reservations can be made seven days a week through the room reservations number: 0870 243 0500. For further details, consult the Hotel Groups page.
**ROOMS:** 29 en suite

## DESBOROUGH, Northamptonshire Map 04 SP88

### *Travelodge*

Harborough Rd NN14 2UG
☎ 01536 762034 📠 01536 762034
***Dir:*** *on A6, southbound*
Travelodge offers good quality, good value, modern accommodation. Ideal for families, the spacious, en suite bedrooms include remote-control TV, tea and coffee-making facilities, luxury beds and free morning newspaper. Meals can be taken at the nearby family restaurant. For further details and the Travelodge phone number, consult the Hotel Groups page.

**ROOMS:** 32 en suite

## DEVIZES, Wiltshire Map 04 SU06

### ★★★64% Bear

Market Place SN10 1HS
☎ 01380 722444 📠 01380 722450
e-mail: beardevizes@aol.com
Dating back to 1599, this attractive building sits to one side of the market place. Bedrooms vary between the older part of the inn to newer rooms but all are comfortable, and there is a lovely lounge and two bars with beams and open fires. Home-made cakes are available throughout the day and meals are complemented by an interesting choice of wines.
**ROOMS:** 24 en suite (5 fmly) s fr £60; d fr £88 (incl. bkfst) * **LB** **FACILITIES:** Solarium **CONF:** Thtr 150 Board 50 **PARKING:** 25 **NOTES:** No smoking in restaurant Closed 25-26 Dec
**CARDS:**

## DEWSBURY, West Yorkshire Map 08 SE22

### ★★★65% Heath Cottage Hotel & Restaurant

Wakefield Rd WF12 8ET
☎ 01924 465399 📠 01924 459405
e-mail: info@heathcottage.co.uk
***Dir:*** *from M1 junct 40 take A638 for 2.5m towards Dewsbury. Hotel just before traffic lights*
Standing in approximately an acre of grounds, Heath Cottage is 2.5 miles from the M1. It has ample parking, and well-appointed modern bedrooms. A converted stable building houses some ground-floor rooms. The lounge bar and restaurant are air-conditioned and service is professional.

**ROOMS:** 23 en suite 6 annexe en suite (3 fmly) No smoking in 18 bedrooms s £52-£59; d £65-£70 (incl. bkfst) * **LB** **CONF:** Thtr 90 Class 50 Board 30 Del from £84 * **PARKING:** 70 **NOTES:** No dogs (ex guide dogs) No smoking in restaurant Civ Wed 90
**CARDS:**

*See advert on opposite page*

### ★★71% Healds Hall

Leeds Rd, Liversedge WF15 6JA
☎ 01924 409112 📠 01924 401895
e-mail: healdshall@ndirect.co.uk
***Dir:*** *on A62 between Leeds and Huddersfield*
This 18th-century house in the heart of West Yorkshire offers comfortable and well-equipped accommodation and excellent hospitality. The hotel has earned a good local reputation for the quality of its food and offers a choice of dining styles with a wide choice of dishes on the various menus.
**ROOMS:** 24 en suite (3 fmly) No smoking in 9 bedrooms s £45-£59; d £60-£75 (incl. bkfst) * **LB** **FACILITIES:** STV **CONF:** Thtr 100 Class 60 Board 80 Del from £85 * **PARKING:** 90 **NOTES:** No smoking in restaurant Closed New Years Day **CARDS:**

## DONCASTER, South Yorkshire Map 08 SE50

### ★★★72% Mount Pleasant

Great North Rd DN11 0HW
☎ 01302 868696 & 868219 📠 01302 865130
e-mail: mountpleasant@fax.co.uk
(For full entry see Rossington)

### ★★★67% Regent

Regent Square DN1 2DS
☎ 01302 364180 📠 01302 322331
e-mail: admin@theregenthotel.co.uk
***Dir:*** *on the corner of the A630 & A638, 1m from racecourse*
The Regent is located in the town centre, overlooking a delightful small square. Bedrooms have been furnished along modern lines, most with co-ordinated colour schemes. The public rooms include a choice of bars, and the refurbished restaurant offers an interesting range of dishes.
**ROOMS:** 50 en suite (4 fmly) s £60-£80; d £72-£86 (incl. bkfst) * **LB** **FACILITIES:** STV Sauna entertainment **CONF:** Thtr 80 Class 50 Board 40 **SERVICES:** Lift **PARKING:** 20 **NOTES:** No smoking in restaurant Closed New Year's Day Xmas Day RS Bank Hols
**CARDS:**

### ★★★65% Grand St Leger

Bennetthorpe DN2 6AX
☎ 01302 364111 🖷 01302 329865
***Dir:*** *follow signs for Doncaster Racecourse, at Racecourse rdbt hotel on corner*

This well-furnished and friendly hotel is located next to the racecourse and is also convenient for the town centre. There is an extensive choice of well-prepared dishes available in the elegant restaurant while bedrooms are thoughtfully equipped.

**ROOMS:** 20 en suite No smoking in all bedrooms **FACILITIES:** STV **CONF:** Thtr 65 Class 40 Board 40 Del from £60 * **PARKING:** 28 **NOTES:** No dogs (ex guide dogs) No smoking in restaurant Closed New Year's Day RS Christmas Day (lunch only) Civ Wed 60 **CARDS:**

### ★★★64% Danum

High St DN1 1DN
☎ 01302 342261 🖷 01302 329034
e-mail: admin@danumhotel.sagehost.co.uk
***Dir:*** *from M18 junct3 A6182 to Doncaster. Cross rdbt, & right at next rdbt. Turn right at Give way sign, left at mini rdbt, & hotel straight ahead*

Situated in the centre of the town, this Edwardian hotel offers spacious public rooms together with soundly equipped accommodation. A very pleasant restaurant on the first floor serves quality dinners. There are good conference facilities.

**ROOMS:** 66 en suite (1 fmly) No smoking in 24 bedrooms s £59-£75; d £79-£105 (incl. bkfst) * **LB** **FACILITIES:** STV Jacuzzi special rates with Cannons health club entertainment Xmas **CONF:** Thtr 350 Class 160 Board 100 Del from £80 * **SERVICES:** Lift **PARKING:** 68 **NOTES:** Civ Wed 250 **CARDS:**

### ⌂ Campanile

Campanile

Doncaster Leisure Park, Bawtry Rd DN4 7PD
☎ 01302 370770 🖷 01302 370813
***Dir:*** *follow signs to Doncaster Leisure Centre and turn left at rdbt before Dome complex*

This modern building offers accommodation in smart, well-equipped bedrooms, all with en suite bathrooms. Refreshments may be taken at the informal Bistro. For further details and the Campanile phone number, consult the Hotel Groups page.

**ROOMS:** 50 en suite d fr £39 * **CONF:** Thtr 35 Class 18 Board 20 Del from £68 *

### ⌂ *Travelodge Doncaster North*

Travelodge

DN8 5GS
☎ 01302 351221 🖷 01302 847711
***Dir:*** *M18 junct 5*

Travelodge offers good quality, good value, modern accommodation. Ideal for families, the spacious, en suite bedrooms include remote-control TV, tea and coffee-making

*continued*

facilities, luxury beds and free morning newspaper. Meals can be taken at the nearby family restaurant. For further details and the Travelodge phone number, consult the Hotel Groups page.

**ROOMS:** 39 en suite

## DONNINGTON See Telford

## DORCHESTER, Dorset

Map 03 SY69

### ★★★64% The Wessex Royale

MINOTEL Great Britain

32 High St DT1 1UP
☎ 01305 262660 🖷 01305 251941
e-mail: info@wessex-royale-hotel.com
***Dir:*** *On the main high street in the centre of Dorchester*

Formerly the family home of the Earl of Ilchester, this period property is situated near the centre of Dorchester. Equally suited to both the business and leisure traveller, the bedrooms vary in size and offer modern facilities. Each evening an interesting selection of dishes is available in the hotel's restaurant, while at lunch time a range of lighter meals is provided.

**ROOMS:** 25 en suite (2 fmly) No smoking in 10 bedrooms s £59-£79; d £79-£99 (incl. bkfst) * **FACILITIES:** STV **CONF:** Thtr 100 Class 40 Board 30 Del from £75 * **PARKING:** 15 **NOTES:** No dogs (ex guide dogs) No smoking in restaurant **CARDS:**

> Popped the question? Hotels with Civ Wed in their entry are licensed for civil wedding ceremonies. Maximum numbers for the ceremony only are shown, e.g. Civ Wed 120

## DORCHESTER-ON-THAMES, Oxfordshire Map 04 SU59

### ★★★66% George

THE CIRCLE
Selected Individual Hotels
GREAT BRITAIN

25 High St OX10 7HH
☎ 01865 340404 🖷 01865 341620
**Dir:** *leave M40 junct6 onto B4009 through Watlington & Benson, take A4074 at BP petrol station, follow signposts to Dorchester. Hotel on left.*

The George dates back to the 15th century with historic features throughout such as a vaulted ceiling in the restaurant. Bedrooms retain the character of the building with beams and furnishings to suit the period. Diners have two options for meals as the hotel has a busy bar and offers a full menu in the restaurant with an excellent wine list.
**ROOMS:** 9 en suite 9 annexe en suite (1 fmly) No smoking in 4 bedrooms **CONF:** Thtr 35 Class 25 Board 26 **PARKING:** 75
**NOTES:** No smoking in restaurant **CARDS:**

### ★★★65% White Hart

High St OX10 7HN
☎ 01865 340074 🖷 01865 341082
e-mail: whitehartdorches@aol.com
**Dir:** *Leave M40 junct 6 , take B4009 through Watlington & Benson to A4074. Follow signs to Dorchester. Hotel on right*
This historic inn, situated on a Thameside village high street, offers good modern cooking in a charming setting. The village is known for its abbey and antique shops. The bar and restaurant are across a courtyard, and the well-equipped bedrooms are available in a variety of shapes and sizes and have recently undergone refurbishment.
**ROOMS:** 20 en suite 4 annexe en suite (2 fmly) No smoking in 6 bedrooms s £75-£95; d £85-£120 (incl. bkfst) * **LB** **FACILITIES:** STV Xmas **CONF:** Thtr 30 Class 20 Board 18 Del from £115 * **PARKING:** 36
**CARDS:**

*See advert under OXFORD*

## DORKING, Surrey Map 04 TQ14

### ★★★★67% The Burford Bridge

Burford Bridge, Box Hill RH5 6BX
☎ 0870 400 8283 🖷 01306 880386
e-mail: heritagehotels_box_hill.burford-bridge@forte-hotels.com
**Dir:** *from M25 junct 9 follow signs for Dorking on A24. Hotel is located on this road on the left hand side*
This hotel is located at the bottom of Box Hill, a landscape feature that was a source of inspiration for poets Keats and Wordsworth. Some of the bedrooms have balconies overlooking the well-tended gardens. There is an elegant lounge, cocktail bar and restaurant also there are extensive conference and banqueting facilities.
**ROOMS:** 57 en suite No smoking in 17 bedrooms d £165-£185 * **LB**
**FACILITIES:** Outdoor swimming (H) Croquet lawn Putting green entertainment Xmas **CONF:** Thtr 300 Class 100 Board 60 **PARKING:** 80
**NOTES:** Civ Wed 120 **CARDS:**

### ★★★64% The White Horse

High St RH4 1BE
☎ 0870 400 8282 🖷 01306 887241
**Dir:** *from M25 junct 9 take A24 S towards Dorking.Hotel is situated in the centre of the town*
Combining a superb location in the centre of town with the charm and character of a Dickensian inn, The White Horse has long been a popular destination for travellers and a favourite haunt for locals. Old oak beams, open log fires and inviting lounges are features in the public areas as are the four poster beds in some bedrooms.
**ROOMS:** 37 en suite 32 annexe en suite (2 fmly) No smoking in 20 bedrooms **CONF:** Thtr 50 Class 30 Board 30 **PARKING:** 73
**CARDS:**

### ★★★63% Gatton Manor Hotel Golf & Country Club

Standon Ln RH5 5PQ
☎ 01306 627555 🖷 01306 627713
e-mail: gattonmanor@enterprise.net
(For full entry see Ockley)

### Travelodge

Reigate Rd RH4 1QB
☎ 01306 740361 🖷 01306 740361
**Dir:** *0.5m E, on A25*
Travelodge offers good quality, good value, modern accommodation. Ideal for families, the spacious, en suite bedrooms include remote-control TV, tea and coffee-making facilities, luxury beds and free morning newspaper. Meals can be taken at the nearby family restaurant. For further details and the Travelodge phone number, consult the Hotel Groups page.

**ROOMS:** 54 en suite

## DORRIDGE, West Midlands Map 07 SP17

### ★★63% Forest Hotel

25 Station Approach B93 8JA
☎ 01564 772120 🖷 01564 770677
**Dir:** *take junct 5 off M42, follow A4141 for 2m, after Knowle village turn right (signed Dorridge) in 1.5m left just before rail bridge, hotel 200yds*
This well-established, privately run hotel is situated in the heart of Dorridge village, 30 minutes from Stratford-upon-Avon and the Cotswolds. Rooms are very well-equipped with modern facilities. Downstairs, a choice of bars serves meals; there is also a restaurant and a function room.
**ROOMS:** 12 en suite (1 fmly) **SERVICES:** air con **PARKING:** 70
**NOTES:** No dogs (ex guide dogs) **CARDS:**

## DOVER, Kent Map 05 TR34

### ★★★75% Wallett's Court

West Cliffe, St Margarets-at-Cliffe CT15 6EW
☎ 01304 852424 0800 0351628 🖷 01304 853430
e-mail: wc@wallettscourt.com
**Dir:** *from Dover, take A258 towards Deal; 1st right to St Margarets-at-Cliffe & West Cliffe, 1m on right opposite West Cliffe church*
This country house hotel has at its core a lovely Jacobean manor. Bedrooms in the original house are traditionally furnished and rooms in the courtyard buildings are more modern, all are

*continued*

equipped to a high standard. The restaurant offers well prepared traditional food.

**ROOMS:** 3 en suite 12 annexe en suite (2 fmly) s £75-£110; d £90-£150 (incl. bkfst) * **LB** **FACILITIES:** **Spa** Indoor swimming (H) Tennis (hard) Riding Sauna Solarium Gym Croquet lawn Putting green Jacuzzi Xmas **CONF:** Thtr 25 Class 25 Board 16 Del from £127.50 * **PARKING:** 32 **NOTES:** No dogs (ex guide dogs) No smoking in restaurant **CARDS:**

### ★★★70% The Churchill

Dover Waterfront CT17 9BP
☎ 01304 203633 🖷 01304 216320
e-mail: enquiries@churchill-hotel.com
***Dir:*** *A20 follow signs for Hoverport, turn left onto seafront, hotel 800yds along*

Located on Dover's waterfront overlooking the harbour, this hotel forms part of the Regency terrace. Bedrooms are furnished to a comfortable standard, some with sea views, and the first floor rooms have balconies. Winston's Restaurant serves enjoyable cooking and there is a well-appointed lounge bar and front terrace.
**ROOMS:** 66 en suite (5 fmly) No smoking in 12 bedrooms s £59; d £79 * **FACILITIES:** STV Sauna Solarium Gym Health Club Hair & Beauty Xmas **CONF:** Thtr 110 Class 60 Board 50 Del £89 * **SERVICES:** Lift **PARKING:** 32 **NOTES:** No dogs (ex guide dogs) No smoking in restaurant Civ Wed 80 **CARDS:**

*See advert on this page*

## DOWNHAM MARKET, Norfolk Map 05 TF60

### ★★71% Castle

High St PE38 9HF
☎ 01366 384311 🖷 01366 384311
e-mail: howards@castle-hotel.com
***Dir:*** *from M11 take A10 for Ely into Downham Market, on reaching town hotel opposite traffic lights, on corner of High St*

This popular coaching inn is situated close to the centre of town and has been welcoming guests for over 300 years. Well-

*continued*



maintained public areas include a cosy lounge bar and two smartly appointed restaurants. Inviting bedrooms, some with four-poster beds, are attractively decorated, thoughtfully equipped and have co-ordinated soft furnishings.
**ROOMS:** 12 en suite s £54-£69; d £69-£95 (incl. bkfst) * **LB** **FACILITIES:** Xmas **CONF:** Thtr 60 Class 30 Board 40 Del from £84 * **PARKING:** 26 **NOTES:** No smoking in restaurant **CARDS:**

## DRIFFIELD (GREAT), East Riding of Yorkshire Map 08 TA05

### ★★★71% Bell

46 Market Place YO25 6AN
☎ 01377 256661 🖷 01377 253228
e-mail: bell@bestwestern.co.uk
***Dir:*** *enter town from A164, turn right at traffic lights. Car park 50yds on left behind black railings*

This 250-year old hotel is furnished with many antique and period pieces. The bedrooms vary in shape and size; all have modern facilities and some have their own sitting rooms. There is a good leisure and natural health centre across the courtyard. The hotel has a relaxed and friendly atmosphere.
**ROOMS:** 16 en suite No smoking in 4 bedrooms s £80-£90; d £110-£120 (incl. bkfst) * **LB** **FACILITIES:** Indoor swimming (H) Squash Snooker Sauna Solarium Gym Jacuzzi Masseur entertainment **CONF:** Thtr 250 Class 200 Board 50 **SERVICES:** Lift **PARKING:** 18 **NOTES:** No dogs (ex guide dogs) No children 15yrs No smoking in restaurant Civ Wed 100 **CARDS:**

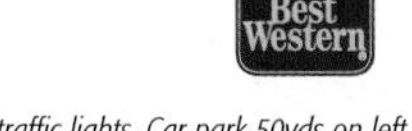

Arriving late? Four and five star hotels have night porters to assist with your luggage, and 24-hour room service.

DROITWICH, Worcestershire Map 03 SO86

★★★★67% **Château Impney**
WR9 0BN
☎ 01905 774411 01905 772371
e-mail: chateau@impney.demon.co.uk
***Dir:*** *on A38, 1m from M5 junct 5 towards Droitwich/Worcester*
Overlooking 120 acres of beautiful parkland, this elegant and imposing French-style château dates back to the 1800s. All bedrooms are furnished and equipped to modern standards, and come in a variety of sizes. The hotel has excellent conference, function and leisure facilities.
**ROOMS:** 67 en suite 53 annexe en suite (10 fmly) s £79.95-£119.95; d £89.95-£139.95 (incl. bkfst) * **FACILITIES:** Tennis (hard) Sauna Solarium Gym ch fac **CONF:** Thtr 1000 Class 550 Board 160 **SERVICES:** Lift **PARKING:** 1000 **NOTES:** No dogs (ex guide dogs) No smoking in restaurant Closed Xmas
**CARDS:**

★★★★65% **Raven**
Victoria Square WR9 8DQ
☎ 01905 772224 01905 797100
e-mail: sales@ravenhotel.demon.co.uk
***Dir:*** *in town centre on A38, 1.5m from M5 junct 5 towards Droitwich/Worcester*
Situated in the heart of the spa town this unique timber framed property dates back to the early 16th century. Considerably extended over the centuries, it now provides modern, well-equipped accommodation. Public areas include a spacious lounge, pleasant lounge bar with pianist, and charming restaurant with exposed beams and wall timbers.
**ROOMS:** 72 en suite (1 fmly) s £79.95-£119.95; d £89.95-£139.95 (incl. bkfst) * **FACILITIES:** ch fac **CONF:** Thtr 150 Class 70 Board 40 Del from £146.85 * **SERVICES:** Lift **PARKING:** 250 **NOTES:** No dogs (ex guide dogs) No smoking in restaurant Closed Xmas
**CARDS:**

★★65% ***The Hadley Bowling Green Inn***
Hadley Heath WR9 0AR
☎ 01905 620294 01905 620771
e-mail: hbginn@backissues.freeserve.co.uk
***Dir:*** *from M5 junct 5 A38 towards Droitwich. Follow Ring Road (A38) towards Worcester. Take next left signed Ombersley/Tenbury and follow hotel signs*

The Hadley Bowling Green Inn

This 16th-century inn claims to have one of the country's oldest crown greens. Guy Fawkes and his confederates reputedly planned the Gunpowder Plot here. There is a choice of bars and a pleasant restaurant. A wide range of food is available. The well-equipped accommodation includes two rooms with four-poster beds, family rooms and bedrooms on the ground floor of a separate building.
**ROOMS:** 11 en suite 3 annexe en suite (2 fmly) **FACILITIES:** Clay pigeon shooting Crown bowling Craft weekends **PARKING:** 100 **NOTES:** Closed 26 Dec pm **CARDS:**

***Travelodge***
Rashwood Hill WR9 8DA
☎ 01527 861545 01527 861545
Travelodge
Travelodge offers good quality, good value, modern accommodation. Ideal for families, the spacious, en suite bedrooms include remote-control TV, tea and coffee-making facilities, luxury beds and free morning newspaper. Meals can be taken at the nearby family restaurant. For further details and the Travelodge phone number, consult the Hotel Groups page.

**ROOMS:** 32 en suite

○ **Express by Holiday Inn**
Eastlake WR9
☎ 0800 897121
Express by Holiday Inn
A modern budget hotel offering comfortable accommodation in refreshing, spacious and comprehensively equipped bedrooms, en suite bathrooms with power showers and continental buffet breakfast included in the room rate. Suitable for business travellers or families. For further details and the Express by Holiday Inn phone number, consult the Hotel Groups page.
**ROOMS:** 100 en suite **NOTES:** Opening 2002

DRONFIELD, Derbyshire Map 08 SK37

★★67% ***Chantry***
Church St S18 1QB
☎ 01246 413014 01246 413014
***Dir:*** *6m from Sheffield and Chesterfield on A61. Opposite church with spire*
Next to an attractive church, this hotel has award-winning gardens and friendly service. Day rooms include a pleasant conservatory coffee shop, a spacious restaurant and a bar. Bedrooms are thoughtfully designed and relatively spacious. Hospitality is a major strength at this hotel.
**ROOMS:** 7 en suite **PARKING:** 28 **CARDS:**

DUDLEY, West Midlands Map 07 SO99
see also Himley

★★★★67% **Copthorne Hotel Merry Hill-Dudley**
The Waterfront, Level St, Brierley Hill DY5 1UR
COPTHORNE
☎ 01384 482882 01384 482773
e-mail: philip.bell@mill-cop.com
***Dir:*** *follow signs for Merry Hill Centre*
The hotel enjoys a waterfront aspect and easy accessibility. Polished marble floors, rich fabrics and striking interior design are features of the stylish public areas which include the informal Faradays bar and restaurant. Bedrooms have up to date facilities and are spacious and well-equipped.
**ROOMS:** 138 en suite (14 fmly) No smoking in 90 bedrooms s £135; d £145 * **LB FACILITIES:** STV Indoor swimming (H) Sauna Solarium Gym Jacuzzi Aerobics Beauty/massage therapists **CONF:** Thtr 570 Class 240 Board 60 Del £170 * **SERVICES:** Lift **PARKING:** 100 **NOTES:** No dogs (ex guide dogs) **CARDS:**

**★★★65% Ward Arms**
Birmingham Rd DY1 4RN
corus
☎ 01384 458070 📠 01384 457502
e-mail: wardarms@corushotels.com
***Dir:*** *on A461. At M5 junct 2 1st left at rdbt, then 3rd exit from next rdbt, proceed for 1.5m. Take 1st exit at 3rd rdbt, hotel 500yds on left*

This busy and popular, modern hotel is within easy reach of the M5. The bedrooms are well-equipped and rooms on the ground floor level are available. Public areas include the traditionally furnished conservatory restaurant and bar, where popular dishes are served. There is also Morriseys, a very popular Irish theme bar. Rooms for functions and conferences are available.
**ROOMS:** 72 en suite No smoking in 14 bedrooms d £65 * **LB** **FACILITIES:** STV ch fac Xmas **CONF:** Thtr 140 Class 50 Board 60 Del £95 * **PARKING:** 150 **CARDS:**

**⌂ *Travelodge***
Dudley Rd, Brierley Hill DY5 1LQ
Travelodge
☎ 01384 481579 📠 01384 481579
***Dir:*** *3m W, on A461*
Travelodge offers good quality, good value, modern accommodation. Ideal for families, the spacious, en suite bedrooms include remote-control TV, tea and coffee-making facilities, luxury beds and free morning newspaper. Meals can be taken at the nearby family restaurant. For further details and the Travelodge phone number, consult the Hotel Groups page.

**ROOMS:** 32 en suite

## DULVERTON, Somerset
Map 03 SS92

### *Premier Collection*

**★★ Ashwick House**
TA22 9QD
☎ 01398 323868 📠 01398 323868
e-mail: ashwickhouse@talk21.com
***Dir:*** *turn left at post office, 3m NW on B3223, over two cattlegrids, signposted on left*
A small Edwardian hotel, peacefully set in six beautiful acres above the breathtaking valley of the River Barle, on the edge of Exmoor. Public areas are extensive, the main feature being the galleried hall with its welcoming log fire. Bedrooms, all on the first floor are spacious and comfortable, with every

*continued*

conceivable facility. Each evening a set menu is served, with a choice of starter and pudding, using the finest local produce.

**ROOMS:** 6 en suite No smoking in 1 bedroom s £70-£84; d £120-£144 (incl. bkfst & dinner) **LB** **FACILITIES:** Solarium Croquet lawn Xmas **PARKING:** 27 **NOTES:** No dogs No children 8yrs No smoking in restaurant

**★★65% Lion**
Bank Square TA22 9BU
☎ 01398 323444 📠 01398 323980
***Dir:*** *turn right from A361 at Tiverton rdbt on to A396. Turn left at Exbridge onto B3223. Over bridge in Dulverton, hotel is in Bank Sq*
A charming, traditional inn in the centre of Dulverton. The bar is popular with locals and visitors alike, offering a variety of real ales and quality meals. Well-equipped bedrooms have benefited from recent improvements and combine comfort with character. This is an ideal base from which to explore Exmoor National Park.
**ROOMS:** 13 en suite (2 fmly) No smoking in 2 bedrooms s £29.50-£32; d £55 (incl. bkfst) * **LB** **FACILITIES:** Xmas **PARKING:** 6 **NOTES:** No smoking in restaurant **CARDS:**

## DUNCHURCH, Warwickshire
Map 04 SP47

**⌂ *Travelodge***
London Rd, Thurlaston CV23 9LG
Travelodge
☎ 01788 521538 📠 01788 521538
***Dir:*** *A45, westbound*
Travelodge offers good quality, good value, modern accommodation. Ideal for families, the spacious, en suite bedrooms include remote-control TV, tea and coffee-making facilities, luxury beds and free morning newspaper. Meals can be taken at the nearby family restaurant. For further details and the Travelodge phone number, consult the Hotel Groups page.

**ROOMS:** 40 en suite

## DUNSTABLE, Bedfordshire
Map 04 TL02

**★★★67% Hanover International Hotel**
Church St LU5 4RT
Hanover International Hotels & Clubs
☎ 01582 662201 📠 01582 696422
e-mail: info@hanover-dunstable.fsnet.co.uk
***Dir:*** *exit M1 at junct 11 and take A505. Hotel 2m on right opposite Priory church*
Well positioned between the town centre and the motorway, this ivy-clad Grade II listed building offers comfortable bedrooms in either period or modern style. Public areas include a comfortably

*continued on p206*

DUNSTABLE, continued

furnished bar lounge and an attractive restaurant serving a daily menu and a varied carte.

*Hanover International Hotel, Dunstable*

**ROOMS:** 68 en suite (7 fmly) No smoking in 21 bedrooms s £105-£136; d £115-£150 * **LB** **FACILITIES:** STV entertainment ch fac **CONF:** Thtr 45 Class 18 Board 26 Del from £111.63 * **SERVICES:** Lift **PARKING:** 70 **NOTES:** No smoking in restaurant Civ Wed 45
**CARDS:**

### ⇧ *Travelodge*
Watling St LU7 9LZ
☎ 01525 211177 🖷 01525 211177
***Dir:*** *3m N, on A5*

Travelodge

Travelodge offers good quality, good value, modern accommodation. Ideal for families, the spacious, en suite bedrooms include remote-control TV, tea and coffee-making facilities, luxury beds and free morning newspaper. Meals can be taken at the nearby family restaurant. For further details and the Travelodge phone number, consult the Hotel Groups page.

**ROOMS:** 28 en suite

## DUNSTER, Somerset
Map 03 SS94

### ★★★64% *The Luttrell Arms*
High St TA24 6SG
☎ 0870 400 8110 🖷 01643 821567
***Dir:*** *20m beyond the Exmoor Visitor Centre on A396, opposite the Yarn Market*

Heritage Hotels

The Luttrell Arms dates back to the 15th century and was formerly the guest house to Cleeve Abbey. Bedrooms vary in size and style, ranging from spacious four poster rooms to more compact rooms. The smart split-level restaurant serves home cooked meals. The bar also serves meals and there is a comfortable, beamed lounge on the first floor.
**ROOMS:** 27 en suite (4 fmly) No smoking in 9 bedrooms **CONF:** Thtr 25 Board 15 **PARKING:** 3 **NOTES:** No smoking in restaurant
**CARDS:**

## DURHAM, Co Durham
Map 12 NZ24
see also Rushyford

### ★★★★74% ◎◎ Durham Marriott Hotel, Royal County
Old Elvet DH1 3JN
☎ 0191 386 6821 🖷 0191 386 0704
e-mail: durhamroyal.marriott@whitbread.com
***Dir:*** *from A1(M) take junct 62 towards Durham, over 1st rdbt, turn left at 2nd rdbt over the bridge. Turn left at traffic lights, hotel on left*

Marriott HOTELS · RESORTS · SUITES

This long established hotel sits by the river in the heart of the city. Bedrooms have all recently been refurbished to a very comfortable standard. Public areas include antiques and paintings. There are two restaurants, with Rosette Award winning cuisine served in the County.

**ROOMS:** 139 en suite (4 fmly) No smoking in 99 bedrooms s £99-£119; d £119-£300 * **LB** **FACILITIES:** STV Indoor swimming (H) Sauna Solarium Gym Jacuzzi Steamroom Plungepool Impulse showers Xmas **CONF:** Thtr 120 Class 50 Board 45 Del from £135 * **SERVICES:** Lift **PARKING:** 80 **NOTES:** Civ Wed 60
**CARDS:**

### ★★★72% ◎◎ *Kings Lodge Hotel & Restaurant*
Flass Vale DH1 4BG
☎ 0191 370 9977 🖷 0191 370 9988
***Dir:*** *A1 J62, ahead at first three rdbts, turn R at fourth. First left then first right, hotel at end of road*

This modern, dynamically styled hotel provides comfortable, well-equipped accommodation. Knights restaurant and champagne bar offers an imaginative menu of innovative dishes cooked with flair and panache. There is a comfortable lounge, and a range of terrace seating is available during the warmer months.
**ROOMS:** 21 en suite (1 fmly) No smoking in all bedrooms **FACILITIES:** STV entertainment **CONF:** Thtr 25 Class 25 Board 18 **SERVICES:** air con **PARKING:** 35 **NOTES:** No smoking in restaurant
**CARDS:**

### ★★★70% Ramside Hall
Carrville DH1 1TD
☎ 0191 386 5282 🖷 0191 386 0399
e-mail: ramsidehal@aol.com
***Dir:*** *take A690 towards Sunderland from A1M/A690 interchange junct 62, 200mtrs after going under railway bridge turn right*

Set in attractive parkland, with its own golf course, driving range and conference centre, just seconds from the motorway. Bedrooms are spacious, very comfortable and very well-equipped. A formal restaurant, less formal grillroom and an informal carvery

*continued*

provide an extensive choice for dining and there are several comfortable lounges.
**ROOMS:** 80 en suite (10 fmly) No smoking in 36 bedrooms s £105-£125; d £125-£145 (incl. bkfst) * **LB** **FACILITIES:** STV Golf 27 Snooker Sauna Putting green Steam room Golf academy Driving Range entertainment ch fac **CONF:** Thtr 400 Class 160 Board 40 Del from £95 * **SERVICES:** Lift **PARKING:** 500 **NOTES:** Civ Wed 450
**CARDS:**

### ★★★69% Swallow Three Tuns

SWALLOW HOTELS

New Elvet DH1 3AQ
☎ 0191 386 4326 🖷 0191 386 1406
e-mail: threetuns.swallow@whitbread.com
**Dir:** *A1(M) junct 62 follow signs for city centre at rdbt, straight over at next rdbt left, over bridge, hotel past lights left*

Dating in part from the 16th century, this city-centre hotel preserves its individuality, and the friendly, attentive staff are the key to its popularity. Bedrooms are well-equipped, the executive rooms being particularly spacious. Guests have use of nearby leisure facilities, and the cathedral and castle are only a few minutes' walk away.
**ROOMS:** 50 en suite (8 fmly) No smoking in 28 bedrooms s £99-£105; d £115-£120 (incl. bkfst) * **LB** **FACILITIES:** STV Complimentary use of leisure facilities nearby Xmas **CONF:** Thtr 250 Class 200 Board 108 Del from £125 * **PARKING:** 60 **CARDS:**

### ★★★60% Bowburn Hall

Bowburn DH6 5NH
☎ 0191 377 0311 🖷 0191 377 3459
**Dir:** *head towards Bowburn, go right at Cooperage Pub, then 0.5 miles along country road to left junct signposted Durham. Hotel on immediate left*
This hotel, in five acres of grounds, lies in a quiet residential area, yet with easy access to the A1 just south of the city. Cosy bedrooms are attractively decorated, and the spacious lounge bar and conservatory overlook the gardens. Bar meals are popular with locals and visitors alike, more formal dining also being available in the restaurant.
**ROOMS:** 19 en suite s £48-£58; d £60-£70 (incl. bkfst) * **LB** **FACILITIES:** STV **CONF:** Thtr 150 Class 80 Board 60 Del from £85 * **PARKING:** 100 **NOTES:** RS 24-26 Dec & 1 Jan
**CARDS:**

### ★★62% Rainton Lodge

Rainton Gate, West Rainton DH4 6QY
☎ 0191 512 0540 🖷 0191 584 1221
**Dir:** *1.5m from junct 62 A1(M) on A690 towards Sunderland*
Enjoying sweeping countryside views, this hotel has an attractive interior. The open plan bar and restaurant feature a good range of dishes, and the fixed price dinner is excellent value. Bedrooms

*continued on p208*

DURHAM, continued

vary in style and size, some furnished in a contemporary style, others with traditional pine.
**ROOMS:** 27 en suite s £38-£42; d £48-£75 (incl. bkfst) *
**FACILITIES:** STV Xmas **CONF:** Thtr 100 Class 40 Board 25 Del from £75 * **PARKING:** 60 **CARDS:**

*See advert on page 207*

### ○ *Travelodge Durham*
☎ 0800 850950
**NOTES:** Opening Winter 2001

Travelodge

DUXFORD, Cambridgeshire Map 05 TL44

### ★★★73% Duxford Lodge
Ickleton Rd CB2 4RU
☎ 01223 836444 01223 832271
e-mail: duxford@btclick.com
***Dir:*** *at M11 junct 10, turn onto A505 to Duxford. Take first turn right at 'T' junction, hotel on left*

A warm welcome is assured at this attractive red brick hotel in the heart of this delightful village. Public areas include a bar, separate lounge, and an attractive restaurant, where an excellent and imaginative menu is offered. The bedrooms are comfortable and smartly appointed.
**ROOMS:** 11 en suite 4 annexe en suite (2 fmly) s £55-£85; d £94-£115 (incl. bkfst) * **LB** **FACILITIES:** Xmas **CONF:** Thtr 30 Class 20 Board 20 **PARKING:** 34 **NOTES:** Closed 26-30 Dec & 1 Jan RS Saturday lunch
**CARDS:**

*See advert under CAMBRIDGE*

EASINGTON, North Yorkshire Map 08 NZ71

### ★★★72% Grinkle Park
TS13 4UB
☎ 01287 640515 01287 641278
e-mail: grinkle.parkhotel@bass.com
***Dir:*** *9m from Guisborough, signed left off the main A171 Guisborough/Whitby Road*
Standing in 35 acres of moor and woodland, this elegant Victorian house has very hospitable staff and delightfully furnished bedrooms. There are comfortable lounges and a gracious restaurant, which serves well presented dishes using the best of local produce and enjoys superb open views.
**ROOMS:** 20 en suite s fr £81.50; d £100-£107 (incl. bkfst) * **LB**
**FACILITIES:** Tennis (hard) Snooker Croquet lawn Xmas **CONF:** Thtr 60 Class 20 Board 25 Del from £100.95 * **PARKING:** 122
**CARDS:**

EASINGWOLD, North Yorkshire Map 08 SE56

### ★★68% George
Market Place YO61 3AD
☎ 01347 821698 01347 823448
e-mail: info@the-george-hotel.co.uk
***Dir:*** *off A19 midway between York & Thirsk, in Market Place*
An old coaching inn facing the cobbled market square. Bedrooms are well-furnished and equipped, and the courtyard rooms have direct external access. An extensive range of well-produced food is available either in the bar or candlelit restaurant. A comfortable lounge is provided, and the owners provide efficient, friendly service.
**ROOMS:** 15 en suite (2 fmly) No smoking in 6 bedrooms s £50-£55; d £65-£69.50 (incl. bkfst) * **LB** **FACILITIES:** Xmas **CONF:** Board 12 Del from £65 * **PARKING:** 10 **NOTES:** No dogs (ex guide dogs) No smoking in restaurant **CARDS:**

EAST AYTON, North Yorkshire Map 08 SE98

### ★★★63% *East Ayton Lodge*
Moor Ln, Forge Valley YO13 9EW
☎ 01723 864227 01723 862680
e-mail: ealodge@cix.co.uk
***Dir:*** *400 yds off A170*
This family-run hotel stands in three acres of grounds close to the River Derwent, off a quiet lane on the edge of East Ayton. Bedrooms are well equipped and those in the courtyard are particularly spacious. A good range of food is available and there are plans to add a leisure centre.
**ROOMS:** 11 en suite 20 annexe en suite (3 fmly) **CONF:** Thtr 46 Class 74 Board 32 **PARKING:** 50 **NOTES:** No smoking in restaurant
**CARDS:**

EASTBOURNE, East Sussex Map 05 TV69

### ★★★★★71% Grand
King Edward's Pde BN21 4EQ
☎ 01323 412345 01323 412233
e-mail: Reservations@GrandEastbourne.co.uk
***Dir:*** *on seafront west of Eastbourne 1m from railway station*

SMALL LUXURY HOTELS OF THE WORLD

Huge investment has returned this famous Victorian hotel back to its former glory. Extensive public rooms, dominated by the Great Hall with its marble columns and high ceiling, are especially spacious and comfortable. The thoughtfully equipped bedrooms, some of which enjoy stunning sea views and own balconies, provide the expected levels of comfort. Guests have a choice of

*continued*

two restaurants, which demonstrate a high standard of cuisine. Service throughout is attentive and the atmosphere relaxed.
**ROOMS:** 152 en suite (20 fmly) s £125-£180; d £159-£210 (incl. bkfst) * **LB** **FACILITIES:** **Spa** Indoor swimming (H) Outdoor swimming (H) Snooker Sauna Solarium Gym Putting green Hairdressing beauty & massage entertainment ch fac Xmas **CONF:** Thtr 350 Class 200 Board 40 **SERVICES:** Lift **PARKING:** 60 **NOTES:** No smoking in restaurant Civ Wed 200 **CARDS:**

★★★71% **Hydro**
Mount Rd BN20 7HZ
☎ 01323 720643 01323 641167
e-mail: Sales@hydrohotel.com
***Dir:*** *proceed to pier/seafront, turn right along Grand Parade, at Grand Hotel you will see a road with the sign Hydro Hotel, proceed up South Cliff 200yds*

This well-established hotel enjoys an elevated position with views of the attractive gardens and the sea beyond. The spacious bedrooms are attractive and well-equipped many with new decoration. In addition to the lounges, guests also have access to fitness facilities and a hairdressing salon.
**ROOMS:** 82 en suite (3 fmly) s £36-£62; d £66-£118 (incl. bkfst) * **LB** **FACILITIES:** STV Outdoor swimming (H) Sauna Gym Croquet lawn Putting green Beauty room Hairdressing Pool table Xmas **CONF:** Thtr 140 Class 90 Board 40 Del from £69.50 * **SERVICES:** Lift **PARKING:** 50 **NOTES:** No smoking in restaurant RS 24-28 & 31 Dec Civ Wed 100 **CARDS:**

★★★71% **Lansdowne**
King Edward's Pde BN21 4EE
☎ 01323 725174 01323 739721
e-mail: thelandsdowne@btinternet.com
***Dir:*** *hotel situated at west end of seafront (B2103) facing Western Lawns*
This hotel occupies a seafront location at the quieter end of the parade. Facilities include several cosy lounge areas, a range of meeting rooms and a games room. Bedrooms are attractively decorated with some superior sized rooms available and many offering sea views.
**ROOMS:** 112 en suite (9 fmly) No smoking in 25 bedrooms s £55-£65; d £87-£112 (incl. bkfst) * **LB** **FACILITIES:** STV Snooker Darts Table tennis Pool table ch fac Xmas **CONF:** Thtr 120 Class 50 Board 50 Del from £90 * **SERVICES:** Lift **PARKING:** 22 **NOTES:** No smoking in restaurant Closed 1-17 Jan **CARDS:**

*See advert on this page*

★★★64% **York House**
14/22 Royal Pde BN22 7AP
☎ 01323 412918 01323 646238
e-mail: frontdesk@yorkhousehotel.co.uk
***Dir:*** *M25, take M23 to Brighton, A27 towards Lewes and then Eastbourne. York House is on the sea front 0.25m east of the pier*
Owned by the Williamson family since 1896, the York House

*continued on p210*





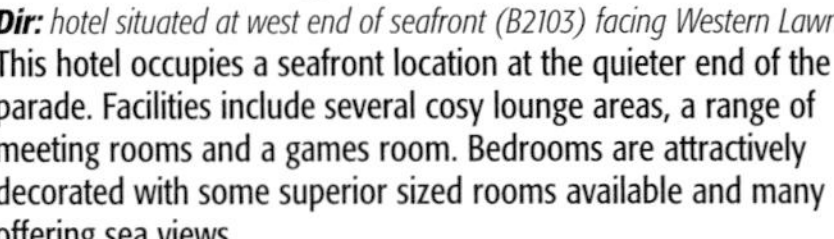

EASTBOURNE, continued

enjoys an enviable location on the seafront. Bedrooms and facilities continue to be upgraded. An open verandah makes the best of the location with sea views. Public areas include a spacious reception hall, cosy bar and separate lounge plus a games room and indoor swimming pool.

*York House, Eastbourne*

**ROOMS:** 88 en suite (8 fmly) s £45-£50; d £90-£100 (incl. bkfst) * **LB** **FACILITIES:** STV Indoor swimming (H) Games room **CONF:** Thtr 100 Class 30 Board 24 **SERVICES:** Lift **NOTES:** Closed 23-29 Dec Civ Wed 40 **CARDS:**

*See advert on page 209*

### ★★★62% Chatsworth

Grand Pde BN21 3YR
☎ 01323 411016 01323 643270
e-mail: stay@chatsworth-hotel.com
***Dir:*** *on seafront between the pier and the bandstand*

CHATSWORTH

Within minutes of the town centre and the pier, this attractive Edwardian hotel enjoys one of the best positions on the seafront. Bedrooms, many of which have sea views, are traditional in style and offer a useful range of in-room facilities. The public areas consist of the cosy Dukes Bar, a spacious lounge and the Devonshire Restaurant.

**ROOMS:** 47 en suite (2 fmly) No smoking in 10 bedrooms s £48-£68; d £88-£118 (incl. bkfst) * **LB** **FACILITIES:** STV entertainment ch fac Xmas **CONF:** Thtr 100 Class 60 Board 30 Del from £102.50 * **SERVICES:** Lift **NOTES:** No smoking in restaurant Civ Wed 140 **CARDS:**

*See advert on opposite page*

Popped the question? Hotels with Civ Wed in their entry are licensed for civil wedding ceremonies. Maximum numbers for the ceremony only are shown, e.g. Civ Wed 120

### ★★★61% *Quality Hotel Eastbourne*

Grand Pde BN21 3YS
☎ 01323 727411 01323 720665
e-mail: admin@gb610.u-net.com
***Dir:*** *take A22 to Eastbourne and follow through to seafront where the hotel is located between the pier and the bandstand*

This hotel benefits from an ideal location on the sea front, a short distance from the pier. Bedrooms vary in size and shape, but all are well-equipped and comfortably furnished. The public areas include a spacious restaurant and a lounge/bar area with sun terrace. There is regular entertainment including bingo and live music.

**ROOMS:** 95 en suite (6 fmly) No smoking in 47 bedrooms **FACILITIES:** STV Gym **CONF:** Thtr 150 Class 80 Board 20 **SERVICES:** Lift **NOTES:** No smoking in restaurant **CARDS:**

### ★★★61% Wish Tower

King Edward's Pde BN21 4EB
☎ 01323 722676 01323 721474
e-mail: wishtower@british-trust-hotels.com
***Dir:*** *follow signs for seafront. Turn right from Devonshire Place into Promenade Rd. Hotel 0.5m along on King Edward's Parade*

WISH TOWER

An established seafront hotel, located opposite the Martello tower. It is convenient for local theatres, amenities and the well known winter gardens. Bedrooms vary, all are practically furnished and most have sea views. Public areas consist of a spacious lounge/bar and downstairs dining room.

**ROOMS:** 54 en suite No smoking in 15 bedrooms s £62.50; d £95 (incl. bkfst) * **LB** **FACILITIES:** entertainment Xmas **CONF:** Thtr 50 Class 20 Board 30 Del from £75 * **SERVICES:** Lift **PARKING:** 3 **NOTES:** No smoking in restaurant **CARDS:**

### ★★70% West Rocks

Grand Pde BN21 4DL
☎ 01323 725217 01323 720421
***Dir:*** *on seafront western end*

Located in a prime position on the Grand Parade, this family run hotel is convenient for the seafront, local attractions and only a short walk from the town centre shops. Bedrooms vary with many offering sea views; all are furnished and decorated to a good standard. Guests have the choice of two comfortable lounges and a bar in which to relax.

**ROOMS:** 45 en suite (4 fmly) s fr £40; d fr £64 (incl. bkfst) **LB** **FACILITIES:** entertainment **CONF:** Thtr 50 Class 26 Board 20 **SERVICES:** Lift **NOTES:** No dogs No children 3yrs No smoking in restaurant Closed mid Nov-end Feb **CARDS:**

TV dinner? Room service at three stars and above.

**★★69% New Wilmington**
25 Compton St BN21 4DU
☎ 01323 721219 Fax 01323 746255
e-mail: info@new-wilmington-hotel.co.uk
***Dir:*** *A22 to Eastbourne along the seafront, turn right along Promenade until Wish Tower. Turn right off Promenade and hotel is on the first left*
This family-run hotel is conveniently located close to the town centre and the seafront. Bedrooms are comfortably appointed and tastefully decorated with some suitable for family accommodation. Public areas include a cosy bar, no-smoking lounge and a spacious, informal restaurant.
**ROOMS:** 40 en suite (8 fmly) s £35-£41; d £61-£73 (incl. bkfst) * **LB**
**FACILITIES:** entertainment Xmas **CONF:** Thtr 80 Class 40
**SERVICES:** Lift **PARKING:** 2 **NOTES:** No smoking in restaurant Closed Jan & Feb **CARDS:**

**★★68% The Downland Hotel & Restaurant**
37 Lewes Rd BN21 2BU
☎ 01323 732689 Fax 01323 720321
***Dir:*** *on A22, take 1st exit at Willingdon rdbt, follow sign to seafront, go past college and hospital straight over rdbt. Hotel in 0.5m*
High standards of hospitality and service are maintained at this family-run hotel, which is set just out of the town centre. Bedrooms are generally spacious with good facilities. The dining room offers a daily-changing menu of dishes, all cooked to order.
**ROOMS:** 12 en suite (2 fmly) No smoking in 4 bedrooms s £25-£35; d £50-£70 (incl. bkfst) * **LB** **PARKING:** 10 **NOTES:** No dogs (ex guide dogs) No children 10yrs No smoking in restaurant **CARDS:**

**★★68% *Stanley House Hotel***
9/10 Howard Square BN21 4BQ
☎ 01323 731393 Fax 01323 738823
This family run hotel is close to the bandstand and pier continues to be popular for holidays. The good value accommodation offers all the expected modern comforts in an attractive setting. Public areas include a small bar, choice of lounges and smart dining room which offers a selection of dishes.
**ROOMS:** 25 en suite (3 fmly) **FACILITIES:** entertainment
**SERVICES:** Lift **NOTES:** No dogs No smoking in restaurant Closed Jan-Feb **CARDS:**

**★★66% Farrar's Hotel**
Wilmington Gardens BN21 4JN
☎ 01323 723737 Fax 01323 732902
***Dir:*** *turn off seafront by Wish Tower, hotel opposite Congress Theatre*
This small, privately owned hotel is located just opposite Devonshire Park and is only minutes away from the seafront. Bedrooms are furnished and decorated to a good standard and feature a good range of facilities. Public areas have been redecorated to a high standard and include a cosy bar, separate lounge areas and an attractive downstairs dining room.
**ROOMS:** 45 en suite (4 fmly) s £32-£36; d £64-£72 (incl. bkfst) * **LB**
**CONF:** Thtr 80 **SERVICES:** Lift **PARKING:** 35 **NOTES:** No smoking in restaurant Closed Jan **CARDS:**

**★★66% Langham**
Royal Pde BN22 7AH
☎ 01323 731451 Fax 01323 646623
e-mail: info@langhamhotel.co.uk
***Dir:*** *from A22, A27 or A259 to Eastbourne follow signs for the seafront, hotel half a mile E of the pier, near the Redoubt Fortress*
This popular hotel enjoys a prime seafront location. Bedrooms are neatly appointed with modern facilities and are gradually being refurbished. Spacious public areas include a sea-facing terrace

*continued*

MINOTEL Great Britain



restaurant, lounge area and Grand Parade bar. The main dining room offers seasonal dishes.
**ROOMS:** 87 en suite (5 fmly) s £27-£44; d £54-£88 (incl. bkfst) * **LB**
**FACILITIES:** Temporary membership of Sovereign Club entertainment ch fac Xmas **CONF:** Thtr 80 Class 40 Board 24 Del from £55 *
**SERVICES:** Lift **PARKING:** 4 **NOTES:** No smoking in restaurant Closed 2 Jan-15 Feb **CARDS:**

**★★65% Ashley Grange Hotel**
Lewes Rd BN21 2BY
☎ 01323 721550 Fax 01323 721550
e-mail: ashleygrange@hotmail.com
***Dir:*** *on A22 turn left at Willingdon rdbt, go past Hospital on King's Drive, pass School on left, Hotel is approx. 100 mtrs on left*
Located on the edge of the town centre, this small friendly hotel offers comfortably furnished, well-equipped bedrooms. Smartly appointed public areas include a cosy bar and attractive dining room with access to a large rear garden with a "fun splasher pool".
**ROOMS:** 6 rms (5 en suite) s £34-£40; d £50-£60 (incl. bkfst) * **LB**
**FACILITIES:** Fun pool-"Splasher" **PARKING:** 6 **NOTES:** No dogs No children 10yrs Closed 24-27 Dec **CARDS:**

THE CIRCLE
Selected Individual Hotels
GREAT BRITAIN

**★★64% Oban**
King Edward's Pde BN21 4DS
☎ 01323 731581 Fax 01323 721994
***Dir:*** *opposite Wish Tower seafront area*
This privately owned, friendly hotel is located on the seafront and overlooks well-kept lawns. Bedrooms are well cared for, cheerfully decorated and offer a good range of in room facilities. Public areas include a spacious lounge/bar overlooking the seafront and

*continued on p212*

EASTBOURNE, continued

an attractively decorated downstairs dining room retaining many period features.
**ROOMS:** 31 en suite (2 fmly) s £34-£40; d £68-£80 (incl. bkfst) * LB
**FACILITIES:** Lounge bar activities entertainment Xmas **SERVICES:** Lift
**NOTES:** No smoking in restaurant Closed Dec-Feb (ex Xmas)
**CARDS:**

★★62% **Queens Hotel**
Marine Pde BN21 3DY
☎ 01323 722822 01323 731056

Popular with tour groups, this long established hotel enjoys a central, seafront location overlooking the pier. Bedrooms are comfortably appointed with many enjoying seaviews. Spacious public areas include a choice of lounges and regular entertainment is also provided.
**ROOMS:** 122 en suite (1 fmly) s £28-£37; d £46-£66 (incl. bkfst) * LB
**FACILITIES:** Snooker entertainment Xmas **CONF:** Thtr 100 Class 56 Board 40 Del from £65 * **SERVICES:** Lift **PARKING:** 50 **NOTES:** No dogs (ex guide dogs) No smoking in restaurant Closed Jan-mid Feb RS Nov-Dec & mid Feb-Mar (weekdays only) **CARDS:**

## EAST GRINSTEAD, West Sussex Map 05 TQ33

### Premier Collection

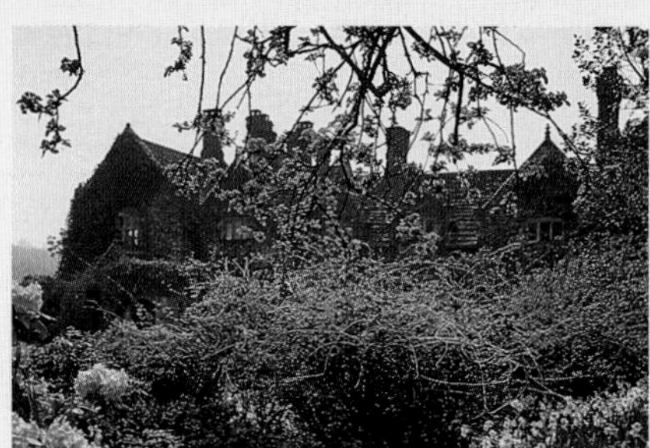

★★★ ®®® **Gravetye Manor**
RH19 4LJ
☎ 01342 810567 01342 810080
e-mail: info@gravetyemanor.co.uk
***Dir:** B2028 towards Haywards Heath. 1m after Turners Hill, take left fork towards Sharpthorne, then 1st left into Vowels Lane*

RELAIS & CHATEAUX.

This Elizabethan stone mansion was built in 1598. It was one of the first country house hotels and remains a shining example in its class. The day rooms are comfortably furnished, and the bedrooms are decorated in traditional English style: furnished with antiques, including many thoughtful extras. The cuisine uses home-grown fruit and vegetables as well as local spring water. The local area has an abundance of historic houses and gardens to visit.
**ROOMS:** 18 en suite s £95-£150; d £190-£320 *
**FACILITIES:** Fishing Croquet lawn **CONF:** Del from £235 *
**PARKING:** 35 **NOTES:** No dogs No children 7yrs No smoking in restaurant RS 25 Dec **CARDS:**

Late for dinner? Quality Standards star rating means that last orders for dinner should be no earlier than:
★ 6.30pm ★★ 7.00pm ★★★ 8.00pm
★★★★ 9.00pm ★★★★★ 10.00pm

★★★64% **Woodbury House**
Lewes Rd RH19 3UD
☎ 01342 313657 01342 314801
e-mail: stay@woodbury-house.demon.co.uk
***Dir:** 0.5m S of town on A22*

Best Western

This well-furnished hotel offers comfortable accommodation in well-equipped bedrooms. Guests are provided with a choice of eating options in the hotel restaurant or the more informal bistro. Service is both friendly and attentive from the dedicated team of staff.
**ROOMS:** 14 en suite (1 fmly) No smoking in 2 bedrooms s £75-£85; d £85-£110 (incl. bkfst) * LB **FACILITIES:** STV ch fac Xmas
**CONF:** Thtr 40 Class 30 Board 24 Del £112.50 * **PARKING:** 52
**NOTES:** No smoking in restaurant Civ Wed 80
**CARDS:**

*See advert on opposite page*

## EAST HORNDON, Essex Map 05 TQ68

**Travelodge**
CM13 3LL
☎ 01277 810819 01277 810819
***Dir:** on A127, eastbound 4m off junct 29 M25*

Travelodge

Travelodge offers good quality, good value, modern accommodation. Ideal for families, the spacious, en suite bedrooms include remote-control TV, tea and coffee-making facilities, luxury beds and free morning newspaper. Meals can be taken at the nearby family restaurant. For further details and the Travelodge phone number, consult the Hotel Groups page.

**ROOMS:** 22 en suite

## EASTLEIGH, Hampshire Map 04 SU41

★★★68% ***Posthouse Eastleigh/Southampton***
Leigh Rd SO50 9PG
☎ 0870 400 9075 023 8064 3945
***Dir:** follow A335 to Eastleigh, hotel on right*

Posthouse

Located close to junction 13 of the M3 motorway, this well sited hotel is suitable for both business and leisure traveller. Recent refurbishment now provides a pleasant restaurant area with varied menus. Bright modern accommodation is offered in very well-equipped bedrooms. The popular leisure area includes swimming pool, spa baths and weight facilities.
**ROOMS:** 116 en suite (3 fmly) No smoking in 86 bedrooms
**FACILITIES:** Indoor swimming (H) Sauna Gym Jacuzzi Beauty treatment Leisure club **CONF:** Thtr 250 Class 90 Board 90 **SERVICES:** Lift
**PARKING:** 160 **CARDS:**

**Travelodge**
Twyford Rd SO50 4LF
☎ 023 8061 6813 023 8061 6813
***Dir:** off junct 12 on M3 on A335*

Travelodge

Travelodge offers good quality, good value, modern accommodation. Ideal for families, the spacious, en suite bedrooms include remote-control TV, tea and coffee-making facilities, luxury beds and free morning newspaper. Meals can be taken at the nearby family restaurant. For further details and the Travelodge phone number, consult the Hotel Groups page.

**ROOMS:** 32 en suite

TV dinner? Room service at three stars and above.

EAST MIDLANDS AIRPORT, Leicestershire Map 08 SK42

**★★★73% Yew Lodge Hotel & Conference Centre**

Best Western

Packington Hill, Kegworth DE74 2DF

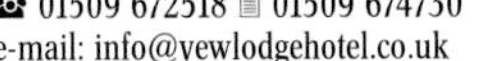

☎ 01509 672518 01509 674730
e-mail: info@yewlodgehotel.co.uk

***Dir:*** *leave M1 at junc 24, then follow signs to Loughborough & Kegworth on the A6. At the bottom of the hill, first right, 400yds Yew Lodge on right*

Significant investment has been made in this smart, family-owned hotel which is very conveniently and peacefully located. Bedrooms and public areas are well-appointed and thoughtfully equipped. At the time of our inspection, fellow guests were full of praise for the award-winning food.

**ROOMS:** 64 en suite (3 fmly) No smoking in 18 bedrooms s fr £45; d £65-£110 * **LB FACILITIES:** STV ch fac Xmas **CONF:** Thtr 150 Class 60 Board 36 Del from £115 * **SERVICES:** Lift **PARKING:** 120 **NOTES:** No smoking in restaurant Civ Wed 150 **CARDS:**

**★★★70% Donington Manor**

High St, Castle Donington DE74 2PP
☎ 01332 810253 01332 850330
e-mail: cngrist@dmhgrist.demon.co.uk

***Dir:*** *1m into village on B5430 situated on left at traffic lights*

Just off the village centre, this refined Georgian building offers high standards of hospitality and a professional service. Many of the original architectural features have been preserved; the elegant dining room is particularly appealing. Bedrooms are individually designed, and the newer suites are especially comfortable and well-equipped. One of the luxurious bathrooms once belonged to Elvis Presley.

**ROOMS:** 25 en suite 1 annexe en suite (1 fmly) s £68-£85; d £82-£105 (incl. bkfst) * **LB FACILITIES:** STV **CONF:** Thtr 80 Class 50 Board 20 Del from £98 * **PARKING:** 40 **NOTES:** No dogs (ex guide dogs) Closed 24-30 Dec RS Sat Civ Wed 120 **CARDS:**

**★★★69% The Priest House on the River**

Arcadian Hotels Distinctly Different

Kings Mills, Castle Donington DE74 2RR
☎ 01332 810649 01332 811141

***Dir:*** *M1 junct 23A towards airport, pass airport entrance, after 1.5m turn right into Castle Donington. At 1st traffic lights turn left & follow road*

An historic hotel nestling peacefully in a picturesque riverside setting. The hotel itself is now mostly contemporary in style, with bedrooms in converted cottages and the main building; bedrooms in the main building offer particularly high levels of comfort. Guests have the choice of a fine dining restaurant or a brasserie option.

**ROOMS:** 25 en suite 20 annexe en suite (1 fmly) No smoking in 1 bedroom s £80-£90; d £100-£150 (incl. bkfst) * **LB FACILITIES:** STV Fishing Xmas **CONF:** Thtr 130 Class 40 Board 50 Del from £150 * **PARKING:** 150 **NOTES:** No smoking in restaurant Civ Wed 90 **CARDS:**

*See advert on this page*

## EAST MIDLANDS AIRPORT, continued

### ★★66% Tudor Hotel & Restaurant

Bond Gate, Castle Donington DE74 2NR
☎ 01332 810875 🖷 01332 850883
e-mail: tudorinn@commodoreinternational.co.uk
***Dir:*** *M1 junct 24 follow A50 to Derby, turn left for Long Eaton at rdbt take turning for Castle Donnington*

This Tudor style hotel is close to Donington race track and the West Midlands airport. Bedrooms have been tastefully refurbished and are comfortable and very well-equipped. Downstairs there is a large restaurant, a character bar and a beer garden.

**ROOMS:** 7 en suite (2 fmly) No smoking in all bedrooms s £38; d £50 (incl. bkfst) * **LB** **FACILITIES:** STV Xmas **CONF:** Thtr 30 Class 30 Board 30 **PARKING:** 60 **NOTES:** No dogs (ex guide dogs) **CARDS:**

### ⌂ Express by Holiday Inn

Pegasus Business Park, Castle Donington DE74 2TQ
☎ 01509 678000 🖷 01509 670954
e-mail: ema@expressbyholidayinn.net
***Dir:*** *follow signs for East Midlands Airport, turn right into Pegasus Business Park, hotel on left*

A modern budget hotel offering comfortable accommodation in refreshing, spacious and comprehensively equipped bedrooms, en suite bathrooms with power showers and continental buffet breakfast included in the room rate. Suitable for business travellers or families. For further details and the Express by Holiday Inn phone number, consult the Hotel Groups page.

**ROOMS:** 90 en suite **CONF:** Thtr 45 Class 30 Board 30

### ⌂ *Travelodge*

Castle Donnington DE74 2TN
☎ 08700 850950

Travelodge offers good quality, good value, modern accommodation. Ideal for families, the spacious, en suite bedrooms include remote-control TV, tea and coffee-making facilities, luxury beds and free morning newspaper. Meals can be taken at the nearby family restaurant. For further details and the Travelodge phone number, consult the Hotel Groups page.

## EAST RETFORD, Nottinghamshire — Map 08 SK78

### ★★★64% West Retford

24 North Rd DN22 7XG
☎ 01777 706333 🖷 01777 709951
***Dir:*** *From A1 take A620 to Ranby and Retford, turn left at rdbt into North road (A638). Hotel on right*

Set in attractive grounds close to the town centre, this 18th-century manor house offers a good range of well-equipped meeting facilities. The spacious, well laid out bedrooms and suites are located in separate buildings.

**ROOMS:** 62 annexe en suite (37 fmly) No smoking in 36 bedrooms s fr £68; d fr £80 * **LB** **FACILITIES:** STV Croquet lawn **CONF:** Thtr 150 Class 40 Board 43 Del from £99 * **PARKING:** 100 **NOTES:** No smoking in restaurant Civ Wed 120 **CARDS:**

## EGHAM, Surrey — Map 04 TQ07

### ★★★★73% ⊛⊛ Runnymede Hotel & Spa

Windsor Rd TW20 0AG
☎ 01784 436171 🖷 01784 436340
e-mail: info@runnymedehotel.com
***Dir:*** *M25 junct 13, onto A308 towards Windsor*

Within easy reach of Heathrow and the motorways, and enjoying a riverside location, there is no wonder that this hotel is so popular. Bedrooms and conference facilities have undergone a full refurbishment programme, and all are air conditioned. Two dining options and riverside terrace are some of the features of the public areas.

**ROOMS:** 180 en suite (19 fmly) No smoking in 116 bedrooms s £163-£183; d £200-£225 * **LB** **FACILITIES:** STV Indoor swimming (H) Tennis (hard & grass) Snooker Sauna Solarium Gym Croquet lawn Putting green Jacuzzi Beauty Salon Dance studio Hairdressers entertainment ch fac **CONF:** Thtr 300 Class 250 Board 76 Del from £245 * **SERVICES:** Lift air con **PARKING:** 280 **NOTES:** No dogs (ex guide dogs) RS Restaurant closed Sat lunch/Sun dinner Civ Wed 150 **CARDS:**

*See advert under WINDSOR*

## ELLESMERE PORT, Cheshire — Map 07 SJ47

### ★★★66% Quality Hotel Chester

Welsh Road/Berwick Rd, Little Sutton CH66 4PS
☎ 0151 339 5121 🖷 0151 339 3214
e-mail: admin@gb066.u-net.com
***Dir:*** *M53 junct 5 turn left at rdbt at 2nd set of traffic lights, turn right onto A550 over the hump back bridge turn left into Berwick Road*

Conveniently located close to the M53, yet in an attractive and tranquil setting. This friendly hotel offers modern, well equipped accommodation and the refurbished public areas are popular for large parties. There is a good range of facilities, including a leisure complex and versatile banqueting and conference suites.

**ROOMS:** 53 en suite (8 fmly) No smoking in 18 bedrooms s fr £80; d £95-£103 * **LB** **FACILITIES:** STV Indoor swimming (H) Sauna Steam room Exercise equipment entertainment Xmas **CONF:** Thtr 300 Class 150 Board 100 Del from £100 * **PARKING:** 200 **NOTES:** No smoking in restaurant Civ Wed 100 **CARDS:**

Bad hair day? Hairdryers in all rooms three stars and above.

**★★64% Woodcote Hotel & Restaurant**
3 Hooton Rd CH66 1QU
☎ 0151 327 1542 📠 0151 328 1328
**Dir:** *M53 junc 5, take A41 towards Chester, first traffic lights turn right towards Willaston. Hotel 300 yards on left*
This popular commercial hotel offers generally spacious, well-equipped rooms, many of which are located in a separate building. The bars and restaurant are attractively decorated and there is a separate breakfast room. A range of popular, reasonably priced dishes are on offer.
**ROOMS:** 10 en suite 11 annexe en suite (1 fmly) s £25-£32; d £32 * **FACILITIES:** entertainment **CONF:** Thtr 90 Class 50 Board 48 **PARKING:** 35 **NOTES:** No dogs (ex guide dogs) RS Sundays
**CARDS:**

## ELSTREE, Hertfordshire
Map 04 TQ19

**★★★75% Edgwarebury**
corus
Barnet Ln WD6 3RE
☎ 020 8953 8227 📠 020 8207 3668
e-mail: edgwarebury@corushotels.com
**Dir:** *M1 junct 5 follow A41 to Harrow, turn left onto A411 into Elstree cont through crossroads into Barnet Ln, hotel entrance is on the right*

An hotel with abundant charm and character, with its Tudor style exterior and traditional interior design all set in 10 acres of landscaped gardens and natural woodland. Both the oak-panelled Terrace bar with its two large fireplaces and the stately Cavendish Restaurant have a southerly aspect with views over the gardens and the lights of the city beyond.
**ROOMS:** 47 en suite (1 fmly) No smoking in 19 bedrooms s £75-£130; d £95-£215 * **LB** **FACILITIES:** STV Xmas **CONF:** Thtr 80 Class 50 Board 10 Del from £140 * **PARKING:** 100 **NOTES:** No smoking in restaurant Civ Wed 100 **CARDS:**

## ELTERWATER, Cumbria
Map 07 NY30

***★★★72% Langdale Hotel & Country Club***
LA22 9JD
☎ 01539 437302 📠 01539 437694
e-mail: itsgreat@langdale.co.uk
**Dir:** *follow road into Langdale, hotel part of private estate on left in the bottom of the valley*
An extensive modern hotel offering a wide range of comfortable and well-equipped bedrooms, of which five rooms are in the main hotel and others in attractive slate buildings arranged within the surrounding woodland. Many bathrooms have spa baths. Extensive new leisure facilities feature a large indoor pool and a well-equipped gym. A wide range of dishes is served within either of the two stylish restaurants.

*continued*

**ROOMS:** 5 en suite 60 annexe en suite (8 fmly) **FACILITIES:** STV Indoor swimming (H) Tennis (hard) Fishing Squash Sauna Solarium Gym Jacuzzi Steam room Hair & beauty salon Cycle hire entertainment ch fac **CONF:** Thtr 100 Class 66 Board 50 **PARKING:** 65 **NOTES:** No dogs No smoking in restaurant RS Oct-Dec & Jan-Apr
**CARDS:**

**★★68% Eltermere Country House**
LA22 9HY
☎ 01539 437207 📠 01539 437540
e-mail: colin@hensington.demon.co.uk
**Dir:** *on unclass road between A593 & B5343, turn left after cattle grid through village of Elterwater, cross bridge 100mtrs on left*
This Georgian country house hotel, dating back to 1756, is peacefully located on the edge of the village, beside Elterwater Lake. The lounge, bar and dining room enjoy panoramic views over the lake and valley, as do superior bedrooms. Guests have complimentary use of a nearby leisure club.
**ROOMS:** 19 rms (14 en suite) (4 fmly) s £50-£65; d £100-£130 (incl. bkfst & dinner) * **LB** **FACILITIES:** Fishing Putting green Use of facilties at Langdale Hotel Xmas **PARKING:** 20 **NOTES:** No dogs (ex guide dogs) No smoking in restaurant **CARDS:**

**★66% Britannia Inn**
LA22 9HP
☎ 01539 437210 📠 01539 437311
e-mail: info@britinn.co.uk
**Dir:** *from A593 at Skelwith Bridge Hotel turn right onto B5343 after crossing cattle grid on main road take left turn into village of Elterwater*
This country inn is located adjacent to the village green. Bedrooms are tastefully furnished and thoughtfully equipped, some being housed in an adjacent cottage. Traditional public areas have oak beams and are furnished with period pieces. Home cooking can be enjoyed in the dining room and there is a comfortable residents lounge in addition to the public bar.
**ROOMS:** 9 rms (8 en suite) 4 annexe rms (1 en suite) s £28-£30; d £56-£78 (incl. bkfst) * **LB** **FACILITIES:** entertainment **PARKING:** 10 **NOTES:** No smoking in restaurant Closed 25 & 26 Dec
**CARDS:**

## ELY, Cambridgeshire
Map 05 TL58

***★★★66% Lamb***
OLD ENGLISH INNS
2 Lynn Rd CB7 4EJ
☎ 01353 663574 📠 01353 662023
**Dir:** *enter Ely on A10, hotel in centre of city near Cathedral on the corner of Lynn Rd & the High St*
This pleasant 15th-century coaching inn has been sympathetically developed to provide good all round comforts. Informal snacks are served in the smart bars and traditional British cooking

*continued on p216*

ELY, continued

features on the menu in the Octagon Restaurant. Bedrooms offer co-ordinated soft furnishings and decor and modern light wood furniture.
**ROOMS:** 32 en suite (6 fmly) **FACILITIES:** STV **CONF:** Thtr 45 Class 28 Board 30 **PARKING:** 20 **NOTES:** No smoking in restaurant
**CARDS:**

### ⌂ *Travelodge*
Witchford Rd CB6 3NN
☎ 01353 668499 01353 668499
***Dir:*** *at roundabout A10/A142*

Travelodge

Travelodge offers good quality, good value, modern accommodation. Ideal for families, the spacious, en suite bedrooms include remote-control TV, tea and coffee-making facilities, luxury beds and free morning newspaper. Meals can be taken at the nearby family restaurant. For further details and the Travelodge phone number, consult the Hotel Groups page.

**ROOMS:** 39 en suite

## EMBLETON, Northumberland — Map 12 NU22

### ★★70% Dunstanburgh Castle Hotel
NE66 3UN
☎ 01665 576111
e-mail: stay@dunstanburghcastlehotel.co.uk
***Dir:*** *from A1, take B1240 to Denwick then 3m past Rennington & Masons Arms. Next right signed Embleton & continue into village*

The young owners of this immaculately kept inn, a few minutes' walk from the sea, offer friendly hospitality and total guest care. Good food is served in both the restaurant and grill room, and two comfortable lounges include open fires in the season.
**ROOMS:** 17 en suite (4 fmly) s £30-£33; d £60-£66 (incl. bkfst) * LB **PARKING:** 16 **NOTES:** No smoking in restaurant Closed Nov-Feb
**CARDS:**

## EMPINGHAM, Rutland — Map 04 SK90

### ★★67% The White Horse Inn
Main St LE15 8PR
☎ 01780 460221 & 460521 01780 460521
e-mail: info@the-white-horse.co.uk
***Dir:*** *on A606, Oakham-Stamford road*

This attractive stone-built inn has bright and well equipped bedrooms that are located either across the courtyard or inside the inn, where the rooms are en suite. A wide range of meals is served in the various rooms that make up the bar, and a full menu is available in the comfortable Basil's Bistro. Service is relaxed and friendly.
**ROOMS:** 4 en suite 9 annexe en suite (3 fmly) No smoking in 1 bedroom s £50; d £63-£70 (incl. bkfst) * LB **FACILITIES:** Xmas **CONF:** Thtr 60 Class 60 Board 34 Del £60 * **PARKING:** 60 **NOTES:** No smoking in restaurant **CARDS:**

## EMSWORTH, Hampshire — Map 04 SU70

### ★★★68% Brookfield
Havant Rd PO10 7LF
☎ 01243 373363 & 376383 01243 376342
***Dir:*** *Emsworth junct off A27, turn onto B529, hotel is 0.5m on the left on the way into Emsworth*

This well-established family run hotel has spacious public areas with popular conference and banqueting facilities. Bedrooms are in a modern style, and comfortably furnished. The popular Hermitage Restaurant offers a seasonally changing menu and an award-winning wine list.
**ROOMS:** 40 en suite (4 fmly) No smoking in 20 bedrooms **FACILITIES:** STV **CONF:** Thtr 100 Class 60 Board 40 Del from £125 * **PARKING:** 80 **NOTES:** No dogs (ex guide dogs) Closed 25 Dec-1 Jan
**CARDS:**

### ⌂ *Travelodge*
PO10 7RB
☎ 01243 370877 01243 370877
***Dir:*** *A27*

Travelodge

Travelodge offers good quality, good value, modern accommodation. Ideal for families, the spacious, en suite bedrooms include remote-control TV, tea and coffee-making facilities, luxury beds and free morning newspaper. Meals can be taken at the nearby family restaurant. For further details and the Travelodge phone number, consult the Hotel Groups page.

**ROOMS:** 36 en suite

## ENFIELD, Greater London — Map 04 TQ39

### ★★★71% Royal Chace
The Ridgeway EN2 8AR
☎ 020 8884 8181 020 8884 8150
e-mail: royal.chace@dial.pipex.com
***Dir:*** *from junct 24 off M25 take A1005 towards Enfield. Hotel 3m on right*

This privately owned hotel enjoys a peaceful North London location with open fields to the rear. Bedrooms are tastefully decorated, furnished to a good standard and feature good facilities. The spacious public areas include a variety of versatile function rooms.
**ROOMS:** 92 en suite (2 fmly) No smoking in 34 bedrooms s fr £110; d fr £125 (incl. bkfst) * **FACILITIES:** STV Outdoor swimming (H) Free access to local leisure centre **CONF:** Thtr 250 Class 100 Board 40 **PARKING:** 200 **NOTES:** No dogs (ex guide dogs) No smoking in restaurant Closed 24-30 Dec RS Restaurant closed lunchtime/Sun eve Civ Wed 220 **CARDS:**

### ★★71% Oak Lodge
80 Village Rd, Bush Hill Park EN1 2EU
☎ 020 8360 7082
e-mail: oaklodge@fsmail.net
***Dir:*** *turn right at 11th set of lights from M25, exit 25. Turn right at next lights onto A105. Hotel is located 0.25m on the right*

This charming and privately-run hotel is located in a leafy, suburban area. Both the service and hospitality continue to be

*continued*

particularly noteworthy and a warm welcome is offered to all guests. Public areas are comfortable and the availability of car parking is an added bonus.
**ROOMS:** 7 en suite (1 fmly) No smoking in 6 bedrooms s £80-£94; d £110-£135 (incl. bkfst) * **FACILITIES:** Special arrangement with David Lloyd Sports Centre entertainment Xmas **CONF:** Class 16 Board 16 **PARKING:** 4 **NOTES:** No dogs (ex guide dogs) No smoking in restaurant
**CARDS:**

## EPPING, Essex Map 05 TL40

### ★★★62% *Posthouse Epping*

Posthouse

High Rd, Bell Common CM16 4DG
☎ 0870 400 9027 📠 01992 560402
***Dir:*** *on B1393*
Situated just a short drive from the town centre and railway station, this busy hotel offers spacious bedrooms, and public areas include a small popular bar and the Junction restaurant which offers a range of modern dishes.
**ROOMS:** 79 annexe en suite (22 fmly) No smoking in 32 bedrooms **CONF:** Thtr 85 Class 50 Board 32 **PARKING:** 95
**CARDS:**

## EPSOM, Surrey Map 04 TQ26

### ★★★70% ® Chalk Lane Hotel

Chalk Ln, Woodcote End KT18 7BB
☎ 01372 721179 📠 01372 727878
e-mail: chalklane@compuserve.com

This delightful hotel is privately owned and is only a ten-minute walk from the famous Derby racecourse. All staff are committed to providing a warm and caring atmosphere, with every effort made to help one relax. Bedrooms are spacious, attractively furnished and thoughtfully equipped, while the restaurant offers an imaginative selection of dishes.
**ROOMS:** 22 rms (19 en suite) d £100-£155 (incl. bkfst) * **FACILITIES:** STV **CONF:** Thtr 140 Class 40 Board 30 Del £145 * **PARKING:** 100 **NOTES:** No smoking in restaurant
**CARDS:**

### ⌂ Premier Lodge (Epsom)

PREMIER LODGE

272 Kingston Rd, Ewell KT19 0SH
☎ 0870 700 1436 📠 0870 700 1437
***Dir:*** *Hotel located on A240 between A3 & A24 ,7m from junct 8&9 of M25*
Premier Lodge offers modern, well-equipped, en suite accommodation suitable for both business and leisure travellers. Meals can be taken at the adjacent popular restaurant and bar, which is fully licensed. For further details, consult the Hotel Groups page.
**ROOMS:** 29 en suite d £49.95 *

## EPWORTH, Lincolnshire Map 08 SE70

### ★★64% Red Lion Hotel

Market Place DN9 1EU
☎ 01427 872208 📠 01427 875214
***Dir:*** *leave M180 junc 2 onto A161. Hotel located after 3 miles*
Standing in the heart of the village, this coaching inn is very popular with locals and is quite a meeting place. It provides a wide range of food either in the bar or the cosy dining room and the staff are friendly and attentive. Bedrooms are bright and fresh and there is also a fitness centre within the hotel complex.
**ROOMS:** 15 en suite 4 annexe en suite (3 fmly) s £35-£50; d £55-£72 (incl. bkfst) * **LB** **FACILITIES:** Sauna Solarium Gym **CONF:** Thtr 50 Class 20 Board 20 **PARKING:** 30 **NOTES:** No dogs (ex guide dogs)
**CARDS:**

## ESCRICK, North Yorkshire Map 08 SE64

### ★★★73% ®® Parsonage Country House

York Rd YO19 6LF
☎ 01904 728111 📠 01904 728151
e-mail: reservations@parsonagehotel.co.uk
***Dir:*** *next to St Helens Church on A19*

An early 19th-century parsonage with a charming country house atmosphere, standing in well-tended grounds. Lounges are comfortable and now include a spacious conservatory. The bedrooms are well-equipped and attractive while staff are caring and professional. Good conference facilities are available.
**ROOMS:** 12 en suite 9 annexe en suite (3 fmly) No smoking in 13 bedrooms s fr £95; d fr £110 (incl. bkfst) * **LB** **FACILITIES:** STV Xmas **CONF:** Thtr 160 Class 80 Board 80 Del from £120 * **PARKING:** 100 **NOTES:** No dogs (ex guide dogs) No smoking in restaurant Civ Wed 50
**CARDS:**

## ESKDALE GREEN, Cumbria Map 06 NY10

### ★★62% Bower House Inn

CA19 1TD
☎ 019467 23244 📠 019467 23308
e-mail: Info@bowerhouseinn@freeserve.co.uk
***Dir:*** *4m off A595 1/2 mile west of Eskdale Green*
This former farmhouse enjoys a countryside location with delightful mountain views and offers true peace and relaxation. The traditional bar and restaurant reflect the coaching inn origins of the house while the formal dining room is more akin to that of a country house. Bedrooms are found in a smartly converted barn,

*continued on p218*

E

ESKDALE GREEN, continued

a secluded garden house and inside the original inn; all rooms are well-appointed and comfortable.

BOWER
HOUSE
INN

*Bower House Inn, Eskdale Green*

**ROOMS:** 5 en suite 19 annexe en suite (3 fmly) s fr £51.50; d fr £74 (incl. bkfst) * LB **FACILITIES:** ch fac Xmas **CONF:** Thtr 50 Class 50 Board 40 **PARKING:** 60 **NOTES:** No dogs (ex guide dogs) No smoking in restaurant Civ Wed 60 **CARDS:**

## EVERSHOT, Dorset

Map 03 ST50

### Premier Collection

### ★★★ Summer Lodge

RELAIS & CHATEAUX.

DT2 0JR
☎ 01935 83424 01935 83005
e-mail: enquiries@summerlodgehotel.com
***Dir:*** *1m W of A37 halfway between Dorchester & Yeovil*
Situated in a picture book village with deepest Dorset all around, it's no wonder that Summer Lodge is the ideal retreat away from it all. A typical country house atmosphere prevails with a caring team of staff on hand to cater to your every need. Try to arrive for afternoon tea, which is a highlight of any visit. Bedrooms are individually decorated with excellent levels of comfort; most are spacious with views over the gardens.
**ROOMS:** 11 en suite 7 annexe en suite (2 fmly) s £135-£175; d £205-£395 (incl. bkfst & dinner) * LB **FACILITIES:** Outdoor swimming (H) Tennis (hard & grass) Croquet lawn ch fac Xmas **CONF:** Thtr 20 Board 20 **PARKING:** 40 **NOTES:** No smoking in restaurant Civ Wed **CARDS:**

Early start? Hotels at all star levels should provide in-room alarm clocks and/or alarm calls.

## EVESHAM, Worcestershire

Map 04 SP04

see also Fladbury

### ★★★★75% ***Wood Norton Hall***

Wood Norton WR11 4YB
☎ 01386 420007 01386 420190
e-mail: woodnorton.hall@bbc.co.uk
***Dir:*** *2m from Evesham on the A4538, after the village of Chadbury travelling westwards or 4m after Wyre Piddle travelling eastwards*
This impressive Victorian hall stands in a 170-acre estate and provides excellent accommodation along with fine cuisine. The bedrooms have all been thoughtfully furnished and include a wealth of extras. Public areas are comfortable and feature fine wooden carvings and panelling throughout.
**ROOMS:** 15 en suite 30 annexe en suite No smoking in 40 bedrooms **FACILITIES:** STV Tennis (hard) Fishing Squash Snooker Gym Croquet lawn **CONF:** Thtr 70 Class 35 Board 32 **PARKING:** 300 **NOTES:** No dogs (ex guide dogs) No smoking in restaurant Closed 26 Dec-4 Jan Civ Wed 60 **CARDS:**

### ★★★71% **The Evesham**

Coopers Ln, Off Waterside WR11 6DA
☎ 01386 765566 & 0800 716969 (Res) 01386 765443
e-mail: reception@eveshamhotel.com
***Dir:*** *Coopers Lane is off the road alongside the River Avon*
Originally built in 1540 and set in two and a half acres of grounds, this delightful hotel has well-equipped accommodation that includes family suites. The hotel has a deserved reputation for its food. Facilities include a conference room and an indoor pool, there are lots of things to keep children amused, making the hotel ideal for families.
**ROOMS:** 39 en suite 1 annexe en suite (3 fmly) No smoking in 5 bedrooms s £65-£75; d £103 (incl. bkfst) * LB **FACILITIES:** Indoor swimming (H) Croquet lawn Putting green ch fac **CONF:** Thtr 12 Class 12 Board 12 Del from £111 * **PARKING:** 50 **NOTES:** No smoking in restaurant Closed 25 & 26 Dec **CARDS:**

### ★★★69% **Waterside**

56 Waterside WR11 6JZ
☎ 01386 442420 01386 446272
***Dir:*** *A44/A435 junc 40yds on right alongside river*
This friendly hotel stands in a prominent position overlooking the River Avon and is within easy reach of the town centre. Bedrooms are attractively furnished and well-equipped. Public areas include the popular Strollers restaurant and bar, which has an American theme and provides a wide variety of dishes. Cream teas are served in the riverside gardens on sunny days.
**ROOMS:** 15 en suite (2 fmly) s £57; d £68 (incl. bkfst) * LB **FACILITIES:** Fishing ch fac **PARKING:** 30 **CARDS:**

### ★★★68% ***Northwick Hotel***

Best Western

Waterside WR11 6BT
☎ 01386 40322 01386 41070
***Dir:*** *turn off A46 onto A44 over traffic lights to next set turn right along B4035 past hospital hotel on right side opposite river*
Standing opposite the River Avon this former coaching inn is within easy walking distance of the centre of Evesham. Bedrooms are tastefully decorated and well-equipped, with one specially adapted for disabled guests. The recently refurbished public areas offer a choice of bars, meeting rooms and restaurant.
**ROOMS:** 31 en suite (4 fmly) No smoking in 10 bedrooms **FACILITIES:** Hot air ballooning Clay pigeon shooting Archery Paint balling **CONF:** Thtr 240 Class 150 Board 80 **PARKING:** 200 **NOTES:** No smoking in restaurant **CARDS:**

### ★★80% The Mill at Harvington

Anchor Ln, Harvington WR11 5NR
☎ 01386 870688 Fax 01386 870688
e-mail: millatharvington@aol.com
***Dir:*** *Harvington is 4m NE of Evesham. The hotel is on the banks of the Avon, reached by a bridge over the new A46 and not in village*

This delightful small hotel, once a Georgian house and mill, stands in extensive grounds on the banks of the River Avon in tranquil rural surroundings. It provides a comfortable lounge with fine views, a conservatory bar and an elegant restaurant. Bedrooms, which include rooms on ground floor level, are for the most part well proportioned and have been thoughtfully equipped. Six spacious rooms are set in a separate building. Facilities include an outdoor swimming pool and a tennis court.

**ROOMS:** 15 en suite 6 annexe en suite s £63-£75; d £85-£125 (incl. bkfst) * **LB** **FACILITIES:** Outdoor swimming (H) Fishing Croquet lawn **CONF:** Thtr 15 Class 10 Board 10 Del from £105 * **PARKING:** 50 **NOTES:** No dogs (ex guide dogs) No children 10yrs No smoking in restaurant Closed 24-27 Dec **CARDS:**

### ★★72% Riverside

The Parks, Offenham Rd WR11 5JP
☎ 01386 446200 Fax 01386 40021
e-mail: riversidehotel@theparksoffenham.freeserve.co.uk
***Dir:*** *off the A46 follow signs for Offenham. Take turning on right B4510 (Offenham) 1/2 mile turn left along private drive called The Parks to end*

This family-owned and run hotel stands in three acres of gardens sloping down to the River Avon. The lounge, restaurant and many of the comfortable bedrooms overlook the river. Cooking remains a strength here, with a menu of imaginative dishes based on really good produce.

**ROOMS:** 7 en suite s £65; d £95 (incl. bkfst) * **LB** **FACILITIES:** Fishing **PARKING:** 40 **NOTES:** No dogs (ex guide dogs) No smoking in restaurant Closed 25 Dec, Sun night & Mon RS 2-20 Jan (wknds only) **CARDS:**

## EWEN, Gloucestershire — Map 04 SU09

### ★★70% Wild Duck Inn

Drakes Island GL7 6BY
☎ 01285 770310 Fax 01285 770924
e-mail: wduckinn@aol.com
***Dir:*** *from Cirencester take A429 on reaching Kemble take left turn to Ewen keep driving to the centre of the village*

A bustling, ever popular inn dating back to the early 16th century. Open fires, old beams and rustic pine tables lend character to the bar and restaurant, where imaginative, robust cooking and cheerful service are further strengths.

**ROOMS:** 11 en suite s fr £55; d £75-£90 (incl. cont bkfst) * **FACILITIES:** Discounted leisure facilities within 3m **PARKING:** 50 **NOTES:** RS 25 Dec **CARDS:**

*See advert under CIRENCESTER*

## EXETER, Devon — Map 03 SX99

### ★★★★70% The Southgate

Southernhay East EX1 1QF
☎ 0870 400 8333 Fax 01392 413549
e-mail: heritagehotels-exeter.southgate@forte-hotels.com
***Dir:*** *on Southernhay roundabout near cathedral*

This attractive modern hotel is situated close to the town centre and across from the quay. Smart bedrooms offer a good level of comfort and are equipped with such extra facilities as trouser presses and mini bars. The public rooms are elegantly furnished, with a choice of dining options now available.

**ROOMS:** 110 en suite (6 fmly) No smoking in 55 bedrooms d £110 * **LB** **FACILITIES:** STV Indoor swimming (H) Sauna Solarium Gym Jacuzzi entertainment Xmas **CONF:** Thtr 150 Class 70 Board 50 Del from £110 * **SERVICES:** Lift **PARKING:** 115 **NOTES:** No smoking in restaurant RS Sat (restaurant closed for lunch) Civ Wed 80 **CARDS:**

### ★★★73% Barton Cross Hotel & Restaurant

Huxham, Stoke Canon EX5 4EJ
☎ 01392 841245 Fax 01392 841942
***Dir:*** *0.5m off A396 at Stoke Canon just 3 miles north of Exeter*

'Seventeenth-century charm with 20th-century luxury' perfectly sums up this lovely countryside hotel. The eight bedrooms are spacious, tastefully decorated and well-maintained. Public areas include the cosy first floor lounge, in addition to the lounge/bar

*continued on p220*

EXETER, continued

with its warming log fire. The restaurant offers a seasonally changing menu and consistently fine cuisine.
**ROOMS:** 9 en suite (2 fmly) No smoking in 2 bedrooms s £65.50-£75; d £90-£110 (incl. bkfst) * **LB** **FACILITIES:** STV ch fac Xmas **CONF:** Board 12 **PARKING:** 35 **NOTES:** No smoking in restaurant
**CARDS:**

*See advert on page 219*

**★★★71% Royal Clarence**
Cathedral Yard EX1 1HD

REGAL
☎ 01392 319955 01392 439423
***Dir:*** *facing cathedral*

This historic, 14th century building is a landmark in Exeter, situated opposite the Cathedral. Bedrooms range from compact to grand, some with views over the Cathedral green. No visit here is complete without dinner at Michael Caines' restaurant within the hotel, booking is strongly advised. The Café Bar, also run by Michael Caines, is a less formal option and open most of the day.
**ROOMS:** 56 en suite (6 fmly) No smoking in 16 bedrooms s £99-£109; d £125-£135 * **LB** **FACILITIES:** Xmas **CONF:** Thtr 120 Class 50 Board 50 Del from £136 * **SERVICES:** Lift **PARKING:** 15 **NOTES:** No dogs (ex guide dogs) No smoking in restaurant Civ Wed 50
**CARDS:**

**★★★71% St Olaves Court Restaurant & Hotel**
Mary Arches St EX4 3AZ
☎ 01392 217736 01392 413054
e-mail: info@olaves.co.uk
***Dir:*** *drive to City centre, follow signs to Mary Arches Parking. Hotel entrance is directly opposite car park entrance*
This hotel is just a short stroll from the cathedral, shops and medieval centre of Exeter. Bedrooms are smart and include thoughtful extras such as a complimentary decanter of sherry. The intimate Golsworthy's Restaurant offers a high standard of cuisine with an imaginative carte.
**ROOMS:** 11 en suite 4 annexe en suite (2 fmly) **FACILITIES:** Croquet lawn ch fac **CONF:** Thtr 45 Class 35 Board 35 Del £125 * **PARKING:** 15 **NOTES:** No smoking in restaurant Civ Wed 150
**CARDS:**

*See advert on opposite page*

**★★★70% Devon**
Exeter Bypass, Matford EX2 8XU
☎ 01392 259268 01392 413142
e-mail: info@devonhotel.co.uk
***Dir:*** *leave M5 at junct 30, follow signpost to Marsh Barton Ind Est A379, hotel is on main A38 rdbt*
Conveniently situated for the city centre and with easy access to the M5, this hotel offers modern, comfortable accommodation. The brasserie is popular with locals and visitors alike, offering a wide range of dishes as well as a more traditional carvery. Service is friendly and efficient, and extensive meeting and rooms are available.
**ROOMS:** 41 annexe en suite (3 fmly) s £49-£69; d £59-£69 * **LB** **FACILITIES:** STV entertainment ch fac Xmas **CONF:** Thtr 150 Class 150 Board 150 **PARKING:** 250 **NOTES:** No smoking in restaurant Civ Wed 100 **CARDS:**

**★★★68% Lord Haldon Country House**
Dunchideock EX6 7YF
☎ 01392 832483 01392 833765
e-mail: lordhaldon@eclipse.co.uk
***Dir:*** *from M5 junct 31 or A30 follow signs to Ide then continue through village for 2.5m. After red telephone box turn left. In 0.5m pass under stone bridge turn left*
Offering a warm welcome and comfortable accommodation, this family owned establishment is situated in some of Devon's most picturesque countryside. Many of the individually furnished and well-equipped bedrooms have the benefit of stunning views, while in the restaurant an interesting selection of popular dishes is prepared with care.
**ROOMS:** 19 en suite (3 fmly) No smoking in 10 bedrooms s £48-£55; d £68-£120 (incl. bkfst) * **LB** **FACILITIES:** STV ch fac Xmas **CONF:** Thtr 300 Class 150 Board 60 Del £95 * **PARKING:** 60 **NOTES:** No smoking in restaurant Civ Wed 120
**CARDS:**

*See advert on opposite page*

**★★★68% Queens Court**
Bystock Ter EX4 4HY

THE CIRCLE
Selected Individual Hotels
GREAT BRITAIN
☎ 01392 272709 01392 491390
e-mail: sales@queenscourt-hotel.co.uk

QUEENS COURT HOTEL

Quietly located within walking distance of the city centre, this recently refurbished hotel provides every service that the modern traveller could need. Both public areas and bedrooms are furnished in contemporary style. The adjacent Olive Tree restaurant offers an interesting selection of Mediterranean influenced dishes.
**ROOMS:** 18 en suite No smoking in 9 bedrooms s £59-£69; d £59-£79 * **LB** **FACILITIES:** STV **CONF:** Thtr 80 Class 30 Board 40 **SERVICES:** Lift **PARKING:** 6 **NOTES:** No dogs (ex guide dogs)
**CARDS:**

***★★★67% Buckerell Lodge***
Topsham Rd EX2 4SQ
☎ 01392 221111 01392 491111
***Dir:*** *M5 junct 30 follow signs for City Centre, hotel is located on the main Topsham Rd approx 0.5m from Exeter*
Although situated outside the city centre, the hotel has good access either by car or public transport. Accommodation is

*continued*

comfortable, fairly spacious and generally quiet. Public areas include a variety of function rooms, a popular bar and restaurant.

**ROOMS:** 53 en suite (2 fmly) No smoking in 15 bedrooms
**FACILITIES:** STV Jacuzzi **CONF:** Thtr 50 Class 35 Board 30
**PARKING:** 100 **NOTES:** No smoking in restaurant
**CARDS:** 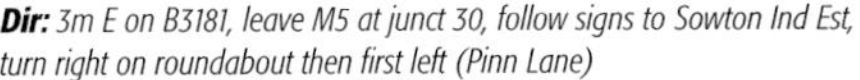

★★★66% **Gipsy Hill**
Gipsy Hill Ln, Pinn Ln, Monkerton EX1 3RN
☎ 01392 465252 🖹 01392 464302
e-mail: gipsyhill@bestwestern.co.uk
***Dir:*** *3m E on B3181, leave M5 at junct 30, follow signs to Sowton Ind Est, turn right on roundabout then first left (Pinn Lane)*
A popular hotel, just outside Exeter, and close to the M5 and the airport. Set in attractive, well-tended gardens with country views, the hotel offers conference and function rooms with comfortable bedroom accommodation and modern facilities. An intimate bar

*continued on p222*

# St Olaves Hotel & Restaurant

**Mary Arches Street, Exeter, Devon EX4 3AZ**
**Tel: 01392 217736 Fax: 01392 413054**
**Web: www.olaves.co.uk**
**Email: info@olaves.co.uk**

This hotel is just a short stroll from the cathedral, shops and medieval centre of Exeter.
Bedrooms are smart and include thoughtful extras such as a complimentary decanter of sherry.
The intimate Golsworthy's Restaurant offers a high standard of cuisine with

AA★★★
GIPSY HILL

**COUNTRY HOUSE HOTEL**
**Gipsy Hill Lane, Monkerton, Exeter, Devon EX1 3RN**
**Tel: 01392 465252 Fax: 01392 464302**
**Email: gipsyhill@bestwestern.co.uk**

The hotel is situated on the eastern edge of the historic city of Exeter, close to the M5, junction 29. Built in the early part of this century it became an hotel just after the Second World War. The hotel still retains its former style and charm, the bedrooms are all individually furnished, decorated and have en suite facilities.
The popular restaurant overlooks the gardens and the Devon countryside.

Best Western

**www.gipsyhillhotel.co.uk**

# The Lord Haldon Hotel

AA ★★★

**DUNCHIDEOCK, EXETER, DEVON EX6 7YF**
**Tel: 01392 832483 Fax: 01392 833765**
**Email: lordhaldon@eclipse.co.uk**

Described as a Pearl in the Heart of the Devon countryside, this small comfortable family-run hotel attracts many guests back year after year. They come for good food, pleasant company and friendly staff.
As well as the lovely setting in five acres of secluded gardens with breathtaking views over the Exe Valley, the hotel is a short distance from the Cathedral City of Exeter. Horse riding, walking, birds of prey are but some of the local attractions of staying at the hotel.

***Free colour brochure on request.***
Recommended by Johansens, and Relais Du Silence.

EXETER, continued

and lounge are next to the elegant restaurant, daily and carte menus are available.
**ROOMS:** 20 en suite 17 annexe en suite (5 fmly) No smoking in 6 bedrooms s £80; d £103 (incl. bkfst) * **LB** **FACILITIES:** ch fac **CONF:** Thtr 120 Class 55 Board 36 Del £75 * **PARKING:** 100 **NOTES:** No smoking in restaurant Closed 25-30 Dec Civ Wed 120 **CARDS:**

*See advert on page 221*

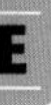

### ★★69% Fairwinds Hotel
Kennford EX6 7UD
☎ 01392 832911 01392 832911
***Dir:*** *4m S of Exeter, from M5 junct 31, continue along A38, after 2m turn left at sign for Kennford. First hotel on the left*
A warm and genuine welcome is assured at this conveniently situated hotel, which lies within easy reach of Exeter, Torbay and Plymouth. Being a strictly non-smoking hotel throughout, guests are therefore assured of a pleasant environment in which to relax and unwind. A small bar-lounge is available adjacent to the restaurant, where enjoyable and interesting home-made dishes are served. Bedrooms are well-maintained, combining comfort with useful facilities, four rooms being available on the ground floor.
**ROOMS:** 6 en suite (1 fmly) No smoking in all bedrooms s £37-£39; d £52-£56 (incl. bkfst) * **LB** **PARKING:** 8 **NOTES:** No dogs No smoking in restaurant Closed 19 Nov-31 Dec **CARDS:**

### ★★66% Comfort Inn
A38 (Kennford) EX6 7UX
☎ 01392 832121 01392 833590
e-mail: admin@gb056.u-net.com
***Dir:*** *on A38 turn off for Kennford Services follow hotel signs*
Conveniently located for both the city and the M5, this hotel is popular with all types of guest. Bedrooms, all located in adjacent motel style buildings, are comfortably appointed and well-equipped. Public areas include an open plan bar and restaurant, and conference facilities.
**ROOMS:** 63 en suite (5 fmly) No smoking in 37 bedrooms s fr £44; d fr £55 * **LB** **FACILITIES:** STV Tennis (hard) **CONF:** Thtr 120 Class 80 Board 60 **PARKING:** 250 **NOTES:** No smoking in restaurant **CARDS:**

### ★★65% Ebford House
Exmouth Rd EX3 0QH
☎ 01392 877658 01392 874424
e-mail: ebford@eclipse.co.uk
***Dir:*** *1m E of Topsham on A376*
This charming Georgian house lies between Exeter and Exmouth and offers a choice of dining options - the elegant surroundings of the formal restaurant or the informality of the bistro, offering interesting home-cooked dishes and other blackboard specials. Bedrooms are individual in style and size and include many modern facilities.
**ROOMS:** 16 en suite No smoking in 6 bedrooms s £55-£60; d £78-£87 (incl. bkfst) * **LB** **FACILITIES:** STV Sauna Gym **CONF:** Thtr 25 Class 10 Board 18 Del from £85 * **PARKING:** 45 **NOTES:** No dogs (ex guide dogs) Closed 23 Dec-28 Dec **CARDS:**

### ★★62% Red House
2 Whipton Village Rd EX4 8AR
☎ 01392 256104 01392 666145
e-mail: red.house.hotel@eclipse.co.uk
***Dir:*** *junct 30 M5, left before services signed Middlemoor, right at rdbt towards Pinhoe & University, in 0.75m left to Whipton/University, hotel 1m on right*

This family-owned hotel is located on the edge of the city, and offers an extensive menu, including a carvery, served either in the popular bar or in the adjacent dining room. The bedrooms are modern and well-equipped offering accommodation that is suitable for all types of guest.
**ROOMS:** 12 en suite (2 fmly) No smoking in 8 bedrooms s £38-£40; d £49-£54 (incl. bkfst) * **LB** **FACILITIES:** STV **CONF:** Class 50 Board 20 **PARKING:** 28 **CARDS:**

## *Town House*

### ★★★★ Hotel Barcelona
Magdalen St EX2 4HY
☎ 01392 281000 01392 281001
e-mail: info@hotelbarcelona-uk.com
Designed to impress, Hotel Barcelona is a very special place to stay. Situated within walking distance of the city centre, this former eye hospital has been transformed and now provides stylish accommodation with a glamorous atmosphere. Other attractions include Café Paradiso, a smart yet informal eatery with a varied menu, Kino, a night-club straight out of a classic film, a range of quiet meeting rooms and a delightful garden terrace ideal for al fresco dining.
**ROOMS:** 48 en suite s £70; d £80-£90 * **FACILITIES:** no TV in bdrms **CONF:** Thtr 40 Class 18 Board 18 Del £120 * **SERVICES:** Lift **PARKING:** 35 **NOTES:** No smoking in restaurant **CARDS:**

*See advert on opposite page*

### Express by Holiday Inn Exeter
Guardian Rd EX1 3PE
☎ 01392 261000 01392 261061
***Dir:*** *turn off M5 at junct 29 and follow signs for Exeter City Centre. Hotel located on 1st rdbt*
A modern budget hotel offering comfortable accommodation in refreshing, spacious and comprehensively equipped bedrooms, en suite bathrooms with power showers and continental buffet breakfast included in the room rate. Suitable for business

*continued*

travellers or families. For further details and the Express by Holiday Inn phone number, consult the Hotel Groups page.

**ROOMS:** 122 en suite (incl. cont bkfst) d fr £55 * **CONF:** Thtr 32 Class 30 Board 24

### *Travelodge*

Moor Ln, Sandygate EX2 4AR
☎ 01392 74044 ▤ 01392 410406
***Dir:*** *M5 jnct 30*
Travelodge offers good quality, good value, modern accommodation. Ideal for families, the spacious, en suite bedrooms include remote-control TV, tea and coffee-making facilities, luxury beds and free morning newspaper. Meals can be taken at the nearby family restaurant. For further details and the Travelodge phone number, consult the Hotel Groups page.

**ROOMS:** 74 en suite **CONF:** Thtr 80 Class 18 Board 25

## EXFORD, Somerset — Map 03 SS83

### ★★★72% Crown

TA24 7PP
☎ 01643 831554 ▤ 01643 831665
e-mail: info@crownhotelexmore.co.uk
***Dir:*** *leave M5 junct 25 and follow signs for Taunton. Take the A358 out of Taunton, then the B3224 via Wheddon Cross into Exford*
Guest comfort is paramount in this corner of Somerset and it shines through the Crown Hotel. Afternoon teas served in the lounge beside a roaring fire and tempting menus in the bar and restaurant are all part of the charm of this delightful old coaching inn. Bedrooms offer space, comfort and modern facilities, many with views of the pretty moorland village.
**ROOMS:** 17 en suite s fr £47.50; d £80-£116 (incl. bkfst) * **LB**
**FACILITIES:** Fishing Riding Shooting Xmas **PARKING:** 30
**CARDS:**

## EXMOUTH, Devon — Map 03 SY08

### ★★★67% Royal Beacon

The Beacon EX8 2AF
☎ 01395 264886 ▤ 01395 268890
e-mail: reception@royalbeaconhotel.co.uk
***Dir:*** *from M5 and Exeter along A376 enter marine way. Follows signs for sea front . On Imperial Road turn left at T junc & 1st right. Hotel is 100yds on left).*
A welcoming hotel, the Royal Beacon is an elegant Georgian property overlooking both the town of Exmouth and the beautiful

*continued on p224*

EXMOUTH, continued

Devon coastline. The hotel enjoys fine views, an inviting bar and restaurant, well-appointed rooms and an impressive function suite.

*Royal Beacon, Exmouth*

**ROOMS:** 30 en suite (2 fmly) No smoking in 4 bedrooms s £45-£55; d £85-£95 (incl. bkfst) * **LB** **FACILITIES:** Xmas **CONF:** Thtr 150 Class 100 Board 40 Del from £65 * **SERVICES:** Lift **PARKING:** 10 **NOTES:** No smoking in restaurant Civ Wed 150
**CARDS:**

*See advert on page 223*

### ★★68% Barn

Foxholes Hill, Marine Dr EX8 2DF
☎ 01395 224411 🖷 01395 225445
e-mail: Info@barnhotel.co.uk
***Dir:*** *M5 junct 30 follow signs for Exmouth A376, to seafront in an easterly direction, next rdbt last exit into Foxholes Hill. Hotel on right*
This unique Grade II listed property is quietly situated, just a couple of minutes walk from the beach. The views from the elegant public areas and most of the bedrooms are simply breathtaking, across the gardens to the shimmering sea beyond. Akin to a country house hotel, the atmosphere is relaxed and hospitable with every effort made to ensure an enjoyable stay.
**ROOMS:** 11 en suite (4 fmly) No smoking in all bedrooms s £26-£37; d £52-£74 (incl. bkfst) * **LB** **FACILITIES:** Outdoor swimming Putting green **CONF:** Class 40 Board 20 **PARKING:** 24 **NOTES:** No dogs No smoking in restaurant Closed 23 Dec-10 Jan
**CARDS:**

### ★★62% Cavendish Hotel

11 Morton Crescent, The Esplanade EX8 1BE
☎ 01395 272528 🖷 01395 268221
Leisureplex
e-mail: cavendish@leisureplex.fsbusiness.co.uk
***Dir:*** *Follow signs to seafront, hotel is situated in the centre of the large crescent overlooking the river and sea.*
Situated on the seafront, this terraced hotel attracts many groups from around the country. With fine views out to sea, the hotel is within walking distance of the town centre. The bedrooms are neatly presented; front facing rooms are always popular. Entertainment is provided on some evenings during the summer months.
**ROOMS:** 72 en suite (3 fmly) s fr £30; d fr £60 (incl. bkfst) * **FACILITIES:** Snooker entertainment Xmas **SERVICES:** Lift **PARKING:** 25 **NOTES:** No dogs (ex guide dogs) No smoking in restaurant Closed part Nov & Dec-Mar (ex Xmas)
**CARDS:**

> Early start? Hotels at all star levels should provide in-room alarm clocks and/or alarm calls.

### ★★62% Manor

The Beacon EX8 2AG
☎ 01395 272549 & 274477 🖷 01395 225519
***Dir:*** *M5 junct 30 take A376 to Exmouth take signs for seafront, hotel 300yds from seafront by Tourist Information Office*
Traditional hospitality is the hallmark of this friendly, family-run hotel. The convenience of the location, overlooking the town centre and the sea, is a factor which brings back guests year after year. The well-equipped bedrooms vary in style and size, with many offering the added bonus of far reaching views. The table d'hôte menu offers a selection of traditional dishes, after which a drink can be enjoyed in the convivial surroundings of the lounge bar.
**ROOMS:** 38 en suite (3 fmly) s £29.50-£32.50; d £56-£61 (incl. bkfst) * **LB** **FACILITIES:** Xmas **CONF:** Thtr 100 **SERVICES:** Lift **PARKING:** 15 **NOTES:** No dogs (ex guide dogs) No smoking in restaurant
**CARDS:**

## FAIRFORD, Gloucestershire

Map 04 SP10

### ★★65% Bull Hotel

The Market Place GL7 4AA
☎ 01285 712535 & 712217 🖷 01285 713782
e-mail: info@thebullhotelfairford.co.uk
***Dir:*** *on the A417 in the market square adjacent to the post office*
Located in the picturesque Cotswold market town, this family-run inn retains its period character and charm. The bar is a popular meeting place, with a wide range of meals on offer; while in the restaurant, an interesting selection of dishes is available. Many of the well-equipped bedrooms overlook the square.
**ROOMS:** 22 rms (20 en suite) (1 fmly) s £48-£70; d £70-£100 (incl. bkfst) * **LB** **FACILITIES:** Fishing **CONF:** Thtr 60 Class 40 Board 40 **PARKING:** 10 **NOTES:** No smoking in restaurant
**CARDS:**

*See advert on opposite page*

## FAKENHAM, Norfolk

Map 09 TF92

### ★★68% Crown

6 Market Place NR21 9BP
☎ 01328 851418 🖷 01328 862433
***Dir:*** *A148, A1065,A1065 to Fakenham town centre, follow signs to Market Place*

THE CROWN HOTEL

Originally a coaching inn and focal point of this old market town, parts of The Crown date back to the 16th century. Bedrooms are attractively decorated and well-equipped, and one has a four-poster bed. The bar menu and blackboard offer a range of snacks whilst the restaurant has a carte menu.
**ROOMS:** 12 en suite (2 fmly) No smoking in 1 bedroom s £45-£75; d £65-£95 (incl. bkfst) * **LB** **FACILITIES:** Garage lock up for bicycles **CONF:** Class 35 Board 22 Del from £100 * **PARKING:** 25 **NOTES:** No dogs (ex guide dogs) **CARDS:**

★★66% ***Sculthorpe Mill***

Lynn Rd, Sculthorpe NR21 9QG
☎ 01328 856161 🖹 01328 856651
***Dir:*** *turn off A148 from Fakenham to Kings Lynn, just beyond village of Sculthorpe*
An 18th-century watermill situated within easy striking distance of the town centre in an idyllic and tranquil position. With its open fires, low beams and nooks and crannies, it is popular both as a watering hole for locals and a fine dining venue. The bedrooms are spacious and well-equipped; one has a four-poster bed.
**ROOMS:** 6 en suite (1 fmly) No smoking in all bedrooms
**FACILITIES:** ch fac **CONF:** Thtr 25 Class 16 Board 16 **PARKING:** 60
**NOTES:** No smoking in restaurant RS Oct-Good Fri Mon-Fri closed 3-6pm Civ Wed 120 **CARDS:**

FALMOUTH, Cornwall & Isles of Scilly Map 02 SW83
see also Mawnan Smith

★★★★70% ❀❀ **Royal Duchy**
Cliff Rd TR11 4NX
☎ 01326 313042 🖹 01326 319420
e-mail: info@royalduchy.co.uk
***Dir:*** *located on Cliff Rd, along Falmouth Sea Front*
Situated on the sea front, just a short walk from the town centre, this hotel continues to attract a regular clientele. The lounges enjoy spectacular views, as does the restaurant, where carefully

*continued on p226*

Falmouth's Only 4-star Hotel
Situated in a prime location on Falmouth's seafront, The Royal Duchy Hotel enjoys panoramic views across Falmouth's famous bay.
Renowned cuisine is matched by the hotel's lavish accommodation. Every bedroom enjoys private bathroom en-suite, Satellite reception and direct dial telephone.
A lift provides easy access to all floors.
Facilities include heated indoor swimming pool complex with sauna, solarium, spa bath, family games room and private function room.
The Royal Duchy Hotel
AA ★★★★
The Royal Duchy Hotel, Cliff Road, Falmouth, Cornwall TR11 4NX
Tel: (01326) 313042 Fax: (01326) 319420
e-mail: info@royalduchy.co.uk
www.royalduchy.co.uk
Brend Hotels

A PLACE OF PEACE AND BEAUTY
...where the gardens sweep down to the sea
Family run Country House Hotel specialists in local seafood, traditional service, cosseted comforts, antiques, log fires and fresh flowers.
Meudon
GOLF IS FREE
Please see full entry under Mawnan Smith
Tel 01 326 250541 • Fax 250543
www.meudon.co.uk

FALMOUTH, continued

prepared dishes are served. Bedrooms vary in size and aspect, with sea facing rooms always being in demand.

*Royal Duchy, Falmouth*

**ROOMS:** 43 en suite (6 fmly) s £62-£88; d £116-£196 (incl. bkfst) * **LB** **FACILITIES:** Spa STV Indoor swimming (H) Sauna Solarium Table tennis entertainment ch fac Xmas **CONF:** Thtr 50 Class 50 Board 50 **SERVICES:** Lift **PARKING:** 50 **NOTES:** No dogs (ex guide dogs) Civ Wed 100 **CARDS:**

*See advert on page 225*

### ★★★75% Penmere Manor

Mongleath Rd TR11 4PN
☎ 01326 211411 📠 01326 317588
e-mail: reservations@penmere.co.uk
***Dir:*** *turn right off Hillhead roundabout and follow road for approx 1m then turn left into Mongleath Road*

Best Western

Quietly located within five acres of gardens and woodlands, this family-owned hotel is a popular choice. A wide range of bedrooms are offered with the spacious garden wing rooms being furnished and equipped to a particularly high standard. Imaginative dishes using local produce are served in Bolitho's Restaurant. Fountains Bar, part of the leisure club, offers light meals and snacks in a more informal setting.

**ROOMS:** 37 en suite (12 fmly) No smoking in 29 bedrooms s £58-£60; d £90-£130 (incl. bkfst) * **LB** **FACILITIES:** STV Indoor swimming (H) Outdoor swimming (H) Sauna Solarium Gym Croquet lawn Jacuzzi Boules Pool table entertainment Xmas **CONF:** Thtr 40 Class 20 Board 30 Del from £75 * **PARKING:** 50 **NOTES:** No smoking in restaurant Closed 24-27 Dec Civ Wed 80 **CARDS:**

*See advert on opposite page*

### ★★★72% Falmouth Beach Resort Hotel

Gyllyngvase Beach, Seafront TR11 4NA
☎ 01326 312999 📠 01326 319147
e-mail: info@falmouthbeachhotel.co.uk
***Dir:*** *from A39 to Falmouth follow signs to seafront & Gyllyngvase Beach, hotel opposite Gyllyngvase Beach, near tennis courts*

Best Western

This large, popular hotel continues to build upon its reputation for a friendly and enjoyable atmosphere. Bedrooms vary in size, all offering good standards of comfort; with many having wonderful sea views. A range of dining options is available to suit all tastes and appetites! Leisure facilities include heated indoor pool and well-equipped gym.

**ROOMS:** 111 rms (94 en suite) 7 annexe rms (6 en suite) (20 fmly) No smoking in 94 bedrooms s £70.50; d £113-£127 (incl. bkfst & dinner) * **LB** **FACILITIES:** Spa STV Indoor swimming (H) Tennis (hard) Sauna Solarium Gym Jacuzzi Steam room entertainment Xmas **CONF:** Thtr 300 Class 200 Board 150 Del £72 * **SERVICES:** Lift **PARKING:** 95 **NOTES:** No smoking in restaurant Civ Wed 300 **CARDS:**

*See advert on opposite page*

### ★★★71% Falmouth

Castle Beach TR11 4NZ
☎ 01326 312671 0800 0193121 📠 01326 319533
e-mail: info@falmouthhotel.com
***Dir:*** *from Exeter take A30 to Truro then A390 to Falmouth. Hotel on the seafront near Pendennis Castle*

This grand Victorian hotel is set within five acres of gardens overlooking Castle Beach and just a short walk from the town centre. All bedrooms offer good levels of comfort and facilities and include family, non-smoking and balconied rooms. A choice of seaward facing lounges, an elegant restaurant, large ballroom and

*continued on p228*

What a position to be in!
AA
★★★
72%

. . . sunbathing on the beautiful beach right outside the hotel, swimming in the pool at 'The Beach Club', or sampling our wonderful food, maybe on the sun terrace overlooking the sea.

Live music, free tennis.
Enjoy Falmouth with all its history, attractions and facilities . . . shops, golf, sailing, fishing, beautiful gardens.
Just be in the right position to enjoy it.

Best Western
FALMOUTH BEACH
RESORT HOTEL & Conference Centre

**The Falmouth Beach Resort Hotel.**
Gyllyngvase Beach, Falmouth, Cornwall.
**Tel: 01326 312999 Fax: 319147**
Email: info@falmouthbeachhotel.co.uk
Website: www.famouthbeachhotel.co.uk

Best Western

An oasis of gracious living in 5 acres of gardens and woodland offering the last word in comfort, friendliness and attentive service, a real home away from home.

Best Western
*Penmere*
MANOR
FALMOUTH, CORNWALL UK

Mongleath Road, Falmouth,
Cornwall TR11 4PN
**FREEPHONE 0800 980 4611**
Web: www.penmere.co.uk
Email: reservations@penmere.co.uk

★★★
Trelawne Hotel

In a beautiful, peaceful and tranquil corner of Cornwall, this fine country house hotel nestles on the coastline between the Helford and the Fal rivers with magnificent views across Falmouth Bay. The Trelawne is ideally situated for endless coastal walks, exploring sandy beaches and coves, visiting many National Trust properties and free entry into some of Cornwall's famous gardens.

**Mawnan Smith, Falmouth,**
**Cornwall TR11 5HS**
**Tel: (01326) 250226 Fax: (01326) 250909**

The Falmouth Hotel

**CASTLE BEACH**
**FALMOUTH**
**CORNWALL**
**TR11 4NZ**
**Fax: 01326 319533**
**Email: info@falmouthhotel.com**
**Website: www.falmouthhotel.com**

AA ★★★

A beautiful hotel commanding an unrivalled seafront position. 100 luxurious bedrooms, apartments and cottages, some with balconies and jacuzzis. Delightful restaurants, bars and lounges with stunning views and a wonderfully relaxing ambience. Superb leisure complex with pool, sauna, jacuzzi, solarium and gymnasium. The perfect location for business or holiday as well as a delightful venue for weddings, conferences and all functions.

*Please call for a brochure and tariff.*

**FREEPHONE: 0800 0193121**

F

FALMOUTH, continued

leisure club complete the amenities. Self-catering apartments are available in the grounds.
**ROOMS:** 69 en suite 34 annexe en suite (13 fmly) No smoking in 18 bedrooms s £37-£45; d £65-£132 * **LB** **FACILITIES:** STV Indoor swimming (H) Snooker Sauna Solarium Gym Putting green Free m/ship tennis/squash club ch fac **CONF:** Thtr 250 Class 150 Board 100 Del from £59 * **SERVICES:** Lift **PARKING:** 175 **NOTES:** Closed 23 Dec-30 Dec Civ Wed 250 **CARDS:**

*See advert on page 227*

### ★★★69% The Greenbank

Harbourside TR11 2SR
☎ 01326 312440 01326 211362
e-mail: sales@greenbank-hotel.com
***Dir:*** *500yds past Falmouth Marina on Penryn River*

This harbourside hotel has a private 17th-century quay. Refurbishment has sensitively combined contemporary expectations with the charm and elegance of yesteryear. Bedrooms are spacious and well-equipped, many having sea views. Unrivalled views across the water are best enjoyed in the stylish restaurant, which offers an interesting choice of tempting dishes.
**ROOMS:** 59 en suite (4 fmly) No smoking in 10 bedrooms s £57-£72; d £98-£145 (incl. bkfst) * **LB** **CONF:** Thtr 60 Class 45 Board 20 Del from £79 * **SERVICES:** Lift **PARKING:** 68 **NOTES:** No smoking in restaurant Civ Wed 60 **CARDS:**

### ★★★67% Green Lawns

Western Ter TR11 4QJ
☎ 01326 312734 01326 211427
e-mail: info@greenlawnshotel.com
***Dir:*** *on A39*

Popular with both business and leisure guests, this established hotel offers extensive facilities, including a spacious function room and an attractive split-level restaurant where both a table d'hôte and a carte menu is available to guests and non-residents alike. Bedrooms vary in size and style, although all offer many modern facilities and comforts.
**ROOMS:** 39 en suite (8 fmly) No smoking in 8 bedrooms s £55-£105; d £110-£150 (incl. bkfst) **LB** **FACILITIES:** STV Indoor swimming (H) Tennis (hard & grass) Squash Sauna Solarium Gym Jacuzzi entertainment **CONF:** Thtr 200 Class 80 Board 100 Del from £95 * **PARKING:** 69 **NOTES:** No smoking in restaurant Closed 24-30 Dec Civ Wed 60 **CARDS:**

Packed in a hurry? Ironing facilities should be available at all star levels, either in rooms or on request.

### ★★★67% Penmorvah Manor

MINOTEL Great Britain

Budock Water TR11 5ED
☎ 01326 250277 01326 250509
e-mail: reception@penmorvah.co.uk
***Dir:*** *take A39 to Hillhead roundabout take 2nd exit. At Falmouth Football Club turn right, through Budock, hotel opposite Penjerrick Gardens*

This extended Victorian manor house is peacefully set in six acres of private woodland and gardens. Activity holidays and leisure breaks are available, including painters' workshop, and garden and golfing holidays. Most of the rooms are located in a modern wing. In the candlelit restaurant an interesting fixed-price menu is offered.
**ROOMS:** 27 en suite (1 fmly) No smoking in all bedrooms s fr £55; d £77.50-£120 (incl. bkfst) * **LB** **FACILITIES:** Croquet lawn Pool table ch fac Xmas **CONF:** Thtr 250 Class 100 Board 56 Del from £93.75 * **PARKING:** 150 **NOTES:** No smoking in restaurant
**CARDS:**

### ★★★61% Gyllyngdune Manor

Melvill Rd TR11 4AR
☎ 01326 312978 01326 211881
***Dir:*** *from A39 follow signs for beaches and docks. Hotel 200yds beyond Pavilion and Beer Garden on right*

This imposing Georgian manor house, situated above the town in its own mature grounds, has fine views of Falmouth Bay. The hotel has friendly staff and comfortable public areas in addition to an indoor swimming pool, games room and gymnasium. Bedrooms include ground floor, four-poster, and family options.
**ROOMS:** 30 en suite (3 fmly) s £46-£50 (incl. bkfst) * **LB** **FACILITIES:** Indoor swimming (H) Sauna Solarium Gym Table tennis entertainment ch fac Xmas **PARKING:** 27 **NOTES:** No smoking in restaurant Closed 27 Dec-11 Jan **CARDS:**

### ★★★60% St Michaels of Falmouth

REGAL

Gyllyngvase Beach, Seafront TR11 4NB
☎ 01326 312707 01326 211772
***Dir:*** *follow the A39 into Falmouth, at 2nd rdbt, take Melville Rd, then take the 3rd right turn and right again into Stracey Rd*

St Michaels is in a great location overlooking the sea and small

*continued*

bay. Spacious public areas include a lounge with super views, landscaped gardens and a leisure centre. Bedrooms vary in size and style; some have sea views.
**ROOMS:** 57 en suite 8 annexe en suite (2 fmly) No smoking in 4 bedrooms s £33-£46; d £66-£92 (incl. bkfst) * **LB** **FACILITIES:** STV Indoor swimming (H) Sauna Solarium Gym Jacuzzi Concessionary golf rates Xmas **CONF:** Thtr 200 Class 150 Board 120 Del from £70 * **PARKING:** 30 **NOTES:** No dogs (ex guide dogs) No smoking in restaurant Civ Wed 100 **CARDS:**

★★70% **Crill Manor**
Maen Valley, Budock Water TR11 5BL
☎ 01326 211880 ▤ 01326 211229
e-mail: info@crillmanor.com
***Dir:*** *2.5m W on unclass rd*
This delightful family-run hotel lies in an idyllic spot two miles from Falmouth, set in attractive gardens, surrounded by an area of outstanding natural beauty. Bedrooms are stylishly decorated, well-equipped with modern facilities, and two are located in an adjoining building. The open-plan lounge and bar look out over the swimming pool and gardens.
**ROOMS:** 12 en suite 2 annexe en suite No smoking in all bedrooms s £29-£39; d £58-£78 (incl. bkfst) * **LB** **FACILITIES:** Xmas **PARKING:** 14 **NOTES:** No dogs No children 10yrs No smoking in restaurant **CARDS:**

★★66% **Broadmead**
66-68 Kimberley Park Rd TR11 2DD
☎ 01326 315704 & 318036 ▤ 01326 311048
e-mail: Broadmeadhotel@aol.com

THE CIRCLE
Selected Individual Hotels
GREAT BRITAIN

***Dir:*** *turn off A39 at traffic lights by Riders Garage, towards town centre, hotel 150yds on left*
Within easy walking distance of the town centre, this informal, family-run hotel overlooks the attractive Kimberley Park. Ideally suited for both business and leisure guests, the bedrooms are well-appointed. A choice of comfortable lounges is available, together with a small bar and smart dining room where a fixed price menu is offered.
**ROOMS:** 12 rms (11 en suite) (1 fmly) s £23-£30; d £56-£64 (incl. bkfst) * **LB** **PARKING:** 8 **NOTES:** No dogs No smoking in restaurant Closed 20 Dec-3 Jan **CARDS:**

★★66% **Park Grove**
Kimberley Park Rd TR11 2DD
☎ 01326 313276 ▤ 01326 211926
e-mail: reception@parkgrovehotel.com
***Dir:*** *turn off A39 at traffic lights by Riders Garage, towards harbour. Hotel is 400yds on left opposite the park*
A long established family-run hotel, conveniently situated opposite Kimberley Gardens within walking distance of Falmouth town centre. Relaxed, friendly service is provided by a small team of loyal staff. Bedrooms are neat and comfortably furnished with many modern facilities. Each evening a four-course meal is served in the dining room, next to the bar.
**ROOMS:** 17 en suite (6 fmly) s £26-£36; d £52-£62 (incl. bkfst) * **LB** **PARKING:** 25 **NOTES:** No smoking in restaurant **CARDS:**

★★63% **Maderia Hotel**
Cliff Rd TR11 4NY
☎ 01326 313531 ▤ 01326 319143

Leisureplex

Boasting superb views across Falmouth Bay, this popular hotel enjoys a prime position on the seafront, fronted by well-tended gardens. Extensive sun lounges are popular haunts in which to enjoy the views, whilst additional facilities include an oak panelled cocktail bar. Many of the bedrooms have sea views, some also with balconies.
**ROOMS:** 50 en suite (8 fmly) s £28-£37; d £48-£66 (incl. bkfst) * **LB** **FACILITIES:** entertainment Xmas **SERVICES:** Lift **PARKING:** 11 **NOTES:** No dogs (ex guide dogs) No smoking in restaurant Closed Dec-Feb RS Nov/Mar (open Mon-Thu nights only) **CARDS:**

★★63% **Rosslyn**
110 Kimberley Park Rd TR11 2JJ
☎ 01326 312699 ▤ 01326 312699
On the northern edge of Falmouth, this family-run hotel is popular with tour groups. Public areas are spacious and comfortable with a choice of lounges, one specifically for non-smokers. The attractive gardens at the rear of the property are well-tended and peaceful. Bedrooms vary in size and are freshly decorated.
**ROOMS:** 27 rms (21 en suite) (2 fmly) No smoking in all bedrooms **FACILITIES:** Putting green Table tennis Darts Pool table **CONF:** Class 60 **PARKING:** 10 **NOTES:** No children No smoking in restaurant RS 24 Dec-28 Feb **CARDS:**

★★62% **Membly Hall**
Sea Front, Cliff Rd TR11 4NT
☎ 01326 312869 & 311115 ▤ 01326 211751
e-mail: memblyhallhotel@netscapeonline.co.uk
***Dir:*** *from A30 turn onto A3076 for Truro then follow A39 to Falmouth. At Falmouth follow signs for seafront and beaches. Hotel located middle of seafront*

This holiday hotel lies on the seafront with superb views over Falmouth Bay. Bedrooms are decorated with pretty wallpapers and are well-equipped. Several rooms are located at ground-floor level and many are suitable for families. Public areas are spacious and live entertainment is held regularly.
**ROOMS:** 37 en suite (3 fmly) s £24-£40; d £48-£80 (incl. bkfst) * **LB** **FACILITIES:** STV Putting green Indoor short bowls Table tennis P/table entertainment **CONF:** Thtr 150 Class 130 Board 60 Del from £50 * **SERVICES:** Lift **PARKING:** 30 **NOTES:** No smoking in restaurant Closed Xmas week RS Dec-Feb

## FAREHAM, Hampshire — Map 04 SU50

★★★★73% ❀ **Solent**
Rookery Av, Whiteley PO15 7AJ
☎ 01489 880000 ▤ 01489 880007
e-mail: solent@shireinns.co.uk

SHIRE INNS

***Dir:*** *on Solent Business Park just off junct 9 on M27*
Although close to the M27, this smart, purpose-built hotel enjoys a peaceful location. Bedrooms are well appointed and public areas include a good range of meeting and leisure facilities. There is a pub in the grounds which serves real ale and home-cooked food,

*continued on p230*

FAREHAM, continued

and the hotel also has a more formal restaurant, Woodlands. Staff are friendly and helpful.
**ROOMS:** 111 en suite (9 fmly) No smoking in 30 bedrooms s fr £125; d fr £145 (incl. bkfst) * **LB** **FACILITIES:** STV Indoor swimming (H) Tennis (hard) Squash Sauna Solarium Gym Jacuzzi Steam room Childrens splash pool Xmas **CONF:** Thtr 250 Class 120 Board 80 Del £160 * **SERVICES:** Lift **PARKING:** 200 **NOTES:** Civ Wed 250
**CARDS:**

### ★★★68% Posthouse Fareham

Posthouse

Cartwright Dr, Titchfield PO15 5RJ
☎ 0870 400 9028 📠 01329 844666
***Dir:*** *exit M27 at junct 9 and follow signs for A27. Continue across Segensworth roundabout following road for 1.5m, turn left at next roundabout*
This well established Posthouse continues to attract both business and leisure markets. Bedrooms are modern and well-equipped, including a mini-bar. Spacious public areas include several conference rooms, newly refurbished leisure centre with pool and large restaurant.
**ROOMS:** 125 en suite (25 fmly) No smoking in 78 bedrooms s £79-£89; d £79-£89 * **LB** **FACILITIES:** Indoor swimming (H) Sauna Solarium Gym Jacuzzi Childrens play area Xmas **CONF:** Thtr 160 Class 80 Board 50 Del from £130 * **PARKING:** 130 **NOTES:** No smoking in restaurant
**CARDS:**

### ★★★64% ◎ Lysses House

51 High St PO16 7BQ
☎ 01329 822622 📠 01329 822762
e-mail: lysses@lysses.co.uk
***Dir:*** *take M27 junct 11 and stay in left hand lane till rdbt, take third exit in to East St and follow into High St. Hotel is at top on right*
Attractive Georgian hotel in a quiet location on the edge of the town centre. Rooms are spacious and well-equipped. There are conference facilities and a lounge bar serving a range of snacks. The Richmond Restaurant has an interesting selection of dishes on set and carte menus.
**ROOMS:** 21 en suite s £68; d £85 (incl. bkfst) * **CONF:** Thtr 95 Class 42 Board 28 Del from £100 * **SERVICES:** Lift **PARKING:** 30 **NOTES:** No dogs (ex guide dogs) No smoking in restaurant Closed 25 Dec-1 Jan RS 24 Dec Civ Wed 95
**CARDS:**

## FARINGDON, Oxfordshire

Map 04 SU29

### ★★★73% ◎ Sudbury House Hotel & Conference Centre

Best Western

London St SN7 8AA
☎ 01367 241272 📠 01367 242346
e-mail: sudburyhouse@cix.co.uk
***Dir:*** *off A420, signposted Folly Hill*
Sudbury House lies on the edge of the Cotswolds between Oxford and Swindon. Bedrooms are attractive, decorated in warm colour schemes, spacious and well-equipped. Dining options include the restaurant, bar and a comprehensive room service menu.

*continued*

Conference facilities, a small fitness room and private dining rooms are also available.

**ROOMS:** 49 en suite (2 fmly) No smoking in 22 bedrooms s £65-£85; d £75-£95 (incl. bkfst) * **LB** **FACILITIES:** STV Gym Croquet lawn Putting green Pitch & Putt Badminton Xmas **CONF:** Thtr 90 Class 90 Board 40 Del from £126 * **SERVICES:** Lift **PARKING:** 100 **NOTES:** No smoking in restaurant Civ Wed 130
**CARDS:**

*See advert on opposite page*

### ★★62% Faringdon

1 Market Place SN7 7HL
☎ 01367 240536 📠 01367 243250
***Dir:*** *M4 junct 15 A419 take A420 signposted to Oxford for 10m follow signs for Faringdon, hotel next to All Saints Church*
Opposite the 12th Century parish church, Faringdon Hotel occupies a lovely spot in the Market Place of this small town. The hotel itself has much history and it is believed that it stands on what was the site of the Royal Palace of Alfred the Great. Bedrooms offer good facilities and are spacious, with some four-poster rooms available. Ideal for business or pleasure guests can relax after a hard day and enjoy the hotel bar and dinner in the Surin Thai Restaurant.
**ROOMS:** 15 en suite 5 annexe en suite (3 fmly) s £60-£65; d £70-£75 (incl. bkfst) * **LB** **CONF:** Thtr 30 Class 15 Board 20
**CARDS:**

## FARNBOROUGH, Hampshire

Map 04 SU85

### ★★★68% Posthouse Farnborough

Posthouse

Lynchford Rd GU14 6AZ
☎ 0870 400 9029 📠 01252 377210
***Dir:*** *from M3 junct 4, follow A325 for Farnborough. Take A325 through Farnborough town centre towards Aldershot. Hotel on the left at The Queen's rdbt*
Combining a mixture of modern and traditional styles, this hotel is well-located for local railway and motorway links. Modern bedrooms are tastefully decorated and equipped with a useful range of extras. The hotel has a number of function rooms and a well-appointed health club.
**ROOMS:** 143 en suite (39 fmly) No smoking in 80 bedrooms d £129-£139 * **FACILITIES:** Indoor swimming (H) Sauna Solarium Gym Jacuzzi Health & fitness centre **CONF:** Thtr 180 Class 80 Board 80 Del from £155 * **PARKING:** 175 **CARDS:**

### ★★★63% *Falcon*

68 Farnborough Rd GU14 6TH
☎ 01252 545378 📠 01252 522539
***Dir:*** *on A325 opposite Aerospace Centre Airfield*
Conveniently located for local business centres, the motorway network and mainline railway links, the hotel is popular with business travellers. Modern bedrooms are practically furnished

*continued*

and equipped with a useful range of extras. Public rooms include the conservatory restaurant and the bar and lounge which have a pleasant club-style decor.

**ROOMS:** 30 en suite (1 fmly) **FACILITIES:** STV **CONF:** Thtr 25 Class 10 Board 16 Del from £85.50 * **PARKING:** 30 **NOTES:** No dogs (ex guide dogs) RS Xmas & New Year **CARDS:**

FARNHAM, Surrey — Map 04 SU84

see also Churt

★★★72% **Bishop's Table**

27 West St GU9 7DR

☎ 01252 710222 01252 733494

e-mail: welcome@bishopstable.com

***Dir:*** *take the A331 (from M3 J4), or A31 (from A3) and follow signs for town centre, hotel is located next to the library*

A family run friendly Georgian townhouse hotel in the centre of town. Bedrooms, some of which occupy a restored coach house,

*continued on p232*

FARNHAM, continued

are all individual in style and tastefully appointed. Public areas include a cosy bar and an elegant restaurant offering an interesting range of carefully prepared dishes. Service is both friendly and attentive.

**ROOMS:** 9 en suite 8 annexe en suite No smoking in 1 bedroom s £105-£115; d £115-£165 (incl. bkfst) * **LB** **FACILITIES:** free use of nearby gym **CONF:** Thtr 26 Class 30 Board 15 Del from £165 * **NOTES:** No dogs (ex guide dogs) No children 16yrs No smoking in restaurant Closed 25 Dec-3 Jan RS Closed for lunch Mon **CARDS:**

*See advert on page 231*

### ★★★65% The Bush

The Borough GU9 7NN
☎ 0870 400 8225 01252 733530
e-mail: heritagehotels_farnham.bush@forte-hotels.com
***Dir:*** *join A31 Farnham follow signs for town centre. At crossroads left and hotel on the right*

Mentioned in Thackeray's novel, 'The Virginians', this attractive coaching inn dates back to the 17th century. Bedrooms are split between the main building and the more modern extension, all are traditionally furnished and decorated offering a range of modern facilities. Public rooms include the grand room, where the original frescoes have been preserved, and the oak-beamed Coachman's Bar.

**ROOMS:** 83 en suite No smoking in 48 bedrooms s £150; d £150-£190 * **LB** **FACILITIES:** Croquet lawn Xmas **CONF:** Thtr 60 Class 30 Board 30 Del from £140 * **PARKING:** 60 **NOTES:** No smoking in restaurant Civ Wed 90 **CARDS:**

### ★★★59% Farnham House

Alton Rd GU10 5ER
☎ 01252 716908 01252 722583
e-mail: mail@farnhamhousehotel.com
***Dir:*** *1m from town, off A31 Alton road*

Popular for conferences and weddings, Farnham House is surrounded by five acres of grounds. The Victorian architecture is part Tudor, part baronial in style, and features an oak-panelled bar with an inglenook fireplace. Comfortable, well-appointed bedrooms enjoy views over tranquil countryside.

**ROOMS:** 25 en suite (1 fmly) No smoking in 5 bedrooms s £75-£80; d £80 * **LB** **FACILITIES:** STV Outdoor swimming (H) Tennis (hard) **CONF:** Thtr 65 Class 15 Board 24 Del from £130 * **PARKING:** 75 **NOTES:** No dogs (ex guide dogs) RS 25 & 26 Dec Civ Wed 70 **CARDS:**

## FAVERSHAM, Kent — Map 05 TR06

### *Travelodge*

Thanet Way ME8 9EL
☎ 01227 770980
***Dir:*** *from junc 7 M2, take A299*

Travelodge

Travelodge offers good quality, good value, modern accommodation. Ideal for families, the spacious, en suite bedrooms include remote-control TV, tea and coffee-making facilities, luxury beds and free morning newspaper. Meals can be taken at the nearby family restaurant. For further details and the Travelodge phone number, consult the Hotel Groups page.

**ROOMS:** 40 en suite

### *Travelodge*

A 299, Thanet Way ME8 9EL
☎ 01227 770980

Travelodge

Travelodge offers good quality, good value, modern accommodation. Ideal for families, the spacious, en suite bedrooms include remote-control TV, tea and coffee-making facilities, luxury beds and free morning newspaper. Meals can be taken at the nearby family restaurant. For further details and the Travelodge phone number, consult the Hotel Groups page.

## FEERING, Essex — Map 05 TL82

### *Travelodge*

A12 London Rd Northbound CO5 9EL
☎ 08700 850950

Travelodge

Travelodge offers good quality, good value, modern accommodation. Ideal for families, the spacious, en suite bedrooms include remote-control TV, tea and coffee-making facilities, luxury beds and free morning newspaper. Meals can be taken at the nearby family restaurant. For further details and the Travelodge phone number, consult the Hotel Groups page.

**ROOMS:** 39 en suite

## FELIXSTOWE, Suffolk — Map 05 TM33

### ★★★68% Orwell

Hamilton Rd IP11 7DX
☎ 01394 285511 01394 670687
e-mail: office@orwellhotel.co.uk
***Dir:*** *approaching on A14, straight across Dock rdbt & next rdbt, 4th exit off third rdbt into Peartrice Avenue, proceed to end of road. Hotel on other side of rdbt*

Situated close to the town centre, this imposing Victorian hotel dates back to 1898. The spacious public areas are traditionally decorated and have a wealth of charm and elegance. The well-equipped, smartly decorated bedrooms include several large 'Superior' rooms which are well worth booking. Guests have a choice of two bars, and for meals, an informal buttery or the spacious restaurant.

**ROOMS:** 58 en suite (8 fmly) s fr £60; d fr £70 * **LB** **FACILITIES:** STV entertainment Xmas **CONF:** Thtr 200 Class 100 Board 60 Del from £90 * **SERVICES:** Lift **PARKING:** 70 **NOTES:** No dogs (ex guide dogs) No smoking in restaurant **CARDS:**

### ★★64% Marlborough

Sea Front IP11 2BJ
☎ 01394 285621 01394 670724
e-mail: hsm@marlborough-hotel-felix.com
***Dir:*** *from A14 follow for Docks. Go straight on at Dock rdbt, over railway crossing & traffic lights. Turn left at 'T' junc, Hotel 400mtrs on left*

Traditional resort hotel situated on the seafront within easy walking distance of the pier leisure complex. Public areas include the smart Rattan Restaurant, Flying Boat Bar and L'Aperitif lounge. Bedrooms are pleasantly decorated and equipped with a good range of useful extras, many of the rooms have lovely sea views.

**ROOMS:** 49 en suite No smoking in 3 bedrooms s £37-£47; d £52-£72 (incl. bkfst) * **LB** **FACILITIES:** STV Pool table Xmas **CONF:** Thtr 80 Class 60 Board 40 Del from £64 * **SERVICES:** Lift **PARKING:** 16 **NOTES:** No dogs (ex guide dogs) No smoking in restaurant **CARDS:**

## ENNY BENTLEY, Derbyshire Map 07 SK14

**★66% The Bentley Brook Inn & Fenny's Restaurant**
)E6 1LF
☎ 01335 350278 📠 01335 350422
-mail: all@bentleybrookinn.co.uk
*Dir: 2m north of Asbourne at junct A515 & B5056*
his busy, family-run country inn lies within the Peak District Jational Park. It is a charming half-timbered building with an ttractive terrace and sweeping lawns. Trout fishing is available. A well-appointed restaurant dominates the ground floor, and the haracter bar is open throughout the day for informal dining. edrooms, which vary in styles and sizes, are well-equipped. An n-site brewery, Leatherbritches, supplies award-winning real ales o the bar.
**ROOMS:** 9 rms (6 en suite) 1 annexe en suite (1 fmly) No smoking in 1 edroom s £35-£45; d £50-£65 (incl. bkfst) * **LB** **FACILITIES:** Fishing oules Skittles,Brewery tour Xmas **CONF:** Class 28 Board 18 Del £65 * **PARKING:** 60 **NOTES:** No smoking in restaurant
**CARDS:**

## ENSTANTON, Cambridgeshire Map 04 TL36

**Travelodge**
PE18 9JF
☎ 01954 230919 📠 01954 230919
*Dir: 4m SE of Huntingdon, on A14 eastbound*
Travelodge

Travelodge offers good quality, good value, modern accommodation. Ideal for families, the spacious, en suite bedrooms include remote-control TV, tea and coffee-making facilities, luxury beds and free morning newspaper. Meals can be taken at the nearby family restaurant. For further details and the Travelodge phone number, consult the Hotel Groups page.

**ROOMS:** 40 en suite

## FERNDOWN, Dorset Map 04 SU00

**★★★★70% Dormy**
New Rd BH22 8ES
☎ 01202 872121 📠 01202 895388
e-mail: devere.dormy@airtime.co.uk
*Dir: off A347 from Bournemouth*
De Vere Hotels

Set in attractive grounds, this popular, well-established hotel offers several dining options, including Hennessys, the new fine dining restaurant, providing a high standard of cuisine and service. Bedrooms are located both in the main building and in several

continued

nearby cottage wings. Public rooms feature traditional wood panelling and open fires.
**ROOMS:** 115 en suite (15 fmly) No smoking in 28 bedrooms s £110-£220; d £145-£255 (incl. bkfst) * **LB** **FACILITIES:** Spa STV Indoor swimming (H) Tennis (hard) Squash Snooker Sauna Solarium Gym Putting green Jacuzzi Beauty salon,Toning tables,dance classes entertainment ch fac Xmas **CONF:** Thtr 250 Class 150 Board 60 **SERVICES:** Lift **PARKING:** 220 **NOTES:** No smoking in restaurant Civ Wed **CARDS:**

## FERRYBRIDGE SERVICE AREA, West Yorkshire Map 08 SE42

**Travelodge**
WF11 0AF
☎ 01977 672767
*Dir: A1/M62 jnct 33*
Travelodge

Travelodge offers good quality, good value, modern accommodation. Ideal for families, the spacious, en suite bedrooms include remote-control TV, tea and coffee-making facilities, luxury beds and free morning newspaper. Meals can be taken at the nearby family restaurant. For further details and the Travelodge phone number, consult the Hotel Groups page.

**ROOMS:** 36 en suite

## FILEY, North Yorkshire Map 08 TA18

**★★74% Downcliffe House Hotel**
6 The Beach YO14 9LA
☎ 01723 513310 📠 01723 513773
e-mail: paulmanners@onyxnet.co.uk
*Dir: leave A165 & join A1039 into centre of Filey, continue through centre along Cargate Hill & turn right. Hotel is approx 200yds along sea front*
The Downcliffe House Hotel is set right on the sea front. A friendly welcome awaits you at this hotel, which has inviting public areas including an attractive restaurant serving an excellent range of freshly prepared meals, and a bar. The hotel is furnished to a very high standard, and you can be sure that bedrooms are smart and suitably well-equipped.
**ROOMS:** 11 en suite (2 fmly) s £38-£77; d £76-£120 (incl. bkfst) * **LB** **PARKING:** 4 **NOTES:** No smoking in restaurant Closed mid Dec-Jan
**CARDS:**

## FIR TREE, Co Durham Map 12 NZ13

**★★★64% Helme Park Hall Hotel**
DL13 4NW
☎ 01388 730970 📠 01388 731799
*Dir: 1m N of roundabout at A689/A68 intersection between Darlington and Corbridge*
Dating back to the 13th century, this very friendly family-owned hotel commands superb panoramic views up the Wear Valley. The comfortable lounge bar is extremely popular for its comprehensive selection of bar meals, and the restaurant offers both set and a la carte menus. The bedrooms are modern in style and vary in size.
**ROOMS:** 13 en suite (1 fmly) s £40-£45; d £65-£75 * **LB** **FACILITIES:** Xmas **CONF:** Thtr 200 Class 160 Board 140 Del from £40 * **PARKING:** 70 **NOTES:** No smoking in restaurant Civ Wed 140
**CARDS:**

## FIVE OAKS, West Sussex
Map 04 TQ02

### ⌂ *Travelodge*
Travelodge

Staines St RH14 9AE
☎ 01403 782711 🖷 01403 782711
***Dir:*** *on A29, northbound, 1m N of Billingshurst*
Travelodge offers good quality, good value, modern accommodation. Ideal for families, the spacious, en suite bedrooms include remote-control TV, tea and coffee-making facilities, luxury beds and free morning newspaper. Meals can be taken at the nearby family restaurant. For further details and the Travelodge phone number, consult the Hotel Groups page.

**ROOMS:** 26 en suite

F

## FLADBURY, Worcestershire
Map 03 SO94

### ★★66% *The Chequers Inn*
Chequers Ln WR10 2PZ
☎ 01386 860276 & 860527 🖷 01386 861286
***Dir:*** *off A4538 between Evesham & Pershore. Once in village pass the church, right at War Memorial into Chequers Lane*
This charming old inn, which dates from the 14th century, stands in the centre of this rural village. Features include a bar with beamed ceiling and real open fires. A wide selection of meals is available in the traditionally furnished restaurant and quaint bar. The bedrooms are equipped with modern facilities.
**ROOMS:** 8 en suite (2 fmly) **FACILITIES:** Fishing **PARKING:** 24
**CARDS:**

## FLAMBOROUGH, East Riding of Yorkshire
Map 08 TA26

### ★★70% North Star
North Marine Dr YO15 1BL
☎ 01262 850379
***Dir:*** *in town follow signs for 'North Landing'. Hotel 100yds from the sea*
Standing close to the North Landing of Flamborough Head, this family-run hotel overlooks delightful countryside. The hotel has been tastefully furnished and provides excellent bedrooms together with a busy bar. A good range of well produced food is available in both the bar and the spacious dining room.
**ROOMS:** 7 en suite s fr £40; d £60-£70 (incl. bkfst) * **LB**
**PARKING:** 30 **NOTES:** No dogs (ex guide dogs) No smoking in restaurant Closed Xmas **CARDS:**

### ★★65% Flaneburg
North Marine Rd YO15 1LF
☎ 01262 850284 🖷 01262 850284
e-mail: stay@flaneburghotel.co.uk
***Dir:*** *from the centre of Flamborough, follow the signs for hotel & North Landing. The hotel is situated on the very edge of the village on the left*
This friendly good-value hotel, on the North Landing of Flamborough Head, is popular with bird watchers and golfers. The traditional-style bedrooms are pleasantly furnished and the public rooms are comfortable and cosy. A good range of well-prepared dishes is provided in the bar and dining room. Hotel service is friendly and attentive.
**ROOMS:** 14 en suite (3 fmly) No smoking in 5 bedrooms s fr £37; d fr £59 (incl. bkfst) * **LB** **FACILITIES:** Sauna Gym Jacuzzi Xmas **CONF:** Thtr 30 Class 30 Board 20 **PARKING:** 50 **NOTES:** No smoking in restaurant Closed X mas **CARDS:**

Early start? Hotels at all star levels should provide in-room alarm clocks and/or alarm calls.

## FLEET, Hampshire
Map 04 SU8

### ★★★63% Lismoyne
Church Rd GU51 5NE
☎ 01252 628555 🖷 01252 811761
***Dir:*** *approach town on B3013, cross over railway bridge and continue to town centre. Pass through traffic lights & take fourth right. Hotel 0.25m on le*

In its own extensive grounds this attractive hotel is close to the town centre. Public rooms include a comfortable lounge and pleasant bar with a conservatory overlooking the garden. Accommodation is divided between the bedrooms in the original building and those in the more modern extension, all are well-equipped and comfortable.
**ROOMS:** 44 en suite (3 fmly) No smoking in 13 bedrooms **CONF:** Thtr 150 Class 105 Board 50 Del from £130 * **PARKING:** 120 **NOTES:** No smoking in restaurant Civ Wed 200
**CARDS:**

## FLEET MOTORWAY SERVICE AREA (M3), Hampshire
Map 04 SU7

### ⌂ Days Inn
DAYS INN

Fleet Services RG27 8BN
☎ 01252 815587 🖷 01252 815587
e-mail: Fleet.hotel@welcomebreak.co.uk
***Dir:*** *Welcome Break Fleet Motorway Service area between junct 4a & 5 southbound on the M3*
This modern building offers accommodation in smart, spacious and well-equipped bedrooms, suitable for families and business travellers, and all with en suite bathrooms. Continental breakfast i available and other refreshments may be taken at the nearby family restaurant. For further details and the Days Inn phone number, consult the Hotel Groups page.
**ROOMS:** 58 en suite s fr £55; d fr £55 * **CONF:** Thtr 10

## FLITWICK, Bedfordshire
Map 04 TL0

### ★★★81% ⊛⊛ Menzies Flitwick Manor
MENZIES HOTELS

Church Rd MK45 1AE
☎ 0870 6003013 🖷 01332 511144
e-mail: info@menzies-hotels.co.uk
***Dir:*** *on A5120, 2m from M1 exit 12 towards Ampthill*
Although close to the M1 this delightful Georgian house is peacefully set in extensive parkland and gardens. Individually decorated bedrooms are extremely comfortable and equipped with a host of useful extras. Guests are warmly welcomed and we cared for and meals in the restaurant are a highlight of any stay.
**ROOMS:** 17 en suite s £120; d £145 * **LB** **FACILITIES:** Tennis (hard) Croquet lawn Putting green Xmas **CONF:** Thtr 40 Class 30 Board 24 Del from £215 * **PARKING:** 50 **NOTES:** No smoking in restaurant Civ Wed 50 **CARDS:**

## FLORE, Northamptonshire — Map 04 SP66

### ★★★72% Courtyard by Marriott Daventry

High St NN7 4LP
☎ 01327 349022 🖷 01327 349017
**Dir:** *from M1 junct 16, follow A45 towards Daventry. Hotel 1m on right between Upper Heyford and Flore*

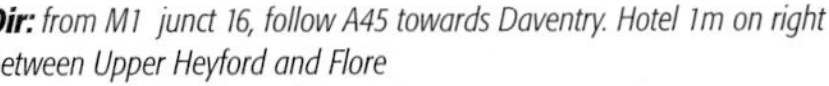

COURTYARD
Marriott

Just off the M1 motorway in rural surroundings, this modern hotel is particularly suited to the business guest. Bedrooms provide smart decor, together with thoughtful design of useful workspaces. Public rooms are bright though compact. The friendly team of staff provide a warm welcome and helpful service.
**ROOMS:** 53 en suite (7 fmly) No smoking in 19 bedrooms d £75-£95 * LB **FACILITIES:** STV Gym Xmas **CONF:** Thtr 80 Class 40 Board 48 Del from £95 * **PARKING:** 120 **NOTES:** No dogs (ex guide dogs) Civ Wed 100 **CARDS:**

## FOLKESTONE, Kent — Map 05 TR23

### ★★★70% Clifton

The Leas CT20 2EB
☎ 01303 851231 🖷 01303 851231
e-mail: reservations@thecliftonhotel.com
**Dir:** *from M20 junct 13, 0.25m W of town centre on A259*

This privately owned Victorian-style hotel occupies a prime location with far reaching views across the English Channel. The bedrooms are all comfortable and most have views of the sea. The public areas include a comfortable, traditionally furnished lounge, a popular bar with a good range of beers and several well-appointed conference rooms.
**ROOMS:** 80 en suite (5 fmly) No smoking in 13 bedrooms s £59; d £79 (incl. bkfst) * **LB** **FACILITIES:** STV Solarium Games room ch fac Xmas **CONF:** Thtr 80 Class 36 Board 32 Del from £97.50 * **SERVICES:** Lift **CARDS:**

*See advert on this page*

### ★★80% 🏵🏵🏵 Sandgate Hotel et Restaurant La Terrasse

The Esplanade, Sandgate CT20 3DY
☎ 01303 220444 🖷 01303 220496
**Dir:** *exit M20 junct 12 (Cheriton/Tunnel) towards Sandgate, go through Sandgate on A249 towards Hythe, hotel on right facing sea*
Elegant terrace property overlooking the beach and sea beyond, yet with a French country house feel. The comfortable bedrooms, some with balconies are attractively decorated in pastel shades and tastefully furnished. The restaurant is the focal point and the tiered terrace is perfect for breakfast, tea and pre-dinner drinks.
**ROOMS:** 14 en suite s £45-£71; d £58-£76 (incl. bkfst) * **LB** **FACILITIES:** Xmas **SERVICES:** Lift **PARKING:** 4 **NOTES:** No dogs (ex guide dogs) No smoking in restaurant Closed Jan, 2nd wk Oct, Sun evenings **CARDS:**

## FONTWELL, West Sussex — Map 04 SU90

### ⌂ *Travelodge*

Travelodge

BN18 0SB
☎ 01243 543973 🖷 01243 543973
**Dir:** *on A27/A29 roundabout*
Travelodge offers good quality, good value, modern accommodation. Ideal for families, the spacious, en suite bedrooms include remote-control TV, tea and coffee-making facilities, luxury beds and free morning newspaper. Meals can be taken at the nearby family restaurant. For further details and the Travelodge phone number, consult the Hotel Groups page.

**ROOMS:** 63 en suite

## FORDINGBRIDGE, Hampshire Map 04 SU11

**★★72% ❀ Ashburn Hotel & Restaurant**
Station Rd SP6 1JP
☎ 01425 652060 📠 01425 652150
e-mail: ashburn@mistral.co.uk
***Dir:*** *from Fordingbridge High St follow road signposted Damerham. Pass police and fire station and hotel is 400yds on left-hand side*

MINOTEL Great Britain

In a slightly elevated position, on the edge of the village, this family-run hotel enjoys distant views of the New Forest. The comfortable, well-equipped bedrooms include one ground floor suite. Imaginative, carefully cooked meals are served in the attractive dining room. In addition to the bar, a cosy lounge is provided.

**ROOMS:** 20 en suite (3 fmly) No smoking in 10 bedrooms s £39.50-£49.50; d £76-£88 (incl. bkfst) * **LB** **FACILITIES:** Outdoor swimming (H) ch fac Xmas **CONF:** Thtr 150 Class 80 Board 50 Del from £63 * **PARKING:** 60 **NOTES:** No smoking in restaurant Civ Wed 180 **CARDS:**

## FOREST ROW, East Sussex Map 05 TQ43

**Premier Collection**

**★★★★ ❀❀ Ashdown Park Hotel and Country Club**
Wych Cross RH18 5JR
☎ 01342 824988 📠 01342 826206
e-mail: reservations@ashdownpark.com
***Dir:*** *A264 to East Grinstead, then A22 to Eastbourne, 2m S of Forest Row at Wych Cross, traffic lights turn left to Hartfield, hotel on right 0.75 miles down road*

SLH Small Luxury Hotels of the World

An impressive country house hotel in a secluded forest setting, with 165 acres of landscaped Sussex countryside to explore. The traditionally styled bedrooms offer superior comfort. A recent addition is twelve newly built rooms with views over the golf course. Features include a chapel converted into a conference room, a leisure club and a well-established restaurant.

**ROOMS:** 107 en suite s fr £125; d fr £159 (incl. bkfst) * **LB**
**FACILITIES:** Spa STV Indoor swimming (H) Golf 18 Tennis (hard) Snooker Sauna Solarium Gym Croquet lawn Putting green Jacuzzi Beauty/Hair salon, Aerobics, Treatment room Xmas **CONF:** Thtr 150 Class 60 Board 60 Del from £215 * **SERVICES:** Lift **PARKING:** 200 **NOTES:** No dogs (ex guide dogs) No smoking in restaurant Civ Wed 140 **CARDS:**

Packed in a hurry? Ironing facilities should be available at all star levels, either in rooms or on request.

## FORMBY, Merseyside Map 07 SD30

**★★★62% Tree Tops**
Southport Old Rd L37 0AB
☎ 01704 572430 📠 01704 572430
***Dir:*** *off A565 Southport to Liverpool road*

This privately owned hotel, set in five acres of wooded grounds, offers chalet-style accommodation, a pleasant lounge bar and an outdoor swimming pool. Bedrooms are well-equipped and some larger rooms are particularly suitable for families. Carefully prepared meals are served in the restaurant with conservatory extension.

**ROOMS:** 11 en suite (2 fmly) s fr £53; d fr £90 (incl. bkfst) * **LB** **FACILITIES:** Outdoor swimming (H) **CONF:** Thtr 200 Class 80 Board 40 **PARKING:** 100 **NOTES:** No dogs No smoking in restaurant Civ Wed 60 **CARDS:**

*See advert under SOUTHPORT*

## FORTON MOTORWAY SERVICE AREA (M6), Lancashire Map 07 SD55

**⌂ *Travelodge***
White Carr Ln, Bay Horse LA2 9DU
☎ 01524 792227 📠 01524 791703
***Dir:*** *between juncts 32 & 33 M6*

Travelodge

Travelodge offers good quality, good value, modern accommodation. Ideal for families, the spacious, en suite bedrooms include remote-control TV, tea and coffee-making facilities, luxury beds and free morning newspaper. Meals can be taken at the nearby family restaurant. For further details and the Travelodge phone number, consult the Hotel Groups page.

**ROOMS:** 53 en suite

## FOSSEBRIDGE, Gloucestershire Map 04 SP01

**★★68% ❀ Fossebridge Inn**
GL54 3JS
☎ 01285 720721 📠 01285 720793
e-mail: fossebridgeinn@compuserve.com
***Dir:*** *from M4 junct 15 take A419 towards Cirencester, then take A429 towards Stow. Hotel approx 7m on left.*

The Bridge Bar dates from the 15th century, and has particular character to offer with old beams, Yorkstone floors and an inglenook fireplace. There are good bar meals, and the restaurant offers imaginative cooking. Bedrooms are divided between the main inn and a converted stable block.

**ROOMS:** 11 en suite (1 fmly) No smoking in all bedrooms s fr £55; d fr £80 (incl. bkfst) * **LB** **FACILITIES:** Fishing Xmas **CONF:** Thtr 60 Class 30 Board 30 **PARKING:** 60 **NOTES:** No smoking in restaurant RS 24-26 Dec Civ Wed 75 **CARDS:**

## FOUR MARKS, Hampshire Map 04 SU63

**⌂ *Travelodge***
156 Winchester Rd GU34 5HZ
☎ 01420 562659 📠 01420 562659
***Dir:*** *5m S of Alton on the A31, northbound*

Travelodge

Travelodge offers good quality, good value, modern accommodation. Ideal for families, the spacious, en suite bedrooms include remote-control TV, tea and coffee-making facilities, luxury beds and free morning newspaper. Meals can be taken at the nearby family restaurant. For further details and the Travelodge phone number, consult the Hotel Groups page.

**ROOMS:** 31 en suite

OWEY, Cornwall & Isles of Scilly Map 02 SX15

**★★★79% ◎◎ Fowey Hall**
Ianson Dr PL23 1ET
☎ 01726 833866 🖷 01726 834100
-mail: info@foweyhall.com
***ir:*** *on arriving in Fowey cross mini rdbt continue until you descend into own centre. Pass school on right after 400mtrs right into Hanson Drive*

his listed mansion above the estuary looks out onto the English 'hannel. Imaginatively designed bedrooms offer charm and umptuous comfort. Beautifully appointed public rooms include ne wood-panelled dining room where accomplished cuisine is erved. Families are a priority with a range of facilities to entertain hildren of all ages. The grounds have a covered pool and unbathing area.
**OOMS:** 16 en suite 8 annexe en suite (18 fmly) d £195-£375 (incl. kfst & dinner) * **LB** **FACILITIES:** STV Indoor swimming (H) Croquet wn Childrens play area Table tennis Xmas **CONF:** Thtr 30 Class 14 oard 14 Del from £130 * **PARKING:** 40 **NOTES:** No smoking in estaurant Civ Wed 40 **CARDS:**

*See advert on this page*

**★★★73% ◎◎ Fowey**
'he Esplanade PL23 1HX
☎ 01726 832551 🖷 01726 832125
-mail: fowey@richardsonhotels.co.uk
***ir:*** *from M5 take A3 to Okehampton,continue on road to Bodmin. At odmin, B3269 to Fowey, continue for 1m & on r/h bend take left junct hen right into Dagands road. Hotel 200m on left.*

Best Western

'his attractive hotel stands proudly above the estuary, with narvellous views of the river from the public areas and the najority of the bedrooms. High standards are evident throughout, nd the atmosphere is welcoming. There is a spacious bar, elegant estaurant and smart drawing room. Imaginative dinners make ood use of local ingredients.
**OOMS:** 27 en suite (1 fmly) No smoking in 1 bedroom s £52-£89; £104-£178 (incl. bkfst & dinner) * **LB** **FACILITIES:** Spa Fishing ch fac mas **CONF:** Thtr 100 Class 60 Board 20 Del from £80 *
**ERVICES:** Lift **PARKING:** 13 **NOTES:** No smoking in restaurant
**ARDS:**

**★★69% Marina**
Esplanade PL23 1HY
☎ 01726 833315 🖷 01726 832779
e-mail: marina.hotel@dial.pipex.com
***Dir:*** *drive into town down Lostwithiel Street, near bottom of hill turn right into Esplanade*

Many guests return year after year to enjoy the delights of this charming Georgian property. High standards of contemporary comfort are offered yet many original features have been retained. Public areas consist of the Waterside Restaurant, separate lounges and a bar. Bedrooms are well-equipped and some have balconies from which lovely sea views can be enjoyed.
**ROOMS:** 13 en suite (1 fmly) s £80-£118; d £80-£118 (incl. bkfst) * **LB** **FACILITIES:** Fishing Sailing Xmas **NOTES:** No dogs (ex guide dogs) No smoking in restaurant **CARDS:**

Bad hair day? Hairdryers in all rooms three stars and above.

## FOWNHOPE, Herefordshire
Map 03 SO53

### ★★67% Green Man Inn
HR1 4PE
☎ 01432 860243 🖹 01432 860207
***Dir:*** *on B4224 midway between Ross-on-Wye and Hereford*
This charming 15th-century village inn has a wealth of character. Well-equipped accommodation includes bedrooms on ground-floor level and one room with a four-poster bed. Some bedrooms are located in two separate cottage-style buildings. There are two lounges, a choice of bars, and a restaurant with a beamed ceiling. Other facilities include a play area for children and a modern health & leisure centre complete with beauty therapist.
**ROOMS:** 10 en suite 9 annexe en suite (3 fmly) s £37.50-£38.50; d £62-£65 (incl. bkfst) * **LB** **FACILITIES:** **Spa** STV Indoor swimming (H) Fishing Sauna Solarium Gym Jacuzzi ch fac Xmas **CONF:** Thtr 40 Class 60 Board 30 Del £79.50 * **PARKING:** 75 **NOTES:** No smoking in restaurant **CARDS:**

## FRANKLEY MOTORWAY SERVICE AREA (M5), West Midlands
Map 07 SO98

### ⇧ *Travelodge*
Travelodge
Illey Ln, Frankley Motorway Service Area, Frankley B32 4AR
☎ 0121 550 3131
***Dir:*** *between junc 3 and 4 on southbound carriageway of M5*
Travelodge offers good quality, good value, modern accommodation. Ideal for families, the spacious, en suite bedrooms include remote-control TV, tea and coffee-making facilities, luxury beds and free morning newspaper. Meals can be taken at the nearby family restaurant. For further details and the Travelodge phone number, consult the Hotel Groups page.

**ROOMS:** 62 en suite

## FRIMLEY, Surrey

### ○ Innkeeper's Lodge Frimley
Innkeeper's Lodge
Portsmouth Rd GU15 1HS
A new concept in the travel accommodation market. Smart rooms meet essential business requirements but also have home comforts. Dining options include all-day menus plus the added advantage of breakfast, which is included in the room price. Reservations can be made seven days a week through the room reservations number: 0870 243 0500. For further details, consult the Hotel Groups page.
**ROOMS:** 43 en suite

## FRINTON-ON-SEA, Essex
Map 05 TM21

### ★★72% Maplin
THE CIRCLE Selected Individual Hotels GREAT BRITAIN
Esplanade CO13 9EL
☎ 01255 673832 🖹 01255 673832
e-mail: maplin@globalnet.co.uk
***Dir:*** *from A133 towards Clacton, follow local signs to Frinton B1033. Turn at level crossing on to Connaught Av at end turn right onto Esplanade*
At the quiet end of the esplanade, overlooking the sea, stands this impressive house, which was built in 1911. The bedrooms are attractively furnished to a high standard and equipped with many useful extras; some rooms have spa baths. Day rooms feature beautiful oak panelling and leaded windows.
**ROOMS:** 11 rms (10 en suite) (2 fmly) s £59.50-£85; d £95-£110 (incl. bkfst) * **LB** **FACILITIES:** Outdoor swimming (H) Xmas **CONF:** Thtr 35 Class 20 Board 30 Del from £85 * **PARKING:** 12 **NOTES:** No smoking in restaurant Closed Jan **CARDS:**

Popped the question? Hotels with Civ Wed in their entry are licensed for civil wedding ceremonies. Maximum numbers for the ceremony only are shown, e.g. Civ Wed 120

## FRITTON, Norfolk
Map 05 TG4

### ★★★71% *Caldecott Hall Golf & Leisure*
Caldecott Hall, Beccles Rd NR31 9EY
☎ 01493 488488 🖹 01493 488561
Close to Fritton Lake in its own landscaped grounds is this small privately owned hotel. The spacious bedrooms are individually decorated with bright fabrics and have many useful extras. Public areas include a smart sitting room, a lounge bar, restaurant and leisure facilities. There is also an 18 hole golf course with clubhouse as well as banqueting and conference facilities.
**ROOMS:** 8 en suite (6 fmly) No smoking in all bedrooms
**FACILITIES:** Golf 27 Driving range Pitch & Putt **CONF:** Thtr 100 Class 80 Board 20 **PARKING:** 100 **NOTES:** No dogs (ex guide dogs) No smoking in restaurant **CARDS:**

## FRODSHAM, Cheshire
Map 07 SJ5

### ★★★67% Forest Hill Hotel & Leisure Complex
Overton Hill WA6 6HH
☎ 01928 735255 🖹 01928 735517
e-mail: info@foresthillshotel.com
***Dir:*** *at Frodsham turn onto B5151 after 1m turn right into Manley Rd after 0.5m turn right into Simons Ln. Hotel 0.5m along road past Frodsham golf course following brown tourist info signs*
Situated high on Overton Hill, enjoying panoramic views across the Cheshire plain and over to the distant Welsh hills, this modern hotel offers spacious and well-equipped bedrooms, many of which have been redecorated and refurbished. There is a choice of bars for guests to relax in, conference facilities and a leisure centre.
**ROOMS:** 58 en suite (4 fmly) No smoking in 5 bedrooms s £65-£90; d £65-£90 * **LB** **FACILITIES:** STV Indoor swimming (H) Snooker Sauna Solarium Gym Jacuzzi Nightclub entertainment ch fac Xmas
**CONF:** Thtr 200 Class 80 Board 48 Del from £80 * **PARKING:** 350
**NOTES:** No smoking in restaurant Civ Wed 150
**CARDS:**

## FROME, Somerset
Map 03 ST7

### ★★65% The George at Nunney
11 Church St BA11 4LW
☎ 01373 836458 🖹 01373 836565
e-mail: georgenunneyhotel@barbox.net
(For full entry see Nunney)

## GARFORTH, West Yorkshire
Map 08 SE4

### ★★★70% Milford Lodge
Best Western
A1 Great North Rd, Peckfield LS25 5LQ
☎ 01977 681800 🖹 01977 681245
e-mail: enquires@mlh.co.uk
***Dir:*** *on the southbound carriageway of the A1, E of Leeds where A63 joins A1 from Leeds*
This welcoming hotel is situated alongside the A1 at its junction with the A63. The comfortable bedrooms are particularly spacious and have been insulated against traffic noise. The Watermill Restaurant and Bar, which features a working water wheel,

continued

rovides a high standard of cuisine, friendly service and omfortable surroundings.

MILFORD LODGE

**ROOMS:** 47 en suite (10 fmly) No smoking in 19 bedrooms d £49-£59 * **LB FACILITIES:** STV Xmas **CONF:** Thtr 70 Class 35 Board 30 Del £95 **SERVICES:** air con **PARKING:** 80 **CARDS:**

## GARSTANG, Lancashire Map 07 SD44

### ★★★70% Pickerings

Garstang Rd, Catterall PR3 0HD
☎ 01995 600999 🖷 01995 602100
e-mail: hotel@pickeringpark.demon.co.uk

MINOTEL Great Britain

***Dir:** from S M6 junct 32 take A6 N, after Esso garage turn right onto B6430 then right after bus shelter*

This friendly hotel dates back to the 17th century and is set in carefully tended grounds that include a lovely children's play area. Bedrooms are spacious and include several smart four-poster rooms. Public areas include an inviting bar lounge; two elegant dining rooms and a purpose built conference suite.

**ROOMS:** 12 en suite (1 fmly) s fr £35; d fr £50 (incl. bkfst) * **LB FACILITIES:** ch fac Xmas **CONF:** Thtr 65 Class 50 Board 35 **PARKING:** 50 **NOTES:** No dogs (ex guide dogs) No smoking in restaurant Civ Wed 60 **CARDS:**

## GATESHEAD, Tyne & Wear Map 12 NZ26

See also Beamish & Whickham

### ★★★★68% *Newcastle Marriott Hotel MetroCentre*

Metro Centre NE11 9XF
☎ 0191 493 2233 🖷 0191 493 2030

Marriott HOTELS · RESORTS · SUITES

***Dir:** on A1 follow signs for Metro Centre & then signs for Marriott Hotel*

Conveniently situated just off the A1, this smart hotel is close to the Metro Centre. Bedrooms are comprehensively equipped and very comfortable. More formal dining is available in the main restaurant, and the café-bar serves a range of popular dishes.

*continued*

Leisure facilities are superb, as are the extensive conference and banqueting rooms.

**ROOMS:** 148 en suite (136 fmly) No smoking in 75 bedrooms **FACILITIES:** STV Indoor swimming (H) Sauna Solarium Gym Jacuzzi Health & beauty clinic Dance studio **CONF:** Thtr 450 Class 190 Board 40 **SERVICES:** Lift air con **PARKING:** 300 **NOTES:** No dogs (ex guide dogs) Civ Wed 100 **CARDS:**

### ★★★67% Swallow Hotel

High West St NE8 1PE
☎ 0191 477 1105 🖷 0191 478 7214
e-mail: info@swallowhotels.com

SWALLOW HOTELS

***Dir:** A1, A184 to Gateshead, follow signs for centre. At mini rdbt turn right, pass bus stn, lights, and two rdbts. Take 3rd left, hotel at bottom of road*

Just across the Tyne from the centre of Newcastle, this purpose-built hotel offers a wide range of services. The attractive, modern bedrooms are compact and very well-equipped. Guests wishing to relax can enjoy the pool and leisure facilities, or alternatively work off some of the good food found in the restaurant in the smartly converted gym. Parking facilities are secure.

**ROOMS:** 103 en suite (12 fmly) No smoking in 60 bedrooms s £55-£105; d £65-£115 (incl. bkfst) * **LB FACILITIES:** STV Indoor swimming (H) Sauna Solarium Gym Jacuzzi Sunbeds Xmas **CONF:** Thtr 350 Class 150 Board 100 Del from £87 * **SERVICES:** Lift **PARKING:** 190 **NOTES:** No smoking in restaurant **CARDS:**

### ★★76% Eslington Villa

8 Station Rd, Low Fell NE9 6DR
☎ 0191 487 6017 & 420 0666 🖷 0191 420 0667
e-mail: admin@eslingtonvilla.fsnet.co.uk

***Dir:** turn off A1 onto Team Valley Trading Estate, take 2nd rdbt turn right along Eastern Av then turn left just past Belle Vue Motors, hotel on left*

Situated in a quiet conservation area, with easy access to the A1, this hotel's public rooms retain their Victorian character. Bedrooms offer good levels of comfort and space. Service throughout is friendly and attentive, and a wide range of dishes is available in the dining room which overlooks well-maintained grounds.

**ROOMS:** 17 en suite (2 fmly) s £45-£59.50; d £54.50-£69.50 (incl. bkfst) * **CONF:** Thtr 36 Class 30 Board 25 Del from £95 * **PARKING:** 15 **NOTES:** No dogs (ex guide dogs) No smoking in restaurant Closed 25-26 Dec RS Sun/BHs (restricted restaurant service) Civ Wed 40 **CARDS:**

### Express by Holiday Inn

Clasper Way, Riverside Way, Derwenthaugh NE16 3BE
☎ 01207 541100 🖷 0191 414 6967

Express by Holiday Inn

***Dir:** Hotel is on A1114 next to TGI Fridays & opposite Shell/Honda garage*

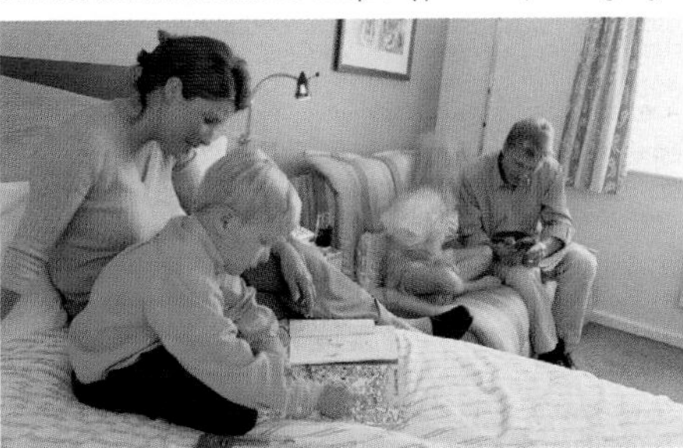

A modern budget hotel offering comfortable accommodation in refreshing, spacious and comprehensively equipped bedrooms, en suite bathrooms with power showers and continental buffet

*continued*

G

GATESHEAD, continued

breakfast included in the room rate. Suitable for business travellers or families. For further details and the Express by Holiday Inn phone number, consult the Hotel Groups page.
**ROOMS:** 100 en suite

### ⇧ *Premier Lodge*

Lobley Hill Rd NE11 9NA

☎ 0870 700 1508 🖹 0870 700 1509
Premier Lodge offers modern, well-equipped, en suite accommodation suitable for both business and leisure travellers. Meals can be taken at the adjacent popular restaurant and bar, which is fully licensed. For further details, consult the Hotel Groups page.
**ROOMS:** 40 en suite

## GATWICK AIRPORT (LONDON), West Sussex Map 04 TQ24

see also Dorking, East Grinstead & Reigate

### ★★★★70% ֍֍ Copthorne Hotel London Gatwick

Copthorne Way RH10 3PG
☎ 01342 348800 & 348888 🖹 01342 348833
e-mail: coplgw@mill-cop.com
***Dir:*** *on A264, 2m E of A264/B2036 rdbt*
This well-run hotel is set in 100 acres of wooded, landscaped gardens, which contain jogging tracks, a putting green and even a petanque pit. The sprawling building is built around a 16th-century farmhouse and has comfortable, well-maintained bedrooms. In addition to the brasserie there is a more formal restaurant.
**ROOMS:** 227 en suite (10 fmly) No smoking in 136 bedrooms s £139-£164; d £139-£164 * **LB** **FACILITIES:** **Spa** STV Indoor swimming (H) Tennis (hard) Squash Solarium Gym Croquet lawn Putting green Jacuzzi Petanque pit Aerobic studio entertainment **CONF:** Thtr 150 Class 65 Board 40 Del from £135 * **SERVICES:** Lift **PARKING:** 300 **NOTES:** Civ Wed 100 **CARDS:**

### ★★★★69% Le Meridien London Gatwick

North Terminal RH6 0PH
☎ 0870 4008494 🖹 01293 567739
e-mail: reservations.gatwick@lemeridien-hotels.com
***Dir:*** *M23 junct 9, follow dual carriageway to second rdbt, hotel is large white building straight ahead*
This bright, modern, purpose built hotel is located only minutes from the airport terminals. Bedrooms are contemporary in style and offer an excellent range of facilities for today's traveller. Guests have a choice of eating options including a French-style café, Brasserie and Oriental restaurant.
**ROOMS:** 494 en suite (36 fmly) No smoking in 228 bedrooms d £180-£200 * **FACILITIES:** STV Indoor swimming (H) Sauna Solarium Gym **CONF:** Thtr 220 Class 200 Board 120 Del £179 * **SERVICES:** Lift air con **PARKING:** 120 **NOTES:** Civ Wed 220
**CARDS:** 

Popped the question? Hotels with Civ Wed in their entry are licensed for civil wedding ceremonies. Maximum numbers for the ceremony only are shown, e.g. Civ Wed 120

### ★★★★65% Copthorne Hotel Effingham Park Gatwick

West Park Rd RH10 3EU
☎ 01342 714994 🖹 01342 716039
e-mail: sales.effingham@mill-cop.com
***Dir:*** *from M23 junct 10, take A264 towards East Grinstead. Go straight over rdbt, at 2nd rdbt turn left along B2028. Effingham Park is on right*
A former stately home, set in 40 acres of grounds, this hotel is popular with conference organisers and for weekend functions. The main restaurant is an open-plan, Mediterranean-themed brasserie, and snacks are also available in the bar. Both categorie of bedroom are spacious and well-cared for.
**ROOMS:** 122 en suite (6 fmly) No smoking in 48 bedrooms s £139; d £139 * **LB** **FACILITIES:** STV Indoor swimming (H) Golf 9 Tennis (hard) Sauna Solarium Gym Croquet lawn Putting green Jacuzzi Aerobic studio Bowls Croquet **CONF:** Thtr 600 Class 250 Board 30 Del from £135 * **SERVICES:** Lift **PARKING:** 500 **NOTES:** No dogs (ex gui dogs) No smoking in restaurant Civ Wed 140
**CARDS:** 

### ★★★79% ֍֍ Langshott Manor

Langshott Ln RH6 9LN
☎ 01293 786680 🖹 01293 783905
e-mail: admin@langshottmanor.com
***Dir:*** *from A23 take Ladbroke Rd, turn off the Chequers rdbt to Langshott, proceed for 0.75 miles, entrance to hotel on right*

This classic timber-framed Tudor house dates back to 1580 and is set in beautifully maintained gardens. The interior boasts cosy lounges with polished oak panelling, exposed beams and log fires Bedrooms combine the most up to date modern comforts with flair, individuality and traditional elegance. The newly extended Mulberry restaurant overlooks the pond and offers a fine menu.
**ROOMS:** 7 en suite 8 annexe en suite No smoking in all bedrooms s £155-£245; d £175-£275 (incl. bkfst) * **LB** **FACILITIES:** Croquet lawn ch fac Xmas **CONF:** Thtr 40 Class 20 Board 22 Del from £188 * **PARKING:** 25 **NOTES:** No dogs (ex guide dogs) No smoking in restaurant Civ Wed 60 **CARDS:**

### ★★★67% Stanhill Court

Stanhill Rd, Charlwood RH6 0EP
☎ 01293 862166 🖹 01293 862773
e-mail: enquiries@stanhillcourthotel.co.uk
***Dir:*** *N of Charlwood towards Newdigate*
Dating back to 1881, this hotel enjoys a secluded location in 35 acres of well-tended grounds with views over the Downs. Bedrooms are individually furnished and decorated, many having four-poster beds. Public areas include a library, a Mediterranean-style bar and a traditional style wood panelled restaurant.
**ROOMS:** 14 en suite (3 fmly) No smoking in 2 bedrooms s £99-£121.50 d £125-£148 (incl. bkfst) * **LB** **FACILITIES:** STV Fishing Croquet lawn Putting green **CONF:** Thtr 250 Class 100 Board 60 **PARKING:** 100 **NOTES:** No dogs (ex guide dogs) No smoking in restaurant Civ Wed 160
**CARDS:**

### ★★★63% Gatwick Worth Hotel
Crabbet Park, Turners Hill Rd, Worth RH10 4ST
☎ 01293 884806 🖹 01293 882444
e-mail: gatwickworth@aol.com
***Dir:*** *Exit M23 at junct 10, turn left to A264. At 1st rdbt turn right (signposted to Maidenbower). Take 1st left into Old Hollow Rd and follow to the end. At T junct turn right. Hotel 200 yds right*
This purpose built hotel is ideally placed for access to Gatwick airport. The bedrooms are spacious and suitably appointed with good facilities. Public areas consist of a light and airy bar area, a Brasserie style restaurant offering good value meals; conferencing, and the use of the superb leisure club next door.
**ROOMS:** 118 en suite (9 fmly) No smoking in 57 bedrooms s £55-£90; d £65-£100 * **FACILITIES:** Cannon's fitness centre adjacent to hotel. **CONF:** Thtr 200 Class 100 Board 60 Del from £75 * **NOTES:** No smoking in restaurant Civ Wed 150
**CARDS:**

### ★★★63% Posthouse Gatwick Airport
Posthouse
Povey Cross Rd RH6 0BA
☎ 0870 400 9030 🖹 01293 771054
***Dir:*** *from M23 junct 9 follow signs for Gatwick, then Reigate. Hotel on left after 3rd rdbt*
This busy hotel is well situated for access to the airport and is popular with both business and leisure travellers. Bedrooms are bright, modern and well-equipped. The availability of a large secure car park is a bonus for drivers.
**ROOMS:** 210 en suite (19 fmly) No smoking in 105 bedrooms d £80-£129 (incl. bkfst) * **LB** **CONF:** Thtr 160 Class 90 Board 60 Del £150 * **SERVICES:** Lift **PARKING:** 300 **NOTES:** No smoking in restaurant
**CARDS:**

### ⌂ *Premier Lodge (Gatwick)*
PREMIER LODGE
Goffs Park Rd RH11 8AX
☎ 0870 700 1390 🖹 0870 700 1391
Premier Lodge offers modern, well-equipped, en suite accommodation suitable for both business and leisure travellers. Meals can be taken at the adjacent popular restaurant and bar, which is fully licensed. For further details, consult the Hotel Groups page.
**ROOMS:** 56 en suite **CONF:** Thtr 120 Class 70 Board 40

### ⌂ *Travelodge*
Travelodge
Church Rd, Lowfield Heath RH11 0PQ
☎ 01293 533441 🖹 01293 535369
***Dir:*** *1m S, off A23 junc 10 M23*

Travelodge offers good quality, good value, modern accommodation. Ideal for families, the spacious, en suite bedrooms include remote-control TV, tea and coffee-making facilities, luxury beds and free morning newspaper. Meals can be taken at the nearby family restaurant. For further details and the Travelodge phone number, consult the Hotel Groups page.

**ROOMS:** 126 en suite **CONF:** Thtr 60 Class 25 Board 25

### ⌂ Express by Holiday Inn Crawley
Express by Holiday Inn
Haslett Av East RH10 1UG
☎ 01293 525523 🖹 01293 525529
A modern budget hotel offering comfortable accommodation in refreshing, spacious and comprehensively equipped bedrooms, en suite bathrooms with power showers and continental buffet breakfast included in the room rate. Suitable for business travellers or families. For further details and the Express by Holiday Inn phone number, consult the Hotel Groups page.

**ROOMS:** 74 en suite (incl. cont bkfst) s £57.50; d £57.50 * **CONF:** Thtr 30 Class 20 Board 16

Early start? Hotels at all star levels should provide in-room alarm clocks and/or alarm calls.

GATWICK AIRPORT (LONDON), continued

### Hotel Ibis

London Rd, County Oak RH10 9GY
☎ 01293 590300 📠 01293 590310
e-mail: H1889@accor-hotels.com

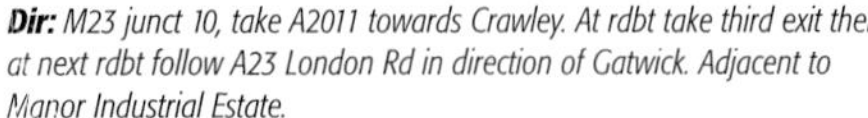

***Dir:** M23 junct 10, take A2011 towards Crawley. At rdbt take third exit then at next rdbt follow A23 London Rd in direction of Gatwick. Adjacent to Manor Industrial Estate.*

Modern, budget hotel offering comfortable accommodation in bright and practical bedrooms. Breakfast is self-service and dinner is available in the restaurant. For further details, consult the Hotel Groups page.

**ROOMS:** 141 en suite s £39.95-£49.95; d £39.95-£49.95 *

### Premier Lodge

PREMIER LODGE

London Rd, Lowfield Heath RH10 2ST
☎ 0870 700 1388 📠 0870 700 1389

Premier Lodge offers modern, well-equipped, en suite accommodation suitable for both business and leisure travellers. Meals can be taken at the adjacent popular restaurant and bar, which is fully licensed. For further details, consult the Hotel Groups page.

**ROOMS:** 100 en suite d fr £49.95 * **CONF:** Thtr 200 Class 100 Board 80 Del from £105 *

### ○ Three Bridges Lodge

190 Three Bridges Rd, Gatwick RH10 1LN
☎ 01293 612190

At the time of going to press, the star classification for this hotel was not confirmed. Please refer to the AA internet site www.theAA.com for current information.

---

GERRARDS CROSS, Buckinghamshire — Map 04 TQ08

### ★★★70% Bull

Oxford Rd SL9 7PA
☎ 01753 885995 📠 01753 885504
e-mail: bull@sarova.co.uk

***Dir:** from M40 junct 2 follow signs for Beaconsfield (A355). After 0.5m at rdbt take 2nd exit signed A40 Gerrards Cross for 2m to The Bull on right*

This 17th-century inn, once the haunt of highwaymen, has been sympathetically refurbished. Spacious bedrooms are tastefully furnished and provide an excellent range of facilities. Guests have the use of the popular Jack Shrimpton bar or the attractive cocktail bar and meals are served in the comfortable restaurant.

**ROOMS:** 111 en suite (3 fmly) No smoking in 74 bedrooms s £160-£190; d £180-£210 * **LB** **FACILITIES:** STV Leisure facilities available nearby entertainment Xmas **CONF:** Thtr 200 Class 90 Board 50 Del from £130 * **SERVICES:** Lift **PARKING:** 200 **NOTES:** No dogs (ex guide dogs) No smoking in restaurant Civ Wed 200

**CARDS:**

*See advert on opposite page*

### ★★65% Ethorpe

SCOTTISH NEWCASTLE
hotels

Packhorse Rd SL9 8HY
☎ 01753 882039 📠 01753 887012

***Dir:** M40 junct 2. Head towards Beaconsfield. At next island turn right onto A40 towards Gerrards Cross. At traffic lights, turn left into Packhouse Road hotel is at end of the high street on the left.*

This attractive hotel is located in the centre of town and is within easy reach of the motorway network and Heathrow Airport.

*continued*

Bedrooms are well-equipped and offer a good range of extra facilities. Meals may be taken in the bar or restaurant.

**ROOMS:** 34 rms (31 en suite) (2 fmly) s £95-£106; d £115-£135 * **LB** **FACILITIES:** STV Xmas **CONF:** Thtr 30 Class 30 Board 18 **PARKING:** 80 **NOTES:** No dogs (ex guide dogs) **CARDS:**

---

GILLAN, Cornwall & Isles of Scilly — Map 02 SW72

### ★★80% Tregildry

TR12 6HG
☎ 01326 231378 📠 01326 231561
e-mail: trgildry@globalnet.co.uk

***Dir:** from Helston join the A3083 Lizard Rd and take first turning left for St Keverne and follow signs for Manaccan and Gillan*

From its unspoilt and peaceful location Tregildry is blessed with both sea and river views. The tastefully furnished bedrooms and lounges make the most of the wonderful views. The dining room provides the perfect environment to enjoy the imaginative and innovative menus. There is direct access to the beach and adjacent coastal footpath.

**ROOMS:** 10 en suite No smoking in all bedrooms s £80-£85; d £160-£170 (incl. bkfst & dinner) * **LB** **FACILITIES:** Boat hire Windsurfing **PARKING:** 15 **NOTES:** No children 8yrs No smoking in restaurant Closed Nov-Feb **CARDS:**

---

GILLINGHAM, Kent — Map 05 TQ76

### *Travelodge*

Medway Motorway Service Area, Rainham ME8 8PQ
☎ 01634 233343 📠 01634 360848

***Dir:** between juncts 4 & 5 M2*

Travelodge offers good quality, good value, modern accommodation. Ideal for families, the spacious, en suite bedrooms include remote-control TV, tea and coffee-making facilities, luxury beds and free morning newspaper. Meals can be taken at the nearby family restaurant. For further details and the Travelodge phone number, consult the Hotel Groups page.

**ROOMS:** 58 en suite

---

GLENRIDDING, Cumbria — Map 11 NY31

### ★★★70% Glenridding

CA11 0PB
☎ 017684 82228 📠 017684 82555
e-mail: glenridding@bestwestern.co.uk

***Dir:** on A592 in village*

A friendly, welcoming village hotel with views of the lake and surrounding mountains. There is a wide choice of accommodation, with newly refurbished rooms offering very good quality. The smart leisure facilities boast a heated indoor pool, children's pool and sauna. Well-equipped conference facilities are also available. The hotel has a formal restaurant, a friendly pub with traditional hearty dishes, and a cosy coffee shop.

**ROOMS:** 36 en suite (6 fmly) s £74-£81; d £102-£110 (incl. bkfst) * **LB** **FACILITIES:** STV Indoor swimming (H) Sauna Jacuzzi Billiards 3/4 Snooker table Table tennis ch fac Xmas **CONF:** Thtr 30 Class 30 Board 20 Del from £85 * **SERVICES:** Lift **PARKING:** 38 **NOTES:** No smoking in restaurant Civ Wed 60 **CARDS:**

★★★68% **The Inn on the Lake**
Lake Ullswater, Glenridding CA11 0PE
☎ 017684 82444 017684 82303
e-mail: info@innonthelakeullswater.co.uk
***Dir:*** *M6 junct 40 and follow A66 towards Keswick. At roundabout take A592 to Ullswater lake. Follow road along lake to Glenridding. Hotel on left on entering village.*

Enjoying an idyllic, peaceful, lakeside position this Victorian hotel provides very stylish accommodation. Superb Lakeland views may be enjoyed from the bedrooms that face either the open lake or towering fells, and afternoon teas can be served on the garden terrace during warmer months. The lake-facing restaurant serves imaginative dishes. Well-equipped conference facilities are also provided.
**ROOMS:** 46 en suite (6 fmly) No smoking in 15 bedrooms s £49; d £78 (incl. bkfst) * **LB** **FACILITIES:** STV Tennis (grass) Fishing Sauna Solarium Gym Croquet lawn Putting green Jacuzzi Sailing Xmas **CONF:** Thtr 120 Class 60 Board 40 Del £75 * **SERVICES:** Lift **PARKING:** 200 **NOTES:** No smoking in restaurant
**CARDS:**

*See advert on this page*

GLOSSOP, Derbyshire Map 07 SK09

★★77% **Wind in the Willows**
Derbyshire Level, Sheffield Rd SK13 7PT
☎ 01457 868001 01457 853354
e-mail: info@windinthewillows.co.uk
***Dir:*** *1m E on A57 opposite the Royal Oak*
A warm relaxed atmosphere prevails at this small hotel. Bedrooms are comfortable and individually decorated, and offer many thoughtful extras. There are two comfortable lounges and a dining room that overlooks the pretty garden.
**ROOMS:** 12 en suite s £74-£94; d £99-£121 (incl. bkfst) * **LB** **FACILITIES:** Fishing **CONF:** Thtr 40 Class 12 Board 16 Del from £135 * **PARKING:** 16 **NOTES:** No dogs No children 10yrs No smoking in restaurant **CARDS:**

GLOUCESTER, Gloucestershire Map 03 SO81

★★★72% **Hatton Court**
Upton Hill, Upton St Leonards GL4 8DE
☎ 01452 617412 01452 612945
e-mail: res@hatton-court.co.uk
***Dir:*** *leave Gloucester on B4073 Painswick Rd. Hotel at top of hill on right*
This beautifully preserved 17th-century Cotswold manor house is set in seven acres of well-kept gardens. It stands at the top of Upton Hill and commands truly spectacular views of the Severn Valley. Bedrooms are comfortable and tastefully furnished with many extras. The elegant Carringtons Restaurant offers a varied

*continued on p244*

GLOUCESTER, continued

choice of menus, there is a traditionally furnished bar, as well as a very comfortable foyer lounge.
**ROOMS:** 17 en suite 28 annexe en suite No smoking in 11 bedrooms s £95-£155; d £110-£180 (incl. bkfst) * **LB** **FACILITIES:** STV Sauna Gym Croquet lawn Jacuzzi Xmas **CONF:** Thtr 60 Class 30 Board 30 Del from £139 * **PARKING:** 80 **NOTES:** No dogs (ex guide dogs) No smoking in restaurant Civ Wed 80
**CARDS:**

*See advert on opposite page*

### ★★★68% *Posthouse Gloucester*

Posthouse

Crest Way, Barnwood GL4 7RX
☎ 0870 400 9034 Fax 01452 371036
***Dir:*** *on A417 ring road to Barnwood, next to Cheltenham & Gloucester building*
This modern hotel is conveniently located close to many local attractions. Bedrooms are all spacious, attractively designed and benefit from a number of first rate features. Guests can enjoy a varied range of food and drinks in the stylish bar and restaurant, and there is an excellent range of leisure facilities.
**ROOMS:** 122 en suite (25 fmly) No smoking in 60 bedrooms **FACILITIES:** STV Indoor swimming (H) Sauna Solarium Gym Jacuzzi Spa pool Sauna Dance Studio **CONF:** Thtr 100 Class 45 Board 40 **PARKING:** 135 **NOTES:** No smoking in restaurant
**CARDS:**

### ★★★67% New County

Best Western

44 Southgate St GL1 2DU
☎ 01452 307000 Fax 01452 500487
e-mail: newcounty@meridianleisure.com
***Dir:*** *follow signs for City & Docks along A38. Along Bristol Rd for 2m, passing docks on left. At lights take right hand lane into one way system, then left lane turning left at Black Swan Inn into Southgate St. Hotel 100yds on left opposite St Mary de Crypt church.*

THE NEW COUNTY HOTEL
NEW COUNTY HOTEL

This character hotel in the heart of the city has been refurbished to offer modern comforts and bright well furnished bedrooms with good facilities. Public rooms include a bistro-style restaurant, a bar and a ballroom/function suite. Complementary parking is available within close proximity of the hotel.
**ROOMS:** 39 en suite (3 fmly) s £60-£65; d £70-£80 (incl. bkfst) * **LB** **FACILITIES:** Xmas **CONF:** Thtr 130 Class 60 Board 60 Del from £95 * **NOTES:** No smoking in restaurant **CARDS:**

*See advert on opposite page*

> Late for dinner? Quality Standards star rating means that last orders for dinner should be no earlier than:
> ★ 6.30pm ★★ 7.00pm ★★★ 8.00pm
> ★★★★ 9.00pm ★★★★★ 10.00pm

### ★★★65% *Hatherley Manor*

Down Hatherley Ln GL2 9QA
☎ 01452 730217 Fax 01452 731032
***Dir:*** *from Gloucester, go through the village of Twigworth on the A38 & take turning for Down Hatherley, hotel 0.25m on left*
Within easy striking distance of the M5, Gloucester, Cheltenham and the Cotswolds, this stylish 17th-century manor remains popular. Hatherley Manor has both bedrooms in the original building, as well as purpose-built rooms. The restaurant offers an imaginative selection of dishes using fresh ingredients.
**ROOMS:** 56 en suite No smoking in 6 bedrooms **FACILITIES:** In-house movies **CONF:** Thtr 300 Class 90 Board 70 **PARKING:** 350 **NOTES:** No smoking in restaurant Civ Wed 300 **CARDS:**

### ⌂ *Express by Holiday Inn Gloucester South*

Express
by Holiday Inn

Waterwells Business Park, Quedgeley GL2 4SA
☎ 01452 726400 Fax 722922

A modern budget hotel offering comfortable accommodation in refreshing, spacious and comprehensively equipped bedrooms, en suite bathrooms with power showers and continental buffet breakfast included in the room rate. Suitable for business travellers or families. For further details and the Express by Holiday Inn phone number, consult the Hotel Groups page.
**ROOMS:** 106 en suite **CONF:** Thtr 35 Class 15 Board 20

### ⌂ *Premier Lodge (Gloucester North)*

PREMIER LODGE

Tewkesbury Rd, Twigworth GL2 9PG
☎ 0870 700 1404 Fax 0870 700 1405
Premier Lodge offers modern, well-equipped, en suite accommodation suitable for both business and leisure travellers. Meals can be taken at the adjacent popular restaurant and bar, which is fully licensed. For further details, consult the Hotel Groups page.
**ROOMS:** 52 en suite

GOATHLAND, North Yorkshire — Map 08 NZ80

### ★★72% *Mallyan Spout*

YO22 5AN
☎ 01947 896486 Fax 01947 896327
e-mail: mallyan@ukgateway.net
***Dir:*** *off A169*
Friendly, efficient service is a key feature of this welcoming hotel, set on the edge of a popular moorland village. Bedrooms are well-equipped and there is a choice of lounges. A good range of dishes is served in both the inviting restaurant and the cosy, characterful bar.
**ROOMS:** 20 en suite 4 annexe en suite **CONF:** Thtr 70 Class 70 Board 40 **PARKING:** 50 **NOTES:** Closed 25 & 26 Dec
**CARDS:**

*See advert on opposite page*

## STONEHOUSE COURT HOTEL

AA ★★★ 72% 

STONEHOUSE, GLOUCESTERSHIRE GL10 3RA
TEL: 01453 825155 FAX: 01453 824611
Email: stonehouse.court@pageant.co.uk
www.pageant.co.uk

Stonehouse Court is a superb Grade II Listed manor house which has been wonderfully transformed into a delightful hotel.
Set in six acres of mature gardens on the edge of the Cotswolds the hotel offers award winning cuisine and is the perfect venue for either business or pleasure. Situated close to junction 13 of the M5, the hotel is ideal for visiting Slimbridge Wildfowl Trust, Gloucester Cathedral, Regency Cheltenham and Berkeley Castle where King Edward II was murdered.

## getaway

**Set in the midst of the Cotswolds, near Cheltenham Spa, this luxurious property has exceptional views across the Severn Valley. Built in the 17th Century, careful and extensive refurbishment combines modern day standards of comfort and sophistication with the charm and character of a bygone age.**

Upton Hill
Upton St Leonards
Nr Cheltenham
GL4 8DE

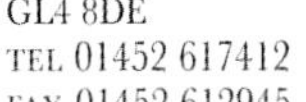

TEL 01452 617412
FAX 01452 612945
E-MAIL res@hatton-court.co.uk
www.hatton-court.co.uk

## HATTON COURT

## Mallyan Spout Hotel

AA ★★

**Goathland, Whitby
N Yorkshire
YO22 5AN
Tel: (01947) 896486
Fax: (01947) 896327**

A stone-built, ivy clad building situated on the green of a beautiful Yorkshire village overlooking the wide expanses of the famous moors. The hotel takes its name from a small picturesque waterfall flowing into a wooded valley, a short walk below the hotel. Three spacious lounges command a view of the garden, moors and the beautiful Esk Valley, and in the winter you are warmed by roaring fires. Mallyan Spout is an ideal location for outdoor pursuits or the peaceful pleasures of the fine food, good wines and friendly hospitality. 22 cottage style bedrooms with private bath, four large rooms with balconies and superb views.

## THE NEW COUNTY HOTEL

AA ★★★ ETC Best Western

Gloucester City Centre

**44 Southgate Street, Gloucester GL1 2DU
Tel: 01452 307000 Fax: 01452 500487
Email: newcounty@meridianleisure.com
www.meridianleisure.com**

- Ideally situated in the heart of Gloucester city, this 19th century hotel combines many of the original features with all modern amenities to create a fine modern day hotel
- City Centre located with free car parking adjacent
- All 39 bedrooms are en-suite and decorated to the highest standards
- A perfect venue for Weddings, Conferences and Special Occasion Dining
- Special Leisure Breaks Packages available

THE NEW COUNTY HOTEL
NEW COUNTY HOTEL

## GOMERSAL, West Yorkshire
Map 08 SE22

**★★★70% Gomersal Park**
Moor Ln BD19 4LJ
☎ 01274 869386 📠 01274 861042
e-mail: gomersal@bestwestern.co.uk
***Dir:*** *take A62 towards Huddersfield, at junct with A651 (by Greyhound Pub) turn right, after approx 1m take first right after Oakwell Hall*
Built around a 19th century house, this modern hotel enjoys a peaceful location and pleasant grounds. A comfortable lounge is provided, and imaginative meals are served in the Harlequin restaurant. The well-equipped bedrooms have been recently refurbished to provide high quality and comfort. Extensive public areas include a well equipped leisure complex and pool, and a wide variety of conference rooms.
**ROOMS:** 52 en suite (4 fmly) No smoking in 35 bedrooms s £83-£89; d £94-£99 * **LB** **FACILITIES:** STV Indoor swimming (H) Sauna Solarium Gym Jacuzzi 5 a side football pitch Xmas **CONF:** Thtr 220 Class 130 Board 60 Del from £110 * **PARKING:** 220 **NOTES:** No smoking in restaurant Civ Wed 120 **CARDS:**

**★★65% *Gomersal Lodge***
Spen Ln BD19 4PJ
☎ 01274 861111 📠 01274 861111
***Dir:*** *M62 junct 26, take A638 to Cleckheaton, 2nd lights turn left along Peg Lane leading to Spen Lane. Hotel on left just after Old Saw Pub on right*
Gomersal Lodge Hotel stands centrally in five acres of grounds and gardens. This 19th-century house offers well-furnished bedrooms together with a cosy bar. There is a popular restaurant in which a skilfully prepared, contemporary menu is served.
**ROOMS:** 9 en suite (1 fmly) No smoking in 4 bedrooms **CONF:** Thtr 20 Class 12 Board 12 **PARKING:** 70 **NOTES:** No dogs (ex guide dogs) No smoking in restaurant **CARDS:**

## GOODRICH, Herefordshire
Map 03 SO51

**★★70% *Ye Hostelrie***
HR9 6HX
☎ 01600 890241 📠 01600 890838
e-mail: ye_hostelrie@lineone.net
***Dir:*** *1m off the A40, between Ross-on-Wye & Monmouth, within 100yds of Goodrich Castle*

Parts of this unusual building are reputed to date back to 1625. Considerable improvements to both accommodation and public areas have been made in the last few years, and there is a pleasant garden and patio area.
**ROOMS:** 6 en suite (2 fmly) **CONF:** Thtr 60 Class 40 Board 30 **PARKING:** 32 **NOTES:** No smoking in restaurant
**CARDS:**

*See advert under ROSS-ON-WYE*

## GOODRINGTON See Paignton

## GOODWOOD, West Sussex
Map 04 SU80

**★★★★72% Marriott Goodwood Park Hotel & Country Club**
PO18 0QB
☎ 01243 775537 📠 01243 520120
***Dir:*** *off the A285, 3m NE of Chichester*

This hotel offers extensive indoor and outdoor leisure facilities. Recent refurbishment ensures the bedrooms are furnished to a high standard, some in the old part of the building. Quality cuisine is served in the Richmond restaurant; there is also a smart cocktail bar and excellent conference facilities.
**ROOMS:** 94 en suite (1 fmly) No smoking in 54 bedrooms s £84-£99; d £104-£128 (incl. bkfst) * **LB** **FACILITIES:** STV Indoor swimming (H) Golf 18 Tennis (hard) Sauna Solarium Gym Putting green Jacuzzi Beauty salons Xmas **CONF:** Thtr 150 Class 60 Board 60 Del from £160 * **PARKING:** 250 **NOTES:** No dogs (ex guide dogs) No smoking in restaurant Civ Wed 120 **CARDS:**

## GOOLE, East Riding of Yorkshire
Map 08 SE72

**★★71% Clifton**
155 Boothferry Rd DN14 6AL
☎ 01405 761336 📠 01405 762350
e-mail: cliftonhotel@telinco.co.uk
***Dir:*** *leave M62 junct 36 & follow town centre signs. At 2nd set of traffic lights turn right into Boothferry Rd. Hotel is on left*
This delightful small hotel provides a high level of service and hospitality from friendly, attentive and willing staff. Bedrooms are attractively decorated and particularly well-equipped and the comfortable public rooms include a separate guests' lounge and a small bar. The pleasantly appointed restaurant offers a good choice of dishes.
**ROOMS:** 9 rms (8 en suite) (1 fmly) s £42; d £49 (incl. bkfst) * **LB** **CONF:** Thtr 40 Class 20 Board 20 **PARKING:** 8 **NOTES:** No smoking in restaurant **CARDS:**

## GORDANO MOTORWAY SERVICE AREA (M5), Somerset
Map 03 ST57

**⇧ Days Inn**
M5 Motorway BS20 7XG
☎ 01275 373709 & 373624 📠 01275 374104
e-mail: gordano.hotel@welcomebreak.co.uk
***Dir:*** *M5 junct 19, follow signs for Gordano services*
This modern building offers accommodation in smart, spacious and well-equipped bedrooms, suitable for families and business travellers, and all with en suite bathrooms. Continental breakfast is available and other refreshments may be taken at the nearby

*continued*

family restaurant. For further details and the Days Inn phone number, consult the Hotel Groups page.
**ROOMS:** 60 en suite s fr £49; d fr £49 * **CONF:** Board 12

GORLESTON-ON-SEA See Great Yarmouth

## GOSFORTH, Cumbria Map 11 NY00

### ★★71% Westlakes
CA20 1HP
☎ 019467 25221 🖷 019467 25099
e-mail: westlakeshotel@compuserve.com
***Dir:*** *junc of A595 and B5344*
A Georgian country house set in tranquil, mature gardens; careful refurbishment has resulted in a popular intimate hotel that is full of character. There is a compact lounge bar, and an attractive dining room comprising of three rooms, one of which is ideal for private dining or meetings. Bedrooms vary in style, but are all thoughtfully equipped.
**ROOMS:** 9 en suite (1 fmly) s £50-£52; d £66.50-£68 (incl. bkfst) * **FACILITIES:** STV Croquet lawn ch fac **PARKING:** 25 **NOTES:** No dogs (ex guide dogs) No smoking in restaurant RS Christmas & New Year
**CARDS:**

## GOSPORT, Hampshire Map 04 SZ69

### ★★★62% Belle Vue
39 Marine Pde East, Lee-on-Solent PO13 9BW
☎ 023 9255 0258 🖷 023 9255 2624
e-mail: information@bellevue-hotel.co.uk
***Dir:*** *M27 junct 9/11 to Fareham follow signs to Lee-on-Solent, hotel is on seafront*
Located on the sea front overlooking the beach with stunning views of the Solent. Bedrooms are attractively decorated, comfortably furnished and well-equipped, many rooms have lovely sea views. Public rooms include the spacious Promenade Bar and the smart Seasons Restaurant.
**ROOMS:** 24 en suite 3 annexe en suite (4 fmly) s £52; d £75-£82 * LB **FACILITIES:** STV entertainment **CONF:** Thtr 150 Class 60 Board 40 Del from £89.50 * **PARKING:** 55 **NOTES:** Closed 25-26 Dec RS 24 Dec
**CARDS:**

## GRANGE-OVER-SANDS, Cumbria Map 07 SD47

### ★★★69% Netherwood
Lindale Rd LA11 6ET
☎ 015395 32552 🖷 015395 34121
e-mail: blawith@aol.com
***Dir:*** *on B5277 just before the station*
Overlooking Morecambe Bay, this stylish hotel dating back to the 1800s is set in its own extensive, landscaped grounds. It provides modern facilities such as a spa and leisure club, as well as various function rooms, yet still manages to retain many original features such as oak-panelled rooms and open fires. Bedrooms vary in size but all are stylishly furnished and decorated, and have modern, fully tiled bathrooms.
**ROOMS:** 28 en suite (5 fmly) No smoking in 14 bedrooms s £55-£65; d £110-£130 (incl. bkfst) * LB **FACILITIES:** Indoor swimming (H) Solarium Gym Croquet lawn Jacuzzi Beauty salon Steam room ch fac **CONF:** Thtr 150 Class 30 Board 40 Del from £94 * **SERVICES:** Lift **PARKING:** 160 **NOTES:** No smoking in restaurant Civ Wed 150
**CARDS:**

Weekend away? Hotels with LB in their entry offer leisure breaks.

### ★★★64% Graythwaite Manor
Fernhill Rd LA11 7JE
☎ 015395 32001 & 33755 🖷 015395 35549
e-mail: enquiries@graythwaitemanor.co.uk
***Dir:*** *follow B5277 through Grange, Fernhill Road opposite fire station behind small traffic island, hotel first left*

In superb gardens above the town, this hotel enjoys lovely views. The comfortable bedrooms vary in size and style, and there is a choice of lounges and a restaurant. The ambitious cooking remains a real highlight.
**ROOMS:** 21 en suite (2 fmly) s £55-£75; d £99-£110 (incl. bkfst) * LB **FACILITIES:** Tennis (hard) Fishing Putting green 3/4 size billiard table Xmas **CONF:** Thtr 30 Board 20 Del from £85 * **SERVICES:** Lift **PARKING:** 32 **NOTES:** No dogs (ex guide dogs) No smoking in restaurant **CARDS:**

### ★★67% Hampsfell House
Hampsfell Rd LA11 6BG
☎ 015395 32567 🖷 015395 35995
e-mail: hampsfellhotel@email.msn.com
***Dir:*** *M6 junct 36, take exit A590 signed Barrow-in-Furness. Continue to junct with B5277 and follow to Grange-over-Sands. Left at rndbt into Main Street, continue to second rdbt turn right & at cross roads turn right. At Hampsfell Rd turn left*
Handy for the town and local amenities, this friendly hotel is situated in its own gardens off a quiet wooded lane. There are two cosy lounges served by one bar, and the well-maintained bedrooms are bright and cheerful.
**ROOMS:** 9 en suite (1 fmly) No smoking in 3 bedrooms s £38-£48; d £76-£82 (incl. bkfst) * LB **FACILITIES:** Xmas **PARKING:** 12 **NOTES:** No children 5yrs No smoking in restaurant
**CARDS:**

### ★78% ⊛ Clare House
Park Rd LA11 7HQ
☎ 015395 33026 & 34253
e-mail: ajread@clarehouse.fsbusiness.co.uk
***Dir:*** *turn off A590 onto B5277, through Lindale into Grange, keep left, hotel 0.5m on left past Crown Hill/St Paul's Church*
A warm, friendly welcome awaits guests at this elegant, family-run, Victorian country house hotel. Standing in its own secluded gardens, it provides a peaceful retreat in which to relax and to enjoy stunning views of the grounds and across Morecambe Bay. Bedrooms and public areas are comfortable and attractively furnished. Carefully prepared meals can be enjoyed in the charming dining room, and excellent, substantial breakfasts are not to be missed.
**ROOMS:** 17 rms (16 en suite) (1 fmly) s £30-£32; d £60-£64 (incl. bkfst) * LB **FACILITIES:** Croquet lawn Putting green **PARKING:** 18 **NOTES:** No dogs (ex guide dogs) No children 5yrs No smoking in restaurant Closed Dec-Mar RS Oct - Nov **CARDS:**

## GRANTHAM, Lincolnshire

Map 08 SK93

### ★★★74% Grantham Marriott

Swingbridge Rd NG31 7XT

☎ 01476 593000 🖷 01476 592592

**Dir:** *Exit off A1 at junct Grantham/Melton Mowbray A607. From N take 1st exit at mini rdbt, hotel is located on right. From S at T junct turn right towards Grantham. Under A1, take the next left signposted Marriott Hotel*

This smart, modern hotel offers comfortable and spacious public rooms; in the summer they extend into a pretty courtyard. Bedrooms are roomy, attractively furnished and well-equipped. There is also a full range of conference and leisure facilities and good car parking.

**ROOMS:** 90 en suite No smoking in 68 bedrooms d £89-£99 (incl. bkfst) * **LB** **FACILITIES:** STV Indoor swimming (H) Sauna Gym Jacuzzi Steam room entertainment Xmas **CONF:** Thtr 200 Class 90 Board 50 Del from £115 * **PARKING:** 150 **NOTES:** No smoking in restaurant

**CARDS:**

### ★★★68% Kings

North Pde NG31 8AU

☎ 01476 590800 🖷 01476 590800

e-mail: kingshotel@compuserve.com

**Dir:** *turn off A1 at rdbt northern end of Grantham onto B1174, follow road for 2m. Hotel on left by rail bridge*

An extended Georgian house, set back from the main road. Bedrooms are attractively decorated and furnished in modern light oak. A popular alternative to the more formal Victorian restaurant, the Orangery serves as both coffee shop and breakfast room. There is also a smart open-plan foyer lounge and bar.

**ROOMS:** 21 en suite (1 fmly) s £50-£65; d £60-£80 (incl. bkfst) * **LB** **FACILITIES:** STV Tennis (hard) **CONF:** Thtr 100 Class 50 Board 40 Del from £66.50 * **PARKING:** 36 **NOTES:** No smoking in restaurant

**CARDS:**

### ⌂ *Travelodge*

Travelodge

Grantham Service Area, Grantham North, Gonerby Moor NG32 2AB

☎ 01476 577500

**Dir:** *4m N on A1*

Travelodge offers good quality, good value, modern accommodation. Ideal for families, the spacious, en suite bedrooms include remote-control TV, tea and coffee-making facilities, luxury beds and free morning newspaper. Meals can be taken at the nearby family restaurant. For further details and the Travelodge phone number, consult the Hotel Groups page.

**ROOMS:** 40 en suite

## GRASMERE, Cumbria

Map 11 NY30

### ★★★★67% Wordsworth

LA22 9SW

☎ 015394 35592 🖷 015394 35765

e-mail: enquiry@wordsworth-grasmere.co.uk

**Dir:** *in centre of village adjacent to St Oswalds Church*

With fells rising in the background, The Wordsworth is a busy hotel in the heart of Grasmere village. There are a host of leisure facilities, a pub and plenty of spacious lounge areas. Bedrooms are individually and traditionally styled.

**ROOMS:** 37 en suite (3 fmly) s £120-£200; d £190-£300 (incl. bkfst & dinner) * **LB** **FACILITIES:** STV Indoor swimming (H) Sauna Solarium Gym Croquet lawn Jacuzzi entertainment ch fac Xmas **CONF:** Thtr 130 Class 50 Board 40 Del from £135 * **SERVICES:** Lift **PARKING:** 60 **NOTES:** No dogs (ex guide dogs) No smoking in restaurant Civ Wed 120

**CARDS:**

*See advert on opposite page*

## *Premier Collection*

### ★★★ Michael's Nook Country House

LA22 9RP

☎ 015394 35496 🖷 015394 35645

e-mail: m-nook@wordsworth-grasmere.co.uk

**Dir:** *turn off A591 between The Swan Hotel and its car park just North of village. Hotel 400yds on right*

Michael's Nook is a unique Victorian country house hotel, which occupies a fine elevated position in its own landscaped gardens, close to Dove Cottage. The public areas are elegant and spacious, and are furnished with fine period and antique pieces. Bedrooms, all individually designed, are equipped with a host of luxurious extras and include a split-level suite and

*continued*

rooms with private patios. Dinner is a memorable experience not to be missed.
**ROOMS:** 14 en suite s fr £148; d fr £190 (incl. bkfst & dinner) * **LB** **FACILITIES:** Croquet lawn Leisure fac at Wordsworth Hotel Xmas **CONF:** Thtr 24 Board 20 **PARKING:** 20 **NOTES:** No dogs (ex guide dogs) No smoking in restaurant Civ Wed 30
**CARDS:**

### ★★★73% Gold Rill Country House

Red Bank Rd LA22 9PU
☎ 015394 35486 📠 015394 35486
e-mail: enquiries@gold-rill.com
***Dir:*** *turn off A591 into village centre, turn into road opposite St Oswalds Church. Hotel 300yds on left*

With spectacular views of the mountain and lake, this relaxed and friendly hotel offers elegant, traditional service. There are comfortable lounges and an attractive restaurant, where irresistible steamed puddings are a speciality. Many guests return two or three times a year.
**ROOMS:** 25 en suite 3 annexe en suite (2 fmly) s £59-£65; d £118-£130 (incl. bkfst & dinner) * **LB** **FACILITIES:** STV Outdoor swimming (H) Croquet lawn Putting green Xmas **PARKING:** 35 **NOTES:** No dogs No smoking in restaurant Closed mid Dec-mid Jan (open Xmas & New Year)
**CARDS:**

### ★★★71% *Rothay Garden*

Broadgate LA22 9RJ
☎ 015394 35334 📠 015394 35723
e-mail: rothay@grasmere.com
***Dir:*** *turn off A591, opposite Swan Hotel, into Grasmere village, 300 yds on left*

Located on the northern approach to this unspoilt Cumbrian village, this hotel offers comfortable bedrooms, including some with four-posters and whirlpool baths. There is a choice of relaxing lounges and a cosy cocktail bar, as well as a conservatory restaurant, which enjoys magnificent views across the lawns up into the fells.
**ROOMS:** 25 en suite (2 fmly) **FACILITIES:** STV Fishing Jacuzzi use of local leisure club ch fac **CONF:** Thtr 16 Class 16 Board 16 Del from £95 * **PARKING:** 38 **NOTES:** No smoking in restaurant
**CARDS:**

### ★★★70% Red Lion

Red Lion Square LA22 9SS
☎ 015394 35456 📠 015394 35579
e-mail: enquires@hotelgrasmere.uk.com
***Dir:*** *turn off A591, signposted Grasmere Village, hotel is in centre of the village*

This former coaching inn, in the heart of the village is now a spacious, smart hotel. Tasteful bedrooms are well-equipped and all have smart bathrooms. Guests can choose between the buzzing

*continued on p250*

G

GRASMERE, continued

Lamb Inn pub serving traditional ales or the quieter, comfortable conservatory lounge bar where snacks and afternoon teas are also served.

*Red Lion, Grasmere*

**ROOMS:** 47 en suite (4 fmly) No smoking in 12 bedrooms s £48.50-£56.50; d £97-£113 (incl. bkfst) **FACILITIES:** Spa STV Sauna Solarium Gym Jacuzzi Hairdressing ch fac Xmas **CONF:** Thtr 60 Class 30 Board 30 Del from £80 * **SERVICES:** Lift **PARKING:** 38 **NOTES:** No smoking in restaurant **CARDS:**

See advert on page 249

### ★★★70% The Swan

LA22 9RF
☎ 0870 400 8132 015394 35741
e-mail: heritagehotels-grasmere.swan@forte-hotels.com
***Dir:*** *M6 junct 36, take A590 past Windermere, follow signs for Grasmere and Keswick. Hotel is on outskirts of village. Do not go into Grasmere village instead follow road to Keswick*

Occupying a prominent position on the edge of the village close to Dove Cottage, this 300-year-old inn was mentioned by Wordsworth in his poem 'The Waggoner'. Attractive public areas are spacious and comfortable with fresh flowers and real fires in winter. Bedrooms are equally stylish and are all equipped with CD players. A good range of bar meals are available, whilst the elegant restaurant offers more formal dining.

**ROOMS:** 38 en suite No smoking in 20 bedrooms s £70-£115; d £140-£190 (incl. bkfst & dinner) * LB **FACILITIES:** Xmas **PARKING:** 40 **NOTES:** No smoking in restaurant **CARDS:**

### ★★74% Grasmere

Broadgate LA22 9TA
☎ 015394 35277 015394 35277
e-mail: grashotel@aol.com
***Dir:*** *take A591 from Ambleside, then second turning left into town centre. Follow road over humpbacked bridge, past playing field. Hotel on left*

Attentive and hospitable service make for a good atmosphere at this family-run hotel set in secluded gardens bordered by the River Rothay. There are two inviting lounges (one with residents' bar) and an attractive dining room looking onto the garden. The thoughtfully chosen dinner menu makes careful use of fresh ingredients. Smart pine is featured in most bedrooms.

**ROOMS:** 12 en suite **FACILITIES:** STV Croquet lawn Putting green **PARKING:** 16 **NOTES:** No children 6yrs No smoking in restaurant Closed Jan-8 Feb **CARDS:**

Packed in a hurry? Ironing facilities should be available at all star levels, either in rooms or on request.

### ★★71% Oak Bank

Broadgate LA22 9TA
☎ 015394 35217 015394 35685
e-mail: info@lakedistricthotel.co.uk
***Dir:*** *in centre of village just off A591*

A relaxed and welcoming atmosphere prevails at this comfortable holiday hotel in the centre of the village. Bedrooms vary in size, have pleasing colour schemes and are comfortably furnished in antique pine. There is a choice of stylish lounges, a well-stocked bar and an attractive restaurant with conservatory extension.

**ROOMS:** 15 en suite (1 fmly) s £47; d £84-£104 (incl. bkfst & dinner) * LB **FACILITIES:** Jacuzzi Xmas **PARKING:** 15 **NOTES:** No smoking in restaurant **CARDS:**

## Premier Collection

### ★ White Moss House

Rydal Water LA22 9SE
☎ 015394 35295 015394 35516
e-mail: sue@whitemoss.com
***Dir:*** *on A591, 1m S of Grasmere*

This traditional Lakeland house was once bought by Wordsworth for his son. It benefits from a central location and a loyal following. The individually styled bedrooms are comfortable and thoughtfully equipped. There is also a two-room suite in a cottage on the hillside above the hotel. Peter Dixon's five-course set dinner makes good use of the quality local ingredients. Afternoon tea and pre-dinner drinks are served in the inviting lounge.

**ROOMS:** 7 en suite 2 annexe en suite s £69-£89; d £138-£178 (incl. bkfst & dinner) * LB **FACILITIES:** Free use local leisure club, Free fishing at local waters **PARKING:** 10 **NOTES:** No dogs No smoking in restaurant Closed Dec-Jan RS Sun **CARDS:**

GRASSINGTON, North Yorkshire Map 07 SE06

### ★★63% Grassington House

5 The Square BD23 5AQ
☎ 01756 752406 01756 752135
***Dir:*** *Take B6265 from Skipton, on right hand side of village square*

Centrally located in the main square, this popular, family-owned hotel offers homely and welcoming accommodation. Day rooms are spacious and pleasant to relax in. Service is willing and friendly, and a good range of food is provided in either the informal bar or the elegant dining room.

**ROOMS:** 9 en suite (2 fmly) No smoking in all bedrooms s £29-£35; d fr £59 (incl. bkfst) * LB **FACILITIES:** ch fac Xmas **PARKING:** 20 **NOTES:** No smoking in restaurant **CARDS:**

Bad hair day? Hairdryers in all rooms three stars and above.

GRAVESEND, Kent Map 05 TQ67

★★★72% **Manor Hotel**
Hever Court Rd DA12 5UQ
☎ 01474 353100 🖷 01474 354978
e-mail: manorhotel@clara.net
***Dir:*** *A2 Gravesend East turn off, hotel at this junction*
Modern privately owned hotel conveniently located close to the A2 with its links to the motorways, channel ports and tunnel. The spacious bedrooms are attractively decorated and thoughtfully equipped with many useful extras. Public rooms include a large open plan lounge bar and a smart restaurant. There is also a health club with a swimming pool, sauna and gymnasium.
**ROOMS:** 52 en suite (3 fmly) No smoking in 37 bedrooms s fr £78; d fr £88 (incl. bkfst) * **FACILITIES:** STV Indoor swimming (H) Sauna Solarium Gym **CONF:** Thtr 200 Class 100 Board 25 Del from £105 * **PARKING:** 100 **NOTES:** No dogs (ex guide dogs)
**CARDS:**

***Premier Lodge***
Hevercourt Rd, Singlewell DA12 5UQ
☎ 0870 700 1382 🖷 0870 700 1383
Premier Lodge offers modern, well-equipped, en suite accommodation suitable for both business and leisure travellers. Meals can be taken at the adjacent popular restaurant and bar, which is fully licensed. For further details, consult the Hotel Groups page.
**ROOMS:** 31 en suite

GREAT CHESTERFORD, Essex Map 05 TL54

★★68% **The Crown House**
CB10 1NY
☎ 01799 530515 🖷 01799 530683
***Dir:*** *on B1383 1m from junct 9 on M11*
This pleasantly furnished hotel dates back to Tudor times and offers bedrooms of character in the main house while the rooms in the courtyard are more modern in style. The newly refurbished lounge bar is a delightful room as are two dining rooms. Staff are friendly and attentive.
**ROOMS:** 8 en suite 10 annexe en suite (1 fmly) s £63; d £85-£120 (incl. bkfst) * **LB** **CONF:** Thtr 38 Class 40 Board 30 Del from £99.50 * **PARKING:** 30 **NOTES:** No smoking in restaurant Civ Wed 40
**CARDS:**

GREAT DUNMOW, Essex Map 05 TL62

★★63% **The Saracen's Head**
High St CM6 1AG
☎ 01371 873901 🖷 01371 875743
***Dir:*** *take A120 towards Colchester turn left at 2nd rndbt, hotel 0.50m downhill*

SARACEN'S HEAD HOTEL

Situated at the heart of an attractive market town, this former coaching inn is conveniently located for Stanstead Airport. Much of the original character of the building has been preserved in the beamed public rooms. The spacious bedrooms are decorated in traditional style and equipped with a useful range of extras.
**ROOMS:** 4 en suite 20 annexe en suite (3 fmly) No smoking in 5 bedrooms s £77; d £90 * **LB** **CONF:** Thtr 50 Class 30 Board 34 Del from £85 * **PARKING:** 65 **NOTES:** No dogs (ex guide dogs) No smoking in restaurant **CARDS:**

GREAT LANGDALE See Elterwater

GREAT MILTON, Oxfordshire Map 04 SP60

*Premier Collection*

★★★★ @@@@@ **Le Manoir Aux Quat' Saisons**
OX44 7PD
☎ 01844 278881 🖷 01844 278847
e-mail: lemanoir@blanc.co.uk
***Dir:*** *from A329 take 2nd right turn to Great Milton Manor, hotel 200yds on right*
One of Britain's great dining destinations, Le Manoir also offers superb accommodation. A walk round the gardens rewards the guest with captivating vistas and an abundance of bronze sculptures to admire. The kitchen gardens provide much of Le Manoir's produce and are the envy of any gardener. Bedrooms are individual in style, some quite fantastic, others more conventional. Public rooms are furnished and decorated with great taste, and offer high standards of comfort and luxury.
**ROOMS:** 32 rms (9 en suite) s £245-£750; d £245-£750 (incl. cont bkfst) * **LB** **FACILITIES:** STV Croquet lawn Cookery School Water Gardens ch fac Xmas **CONF:** Thtr 24 Board 20 **PARKING:** 60 **NOTES:** No dogs (ex guide dogs) No smoking in restaurant Civ Wed 55 **CARDS:**

GREAT YARMOUTH, Norfolk Map 05 TG50

★★★74% **Cliff**
Cliffe Hill, Gorleston NR31 6DH
☎ 01493 662179 🖷 01493 653617
***Dir:*** *M11. A11 to Norwich, A47 to Gt Yarmouth, situated at north end Gorleston's Upper Marine Parade*
Overlooking the sea close to the centre of Gorleston is this hotel which offers excellent accommodation. Public rooms feature a smart restaurant, a choice of bars and an attractive lounge. Although the bedrooms vary in style they are all furnished to a good standard, with well-matched furnishings.
**ROOMS:** 39 en suite (2 fmly) No smoking in 2 bedrooms s £71-£120; d £100-£150 (incl. bkfst) **LB** **FACILITIES:** STV entertainment Xmas **CONF:** Thtr 170 Class 150 Board 80 Del from £95 * **PARKING:** 70 **NOTES:** Civ Wed 120 **CARDS:**

GREAT YARMOUTH, continued

**★★★68% Imperial**
North Dr NR30 1EQ
☎ 01493 842000 01493 852229
e-mail: imperial@scs-datacom.co.uk
***Dir:*** *follow signs to seafront and turn left, Hotel opposite tennis courts*
A spacious hotel situated at the quieter end of the seafront and within easy walking distance of the town centre. The extensive public areas include banqueting rooms, the comfortable Savoie Lounge Bar, and the Rambouillet Restaurant and Brasserie. The colour co-ordinated accommodation is attractive and well-equipped.
**ROOMS:** 39 en suite (4 fmly) No smoking in 12 bedrooms s £50-£70; d £60-£86 (incl. bkfst) * **LB** **FACILITIES:** STV ch fac Xmas **CONF:** Thtr 120 Class 30 Board 30 Del from £65 * **SERVICES:** Lift **PARKING:** 50
**CARDS:**

G

**★★★68% Star**
Hall Quay NR30 1HG
☎ 01493 842294 01493 330215
e-mail: starhotel@westerfieldhotels.co.uk
***Dir:*** *from Norwich A47 continue straight over 1st rdbt onto 2nd rdbt and take 3rd exit. Continue & hotel on left*
Overlooking the quayside, this friendly, tastefully furnished hotel has a fascinating history. The intimate public rooms are richly decorated and welcoming. The bedrooms are freshly decorated and have vibrant interior design as well as good facilities.
**ROOMS:** 40 en suite (1 fmly) No smoking in 13 bedrooms s £70-£120; d £85-£140 (incl. bkfst) * **LB** **FACILITIES:** STV Xmas **CONF:** Thtr 75 Class 30 Board 30 Del from £85 * **SERVICES:** Lift **PARKING:** 20
**CARDS:**

**★★★67% Regency Dolphin**
Albert Square NR30 3JH
☎ 01493 855070 01493 853798
e-mail: regency@meridianleisure.com
***Dir:*** *proceed along seafront and turn right at Wellington Pier, turn right into Kimberley Terr, follow road and turn left into Albert Sq, hotel is on left*

Regency Dolphin Hotel
HOTEL

A smart hotel situated in a side road close to the seafront, pier and local attractions. The bedrooms are generally quite spacious, tastefully decorated and well-equipped; many rooms have sea views. Public rooms include a comfortable lounge, a bar and intimate restaurant. The hotel also has an outdoor swimming pool.
**ROOMS:** 48 en suite (6 fmly) No smoking in 8 bedrooms s £65; d £75 (incl. bkfst) * **LB** **FACILITIES:** STV Outdoor swimming (H) Xmas **CONF:** Thtr 140 Class 50 Board 30 Del from £75 * **PARKING:** 20
**NOTES:** No smoking in restaurant Civ Wed 120
**CARDS:**

*See advert on opposite page*

**★★72% *The Arden Court Hotel***
93-94 North Denes Rd NR30 4LW
☎ 01493 855310 01493 855310
***Dir:*** *follow signs to seafront. At seafront turn left along North Drive. At boating lake turn left. At mini rdbt take 2nd right into North Denes rd*
Guests are assured of a warm welcome at the Arden Court, with genuine courtesy and care provided. Service is both attentive and efficient, with lounge and room service readily available. Public rooms are attractively presented, and the restaurant offers freshly prepared home-cooked dishes. Bedrooms are thoughtfully equipped and pleasantly appointed.
**ROOMS:** 14 en suite (4 fmly) No smoking in 5 bedrooms **PARKING:** 12
**NOTES:** No dogs (ex guide dogs) No smoking in restaurant
**CARDS:**

**★★67% Knights Court Hotel**
22 North Dr NR30 4EW
☎ 01493 843089 01493 850780
***Dir:*** *follow seafront signs. Hotel opposite Venetian Waterways & Gardens*
Immaculately maintained, this small, privately owned hotel overlooks the Venetian waterways and the sea. Bedrooms are generally quite spacious and thoughtfully equipped; many rooms have lovely sea views. Breakfast is served in the smart dining room and guests also have the use of a cosy lounge bar.
**ROOMS:** 14 en suite (3 fmly) **CONF:** Class 20 **PARKING:** 18
**NOTES:** No smoking in restaurant Closed mid Oct-mid Mar
**CARDS:**

**★★67% Regency**
5 North Dr NR30 1ED
☎ 01493 843759 01493 330411
e-mail: regency35@hotmail.com
***Dir:*** *on sea front*
This traditional hotel is situated at the quiet end of town overlooking the seafront. The hotel has been owned and run by the same family for a number of years and the regular guests appreciate the friendly ambience and high standards. Although the bedrooms vary in size and style they all have good facilities.
**ROOMS:** 14 en suite (2 fmly) s £36; d £54 (incl. bkfst) * **LB** **FACILITIES:** Xmas **PARKING:** 10 **NOTES:** No dogs (ex guide dogs) No children 7yrs No smoking in restaurant Closed Jan
**CARDS:**

**★★66% Burlington Palm Court**
11 North Dr NR30 1EG
☎ 01493 844568 & 842095 01493 331848
e-mail: enquiries@burlington-hotel.co.uk
***Dir:*** *A12 to sea front, turn left at Britannia Pier. Hotel close to tennis courts*
This privately owned hotel is at the quiet end of the resort and overlooks the sea. The pleasant, well equipped bedrooms come in a variety of sizes and styles. Sister properties, the Burlington and the Palm Court provide joint facilities for all residents.
**ROOMS:** 71 en suite (9 fmly) No smoking in 14 bedrooms s £50-£70; d £76-£98 (incl. bkfst) * **LB** **FACILITIES:** STV Indoor swimming (H) Jacuzzi Turkish steam room entertainment Xmas **CONF:** Thtr 120 Class 60 Board 30 Del from £50 * **SERVICES:** Lift **PARKING:** 70
**NOTES:** No dogs (ex guide dogs) Closed Jan-Feb RS Dec (group bookings only) **CARDS:**

*See advert on opposite page*

**★★64% Furzedown**
19-20 North Dr NR30 4EW
☎ 01493 844138 01493 844138
e-mail: PaulG@Furzedownhotel.freeserve.co.uk
***Dir:*** *At end of A47 or A12, head for seafront, turn left, hotel is opposite Waterways*
Situated at the north end of the seafront, this privately owned

*continued*

hotel overlooks the beach and Venetian waterways. Bedrooms are well-equipped, brightly decorated and represent good value for money. Fresh floral displays feature in the day rooms, which include a bar and a TV lounge. Set price and carte menus are offered for dinner.

**ROOMS:** 23 rms (19 en suite) (11 fmly) s £40-£48; d £53-£67 (incl. bkfst) * **LB** **FACILITIES:** STV **CONF:** Thtr 100 Class 100 Board 100 Del from £22.50 * **PARKING:** 15 **NOTES:** No smoking in restaurant **CARDS:**

### ★★62% New Beach Hotel

Leisureplex

67 Marine Pde NR30 2EJ
☎ 01493 332300 🖷 01493 331880
An impressive Victorian building centrally located on the seafront overlooking Britannia Pier and the sandy beach. Bedrooms are pleasantly decorated and equipped with modern facilities, many rooms have lovely sea views. Dinner is taken in the first floor restaurant which doubles as the ballroom and guests can also relax in the bar or sunny lounge.
**ROOMS:** 75 en suite (3 fmly) s £25-£30; d £42-£58 (incl. bkfst) * **FACILITIES:** entertainment Xmas **SERVICES:** Lift **NOTES:** No dogs (ex guide dogs) No smoking in restaurant Closed Jan-Feb, part Nov/Mar RS part Nov/Mar (open weekdays only) **CARDS:**

---

## GREENFORD, Greater London
See LONDON SECTION plan 1 B4

### ★★★69% The Bridge

Western Av UB6 8ST
☎ 020 8566 6246 🖷 020 8566 6140
e-mail: bridgehotel@youngs.co.uk
Ideally located for access to and from central London, this hotel remains a popular choice. Spacious bedrooms offer a good range of facilities and some have four-poster beds. There is a popular bar and bistro-style restaurant. Secure car parking is an added bonus for car users.
**ROOMS:** 68 en suite (4 fmly) No smoking in 44 bedrooms s £68-£96; d £74-£110 (incl. bkfst) * **FACILITIES:** STV Arrangement with local leisure centre **CONF:** Thtr 130 Class 60 Board 60 **SERVICES:** Lift **PARKING:** 68 **NOTES:** No dogs (ex guide dogs) No smoking in restaurant Civ Wed 120 **CARDS:**

---

## GRIMSBY, Lincolnshire
Map 08 TA20

### ★★★65% Beeches

42 Waltham Rd, Scartho DN33 2LX
☎ 01472 278830 🖷 01472 278830
e-mail: joeramsden@freeuk.com
In the suburb of Scartho, not far from the town centre, this contemporary hotel offers good modern accommodation and pleasing public rooms. Bedrooms are inviting and nicely equipped

*continued on p254*

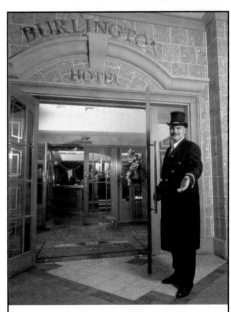

GRIMSBY, continued

with a thoughtful range of facilities. There is a popular brasserie and a comfortable lounge bar.
**ROOMS:** 10 en suite No smoking in all bedrooms s fr £43; d fr £63 (incl. bkfst) * **LB** **CONF:** Del from £78.50 * **SERVICES:** Lift **PARKING:** 70 **NOTES:** No dogs (ex guide dogs) No smoking in restaurant **CARDS:**

### ★★★64% Humber Royal

Littlecoates Rd DN34 4LX
☎ 01472 240024 01472 241354
e-mail: enquiries@humberroyal.co
***Dir:*** *take A1136 signed Greatcoates, left at first rdbt right at second rdbt. Hotel is on right 200 metres down*
Bedrooms at this pleasantly situated hotel are equipped with all modern comforts and many have large windows and balconies overlooking the adjoining golf course; this view is also shared by the popular restaurant. There is a large banqueting suite in addition to the smaller meeting and conference rooms. 24 hour room service is available.
**ROOMS:** 52 en suite (4 fmly) No smoking in 27 bedrooms s fr £60; d fr £70 (incl. bkfst) * **LB** **FACILITIES:** Xmas **CONF:** Thtr 300 Class 100 Board 60 Del £89 * **SERVICES:** Lift **PARKING:** 200 **NOTES:** Civ Wed **CARDS:**

G

GRIMSTON, Norfolk Map 09 TF72

## Premier Collection

### ★★★ Congham Hall Country House

Lynn Rd PE32 1AH
☎ 01485 600250 01485 601191
e-mail: reception@conghamhallhotel.com
***Dir:*** *A149/A148 interchange north east of King's Lynn, follow A148 to Sandringham/Fakenham/Cromer for 100yds. Turn right to Grimston, hotel 2.5m on left*
An elegant 18th-century Georgian manor set amidst 30 acres of paddocks, parkland and neat lawns. The public rooms provide a range of beautifully furnished and comfortable areas in which to sit and relax. Quality cuisine is served in the Orangery Restaurant, which has an intimate atmosphere and panoramic views of the gardens. The bedrooms are mostly furnished in period style but have modern facilities and many thoughtful touches. Service is attentive and extremely friendly.
**ROOMS:** 14 en suite No smoking in all bedrooms s £85-£135; d £130-£240 (incl. bkfst) * **LB** **FACILITIES:** Outdoor swimming (H) Tennis (hard) Croquet lawn Putting green Jacuzzi Cricket, shooting Xmas **CONF:** Thtr 50 Class 20 Board 30 **PARKING:** 50 **NOTES:** No dogs (ex guide dogs) No children 7yrs No smoking in restaurant Civ Wed 60 **CARDS:**

GRINDLEFORD, Derbyshire Map 08 SK27

### ★★★68% Maynard Arms

Main Rd S32 2HE
☎ 01433 630321 01433 630445
e-mail: info@maynardarms.co.uk
***Dir:*** *leave Sheffield on the A625 towards Castleton. Turn left into Grindleford on the B6521 after the Fox House. Hotel is on left*
A delightful country mansion in attractive gardens with fine views. Bedrooms are very tastefully furnished and decorated, some have four-poster beds and two have separate sitting rooms. A very comfortable lounge is situated on the first floor, overlooking the garden, and the restaurant has similar views. Bar food is available at both lunch and dinner.
**ROOMS:** 10 en suite s £69-£89; d £79-£99 (incl. bkfst) * **LB** **FACILITIES:** STV Xmas **CONF:** Thtr 140 Class 80 Board 60 Del from £92 * **PARKING:** 80 **NOTES:** No smoking in restaurant Civ Wed 120 **CARDS:**

GUILDFORD, Surrey Map 04 SU94

### ★★★75% The Angel Posting House and Livery

91 High St GU1 3DP
☎ 01483 564555 01483 533770
e-mail: angelhotel@hotmail.com

POSTING HOUSE.
LIVERY STABLES.

This historic coaching inn offers friendly service. Many of the bedroom suites are beamed, and all are equipped with thoughtful extras. Cosy public areas retain original features such as a Jacobean fireplace and 17th-century parliament clock. The 13th-century, stone-vaulted Crypt Restaurant serves tempting dishes with high quality ingredients.
**ROOMS:** 11 en suite 10 annexe en suite (4 fmly) s £135-£200; d £135-£200 * **LB** **FACILITIES:** STV **CONF:** Thtr 80 Class 20 Board 40 Del from £221 * **SERVICES:** Lift **NOTES:** No smoking in restaurant **CARDS:**

*See advert on opposite page*

### ★★★70% The Manor

Newlands Corner GU4 8SE
☎ 01483 222624 01483 211389
e-mail: mail@hollybournehotels.com
***Dir:*** *3.5m on A25 to Dorking*
With its quiet yet convenient location and attractive grounds, this hotel, dating back to the 1890s, is a popular venue for conferences and weddings. Bedrooms are fairly modern, tastefully furnished and decorated and feature a good range of facilities. The public areas consist of a variety of meeting rooms, a spacious lounge area and an attractive restaurant and bar.
**ROOMS:** 45 en suite (4 fmly) No smoking in 4 bedrooms s fr £79; d fr £95 * **LB** **FACILITIES:** Croquet lawn **CONF:** Thtr 150 Class 50 Board 50 **PARKING:** 100 **NOTES:** No smoking in restaurant Civ Wed 120 **CARDS:**

### ★★★69% *Posthouse Guildford*

Posthouse

Egerton Rd GU2 5XZ
☎ 0870 400 9036 🖹 01483 302960
***Dir:*** *exit A3 for Hospital and Cathedral, take third exit at rdbt then second exit at next*
Located near the cathedral and university, this large, modern hotel has smartly appointed bedrooms, all of which are spacious and well-equipped. Public areas include a large, comfortable bar lounge and a health club.
**ROOMS:** 162 en suite (100 fmly) No smoking in 71 bedrooms
**FACILITIES:** STV Indoor swimming (H) Sauna Solarium Gym
**CONF:** Thtr 200 Class 100 Board 45 **PARKING:** 220
**CARDS:**

## GUISBOROUGH, North Yorkshire — Map 08 NZ61

### ★★63% *Cross Keys*

Scottish Newcastle hotels

Upsall TS14 6RW
☎ 01287 610035 🖹 01287 639037
This large, stone-built property is in open countryside in a main road location. There are extensive dining areas offering a wide range of dishes. Lodge-style bedrooms are modern and well-equipped.
**ROOMS:** 20 en suite (2 fmly) No smoking in 10 bedrooms
**FACILITIES:** entertainment **PARKING:** 300 **NOTES:** No dogs (ex guide dogs) No smoking in restaurant **CARDS:**

### ○ *Guisborough Hall*

Whitby Rd TS14 6PT
☎ 0870 4008191
At the time of going to press, the star classification for this hotel was not confirmed. Please refer to the AA internet site www.theAA.com for current information.
**ROOMS:** 71 en suite **NOTES:** Opening December 2001

## GULWORTHY, Devon — Map 02 SX47

### ★★★77% ®®® Horn of Plenty

PL19 8JD
☎ 01822 832528 🖹 01822 832528
e-mail: enquiries@thehornofplenty.co.uk
***Dir:*** *from Tavistock take A390 W for 3m and turn right at Gulworthy Cross. After 400yds turn left and continue for a further 400yds to hotel on right*

Set above the Tamar Valley, this beautiful country house enjoys stunning views across to Bodmin Moor. All bedrooms are well-equipped and have many thoughtful extras. The elegantly furnished public rooms are comfortable and the renowned restaurant benefits from excellent views. The cuisine has flair and imagination. There is a well-tended, walled garden.
**ROOMS:** 4 en suite 6 annexe en suite (3 fmly) No smoking in 1 bedroom s £105-£190; d £115-£200 (incl. bkfst) * **LB**
**FACILITIES:** ch fac Xmas **CONF:** Thtr 20 Class 20 Board 12 Del from £134 * **PARKING:** 25 **NOTES:** No smoking in restaurant Closed 24-26 Dec Civ Wed 120 **CARDS:**

## GUNTHORPE, Nottinghamshire — Map 08 SK64

### ★★70% *Unicorn*

Gunthorpe Bridge NG14 7FB
☎ 0115 966 3612 🖹 0115 966 4801
***Dir:*** *on A6097, between Lowdham and Bingham*
This popular and characterful riverside inn offers a light and airy restaurant and bars featuring exposed timbers and brickwork. Spacious, comfortable bedrooms are thoughtfully equipped with many extra facilities. Both the bar and restaurant menus centre on good home-cooked food, with friendly, informal service.
**ROOMS:** 16 en suite (3 fmly) **FACILITIES:** STV Fishing **PARKING:** 200
**NOTES:** No dogs (ex guide dogs) **CARDS:**

## HACKNESS, North Yorkshire — Map 08 SE99

### ★★★70% ® *Hackness Grange Country House*

Best Western

North York National Park YO13 0JW
☎ 01723 882345 🖹 01723 882391
***Dir:*** *A64 to Scarborough and then A171 to Whitby/Scalby, follow signs to Hackness/Forge Valley National Park, through Hackness village on left hand side*
Close to Scarborough, and set in the North Yorkshire Moors National Park, Hackness Grange is surrounded by well-tended gardens. Comfortable bedrooms have views of the open countryside; those in the cottages are ideally suited to families, and the courtyard rooms include disabled facilities. Lounges and the restaurant are spacious and relaxing.
**ROOMS:** 33 en suite (5 fmly) **FACILITIES:** STV Indoor swimming (H) Tennis (hard) Croquet lawn Putting green Jacuzzi 9 hole pitch & putt
**CONF:** Thtr 15 Class 8 Board 8 **PARKING:** 60 **NOTES:** No dogs (ex guide dogs) No smoking in restaurant
**CARDS:**

## HADLEY WOOD, Greater London Map 04 TQ29

### ★★★★71% West Lodge Park

Cockfosters Rd EN4 0PY
☎ 020 8216 3900 020 8216 3937
e-mail: info@westlodgepark.com
***Dir:*** *on A111, 1m S of exit 24 on M25*

An impressive country house hotel set in parkland and gardens, yet only 12 miles from London's West End. Bedrooms are individually furnished and decorated, offering a comprehensive range of in-room facilities. The Cedar Restaurant offers a range of interesting, Rosette worthy dishes.

**ROOMS:** 46 en suite 9 annexe en suite (1 fmly) No smoking in 19 bedrooms s £98-£120; d £120-£215 * **LB** **FACILITIES:** **Spa** STV Croquet lawn Putting green Free membership of sports academy Xmas **CONF:** Thtr 80 Class 24 Board 30 **SERVICES:** Lift **PARKING:** 200 **NOTES:** No dogs (ex guide dogs) No smoking in restaurant Civ Wed 40 **CARDS:**

## HAILSHAM, East Sussex Map 05 TQ50

### ★★★65% Boship Farm

Forestdale Hotels

Lower Dicker BN27 4AT
☎ 01323 844826 01323 843945
e-mail: Boship.farm@forestdale.com
***Dir:*** *on A22 at Boship roundabout, junct of A22/A267/A271*

Dating back to 1652, this lovely old farmhouse forms the hub of the hotel and is set in 17 acres of well-tended grounds. Guests have the use of an all-weather tennis court and outdoor pool; croquet is also available. Bedrooms are smartly appointed and well-equipped; most have views across the fields and countryside beyond.

**ROOMS:** 47 annexe en suite (5 fmly) No smoking in 17 bedrooms s £60-£70; d £120-£140 (incl. bkfst & dinner) * **LB** **FACILITIES:** Outdoor swimming (H) Tennis (hard) Gym Croquet lawn Jacuzzi Xmas **CONF:** Thtr 175 Class 40 Board 46 Del £95 * **PARKING:** 100 **NOTES:** No smoking in restaurant Civ Wed **CARDS:**

### ★★69% The Olde Forge Hotel & Restaurant

Magham Down BN27 1PN
☎ 01323 842893 01323 842893
e-mail: theoldeforgehotelandrestaurant@tesco.net
***Dir:*** *off Boship rdbt on A271 to Bexhill. 3m on left, opposite The Red Lion Public House*

In the heart of the Wealdon countryside, this family-run hotel offers a warm friendly welcome with an informal atmosphere. The bedrooms are attractively decorated with thoughtful extras. The restaurant, with its timbered beams and log fires, once the home of a 16th-century forge, is gaining a growing reputation for its cuisine and service.

**ROOMS:** 7 en suite s £45; d £65-£75 (incl. bkfst) * **LB** **FACILITIES:** ch fac **PARKING:** 11 **NOTES:** No smoking in restaurant **CARDS:**

### ⇧ *Travelodge*

Travelodge

Boship Roundabout, Hellingly BN27 4DT
☎ 01323 844556 01323 844556
***Dir:*** *on A22 at Boship roundabout*

Travelodge offers good quality, good value, modern accommodation. Ideal for families, the spacious, en suite bedrooms include remote-control TV, tea and coffee-making facilities, luxury beds and free morning newspaper. Meals can be taken at the nearby family restaurant. For further details and the Travelodge phone number, consult the Hotel Groups page.

**ROOMS:** 40 en suite

## HALIFAX, West Yorkshire Map 07 SE02

### ★★★76% Holdsworth House

Holdsworth HX2 9TG
☎ 01422 240024 01422 245174
e-mail: info@holdsworthhouse.co.uk
***Dir:*** *From town centre take A629 Keighley Rd. Turn right at garage up Shay Lane after 1.5m. Hotel on right after 1m.*

This delightful 17th century Jacobean manor house is set in manicured gardens and has been extended to provide individually decorated, thoughtfully equipped rooms. Guests can relax in front of a real fire in one of the many cosy lounges. Dinner provides the highlight of any stay with traditional dishes benefiting from a modern, skilled approach.

**ROOMS:** 40 en suite (2 fmly) No smoking in 15 bedrooms s £87-£122; d £107-£138 (incl. cont bkfst) * **LB** **FACILITIES:** STV ch fac **CONF:** Thtr 150 Class 75 Board 50 Del £122.50 * **PARKING:** 60 **NOTES:** No smoking in restaurant Civ Wed 118 **CARDS:**

### ★★★67% Rock Inn

Holywell Green HX4 9BS
☎ 01422 379721 01422 379110
e-mail: the.rock@dial.pipex.com
***Dir:*** *junct 24 off M62, signs for Blackley, left at crossroads approx 1/2m on left*

Situated in a quiet village, close to the town, this hotel offers a variety of bedrooms. The newer rooms are particularly innovative with attractive design features. The brasserie serves a wide range of dishes and is popular with locals and residents alike.

**ROOMS:** 30 en suite (5 fmly) No smoking in 15 bedrooms s £55-£120; d £55-£120 (incl. bkfst) * **LB** **FACILITIES:** STV Xmas **CONF:** Thtr 200 Class 100 Board 100 Del £99 * **PARKING:** 122 **NOTES:** No smoking in restaurant Civ Wed 200 **CARDS:**

### ★★★63% *The Imperial Crown*

corus

42/46 Horton St HX1 1QE
☎ 01422 342342 01422 349866
e-mail: imperialcrown@corushotels.com
***Dir:*** *opposite Railway Station*

This friendly, traditional hotel is situated in the town centre opposite the main railway station and the Eureka children's museum. Some of its modern bedrooms are located above the hotel's American diner opposite. The more formal Wallis Simpson

*continued*

Restaurant, together with a comfortable bar, are in the main building.

**ROOMS:** 41 en suite 15 annexe en suite (3 fmly) No smoking in 10 bedrooms **FACILITIES:** STV entertainment **CONF:** Thtr 150 Class 120 Board 70 **PARKING:** 63 **NOTES:** Civ Wed 200
**CARDS:**

### *Premier Lodge*

Salterhebble Hill, Huddersfield Rd HX3 0QT
☎ 0870 700 1410 📠 0870 700 1411
Premier Lodge offers modern, well-equipped, en suite accommodation suitable for both business and leisure travellers. Meals can be taken at the adjacent popular restaurant and bar, which is fully licensed. For further details, consult the Hotel Groups page.
**ROOMS:** 31 en suite

### *Travelodge (Halifax Central)*

Travelodge

Dean Clough Park HX3 5AX
☎ 01422 362271 📠 01422 362669
Travelodge offers good quality, good value, modern accommodation. Ideal for families, the spacious, en suite bedrooms include remote-control TV, tea and coffee-making facilities, luxury beds and free morning newspaper. Meals can be taken at the nearby family restaurant. For further details and the Travelodge phone number, consult the Hotel Groups page.

**ROOMS:** 52 en suite

## HAMBLETON, North Yorkshire Map 08 SE53

### ★★64% Owl

Main Rd YO8 9JH
☎ 01757 228374 📠 01757 228125
e-mail: owlhotel@talk21.co.uk
***Dir:*** *4m W on A63*
Standing in the centre of the village, this modern and very well-equipped hotel serves a very extensive range of popular food. Bedrooms, some of which are located in a nearby wing, are pleasantly decorated and thoughtfully furnished.
**ROOMS:** 7 en suite 15 annexe en suite (2 fmly) s £42.50; d £59.95 (incl. bkfst) * **LB FACILITIES:** STV **CONF:** Thtr 80 Class 40 Board 50 Del from £65 * **PARKING:** 101 **NOTES:** No dogs (ex guide dogs) No smoking in restaurant **CARDS:**

Popped the question? Hotels with Civ Wed in their entry are licensed for civil wedding ceremonies. Maximum numbers for the ceremony only are shown, e.g. Civ Wed 120

## HAMPSON GREEN, Lancashire Map 07 SD45

### ★★63% Hampson House

Hampson Ln LA2 0JB
☎ 01524 751158 📠 01524 751779
e-mail: info@hampsonhousehotellancaster.com
***Dir:*** *leave Junc 33 M6, follow for Garstang 1st left into Hampson Lane, the Hotel is 400yds on the left*
Conveniently situated close to the M6, this traditional hotel nestles in over an acre of mature gardens, and part of the building dates back to 1666. An imaginative choice of dishes is offered in the open-plan restaurant, and the bedrooms are bright and well equipped.
**ROOMS:** 12 en suite 2 annexe en suite (4 fmly) **CONF:** Thtr 90 Class 40 Board 26 Del from £56 * **PARKING:** 60 **NOTES:** Civ Wed 70
**CARDS:**

## HAMPTON COURT, Greater London

See LONDON SECTION plan 1 B1

### ★★★★67% The Carlton Mitre

Hampton Court Rd KT8 9BN
☎ 020 8979 9988 📠 020 8979 9777
e-mail: mitre@carltonhotels.co.uk
***Dir:*** *from M3 junct 1 follow signs to Sunbury & Hampton Court Palace, continue until Hampton Court Palace rdbt, turn right & The Mitre is on the right*

Dating back in parts to 1665 and located on the Thames, this hotel originally served as lodging for courtiers who could not be accommodated at Hampton Court Palace opposite. The riverside terrace, restaurant and brasserie all command good views. Bedrooms are generally spacious with good facilities, some also with views. Parking is limited.
**ROOMS:** 36 en suite (2 fmly) No smoking in 16 bedrooms d £140-£170 * **LB FACILITIES:** STV Jacuzzi entertainment Xmas **CONF:** Thtr 30 Class 15 Board 20 Del from £195 * **SERVICES:** Lift **PARKING:** 13 **NOTES:** Civ Wed 36 **CARDS:**

### ★★★63% Menzies Liongate

MENZIES HOTELS

Hampton Court Rd KT8 9DD
☎ 0870 6003012 📠 01332 511144
e-mail: info@menzies-hotels.co.uk
***Dir:*** *from London approach via A3 and A308. From SW leave M3 at junct 1 and follow A308*
Well situated, opposite the Lion Gate entrance to Hampton Court and beside the entrance to Bushy Park, this hotel has well equipped bedrooms and friendly staff. In addition to those in the main house there are rooms in a small mews across the road. The hotel also has a modern open-plan restaurant and bar.
**ROOMS:** 29 en suite d £120 * **LB FACILITIES:** STV Xmas **CONF:** Thtr 60 Class 30 Board 30 Del from £150 * **PARKING:** 30 **NOTES:** No smoking in restaurant Civ Wed 60
**CARDS:**

HANDFORTH See Manchester Airport

HARLESTON, Norfolk Map 05 TM28

★★63% ***The Swan Hotel***
The Thoroughfare IP20 9AS
☎ 01379 852221 ▯ 01379 854817
e-mail: swan@norfolk-hotels.co.uk
***Dir:*** *turn off A140 onto B1134 signed 'The Pulhams'. Through Pulham villages to Starston, then Harleston. Hotel at end of Swan Lane on left*
This hotel dates back to the 15th century and was once a stopping place for the London to Great Yarmouth coaches. It is situated in the heart of town and popular with the locals for its warm atmosphere. Bedrooms come in a variety of sizes and styles and are all attractively decorated and well-equipped.
**ROOMS:** 15 en suite (2 fmly) **FACILITIES:** entertainment **CONF:** Thtr 60 Class 30 Board 10 **PARKING:** 30 **NOTES:** No smoking in restaurant
**CARDS:**

HARLOW, Essex Map 05 TL41

★★★73% **Swallow Churchgate Hotel**
Churchgate St Village, Old Harlow CM17 0JT
☎ 01279 420246 ▯ 01279 420246
e-mail: info@swallowhotels.com
***Dir:*** *on B183, NE of Old Harlow. Exit M11 Junc 7 for Harlow. At 4th rdbt turn right on B183 follow signs for Churchgate Street*

SWALLOW
HOTELS

This Jacobean house is situated in a quiet village location to the north-east of Old Harlow. The bedrooms are generally quite spacious and feature several 'Executive' rooms. Public areas include a comfortable lounge bar, the elegant Manor Restaurant and a leisure club.
**ROOMS:** 85 en suite (6 fmly) No smoking in 41 bedrooms s fr £95; d £125-£170 * **LB** **FACILITIES:** Spa STV Indoor swimming (H) Sauna Solarium Gym Jacuzzi Xmas **CONF:** Thtr 180 Class 70 Board 40 Del from £110 * **PARKING:** 120 **NOTES:** No smoking in restaurant Closed 27-29 Dec Civ Wed 80 **CARDS:**

★★★65% **Green Man**
Mulberry Green, Old Harlow CM17 0ET
☎ 01279 442521 ▯ 01279 626113
***Dir:*** *exit M11 Junc 7 onto A414. At 4th rdbt turn right. After rdbt turn left into Mulberry Green, hotel is on left*
corus
This popular coaching inn dating back to the 14th century is situated close to the town centre. The busy lounge bar is an enjoyable place to drink, and there is also a trendy brasserie style restaurant offering a carte or daily changing menus. Modern, well-equipped bedrooms are located to the rear of the property.

**ROOMS:** 55 annexe en suite No smoking in 27 bedrooms s £93; d £99 * **LB** **FACILITIES:** Xmas **CONF:** Thtr 60 Class 26 Board 30 Del from £110 * **PARKING:** 75 **NOTES:** No smoking in restaurant
**CARDS:**

⌂ ***Travelodge Harlow East***
A414 Eastbound, Tylers Green, North Weald CM16 6BJ
☎ 01992 523276
Travelodge
Travelodge offers good quality, good value, modern accommodation. Ideal for families, the spacious, en suite bedrooms include remote-control TV, tea and coffee-making facilities, luxury beds and free morning newspaper. Meals can be taken at the nearby family restaurant. For further details and the Travelodge phone number, consult the Hotel Groups page.

HAROME See Helmsley

HARPENDEN, Hertfordshire Map 04 TL11

★★★70% **Hanover International Hotel**
1 Luton Rd AL5 2PX
☎ 01582 760271 ▯ 01582 460819
e-mail: hih.harpenden@virgin.net
***Dir:*** *Leave junct 10 of M1 towards Luton Airport at next rdbt turn right for Harpenden(A1081).After 5 miles enter hotel on right beyond Oggelsbys Vauxhall garage*

EXIT

The hotel is situated in a quiet location at the edge of town and within a few miles of the M1. Good sized and well-equipped bedrooms provide guests with a very comfortable environment. A variety of function rooms are available for corporate or private use.
**ROOMS:** 60 en suite (12 fmly) No smoking in 25 bedrooms s fr £98; d £115-£160 * **LB** **FACILITIES:** STV Free membership of local leisure club **CONF:** Thtr 150 Class 60 Board 44 Del from £125 * **SERVICES:** Lift **PARKING:** 85 **NOTES:** Civ Wed 120
**CARDS:**

★★★68% **Harpenden House**
18 Southdown Rd AL5 1PE
☎ 01582 449955 🖹 01582 769858
e-mail: harpendenhouse@corushotels.com
***Dir:*** *M1 junct 10 turn left at rdbt. At next rdbt (J10A) turn right onto A1081.Proceed towards Harpenden,straight over mini rdbt through town centre over next mini rdbt. Left at next rdbt, hotel 200yds on left.*

REGAL

Overlooking Harpenden green, this attractive Grade II listed Georgian building has had some comfortable new bedrooms added to its annexe wing. Frequented by visitors to the many businesses in the area, the hotel is well geared to the commercial guest. Public areas include the restaurant with an interesting mural ceiling.
**ROOMS:** 17 en suite 59 annexe en suite (13 fmly) No smoking in 49 bedrooms s £120-£140; d £150-£200 * **LB** **FACILITIES:** STV
**CONF:** Thtr 150 Class 60 Board 60 Del from £90 * **PARKING:** 80
**NOTES:** RS Weekends & Bank Holiday Civ Wed 50
**CARDS:**

HARROGATE, North Yorkshire — Map 08 SE35
see also Hazlewood & Knaresborough

★★★★78% ®® **Rudding Park Hotel & Golf**
Rudding Park, Follifoot HG3 1JH
☎ 01423 871350 🖹 01423 872286
e-mail: sales@ruddingpark.com
***Dir:*** *from A61, at rdbt with A658 take exit for York and follow brown signs to Rudding Park*

Part of a 230-acre estate, this hotel is elegant and welcoming. The well-equipped and very comfortable bedrooms are stylish yet simple. Public areas include the contemporary Clocktower Restaurant and Bar, a sunny atrium and separate residents' drawing room.
**ROOMS:** 50 en suite No smoking in 31 bedrooms s £115-£270; d £145-£270 (incl. bkfst) * **LB** **FACILITIES:** STV Golf 18 Croquet lawn Jogging trail Membership of local gym ch fac Xmas **CONF:** Del from £170 * **SERVICES:** Lift **PARKING:** 150 **NOTES:** No dogs (ex guide dogs) No smoking in restaurant Civ Wed **CARDS:**

*See advert on this page*

HARROGATE, continued

**★★★★69% The Majestic**
Ripon Rd HG1 2HU
☎ 01423 700300 Fax 01423 521332
e-mail: majestic@paramount-hotels.co.uk
PARAMOUNT GROUP OF HOTELS
***Dir:*** *from M1 continue on A1(M) link road, on leaving A1 at Wetherby take A661 to Harrogate. Hotel in town centre opposite The Royal Hall*

This grand Victorian hotel is centrally located and is within easy walking distance of the town centre. The impressive public rooms feature chandeliers, murals, paintings and beautiful wood panelling. The bedrooms, many of which have been recently refurbished, are comfortable, well-equipped and include several spacious suites. Wide-ranging conference and function facilities make this hotel popular for weddings.
**ROOMS:** 156 en suite (11 fmly) No smoking in 86 bedrooms s fr £104; d fr £143 * **LB** **FACILITIES:** STV Indoor swimming (H) Tennis (hard) Squash Snooker Sauna Solarium Gym Jacuzzi Golf practise net entertainment Xmas **CONF:** Thtr 500 Class 250 Board 70 Del from £140 * **SERVICES:** Lift **PARKING:** 250 **NOTES:** No smoking in restaurant Civ Wed 300 **CARDS:**

**★★★★66% Cedar Court**
Queens Buildings, Park Pde HG1 5AH
☎ 01423 858585 858595(reservations)
Fax 01423 504950
e-mail: cedarcourt@bestwestern.co.uk
Best Western
***Dir:*** *A1(M) follow signs to Harrogate on A661 past Sainsburys, at rdbt turn left to A6040.Hotel right after church.*

CEDAR COURT HOTEL ENTRANCE
CEDAR COURT HOTEL ENTRANCE

Set quietly back from the road, just minutes' walk from the centre of town, this Grade II listed building has been completely refurbished to a high standard. Attractive, spacious, well equipped bedrooms and public areas that include an elegant restaurant, a gymnasium, ample meeting rooms and two large banqueting halls are features at this hotel.
**ROOMS:** 100 en suite (8 fmly) No smoking in 75 bedrooms s £105; d £115 * **LB** **FACILITIES:** STV Gym Residents gym Xmas **CONF:** Thtr 323 Class 90 Board 80 Del from £125 * **SERVICES:** Lift air con **PARKING:** 150 **NOTES:** No dogs (ex guide dogs) Civ Wed 171 **CARDS:**

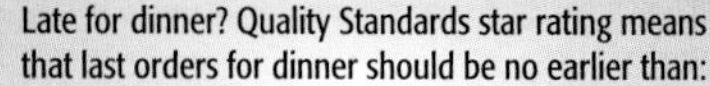
Late for dinner? Quality Standards star rating means that last orders for dinner should be no earlier than:
★ 6.30pm ★★ 7.00pm ★★★ 8.00pm
★★★★ 9.00pm ★★★★★ 10.00pm

**★★★★60% Old Swan**
Swan Rd HG1 2SR
☎ 01423 500055 Fax 01423 501154
e-mail: info@oldswan.macdonald-hotels.co.uk
***Dir:*** *follow Town Centre & Harrogate International Centre signs onto the Ripon Rd, through traffic lights, 2nd left turning into Swan Rd, 300yrds on right*
One of the town's oldest hotels, the Old Swan is renowned for its connection with Agatha Christie when she "disappeared" in 1926. *Agatha* was filmed at the hotel. The elegant Wedgwood and Library restaurants provide comfortable venues in which to dine. A wide range of conference rooms is also available.
**ROOMS:** 125 en suite (1 fmly) s £75-£105; d £95-£130 * **LB** **FACILITIES:** STV ch fac Xmas **CONF:** Thtr 500 Class 180 Board 80 Del £136 * **SERVICES:** Lift **PARKING:** 200 **NOTES:** Civ Wed 450 **CARDS:**

**★★★77% ֍֍ The Boar's Head Hotel**
Ripley Castle Estate HG3 3AY
☎ 01423 771888 Fax 01423 771509
e-mail: reservations@boarsheadripley.co.uk
***Dir:*** *on the A61 Harrogate/Ripon road, the hotel is in the centre of Ripley Village*

In the private village of Ripley Castle estate, this charming hotel is renowned for its warm hospitality, traditional hostelry and the restaurant with its mix of modern dishes and traditional classics. Bedrooms offer many comforts, and the opulent day rooms feature works of art from the nearby castle.
**ROOMS:** 13 en suite 12 annexe en suite (2 fmly) No smoking in 3 bedrooms s £120; d £140 (incl. bkfst) * **LB** **FACILITIES:** STV Tennis (hard) Fishing Clay pigeon shooting Xmas **CONF:** Thtr 60 Class 35 Board 30 Del from £120 * **PARKING:** 53 **NOTES:** Civ Wed 100 **CARDS:**

**★★★71% Grants**
3-13 Swan Rd HG1 2SS
☎ 01423 560666 Fax 01423 502550
e-mail: enquires@grantshotel-harrogate.com
***Dir:*** *off A61*
A delightful family run hotel with an attractive flower-covered front patio. Tastefully decorated bedrooms, including some with four-poster beds, a comfortable lounge bar with lots of interesting old

*continued*

photographs and imaginative food in the colourful Chimney Pots Bistro are just some of the features of this friendly hotel.

**ROOMS:** 42 en suite (2 fmly) s £65-£114; d £90-£170 (incl. bkfst) * **LB** **FACILITIES:** Use of local Health & Leisure Club Xmas **CONF:** Thtr 70 Class 20 Board 30 **SERVICES:** Lift **PARKING:** 26 **NOTES:** No smoking in restaurant **CARDS:**

*See advert on this page*

**★★★66% Studley**

Swan Rd HG1 2SE

☎ 01423 560425 01423 530967

e-mail: studleyhotel@faxdoc.net

***Dir:*** *Adjacent to the Valley Gardens on Swan Rd*

This welcoming hotel, close to the town centre and Valley Gardens, is renowned for its friendly and attentive service. The popular Orchid Restaurant provides a dynamic and authentic approach to Pacific Rim and Asian cuisine. Bedrooms are well-

*continued on p262*

HARROGATE, continued

equipped and vary in size. Sizeable day rooms are comfortably furnished.

**ROOMS:** 36 en suite (2 fmly) s £59-£68; d £77-£88 (incl. bkfst) * **LB** **FACILITIES:** STV Xmas **CONF:** Thtr 15 Class 15 Board 12 Del from £64 * **SERVICES:** Lift **PARKING:** 15 **NOTES:** No smoking in restaurant **CARDS:**

### ★★★66% Swallow St George Hotel

SWALLOW
HOTELS

1 Ripon Rd HG1 2SY
☎ 01423 561431 🖷 01423 530037
e-mail: info@swallowhotels.com
***Dir:*** *on A61 opposite the Royal Hall, Conference Centre*

Situated in the town centre, close to the conference centre, this well furnished hotel offers comfortable, well-equipped accommodation. Bedrooms, which include a ground-floor suite and a number of family rooms, vary in size and outlook. There is a leisure centre with pool, good conference and meeting facilities and elegant, comfortable lounges.

**ROOMS:** 90 en suite (14 fmly) No smoking in 35 bedrooms s £70-£105; d £105-£115 (incl. bkfst) * **LB** **FACILITIES:** **Spa** STV Indoor swimming (H) Sauna Solarium Gym Boutique, Beautician, Masseuse Steamroom, Cardio-vascular room entertainment Xmas **CONF:** Thtr 200 Class 80 Board 50 Del from £80 * **SERVICES:** Lift **PARKING:** 60 **NOTES:** No smoking in restaurant Civ Wed 140
**CARDS:**

### ★★★65% *Imperial*

Prospect Place HG1 1LA
☎ 01423 565071 🖷 01423 508427
***Dir:*** *follow A61 into town centre. Hotel opposite Betty's Tea Rooms*

Friendly and hospitable staff welcome guests to this grand hotel, which boasts a pleasant aspect overlooking lawns and gardens close to the town centre. Bedrooms are modern and elegant; public rooms are well-proportioned and comfortable. Main meals can be taken in the restaurant, supplemented by all day lounge service.

**ROOMS:** 83 en suite **CONF:** Thtr 200 Class 80 Board 40
**SERVICES:** Lift **PARKING:** 12 **NOTES:** No smoking in restaurant
**CARDS:**

### ★★★63% The Harrogate Spa Hotel

PEEL HOTELS

Prospect Place, West Park HG1 1LB
☎ 01423 564601 🖷 01423 507508
e-mail: info@spa-hotel-harrogate.com
***Dir:*** *from A61 Leeds/Ripon Road, continue along West Park towards City Centre. Right at traffic lights into Albert St & 1st right to hotel*

The Stray - 200 acres of tree-lined lawns - provides a delightful backdrop for this hotel. Its traditionally furnished bedrooms are equipped with a useful range of extras. Public rooms include the David Copperfield bar, popular with residents and locals alike, and the beamed Oliver Twist restaurant.

**ROOMS:** 71 en suite (5 fmly) No smoking in 9 bedrooms s £70-£97; d £80-£108 (incl. bkfst) * **LB** **FACILITIES:** Pool Table Xmas **CONF:** Thtr 150 Class 75 Board 58 Del from £80 * **SERVICES:** Lift **PARKING:** 40 **NOTES:** No smoking in restaurant **CARDS:**

### ★★★59% The Crown

REGAL

Crown Place HG1 2RZ
☎ 01423 567755 🖷 01423 502284
e-mail: thecrown@corushotels.com
***Dir:*** *take A61 into Harrogate continue down Parliament St to traffic lights by Royal Hall, left towards Valley Gardens, 1st left to rdbt, hotel on right*

Centrally situated, this hotel has been in existence for the past 250 years. Bedrooms are mixed in standard and size. All have good facilities such as a movie channel and modem links. Public areas have all the hallmarks of a bygone era, tall ceilings with columns and plenty of space.

**ROOMS:** 121 en suite (8 fmly) No smoking in 61 bedrooms s £70-£104; d £90-£147 (incl. bkfst) * **LB** **FACILITIES:** free use of local sports club Xmas **CONF:** Thtr 400 Class 200 Board 80 Del £150 * **SERVICES:** Lift **PARKING:** 50 **NOTES:** No smoking in restaurant Civ Wed 400
**CARDS:**

> Need to unwind? Look out for hotels with Spa in their entry.

> Late for dinner? Quality Standards star rating means that last orders for dinner should be no earlier than:
> ★ 6.30pm ★★ 7.00pm ★★★ 8.00pm
> ★★★★ 9.00pm ★★★★★ 10.00pm

**★★71% Ascot House**

MINOTEL
Great Britain

53 Kings Rd HG1 5HJ
☎ 01423 531005 📠 01423 503523
e-mail: admin@ascothouse.com
***Dir:*** *follow signs to town centre/conference and exhibition centre. At Kings Rd, drive past conference centre, Ascot House on left immediately after park*

This late-Victorian house has been tastefully transformed into a very relaxing, informal, family-owned hotel. Situated a short distance from the International Conference Centre, it provides comfortable, well-appointed bedrooms, including one with a four-poster bed. There is an elegant dining room, a cosy lounge and a spacious bar lounge.

**ROOMS:** 19 en suite (2 fmly) s £51-£61; d £76-£86 (incl. bkfst) * **LB** **FACILITIES:** ch fac Xmas **CONF:** Thtr 80 Class 36 Board 36 Del from £80 * **PARKING:** 14 **NOTES:** Closed 28 Dec-1 Jan & 27 Jan-10 Feb Civ Wed 90 **CARDS:**

**★★64% *Harrogate Brasserie Hotel & Bar***

28-30 Cheltenham Pde HG1 1DB
☎ 01423 505041 📠 01423 722300
e-mail: harrogate.brasserie@zoom.co.uk
***Dir:*** *on A61 Town Centre behind Theatre*

This town centre hotel is distinctly continental in style and advertises itself as a 'restaurant with rooms'. The popular brasserie features live jazz on busy nights and an eclectic menu that makes good use of seasonal produce. Many bedrooms have been thoughtfully refurbished and offer stylish standards of appointment.

**ROOMS:** 13 en suite (3 fmly) **FACILITIES:** STV entertainment **PARKING:** 12 **CARDS:**

*See advert on this page*

**○ Cutlers on the Stray**

19 West Park HGI 1BL
☎ 01423 524471

At the time of going to press, the star classification for this hotel was not confirmed. Please refer to the AA internet site www.theaa.com for current information.

**○ Innkeeper's Lodge Harrogate West**

Innkeeper's Lodge

Otley Rd, Beckwith Knowle HG3 1PR

A new concept in the travel accommodation market. Smart rooms meet essential business requirements but also have home comforts. Dining options include all-day menus plus the added advantage of breakfast, which is included in the room price. Reservations can be made seven days a week through the room reservations number: 0870 243 0500. For further details, consult the Hotel Groups page.

**ROOMS:** 11 en suite **NOTES:** Open now

HARROW, Greater London
See LONDON SECTION plan 1 B5

### ★★★67% Cumberland

1 St Johns Rd HA1 2EF
☎ 020 8863 4111 🖹 020 8861 5668
e-mail: sforsdyke@cumberlandhotel.co.uk
***Dir:*** *From A404 or A409 turn into Gayton Road, then into Lyon Road. Hotel at end of road*

This town centre hotel offers modern, yet practical bedrooms with a good range of in-room facilities, located in the main house and in two other separate wings. Public areas include a range of meeting rooms, a popular bar, a quiet lounge and an attractive, modern restaurant.
**ROOMS:** 31 en suite 53 annexe en suite (5 fmly) No smoking in 51 bedrooms s £95; d £107 (incl. bkfst) * **LB** **FACILITIES:** STV Sauna Gym Small Fitness Room **CONF:** Thtr 130 Class 70 Board 62 Del £130 * **PARKING:** 57 **NOTES:** No dogs (ex guide dogs)
**CARDS:**

*See advert on page 263*

### ★★★67% Quality Harrow Hotel

12-22 Pinner Rd HA1 4HZ
☎ 020 8427 3435 🖹 020 8861 1370
e-mail: info@harrowhotel.co.uk
***Dir:*** *off rdbt on A404 at junction with A312*

A privately owned, commercial hotel consisting of three interlinked houses dating back to the early 20th century. Bedrooms are comfortably appointed, well-equipped and include a new wing offering superior rooms. Public areas comprise a bar, conservatory lounge, meeting rooms and a smart conservatory restaurant
**ROOMS:** 79 en suite 23 annexe en suite (2 fmly) No smoking in 48 bedrooms s £98; d £123 * **FACILITIES:** STV **CONF:** Thtr 160 Class 60 Board 60 Del from £130 * **SERVICES:** Lift **PARKING:** 70 **NOTES:** No smoking in restaurant RS Xmas (limited service) Civ Wed 120
**CARDS:**

*See advert on opposite page*

### ★★★65% Menzies Northwick Park

2-12 Northwick Park Rd HA1 2NT
☎ 0870 600 3013 🖹 01332 511144
e-mail: info@menzies-hotels.co.uk
***Dir:*** *off A4006*

The hotel is located in a quiet residential street of this north-London suburb, yet ideally situated for road and rail links. The attractions of central London are only 30 minutes away and the historic city of St Albans is a short drive. Bedrooms are divided between the main house and the adjacent wing.
**ROOMS:** 75 en suite (3 fmly) No smoking in 30 bedrooms d £80 * **FACILITIES:** STV Xmas **CONF:** Thtr 180 Class 80 Board 50 Del from £120 * **PARKING:** 65 **NOTES:** No smoking in restaurant
**CARDS:**

### ★★55% The Lindal Hotel

2 Hindes Rd HA1 1SJ
☎ 020 8863 3164 🖹 020 8427 5435
***Dir:*** *off A409, opposite Tesco Superstore*
This family-run hotel is conveniently located for the local shopping centre and provides good transport links to the centre of London. Bedrooms are modern and attractively furnished. Day rooms consist of a combined bar-lounge area and dining room.
**ROOMS:** 21 en suite (3 fmly) No smoking in 9 bedrooms s £48-£55; d £65-£70 (incl. bkfst) * **PARKING:** 21 **NOTES:** No dogs (ex guide dogs) No children 6yrs No smoking in restaurant
**CARDS:**

HARROW WEALD, Greater London
See LONDON SECTION plan 1 B6

### ★★★66% Grim's Dyke

Old Redding HA3 6SH
☎ 020 8385 3100 🖹 020 8954 4560
e-mail: enquiries@grimsdyke.com
Once home to Sir William Gilbert, this Grade II mansion contains many references to well known Gilbert and Sullivan productions. The attractive house is set in over 40 acres of beautiful parkland and gardens. Main house rooms are elegant and traditional, while those in the Garden Lodge are more suited to corporate use.
**ROOMS:** 9 en suite 35 annexe en suite s fr £123; d fr £149 (incl. bkfst) * **LB** **FACILITIES:** STV Croquet lawn entertainment Xmas **CONF:** Thtr 70 Class 24 Board 24 Del from £155 * **PARKING:** 97
**NOTES:** Civ Wed 85 **CARDS:**

HARTLEBURY, Worcestershire — Map 07 SO87

### *Travelodge*

Shorthill Nurseries DY13 9SH
☎ 01299 250553 🖹 01299 250553
***Dir:*** *A449 southbound*
Travelodge offers good quality, good value, modern accommodation. Ideal for families, the spacious, en suite bedrooms

*continued*

include remote-control TV, tea and coffee-making facilities, luxury beds and free morning newspaper. Meals can be taken at the nearby family restaurant. For further details and the Travelodge phone number, consult the Hotel Groups page.

**ROOMS:** 32 en suite

## HARTLEPOOL, Co Durham — Map 08 NZ53

### ★★★65% *The Grand*

Swainson St TS24 8AA
☎ 01429 266345 🖷 01429 265217
***Dir:*** *opposite shopping centre, adjacent to Civic Centre*
Centrally situated, this splendid Victorian building has an impressive facade. Refurbished public areas are smart and spacious, whilst accommodation offers a choice of superior or standard rooms. A good range of food is available both in the restaurant and Pullman Bistro.
**ROOMS:** 47 en suite (4 fmly) No smoking in 1 bedroom **FACILITIES:** STV Free use of adjacent local leisure centre **CONF:** Thtr 200 Class 150 Board 35 **SERVICES:** Lift **PARKING:** 50 **NOTES:** No dogs (ex guide dogs) Civ Wed 200 **CARDS:**

## HARTSHEAD MOOR SERVICE AREA, West Yorkshire — Map 07 SE12

### ⇧ Days Inn

DAYS INN

Hartshead Moor Service Area, Clifton HD6 4JX
☎ 01274 851706 🖷 01274 855169
e-mail: hartsheadmoor.hotel@welcomebreak.co.uk
***Dir:*** *M62 eastbound between junct 25 & 26*
This modern building offers accommodation in smart, spacious and well-equipped bedrooms, suitable for families and business travellers, and all with en suite bathrooms. Continental breakfast is available and other refreshments may be taken at the nearby family restaurant. For further details and the Days Inn phone number, consult the Hotel Groups page.
**ROOMS:** 38 en suite s £45-£50; d £45-£50 * **CONF:** Board 10

## HARVINGTON (NEAR EVESHAM), Worcestershire — Map 04 SP04

### ★★80% The Mill At Harvington

Anchor Ln, Harvington WR11 5NR
☎ 01386 870688 🖷 01386 870688
e-mail: millatharvington@aol.com
***Dir:*** *Harvington is 4m NE of Evesham. The hotel is on the banks of the Avon, reached by a bridge over the new A46 and not in village*
This delightful small hotel, once a Georgian house and mill, stands in extensive grounds on the banks of the River Avon in tranquil rural surroundings. It provides a comfortable lounge with fine views, a conservatory bar and an elegant restaurant. Bedrooms, which include rooms on ground floor level, are for the most part well proportioned and have been thoughtfully equipped. Six spacious rooms are set in a separate building. Facilities include an outdoor swimming pool and a tennis court.
**ROOMS:** 15 en suite 6 annexe en suite s £63-£75; d £85-£125 (incl. bkfst) * **LB** **FACILITIES:** Outdoor swimming (H) Fishing Croquet lawn **CONF:** Thtr 15 Class 10 Board 10 Del from £105 * **PARKING:** 50 **NOTES:** No dogs (ex guide dogs) No children 10yrs No smoking in restaurant Closed 24-27 Dec **CARDS:**

> Arriving late? Four and five star hotels have night porters to assist with your luggage, and 24-hour room service.



## HARWICH, Essex — Map 05 TM23

### ★★★70% ❀❀ The Pier at Harwich

The Quay CO12 3HH
☎ 01255 241212 🖷 01255 551922
e-mail: reception@thepieratharwich.co.uk
***Dir:*** *from A12, take A120 to the Quay, hotel is opposite the Lifeboat Station*

PIER HOTEL
HA'PENNY BISTRO

Just across the road from the harbourside, most rooms at this lovely hotel offer a sea view. The Harbourside Restaurant specialises in seafood and serves Rosette-worthy dishes. There is also a second, less formal, bistro-style restaurant and an attractive modern bar.
**ROOMS:** 7 en suite 7 annexe en suite (5 fmly) s £63-£100; d £80-£150 (incl. cont bkfst) * **LB** **FACILITIES:** STV entertainment ch fac Xmas **CONF:** Thtr 50 Class 50 Board 24 Del from £93.30 * **PARKING:** 10 **NOTES:** No dogs (ex guide dogs) Civ Wed 50
**CARDS:**

HARWICH, continued

### ★★64% *Hotel Continental*

28/29 Marine Pde, Dovercourt CO12 3RG
☎ 01255 551298 📠 01255 551698
e-mail: hotconti@aol.com
***Dir:*** *turn off A120 at Ramsay rdbt onto B1352, continue until reaching a pedestrian crossing & Co-op store on right, turn right here into Fronks Rd*

Hotel Continental

Ideally situated overlooking the sea, this small privately owned hotel is within easy striking distance of the ferry terminals. Although the bedrooms vary in size and style they feature many innovative decorative touches, some rooms also have sea views. The bar is popular with residents and locals alike and there is also a comfortable non-smoking residents lounge.
**ROOMS:** 13 en suite (2 fmly) No smoking in 1 bedroom
**FACILITIES:** STV **CONF:** Thtr 30 Board 20 **PARKING:** 4 **NOTES:** No smoking in restaurant **CARDS:**

### ★★63% Cliff

Marine Pde, Dovercourt CO12 3RE
☎ 01255 503345 & 507373 📠 01255 240358
***Dir:*** *A120 to Parkeston rdbt, take road to Dovercourt, on seafront after Dovercourt town centre*
Ideally placed overlooking the sea, the Cliff is just a few minutes drive from the ferry terminals and railway station. Public rooms include the Shade Bar, lounge, restaurant and a Marine Bar with views of Dovercourt Bay. Bedrooms vary in style and size but are modern and offer a good range of facilities.
**ROOMS:** 26 en suite (3 fmly) No smoking in 1 bedroom s £50-£56; d £60-£66 (incl. bkfst) * **LB FACILITIES:** STV Jacuzzi **CONF:** Thtr 200 Class 150 Board 40 Del from £64.50 * **PARKING:** 50 **NOTES:** RS Xmas & New Year **CARDS:**

## HASLEMERE, Surrey — Map 04 SU93

### ★★★★65% Lythe Hill

Petworth Rd GU27 3BQ
☎ 01428 651251 📠 01428 644131
e-mail: lythe@lythehill.co.uk
***Dir:*** *turn left from Haslemere High St onto B2131. Lythe Hill 1.25m on right*
Set in 20 acres of grounds including a bluebell wood and several lakes, this hotel is a cluster of 15th-century buildings. Many of the individually styled bedrooms are designed around the original features. There are separate garden suites and five rooms in the original timbered house with its jetted upper storey. There are two

*continued*

restaurants and the oak-panelled Auberge de France serves consistently rewarding cuisine.

**ROOMS:** 41 en suite (8 fmly) s £98-£235; d £120-£235 * **LB**
**FACILITIES:** STV Tennis (hard) Fishing Croquet lawn Boules Games Room Xmas **CONF:** Thtr 60 Class 40 Board 30 **PARKING:** 200
**NOTES:** No smoking in restaurant Civ Wed 128
**CARDS:**

### ★★★65% Georgian House Hotel

High St GU27 2JY
☎ 01428 656644 📠 01428 645600
e-mail: mail@georgianhousehotel.com
***Dir:*** *A3 follow signs to Milford then Haslemere*
An impressive, refurbished Georgian building situated on the High Street. The bedrooms feature good-quality furnishings enhanced by good facilities. The modern dining room and bar serves a selection of meals, from snacks to a three-course meal.
**ROOMS:** 53 en suite d £75-£95 * **LB FACILITIES:** STV Indoor swimming (H) Sauna Solarium Gym Jacuzzi **CONF:** Thtr 100 Class 50 Board 30 Del £120 * **PARKING:** 30 **NOTES:** No dogs (ex guide dogs) Civ Wed 60 **CARDS:**

## HASTINGS & ST LEONARDS, East Sussex — Map 05 TQ80

### ★★★66% Cinque Ports Hotel

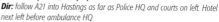

THE CIRCLE *Selected Individual Hotels* GREAT BRITAIN

Bohemia Rd TN34 1ET
☎ 01424 439222 📠 01424 437277
e-mail: enquires@cinqueports.co.uk
***Dir:*** *follow A21 into Hastings as far as Police HQ and courts on left. Hotel next left before ambulance HQ*
Old flagstone floors, oriental rugs, hanging tapestries, beams and open fireplaces feature in the public areas of this modern hotel. Bedrooms are well-equipped and offer a good degree of comfort throughout. The hotel also offers all-day room service, which includes early morning tea.
**ROOMS:** 40 en suite (8 fmly) No smoking in 6 bedrooms s £55-£65; d £65-£85 (incl. bkfst) * **LB FACILITIES:** STV free m/ship at next door leisure centre Xmas **CONF:** Thtr 200 Class 130 Board 60 Del from £65 * **PARKING:** 80 **NOTES:** No smoking in restaurant
**CARDS:**

### ★★★68% Beauport Park

Battle Rd TN38 8EA
☎ 01424 851222 📠 01424 852465
e-mail: reservations@beauportprkhotel.demon.co.uk
***Dir:*** *3m N off A2100*
An elegant Georgian manor house set in 40 acres just outside Hastings. The bedrooms are tastefully decorated and well-equipped. Public rooms convey much of the original character of the building; a large conservatory provides an ideal setting to

*continued*

enjoy the well-tended gardens and the restaurant offers an extensive range of dishes.

**ROOMS:** 25 en suite (2 fmly) No smoking in 11 bedrooms s £85; d £110 (incl. bkfst) * **LB** **FACILITIES:** STV Outdoor swimming (H) Golf 18 Tennis (hard) Riding Croquet lawn Putting green entertainment ch fac Xmas **CONF:** Thtr 70 Class 25 Board 30 **PARKING:** 60 **NOTES:** No smoking in restaurant Civ Wed 65
**CARDS:**

*See advert on this page*

### ★★★65% *High Beech*

Battle Rd TN37 7BS
☎ 01424 851383 📠 01424 854265
***Dir:*** *400yds from A2100 between Hastings and Battle*

Bedrooms at this privately-owned hotel are generally of a good size and come with complimentary wine and snacks. The Mountbatten Bar doubles as the lounge area and the elegant Wedgwood Restaurant serves a good cooked breakfast. Self-catering suites are available.
**ROOMS:** 17 en suite (3 fmly) **FACILITIES:** STV **CONF:** Thtr 250 Class 192 Board 146 **PARKING:** 65 **NOTES:** No dogs (ex guide dogs)
**CARDS:**

*See advert on this page*

### ★★★65% Royal Victoria

Best Western

Marina, St Leonards-on-Sea TN38 0BD
☎ 01424 445544 📠 01424 721995
e-mail: reception@royal-vic-hotel.demon.co.uk
***Dir:*** *on western seafront off A21*
The Royal Victoria hotel dates back to 1828 and has welcomed many famous visitors during its history including Queen Victoria herself. Situated in a prime position on the seafront, this hotel offers traditional hospitality along with a friendly atmosphere. A fine marble staircase leads up from the lobby to the main public

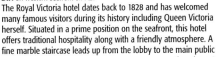

*continued on p268*

HASTINGS & ST LEONARDS, continued

areas on the first floor. The well-equipped bedrooms are very spacious and include a number of duplex and family suites.

*Royal Victoria, Hastings & St Leonards*

**ROOMS:** 50 en suite (15 fmly) s fr £85; d fr £110 (incl. bkfst) * **LB** **FACILITIES:** entertainment Xmas **SERVICES:** Lift **PARKING:** 6 **NOTES:** Civ Wed 50 **CARDS:**

*See advert on opposite page*

## HATFIELD, Hertfordshire — Map 04 TL20

### ★★★67% Bush Hall

Mill Green AL9 5NT
☎ 01707 271251 01707 272289
e-mail: enquiries@bush-hall.com

Bush Hall stands as part of the Hatfield Estate. The grounds not only reflect the period of the property, they also include ponds and a river, as well as outdoor pursuits. Bedrooms are comfortable, with a range of facilities. Kipling's restaurant offers an interesting range of dishes on its fine dining and house menus. Meeting and function rooms are many and varied in scope with most enjoying river frontages.

**ROOMS:** 25 en suite (3 fmly) s £80-£90; d £100-£145 * **FACILITIES:** Shooting, road karting for groups **CONF:** Thtr 150 Class 70 Board 50 Del £145 * **PARKING:** 100 **NOTES:** No dogs (ex guide dogs) Closed 26 Dec-3Jan Civ Wed 150 **CARDS:**

### ★★★62% Quality Hotel Hatfield

Quality Hotel

Roehyde Way AL10 9AF
☎ 01707 275701 01707 266033
e-mail: admin@gb059.u-net.com

***Dir:*** *M25 junct 23 take A1(M) northbound to junct 2, at rdbt take exit left, hotel in 0.5m on right*

The well equipped rooms at this hotel feature extras such as trouser presses and modem access. Executive rooms are very spacious. Room service is 24 hour, or guests may dine in the brasserie or main restaurant, where service is informal and friendly.

**ROOMS:** 76 en suite (14 fmly) No smoking in 39 bedrooms d £95-£115 * **LB** **FACILITIES:** STV Xmas **CONF:** Thtr 120 Class 60 Board 50 Del from £115 * **PARKING:** 120 **NOTES:** No smoking in restaurant **CARDS:**

## HATHERSAGE, Derbyshire — Map 08 SK28

### ★★★71% The George at Hathersage

Main Rd S32 1BB
☎ 01433 650436 01433 650099
e-mail: info@george-hotel.net

***Dir:*** *in village centre on A6187 SW of Sheffield*

The George is a relaxing historic hostelry in the heart of this picturesque town. The beamed bar lounge has much character, and the partitioned restaurant is full of antique charm. Upstairs the decor is simpler with lots of light hues; the split-level and four-poster rooms are especially appealing. Cooking skills are very good with much fresh local produce used.

**ROOMS:** 19 en suite (2 fmly) s £69.50-£109.50; d £99.50-£119.50 (incl. bkfst) * **LB** **FACILITIES:** Xmas **CONF:** Thtr 80 Class 20 Board 36 Del from £115 * **PARKING:** 40 **NOTES:** No smoking in restaurant Civ Wed 90 **CARDS:**

## HAWES, North Yorkshire — Map 07 SD88

### ★★73% Simonstone Hall

Simonstone DL8 3LY
☎ 01969 667255 01969 667741
e-mail: simonstonehall@demon.co.uk

***Dir:*** *1.5m N on road signed to Muker and Buttertubs*

This former hunting lodge provides professional, friendly service in a relaxed atmosphere. There is an inviting drawing room, stylish restaurant and character bar serving value-for-money pub food. Bedrooms reflect the style of the house and are generally spacious. The creative dinner menu makes excellent use of local game, fish and delicious cheeses.

**ROOMS:** 20 en suite (10 fmly) No smoking in all bedrooms s £55-£65; d £100-£170 (incl. bkfst) * **LB** **FACILITIES:** Fishing ch fac Xmas **CONF:** Thtr 40 Class 20 Board 20 Del from £120 * **PARKING:** 40 **NOTES:** No smoking in restaurant Civ Wed 65 **CARDS:**

### ★★71% Stone House

Sedbusk DL8 3PT
☎ 01969 667571 01969 667720
e-mail: daleshotel@aol.com

***Dir:*** *from Hawes take road signposted 'Muker & The Buttertubs' to T-junct then right towards Sedbusk & Askrigg. Hotel 500yds on left*

With panoramic views across green fields, this stylish Edwardian hotel retains the charm and character of a bygone age. Carefully

*continued*

prepared Yorkshire dinners are served each evening in the restaurant. The thoughtfully furnished bedrooms come in two styles; modern and original. Staff are friendly and obliging.
**ROOMS:** 18 rms (17 en suite) 4 annexe en suite (1 fmly) No smoking in all bedrooms s £39.50-£79; d £79-£92 (incl. bkfst) * **LB**
**FACILITIES:** Tennis (grass) Croquet lawn Billiards table ch fac Xmas
**CONF:** Thtr 35 Class 35 Board 35 **PARKING:** 30 **NOTES:** No smoking in restaurant Closed Jan RS mid Nov-Dec & Feb
**CARDS:**

HAWKHURST, Kent Map 05 TQ73

### ★★★66% *Tudor Court*

Rye Rd TN18 5DA
☎ 01580 752312 01580 753966
e-mail: tudor-court@kentindex.com
***Dir:*** *approx 1m from Hawkhurst on the Rye A268 road*
This quiet hotel offers comfortably furnished bedrooms equipped with good facilities. The public areas include bars, a comfortable lounge and an attractive restaurant overlooking the garden. Guests have use of hard tennis courts opposite.
**ROOMS:** 18 en suite (2 fmly) No smoking in 2 bedrooms
**FACILITIES:** Tennis (hard) Croquet lawn Putting green Clock golf Childrens play area **CONF:** Thtr 60 Class 40 Board 32 **PARKING:** 50
**NOTES:** No dogs (ex guide dogs) No smoking in restaurant
**CARDS:**

HAWKSHEAD (NEAR AMBLESIDE), Cumbria Map 07 SD39

### ★★75% Highfield House Country Hotel

Hawkshead Hill LA22 0PN
☎ 015394 36344 015394 36793
e-mail: rooms@highfield-hawkshead.com
***Dir:*** *on B5285 towards Coniston 0.5m from Hawkshead village*

Set in its own mature gardens, this well maintained country house enjoys magnificent views of the Cumbrian countryside. Bedrooms vary in size and style but are all attractively furnished and decorated. Public areas include an inviting lounge, a cosy bar and an elegant dining room where carefully prepared meals are served.
**ROOMS:** 11 en suite (2 fmly) No smoking in 8 bedrooms s £60-£64; d £124-£135 (incl. bkfst & dinner) * **LB** **FACILITIES:** ch fac Xmas
**PARKING:** 15 **NOTES:** No dogs (ex guide dogs) No smoking in restaurant Closed 3-31 Jan **CARDS:**

Popped the question? Hotels with Civ Wed in their entry are licensed for civil wedding ceremonies. Maximum numbers for the ceremony only are shown, e.g. Civ Wed 120

HAWKSHEAD (NEAR AMBLESIDE), continued

**★★68% Queen's Head**
Main St LA22 0NS
☎ 015394 36271 015394 36722
e-mail: enquires@queensheadhotel.co.uk
***Dir:*** *leave M6 at junct 36, then A590 to Newby Bridge. Take 2nd right and continue 8m into Hawkshead*

This 16th-century inn features a wood-panelled bar with low, oak-beamed ceilings and an open log fire. Substantial, carefully prepared meals are served in the bar and in the pretty dining room. The bedrooms, three of which are in an adjacent cottage, are attractively furnished and include some four-poster rooms.
**ROOMS:** 10 rms (8 en suite) 3 annexe en suite (2 fmly) No smoking in all bedrooms s £45-£47; d £74 (incl. bkfst) * **LB** **FACILITIES:** Xmas **NOTES:** No dogs (ex guide dogs) No smoking in restaurant
**CARDS:**

*See advert on page 269*

HAWORTH, West Yorkshire Map 07 SE03

**★★67% Old White Lion**
6 West Ln BD22 8DU
☎ 01535 642313 01535 646222
e-mail: enquiries@oldwhitelionhotel.com
***Dir:*** *turn off A629 onto B6142, hotel 0.5m past Haworth Station*

Almost 300 years old, this historic hotel is situated at the top of an old cobbled street. There is an oak-panelled lounge and a choice of bars, serving a range of snacks and meals. More formal dining is available in the popular restaurant. Comfortably furnished bedrooms vary in size and style.
**ROOMS:** 15 en suite (3 fmly) s £46-£60; d £62-£82 (incl. bkfst) * **LB** **FACILITIES:** STV Xmas **CONF:** Thtr 90 Class 20 Board 38 **PARKING:** 10 **NOTES:** No dogs (ex guide dogs)
**CARDS:**

*See advert under BRADFORD*

***★★65% Three Sisters***
Brow Top Rd BD22 9PH
☎ 01535 643458 01535 646842
***Dir:*** *from A629 Keighley/Halifax road take B6144 at Flappit Corner. Hotel 0.75m on right*
Once a Victorian farmhouse, this popular hotel and inn now offers modern, spacious bedrooms. A wide selection of freshly prepared meals and snacks is served, in generous portions, in either the bar or the restaurant, which enjoys fine views over Haworth and the surrounding area.
**ROOMS:** 9 en suite (1 fmly) **FACILITIES:** STV entertainment **CONF:** Thtr 250 Class 200 Board 100 **PARKING:** 300 **NOTES:** No dogs (ex guide dogs) No smoking in restaurant **CARDS:**

HAYDOCK, Merseyside Map 07 SJ59

**★★★66% Posthouse Haydock**
Posthouse
Lodge Ln WA12 0JG
☎ 0870 400 9039 01942 718419
e-mail: gm1117@forte-hotels.com
***Dir:*** *adj to M6 junct 23, on A49. From junct 23 on M6, take the A49 to Ashton in Nakerfield. The Posthouse is 0.25m on the right by the racecourse*
The hotel has an ideal location adjacent to Haydock racecourse and within easy reach of most north-west cities and attractions. A variety of bedrooms is available, including smart executive and impressive superior rooms. Public areas include extensive meeting and conference facilities, a smart Spirit health and leisure club and a spacious bar and restaurant.
**ROOMS:** 138 en suite (41 fmly) No smoking in 74 bedrooms s £109; d £89-£119 * **LB** **FACILITIES:** **Spa** Indoor swimming (H) Snooker Sauna Solarium Gym Jacuzzi ch fac Xmas **CONF:** Thtr 180 Class 100 Board 60 Del from £79 * **SERVICES:** Lift **PARKING:** 197 **NOTES:** Civ Wed 180 **CARDS:**

***Travelodge***
Travelodge
Piele Rd WA11 9TL
☎ 01942 272055 01942 272055
***Dir:*** *2m W of junct 23 on M6, on A580 westbound*
Travelodge offers good quality, good value, modern accommodation. Ideal for families, the spacious, en suite bedrooms include remote-control TV, tea and coffee-making facilities, luxury beds and free morning newspaper. Meals can be taken at the nearby family restaurant. For further details and the Travelodge phone number, consult the Hotel Groups page.

**ROOMS:** 40 en suite

HAYES Hotels are listed under Heathrow Airport

HAYTOR VALE, Devon Map 03 SX77

**★★74% Rock Inn**
TQ13 9XP
☎ 01364 661305 & 661465 01364 661242
e-mail: rockinn@eclipse.co.uk
***Dir:*** *turn off A38 onto A382 as far as Bovey Tracey, approx 0.5m turn left and join B3387 to Haytor*
A coaching inn dating back to the 1750s, located in a pretty hamlet on the edge of Dartmoor. Each named after a Grand National winner, the individually decorated bedrooms have good facilities and some nice extra touches. A wide range of dishes is served and the bars are full of character, with flagstone floors and old beams.
**ROOMS:** 9 en suite (2 fmly) No smoking in 2 bedrooms **FACILITIES:** STV **PARKING:** 20 **NOTES:** No dogs (ex guide dogs) **CARDS:**

## HAYWARDS HEATH, West Sussex Map 05 TQ32

### ★★★67% The Birch Hotel

Lewes Rd RH17 7SF
☎ 01444 451565 01444 440109
e-mail: info@birch-hotel
***Dir:*** *on A272 opposite Princess Royal Hospital and behind Shell Garage*
Attractive Victorian property, carefully extended to combine modern facilities with historic charm. The spacious bedrooms are pleasantly decorated and equipped with many useful extras. Public rooms feature the newly refurbished conservatory-style restaurant. In addition guests have the use of a delightful open plan lounge and a brasserie style bar serving a range of snacks
**ROOMS:** 51 en suite (3 fmly) No smoking in 23 bedrooms s fr £85; d fr £95 (incl. bkfst) * **FACILITIES:** STV **CONF:** Thtr 60 Class 30 Board 26 Del from £120 * **PARKING:** 60 **NOTES:** No dogs (ex guide dogs) No smoking in restaurant **CARDS:**

## HEATHROW AIRPORT (LONDON), Greater London Map 04 TQ07

see also Slough & Staines

### ★★★★75% Crowne Plaza London - Heathrow

Stockley Rd UB7 9NA
☎ 01895 445555 01895 445122
e-mail: cplhr@netscapeonline.co.uk
***Dir:*** *leave M4 junct 4 follow signs to Uxbridge on A408, hotel entrance approx 400yds on left*
This modern hotel is conveniently located for access to Heathrow Airport and the motorway network. A very good range of facilities is available for guests including versatile conference and meeting rooms, golfing and a 24-hour leisure complex. Guests have the choice of two bars, both serving food, and two restaurants. Air-conditioned bedrooms are furnished and decorated to a high standard and feature a comprehensive range of extra facilities.
**ROOMS:** 458 en suite (220 fmly) No smoking in 187 bedrooms d £144-£250 * **LB** **FACILITIES:** Spa STV Indoor swimming (H) Golf 9 Sauna Solarium Gym Jacuzzi Beauty room Helipad kids playground Xmas **CONF:** Thtr 200 Class 120 Board 75 Del £235 * **SERVICES:** Lift air con **PARKING:** 410 **NOTES:** No dogs (ex guide dogs) **CARDS:**

### ★★★★74% London Marriott Hotel Heathrow

Bath Rd UB3 5AN
☎ 020 8990 1100 020 8990 1110
***Dir:*** *leave M4 junct 4, follow for Terms 1 2 & 3 via M4/Heathrow airport access road, left ar rdbt sign posted A4/London , hotel left 0.5 miles through 2 sets of lights*

This smart hotel meets all expectations of a modern airport hotel. The light and airy atrium offers several eating and drinking options each with different themes. Spacious bedrooms are appointed to a good standard with an excellent range of facilities. The hotel has secure car parking and some indoor leisure.
**ROOMS:** 390 en suite (140 fmly) No smoking in 327 bedrooms s £149-£190; d £149-£190 * **FACILITIES:** Spa STV Indoor swimming (H) Sauna Solarium Gym Steam Room entertainment Xmas **CONF:** Thtr 540 Class 214 Board 62 Del from £155 * **SERVICES:** Lift air con **PARKING:** 220 **NOTES:** No dogs (ex guide dogs) **CARDS:**

### ★★★★69% Sheraton Skyline

Bath Rd UB3 5BP
☎ 020 8759 2535 020 8750 9150
e-mail: mary.casey@sheraton.com
***Dir:*** *leave M4 junct 4 for Heathrow, follow for Terminals 1,2 & 3. Before Airport entrance take slip road to left for 0.25m signed A4 Cen London*
Within easy access of all terminals, this hotel offers spacious, well-equipped and air-conditioned bedrooms, some of which have been recently refurbished. Guests can enjoy a varied range of food and drinks in various bars and restaurants catering for all tastes. An excellent range of function rooms, a business centre, gym and convenient parking are also available.
**ROOMS:** 352 en suite (12 fmly) No smoking in 253 bedrooms s £105-£205; d £105-£205 * **LB** **FACILITIES:** STV Indoor swimming (H) Gym Pool table Xmas **CONF:** Thtr 500 Class 325 Board 100 Del from £150 * **SERVICES:** Lift air con **PARKING:** 300 **NOTES:** RS Restaurant closed Bank Holidays Civ Wed 200 **CARDS:**

### ★★★★68% *Slough/Windsor Marriott Hotel*

Ditton Rd, Langley SL3 8PT
☎ 01753 544244 01753 540272
***Dir:*** *from junct 5 of M4/A4, follow 'Langley' signs and turn left at traffic lights into Ditton Road*

This busy and popular hotel enjoys good access to the motorway network and Heathrow Airport. Bedrooms are spacious with attractive colour schemes and excellent facilities. Guests can enjoy a varied range of food and drinks in various bars and restaurants. An excellent range of function rooms and secure car park are additional features.
**ROOMS:** 380 en suite (149 fmly) No smoking in 231 bedrooms **FACILITIES:** STV Indoor swimming (H) Tennis (hard) Sauna Solarium Gym Beautician entertainment **CONF:** Thtr 300 Class 150 Board 10 **SERVICES:** Lift air con **PARKING:** 600 **NOTES:** No dogs (ex guide dogs) **CARDS:**

### ★★★★67% *Posthouse Premier Heathrow*

Sipson Rd UB7 0JU
☎ 020 8759 2323 020 8897 8659
***Dir:*** *M4 junct4, keep left, take first left into Holloway Lane, left at mini rdbt then immediately left through hotel gates*
This modern hotel is the largest in the Heathrow area, catering well for the needs of the international traveller. Facilities include several meeting rooms, four restaurants, two bars and business

continued on p272

H

HEATHROW AIRPORT (LONDON), continued

services. There is a range of bedroom types, all equipped with useful extras.
**ROOMS:** 610 en suite (284 fmly) No smoking in 359 bedrooms **FACILITIES:** STV **CONF:** Thtr 130 Class 60 Board 60 **SERVICES:** Lift **PARKING:** 478 **NOTES:** No dogs (ex guide dogs)
**CARDS:**

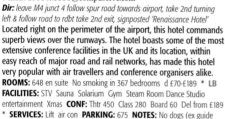

### ★★★★65% Le Meridien Excelsior

Bath Rd UB7 0DU
☎ 0870 400 8899 🖷 020 8759 3421
e-mail: excelsior@lemeridien.co.uk
***Dir:*** *adjacent to M4 spur at junct with A4*
This convenient, large corporate hotel offers a wide range of facilities including a choice of bars and restaurants, conference rooms and a health club. Bedrooms vary from the Standard type to the recently refurbished Executives and Crown Clubrooms.
**ROOMS:** 537 en suite (43 fmly) No smoking in 259 bedrooms d £141-£212 * **LB** **FACILITIES:** STV Indoor swimming (H) Sauna Solarium Gym Jacuzzi **CONF:** Thtr 250 Class 135 Board 60 Del £175 * **SERVICES:** Lift air con **PARKING:** 500 **NOTES:** No dogs (ex guide dogs) Civ Wed 200 **CARDS:**

### ★★★★65% The Renaissance London Heathrow Hotel

Bath Rd TW6 2AQ
☎ 020 8897 6363 🖷 020 8897 1113
e-mail: 106047.3556@compuserve.com
***Dir:*** *leave M4 junct 4 follow spur road towards airport, take 2nd turning left & follow road to rdbt take 2nd exit, signposted 'Renaissance Hotel'*
Located right on the perimeter of the airport, this hotel commands superb views over the runways. The hotel boasts some of the most extensive conference facilities in the UK and its location, within easy reach of major road and rail networks, has made this hotel very popular with air travellers and conference organisers alike.
**ROOMS:** 648 en suite No smoking in 367 bedrooms d £70-£189 * **LB** **FACILITIES:** STV Sauna Solarium Gym Steam Room Dance Studio entertainment Xmas **CONF:** Thtr 450 Class 280 Board 60 Del from £189 * **SERVICES:** Lift air con **PARKING:** 675 **NOTES:** No dogs (ex guide dogs) Civ Wed 400 **CARDS:**

### ★★★70% Novotel Heathrow

NOVOTEL

Junction 4 M4, Cherry Ln UB7 9HB
☎ 01895 431431 🖷 01895 431221
e-mail: H1551@accor-hotels.com
***Dir:*** *leave M4 junct 4 follow signs for Uxbridge(A408), keep left & take 2nd exit off traffic island into Cherry Ln signed West Drayton. Hotel on left*
This modern hotel is conveniently located for the airport and motorway network. Bedrooms are spacious and feature a good range of facilities. Five rooms also have facilities for disabled guests. The huge indoor atrium is airy and stylish and creates a sense of space in the public areas, which include a cocktail bar, meeting rooms, fitness centre and indoor swimming pool.
**ROOMS:** 178 en suite (34 fmly) No smoking in 112 bedrooms d £115-£125 * **LB** **FACILITIES:** STV Indoor swimming (H) Gym **CONF:** Thtr 250 Class 100 Board 90 Del from £139 * **SERVICES:** Lift **PARKING:** 100 **CARDS:**

### ★★★68% Posthouse Heathrow Airport

118 Bath Rd UB3 5AJ
☎ 0870 400 9040 🖷 020 8564 9265
***Dir:*** *leave M4 junct 4, take spur road to Heathrow Airport, 1st left off towards A4, on to A4 Bath Road, through 3 traffic lights, hotel on left*
This smartly presented hotel is ideally situated for the traveller and the business guest. The bar/lounge and Rotisserie Restaurant are attractively furnished and well appointed, as are the bedrooms. For the conference delegate, the Academy meeting rooms fulfil a range of needs.

**ROOMS:** 186 en suite No smoking in 100 bedrooms d £169 * **FACILITIES:** Xmas **CONF:** Thtr 60 Class 10 Board 35 Del from £65 * **SERVICES:** Lift **PARKING:** 105 **CARDS:**

### ★★★65% Osterley Four Pillars Hotel

FOUR PILLARS HOTELS

764 Great West Rd TW7 5NA
☎ 020 8568 9981 🖷 020 8569 7819
e-mail: enquiries@four-pillars.co.uk
(For full entry see Osterley)

### ★★★64% Master Robert

366 Great West Rd TW5 0BD
☎ 020 8570 6261 🖷 020 8569 4016
e-mail: stay@masterrobert.co.uk
The Master Robert is conveniently located three-and-a-half miles from Heathrow on the A4 towards London. The well-equipped bedrooms are modern in style and are set in motel-style buildings behind the main hotel. There is a residents' lounge bar, a restaurant and a popular pub.
**ROOMS:** 94 annexe en suite (10 fmly) No smoking in 15 bedrooms s £92.50-£104; d £104-£124 * **FACILITIES:** STV **CONF:** Thtr 150 Class 60 Board 40 Del from £99 * **PARKING:** 200 **NOTES:** No dogs (ex guide dogs) **CARDS:**

### ⌂ *Travelodge*

Bath Rd UB7 0DU
☎ 020 88977775
Travelodge offers good quality, good value, modern accommodation. Ideal for families, the spacious, en suite bedrooms include remote-control TV, tea and coffee-making facilities, luxury beds and free morning newspaper. Meals can be taken at the nearby family restaurant. For further details and the Travelodge phone number, consult the Hotel Groups page.

### ⌂ Hotel Ibis Heathrow

112/114 Bath Rd UB3 5AL
☎ 020 8759 4888 🖷 020 8564 7894
e-mail: H0794@accor-hotels.com
***Dir:*** *follow signs for Heathrow terminals 1,2,3. Take the spur road, turn off at sign for A4 Central London, hotel 0.5m on left*
Modern, budget hotel offering comfortable accommodation in bright and practical bedrooms. Breakfast is self-service and dinner is available in the restaurant. For further details, consult the Hotel Groups page.
**ROOMS:** 354 en suite (incl. cont bkfst) d £60 *

### ○ *The Radisson Edwardian*

Bath Rd UB3 5AW
☎ 020 8759 6311 🖷 020 8759 4559
At the time of going to press, the star classification for this hotel was not confirmed. Please refer to the AA internet site www.theAA.com for current information.
**ROOMS:** 459 en suite (14 fmly) No smoking in 75 bedrooms **FACILITIES:** STV Indoor swimming (H) Sauna Solarium Gym Jacuzzi entertainment **CONF:** Thtr 700 Class 300 Board 70 **SERVICES:** Lift air con **PARKING:** 242 **CARDS:**

## HEBDEN BRIDGE, West Yorkshire
Map 07 SD92

### ★★★66% Carlton
Albert St HX7 8ES
☎ 01422 844400 🖷 01422 843117
e-mail: ctonhotel@aol.com
***Dir:*** *turn right at cinema for hotel at top of Hope St*
Formerly the general store of Hebden Bridge, a collection of shops remains on the ground floor of this Victorian building. Individually designed bedrooms are attractively furnished, whilst public areas are smart, peaceful and comfortable. Diners can choose between lounge service snacks, or extensive high quality cuisine in the elegant dining room.
**ROOMS:** 16 en suite s fr £56; d fr £75 (incl. bkfst) * **LB**
**FACILITIES:** STV **CONF:** Thtr 120 Class 40 Board 40 Del from £90 *
**SERVICES:** Lift **NOTES:** No smoking in restaurant Civ Wed 90
**CARDS:**

### ★★68% Hebden Lodge Hotel
6-10 New Rd HX7 8AD
☎ 01422 845272 🖷 01422 842959
***Dir:*** *on A646 opposite Hebden Bridge Marina*
Situated across from the Rochdale canal marina, this hospitable, family-owned hotel offers a range of well-equipped bedrooms. Restyled public rooms are light and modern. Staff are friendly and attentive.
**ROOMS:** 12 en suite (1 fmly) s £28-£33; d £55 (incl. bkfst) * **LB**
**FACILITIES:** Xmas **NOTES:** RS 24-26 Dec
**CARDS:**

## HECKFIELD, Hampshire
Map 04 SU76

### ★★68% New Inn
RG27 0LE
☎ 0118 932 6374 🖷 0118 932 6550
e-mail: newinn@heckfieldl.freeserve.co.uk
***Dir:*** *turn off A33 onto B3349, turn right at island and continue straight over next on B3349 to hotel 0.5m on left*
Dating back to the 15th century in parts, this characterful inn offers spacious bedrooms designed to meet the needs of business and leisure travellers alike. A wide range of popular dishes is served in the restaurant; the same menu is also available in the beamed bar.
**ROOMS:** 16 en suite (1 fmly) s fr £75; d fr £85 (incl. bkfst) * **LB**
**CONF:** Thtr 30 Class 25 Board 16 Del from £105 * **PARKING:** 80
**NOTES:** No smoking in restaurant Closed 25 Dec
**CARDS:**

## HEDDON'S MOUTH, Devon
Map 03 SS64

### ★★76% Heddon's Gate Hotel
EX31 4PZ
☎ 01598 763313 🖷 01598 763363
e-mail: info@hgate.co.uk
***Dir:*** *3.5m W of Lynton on A39 turn R, signs Martinhoe & Woody Bay. Follow signs for Hunter's Inn & Heddon's Mouth, hotel on R 0.25m before Hunter's Inn*
The proprietors take great care of their guests at this personally run hotel, standing in the heart of Exmoor. Food is of great importance and quality local ingredients are carefully prepared. Bedrooms are individually designed and comfortable. Day rooms

*continued*



include a bar, a Victorian morning room/library and an Edwardian sitting room.

**ROOMS:** 11 en suite 3 annexe en suite s £70-£87; d £140-£168 (incl. bkfst & dinner) * **LB** **PARKING:** 20 **NOTES:** No smoking in restaurant Closed Nov-Etr **CARDS:**

*See advert on this page*

## HELLAND BRIDGE, Cornwall & Isles of Scilly
Map 02 SX07

### ★★★68% Tredethy House
THE CIRCLE Selected Individual Hotels GREAT BRITAIN
Tredethy PL30 4QS
☎ 01208 841262 🖷 01208 841707
e-mail: bookings@tredethyhouse.co.uk
***Dir:*** *Follow signs to Helland and then Tredethy*
Set in nine acres of grounds, Tredethy House was formerly home to Prince and Princess Chula of Thailand. The spacious public areas mainly look out over the surrounding countryside and are furnished with an interesting mix of period and African artefacts.

*continued on p274*

HELLAND BRIDGE, continued

Bedrooms vary in size and style, some are located around a courtyard at the rear of the property.

*Tredethy House, Helland Bridge*

**ROOMS:** 11 en suite 4 annexe en suite (5 fmly) No smoking in all bedrooms s £50-£115; d £80-£145 (incl. bkfst) * **LB** **FACILITIES:** Outdoor swimming (H) ch fac Xmas **CONF:** Class 20 Board 20 Del from £70 * **PARKING:** 20 **NOTES:** No smoking in restaurant Closed early Jan- early Feb **CARDS:**

## HELLIDON, Northamptonshire

Map 04 SP55

### ★★★★67% *Hellidon Lakes Hotel & Country Club*

MARSTON HOTELS

NN11 6GG
☎ 01327 262550 01327 262559
e-mail: stay@hellidon.demon.co.uk

***Dir:*** *signposted, off A361 between Daventry and Banbury*

Set in grounds including 12 lakes and an 18- and nine-hole golf course, this hotel offers spacious, well equipped bedrooms furnished in striking tulip wood. Facilities include a beauty salon, video golf and bowling alley. The Lake restaurant, overlooking the Holly Lake and the 18th hole, serves modern British cuisine, whilst the Brunswick bar offers lighter meals throughout the day.

**ROOMS:** 71 en suite **FACILITIES:** STV Indoor swimming (H) Golf 27 Tennis (hard) Fishing Solarium Gym Putting green Jacuzzi Beautician Ten Pin Bowling Golf simulator Steam room **CONF:** Thtr 150 Class 70 Board 50 **PARKING:** 140 **NOTES:** No dogs (ex guide dogs) No smoking in restaurant **CARDS:**

## HELMSLEY, North Yorkshire

Map 08 SE68

### ★★★75% The Black Swan

Market Place YO62 5BJ
☎ 0870 400 8112 01439 770174
e-mail: HeritageHotels_Helmsley.BlackSwan@forte-hotels.com

***Dir:*** *follow A170 towards Scarborough into Helmsley and hotel at top of Market Square*

The face of this former coaching inn is a blend of Elizabethan, Georgian and Tudor, all of it charming, with warm, welcoming interiors of candlelight, oak beams and open fireplaces. There are six guest lounges and plenty of cosy nooks for quiet conversation. The hotel has 45 comfortable, individually decorated bedrooms and a popular restaurant.

**ROOMS:** 45 en suite (4 fmly) No smoking in 13 bedrooms d £120-£180 (incl. bkfst) * **LB** **FACILITIES:** Croquet lawn ch fac Xmas **CONF:** Thtr 60 Class 16 Board 22 Del £135 * **PARKING:** 50 **NOTES:** No smoking in restaurant **CARDS:**

### ★★★70% Feversham Arms

Best Western

1 High St YO62 5AG
☎ 01439 770766 01439 770346
e-mail: fevershamarms@hotmail.com

***Dir:*** *take A168 'Thirsk' from A1 then A170. Alternative: Take A64 'York' from A1 to York North & then B1363 to Helmsley. Hotel 125mtrs from Mkt Pl*

This well-furnished, comfortable hotel has been popular with guests for many years. Each summer a colourful display of roses adorns the façade. Both the restaurant and bar menus offer a good selection of dishes. The comfortable bedrooms are well-equipped and hospitality is very good.

**ROOMS:** 17 en suite (5 fmly) No smoking in all bedrooms s £70-£90; d £90-£110 (incl. bkfst) * **LB** **FACILITIES:** STV Outdoor swimming (H) Tennis (hard) Gym Xmas **CONF:** Thtr 30 Class 30 Board 24 Del £125 * **PARKING:** 50 **NOTES:** No smoking in restaurant **CARDS:**

### ★★★70% Pheasant

Harome YO62 5JG
☎ 01439 771241 01439 771744

***Dir:*** *2.5m SE, leave A170 after 0.25m, turn right signposted Harome for further 2m*

Enjoying a charming setting next to the village pond, this welcoming hotel has attractive, comfortable bedrooms. The beamed, flagstoned bar leads into the extended conservatory dining room, where wholesome English food is served. There is a comfortable lounge in which to relax.

**ROOMS:** 12 en suite 2 annexe en suite s £63-£67; d £126-£134 (incl. bkfst & dinner) * **LB** **FACILITIES:** Indoor swimming (H) **PARKING:** 20 **NOTES:** No children 12yrs Closed Xmas & Jan-Feb **CARDS:**

### ★★68% Carlton Lodge

Bondgate YO62 5EY
☎ 01439 770557 01439 770623
e-mail: aa.enquiries@carlton-lodge.com

***Dir:*** *on the A170 Scarborough road, close to Market Sq*

A friendly, welcoming hotel on the edge of the town and offering comfortable, well-furnished bedrooms. Public areas include an inviting lounge with an open fire, and a well-appointed dining room where good quality, home-cooked evening meals are served.

**ROOMS:** 7 rms (6 en suite) 4 annexe en suite (1 fmly) s £27.50-£37.50; d £55-£70 (incl. bkfst) * **LB** **FACILITIES:** Xmas **CONF:** Thtr 150 Class 60 Board 50 Del from £49.50 * **PARKING:** 45 **NOTES:** No smoking in restaurant Civ Wed 160 **CARDS:**

### ★★68% Crown

Market Square YO62 5BJ
☎ 01439 770297 01439 771595

***Dir:*** *on A170*

A 16th-century inn with lots of character, standing in the market square and noted for its colourful flower arrangements. Bedrooms

*continued*

are individual and thoughtfully equipped. Public areas are pleasantly traditional and include cosy bars, a residents' lounge and a dining room serving wholesome dishes in generous portions.
**ROOMS:** 12 en suite (1 fmly) s £30-£36; d £60-£72 (incl. bkfst) * **LB**
**FACILITIES:** Xmas **PARKING:** 20 **CARDS:**

**★★64% Feathers**
Market Place YO62 5BH
☎ 01439 770275 🖷 01439 771101
***Dir:*** *in Helmsley market place on A170*
This 15th century, creeper-clad hotel and inn offers very pleasant, well-equipped bedrooms. An extensive range of food is available in either the bar, or the dining room. The bars are particularly popular, especially with the friendly locals, and there are gardens to the rear.
**ROOMS:** 14 en suite (3 fmly) s £45; d £60 (incl. bkfst) * **LB**
**FACILITIES:** Xmas **CONF:** Thtr 100 Class 50 Board 50 **PARKING:** 24
**CARDS:**

## HELSTON, Cornwall & Isles of Scilly — Map 02 SW62

**★★79% ®® Nansloe Manor**
Meneage Rd TR13 0SB
☎ 01326 574691 🖷 01326 564680
e-mail: info@nansloe-manor.co.uk
***Dir:*** *300yds on the left from Helston/Lizard roundabout A394/A3083*

A haven of tranquillity and understated elegance, this Georgian Grade II listed property dates back to 1735. Service is thoughtful and attentive, and bedrooms have character and are equipped with many personal touches. Guests can wander in the grounds, which include a wonderful, walled garden. Imaginative cuisine is a high priority.
**ROOMS:** 7 rms (6 en suite) s £59-£80; d £110-£140 (incl. bkfst) * **LB**
**FACILITIES:** Croquet lawn Xmas **PARKING:** 40 **NOTES:** No dogs No children 10yrs No smoking in restaurant **CARDS:**

**★★64% The Gwealdues**
Falmouth Rd TR13 8JX
☎ 01326 572808 🖷 01326 561388
e-mail: gwealdueshotel@btinternet.com
***Dir:*** *Hotel is on approach into Helston on A394, coming from Truro or Falmouth*
On the outskirts of town, this friendly, family-run hotel is popular with business and leisure guests. Bedrooms are comfortable and feature many additional useful facilities. Authentic Thai cuisine is offered in the attractive restaurant, with other European dishes also available. For yachting enthusiasts, a 42' motor sailing yacht is available for hire.
**ROOMS:** 17 en suite (2 fmly) No smoking in 5 bedrooms s fr £37; d fr £55 (incl. bkfst) * **LB** **FACILITIES:** Sailing on own yacht Xmas
**CONF:** Del from £55 * **PARKING:** 50 **NOTES:** No dogs (ex guide dogs) No smoking in restaurant **CARDS:**

## HEMEL HEMPSTEAD, Hertfordshire — Map 04 TL00

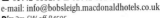

**★★★68% Posthouse Hemel Hempstead**
Breakspear Way HP2 4UA
**Posthouse**
☎ 0870 400 9041 🖷 01442 211812
***Dir:*** *exit junct 8 of M1, straight over roundabout and 1st left after BP garage*
Within easy access of the motorway network, this modern hotel is well-suited to its largely business clientele. The bedrooms are practically furnished and decorated, offering many in-room facilities. There is a well-equipped health club and a range of meeting rooms.
**ROOMS:** 145 en suite (33 fmly) No smoking in 76 bedrooms s £163; d £129-£183 * **LB** **FACILITIES:** Indoor swimming (H) Sauna Solarium Gym Jacuzzi Kids playroom/play area at wknds Xmas **CONF:** Thtr 60 Class 22 Board 30 **SERVICES:** Lift **PARKING:** 195
**CARDS:**

**★★★66% The Bobsleigh Inn**
Hempstead Rd, Bovingdon HP3 0DS
☎ 01442 833276 🖷 01442 832471
e-mail: info@bobsleigh.macdonaldhotels.co.uk
***Dir:*** *2m SW off B4505*

MACDONALD
HOTELS

This friendly hotel enjoys a rural setting. Bedrooms, which vary in shape and size, have been smartly refurbished. The popular restaurant offers a good range of interesting dishes. There is also an indoor pool which is open nine months of the year.
**ROOMS:** 47 en suite (6 fmly) No smoking in 40 bedrooms s £77-£110; d £95-£120 * **LB** **FACILITIES:** **Spa** STV Indoor swimming (H) Jacuzzi ch fac Xmas **CONF:** Thtr 60 Class 50 Board 45 Del from £140 *
**PARKING:** 72 **NOTES:** No smoking in restaurant Civ Wed
**CARDS:**

**★★★64% Watermill**
London Rd, Bourne End HP1 2RJ
☎ 01442 349955 🖷 01442 866130
e-mail: watermill@sarova.co.uk
***Dir:*** *from M1 junct 8 or M25 junct 20 follow signs to & join A41 for Aylesbury then A4251 to Bourne End*
Built around a former flour mill adjacent to the Grand Union Canal, the Watermill is a peaceful countryside retreat. The various annexe wings feature modern, well-equipped rooms, some overlooking the river. A large bar with superb river views serves snacks throughout the day.
**ROOMS:** 75 annexe en suite (9 fmly) No smoking in 26 bedrooms s £85-£105; d £90-£110 * **LB** **FACILITIES:** STV Fishing **CONF:** Thtr 100 Class 60 Board 50 **PARKING:** 100 **NOTES:** No dogs (ex guide dogs) No smoking in restaurant Civ Wed 100
**CARDS:**

TV dinner? Room service at three stars and above.

HEMEL HEMPSTEAD, continued

### ⇧ *Travelodge*
Wolsey House, Wolsey Rd HP2 4SS
☎ 01422 244450
Travelodge offers good quality, good value, modern accommodation. Ideal for families, the spacious, en suite bedrooms include remote-control TV, tea and coffee-making facilities, luxury beds and free morning newspaper. Meals can be taken at the nearby family restaurant. For further details and the Travelodge phone number, consult the Hotel Groups page.

Travelodge

## HENLEY-ON-THAMES, Oxfordshire — Map 04 SU78
see also Stonor

### ★★★71% Red Lion
Hart St RG9 2AR
☎ 01491 572161 📠 01491 410039
e-mail: reservations@redlionhenley.co.uk
***Dir:*** *adjacent to Henley Bridge*
The front rooms of this 16th-century Thames-side hotel offer fabulous views of the river. Bedrooms and public areas retain original features such as wood panelling, flagstone floors and beams. Bedrooms, decorated to a high standard, feature period furniture. Beds are new and extremely comfortable.
**ROOMS:** 26 en suite (1 fmly) s £99-£135; d £145-£170 * **FACILITIES:** STV **CONF:** Thtr 60 Class 20 Board 30 Del from £184 * **PARKING:** 25 **NOTES:** No dogs **CARDS:**

## HEREFORD, Herefordshire — Map 03 SO54
see also Much Birch

**Premier Collection**

Castle House

### ★★★ Castle House
Castle St HR1 2NW
☎ 01432 356321 📠 01432 365909
e-mail: info@castlehse.co.uk
***Dir:*** *follow signs for city centre & city centre east, pass town hall, where St Owen's St narrows turn sharp right twice into St Ethelbert St*
This riverside Victorian town mansion was once the home of the Bishop of Hereford. The superb bedrooms are equipped with every luxury and the elegant public rooms are of the highest quality. The attractive restaurant décor complements the topiary garden, and the smartly attired young staff provide excellent service in serving the exceptionally good cuisine.
**ROOMS:** 15 en suite s fr £90; d £165-£210 (incl. cont bkfst) * **LB** **FACILITIES:** STV Xmas **SERVICES:** Lift **PARKING:** 15 **CARDS:**

*See advert on opposite page*

### ★★★67% Three Counties Hotel
Belmont Rd HR2 7BP
☎ 01432 299955 📠 01432 275114
e-mail: enquiries@threecountieshotel.co.uk
***Dir:*** *on A465 Abergavenny Rd*
A mile west of the city centre, this large, modern complex has well-equipped, spacious bedrooms, many of which are located in separate single-storey buildings around the extensive car park. There is a spacious, comfortable lounge, a traditional bar and an attractive restaurant.
**ROOMS:** 28 en suite 32 annexe en suite (4 fmly) No smoking in 23 bedrooms s £38.50-£62; d £56-£80 (incl. bkfst) * **LB** **FACILITIES:** STV Xmas **CONF:** Thtr 300 Class 100 Board 60 Del from £79 * **PARKING:** 250 **NOTES:** Civ Wed 200 **CARDS:**

*See advert on opposite page*

### ★★★64% *The Green Dragon*
Broad St HR4 9BG
☎ 0870 400 8113 📠 01432 352139
e-mail: HeritageHotels_HerefordGreenDragon@forte-Hotels.com
***Dir:*** *follow signs for Cathedral and Mappa Mundi to rdbt. First exit, then 2nd left into West St, then 2nd right into Aubrey St and hotel garage*
Close to the cathedral, this landmark hotel is on the one-way city-centre road system. Impressive public areas have the appealing charm of an elegant bygone era. The comfortable lounges are popular for leisurely afternoon tea. There is a large function room and a secure car park.
**ROOMS:** 83 en suite (22 fmly) No smoking in 29 bedrooms **FACILITIES:** N **CONF:** Thtr 200 Class 60 Board 40 **SERVICES:** Lift **PARKING:** 110 **CARDS:**

### ★★★62% Belmont Lodge & Golf Course
Belmont HR2 9SA
☎ 01432 352666 📠 01432 358090
e-mail: info@belmontlodge.co.uk
***Dir:*** *from city centre turn off A465 to Abergavenny into Ruckhall Lane, hotel located on right in approx 0.5m*
This hotel and golfing complex occupies a superb location above the River Wye. The modern, well-equipped bedrooms are in a purpose-built lodge, and the restaurant and bar are located in the clubhouse, in the Grade II listed Belmont House.
**ROOMS:** 30 en suite (4 fmly) No smoking in 15 bedrooms s £47.50-£52; d £72.50-£67.50 (incl. bkfst) * **LB** **FACILITIES:** Golf 18 Tennis (hard) Fishing Snooker Putting green Bowls Darts **CONF:** Thtr 60 Class 14 Board 25 Del from £59.50 * **PARKING:** 150 **NOTES:** No dogs (ex guide dogs) No smoking in restaurant **CARDS:**

### ★★★60% Graftonbury Garden Hotel
Grafton Ln HR2 8BN
☎ 01432 268826 📠 01432 354633
e-mail: sales@graftonbury.co.uk
***Dir:*** *2m S of Hereford, 0.5m off A49 to Ross-on-Wye*
In a secluded location to the south of Hereford, this hotel is conveniently located for the city. It benefits from bright public areas, including a bar, lounge and bistro, as well as extensive

*continued*

function/conference rooms. Bedrooms are comfortable and well-equipped.

**ROOMS:** 15 en suite 11 annexe en suite (3 fmly) s £40; d £55-£90 (incl. bkfst) * **LB** **CONF:** Thtr 200 Class 150 Board 35 Del from £75 * **PARKING:** 90 **NOTES:** No smoking in restaurant Closed 25 & 26 Dec Civ Wed 60 **CARDS:**

★★71% ®® ***Ancient Camp Inn***
Ruckhall HR2 9QX
☎ 01981 250449 📠 01981 251581
***Dir:*** *A465, turn right to Belmont Abbey, 2.5m to hotel*
In a superb location above the River Wye and enjoying stunning views, this inn is named after a nearby Iron Age fort. It features flagstone floors, exposed beams and real fires in the bar and dining room. Cuisine is rustic in style.
**ROOMS:** 5 en suite (1 fmly) **FACILITIES:** Fishing **PARKING:** 30 **NOTES:** No dogs (ex guide dogs) No children 12 No smoking in restaurant Closed 1-14 Jan RS Mon **CARDS:**

## HERTFORD, Hertfordshire

Map 04 TL31

### ★★★65% The White Horse

Hertingfordbury SG14 2LB
☎ 0870 400 8114 📠 01992 550809
e-mail: heritagehotelshertingfordbury.whitehorse@forte-hotels.com
***Dir:*** *1m W of Hertford on A414*

The Georgian facade of this former coaching inn belies a much older interior with parts of the building dating back to the 17th century. Today, most of the tastefully decorated bedrooms are located in a more modern extension to the property, with many overlooking the attractive gardens. The beamed bar, with its open fire, is a popular venue for locals and residents alike.

**ROOMS:** 42 en suite No smoking in 14 bedrooms s £83-£110; d £98-£121 (incl. bkfst) * **LB** **FACILITIES:** Xmas **CONF:** Thtr 60 Class 30 Board 30 Del from £100 * **PARKING:** 60 **NOTES:** No smoking in restaurant **CARDS:**

## HESTON MOTORWAY SERVICE AREA (M4), Greater London See LONDON SECTION plan 1 A3

### Travelodge

Travelodge

Phoenix Way TW5 9NB
☎ 08700 850950 📠 01384 78578
***Dir:*** *M4 junc 2&3 westbound*

Travelodge offers good quality, good value, modern accommodation. Ideal for families, the spacious, en suite bedrooms include remote-control TV, tea and coffee-making facilities, luxury beds and free morning newspaper. Meals can be taken at the nearby family restaurant. For further details and the Travelodge phone number, consult the Hotel Groups page.

**ROOMS:** 95 en suite

### ○ Travelodge

Travelodge

M4 J2/3 South TW5 9NB
☎ 020 8580 2101
**ROOMS:** 40 en suite **NOTES:** Open now

## HETHERSETT, Norfolk

Map 05 TG10

### ★★★73% Park Farm

NR9 3DL
☎ 01603 810264 📠 01603 812104
e-mail: enq@parkfarm-hotel.co.uk
***Dir:*** *5m S of Norwich, off A11 on B1172*

An elegant Georgian farmhouse situated amidst landscaped grounds and surrounded by 200 acres of open countryside. The attractive bedrooms are individually decorated with co-ordinated fabrics, tastefully furnished and well-equipped. Public rooms include a smart conservatory, a lounge, a bar and an intimate restaurant as well as a superb leisure club. Banqueting and conference rooms are also available.

**ROOMS:** 5 en suite 42 annexe en suite (20 fmly) s £80-£105; d £110-£140 (incl. bkfst) * **LB** **FACILITIES:** Indoor swimming (H) Sauna Solarium Gym Jacuzzi Beauty salon Hairdressing Xmas **CONF:** Thtr 120 Class 50 Board 50 Del £112.50 * **PARKING:** 150 **NOTES:** No dogs (ex guide dogs) No smoking in restaurant
**CARDS:**

## HEVERSHAM, Cumbria

Map 07 SD4

### ★★★69% *Blue Bell*

Prince's Way LA7 7EE
☎ 015395 62018 📠 015395 62455
***Dir:*** *1m N of Milnthorpe, on A6*

Originally the old vicarage, this Jacobean inn dates back to 1460. Public areas are full of character and include an old beamed lounge bar where a wide selection of bar meals is available, two comfortable lounges and a spacious restaurant. Well-appointed bedrooms vary in style and refurbished rooms have lovely smart bathrooms. Staff are particularly friendly and attentive.

**ROOMS:** 21 en suite (4 fmly) **CONF:** Thtr 85 Class 35 Board 25
**PARKING:** 100 **NOTES:** No smoking in restaurant
**CARDS:**

## HEXHAM, Northumberland

Map 12 NY9

### ★★★★71% De Vere Slaley Hall

De Vere Hotels

Slaley NE47 0BY
☎ 01434 673350 📠 01434 673962
e-mail: slaley.hall@devere-hotels.com
***Dir:*** *A1 from south to A68 link road follow signs for Slaley Hall.*

Superbly situated in 1000 acres which includes two championship golf courses, this smart hotel offers thoughtfully equipped air-conditioned bedrooms and suites. There is an excellent health spa and leisure club. The food served in Fairways Brasserie is well deserving of its Rosette Award.

**ROOMS:** 139 en suite (22 fmly) No smoking in 101 bedrooms s £69-£130; d £88-£170 (incl. bkfst) * **LB** **FACILITIES:** Spa STV Indoor swimming (H) Golf 18 Sauna Solarium Gym Jacuzzi Quad bikes, archery, clay pigeon shooting ch fac Xmas **CONF:** Thtr 300 Class 220 Board 150 Del from £110 * **SERVICES:** Lift air con **PARKING:** 500 **NOTES:** No smoking in restaurant **CARDS:**

### ★★★69% Langley Castle

Langley on Tyne NE47 5LU
☎ 01434 688888 📠 01434 684019
e-mail: manager@langleycastle.com
***Dir:*** *from A69 S on A686 for 2m. Castle on right*

Langley is a magnificent 14th-century fortified castle in ten acres of parkland. There is a restaurant, a comfortable drawing room and cosy bar. The bedrooms in the castle are furnished with period

*continued*

pieces and most feature window seats set into thick, exposed stone walls. Restored buildings in the grounds have been converted into very smart bedrooms called "Castle View" rooms.
**ROOMS:** 8 en suite 10 annexe en suite (4 fmly) s £100-£135; d £120-£189 (incl. bkfst) * **LB** **FACILITIES:** STV ch fac Xmas **CONF:** Thtr 120 Class 60 Board 40 Del from £115 * **PARKING:** 60 **NOTES:** No smoking in restaurant Civ Wed 120 **CARDS:**

*See advert on this page*

**★★★68% Beaumont**
Beaumont St NE46 3LT
☎ 01434 602331 01434 606184
e-mail: beaumont.hotel@btinternet.com
***Dir:*** *on A69 towards Hexham*

The Beaumont overlooks the park in Hexham town centre. Its bright attractive bedrooms are well equipped. There are two bars, a relaxing foyer lounge and a first-floor restaurant featuring regional and seasonal produce.
**ROOMS:** 25 en suite (3 fmly) No smoking in 18 bedrooms s £65-£75; d £85-£95 * **LB** **FACILITIES:** STV Snooker Solarium ch fac **CONF:** Thtr 100 Class 60 Board 40 Del from £65 * **SERVICES:** Lift **PARKING:** 16 **NOTES:** No dogs No smoking in restaurant Closed 25-26 Dec & 1 Jan
**CARDS:**

*See advert on this page*

## HICKSTEAD, West Sussex
Map 04 TQ22

**★★★62% *The Hickstead Hotel***
Jobs Ln, Bolney RH17 5PA
☎ 01444 248023 01444 245280
***Dir:*** *0.25m E of A23 turn off at Hickstead village towards Burgess Hill*
Set in the heart of West Sussex this hotel enjoys a peaceful location not far from the A23. The bedrooms are modern in style and comfortably furnished. Lounge and bar areas are compact but the hotel benefits from an indoor leisure centre, conference rooms and ample car parking.
**ROOMS:** 50 en suite (8 fmly) No smoking in 25 bedrooms
**FACILITIES:** STV Indoor swimming (H) Sauna Solarium Gym Jacuzzi
**CONF:** Thtr 120 Class 60 Board 40 **PARKING:** 150 **NOTES:** No smoking in restaurant **CARDS:**

**⇧ *Travelodge***
Jobs Ln RH17 5NX
☎ 01444 881377 01444 881377
***Dir:*** *A23 southbound*
Travelodge offers good quality, good value, modern accommodation. Ideal for families, the spacious, en suite bedrooms include remote-control TV, tea and coffee-making facilities, luxury beds and free morning newspaper. Meals can be taken at the nearby family restaurant. For further details and the Travelodge phone number, consult the Hotel Groups page.

**ROOMS:** 40 en suite

HIGHBRIDGE, Somerset Map 03 ST34

**★★62% Sundowner**
74 Main Rd, West Huntspill TA9 3QU
☎ 01278 784766 01278 794133
e-mail: runnalls@msn.com
***Dir:*** *3m south on A38 from M5 junct 22 or 3m N on A38 from M5 junct 23*
The friendly service and informal atmosphere of this cosy hotel make the Sundowner a particularly pleasant place to stay. The open-plan lounge/bar is a comfortable area in which to relax, and an extensive menu is offered in the popular restaurant.
**ROOMS:** 8 en suite (1 fmly) s £36-£40; d £49-£54 (incl. bkfst) * **CONF:** Thtr 40 Board 24 Del from £59.95 * **PARKING:** 18 **NOTES:** No smoking in restaurant **CARDS:**

HIGH WYCOMBE, Buckinghamshire Map 04 SU89
see also Stokenchurch

**★★★66% Posthouse High Wycombe**
Handy Cross HP11 1TL
Posthouse
☎ 0870 400 9042 01494 439071
***Dir:*** *Exit M40 Junct 4, take A4010 towards Aylesbury.*
A modern, purpose-built hotel, convenient for the motorway networks. Bedrooms are spacious and well-equipped for the business traveller, featuring a comprehensive range of extra facilities. Guests have a choice of eating options, including the Junction Restaurant and the more informal Mongolian Barbecue.
**ROOMS:** 109 en suite (4 fmly) No smoking in 55 bedrooms d £129-£139 * **LB** **FACILITIES:** Xmas **CONF:** Thtr 200 Class 100 Board 40 Del from £95 * **PARKING:** 173 **NOTES:** No dogs (ex guide dogs) **CARDS:**

HILLINGTON, Norfolk Map 09 TF72

**★★67% Ffolkes Arms**
Lynn Rd PE31 6BJ
☎ 01485 600210 01485 601196
e-mail: ffolkespub@aol.com
***Dir:*** *on main A149 at Knights Hill rdbt turn right onto A148 towards Cromer. Hotel is 6m along A148 at Hillington*
This popular 17th-century coaching inn, ideally situated for many of west Norfolk's attractions, has been sympathetically adapted. Facilities include a bar, restaurant and lounge area. The courtyard boasts a popular function suite and social club. The spacious bedrooms are situated in a modern wing.
**ROOMS:** 20 annexe en suite (2 fmly) No smoking in all bedrooms s £35; d £50 (incl. bkfst) * **LB** **FACILITIES:** Pool table Xmas **CONF:** Thtr 200 Class 60 Board 50 Del £60 * **PARKING:** 200 **NOTES:** No dogs (ex guide dogs) No smoking in restaurant **CARDS:**

HILTON PARK MOTORWAY SERVICE AREA (M6), West Midlands Map 07 SJ90

**☖ *Travelodge***
Hilton Park Services (M6), Essington WV11 2DR
Travelodge
☎ 08700 850950 01922 701967
***Dir:*** *on M6 between juncts 10a & 11*
Travelodge offers good quality, good value, modern accommodation. Ideal for families, the spacious, en suite bedrooms include remote-control TV, tea and coffee-making facilities, luxury beds and free morning newspaper. Meals can be taken at the nearby family restaurant. For further details and the Travelodge phone number, consult the Hotel Groups page.

**ROOMS:** 64 en suite

Late for dinner? Quality Standards star rating means that last orders for dinner should be no earlier than:
★ 6.30pm ★★ 7.00pm ★★★ 8.00pm
★★★★ 9.00pm ★★★★★ 10.00pm

HIMLEY, Staffordshire Map 07 SO89

**★★★63% *Himley Country Hotel***
School Rd DY3 4LG
corus
☎ 01902 896716 01902 896668
e-mail: himleycountryhotel@corushotels.com
***Dir:*** *100yds off A449*

This modern hotel has been tastefully built around a 19th-century village schoolhouse. Bedrooms are well-equipped with many offering extra space. Day rooms include a stylish conservatory restaurant in which wide-ranging menus are accompanied by traditional buffet roasts.
**ROOMS:** 73 en suite (1 fmly) No smoking in 38 bedrooms **FACILITIES:** STV **CONF:** Thtr 150 Class 80 Board 50 Del from £82.50 * **PARKING:** 100 **NOTES:** No smoking in restaurant Civ Wed 100 **CARDS:**

**★★63% Himley House Hotel**
Stourbridge Rd DY3 4LD
Scottish Newcastle hotels
☎ 01902 892468 01902 892604
e-mail: himleyhouse@hotmail.com
***Dir:*** *on A449 N of Stourbridge*
Dating back to the 17th century, this one-time lodge house for the nearby Himley Hall offers well-equipped and comfortable accommodation. Bedrooms of varying sizes are located both in the main house and separate buildings around the hotel, and the busy restaurant offers a wide selection of dishes.
**ROOMS:** 24 en suite (2 fmly) s £38; d £42 * **LB** **FACILITIES:** ch fac **CONF:** Thtr 50 Class 30 Board 22 Del from £90 * **PARKING:** 162 **NOTES:** No dogs (ex guide dogs) **CARDS:**

HINCKLEY, Leicestershire Map 04 SP49

**★★★★60% Hanover International Hotel & Club**
Watling St (A5) LE10 3JA
Hanover International Hotels & Clubs
☎ 01455 631122 01455 634536
e-mail: hisland@webleicester.co.uk
***Dir:*** *on A5, S of junct 1 on M69*
A large hotel offering excellent facilities for conference and business guests. Bedrooms are large with the Club Floor offering high levels of comfort, such as leather seating at large desks. The

continued

large leisure centre has been refurbished, as have the new-look Brasserie and Conservatory restaurants.

**ROOMS:** 350 en suite (47 fmly) No smoking in 197 bedrooms d £105 * LB **FACILITIES:** STV Indoor swimming (H) Snooker Sauna Solarium Gym Jacuzzi Xmas **CONF:** Thtr 400 Class 190 Board 40 Del £160 * **SERVICES:** Lift air con **PARKING:** 600 **NOTES:** No dogs (ex guide dogs) No smoking in restaurant Civ Wed 250
**CARDS:**

## ★★★76% Sketchley Grange

Sketchley Ln, Burbage LE10 3HU
☎ 01455 251133 01455 631384
e-mail: sketchleygrange@btinternet.com
***Dir:*** *SE of town, off A5, take B4109 (Hinckley) turn left at 2nd rdbt. First right onto Sketchley Lane*

Centrally located near the Warwickshire and Leicestershire border, this country house hotel is set in its own landscaped gardens. The hotel has an excellent range of facilities, including the popular Roman's Health and Leisure Club, which also has crèche facilities for "little Romans". There is also a choice of bars and eating options including Willows Restaurant and the more informal Terrace Bistro.
**ROOMS:** 55 en suite (9 fmly) No smoking in 15 bedrooms d £99 * LB **FACILITIES:** Spa STV Indoor swimming (H) Sauna Solarium Gym Steam room Hairdressing Creche ch fac **CONF:** Thtr 300 Class 150 Board 50 Del from £130 * **SERVICES:** Lift **PARKING:** 200 **NOTES:** No smoking in restaurant Civ Wed 250
**CARDS:**

*See advert on this page*

## ★★72% Kings Hotel & Restaurant

13/19 Mount Rd LE10 1AD
☎ 01455 637193 01455 636201
e-mail: kingshinck@aol.com
***Dir:*** *follow A447 signposted to Hinckley. Under railway bridge and turn right at rdbt. First road left opposite railway station and then third right*
Friendly hotel situated in a quiet road, yet within easy walking distance of the town centre and station. The bedrooms are tastefully decorated and have attractive furnishings as well as beautifully tiled bathrooms. The public rooms include a cosy lounge bar with striking Chinese style wallpaper and a large restaurant with a baby grand piano, lounge seating and a Victorian fireplace.

**ROOMS:** 7 en suite No smoking in all bedrooms s £64.90-£74.90; d £74.90-£84.90 (incl. bkfst) * LB **FACILITIES:** STV **CONF:** Thtr 30 Class 40 Board 20 Del from £80 * **PARKING:** 20 **NOTES:** No dogs No children 10yrs No smoking in restaurant
**CARDS:**



Late for dinner? Quality Standards star rating means that last orders for dinner should be no earlier than:
★ 6.30pm ★★ 7.00pm ★★★ 8.00pm
★★★★ 9.00pm ★★★★★ 10.00pm

*continued*

H

HINDON, Wiltshire Map 03 ST93

★★72% The Grosvenor Arms

High St SP3 6DJ

☎ 01747 820696 01747 820869

***Dir:** village centre 1.5m from A303 & A350, through village B3089 to Salisbury*

This small hotel has been decorated to a high standard; bedrooms are smartly appointed with co-ordinating furnishings and fabrics. Public areas include a cosy lounge, spacious bar with a log fire and an attractive dining room where guests can watch the chefs work in the open plan kitchen.

**ROOMS:** 7 en suite (2 fmly) No smoking in all bedrooms **FACILITIES:** Fishing **PARKING:** 18 **NOTES:** No children 5yrs No smoking in restaurant **CARDS:**

★★72% **Lamb at Hindon**

SP3 6DP

☎ 01747 820573 01747 820605

***Dir:** 1m from A303 & A350, on B3089 in the centre of the village*

This welcoming, stone-built free house dates back to the 17th century. Bedrooms retain a pleasing element of simplicity but are comfortable and well-equipped. There are beamed bars with open fireplaces, a quiet lounge and the attractive dining room features a roaring fire on cooler evenings. The set menu offers a selection of interesting dishes, and there is always a sophisticated choice of bar snacks on the blackboard.

**ROOMS:** 14 en suite s fr £45; d fr £75 (incl. bkfst) * **LB** **FACILITIES:** Fishing Shooting Mountain bikes ch fac **CONF:** Thtr 35 Class 30 Board 20 Del from £82 * **PARKING:** 26 **NOTES:** No smoking in restaurant **CARDS:**

Early start? Hotels at all star levels should provide in-room alarm clocks and/or alarm calls.

HINTLESHAM, Suffolk Map 05 TM04

## Premier Collection

★★★★ **Hintlesham Hall**

IP8 3NS

☎ 01473 652334 & 652268 01473 652463

e-mail: reservations@hintlesham-hall.co.uk

***Dir:** 4m W of Ipswich on A1071 to Sudbury*

A fine Grade I country house hotel, surrounded by 175 acres of countryside, and offering attentive and friendly service. The magnificent Georgian façade belies the Tudor origins of this grand house. The main dining room is an elegant room serving fine classical cuisine. Bedrooms vary in style and design, each is well-appointed and attractive, with individual decor. Guests may take advantage of the 18-hole golf facilities for a fee, or enjoy the new health complex.

**ROOMS:** 33 en suite (1 fmly) s £97-£120; d £120-£230 (incl. cont bkfst) * **LB** **FACILITIES:** **Spa** Outdoor swimming (H) Golf 18 Tennis (hard) Snooker Sauna Gym Croquet lawn Putting green Jacuzzi Health & beauty suite & treatments entertainment Xmas **CONF:** Thtr 80 Class 50 Board 32 Del from £175 * **PARKING:** 100 **NOTES:** No smoking in restaurant RS Sat Civ Wed 120 **CARDS:**

HINTON CHARTERHOUSE, Somerset Map 03 ST75

## Premier Collection

★★★ **Homewood Park**

BA2 7TB

☎ 01225 723731 01225 723820

e-mail: res@homewoodpark.com

***Dir:** 6m SE of Bath on A36, turn left at 2nd sign for Freshford*

A warm welcome awaits at this unassuming yet stylish Georgian house. Set in delightful grounds, Homewood Park

continued

offers relaxed surroundings and maintains high standards of quality and comfort throughout. Bedrooms, all individually decorated, include thoughtful extras to ensure a comfortable stay. The hotel has a reputation for its excellent standard of cuisine - with an imaginative interpretation of classical dishes featuring an impressive, not to be missed, eight-course tasting dinner.
**ROOMS:** 19 en suite s fr £109; d £139-£180 (incl. bkfst) * LB **FACILITIES:** STV Outdoor swimming (H) Tennis (hard) Croquet lawn Xmas **CONF:** Thtr 40 Class 30 Board 25 Del from £165 * **PARKING:** 30 **NOTES:** No dogs No smoking in restaurant Civ Wed 50 **CARDS:**

## HITCHIN, Hertfordshire — Map 04 TL12

**★★66% Firs**
83 Bedford Rd SG5 2TY
☎ 01462 422322 📠 01462 432051
e-mail: info@firshotel.co.uk
***Dir:*** *turn off A505 onto A600. Hotel 1m on left next to Shell petrol station*
This family owned and run hotel is situated on the northern edge of town and caters well for business as well as leisure guests. Spacious public areas include a lounge bar, conference room and Italian-styled restaurant. Well-equipped bedrooms vary in size and style and many have been tastefully refurbished, boasting smart fully tiled bathrooms.
**ROOMS:** 30 en suite (3 fmly) No smoking in 9 bedrooms s £42-£52; d £57-£62 (incl. bkfst) * **CONF:** Class 24 Board 20 Del from £95 * **PARKING:** 30 **NOTES:** No dogs (ex guide dogs) No smoking in restaurant **CARDS:**

## HOCKLEY HEATH, West Midlands — Map 07 SP17

**Premier Collection**

**★★★ 🏵🏵🏵 Nuthurst Grange Country House**
Nuthurst Grange Ln B94 5NL
☎ 01564 783972 📠 01564 783919
e-mail: info@nuthurst-grange.com
***Dir:*** *0.5m S on A3400*
The approach to this period country house is a stunning avenue drive. The hotel enjoys views over rolling countryside and several acres of manicured gardens, woodland and ponds. Public areas include restful lounges, meeting rooms and a sunny restaurant. Bedrooms benefit not only from being spacious but also from considerable luxury and comfort. The restaurant team produces highly imaginative British and French cuisine, using quality local produce.
**ROOMS:** 15 en suite (2 fmly) s fr £135; d £155-£185 (incl. bkfst) * LB **FACILITIES:** STV Croquet lawn Helipad ch fac **CONF:** Thtr 100 Class 50 Board 45 Del £179 * **PARKING:** 86 **NOTES:** No smoking in restaurant Civ Wed 100 **CARDS:**

## HODNET, Shropshire — Map 07 SJ62

**★★65% Bear**
Nr Market Drayton TF9 3NH
☎ 01630 685214 📠 01630 685787
e-mail: info@bearhotel.org
***Dir:*** *junct of A53 & A442 on sharp corner in middle of small village*
This 16th-century former coaching inn provides bedrooms equipped with all modern comforts. The public areas have a wealth of charm and character, enhanced by features such as exposed beams. There is a large baronial-style function room and medieval banquets are something of a speciality here.
**ROOMS:** 6 en suite 2 annexe en suite (2 fmly) s £42.50-£45; d £65-£70 (incl. bkfst) LB **FACILITIES:** Ten-pin & Skittles Medieval banquets entertainment Xmas **CONF:** Thtr 100 Class 50 Board 40 **PARKING:** 70 **NOTES:** No dogs (ex guide dogs) Civ Wed 70 **CARDS:**

## HOLCOMBE, Somerset — Map 03 ST64

**★★70% 🏵 The Ring O' Roses Country Inn**
Stratton Rd BA3 5EB
☎ 01761 232478 📠 01761 233737
e-mail: ringorosesholcombe@tesco.net
***Dir:*** *Off A367 rdbt with white post onto B3139 to Trowbridge, straight over rdbt towards Shepton Mallet, turn left into Watery Ln then left opposite Church Farm continue for 1m*
Rurally located with views of Downside Abbey in the distance, the inn dates back to the 16th century. A friendly and relaxing atmosphere is created by the attentive owners and staff. The individually furnished and decorated bedrooms are comfortable and feature many thoughtful extras. In the restaurant, an imaginative carte is offered, using local ingredients wherever possible.
**ROOMS:** 8 en suite No smoking in all bedrooms s £55-£65; d £69-£85 (incl. bkfst) * LB **FACILITIES:** Xmas **CONF:** Thtr 40 Class 40 Board 14 Del from £86.50 * **PARKING:** 35 **NOTES:** No smoking in restaurant **CARDS:**

## HOLFORD, Somerset — Map 03 ST14

**★★72% Combe House**
TA5 1RZ
☎ 01278 741382 📠 01278 741322
e-mail: enquires@combehouse.co.uk
***Dir:*** *from A39 in Holford take road beside Plough Inn, bear left at fork and continue for 0.25m to Holford Combe*
Once a tannery, this charming, 17th-century house is set in the Quantock Hills. The resident proprietors and friendly staff welcome guests to this haven. Delightful public rooms retain original features, and comfortable bedrooms are equipped with all expected modern facilities. In the dining room, the focus is on good honest cooking from fresh.
**ROOMS:** 16 en suite (2 fmly) No smoking in 10 bedrooms s £38; d £76-£87 (incl. bkfst) * LB **FACILITIES:** Indoor swimming (H) Tennis (hard) Xmas **PARKING:** 17 **NOTES:** No smoking in restaurant Closed Jan RS Nov,Dec & Feb **CARDS:**

## HOLMES CHAPEL, Cheshire
Map 07 SJ76

### ★★★65% Holly Lodge Hotel & "Truffles" Restaurant
70 London Rd CW4 7AS
☎ 01477 537033 01477 535823
e-mail: sales@hollylodgehotel.co.uk
***Dir:*** *A50/A54 crossroads, 1m from junct 18 of M6*
Situated close to the centre of Holmes Chapel, the Holly Lodge Hotel caters for both business and leisure guests. Accommodation varies in style, with particularly comfortably furnished bright modern bedrooms located in an adjacent cottage. A carefully prepared menu is served in Truffles restaurant and several function rooms are also available.
**ROOMS:** 17 en suite 25 annexe en suite (3 fmly) No smoking in 17 bedrooms s fr £77; d fr £89.50 (incl. bkfst) * **LB** **FACILITIES:** STV Xmas **CONF:** Thtr 120 Class 60 Board 60 Del from £99.95 * **PARKING:** 90 **NOTES:** No smoking in restaurant Civ Wed 140
**CARDS:**

### ★★★65% Old Vicarage
Knutsford Rd CW4 8EF
☎ 01477 532041 01477 535728
e-mail: oldvichotel@aol.com
***Dir:*** *on the A50, 1m from junct 18 on the M6*
This Grade II listed building dates back to the 17th century. Bedrooms are well-equipped and most are situated in the newer wing, overlooking the River Dane. An atmospheric open-beamed bar leads into the restaurant, which offers a wide range of freshly prepared dishes. There is also a spacious lounge bar for guests to relax in after dinner.
**ROOMS:** 29 en suite No smoking in 4 bedrooms s £42-£70.50; d £58-£82 (incl. bkfst) * **LB** **FACILITIES:** STV ch fac **CONF:** Thtr 36 Class 14 Board 22 Del from £110 * **PARKING:** 70 **NOTES:** No dogs (ex guide dogs) No smoking in restaurant **CARDS:**

## HOLMFIRTH, West Yorkshire
Map 07 SE10

### ★★64% *Old Bridge*
Market Walk HD7 1DA
☎ 01484 681212 01484 687978
e-mail: oldbridgehotel@enterprise.net
***Dir:*** *At lights on A6024/A635 in the centre of Holmfirth, turn into Victoria St for 20m, left immediately after bank and shops into hotel car park*
Located centrally in the town and with convenient parking facilities, this stone built hotel offers well-equipped bedrooms and spacious public rooms. There is a wide range of food available both in the attractive restaurant and the cosy bars.
**ROOMS:** 20 en suite **CONF:** Thtr 80 Class 50 Board 40 **PARKING:** 30
**CARDS:**

## HOLSWORTHY, Devon
Map 02 SS30

### ★★72% Court Barn Country House
Clawton EX22 6PS
☎ 01409 271219 01409 271309
e-mail: courtbarnhotel@talk21.com
***Dir:*** *2.5m S of Holsworthy off A388 Tamerton road next to Clawton church*
This Victorian country house is set within five tranquil and peaceful acres of attractive gardens and grounds with a 9-hole putting course and croquet. Comfortable bedrooms are individually furnished, incorporating many thoughtful extras. A four-course dinner is served in the spacious restaurant, featuring fresh local produce and an impressive wine list. Leisurely breakfasts are served in a separate room overlooking the garden; additionally two comfortable lounges are available.
**ROOMS:** 8 rms (7 en suite) (1 fmly) No smoking in all bedrooms s £35-£45; d £60-£80 (incl. bkfst) * **LB** **FACILITIES:** Tennis (grass) Croquet lawn Putting green Xmas **CONF:** Thtr 25 Board 8 Del from £75 * **PARKING:** 13 **NOTES:** No smoking in restaurant
**CARDS:**

## HONILEY, Warwickshire
Map 04 SP2

### ★★★67% Honiley Court
corus

CV8 1NP
☎ 01926 484234 01926 484474
***Dir:*** *from M40 junc 15, take A46 then A4177 to Solihull, at 1st main rdbt turn right to hotel approx 2m on left*

An extension of the Old Boot Inn, this modern hotel is within easy reach of the motorways and airport. Restyled open-plan public areas are smart and modern with vibrant colour schemes and comfortable furnishings. A dedicated conference team serves a range of meeting rooms. Bedrooms are spacious, comfortable and well-equipped.
**ROOMS:** 62 en suite (4 fmly) No smoking in 31 bedrooms s £60-£95; d £70-£110 * **LB** **FACILITIES:** STV Xmas **CONF:** Thtr 170 Class 60 Board 45 Del from £125 * **SERVICES:** Lift **PARKING:** 250 **NOTES:** No smoking in restaurant Civ Wed 160
**CARDS:**

## HONITON, Devon
Map 03 ST1

see also Yarcombe

### ★★★78% Combe House Hotel at Gittisham
Gittisham EX14 3AD
☎ 01404 540400 01404 46004
e-mail: stay@thishotel.com
***Dir:*** *turn off A30 1m S of Honiton, follow Gittisham Heathpark signs*

Set within thousands of acres of woodland, meadow and pasture, this beautiful Elizabethan mansion exudes a sense of serene splendour. Bedrooms are individually styled, offer a high level of

continued

omfort, and many enjoy far-reaching views across the urrounding countryside. The pretty restaurant offers interesting menus featuring local produce.
**ROOMS:** 15 en suite s fr £85 (incl. bkfst) * LB **FACILITIES:** Fishing croquet lawn Jacuzzi ch fac Xmas **CONF:** Thtr 60 Class 40 Board 26 el from £162 * **PARKING:** 51 **NOTES:** No smoking in restaurant iv Wed 100 **CARDS:**

★★69% **Home Farm**
Wilmington EX14 9JR
☎ 01404 831278 📠 01404 831411
e-mail: homefarmhotel@breathemail.net
*Dir: 3m E on A35 in village of Wilmington*
This thatched, 16th-century former farmhouse retains many original features. All rooms, both in the main house and in the old stable block around the cobbled courtyard, are traditionally furnished and comfortably equipped. Guests can dine in the bar, or in the more intimate restaurant; the standard of cooking is high in both.
**ROOMS:** 8 en suite 5 annexe en suite (4 fmly) s £40-£50; d £65-£85 (incl. bkfst) * LB **PARKING:** 20 **NOTES:** No smoking in restaurant Closed 1-14 Jan **CARDS:**

★★64% **Honiton Motel**
Turks Head Corner, Exeter Rd EX14 1BL
☎ 01404 43440 📠 01404 47767
*Dir: off A30*

HONITON MOTEL

The Honiton Motel offers well maintained budget accommodation with modern facilities. All rooms have their own access and are set round the large car park. In the main building, additional features include bars, restaurant, function suite and fast-food bar.
**ROOMS:** 14 annexe en suite (3 fmly) s £35-£40; d £50-£55 (incl. bkfst) LB **PARKING:** 50 **CARDS:**

HOOK, Hampshire — Map 04 SU75

★★71% **Hook House**
London Rd RG27 9EQ
☎ 01256 762630 📠 01256 760232
*Dir: 1m E of Hook on A30*
This charming hotel set in several acres of landscaped grounds has a reputation for warmth and good service. Bedrooms are quiet, attractive and well-equipped; the refurbished rooms are exceptionally well-presented.
**ROOMS:** 17 rms (13 en suite) s £72.50-£79.50; d £77.50-£84.50 (incl. bkfst) * **FACILITIES:** Croquet lawn **CONF:** Thtr 40 Class 20 Board 20 Del £109.50 * **PARKING:** 20 **NOTES:** No dogs No smoking in restaurant Closed Xmas Civ Wed 50
**CARDS:**

Bad hair day? Hairdryers in all rooms three stars and above.

HOPE COVE, Devon — Map 03 SX64

★★69% **Lantern Lodge**
TQ7 3HE
☎ 01548 561280 📠 01548 561736
*Dir: turn right off A381 Kingsbridge-Salcombe road, take first right after passing Hope Cove sign then first left along Grand View Rd*
This attractive, small hotel close to the South Devon coastal path benefits from a friendly team of loyal staff. Bedrooms are well-furnished; some have balconies which overlook the rugged coastline. An imaginative range of home cooked meals is available. There is a choice of lounges and a pretty enclosed garden with putting green. The indoor pool has large doors opening to the garden.
**ROOMS:** 14 en suite (1 fmly) s £60-£82; d £100-£136 (incl. bkfst & dinner) * LB **FACILITIES:** Indoor swimming (H) Sauna Putting green Multi-gym **PARKING:** 15 **NOTES:** No dogs (ex guide dogs) No children 12yrs No smoking in restaurant Closed Dec-Feb
**CARDS:**

★★68% **Cottage**
TQ7 3HJ
☎ 01548 561555 📠 01548 561455
e-mail: info@hopecove.com
*Dir: from Kingsbridge A381 towards Salcombe, it is suggested you take 2nd right at village of Marlborough continue & turn left for Inner Hope*
With stunning coastal views, this friendly, family-owned hotel has a relaxed and comfortable atmosphere. Bedrooms vary in size and standard, the deluxe balcony rooms feature such extras as videos. Three lounges are available for guests, together with an original cabin bar. The menu offers a good choice of home-cooked dishes and is complemented by a varied wine list.
**ROOMS:** 35 rms (25 en suite) (5 fmly) s £52.75-£68.75; d £95.50-£117.50 (incl. bkfst & dinner) * LB **FACILITIES:** STV Table Tennis ch fac Xmas **CONF:** Thtr 50 Class 20 Board 24 Del from £47.65 * **PARKING:** 50 **NOTES:** No smoking in restaurant Closed 3-30 Jan
**CARDS:**

HORLEY Hotels are listed under Gatwick Airport

HORNBY, Lancashire

○ **Castle Hotel**
Main St LA28 8JT
☎ 01524 221204
At the time of going to press, the star classification for this hotel was not confirmed. Please refer to the AA internet site www.theAA.com for current information.

HORNCASTLE, Lincolnshire — Map 08 TF26

★★71% **Admiral Rodney**
North St LN9 5DX
☎ 01507 523131 📠 01507 523104
e-mail: reception@admiralrodney.com
*Dir: off A153*
Best Western
This smart, well-furnished hotel stands in the centre of this popular town. The Rodney bar is in the style of an old galleon and the informal Courtyard restaurant serves a wide range of food and snacks. Modern bedrooms are well-appointed, thoughtfully equipped and generally spacious.
**ROOMS:** 31 en suite (3 fmly) No smoking in 10 bedrooms s £50-£55; d £69-£79 (incl. bkfst) * LB **FACILITIES:** STV Xmas **CONF:** Thtr 140 Class 60 Board 50 Del from £75 * **SERVICES:** Lift **PARKING:** 60 **NOTES:** No dogs (ex guide dogs) **CARDS:**

H

## HORNING, Norfolk Map 09 TG31

### ★★★64% Petersfield House

Lower St NR12 8PF
☎ 01692 630741 📠 01692 630745
e-mail: reception@petersfieldhotel.co.uk
***Dir:*** *from Wroxham take A1062, follow for 2½ miles then turn right into Horning village, hotel in centre of village on left*
Situated in the heart of this delightful riverside village amidst its own attractive landscaped grounds, this property was built in the 1920s as a large private residence. Although the bedrooms vary in size and style they are all comfortably furnished and most rooms enjoy views over the pretty gardens. Public areas include a large lounge, a bar and a restaurant.
**ROOMS:** 18 en suite (1 fmly) s £60-£65; d £80-£90 (incl. bkfst) **LB** **FACILITIES:** Fishing Putting green Boating entertainment Xmas **CONF:** Thtr 50 Class 40 Board 30 Del from £95 * **PARKING:** 70 **CARDS:**

## HORNINGSHAM, Wiltshire Map 03 ST84

### ★★63% *The Bath Arms*

Longleat Estate BA12 7LY
☎ 01985 844308 📠 01985 844150
Situated by the driveway of Longleat House, the Bath Arms is an ideal centre from which to explore the many attractions of the area. An imaginative menu is available in the restaurant and the bar menu extends the options open to guests. During summer the beer garden is popular. Bedrooms are well-appointed and comfortable. A two bedroomed, self-catering cottage adjoins the hotel and is especially suitable for families.
**ROOMS:** 6 en suite 2 annexe en suite (1 fmly) **PARKING:** 15 **NOTES:** No smoking in restaurant RS Xmas & New Year **CARDS:**

## HORSHAM, West Sussex Map 04 TQ13

### ★★★★ ®®® South Lodge

Brighton Rd RH13 6PS
☎ 01403 891711 📠 01403 891766
e-mail: enquiries@southlodgehotel.co.uk
(For full entry see Lower Beeding)

### ★★67% Ye Olde King's Head

Carfax RH12 1EG
☎ 01403 253126 📠 01403 242291
***Dir:*** *close to town hall, 0.5m from railway station, at junction of Carfax & East St*
In the centre of Horsham, this 14th-century former coaching inn retains many original features. The smart, well-equipped bedrooms vary in size and there is an attractive restaurant, cosy bar and wine cellar and a popular coffee shop, a buzz of activity throughout the day.
**ROOMS:** 42 rms (41 en suite) (1 fmly) No smoking in 17 bedrooms s £83-£93; d £98-£108 (incl. bkfst) * **LB** **FACILITIES:** STV **CONF:** Thtr 40 Class 40 Board 30 Del from £110 * **PARKING:** 40 **NOTES:** No smoking in restaurant **CARDS:**

## HORTON-CUM-STUDLEY, Oxfordshire Map 04 SP51

### ★★★77% ®®® Studley Priory

OX33 1AZ
☎ 01865 351203 & 351254 📠 01865 351613
e-mail: res@studley-priory.co.uk
***Dir:*** *2.5m off B4027 between Wheatley and Islip*
Rising proudly above the rolling countryside, this Elizabethan house was founded in the 12th century as a Benedictine nunnery, and extended by the Croke family, who acquired the property after the Dissolution of the Monasteries. A professional, friendly welcome awaits, and comfortable bedrooms have a host of thoughtful extras. Dinner provides the highlight of any stay, offering exciting, dynamic dishes.
**ROOMS:** 18 en suite No smoking in 4 bedrooms s fr £110; d fr £150 (incl. cont bkfst) * **LB** **FACILITIES:** STV Tennis (hard & grass) Croquet lawn ch fac Xmas **CONF:** Thtr 50 Board 25 Del from £165 * **PARKING:** 100 **NOTES:** No dogs No smoking in restaurant Civ Wed 50 **CARDS:**

## HORWICH, Greater Manchester Map 07 SD6

### ★★★★70% De Vere White's Hotel

De Havilland Way BL6 6SF
☎ 01204 667788 📠 01204 673721
e-mail: whites@devere-hotels.com
***Dir:*** *Turn off M61 at junct 6. Take the 3rd right exit from the sliproad rndbt onto A6027 Mansell Way. Follow visitors carpark A for Hotel*
This impressive new hotel enjoys a rather unique location as part of the Reebok Stadium. Bedrooms, some of which overlook the stadium, are stylishly appointed and well-equipped with modern technology. Public areas include a choice of eating options, spacious bar/lounge, indoor leisure club and extensive conference and banqueting facilities.
**ROOMS:** 125 en suite (1 fmly) No smoking in 99 bedrooms s £110; d £125 (incl. bkfst) * **LB** **FACILITIES:** Spa STV Indoor swimming (H) Sauna Solarium Gym Jacuzzi Xmas **CONF:** Thtr 1800 Class 1000 Board 250 Del from £95 * **SERVICES:** Lift **PARKING:** 2750 **NOTES:** No dogs (ex guide dogs) No smoking in restaurant Civ Wed 550 **CARDS:**

## HOUGHTON-LE-SPRING, Tyne & Wear Map 12 NZ3

### ★★66% Chilton Lodge

Black Boy Rd, Chilton Moor, Fencehouses DH4 6LX
☎ 0191 385 2694 📠 0191 385 6762
***Dir:*** *leave A1(M) at junct 62, then A690 towards Sunderland. Turn left at Rainton Bridge/Fencehouses sign, cross rdbt and take 1st left*
Set in open countryside near the village of Fencehouses, this complex evolved from original farm cottages, and now provides a country pub and spacious ballroom catering for functions and weddings. There is a wide choice of bar and dining room meals. Accommodation is modern and comfortable.
**ROOMS:** 25 en suite (7 fmly) No smoking in 7 bedrooms s £38-£52; d £48-£62 (incl. bkfst) * **LB** **FACILITIES:** STV Horse riding entertainment Xmas **CONF:** Thtr 60 Class 50 Board 30 **PARKING:** 100 **NOTES:** No dogs (ex guide dogs) **CARDS:**

*See advert on page 20*

## HOUNSLOW Hotels are listed under Heathrow Airport

## HOVE See Brighton & Hove

## HOVINGHAM, North Yorkshire Map 08 SE6

### ★★★67% ®® Worsley Arms

High St YO62 4LA
☎ 01653 628234 📠 01653 628130
e-mail: worsleyarms@aol.com
***Dir:*** *From the South take A64. Follow signs to York. Head towards Malton. When road becomes dual carriageway turn left towards Hovingham. Upon reaching village of Slingsby turn left and Hovingham is 2m ahead. Hotel situated on main street through Hovingham.*
Overlooking the village green, this hotel has comfortable and attractive lounges with welcoming open fires, and comfortable

*continued*

edrooms. The restaurant provides good quality cooking, with less rmal dining in the Cricketers Bar and Bistro to the rear. Several edrooms are contained in cottages across the green.
**OOMS:** 11 en suite 8 annexe en suite No smoking in all bedrooms £80-£90; d £130-£140 (incl. bkfst & dinner) * **LB** **FACILITIES:** Tennis ard) Squash Shooting ch fac Xmas **CONF:** Thtr 40 Class 40 Board 20 el from £110 * **PARKING:** 25 **NOTES:** No smoking in restaurant iv Wed 90 **CARDS:**

OWTOWN (NEAR POOLEY BRIDGE), umbria — Map 12 NY41

## Premier Collection

★★★ @@@ **Sharrow Bay Country House**
Sharrow Bay CA10 2LZ
☎ 017684 86301 & 86483 017684 86349
e-mail: enquiries@sharrow-bay.com
***Dir:*** *at Pooley Bridge take right hand fork by church towards Howtown. At crossroad turn right and follow Lakeside Road for 2m.*
Standing serenely at the water's edge, with stunning views across the lake to the mountains, Sharrow Bay is often described as the first country house hotel - a fair title for an establishment of such opulence and charm. Individually furnished bedrooms are split between the main house and the Elizabethan farmhouse, complete with its own service staff, lounges and breakfast room. There is a choice of inviting lounges to relax in over tea and home-baked scones.
**ROOMS:** 8 en suite 16 annexe en suite s £145-£190; d £150-£210 (incl. bkfst & dinner) * **LB** **CONF:** Class 30 Board 20 Del from £200 * **PARKING:** 35 **NOTES:** No dogs No children 13yrs No smoking in restaurant Closed 4 Dec-2 Mar Civ Wed 35
**CARDS:**

IUCKNALL, Nottinghamshire — Map 08 SK54

***Premier Lodge (Nottingham North West)***
Nottingham Rd NG15 7PY
☎ 0870 700 1530 0870 700 1531
Premier Lodge offers modern, well-equipped, en suite ccommodation suitable for both business and leisure travellers. Meals can be taken at the adjacent popular restaurant and bar, which is fully licensed. For further details, consult the Hotel Groups page.
**ROOMS:** 34 en suite

HUDDERSFIELD, West Yorkshire — Map 07 SE11

★★★69% **Old Golf House Hotel**
New Hey Rd, Outlane HD3 3YP
☎ 01422 379311 01422 372694
e-mail: oldgolfhouse@corushotels.com
***Dir:*** *leave M62 at junct 23 (Eastbound only), or junct 24 & follow A640 towards Rochdale. Hotel on A640 (New Hey Rd) at Outlane*

Situated close to the M62, this traditionally styled hotel offers bedrooms which are well equipped to a good modern standard. A wide choice of dishes is served in the restaurant, and lighter meals are available in the comfortable lounge bar. The hotel is a popular venue for weddings.
**ROOMS:** 52 en suite (4 fmly) No smoking in 30 bedrooms d £60-£70 * **LB** **FACILITIES:** STV Putting green 5 Hole pitch & putt Xmas **CONF:** Thtr 100 Class 50 Board 40 Del £99.50 * **PARKING:** 100 **NOTES:** No smoking in restaurant Civ Wed 180
**CARDS:**

★★★65% **Bagden Hall**
Wakefield Rd, Scissett HD8 9LE
☎ 01484 865330 01484 861001
e-mail: info@bagdenhall.demon.co.uk
***Dir:*** *on A636, between Scissett and Denby Dale*

Set in well-tended grounds, with a par three nine-hole golf course, this elegant mansion house is close to the village of Scissett. The traditional public rooms include a bright conservatory where light meals are served, and a versatile conference/function room. Bedrooms vary in size, and all are well equipped and pleasantly furnished.
**ROOMS:** 17 en suite (3 fmly) s £56-£60; d £72-£100 (incl. bkfst) * **FACILITIES:** STV Golf 9 Putting green ch fac **CONF:** Thtr 80 Class 40 Board 30 Del £105 * **PARKING:** 96 **NOTES:** No dogs (ex guide dogs) No smoking in restaurant RS 24-25 Dec Civ Wed 76
**CARDS:**

HUDDERSFIELD, continued

**★★★65% George**
St George's Square HD1 1JA
☎ 01484 515444 Fax 01484 435056
e-mail: george@brook-hotels.co.uk
***Dir:*** *adjacent to Huddersfield Railway Station in centre of town*
Situated in the main town square, the Italianate façade of this elegant Grade II listed Victorian building complements its neighbour, the railway station. The hotel is famous as the birthplace of Rugby League football; the meeting that founded it was held here in 1895. Today the hotel bar continues to display rugby league memorabilia.
**ROOMS:** 60 en suite (1 fmly) No smoking in 15 bedrooms s £80-£90; d £90-£100 * **LB** **FACILITIES:** STV Xmas **CONF:** Thtr 180 Board 50 Del £120 * **SERVICES:** Lift **PARKING:** 22 **NOTES:** No smoking in restaurant **CARDS:**

**★★★65% *Huddersfield***
33-47 Kirkgate HD1 1QT
☎ 01484 512111 Fax 01484 435262
e-mail: enquiries@huddersfieldhotel.com
***Dir:*** *on A62 ring road, below parish church, opposite sports centre*
This modern, popular town centre hotel offers comfortable and attractively furnished bedrooms, including some with four-poster beds. A choice of bars and restaurants is available, with an all-day brasserie and evening bistro for meals and snacks. Friendly staff provide good levels of service and attention.
**ROOMS:** 50 en suite (6 fmly) **FACILITIES:** STV entertainment **SERVICES:** Lift **PARKING:** 70 **CARDS:**

**★★72% ❀ Lodge**
48 Birkby Lodge Rd, Birkby HD2 2BG
☎ 01484 431001 Fax 01484 421590
***Dir:*** *junct 24 of M62, then exit A629 for Birkby. Turn right at Nuffield Hospital down Birkby Lodge Road, hotel 200yds on left*

This family-run hotel successfully provides a relaxed ambience in a quiet residential area close to the city centre. Smart public areas include two comfortable lounges and an inviting restaurant where carefully prepared meals are served. Bedrooms vary in size and style and are well-equipped, with one boasting a grand four-poster bed. A wood-panelled meeting room is available; service is friendly and efficient.
**ROOMS:** 12 en suite (2 fmly) No smoking in all bedrooms s £60-£65; d £75-£85 (incl. bkfst) * **CONF:** Thtr 40 Class 20 Board 20 **PARKING:** 41 **NOTES:** No smoking in restaurant Closed 25-27 Dec **CARDS:**

**★★67% Pennine Manor**
Nettleton Hill Rd, Scapegoat Hill HD7 4NY
☎ 01484 642368 Fax 01484 642866
e-mail: penninemanor@bestwestern.co.uk
***Dir:*** *junct 24 M62 follow signs for Rochdale-Outlane Village, left after Highlander onto Round Ings Rd, top of hill turn left onto Nettleton Hill Rd*
High in the Pennines, this attractive stone-built hotel enjoys magnificent panoramic views. Bedrooms are compact in some cases but all are well-equipped. There is a popular bar and restaurant, offering a good selection of snacks and meals, and modern meeting facilities.
**ROOMS:** 31 en suite (4 fmly) No smoking in 10 bedrooms s £65; d £75 (incl. bkfst) * **LB** **FACILITIES:** STV **CONF:** Thtr 132 Class 56 Board 30 Del £85 * **PARKING:** 115 **NOTES:** Civ Wed 100
**CARDS:**

**⌂ *Premier Lodge***
New Hey Rd, Ainley Top HD2 2EA
☎ 0870 700 1408 Fax 0870 700 1409
Premier Lodge offers modern, well-equipped, en suite accommodation suitable for both business and leisure travellers. Meals can be taken at the adjacent popular restaurant and bar, which is fully licensed. For further details, consult the Hotel Groups page.
**ROOMS:** 40 en suite

**⌂ *Travelodge***
Leeds Rd, Mirfield WF14 0BY
☎ 01924 489921
***Dir:*** *M62 junct 25, follow A62 across two roundabouts. Lodge on right*
Travelodge offers good quality, good value, modern accommodation. Ideal for families, the spacious, en suite bedrooms include remote-control TV, tea and coffee-making facilities, luxury beds and free morning newspaper. Meals can be taken at the nearby family restaurant. For further details and the Travelodge phone number, consult the Hotel Groups page.

**ROOMS:** 27 en suite

HULL, East Riding of Yorkshire — Map 08 TA0
see also Little Weighton

**★★★72% ❀ Willerby Manor**
Well Ln HU10 6ER
☎ 01482 652616 Fax 01482 653901
e-mail: info@willerbymanor.co.uk
(For full entry see Willerby)

**★★★68% *Posthouse Hull Marina***
The Marina, Castle St HU1 2BX
☎ 0870 400 9043 Fax 01482 213299
***Dir:*** *from M62 join A63 to Hull. Follow signs for 'Marina and Ice Arena'. Hotel on left next to Ice Arena*
This modern hotel overlooks Hull Marina and is close to the centre of the city. Bedrooms are well-appointed and many have views over the waterfront. The restaurant offers both international and British dishes in a pleasant and relaxed atmosphere. Secretarial services can be provided and there is also a well equipped health and fitness club.
**ROOMS:** 99 en suite (12 fmly) No smoking in 66 bedrooms **FACILITIES:** Indoor swimming (H) Sauna Solarium Gym **CONF:** Thtr 150 Class 60 Board 50 **SERVICES:** Lift **PARKING:** 130 **NOTES:** No smoking in restaurant **CARDS:**

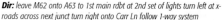

### ★★★67% Portland
Paragon St HU1 3JP
☎ 01482 326462 🖷 01482 213460
e-mail: info@portland.co.uk
***Dir:*** *leave M62 onto A63 to 1st main rdbt at 2nd set of lights turn left at x-roads across next junct turn right onto Carr Ln follow 1-way system*
A modern hotel situated in the city centre providing a good range of accommodation. Most of the public rooms are on the first floor and include the Wilberforce Restaurant and the Humber Bar and Lounge. In addition the Bay Tree Café is open during the day and evening. Staff are friendly and helpful, and car parking is taken care of by a team of porters.
**ROOMS:** 106 en suite (4 fmly) No smoking in 22 bedrooms s £90; d £105 * **FACILITIES:** STV Complimentary use of nearby health & fitness centre ch fac Xmas **CONF:** Thtr 220 Class 100 Board 500 **SERVICES:** Lift **PARKING:** 12 **CARDS:**

### ★★★65% Quality Hotel Hull
170 Ferensway HU1 3UF
☎ 01482 325087 🖷 01482 323172
e-mail: admin@gb611.u-net.com
***Dir:*** *M62 becomes A63 into Hull, follow flyover then turn left at 2nd set of traffic lights follow signposts to the railway station. Hotel located on left at second set of traffic lights*

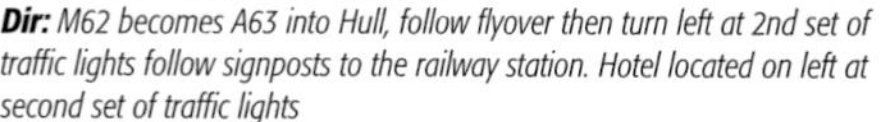

A former Victorian railway hotel modernised in recent years, overlooking the station concourse in the centre of the city. Bedrooms are very well-equipped and include a number of Premier rooms offering higher standards. A spacious lounge provides an ideal setting for light meals, drinks and relaxation. There are extensive banqueting and conference facilities, an adjacent leisure club and a free car park.
**ROOMS:** 155 en suite No smoking in 85 bedrooms s £80-£95; d £110-£115 * **LB** **FACILITIES:** **Spa** STV Indoor swimming (H) Sauna Solarium Gym Jacuzzi Steamroom Xmas **CONF:** Thtr 450 Class 150 Board 105 Del from £100 * **SERVICES:** Lift **PARKING:** 130 **NOTES:** Civ Wed 450 **CARDS:**

### ★★★62% Humber Crown
Ferriby High Rd HU14 3LG
☎ 01482 645212 🖷 01482 643332
e-mail: enquiries@humbercrown.co.uk
(For full entry see North Ferriby)

### ★★68% *The Rowley Manor*
Rowley Rd HU20 3XR
☎ 01482 848248 🖷 01482 849900
(For full entry see Little Weighton)

### ★★57% Comfort Inn
11 Anlaby Rd HU1 2PJ
☎ 01482 323299 🖷 01482 214730
e-mail: admin@gb631.u-net.com
***Dir:*** *follow signs to Railway Station*

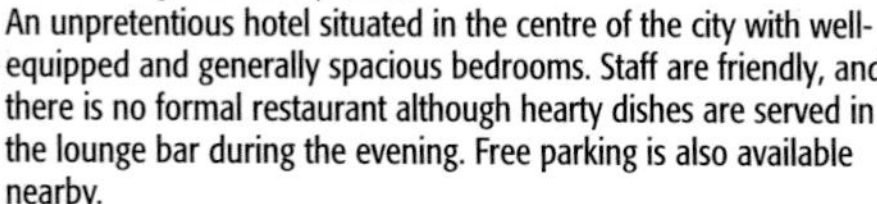

An unpretentious hotel situated in the centre of the city with well-equipped and generally spacious bedrooms. Staff are friendly, and there is no formal restaurant although hearty dishes are served in the lounge bar during the evening. Free parking is also available nearby.
**ROOMS:** 59 en suite (5 fmly) No smoking in 29 bedrooms d £35-£50 * **LB** **FACILITIES:** STV leisure facilities at sister Hotel Xmas **CONF:** Thtr 140 Class 80 Board 45 Del from £50 * **SERVICES:** Lift **PARKING:** 100 **NOTES:** No smoking in restaurant **CARDS:**

### ⌂ *Travelodge*
Beacon Service Area HU15 1RZ
☎ 01430 424455 🖷 01430 424455
(For full entry see South Cave)

Travelodge

### ⌂ Campanile
Beverley Rd, Freetown Way HU2 9AN
☎ 01482 325530 🖷 01482 587538
***Dir:*** *From M62 follow A63 into Hull city centre, pass Humber Bridge on right and continue over flyover. Follow signs for railway station A1079 which will take you onto Ferensway. Hotel situated at bottom of Ferensway on Beverley Rd.*

HOTEL
Campanile
RESTAURANT

This modern building offers accommodation in smart, well-equipped bedrooms, all with en suite bathrooms. Refreshments may be taken at the informal Bistro. For further details and the Campanile phone number, consult the Hotel Groups page.
**ROOMS:** 50 annexe en suite d £39.95 * **CONF:** Thtr 35 Class 18 Board 20 Del from £65 *

## HUNMANBY, North Yorkshire — Map 08 TA07

### ★★68% Wrangham House Hotel
10 Stonegate YO14 0NS
☎ 01723 891333 🖷 01723 892973
e-mail: mervynpoulter@lineone.net
***Dir:*** *from main A64 road, follow the A1039 to Filey, turning right onto Hunmanby road, the hotel is behind All Saints Church in Hunmanby village*

Standing in delightful gardens next to the church, this former vicarage is now a comfortable, well-furnished hotel. The attractive bedrooms are thoughtfully equipped. Two comfortable lounges are available, and a good selection of well-produced dishes is served in the elegant dining room.
**ROOMS:** 8 en suite 4 annexe en suite No smoking in all bedrooms s £38.50-£43.50; d £77 (incl. bkfst) * **LB** **FACILITIES:** Xmas **CONF:** Thtr 50 Class 20 Board 20 **PARKING:** 20 **NOTES:** No children 12yrs No smoking in restaurant **CARDS:**

Packed in a hurry? Ironing facilities should be available at all star levels, either in rooms or on request.

## HUNSTANTON, Norfolk Map 09 TF64

### ★★★67% Le Strange Arms
Golf Course Rd, Old Hunstanton PE36 6JJ
☎ 01485 534411 🖹 01485 534724
e-mail: reception@lestrangearms.co.uk
***Dir:*** *turn off A149 1m N of Hunstanton town. Road bends sharply right and access road to hotel is on bend*

This hotel enjoys magnificent views from the wide lawns down to the sandy beach and across the wash. A choice of menus is served in the attractive restaurant. Bedrooms come in a range of styles, from original rooms in the main house with period furnishings, to more contemporary rooms in the new wing.

**ROOMS:** 36 en suite (4 fmly) s £57.50-£65; d £88-£103 (incl. bkfst) * **LB** **FACILITIES:** Snooker Xmas **CONF:** Thtr 180 Class 150 Board 50 Del from £98 * **PARKING:** 80 **NOTES:** No smoking in restaurant Civ Wed 150 **CARDS:**

*See advert on opposite page*

### ★★74% Caley Hall
Old Hunstanton Rd PE36 6HH
☎ 01485 533486 🖹 01485 533348
***Dir:*** *1m from Hunstanton, on A149*

This 17th-century manor house, originally part of a working farm, offers relaxing public areas including a cosy bar, an open-plan lounge, a billiard room and a spacious restaurant serving a daily-changing menu. The pleasantly furnished bedrooms are in courtyard style blocks, tastefully converted from the authentic buildings.

**ROOMS:** 33 annexe en suite (5 fmly) s £42-£45; d £64-£70 (incl. bkfst) * **LB** **FACILITIES:** STV Snooker Xmas **CONF:** Board 40 **PARKING:** 70 **NOTES:** No smoking in restaurant Closed Jan-Feb **CARDS:**

### ★★70% The Lodge Hotel & Restaurant
Old Hunstanton Rd PE36 6HX
☎ 01485 532896 🖹 01485 535007
e-mail: reception@thelodge-hotel.co.uk
***Dir:*** *1m E of Hunstanton on A149*

A friendly hotel within easy reach of the beach and town centre. The attractive bedrooms are generally spacious, well-maintained and offer good facilities. Six new bedrooms have been added to the rear. There is a large garden in which to enjoy cream teas, a popular restaurant, food-serving bar and a comfortable lounge.

**ROOMS:** 16 en suite 6 annexe en suite (3 fmly) No smoking in 6 bedrooms s £35-£52; d £70-£100 (incl. bkfst) * **LB** **FACILITIES:** Darts, Pool table Xmas **CONF:** Thtr 40 Class 40 Board 40 Del from £60 * **PARKING:** 70 **NOTES:** No smoking in restaurant **CARDS:**

*See advert on opposite page*

## HUNSTRETE, Somerset Map 03 ST66

### ★★★77% ®® Hunstrete House
BS39 4NS
☎ 01761 490490 🖹 01761 490732
e-mail: user@hunstretehouse.co.uk
***Dir:*** *from Bath take A4 towards Bristol to Globe Inn rdbt. Take 2nd left(A368)towards Wells. Approx 1m after Marksbury next turning right for Hunstrete village, hotel next turning left.*

This delightful Georgian house enjoys a stunning setting, located in 92 acres of deer park and woodland on the edge of the Mendip Hills. The individual bedrooms have modern facilities and enjoy tranquil views. Public areas feature antiques, paintings and fine china. The restaurant enjoys a well-deserved reputation for fine food and utilises much home grown produce from the walled gardens of the house.

**ROOMS:** 22 en suite (2 fmly) No smoking in 11 bedrooms s £115; d £135-£165 (incl. bkfst) * **LB** **FACILITIES:** STV Outdoor swimming (H) Tennis (hard) Croquet lawn mini gym/fitness room ch fac Xmas **CONF:** Thtr 50 Class 40 Board 30 Del £175 * **PARKING:** 75 **NOTES:** No dogs (ex guide dogs) No smoking in restaurant Civ Wed 50 **CARDS:**

## HUNTINGDON, Cambridgeshire Map 04 TL27

### ★★★★72% Huntingdon Marriott Hotel

Marriott
HOTELS · RESORTS · SUITES

Kingfisher Way, Hinchingbrooke Business Park PE29 6FL
☎ 01480 446000 🖹 01480 451111
***Dir:*** *situated 1m from the centre of Huntington on the A14, close to Brampton racecourse*

The Huntingdon Marriott offers all the comforts of a modern, well-designed hotel. The first-class, air-conditioned bedrooms are very comfortable and well equipped. There is a smart, open-plan lounge bar, and the pleasant restaurant includes a carvery option. A good range of services is provided by the smartly uniformed staff.

**ROOMS:** 150 en suite No smoking in 60 bedrooms d £99-£125 * **LB** **FACILITIES:** STV Indoor swimming (H) Gym Jacuzzi entertainment Xmas **CONF:** Thtr 300 Class 150 Board 100 Del from £145 * **SERVICES:** Lift air con **PARKING:** 250 **NOTES:** No smoking in restaurant Civ Wed 250 **CARDS:**

### ★★★76% ®® The Old Bridge
1 High St PE29 3TQ
☎ 01480 424300 🖹 01480 411017
e-mail: oldbridge@huntsbridge.co.uk
***Dir:*** *from A14 or A1 follow signs for 'Huntingdon'. The Old Bridge is clearly visible from the inner ring road*

A delightful 18th-century hotel combining classical architecture with modern facilities. The two eating areas, the convivial terrace and the more formal restaurant, offer the same appealing menu.

*continued*

Individual rooms are designed with style and include many useful extras. There is a particularly good business centre with secretarial services.

**ROOMS:** 24 en suite (3 fmly) s £80-£125; d £100-£160 (incl. bkfst) * LB **FACILITIES:** STV Fishing Private mooring for boats ch fac Xmas **CONF:** Thtr 50 Class 20 Board 24 Del from £145 * **PARKING:** 50 **NOTES:** No smoking in restaurant Civ Wed 80 **CARDS:**

★★65% ***The Stukeleys Country Hotel***
Ermine St, Great Stukeley PE17 5AF
☎ 01480 456927 01480 450260
e-mail: janmick@stukeleys.freeservenet.co.uk
***Dir:*** *on B1043, off A1/A14 junction*
This attractive 16th-century coaching inn offers comfortable accommodation with exposed beams and open fireplaces. The spacious bedrooms are individually decorated and tastefully

*continued on p292*

HUNTINGDON, continued

furnished in pine. On the ground floor there is a cosy lounge bar and dining area as well as a smart restaurant.
**ROOMS:** 8 en suite (1 fmly) **PARKING:** 30 **NOTES:** No dogs (ex guide dogs) **CARDS:**

## HYDE, Cheshire
Map 07 SJ99

### Premier Lodge (Manchester East)
PREMIER LODGE
Stockport Rd, Mottram SK14 3AU
☎ 0870 700 1478 Fax 0870 700 1479
***Dir:*** *3rd exit off rdbt at end of M67 just behind McDonalds*
Premier Lodge offers modern, well-equipped, en suite accommodation suitable for both business and leisure travellers. Meals can be taken at the adjacent popular restaurant and bar, which is fully licensed. For further details, consult the Hotel Groups page.
**ROOMS:** 82 en suite d £42 *

H

## HYTHE, Kent
Map 05 TR13

### ★★★★77% The Hythe Imperial
MARSTON HOTELS
Princes Pde CT21 6AE
☎ 01303 267441 Fax 01303 264610
e-mail: hytheimperial@marstonhotels.com
***Dir:*** *M20, junct 11 take A261. When in Hythe, follow signs to Folkestone. For hotel turn right into Twiss Road*
In a 50-acre seafront estate, this magnificent building, evocative of a bygone era, is surrounded by a golf course and beautiful gardens. Spacious, well-equipped bedrooms have lovely views of the grounds or the sea. Professional, friendly staff serve a wide range of carefully prepared dishes in the restaurant. Lighter dishes are available in the sunny Bistro Bar. Leisure facilities are excellent.
**ROOMS:** 100 en suite (5 fmly) No smoking in 38 bedrooms s £87-£119; d £120-£160 * **LB** **FACILITIES:** STV Indoor swimming (H) Golf 9 Tennis (hard & grass) Squash Snooker Sauna Solarium Gym Croquet lawn Putting green Jacuzzi Beauty salon Fitness assessments ch fac Xmas **CONF:** Thtr 250 Class 120 Board 80 **SERVICES:** Lift **PARKING:** 201 **NOTES:** No dogs (ex guide dogs) No smoking in restaurant Civ Wed 200 **CARDS:**

### ★★★73% Stade Court
MARSTON HOTELS
West Pde CT21 6DT
☎ 01303 268263 Fax 01303 261803
e-mail: stadecourt@marstonhotels.com
***Dir:*** *M20, junc 11 on A261*
A comfortable base from which to explore the local area. Attractive bedrooms are well-equipped and a number have additional seating overlooking the channel. The committed team offer smooth service and genuine hospitality. Leisure facilities are available at the sister hotel, the Hythe Imperial.
**ROOMS:** 42 en suite (5 fmly) No smoking in 7 bedrooms s £59-£69; d £79 * **LB** **FACILITIES:** STV Indoor swimming (H) Golf 9 Tennis (hard & grass) Squash Snooker Sauna Solarium Gym Croquet lawn Putting green Jacuzzi All leisure facilities at sister hotel Xmas **CONF:** Thtr 60 Class 50 Board 30 **SERVICES:** Lift **PARKING:** 13 **NOTES:** No smoking in restaurant **CARDS:**

Popped the question? Hotels with Civ Wed in their entry are licensed for civil wedding ceremonies. Maximum numbers for the ceremony only are shown, e.g. Civ Wed 120

## ILFORD, Greater London
See LONDON SECTION plan 1 H5

### *Travelodge*
Travelodge
Beehive Ln, Gants Hill IG4 5DR
☎ 020 8550 4248 Fax 020 8550 4248
Travelodge offers good quality, good value, modern accommodation. Ideal for families, the spacious, en suite bedrooms include remote-control TV, tea and coffee-making facilities, luxury beds and free morning newspaper. Meals can be taken at the nearby family restaurant. For further details and the Travelodge phone number, consult the Hotel Groups page.

**ROOMS:** 32 en suite

## ILFRACOMBE, Devon
Map 02 SS54

### ★★71% Elmfield
Torrs Park EX34 8AZ
☎ 01271 863377 Fax 01271 866828
***Dir:*** *take A361 to Ilfracombe left at 1st traffic lights, left again at 2nd traffic lights, after 10yds left again hotel near top of hill on left*
With glorious views over the town, this well maintained Victorian property is set in pleasant terraced gardens. Good home-cooked meals that use fresh, local ingredients are served in the traditional dining room; there is a cosy bar and comfortable lounge with a small games room. The bedrooms are spacious and well-equipped.
**ROOMS:** 11 en suite 2 annexe en suite s £40-£45; d £80-£90 (incl. bkfst & dinner) * **LB** **FACILITIES:** Indoor swimming (H) Sauna Solarium Gym Jacuzzi Darts Pool table Xmas **PARKING:** 14 **NOTES:** No dogs No children 8yrs No smoking in restaurant Closed Nov-Mar ex Xmas
**CARDS:**
*See advert on opposite page*

### ★★67% Ilfracombe Carlton
Runnacleave Rd EX34 8AR
☎ 01271 862446 & 863711 Fax 01271 865379
***Dir:*** *take A361 to Ilfracombe left at traffic lights, left at next lights follow brown sign 'tunnels, beaches'*

Situated in the centre of the town, this well-maintained hotel has a loyal following. The spacious public areas include two lounges and a bar with an entertainment area. The comfortable bedrooms are attractively decorated and well-equipped. In the bright and airy dining room a short set-price menu is offered each evening.
**ROOMS:** 48 en suite (8 fmly) No smoking in all bedrooms s £27.50-£29.50; d £45-£50 (incl. bkfst) * **LB** **FACILITIES:** entertainment Xmas **CONF:** Thtr 50 Class 50 Board 50 Del from £39 * **SERVICES:** Lift **PARKING:** 25 **NOTES:** No dogs (ex guide dogs) No smoking in restaurant Closed Jan RS Feb **CARDS:**
*See advert on opposite page*

★★65% **St Helier**
Hillsborough Rd EX34 9QQ
☎ 01271 864906 01271 864906
e-mail: st_helier_hotel@yahoo.co.uk
***Dir:*** *leave M5 junct 27 onto A361 continue to Ilfracombe, then take Combe Martin road through High St hotel opposite 'Old Thatched Inn'*
Within walking distance of the town centre and the harbour, this small hotel has been in the same family ownership for over sixty years. Some of the bedrooms have views of the sea. The public areas include a comfortable reception/lounge, a convivial Cellar Bar and a separate dining room.
**ROOMS:** 10 en suite (2 fmly) s £26-£28; d £50-£54 (incl. bkfst) * **LB**
**PARKING:** 29 **NOTES:** No smoking in restaurant Closed Nov to Apr
**CARDS:**

★★64% **Imperial Hotel**
Wilder Rd EX34 9AL
☎ 01271 862536 01271 862571
Leisureplex
***Dir:*** *hotel opposite Landmark Theatre*
Occupying a prime position overlooking gardens and the sea, this popular hotel is just a short walk from the shops and harbour. Public areas include the spacious sun lounge, a wonderful place to sit and enjoy the excellent views and watch the world go by. Comfortable bedrooms are well-equipped with many having the added bonus of sea views.
**ROOMS:** 104 en suite (6 fmly) s £25-£30; d £42-£58 (incl. bkfst) * **LB**
**FACILITIES:** entertainment **SERVICES:** Lift **PARKING:** 10 **NOTES:** No dogs (ex guide dogs) No smoking in restaurant Closed Nov-Mar (ex Xmas) **CARDS:**

★69% **Westwell Hall Hotel**
Torrs Park EX34 8AZ
☎ 01271 862792 01271 862792
e-mail: colin.lomas@westwellhall.freeserve.co.uk
***Dir:*** *along Ilfracombe High Street, onto Worthfield road at lights, then L up Torrs Park. Turn R (Upper Torrs). Westwell Hall is 3rd drive on the left*
Conveniently located for both the beaches and the shops, this fine Victorian property is set in large gardens overlooking the town. The well equipped, individually decorated bedrooms are comfortable and the majority of rooms benefit from delightful views. There is a lounge and a restaurant, and an intimate bar for guests.
**ROOMS:** 10 en suite s £22-£24; d £44-£48 (incl. bkfst) * **PARKING:** 10
**NOTES:** No smoking in restaurant Closed Nov to Easter
**CARDS:**

★65% **Torrs**
Torrs Park EX34 8AY
☎ 01271 862334 01271 862334
***Dir:*** *from Barnstaple (A361), 1st set of lights in Ilfracombe left into Wilder Road. Next set of lights. Turn left then left again. Hotel 320yds on right*
Standing in its own gardens, this personally run, detached hotel benefits from views over both the town and surrounding countryside. The light and airy bedrooms are comfortable and equipped with the expected modern amenities.
**ROOMS:** 14 en suite (5 fmly) s £20-£25; d £40-£50 (incl. bkfst) * **LB**
**PARKING:** 14 **NOTES:** No children 5yrs No smoking in restaurant Closed mid Nov-mid Feb **CARDS:**

Late for dinner? Quality Standards star rating means that last orders for dinner should be no earlier than:
★ 6.30pm ★★ 7.00pm ★★★ 8.00pm
★★★★ 9.00pm ★★★★★ 10.00pm

## ILKLEY, West Yorkshire

Map 07 SE14

### ★★★70% Rombalds

11 West View, Wells Rd LS29 9JG
☎ 01943 603201 01943 816586
e-mail: reception@rombalds.demon.co.uk
***Dir:*** *on Leeds/Skipton road A65, left at 2nd main lights, follow signs Ilkley Moor. Right at HSBC Bank onto Wells Road. Hotel is 600yds on left*

Located on a quiet terrace between the town and the moors, this elegantly furnished hotel provides comfortable lounges and well-equipped bedrooms. The attractive restaurant serves well-produced imaginative meals.
**ROOMS:** 15 en suite (2 fmly) No smoking in 6 bedrooms s £70-£100; d £89-£119 (incl. bkfst) * LB **FACILITIES:** STV Xmas **CONF:** Thtr 70 Class 40 Board 25 Del from £105 * **PARKING:** 28 **NOTES:** No smoking in restaurant Civ Wed 70 **CARDS:**

### ★★★68% The Craiglands

Cowpasture Rd LS29 8RQ
☎ 01943 430001 01943 430002
e-mail: reservations@craiglandshotel.co.uk
***Dir:*** *Turn off A65 into Ilkley. At T junct turn left. Proceed past railway station and fork right into Cowpasture Rd. Hotel situated opposite school*
This grand Victorian hotel nestles in mature, landscaped grounds, close to the town centre and rail links. Public rooms are light and airy, and include an elegant restaurant and traditionally styled bar and lounge. Bedrooms vary in size and style but all are comfortably furnished, many having been upgraded.
**ROOMS:** 60 en suite (5 fmly) s £65-£85; d £90-£120 (incl. bkfst) LB **FACILITIES:** STV ch fac Xmas **CONF:** Thtr 500 Class 200 Board 100 Del from £105 * **SERVICES:** Lift **PARKING:** 200 **NOTES:** Civ Wed 500 **CARDS:**

### ○ Innkeeper's Lodge Ilkley

Hangingstone Rd LS29 8BT
A new concept in the travel accommodation market. Smart rooms meet essential business requirements but also have home comforts. Dining options include all-day menus plus the added advantage of breakfast, which is included in the room price. Reservations can be made seven days a week through the room reservations number: 0870 243 0500. For further details, consult the Hotel Groups page.
**ROOMS:** 16 en suite **NOTES:** Open Now

## ILMINSTER, Somerset

Map 03 ST31

### ★★★67% *Pheasant Hotel & Restaurant*

Water St, Seavington St Mary TA19 0QH
☎ 01460 240502 01460 242388
***Dir:*** *3m E of Ilminster, off B3168*
A delightful, part thatched former farmhouse in well-tended gardens, close to the Dorset-Devon border. There is character in abundance here, with oak beams and splendid inglenook fireplaces. Individually styled bedrooms, some in stone-built cottages around the main house, are equipped with modern comforts and thoughtful extras.
**ROOMS:** 2 en suite 6 annexe en suite **FACILITIES:** STV ch fac **CONF:** Thtr 28 Board 12 **PARKING:** 30 **NOTES:** No smoking in restaurant Closed 24 Dec, 26 Dec & 1 Jan RS BH's (bed & breakfast only) **CARDS:**

### ★★★66% Shrubbery

TA19 9AR
☎ 01460 52108 01460 53660
e-mail: stuart@shrubberyhotel.demon.co.uk
***Dir:*** *half a mile from A303 towards Ilminster town centre*
Set in attractive terraced gardens, this Victorian hotel offers well-equipped bedrooms of various sizes, including three on the ground floor. A choice of menus is offered at dinner, along with a selection of fish dishes. Less formal bar meals are available at lunch. Guests can take a dip in the heated outdoor pool on warmer days.
**ROOMS:** 17 en suite (3 fmly) s £65-£75; d £71-£97 (incl. bkfst) * LB **FACILITIES:** STV Outdoor swimming (H) Tennis (grass) ch fac **CONF:** Thtr 250 Class 120 Board 80 Del from £95 * **PARKING:** 100 **NOTES:** Civ Wed 200 **CARDS:**

### ⌂ *Travelodge*

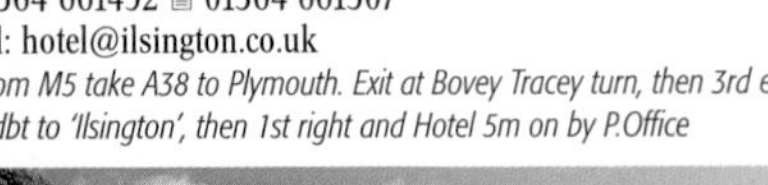
Travelodge

Southfields Roundabout, Horton Cross TA19 9PT
☎ 01460 53748 01460 53748
***Dir:*** *on A303*
Travelodge offers good quality, good value, modern accommodation. Ideal for families, the spacious, en suite bedrooms include remote-control TV, tea and coffee-making facilities, luxury beds and free morning newspaper. Meals can be taken at the nearby family restaurant. For further details and the Travelodge phone number, consult the Hotel Groups page.

**ROOMS:** 32 en suite

## ILSINGTON, Devon

Map 03 SX77

### ★★★70% The Ilsington Country House

Ilsington Village TQ13 9RR
☎ 01364 661452 01364 661307
e-mail: hotel@ilsington.co.uk
***Dir:*** *from M5 take A38 to Plymouth. Exit at Bovey Tracey turn, then 3rd exit from rdbt to 'Ilsington', then 1st right and Hotel 5m on by P.Office*

This friendly, peaceful hotel on the southern slopes of Dartmoor is approached along four miles of winding country roads. Bedrooms are individually furnished, some are on the ground floor. The daily

continued

changing menu offers innovative dishes using local fish, meat and game. Leisure facilities are good.
**ROOMS:** 25 en suite (2 fmly) s £70-£96; d £109-£155 (incl. bkfst & dinner) * LB **FACILITIES:** Spa STV Indoor swimming (H) Tennis (hard) Sauna Solarium Gym Croquet lawn Jacuzzi Beautician ch fac Xmas **CONF:** Thtr 35 Class 30 Board 30 Del from £85 * **SERVICES:** Lift **PARKING:** 100 **NOTES:** No smoking in restaurant
**CARDS:**

## IMMINGHAM, Lincolnshire
Map 08 TA11

### ★★65% Old Chapel Hotel & Restaurant
50 Station Rd, Habrough DN40 3AY
☎ 01469 572377 🖷 01469 577883
e-mail: bewick18@aol.com
***Dir:*** *M180/A180 turn off A180 onto A160 (Killingholme/Immingham) right at 1st rdbt to Harbrough. Straight over mini rdbt, 500mtrs on right after flyover*
This converted early 19th-century chapel offers comfortable, well equipped bedrooms and a friendly atmosphere. Day rooms include a small bar, a bright conservatory lounge and a cosy beamed restaurant where a range of popular dishes is served.
**ROOMS:** 14 en suite (1 fmly) s £40-£50; d £50-£55 (incl. bkfst) * **PARKING:** 20 **NOTES:** No smoking in restaurant
**CARDS:**

## INGATESTONE, Essex
Map 05 TQ69

### ★★★66% The Heybridge
Roman Rd CM4 9AB
☎ 01277 355355 🖷 01277 353288
***Dir:*** *follow M25/A12. Take B1002 exit (Ingatestone). Through Mountnessing and bridge over A12, 1st right (A12 London & Heybridge). Hotel 200yds on left*
This friendly family-run hotel is situated within easy reach of the major road networks and is therefore ideally placed for touring Essex or visiting London. Parts of the main building date back to the 15th century and retain much of their original character. The spacious well-equipped bedrooms are located in two courtyard style wings. Public areas include a lounge, two bars and a smart traditional style restaurant.
**ROOMS:** 22 en suite (3 fmly) No smoking in 2 bedrooms s £83-£94; d £94-£104 * **FACILITIES:** STV entertainment Xmas **CONF:** Thtr 600 Class 400 Board 70 Del from £136 * **PARKING:** 220 **NOTES:** No dogs Civ Wed 200 **CARDS:**

## INSTOW, Devon
Map 02 SS43

### ★★★74% Commodore
Marine Pde EX39 4JN
☎ 01271 860347 🖷 01271 861233
e-mail: admin@the-commodore.freeserve.co.uk
***Dir:*** *leave M5 junct 27 follow N Devon link road to Bideford. Turn right before bridge to Instow hotel 3m from bridge*
The majority of this hotel's well-equipped bedrooms have balconies that take advantage of its delightful location overlooking the sandy beach at the mouth of the Taw and Torridge Estuaries. An extensive range of bar meals is served in the Quarter Deck Bar,

*continued*

and the restaurant offers a fixed-price menu and seasonally changing carte.

**ROOMS:** 20 en suite s £65-£75; d £115-£131 (incl. bkfst & dinner) * LB **CONF:** Thtr 250 Class 250 Board 80 Del from £74 * **PARKING:** 200 **NOTES:** No dogs No smoking in restaurant
**CARDS:**

## IPSWICH, Suffolk
Map 05 TM14

### ★★★★ ⊛⊛⊛ Hintlesham Hall
IP8 3NS
☎ 01473 652334 & 652268 🖷 01473 652463
e-mail: reservations@hintlesham-hall.co.uk
(For full entry see Hintlesham)

SLH

### ★★★73% Swallow Belstead Brook Hotel
Belstead Rd IP2 9HB
☎ 01473 684241 🖷 01473 681249
e-mail: info@swallowhotels.com

SWALLOW HOTELS

***Dir:*** *take A1214 from A12/A14 interchange rdbt & follow signs to hotel*
Set in eight acres of landscaped grounds on the outskirts of the town centre, this hotel provides comfortable bedrooms equipped with modern facilities and many thoughtful touches. Public areas include a lounge area, bar and wood-panelled restaurant, in addition to extensive leisure facilities.
**ROOMS:** 76 en suite 12 annexe en suite (2 fmly) No smoking in 65 bedrooms s £99; d £109 (incl. bkfst) * LB **FACILITIES:** STV Indoor swimming (H) Sauna Solarium Gym Croquet lawn Steam Room entertainment Xmas **CONF:** Thtr 180 Class 75 Board 50 Del from £135 * **SERVICES:** Lift **PARKING:** 120 **NOTES:** No smoking in restaurant Civ Wed 130 **CARDS:**

### ★★★71% ⊛ Marlborough
Henley Rd IP1 3SP
☎ 01473 226789 🖷 01473 226927
e-mail: reception@themarlborough.co.uk
***Dir:*** *take A1156 from A14 or A1214 from A12 turn right at Henley Rd/ A1214 x-rds*
A delightful 19th-century building with a country house atmosphere situated in a quiet residential area. The attractive bedrooms are tastefully decorated and thoughtfully equipped. Drinks are served in the contemporary bar, and the smart

*continued on p296*

IPSWICH, continued

restaurant overlooks the well-tended gardens. The adventurous cooking makes excellent use of good local produce.

*Marlborough, Ipswich*

**ROOMS:** 22 en suite (3 fmly) s fr £69; d £84-£91 * **LB** **FACILITIES:** STV Xmas **CONF:** Thtr 40 Class 20 Board 26 Del from £118 * **PARKING:** 60 **NOTES:** No smoking in restaurant Civ Wed 120 **CARDS:**

*See advert on opposite page*

### ★★★69% Courtyard by Marriott Ipswich

The Havens, Ransomes Europark IP3 9SJ
☎ 01473 272244 📠 01473 272484

***Dir:*** *just off A14 Ipswich bypass at 1st jnct after Orwell Bridge signed Ransomes Europark when travelling towards Felixstowe, hotel faces the slip road*

Conveniently situated within easy striking distance of the town centre and major road networks, this modern well-maintained hotel offers stylish accommodation with attractive, spacious bedrooms. The open plan public rooms include a restaurant, bar and a suite of conference rooms. Guests also have the use of a small fitness studio.

**ROOMS:** 60 en suite (28 fmly) No smoking in 44 bedrooms s £88-£94; d £95-£101 (incl. bkfst) * **LB** **FACILITIES:** STV Gym Xmas **CONF:** Thtr 160 Class 70 Board 55 Del £120 * **SERVICES:** Lift **PARKING:** 150 **NOTES:** No dogs (ex guide dogs) Civ Wed 70 **CARDS:**

### ★★★66% County Hotel Ipswich

London Rd, Copdock IP8 3JD
☎ 01473 209988 📠 01473 730801

***Dir:*** *close to the A12/A14 interchange S of Ipswich. Exit A12 at junct signposted Washbrook/Copdock. Hotel on old A12 1m on left*

This modern hotel is popular with both business and leisure guests. The spacious bedrooms offer a good level of comfort and are equipped with modern facilities. The bar and restaurant have an informal atmosphere and room service is actively promoted.

**ROOMS:** 76 en suite (51 fmly) No smoking in 38 bedrooms s £45-£85; d £55-£95 * **LB** **FACILITIES:** Indoor swimming (H) Sauna Solarium Gym Jacuzzi Xmas **CONF:** Thtr 500 Class 200 Board 35 Del £99 * **SERVICES:** Lift **PARKING:** 360 **NOTES:** No smoking in restaurant Civ Wed 120 **CARDS:**

### ★★★65% Novotel Ipswich

NOVOTEL

Greyfriars Rd IP1 1UP
☎ 01473 232400 📠 01473 232414
e-mail: h0995@accor.hotels.com

***Dir:*** *from A14 towards Felixstowe turn left onto A137 & follow for 2m into centre of town, hotel on double rdbt by Stoke Bridge*

Situated close to the town centre this modern continental style redbrick hotel is popular as a business and meeting venue. The open plan public areas include a Mediterranean style restaurant and a bar with a small games area. Smartly refurbished bedrooms are simple in decor, well-designed for most needs and equipped to a modern standard; three are suitable for disabled people.

**ROOMS:** 100 en suite (6 fmly) No smoking in 76 bedrooms d £78 * **LB** **FACILITIES:** STV pool table ch fac **CONF:** Thtr 180 Class 75 Board 45 Del £99 * **SERVICES:** Lift air con **PARKING:** 50 **CARDS:**

### ★★★63% *Posthouse Ipswich*

Posthouse

London Rd IP2 0UA
☎ 0870 400 9045 📠 01473 680412

***Dir:*** *from A12/A45, go on A1214. At Tesco's go straight over 1st rndbt and hotel is 200yds on left*

This pleasant, modern hotel is located to the west of the town centre. Bedrooms and public areas are suited to the needs of both business and leisure guests, and there is a useful leisure club.

**ROOMS:** 109 en suite (48 fmly) No smoking in 66 bedrooms **FACILITIES:** Indoor swimming (H) ch fac **CONF:** Thtr 120 Class 50 Board 40 **PARKING:** 200 **CARDS:**

### ★★69% Claydon Country House

Best Western

16-18 Ipswich Rd, Claydon IP6 0AR
☎ 01473 830382 📠 01473 832476
e-mail: kayshotels@aol.com

***Dir:*** *from A14, north west of Ipswich 4m take Great Blakenham road, B1113 then turn off to Claydon, hotel on left*

Ideally situated just off the A14, this hotel is a short drive form the centre of Ipswich. The bedrooms are modern, well-equipped and include a spacious, attractively furnished four-poster room. The smart restaurant offers a wide choice of appealing dishes and guests also have the use of a relaxing lounge bar.

**ROOMS:** 14 en suite (2 fmly) No smoking in 4 bedrooms s £59-£64; d £74-£79 (incl. bkfst) * **LB** **FACILITIES:** STV Xmas **CONF:** Thtr 50 Class 30 Board 28 **PARKING:** 60 **NOTES:** No dogs (ex guide dogs) No smoking in restaurant **CARDS:**

Popped the question? Hotels with Civ Wed in their entry are licensed for civil wedding ceremonies. Maximum numbers for the ceremony only are shown, e.g. Civ Wed 120

**⇧ Express by Holiday Inn Ipswich**
Old Hadleigh Rd, Sproughton IP8 3AR
☎ 01473 222279 🖷 01473 222297
***Dir:*** *From A12/A14 interchange follow directions for Town Centre on A1214. At traffic lights with Post House turn left onto the A1071. At mini rdbt turn Right onto B113. Hotel is on the right*

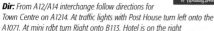

Express by Holiday Inn

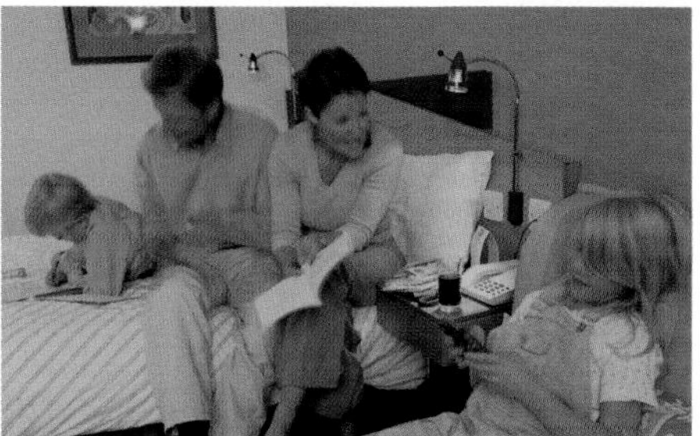

A modern budget hotel offering comfortable accommodation in refreshing, spacious and comprehensively equipped bedrooms, en suite bathrooms with power showers and continental buffet breakfast included in the room rate. Suitable for business travellers or families. For further details and the Express by Holiday Inn phone number, consult the Hotel Groups page.
**ROOMS:** 49 en suite (incl. cont bkfst) s £41-£53; d £41-£53 *
**CONF:** Thtr 30 Class 16 Board 16

**⇧ *Travelodge***
Capel St Mary IP9 2JP
☎ 01473 312157 🖷 01473 312157
***Dir:*** *5m S on A12*

Travelodge

Travelodge offers good quality, good value, modern accommodation. Ideal for families, the spacious, en suite bedrooms include remote-control TV, tea and coffee-making facilities, luxury beds and free morning newspaper. Meals can be taken at the nearby family restaurant. For further details and the Travelodge phone number, consult the Hotel Groups page.

**ROOMS:** 32 en suite

ISLE OF Places incorporating the words 'Isle of' or 'Isle' will be found under the actual name - eg Isle of Wight is listed under Wight, Isle of.

IVYBRIDGE, Devon Map 02 SX65

**★★74% ® Glazebrook House Hotel & Restaurant**
TQ10 9JE
☎ 01364 73322 🖷 01364 72350
***Dir:*** *turn off A38 at Avonwick, South Brent jct. proceed 1.5m to South Brent. Pass the London Inn, in 100yds the jct for Glazebrook is on the right*
An elegant mid-Victorian country house surrounded by four acres of gardens standing on the southern slopes of the Dartmoor

*continued on p298*

IVYBRIDGE, continued

National Park. Bedrooms are decorated in pleasing colour schemes, and extra little touches add to a feeling of comfort.

*Glazebrook House, Ivybridge*

**ROOMS:** 11 en suite (1 fmly) s £50; d £72-£125 (incl. bkfst) * **LB**
**CONF:** Thtr 100 Class 80 Board 60 Del from £70 * **PARKING:** 50
**NOTES:** No dogs (ex guide dogs) No smoking in restaurant
**CARDS:**

See advert on page 297

**★★65% Sportsmans Inn Hotel & Restaurant**
Exeter Rd PL21 0BQ
☎ 01752 892280 🖹 01752 690714
e-mail: info@thesportsmaninn.co.uk
***Dir:*** *turn off A38 Devon expressway at Ivybridge exit, follow main road through town, hotel on the main road*
This ever popular inn attracts a healthy trade from both locals and visitors alike with a wide choice of meals and snacks available in its open-plan bar and restaurant. Bedrooms are well-equipped and include a ground floor room and an impressive four-poster.
**ROOMS:** 14 en suite s fr £40; d fr £50 (incl. bkfst) * **LB**
**FACILITIES:** entertainment **PARKING:** 50 **NOTES:** No dogs (ex guide dogs) RS X-mas day **CARDS:**

KEGWORTH See East Midlands Airport

KEIGHLEY, West Yorkshire — Map 07 SE04

**★★66% Dalesgate**
406 Skipton Rd, Utley BD20 6HP
☎ 01535 664930 🖹 01535 611253
e-mail: Stephen.E.Atha@btinternet.com
***Dir:*** *from town centre follow A629 over rdbt. After 3/4 mile turn right into St. John's Road and 1st right into Hotel car park*
Originally the residence of a local chapel minister, this modern hotel has been expanded with the addition of a new wing to provide well-equipped, comfortable bedrooms. The hotel also has a cosy bar and pleasant restaurant, serving a good range of well-produced dishes. There is ample car parking to the rear.
**ROOMS:** 20 en suite (2 fmly) s £35-£45; d £50-£65 (incl. bkfst) * **LB**
**FACILITIES:** ch fac **PARKING:** 25 **CARDS:**

KENDAL, Cumbria — Map 07 SD59
see also Crooklands

**★★★75% The Castle Green Hotel in Kendal**
LA9 6RG
☎ 01539 734000 🖹 01539 735522
e-mail: reception@castlegreen.co.uk
***Dir:*** *from M6 junc 36, head for Kendal. Right at 1st traffic lights, left at rdbt to "K" Village then right for 0.75m to hotel at T-junct*
Commanding views of the distant fells, this new hotel provides a peaceful location for both business and leisure guests. Bedrooms are stylish and well-equipped, and many enjoy fine views. The Greenhouse Restaurant provides imaginative and skilfully prepared dishes, and a business centre offers an array of conference facilities.
**ROOMS:** 100 en suite (3 fmly) s £75; d £99 (incl. bkfst) * **LB**
**FACILITIES:** STV Indoor swimming (H) Solarium Gym Steam Room Aerobics, Yoga, Beauty Salon entertainment ch fac **CONF:** Thtr 350 Class 200 Board 120 Del from £114.57 * **SERVICES:** Lift **PARKING:** 200
**NOTES:** No dogs (ex guide dogs) No smoking in restaurant Civ Wed
**CARDS:**

**★★★68% Riverside Hotel**
Stramongate Bridge LA9 4BZ
☎ 01539 734861 🖹 01539 734863
e-mail: riverside@macdonald-hotels.co.uk
***Dir:*** *M6 junct 36 follow A590 to A591,follow signs for Kendal*
Centrally located in this market town, and enjoying a peaceful riverside location, this 17th-century tannery provides an ideal base for both business people and tourists. The comfortable bedrooms are well equipped whilst open plan day rooms include the attractive restaurant and bar. Conferencing and leisure facilities are also available. Staff throughout are friendly and professional.
**ROOMS:** 47 en suite (11 fmly) No smoking in 20 bedrooms s £70-£95; d £75-£115 (incl. bkfst) * **LB** **FACILITIES:** STV Gym Sports Hall ch fac Xmas **CONF:** Thtr 140 Del from £85 * **SERVICES:** Lift **PARKING:** 35
**NOTES:** No smoking in restaurant **CARDS:**

**★★64% Garden House**
Fowl-Ing Ln LA9 6PH
☎ 01539 731131 🖹 01539 740064
e-mail: gardenhouse.hotel@virgin.net
***Dir:*** *leave M6 junct 36 follow signs for A6 north & turn right at Duke of Cumberland after 200yds take 2nd right, next to secondhand car show room*
An early 19th-century country house situated in wooded grounds and formal gardens close to the centre of the town. Bedrooms vary in style but all are well-equipped and individually furnished and some have four-posters. The conservatory restaurant, with a mural of the hotel on one wall, looks out over the garden.
**ROOMS:** 11 en suite (2 fmly) No smoking in 4 bedrooms s fr £49.50; d fr £75 (incl. bkfst) * **LB** **FACILITIES:** Croquet lawn Putting green
**CONF:** Thtr 60 Class 40 Board 30 **PARKING:** 30 **NOTES:** No smoking in restaurant RS 26-30 Dec **CARDS:**

KENILWORTH, Warwickshire — Map 04 SP27

**★★★★65% Chesford Grange**
Chesford Bridge CV8 2LD
☎ 01926 859331 🖹 01926 859075
e-mail: sales.chesford@btinternet.com
***Dir:*** *0.5m SE junct A46/A452 at rdbt take right exit signed Leamington Spa. After approx 250yds at x-rds turn right hotel on left*
Situated in 17 acres of private grounds in the Warwickshire countryside, yet only twenty minutes away from Birmingham International Airport and the NEC, the hotel benefits from good transport links and extensive facilities. The tastefully decorated bedrooms range from standard to executive rooms. Public rooms include well-equipped leisure facilities and an extensive range of meeting rooms.
**ROOMS:** 145 en suite 9 annexe en suite (12 fmly) No smoking in 80 bedrooms s £90-£125; d £100-£145 (incl. bkfst) * **LB** **FACILITIES:** STV Indoor swimming (H) Fishing Sauna Solarium Gym Jacuzzi entertainment Xmas **CONF:** Thtr 860 Class 300 Board 50 Del £160 *
**SERVICES:** Lift **PARKING:** 550 **NOTES:** No smoking in restaurant Civ Wed 80 **CARDS:**

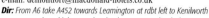

**★★★★65% De Montfort**
Abbey End CV8 1ED
☎ 01926 855944 01926 857830
e-mail: demontfort@macdonald-hotels.co.uk
***Dir:*** *From A6 take A452 towards Leamington at rdbt left to Kenilworth town centre, down high street, hotel at bottom opposite clock tower*
Located in the heart of Shakespeare country the De Montfort Hotel offers accommodation of a high standard. Its public areas include a smart café bar and a restaurant, as well as an extensive range of meeting and function rooms. Friendly staff offer a warm welcome.
**ROOMS:** 108 en suite (15 fmly) No smoking in 55 bedrooms s £70-£100; d £90-£120 * **LB** **FACILITIES:** STV Free use of nearby pool and gym Xmas **CONF:** Thtr 300 Class 100 Board 100 Del from £95 *
**SERVICES:** Lift **PARKING:** 65 **NOTES:** No smoking in restaurant
**CARDS:**

**★★68% Clarendon House**
Old High St CV8 1LZ
☎ 01926 857668 01926 850669
e-mail: clarendon@nuthurst-grange.com
***Dir:*** *from A452 pass castle, then left and continue into High Street*
Situated in the old part of the town, this building incorporates the original 15th-century timber-framed Castle Tavern, which was supported by an oak tree. The public rooms have been totally transformed with modern appointments tastefully introduced through a lounge bar and brasserie. Bedroom styles and sizes vary, but all are equipped with modern facilities.
**ROOMS:** 30 en suite (1 fmly) No smoking in 6 bedrooms s £58-£70; d £80-£90 (incl. bkfst) * **LB** **CONF:** Thtr 150 Class 100 Board 70
**PARKING:** 30 **NOTES:** Closed 1 week Xmas Civ Wed 150
**CARDS:**

## KESWICK, Cumbria Map 11 NY22

**★★★74% Dale Head Hall Lakeside**
Lake Thirlmere CA12 4TN
☎ 017687 72478 017687 71070
e-mail: onthelakeside@dale-head-hall.co.uk
***Dir:*** *mid-way between Keswick & Grasmere, off A591, onto private drive to shores of Lake Thirlmere*

Dating from the 16th century, this hotel is located on the shores of the lake. There are two inviting lounges commanding spectacular views, and tastefully decorated bedrooms. Dinner features the best of British produce, good cooking and a recommended wine list.
**ROOMS:** 14 en suite (1 fmly) No smoking in all bedrooms s £65-£75; d £80-£100 (incl. bkfst) * **LB** **FACILITIES:** no TV in bdrms Fishing Croquet lawn ch fac Xmas **PARKING:** 31 **NOTES:** No dogs (ex guide dogs) No smoking in restaurant Closed 31 Dec-31 Jan
**CARDS:**

*See advert on page 301*

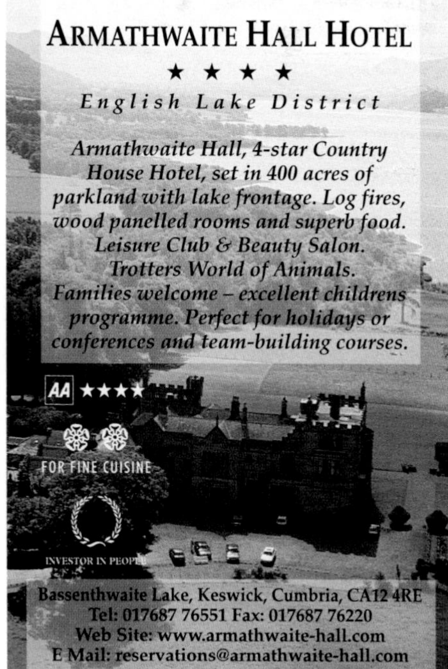
ARMATHWAITE HALL HOTEL
★★★★
English Lake District
Armathwaite Hall, 4-star Country House Hotel, set in 400 acres of parkland with lake frontage. Log fires, wood panelled rooms and superb food. Leisure Club & Beauty Salon. Trotters World of Animals. Families welcome – excellent childrens programme. Perfect for holidays or conferences and team-building courses.
AA ★★★★
FOR FINE CUISINE
Bassenthwaite Lake, Keswick, Cumbria, CA12 4RE
Tel: 017687 76551 Fax: 017687 76220
Web Site: www.armathwaite-hall.com
E Mail: reservations@armathwaite-hall.com

KESWICK, continued

### ★★★74% Derwentwater

Portinscale CA12 5RE
☎ 017687 72538 🖷 017687 71002
e-mail: info@derwentwater-hotel.co.uk
***Dir:*** *off A66 turn into village of Portinscale, follow signs*

A popular and friendly holiday hotel with gardens that stretch down to the shores of Derwentwater. It offers a wide range of bedrooms, all thoughtfully equipped and some with good views of the lake. Public areas include a conservatory lounge, games room and shop.

**ROOMS:** 46 en suite (1 fmly) s £79-£95; d £130-£190 (incl. bkfst) * **LB** **FACILITIES:** Fishing Putting green entertainment ch fac Xmas **CONF:** Thtr 10 Class 10 Board 15 Del from £130 * **SERVICES:** Lift **PARKING:** 120 **NOTES:** No smoking in restaurant
**CARDS:**

*See advert on opposite page*

### ★★★70% ◎◎ *Kings Head Hotel & Inn*

Thirlspot, Thirlmere CA12 4TN
☎ 017687 72393 🖷 017687 72309
e-mail: kings@lakelandsheart.demon.co.uk
***Dir:*** *from M6 junct 40 take A66 to Keswick, then A591 towards Grasmere to hotel in 4m*

Located in a delightful, peaceful valley between Grasmere and Keswick, this traditionally styled inn provides a comfortable base from which to tour the Lake District. Having just completed refurbishment, the smart bedrooms are well-equipped, and the cosy day rooms ideal venues in which to relax. Cooking provides a highlight of any stay and creative dishes make super use of local, seasonal produce.

**ROOMS:** 17 en suite No smoking in 10 bedrooms **FACILITIES:** STV Free use of local Leisure Centre entertainment **CONF:** Thtr 100 Class 40 Board 20 **PARKING:** 60 **NOTES:** No smoking in restaurant
**CARDS:**

*See advert on page 303*

### ★★★66% Skiddaw

Main St CA12 5BN
☎ 017687 72071 🖷 017687 74850
e-mail: reservations@skiddawhotel.co.uk
***Dir:*** *A66 to Keswick follow signs for town centre. Hotel in the Market Square in heart of the town*

Centrally located overlooking the market square, this hotel boasts smartly furnished bedrooms including some family suites. Food is available throughout the day in the lounge bar, and dinner is served in the restaurant.

**ROOMS:** 40 en suite (7 fmly) No smoking in 10 bedrooms s £44-£51; d £82-£96 (incl. bkfst) * **LB** **FACILITIES:** STV Sauna Free use of out of town leisure fac ch fac Xmas **CONF:** Thtr 70 Class 60 Board 40 **SERVICES:** Lift **PARKING:** 22 **NOTES:** No dogs (ex guide dogs) No smoking in restaurant Civ Wed 140 **CARDS:**

*See advert on page 303*

### ★★★65% Keswick Country House

PRINCIPAL HOTELS

Station Rd CA12 4NQ
☎ 017687 72020 🖷 017687 71300
***Dir:*** *adjacent to Keswick Leisure Pool*

This impressive Victorian hotel is set amid beautiful landscaped gardens. Eight superior bedrooms have been created in the Station Wing, which is accessed through the Victorian conservatory. Main house rooms are comfortably modern in style and offer a good range of amenities. Public areas include a well-stocked bar, a spacious and relaxing lounge, and a popular restaurant.

**ROOMS:** 74 en suite (10 fmly) s fr £82; d fr £115 (incl. bkfst) * **LB** **FACILITIES:** STV Snooker Croquet lawn Putting green Pitch & putt entertainment Xmas **CONF:** Thtr 80 Class 35 Board 35 Del £115 * **SERVICES:** Lift **PARKING:** 70 **NOTES:** No smoking in restaurant Civ Wed 130 **CARDS:**

### ★★75% Lyzzick Hall Country House

Under Skiddaw CA12 4PY
☎ 017687 72277 🖷 017687 72278
e-mail: lyzzickhall@netscapeonline.co.uk
***Dir:*** *from M6 junct 40, A66 Keswick do not enter town keep to Keswick by-pass, 3rd exit off rdbt onto A591 to Carlisle, hotel is 1.5m on right*

Among the foothills of Skiddaw, this popular country house boasts lovely views across the valley. There are two spacious lounges, a small bar area and an attractive restaurant in which a wide range of international dishes is served at lunch and dinner. Bedrooms are well-equipped and thoughtfully decorated.

**ROOMS:** 28 en suite 1 annexe en suite (3 fmly) s £46-£48; d £91-£95 (incl. bkfst) * **LB** **FACILITIES:** Indoor swimming (H) Sauna Jacuzzi ch fac **CONF:** Board 15 **PARKING:** 40 **NOTES:** No dogs No smoking in restaurant Closed 24-26 Dec & mid Jan-mid Feb
**CARDS:**

DALE HEAD HALL

*on the lakeside*

For those Special moments in your life

TEL: 017687 72478

email: onthelakeside@dale-head-hall.co.uk
http://www.dale-head-hall.co.uk
AA★★★ 74% - Red Rosette for Cuisine
ETC ★★★ - Silver Award for Excellence

RECOMMENDED BY LEADING HOTEL GUIDES

## Keswick – Unrivalled Lakeshore Location – Lake District

AA
★★★

# *The Derwentwater Hotel*

Remaining in private hands The Derwentwater is the epitome of a Lakeland Country House Hotel without being the least pretentious. A relaxing haven on the shores of Lake Derwentwater in 16 acres of conservation grounds (designated European area of special conservation). Fabulous lake and fell views from our conservatory and many bedrooms.

Be pampered in our Deluxe Rooms, which come complete with Fridge, CD and Video player, Slippers and Bathrobe, Sherry Decanter, lounge area and much much more.

Quality local produce is prepared with skill and care in our Deers Leap Restaurant.

Award Winning Hospitality, Customer Care and Environmental Policy.

*Dedicated to realising the true art of RELAXATION.*

Telephone 017687 72538

Visit our website: www.derwentwater-hotel.co.uk

***The Derwentwater – Realising the true art of relaxation.***

KESWICK, continued

**★★73% Highfield**
The Heads CA12 5ER
☎ 017687 72508 017687 80634
e-mail: highfieldkeswick@talk21.com
***Dir:*** *M6 junct 40, take A66 2nd exit at rdbt, turn left follow road to T-junct left again & right at mini rdbt, The Heads is 4th turning on right*
This attractive hotel enjoys a peaceful setting with stunning mountain views. Bedrooms are stylishly furnished and thoughtfully equipped. Guests can relax in a choice of homely lounges which look out onto the well-tended gardens. Hotel cuisine is of a high standard with an interesting range of carefully prepared dishes.
**ROOMS:** 18 en suite (1 fmly) No smoking in all bedrooms s £52-£60; d £88-£104 (incl. bkfst) **LB** **PARKING:** 19 **NOTES:** No dogs No children 8yrs No smoking in restaurant Closed Dec-Jan excl. Xmas & New Year
**CARDS:**

**★★72% Lairbeck**
Vicarage Hill CA12 5QB
☎ 017687 73373 017687 73144
e-mail: aa@lairbeckhotel-keswick.co.uk
***Dir:*** *follow A66 to rdbt with A591 turn left then immediately right onto Vicarage Hill, hotel 150 yds on right*
Immaculately maintained, this fine Victorian country house is situated close to the town but peacefully secluded in attractive gardens. There is a welcoming residents' bar and a comfortable dining room in which a range of freshly prepared dishes is served each day. Bedrooms are all individual and most appealing.
**ROOMS:** 14 en suite (1 fmly) No smoking in all bedrooms s fr £38.50; d fr £77 (incl. bkfst) * **LB** **PARKING:** 16 **NOTES:** No dogs No children 5yrs No smoking in restaurant Closed Jan & Feb RS Dec
**CARDS:**

**★★70% *Applethwaite Country House Hotel***
Applethwaite, Underskiddaw CA12 4PL
☎ 017687 72413 017687 75706
e-mail: ryan@applethwaite.freeserve.co.uk
***Dir:*** *from M6 follow A66 to Keswick. Do not take left turn into Keswick but continue to rdbt then right A591 to Carlisle and 1st right signed Underscar*
A friendly welcome awaits at this impressive Victorian residence, set in beautiful gardens, in the shadow of Skiddaw. Elegant public rooms enjoy stunning views of the Borrowdale Valley and include comfortable non-smoking sitting rooms. Home cooking is served in the dining room. Bedrooms are attractively decorated and furnished.
**ROOMS:** 12 en suite (2 fmly) No smoking in all bedrooms
**FACILITIES:** Croquet lawn Putting green Bowling green **PARKING:** 10 **NOTES:** No dogs (ex guide dogs) No children 5yrs No smoking in restaurant Closed Dec-10 Feb **CARDS:**

**★★70% Thwaite Howe**
Thornthwaite CA12 5SA
☎ 017687 78281 017687 78529
***Dir:*** *follow signs to Thornthwaite Gallery from A66 approx 3 miles from Keswick. Hotel is signposted from outside Gallery*
This Victorian country house enjoys an idyllic setting and magnificent views across the valley and distant hills. Public rooms feature a cosy residents' bar, comfortable lounge with a real fire, and an attractive dining room. Bedrooms are all individually furnished and well-equipped.

**ROOMS:** 8 en suite (1 fmly) No smoking in all bedrooms s £52-£62; d £104 (incl. bkfst & dinner) * **LB** **PARKING:** 11 **NOTES:** No children 12yrs No smoking in restaurant Closed Dec-Feb
**CARDS:**

**★★69% Chaucer House**
THE CIRCLE Selected Individual Hotels GREAT BRITAIN
Derwentwater Place CA12 4DR
☎ 017687 72318 & 73223 017687 75551
e-mail: enquiries@chaucer-house.demon.co.uk
***Dir:*** *turn right off A591 into Manor Brow, continue down hill, past Castlerigg Catholic Training Centre and sharp double bend, hotel on right*
A relaxed and welcoming atmosphere prevails at this comfortable family-run hotel which is situated in a residential area just a short walk from central amenities. Bedrooms are comfortably modern in style and offer the expected facilities. Public areas include a choice of inviting lounges, a well-stocked bar and separate dining room where the varied menus offer a wide range of tempting dishes.
**ROOMS:** 33 rms (31 en suite) (4 fmly) s £42; d £78-£93 (incl. bkfst) * **LB** **FACILITIES:** STV **SERVICES:** Lift **PARKING:** 25 **NOTES:** No smoking in restaurant Closed Dec-Jan **CARDS:**

**★★67% Crow Park**
The Heads CA12 5ER
☎ 017687 72208 017687 74776
A welcoming atmosphere prevails at this hotel, which enjoys views towards the lake and the Borrowdale Valley. Attractive day rooms include a lounge, residents' bar and a dining room featuring photos of historic lakeland scenes. Bedrooms come in a variety of sizes and offer a good range of amenities.
**ROOMS:** 26 en suite (1 fmly) No smoking in 1 bedroom s £25-£32; d £49-£63 (incl. bkfst) * **LB** **FACILITIES:** STV ch fac Xmas
**PARKING:** 27 **NOTES:** No smoking in restaurant **CARDS:**

**★★65% Horse & Farrier Inn**
Threlkeld CA12 4SQ
☎ 017687 79688 017687 79824
***Dir:*** *12m from Penrith M6, just off A66 4m from Keswick*
This attractive, recently refurbished inn offers smart, stylish, good value accommodation. Open plan day rooms retain much original character and guests can enjoy an interesting range of carefully prepared dishes served in the informal restaurant.
**ROOMS:** 9 en suite No smoking in all bedrooms s fr £30; d fr £60 (incl. bkfst) * **PARKING:** 60 **NOTES:** No smoking in restaurant
**CARDS:**

KESWICK, continued

### ★★64% Ladstock Country House

Thornthwaite CA12 5RZ
☎ 017687 78210 017687 78088
e-mail: enquiries@keswickhotel.co.uk
***Dir:*** *Turn off M6 at Junct40 to A66. 1m after Keswick turn left at Braithwaite off A66 to Thornthwaite and Gallery Ladstock 0.5m on left*

This traditional country house hotel is set in pretty gardens overlooking Bassenthwaite and the valley towards Skiddaw. Once the local parsonage, the house contains splendid oak panelling and mullioned windows designed by Sir Edwin Lutyens.

**ROOMS:** 18 en suite (2 fmly) s fr £45; d fr £70 (incl. bkfst) * **CONF:** Thtr 200 Class 100 Board 60 **PARKING:** 10 **NOTES:** No dogs Civ Wed 200 **CARDS:**

### ★82% Swinside Lodge

Grange Rd, Newlands CA12 5UE
☎ 017687 72948 017687 72948
e-mail: info@swinsidelodge-hotel.co.uk
***Dir:*** *off A66 turn left at Portinscale & follow road to Grange for 2m. Ignore signs to Swinside & Newlands Valley*

A delightful Victorian house, set in attractive gardens at the foot of Catbells, a short stroll from Derwentwater. The house has a choice of inviting lounges, packed with reading material and board games. Smartly furnished, attractively decorated bedrooms are thoughtfully equipped, with extra touches such as mineral water, sweets and home-made biscuits. Cooking is of a high standard and makes good use of local produce.

**ROOMS:** 7 en suite No smoking in all bedrooms s £40-£70; d £94-£124 (incl. bkfst & dinner) * **LB** **FACILITIES:** Xmas **PARKING:** 12 **NOTES:** No dogs (ex guide dogs) No children 10yrs No smoking in restaurant **CARDS:**

K

## KETTERING, Northamptonshire — Map 04 SP87

### ★★★★72% Kettering Park

SHIRE INNS

Kettering Parkway NN15 6XT
☎ 01536 416666 01536 416171
e-mail: kpark@shireinns.co.uk
***Dir:*** *just off junct 9 A14, M1 to A1 link road, on Kettering Venture Park*

This modern, stylish hotel provides a warm welcome and spacious well-equipped and meticulously maintained bedrooms. Equally impressive are the wide-ranging leisure facilities that include a large indoor pool. Dining in the open plan restaurant is largely informal and guests can choose from a lengthy menu of both classical and contemporary dishes.

**ROOMS:** 119 en suite (28 fmly) No smoking in 60 bedrooms s £125; d £145 (incl. bkfst) * **LB** **FACILITIES:** STV Indoor swimming (H) Squash Snooker Sauna Solarium Gym Jacuzzi Steam rooms Childrens splash pool Xmas **CONF:** Thtr 260 Class 120 Board 40 Del £170 * **SERVICES:** Lift air con **PARKING:** 200 **NOTES:** Civ Wed 200 **CARDS:**

### ⌂ *Travelodge*

Travelodge

On the A14 (Westbound) NN14 1WR
☎ 08700 850950

Travelodge offers good quality, good value, modern accommodation. Ideal for families, the spacious, en suite bedrooms include remote-control TV, tea and coffee-making facilities, luxury beds and free morning newspaper. Meals can be taken at the nearby family restaurant. For further details and the Travelodge phone number, consult the Hotel Groups page.

## KIDDERMINSTER, Worcestershire — Map 07 SO87

### ★★★★67% Stone Manor

Stone DY10 4PJ
☎ 01562 777555 01562 777834
e-mail: enquiries@stonemanorhotel.co.uk
***Dir:*** *2m SE on A448*

A converted, much extended former manor house, standing in 25 acres of impressive grounds and gardens. The well-equipped accommodation includes rooms with four-poster beds and bedrooms on ground floor level. There are also some newly created, luxuriously appointed annexe bedrooms. The hotel is a popular venue for wedding receptions and there are four conference suites.

**ROOMS:** 52 en suite 5 annexe en suite No smoking in 11 bedrooms d £95-£135 * **LB** **FACILITIES:** **Spa** STV Outdoor swimming Tennis (hard) Croquet lawn Putting green ch fac Xmas **CONF:** Thtr 150 Class 48 Board 60 Del £140 * **PARKING:** 400 **NOTES:** No smoking in restaurant Civ Wed 150 **CARDS:**

### ★★★63% Gainsborough House

Bewdley Hill DY11 6BS
☎ 01562 820041 01562 66179
e-mail: reservations@gainsboroughhotel.co.uk
***Dir:*** *on A456 Kidderminster/Bewdley road, at General Hospital, straight over at traffic lights, hotel 200yds on right-hand side*

This listed Georgian building, situated on the edge of the town, has benefited from substantial improvements to public areas. Bedrooms are well-equipped and comfortable. Additional features include a bar lounge, carvery and attractive function rooms.

**ROOMS:** 43 en suite (8 fmly) No smoking in 12 bedrooms s fr £70; d fr £90 * **LB** **FACILITIES:** Xmas **CONF:** Thtr 250 Class 80 Board 60 Del from £99 * **PARKING:** 130 **NOTES:** No smoking in restaurant Civ Wed 250 **CARDS:**

### ★★66% Cedars

MINOTEL Great Britain

Mason Rd DY11 6AG
☎ 01562 515595 01562 751103
e-mail: reservations@cedars-hotel.co.uk
***Dir:*** *on ring road follow signs to Bridgnorth (A442) take left turn from last rdbt signed Habberley, 400 metres on left opposite Police Station*

The Cedars is a discreet private hotel situated in a residential suburb close to the centre of town. Bedrooms are well-equipped and comfortable. Additional facilities include a dining room and a lounge bar with an adjacent conservatory lounge overlooking a delightful garden.

**ROOMS:** 21 en suite (3 fmly) No smoking in 7 bedrooms s £48-£58; d £59-£79 (incl. bkfst) * **LB** **FACILITIES:** STV **CONF:** Thtr 20 Class 10 Board 14 Del from £75 * **PARKING:** 21 **NOTES:** No dogs (ex guide dogs) No smoking in restaurant Closed 24 Dec-2 Jan **CARDS:**

## KINGHAM, Oxfordshire — Map 04 SP22

### ★★★70% Mill House Hotel & Restaurant

OX7 6UH
☎ 01608 658188 01608 658492
e-mail: stay@millhousehotel.co.uk
***Dir:*** *turn off A44 at Chipping Norton or Stow-on-the-Wold onto B4450, hotel on outskirts of Kingham village signposted by brown tourist signs*

This Cotswold stone hotel is set in extensive well-kept grounds, bordered by its own trout stream. Bedrooms are individually decorated and thoughtfully equipped. Guests may relax in the

*continued*

lounge or in the bar with its log burning fire. The restaurant is popular with locals and guests alike.

**ROOMS:** 21 en suite 2 annexe en suite (1 fmly) s £80-£90; d £156-£176 (incl. bkfst & dinner) * **LB FACILITIES:** STV Fishing Croquet lawn ch fac Xmas **CONF:** Thtr 70 Class 24 Board 20 **PARKING:** 62 **NOTES:** No smoking in restaurant **CARDS:**

KINGSBRIDGE, Devon — Map 03 SX74

**★★★79% Buckland-Tout-Saints**
Goveton TQ7 2DS
☎ 01548 853055 01548 856261
e-mail: buckland@tout-saints.co.uk
***Dir:*** *turn off A381 Totnes/Kingsbridge Rd towards Goveton, left into Goveton and up hill towards St Peters Church, hotel 2nd right after church*

This Queen Anne manor house stands in seven acres of grounds. Bedrooms are individual in style and size and day rooms include an intimate restaurant, a choice of lounges, and a bar-lounge. There is also a function room and the hotel has a licence for civil weddings.
**ROOMS:** 10 en suite (1 fmly) No smoking in 1 bedroom s £65-£120; d £130-£240 (incl. bkfst) * **FACILITIES:** Croquet lawn Putting green Petanque pitch ch fac Xmas **CONF:** Thtr 150 Class 100 Board 70 Del from £90 * **PARKING:** 42 **NOTES:** No smoking in restaurant Civ Wed 130 **CARDS:**

*See advert on this page*

KINGS LANGLEY, Hertfordshire — Map 04 TL00

**Premier Lodge**
Hempstead Rd WD4 8BR
☎ 0870 700 1568 0870 700 1569
PREMIER LODGE
Premier Lodge offers modern, well-equipped, en suite accommodation suitable for both business and leisure travellers. Meals can be taken at the adjacent popular restaurant and bar, which is fully licensed. For further details, consult the Hotel Groups page.
**ROOMS:** 60 en suite d £49 *

KING'S LYNN, Norfolk — Map 09 TF62

**★★★ Congham Hall Country House**
Lynn Rd PE32 1AH
☎ 01485 600250 01485 601191
e-mail: reception@conghamhallhotel.com
(For full entry see Grimston)

**★★★69% Knights Hill**
Knights Hill Village, South Wootton PE30 3HQ
☎ 01553 675566 01553 675568
e-mail: reception@knightshill.co.uk
***Dir:*** *junct A148/A149*

Best Western

Knights Hill is a hotel village complex, set around a 16th-century site. In the main house and the surrounding buildings, historical charm has been combined with modern facilities such as conference and banqueting suites and a smart indoor leisure centre. The accommodation is mainly in extensions to the original hunting lodge. Dining options include formal meals in the Garden Restaurant, or informal choices in the Farmers Arms pub.
**ROOMS:** 43 en suite 18 annexe en suite No smoking in 16 bedrooms s £47-£62; d £94 (incl. bkfst) * **LB FACILITIES:** STV Indoor swimming (H) Tennis (hard) Sauna Solarium Gym Croquet lawn Jacuzzi Heli-pad Xmas **CONF:** Thtr 299 Class 150 Board 30 **PARKING:** 350 **NOTES:** No smoking in restaurant Civ Wed 75
**CARDS:** 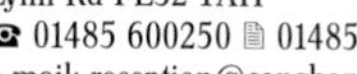

Early start? Hotels at all star levels should provide in-room alarm clocks and/or alarm calls.

KING'S LYNN, continued

### ★★★66% Butterfly
Beveridge Way, Hardwick Narrows PE30 4NB
☎ 01553 771707 📠 01553 768027
e-mail: kingsbutterfly@lineone.net
***Dir:*** *situated on A10/A47 roundabout, exit for Hardwick Narrows Industrial Estate*
This popular modern hotel is ideal for business travellers. A variety of well-equipped bedroom types is available; ladies', studio and ground floor rooms are all provided. The lounge areas and Walt's Restaurant and Bar are both popular venues.
**ROOMS:** 50 en suite (2 fmly) No smoking in 10 bedrooms d £75 * **LB** **FACILITIES:** STV **CONF:** Thtr 40 Class 21 Board 22 Del £97.50 * **PARKING:** 70 **NOTES:** No dogs (ex guide dogs) No smoking in restaurant **CARDS:**

### ★★★64% The Duke's Head
REGAL
Tuesday Market Place PE30 1JS
☎ 01553 774996 📠 01553 763556
e-mail: dukeshead@corushotels.com
***Dir:*** *in town centre one-way system go left when road splits then left at lights, along St Anns St into Chapel St, hotel just past carpark on right*

A 16th-century coaching inn, overlooking the Tuesday Market Place. Bedrooms are soundly furnished and well-equipped. Public areas include a spacious lounge, a non-smoking lounge bar and a public bar. A choice of dining options is available: informal dining in Griffins restaurant, and a more formal menu in the main restaurant.
**ROOMS:** 71 en suite (2 fmly) No smoking in 33 bedrooms s £80-£100; d £98-£118 * **LB** **FACILITIES:** Xmas **CONF:** Thtr 240 Class 120 Board 60 Del from £67 * **SERVICES:** Lift **PARKING:** 41 **NOTES:** No smoking in restaurant Civ Wed 100 **CARDS:**

### ★★67% Russet House
53 Goodwins Rd PE30 5PE
☎ 01553 773098 📠 01553 773098
e-mail: russethouse@freenet.co.uk
***Dir:*** *follow town centre signs along Hardwick Rd at small rdbt just before Southgates turn right into Vancouver Av after short drive hotel on left*
Russet House dates back to 1890, and is just a short walk from the River Ouse and King's Lynn town centre. Bedrooms are neatly decorated and have a bright airy feel. The public rooms feature a lounge with open fire and French windows which open onto the gardens.
**ROOMS:** 13 en suite (2 fmly) No smoking in 1 bedroom s fr £38; d fr £48 (incl. bkfst) * **LB** **PARKING:** 20 **NOTES:** No smoking in restaurant **CARDS:**

*See advert on opposite page*

### ★★67% Stuart House
35 Goodwins Rd PE30 5QX
☎ 01553 772169 📠 01553 774788
e-mail: stuarthousehotel@btinternet.com
***Dir:*** *At A47/A10/A149 rdbt follow signs for King's Lynn Town Centre. Pass under the Southgate Arch right into Guanock Ter. Right Goodwins Rd*

In a quiet area close to the town, this comfortable hotel offers informal public rooms. Guests may choose between meals in the popular bar, or the carte menu and daily specials on offer in the elegant restaurant. The accommodation comes in a variety of sizes and is attractively appointed.
**ROOMS:** 18 en suite (2 fmly) No smoking in 4 bedrooms s £50-£70; d £70-£90 * **LB** **FACILITIES:** STV Jacuzzi entertainment **CONF:** Thtr 50 Class 30 Board 20 Del from £70 * **PARKING:** 30 **NOTES:** No dogs (ex guide dogs) No smoking in restaurant RS 25/26 Dec 1 Jan
**CARDS:**

### ★★64% The Tudor Rose
St Nicholas St, Tuesday Market Place PE30 1LR
☎ 01553 762824 📠 01553 764894
e-mail: KLTudorRose@aol.com
***Dir:*** *Hotel is off Tuesday Market Place in the centre of King's Lynn*
A Grade II listed building dating back to before the 14th century. There are exposed beams in the restaurant, and the entire hotel has a pleasant atmosphere. Public rooms include a small reception lounge and two bars, where real ales and informal fare are served. Bedroom styles and sizes vary and each room is well-equipped.
**ROOMS:** 13 rms (11 en suite) s fr £39; d fr £50 (incl. bkfst) * **LB** **NOTES:** No smoking in restaurant **CARDS:**

### ★★63% *Grange*
Willow Park, South Wootton Ln PE30 3BP
☎ 01553 673777 & 671222 📠 01553 673777
e-mail: grange@btinternet.com
***Dir:*** *take A148 towards King's Lynn for 1.5m at traffic lights turn left into Wootton Rd 400yds on right South Wootton Ln hotel 1st on left*
This imposing yet welcoming Edwardian house sits in a quiet residential area, surrounded by its own gardens. Most of the bedrooms are in the main house, with some in an adjacent courtyard-style wing. All the accommodation is comfortably appointed.
**ROOMS:** 5 en suite 4 annexe en suite (2 fmly) **CONF:** Thtr 20 Class 15 Board 12 **PARKING:** 15 **NOTES:** No smoking in restaurant
**CARDS:**

TV dinner? Room service at three stars and above.

KINGSTON UPON THAMES, Greater London
See LONDON SECTION plan 1 C1

### ★★★70% Kingston Lodge

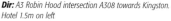

Kingston Hill KT2 7NP
☎ 0870 400 8115 📠 020 8547 1013
***Dir:*** *A3 Robin Hood intersection A308 towards Kingston. Hotel 1.5m on left*
This friendly and popular hotel commands a quiet location just on the edge of Kingston. Bedrooms are spacious and attractively furnished, with many thoughtful facilities as standard. Public rooms are inviting and the Burnt Orange brasserie provides a modern style of eating in an informal atmosphere.
**ROOMS:** 63 en suite No smoking in 38 bedrooms d £150-£180 * LB
**CONF:** Thtr 70 Class 30 Board 26 Del £175 * **PARKING:** 70
**CARDS:**

### ○ *Travelodge Kingston-upon-Thames*

Travelodge

☎ 0800 850950
**NOTES:** Opening Winter 2001

KINGTON, Herefordshire — Map 03 SO25

### ★★67% *Burton*

Mill St HR5 3BQ
☎ 01544 230323 📠 01544 230323
e-mail: burton@hotelkington.kc31td.co.uk
***Dir:*** *at rdbt of A44/A411 interchange take road signed town centre*
This friendly, privately-owned hotel, located in the town centre, offers spacious and well-equipped bedrooms. Facilities include a lounge bar, a small lounge and a pleasant restaurant. There is also a meeting room and a large ballroom.
**ROOMS:** 16 en suite (5 fmly) **CONF:** Thtr 150 Class 100 Board 20
**PARKING:** 50 **CARDS:**

KIRKBURTON, West Yorkshire — Map 07 SE11

### ○ Innkeeper's Lodge Huddersfield

Innkeeper's Lodge

36a Penistone Rd, Kirkburton HD8 0PQ
A new concept in the travel accommodation market. Smart rooms meet essential business requirements but also have home comforts. Dining options include all-day menus plus the added advantage of breakfast, which is included in the room price. Reservations can be made seven days a week through the room reservations number: 0870 243 0500. For further details, consult the Hotel Groups page.
**ROOMS:** 23 en suite **NOTES:** Opening Autumn 2001

KIRKBY LONSDALE, Cumbria — Map 07 SD67

### ★★69% Pheasant Inn

LA6 2RX
☎ 015242 71230 📠 015242 71230
e-mail: pheasant.casterton@eggconnect.net
***Dir:*** *leave M6 junc36 onto A65, turn left at A683 1m onwards in centre of village*
A family run inn, located in the village of Casterton north of Kirkby Lonsdale. Public areas include a choice of cosy bars and a panelled restaurant, where a range of home-cooked fare is offered
*continued*

at competitive prices. Bedrooms are variable in size with both modern and traditional furnishings.

**ROOMS:** 11 en suite **PARKING:** 40 **NOTES:** No smoking in restaurant Closed 4-6 Jan **CARDS:**

### ★★59% Plough Hotel

Cow Brow LA6 1PJ
☎ 015395 67227 📠 015395 67848
***Dir:*** *turn off junc 36 M6, head for Skipton/Kirkby Lonsdale, 1m from M6*
An old roadside coaching inn which combines traditional values with many modern amenities. Bedrooms vary in size, but are comfortable, soundly furnished and suitably equipped. A wide range of food is available including snacks in the bar, a choice
*continued on p308*

KIRKBY LONSDALE, continued

from the restaurant menu and the daily-changing blackboard selections.

*Plough Hotel, Kirkby Lonsdale*

**ROOMS:** 12 en suite (2 fmly) **FACILITIES:** Fishing **CONF:** Thtr 100 Class 100 Board 60 Del from £35 * **PARKING:** 72
**CARDS:**

## *Premier Collection*

### ★ Hipping Hall

Cowan Bridge LA6 2JJ
☎ 015242 71187 🖷 015242 72452
e-mail: hippinghal@aol.com
***Dir:*** *0.5m E of Cowan Bridge on A65*

Enthusiastic new owners have made further improvements to this already comfortable 15th-century house. All of the bedrooms are spacious and attractively furnished. There are also two cottage suites, which have spiral staircases from the lounge to the bedroom. Public areas include an original 'great hall' and a cosy drawing room. There is a dining room adjacent to the drawing room. The service at Hipping Hall is very friendly and attentive.

**ROOMS:** 5 en suite 2 annexe en suite No smoking in 5 bedrooms s £74; d £92 (incl. bkfst) * **LB** **FACILITIES:** Croquet lawn Putting green **CONF:** Thtr 14 Class 14 Board 14 Del £125 * **PARKING:** 20 **NOTES:** No smoking in restaurant Closed Dec-Feb
**CARDS:**

KIRKBYMOORSIDE, North Yorkshire — Map 08 SE68

### ★★65% George & Dragon Hotel

17 Market Place YO62 6AA
☎ 01751 433334 🖷 01751 432933
***Dir:*** *off A170 between Thirsk/Scarborough, in centre of market town*

A popular 17th-century coaching inn located centrally within the town. The pub, with its blazing fire and sporting theme provides a cosy, welcoming atmosphere. A wide range of hearty dishes is offered from the carte and the blackboard. Spacious bedrooms are individually furnished and housed in two nearby wings.

**ROOMS:** 11 en suite 7 annexe en suite (2 fmly) s £49; d fr £79 (incl. bkfst) * **LB** **FACILITIES:** Gym ch fac Xmas **CONF:** Thtr 50 Class 20 Board 20 Del from £75 * **PARKING:** 20 **NOTES:** No smoking in restaurant **CARDS:**

KIRKHAM, Lancashire — Map 07 SD43

### ⌂ *Premier Lodge (Blackpool East)*

Fleetwood Rd, Greenhalgh PR4 3HE
☎ 0870 700 1510 🖷 0870 700 1511

Premier Lodge offers modern, well-equipped, en suite accommodation suitable for both business and leisure travellers. Meals can be taken at the adjacent popular restaurant and bar, which is fully licensed. For further details, consult the Hotel Groups page.

**ROOMS:** 28 en suite

KNARESBOROUGH, North Yorkshire — Map 08 SE35

### ★★★69% Dower House

Bond End HG5 9AL
☎ 01423 863302 🖷 01423 867665

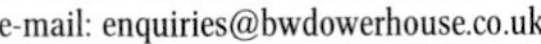

e-mail: enquiries@bwdowerhouse.co.uk

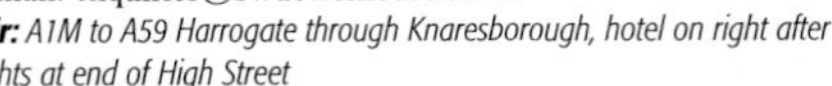

***Dir:*** *A1M to A59 Harrogate through Knaresborough, hotel on right after lights at end of High Street*

An attractive 15th-century house situated in pleasant gardens on the edge of the town. Bedrooms vary in size and style, but are well-equipped with expected extras. The Terrace Restaurant, open for lunch and dinner, overlooks the garden and has a relaxed and comfortable atmosphere. There are two main function rooms and a popular health and leisure club.

**ROOMS:** 28 en suite 3 annexe en suite (2 fmly) No smoking in 20 bedrooms s £76-£94; d £84-£105 (incl. bkfst) **LB** **FACILITIES:** Spa Indoor swimming (H) Sauna Gym Jacuzzi ch fac Xmas **CONF:** Thtr 65 Class 35 Board 40 Del £110 * **PARKING:** 80 **NOTES:** No smoking in restaurant **CARDS:**

### ★★★66% General Tarleton Inn

Boroughbridge Rd, Ferrensby HG5 0QB
☎ 01423 340284 🖷 01423 340288
e-mail: gti@generaltarleton.co.uk
***Dir:*** *on A6055, on crossroad in Ferrensby*

This hotel is renowned for its high standard of cooking, not only in its formal restaurant but also in its bars in which a wide range of dishes is available. Once an 18th-century coaching inn, 14 modern bedrooms are housed in a sympathetic extension and a covered courtyard has been added.

**ROOMS:** 14 en suite s £75; d £85 (incl. bkfst) * **LB** **FACILITIES:** Xmas **CONF:** Thtr 60 Class 35 Board 28 Del from £125 * **PARKING:** 80 **NOTES:** No smoking in restaurant Closed 25 Dec only
**CARDS:**

### ○ Innkeeper's Lodge Harrogate East

Wetherby Rd, Plompton HG5 8LY

A new concept in the travel accommodation market. Smart rooms meet essential business requirements but also have home comforts. Dining options include all-day menus plus the added advantage of breakfast, which is included in the room price. Reservations can be made seven days a week through the room reservations number: 0870 243 0500. For further details, consult the Hotel Groups page.

**ROOMS:** 11 en suite **NOTES:** Open now

## KNOWLE, West Midlands

### ○ Innkeeper's Lodge Knowle

Warwick Rd, Knowle B93 0EE

A new concept in the travel accommodation market. Smart rooms meet essential business requirements but also have home comforts. Dining options include all-day menus plus the added advantage of breakfast, which is included in the room price. Reservations can be made seven days a week through the room reservations number: 0870 243 0500. For further details, consult the Hotel Groups page.

**ROOMS:** 13 en suite **NOTES:** Opening Autumn 2001

## KNUTSFORD, Cheshire

Map 07 SJ77

### ★★★★69% Mere Court Hotel & Conference Centre

Warrington Rd, Mere WA16 0RW

☎ 01565 831000 01565 831001

e-mail: sales@merecourt.co.uk

Conveniently located and set in its own well-tended grounds, Mere Court combines a high standard of accommodation with extensive

continued

conference facilities. Bedrooms are especially impressive both in terms of high quality decoration and excellent facilities.

**ROOMS:** 34 en suite (24 fmly) No smoking in 5 bedrooms s £75-£115; d £85-£135 * **FACILITIES:** STV Croquet lawn Jacuzzi **CONF:** Thtr 100 Class 60 Board 35 **SERVICES:** Lift **PARKING:** 150 **NOTES:** No smoking in restaurant Civ Wed 80 **CARDS:**

*See advert on this page*

### ★★★★67% Cottons

SHIRE INNS

Manchester Rd WA16 0SU

☎ 01565 650333 01565 755351

e-mail: cottons@shireinns.co.uk

***Dir:*** *on A50 1m from junct 19 of M6*

Super leisure facilities and a quiet location are an attraction for all types of business at this hotel just a short distance from Manchester Airport. Bedrooms are smartly appointed in a number of styles, executive rooms having very good working areas.

**ROOMS:** 99 en suite (4 fmly) No smoking in 44 bedrooms s £125; d £145 (incl. bkfst) * **LB** **FACILITIES:** STV Indoor swimming (H) Tennis (hard) Squash Sauna Solarium Gym Jacuzzi Xmas **CONF:** Thtr 200 Class 120 Board 30 Del £155 * **SERVICES:** Lift **PARKING:** 180 **NOTES:** Civ Wed **CARDS:**

### ★★74% The Longview Hotel & Restaurant

55 Manchester Rd WA16 0LX

☎ 01565 632119 01565 652402

e-mail: enquiries@longviewhotel.com

***Dir:*** *from M6 junct 19 take A556 W towards Chester. Left at lights onto A5033 1.5m to rdbt then left. Hotel 200yds on right*

A friendly Victorian hotel with high standards of service. Attractive public areas include a cellar bar and foyer lounge. The restaurant

*continued on p310*

KNUTSFORD, continued

has a Victorian feel and offers an imaginative selection of dishes. Bedrooms offer a great range of thoughtful amenities.

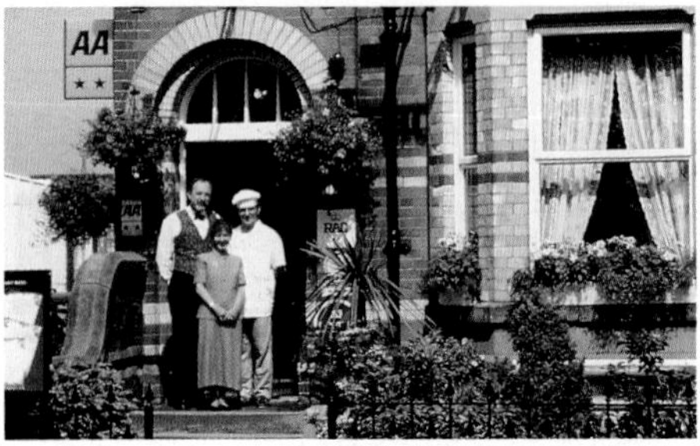

*The Longview Hotel & Restaurant, Knutsford*

**ROOMS:** 13 en suite 13 annexe en suite (1 fmly) s £70-£100; d £83-£135 (incl. bkfst) **LB** **FACILITIES:** Free use of local fitness club ch fac **PARKING:** 29 **NOTES:** No smoking in restaurant Closed 24 Dec-8 Jan
**CARDS:**

### ⇧ Premier Lodge (Knutsford North West)

PREMIER LODGE
THE BEST. BEST ASSURED.

Warrington Rd, Hoo Green, Mere WA16 0PZ
☎ 0870 700 1482 🖷 0870 700 1483
***Dir:*** *Turn onto A556 off M6 junct 19. Left at traffic lights onto A50. Hotel 1m on right*
Premier Lodge offers modern, well-equipped, en suite accommodation suitable for both business and leisure travellers. Meals can be taken at the adjacent popular restaurant and bar, which is fully licensed. For further details, consult the Hotel Groups page.
**ROOMS:** 28 en suite d £46 *

### ⇧ *Travelodge*

Travelodge

Chester Rd, Tabley WA16 0PP
☎ 01565 652187 🖷 01565 652187
***Dir:*** *on A556, northbound just E of junct 19 on M6*
Travelodge offers good quality, good value, modern accommodation. Ideal for families, the spacious, en suite bedrooms include remote-control TV, tea and coffee-making facilities, luxury beds and free morning newspaper. Meals can be taken at the nearby family restaurant. For further details and the Travelodge phone number, consult the Hotel Groups page.

**ROOMS:** 32 en suite

---

## LANCASTER, Lancashire

Map 07 SD46

see also Hampson Green

### ★★★★67% Lancaster House

Best Western

Green Ln, Ellel LA1 4GJ
☎ 01524 844822 🖷 01524 844766
e-mail: lancaster@elhmail.co.uk
***Dir:*** *M6 junct 33 N towards Lancaster. Through Galgate village, into Green Lane. Hotel just before University entrance on right*
This modern hotel has a peaceful, rural setting. The attractive, open plan, balconied reception and lounge, has flagstone floors and a real fire. Bedrooms are spacious and particularly well-equipped for business guests. The excellent business and leisure facilities make this hotel a popular conference venue.
**ROOMS:** 80 en suite (10 fmly) No smoking in 16 bedrooms d £77-£129 * **LB** **FACILITIES:** STV Indoor swimming (H) Sauna Gym Jacuzzi Activity centre 1 mile ch fac Xmas **CONF:** Thtr 120 Class 50 Board 48 Del from £119 * **PARKING:** 100 **NOTES:** No smoking in restaurant
**CARDS:**

### ★★★68% Menzies Royal Kings Arms

MENZIES HOTELS

Market St LA1 1HP
☎ 0870 6003013 🖷 01332 511144
e-mail: info@menzies-hotels.co.uk
***Dir:*** *follow 'City Centre' signs from M6, then 'Castle & Railway Station', turn off before traffic lights next to Waterstones bookshop*
This traditional, city-centre hotel is well located close to the castle and other local attractions and is staffed by a friendly team. The hotel has kept many of its 19th-century features, including the galleried restaurant. Bedrooms come in a variety of styles, and all have modern facilities.
**ROOMS:** 55 en suite (2 fmly) No smoking in 15 bedrooms s £70; d £80 * **LB** **FACILITIES:** STV entertainment Xmas **CONF:** Thtr 100 Class 50 Board 60 Del from £95 * **SERVICES:** Lift **PARKING:** 20 **NOTES:** No smoking in restaurant Civ Wed 100
**CARDS:**

### ★★★67% Posthouse Lancaster

Posthouse

Waterside Park, Caton Rd LA1 3RA
☎ 0870 400 9047 🖷 01524 841265
***Dir:*** *take junct 34 off M6, turn towards Lancaster, hotel first on right*
This modern hotel is conveniently located only minutes from the M6. Bedrooms vary in style and include stylish, thoughtfully equipped, superior rooms as well as rooms suitable for families. Smart leisure facilities and extensive meeting rooms make this a busy, popular hotel.
**ROOMS:** 157 en suite (82 fmly) No smoking in 73 bedrooms d fr £75 * **LB** **FACILITIES:** STV Indoor swimming (H) Sauna Gym Jacuzzi Health & fitness centre Xmas **CONF:** Thtr 120 Class 60 Board 60 Del from £100 * **SERVICES:** Lift **PARKING:** 300
**CARDS:**

### ★★63% Hampson House

Hampson Ln LA2 0JB
☎ 01524 751158 🖷 01524 751779
e-mail: info@hampsonhousehotellancaster.com
(For full entry see Hampson Green)

### ★★61% Scarthwaite Country House

Crook O Lune, Caton LA2 9HR
☎ 01524 770267 🖷 01524 770711
***Dir:*** *leave M6 at junct 34 onto A683 towards Caton, hotel 1.5m on right*
An early Victorian country house situated in the attractive Lune Valley and close to junction 34 of the M6 motorway. Facilities include comfortably appointed bedrooms, a small guests' lounge, a traditional bar and small dining room in which brasserie style meals can be enjoyed. Weddings are a speciality. Staff throughout are helpful and friendly.
**ROOMS:** 7 en suite (1 fmly) No smoking in 2 bedrooms s £40; d £58 (incl. bkfst) * **LB** **CONF:** Thtr 180 Class 110 Board 80 **PARKING:** 65 **NOTES:** No dogs (ex guide dogs) **CARDS:**

---

## LAND'S END, Cornwall & Isles of Scilly

Map 02 SW32

see also Sennen

### ★★★65% The Land's End Hotel

TR19 7AA
☎ 01736 871844 🖷 01736 871599
e-mail: info@landsend-landmark.co.uk
***Dir:*** *from Penzance follow A30 & signs to Land's End. After Sennen continue for 1m to Land's End*
With its famous clifftop location the hotel commands views across the Atlantic and over to the Longships lighthouse. The recently opened Longships Restaurant and Bar uses fresh local produce

*continued*

and fish dishes are a speciality. All bedrooms are comfortably furnished with modern facilities.

**ROOMS:** 33 en suite (2 fmly) s £54-£80; d £88-£140 (incl. bkfst) * **LB** **FACILITIES:** Free entry Lands End visitor centre entertainment ch fac Xmas **CONF:** Thtr 200 Class 100 Board 50 Del from £60 * **PARKING:** 1000 **NOTES:** No smoking in restaurant Closed Nov-Feb Civ Wed 110 **CARDS:**

## LANGAR, Nottinghamshire — Map 08 SK73

### ★★★69% Langar Hall

NG13 9HG
☎ 01949 860559 📠 01949 861045
e-mail: langarhall-hotel@ndirect.co.uk
***Dir:*** *accessible via Bingham on the A52 or Cropwell Bishop from the A46, both signposted, the house adjoins the church and is hidden behind it*

A country house hotel, where the majority of bedrooms have fine antique furniture, paintings and quality soft furnishings. Drinks are served in an elegant lounge, and excellent meals are available in the pillared hall dining room. There are also two private dining rooms leading out onto the garden.

**ROOMS:** 12 en suite (1 fmly) No smoking in all bedrooms s £75-£98; d £100-£185 (incl. bkfst) **LB** **FACILITIES:** Fishing Croquet lawn ch fac **CONF:** Thtr 20 Class 20 Board 20 Del from £155 * **PARKING:** 20 **NOTES:** No smoking in restaurant Civ Wed 40 **CARDS:**

## LANGHO, Lancashire — Map 07 SD73

### ★★★70% Northcote Manor

Northcote Rd BB6 8BE
☎ 01254 240555 📠 01254 246568
e-mail: admin@northcotemanor.com
***Dir:*** *M6 junct 31, 8m to Northcote, follow signs to Clitheroe, Hotel is set back on the left just before the rdbt*

Northcote Manor is full of character and provides a very comfortable environment in which to sample the delights of its famous restaurant. Excellent cooking includes much of Lancashire's finest fare. Drinks can be enjoyed in the comfortable, elegantly furnished lounges and bar. Bedrooms have been individually furnished and thoughtfully equipped.

**ROOMS:** 14 en suite s £100-£110; d £130-£150 (incl. bkfst) * **LB** **FACILITIES:** STV Croquet lawn Xmas **CONF:** Thtr 40 Class 20 Board 26 **PARKING:** 50 **NOTES:** No dogs (ex guide dogs) No smoking in restaurant Closed Xmas day, New year day & most BH Civ Wed 40 **CARDS:**

Early start? Hotels at all star levels should provide in-room alarm clocks and/or alarm calls.

## LANGTOFT, East Riding of Yorkshire — Map 08 TA06

### ★★70% Old Mill Hotel & Restaurant

MINOTEL Great Britain

Mill Ln YO25 3BQ
☎ 01377 267383 📠 01377 267383
***Dir:*** *6m N of Driffield, on B1249, through village of Langtoft on B1249 approx 1m N, turn left at hotel sign, hotel straight ahead*

Standing in open countryside, this modern hotel has been very well-furnished throughout. It provides thoughtfully equipped bedrooms, and a popular bar-lounge where a good range of well produced food is available. There is also a charming restaurant.

**ROOMS:** 9 en suite (1 fmly) s £46-£54; d £56-£64 (incl. bkfst) * **LB** **CONF:** Thtr 40 Class 20 Board 20 Del from £80 * **PARKING:** 30 **NOTES:** No dogs (ex guide dogs) No children 12yrs No smoking in restaurant **CARDS:**

## LASTINGHAM, North Yorkshire — Map 08 SE79

### ★★★72% *Lastingham Grange*

YO62 6TH
☎ 01751 417345 & 417402 📠 01751 417358
e-mail: lastinghamgrange@aol.com
***Dir:*** *2m E on A170 towards Scarborough, onto Lastingham, in village turn left uphill towards Moors. Hotel can be found on right*

This charming hotel dating from the 17th century remains a very popular place to stay. Fine antiques are displayed, both in the attractively decorated bedrooms, and in the public areas. Quality home cooking is offered and there is a welcoming lounge. The colourful grounds feature a sunken rose garden.

**ROOMS:** 12 en suite (2 fmly) **FACILITIES:** Large adventure playground ch fac **PARKING:** 32 **NOTES:** No smoking in restaurant Closed Dec-Feb

## LAUNCESTON, Cornwall & Isles of Scilly — Map 02 SX38

see also Lifton

### ★★75% *Penhallow Manor Country House*

THE INDEPENDENTS

PL15 7SJ
☎ 01566 86206 📠 01566 86179
e-mail: penhallow@ukonline.co.uk
(For full entry see Altarnun)

### ★★64% *Eagle House*

Castle St PL15 8BA
☎ 01566 772036 📠 01566 772036

Next to the castle, this elegant Georgian house dating back to 1767 is within walking distance of all local amenities. Many of the bedrooms have views over the Cornish countryside. A fixed-price menu is served in the restaurant, and on Sunday evenings a more modest menu is available.

**ROOMS:** 14 en suite (1 fmly) **FACILITIES:** STV **CONF:** Thtr 190 Class 190 Board 190 **PARKING:** 100 **NOTES:** No dogs (ex guide dogs) **CARDS:**

LAVENHAM, Suffolk Map 05 TL94

**★★★★66% The Swan**
High St CO10 9QA
☎ 0870 400 8116 01787 248286
e-mail: HeritageHotels_Lavenham.Swan@forte-hotels.com
***Dir:*** *in centre of village on A134 Bury St Edmunds/Hadleigh*
The Swan has been impressively upgraded whilst retaining much of its original character. Bedrooms have been furnished to a high standard and feature thoughtful touches such as CD players and mini bars. Public areas offer open fire places and a choice of bars. Guests can enjoy modern cooking in the beamed restaurant.
**ROOMS:** 51 en suite No smoking in 15 bedrooms s £95-£125; d £105-£175 * **LB** **FACILITIES:** STV entertainment Xmas **CONF:** Thtr 40 Class 20 Board 20 Del from £140 * **PARKING:** 60 **NOTES:** No smoking in restaurant RS Xmas Civ Wed 40 **CARDS:**

**★★68% Angel**
Market Place CO10 9QZ
☎ 01787 247388 01787 248344
e-mail: angellav@aol.com
***Dir:*** *from A14 take Bury East/Sudbury turn off A143, after 4m take A1141 to Lavenham, Angel is off the High Street*
A 15th-century inn in the town centre. Well known for its cuisine, it offers an imaginative menu based on fresh ingredients. Each bedroom is individually furnished, attractively decorated and equipped with many useful extras. The spacious first floor lounge has a magnificent ceiling.
**ROOMS:** 8 en suite (1 fmly) s fr £45; d fr £70 (incl. bkfst) * **LB**
**FACILITIES:** Use of Lavenham Tennis Club facilities entertainment ch fac
**PARKING:** 5 **NOTES:** Closed 25-26 Dec
**CARDS:**

LEA MARSTON, Warwickshire Map 04 SP29

**★★★72% Lea Marston Hotel & Leisure Complex**
Haunch Ln B76 0BY
☎ 01675 470468 01675 470871
e-mail: leamarstonhotel@btinternet.com
***Dir:*** *leave M42 at junct 9 and take A4097 towards Kingsbury. Hotel signposted 1.5m on right*

Conveniently positioned for Birmingham, this hotel is not only popular with the leisure market but also with conference delegates. Bedrooms are comfortable and have excellent facilities. A good range of bars, eating options, function rooms, a business centre, leisure complex, golf course and secure car park are additional features.
**ROOMS:** 83 en suite No smoking in 26 bedrooms s £110; d £130 (incl. bkfst) * **LB** **FACILITIES:** STV Indoor swimming (H) Golf 9 Tennis (hard) Sauna Solarium Gym Croquet lawn Putting green Jacuzzi Golf driving range Beauty Salon entertainment ch fac Xmas **CONF:** Thtr 120 Class 50 Board 18 Del £149.50 * **SERVICES:** Lift **PARKING:** 220
**NOTES:** No dogs (ex guide dogs) No smoking in restaurant
**CARDS:**

*See advert on opposite page*

LEAMINGTON SPA (ROYAL), Warwickshire Map 04 SP36

## *Premier Collection*

**★★★ Mallory Court**
Harbury Ln, Bishop's Tachbrook CV33 9QB
☎ 01926 330214 01926 451714
e-mail: reception@mallory.co.uk
***Dir:*** *2m S off B4087 towards Harbury*
Tranquillity and elegance best describe this English country house set amidst ten acres of beautifully landscaped gardens and grounds. Most of the tastefully appointed, spacious bedrooms enjoy magnificent views over the gardens, and each one is individually styled. Public areas include two elegant and comfortable lounges, a drawing room, conservatory, private dining room and an impressive panelled restaurant serving contemporary European dishes. All of the staff combine friendly warmth with seamless service.
**ROOMS:** 18 en suite (1 fmly) s £175-£275; d £185-£320 (incl. cont bkfst) * **LB** **FACILITIES:** STV Outdoor swimming Tennis (hard) Croquet lawn Xmas **CONF:** Thtr 20 Board 20 Del from £205.62 *
**PARKING:** 52 **NOTES:** No children 9yrs Civ Wed 22
**CARDS:**

**★★★69% Courtyard by Marriott Leamington Spa**
Olympus Av, Tachbrook Park CV34 6RJ
☎ 01926 425522 01926 881322
***Dir:*** *From town centre follow signs for M40/A452(Tachbrook Park)at rdbt go straight on into Europa Way, turn left to Olympus Ave*
This modern hotel, situated on the edge of the town, is well located for nearby Stratford and Warwick. Bedrooms are attractively decorated, with guest comfort a priority. Public areas,

*continued*

though compact, are bright and modern. Function and meeting rooms are smart and well equipped.

**ROOMS:** 91 en suite (14 fmly) No smoking in 48 bedrooms s fr £89; d fr £99 (incl. bkfst) * **LB** **FACILITIES:** STV Gym Xmas **CONF:** Thtr 70 Class 35 Board 30 Del from £110 * **SERVICES:** Lift **PARKING:** 150 **CARDS:**

### ★★★67% Falstaff

16-20 Warwick New Rd CV32 5JQ
☎ 01926 312044 📠 01926 450574
e-mail: falstaff@meridianleisure.com
***Dir:*** *from M40 junct 13/14 follow signs for Leamington Spa over 4 rdbts then under bridge. Left into Princes Drive, then right at mini-rdbt*

The bedrooms at the Falstaff Hotel come in a variety of sizes and styles, and are all well-equipped. An interesting range of dishes, both English and continental, are offered in the smartly appointed lounge bar and restaurant. There are also extensive conference and banqueting facilities available. Bedrooms include many thoughtful extras such as trouser presses as well as 24 hour room service.

**ROOMS:** 63 en suite (2 fmly) No smoking in 12 bedrooms s £50-£70; d £60-£80 (incl. bkfst) * **LB** **FACILITIES:** STV Arrangement with local Health Club Xmas **CONF:** Thtr 60 Class 40 Board 32 Del from £95 * **PARKING:** 50 **NOTES:** No smoking in restaurant Civ Wed 46 **CARDS:**

*See advert on this page*

### ★★★65% The Leamington Hotel & Bistro

64 Upper Holly Walk CV32 4JL
☎ 01926 883777 📠 01926 330467
e-mail: leamington@bestwestern.co.uk
***Dir:*** *exit M40 junct 13 take Leamington Spa road A452*

Public rooms at The Leamington Hotel include a welcoming residents' lounge with a high ceiling and ornate plasterwork. The modern bistro-style menu combines traditional English and French

*continued on p314*

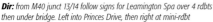

LEAMINGTON SPA, continued

cuisine with a modern twist. Bedrooms are generally spacious, each with a range of thoughtful extras and modern facilities.
**ROOMS:** 30 en suite (6 fmly) No smoking in 4 bedrooms s £70-£80; d £80-£90 (incl. cont bkfst) * **LB** **FACILITIES:** Xmas **CONF:** Thtr 45 Class 32 Board 24 **PARKING:** 22 **NOTES:** No dogs (ex guide dogs) Civ Wed 40 **CARDS:**

### ★★★63% Angel
143 Regent St CV32 4NZ
☎ 01926 881296 📠 01926 881296
e-mail: angelhotel143@hotmail.com
***Dir:*** *in the town centre at junct of Regent Street and Holly Walk*
This well-established hotel comes in two parts - the original inn and a modern extension. Public rooms include a comfortable foyer lounge area, a smart restaurant and an informal bar. Bedrooms are individual in style, and, whether modern or traditional, have all the expected facilities.
**ROOMS:** 50 en suite (3 fmly) s £45-£65; d £60-£75 (incl. bkfst) * **LB** **FACILITIES:** STV Xmas **CONF:** Thtr 70 Class 40 Board 40 Del from £75 * **SERVICES:** Lift **PARKING:** 38 **NOTES:** No smoking in restaurant
**CARDS:**

### ★★★58% Manor House
REGAL
Avenue Rd CV31 3NJ
☎ 01926 423251 📠 01926 425933
***Dir:*** *from M40 follow signs for A452. At rdbt take 3rd exit for Leamington. Follow signs for station. Hotel directly behind station*

Near the town centre, this Victorian hotel offers well-equipped bedrooms which vary in style and size, some benefiting from refurbishment. The spacious lounge and bar and the light and airy restaurant all add to the character of the building. Service is friendly and welcoming.
**ROOMS:** 53 en suite (2 fmly) No smoking in 19 bedrooms s £65-£85; d £75-£100 * **LB** **FACILITIES:** Reduced price at nearby leisure club Xmas **CONF:** Thtr 200 Class 60 Board 50 Del from £95 * **SERVICES:** Lift **PARKING:** 70 **NOTES:** No smoking in restaurant Civ Wed 96
**CARDS:**

### ★★73% ® Lansdowne
THE CIRCLE Selected Individual Hotels GREAT BRITAIN
87 Clarendon St CV32 4PF
☎ 01926 450505 📠 01926 421313
***Dir:*** *town centre at junct of Clarendon St & Warwick St*
The Landsdowne Hotel is a traditional Georgian house, from the china-laden entrance hall to each of the individually styled bedrooms. Attic rooms occupy the best space under the eaves and are full of character. The restaurant, while small, offers food which packs a punch, and good quality ingredients combine with talent to provide delicious meals.
**ROOMS:** 14 en suite (2 fmly) s £44.95-£54.95; d £58-£68 (incl. bkfst) * **LB** **PARKING:** 11 **NOTES:** No dogs (ex guide dogs) No children 5yrs No smoking in restaurant RS 26 Dec-2 Jan
**CARDS:**

### ★★70% Adams
22 Avenue Rd CV31 3PQ
☎ 01926 450742 📠 01926 313110
***Dir:*** *situated near Library on A452*
Adams Hotel is a converted Regency house just south of the town centre and close to the railway station. It is welcoming and family-run with relaxing public areas, including a lounge with comfortable leather chairs and a residents bar. Home cooked fare is served in the adjacent elegant dining room. Bedrooms are tastefully furnished and offer a good range of accessories.
**ROOMS:** 12 en suite s £52-£70; d £64-£76 (incl. bkfst) * **CONF:** Thtr 20 Class 14 Board 12 Del from £95 * **PARKING:** 14 **NOTES:** No dogs No smoking in restaurant **CARDS:**

## LEATHERHEAD, Surrey — Map 04 TQ15

### ★★62% Bookham Grange
Little Bookham Common, Bookham KT23 3HS
☎ 01372 452742 📠 01372 450080
e-mail: bookhamgrange@easynet.co.uk
***Dir:*** *off A246 at Bookham High Street, carry on into Church Road, take first turning right after Bookham railway station*
Quietly situated in 2.5 acres, this family-run hotel has the style of an English country house. As well as two function and meeting rooms, there is a beamed bar, central sitting area and restaurant. The bedrooms are well-equipped.
**ROOMS:** 27 en suite (5 fmly) s £75-£80; d £85-£90 (incl. bkfst) * **LB** **FACILITIES:** Xmas **CONF:** Thtr 80 Class 24 Board 24 Del from £117 * **PARKING:** 100 **NOTES:** No smoking in restaurant Civ Wed 100
**CARDS:**

## LEDBURY, Herefordshire — Map 03 SO73

### ★★★72% ® Feathers
High St HR8 1DS
☎ 01531 635266 📠 01531 638955
e-mail: mary@feathers-ledbury.co.uk
***Dir:*** *S from Worcester A449, E from HerefordA438, N from Gloucester A417, hotel is situated in the High Street*

Standing in the centre of town, this timber-framed coaching inn has a wealth of charm and character. There is a comfortable lounge and 'Fuggles' bar/bistro, where a range of soundly prepared dishes is available. Facilities include a leisure centre and a function suite. The bedrooms are individually styled and well-equipped.
**ROOMS:** 19 en suite (2 fmly) No smoking in 2 bedrooms s £72-£80; d £95-£135 (incl. bkfst) * **LB** **FACILITIES:** STV Indoor swimming (H) Solarium Gym Jacuzzi Steam room Xmas **CONF:** Thtr 140 Class 80 Board 40 Del £130 * **PARKING:** 30 **NOTES:** Civ Wed 90
**CARDS:**

*See advert on opposite page*

**★★68% The Verzons Country Inn & Restaurant**
Hereford Rd, Trumpet HR8 2PZ
☎ 01531 670381 🖷 01531 670830
***Dir:*** *2m W of Ledbury A438*
This large country house dates back to 1790, and stands in extensive gardens near Ledbury. It changed hands at the beginning of 2001 and at the time of our last inspection, the new owners had made many improvements. Bedrooms are well-equipped, and some have views of the Malvern Hills. A family room and a room with a four-poster bed are both available. Facilities here include a room for functions and meetings.
**ROOMS:** 8 en suite (1 fmly) s £49-£59; d £68-£78 (incl. bkfst) * **LB** **FACILITIES:** STV ch fac Xmas **CONF:** Thtr 50 Class 25 Board 20 Del from £84 * **PARKING:** 60 **NOTES:** No dogs (ex guide dogs)
**CARDS:**

LEEDS, West Yorkshire Map 08 SE33
see also Gomersal & Shipley

**★★★★★60% Oulton Hall**
Rothwell Ln, Oulton LS26 8HN
☎ 0113 282 1000 🖷 0113 282 8066
e-mail: oulton.hall@devere-hotels.com
***Dir:*** *2m from M62 junct 30/A639 on the left hand side, or 1m from M1 junct 44 then follow signs to Castleford/Pontefract A639*

This elegant 19th-century house is set in gardens and parkland, within easy reach of the city centre. The graceful public rooms in the original house include the impressive galleried Great Hall, to which meeting and leisure facilities have been added. A well-rounded hotel, which proves popular with both business and leisure guests.
**ROOMS:** 152 en suite No smoking in 128 bedrooms s fr £140; d fr £160 (incl. bkfst) * **LB** **FACILITIES:** STV Indoor swimming (H) Golf 27 Sauna Solarium Gym Croquet lawn Jacuzzi Beauty therapy Aerobics ch fac Xmas **CONF:** Thtr 350 Class 150 Board 40 Del from £145 * **SERVICES:** Lift **PARKING:** 260 **NOTES:** No smoking in restaurant
**CARDS:**

**★★★★70% Crowne Plaza Leeds**
Wellington St LS1 4DL
☎ 0113 244 2200 🖷 0113 244 0460
e-mail: riches.angela@hiw.com
***Dir:*** *from M1 follow signs to City Centre, at City Square left into Wellington Street*
Within easy distance of the motorway and city centre, this modern hotel is an ideal choice for the business traveller. Bedrooms are all well-proportioned with excellent facilities. Leisure facilities include a good sized pool and large gym; both are well worth a visit.
**ROOMS:** 135 en suite (38 fmly) No smoking in 90 bedrooms d £60-£175 * **LB** **FACILITIES:** STV Indoor swimming (H) Sauna Solarium Gym Jacuzzi Steam room Childrens playroom Xmas **CONF:** Thtr 200 Class 100 Board 60 Del from £140 * **SERVICES:** Lift air con **PARKING:** 125 **NOTES:** Civ Wed 150 **CARDS:**

**★★★★69% Le Meridien Queen's**
City Square LS1 1PL
☎ 0113 243 1323 & 0870 4008696
🖷 0113 242 5154
***Dir:*** *follow signs for City Centre, hotel adjacent to the railway station in City Square*
Standing in the heart of Leeds, this former railway hotel has retained much of its original splendour while benefiting from sympathetic and careful modernisation. Public rooms include the comfortable Palm Court Lounge, the elegant Harewood Restaurant, the Carvery Restaurant and the popular Piano Bar. Bedrooms are mostly spacious and well-furnished. A good variety of banqueting and meeting rooms are available.
**ROOMS:** 199 en suite No smoking in 72 bedrooms s £53-£125; d £86-£135 * **LB** **FACILITIES:** STV entertainment Xmas **CONF:** Thtr 600 Class 160 Board 40 Del from £90 * **SERVICES:** Lift **PARKING:** 88 **NOTES:** Civ Wed 400 **CARDS:**

**★★★★68% Leeds Marriott Hotel**
4 Trevelyan Square, Boar Ln LS1 6ET
☎ 0113 236 6366 🖷 0113 236 6367
***Dir:*** *From M621/M1 exit junct 3. Follow signs for centre (A653) staying in right hand lane. Energis building on left turn right to follow signs to Marriott hotel*
A large, modern hotel in a pedestrianised square in the city centre, offering mostly spacious bedrooms which are comfortably furnished and equipped. John T's restaurant provides a modern

Marriott
HOTELS·RESORTS·SUITES

*continued on p316*

LEEDS, continued

informal style menu; service is both attentive and friendly. A variety of smart function rooms and a leisure centre are also available.

*Leeds Marriott Hotel, Leeds*

**ROOMS:** 244 en suite (26 fmly) No smoking in 194 bedrooms d £117 * **LB** **FACILITIES:** STV Indoor swimming (H) Sauna Solarium Gym Jacuzzi Subsidised use of NCP car park Xmas **CONF:** Thtr 280 Class 120 Board 80 **SERVICES:** Lift air con **NOTES:** No dogs (ex guide dogs) Civ Wed 280 **CARDS:**

**★★★★57% Hotel Metropole**
King St LS1 2HQ
☎ 0113 245 0841 🖷 0113 242 5156
***Dir:*** *from M1/M62/M621 follow signs for City Centre. Take A65 Airport into Wellington St, at first traffic island turn right into King St, Hotel on right*

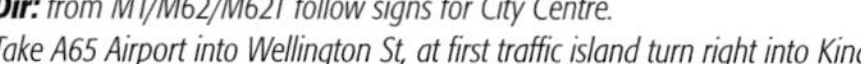

This splendid terracotta-fronted hotel stands in the heart of the city, close to the railway. The accommodation is well-equipped, spacious and stylish. Public areas include a very smart foyer and lounge. All of the staff at the Metropole are cheerful and helpful.
**ROOMS:** 118 en suite No smoking in 98 bedrooms s fr £105; d fr £125 * **LB** **FACILITIES:** STV **CONF:** Thtr 250 Class 100 Board 80 Del from £150 * **SERVICES:** Lift **PARKING:** 40 **NOTES:** No dogs (ex guide dogs) No smoking in restaurant RS 24 Dec-1 Jan Civ Wed 200 **CARDS:**

**★★★80% ◎◎ Haley's Hotel & Restaurant**
Shire Oak Rd, Headingley LS6 2DE
☎ 0113 278 4446 🖷 0113 275 3342
e-mail: info@haleys.co.uk
***Dir:*** *from city centre follow local signs to University on A660, 1.5m turn right in Headingley between HSBC and Yorkshire Banks*

Convenient for the cricket ground and the city centre, this conversion of Victorian houses is quietly situated, almost hidden away, in a tree lined cul-de-sac. Bedrooms, some situated in an adjacent Grade II listed property, are individually designed and, like the public rooms, offer good guest comfort. Service is both friendly and attentive, whilst dinner remains the highlight of any stay at this hotel.
**ROOMS:** 22 en suite 7 annexe en suite (3 fmly) No smoking in 10 bedrooms s £95-£110; d £125-£140 (incl. bkfst) * **LB** **FACILITIES:** STV **CONF:** Thtr 30 Class 20 Board 25 Del from £100 * **PARKING:** 25 **NOTES:** No dogs (ex guide dogs) No smoking in restaurant Closed 26-30 Dec RS Sun evening Civ Wed 85 **CARDS:**

*See advert on opposite page*

**★★★77% ◎◎ Hazlewood Castle**
Paradise Ln, Hazlewood LS24 9NJ
☎ 01937 535353 🖷 01937 530630
e-mail: info@hazlewood-castle.co.uk
(For full entry see Tadcaster)

**★★★73% Malmaison Hotel**
Sovereign Quay LS1 1DQ
☎ 0113 398 1000 🖷 0113 398 1002
e-mail: leeds@malmaison.com

***Dir:*** *follow signs for 'City Centre', turn into Sovereign Street, go past the KPMG office. Hotel is at end of street on right*
Close to the waterfront, this stylish property offers striking bedrooms with CD players and air conditioning. The bar leads into a brasserie, where guests can choose between a full three-course meal or a substantial snack. Service is both willing and friendly. A small fitness centre and impressive meeting rooms complete the package.
**ROOMS:** 100 en suite No smoking in 70 bedrooms s £89; d £115 * **LB** **FACILITIES:** STV Gym Xmas **CONF:** Thtr 40 Class 20 Board 28 Del £160 * **SERVICES:** Lift air con **NOTES:** No dogs (ex guide dogs) **CARDS:**

**★★★70% Milford Lodge Hotel**
A1 Great North Rd, Peckfield LS25 5LQ
☎ 01977 681800 🖷 01977 681245
e-mail: enquires@mlh.co.uk
(For full entry see Garforth)

**★★★68% The Merrion**
Merrion Centre LS2 8NH
☎ 0113 243 9191 🖷 0113 242 3527
e-mail: info@merrion-hotel-leeds.com

PEEL HOTELS

***Dir:*** *from the M1/M62/A61 join city loop road to junct 7, the Hotel is situated on Wade Lane adjoining the Merrion Centre*
In the heart of the city, this smart hotel is ideally located on the edge of the commercial and financial district. Leisure guests too have an ideal base from which to explore the countryside, or the city's shops and museums. Bedrooms are attractively decorated, well-designed and equipped with an excellent range of facilities.
**ROOMS:** 109 en suite No smoking in 76 bedrooms s fr £99; d fr £115 * **LB** **FACILITIES:** STV Xmas **CONF:** Thtr 80 Class 25 Board 25 Del £140 * **SERVICES:** Lift **CARDS:**

**★★★67% Golden Lion**
2 Lower Briggate LS1 4AE
☎ 0113 243 6454 🖷 0113 242 9327
e-mail: info@goldenlion-hotel-leeds.com
PEEL HOTELS
***Dir:*** *between junct 16 (Bridge End) and 17 (Sovereign Street). Hotel situated on junct of Lower Briggate & Swinegate*
This smartly presented Victorian hotel enjoys a central location within the city. Bedrooms have been refurbished and provide a wide range of modern facilities. Staff are friendly and helpful, ensuring a warm and informal welcome. Meeting and conference

*continued*

facilities are available and free overnight parking is provided in a 24-hour car park just a minute's walk from the hotel.
**ROOMS:** 89 en suite (5 fmly) No smoking in 46 bedrooms s £99-£110; d £109-£120 (incl. bkfst) * **LB** **FACILITIES:** STV Xmas **CONF:** Thtr 120 Class 65 Board 45 Del from £85 * **SERVICES:** Lift
**CARDS:**

**★★69% Aragon**
250 Stainbeck Ln LS7 2PS
☎ 0113 275 9306 📠 0113 275 7166
e-mail: aragon@onmail.co.uk
***Dir:*** *from A61 Harrogate follow from City Centre this turns into Scott Hall Road at 2nd rdbt turn left into Stainbeck Lane half mile on right*
This smart privately run hotel has a peaceful location in a leafy suburb of Leeds. Well-appointed bedrooms vary in style and many have been attractively refurbished and are particularly well co-ordinated. There is a comfortable lounge and small bar that overlook the carefully tended gardens. Home cooked meals as well as a good selection of bar snacks are available. This establishment is totally non-smoking throughout.
**ROOMS:** 12 en suite (2 fmly) No smoking in all bedrooms s fr £47; d £57-£64 (incl. bkfst) * **LB** **PARKING:** 20 **NOTES:** No dogs No smoking in restaurant Closed 25 Dec-1 Jan
**CARDS:**

## *Town House*

**★★★★ 42 The Calls**
LS2 7EW
☎ 0113 244 0099 📠 0113 234 4100
e-mail: hotel@42thecalls.co.uk
***Dir:*** *leave city centre loop road at junct 15 (The Calls). Hotel next to Calls Landing*
Located on the edge of the River Aire in a peaceful area of the city, this stylish hotel has been carefully converted from an old warehouse. Individually designed bedrooms range from a penthouse suite to the more compact studio rooms. All are particularly thoughtfully equipped with every convenience imaginable. Meals can be taken in one of two adjacent stylish restaurants, or alternatively there is a good room service menu.
**ROOMS:** 41 en suite No smoking in 6 bedrooms s £105-£275; d £138-£275 * **LB** **FACILITIES:** STV Fishing **CONF:** Thtr 70 Class 50 Board 40 Del from £193.50 * **SERVICES:** Lift **PARKING:** 28 **NOTES:** Closed Tba **CARDS:**

Arriving late? Four and five star hotels have night porters to assist with your luggage, and 24-hour room service.



**Express by Holiday Inn Leeds**
Cavendish St LS3 1LY
☎ 0113 242 6200 📠 0113 242 6300
e-mail: leeds@premierhotels.co.uk
***Dir:*** *M621 junct 2, take A643 towards city centre. At large rdbt take 3rd exit signposted A58(M). First left to A65 and turn left. Hotel on right*

Express by Holiday Inn

A modern budget hotel offering comfortable accommodation in refreshing, spacious and comprehensively equipped bedrooms, en suite bathrooms with power showers and continental buffet breakfast included in the room rate. Suitable for business travellers or families. For further details and the Express by Holiday Inn phone number, consult the Hotel Groups page.
**ROOMS:** 112 en suite (incl. bkfst) d £63 * **CONF:** Thtr 45 Class 20 Board 25

Weekend away? Hotels with LB in their entry offer leisure breaks.

L

LEEDS, continued

### ⇧ *Premier Lodge (Leeds City West)*

City West One Office Park, Gelderd Rd LS12 6SN
☎ 0870 700 1414 🖷 0870 700 1415
Premier Lodge offers modern, well-equipped, en suite accommodation suitable for both business and leisure travellers. Meals can be taken at the adjacent popular restaurant and bar, which is fully licensed. For further details, consult the Hotel Groups page.
**ROOMS:** 125 en suite

### ⇧ *Travelodge*

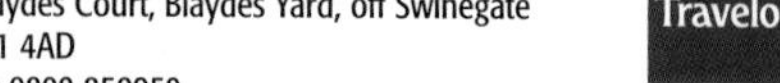

Blaydes Court, Blaydes Yard, off Swinegate LS1 4AD
☎ 0800 850950

Travelodge offers good quality, good value, modern accommodation. Ideal for families, the spacious, en suite bedrooms include remote-control TV, tea and coffee-making facilities, luxury beds and free morning newspaper. Meals can be taken at the nearby family restaurant. For further details and the Travelodge phone number, consult the Hotel Groups page.

### ⇧ Express by Holiday Inn Leeds East

Aberford Rd, Oulton LS26 8EJ
☎ 0113 282 6201 🖷 288 7210
***Dir:** Hotel is 0.5m on A642, situated on the 1st rdbt*

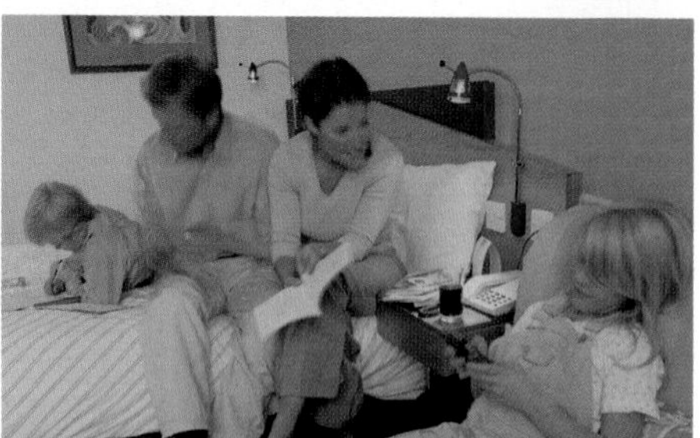

A modern budget hotel offering comfortable accommodation in refreshing, spacious and comprehensively equipped bedrooms, en suite bathrooms with power showers and continental buffet breakfast included in the room rate. Suitable for business travellers or families. For further details and the Express by Holiday Inn phone number, consult the Hotel Groups page.
**ROOMS:** 77 en suite **CONF:** Thtr 30 Class 20 Board 16

Bad hair day? Hairdryers in all rooms three stars and above.

### ○ Innkeeper's Lodge Leeds North

Bruntcliffe Rd, Morley LS27 0LY
A new concept in the travel accommodation market. Smart rooms meet essential business requirements but also have home comforts. Dining options include all-day menus plus the added advantage of breakfast, which is included in the room price. Reservations can be made seven days a week through the room reservations number: 0870 243 0500. For further details, consult the Hotel Groups page.
**ROOMS:** 32 en suite

### ○ *The Thorpe Park Hotel*

Century Way, Thorpe Park LS15
☎ 0113 264 1000
At the time of going to press, the star classification for this hotel was not confirmed. Please refer to the AA internet site www.theAA.com for current information.
**ROOMS:** 123 en suite **NOTES:** Opening May 2002

### ○ *Travelodge Leeds East*

☎ 0800 850950
**NOTES:** Opening Winter 2001

LEEK, Staffordshire — Map 07 SJ95

### ★★★63% *Hotel Rudyard*

Lake Rd, Rudyard ST13 8RN
☎ 01538 306208 🖷 01538 306208
A large stone-built Victorian property, now a private hotel, set in extensive wooded grounds in the centre of Rudyard village. It provides modern and well-equipped accommodation, a room with a four-poster bed is also available. There is a function room, a large carvery restaurant and a traditionally furnished bar.
**ROOMS:** 15 en suite (2 fmly) No smoking in 2 bedrooms **CONF:** Thtr 80 Class 60 Board 40 **PARKING:** 100 **NOTES:** No smoking in restaurant
**CARDS:**

### ★★68% ® *Three Horseshoes Inn & Restaurant*

Buxton Rd, Blackshaw Moor ST13 8TW
☎ 01538 300296 🖷 01538 300320
***Dir:** 2m N of Leek on the A53 Leek/Buxton Road*

A family owned hostelry in spacious grounds, which include a beer garden and children's play area. The non-smoking bedrooms are tastefully appointed and furnished in style with the character of the hotel. The public areas are traditional in style and include a choice of bars and eating options.
**ROOMS:** 6 en suite No smoking in all bedrooms
**FACILITIES:** entertainment **PARKING:** 80 **NOTES:** No dogs (ex guide dogs) No smoking in restaurant Closed 24 Dec-1 Jan
**CARDS:**

## LEICESTER, Leicestershire
Map 04 SK50

see also Rothley

### ★★★74% Belmont House
De Montfort St LE1 7GR
☎ 0116 254 4773 Fax 0116 247 0804
e-mail: info@belmonthotel.co.uk
***Dir:*** *from A6 London Road, take first right after railway station. Hotel 200yds on left*

Attractive property situated within easy walking distance of the railway station and city centre. The individually decorated bedrooms are tastefully furnished and equipped to suit the needs of the business user or leisure guest. The extensive public rooms are smartly appointed and include a superb conservatory walkway, Bowie's Bistro, Cherry's restaurant, Jamie's bar and Will's lounge bar.

**ROOMS:** 77 en suite (7 fmly) No smoking in 54 bedrooms s £89-£99; d £97-£107 * **LB** **FACILITIES:** Gym entertainment **CONF:** Thtr 175 Class 75 Board 65 Del from £129 * **SERVICES:** Lift **PARKING:** 75 **NOTES:** No smoking in restaurant Closed 25-26 Dec Civ Wed 140 **CARDS:**

*See advert on this page*

### ★★★68% Posthouse Leicester
Posthouse

Braunstone Ln East LE3 2FW
☎ 0870 400 9051 0870 4009051
Fax 0116 282 3623
e-mail: GM1124@forte-hotels.com
***Dir:*** *from junct 21 of M1 at M69 interchange take A5460 and continue towards city to hotel, 1m and turn right at traffic lights*

A hallmark of this recently refurbished hotel is the warmth and friendliness reflected by staff throughout. Additional features include 24-hour room service and an all day lounge menu. Meeting and conference facilities are available.

**ROOMS:** 172 en suite (35 fmly) No smoking in 110 bedrooms d £69-£109 * **LB** **FACILITIES:** Xmas **CONF:** Thtr 100 Class 54 Board 45 Del from £120 * **SERVICES:** Lift **PARKING:** 300 **NOTES:** No smoking in restaurant **CARDS:**

### ★★★66% Hermitage
REGAL

Wigston Rd, Oadby LE2 5QE
☎ 0116 256 9955 Fax 0116 272 0559/272 0686
***Dir:*** *from city centre follow A6 Market Harborough. After 4m pass ASDA on left turn right at lights for Oadby Village and over rdbt to hotel on left*

Located in a residential area, this modern hotel appeals to business guests. Bedrooms are well-equipped and there is a good range of meeting and function suites. Public areas have recently

*continued on p320*

LEICESTER, continued

been refurbished, these include a comfortable foyer lounge and a carvery restaurant.

*Hermitage, Leicester*

**ROOMS:** 56 en suite (3 fmly) No smoking in 24 bedrooms d £50 * **LB** **FACILITIES:** Xmas **CONF:** Thtr 250 Class 100 Board 60 **SERVICES:** Lift **PARKING:** 160 **NOTES:** No smoking in restaurant Civ Wed 200 **CARDS:**

### ★★★66% Regency

360 London Rd LE2 2PL
☎ 0116 270 9634 📠 0116 270 1375
e-mail: info@the-regency-hotel.com
***Dir:*** *on the A6 London Road 1.5m from the city centre, near outer ring road which leads to the M1 & M9 approx 4m away*

Originally a convent, this modernised hotel provides bright and well-equipped accommodation. The pleasantly appointed bedrooms are attractively decorated. A conservatory brasserie, next to the lounge bar, is an informal alternative to the restaurant, which offers more formal dining.
**ROOMS:** 32 en suite (4 fmly) s £46-£52; d £62-£67 (incl. bkfst) * **FACILITIES:** STV entertainment Xmas **CONF:** Thtr 70 Class 50 Board 30 Del £82 * **PARKING:** 40 **NOTES:** No dogs (ex guide dogs) **CARDS:**

### ★★★66% Time Out Hotel & Leisure

corus

Enderby Rd, Blaby LE8 4GD
☎ 0116 278 7898 📠 0116 278 1974
e-mail: timeout@corushotels.co.uk
***Dir:*** *M1 junct 21, A5460 Leicester take 4th exit at 1st rdbt, ahead at 2nd, left at 3rd follow signs to Blaby, over 4th rdbt Hotel on left*
Adjacent to the link road on the outskirts of the city, this pleasant hotel provides spacious and comfortable bedrooms, a bustling open plan restaurant and two bars; executive and superior rooms

*continued*

are particularly desirable. The modern leisure complex is a popular attraction for both corporate and weekend guests.

**ROOMS:** 48 en suite (5 fmly) No smoking in 30 bedrooms s £90-£95; d £100-£120 * **LB** **FACILITIES:** **Spa** STV Indoor swimming (H) Sauna Solarium Gym Steam room Xmas **CONF:** Thtr 70 Class 30 Board 36 Del £137.50 * **PARKING:** 110 **NOTES:** Civ Wed 70 **CARDS:**

### ★★★64% Leicester Stage Hotel

Best Western

Leicester Rd, Wigston LE18 1JW
☎ 0116 288 6161 📠 0116 257 3900
e-mail: reservations@stagehotel.co.uk
***Dir:*** *from M69/M1 junct 21 take ring road South Leicester. Follow signs for Oadby & Wigston,turn right onto A5199 towards Northampton. Hotel on left*
An imposing glass-fronted building to the south of the city centre. In recent years, major investment has dramatically upgraded the conference and leisure facilities and main ground floor public areas. Executive rooms and four-poster bridal suites are worth requesting.
**ROOMS:** 75 en suite (10 fmly) No smoking in 30 bedrooms s £70-£85; d £80-£99 (incl. bkfst) * **LB** **FACILITIES:** STV Indoor swimming (H) Sauna Gym Jacuzzi Xmas **CONF:** Thtr 450 Class 200 Board 100 Del from £100 * **PARKING:** 200 **NOTES:** No dogs (ex guide dogs) Civ Wed 300 **CARDS:**

### ★★67% Charnwood

48 Leicester Rd, Narborough LE9 5DF
☎ 0116 286 2218 📠 0116 275 0119
e-mail: info@thecharnwood.co.uk
***Dir:*** *junct 21 of M1 follow B4114 to Narborough*
Public rooms at the Charnwood are smart and cheerful, including an attractive restaurant with small bar and a lounge bar. Bar meals supplement the carte which offers traditional and international dishes. The hotel is a popular venue for weddings.
**ROOMS:** 20 en suite s £45; d £65 (incl. bkfst) * **CONF:** Thtr 50 Class 20 Board 30 Del £83.50 * **PARKING:** 30 **NOTES:** No children Closed 26 Dec-3 Jan Civ Wed 150 **CARDS:**

### ★★65% Red Cow

Hinckley Rd, Leicester Forest East LE3 3PG
☎ 0116 238 7878 📠 0116 238 6539
e-mail: redcowhotel@aol.com
***Dir:*** *follow A47 out of Leicester towards Hinckley, hotel is on right approx 4m from city centre*
To the west of Leicester, the Red Cow is a modern and popular pub restaurant with an adjacent bedroom block. A good range of food is available in the bar, restaurant and conservatory; the latter overlooks a rear garden and is set aside for families. The accommodation is modern and well-equipped.
**ROOMS:** 31 en suite (26 fmly) No smoking in 23 bedrooms d fr £40 * **PARKING:** 120 **NOTES:** No dogs (ex guide dogs) No smoking in restaurant **CARDS:**

### ★★58% Gables
368 London Rd LE2 2PN
☎ 0116 270 6969 📠 0116 270 3988
***Dir:*** *0.5m city side of junction A563 (South East) and A6*
This privately owned commercial hotel is located south of the city centre and conveniently placed for the university. The public rooms include a restaurant and a cosy lounge bar; an adjoining room serves as a popular venue for business meetings and local functions.
**ROOMS:** 30 en suite (9 fmly) s £34-£40; d £44-£50 (incl. bkfst) *
**CONF:** Thtr 60 Class 20 Board 30 Del from £75 * **PARKING:** 29
**NOTES:** No dogs (ex guide dogs) No smoking in restaurant
**CARDS:**

### Hotel Ibis
Constitution Hill, St Georges Way LE1 1PL
☎ 0116 248 7200 📠 0116 262 0880
e-mail: H3061@accor-hotels.com
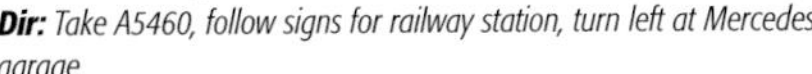
***Dir:*** *Take A5460, follow signs for railway station, turn left at Mercedes garage*
Modern, budget hotel offering comfortable accommodation in bright and practical bedrooms. Breakfast is self-service and dinner is available in the restaurant. For further details, consult the Hotel Groups page.
**ROOMS:** 94 en suite d £45 *

### Premier Lodge (Leicester West)
Leicester Rd, Glenfield LE3 8HB
☎ 0870 700 1416 📠 0870 700 1417
***Dir:*** *Situated off A50, 4m from Leicester city centre. Hotel is on the slip road that leads to County Hall*
Premier Lodge offers modern, well-equipped, en suite accommodation suitable for both business and leisure travellers. Meals can be taken at the adjacent popular restaurant and bar, which is fully licensed. For further details, consult the Hotel Groups page.
**ROOMS:** 43 en suite d £46 * **CONF:** Thtr 30 Class 20 Board 20

### *Premier Lodge (Leicester Central)*
Groby Rd
☎ 0870 700 1420 📠 0870 700 1421
Premier Lodge offers modern, well-equipped, en suite accommodation suitable for both business and leisure travellers. Meals can be taken at the adjacent popular restaurant and bar, which is fully licensed. For further details, consult the Hotel Groups page.

### Premier Lodge (Leicester South)
Glen Rise, Oadby LE2 4RG
☎ 0870 700 1418 📠 0870 700 1419
***Dir:*** *Situated off junct 21 on the M1. Follow A563 to Market Harbour and Leicester Racecourse. At A6 junct follow A6 through Oadby, and the Horse and Hounds is on the right*
Premier Lodge offers modern, well-equipped, en suite accommodation suitable for both business and leisure travellers. Meals can be taken at the adjacent popular restaurant and bar, which is fully licensed. For further details, consult the Hotel Groups page.
**ROOMS:** 30 en suite d £46 * **CONF:** Thtr 10 Class 8 Board 10 Del from £80 *

> Packed in a hurry? Ironing facilities should be available at all star levels, either in rooms or on request.

## LEICESTER FOREST SERVICE AREA (M1), Leicestershire — Map 04 SK50

### Days Inn
Leicester Forest East, Junction 21 M1 LE3 3GB
☎ 0116 239 0534 📠 0116 239 0546
e-mail: leicester.hotel@welcomebreak.co.uk
***Dir:*** *situated on M1 motorway N/bound between junct 21 & 21A*
This modern building offers accommodation in smart, spacious and well-equipped bedrooms, suitable for families and business travellers, and all with en suite bathrooms. Continental breakfast is available and other refreshments may be taken at the nearby family restaurant. For further details and the Days Inn phone number, consult the Hotel Groups page.
**ROOMS:** 92 en suite s £45-£60; d £45-£60 * **CONF:** Board 10

## LEIGH DELAMERE MOTORWAY SERVICE AREA (M4), Wiltshire — Map 03 ST87

### *Travelodge*
SN14 6LB
☎ 08700 850950 📠 01666 837112
***Dir:*** *Between junc 17 & 18 on the M4*
Travelodge offers good quality, good value, modern accommodation. Ideal for families, the spacious, en suite bedrooms include remote-control TV, tea and coffee-making facilities, luxury beds and free morning newspaper. Meals can be taken at the nearby family restaurant. For further details and the Travelodge phone number, consult the Hotel Groups page.

**ROOMS:** 70 en suite

## LENHAM, Kent — Map 05 TQ85

### ★★★★73% Chilston Park
Sandway ME17 2BE
☎ 01622 859803 📠 01622 858588
e-mail: chilstonpark@arcadianhotels.co.uk
***Dir:*** *turn right at x-roads in Lenham. Then left after 0.5m into Boughton Road. Straight over x-roads, and hotel is on left*

Standing in extensive well-cared-for grounds, this antique-filled country house is of somewhat eccentric but lovingly constructed and thoroughly stylish taste. Many of the bedrooms have four-poster beds and all are furnished in unique style. Public areas include meeting rooms and lounges that are comfortable and smart. Stylish modern European food is served in a candle-lit cavernous dining room.
**ROOMS:** 30 en suite 23 annexe en suite (2 fmly) d £85-£105 * **LB**
**FACILITIES:** STV Tennis (hard) Fishing Snooker Croquet lawn Xmas
**CONF:** Thtr 120 Class 40 Board 44 Del from £185 * **SERVICES:** Lift
**PARKING:** 100 **NOTES:** No smoking in restaurant Civ Wed 80
**CARDS:**

## LEOMINSTER, Herefordshire

Map 03 SO45

**★★★65% Talbot**
West St HR6 8EP
☎ 01568 616347 ▯ 01568 614880
***Dir:*** *approach either from A49, A44 or A4112, the Hotel can be found at the centre of the town*
The charm and character of this former coaching inn are enhanced by exposed ceiling beams, antique furniture in the bars, and welcoming fires. Bedrooms are well-equipped and many have recently been refurbished. Facilities are available for private functions and conferences.
**ROOMS:** 20 en suite (3 fmly) s £42-£47; d £58-£64 * LB
**FACILITIES:** Xmas **CONF:** Thtr 150 Class 25 Board 28 Del from £80 *
**PARKING:** 20 **NOTES:** No smoking in restaurant
**CARDS:**

**★★62% Royal Oak**
South St HR6 8JA
☎ 01568 612610 ▯ 01568 612710
***Dir:*** *junct A44/A49 in town centre*
This privately owned hotel is conveniently located in the town centre. It is personally run in an informal manner and provides warm and friendly hospitality. Public areas have charm and character and include a bistro style restaurant, public bar, and several function rooms. Bedrooms are currently being refurbished.
**ROOMS:** 17 en suite 1 annexe en suite (2 fmly) No smoking in 2 bedrooms s fr £42; d fr £56 (incl. bkfst) * LB **CONF:** Thtr 220 Class 100 Board 50 Del £72 * **PARKING:** 25 **NOTES:** No smoking in restaurant **CARDS:**

*See advert on opposite page*

## LEWDOWN, Devon

Map 02 SX48

*Premier Collection*

**★★★ Lewtrenchard Manor**
EX20 4PN
☎ 01566 783256 & 783222
▯ 01566 783332
e-mail: s&j@lewtrenchard.co.uk
***Dir:*** *A30 from Exeter turn on to Plymouth/Tavistock road. T-junct right and immediately left onto old A30 Lewdown 6m turn left signposted Lewtrenchard*
Lewtrenchard is located in beautiful countryside close to the northern edge of Dartmoor. This Jacobean mansion was built by the Monk family in the 1600s and has many interesting architectural features. There are many public rooms, which include a fine gallery, as well as magnificent carvings and oak panelling. Meals can be taken in the panelled dining room where imaginative and carefully prepared dishes are served. The bedrooms are comfortably furnished and spacious.
**ROOMS:** 9 en suite s £100-£110; d fr £125 (incl. bkfst) LB
**FACILITIES:** Fishing Croquet lawn Clay pigeon shooting Xmas
**CONF:** Thtr 50 Class 40 Board 30 **PARKING:** 50 **NOTES:** No children 7yrs No smoking in restaurant Civ Wed 100
**CARDS:**

## LEWES, East Sussex

Map 05 TQ41

**★★★76% Shelleys Hotel**
High St BN7 1XS
☎ 01273 472361 ▯ 01273 483152
e-mail: info@shelleys-hotel-lewes.com
***Dir:*** *follow A23 to Brighton, turn onto A27 to Lewes. At 1st rdbt turn left for town centre, after crossroads hotel is located on left*
This hotel is steeped in history with previous owners including the Earl of Dorset. Nowadays Shelleys boasts beautifully appointed bedrooms, furnished and decorated in a traditional style. The elegant restaurant overlooks the garden and serves a variety of interesting dishes.
**ROOMS:** 19 en suite (2 fmly) No smoking in 4 bedrooms s £130-£145; d £170-£250 * LB **FACILITIES:** STV Xmas **CONF:** Thtr 50 Class 20 Board 28 Del from £160 * **PARKING:** 25 **NOTES:** No smoking in restaurant Civ Wed 50 **CARDS:**

**★★★63% White Hart**
55 High St BN7 1XE
☎ 01273 476694 ▯ 01273 476695
***Dir:*** *from A27 follow signs for town centre. Hotel opposite County Court*

This historic hotel combines the old and the new. A leisure centre, patio and conservatory have been added to the Tudor bar, lounge and restaurant. Bedrooms vary between the character of the original inn and the more contemporary annexe rooms.
**ROOMS:** 23 en suite 29 annexe en suite (3 fmly) s fr £61; d fr £86 LB
**FACILITIES:** Spa STV Indoor swimming (H) Sauna Solarium Gym Steam room entertainment Xmas **CONF:** Thtr 250 Class 120 Board 90 Del from £85.60 * **PARKING:** 40
**CARDS:**

*See advert on opposite page*

## LEYBURN, North Yorkshire

Map 07 SE19

**★65% Golden Lion**
Market Place DL8 5AS
☎ 01969 622161 ▯ 01969 623836
e-mail: AnneGoldenLion@aol.com
***Dir:*** *set on the A684 in Market Square*
This traditional family inn dates back to 1765 and overlooks Leyburn's well-known market square. Bedrooms are very well-equipped and some have bathrooms adapted specially for

*continued*

disabled guests. The restaurant, decorated with murals of Dales scenes, offers a full range of dishes, and the bar areas also provide meals and snacks.
**ROOMS:** 15 rms (14 en suite) (5 fmly) s £25-£32; d £50-£64 (incl. bkfst) * **LB** **SERVICES:** Lift **NOTES:** Closed 25 & 26 Dec
**CARDS:**

## LICHFIELD, Staffordshire — Map 07 SK10

### ★★★68% Little Barrow
Beacon St WS13 7AR
☎ 01543 414500 01543 415734
***Dir:*** *200 yds from cathedral on right*
Conveniently situated for the cathedral and the city, this friendly hotel provides well-equipped accommodation. The cosy lounge bar, popular with locals and visitors alike, has a range of real ales and a choice of bar meals. More formal dining is offered in the pleasant restaurant. Service is relaxed and attentive.
**ROOMS:** 24 en suite (2 fmly) s fr £65; d fr £80 (incl. bkfst) * **LB** **CONF:** Thtr 80 Class 30 Board 30 Del from £95 * **PARKING:** 70 **NOTES:** No dogs (ex guide dogs) No smoking in restaurant Closed 24-26 Dec Civ Wed 70 **CARDS:**

### ★★66% The Olde Corner House
Walsall Rd, Muckley Corner WS14 0BG
☎ 01543 372182 01543 372211
***Dir:*** *at junct of A5/A461 5 mins from A38*
This coaching inn dates back to the 17th century in parts and retains much of its character. Two dining rooms offer a range of well-prepared dishes, and there is a popular bar and a separate comfortable lounge. Bedrooms are all attractively furnished and well-equipped, including rooms in the newer wing. Service is informal and welcoming.
**ROOMS:** 23 en suite No smoking in all bedrooms s £28.95-£39.95; d £55.95-£75 (incl. bkfst) * **CONF:** Class 18 Del from £50 * **PARKING:** 65 **NOTES:** No dogs **CARDS:**

### ★★64% *Angel Croft*
Beacon St WS13 7AA
☎ 01543 258737 01543 415605
***Dir:*** *situated opposite main west gate entrance to Lichfield Cathedral*
This traditional, family-run, Georgian hotel is close to the cathedral and city centre. A comfortable lounge leads into a nicely appointed dining room; there is also a cosy bar on the lower ground floor. Bedrooms vary but most are spacious, particularly those in the adjacent Westgate House.
**ROOMS:** 10 rms (8 en suite) 8 annexe en suite (1 fmly) **CONF:** Thtr 30 Board 20 **PARKING:** 60 **NOTES:** No dogs (ex guide dogs) No smoking in restaurant Closed 25 & 26 Dec RS Sun evenings
**CARDS:**

### ⌂ *Premier Lodge*
Rykneld St, Fradley WS13 8RD
☎ 0870 700 1318 0870 700 1319

PREMIER LODGE
THE BEST. REST ASSURED.

Premier Lodge offers modern, well-equipped, en suite accommodation suitable for both business and leisure travellers. Meals can be taken at the adjacent popular restaurant and bar, which is fully licensed. For further details, consult the Hotel Groups page.
**ROOMS:** 30 en suite

Early start? Hotels at all star levels should provide in-room alarm clocks and/or alarm calls.

LICHFIELD, continued

### ○ Express by Holiday Inn Lichfield

Wall Island, Shenstone WS16
☎ 0800 897121

Express
by Holiday Inn

A modern budget hotel offering comfortable accommodation in refreshing, spacious and comprehensively equipped bedrooms, en suite bathrooms with power showers and continental buffet breakfast included in the room rate. Suitable for business travellers or families. For further details and the Express by Holiday Inn phone number, consult the Hotel Groups page.
**ROOMS:** 102 rms **NOTES:** Open now

### ○ Innkeeper's Lodge Lichfield

Stafford Rd WS13 8JB
A new concept in the travel accommodation market. Smart rooms meet essential business requirements but also have home comforts. Dining options include all-day menus plus the added advantage of breakfast, which is included in the room price. Reservations can be made seven days a week through the room reservations number: 0870 243 0500. For further details, consult the Hotel Groups page.
**ROOMS:** 10 en suite **NOTES:** Open now

## LIFTON, Devon — Map 02 SX38

### ★★★73% Arundell Arms

PL16 0AA
☎ 01566 784666 📠 01566 784494
e-mail: reservations@arundellarms.com
**Dir:** *40m West of Exeter and M5, 1m off A30 in Lifton Village*

An experienced and efficient team of staff helps to create an overall relaxed and friendly atmosphere at this delightful, 18th century, former coaching inn. A complete refurbishment of the restaurant has now been completed. A varied menu is offered where emphasis is placed upon fresh, high quality, local produce. The hotel offers 20 miles of salmon and trout fishing and other country pursuits.
**ROOMS:** 22 en suite 5 annexe en suite s £47-£77; d £93-£117 (incl. bkfst) * LB **FACILITIES:** STV Fishing Skittle alley Games room **CONF:** Thtr 100 Class 30 Board 40 Del from £110 * **PARKING:** 80 **NOTES:** No smoking in restaurant Closed 3 days Xmas
**CARDS:**

*See advert on opposite page*

### ★★74% Lifton Hall Country House

New Rd PL16 0DR
☎ 01566 784863 & 784263 📠 01566 784770
e-mail: mail@liftonhall.co.uk
**Dir:** *Leave A30 at Liftondown Junction, 2m E of Launceston. Turn right at T-junct signed Lifton, continue through village, hotel on left 1m after T-junct*

This charming small hotel has a traditional country house atmosphere. In addition to the bar and bistro, the civilised dining room is the venue for skilfully prepared and interesting dishes making full use of local produce with fresh fish featuring prominently. Bedrooms are well-equipped and offer a blend of individuality, character and contemporary comforts.
**ROOMS:** 10 en suite (2 fmly) No smoking in 9 bedrooms s fr £50; d fr £75 (incl. bkfst) * LB **FACILITIES:** ch fac Xmas **CONF:** Thtr 25 Class 25 Board 25 Del from £70 * **PARKING:** 16 **NOTES:** No dogs (ex guide dogs) **CARDS:**

## LINCOLN, Lincolnshire — Map 08 SK97

### ★★★72% The Bentley Hotel & Leisure Club

Newark Rd, South Hykeham LN6 9NH
☎ 01522 878000 📠 01522 878001
e-mail: info@thebentleyhotel.uk.com
**Dir:** *from A1 take A46 E towards Lincoln for 10m. Cross 1st rdbt on Lincoln Bypass to hotel 50yds on left*
This smart new hotel, conveniently located on the bypass, offers bright, attractive accommodation. The bedrooms are spacious and well-equipped. There is a stylish leisure suite with gymnasium, sauna, steam room and a large pool with disabled access. For the less energetic there is a beauty salon. Air-conditioning is a bonus.
**ROOMS:** 53 en suite (3 fmly) **FACILITIES:** STV Indoor swimming (H) Sauna Gym Jacuzzi Beauty salon **CONF:** Thtr 350 Class 150 Board 30 Del from £95 **SERVICES:** Lift **PARKING:** 140 **NOTES:** No dogs (ex guide dogs) No smoking in restaurant Civ Wed 100
**CARDS:**

### ★★★71% Washingborough Hall

Church Hill, Washingborough LN4 1BE
☎ 01522 790340 📠 01522 792936
**Dir:** *from B1188 onto B1190. Pass bowling alley, under railway bridge. Carry on along road till small rdbt. Turn right at rdbt & establishment on left*
This Georgian manor stands on the edge of the village and is set in attractive gardens with an outdoor swimming pool. Public

*continued*

rooms are pleasantly furnished and comfortable. The restaurant offers interesting menus and the bedrooms are individually designed, most looking out to the grounds or countryside.

**ROOMS:** 14 en suite (1 fmly) s £58-£65; d £75-£88 (incl. bkfst) * LB **FACILITIES:** Outdoor swimming (H) Snooker Croquet lawn Can arrange golf, tennis & horse riding ch fac Xmas **CONF:** Thtr 50 Class 20 Board 25 Del from £115 * **PARKING:** 50 **NOTES:** No smoking in restaurant Civ Wed 50 **CARDS:**

### ★★★69% Courtyard by Marriott Lincoln

COURTYARD

Brayford Wharf North LN1 1YW
☎ 01522 544244 📠 01522 560805
***Dir:*** *from A46 onto A57 – Lincoln Central. After Tranvics straight ahead at the lights, hotel on left*

Within easy walking distance of the city centre, overlooking Bayford Pool, this smart modern hotel offers spacious bedrooms, many of which look out over the waterfront. The public areas are comfortable and inviting; one of the main features is the restaurant with a gallery which overlooks the lounge bar.
**ROOMS:** 95 en suite No smoking in 47 bedrooms s fr £69; d fr £69 * LB **FACILITIES:** STV Fitness room **CONF:** Thtr 30 Class 20 Board 18 Del from £95 * **SERVICES:** Lift air con **PARKING:** 100 **NOTES:** No dogs (ex guide dogs) **CARDS:**

### ★★★68% Grand Hotel

Best Western

Saint Mary's St LN5 7EP
☎ 01522 524211 📠 01522 537661

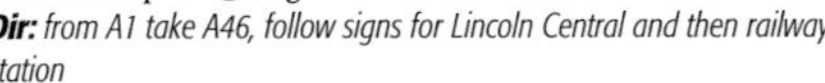

e-mail: reception@thegrandhotel.uk.com
***Dir:*** *from A1 take A46, follow signs for Lincoln Central and then railway station*
Close to the railway station, this friendly family-owned hotel is ideal for exploring the city and its many attractions. The tastefully decorated bedrooms include a number of smart executive rooms,

*continued*



and some four-poster beds. Staff are willing and helpful, and the hotel benefits from two restaurants and bars.

**ROOMS:** 46 en suite (2 fmly) s £52-£67; d £67-£77 (incl. bkfst) * LB **FACILITIES:** STV Xmas **CONF:** Thtr 80 Class 50 Board 30 Del from £84 * **PARKING:** 30 **NOTES:** No dogs (ex guide dogs) **CARDS:**

### ★★★66% The White Hart

Bailgate LN1 3AR
☎ 0870 400 8117 📠 01522 531798
e-mail: HeritageHotels_Lincoln.White-Hart@forte-hotels.com
***Dir:*** *from A15 rdbt on north side of city follow historic Lincoln signs, go through Newport Arch, continue along Bailgate, hotel on corner at bend of road*
The hotel faces Lincoln Cathedral, at the heart of the historic city. The mellow public rooms have antique furnishings and an

*continued on p326*

LINCOLN, continued

impressive display of Rockingham china. Bedrooms are spacious, stylishly decorated and well-equipped.
**ROOMS:** 48 en suite (4 fmly) No smoking in 18 bedrooms s fr £115; d fr £120 * **LB** **FACILITIES:** Xmas **CONF:** Thtr 90 Class 40 Board 30 Del from £130 * **SERVICES:** Lift **PARKING:** 57 **NOTES:** No smoking in restaurant Civ Wed 120 **CARDS:**

### ★★★65% *Posthouse Lincoln*

Posthouse

Eastgate LN2 1PN
☎ 0870 400 9052 📠 01522 510780
***Dir:*** *adjacent to cathedral*
This modern and friendly hotel is opposite Lincoln Cathedral and its grounds contain ruins of the Roman wall and Eastgate. Bedrooms have modern facilities and those facing the cathedral have balconies. The ground floor rooms have patio doors opening onto a secluded garden. Facilities include a spacious restaurant and bar.
**ROOMS:** 70 en suite (7 fmly) No smoking in 46 bedrooms **CONF:** Thtr 90 Class 50 Board 40 **SERVICES:** Lift **PARKING:** 110
**CARDS:**

### ★★72% Castle

MINOTEL Great Britain

Westgate LN1 3AS
☎ 01522 538801 📠 01522 575457
e-mail: reception@thegrandhotel.uk.com
***Dir:*** *follow signs for 'Historic Lincoln' Hotel is at NE corner of the Castle*
The delightful bedrooms at this hotel are named after British castles; the Lincoln suite has a separate lounge. There is a cosy residents' lounge on the first floor and a small bar with an attractive open-plan restaurant. The wide selection of dishes features quality seafood and local game.
**ROOMS:** 17 en suite 3 annexe en suite (1 fmly) No smoking in 10 bedrooms s £62-£82; d £82-£93 (incl. bkfst) * **LB** **FACILITIES:** Xmas **CONF:** Thtr 50 Class 18 Board 22 **PARKING:** 20 **NOTES:** No children 8yrs No smoking in restaurant **CARDS:**

*See advert on opposite page*

### ★★71% Hillcrest

THE CIRCLE Selected Individual Hotels GREAT BRITAIN

15 Lindum Ter LN2 5RT
☎ 01522 510182 📠 01522 510182
e-mail: reservations@hillcrest-hotel.com
***Dir:*** *from A15/Wragby Road, turn into Upper Lindium Road at brown tourist sign. Continue and turn left at bottom. Hotel 200mtrs on right*

The hospitality offered by the proprietor and her staff is one of the strengths of Hillcrest, which sits in a quiet location. The well-equipped bedrooms come in a variety of sizes, and a cosy dining room offers a good range of freshly prepared food. The pleasant conservatory overlooks the adjacent park. A computer room with internet access is available for business users.
**ROOMS:** 15 en suite (4 fmly) No smoking in 6 bedrooms s £52-£59; d £79 (incl. bkfst) * **LB** **FACILITIES:** ch fac **CONF:** Thtr 20 Class 16 Board 12 Del £86 * **PARKING:** 8 **NOTES:** No smoking in restaurant Closed 23 Dec-3 Jan **CARDS:**

### ★★70% Moor Lodge

Best Western

Sleaford Rd LN4 1HU
☎ 01522 791366 📠 01522 794389
e-mail: moorlodge@bestwestern.co.uk
(For full entry see Branston)

### ★★65% Tower Hotel

38 Westgate LN1 3BD
☎ 01522 529999 📠 01522 560596
***Dir:*** *From A46 follow signs to Lincoln north. Follow signs to Bailgate area. Through the arch and 2nd turn on the left is Westgate*

This pleasantly furnished hotel stands facing the Norman castle wall and is in a very convenient location for the city. There are cosy public rooms and interesting dishes are featured on the menu. Hospitality is one of the hotel's key strengths.
**ROOMS:** 14 en suite (1 fmly) No smoking in 2 bedrooms s £40-£52; d £55-£70 (incl. bkfst) * **LB** **FACILITIES:** ch fac **CONF:** Thtr 30 Class 30 Board 30 Del from £61.95 * **PARKING:** 9 **NOTES:** No smoking in restaurant Closed 24-26 Dec **CARDS:**

### ★★63% Loudor

37 Newark Rd, North Hykeham LN6 8RB
☎ 01522 680333 & 500474 📠 01522 680403
e-mail: theloudorhotel@yahoo.co.uk
***Dir:*** *turn off A1 10m on A46 A1434 2m hotel on left opposite Forum shopping centre*
This small privately owned hotel offers bedrooms that are fresh and bright and are suitably equipped with a good standard of facilities. The relaxing public rooms include a cosy lounge, small bar and welcoming restaurant.
**ROOMS:** 9 en suite 1 annexe en suite (1 fmly) No smoking in 5 bedrooms s £35; d £46 (incl. bkfst) * **LB** **PARKING:** 10 **NOTES:** No dogs (ex guide dogs) No smoking in restaurant
**CARDS:**

### Hotel Ibis Lincoln

ibis
ACCOR hotels

Runcorn Rd, off Whisby Rd LN6 3QZ
☎ 01522 698333 📠 698444
e-mail: H3161@accor-hotels.com
***Dir:*** *turn off A46 ringroad onto the Whisby Road. Take 1st turning on the left*
Modern, budget hotel offering comfortable accommodation in bright and practical bedrooms. Breakfast is self-service and dinner is available in the restaurant. For further details, consult the Hotel Groups page.
**ROOMS:** 86 en suite d fr £40 * **CONF:** Thtr 35 Board 25

**Travelodge**
Thorpe on the Hill LN6 9AJ
☎ 08700 850950
**Dir:** *on A46*
Travelodge offers good quality, good value, modern accommodation. Ideal for families, the spacious, en suite bedrooms include remote-control TV, tea and coffee-making facilities, luxury beds and free morning newspaper. Meals can be taken at the nearby family restaurant. For further details and the Travelodge phone number, consult the Hotel Groups page.

**ROOMS:** 32 en suite

LIPHOOK, Hampshire Map 04 SU83

★★★71% **Old Thorns Hotel, Golf & Country Club**
Longmoor Rd, Griggs Green GU30 7PE
☎ 01428 724555 Fax 01428 725036
e-mail: kflockhart@oldthorns.com
**Dir:** *A3 Guildford to Portsmouth, take Griggs Green exit south of Liphook. Signposted*

This smartly presented hotel has many attractions: an 18-hole golf course with golf shop, an indoor pool with sauna and solarium, and spacious bedrooms, some with balconies. Of the two restaurants, the Nippon Kan, is Japanese and specialises in Teppan-Yaki cuisine.
**ROOMS:** 29 en suite 4 annexe en suite No smoking in 9 bedrooms s fr £125; d £145-£165 (incl. bkfst) * LB **FACILITIES:** STV Indoor swimming (H) Golf 18 Tennis (hard) Sauna Solarium Gym Putting green Steam room Beauty treatment rooms Xmas **CONF:** Thtr 100 Class 50 Board 30 Del from £145 * **PARKING:** 80 **NOTES:** Civ Wed 80
**CARDS:**

**Travelodge**
GU30 7TT
☎ 08700 850950
**Dir:** *on northbound carriageway of A3, 1m from Griggs Green exit at Shell services*
Travelodge offers good quality, good value, modern accommodation. Ideal for families, the spacious, en suite bedrooms include remote-control TV, tea and coffee-making facilities, luxury beds and free morning newspaper. Meals can be taken at the nearby family restaurant. For further details and the Travelodge phone number, consult the Hotel Groups page.

**ROOMS:** 40 en suite

Popped the question? Hotels with Civ Wed in their entry are licensed for civil wedding ceremonies. Maximum numbers for the ceremony only are shown, e.g. Civ Wed 120

LISKEARD, Cornwall & Isles of Scilly Map 02 SX26

*Premier Collection*

★★ **Well House**
St Keyne PL14 4RN
☎ 01579 342001 Fax 01579 343891
e-mail: wellhse@aol.com
**Dir:** *from Liskeard A38 take B3254 to St Keyne, at church take left fork signed St Keynewell, hotel 0.5m from church*
Well House is peacefully situated in a fold of the valley. A feature of this charming small hotel is the spacious, attractively furnished and well-equipped bedrooms. The smell of a log burning fire beckons guests to the cosy lounge with an intimate bar or, in the summer, drinks can be taken on

*continued on p328*

LISKEARD, continued

the terrace. Carefully prepared meals, always including a selection of locally landed seafood, are served in the bright dining room.
**ROOMS:** 9 en suite (1 fmly) s £75-£95; d £110-£160 (incl. bkfst) * LB **FACILITIES:** Outdoor swimming (H) Tennis (hard) Croquet lawn Xmas **PARKING:** 30 **NOTES:** No smoking in restaurant
**CARDS:**

### ★★63% Lord Eliot

Castle St PL14 3AU
☎ 01579 342717 01579 347593
***Dir:*** *take A38 into Liskeard, hotel 0.5m on left past St Martins Church*

Conveniently situated on the edge of town, this popular hotel offers a warm and friendly welcome to guests. Bedrooms are comfortable and individually decorated, whilst public areas include a convivial bar and large function room. A range of meals is offered in either the bar or dining room.
**ROOMS:** 15 rms (14 en suite) (1 fmly) No smoking in 2 bedrooms s fr £52; d fr £66 (incl. bkfst) * LB **FACILITIES:** ch fac Xmas **CONF:** Thtr 180 Class 180 Board 180 **PARKING:** 60 **NOTES:** RS 25 Dec, closed evening **CARDS:**

## LITTLE LANGDALE, Cumbria — Map 07 NY30

### ★★68% *Three Shires Inn*

LA22 9NZ
☎ 015394 37215 015394 37127
e-mail: Ian@threeshiresinn.co.uk
***Dir:*** *turn off A593, 2.5m from Ambleside at 2nd junct signposted for the Langdales. 1st left 0.5m, then hotel 1m up lane*

Dating back to 1872, this traditional family-run inn has a welcoming atmosphere. Guests have a choice of light, simple dishes in the well-stocked bar lounge, or a more elaborate, upmarket menu in the attractive restaurant. Bedrooms, all individually designed with bright colour schemes, are comfortably furnished and most enjoy wonderful views over the Tiberthwaite fells.
**ROOMS:** 10 en suite (1 fmly) No smoking in all bedrooms
**PARKING:** 22 **NOTES:** No dogs No smoking in restaurant Closed Jan (ex New Year) RS Dec **CARDS:**

## LITTLE WEIGHTON, East Riding of Yorkshire — Map 08 SE93

### ★★68% *The Rowley Manor*

Rowley Rd HU20 3XR
☎ 01482 848248 01482 849900
***Dir:*** *leave A63 at South Cave/Market Weighton sign into South Cave, turn right into Beverley Rd at the clock tower & follow signs for Rowley*

Rowley Manor is a Georgian country vicarage set in rural gardens and parkland. Bedrooms are traditionally furnished and decorated and many have panoramic views. Some master rooms are particularly spacious. The spacious public rooms feature a magnificent pine-panelled study and are of grand design.
**ROOMS:** 16 en suite (2 fmly) **FACILITIES:** STV Riding Croquet lawn **CONF:** Thtr 90 Class 30 Board 50 **PARKING:** 120 **NOTES:** Civ Wed 100
**CARDS:**

## LIVERPOOL, Merseyside — Map 07 SJ3

see also Blundellsands

### ★★★★72% Liverpool Marriott Hotel City Centre

1 Queen Square L1 1RH
☎ 0151 476 8000 0151 474 5000
***Dir:*** *from City Centre follow signs for Queen Square Parking. Hotel adjacent*

An impressive modern hotel, located in the heart of the city. The elegant public rooms include a lounge, cocktail bar and Oliver's Restaurant which provides cuisine in stylish surroundings. The hotel also boasts a well equipped health club with indoor pool. Bedrooms feature a comprehensive range of facilities and are stylishly furnished and decorated.
**ROOMS:** 146 en suite (29 fmly) No smoking in 90 bedrooms s £109; d £109 * LB **FACILITIES:** STV Indoor swimming (H) Sauna Solarium Gym Jacuzzi entertainment Xmas **CONF:** Thtr 250 Class 90 Board 30 Del from £136 * **SERVICES:** Lift air con **PARKING:** 158 **NOTES:** No smoking in restaurant Civ Wed 250 **CARDS:**

### ★★★★68% Liverpool Marriott Hotel South

Speke Aerodrome L24 8QD
☎ 0151 494 5000 0151 494 5050
e-mail: tiffany.dodd@marriotthotels.co.uk
***Dir:*** *Approach Liverpool on M62 exit 6 south into Knowsley Expressway towards Speke, At rdbt right to A561 towards Liverpool, continue past turning for Speke Hall and Liverpool Airport. Hotel left after Estuary Commerce Park*

The old North Terminal of Liverpool airport has been restored and extended, the art deco architecture has been maintained and the interior design reflects this distinctive look. The spacious hotel rooms are fully air-conditioned and feature a comprehensive

continued

ange of facilities. Feature rooms include the presidential suite in he base of the old control tower.

**ROOMS:** 164 en suite (22 fmly) No smoking in 120 bedrooms s fr £95; d fr £95 * **FACILITIES:** Spa STV Indoor swimming Outdoor swimming (H) Tennis (hard) Squash Sauna Gym Jacuzzi Selected use of David Lloyd Leisure Centre adjacent to hotel Xmas **CONF:** Thtr 250 Class 120 Board 60 Del from £135 * **SERVICES:** Lift air con **PARKING:** 300 **NOTES:** No dogs (ex guide dogs) No smoking in restaurant Civ Wed 200 **CARDS:**

### ★★★65% The Royal

Marine Ter, Waterloo L22 5PR
☎ 0151 928 2332 🖹 0151 949 0320
e-mail: royalhotel@compuserve.com
***Dir:*** *6.5m NW of city centre, turn left off A565 Liverpool/Southport road at monument, hotel at bottom of this road*

ROYAL HOTEL
ROYAL HOTEL

On the outskirts of the city, beside the Marine Gardens, this hotel, dated 1815, commands views of the Wirral and North Wales. Bedrooms are modern and spacious public areas include a conservatory adjacent to the brightly decorated restaurant and the comfortable, newly renovated Seabank lounge. A wide range of interesting dishes is available.
**ROOMS:** 25 en suite (5 fmly) s £45-£65; d £65-£75 (incl. bkfst) * **FACILITIES:** STV ch fac **CONF:** Thtr 120 Class 70 Board 40 **PARKING:** 25 **NOTES:** No dogs (ex guide dogs) **CARDS:**

### ⌂ *Express by Holiday Inn Liverpool*

Express by Holiday Inn

Brittania Pavilion, Albert Dock L3 4AD
☎ 0151 709 1133 🖹 709 1144
e-mail: liverpool@premierhotels.co.uk
***Dir:*** *follow signs for Liverpool City Centre & Albert Dock*
A modern budget hotel offering comfortable accommodation in refreshing, spacious and comprehensively equipped bedrooms, en suite bathrooms with power showers and continental buffet breakfast included in the room rate. Suitable for business

*continued*

travellers or families. For further details and the Express by Holiday Inn phone number, consult the Hotel Groups page.

**ROOMS:** 117 en suite **CONF:** Thtr 35 Class 30 Board 25

### ⌂ Howard Johnson Liverpool

Ribblers Ln, Knowsley, Prescot L34 9HA
☎ 0151 549 2700 🖹 0151 549 2800
e-mail: knowsley@howardjohnson.co.uk
***Dir:*** *N of city centre follow signs Goodison Park Football Stadium, join A580 & continue for approx 5m follow signs for M57/Knowsley Business Pk. 2nd exit from rdbt hotel on left*
**ROOMS:** 86 en suite **CONF:** Thtr 40 Class 20 Board 25

### ⌂ *Premier Lodge (Liverpool City Centre)*

PREMIER LODGE THE BEST. BEST ASSURED.

45 Victoria St L1 6JB
☎ 0870 700 1422 🖹 0870 700 1423
Premier Lodge offers modern, well-equipped, en suite accommodation suitable for both business and leisure travellers. Meals can be taken at the adjacent popular restaurant and bar, which is fully licensed. For further details, consult the Hotel Groups page.
**ROOMS:** 39 en suite

### ⌂ Premier Lodge (Liverpool North)

PREMIER LODGE THE BEST. BEST ASSURED.

Dunningsbridge Rd L30 6YN
☎ 0870 700 1428 🖹 0870 700 1429
***Dir:*** *From M57 or M58 take junct to A5036 towards Bootle and the docks. At 3rd set of traffic lights with a park on the right turn right. Then right again into car park*
Premier Lodge offers modern, well-equipped, en suite accommodation suitable for both business and leisure travellers. Meals can be taken at the adjacent popular restaurant and bar, which is fully licensed. For further details, consult the Hotel Groups page.
**ROOMS:** 62 en suite d £42 * **CONF:** Thtr 220 Class 110 Board 60 Del from £69 *

### ⌂ Premier Lodge (Liverpool South East)

PREMIER LODGE THE BEST. BEST ASSURED.

Roby Rd, Huyton L36 4HD
☎ 0870 700 1426 🖹 0870 700 1427
***Dir:*** *From junct 5 of the M62 turn to A5080(Roby road) towards Huyton town centre. Lodge 500yds right*
Premier Lodge offers modern, well-equipped, en suite accommodation suitable for both business and leisure travellers. Meals can be taken at the adjacent popular restaurant and bar, which is fully licensed. For further details, consult the Hotel Groups page.
**ROOMS:** 53 en suite d £46 * **CONF:** Thtr 35 Class 15 Board 22

L

LIVERPOOL, continued

### ⇧ Campanile

Campanile

Chaloner St, Queens Dock L3 4AJ
☎ 0151 709 8104 🖷 0151 709 8725
***Dir:*** *follow brown tourist signs marked "Albert Dock" Hotel is situated south on the waterfront*

This modern building offers accommodation in smart, well-equipped bedrooms, all with en suite bathrooms. Refreshments may be taken at the informal Bistro. For further details and the Campanile phone number, consult the Hotel Groups page.
**ROOMS:** 103 en suite d £50 * **CONF:** Thtr 25 Class 18 Board 20 Del from £68 *

L

### ○ Hotel Ibis

27 Wapping L1 8DQ
☎ 0151 706 9800
**ROOMS:** 127 rms **NOTES:** Open now

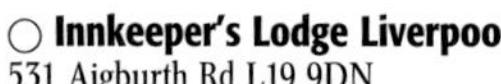

### ○ Innkeeper's Lodge Liverpool

531 Aigburth Rd L19 9DN
☎ 0870 243 0500
A new concept in the travel accommodation market. Smart rooms meet essential business requirements but also have home comforts. Dining options include all-day menus plus the added advantage of breakfast, which is included in the room price. Reservations can be made seven days a week through the room reservations number: 0870 243 0500. For further details, consult the Hotel Groups page.
**ROOMS:** 33 en suite

LIZARD, THE, Cornwall & Isles of Scilly Map 02 SW71

### ★★★68% Housel Bay

Housel Cove TR12 7PG
☎ 01326 290417 & 290917 🖷 01326 290359
e-mail: info@houselbay.com
***Dir:*** *follow A39/A394 to Helston, take the A3083 to the Lizard, at Lizard sign bear left, at school turn left and proceed down Lane to Hotel*
This long-established hotel has stunning views across the Western Approaches, equally enjoyable from the sunny lounge and many of the bedrooms. Most bedrooms have high standards of comfort with modern facilities and extras. Enjoyable cuisine is available in the stylish, wooden-floored dining room, after which a stroll to the end of the garden leads directly onto the Cornwall coastal path.
**ROOMS:** 21 en suite (1 fmly) No smoking in 2 bedrooms s £30-£90; d £60-£120 (incl. bkfst) * **LB** **FACILITIES:** STV Xmas **CONF:** Thtr 20 Class 16 Board 12 Del £150 * **SERVICES:** Lift **PARKING:** 37
**NOTES:** No dogs (ex guide dogs) No smoking in restaurant RS Winter
**CARDS:**

### ★★80% ❀❀ Tregildry

TR12 6HG
☎ 01326 231378 🖷 01326 231561
e-mail: trgildry@globalnet.co.uk
(For full entry see Gillan)

---

LOCKINGTON Hotels are listed under East Midlands Airport

---

LOLWORTH, Cambridgeshire Map 05 TL36

### ⇧ *Travelodge*

Huntingdon Rd CB3 8DR
☎ 01954 781335 🖷 01954 781335
***Dir:*** *on A14 northbound, 3m N of junct 14 on M11*
Travelodge offers good quality, good value, modern accommodation. Ideal for families, the spacious, en suite bedrooms include remote-control TV, tea and coffee-making facilities, luxury beds and free morning newspaper. Meals can be taken at the nearby family restaurant. For further details and the Travelodge phone number, consult the Hotel Groups page.

**ROOMS:** 20 en suite

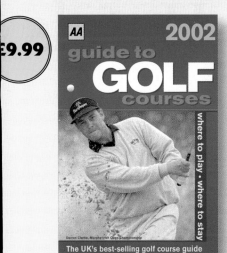

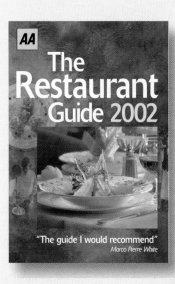

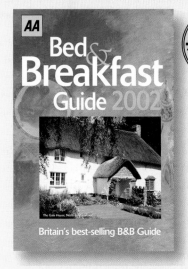

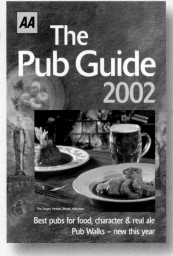

# Index of London Hotels

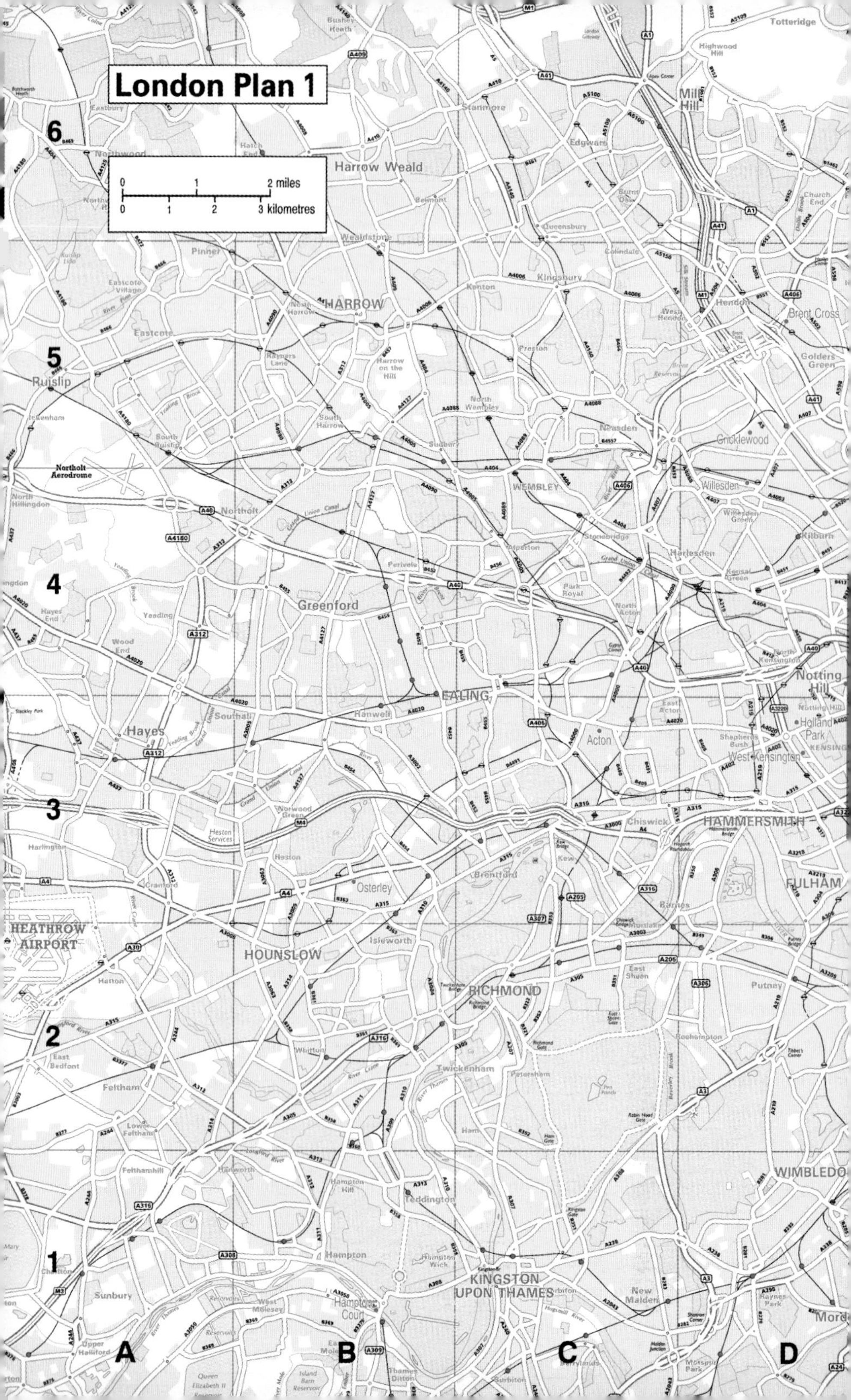
London Plan 1
0 1 2 miles
0 1 2 3 kilometres
A
B
C
D
1
2
3
4
5
6
HARROW
Harrow Weald
Stanmore
Edgware
Mill Hill
Hendon
Brent Cross
Golders Green
Cricklewood
Willesden
Kilburn
Harlesden
WEMBLEY
Greenford
Northolt
Ruislip
Eastcote
Pinner
Northwood
Hayes
Southall
EALING
Acton
Notting Hill
Holland Park
West Kensington
HAMMERSMITH
Chiswick
FULHAM
Putney
Barnes
Brentford
Osterley
HOUNSLOW
Isleworth
RICHMOND
Twickenham
Teddington
Hampton
Hampton Court
KINGSTON UPON THAMES
New Malden
WIMBLEDO
Feltham
Sunbury
HEATHROW AIRPORT
Hatton
Harlington
Heston
Cranford
Northolt Aerodrome
Yeading
Hayes End
Ickenham
North Hillingdon
Greenford
Perivale
Alperton
Park Royal
Neasden
Kingsbury
Kenton
Preston
Sudbury
Colindale
Queensbury
Roehampton
East Sheen
Petersham
Whitton
Hanworth
Lower Feltham
East Bedfont
Norwood Green
Hanwell
Totteridge
Highwood Hill
Church End
Bushey Heath
Belmont
Wealdstone
Rayners Lane
South Harrow
Harrow on the Hill
North Wembley
Surbiton
Raynes Park
Motspur Park

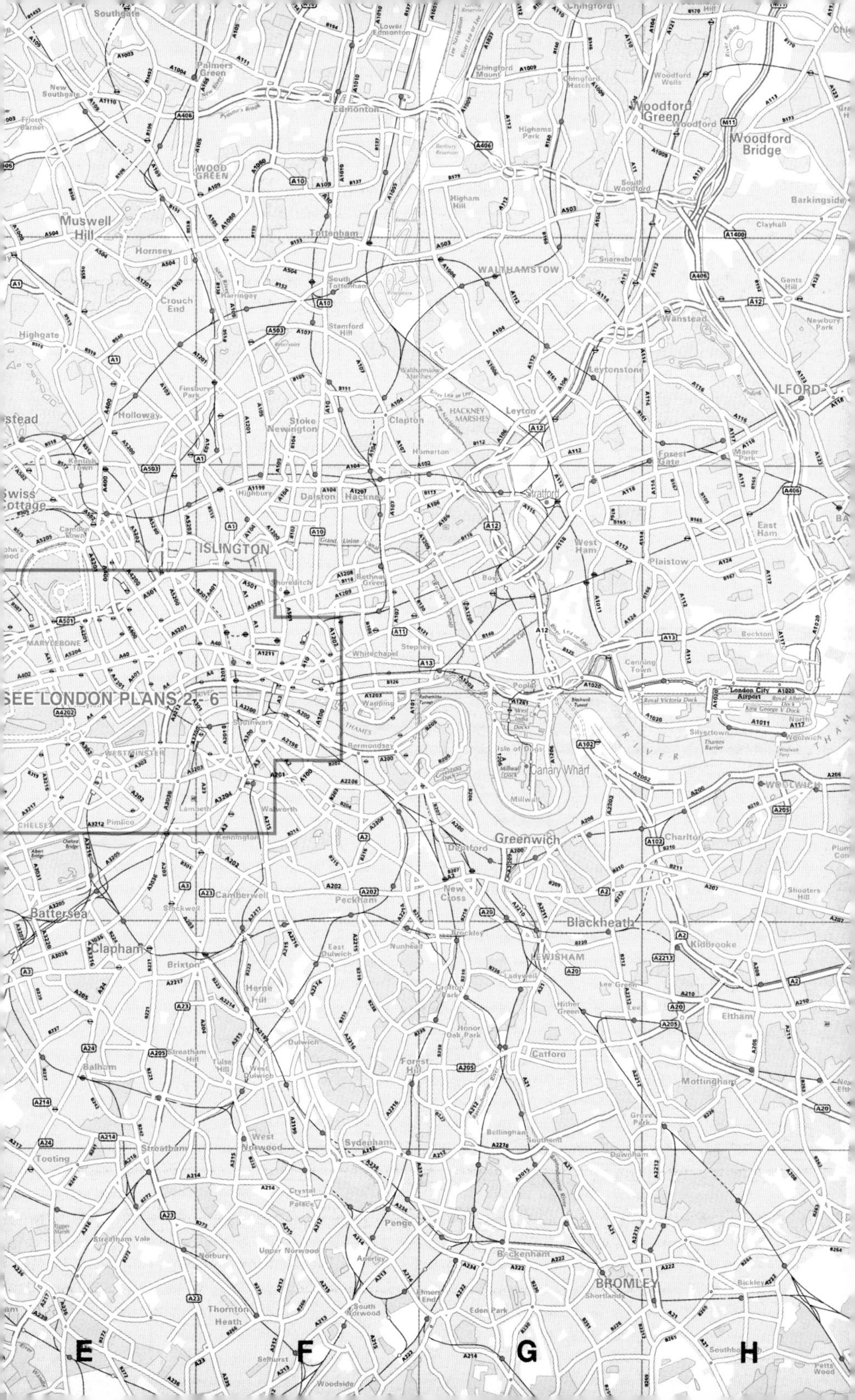
SEE LONDON PLANS 2–6
Southgate
Palmers Green
New Southgate
Friern Barnet
Lower Edmonton
Edmonton
Chingford
Chingford Mount
Chingford Hatch
Woodford Wells
Woodford Green
Woodford
Woodford Bridge
Highams Park
Higham Hill
South Woodford
Barkingside
WOOD GREEN
Muswell Hill
Hornsey
Tottenham
Clayhall
Snaresbrook
Gants Hill
Harringey
Crouch End
South Tottenham
WALTHAMSTOW
Wanstead
Newbury Park
Highgate
Stamford Hill
Walthamstow Marshes
Finsbury Park
Leytonstone
ILFORD
Holloway
Stoke Newington
Clapton
HACKNEY MARSHES
Leyton
Kentish Town
Homerton
Forest Gate
Manor Park
Swiss Cottage
Highbury
Dalston
Hackney
Stratford
Camden Town
ISLINGTON
West Ham
East Ham
Plaistow
Shoreditch
Bethnal Green
Bow
MARYLEBONE
Whitechapel
Stepney
Beckton
Canning Town
Poplar
Wapping
Royal Victoria Dock
London City Airport
Royal Albert Dock
King George V Dock
North Woolwich
Southwark
THAMES
Bermondsey
West India Docks
Isle of Dogs
Silvertown
Thames Barrier
Woolwich
RIVER
WESTMINSTER
Canary Wharf
Millwall
WOOLWICH
Lambeth
Pimlico
Walworth
CHELSEA
Kennington
Greenwich
Deptford
Charlton
Shooters Hill
Camberwell
Peckham
New Cross
Battersea
Stockwell
Blackheath
Clapham
Brixton
East Dulwich
Nunhead
Brockley
LEWISHAM
Kidbrooke
Ladywell
Lee Green
Herne Hill
Crofton Park
Hither Green
Eltham
Dulwich
Honor Oak Park
Catford
Balham
Streatham Hill
Tulse Hill
West Dulwich
Forest Hill
Mottingham
Grove Park
Tooting
Streatham
West Norwood
Sydenham
Bellingham
Southend
Downham
Crystal Palace
Penge
Streatham Vale
Upper Norwood
Anerley
Norbury
Beckenham
BROMLEY
Shortlands
Bickley
Thornton Heath
South Norwood
Elmers End
Eden Park
Selhurst
Woodside
Southborough
Petts Wood
E
F
G
H

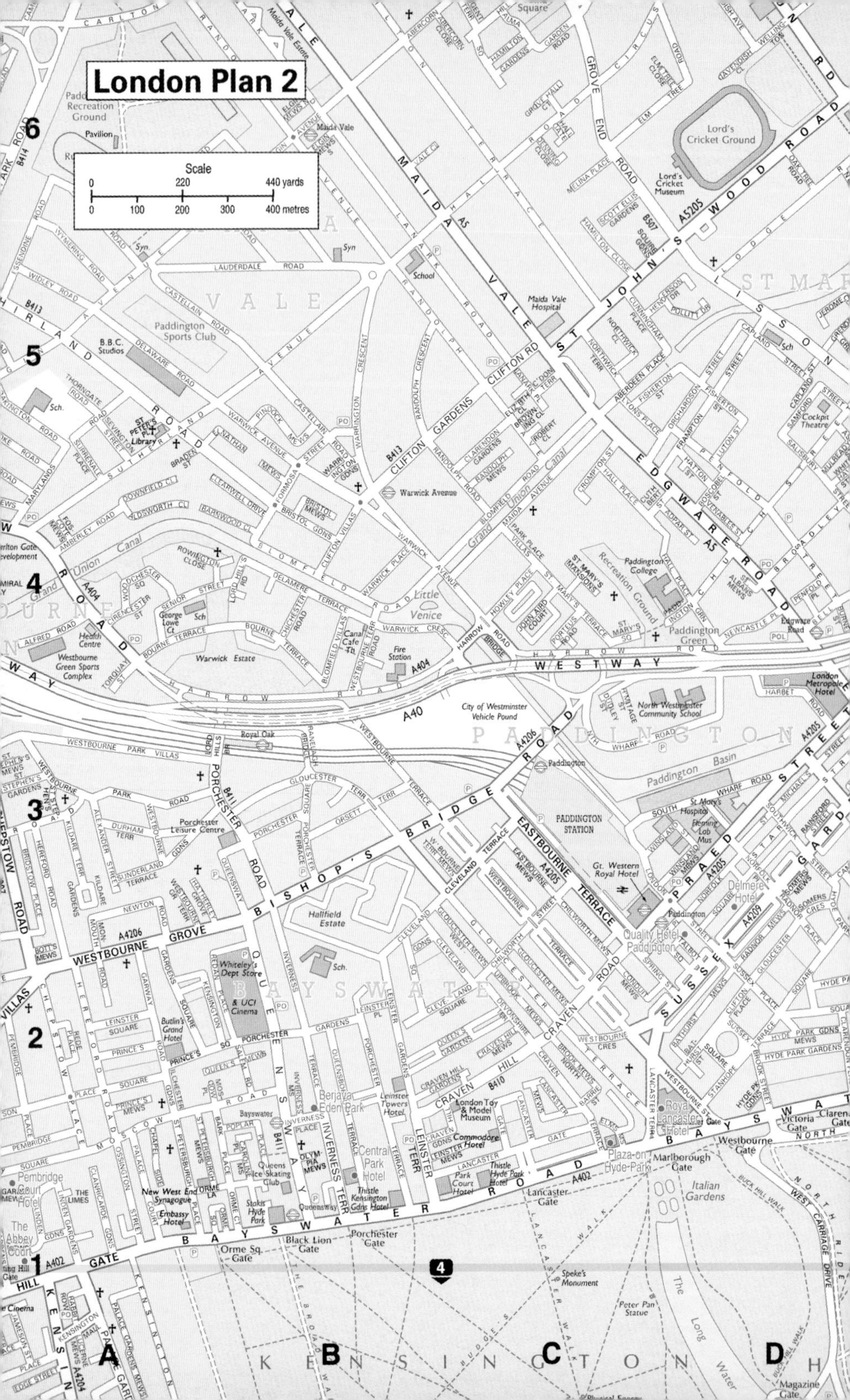
London Plan 2
Scale
0
220
440 yards
0
100
200
300
400 metres
Paddington Recreation Ground
Lord's Cricket Ground
Lord's Cricket Museum
Maida Vale Hospital
Paddington Sports Club
B.B.C. Studios
Warwick Avenue
Little Venice
Paddington College
Recreation Ground
Paddington Green
WESTWAY
City of Westminster Vehicle Pound
North Westminster Community School
London Metropole Hotel
Paddington Basin
PADDINGTON STATION
Gt. Western Royal Hotel
St Mary's Hospital
Fleming Lab Mus
Royal Oak
Porchester Leisure Centre
Hallfield Estate
Whiteley's Dept Store & UCI Cinema
Butlin's Grand Hotel
Quality Hotel Paddington
Delmere Hotel
London Toy & Model Museum
Commodore Hotel
Central Park Hotel
Queens Ice Skating Club
New West End Synagogue
Embassy Hotel
Stakis Hyde Park
Thistle Kensington Gdns Hotel
Thistle Hyde Park Hotel
Park Court Hotel
Royal Lancaster Hotel
Plaza-on-Hyde-Park
Pembridge Court Hotel
The Abbey Court
Italian Gardens
Speke's Monument
Peter Pan Statue
Marlborough Gate
Lancaster Gate
Victoria Gate
Westbourne Gate
Black Lion Gate
Porchester Gate
Orme Sq. Gate
Magazine Gate
BAYSWATER ROAD
MAIDA VALE
EDGWARE ROAD
ST JOHN'S WOOD ROAD
BISHOP'S BRIDGE ROAD
WESTBOURNE GROVE
PRAED STREET
SUSSEX GARDENS
HARROW ROAD
KENSINGTON
PADDINGTON
BAYSWATER
1
2
3
4
5
6
A
B
C
D

REGENTS PARK
Winfield House
London Central Mosque
Hanover Gate
Boat House
Boating Lake
Open Air Theatre
Queen Mary's Garden
INNER CIRCLE
The Holme
Regent's College
Tennis Courts
Cumberland Gate
CHESTER ROAD
THE BROAD WALK
OUTER CIRCLE
Royal College of Physicians
Royal College of Obstetricians & Gynaecologists
Rudolf Steiner Hall
Clarence Gate
Cornwall Terrace
YORK BRIDGE
Park Square
Regent's Park
PARK CRESCENT
Central London County Court
Royal Academy of Music
L.T. Lost Property Office
Madame Tussaud's
Planetarium
Baker Street
Sherlock Holmes Mus
Regents Park Hotel
Marylebone
MARYLEBONE STATION
MARYLEBONE ROAD
University of Westminster
Princess Grace Hosp
London Clinic
Town Hall
Liby
Landmark
Harewood Hotel
Western Ophthalmic Hosp
Samaritan Hosp
GLOUCESTER PLACE
BAKER STREET
PADDINGTON STREET
MARYLEBONE HIGH STREET
King Edward VII's Hosp
Heart Hospital
RIBA
BBC
Visitor Centre
All Souls' Ch
PORTLAND PLACE
GREAT PORTLAND STREET
Melia White House Regents Park
Thames TV Centre
EUSTON
Royal Nat Orth Hosp
Posthouse Premier Regents Park
Grange Fitzrovia
Kingsway College
ALBANY STREET
Library
Play Area
Seymour Leisure Centre
Fitzroy Nuffield Hosp
Wallace Collection
Jury's Clifton-Ford
British Dental Association
Wigmore Hall
Londoner Hotel
Mandeville Hotel
Royal Society of Medicine
University of Westminster
St Georges Hotel
CAVENDISH
MORTIMER STREET
REGENT STREET
Oxford Circus
Radisson SAS Portman Hotel
Churchill Inter-Continental
The Montcalm Hotel Nikko London
Mostyn Hotel
Selfridge Hotel
Radisson Edwardian Berkshire
Bryanston Court Hotel
London Marriott Hotel Marble Arch
WIGMORE STREET
SEYMOUR STREET
OXFORD STREET
Thistle Marble Arch Hotel
The Cumberland
Odeon
Marble Arch
MARBLE ARCH
Bond Street
NEW BOND STREET
Stanhope Gate
Albion Gate
Speakers Corner
Entrance and Exit to Underground Car Park
Brook Gate
Grosvenor Gate
PARK LANE
London Marriott Hotel Grosvenor Square
Roosevelt Memorial
US Embassy
Claridges
St Georges Church
The Westbury
Millennium Hotel London Mayfair
Connaught Hotel
Grosvenor House
MAYFAIR
Royal Inst. (Faraday Mus.)
Museum of Mankind
Brown's Hotel
Agnew's Gallery
May Fair Inter-Continental London
Chesterfield Hotel
Washington Mayfair Hotel
Flemings Mayfair
Ritz Hotel
Green Park
The Dorchester
RING ROAD
A4202
A501
A41
A5
A402
A5204
B524
B406
A4201
E
F
G
H

London Plan 3
Somers Town
Euston Station
British Library
St Pancras Station
King's Cross St Pancras
Euston Road
Camden Town Hall & St Pancras Liby
St Pancras International Youth Hostel
National Temperance Hospital
Kennedy Hotel
Ibis London Euston
Elizabeth Garrett Anderson Hosp.
London Euston Travel Inn
New Ambassadors Hotel
County Hotel
Euston Plaza Hotel
Friends House
Wellcome Inst
Euston Square
Euston Tower
Euston Centre
Thames TV Centre
Melia White House Regents Park
Kingsway College
Play Area
Library
St Pancras
St George's Gardens
Thomas Coram Foundation
Coram's Fields Playground
Brunswick Housing & Shopping Centre
Renoir Cinema
Posthouse Premier Bloomsbury
British Medical Assoc
Tavistock Hotel
Royal National Hotel
University of London
Russell Square
Hotel Russell
President Hotel
National Hosp
Royal London Homeopathic Hospital
Hospital for Sick Children
Imperial Hotel
Waverley House Hotel
Bedford Hotel
Bloomsbury Park Hotel
The Bonnington in Bloomsbury
Bloomsbury
University College
University College Hosp.
Bloomsbury Theatre
Percival David Foundation of Chinese Art
Maternity & Childrens Hosp.
Obstetrics Hosp
Vanbrugh Th.
R.A.D.A.
Academy Hotel
Drill Hall
Building Centre
Myhotel
Montague on the Gardens
British Museum
Blooms Hotel
Radisson Edwardian Kenilworth
Radisson Edwardian Marlborough
Kingsley Hotel
Great Russell Street
Warren Street
Grafton Hotel
London Foot Hosp
Great Portland Street
Royal Nat. Orth. Hosp
Posthouse Premier Regents Park
Grange Fitzrovia
British Telecom Tower
Middlesex Hospital
Pollock's Toy Museum
Goodge Street
Middlesex Hosp
Rathbone Hotel
ABC
RIBA
BBC
Visitor Centre
All Souls' Ch
St Georges Hotel
Soho Poly
Mag. Court
University of Westminster
Oxford Circus
Palladium
Tottenham Court Road
Astoria
YMCA
Dominion
St Giles Circus
Centre Pt
The Berners
House of St Barnabas
Princes Circus
Shaftesbury Th
Oasis Sports Centre
Drury Lane Moathouse Hotel
Holborn Town Hall
Kingsway Hall
New Connaught Rooms
Freemason's Hall
New London Theatre
Shaftesbury Hosp.
Contemp Applied Arts
St Donmar Th.
Radisson Edwardian Mountbatten
New Ambass. Th
Cambridge Th
Seven Dials
Royal Opera House
Theatre Mus.
London Transport Mus
Fortune Th
Covent Garden
Africa Centre
St Paul's
St Peter's Hosp.
Jubilee Mkt.
Strand Palace
Vaudeville Th
Adelphi Th
Savoy Th
Royal Society of Arts
Marshall Street Leisure Centre
Soho
Health Centre
Prince Edward Th
Palace Th
Curzon (Soho)
Fire Sta
Gielgud Th
Queens Th
Apollo Th
Lyric Th
Trocadero Centre
UGC
Prince Charles
St John's Hosp
Hippodrome
Warner
Empire
MGM (Swiss Centre)
Leicester Square
Leicester Square Theatre Booking Off
Odeon
Capital Radio
Hunt's
Wyndhams
Duke of York Th
Albery
County Ct
Coliseum
Garrick
St Martin's
Arts Th
Photo
London Pavilion
Piccadilly Circus
Criterion Th
Prince of Wales Th
Odeon (West End)
Comedy Th
Thistle Trafalgar Sq Hotel
Hants Hotel
National Portrait Gallery
National Gallery
St Martin-in-the Fields
Charing Cross Hotel
Charing Cross Sta
Players Th
York Water Gate
Embankment
Victoria Embankment Gardens
Trafalgar Square
Nelson's Column
Canada Hse
S Africa House
Northumberland Av
Government Offices
Min of Agriculture
Admiralty Arch
Mall Gallery
Her Majesty's Th
Th Royal Haymarket
Haymarket
Britain Visitor Centre
Piccadilly
Le Meridien Piccadilly
Royal Academy of Arts
Museum of Mankind
Royal Inst. (Faraday Mus.)
Brown's Hotel
Agnew's Gallery
May Fair Inter-Continental London
Chesterfield Hotel
Washington Mayfair Hotel
Flemings Mayfair
Ritz Hotel
Green Park
Cavendish St James's
St James's Church
22 Jermyn Street
Plaza Cin
St James's
The Westbury
St Georges Church
Hanover Square
Mayfair
Regent Street
Oxford Street
New Oxford Street
High Holborn
Shaftesbury Avenue
Charing Cross Road
Tottenham Court Road
Gower Street
Strand
Piccadilly
Pall Mall
Long Acre
Kingsway
Southampton Row
Gray's Inn Road
A B C D
1 2 3 4 5 6

Scale
0 220 440 yards
0 100 200 300 400 metres
PENTONVILLE
FINSBURY
CLERKENWELL
ST LUKE'S
PENTON RISE
Kingsway College
Royal Scot Hotel
Magistrates Court
London Ryan Hotel
Holiday Inn Kings Cross Bloomsbury
Mount Pleasant (Postal Sorting Office)
Lilian Baylis Theatre
Sadlers Wells Theatre
Town Hall
London Records Office
Kingsway College
House of Detention
Clerkenwell Heritage Centre
Museum of the Order of St John
St Bartholomew's Medical School
Charterhouse
Dallington Square
Barbican Hotel
Finsbury Leisure Complex
Exhibition Halls
Barbican Centre
The Barbican
Guildhall School of Music & Drama
Barbican
Farringdon
Gray's Inn
School
St Alban's
Chancery Lane
Stationery Office
St Etheldreda's Ch
Central London Markets
Founders' Hall
St Bart the Great
Butcher's Hall
St Bartholomew's Hospital
Holy Sepulchre
Ironmongers Hall
Barber Surgeons' Hall
Mus of London
Roman Wall
Salters' Hall
St Giles
Brewers' Hall
Girdlers' Hall
Plaisterers' Hall
Pewterers' Hall
Clock Museum
Haberdashers' Hall
Guildhall
Goldsmiths Hall
Waxchandlers' Hall
Saddlers Hall
St Lawrence Jewry
St Botolph's
Postman's Park
BT Centre
Staple Inn
London Silver Vaults
Daily Mirror Offices
Patent Office
Science Ref. Lib
Lincoln's Inn
Lincoln's Inn Fields
Royal College of Surgeons
Old Curiosity Shop
Public Record Office
Library
Dr Johnson's House
City Temple
Central Criminal Court
City Thameslink Station
Cutlers' Hall
Stationers Hall
St Martin's
St Paul's Cathedral
Bank of England Extension
St Mary le Bow
St Mary Aldermary
Temple of Mithras
Mansion House
Royal Courts of Justice
London School of Economics
Prince Henry's Room
Temple Church
St Clement Danes
Australia House
Bush House (B.B.C.)
St Mary-le-Strand
Inns of Court and Chancery
Middle Temple Hall
Inner Temple
Middle Temple
Temple
Somerset House
Courtauld Institute Galleries
Roman Bath
Howard Hotel
King's College
Gilbert Collection
St Brides
The Bridewell Th
Apothecaries' Hall
Youth Hostel
Faraday Building
College of Arms
Blackfriars
Mermaid Theatre
Salvation Army Heritage Centre
City of London School
Painters' Hall
Vintners Hall
Innholders' Hall
Livery Halls
Thames Police Station
Entrance to Strand Underpass (northbound only)
HQS Wellington (Master Mariners)
HMS President
Blackfriars Millennium Pier
BLACKFRIARS STATION
Blackfriars Pier
Millennium Bridge
Queenhithe Stairs
Southwark Br. Stairs
Three Cranes Walk
Bankside Jetty
Old Barge House Stairs
Oxo Tower Wharf
Bankside Gallery
Tate Modern
Globe Th Shakespeare Globe Exhibition
Financial Times
Vinopolis City of Wine
The London Television Centre (LWT)
Royal National Theatre
National Film Th.
Queen Elizabeth Hall
Purcell Room
London Nautical Sch
Express by Holiday Inn Southwark
St Christopher House
RIVER
NORTH SOUTHWARK
HOLBORN
HOLBORN VIADUCT
CLERKENWELL ROAD
FARRINGDON ROAD
FARRINGDON STREET
GRAY'S INN ROAD
ROSEBERY AVENUE
GOSWELL ROAD
ALDERSGATE STREET
OLD STREET
CITY ROAD
NEWGATE STREET
CHEAPSIDE
LONDON WALL
FLEET STREET
LUDGATE HILL
LUDGATE CIRCUS
STRAND
ALDWYCH
CHANCERY LANE
FETTER LANE
QUEEN VICTORIA STREET
CANNON STREET
UPPER THAMES STREET
VICTORIA EMBANKMENT
BLACKFRIARS BRIDGE
SOUTHWARK BRIDGE
WATERLOO BRIDGE
STAMFORD STREET
SOUTHWARK STREET
CHARTERHOUSE STREET
BEECH STREET
ST JOHN STREET
KING'S CROSS ROAD
PENTONVILLE ROAD
SKINNER STREET
LEVER STREET
A501 A401 A5201 A5200 A40 A201 A4 A3211 A3200 A300 A301 A1211 A1 B502 B501 B100 B144 B400 B521
5
6
7
E F G H

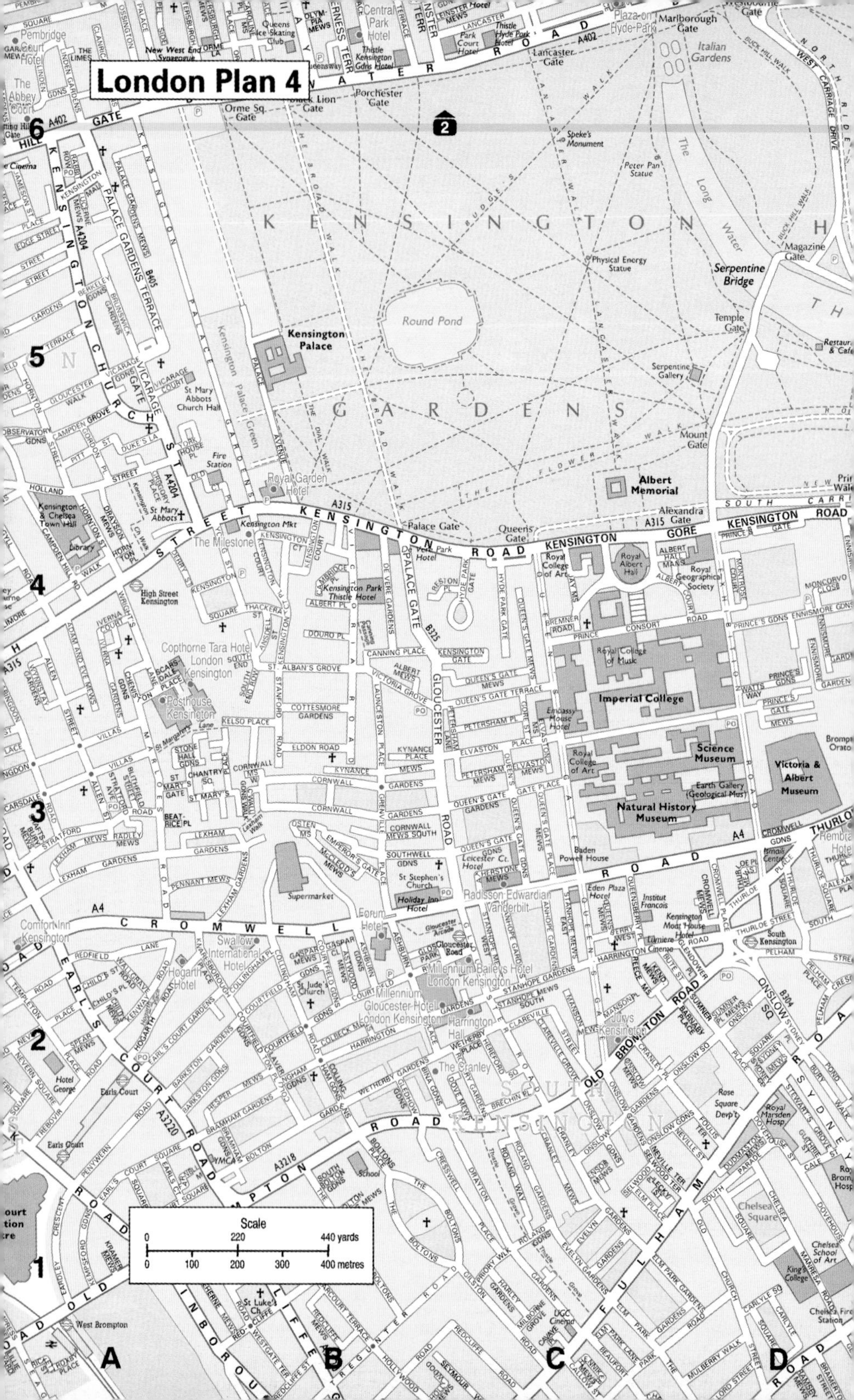
London Plan 4
KENSINGTON GARDENS
Kensington Palace
Round Pond
Albert Memorial
Royal Albert Hall
Royal College of Music
Imperial College
Science Museum
Natural History Museum
Victoria & Albert Museum
Serpentine Bridge
The Long Water
Italian Gardens
Kensington Mkt
The Milestone
High Street Kensington
Kensington & Chelsea Town Hall
Earls Court
Gloucester Road
South Kensington
West Brompton
SOUTH KENSINGTON
KENSINGTON ROAD
KENSINGTON GORE
CROMWELL ROAD
BAYSWATER ROAD
KENSINGTON HIGH STREET
KENSINGTON CHURCH STREET
EARL'S COURT ROAD
OLD BROMPTON ROAD
FULHAM ROAD
Scale
0 220 440 yards
0 100 200 300 400 metres
A B C D
1 2 3 4 5 6

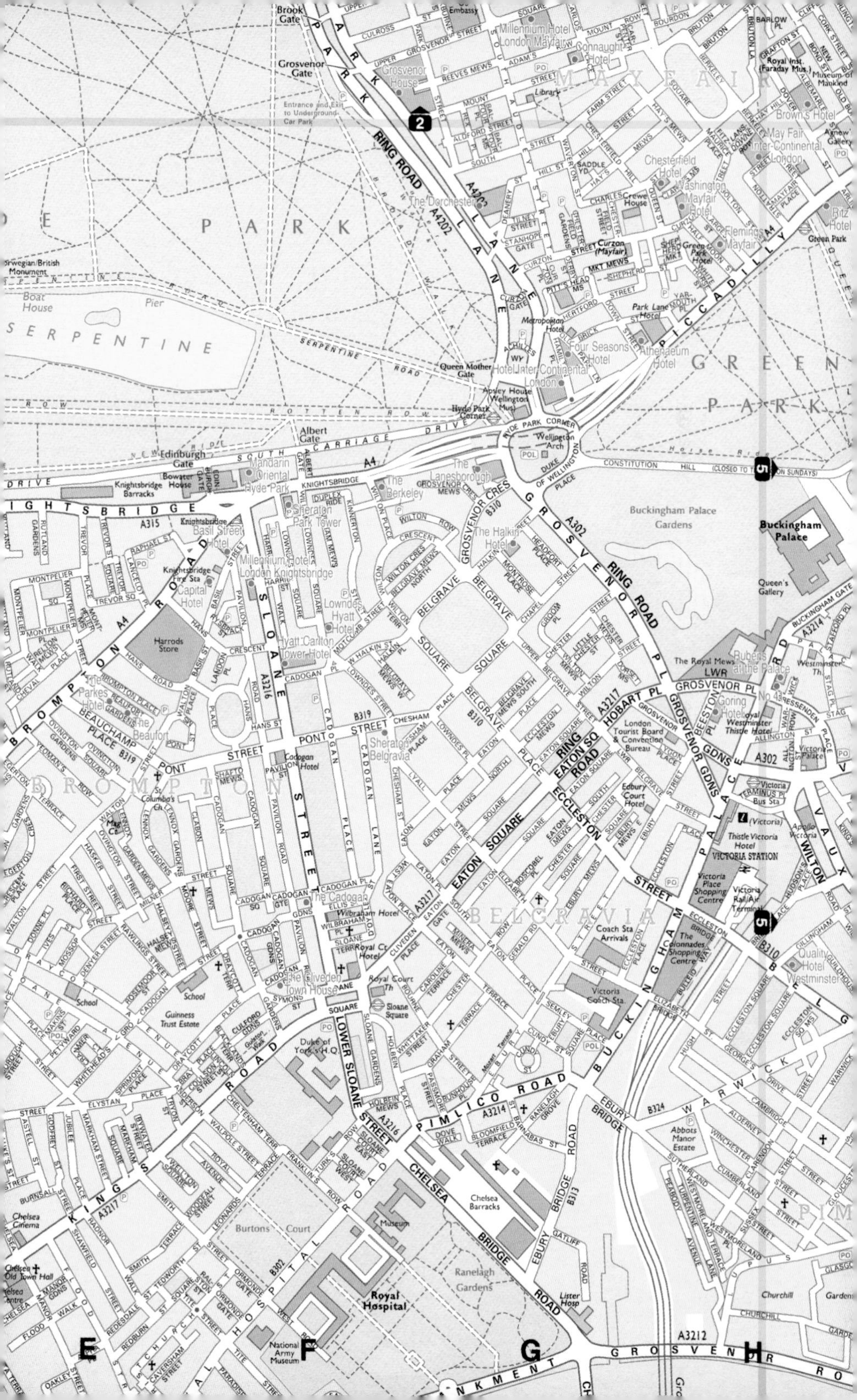

Brook Gate
Grosvenor Gate
PARK LANE
RING ROAD
A4202
Grosvenor House
Entrance and Exit to Underground Car Park
Embassy
Millennium Hotel London Mayfair
Connaught Hotel
MAYFAIR
Royal Inst. (Faraday Mus.)
Museum of Mankind
Brown's Hotel
May Fair Inter-Continental London
Agnew's Gallery
Chesterfield Hotel
Washington Mayfair Hotel
Crewe House
The Dorchester
Flemings Mayfair
Ritz Hotel
Green Park
Curzon (Mayfair)
Green Park Hotel
Park Lane Hotel
Metropolitan Hotel
Four Seasons Hotel
Athenaeum Hotel
PICCADILLY
HYDE PARK
Norwegian/British Monument
Boat House
Pier
SERPENTINE
SERPENTINE ROAD
ROTTEN ROW
Queen Mother Gate
Hotel Inter-Continental London
Apsley House (Wellington Mus)
Hyde Park Corner
HYDE PARK CORNER
Wellington Arch
Albert Gate
SOUTH CARRIAGE DRIVE
Edinburgh Gate
Mandarin Oriental Hyde Park
Knightsbridge Barracks
Bowater House
KNIGHTSBRIDGE
A4
A315
The Lanesborough
The Berkeley
GREEN PARK
CONSTITUTION HILL (CLOSED TO TRAFFIC ON SUNDAYS)
Buckingham Palace Gardens
Buckingham Palace
Queen's Gallery
Sheraton Park Tower
The Halkin Hotel
Knightsbridge
Basil Street Hotel
Millennium Hotel London Knightsbridge
Knightsbridge Fire Sta
Capital Hotel
Harrods Store
Lowndes Hyatt Hotel
Hyatt Carlton Tower Hotel
BELGRAVE SQUARE
GROSVENOR PLACE
A302
The Royal Mews
Rubens at the Palace
Westminster Th.
Goring Hotel
Royal Westminster Thistle Hotel
Victoria Palace
London Tourist Board & Convention Bureau
BROMPTON ROAD
The Parkes Hotel
The Beaufort
BEAUCHAMP PLACE
SLOANE STREET
A3216
PONT STREET
Cadogan Hotel
Sheraton Belgravia
EATON SQUARE
ECCLESTON STREET
Ebury Court Hotel
Thistle Victoria Hotel
VICTORIA STATION
Victoria Place Shopping Centre
Victoria Rail/Air Terminal
Apollo Victoria
BROMPTON
St Columba's Ch
The Cadogan
Wilbraham Hotel
Royal Ct Hotel
BELGRAVIA
Coach Sta Arrivals
The Colonnades Shopping Centre
Quality Hotel Westminster
The Cliveden Town House
Royal Court Th
Sloane Square
Victoria Coach Sta.
BUCKINGHAM PALACE ROAD
School
Guinness Trust Estate
Duke of York's H.Q.
LOWER SLOANE STREET
PIMLICO ROAD
A3214
EBURY BRIDGE
B324
Abbots Manor Estate
KING'S ROAD
A3217
Chelsea Cinema
Chelsea Barracks
Burtons Court
Museum
CHELSEA BRIDGE ROAD
Ranelagh Gardens
Royal Hospital
Chelsea Old Town Hall
National Army Museum
Lister Hosp
ROYAL HOSPITAL ROAD
B302
GROSVENOR ROAD
A3212
Churchill Gardens
EMBANKMENT
E
F
G
H
2
5

London Plan 5
Buckingham Palace
St James's Park
Green Park
Westminster Abbey
Houses of Parliament
Big Ben
National Gallery
Trafalgar Square
Victoria Station
Westminster Cathedral
Tate Gallery of British Art
Pimlico
Westminster
Lambeth Bridge
Westminster Bridge
Vauxhall Bridge
Piccadilly
Pall Mall
Whitehall
Victoria Street
Victoria Embankment
Millbank
Horse Guards Parade
Treasury
Foreign & Commonwealth Office
Ministry of Defence
Old Admiralty
St James's Palace

HQS Wellington (Master Mariners)
Thames Police Station
Entrance to Strand Underpass (northbound only)
Blackfriars Bridge
Millennium Bridge
Queenhithe Stairs
Southwark Br. Stairs
River
Old Barge House Stairs
Oxo Tower Wharf
Bankside Jetty
Bankside Gallery
Riverside Walk
Waterloo Bridge
The London Television Centre (LWT)
Royal National Theatre
National Film Th.
Queen Elizabeth Hall
Purcell Room
Hayward Gallery
Tate Modern
Globe Th Shakespeare Globe Exhibition
Financial Times
Vinopolis City of Wine
North Southwark
Stamford Street
Upper Ground
London Nautical Sch
Schiller International University
IMAX Cinema
Express by Holiday Inn Southwark
St Christopher House
Mercure London City Bankside
Southwark Street
Sumner Street
Union Street
Waterloo (East) Station
Waterloo
Southwark
Waterloo Station
International Rail Terminal
Shell Centre
London Marriott County Hall
County Hall
Forum Magnum Square
Young Vic Theatre
Southwark College
The Cut
Old Vic Theatre
Crown Court at the Borough
Fire Brigade Mus
Fire Stn
Southwark Th
Borough
Marshalsea Road
Borough High Street
Blackfriars Road
Waterloo Road
York Road
Library
Health Centre
Westminster Bridge Road
Lambeth North
St George's Cathedral
St George's Circus
Borough Road
South Bank University
Mathieson Court
Inner London Sessions House (Crown Court)
Newington Gardens
Newington Causeway
London Road
Elephant & Castle
Imperial War Museum
Geraldine Mary Harmsworth Park
Imperial War Museum Annexe
Days Inn Waterloo
Archbishop's Park
Lambeth Road
Kennington Road
St George's Road
London College of Printing
Metropolitan Tabernacle
Recreation Centre
Elephant & Castle Shopping Centre
Coronet Film Centre
New Kent Road
Heygate Estate
London Park Hotel
Draper Estate
Newington Butts
Walworth Road
Walworth Town Hall
The Cuming Museum
John Smith House
Novotel London Waterloo
Lambeth Walk Open Space
Lilian Baylis School
Ethelred Estate
Cotton Gardens Estate
Kennington Lane
Kennington Park Road
Kennington
Lambeth County Court
Kennings Estate
Art School
College
Kennington Road
Kennington Lane
Newington
Kennington
Lambeth
Southwark
Scale
0 220 440 yards
0 100 200 300 400 metres
E
F
G
H
3
9

London Plan 6
Scale
0
220
440 yards
0
100
200
300
400 metres
6
5
4
3
2
1
A
B
C
D
The Barbican
Barbican Centre
Guildhall School of Music & Drama
Moorgate
Broadgate
Liverpool Street Station
Spitalfields Market Hall
London Guildhall University
Bank of England (& Mus)
Bank of England Extension
Royal Exchange
Stock Exchange
Mansion House
Lloyd's
Leadenhall Market
Fenchurch Street Station
Cannon Street Sta
Monument
Custom House
Tower of London
Tower Hill
Tower Bridge
Tower Pier
HMS Belfast
London Bridge City Pier
London Bridge Station
Southwark Cathedral
Guy's Hospital
Borough Market
Globe Th Shakespeare Globe Exhibition
Financial Times
Vinopolis City of Wine
Clink Exhibition
London Dungeon
Britain at War Museum
Hays Galleria
Tower Bridge Museum
Millennium Bridge
Area Under Development
Greater London Authority Headquaters
Cheapside
Threadneedle Street
Cornhill
Leadenhall Street
Fenchurch Street
Bishopsgate
Houndsditch
Whitechapel
Lwr Thames Street
Upper Thames Street
Cannon Street
Queen Victoria Street
King William Street
London Bridge
Southwark Bridge
Borough High Street
Tooley Street
St Thomas Street
Bermondsey Street
Long Lane
Tower Bridge Road
Druid Street
Aldersgate Street
London Wall
Chiswell Street
Commercial Street
Middlesex Street (Petticoat Lane)
Minories
River Thames
North Southwark
Spitalfields

LONDON Greater London Plans 1-6, pages 336-346. (Small scale maps 4 & 5 at back of book.) Hotels are listed below in postal district order, commencing East, then North, South and West, with a brief indication of the area covered. Detailed plans 2-6 show the locations of AA-appointed hotels within the Central London postal districts. If you do not know the postal district of the hotel you want, please refer to the index preceding the street plans for the entry and map pages.

## E1 STEPNEY AND EAST OF THE TOWER OF LONDON

### ⌂ *Travelodge (London City)*

Harrow Place E1 7DB
☎ 08700 850950
Travelodge offers good quality, good value, modern accommodation. Ideal for families, the spacious, en suite bedrooms include remote-control TV, tea and coffee-making facilities, luxury beds and free morning newspaper. Meals can be taken at the nearby family restaurant. For further details and the Travelodge phone number, consult the Hotel Groups page.

## E4 CHINGFORD

### ○ Express by Holiday Inn

Chingford E4
☎ 0800 897121
A modern budget hotel offering comfortable accommodation in refreshing, spacious and comprehensively equipped bedrooms, en suite bathrooms with power showers and continental buffet breakfast included in the room rate. Suitable for business travellers or families. For further details and the Express by Holiday Inn phone number, consult the Hotel Groups page.
**ROOMS:** 91 en suite **NOTES:** Opening December 2001

## E14 CANARY WHARF & LIMEHOUSE
See LONDON plan 1 G3

### ★★★★★74% Four Seasons Hotel Canary Wharf

Westferry Circus, Canary Wharf E14 8RS
☎ 020 7510 1999 Fax 020 7510 1998
***Dir:** Leave A13 and follow signs to Canary Wharf/Isle of Dogs/Westferry Circus.Hotel is located off the 3rd exit of Westferry Circus r/about*
This stylish, modern hotel is in a superb riverside location and enjoys stunning views of the London skyline. The well-equipped bedrooms have been thoughtfully designed and decorated to a high standard. Staff are friendly and provide impeccable service.
**ROOMS:** 142 en suite No smoking in 99 bedrooms s £245-£260; d £265-£280 * **FACILITIES:** STV Indoor swimming (H) Tennis (hard) Sauna Solarium Gym Jacuzzi entertainment Xmas **CONF:** Thtr 200 Class 120 Board 56 **SERVICES:** Lift air con **PARKING:** 29
**NOTES:** Civ Wed 200 **CARDS:**

### ⌂ Hotel Ibis London Docklands

1 Baffin Way E14 9PE
☎ 020 7517 1100 Fax 020 7987 5916
e-mail: H2177@accor-hotels.com
***Dir:** From Tower Bridge follow signs City Airport/ Royal Docks, take exit 'Isle of Dogs'. Hotel is on 1st Left opposite McDonalds*
Modern, budget hotel offering comfortable accommodation in bright and practical bedrooms. Breakfast is self-service and dinner is available in the restaurant. For further details, consult the Hotel Groups page.
**ROOMS:** 87 en suite d £65 *

### ⌂ *Travelodge*

Travelodge

Coriander Av, East India Dock Rd E14 2AA
☎ 020 7531 9705
***Dir:** fronts A13 at East India Dock Road*

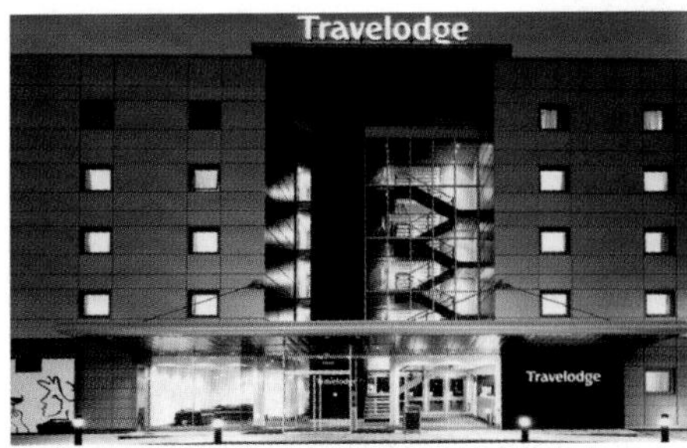
Travelodge

Travelodge offers good quality, good value, modern accommodation. Ideal for families, the spacious, en suite bedrooms include remote-control TV, tea and coffee-making facilities, luxury beds and free morning newspaper. Meals can be taken at the nearby family restaurant. For further details and the Travelodge phone number, consult the Hotel Groups page.

**ROOMS:** 132 en suite

## E15 STRATFORD See LONDON plan 1 G4

### ⌂ Hotel Ibis

Romford Rd, Stratford E15 4LJ
☎ 020 8536 3700 Fax 020 8519 5161
e-mail: H3099@accor-hotels.com
Modern, budget hotel offering comfortable accommodation in bright and practical bedrooms. Breakfast is self-service and dinner is available in the restaurant. For further details, consult the Hotel Groups page.
**ROOMS:** 108 en suite s £59.95; d £59.95 *

## E16 SILVERTOWN

### ○ Express by Holiday Inn London Royal Docks

Express
by Holiday Inn

1 Silvertown Way, Silvertown E16 1EA
☎ 020 7540 4040 Fax 020 7540 4050
A modern budget hotel offering comfortable accommodation in refreshing, spacious and comprehensively equipped bedrooms, en suite bathrooms with power showers and continental buffet breakfast included in the room rate. Suitable for business travellers or families. For further details and the Express by Holiday Inn phone number, consult the Hotel Groups page.
**ROOMS:** 88 rms **NOTES:** Open Now

## EC1 CITY OF LONDON

### ⌂ *Express by Holiday Inn London City*

275 Old St EC1V 9LN
☎ 020 7300 4300 Fax 020 7300 4400
e-mail: reservationsfc@holidayinnlondon.demon.co.uk
A modern budget hotel offering comfortable accommodation in refreshing, spacious and comprehensively equipped bedrooms, en suite bathrooms with power showers and continental buffet

*continued on p348*

## EC1 CITY OF LONDON, continued

breakfast included in the room rate. Suitable for business travellers or families. For further details and the Express by Holiday Inn phone number, consult the Hotel Groups page.

*Express by Holiday Inn, EC1 City of London*

**ROOMS:** 224 en suite **CONF:** Thtr 90 Class 40 Board 36

### ○ Malmaison London

Malmaison
HOTELS

18-21 Charterhouse Square EC1
☎ 01737 780 200 (reservations)
At the time of going to press, the star classification for this hotel was not confirmed. Please refer to the AA internet site www.theAA.com for current information.
**ROOMS:** 100 rms **NOTES:** Due to open Summer 2002

## EC2

### ★★★★★71% Great Eastern Hotel

Liverpool St EC2M 7QN
☎ 020 7618 5000 020 7618 5001
e-mail: sales@great-eastern-hotel.co.uk
This stylish Liverpool Street hotel continues to impress. Smart modern bedrooms are stylishly simple, with DVD and CD players and air conditioning adding comfort. The four restaurants ensure that long term guests don't get bored, and include a fine dining option - Aurora, a fish restaurant with Champagne bar, a Japanese restaurant and a traditionally themed pub. Personal trainers and beauty treatment rooms are available in the gym; and there are extensive conference and business facilities.
**ROOMS:** 267 en suite s £225-£515; d £260-£515 * **LB** **FACILITIES:** STV Gym steam room **CONF:** Thtr 200 Class 120 **SERVICES:** Lift air con **CARDS:**

## EC3 CHEAPSIDE

### ★★★71% Novotel London Tower Bridge

10 Pepys St EC3N 2NR
☎ 020 7265 6000 020 7265 6060
e-mail: H3107@accor-hotels.com

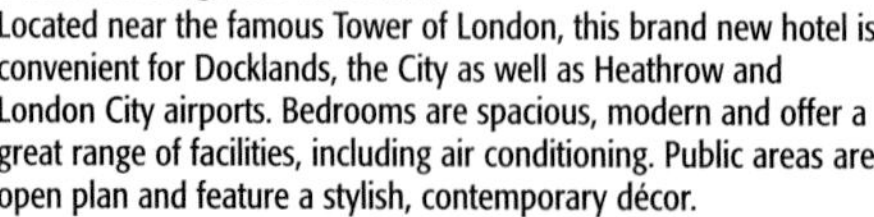

Located near the famous Tower of London, this brand new hotel is convenient for Docklands, the City as well as Heathrow and London City airports. Bedrooms are spacious, modern and offer a great range of facilities, including air conditioning. Public areas are open plan and feature a stylish, contemporary décor.
**ROOMS:** 203 en suite (77 fmly) No smoking in 145 bedrooms s fr £155; d fr £175 * **LB** **FACILITIES:** no TV in bdrms STV Sauna Gym Steam Room **CONF:** Thtr 72 Class 32 Board 28 Del from £199 * **SERVICES:** Lift air con **CARDS:**

## EC4

### ○ Crowne Plaza London - The City

19 New Bridge St EC4V 6BD
☎ 020 7329 2049
At the time of going to press, the star classification for this hotel was not confirmed. Please refer to the AA internet site www.theAA.com for current information.
**ROOMS:** 203 rms **NOTES:** Due to open Winter 2001

## N1 ISLINGTON See LONDON plan 1 F4

### ★★★62% Jurys Inn London

60 Pentonville Rd, Islington N1 9LA
☎ 020 7282 5500 020 7282 5511
e-mail: london_inn@jurysdoyle.com
***Dir:*** *from A1 turn right onto A501, turn right and continue onto Pentonville Road*
The Jurys Inn concept is based on good value rooms, that can easily be adapted to family use. All the rooms have a double bed and air-conditioning. Other facilities and services are fairly low-key. The Angel Tube station is nearby and there are several car parks in the neighbourhood.
**ROOMS:** 229 en suite (116 fmly) No smoking in 135 bedrooms d fr £89 * **FACILITIES:** STV **CONF:** Thtr 50 Class 24 Board 28 Del £160 * **SERVICES:** Lift air con **NOTES:** No dogs (ex guide dogs) Closed 24-27 Dec **CARDS:**

*See advert on opposite page*

## N10 MUSWELL HILL See LONDON plan 1 E6

### ★★★66% Raglan Hall

8-12 Queens Ave, Muswell Hill N10 3NR
☎ 020 8883 9836 020 8883 5002
e-mail: raglanhall@aol.com
***Dir:*** *North Circ B550 for Muswell Hill. At roundabout take last exit to Queens Avenue. Hotel is 75yds on the right.*
Located on an elegant tree lined avenue in North London, this hotel is well-situated for access to major road and rail networks. Bedrooms vary in size and style, with some suitable for family accommodation. Limited off street parking is also available.
**ROOMS:** 46 en suite (8 fmly) No smoking in 12 bedrooms s £69-£109; d £89-£114 * **FACILITIES:** STV **CONF:** Thtr 120 Class 40 Board 50 Del from £100 * **PARKING:** 12 **NOTES:** No dogs (ex guide dogs) Civ Wed 100 **CARDS:**

## N14 SOUTHGATE

### ○ Innkeeper's Lodge Southgate

The Green, Southgate N14 6EN
A new concept in the travel accommodation market. Smart rooms meet essential business requirements but also have home comforts. Dining options include all-day menus plus the added advantage of breakfast, which is included in the room price. Reservations can be made seven days a week through the room reservations number: 0870 243 0500. For further details, consult the Hotel Groups page.
**ROOMS:** 19 en suite **NOTES:** Opening Summer 2001

> Fancy a Singapore Sling? Bar staff in five star hotels should be skilled cocktail mixers.

London

NW1 REGENT'S PARK See LONDON plan 1 E4

## *Premier Collection*

### ★★★★★ Landmark

222 Marylebone Rd NW1 6JQ
☎ 020 7631 8000 020 7631 8080
e-mail: reservations@thelandmark.co.uk
***Dir:*** *located on Marylebone Road in front of Marylebone Station*

Landmark Hotel has a spectacular eight storey central atrium complete with palm trees, where light meals and refreshments are available throughout the day. The downstairs Cellars restaurant offers a relaxed atmosphere, while the more formal main restaurant now benefits from the considerable talents of John Burton-Race. The bedrooms are extremely stylish, generously proportioned and air-conditioned, with marble bathrooms offering deep tubs and separate showers. The hotel is located close to Hyde Park and Regents Park.

**ROOMS:** 299 en suite (60 fmly) No smoking in 147 bedrooms s fr £359; d fr £388 * **LB** **FACILITIES:** Spa STV Indoor swimming (H) Sauna Gym Health club Massage Steam room Whirlpool Reflexology Personal Training Xmas **CONF:** Thtr 380 Class 180 Board 50 **SERVICES:** Lift air con **PARKING:** 90 **NOTES:** No dogs (ex guide dogs) Civ Wed 300
**CARDS:**

### ★★★★71% *Meliá White House Regents Park*

Albany St, Regents Park NW1 3UP
☎ 020 7387 1200 020 7388 0091
e-mail: melia.white.house@solmelia.es
***Dir:*** *opposite Gt Portland St Underground and set slightly back from Marylebone & Euston Rd*

This delightful hotel, which began life as an apartment building in 1936, offers high standards of comfort and service. Bedrooms are well-equipped and smartly presented. Impressive facilities include

*continued on p350*

London

NW1 REGENT'S PARK, continued

the Garden Café, a fine dining restaurant and The Wine Press, often used for private parties.
**ROOMS:** 582 en suite (1 fmly) No smoking in 166 bedrooms
**FACILITIES:** STV Sauna Gym **CONF:** Thtr 120 Class 45 Board 40
**SERVICES:** Lift air con **PARKING:** 7 **NOTES:** No dogs (ex guide dogs)
**CARDS:**

*See advert on page 349*

### ★★65% Regents Park Hotel
156 Gloucester Place NW1 6DT
☎ 020 7258 1911 020 7258 0288
e-mail: rph-reservation@usa.net
***Dir:*** *R at Baker St tube, R at petrol station, pass Dorset Sq, hotel on R*
This privately owned hotel is ideally located in the heart of London and close to Baker Street tube. Bedrooms are smartly furnished, equipped with a good range of facilities and modern en suite bathrooms. The attractively presented restaurant serves authentic Singaporean cuisine.
**ROOMS:** 17 en suite 12 annexe en suite (3 fmly) s £80; d £99 (incl. bkfst) * **FACILITIES:** STV **NOTES:** No dogs (ex guide dogs)
**CARDS:**

*See advert on opposite page*

### Hotel Ibis London Euston
3 Cardington St NW1 2LW
☎ 020 7388 7777 020 7388 0001
e-mail: H0921@accor-hotels.com
***Dir:*** *from Euston station R to Melton St leading to Cardington St*
Modern, budget hotel offering comfortable accommodation in bright and practical bedrooms. Breakfast is self-service and dinner is available in the restaurant. For further details, consult the Hotel Groups page.
**ROOMS:** 380 en suite d £70 * **CONF:** Thtr 100 Class 50 Board 50

NW2 CRICKLEWOOD

### ★★66% The Garth Hotel
64-76 Hendon Way NW2 2NL
☎ 020 8209 1511 020 8455 4744

NW3 HAMPSTEAD AND SWISS COTTAGE
See LONDON plan 1 E5/E4

### ★★★★71% London Marriott Hotel Regents Park
128 King Henry's Rd NW3 3ST
☎ 020 7722 7711 020 7586 5822
***Dir:*** *at the junct of Adelaide Rd and King Henry's Rd. Approximately 200yds off Finchley Rd, A41*

This large, modern hotel has recently been extensively refurbished to a high standard. Smart public areas comprise an open plan marbled lobby, bar-lounge, leisure club and new Mediteranno restaurant. Air conditioned bedrooms are modern in style and very well-equipped.
**ROOMS:** 303 en suite (157 fmly) No smoking in 190 bedrooms
s fr £158; d £150-£205 * **FACILITIES:** STV Indoor swimming (H) Sauna Solarium Gym Hair & Beauty salon entertainment **CONF:** Thtr 300 Class 150 Board 90 Del from £225 * **SERVICES:** Lift air con **PARKING:** 150
**NOTES:** No dogs (ex guide dogs) Civ Wed 250
**CARDS:**

### ★★★66% *Posthouse Hampstead*
Posthouse
215 Haverstock Hill NW3 4RB
☎ 0870 400 9037 020 7435 5586
***Dir:*** *take A41 to Swiss Cottage just before this junction take feeder road left into Buckland Cres onto Belsize Av left into Haverstock Hill*
Exciting developments are taking place at this central Hampstead hotel. The arrival of Marco Pierre White's MPW restaurant makes it a popular venue for locals as well as residents. Stylish bedrooms feature alongside the more traditional rooms - all are well-equipped - and the lobby is particularly smart.
**ROOMS:** 140 en suite No smoking in 70 bedrooms **CONF:** Thtr 35 Board 20 **SERVICES:** Lift **PARKING:** 70
**CARDS:**

NW6 MAIDA VALE

### ★★★★66% *London Marriott Hotel Maida Vale*

Plaza Pde, Maida Vale NW6 5RP
☎ 020 7543 6000 020 7543 2100
e-mail: regentsplaza@btinternet.com

Situated at Maida Vale, this large, modern hotel has spacious bedrooms, air conditioning and excellent facilities. Smart public areas comprise a marbled lobby and a choice of restaurants. The hotel also offers valet parking, an impressive leisure club and a range of conference rooms.
**ROOMS:** 221 en suite (6 fmly) No smoking in 110 bedrooms
**FACILITIES:** Indoor swimming (H) Sauna Gym **CONF:** Thtr 200 Class 90 Board 40 **SERVICES:** Lift air con **PARKING:** 26 **NOTES:** No dogs (ex guide dogs) **CARDS:**

NW7 MILL HILL See LONDON plan1 D6

### *Welcome Lodge*
Welcome Break Service Area, London Gateway, M1, Mill Hill NW7 3HB
☎ 020 8906 0611 020 8906 3654
***Dir:*** *on M1, between junct 2 & 3 - northbound. Accessible from southbound carriageway*
This modern building offers accommodation in smart, spacious and well-equipped bedrooms, suitable for families and business travellers, and all with en suite bathrooms. Refreshments may be

*continued*

London

taken at the nearby family restaurant. For further details and the Welcome Break phone number, consult the Hotel Groups page.
**ROOMS:** 101 en suite **CONF:** Thtr 40 Board 20

## NW10 WILLESDEN See LONDON plan 1 C4/D4

### *Howard Johnson Wembley*
North Circular Rd NW10 7UG
☎ 020 8965 9200 020 8965 9300
e-mail: wembley@howardjohnson.co.uk
***Dir:*** *located on the A406 North Circular Road, next to Wembley Stadium*
**ROOMS:** 120 en suite **CONF:** Thtr 20 Class 15 Board 15

## SE1 SOUTHWARK AND WATERLOO

### ★★★★★69% London Marriott Hotel County Hall
Marriott HOTELS · RESORTS · SUITES

Westminster Bridge Rd, County Hall SE1 7PB
☎ 020 7928 5200 020 7928 5300
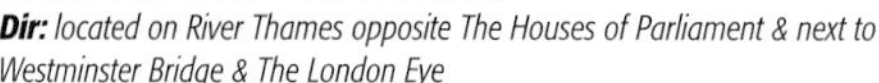
***Dir:*** *located on River Thames opposite The Houses of Parliament & next to Westminster Bridge & The London Eye*
Situated in the very heart of London, on the banks of the Thames, this beautiful hotel occupies the majority of the impressive and historic buildings of London's County Hall. Leisure facilities are extensive and include a superb 25-meter swimming pool and 6000 square feet of gymnasium. There are 200 air-conditioned bedrooms, many of which have views over the Thames.

continued

**ROOMS:** 200 en suite (60 fmly) No smoking in 147 bedrooms d fr £255 * **LB FACILITIES:** **Spa** STV Indoor swimming (H) Sauna Solarium Gym Jacuzzi entertainment ch fac Xmas **CONF:** Thtr 72 Class 34 Board 30 **SERVICES:** Lift air con **PARKING:** 120 **NOTES:** No dogs (ex guide dogs) Civ Wed 85 **CARDS:**

### ★★★71% Mercure London City Bankside
NOVOTEL

75-79 Southwark St SE1 0JA
☎ 020 7902 0800 020 7902 0810
e-mail: H2814@accor-hotels.com
The South Bank has seen a remarkable return to popularity over recent years. This smart, modern hotel has stylish, contemporary décor in bedrooms and public rooms. There is a small fitness room, a range of meeting rooms and a popular restaurant.
**ROOMS:** 144 en suite (24 fmly) No smoking in 88 bedrooms s £135; d £155 * **LB FACILITIES:** STV Gym **CONF:** Thtr 50 Class 30 Board 30 Del from £177 * **SERVICES:** Lift air con
**CARDS:**

London

SE1 SOUTHWARK AND WATERLOO, continued

### ★★★70% Novotel London Waterloo
113 Lambeth Rd SE1 7LS
☎ 020 7793 1010 🖹 020 7793 0202
e-mail: h1785@accor-hotels.com
***Dir:*** *opp Houses of Parliament on S bank of the R Thames, situated just off Lambeth Bridge, opp Lambeth Palace on Lambeth Rd*
This modern hotel is close to Waterloo station. Bedrooms are spacious and include air conditioning. Ten rooms have facilities for disabled guests. The open plan public areas include a garden brasserie, the Flag and Whistle Pub, a small shop and leisure facilities.
**ROOMS:** 187 en suite (80 fmly) No smoking in 158 bedrooms s fr £130; d fr £150 * **LB** **FACILITIES:** STV Sauna Gym Steam room **CONF:** Thtr 40 Class 24 Board 24 Del £194 * **SERVICES:** Lift air con
**PARKING:** 40 **CARDS:**

### ⇧ *Days Inn Waterloo*
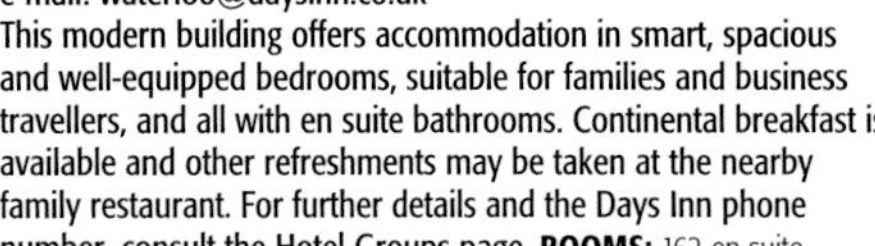
54 Kennington Rd SE1 7BG
☎ 020 7922 1331 🖹 020 7922 1441
e-mail: waterloo@daysinn.co.uk
This modern building offers accommodation in smart, spacious and well-equipped bedrooms, suitable for families and business travellers, and all with en suite bathrooms. Continental breakfast is available and other refreshments may be taken at the nearby family restaurant. For further details and the Days Inn phone number, consult the Hotel Groups page. **ROOMS:** 162 en suite

### ⇧ *Express by Holiday Inn Southwark*
103-109 Southwark St SE1 0JQ
☎ 020 7401 2525 🖹 020 7401 3322
e-mail: stay@expresssouthwark.co.uk
***Dir:*** *Follow A20/A2 to City Centre. Head towards Elephant & Castle. Right before Blackfriars bridge at 1st large t/light intersection*

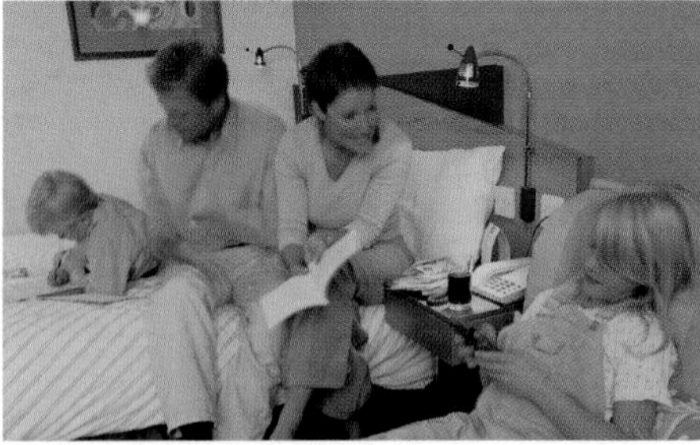

A modern budget hotel offering comfortable, refreshing, spacious and comprehensively equipped bedrooms, en suite bathrooms with power showers and continental buffet breakfast included in the room rate. Suitable for business travellers or families. For further details and the Express by Holiday Inn phone number, consult the Hotel Groups page. **ROOMS:** 88 en suite

SE3 BLACKHEATH See LONDON plan 1 G3

### ★★★65% Bardon Lodge

MINOTEL
Great Britain
15-17 Stratheden Rd, Blackheath SE3 7TH
☎ 020 8853 7000 🖹 020 8858 7387
e-mail: bardonlodge@btclick.com
On the edge of the pretty village of Blackheath, this friendly hotel is popular for small conferences and corporate business during the week and is equally in demand by weekend visitors.
**ROOMS:** 32 en suite (4 fmly) s fr £85; d fr £110 (incl. bkfst) * **LB**
**FACILITIES:** STV Jacuzzi Xmas **CONF:** Thtr 45 Class 20 Board 20
**PARKING:** 16 **NOTES:** No smoking in restaurant
**CARDS:**

### ★★65% Clarendon
8-16 Montpelier Row, Blackheath SE3 0RW
☎ 020 8318 4321 🖹 020 8318 4378
e-mail: relax@clarendonhotel.com
***Dir:*** *A2, turn off at Blackheath junct, hotel on left just before village overlooking Blackheath & Greenwich Royal Park*

This impressive Georgian building offers views over Blackheath and on to the city. Bedrooms vary in size and décor, there are some suites available. There is use of a local health club and several conference rooms on site.
**ROOMS:** 182 en suite (3 fmly) No smoking in 22 bedrooms s £70-£85; d £80-£95 (incl. bkfst) * **LB** **FACILITIES:** STV Reduce rate at David Lloyds centre entertainment Xmas **CONF:** Thtr 150 Class 50 Board 80 Del from £95 * **SERVICES:** Lift **PARKING:** 80 **NOTES:** Civ Wed 50
**CARDS:**

*See advert on opposite page*

SE10 GREENWICH See LONDON plan 1 G3

### ★★69% Hamilton House
14 West Grove, Greenwich SE10 8QT
☎ 020 8694 9899 🖹 020 8694 2370
e-mail: reception@hamiltonhousehotel.co.uk
***Dir:*** *Cross Blackheath common on A2 heading E to W towards central London, 2nd right after the Blackheath Tea Hut into Hyde Vale. West Grove is immediate Left*
This small Georgian hotel offers style and character with some impressive views of the Docklands. Bedrooms are individually appointed with some antique pieces of furniture. The restaurant is bright with a modern menu. There is a cosy lounge and the bar area opens out to an attractive garden with seating. There is some parking.
**ROOMS:** 9 en suite (8 fmly) No smoking in 4 bedrooms s £90-£120; d £100-£150 (incl. bkfst) * **LB** **FACILITIES:** STV **CONF:** Thtr 35 Class 22 Board 20 Del from £110 * **PARKING:** 8 **NOTES:** No dogs (ex guide dogs) No smoking in restaurant Civ Wed 65
**CARDS:**

### ⇧ *Express by Holiday Inn Greenwich*
Bugsby's Way, Greenwich SE10 0GD
☎ 020 8269 5000 🖹 020 8269 5069
e-mail: greenwich@stannifer-hotels.com
***Dir:*** *just S of Blackwell Tunnel off A102, on Greenwich Peninsula, near The Millennium Dome*
A modern budget hotel offering comfortable accommodation in refreshing, spacious and comprehensively equipped bedrooms, en suite bathrooms with power showers and continental buffet breakfast included in the room rate. Suitable for business

*continued*

travellers or families. For further details and the Express by Holiday Inn phone number, consult the Hotel Groups page.

**ROOMS:** 162 en suite **CONF:** Thtr 75 Class 45 Board 45

### ⇧ Hotel Ibis London Greenwich

30 Stockwell St, Greenwich SE10 9JN
☎ 020 8305 1177 🖹 020 8858 7139
e-mail: H0975@accor-hotels.com

***Dir:*** *From centre of London, follow Waterloo Bridge, Elephant and Castle, New Cross and A2 to Greenwich. From M25 follow A2 to central London*

Modern, budget hotel offering comfortable accommodation in bright and practical bedrooms. Breakfast is self-service and dinner is available in the restaurant. For further details, consult the Hotel Groups page.

**ROOMS:** 82 en suite d £58-£65 *

## SW1 WESTMINSTER

## Premier Collection

### ★★★★★ ◎◎◎ The Berkeley

Wilton Place, Knightsbridge SW1X 7RL
☎ 020 7235 6000 🖹 020 7235 4330
e-mail: info@the-berkeley.co.uk

The Savoy Group

***Dir:*** *300mtrs along Knightsbridge from Hyde Park Corner*

The Berkeley continues to impress, bedrooms are furnished with care and attention to detail. The stylish reception rooms are enhanced by the striking new Blue Bar. The impressive Spa offers a range of treatment rooms and has a stunning rooftop pool. The restaurants offer a complete contrast of style: modern, influenced by South East Asia at Vong and French cuisine at La Tante Claire.

**ROOMS:** 168 en suite No smoking in 28 bedrooms s fr £347; d fr £418 * LB **FACILITIES:** Spa STV Indoor swimming (H) Sauna Solarium Gym Beauty/therapy treatments Xmas **CONF:** Thtr 220 Class 100 Board 50 **SERVICES:** Lift air con **PARKING:** 50 **NOTES:** No dogs (ex guide dogs) Civ Wed 160 **CARDS:**

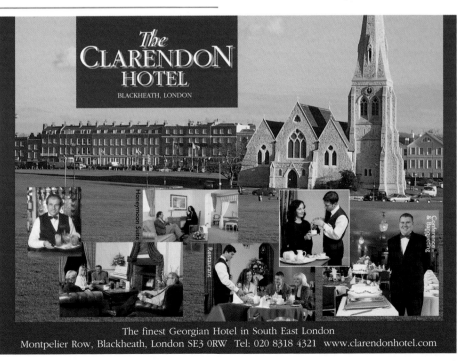



London

SW1 WESTMINSTER, continued

## Premier Collection

★★★★★ ®® **Lanesborough**
Hyde Park Corner SW1X 7TA
☎ 020 7259 5599 020 7259 5606
e-mail: info@lanesborough.co.uk
***Dir:*** *follow signs to central London and Hyde Park Corner*
Occupying an enviable position on Hyde Park Corner, the Lanesborough offers the highest levels of comfort in bedrooms and suites. Twenty-four-hour service from a personal butler ensures that guests are well cared for, and the reception rooms, with their lavish furnishings and magnificent flower arrangements, are a delight to use. Choose from a wonderful selection of vintage cognac, whiskies and ports in the popular cocktail bar and dine in the pleasant surroundings of the conservatory restaurant.
**ROOMS:** 95 en suite No smoking in 24 bedrooms s £312-£376; d £435-£528 * LB **FACILITIES:** STV Gym Fitness studio entertainment Xmas **CONF:** Thtr 90 Class 60 Board 50 **SERVICES:** Lift air con **PARKING:** 38 **NOTES:** Civ Wed
**CARDS:**

Popped the question? Hotels with Civ Wed in their entry are licensed for civil wedding ceremonies. Maximum numbers for the ceremony only are shown, e.g. Civ Wed 120

## Premier Collection

★★★★★ ®®®® **Mandarin Oriental Hyde Park**
66 Knightsbridge SW1X 7LA
☎ 020 7235 2000 020 7235 4552
e-mail: reserve-molon@mohg.com
***Dir:*** *after passing Harrods, on the righthand side, the hotel is 0.5m on the left opposite Harvey Nichols department store*
Situated between the fashionable shopping district of Knightsbridge and the peaceful green expanse of Hyde Park, this famous hotel offers a luxurious atmosphere. The stylish cocktail lounge is very popular with guests and has live jazz every evening. There are two dining options - The Park restaurant, offering light brasserie-style dishes; and Foliage, offering the highest standard of cuisine. There is also a spa which offers a range of high quality treatments in a stylish setting.
**ROOMS:** 200 en suite No smoking in 72 bedrooms s fr £355 * LB **FACILITIES:** Spa STV Sauna Gym Jacuzzi Fitness centre, steam room, relaxation area entertainment Xmas **CONF:** Thtr 250 Class 120 Board 60 **SERVICES:** Lift air con **NOTES:** No dogs (ex guide dogs) Civ Wed 400 **CARDS:**

★★★★★71% ®® **Hyatt Carlton Tower**
Cadogan Place SW1X 9PY
☎ 020 7235 1234 020 7235 9129
e-mail: ctower@hytlondon.co.uk
***Dir:*** *turn down Sloane St, Cadogan Place is the second turning on the left immediately before Pont St*
In the heart of Knightsbridge, the Hyatt Carlton Tower offers modern bedrooms, stylish public areas and impressive facilities. The ground floor houses the Chinoiserie lounge and Rib Room restaurant with its clubby bar. Modern Italian cooking is on offer in the friendly Grissini restaurant.
**ROOMS:** 220 en suite No smoking in 106 bedrooms **FACILITIES:** STV Indoor swimming (H) Tennis (hard) Sauna Solarium Gym Jacuzzi Beauty treatment Health club Hair salon Massage entertainment Xmas **CONF:** Thtr 400 Class 250 Board 80 **SERVICES:** Lift air con **PARKING:** 80 **NOTES:** No dogs (ex guide dogs) Civ Wed 360
**CARDS:**

★★★★★67% ®®® **Sheraton Park Tower**
The Luxury Collection
101 Knightsbridge SW1X 7RN
☎ 020 7235 8050 020 7235 8231
e-mail: morten.ebbesen@luxurycollection.com
***Dir:*** *close to Knightsbridge Underground Station,next door to Harvey Nichols*
This unique, circular, modern hotel has good standard-sized bedrooms; higher tariffs have better views and facilities, up to full

*continued*

London

butler service. Public areas have a lively atmosphere; the main bar off the lobby has a 'clubby' feel with tasteful polo prints. Afternoon tea can be taken in the Rotunda Lounge. Restaurant One-O-One serves sea food, meeting a very high standard of cooking.
**ROOMS:** 289 en suite (289 fmly) No smoking in 80 bedrooms s fr £382; d fr £405 * **FACILITIES:** STV Gym Fitness room entertainment Xmas **CONF:** Thtr 60 Class 50 Board 30 Del from £331 * **SERVICES:** Lift air con **PARKING:** 90 **NOTES:** No dogs (ex guide dogs)
**CARDS:**

## Premier Collection

### ★★★★ ◎◎ Goring

PRIDE OF BRITAIN
MEMBER

Beeston Place, Grosvenor Gardens
SW1W 0JW
☎ 020 7396 9000 📠 020 7834 4393
e-mail: reception@goringhotel.co.uk
***Dir:*** *behind Buckingham Palace, right off Lower Grosvenor Place, just prior to the Royal Mews on the left*
Situated in central London, this hotel is within walking distance of the Royal Parks and the principal shopping areas. The Goring offers well-equipped bedrooms that are traditionally furnished and boast high levels of comfort and quality. Stylish reception rooms include the garden bar and the drawing room, both popular for afternoon tea and cocktails. The restaurant menu has a classic repertoire but also has a well-deserved reputation for its contemporary British cuisine.
**ROOMS:** 74 en suite s £218-£264; d £264-£323 * LB **FACILITIES:** STV Free membership of nearby Health Club entertainment ch fac Xmas **CONF:** Thtr 60 Class 30 Board 30 **SERVICES:** Lift air con **PARKING:** 8 **NOTES:** No dogs Civ Wed 50
**CARDS:**

## Premier Collection

### ★★★★ ◎◎◎ The Halkin Hotel

Halkin St, Belgravia SW1X 7DJ
☎ 020 7333 1000 📠 020 7333 1100
e-mail: sales@halkin.co.uk
***Dir:*** *Hotel located between Belgrave Sq & Grosvenor Place. Access via Chapel St into Headfort Pl & turn left into Halkin St*
Modern in design, this individual hotel is located in a peaceful area just a stroll away from Hyde Park. The Halkin Hotel is minutes from the exclusive boutiques of Knightsbridge. The stylish, fully air-conditioned bedrooms combine comfort with practicality and many include state of the art communications
*continued*
for business visitors. New chef, Australian David Thompson, is an expert in Thai cuisine.

**ROOMS:** 41 en suite No smoking in 9 bedrooms d £335-£735 * LB **FACILITIES:** STV **CONF:** Thtr 30 Class 15 Board 26 **SERVICES:** Lift air con **NOTES:** No dogs (ex guide dogs)
**CARDS:**

## Premier Collection

### ★★★★ ◎◎ The Stafford

16-18 St James's Place SW1A 1NJ
☎ 020 7493 0111 📠 020 7493 7121
e-mail: info@thestaffordhotel.co.uk
***Dir:*** *turn off Pall Mall into St James's Street, take second left turn into St James's Place*
Quietly located in exclusive St James's, this charming hotel retains the understated luxury that has been its trademark for decades. Afternoon tea is a long-standing tradition in the comfortable drawing room and the American Bar is famous for its collection of celebrity photos, caps and ties. In the restaurant, menus balance traditional grills with more creative dishes. There are several private dining rooms and 350-year-old wine cellars. Service and hospitality demonstrate a serious commitment to customer care.
**ROOMS:** 81 en suite s £275-£700 * **FACILITIES:** STV Membership of Fitness Club available Xmas **CONF:** Thtr 40 Board 24 **SERVICES:** Lift air con **NOTES:** No dogs No smoking in restaurant Civ Wed 60 **CARDS:**

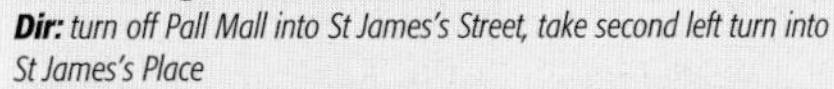

### ★★★★77% ◎◎ The Cadogan Hotel

75 Sloane St SW1X 9SG
☎ 020 7235 7141 📠 020 7245 0994
e-mail: info@cadogan.com
This delightful Victorian hotel overlooks the gardens in Cadogan Place and lists Lillie Langtry and Oscar Wilde as two of its most celebrated visitors. Bedrooms, mostly air-conditioned, are
*continued on p356*

London

SW1 WESTMINSTER, continued

tastefully furnished and feature a host of thoughtful extras. The elegant drawing room is popular for afternoon tea and the Edwardian restaurant is the setting for imaginative food.
**ROOMS:** 65 en suite (1 fmly) No smoking in 16 bedrooms s £223; d £223-£282 * **FACILITIES:** STV Tennis (hard) Xmas **CONF:** Thtr 50 Class 12 Board 20 **SERVICES:** Lift **NOTES:** No dogs (ex guide dogs) RS Saturdays **CARDS:**

### ★★★★73% The Rubens at the Palace

39 Buckingham Palace Rd SW1W 0PS
☎ 020 7834 6600 🖷 020 7233 6037
e-mail: reservations@rubens.redcarnationhotels.com
***Dir:*** *opposite the Royal Mews, 100m away from Buckingham Palace*
Overlooking the Royal Mews, behind Buckingham Palace and close to Victoria Station, the Rubens offers stylish bedrooms and comfortable public rooms, all of which have been recently refurbished. Dining options include the award winning Library restaurant, as well as an extensive lounge and room service menu.
**ROOMS:** 173 en suite No smoking in 80 bedrooms s fr £200; d fr £247 (incl. bkfst) * **FACILITIES:** STV Health clubs locally entertainment Xmas **CONF:** Thtr 90 Class 40 Board 30 Del from £220 * **SERVICES:** Lift air con **NOTES:** No dogs (ex guide dogs) No smoking in restaurant **CARDS:**

### ★★★★70% *The Royal Horseguards*

Whitehall Court SW1A 2EJ
☎ 020 7839 3400 🖷 020 7925 2263
e-mail: royal.horseguards@thistle.co.uk
Set in the heart of Whitehall, this impressive hotel is only a short walk from Trafalgar Square. Spacious bedrooms offer high standards and many overlook the River Thames. There is also an alliance with the magnificent meeting facilities of the adjacent One Whitehall, owned by the same company.
**ROOMS:** 280 en suite No smoking in 180 bedrooms **FACILITIES:** STV Gym **CONF:** Thtr 60 Class 30 Board 24 **SERVICES:** Lift air con **NOTES:** No dogs **CARDS:**

### ★★★★69% *Crowne Plaza London St James*

Buckingham Gate SW1E 6AF
☎ 020 7834 6655 🖷 020 7630 7587
e-mail: westres@bankrestaurants.com
***Dir:*** *Facing Buckingham Palace, take Buckingham Gate to left, continue for 100m and hotel is on right*
This elegant Victorian hotel is situated in the heart of Westminster. Spacious, air conditioned bedrooms are decorated to a high standard and feature a wide range of facilities. Impressive public areas feature a leisure club, business centre, and three restaurants.
**ROOMS:** 342 en suite No smoking in 180 bedrooms **FACILITIES:** STV Sauna Solarium Gym Jacuzzi **CONF:** Thtr 180 Class 95 Board 50 **SERVICES:** Lift air con **NOTES:** No dogs **CARDS:**

### ★★★★69% Millennium Hotel London Knightsbridge

17 Sloane St, Knightsbridge SW1X 9NU
☎ 020 7235 4377 🖷 020 7235 3705
e-mail: reservations.knightsbridge@mill-cop.com
***Dir:*** *Knightsbridge tube, Sloane Street exit, hotel 70 m right*
This modern, stylish hotel is located just a short walk from Harrods and Harvey Nichols. Bedrooms are decorated to a high standard and offer an excellent range of modern facilities. The lounge is popular for coffee or snacks and the open-plan Chelsea restaurant is the ideal venue for the modern, skilled cooking.
**ROOMS:** 222 en suite No smoking in 86 bedrooms d £99-£264 * **FACILITIES:** STV **CONF:** Thtr 110 Class 70 Board 50 **SERVICES:** Lift air con **PARKING:** 6 **NOTES:** No dogs (ex guide dogs) **CARDS:**

### ★★★★66% The Cavendish St James's

81 Jermyn St SW1Y 6JF
☎ 020 7930 2111 🖷 020 7839 2125
***Dir:*** *follow signs for Marble Arch along Park Lane to Hyde Park Corner left to Piccadilly. Past Ritz right down Dukes St Behind Fortnum and Mason*
Close to Piccadilly and Green Park, this busy hotel is particularly popular with business guests. The Sub Rosa Bar is a cosy, club-like venue next to the lobby, and there is a spacious lounge on the first floor. '81' Restaurant offers a European-style menu with hints of Spanish influence.
**ROOMS:** 251 en suite No smoking in 195 bedrooms s £199; d £239 * **LB** **FACILITIES:** STV Xmas **CONF:** Thtr 100 Class 50 Board 40 Del £249 * **SERVICES:** Lift **PARKING:** 65 **NOTES:** No dogs (ex guide dogs) **CARDS:**

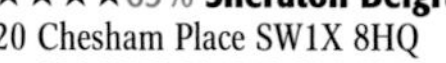

### ★★★★65% Sheraton Belgravia

20 Chesham Place SW1X 8HQ
☎ 020 7235 6040 🖷 020 7259 6243
e-mail: judy-kent@sheraton.com
***Dir:*** *A4 Brompton Rd into Central London. After Brompton Oratory right into Beauchamp Place. Follow into Pont St. Cross Sloane St & hotel on corner*
Situated in the heart of Belgravia, the shops of Knightsbridge, Kings Road and Sloane Street are just a short walk away. The facade is modern, the interiors very elegant. Accommodation features textured fabrics ranging from rich russets to warm yellows and there is a comprehensive range of in-room facilities.
**ROOMS:** 89 en suite (16 fmly) No smoking in 37 bedrooms s £270; d £246-£323 * **FACILITIES:** STV comp membership to local healthspa entertainment **CONF:** Thtr 35 Class 14 Board 20 **SERVICES:** Lift air con **NOTES:** No dogs (ex guide dogs) **CARDS:**

### ★★★66% Quality Hotel Westminster

82-83 Eccleston Square SW1V 1PS
☎ 020 7834 8042 🖷 020 7630 8942
e-mail: admin@gb614.u-net.com
This hotel is conveniently close to Victoria Station. Bedrooms, which vary in shape and size, are all comfortably furnished. Public areas include a small foyer bar, a range of meeting rooms and a brasserie-style restaurant.
**ROOMS:** 107 en suite (3 fmly) No smoking in 48 bedrooms s fr £99; d £108-£140 * **LB** **FACILITIES:** STV **CONF:** Thtr 150 Class 65 Board 40 Del from £144 * **SERVICES:** Lift **NOTES:** No smoking in restaurant **CARDS:**

## *Premier Collection Town House*

### ★★★★★ No 41

41 Buckingham Palace Rd SW1W 0PS
☎ 020 7300 0041 🖷 020 7300 0141
Discreetly located directly opposite the Royal Mews, No 41 is a stunning new townhouse. Bedrooms, furnished in contemporary black and white, combine high standards of comfort with state of the art technology. Guests can relax in the elegant split-level, executive lounge where

*continued*

meals and beverages are offered. Butler service is highly professional, attentive and friendly throughout.
**ROOMS:** 18 en suite s £346; d £346 (incl. bkfst) *
**FACILITIES:** STV use of 2 health clubs **CONF:** Board 12 Del from £342 * **SERVICES:** Lift air con **NOTES:** No dogs (ex guide dogs)
**CARDS:**

## Town House

### ★★★★ The Lowndes Hyatt Hotel

21 Lowndes St SW1X 9ES
☎ 020 7823 1234 020 7235 1154
e-mail: lowndes@hyattintl.com
***Dir:*** *follow A4 from M4 into London, left from Brompton Road into Sloane Street. Left into Pont Street, Lowndes Street next left, Hotel on right*
This small hotel is located in a salubrious part of town, within walking distance of Harrods. Bedrooms have a modern feel with good facilities including high-tech modem points. Small public areas are attractive including a Brasserie restaurant and meeting room.
**ROOMS:** 78 en suite No smoking in 31 bedrooms **FACILITIES:** STV Indoor swimming (H) Tennis (hard) Sauna Gym Jacuzzi
**CONF:** Thtr 25 Board 18 **SERVICES:** Lift air con **NOTES:** No dogs (ex guide dogs) **CARDS:**

## Town House

### ★★★★★ 22 Jermyn Street

St James's SW1Y 6HL
☎ 020 7734 2353 020 7734 0750
e-mail: office@22jermyn.com
***Dir:*** *follow A4 into Piccadilly, right into Duke Street, left into King Street, through St. James' Sq to Charles II St, left into Regent St & left again*
Jermyn Street is in the heart of one of the most fashionable and exclusive areas in London. Bedrooms and suites in this town house are traditional in style and offer the highest standards of comfort. The hotel provides 24-hour room service, mini bar and a wide range of secretarial and business services. There is no dining room in the hotel, however there are several outstanding restaurants in the area.
**ROOMS:** 18 en suite (13 fmly) d £210-£335 * **FACILITIES:** STV Membership of nearby Health Club **CONF:** Thtr 15 Class 15 Board 10 **SERVICES:** Lift air con **NOTES:** No smoking in restaurant
**CARDS:**

TV dinner? Room service at three stars and above.

### *Express by Holiday Inn London Victoria*

106 - 110 Belgrave Rd, Victoria SW1V 2BJ
☎ 020 7630 8888 020 7828 0441
e-mail: ligatom@expressvictoria.co.uk
***Dir:*** *from A13 (Tilbury Road) take A1011 towards Airport. Immediately turn off Canning Town. Underground on right, hotel 20 metres on left*

A modern budget hotel offering comfortable accommodation in refreshing, spacious and comprehensively equipped bedrooms, en suite bathrooms with power showers and continental buffet breakfast included in the room rate. Suitable for business travellers or families. For further details and the Express by Holiday Inn phone number, consult the Hotel Groups page.
**ROOMS:** 52 en suite

### ○ Corona

87 Belgrave Rd, Victoria SW1V 2BQ
☎ 020 7828 9279
At the time of going to press, the star classification for this hotel was not confirmed. Please refer to the AA internet site www.theAA.com for current information.
**ROOMS:** 51 rms **NOTES:** Opening July 2001

## SW3 CHELSEA, BROMPTON

## Premier Collection

### ★★★★ Capital

Basil St, Knightsbridge SW3 1AT
☎ 020 7589 5171 020 7225 0011
e-mail: reservations@capitalhotel.co.uk
Located in the heart of Knightsbridge, this hotel is close to the Royal Parks, famous South Kensington museums, Harrods and Harvey Nichols. A small, family run, luxurious hotel, it offers a warm and inviting environment to all its guests. The award-winning restaurant offers cuisine at a high level, booking is essential. Bedrooms are all individually designed

*continued on p358*

London

SW3 CHELSEA, BROMPTON, continued

with antique furniture; quality fabrics and marble bathrooms, which create a stylish, traditional feel.
**ROOMS:** 48 en suite No smoking in 12 bedrooms s fr £223; d fr £288 * LB **FACILITIES:** STV **CONF:** Thtr 30 **SERVICES:** Lift air con **PARKING:** 15 **CARDS:**

★★★70% **Basil Street**
Basil St, Knightsbridge SW3 1AH
☎ 020 7581 3311 020 7581 3693
e-mail: info@TheBasil.com
***Dir:*** *from M4 & A4 Brompton Road, turn right immediately before Harrods, the left into Basil Street. Hotel is on left*
A traditional and friendly hotel located in the heart of this shoppers' paradise. The public rooms are full of character with antiques, parquet floors, fine paintings and tapestries. Bedrooms continue to be in keeping with the original style of the property with the addition of up-to-date facilities.
**ROOMS:** 80 en suite (4 fmly) No smoking in 40 bedrooms s £150; d £223 * LB **FACILITIES:** STV entertainment Xmas **CONF:** Thtr 30 Class 16 Board 20 Del from £209.29 * **SERVICES:** Lift **PARKING:** 2 **CARDS:**

***Town House***

★★★★ **The Beaufort**
33 Beaufort Gardens SW3 1PP
☎ 020 7584 5252 020 7589 2834
e-mail: enquiries@beaufort.co.uk
***Dir:*** *100yds from Harrods*
In a tranquil, leafy location, yet just 100 yards from Harrods, the Beaufort offers the highest levels of hospitality. Luxurious bedrooms provide many extras such as chocolates, fresh flowers, videos and CD players. The attentive service leaves guests feeling relaxed and pampered.
**ROOMS:** 28 en suite (7 fmly) No smoking in 6 bedrooms s £182-£194; d £212-£306 (incl. cont bkfst) * **FACILITIES:** STV Complimentary entry to local health club **SERVICES:** Lift air con **NOTES:** No dogs (ex guide dogs)
**CARDS:**

***Town House***

★★★★★ ***Cliveden Townhouse***
26 Cadogan Gardens SW3 2RP
☎ 020 7730 6466 020 7730 0236
Only yards from Sloane Square, this town house bears all the hallmarks of quality and style. Luxurious bedrooms are beautifully furnished and day rooms comprise two lounges, where refreshments are served. There is also a sheltered garden. A complimentary executive car chauffeurs guests to the City twice each morning.
**ROOMS:** 35 en suite (9 fmly) No smoking in 30 bedrooms **FACILITIES:** STV Gym Beauty treatment Massage **CONF:** Board 12 **SERVICES:** Lift air con **CARDS:**

***Town House***

★★★★ **Parkes**
41 Beaufort Gardens, Knightsbridge SW3 1PW
☎ 020 7581 9944 020 7581 1999
e-mail: reception@parkeshotel.com
***Dir:*** *off Brompton Road, 150yds from Harrods*
Only five minutes from Knightsbridge, this charming little hotel, situated in the oasis of a peaceful square, offers every modern comfort yet retains the atmosphere of an elegant home. Its well-equipped suites come in a range of sizes, and many have a kitchenette. Breakfast is served in an attractive dining room and there is a small lounge.
**ROOMS:** 33 en suite (16 fmly) s fr £176; d £206-£411 * **FACILITIES:** STV **SERVICES:** Lift air con **NOTES:** No dogs (ex guide dogs) **CARDS:**

SW4 CLAPHAM See LONDON plan 1 E2

★★★69% **The Windmill on The Common**
Southside, Clapham Common SW4 9DE
☎ 020 8673 4578 020 8675 1486
Located on the edge of Clapham Common this hotel has much to offer. Spacious bedrooms are well-presented with all the modern facilities. There is a cosy guest lounge and wood panelled dining room. The Windmill bar is very popular, and the light airy conservatory can be used for functions.
**ROOMS:** 29 en suite No smoking in 15 bedrooms s £96; d £110-£130 (incl. bkfst) * LB **FACILITIES:** STV **CONF:** Thtr 40 Class 25 Board 20 **SERVICES:** air con **PARKING:** 16
**CARDS:**

SW5 EARLS COURT

★★★★67% **Swallow International**
Cromwell Rd SW5 0TH
☎ 020 7973 1000 020 7244 8194
e-mail: international@swallow-hotels.co.uk
***Dir:*** *on the A4, opposite Cromwell Road hospital*

SWALLOW
HOTELS

Swallow International Hotel

Well located for road access to the city, this hotel is one of the few in central London with its own car park. Bedrooms are modern in style and equipped with a comprehensive range of facilities. Public

*continued*

rooms include two restaurants, Hunters and the more formal Blayney's where diners are entertained nightly by a pianist.
**ROOMS:** 331 en suite (36 fmly) No smoking in 76 bedrooms s £99-£165; d £99-£165 * **LB** **FACILITIES:** STV Indoor swimming (H) Sauna Solarium Gym Jacuzzi **CONF:** Thtr 200 Class 100 Board 60 Del from £165 * **SERVICES:** Lift air con **PARKING:** 50 **NOTES:** No dogs (ex guide dogs) **CARDS:**

### ★★★73% The Hogarth

33 Hogarth Rd, Kensington SW5 0QQ
☎ 020 7370 6831 020 7373 6179
e-mail: hogarth@marstonhotels.com
***Dir:*** *turn into Earls Court Rd from Cromwell Rd (A4), take 3rd left into Hogarth Rd. Hotel is at the end of the rd on the left*
A purpose built hotel, conveniently located for the exhibition centre, the West End and local transport links. Bedrooms are tastefully furnished and decorated, offering guests a comprehensive range of modern facilities and amenities. The Terrace Bistro has an informal atmosphere and offers wholesome, uncomplicated cuisine.
**ROOMS:** 85 en suite (12 fmly) No smoking in 18 bedrooms s £99-£109; d £120-£140 * **LB** **FACILITIES:** STV **CONF:** Thtr 50 Class 20 Board 24 Del from £95 * **SERVICES:** Lift **PARKING:** 20 **NOTES:** No smoking in restaurant **CARDS:**

### ★★65% Comfort Inn Kensington

22-32 West Cromwell Rd, Kensington SW5 9QJ
☎ 020 7373 3300 020 7835 2040
e-mail: admin@gb043.u-net.com
***Dir:*** *on the Northern side of West Cromwell Rd, between juncts of Cromwell Rd, Earls Court Rd & Warwick Rd*
Convenient for Earl's Court, this cheerful, modern hotel offers smartly-kept bedrooms of varying sizes, with a range of amenities. The welcoming public areas are bright and comfortable.
**ROOMS:** 125 en suite (2 fmly) No smoking in 48 bedrooms s £100-£120; d £120-£140 * **LB** **FACILITIES:** STV **CONF:** Thtr 70 Class 35 Board 40 Del from £135.50 * **SERVICES:** Lift air con **NOTES:** No dogs (ex guide dogs) No smoking in restaurant **CARDS:**

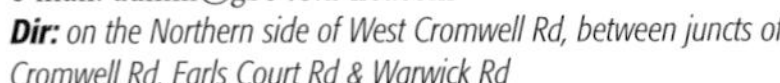

## *Town House*

### ★★★★ Cranley Hotel

10-12 Bina Gardens, South Kensington SW5 OLA
☎ 020 7373 0123 020 7373 9497
e-mail: info@thecranley.com
***Dir:*** *Walking down Gloucester Rd towards Old Brompton Rd from Gloucester Rd Tube Station. Take the 3rd Street on right into Hereford Square, then 3rd street on the Left into Bina Gardens*
This splendid and friendly Victorian town house is set in a quiet residential area of South Kensington. The bedrooms, including five suites, are attractively decorated and well-furnished, with many antiques and thoughtful extras as a standard. Complimentary afternoon tea along with aperitifs and canapés in the evening are served daily.
**ROOMS:** 38 en suite (2 fmly) s fr £182; d fr £259 * **LB** **FACILITIES:** STV **SERVICES:** Lift air con **NOTES:** No dogs (ex guide dogs) **CARDS:**

### ○ Burns

18-26 Barkston Gardens, Kensingston SW5 0EN
☎ 020 7373 3151
At the time of going to press, the star classification for this hotel was not confirmed. Please refer to the AA internet site www.theAA.com for current information.

## SW6 FULHAM See LONDON plan 1 D3

### ★★★★68% *Chelsea Village*

Stamford Bridge, Fulham Rd SW6 1HS
☎ 020 7565 1400 020 7565 1450
e-mail: reservation@chelseavillage.co.uk
This stylish eye-catching hotel forms part of the ambitious development at Chelsea Football Club and is a bold modern structure adjacent to the ground. The spacious bedrooms are well-equipped and the range of public areas includes five different styles of eating option that will satisfy the many varied markets of the hotel.
**ROOMS:** 160 en suite (64 fmly) No smoking in 56 bedrooms **FACILITIES:** STV **CONF:** Thtr 50 Class 25 Board 30 **SERVICES:** Lift air con **PARKING:** 250 **NOTES:** No dogs (ex guide dogs) **CARDS:**

### ★★★64% Paragon Hotel

47 Lillie Rd SW6 1UD
☎ 020 7385 1255 020 7381 0215
e-mail: sales@paragonhotel.co.uk
***Dir:*** *A4 to central London,0.5m after Hammersmith flyover turn right at traffic lights into North End Rd follow for 0.5m to mini rdbt left into Lillie Rd*
Conveniently located for the Earls Court Exhibition Centre, this large, modern hotel is gradually being upgraded. Bedrooms are comfortable and well-equipped. Two restaurants offer a choice of light meals and pizzas or more formal traditional menus. There are also extensive conference facilities and an underground car park.
**ROOMS:** 503 en suite No smoking in 96 bedrooms s £95-£150 (incl. bkfst) * **LB** **FACILITIES:** STV entertainment **CONF:** Thtr 1750 Class 900 Board 50 Del from £145 * **SERVICES:** Lift **PARKING:** 120 **NOTES:** No dogs (ex guide dogs) No smoking in restaurant **CARDS:**

## SW7 SOUTH KENSINGTON

### ★★★★75% Millennium Gloucester Hotel London Kensington

4-18 Harrington Gardens SW7 4LH
☎ 020 7373 6030 020 7373 0409
e-mail: sales.gloucester@mill-cop.com
***Dir:*** *opposite Gloucester Road underground station*
This stylish hotel rightly deserves its fine reputation. Bedrooms are furnished in contemporary styles with marble bathrooms and air conditioning. Additional amenities are provided in Club rooms

*continued on p360*

London

SW7 SOUTH KENSINGTON, continued

which have a dedicated lounge. There is a wide range of eating options including informal snacks, Singaporean cuisine and more formal Italian food.

*Millennium Gloucester Hotel, South Kensington*

**ROOMS:** 610 en suite (6 fmly) No smoking in 439 bedrooms d £240-£295 * **LB** **FACILITIES:** STV Gym **CONF:** Thtr 500 Class 300 Board 40 Del from £195 * **SERVICES:** Lift air con **PARKING:** 110 **NOTES:** No dogs (ex guide dogs) Civ Wed 300 **CARDS:**

### ★★★★72% Harrington Hall

5-25 Harrington Gardens SW7 4JW
☎ 020 7396 9696 📠 020 7396 9090
e-mail: harringtonsales@compuserve.com
***Dir:*** *head towards Knightsbridge into Gloucester Rd. Take 2nd right into Harrington Gdns hotel on the left*

Behind this classic Victorian façade can be found a modern and elegant hotel. Bedrooms are spacious, well equipped and air-conditioned. Additional features include a multi-gym, extensive meeting rooms and the stylish restaurant which serves an imaginative choice of carefully prepared dishes.

**ROOMS:** 200 en suite No smoking in 132 bedrooms s £130-£185; d £140-£195 * **LB** **FACILITIES:** STV Sauna Gym entertainment Xmas **CONF:** Thtr 200 Class 80 Board 25 Del £205 * **SERVICES:** Lift air con **NOTES:** No dogs (ex guide dogs) **CARDS:**

### ★★★★68% *Radisson Edwardian Vanderbilt*

Radisson Edwardian

68/86 Cromwell Rd SW7 5BT
☎ 020 7761 9000 📠 020 7761 9001
e-mail: resvand@radisson.com
***Dir:*** *A4 into Central London, past the junc with Gloucester Rd, hotel on left 100m beyond the traffic lights*

Situated almost opposite South Kensington tube station, this hotel is an ideal base for visitors to the capital. The interior is both cheerful and contemporary. Room facilities are superb - all have air conditioning, modems, several telephone lines, safes and mini-bars. Dining options include Restaurant 68-86 and Cleo's, which has a popular local following at lunchtime.

**ROOMS:** 215 en suite (15 fmly) No smoking in 90 bedrooms **FACILITIES:** STV Gym **CONF:** Thtr 120 Class 36 Board 40 **SERVICES:** Lift air con **NOTES:** No dogs (ex guide dogs) **CARDS:**

### ★★★★67% Jurys Kensington Hotel

Jurys Doyle Hotels

109-113 Queensgate, South Kensington SW7 5LR
☎ 020 7589 6300 📠 020 7581 1492
e-mail: Kensington_hotel@jurysdoyle.com
***Dir:*** *from A3218 (Old Bromton Rd), hotel is approx 300 yards on left at junction with Queensgate*

This fine hotel has been extensively upgraded and offers a traditional Irish welcome. Newly air-conditioned bedrooms are well-equipped and have recently been refurbished. Smartly appointed public areas include an open plan lobby/bar, Copplestones restaurant with adjoining library lounge and the lively Kavanagh's bar.

**ROOMS:** 173 annexe en suite (10 fmly) No smoking in 65 bedrooms s £150-£200; d £150-£200 * **FACILITIES:** STV Facilities available locally at discounted rate entertainment Xmas **CONF:** Thtr 80 Class 45 Board 35 Del from £190 * **SERVICES:** Lift air con **NOTES:** No dogs (ex guide dogs) Closed 23-26 Dec **CARDS:**

### ★★★★65% Millennium Baileys Hotel London Kensington

MILLENNIUM HOTELS AND RESORTS

140 Gloucester Rd SW7 4QH
☎ 020 7373 6000 📠 020 7370 3760
e-mail: baileys@mill-cop.com
***Dir:*** *M4, take A4 which turns into Cromwell Road, turn right onto Gloucester Road, hotel on the right opposite tube station*

Purpose-built in 1876 and given a new lease of life by its current owners, the Millenium Baileys has modern bedrooms with useful facilities such as air-conditioning, mini bars, and in the larger rooms, DVD players. Its cosmopolitan restaurant, Olives, produces enjoyable food in contemporary style.

**ROOMS:** 212 en suite No smoking in 80 bedrooms d £255 * **FACILITIES:** STV Gym **CONF:** Thtr 20 Class 18 Board 16 **SERVICES:** Lift air con **PARKING:** 70 **NOTES:** No dogs (ex guide dogs) **CARDS:**

### ★★★★63% Forum

INTER-CONTINENTAL HOTELS AND RESORTS

97 Cromwell Rd SW7 4DN
☎ 020 7370 5757 📠 020 7373 1448
e-mail: forumlondon@interconti.com
***Dir:*** *from South Circular onto North Circular at Chiswick Flyover, join A4 Cromwell Rd as far as the Gloucseter Rd*

London's tallest hotel enjoys panoramic views over the city from many of its smartly decorated and well-equipped bedrooms. Facilities include a business centre, a gymnasium, a large shop and a variety of eating outlets. Extensive conference and function suites are also available.

**ROOMS:** 910 en suite (36 fmly) No smoking in 395 bedrooms s fr £200; d fr £220 * **LB** **FACILITIES:** STV Fitness room entertainment Xmas **CONF:** Thtr 400 Class 200 Board 35 Del £205 * **SERVICES:** Lift air con **PARKING:** 75 **NOTES:** No dogs (ex guide dogs) **CARDS:**

### ★★★★62% Rembrandt

11 Thurloe Place SW7 2RS
☎ 020 7589 8100 📠 020 7225 3363
e-mail: rembrandt@sarova.co.uk
***Dir:*** *Follow M4/A4 Cromwell Rd into central London. The Rembrandt is opposite Victoria & Albert Museum*

The ornate architecture of the Rembrandt connects it stylistically to nearby Harrods. A strength of this plush, comfortable hotel is the leisure centre, designed in a style reminiscent of ancient Rome.

**ROOMS:** 195 en suite (16 fmly) No smoking in 65 bedrooms s £175; d £200 * **LB** **FACILITIES:** **Spa** STV Indoor swimming (H) Sauna Solarium Gym Jacuzzi Health, fitness & beauty centre entertainment Xmas **CONF:** Thtr 180 Class 84 Board 80 Del from £210 * **SERVICES:** Lift **NOTES:** No dogs (ex guide dogs) Civ Wed 180 **CARDS:**

Early start? Hotels at all star levels should provide in-room alarm clocks and/or alarm calls.

continued

## SW8 VAUXHALL

### ○ *Comfort Inn Vauxhall*
87 South Lambeth Rd, Vauxhall SW8 1RN
☎ 020 7735 9494
At the time of going to press, the star classification for this hotel was not confirmed. Please refer to the AA internet site www.theAA.com for current information.
**ROOMS:** 94 en suite **NOTES:** Open Now

## SW10 WEST BROMPTON See LONDON plan 1 E3

### ★★★★★66% ® Conrad London
Chelsea Harbour SW10 0XG
☎ 020 7823 3000 📠 020 7351 6525
e-mail: LONCH_DS@hilton.com
***Dir:*** *A4 Earls Court Rd south towards river. Right into Kings Rd left down Lots Rd Chelsea Harbour is in front of you*
This modern hotel is in a smart development overlooking a small marina at Chelsea Harbour. Accommodation takes the form of superbly equipped private suites. There is an excellent range of leisure facilities and meeting rooms. The restaurant is informal and has a modern menu with fusion influences.
**ROOMS:** 160 en suite (41 fmly) No smoking in 82 bedrooms s £170-£350; d £200-£380 * **LB** **FACILITIES:** STV Indoor swimming (H) Sauna Solarium Gym Steam room Massage therapist entertainment Xmas **CONF:** Thtr 200 Class 120 Board 50 Del from £269 * **SERVICES:** Lift air con **PARKING:** 88 **NOTES:** Civ Wed 200
**CARDS:**

## SW11 BATTERSEA See LONDON plan 1 E3

### ⌂ *Travelodge*
200 York Rd, Battersea SW11 3SA
☎ 020 7228 5508
***Dir:*** *from Wandsworth Bridge southern rdbt, take York Road A3205 towards Battersea. Travelodge 0.5m on left*
Travelodge offers good quality, good value, modern accommodation. Ideal for families, the spacious, en suite bedrooms include remote-control TV, tea and coffee-making facilities, luxury beds and free morning newspaper. Meals can be taken at the nearby family restaurant. For further details and the Travelodge phone number, consult the Hotel Groups page.

**ROOMS:** 80 en suite

## SW15 PUTNEY

### ○ The Lodge
52 -54 Upper Richmond Rd, Putney SW15 2RN
☎ 0181 874 1598
At the time of going to press, the star classification for this hotel was not confirmed. Please refer to the AA internet site www.theAA.com for current information.

## SW18 WANDSWORTH

### ○ Express by Holiday Inn Wandsworth
Smugglers Way, Wandsworth SW18 1EG
☎ 0800 897121
A modern budget hotel offering comfortable accommodation in refreshing, spacious and comprehensively equipped bedrooms, en suite bathrooms with power showers and continental buffet breakfast included in the room rate. Suitable for business travellers or families. For further details and the Express by Holiday Inn phone number, consult the Hotel Groups page.

**ROOMS:** 148 rms **NOTES:** Open now

## SW19 WIMBLEDON See LONDON plan 1 D1

### ★★★★74% ®® *Cannizaro House*
West Side, Wimbledon Common SW19 4UE
☎ 020 8879 1464 📠 020 8879 7338
e-mail: cannizaro.house@thistle.co.uk
***Dir:*** *approaching from A3 follow A219 signed Wimbledon into Parkside and past old fountain sharp right then 2nd on right*
This impressive, 18th-century house has a long tradition of hosting the rich and famous of London society. A few miles from the city centre, the landscaped grounds provide a peaceful haven. Oil paintings, murals and stunning fireplaces feature throughout. Spacious bedrooms are decorated in a country house style.
**ROOMS:** 45 en suite No smoking in 19 bedrooms **FACILITIES:** STV Croquet lawn Massage treatments entertainment **CONF:** Thtr 80 Class 34 Board 40 **SERVICES:** Lift **PARKING:** 60 **NOTES:** No dogs (ex guide dogs) Civ Wed 60 **CARDS:**

### ⌂ Express by Holiday Inn Wimbledon
200 High St, Colliers Wood, Wimbledon SW19 2BH
☎ 020 8545 7300 📠 020 8545 7301
***Dir:*** *M25 junct10. A3 to Central London, follow to Merton turn off at A238, past S Wimbledon underground on right. Proceed through t/lights, hotel on left*

A modern budget hotel offering comfortable accommodation in refreshing, spacious and comprehensively equipped bedrooms, en suite bathrooms with power showers and continental buffet breakfast included in the room rate. Suitable for business travellers or families. For further details and the Express by Holiday Inn phone number, consult the Hotel Groups page.
**ROOMS:** 83 en suite (incl. cont bkfst) d fr £89 * **CONF:** Thtr 60 Class 25 Board 25

London

W1 WEST END

## Premier Collection

CLARIDGES

★★★★★ ◎◎ **Claridge's**

The Savoy Group

Brook St W1A 2JQ
☎ 020 7629 8860 🖷 020 7499 2210
e-mail: info@claridges.co.uk
***Dir:*** *between Grosvenor Square and New Bond Street parallel with Oxford Street*

Claridges has always showcased the work of top architects and designers. The tradition continues with the newly refurbished bedrooms in art deco and Victorian styles. Six stunning new suites feature plasma screen TV and DVD/CD sound systems. The sleek new cocktail bar is a popular meeting place and the stylish art deco foyer and reading room are ideal for afternoon tea. The highly professional staff combine attentive service with warm hospitality and excellent guest care.

**ROOMS:** 203 en suite No smoking in 18 bedrooms s £370-£405; d £435-£580 * **LB** **FACILITIES:** STV Gym Tennis at the Vanderbilt Club entertainment Xmas **CONF:** Thtr 250 Class 130 Board 60 **SERVICES:** Lift air con **NOTES:** No dogs (ex guide dogs) Civ Wed 250 **CARDS:**

## Premier Collection

★★★★★ ◎◎ **Connaught**

The Savoy Group

Carlos Place W1K 2AL
☎ 020 7499 7070 🖷 020 7495 3262
e-mail: info@the-connaught.co.uk

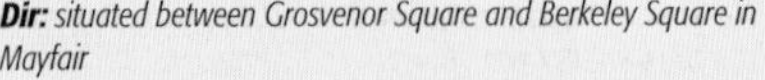

***Dir:*** *situated between Grosvenor Square and Berkeley Square in Mayfair*

The Connaught stands in the heart of fashionable Mayfair. It is the archetypal bastion of tradition, offering exemplary standards of service to ensure that every visit is memorable. Butlers and valets respond at the touch of a button and

*continued*

nothing is too much trouble. The Restaurant and Grill provide comprehensive, classical menus served by a highly skilled team of professionals. A new, well-equipped fitness studio provides a healthy option for more athletic guests.

**ROOMS:** 92 en suite s £329-£353; d £447-£500 * **LB** **FACILITIES:** STV Gym Health club facilities at sister hotels **CONF:** Board 18 **SERVICES:** Lift air con **NOTES:** No dogs **CARDS:**

## Premier Collection

The Dorchester

★★★★★ ◎◎◎ **The Dorchester**

Park Ln W1A 2HJ
☎ 020 7629 8888 🖷 020 7409 0114
e-mail: reservations@dorchesterhotel.com
***Dir:*** *half way along Park Lane between Hyde Park Corner & Marble Arch, overlooking Hyde Park on corner of Park Lane & Deanery St*

One of London's finest hotels, the Dorchester is sumptuously decorated. Bedrooms have individual design schemes, are beautifully furnished, and have huge luxurious baths. Leading off from the foyer, the Promenade is the perfect setting for afternoon tea or drinks. In the evenings there is live jazz in the famous bar which specialises in Italian dishes and cocktails. The Grill is a restaurant in the traditional style and there is also a Cantonese restaurant, the Oriental.

**ROOMS:** 250 en suite No smoking in 34 bedrooms s £335-£359; d £376-£412 * **LB** **FACILITIES:** **Spa** STV Sauna Solarium Gym Jacuzzi The Dorchester Spa Health club entertainment ch fac Xmas **CONF:** Thtr 550 Class 300 Board 42 **SERVICES:** Lift air con **PARKING:** 21 **NOTES:** No dogs (ex guide dogs) Civ Wed 500 **CARDS:**

## Premier Collection

★★★★★ ◎◎ **Four Seasons**

Hamilton Place, Park Ln W1A 1AZ
☎ 020 7499 0888 🖷 020 7493 6629
e-mail: fsh.london@fourseasons.com
***Dir:*** *From Piccadilly, turn left on Old Park Lane continue to the end of this road and around rdbt to Hamilton Place.*

Now firmly established as one of London's top hotels, the Four Seasons is an unimposing building occupying an excellent position just off Park Lane. The staff are genuinely friendly and provide guests with attentive service of the highest standards. The guestrooms, suites and conservatory rooms are all equipped with an excellent range of modern

*continued*

London

facilities and are decorated with a timeless style and elegance. Public rooms include the contemporary Lane's restaurant and adjoining cocktail bar.

**ROOMS:** 220 en suite No smoking in 96 bedrooms s £335-£370; d £388-£400 * **LB** **FACILITIES:** STV Gym Fitness club entertainment Xmas **CONF:** Thtr 500 Class 180 Board 70 **SERVICES:** Lift air con **PARKING:** 72 **NOTES:** Civ Wed 500 **CARDS:**

### ★★★★★78% The Ritz

150 Piccadilly W1J 9BR
☎ 020 7493 8181 020 7493 2687
e-mail: theritzlondon.com
***Dir:*** *from Hyde Park Corner travel E on Piccadilly. The Ritz is the first building on the right immediately after Green Park*

The Ritz continues its stately progress into the third millennium, having recaptured much of its former glory. All bedrooms are comfortably furnished in Louis XVI style and have fine marble bathrooms and every imaginable comfort. Elegant reception rooms include the Palm Court with its famous afternoon teas, and the sumptuous Ritz Restaurant with its gold chandeliers and extraordinary trompe-l'oeil decoration.

**ROOMS:** 133 en suite No smoking in 20 bedrooms s £347-£2174; d £405-£2174 * **LB** **FACILITIES:** STV Gym entertainment Xmas **CONF:** Thtr 60 Class 25 Board 30 **SERVICES:** Lift air con **NOTES:** No dogs (ex guide dogs) Civ Wed 50 **CARDS:**

### ★★★★★72% Churchill Inter-Continental

30 Portman Square W1A 4ZX
☎ 020 7486 5800 020 7486 1255
e-mail: churchill@interconti.com

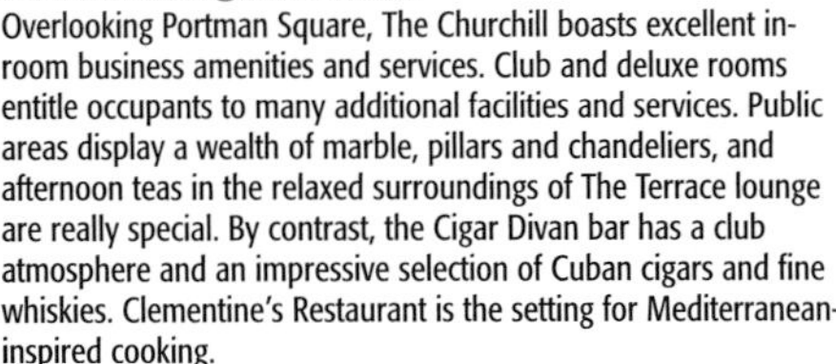

Overlooking Portman Square, The Churchill boasts excellent in-room business amenities and services. Club and deluxe rooms entitle occupants to many additional facilities and services. Public areas display a wealth of marble, pillars and chandeliers, and afternoon teas in the relaxed surroundings of The Terrace lounge are really special. By contrast, the Cigar Divan bar has a club atmosphere and an impressive selection of Cuban cigars and fine whiskies. Clementine's Restaurant is the setting for Mediterranean-inspired cooking.

**ROOMS:** 445 en suite No smoking in 156 bedrooms s £159-£376; d £169-£399 * **LB** **FACILITIES:** STV Tennis (hard) Sauna Gym entertainment Xmas **CONF:** Thtr 250 Class 160 Board 65 Del £75 * **SERVICES:** Lift air con **PARKING:** 50 **NOTES:** No dogs (ex guide dogs) Civ Wed 180 **CARDS:**

Packed in a hurry? Ironing facilities should be available at all star levels, either in rooms or on request.

### ★★★★★72% Le Meridien Piccadilly

21 Piccadilly W1J 0BH
☎ 0870 400 8400 020 7437 3574
e-mail: lmpiccres@lemeridien-hotels.com
***Dir:*** *100mtrs from Piccadilly Circus*

Enjoying a fabulous location in the very heart of the capital, with the very best in shopping and entertainment just a stone's throw away. There are a variety of room types, smartly decorated and equipped with a comprehensive range of facilities and accessories. Hotel facilities include the renowned Champneys Health Club, the acclaimed Oak Room restaurant and the conservatory-style Terrace restaurant overlooking the hubbub of Piccadilly.

**ROOMS:** 267 en suite (19 fmly) No smoking in 91 bedrooms s £206-£347; d £230-£371 * **LB** **FACILITIES:** STV Indoor swimming (H) Squash Sauna Solarium Gym Jacuzzi Beauty treatments Aerobics Massage Xmas **CONF:** Thtr 250 Class 160 Board 80 Del from £75 * **SERVICES:** Lift air con **NOTES:** No dogs (ex guide dogs) Civ Wed 200 **CARDS:**

### ★★★★★72% Hotel Inter-Continental London

1 Hamilton Place, Hyde Park Corner W1J 7QY
☎ 020 7409 3131 020 7493 3476
e-mail: london@interconti.com
***Dir:*** *situated at Hyde Park Corner, on the corner of Park Lane & Piccadilly*

Situated in a prominent position on Hyde Park Corner, this fine hotel has excellent views of the surrounding area from upper floors and lounges. Bedrooms vary from inner courtyard rooms to spacious suites. The smart, marbled foyer houses the Observatory lounge for light meals and afternoon teas, and the Coffee House for breakfast and all-day dining. The jewel in the hotel's crown is Le Soufflé Restaurant.

**ROOMS:** 458 en suite No smoking in 312 bedrooms s fr £359; d fr £359 * **LB** **FACILITIES:** STV Sauna Gym Jacuzzi Beauty treatments Health Club entertainment Xmas **CONF:** Thtr 750 Class 340 Board 66 **SERVICES:** Lift air con **PARKING:** 100 **NOTES:** No dogs (ex guide dogs) Civ Wed 750 **CARDS:**

London

### ★★★★★69% Grosvenor House

Park Ln W1A 3AA
☎ 0870 400 8500 020 7493 3341
e-mail: gros.house@virgin.net
***Dir:*** *Marble Arch, halfway down Park Lane*

Majestically positioned on Park Lane, this internationally recognised hotel offers thoughtfully equipped accommodation including a number of impressive suites. Executive Crown Club rooms boasts a range of extra services and facilities. Guests have the choice between the award winning Chez Nico restaurant or, within the hotel, La Terrazza, which offers a more informal dining experience, with an Italian theme.

**ROOMS:** 453 en suite (140 fmly) No smoking in 154 bedrooms s fr £405; d fr £435 * **LB** **FACILITIES:** STV Indoor swimming (H) Sauna Solarium Gym Jacuzzi Health & Fitness centre entertainment Xmas **CONF:** Thtr 110 Class 60 Board 36 **SERVICES:** Lift air con **PARKING:** 95 **NOTES:** No dogs (ex guide dogs) Civ Wed 100 **CARDS:**

### ★★★★★63% May Fair Inter-Continental London

Stratton St W1J 8LL
☎ 020 7629 7777 020 7629 1459
e-mail: mayfair@interconti.com
***Dir:*** *from Hyde Park Corner/Piccadilly turn left onto Stratton St & hotel is on left*

This well established hotel has an intimate atmosphere. Air-

*continued on p364*

W1 WEST END, continued

conditioned bedrooms are of varying sizes including suites and business-dedicated rooms with a useful range of amenities. The choice of eating options includes the Opus 70 restaurant, a showcase for the hotel's modern British cuisine. There is also a staffed business centre and a conference auditorium.
**ROOMS:** 289 en suite (14 fmly) No smoking in 148 bedrooms s fr £315; d fr £315 * LB **FACILITIES:** STV Indoor swimming (H) Sauna Solarium Gym entertainment Xmas **CONF:** Thtr 292 Class 108 Board 60 **SERVICES:** Lift air con **NOTES:** No dogs (ex guide dogs) Civ Wed 250 **CARDS:**

## Premier Collection

### ★★★★ Athenaeum

116 Piccadilly W1J 7BJ
☎ 020 7499 3464 020 7493 1860
e-mail: info@athenaeumhotel.com
***Dir:*** *located on Piccadilly, overlooking Green Park*
A discreet address in the heart of Mayfair, this well loved hotel has become a favourite with many repeat guests for its efficient service and excellent hospitality. Bedrooms are decorated to the highest standard and some have views over Green Park. The spacious and well-appointed apartments offer guests the convenience of a townhouse, with all the services of a deluxe hotel. Public rooms include Bullochs Restaurant, Windsor lounge and a cosy cocktail bar specialising in malt whisky.
**ROOMS:** 157 en suite No smoking in 58 bedrooms s fr £294; d fr £317 * LB **FACILITIES:** Spa STV Sauna Gym Jacuzzi Massage treatment Steam rooms **CONF:** Thtr 55 Class 35 Board 36 Del from £230 * **SERVICES:** Lift air con **NOTES:** No dogs (ex guide dogs) Civ Wed 55 **CARDS:**

### ★★★★77% The Montcalm-Hotel Nikko London

Great Cumberland Place W1H 7TW
☎ 020 7402 4288 020 7724 9180
e-mail: reservations@montcalm.co.uk
***Dir:*** *by Marble Arch*
Situated on a secluded crescent close to Marble Arch, this charming Georgian property is named after the famous General Montcalm. A Japanese-owned hotel, it offers extremely comfortable accommodation, ranging from standard to duplex 'junior' and penthouse suites. Staff are attentive and the stylish restaurant has a reputation for good modern cooking. Lunch is particularly good value for money. A low allergy room is specially designed for sufferers of asthma and related allergies.

**ROOMS:** 120 en suite No smoking in 28 bedrooms s £230; d £250 * LB **FACILITIES:** STV **CONF:** Thtr 80 Class 36 Board 36 Del from £230 * **SERVICES:** Lift air con **PARKING:** 10 **NOTES:** No dogs (ex guide dogs) **CARDS:**

### ★★★★76% Brown's

Albemarle St, Mayfair W1S 4BP
☎ 020 7493 6020 020 7493 9381
e-mail: brownshotel@brownshotel.com
***Dir:*** *from Green Park Underground Station on Piccadilly, take third left into Albemarle Street*
Brown's is famous for its English country-house style and traditional emphasis on comfortable furnishings and quality appointments. Accommodation is excellent and rooms are particularly spacious for the Mayfair setting. There is a smartly decorated restaurant, the oldest hotel restaurant in London, with an imaginative menu. The hotel is a deservedly popular refuge for afternoon tea.
**ROOMS:** 118 en suite (15 fmly) s fr £318; d fr £359 (incl. bkfst) * LB **FACILITIES:** STV Gym entertainment Xmas **CONF:** Thtr 70 Class 30 Board 35 **SERVICES:** Lift air con **NOTES:** No dogs (ex guide dogs) Civ Wed 70 **CARDS:**

### ★★★★74% The Washington Mayfair Hotel

5-7 Curzon St, Mayfair W1J 5HE
☎ 020 7499 7000 020 7495 6172
e-mail: sales@washington-mayfair.co.uk
***Dir:*** *From Green Park station take Piccadilly exit and turn right. Take 4th street on right*
This smart and modern hotel offers a very high standard of accommodation. Bedrooms are all attractively furnished and provide high levels of comfort. Light refreshments are served in the marbled and wood-panelled public areas.
**ROOMS:** 173 en suite No smoking in 94 bedrooms s £230-£470; d £230-£470 * **FACILITIES:** STV entertainment Xmas **CONF:** Thtr 90 Class 40 Board 36 Del from £252 * **SERVICES:** Lift air con **NOTES:** No dogs (ex guide dogs) **CARDS:**

*See advert on opposite page*

### ★★★★73% London Marriott Hotel Grosvenor Square

Marriott HOTELS · RESORTS · SUITES

Grosvenor Square W1K 6JP
☎ 020 7493 1232 020 7491 3201
e-mail: businesscentrre@londonmarriott.co.uk
***Dir:*** *M4 east to Cromwell Rd through Knightsbridge to Hyde Park Corner, Park Lane right at Brook Gate onto upper Brook St to Grosvenor Sq/ Duke St*
This smart hotel is situated in the heart of Mayfair and provides a high standard of accommodation and public rooms. Friendly staff

*continued*

London

remain unfailingly helpful and willing to please. Excellent food is served in the Diplomat Restaurant overlooking the gardens of Grosvenor Square.

**ROOMS:** 221 en suite (26 fmly) No smoking in 120 bedrooms s fr £210; d fr £260 * **LB** **FACILITIES:** STV Gym Exercise & fitness centre Xmas **CONF:** Thtr 1000 Class 550 Board 120 **SERVICES:** Lift air con **PARKING:** 80 **NOTES:** No dogs (ex guide dogs)
**CARDS:**

★★★★73% ***Radisson Edwardian Berkshire***

Radisson Edwardian

350 Oxford St W1N 0BY
☎ 020 7629 7474 020 7629 8156
e-mail: resberk@radisson.com
***Dir:*** *central London, on Oxford Street opposite Bond Street Underground Station*

Sandwiched between Oxford Street's department stores, this is an ideal hotel for grand-scale shopping. Intimate, warm and friendly, the hotel attracts an international business clientele. Bedrooms, though not over-large, are stylishly decorated. Public rooms include the newly refurbished, contemporary drawing room and the Ascot cocktail bar restaurant.
**ROOMS:** 147 en suite (2 fmly) No smoking in 44 bedrooms **FACILITIES:** STV **CONF:** Thtr 45 Class 20 Board 26 **SERVICES:** Lift air con **NOTES:** No dogs (ex guide dogs)
**CARDS:**

★★★★72% **The Westbury**

New Bond St W1S 2YF
☎ 020 7629 7755 020 7495 1163
e-mail: westburyhotel@compuserve.com
***Dir:*** *from Oxford Circus south down Regent St turn right onto Conduit St, hotel at junct of Conduit St & Bond St*

In the heart of one of London's best known shopping districts, this distinctive hotel benefits from an unhurried, relaxing atmosphere. Standards of accommodation are high throughout, attracting an international clientele. Reception rooms include the Polo Lounge

*continued on p366*

London

W1 WEST END, continued

and The Restaurant, serving traditional dishes at lunchtime and offering a more adventurous evening menu.
**ROOMS:** 254 en suite No smoking in 150 bedrooms s £265; d £282-£340 * **LB** **FACILITIES:** STV Fitness centre entertainment Xmas **CONF:** Thtr 120 Class 65 Board 36 Del from £300 * **SERVICES:** Lift air con **NOTES:** No dogs (ex guide dogs)
**CARDS:**

*See advert on page 365*

### ★★★★71% The Chesterfield

35 Charles St, Mayfair W1X 8LX
☎ 020 7491 2622 ▯ 020 7491 4793
e-mail: reservations@chesterfield.redcarnationhotels.com
***Dir:*** *Hyde Park corner along Picadilly, turn left into Half Moon St. At the end turn left and first right into Queens St, then turn right onto Charles St*
Quiet elegance and an atmosphere of exclusivity characterise this hotel. The lobby, with its marble floor, glittering chandelier and fluted pillars, leads into a library lounge and clubby bar. The restaurant is traditional in decor and provides a modern menu. Stylish bedrooms have direct internet access via the TV.
**ROOMS:** 110 en suite (7 fmly) No smoking in 34 bedrooms s fr £229; d fr £240 * **LB** **FACILITIES:** STV entertainment Xmas **CONF:** Thtr 120 Class 50 Board 45 **SERVICES:** Lift air con **NOTES:** Civ Wed 120
**CARDS:**

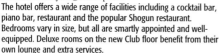

### ★★★★71% Millennium Hotel London Mayfair

Grosvenor Square W1K 2HP
☎ 020 7629 9400 ▯ 020 7629 7736
e-mail: sales.mayfair@mill-cop.com

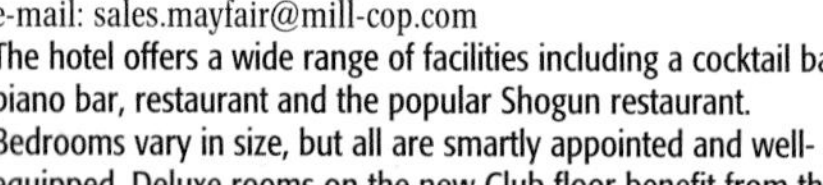

The hotel offers a wide range of facilities including a cocktail bar, piano bar, restaurant and the popular Shogun restaurant. Bedrooms vary in size, but all are smartly appointed and well-equipped. Deluxe rooms on the new Club floor benefit from their own lounge and extra services.
**ROOMS:** 348 en suite No smoking in 145 bedrooms s £170-£255; d £255-£290 * **LB** **FACILITIES:** STV Gym entertainment ch fac Xmas **CONF:** Thtr 450 Class 250 Board 40 **SERVICES:** Lift air con **NOTES:** No dogs (ex guide dogs) Civ Wed 400
**CARDS:**

### ★★★★71% Radisson SAS Portman

22 Portman Square W1H 7BG
☎ 020 7208 6000 ▯ 020 7208 6001
e-mail: portman@lonza.rdsas.com
***Dir:*** *100mtrs N of Oxford St and 500mtrs E of Edgware Rd*
Located in a quieter area of the city and just a short stroll from Oxford Street. There are five styles of bedroom, ranging from Oriental through to classical; the new Italian décor is receiving enthusiastic reviews. The new Talavera restaurant offers a contemporary Mediterranean menu. Parking is available in the car park adjacent.
**ROOMS:** 272 en suite (21 fmly) No smoking in 129 bedrooms **FACILITIES:** STV Tennis (hard) Sauna Solarium Gym entertainment Xmas **CONF:** Thtr 700 Class 350 Board 65 **SERVICES:** Lift air con **PARKING:** 400 **NOTES:** No dogs (ex guide dogs) Civ Wed 450
**CARDS:**

Early start? Hotels at all star levels should provide in-room alarm clocks and/or alarm calls.

### ★★★★68% The Berners Hotel

Berners St W1A 3BE
☎ 020 7666 2000 ▯ 020 7666 2001
e-mail: berners@berners.co.uk
***Dir:*** *head towards Central London. At Baker Street turn left into Oxford Street*
Well positioned in the heart of London's West End, just off Oxford Street, this traditional hotel has an elegant, classical marble-columned foyer with a comfortable lounge - popular for afternoon tea - and attractive restaurant. Bedrooms are all equipped with modern comforts and thoughtful extras.
**ROOMS:** 216 en suite No smoking in 100 bedrooms s fr £190; d fr £215 * **FACILITIES:** STV **CONF:** Thtr 150 Class 80 Board 36 Del from £169 * **SERVICES:** Lift **NOTES:** No dogs (ex guide dogs) Civ Wed 100
**CARDS:**

### ★★★★68% *Jurys Clifton-Ford*

47 Welbeck St W1M 8DN
☎ 020 7486 6600 ▯ 020 7486 7492
e-mail: sales@cliftonf.itsnet.co.uk
***Dir:*** *from Portland Place, turn into New Cavendish Street. Welbeck Street is last turning on the left.*
Centrally located, this smart hotel offers outstanding bedrooms with excellent facilities. Refurbishment has provided extensive leisure amenities and a range of conference suites. The lounge and bar offer elegant surroundings and the restaurant caters for a variety of tastes.
**ROOMS:** 255 en suite (7 fmly) **FACILITIES:** STV Indoor swimming (H) Sauna Solarium Gym Jacuzzi Fully equipped leisure club **CONF:** Thtr 200 Class 70 Board 40 **SERVICES:** Lift air con **PARKING:** 9
**CARDS:**

### ★★★★68% London Marriott Hotel Marble Arch

134 George St W1H 6DN
☎ 020 7723 1277 ▯ 020 7402 0666
e-mail: salesadmin.marblearch@marriotthotels.co.uk
***Dir:*** *from Marble Arch turn into the Edgware Road then take 4th turning on right into George St. Turn immediate left into Forset Street for main entrance*

This modern hotel, conveniently situated just off the Edgware Road, and close to Oxford Street shops, offers a good standard of accommodation. Bedrooms are well-equipped and furnished with quality fittings. Public areas are not overly spacious, but the bar and restaurant have recently undergone a stylish refurbishment. Parking is also a bonus.
**ROOMS:** 240 en suite (100 fmly) No smoking in 120 bedrooms **FACILITIES:** STV Indoor swimming (H) Sauna Solarium Gym Jacuzzi Xmas **CONF:** Thtr 150 Class 75 Board 80 Del from £270 * **SERVICES:** Lift air con **PARKING:** 80 **NOTES:** No dogs (ex guide dogs)
**CARDS:**

London

### ★★★★67% *The Cumberland*

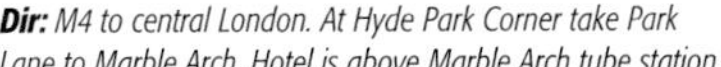

Marble Arch W1H 8DP
☎ 0870 400 8701 📠 020 7724 4621
***Dir:*** *M4 to central London. At Hyde Park Corner take Park Lane to Marble Arch. Hotel is above Marble Arch tube station*
In an unrivalled location near Hyde Park, the hotel provides a range of eating and drinking options, including cafés, oriental dining in Sampans, the ever popular Carvery, and Callaghan's bar and restaurant for fresh Irish fare and nightly live music. The excellent, staffed business complex has 17 conference rooms. Bedrooms are comfortable and modern; Premier Club rooms provide extra comfort and amenities.
**ROOMS:** 917 en suite (21 fmly) No smoking in 480 bedrooms
**FACILITIES:** STV entertainment **CONF:** Thtr 750 Class 350 Board 80
**SERVICES:** Lift **NOTES:** No dogs (ex guide dogs)
**CARDS:**

### ★★★★64% *Flemings Mayfair*

7-12 Half Moon St, Mayfair W1Y 7RA
☎ 020 7499 2964 📠 020 7491 8866
e-mail: sales@flemings-mayfair.co.uk
The second oldest hotel in London offers traditional décor with a cosy atmosphere. Whilst public areas are compact, good quality is apparent with chandeliers and feature fireplaces. Bedrooms vary in size but are all being upgraded and are equipped with an excellent range of facilities.
**ROOMS:** 121 en suite (11 fmly) No smoking in 25 bedrooms
**FACILITIES:** STV **CONF:** Thtr 55 Class 30 Board 30 **SERVICES:** Lift air con **NOTES:** No dogs (ex guide dogs)
**CARDS:**

### ★★★68% Posthouse Premier Regents Park

Carburton St, Regents Park W1W 5EE
☎ 0870 400 9111 📠 020 7387 2806
e-mail: gm1262@forte-hotels.com
This modern hotel enjoys a central location and is not only popular with the corporate market, but also with leisure guests. The bedrooms do tend to vary in size and style, but all are comfortable and well designed. There is 24-hour room service, an all-day lounge menu and convenient parking.
**ROOMS:** 333 en suite No smoking in 199 bedrooms s £139-£169; d £139-£169 * **FACILITIES:** STV Xmas **CONF:** Thtr 350 Class 180 Board 50 Del from £176 * **SERVICES:** Lift **PARKING:** 85 **NOTES:** No dogs (ex guide dogs) **CARDS:**

### ★★★66% Mostyn

4 Bryanston St W1H 7BY
☎ 020 7935 2361 📠 020 7487 2759
e-mail: info@mostynhotel.co.uk
***Dir:*** *Accessible via A40(M) Marylebone Rd close to Marble Arch and Bond Street tube*

With a prime location from which to explore London and an on-going refurbishment programme, this hotel has much to offer

*continued on p368*



London

W1 WEST END, continued

guests. Bedrooms are bright and well-appointed, suites and large single rooms are available. The open-plan lounge and cocktail bar area is ideal for enjoying drinks and snacks.
**ROOMS:** 121 en suite (15 fmly) No smoking in 54 bedrooms s £124-£135; d £135-£165 * **FACILITIES:** STV **CONF:** Thtr 140 Class 80 Board 60 Del from £115 * **SERVICES:** Lift air con **NOTES:** No dogs (ex guide dogs) **CARDS:**

*See advert on page 367*

### ★★★65% *Mandeville*
Mandeville Place W1M 6BE
☎ 020 7935 5599 🖷 020 7935 9588
e-mail: info@mandeville.co.uk
***Dir:*** *off Oxford Street & Wigmore St near Bond St underground station*
This quiet hotel is only a short walk from Oxford Street. The language skills of reception staff, plus the helpful concierge desk, have made it popular with foreign visitors. The Orangery Restaurant offers well-cooked dishes, and bar meals are available in Boswells. There are also good business and conference facilities.
**ROOMS:** 165 en suite No smoking in 30 bedrooms **FACILITIES:** STV **CONF:** Thtr 35 Class 30 Board 20 **SERVICES:** Lift **NOTES:** No dogs (ex guide dogs) **CARDS:**

*See advert on page 367*

## *Town House*

### ★★★★ Grange Fitzrovia
20-28 Bolsover St W1W 5NB
☎ 020 7467 7000 🖷 020 7636 5085
e-mail: fitzrovia@grangehotels.co.uk
Nestling in a quiet street in the very heart of the city centre, this hotel is a super retreat from the capital's hustle and bustle. Bedrooms are richly decorated and feature polished wood furnishings and marbled bathrooms. An atmosphere of quiet luxury and comfort prevails in the cosy public rooms.
**ROOMS:** 88 en suite No smoking in 40 bedrooms s £145-£190; d £155-£215 * **FACILITIES:** STV **CONF:** Thtr 100 Class 45 Board 40 Del from £235 * **SERVICES:** Lift **NOTES:** No dogs (ex guide dogs) **CARDS:**

### ○ *Radisson Edwardian Grafton Hotel*
130 Tottenham Court Rd W1P 9HP
Radisson Edwardian
☎ 020 7388 4131 🖷 020 7387 7394
e-mail: resgrafton@radisson.com
***Dir:*** *central London, along Euston Road, turn into Tottenham Court Road. Past Warren Street Tube*
The Grafton is currently undergoing a massive 20 million pound refurbishment programme which will lift standards in all areas. Already completed are the well thought-out public areas, which include the contemporary Astons bar and restaurant. The hotel is well placed opposite Warren Street tube station.
**ROOMS:** 324 en suite (8 fmly) No smoking in 163 bedrooms **FACILITIES:** Gym **CONF:** Thtr 100 Class 50 Board 30 **SERVICES:** Lift **NOTES:** No dogs (ex guide dogs) **CARDS:**

## W2 BAYSWATER, PADDINGTON

### ★★★★73% Royal Lancaster
Lancaster Ter W2 2TY
☎ 020 7262 6737 🖷 020 7724 3191
e-mail: book@royallancaster.com
***Dir:*** *directly above Lancaster Gate Underground Station*
Overlooking Hyde Park and Kensington Gardens, the Royal Lancaster's upper storeys offer fine views across London. The choice of eating ranges from the lounge, the Pavement Café, the smart Park Restaurant or the exotic and authentic Nipa Thai. Bedrooms are all attractively presented and conference facilities remain impressive.
**ROOMS:** 416 en suite (11 fmly) No smoking in 111 bedrooms s £271-£359; d £271-£359 * **LB** **FACILITIES:** STV entertainment Xmas **CONF:** Thtr 1500 Class 650 Board 40 **SERVICES:** Lift air con **PARKING:** 100 **NOTES:** No dogs (ex guide dogs) **CARDS:**

### ★★★67% Plaza on Hyde Park
1-7 Lancaster Gate W2 3LG
corus
☎ 020 7262 5022 🖷 020 7724 8666
e-mail: plazaonhydepark@corushotels.com
***Dir:*** *200yds from Lancaster Gate Underground Station. 0.25m from Paddington Station*
The hotel has almost completed a massive refurbishment programme, some of which has been designed in Laura Ashley style. New bedrooms have been fitted out to the new Corus standard, with modern colour schemes, good lighting and attention to detail. Public areas include the popular Olio's restaurant complete with genuine pizza oven.
**ROOMS:** 401 en suite (10 fmly) No smoking in 200 bedrooms s £115; d £135 * **LB** **FACILITIES:** STV **CONF:** Thtr 20 Class 12 Board 20 **SERVICES:** Lift **NOTES:** No dogs (ex guide dogs) **CARDS:**

### ★★★63% Berjaya Eden Park Hotel
35-39 Inverness Ter, Bayswater W2 3JS
☎ 020 7221 2220 🖷 020 7221 2286
e-mail: edenpark@dircon.co.uk
***Dir:*** *from Marble Arch, straight across main rdbt onto Bayswater Rd, turn right into Queensway, the first turn left into Inverness Terrace*

This friendly hotel is close to Queensway Underground and within easy reach of the West End. Bedrooms are attractively furnished and well-equipped. Public rooms feature a spacious restaurant and cosy bar.
**ROOMS:** 75 rms (67 en suite) 62 annexe en suite (8 fmly) s £80; d £120 * **FACILITIES:** STV **CONF:** Thtr 50 Class 50 Board 25 **SERVICES:** Lift **NOTES:** No dogs (ex guide dogs) **CARDS:**

### ★★★63% Quality Hotel Paddington
8-14 Talbot Square W2 1TS
Quality Hotel
☎ 020 7262 6699 🖷 020 7723 3233
e-mail: quality@lth-hotels.com
***Dir:*** *From Bayswater Rd turn right on to Sussex Gdns*
This well presented hotel is ideally located close to Paddington Station. Modern styled bedrooms are comfortably appointed and

*continued*

London

particulary well-equipped. Public areas include a compact bar and lounge, and basement restaurant where all meals are served.
**ROOMS:** 73 en suite No smoking in 20 bedrooms s £95; d £160 (incl. cont bkfst) * **LB** **FACILITIES:** STV **SERVICES:** Lift **NOTES:** No smoking in restaurant **CARDS:**

**★★★62% Central Park**
Queensborough Ter W2 3SS
☎ 020 7229 2424 020 7229 2904
e-mail: cph@centralparklondon.co.uk
Central Park is a popular hotel just off the Bayswater Road and close to London's West End. Bedrooms offer all the expected modern comforts, and there are spacious public areas. Garage parking is also a bonus.
**ROOMS:** 255 en suite **CONF:** Thtr 100 Class 30 Board 30 Del from £120 * **SERVICES:** Lift **PARKING:** 30 **NOTES:** Civ Wed 120
**CARDS:**

*See advert on this page*

**★★70% Delmere**
130 Sussex Gardens, Hyde Park W2 1UB
☎ 020 7706 3344 020 7262 1863
e-mail: delmerehotel@compuserve.com

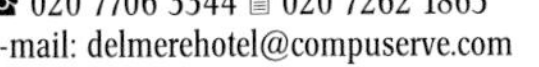

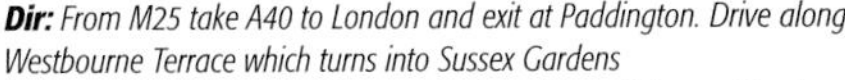

***Dir:*** *From M25 take A40 to London and exit at Paddington. Drive along Westbourne Terrace which turns into Sussex Gardens*
Delmere Hotel is located in a central position of Sussex Gardens and within easy reach of the West End. This friendly and privately owned hotel has bedrooms that make good use of space, and are well-equipped. Public rooms include a jazz-theme bar and a comfortable lounge.
**ROOMS:** 35 en suite (1 fmly) s £86-£97; d £107-£122 (incl. cont bkfst) * **LB** **SERVICES:** Lift **PARKING:** 2 **NOTES:** No dogs (ex guide dogs)
**CARDS:**

## *Town House*

**★★★★ The Abbey Court**
20 Pembridge Gardens, Kensington W2 4DU
☎ 020 7221 7518 020 7792 0858
e-mail: info@abbeycourthotel.co.uk
***Dir:*** *2 minute walk from Notting Hill Gate Underground station*
Situated in Notting Hill and close to Kensington, this elegant, five-storey town house is in a quiet side road. Rooms are individually decorated and furnished to a high standard and there is room service of light snacks. Breakfast is taken in the conservatory.
**ROOMS:** 22 en suite (1 fmly) No smoking in 10 bedrooms s £105-£145; d £155-£175 (incl. cont bkfst) * **FACILITIES:** STV
**NOTES:** No dogs (ex guide dogs)
**CARDS:**

Read all about it! Newspapers delivered to bedrooms in four and five star hotels.

Late for dinner? Quality Standards star rating means that last orders for dinner should be no earlier than:
★ 6.30pm ★★ 7.00pm ★★★ 8.00pm
★★★★ 9.00pm ★★★★★ 10.00pm

## *Town House*

**★★★★ Pembridge Court**
34 Pembridge Gardens W2 4DX
☎ 020 7229 9977 020 7727 4982
e-mail: reservations@pemct.co.uk
***Dir:*** *off the Bayswater Rd at Notting Hill Gate by underground Station*

This attractive Victorian town house is just minutes from the Portobello Market and Notting Hill Gate tube. Bedrooms are all individual, stylish, comfortable and thoughtfully equipped. Staff are friendly and provide high levels of service including 24-hour room service.
**ROOMS:** 20 en suite (4 fmly) s £125-£165; d £160-£195 (incl. bkfst) * **FACILITIES:** STV Membership of local Health Club **SERVICES:** Lift air con **PARKING:** 2 **CARDS:**

London

W3 ACTON

### ○ *Comfort Inn*

5-7 Princes Square, Bayswater W2 4NP
☎ 020 7792 1414
At the time of going to press, the star classification for this hotel was not confirmed. Please refer to the AA internet site www.theAA.com for current information.
**ROOMS:** 65 en suite **NOTES:** Open Now

### ⌂ *Travelodge (London Park Royal)*

A40 Western Ave, Acton W3 0TE
☎ 08700 850950
Travelodge offers good quality, good value, modern accommodation. Ideal for families, the spacious, en suite bedrooms include remote-control TV, tea and coffee-making facilities, luxury beds and free morning newspaper. Meals can be taken at the nearby family restaurant. For further details and the Travelodge phone number, consult the Hotel Groups page.

W6 HAMMERSMITH See LONDON plan 1 D3

### ★★★69% Novotel London West

1 Shortlands W6 8DR
☎ 020 8741 1555 ▤ 020 8741 2120
e-mail: h0737@accor-hotels.com
***Dir:*** *turn off A4 onto Hammersmith Broadway, then follow signs for City Centre, take first left and hotel is on the left*
This large and purpose-built hotel is located in the heart of Hammersmith and is easily accessible from the M4 or Underground. Practical and spacious bedrooms are equipped with a range of modern facilities including air conditioning. Newly refurbished public areas include a choice of restaurants and bars, a useful shop and extensive conference and banquetting facilities. Secure parking is also a bonus.
**ROOMS:** 629 en suite (73 fmly) No smoking in 421 bedrooms s fr £145; d fr £165 * **LB** **FACILITIES:** STV Fitness pool Pool table **CONF:** Thtr 900 Class 600 Board 750 Del from £200 * **SERVICES:** Lift air con **PARKING:** 240 **NOTES:** Civ Wed 1000
**CARDS:**

### ★★★63% Vencourt

255 King St, Hammersmith W6 9LU
☎ 020 8563 8855 ▤ 020 8563 9988
e-mail: vencourt@bestwestern.co.uk
***Dir:*** *from Central London-A4 to Hammersmith then follow A315 towards Chiswick*
Good value accommodation with city views from the higher floors. The hotel has open-plan public areas including a lounge bar, where snacks are served all day, and a small restaurant for more substantial meals.
**ROOMS:** 120 en suite (25 fmly) No smoking in 18 bedrooms s £89-£109; d £99-£109 * **LB** **FACILITIES:** STV Xmas **CONF:** Thtr 50 Class 45 Board 32 **SERVICES:** Lift **PARKING:** 27
**CARDS:**

### ○ Express by Holiday Inn London Hammersmith

120-124 King St, Hammersmith W6 0QU
☎ 020 8746 5100
A modern budget hotel offering comfortable accommodation in refreshing, spacious and comprehensively equipped bedrooms, en suite bathrooms with power showers and continental buffet breakfast included in the room rate. Suitable for business travellers or families. For further details and the Express by Holiday Inn phone number, consult the Hotel Groups page.

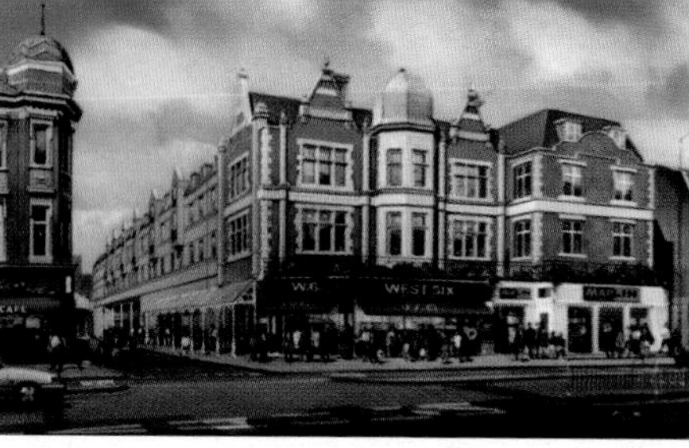

**ROOMS:** 135 en suite **NOTES:** Opened July 2001

W8 KENSINGTON See LONDON plan 1 D3

### ★★★★★75% ®®® Royal Garden Hotel

2-24 Kensington High St W8 4PT
☎ 020 7937 8000 ▤ 020 7361 1991
e-mail: sales@royalgardenhotel.co.uk
***Dir:*** *next to Kensington Palace*
This tall, modern hotel provides guests with the expected international levels of comfort and service. The smart, modern rooms overlook either Hyde Park or the Kensington rooftops. The hotel's showcase restaurant - The Tenth - is contemporary, with great views; the cooking style has its base in the classical repertoire but skilfully injects modern and Oriental ideas.
**ROOMS:** 396 en suite (19 fmly) No smoking in 164 bedrooms s £210-£310; d £250-£375 * **FACILITIES:** STV Sauna Solarium Gym Health & fitness centre entertainment Xmas **CONF:** Thtr 550 Class 260 Board 80 **SERVICES:** Lift air con **PARKING:** 160 **NOTES:** No dogs (ex guide dogs) Civ Wed 400 **CARDS:**

*See advert on opposite page*

### ★★★★63% Copthorne Tara Hotel London Kensington

COPTHORNE

Scarsdale Place, Wrights Ln W8 5SR
☎ 020 7937 7211 ▤ 020 7937 7100
e-mail: tara.sales@mill-cop.com
***Dir:*** *located just off Kensington High Street*
One of the city's larger hotels and popular with continental tours and conferences. Located in a quiet residential area, off Kensington High Street. Public areas have a bustling and smart atmosphere, and include the relaxing setting of Café Mozart or the Brasserie. Bedrooms fall into two grades, Classic and Connoisseur; there are a number of very well-appointed rooms for disabled guests. All bedrooms are air-conditioned.
**ROOMS:** 834 en suite No smoking in 265 bedrooms s £205; d £205 * **LB** **FACILITIES:** STV Xmas **CONF:** Thtr 280 Class 160 Board 80 Del £205 * **SERVICES:** Lift air con **PARKING:** 86 **NOTES:** No dogs (ex guide dogs) **CARDS:**

### ★★★70% Posthouse Kensington

Posthouse

Wright's Ln, Kensington W8 5SP
☎ 0870 400 9000 ▤ 020 7937 8289
e-mail: gm1253@forte-hotels.com
***Dir:*** *off Kensington High Street*
Positioned close to Kensington High Street, this hotel offers an extensive range of facilities; these include the refurbished leisure club, the 'Academy' conference rooms and a choice of dining

*continued*

options. Bedrooms vary in style and although some rooms are quite compact, they all offer good facilities.
**ROOMS:** 550 en suite No smoking in 150 bedrooms s £79-£139; d £79-£159 * LB **FACILITIES:** STV Indoor swimming (H) Squash Sauna Solarium Gym Jacuzzi Health & Fitness centre **CONF:** Thtr 180 Class 80 Board 60 Del from £170 * **SERVICES:** Lift **PARKING:** 70 **NOTES:** No dogs (ex guide dogs) **CARDS:**

Premier Collection
Town House

**★★★★★ Milestone Hotel & Apartments**

Red Carnation HOTELS

1 Kensington Court W8 5DL
☎ 020 7917 1000 020 7917 1010
e-mail: guestservices@milestone.redcarnationhotels.com
***Dir:*** *from M4 follow into Central London. Turn into Warwick Road and then right into Kensington High St. Hotel 400yds past Kensington Underground*
Much care has been lavished on this town house, which enjoys views of Kensington Palace and Gardens. Themed bedrooms are of a high standard and facilities include DVD players. There are superb suites and some duplex such as the Safari, complete with colonial fan and safari print fabrics. Staff are very friendly, and the bar and kitchen produce excellent cocktails and meals. There is a snug bar with a conservatory extension and a luxurious lounge.
**ROOMS:** 57 en suite No smoking in 10 bedrooms s £250-£270; d £250-£270 * **FACILITIES:** STV Sauna Gym Jacuzzi Health Club entertainment Xmas **CONF:** Thtr 28 Class 12 Board 16 **SERVICES:** Lift air con **NOTES:** Civ Wed 30
**CARDS:**

## W11 HOLLAND PARK, NOTTING HILL
See LONDON plan 1 D3/D4

**★★★★75% Halcyon**
81 Holland Park W11 3RZ
☎ 020 7727 7288 020 7229 8516
e-mail: information@thehalcyon.com
***Dir:*** *From M40 follow signs to West London,when reaching Shepherds Bush rdbt take first left onto Holland Park Avenue*

Faithfully restored and situated in the fashionable Holland Park area, this elegant hotel provides amply proportioned bedrooms equipped with every comfort. Friendly staff provide round-the-clock attentive and cheery service. 'Aix en Provence' is the hotel's stylish venue for flavour packed dishes with a distinctive rustic French theme.
**ROOMS:** 42 en suite No smoking in 6 bedrooms s £211; d £329 * **FACILITIES:** STV Membership of nearby club Xmas **CONF:** Class 20 Board 10 **SERVICES:** Lift air con **NOTES:** No dogs (ex guide dogs)
**CARDS:**

## WC1 BLOOMSBURY, HOLBORN

**★★★★★71% Renaissance London Chancery Court**

RENAISSANCE

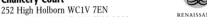

252 High Holborn WC1V 7EN
☎ 020 7829 9888 020 7829 9889
***Dir:*** *Follow A4 along Piccadilly & onto Shaftesbury Avenue, into High Holborn, hotel on right*
There is a grand new addition to London's hotel scene. Craftsmen have meticulously restored the sweeping marble staircases, grand archways and stately public rooms of the 1914 building. The result is a grand, yet relaxed hotel offering everything from stylish, luxuriously appointed bedrooms to a health club and state of the art meeting rooms.
**ROOMS:** 357 en suite No smoking in 170 bedrooms s £180-£325; d £180-£325 (incl. bkfst) * **FACILITIES:** no TV in bdrms Xmas **CONF:** Thtr 450 Class 252 Board 60 **SERVICES:** Lift air con **NOTES:** Civ Wed **CARDS:**

**★★★★70% *Radisson Edwardian Kenilworth***

Radisson Edwardian

Great Russell St WC1B 3LB
☎ 020 7637 3477 020 7631 3133
e-mail: resmarl@radisson.com
***Dir:*** *continue past Oxford Street and down New Oxford Street. Turn into Bloomsbury Street*
Following extensive refurbishment, the hotel has been completely transformed and now features the stylish, contemporary Glass Bar and Restaurant with its theatre kitchen as well as a range of

*continued on p372*

London

WC1 BLOOMSBURY, HOLBORN, continued

meeting rooms and a small leisure facility. Air-conditioned bedrooms are modern in style and feature a multitude of useful extras.
**ROOMS:** 187 en suite No smoking in 20 bedrooms **FACILITIES:** STV **CONF:** Thtr 150 Class 50 Board 50 **SERVICES:** Lift
**CARDS:**

### ★★★★70% *Radisson Edwardian Marlborough*

Bloomsbury St WC1B 3QD
☎ 020 7636 5601 020 7636 0532
e-mail: resmarl@radisson.com
***Dir:*** *continue past Oxford Street and down New Oxford Street turn into Bloomsbury Street*
Within sight of the British Museum, this smart modern hotel is ideal for cultural visits to London. The theatre district is five minutes' walk away. Public areas feature a choice of bars and the modern Glass Restaurant, while spacious bedrooms offer high standards of comfort.
**ROOMS:** 173 en suite (3 fmly) No smoking in 57 bedrooms **CONF:** Thtr 250 Class 90 Board 50 **SERVICES:** Lift
**CARDS:**

### ★★★★68% Jurys Great Russell Street

16-22 Great Russell St WC1B 3NN
☎ 020 7347 1000 020 7347 1001
e-mail: sales@jurysdoyle.com
This carefully restored property was originally built in 1929 and was designed by the renowned Sir Edwin Lutyens. Many of the original features have been retained including the grand reception, lobby and spacious meeting rooms. Both the restaurant and bar offer the same traditional elegance seen throughout the hotel and bedrooms are attractively appointed.
**ROOMS:** 169 en suite No smoking in 67 bedrooms s £205-£225; d £205-£225 * LB **FACILITIES:** STV **CONF:** Thtr 280 Class 140 Board 50 Del £230 * **SERVICES:** Lift air con **NOTES:** No dogs (ex guide dogs)
**CARDS:**

### ★★★★68% The Montague on the Gardens

15 Montague St, Bloomsbury WC1B 5BJ
☎ 020 7637 1001 020 7637 2516
e-mail: reservations@montague.redcarnationhotels.com
***Dir:*** *Next to British Museum.*
This stylish central London hotel benefits from an al fresco garden terrace overlooking a peaceful garden. Other public areas include the elegant Blue Door Bistro, a bar lounge and airy conservatory where traditional afternoon teas are served and an excellent range of meeting rooms. Luxuriously appointed accommodation ranges from compact bedrooms to spacious split-level suites.
**ROOMS:** 104 en suite No smoking in 20 bedrooms s £150-£180; d £170-£210 * LB **FACILITIES:** STV Sauna Gym Jacuzzi entertainment Xmas **CONF:** Thtr 120 Class 50 Board 50 **SERVICES:** Lift air con **NOTES:** No dogs (ex guide dogs) Civ Wed 120
**CARDS:**

### ★★★★66% *Holiday Inn Kings Cross/Bloomsbury*

1 Kings Cross Rd WC1X 9HX
☎ 020 7833 3900 020 7917 6163
e-mail: peterstubbs@axford.com
***Dir:*** *0.50m from Kings Cross station on the corner of King Cross Rd and Calthorpe St*
Conveniently located for Kings Cross station and the City, this modern hotel offers smart accommodation with a wide range of facilities. The hotel has two restaurants, one of which is Indian, limited lounge seating, versatile meeting rooms, a cosy bar and a small, well-equipped fitness centre.
**ROOMS:** 405 en suite (163 fmly) No smoking in 160 bedrooms **FACILITIES:** STV Indoor swimming (H) Sauna Solarium Gym Jacuzzi Hair & Beauty salon **CONF:** Thtr 220 Class 120 Board 30 **SERVICES:** Lift air con **PARKING:** 12 **NOTES:** No dogs (ex guide dogs)
**CARDS:**

### ★★★★65% Hotel Russell

Russell Square WC1B 5BE
☎ 020 7837 6470 020 7837 2857
e-mail: reservations.russell@principalhotels.co.uk
This landmark Victorian hotel has recently undergone a multi-million pound transformation, which has seen most bedrooms completely refurbished to a very high standard. The grandeur of the public rooms has also been recaptured and further improvements are planned. The hotel itself is superbly located and is within walking distance of the theatre district and a short distance from the city of London.
**ROOMS:** 380 en suite No smoking in 80 bedrooms s £178-£236; d £198-£273 (incl. cont bkfst) * LB **FACILITIES:** STV Xmas **CONF:** Thtr 450 Class 200 Board 40 Del from £195 * **SERVICES:** Lift air con
**CARDS:**

*See advert on opposite page*

### ★★★71% The Bonnington in Bloomsbury

92 Southampton Row WC1B 4BH
☎ 020 7242 2828 020 7831 9170
e-mail: sales@bonnington.com
***Dir:*** *from M40 Euston Rd opposite Stn turn south into Upper Woburn Place past Russell Sq into Southampton Row. Bonnington on left*
Within easy access of the City and West End, this hotel offers traditional service and modern comfort. Bedrooms are well-laid out with many extras including air conditioning as a standard. Meals can be enjoyed in either the attractive Waterfalls restaurant or in the popular bar.
**ROOMS:** 215 en suite (4 fmly) No smoking in 87 bedrooms s £80-£117; d £120-£149 (incl. bkfst) * **FACILITIES:** STV **CONF:** Thtr 250 Class 80 Board 100 Del from £120 * **SERVICES:** Lift air con
**CARDS:**

### ★★★66% *Posthouse Premier Bloomsbury*

Coram St WC1N 1HT
☎ 0870 400 9222 020 7837 5374
***Dir:*** *off Upper Woburn Place near to Russell Square*
The central location of this modern hotel makes it an ideal base for both business and leisure travellers. Public areas have been extensively refurbished and include a range of meeting rooms and an Irish-themed bar. Bedrooms vary in size and style, all offering a good range of facilities and amenities.
**ROOMS:** 284 en suite (29 fmly) No smoking in 211 bedrooms **FACILITIES:** STV **CONF:** Thtr 200 Class 140 Board 22 **SERVICES:** Lift **PARKING:** 80 **NOTES:** No dogs (ex guide dogs)
**CARDS:**

## *Town House*

### ★★★★ Blooms

7 Montague St WC1B 5BP
☎ 020 7323 1717 020 7636 6498
e-mail: blooms@mermaid.co.uk
***Dir:*** *off Russell Square*
Part of an 18th-century terrace, this elegant town house is just around the corner from the British Museum. Bedrooms are

*continued*

London

furnished in Regency style and day rooms consist of a lobby lounge, a garden terrace, a breakfast room and cocktail bar, all graced with antique pieces, paintings and flowers. The lounge menu is also available as room service, and meals can be delivered from some of the local restaurants.

**ROOMS:** 27 en suite s £130-£135; d £205-£210 * **LB**
**FACILITIES:** STV Xmas **CONF:** Thtr 20 Class 10 Board 18 Del from £180 * **SERVICES:** Lift **NOTES:** No dogs (ex guide dogs) Civ Wed 20 **CARDS:**

*See advert on this page*

### Grange Holborn

50-60 Southampton Rd WC1B 4AR
☎ 020 7242 1800 020 7242 0057
e-mail: holborn@grangehotels.co.uk
At the time of going to press, the star classification for this hotel was not confirmed. Please refer to the AA internet site www.theAA.com for current information.
**ROOMS:** 200 en suite **CONF:** Thtr 220 Class 120 Board 60 Del £265 *

### Grange Whitehall

2-5 Montague St WC1B 5BP
☎ 020 7580 2224 020 7580 5554
e-mail: whitehall@grangehotel.co.uk
At the time of going to press, the star classification for this hotel was not confirmed. Please refer to the AA internet site www.theAA.com for current information.
**ROOMS:** 56 en suite **CONF:** Thtr 90 Class 45 Board 45 Del from £235 *

### Ambassador in Bloomsbury

12 Upper Woburn Place WC1H 0HX
☎ 0207 387 1456
At the time of going to press, the star classification for this hotel was not confirmed. Please refer to the AA internet site www.theAA.com for current information.



London

WC2 SOHO, STRAND

## Premier Collection

SAVOY

### ★★★★★ The Savoy

Strand WC2R 0EU
☎ 020 7836 4343 020 7240 6040
e-mail: info@the-savoy.co.uk

The Savoy Group

***Dir:*** *situated halfway along The Strand between Trafalgar Square and Aldwych*

There is a feeling of great anticipation as one arrives at this internationally renowned hotel. Services flow smoothly and bedrooms offer excellent levels of comfort; many have fine views along the river. The choice of dining areas presents a predicament - whether to opt for the Grill, the River Room or the more informal Upstairs Restaurant. No visit would be complete without experiencing afternoon tea in the Thames Foyer, perhaps enjoying the regular Sunday afternoon tea dance.

**ROOMS:** 263 en suite (6 fmly) No smoking in 55 bedrooms s £320-£1125; d £375-£1250 * **LB** **FACILITIES:** STV Indoor swimming (H) Sauna Gym entertainment Xmas **CONF:** Thtr 500 Class 200 Board 32 **SERVICES:** Lift air con **PARKING:** 65 **NOTES:** No dogs (ex guide dogs) Civ Wed 300 **CARDS:**

### ★★★★★74% *One Aldwych*

1 Aldwych WC2B 4BZ
☎ 020 7300 1000 020 7300 1001
e-mail: sales@onealdwych.co.uk

***Dir:*** *at the point where the Aldwych meets the Strand, near Waterloo Bridge*

From its position on the corner of the Aldwych, this magnificent hotel enjoys commanding views across Waterloo Bridge and Covent Garden. The building has been carefully restored and now combines all the expected modern comforts with the charm of the original architecture. Accommodation is bright, stylish and fully air-conditioned. All rooms are equipped with CD player and voicemail. The Axis and Indigo restaurants provide quality dining, and the cocktail bar is a popular meeting place.

**ROOMS:** 105 en suite No smoking in 39 bedrooms **FACILITIES:** STV Indoor swimming (H) Sauna Gym Steam room 2 Treatment rooms **CONF:** Thtr 60 Board 40 **SERVICES:** Lift air con **NOTES:** No dogs (ex guide dogs) Civ Wed 60 **CARDS:**

### ★★★★★67% Le Meridien Waldorf

Aldwych WC2B 4DD
☎ 0870 400 8484 020 7836 7244

Le Meridien Hotels & Resorts

***Dir:*** *from Trafalgar Sq follow The Strand all the way to the end, when the one way system brings you into Aldwych*

A traditional English hotel enjoying an enviable central location at the gateway to the City of London itself. The Palm Court is the heart of the hotel, a stunning venue for all day dining, including the famous afternoon tea-dances hosted here at weekends. Other public rooms include the Club Bar and the Footlights Bar, and an informal bistro. Bedrooms are decorated in an authentic Edwardian style, bathrooms are marble and generally spacious.

**ROOMS:** 292 en suite (6 fmly) No smoking in 150 bedrooms s £275; d £275 * **LB** **FACILITIES:** STV Health & Fitness Club entertainment Xmas **CONF:** Thtr 250 Class 120 Board 70 **SERVICES:** Lift air con **NOTES:** No dogs (ex guide dogs) Civ Wed 400 **CARDS:**

### ★★★★76% *Radisson Edwardian Mountbatten*

Monmouth St, Seven Dials, Covent Garden WC2H 9HD
☎ 020 7836 4300 020 7240 3540
e-mail: resmoun@radisson.com

Radisson Edwardian

***Dir:*** *just off Shaftesbury Av, on the corner of Seven Dials rdbt*

This hotel is named after Lord Mountbatten and contains many items of memorabilia. Its excellent location in London's Theatreland, above average service and super hospitality prove popular with a loyal following of regular guests. The smart, air-conditioned bedrooms are not over-large but are very comfortable.

**ROOMS:** 128 en suite No smoking in 64 bedrooms **FACILITIES:** STV Gym entertainment **CONF:** Thtr 90 Class 45 Board 32 **SERVICES:** Lift air con **CARDS:**

### ★★★★72% Kingsway Hall

Great Queen St, Covent Garden WC2B 5BX
☎ 020 7309 0909 020 7309 9696
e-mail: kingswayhall@compuserve.com

***Dir:*** *from Holborn Underground Station follow Kingsway towards Aldwych At first lights turn right. Hotel 50mtrs on left*

Situated in Covent Garden, this smart hotel offers a high standard of accommodation. Air-conditioned bedrooms have been well-

continued

London

designed and feature excellent facilities. The lounge bar is a stylish setting for drinks and lighter meals and the Harlequin restaurant features accomplished cooking.
**ROOMS:** 170 en suite No smoking in 114 bedrooms s fr £230; d fr £240 * **FACILITIES:** STV Gym, sauna and jacuzzi ready late 2001 Xmas **CONF:** Thtr 150 Class 90 Board 50 **SERVICES:** Lift air con **NOTES:** No dogs (ex guide dogs) **CARDS:**

*See advert on this page*

### ★★★66% *Strand Palace*
Strand WC2R 0JJ
☎ 0870 400 8702 Fax 020 7836 2077
This large and prominently positioned hotel has a wide range of restaurants and facilities, which are tailored to suit most guests' needs and requirements. Bedrooms vary, with the newly refurbished examples being particularly smart and the 'Academy' provides state-of-the-art conference and banqueting suites.
**ROOMS:** 783 en suite No smoking in 305 bedrooms **FACILITIES:** STV Discount at nearby Health Club **CONF:** Thtr 160 Class 85 Board 40 **SERVICES:** Lift **NOTES:** No dogs (ex guide dogs)
**CARDS:**

### ○ *Radisson Edwardian Hampshire Hotel*
Leicester Square WC2H 7LH
Radisson Edwardian
☎ 020 7839 9399 Fax 020 7930 8122
e-mail: reshamp@radisson.com
***Dir:*** *situated on Leicester Square*
This popular hotel is superbly situated in Leicester Square. Public areas have been smartly refurbished and the air-conditioned bedrooms are both comfortable and very thoughtfully equipped. Good food can be enjoyed in the stylish Apex restaurant.
**ROOMS:** 124 en suite No smoking in 20 bedrooms **FACILITIES:** STV Gym **CONF:** Thtr 100 Class 40 Board 34 **SERVICES:** Lift air con
**CARDS:**

### ○ *Radisson Edwardian Pastoria Hotel*
3-6 St Martins St WC2H 7HL
Radisson Edwardian
☎ 020 7930 8641 Fax 020 7925 0551
e-mail: reshamp@radisson.com
***Dir:*** *S side of Leicester Square*
In a discreet side street off Leicester Square, this small hotel has smart public areas and an informal restaurant. The bedrooms are tastefully furnished and comfortable, and offer room service. Those on the top floor are more spacious and have marble bathrooms. Staff go out of their way to ensure guests are well looked after.
**ROOMS:** 58 en suite No smoking in 16 bedrooms **FACILITIES:** STV **CONF:** Thtr 60 Class 28 Board 26 **SERVICES:** Lift **NOTES:** No dogs (ex guide dogs) **CARDS:**



## LONDON AIRPORTS See under Gatwick & Heathrow

## LONDON COLNEY, Hertfordshire

### ○ Innkeeper's Lodge St Albans
Barnet Rd, London Colney AL2 1BL
Innkeeper's Lodge
A new concept in the travel accommodation market. Smart rooms meet essential business requirements but also have home comforts. Dining options include all-day menus plus the added advantage of breakfast, which is included in the room price. Reservations can be made seven days a week through the room reservations number: 0870 243 0500. For further details, consult the Hotel Groups page.
**ROOMS:** 12 en suite **NOTES:** Opening Autumn 2001

London

LONG EATON, Derbyshire Map 08 SK43
see also Sandiacre

### ★★★66% Novotel Nottingham

Bostock Ln NG10 4EP
☎ 0115 946 5111 🖹 0115 946 5900
e-mail: H0507@accor.hotels.com
*Dir: M1 junct 25. Take B6002 to Long Eaton, hotel is 400 yds on left*
A purpose-built hotel, close to J25 of the M1. Bedrooms are uniform in size and layout, offering the range of facilities and comfort associated with this international brand. Two rooms have suitable facilities for disabled guests. Services are efficiently provided by a young and friendly team.
**ROOMS:** 108 en suite (31 fmly) No smoking in 58 bedrooms d £62 * **LB** **FACILITIES:** STV Outdoor swimming (H) **CONF:** Thtr 220 Class 100 Board 100 Del from £99 * **SERVICES:** Lift **PARKING:** 180
**CARDS:**

### ★★64% *Europa*

20-22 Derby Rd NG10 1LW
☎ 0115 972 8481 🖹 0115 946 0229
*Dir: on A6005, in the centre of Long Eaton*
Convenient for the town centre and the M1, this commercial hotel offers clean, brightly furnished bedrooms. In addition to the restaurant, light refreshments are available throughout the day in the conservatory. Cheerful, informal service is provided by friendly staff.
**ROOMS:** 15 en suite (2 fmly) **CONF:** Thtr 35 Class 35 Board 28 **PARKING:** 24 **NOTES:** No dogs (ex guide dogs) No smoking in restaurant **CARDS:**

LONGHORSLEY, Northumberland Map 12 NZ19

### ★★★70% Linden Hall

NE65 8XF
☎ 01670 500000 🖹 01670 500001
e-mail: stay@lindenhall.co.uk
*Dir: 1m N on A697*
This impressive Georgian mansion, standing in 400 acres of park and woodlands, offers extensive leisure and function facilities. Bedrooms, generally spacious, are equipped to suit the needs of business and leisure visitors alike. An imaginative choice of dishes is available in the Dobson restaurant, diners also having the alternative of lighter fare in the Linden Tree pub in the grounds.
**ROOMS:** 50 en suite (4 fmly) s £73-£84; d £104-£125 (incl. bkfst) * **LB** **FACILITIES:** STV Indoor swimming (H) Golf 18 Tennis (hard) Snooker Sauna Solarium Gym Croquet lawn Putting green Jacuzzi Hairdressing Health/beauty spa steamroom Xmas **CONF:** Thtr 300 Class 100 Board 40 Del from £130 * **SERVICES:** Lift **PARKING:** 260 **NOTES:** No smoking in restaurant Civ Wed 120 **CARDS:**

*See advert on opposite page*

LONG MELFORD, Suffolk Map 05 TL84

### ★★★67% *The Bull*

Hall St CO10 9JG
☎ 01787 378494 🖹 01787 880307
*Dir: 3m N of Sudbury on the A134*
Fifteenth century building full of character with a wealth of exposed beams, carvings and heraldic markings. The well-equipped bedrooms have many original features and offer a good degree of comfort. There is a bar, restaurant and two lounges to relax in, one of which is non smoking.
**ROOMS:** 25 en suite (3 fmly) No smoking in 11 bedrooms **CONF:** Thtr 60 Class 30 Board 35 **PARKING:** 30 **NOTES:** No smoking in restaurant Civ Wed 50 **CARDS:**

### ★★72% The Black Lion

Church Walk, The Green CO10 9DN
☎ 01787 312356 🖹 01787 374557
*Dir: at junct of A134/A1092. Overlooking the green.*
This 15th-century hotel offers a great deal of charm and character. Each bedroom is individually decorated, all are spacious and comfortable with a number of thoughtful extras. Guests may choose to dine in the bar or opt for the more formal restaurant.
**ROOMS:** 10 en suite (3 fmly) s £69-£85; d £90-£115 (incl. bkfst) * **LB** **FACILITIES:** Xmas **CONF:** Thtr 50 Class 28 Board 28 **PARKING:** 10 **NOTES:** No smoking in restaurant **CARDS:**

LONGRIDGE, Lancashire Map 07 SD6

### ★★65% Ferrari's Country House

Chipping Rd, Thornley PR3 2TB
☎ 01772 783148 🖹 01772 786174
*Dir: from Longridge centre follow signs for Chipping past Safeway, along Chipping Lane for 1m, past Derby Arms to hotel 50yds on left*
A delightful privately-owned country house situated in splendid gardens in the heart of rural Lancashire. Most of the spacious bedrooms have been refurbished in recent years, many with beautiful antique furniture. An attractively appointed restaurant and comfortable lounge bar are also features. The setting is ideal for weddings.
**ROOMS:** 11 en suite (2 fmly) s fr £45; d fr £60 (incl. bkfst) * **LB** **FACILITIES:** Xmas **CONF:** Thtr 60 Class 30 Board 30 **PARKING:** 50 **NOTES:** Civ Wed 120 **CARDS:**

LONG SUTTON, Lincolnshire Map 09 TF4

### ⌂ *Travelodge*

Wisbech Rd PE12 9AG
☎ 01406 362230 🖹 01406 362230
*Dir: on junct A17/A1101 roundabout*
Travelodge offers good quality, good value, modern accommodation. Ideal for families, the spacious, en suite bedrooms include remote-control TV, tea and coffee-making facilities, luxury beds and free morning newspaper. Meals can be taken at the nearby family restaurant. For further details and the Travelodge phone number, consult the Hotel Groups page.

**ROOMS:** 40 en suite

LOOE, Cornwall & Isles of Scilly Map 02 SX2

### ★★★64% Hannafore Point

Marine Dr, West Looe PL13 2DG
☎ 01503 263273 🖹 01503 263272
e-mail: hannafore@aol.com
*Dir: on A38 Plymouth road turn left onto A385 to Looe across bridge and take immediate left. Hotel is half mile on left*
With panoramic coastal views embracing St George's Island around to Rame Head, this popular hotel provides a warm welcome. The spacious restaurant shares the view, where a choice of menus is offered, served by a friendly team of staff. Additional facilities include heated indoor pool, squash court and gymnasium.
**ROOMS:** 37 en suite (5 fmly) s £50-£56; d £100-£112 (incl. bkfst & dinner) * **LB** **FACILITIES:** Indoor swimming (H) Squash Sauna Solarium Gym Jacuzzi 3/4 billiard table entertainment Xmas **CONF:** Thtr 100 Class 120 Board 40 **SERVICES:** Lift **PARKING:** 32 **NOTES:** No smoking in restaurant Civ Wed 160
**CARDS:**

*See advert on opposite pag*

★★75% **Fieldhead**
Portuan Rd, Hannafore PL13 2DR
☎ 01503 262689 📠 01503 264114
e-mail: field.head@virgin.net

MINOTEL
Great Britain

*Dir: Arriving in Looe from East or West take road along harbour side signposted 'Hannafore'. Follow along past the small waterside church up the hill to seafront. Take the 1st right and then right again*

A warm and genuine welcome is assured, with a relaxed and civilised atmosphere pervading. Bedrooms are furnished with care, many having a window-full of sea view! Smartly presented public areas include a convivial bar and restaurant, whilst moving outside a palm-filled garden leads to a secluded patio and swimming pool. The fixed-price menu changes daily and features quality local produce.

**ROOMS:** 14 en suite (2 fmly) s £45-£55; d £75-£100 (incl. bkfst) * **LB**
**FACILITIES:** Outdoor swimming (H) ch fac Xmas **PARKING:** 15
**NOTES:** No smoking in restaurant **CARDS:**

*See advert on this page*

LOOE, continued

**★★62% Rivercroft Hotel**
Station Rd PL13 1HL
☎ 01503 262251 ▤ 01503 265494
e-mail: rivercroft.hotel@virgin.net
***Dir:*** *From A38 take B387 to Looe. Hotel on left near bridge*

Standing high above the river, this family run hotel is conveniently located, just a short walk from the town centre and beach. Bedrooms are comfortably furnished and well-equipped, many enjoying wonderful views of the varied activity below. An extensive menu is offered in the Croft Restaurant, or alternatively, meals can be enjoyed in the convivial atmosphere of the bar.
**ROOMS:** 15 en suite (8 fmly) **FACILITIES:** ch fac **NOTES:** No dogs No smoking in restaurant **CARDS:**

L

LOSTWITHIEL, Cornwall & Isles of Scilly Map 02 SX15

**★★★65% Restormel Lodge**
Hillside Gardens PL22 0DD
☎ 01208 872223 ▤ 01208 873568
e-mail: restlodge@aol.com
***Dir:*** *on A390 in Lostwithiel*

Best Western

Under the same family ownership for over 30 years, this hotel offers a friendly welcome to all visitors. The original building, housing the bar, restaurant and lounges, has kept much of its character. Bedrooms are comfortably furnished, and a number overlook the outdoor pool.
**ROOMS:** 21 en suite 12 annexe en suite (3 fmly) No smoking in 24 bedrooms s £52-£58; d £80-£84 (incl. bkfst) * **LB** **FACILITIES:** STV Outdoor swimming (H) ch fac Xmas **CONF:** Thtr 100 Class 80 Board 60 **PARKING:** 40 **CARDS:**

**★★★61% Lostwithiel Hotel Golf & Country Club**
Lower Polscoe PL22 0HQ
☎ 01208 873550 ▤ 01208 873479
e-mail: info@golf-hotel.co.uk
***Dir:*** *turn off A38 at Dobwalls onto the A390, on entering Lostwithiel turn right - signposted from main road*

Established as a leisure resort in its own right, Lostwithiel offers a wide range of activities in addition to its challenging 18-hole golf course. The well-equipped bedrooms are housed in attractive Cornish stone buildings. A range of interesting meals are served in the Sportsman's Bar and the Black Prince restaurant.
**ROOMS:** 19 en suite s £29-£42; d £58-£78 (incl. bkfst) * **LB** **FACILITIES:** Indoor swimming (H) Golf 18 Tennis (hard) Fishing Snooker Gym Putting green Undercover floodlit driving range Xmas **CONF:** Thtr 200 Class 60 Board 40 Del from £52 * **PARKING:** 120 **CARDS:**

LOUGHBOROUGH, Leicestershire Map 08 SK

**★★★★70% Quorn Country Hotel**
Charnwood House, 66 Leicester Rd LE12 8BB
☎ 01509 415050 ▤ 01509 415557
e-mail: quorncountry.hotel@virgin.net
(For full entry see Quorn)

**★★★64% The Quality Hotel**
New Ashby Rd LE11 4EX
☎ 01509 211800 ▤ 01509 211868
e-mail: admin@gb613.u-net.com
***Dir:*** *leave M1 at junct 23 and take A512 towards Loughborough. Hotel 1 on left*

Quality Hotel

This popular, modern hotel offers comfortable, well-equipped accommodation. All the bedrooms offer a spacious work area, ar some rooms have small lounges and kitchenettes, ideal for the longer stay or families. There is a small leisure centre and versati conference facilities.
**ROOMS:** 94 en suite (12 fmly) No smoking in 47 bedrooms s £80-£90, d £90-£115 * **LB** **FACILITIES:** STV Indoor swimming (H) Sauna Solarium Gym Jacuzzi ch fac Xmas **CONF:** Thtr 225 Class 120 Board 80 Del from £90 * **PARKING:** 160 **NOTES:** No smoking in restaurant Civ Wed 80 **CARDS:**

**★★67% Cedars Hotel**
Cedar Rd LE11 2AB
☎ 01509 214459 ▤ 01509 233573
e-mail: goodman@cedars01.freeserve.co.uk
***Dir:*** *leaving Loughborough for Leicester on the A6, Cedar Road is last road on the left opposite Crematorium*

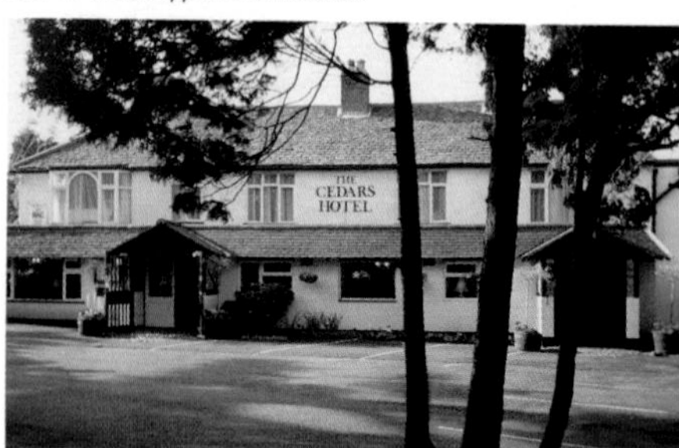
THE
CEDARS
HOTEL

This popular well maintained hotel is located in a peaceful residential area south of the town centre. Its well-equipped, comfortable bedrooms offer the ideal spot to relax and enjoy a meal in the light and airy restaurant or a quiet drink in the cosy bar.
**ROOMS:** 36 en suite (4 fmly) s £45-£65; d £65-£80 (incl. bkfst) * **FACILITIES:** Outdoor swimming (H) Sauna **CONF:** Thtr 30 Class 30 Board 28 Del from £95 * **PARKING:** 50 **NOTES:** No smoking in restaurant **CARDS:**

**★★61% Great Central**
Great Central Rd LE11 1RW
☎ 01509 263405 ▤ 01509 264130
e-mail: reception@greatcentralhotel.co.uk
***Dir:*** *from town centre take A60 towards Nottingham then first right. Hotel on left*

This aptly-named hotel is near the Great Central Steam Railway. It high-ceilinged, Victorian-style bar has a convivial atmosphere and is decorated with railway memorabilia. Most of the attractive

*continue*

·edrooms have pine furniture and cheerful colour schemes; everal four-poster bedrooms are also available.
**OOMS:** 22 en suite (5 fmly) s £35; d £50 (incl. bkfst) * **LB**
**ACILITIES:** STV Xmas **CONF:** Thtr 100 Class 100 Board 40 Del from 60 * **PARKING:** 40 **CARDS:**

OUTH, Lincolnshire Map 08 TF38

### ★★★71% Brackenborough Arms Hotel

Cordeaux Corner, Brackenborough LN11 0SZ
☎ 01507 609169 🖷 01507 609413
-mail: ashley@brackenborough.force9.co.uk
**Dir:** *off A16 2m N of Louth*

et amidst well tended gardens and patios, this hotel offers ttractive bedrooms individually decorated with co-ordinated urnishings and many extras. There is a cocktail bar, and the ippler's Retreat lounge bar, famous for its fish and chips. rackens Restaurant offers an interesting range of more dventurous dishes.
**OOMS:** 24 en suite (1 fmly) No smoking in 6 bedrooms s £59-£62; £70-£75 (incl. bkfst) * **LB** **FACILITIES:** STV ch fac **CONF:** Thtr 34 lass 24 Board 30 **PARKING:** 90 **NOTES:** No dogs (ex guide dogs) losed 25-26 Dec Civ Wed 34 **CARDS:**

### ★★★69% Beaumont

6 Victoria Rd LN11 0BX
☎ 01507 605005 🖷 01507 607768
-mail: enquiries@thebeaumont.freeserve.co.uk

n a peaceful residential street close to the town centre, this ersonally-run private hotel provides spacious, individually ecorated bedrooms. A couple of small single rooms are also vailable. The lounge is comfortable and the restaurant offers set-riced and carte menus that includes a wide range of fresh pasta ishes.
**OOMS:** 16 en suite (2 fmly) s £45-£55; d £65-£80 (incl. bkfst) *
**ACILITIES:** STV ch fac **CONF:** Thtr 80 Class 50 Board 46
**ERVICES:** Lift **PARKING:** 70 **NOTES:** RS Sun
**ARDS:**

### ★★★68% Kenwick Park

Kenwick Park LN11 8NR
☎ 01507 608806 🖷 01507 608027
-mail: enquiries@kenwick-park.co.uk
**Dir:** *follow A16 from Grimsby, then A157 Mablethorpe/Manby road. Hotel s 400mtrs down hill on right*

Best Western

his elegant Georgian house is situated on the 500 acre Kenwick ark estate adjacent to the golf course. The bedrooms are enerally quite spacious and offer a good degree of comfort as vell as many modern facilities. Public areas include a restaurant nd a conservatory bar which overlooks the golf course, there is lso an excellent leisure centre.
**OOMS:** 29 en suite 5 annexe en suite (3 fmly) No smoking in 11 edrooms s £65-£80; d £75-£98 (incl. bkfst) * **LB** **FACILITIES:** **Spa** TV Indoor swimming (H) Golf 18 Tennis (hard) Squash Snooker Sauna olarium Gym Putting green Jacuzzi Health & Beauty Centre ch fac mas **CONF:** Thtr 100 Class 40 Board 40 Del from £100 *
**ARKING:** 50 **NOTES:** No smoking in restaurant Civ Wed 70
**ARDS:**

*See advert on this page*



LOWER ANSTY, Dorset Map 03 ST70

### ★★67% The Fox Inn

DT2 7PN
☎ 01258 880328 🖷 01258 881440
e-mail: hotel@fox-inn-ansty.co.uk
**Dir:** *From Dorchester A35 towards Poole after 4m exit at Northbrook Junction to Piddlehinton, 1st exit & continue for 200mtrs, turn right for Cheselbourne stay on this road for Ansty*

Set in the heart of Hardy's Wessex, The Fox Inn was formerly the home of the Woodhouse family, renowned in the area for their brewing. An imaginative range of dishes is offered from both the carte and from the blackboard and are served either in the bar or in the restaurant. Bedrooms vary in size but each is comfortable and well-equipped.
**ROOMS:** 14 en suite (1 fmly) s £45; d £70 (incl. bkfst) * **LB**
**FACILITIES:** Outdoor swimming (H) Xmas **CONF:** Thtr 40 Class 20 Board 30 Del from £85 * **PARKING:** 30 **NOTES:** No smoking in restaurant **CARDS:**

Early start? Hotels at all star levels should provide in-room alarm clocks and/or alarm calls.

L

LOWER BEEDING, West Sussex Map 04 TQ22

## Premier Collection

### ★★★★ South Lodge

Brighton Rd RH13 6PS
☎ 01403 891711 01403 891766
e-mail: enquiries@southlodgehotel.co.uk

***Dir:*** *on A23 left onto B2110 'Handcross'. Turn right through Handcross and follow B2110, until A281 junct. Turn left and Hotel entrance on right*

Enjoying splendid views over the Downs, this fine Victorian mansion stands in 90 acres of well-established gardens and grounds. Character public rooms include the delightful wood panelled Camellia restaurant, named after the 100-year-old camellia, which grows against the Tudor terrace wall. The kitchen team offer well executed and interesting cuisine through set priced and carte menus. Bedrooms are individually furnished and comfortably appointed, well-equipped and with many thoughtful personal touches provided.

**ROOMS:** 41 en suite s £160; d £185-£360 * LB **FACILITIES:** STV Golf 36 Tennis (hard) Snooker Gym Croquet lawn Putting green Can organise riding, shooting & fishing entertainment Xmas **CONF:** Thtr 85 Class 40 Board 30 Del from £210 * **PARKING:** 80 **NOTES:** No dogs (ex guide dogs) No smoking in restaurant Civ Wed 65 **CARDS:**

*See advert on opposite page*

LOWER SLAUGHTER, Gloucestershire Map 04 SP12

## Premier Collection

### ★★★ Lower Slaughter Manor

GL54 2HP
☎ 01451 820456 01451 822150
e-mail: lowsmanor@aol.com

***Dir:*** *off A429 signposted "The Slaughters", the manor is 0.5m on right entering village*

This charming Grade II listed manor dates mainly from the 17th century and enjoys a tranquil location at the heart of one of the Cotswolds' most famous villages. The manor was largely rebuilt in 1658 and features spacious bedrooms which are tastefully furnished and thoughtfully equipped. The appealing public areas include an inviting lounge and drawing room with log fires in season; leisure facilities include both heated indoor pool and tennis court.

**ROOMS:** 11 en suite 5 annexe en suite s £175-£350; d £200-£400 (incl. bkfst) * **FACILITIES:** Indoor swimming (H) Tennis (hard) Xmas **CONF:** Thtr 36 Class 20 Board 18 Del from £225 * **PARKING:** 30 **NOTES:** No dogs No children 12yrs No smoking in restaurant **CARDS:**

### ★★★77% Washbourne Court

GL54 2HS
☎ 01451 822143 01451 821045
e-mail: washbourne@msn.com

***Dir:*** *turn off A429 at signpost 'The Slaughters', between Stow-on-the-Wold and Bourton-on-the-Water. Hotel is in the centre of village*

Beamed ceilings, log fires and flagstone floors are just some of the attractive features of this 17th-century hotel, set in four acres of grounds beside the River Eye. Bedrooms, in the main house and self-contained cottages, are smartly decorated. There is a character bar, and the elegant dining room serves an interesting menu enhanced by a comprehensive list of wines.

**ROOMS:** 15 en suite 13 annexe en suite s £145-£215; d £200-£270 (incl. bkfst & dinner) * LB **FACILITIES:** Tennis (hard) Xmas **CONF:** Thtr 30 Board 20 **PARKING:** 40 **NOTES:** No dogs (ex guide dogs) No children 7yrs **CARDS:**

*See advert on opposite page*

LOWESTOFT, Suffolk Map 05 TM59

### ★★★75% Ivy House Farm Hotel

Ivy Ln, Beccles Rd, Oulton Broad NR33 8HY
☎ 01502 501353 & 588144 01502 501539
e-mail: admin@ivyhousefarm.co.uk

***Dir:*** *on A146 SW of Oulton Broad turn into Ivy Ln beside Esso petrol station, over small railway bridge & follow private driveway into car park*

The hotel centres around the restored Crooked Barn restaurant which is the focal point of this popular venue. The attractive bedrooms are spacious and comfortably furnished, with bright

*continued on p38*

LOWESTOFT, continued

modern fabrics. All rooms enjoy views of the garden or neighbouring fields, which are a home to a variety of wildfowl.
**ROOMS:** 19 annexe en suite (1 fmly) No smoking in 6 bedrooms s £73-£93; d £93-£125 (incl. bkfst) * **LB** **FACILITIES:** Arrangement with neighbouring leisure club for reduced rates **CONF:** Thtr 55 Board 22 Del from £115 * **PARKING:** 50 **NOTES:** No smoking in restaurant Closed 23 Dec-2Jan **CARDS:**

*See advert on page 381*

### ★★★66% Wherry Hotel

Bridge Rd, Oulton Broad NR32 3LN
☎ 01502 516845 & 516846 📠 01502 501350
e-mail: wherry@wherry.force9.net
***Dir:*** *Hotel is situated just north of the bridge in the centre of Oulton Broad on A146*

WHERRY HOTEL
WAVENEY RIVER

Built around 1900, the Wherry is named after the sailing barges typical of the Norfolk Broads area. Many original features can be seen in the bustling public areas, which overlook the waterfront. Well-equipped bedrooms come in a variety of sizes and styles, and there is a carvery-style restaurant, as well as public and lounge bars.
**ROOMS:** 29 en suite (5 fmly) s £49-£59; d £69 (incl. bkfst) * **LB** **FACILITIES:** STV **CONF:** Thtr 250 Class 150 Board 80 Del £70 * **SERVICES:** Lift **PARKING:** 185 **NOTES:** No smoking in restaurant Closed 24-26 Dec **CARDS:**

### ★★★65% *Hotel Hatfield*

Best Western

The Esplanade NR33 0QP
☎ 01502 565337 📠 01502 511885
e-mail: enquiries@hotelhatfield.co.uk
***Dir:*** *from town centre follow signs for 'South Beach' (A12 Ipswich). Hotel 200yds on left*

Situated on the esplanade overlooking the sandy beaches and the sea beyond. The lively bar serves a range of snacks and a choice of real ales, whereas the sea-facing Chaplins restaurant offers

*continued*

international dishes to suit most tastes. Bedrooms are spacious and well-equipped.
**ROOMS:** 33 en suite (1 fmly) **FACILITIES:** STV **CONF:** Thtr 100 Class 50 Board 40 **SERVICES:** Lift **PARKING:** 26 **NOTES:** No dogs (ex guide dogs) No smoking in restaurant Civ Wed 200
**CARDS:**

## LOWESWATER, Cumbria — Map 11 NY12

### ★71% Grange Country House

CA13 0SU
☎ 01946 861211 & 861570
***Dir:*** *turn left off A5086 for Mockerkin, through village and after 2m turn left for Loweswater Lake. Hotel at bottom of hill on left*
This delightful country hotel sits in a quiet valley at the north-western end of Loweswater and continues to prove popular with guests seeking a peace-and-quiet break. It has a friendly and relaxed atmosphere and cosy public areas. There is a small bar, a residents' lounge, and an attractive dining room. The bedrooms are well equipped and comfortable.
**ROOMS:** 8 rms (7 en suite) 2 annexe en suite (2 fmly) s £30-£40; d £60-£74 (incl. bkfst) * **FACILITIES:** National Trust boats & fishing Xmas **CONF:** Thtr 25 Class 25 Board 25 Del from £65 * **PARKING:** 22 **NOTES:** No smoking in restaurant RS Jan-Feb

## LUDLOW, Shropshire — Map 07 SO57

### ★★★78% ®®® Overton Grange

Hereford Rd SY8 4AD
☎ 01584 873500 📠 01584 873524
***Dir:*** *turn off A49 at B4361 Richards Castle, Ludlow and hotel is 200yds on left*

An Edwardian mansion situated above Ludlow with stunning views across the Shropshire countryside. Well-manicured gardens and abundant fresh flowers create a pleasant appearance. There is a comfortable lounge and bar, and the restaurant offers a high standard of cuisine with classical flair.
**ROOMS:** 14 en suite (2 fmly) No smoking in all bedrooms s fr £60; d fr £95 (incl. bkfst) * **LB** **FACILITIES:** Croquet lawn Xmas **CONF:** Thtr 160 Class 80 Board 50 Del from £135 * **PARKING:** 80 **NOTES:** No dogs (ex guide dogs) No smoking in restaurant Closed 2nd week in Jan
**CARDS:**

*See advert on opposite page*

### ★★★72% ®® Dinham Hall

By the Castle SY8 1EJ
☎ 01584 876464 📠 01584 876019
e-mail: info@dinhamhall.co.uk
***Dir:*** *opposite the castle*
Built in 1792, this lovely old house in attractive gardens stands immediately opposite Ludlow Castle. It has a well-deserved reputation for warm hospitality and fine cuisine. Well-equipped

*continued*

edrooms include two in a converted cottage and some four-posters. The comfortable public rooms are elegantly appointed.
**ROOMS:** 14 en suite (3 fmly) s £70-£100; d £120-£170 (incl. bkfst) * LB **FACILITIES:** Xmas **CONF:** Thtr 28 Class 28 Board 24 Del from £130 **PARKING:** 16 **NOTES:** No smoking in restaurant Civ Wed 50 **CARDS:**

★★64% **The Feathers at Ludlow**
Bull Ring SY8 1AA

REGAL
☎ 01584 875261 📠 01584 876030
**Dir:** *in the centre of Ludlow. Leave A49 & follow signs for town centre. Hotel on left*

THE FEATHERS

Famous for the carved woodwork outside and in, this picturesque, 17th century hotel is one of the town's best-known landmarks and is in an excellent location. Bedrooms are traditional in style and décor. Public areas have retained some of the charm of days gone by; the first-floor lounge is particularly stunning. Limited car parking is available.
**ROOMS:** 40 en suite (3 fmly) No smoking in 19 bedrooms s fr £70; d £90-£120 * LB **FACILITIES:** Xmas **CONF:** Thtr 80 Class 40 Board 40 **SERVICES:** Lift **PARKING:** 39 **NOTES:** No smoking in restaurant Civ Wed 80 **CARDS:**

★★66% **Cliffe**
Dinham SY8 2JE
☎ 01584 872063 📠 01584 873991
e-mail: cliffhotel@lineone.net
**Dir:** *through Ludlow town centre to Castle turn left at castle gates to Dinham, follow road beneath castle over bridge, hotel sign 100yds from bridge*
Built in the last century and standing in extensive grounds and gardens, this privately owned and personally run hotel is quietly located close to the castle and the river. It provides well-equipped accommodation, and facilities include a lounge bar, a pleasant restaurant and a patio overlooking the garden.
**ROOMS:** 9 en suite (2 fmly) No smoking in all bedrooms s £35-£40; d £60-£70 (incl. bkfst) * LB **PARKING:** 22 **NOTES:** No smoking in restaurant **CARDS:**

***Travelodge***
Woofferton SY8 4AL
Travelodge
☎ 01584 711695 📠 01584 711695
**Dir:** *on A49 at junct A456/B4362*
Travelodge offers good quality, good value, modern accommodation. Ideal for families, the spacious, en suite bedrooms include remote-control TV, tea and coffee-making facilities, luxury beds and free morning newspaper. Meals can be taken at the nearby family restaurant. For further details and the Travelodge phone number, consult the Hotel Groups page.
**ROOMS:** 32 en suite

LULWORTH COVE See West Lulworth



LUTON, Bedfordshire Map 04 TL02

★★★57% **The Chiltern**
Waller Av LU4 9RU

REGAL
☎ 01582 575911 📠 01582 581859
**Dir:** *M1 junct 11 take A505 to Luton go past two sets of lights over rdbt left filter lane left at lights hotel on right*

Conveniently close to the M1, this hotel is geared towards the business guest. It has a range of conference and meeting rooms. Bedrooms offer good desk space, and room service is a bonus. The busy bar is at the hub of the hotel.
**ROOMS:** 91 en suite (6 fmly) No smoking in 63 bedrooms d £85-£95 * LB **FACILITIES:** STV Xmas **CONF:** Thtr 180 Class 80 Board 30 Del from £110 * **SERVICES:** Lift **PARKING:** 150
**CARDS:**

Bad hair day? Hairdryers in all rooms three stars and above.

LUTON, continued

### ⇧ *Travelodge*

641 Dunstable Rd LU4 8RQ
☎ 01582 575955 📠 01582 490065
***Dir:*** *from M1 junct 11 travel towards Luton, hotel on right within 100yds*

Travelodge offers good quality, good value, modern accommodation. Ideal for families, the spacious, en suite bedrooms include remote-control TV, tea and coffee-making facilities, luxury beds and free morning newspaper. Meals can be taken at the nearby family restaurant. For further details and the Travelodge phone number, consult the Hotel Groups page.

**ROOMS:** 109 en suite **CONF:** Thtr 80 Class 40 Board 30

LUTON AIRPORT, Bedfordshire Map 04 TL12

### ⇧ Hotel Ibis

Spittlesea Rd LU2 9NH
☎ 01582 424488 📠 01582 455511
e-mail: H1040@accor-hotels.com
***Dir:*** *from junct 10 on M1 follow signs to Airport,hotel is 1km before airport*

Modern, budget hotel offering comfortable accommodation in bright and practical bedrooms. Breakfast is self-service and dinner is available in the restaurant. For further details, consult the Hotel Groups page.

**ROOMS:** 98 en suite d £58 * **CONF:** Thtr 80 Class 40 Board 40

### ○ Express by Holiday Inn

LU2
☎ 0800 897121

A modern budget hotel offering comfortable accommodation in refreshing, spacious and comprehensively equipped bedrooms, en suite bathrooms with power showers and continental buffet breakfast included in the room rate. Suitable for business travellers or families. For further details and the Express by Holiday Inn phone number, consult the Hotel Groups page.

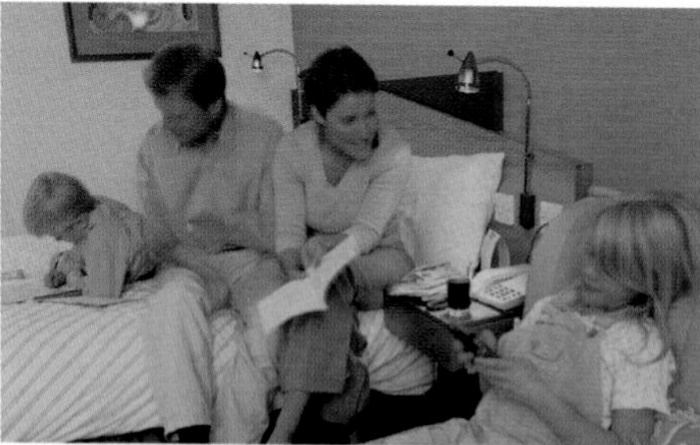

**ROOMS:** 86 en suite **NOTES:** Opening 2002

LYDFORD, Devon Map 02 SX58

### ★★71% Lydford House

EX20 4AU
☎ 01822 820347 📠 01822 820442
e-mail: relax@lydfordhouse.co.uk
***Dir:*** *turn off A386 halfway between Okehampton and Tavistock, signpost Lydford, 0.25m on right hand side*

This impressive Victorian country house is located on the edge of Dartmoor. The comfortable bedrooms are attractively decorated and, in addition to the conservatory lounge, a separate lounge is available. There are riding stables adjacent to the hotel which are run by the proprietors, so guests can take lessons or accompanied rides over the moors.

**ROOMS:** 12 rms (11 en suite) (4 fmly) s £33-£39; d £67-£79 (incl. bkfst) * **LB** **FACILITIES:** Riding **CONF:** Thtr 25 Class 25 Board 20 Del from £62 * **PARKING:** 30 **NOTES:** No smoking in restaurant Closed 25 Dec-31 Jan **CARDS:**

LYME REGIS, Dorset Map 03 SY

### ★★★70% Alexandra

Pound St DT7 3HZ
☎ 01297 442010 📠 01297 443229
e-mail: enquiries@hotelalexandra.co.uk
***Dir:*** *from A30 turn onto A35 and then follow A358. Turn off onto A3052 Lyme Regis*

Built in 1735 and Grade II listed, this welcoming family run hotel features an elegant restaurant with picture windows taking in the magnificent views. Bedrooms have pretty chintz fabrics and attractive furniture. Breakfast is taken in the south-facing conservatory, which opens onto well-tended gardens. During the winter log fires burn in the lounge.

**ROOMS:** 25 en suite 1 annexe en suite (8 fmly) s £50-£80; d £86-£12 (incl. bkfst) * **LB** **PARKING:** 18 **NOTES:** No smoking in restaurant Closed Xmas & Jan **CARDS:**

### ★★77% Swallows Eaves

EX24 6QJ
☎ 01297 553184 📠 01297 553574
(For full entry see Colyford)

### ★★74% Mariners Hotel

Silver St DT7 3HS
☎ 01297 442753 📠 01297 442431
e-mail: mariners@ukgateway.net
***Dir:*** *W of town on A3052, turn right on B3070*

With period character and charm, this small, friendly hotel has a happy, relaxed atmosphere. The individually, decorated bedroom are comfortable; some rooms benefit from stunning views over the town. A beamed bar and choice of lounges is provided for guests; while in the restaurant both set price and carte menus ar offered.

**ROOMS:** 12 en suite No smoking in 6 bedrooms s £39-£42; d £78-£84 (incl. bkfst) * **LB** **FACILITIES:** ch fac **PARKING:** 20 **NOTES:** No smoking in restaurant Closed Xmas & New Year **CARDS:**

Arriving late? Four and five star hotels have night porters to assist with your luggage, and 24-hour room service.

**★★70% Buena Vista**
Pound St DT7 3HZ
☎ 01297 442494 ▤ 01297 444670
e-mail: buenavista@amserve.net
***Dir:*** *W on A3052 out of town*

This Regency-styled hotel is set in award-winning gardens, overlooking the Cobb, harbour and the Dorset coast. Many bedrooms overlook the sea, some have balconies and several are on the ground floor. Guests have a choice of lounges, or during the summer months, they can relax on the terrace or sundeck.
**ROOMS:** 18 rms (17 en suite) (1 fmly) d £70-£100 (incl. bkfst) * **LB**
**PARKING:** 18 **NOTES:** No smoking in restaurant Closed Dec-Jan
**CARDS:**

**★★66% Bay**
Marine Pde DT7 3JQ
☎ 01297 442059 ▤ 01297 444642
***Dir:*** *on the seafront in the centre of Lyme Regis*
Guests are assured a relaxed and friendly atmosphere at this sea front hotel. An interesting menu, featuring local seafood is served in the brightly decorated dining room. The spacious, first floor lounge, with its billiard table, is the ideal spot to relax after a day exploring the area. Bedrooms are stylish and comfortable.
**ROOMS:** 19 en suite (2 fmly) s £40-£55; d £75-£90 (incl. bkfst) * **LB**
**FACILITIES:** Snooker Sun lounge beach front balcony ch fac Xmas
**CONF:** Thtr 30 Class 30 **PARKING:** 20 **NOTES:** No smoking in restaurant **CARDS:**

*See advert on this page*

**★★63% Royal Lion**
Broad St DT7 3QF
☎ 01297 445622 ▤ 01297 445859
Built as a coaching inn in 1601, the Royal Lion retains much character. Bedrooms in the newer wing are more spacious, some have balconies, sea views or a private terrace. There are a number of lounge areas. The elegant dining room provides an extensive range of dishes.
**ROOMS:** 30 en suite (4 fmly) s £35-£44; d £70-£88 (incl. bkfst) * **LB**
**FACILITIES:** Indoor swimming (H) Snooker Sauna Gym Jacuzzi Games room Table tennis ch fac Xmas **PARKING:** 36 **NOTES:** Closed 3 days Xmas **CARDS:**

## LYMINGTON, Hampshire

Map 04 SZ39

**★★★74% Passford House**
Mount Pleasant Ln SO41 8LS
☎ 01590 682398 ▤ 01590 683494
e-mail: sales@passfordhousehotel.co.uk
***Dir:*** *from A337 at Lymington straight on at mini rdbt, then first right at Tollhouse public house, then after 1m right into Mount Pleasant Lane*
A peaceful hotel set in attractive grounds on the edge of town. Bedrooms vary in size but all are comfortably furnished and well-

*continued on p386*

LYMINGTON, continued

equipped. Extensive public areas include lounges, a smartly appointed bar and restaurant and leisure facilities. Attentive service is provided by a friendly and well motivated team.
**ROOMS:** 53 en suite 2 annexe en suite (2 fmly) No smoking in 5 bedrooms s £65-£95; d £90-£130 (incl. bkfst) * **LB** **FACILITIES:** Spa Indoor swimming (H) Outdoor swimming (H) Tennis (hard) Sauna Solarium Gym Croquet lawn Putting green Petanque Table tennis Helipad pool table Xmas **CONF:** Thtr 80 Class 30 Board 30 Del from £120 * **PARKING:** 100 **NOTES:** No smoking in restaurant
**CARDS:**

★★★66% **String of Horses**
Mead End Rd SO41 6EH
☎ 01590 682631 01590 682911
e-mail: relax@stringofhorses.co.uk
(For full entry see Sway)

★★69% ***Gordleton Mill Hotel & Restaurant***
Silver St, Hordle SO41 6DJ
☎ 01590 682219 01590 683073
***Dir:*** *on Sway Rd which becomes Silver St*

A delightful 17th-century watermill on the banks of the River Avon. The restaurant takes full advantage of the hotel's position and serves an extensive range of dishes at lunch and dinner. The picturesque gardens are popular for al fresco dining during the warmer months and the attractive bedrooms are equipped with whirlpool baths.
**ROOMS:** 9 en suite (1 fmly) No smoking in 5 bedrooms **PARKING:** 60 **NOTES:** No dogs (ex guide dogs) No children 8yrs No smoking in restaurant **CARDS:**

○ **Elmers Court**
South Baddesley Rd SO41 5ZB
☎ 01590 676011 01590 679780

MACDONALD
HOTELS

At the time of going to press, the star classification for this hotel was not confirmed. Please refer to the AA internet site www.theAA.com for current information.
**ROOMS:** 42 rms **NOTES:** Open now

LYMM, Cheshire Map 07 SJ68

★★★66% ***Lymm Hotel***
Whitbarrow Rd WA13 9AQ
☎ 01925 752233 01925 756035
***Dir:*** *turn off motorway and follow B5158 to Lymm village at junct left and first right at mini rdbt left into Brookfield Rd third left into Whitbarrow Rd*

MACDONALD HOTELS

Situated in a quiet residential area, but conveniently close to several motorways, this hotel offers comfortable bedrooms equipped for both the business and leisure guest. Public areas include a cosy bar and an elegant restaurant in which creative dinners can be enjoyed.
**ROOMS:** 15 en suite 48 annexe en suite (5 fmly) No smoking in 34 bedrooms **FACILITIES:** STV **CONF:** Thtr 120 Class 80 Board 50 Del from £125 * **PARKING:** 120 **NOTES:** No smoking in restaurant
**CARDS:**

⌂ ***Travelodge***
Granada Services A50, Cliffe Ln WA13 0SP
☎ 08700 850950

Travelodge

Travelodge offers good quality, good value, modern accommodation. Ideal for families, the spacious, en suite bedrooms include remote-control TV, tea and coffee-making facilities, luxury beds and free morning newspaper. Meals can be taken at the nearby family restaurant. For further details and the Travelodge phone number, consult the Hotel Groups page.

LYMPSHAM, Somerset Map 03 ST35

★★70% **Batch Country Hotel**
Batch Ln BS24 0EX
☎ 01934 750371 01934 750501
***Dir:*** *off A370. Follow Tourist Board signs for 1.5m through village to hotel*

MINOTEL
Great Britain

Midway between the resorts of Weston-super-Mare and Burnham-on-Sea, this attractive property offers relaxed and friendly service in a tranquil environment. The comfortable bedrooms have countryside views to the Mendip and Quantock Hills. Spacious lounges overlook the gardens and an extensive range of dishes is served in the beamed dining room.
**ROOMS:** 10 en suite (6 fmly) No smoking in 2 bedrooms s £46-£50; d £70-£80 (incl. bkfst) * **LB** **FACILITIES:** Fishing **CONF:** Thtr 80 Class 60 Board 100 Del from £78 * **PARKING:** 80 **NOTES:** No dogs No smoking in restaurant Closed Xmas Civ Wed 120
**CARDS:**

*See advert under WESTON-SUPER-MARE*

LYNDHURST, Hampshire Map 04 SU30

★★★79% **Le Poussin at Parkhill**
Beaulieu Rd SO43 7FZ
☎ 023 8028 2944 023 8028 3268
e-mail: sales@lepoussinparkhill.co.uk
***Dir:*** *turn off A35 onto B3056 Beaulieu, Hotel 1m on left*
Set amidst unspoilt park and woodland, this Georgian country house offers elegant public rooms, with open fires during the cooler months. Bedrooms are individually furnished and decorated, most have delightful views over the forest. A meal in

*continued*

the renowned restaurant is the highlight of any stay, featuring local seasonal ingredients. Service is efficient and professional.

**ROOMS:** 15 en suite 5 annexe en suite (2 fmly) No smoking in 16 bedrooms s £75-£180; d £120-£150 (incl. cont bkfst) * **FACILITIES:** Outdoor swimming (H) Fishing Croquet lawn Putting green Outdoor chess Xmas **CONF:** Thtr 20 Class 20 Board 20 Del from £100 * **PARKING:** 75 **NOTES:** No smoking in restaurant 2 Jan-15 Jan Civ Wed 60 **CARDS:**

*See advert on this page*

★★★68% **Crown**

High St SO43 7NF

☎ 023 8028 2922 023 8028 2751

e-mail: reception@crownhotel-lyndhurst.co.uk

***Dir:*** *in the centre of the village, opposite the church*

Informally referred to as the capital of the New Forest, the village is an ideal base from which to explore the national park. The Crown, with its stone mullioned windows, panelled rooms and

*continued on p388*

LYNDHURST, continued

elegant period decor evokes the style of an English country house and has been welcoming visitors to the area for generations.

The Crown Hotel

Crown, Lyndhurst

**ROOMS:** 39 en suite (8 fmly) s £80-£90; d £130-£150 (incl. bkfst) * **LB** **FACILITIES:** STV Xmas **CONF:** Thtr 70 Class 30 Board 45 Del from £95 * **SERVICES:** Lift **PARKING:** 60 **NOTES:** No smoking in restaurant Civ Wed 30 **CARDS:**

*See advert on page 387*

### ★★★67% Bell Inn

SO43 7HE
☎ 023 8081 2214 023 8081 3958
e-mail: bell@bramshaw.co.uk
(For full entry see Brook (Near Cadnam))

### ★★★66% Forest Lodge

Best Western

Pikes Hill, Romsey Rd SO43 7AS
☎ 023 8028 3677 023 8028 2940
e-mail: reservations@carehotels.co.uk
***Dir:*** *exit M27 at junct 1 and join A337 towards Lyndhurst. On approaching village, police station/courts on right, take first right into Pikes Hill*
Situated on the edge of Lyndhurst, this well-maintained hotel has spacious, well-presented bedrooms, many ideal for families. Public areas are cosy and attractive. The leisure centre offers not only a pool, but also sauna and gym. Staff here are friendly yet efficient.
**ROOMS:** 28 en suite (7 fmly) s £65-£80; d £115-£130 (incl. bkfst) * **LB** **FACILITIES:** Indoor swimming (H) Sauna Gym ch fac Xmas **CONF:** Thtr 100 Class 70 Board 50 Del from £90 * **PARKING:** 50 **NOTES:** No smoking in restaurant Civ Wed 100 **CARDS:**

### ★★★64% Lyndhurst Park

Forestdale Hotels

High St SO43 7NL
☎ 023 8028 3923 023 8028 3019
e-mail: lyndhurst.park@forestdale.com
***Dir:*** *M27 Junct 1-3 to A35 to Lyndhurst. Hotel is situated at bottom of High Street*
A short walk from the high street, this extended Georgian house, set in five acres of mature grounds, is ideally placed for exploring the New Forest. There are two bars and a cosy oak-panelled restaurant with a sunny conservatory addition. Bedrooms vary in size and style and include several with four-posters.
**ROOMS:** 59 en suite (3 fmly) No smoking in 3 bedrooms s £62-£72; d £124-£144 (incl. bkfst & dinner) * **LB** **FACILITIES:** Outdoor swimming (H) Tennis (hard) Snooker Sauna Table tennis Xmas **CONF:** Thtr 300 Class 120 Board 80 Del £110 * **SERVICES:** Lift **PARKING:** 100 **NOTES:** Civ Wed **CARDS:**

### ★71% Knightwood Lodge

MINOTEL Great Britain

Southampton Rd SO43 7BU
☎ 023 8028 2502 023 8028 3730
***Dir:*** *on A35*
This friendly, family-run hotel is situated on the outskirts of Lyndhurst. Comfortable bedrooms are modern in style and well-equipped with many useful extras. The hotel offers an excellent range of facilities, which are free to residents.
**ROOMS:** 14 en suite 4 annexe en suite (2 fmly) s £30-£50; d £60-£90 (incl. bkfst) * **LB** **FACILITIES:** STV Indoor swimming (H) Sauna Solarium Gym Jacuzzi Steam room **PARKING:** 15 **NOTES:** No smoking in restaurant **CARDS:**

## LYNMOUTH, Devon

Map 03 SS74

see also Lynton

### ★★★66% Tors

EX35 6NA
☎ 01598 753236 01598 752544
e-mail: torshotel@torslynmouth.co.uk
***Dir:*** *adjacent to A39 on Countisbury Hill just before you enter Lynmouth*
In an elevated position overlooking Lynmouth Bay, this friendly hotel is set in five acres of woodland. The majority of the soundly furnished bedrooms benefit from the superb views, as do the public areas. A choice of comfortable, well-presented lounges is provided. Both fixed-price and short carte menus are offered in the restaurant.
**ROOMS:** 33 en suite (7 fmly) s £40-£85; d £70-£110 (incl. bkfst) * **LB** **FACILITIES:** Outdoor swimming (H) Table tennis Pool table ch fac Xmas **CONF:** Thtr 60 Class 40 Board 25 Del from £57 * **SERVICES:** Lift **PARKING:** 40 **NOTES:** No smoking in restaurant Closed 4-31 Jan RS Feb-5 Mar (wknds only) **CARDS:**

### ★★76% Rising Sun

Harbourside EX35 6EQ
☎ 01598 753223 01598 753480
e-mail: risingsunlynmouth@easynet.co.uk
***Dir:*** *leave M5 at junct 23 (Minehead), follow A39 to Lynmouth. Hotel is located on Harbourside*
This historic former smugglers' inn nestles on the harbour front and benefits from a popular bar and a good restaurant. The individually designed bedrooms with modern facilities are located within the inn or in the adjoining cottage rooms. In addition to the convivial bar, there is a comfortable, quiet lounge.
**ROOMS:** 11 en suite 5 annexe en suite No smoking in 11 bedrooms s £63; d £94-£150 (incl. bkfst) * **LB** **FACILITIES:** Fishing Xmas **NOTES:** No dogs (ex guide dogs) No children 8yrs No smoking in restaurant **CARDS:**

### ★★67% Bath

Sea Front EX35 6EL
☎ 01598 752238 01598 752544
e-mail: bathhotel@torslynmouth.co.uk
***Dir:*** *M5 junct 25 follow A39 to Minehead then Porlock and Lynmouth*
This well established hotel stands near the harbour, and its sea-facing bedrooms are particularly attractive. Local fish in season features on the restaurant menu and cream teas are served in the sun lounge.
**ROOMS:** 24 en suite (9 fmly) s £27-£46; d £54-£84 (incl. bkfst) * **LB** **FACILITIES:** ch fac **PARKING:** 13 **NOTES:** No smoking in restaurant Closed Jan & Dec RS Nov-Mar **CARDS:**

## LYNTON, Devon
Map 03 SS74

see also Lynmouth

### ★★★65% Lynton Cottage
North Walk EX35 6ED

☎ 01598 752342 📠 01598 752597

e-mail: enquiries@lynton-cottage.co.uk

***Dir:*** *turn into North Walk by St Mary's Church, hotel is 100mtrs on right*

The Lynton Cottage Hotel has an enviable position, enjoying stunning views over Lynmouth Bay and the Bristol Channel. A fixed-priced menu is available in the restaurant and offers a balanced selection of tempting dishes at both lunch and dinner time. A spacious lounge and separate bar are complemented by a terrace that overlooks the idyllic scenery.

**ROOMS:** 17 en suite No smoking in 2 bedrooms s £29-£75; d £58-£150 (incl. bkfst) * **LB** **PARKING:** 17 **NOTES:** No dogs No children 14yrs No smoking in restaurant Closed Jan & Dec **CARDS:**

### ★★63% Sandrock
Longmead EX35 6DH

☎ 01598 753307 📠 01598 752665

***Dir:*** *follow signs to 'The Valley of the Rocks'*

On the edge of the village and at the head of the Valley of the Rocks, this family-run hotel offers light, airy, modern bedrooms. It has a popular public bar and a comfortable residents' lounge on the first floor.

**ROOMS:** 8 en suite (3 fmly) s £24-£25; d £47-£50 (incl. bkfst) * **LB** **PARKING:** 9 **NOTES:** No smoking in restaurant Closed Nov-Jan **CARDS:**

### ★73% Seawood
North Walk EX35 6HJ

☎ 01598 752272 📠 01598 752272

e-mail: seawoodhotel@tinyworld.com

With spectacular views over Lynmouth Bay, this charming hotel nestles on wooded cliffs some 400 feet above the sea. The individually furnished and decorated bedrooms are well-equipped; some rooms feature four-poster beds. Public areas are comfortable and well-appointed, while in the dining room, the daily changing menu continues to be popular with the hotel's regular clientele.

**ROOMS:** 12 en suite s £27-£31; d £54-£62 (incl. bkfst) **LB** **PARKING:** 10 **NOTES:** No children 11yrs No smoking in restaurant Closed Nov-Easter

## LYTHAM ST ANNES, Lancashire
Map 07 SD32

### ★★★★64% Clifton Arms
West Beach, Lytham FY8 5QJ

☎ 01253 739898 📠 01253 730657

e-mail: welcome@cliftonarms.demon.co.uk

***Dir:*** *on the A584 along the seafront*

This long established hotel commands fine views over Lytham green and the Ribble estuary beyond. Bedrooms are particularly

*continued*

large and comfortable and include one room with a four-poster bed. The elegant restaurant offers a wide choice of delectable dishes and a selection of fine wines.

**ROOMS:** 48 en suite No smoking in 4 bedrooms s fr £91; d fr £115 (incl. bkfst) * **LB** **FACILITIES:** STV ch fac Xmas **CONF:** Thtr 300 Class 200 Board 100 Del £120 * **SERVICES:** Lift **PARKING:** 50 **NOTES:** No dogs (ex guide dogs) No smoking in restaurant

**CARDS:**

*See advert on this page*

### ★★★67% Chadwick
South Promenade FY8 1NP

☎ 01253 720061 📠 01253 714455

e-mail: sales@chadwickhotel.com

***Dir:*** *M6 Junct 32 take M55 Blackpool A5230 South Shore and follow signs for St Annes*

A comfortable, traditional, family run seafront hotel with friendly, willing and dedicated staff. Bedrooms vary in shape and size, but

*continued on p390*

LYTHAM ST ANNES, continued

are very well-equipped and those at the front have splendid views over the sea. Some also have four-poster beds. Public rooms are spacious and very comfortably furnished.

*Chadwick, Lytham St Annes*

**ROOMS:** 75 en suite (28 fmly) s £45-£48; d £60-£68 (incl. bkfst) * **LB** **FACILITIES:** STV Indoor swimming (H) Sauna Solarium Gym Jacuzzi Turkish bth Games rm Soft play adv area entertainment ch fac Xmas **CONF:** Thtr 72 Class 24 Board 28 Del from £64 * **SERVICES:** Lift **PARKING:** 40 **NOTES:** No dogs (ex guide dogs) No smoking in restaurant **CARDS:**

*See advert on opposite page*

L

### ★★★63% Bedford

307-311 Clifton Dr South FY8 1HN
☎ 01253 724636 📠 01253 729244
e-mail: reservations@bedford-hotel.com
***Dir:*** *from M55 follow signs for airport to last set of lights. Turn left, through 2 sets of lights hotel is 300yds on left*

This family-run hotel is close to the town centre and the seafront. Bedrooms, varying in size, are attractively furnished and well-equipped. Facilities include a conference and function suite, the Cartland Restaurant, a popular coffee shop and Kitty's public bar offering regular entertainment.

**ROOMS:** 35 en suite (6 fmly) s £45-£55; d £68-£75 (incl. bkfst) * **LB** **FACILITIES:** STV Sauna Solarium Gym Jacuzzi Steam room entertainment Xmas **CONF:** Thtr 150 Class 100 Board 40 **SERVICES:** Lift **PARKING:** 20 **NOTES:** No dogs (ex guide dogs) No smoking in restaurant Civ Wed 120 **CARDS:**

*See advert on opposite page*

### ★★68% Glendower

North Promenade FY8 2NQ
☎ 01253 723241 📠 01253 640069

e-mail: glendowerhotel@bestwestern.co.uk
***Dir:*** *M55 follow airport signs turn left at Promenade to St Annes. Hotel situated on St Annes promenade 500yds from the pier*

Conveniently located on the seafront and with easy access to the town centre, this popular, friendly hotel offers comfortably furnished, well-equipped accommodation. Bedrooms vary in size, with four-poster and family rooms among the larger ones. Public areas include a choice of smart, comfortable lounges, a bright, modern leisure club and function facilities.

**ROOMS:** 60 en suite (17 fmly) s £39-£49; d £70-£89 (incl. bkfst) * **LB** **FACILITIES:** STV Indoor swimming (H) Snooker Sauna Solarium Gym Jacuzzi Childrens playroom Xmas **CONF:** Thtr 150 Class 120 Board 40 Del from £65 * **SERVICES:** Lift **PARKING:** 45 **NOTES:** No smoking in restaurant **CARDS:**

### ★★68% Lindum

63-67 South Promenade FY8 1LZ
☎ 01253 721534 & 722516 📠 01253 721364
e-mail: info@lindumhotel.co.uk
***Dir:*** *from airport, continue to seafront lights and turn left. Continue onto 2nd set of lights & turn right, then left at jct. Hotel on left*

This friendly seafront hotel has been run by the same family for over 40 years. Bedrooms are generally spacious, comfortable and well-equipped, with some enjoying fine sea views. There are several lounges, one with a large screen TV, a games room and a health suite. The airy restaurant offers a wide choice of dishes.

**ROOMS:** 76 en suite (25 fmly) No smoking in 4 bedrooms s £35-£49; d £60-£88 (incl. bkfst) * **LB** **FACILITIES:** Sauna Solarium Jacuzzi Xmas **CONF:** Thtr 80 Class 30 Board 25 Del from £60 * **SERVICES:** Lift air con **PARKING:** 20 **NOTES:** No smoking in restaurant **CARDS:**

### ★★67% *New England*

314 Clifton Dr North, St Annes on Sea FY8 2PB
☎ 01253 722355 📠 01253 726122
***Dir:*** *200 yards from pier*

Jay D's American style Bistro and Bar are features of this hotel, conveniently and centrally situated, which also offers spacious, well-equipped and comfortable bedroom accommodation. Resident guests also have access to the hotel's private members' sports bar. A private car park is situated at the front of the hotel.

**ROOMS:** 10 en suite (5 fmly) **PARKING:** 14 **NOTES:** No dogs **CARDS:**

### ⌂ *Premier Lodge*

Church Rd FY8 5LH
☎ 0870 700 1424 📠 0870 700 1425

Premier Lodge offers modern, well-equipped, en suite accommodation suitable for both business and leisure travellers. Meals can be taken at the adjacent popular restaurant and bar, which is fully licensed. For further details, consult the Hotel Groups page.

**ROOMS:** 21 en suite

MACCLESFIELD, Cheshire — Map 07 SJ97

### ★★★★64% Shrigley Hall Hotel Golf & Country Club

Shrigley Park, Pott Shrigley SK10 5SB
☎ 01625 575757 📠 01625 573323
e-mail: shrigleyhall@paramount-hotels.co.uk
***Dir:*** *turn off A523 at Legh Arms, towards Pott Shrigley, hotel is 2m on left just before village*

Originally built in 1825, Shrigley Hall is an impressive hotel set in 262 acres of mature parkland featuring its own championship golf course. There is a wide choice of room size and style. Spacious public areas include a newly refurbished restaurant, courtyard

*continued*

lounge, leisure club and a range of conferences suites; of which the Tilden enjoys a rather unique setting within the original adjoining church.
**ROOMS:** 150 en suite (8 fmly) No smoking in 28 bedrooms s fr £119; d fr £149 (incl. bkfst) * **LB** **FACILITIES:** STV Indoor swimming (H) Golf 18 Tennis (hard) Fishing Sauna Solarium Gym Putting green Jacuzzi Beauty salon entertainment Xmas **CONF:** Thtr 280 Class 140 Board 50 Del £165 * **SERVICES:** Lift **PARKING:** 300 **NOTES:** No smoking in restaurant Civ Wed 220 **CARDS:**

### ★★★68% Belgrade Hotel & Restaurant

Best Western

Jackson Ln, Kerridge, Bollington SK10 5BG
☎ 01625 573246 🖹 01625 574791
e-mail: belgradehotel@btinternet.com
***Dir:*** *off A523, 2m along B5090*
Set in the peaceful Cheshire countryside, this hotel is convenient for Manchester Airport (courtesy transport available). The main building has an impressive carved staircase, high ceilings, a restaurant and a lounge. Attractively furnished accommodation is situated in a modern extension.
**ROOMS:** 54 en suite (2 fmly) No smoking in 36 bedrooms d £60-£70 * **LB** **FACILITIES:** STV Free use neighbouring Leisure Club **CONF:** Thtr 80 Class 50 Board 50 **PARKING:** 200 **NOTES:** No dogs (ex guide dogs) Civ Wed 50 **CARDS:**

### ⌂ *Premier Lodge*

PREMIER LODGE

Congleton Rd, Gawsworth SK11 7XD
☎ 0870 700 1466 🖹 0870 700 1467
Premier Lodge offers modern, well-equipped, en suite accommodation suitable for both business and leisure travellers. Meals can be taken at the adjacent popular restaurant and bar, which is fully licensed. For further details, consult the Hotel Groups page.
**ROOMS:** 28 en suite

MAIDENCOMBE See Torquay

## MAIDENHEAD, Berkshire

Map 04 SU88

see also Bray

### *Premier Collection*

RECEPTION

### ★★★★ ®®® Fredrick's

Shoppenhangers Rd SL6 2PZ
☎ 01628 581000 🖹 01628 771054
e-mail: reservations@fredricks-hotel.co.uk
***Dir:*** *M4 junct 8/9 A404(M) direction Maidenhead West/Henley. Take 1st exit White Waltham turn left into Shoppenhangers Road towards M'Head*
This delightful hotel is set in a quiet location, in easy reach of the M4 and 30 minutes from London. The bedrooms are all

*continued on p392*

MAIDENHEAD, continued

individually decorated, and are all very well equipped. The enthusiastic staff in this hotel are friendly and efficient, and a highlight of any visit is a meal in the restaurant, which serves memorable modern cuisine. Local attractions include Wentworth and Sunningdale golf courses, which are both within 20 minutes drive from the hotel.
**ROOMS:** 37 en suite s £195-£215; d £240-£260 (incl. bkfst) * **FACILITIES:** STV Croquet lawn **CONF:** Thtr 120 Class 80 Board 60 Del from £280 * **PARKING:** 90 **NOTES:** No dogs (ex guide dogs) Closed 24 Dec-3 Jan Civ Wed 120 **CARDS:**

### ★★★69% Thames Riviera
At the Bridge SL6 8DW
☎ 01628 674057 🖹 01628 776586
e-mail: thamesriv.sales@dial.pipex.com
***Dir:*** *turn off A4 by Maidenhead Historic Bridge, the hotel is situated by the bridge*

Enjoying an enviable position on the banks of the Thames, this attractive hotel is well located for London, Heathrow, local tourist attractions and motorway networks. Many of the well-equipped bedrooms have balconies and river views. Jerome's Riverside Restaurant, the bar and coffee shop offer a variety of eating options.
**ROOMS:** 34 en suite 18 annexe en suite (1 fmly) No smoking in 4 bedrooms s £110-£125; d £130-£140 **LB** **FACILITIES:** STV **CONF:** Thtr 50 Class 30 Board 20 Del from £160 * **PARKING:** 60 **NOTES:** No dogs (ex guide dogs) Closed 26-30 Dec
**CARDS:**

### ★69% Elva Lodge
Castle Hill SL6 4AD
☎ 01628 622948 🖹 01628 778954
e-mail: reservations@elvalodgehotel.demon.co.uk
***Dir:*** *take A4 out of Maidenhead towards Reading. Hotel at top of hill on left*

ELVA
LODGE
HOTEL

Located just minutes from the town centre, this family-run hotel offers a warm welcome. Bedrooms are comfortable and well equipped. Spacious public areas include a lounge bar and the Lion's Brasserie, which offers a wide range of popular dishes.
**ROOMS:** 26 rms (23 en suite) (2 fmly) No smoking in 3 bedrooms s £50-£105; d £65-£115 (incl. bkfst) * **FACILITIES:** **Spa** Reduced rates at local Leisure Centre **CONF:** Thtr 50 Class 30 Board 30 **PARKING:** 32 **NOTES:** No smoking in restaurant Closed 24-30 Dec Civ Wed 60
**CARDS:**

MAIDSTONE, Kent Map 05 TQ75

### ★★★★70% Marriott Tudor Park Hotel & Country Club
Marriott HOTELS · RESORTS · SUITES
Ashford Rd, Bearsted ME14 4NQ
☎ 01622 734334 🖹 01622 735360
e-mail: tudorpark@marriotthotels.co.uk
***Dir:*** *leave M20 at junct 8 Lenham. At rdbt turn right and head to Bearsted and Maidstone on A20 . Hotel is situated 1m on the left hand side*

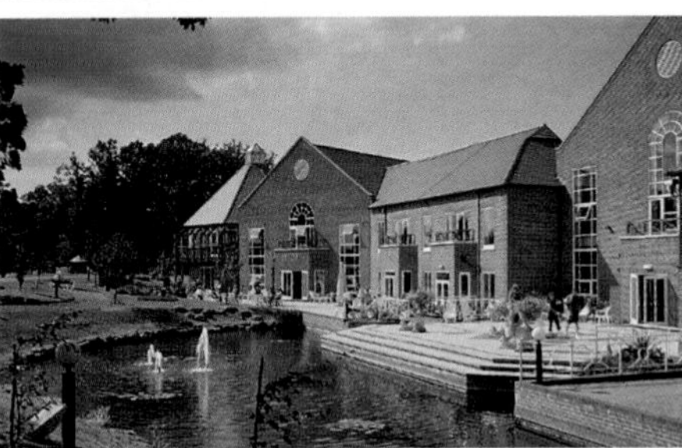

This fine country hotel provides good levels of comfort. Guests can dine in the main restaurant, Fairviews, which offers uncomplicated dishes, or the more relaxed environment of the Long Weekend Brasserie. Take time to enjoy the excellent range of leisure options, be it golf, a workout, swim or the beauty salon.
**ROOMS:** 120 en suite (48 fmly) No smoking in 65 bedrooms s £74-£79; d £98-£108 (incl. bkfst) * **FACILITIES:** STV Indoor swimming (H) Golf 18 Tennis (hard) Sauna Solarium Gym Putting green Jacuzzi Driving range, Beauty salon, Steam room entertainment Xmas **CONF:** Thtr 250 Class 120 Board 60 Del from £145 * **SERVICES:** Lift **PARKING:** 250 **NOTES:** No dogs (ex guide dogs) No smoking in restaurant Civ Wed 180
**CARDS:**

### ★★★66% Larkfield Priory
REGAL
London Rd, Larkfield ME20 6HJ
☎ 01732 846858 🖹 01732 846786
***Dir:*** *M20 junct 4 take A228 to W Malling at traffic lights turn left signposted to Maidstone (A20), after 1m hotel on left*

Dating from 1890, this hotel has been upgraded to provide the levels of comfort demanded by today's business travellers. All the bedrooms are bright and smart. The restaurant boasts a conservatory annexe, and the bar lounge is a pleasant alternative for lighter meals and snacks.
**ROOMS:** 52 en suite No smoking in 24 bedrooms s fr £80; d fr £90 * **LB** **FACILITIES:** Xmas **CONF:** Thtr 80 Class 36 Board 30 Del from £85 * **PARKING:** 80 **NOTES:** No smoking in restaurant
**CARDS:**

★★★61% **Russell**
136 Boxley Rd ME14 2AE
☎ 01622 692221 📠 01622 762084
e-mail: russhotel@aol.com

Best Western

This attractive former Carmelite convent is set in two acres of grounds on the edge of Maidstone. Bedrooms have modern facilities and the attractive restaurant offers good home-cooked food, attracting a strong local following. The hotel is a popular venue for wedding receptions and meetings. Service is enthusiastic and attentive.
**ROOMS:** 42 en suite (5 fmly) s fr £70; d fr £90 (incl. bkfst) * **LB**
**FACILITIES:** Jacuzzi Xmas **CONF:** Thtr 250 Class 100 Board 100
**PARKING:** 100 **NOTES:** No dogs (ex guide dogs) Civ Wed 80
**CARDS:**

★★67% **Grange Moor**
St Michael's Rd ME16 8BS
☎ 01622 677623 📠 01622 678246
e-mail: reservations@grangemoor.co.uk
***Dir:*** *off A26, Tonbridge Road. Church on lft, turn left hotel on right*
Bedrooms at this friendly, family-run hotel are well-appointed with good facilities. The quaint bar offers a good range of meals and the restaurant provides a fixed price and an a la carte menu. There is a small lounge and several dining and function rooms.
**ROOMS:** 51 en suite (6 fmly) No smoking in 16 bedrooms s £44-£48; d £52-£54 (incl. bkfst) * **LB** **CONF:** Thtr 100 Class 60 Board 40 Del from £85 * **PARKING:** 60 **NOTES:** Closed last week Dec
**CARDS:**

○ **Innkeeper's Lodge Maidstone**
Sandling Rd ME14 2RF
A new concept in the travel accommodation market. Smart rooms meet essential business requirements but also have home comforts. Dining options include all-day menus plus the added advantage of breakfast, which is included in the room price. Reservations can be made seven days a week through the room reservations number: 0870 243 0500. For further details, consult the Hotel Groups page.
**ROOMS:** 11 en suite **NOTES:** Open now

MALDON See Tolleshunt Knights

Popped the question? Hotels with Civ Wed in their entry are licensed for civil wedding ceremonies. Maximum numbers for the ceremony only are shown, e.g. Civ Wed 120

MALHAM, North Yorkshire Map 07 SD96

**★★65% The Buck Inn**
BD23 4DA
☎ 01729 830317 01729 830670
***Dir:*** *from Skipton, take A65 to Gargrave, signposted in village centre, for 7 miles*
Located in the centre of the village, this stone-built inn provides attractively furnished and comfortable bedrooms. Imaginitive menus are provided in the traditional dining room, and a wide choice of homemade dishes is available in the two cosy bars.
**ROOMS:** 10 en suite (3 fmly) s £30-£35; d £60-£75 (incl. bkfst) * LB **FACILITIES:** Spa Riding Xmas **PARKING:** 25 **NOTES:** No dogs (ex guide dogs) No smoking in restaurant **CARDS:**

MALMESBURY, Wiltshire Map 03 ST98

**★★★74% Old Bell**
Abbey Row SN16 0AG
☎ 01666 822344 01666 825145
e-mail: info@oldbellhotel.com
***Dir:*** *off A429, in centre of Malmesbury, adjacent to the Abbey*

RAC

This hotel is reputed to be the oldest in England. Many original features have been retained and are combined with modern facilities. There is a choice of comfortable lounges in which to relax. Bedrooms are varied in size and style, ranging from character rooms to stylish Japanese-inspired rooms.
**ROOMS:** 16 en suite 15 annexe en suite (3 fmly) s £68-£75; d £100-£190 (incl. bkfst) * LB **FACILITIES:** STV Childrens playroom, Cyber room with internet access/Nintendo games ch fac Xmas **CONF:** Thtr 45 Class 10 Board 24 Del from £130 * **PARKING:** 30 **NOTES:** No smoking in restaurant RS 23 Dec-2 Jan Civ Wed 45
**CARDS:**

*See advert on opposite page*

**★★★68% Knoll House**
MINOTEL Great Britain
Swindon Rd SN16 9LU
☎ 01666 823114 01666 823897
e-mail: knollhotel@malmesbury64.freeserve.co.uk
***Dir:*** *from M4 junct 17 follow A429 towards Cirencester, at first rdbt after 5m turn right, 3rd exit. Hotel is on left at top of hill along B4042*
Well-tended gardens surround this small hotel, just outside Malmesbury, with views over the Wiltshire countryside. Whether in the main house or separate wing, bedrooms are well-decorated and equipped, many having benefited from recent refurbishment.

*continued*

In addition to the pleasant dining room there is a comfortable lounge and bar.

**ROOMS:** 12 en suite 10 annexe en suite (1 fmly) s fr £70; d fr £90 (incl. bkfst) * LB **FACILITIES:** Outdoor swimming (H) Croquet lawn ch fac Xmas **CONF:** Thtr 50 Class 24 Board 30 Del £135 * **PARKING:** 40 **NOTES:** No smoking in restaurant **CARDS:**

**★★74% Mayfield House**
Best Western
Crudwell SN16 9EW
☎ 01666 577409 & 577198 01666 577977
e-mail: mayfield@callnetuk.com
***Dir:*** *3m N on A429 from Malmesbury*
A warm welcome is assured at this charming hotel on the edge of the Cotswolds. There is a foyer lounge, a bar offering a wide range of dishes and a restaurant with an imaginative menu. Bedrooms, some on the ground floor, are all equipped with modern facilities.
**ROOMS:** 21 en suite 3 annexe en suite (2 fmly) No smoking in 4 bedrooms s £60-£62; d £82-£84 (incl. bkfst) * LB **FACILITIES:** Xmas **CONF:** Thtr 40 Class 30 Board 25 Del from £88.50 * **PARKING:** 50 **NOTES:** No smoking in restaurant **CARDS:**

*See advert on opposite page*

MALTON, North Yorkshire Map 08 SE77

**★★★72% *Burythorpe House***
Burythorpe YO17 9LB
☎ 01653 658200 01653 658204
***Dir:*** *4m S of Malton, just outside the village of Burythorpe and 4m from A64 York to Scarborough*
This charming house offers generally spacious and individually furnished bedrooms. Five rooms in a rear courtyard have small kitchens, and two of these rooms are equipped for disabled guests. There is a comfortable lounge and an oak-panelled dining room. Meals are skilfully prepared by Mr Austin and his daughter.
**ROOMS:** 11 en suite 5 annexe en suite (2 fmly) **FACILITIES:** Indoor swimming (H) Tennis (hard) Snooker Sauna Solarium Gym **PARKING:** 50 **NOTES:** No smoking in restaurant
**CARDS:**

**★★★61% Green Man**
15 Market St YO17 7LY
☎ 01653 600370 01653 696006
e-mail: greenman@englishrosehotels.co.uk
***Dir:*** *from A64 follow signs fo Malton town centre, turn left into Market St, hotel on left*
This charming hotel set in the centre of town includes an inviting reception lounge where a log fire burns in winter. There is also a cosy bar. Dining takes place in the traditional style restaurant at the rear. Bedrooms are thoughtfully equipped.
**ROOMS:** 24 en suite (4 fmly) s £40-£60; d £65-£100 (incl. bkfst) * LB **FACILITIES:** Xmas **CONF:** Thtr 40 Class 20 Board 40 Del from £60 * **PARKING:** 40 **NOTES:** No dogs (ex guide dogs) No smoking in restaurant **CARDS:**

★★67% ***Talbot***
Yorkersgate YO17 7AJ
☎ 01653 694031 📠 01653 693355
***Dir:*** *off A64 towards Malton. The Talbot is on the right*
This long established, creeper-covered hotel, although on the main road, looks out towards the River Derwent and open countryside. Bedrooms come in various sizes, and the comfortable lounge is the focus of the traditional public rooms.
**ROOMS:** 31 en suite (3 fmly) **CONF:** Thtr 80 Class 40 Board 40 **PARKING:** 30 **NOTES:** No dogs (ex guide dogs) No smoking in restaurant **CARDS:**

*See advert on this page*

★62% **Wentworth Arms**
111 Town St, Old Malton YO17 7HD
☎ 01653 692618 📠 01653 692618
***Dir:*** *turn off A64 onto A169 to Malton. Hotel 400yds on right*
This friendly inn, which stands in the centre of the village, has a 'home from home' atmosphere. It has comfortable, well-equipped bedrooms. Generous, home cooked meals can be taken either in the smart dining room, with its exposed stone walls and old beams, or in the bar. The inn has undergone much refurbishment by its enthusiastic new owners.
**ROOMS:** 5 rms (4 en suite) s £25; d £50 (incl. bkfst) * **PARKING:** 30 **NOTES:** No dogs **CARDS:**

Popped the question? Hotels with Civ Wed in their entry are licensed for civil wedding ceremonies. Maximum numbers for the ceremony only are shown, e.g. Civ Wed 120

## MALVERN, Worcestershire

Map 03 SO74

### ★★★75% Colwall Park

Walwyn Rd, Colwall WR13 6QG
☎ 01684 540000 01684 540847
e-mail: hotel@colwall.com
**Dir:** *3m SW on B4218*

Standing in extensive gardens on the western side of the Malvern Hills, this hotel was purpose built in the early 20th century to serve the local railway station. The present-day proprietors and loyal staff provide high levels of hospitality, service and cuisine, for which the hotel has a well-deserved reputation. Bedrooms have been refurbished and are well-equipped.

**ROOMS:** 22 en suite (6 fmly) No smoking in 3 bedrooms s £65-£80; d £110-£150 (incl. bkfst) * **LB** **FACILITIES:** STV Croquet lawn Boule Xmas **CONF:** Thtr 120 Class 80 Board 50 Del from £130 * **PARKING:** 40 **NOTES:** No smoking in restaurant **CARDS:**

*See advert on opposite page*

### ★★★74% Cottage in the Wood

Holywell Rd, Malvern Wells WR14 4LG
☎ 01684 575859 01684 560662
e-mail: proprietor@cottageinthewood.co.uk
**Dir:** *3m S of Great Malvern off A449 500yds N of B4209 turning on opposite side of road*

This delightful family owned and run hotel stands high up on the eastern slopes of the Malvern Hills and enjoys magnificent views across the Severn Valley. The cosy bedrooms are divided between the main house, Beech Cottage and the Coach House. All are well-equipped with lots of thoughtful extras. Public rooms are elegantly appointed and feature real fires, deep-cushioned sofas and fresh flowers. The hotel has a well-deserved high reputation for its food.

**ROOMS:** 8 en suite 12 annexe en suite s £75-£85; d £95-£145 (incl. bkfst) * **LB** **FACILITIES:** Xmas **CONF:** Thtr 20 Class 16 Board 14 Del from £135 * **PARKING:** 40 **NOTES:** No smoking in restaurant **CARDS:**

*See advert on opposite page*

### ★★★70% Foley Arms

14 Worcester Rd WR14 4QS
☎ 01684 573397 01684 569665
e-mail: reservations@foleyarmshotel.com
**Dir:** *M5 exit 7 north or 8 south, M50 exit 1, proceed to Great Malvern on A449*

The oldest hotel in Malvern, the Foley Arms is situated in the heart of town overlooking the Severn Valley. The bedrooms are comfortable and tastefully decorated with period furnishings and modern facilities. Elgar's Restaurant serves fine food, and there is a popular bar and a choice of comfortable lounges.

**ROOMS:** 28 en suite (2 fmly) No smoking in 5 bedrooms s £74; d £98-£110 (incl. bkfst) * **LB** **FACILITIES:** STV Free use leisure cent pool, gym & sauna entertainment ch fac Xmas **CONF:** Thtr 150 Class 40 Board 45 Del £102 * **PARKING:** 64 **NOTES:** No smoking in restaurant Civ Wed 120 **CARDS:**

*See advert on opposite page*

### ★★★66% Abbey

Abbey Rd WR14 3ET
☎ 01684 892332 01684 892662
e-mail: abbey@sarova.co.uk
**Dir:** *M5 junct 7, take A449 into Malvern, left (by Barclays Bank) into Church St, right at traffic lights and first right into Abbey Rd*

This large and impressive hotel stands in the centre of Great Malvern, next to the Abbey and close to the theatre. It provides well-equipped modern accommodation equally suitable for business people and tourists. Facilities here include a good range of function rooms and the hotel is a popular venue for large and small conferences. It is popular with coach tour parties during the summer months.

**ROOMS:** 103 en suite (5 fmly) No smoking in 24 bedrooms s £90-£110; d £100-£120 (incl. bkfst) * **LB** **FACILITIES:** STV Free entry to Malvern Leisure Complex Xmas **CONF:** Thtr 300 Class 180 Board 65 Del from £110 * **SERVICES:** Lift **PARKING:** 90 **NOTES:** No smoking in restaurant Civ Wed 100 **CARDS:**

### ★★76% Holdfast Cottage

Little Malvern WR13 6NA
☎ 01684 310288 01684 311117
e-mail: holdcothot@aol.com
**Dir:** *on A4104 midway between Welland and Little Malvern*

This charming, personally run hotel lies in extensive grounds with impressive views of the Malvern Hills. Accommodation is full of charm and character, with all expected comforts. The Victorian-style bar, comfortable lounge and dining room are all furnished in period style. The bedrooms are well equipped and have modern

*continued on p398*

M

*Cottage in the Wood, Malvern*

MALVERN, continued

facilities. The hotel has a well deserved reputation for its award winning cuisine.

*Holdfast Cottage, Malvern*

**ROOMS:** 8 en suite (1 fmly) No smoking in all bedrooms s £50-£52; d £84-£94 (incl. bkfst) * **LB** **FACILITIES:** Croquet lawn Xmas **PARKING:** 15 **NOTES:** No smoking in restaurant Closed first two weeks of Jan **CARDS:**

*See advert on opposite page*

### ★★68% Cotford

51 Graham Rd WR14 2HU
☎ 01684 572427 📠 01684 572952
e-mail: reservations@catfordhotel.co.uk
***Dir:*** *from Worcester follow signs to Malvern on A449. Left into Graham Rd signed town centre hotel on right*

This delightful house built in 1851, reputedly for the Bishop of Worcester, stands in spacious gardens, within easy reach of Malvern. All rooms are tastefully decorated with modern facilities. Additional features include a bar, a cosy lounge and a pleasant restaurant.

**ROOMS:** 17 en suite (4 fmly) s £50-£60; d £70-£80 (incl. bkfst) * **LB** **FACILITIES:** STV **CONF:** Thtr 26 Class 26 Del from £65 * **PARKING:** 18 **NOTES:** No smoking in restaurant **CARDS:**

### ★★68% The Malvern Hills

Wynds Point WR13 6DW
☎ 01684 540690 📠 01684 540327
e-mail: malhilhotl@aol.com
***Dir:*** *4m S, at junct of A449 with B4232*

This privately-owned, 19th-century hostelry is situated to the west of Malvern, opposite the British Camp, which was fortified and occupied by the Ancient Britons. Facilities include a choice of bars and a sun terrace from which customers can enjoy spectacular sunsets. The hotel is popular with walkers as well as business guests.

**ROOMS:** 14 en suite (3 fmly) No smoking in 4 bedrooms s £40-£50; d £75-£85 (incl. bkfst) * **LB** **FACILITIES:** pool table entertainment Xmas **CONF:** Thtr 40 Class 40 Board 30 Del from £58.50 * **PARKING:** 30 **NOTES:** No smoking in restaurant **CARDS:**

### ★★66% Great Malvern

Graham Rd WR14 2HN
☎ 01684 563411 📠 01684 560514
e-mail: sutton@great-malvern-hotel.co.uk
***Dir:*** *from Worcester on A449, turn left just beyond the fire station into Graham Rd. Hotel is at the end of Graham Rd on the right*

This town-centre hotel is close to many cultural and scenic attractions. Popular with both business and leisure travellers, the hotel features well-equipped and comfortable accommodation, a busy bar, a brasserie and meeting rooms.

**ROOMS:** 14 rms (13 en suite) (3 fmly) s £45-£55; d £70-£80 (incl. bkfst) * **LB** **FACILITIES:** ch fac **CONF:** Thtr 60 Class 20 Board 30 Del from £59.95 * **SERVICES:** Lift **PARKING:** 9 **NOTES:** No dogs (ex guide dogs) **CARDS:**

### ★★66% Mount Pleasant

THE CIRCLE Selected Individual Hotels GREAT BRITAIN

Belle Vue Ter WR14 4PZ
☎ 01684 561837 📠 01684 569968
e-mail: mountpleasanthotel@freeserve.co.uk
***Dir:*** *on A449, 0.5m from Great Malvern station*

This attractive Georgian house overlooks the picturesque Severn Valley and the Priory Church. Well presented bedrooms vary in style and provide comfortable accommodation. There is a quiet

*continued*

lounge for residents, a lounge bar and the pleasant Café el Sol restaurant, which doubles as a coffee shop during the day.

**ROOMS:** 15 rms (14 en suite) s £49-£60; d £79-£92 (incl. bkfst) * **LB** **CONF:** Thtr 90 Class 40 Board 50 Del from £83 * **PARKING:** 20 **NOTES:** No dogs (ex guide dogs) No smoking in restaurant **CARDS:**

*See advert on this page*

## MANCHESTER, Greater Manchester — Map 07 SJ89

see also Manchester Airport, Sale & Salford

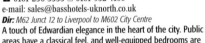

### ★★★★74% Crowne Plaza Manchester - The Midland

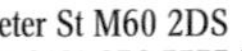

Peter St M60 2DS
☎ 0161 236 3333 Fax 0161 932 4100
e-mail: sales@basshotels-uknorth.co.uk
***Dir:*** *M62 Junct 12 to Liverpool to M602 City Centre*

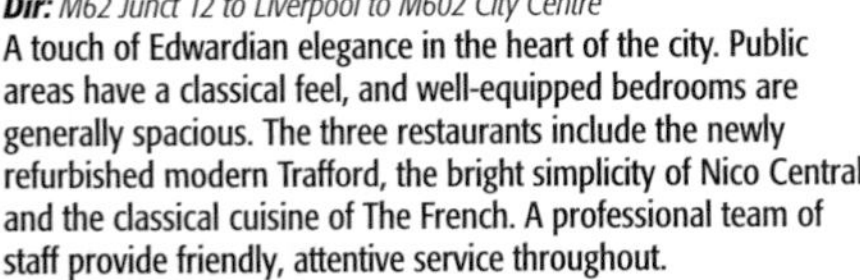

A touch of Edwardian elegance in the heart of the city. Public areas have a classical feel, and well-equipped bedrooms are generally spacious. The three restaurants include the newly refurbished modern Trafford, the bright simplicity of Nico Central, and the classical cuisine of The French. A professional team of staff provide friendly, attentive service throughout.
**ROOMS:** 303 en suite (62 fmly) No smoking in 180 bedrooms d £160 * **LB** **FACILITIES:** STV Indoor swimming (H) Squash Sauna Solarium Gym Jacuzzi Hairdressing/beauty salon entertainment Xmas **CONF:** Thtr 500 Class 360 Board 40 **SERVICES:** Lift air con **CARDS:**

### ★★★★73% Palace

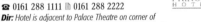

Oxford St M60 7HA
☎ 0161 288 1111 Fax 0161 288 2222
***Dir:*** *Hotel is adjacent to Palace Theatre on corner of Oxford St & Whitworth St and opposite Oxford Road railway station*

Established in 1890 as the headquarters for the Refuge Assurance Company, the Gothic style of the building has made it an impressive city landmark. The interior is enhanced by richly glazed decorative tiles, panelling and plaster work. Today the building, restored to its former glory, is a hotel with stylish bedrooms, an impressive ballroom, a business centre, restaurant and two bars.
**ROOMS:** 252 en suite (59 fmly) No smoking in 30 bedrooms s £109-£149; d £119-£159 * **LB** **FACILITIES:** STV entertainment **CONF:** Thtr 1000 Class 450 Board 100 **SERVICES:** Lift **NOTES:** No dogs (ex guide dogs) Civ Wed 100 **CARDS:**

*See advert on page 401*

Late for dinner? Quality Standards star rating means that last orders for dinner should be no earlier than:
★ 6.30pm ★★ 7.00pm ★★★ 8.00pm
★★★★ 9.00pm ★★★★★ 10.00pm

M

MANCHESTER, continued

**★★★★71% ◎ Marriott Worsley Park Hotel & Country Club**

Worsley Park, Worsley M28 2QT
☎ 0161 975 2000 📠 0161 799 6341
e-mail: salesadmin.worsleypark@marriotthotels.co.uk
***Dir:*** *junct 13 M60, go straight on at 1st rdbt take A575 hotel 400yds on left*

Set in extensive grounds (which include a championship golf club), this hotel was once part of a farm, converted to offer modern, attractively furnished, thoughtfully equipped accommodation. The restaurant offers a good standard of carefully prepared dishes.
**ROOMS:** 158 en suite (5 fmly) No smoking in 116 bedrooms d £109-£119 * **LB** **FACILITIES:** STV Indoor swimming (H) Golf 18 Sauna Solarium Gym Putting green Jacuzzi Steam room Health & Beauty salon Xmas **CONF:** Thtr 200 Class 150 Board 100 Del from £165 * **SERVICES:** Lift **PARKING:** 400 **NOTES:** No dogs (ex guide dogs) Civ Wed 200 **CARDS:**

**★★★★71% Le Meridien Victoria & Albert**

Water St M3 4JQ
☎ 0870 400 8585 📠 0161 834 2484
e-mail: frontoffice1452@lemeridien.co.uk
***Dir:*** *M602 to A57 through lights on Regent Rd pass Sainsbury's then left at lights into Water St go over lights and hotel is on the left*
Created from former warehouses on the banks of the River Irwell, this impressive hotel, situated opposite the Granada Studios, is a few minutes' walk from the city centre. Beautifully decorated, thoughtfully equipped bedrooms are named after Granada productions with pictures to match. The interior features exposed brick walls, iron pillars and wooden beams. Guests eat in Café Maigret, a lively, bustling brasserie. There is valet parking.
**ROOMS:** 158 en suite (2 fmly) No smoking in 60 bedrooms d £165-£185 * **LB** **FACILITIES:** STV Access to Livingwell Health Club entertainment ch fac Xmas **CONF:** Thtr 250 Class 120 Board 72 Del from £159 * **SERVICES:** Lift air con **PARKING:** 120 **NOTES:** No dogs (ex guide dogs) Civ Wed 200 **CARDS:**

*See advert on opposite page*

**★★★★65% Copthorne Hotel Manchester**

Clippers Quay, Salford Quays M5 2XP
☎ 0161 873 7321 📠 0161 873 7318
e-mail: manchester@mill-cop.com
***Dir:*** *from M602 follow signs for Salford Quays/Trafford Park (A5063)-Trafford Road, hotel is 3/4 mile along road on right*
Located within the redeveloped Salford Quays, this modern hotel is conveniently connected to the city by the Metro Link. Bedrooms are comfortable especially the Connoisseur rooms, and many of which overlook the quay. Stylishly furnished public areas include the formal Chandlers restaurant and the informal Clippers restaurant.
**ROOMS:** 166 en suite (6 fmly) No smoking in 80 bedrooms d £145-£170 * **LB** **FACILITIES:** STV Indoor swimming (H) Sauna Gym Jacuzzi Steam room **CONF:** Thtr 150 Class 70 Board 70 Del from £115 * **SERVICES:** Lift **PARKING:** 120 **NOTES:** No dogs (ex guide dogs) **CARDS:**

**★★★72% Malmaison**

Piccadilly M1 3AQ
☎ 0161 278 1000 📠 0161 278 1002
e-mail: manchester@malmaison.com
***Dir:*** *follow signs to city centre then Piccadilly station, hotel opposite station, at bottom of station approach*
Malmaison continues to deliver a chic and stylish experience. Recently extended to offer a further 60 bedrooms all of which are thoughtfully designed and air-conditioned. Public areas are complemented by Gymtonic and Petit Spa offering a wide range of spa treatments. The Brasserie delivers a French inspired menu with many firm favourites on offer.
**ROOMS:** 167 en suite d £115 * **FACILITIES:** **Spa** STV Sauna Solarium Gym Jacuzzi **CONF:** Thtr 75 Class 48 Board 30 Del £160 * **SERVICES:** Lift air con **NOTES:** No dogs (ex guide dogs) **CARDS:**

**★★★70% ◎◎ Golden Tulip Manchester**

Waters Reach, Trafford Park M17 1WS
☎ 0161 873 8899 📠 0161 872 6556
e-mail: goldentulipmanchester.com
***Dir:*** *From A56 onto Sir Matt Busby Way follow past Manchester United stadium to traffic lights hotel directly right.*
Situated opposite Old Trafford, close to the city centre and within easy reach of the airport and national road network. The rooms are spacious and comfortable and equipped with all modern requirements and accessories. Rhodes & Co Brasserie and Bar are located within the hotel and conference facilities are available.
**ROOMS:** 111 en suite (22 fmly) No smoking in 70 bedrooms d £85-£100 * **LB** **FACILITIES:** STV Xmas **CONF:** Thtr 120 Class 70 Board 40 Del from £140 * **SERVICES:** Lift **PARKING:** 160 **NOTES:** No dogs (ex guide dogs) **CARDS:**

**★★★67% Old Rectory Hotel**

Meadow Ln, Haughton Green, Denton M34 7GD
☎ 0161 336 7516 📠 0161 320 3212
e-mail: reservations@oldrectoryhotelmanchester.co.uk

A former Victorian rectory with modern well-appointed bedrooms, set around an enclosed garden in a peaceful location, only a short distance from Manchester. Staff are friendly and helpful, and the attractive restaurant enjoys a good local reputation. There are

continued

conference and banqueting facilities, and weddings can also be catered for.
**ROOMS:** 30 en suite 6 annexe en suite (1 fmly) No smoking in 3 bedrooms **FACILITIES:** STV Games room Xmas **CONF:** Thtr 100 Class 45 Board 50 Del from £100 * **PARKING:** 50 **NOTES:** No smoking in restaurant **CARDS:**

### ★★★67% Willow Bank Hotel
340-342 Wilmslow Rd, Fallowfield M14 6AF
☎ 0161 224 0461 Fax 0161 257 2561
e-mail: willowbankhotel@feathers.uk.com
***Dir:*** *situated 3m S of Manchester City Centre on B5093*
Conveniently located within three miles of the city centre and close to the universities, this hotel has undergone a transformation. The result is spacious, elegant public areas and a number of bright, attractive bedrooms. New rooms are thoughtfully equipped with CD players, satellite TV and PlayStations.
**ROOMS:** 118 en suite (4 fmly) s £60-£70; d £80-£100 (incl. bkfst) * **LB** **FACILITIES:** STV ch fac Xmas **CONF:** Thtr 125 Class 60 Board 70 Del from £75 * **PARKING:** 100 **NOTES:** No dogs (ex guide dogs) Civ Wed 125 **CARDS:**

### ★★★66% Novotel Manchester West

NOVOTEL
Worsley Brow M28 2YA
☎ 0161 799 3535 Fax 0161 703 8207
e-mail: H0907@accor-hotels.com
(For full entry see Worsley)

### ★★★64% Jury's Inn Manchester
JURYS DOYLE HOTELS
56 Great Bridgwater St M1 5LE
☎ 0161 953 8888 Fax 0161 953 9090
e-mail: manchester_inn@jurysdoyle.com
***Dir:*** *In city centre next to G-Mex centre & Bridgewater mall*
Enjoying a prime central location, Jurys Inn offers good value, air-conditioned accommodation ideal for both business travellers and families. Public areas include a smart, spacious lobby, the Inn pub and Arches restaurant. There are several car parks close by.
**ROOMS:** 265 en suite (5 fmly) No smoking in 230 bedrooms d £63 * **FACILITIES:** STV **CONF:** Thtr 50 Class 40 Board 25 Del £125 * **SERVICES:** Lift air con **NOTES:** No dogs Closed 24-26 Dec **CARDS:**

### ★★★64% *Posthouse Manchester*
Posthouse
Palatine Rd, Northenden M22 4FH
☎ 0870 400 9056 Fax 0161 946 0139
***Dir:*** *S M56 junct 3A signed City Centre A5103. Follow signs Northenden B5166 and rt at lights. N M60 junct 5 signed Airport to Northenden exit.*
Many of the bedrooms of this modern hotel, conveniently situated for the city and International Airport, have panoramic views of the surrounding area. An all day lounge menu and 24 hour room service together with secure car parking are also features of the hotel. The popular "Traders" restaurant is open for both lunch and dinner.
**ROOMS:** 190 en suite (5 fmly) No smoking in 67 bedrooms **FACILITIES:** Free admittance to local Leisure Centre **CONF:** Thtr 120 Class 60 Board 80 **SERVICES:** Lift **PARKING:** 370 **CARDS:**

### ★★★62% Waterside
Wilmslow Rd, Didsbury M20 5WZ
☎ 0161 445 0225 Fax 0161 446 2090
e-mail: office@watersidehotel.co.uk
***Dir:*** *M60 junct 3, A34 Disbury, at 3rd set of lights turn left, then left again on B5095 towards Cheadle. Hotel 2nd turning on right*
Centrally located for both the motorway network and the city

*continued on p402*

MANCHESTER, continued

centre, this modern hotel has an exceptionally well equipped leisure centre. The brasserie and adjacent café bar, overlooking the river, offer a wide choice of meals and snacks. Staff are friendly and keen to please.
**ROOMS:** 46 en suite (1 fmly) No smoking in 18 bedrooms s £79-£84; d £96-£106 * **FACILITIES:** STV Indoor swimming (H) Tennis (hard) Sauna Solarium Gym Jacuzzi Beauty salon Xmas **CONF:** Thtr 160 Class 90 Board 56 Del from £125 * **PARKING:** 250 **NOTES:** No dogs (ex guide dogs) **CARDS:**

### ★★64% Comfort Friendly Inn

Hyde Rd, Birch St, West Gorton M12 5NT
☎ 0161 220 8700 0161 220 8848
e-mail: admin@gb615.u-net.com
***Dir:*** *3m SE on A57*
A warm welcome is offered by the friendly and attentive staff of this hotel, just 3 miles from the city centre. The modest yet practical bedrooms offer value-for-money accommodation and modern facilities. Public areas include a lounge bar serving snacks all day and an attractive restaurant serving good value meals.
**ROOMS:** 90 en suite (5 fmly) No smoking in 45 bedrooms s £40-£49.50; d £40-£49.50 * **LB** **FACILITIES:** STV Xmas **CONF:** Thtr 100 Class 50 Board 50 Del from £70 * **PARKING:** 70 **NOTES:** No smoking in restaurant **CARDS:**

### ★★61% Manchester Conference Centre and Hotel

Weston Building, Sackville St M1 3BB
☎ 0161 955 8000 0161 955 8050
e-mail: weston@umist.ac.uk
***Dir:*** *Located on Sackville Street between Whitworth Street & Mancunian Way (A57m)*
A modern, state-of-the-art conference centre with well-equipped comfortable rooms, set in the heart of the UMIST university buildings. Public areas include a bar and spacious restaurant, as well as an extensive range of conference and meeting rooms.
**ROOMS:** 133 en suite (2 fmly) No smoking in 106 bedrooms d £75 * **CONF:** Thtr 300 Class 30 Board 40 Del £141 * **SERVICES:** Lift **PARKING:** 700 **NOTES:** No dogs (ex guide dogs) No smoking in restaurant **CARDS:**

### Express by Holiday Inn Manchester

Waterfront Quay, Salford Quays M5 2XW
☎ 0161 868 1000 0161 868 1068
e-mail: managersalfordquays@expressholidayinn.co.uk
***Dir:*** *from M62 take M602 to Manchester. End of M602 take left lane towards A5063 Trafford Park. At 2nd t/lights on A5063 turn right. Hotel straight ahead across tram lines*

A modern budget hotel offering comfortable accommodation in refreshing, spacious and comprehensively equipped bedrooms, en suite bathrooms with power showers and continental buffet breakfast included in the room rate. Suitable for business travellers or families. For further details and the Express by Holiday Inn phone number, consult the Hotel Groups page.
**ROOMS:** 120 en suite (incl. cont bkfst) d £60 * **CONF:** Thtr 25 Class 15 Board 10

### Express by Holiday Inn Manchester East

Debdale Park, Hyde Rd M18 7LJ
☎ 0161 231 9900 0161 220 8555
e-mail: manchestereast@premierhotels.co.uk
***Dir:*** *3m from Manchester City Centre on left hand side of A57 at Debdale Park*

Express
by Holiday Inn

A modern budget hotel offering comfortable accommodation in refreshing, spacious and comprehensively equipped bedrooms, en suite bathrooms with power showers and continental buffet breakfast included in the room rate. Suitable for business travellers or families. For further details and the Express by Holiday Inn phone number, consult the Hotel Groups page.
**ROOMS:** 97 en suite (incl. cont bkfst) d £53 * **CONF:** Thtr 35 Class 15 Board 20 Del £75 *

### *Campanile*

55 Ordsall Ln, Salford M5 4RS
☎ 0161 833 1845 0161 833 1847
***Dir:*** *take M602 towards Manchester, then A57, after large rdbt Sainsbury's on left turn left at next traffic lights, hotel on right*

This modern building offers accommodation in smart, well-equipped bedrooms, all with en suite bathrooms. Refreshments may be taken at the informal Bistro. For further details and the Campanile phone number, consult the Hotel Groups page.
**ROOMS:** 105 en suite **CONF:** Thtr 50 Class 40 Board 30

### *Travelodge*

Townbury House, Blackfriars St M3 5AB
☎ 08700 850950
Travelodge offers good quality, good value, modern accommodation. Ideal for families, the spacious, en suite

continued

bedrooms include remote-control TV, tea and coffee-making facilities, luxury beds and free morning newspaper. Meals can be taken at the nearby family restaurant. For further details and the Travelodge phone number, consult the Hotel Groups page.

### ⇧ *Premier Lodge (City Centre GMEX)*
7-11 Lower Mosley St M2 3DW
☎ 0870 700 1476 🖹 0870 700 1477
Premier Lodge offers modern, well-equipped, en suite accommodation suitable for both business and leisure travellers. Meals can be taken at the adjacent popular restaurant and bar, which is fully licensed. For further details, consult the Hotel Groups page.
**ROOMS:** 147 en suite

### ○ Hotel Ibis

ibis
Accor hotels

Charles St M1 7DL
☎ 0161 272 5000
**ROOMS:** 127 rms **NOTES:** Open now

### ○ Hotel Ibis Manchester Portland

ibis
Accor hotels

Portland St
**ROOMS:** 127 rms **NOTES:** Opening September 2001

## MANCHESTER AIRPORT, Greater Manchester Map 07 SJ88
see also Altrincham

### ★★★★68% ◎◎ Radisson SAS Hotel Manchester Airport
Chicago Av M90 3RA
☎ 0161 490 5000 🖹 0161 490 5100
e-mail: sales@manzq.rdsas.com
***Dir:** M56 junct 5, follow signs for Airport Terminal 2. At rdbt, take 2nd left and follow signs for railway station. Hotel next to station*
This stylish, modern hotel, directly connected to all terminals, offers excellent amenities. Bedrooms are air-conditioned and thoughtfully equipped with every modern convenience. Public areas include extensive leisure and conference facilities as well as a choice of eating and drinking options with The Phileas Fogg Restaurant offering carefully prepared dishes.
**ROOMS:** 360 en suite (2 fmly) No smoking in 220 bedrooms d £79-£150 * **LB** **FACILITIES:** STV Indoor swimming (H) Sauna Solarium Gym Steam room sun beds Xmas **CONF:** Thtr 350 Class 180 Board 50 Del from £155 * **SERVICES:** Lift air con **PARKING:** 225 **NOTES:** No dogs (ex guide dogs) Civ Wed 60 **CARDS:**

### ★★★★65% ◎ Belfry House
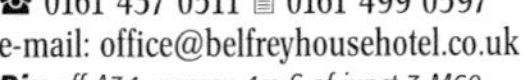

Stanley Rd SK9 3LD
☎ 0161 437 0511 🖹 0161 499 0597
e-mail: office@belfreyhousehotel.co.uk
***Dir:** off A34, approx 4m S of junct 3 M60*
Belfry House offers high standards of service and hospitality. A new café-bar has opened, serving light meals. Bedrooms are well-equipped and traditionally furnished, and conference and function facilities are available. A leisure centre is under construction.
**ROOMS:** 80 en suite (2 fmly) No smoking in 40 bedrooms s fr £90; d fr £106 * **LB** **FACILITIES:** Spa STV Indoor swimming (H) Sauna Solarium Gym Jacuzzi entertainment Xmas **CONF:** Thtr 120 Class 70 Board 50 Del from £125 * **SERVICES:** Lift **PARKING:** 150 **NOTES:** No dogs (ex guide dogs) No smoking in restaurant Civ Wed 60
**CARDS:**

Packed in a hurry? Ironing facilities should be available at all star levels, either in rooms or on request.

### ★★★★64% Manchester Airport Marriott

Marriott
HOTELS · RESORTS · SUITES

Hale Rd, Hale Barns WA15 8XW
☎ 0161 904 0301 🖹 0161 980 1787
e-mail: info@swallowhotels.com

A modern hotel with good airport links, noteworthy leisure and business facilities and secure parking arrangements. Bedrooms are situated around open courtyards and offer comfortable acommodation. There is a good choice of bars and restaurants.
**ROOMS:** 142 en suite (16 fmly) No smoking in 64 bedrooms d £109-£124 * **LB** **FACILITIES:** STV Indoor swimming (H) Sauna Gym Jacuzzi **CONF:** Thtr 200 Class 90 Board 50 Del from £160 * **SERVICES:** Lift **PARKING:** 480 **NOTES:** No dogs (ex guide dogs) Civ Wed 100
**CARDS:**

### ★★★73% ◎◎ Etrop Grange
Thorley Ln M90 4EG
☎ 0161 499 0500 🖹 0161 499 0790
e-mail: etropgrange@corushotels.com
***Dir:** M56 junct 5 follow signs for Terminal 2, go up slip rd to rdbt take 1st exit, take immediate left, hotel is 400yds ahead*

This Georgian country house-style hotel is close to Terminal 2 but one would never know once inside. Smart bedrooms offer all modern comforts and good business facilities. Comfortable, elegant day rooms include the Coach House Restaurant, serving a high standard of cuisine. A chauffeured limousine service is available for airport passengers.
**ROOMS:** 64 en suite No smoking in 10 bedrooms s £70-£155; d £90-£175 * **LB** **FACILITIES:** STV **CONF:** Thtr 80 Class 30 Board 36 Del from £99 * **PARKING:** 80 **NOTES:** No smoking in restaurant Civ Wed 90 **CARDS:**

### ★★★73% ◎◎ Stanneylands
Stanneylands Rd SK9 4EY
☎ 01625 525225 🖹 01625 537282
e-mail: reservations@stanneylands.co.uk
***Dir:** leave M56 at Airport turn off, follow signs to Wilmslow, turn left into Station Rd, onto Stanneylands Rd, hotel is on the right*
Now under new ownership this traditional hotel is being tastefully
continued on p404

MANCHESTER AIRPORT, continued

transformed thanks to the sympathetic refurbishment of the well-equipped bedrooms and delightful, comfortable day rooms. The cuisine on offer in the restaurant is of a high standard and ranges from traditional favourites to more imaginative contemporary dishes. Staff throughout are friendly and nothing is too much trouble.
**ROOMS:** 32 en suite (2 fmly) No smoking in 10 bedrooms s £94-£118; d £108-£118 * **LB** **FACILITIES:** STV **CONF:** Thtr 100 Class 50 Board 40 Del from £130 * **PARKING:** 80 **NOTES:** No dogs (ex guide dogs) Civ Wed 100 **CARDS:**

*See advert on opposite page*

★★★67% ***Posthouse Manchester Airport***
Ringway Rd, Wythenshawe M90 3NS
Posthouse
☎ 0870 400 9055 🖹 0161 436 2340
A modern airport hotel with well-appointed bedrooms, several in the new style. "Sampans", an additional eating option serving Oriental dishes, is a recent addition, alongside an Irish Theme Bar. Other features include 24 hour room service and an all-day lounge menu. Transport to the various airport terminals is also provided.
**ROOMS:** 290 en suite (6 fmly) No smoking in 80 bedrooms **FACILITIES:** STV Indoor swimming (H) Sauna Solarium Gym Health & fitness centre **CONF:** Thtr 80 Class 26 Board 30 **SERVICES:** Lift air con **PARKING:** 290 **CARDS:**

⌂ ***Premier Lodge (Manchester Airport)***
30 Wilmslow Rd SK9 3EW
PREMIER LODGE
☎ 0870 700 1486 🖹 0870 700 1487
Premier Lodge offers modern, well-equipped, en suite accommodation suitable for both business and leisure travellers. Meals can be taken at the adjacent popular restaurant and bar, which is fully licensed. For further details, consult the Hotel Groups page.
**ROOMS:** 35 en suite

MANSFIELD, Nottinghamshire — Map 08 SK56

★★66% **Pine Lodge**
281-283 Nottingham Rd NG18 4SE
☎ 01623 622308 🖹 01623 656819
e-mail: enquiries@pinelodge-hotel.co.uk
***Dir:*** *on A60 Nottingham to Mansfield road*
Located on the edge of Mansfield, this hotel offers welcoming and personal service to its guests, many of whom return time and again. The public rooms include a comfortable lounge bar, a cosy restaurant and a choice of meeting and function rooms. Bedrooms are thoughtfully equipped.
**ROOMS:** 20 en suite (2 fmly) No smoking in 5 bedrooms s £43-£55; d £65 (incl. bkfst) * **LB** **FACILITIES:** STV Sauna **CONF:** Thtr 50 Class 30 Board 35 Del from £78 * **PARKING:** 40 **NOTES:** No dogs No smoking in restaurant Closed 25-26 Dec
**CARDS:**

★★65% **Portland Hall**
Carr Bank Park, Windmill Ln NG18 2AL
☎ 01623 452525 🖹 01623 452550
***Dir:*** *from town centre take A60 towards Worksop for 100yds then right at Pelican Crossing into Nursery Street - Carr Bank Park 50yds on right*
Portland Hall, a former Georgian mansion, sits in 15 acres of parkland. The house retains some fine examples of its past, with original plasterwork and friezes in the cosy lounge bar, and around the domed skylight over the spiral stairs. There is an attractive restaurant in which carvery and carte menus offer a flexible choice to diners.
**ROOMS:** 11 en suite (1 fmly) No smoking in 7 bedrooms s £47; d £59 (incl. bkfst) * **FACILITIES:** Bowls entertainment Xmas **CONF:** Thtr 60 Class 30 Board 30 Del from £60 * **PARKING:** 150 **NOTES:** No smoking in restaurant Civ Wed 70 **CARDS:**

MARAZION, Cornwall & Isles of Scilly — Map 02 SW53

★★72% ® **Mount Haven**
Turnpike Rd TR17 0DQ
MINOTEL Great Britain
☎ 01736 710249 🖹 01736 711658
e-mail: aa@mounthaven.co.uk
***Dir:*** *approaching Penzance from A30 (E), at rdbt take Helston exit (A394). At next rdbt take right hand exit into Marazion, Hotel on left*

A former coaching inn set on the outskirts of Marazion, Mount Haven offers bright and cheerful bedrooms with modern facilities. Those at the front enjoy views of St. Michael's Mount. The split-level restaurant offers a set-price menu and a short carte.
**ROOMS:** 17 en suite (5 fmly) s £40-£65; d £68-£89 (incl. bkfst) **LB** **FACILITIES:** ch fac **PARKING:** 30 **NOTES:** No smoking in restaurant Closed 25 & 26 Dec **CARDS:**

*See advert under PENZANCE*

★★69% **Godolphin Arms**
TR17 0EN
☎ 01736 710202 🖹 01736 710171
e-mail: enquires@godolphinarms.co.uk
***Dir:*** *from A30 follow Marazion signs for 1m to hotel at the end of the causeway to St Michael's Mount*
This 170-year-old waterside hotel is in a prime location. Stunning views of St Michael's Mount provide a backdrop for the restaurant and lounge bar. Bedrooms are colourful, comfortable and spacious. A choice of menu is offered in the main restaurant and the Gig Bar, with an emphasis on local seafood.
**ROOMS:** 10 en suite (2 fmly) s £43-£48; d £65-£75 (incl. bkfst) * **LB** **FACILITIES:** STV **PARKING:** 48 **NOTES:** No smoking in restaurant
**CARDS:**

MARCH, Cambridgeshire — Map 05 TL49

★★64% ***Olde Griffin***
High St PE15 9JS
☎ 01354 652517 🖹 01354 650086
***Dir:*** *March is on A141/142 north of Ely Cambs and off A47 east of Peterborough towards Norwich*
Situated overlooking the town square, this former coaching inn dates back to the 16th century. Bedrooms vary in size and style and all are fully equipped with creature comforts. Meals are

*continued*

available in the lounge and bar areas and there is a restaurant for more formal dining.
**ROOMS:** 20 rms (19 en suite) (1 fmly) **CONF:** Thtr 100 Class 50 Board 36 **PARKING:** 50 **NOTES:** No dogs (ex guide dogs)
**CARDS:**

## MARKET DRAYTON, Shropshire Map 07 SJ63

### ★★★70% Goldstone Hall
Goldstone TF9 2NA
☎ 01630 661202 & 661487 📠 01630 661585
e-mail: enquiries@GoldstoneHall.com
***Dir:*** *4m S of Market Drayton off A529 signposted Goldstone Hall Gardens. 4m N of Newport signed off A41*

Situated in extensive grounds, this charming period property is a family-run hotel. It provides traditionally furnished, well-equipped accommodation, with some more contemporary artistic touches. Public rooms are extensive and include a choice of lounges, a snooker room and a conservatory. The hotel has a well deserved reputation for good food.
**ROOMS:** 8 en suite s £70; d £95-£105 (incl. bkfst) * LB **FACILITIES:** Fishing Snooker ch fac **CONF:** Thtr 50 Board 30 Del from £105 * **PARKING:** 60 **NOTES:** No dogs (ex guide dogs) Civ Wed 60
**CARDS:**

### ★★69% Rosehill Manor
Rosehill, Ternhill TF9 2JF
☎ 01630 638532 📠 01630 637008
***Dir:*** *from the rdbt at Ternhill A53/41 head south towards Newport or M54 hotel 2m on right*

Parts of this charming, privately owned house, set in mature gardens, date back to the 16th century. The well-equipped accommodation includes family rooms. Public areas comprise a pleasant restaurant, a bar and a comfortable lounge. There is also a recently constructed conservatory, which is available for functions. The hotel has a well-deserved reputation for its food.
**ROOMS:** 9 en suite (2 fmly) s £42-£50; d £70 (incl. bkfst) * LB **FACILITIES:** Croquet lawn **PARKING:** 80 **NOTES:** No smoking in restaurant Civ Wed 90 **CARDS:**

## MARKET HARBOROUGH, Leicestershire Map 04 SP78
see also Marston Trussell

### ★★★72% Three Swans
21 High St LE16 7NJ
☎ 01858 466644 📠 01858 433101
e-mail: sales@threeswans.co.uk
***Dir:*** *at junct 20 take A4304 to Market Harborough. Passing through town centre on A6 from Leicester, the Hotel is on right*

This former coaching inn has been refurbished and extended to improve guests' comfort. Bold, warm colour schemes are used throughout the bars, reception and lounge area. The formal restaurant serves good food in a professional, attentive manner. A new bedroom wing houses modern executive rooms, which are well-equipped and comfortably appointed and a large attractive conference/ballroom has recently opened.
**ROOMS:** 18 en suite 43 annexe en suite (8 fmly) No smoking in 32 bedrooms s fr £75; d fr £95 (incl. bkfst) * LB **FACILITIES:** STV Jacuzzi **CONF:** Thtr 200 Class 120 Board 120 Del from £135 * **SERVICES:** Lift **PARKING:** 100 **NOTES:** No dogs (ex guide dogs) No smoking in restaurant Civ Wed 160 **CARDS:**

Early start? Hotels at all star levels should provide in-room alarm clocks and/or alarm calls.



### ★★★68% Menzies Angel
37 High St LE16 7NL
☎ 0870 6003013 📠 01332 511144
e-mail: info@menzies-hotels.co.uk
***Dir:*** *on A6*

A former coaching inn on the town's main street, this property has been totally refurbished. Public areas include a cheerful brasserie, more traditional bar and a separate lounge. Bedroom sizes vary, all are furnished to a high standard and have a range of facilities to suit the regular traveller.
**ROOMS:** 37 en suite s £65; d £75 * LB **FACILITIES:** Jacuzzi Xmas **CONF:** Thtr 24 Class 12 Board 14 Del from £105 * **PARKING:** 30 **NOTES:** No smoking in restaurant Civ Wed 75
**CARDS:**

## MARKFIELD, Leicestershire Map 08 SK41

### ⇧ *Travelodge*
Littleshaw Ln LE67 0PP
☎ 08700 850950
***Dir:*** *on A50 fom junct22 with M1*

Travelodge offers good quality, good value, modern accommodation. Ideal for families, the spacious, en suite bedrooms include remote-control TV, tea and coffee-making facilities, luxury beds and free morning newspaper. Meals can be taken at the nearby family restaurant. For further details and the Travelodge phone number, consult the Hotel Groups page.
**ROOMS:** 40 en suite

TV dinner? Room service at three stars and above.

## MARKHAM MOOR, Nottinghamshire — Map 08 SK77

### Travelodge
DN22 0QU
☎ 01777 838091 01777 838091
***Dir:*** *on A1 northbound*

Travelodge offers good quality, good value, modern accommodation. Ideal for families, the spacious, en suite bedrooms include remote-control TV, tea and coffee-making facilities, luxury beds and free morning newspaper. Meals can be taken at the nearby family restaurant. For further details and the Travelodge phone number, consult the Hotel Groups page.

**ROOMS:** 40 en suite

## MARKINGTON, North Yorkshire — Map 08 SE26

### ★★★76% Hob Green
HG3 3PJ
☎ 01423 770031 01423 771589
e-mail: info@hobgreen.com
***Dir:*** *exit A61 4m after Harrogate and turn left at Wormald Green and follow brown hotel signs*

An elegant 18th-century country house hotel nestling amongst 800 acres of beautiful rolling countryside, not far from Harrogate and Ripon. Comfortable lounges have open fires in winter. Bedrooms are furnished with antiques and retain many original features. The restaurant enjoys a fine reputation thanks to creative and skillfully prepared menus. Staff are friendly and helpful.

**ROOMS:** 12 en suite (1 fmly) s £90-£115; d £140-£150 (incl. bkfst & dinner) * **LB** **FACILITIES:** Croquet lawn Xmas **CONF:** Thtr 15 Class 10 Board 10 Del from £95 * **PARKING:** 40 **NOTES:** Civ Wed 30
**CARDS:**

*See advert under HARROGATE*

## MARLBOROUGH, Wiltshire — Map 04 SU16

### ★★★74% Ivy House Hotel
High St SN8 1HJ
☎ 01672 515333 01672 515338
e-mail: ivyhouse@btconnect.com
***Dir:*** *M4 junct 15 take A346 to Marlborough hotel is situated on High St*

A grade II listed Georgian property, built for the Earl of Aylesbury in 1707. The well-equipped bedrooms are individually decorated. Facilities include the Beeches conference suite, lounges and the elegant Scott's restaurant, serving both fixed price and carte menus, offering a mix of traditional and more contemporary cuisine.

**ROOMS:** 28 en suite (3 fmly) No smoking in 21 bedrooms s £69-£79; d £84-£98 (incl. bkfst) * **LB** **FACILITIES:** STV ch fac **CONF:** Thtr 60 Class 40 Board 30 Del from £115 * **PARKING:** 36 **NOTES:** No dogs (ex guide dogs) No smoking in restaurant **CARDS:**

*See advert on opposite page*

### ★★★68% *The Castle & Ball*
High St SN8 1LZ
☎ 01672 515201 01672 515895
***Dir:*** *both the A338 and A4 lead into Marlborough and eventually into the High St*

Now under new ownership, this traditional town centre coaching inn has been extensively upgraded. Spacious bedrooms have been tastefully refurbished and are well-equipped. Open plan public areas include a comfortable bar/lounge area and a smartly appointed restaurant, which serves food all day. Meeting rooms and parking are also available.

**ROOMS:** 34 en suite (1 fmly) No smoking in 13 bedrooms
**FACILITIES:** STV **CONF:** Thtr 45 Class 20 Board 30 **PARKING:** 48
**NOTES:** No smoking in restaurant **CARDS:**

## MARLOW, Buckinghamshire — Map 04 SU88

### ★★★★73% Danesfield House

Henley Rd SL7 2EY
☎ 01628 891010 01628 890408
e-mail: sales@danesfieldhouse.co.uk
***Dir:*** *2m from Marlow on A4155 towards Henley*

Set in sixty-five acres of landscaped grounds, the hotel enjoys stunning views. The spacious bedrooms are furnished and decorated to a high standard and boast a comprehensive range of facilities. The public areas are no less impressive, the Great Hall is almost cathedral-like and the panelled Oak Room Restaurant is a good setting for fine dining. The Orangery offers a less formal dining option with lovely views over the Thames.

**ROOMS:** 87 en suite (3 fmly) No smoking in 5 bedrooms s £175-£275; d £205-£300 (incl. bkfst) * **LB** **FACILITIES:** STV Indoor swimming (H) Outdoor swimming (H) Tennis (hard) Snooker Sauna Solarium Gym Croquet lawn Putting green Jacuzzi Jogging trail,Fitness centre,Steam room,Hydrotherapy room entertainment Xmas **CONF:** Thtr 100 Class 60 Board 50 **SERVICES:** Lift **PARKING:** 100 **NOTES:** No dogs (ex guide dogs) No smoking in restaurant Civ Wed 100
**CARDS:**

*See advert on opposite page*

### ★★★★71% The Compleat Angler
Marlow Bridge SL7 1RG
☎ 0870 400 8100 01628 486388
***Dir:*** *from M40 junct 4 follow A404 to Bisham rdbt, right through Bisham Village. Hotel is on right before Marlow Bridge*

This well-established hotel enjoys an enviable position on the Thames overlooking Marlow Weir. Bedrooms, which come in various shapes and sizes, are all tastefully appointed and thoughtfully equipped. Guests can choose from two eating options including the award winning cuisine of the Riverside Restaurant.

**ROOMS:** 64 en suite (20 fmly) No smoking in 23 bedrooms s fr £215; d fr £235 * **LB** **FACILITIES:** STV Fishing Croquet lawn Boating entertainment Xmas **CONF:** Thtr 120 Class 60 Board 45 Del from £250 * **SERVICES:** Lift **PARKING:** 100 **NOTES:** Civ Wed 120
**CARDS:**

*See advert on opposite page*

MARSTON MORETAINE, Bedfordshire Map 04 SP94

**Travelodge**

Travelodge

Beancroft Rd Junction MK43 0PZ
☎ 01234 766755 📠 01234 766755
**Dir:** *on A421, northbound*

Travelodge offers good quality, good value, modern accommodation. Ideal for families, the spacious, en suite bedrooms include remote-control TV, tea and coffee-making facilities, luxury beds and free morning newspaper. Meals can be taken at the nearby family restaurant. For further details and the Travelodge phone number, consult the Hotel Groups page.

**ROOMS:** 32 en suite

MARSTON TRUSSELL, Northamptonshire Map 04 SP68

★★71% **The Sun Inn**

Main St LE16 9TY
☎ 01858 465531 📠 01858 433155
e-mail: manager@suninn.com
**Dir:** *from M1 junct 20 take A4304. After Theddingworth, right to Marston Trussell (looks like a layby). Hotel on right of Main St*

This pleasant inn successfully combines a mixture of modern facilities and accommodation with the classical traditions of the rural English inn. There are two separate dining areas, including a popular restaurant, and a locally popular bar; friendly informal service. Bedrooms, recently refurbished to a good standard, are comfortable and well-appointed; good modern bathrooms.

**ROOMS:** 20 en suite (3 fmly) No smoking in 10 bedrooms d £69 (incl. bkfst) * **LB FACILITIES:** Fishing Rambling trails Xmas **CONF:** Thtr 60 Class 40 Board 28 Del £85 * **PARKING:** 60
**CARDS:**

MARTINHOE, Devon Map 03 SS64

**★★73% ® The Old Rectory**
EX31 4QT
☎ 01598 763368 ▤ 01598 763567
e-mail: reception@oldrectoryhotel.co.uk
***Dir:*** *exit M5 jnct 27 onto A361, right onto A399 Blackmoor Gate, right onto A39 bypass Parracombe, take 2nd left to Martinhoe & follow signs*
An ideal base for exploring Exmoor, within 500 yards of the coastal footpath. In addition to the comfortable lounge, guests can relax in the vinery, overlooking the delightful gardens. Interesting menus are served in the spacious dining room. Each bedroom is tastefully decorated, two are on the ground floor and there are also two self-catering cottages.
**ROOMS:** 8 en suite No smoking in all bedrooms s £73-£86; d £124-£150 (incl. bkfst & dinner) * **LB** **PARKING:** 8 **NOTES:** No dogs No children 14yrs No smoking in restaurant Closed Dec-Feb RS Mar & Nov (weekends only) **CARDS:**

MARTOCK, Somerset Map 03 ST41

**★★★71% The Hollies**
Bower Hinton TA12 6LG
☎ 01935 822232 ▤ 01935 822249
e-mail: theholllieshotel@ukonline.co.uk
***Dir:*** *on B3165 S of town centre just off A303*
Within easy access of the A303, the bar and restaurant of this popular venue are housed in an attractive 17th-century farmhouse. Bar meals are available in addition to the interesting carte menu. Located at the rear of the property in a purpose-built wing, the spacious, well-equipped bedrooms include both suites and mini-suites.
**ROOMS:** 32 annexe en suite (2 fmly) No smoking in 4 bedrooms s £60-£95; d £75-£110 (incl. bkfst) * **LB** **FACILITIES:** STV ch fac **CONF:** Thtr 150 Class 80 Board 60 Del from £100 * **PARKING:** 80 **NOTES:** No dogs (ex guide dogs) No smoking in restaurant RS Xmas & New Year
**CARDS:**

MASHAM, North Yorkshire Map 08 SE28

**★★★★76% ®® Swinton Park**
HG4 4JH
☎ 01765 680900 ▤ 01765 680901
e-mail: enquiries@swintonpark.com
***Dir:*** *turn off A1 onto B6207 signed Masham/Thirsk. Follow into Masham, pass Market Square, right onto Swinton Terrace and follow road for 1m*

This historic castle, dating back as far as 1695, has been in the Cunliffe-Lister family since 1882. It has been carefully transformed and restored into a luxurious country house hotel sitting in extensive parklands with its own ornamental lake. Spacious bedrooms and public areas are beautifully appointed and thoughtfully equipped to the highest standard. Carefully prepared meals served in the delightful south facing dining room are a highlight.
**ROOMS:** 20 en suite s £95-£350; d £95-£350 (incl. bkfst) * **LB**
**FACILITIES:** STV Fishing Riding Snooker Gym Croquet lawn Jacuzzi Shooting Falconry Pony Trekking Xmas **CONF:** Thtr 100 Class 50 Board 40 Del £170 * **SERVICES:** Lift **PARKING:** 50 **NOTES:** No smoking in restaurant **CARDS:**

**★★68% *The Kings Head***
Market Place HG4 4EF
☎ 01765 689295 ▤ 01765 689070
***Dir:*** *off the A6108 Ripon to Leyburn Rd in centre of village*
SCOTTISH NEWCASTLE hotels
This historic, stone-built hotel, with its uneven floors, beamed bars and attractive window boxes, looks out over the large Market Square. Bedrooms are elegantly furnished, thoughtfully equipped and continue to reflect the high standards of a recent refurbishment. Public areas have also been extensively upgraded and include a popular bar and smartly appointed restaurant.
**ROOMS:** 10 en suite **CONF:** Thtr 40 Class 20 Board 20 **NOTES:** No dogs (ex guide dogs) **CARDS:**

MATFEN, Northumberland Map 12 NZ07

**★★★70% Matfen Hall**
NE20 0RH
☎ 01661 886500 ▤ 01661 886055
e-mail: info@matfenhall.com
***Dir:*** *Turn off A69 to B6318. Hotel is situated just before the village*
This fine mansion house is set amidst landscaped parkland. Bedrooms vary from the standard to the luxurious and comfortable superior rooms. Apart from the golfers' bar, there is a splendid drawing room and library restaurant, both boasting carved wood fire surrounds and interesting plaster relief ceilings.
**ROOMS:** 31 en suite (5 fmly) No smoking in 18 bedrooms s £60-£95; d £80-£120 (incl. bkfst) * **FACILITIES:** STV Golf 18 Putting green ch fac Xmas **CONF:** Thtr 100 Class 60 Board 40 Del £120 * **PARKING:** 150 **NOTES:** No smoking in restaurant Civ Wed 120
**CARDS:**

MATLOCK, Derbyshire Map 08 SK36

**★★★75% ®® Riber Hall**
DE4 5JU
☎ 01629 582795 ▤ 01629 580475
e-mail: info@riber-hall.co.uk
***Dir:*** *1m off A615 at Tansley*

This charming Elizabethan manor house sits in tranquil countryside high above Matlock. Public rooms are all tastefully appointed with period furnishings, and a new lounge has further

continued

enhanced the levels of comfort. The interesting menus are complemented by an excellent wine list. Individual and beautifully furnished bedrooms have oak four-poster beds and comfortable sitting areas.
**ROOMS:** 3 en suite 11 annexe en suite No smoking in 4 bedrooms s £97-£112; d £127-£170 (incl. cont bkfst) * **LB** **FACILITIES:** STV Tennis (hard) Croquet lawn **CONF:** Thtr 20 Class 20 Board 20 Del from £148 * **PARKING:** 50 **NOTES:** No children 10yrs No smoking in restaurant Civ Wed 45 **CARDS:**

### ★★★71% New Bath
New Bath Rd DE4 3PX
☎ 0870 400 8119 📠 01629 580268
e-mail: HeritageHotels_Bath.Matlock.New_Bath@forte-hotels.com
***Dir:*** *M1 junct 28 to Alfreton follow signs for Matlock and then Matlock Bath. Hotel is on the A6 just after Matlock Bath on the right*
Set in five acres of grounds in the beautiful Derwent Gorge, the hotel has indoor and outdoor pools fed by natural thermal springs. The medicinal properties of the springs were first recognised in Regency times and the original building on the site was built to take advantage of them. Bedrooms are tastefully furnished and decorated, two rooms have four-poster beds, and some have balconies.
**ROOMS:** 55 en suite (5 fmly) No smoking in 11 bedrooms s £100-£110; d £120-£150 * **LB** **FACILITIES:** Indoor swimming (H) Outdoor swimming Tennis (hard) Sauna Solarium Xmas **CONF:** Thtr 180 Class 60 Board 50 Del from £110 * **PARKING:** 200 **NOTES:** No smoking in restaurant Civ Wed 50 **CARDS:**

### ★★74% Red House
Old Rd, Darley Dale DE4 2ER
☎ 01629 734854 📠 01629 734885
e-mail: redhouse@aol.com
***Dir:*** *just off A6 onto Old Road signposted Carriage Museum, 2.5m N of Matlock*

A peaceful country retreat set in lovely gardens just outside Matlock. Rich colour schemes are used to excellent effect throughout. Well-equipped bedrooms include three ground floor rooms in the adjacent coach house. A comfortable lounge with delightful rural views is available for refreshments and pre-dinner drinks; service is friendly and attentive. Attractively presented meals are served in the dining room.
**ROOMS:** 7 en suite 3 annexe en suite (1 fmly) No smoking in 8 bedrooms s £63; d £85 (incl. bkfst) * **LB** **FACILITIES:** Xmas **CONF:** Class 60 Board 12 Del from £80 * **PARKING:** 15 **NOTES:** No dogs (ex guide dogs) No smoking in restaurant
**CARDS:**

## MAWGAN PORTH, Cornwall & Isles of Scilly Map 02 SW86

### ★★68% *Tredragon*
TR8 4DQ
☎ 01637 860213 📠 01637 860269
e-mail: tredragon@btinternet.com

TREDRAGON HOTEL
MAWGAN PORTH
Nr. NEWQUAY, CORNWALL
Telephone St. Mawgan (0637) 860213

The Tredragon enjoys panoramic views over the sea to the hills beyond, and has been run by the same family for many years. Bedrooms vary in size and style, and in the hotel's dining room, guests can enjoy a variety of home-cooked dishes. Special residential courses are arranged, including lace-making, cooking and painting.
**ROOMS:** 26 en suite (15 fmly) **FACILITIES:** Indoor swimming (H) Sauna Solarium ch fac **CONF:** Thtr 50 Class 40 Board 30 **PARKING:** 30 **NOTES:** No smoking in restaurant **CARDS:**

## MAWNAN SMITH, Cornwall & Isles of Scilly Map 02 SW72

### ★★★★72% Budock Vean - The Hotel on the River
TR11 5LG
☎ 01326 252100 & Freephone 0800 833927 📠 01326 250892
e-mail: relax@budockvean.co.uk
***Dir:*** *from A39 Truro/Falmouth road follow the brown tourist info signs to Trebah Gdns, then continue for 0.5m to the hotel*

Peacefully located in 65 acres of mature grounds beside the River Helford, this impressive hotel is the ideal venue for rest and relaxation. Extensive leisure facilities are offered in addition to the modern health spa centre. Most bedrooms benefit from views over the verdant valley and golf course.
**ROOMS:** 58 en suite (4 fmly) No smoking in 6 bedrooms s £52-£89; d £104-£178 (incl. bkfst & dinner) * **LB** **FACILITIES:** Spa STV Indoor swimming (H) Golf 9 Tennis (hard) Fishing Snooker Putting green entertainment ch fac Xmas **CONF:** Thtr 100 Class 100 Board 80 Del from £87 * **SERVICES:** Lift **PARKING:** 100 **NOTES:** No smoking in restaurant Civ Wed 100 **CARDS:**

MAWNAN SMITH, continued

★★★76% **Meudon**
TR11 5HT
☎ 01326 250541 📠 01326 250543
e-mail: info@meudon.co.uk
***Dir:*** *leave A39 at Hillhead rdbt and follow signs to Maenporth beach, Meudon on left one mile after beach*

This late-Victorian mansion boasts over nine acres of grounds, including lush sub-tropical gardens, which lead down to Bream Cove. A relaxed atmosphere and warm welcome are assured. Public rooms include a choice of lounges and an intimate bar. Bedrooms are spacious, offering comfort and quality in equal measures. The conservatory restaurant overlooks the glorious gardens and offers a fixed-price dinner.
**ROOMS:** 29 en suite (2 fmly) s £95-£105; d £190-£200 (incl. bkfst & dinner) * **LB** **FACILITIES:** **Spa** Fishing Riding Private beach Hair salon Subtrop gdns ch fac Xmas **CONF:** Thtr 30 Class 20 Board 15 **SERVICES:** Lift **PARKING:** 52 **NOTES:** No smoking in restaurant Closed 4 Jan-1 Feb **CARDS:**

*See advert under FALMOUTH*

★★★68% ◎◎ ***Trelawne***
TR11 5HS
☎ 01326 250226 📠 01326 250909
***Dir:*** *A39 towards Falmouth, right at Hillhead rdbt take exit signed Maenporth past beach and up the hill, hotel on left overlooking Falmouth Bay*

The Trelawne is surrounded by attractive lawns and gardens from which superb coastal views can be enjoyed. An informal atmosphere prevails, and many guests return year after year. The hotel provides neat and well-equipped bedrooms and comfortable public areas. Dinner features quality local produce in imaginative dishes.
**ROOMS:** 14 en suite (2 fmly) **FACILITIES:** Indoor swimming (H) **PARKING:** 20 **NOTES:** No smoking in restaurant Closed 23 Dec-12 Feb **CARDS:**

*See advert under FALMOUTH*

MELKSHAM, Wiltshire Map 03 ST96

★★68% ◎ **Shaw Country**
Bath Rd, Shaw SN12 8EF
☎ 01225 702836 & 790321 📠 01225 790275
e-mail: info@shawcountryhotel.fsnet.co.uk
***Dir:*** *1m from Melksham, 9m from Bath on A365*
Situated in an Area of Outstanding Natural Beauty, within easy driving distance of Bath and the M4, Shaw Country Hotel provides a warm welcome and very well-equipped, comfortable bedrooms. There is a residents' lounge and bar and the Mulberry Restaurant offers a good choice of well-cooked dishes. Friendly staff are always on hand to help.
**ROOMS:** 13 en suite (2 fmly) s £46-£54; d £66-£85 (incl. bkfst) * **LB** **FACILITIES:** Jacuzzi ch fac **CONF:** Thtr 30 Class 20 Board 15 **PARKING:** 30 **NOTES:** No smoking in restaurant Closed 26-27 Dec **CARDS:**

*See advert under BATH*

★★63% ***Conigre Farm Hotel***
Semington Rd SN12 6BZ
☎ 01225 702229 📠 01225 707392
e-mail: enq@cfhotel.co.uk
***Dir:*** *Turn off A350 onto Semington Road, hotel is 0.5m on left after fire station*

Conigre
Farm
Hotel

The varied restaurant menu with much emphasis on fresh ingredients plays an important part in the enjoyment of any stay at this stone-built 17th-century former farmhouse. Bedrooms are well-equipped and include some welcome extras. In addition to a small lounge with bar, there is a pleasant and comfortably furnished Victorian conservatory.
**ROOMS:** 3 en suite 5 annexe en suite (1 fmly) No smoking in 4 bedrooms **FACILITIES:** STV **CONF:** Thtr 45 Board 25 **PARKING:** 15 **NOTES:** No smoking in restaurant **CARDS:**

MELTON MOWBRAY, Leicestershire Map 08 SK71

## *Premier Collection*

★★★★ ◎◎ **Stapleford Park**
Stapleford LE14 2EF
☎ 01572 787522 📠 01572 787651
e-mail: reservations@stapleford.co.uk
***Dir:*** *1m SW of B676 4m E of Melton Mowbray and 9m W of Colsterworth*
Set in 500 acres of parkland and woods, Stapleford Park overlooks a tranquil lake. The house dates back to the 14th century, with later additions. Main reception rooms are sumptuously decorated and furnished in grand country-house style. The dining room features carvings by Grinling Gibbons and makes a fine setting for the daily-changing menu.

*continued*

Bedrooms are very individual, stylish and thoughtfully equipped. Leisure activities include therapy rooms, Clarins spa and a championship golf course.

**ROOMS:** 44 en suite 7 annexe en suite No smoking in 44 bedrooms s £206-£595; d £206-£595 (incl. bkfst) * **FACILITIES:** Spa STV Indoor swimming (H) Golf 18 Tennis (hard) Fishing Riding Sauna Solarium Gym Croquet lawn Putting green Jacuzzi Shooting Falconry Archery Petanque entertainment ch fac Xmas **CONF:** Thtr 200 Class 140 Board 80 Del from £225 * **SERVICES:** Lift **PARKING:** 120 **NOTES:** No smoking in restaurant Civ Wed 150
**CARDS:**

★★★69% **Sysonby Knoll**
Asfordby Rd LE13 0HP
☎ 01664 563563 📠 01664 410364
e-mail: sysonby.knoll@btinternet.com
***Dir:*** *0.5m from town centre beside A6006*
Situated just on the outskirts of Melton Mowbray, this Edwardian country house is set in beautiful grounds leading to the River Eye. Bedrooms are attractively furnished with a good range of facilities. The charming bar, restaurant and conservatory are the focal point, serving good food.
**ROOMS:** 23 en suite 1 annexe en suite (1 fmly) s £51-£61; d £65-£78 (incl. bkfst) * LB **FACILITIES:** STV Outdoor swimming Fishing Croquet lawn **CONF:** Thtr 30 Class 16 Board 24 **PARKING:** 40 **NOTES:** No smoking in restaurant Closed 25 Dec-1 Jan
**CARDS:**

*See advert on this page*

★★★64% **Quorn Lodge**
46 Asfordby Rd LE13 0HR
☎ 01664 566660 & 562590 📠 01664 480660
e-mail: quornlodge@aol.com
***Dir:*** *from town centre take A6006, hotel 300yds from junct of A606/A607 on right*
Popular for its friendly and welcoming atmosphere, this appealing hotel was originally a hunting lodge. Bedrooms are individually decorated and thoughtfully designed. The public rooms offer an

*continued on p412*

MELTON MOWBRAY, continued

elegant restaurant, a cosy lounge bar and a modern function suite. High standards are maintained throughout.

*Quorn Lodge, Melton Mowbray*

**ROOMS:** 19 en suite (2 fmly) No smoking in 11 bedrooms s £46-£53.50; d £62-£75 (incl. bkfst) * **LB** **FACILITIES:** STV **CONF:** Thtr 90 Class 60 Board 85 Del from £86 * **PARKING:** 33 **NOTES:** No dogs No smoking in restaurant **CARDS:**

★★65% **Harboro Hotel**
49 Burton St LE13 1AF
☎ 01664 560121 📠 01664 564296
***Dir:*** *in town centre between church and railway station on A606 Oakham road*

HARBORO HOTEL

Just a short walk from the town centre, this well established hotel provides friendly service and sound accommodation. Bedrooms vary in size and style, with a good selection of furnishings and facilities. The public rooms are relaxed and informal, with a range of meals available in the lounge bar or more formal restaurant.
**ROOMS:** 27 en suite (3 fmly) No smoking in 4 bedrooms s £50; d £60 (incl. bkfst) * **LB** **FACILITIES:** Xmas **CONF:** Thtr 35 Board 15 **PARKING:** 50 **CARDS:**

MEMBURY MOTORWAY SERVICE AREA (M4), Berkshire — Map 04 SU37

⌂ **Days Inn**
Membury Service Area RG17 7TZ
☎ 01488 72336 📠 01488 72336
e-mail: membury.hotel@welcomebreak.co.uk
***Dir:*** *M4 between junct 14 & 15 westbound*
This modern building offers accommodation in smart, spacious and well-equipped bedrooms, suitable for families and business travellers, and all with en suite bathrooms. Continental breakfast is available and other refreshments may be taken at the nearby family restaurant. For further details and the Days Inn phone number, consult the Hotel Groups page.
**ROOMS:** 38 en suite s fr £49; d fr £49 * **CONF:** Thtr 10 Class 10 Board 10

MERIDEN, West Midlands — Map 04 SP28

★★★★72% **Marriott Forest of Arden Hotel & Country Club**
Maxstoke Ln CV7 7HR
☎ 01676 522335 📠 01676 523711
***Dir:*** *M42 junct 6 onto A45 towards Coventry straight on at Stonebridge flyover, after 0.75m turn left into Shepherds Lane, hotel 1.5m on left*

The ancient oaks, rolling hills and natural lakes of the 10,000 acre Forest of Arden estate provide an idyllic backdrop for this modern hotel and country club. The hotel boasts an excellent range of leisure facilities and is regarded as one of the finest golfing destinations in the UK. Bedrooms provide every modern convenience and a full range of facilities.
**ROOMS:** 214 en suite (4 fmly) No smoking in 135 bedrooms s £132-£199; d £132-£199 * **LB** **FACILITIES:** STV Indoor swimming (H) Golf 18 Tennis (hard) Fishing Sauna Solarium Gym Croquet lawn Putting green Jacuzzi Health & Beauty salon Xmas **CONF:** Thtr 360 Class 200 Board 40 Del from £175 * **SERVICES:** Lift air con **PARKING:** 300 **NOTES:** No smoking in restaurant Civ Wed 150
**CARDS:**

★★★74% **Manor**
Main Rd CV7 7NH
☎ 01676 522735 📠 01676 522186
e-mail: reservations@manorhotelmeriden.co.uk
***Dir:*** *from M42 junct 6, take A45 towards Coventry, after approx 2m cross dual carriageway onto B4104 for Meriden. Straight ahead at mini-rdbt*
A sympathetically extended Georgian manor in the heart of this sleepy village. The Regency Restaurant offers modern dishes, while the Triumph Buttery serves lighter meals and snacks. Bedroom styles vary considerably; the delightful Executive rooms are very smart and well-equipped. The service is provided by professional, friendly and attentive staff.
**ROOMS:** 114 en suite No smoking in 54 bedrooms s £75-£155; d £85-£165 (incl. bkfst) * **LB** **CONF:** Thtr 250 Class 150 Board 60 Del from £95 * **SERVICES:** Lift **PARKING:** 200 **NOTES:** No smoking in restaurant
**CARDS:**

MEVAGISSEY, Cornwall & Isles of Scilly — Map 02 SX04

★★71% **Tremarne**
Polkirt PL26 6UY
☎ 01726 842213 📠 01726 843420
e-mail: tremarne@talk21.com
***Dir:*** *from A390 at St Austell take B3273 to Mevagissey, follow Portmellon signs through Mevagissey, at top of Polkirt Hill turn right*
On the edge of the village, this relaxing, comfortable hotel is an ideal choice for those looking to unwind. Many of the thoughtfully equipped bedrooms have extensive views across the countryside to the sea beyond. Enjoy a drink in the lounge beside the

*continued*

flickering wood burner before moving through to sample the accomplished cuisine in the restaurant.
**ROOMS:** 14 en suite (2 fmly) No smoking in all bedrooms s £33-£38; d £62-£72 (incl. bkfst) * **LB FACILITIES:** Outdoor swimming (H) Xmas **PARKING:** 14 **NOTES:** No smoking in restaurant Closed 28-29 Dec **CARDS:**

★★66% **Spa Hotel**
Polkirt Hill PL26 6UY
☎ 01726 842244 ⎙ 01726 842244
e-mail: Alan@the-spa-hotel.fsnet.co.uk
***Dir:*** *From St Austell follow signs for Mevagissey then signs to Portmellon, sign for Spa Hotel on right*
In an elevated position, the Spa enjoys wonderful coastal views. There is a wide choice of bedroom size; all are light, airy and colourful, and some have patio areas leading onto well-tended gardens. A comfortable, cane-furnished lounge and a cosy bar are provided.
**ROOMS:** 11 en suite (5 fmly) No smoking in 7 bedrooms s £25-£32; d £50-£60 (incl. bkfst) * **LB FACILITIES:** Putting green ch fac **PARKING:** 12 **NOTES:** No smoking in restaurant **CARDS:**

## MICHAEL WOOD MOTORWAY SERVICE AREA (M5), Gloucestershire — Map 03 ST79

⇧ **Days Inn**
Lower Wick, Michaelwood Service Area GL11 6DD
☎ 01454 261513 ⎙ 01454 269150
e-mail: michaelwood.hotel@welcomebreak.co.uk
***Dir:*** *M5 northbound between junct 13 & 14*
This modern building offers accommodation in smart, spacious and well-equipped bedrooms, suitable for families and business travellers, and all with en suite bathrooms. Continental breakfast is available and other refreshments may be taken at the nearby family restaurant. For further details and the Days Inn phone number, consult the Hotel Groups page.
**ROOMS:** 38 en suite s £45-£50; d £45-£50 * **CONF:** Class 10 Board 10

## MIDDLEHAM, North Yorkshire — Map 07 SE18

★★64% ***The White Swan***
Market Place DL8 4PE
☎ 01969 622093 ⎙ 01969 624551
e-mail: whiteswan@easynet.co.uk
***Dir:*** *exit A1 at Leeming Bar, take A684 to Leyburn, before Leyburn Centre take A6108 to Ripon, Middleham is 1.5m from this junct, in the Market Place*
This charming country inn has a reputation for its cosmopolitan cuisine and endearing, traditional values. Appealing bedrooms are well-equipped and smartly decorated with many thoughtful touches. An open wood burning stove welcomes you to the bar, and service throughout the hotel is very friendly.
**ROOMS:** 11 en suite (2 fmly) **PARKING:** 5
**CARDS:**

★79% ***Waterford House***
Kirkgate DL8 4PG
☎ 01969 622090 ⎙ 01969 624020
***Dir:*** *A1 to B6267 via Masham to Middleham. Hotel in right corner of Market Sq or A1 to Scotch Corner via Richmond & Leyburn to Middleham, Hotel at hilltop*
This delightful restaurant with rooms, furnished with antiques, china and silver, has a warm, restful atmosphere. Individually styled bedrooms are furnished with period and antique pieces and are equipped with a thoughtful range of extras such as complimentary sherry and homemade shortbread. Fine cooking is complemented by a carefully selected extensive wine list.
**ROOMS:** 5 en suite **FACILITIES:** ch fac **PARKING:** 8 **NOTES:** No smoking in restaurant Civ Wed 24 **CARDS:**

## MIDDLETON, Greater Manchester — Map 07 SD80

⇧ ***Premier Lodge (Manchester North)***
818 Manchester Old Rd, Rhodes M24 4RF
☎ 0870 700 1474 ⎙ 0870 700 1475
Premier Lodge offers modern, well-equipped, en suite accommodation suitable for both business and leisure travellers. Meals can be taken at the adjacent popular restaurant and bar, which is fully licensed. For further details, consult the Hotel Groups page.
**ROOMS:** 42 en suite

## MIDDLETON STONEY, Oxfordshire — Map 04 SP52

★★70% **Jersey Arms**
OX6 8SE
☎ 01869 343234 & 343505 ⎙ 01869 343565
e-mail: jerseyarms@bestwestern.co.uk
***Dir:*** *on the B430 10m N of Oxford, between junct 9 & 10 of M40*
This family-run hotel close to Bicester and the M40 is a former coaching inn with a long tradition of hospitality. Bedrooms are either in the main house or in buildings round the courtyard. The cosy bar is full of village atmosphere and meals may be taken here or in the more formal setting of the restaurant.
**ROOMS:** 6 en suite 14 annexe en suite (3 fmly) s fr £79; d fr £92 (incl. bkfst) * **LB FACILITIES:** Xmas **CONF:** Board 12 Del from £115 * **PARKING:** 55 **NOTES:** No dogs (ex guide dogs) No smoking in restaurant **CARDS:**

## MIDDLE WALLOP, Hampshire — Map 04 SU23

★★★70% **Fifehead Manor**
SO20 8EG
☎ 01264 781565 ⎙ 01264 781400
e-mail: fifeheadmanorhotel@ukonline.co.uk
***Dir:*** *from M3 exit at junct 8 onto A303 to Andover, then take A343 S for 6m to Middle Wallop*
This 11th-century manor house retains many of its original features. Bedrooms are comfortably furnished, well-equipped and feature many thoughtful touches. Public areas include a well-stocked bar, elegant lounge and charming restaurant, which offers a high standard of cuisine. Service is attentive from the friendly team of staff.
**ROOMS:** 8 en suite 8 annexe en suite s £70-£90; d £110-£150 (incl. bkfst) * **FACILITIES:** STV Croquet lawn ch fac **CONF:** Thtr 40 Class 20 Board 24 Del from £137 * **PARKING:** 40 **NOTES:** No dogs (ex guide dogs) No smoking in restaurant Civ Wed 120
**CARDS:**

*See advert under ANDOVER*

## MIDDLEWICH, Cheshire — Map 07 SJ76

⇧ ***Travelodge***
M6 Junction 18, A54 CW10 0JZ
☎ 08700 850950
Travelodge offers good quality, good value, modern accommodation. Ideal for families, the spacious, en suite bedrooms include remote-control TV, tea and coffee-making

*continued on p414*

MIDDLEWICH, continued

facilities, luxury beds and free morning newspaper. Meals can be taken at the nearby family restaurant. For further details and the Travelodge phone number, consult the Hotel Groups page.

**ROOMS:** 32 en suite

MIDHURST, West Sussex — Map 04 SU82

### ★★★70% Southdowns Country

Dumpford Ln, Trotton GU31 5JN
☎ 01730 821521 01730 821790
e-mail: reception@southdownshotel.freeserve.co.uk
***Dir:*** *on A272, after town turn left at Keepers Arms*

In peaceful rural surroundings, this hotel offers good conference and meeting facilities and is a popular wedding venue. Most bedrooms have lovely views over the countryside and all are tastefully furnished and decorated. The Tudor bar offers a good selection of snacks and light meals, and the restaurant offers more substantial fare.
**ROOMS:** 20 en suite (2 fmly) No smoking in 4 bedrooms s £70-£90; d £80-£120 (incl. bkfst) * LB **FACILITIES:** Indoor swimming (H) Tennis (hard) Sauna Solarium Croquet lawn Exercise equipment Xmas **CONF:** Thtr 100 Class 30 Board 30 Del from £85 * **PARKING:** 70 **NOTES:** No children 10yrs No smoking in restaurant Civ Wed 100
**CARDS:**

*See advert under PETERSFIELD*

MIDSOMER NORTON, Somerset — Map 03 ST65

### ★★★70% Centurion

Charlton Ln BA3 4BD
☎ 01761 417711 01761 418357
e-mail: enquiries@centurionhotel.co.uk
***Dir:*** *off A367, 10m S of Bath*

This family-run hotel incorporates the adjacent Fosseway Country Club with its nine-hole golf course and other extensive leisure amenities. Comfortable bedrooms are equipped and furnished to a high standard with co-ordinating fabrics. Public areas include a choice of bars, an attractive lounge and a range of meeting/function rooms.
**ROOMS:** 44 en suite (4 fmly) s fr £62; d fr £80 (incl. bkfst) * LB **FACILITIES:** STV Indoor swimming (H) Golf 9 Sauna Gym Jacuzzi Bowling green Sports field **CONF:** Thtr 180 Class 70 Board 50 Del from £100 * **PARKING:** 100 **NOTES:** No dogs (ex guide dogs) No smoking in restaurant Closed 24-26 Dec Civ Wed 80
**CARDS:**

MILDENHALL, Suffolk — Map 05 TL77

### ★★★76% Riverside

Mill St IP28 7DP
☎ 01638 717274 01638 715997
e-mail: bookings@riverside-hotel.net
***Dir:*** *from A11 at Fiveways rdbt take A1101 in Mildenhall Town. Turn left at mini-rdbt along High St, hotel is last building on left before bridge*
An imposing 18th-century red brick building situated on the banks of the River Lark. The public rooms feature a restaurant, which overlooks the river and attractive gardens to the rear. The recently refurbished bedrooms vary in size and style.
**ROOMS:** 18 en suite 11 annexe en suite (4 fmly) s £65-£110; d £88-£150 (incl. bkfst) * LB **FACILITIES:** Spa Fishing Sauna Gym Jacuzzi entertainment ch fac Xmas **CONF:** Thtr 150 Class 60 Board 40 Del from £78 * **SERVICES:** Lift **PARKING:** 60 **NOTES:** Civ Wed 150
**CARDS:**

### ★★★64% The Smoke House

Beck Row IP28 8DH
☎ 01638 713223 01638 712202
e-mail: enquiries@smoke-house.co.uk
***Dir:*** *A1101 into Mildenhall, follow Beck Row signs. Hotel located immediately after mini-rdbt through Beck Row on right-hand side*

This busy complex is popular with tour parties and visitors to the nearby airbases, it has a shopping mall and conference centre. Public areas owe their character to 16th century origins, with open log fires, beams and exposed brickwork. There are two bars and a choice of dining options. The accommodation is mainly based around modern wings of well-proportioned bedrooms.
**ROOMS:** 94 en suite 2 annexe en suite s £95-£135; d £120-£165 (incl. bkfst) * LB **FACILITIES:** entertainment Xmas **CONF:** Thtr 120 Class 80 Board 50 Del £98 * **PARKING:** 100 **NOTES:** No dogs (ex guide dogs) No smoking in restaurant **CARDS:**

*See advert on opposite page*

Arriving late? Four and five star hotels have night porters to assist with your luggage, and 24-hour room service.

MILFORD ON SEA, Hampshire Map 04 SZ29

**★★★80% Westover Hall**
Park Ln SO41 0PT
☎ 01590 643044 01590 644490
e-mail: westoverhallhotel@barclays.net
***Dir:*** *M3/M27 W A337 to Lymington. Follow signs from Lymington to Milford-on-Sea, (B3058) hotel is just outside village centre towards cliff*

This late-Victorian mansion has uninterrupted views across Christchurch Bay and is just a few moments walk from the beach. Architectural delights include dramatic stained-glass windows, extensive oak panelling and a galleried entrance hall, and bedrooms have been decorated with great panache and originality. Meals are prepared with skill, and hospitality is relaxed yet attentive.
**ROOMS:** 14 en suite (1 fmly) s £65-£70; d £120-£160 (incl. bkfst) * **LB**
**FACILITIES:** Beach Hut Xmas **CONF:** Thtr 50 Class 30 Board 25
**PARKING:** 50 **NOTES:** No smoking in restaurant Civ Wed 50
**CARDS:**

*See advert under LYMINGTON*

**★★★72% South Lawn**
Lymington Rd SO41 0RF
☎ 01590 643911 01590 644820
e-mail: enquiries@southlawn.co.uk
***Dir:*** *turn left off A337 at Everton onto B3058. Hotel approx 0.5m on right*

Owned by the same family since 1970, this former dower house offers good service provided by friendly staff. The hotel is situated close to the sea and is set in four acres of very well-tended grounds. Bedrooms are spacious and attractively decorated. The bright dining room serves a good range of local produce prepared with care.
**ROOMS:** 24 en suite No smoking in all bedrooms s £45-£65; d £80-£120 (incl. bkfst) * **LB** **FACILITIES:** STV **PARKING:** 60 **NOTES:** No dogs No children 7yrs No smoking in restaurant Closed 20 Dec-18 Jan
**CARDS:**

*See advert under LYMINGTON*

MILTON COMMON, Oxfordshire Map 04 SP60

**★★★★72% The Oxford Belfry**
OX9 2JW
MARSTON HOTELS
☎ 01844 279381 01844 279624
e-mail: oxfordbelfry@marstonhotels.com
***Dir:*** *M40 junct 7 - A329 to Thame. Left onto A40 by 3 Pigeons pub. Hotel 300yds on right*
Conveniently placed for the M40, the Oxford Belfry is set in extensive grounds and offers an impressive choice of well-appointed accommodation. Public areas are both smart and inviting and include conference rooms and a leisure club. The spacious restaurant offers an interesting range of carefully prepared dishes.
**ROOMS:** 130 en suite (10 fmly) No smoking in 68 bedrooms s £99-£119; d £120-£160 * **LB** **FACILITIES:** STV Indoor swimming (H) Tennis (hard) Sauna Solarium Gym Croquet lawn ch fac Xmas **CONF:** Thtr 370 Class 220 Board 120 **SERVICES:** Lift **PARKING:** 200 **NOTES:** No dogs (ex guide dogs) No smoking in restaurant Civ Wed 250
**CARDS:**

MILTON KEYNES, Buckinghamshire Map 04 SP83
see also Flitwick

**★★★70% Courtyard by Marriott Milton Keynes**

COURTYARD

London Rd, Newport Pagnell MK16 0JA
☎ 01908 613688 01908 617335
***Dir:*** *0.5m from M1 junct 14 on the A509, towards Newport Pagnell*
Conveniently positioned for the M1, yet in a rural setting, this popular hotel is designed around a handsome three-story Georgian House and a pretty courtyard. Public rooms include a

*continued on p416*

MILTON KEYNES, continued

pretty conservatory restaurant, and a bar and lounge, suitable for casual meetings. All are pleasantly appointed and inviting. Bedrooms are smartly decorated, thoughtfully designed and offer a good range of facilities.

COURTYARD

*Courtyard by Marriott, Milton Keynes*

**ROOMS:** 49 en suite (1 fmly) No smoking in 26 bedrooms **FACILITIES:** STV Gym entertainment **CONF:** Thtr 200 Class 90 Board 50 **PARKING:** 160 **NOTES:** No dogs (ex guide dogs) No smoking in restaurant **CARDS:**

★★★63% ***Posthouse Milton Keynes***
500 Saxon Gate West MK9 2HQ
☎ 0870 400 9057 📠 01908 674714
**Posthouse**
***Dir:*** *M1 junct 14 over 7 roundabouts right at 8th hotel on left*
This large modern hotel is situated in the city centre, and offers opulent public areas, with glass-sided lifts overlooking the lounges and restaurants. Bedrooms are comfortably appointed and include several designed for women; a wing of bedrooms has recently been upgraded.
**ROOMS:** 150 en suite No smoking in 79 bedrooms **FACILITIES:** STV Indoor swimming (H) Sauna Solarium Gym Health & fitness centre entertainment **CONF:** Thtr 150 Class 85 Board 35 **SERVICES:** Lift **PARKING:** 80 **CARDS:**

★★★63% **Quality Hotel & Suites Milton Keynes**
Monks Way, Two Mile Ash MK8 8LY
☎ 01908 561666 📠 01908 568303
e-mail: admin@gb616.u-net.com
***Dir:*** *junct A5/A422*
Bedrooms at this purpose-built hotel are particularly well-equipped, having extra phones and mini-bars. There are also a number of suites with fax machines. All-day room and lounge service are additional eating options to the French-style rôtisserie.
**ROOMS:** 88 en suite (15 fmly) No smoking in 44 bedrooms s £80-£105; d £80-£105 * **LB** **FACILITIES:** **Spa** STV Indoor swimming (H) Sauna Solarium Gym Jacuzzi Steam room Whirlpool spa Xmas **CONF:** Thtr 120 Class 70 Board 50 Del from £125 * **PARKING:** 200 **NOTES:** No dogs (ex guide dogs) No smoking in restaurant Civ Wed 90
**CARDS:**

★★68% **Different Drummer**
94 High St, Stony Stratford MK11 1AH
☎ 01908 564733 📠 01908 260646
This attractive townhouse hotel on historic Stony Stratford's high street offers a warm welcome to its guests. The smart Italian restaurant is a popular dining spot and enjoys a good local reputation. Bedrooms are generally spacious, and the hotel lounge incorporates a bar and is particularly comfortable.

**ROOMS:** 15 en suite 8 annexe en suite (2 fmly) No smoking in 14 bedrooms s £49-£77; d £77-£120 (incl. bkfst) * **NOTES:** No dogs (ex guide dogs) **CARDS:**

★★66% **Swan Revived**
High St, Newport Pagnell MK16 8AR
☎ 01908 610565 📠 01908 210995
e-mail: swanrevived@btinternet.com
***Dir:*** *M1 junct 14, A509 (B526) into Newport Pagnell (2m) Hotel is on the High Street*
This busy coaching inn at the heart of the town offers a relaxing and informal base for leisure or business guests. The popular public bar caters well for the mix of guests. Bedrooms are comfortable.
**ROOMS:** 42 en suite (2 fmly) s £74; d £85 (incl. bkfst) * **LB** **FACILITIES:** STV **CONF:** Thtr 70 Class 30 Board 28 Del from £109 * **SERVICES:** Lift **PARKING:** 18 **NOTES:** No smoking in restaurant RS 25 Dec-1 Jan Civ Wed 75 **CARDS:**

⌂ **Campanile**
40 Penn Rd, Fenny Stratford, Bletchley MK2 2AU
☎ 01908 649819 📠 01908 649818
Campanile
***Dir:*** *M1 junct 14, follow for A4146 to A5. A5 southbound to 1st rdbt take fourth exit to Fenny Stratford. Hotel 500yds on left*

This modern building offers accommodation in smart, well-equipped bedrooms, all with en suite bathrooms. Refreshments may be taken at the informal Bistro. For further details and the Campanile phone number, consult the Hotel Groups page.
**ROOMS:** 80 en suite s £40.95; d £40.95 * **CONF:** Thtr 40 Class 30 Board 25 Del from £68 *

### ⇧ Premier Lodge (Central)

Shirwell Crescent, Furzton MK4 1GA
☎ 0870 700 1494 🖷 0870 700 1495
***Dir:*** *M1 junct 14, follow A509 to central Milton Keynes. Straight over 8th rdbt at 9th 'North Grafton' rdbt turn left onto V6. Right at Leadenhall rdbt onto H7. Over 'The Bowl' rdbt Furzton lake on left*
Premier Lodge offers modern, well-equipped, en suite accommodation suitable for both business and leisure travellers. Meals can be taken at the adjacent popular restaurant and bar, which is fully licensed. For further details, consult the Hotel Groups page.
**ROOMS:** 120 en suite s fr £49.95; d fr £49.95 *

### ⇧ Premier Lodge (Milton Keynes South)

Bletcham Way, Caldecotte MK7 8HP
☎ 0870 700 1492 🖷 0870 700 1493
***Dir:*** *M1 junct 14, A509 towards Milton Keynes. At 1st rdbt, take A4146, left at 2nd rdbt, straight over 3rd rdbt and right at 4th. Lodge located across next rdbt on right*
Premier Lodge offers modern, well-equipped, en suite accommodation suitable for both business and leisure travellers. Meals can be taken at the adjacent popular restaurant and bar, which is fully licensed. For further details, consult the Hotel Groups page.
**ROOMS:** 40 en suite s £49.95; d £49.95 * **CONF:** Board 12

### ⇧ *Travelodge*

109 Grafton Gate MK9 1AL
☎ 08700 850950
Travelodge offers good quality, good value, modern accommodation. Ideal for families, the spacious, en suite bedrooms include remote-control TV, tea and coffee-making facilities, luxury beds and free morning newspaper. Meals can be taken at the nearby family restaurant. For further details and the Travelodge phone number, consult the Hotel Groups page.

**ROOMS:** 80 en suite

### ⇧ Welcome Lodge

Newport Pagnell Service Area MK16 8DS
☎ 01908 610878 🖷 01908 216539
e-mail: newport.hotel@welcomebreak.co.uk
This modern building offers accommodation in smart, spacious and well-equipped bedrooms, suitable for families and business travellers, and all with en suite bathrooms. Refreshments may be taken at the nearby family restaurant. For further details and the Welcome Break phone number, consult the Hotel Groups page.
**ROOMS:** 90 en suite s fr £45; d fr £45 * **CONF:** Thtr 30 Class 12 Board 16

## MINEHEAD, Somerset — Map 03 SS94

### ★★★67% Northfield

Northfield Rd TA24 5PU
☎ 01643 705155 🖷 01643 707715
e-mail: reservations@northfield-hotel.co.uk
***Dir:*** *exit M5 junct 23, follow A38 to Bridgwater & join A39 to Minehead.*
Set in delightfully maintained gardens, this hotel is located near the town centre and seafront. There are a range of comfortable sitting rooms and leisure facilities provided at Northfield Hotel, including a heated indoor swimming pool. A fixed price menu is served every evening in the oak-panelled dining room. The

*continued*



attractively co-ordinated bedrooms vary in size and are equipped to a good standard.
**ROOMS:** 25 en suite (7 fmly) s £51-£59; d £102-£118 (incl. bkfst & dinner) **LB** **FACILITIES:** STV Indoor swimming (H) Gym Putting green Jacuzzi Steam room ch fac Xmas **CONF:** Thtr 70 Class 45 Board 30 **SERVICES:** Lift **PARKING:** 44 **NOTES:** No smoking in restaurant
**CARDS:**

### ★★77% Channel House Hotel

Church Path TA24 5QG
☎ 01643 703229 🖷 01643 708925
e-mail: channel.house@virgin.net
***Dir:*** *from A39, at rdbt turn right to seafront, then left onto promenade, 1st right, then 1st left to Blenheim Gardens 1st right Northfield Road*

Set in two acres of well tended, colourful gardens, this charming and well-run hotel offers relaxing and tranquil surroundings. Many of the exceptionally well-equipped bedrooms have wonderful views, whilst the dining room is the venue for imaginative menus

*continued on p418*

MINEHEAD, continued

using the best of local produce. The South West coastal path starts from the hotel garden.
**ROOMS:** 8 en suite (1 fmly) No smoking in all bedrooms s £74-£84; d £118-£138 (incl. bkfst & dinner) * LB **FACILITIES:** Xmas **SERVICES:** air con **PARKING:** 10 **NOTES:** No dogs No children 10yrs No smoking in restaurant Closed 6 Nov-16 Mar (ex Xmas)
**CARDS:**

*See advert on page 417*

### ★★75% Periton Park
Middlecombe TA24 8SN
☎ 01643 706885 01643 706885
***Dir:*** *on S side of A39 from Minehead*
In wooded grounds on the edge of Exmoor, this delightful country house offers genuine hospitality and relaxed, friendly service. Spacious bedrooms are decorated in rich fabrics, whilst lounges feature deeps sofas for rest and relaxation! The seasonally changing menu offers interesting dishes based on fresh local produce.
**ROOMS:** 8 en suite No smoking in 3 bedrooms s £54-£59.50; d £88-£99 (incl. bkfst) * LB **FACILITIES:** Riding Croquet lawn Xmas **CONF:** Thtr 24 Board 16 Del £95 * **PARKING:** 12 **NOTES:** No children 12yrs No smoking in restaurant Closed Jan **CARDS:**

## MONK FRYSTON, North Yorkshire — Map 08 SE52

### ★★★70% Monk Fryston Hall
LS25 5DU
☎ 01977 682369 01977 683544
e-mail: reception@monkfryston-hotel.com
***Dir:*** *A1/A63 junct towards Selby. Left-hand side in centre of Monk Fryston*
Dating back to the 16th century, this mansion house is quietly situated in 30 acres of grounds yet is only a few minutes from the main motorway network. Bedrooms, most recently refurbished, are comfortable and equipped to meet the needs of business and leisure guests alike. Many original features have been retained in the characterful public areas and traditional home cooking is offered in the light and airy restaurant.
**ROOMS:** 30 en suite (3 fmly) No smoking in 10 bedrooms s £85-£140; d £105-£165 (incl. bkfst) LB **FACILITIES:** STV Riding Croquet lawn Putting green ch fac Xmas **CONF:** Thtr 100 Class 40 Board 30 Del £119 * **PARKING:** 100 **NOTES:** No smoking in restaurant Civ Wed 80
**CARDS:**

## MORCOTT, Rutland — Map 04 SK90

### *Travelodge*
Uppingham LE15 9DL
☎ 01572 747719 01572 747719
***Dir:*** *on A47, eastbound*

Travelodge

Travelodge offers good quality, good value, modern accommodation. Ideal for families, the spacious, en suite bedrooms include remote-control TV, tea and coffee-making facilities, luxury beds and free morning newspaper. Meals can be taken at the nearby family restaurant. For further details and the Travelodge phone number, consult the Hotel Groups page.
**ROOMS:** 40 en suite

## MORDEN, Greater London
See LONDON SECTION plan 1 D1

### *Travelodge*
Epsom Rd SM4 5PH
☎ 020 8640 8227 020 8640 8227
***Dir:*** *on A24*

Travelodge

Travelodge offers good quality, good value, modern accommodation. Ideal for families, the spacious, en suite bedrooms include remote-control TV, tea and coffee-making facilities, luxury beds and free morning newspaper. Meals can be taken at the nearby family restaurant. For further details and the Travelodge phone number, consult the Hotel Groups page.

**ROOMS:** 32 en suite

## MORECAMBE, Lancashire — Map 07 SD46

### ★★★65% Elms
Bare Village LA4 6DD
☎ 01524 411501 01524 831979
Centrally located just off the North Promenade, this well established hotel is popular with business and leisure guests. Bedrooms are smartly presented and there are a number with four-poster beds. Public rooms include a spacious lounge bar, an elegant Victorian-style restaurant and extensive function facilities.
**ROOMS:** 40 en suite (3 fmly) s fr £61; d fr £90 (incl. bkfst) * LB **FACILITIES:** Xmas **CONF:** Thtr 200 Class 72 Board 60 Del from £56 * **SERVICES:** Lift **PARKING:** 80 **NOTES:** No smoking in restaurant Civ Wed 100 **CARDS:**

### ★★★62% Strathmore
East Promenade LA4 5AP
☎ 01524 421234 01524 414242
e-mail: info@strathmore-hotel.co.uk
***Dir:*** *from Lancaster A589 to Morecambe 3rd rdbt follow signs for the Promenade on reaching coast road turn left and hotel on the left*

STRATHMORE
HOTEL

Situated on the promenade, this friendly hotel provides spacious and comfortable public rooms. At the time of going to press, an extensive refurbishment plan was sweeping through the smart bedrooms and stylish public areas. A skilfully prepared range of food is available.
**ROOMS:** 48 en suite (1 fmly) No smoking in 34 bedrooms s £55; d £75 (incl. bkfst) * LB **FACILITIES:** STV ch fac Xmas **CONF:** Thtr 180 Class 100 Board 50 Del £75 * **SERVICES:** Lift **PARKING:** 19 **NOTES:** No dogs (ex guide dogs) No smoking in restaurant Civ Wed 100
**CARDS:**

**★58% Clarendon**
76 Marine Rd West, West End Promenade LA4 4EP
☎ 01524 410180 🖷 01524 421616
***Dir:*** *Exit M6 junct 34 follow signs to Morecambe till large rdbt with the Shrimp pub on the corner, 1st exit to Westgate, stay on road to seafront, right at lights hotel 3rd block along*
This popular resort hotel overlooking the promenade is just a short walk from the local attractions. Public areas include a stylish dining room, a residents' lounge and a popular lounge bar where a good range of food is served. Bedrooms come in a range of sizes and styles, some with sea views.
**ROOMS:** 29 en suite (4 fmly) No smoking in 10 bedrooms s £45; d £65 (incl. bkfst) * **LB** **FACILITIES:** ch fac Xmas **CONF:** Thtr 90 Class 40 Board 40 Del from £56 * **SERVICES:** Lift **PARKING:** 22
**CARDS:**

## MORETON, Merseyside — Map 07 SJ28

**★★★67% Leasowe Castle**
Leasowe Rd CH46 3RF
☎ 0151 606 9191 🖷 0151 678 5551
e-mail: leasowe.castle@mail.cybase.co.uk
***Dir:*** *leave M53 junct 1 take 1st exit from rdbt at 1st slip road join A551, hotel 0.75m on right*

Partly dating back to 1592, this hotel was built to allow the owner to watch horseracing on the sands. Many impressive features remain, including ornately carved wall panels and a ceiling brought from the Palace of Westminster. Bedrooms are well equipped and comfortable. The beamed bar offers a range of meals and there is also a more formal restaurant.
**ROOMS:** 47 en suite (3 fmly) No smoking in 3 bedrooms s £65-£110; d £75-£150 (incl. bkfst) * **LB** **FACILITIES:** STV Water sports Sea Fishing Sailing Xmas **CONF:** Thtr 400 Class 200 Board 40 Del from £90 * **SERVICES:** Lift **PARKING:** 200 **NOTES:** No dogs (ex guide dogs) Civ Wed 120 **CARDS:**

## MORETONHAMPSTEAD, Devon — Map 03 SX78

**★★★★67% ❀ Manor House**
PRINCIPAL HOTELS
TQ13 8RE
☎ 01647 440355 🖷 01647 440961
e-mail: manorhouse@principalhotels.co.uk
***Dir:*** *2m from Moretonhampstead towards Princetown on B3212*
Set within beautifully maintained grounds, including a championship golf course and a lake, this substantial Victorian manor house was formerly the home of the W H Smith family. In keeping with the style and age of the property, the inviting bedrooms are well-equipped. The Hambledon Restaurant serves an interesting choice of dishes that are prepared and served with considerable flair.
**ROOMS:** 90 en suite (5 fmly) s £79; d £89 (incl. bkfst & dinner) * **LB** **FACILITIES:** STV Golf 18 Tennis (hard) Fishing Snooker Croquet lawn Putting green Xmas **CONF:** Thtr 100 Class 50 Board 40 **SERVICES:** Lift **PARKING:** 100 **NOTES:** Civ Wed 100 **CARDS:**

## MORETON-IN-MARSH, Gloucestershire — Map 04 SP23

**★★63% White Hart Royal**

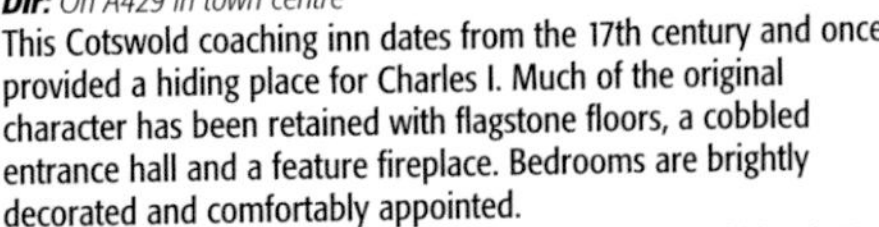
OLD ENGLISH INNS

High St GL56 0BA
☎ 01608 650731 🖷 01608 650880
***Dir:*** *On A429 in town centre*
This Cotswold coaching inn dates from the 17th century and once provided a hiding place for Charles I. Much of the original character has been retained with flagstone floors, a cobbled entrance hall and a feature fireplace. Bedrooms are brightly decorated and comfortably appointed.
**ROOMS:** 19 en suite (2 fmly) s £70-£85; d £70-£85 (incl. bkfst) * **LB** **FACILITIES:** STV Xmas **CONF:** Thtr 80 **PARKING:** 20 **NOTES:** No smoking in restaurant **CARDS:**

## MORLEY, West Yorkshire — Map 08 SE22

**★★65% The Old Vicarage**
Bruntcliffe Rd LS27 0JZ
☎ 0113 253 2174 🖷 0113 253 3549
e-mail: oldvicarage@btinternet.com
***Dir:*** *follow signs for A650, go through traffic lights and pass two garages on the left. Hotel is located just before St Andrew's Church*
This sympathetically extended Victorian vicarage offers spacious, traditional bedrooms in the original house and more modern rooms in a newer wing. Antiques and bric-a-brac abound. Service is friendly and informal and guests can relax in the cosy bar or in the large lounge. Hearty meals are served in the pleasant dining room.
**ROOMS:** 21 en suite (1 fmly) No smoking in 14 bedrooms s £48; d £62 (incl. bkfst) * **PARKING:** 21 **NOTES:** No dogs (ex guide dogs) No smoking in restaurant **CARDS:**

## MORPETH, Northumberland

**★★★70% Linden Hall**
NE65 8XF
☎ 01670 500000 🖷 01670 500001
e-mail: stay@lindenhall.co.uk
(For full entry see Longhorsley)

## MORTEHOE, Devon — Map 02 SS44

**★★66% Lundy House Hotel**
Chapel Hill EX34 7DZ
☎ 01271 870372 🖷 01271 871001
e-mail: info@lundyhousehotel.co.uk
***Dir:*** *take A361 to Braunton/Ilfracombe. Then Woolacombe exit at rdbt. In village right along esplanade and uphill towards Mortehoe, hotel on left*
Facing south across the rugged North Devon coastline to Lundy Island in the distance, this personally-run hotel offers a warm, friendly welcome. In the dining room, honest home cooking is served; vegetarians are particularly welcome. Very much a 'dog-friendly' hotel, there is direct access to the coastal path from the hotel's terraced gardens.
**ROOMS:** 9 en suite (4 fmly) No smoking in all bedrooms s fr £34; d £48-£68 (incl. bkfst) * **LB** **PARKING:** 9 **NOTES:** No smoking in restaurant Closed Nov-Mar **CARDS:**

> Late for dinner? Quality Standards star rating means that last orders for dinner should be no earlier than:
> ★ 6.30pm ★★ 7.00pm ★★★ 8.00pm
> ★★★★ 9.00pm ★★★★★ 10.00pm

M

## MOUSEHOLE, Cornwall & Isles of Scilly — Map 02 SW42

★★69% ◎ **Old Coastguard Hotel**
The Parade TR19 6PR
☎ 01736 731222 ▤ 01736 731720
e-mail: bookings@oldcoastguardhotel.co.uk
**Dir:** *A30 to Penzance, coast road to Newlyn then Mousehole. 1st building on left as enter into village*

OLD COASTGUARD INN
& SEAFOOD

Situated on the edge of Mousehole, this friendly and charming hotel offers comfortable accommodation and modern facilities. Bedrooms are simply styled, many boast sea views. An imaginative menu is offered, several dishes are based on fresh fish from nearby Newlyn. The stylish bar, restaurant and sun lounge provide both wonderful views and a lively atmosphere.
**ROOMS:** 14 en suite 8 annexe rms (7 en suite) (2 fmly) s £35-£64; d £70-£90 (incl. bkfst) * LB **PARKING:** 12 **NOTES:** Closed Xmas day RS Nov-1 Apr **CARDS:**

## MUCH BIRCH, Herefordshire — Map 03 SO53

★★★64% **Pilgrim**
Ross Rd HR2 8HJ
☎ 01981 540742 ▤ 01981 540620
e-mail: pilgrim540@aol.com
**Dir:** *midway between Hereford and Ross-on-Wye off A49*
This much extended former rectory, surrounded by extensive grounds, provides bedrooms equipped with modern comforts. There is a pleasant character bar, a traditionally furnished restaurant and a comfortable lounge. Other facilities include a small function room and a pitch and putt course.
**ROOMS:** 20 en suite (3 fmly) No smoking in 5 bedrooms **FACILITIES:** Croquet lawn Putting green Pitch & putt Badminton **CONF:** Thtr 45 Class 45 Board 25 **PARKING:** 40 **NOTES:** No smoking in restaurant **CARDS:**

## MUCH WENLOCK, Shropshire — Map 07 SO69

★★★73% ◎◎ ***Raven***
Barrow St TF13 6EN
☎ 01952 727251 ▤ 01952 728416
**Dir:** *M54 junct 4 or 5, take the A442 S, then A4169 to Much Wenlock*
This town centre hotel is spread across several historic buildings with a 17th-century coaching inn at its centre. Accommodation is well furnished and equipped to offer modern comfort, with some ground floor rooms available. Public areas feature an interesting collection of prints and other memorabilia connected with the Olympic Games.
**ROOMS:** 8 en suite 7 annexe en suite **FACILITIES:** STV **CONF:** Thtr 16 Board 14 **PARKING:** 30 **NOTES:** No dogs (ex guide dogs) No smoking in restaurant **CARDS:**

★★67% **Wheatland Fox**
TF13 6AD
☎ 01952 727292 ▤ 01952 727301
e-mail: wheatlandfox@muchwenlock42.freeserve.co.uk
**Dir:** *just off A458 Shrewsbury/Bridgnorth road turn into High Street Much Wenlock*
The original part of this Grade II listed building dates back to 1669. The modern, smartly equipped accommodation includes rooms with four-poster beds and a family bedded room. Service at the privately owned and personally run hotel is friendly and courteous.
**ROOMS:** 7 en suite s £40-£45; d £55-£60 (incl. bkfst) * LB
**PARKING:** 12 **NOTES:** No smoking in restaurant
**CARDS:**

## MUDEFORD See Christchurch

## MULLION, Cornwall & Isles of Scilly — Map 02 SW61

★★★71% **Polurrian**
TR12 7EN
☎ 01326 240421 ▤ 01326 240083
e-mail: polurotel@aol.com
**Dir:** *exit A30 onto A3076 to Truro. Follow signs for Helston A39 then A394 to The Lizard & Mullion*
This long established hotel is set in twelve acres of landscaped gardens, three hundred feet above the restless ocean. Spectacular views over Mullion Cove will remain long in the memory, with sunsets a treat to behold. Public areas are spacious and comfortable, there is a well-equipped leisure centre, and many of the individually styled bedrooms enjoy lovely views.
**ROOMS:** 39 en suite (22 fmly) s £65-£105; d £130-£210 (incl. bkfst & dinner) * LB **FACILITIES:** STV Indoor swimming (H) Outdoor swimming (H) Tennis (hard) Squash Snooker Sauna Solarium Gym Croquet lawn Putting green Jacuzzi Cricket net Whirlpool Mountain bikes entertainment ch fac Xmas **CONF:** Thtr 100 Class 60 Board 30 Del from £55 * **PARKING:** 80 **NOTES:** No smoking in restaurant
**CARDS:**

*See advert on opposite page*

★★★68% ◎ **Mullion Cove Hotel**
TR12 7EP
☎ 01326 240328 ▤ 01326 240998
e-mail: mullion.cove@btinternet.com
**Dir:** *From Helston follow signs to The Lizard, right at Mullion Holiday Park. Through village & turn left for Cove & Hotel. Cove is approx 1m from Mullion, on approaching Cove turn right. Hotel on top of hill*

Built at the turn of the last century, this imposing hotel enjoys breathtaking views from its cliff-top setting above the working harbour of Mullion Cove. A range of freshly prepared dishes is served in the stylish restaurant, while lighter meals are available in

*continued*

the informal conservatory bar. Bedrooms come in a variety of sizes and styles; all are equipped with modern facilities.
**ROOMS:** 28 en suite (9 fmly) s £45-£136; d £82-£194 (incl. bkfst & dinner) * **LB** **FACILITIES:** Outdoor swimming (H) Sauna Solarium Beauty treatments ch fac Xmas **CONF:** Thtr 35 Board 12 Del from £90 * **PARKING:** 60 **NOTES:** No smoking in restaurant
**CARDS:**

MUNDFORD, Norfolk Map 05 TL89

### ★★★68% Lynford Hall

Lynford Hall IP26 5HW
☎ 01842 878351 📠 01842 878252

In a peaceful location at the end of a long drive, this delightful country hotel has attractive, well-tended gardens. The public rooms are very elegant and feature a large open plan hallway. In addition there is a comfortable lounge bar and the Duvernay restaurant. The spacious bedrooms are tastefully decorated and equipped with many useful extras.
**ROOMS:** 21 en suite (3 fmly) No smoking in all bedrooms s £79; d £99 (incl. bkfst) * **LB** **FACILITIES:** Fishing Croquet lawn Xmas **CONF:** Thtr 500 Class 250 Board 150 Del from £135 * **PARKING:** 150 **NOTES:** No dogs (ex guide dogs) No smoking in restaurant Civ Wed 400
**CARDS:**

MUNGRISDALE, Cumbria Map 11 NY33

### ★76% The Mill

CA11 0XR
☎ 01768 779659 📠 01768 779155
e-mail: quinlan.themill@bushinternet.com
***Dir:*** *exit M6 junct 40, 2m N of A66*
Set amidst magnificent rural scenery, formerly a mill cottage dating from 1651, this charming hotel and restaurant lies beside the old millstream. Inside there are cosy lounges, low ceilings and a plethora of books, antiques, paintings and period pieces. Dinner is served at 7pm and is a special occasion. The cooking is excellent, and the full five courses will satisfy the heartiest of Lakeland appetites.
**ROOMS:** 7 rms (5 en suite) d £108-£150 (incl. bkfst & dinner) * **FACILITIES:** Fishing Games room **PARKING:** 15 **NOTES:** Closed Nov-Feb Civ Wed 25

NAILSWORTH, Gloucestershire Map 03 ST89

### ★★70% Egypt Mill

GL6 0AE
☎ 01453 833449 📠 01453 836098
***Dir:*** *on A46*
This former corn mill dates back to the 17th century. It offers a restaurant with adjoining bar, and a cellar bar with a popular bistro. The millstones and lifting equipment are still in evidence, as

*continued*

well as working waterwheels. There is also a riverside patio and gardens. Bedrooms are well-equipped and tastefully furnished.
**ROOMS:** 8 en suite 10 annexe en suite (2 fmly) s £47-£49; d fr £75 (incl. bkfst) * **LB** **FACILITIES:** Xmas **CONF:** Thtr 100 Class 80 Board 80 Del from £90 * **PARKING:** 120 **NOTES:** No dogs (ex guide dogs) No smoking in restaurant **CARDS:**

NANTWICH, Cheshire Map 07 SJ65

### ★★★77% Rookery Hall

Main Rd, Worleston CW5 6DQ
☎ 01270 610016 📠 01270 626027
e-mail: rookery@arcadianhotels.co.uk
***Dir:*** *take B5074 off the 4th rdbt on the Nantwich by-pass. Rookery Hall is 1.5m on the right*

ARCADIAN HOTELS *Distinctly Different*

Partly dating back to 1816, this fine mansion has been extended over the years. Spacious bedrooms, some in an adjacent coach house, are both comfortable and luxurious. There is a light and

*continued on p422*

NANTWICH, continued

airy salon, and a bar leading out on to the patio. Dinner is served in the mahogany-panelled dining room, overlooking gardens and pastureland. All enhanced by friendly and efficient staff with guest comfort in mind.
**ROOMS:** 30 en suite 15 annexe en suite s £85-£110; d £110-£140 (incl. bkfst) * **LB** **FACILITIES:** STV Tennis (hard) Croquet lawn Xmas **CONF:** Thtr 90 Class 40 Board 40 Del from £130 * **SERVICES:** Lift **PARKING:** 80 **NOTES:** No smoking in restaurant Civ Wed 60
**CARDS:**

### ★★69% Crown
High St CW5 5AS
☎ 01270 625283 01270 628047
e-mail: crownhotel@highstnantwich.freeserve.co.uk
***Dir:*** *take A52 to Nantwich hotel in centre of town*
A Grade I listed building and 16th-century coaching inn, this hotel is centrally situated within the pedestrianised main street. The hotel has much original character with exposed beams, uneven floors and narrow corridors. Rooms vary in size but all are neatly furnished and well-equipped. The popular restaurant offers an extensive Italian menu.
**ROOMS:** 18 en suite (2 fmly) No smoking in 2 bedrooms s £59-£62; d £69-£72 * **LB** **CONF:** Thtr 200 Class 150 Board 70 **PARKING:** 18 **NOTES:** Civ Wed 150 **CARDS:**

Best Western

### ⇧ *Premier Lodge*
221 Crewe Rd CW5 6NE
☎ 0870 700 1496 0870 700 1497
Premier Lodge offers modern, well-equipped, en suite accommodation suitable for both business and leisure travellers. Meals can be taken at the adjacent popular restaurant and bar, which is fully licensed. For further details, consult the Hotel Groups page.
**ROOMS:** 37 en suite

PREMIER LODGE
THE BEST. BEST ASSURED.

N

## NEEDHAM MARKET, Suffolk — Map 05 TM05

### ⇧ *Travelodge*
Beacon Hill IP6 8NY
☎ 01449 721640 01449 721640
***Dir:*** *A14/A140*
Travelodge offers good quality, good value, modern accommodation. Ideal for families, the spacious, en suite bedrooms include remote-control TV, tea and coffee-making facilities, luxury beds and free morning newspaper. Meals can be taken at the nearby family restaurant. For further details and the Travelodge phone number, consult the Hotel Groups page.

**ROOMS:** 40 en suite

Travelodge

## NESSCLIFFE, Shropshire — Map 07 SJ31

### ★★70% *Nesscliffe*
Nesscliffe SY4 1DB
☎ 01743 741430 01743 741104
e-mail: mike@wright70.co.uk
***Dir:*** *on A5 between Shrewsbury/Oswestry*
This Grade II listed property, dating back to the early 19th century, provides good quality, tastefully appointed and well-equipped accommodation, including two rooms with four-poster beds. The open plan public areas include an attractive lounge bar and a very pleasant restaurant area.
**ROOMS:** 8 en suite (1 fmly) **FACILITIES:** STV ch fac **PARKING:** 50 **NOTES:** No dogs (ex guide dogs) No smoking in restaurant
**CARDS:**

## NETHER STOWEY, Somerset — Map 03 ST13

### ★★66% Apple Tree
Keenthorne TA5 1HZ
☎ 01278 733238 01278 732693
***Dir:*** *on A39 approx. 7m W of Bridgwater and 2m E of Nether Stowey*
Comfortable and well equipped accommodation is provided at this attractive roadside inn. Bedrooms are smartly presented with several located in an adjoining wing overlooking the garden. A friendly, relaxed atmosphere prevails throughout; the bar, attractive conservatory and lounge offer areas in which to enjoy a quiet drink and home-cooked meal.
**ROOMS:** 15 en suite (1 fmly) No smoking in 3 bedrooms s fr £42.50; d fr £52.50 (incl. bkfst) * **CONF:** Board 10 **PARKING:** 60 **NOTES:** No dogs (ex guide dogs) No smoking in restaurant **CARDS:**

## NETHER WASDALE, Cumbria — Map 06 NY10

### ★★73% Low Wood Hall Hotel & Restaurant
CA20 1ET
☎ 019467 26100 019467 26111
e-mail: reservations@lowwoodhall.co.uk
***Dir:*** *turn off A595 at Gosforth and bear left for Wasdale, after 3m turn right for Nether Wasdale*
Guests can be sure of a warm welcome at this delightful country house hotel. Set in five acres of woodlands and landscaped gardens, this tranquil haven offers breathtaking views over Whinn Rigg and Irton Fell. Sumptuous public areas are enhanced by stained glass windows and wooden floors. All rooms are thoughtfully equipped and those in the main house are particularly impressive. Carefully prepared meals are a highlight.
**ROOMS:** 6 en suite 6 annexe en suite (2 fmly) No smoking in all bedrooms s £45-£75; d £55-£120 (incl. bkfst) * **LB** **FACILITIES:** Xmas **CONF:** Thtr 30 Class 30 Board 20 **PARKING:** 20 **NOTES:** No dogs (ex guide dogs) No smoking in restaurant **CARDS:**

## NEWARK-ON-TRENT, Nottinghamshire — Map 08 SK75

### ★★74% South Parade
117-119 Baldertongate NG24 1RY
☎ 01636 703008 & 703030 01636 605593
e-mail: enquiries@southparadehotel.co.uk
***Dir:*** *A1 onto B6326, travel approx 2 m into Newark, right at lights on x-rd next to gardens, then 1st right. Hotel approx 200 yds on left*
This welcoming hotel is situated just a few minutes walk from the town centre and is a Grade II listed Georgian building. Bedrooms offer attractively decorated and comfortably appointed accommodation, that has a good range of useful facilities. In addition to the homely lounge, there is a bar and restaurant on the lower ground floor.
**ROOMS:** 13 en suite (3 fmly) No smoking in 11 bedrooms s £42-£54; d £64-£75 (incl. bkfst) * **LB** **CONF:** Thtr 25 Class 25 Board 25 **PARKING:** 14 **NOTES:** No smoking in restaurant
**CARDS:**

### ★★68% The Grange Hotel
73 London Rd NG24 1RZ
☎ 01636 703399 01636 702328
e-mail: info@grangenewark.co.uk
***Dir:*** *From A1 follow signs to town centre. At the castle rdbt follow signs to Balderton. Straight on at 2 sets of lights. Hotel 0.25m on left*
This pleasant hotel is situated in a residential area and offers high standards of hospitality. Public rooms include a smart lounge bar, a quiet comfortable lounge, and a restaurant, which offers daily and carte menus. Bedrooms, some of which are located in an

*continued on p424*

THE

vineyard

RESTAURANT • SUITES • SPA

AA ★★★★★

* All 31 luxuriously furnished rooms and suites are individually named after wines, offering the ultimate in comfort with distinctive character. Voted 'English Tourism Council Hotel of the Year', the cuisine has been awarded 3 AA Rosettes, and superb wine list voted the Best in the UK by the AA.

* At the end of a long day, relax in The Vineyard Spa and enjoy a treatment in one of our beautiful dedicated suites. Exercise in the gym, revitalise with a swim and unwind in the sauna or steam room. Play golf at our own challenging 18-hole, par 71 golf course at the Donnington Valley Hotel, only two miles away.

The Vineyard at Stockcross
Newbury Berkshire RG20 8JU
telephone: (01635) 528770
facsimile: (01635) 528398
email: general@
the-vineyard.co.uk website:
www.the-vineyard.co.uk

N

---

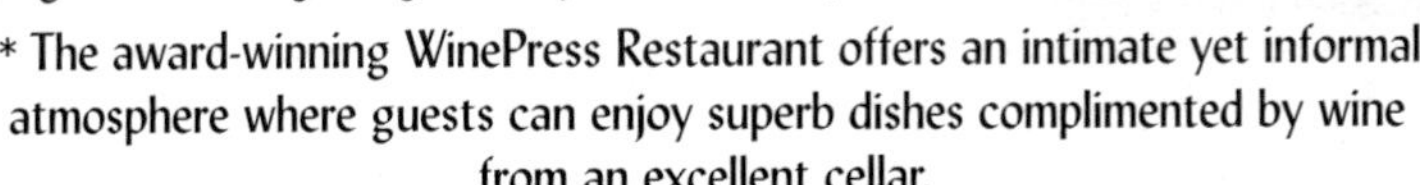
donnington Valley

HOTEL • RESTAURANT • GOLF

* Each of the 58 individually designed and thoughtfully equipped bedrooms are of uncompromising quality, most enjoying views over golfing fairways and countryside.

* The award-winning WinePress Restaurant offers an intimate yet informal atmosphere where guests can enjoy superb dishes complimented by wine from an excellent cellar.

* The hotel's own golf course is a challenging 18-hole, 6353 yard, par 71 course unequalled in terms of beauty accessibility and amenities.

The Donnington Valley Hotel Old Oxford Road
Donnington Newbury Berkshire RG14 3AG

telephone: (01635) 551199
facsimile (01635) 551123
email: general@
donningtonvalley.co.uk
website:
www.donningtonvalley.co.uk

NEWARK-ON-TRENT, continued

adjacent house, are comfortably furnished, well-equipped and pleasantly decorated.
**ROOMS:** 10 en suite 5 annexe en suite (1 fmly) No smoking in 10 bedrooms s £49-£55; d £69-£80 (incl. bkfst) * **LB** **CONF:** Board 14 Del from £90 * **PARKING:** 17 **NOTES:** No dogs (ex guide dogs) No smoking in restaurant **CARDS:**

NEWBURY, Berkshire Map 04 SU46

### ★★★★★79% The Vineyard at Stockcross

Stockcross RG20 8JU
☎ 01635 528770 01635 528398
e-mail: general@the-vineyard.co.uk
***Dir:*** *From M4 take A34 towards Newbury, exit at 3rd junct for Speen, take A4 towards Hungerford, at rdbt take 2nd exit to Stockcross.*

The Vineyard at Stockcross is set in rolling Berkshire countryside. Guests can enjoy first class service and food at this stylish hotel and restaurant, which has a very special atmosphere created by the well-drilled, discreet and naturally friendly staff. A great deal of thought has been put into the artistic design of the grounds, public rooms and bedrooms. The outstanding wine list complements the seasonal cooking perfectly.
**ROOMS:** 31 en suite No smoking in 10 bedrooms s £180-£604 (incl. bkfst) * **LB** **FACILITIES:** **Spa** STV Indoor swimming (H) Sauna Gym Jacuzzi Treatment rooms entertainment **CONF:** Thtr 60 Class 50 Board 30 Del from £280 * **SERVICES:** Lift air con **PARKING:** 60 **NOTES:** No dogs (ex guide dogs) Closed Xmas period (to be advised) Civ Wed
**CARDS:**

### ★★★★76% Donnington Valley

Old Oxford Rd, Donnington RG14 3AG
☎ 01635 551199 01635 551123
e-mail: general@donningtonvalley.co.uk
***Dir:*** *exit M4 junct 13, take A34 southbound and exit at Donnington Castle. Turn right over bridge then left hotel is 1m on right*

This friendly hotel stands in its own 18-hole golf course and provides excellent accommodation. Public rooms are furnished to a high standard and the well-equipped meeting rooms, much in demand for conferences, give character to the striking modern structure of the building.
**ROOMS:** 58 en suite (11 fmly) No smoking in 30 bedrooms s £139-£199 * **LB** **FACILITIES:** STV Golf 18 Putting green Leisure fac available at sister hotel entertainment Xmas **CONF:** Thtr 140 Class 60 Board 40 Del from £95 * **SERVICES:** Lift **PARKING:** 160 **NOTES:** No dogs (ex guide dogs) Civ Wed 85 **CARDS:**

*See advert on page 423*

### ★★★★75% Regency Park Hotel

Bowling Green Rd, Thatcham RG18 3RP
☎ 01635 871555 01635 871571
e-mail: info@regencypark.co.uk
***Dir:*** *from Newbury take A4 signed Thatcham/Reading. At 2nd rdbt follow signs to Cold Ash. Hotel 1m on the left*

Peacefully situated in five acres of grounds, within easy reach of the M3 and M4, this hotel has been extended to add a smart leisure club, a further 36 bedrooms and a state-of-the-art function suite. Accommodation is spacious, modern and well-equipped; the new executive rooms are particularly impressive. Day rooms include the stylish Watermark restaurant.
**ROOMS:** 82 en suite (7 fmly) No smoking in 52 bedrooms s £135-£305; d £155-£325 * **LB** **FACILITIES:** **Spa** STV Indoor swimming (H) Tennis (hard) Sauna Solarium Gym Jacuzzi 4 Health & Beauty rooms Xmas **CONF:** Thtr 200 Class 80 Board 70 Del £155 * **SERVICES:** Lift **PARKING:** 160 **NOTES:** No dogs (ex guide dogs) No smoking in restaurant Civ Wed 90 **CARDS:**

*See advert on opposite page*

### ★★★65% The Chequers

6-8 Oxford St RG14 1JB
☎ 01635 38000 01635 37170
***Dir:*** *Off A34 at Newbury follow signs Newbury town centre. At 2nd mini rdbt turn right hotel immediately on right hand side*

REGAL

In an enviable town centre location with parking, this hotel offers bedrooms of varying sizes and outlook; most are in the original buildings but some are in modern wings. All have good facilities and offer high levels of comfort.
**ROOMS:** 46 en suite 10 annexe en suite (3 fmly) No smoking in 41 bedrooms s £125; d £135 * **LB** **FACILITIES:** STV **CONF:** Thtr 100 Class 50 Board 40 Del from £90 * **PARKING:** 60 **NOTES:** No dogs (ex guide dogs) No smoking in restaurant Closed 24 Dec-2 Jan
**CARDS:**

### Premier Lodge
Bath Rd, Midgham RG7 5UX
☎ 0870 700 1498 📠 0870 700 1499
Premier Lodge offers modern, well-equipped, en suite accommodation suitable for both business and leisure travellers. Meals can be taken at the adjacent popular restaurant and bar, which is fully licensed. For further details, consult the Hotel Groups page.
**ROOMS:** 29 en suite

### Travelodge
Chieveley, Oxford Rd RG18 9XX
☎ 01635 248024
***Dir:*** *on A34/off junc 13 M4*
Travelodge offers good quality, good value, modern accommodation. Ideal for families, the spacious, en suite bedrooms include remote-control TV, tea and coffee-making facilities, luxury beds and free morning newspaper. Meals can be taken at the nearby family restaurant. For further details and the Travelodge phone number, consult the Hotel Groups page.

**ROOMS:** 64 en suite

### Travelodge (Newbury South)
Tot Hill Services (A34), Newbury by-pass RG20 9ED
☎ 01635 278169
***Dir:*** *Tot Hill Services A34*
Travelodge offers good quality, good value, modern accommodation. Ideal for families, the spacious, en suite bedrooms include remote-control TV, tea and coffee-making facilities, luxury beds and free morning newspaper. Meals can be taken at the nearby family restaurant. For further details and the Travelodge phone number, consult the Hotel Groups page.

## NEWBY BRIDGE, Cumbria — Map 07 SD38

### ★★★★75% ❀ Lakeside
Lakeside LA12 8AT
☎ 015395 30001 📠 015395 31699
e-mail: sales@lakesidehotel.co.uk
***Dir:*** *from M6 junct 36 join A590 to Barrow and follow signs to Newby Bridge. Turn right over the bridge, the hotel is 1m along on the right or follow signs for Lakeside Steamers from junct 36*
This impressive hotel has an enviable location on the southern edge of Lake Windermere. Bedrooms are tastefully and individually styled, many with patios and wonderful lake views. Spacious lounges and a choice of restaurants are available. The addition of a luxury spa complex completes the picture.
**ROOMS:** 80 en suite (7 fmly) No smoking in 34 bedrooms s £99.87-£230; d £110-£230 (incl. bkfst) * **LB** **FACILITIES:** **Spa** STV Indoor swimming (H) Fishing Sauna Croquet lawn Jacuzzi Private jetty Use of Health club entertainment Xmas **CONF:** Thtr 100 Class 50 Board 40 Del £152.75 * **SERVICES:** Lift **PARKING:** 200 **NOTES:** No smoking in restaurant Civ Wed 100 **CARDS:**

### ★★★★68% Swan
LA12 8NB
☎ 015395 31681 📠 015395 31917
e-mail: swanhotel@aol.com
***Dir:*** *From M6 junct 36 follow A590 sigposted Barrow for 16m, hotel on right of the old 5- arch bridge, at Newby Bridge*
Completion of a major renovation programme has completely transformed this delightful business and tourist hotel, which enjoys a spectacular setting on the banks of the River Leven. Most
*continued*

AA
★★★★

Best Western

REGENCY
PARK HOTEL

of the stylishly refurbished bedrooms are well- proportioned and offer a wide range of accessories. Inviting public areas include a range of relaxing lounges, a well-stocked bar, formal and informal eating options, and a smart new health and fitness centre.

**ROOMS:** 55 en suite (4 fmly) No smoking in 16 bedrooms s £70-£91; d £120-£150 (incl. bkfst) * **LB** **FACILITIES:** STV Indoor swimming (H) Fishing Sauna Gym Jacuzzi Beauty treatment ch fac Xmas **CONF:** Thtr 90 Class 60 Board 50 Del from £110 * **SERVICES:** Lift **PARKING:** 100 **NOTES:** No dogs (ex guide dogs) No smoking in restaurant Civ Wed 80 **CARDS:**

### ★★★65% Whitewater
The Lakeland Village LA12 8PX
☎ 015395 31133 📠 015395 31881
e-mail: enquiries@whitewater-hotel.co.uk
***Dir:*** *leave M6 junct 36 follow signs for A590 Barrow 1m through Newby Bridge, turn right at signpost for Lakeland Village, hotel on left*
This stylish converted mill is peacefully located on the banks of the
*continued on p426*

NEWBY BRIDGE, continued

River Leven. Spacious bedrooms have exposed natural stone and are equipped to a high standard. Public areas offer guests a host of amenities ranging from spa and leisure to mountain bikes and tennis courts. River views are enjoyed from both the elegant restaurant and the public bar, where a good range of lighter meals and snacks are served.

*Whitewater, Newby Bridge*

**ROOMS:** 35 en suite (10 fmly) s £75-£90; d £125-£150 (incl. bkfst) * **LB FACILITIES:** Spa STV Indoor swimming (H) Tennis (hard) Squash Sauna Solarium Gym Putting green Beauty treatment, table tennis,steam room,golf driving net entertainment Xmas **CONF:** Thtr 80 Class 32 Board 40 Del from £90 * **SERVICES:** Lift **PARKING:** 50 **NOTES:** No dogs (ex guide dogs) No smoking in restaurant Civ Wed 100
**CARDS:**

NEWCASTLE-UNDER-LYME, Staffordshire Map 07 SJ84

N

### ★★★67% Posthouse Stoke-on-Trent

Clayton Rd ST5 4DL

Posthouse

☎ 0870 400 9077 01782 717138

***Dir:*** *on A519 at junct 15 of M6*

This modern hotel is situated in spacious grounds. Facilities include a Spa leisure centre and popular Traders restaurant. Bedrooms are comfortably furnished and include interactive TV, hairdryers and trouser presses. Extended room service and all-day lounge service are available. Staff are professional, friendly and willing.

**ROOMS:** 119 en suite (41 fmly) No smoking in 54 bedrooms s £69-£109; d £69-£109 * **LB FACILITIES:** Indoor swimming (H) Sauna Solarium Gym Jacuzzi Xmas **CONF:** Thtr 70 Class 40 Board 34 Del from £104 * **PARKING:** 128 **NOTES:** Civ Wed 55
**CARDS:**

### ★★62% Comfort Inn

Liverpool Rd, Cross Heath ST5 9DX

Comfort Inn

☎ 01782 717000 01782 713669

e-mail: admin@gb617.u-net.com

***Dir:*** *M6 junct 16 onto A500 towards Stoke-on-Trent. Take A34 to Newcastle-under-Lyme, hotel on right after 1.5m*

Some of the well-equipped bedrooms at this purpose built hotel are in a separate block at the rear. There is a large lounge bar, an attractively appointed restaurant and a small gymnasium.

**ROOMS:** 43 en suite 24 annexe en suite (6 fmly) No smoking in 25 bedrooms s £50; d £50 * **LB FACILITIES:** STV Xmas **CONF:** Thtr 130 Class 80 Board 50 Del £74 * **PARKING:** 160 **NOTES:** No smoking in restaurant Civ Wed 100 **CARDS:**

NEWCASTLE UPON TYNE, Tyne & Wear Map 12 NZ2
see also Seaton Burn & Whickham

### ★★★★78% Newcastle Marriott Hotel Gosforth Park

Marriott HOTELS · RESORTS · SUITES

High Gosforth Park, Gosforth NE3 5HN

☎ 0191 236 4111 0191 236 8192

e-mail: Marriott/Hotels/Whitbread@Whitbread,Gosforthpark

***Dir:*** *A1 North & South bound, exit A1056 Killingworth/Wideopen 3rd exit to Gosforth Park hotel ahead*

Marriott HOTEL

Set in twelve and a half acres of woodland and attractive gardens, with easy access to the A1, the racecourse and the airport, the hotel has its own helipad. Bedrooms are comfortable and very well-equipped. The Brandling Restaurant serves classical and modern dishes, while Chats is the less formal dining option.

**ROOMS:** 178 en suite No smoking in 96 bedrooms s £105-£175; d £105-£175 * **FACILITIES:** Spa STV Indoor swimming (H) Tennis (hard) Squash Sauna Solarium Gym Jacuzzi Trim & jogging trail in hotel grounds entertainment **CONF:** Thtr 600 Class 280 Board 50 Del from £151 * **SERVICES:** Lift **PARKING:** 340 **NOTES:** RS X-mas & new year Civ Wed 150 **CARDS:**

### ★★★★76% Vermont

Castle Garth NE1 1RQ

☎ 0191 233 1010 0191 233 1234

e-mail: info@vermont-hotel.co.uk

***Dir:*** *city centre by the high level bridge & Castle Keep*

The Vermont presents a striking facade and sits adjacent to Castle Keep and the Tyne Bridge in the heart of the city. Bedrooms are comfortable and spacious and are very well-equipped. There are a number of relaxing dining and drinking venues, from the informal Martha's bar and an all day Brasserie to the sedate Blue Room where award winning cuisine is served.

**ROOMS:** 101 en suite (12 fmly) No smoking in 20 bedrooms s £145-£165; d £165-£190 * **LB FACILITIES:** STV Solarium Gym entertainment Xmas **CONF:** Thtr 210 Class 60 Board 36 **SERVICES:** Lift **PARKING:** 100 **NOTES:** Civ Wed 200
**CARDS:**

### ★★★★71% Copthorne Hotel Newcastle

The Close, Quayside NE1 3RT

COPTHORNE

☎ 0191 222 0333 0191 230 4148

e-mail: sales@newcastlemill-cop.com

***Dir:*** *follow signs for Newcastle city centre. Take B1600 Quayside exit, hotel on right*

Set on the banks of the River Tyne, yet close to the city centre, this hotel provides modern comforts, a leisure centre and a range of conference facilities. Many bedrooms have views overlooking the

continued

ver and there is a floor of 'Connoisseur' rooms with their own xclusive lounge and business support services.
**OOMS:** 156 en suite No smoking in 85 bedrooms s £155-£180; d £180-205 * **FACILITIES: Spa** STV Indoor swimming (H) Sauna Solarium ym Jacuzzi Steam roomBeauty treatment room Xmas **CONF:** Thtr 200 lass 85 Board 60 **SERVICES:** Lift air con
**ARDS:**

★★★★68% ***Newcastle Marriott Hotel MetroCentre***

Marriott
HOTELS · RESORTS · SUITES

Metro Centre NE11 9XF
☎ 0191 493 2233 🖷 0191 493 2030
(For full entry see Gateshead)

★★★77% **Malmaison**
Quayside NE1 3DX
☎ 0191 245 5000 🖷 0191 245 4545
-mail: newcastle@malmaison.com
***ir:** follow signs for Newcastle city centre. Take road for Quayside/Law ourts. Hotel is approx 100yds past the Law Courts overlooking the river*
Overlooking the river in the redeveloped quayside, this striking modern hotel is popular with guests looking for a change from raditional accommodation. Bedrooms are spacious and ontemporary in style, offering large beds, music and ommunications systems as standard. Public areas include a spa nd gym facility, some meeting rooms and the popular riverside rasserie.
**OOMS:** 116 en suite (10 fmly) s £115-£125; d £115-£125 * **LB** **ACILITIES:** STV Sauna Solarium Gym **CONF:** Thtr 50 Class 10 Board 4 Del from £150 * **SERVICES:** Lift **PARKING:** 50 **NOTES:** No dogs ex guide dogs) **CARDS:**

★★★67% ***Posthouse Newcastle City***
New Bridge St NE1 8BS
☎ 0870 400 9058 🖷 0191 261 8529
***Dir:** follow signs for Gateshead/Newcastle A167M over yne Bridge take A193 Wallsend and City Centre left to Carliol Sq hotel n corner*
This is the largest hotel in the heart of the city and offers a choice of bedroom styles and dining options. Other facilities include a staffed business centre, wide choice of meeting and function rooms and an impressive leisure club. Secure parking is provided n the adjacent multi-storey car park.
**ROOMS:** 166 en suite (2 fmly) No smoking in 108 bedrooms **FACILITIES:** Indoor swimming (H) Sauna Solarium Gym Jacuzzi adjoining leisure club **CONF:** Thtr 600 Class 350 Board 50 **SERVICES:** Lift **PARKING:** 132 **CARDS:**

★★★67% ***Posthouse Newcastle/ Washington***
Emerson District 5 NE37 1LB
☎ 0870 400 9084 🖷 0191 415 3371
(For full entry see Washington)

★★★67% **Swallow Hotel**

SWALLOW
HOTELS

High West St NE8 1PE
☎ 0191 477 1105 🖷 0191 478 7214
e-mail: info@swallowhotels.com
(For full entry see Gateshead)

★★★66% **Novotel Newcastle-upon-Tyne**
Ponteland Rd, Kenton NE3 3HZ
☎ 0191 214 0303 🖷 0191 214 0633
e-mail: H1118@accor-hotels.com
***Dir:** off A1(M) Airport junct - A696, take Kingston Park exit*
Convenient for the airport and the bypass, this bright, modern hotel offers stylish public areas and spacious, well-equipped accommodation. Four rooms have facilities for disabled guests. The Garden Brasserie is open for meals until late.
**ROOMS:** 126 en suite (126 fmly) No smoking in 82 bedrooms s £75; d £75 * **LB** **FACILITIES:** STV Indoor swimming (H) Sauna Gym **CONF:** Thtr 200 Class 90 Board 100 Del from £125 * **SERVICES:** Lift **PARKING:** 260 **CARDS:**

★★★66% **Swallow Imperial Hotel**
Jesmond Rd NE2 1PR
☎ 0191 281 5511 🖷 0191 281 8472
e-mail: jesmond@swallow-hotels.co.uk
***Dir:** turn off A167(M) onto A1058 (Tynemouth/East Coast). Hotel 0.25m on left just after second mini rdbt*

This hotel is well-located on the coast road just east of the city centre, and only minutes away from a Metro station. It has good meeting rooms, a well-equipped leisure centre, comfortable club-style lounge, and ample secure parking.
**ROOMS:** 122 en suite (6 fmly) No smoking in 77 bedrooms s £90; d £110 (incl. bkfst) * **LB** **FACILITIES:** STV Indoor swimming (H) Sauna Solarium Gym Jacuzzi Steam room entertainment Xmas **CONF:** Thtr 150 Class 60 Board 50 Del £120 * **SERVICES:** Lift **PARKING:** 100 **NOTES:** No smoking in restaurant Civ Wed 135
**CARDS:**

★★★65% **George Washington County Hotel**
Stone Cellar Rd, District 12, High Usworth NE37 1PH
☎ 0191 402 9988 🖷 0191 415 1166
e-mail: reservations@corushotels.com
(For full entry see Washington)

★★★65% **New Kent Hotel**
127 Osborne Rd NE2 2TB
☎ 0191 281 7711 🖷 0191 281 3369
***Dir:** beside B1600, opposite St Georges Church*
This relaxed and friendly business hotel serves generous meals in its bright, cheerful restaurant. Bedrooms are well-equipped and come in a variety of sizes.
**ROOMS:** 32 en suite (4 fmly) s £48-£70; d £70-£80 (incl. bkfst) * **LB** **FACILITIES:** STV Xmas **PARKING:** 22 **NOTES:** No smoking in restaurant Civ Wed 90 **CARDS:**

★★★63% **The Caledonian Hotel, Newcastle**

PEEL HOTELS

64 Osborne Rd, Jesmond NE2 2AT
☎ 0191 281 7881 🖷 0191 281 6241
e-mail: info@caledonian-hotel-newcastle.com
***Dir:** from A1 follow signs to Newcastle city, cross the Tyne Bridge and continue to Tynemouth, left at r/about at Osborne Rd, hotel on right*
Situated on the East Side of the city, this business and conference

*continued on p428*

N

NEWCASTLE UPON TYNE, continued

hotel provides comfortable well-equipped bedrooms along with a friendly informal atmosphere. The new style bar bistro is proving popular.
**ROOMS:** 89 en suite (6 fmly) No smoking in 32 bedrooms s £89-£99; d £99-£109 (incl. bkfst) * **LB** **FACILITIES:** STV Xmas **CONF:** Thtr 100 Class 50 Board 50 Del from £95 * **SERVICES:** Lift **PARKING:** 35
**CARDS:**

**★★★61% Quality**
Newgate St NE1 5SX
☎ 0191 232 5025 📠 0191 232 8428
e-mail: admin@gb077.u-net.com
***Dir:*** *A1(M) take A184 Gateshead and Newcastle centre, follow A6082*
In a tremendous location in the heart of the city and having the advantage of secure car parking, this hotel offers a rooftop restaurant and bar with fine views over the city. Bedrooms, although compact are well equipped and those recently refurbished are most comfortable.
**ROOMS:** 93 en suite (4 fmly) No smoking in 42 bedrooms s £95; d £110 * **LB** **FACILITIES:** STV entertainment Xmas **CONF:** Thtr 100 Class 40 Board 40 Del £110 * **SERVICES:** Lift **PARKING:** 120
**NOTES:** No smoking in restaurant **CARDS:**

**★★76% Eslington Villa**
8 Station Rd, Low Fell NE9 6DR
☎ 0191 487 6017 & 420 0666 📠 0191 420 0667
e-mail: admin@eslingtonvilla.fsnet.co.uk
(For full entry see Gateshead)

**★★64% *Whites***
38-42 Osborne Rd, Jesmond NE2 2AL
☎ 0191 281 5126 📠 0191 281 9953
e-mail: apuri80741@aol.com
***Dir:*** *1m N, travelling from N or S follow A1058 signs for coast and turn left into Osborne Road at first rdbt*
This commercial hotel in Jesmond has the benefit of a secure car park and good transport links. Service is cheery, and the bedrooms are well-equipped. Good value meals are offered in the restaurant.
**ROOMS:** 39 rms (38 en suite) (3 fmly) No smoking in 3 bedrooms
**FACILITIES:** STV **CONF:** Thtr 75 Class 50 Board 40 **PARKING:** 40
**CARDS:**

**★★59% Cairn**
97/103 Osborne Rd, Jesmond NE2 2TJ
☎ 0191 281 1358 📠 0191 281 9031
Situated in the suburb of Jesmond, east of the city centre, this commercial hotel offers friendly informal service and well-equipped bedrooms. Public areas feature a colonial-style restaurant and smart, trendy bar.
**ROOMS:** 50 en suite (2 fmly) s £40-£59; d £55-£69 (incl. bkfst) * **LB**
**FACILITIES:** STV Xmas **CONF:** Thtr 150 Class 110 Board 100
**PARKING:** 22 **NOTES:** Civ Wed **CARDS:**

*See advert on opposite page*

**★65% Hadrian Lodge Hotel**
Hadrian Rd, Wallsend NE28 6HH
☎ 0191 262 7733 📠 0191 263 0714
e-mail: Claire.Stubbs@barbox.net
***Dir:*** *from Tyne tunnel (A19) take A187 to Wallsend follow this route for 1.5m, hotel on left opposite Hadrian Road Metro Station*
Conveniently situated near the metro system with easy access to the city centre, airport and railway station, this hotel offers modern accommodation, ground floor bedrooms tending to be somewhat larger. Service is friendly and a wide range of English and Italian dishes is available either in the spacious bar or in Pino's restaurant.

**ROOMS:** 24 en suite (1 fmly) No smoking in 6 bedrooms s £30-£43; d £49 (incl. bkfst) * **FACILITIES:** Xmas **CONF:** Class 15 Board 15
**PARKING:** 60 **CARDS:**

**Premier Lodge**
The Quayside NE1 3DW
☎ 0870 700 1504 📠 0870 700 1505
***Dir:*** *A167M then A186 & B1600, hotel is situated on B1600 next to Tyne bridge*
Premier Lodge offers modern, well-equipped, en suite accommodation suitable for both business and leisure travellers. Meals can be taken at the adjacent popular restaurant and bar, which is fully licensed. For further details, consult the Hotel Groups page.
**ROOMS:** 136 en suite s £49.95; d £49.95 * **CONF:** Thtr 50 Class 30 Board 30 Del £99 *

***Travelodge***
Foster St NE1 2NH
☎ 08700 850950

Travelodge offers good quality, good value, modern accommodation. Ideal for families, the spacious, en suite bedrooms include remote-control TV, tea and coffee-making facilities, luxury beds and free morning newspaper. Meals can be taken at the nearby family restaurant. For further details and the Travelodge phone number, consult the Hotel Groups page.

**○ Innkeeper's Lodge Newcastle**
Kenton Bank NE3 3TY
A new concept in the travel accommodation market. Smart rooms meet essential business requirements but also have home comforts. Dining options includ all-day menus plus the added advantage of breakfast, which is

*continue*

ıcluded in the room price. Reservations can be made seven days week through the room reservations number: 0870 243 0500. or further details, consult the Hotel Groups page.
**OOMS:** 30 en suite

**Menzies Silverlink Park**
ilverlink, Coast Rd NE28 9HP
☎ 0191 202 9955 📠 0191 263 4172
-mail: silverlinkpark@menzies-hotels.co.uk

MENZIES HOTELS

his hotel was acquired by Menzies as the guide went to press. ublic areas are being upgraded and the company's brasserie estaurant concept is being introduced. Please refer to the AA nternet site www.theAA.com for current information.
**OOMS:** 119 rms **NOTES:** Open now

NEWCASTLE UPON TYNE AIRPORT, Tyne & Wear — Map 12 NZ17

**Premier Lodge**
allerton Ln Ends, Woolsington NE13 8DF
☎ 0870 700 1506 📠 0870 700 1507

PREMIER LODGE

**ir:** *Turn off A1 onto A696 Jedburgh Rd towards Newcastle airport, take 2nd slip road signed Throckley & Woolsington turn ight at the top of the road 2 rdbts over level x-ing, hotel on left)*
remier Lodge offers modern, well-equipped, en suite accommodation suitable for both business and leisure travellers. Meals can be taken at the adjacent popular restaurant and bar, which is fully licensed. For further details, consult the Hotel Groups page.
**ROOMS:** 42 en suite 10 annexe en suite s £42; d £42 * **CONF:** Thtr 60 Class 20 Board 26 Del £77.50 *

NEWICK, East Sussex — Map 05 TQ42

★★★81% ⚙⚙ ***Newick Park Country Estate***
BN8 4SB
☎ 01825 723633 📠 01825 723969
e-mail: bookings@newickpark.co.uk
**Dir:** *turn S off A272 in Newick between Haywards Heath and Uckfield, pass the church and turn left at junct, entrance to Newick Park is 0.25m on right*
This Grade II listed property is set in 250 acres of Sussex parkland. The lounge offers views over the lake, a truly secluded location. Bedrooms are tastefully furnished with some beautiful furniture and good facilities. Cuisine offers choice and quality and is enjoyed in the elegant restaurant.
**ROOMS:** 13 en suite 3 annexe en suite (5 fmly) No smoking in 12 bedrooms **FACILITIES:** STV Outdoor swimming (H) Tennis (hard) Fishing Croquet lawn Badminton **CONF:** Thtr 80 Class 80 Board 25 **PARKING:** 52 **NOTES:** No smoking in restaurant Civ Wed 70
**CARDS:**

*See advert on this page*



N

## NEWMARKET, Suffolk
Map 05 TL66

**★★★77% Bedford Lodge**
Bury Rd CB8 7BX
☎ 01638 663175 01638 667391
e-mail: info@bedfordlodgehotel.co.uk
***Dir:** take Bury St Edmunds road from town centre, hotel half a mile on left*
In three acres of secluded gardens a short drive from Newmarket race track, this 18th-century Georgian hunting lodge was originally built for the Duke of Bedford. Most of the bedrooms have recently been fully refurbished in a clean modern style, with bathrooms equipped to a high standard; a selection of suites are available. Guests can dine in the bar or in the smartly restyled restaurant which offers a wide variety of freshly prepared dishes. A modern leisure complex proves popular.
**ROOMS:** 56 en suite (3 fmly) **FACILITIES:** Indoor swimming (H) Sauna Solarium Gym Jacuzzi Steam room & beauty salon **CONF:** Thtr 200 Class 80 Board 60 **SERVICES:** Lift **PARKING:** 90
**CARDS:**

**★★★73% Swynford Paddocks Hotel**
CB8 0UE
☎ 01638 570234 01638 570283
e-mail: info@swynfordpaddocks.com
(For full entry see Six Mile Bottom)

**★★★68% Heath Court**
Moulton Rd CB8 8DY
☎ 01638 667171 01638 666533
e-mail: quality@heathcourt-hotel.co.uk
***Dir:** from A14 leave at Newmarket/Ely exit (A142) follow town centre signs through mini-rdbt at clocktower turn immediately left into Moulton Rd*
Close to Newmarket Heath, this modern red-brick hotel is popular for its pleasant facilities. Bedrooms are spacious and smartly presented and informal meals can be taken in the lounge bar. Alternatively a good carte is served in the restaurant.
**ROOMS:** 41 en suite (2 fmly) No smoking in 11 bedrooms s £82-£98; d £102-£125 (incl. bkfst) * **LB** **FACILITIES:** STV **CONF:** Thtr 150 Class 40 Board 40 Del from £85 * **SERVICES:** Lift **PARKING:** 50
**NOTES:** Civ Wed 80 **CARDS:**

Late for dinner? Quality Standards star rating means that last orders for dinner should be no earlier than:
★ 6.30pm ★★ 7.00pm ★★★ 8.00pm
★★★★ 9.00pm ★★★★★ 10.00pm



## NEW MILTON, Hampshire
Map 04 SZ2

**Premier Collection**

**★★★★★ Chewton Glen**
Christchurch Rd BH25 6QS
☎ 01425 275341 01425 272310
e-mail: reservations@chewtonglen.com
***Dir:** on A35 from Lyndhurst, drive 10 miles and turn left at staggered junct. Following brown tourist sign for hotel through Walkford, take second left*
Once past the front door the guest is transported into a world of luxury. Log fires and afternoon tea are part of the tradition here; lounges enjoy fine views over the gardens. Grounds include a number of outdoor pleasures, including a path to the sea. The spa and leisure facilities are amongst the best in the country. Dining is a treat in the conservatory style restaurant, and extensive wine lists are a must for enthusiasts.
**ROOMS:** 62 en suite s £275-£720; d £275-£720 * **LB**
**FACILITIES:** **Spa** STV Indoor swimming (H) Outdoor swimming (H) Golf 9 Tennis (hard) Snooker Sauna Gym Croquet lawn Putting green Jacuzzi Steam&Treatment rooms, Hairdresser,indoor tennis courts entertainment Xmas **CONF:** Thtr 150 Class 70 Board 40 Del £330 * **PARKING:** 100 **NOTES:** No dogs (ex guide dogs) No children 6yrs No smoking in restaurant Civ Wed 120
**CARDS:**

## NEWPORT, Shropshire
Map 07 SJ7

**★★63% Royal Victoria**
St Mary's St TF10 7AB
☎ 01952 820331 01952 820209
e-mail: info@royal-victoria.com.uk
***Dir:** turn off A41 at 2nd Newport by-pass rdbt towards town centre turn right at 1st traffic lights. Hotel car park 150 metres on left*
This town centre hotel stands behind St Nicholas church. It dates back to Georgian times and its name derives from a visit by Princess Victoria, in 1832. The hotel provides well-equipped, modern accommodation. Facilities here include an attractively appointed restaurant, a choice of bars and a large function/conference suite.
**ROOMS:** 24 en suite (2 fmly) s £44; d £59 (incl. bkfst) * **CONF:** Del from £71 * **PARKING:** 57 **CARDS:**

## NEWQUAY, Cornwall & Isles of Scilly
Map 02 SW8

**★★★72% Headland**
Fistral Beach TR7 1EW
☎ 01637 872211 01637 872212
e-mail: office@headland.hotel.co.uk
***Dir:** turn off A30 onto A392 at Indian Queens, on approaching Newquay follow signs for Fistral Beach, the hotel is adjacent*
Surrounded on three sides by the sea, this unique Victorian hotel
continued

built in one of the most spectacular settings in Cornwall. Most of e bedrooms benefit from the splendid views and all offer odern facilities. In addition to the formal dining options, the arden Room' offer lighter meals. Facilities include indoor and ıtdoor pools and tennis courts.

**OOMS:** 108 en suite (56 fmly) s £55-£79; d £78-£159 (incl. bkfst) * **B FACILITIES: Spa** Indoor swimming (H) Outdoor swimming (H) Golf Tennis (hard) Snooker Sauna Gym Croquet lawn Putting green cuzzi Children's indoor/outdoor play area entertainment ch fac **ONF:** Thtr 250 Class 120 Board 50 Del from £99 * **SERVICES:** Lift **ARKING:** 400 **NOTES:** No smoking in restaurant Closed 23-27 Dec v Wed 250 **CARDS:**

### ★★★70% *Barrowfield*

Hilgrove Rd TR7 2QY
☎ 01637 878878 📠 01637 879490
-mail: booking@barrowfield.prestel.co.uk
**ir:** *take A3058 to Newquay towards Quintrell Downs, turn right at rdbt ontinue into town and turn left at Shell garage*

onveniently located close to the town centre and the beaches, ıis ever popular hotel is equally suited for all guests' needs. ublic areas include an elegant restaurant, spacious foyer lounge, ttractive coffee shop and intimate 'Piano Bar'. Some of the omfortable bedrooms have the benefit of sea views, all offer ıodern facilities.

**OOMS:** 81 en suite 2 annexe en suite (18 fmly) **FACILITIES:** STV ıdoor swimming (H) Outdoor swimming (H) Snooker Sauna Solarium ym Jacuzzi Table tennis **CONF:** Thtr 150 Class 60 Board 40 **ERVICES:** Lift **PARKING:** 70 **NOTES:** No smoking in restaurant iv Wed 150 **CARDS:**

### ★★★69% Hotel Bristol

Best Western

Narrowcliff TR7 2PQ
☎ 01637 875181 📠 01637 879347
-mail: info@hotelbristol.co.uk
**ir:** *turn off A30 onto A392, then onto A3058. Hotel is located 2.5m on left*

The Hotel Bristol is conveniently situated opposite the Barrowfields ınd with fine views over the sea. Many of the comfortable

*continued on p432*

N

NEWQUAY, continued

bedrooms enjoy excellent views, as do the spacious public areas. A choice of lounges is available, ideal for relaxing, prior to enjoying a meal in the elegant restaurant. The friendly team of committed staff provide a professional service.
**ROOMS:** 74 en suite (23 fmly) s £53-£68; d £86-£96 * **LB**
**FACILITIES:** Indoor swimming (H) Snooker Sauna Solarium Table tennis ch fac Xmas **CONF:** Thtr 200 Class 80 Board 20 Del from £75 *
**SERVICES:** Lift **PARKING:** 105 **NOTES:** No smoking in restaurant
**CARDS:**

*See advert on page 431*

### ★★★68% Trebarwith
Trebarwith Crescent TR7 1BZ
☎ 01637 872288 01637 875431
e-mail: trebahotel@aol.com
***Dir:*** *from A3058 forward until Mount Wise Rd then 3rd right down Marcus Hill and across East St into Trebarwith Crescent. Hotel at end*

With stunning views along the North Cornish coastline, this family run hotel is set in its own grounds, close to the town centre and with a path leading to the beach. The public rooms include a lounge, a ballroom, a restaurant and a unique cinema. The comfortable bedrooms include both four-poster and family rooms, many benefiting from the views.
**ROOMS:** 41 en suite (8 fmly) s £35-£59; d £70-£120 (incl. bkfst & dinner) * **LB** **FACILITIES:** Indoor swimming (H) Fishing Snooker Sauna Solarium Jacuzzi Video theatre Games room entertainment ch fac
**CONF:** Thtr 45 Del £100 * **PARKING:** 41 **NOTES:** No dogs (ex guide dogs) No smoking in restaurant Closed Nov-8 Apr
**CARDS:**

*See advert on page 431*

### ★★★66% Esplanade Hotel
Esplanade Rd, Pentire TR7 1PS
☎ 01637 873333 01637 851413
e-mail: info@newquay-hotels.co.uk
***Dir:*** *from A30 take A392 at Indian Queens towards Newquay, follow holiday route until rdbt, take left to Pentire, then right hand fork towards beach*
Overlooking Fistral Beach, this hotel offers warm hospitality. There is a choice of bedroom sizes; all have modern facilities and the most popular rooms benefit from stunning sea views. There are a number of bars, a continental-style coffee shop and the more formal surroundings of the Ocean View restaurant.
**ROOMS:** 93 en suite (44 fmly) No smoking in 5 bedrooms s £27-£55; d £50-£110 (incl. bkfst & dinner) * **LB** **FACILITIES:** **Spa** STV Indoor swimming (H) Outdoor swimming (H) Sauna Solarium Jacuzzi Table tennis entertainment ch fac Xmas **CONF:** Thtr 300 Class 180 Board 150
**SERVICES:** Lift **PARKING:** 40 **NOTES:** No smoking in restaurant
**CARDS:**

*See advert on opposite page*

### ★★★63% Hotel Riviera
Lusty Glaze Rd TR7 3AA
☎ 01637 874251 01637 850823
e-mail: a.newton@btinternet.com
***Dir:*** *approaching Newquay from Porth turn right at The Barrowfields. Hotel on right overlooking the sea*
This popular cliff-top hotel enjoys panoramic views across the gardens to the sea beyond. Bedrooms are well-equipped, althou varied in terms of size and style. Comfortable lounges are provided for rest and relaxation; the more energetic may wish to use the squash court, followed by a dip in the heated outdoor pool.
**ROOMS:** 48 en suite (6 fmly) s £35-£45; d £70-£90 (incl. bkfst) * **LB**
**FACILITIES:** STV Outdoor swimming (H) Tennis (hard & grass) Squash Snooker Sauna ch fac Xmas **CONF:** Thtr 200 Class 150 Board 50 Del from £54.95 * **SERVICES:** Lift **PARKING:** 80 **NOTES:** No dogs (ex guide dogs) No smoking in restaurant Civ Wed 200
**CARDS:**

*See advert on opposite pa*

### ★★★56% Kilbirnie
Narrowcliff TR7 2RS
☎ 01637 875155 01637 850769
e-mail: enquirykilbirnie@aol.com
***Dir:*** *on A392*
Overlooking the Barrowfields and the Atlantic Ocean, this family owned hotel has spacious reception rooms, including a ballroom, cocktail bar and a comfortable foyer lounge. Bedrooms vary in size and style and the hotel offers a good range of indoor facilitie the restaurant offers a fixed-price menu.
**ROOMS:** 66 en suite (3 fmly) **FACILITIES:** Indoor swimming (H) Outdoor swimming (H) Snooker Sauna Solarium Jacuzzi Table tennis Xmas **SERVICES:** Lift air con **PARKING:** 68
**CARDS:**

*See advert on opposite pag*

### ★★76% Corisande Manor
Riverside Av, Pentire TR7 1PL
☎ 01637 872042 01637 874557
e-mail: relax@corisande.com
***Dir:*** *from A392 Newquay road follow signs for Pentire*
A Victorian hotel situated in three acres of grounds, with easy access to the town centre. Each evening a short menu offers an innovative choice of dishes, supported by an extensive and well-chosen wine list. The bedrooms offer modern facilities and are decorated and furnished with great care and imagination.
**ROOMS:** 12 en suite s £69-£79; d £118-£138 (incl. bkfst) * **LB**
**FACILITIES:** Croquet lawn Putting green Xmas **PARKING:** 19
**NOTES:** No smoking in restaurant **CARDS:**

### ★★71% Whipsiderry
Trevelgue Rd, Porth TR7 3LY
☎ 01637 874777 01637 874777
e-mail: whipsiderry@cornwall.net
***Dir:*** *turn right onto Padstow road B3276 out of Newquay, in half a mile turn right at Trevelgue Rd*
Benefitting from superb views over Newquay's Porth Beach, this long established, friendly family-run hotel continues to prove popular. Bedrooms vary in size and style; many enjoy superb views. Each evening in the dining room, an imaginative, well balanced menu is provided with the emphasis on fresh, local produce wherever possible. As dusk draws on, badger watching has become a special pastime for guests.
**ROOMS:** 24 rms (19 en suite) (5 fmly) s £38.50-£50.50; d £77-£101 (incl. bkfst & dinner) * **LB** **FACILITIES:** Outdoor swimming (H) Sauna american pool entertainment ch fac Xmas **PARKING:** 30 **NOTES:** No smoking in restaurant Closed Nov-Etr (ex Xmas) **CARDS:**

## *The Esplanade Hotel*

Esplanade Road · Pentire · Newquay
Cornwall TR7 1PS · Tel: (01637) 87333
Fax: (01637) 851413 · www.newquay-hotels.co.uk
Freephone 0500 900950
E-mail: info@newquay-hotels.co.uk

***A warm welcome awaits you at this modern spacious hotel, directly overlooking the magnificent Fistral beach.***

• INDOOR AND OUTDOOR HEATED POOLS •
• SAUNA, SOLARIUM AND SPA BATH • TWO LIFTS •
• BALLROOM BAR • CABARET BAR • FUNCTION SUITE •
• GAMES ROOM • COFFEE SHOP •
• CONCESSIONARY GOLF • PARKING •

All 93 rooms are attractively furnished, all front facing rooms enjoy a sea view. We also offer some business class rooms. A wide range of facilities, excellent cuisine and wine list combined with friendly yet professional service ensure that the Esplanade is an ideal base, whatever the nature of your visit to Newquay.

AA ★★★

## Hotel Riviera

Lusty Glaze Road
Newquay, Cornwall TR7 3AA
Tel: 01637 874251 Fax: 01637 850823
Web: www.hotelrivieranewquay.com
Email: a.newton@btinternet.com

◆

This popular cliff-top hotel enjoys panoramic views across the gardens to the sea beyond.

Bedrooms are well-equipped, although varied in terms of size and style.

Comfortable lounges are provided for rest and relaxation; the more energetic may wish to use the squash court, followed by a dip in the heated outdoor pool.

## Kilbirnie Hotel

**Newquay**
**Cornwall**
**TR7 3RS**

AA ★★★

**Telephone: 01673 875155**
**Fax: 01637 850769**
**E-mail: enquirykilbirnie@aol.com**
**Web: www.connexions.co.uk/Kilbirnie**

Kilbirnie Hotel
AA ★★★ RAC
Kilbirnie Hotel
Kilbirnie

The Kilbirnie Hotel is one of the leading hotels in Newquay, with a superb position overlooking Tolcarne and Lusty Glaze beaches and just five minutes level walk to the town centre.
**Luxury indoor and outdoor heated swimming pools, sauna, solarium and spa bath. Lift to all floors. Ballroom and cocktail bar, entertainment in summer. Games room, snooker and pool tables.**
A friendly and attentive team ensures you a relaxed holiday. Excellent cuisine using the finest, fresh local produce complemented by a fine selection of wines, served in our Ocean Room restaurant.

NEWQUAY, continued

### ★★69% Porth Veor Manor

Porth Way TR7 3LW
☎ 01637 873274 01637 851690
e-mail: booking@porthveor.co.uk
***Dir:*** *on B3276 quarter of a mile from junct with A3058*
Overlooking Porth Beach, this Victorian stone house is set in two acres of gardens and grounds and offers a friendly relaxed atmosphere. Equally well suited to both leisure and business guests, a variety of bedrooms is available. In the dining room, with splendid coastal views from every window, an innovative set-price menu is served.
**ROOMS:** 22 en suite (7 fmly) No smoking in 6 bedrooms s £32-£42; d £64-£84 (incl. bkfst) * **LB** **FACILITIES:** Croquet lawn Putting green Xmas **CONF:** Thtr 36 Class 24 Board 24 **PARKING:** 40 **NOTES:** No smoking in restaurant RS Nov-Feb **CARDS:**

### ★★67% Philema

1 Esplanade Rd, Pentire TR7 1PY
☎ 01637 872571 01637 873188
e-mail: info@philema.demon.co.uk
***Dir:*** *from A30 follow A392 signs then signs for Fistral Beach & Pentire, turn left at rdbt for Pentire. Hotel at bottom of Pentire Rd*
Overlooking Fistral Beach, this family-run hotel prides itself on its hospitality and is situated close to the town centre and shops. With modern facilities, all of the bedrooms are comfortably furnished and some benefit from views of the beach. Public areas are spacious and leisure facilities are provided. Evening meals are served in the pleasant dining room.
**ROOMS:** 29 en suite (16 fmly) s £24-£36; d £48-£72 (incl. bkfst & dinner) * **LB** **FACILITIES:** STV Indoor swimming (H) Snooker Sauna Solarium Jacuzzi Table tennis entertainment **PARKING:** 37 **NOTES:** No smoking in restaurant Closed Nov-Feb **CARDS:**

N

### ★★63% *Cedars*

Mount Wise TR7 2BA
☎ 01637 874225 01637 850421
***Dir:*** *enter Newquay via Narrowcliff follow one way system into Berry Rd & Mountwise approx 500yds on right from Mountwise public car park*
With distant views of the coastline, this family-run hotel remains popular with holidaymakers. Friendly and enthusiastic staff serve in the dining room, and in the spacious lounge/bar entertainment is provided in season. Bedrooms vary in size, shape and style, and some are especially suitable for families.
**ROOMS:** 42 rms (31 en suite) (8 fmly) **FACILITIES:** Outdoor swimming (H) Sauna Solarium Gym Jacuzzi entertainment **PARKING:** 42 **NOTES:** No smoking in restaurant Closed Nov-Mar (ex Xmas & New Year) **CARDS:**

### ★★63% Eliot Cavendish

Leisureplex

Edgcumbe Av TR7 2NH
☎ 01637 878177 01637 852053
***Dir:*** *from A30 take A392 towards Quintrell Downs. Turn right at roundabout onto A3058. Follow road for 4m towards Newquay, left at amusement arcades on to Edgcumbe Av, hotel on left.*
Quietly located and just a short walk from the beaches and shops, this long established hotel is conveniently situated to make the most of Newquay's many and varied attractions. Bedrooms are neatly presented and well-equipped. Facilities include heated outdoor pool, sauna, solarium and games room.
**ROOMS:** 76 en suite (10 fmly) s £25-£30; d £42-£52 (incl. bkfst) * **FACILITIES:** Outdoor swimming (H) Sauna Solarium Jacuzzi entertainment Xmas **SERVICES:** Lift **PARKING:** 20 **NOTES:** No dogs (ex guide dogs) No smoking in restaurant Closed Jan-Feb & Dec (ex Xmas) RS Nov & Mar (open weekdays only) **CARDS:**

### ★★63% Tremont

Pentire Av TR7 1PB
☎ 01637 872984 01637 851984
***Dir:*** *from A30 onto B3902 into Newquay and follow Pentire signs*
Within walking distance of both Fistral Beach and the town centre, this popular hotel continues to have a loyal customer base. Entertainment is held on a regular basis during the summer months in the spacious lounges, and in addition a cosy bar is available for guests. Sensibly furnished, the bedrooms are all equipped with modern facilities.
**ROOMS:** 54 en suite (26 fmly) No smoking in all bedrooms s £24-£35; d £48-£70 (incl. bkfst & dinner) * **LB** **FACILITIES:** Indoor swimming (H) Tennis (hard) Squash Sauna Solarium Gym Putting green Table tennis entertainment ch fac Xmas **SERVICES:** Lift **PARKING:** 60 **NOTES:** No smoking in restaurant **CARDS:**

---

NEWTON ABBOT, Devon — Map 03 SX87
see also Ilsington

### ★★★69% Passage House

Hackney Ln, Kingsteignton TQ12 3QH
☎ 01626 355515 01626 363336
e-mail: mail@passagehousehotel.co.uk
***Dir:*** *leave the A380 for the A381 and follow racecourse signs*
In an enviable position on the Teign estuary, this hotel provides smart, modern bedrooms, meeting rooms and good health and leisure facilities. A choice of menus is available in the restaurant, and guests can also use the well-known historic inn adjacent, under the same management.
**ROOMS:** 38 en suite (32 fmly) No smoking in 9 bedrooms s £68-£78; d £80-£90 (incl. bkfst) * **LB** **FACILITIES:** **Spa** STV Indoor swimming (H) Sauna Solarium Gym ch fac Xmas **CONF:** Thtr 120 Class 50 Board 40 Del from £80 * **SERVICES:** Lift **PARKING:** 300 **NOTES:** No dogs (ex guide dogs) No smoking in restaurant
**CARDS:**

### ★★66% Queens

Best Western

Queen St TQ12 2EZ
☎ 01626 363133 01626 354106
e-mail: queens@bestwestern.co.uk
***Dir:*** *M5 onto A380, follow signs for railway station. Hotel almost directly opposite railway station*
Popular with business clientele during the week and younger customers at weekends in Azarats, the hotel's wine bar, this busy hotel is located opposite the railway station. Guests have the option of dining in the Regency Restaurant or from the extensive bar menu.
**ROOMS:** 20 en suite (2 fmly) No smoking in 6 bedrooms s £52.50-£57.50; d £72.50 (incl. bkfst) * **FACILITIES:** STV **CONF:** Thtr 130 Class 90 Board 40 Del £80 * **PARKING:** 7 **NOTES:** No smoking in restaurant
**CARDS:**

### ★65% Hazelwood Hotel

33a Torquay Rd TQ12 2LW
☎ 01626 366130 01626 365021
***Dir:*** *join A380 until reaching Newton Abbot. At main rdbt right past McDonalds. Keep left through 2 sets of lights. Hotel located on top of hill on right*
Guests are assured of a friendly welcome and a relaxed atmosphere at this small hotel close to the town centre. The pleasantly decorated bedrooms are well maintained, and honest home cooking features in the small panelled dining room. In the lounge, guests can relax in comfort and enjoy a drink from the bar.
**ROOMS:** 7 en suite s £40; d £55 (incl. bkfst) * **CONF:** Board 12 **PARKING:** 7 **NOTES:** No dogs (ex guide dogs) No smoking in restaurant
**CARDS:**

## NEWTON-LE-WILLOWS, Merseyside Map 07 SJ59

### ★★66% *Kirkfield Hotel*

2/4 Church St WA12 9SU
☎ 01925 228196 📠 01925 291540
***Dir:*** *on A49 Newton-le-Willows opposite St Peter's Church*
Situated directly opposite the church, this hotel offers accommodation with straightforward furnishings. A good range of meals is available in the bar or dining room, and the staff create a relaxing and informal atmosphere.
**ROOMS:** 15 en suite (3 fmly) No smoking in 5 bedrooms **CONF:** Thtr 70 Class 60 Board 20 **PARKING:** 50 **NOTES:** No dogs (ex guide dogs) Closed 25 Dec **CARDS:**

## NORMAN CROSS, Cambridgeshire Map 04 TL19

### ★★★63% Posthouse Peterborough

Posthouse

Great North Rd PE7 3TB
☎ 0870 400 9063 📠 01733 244455
***Dir:*** *100 yds from junct 16 A1(m) towards Yaxley om A15*
Situated at the junction of the A1(M) and A15, approximately 6 miles from the town centre, this hotel offers a mixture of traditionally furnished and modern styled bedrooms, which are all well-equipped. A health club is a feature of the hotel, together with the Junction restaurant that serves British and international dishes.
**ROOMS:** 96 en suite No smoking in 47 bedrooms s £59-£79; d £59-£79 * **LB** **FACILITIES:** Indoor swimming (H) Sauna Gym Jacuzzi Steam room Xmas **CONF:** Thtr 50 Class 16 Board 24 Del from £100 * **PARKING:** 150 **NOTES:** RS 24-27 Dec
**CARDS:**

## NORTHALLERTON, North Yorkshire Map 08 SE39

### ★★★67% Solberge Hall

Newby Wiske DL7 9ER
☎ 01609 779191 📠 01609 780472
e-mail: hotel@solberge.freeserve.co.uk
***Dir:*** *3.25kms S of Northallerton on the A167. Hotel is located on the right as you pass through North Otterington*
Set in 16 acres of grounds, this Georgian country house commands views over the Yorkshire dales and moors. Rooms vary in style but all are thoughtfully equipped and several have beautiful four poster beds. Stylish public areas include a bar and elegant lounge as well as the Garden Room Restaurant offering a good selection of carefully prepared dishes.
**ROOMS:** 24 en suite (2 fmly) s £75-£85; d £100-£120 (incl. bkfst) * **LB** **FACILITIES:** STV Croquet lawn Xmas **CONF:** Thtr 100 Class 50 Board 40 **PARKING:** 100 **NOTES:** No smoking in restaurant Civ Wed 100
**CARDS:**

### ★★64% ® The Golden Lion

High St DL7 8PP
☎ 01609 777411 📠 01609 773250
***Dir:*** *take A684 travel approx 5m onto A167 through built-up area 3rd exit at next rdbt to town centre at 3rd rdbt turn left into High St*
A popular hotel in the town centre. Inviting public areas include a lounge and spacious well-stocked bar. The attractive restaurant is noted locally for its gourmet fare. Bedrooms, with pleasing colour schemes, are comfortable and offer a good range of amenities.
**ROOMS:** 25 en suite (2 fmly) No smoking in 18 bedrooms **FACILITIES:** Xmas **CONF:** Thtr 150 Class 80 Board 60 Del from £19.95 * **PARKING:** 100 **NOTES:** No smoking in restaurant Civ Wed 150
**CARDS:**

## NORTHAMPTON, Northamptonshire Map 04 SP76

see also Flore

### ★★★★69% ® Northampton Marriott Hotel

Marriott
HOTELS · RESORTS · SUITES

Eagle Dr NN4 7HW
☎ 01604 768700 📠 01604 769011
e-mail: northampton@marriotthotels.co.uk
***Dir:*** *off A45, between A428 & A508*

Ideal for conferences, this hotel has its own self-contained management centre. Public areas are bright and inviting, and bedrooms are equally appealing, equipped with all modern comforts. Dining options include Spires, an elegant room overlooking the lake, and La Fontana, an Italian restaurant with a more informal atmosphere.
**ROOMS:** 120 en suite (12 fmly) No smoking in 82 bedrooms s fr £99; d fr £99 (incl. bkfst) * **LB** **FACILITIES:** STV Indoor swimming (H) Sauna Solarium Gym Jacuzzi Steam room Xmas **CONF:** Thtr 220 Class 100 Board 36 Del from £142 * **PARKING:** 187 **NOTES:** Civ Wed 80
**CARDS:**

### ★★★69% Lime Trees

8 Langham Place, Barrack Rd NN2 6AA
☎ 01604 632188 📠 01604 233012
e-mail: info@limetrees.co.uk
***Dir:*** *from city centre 0.5m N on A508 Leicester near racecourse park & cathedral*
This charming hotel remains ever popular. Bedrooms are well-equipped and very comfortable. The hotel is popular with business guests throughout the week, who appreciate the efficient and friendly service; the weekends see more leisure guests. The smart restaurant offers a range of carefully prepared and popular dishes. Hospitality is excellent.
**ROOMS:** 27 en suite (2 fmly) s £72-£80; d £90 (incl. bkfst) * **LB** **CONF:** Thtr 50 Class 30 Board 30 Del from £79 * **PARKING:** 24 **NOTES:** No dogs (ex guide dogs) RS 27 Dec-New Year
**CARDS:**

### ★★★68% *Courtyard by Marriott Northampton*

Bedford Rd NN4 7YF
☎ 01604 622777 📠 01604 635454
***Dir:*** *from M1 junct 15 follow A508 towards Northampton. Follow A45 towards Wellingborough for 2m then A428 towards Bedford, hotel on left*
On the eastern edge of the town centre and easily accessible for the business traveller, this modern, purpose-built hotel offers a good standard of facilities and spacious accommodation. The open-plan public areas offer an informal atmosphere and have

*continued on p436*

## NORTHAMPTON, continued

been extended to give more space. Friendly staff provides a good range of services.

*Courtyard by Marriott, Northampton*

**ROOMS:** 104 en suite (55 fmly) No smoking in 50 bedrooms **FACILITIES:** STV Gym **CONF:** Thtr 40 Class 30 Board 30 **SERVICES:** Lift air con **PARKING:** 150 **NOTES:** No dogs (ex guide dogs) No smoking in restaurant **CARDS:**

### ★★★65% *Grand*

CLOSED

ZOFFANY HOTELS

15 Gold St NN1 1RE
☎ 01604 250511 🖷 01604 234534
e-mail: grand@zoffanyhotels.co.uk
***Dir:*** *follow A508 to town centre, over traffic [illegible] the [illegible]arlsberg Brewery, take the road to left, hotel [illegible] on left*

This impressive town centre [illegible] bright and attractive accommodation. The be[illegible] comfortably furnished and well equipped. Public are[illegible] include the Kasbah bar which offers a popular range of [illegible]es at dinner, and the lower ground floor dining ro[illegible] where [illegible]kfast is served.

**ROOMS:** 5[illegible] (2 fmly) No smoking in 21 bedrooms **FACILITIES:** STV **CONF:** Thtr 120 Class 50 Board 40 **SERVICES:** Lift **PARKING:** 72 **NOTES:** No smoking in restaurant **CARDS:**

### ★★★64% Quality Hotel Northampton

Quality Hotel

Ashley Way, Weston Favell NN3 3EA
☎ 01604 739955 🖷 01604 415023
e-mail: admin@gb070.u-net.com
***Dir:*** *leave A45 at junct with A43, towards Weston Favell. After 0.5m bear left to town centre. Turn left at top of slip road, hotel signposted off A4500*

Built in 1914, this established hotel enjoys a quiet residential location on the outskirts of town. Well-equipped bedrooms are split between the main house and an adjoining wing. Attractive public rooms include comfortable lounge areas, smartly appointed restaurant and a number of excellent meeting rooms.

**ROOMS:** 31 en suite 35 annexe en suite (4 fmly) No smoking in 21 bedrooms s £72-£82; d £82-£92 * **LB** **FACILITIES:** STV Croquet lawn entertainment Xmas **CONF:** Thtr 150 Class 65 Board 60 **SERVICES:** Lift **PARKING:** 100 **NOTES:** No smoking in restaurant Civ Wed 150 **CARDS:**

### ⇧ *Travelodge*

Travelodge

Upton Way NN5 6EG
☎ 01604 758395 🖷 01604 758395
***Dir:*** *A45, towards M1 junct 16*

Travelodge offers good quality, good value, modern accommodation. Ideal for families, the spacious, en suite bedrooms include remote-control TV, tea and coffee-making facilities, luxury beds and free morning newspaper. Meals can be taken at the nearby family restaurant. For further details and the Travelodge phone number, consult the Hotel Groups page.

**ROOMS:** 62 en suite

### ⇧ *Premier Lodge (Northampton East)*

PREMIER LODGE

Crown Ln, Great Billing NN3 9DA
☎ 0870 700 1522 🖷 0870 700 1523

Premier Lodge offers modern, well-equipped, en suite accommodation suitable for both business and leisure travellers. Meals can be taken at the adjacent popular restaurant and bar, which is fully licensed. For further details, consult the Hotel Groups page.

**ROOMS:** 60 en suite

### ⇧ Premier Lodge (Northampton South)

PREMIER LODGE

London Rd West, Wootton NN4 0JN
☎ 0870 700 1518 🖷 0870 700 1519
***Dir:*** *M1 junct 15 towards Northampton at A508/A45 junct take 5th exit off rdbt. Lodge is on right*

Premier Lodge offers modern, well-equipped, en suite accommodation suitable for both business and leisure travellers. Meals can be taken at the adjacent popular restaurant and bar, which is fully licensed. For further details, consult the Hotel Groups page.

**ROOMS:** 39 en suite s £46; d £46 * **CONF:** Thtr 80 Class 48 Board 30 Del from £95 *

### ○ Innkeeper's Lodge Northampton South

Innkeeper's Lodge

London Rd, Wootton NN4 0TG

A new concept in the travel accommodation market. Smart rooms meet essential business requirements but also have home comforts. Dining options include all-day menus plus the added advantage of breakfast, which is included in the room price. Reservations can be made seven days a week through the room reservations number: 0870 243 0500. For further details, consult the Hotel Groups page.

**ROOMS:** 31 en suite

## NORTH FERRIBY, East Riding of Yorkshire — Map 08 SE92

### ★★★62% Humber Crown

Ferriby High Rd HU14 3LG
☎ 01482 645212 🖷 01482 643332
e-mail: enquiries@humbercrown.co.uk
***Dir:*** *from M62 join A63 to Hull. Take exit for Humber Bridge. At rdbt follow signs for Leeds continue until signs for North Ferriby hotel 0.5 miles left*

A former post house which commands fine views of the Humber Bridge. Bedrooms are well equipped. Public areas are functional and both the restaurant and lounge bar look out over the Humber. There is ample car parking and also a children's play area at the rear. 24 hour room service is available.

**ROOMS:** 95 en suite (3 fmly) No smoking in 66 bedrooms s fr £55; d fr £65 * **LB** **FACILITIES:** STV Nearly full size pool table ch fac Xmas **CONF:** Thtr 120 Class 45 Board 45 Del from £79.50 * **PARKING:** 140 **NOTES:** No smoking in restaurant Civ Wed 50 **CARDS:**

## NORTH MUSKHAM, Nottinghamshire — Map 08 SK75

### ⇧ *Travelodge*

Travelodge

NG23 6HT
☎ 01636 703635 🖷 01636 703635
***Dir:*** *3m N, on A1 southbound*

Travelodge offers good quality, good value, modern accommodation. Ideal for families, the spacious, en suite bedrooms

*continued*

include remote-control TV, tea and coffee-making facilities, luxury beds and free morning newspaper. Meals can be taken at the nearby family restaurant. For further details and the Travelodge phone number, consult the Hotel Groups page.

**ROOMS:** 30 en suite

NORTH WALSHAM, Norfolk — Map 09 TG23

### ★★81% ꕥꕥ Beechwood

Cromer Rd NR28 0HD
☎ 01692 403231 🖷 01692 407284
***Dir:*** *take B1150 from Norwich, at North Walsham turn left at first set of traffic lights then right at the next*

An elegant ivy-clad 18th-century house, within easy striking distance of the North Norfolk coastline. Lovingly converted, it provides attractively decorated and well laid out accommodation throughout. Bedrooms are tastefully furnished with antique pieces, lovely soft furnishings and many thoughtful touches. The public areas include a cosy sitting room and a smart lounge bar.
**ROOMS:** 10 en suite No smoking in 7 bedrooms s £50-£60; d £74-£94 (incl. bkfst) **LB** **PARKING:** 15 **NOTES:** No children 10yrs No smoking in restaurant **CARDS:**

*See advert on this page*

NORTH WALTHAM, Hampshire — Map 04 SU54

### ⌂ *Premier Lodge (Basingstoke)*

PREMIER LODGE

RG25 2BB
☎ 0870 700 1312 🖷 0870 700 1313
***Dir:*** *on A30 one & a half miles from junc7 M3 follow signs for Basingstoke, then Kings Worthy & Popham*
Premier Lodge offers modern, well-equipped, en suite accommodation suitable for both business and leisure travellers. Meals can be taken at the adjacent popular restaurant and bar, which is fully licensed. For further details, consult the Hotel Groups page.
**ROOMS:** 28 en suite **CONF:** Thtr 80 Class 30 Board 35

NORTHWICH, Cheshire — Map 07 SJ67

### ★★★66% Quality Hotel Northwich

Quality Hotel

London Rd CW9 5HD
☎ 01606 44443 🖷 01606 42596
e-mail: admin@gb618.u-net.com
***Dir:*** *from M6 junct 19 take A556 to Northwich. Follow signs for Chester & 'Salt Museum'. At 2nd rdbt take A533 London Road*
A first in the UK! This floating hotel has been built over the river and a very successful concept it is. The bedrooms are modern and *continued*

well-equipped and there is a carvery restaurant which, not surprisingly, overlooks the river.
**ROOMS:** 60 en suite (2 fmly) No smoking in 30 bedrooms s £40-£71; d £40-£83 * **LB** **FACILITIES:** STV Gym Xmas **CONF:** Thtr 80 Class 40 Board 30 Del from £65 * **SERVICES:** Lift **PARKING:** 110 **NOTES:** No smoking in restaurant Civ Wed 80
**CARDS:**

### ★★66% Wincham Hall

Hall Ln, Wincham CW9 6DG
☎ 01606 43453 🖷 01606 40128
e-mail: sarah@wincham-hall.demon.co.uk
***Dir:*** *leave M6 junct 19 take A556 to Chester. Turn right onto A559 to Northwich. At lights turn right. Hotel 0.5m on left*
This family run hotel offers well presented pine furnished bedrooms. Many of the rooms overlook the five acres of grounds, which include a walled garden and lily pond. Guests can relax in the lounge bar before enjoying a meal.
**ROOMS:** 10 rms (9 en suite) (1 fmly) **FACILITIES:** Croquet lawn **CONF:** Thtr 100 Class 50 Board 30 Del from £85 * **PARKING:** 200 **NOTES:** No smoking in restaurant Civ Wed 110
**CARDS:**

### ⌂ *Premier Lodge*

PREMIER LODGE

520 Chester Rd, Sandiway CW8 2DN
☎ 0870 700 1524 🖷 0870 700 1525
Premier Lodge offers modern, well-equipped, en suite accommodation suitable for both business and leisure travellers. Meals can be taken at the adjacent popular restaurant and bar, which is fully licensed. For further details, consult the Hotel Groups page.
**ROOMS:** 52 en suite

NORTHWICH, continued

### ⌂ Premier Lodge (Northwich South)

London Rd, Leftwich CW9 8EG
☎ 0870 700 1526 📠 0870 700 1527
Premier Lodge offers modern, well-equipped, en suite accommodation suitable for both business and leisure travellers. Meals can be taken at the adjacent popular restaurant and bar, which is fully licensed. For further details, consult the Hotel Groups page.
**ROOMS:** 32 en suite s £42; d £42 * **CONF:** Thtr 25 Class 25 Board 25

NORTHWOLD, Norfolk Map 05 TL79

### ★★67% Comfort Inn Thetford

Thetford Rd IP26 5LQ
☎ 01366 728888 📠 01366 727121
e-mail: admin@gb632.u-net.com
***Dir:*** *W of Mundford on A134*
This modern hotel is situated in a rural location just off the A134. The spacious, well-equipped bedrooms are located in a courtyard-style wing, and the beamed Woodland Inn combines the roles of country pub and hotel restaurant.
**ROOMS:** 34 en suite (12 fmly) No smoking in 17 bedrooms s £50.75-£57.75; d £59-£66 (incl. bkfst) * **LB** **FACILITIES:** STV Gym mini gym Xmas **CONF:** Thtr 150 Class 55 Board 60 Del from £65 * **PARKING:** 250 **NOTES:** No smoking in restaurant Civ Wed 80
**CARDS:**

NORTON, Shropshire Map 07 SJ70

### ★★76% Hundred House Hotel

Bridgnorth Rd TF11 9EE
☎ 01952 730353 📠 01952 730355
e-mail: hphundredhouse@messages.co.uk
***Dir:*** *midway between Telford & Bridgnorth on A442. In centre of Norton village*

Primarily Georgian, but with parts dating back to the 14th century, this friendly family owned and run hotel offers individually styled, well-equipped bedrooms which have period furniture and attractive soft furnishings. Some rooms have romantic swings hanging from the ceiling. Public areas include cosy bars and intimate dining areas where memorable meals are served.
**ROOMS:** 10 en suite (4 fmly) s £69-£85; d £99-£125 (incl. bkfst) * **LB** **FACILITIES:** Xmas **CONF:** Class 20 Board 15 **PARKING:** 30 **NOTES:** RS Sunday evenings **CARDS:**

> Packed in a hurry? Ironing facilities should be available at all star levels, either in rooms or on request.

NORWICH, Norfolk Map 05 TG20
see also South Walsham

### ★★★★75% Marriott Sprowston Manor Hotel & Country Club

Sprowston Park, Wroxham Rd, Sprowston NR7 8RP
☎ 01603 410871 📠 01603 423911
e-mail: sprowston.manor@marriotthotels.co.uk
***Dir:*** *2m NE A1151-from A11 take the Wroxham road A1151 and follow signs to Sprowston Park*

Set in its own attractive grounds, surrounded by parkland and within easy driving distance of Norwich city centre. Impressive building with extensive conference, banqueting and leisure facilities, including a golf course. The spacious bedrooms come in different styles and the restaurant serves an interesting range of dishes.
**ROOMS:** 94 en suite (3 fmly) No smoking in 65 bedrooms s £105-£140; d £105-£140 * **LB** **FACILITIES:** **Spa** STV Indoor swimming (H) Golf 18 Sauna Solarium Gym Croquet lawn Jacuzzi Beauty salon Steam room entertainment Xmas **CONF:** Thtr 120 Class 50 Board 50 Del £134 * **SERVICES:** Lift **PARKING:** 150 **NOTES:** No smoking in restaurant Civ Wed 110 **CARDS:**

### ★★★★66% De Vere Dunston Hall

Ipswich Rd NR14 8PQ
☎ 01508 470444 📠 01508 471499
e-mail: dhreception@devere-hotels.com
***Dir:*** *from A47 , take A140 Ipswich Road, hotel directly off this road on left after approx 0.25m*
Set in 170 acres of landscaped grounds this Grade II listed building stands just two miles south of the city. The extensive range of outdoor facilities includes an 18-hole PGA golf course, two floodlit tennis courts and a floodlit driving range. Indoor facilities include a swimming pool, gym and hairdressing salon. Bedrooms are spacious, comfortably furnished and equipped to a high standard.
**ROOMS:** 130 en suite No smoking in 58 bedrooms s £105-£145; d £140-£190 (incl. bkfst) * **LB** **FACILITIES:** **Spa** STV Indoor swimming (H) Golf 18 Tennis (hard) Snooker Sauna Solarium Gym Putting green Jacuzzi Bowling green Floodlit Golf Driving Range Xmas **CONF:** Thtr 299 Class 140 Board 90 Del from £140 * **SERVICES:** Lift **PARKING:** 500 **NOTES:** No dogs (ex guide dogs) No smoking in restaurant
**CARDS:**

### ★★★75% Annesley House

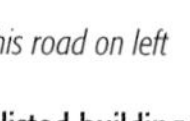

6 Newmarket Rd NR2 2LA
☎ 01603 624553 📠 01603 621577
***Dir:*** *on A11 half a mile before city centre*
Attractive Georgian property situated amidst three acres of landscaped gardens, just a few minuets walk from the city centre. The accommodation is located in three separate houses, two of which are linked by a glass walkway. Bedrooms are attractively

*continued*

decorated, tastefully furnished and thoughtfully equipped. Public rooms feature a smart conservatory restaurant, which overlooks the gardens; guests also have the use of a comfortable lounge bar.
**ROOMS:** 18 en suite 8 annexe en suite (3 fmly) s £75-£80; d £90-£95 (incl. bkfst) * **LB** **FACILITIES:** STV **PARKING:** 25 **NOTES:** No dogs (ex guide dogs) No smoking in restaurant Closed 24-27 & 30-31 Dec
**CARDS:**

### ★★★70% Beeches Hotel & Victorian Gardens

2-6 Earlham Rd NR2 3DB
☎ 01603 621167 01603 620151
e-mail: reception@beeches.co.uk
***Dir:*** *to the W of the City Centre on B1108, next to St Johns RC Cathedral just off inner ring road*
The hotel is located in three separate buildings, each with their own individual character. The tastefully decorated bedrooms come in a variety of styles and are thoughtfully equipped. Public rooms include a smart lounge bar and a bistro-style restaurant. The hotel grounds feature a lovely sunken Victorian garden.
**ROOMS:** 16 en suite 20 annexe en suite No smoking in all bedrooms s £59-£64; d £76-£88 (incl. bkfst) * **LB** **FACILITIES:** Heritage Grade 2 listed Victorian garden of 3 acres **CONF:** Class 20 Board 12 **PARKING:** 34 **NOTES:** No dogs (ex guide dogs) No children 12yrs No smoking in restaurant Closed 22-30 Dec
**CARDS:**

*See advert on this page*

### ★★★68% The George Hotel

10 Arlington Ln, Newmarket Rd NR2 2DA
☎ 01603 617841 01603 663708
e-mail: reservations@georgehotel.co.uk
***Dir:*** *approach on A11, follow City Ctr signs, Newmarket Rd towards city centre. Hotel on left.*

Guests will receive a warm welcome from the friendly team at the George Hotel. The well maintained establishment offers a good standard of accommodation in well-decorated bedrooms. Public areas include an attractive and comfortable lounge bar and small grill-restaurant serving home-cooked meals.
**ROOMS:** 36 en suite 4 annexe en suite (3 fmly) No smoking in 9 bedrooms s fr £65; d £89-£106 (incl. bkfst) **LB** **FACILITIES:** Xmas **CONF:** Thtr 60 Class 25 Board 32 Del from £60 * **PARKING:** 40
**CARDS:**

### ★★★68% *Posthouse Norwich*

Posthouse

Ipswich Rd NR4 6EP
☎ 0870 400 9060 01603 506400
***Dir:*** *take A47, southern bypass, until sign for A140, then turn N into Norwich. Hotel 0.5m on right*
A modern hotel on the outskirts of the city centre. Public areas are comfortably appointed, including The Junction restaurant, a lounge bar and the well-equipped Spa leisure club, which is a

*continued on p440*

N

NORWICH, continued

prominent feature. Bedrooms have every modern facility including mini bars and in-house movies. There is an all-day lounge menu and 24 hour room service.
**ROOMS:** 116 en suite (54 fmly) No smoking in 44 bedrooms **FACILITIES:** Indoor swimming (H) Sauna Gym Jacuzzi Health & fitness centre ch fac **CONF:** Thtr 100 Class 48 Board 40 **PARKING:** 200 **CARDS:**

### ★★★68% Swallow Nelson Hotel

SWALLOW
HOTELS

Prince of Wales Rd NR1 1DX
☎ 01603 760260 📠 01603 620008
e-mail: nelson@swallow-hotels.co.uk
***Dir:*** *follow signs for city centre & football ground & railway station. Hotel is on riverside opposite station*
Situated close to the city centre and railway station overlooking the River Wensum, this pleasant hotel has a nautical theme and features many references to its namesake. Public areas are well-designed and include a range of comfortable seating areas. The choice of eating options, the leisure complex and conference suites make this a popular hotel.
**ROOMS:** 132 en suite No smoking in 60 bedrooms s £92-£106; d £102-£116 * **LB** **FACILITIES:** STV Indoor swimming (H) Sauna Solarium Gym Jacuzzi Xmas **CONF:** Thtr 90 Class 10 Board 44 Del from £115 * **SERVICES:** Lift **PARKING:** 210 **CARDS:**

### ★★★67% Quality Hotel

Quality
Hotel

2 Barnard Rd, Bowthorpe NR5 9JB
☎ 01603 741161 📠 01603 741500
e-mail: admin@gb619.u-net.com
***Dir:*** *take A1074 to Norwich/Cromer. Hotel is situated off A47 Southern Bypass 4m from City Centre*
Situated close to the A47 bypass on the western side of the city centre, this modern hotel gives easy access to routes around Norwich. Bedrooms are generally quite spacious and well-equipped, and there is a good leisure centre and a wide choice of meeting rooms.
**ROOMS:** 80 en suite (13 fmly) No smoking in 40 bedrooms s £89; d £89 * **LB** **FACILITIES:** STV Indoor swimming (H) Sauna Solarium Gym Jacuzzi Steamroom Xmas **CONF:** Thtr 200 Class 80 Board 60 Del from £88 * **PARKING:** 140 **NOTES:** No smoking in restaurant Civ Wed 70 **CARDS:**

### ★★★63% Maids Head

REGAL

Tombland NR3 1LB
☎ 01603 209955 📠 01603 613688
***Dir:*** *follow city centre signs, continue past Norwich Castle, 3rd turning after castle into Upper King St, hotel opposite Norman cathedral*

This 13th-century building situated close to the impressive Norman cathedral and within easy walking distance of the city centre. The bedrooms are well-equipped and smartly furnished, and several rooms feature exposed oak beams. The public areas include a Jacobean bar, a range of seating areas and the Courtyard restaurant. There is a secure car park at the back of the building.
**ROOMS:** 84 en suite (7 fmly) No smoking in 30 bedrooms s £47-£89; d £47-£109 * **LB** **FACILITIES:** Xmas **CONF:** Thtr 300 Class 120 Board 40 Del from £120 * **SERVICES:** Lift **PARKING:** 60 **NOTES:** No smoking in restaurant Civ Wed 100 **CARDS:**

### ★★79% ® The Old Rectory

103 Yarmouth Rd, Thorpe St Andrew NR7 0HF
☎ 01603 700772 📠 01603 300772
e-mail: enquiries@oldrectorynorwich.com
***Dir:*** *from A47 Norwich Southern Bypass, take A1042 towards Norwich N & E. At mini-rdbt bear left (A1242), continue for approx 0.3m, straight over at traffic lights hotel 100mtrs*
Situated in mature gardens in a quiet residential area on the outskirts of the city centre, this elegant Georgian property overlooks the River Yare. The spacious, individually styled bedrooms offer a high degree of comfort and many thoughtful finishing touches. Relax in the drawing room over a pre-dinner drink whilst choosing from the imaginative, daily-changing menu.
**ROOMS:** 5 en suite 3 annexe en suite No smoking in all bedrooms s £63-£73; d £80-£90 (incl. bkfst) * **LB** **FACILITIES:** STV Outdoor swimming (H) **CONF:** Thtr 25 Class 18 Board 16 Del from £104.55 * **PARKING:** 15 **NOTES:** No dogs (ex guide dogs) No smoking in restaurant Closed 23 Dec-11 Jan **CARDS:**

*See advert on opposite page*

### ★★70% The Georgian House

MINOTEL
Great Britain

32-34 Unthank Rd NR2 2RB
☎ 01603 615655 📠 01603 765689
e-mail: reception@georgian-hotel.co.uk
***Dir:*** *follow signs for Roman Catholic Cathedral from city centre the hotel is just off the inner ring road*

Ideally placed for the city centre and close to the Catholic cathedral, this attractive hotel was formerly a pair of Victorian houses. Public areas include a cosy bar, a TV lounge and an elegant restaurant offering a daily changing carte menu. The newly refurbished bedrooms are equipped with many useful extras.
**ROOMS:** 27 en suite (4 fmly) No smoking in 20 bedrooms s £52.50-£60; d £75-£85 (incl. bkfst) * **LB** **CONF:** Thtr 25 Class 20 Board 20 Del from £75 * **PARKING:** 40 **NOTES:** No dogs (ex guide dogs) No smoking in restaurant **CARDS:**

*See advert on opposite page*

Need to unwind? Look out for hotels with Spa in their entry.

**★★70% Stower Grange**
School Rd, Drayton NR8 6EF
☎ 01603 860210 🖷 01603 860464
e-mail: enquiries@stowergrange.co.uk
***Dir:*** *Take Norwich ring road N until ASDA supermarket take A1067 Fakenham Road at village of Drayton trun right at lights along School Rd hotel 150yds on right*

Attractive ivy-clad property, dating back to the 17th century and situated just a few minutes drive from the city centre. The individually decorated bedrooms are tastefully furnished and well-equipped. Public rooms include a bar with an adjacent lounge and a smart restaurant.
**ROOMS:** 11 en suite (1 fmly) s fr £62.50; d fr £80 (incl. bkfst) * **FACILITIES:** Croquet lawn **CONF:** Thtr 100 Class 45 Board 30 Del from £125 * **CARDS:**

79% AA ★★

# The Old Rectory

103 Yarmouth Road, Thorpe St. Andrew
Norwich NR7 0HF
www.oldrectorynorwich.com

Chris and Sally Entwistle invite you to enjoy a relaxed, friendly atmosphere and traditional hospitality in their charming Georgian home, with its delightful view over the Yare valley, on the outskirts of Norwich. Spacious, individually furnished bedrooms offer you every comfort and amenity and our extensive mature gardens, sun terrace and heated swimming pool (summer months) are available for your pleasure. Private meeting and dining facilities also available.

Tel: 01603 700772 Fax: 01603 300772
Email: enquiries@oldrectorynorwich.com

Best Western

# Best Western Abbey Hotel

★★ 71%

**10 Church Street · Wymondham**
**Near Norwich · NR18 0PH**
**Tel: 01953 602148 · Fax: 01953 606247**
**info@abbeyhotels.co.uk**
**www.abbeyhotels.co.uk**

The Wisteria clad hotel is located in a quiet street overlooking the ancient Abbey Grounds. Beyond which is a river walk through the fields, yet the centre of the historic town is just around the corner • The hotel is warm and relaxing with a plethora of original paintings, and art glass. The well established staff pay attention to detail, give an exceptional welcome and do everything to ensure our guests return time and time again • Benims Restaurant menus are modern and traditional. Chef uses fresh local produce when possible. Guests on Getaways, business people, families and groups all compliment us on food, ambience and location. Wymondham is ideally situated for visiting Norwich, Snetterton and touring. The halt for Heritage Railway Wymondham to Dereham line is within walking distance • Pat and Paul Connor, the proprietors, personally run the hotel, and are always striving to introduce new delights.

The
Georgian
House Hotel

**32-34 Unthank Road, Norwich NR2 2RB**
**Web: www.georgian-hotel.co.uk**
**E-mail: reception@georgian-hotel.co.uk**
**Tel: (01603) 615655 Fax: (01603) 765689**

- *Situated in the heart of Norwich, just a short stroll away from the city centre.*
- *Two Georgian town houses tastefully refurbished offering a high standard of accommodation.*
- *Set in beautiful landscaped gardens.*
- *Licensed restaurant and comfortable bar.*
- *Ample free car parking.*

AA ★★

NORWICH, continued

### ★★68% Cumberland
212-216 Thorpe Rd NR1 1TJ
☎ 01603 434550 & 434560 01603 433355
e-mail: cumberland@paston.co.uk
**Dir:** *on A1242, 1m from railway station*
This small hotel provides hospitality and jovial warmth offered from the owner and his friendly team. An interesting choice of dishes is offered in the vibrant restaurant and the welcoming public rooms include a smart lounge bar and a cosy sitting room. Bedroom sizes vary, but all are individually furnished and well-equipped.
**ROOMS:** 22 en suite 3 annexe en suite No smoking in 10 bedrooms **CONF:** Thtr 75 Class 75 Board 40 Del from £74.95 * **PARKING:** 60 **NOTES:** No dogs (ex guide dogs) No children 12yrs No smoking in restaurant Closed 26 Dec-2 Jan **CARDS:**

### *Travelodge*
Thickthorn Service Area, Norwich Southern Bypass NR9 3AU
☎ 01603 457549 01603 457549
**Dir:** *A11/A47 interchange*
Travelodge offers good quality, good value, modern accommodation. Ideal for families, the spacious, en suite bedrooms include remote-control TV, tea and coffee-making facilities, luxury beds and free morning newspaper. Meals can be taken at the nearby family restaurant. For further details and the Travelodge phone number, consult the Hotel Groups page.

**ROOMS:** 40 en suite

NOTTINGHAM, Nottinghamshire Map 08 SK54
see also Langar

### ★★★66% Rutland Square Hotel by the Castle
St James St NG1 6FJ
☎ 0115 941 1114 0115 941 0014
e-mail: rutlandsquare@zoffanyhotels.co.uk
**Dir:** *on entering the city follow brown signs to the castle, hotel on right 50yds on from the castle*
An enviable location in the heart of the city, adjacent to the castle, makes this hotel a popular choice. Behind its Regency facade the hotel is modern and comfortable with good business facilities. The well-equipped bedrooms are tastefully decorated. Public rooms include the informal Terrace Bar and Restaurant and Woods Restaurant.
**ROOMS:** 105 en suite (3 fmly) No smoking in 38 bedrooms s £35-£93; d £70-£110 (incl. bkfst) * **LB** **FACILITIES:** STV Free use of nearby Fitness Club Xmas **CONF:** Thtr 200 Class 70 Board 45 Del from £120 * **SERVICES:** Lift **CARDS:**

*See advert on opposite page*

### ★★★66% The Strathdon
Derby Rd, City Centre NG1 5FT
☎ 0115 941 8501 0115 948 3725
e-mail: info@strathdon-hotel-nottingham.com

PEEL HOTELS

**Dir:** *follow signs to City Centre. Enter one way system proceed down Wollaton street, keep in right lane, next right to hotel*
This popular city centre hotel is conveniently located for the Albert Hall Conference and Exhibition Centre. Bedrooms are modern in style and well-equipped. Public rooms include the popular American Boston Bean Company Bar and Diner, Bobbins Restaurant and a range of meeting rooms.
**ROOMS:** 68 en suite (4 fmly) No smoking in 46 bedrooms s fr £68; d fr £95 * **LB** **FACILITIES:** STV **CONF:** Thtr 150 Class 60 Board 40 Del from £90 * **SERVICES:** Lift **CARDS:**

Popped the question? Hotels with Civ Wed in their entry are licensed for civil wedding ceremonies. Maximum numbers for the ceremony only are shown, e.g. Civ Wed 120

### ★★★66% Westminster Hotel
312 Mansfield Rd, Carrington NG5 2EF
☎ 0115 955 5000 0115 955 5005
e-mail: mail@westminster-hotel.co.uk
**Dir:** *on A60 1m N of town centre*

Best Western

This period property is an ideal base for business and leisure guests alike. All bedrooms are well-equipped and comfortable, however, the new superior rooms are considerably more spacious. The restaurant offers fresh, well-cooked food; the lounge and bar provide less formal surroundings in which to relax.
**ROOMS:** 72 en suite No smoking in 40 bedrooms s £75-£90; d £90-£105 * **LB** **FACILITIES:** STV **CONF:** Thtr 60 Class 30 Board 30 Del from £100 * **SERVICES:** Lift **PARKING:** 66 **NOTES:** No dogs (ex guide dogs) No smoking in restaurant Closed 25 Dec-2 Jan
**CARDS:**

*See advert on opposite page*

### ★★★65% Bestwood Lodge
Bestwood Country Park, Arnold NG5 8NE
☎ 0115 920 3011 0115 967 0409
**Dir:** *3m N off A60 at lights turn left into Oxclose Lane, at next lights, turn right onto Queens Bower Rd then 1st right, where road forks keep right*
A Victorian hunting lodge in 700 acres of parkland, providing contemporary bedrooms of varying sizes and style. A refurbishment programme is on-going. The interior architecture includes Gothic features and high vaulted ceilings in the lounge bar and the gallery. This is a popular venue for weddings and conferences.
**ROOMS:** 39 en suite (5 fmly) s £38-£75; d £76-£130 (incl. bkfst) * **LB** **FACILITIES:** Riding Guided walking ch fac Xmas **CONF:** Thtr 200 Class 65 Board 50 Del £95 * **PARKING:** 120 **NOTES:** No smoking in restaurant RS no accomodation 25 Dec & 1 Jan
**CARDS:**

*See advert on opposite page*

### ★★★65% Nottingham Gateway
Nuthall Rd, Cinderhill NG8 6AZ
☎ 0115 979 4949 0115 979 4744
e-mail: nottingateway@btconnect.com
**Dir:** *M1 junct 26, take A610*
A modern hotel, convenient for the city and the motorway network. Well-equipped bedrooms are comfortable and there is a choice of dining styles available including a carvery and a Thai

*continued on p444*

Best Western THE AA ★★★

# BESTWOOD LODGE HOTEL

Bestwood Country Park

Arnold, Nottingham NG5 8NE

Tel: 0115 920 3011 Fax: 0115 967 0409

Once the former home of Charles II and Nell Gwynn this historic royal hunting lodge is set in 700 acres of beautiful parkland nestling on the edge of Sherwood Forest. All 39 bedrooms are en-suite including 4-poster and executive suites. Dine in the elegant Parkside Restaurant offering superb A La Carte and Table D'hôte menus. Beautiful oak pannelled bar. Extensive conference facilities. Professional tailor-made conference service available. Excellent parking facilities. Ideally located for business or pleasure four miles north of Nottingham City centre. Close to junction 26 of the M1.

# Rutland Square Hotel

*By the Castle*

**NOTTINGHAM**

ZOFFANY HOTELS

*105 fully en-suite bedrooms with executive upgrades*

*Dedicated Conference and Banqueting centre with air conditioning and natural daylight*

•

***Woods,** award winning a la Carte Restaurant and the Terrace Cafe Bar overlooking Nottingham Castle*

ST. JAMES STREET · NOTTINGHAM

Tel: 0115 941 1114 · Fax: 0115 941 0014

Email: rutlandsquare@zoffanyhotels.co.uk

N

★★★

# WESTMINSTER HOTEL

Conveniently located for Nottingham's tourist attractions, its celebrated shopping centres and wealth of sporting venues our family-owned and run hotel is decorated and equipped to the highest standards. Included in our 72 rooms are 2 four-poster bedded rooms and also our 19 superior rooms which are air-conditioned and offer the additional attraction of king-size beds, dedicated PC/Fax connection points and in the bathroom, the luxury of a shower unit which also provides a relaxing steam shower. Dinner in the informal atmosphere of our highly acclaimed restaurant where excellent food and good wines are sensibly priced will simply add to the enjoyment of your stay. The hotel also has 5 meeting rooms including 1 function suite for up to 60, all of which are fully air conditioned.

**312 Mansfield Road, Nottingham NG5 2EF**

Telephone: 0115 955 5000

Fax: 0115 955 5005

Website: www.westminster-hotel.co.uk

Email: mail@westminster-hotel.co.uk

Best Western

NOTTINGHAM, continued

menu. With a number of meeting rooms leading off the glass atrium, this hotel offers a flexible range of facilities.

*Nottingham Gateway, Nottingham*

**ROOMS:** 107 en suite (18 fmly) No smoking in 54 bedrooms s £40-£75; d £50-£80 * LB **FACILITIES:** STV Discounted entrance to David Lloyd H.C Xmas **CONF:** Thtr 300 Class 100 Board 50 Del from £100 * **SERVICES:** Lift **PARKING:** 250 **NOTES:** No dogs (ex guide dogs) **CARDS:**

*See advert on opposite page*

### ★★★64% Comfort Hotel Nottingham

George St NG1 3BP
☎ 0115 947 5641 ⎙ 0115 948 3292
e-mail: admin@gb620.u-net.com

Comfort Inn

***Dir:*** *follow signs to city centre, at top of hill follow road to the right , take left fork onto Talbot St, take left hand lane and right to George St, hotel on the left*

Situated in heart of the city, the hotel began life as a coaching inn in the late 17th century. Bedrooms, all of which have been refurbished, are comfortably appointed. Public areas include a residents' lounge, informal restaurant and public bar. Parking is available at a multi-storey close to the hotel.

**ROOMS:** 70 en suite (3 fmly) No smoking in 22 bedrooms s £60; d £60 * LB **FACILITIES:** STV Xmas **CONF:** Thtr 200 Class 40 Board 35 Del from £65 * **SERVICES:** Lift **NOTES:** No dogs (ex guide dogs) **CARDS:**

### ★★★63% Posthouse Nottingham City

St James's St NG1 6BN
☎ 0870 400 9061 ⎙ 0115 948 4366

Posthouse

***Dir:*** *from M1 junct 24,25,26 follow signs to city centre, then brown tourist signs to Nottingham Castle & Tales of Robin Hood, hotel is located next door*

This city centre hotel is close to all the main attractions of the city. There is a modern business centre, and good conference and function facilities. Behan's Irish Bar is a popular feature and there is also a separate restaurant.

**ROOMS:** 160 en suite (18 fmly) No smoking in 88 bedrooms d fr £89 * LB **FACILITIES:** entertainment ch fac **CONF:** Thtr 600 Class 350 Board 120 **SERVICES:** Lift air con **NOTES:** No smoking in restaurant **CARDS:**

### ★★★59% Swans Hotel & Restaurant

84-90 Radcliffe Rd, West Bridgford NG2 5HH
☎ 0115 981 4042 ⎙ 0115 945 5745
e-mail: enquiries@swanshotel.co.uk

***Dir:*** *on A6011, approached from either A60 or A52 close to Trent Bridge*

Conveniently located for the various sports stadia, this privately owned hotel has recently been refurbished. Bedrooms, varying in size, are equipped to meet the needs of business and leisure visitors alike. An interesting range of dishes is served in the cosy bar or, more formally, in the restaurant.

**ROOMS:** 30 en suite (3 fmly) No smoking in 20 bedrooms s £53-£58; d £63 (incl. bkfst) * LB **FACILITIES:** STV **CONF:** Thtr 50 Class 10 Board 15 Del from £65 * **SERVICES:** Lift **PARKING:** 31 **NOTES:** No dogs (ex guide dogs) No smoking in restaurant Closed 24-28 Dec **CARDS:**

*See advert on opposite page*

### ★★77% Hotel des Clos

Old Lenton Ln NG7 2SA
☎ 0115 986 6566 ⎙ 0115 986 0343
e-mail: danralley@hoteldesclos.com

***Dir:*** *M1 junct 24, take A453 Nottingham south. As road crosses river Trent, centre lane to rdbt, turn left & immediately left again towards river. Hotel on left after bend*

This small hotel, a sympathetic conversion of Victorian farm buildings, is situated on the riverside. The majority of the bedrooms have quality soft furnishings and antique/period furniture; suites and four-poster bedrooms are available. Public rooms are cosy, and the delightful restaurant complements the fine cuisine on offer.

**ROOMS:** 4 en suite 4 annexe en suite (1 fmly) s £79.50-£119.50; d £89.50-£129.50 (incl. bkfst) * LB **FACILITIES:** STV Fishing **CONF:** Thtr 20 Board 14 Del from £134 * **PARKING:** 22 **NOTES:** No dogs (ex guide dogs) No smoking in restaurant Closed 26-30 Dec & 1-7 Jan **CARDS:**

### ★★67% *Windsor Lodge Hotel*

116 Radcliffe Rd, West Bridgford NG2 5HG
☎ 0115 952 8528 ⎙ 0115 952 0020
e-mail: windsor@btinternet.com

***Dir:*** *A6011 & A52 Grantham, 0.5m Trent Bridge Cricket Ground*

This family run hotel has been in the same ownership for almost 30 years. It is conveniently situated for Trent Bridge cricket ground. The bedrooms are spacious and comfortably furnished, whilst public areas include a welcoming bar lounge and a separate billiards room.

**ROOMS:** 47 en suite (8 fmly) **FACILITIES:** STV Snooker **CONF:** Thtr 40 Class 25 Board 24 **PARKING:** 50 **NOTES:** No dogs (ex guide dogs) Closed 25-26 Dec **CARDS:**

*See advert on opposite page*

### ★★65% Balmoral

55-57 Loughborough Rd, West Bridgford NG2 7LA
☎ 0115 955 2992 & 0800 952 2992 ⎙ 0115 955 2991
e-mail: balmoralhotel55@hotmail.com

***Dir:*** *beside A60 Loughborough Road, cross Trent Bridge, past cricket ground, hotel 200mtrs on left*

Ideally placed for the major sporting venues of the city, this popular hotel offers comfortable well-equipped accommodation, including some bedrooms on the ground floor. Service is both

*continued*

friendly and helpful, creating a relaxed atmosphere within the open plan public rooms.
**ROOMS:** 39 en suite (8 fmly) s £35-£37.50; d £45-£47.50 (incl. bkfst) * **FACILITIES:** pool table **CONF:** Thtr 20 Class 20 Board 20 Del £69.50 * **PARKING:** 40 **CARDS:**

**★★65% Rufford**
53 Melton Rd, West Bridgford NG2 7NE
☎ 0115 981 4202 📠 0115 945 5801
***Dir:*** *on A606, near junct A60 Loughborough Road*
Conveniently situated for all the major sporting arenas, this family run hotel offers a bright conservatory bar and wood panelled restaurant serving a good range of popular dishes. There is a choice of bedroom size and layout, with all rooms being comfortably furnished and thoughtfully designed.
**ROOMS:** 34 en suite No smoking in 3 bedrooms s £35-£45; d £55 (incl. bkfst) * **PARKING:** 35 **NOTES:** No dogs (ex guide dogs) Closed Xmas **CARDS:**

**★★61% The Stage**
Gregory Boulevard NG7 6LB
☎ 0115 960 3261 📠 0115 969 1040
e-mail: reservations@stagenottingham.fsnet.co.uk

MINOTEL
Great Britain

***Dir:*** *off the main Mansfield road (A60) approx 1m from City Centre on A6130, opposite Forest Park*
The Stage is situated opposite Forest Park, where the famous Goose Fair is held. Public rooms include a spacious lounge bar, various function rooms and a restaurant serving a menu of popular dishes. Bedroom sizes and styles vary, ranging from

*continued on p446*

N

NOTTINGHAM, continued

executive to standard rooms, but all are well-equipped and generally of comfortable proportions.
**ROOMS:** 52 en suite (5 fmly) No smoking in 4 bedrooms s £44.50-£49.50; d £54.50-£59.50 (incl. bkfst) * LB **FACILITIES:** Xmas **CONF:** Thtr 100 Class 50 Board 35 **PARKING:** 80 **NOTES:** No dogs (ex guide dogs) No smoking in restaurant **CARDS:**

## *Town House*

### ★★★★ Lace Market
29-31 High Pavement NG1 1HE
☎ 0115 852 3232 0115 852 3223
e-mail: reservations@lacemarkethotel.co.uk
***Dir:*** *follow brown tourist information signs for Galleries of Justice which is opposite Hotel*
This smart hotel is located in the centre of the city. Its bedrooms are contemporary in style and very well equipped. Guests may dine in the modern bar or the brasserie-style Merchants restaurant.
**ROOMS:** 29 en suite s £69-£89; d £89-£169 * LB **FACILITIES:** STV Complimentary use of nearby health club. **CONF:** Thtr 35 Class 35 Board 20 Del from £150 * **SERVICES:** Lift **NOTES:** Closed 24 Dec-26 Dec **CARDS:**

### ⇧ *Premier Lodge (Nottingham North)*

101 Mansfield Rd, Daybrook NG5 6BH
☎ 0870 700 1532 0870 700 1533
Premier Lodge offers modern, well-equipped, en suite accommodation suitable for both business and leisure travellers. Meals can be taken at the adjacent popular restaurant and bar, which is fully licensed. For further details, consult the Hotel Groups page.
**ROOMS:** 64 en suite

### ⇧ *Premier Lodge (Nottingham South)*

Loughborough Rd, Ruddington NG11 6LS
☎ 0870 700 1534 0870 700 1535
Premier Lodge offers modern, well-equipped, en suite accommodation suitable for both business and leisure travellers. Meals can be taken at the adjacent popular restaurant and bar, which is fully licensed. For further details, consult the Hotel Groups page.
**ROOMS:** 42 en suite

### ⇧ *Travelodge (Nottingham Riverside)*
Riverside Retail Park NG2 1RT
☎ 0115 985 0934
***Dir:*** *on Riverside Retail Park*
Travelodge offers good quality, good value, modern accommodation. Ideal for families, the spacious, en suite bedrooms include remote-control TV, tea and coffee-making facilities, luxury beds and free morning newspaper. Meals can be taken at the nearby family restaurant. For further details and the Travelodge phone number, consult the Hotel Groups page.

**ROOMS:** 61 en suite

### ○ Innkeeper's Lodge Nottingham
Derby Rd, Wollaton Vale NG8 2NR
A new concept in the travel accommodation market. Smart rooms meet essential business requirements but also have home comforts. Dining options include all-day menus plus the added advantage of breakfast, which is included in the room price. Reservations can be made seven days a week through the room reservations number: 0870 243 0500. For further details, consult the Hotel Groups page.
**ROOMS:** 34 en suite

NUNEATON, Warwickshire Map 04 SP39

### ★★★65% Weston Hall
Weston Ln, Weston in Arden, Bulkington CV12 9RU
☎ 024 7631 2989 024 7664 0846
e-mail: info@westonhallhotel.co.uk
***Dir:*** *M6 junct 2 follow B4065 through Ansty turn left in Shilton, follow Nuneaton signs out of Bulkington, turn into Weston Ln at 30mph sign*
Close to Coventry and the NEC this former dower house, dating from 1580, is set in seven acres of peaceful grounds. Bedrooms are all thoughtfully equipped, but do vary in size. The hotel has extensive conference facilities and service is provided in a friendly and helpful manner.
**ROOMS:** 40 en suite (1 fmly) No smoking in 6 bedrooms s £69.50-£95; d £85-£105 (incl. bkfst) * LB **FACILITIES:** Fishing Riding Sauna Gym Croquet lawn Jacuzzi Steam room entertainment **CONF:** Thtr 200 Class 100 Board 80 Del from £120 * **PARKING:** 300 **NOTES:** No smoking in restaurant Civ Wed 190 **CARDS:**

*See advert under COVENTRY*

### ⇧ *Travelodge*
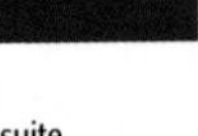
Travelodge
St Nicholas Park Dr CV11 6EN
☎ 024 76353885 024 76353885
***Dir:*** *on A47*
Travelodge offers good quality, good value, modern accommodation. Ideal for families, the spacious, en suite bedrooms include remote-control TV, tea and coffee-making facilities, luxury beds and free morning newspaper. Meals can be taken at the nearby family restaurant. For further details and the Travelodge phone number, consult the Hotel Groups page.

**ROOMS:** 30 en suite

### ⇧ *Travelodge*
Bedworth CV10 7TF
☎ 024 76382541 024 76382541
***Dir:*** *2m S, on A444*
Travelodge offers good quality, good value, modern accommodation. Ideal for families, the spacious, en suite bedrooms include remote-control TV, tea and coffee-making facilities, luxury beds and free morning newspaper. Meals can be taken at the nearby family restaurant. For further details and the Travelodge phone number, consult the Hotel Groups page.

**ROOMS:** 40 en suite

NUNNEY, Somerset Map 03 ST74

**★★65% The George at Nunney**
11 Church St BA11 4LW
☎ 01373 836458 🖹 01373 836565
e-mail: georgenunneyhotel@barbox.net
***Dir:*** *0.5m N off A361 Frome/Shepton Mallet*
Situated in the centre of Nunney, opposite the castle, The George dates back to the 17th century. Guests may choose from an extensive range of bar meals or a selection of dishes offered in the more intimate restaurant. A commendable selection of whiskies is also available. The cosy bedrooms are particularly well-equipped.
**ROOMS:** 9 rms (8 en suite) (2 fmly) No smoking in 2 bedrooms s £40-£52; d £68-£82 (incl. bkfst) * **LB** **FACILITIES:** STV Xmas **PARKING:** 30 **NOTES:** No dogs (ex guide dogs)
**CARDS:**

OAKHAM, Rutland Map 04 SK80

***Premier Collection***

**★★★ Hambleton Hall**
Hambleton LE15 8TH
☎ 01572 756991 🖹 01572 724721
e-mail: hotel@hambletonhall.com
***Dir:*** *3m E off A606*
Hambleton Hall is set in its own landscaped grounds, edging Rutland Water. The epitome of the English country hotel, its stunning public rooms include the bar and elegant drawing room. The restaurant showcases the inspired cuisine with its superb seasonal and locally sourced menu. Bedrooms are stylish and each room is individually decorated.
**ROOMS:** 15 en suite 2 annexe en suite No smoking in 1 bedroom s £150-£335; d £200-£550 (incl. cont bkfst) * **FACILITIES:** STV Outdoor swimming (H) Tennis (hard) ch fac Xmas **CONF:** Thtr 40 Class 40 Board 24 Del from £220 * **SERVICES:** Lift **PARKING:** 40 **NOTES:** No smoking in restaurant Civ Wed 60
**CARDS:**

**★★★72% Barnsdale Lodge**
The Avenue, Rutland Water, North Shore LE15 8AH
☎ 01572 724678 🖹 01572 724961
e-mail: barnsdale.lodge@btconnect.com
***Dir:*** *turn off A1 onto A606. Hotel is located 5m on right, 2m E of Oakham*
A very popular hotel overlooking Rutland Water. Bedrooms are comfortably appointed with excellent beds and period furnishings, enhanced by contemporary, stylish soft furnishings and thoughtful extras. The restaurant, which is a series of three intimate dining rooms, offers a good range of internationally appealing freshly cooked dishes.

*continued*

**ROOMS:** 45 en suite (2 fmly) No smoking in 34 bedrooms s fr £69; d fr £89 (incl. bkfst) * **LB** **FACILITIES:** Spa STV Fishing Shooting Archery Golf arranged Xmas **CONF:** Thtr 330 Class 120 Board 76 **PARKING:** 200 **NOTES:** No smoking in restaurant Civ Wed 100
**CARDS:**

***★★★64% Barnsdale Hall Hotel & Country Club***
Best Western
Barnsdale LE15 8AB
☎ 01572 757901 🖹 01572 756235
e-mail: barnsdale@webleicester.co.uk
***Dir:*** *from A1 take A606 towards Oakham, travel through the villages of Empingham then Whitwell, after approx 1m hotel on left overlooking Rutland Water*
Set in attractive grounds overlooking Rutland Water, this complex offers extensive leisure facilities. Spacious modern bedrooms in separate buildings in the grounds are comfortable and well-equipped; many have the added benefit of a balcony and views. Public rooms provide a choice of modern dining options and a new lounge area.
**ROOMS:** 60 annexe en suite (9 fmly) No smoking in 8 bedrooms **FACILITIES:** STV Indoor swimming (H) Tennis (hard) Squash Snooker Sauna Solarium Gym Croquet lawn Putting green Jacuzzi Boule Bowls **CONF:** Thtr 200 Class 80 Board 50 **SERVICES:** Lift **PARKING:** 100 **NOTES:** No dogs (ex guide dogs) Civ Wed 120
**CARDS:**

**★★★60% Whipper-in Hotel**
BROOK HOTELS
Market Place LE15 6DT
☎ 01572 756971 🖹 01572 757759
e-mail: whipper.in@lineone.net
***Dir:*** *from A1 take B668 for Oakham and head for the Market Square*
This fashionable market town inn is furnished in an English country-house style. An open fire warms the lounge bar, a popular meeting place for locals, and a good range of interesting meals is served in both the modern, informal brasserie and the candlelit restaurant. Each bedroom is individually designed; four-poster and executive rooms are available.
**ROOMS:** 24 en suite No smoking in 4 bedrooms s £69-£74; d £79-£94 (incl. bkfst) * **LB** **FACILITIES:** Xmas **CONF:** Thtr 60 Board 30 Del from £95 * **PARKING:** 40 **NOTES:** No smoking in restaurant
**CARDS:**

Popped the question? Hotels with Civ Wed in their entry are licensed for civil wedding ceremonies. Maximum numbers for the ceremony only are shown, e.g. Civ Wed 120

## OCKLEY, Surrey

Map 04 TQ14

### ★★★63% Gatton Manor Hotel Golf & Country Club

Standon Ln RH5 5PQ
☎ 01306 627555 📠 01306 627713
e-mail: gattonmanor@enterprise.net
**Dir:** *off A29 at Ockley turn into Cat Hill Ln, signposted for 2m hotel entrance on the right*

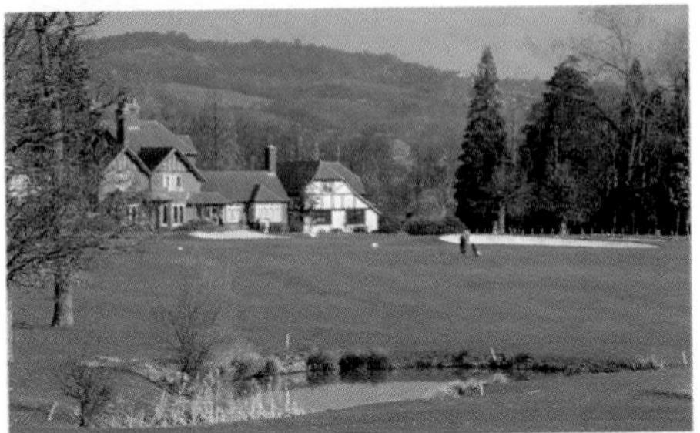

Enjoying a peaceful setting, this popular golf and country club, with an 18-hole professional course, offers a range of comfortable, modern bedrooms. Public areas include the main club bar, a small restaurant and an attractive drawing room.
**ROOMS:** 18 en suite (2 fmly) No smoking in 6 bedrooms s £67.50; d £105 (incl. bkfst) * **LB** **FACILITIES:** STV Golf 18 Fishing Sauna Solarium Gym Putting green Jacuzzi ch fac Xmas **CONF:** Thtr 50 Class 40 Board 30 Del from £120 * **PARKING:** 250 **NOTES:** No dogs (ex guide dogs) No smoking in restaurant Civ Wed 50
**CARDS:**

## ODIHAM, Hampshire

Map 04 SU75

### ★★71% George

High St RG29 1LP
☎ 01256 702081 📠 01256 704213
**Dir:** *from M3 junct 5 follow signs to Alton/Odiham. In Odiham left at mini-rdbt, hotel is on left*

THE GEORGE
HOTEL &
RESTAURANT

The George is over 450 years old and is a fine example of an old English inn. Bedrooms come in a number of styles, the older part of the property having old beams and period features, newer rooms having a more contemporary feel. The seafood restaurant and brasserie style café bar serve good food which is popular with both locals and residents.
**ROOMS:** 19 en suite 9 annexe en suite (1 fmly) No smoking in 14 bedrooms s fr £75; d fr £85 (incl. bkfst) * **LB** **FACILITIES:** STV **CONF:** Thtr 30 Class 10 Board 26 Del from £105 * **PARKING:** 20
**CARDS:**

## OKEHAMPTON, Devon

Map 02 SX59

### ★★67% White Hart

Fore St EX20 1HD
☎ 01837 52730 & 54514 📠 01837 53979
e-mail: graham@whitehartHotel.telme.com
**Dir:** *located in town centre, adjacent to the traffic lights, car park at rear of hotel*
This 17th-century former coaching inn has bedrooms that vary in size; all are well-equipped and furnished in similar style. The public areas retain the original character and charm of the building. A range of bar meals is available, whilst in the restaurant both fixed price and carte menus are offered.
**ROOMS:** 19 en suite (2 fmly) No smoking in 4 bedrooms s £35-£40; d £50-£60 (incl. bkfst) * **LB** **FACILITIES:** Putting green Games room Skittle alley Xmas **CONF:** Thtr 100 Class 80 Board 40 **PARKING:** 22 **NOTES:** No dogs (ex guide dogs) **CARDS:**

*See advert on opposite page*

### ★★65% Ashbury Hotel

Higher Maddaford, Southcott EX20 4NL
☎ 01837 55453 📠 01837 55468
**Dir:** *turn off A30 at Sourton Cross onto A386. Turn left onto A3079 to Bude at Fowley Cross. After 1m turn right to Ashbury. Hotel 0.5m on right*
A golfer's paradise, The Ashbury has three courses and a clubhouse with lounge, bar and dining facilities. The majority of the well-equipped bedrooms are located in the adjacent farmhouse and courtyard-style development around the putting green. Guests can enjoy the many on-site leisure facilities or join the activities available at the adjacent sister hotel.
**ROOMS:** 26 en suite 29 annexe en suite (21 fmly) s £34-£60; d £65-£116 (incl. bkfst & dinner) * **LB** **FACILITIES:** Indoor swimming (H) Golf 63 Tennis (hard) Fishing Snooker Sauna Solarium Putting green Jacuzzi Driving range, Indoor bowls, Ten-pin bowling, table tennis Xmas **PARKING:** 100 **NOTES:** No dogs (ex guide dogs) No smoking in restaurant **CARDS:**

*See advert on opposite page*

### ★★65% Manor House Hotel

Fowley Cross EX20 4NA
☎ 01837 53053 📠 01837 55027
**Dir:** *turn off A30 at Sourton Cross flyover, take right onto A386, hotel is located 1.5m on right*
This popular hotel, set in 17 acres of grounds and about three miles from the town, enjoys stunning views of Dartmoor. The bedrooms are comfortable and well-equipped. It offers an incredible range of amenities and activities, catering exclusively for breaks. Guests can use the golfing facilities at the adjacent hotel.
**ROOMS:** 161 en suite (66 fmly) s £37-£66; d £71-£126 (incl. bkfst & dinner) * **LB** **FACILITIES:** **Spa** Indoor swimming (H) Tennis (hard) Squash Snooker Sauna Gym Croquet lawn Putting green Jacuzzi Craft centre Indoor bowls Shooting range Laser clay pigeon shooting Aerobics ch fac Xmas **PARKING:** 200 **NOTES:** No dogs (ex guide dogs) No smoking in restaurant **CARDS:**

*See advert on opposite page*

### ⌂ *Travelodge*

Travelodge

Whiddon Down EX20 2QT
☎ 01647 231626 📠 01647 231626
**Dir:** *at Merrymeet rdbt on A30/A382*
Travelodge offers good quality, good value, modern accommodation. Ideal for families, the spacious, en suite bedrooms include remote-control TV, tea and coffee-making facilities, luxury beds and free morning newspaper. Meals can be taken at the nearby family restaurant. For further details and the Travelodge phone number, consult the Hotel Groups page.
**ROOMS:** 40 en suite

O

OLDBURY, West Midlands

Map 07 SO98

**Express by Holiday Inn Oldbury**

Birchley Park B69 2BD

☎ 0121 511 0000

***Dir:*** *hotel is located off junct2 of the M5, behind Total garage on the Wolverhampton Rd*

Express
by Holiday Inn

A modern budget hotel offering comfortable accommodation in refreshing, spacious and comprehensively equipped bedrooms, en suite bathrooms with power showers and continental buffet breakfast included in the room rate. Suitable for business travellers or families. For further details and the Express by Holiday Inn phone number, consult the Hotel Groups page.

**ROOMS:** 109 en suite (incl. cont bkfst) s £35-£65; d £35-£65 *

**CONF:** Thtr 40 Class 25 Board 25

Read all about it! Newspapers delivered to bedrooms in four and five star hotels.

O

OLDBURY, continued

### Travelodge

Wolverhampton Rd B69 2BH
☎ 0121 552 2967 0121 552 2967
**Dir:** *on A4123, northbound off junct 2 of M5*
Travelodge offers good quality, good value, modern accommodation. Ideal for families, the spacious, en suite bedrooms include remote-control TV, tea and coffee-making facilities, luxury beds and free morning newspaper. Meals can be taken at the nearby family restaurant. For further details and the Travelodge phone number, consult the Hotel Groups page.

**ROOMS:** 33 en suite

OLDHAM, Greater Manchester Map 07 SD90

### ★★★★64% Menzies Avant

Windsor Rd, Manchester St OL8 4AS
☎ 0870 6003013 01332 511144
e-mail: info@menzies-hotels.co.uk
**Dir:** *hotel is 1 mile from junct 22 of the M60. Follow A62 into Oldham turn right straight after Esso garage*

This modern hotel offers smart well-equipped accommodation. There is a variety of bedrooms sizes; all rooms are very attractive. A covered walkway leads to the public areas which include a bright and comfortable restaurant serving quality cuisine, and a spacious bar. Conference and banqueting suites are also available.
**ROOMS:** 103 en suite (2 fmly) No smoking in 16 bedrooms s £85; d £85 * LB **FACILITIES:** STV Indoor swimming (H) Sauna Solarium Gym Jacuzzi Xmas **CONF:** Thtr 200 Class 100 Board 60 Del from £105 * **SERVICES:** Lift **PARKING:** 120 **NOTES:** No smoking in restaurant Civ Wed 250 **CARDS:**

### ★★★73% Hotel Smokies Park

Ashton Rd, Bardsley OL8 3HX
☎ 0161 785 5000 0161 785 5010
e-mail: sales@smokies.co.uk
**Dir:** *on A627 between Oldham and Ashton-under-Lyne*
This modern, stylish hotel offers smart, comfortable, well-equipped bedrooms and suites. An extensive range of Italian and English dishes is offered in the airy restaurant and there is a welcoming lounge bar with live entertainment at weekends. A small but well-equipped fitness centre is available for use by residents only. There is also a nightclub on site, to which residents gain free admission.
**ROOMS:** 73 en suite (2 fmly) No smoking in 36 bedrooms s fr £75; d fr £85 (incl. bkfst) * LB **FACILITIES:** STV Sauna Solarium Gym Night club Cabaret lounge entertainment **CONF:** Thtr 200 Class 125 Board 50 Del from £115 * **SERVICES:** Lift **PARKING:** 120 **NOTES:** No dogs (ex guide dogs) **CARDS:**

### ★★★66% Bower Hotel

Hollinwood Av, Chadderton OL9 8DE
☎ 0161 682 7254 0161 683 4695
e-mail: events.bower@macdonald-hotels.co.uk
**Dir:** *Follow A62 from Manchester(Oldham road) until Roxy cinema in sight on right, left lane, turn to A6104 Hollinwood, under railway, past Mirror Group to lights, left to hotel's drive.*
Located just off junction 22 of the M60, this hotel provides a comfortable destination for both the business and leisure guest. Bedrooms vary in size and style and are well-equipped with a host of thoughtful extras. Creative menus are served in the restaurant whilst extensive function capabilities make this hotel a popular venue for weddings and conferences.
**ROOMS:** 92 en suite (6 fmly) s £60-£110; d £60-£110 * LB **FACILITIES:** STV ch fac Xmas **CONF:** Thtr 250 Class 60 Board 60 Del from £110 * **PARKING:** 140 **NOTES:** No smoking in restaurant Civ Wed 200 **CARDS:**

### ★★★60% Pennine Way Hotel

Manchester St OL8 1UZ
☎ 0161 624 0555 0161 627 2031
e-mail: mail@penninewayhotel.co.uk
**Dir:** *exit M60 junct 21 and follow signs for town centre*

This large purpose built hotel is close to the centre of town. Bedrooms are well-equipped and staff are friendly and helpful. The ballroom, accommodating up to 350, is one of a choice of rooms for functions and conferences. The hotel is a popular venue for coach tours.
**ROOMS:** 130 en suite (50 fmly) No smoking in 70 bedrooms s £45-£75; d £65-£85 * LB **FACILITIES:** STV Xmas **CONF:** Thtr 320 Class 70 Board 70 Del from £95 * **SERVICES:** Lift **PARKING:** 250 **NOTES:** No smoking in restaurant **CARDS:**

### ★★68% High Point

64 Napier St East OL8 1TR
☎ 0161 624 4130 0161 627 2757
**Dir:** *M62 junct 20 to M627 Oldham onto A627 off at A62 (Manchester) under "Glass Bridge", onto Lee St right at T-junct onto Napier St East*
A friendly hotel in an elevated position, with panoramic views from its restaurant. Bedrooms are very well-equipped and most have been refurbished in a tasteful modern style. Some have jacuzzi baths and four-poster beds. There is a comfortable lounge bar and a small residents' lounge.
**ROOMS:** 19 en suite (3 fmly) No smoking in 2 bedrooms s £42; d £45-£53 (incl. bkfst) * **FACILITIES:** STV Xmas **CONF:** Thtr 30 Class 15 Board 20 Del £69 * **PARKING:** 42 **NOTES:** No dogs (ex guide dogs) **CARDS:**

Fancy a Singapore Sling? Bar staff in five star hotels should be skilled cocktail mixers.

## ORFORD, Suffolk
Map 05 TM45

**★★68% Crown & Castle**
IP12 2LJ
☎ 01394 450205 01394 450176
e-mail: info@crownandcastlehotel.co.uk
***Dir:*** *turn right from B1084 on entering village*
Situated in a picturesque village and overlooking the market square, this popular hotel dates back to Tudor times. Bedrooms are located in the main house and the purpose-built wing; the latter are more spacious and have a patio with direct access to the gardens. Much use of local produce is made in the quality cooking.
**ROOMS:** 7 en suite 11 annexe en suite (1 fmly) s £60-£110; d £80-£110 (incl. bkfst) * LB **FACILITIES:** Xmas **PARKING:** 25
**CARDS:**

## ORMSKIRK, Lancashire
Map 07 SD40

**★★★67% Beaufort**
High Ln, Burscough L40 7SN
☎ 01704 892655 01704 895135
e-mail: info@beaufort.uk.com
***Dir:*** *from M58 junct 3 follow signs for Ormskirk which is 7m. Hotel is situated between Ormskirk and Burscough on A59*
A modern, privately owned hotel with good open-plan lounge, bar and restaurant areas. A wide choice of food is available all day. Bedrooms are well-equipped and comfortable, and conference facilities are available.
**ROOMS:** 20 en suite s £63; d £90 (incl. bkfst) * LB **FACILITIES:** STV Free use of sister hotel's (Stutelea Hotel, Southport - 8m) facilities Xmas **CONF:** Thtr 120 Class 32 Board 30 **PARKING:** 126 **NOTES:** No dogs (ex guide dogs) No smoking in restaurant Civ Wed 120
**CARDS:**

## OSTERLEY, Greater London
See LONDON SECTION plan 1 B3

**★★★65% Osterley Four Pillars Hotel**
FOUR PILLARS HOTELS
764 Great West Rd TW7 5NA
☎ 020 8568 9981 020 8569 7819
e-mail: enquiries@four-pillars.co.uk
***Dir:*** *Hotel at junct of A4 and Wood Lane. 1m past Osterley Tube Station, eastbound on A4. 0.5m past Gillette, westbound on A4*
This well situated hotel has good access to both central London and Heathrow Airport. Bedrooms are well-designed, tastefully decorated and feature a useful range of extra facilities. Public areas include the Gresham's restaurant and bar, as well as a free house pub which is equally popular with locals.
**ROOMS:** 61 en suite (9 fmly) No smoking in 21 bedrooms s £47-£85; d £47-£95 * LB **FACILITIES:** STV entertainment **CONF:** Thtr 250 Class 126 Board 80 Del £130 * **PARKING:** 98 **NOTES:** Closed 26-27 Dec
**CARDS:**

## OSWESTRY, Shropshire
Map 07 SJ22

**★★★74% Pen-y-Dyffryn Hall Country Hotel**
Rhydycroesau SY10 7JD
☎ 01691 653700 01691 650066
e-mail: stay@peny.co.uk
***Dir:*** *from A5 into Oswestry town centre, follow signs to Llansilin on B4580, hotel is 3m W of Oswestry just before Rhydycroesau village*
This charming old house dates back to around 1840, when it was built as a rectory. It is quietly located in five acres of grounds. Staff are hospitable, and the hotel has a well-deserved reputation for its food. Well-equipped accommodation includes a bedroom on ground floor level and a family room. The public rooms are
*continued*

comfortably and tastefully appointed, and warmed by real fires during cold weather.
**ROOMS:** 8 en suite 2 annexe en suite (1 fmly) No smoking in all bedrooms s £63-£66; d £84-£100 (incl. bkfst) * LB **FACILITIES:** Spa Fishing Jacuzzi Guided walks ch fac **PARKING:** 14 **NOTES:** No smoking in restaurant Closed 24 Dec-19 Jan **CARDS:**

**★★★70% Wynnstay**
Best Western
Church St SY11 2SZ
☎ 01691 655261 01691 670606
e-mail: info@wynnstayhotel.com
***Dir:*** *take B4083 to town, then fork left at Honda Garage and right at lights. Hotel opposite parish church*

This Georgian property was once the posting house on the Liverpool to Cardiff route, and it is located close to the town centre. It surrounds a unique Crown Bowling Green which itself is 200 years old. In recent years, a good health, leisure and beauty centre plus extensive function facilities have been added. The well-
*continued on p452*

O

OSWESTRY, continued

equipped bedrooms are all individually styled and decorated. They include several suites and four-poster rooms. The restaurant has an Italian theme and there is also a full range of bar food on offer.
**ROOMS:** 29 en suite (4 fmly) No smoking in 14 bedrooms s £74-£94; d £95-£118 * **LB** **FACILITIES:** **Spa** Indoor swimming (H) Sauna Solarium Gym Jacuzzi Crown green bowling Beauty suite ch fac
**CONF:** Thtr 290 Class 150 Board 50 Del from £99 * **PARKING:** 70
**NOTES:** Civ Wed 90 **CARDS:**

### ★★69% Sebastian's Hotel & Restaurant

45 Willow St SY11 1AQ
☎ 01691 655444 01691 653452
e-mail: sebastians.rest@virgin.net
***Dir:*** *Follow signs to town centre at junct with small pedestrian triangle near Barclays & Midland banks take road towards Selattyn & Llansilin for 300yds into Willow St, hotel on left*
Parts of this town centre property date back to 1640. Now a privately owned and personally run small hotel, it has a wealth of charm and character, enhanced by original features such as exposed beams and oak panelling in the cosy lounge, bar and cottage style restaurant. Bedrooms include four newly constructed to the rear of the main building. Sebastian's has a well-deserved reputation for food.
**ROOMS:** 7 en suite 1 annexe en suite (4 fmly) No smoking in all bedrooms s fr £45; d fr £60 * **FACILITIES:** ch fac **NOTES:** No smoking in restaurant Closed 25-26 Dec & 1 Jan
**CARDS:**

### ⌂ *Travelodge*

Travelodge

Mile End Service Area SY11 4JA
☎ 01691 658178 01691 658178
***Dir:*** *junct A5/A483*
Travelodge offers good quality, good value, modern accommodation. Ideal for families, the spacious, en suite bedrooms include remote-control TV, tea and coffee-making facilities, luxury beds and free morning newspaper. Meals can be taken at the nearby family restaurant. For further details and the Travelodge phone number, consult the Hotel Groups page.

**ROOMS:** 40 en suite

O

## OTTERBURN, Northumberland Map 12 NY89

### ★★★63% The Otterburn Tower Hotel

NE19 1NS
☎ 01830 520620 01830 521504
e-mail: reservations@otterburntower.co.uk
***Dir:*** *on A696 Newcastle to Edinburgh Rd*
Set in grounds and gardens in the centre of the village, parts of this mansion date from 1076 and still display original features despite being totally upgraded two years ago. Service is in the country house mould and all bedrooms are individual in design, well-equipped and furnished with period pieces.
**ROOMS:** 17 en suite (2 fmly) No smoking in 10 bedrooms s £60-£80; d £90-£200 (incl. bkfst) * **LB** **FACILITIES:** STV Fishing Xmas
**CONF:** Thtr 90 Class 90 Board 90 Del from £115 * **PARKING:** 70
**NOTES:** No smoking in restaurant Civ Wed 90
**CARDS:**

Arriving late? Four and five star hotels have night porters to assist with your luggage, and 24-hour room service.

### ★★64% Percy Arms

Best Western

NE19 1NR
☎ 01830 520261 01830 520567
e-mail: percyarms@bestwestern.co.uk
***Dir:*** *centre of Otterburn village on A696*
This 17th-century coaching inn stands in the centre of the village surrounded by beautiful Northumberland moors. Public areas offer comfortable lounges with open fires, and there is a choice of bars and places to eat.
**ROOMS:** 28 en suite (2 fmly) No smoking in 2 bedrooms s £50-£64; d £70-£90 (incl. bkfst) * **LB** **FACILITIES:** Fishing ch fac Xmas
**CONF:** Thtr 70 Class 40 Board 50 Del from £70 * **PARKING:** 74
**CARDS:**

## OTTERSHAW, Surrey Map 04 TQ06

### ★★★★71% Foxhills

Stonehill Rd KT16 0EL
☎ 01932 872050 01932 874762
e-mail: reservations@foxhills.co.uk
***Dir:*** *A320 to Woking from M25. At 2nd rdbt take last exit Chobham Rd, right into Foxhills Rd, right at T-junct, then left into Stonehill Rd*
Although close to the M25 and Heathrow, Foxhills enjoys a wonderfully tranquil setting in a vast expanse of grounds. Leisure facilities ares a primary attraction, and include golf courses and three pools. Bedrooms, built around a courtyard, are spacious and designed with great consideration to comfort. Public areas include lounge, restaurant and conference facilities.
**ROOMS:** 38 en suite (1 fmly) s £150-£300; d £150-£300 * **LB**
**FACILITIES:** STV Indoor swimming (H) Outdoor swimming (H) Golf 45 Tennis (hard) Squash Snooker Sauna Solarium Gym Croquet lawn Putting green Boules, childrens adventure playground ch fac Xmas
**CONF:** Thtr 100 Class 52 Board 56 Del from £210 * **PARKING:** 500
**NOTES:** No dogs (ex guide dogs) **CARDS:**
*See advert under WEYBRIDGE*

## OTTERY ST MARY, Devon Map 03 SY19

### ★★70% *Tumbling Weir Hotel & Restaurant*

EX11 1AQ
☎ 01404 812752 01404 812752
e-mail: 106120.2702@compuserve.com
***Dir:*** *turn off A30, take B3177 into Ottery St Mary, hotel adjoining 'Land of Canaan/long stay carpark'*
Situated between the River Otter and its millstream, this 17th-century cottage has old-world charm and attractive bedrooms. Original character has been retained with beams and candles helping to create an intimate atmosphere in the dining room and cosy lounge.
**ROOMS:** 11 en suite **FACILITIES:** STV Fishing **CONF:** Thtr 95 Class 95 Board 95 **PARKING:** 10 **NOTES:** No smoking in restaurant
**CARDS:**

## OXFORD, Oxfordshire Map 04 SP50

see also Milton Common

### ★★★★ Le Manoir Aux Quat' Saisons

RELAIS & CHATEAUX.

OX44 7PD
☎ 01844 278881 01844 278847
e-mail: lemanoir@blanc.co.uk
(For full entry see Great Milton)

TV dinner? Room service at three stars and above.

**★★★★67% Cotswold Lodge**
66a Banbury Rd OX2 6JP
☎ 01865 512121 🖷 01865 512490
e-mail: cotswoldlodge@netscapeonline.co.uk
***Dir:*** *turn off the A40 Oxford ring road onto the A4165, Banbury Rd - signposted city centre/Summertown. Hotel 2m on left*
This family run hotel is set in a Victorian building close to the centre of Oxford and has undergone a total refurbishment. Bedrooms are smartly presented and well-equipped; the comfortable public areas now have an elegant country house charm. The hotel is popular with business guests and caters for conferences and banquets.
**ROOMS:** 49 en suite No smoking in 40 bedrooms s £125-£145; d £175-£455 (incl. bkfst) * **FACILITIES:** STV **CONF:** Thtr 80 Class 48 Board 30 Del £150 * **PARKING:** 40 **NOTES:** No smoking in restaurant
**CARDS:**

*See advert on this page*

**★★★★67% Oxford Spires Four Pillars Hotel**
Abingdon Rd OX1 4PS
☎ 01865 324324 🖷 01865 324325
e-mail: spires@four-pillars.co.uk
***Dir:*** *M40 junct 8*
This brand new, purpose built hotel is surrounded by extensive parkland, yet is only a short walk to the city centre. Bedrooms are attractively furnished, well-equipped and include several apartments. Smartly appointed public areas include a spacious restaurant, open plan bar/lounge, leisure club and extensive conference facilities.
**ROOMS:** 115 en suite (8 fmly) No smoking in 44 bedrooms s £75-£139; d £96-£169 * **LB FACILITIES: Spa** STV Indoor swimming (H) Gym Beauty, games, steam rooms entertainment Xmas **CONF:** Thtr 266 Class 96 Board 76 Del from £152 * **SERVICES:** Lift **PARKING:** 95 **NOTES:** Civ Wed 140 **CARDS:**

**★★★★67% Oxford Thames Four Pillars Hotel**
Henley Rd, Sandford-on-Thames OX4 4GX
☎ 01865 334444 🖷 01865 334400
e-mail: thames@four-pillars.co.uk
***Dir:*** *M40 junct 8*

An impressive Victorian mansion in extensive grounds. The main house retains its galleried staircase leading to the bedrooms, which are individually decorated and have views of the river and gardens. Many rooms in the new wing have balconies. Public areas include a comfortable lounge, open plan bar and a leisure suite.
**ROOMS:** 60 en suite (4 fmly) s £75-£139; d £96-£169 * **LB FACILITIES: Spa** STV Indoor swimming (H) Tennis (hard) Snooker Sauna Gym steam room entertainment Xmas **CONF:** Thtr 160 Class 80 Board 60 Del from £152 * **PARKING:** 120 **NOTES:** Civ Wed 120
**CARDS:**

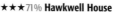

**★★★★67% The Randolph**
Beaumont St OX1 2LN
☎ 0870 400 8200 🖷 01865 791678
e-mail: sales.randolph@heritage-hotels.com
***Dir:*** *from M40 head for A40 Northern Bypass and at Pear Tree rdbt take exit S towards city centre into St Giles. Hotel on corner of Beaumont St*
Superbly located near the centre of town and across from the Ashmolean, The Randolph boasts impressive neo-Gothic architectural features and tasteful décor. Spires Restaurant, with its huge picture windows, is the place to watch the world go by, and the traditional teas served in the lounge are the height of decadence. Refurbished bedrooms are classical in style and have a timeless elegance.
**ROOMS:** 116 en suite No smoking in 60 bedrooms s £140-£150; d £160-£250 * **LB FACILITIES:** STV **CONF:** Thtr 300 Class 120 Board 35 Del from £150 * **SERVICES:** Lift **PARKING:** 64 **NOTES:** No smoking in restaurant Civ Wed 300 **CARDS:**

**★★★77% Studley Priory**
OX33 1AZ
☎ 01865 351203 & 351254 🖷 01865 351613
e-mail: res@studley-priory.co.uk
(For full entry see Horton-cum-Studley)

**★★★71% Hawkwell House**
Church Way, Iffley Village OX4 4DZ
☎ 01865 749988 🖷 01865 748525
e-mail: hawkwellhousehotel@corushotels.com
***Dir:*** *A34 follow signs to Cowley, at Littlemore rdbt take A4158 exit (Iffley Rd), after traffic lights, left to Iffley*
Set in a peaceful residential location, Hawkwell House is just a few minutes' drive from the Oxford ring road. The spacious rooms are

*continued on p454*

OXFORD, continued

modern, attractively decorated and well-equipped. Public areas are tastefully appointed and the conservatory style restaurant offers an interesting choice of dishes. The hotel also has a range of conference and function facilities.

*Hawkwell House, Oxford*

**ROOMS:** 51 en suite (3 fmly) No smoking in 13 bedrooms s £90-£120; d £105-£140 (incl. bkfst) * **LB** **FACILITIES:** STV Croquet lawn Xmas **CONF:** Thtr 200 Class 100 Board 200 Del £140 * **SERVICES:** Lift **PARKING:** 60 **NOTES:** No dogs (ex guide dogs) No smoking in restaurant Civ Wed 200 **CARDS:**

### ★★★69% Fallowfields Country House Hotel

Faringdon Rd, Kingston Bagpuize, Southmoor OX13 5BH
☎ 01865 820416 01865 821275
e-mail: stay@fallowfields.com
***Dir:*** *from A420, take A415 towards Abingdon for 100yds. Right at mini-rdbt, then through Kingston Bagpuize, Southmoor & Longworth and follow signs*

Once home to Begum Aga Khan, this delightful hotel is set in its own grounds and is personally run by friendly proprietors. The spacious, tasteful bedrooms feature many thoughtful touches. There is an elegant drawing room and an attractive conservatory restaurant overlooking the grounds. The hotel has a well-deserved reputation for its food which uses produce from its kitchen garden.
**ROOMS:** 10 en suite (2 fmly) No smoking in all bedrooms s £121-£140; d £140-£200 (incl. bkfst) * **LB** **FACILITIES:** STV Tennis (hard) Croquet lawn **CONF:** Thtr 60 Board 20 Del from £185 * **PARKING:** 21 **NOTES:** No children 8yrs No smoking in restaurant Civ Wed 100 **CARDS:**

> Early start? Hotels at all star levels should provide in-room alarm clocks and/or alarm calls.

### ★★★67% Linton Lodge

Linton Rd OX2 6UJ
☎ 01865 553461 01865 310365
e-mail: LintonLodge@vienna-group.co.uk
***Dir:*** *take Banbury Rd leading out of Oxford city centre. Turn right into Linton Rd after approx 0.5m. Hotel is located opposite St Andrews Church*

Best Western

Located in a side road of a residential area, Linton Lodge is within walking distance of the town centre. Bedrooms are well-equipped and comfortable and all have undergone recent refurbishment and decoration. There are some quaint period features such as the wood-panelled restaurant and a bar overlooking the croquet lawn.
**ROOMS:** 71 en suite (2 fmly) No smoking in 40 bedrooms s £105-£115; d £125-£135 (incl. bkfst) * **LB** **FACILITIES:** STV Croquet lawn Putting green **CONF:** Thtr 120 Class 50 Board 40 Del from £140 * **SERVICES:** Lift **PARKING:** 40 **NOTES:** No smoking in restaurant Civ Wed 100 **CARDS:**

*See advert on opposite page*

### ★★★67% Weston Manor Hotel

OX6 8QL
☎ 01869 350621 01869 350901
e-mail: westonmanor@hotmail.com
(For full entry see Weston-on-the-Green)

### ★★★65% Eastgate

The High, Merton St OX1 4BE
☎ 0870 400 8201 01865 791681
e-mail: HeritageHotels_Oxford.Eastgate@forte-hotels.com
***Dir:*** *follow signs to Headington and Oxford city centre. Hotel is on corner of High St and Merton St after Magdalen Bridge and a set of traffic lights*

As the name suggests, the hotel occupies the site of the medieval East Gate of the city. It is superbly located for the city centre and the historic university buildings. Bedrooms are tastefully furnished and decorated and offer a good range of facilities. Public areas include a popular bar and Café Bohème which serves modern French bistro style cooking.
**ROOMS:** 64 en suite (3 fmly) No smoking in 25 bedrooms s £115-£125; d £135-£145 * **LB** **FACILITIES:** entertainment **SERVICES:** Lift **PARKING:** 27 **CARDS:**

### ★★★65% The Oxford Hotel

Godstow Rd, Wolvercote Roundabout OX2 8AL
☎ 01865 489988 01865 310259
e-mail: oxford@paramount-hotels.co.uk
***Dir:*** *adjacent to A34/A40, 2m from city centre*

PARAMOUNT GROUP OF HOTELS

Conveniently located on the northern edge of the city centre, this purpose-built hotel offers a range of conference and leisure facilities. Bedrooms are neatly appointed and well-equipped with modern facilities. Guests can eat in the restaurant or try the more relaxed bar menu.
**ROOMS:** 173 en suite No smoking in 110 bedrooms s £130; d £150 * **LB** **FACILITIES:** STV Indoor swimming (H) Squash Sauna Solarium Gym Steam room Xmas **CONF:** Thtr 300 Class 100 Board 50 Del £165 * **PARKING:** 170 **NOTES:** No smoking in restaurant **CARDS:**

### ★★66% Victoria

180 Abingdon Rd OX1 4RA
☎ 01865 724536 01865 794909
***Dir:*** *from M40/A40 take Eastern bypass and A4144 into city*

The Victoria is a friendly hotel, a short walk from the city centre and a convenient base for touring the area. Meals have a Southern European flavour. Bedrooms have been refurbished to a

*continued*

high standard, and the addition of a conservatory bar makes for a comfortable area to enjoy a leisurely drink.
**ROOMS:** 15 en suite 5 annexe en suite (1 fmly) s £62-£65; d £75-£85 (incl. bkfst) * **LB** **CONF:** Board 20 **PARKING:** 20 **NOTES:** No smoking in restaurant **CARDS:**

**★★65% The Balkan Lodge Hotel**
315 Iffley Rd OX4 4AG
☎ 01865 244524 Fax 01865 251090
***Dir:*** *from M40/A40 take Eastern bypass, into city on A4158*
Situated to the east of the city, Balkan Lodge offers easy access to the ring road and centre. Now family owned, the property has undergone extensive refurbishment. The bright, attractive bedrooms have modern en suite facilities, and one room has a four-poster bed and a jacuzzi. There is a comfortable guest lounge and a smartly furnished dining room. Parking availability is also a real advantage.
**ROOMS:** 13 en suite No smoking in all bedrooms s £68; d £78 (incl. bkfst) * **LB** **FACILITIES:** STV **PARKING:** 13 **NOTES:** No children No smoking in restaurant Closed 20 Dec-20 Jan **CARDS:**

**★★61% Palace**
250 Iffley Rd OX4 1SE
☎ 01865 727627 Fax 01865 200478
***Dir:*** *on A4158 1m from City Centre*
A small, family-run hotel close to the city centre. The attractive bedrooms are bright and thoughtfully equipped. There is a comfortable lounge and bar/dining facilities are available.
**ROOMS:** 8 en suite (2 fmly) No smoking in all bedrooms s £65-£69; d £75-£80 (incl. bkfst) * **PARKING:** 6 **NOTES:** No dogs Closed 20 Dec-20 Jan **CARDS:**

## *Town House*

**★★★★ *Old Bank***
92-94 High St OX1 4BJ
☎ 01865 799599 Fax 01865 799598
e-mail: info@oldbank-hotel.co.uk
***Dir:*** *Approach city centre via Headington over Magdalen Bridge into High St, hotel 50yds on left*
The tranquillity of this hotel provides a contrast to the bustle of the High Street, just a few minutes away. This skilfully restored former bank offers smart, well-equipped bedrooms, all with thoughtful extras and air conditioning. The Quod brasserie serves meals all day and there is also a peaceful courtyard.
**ROOMS:** 43 en suite (10 fmly) **FACILITIES:** STV ch fac **SERVICES:** Lift air con **PARKING:** 40 **NOTES:** No dogs (ex guide dogs) Closed 25-27 Dec **CARDS:**

## *Town House*

**★★★★ Old Parsonage**
1 Banbury Rd OX2 6NN
☎ 01865 310210 Fax 01865 311262
e-mail: info@oldparsonage-hotel.co.uk
***Dir:*** *from Oxford ring-road, approach city centre via Summertown, last building on right next to St Giles Church before entering city centre*
Situated just north of the city centre, this stylish hotel has great character and, in parts, dates back to the 16th century. Attractively furnished bedrooms, including some spacious suites, are complemented by a cosy lounge. The focal point, though, is the all day bar restaurant, serving a wide range of interesting dishes.
**ROOMS:** 30 en suite (4 fmly) s £130-£175; d £170-£190 (incl. bkfst) * **FACILITIES:** STV **PARKING:** 16 **NOTES:** No dogs (ex guide dogs) Closed 24-27 Dec **CARDS:**





O

OXFORD, continued

### ⌂ *Travelodge*
London Rd, Wheatley OX33 1JH
☎ 01865 875705 📠 01865 875905
***Dir:*** *off A40 next to The Harvester on the outskirts of Wheatley*
Travelodge offers good quality, good value, modern accommodation. Ideal for families, the spacious, en suite bedrooms include remote-control TV, tea and coffee-making facilities, luxury beds and free morning newspaper. Meals can be taken at the nearby family restaurant. For further details and the Travelodge phone number, consult the Hotel Groups page.

**ROOMS:** 36 en suite

### ⌂ Days Inn
OX33 1LJ
☎ 01865 877000 📠 01865 877016
e-mail: oxford.hotel@welcomebreak.co.uk
***Dir:*** *situated at the Welcome Break service area of M40 junct 8A. Access available from both southbound & northbound carriageways*
This modern building offers accommodation in smart, spacious and well-equipped bedrooms, suitable for families and business travellers, and all with en suite bathrooms. Continental breakfast is available and other refreshments may be taken at the nearby family restaurant. For further details and the Days Inn phone number, consult the Hotel Groups page.
**ROOMS:** 59 en suite s fr £59; d fr £59 *

### ⌂ *Travelodge*
Peartree Roundabout, Woodstock Rd OX2 8JZ
☎ 01865 554301 📠 01865 513474
***Dir:*** *junc A34/A43*

O

Travelodge offers good quality, good value, modern accommodation. Ideal for families, the spacious, en suite bedrooms include remote-control TV, tea and coffee-making facilities, luxury beds and free morning newspaper. Meals can be taken at the nearby family restaurant. For further details and the Travelodge phone number, consult the Hotel Groups page.

**ROOMS:** 98 en suite

## PADSTOW, Cornwall & Isles of Scilly — Map 02 SW97
see also Constantine Bay

### ★★★70% The Metropole
Station Rd PL28 8DB
☎ 0870 400 8122 📠 01841 532867
e-mail: heritagehotels_padstow.metropole@forte-hotels.com
***Dir:*** *M5 junct 31, take A3 until it joins the A39 then the A389 following signs for Padstow*
With splendid views over the Camel Estuary, The Metropole enjoys an enviable location in this popular Cornish seaside village. Public rooms offer guests a range of relaxing seating options from the Veranda, with views over the garden and estuary beyond, to the attractive lounges and small bar area. Staff are genuinely willing to please and help to create that special atmosphere that will make guests want to return time and time again.
**ROOMS:** 50 en suite (5 fmly) No smoking in 19 bedrooms s £90-£95; d £128-£175 * LB **FACILITIES:** Outdoor swimming (H) Swimming pool open Jul & Aug only Xmas **SERVICES:** Lift **PARKING:** 38 **NOTES:** No smoking in restaurant **CARDS:**

### ★★★66% *Old Custom House Inn*
South Quay PL28 8ED
☎ 01841 532359 📠 01841 533372
***Dir:*** *A359 from Wadebridge take 2nd right, once in Padstow follow road round hairpin bend at bottom of hill & cont, hotel is 2nd building*
Situated by the harbour, this charming inn continues to be a popular choice for locals and visitors alike. The lively bar serves real ales and good bar meals at lunchtime and in the evening. In the restaurant, locally caught fish and other captivating dishes are featured on the fixed price menu.
**ROOMS:** 27 en suite (8 fmly) **FACILITIES:** STV **CONF:** Board 85
**PARKING:** 9 **CARDS:**

### ★★66% Green Waves
West View Rd, Trevone Bay PL28 8RD
☎ 01841 520114 📠 01841 520568
***Dir:*** *Turn off A39 to Padstow at B3276 signposted to Newquay, Trevone. Follow for 1 mile then take first turning to your right signposted Trevone. Green Waves is at the bottom of the road after the Beach Car Parks.*
This ever-popular, family-run hotel is just a short stroll from the beach and coastal footpaths. Bedrooms are varied in terms of size and style, some located on the ground floor and a number having the added bonus of wonderful sea views. Public areas include a spacious lounge and a separate bar, ideal for enjoying a drink before dinner and swapping a few stories with fellow visitors.
**ROOMS:** 15 en suite s £28-£40; d £56-£86 (incl. bkfst) * LB
**PARKING:** 16 **NOTES:** No dogs (ex guide dogs) No children 4yrs No smoking in restaurant Closed End Nov - March **CARDS:**

*See advert on opposite page*

## PAIGNTON, Devon — Map 03 SX86

### ★★★71% Redcliffe
Marine Dr TQ3 2NL
☎ 01803 526397 📠 01803 528030
e-mail: redclfe@aol.com
***Dir:*** *follow signs for Paignton & sea front, hotel on sea front at Torquay end of Paignton Green*

Standing in three acres of grounds, this well-established hotel enjoys uninterrupted views across Tor Bay. Service is both friendly and attentive and all bedrooms are comfortably furnished, with modern facilities. Spacious public rooms include the 'Dick Francis' suite and a popular leisure centre.
**ROOMS:** 65 en suite (8 fmly) s £50-£55; d £100-£110 (incl. bkfst) *
**FACILITIES:** STV Indoor swimming (H) Outdoor swimming (H) Fishing Sauna Solarium Gym Putting green Jacuzzi Table tennis Carpet Bowls Xmas **CONF:** Thtr 150 Class 50 Board 50 Del from £60 *
**SERVICES:** Lift **PARKING:** 80 **NOTES:** No dogs (ex guide dogs) No smoking in restaurant Civ Wed 150 **CARDS:**

**★★69% Preston Sands**
10/12 Marine Pde TQ3 2NU
☎ 01803 558718 Fax 01803 522875
***Dir:*** *approx 1.5m from Paignton rail station, situated on Preston Beach*
Many of the bedrooms in this small, family-run hotel, situated right on the seafront, benefit from fine sea views. The owners offer a friendly welcome, and a genuinely relaxing atmosphere is apparent throughout the hotel.
**ROOMS:** 31 en suite (3 fmly) s £26-£32; d £48-£56 (incl. bkfst) * **LB** **FACILITIES:** Xmas **PARKING:** 24 **NOTES:** No children 8yrs No smoking in restaurant **CARDS:**

**★★68% Clennon Valley Hotel**
Clennon Rise, Goodrington TQ4 5HG
☎ 01803 550304 Fax 01803 527584
e-mail: clennonvalleyhotel@hotmail.com
***Dir:*** *400yds N of Quay West Water Park*
This pleasant Victorian house is conveniently located on the Dartmouth road, between the town centre and Goodrington's beaches. Equally suited to both business and leisure guests, it provides well equipped accommodation and an informal, relaxed atmosphere. Facilities include an attractive lounge, a small bar and a traditionally furnished dining room.
**ROOMS:** 9 en suite No smoking in all bedrooms s fr £32; d fr £64 (incl. bkfst) * **LB** **FACILITIES:** STV **PARKING:** 8 **NOTES:** No dogs No children 12yrs No smoking in restaurant Closed Nov-Feb
**CARDS:**

**★★67% Sea Verge Hotel**
21 Marine Dr TQ3 2NJ
☎ 01803 557795
Conveniently situated close to the seafront and Preston Green, this family-run hotel continues to benefit from the dedicated approach of the owners. Several of the light and airy bedrooms have balconies, with views of the Channel. Spacious public areas include a comfortable lounge with adjacent sun room, a cosy bar and the soundly appointed restaurant.
**ROOMS:** 10 en suite (1 fmly) s £20-£36; d £36 (incl. bkfst) * **LB** **PARKING:** 14 **NOTES:** No children 9yrs Closed Dec-Feb

**★★66% Tor Sands**
8 Sands Rd TQ4 6EH
☎ 01803 559695 Fax 01803 526786
e-mail: enquiries@torsandatpaignton.co.uk
***Dir:*** *From sea front, follow Esplanade Rd towards harbour. Past multiplex towards rdbt turn right into Sands Rd, hotel on left at next mini rdbt*
Continuing the family tradition, Tor Sands' brother and sister proprietors run a comfortable and friendly hotel, providing regular entertainment and themed events for their guests. Attractive bedrooms all have modern facilities and enjoyable food is served in the dining room.
**ROOMS:** 29 rms (26 en suite) 5 annexe en suite No smoking in all bedrooms s £27-£33; d £54-£66 (incl. bkfst & dinner) * **LB** **FACILITIES:** entertainment Xmas **PARKING:** 15 **NOTES:** No smoking in restaurant Closed 3 Jan-Feb **CARDS:**

**★★65% *Dainton***
95 Dartmouth Rd, Three Beaches, Goodrington TQ4 6NA
☎ 01803 550067 & 525901 Fax 01803 666339
e-mail: Dave@Dainton-hotel.co.uk
***Dir:*** *located on the A379 at Goodrington*
This pleasant Tudor-style property is situated within easy walking distance of the beach and leisure park. Bedrooms and bathrooms are very well-furnished and equipped. Guests can eat in the bar

*continued on p458*

PAIGNTON, continued

or, later in the evening, choose between a fixed-price menu and full carte in the attractive restaurant.
**ROOMS:** 11 en suite (2 fmly) No smoking in all bedrooms
**FACILITIES:** entertainment **PARKING:** 20 **NOTES:** No smoking in restaurant **CARDS:**

### ★★65% Torbay Holiday Motel

Totnes Rd TQ4 7PP
☎ 01803 558226 🖹 01803 663375
e-mail: enquiries@thm.co.uk
***Dir:*** *on A385 Totnes/Paignton road, 2.5m from Paignton*
Leisure facilities, self-catering apartments and motel accommodation are all part of a purpose built, small complex situated between Paignton and Totnes. The comfortable bedrooms are very spacious and well co-ordinated. In the dining room traditional food is served, whilst a less formal menu is available in the bar-lounge.
**ROOMS:** 16 en suite s £33.50-£36.50; d £51-£57 (incl. bkfst) **LB**
**FACILITIES:** STV Indoor swimming (H) Outdoor swimming (H) Sauna Solarium Gym Putting green Crazy golf Adventure playground ch fac
**PARKING:** 150 **NOTES:** RS 24-31 Dec **CARDS:**

*See advert on opposite page*

### ★70% The Commodore Hotel

14 Esplanade Rd TQ4 6EB
☎ 01803 553107 🖹 01803 553107
***Dir:*** *follow A3022 stay in left lane to sea front, just past multiplex cinema complex, hotel on right*

Commodore
AA

Enjoying a prime seafront position, this family-run hotel benefits from the added bonus of lovely views across the bay. Public areas are spacious and well presented, with ample seating in both the lounge and bar lounge. Bedrooms are comfortable and well equipped.
**ROOMS:** 12 en suite (4 fmly) s £22-£24; d £44-£48 (incl. bkfst) *
**FACILITIES:** Xmas **PARKING:** 10 **NOTES:** No dogs (ex guide dogs) No smoking in restaurant Closed Nov-Feb

### ★61% Sattva

Esplanade TQ4 6BL
☎ 01803 557820 🖹 01803 557820
***Dir:*** *hotel located on the seafront by the pier*
Ideally situated on the seafront, the Sattva Hotel is family run and conveniently near to all the resort's attractions. Bedrooms vary in size and style; some of the sea-facing rooms have the benefit of a balcony. Entertainment is provided in the lively bar on a regular basis, during the summer months.
**ROOMS:** 20 en suite (2 fmly) No smoking in 3 bedrooms s £29-£35; d £58-£70 (incl. bkfst) * **LB** **FACILITIES:** Xmas **SERVICES:** Lift
**PARKING:** 10 **NOTES:** No smoking in restaurant Closed Jan-Feb
**CARDS:**

PAINSWICK, Gloucestershire Map 03 SO80

### ★★★78% Painswick

Kemps Ln GL6 6YB
☎ 01452 812160 🖹 01452 814059
e-mail: reservations@painswickhotel.com
***Dir:*** *turn off A46 in centre of village by the church. Hotel is located off 2nd road behind church off Tibbiwell Lane*

This hotel, formerly a rectory built in 1790, is set in beautiful rolling countryside. Bedrooms, all well-equipped, are in the main house and adjacent building. Elegant day rooms feature antiques and high quality furnishings. The restaurant offers fine wines and noteworthy cuisine.
**ROOMS:** 19 en suite (4 fmly) s £85-£125; d £115-£180 (incl. bkfst) * **LB** **FACILITIES:** Croquet lawn ch fac Xmas **CONF:** Thtr 40 Class 20 Board 20 Del £150 * **PARKING:** 25 **NOTES:** No smoking in restaurant Civ Wed 100 **CARDS:**

*See advert on opposite page*

PANGBOURNE, Berkshire Map 04 SU67

### ★★★75% The Copper Inn Hotel and Restaurant

Best Western

RG8 7AR
☎ 0118 984 2244 🖹 0118 984 5542
e-mail: reservations@copper-inn.co.uk
***Dir:*** *from M4 junct 12 take A4 west then A340 to Pangbourne. Hotel located next to Pangbourne parish church at the junction of A329/A340*
This 19th-century coaching inn is well known for its high standards of hotel keeping. Individually decorated bedrooms are comfortable and well-equipped; many overlook the secluded garden and village church. The lovely restaurant has a Mediterranean feel and is a local dining destination.
**ROOMS:** 14 en suite 8 annexe en suite (1 fmly) No smoking in all bedrooms s £90; d £110 * **LB** **FACILITIES:** STV Xmas **CONF:** Thtr 60 Class 24 Board 30 Del from £140 * **PARKING:** 20 **NOTES:** Civ Wed 80
**CARDS:**

### ★★★68% George Hotel

The Square RG8 7AJ
☎ 0118 984 2237 🖹 0118 984 4354
e-mail: info@georgehotelpangbourne.co.uk
***Dir:*** *leave M4 junct 12 towards Newbury, at 2nd rdbt turn right onto A340, continue for 3m into Pangbourne. Right at rdbt, hotel 50yds on left*
This former coaching inn stands right in the centre of Pangbourne and has been comfortably modernised. All of the bedrooms vary in size and outlook, whilst service is informal, friendly and willing.
**ROOMS:** 26 en suite (3 fmly) No smoking in 9 bedrooms s £90-£110; d £100-£125 * **FACILITIES:** STV Xmas **CONF:** Thtr 60 Class 60 Board 50 Del from £135 * **PARKING:** 30 **NOTES:** No smoking in restaurant RS wknds & BH's **CARDS:**

## PARKHAM, Devon

Map 02 SS32

**★★★73% Penhaven Country House**
Rectory Ln EX39 5PL
☎ 01237 451388 & 451711 01237 451878
e-mail: reservations@penhaven.co.uk
***Dir:*** *turn off A39 at Horns Cross and follow signs to Parkham, turn second left after Church into Rectory Lane*

With distant views of Exmoor, this 17th-century hotel offers comfortable accommodation in a friendly, relaxed atmosphere. Bedrooms are in the main building or in cottage suites in the grounds; two ground floor rooms are available for the less mobile. Local produce features on the menu, and vegetarians are especially welcome. Many guests visit this hotel specifically to see the badgers in the evening.

**ROOMS:** 12 en suite s £75-£80; d £150-£160 (incl. bkfst & dinner) * LB **FACILITIES:** Xmas **PARKING:** 50 **NOTES:** No children 10yrs No smoking in restaurant **CARDS:**

## PATELEY BRIDGE, North Yorkshire

Map 07 SE16

**★★70% Grassfields Country House**
Low Wath Rd HG3 5HL
☎ 01423 711412 01423 712844
e-mail: grassfields@nidderdale.co.uk
***Dir:*** *turn off A59 onto B6451 and turn left at Summerbridge onto B6165. Cross bridge and take first right at petrol pumps*

A relaxed and friendly atmosphere prevails at this fine Georgian mansion. One can eat well in the restaurant from an interesting and varied menu, or less formally in the bistro. There is a comfortable drawing room and a cosy bar.

**ROOMS:** 9 en suite (3 fmly) s £31-£44.50; d £59-£75 (incl. bkfst) * LB **FACILITIES:** Xmas **CONF:** Thtr 100 Class 70 Board 50 **PARKING:** 30 **NOTES:** No smoking in restaurant **CARDS:**

## PATTERDALE, Cumbria

Map 11 NY31

**★★60% Patterdale**
CA11 0NN
☎ 017684 82231 017684 82440
***Dir:*** *M6 junct 40, take A592 towards Ullswater, then 10m up Lakeside Rd to Patterdale*

Patterdale is a real tourist destination and this hotel enjoys delightful views of the valley and fells, being located at the southern end of Ullswater. The hotel's current core business is touring and accordingly it offers practical and functional accommodation.

**ROOMS:** 63 en suite (4 fmly) s £32-£39; d £64-£72 (incl. bkfst) * LB **FACILITIES:** Tennis (hard) Fishing entertainment **CONF:** Class 20 **SERVICES:** Lift **PARKING:** 31 **NOTES:** No dogs (ex guide dogs) No smoking in restaurant Closed Jan-Feb Civ Wed 110 **CARDS:**



P

PATTINGHAM, Staffordshire Map 07 SO89

**★★★67% Patshull Park Hotel Golf & Country Club**
Patshull Park WV6 7HR
☎ 01902 700100 01902 700874
e-mail: sales@patshull-park.co.uk
***Dir:*** *1.5m W of Pattingham, at Pattingham Church take the Patshull Rd hotel 1.5m on right*

There has been a manor house here since before the Norman conquest. The present house, dating back to the 1730s, and its 280 acres of parkland now provide a hotel with a golf, fishing, leisure and conference complex. Facilities include a coffee shop and a golf shop, along with extensive conference and banqueting suites. Bedrooms are well-equipped.
**ROOMS:** 49 en suite (2 fmly) s £88-£98; d £98-£118 (incl. bkfst) * **LB**
**FACILITIES:** STV Indoor swimming (H) Golf 18 Fishing Sauna Solarium Gym Putting green Jacuzzi Beauty therapist entertainment Xmas
**CONF:** Thtr 250 Class 75 Board 44 Del from £99 * **PARKING:** 200
**NOTES:** No smoking in restaurant Civ Wed 100
**CARDS:**

*See advert on opposite page*

PEASLAKE, Surrey Map 04 TQ04

**★★★66% ◎ Hurtwood Inn Hotel**
Walking Bottom GU5 9RR
☎ 01306 730851 01306 731390
e-mail: sales@hurtwoodinnhotel.com
***Dir:*** *turn off A25 at Gomshall opposite Jet Filling Station towards Peaslake. After 2.5 turn right at village shop, hotel in village centre*
Situated in the peaceful village of Peaslake between Guildford and Dorking, this hotel offers brightly appointed bedrooms which have benefited from refurbishment. Some are located in an adjacent wing overlooking the hotel garden. Public areas include a cosy bar/lounge with a warming fire and the oak-panelled Oscars restaurant where guests can enjoy a good standard of cuisine.
**ROOMS:** 9 en suite 8 annexe en suite (6 fmly) s fr £70; d £80-£90 *
**LB CONF:** Thtr 40 Class 15 Board 20 Del from £136.95 *
**PARKING:** 21 **NOTES:** No smoking in restaurant
**CARDS:**

PEASMARSH, East Sussex Map 05 TQ82

**★★★74% Flackley Ash**
MARSTON HOTELS
TN31 6YH
☎ 01797 230651 01797 230510
e-mail: flackleyash@marstonhotels.co.uk
***Dir:*** *3m from Rye, beside A268*
This attractive Georgian country house enjoys a peaceful setting in well kept grounds just a short distance to the north of Rye. Spacious bedrooms are individually furnished and feature a full range of modern facilities. The hotel is also equipped with conference facilities and an indoor leisure suite offering various health treatments. Guests can expect efficient, attentive service from a friendly young team.

**ROOMS:** 45 en suite (3 fmly) s fr £79; d fr £119 (incl. bkfst) * **LB**
**FACILITIES:** **Spa** Indoor swimming (H) Sauna Gym Croquet lawn Putting green Beautician aromatherapy reflexology ch fac Xmas
**CONF:** Thtr 100 Class 50 Board 40 Del from £115 * **PARKING:** 70
**NOTES:** No smoking in restaurant Civ Wed 120
**CARDS:**

*See advert under RYE*

PELYNT, Cornwall & Isles of Scilly Map 02 SX25

**★★63% Jubilee Inn**
PL13 2JZ
☎ 01503 220312 01503 220920
e-mail: rickard@jubileeinn.freeserve.co.uk
***Dir:*** *take A390 signposted St Austell at village of East Taphouse turn left onto B3359 signposted Looe & Polperro. Jubilee Inn on left on leaving Pelynt.*
Situated close to Looe, this popular 16th-century inn has great character with flagstone floors and charming, old-fashioned rooms. A choice of bars is available, and menus focus on fresh local produce. Individual in size and decor, the bedrooms provide comfortable accommodation and modern facilities.
**ROOMS:** 11 en suite (3 fmly) s £32-£38.50; d £52-£65 (incl. bkfst) *
**FACILITIES:** Xmas **PARKING:** 80 **NOTES:** No smoking in restaurant
**CARDS:**

PENDLEBURY, Greater Manchester Map 07 SD70

**⌂ *Premier Lodge (Manchester North West)***
PREMIER LODGE
219 Bolton Rd M27 8TG
☎ 0870 700 1470 0870 700 1471
Premier Lodge offers modern, well-equipped, en suite accommodation suitable for both business and leisure travellers. Meals can be taken at the adjacent popular restaurant and bar, which is fully licensed. For further details, consult the Hotel Groups page.
**ROOMS:** 31 en suite

PENKRIDGE, Staffordshire Map 07 SJ91

**★★★66% Quality Hotel Stafford**
Quality Hotel
Pinfold Ln ST19 5QP
☎ 01785 712459 01785 715532
e-mail: admin@gb067.u-net.com
***Dir:*** *from M6 junct 12 A5 towards Telford at 1st rdbt turn right onto A449, 2m into Penkridge turn left just beyond Ford garage, opposite White Hart*
In a quiet backwater of Staffordshire and surrounded by countryside, this hotel is just a few minutes' drive from the M6. Bedrooms are spacious and well-presented with good facilities;

*continued*

some are on ground floor level. There is an attractive lounge and a smart restaurant offering an interesting menu.
**ROOMS:** 47 en suite (1 fmly) No smoking in 25 bedrooms
**FACILITIES:** **Spa** STV Indoor swimming (H) Squash Sauna Solarium Gym entertainment **CONF:** Thtr 300 Class 120 Board 90
**PARKING:** 160 **NOTES:** No smoking in restaurant Civ Wed 70
**CARDS:**

PENRITH, Cumbria Map 12 NY53
see also Shap & Temple Sowerby

★★★★66% **North Lakes**
Ullswater Rd CA11 8QT
☎ 01768 868111 01768 868291
e-mail: nlakes@shireinns.co.uk
SHIRE INNS
***Dir:*** *M6 junct 40 at intersection with A66*
With its great location just off junction 40 of the M6, it is no wonder that this hotel enjoys a busy trade. Amenities include a good range of meeting and function rooms and excellent health and leisure facilities. Themed public areas have a contemporary Nordic country style and offer plenty of comfort.
**ROOMS:** 84 en suite (6 fmly) No smoking in 25 bedrooms d £122-£142 (incl. bkfst) * **LB** **FACILITIES:** STV Indoor swimming (H) Squash Sauna Solarium Gym Jacuzzi Childrens pool,Health & Beauty rooms Xmas
**CONF:** Thtr 200 Class 140 Board 24 Del £138 * **SERVICES:** Lift
**PARKING:** 150 **NOTES:** No smoking in restaurant Civ Wed 200
**CARDS:**

★★★71% **Westmorland Hotel**
Orton CA10 3SB
☎ 015396 24351 015396 24354
e-mail: westmorlandhotel@aol.com
(For full entry and advert see Tebay)

★★★62% **The George**
Devonshire St CA11 7SU
☎ 01768 862696 01768 868223
e-mail: info@georgehotelpenrith.co.uk
***Dir:*** *leave M6 junct 40 & follow route for town centre continue for approx 1m. If travelling from A6/A66 follow route for Penrith town centre*

Experienced new owners are committed to a total upgrade of this long-established town centre hotel, which remains as friendly and as popular as ever. Already many bedrooms have been upgraded to a high standard, whilst public areas retain their old-fashioned charm, the lounges being a venue for morning coffees and afternoon teas.
**ROOMS:** 34 en suite (3 fmly) No smoking in 13 bedrooms s fr £45; d fr £70 (incl. bkfst) * **LB** **FACILITIES:** STV Free use of local pool and gym Xmas **CONF:** Thtr 140 Class 50 Board 40 **PARKING:** 34
**NOTES:** No smoking in restaurant Civ Wed 140
**CARDS:**

*See advert on this page*

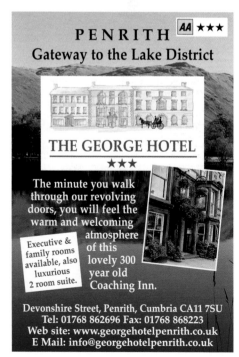

PENRITH, continued

★★67% ***Brantwood Country Hotel***
Stainton CA11 0EP
☎ 01768 862748 🖹 01768 890164
e-mail: brantwood2@aol.com
***Dir:*** *From M6 junct 40 join A66 Keswick road and in 0.5 mile turn left then right signposted Stainton*

Just two minutes' drive from the M6, this family-run hotel enjoys an open outlook to the rear. The traditional bedrooms are individual and cheerful in colour; five rooms are in a converted courtyard building. Good meals are served both in the bar and the restaurant.
**ROOMS:** 6 en suite 5 annexe en suite (3 fmly) No smoking in 5 bedrooms **FACILITIES:** Croquet lawn Putting green **CONF:** Thtr 60 Class 30 Board 30 **PARKING:** 35 **NOTES:** No dogs No smoking in restaurant **CARDS:**

*See advert on opposite page*

★★67% ***Edenhall***
Edenhall CA11 8SX
☎ 01768 881454 🖹 01768 881454
This is a long-established and traditional hotel, which lies in well-tended gardens in a quiet village. Public rooms include a spacious lounge bar with a conservatory, and an attractive dining room, which together with some of the bedrooms, overlook the gardens. Edenhall Hotel offers friendly and attentive service.
**ROOMS:** 21 en suite 8 annexe en suite (3 fmly) **FACILITIES:** Fishing **CONF:** Thtr 50 Class 20 Board 20 **PARKING:** 82 **NOTES:** No dogs (ex guide dogs) No smoking in restaurant **CARDS:**

P

***Travelodge***
Redhills CA11 0DT
☎ 01768 866958 🖹 01768 866958
***Dir:*** *on A66*

Travelodge

Travelodge offers good quality, good value, modern accommodation. Ideal for families, the spacious, en suite bedrooms include remote-control TV, tea and coffee-making facilities, luxury beds and free morning newspaper. Meals can be taken at the nearby family restaurant. For further details and the Travelodge phone number, consult the Hotel Groups page.

**ROOMS:** 40 en suite

PENZANCE, Cornwall & Isles of Scilly — Map 02 SW43

★★★69% **Mount Prospect**
Britons Hill TR18 3AE
☎ 01736 363117 🖹 01736 350970
e-mail: mtpros2000@aol.com
***Dir:*** *from A30 pass heliport on right straight onto next rdbt, bear left for town centre take 3rd right, look for brown sign, hotel is on right*

THE CIRCLE
Selected Individual Hotels
GREAT BRITAIN

A warm welcome is assured from the resident proprietors, who make every effort to ensure guests have an enjoyable, relaxed and memorable stay at this elegant Edwardian house. Bedrooms vary in style, many offering the added bonus of wonderful sea views. An interesting menu makes full use of the excellent local produce.
**ROOMS:** 21 en suite (2 fmly) No smoking in 17 bedrooms s £54-£54; d £80-£100 (incl. bkfst) * **LB** **FACILITIES:** STV Outdoor swimming (H) **CONF:** Thtr 80 Class 50 Board 12 Del from £74 * **PARKING:** 14 **NOTES:** No smoking in restaurant Closed 23 Dec-12 Jan **CARDS:**

★★★66% **Queen's**
The Promenade TR18 4HG
☎ 01736 362371 🖹 01736 350033
e-mail: enquiries@queens-hotel.com
***Dir:*** *A30 to Penzance, follow signs for seafront pass harbour & into promenade, hotel 0.5m on right*

Overlooking the impressive sweep of Mount's Bay, this large Victorian hotel has a long and distinguished history. Bedrooms are individually styled and provide all modern comforts, many benefiting from wonderful views. The dining room provides an elegant venue in which to enjoy the daily changing menu.
**ROOMS:** 70 en suite (10 fmly) s £40-£60; d £76-£128 (incl. bkfst) * **LB** **FACILITIES:** STV Sauna Solarium Gym Xmas **CONF:** Thtr 200 Class 100 Board 80 **SERVICES:** Lift **PARKING:** 50 **NOTES:** No smoking in restaurant Civ Wed 180 **CARDS:**

*See advert on opposite page*

★★★62% **Higher Faugan Country House**
Newlyn TR18 5NS
☎ 01736 362076 🖹 01736 351648
e-mail: reception@higherfaugan-hotel.co.uk
***Dir:*** *off B3115, 0.75m from Newlyn crossroads*
This gracious turn-of-the-century hotel, formerly the home of renowned local artist Stanhope Forbes, is surrounded by acres of well-kept gardens. Personal touches contribute to the 'home from home' atmosphere. Bedrooms are generally spacious, with some offering wonderful views across the countryside to the sea beyond.
**ROOMS:** 11 en suite (2 fmly) s £60-£75; d £80-£115 (incl. bkfst) * **LB** **FACILITIES:** Outdoor swimming (H) Tennis (hard) Snooker Croquet lawn Putting green **PARKING:** 20 **NOTES:** No smoking in restaurant **CARDS:**

★★66% **Tarbert**
11-12 Clarence St TR18 2NU
☎ 01736 363758 & 364317 🖹 01736 331336
e-mail: reception@tarbert-hotel.co.uk
***Dir:*** *take Land's End turning at town approach. At 2nd rdbt turn left, continue past next mini rdbt - 100yds turn right into Clarence St*
Formerly a sea captain's house, dating back to the 1830s, this family-run hotel is located just a short walk from the town centre and promenade. Bedrooms vary in size but all offer good levels of

*continued on p464*

PENZANCE, continued

comfort and character. The bar has a convivial and relaxing atmosphere, whilst the popular restaurant features an interesting menu with good use of local produce.

*Tarbert, Penzance*

**ROOMS:** 12 en suite (2 fmly) No smoking in all bedrooms s £27-£35; d £50-£60 (incl. bkfst) * **LB** **PARKING:** 4 **NOTES:** No dogs No smoking in restaurant Closed Dec-10 Feb
**CARDS:**

★★65% ***Union Hotel***
Chapel St TR18 4AE
☎ 01736 362319 01726 362319
e-mail: unionhotel@hotmail.com
The Union Hotel's Nelson bar is popular with locals and visitors alike, and serves a range of traditional bar meals. The Hamilton Restaurant offers a more formal dining option, with both fixed price and carte menus available. There is a variety of sizes and styles of accommodation, with all bedrooms having modern facilities.
**ROOMS:** 28 rms (22 en suite) (4 fmly) **PARKING:** 15 **NOTES:** No dogs
**CARDS:**

P

★67% **Estoril**
46 Morrab Rd TR18 4EX
☎ 01736 362468 & 367471 01736 367471
e-mail: estorilhotel@aol.com
***Dir:*** *from bus/train station keep left along promenade towards Newlyn, take 1st turning past "The Lugger", Estoril is 300yds along on left*
Ideally situated in a quiet location midway between the town centre and seafront, this is an ideal base for exploring the local area. Great attention is paid to the well-being of guests, and all of the well-equipped bedrooms offer good levels of comfort. Fresh produce is frequently used for meals, which are served in the smart dining room.
**ROOMS:** 9 en suite (2 fmly) No smoking in all bedrooms s £30; d £59 (incl. bkfst) * **LB** **PARKING:** 4 **NOTES:** No dogs No smoking in restaurant Closed 24 25 31 Dec 01 Jan **CARDS:**

PETERBOROUGH, Cambridgeshire — Map 04 TL19
see also Wansford

★★★★65% **Peterborough Marriott**

Marriott
HOTELS · RESORTS · SUITES

Peterborough Business Park, Lynchwood
PE2 6GB
☎ 01733 371111 01733 236725
***Dir:*** *opposite East of England Showground at Alwalton. From A1 turn off at Alwalton Showground, Chesterton. At T-junction turn left and hotel is on your left at next rdbt.*
Opposite the East of England Showground, and next to the Peterborough Business Park, this modern hotel is commercially popular. Bedrooms are well-equipped and comfortable. Public rooms include lounge and cocktail bars, and the brasserie offers a variety of dishes. There is also a formal restaurant. The leisure club includes a children's pool.

**ROOMS:** 157 en suite (8 fmly) No smoking in 108 bedrooms s £85; d £85 * **LB** **FACILITIES:** **Spa** STV Indoor swimming (H) Sauna Solarium Gym Putting green Jacuzzi Beauty therapist, Hairdressing ch fac Xmas **CONF:** Thtr 300 Class 160 Board 45 Del £140 * **PARKING:** 250 **NOTES:** No dogs (ex guide dogs) No smoking in restaurant Civ Wed 200 **CARDS:**

★★★69% **Bell Inn**
Great North Rd PE7 3RA
☎ 01733 241066 01733 245173
e-mail: reception@thebellstitton.co.uk
(For full entry see Stilton)

★★★69% **Orton Hall**
Best Western
Orton Longueville PE2 7DN
☎ 01733 391111 01733 231912
e-mail: reception@ortonhall.co.uk
***Dir:*** *off A605 (East) opposite Orton Mere*
Set in 20 acres of woodland, this impressive country house has spacious and relaxing public areas, with extra facilities dotted around the grounds. Original features include oak panelling in the Huntly Restaurant, the Grand Hall, which is a popular banqueting venue, and some 16th-century terracotta floors. Across the courtyard is the Ramblewood Inn.
**ROOMS:** 65 en suite (2 fmly) No smoking in 42 bedrooms s £70-£95; d £85-£135 * **LB** **FACILITIES:** Three quarter size snooker table Xmas **CONF:** Thtr 120 Class 48 Board 42 Del from £125 * **PARKING:** 200 **NOTES:** No smoking in restaurant Civ Wed 90
**CARDS:**

★★★68% **Bull**
PEEL HOTELS
Westgate PE1 1RB
☎ 01733 561364 01733 557304
***Dir:*** *turn off A1 follow signs to city centre, hotel in heart of city opposite Queensgate shopping centre. Car park is on Broadway next to Library*
A very pleasant city centre hotel, offering well-equipped modern accommodation which includes a new wing of deluxe bedrooms. The public rooms are extensive and include a good range of meeting rooms and conference facilities. An interesting range of dishes is served in the elegant restaurant; alternative informal dining is available within the lounge.
**ROOMS:** 118 rms (115 en suite) (3 fmly) No smoking in 40 bedrooms s fr £75; d fr £85 (incl. bkfst) * **LB** **FACILITIES:** STV **CONF:** Thtr 200 Class 80 Board 60 Del from £125 * **PARKING:** 100 **NOTES:** No smoking in restaurant Civ Wed 80 **CARDS:**

*continued*

### ★★★66% Butterfly
Thorpe Meadows, Longthorpe Parkway PE3 6GA
☎ 01733 564240 📠 01733 565538
e-mail: peterbutterfly@lineone.net
**Dir:** *from A1179 take exit for Thorpe Meadows and city centre, turn right at next two roundabouts*

Sitting in a pretty location beside the international rowing course in Thorpe Meadows, this hotel is near park, lake and river walks, as well as the local steam railway. The refurbished bedrooms are well-designed and properly equipped, with particular consideration for the needs of corporate guests; ground floor, studio and ladies' rooms are also available.

**ROOMS:** 70 en suite (2 fmly) No smoking in 10 bedrooms s £79.50; d £79.50 * **LB FACILITIES:** STV **CONF:** Thtr 80 Class 50 Board 50 Del £97.50 * **PARKING:** 85 **NOTES:** No dogs (ex guide dogs) No smoking in restaurant **CARDS:**

### ★★★63% Posthouse Peterborough
Posthouse

Great North Rd PE7 3TB
☎ 0870 400 9063 📠 01733 244455
(For full entry see Norman Cross)

### ⌂ Express by Holiday Inn Peterborough
Express by Holiday Inn

East of England Way, Alwalton PE2 6HE
☎ 01733 284450 📠 01733 284451
**Dir:** *1m E of the A1 and 4m from city centre on the A605 Oundle Road, adjacent to East of England Showground*

A modern budget hotel offering comfortable accommodation in refreshing, spacious and comprehensively equipped bedrooms, en suite bathrooms with power showers and continental buffet breakfast included in the room rate. Suitable for business travellers or families. For further details and the Express by Holiday Inn phone number, consult the Hotel Groups page.

**ROOMS:** 80 en suite (incl. cont bkfst) s £45-£60; d £45-£60 *
**CONF:** Thtr 25 Class 20 Board 16

### ⌂ *Travelodge*
Travelodge

Great North Rd, Alwalton PE7 3UR
☎ 01733 231109 📠 01733 231109
**Dir:** *on A1, southbound*

Travelodge offers good quality, good value, modern accommodation. Ideal for families, the spacious, en suite bedrooms include remote-control TV, tea and coffee-making facilities, luxury beds and free morning newspaper. Meals can be taken at the nearby family restaurant. For further details and the Travelodge phone number, consult the Hotel Groups page.

**ROOMS:** 32 en suite

## PETERLEE, Co Durham
Map 08 NZ44

### ★★69% *Hardwicke Hall Manor*
Hesleden TS27 4PA
☎ 01429 836326 📠 01429 837676
**Dir:** *NE on B1281, off A19 at the sign for Durham/Blackhall*

This country mansion house majors in business custom and weddings. Its comfortable bedrooms are well furnished and thoughtfully equipped and the public rooms are cosy and inviting.

**ROOMS:** 15 en suite (2 fmly) **CONF:** Thtr 60 Board 20 **PARKING:** 100
**NOTES:** No smoking in restaurant Civ Wed 110
**CARDS:**

## PETERSFIELD, Hampshire
Map 04 SU72

### ★★70% Langrish House
Langrish GU32 1RN
☎ 01730 266941 📠 01730 260543
e-mail: frontdesk@langrishhouse.co.uk
**Dir:** *turn off A3 onto A272 towards Winchester. Hotel signposted 3m on left*

Located in a secluded spot just outside Petersfield, this family home dates back to the 17th century. Rooms offer good levels of comfort with beautiful views over the countryside. The public

*continued on p466*

P

PETERSFIELD, continued

areas consist of a small cosy restaurant, a bar in the vaults, and conference and banqueting rooms that are popular for weddings.

*Langrish House, Petersfield*

**ROOMS:** 13 en suite (1 fmly) s £63-£72; d £96-£104 (incl. bkfst) * **LB** **FACILITIES:** Fishing Xmas **CONF:** Thtr 60 Class 18 Board 25 Del from £115 * **PARKING:** 80 **NOTES:** No smoking in restaurant Civ Wed 60
**CARDS:**

PETTY FRANCE, Gloucestershire Map 03 ST78

### ★★★68% *Petty France*

GL9 1AF
☎ 01454 238361 🖷 01454 238768
e-mail: hotel@pettyfrance.telme.com
***Dir:*** *on A46 S of junct with A433, 6m N of M4 junction 18, A46*
Surrounded by historical sights and the Cotswold countryside lies Petty France. This privately owned hotel features elegant rooms, pretty walled gardens, and a courtyard stable block converted into comfortable, modern bedrooms. Rooms in the main hotel reflect country house style. The attractive bar, lounge and restaurant have open fires which add to the atmosphere of this friendly country home.
**ROOMS:** 8 en suite 12 annexe en suite (1 fmly) No smoking in 1 bedroom **FACILITIES:** Croquet lawn Bicycle hire **CONF:** Thtr 55 Class 20 Board 24 **PARKING:** 70 **NOTES:** No smoking in restaurant Civ Wed
**CARDS:**

PICKERING, North Yorkshire Map 08 SE78

### ★★★69% Forest & Vale

Best Western

Malton Rd YO18 7DL
☎ 01751 472722 🖷 01751 472972
e-mail: reception@forestandvalehotel.co.uk
***Dir:*** *on A169 between York & Pickering at a rdbt on the outskirts of Pickering*

A warm welcome is assured at this pleasantly appointed hotel. The newly refurbished bedrooms are comfortable and include some spacious superior rooms, one with a four-poster bed. A good range of food is available, served either in the bar or in the restaurant; room service is another alternative.
**ROOMS:** 13 en suite 5 annexe en suite (5 fmly) No smoking in 6 bedrooms s £58-£72; d £80-£104 (incl. bkfst) * **LB** **FACILITIES:** STV Xmas **CONF:** Thtr 120 Class 50 Board 50 Del £95 * **PARKING:** 70 **NOTES:** No dogs (ex guide dogs) No smoking in restaurant Civ Wed 100
**CARDS:**

### ★★72% White Swan

Market Place YO18 7AA
☎ 01751 472288 🖷 01751 475554
e-mail: welcome@white-swan.co.uk
***Dir:*** *in the market place between the Church and the Steam Railway Station*
This delightful 16th-century coaching inn offers very well equipped, comfortable bedrooms, one with its own sitting room. Service is friendly and attentive and the standard of cuisine high, in both the attractive restaurant and the cosy bars where log fires burn. The extensive wine list offers many fine vintages. There is a separate, stylishly furnished drawing room.
**ROOMS:** 12 en suite (3 fmly) No smoking in all bedrooms s £60-£85; d £90-£140 (incl. bkfst) * **LB** **FACILITIES:** Motorised Treasure hunt Bike hire ch fac Xmas **CONF:** Thtr 80 Class 100 Board 25 Del from £99 * **PARKING:** 35 **NOTES:** No smoking in restaurant
**CARDS:**

### ★★68% Appleton Hall Country House Hotel

YO62 6TF
☎ 01751 417227 🖷 01751 417540
***Dir:*** *1.5m off A170 between Helmsley & Pickering*
Set in extensive gardens, this well maintained gracious Victorian country house offers a comfortable lounge with a real fire in a marble fireplace, a cosy residents' bar and an elegant dining room, where interesting traditional cooking is served. Bedrooms are all individually and attractively decorated, well-equipped, and two have their own lounges.
**ROOMS:** 9 en suite No smoking in all bedrooms s £64-£74; d £128-£166 (incl. bkfst & dinner) * **FACILITIES:** Croquet lawn **SERVICES:** Lift **PARKING:** 12 **NOTES:** No dogs (ex guide dogs) No children 14yrs No smoking in restaurant **CARDS:**

PICKHILL, North Yorkshire Map 08 SE38

### ★★67% Nags Head Country Inn

YO7 4JG
☎ 01845 567391 & 567570 🖷 01845 567212
e-mail: reservations@nagsheadpickhill.freeserve.co.uk
***Dir:*** *4m SE of Leeming Bar, 1.25m E of A1*
Convenient for the A1, this country inn offers an extensive range of food either in the bar or the newly refurbished and attractive restaurant. The bars are full of character and feature an extensive collection of ties. Bedrooms are well-equipped and modern while service is friendly and attentive.
**ROOMS:** 8 en suite 7 annexe en suite s £40; d £60 (incl. bkfst) * **LB** **FACILITIES:** Putting green Quoits pitch **CONF:** Thtr 36 Class 18 Board 24 Del from £65 * **PARKING:** 50 **NOTES:** No smoking in restaurant
**CARDS:**

Late for dinner? Quality Standards star rating means that last orders for dinner should be no earlier than:
★ 6.30pm ★★ 7.00pm ★★★ 8.00pm
★★★★ 9.00pm ★★★★★ 10.00pm

PINNER, Greater London
See LONDON SECTION plan 1 A5

**★★72% Tudor Lodge**
50 Field End Rd, Eastcote HA5 2QN
☎ 020 8429 0585 020 8429 0117
e-mail: tudorlodge@meridianleisure.com
***Dir:*** *turn off A40 at Swakeleys rdbt to Ickenham, turn onto A312 to Harrow, left at Northholt Station to Eastcote*

This friendly hotel, set in its own grounds, is located a short walk from Eastcote station, convenient for Heathrow Airport and many local golf courses. Bedrooms vary in size, all are well-equipped and some are suitable for families. As an alternative to the main restaurant a good range of bar snacks is offered.
**ROOMS:** 24 en suite 8 annexe en suite (10 fmly) s £84; d £89 (incl. bkfst) * **LB** **FACILITIES:** STV Xmas **CONF:** Thtr 60 Class 20 Board 26 Del £105 * **PARKING:** 30 **NOTES:** No smoking in restaurant
**CARDS:**

*See advert on this page*

PLYMOUTH, Devon — Map 02 SX45
see also St Mellion

**★★★★64% Copthorne Hotel Plymouth**
Armada Way PL1 1AR
☎ 01752 224161 01752 670688 COPTHORNE
e-mail: sales.plymouth@mill-cop.com
***Dir:*** *from M5, follow A38 to Plymouth city centre. Follow continental ferryport signs over 3 rdbts. Hotel visible on first exit left before 4th rdbt*
Located right in the city centre, this hotel possesses plentiful conference facilities and parking. Suites, Connoisseur and classic rooms are available; all are spacious and well-equipped. Non-smoking rooms can be requested. Public areas are divided over two floors and include Bentley's brasserie and bar, plus a small leisure centre with pool and gym.
**ROOMS:** 135 en suite (29 fmly) No smoking in 38 bedrooms s £60-£150; d £60-£170 **LB** **FACILITIES:** STV Indoor swimming (H) Gym Steam room Xmas **CONF:** Thtr 140 Class 60 Board 60 Del £133 * **SERVICES:** Lift **PARKING:** 50 **NOTES:** No dogs (ex guide dogs) Civ Wed 100 **CARDS:**

**★★★73% Kitley House Hotel**
Yealmpton PL8 2NW
☎ 01752 881555 01752 881667
e-mail: reservations@kitleyhousehotel.com
***Dir:*** *from Plymouth take A379 to Kingsbridge. Hotel on right after Brixton & before Yealmpton.*
A mile-long tree-lined drive leads to this fine house built of Devonshire granite and set in 300 acres of peaceful wooded parkland. Large bedrooms and suites are traditionally furnished to a high standard. The impressive public areas have a timeless

*continued on p468*

PLYMOUTH, continued

elegance. The dining room is housed in the former library and the cooking makes imaginative use of local produce.

*Kitley House Hotel, Plymouth*

**ROOMS:** 20 en suite (8 fmly) s £85-£115; d £110-£130 (incl. bkfst) * LB **FACILITIES:** STV Fishing Croquet lawn Beauty salon ch fac Xmas **CONF:** Thtr 70 Class 40 Board 35 Del from £95 * **PARKING:** 100 **NOTES:** No smoking in restaurant Civ Wed 80 **CARDS:**

*See advert on page 467*

### ★★★68% Duke of Cornwall

Best Western

Millbay Rd PL1 3LG
☎ 01752 275850 01752 275854
e-mail: duke@B'here.co.uk
***Dir:*** *follow signs to city centre then to Plymouth Pavilions Conference & Leisure Centre which leads you past hotel*

For those who prefer more character in their hotels, this Victorian Gothic building has a variety of period features. Individually designed bedrooms vary in size, many with their own seating area, and continuous refurbishment ensures high levels of comfort. The restaurant contains a stunning chandelier originating from the 1860s.
**ROOMS:** 71 en suite (6 fmly) No smoking in 20 bedrooms s £85-£99; d £90-£135 (incl. bkfst) * LB **FACILITIES:** Xmas **CONF:** Thtr 300 Class 125 Board 84 Del from £100 * **SERVICES:** Lift **PARKING:** 50 **NOTES:** No smoking in restaurant Civ Wed 120 **CARDS:**

### ★★★68% New Continental

Millbay Rd PL1 3LD
☎ 01752 220782 01752 227013
e-mail: newconti@aol.com
***Dir:*** *from A38 expressway follow City Centre signs for the Pavilions which are adjacent to hotel*
Within easy reach of the city centre and the Hoe, this privately owned hotel offers high standards of service and hospitality. Bedrooms vary in size and style, but all share the same levels of equipment and comfort. The hotel has a number of conference/function rooms together with leisure facilities.
**ROOMS:** 99 en suite (20 fmly) No smoking in 28 bedrooms **FACILITIES:** STV Indoor swimming (H) Sauna Solarium Gym Steam Room Beautician **CONF:** Thtr 400 Class 100 Board 70 Del from £70 * **SERVICES:** Lift **PARKING:** 100 **NOTES:** Closed 24 Dec-2 Jan Civ Wed 130 **CARDS:**

*See advert on opposite page*

### ★★★66% Grosvenor Park

114-116 North Rd East PL4 6AH
☎ 01752 229312 01752 252777
***Dir:*** *nearest hotel to Plymouth Station, approx 150yds from the main entrance in the heart of the city*
This friendly, small hotel is conveniently situated for both the city centre and the railway station. Public areas comprise a comfortable lounge, separate bar and dining room where a range of popular dishes is on offer.
**ROOMS:** 16 rms (11 en suite) (1 fmly) No smoking in 3 bedrooms s £22-£33; d £44-£44 (incl. bkfst) * **FACILITIES:** STV **PARKING:** 6 **NOTES:** No dogs (ex guide dogs) No smoking in restaurant **CARDS:**

### ★★★66% Posthouse Plymouth

Posthouse

Cliff Rd, The Hoe PL1 3DL
☎ 0870 400 9064 01752 660974
***Dir:*** *turn off A38 at Plymouth follow signs for City Centre, then follow signs for Hoe, the Hotel is situated on Cliff Road West Hoe*
This purpose-built hotel commands superb views over Plymouth Sound. The bedrooms are comfortable and well-equipped, and some superior rooms are available. There is lounge service throughout the day, and dinner is served in the Mayflower Restaurant.
**ROOMS:** 113 en suite No smoking in 65 bedrooms s £79-£109; d £79-£109 * LB **FACILITIES:** Spa STV Childrens play area ch fac Xmas **CONF:** Thtr 90 Class 30 Board 40 Del from £99 * **SERVICES:** Lift **PARKING:** 149 **NOTES:** No smoking in restaurant Civ Wed **CARDS:**

### ★★★65% Novotel Plymouth

NOVOTEL

Marsh Mills PL6 8NH
☎ 01752 221422 01752 223922
e-mail: h0508@accor-hotels.com

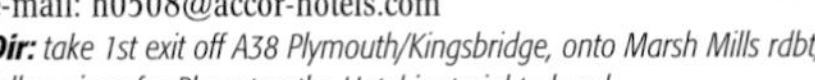

***Dir:*** *take 1st exit off A38 Plymouth/Kingsbridge, onto Marsh Mills rdbt, follow signs for Plympton the Hotel is straight ahead*
Located on the outskirts of the city, this modern hotel offers good value accommodation that caters for all types of guest. All rooms are spacious and adapted for family use. Public areas are open-plan and meals are available throughout the day in either the Garden Brasserie, the bar, or from room service. There is a heated outdoor swimming pool.
**ROOMS:** 100 en suite (18 fmly) No smoking in 50 bedrooms s fr £59; d fr £64 * LB **FACILITIES:** STV Outdoor swimming (H) ch fac Xmas **CONF:** Thtr 300 Class 120 Board 100 Del from £89 * **SERVICES:** Lift **PARKING:** 140 **CARDS:**

### ★★★64% *Boringdon Hall*

Colebrook, Plympton PL7 4DP
☎ 01752 344455 01752 346578
***Dir:*** *A38 at Marsh Mills rdbt follow signs for Plympton along dual carriageway to small island turn left over bridge and follow brown tourist signs*
Set in ten acres of grounds, this historic, listed property is only six miles from the city centre and retains much original character. Most of the comfortable bedrooms, some with four-poster beds,

*continued*

are set round a central courtyard. Meals using local produce are served in the Gallery Restaurant overlooking the Great Hall.
**ROOMS:** 41 en suite (5 fmly) No smoking in 16 bedrooms
**FACILITIES:** STV Indoor swimming (H) Tennis (hard) Sauna Gym pitch & putt 9 hole **CONF:** Thtr 120 Class 40 Board 50 **PARKING:** 200
**NOTES:** No smoking in restaurant **CARDS:**

## ★★★64% Grand

Elliot St, The Hoe PL1 2PT
☎ 01752 661195 🖷 01752 600653
e-mail: info@plymouthgrand.com
***Dir:*** *A38 to city centre, turn left at "Barbican" sign, follow road until 4th set traffic lights, turn left at Walrus pub into Atheneum St., straight ahead at crossroads into Elliot St, hotel is at top on right*

Originally built in 1879, this gracious hotel reflects the grandeur of Victorian architecture. Spectacular views over The Hoe and Plymouth Sound are an attractive feature. Some of the bedrooms have balconies; not surprisingly, front-facing bedrooms are always

*continued on p470*

PLYMOUTH, continued

in high demand. Public areas include a restaurant, bar and small lounge.
**ROOMS:** 77 en suite (6 fmly) No smoking in 45 bedrooms s £85-£135; d £95-£145 (incl. bkfst) * **LB** **FACILITIES:** STV archery, clays, sailing, riding for groups entertainment Xmas **CONF:** Thtr 70 Class 35 Board 30 Del from £65 * **SERVICES:** Lift **PARKING:** 60 **NOTES:** No smoking in restaurant **CARDS:**

### ★★★60% *Strathmore*
Elliot St, The Hoe PL1 2PR
☎ 01752 662101 🖹 01752 223690
***Dir:*** *off A38 at Marsh Mills and head for city centre, when you come to Exeter St, follow signs to the 'Hoe', hotel is at end opposite the 'Grand Hotel'*
The city centre and The Hoe are in easy walking distance of this hotel. Bedrooms come in a variety of shapes and sizes, but all are equipped to a similar standard. The smartly decorated restaurant offers a sensible menu, often featuring locally caught fish.
**ROOMS:** 54 en suite (6 fmly) **FACILITIES:** STV **CONF:** Thtr 60 Class 40 Board 20 **SERVICES:** Lift **CARDS:**

### ★★69% Invicta
11-12 Osborne Place, Lockyer St, The Hoe PL1 2PU
☎ 01752 664997 🖹 01752 664994
e-mail: info@invictahotel.co.uk
***Dir:*** *approaching Plymouth from A38, follow signs for City Centre, then look for the Hoe park, the hotel is situated opposite the park entrance*
An elegant Victorian building, opposite the famous bowling green, and just a short stroll from the city centre and Barbican. The atmosphere is relaxed and friendly and every effort is made to ensure an enjoyable and relaxing stay. Bedrooms are well-equipped and attractively decorated, ideally suited for both business and leisure guests. An extensive menu is offered in the dining room.
**ROOMS:** 23 en suite (6 fmly) No smoking in 14 bedrooms s £44-£52; d £54-£62 (incl. bkfst) * **LB** **CONF:** Thtr 35 Class 40 Board 60 Del from £57 * **PARKING:** 10 **NOTES:** No dogs (ex guide dogs) No smoking in restaurant Closed 24 Dec-3 Jan
**CARDS:**

P

### ★★68% Langdon Court
Down Thomas PL9 0DY
☎ 01752 862358 🖹 01752 863428
e-mail: enquiries@langdoncourt.co.uk
***Dir:*** *follow HMS Cambridge signs from Elburton and brown tourist signs on A379*

Surrounded by seven acres of lush countryside, private woodland and gardens, Langdon Court is the perfect choice for a peaceful break. Once owned by Henry VIII, there is history at every turn. The convivial bar is very popular and a good range of bar meals is

*continued*

offered. For more formal dining, both fixed-price and carte menus are available in the elegant restaurant. The well-equipped bedrooms are individual in style and some have lovely views.
**ROOMS:** 18 en suite (4 fmly) s £40-£57; d £68-£78 (incl. bkfst) * **LB** **FACILITIES:** Xmas **CONF:** Thtr 60 Board 20 Del £80 * **PARKING:** 100 **NOTES:** No smoking in restaurant Civ Wed 75
**CARDS:**

### ★★66% Camelot
5 Elliot St, The Hoe PL1 2PP
☎ 01752 221255 & 669667 🖹 01752 603660
e-mail: camelotuk@supanet.com
***Dir:*** *from the A38 follow signs fot the city centre, The Hoe, Citadel Rd and then onto Elliot St*
Located within easy walking distance of the city centre and the Barbican, the Camelot Hotel offers a genuinely friendly atmosphere. Bedrooms are comfortable and equipped with modern facilities. There is a well-stocked bar and separate lounge for guests, with the restaurant offering both fixed-price and carte menus.
**ROOMS:** 17 en suite (4 fmly) s £39; d £50 (incl. bkfst) * **LB** **CONF:** Thtr 60 Class 40 Board 20 **NOTES:** No dogs (ex guide dogs) No smoking in restaurant **CARDS:**

### ★★64% *Grosvenor*
7-9 Elliot St, The Hoe PL1 2PP
☎ 01752 260411 🖹 01752 668878
***Dir:*** *when approaching city centre turn left marked "Barbican", follow this road until the Walrus Pub, turn left, go over crossroads, hotel is on the left*
Converted from two adjoining Victorian buildings, the Grosvenor offers easy access to the city centre, the Hoe and the Barbican. Guests have a choice of dining options, with the Lemon Tree bistro offering carefully prepared meals from excellent local produce.
**ROOMS:** 28 en suite (2 fmly) **FACILITIES:** STV **PARKING:** 3 **NOTES:** Closed 24 Dec-1 Jan **CARDS:**

### ★73% Victoria Court
62/64 North Rd East PL4 6AL
☎ 01752 668133 🖹 01752 668133
e-mail: victoria.court@btinternet.com
***Dir:*** *from A38 follow signs for city centre, past railway station follow North Road East for approx 200yds hotel on left*
Situated within walking distance of the city centre and railway station, this family run hotel offers impeccably presented accommodation. The public areas retain the Victorian character of the building, and include a comfortable lounge, bar and dining area. The attractively decorated bedrooms are well-maintained with modern facilities.
**ROOMS:** 13 en suite (4 fmly) s £39-£42; d £49-£55 (incl. bkfst) * **LB** **PARKING:** 6 **NOTES:** No dogs No smoking in restaurant Closed 22 Dec-1 Jan **CARDS:**

### ★68% Imperial
Lockyer St, The Hoe PL1 2QD
☎ 01752 227311 🖹 01752 674986
***Dir:*** *centrally located between Hoe Promenade & City Centre*
Close to the city centre, this Grade II listed hotel is suitable for both commercial and leisure travellers. The family proprietors offer old-fashioned hospitality in a friendly and convivial atmosphere. Guests can relax in either the cosy bar or TV lounge, both before and after sampling a menu which offers a varied selection of dishes.
**ROOMS:** 22 rms (18 en suite) (4 fmly) **CONF:** Thtr 25 Class 25 Board 16 **PARKING:** 14 **NOTES:** No dogs (ex guide dogs) Closed 25-31 Dec
**CARDS:**

★65% **Drake**
1 & 2 Windsor Villas, Lockyer St, The Hoe
PL1 2QD
☎ 01752 229730 🖹 01752 255092
e-mail: drakehotel@themutual.net
***Dir:*** *follow City Centre signs, left at Theatre Royal, last left, first right*
Two adjoining Victorian houses have been linked to form this comfortable, family run hotel. Bedrooms are well-equipped, and public areas offer a lounge, bar and spacious dining room. The convenient location, just a short walk from the city centre and the Hoe, make this a popular choice for both business and leisure guests.
**ROOMS:** 35 rms (30 en suite) (3 fmly) s £34-£42; d £48-£54 (incl. bkfst) * **LB** **PARKING:** 25 **NOTES:** No dogs (ex guide dogs) No smoking in restaurant Closed 24 Dec-3 Jan
**CARDS:**

⌂ **Hotel Ibis**
Marsh Mills, Longbridge Rd, Forder Valley PL6 8LD
☎ 01752 601087 🖹 01752 223213
e-mail: H2093@accor-hotels.com
***Dir:*** *A38 towards Plymouth, 1st exit over the fly over toward Estover, Leigham and Parkway industrial estate. At rdbt, hotel on 4th exit*
Modern, budget hotel offering comfortable accommodation in bright and practical bedrooms. Breakfast is self-service and dinner is available in the restaurant. For further details, consult the Hotel Groups page.
**ROOMS:** 51 en suite s £39.95; d £39.95 * **CONF:** Thtr 20 Class 20 Board 20

○ **Express by Holiday Inn Plymouth North**
☎ 0800 897121
A modern budget hotel offering comfortable accommodation in refreshing, spacious and comprehensively equipped bedrooms, en suite bathrooms with power showers and continental buffet breakfast included in the room rate. Suitable for business travellers or families. For further details and the Express by Holiday Inn phone number, consult the Hotel Groups page.
**ROOMS:** 37 en suite **NOTES:** Opening 2002

## POCKLINGTON, East Riding of Yorkshire — Map 08 SE84

★★65% **Yorkway Motel**
Hull-York Rd YO42 2NX
☎ 01759 303071 🖹 01759 305215
e-mail: info@yorkway-motel.co.uk
***Dir:*** *between Beverley & York on the A1079 with the junc of B1247*
This family owned and run motel and diner is close to the village of Pocklington and offers value-for-money accommodation. Bedrooms are thoughtfully equipped and public rooms include a bar and cosy dining room, where a good range of food is served all day. The single room price includes breakfast.
**ROOMS:** 15 annexe en suite (6 fmly) d £36-£40 * **LB** **CONF:** Thtr 30 Class 12 Board 16 **PARKING:** 40 **NOTES:** No dogs (ex guide dogs)
**CARDS:**

## PODIMORE, Somerset — Map 03 ST52

⌂ ***Travelodge***
BA22 8JG
☎ 01935 840074 🖹 01935 840074
***Dir:*** *on A303, near junct with A37*
Travelodge offers good quality, good value, modern accommodation. Ideal for families, the spacious, en suite bedrooms include remote-control TV, tea and coffee-making

*continued*

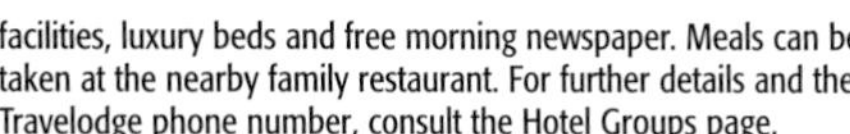

facilities, luxury beds and free morning newspaper. Meals can be taken at the nearby family restaurant. For further details and the Travelodge phone number, consult the Hotel Groups page.

**ROOMS:** 31 en suite

## POLPERRO, Cornwall & Isles of Scilly — Map 02 SX25

★★★75% **Talland Bay**
PL13 2JB
☎ 01503 272667 🖹 01503 272940
e-mail: tallandbay@aol.com
***Dir:*** *signposted from crossroads on A387 Looe/Polperro road*
Dating back to the 16th century, this Cornish stone manor house stands in two acres of sub-tropical gardens. The views across to the restless ocean are spectacular. Bedrooms are charmingly furnished and decorated and each has its own character. The restaurant menu incorporates the finest regional produce and seafood features strongly.
**ROOMS:** 16 en suite 6 annexe en suite (2 fmly) s £67-£99; d £134-£198 (incl. bkfst & dinner) * **LB** **FACILITIES:** Spa Outdoor swimming (H) Sauna Croquet lawn Putting green Games room Xmas **CONF:** Thtr 30 Board 30 Del from £80 * **PARKING:** 20 **NOTES:** No smoking in restaurant Closed 2 Jan-late Feb **CARDS:**

## PONTEFRACT, West Yorkshire — Map 08 SE42

★★★65% **Rogerthorpe Manor Hotel**
Thorpe Ln, Badsworth WF9 1AB
☎ 01977 643839 🖹 01977 641571
e-mail: ops@rogerthorpemanor.co.uk
***Dir:*** *From motorway take A639 from Pontefract to Badsworth. Follow the B6474 through Thorpe Audlin, the hotel is on the L handside at the end of Thorpe Audlin village*

This Jacobean manor is situated in extensive grounds and gardens, surrounded by delightful countryside yet close to the motorway network. It specialises in all kinds of banquets, conferences and functions. Many of the bedrooms are furnished in antique style. Formal meals can be enjoyed in the oak-panelled restaurant or, more informally, in the popular Jacobean Bar.
**ROOMS:** 23 en suite (3 fmly) No smoking in 8 bedrooms s fr £80; d fr £95 (incl. bkfst) * **LB** **FACILITIES:** STV Croquet lawn Xmas **CONF:** Thtr 200 Class 150 Board 50 Del from £105 * **PARKING:** 90 **NOTES:** No dogs (ex guide dogs) No smoking in restaurant Civ Wed 300
**CARDS:**

> Popped the question? Hotels with Civ Wed in their entry are licensed for civil wedding ceremonies. Maximum numbers for the ceremony only are shown, e.g. Civ Wed 120

POOLE, Dorset Map 04 SZ09

### ★★★★73% Haven

Banks Rd, Sandbanks BH13 7QL
☎ 01202 707333 01202 708796
e-mail: reservations@havenhotel.co.uk
***Dir:*** *take the B3965 towards Poole Bay and turn left onto the Peninsula. Hotel 1.5m on left next to the Swanage Toll Ferry point*

Overlooking Poole Bay and the Sandbanks ferry, this attractive hotel has enviable views. There are ample lounge areas, a waterside restaurant and a brasserie. Bedrooms vary in style and size, some have sea views and balconies. The restaurant and La Roche fish restaurant serve carefully prepared dishes, and lighter meals are available in the conservatory.
**ROOMS:** 94 en suite (4 fmly) s £82-£165; d £164-£295 (incl. bkfst) * **LB** **FACILITIES:** **Spa** STV Indoor swimming (H) Outdoor swimming (H) Tennis (hard) Sauna Solarium Gym Jacuzzi Steam room, Hair salon, Health & beauty suite Xmas **CONF:** Thtr 160 Class 70 Board 50 Del from £145 * **SERVICES:** Lift **PARKING:** 160 **NOTES:** No dogs (ex guide dogs) No smoking in restaurant Civ Wed 80
**CARDS:**

### ★★★80% Mansion House

Best Western
Thames St BH15 1JN
☎ 01202 685666 01202 665709
e-mail: enquiries@themansionhouse.co.uk
***Dir:*** *A31 to Poole, follow signs to channel ferry, turn left at Poole bridge onto Poole Quay, take first left (Thames St), hotel is opposite St James church*

Tucked away off the Old Quay, this sophisticated hotel provides individually designed bedrooms and pleasant public areas which include a flagstoned entrance and a quiet drawing room. Guest care and comfort is of particular importance at this efficiently run hotel. The comfortable restaurant and the bistro serve a selection of award winning cuisine.
**ROOMS:** 32 en suite (2 fmly) No smoking in 4 bedrooms s £65-£90; d £100-£130 (incl. bkfst) * **LB** **FACILITIES:** STV facilities available locally Watersports Xmas **CONF:** Thtr 40 Class 18 Board 20 Del from £110 * **PARKING:** 46 **NOTES:** No dogs No smoking in restaurant Civ Wed 35
**CARDS:**

### ★★★80% Salterns

Best Western
38 Salterns Way, Lilliput BH14 8JR
☎ 01202 707321 01202 707488
e-mail: reception@salterns.co.uk
***Dir:*** *in Poole follow B3369 Sandbanks road. In 1m at Lilliput shops turn into Salterns Way by Barclays Bank*
Situated beside its own marina and enjoying splendid views across to Brownsea Island, this hotel has an enviable reputation. The bedrooms are mostly spacious and comfortably furnished including many welcome extras. In the restaurant an interesting menu makes good use of local game and fish. A bistro is also available where lighter meals may be enjoyed.
**ROOMS:** 20 en suite (4 fmly) No smoking in 3 bedrooms s £86-£96; d £126-£146 * **LB** **FACILITIES:** STV Fishing Leis facs available at sister hotel ch fac Xmas **CONF:** Thtr 100 Class 50 Board 50 Del from £120 * **PARKING:** 300 **NOTES:** Civ Wed 120
**CARDS:**

*See advert on opposite page*

### ★★★74% Sandbanks

15 Banks Rd, Sandbanks BH13 7PS
☎ 01202 707377 01202 708885
e-mail: reservations@sandbankshotel.co.uk
***Dir:*** *follow A338 from Bournemouth onto Wessex Way to Liverpool Victoria rdbt. Keep left & take 2nd exit - B3965 to Sandbanks Peninsula Hotel on left*

Popular with both leisure and business guests, this large hotel has direct access to a blue flag beach and stunning views across Poole Harbour. In addition to the main restaurant, Sands Brasserie serves an imaginative selection of dishes. Many of the well-equipped bedrooms have balconies and there is an extensive range of leisure facilities ideal for entertaining families.
**ROOMS:** 116 en suite (31 fmly) No smoking in 40 bedrooms s £60-£92; d £120-£184 (incl. bkfst & dinner) * **LB** **FACILITIES:** **Spa** STV Indoor swimming (H) Sauna Solarium Gym Putting green Jacuzzi Sailing,Mntn bikes,kids play area. entertainment ch fac Xmas **CONF:** Thtr 150 Class 40 Board 25 Del from £90 * **SERVICES:** Lift **PARKING:** 150 **NOTES:** No dogs (ex guide dogs) No smoking in restaurant
**CARDS:**

**★★★63% *Arndale Court***
‚2/66 Wimborne Rd BH15 2BY
☎ 01202 683746 🖹 01202 668838
***ir:** on th A349 close to Town Centre, opposite Poole Stadium entrance*

'his small, privately owned hotel is conveniently located for access o the town centre and to the ferry terminal. For car users, the arge car park to the rear of the hotel is a bonus. Bedrooms are raditionally furnished and decorated and offer a good range of acilities. Public rooms include a cosy bar and restaurant.
**ROOMS:** 39 en suite (7 fmly) **FACILITIES:** STV **CONF:** Thtr 50 Class 35 3oard 35 **PARKING:** 32 **NOTES:** No smoking in restaurant
**CARDS:**

**★★63% Norfolk Lodge**
1 Flaghead Rd, Canford Cliffs BH13 7JL
☎ 01202 708614 🖹 01202 708661
e-mail: allnmartin@aol.com
***Dir:** between Poole & Bournemouth hotel on corner of Haven & Flaghead Rd*
The Norfolk Lodge is a delightful family run property in a quiet residential area, only minutes from the beach. Bedrooms are well-equipped. Public areas offer a choice of dining options and sitting areas, most of which overlook the attractive gardens.
**ROOMS:** 19 rms (17 en suite) (4 fmly) s £48-£50; d £62-£65 (incl. bkfst) * **LB** **FACILITIES:** ch fac **PARKING:** 16 **NOTES:** No smoking in restaurant **CARDS:**

**⇧ Express by Holiday Inn**
Walking Field Ln BH15 1TJ
☎ 01202 649222 🖹 01202 649666
e-mail: poole@premierhotels.co.uk

***Dir:** Take A350 to town centre, pass bus station, turn right at next rdbt & take slip road to the left. Hotel is next to the Dolphin Swimming Pool*
A modern budget hotel offering comfortable accommodation in refreshing, spacious and comprehensively equipped bedrooms, en suite bathrooms with power showers and continental buffet

*continued on p474*

POOLE, continued

breakfast included in the room rate. Suitable for business travellers or families. For further details and the Express by Holiday Inn phone number, consult the Hotel Groups page.

*Express by Holiday Inn, Poole*

**ROOMS:** 85 en suite **CONF:** Thtr 35 Class 20 Board 20

### ○ Harbour Heights

73 Haven Rd, Sandbanks BH13 7LW
☎ 01202 707272 🖷 01202 708594
At the time of going to press, the star classification for this hotel was not confirmed. Please refer to the AA internet site www.theAA.com for current information.

---

PORLOCK, Somerset Map 03 SS84

### ★★★67% Anchor Hotel & Ship Inn

Porlock Harbour TA24 8PB
☎ 01643 862753 🖷 01643 862843
e-mail: anchorhotel@clara.net
***Dir:*** *from A39 take the B3225 Porlock Weir road. Hotel is located after 1.5m in a cul-de-sac*

This long established hotel overlooks the harbour and the Bristol Channel to Wales in the distance. Bedrooms in the original, 16th-century Ship Inn are full of traditional character, while those in the main hotel are more spacious. The Harbour Restaurant offers set price and carte menus; bar meals are also available.
**ROOMS:** 14 en suite 6 annexe en suite (2 fmly) d £130-£162 (incl. bkfst & dinner) * **LB** **FACILITIES:** Xmas **CONF:** Thtr 20 Board 12 **PARKING:** 20 **NOTES:** RS Jan & Feb **CARDS:**

*See advert on opposite page*

P

## Premier Collection

### ★★ The Oaks

TA24 8ES
☎ 01643 862265 🖷 01643 863131
e-mail: oakshotel@aol.com
This relaxing Edwardian country house enjoys views across the town to Porlock Weir and Exmoor in the distance. Bedrooms vary in size, with many thoughtful extras, and most benefit from the fabulous views. Public rooms are attractively furnished with period pieces. In winter coal fires create a delightful atmosphere, while during the summer, the garden is the perfect place to enjoy a drink before enjoying a delicious meal prepared from the best of local produce.

**ROOMS:** 9 en suite No smoking in all bedrooms s £80; d £140 (incl. bkfst & dinner) * **LB** **FACILITIES:** Xmas **PARKING:** 12 **NOTES:** No children 8yrs No smoking in restaurant Closed Nov-Mar (excl. Xmas) **CARDS:**

---

PORT GAVERNE, Cornwall & Isles of Scilly Map 02 SX08

### ★★70% Port Gaverne

PL29 3SQ
☎ 01208 880244 🖷 01208 880151
e-mail: pghotel@telinco.co.uk
***Dir:*** *signposted from B3314*

Retaining its flagged floors, beamed ceilings and steep stairways, this charming, traditional inn has something of a following. Half a mile from the old fishing village of Port Isaac and set back from a spectacular small cove, the Port Gaverne has a relaxed atmosphere. Local produce often features on the hotel menus, which include bar meals.
**ROOMS:** 16 en suite (4 fmly) s £45-£55; d £70-£90 (incl. bkfst) * **LB** **PARKING:** 30 **NOTES:** No smoking in restaurant Closed 5 Jan-11 Feb **CARDS:**

---

PORT ISAAC, Cornwall & Isles of Scilly Map 02 SW98

### ★★68% Castle Rock

4 New Rd PL29 3SB
☎ 01208 880300 🖷 01208 880219
e-mail: info@castlerockhotel.co.uk
***Dir:*** *from A30 turn off after Launceston onto A395. Turn left at junction with A39 then take first right signposted Port Isaac, follow signs to village*

With spectacular views of the rugged Cornish coastline, this friendly hotel is an ideal base for holidaymakers. It has comfortable and spacious accommodation, with all the public areas benefiting from the wonderful sea views. In addition to the carte and fixed price menus, an extensive range of dishes is served in the bar or on the terrace.
**ROOMS:** 15 en suite 3 annexe en suite (2 fmly) s £29-£35; d £58-£76 (incl. bkfst) * **LB** **PARKING:** 18 **CARDS:**

*See advert on opposite page*

Fancy a Singapore Sling? Bar staff in five star hotels should be skilled cocktail mixers.

## PORTSCATHO, Cornwall & Isles of Scilly — Map 02 SW83

### Premier Collection

★★★ Rosevine
TR2 5EW
☎ 01872 580206 01872 580230
e-mail: info@makepeacehotels.co.uk
**Dir:** *from St Austell take A390 for Truro and turn left onto B3287 to Tregony. Leave Tregony by A3078 through Ruan High Lanes. Hotel third turning left*

Situated on the coast of the spectacular Roseland Peninsula, this family-run Georgian country house offers high standards of comfort combined with polished service and a keen hospitality. Bedrooms are spacious, relaxing and enhanced with many extras, such as flowers, fruit and magazines; most of those in the main building have lovely views across the gardens to the sea. Day rooms include a choice of lounges and a spacious dining room, which offers accomplished cuisine and occasional live piano. A heated indoor pool is also available with an adjacent paddling pool for the younger members of the family.

**ROOMS:** 11 en suite 6 annexe en suite (7 fmly) s £108-£126; d £144-£168 (incl. bkfst) * LB **FACILITIES:** Indoor swimming (H) Table tennis Childrens playroom entertainment ch fac Xmas **PARKING:** 20 **NOTES:** No smoking in restaurant Closed Nov-11 Feb (ex Xmas) **CARDS:** 

## PORTSMOUTH, Hampshire — Map 04 SZ69

★★★★65% **Portsmouth Marriott Hotel**
North Harbour PO6 4SH
☎ 023 9238 3151 023 9238 8701
**Dir:** *from M27 junct 12 - keep left, hotel on left*

Marriott HOTELS · RESORTS · SUITES

Marriott

Overlooking Port Solent and Porchester Castle, this modern hotel is close to the city centre and continental ferryport. Conveniently laid out and spacious bedrooms offer a comprehensive range of

continued on p476

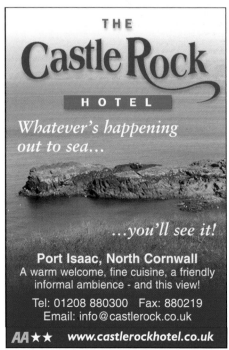

P

PORTSMOUTH, continued

in-room facilities. The hotel has some interesting features such as the lounge and restaurant area with its lofty four-storey high ceiling.
**ROOMS:** 170 en suite (76 fmly) No smoking in 122 bedrooms s £59-£130; d £70-£140 (incl. bkfst) * **LB FACILITIES:** Spa STV Indoor swimming (H) Sauna Solarium Gym Jacuzzi Sunbed & exercise studio entertainment Xmas **CONF:** Thtr 350 Class 180 Board 36 Del from £135 * **SERVICES:** Lift air con **PARKING:** 300 **NOTES:** Civ Wed 100 **CARDS:**

### ★★★69% Queen's Hotel

Clarence Pde, Southsea PO5 3LJ
☎ 023 9282 2466 023 9282 1901
e-mail: reservations@queenshotel-southsea.co.uk
***Dir:*** *from M27 take junct 12 onto M275 and follow signs for Southsea seafront. Hotel is located opp. Hovercraft terminal*

Best Western

QUEENS
HOTEL

This elegant Edwardian hotel has dominated the Southsea seafront for over 100 years and enjoys magnificent views over the Solent. Bedrooms vary, there is a choice of room categories from family rooms to single rooms; all rooms are traditionally furnished and decorated. Public areas include a restaurant, garden and pool, two comfortable bars and a nightclub.
**ROOMS:** 73 en suite (4 fmly) No smoking in 43 bedrooms s £65-£85; d £85-£125 (incl. bkfst) * **LB FACILITIES:** STV Outdoor swimming (H) Private garden Xmas **CONF:** Thtr 150 Class 120 Board 35 Del from £89.50 * **SERVICES:** Lift **PARKING:** 70 **NOTES:** No dogs (ex guide dogs) **CARDS:**

### ★★★68% *Westfield Hall*

65 Festing Rd, Southsea PO4 0NQ
☎ 023 9282 6971 023 9287 0200
e-mail: jdanie@westfield-hall-hotel.co.uk
***Dir:*** *follow signs Seafront, bear left at South Parade Pier then 3rd turning left*
Westfield Hall is situated in a quiet side road close to the seafront and town centre. The accommodation is split between two identical houses; all rooms are smartly appointed and well-equipped. Public rooms are attractively decorated and include three lounges, a bar and a restaurant.
**ROOMS:** 16 en suite 11 annexe en suite (5 fmly) No smoking in 14 bedrooms **FACILITIES:** STV **PARKING:** 18 **NOTES:** No dogs No smoking in restaurant **CARDS:**

### ★★★65% Innlodge Hotel

Burrfields Rd PO3 5HH
☎ 023 9265 0510 023 9269 3458
e-mail: Innlodge@bestwestern.co.uk
***Dir:*** *from A3(M) & M27 follow A27, take Southsea exit and follow A2030. At 3rd set of traffic lights. Turn right into Burrfields Rd-hotel on left*

Best Western

Located on the eastern fringe of the city, this purpose-built hotel is conveniently located for all major routes. The modern bedrooms

continued

are spacious, well-appointed and equipped with a useful range of extras. Guests have two eating options: Beiderbecks restaurant and the Farmhouse Inn. The hotel also boasts a large covered children's play area.
**ROOMS:** 74 en suite (10 fmly) No smoking in 40 bedrooms s £57-£67; d £57-£67 * **LB FACILITIES:** Spa STV Indoor fun factory & outdoor kids play area,pool tables entertainment ch fac Xmas **CONF:** Thtr 150 Class 72 Board 40 **PARKING:** 200 **NOTES:** No dogs (ex guide dogs) **CARDS:**

### ★★★62% *Posthouse Portsmouth*

Pembroke Rd PO1 2TA
☎ 0870 400 9065 023 9275 6715
***Dir:*** *from M275, follow signs for Southsea and I.O.W Hovercraft for 1 mile, at Southsea Common the Hotel can be found on the right*

Posthouse

Conveniently located for the seafront, local shops and city centre, the hotel is a popular venue for functions at weekends. Bedrooms are gradually being refurbished, and are well equipped. The smart bar and lounge serves meals and snacks, the new Junction restaurant offers interesting menus. The hotel has good leisure facilities, a range of meeting rooms and a business centre.
**ROOMS:** 167 en suite (12 fmly) No smoking in 82 bedrooms **FACILITIES:** Indoor swimming (H) Sauna Solarium Gym Jacuzzi Turkish steam room, Beauty Room, Pool room, Play room **CONF:** Thtr 220 Class 120 Board 80 **SERVICES:** Lift **PARKING:** 80 **NOTES:** No smoking in restaurant **CARDS:**

### ★★★59% Royal Beach

South Pde, Southsea PO4 0RN
☎ 023 9273 1281 023 9281 7572
e-mail: info@royalbeach-hotel-portsmouth.com
***Dir:*** *follow M27 to M275, then follow signs to seafront, hotel is situated on seafront*

Peel Hotels

This hotel enjoys a seafront location with views over the South Parade Pier. The impressive building offers comfortable accommodation with good facilities. Public areas consist of a hotel bar, various conference rooms and a large dining room, serving a good choice of meals.
**ROOMS:** 115 en suite (9 fmly) No smoking in 30 bedrooms s £40-£75; d £50-£85 (incl. bkfst) * **LB FACILITIES:** STV Xmas **CONF:** Thtr 250 Class 160 Board 30 Del from £68 * **SERVICES:** Lift **PARKING:** 62 **NOTES:** No smoking in restaurant **CARDS:**

### ★★72% The Beaufort

71 Festing Rd, Southsea PO4 0NQ
☎ 023 9282 3707 023 9287 0270
e-mail: res/enq@beauforthotel.co.uk
***Dir:*** *follow signs for seafront at South Parade Pier take left fork, Festing Rd is fourth turning on left*

The Independents

Situated close to the sea, which is visible from some rooms, this hotel offers well-presented public areas and accommodation. Bedrooms have good quality fabrics and facilities. Home cooked,

continued

freshly prepared food is served in the dining room on the lower ground floor, where there is also a bar.
**ROOMS:** 19 en suite (1 fmly) No smoking in 10 bedrooms s £48-£54; d £58-£80 (incl. bkfst) * **LB** **FACILITIES:** STV Xmas **CONF:** Class 20 **PARKING:** 10 **NOTES:** No dogs No smoking in restaurant
**CARDS:**

### ★★70% Seacrest

11/12 South Pde, Southsea PO5 2JB
☎ 023 9273 3192 📠 023 9283 2523
e-mail: seacrest@mccail.com
***Dir:*** *from M27 follow signs for seafront, Pyramids, Sea Life Centre, Hotel opposite Rock Gardens and the Pyramids*

MINOTEL Great Britain

In a premier seafront location, this smart hotel provides the ideal base for exploring the town. Bedrooms, many benefiting from sea views, are decorated to a high standard with good facilities. Guests can relax in either the south-facing lounge, furnished with large leather sofas, or the adjacent cosy bar, before enjoying a meal in the downstairs dining room.
**ROOMS:** 28 en suite (3 fmly) No smoking in 10 bedrooms s £45-£50; d £60-£85 (incl. bkfst) * **LB** **FACILITIES:** STV Xmas **SERVICES:** Lift **PARKING:** 12 **NOTES:** No smoking in restaurant
**CARDS:**

### ★★59% Sandringham

7 Osborne Rd, Clarence Pde, Southsea PO5 3LR
☎ 023 9282 6969 & 9282 2914 📠 023 9282 2330
e-mail: reception@sandringham-hotel.co.uk
***Dir:*** *turn off M275 at Portsmouth junct, follow signs to historic ships, then to Southsea, along seafront, hotel on left, opposite council car park*
This traditional resort hotel is situated close to the seafront, Southsea Common and town centre. Bedrooms are pleasantly decorated and equipped with many useful extras. Public rooms offer a wide choice of areas in which to relax and feature two bars, a choice of lounges, a restaurant and banqueting facilities.
**ROOMS:** 44 en suite (7 fmly) s £35-£45; d £45-£56 (incl. bkfst) * **LB** **FACILITIES:** Xmas **CONF:** Thtr 180 Class 80 Board 50 Del from £75 * **SERVICES:** Lift **NOTES:** No dogs (ex guide dogs) No smoking in restaurant Civ Wed 100 **CARDS:**

### ⇧ *Travelodge*

Kingston Crescent, North End PO62 8AB
☎ 012 9263 9118

Travelodge

Travelodge offers good quality, good value, modern accommodation. Ideal for families, the spacious, en suite bedrooms include remote-control TV, tea and coffee-making

*continued*

facilities, luxury beds and free morning newspaper. Meals can be taken at the nearby family restaurant. For further details and the Travelodge phone number, consult the Hotel Groups page.

### ⇧ Hotel Ibis

Winston Churchill Av PO1 2LX
☎ 023 9264 0000 📠 023 9264 1000
e-mail: h1461@accor-hotels.com

ibis Accor hotels

***Dir:*** *M27 junct 2 onto M275 and follow signs first for city centre, then Sealife Centre, then Guildhall. Turn right at rdbt into Winston Churchill Ave*
Modern, budget hotel offering comfortable accommodation in bright and practical bedrooms. Breakfast is self-service and dinner is available in the restaurant. For further details, consult the Hotel Groups page.
**ROOMS:** 144 en suite s £39.95-£44.95; d £39.95-£44.95 * **CONF:** Thtr 40 Class 30 Board 30

### ○ Innkeeper's Lodge Portsmouth

Copnor Rd, Hilsea PO3 5HS
☎ 0870 243 0500

Innkeeper's Lodge

A new concept in the travel accommodation market. Smart rooms meet essential business requirements but also have home comforts. Dining options include all-day menus plus the added advantage of breakfast, which is included in the room price. Reservations can be made seven days a week through the room reservations number: 0870 243 0500. For further details, consult the Hotel Groups page.
**ROOMS:** 33 en suite

## PRESTBURY, Cheshire — Map 07 SJ97

### ★★★69% Bridge

The Village SK10 4DQ
☎ 01625 829326 📠 01625 827557
e-mail: reception@bridge-hotel.co.uk
***Dir:*** *off A538 through village, hotel next to church*
Dating in parts from the 17th century, this delightful hotel stands sideways to the village street, between the River Bollin and the ancient church. The cocktail bar provides the ideal place to relax before a satisfying meal in the restaurant. A wide range of

*continued on p478*

P

PRESTBURY, continued

bedrooms is available in the original building and a rear extension.

*Bridge, Prestbury*

**ROOMS:** 23 en suite (1 fmly) No smoking in 5 bedrooms s £85-£90; d £90-£100 * **LB** **FACILITIES:** STV entertainment **CONF:** Thtr 100 Class 56 Board 48 Del £107.50 * **PARKING:** 52 **NOTES:** No dogs (ex guide dogs) Civ Wed 110 **CARDS:**

## *Town House*

### ★★★★ White House Manor

New Rd SK10 4HP
☎ 01625 829376 🖹 01625 828627
e-mail: info@thewhitehouse.uk.com
***Dir:*** *on the A538 Macclesfield Road*

This elegant Georgian house, situated in attractive gardens on the edge of the village, offers charming individually styled bedrooms, many with four-poster beds. Meals can be ordered from the room service menu and breakfast is served in the conservatory. The White House restaurant, under the same ownership, is just a short walk away but guests may be driven there if needed.

**ROOMS:** 11 en suite No smoking in all bedrooms s £75-£95; d £100-£120 * **FACILITIES:** STV Jacuzzi Xmas **CONF:** Thtr 60 Class 40 Board 26 Del from £110 * **PARKING:** 11 **NOTES:** No dogs (ex guide dogs) No children 10yrs Closed 24 Dec - 26 Dec **CARDS:**

PRESTON, Lancashire Map 07 SD52
see also Barton

### ★★★★67% Preston Marriott Hotel

Garstang Rd, Broughton PR3 5JB
☎ 01772 864087 🖹 01772 861728
e-mail: reservations.preston@marriotthotels.co.uk
***Dir:*** *M6 junct 32 onto M55 junct 1, follow A6 towards Garstang, the Hotel is 0.05m on the right*

Set in tranquil grounds, yet close to the M6, this former farmhouse has been carefully extended to provide attractive, thoughtfully equipped accommodation. There is an elegant restaurant, an informal poolside café bar, an impressive leisure club, and a spacious conservatory lounge and bar. Guests in executive rooms have exclusive free use of a private lounge.

**ROOMS:** 150 en suite (40 fmly) No smoking in 94 bedrooms s £95; d £103 (incl. bkfst) * **LB** **FACILITIES:** **Spa** STV Indoor swimming (H) Sauna Solarium Gym Croquet lawn Steam room Beauty salon/hairdressing Xmas **CONF:** Thtr 200 Class 120 Board 70 **SERVICES:** Lift **PARKING:** 250 **NOTES:** No dogs (ex guide dogs) No smoking in restaurant Civ Wed 180 **CARDS:**

### ★★★70% Barton Grange

Garstang Rd PR3 5AA
☎ 01772 862551 🖹 01772 861267
e-mail: stay@bartongrangehotel.com
(For full entry see Barton)

### ★★★70% Pines

570 Preston Rd, Clayton-Le-Woods PR6 7ED
☎ 01772 338551 🖹 01772 629002
e-mail: info@thepineshotel.co.uk
***Dir:*** *on A6, 1m S of M6 junc 29*

Entrance

This privately owned hotel is set in four acres of mature grounds, yet is convenient for all the local motorway networks. Comfortable bedrooms are thoughtfully equipped. Public areas include Haworths Brasserie, offering an interesting selection of carefully prepared dishes, as well as fine dining by prior arrangement in the elegant Crystal room. Meeting and function suites are available and there are regular cabaret nights.

**ROOMS:** 37 en suite (12 fmly) No smoking in 11 bedrooms s £60-£95; d £70-£110 (incl. bkfst) * **LB** **FACILITIES:** STV Jacuzzi Xmas **CONF:** Thtr 150 Class 300 Board 60 Del from £96.50 * **PARKING:** 120 **NOTES:** No dogs (ex guide dogs) Civ Wed 150 **CARDS:**

★★66% **Mill Hotel**
oor Rd, Croston PR25 9HP
☎ 01772 600110 🖹 01772 601623
mail: millhotelcroston@ukonline.co.uk
*ir: M6 junct 28 exit for Leyland, right off slip road, right at lights following igan A49. After 2.5m turn right at mini- rdbt A581 Southport/Croston. The otel is 3.5m on right*
modern hotel with rustic charm, peacefully yet conveniently cated for visiting the nearby towns of Preston, Southport and ackpool. Spacious public areas include two bars and a pleasant staurant. Bright, well-equipped bedrooms are comfortably rnished and staff are friendly and attentive.
**OOMS:** 46 en suite (3 fmly) No smoking in 4 bedrooms s fr £50; fr £65 (incl. bkfst) * **FACILITIES:** Xmas **CONF:** Thtr 150 Class 50 oard 25 Del £70 * **PARKING:** 130 **NOTES:** Civ Wed 150
**ARDS:**

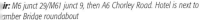

★★64% **Novotel Preston**
eedfield Place, Walton Summit PR5 8AA
☎ 01772 313331 🖹 01772 627868
mail: H0838@accor-hotels.com
*ir: M6 junct 29/M61 junct 9, then A6 Chorley Road. Hotel is next to amber Bridge roundabout*
popular modern hotel conveniently situated close to busy otorway junctions. Spacious bedrooms have good facilities and e well insulated against traffic noise. A children's indoor play rea, conference and meeting rooms make this ideal for leisure nd business purposes alike.
**OOMS:** 98 en suite (22 fmly) No smoking in 49 bedrooms s fr £55; fr £55 * **LB** **FACILITIES:** STV Outdoor swimming (H) **CONF:** Thtr 180 lass 80 Board 52 Del from £69 * **SERVICES:** Lift **PARKING:** 140
**ARDS:**

★★64% **Swallow Hotel**
reston New Rd, Samlesbury PR5 0UL
☎ 01772 877351 🖹 01772 877424
-mail: info@swallowhotelseurope.com
*ir: 1m from M6, on A59/A677 junct*

SWALLOW
HOTELS

qually well-suited to the business, conference or leisure guest, his hotel is easily accessible from the M6. The modern bedrooms re equipped to a high standard, and there is a good range of eisure facilities and spacious reception areas.
**OOMS:** 78 en suite No smoking in 24 bedrooms s £85-£105; d £115-120 (incl. bkfst) * **LB** **FACILITIES:** STV Indoor swimming (H) Sauna olarium Gym Jacuzzi Steam Rm, New Gym. Xmas **CONF:** Thtr 250 lass 100 Board 60 **SERVICES:** Lift **PARKING:** 190
**ARDS:**

★★★63% ***Tickled Trout***
Preston New Rd, Samlesbury PR5 0UJ
☎ 01772 877671 🖹 01772 877463
***Dir:** close to M6 junct 31*

MACDONALD
HOTELS

This amusingly named hotel is suitable for business and leisure guests, as well as families. Rooms are thoughtfully equipped and a large number of executive rooms are available. The open plan lounge bar offers refreshments and snacks throughout the day and conferences and meetings are well catered for.
**ROOMS:** 72 en suite (56 fmly) No smoking in 40 bedrooms
**FACILITIES:** STV Fishing Sauna Solarium Plunge pool **CONF:** Thtr 150 Class 60 Board 50 **PARKING:** 150 **NOTES:** No smoking in restaurant Civ Wed 120 **CARDS:**

★★★62% ***Posthouse Preston***
Ringway PR1 3AU
☎ 0870 400 9066 🖹 01772 201923
***Dir:** M6 junct 31 follow A59 signs for the Town Centre right at T junct, Forte Posthouse is on the left*
With a prime town-centre location, this modern hotel offers thoughtfully equipped accommodation, with several impressive, well appointed, superior rooms available. The Junction restaurant and adjacent bar, offering an all-day lounge menu, are located on the first floor. 24 hour room service is also available.
**ROOMS:** 119 en suite (11 fmly) No smoking in 73 bedrooms
**CONF:** Thtr 120 Class 50 Board 40 **SERVICES:** Lift **PARKING:** 30
**NOTES:** No smoking in restaurant **CARDS:**

★★66% **Claremont**
516 Blackpool Rd, Ashton-on-Ribble PR2 1HY
☎ 01772 729738 🖹 01772 726274
***Dir:** from M6 junct 31 take A59 towards Preston. At hilltop rdbt turn right onto A583. Hotel can be seen on the right just past pub and over bridge*
This friendly hotel is convenient for Preston town centre and the motorways. Bedrooms are bright, thoughtfully equipped, and include a four poster room. Public areas include a cosy lounge, as well as a comfortable bar, adjacent to the dining room. The self-contained function room is nicely presented and the rear garden is very attractive.
**ROOMS:** 14 en suite **CONF:** Thtr 85 Class 45 Board 50 **PARKING:** 27
**NOTES:** No dogs (ex guide dogs) **CARDS:**

⌂ **Hotel Ibis**
Garstang Rd, Broughton PR3 5JE
☎ 01772 861800 🖹 01772 861900
e-mail: H3162@accor-hotels.com
***Dir:** M6 junct32, then M55. Take left lane & pick up A6 sign. At slip road turn left, left again at mini-rdbt. Take 2nd turning. Hotel on right past pub*
Modern, budget hotel offering comfortable accommodation in bright and practical bedrooms. Breakfast is self-service and dinner is available in the restaurant. For further details, consult the Hotel Groups page.
**ROOMS:** 82 en suite s £42; d £52 * **CONF:** Thtr 30 Class 20 Board 20

P

PRESTON, continued

### Premier Lodge

Lostock Ln, Bamber Bridge PR5 6BA
☎ 0870 700 1512 📠 0870 700 1513
**Dir:** *Exit junct 1 M65,0.5miles from junct 29 of M6 close to rdbt of A582 & A6*

Premier Lodge offers modern, well-equipped, en suite accommodation suitable for both business and leisure travellers. Meals can be taken at the adjacent popular restaurant and bar, which is fully licensed. For further details, consult the Hotel Groups page.

**ROOMS:** 40 en suite s £42; d £42 * **CONF:** Thtr 30 Board 30

### Express by Holiday Inn

☎ 0800 897121

A modern budget hotel offering comfortable accommodation in refreshing, spacious and comprehensively equipped bedrooms, en suite bathrooms with power showers and continental buffet breakfast included in the room rate. Suitable for business travellers or families. For further details and the Express by Holiday Inn phone number, consult the Hotel Groups page.

**ROOMS:** 74 en suite **NOTES:** Opening 2002

PUDDINGTON, Cheshire Map 07 SJ37

### ★★★★67% Craxton Wood

Parkgate Rd, Ledsham CH66 9PB
☎ 0151 347 4000 📠 0151 347 4040
e-mail: info@craxton.macdonald.co.uk
**Dir:** *leave M6 take M56 direction North Wales, take A5117, A540 direction Hoylake, hotel is 200yds past the traffic lights*

Significant investment in the form of smart new bedrooms, which are both spacious and very thoughtfully equipped, as well as the addition of extensive meeting and leisure facilities make for a well-rounded hotel. A bit of theatre is available in the restaurant, where traditional favourites such as crêpe suzette are served.

**ROOMS:** 73 en suite (8 fmly) No smoking in 40 bedrooms s £70-£105; d £90-£130 * **LB** **FACILITIES:** **Spa** STV Indoor swimming (H) Sauna Solarium Gym Xmas **CONF:** Thtr 300 Class 150 Board 60 **SERVICES:** Lift **PARKING:** 220 **NOTES:** No smoking in restaurant Civ Wed 400 **CARDS:**

### *Premier Lodge (Wirral South)*

Parkgate Rd, Two Mills L66 9PD
☎ 0870 700 1580 📠 0870 700 1581

Premier Lodge offers modern, well-equipped, en suite accommodation suitable for both business and leisure travellers. Meals can be taken at the adjacent popular restaurant and bar, which is fully licensed. For further details, consult the Hotel Groups page.

**ROOMS:** 31 en suite

PUDSEY, West Yorkshire

### *Travelodge*

1 Mid Point, Dick Ln BD3 8QD
☎ 01274 665436
**ROOMS:** 40 en suite **NOTES:** Open now

Bad hair day? Hairdryers in all rooms three stars and above.

PULBOROUGH, West Sussex Map 04 TQ0

### ★★★66% Chequers

Old Rectory Ln RH20 1AD
☎ 01798 872486 📠 01798 872715
e-mail: chequershotel@btinternet.com
**Dir:** *100m mtrs N of junct of A283/A29 opposite church in Pulborough*

Personally run by friendly owners, this charming Grade II listed hotel is located just north of Pulborough overlooking the South Downs. All rooms are individual in style with character and good facilities. Public areas include two cosy lounges where drinks are served and also a conservatory coffee shop. The restaurant serves carefully prepared dishes using quality fresh produce.

**ROOMS:** 10 en suite (3 fmly) No smoking in all bedrooms s £49.50-£59.50; d £85-£95 (incl. bkfst) * **LB** **FACILITIES:** Xmas **CONF:** Thtr 20 Class 20 Board 20 **PARKING:** 15 **NOTES:** No smoking in restaurant **CARDS:**

PURTON, Wiltshire Map 04 SU0

### ★★★78% The Pear Tree at Purton

Church End SN5 4ED
☎ 01793 772100 📠 01793 772369
e-mail: stay@peartreepurton.co.uk
**Dir:** *from junct 16 of M4 follow signs to Purton, at Spar grocers turn right hotel is 0.25m on left*

Parts of this former vicarage date back to the early 15th century. Today, this charming Cotswold stone house has been transformed into an elegant country retreat with stunning gardens overlooked by the conservatory restaurant. Bedrooms are spacious and individually styled, featuring thoughtful extra touches like fresh fruit and sherry.

**ROOMS:** 18 en suite (2 fmly) s £110-£130; d £110-£130 (incl. bkfst) * **FACILITIES:** STV Croquet lawn Pool table **CONF:** Thtr 70 Class 30 Board 30 Del from £150 * **PARKING:** 60 **NOTES:** Civ Wed 50 **CARDS:**

QUORN, Leicestershire Map 08 SK5

### ★★★★70% Quorn Country

Charnwood House, 66 Leicester Rd LE12 8BB
☎ 01509 415050 📠 01509 415557
e-mail: quorncountry.hotel@virgin.net
**Dir:** *M1 junct 23-A512 into Loughborough and follow A6 signs. At 1st rdbt after town follow signs for Quorn, through lights-hotel 500yds from 2nd rdbt*

This pleasant hotel is set in four acres of landscaped grounds. There are two restaurants: the Shires and the conservatory style

continued

Orangery. Bedrooms are divided between the main house and appealing new suites.
**ROOMS:** 23 en suite (1 fmly) No smoking in 3 bedrooms s fr £102; d fr £115 * LB **FACILITIES:** STV Fishing **CONF:** Thtr 120 Class 60 Board 40 Del from £135 * **SERVICES:** air con **PARKING:** 100 **NOTES:** No dogs (ex guide dogs) Civ Wed 120
**CARDS:**

*See advert under LEICESTER*

RAINHILL, Merseyside Map 07 SJ49

### ★ 62% Rockland

View Rd L35 0LG
☎ 0151 426 4603 📠 0151 426 0107
***Dir:*** *leave M62 junc 7, take A57 towards Rainhill,after 1m turn left into View Rd, hotel 0.25m on left*
This former Victorian residence is situated within attractive grounds and gardens, in a quiet residential area, only a short distance from junction 7 of the M62. A friendly, family run hotel, its spacious and well-equipped bedrooms provide good value for money in pleasant informal surroundings.
**ROOMS:** 11 rms (10 en suite) (2 fmly) s £21-£33; d £29-£42 (incl. bkfst) * LB **PARKING:** 30 **CARDS:**

### *Premier Lodge (Liverpool East)*

PREMIER LODGE

804 Warrington Rd L35 6PE
☎ 0870 700 1430 📠 0870 700 1431
Premier Lodge offers modern, well-equipped, en suite accommodation suitable for both business and leisure travellers. Meals can be taken at the adjacent popular restaurant and bar, which is fully licensed. For further details, consult the Hotel Groups page.
**ROOMS:** 34 en suite

RAMSGATE, Kent Map 05 TR36

### ★★★ 66% San Clu

MINOTEL Great Britain

Victoria Pde, East Cliff CT11 8DT
☎ 01843 592345 📠 01843 580157
e-mail: sancluhotel@lineone.net
***Dir:*** *opposite Granville Theatre*
This Victorian hotel stands on the seafront, close to the ferry and the town. Bedrooms, some with balconies, are generously sized and well-equipped. Meals are served both in the bar lounge and in the restaurant.
**ROOMS:** 44 en suite (14 fmly) s fr £50; d fr £80 (incl. bkfst) * LB **FACILITIES:** Xmas **CONF:** Thtr 180 Class 100 Board 100 **SERVICES:** Lift **PARKING:** 16 **NOTES:** No smoking in restaurant
**CARDS:**

RAMSGILL, North Yorkshire Map 07 SE17

### ★★ 75% Yorke Arms

HG3 5RL
☎ 01423 755243 📠 01423 755330
e-mail: enquiries@yorke-arms.co.uk
***Dir:*** *turn off B6265 at Pateley Bridge at the Nidderdale filling station onto Low Wath road, signed to Ramsgill, continue for 4.5m*
No tour of the Dales is complete until one has experienced the genuine warmth of hospitality, slick service and award-winning cuisine of this smartly presented hotel. Thoughtfully equipped bedrooms vary in size and style and many enjoy delightful country views. Dinner provides the highlight of any stay with skilfully prepared dishes making the very best of local, quality produce.

**ROOMS:** 13 en suite 1 annexe en suite (2 fmly) s £90-£110; d £170-£210 (incl. bkfst & dinner) * LB **FACILITIES:** shooting,mountain biking Xmas **CONF:** Class 20 Board 10 **PARKING:** 20 **NOTES:** No dogs (ex guide dogs) No smoking in restaurant RS Sun
**CARDS:**

RANGEWORTHY, Gloucestershire Map 03 ST68

### ★★ 70% Rangeworthy Court

Church Ln BS37 7ND
☎ 01454 228347 📠 01454 228945
e-mail: hotel@rangeworthy.demon.co.uk
***Dir:*** *signposted off B4058*

This peacefully located, welcoming manor house hotel is within easy reach of the motorway network. It offers a choice of comfortable lounges, and bedrooms equipped to modern standards. Its relaxing restaurant provides a varied and interesting menu.
**ROOMS:** 13 en suite (4 fmly) s £65-£70; d £75-£90 (incl. bkfst) * LB **FACILITIES:** STV Outdoor swimming (H) Xmas **CONF:** Thtr 22 Class 14 Board 16 Del £98 * **PARKING:** 40 **NOTES:** No smoking in restaurant Civ Wed 60 **CARDS:**

RAVENSCAR, North Yorkshire Map 08 NZ90

### ★★★ 65% Raven Hall Country House

YO13 0ET
☎ 01723 870353 📠 01723 870072
e-mail: enquiries@ravenhall.co.uk
***Dir:*** *from Scarborough take A171 to Whitby Rd, go through Cloughton Village turn right to Ravenscar*
Occupying a dramatic cliff-top location in extensive gardens, Raven Hall offers superb views towards Robin Hood's Bay. The bedrooms are traditional in style and public areas are in keeping with a

*continued on p482*

R

RAVENSCAR, continued

'country mansion' feel. Leisure facilities, meeting rooms and banqueting facilities are provided.
**ROOMS:** 53 en suite (22 fmly) No smoking in 1 bedroom d £100-£200 (incl. bkfst) * **LB** **FACILITIES:** Indoor swimming (H) Golf 9 Tennis (hard) Snooker Sauna Croquet lawn Putting green Crown green bowls Giant chess entertainment ch fac Xmas **CONF:** Thtr 160 Class 100 Board 60 Del from £85 * **PARKING:** 200 **NOTES:** No dogs (ex guide dogs) No smoking in restaurant Civ Wed 120
**CARDS:**

*See advert under SCARBOROUGH*

## RAVENSTONEDALE, Cumbria — Map 07 NY70

### ★★66% Black Swan

CA17 4NG
☎ 015396 23204 Fax 015396 23604
e-mail: reservations@blackswanhotel.com
***Dir:*** *40 mins from Scotch Corner via A66 & A685*
Peacefully located in the centre of the village, this friendly hotel is only ten minutes' drive from the M6. A wide range of meals is served in the traditional dining room or in the cosy well-stocked bar with its real ales. Thoughtfully equipped bedrooms vary in style and include ground floor chalet style rooms.
**ROOMS:** 13 en suite 4 annexe en suite (1 fmly) s £45-£50; d £75-£85 (incl. bkfst) * **LB** **FACILITIES:** Tennis (hard) Fishing free golf at nearby gc ch fac Xmas **PARKING:** 30 **NOTES:** No smoking in restaurant
**CARDS:**

### ★★65% *The Fat Lamb*

Crossbank CA17 4LL
☎ 01539 623242 Fax 01539 623285
e-mail: fatlamb@cumbria.com
***Dir:*** *on A683, between Kirkby Stephen/Sedbergh*
Dating back to the 1600s, this stone inn is peacefully located on its own private nature reserve. The traditional bar has open fires and offers an extensive bar menu, while freshly prepared food is also available in the restaurant. Accommodation includes spacious family rooms and facilities for the disabled.
**ROOMS:** 12 en suite (4 fmly) No smoking in all bedrooms **FACILITIES:** Fishing Private 5 acre nature reserve **PARKING:** 60 **NOTES:** No smoking in restaurant **CARDS:**

## READING, Berkshire — Map 04 SU77

see also Swallowfield & Wokingham

### ★★★★75% Millennium Madejski Hotel Reading

Madejski Stadium RG2 0FL
☎ 0118 925 3500 Fax 0118 925 3501
e-mail: sales.reading@mill-cop.com
***Dir:*** *M4 junct 11 onto A33, follow signs for Madejski Complex*
This stylish new property is part of the Reading Madejski Football Stadium. Features include the fine dining restaurant Cilantro and Atrium lobby with specially commissioned water sculpture. Bedrooms have similar high style with spacious work stations and plenty of amenities. A choice of suites and a club floor with its own lounge give additional choice.
**ROOMS:** 140 en suite (4 fmly) No smoking in 92 bedrooms s £190-£260; d £190-£260 * **LB** **FACILITIES:** **Spa** STV Indoor swimming (H) Sauna Solarium Gym Jacuzzi **SERVICES:** Lift air con **PARKING:** 150
**CARDS:**

### ★★★69% *Posthouse Reading*

Posthouse

Basingstoke Rd RG2 0SL
☎ 0870 400 9067 Fax 0118 931 1958
Situated close to both Reading and the M4, this bright hotel provides modern accommodation ideal for leisure and business markets. Meals are served in the Rotisserie restaurant, or snacks are available in the lounge. The leisure centre and 'Academy' meeting rooms are a bonus.
**ROOMS:** 202 en suite (56 fmly) No smoking in 94 bedrooms **FACILITIES:** Indoor swimming (H) Sauna Solarium Gym Jacuzzi Health & fitness centre ch fac **CONF:** Thtr 100 Class 50 Board 45 **PARKING:** 450 **CARDS:**

### ★★★68% Courtyard by Marriott Reading

Bath Rd, Padworth RG7 5HT
☎ 0118 971 4411 Fax 0118 971 4442
***Dir:*** *leave the M4 at junct 12 and follow A4 towards Newbury, hotel is 3.5m on left*

A modern purpose-built hotel whose air-conditioned bedrooms are comfortably furnished, well-equipped and suitable for business guests. The reception area features an attractive gallery lounge and there is a small gym. Popular dishes from the branded menu are offered in the conservatory-style dining room.
**ROOMS:** 50 en suite No smoking in 30 bedrooms s £115-£125; d £115-£125 * **LB** **FACILITIES:** STV Gym Fitness room Xmas **CONF:** Thtr 200 Class 100 Board 80 Del from £145 * **SERVICES:** air con **PARKING:** 200 **NOTES:** No dogs (ex guide dogs) No smoking in restaurant Civ Wed 120
**CARDS:**

### ★★★67% Hanover International Hotel & Club

Pingewood RG30 3UN
☎ 0118 950 0885 Fax 0118 939 1996
e-mail: reading@hanover-international.com
***Dir:*** *A33 towards Basingstoke,at Three Mile Cross rdbt, turn right signposted Burghfield, continue 300m, 2nd right, over M4, cross lights, hotel on left*
Quietly located a short distance south of Reading, with convenient access to the major routes, this modern hotel has the attractive feature of being built around a man-made lake, occasionally used for water sports. Bedrooms are generally spacious with good facilities and have balconies overlooking the lake. Public areas

*continued*

include the newly refurbished brasserie 209 and a leisure club with adjacent bar.

**ROOMS:** 81 en suite (43 fmly) No smoking in 46 bedrooms s £110-£170; d £110-£170 * **LB** **FACILITIES:** STV Indoor swimming (H) Tennis (hard) Squash Sauna Gym Jacuzzi Beauty treatment water & jet skiing **CONF:** Thtr 110 Class 50 Board 45 Del from £150 * **SERVICES:** Lift **PARKING:** 250 **NOTES:** No dogs (ex guide dogs) No smoking in restaurant Civ Wed 80 **CARDS:**

### ★★★65% Calcot Hotel

98 Bath Rd, Calcot RG31 7QN
☎ 0118 941 6423 🖷 0118 941 1223
e-mail: calcothotel@zoom.co.uk
***Dir:*** *M4 junct 12 onto A4 towards Reading, hotel is located in 0.5m on southside of A4*

The Calcot Hotel enjoys good road access, and is conveniently located for both London and the motorway. Bedrooms are well-equipped and tastefully decorated, and the restaurant provides enjoyable food in welcoming surroundings. Attractive public rooms and function suites are additional features.

**ROOMS:** 66 en suite (2 fmly) No smoking in 22 bedrooms s £73.50-£100; d £73.50-£100 * **FACILITIES:** STV entertainment **CONF:** Thtr 120 Class 35 Board 35 Del from £130.50 * **PARKING:** 130 **NOTES:** No dogs (ex guide dogs) Closed 25-27 Dec
**CARDS:**

### ★★★64% Royal County Hotel

4-8 Duke St RG1 4RY
☎ 0118 958 3455 🖷 0118 950 4450
e-mail: royalcountyhotel@bestwestern.co.uk

Situated in the city centre with handy parking, this hotel has a strong commercial following. The bedrooms are smart, well-appointed and comfortable. The public rooms are all decorated in a modern style and the new 'Fusion' Brasserie is already proving a popular venue.

**ROOMS:** 52 en suite (2 fmly) No smoking in 24 bedrooms s £95-£120; d £105-£120 * **LB** **FACILITIES:** STV **CONF:** Thtr 90 Class 40 Board 40 Del from £149.22 * **PARKING:** 19 **NOTES:** No dogs (ex guide dogs)
**CARDS:**

### ★★★62% Quality Hotel Reading

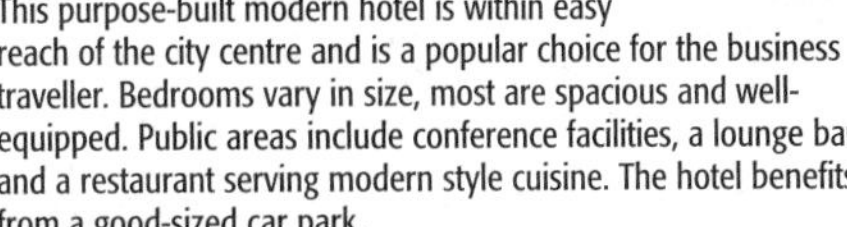
Quality Hotel

648-654 Oxford Rd RG30 1EH
☎ 0118 950 0541 🖷 0118 956 7220

This purpose-built modern hotel is within easy reach of the city centre and is a popular choice for the business traveller. Bedrooms vary in size, most are spacious and well-equipped. Public areas include conference facilities, a lounge bar and a restaurant serving modern style cuisine. The hotel benefits from a good-sized car park.

**ROOMS:** 95 en suite (9 fmly) No smoking in 28 bedrooms s £95-£105; d £95-£105 * **CONF:** Thtr 100 Class 50 Board 40 Del from £125 * **SERVICES:** Lift **PARKING:** 40 **NOTES:** No dogs (ex guide dogs) No smoking in restaurant **CARDS:**

### ★★70% *The Mill House*

Old Basingstoke Rd, Swallowfield RG7 1PY
☎ 0118 988 3124 🖷 0118 988 5550
e-mail: info@themillhousehotel.co.uk
(For full entry see Swallowfield)

### ★★66% Rainbow Corner

132-138 Caversham Rd RG1 8AY
☎ 0118 955 6902 & 958 8140 🖷 0118 958 6500
e-mail: info@rainbowhotel.co.uk
***Dir:*** *from junct 11 of M4 take A327 to town centre then follow signs to Caversham*

This friendly, privately owned hotel is close to the city centre and station. Bedrooms are well equipped and smartly presented, and the cosy bar is the focus of activity in the evenings. The car park is a bonus.

**ROOMS:** 24 en suite (1 fmly) No smoking in all bedrooms s £39-£70; d £49-£91 * **LB** **FACILITIES:** STV **CONF:** Thtr 30 Class 30 Board 20 **PARKING:** 15 **NOTES:** No smoking in restaurant
**CARDS:**

### ★★64% Abbey House

118 Connaught Rd RG30 2UF
☎ 0118 959 0549 🖷 0118 956 9299
e-mail: ahh@fardellhotels.com
***Dir:*** *from town centre take A329 towards Pangborne after Reading West Railway bridge take 3rd left*

This friendly and privately run hotel located in a quiet residential area is close to the city centre. Bedrooms are well-equipped, comfortable and soundly maintained. Other facilities include a cosy lounge, a small bar, a pleasant dining room and convenient car park.

**ROOMS:** 15 rms (14 en suite) 5 annexe en suite (4 fmly) No smoking in all bedrooms **FACILITIES:** STV **CONF:** Thtr 28 Class 12 Board 16 Del from £95 * **PARKING:** 4 **NOTES:** No dogs (ex guide dogs) No smoking in restaurant **CARDS:**

### ⌂ *Premier Lodge*

PREMIER LODGE

Grazeley Rd RG7 1LS
☎ 0870 700 1500 🖷 0870 700 1501

Premier Lodge offers modern, well-equipped, en suite accommodation suitable for both business and leisure travellers. Meals can be taken at the adjacent popular restaurant and bar, which is fully licensed. For further details, consult the Hotel Groups page.

**ROOMS:** 32 en suite

### ⌂ *Travelodge (Reading Central)*

Travelodge

Oxford Rd RG1 7LT
☎ 0118 950 3179

Travelodge offers good quality, good value, modern accommodation. Ideal for families, the spacious, en suite

*continued on p484*

R

READING, continued

bedrooms include remote-control TV, tea and coffee-making facilities, luxury beds and free morning newspaper. Meals can be taken at the nearby family restaurant. For further details and the Travelodge phone number, consult the Hotel Groups page.

### ⇧ *Travelodge (Eastbound)*

Burghfield RG30 3UQ
☎ 0118 956 6966 📠 0118 959 5444
***Dir:*** *M4 between junc 11&12*
Travelodge offers good quality, good value, modern accommodation. Ideal for families, the spacious, en suite bedrooms include remote-control TV, tea and coffee-making facilities, luxury beds and free morning newspaper. Meals can be taken at the nearby family restaurant. For further details and the Travelodge phone number, consult the Hotel Groups page.

**ROOMS:** 45 en suite **CONF:** Thtr 20 Class 20 Board 20

### ⇧ *Travelodge*

387 Basingstoke Rd RG2 0JE
☎ 0118 975 0618 📠 0118 975 0618
***Dir:*** *on A33, southbound*
Travelodge offers good quality, good value, modern accommodation. Ideal for families, the spacious, en suite bedrooms include remote-control TV, tea and coffee-making facilities, luxury beds and free morning newspaper. Meals can be taken at the nearby family restaurant. For further details and the Travelodge phone number, consult the Hotel Groups page.

**ROOMS:** 36 en suite

### ○ Express by Holiday Inn

Richfield Av RG1 8EQ
☎ 0800 897121
A modern budget hotel offering comfortable accommodation in refreshing, spacious and comprehensively equipped bedrooms, en suite bathrooms with power showers and continental buffet breakfast included in the room rate. Suitable for business travellers or families. For further details and the Express by Holiday Inn phone number, consult the Hotel Groups page.

**ROOMS:** 74 en suite **NOTES:** Opened September 2001

> Read all about it! Newspapers delivered to bedrooms in four and five star hotels.

REDDITCH, Worcestershire Map 07 SP06

### ★★★72% The Abbey Hotel Golf & Country Club

Hither Green Ln, Dagnell End Rd, Bordesley B98 9BE
☎ 01527 406600 📠 01527 406514
e-mail: theabbeyhotel@bestwestern.co.uk
***Dir:*** *from M42 junct 2 take A441 to Redditch, at end dual carriageway turn left still on A441, Dagnell End Rd is on the left, hotel approx 600yds right*

This large modern hotel complex is close to junction 2 of the M42. Rooms are well-equipped, spacious and attractively decorated. Public areas include a cosy restaurant with adjacent cocktail bar as well as a public bar. There are good leisure facilities.
**ROOMS:** 72 en suite (2 fmly) No smoking in 10 bedrooms s £50-£110; d £60-£130 (incl. bkfst) * **LB** **FACILITIES:** STV Indoor swimming (H) Golf 18 Fishing Sauna Solarium Gym Putting green Jacuzzi Beauty Salon,Golf driving range ch fac Xmas **CONF:** Thtr 150 Class 60 Board 30 Del £149.50 * **PARKING:** 170 **NOTES:** No dogs (ex guide dogs) No smoking in restaurant **CARDS:**

*See advert on opposite page*

### ★★★66% Quality Hotel

Pool Bank, Southcrest B97 4JS
☎ 01527 541511 📠 01527 402600
e-mail: admin@gb646.u-net.com
***Dir:*** *follow signs to hotel, 2nd on right after B&Q DIY store. Follow signs for Redditch, A441, on reaching Redditch, follow signs for all other Redditch Districts until Southcrest is signposted. From that point on follow signs for hotel*
Originally a country house, this hotel enjoys a peaceful location set in extensive wooded grounds. Bedrooms vary in size and style, but are all well-appointed and equipped. Both restaurant and bar/conservatory overlook the attractive gardens.
**ROOMS:** 73 en suite (4 fmly) No smoking in 16 bedrooms s fr £78; d fr £95 * **LB** **FACILITIES:** STV **CONF:** Thtr 100 Class 25 Board 50 Del £122 * **PARKING:** 100 **NOTES:** No smoking in restaurant Civ Wed 100
**CARDS:**

### ★★62% Montville

101 Mount Pleasant, Southcrest B97 4JE
☎ 01527 544411 & 402566 📠 01527 544341
e-mail: sales@montvillehotel.co.uk
***Dir:*** *off M42 at junct 3 (A435) follow signs towards Redditch centre, then signs towards Southcrest (A441)*
This small and privately owned hotel lies less than half a mile from the town centre. It provides modern furnished and well-equipped accommodation suitable for both business and leisure guests.

*continued*

Public areas include the pleasant Granny's restaurant, a quaint bar and a homely lounge.
**ROOMS:** 14 en suite (2 fmly) No smoking in 5 bedrooms s £40-£50; d £55-£70 (incl. bkfst) * **CONF:** Thtr 60 Class 30 Board 24 Del from £74 * **PARKING:** 12 **NOTES:** No smoking in restaurant
**CARDS:**

### Premier Lodge

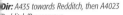

Birchfield Rd B97 6PX

PREMIER LODGE
☎ 0870 700 1320 🖷 0870 700 1321
Premier Lodge offers modern, well-equipped, en suite accommodation suitable for both business and leisure travellers. Meals can be taken at the adjacent popular restaurant and bar, which is fully licensed. For further details, consult the Hotel Groups page.
**ROOMS:** 33 en suite s £46; d £46 *

### Campanile

Far Moor Ln, Winyates Green B98 0SD

Campanile
☎ 01527 510710 🖷 01527 517269
***Dir:*** *A435 towards Redditch, then A4023 Redditch/Bromsgrove*

HOTEL
Campanile

This modern building offers accommodation in smart, well-equipped bedrooms, all with en suite bathrooms. Refreshments may be taken at the informal Bistro. For further details and the Campanile phone number, consult the Hotel Groups page.
**ROOMS:** 50 annexe en suite s fr £38.50; d fr £38.50 * **CONF:** Thtr 35 Class 18 Board 20

## REDHILL, Surrey — Map 04 TQ25

### ★★★★71% Nutfield Priory

Nutfield RH1 4EL
☎ 01737 824400 🖷 01737 823321
e-mail: nutpriory@aol.com
***Dir:*** *exit M25 junct 6 & follow signs to Redhill via Godstone on A25. Hotel 1m on left after Nutfield Village*

Built in 1872 as an extravagant folly, this Victorian country house is
*continued*

set in forty acres of grounds and has wonderful views over the Surrey and Sussex countryside. Bedrooms are individually styled and equipped with a comprehensive range of facilities. Public areas include the impressive grand hall, Cloisters restaurant, the library, and a cosy lounge bar area.
**ROOMS:** 60 en suite (4 fmly) No smoking in 24 bedrooms s fr £105; d fr £150 * **LB** **FACILITIES:** STV Indoor swimming (H) Squash Sauna Solarium Gym Jacuzzi Steam room Beauty therapy Hairdressing Xmas **CONF:** Thtr 80 Class 45 Board 40 Del from £215 * **SERVICES:** Lift **PARKING:** 130 **NOTES:** No smoking in restaurant Civ Wed 80
**CARDS:**

R

### Innkeeper's Lodge Redhill

Redstone Hill RH1 4BL
A new concept in the travel accommodation market. Smart rooms meet essential business requirements but also have home comforts. Dining options include all-day menus plus the added advantage of breakfast, which is included in the room price. Reservations can be made seven days a week through the room reservations number: 0870 243 0500. For further details, consult the Hotel Groups page.
**ROOMS:** 37 en suite

## REDRUTH, Cornwall & Isles of Scilly — Map 02 SW64

### ★★★65% Penventon

TR15 1TE
☎ 01209 203000 🖷 01209 203001
e-mail: manager@penventon.com
***Dir:*** *turn off A30 at Redruth, hotel is 1m South*
This Georgian mansion is conveniently located for the A30 and a short walk from Redruth town centre. Public areas are luxurious,
*continued on p486*

REDRUTH, continued

and additional facilities include a health spa and the lively Spice of Life bar. There is a wide choice of bedrooms, with the largest incorporating separate sitting areas. The restaurant, featuring a pianist, offers extensive menus of Italian, French, British and Cornish dishes.

*Penventon, Redruth*

**ROOMS:** 50 en suite (3 fmly) No smoking in 6 bedrooms s £39.50-£69; d £66-£99 (incl. bkfst) * **LB** **FACILITIES:** **Spa** Indoor swimming (H) Sauna Solarium Gym Jacuzzi Masseuse Steam bath Pool table entertainment ch fac Xmas **CONF:** Thtr 200 Class 100 Board 60 Del from £58 * **PARKING:** 100 **NOTES:** No smoking in restaurant Civ Wed 200 **CARDS:**

### ★★69% Aviary Court

Mary's Well, Illogan TR16 4QZ
☎ 01209 842256 01209 843744
e-mail: aviarycourt@connexions.co.uk
***Dir:*** *turn off A30 at sign A3047 Camborne, Pool & Portreath. Follow Portreath & Illogan signs for approx 2m to Alexandra Rd*

Peace and tranquillity are assured at this charming property set in well-tended gardens on the edge of Illogan Woods. Bedrooms are individually furnished and decorated and include many thoughtful extras. The generous meals make full use of Cornish produce; Sunday lunches are a speciality and booking is essential.
**ROOMS:** 6 en suite (1 fmly) s £45; d £64 (incl. bkfst) * **FACILITIES:** Tennis (hard) **PARKING:** 25 **NOTES:** No dogs No children 3yrs No smoking in restaurant **CARDS:**

### ★★65% Crossroads

Scorrier TR16 5BP
☎ 01209 820551 01209 820392
e-mail: crossroads.hotel@talk21.com
***Dir:*** *two miles east of Redruth off A30, Scorrier/Helston exit*

Conveniently located close to the A30, this purpose-built hotel provides a variety of bedroom styles, with nine executive rooms offering extra space and facilities. The convivial bar is popular with locals and visitors alike, and the intimate restaurant offers an interesting choice of dishes. Extensive conference facilities are also available.
**ROOMS:** 35 en suite (4 fmly) No smoking in 5 bedrooms s £34-£49; d £46-£60 (incl. bkfst) * **LB** **CONF:** Thtr 100 Class 30 Board 30 **SERVICES:** Lift **PARKING:** 140 **CARDS:**

> Late for dinner? Quality Standards star rating means that last orders for dinner should be no earlier than:
> ★ 6.30pm ★★ 7.00pm ★★★ 8.00pm
> ★★★★ 9.00pm ★★★★★ 10.00pm

REDWORTH, Co Durham — Map 08 NZ2

### ★★★★71% Redworth Hall Hotel

DL5 6NL
☎ 01388 770600 01388 770654
e-mail: redworthhall@paramount-hotels.co.uk
***Dir:*** *from A1(M) junct 58 take A68 'Corbridge'. Follow brown hotel signs*

PARAMOUN GROUP OF HOTEL

This grand Elizabethan style hotel and health club makes a fine impression. There are several spacious, comfortable lounges and two restaurants, of which the Blue Room is the best showcase for the chef's talents. Bedrooms are comfortable, stylish and well-equipped. Leisure, conference and banqueting facilities are very popular.
**ROOMS:** 100 en suite (8 fmly) No smoking in 45 bedrooms s fr £110; d fr £145 (incl. bkfst) * **LB** **FACILITIES:** STV Indoor swimming (H) Tennis (hard) Sauna Solarium Gym Croquet lawn Jacuzzi Bodysense Health & Beauty Club entertainment Xmas **CONF:** Thtr 300 Class 150 Board 100 Del from £145 * **SERVICES:** Lift **PARKING:** 300 **NOTES:** Civ Wed 220 **CARDS:**

REEPHAM, Norfolk — Map 09 TG1

### ★★68% The Old Brewery House Hotel

Market Place NR10 4JJ
☎ 01603 870881 01603 870969
e-mail: oldbrewery@norfolk-hotels.co.uk
***Dir:*** *off A1067 Norwich-Fakenham. Take B1145 sigposted Reepham*

The Old Brewery House is situated in the Market Square and is the focal point of Reepham, with both guests and locals enjoying the relaxed atmosphere. Bedrooms are generally spacious and equipped with many useful extras; some rooms have four-poster beds. Public areas include a well-equipped leisure centre, a new conservatory restaurant and a cosy lounge.
**ROOMS:** 23 en suite (2 fmly) No smoking in 7 bedrooms s fr £47.50; d fr £75 (incl. bkfst) * **LB** **FACILITIES:** Indoor swimming (H) Squash Sauna Solarium Gym Aerobics & Steps Swimming lessons entertainment Xmas **CONF:** Thtr 200 Class 150 Board 100 Del from £67.50 * **PARKING:** 60 **NOTES:** No dogs (ex guide dogs) No smoking in restaurant Civ Wed 200 **CARDS:**

REIGATE, Surrey — Map 04 TQ2

### ★★★66% Reigate Manor Hotel

Reigate Hill RH2 9PF
☎ 01737 240125 01737 223883
e-mail: hotel@reigatemanor.co.uk
***Dir:*** *on A217, 1m S of junct 8 on M25*

Best Western

On the slopes of Reigate Hill, the hotel is ideally located for access to the town and for local motorway links. Bedrooms are divided between the more traditional rooms in the old house and

continued

contemporary rooms in the newer wing. There is a variety of function rooms available.
**ROOMS:** 50 en suite No smoking in 30 bedrooms s £98-£120; d £120-£140 **LB** **FACILITIES:** STV Sauna Solarium Gym **CONF:** Thtr 200 Class 80 Board 50 Del from £135 * **PARKING:** 130 **NOTES:** No dogs (ex guide dogs) No smoking in restaurant Civ Wed 210
**CARDS:**

**★★★63% Bridge House**
Reigate Hill RH2 9RP
☎ 01737 246801 & 244821 🖹 01737 223756
***Dir:*** *on A217 between M25 and Reigate*
Perched high on Reigate Hill and commanding fine countryside views, this well-established hotel offers a selection of modern, well-equipped bedrooms including family rooms and premier rooms. There is a Mediterranean-style restaurant and live music and dancing are to be had on most nights.
**ROOMS:** 39 en suite (3 fmly) s £50-£90; d £85-£135 *
**FACILITIES:** STV entertainment Xmas **CONF:** Thtr 100 Class 70 Board 60 Del £135.50 * **PARKING:** 110 **NOTES:** No dogs (ex guide dogs) RS Bank Holidays **CARDS:**

*See advert on this page*

RENISHAW, Derbyshire Map 08 SK47

**★★★64% *Sitwell Arms***
Station Rd S21 3WF
☎ 01246 435226 🖹 01246 433915
***Dir:*** *on A6135 to Sheffield, W of junct 30 of M1*

This stone-built hotel, parts of which date back to the 18th century, is conveniently situated close to the M1 and offers good value accommodation. Bedrooms are of a comfortable size and include the expected range of facilities and appointments. The public rooms offer a choice of bars and a restaurant, which provides a range of popular dishes and grills.
**ROOMS:** 30 en suite (6 fmly) No smoking in 10 bedrooms **CONF:** Thtr 160 Class 60 Board 60 **PARKING:** 150 **NOTES:** No dogs (ex guide dogs) **CARDS:**

*See advert under SHEFFIELD*

RICHMOND, North Yorkshire Map 07 NZ10

**★★68% King's Head**
Best Western
Market Place DL10 4HS
☎ 01748 850220 🖹 01748 850635
e-mail: res@kingsheadrichmond.co.uk
***Dir:*** *in Richmond Market Place, 5m from A1/A66 at Scotch Corner on the A6108*
Centrally situated in the historic market square, The King's Head offers a range of well equipped, modern bedrooms. Its lounges, furnished with deep sofas, display an interesting collection of antique clocks. Afternoon tea is worth sampling and the restaurant offers a good choice at dinner and breakfast.

KINGS HEAD

**ROOMS:** 26 en suite 4 annexe en suite (1 fmly) No smoking in 11 bedrooms **FACILITIES:** STV Xmas **CONF:** Thtr 180 Class 80 Board 50 Del from £77 * **PARKING:** 25 **NOTES:** No smoking in restaurant
**CARDS:**

**★★65% Frenchgate**
59-61 Frenchgate DL10 7AE
☎ 01748 822087 🖹 01748 823596
***Dir:*** *turn off at Scotch Corner on the A6108 Richmond. Through Richmond to New Queens Road rdbt, turn left into Dundas St and left again into Frenchgate*
This elegant townhouse is situated in a quiet area with a secluded garden at the rear. Most bedrooms have been refurbished and all are particularly well equipped. Public areas are also comfortably furnished. At dinner there is a good choice of freshly prepared

*continued on p488*



R

RICHMOND, continued

dishes. Bar meals can also be taken in the evenings and at lunchtime.
**ROOMS:** 10 en suite 1 annexe en suite (1 fmly) No smoking in all bedrooms s £39-£55; d £65-£70 (incl. bkfst) * **LB FACILITIES:** Award winning gardens ch fac Xmas **CONF:** Del from £71 * **PARKING:** 9 **NOTES:** No smoking in restaurant **CARDS:**

RICHMOND UPON THAMES, Greater London See LONDON SECTION plan 1 C2

### ★★★★ 74% Richmond Gate

Richmond Hill TW10 6RP
☎ 020 8940 0061 020 8332 0354
e-mail: richmondgate@corus.co.uk
***Dir:*** *from Richmond head to the top of Richmond hill and the hotel on left opposite the Star & Garter home at Richmond gate exit*

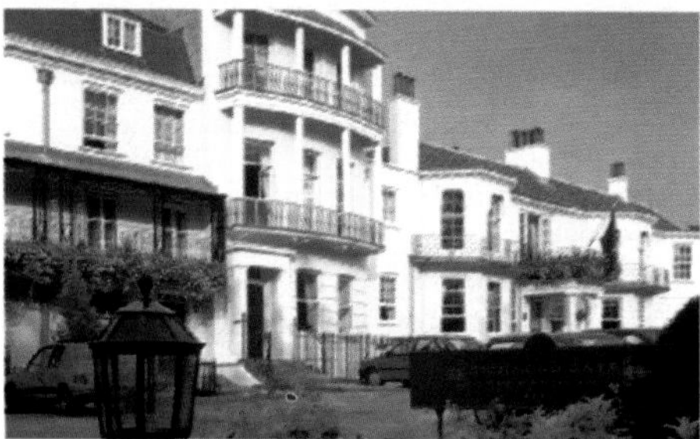

This smart Georgian hotel sits at the top of Richmond Hill opposite the park. Stylish bedrooms are equipped to a very high standard and include luxury doubles, spacious suites and smaller, more compact garden wing rooms. The Park Restaurant provides the highlight of any visit with bold contemporary cuisine very much to the fore; enthusiasts of this style of cooking can join the hotel's dining club.
**ROOMS:** 68 en suite (2 fmly) No smoking in 11 bedrooms s £115-£145; d £145-£172 (incl. bkfst) * **LB FACILITIES:** STV Indoor swimming (H) Sauna Solarium Gym Jacuzzi Health & beauty suite Steam room Xmas **CONF:** Thtr 50 Class 25 Board 30 Del £210 * **PARKING:** 50 **NOTES:** No dogs (ex guide dogs) No smoking in restaurant Civ Wed 70 **CARDS:**

R

### ★★★ 69% Richmond Hill

corus

Richmond Hill TW10 6RW
☎ 020 8940 2247 020 8940 5424
e-mail: richmondhill@corushotels.co.uk
***Dir:*** *located at top of Richmond Hill on B321*

An imposing Georgian manor house built in 1726 on Richmond Hill, enjoying views of the Thames and open parkland. Rooms come in a variety of sizes and styles. The restaurant offers a fixed price menu and an impressive array of dishes. The stylish, well-designed health club with large pool is shared with sister hotel the Richmond Gate.
**ROOMS:** 138 en suite (2 fmly) No smoking in 48 bedrooms s £80-£137; d £90-£167 (incl. bkfst) * **LB FACILITIES: Spa** STV Indoor swimming (H) Sauna Solarium Gym Jacuzzi Steam room Health & beauty suite entertainment Xmas **CONF:** Thtr 180 Class 100 Board 50 Del from £202 * **SERVICES:** Lift **PARKING:** 150 **NOTES:** Civ Wed 200 **CARDS:**

### ★★★ 61% *Bingham Hotel*

61-63 Petersham Rd TW10 6UT
☎ 020 8940 0902 020 8948 8737
e-mail: reservation@binghamhotel.co.uk
***Dir:*** *on A307*
This Georgian period building overlooks the Thames and is within walking distance of the town centre. Bedrooms vary in size and style and some have views of the river. Limited parking is a bonus.
**ROOMS:** 23 en suite **CONF:** Thtr 35 Class 14 Board 18 **PARKING:** 8 **CARDS:**

RINGWOOD, Hampshire Map 04 SU10

### ★★★ 69% Tyrrells Ford Country House

Avon BH23 7BH
☎ 01425 672646 01425 672262
***Dir:*** *turn off A31 to Ringwood. Follow B3347, Hotel 3m S on left at Avon*
Set in the New Forest, this delightful family-run hotel has much to offer. Bedrooms have views over woodland and the open country. Diners may eat in the formal restaurant, or sample the wide range of bar meals, all prepared using fresh local produce. The Gallery lounge is a peaceful area in which to relax.
**ROOMS:** 16 en suite s £70-£80; d £120-£140 (incl. bkfst) * **LB FACILITIES:** Xmas **CONF:** Thtr 40 Class 20 Board 20 Del from £120 * **PARKING:** 100 **NOTES:** No dogs (ex guide dogs) No smoking in restaurant Civ Wed 60 **CARDS:**

### ★★ 71% Moortown Lodge Hotel

244 Christchurch Rd BH24 3AS
☎ 01425 471404 01425 476052
e-mail: hotel@moortownlodge.co.uk
***Dir:*** *off A31 onto B3347. Hotel 1.5m S on right*
This delightful little hotel is personally run by its proprietors enabling them to provide a particularly warm welcome to their guests. The attractively decorated bedrooms are cosy, well-maintained and have several thoughtful, extra features. Each evening, an excellent fixed price menu is served, featuring honest cooking and using local produce wherever possible.
**ROOMS:** 6 rms (5 en suite) (1 fmly) No smoking in 3 bedrooms s £50-£70; d £65-£90 (incl. bkfst) * **LB PARKING:** 8 **NOTES:** No dogs No smoking in restaurant Closed 24 Dec-mid Jan
**CARDS:**

### ★★ 62% *Candlesticks Inn*

136 Christchurch Rd BH24 3AP
☎ 01425 472587 01425 471600
e-mail: royconway@hotmail.com
***Dir:*** *from M27/A31,take B3347 towards Christchurch, hotel on right hand side approx 0.5m from intersection/flyover*
This pretty 15th-century thatched inn, a consistent winner of 'Ringwood in Bloom', is conveniently located for the New Forest. The well-equipped bedrooms are located in a modern lodge to the rear, and include ground-floor rooms and one equipped for disabled guests. There is a bright conservatory bar-lounge where

continued

snacks can be taken, and a cosy beamed restaurant serving a more extensive menu.
**ROOMS:** 8 en suite (1 fmly) **PARKING:** 45 **NOTES:** No dogs No children 2yrs Closed 23 Dec-9 Jan **CARDS:**

## RIPON, North Yorkshire Map 08 SE37

### ★★★ 69% Ripon Spa

Park St HG4 2BU
☎ 01765 602172 🖷 01765 690770
e-mail: spahotel@bronco.co.uk
***Dir:*** *follow signs to the B6265, at T junct to join this road, turn right back towards Ripon, hotel on this section of B6265*

Boasting acres of attractive gardens whilst being just a short walk from the city centre, this hotel provides comfortable and traditional accommodation in a pleasant and relaxing environment. There are comfortable lounges, a terrace overlooking the gardens and the popular Turf Tavern. Traditional English cooking is served in the elegant main restaurant.
**ROOMS:** 40 en suite (5 fmly) s £80-£95; d £89-£102 (incl. bkfst) * **LB**
**FACILITIES:** STV Croquet lawn Xmas **CONF:** Thtr 150 Class 35 Board 40 Del from £105 * **SERVICES:** Lift **PARKING:** 60
**NOTES:** Civ Wed 150 **CARDS:**

*See advert under HARROGATE*

### ★★ 62% Unicorn

Market Place HG4 1BP
☎ 01765 602202 🖷 01765 690734
e-mail: info@unicorn-hotel.co.uk
***Dir:*** *on south east corner of Market Place, 4m from A1 on A61*
Situated in Ripon's ancient market place the Unicorn Hotel dates back five hundred years, when it was a coaching house. The bedrooms are traditionally furnished, and the renamed "Bricants" restaurant serves tantalising dishes in historical surrounds. A huge mural and a wide range of meals are features of the bar.
**ROOMS:** 33 en suite (4 fmly) s £48; d £68 (incl. bkfst) * **LB**
**FACILITIES:** entertainment **CONF:** Thtr 60 Class 10 Board 26 Del £81.50 * **PARKING:** 20 **NOTES:** No smoking in restaurant Closed 24-25 Dec
**CARDS:**

## RISLEY, Derbyshire Map 08 SK43

### ★★★ 72% Risley Hall

Derby Rd DE72 3SS
☎ 0115 939 9000 🖷 0115 939 7766
***Dir:*** *off junct 25 on M1, Sandiacre exit, left at T junct, 0.5m on left*
This impressive manor house, dating from the 11th century, is set in beautiful listed gardens. Relaxing areas include a choice of bars, morning room, private dining rooms and a grand baronial hall. Many of the individually styled bedrooms boast antique furnishings, exposed beams and wall timbers. An interesting menu is served, supplemented by daily dishes.

**ROOMS:** 16 en suite (8 fmly) s £85-£105; d £105-£125 * **LB**
**FACILITIES:** Spa STV Indoor swimming (H) Snooker Sauna Gym Croquet lawn Jacuzzi Archery Xmas **CONF:** Thtr 150 Class 80 Board 60 Del from £145 * **SERVICES:** Lift **PARKING:** 120 **NOTES:** No dogs (ex guide dogs) No smoking in restaurant Civ Wed 120
**CARDS:**

*See advert under DERBY*

## ROCHDALE, Greater Manchester Map 07 SD81

### ★★★★ 64% Norton Grange

Manchester Rd, Castleton OL11 2XZ
☎ 01706 630788 🖷 01706 649313
***Dir:*** *M62 junct 20 follow signs for A627 (M) Oldham then A664 Middleton/Manchester then follow signs for Castleton on A664 on left*

Situated in nine acres of grounds this Victorian house provides comfort in elegant surroundings. The well-equipped bedrooms have recently been refurbished. Public areas include the Pickwick Bistro and Bar and a smart restaurant, both offering a wide choice of freshly prepared dishes.
**ROOMS:** 51 en suite (28 fmly) No smoking in 25 bedrooms
**FACILITIES:** STV Xmas **CONF:** Thtr 250 Class 80 Board 60 Del from £100 * **SERVICES:** Lift **PARKING:** 150 **NOTES:** Civ Wed 250
**CARDS:**

## ROCHESTER, Kent Map 05 TQ76

### ★★★ 65% *Posthouse Rochester*

Maidstone Rd ME5 9SF
☎ 0870 400 9069 🖷 01634 684512
***Dir:*** *on A229 1m N of M2 jnct 3-from A229 head straight on over rdbt. Hotel and airport are signposted 100yds on the left*
This conveniently located hotel provides modern, well laid out bedrooms. At the time of our last inspection, there were plans to

*continued on p490*

ROCHESTER, continued

refurbish all ground-floor public areas, to introduce comfortable, modern facilities that complement the accommodation.
**ROOMS:** 145 en suite (45 fmly) No smoking in 93 bedrooms **FACILITIES:** Indoor swimming (H) Sauna Solarium Gym Jacuzzi Steam room Beautician available at charge **CONF:** Thtr 110 Class 48 Board 40 **SERVICES:** Lift **PARKING:** 250 **CARDS:**

### ★66% Royal Victoria & Bull Hotel

16-18 High St ME1 1PX
☎ 01634 846266 01634 832312
e-mail: reservations@ruandb.co.uk
***Dir:*** *from M25 or London follow A2 into Rochester. Take second right after large bridge (over Medway River) then first right. Hotel located on the left*
A historic coaching inn, once frequented by Charles Dickens. The large bar is popular with locals, as is the hotel's Italian restaurant. Bedrooms are spacious and well-equipped. Off street car parking is a bonus.
**ROOMS:** 28 rms (24 en suite) (2 fmly) s £52.50-£62.25; d £57.50-£90 (incl. bkfst) * **FACILITIES:** STV Jacuzzi **CONF:** Thtr 100 Class 60 Board 40 Del from £90 * **PARKING:** 25 **NOTES:** Closed 24 Dec-4 Jan
**CARDS:**

## ROCHFORD, Essex — Map 05 TQ89

### ★★★69% Hotel Renouf

Bradley Way SS4 1BU
☎ 01702 541334 01702 549563
e-mail: reception@hotelrenouf.fsnet.co.uk
***Dir:*** *turn off A127 onto B1013 to Rochford, at 3rd mini-rdbt turn right & keep right*

Owned and run by the Renouf family this modern style hotel is situated in the centre of town adjacent to the car park. There is a comfortable bar filled with cricket and sporting memorabilia as well as an attractive French restaurant overlooking the garden. Bedrooms are spacious, modern in style and well equipped.
**ROOMS:** 24 en suite (2 fmly) s £71.50-£81.50; d fr £81.50 (incl. cont bkfst) * **FACILITIES:** STV **CONF:** Thtr 30 Class 30 Board 20 **PARKING:** 25 **NOTES:** No smoking in restaurant Closed 26-31 Dec
**CARDS:**

*See advert on opposite page*

## ROMALDKIRK, Co Durham — Map 12 NY92

### ★★79% Rose & Crown

DL12 9EB
☎ 01833 650213 01833 650828
e-mail: hotel@rose-and-crown.co.uk
***Dir:*** *6m NW from Barnard Castle on B6277*
Located in a small village, this splendid Jacobean inn retains much of its original charm and character. It boasts a cosy pub with great

*continued*

bar food, a smart restaurant and a cosy lounge with lots to read. Stylish accommodation, all with luxurious bathrooms, includes refurbished bedrooms, two suites, and a stone-built row of spacious chalet-style rooms.

**ROOMS:** 7 en suite 5 annexe en suite (1 fmly) s £62; d £86 (incl. bkfst) * **LB** **FACILITIES:** STV **PARKING:** 20 **NOTES:** No smoking in restaurant Closed 24-26 Dec **CARDS:**

## ROMFORD, Greater London — Map 05 TQ58

### *Premier Lodge*

Whalebone Ln North, Chadwell Heath RM6 6QU
☎ 0870 700 1378 0870 700 1379

PREMIER LODGE

Premier Lodge offers modern, well-equipped, en suite accommodation suitable for both business and leisure travellers. Meals can be taken at the adjacent popular restaurant and bar, which is fully licensed. For further details, consult the Hotel Groups page.
**ROOMS:** 40 en suite

## ROMSEY, Hampshire — Map 04 SU32

### ★★★66% Potters Heron

Winchester Rd, Ampfield SO51 9ZF
☎ 023 8026 6611 023 8025 1359
e-mail: pottersheron@corushotels.com

corus

***Dir:*** *M3 junct 12 follow signs for Chandlers Ford at rdbt take 2nd exit, follow signs for Ampfield, go over crossrds, hotel is on left hand side after 1m*

This distinctive thatched hotel retains many original features. Extensive refurbishment has taken place to offer modern, stylish accommodation and spacious public areas. The re-styled pub and restaurant offers an interesting range of dishes to suit all tastes.
**ROOMS:** 54 en suite No smoking in 32 bedrooms s fr £53; d fr £106 (incl. bkfst) * **LB** **FACILITIES:** STV Sauna Xmas **CONF:** Thtr 120 Class 50 Board 45 Del from £105 * **SERVICES:** Lift **PARKING:** 150 **NOTES:** No smoking in restaurant Civ Wed 60
**CARDS:**

★★★60% **The White Horse**
Market Place SO51 8ZJ
☎ 0870 400 8123 🖷 01794 517485
e-mail: HeritageHotels_Romsey.White_Horse@Forte-Hotels.com
***Dir:*** *from M27 junct 3, follow A3057 to Romsey, then signs to town centre. Hotel can be seen on left, car park found on next turn in Latimer St*
Set in the heart of this historic town, the White Horse dates back to Elizabethan times. Bedrooms are very well-equipped and the hotel is about to benefit from a major refurbishment programme throughout bedrooms and public areas. The popular restaurant and the relaxing, characterful lounge are two particular attractions.
**ROOMS:** 26 en suite 7 annexe en suite (7 fmly) No smoking in 10 bedrooms s £70-£90; d £90-£110 * **LB** **FACILITIES:** Complimentary tickets for nearby leisure facilities Xmas **CONF:** Thtr 90 Class 60 Board 40 Del from £90 * **PARKING:** 40 **NOTES:** No smoking in restaurant
**CARDS:**

⌂ **Premier Lodge (Southampton)**
Romsey Rd, Ower SO51 6ZJ
☎ 0870 700 1542 🖷 0870 700 1543
***Dir:*** *Off M27 junct 2,follow A36 towards Salisbury, brown tourist sign saying'The Vine Inn'. 200yds on Romsey Rd on right*

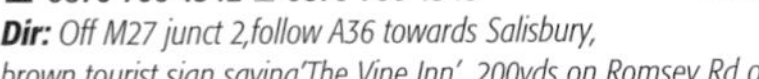

Premier Lodge offers modern, well-equipped, en suite accommodation suitable for both business and leisure travellers. Meals can be taken at the adjacent popular restaurant and bar, which is fully licensed. For further details, consult the Hotel Groups page.
**ROOMS:** 50 en suite s fr £46; d fr £46 * **CONF:** Thtr 150 Class 80 Board 60 Del from £85 *

ROSEDALE ABBEY, North Yorkshire — Map 08 SE79

★★★68% ***Blacksmith's Country Inn***
Hartoft End YO18 8EN
☎ 01751 417331 🖷 01751 417167
e-mail: blacksmiths.rosedale@virgin.net
***Dir:*** *A64 from York turn off for Pickering A169. In Pickering turn left for Thirsk A170. Turn left at Wrelton sign post to Hartoft 5m*

Set amongst the wooded valleys and hillsides of the Yorkshire Moors, this charming hotel offers a choice of popular bars and intimate, cosy lounges. A spacious restaurant serves excellent cuisine, and bedrooms, which vary in size, are all equipped to modern comfortable standards.
**ROOMS:** 18 en suite (1 fmly) **PARKING:** 60 **NOTES:** No smoking in restaurant **CARDS:**

*See advert on this page*

Early start? Hotels at all star levels should provide in-room alarm clocks and/or alarm calls.

*Hotel Renouf & Restaurant*

*is situated in Rochford, Essex and stands in one acre of landscaped gardens and blends easily into the architecture of the old town. With 23 bedrooms and suites, the hotel offers the height of luxury and comfort to match any in the country. The restaurant serves food of the highest standard with a two-tier menu to suit all pallets. There is also a set two or three course menu available Monday to Saturday. With a wide and varied selection of wines to compliment your meal, your enjoyment is assured. All bedrooms are tastefully decorated and have en-suite facilities (some with jacuzzi), colour TV with terrestrial and Sky channels. There are also tea and coffee making facilities.*

HOTEL
HR
RENOUF

**Hotel Renouf**
**Bradley Way, Rochford**
**Essex SS4 1BU**
**Tel: 01702 541334**
**Fax: 01702 549563**

RENOUF'S
RR
RESTAURANT

The
**Blacksmith's Country Inn**

ROSEDALE

Hartoft End, Rosedale Abbey
Pickering, North Yorkshire YO18 8EN
**Tel: (01751) 417331 Fax: (01751) 417167**

Set in the heart of the North Yorkshire Moors, this lovely 16th century hostelry has been fully refurbished to provide modern facilities yet retain all the original ambiance of years past. Cosy lounges, log fires. Enjoy superb food and wine in wonderful surroundings. Quality individual ensuite bedrooms some ground floor. Views over moors and forest. Resident owners.

R

ROSEDALE ABBEY, continued

**★★72% ◎◎ *Milburn Arms***
YO18 8RA
☎ 01751 417312 Fax 01751 417312
e-mail: info@milburnarms.com
***Dir:*** *7m N off A170 from Wrelton village*
Imagine a hotel serving high quality food, with no reception for mobile phones, nestling in a basin between the panoramic hills of North Yorkshire. Soft sofas, log fires, comfortable bedrooms and parts dating back to the 16th century create an idyllic retreat.
**ROOMS:** 3 en suite 8 annexe en suite (2 fmly) **CONF:** Thtr 48 Board 16 **PARKING:** 35 **NOTES:** No children 8yrs No smoking in restaurant Closed 23-27 Dec & 12-29 Jan Civ Wed 65 **CARDS:**

**★★65% White Horse Farm**
YO18 8SE
☎ 01751 417239 Fax 01751 417781
e-mail: sales@whitehorsefarmhotel.co.uk
***Dir:*** *turn off A170, follow signs to Rosedale for approx 7m, hotel sign points up steep hill out of village, hotel 300yds on left*
From its position above the village, this hotel enjoys lovely views over the moors. Bedrooms, whether in the main house or an adjoining building in the gardens, are individually and attractively decorated. Meals are served in the bar or in the restaurant, and there is also a cosy residents' lounge.
**ROOMS:** 11 en suite 4 annexe en suite (3 fmly) s £33-£47; d £75-£87 (incl. bkfst) * **LB** **FACILITIES:** pool,darts,dominoes ch fac Xmas **PARKING:** 100 **NOTES:** No smoking in restaurant
**CARDS:**

ROSSINGTON, South Yorkshire — Map 08 SK69

**★★★72% Mount Pleasant**
Great North Rd DN11 0HW
☎ 01302 868696 & 868219 Fax 01302 865130
e-mail: mountpleasant@fax.co.uk
***Dir:*** *on A638 Great North Rd between Bawtry and Doncaster*
This charming house dates back to the 18th century and stands in 100 acres of wooded parkland. The spacious bedrooms have been thoughtfully equipped and pleasantly furnished, the new Premier bedrooms being particularly comfortable. There are cosy lounges, a small bar and a traditionally styled restaurant.
**ROOMS:** 42 en suite (15 fmly) No smoking in all bedrooms s £59-£85; d £75-£99 * **LB** **CONF:** Thtr 100 Class 60 Board 60 Del £115 * **PARKING:** 100 **NOTES:** No dogs (ex guide dogs) No smoking in restaurant Closed 25 Dec Civ Wed 120
**CARDS:**

ROSS-ON-WYE, Herefordshire — Map 03 SO62
see also Goodrich and Symonds Yat

**★★★77% ◎◎ Pengethley Manor**
Pengethley Park HR9 6LL
☎ 01989 730211 Fax 01989 730238
e-mail: reservations@pengethleymanor.co.uk
***Dir:*** *4m N on A49 Hereford road*
This fine Georgian mansion is set in extensive grounds with two vineyards. The accommodation is tastefully appointed and there is a wide variety of bedroom styles, all similarly well-equipped. The elegant public rooms are furnished in a style sympathetic to the character of the house.

**ROOMS:** 11 en suite 14 annexe en suite (3 fmly) s £75-£115; d £120-£160 (incl. bkfst) * **LB** **FACILITIES:** Outdoor swimming (H) Golf 9 Fishing Snooker Croquet lawn Golf improvement course ch fac Xmas **CONF:** Thtr 50 Class 25 Board 28 Del £123.37 * **PARKING:** 70 **NOTES:** No smoking in restaurant Civ Wed 70
**CARDS:**

*See advert on opposite page*

**★★★71% ◎ *Hunsdon Manor***
Gloucester Rd, Weston under Penyard HR9 7PE
☎ 01989 562748 & 563376 & 768348 Fax 01989 768348
e-mail: hunsdon_manor@hotmail.com
***Dir:*** *two miles east of M50 on the A40 road to Gloucester*

Hunsdon Manor is built of mellow local sandstone and dates back to Elizabethan times. Set in extensive grounds, it stands in the village of Weston under Penyard and offers accommodation ranging from rooms large enough for family use, to some with four-posters, and some on the ground and first floors of cleverly converted buildings near the main house. Public rooms include a pleasant bar and a very attractive restaurant. A very popular venue for conferences.
**ROOMS:** 12 en suite 13 annexe en suite (3 fmly) **CONF:** Thtr 60 Class 46 Board 36 **PARKING:** 55 **CARDS:**

*See advert on opposite page*

**★★★69% ◎ Chase**
Gloucester Rd HR9 5LH
☎ 01989 763161 Fax 01989 768330
e-mail: info@chasehotel.co.uk
***Dir:*** *M50 junct 4, 1st left exit towards rdbt, left at rdbt towards A40. Right at 2nd rdbt towards Ross-on-Wye town centre, hotel 0.5m on left*
Just a short distance from the town centre this Regency mansion is set in extensive grounds and gardens. Bedrooms vary in size, all have modern furnishings and are well-equipped. Four-poster rooms are available. Public rooms include a bar and lounge and
*continued*

an attractive restaurant. Other facilities include conference rooms and a large function suite.

**ROOMS:** 36 en suite (1 fmly) No smoking in 10 bedrooms s fr £105; d fr £120 (incl. bkfst) * **LB** **FACILITIES:** STV fitness room **CONF:** Thtr 300 Class 100 Board 50 Del from £112.50 * **PARKING:** 200 **NOTES:** No dogs (ex guide dogs) No smoking in restaurant Closed 26-30 Dec Civ Wed 300 **CARDS:**

### ★★★68% Pencraig Court

Pencraig HR9 6HR
☎ 01989 770306 01989 770040
e-mail: mike@pencraig-court.co.uk
***Dir:*** *off A40, 4m S of Ross-on-Wye*

This large Georgian house stands in extensive grounds, with impressive views of the River Wye. Personally run, it provides well-equipped, traditionally furnished accommodation, including a

*continued on p494*

ROSS-ON-WYE, continued

room with a four-poster. There is no bar, but drinks are dispensed in both lounges and the restaurant.
**ROOMS:** 11 en suite (1 fmly) s £50-£53; d £70-£75 (incl. bkfst) * **LB** **FACILITIES:** Fishing Riding Croquet lawn ch fac **CONF:** Del from £100 * **PARKING:** 20 **NOTES:** No smoking in restaurant
**CARDS:**

*See advert on opposite page*

### ★★★66% The Royal

Palace Pound HR9 5HZ
☎ 01989 565105 01989 768058
***Dir:*** *at end of M50 take A40 'Monmouth'. At 3rd rdbt, take left to Ross, over bridge and take road signed 'The Royal Hotel' after left hand bend*

A new owner took over this hotel at the beginning of 2000 and at the time of our last inspection, he had made a lot of improvements to the public areas and bedrooms. The hotel enjoys a delightful location overlooking the River Wye and just a few minutes' walk from the town centre. Facilities here include a comfortable lounge, an attractively appointed restaurant and a lovely garden
**ROOMS:** 42 en suite (3 fmly) No smoking in 18 bedrooms s £65-£85; d £95-£135 (incl. bkfst) * **LB** **FACILITIES:** STV Xmas **CONF:** Thtr 85 Class 20 Board 28 Del from £100 * **PARKING:** 38 **NOTES:** No smoking in restaurant Civ Wed 60 **CARDS:**

### ★★74% Glewstone Court

Glewstone HR9 6AW
☎ 01989 770367 01989 770282
e-mail: glewstone@aol.com
***Dir:*** *from Ross Market Place take A40/A49 Monmouth/Hereford, over Wilton Bridge to rdbt, turn left onto A40 to Monmouth, after 1m turn right for Glewstone*

This charming hotel is set in delightful grounds and provides a friendly and relaxed environment for both leisure and business guests. The kitchen offers a thoughtful menu of well-executed dishes. Throughout, the hotel is decorated and furnished with great flair.
**ROOMS:** 8 en suite (2 fmly) s £45-£60; d £75-£90 (incl. bkfst) * **LB** **FACILITIES:** Croquet lawn ch fac **CONF:** Thtr 35 Board 16 Del from £95 * **PARKING:** 25 **NOTES:** Closed 25-27 Dec
**CARDS:**

### ★★71% Wilton Court Hotel

Wilton Ln HR9 6AQ
☎ 01989 562569 01989 768460
e-mail: info@wiltoncourthotel.com
***Dir:*** *M50 junct 4 onto A40 towards Monmouth at 3rd rdbt turn left signed Ross then take 1st right, hotel on right facing river*
This personally-run 16th-century inn has a wealth of charm and character. It stands on the northern bank of the River Wye, looking towards Ross-on-Wye. The bedrooms are comfortable, tastefully furnished and well-equipped. Public areas include a comfortable lounge, a traditional bar and a pleasant restaurant with a conservatory extension, overlooking the garden.
**ROOMS:** 11 en suite (1 fmly) s £45-£70; d £65-£95 (incl. bkfst) * **LB** **FACILITIES:** Fishing Xmas **PARKING:** 24 **CARDS:**

### ★★70% Castle Lodge Hotel

Wilton HR9 6AD
☎ 01989 562234 01989 768322
e-mail: carlos@castlelodge.co.uk
***Dir:*** *on rdbt at junct of A40/A49, 0.5m from centre of Ross-on-Wye*
Considerable upgrading and improvements have been made to this personally run hotel over the last two or three years. It dates back to the 16th century and provides pleasant bedrooms, all of which are well-equipped. A good range of bar meals is offered, together with a varied restaurant menu. Fish dishes are something of a speciality here. A large function room is available.
**ROOMS:** 10 en suite (3 fmly) s fr £39.95; d fr £48.95 * **LB** **FACILITIES:** tennis courts(0.5m) **CONF:** Thtr 100 Class 80 Board 60 **PARKING:** 40 **CARDS:**

### ★★66% Bridge House

Wilton HR9 6AA
☎ 01989 562655 01989 567652
e-mail: alison@bhhotel.fsnet.co.uk
***Dir:*** *0.5m N of Ross-on-Wye, at joining of A40/A49 is a rdbt at Wilton, hotel 200yds from rdbt, towards Ross, at end of Wilton Bridge*
This Georgian house has a large garden extending to the bank of the River Wye. The privately owned and personally run hotel has a well-deserved reputation for friendliness. Modern equipped accommodation includes several spacious rooms, and one with a four-poster bed.
**ROOMS:** 8 en suite (1 fmly) s £37.50-£39.95; d £56-£58 (incl. bkfst) **LB** **FACILITIES:** Xmas **PARKING:** 14 **NOTES:** No smoking in restaurant
**CARDS:**

### ★★66% Chasedale

Walford Rd HR9 5PQ
☎ 01989 562423 01989 567900
e-mail: chasedale@supanet.com
***Dir:*** *from Ross-on-Wye town centre head south on B4234, hotel 0.5m on left*
A large, mid-Victorian country house in extensive gardens, the Chasedale provides well-equipped accommodation, including ground floor and family rooms. There is a spacious lounge, and the restaurant offers a good selection of wholesome food.
**ROOMS:** 10 en suite (2 fmly) No smoking in 1 bedroom s £31.50-£34.50; d £63-£69 (incl. bkfst) * **LB** **FACILITIES:** Xmas **CONF:** Thtr 40 Class 30 Board 25 **PARKING:** 14 **NOTES:** No smoking in restaurant
**CARDS:**

R

**★★65% Orles Barn**
Wilton HR9 6AE
☎ 01989 562155 🖹 01989 768470
e-mail: orles.barn@clara.net
***Dir:*** *off junct A40/A49*

THE CIRCLE
Selected Individual Hotels
GREAT BRITAIN

This privately owned and personally run hotel stands in extensive gardens, which include an outdoor heated swimming pool. Bedrooms are well maintained and well-equipped. The owners' South African heritage is reflected in the restaurant menu.
**ROOMS:** 9 en suite (1 fmly) s fr £41; d fr £53 * **LB**
**FACILITIES:** Outdoor swimming (H) Fishing ch fac **CONF:** Board 16
**PARKING:** 16 **NOTES:** No smoking in restaurant
**CARDS:**

○ ***King's Head***
8 High St HR9 5HL
☎ 01989 763174 🖹 01989 769578
e-mail: enquiries@kingshead.co.uk
***Dir:*** *near Ancient Town Centre on the High St*
At the time of going to press, the star classification for this hotel was not confirmed. Please refer to the AA internet site www.theAA.com for current information.
**ROOMS:** 14 en suite 11 annexe en suite (6 fmly) **PARKING:** 26
**NOTES:** No smoking in restaurant Closed 24-26 Dec
**CARDS:**

## ROSTHWAITE, Cumbria — Map 11 NY21
see also Borrowdale

**★★63% Scafell**
CA12 5XB
☎ 017687 77208 🖹 017687 77280
e-mail: info@scafell.ws
***Dir:*** *6m S of Keswick on B5289*

This friendly hotel is run by experienced staff. A good range of imaginative dishes is presented in the spacious dining room, or you can enjoy meals all day during the summer in the less formal Riverside Inn pub. There is a wide choice of accommodation, the most stylish rooms being in the main house.
**ROOMS:** 24 en suite (2 fmly) s £64; d £127 (incl. bkfst & dinner) * **LB**
**FACILITIES:** Xmas **PARKING:** 50 **NOTES:** No smoking in restaurant Civ Wed 75 **CARDS:**

## ROTHERHAM, South Yorkshire — Map 08 SK49

**★★★★62% Hellaby Hall**
Old Hellaby Ln, Hellaby S66 8SN
☎ 01709 702701 🖹 01709 700979
e-mail: hellabyhallreservations@paramount-hotels.co.uk
PARAMOUNT GROUP OF HOTELS
***Dir:*** *1m off M18 junct 1 onto the A631 towards Bawtry from Rotherham, in village of Hellaby*
This 17th-century hotel was built according to a Flemish design
*continued on p496*

R

ROTHERHAM, continued

with high, beamed ceilings and staircases which lead off to a series of oak-panelled lounges. Bedrooms are all elegant. Guests can dine in the Attic Restaurant or Rizzio's.
**ROOMS:** 52 en suite (4 fmly) No smoking in 15 bedrooms s fr £90; d fr £105 * LB **FACILITIES:** Spa STV Indoor swimming (H) Sauna Solarium Gym Croquet lawn Putting green Jacuzzi entertainment Xmas **CONF:** Thtr 140 Class 75 Board 40 Del from £125 * **SERVICES:** Lift **PARKING:** 235 **NOTES:** No smoking in restaurant Civ Wed 100
**CARDS:**

### ★★★ 74% Consort

Brampton Rd, Thurcroft S66 9JA
☎ 01709 530022 01709 531529
e-mail: info@consorthotel.com
***Dir:*** *M18 J1, R twds Bawtry on A631 50yds turn R, 1.5m x-rds, hotel opp.*
Bedrooms at this modern, friendly hotel are comfortable and attractive, and include a new wing of ten superior rooms. A wide range of dishes is served in the bar and restaurant, and entertainment evenings are often hosted here.
**ROOMS:** 27 en suite (2 fmly) No smoking in 6 bedrooms s £42-£72; d £62-£82 (incl. bkfst) * LB **FACILITIES:** STV **CONF:** Thtr 300 Class 120 Board 50 Del from £56 * **PARKING:** 90 **NOTES:** No dogs (ex guide dogs) No smoking in restaurant
**CARDS:**

*See advert on opposite page*

### ★★★ 68% Best Western Elton

Main St, Bramley S66 2SF
☎ 01709 545681 01709 549100
e-mail: bestwestern.eltonhotel@btinternet.com
***Dir:*** *0.5m E A631, from M18 junct 1 follow A631 Rotherham, turn right to Ravenfield, hotel at end Bramley village*

Within easy reach of the M18, this welcoming, stone-built hotel has well-tended gardens. It offers good modern accommodation; the larger rooms located in a separate building are particularly comfortable and well-equipped.
**ROOMS:** 13 en suite 16 annexe en suite (4 fmly) No smoking in 11 bedrooms s £60-£80; d £98 (incl. bkfst) * LB **FACILITIES:** STV **CONF:** Thtr 55 Class 24 Board 26 Del from £85 * **PARKING:** 48 **NOTES:** Civ Wed 50 **CARDS:**

### ★★★ 68% Courtyard by Marriott, Rotherham

West Bawtry Rd S60 4NA
☎ 01709 830630 01709 830549
e-mail: rotherham@courtyardhotels.co.uk
***Dir:*** *M1 junct 33, A630 towards Rotherham, hotel 0.5m on R*
Stylish and contemporary, this modern hotel is well located, being just five minutes from the motorway. Bedrooms are spacious with an excellent range of facilities. Guests have the use of the popular leisure club with its swimming pool, spa bath and steam room.

*continued*

**ROOMS:** 100 en suite (6 fmly) No smoking in 71 bedrooms s £83; d £83 * LB **FACILITIES:** Spa STV Indoor swimming (H) Solarium Gym Jacuzzi Steam room Childrens pool Xmas **CONF:** Thtr 300 Class 120 Board 40 Del £130 * **SERVICES:** Lift **PARKING:** 222 **NOTES:** No dogs (ex guide dogs) Civ Wed 100 **CARDS:**

### ★★★ 59% Carlton Park

102/104 Moorgate Rd S60 2BG
☎ 01709 849955 01709 368960
e-mail: 114317.2341@compuserve.com
***Dir:*** *M1 J33, R onto A631 and L onto A618. Hotel 800yds past Hospital*

This modern hotel is situated in a pleasant residential area. Bedrooms are furnished in a modern style and three have separate sitting rooms. The "Nelsons" Restaurant and Bar is lively.
**ROOMS:** 76 en suite (6 fmly) No smoking in 33 bedrooms s £79; d £79 * LB **FACILITIES:** STV Sauna Solarium Gym Jacuzzi entertainment Xmas **CONF:** Thtr 250 Class 160 Board 60 Del £99 * **SERVICES:** Lift **PARKING:** 120 **NOTES:** Civ Wed 100 **CARDS:**

### Campanile

Hellaby Industrial Estate, Lowton Way, Denby Way S66 8RY
☎ 01709 700255 01709 545169
***Dir:*** *M18 junct 1. Follow Maltby off rdbt. L at lights, 2nd rd on L*

HOTEL
Campanile

This modern building offers accommodation in smart, well-

*continued*

equipped bedrooms, all with en suite bathrooms. Refreshments may be taken at the informal Bistro. For further details and the Campanile phone number, consult the Hotel Groups page.
**ROOMS:** 50 en suite s £38.50; d £38.50 * **CONF:** Thtr 35 Class 18 Board 20

### Hotel Ibis

ibis
Accor hotels

Moorhead Way, Bramley S66 1YY
☎ 01709 730333 01709 730444
e-mail: H3163@accor-hotels.com
**Dir:** *M18 junct 1, left at rdbt & left at 1st t/lights. Hotel next to supermarket*
Modern, budget hotel offering comfortable accommodation in bright and practical bedrooms. Breakfast is self-service and dinner is available in the restaurant. For further details, consult the Hotel Groups page.
**ROOMS:** 86 en suite s £42; d £42 * **CONF:** Thtr 40 Class 12 Board 20 Del £80 *

## ROTHERWICK, Hampshire — Map 04 SU75

### Premier Collection

### ★★★★ Tylney Hall

RG27 9AZ
☎ 01256 764881 01256 768141
e-mail: sales@tylneyhall.com
**Dir:** *M3 junct 5-A287 to Basingstoke, over junct with A30, over railway bridge, towards Newnham. Right at Newnham Green. Hotel 1m on left*
Tylney Hall Hotel is a splendid Grade II listed Victorian country house set in 66 acres of beautiful parkland. It offers very high standards of comfort in the most elegant surroundings. The restored water gardens, which were originally laid out by Gertrude Jekyll, are stunning. Public rooms feature the Wedgwood drawing room and panelled Oak Room, filled with fresh flowers and warmed by log fires. The comfortable bedrooms are traditionally furnished.
**ROOMS:** 35 en suite 75 annexe en suite (1 fmly) s £125-£385; d £159-£410 (incl. bkfst) * **LB** **FACILITIES:** STV Indoor swimming (H) Outdoor swimming (H) Tennis (hard) Snooker Sauna Gym Croquet lawn Jacuzzi Clay pigeon shooting Archery Falconry Xmas **CONF:** Thtr 110 Class 70 Board 40 **PARKING:** 120 **NOTES:** No dogs (ex guide dogs) No smoking in restaurant Civ Wed 100
**CARDS:**

## ROTHLEY, Leicestershire — Map 08 SK51

### ★★★64% *Rothley Court*

OLD ENGLISH INNS

Westfield Ln LE7 7LG
☎ 0116 237 4141 0116 237 4483
**Dir:** *on B5328*
Located at the end of a sweeping drive in six acres of grounds, this hotel dates from the 1500s and has a wealth of historic features. Approximately half the bedrooms are in the main house, the remainder being in the old stable block. As well as an oak-panelled restaurant, the hotel has private dining facilities and function rooms.
**ROOMS:** 13 en suite 21 annexe en suite No smoking in 14 bedrooms **CONF:** Thtr 100 Class 35 Board 35 **PARKING:** 100 **NOTES:** No smoking in restaurant **CARDS:**

Popped the question? Hotels with Civ Wed in their entry are licensed for civil wedding ceremonies. Maximum numbers for the ceremony only are shown, e.g. Civ Wed 120

R

ROTHLEY, continued

**★★72% The Limes**
35 Mountsorrel Ln LE7 7PS
☎ 0116 230 2531
***Dir:*** *turn of old A6, Hotel off village green*
The Limes is owned and run by enthusiastic proprietors. Public areas offer a comfortable lounge bar and a smart restaurant. The well-maintained accommodation is equipped for the needs of the predominantly business clientele, with excellent facilities and comfortable executive swivel chairs. Secure car parking is a bonus.
**ROOMS:** 11 en suite s £42.50-£45; d fr £55 (incl. bkfst) *
**FACILITIES:** STV **SERVICES:** air con **PARKING:** 15 **NOTES:** No dogs (ex guide dogs) No children 14yrs Closed 23 Dec-2 Jan
**CARDS:**

## ROWSLEY, Derbyshire Map 08 SK26

**★★★74% East Lodge Country House**
DE4 2EF
☎ 01629 734474 01629 733949
e-mail: info@eastlodge.com
***Dir:*** *A6, Rowsley Village, 3m from Bakewell, 5m from Matlock*

A delightful country house hotel situated in ten acres of attractive grounds and gardens. Public areas and most bedrooms are furnished to a very comfortable standard and a new conservatory lounge has been added to the front of the hotel. The main restaurant, which is well known for the quality of its cuisine, is open for lunch and dinner and lighter meals are available in the lounges.
**ROOMS:** 15 en suite (2 fmly) s £75-£90; d £95-£130 (incl. bkfst) * LB
**FACILITIES:** Croquet lawn Xmas **CONF:** Thtr 75 Class 20 Board 22 Del from £130 * **PARKING:** 25 **NOTES:** No dogs No smoking in restaurant Civ Wed 74 **CARDS:**
*See advert under BAKEWELL*

## RUAN HIGH LANES, Cornwall & Isles of Scilly Map 02 SW93

**★★73% Hundred House**
TR2 5JR
☎ 01872 501336 01872 501151
e-mail: eccles@hundredhousehotel.co.uk
***Dir:*** *from A390, 4m W of St Austell turn left onto B3287 to Tregony/St Mawes, turn left onto A3078 to St Mawes, hotel 4m along on right*
This Edwardian house on the Roseland Peninsula lies in one of the prettiest parts of Cornwall. The grounds and gardens are beautifully kept and include a croquet lawn. The house is tastefully furnished with fine antiques and pictures, and the bedrooms offer modern comforts and facilities. Guests meet in the bar before enjoying fine cuisine in the restaurant.
**ROOMS:** 10 en suite No smoking in all bedrooms s £64-£71; d £128-£142 (incl. bkfst & dinner) * LB **FACILITIES:** Croquet lawn
**PARKING:** 15 **NOTES:** No children 8yrs No smoking in restaurant Closed Nov-Feb **CARDS:**

## RUGBY, Warwickshire Map 04 SP57

**★★★66% *Brownsover Hall***
Brownsover Ln, Old Brownsover CV21 1HU REGAL
☎ 01788 546100 01788 579241
***Dir:*** *come off M6 junct 1 and follow signs to Rugby A426, follow dual carriageway for 0.5m until slip road to right, follow for 400m, hotel on right*

A mock-Gothic hall in seven acres of wooded parkland. Bedrooms are spacious and well-equipped, the sixteen new rooms in the converted stable block are a delight. The former chapel makes a stylish restaurant with mullion windows and stately chandeliers. For a less formal meal or a relaxing drink, the rugby themed bar is popular.
**ROOMS:** 27 en suite 20 annexe en suite (3 fmly) No smoking in 31 bedrooms **FACILITIES:** STV **CONF:** Thtr 70 Class 36 Board 35
**PARKING:** 100 **NOTES:** No smoking in restaurant Civ Wed 56
**CARDS:**

**★★★64% *Posthouse Northampton/Rugby*** Posthouse
NN6 7XR
☎ 0870 400 9059 01788 823955
(For full entry see Crick)

**★★★58% *Grosvenor Hotel Rugby***
81-87 Clifton Rd CV21 3QQ
☎ 01788 535686 01788 541297
***Dir:*** *M6 junct 1, turn right on to A426 towards Rugby centre, at first rdbt turn left continue to T junct and turn right onto B5414 hotel in 2m on right*

Close to the town centre, this family owned hotel is popular with
*continued*

both business and leisure guests. Bedrooms come in a variety of styles and sizes, including several new rooms. The public rooms are cosy, inviting and pleasantly furnished and service is both friendly and attentive.
**ROOMS:** 26 en suite (3 fmly) **FACILITIES:** Indoor swimming (H) Sauna Solarium Jacuzzi **CONF:** Thtr 30 Class 20 Board 30 **PARKING:** 50
**NOTES:** No dogs (ex guide dogs) **CARDS:**

### ★★65% *Hillmorton Manor*
78 High St, Hillmorton CV21 4EE
☎ 01788 565533 & 572403 📠 01788 540027
***Dir:*** *leave M1 junct 18 & onto A428 to Rugby*
This Victorian manor house on the outskirts of Rugby offers a delightful combination of home and hotel, with an attractive airy restaurant, and a comfortable bar and lounge. The bedrooms vary in size and are comfortable and well-equipped.
**ROOMS:** 11 en suite (1 fmly) **CONF:** Class 30 Board 65 **PARKING:** 40
**NOTES:** No smoking in restaurant **CARDS:**

### ★★64% *Whitefields Hotel Golf & Country Club*
MINOTEL Great Britain
Coventry Rd, Thurlaston CV23 9JR
☎ 01788 521800 & 522393 📠 01788 521695
***Dir:*** *4m SW close to junc 1 M45*

A purpose-built hotel situated on an 18-hole golf course. Bedrooms come in varying styles and sizes, with ground-floor rooms being generally more spacious; a new wing of bedrooms is now complete. An open-plan bar and lounge offers comfortable seating, and there are several well-equipped conference suites available; public areas are shared with golf club members.
**ROOMS:** 34 en suite (2 fmly) No smoking in all bedrooms
**FACILITIES:** STV Golf 18 Fishing Putting green Driving range
**CONF:** Thtr 80 Class 50 Board 45 **PARKING:** 150 **NOTES:** No dogs (ex guide dogs) **CARDS:**

### ⌂ Express by Holiday Inn Rugby
Express by Holiday Inn
Brownsover Rd CV21 1HL
☎ 01788 550333 📠 01788 550666
A modern budget hotel offering comfortable accommodation in refreshing, spacious and comprehensively equipped bedrooms, en suite bathrooms with power showers and continental buffet breakfast included in the room rate. Suitable for business travellers or families. For further details and the Express by Holiday Inn phone number, consult the Hotel Groups page.

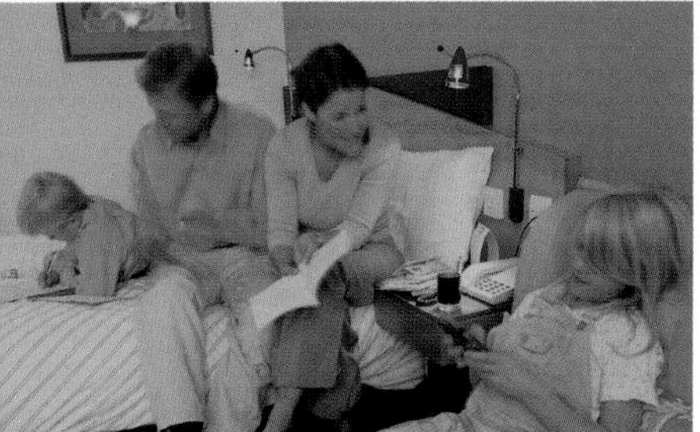

**ROOMS:** 49 en suite (incl. cont bkfst) s £50-£53; d £50-£53 *
**CONF:** Thtr 30 Class 12 Board 16

### ○ Golden Lion Inn
Easenhall CV23 0JA
☎ 01788 832265
At the time of going to press, the star classification for this hotel was not confirmed. Please refer to the AA internet site www.theAA.com for current information.

### ○ Innkeeper's Lodge Rugby
Innkeeper's Lodge
The Green, Dunchurch CV22 6NJ
A new concept in the travel accommodation market. Smart rooms meet essential business requirements but also have home comforts. Dining options include all-day menus plus the added advantage of breakfast, which is included in the room price. Reservations can be made seven days a week through the room reservations number: 0870 243 0500. For further details, consult the Hotel Groups page.
**ROOMS:** 16 en suite **NOTES:** Opening Summer 2001

## RUGELEY, Staffordshire
Map 07 SK01

### ⌂ *Travelodge*
Travelodge
Western Springs Rd WS15 2AS
☎ 01889 570096 📠 01889 570096
***Dir:*** *on A51/B5013*
Travelodge offers good quality, good value, modern accommodation. Ideal for families, the spacious, en suite bedrooms include remote-control TV, tea and coffee-making facilities, luxury beds and free morning newspaper. Meals can be taken at the nearby family restaurant. For further details and the Travelodge phone number, consult the Hotel Groups page.

**ROOMS:** 32 en suite

Late for dinner? Quality Standards star rating means that last orders for dinner should be no earlier than:
★ 6.30pm ★★ 7.00pm ★★★ 8.00pm
★★★★ 9.00pm ★★★★★ 10.00pm

R

RUISLIP, Greater London
See LONDON SECTION plan 1 A5

### ★★★65% Barn Hotel
West End Rd HA4 6JB
☎ 01895 636057 01895 638379
e-mail: info@thebarnhotel.co.uk
**Dir:** *take A4180 (Polish War Memorial) exit off the A40 to Ruislip, 2m to hotel entrance off a mini rdbt before Ruislip Underground Station*

The oldest parts of this sympathetically extended hotel date back to 1628. Today, there is a mixture of older rooms, with beams and uneven floors, and recently added modern rooms. All are comfortable and feature a good range of extra facilities. Snacks are served in the informal bar or meals can be taken in the Leaning Barn Restaurant.
**ROOMS:** 59 en suite (3 fmly) No smoking in 3 bedrooms s fr £125; d fr £160 (incl. bkfst) * LB **FACILITIES:** STV Xmas **CONF:** Thtr 80 Class 50 Board 30 Del from £110 * **PARKING:** 42 **NOTES:** No dogs No smoking in restaurant Civ Wed 65
**CARDS:**

*See advert on page 499*

RUNCORN, Cheshire Map 07 SJ58

### ★★★66% Posthouse Warrington/Runcorn
Posthouse
Wood Ln, Beechwood WA7 3HA
☎ 0870 400 9070 01928 714611
**Dir:** *M56 junct 12, turn left at roundabout then 100 yards on left turn into Halton Station Road under a railway bridge and continue into Wood Lane*
This modern hotel offers extensive conference, meeting and leisure facilities. Bedrooms, some of which have recently been upgraded, are well-equipped. The spacious restaurant is open for lunch and dinner and an all day menu is provided in the lounge and bar. Twenty-four hour room service is also available.
**ROOMS:** 150 en suite No smoking in 112 bedrooms s £79-£99; d £79-£99 * LB **FACILITIES:** Spa STV Indoor swimming (H) Sauna Solarium Gym Jacuzzi Steam room Xmas **CONF:** Thtr 500 Class 60 Board 36 Del £125 * **SERVICES:** Lift **PARKING:** 210 **NOTES:** Civ Wed 200
**CARDS:**

### ⇧ Campanile
Campanile
Lowlands Rd WA7 5TP
☎ 01928 581771 01928 581730
**Dir:** *leave M56 at junct 12, take A557, then follow signs for Runcorn railway station*
This modern building offers accommodation in smart, well-equipped bedrooms, all with en suite bathrooms. Refreshments

*continued*

may be taken at the informal Bistro. For further details and the Campanile phone number, consult the Hotel Groups page.

**ROOMS:** 53 en suite **CONF:** Thtr 35 Class 28 Board 20 Del £68 *

RUSHDEN, Northamptonshire Map 04 SP96

### ⇧ *Travelodge*
Travelodge
Saunders Lodge NN10 9AP
☎ 01933 57008 01933 57008
**Dir:** *on A45, eastbound*
Travelodge offers good quality, good value, modern accommodation. Ideal for families, the spacious, en suite bedrooms include remote-control TV, tea and coffee-making facilities, luxury beds and free morning newspaper. Meals can be taken at the nearby family restaurant. For further details and the Travelodge phone number, consult the Hotel Groups page.

**ROOMS:** 40 en suite

RUSHYFORD, Co Durham Map 08 NZ22

### ★★★68% Swallow Eden Arms Hotel
SWALLOW HOTELS
DL17 0LL
☎ 01388 720541 01388 721871
e-mail: edenarms.swallow@whitbread.com
**Dir:** *follow A689 to Rushyford rbt. Hotel on opposite side of rbt*

Eden Arms

Nestling between the city of Durham and the North York Moors, this 17th-century coaching inn is an ideal venue for a complete break. The hotel also offers well-equipped leisure facilities for those guests who don't want to venture too far. It has excellent transport links and is easily accessible by road, rail and air.
**ROOMS:** 45 en suite (4 fmly) No smoking in 20 bedrooms s fr £85; d £115-£140 (incl. bkfst) * LB **FACILITIES:** Spa STV Indoor swimming (H) Sauna Solarium Gym Steam room Plunge Pool entertainment Xmas **CONF:** Thtr 100 Class 40 Board 50 Del from £100 * **PARKING:** 200 **NOTES:** No dogs (ex guide dogs) No smoking in restaurant Civ Wed 120
**CARDS:**

RUSTINGTON, West Sussex Map 04 TQ00

### Travelodge

Worthing Rd BN17 6JN
☎ 01903 733150 01903 733150
***Dir:*** *on A259, 1m E of Littlehampton*
Travelodge offers good quality, good value, modern accommodation. Ideal for families, the spacious, en suite bedrooms include remote-control TV, tea and coffee-making facilities, luxury beds and free morning newspaper. Meals can be taken at the nearby family restaurant. For further details and the Travelodge phone number, consult the Hotel Groups page.

**ROOMS:** 36 en suite

RYDE See Wight, Isle of

RYE, East Sussex Map 05 TQ92

### ★★★74% Flackley Ash

TN31 6YH
☎ 01797 230651 01797 230510
e-mail: flackleyash@marstonhotels.co.uk
(For full entry see Peasmarsh)

### ★★★69% Mermaid Inn

Mermaid St TN31 7EY
☎ 01797 223065 & 223788 01797 225069
e-mail: mermaidinnrye@btclick.com
***Dir:*** *A259, follow signposts to town centre then up Mermaid St*
This famous smugglers' inn is steeped in history and is now a beautifully presented hotel. The interior has ancient beamed ceilings and attractive stone work. The bedrooms vary in size and shape but are all furnished with antique furniture. The attractive public rooms include cosy lounge areas and the restaurant.
**ROOMS:** 31 en suite (5 fmly) s £70-£75; d £140-£160 (incl. bkfst) * **LB**
**FACILITIES:** Xmas **CONF:** Thtr 80 Class 50 Board 40 Del from £125 *
**PARKING:** 25 **NOTES:** No dogs No smoking in restaurant
**CARDS:**

### ★★★62% The George

High St TN31 7JP
☎ 01797 222114 01797 224065
Right in the heart of this historic town, near the myriad of small specialist shops, The George is full of character with cosy public rooms reflecting the period of the building. The majority of bedrooms have been sympathetically modernised and are well-equipped. Although the restaurant is small, it blends in well with the architecture and style of the building.
**ROOMS:** 22 en suite No smoking in 5 bedrooms **CONF:** Thtr 100 Class 40 Board 40 **PARKING:** 7 **NOTES:** No smoking in restaurant
**CARDS:**

### ★★71% Broomhill Lodge

Rye Foreign TN31 7UN
☎ 01797 280421 01797 280402
***Dir:*** *1.5m N on A268*
Built in the 1820s and set in its own grounds of three acres, this hotel is within easy reach of the historic Cinque Ports town of Rye. Bedrooms are individually decorated, comfortably furnished and well-equipped. There are two lounges and an attractive restaurant.
**ROOMS:** 12 en suite **FACILITIES:** Sauna Mini gym **CONF:** Thtr 60 Class 60 Board 30 **PARKING:** 20 **NOTES:** No dogs No smoking in restaurant
**CARDS:**



ST AGNES, Cornwall & Isles of Scilly Map 02 SW75

### ★★★70% Rose in Vale Country House

Rose in Vale, Mithian TR5 0QD
☎ 01872 552202 01872 552700
e-mail: reception@rose-in-vale-hotel.co.uk
***Dir:*** *From A30 onto B3284 towards Perranporth, cross A3075 after 0.75m take 3rd left for Rose-in-Vale, hotel 0.5m on left*
Peacefully located in a wooded valley, this Georgian manor house is set in spacious gardens including a pond with waterfowl and an area for croquet. The majority of rooms overlook the gardens, accommodation varies in size and style; several rooms are situated on the ground floor. Each evening in the spacious restaurant, an imaginative fixed price menu and a carte are offered. A warm welcome is assured to guests by the resident proprietors and their loyal team of staff.
**ROOMS:** 18 en suite (4 fmly) s £54.50; d £93-£113 (incl. bkfst) * **LB**
**FACILITIES:** Outdoor swimming (H) Sauna Solarium Croquet lawn Jacuzzi Badminton Table tennis Billiards Scenic flights in hotel's own aeroplane Xmas **CONF:** Thtr 65 Class 50 Board 40 Del from £79 *
**PARKING:** 40 **NOTES:** No smoking in restaurant Closed Jan-Feb Civ Wed 75 **CARDS:**

### ★★70% Rosemundy House

Rosemundy Hill TR5 0UF
☎ 01872 552101 01872 554000
e-mail: info@rosemundy.co.uk
***Dir:*** *turn off A30 to St Agnes continue for approx 3m on entering village take 1st turning on the right signposted Rosemundy, hotel is at foot of the hill*
Sympathetically extended to provide comfortable accommodation, this elegant Queen Anne house is quietly located within well-

*continued on p502*

S

ST AGNES, continued

maintained gardens. Guests can be assured of friendly and relaxed service from the mainly local staff. In the restaurant, both fixed price and carte menus are offered, using fresh local produce.

*Rosemundy House, St Agnes*

**ROOMS:** 43 en suite (10 fmly) s £25-£43; d £50-£86 (incl. bkfst) * **LB** **FACILITIES:** Outdoor swimming (H) Croquet lawn Putting green Xmas **PARKING:** 50 **NOTES:** No dogs (ex guide dogs) **CARDS:**

### ★★67% Sunholme

Goonvrea Rd TR5 0NW
☎ 01872 552318 📠 01872 552318
e-mail: jefferies@sunholme.co.uk
***Dir:*** *on B3277, Museum on left at mini rdbt, follow brown & white signs*

Enjoying spectacular views over the surrounding countryside to the sea, this personally run hotel is set in attractive grounds on the southern slopes of St Agnes Beacon. Guests are assured of a friendly welcome, and many return on a regular basis to partake of the relaxed atmosphere. Bedrooms are well-equipped and offer good levels of comfort. The intimate bar is an ideal venue for guests to meet before dinner before retiring to relax in the lounge.
**ROOMS:** 10 en suite (3 fmly) No smoking in 9 bedrooms s £24-£45; d £48-£70 (incl. bkfst) * **LB** **FACILITIES:** Xmas **PARKING:** 12 **NOTES:** No smoking in restaurant **CARDS:**

## ST ALBANS, Hertfordshire Map 04 TL10

### ★★★★74% Sopwell House Hotel, Country Club & Spa

Cottonmill Ln, Sopwell AL1 2HQ
☎ 01727 864477 📠 01727 844741/845636
e-mail: enquiries@sopwellhouse.co.uk
***Dir:*** *Exit M25 junct 22 following signs A1081 St Albans. At grill bar traffic lights, turn left, over mini rndbt into Cottonmill Lane*

Sopwell House is an imposing country house hotel, which although extensive, maintains an exclusive ambience. Whether enjoying the manicured grounds, an afternoon in the spa or a meal in either the brassiere or conservatory restaurant, staff are warm and courteous. Bedrooms vary in style, although all ensure that guests relax in comfort. Meeting and function rooms are across the courtyard from both the hotel and the self-contained cottages within the Sopwell Mews.
**ROOMS:** 112 en suite 16 annexe en suite (6 fmly) s £125; d £165 * **LB** **FACILITIES:** **Spa** STV Indoor swimming (H) Sauna Solarium Gym Jacuzzi Hairdressing salon Xmas **CONF:** Thtr 400 Class 220 Board 90 Del from £199 * **SERVICES:** Lift **PARKING:** 360 **NOTES:** No smoking in restaurant Civ Wed 300 **CARDS:**

### ★★★77% St Michael's Manor

Fishpool St AL3 4RY
☎ 01727 864444 📠 01727 848909
e-mail: smmanor@globalnet.co.uk
***Dir:*** *from St Albans Abbey follow Fishpool Street toward St Michael's village. Hotel located 0.5m on left hand side*

PRIDE OF BRITAIN MEMBER

Fishpool Street boasts one of the finest selections of listed buildings, mills and ancient inns in England. This is where 'a historic street meets a secret garden', which is five acres of hotel grounds. The hotel is furnished and decorated to a very high standard throughout, creating a real sense of luxury. The award winning restaurant overlooks immaculate gardens and the lake. Staff combine warmth and informality to really accentuate the high standards.
**ROOMS:** 23 en suite No smoking in 3 bedrooms s £125-£155; d £160-£260 (incl. bkfst) **LB** **FACILITIES:** STV Croquet lawn Xmas **CONF:** Thtr 30 Class 18 Board 20 Del from £195 * **PARKING:** 70 **NOTES:** No dogs (ex guide dogs) No smoking in restaurant Civ Wed 90 **CARDS:**

*See advert on opposite page*

### ★★★61% Quality Hotel St Albans

Quality Hotel

234 London Rd AL1 1JQ
☎ 01727 857858 📠 01727 855666
e-mail: st.albans@quality-hotels.net
***Dir:*** *junct 22 off M25 follow A1081 to St Albans, after Colney rdbt hotel is 1m on left*

This hotel offers convenient access to and from the motorway network and the railway station in the town centre. The smart bedrooms are well-equipped and for relaxation, there is a comfortable bar and restaurant.
**ROOMS:** 43 en suite (2 fmly) No smoking in 18 bedrooms s £65-£78; d £80-£89 (incl. bkfst) * **FACILITIES:** STV **CONF:** Thtr 220 Class 40 Board 50 Del from £100 * **PARKING:** 70 **NOTES:** No dogs (ex guide dogs) No smoking in restaurant **CARDS:**

> Packed in a hurry? Ironing facilities should be available at all star levels, either in rooms or on request.

**★★67% Apples Hotel**
133 London Rd AL1 1TA
☎ 01727 844111 📠 01727 861100
***Dir:*** *sited on the main A1081, 0.5m from city centre*

A small hotel that is well-located for access to the mainline station and local motorway network. The bedrooms are thoughtfully laid out and offer a comprehensive range of extra facilities. Guests have the use of a quiet lounge, a small bar overlooking the attractive garden and an outdoor swimming pool in the summer months.
**ROOMS:** 9 en suite (1 fmly) No smoking in 2 bedrooms s £43-£50; d £60-£71 (incl. bkfst) * **LB FACILITIES:** Outdoor swimming (H) **CONF:** Thtr 20 Class 15 Board 12 **PARKING:** 9 **NOTES:** No smoking in restaurant **CARDS:**

**⇧ Express by Holiday Inn St Albans**
London Rd, Flamstead AL3 8HT
☎ 01582 841332
A modern budget hotel offering comfortable accommodation in refreshing, spacious and comprehensively equipped bedrooms, en suite bathrooms with power showers and continental buffet breakfast included in the room rate. Suitable for business travellers or families. For further details and the Express by Holiday Inn phone number, consult the Hotel Groups page.
**ROOMS:** 75 en suite (incl. cont bkfst) s £45-£57.50; d £45-£57.50 *
**CONF:** Thtr 30 Class 16 Board 12

## ST ANNES See Lytham St Annes

## ST AUSTELL, Cornwall & Isles of Scilly

Map 02 SX05

**★★★★74% ❀ Carlyon Bay**
Sea Rd, Carlyon Bay PL25 3RD
☎ 01726 812304 📠 01726 814938
e-mail: info@carlyonbay.co.uk
***Dir:*** *from St Austell, follow signs for Charlestown Carlyon Bay is signposted on left, hotel lies at end of Sea Road*

Set in 250 acres of grounds and renowned for its leisure facilities, Carlyon Bay Hotel has established a loyal following. It is especially suited to the leisure visitor but can also cater for small conferences and business guests. Sea-facing rooms are always in demand for their marvellous views of St Austell Bay and fresh fruit and flowers are provided in the best bedrooms. There is a choice of lounges and bars.
**ROOMS:** 73 en suite (14 fmly) s £74-£95; d £150-£224 (incl. bkfst) * **LB FACILITIES: Spa** STV Indoor swimming (H) Outdoor swimming (H) Golf 18 Tennis (hard) Snooker Sauna Solarium Putting green Jacuzzi Table tennis 9-hole approach course entertainment ch fac Xmas **CONF:** Thtr 100 **SERVICES:** Lift **PARKING:** 100 **NOTES:** No dogs (ex guide dogs) Civ Wed **CARDS:**

*See advert on this page*

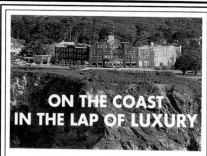

ST AUSTELL, continued

**★★★65% Cliff Head**
Sea Rd, Carlyon Bay PL25 3RB
☎ 01726 812345 🖷 01726 815511
e-mail: cliffheadhotel@btconnect.com
***Dir:*** *2m E off A390*
Set in extensive grounds and conveniently located for visiting the Eden Project, the hotel faces south and enjoys views over Carlyon Bay. A choice of lounges is provided, together with swimming pool and solarium. A range of menus is offered in 'Expressions' restaurant, featuring an interesting selection of dishes.
**ROOMS:** 60 rms (59 en suite) (2 fmly) s £50-£60; d fr £82 (incl. bkfst) * **LB** **FACILITIES:** Indoor swimming Sauna Solarium Gym entertainment Xmas **CONF:** Thtr 150 Class 130 Board 170 Del from £80 * **PARKING:** 60 **NOTES:** No dogs (ex guide dogs) No smoking in restaurant Civ Wed 130 **CARDS:**

**★★★64% Porth Avallen**
Sea Rd, Carlyon Bay PL25 3SG
☎ 01726 812802 🖷 01726 817097
e-mail: info@porthavallen.co.uk
***Dir:*** *leave A30 onto A391. Follow signs to St Austell and then Charlestown and then Carlyon Bay. Turn right into Sea Rd*
This traditional hotel boasts panoramic views over the rugged Cornish coastline and Carlyon Bay. A comprehensive refurbishment programme is underway, including upgrading of the spacious bedrooms, many of which benefit from the wonderful outlook. The atmosphere here is friendly and welcoming and both the oak panelled lounge and conservatory are ideal for quiet relaxation. In addition to the convivial bar area, a function room is available for private parties. Both fixed price and carte menus are offered each evening in the dining room.
**ROOMS:** 24 en suite (5 fmly) No smoking in 3 bedrooms s £64-£105; d £100-£162 (incl. bkfst) * **CONF:** Thtr 82 Class 82 Board 82 Del £80.50 * **PARKING:** 40 **NOTES:** No dogs (ex guide dogs) No smoking in restaurant Closed 23 Dec-4 Jan **CARDS:**

*See advert on opposite page*

**★★78% Boscundle Manor**
Tregrehan PL25 3RL
☎ 01726 813557 🖷 01726 814997
e-mail: stay@boscundlemanor.co.uk
***Dir:*** *2m E on A390 200yds up road signposted 'Tregrehan'*
Comfort and quality are evident throughout this handsome 18th-century, stone-built manor. Bedrooms are spacious and equipped with many thoughtful extras. The beautiful grounds extend to over ten acres and include secluded corners, ponds and woodland walkways. There is also a games room and both indoor and outdoor swimming pools.
**ROOMS:** 9 en suite 3 annexe en suite (1 fmly) s £70-£90; d £120-£140 (incl. bkfst) * **FACILITIES:** Indoor swimming (H) Outdoor swimming (H) Golf 2 Snooker Gym Croquet lawn Golf practice area Table Tennis Badminton **PARKING:** 15 **NOTES:** No smoking in restaurant Closed end Oct-end Mar RS Sun **CARDS:**

**★★70% Pier House**
Harbour Front, Charlestown PL25 3NJ
☎ 01726 67955 🖷 01726 69246
***Dir:*** *follow A390 to St Austell, Mt Charles rdbt turn left down Charlestown Road*
Formerly two cottages, built in 1794 and overlooking the working port, this friendly and relaxed hotel is situated on the picturesque harbour at Charlestown. Many bedrooms have sea views, and the public bar is popular with locals and tourists alike. Locally caught fish regularly features on the varied and interesting menu in the restaurant.
**ROOMS:** 26 en suite (4 fmly) No smoking in 5 bedrooms **PARKING:** 56 **NOTES:** No dogs (ex guide dogs) No smoking in restaurant Closed 24-25 Dec **CARDS:**

**★★68% Victoria Inn & Lodge**
Victoria, Roche PL26 8LQ
☎ 01726 890207 🖷 01726 891233
e-mail: victorian@talk21.com
***Dir:*** *6m W of Bodmin on A30. Turn 1st left after garage, Victoria Inn approx 500yds on right*
Situated on the A30, midway between Bodmin and Newquay, this is a convenient choice for both the business and leisure traveller. Purpose built, lodge-style bedrooms are well-equipped, spacious and comfortable. Guests have a choice of dining options with the conviviality of the inn, or the more formal surroundings of the restaurant.
**ROOMS:** 28 en suite (7 fmly) No smoking in all bedrooms s £40; d £40 * **LB** **FACILITIES:** STV **CONF:** Thtr 30 Class 18 Board 18 Del £90 * **PARKING:** 100 **NOTES:** No dogs (ex guide dogs) No smoking in restaurant RS 24-26 Dec **CARDS:**

**★★63% *White Hart***
Church St PL25 4AT
☎ 01726 72100 🖷 01726 74705
Situated in the town centre this 18th-century, stone-built inn is popular with both visitors and locals. There is a choice of bars, both offer a lively atmosphere and a range of local ales. Alternative seating is available in the foyer lounge, where cream teas can be taken. Meals are available at the bar or from a fixed price menu in the restaurant.
**ROOMS:** 18 en suite **FACILITIES:** STV **CONF:** Thtr 50 Board 20 **NOTES:** No dogs (ex guide dogs) Closed 25 & 26 Dec
**CARDS:**

ST HELENS, Merseyside — Map 07 SJ59
see also Rainhill

**★★★66% Posthouse Haydock**
Lodge Ln WA12 0JG
Posthouse
☎ 0870 400 9039 🖷 01942 718419
e-mail: gm1117@forte-hotels.com
(For full entry see Haydock)

**⌂ Premier Lodge**
Garswood Old Rd, East Lancs Rd WA11 9AB
PREMIER LODGE
☎ 0870 700 1544 🖷 0870 700 1545
***Dir:*** *3 miles from junct 23 M6,on A580 towards Liverpool*
Premier Lodge offers modern, well-equipped, en suite accommodation suitable for both business and leisure travellers. Meals can be taken at the adjacent popular restaurant and bar, which is fully licensed. For further details, consult the Hotel Groups page.
**ROOMS:** 43 en suite s £46; d £46 * **CONF:** Thtr 85 Class 30 Board 40 Del from £80 *

ST IVES, Cambridgeshire — Map 04 TL37

**★★★69% Olivers Lodge**
Needingworth Rd PE27 5JP
THE CIRCLE Selected Individual Hotels GREAT BRITAIN
☎ 01480 463252 🖷 01480 461150
e-mail: reception@oliverslodge.co.uk
***Dir:*** *follow A14 towards Huntingdon/Cambridge, take B1040 to St Ives. Cross 1st rdbt, left at 2nd then 1st right. Hotel 500m on right*
Olivers Lodge is a popular and well run hotel, set in quiet

continued

residential surroundings on the edge of St Ives. The welcoming public rooms include a conservatory dining area and breakfast room, a lounge bar and a restaurant. There are bedrooms in both the main house and an adjoining wing, with modern appointments and good facilities.
**ROOMS:** 12 en suite 5 annexe en suite (3 fmly) No smoking in 3 bedrooms s £69-£79; d £75-£95 (incl. bkfst) * **LB** **FACILITIES:** STV Croquet lawn Free use of local health club,motor cruiser for hire entertainment **CONF:** Thtr 65 Class 45 Board 40 Del from £75 * **PARKING:** 30 **NOTES:** Civ Wed 85 **CARDS:**

### ★★★69% Slepe Hall

Ramsey Rd PE27 5RB
☎ 01480 463122 ⎙ 01480 300706
e-mail: mail@slepehall.co.uk
***Dir:*** *leave A14 on A1096 & follow by-pass signed Huntingdon towards St Ives, turn into Ramsey Rd at set of traffic lights by Toyota garage*
A pleasant hotel with a friendly atmosphere and caring staff, close to the town centre. A wide range of food is offered, from lighter meals in the bar to a choice of menus in the more formal restaurant. Bedroom styles range between traditional in the main house and modern in the new wing, but all rooms offer good accommodation.
**ROOMS:** 16 en suite (1 fmly) s £50-£75; d £65-£100 (incl. bkfst) * **LB** **FACILITIES:** STV ch fac **CONF:** Thtr 200 Class 80 Board 60 Del from £95 * **PARKING:** 70 **NOTES:** No dogs (ex guide dogs) No smoking in restaurant Closed 26-30 Dec Civ Wed 60
**CARDS:**

### ★★★66% Dolphin

London Rd PE27 5EP
☎ 01480 466966 ⎙ 01480 495597
***Dir:*** *leave A14 between Huntingdon & Cambridge on A1096 towards St Ives. Left at first rdbt & immediately right and Hotel is on left after about 0.5m*

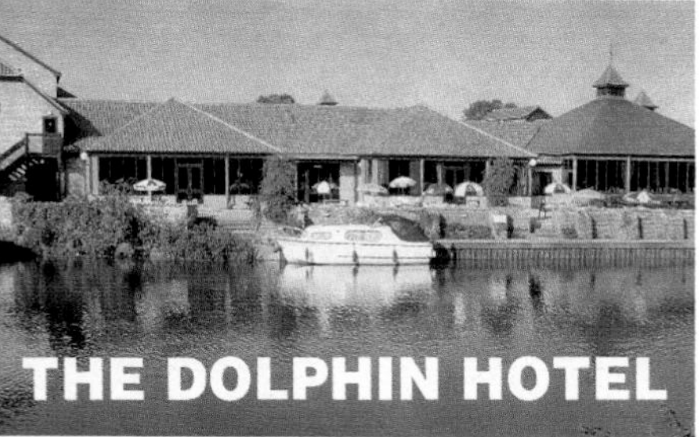
THE DOLPHIN HOTEL

A modern hotel on the River Ouse with a pedestrian bridge leading to the town centre. Open-plan public rooms include a choice of bars and a pleasant restaurant offering enjoyable cuisine. Bedrooms are divided between the hotel and an adjacent wing. There are modern conference and function suites, and secure parking is available.
**ROOMS:** 30 en suite 37 annexe en suite (4 fmly) No smoking in 36 bedrooms **FACILITIES:** STV Fishing Sauna Gym **CONF:** Thtr 150 Class 50 Board 50 Del from £98 * **PARKING:** 400 **NOTES:** No dogs (ex guide dogs) Civ Wed 60 **CARDS:**

*See advert on this page*

Early start? Hotels at all star levels should provide in-room alarm clocks and/or alarm calls.

S

ST IVES, Cornwall & Isles of Scilly Map 02 SW54

**★★★73% ® Carbis Bay**
Carbis Bay TR26 2NP
☎ 01736 795311 ▤ 01736 797677
e-mail: carbisbayhotel@talk21.com
***Dir:*** *From M5 junct 31, take A30 then A3074. After 2m through Helant village, pass garage on right. Take the next right (Porthreptor Rd) and continue down to the sea to the hotel*

This established, professionally run hotel enjoys a superb location with wonderful views overlooking its own sandy beach. The hotel has spacious, newly refurbished public rooms. Upgraded bedrooms provide comfort, quality and modern facilities; the attentive, natural hospitality is an attraction.
**ROOMS:** 35 en suite (9 fmly) No smoking in 5 bedrooms s £60-£120; d £80-£140 (incl. bkfst) * **LB** **FACILITIES:** **Spa** Outdoor swimming (H) Fishing Snooker Private beach entertainment **CONF:** Thtr 120 Class 80 Board 100 Del from £40 * **PARKING:** 200 **NOTES:** No smoking in restaurant Closed Jan Civ Wed 140
**CARDS:**

*See advert on opposite page*

**★★★71% Porthminster**
The Terrace TR26 2BN
☎ 01736 795221 ▤ 01736 797043
e-mail: reception@porthminster-hotel.co.uk
***Dir:*** *on A3074)*
With its enviable position overlooking the sandy beach, this long-established hotel continues to provide excellent hospitality together with facilities for all the family. Many guests holiday at the hotel on a regular basis. Bedrooms are both comfortable and well-equipped, whilst public rooms are spacious and benefit from spectacular views over the bay.
**ROOMS:** 43 en suite (14 fmly) s £44-£66; d £88-£132 (incl. bkfst) * **LB** **FACILITIES:** Indoor swimming (H) Outdoor swimming (H) Sauna Solarium Gym Jacuzzi Xmas **CONF:** Thtr 130 Class 20 Board 35 **SERVICES:** Lift **PARKING:** 43 **NOTES:** Closed 2-11 Jan Civ Wed 130
**CARDS:**

*See advert on opposite page*

**★★★67% ®® Garrack**
Burthallan Ln, Higher Ayr TR26 3AA
☎ 01736 796199 ▤ 01736 798955
e-mail: garrack@accuk.co.uk
***Dir:*** *turn off A30 for St Ives. Follow yellow holiday route signs on B3311. In St Ives, hotel is signposted from first mini rdbt*
The Garrack provides superb views over Porthmeor beach and stands in extensive grounds. Bedrooms are available in both the modern wing and in the original building; all are well-equipped and comfortably furnished. The restaurant offers fixed price and *continued* carte menus featuring skilfully prepared dishes, making good use of home grown produce and local seafood.

**ROOMS:** 16 en suite 2 annexe en suite (2 fmly) s fr £63.50; d fr £127 (incl. bkfst) * **LB** **FACILITIES:** Indoor swimming (H) Sauna Solarium Gym Jacuzzi ch fac Xmas **CONF:** Thtr 30 Board 12 **PARKING:** 30 **NOTES:** No smoking in restaurant **CARDS:**

*See advert on opposite page*

**★★★67% Tregenna Castle Hotel**
TR26 2DE
☎ 01736 795254 ▤ 01736 796066
e-mail: tregenna-castle@demon.co.uk
***Dir:*** *main A30 from Exeter to Penzance, at Lelant just west of Hayle take A3074 to St Ives, through Carbis Bay, signposted main entrance on left*
The Tregenna Castle has spectacular views of St Ives and its beaches, sitting at the top of the town in beautiful landscaped gardens. Bedrooms are generally spacious with super views. A carte menu or carvery buffet are offered in the restaurant; there is also an Italian bistro adjacent to the golf course.
**ROOMS:** 84 en suite (12 fmly) No smoking in 49 bedrooms s £45-£80; d £90-£186 (incl. bkfst & dinner) * **FACILITIES:** **Spa** STV Indoor swimming (H) Outdoor swimming (H) Golf 18 Tennis (hard) Squash Sauna Solarium Gym Putting green Jacuzzi Steam room Xmas **CONF:** Thtr 300 Class 150 Del from £75 * **SERVICES:** Lift **PARKING:** 200 **NOTES:** No dogs (ex guide dogs) No smoking in restaurant Civ Wed 100 **CARDS:**

**★★74% ® Pedn-Olva**
West Porthminster Beach TR26 2EA
☎ 01736 796222 ▤ 01736 797710
e-mail: pednolvahotel@cornwall-county.com
***Dir:*** *take A30 to Hayle, then A3074 to St Ives. At St Ives turn sharp right at Bus Station into Railway Station car park, go down steps into Hotel*
Perched on the water's edge, this professionally-managed hotel has benefited from extensive refurbishment. Results are impressive with stylish public areas designed to take full advantage of the unique location. Bedrooms combine comfort with quality, the majority boasting spectacular views across the bay. In the restaurant, an imaginative, fixed-price menu is offered; during the summer, lighter meals are served on the terraces.
**ROOMS:** 26 en suite 4 annexe en suite (4 fmly) No smoking in all bedrooms s £48-£55; d £96-£110 (incl. bkfst) * **LB** **FACILITIES:** STV Outdoor swimming (H) Xmas **CONF:** Thtr 25 Class 20 Board 16 Del from £68 * **PARKING:** 17 **NOTES:** No dogs (ex guide dogs) No smoking in restaurant **CARDS:**

*See advert on opposite page*

Need to unwind? Look out for hotels with **Spa** in their entry.

S

S

ST IVES, continued

**★★71% Chy-an-Albany**
Albany Ter TR26 2BS
☎ 01736 796759 01736 795584
e-mail: info@chy-an-albanyhtl.demon.co.uk
***Dir:*** *turn of A30 onto A3074 signposted St Ives, hotel on left just before junction*
Refurbished to a high standard throughout, this hotel benefits from spectacular views over St Ives Bay and Porthminster Beach. The comfortable bedrooms are well furnished and equipped, and the rooms with sea views are always popular. A fixed-price menu is offered in the attractive dining room, adjacent to the comfortable lounges and intimate bar.
**ROOMS:** 40 en suite (11 fmly) No smoking in all bedrooms s £35-£46; d £70-£92 (incl. bkfst) * LB **FACILITIES:** entertainment Xmas **CONF:** Thtr 80 Class 40 Board 30 Del from £70 * **SERVICES:** Lift **PARKING:** 37 **NOTES:** No dogs (ex guide dogs) No smoking in restaurant Civ Wed 60 **CARDS:**

**★★69% *Chy-an-Dour***
Trelyon Av TR26 2AD
☎ 01736 796436 01736 795772
e-mail: chyndour@aol.com
***Dir:*** *turn off A30 onto A3074, follow signs to St Ives for approx 3m, hotel on the right just past Ford garage*
Built in 1890, this delightful family-owned hotel has inspiring views over St Ives, the harbour and Porthminster Beach. Good home cooking is provided in the restaurant at both dinner and breakfast. The four-course dinner menu changes daily, often using fresh local produce. Most of the bedrooms enjoy the splendid views, and all the rooms are well-equipped.
**ROOMS:** 23 en suite (2 fmly) No smoking in all bedrooms **SERVICES:** Lift **PARKING:** 23 **NOTES:** No dogs (ex guide dogs) No children 5yrs No smoking in restaurant **CARDS:**

**★★66% Hotel St Eia**
Trelyon Av TR26 2AA
☎ 01736 795531 01736 793591
e-mail: hotelsteia@tinyonline.co.uk
***Dir:*** *turn off A30 onto A3074, follow signs to St Ives, when approaching St Ives, the hotel is prominently on the right hand side*
This conveniently located hotel offers a warm welcome and spectacular views over St Ives, the harbour and Porthminster Beach. Guests can relax with a drink from the well-stocked bar before dining in the attractive restaurant. A roof top terrace is also available, which boasts one of the best views in town!
**ROOMS:** 18 en suite (3 fmly) No smoking in all bedrooms s £28.50-£36.50; d £57-£73 (incl. bkfst) * **PARKING:** 16 **NOTES:** No dogs (ex guide dogs) No smoking in restaurant Closed Dec-Jan
**CARDS:**

**★★66% Skidden House**
THE CIRCLE Selected Individual Hotels GREAT BRITAIN
Skidden Hill TR26 2DU
☎ 01736 796899 01736 798619
e-mail: skiddenhouse@x-stream.co.uk
***Dir:*** *turn off A30 at St Erth rdbt, follow road sign A3074 to St Ives & railway station 1st right after rail/bus station*
Situated in the town centre, Skidden House has an interesting history and is purported to be the oldest hotel in St Ives. Its cosy bedrooms are well-equipped with modern facilities. A fixed-price menu is offered in the bistro-style dining room, often using fresh local produce. There is also a cosy bar and lounge.
**ROOMS:** 7 en suite No smoking in 2 bedrooms s £40-£45; d £70-£84 (incl. bkfst) * LB **PARKING:** 7 **NOTES:** No smoking in restaurant
**CARDS:**

**★★65% Cottage Hotel**
Leisureplex
Boskerris Rd, Carbis Bay TR26 2PE
☎ 01736 795252 01736 798636
***Dir:*** *from A30 take A3074 to Carbis Bay. Take right turn into Porthrepta Rd. Just before railway bridge turn left through railway car park and into hotel car park*
Boasting superb views across Carbis Bay, this quietly situated hotel is an ideal choice for those wishing to explore nearby St Ives. Many bedrooms, together with the spacious lounges and dining room, take full advantage of the spectacular sea views. Additional facilities include ballroom, snooker table and heated outdoor swimming pool.
**ROOMS:** 80 en suite (7 fmly) s £25-£33; d £42-£58 (incl. bkfst) * **FACILITIES:** Outdoor swimming (H) Squash Snooker Sauna Gym entertainment Xmas **SERVICES:** Lift **PARKING:** 10 **NOTES:** No dogs (ex guide dogs) No smoking in restaurant Closed Dec-Feb RS Nov/Mar (open Mon-Fri only) **CARDS:**

**★★64% Boskerris**
Boskerris Rd, Carbis Bay TR26 2NQ
☎ 01736 795295 01736 798632
e-mail: Boskerris.Hotel@btinternet.com
***Dir:*** *upon entering Carbis Bay take 3rd turning right after petrol station*
With magnificent views over Carbis Bay, Boskerris Hotel is set in an acre and a half of gardens, in a quiet area. Comfortable lounge areas and an attractive dining room are provided, and there is also an outdoor swimming pool. Bedrooms vary in size and style, each being well decorated and equipped.
**ROOMS:** 16 en suite (2 fmly) No smoking in 4 bedrooms s £70-£85; d £88-£110 (incl. bkfst) * LB **FACILITIES:** Outdoor swimming (H) Table tennis **PARKING:** 20 **NOTES:** No smoking in restaurant Closed Nov-Etr
**CARDS:**

**★64% Dunmar**
Pednolver Ter TR26 2EL
☎ 01736 796117 01736 796117
e-mail: enquiries@dumar-hotel.co.uk
***Dir:*** *take A3074 and fork left at the Porthminster Hotel into Albert Road. Hotel is 200yds along at junction of Pednolver and Porthminster Terrace*

DUNMAR
HOTEL

In an elevated position above the town and close to the centre, this popular hotel offers a warm welcome to all. Bedrooms are comfortable and most have sea views. Traditional English food is served in the dining room and the attractive lounge bar enjoys views over St Ives and the ocean. The hotel is within close proximity to a family beach.
**ROOMS:** 15 en suite (3 fmly) s £25-£35; d £50-£70 (incl. bkfst) * LB **FACILITIES:** Xmas **PARKING:** 20 **NOTES:** No smoking in restaurant
**CARDS:**

Weekend away? Hotels with LB in their entry offer leisure breaks.

S

## ST KEYNE, Cornwall & Isles of Scilly  Map 02 SX26

### ★★79% Old Rectory House
PL14 4RL
☎ 01579 342617 01579 342293
e-mail: savillelyons@freenet.co.uk
**Dir:** *turn off A38 at Liskeard, take B3254 following signs to St Keyne, pass church on left, hotel is 500yds on left*

CLOSED

This secluded and peaceful hideaway is the perfect choice for those looking to relax and unwind in beautiful surroundings. Built in 1820 and added to since, this delightful house is a fusion of both Edwardian and Victorian architecture. Cuisine is taken seriously here, the daily changing menu making optimum use of local produce.
**ROOMS:** 6 en suite No smoking in all bedrooms s £95; d £110-£130 (incl. bkfst) * **LB FACILITIES:** Croquet lawn **PARKING:** 30 **NOTES:** No dogs (ex guide dogs) No children 16yrs No smoking in restaurant Closed Xmas & New Year **CARDS:**

## ST LAWRENCE See Wight, Isle of

## ST LEONARDS-ON-SEA See Hastings & St Leonards

## ST MARTIN'S See Scilly, Isles of

## ST MARY CHURCH See Torquay

## ST MARY'S See Scilly, Isles of

## ST MAWES, Cornwall & Isles of Scilly  Map 02 SW83

### ★★★77% Idle Rocks
Harbour Side TR2 5AN
☎ 01326 270771 01326 270062
e-mail: reservations@idlerocks.co.uk
**Dir:** *turn off A390 onto A3078, continue for 14 miles until you reach St Mawes. Idle Rocks is situated on the left hand side*
Overlooking the quayside to the sea beyond, this smart, friendly hotel offers wonderful views from many of its bedrooms and its popular waterfront terrace. Bedrooms are individually styled and tastefully furnished to a high standard; the rooms in nearby Bohella House and the waterside cottage are particularly spacious. Cuisine is impressive with local seafood featuring prominently on the daily changing menu.
**ROOMS:** 17 en suite 10 annexe en suite s £88-£159; d £126-£238 (incl. bkfst & dinner) **LB FACILITIES:** Xmas **PARKING:** 4 **NOTES:** No smoking in restaurant **CARDS:**

*See advert on this page*

Read all about it! Newspapers delivered to bedrooms in four and five star hotels.

### ★★71% *Rising Sun*
TR2 5DJ
☎ 01326 270233 01326 270198
**Dir:** *from A39 take A3078 signposted St Mawes, hotel is in centre of village*
The haunt of artists and popular with the yachting fraternity, the pretty harbour of St Mawes is the setting for this charming hotel. The bar is a focal point of village life, and the brasserie and lounge bar offer imaginative cooking featuring local seafood. Stylish bedrooms are individually decorated.
**ROOMS:** 9 en suite (1 fmly) **PARKING:** 6 **NOTES:** No smoking in restaurant **CARDS:**

## ST MELLION, Cornwall & Isles of Scilly  Map 02 SX36

### ★★★72% St Mellion International
American Golf (UK) Ltd PL12 6SD
☎ 01579 351351 01579 350537
e-mail: stmellion@americangolf.uk.com
**Dir:** *from M5/A38 towards Plymouth & Saltash. St Mellion is located off A38 on A388 towards Callington and Launceston*
This purpose built hotel, golfing and leisure complex is surrounded by 450 acres of land with two 18 hole golf courses. The bedrooms generally have views over the courses, but with the vast array of leisure facilities on offer, most guests spend little time in their rooms! Public areas include a choice of bars and eating options. Other facilities include function suites for up to 180 people.
**ROOMS:** 39 annexe en suite (15 fmly) s £63-£104; d £76-£158 (incl. bkfst) * **LB FACILITIES:** Spa Indoor swimming (H) Golf 36 Tennis (hard) Squash Snooker Sauna Solarium Gym Putting green Jacuzzi Steam room Skincare ch fac Xmas **CONF:** Thtr 350 Class 140 Board 80 Del from £115 * **SERVICES:** Lift **PARKING:** 400 **NOTES:** No dogs (ex guide dogs) No smoking in restaurant Civ Wed 120
**CARDS:**

S

ST NEOTS, Cambridgeshire Map 04 TL16

### ★★69% Abbotsley Golf Hotel

Potton Rd, Eynesbury Hardwicke PE19 6XN
☎ 01480 474000 🖷 01480 471018
e-mail: abbotsley@americangolf.uk.com
***Dir:*** *A1/M onto A428 towards Cambridge*

This purpose-built hotel caters well for its many avid golfing guests with a 250-acre estate encompassing two courses, a golf school and leisure complex. A major refurbishment programme is adding more rooms, upgrading the existing ones, and revamping public areas. The bedrooms are generally spacious and surround a pleasing courtyard garden with a putting green. Public rooms overlook the adjacent greens.

**ROOMS:** 42 annexe en suite (2 fmly) s £49-£59; d £75 (incl. bkfst) * LB **FACILITIES:** Spa Golf 36 Squash Solarium Gym Putting green Holistic Health & Beauty Salon,pool table Xmas **CONF:** Thtr 60 Class 30 Board 30 Del from £85 * **PARKING:** 80 **NOTES:** No smoking in restaurant **CARDS:**

### ⇧ *Premier Lodge*

Great North Rd, Eaton Socon PE19 8EN
☎ 0870 700 1368 🖷 0870 700 1369

Premier Lodge offers modern, well-equipped, en suite accommodation suitable for both business and leisure travellers. Meals can be taken at the adjacent popular restaurant and bar, which is fully licensed. For further details, consult the Hotel Groups page.

**ROOMS:** 63 en suite

SALCOMBE, Devon Map 03 SX73
see also Hope Cove, Kingsbridge & Thurlestone

### ★★★★72% ❀ Thurlestone Hotel

TQ7 3NN
☎ 01548 560382 🖷 01548 561069
e-mail: enquiries@thurlestone.co.uk
(For full entry see Thurlestone)

### ★★★★67% Menzies Marine

MENZIES HOTELS

Cliff Rd TQ8 8JH
☎ 0870 600 3013 (Res) 🖷 01332 511144
e-mail: info@menzies-hotels.co.uk
***Dir:*** *from A38 Exeter take A384 to Totnes then follow A381 direct to Kingsbridge and Salcombe*

This splendid hotel enjoys a wonderful waterside location with stunning views of the estuary from its public areas. All the bedrooms are well-equipped and stylishly furnished, many having balconies. Appetising food is served in the restaurant. There is an excellent leisure complex.

**ROOMS:** 53 en suite (10 fmly) s £75; d £150 (incl. bkfst) * LB **FACILITIES:** STV Indoor swimming (H) Sauna Solarium Gym Jacuzzi Xmas **SERVICES:** Lift **PARKING:** 50 **NOTES:** No smoking in restaurant Civ Wed 70 **CARDS:**

## *Premier Collection*

### ★★★❀❀ Soar Mill Cove

Soar Mill Cove, Malborough TQ7 3DS
☎ 01548 561566 🖷 01548 561223
e-mail: info@makepeacehotels.co.uk
***Dir:*** *3m W of town off A381 at Malborough. Follow signs 'Soar'*

At the head of a tranquil small cove, this family run-hotel offers keen standards of hospitality and service, and fine attention to detail. The gardens, public rooms and most accommodation take full advantage of the marvellous views of sea and headland. Bedrooms are all ground floor, spacious, very well-equipped and have deep comfortable armchairs. Cooking is consistently good at all meals, so do not refuse the complimentary cream tea.

**ROOMS:** 21 en suite (5 fmly) No smoking in all bedrooms s £74-£111; d £148-£240 (incl. bkfst) * LB **FACILITIES:** Indoor swimming (H) Outdoor swimming (H) Tennis (grass) Snooker Sauna Table tennis, Games room, 9 hole Pitch n putt entertainment ch fac Xmas **CONF:** Board 25 Del from £100 * **PARKING:** 30 **NOTES:** No smoking in restaurant Closed 2 Jan-8 Feb
**CARDS:**

### ★★★80% ❀❀ *Tides Reach*

South Sands TQ8 8LJ
☎ 01548 843466 🖷 01548 843954
e-mail: enquire@tidesreach.com
***Dir:*** *turn off the A38 at Buckfastleigh towards Totnes. At Totnes join A381 then into Salcombe follow signs to South Sands*

With its delightful, waterside location, this personally run hotel enjoys a regular following. Staff are friendly and professionally efficient. Many of the spacious bedrooms have balconies and the Garden Room restaurant offers high quality cuisine and pleasant views. Particularly comfortable public areas include a leisure complex and a hair and beauty salon.

**ROOMS:** 35 en suite (7 fmly) No smoking in 2 bedrooms **FACILITIES:** Indoor swimming (H) Squash Snooker Sauna Solarium Gym Jacuzzi Windsurfing Dingy sailing Water skiing entertainment **SERVICES:** Lift **PARKING:** 100 **NOTES:** No children 8yrs No smoking in restaurant Closed Jan-early Feb **CARDS:**

*See advert on opposite page*

### ★★★75% Bolt Head

TQ8 8LL
☎ 01548 843751 🖷 01548 843061
e-mail: info@bolthead.com
***Dir:*** *follow signs to South Sands*

Built in 1901, the hotel is at the entrance to the National Trust-owned Sharpitor and enjoys magnificent views of Salcombe estuary. The restaurant has a local reputation for fine seafood and

*continued*

fish. Pine furniture and well-chosen colour schemes make the bedrooms comfortable and attractive.
**ROOMS:** 28 en suite (6 fmly) s £49-£75; d £98-£150 * LB
**FACILITIES:** Outdoor swimming (H) **PARKING:** 30 **NOTES:** No smoking in restaurant Closed mid Nov-mid Mar **CARDS:**

*See advert on this page*

### ★★★69% *South Sands*

South Sands TQ8 8LL
☎ 01548 843741 📠 01548 842112
e-mail: enquire@southsands.com
***Dir:*** *off A38 at Buckfastleigh, travel to Totnes and follow A381 to Salcombe, then follow signs to South Sands*

A popular family hotel on the Salcombe estuary. Facilities include an indoor swimming pool and children's playroom. Bedrooms are comfortably furnished and equipped, many with superb views. The waterside dining room offers a range of interesting dishes, while the beachside Terrace bar is a more informal setting.
**ROOMS:** 30 en suite (10 fmly) **FACILITIES:** STV Indoor swimming (H) Jacuzzi ch fac **PARKING:** 50 **NOTES:** No smoking in restaurant Closed Nov-Mar **CARDS:**

> Fancy a Singapore Sling? Bar staff in five star hotels should be skilled cocktail mixers.

> Popped the question? Hotels with Civ Wed in their entry are licensed for civil wedding ceremonies. Maximum numbers for the ceremony only are shown, e.g. Civ Wed 120

SALCOMBE, continued

**★★71% Grafton Towers**
Moult Rd TQ8 8LG
☎ 01548 842882 01548 842857
e-mail: graftontowers.salcombe@virgin.net
***Dir:*** *approach Salcombe from Kingsbridge, follow signs for South Sands, look for Hotel sign*
Quietly located in an elevated, residential area, with stunning views over the estuary, this family-owned hotel offers bright, cheerful accommodation. Both of the comfortable lounges benefit from the view, and there is a cosy bar. A well-balanced, fixed-price dinner menu is offered, using predominantly local produce.
**ROOMS:** 12 en suite s £33.50-£39; d £72-£104 (incl. bkfst) * **LB** **FACILITIES:** Croquet lawn **PARKING:** 13 **NOTES:** No children 14yrs No smoking in restaurant Closed Nov-Feb **CARDS:**

**★★67% *Sunny Cliff***
Cliff Rd TQ8 8JX
☎ 01548 842207 01548 843388
e-mail: The SunnyC@aol.com
***Dir:*** *A381 into Salcombe follow road down hill, sharp left to South Sands, hotel 150m on left*
This small, friendly hotel enjoys an enviable position above the water's edge. The bar/lounge has been moved to the ground floor and has marvellous views, shared by the dining room and all the bedrooms. The gardens lead down to the outdoor heated pool and the hotel's six private moorings. Bedrooms are generally spacious with light decor and modern facilities.
**ROOMS:** 9 en suite 4 annexe en suite (6 fmly) **FACILITIES:** Outdoor swimming (H) Fishing Moorings and Landing stage **PARKING:** 17 **NOTES:** No smoking in restaurant Closed Jan RS Nov-Mar
**CARDS:**

SALE, Greater Manchester — Map 07 SJ79

**★★★★71% Belmore Hotel**
143 Brooklands Rd M33 3QN
☎ 0161 973 2538 0161 973 2665
e-mail: belmore-hotel@hotmail.com
***Dir:*** *from A56 turn onto A6144. At traffic lights (Brooklands Station on right) turn right into Brooklands Road*

Dating back to 1875 in parts, this small privately-owned hotel is a delightful surprise in this residential area of Sale. Smart public areas include a choice of eating options. Cooking in the fine dining Classic restaurant is imaginative and prepared with skill and care. Bedrooms are tastefully furnished and well-maintained.
**ROOMS:** 23 en suite (2 fmly) No smoking in 13 bedrooms s £90-£190; d £100-£215 (incl. bkfst) * **FACILITIES:** STV Free access to local Health Club ch fac Xmas **CONF:** Thtr 100 Class 50 Board 40 Del from £117 * **PARKING:** 38 **NOTES:** No smoking in restaurant Civ Wed 60
**CARDS:**

SALISBURY, Wiltshire — Map 04 SU12

**★★★70% Milford Hall**
206 Castle St SP1 3TE
☎ 01722 417411 01722 419444
e-mail: milfordhallhotel@compuserve.com
***Dir:*** *hotel is a few hundred yds from the conjunction of Castle St, the A30 ring road and the A345 Amesbury Rd. It is 0.5m from Market Sq*
Within easy walking distance of the city centre, this hotel benefits from a reputation for good hospitality. There are two categories of bedroom, traditional rooms in the original Georgian house and spacious, modern rooms, all are well-equipped. The brasserie restaurant was being re-sited as we went to press.
**ROOMS:** 35 en suite (1 fmly) No smoking in 6 bedrooms s £90-£105; d £100-£125 (incl. bkfst) * **LB** **FACILITIES:** STV Free facilities at local leisure centre ch fac **CONF:** Thtr 90 Class 70 Board 40 Del from £115 * **PARKING:** 60 **NOTES:** No smoking in restaurant Civ Wed 80
**CARDS:**

**★★★70% Red Lion**
Milford St SP1 2AN
☎ 01722 323334 01722 325756
e-mail: reception@the-redlion.co.uk
***Dir:*** *in city centre off Market Sq*

Best Western

Enjoying a central location, this 13th-century coaching inn is one of the oldest buildings in Salisbury. Bedrooms and public areas offer modern levels of comfort, and decor styles keep to the traditional. Dining options include the restaurant and the lounge which is popular for lunches. The Frothblowers Arms is a recent addition to the hotel.
**ROOMS:** 52 en suite (2 fmly) No smoking in 36 bedrooms **CONF:** Thtr 100 Class 50 Board 40 **SERVICES:** Lift **PARKING:** 10 **NOTES:** No dogs (ex guide dogs) **CARDS:**

*See advert on opposite page*

**★★★70% The White Hart**
St John St SP1 2SD
☎ 0870 400 8125 01722 412761
e-mail: heritagehotels_salisbury.white_hart@forte-hotels.com
***Dir:*** *from M3 junct 7/8 take A303 to A343 for Salisbury then A30. Follow signs for City Centre on Ring Road then north up Exeter St, leads into St John Street & hotel*
A well known landmark in this historical city, as there has been a hotel on this site since the 16th century. Bedrooms vary in size but all have good levels of comfort and are well-suited to both

*continued*

business and leisure visitors. The traditional bar and lounge are popular for morning coffee and afternoon tea.
**ROOMS:** 68 en suite (7 fmly) No smoking in 28 bedrooms s £80-£100; d £110-£140 (incl. bkfst) * **LB** **FACILITIES:** STV Xmas **CONF:** Thtr 80 Class 40 Board 40 Del from £120 * **PARKING:** 90 **NOTES:** No smoking in restaurant Civ Wed 80 **CARDS:**

### ★★★66% Grasmere House

MINOTEL Great Britain

Harnhan Rd SP2 8JN
☎ 01722 338388 🖷 01722 333710
e-mail: grasmerehotel@mistral.co.uk
***Dir:*** *on A3094 on S side of Salisbury next to All Saints Church in Harnham*
This Victorian house is in an ideal location. Attractive bedrooms vary in size; those in the older part of the house are especially appealing. The ground-floor rooms are well suited for visitors with disabilities. There is a spacious conservatory, comfortable lounge, cosy bar and a restaurant serving a daily-changing menu of appetising dishes.
**ROOMS:** 4 en suite 16 annexe en suite (2 fmly) No smoking in 4 bedrooms s £92.50-£95.50; d £125-£165 (incl. bkfst) * **LB** **FACILITIES:** Fishing Croquet lawn ch fac Xmas **CONF:** Thtr 110 Class 45 Board 45 Del from £105.50 * **PARKING:** 36 **NOTES:** Civ Wed 120 **CARDS:**

*See advert on this page*

### ★★★65% Rose & Crown

REGAL

Harnham Rd, Harnham SP2 8JQ
☎ 01722 399955 🖷 01722 339816
***Dir:*** *M3 junct 8 to A303 then A30 to centre of Salisbury*

Set on the banks of the River Avon, with delightful views of the cathedral, this attractive, cosy hotel offers well-designed bedrooms, in either the main house or the new wing. The riverside Pavilions restaurant serves an evening fixed-price menu, and the two bars benefit from log fires during the cooler months.
**ROOMS:** 28 en suite (5 fmly) No smoking in 10 bedrooms s £110; d £140 * **LB** **FACILITIES:** STV Fishing Xmas **CONF:** Thtr 80 Class 40 Board 40 Del from £115 * **PARKING:** 42 **NOTES:** No smoking in restaurant Civ Wed 90 **CARDS:**

Arriving late? Four and five star hotels have night porters to assist with your luggage, and 24-hour room service.

Late for dinner? Quality Standards star rating means that last orders for dinner should be no earlier than:
★ 6.30pm ★★ 7.00pm ★★★ 8.00pm
★★★★ 9.00pm ★★★★★ 10.00pm

S

SALISBURY, continued

## Premier Collection

### ★★ ®®® Howard's House

Teffont Evias SP3 5RJ
☎ 01722 716392 01722 716820
e-mail: enq@howardshousehotel.com
**Dir:** *turn off B3089 at Teffont Magna follow signs to Howards House*
This charming hotel is located in the quintessential English village of Teffont Evias, where time seems to have stood still. Howard's House was built in 1623, has two acres of glorious gardens and is easily accessible by road or rail. Spacious bedrooms are comfortably furnished, with thoughtful extras like fresh fruit, home-made biscuits and magazines. The popular cooking is a combination of excellent ingredients and experienced culinary skills.
**ROOMS:** 9 en suite (1 fmly) s £85; d £135-£155 (incl. bkfst) * **LB** **FACILITIES:** Croquet lawn **CONF:** Class 20 Board 12 **PARKING:** 23 **NOTES:** No smoking in restaurant Closed 24-27 Dec
**CARDS:**

SALTASH, Cornwall & Isles of Scilly — Map 02 SX45

### *Travelodge*

Travelodge

Callington Rd, Carkeel PL12 6LF
☎ 08700 850950 01752 849028
**Dir:** *on A38 Saltash By-Pass - 1m from Tamar Bridge*
Travelodge offers good quality, good value, modern accommodation. Ideal for families, the spacious, en suite bedrooms include remote-control TV, tea and coffee-making facilities, luxury beds and free morning newspaper. Meals can be taken at the nearby family restaurant. For further details and the Travelodge phone number, consult the Hotel Groups page.

**ROOMS:** 31 en suite **CONF:** Thtr 25 Class 15 Board 12

SALTBURN-BY-THE-SEA, North Yorkshire — Map 08 NZ62

### ★★63% Hunley Hall Golf Club & Hotel

Ings Ln, Brotton TS12 2QQ
☎ 01287 676216 01287 678250
e-mail: enquiries@hunleyhall.co.uk
**Dir:** *From A1 bypass take left at rdbt with monument at T-junct turn left pass church turn right. 50yds turn right & proceed through housing estate*
Spectacularly set on the cliff tops between Saltburn and Whitby Hunley Hall overlooks a 27-hole golf course and the North Sea. The Members Bar is licensed and serves snacks all day, and the restaurant serves a wide choice of food. Bedrooms are very well-equipped. Golf course (special rates) ranges from par 73 to par 68.

**ROOMS:** 8 en suite (1 fmly) No smoking in all bedrooms s £30-£40; d £56-£60 (incl. bkfst) * **LB** **FACILITIES:** Golf Putting green Pool table **CONF:** Thtr 70 Class 50 Board 24 Del from £68.20 * **PARKING:** 88 **NOTES:** No dogs (ex guide dogs) No smoking in restaurant
**CARDS:**

SAMPFORD PEVERELL, Devon — Map 03 ST01

### ★★67% Parkway House

32 Lower Town EX16 7BJ
☎ 01884 820255 01884 820780
**Dir:** *exit M5 junct 27 towards Tiverton and after 0.25m take road to Sampford Peverell. Follow into village, hotel is large white bldg on right*
Lying in landscaped gardens, this hotel benefits from extensive views across the Culm Valley. Bedrooms are smartly presented and offer high levels of equipment. A tempting menu is served in Cezanne's Restaurant. Additional facilities include a choice of function rooms.
**ROOMS:** 10 en suite (2 fmly) s £37.50; d £55 (incl. bkfst) * **LB** **FACILITIES:** STV Golf ch fac **CONF:** Thtr 120 Class 50 Board 40 Del from £58.50 * **PARKING:** 100 **NOTES:** No dogs (ex guide dogs) No smoking in restaurant Civ Wed 100 **CARDS:**

### *Travelodge*

Travelodge

Sampford Peverell Service Area EX16 7HD
☎ 01884 821087
**Dir:** *junc 27, M5*
Travelodge offers good quality, good value, modern accommodation. Ideal for families, the spacious, en suite bedrooms include remote-control TV, tea and coffee-making facilities, luxury beds and free morning newspaper. Meals can be taken at the nearby family restaurant. For further details and the Travelodge phone number, consult the Hotel Groups page.

**ROOMS:** 40 en suite

SANDBACH, Cheshire — Map 07 SJ76

### ★★★65% Chimney House

REGAL

Congleton Rd CW11 4ST
☎ 01270 764141 01270 768916
e-mail: chimneyhouse@corushotels.com
**Dir:** *on A534, 1m from M6 junct 17 heading for Congleton*
Set in eight acres of attractive grounds, this half-timbered Tudor style building is conveniently located close to junction 17 of the M6 motorway. Bedrooms are bright, modern and well equipped with more spacious rooms being located in the older wing. Dinner

continued

is served in the attractive Patio restaurant. Meeting and function suites are available, together with a sauna and spa bath.

**ROOMS:** 48 en suite (15 fmly) No smoking in 33 bedrooms s £75-£85; d £85-£95 * **LB** **FACILITIES:** STV Sauna Putting green entertainment **CONF:** Thtr 120 Class 40 Board 40 Del from £90 * **PARKING:** 110 **NOTES:** No dogs (ex guide dogs) No smoking in restaurant Civ Wed 60 **CARDS:**

SANDBANKS See Poole

## SANDIACRE, Derbyshire
Map 08 SK43

### ★★★66% *Posthouse Nottingham/Derby*
Bostocks Ln NG10 5NJ
**Posthouse**
☎ 0870 400 9062 📠 0115 9490469
***Dir:*** *M1 J25 follow exit to Sandiacre, hotel on right*
Bedrooms at this modern hotel offer a good standard of contemporary furnishings. Public areas are well-maintained and comfortable. Staff are friendly and helpful, and an all-day lounge menu and 24-hour room service are available.
**ROOMS:** 93 en suite (6 fmly) No smoking in 50 bedrooms **FACILITIES:** Day membership to David Lloyd Leisure **CONF:** Thtr 60 Class 26 Board 28 **PARKING:** 180 **CARDS:**

## SANDIWAY, Cheshire
Map 07 SJ67

**Premier Collection**

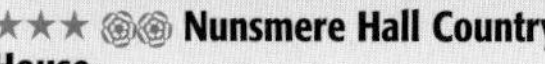

### ★★★ ◎◎ Nunsmere Hall Country House
Tarporley Rd CW8 2ES
☎ 01606 889100 📠 01606 889055
e-mail: reservations@nunsmere.co.uk
***Dir:*** *from Chester follow A51, A556-Manchester, reach intersection at A49 turn right to Whitchurch, Nunsmere Hall is 1m on left hand side*
This impeccably maintained, lakeside house dates back to 1900. The bedrooms are individually styled, tastefully appointed to a very high standard and thoughtfully equipped. Guests can relax in a choice of elegant lounges, the library or the oak-panelled bar. In the restaurant, the menu offers a cosmopolitan range of dishes.
**ROOMS:** 36 en suite No smoking in 10 bedrooms s £122.50-£142.50; d £170-£195 * **LB** **FACILITIES:** Fishing Snooker Croquet lawn Putting green Archery Air rifle & Clay pigeon shooting Falconry entertainment Xmas **CONF:** Thtr 50 Class 24 Board 32 Del from £197.50 * **SERVICES:** Lift **PARKING:** 80 **NOTES:** No dogs (ex guide dogs) No smoking in restaurant RS Sun Civ Wed 70 **CARDS:**

SANDOWN See Wight, Isle of

## SANDWICH, Kent
Map 05 TR35

### ★★65% The Blazing Donkey Country Hotel & Inn
Hay Hill, Ham CT14 0ED
☎ 01304 617362 📠 01304 615264
e-mail: info@blazingdonkey.co.uk
***Dir:*** *turn off A256 at Eastry into the village, turn right at the Five Bells public house, hotel is 0.75m along the lane situated on the left*
The Blazing Donkey is set in the heart of Kentish farmland. A former labourer's cottage and barn, it is now a distinctive inn of character. The atmosphere is convivial and informal. Bedrooms are big and arranged around a courtyard. Ideal for golfers, the hotel is close to Royal St George's.
**ROOMS:** 19 en suite 3 annexe en suite (2 fmly) No smoking in 5 bedrooms s £65-£70; d £79.50-£150 (incl. cont bkfst) * **LB** **FACILITIES:** STV Croquet lawn Putting green Childrens playground ch fac Xmas **SERVICES:** air con **PARKING:** 108 **NOTES:** No smoking in restaurant Civ Wed 350 **CARDS:**

## SAUNDERTON, Buckinghamshire
Map 04 SP70

### ★★64% Rose & Crown
Wycombe Rd HP27 9NP
☎ 01844 345299 📠 01844 343140
e-mail: rose.crown@btinternet.com
***Dir:*** *on A4010, 6m from M40 junct 4*
The Rose and Crown has been offering hospitality to travellers for over a century. Rooms are comfortable, with a range of extra facilities. The bar, with its log fire, is the focal point of the hotel. Guests may choose dinner from an extensive blackboard menu, with meals taken in the bar or the restaurant which overlooks the attractive patio gardens.
**ROOMS:** 15 en suite No smoking in 5 bedrooms s £73.25; d fr £87 (incl. bkfst) * **LB** **FACILITIES:** Xmas **CONF:** Thtr 35 Class 20 Board 50 Del from £150 * **PARKING:** 50 **NOTES:** No dogs (ex guide dogs) No smoking in restaurant **CARDS:**

## SAUNTON, Devon
Map 02 SS43

### ★★★★70% Saunton Sands
EX33 1LQ
*Brend Hotels*
☎ 01271 890212 📠 01271 890145
e-mail: info@sauntonsands.co.uk
***Dir:*** *turn off A361 at Braunton, signposted Croyde B3231 hotel 2m on left*
With direct access to five miles of sandy beach, this popular hotel enjoys stunning sea views. Bedrooms vary in size, several have private balconies and a number are especia[lly suited for family] occupation. All of the public areas benefit fr[om] ... A choice of comfortable lounges is provide[d] ... entertainment arranged on certain evening[s] ...

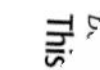

SAUNTON, continued

facilities are available, including both indoor and outdoor swimming pools and a supervised nursery.

*Saunton Sands, Saunton*

**ROOMS:** 92 en suite (39 fmly) s £68-£102; d £136-£216 (incl. bkfst) * **LB** **FACILITIES:** **Spa** STV Indoor swimming (H) Outdoor swimming (H) Tennis (hard) Squash Snooker Sauna Solarium Gym Putting green Table tennis entertainment ch fac Xmas **CONF:** Thtr 150 **SERVICES:** Lift **PARKING:** 142 **NOTES:** No dogs (ex guide dogs) No smoking in restaurant Civ Wed 100 **CARDS:**

*See advert on opposite page*

### ★★74% Preston House

EX33 1LG
☎ 01271 890472 01271 890555
e-mail: prestonhouse-saunton@zoom.co.uk

Preston House occupies a stunning elevated position and has an outdoor heated pool and direct access to Saunton beach. The bedrooms are equipped with modern comforts and most benefit from the best of the views. There is an elegant sitting room, a sunny conservatory where breakfast is served and an impressive dining room where guests can sample imaginative dishes.

**ROOMS:** 12 en suite No smoking in all bedrooms s £55-£75; d £110-£140 (incl. bkfst) * **LB** **FACILITIES:** Outdoor swimming (H) Sauna Solarium Jacuzzi **PARKING:** 16 **NOTES:** No dogs (ex guide dogs) No children 15yrs No smoking in restaurant Closed 21 Dec-Jan **CARDS:**

## SCARBOROUGH, North Yorkshire   Map 08 TA08

### ★★★71% *Ox Pasture Hall Country Hotel*

Lady Ediths Dr, Raincliffe Woods YO12 5TD
☎ 01723 365295 01723 355156
e-mail: hawksmoor@oxpasture.freeserve.co.uk

***Dir:** A171 out of Scarborough, after passing hospital, follow tourist sign for "Forge Valley & Raincliffe Woods" turn left, hotel 1.5m on right*

This delightful country hotel is a lovely conversion of a farmhouse in the North Riding Forest Park. Three bedrooms are in the main house and the others around an attractive garden courtyard. Public areas include a split-level bar, a quiet lounge, and attractive restaurant offering both a carte and a fixed-price menu.

**ROOMS:** 23 en suite (4 fmly) No smoking in 4 bedrooms **FACILITIES:** Fishing Croquet lawn Putting green **PARKING:** 30 **NOTES:** No smoking in restaurant **CARDS:**

### ★★★70% *Wrea Head Country Hotel*

Scalby YO13 0PB
☎ 01723 378211 01723 371780
e-mail: wreahead@englishrosehotels.co.uk

***Dir:** from Scarborough follow A171 until hotel signpost on left, turn into ·rmoor Lane, hotel drive is on left*

·legant Victorian country house is situated in 14 acres of

landscaped grounds and gardens amongst splendid scenery on the edge of the town. The comfortable bedrooms are individually furnished and decorated, many of them with fine views. Public rooms include the oak-panelled lounge with an inglenook fireplace and a beautiful library lounge, full of books and games. Staff are friendly, helpful and enthusiastic.

**ROOMS:** 20 en suite (2 fmly) **FACILITIES:** STV Croquet lawn Putting green **CONF:** Thtr 30 Class 16 Board 20 **PARKING:** 50 **NOTES:** No dogs (ex guide dogs) No smoking in restaurant Civ Wed 60 **CARDS:**

*See advert on page 519*

### ★★★69% Beiderbecke's Hotel

1-3 The Crescent YO11 2PW
☎ 01723 365766 01723 367433
e-mail: info@beiderbeckes.com

An elegant Georgian building, close to the town centre and with its own car parking. The recently refurbished bedrooms are well-equipped, and the public rooms include a spacious oak-panelled bar and Marmalades restaurant. A good range of food is also available in the bar/brasserie.

**ROOMS:** 27 en suite (1 fmly) No smoking in 10 bedrooms s £40-£70; d £60-£120 (incl. bkfst) * **LB** **FACILITIES:** Snooker entertainment Xmas **SERVICES:** Lift **PARKING:** 18 **NOTES:** No dogs (ex guide dogs) **CARDS:**

### ★★★65% Esplanade

Belmont Rd YO11 2AA
☎ 01723 360382 01723 376137

***Dir:** from Scarborough town centre cross Valley Bridge, left after bridge then immediate right onto Belmont Rd, hotel 100mtrs on right*

This large hotel enjoys a superb position overlooking South Bay and the harbour. Both the terrace leading off the lounge bar and the restaurant, with its striking oriel window, benefit from these views. Bedrooms are well-furnished to a stylish modern standard and are well-equipped.

**ROOMS:** 73 en suite (9 fmly) s £47; d £88-£98 (incl. bkfst) * **LB** **FACILITIES:** Table tennis Xmas **CONF:** Thtr 140 Class 100 Board 40 Del from £45 * **SERVICES:** Lift **PARKING:** 20 **NOTES:** No smoking in restaurant Closed 2 Jan-4 Feb **CARDS:**

### ★★★64% Palm Court

St Nicholas Cliff YO11 2ES
☎ 01723 368161 01723 371547

***Dir:** follow signs for Town Centre and Town Hall, hotel is on route to Town Hall situated on right hand side*

The public rooms are spacious and comfortable at this modern town centre hotel and the bedrooms are well-equipped. Traditional cooking is provided in the attractive restaurant while staff are friendly and helpful. Garage parking is guaranteed.

**ROOMS:** 46 en suite (7 fmly) s £41-£46; d £76-£86 (incl. bkfst) * **LB** **FACILITIES:** Indoor swimming (H) Table tennis entertainment Xmas **CONF:** Thtr 200 Class 100 Board 60 Del from £52 * **SERVICES:** Lift **PARKING:** 80 **NOTES:** No dogs (ex guide dogs) **CARDS:**

*See advert on opposite page*

### ★★★64% Hotel St Nicholas

St Nicholas Cliff YO11 2EU
☎ 01723 364101 01723 500538
e-mail: stnicholas@british-trust-hotels.com

***Dir:** in town centre, railway station on right, turn right at traffic lights, left at next set, follow road along, across rdbt, take next left*

A splendid Victorian hotel with fine views over the sea and with easy access to the town. Bedrooms are well-equipped and there is a wide choice in room size. There are good lounge and bar

*continued on p518*

S

SCARBOROUGH, continued

facilities as well as a leisure club. Traditional food is served in the restaurant and there is also a themed pub.

Hotel St Nicholas, Scarborough

**ROOMS:** 144 en suite (17 fmly) No smoking in 4 bedrooms s £71; d £95 (incl. bkfst) * **LB** **FACILITIES:** STV Indoor swimming (H) Snooker Sauna Solarium Gym Supervised children's club during school holidays entertainment ch fac Xmas **CONF:** Thtr 400 Class 500 Board 50 **SERVICES:** Lift **PARKING:** 24 **NOTES:** No dogs (ex guide dogs) No smoking in restaurant Civ Wed 300 **CARDS:**

**★★★63% Crown**
Esplanade YO11 2AG
☎ 01723 357400 01723 362271
e-mail: reservations@ScarboroughHotel.com
***Dir:*** *On A64 follow town centre signs to traffic lights opposite railway station, turn right across Valley Bridge, then 1st left and right up Belmont Rd to cliff top*

Occupying a prime position on the South Cliff, this elegant hotel overlooks the sea and is only a short walk from the town centre. Several bedrooms enjoy spectacular views over Scarborough Bay. The hotel has comfortable lounges, extensive conference facilities, and an impressive new leisure centre.
**ROOMS:** 83 en suite (7 fmly) s £43-£65; d £66-£116 (incl. bkfst) * **LB** **FACILITIES:** Indoor swimming (H) Snooker Sauna Solarium Gym Jacuzzi ch fac Xmas **CONF:** Thtr 180 Class 100 Board 100 Del from £60 * **SERVICES:** Lift **NOTES:** No smoking in restaurant Civ Wed 70 **CARDS:**

*See advert on page 521*

**★★★62% Ambassador**
Centre of the Esplanade YO11 2AY
☎ 01723 362841 01723 366166
***Dir:*** *A64, right at 1st small rdbt opposite, then right at next small rdbt, take immediate left down Avenue Victoria to the Cliff Top*
Standing on the South Cliff with excellent views over the bay, this friendly hotel offers well-equipped bedrooms, some of which are executive rooms. A 40' indoor pool, sauna and solarium are available, and residents can also use the facilities at the Crown Hotel just along the road. Entertainment is provided during high season.
**ROOMS:** 59 en suite (10 fmly) s fr £24; d fr £48 (incl. bkfst) * **LB** **FACILITIES:** **Spa** STV Indoor swimming (H) Sauna Solarium Steam room hot tub Aroma room entertainment Xmas **CONF:** Thtr 140 Class 90 Board 60 Del from £40 * **SERVICES:** Lift
**CARDS:**

*See advert on page 521*

**★★★61% Clifton**
Queens Pde, North Cliff YO12 7HX
☎ 01723 375691 01723 364203
e-mail: clifton@englishrosehotels.co.uk
***Dir:*** *on entering the town centre, follow signs for North Bay*
Standing in an impressive position overlooking the bay, this large holiday hotel is convenient for Peasholm Park and other local leisure attractions. Bedrooms are pleasant and entertainment is provided in the spacious public rooms during the season.
**ROOMS:** 71 en suite (11 fmly) s £35-£55; d £75-£90 (incl. bkfst) * **LB** **FACILITIES:** Sauna Solarium Xmas **CONF:** Thtr 120 Class 50 Board 50 Del from £65 * **SERVICES:** Lift **PARKING:** 45 **NOTES:** No dogs (ex guide dogs) No smoking in restaurant
**CARDS:**

*See advert on opposite page*

**★★74% Gridley's Crescent**
The Crescent YO11 2PP
☎ 01723 360929 & 507507 01723 354126
e-mail: reception@crescent-hotel.co.uk
***Dir:*** *on entering Scarborough travel towards railway station then follow signs to Brunswick Pavilion, at traffic lights turn into Crescent*
This smartly presented listed building sits just a short distance from the town centre. The modern accommodation is thoughtfully equipped with a useful range of facilities. A choice of dining options and bars is another bonus. There is an elegant restaurant serving a set price menu and carte, and a separate carvery offering a less formal option. Service is friendly and attentive.
**ROOMS:** 20 en suite No smoking in 7 bedrooms s fr £45; d fr £80 (incl. bkfst) * **LB** **CONF:** Thtr 40 Board 15 Del from £73 * **SERVICES:** Lift **NOTES:** No dogs (ex guide dogs) No children 6yrs No smoking in restaurant **CARDS:**

**★★71% *The Mount***
Cliff Bridge Ter, Saint Nicholas Cliff YO11 2HA
☎ 01723 360961 01723 360961
Standing in a superb, elevated position enjoying magnificent views of the bay, this elegant Regency hotel is personally owned and managed to a high standard. The richly furnished and comfortable public rooms are inviting, and the well-equipped bedrooms have been attractively decorated. The de luxe rooms are mini-suites and are most comfortable.
**ROOMS:** 50 en suite (5 fmly) No smoking in 2 bedrooms **FACILITIES:** **SERVICES:** Lift **NOTES:** Closed Jan-mid Mar **CARDS:**

*See advert on page 517*

**★★68% Park Manor**
Northstead Manor Dr YO12 6BB
☎ 01723 372090 01723 500480
Enjoying a peaceful residential setting to the north of town, this smartly presented hotel provides the seaside tourist with a wide range of facilities. Bedrooms vary in size and style but all are smartly furnished and well equipped. Day rooms include a spacious lounge, smart restaurant and a games room suitable for

*continued on p520*

S

# ENGLISH ROSE HOTELS

# WREA HEAD COUNTRY HOUSE HOTEL

Sample the delights of this beautifully restored Victorian Country House set in acres of glorious gardens and park lands at the edge of the North York Moors National Park. Twenty individually styled bedrooms. Award winning Four Seasons restaurant offers superb cuisine using fresh local produce. Ample free car parking. Situated three miles north of Scarborough – a perfect base for touring the heritage coast. Meeting facilities for up to 20 persons in privacy and seclusion.

**For details ring 01723 378211**
**Barmoor Lane, Scalby**
**Scarborough YO13 0PB**
**Fax: 01723 355936**

AA

★★★

# HACKNESS GRANGE COUNTRY HOTEL

AA ★★★

**North Yorkshire Moors National Park**
**nr Scarborough YO13 0JW**

Situated on the outskirts of Scarborough, this gracious Country House is set in acres of beautiful gardens and grounds beside the River Derwent, within the North York Moors National Park. Excellent leisure choices - indoor heated swimming pool with jacuzzi, tennis court, trout fishing (in season), croquet and nine hole pitch 'n putt. 33 delightful en-suite bedrooms, many with scenic country views, and award winning restaurant renowned for good food. Some ground floor rooms available. Perfect location for Board Meetings and available for exclusive use for corporated events and activities.

*See entry under Hackness*

**Tel: 01723 882345 Fax: 01723 882391**

CLIFTON HOTEL

# THE CLIFTON HOTEL

**QUEENS PARADE, NORTH SHORE**
**SCARBOROUGH YO12 7HX**
**Tel: 01723 375691 Fax: 01723 364203**

AA ★★★

The finest location on Scarborough's North Shore with many of the 71 en-suite bedrooms having panoramic sea views over the Bay and Scarborough Castle headland.
Excellent food with good old fashioned Yorkshire portions! Free private car parking.
Adjacent to Alexander Bowls Centre and Scarborough Cricket Ground.

ENGLISH ROSE HOTELS

SCARBOROUGH, continued

both adults and children; a heated indoor pool and steam room also prove popular. Staff throughout are very friendly.
**ROOMS:** 42 en suite (6 fmly) s £31.50-£36.50; d £63-£79 (incl. bkfst) * **LB** **FACILITIES:** Indoor swimming (H) Solarium Jacuzzi Pool table Steam room Xmas **CONF:** Thtr 25 Class 20 Board 80 Del from £55 * **SERVICES:** Lift **PARKING:** 20 **NOTES:** No dogs No children 3yrs **CARDS:**

### ★★66% Red Lea

Prince of Wales Ter YO11 2AJ
☎ 01723 362431 📠 01723 371230
e-mail: redlea@globalnet.co.uk
***Dir:*** *follow signs for South Cliff, Prince of Wales Terrace leads off the esplanade opp the cliff lift*

A traditional, friendly, family-owned hotel situated close to the cliff lift. Bedrooms are well-equipped and comfortably furnished, and many at the front have views of the picturesque coast. There are two main lounges and a spacious dining room in which good-value, five-course meals are served.
**ROOMS:** 67 en suite (7 fmly) s £33-£37; d £66-£74 (incl. bkfst) * **LB** **FACILITIES:** Indoor swimming (H) Sauna Solarium Gym Xmas **CONF:** Thtr 40 Class 25 Board 25 Del from £60 * **SERVICES:** Lift **NOTES:** No dogs (ex guide dogs) No smoking in restaurant **CARDS:**

### ★★65% *Bradley Court Hotel*

Filey Rd, South Cliff YO11 2SE
☎ 01723 360476 📠 01723 376661
e-mail: bradley@yorkshirecoast.co.uk
***Dir:*** *from A64 enter Scarborough Town limits, at 1st rdbt turn right signposted Filey & South Cliff, at next rdbt turn left, hotel 50yds on left*

This popular hotel is only a short walk from both the town centre and the South Cliff. Bedrooms are well-equipped and there are spacious public rooms which include a bar lounge and a large, modern function room suitable for weddings and conferences.
**ROOMS:** 40 en suite (4 fmly) No smoking in 6 bedrooms **CONF:** Thtr 160 Class 100 Board 60 **SERVICES:** Lift **PARKING:** 20 **NOTES:** No dogs No smoking in restaurant **CARDS:**

### ★★63% Southlands

15 West St, South Cliff YO11 2QW
☎ 01723 361461 📠 01723 376035
e-mail: sales@southlandshotel.co.uk
***Dir:*** *in Scarborough, follow town centre signs, turn right at railway station, at 2nd set of traffic lights turn left, car park is 200yds on left*

This hotel, popular with tour groups, is situated in a quiet area close to the South Cliff. Bedrooms are spacious and the newly refurbished public rooms are bright and airy. Friendly and attentive service is provided by a pleasant and well managed team.
**ROOMS:** 58 en suite (8 fmly) No smoking in 2 bedrooms s £31-£47 (incl. bkfst & dinner) * **LB** **FACILITIES:** entertainment Xmas **CONF:** Thtr 120 Class 30 Board 30 Del from £70 * **SERVICES:** Lift **PARKING:** 35 **NOTES:** No smoking in restaurant **CARDS:**

### ★★61% Manor Heath Hotel

67 Northstead Manor Dr YO12 6AF
☎ 01723 365720 📠 01723 365720
e-mail: enquiries@manorheath.co.uk
***Dir:*** *follow signs for North Bay and Peasholm Park*

A warm welcome is offered at this pleasant traditional private hotel, situated on the North Bay beside Peasholm Park. Public areas include a cosy bar and comfortable lounge together with a relaxing dining room. The bedrooms vary in size and style but all are modern and bright and offer all the expected comforts.
**ROOMS:** 14 en suite (6 fmly) s £23; d £46 (incl. bkfst) * **LB** **PARKING:** 16 **NOTES:** No smoking in restaurant Closed Dec-1 Jan1 **CARDS:**

### ★★60% Brooklands

Esplanade Gardens, South Cliff YO11 2AW
☎ 01723 376576 📠 01723 376576
***Dir:*** *from A64 York turn left at B&Q rdbt, right at next mini rdbt then 1st left onto Victoria Av, at the end turn left then 2nd left*

BROOKLANDS

The Brooklands is a traditional, family owned and run seaside hotel. It successfully caters for tours and offers sound value for money. The hotel stands on the South Cliff overlooking Esplanade Gardens, and is within close access to the sea. There are ample lounges to relax in and wholesome home cooking to enjoy.
**ROOMS:** 63 rms (62 en suite) (11 fmly) s £20-£34; d £40-£68 (incl. bkfst) * **LB** **FACILITIES:** Riding entertainment ch fac Xmas **CONF:** Thtr 120 Class 80 Board 30 Del from £30 * **SERVICES:** Lift **PARKING:** 1 **NOTES:** No dogs (ex guide dogs) No smoking in restaurant Closed Jan RS Feb **CARDS:**

## SCILLY, ISLES OF — Map 02

## BRYHER — Map 02

### ★★★72% Hell Bay Hotel

TR23 0PR
☎ 01720 422947 📠 01720 423004
e-mail: hellbay@aol.com
***Dir:*** *island location means it is only accessible by helicopter from Penzance, ship from Penzance or plane from Bristol, Exeter, Plymouth or Land's End*

This friendly hotel is located on the smallest of the inhabited islands and provides a wonderful setting for rest, relaxation and peace. Spacious bedrooms have a seating area and access to the garden; many have marvellous sea views. Public areas include a comfortable lounge and stylish restaurant.
**ROOMS:** 17 en suite (3 fmly) **FACILITIES:** Croquet lawn Putting green Boules ch fac **NOTES:** No dogs (ex guide dogs) No smoking in restaurant Closed 29 Oct-12 Mar **CARDS:**

*See advert on opposite page*

Late for dinner? Quality Standards star rating means that last orders for dinner should be no earlier than:
★ 6.30pm ★★ 7.00pm ★★★ 8.00pm
★★★★ 9.00pm ★★★★★ 10.00pm

Tregarthen's Hotel
ST. MARY'S, ISLES OF SCILLY TR21 0PP
Telephone: 01720 422 540 Facsimile: 01720 422 089
Genuine Island Hospitality for over 150 years!
TREGARTHENS

*Tregarthen's Hotel was founded by the good Captain F B Tregarthen over 150 years ago when he brought visitors to St. Mary's on his steam packet together with the Islands' provisions. His guests weren't allowed to leave until more supplies were needed!*

*Today we continue his tradition of superb comfort, wonderful hospitality, excellent food and attentive service. The hotel has panoramic views of the 'off islands', a commanding position over the quay and is just a few minutes walk from the main shopping centre. Stay in one of our 33 en-suite bedrooms, with colour TV, tea and coffee facilities and telephone. We promise that you will enjoy your visit.*

AA
★★

*website: www.tregarthens-hotel.co.uk*
*email: reception@tregarthens-hotel.co.uk*

*Ring (01720) 422 540 or write for your FREE colour brochure*

# Hell Bay Hotel

**Bryher**
**Isle of Scilly TR23 0PR**
**Tel: 01720 422947 Fax: 01720 423004**
**Web: www.hellbay.co.uk**
**Email: hellbay@aol.com**

This friendly hotel is located on the smallest of the inhabited islands and provides a wonderful setting for rest, relaxation and peace.

Spacious bedrooms include a seating area and access to the garden; many have marvellous sea views.

Public areas include a comfortable lounge and stylish restaurant.

# Ambassador Hotel

Centre of the Esplanade
Scarborough YO11 2AY
Tel: 01723 362841 Fax: 01723 366166
www.scarboroughhotel.co.uk

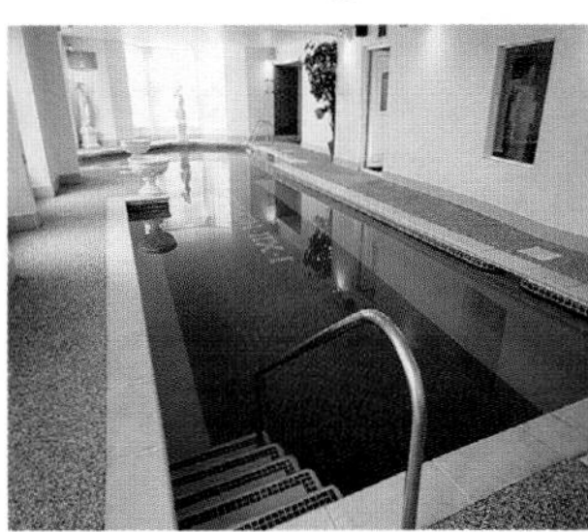

Standing on the South Cliff with excellent views over the bay, this friendly hotel well-equipped bedrooms, some of which are executive rooms. A 40' indoor pool, sauna and solarium are available, and residents can also use the facilities at the Crown Hotel just along the road. Entertainment is provided during high season.

# Crown Hotel

Esplanade, Scarborough YO11 2AG
Tel: 01723 357400 Fax: 01723 362271
reservations@ScarboroughHotel.com
www.ScarboroughHotel.com

Occupying a prime position on the South Cliff, this elegant hotel overlooks the sea and is only a short walk from the town centre. Several bedrooms enjoy spectacular views over Scarborough Bay.
The hotel has comfortable lounges, extensive conference facilities, and a new impressive leisure centre.

S

## ST MARTIN'S Map 02

**Premier Collection**

### ★★★ ®®® St Martin's on the Isle

Lower Town TR25 0QW
☎ 01720 422090 📠 01720 422298
e-mail: stay@stmartinshotel.co.uk
***Dir:*** *20 minute helicopter flight to St Marys, then 20 minute launch to St Martin's*

PRIDE OF BRITAIN MEMBER

St Martin's is an ideal island hideaway. It is the perfect choice for those who are seeking a peaceful and relaxing break. The hotel has its own beach, jetty and yacht, and enjoys an unrivalled panorama across the waves. The bedrooms are all individually decorated and furnished, while the public rooms offer comfort and quality in equal measure. Accomplished cuisine continues to impress, particularly after all that fresh air!
**ROOMS:** 30 en suite (10 fmly) s £85-£120; d £170-£240 (incl. bkfst & dinner) * **LB** **FACILITIES:** Indoor swimming (H) Tennis (hard) Snooker Clay pigeon shooting Boating Bikes Snorkelling ch fac **CONF:** Thtr 50 Class 50 Board 50 **NOTES:** No smoking in restaurant Closed Nov-Mar Civ Wed 60
**CARDS:**

## ST MARY'S Map 02

### ★★★70% ® Star Castle

The Garrison TR21 0JA
☎ 01720 422317 & 423342 📠 01720 422343
e-mail: recep@starcastlescilly.demon.co.uk
***Dir:*** *overlooking the Harbour.*

Built in 1593 as a fortress, this historic landmark now houses a comfortable hotel complete with modern facilities and panoramic views over St Mary's and the surrounding islands. Bedrooms vary in style and size, and most have sea views. The garden apartments are the most spacious whilst the castle rooms include four-poster beds and oak beamed ceilings. The cuisine is a strong feature of the hotel, and guests can choose between a bar meal on the ramparts, a seafood extravaganza in the garden conservatory or a traditional dinner from the carte menu in the castle restaurant.
**ROOMS:** 10 en suite 23 annexe en suite (17 fmly) s £76-£84.50; d £200-£216 (incl. bkfst & dinner) * **LB** **FACILITIES:** Indoor swimming (H) Tennis (grass) Games room ch fac **PARKING:** 6 **NOTES:** No smoking in restaurant Closed end Oct-Feb **CARDS:**

### ★★76% *Tregarthens*

Hugh Town TR21 0PP
☎ 01720 422540 📠 01720 422089
e-mail: reception@tregarthens-hotel.co.uk
***Dir:*** *100yds from the quay*

This well-established hotel was opened in 1848 by Captain Tregarthen, a steam packet owner. It overlooks St Mary's harbour and some of the many islands, including Tresco and Bryher. Many bedrooms benefit from marvellous views out to sea; all are well-equipped and neatly furnished. Traditional cuisine, with some wonderful home-made desserts, is served in the restaurant.
**ROOMS:** 32 en suite 1 annexe en suite (5 fmly) **NOTES:** No dogs No smoking in restaurant Closed late Oct-mid Mar
**CARDS:**

*See advert on previous page*

## TRESCO Map 02

### ★★★79% ® The Island

TR24 0PU
☎ 01720 422883 📠 01720 423008
e-mail: islandhotel@tresco.co.uk
***Dir:*** *helicopter service Penzance to Tresco, hotel on north east side of island*

The magnificent island setting and stunning gardens are just two of many reasons for visiting this splendid hotel. Sunny public rooms include a popular lounge and bar, together with a quiet library for residents. Bedroom accommodation has been designed to make the best of the spectacular sea views. Local fish and shellfish are staples on the regularly-changing menus.
**ROOMS:** 48 en suite (27 fmly) **FACILITIES:** Outdoor swimming (H) Tennis (hard) Fishing Croquet lawn Boating Table tennis Bowls ch fac **NOTES:** No dogs (ex guide dogs) No smoking in restaurant Closed Nov-Feb **CARDS:**

### ★★76% ® New Inn

TR24 0QQ
☎ 01720 422844 📠 01720 423200
e-mail: newinn@tresco.co.uk
***Dir:*** *by New Grimsby Quay*

One of the few hostelries on the island, it provides good cheer, a warm welcome and comfortable surroundings in equal measures. The restaurant and the bar provide a good range of tasty meals, with a new bistro eating option proving popular. Bedrooms are well-maintained, smart and well suited to guests' needs.
**ROOMS:** 14 en suite s £81-£122; d £124-£188 (incl. bkfst & dinner) * **LB** **FACILITIES:** **Spa** Outdoor swimming (H) Tennis (hard) Sea fishing Xmas **NOTES:** No dogs No smoking in restaurant
**CARDS:**

## SCOTCH CORNER (NEAR RICHMOND), North Yorkshire Map 08 NZ20

### ★★★64% Quality Hotel, Scotch Corner

Quality Hotel

DL10 6NR
☎ 01748 850900 📠 01748 825417
e-mail: admin@gb609.u-net.com
***Dir:*** *at A1/A66 junct turn off towards Penrith*

Well located with good parking facilities, this hotel offers spacious lounges, conference facilities and a leisure club. The bedrooms fall into two well-equipped and comfortable categories: Standard and Premier Plus. Food is served all day in the lounges and the restaurant, where there is a choice of evening menus.
**ROOMS:** 90 en suite (5 fmly) No smoking in 45 bedrooms s £55-£91; d £50-£108 (incl. bkfst) * **LB** **FACILITIES:** **Spa** STV Indoor swimming (H) Sauna Solarium Gym Jacuzzi Beauty Therapist Physiotherapy Suite Dance Studio entertainment Xmas **CONF:** Thtr 280 Class 110 Board 40 Del from £72 * **SERVICES:** Lift **PARKING:** 200 **NOTES:** No smoking in restaurant Civ Wed 200 **CARDS:**

TV dinner? Room service at three stars and above.

*continued*

S

### ⇧ *Travelodge*
Skeeby DL10 5EQ
☎ 01748 823768 🖷 01748 823768
***Dir:*** *0.5m S on A1*

Travelodge

Travelodge offers good quality, good value, modern accommodation. Ideal for families, the spacious, en suite bedrooms include remote-control TV, tea and coffee-making facilities, luxury beds and free morning newspaper. Meals can be taken at the nearby family restaurant. For further details and the Travelodge phone number, consult the Hotel Groups page.

**ROOMS:** 40 en suite

### ⇧ *Travelodge*
Middleton Tyas Ln DL10 6PQ
☎ 01325 377177 🖷 01325 377890
***Dir:*** *A1/A66*

Travelodge

Travelodge offers good quality, good value, modern accommodation. Ideal for families, the spacious, en suite bedrooms include remote-control TV, tea and coffee-making facilities, luxury beds and free morning newspaper. Meals can be taken at the nearby family restaurant. For further details and the Travelodge phone number, consult the Hotel Groups page.

**ROOMS:** 50 en suite

## SCUNTHORPE, Lincolnshire — Map 08 SE81

### ★★★★70% Forest Pines Hotel
Ermine St, Broughton DN20 0AQ
☎ 01652 650770 🖷 01652 650495
e-mail: enquiries@forestpines.co.uk
***Dir:*** *200yds from junct 4 on the M180, on the Brigg-Scunthorpe rdbt*

Best Western

This large, well-furnished hotel provides many attractions, including extensive leisure facilities. Service and hospitality are caring and attentive, while the bedrooms are well-equipped and spacious. Quality cooking is available in the elegant restaurant and a second option gives a choice of styles.
**ROOMS:** 86 en suite (40 fmly) No smoking in 50 bedrooms s £70-£90; d £90-£100 (incl. bkfst) * **LB** **FACILITIES:** STV Indoor swimming (H) Golf 27 Sauna Gym Putting green Jacuzzi Mountain bikes Jogging track entertainment ch fac Xmas **CONF:** Thtr 220 Class 100 Board 60 Del from £136 * **SERVICES:** Lift **PARKING:** 300 **NOTES:** No dogs (ex guide dogs) No smoking in restaurant Civ Wed 120
**CARDS:**

### ★★★67% Menzies Royal
Doncaster Rd DN15 7DE
☎ 0870 6003013 🖷 01332 511144
e-mail: info@menzies-hotels.co.uk
***Dir:*** *from M181, follow A18 to Scunthorpe centre, hotel is on left at a crossroads*

MENZIES HOTELS

This recently refurbished hotel provides modern, freshly decorated bedrooms and attentive service. There is an extensive range of conference and banqueting facilities and a small gym.
**ROOMS:** 33 en suite (1 fmly) No smoking in 10 bedrooms s £69.50; d £79.50 * **LB** **FACILITIES:** Gym Xmas **CONF:** Thtr 240 Class 200 Board 100 Del from £95 * **PARKING:** 33 **NOTES:** No smoking in restaurant Civ Wed 240 **CARDS:**

## SEAHAM, Co Durham — Map 12 NZ44
see also Rushyford

### ★★★★78% Seaham Hall Hotel
Lord Byron's Walk SR7 7AG
☎ 0191 516 1400 🖷 0191 516 1410
e-mail: reservations@seahamhall.com
***Dir:*** *Leave A19 at 1st exit marked B1404 Seaham, at junct turn left into Seaham, at traffic lights straight ahead over level crossing. Hotel approx 0.25m on right*

On a clifftop promontory overlooking the North Sea, this one-time home to Lord Byron has been beautifully restored. Bedrooms are individually designed and include three suites. The hotel offers extensive state-of-the-art conference facilities, landscaped gardens, and a large Oriental Spa, due to open in January 2002. Customer care is a priority throughout.
**ROOMS:** 19 en suite No smoking in all bedrooms s £185-£600; d £195-£600 (incl. cont bkfst) * **LB** **FACILITIES:** ch fac Xmas **CONF:** Thtr 140 Class 60 Board 25 Del from £200 * **SERVICES:** Lift air con **PARKING:** 122 **NOTES:** No dogs (ex guide dogs) No smoking in restaurant Civ Wed 100 **CARDS:**

## SEAHOUSES, Northumberland — Map 12 NU23

### ★★74% Olde Ship
NE68 7RD
☎ 01665 720200 🖷 01665 721383
e-mail: theoldeship@seahouses.co.uk
***Dir:*** *lower end of main street above harbour*
Set close to the harbour, this friendly family-run hotel has tremendous character with many areas adorned with nautical memorabilia. There is a cabin bar as well as the popular saloon

*continued on p524*

S

SEAHOUSES, continued

bar, a cosy dining room and a quiet upstairs lounge. Bedrooms come in mixed sizes, are well-equipped and decorated to a high standard. The flagship of the accommodation however is two stunningly impressive apartment rooms in an adjacent building right above the harbour.
**ROOMS:** 12 en suite 6 annexe en suite s £35-£42; d £70-£84 (incl. bkfst) * **LB** **FACILITIES:** STV Putting green **PARKING:** 19 **NOTES:** No dogs No children 10yrs No smoking in restaurant Closed Dec-Jan
**CARDS:**

★★69% **Bamburgh Castle**
NE68 7SQ
☎ 01665 720283 01665 720848
e-mail: bamburghcastlehotel@talk21.com
***Dir:*** *from A1 follow signs for Seahouses*
Situated on the harbour front with splendid views of Bamburgh Castle, the Farne Islands and Lindisfarne, this privately owned hotel is well located for visiting local tourist attractions. Bedrooms vary in size and style, all are thoughtfully equipped and superior rooms are particularly spacious and attractively appointed. Guests have a choice of several comfortable lounges including one that is non-smoking.
**ROOMS:** 20 en suite (3 fmly) No smoking in 5 bedrooms s £40-£45; d £75-£92 (incl. bkfst) * **LB** **FACILITIES:** Putting green Outdoor table tennis **CONF:** Thtr 40 Class 20 Board 25 **PARKING:** 30 **NOTES:** Closed 24-26 Dec & 2wks mid Jan

★★69% **Beach House**
Sea Front NE68 7SR
☎ 01665 720337 01665 720921
e-mail: beach.house.hotel.seahouses@tinyonline.co.uk
***Dir:*** *Seahouses signposted from A1 between Alnwick and Berwick*
A warm welcome awaits guests at this relaxed, non-smoking hotel, enjoying wonderful views of the Farne Islands. Comfortable bedrooms are thoughtfully equipped and newer refurbished rooms benefit from beautiful furnishings and elegant decor. A fabulous four-poster room is available as well as rooms suitable for families. Public areas include a choice of lounges and freshly cooked, local specialities can be enjoyed at breakfast and dinner in the traditional dining room.
**ROOMS:** 14 en suite (5 fmly) No smoking in all bedrooms s £30-£48; d £60-£96 (incl. bkfst) * **PARKING:** 16 **NOTES:** No dogs No smoking in restaurant Closed Jan **CARDS:**

S

SEATON, Devon Map 03 SY29

★★69% **Seaton Heights Hotel**
Seaton Down Hill EX12 2TF
☎ 01297 20932 & 0800 9758474 01297 24839
e-mail: seatonheightshotel@eclipse.co.uk
***Dir:*** *located on A3052 at Tower Cross, Seaton*
With glorious views over the Axe Valley, Seaton Heights Hotel has a relaxed and friendly atmosphere. Each of the well-equipped bedrooms benefits from the splendid views, particularly those on the first floor. In the restaurant, imaginative cooking is the order of the day, with the use of fresh, local ingredients wherever possible.
**ROOMS:** 26 en suite (8 fmly) s £33-£56; d £66-£112 (incl. bkfst) * **LB** **FACILITIES:** Outdoor swimming (H) Squash Snooker Sauna Solarium Gym Croquet lawn Badminton Basketball Table tennis entertainment ch fac Xmas **CONF:** Thtr 500 Class 80 Board 40 Del from £65 * **PARKING:** 128 **NOTES:** No smoking in restaurant
**CARDS:**

SEATON BURN, Tyne & Wear Map 12 NZ27

***Travelodge (Newcastle North)***
Front St NE13 6ED
☎ 0191 217 0107
Travelodge offers good quality, good value, modern accommodation. Ideal for families, the spacious, en suite bedrooms include remote-control TV, tea and coffee-making facilities, luxury beds and free morning newspaper. Meals can be taken at the nearby family restaurant. For further details and the Travelodge phone number, consult the Hotel Groups page.

Travelodge

**ROOMS:** 40 en suite

SEAVIEW See Wight, Isle of

SEDGEFIELD, Co Durham Map 08 NZ32

★★★65% **Hardwick Hall**
TS21 2EH
☎ 01740 620253 01740 622771
***Dir:*** *off A1M junct 60 towards Sedgefield, left at 1st rdbt hotel 400m on left*
This mansion house was built in the mid 18th century and has undergone various alterations since that time. New bedrooms and a conference venue are the most recent additions. Set in extensive parkland, it is an ideal place for a special occasion, where you can dine in the elegant surroundings of the restaurant, or more informally in the bar.
**ROOMS:** 51 en suite (2 fmly) s £68-£120; d £78-£135 (incl. bkfst) * **LB** **FACILITIES:** STV **CONF:** Thtr 450 Board 40 Del from £89 * **SERVICES:** Lift **PARKING:** 200 **NOTES:** No dogs (ex guide dogs) Civ Wed 75 **CARDS:**

***Travelodge***
TS21 2JX
☎ 01740 623399 01740 623399
***Dir:*** *on A689, 3m E of junct A1M*
Travelodge offers good quality, good value, modern accommodation. Ideal for families, the spacious, en suite bedrooms include remote-control TV, tea and coffee-making facilities, luxury beds and free morning newspaper. Meals can be taken at the nearby family restaurant. For further details and the Travelodge phone number, consult the Hotel Groups page.

Travelodge

**ROOMS:** 40 en suite

SEDGEMOOR MOTORWAY SERVICE AREA (M5), Somerset Map 03 ST35

**Welcome Lodge**
BS24 0JL
☎ 01934 750831 01934 750808
e-mail: sedgemoor.hotel@welcomebreak.co.uk
***Dir:*** *between junct 22 & 21 M5 northbound*
This modern building offers accommodation in smart, spacious and well-equipped bedrooms, suitable for families and business travellers, and all with en suite bathrooms. Refreshments may be taken at the nearby family restaurant. For further details and the Welcome Break phone number, consult the Hotel Groups page.

Welcome Break

**ROOMS:** 40 en suite s fr £45; d fr £45 * **CONF:** Board 10

SEDLESCOMBE, East Sussex Map 05 TQ71

★★★68% **Brickwall**
The Green TN33 0QA
☎ 01424 870253 🖹 01424 870785
e-mail: reception@brickwallhotel.totalserve.co.uk
**Dir:** *off A21 on B2244 at top of Sedlescombe Green*
Dating in part from 1597, the original house here retains its Tudor character and a sympathetic extension houses modern bedrooms. The attractive wood-panelled and oak-beamed restaurant and lounge bar offer a fixed-price four-course menu of traditionally cooked food.
**ROOMS:** 26 en suite (2 fmly) No smoking in 9 bedrooms s £50-£55; d £74-£88 (incl. bkfst) * **LB** **FACILITIES:** STV Outdoor swimming (H) Xmas **CONF:** Thtr 30 Class 40 Board 30 **PARKING:** 50 **NOTES:** No smoking in restaurant **CARDS:**

SELBY, North Yorkshire Map 08 SE63

★★64% **Owl**
Main Rd YO8 9JH
☎ 01757 228374 🖹 01757 228125
e-mail: owlhotel@talk21.co.uk
(For full entry see Hambleton (4m W A63))

SENNEN, Cornwall & Isles of Scilly Map 02 SW32

★★67% **Old Success Inn**
Sennen Cove TR19 7DG
☎ 01736 871232 🖹 01736 871457
e-mail: oldsuccess@hotmail.com
**Dir:** *turn right off the A30 approx 1mile before Land's End, signposted Sennen Cove. The Hotel is situated on the left at the bottom of the hill*
Situated on a well known cove, popular with surfers and walkers, this 17th-century inn offers a number of rooms with spectacular sea views. There is a comfortable lounge and a bar around which village and hotel life revolves and where bar meals are served. The restaurant offers traditional dishes and fish specialities.
**ROOMS:** 12 en suite (1 fmly) s £28-£44; d £80-£88 (incl. bkfst) * **LB** **FACILITIES:** entertainment Xmas **PARKING:** 12 **NOTES:** No smoking in restaurant **CARDS:**

SEVENOAKS, Kent Map 05 TQ55

★★★68% **Donnington Manor**
London Rd, Dunton Green TN13 2TD
☎ 01732 462681 🖹 01732 458116
e-mail: donningtonmanor@btconnect.com
**Dir:** *M25 junct 4, follow signs for Bromley/Orpington to rdbt. Turn left onto A224(Dunton Green) and left at 2nd rdbt. At Rose & Crown public house turn left, hotel 300yds on the right*
Located in Dunton Green near Sevenoaks, the hotel centres on a 15th-century manor with modern extensions. The attractive oak-beamed restaurant maintains its historic character, and the smart well-equipped bedrooms are housed in the extension. The leisure complex offers squash, gym and pool facilities.
**ROOMS:** 60 en suite (2 fmly) No smoking in 20 bedrooms s £80; d £90 * **LB** **FACILITIES:** STV Indoor swimming (H) Squash Sauna Gym Jacuzzi Xmas **CONF:** Thtr 180 Class 60 Board 40 Del from £105 * **PARKING:** 120 **NOTES:** No dogs (ex guide dogs) No smoking in restaurant Civ Wed 100 **CARDS:**

★★★65% **Royal Oak**
Upper High St TN13 1HY
☎ 01732 451109 🖹 01732 740187
e-mail: info@royaloak.demon.co.uk
**Dir:** *on A225, through Town Centre on the right, opposite Sevenoaks School*
Situated in the centre of Sevenoaks this flint-fronted hotel provides a good base from which to visit the locality. Bedrooms are divided between the main building and an adjacent wing, all are well-appointed and equipped. Public areas include a newly refurbished bar and brasserie style restaurant which offers an interesting range of carefully prepared dishes.
**ROOMS:** 21 en suite 16 annexe en suite (2 fmly) No smoking in 6 bedrooms s £85; d £95 * **LB** **FACILITIES:** STV Tennis (hard) Xmas **CONF:** Thtr 35 Class 14 Board 20 Del from £130 * **PARKING:** 50 **NOTES:** No smoking in restaurant **CARDS:**

SEVERN VIEW MOTORWAY SERVICE AREA (M4), Gloucestershire Map 03 ST58

***Travelodge***
M48 Motorway, Severn Bridge BS12 3BH
☎ 0800 850950 🖹 01454 632482
**Dir:** *junct 21 M48*
Travelodge offers good quality, good value, modern accommodation. Ideal for families, the spacious, en suite bedrooms include remote-control TV, tea and coffee-making facilities, luxury beds and free morning newspaper. Meals can be taken at the nearby family restaurant. For further details and the Travelodge phone number, consult the Hotel Groups page.

**ROOMS:** 51 en suite

SHAFTESBURY, Dorset Map 03 ST82

★★★67% **Royal Chase**
Royal Chase Roundabout SP7 8DB
☎ 01747 853355 🖹 01747 851969
e-mail: royalchasehotel@btinternet.com
**Dir:** *take A303 to within 7m of town and then A350 signposted Blandford Forum. Avoid town centre and follow road to 3rd rdbt*
A well known local landmark, close to the famous Gold Hill, the hotel is a popular place to stay for both leisure and business guests. There are two categories of bedroom - standard and 'crown'. There are also good conference and leisure facilities.
**ROOMS:** 35 en suite (13 fmly) No smoking in 10 bedrooms s £84-£95; d £100-£115 * **LB** **FACILITIES:** Spa STV Indoor swimming (H) Turkish steam bath ch fac Xmas **CONF:** Thtr 140 Class 90 Board 50 Del from £99.50 * **PARKING:** 100 **NOTES:** No smoking in restaurant Civ Wed 78 **CARDS:**

SHALDON See Teignmouth

SHANKLIN See Wight, Isle of

SHAP, Cumbria Map 12 NY51

★★★66% **Shap Wells**
CA10 3QU
☎ 01931 716628 🖹 01931 716377
e-mail: manager@shapwells.com
**Dir:** *from M6 junct 39, follow signs for Kendal, turn left at A6, after approx 1m turn left into hotel drive, hotel is situated about 1m down*
This former therapeutic centre is now a popular hotel, set in 33 acres of grounds within a short drive of the M6. Public areas include a well-stocked bar, a choice of inviting lounges, a

*continued on p526*

SHAP, continued

restaurant and good banqueting facilities. Bedrooms come in mixed sizes and styles and offer all the expected comforts. Staff are friendly and willing to please.

*Shap Wells, Shap*

**ROOMS:** 91 en suite 7 annexe en suite (10 fmly) s £55-£60; d £80-£90 (incl. bkfst) * **LB** **FACILITIES:** Tennis (hard) Snooker Games room ch fac Xmas **CONF:** Thtr 170 Class 80 Board 40 Del from £50 * **SERVICES:** Lift **PARKING:** 200 **NOTES:** Closed 23-29 Dec & 5 Jan-14 Feb Civ Wed 150 **CARDS:**

*See advert under KENDAL*

## SHAPWICK, Somerset — Map 03 ST43

### ★★68% Shapwick House

Monks Dr TA7 9NL
☎ 01458 210321 01458 210729
e-mail: keith@shapwickhouse.free-on-line.co.uk
***Dir:*** *from M5 junct 23 turn left heading towards Glastonbury. Left again at junct onto A39 still heading Glastonbury. After 5m hotel signposted on left*

Dating back to the 15th century, this stone manor house was originally built by Glastonbury Abbey. The main hall, with its splendid fireplace, provides comfortable seating, an ideal place to relax after a busy day exploring the area. Bedrooms are spacious, well-equipped and feature modern facilities. The Georgian dining room offers an imaginative, fixed-price menu accompanied by a good wine list.

**ROOMS:** 12 en suite No smoking in 10 bedrooms s £52.50; d £75-£105 (incl. bkfst) * **LB** **CONF:** Thtr 40 Class 25 Board 15 Del from £100 * **PARKING:** 40 **NOTES:** No children 10yrs No smoking in restaurant RS Xmas day-New Years day **CARDS:**

*See advert under BRIDGWATER*

## SHARDLOW, Derbyshire — Map 08 SK43

### Days Inn

DAYS INN

Welcome Break Services DE72 2HA
☎ 01332 799666 01332 794166
e-mail: derby.hotel@welcomebreak.co.uk
***Dir:*** *A 50 West*

This modern building offers accommodation in smart, spacious and well-equipped bedrooms, suitable for families and business travellers, and all with en suite bathrooms. Continental breakfast is available and other refreshments may be taken at the nearby family restaurant. For further details and the Days Inn phone number, consult the Hotel Groups page.

**ROOMS:** 48 en suite s £35-£50; d £35-£50 * **CONF:** Board 12

## SHEDFIELD, Hampshire — Map 04 SU51

### ★★★★65% Marriott Meon Valley Hotel & Country Club

Marriott HOTELS · RESORTS · SUITES

Sandy Ln SO32 2HQ
☎ 01329 833455 01329 834411
***Dir:*** *from W, M27 junct7 take A334 then towards Wickham and Botley. Sandy Lane is on left 2m from Botley*

A smartly appointed hotel and country club with golf course, providing spacious, modern bedrooms with excellent facilities. Leisure and fitness facilities are extensive and there is a choice of restaurants and bars. The hotel is ideally placed for conferences.

**ROOMS:** 113 en suite No smoking in 80 bedrooms s fr £90; d fr £90 * **LB** **FACILITIES:** **Spa** STV Indoor swimming (H) Golf 27 Tennis (hard) Sauna Solarium Gym Putting green Jacuzzi Cardio-Vascular Aerobics Health & Beauty salon Xmas **CONF:** Thtr 90 Class 50 Board 36 Del from £130 * **SERVICES:** Lift **PARKING:** 320 **NOTES:** No dogs (ex guide dogs) No smoking in restaurant Civ Wed 80

**CARDS:**

## SHEFFIELD, South Yorkshire — Map 08 SK38

### ★★★★65% Sheffield Marriott Hotel

Marriott HOTELS · RESORTS · SUITES

Kenwood Rd S7 1NQ
☎ 0114 258 3811
0114 250 0138/0114 255 4744
e-mail: info@swallowhotels.com
***Dir:*** *Follow A61 past Red Tape Studios on right ,at 2nd set of lights turn right into St Marys Rd. At rdbt straight across then bear left into London Rd, then right at lights and at top of hill straight across 1st and 2nd rdbt*

Set in eleven acres of gardens and parkland, the hotel is conveniently located in a quiet residential area. Bedrooms range from spacious rooms with private balconies overlooking the ornamental lake, to refurbished rooms with much character in the original house. An extensive range of leisure and meeting facilities

*continued*

is available. The hotel is at present undergoing extensive refurbishment to all areas.
**ROOMS:** 114 en suite (33 fmly) No smoking in 89 bedrooms s £89-£109; d £89-£109 * **LB** **FACILITIES:** **Spa** STV Indoor swimming (H) Fishing Sauna Solarium Gym Jacuzzi Steam room ch fac Xmas **CONF:** Thtr 200 Class 100 Board 60 Del from £135 * **SERVICES:** Lift **PARKING:** 200 **NOTES:** No smoking in restaurant Civ Wed 120 **CARDS:**

### ★★★71% Beauchief

corus

161 Abbeydale Rd South S7 2QW
☎ 0114 262 0500 Fax 0114 235 0197
***Dir:*** *from City Centre 2m on A621 signed Bakewell*

On the southern outskirts of the city, this busy property attracts both resident and local business. The popular restaurant and Merchant's bar have an excellent reputation in the area for good food and hospitality. Bedrooms are well-proportioned with many extras such as movie channels on the TV.
**ROOMS:** 50 en suite No smoking in 30 bedrooms s £85-£95; d £95-£105 * **LB** **FACILITIES:** STV **CONF:** Thtr 100 Class 50 Board 50 Del from £105 * **PARKING:** 200 **NOTES:** No smoking in restaurant Civ Wed 120 **CARDS:**

### ★★★70% Charnwood

10 Sharrow Ln S11 8AA
☎ 0114 258 9411 Fax 0114 255 5107
e-mail: king@charnwood.force9.co.uk
***Dir:*** *Sharrow Lane is near London Rd/Abbeydale Rd junction, on A621, 1.5m SW of city centre*

The Charnwood is within walking distance of the city centre, just off the London Road. It was once a Georgian mansion house owned by a Master Cutler. The bedrooms are well-equipped; lounges and bars are well furnished and comfortable. Leo's Brasserie is an informal restaurant serving freshly cooked and interesting meals.
**ROOMS:** 22 en suite No smoking in 16 bedrooms s £58-£83; d £73-£98 (incl. bkfst) * **LB** **FACILITIES:** STV **CONF:** Thtr 90 Class 40 Board 35 Del from £105 * **PARKING:** 22 **NOTES:** No dogs (ex guide dogs) Closed 24-31 Dec Civ Wed 100 **CARDS:**

### ★★★69% Whitley Hall

Elliott Ln, Grenoside S35 8NR
☎ 0114 245 4444 Fax 0114 245 5414
e-mail: reservations@whitleyhall.com
***Dir:*** *A61 past football ground and 2m further, turn right just before Norfolk Arms, turn left at bottom of hill. Hotel is on left*

This 16th-century house stands in 30 acres of well-tended, landscaped grounds and gardens. Public rooms are full of

*continued on p528*

SHEFFIELD, continued

character, with an impressive gallery, and oak-panelled restaurant, bar and lounge. Bedrooms are individually furnished in a style in keeping with this country house setting; each room is equipped with a range of modern facilities and useful extras.
**ROOMS:** 19 en suite (1 fmly) s £75-£85; d £95-£105 (incl. bkfst) * **LB** **FACILITIES:** Croquet lawn Putting green entertainment **CONF:** Thtr 70 Class 50 Board 40 Del from £120 * **PARKING:** 100 **NOTES:** No smoking in restaurant RS Sat - No lunch Civ Wed 80
**CARDS:**

★★★67% **Novotel Sheffield**
50 Arundel Gate S1 2PR
☎ 0114 278 1781 📠 0114 278 7744
e-mail: h1348@accor-hotels.com
***Dir:*** *between Registry Office and Crucible/Lyceum Theatres, follow signs to Town Hall/Theatres & Hallam University*
A modern hotel situated in the centre of the city close to the Lyceum and Crucible theatres. Bedrooms are well-proportioned and suitable for families as well as being appropriately equipped for business guests. Public areas are spaciously designed and include an attractive restaurant, banqueting and meeting rooms and an indoor heated swimming pool.
**ROOMS:** 144 en suite (40 fmly) No smoking in 108 bedrooms s £79-£82; d £79-£82 * **LB** **FACILITIES:** STV Indoor swimming (H) Local gym facilities for residents free of charge **CONF:** Thtr 200 Class 30 Board 100 Del £110 * **SERVICES:** Lift **PARKING:** 44 **NOTES:** RS 24 Dec-2 Jan
**CARDS:**

★★★67% **The Regency**
High St, Ecclesfield S35 9XB
☎ 0114 246 7703 📠 0114 240 0081
***Dir:*** *A629 to Chapeltown, turn left onto Nether Ln, straight across traffic lights, left into Church St, turn left opp church, left again, hotel on right*
This thoughtfully extended mansion house stands in the centre of Ecclesfield to the north of Sheffield. The restaurant serves a wide range of popular dishes and is popular locally. Well-equipped bedrooms offer good levels of comfort, and the dedicated staff provide good hospitality.
**ROOMS:** 19 en suite (1 fmly) **FACILITIES:** STV **CONF:** Thtr 250 Class 120 Board 40 **PARKING:** 80 **NOTES:** No dogs (ex guide dogs) Closed 25-26 Dec, 1 Jan Civ Wed 180 **CARDS:**

★★★66% **Mosborough Hall**
High St, Mosborough S20 5EA
☎ 0114 248 4353 📠 0114 247 7042
e-mail: hotel@mosboroughhall.co.uk
***Dir:*** *after leaving M1 at junct 30, travel 7m SE on A6135*
This 16th-century, Grade II listed manor house, is set in gardens not far from the M1 and convenient for the city centre. Bedrooms vary from modern to characterful, and some are very spacious. There is a galleried bar and conservatory lounge, and freshly prepared dishes are served in the brightly furnished dining room.
**ROOMS:** 23 en suite (1 fmly) s £65-£76; d £70-£84 * **LB** **CONF:** Thtr 85 Class 50 Board 50 Del from £87 * **PARKING:** 100 **NOTES:** No smoking in restaurant Civ Wed 90 **CARDS:**

★★★65% **Menzies Rutland**
452 Glossop Rd S10 2PY
☎ 0870 6003013 📠 01332 511144
e-mail: info@menzies-hotels.co.uk
***Dir:*** *on A57, located next to the Royal Hallamshire Hospital*
The hotel is well placed for the city centre and university but in a relatively quiet location. Bedrooms have been enhanced with modern facilities. The self contained conference centre with bedrooms is proving to be popular.
**ROOMS:** 63 en suite 13 annexe en suite (5 fmly) No smoking in 10 bedrooms s £65; d £75 * **LB** **FACILITIES:** STV Xmas **CONF:** Thtr 100 Class 40 Board 40 Del from £95 * **SERVICES:** Lift **PARKING:** 80 **NOTES:** No smoking in restaurant Civ Wed 100
**CARDS:**

★★★61% ***Posthouse Sheffield***
Manchester Rd, Broomhill S10 5DX
☎ 0870 400 9071 📠 0114 268 2620
***Dir:*** *M1 J23, follow signs to city centre, then A57 Glossop. Hotel on L after 2.5 miles*
This high rise hotel dominates the skyline west of the city centre, and is situated in a residential area within easy reach of central Sheffield. The majority of bedrooms have fine views. The hotel features a Spa Leisure Club, the Hallam Banqueting Suite and a range of meeting and conference rooms. The restaurant is open for lunch and dinner, and there is an all day lounge menu plus, 24-hour room service.
**ROOMS:** 136 en suite No smoking in 70 bedrooms **FACILITIES:** Indoor swimming (H) Sauna Solarium Gym Jacuzzi Health & fitness centre **CONF:** Thtr 300 Class 130 Board 80 **SERVICES:** Lift **PARKING:** 120
**CARDS:**

★★65% **Cutlers Hotel**
George St S1 2PF
☎ 0114 273 9939 📠 0114 276 8332
e-mail: enquiries@cutlershotel.co.uk
***Dir:*** *city centre adjacent to Crucible Theatre*
Situated close to the Crucible Theatre in the city centre, this hotel offers accommodation in well-equipped bedrooms and extras including hairdryers, trouser presses and business facilities. Public areas include a lower ground floor bistro although room service is available if required. Small meeting rooms are also available. Free overnight parking is provided in the nearby public car park.
**ROOMS:** 50 en suite No smoking in 16 bedrooms s £48.50-£53.50; d £59.50-£64.50 (incl. bkfst) * **LB** **CONF:** Thtr 25 Board 20 **SERVICES:** Lift **NOTES:** No dogs (ex guide dogs) Closed 24 Dec-3 Jan
**CARDS:**

⌂ **Hotel Ibis Sheffield**
Shude Hill S1 2AR
☎ 0114 241 9600 📠 0114 241 9610
e-mail: H2891@accor-hotels.com
***Dir:*** *M1 junct 33, follow signs to Sheffield City Centre and in 7m at rdbt take 5th exit, signed Ponds Forge, for hotel*
Modern, budget hotel offering comfortable accommodation in bright and practical bedrooms. Breakfast is self-service and dinner is available in the restaurant. For further details, consult the Hotel Groups page.
**ROOMS:** 95 en suite s £42; d £42 *

⌂ ***Travelodge***
340 Prince of Wales Rd S2 1FF
☎ 0114 253 0935 📠 0114 253 0935
***Dir:*** *follow A630, take turn off for ring road & services*
Travelodge offers good quality, good value, modern accommodation. Ideal for families, the spacious, en suite bedrooms include remote-control TV, tea and coffee-making facilities, luxury beds and free morning newspaper. Meals can be taken at the nearby family restaurant. For further details and the Travelodge phone number, consult the Hotel Groups page.

**ROOMS:** 60 en suite **CONF:** Thtr 30 Board 20

### ○ Innkeeper's Lodge Sheffield South

Hathersage Rd, Longshaw S11 7TY

A new concept in the travel accommodation market. Smart rooms meet essential business requirements but also have home comforts. Dining options include all-day menus plus the added advantage of breakfast, which is included in the room price. Reservations can be made seven days a week through the room reservations number: 0870 243 0500. For further details, consult the Hotel Groups page.

**ROOMS:** 11 en suite **NOTES:** Opening Autumn 2001

## SHEPTON MALLET, Somerset — Map 03 ST64

**Premier Collection**

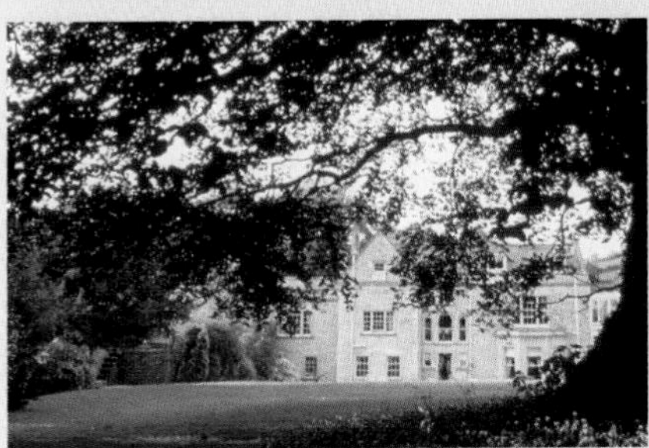

### ★★★ ⊛⊛⊛ Charlton House

Charlton Rd BA4 4PR

☎ 01749 342008 🖹 01749 346362

e-mail: enquiry@charltonhouse.com

***Dir:*** *on A361, 1m beyond Shepton Mallet Town Centre, travelling towards Frome*

Charlton House is situated in beautifully landscaped grounds just outside of the town. Parts of this delightful country house date back to the 1500s. The bedrooms and public areas are decorated with high quality fabrics and furnishings. All of the staff are friendly and professional, and the surroundings conducive to relaxing and being pampered. The restaurant provides some very accomplished and distinctive cooking, with a focus on high quality local ingredients.

**ROOMS:** 11 en suite 5 annexe en suite (1 fmly) s £105-£140; d £140-£300 (incl. cont bkfst) * **LB** **FACILITIES:** STV Indoor swimming (H) Tennis (hard) Fishing Sauna Croquet lawn Archery Clay pigeon shooting Ballooning Xmas **CONF:** Thtr 50 Class 18 Board 20 Del £160 * **PARKING:** 41 **NOTES:** No dogs (ex guide dogs) No smoking in restaurant Civ Wed 70 **CARDS:**

### ★★72% Shrubbery

Commercial Rd BA4 5BU

☎ 01749 346671 🖹 01749 346581

***Dir:*** *turn off A37 at Shepton Mallet onto A371 Wells Rd, hotel 50mtrs past traffic lights in town centre*

This very attractive town centre hotel is an elegant and thoroughly charming place of relaxation and fine food. The bedrooms, including some recently completed high-quality additions in an annexe building, have rich fabrics and co-ordinating colour schemes. The intimate restaurant overlooks a delightful award-

*continued*

winning garden and offers a varied choice of well-presented dishes.

**ROOMS:** 8 en suite 4 annexe en suite (1 fmly) No smoking in 4 bedrooms s £52.50; d £75 (incl. bkfst) * **LB** **FACILITIES:** Xmas **CONF:** Thtr 36 Class 30 Board 24 Del £95 * **PARKING:** 30 **NOTES:** No smoking in restaurant RS Sun evenings **CARDS:**

## SHERBORNE, Dorset — Map 03 ST61

### ★★★69% ⊛ Eastbury

Long St DT9 3BY

☎ 01935 813131 🖹 01935 817296

e-mail: eastbury.sherborne@virgin.net

***Dir:*** *turn left off A30, westbound, into Cheap St, at the bottom turn left 800yds along on the right is the Eastbury hotel*

Situated close to the centre of the town, this quiet, charming hotel is run by a young and professional team. The restaurant and bar overlook the walled garden at the rear, perfect for enjoying the award winning cuisine. Bedrooms are individually furnished, with many thoughtful extras including bathrobes, fresh flowers and mineral water.

**ROOMS:** 15 en suite (1 fmly) No smoking in 3 bedrooms **FACILITIES:** STV Croquet lawn Xmas **CONF:** Thtr 80 Class 40 Board 28 Del £102.50 * **PARKING:** 50 **NOTES:** No dogs (ex guide dogs) Civ Wed 120 **CARDS:**

### ★★★60% Antelope

THE CIRCLE Selected Individual Hotels GREAT BRITAIN

Greenhill DT9 4EP

☎ 01935 812077 🖹 01935 816473

***Dir:*** *stay on the A30 into Sherborne, hotel is located at the top of town with parking at rear*

Formerly a coaching inn dating back to the 18th century, this hotel is centrally located in Sherborne and an ideal base for exploring Hardy country. Many bedrooms have retained their original beams and fireplaces; some have their own access from the courtyard. The San Marino Restaurant serves a range of Italian dishes and together with the bar is popular with locals and residents alike.

**ROOMS:** 19 en suite (1 fmly) No smoking in 1 bedroom s £44-£70; d £49.95-£95 (incl. bkfst) * **LB** **FACILITIES:** Xmas **CONF:** Thtr 80 Class 60 Board 40 **PARKING:** 22 **CARDS:**

## SHERINGHAM, Norfolk — Map 09 TG14

### ★★71% Roman Camp Inn

Holt Rd, Aylmerton NR11 8QD

☎ 01263 838291 🖹 837071

e-mail: Romancamp@lineone.net

***Dir:*** *located on the A148 between Sheringham and Cromer, approx 1.5 miles from Cromer*

This popular inn is situated at one of the highest points of the North Norfolk coast. The spacious bedrooms are individually decorated and equipped with many useful extras. Public rooms feature an attractive conservatory style restaurant, a comfortable lounge, a smart bar and a further dining room on the first floor.

**ROOMS:** 16 en suite No smoking in 2 bedrooms s fr £50; d fr £76 * **LB** **CONF:** Thtr 25 Class 6 Board 12 Del from £69 * **PARKING:** 50 **NOTES:** No dogs (ex guide dogs) No smoking in restaurant Closed 25 Dec **CARDS:**

Bad hair day? Hairdryers in all rooms three stars and above.

S

SHERINGHAM, continued

### ★★70% Beaumaris

South St NR26 8LL
☎ 01263 822370 📠 01263 821421
e-mail: beauhotel@aol.com
***Dir:*** *turn off A148, turn left at rdbt, 1st right over railway bridge, 1st left by church, 1st left into South Street*

This very pleasant hotel has been in the same family since 1947 and has many loyal guests who regularly return to enjoy the friendly hospitality. In quiet residential surroundings with well kept gardens, it is just five minutes' walk from the seafront, town centre and the golf course. Public rooms include two quiet lounges, an inviting bar, and a spacious dining room serving well-produced food.
**ROOMS:** 21 en suite (5 fmly) s £38-£45; d £76-£90 (incl. bkfst) * **LB FACILITIES:** ch fac **CONF:** Board 12 Del from £70 * **PARKING:** 25 **NOTES:** No smoking in restaurant Closed mid Dec-1 Mar
**CARDS:**

### ★★68% Southlands

South St NR26 8LL
☎ 01263 822679 📠 01263 822679
***Dir:*** *from A1082, turn left at rdbt. Take 1st right & then 1st left at St Peters Church. Then 1st left again & hotel is on the left*
This pleasant, homely hotel attracts many loyal regulars. A short walk from the town centre, it offers well-maintained and attractively decorated accommodation. The large downstairs rooms include open-plan lounges and several dining areas. A short but appetising menu is offered.
**ROOMS:** 17 en suite (3 fmly) s fr £34; d fr £67 (incl. bkfst) * **PARKING:** 20 **NOTES:** No smoking in restaurant Closed Oct-Etr
**CARDS:**

S

SHIFNAL, Shropshire Map 07 SJ70

### ★★★★63% Park House

MACDONALD HOTELS ★★★★

Park St TF11 9BA
☎ 01952 460128 📠 01952 461658
e-mail: parkhouse@macdonald-hotels.co.uk
***Dir:*** *leave M54 at junct 4 follow A464 Wolverhampton Rd for approx 2m, under railway bridge and hotel is 100yds on left*
Service is friendly at this sympathetically extended hotel. Originally two separate 17th-century houses, the hotel sits on the edge of this historic market town, within easy reach of M54(J4). Accommodation is spacious and well-appointed. Elegant public areas include a good choice of meeting facilities, as well as a health club.

**ROOMS:** 38 en suite 16 annexe en suite (4 fmly) No smoking in 24 bedrooms s £70-£115; d £70-£115 * **LB FACILITIES:** STV Indoor swimming (H) Sauna Solarium Jacuzzi Xmas **CONF:** Thtr 180 Class 100 Board 40 **SERVICES:** Lift **PARKING:** 200 **NOTES:** No smoking in restaurant Civ Wed 130 **CARDS:**

SHIPHAM, Somerset Map 03 ST45

### ★★★74% Daneswood House

Cuck Hill BS25 1RD
☎ 01934 843145 & 843945 📠 01934 843824
e-mail: info@daneswoodhotel.co.uk
***Dir:*** *turn off A38 towards Cheddar, travel through village, hotel on left*
With wonderful views over the surrounding countryside, to the Bristol Channel and Wales in the distance, this charming Edwardian hotel is set in its own grounds. Each individually decorated bedroom is well-equipped; the cottage suites having the benefit of private lounges. Public areas include a breakfast conservatory, comfortable lounge and inter-connecting dining area.
**ROOMS:** 14 en suite 3 annexe en suite (3 fmly) No smoking in 4 bedrooms s fr £89.50; d fr £105 (incl. bkfst) * **LB FACILITIES:** ch fac **CONF:** Thtr 40 Board 24 Del from £140 * **PARKING:** 27 **NOTES:** No dogs (ex guide dogs) No smoking in restaurant RS 24 Dec-6 Jan
**CARDS:**

SHIPLEY, West Yorkshire Map 07 SE13

### ★★★★70% Marriott Hollins Hall Hotel & Country Club

Marriott HOTELS · RESORTS · SUITES

Hollins Hill, Baildon BD17 7QW
☎ 01274 530053 📠 01274 530187
e-mail: reservations.hollinshall@marriotthotels.co.uk
***Dir:*** *from A650 follow signs to Salt Mill. At lights in Shipley take A6038. Hotel is 3m on left*

This Elizabethan-style hotel was built during the 19th century. Set

*continued*

in over 200 acres of beautiful countryside, its extensive leisure facilities include a golf course and a well-equipped gymnasium. Guests have a choice of dining options including the lively Long Weekend Café Bar and the more formal restaurant, Heathcliff's.
**ROOMS:** 122 en suite (6 fmly) No smoking in 75 bedrooms s £109-£159; d £119-£159 (incl. bkfst) * **LB** **FACILITIES:** **Spa** STV Indoor swimming (H) Golf 18 Sauna Solarium Gym Croquet lawn Putting green Jacuzzi Creche Internet cafe Xmas **CONF:** Thtr 200 Class 90 Board 60 Del £155 * **SERVICES:** Lift **PARKING:** 260 **NOTES:** No dogs (ex guide dogs) No smoking in restaurant Civ Wed 120
**CARDS:**

### Hotel Ibis Bradford

ibis
Accor

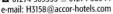

Quayside, Salts Mill Rd BD18 3ST
☎ 01274 589333 01274 589444
e-mail: H3158@accor-hotels.com
***Dir:*** *Follow tourist signs all the way for Salts Mill. Pick up A650 signs through & out of Bradford for approx 5m to Shipley. Hotel on Salts Mill Rd*
Modern, budget hotel offering comfortable accommodation in bright and practical bedrooms. Breakfast is self-service and dinner is available in the restaurant. For further details, consult the Hotel Groups page.
**ROOMS:** 78 en suite s £35-£42; d £35-£42 * **CONF:** Thtr 35 Class 20 Board 20

## SHREWSBURY, Shropshire — Map 07 SJ41

see also Church Stretton & Nesscliffe

### ★★★★63% Albrighton Hall

MACDONALD HOTELS

Albrighton SY4 3AG
☎ 01939 291000 01939 291123
e-mail: info@albrightonmacdonaldhotels.co.uk
***Dir:*** *From S M6 junct 10a to M54 to end. From N M6 junct 12 to M5 then M54. Follow signs Harlescott & Ellesmere to A528*

Set in 14 acres of grounds, this 17th-century country house has elegant public rooms with beautiful oak panelling. Bedrooms in the main house are mostly spacious and have been refurbished; several have four-poster beds and the attic rooms are popular for their sloping beams. There is also a leisure centre and extensive conference facilities.
**ROOMS:** 29 en suite 42 annexe en suite (2 fmly) No smoking in 30 bedrooms **FACILITIES:** **Spa** STV Indoor swimming (H) Squash Snooker Sauna Solarium Gym Beauty treatment rooms **CONF:** Thtr 400 Class 120 Board 60 Del £145 * **SERVICES:** Lift **PARKING:** 120 **NOTES:** No smoking in restaurant Civ Wed 200
**CARDS:**

### ★★★77% Albright Hussey

Ellesmere Rd SY4 3AF
☎ 01939 290571 & 290523 01939 291143
e-mail: abbhotel@aol.com
***Dir:*** *2.5m N of Shrewsbury on A528, follow signs for Ellesmere*

Converted from a classic farmhouse, this timber-framed Tudor building offers a choice of accommodation: spacious and lavishly furnished bedrooms in the older part of the building and well-equipped modern rooms in a new wing. Dinner is taken in the fine, beamed restaurant. A comfortable cocktail bar and lounge are available, as well as a function suite.
**ROOMS:** 14 en suite (4 fmly) No smoking in 3 bedrooms s £65-£93.50; d £95-£148.50 (incl. bkfst) * **LB** **FACILITIES:** **Spa** Croquet lawn Jacuzzi Xmas **CONF:** Thtr 250 Class 180 Board 80 Del from £110 * **PARKING:** 85 **NOTES:** No children 3yrs No smoking in restaurant Civ Wed 200 **CARDS:**

### ★★★74% Rowton Castle Hotel

Halfway House SY5 9EP
☎ 01743 884044 01743 884949
e-mail: post@rowtoncastle.com

Standing in 17 acres of grounds on the site of a Roman fort, this hotel dates back in parts to 1696. Many original features remain, including the oak-panelling in the restaurant and a magnificent 17th-century carved oak fireplace. Most of the bedrooms are spacious and all are equipped with modern facilities. The hotel has lovely formal gardens.
**ROOMS:** 19 en suite (3 fmly) s fr £59; d fr £79 (incl. bkfst) * **LB** **FACILITIES:** Fishing Croquet lawn **CONF:** Thtr 80 Class 40 Board 40 Del from £115 * **PARKING:** 100 **NOTES:** No dogs (ex guide dogs) No smoking in restaurant Civ Wed 110 **CARDS:**

S

SHREWSBURY, continued

**★★★71% Prince Rupert**
Butcher Row SY1 1UQ
☎ 01743 499955 🖹 01743 357306
e-mail: post@prince-rupert-hotel.co.uk
***Dir:*** *follow signs to Town Centre, drive over English Bridge and Wyle Cop Hill. Turn right into Fish St and continue for 200 yds till hotel is in view*

This popular town centre hotel dates back, in parts, to medieval times. Many bedrooms have exposed beams and attractive wood panelling. In addition to the main 'Royalist' restaurant, diners can eat in 'Chambers' bar-bistro. The refurbished bedrooms include four luxury suites, family rooms and rooms with four-poster beds. The hotel's car parking service is recommended.
**ROOMS:** 70 en suite (4 fmly) s £75; d £95-£160 * **LB**
**FACILITIES:** Snooker Sauna Gym Jacuzzi Weight training room Beauty Salon Xmas **CONF:** Thtr 120 Class 80 Board 20 Del from £95 *
**SERVICES:** Lift **PARKING:** 70 **CARDS:**

*See advert on opposite page*

**★★★66% Lord Hill**
Abbey Foregate SY2 6AX
☎ 01743 232601 🖹 01743 369734
e-mail: reservations@lordhill.u-net.com
***Dir:*** *from M54 take A5, at 1st rdbt left then right into London Rd. At next rdbt (Lord Hill Column) take 3rd exit for hotel on left*
A pleasant, attractively appointed hotel close to the town centre. Most of the bedrooms are located in a purpose-built, separate building but those in the main building include one with a four-poster and a recently created suite. There is also a conservatory restaurant and a large function suite.
**ROOMS:** 12 en suite 24 annexe en suite (1 fmly) No smoking in 18 bedrooms s £55-£63.50; d £73-£82 (incl. bkfst) * **LB**
**FACILITIES:** Xmas **CONF:** Thtr 300 Class 120 Board 150 **PARKING:** 120
**NOTES:** Civ Wed 100 **CARDS:**

**★★★64% The Lion**
Wyle Cop SY1 1UY
REGAL
☎ 01743 353107 🖹 01743 352744
e-mail: thelion@corushotels.com
***Dir:*** *from S: cross English Bridge, take right fork, hotel at top of hill on left. From N: to town centre, follow Castle St into Dogpole, hotel is ahead*
Charles Dickens and other famous people have stayed at this 14th-century coaching inn. Public areas are elegant and comfortable,

*continued*

particularly the Tapestry Lounge. Bedrooms have modern equipment and are decorated and furnished to a good standard.

Lion Hotel

**ROOMS:** 59 en suite (3 fmly) No smoking in 30 bedrooms s fr £75; d fr £95 * **LB** **FACILITIES:** use of local gym Xmas **CONF:** Thtr 200 Class 80 Board 60 Del from £90 * **SERVICES:** Lift **PARKING:** 70
**NOTES:** Civ Wed 50 **CARDS:**

**★★65% Lion & Pheasant**
49-50 Wyle Cop SY1 1XJ
☎ 01743 236288 🖹 01743 244475
e-mail: info@lionandpheasant.co.uk
***Dir:*** *town centre, by English Bridge, 2m from M54 motorway link*

FREE HOUSE
FOOD
ROOMS

Privately owned and personally run, this 16th-century coaching inn is close to the town centre. The accommodation is well-equipped and the public areas are full of character, with exposed beams and wall timbers.
**ROOMS:** 20 rms (17 en suite) (1 fmly) s £45; d £60 (incl. bkfst) * **LB**
**CONF:** Thtr 25 Class 30 Board 18 Del £67 * **PARKING:** 20
**NOTES:** No smoking in restaurant **CARDS:**

*See advert on opposite page*

**★★64% Mytton & Mermaid**
Atcham SY5 6QG
☎ 01743 761220 🖹 01743 761292
***Dir:*** *from Shrewsbury cross old bridge in Atcham. Hotel beside River Severn opposite main entrance to Attingham Park*
Convenient for Shrewsbury, this ivy-clad former coaching inn enjoys a pleasant location beside the River Severn. Some bedrooms, including family suites, are in a converted stable block adjacent to the hotel. The large lounge bar has been recently refurbished, and there is also a brasserie and cosy guest lounge.
**ROOMS:** 11 en suite 7 annexe en suite (1 fmly) s £40-£80; d £60-£80 (incl. bkfst) * **FACILITIES:** Fishing Xmas **CONF:** Thtr 70 Class 24 Board 28 **NOTES:** Civ Wed 50 **CARDS:**

★★63% **Abbots Mead**
9 St Julian's Friars SY1 1XL
☎ 01743 235281 Fax 01743 369133
e-mail: res@abbotsmeadhotel.co.uk
***Dir:*** *first left after English Bridge coming into Shrewsbury from S*
This neatly maintained Georgian town house lies in a quiet cul-de-sac near the English Bridge, close to both the river and town centre. Bedrooms are compact but neatly decorated and well-equipped. The hotel also has a bright dining room, overlooking the garden, and a bar with walls adorned by horse racing pictures.
**ROOMS:** 15 en suite (1 fmly) s £40-£45; d £52-£56 (incl. bkfst) * LB
**PARKING:** 10 **NOTES:** No smoking in restaurant
**CARDS:**

⇧ ***Travelodge***
Bayston Hill Services SY3 0DA
☎ 01743 874256 Fax 01743 874256
***Dir:*** *A5/A49 junct*
Travelodge offers good quality, good value, modern accommodation. Ideal for families, the spacious, en suite bedrooms include remote-control TV, tea and coffee-making facilities, luxury beds and free morning newspaper. Meals can be taken at the nearby family restaurant. For further details and the Travelodge phone number, consult the Hotel Groups page.

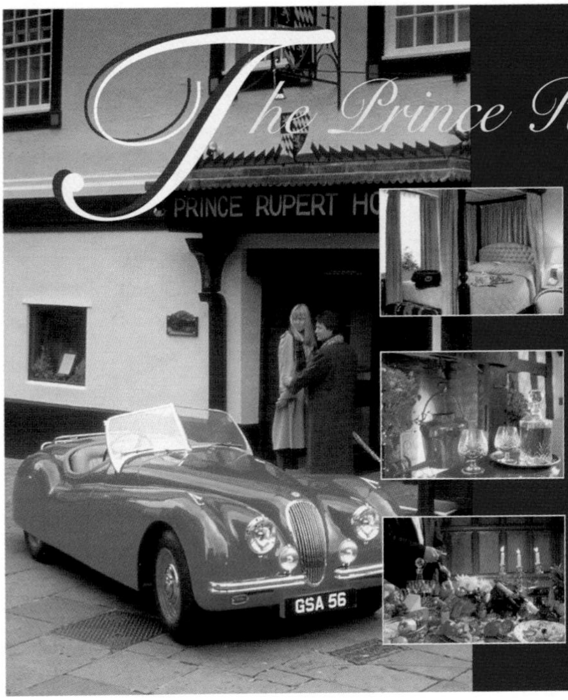

Travelodge

**ROOMS:** 40 en suite

Popped the question? Hotels with Civ Wed in their entry are licensed for civil wedding ceremonies. Maximum numbers for the ceremony only are shown, e.g. Civ Wed 120

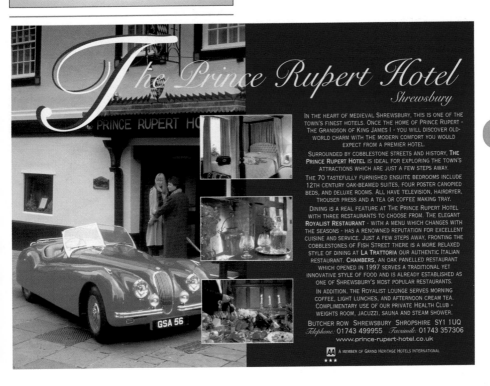

SIDMOUTH, Devon Map 03 SY18

**★★★★74% Riviera**

The Esplanade EX10 8AY
☎ 01395 515201 01395 577775
e-mail: enquiries@hotelriviera.co.uk
***Dir:*** *leave M5 junc 30 & follow A3052*

Situated in a prime location overlooking the sea, the Riviera is a fine Regency building, offering high standards of both service and hospitality. Bedrooms combine comfort with quality, many also benefiting from wonderful views. The daily changing menu places an emphasis upon fresh local produce, served by friendly staff within the elegant dining room.

**ROOMS:** 27 en suite (6 fmly) s £90-£118; d £160-£216 (incl. bkfst & dinner) * **LB** **FACILITIES:** STV entertainment Xmas **CONF:** Thtr 85 Class 60 Board 30 **SERVICES:** Lift **PARKING:** 26 **NOTES:** No smoking in restaurant **CARDS:**

*See advert on page 537*

**★★★★72% Victoria**

The Esplanade EX10 8RY
☎ 01395 512651 01395 579154
e-mail: info@victoriahotel.co.uk
***Dir:*** *on Sidmouth seafront*

Completed around the turn of the last century, this imposing building, set within its own manicured gardens, occupies the prime position on the esplanade. Fine sea views are enjoyed by many of the comfortable bedrooms and elegant public areas. Carefully prepared meals are served, in a professional yet friendly way, in the refurbished air-conditioned restaurant.

**ROOMS:** 61 en suite (18 fmly) s £72-£109; d £120-£236 (incl. bkfst) * **LB** **FACILITIES:** **Spa** STV Indoor swimming (H) Outdoor swimming (H) Tennis (hard) Snooker Sauna Solarium Putting green entertainment ch fac Xmas **CONF:** Thtr 60 **SERVICES:** Lift **PARKING:** 104 **NOTES:** No dogs (ex guide dogs) No smoking in restaurant **CARDS:**

*See advert on opposite page*

**★★★★69% Belmont**

The Esplanade EX10 8RX
☎ 01395 512555 01395 579101
e-mail: info@belmont-hotel.co.uk
***Dir:*** *on Sidmouth seafront*

Prominently positioned on the sea front, within a few minutes walk from the town centre, this traditional hotel continues to retain a regular following. A choice of comfortable lounges is offered and in the air conditioned restaurant, a pianist plays while guests dine. Bedrooms are attractively furnished and many enjoy fine views over the esplanade. Leisure facilities are available to residents at the sister hotel adjacent, the Victoria.

**ROOMS:** 50 en suite (4 fmly) s £62-£109; d £106-£218 (incl. bkfst) * **LB** **FACILITIES:** STV Putting green entertainment ch fac Xmas **CONF:** Thtr 50 **SERVICES:** Lift **PARKING:** 45 **NOTES:** No dogs (ex guide dogs) No smoking in restaurant Civ Wed 110 **CARDS:**

*See advert on opposite page*

**★★★79% Westcliff**

Manor Rd EX10 8RU
☎ 01395 513252 01395 578203
e-mail: stay@westcliffhotel.co.uk
***Dir:*** *turn off A3052 to Sidmouth and proceed to the seafront and esplanade, turn right, hotel is directly ahead*

This charming hotel is within walking distance of the Promenade and standards here have certainly benefited from it having been run by the same family for more than 35 years. Elegant lounges and the cocktail bar open onto a terrace leading to the pool and croquet lawn. Bedrooms, several with balconies and glorious sea views, are spacious and the restaurant offers an interesting choice of dishes from a selection of menus.

**ROOMS:** 40 en suite (4 fmly) No smoking in 4 bedrooms s £61-£81; d £110-£214 (incl. bkfst & dinner) * **LB** **FACILITIES:** STV Outdoor swimming (H) Snooker Gym Croquet lawn Putting green Jacuzzi Mini tennis PoolTable entertainment **SERVICES:** Lift **PARKING:** 40 **NOTES:** No dogs No children 6yrs No smoking in restaurant Closed Nov-Mar **CARDS:**

*See advert on page 537*

The Victoria Hotel

AA ★★★★
Rosette ❄ for cuisine

The Belmont Hotel
AA ★★★★

# *The most luxurious choice in East Devon*

Perfectly positioned on Sidmouth's famous esplanade, the Victoria is one of the resorts finest and most picturesque hotels. It's extensive leisure facilities include indoor and outdoor pools, sauna, solarium, spa bath, hairdressing salon, putting green, tennis courts and snooker.

**Telephone : 01395 512651**

www.victoriahotel.co.uk Email: info@victoriahotel.co.uk

The Belmont too commands spectacular views from the famous esplanade. As inviting in January as July, the Belmont offers fine cusine and superlative service that brings guests back year after year. With the indoor and outdoor leisure facilities of the adjacent Victoria Hotel at your disposal, the Belmont provides the perfect location for your holiday.

**Telephone: 01395 512555**

www.belmont-hotel.co.uk Email: info@belmont-hotel.co.uk

PRB
Brend Hotels

**The Westcountry's Leading Hotel Group**

SIDMOUTH, continued

### ★★★68% Salcombe Hill House

Beatlands Rd EX10 8JQ
☎ 01395 514697 & 514398 🖷 01395 578310
e-mail: salcombehillhousehotel@eclipse.co.uk
***Dir:*** *At Radway Cinema in town centre turn left, go over bridge, turn sharp right then left into Beatlands Road. Hotel is 50yds on left*

Just a short walk from the seafront, this family-run hotel stands in attractive and spacious gardens. Given their south-facing aspect, the lounge and patio get the best of the sun and provide the ideal places to relax with a book or paper. Bedrooms are bright and spacious, and served by a lift.

**ROOMS:** 28 en suite (7 fmly) s £38-£65; d £76-£130 (incl. bkfst & dinner) * **LB** **FACILITIES:** Outdoor swimming (H) Tennis (grass) Putting green Games room ch fac **SERVICES:** Lift **PARKING:** 39 **NOTES:** No smoking in restaurant Closed 20 Nov-1 Mar **CARDS:**

### ★★★64% Royal Glen

Glen Rd EX10 8RW
☎ 01395 513221 & 513456 🖷 01395 514922
e-mail: sidmouthroyalglen.hotel@virgin.net
***Dir:*** *take A303 to Honiton, turn onto A375 to Sidford, then onto the A175 to Sidmouth, follow seafront signs, turn right onto esplanade, turn right at end*

This historic, family owned, 19th-century hotel has associations with Queen Victoria. The connection is emphasised in the names of the comfortable bedrooms which are furnished in period style. Well-prepared food is served in the dining room. A heated indoor pool is available for guests, together with peaceful, well-maintained gardens.

**ROOMS:** 32 en suite (4 fmly) s £41-£44 (incl. bkfst) * **LB** **FACILITIES:** Indoor swimming (H) **PARKING:** 24 **NOTES:** No smoking in restaurant RS 2-31 Jan **CARDS:**

### ★★★61% Fortfield

Station Rd EX10 8NU
☎ 01395 512403 🖷 01395 512403
e-mail: reservations@fortfield-hotel.demon.co.uk

Just a short walk from the town centre, the hotel offers good standards of service, hospitality and cuisine. There are spacious lounges and a bar with a maritime theme. Some of the comfortable bedrooms have sea views.

**ROOMS:** 52 en suite 3 annexe en suite (7 fmly) s £64-£67; d £127-£133 (incl. bkfst & dinner) * **LB** **FACILITIES:** Indoor swimming (H) Sauna Health & beauty salon entertainment ch fac Xmas **CONF:** Thtr 70 Class 40 Board 20 Del from £39 * **SERVICES:** Lift **PARKING:** 60 **NOTES:** No smoking in restaurant **CARDS:**

### ★★77% Brownlands

Sid Rd EX10 9AG
☎ 01395 513053 🖷 01395 513053
e-mail: brownlands.hotel@virgin.net
***Dir:*** *turn off A3052 at Sidford, at Fortescue/Sidford sign, hotel 1m on left*

This fine Victorian country hotel, set peacefully on the wooded slopes of Salcombe Hill, has superb views to the town and sea. The smartly decorated bedrooms are well-equipped, and guests have a choice of comfortable sitting rooms and a separate bar. Five-course dinner is served in the dining room, which is spacious and enjoys the best of the view.

**ROOMS:** 14 en suite s £70-£73; d £120-£145 (incl. bkfst & dinner) * **LB** **FACILITIES:** Tennis (hard) Putting green Xmas **PARKING:** 25 **NOTES:** No children 8yrs No smoking in restaurant Closed Nov-mid Mar RS Dec

### ★★75% Kingswood

The Esplanade EX10 8AX
☎ 01395 516367 🖷 01395 513185
e-mail: enquiries@kingswood-hotel.co.uk
***Dir:*** *in the centre of the Esplanade*

Kingswood is a family run hotel. All bedrooms have modern facilities and many have marvellous sea views. The two lounges offer comfort and space and the attractive dining room serves good traditional cooking.

**ROOMS:** 26 rms (25 en suite) (7 fmly) No smoking in all bedrooms s £50-£60; d £100-£120 (incl. bkfst & dinner) * **LB** **SERVICES:** Lift **PARKING:** 17 **NOTES:** No smoking in restaurant Closed Dec-25 Feb **CARDS:**

### ★★74% Royal York & Faulkner

The Esplanade EX10 8AZ
☎ 01395 513043 & 0800 220714 (Freephone) 🖷 01395 577472
e-mail: yorkhotel@eclipse.co.uk
***Dir:*** *From M5 take A3052, travel 10m to Sidmouth, the hotel is at the centre of the esplanade*

This fine Regency building, facing the sea on the esplanade, has been owned and operated by the Hook family for generations. Bedrooms vary in size and style, some have balconies and sea views and all have modern facilities. Traditional dishes are served in the restaurant, and a wide range of leisure facilities is available.

**ROOMS:** 68 en suite (8 fmly) s £44-£60; d £88-£120 (incl. bkfst & dinner) * **LB** **FACILITIES:** **Spa** Snooker Sauna Solarium Gym Jacuzzi Indoor short mat bowls Free swim at local pool entertainment Xmas **SERVICES:** Lift **PARKING:** 20 **NOTES:** No smoking in restaurant Closed Jan **CARDS:**

### ★★72% Mount Pleasant

Salcombe Rd EX10 8JA
☎ 01395 514694
***Dir:*** *turn off A3052 at Sidford x-rds after 1.25 miles turn left into Salcombe Rd, hotel opposite Radway Cinema*

A sympathetically modernised Georgian hotel, a short walk from the town centre and sea front, offering comfortable accommodation and a relaxed atmosphere. The dining room features a short fixed-price menu of home-cooked dishes, special requests are willingly catered for.

**ROOMS:** 16 en suite (2 fmly) No smoking in 12 bedrooms s £41-£48; d £81-£95 (incl. bkfst & dinner) * **LB** **FACILITIES:** Putting green **PARKING:** 20 **NOTES:** No children 8yrs No smoking in restaurant Closed Nov-Feb

**★★71% Devoran**
Esplanade EX10 8AU
☎ 01395 513151 & 0800 317171 Fax 01395 579929
e-mail: devoran@cosmic.org.uk
***Dir:*** *turn off B3052 at Bowd Inn follow Sidmouth sign for approx 2m turn left onto sea front, hotel is 50yds along at the centre of Esplanade*
Known locally as the 'pink hotel on the seafront', the Devoran has comfortable and attractively decorated bedrooms, some with their own balconies and sea views. Well-maintained public rooms include a large dining room, where guests can enjoy a five-course dinner, and a comfortable lounge and bar.
**ROOMS:** 23 en suite (4 fmly) No smoking in all bedrooms s £35-£45; d £70-£90 (incl. bkfst) * **LB** **SERVICES:** Lift **PARKING:** 4 **NOTES:** No smoking in restaurant Closed mid Nov-mid Mar RS Dec-Mar
**CARDS:**

**★★68% *Hunters Moon***
Sid Rd EX10 9AA
☎ 01395 513380 Fax 01395 514270
e-mail: huntersmoon.hotel@virgin.net
***Dir:*** *from A3052 to Sidford, pass Blue Ball Pub, then next turn on right at Fortescue, hotel 1 mile from turning*
This comfortable, personally owned and run Georgian manor house is set in three acres of grounds within level walking distance of the town centre and the esplanade. Accommodation is
*continued on p538*

SIDMOUTH, continued

traditional in style but facilities are modern, and the restaurant serves imaginative, carefully prepared meals.

*Hunters Moon, Sidmouth*

**ROOMS:** 21 en suite (6 fmly) No smoking in all bedrooms **FACILITIES:** Putting green **PARKING:** 20 **NOTES:** No smoking in restaurant Closed Jan-Feb (ex Xmas) RS Dec **CARDS:**

### ★★65% Westbourne

Manor Rd EX10 8RR
☎ 01395 513774 📠 01395 512231
e-mail: jan@westbournehotelsidmouth.co.uk
***Dir:*** *200yds from Connaught Gardens*

Quietly situated, this family owned and run hotel is convenient for the town centre and the seafront. Set in well-tended gardens, the hotel offers an elegant drawing room and a spacious dining room, where both a daily menu and carte are available. Bedrooms vary in size and style, most benefiting from views over the town and surrounding countryside.

**ROOMS:** 11 rms (9 en suite) (1 fmly) s £40-£46; d fr £81.95 (incl. bkfst & dinner) * **LB** **FACILITIES:** Croquet lawn Garden with sun terrace **PARKING:** 14 **NOTES:** No smoking in restaurant Closed Nov-Feb

## SILCHESTER, Hampshire — Map 04 SU66

### ★★★74% ❀ Romans

Little London Rd RG7 2PN
☎ 0118 970 0421 📠 0118 970 0691
e-mail: romanhotel@hotmail.com
***Dir:*** *A340 Basingstoke to Reading, hotel is signposted*

Best Western

Romans Country House Hotel is located in the quiet village of

Silchester. It is a Lutyens style manor house with smartly presented bedrooms, both in the main house and a separate wing. Public rooms include a number of function rooms, a comfortable lounge and the period style restaurant.

**ROOMS:** 11 en suite 14 annexe en suite (1 fmly) No smoking in 2 bedrooms s £80-£95; d £105-£140 (incl. bkfst) * **LB** **FACILITIES:** STV Outdoor swimming (H) Sauna Gym Xmas **CONF:** Thtr 60 Class 30 Board 24 Del from £125 * **PARKING:** 60 **NOTES:** No smoking in restaurant Closed 1-7 Jan Civ Wed 65
**CARDS:**

*See advert under BASINGSTOKE*

## SILLOTH, Cumbria — Map 11 NY15

### ★★★61% The Skinburness

CA5 4QY
☎ 016973 32332 📠 016973 32549
***Dir:*** *M6 junct 41, take B5305 to Wigton, then B5302 to Silloth. M6 junct 44, take A595 to Carlisle then on to Wigton, then the B5302 to Silloth*

Enviably located on the peaceful Solway Estuary, close to sandy beaches and coastal walks, this popular hotel provides traditionally furnished bedrooms with a host of modern facilities. There is also a leisure complex with pool and spa. Good meals are available in the Mediterranean styled bar and the pleasing hotel restaurant.

**ROOMS:** 33 en suite (2 fmly) No smoking in 6 bedrooms s £55-£70; d £90-£120 (incl. bkfst) * **LB** **FACILITIES:** **Spa** STV Indoor swimming (H) Fishing Sauna Solarium Gym Jacuzzi entertainment Xmas **CONF:** Thtr 120 Class 100 Board 60 Del from £47.50 * **PARKING:** 120 **CARDS:**

### ★★64% Golf Hotel

Criffel St CA5 4AB
☎ 016973 31438 📠 016973 32582
***Dir:*** *off B5302, in Silloth at T-junct turn left hotel overlooks the corner of the green*

This long-established, family-run hotel beside the village green has a relaxed and welcoming atmosphere. Its bedrooms are generally modern in style and benefit from ongoing refurbishment. Public areas include a spacious bar, restaurant, lounge and games room. The varied menus offer a wide selection of dishes.

**ROOMS:** 22 en suite (4 fmly) s £35-£51; d £57-£81 (incl. bkfst) * **LB** **FACILITIES:** Snooker **CONF:** Thtr 100 Class 40 Board 40 **NOTES:** Closed 25 Dec **CARDS:**

## SIX MILE BOTTOM, Cambridgeshire — Map 05 TL55

### ★★★73% ❀ Swynford Paddocks

CB8 0UE
☎ 01638 570234 📠 01638 570283
e-mail: info@swynfordpaddocks.com
***Dir:*** *M11 junct 9, take A11 towards Newmarket, turn onto the A1304 to Newmarket, hotel is on left 0.75m along*

Ideally situated amidst its own attractive gardens, this pleasant

*continued*

country house is located between Newmarket and Cambridge. The relaxing accommodation comes in a variety of shapes and styles, ranging from comfortably appointed quarters to regal bedrooms, with several offering four-poster beds. The hotel restaurant provides an excellent choice of modern dishes in elegant surroundings.
**ROOMS:** 15 en suite s fr £110; d £135-£175 (incl. bkfst) * **LB**
**FACILITIES:** STV Tennis (hard) Croquet lawn Putting green ch fac Xmas
**CONF:** Thtr 30 Class 20 Board 22 Del from £135 * **PARKING:** 180
**NOTES:** No smoking in restaurant Civ Wed 40
**CARDS:**

*See advert under NEWMARKET*

## SKEGNESS, Lincolnshire — Map 09 TF56

### ★★★64% Crown
Drummond Rd, Seacroft PE25 3AB
☎ 01754 610760 Fax 01754 610847
***Dir:*** *take A52 to town centre, hotel 1m from clock tower*
The Crown is ideally situated just a short walk from the seafront and town centre. The bedrooms are attractively decorated, well-maintained and thoughtfully equipped. A wide selection of enjoyable dishes is available either in the attractive modern bar or in the more formal restaurant.
**ROOMS:** 27 en suite (7 fmly) s fr £50; d fr £50 (incl. bkfst) * **LB**
**FACILITIES:** STV Indoor swimming (H) **CONF:** Thtr 120 Class 130 Board 120 **SERVICES:** Lift **PARKING:** 90 **NOTES:** No dogs (ex guide dogs) Civ Wed 80 **CARDS:**

*See advert on this page*

### ★★★63% Vine Hotel
Vine Rd, Seacroft PE25 3DB
☎ 01754 763018 & 610611 Fax 01754 769845
***Dir:*** *A52 to Skegness, head S towards Gibraltar Point, hotel is approx 1m from the clocktower*
Owned by the local brewery, this is reputedly the second oldest building in Skegness. Recently refurbished, it has spacious, comfortable bedrooms. There are two bars, the Tennyson Lounge (the poet wrote some of his works in the garden), and the Oak Room with open fire and excellent beers. Freshly prepared dishes are served in the bar and restaurant.
**ROOMS:** 20 en suite (6 fmly) No smoking in 8 bedrooms s £55-£65; d £75-£85 (incl. bkfst) * **LB** **FACILITIES:** Bowling green ch fac Xmas
**CONF:** Thtr 100 Class 80 Board 50 **PARKING:** 50
**CARDS:**

### ★★66% North Shore
North Shore Rd PE25 1DN
☎ 01754 763298 Fax 01754 761902
e-mail: golf@north-shore.co.uk
***Dir:*** *1m N of town centre on A52 Ingoldmells Rd, right opposite Fenland laundry*
North Shore Golf Hotel is part of a championship course complex. There are ample public rooms including a superb conservatory and busy bar where simple informal fare is served. The restaurant

*continued on p540*

CROWN
HOTEL

SKEGNESS, continued

offers daily changing set menus. The bedrooms vary in size and style but all are smartly decorated and well-equipped.

*North Shore, Skegness*

**ROOMS:** 33 en suite 3 annexe en suite (4 fmly) s £50-£55; d £80-£90 (incl. bkfst & dinner) * **LB** **FACILITIES:** Golf 18 Snooker Putting green Xmas **CONF:** Thtr 220 Class 60 Board 60 Del from £65 * **PARKING:** 200 **NOTES:** No dogs (ex guide dogs) No smoking in restaurant Civ Wed 200 **CARDS:**

## SKIPTON, North Yorkshire

Map 07 SD95

### ★★★69% *Coniston Hall Lodge*

Coniston Cold BD23 4EB
☎ 01756 748080 01756 749487
e-mail: conistonhall@clara.net
***Dir:*** *on A65, 5m NW of Skipton*

Part of a 1200-acre estate, the grounds of Coniston Hall Lodge are dominated by a vast 24-acre lake. Here you can try trout fly-fishing, or rough shooting in the adjacent woodland. The modern bedrooms are spacious and comfortable; most have king-size beds. Cuisine is highly skilled and offers a wide selection of dishes featuring the excellent local produce. Macleod's Bar and the Buttery both offer all-day meals.

**ROOMS:** 40 en suite (4 fmly) **FACILITIES:** STV Fishing 4 wheel drive Clay pigeon shooting Paintball Falconry Archery **CONF:** Thtr 100 Class 50 Board 20 **PARKING:** 120 **NOTES:** Civ Wed 50 **CARDS:**

*See advert on opposite page*

### ★★★66% Hanover International

Keighley Rd BD23 2TA
☎ 01756 700100 01756 700107
e-mail: hihskipton@totalise.co.uk
***Dir:*** *on A629, 1m from town*

A modern building situated just outside town, with a canal path to walk along. Bedrooms are well-equipped and spacious with stunning views over the countryside. Added attractions are the comprehensive leisure facilities and children's areas. The hotel also caters for business people, with conference and training facilities.

**ROOMS:** 75 en suite (10 fmly) No smoking in 14 bedrooms s £80-£88; d £90-£98 * **LB** **FACILITIES:** STV Indoor swimming (H) Squash Sauna Solarium Gym Jacuzzi Whirlpool spa Steam room ch fac Xmas **CONF:** Thtr 400 Class 180 Board 120 Del from £85 * **SERVICES:** Lift **PARKING:** 150 **NOTES:** No smoking in restaurant Civ Wed 200 **CARDS:**

### ★★66% Herriots

Broughton Rd BD23 1RT
☎ 01756 792781 01756 793967
***Dir:*** *off A59, opposite railway station*

Close to the centre of the town and on the doorstep of the Yorkshire Dales National Park, this friendly hotel offers brightly decorated bedrooms. The stylish open-plan brasserie is a relaxing place in which to dine from the varied menu; meals and snacks are also available in the bar. Entertainment is normally provided on Sunday evenings.

**ROOMS:** 13 en suite (2 fmly) No smoking in 8 bedrooms s £55-£65; d fr £75 (incl. bkfst) * **LB** **FACILITIES:** Xmas **CONF:** Thtr 20 Class 15 Board 14 Del from £75 * **PARKING:** 26 **NOTES:** No smoking in restaurant **CARDS:**

### *Travelodge*

Travelodge

Gargrave Rd BD23 1UD
☎ 01756 798091 01756 798091
***Dir:*** *A65/A59 roundabout*

Travelodge offers good quality, good value, modern accommodation. Ideal for families, the spacious, en suite bedrooms include remote-control TV, tea and coffee-making facilities, luxury beds and free morning newspaper. Meals can be taken at the nearby family restaurant. For further details and the Travelodge phone number, consult the Hotel Groups page.

**ROOMS:** 32 en suite

## SLEAFORD, Lincolnshire

Map 08 TF04

### ★★★65% The Lincolnshire Oak

East Rd NG34 7EH
☎ 01529 413807 01529 413710
e-mail: reception@linconshire-oak.co.uk

This pleasant, hospitable Victorian house is set in grounds on the

*continued*

edge of town. It offers modern, well-furnished bedrooms and comfortable public rooms. Ample function rooms are available.

**ROOMS:** 17 en suite No smoking in 12 bedrooms s £55-£69; d £69-£84 (incl. bkfst) * **LB** **FACILITIES:** STV ch fac **CONF:** Thtr 140 Class 70 Board 50 Del from £80 * **PARKING:** 80 **NOTES:** No dogs No smoking in restaurant Civ Wed 50 **CARDS:**

★★69% **Carre Arms**
1 Mareham Ln NG34 7JP
☎ 01529 303156 ▤ 01529 303139
***Dir:*** *take A153 to Sleaford, hotel on right at level crossing*
This welcoming hotel is close to the station and offers well-equipped bedrooms. A range of food is offered in the Brasserie; bar food is also available. There is no lounge, but the bars are comfortable and the conservatory is a riot of colour during the summer. The old stables house a spacious function room.
**ROOMS:** 13 en suite (1 fmly) s £50; d £70 (incl. bkfst) * **CONF:** Thtr 150 Class 20 Board 30 **PARKING:** 100 **NOTES:** No dogs (ex guide dogs) **CARDS:**

⌂ ***Travelodge***
Holdingham NG34 8NP
☎ 01529 414752 ▤ 01529 414752
***Dir:*** *1m N, at roundabout A17/A15*
Travelodge offers good quality, good value, modern accommodation. Ideal for families, the spacious, en suite bedrooms include remote-control TV, tea and coffee-making facilities, luxury beds and free morning newspaper. Meals can be taken at the nearby family restaurant. For further details and the Travelodge phone number, consult the Hotel Groups page.

**ROOMS:** 40 en suite

## SLOUGH, Berkshire

Map 04 SU97

★★★★66% **Copthorne Hotel Slough/Windsor**
400 Cippenham Ln SL1 2YE
☎ 01753 516222 ▤ 01753 516237
e-mail: sales.slough@mill-cop.com
***Dir:*** *leave M4 junct 6 & follow A355 to Slough at next rdbt turn left & left again for hotel entrance*
This is a modern property just off the M4 with views over to Heathrow and Windsor. Public areas include two dining options and a good leisure centre. Bedrooms are spacious with excellent facilities. The hotel is popular for weekend breaks; special vouchers are issued offering discounts to various attractions in the area.
**ROOMS:** 219 en suite (47 fmly) No smoking in 148 bedrooms s £150-£175; d £150-£175 * **FACILITIES:** STV Indoor swimming (H) Sauna Gym Jacuzzi Xmas **CONF:** Thtr 250 Class 160 Board 60 **SERVICES:** Lift air con **PARKING:** 300 **NOTES:** No dogs (ex guide dogs) No smoking in restaurant **CARDS:**

★★★68% **Courtyard by Marriott Slough/Windsor**
Church St SL1 2NH
☎ 01753 551551 ▤ 01753 553333
***Dir:*** *from junct 6 of M4 follow A355 to rdbt, turn right hotel approx 50 yds on right*

Location is a benefit for this modern hotel, with Heathrow Airport and local motorway networks easily accessible by car. Bedrooms feature a comprehensive range of facilities. The public areas are lively, modern and have an informal atmosphere.
**ROOMS:** 150 en suite (74 fmly) No smoking in 108 bedrooms s £125-£145; d £125-£145 * **LB** **FACILITIES:** STV Gym Xmas **CONF:** Thtr 45 Class 18 Board 24 Del from £149 * **SERVICES:** Lift air con **PARKING:** 162 **NOTES:** No dogs (ex guide dogs) No smoking in restaurant **CARDS:**

SLOUGH, continued

★★★65% **Quality Hotel Heathrow**
London Rd, Brands Hill SL3 8QB
☎ 01753 684001 📠 01753 685767
e-mail: info@qualityheathrow.com

***Dir:*** *exit junct 5 M4,follow directions Colnbrook. Hotel approx 250mtrs on right*
A smart modern hotel ideally located for Heathrow Airport, and for commercial visitors to Slough. Bedrooms have good facilities, backed up by all day room service. There is a bright and airy restaurant, bar and lounge. Transport is available to and from the airport.
**ROOMS:** 123 en suite (23 fmly) No smoking in 60 bedrooms s £115-£140; d £115-£140 * **LB** **FACILITIES:** STV **SERVICES:** Lift **PARKING:** 100 **NOTES:** No dogs (ex guide dogs)
**CARDS:**

★★★64% ***Comfort Inn Heathrow***
Sheppiston Ln UB3 1LP
☎ 020 8573 6162
The Comfort Inn is a new addition to Heathrow's many hotels, having been totally rebuilt. It is located a little way from the airport, so guests may prefer this quieter position. A frequent bus service runs throughout the day. Bedrooms are well-equipped with extras. The new air-conditioned conference room is popular.
**ROOMS:** 184 rms **FACILITIES:** no TV in bdrms **NOTES:** Open

○ **Innkeeper's Lodge Slough/Windsor**
London Rd, Langley SL3 8PS
A new concept in the travel accommodation market. Smart rooms meet essential business requirements but also have home comforts. Dining options include all-day menus plus the added advantage of breakfast, which is included in the room price. Reservations can be made seven days a week through the room reservations number: 0870 243 0500. For further details, consult the Hotel Groups page.
**ROOMS:** 57 en suite

SOLIHULL, West Midlands — Map 07 SP17
see also Dorridge

★★★★66% **Renaissance Solihull**
651 Warwick Rd B91 1AT
☎ 0121 711 3000
📠 0121 705 6629/0121 711 3963
e-mail: nina.faulkner@whitbread.com
***Dir:*** *leave M42 junct 5 & follow signs for Solihull centre. At small rdbt 2nd left - Warwick Rd. Straight over 3 sets traffic lights. Barley Mow pub left on approaching large roundabout. Proceed straight ahead, hotel on right.*

This hotel has easy access to main arterial routes and is convenient for the NEC and airport. An attractive modern hotel, with bright, spacious reception rooms, it is popular with business guests. There are excellent leisure, conference and in room facilities. The 651 restaurant offers a contemporary brasserie menu.
**ROOMS:** 175 en suite (6 fmly) No smoking in 87 bedrooms s £110-£160; d £110-£160 * **LB** **FACILITIES:** Spa STV Indoor swimming (H) Sauna Solarium Gym Jacuzzi Beauty therapist Large screen TV entertainment Xmas **CONF:** Thtr 700 Class 350 Board 60 Del from £115 * **SERVICES:** Lift **PARKING:** 300 **NOTES:** Civ Wed 70
**CARDS:**

★★★66% **Regency**
Stratford Rd, Shirley B90 4EB

REGAL
☎ 0121 745 6119 📠 0121 733 3801
***Dir:*** *beside A34, 0.5m from junct 4 of M42*

THE REGENCY HOTEL

This popular business hotel offers a blend of tradition and friendly informal service. Morrissey's Irish Bar provides a lively venue with music, and the lounge, bar and restaurant offer more comfortable surroundings in which to enjoy a meal or leisurely drink. Bedrooms vary in style and size although all offer the space to work or relax.
**ROOMS:** 112 en suite (6 fmly) No smoking in 17 bedrooms **FACILITIES:** STV Indoor swimming (H) Sauna Solarium Gym Jacuzzi Beauty health salon entertainment Xmas **CONF:** Thtr 180 Class 80 Board 60 **SERVICES:** Lift **PARKING:** 275 **NOTES:** No smoking in restaurant **CARDS:**

★★61% **Flemings**
141 Warwick Rd, Olton B92 7HW
☎ 0121 706 0371 📠 0121 706 4494
e-mail: reservations@flemingshotel.co.uk
***Dir:*** *on A41, near Olton Station*
This privately owned hotel is close to the NEC and Birmingham International Airport. There are some ground-floor rooms, and some suitable for family use. Facilities include a small bistro adjacent to the bar, as an alternative to the main dining room, and a snooker room.
**ROOMS:** 77 en suite (6 fmly) No smoking in 4 bedrooms s £25-£50; d £40-£56 (incl. bkfst) * **LB** **FACILITIES:** Snooker **CONF:** Thtr 40 Class 40 Board 22 **PARKING:** 80 **NOTES:** No smoking in restaurant Closed 24-28 Dec **CARDS:**

SONNING, Berkshire — Map 04 SU77

★★★77% ®® **French Horn**
RG4 6TN
☎ 0118 969 2204 📠 0118 944 2210
e-mail: thefrenchhorn@compuserve.com
***Dir:*** *turn left off A4 into Sonning follow road through village over bridge, hotel on right, car park on left*
This long established Thames-side restaurant with rooms has a

continued

lovely village setting and retains the traditions of classical hotel-keeping. The restaurant is a particular attraction where the signature dish is duck, spit-roasted in front of the fire in the bar, and carved at the table. Bedrooms are spacious and comfortable, many offering stunning views over the river. There are also four cottage suites. A private board room and dining facilities are attractive to corporate guests.
**ROOMS:** 12 en suite 8 annexe en suite s £110-£150; d £120-£175 (incl. bkfst) * **FACILITIES:** Fishing **CONF:** Board 16 Del £200 * **PARKING:** 40 **NOTES:** No dogs (ex guide dogs) Closed 26 Dec-2 Jan & Good Fri **CARDS:**

SOURTON, Devon Map 02 SX59

★★71% ***Collaven Manor***
EX20 4HH
☎ 01837 861522 📠 01837 861614
***Dir:*** *turn off A30 onto A386 to Tavistock hotel 2m on right*

Set in five acres of well-tended gardens, this delightful 15th-century manor house benefits from stunning rural views. The comfortable bedrooms are individually designed and well-equipped. Stone walls, old beams and inglenook fireplaces enhance the character of the cosy sitting rooms, one of which has a well-stocked bar. Each evening an imaginative, fixed price menu is offered, using fresh local produce.
**ROOMS:** 9 en suite (1 fmly) **FACILITIES:** Croquet lawn Bowls Badminton **CONF:** Thtr 30 Class 20 Board 16 **PARKING:** 50 **NOTES:** No smoking in restaurant **CARDS:**

SOURTON CROSS, Devon Map 02 SX59

⌂ ***Travelodge***
EX20 4LY
☎ 01837 52124 📠 01837 52124
***Dir:*** *4m W, at junct of A30/A386*

Travelodge

Travelodge offers good quality, good value, modern accommodation. Ideal for families, the spacious, en suite bedrooms include remote-control TV, tea and coffee-making facilities, luxury beds and free morning newspaper. Meals can be taken at the nearby family restaurant. For further details and the Travelodge phone number, consult the Hotel Groups page.

**ROOMS:** 42 en suite

Late for dinner? Quality Standards star rating means that last orders for dinner should be no earlier than:
★ 6.30pm ★★ 7.00pm ★★★ 8.00pm
★★★★ 9.00pm ★★★★★ 10.00pm



S

## SOUTHAMPTON, Hampshire

Map 04 SU41

see also Shedfield

### ★★★★★57% De Vere Grand Harbour

West Quay Rd SO15 1AG

De Vere Hotels

☎ 023 8063 3033 🖷 023 8063 3066

e-mail: grandharbour@devere-hotels.com

***Dir:*** *leave M27 junct 3 follow Waterfront signs keep in left hand lane of dual carriageway,then follow signs Heritage & Waterfront to old town & waterfront onto West Quay Rd*

Located in West Quay, this impressive, modern hotel is ideally placed for the city's business district, shopping centres, waterfront and tourist attractions. Bedrooms and suites, some with balconies, are both comfortably furnished and thoughtfully equipped. Guests have a choice between two restaurants. The hotel also offers an extensive range of conference and banqueting facilities, and a superb leisure centre, which stands in a glass pyramid.

**ROOMS:** 172 en suite No smoking in 139 bedrooms s £155; d £175 (incl. bkfst) * **LB** **FACILITIES:** STV Indoor swimming (H) Snooker Sauna Solarium Gym Jacuzzi Steam room Beauty treatments entertainment ch fac Xmas **CONF:** Thtr 500 Class 270 Board 48 Del from £175 * **SERVICES:** Lift air con **PARKING:** 200 **NOTES:** No dogs (ex guide dogs) No smoking in restaurant

**CARDS:**

### ★★★★67% Botleigh Grange

Hedge End SO30 2GA

Best Western

☎ 01489 787700 🖷 01489 788535

e-mail: enquiries@botleighgrangehotel.co.uk

***Dir:*** *follow A334 to Botley & hotel is on the left just before Botley*

A recent upgrade of this impressive mansion ensures good quality throughout. The bedrooms are newly decorated and have a good range of facilities. Public areas are well-appointed with views overlooking the gardens and lake. The restaurant offers interesting menus to a good standard; there is significant conferencing available.

**ROOMS:** 56 en suite (8 fmly) No smoking in 20 bedrooms s £75-£87; d £95-£117 (incl. bkfst) * **LB** **FACILITIES:** STV Fishing Putting green Coarse fishing Xmas **CONF:** Thtr 500 Class 175 Board 60 Del from £115 * **SERVICES:** Lift **PARKING:** 200 **NOTES:** No dogs (ex guide dogs) No smoking in restaurant Civ Wed 200

**CARDS:**

*See advert on opposite page*

### ★★★72% The Woodlands Lodge

Bartley Rd, Woodlands SO40 7GN

☎ 023 8029 2257 🖷 023 8029 3090

e-mail: woodlands@nortels.ltd.uk

***Dir:*** *take A326 towards Fawley. 2nd rdbt turn right, after 0.25m turn left by White Horse PH. In 1.5m cross cattle grid, hotel is 70mtrs on left*

This beautifully restored 18th-century hunting lodge is set in four acres of attractive grounds on the edge of the New Forest.

*continued*

Bedrooms are furnished and decorated to a high standard, and there is a pleasant lounge and bar, both opening onto the gardens. The restaurant, with its handpainted ceiling, serves delicious award winning cuisine.

**ROOMS:** 16 en suite (1 fmly) No smoking in 2 bedrooms s £69-£93; d £118-£186 (incl. bkfst) * **LB** **FACILITIES:** STV Jacuzzi Xmas **CONF:** Thtr 55 Class 16 Board 20 Del £116 * **PARKING:** 31 **NOTES:** No smoking in restaurant Civ Wed 60

**CARDS:**

### ★★★65% Novotel Southampton

1 West Quay Rd SO15 1RA

Novotel

☎ 023 8033 0550 🖷 023 8022 2158

e-mail: H1073@accor-hotels.com

***Dir:*** *from M27 junct 3 follow for City Centre (A33). After 1m take right hand lane for West Quay & Dock Gates 4-10. Hotel entrance on right*

This modern, purpose built hotel is conveniently located in the heart of the new city centre, close to both the railway station and road network. The spacious bedrooms are brightly appointed and ideal for both families and business guests. Four bedrooms have facilities for disabled guests. Public areas include the garden brasserie and bar which is open throughout the day, a leisure complex, and extensive conference and banqueting facilities.

**ROOMS:** 121 en suite (50 fmly) No smoking in 71 bedrooms s £79; d £79 * **LB** **FACILITIES:** STV Indoor swimming (H) Sauna Gym **CONF:** Thtr 500 Class 300 Board 150 Del from £99 * **SERVICES:** Lift air con **PARKING:** 300 **CARDS:**

### ★★★64% Highfield House

Highfield Ln, Portswood SO17 1AQ

Zoffany Hotels

☎ 023 8035 9955 🖷 023 8058 3910

e-mail: highfield@zoffanyhotels.co.uk

***Dir:*** *from M27 junct 5 take A335 to city centre,at 5th set of traffic lights follow signs for Portswood/University, hotel on right after Shaftesbury Avenue*

Close to the university and within easy reach of the motorway, this hotel remains a popular choice with all guests. New owners have initiated a major refurbishment programme. Bedrooms and public areas have all been upgraded.

**ROOMS:** 66 en suite (6 fmly) No smoking in 30 bedrooms s £90-£130; d £95-£150 (incl. bkfst) * **LB** **FACILITIES:** STV Xmas **CONF:** Thtr 200 Class 100 Board 60 Del from £105 * **PARKING:** 85 **NOTES:** No smoking in restaurant **CARDS:**

### ★★★64% *Posthouse Southampton*

Herbert Walker Av SO15 1HJ

Posthouse

☎ 0870 400 9073 🖷 023 8033 2510

***Dir:*** *from M27 follow signs for 'Western Docks 1-10'. Posthouse situated next to Dock Gate 8*

Conveniently located for both the port and the town centre, this modern hotel is popular with all types of guests. The well equipped bedrooms are comfortably furnished and modern in style. Public areas include an informal lounge bar and the Traders Restaurant which offers an extensive range of popular dishes. Conference facilities are available.

**ROOMS:** 128 en suite (14 fmly) No smoking in 75 bedrooms **FACILITIES:** Indoor swimming (H) Sauna Solarium Gym Jacuzzi Beauty therapy room **CONF:** Thtr 250 Class 80 Board 50 **SERVICES:** Lift **PARKING:** 250 **CARDS:**

Popped the question? Hotels with Civ Wed in their entry are licensed for civil wedding ceremonies. Maximum numbers for the ceremony only are shown, e.g. Civ Wed 120

★★★64% **Southampton Park**
Cumberland Place SO15 2WY
☎ 023 8034 3343 📠 023 8033 2538
e-mail: southampton.park@forestdale.com
**Dir:** *hotel at northern end of the Inner Ring Rd opposite Watts Park & Civic Centre*

Forestdale Hotels

Located in the heart of the city opposite Watts Park, this modern hotel provides well equipped, smartly appointed bedrooms with comfortable furnishings. The public areas include a good leisure centre, spacious bar and lounge, and a choice of eating options. Parking is available in the multi-storey car park behind the hotel.
**ROOMS:** 72 en suite (10 fmly) No smoking in 20 bedrooms s fr £80; d fr £95 (incl. bkfst) * **LB** **FACILITIES:** STV Indoor swimming (H) Sauna Solarium Gym Jacuzzi Massage Jet Steam room **CONF:** Thtr 200 Class 60 Board 70 Del £125 * **SERVICES:** Lift **NOTES:** No smoking in restaurant Closed 25 & 26 Dec nights **CARDS:**

★★67% **Elizabeth House**
43-44 The Avenue SO17 1XP
☎ 023 8022 4327 📠 023 8022 4327
e-mail: enquiries@elizabethhousehotel.com
**Dir:** *on the A33, left hand side travelling towards city centre, after Southampton Common, before main traffic lights*

The Elizabeth House is conveniently situated on The Avenue, and as such provides an ideal base for both business and leisure guests. Bedrooms are attractively furnished with comfort in mind. Dinner may be taken in the dining room or the more informal bar. Service is provided by friendly, helpful staff.
**ROOMS:** 21 en suite (4 fmly) s £48; d £58 (incl. bkfst) * **CONF:** Thtr 40 Class 24 Board 24 Del from £80 * **PARKING:** 23 **NOTES:** No smoking in restaurant **CARDS:**

★★65% **The Star Hotel & Restaurant**
26 High St SO14 2NA
☎ 023 8033 9939 📠 023 8033 5291
**Dir:** *enter city from A33 follow signs for city centre at Isle of Wight ferry terminal turn into High St, hotel on right just beyond zebra crossing*

This friendly city centre hotel continues to grow in popularity. The bedrooms are bright and comfortably furnished, while public areas include a popular bar, smart reception area and dining room. There are several function rooms including a self-contained conference suite, secure parking is available.
**ROOMS:** 43 rms (37 en suite) (2 fmly) No smoking in 7 bedrooms s fr £59; d £80-£90 (incl. bkfst) * **LB** **FACILITIES:** STV entertainment **CONF:** Thtr 60 Class 60 Board 45 Del from £80 * **SERVICES:** Lift **PARKING:** 24 **NOTES:** Closed 24 Dec-1 Jan **CARDS:**

★★64% ***Busketts Lawn***
174 Woodlands Rd, Woodlands SO40 7GL
☎ 023 8029 2272 & 8029 2077 📠 023 8029 2487
**Dir:** *A35 W of city through Ashurst, over railway bridge, sharp right into Woodlands Road*

A relaxing and informal hotel in a tranquil setting on the edge of the New Forest. Bedrooms vary in size although all include many thoughtful extras. There is a cosy lounge and a small separate bar. The hotel is a popular venue for both conferences and weddings.
**ROOMS:** 14 en suite (3 fmly) **FACILITIES:** Outdoor swimming (H) Croquet lawn Putting green Football **CONF:** Thtr 150 Class 75 Board 40 **PARKING:** 50 **NOTES:** No smoking in restaurant **CARDS:**

Early start? Hotels at all star levels should provide in-room alarm clocks and/or alarm calls.





S

SOUTHAMPTON, continued

### ★★64% Rosida Garden
25-27 Hill Ln SO15 5AB
☎ 023 8022 8501 ▯ 023 8063 5501
e-mail: enquiries@rosidagarden.co.uk
***Dir:*** *M3, A33 exit, rdbt 2nd exit, next rdbt 2nd exit, 1st exit next rdbt, straight across mini rdbt, 1.5m ahead, hotel on left*
Situated close to the city centre, this hotel is conveniently located for both the docks and ferry ports. The bedrooms are comfortably furnished, and guests can enjoy hearty home-cooked food in the well-presented dining room. There is also a TV lounge and a licensed bar.
**ROOMS:** 27 en suite (6 fmly) s £51-£63; d £63-£71 (incl. bkfst) * **LB**
**FACILITIES:** Outdoor swimming (H) **CONF:** Thtr 35 Class 20 Board 20
**PARKING:** 50 **CARDS:**

### ⇧ Express by Holiday Inn
Adanac Park, Redbridge Ln, Nursling SO16 0XU
☎ 023 8074 3100 ▯ 023 8073 1827
e-mail: southampton@premierhotels.co.uk
***Dir:*** *ake M271 from M27 junct 3 hotel on left at junct 1 (Lordshill Interchange) via Redbridge Lane*

A modern budget hotel offering comfortable accommodation in refreshing, spacious and comprehensively equipped bedrooms, en suite bathrooms with power showers and continental buffet breakfast included in the room rate. Suitable for business travellers or families. For further details and the Express by Holiday Inn phone number, consult the Hotel Groups page.
**ROOMS:** 105 en suite

### ⇧ *Travelodge*
Lodge Rd SO17 1XS
☎ 023 8022 9023
Travelodge offers good quality, good value, modern accommodation. Ideal for families, the spacious, en suite bedrooms include remote-control TV, tea and coffee-making facilities, luxury beds and free morning newspaper. Meals can be taken at the nearby family restaurant. For further details and the Travelodge phone number, consult the Hotel Groups page.

**ROOMS:** 48 en suite

### ⇧ Hotel Ibis
West Quay Rd, Western Esplanade SO15 1RA
☎ 023 8063 4463 ▯ 023 8022 3273
e-mail: H1039@accor-hotels.com
***Dir:*** *M27 junct 3 joining M271. Turn left to Southampton City A35,follow Old Town Waterfront until 4th lights,left,then left again,hotel opposite station*
Modern, budget hotel offering comfortable accommodation in bright and practical bedrooms. Breakfast is self-service and dinner is available in the restaurant. For further details, consult the Hotel Groups page.
**ROOMS:** 93 en suite s fr £52; d fr £52 * **CONF:** Thtr 70 Class 50 Board 40

SOUTHBOROUGH, Kent

### ○ Innkeeper's Lodge Tunbridge
London Rd, Southborough TN4 0RL
☎ 0870 243 0500
A new concept in the travel accommodation market. Smart rooms meet essential business requirements but also have home comforts. Dining options include all-day menus plus the added advantage of breakfast, which is included in the room price. Reservations can be made seven days a week through the room reservations number: 0870 243 0500. For further details, consult the Hotel Groups page.
**ROOMS:** 15 en suite

SOUTH BRENT, Devon Map 03 SX6

### ★★75% *Brookdale House Restaurant & Hotel*
North Huish TQ10 9NR
☎ 01548 821661 ▯ 01548 821606
e-mail: Brookdalehouse@yahoo.com
***Dir:*** *from A38 follow Avonwich signs, turn right at Avon Inn, next left at telephone box then right at hotel sign to bottom of valley*
This charming Tudor-style residence stands next to the river, with sloping gardens and a tumbling waterfall. Bedrooms are individually named, and furnished largely with antique pieces; many thoughtful touches including mineral water and fresh flowers further enhance their comfort. Enjoyable cuisine is served in the restaurant.
**ROOMS:** 6 en suite 2 annexe en suite No smoking in 2 bedrooms
**CONF:** Thtr 50 Class 30 Board 30 **NOTES:** No children 12yrs Civ Wed 120 **CARDS:**

SOUTH CAVE, East Riding of Yorkshire Map 08 SE9

### ⇧ *Travelodge*
Beacon Service Area HU15 1RZ
☎ 01430 424455 ▯ 01430 424455
***Dir:*** *A63 eastbound*
Travelodge offers good quality, good value, modern accommodation. Ideal for families, the spacious, en suite bedrooms include remote-control TV, tea and coffee-making facilities, luxury beds and free morning newspaper. Meals can be taken at the nearby family restaurant. For further details and the Travelodge phone number, consult the Hotel Groups page.

**ROOMS:** 40 en suite

SOUTHEND-ON-SEA, Essex Map 05 TQ8

### ★★★68% Westcliff
Westcliff Pde, Westcliff-on-Sea SS0 7QW
☎ 01702 345247 ▯ 01702 431814
e-mail: westcliff@zoffanyhotels.co.uk
***Dir:*** *M25 J29, A127 towards Southend, follow signs for Cliffs Pavillion whe approaching town centre*
An imposing Grade II listed Victorian building overlooking the cliffs, gardens and sea beyond. Bedrooms are generally quite spacious, tastefully decorated and offer a good range of useful extras. Public rooms feature a conservatory style restaurant with

*continue*

magnificent views of the estuary, a spacious lounge and a range of function rooms.

**ROOMS:** 55 en suite (3 fmly) No smoking in 21 bedrooms s £75-£90; d £90-£130 (incl. bkfst) * **LB** **FACILITIES:** STV entertainment Xmas **CONF:** Thtr 225 Class 90 Board 64 Del £99 * **SERVICES:** Lift **NOTES:** No dogs (ex guide dogs) No smoking in restaurant Civ Wed 60 **CARDS:**

*See advert on this page*

### ★★★66% Roslin Hotel

Thorpe Esplanade SS1 3BG
☎ 01702 586375 01702 586663
e-mail: frontoffice@roslinhtl.demon.co.uk

This charming hotel is ideally situated at the far end of the Esplanade and overlooks the beach. The pleasantly decorated bedrooms are generally quite spacious and equipped with a good range of useful extras; some have sea views. Public rooms include a large lounge bar and the attractive Mulberry restaurant, which overlooks the sea.
**ROOMS:** 39 rms (35 en suite) (4 fmly) s £38-£67; d £68-£80 (incl. bkfst) * **LB** **FACILITIES:** STV Temp membership of local sports centre **CONF:** Thtr 40 Class 30 Board 30 **PARKING:** 34 **CARDS:**

### ★★70% Balmoral

34 Valkyrie Rd, Westcliff-on-Sea SS0 8BU
☎ 01702 342947 01702 337828
e-mail: balmoralhotel@netscapeonline.co.uk
***Dir:*** *off A13*
Charming hotel situated just a short walk from Westcliff's main shopping centre, railway station and sea front. The attractively decorated bedrooms are tastefully furnished and equipped with many thoughtful touches. The public rooms include a small cocktail bar, a smart restaurant and a further seating area in reception.
**ROOMS:** 29 en suite (4 fmly) s £44-£90; d £69-£120 (incl. bkfst) * **LB** **FACILITIES:** STV Arrangement with nearby health club **PARKING:** 23 **NOTES:** Closed Xmas **CARDS:**

### ★★70% Camelia

178 Eastern Esplanade, Thorpe Bay SS1 3AA
☎ 01702 587917 01702 585704
e-mail: cameliahotel@fsbdial.co.uk
***Dir:*** *from A13 or A127 follow signs to Southend seafront, on seafront turn left, hotel 1m east of the pier*

Attractive privately owned hotel situated at the quiet end of the seafront overlooking the beach. Bedrooms are smartly decorated and have modern facilities; many rooms have superb sea views. The air-conditioned public areas include a cosy lounge bar, an informal restaurant and a coffee lounge.
**ROOMS:** 21 en suite (1 fmly) No smoking in 19 bedrooms s £46-£65; d £60-£90 (incl. bkfst) * **LB** **FACILITIES:** STV Jacuzzi Cycle hire and tours arranged entertainment **PARKING:** 102 **NOTES:** No dogs (ex guide dogs) No smoking in restaurant **CARDS:**

S

SOUTHEND-ON-SEA, continued

### ★★66% Erlsmere

24/32 Pembury Rd, Westcliff-on-Sea SS0 8DS
☎ 01702 349025 🖷 01702 337724
***Dir:*** *Exit M25 junct 29 to A127 to Southend after passing Kent Elms Corner exit next set of lights to A1158 to Westbourne Grove signposted seafront. At next main junct(A13) proceed straight to Chalkwell Avenue, under railway bridge left, 4th turning right.*

Friendly family run hotel situated in a peaceful side road just a short walk from the seafront and shops. The pleasantly decorated, well-equipped bedrooms come in a variety of styles. Dinner is served in the Knights restaurant and guests also have the use of the Patio bar and a cosy lounge.
**ROOMS:** 30 en suite 2 annexe en suite (2 fmly) s £44-£48; d £64-£68 (incl. bkfst) * **LB** **CONF:** Thtr 120 Class 40 Board 60 Del £75 * **PARKING:** 12 **NOTES:** No dogs (ex guide dogs)
**CARDS:**

SOUTH MIMMS, Hertfordshire Map 04 TL20

### ★★★66% *Posthouse South Mimms*

Posthouse

EN6 3NH
☎ 0870 400 9072 🖷 01707 646728
***Dir:*** *junc 23 on M25 & A1 take services exit off main rdbt then 1st left & follow hotel signs*
Within easy reach of local motorways, this hotel offers a range of conference and meeting rooms, meeting the needs of its clientele. Bedrooms vary, with the newer bedrooms being particularly smart and modern; all feature a good range of in-room facilities. Public rooms have also benefited from a recent refurbishment.
**ROOMS:** 143 en suite (25 fmly) No smoking in 70 bedrooms **FACILITIES:** Indoor swimming (H) Sauna Solarium Gym Jacuzzi Outdoor childrens play area **CONF:** Thtr 170 Class 85 Board 40 **PARKING:** 200 **CARDS:**

### ⌂ Days Inn

DAYS INN

South Mimms Service Area, Bignells Corner EN6 3QQ
☎ 01707 665440 🖷 01707 660189
e-mail: southmimmshotel@welcomebreak.co.uk
***Dir:*** *junct 23 on M25,follow signs for South Mimms service area*
This modern building offers accommodation in smart, spacious and well-equipped bedrooms, suitable for families and business travellers, and all with en suite bathrooms. Continental breakfast is available and other refreshments may be taken at the nearby family restaurant. For further details and the Days Inn phone number, consult the Hotel Groups page.
**ROOMS:** 74 en suite s £59-£74; d £59-£74 * **CONF:** Board 10

SOUTH MOLTON, Devon Map 03 SS72

### ★★70% The George Hotel

1 Broad St EX36 3AB
☎ 01769 572514 🖷 01769 572514
e-mail: george@s-molton.freeserve.co.uk
***Dir:*** *turn off A361 at road island signposted 'South Molton 1.5m' to town centre, hotel is in square*
This charming 17th-century hotel has a long tradition of hospitality and has recently been very well restored. It stands in the town centre and attracts both business and leisure guests. Service is friendly and informal, and there is a good selection of food in the bar as well as in the restaurant.
**ROOMS:** 7 en suite (2 fmly) s £40-£45; d £55-£60 (incl. bkfst) * **LB** **CONF:** Thtr 100 Class 20 Board 30 **PARKING:** 12 **NOTES:** No dogs (ex guide dogs) **CARDS:**

SOUTH NORMANTON, Derbyshire Map 08 SK45

### ★★★★68% ® Renaissance Derby/Nottingham

RENAISSANCE

Carter Ln East DE55 2EH
☎ 01773 812000 🖷 01773 580032
e-mail: derby@renaissancehotels.co.uk
***Dir:*** *situated on the E side of M1 junct 28 on A38 to Mansfield*

Bedrooms are stylishly furnished and decorated, with a comprehensive range of extras provided. Public rooms include a smart leisure centre and two restaurants: Chatterleys, and the more formal Pavilion.
**ROOMS:** 158 en suite (7 fmly) No smoking in 100 bedrooms s £66-£89; d £89-£109 (incl. bkfst) * **LB** **FACILITIES:** STV Indoor swimming (H) Sauna Solarium Gym Jacuzzi Whirlpool,Steam room Xmas **CONF:** Thtr 220 Class 100 Board 60 Del from £145 * **PARKING:** 220 **NOTES:** No dogs (ex guide dogs) No smoking in restaurant Civ Wed 180
**CARDS:**

SOUTHPORT, Merseyside Map 07 SD31
see also Formby

### ★★★70% Scarisbrick

Lord St PR8 1NZ
☎ 01704 543000 🖷 01704 533335
e-mail: scarisbrickhotel@talk21.com
***Dir:*** *from South: M6 junct 26, M58 to Ormskirk then onto Southport. from North: A59 from Preston, well signposted. Also junct 26 M6, then M58 junct A570*
Centrally located on Southport's famous Lord Street, this privately owned hotel offers a high standard of attractively furnished, thoughtfully equipped accommodation. A wide range of eating options is available, from the bistro style of Maloney's Kitchen to

continued

S

the more formal Knightsbridge restaurant. An attractive new leisure centre is a recent addition.
**ROOMS:** 90 en suite (5 fmly) s £28-£87; d £56-£99 (incl. bkfst) * LB **FACILITIES:** STV Indoor swimming (H) Sauna Solarium Gym Jacuzzi Use of private leisure centre entertainment Xmas **CONF:** Thtr 200 Class 100 Board 80 Del from £75 * **SERVICES:** Lift **PARKING:** 73 **NOTES:** No smoking in restaurant Civ Wed 170
**CARDS:**

### ★★★68% Royal Clifton

Promenade PR8 1RB
☎ 01704 533771 🖹 01704 500657
e-mail: sales@royalclifton.co.uk
***Dir:*** *hotel on Promenade adjacent to Marine Lake*
This large popular hotel benefits from a prime location on the promenade. Bedrooms range in size and style, but all are comfortable, modern and thoughtfully equipped. Public areas include the lively Bar C, the elegant Pavilion Restaurant, a leisure club, and function and banqueting facilities.
**ROOMS:** 110 en suite (22 fmly) No smoking in 10 bedrooms s £75-£85; d £99-£175 (incl. bkfst) * LB **FACILITIES:** STV Indoor swimming (H) Sauna Solarium Gym Jacuzzi Hair & beauty Steam room, Aromatherapy entertainment Xmas **CONF:** Thtr 250 Class 100 Board 65 Del from £69.33 * **SERVICES:** Lift **PARKING:** 60 **NOTES:** No dogs (ex guide dogs) No smoking in restaurant Civ Wed 150
**CARDS:**

### ★★★68% Stutelea Hotel & Leisure Club

Alexandra Rd PR9 0NB
☎ 01704 544220 🖹 01704 500232
e-mail: info@stutelea.co.uk
***Dir:*** *off the promenade near town & Hesketh Park*
This family owned and run hotel is located in a quiet residential area minutes' walk from Lord Street and The Promenade. Bedrooms vary in style and include family suites, ground floor rooms and rooms with balconies that overlook the attractive rear gardens. The elegant restaurant has an international theme; alternatively, the fully equipped leisure centre has its own Garden bar that serves snacks throughout the day.
**ROOMS:** 20 en suite (4 fmly) s £65-£70; d £95-£99 (incl. bkfst) * LB **FACILITIES:** STV Indoor swimming (H) Sauna Solarium Gym Jacuzzi Games room Keep fit classes Steam room Xmas **SERVICES:** Lift **PARKING:** 18 **NOTES:** No dogs (ex guide dogs) No smoking in restaurant **CARDS:**

### ★★71% Balmoral Lodge

41 Queens Rd PR9 9EX
☎ 01704 544298 & 530751 🖹 01704 501224
e-mail: balmorallg@aol.com
***Dir:*** *edge of town on A565 Preston road*

Balmoral Lodge

Situated in a quiet residential area close to Lord Street, this friendly hotel is particularly popular with golfers. Rooms are nicely continued

TREETOPS
RESTAURANT & HOTEL



furnished and well-equipped, some with private patios overlooking the attractive gardens. There is a cosy bar and a comfortable residents lounge. The restaurant offers good, freshly cooked food.
**ROOMS:** 15 en suite (1 fmly) s £30-£52; d £60-£65 (incl. bkfst) * LB **FACILITIES:** STV Sauna **PARKING:** 12 **NOTES:** No dogs
**CARDS:**

### ★★68% *Bold*

585 Lord St PR9 0BE
☎ 01704 532578 🖹 01704 532528
***Dir:*** *near M57 & M58, at the top end of Lord Street near the Casino*
With a central location, this family hotel is a minute's walk from the promenade and local attractions. Thoughtfully equipped, spacious bedrooms are suitable for both business and leisure guests as well as families. Public areas include a bar and bistro, as well as a nightclub that opens on Friday and Saturday evenings.
**ROOMS:** 23 rms (20 en suite) (4 fmly) **FACILITIES:** Special rates for local squash club entertainment **CONF:** Thtr 40 Class 40 Board 11 **SERVICES:** air con **PARKING:** 15 **NOTES:** No dogs (ex guide dogs)
**CARDS:**

### ★★68% Shelbourne

1 Lord St West PR8 2BH
☎ 01704 541252 🖹 01704 501293
e-mail: info@shelbourne-hotel.co.uk
***Dir:*** *Either A570 or A565 to Southport town centre,hotel on rdbt at Liverpool end of Lord Street A565*
In a prime location at the top of Lord Street, a friendly welcome awaits guests at this family run hotel. Bedrooms vary in style, but
continued on p550

SOUTHPORT, continued

all are well-equipped. Public areas include a real ale bar, a comfortable lounge and an impressive function suite.
**ROOMS:** 23 en suite (4 fmly) No smoking in 4 bedrooms s £35-£55; d £60-£75 (incl. bkfst) * **LB** **CONF:** Thtr 150 Class 75 Board 50 Del from £40 * **PARKING:** 20 **CARDS:**

★★65% **Metropole**
Portland St PR8 1LL
☎ 01704 536836 📠 01704 549041
e-mail: metropole.southport@btinternet.com
***Dir:*** *turn left off Lord St after Prince of Wales Hotel & Metropole is directly behind Prince of Wales*
This family-run hotel, popular with golfers, is located just 100 yards from the famous Lord Street. Accommodation is bright and modern with family rooms available. In addition to the restaurant that offers a selection of freshly prepared dishes, there is a choice of lounges including a popular bar-lounge.
**ROOMS:** 23 en suite (4 fmly) s £30-£35; d £56-£60 (incl. bkfst) * **LB**
**FACILITIES:** Snooker Golf can be arranged at 8 local courses Xmas
**PARKING:** 12 **NOTES:** No smoking in restaurant
**CARDS:**

SOUTHSEA See Portsmouth & Southsea

SOUTH SHIELDS, Tyne & Wear Map 12 NZ36

★★★65% **Sea**
Sea Rd NE33 2LD
☎ 0191 427 0999 📠 0191 454 0500
e-mail: sea@bestwestern.co.uk
***Dir:*** *Follow the A1(M) past Washington Services to A194. Continue along A194 and take A183 through South Shields town centre along Ocean Rd. Hotel on sea front*
Situated on the promenade overlooking the Tyne estuary, this long-established hotel dates from the 1930s. Now a popular business hotel, it has a relaxed and friendly atmosphere. The restaurant and bar serve a good range of generous dishes.
**ROOMS:** 32 en suite (5 fmly) No smoking in 4 bedrooms s fr £49; d fr £59 (incl. bkfst) * **FACILITIES:** STV **CONF:** Thtr 200 Class 100 Board 50 Del from £70 * **PARKING:** 70
**CARDS:**

SOUTHWAITE MOTORWAY SERVICE AREA (M6), Cumbria Map 12 NY44

***Travelodge***
Broadfield Site CA4 0NT
☎ 08700 850950 📠 01525 878450
***Dir:*** *on M6 junc 41/42*
Travelodge offers good quality, good value, modern accommodation. Ideal for families, the spacious, en suite bedrooms include remote-control TV, tea and coffee-making facilities, luxury beds and free morning newspaper. Meals can be taken at the nearby family restaurant. For further details and the Travelodge phone number, consult the Hotel Groups page.

**ROOMS:** 39 en suite

TV dinner? Room service at three stars and above.

SOUTH WITHAM, Lincolnshire Map 08 SK91

***Travelodge***
New Fox NG33 5LN
☎ 01572 767586 📠 01572 767586
***Dir:*** *on A1, northbound*
Travelodge offers good quality, good value, modern accommodation. Ideal for families, the spacious, en suite bedrooms include remote-control TV, tea and coffee-making facilities, luxury beds and free morning newspaper. Meals can be taken at the nearby family restaurant. For further details and the Travelodge phone number, consult the Hotel Groups page.

**ROOMS:** 32 en suite

SOUTHWOLD, Suffolk Map 05 TM57

★★★71% ***Swan***
Market Place IP18 6EG
☎ 01502 722186 📠 01502 724800
***Dir:*** *take A1095 to Southwold, hotel is located in the centre of town, parking is via an archway to the left of the building*
Delightful hotel situated in the centre of town overlooking the busy market place. The property dates back to the 17th century and was once a coaching inn. The public rooms feature an elegant restaurant, a lovely drawing room and a cosy lounge bar. Bedrooms in the main building are attractively decorated and well-equipped.
**ROOMS:** 26 rms (25 en suite) 17 annexe en suite (2 fmly)
**FACILITIES:** Croquet lawn **CONF:** Thtr 50 Class 32 Board 12
**SERVICES:** Lift **PARKING:** 35 **NOTES:** No smoking in restaurant RS Nov-Mar **CARDS:**

★★70% ***The Crown***
90 High St IP18 6DP
☎ 01502 722275 📠 01502 727263
***Dir:*** *off A12 take A1094 to Southwold, stay on main road into town centre, hotel on left in High St*
This old posting inn is a combination of pub, wine bar and an intimate restaurant with accommodation. Bedrooms are attractively decorated with co-ordinated soft furnishings and well-equipped. Public rooms also include a back room bar serving traditional Adnams ales and an elegant first floor lounge.
**ROOMS:** 12 rms (9 en suite) (1 fmly) **CONF:** Thtr 40 Class 20 Board 20
**PARKING:** 23 **NOTES:** No dogs (ex guide dogs) No smoking in restaurant Closed 1st or 2nd wk Jan **CARDS:**

★★65% ***The Blyth Hotel***
Station Rd IP18 6AY
☎ 01502 722632 📠 01502 724123
e-mail: accommodation@blythhotel.co.uk
***Dir:*** *A12 onto A1045, on entering the town Mights Bridge & at the mini rdbt hotel ahead*
This friendly hotel is situated just a short walk from the centre of this upmarket seaside town. The downstairs rooms include two different bar areas serving the local Adnams ales, as well as a smart restaurant with scrubbed pine tables. Upstairs the bedrooms come in a variety of styles and sizes, making the best use of the building's original charm.
**ROOMS:** 12 en suite (1 fmly) No smoking in all bedrooms
**FACILITIES:** Boule pitch **CONF:** Thtr 20 Class 10 Board 12 **PARKING:** 8
**NOTES:** No dogs (ex guide dogs) No smoking in restaurant
**CARDS:**

SOUTH ZEAL, Devon Map 03 SX69

**★★67% Oxenham Arms**
EX20 2JT
☎ 01837 840244 & 840577 Fax 01837 840791
e-mail: jhenry1928@aol.com
***Dir:*** *just off A30 4m E of Okehampton in centre of village*
Dating back to the 12th century, the creeper-clad Oxenham Arms features an even more ancient standing stone. Beams, low doorways and flagstone floors all add to the character and charm of this popular inn. In the comfortable lounge a welcoming open fire crackles during cooler months. The individually furnished and decorated bedrooms are equipped with modern facilities.
**ROOMS:** 8 rms (7 en suite) (3 fmly) s £40-£45; d £50-£60 (incl. bkfst) * **LB** **FACILITIES:** ch fac Xmas **PARKING:** 8 **NOTES:** No smoking in restaurant **CARDS:**

SPALDING, Lincolnshire Map 08 TF22

**★★70% Cley Hall**
22 High St PE11 1TX
☎ 01775 725157 Fax 01775 710785
e-mail: cleyhall@enterprise.net
***Dir:*** *remain on A16 to B1165, take 1st turning on rdbt across mini-rdbt to river turn left*
A Georgian house overlooking the River Welland. The refurbished bedrooms are very smart and offer high standards of comfort. Guests have a choice of places to dine; the informal bistro has a warm, welcoming Mediterranean feel, while the Garden Restaurant offers award-winning 'fine dining' menus supplemented by daily changing fish 'blackboard specials'.
**ROOMS:** 4 en suite 8 annexe en suite (4 fmly) s £55-£65; d £70-£85 (incl. bkfst) * **FACILITIES:** STV ch fac **CONF:** Thtr 35 Class 20 Board 18 **PARKING:** 20 **NOTES:** No smoking in restaurant Civ Wed 35
**CARDS:**

SPENNYMOOR, Co Durham Map 08 NZ23

**★★★76% Whitworth Hall**
Stanners Ln DL16 7QX
☎ 01388 811772 Fax 01388 818669
e-mail: hotel@whitworthhall.co.uk
This estate house dates back to Norman times and is located in the centre of a deer park. It was the family home of the legendary Bobbie Shaftoe. The stylish bedrooms are spacious and well-equipped whilst the public rooms include a brasserie, meeting rooms, several comfortable lounges and an elegant dining room. A Georgian church in the grounds is popular for weddings.
**ROOMS:** 29 en suite (3 fmly) No smoking in all bedrooms s £99; d £115 (incl. bkfst) * **LB** **FACILITIES:** STV Fishing Xmas **CONF:** Thtr 100 Class 50 Board 30 Del £120 * **PARKING:** 100 **NOTES:** No dogs (ex guide dogs) No smoking in restaurant Civ Wed 120
**CARDS:**

*See advert on this page*

STAFFORD, Staffordshire Map 07 SJ92

**★★★★70% The Moat House**
Lower Penkridge Rd, Acton Trussell ST17 0RJ
☎ 01785 712217 Fax 01785 715344
e-mail: info@moathouse.co.uk
***Dir:*** *off M6 junct 13 onto the A449 through the village of Acton Trussell. The hotel is on the right hand side on the way out of the village*
This 17th-century timbered building, with a peaceful canal-side setting, has been skilfully extended. Bedrooms are attractively decorated, well-equipped and comfortable. The bar offers a wide

*continued on p552*

Whitworth Hall, Spennymoor

STAFFORD, continued

range of snacks, which supplement the interesting carte served in the main restaurant.

*The Moat House, Stafford*

**ROOMS:** 32 en suite (4 fmly) No smoking in 22 bedrooms s £110-£178; d £125-£199 (incl. bkfst) * **LB** **FACILITIES:** STV Fishing Private shoot **CONF:** Thtr 200 Class 60 Board 50 Del from £135 * **PARKING:** 200 **NOTES:** No dogs (ex guide dogs) No smoking in restaurant Closed 25-26 Dec & 1-2 Jan Civ Wed 120 **CARDS:**

*See advert on page 551*

### ★★★66% *Tillington Hall*

Eccleshall Rd ST16 1JJ
☎ 01785 253531 📠 01785 259223
***Dir:*** *exit M6 junc 14 take A5013 to Stafford*

This large, privately owned hotel is convenient for the M6. The well equipped accommodation includes bedrooms on ground floor level, no smoking bedrooms and family bedrooms, which interconnect. It offers a selection of rooms for functions and conferences and the newly refurbished restaurant, which was about to open at the time of our last visit.

**ROOMS:** 91 en suite (31 fmly) No smoking in 37 bedrooms **FACILITIES:** STV Indoor swimming (H) Tennis (hard) Sauna Solarium Gym Jacuzzi **CONF:** Thtr 200 Class 80 Board 40 **SERVICES:** Lift **PARKING:** 200 **NOTES:** No smoking in restaurant **CARDS:**

### ★★★65% Garth

Wolverhampton Rd, Moss Pit ST17 9JR
☎ 01785 256124 📠 01785 255152
e-mail: thegarth@regalhotels.com
***Dir:*** *exit M6 at Junc 13 take A449*

Conveniently located close to the M6, this hotel complex has been developed from what was originally the home of an Edwardian industrialist. Set in pleasant gardens, it offers comfortable, well-equipped and attractively furnished bedrooms. Light meals and snacks are served in the popular bar, where real ales are also available. More substantial fare can be had in the restaurant.

**ROOMS:** 60 en suite (4 fmly) No smoking in 42 bedrooms s £79; d £89 * **LB** **FACILITIES:** STV Xmas **CONF:** Thtr 175 Class 50 Board 50 Del from £108 * **PARKING:** 175 **NOTES:** No smoking in restaurant RS 25-26 Dec Civ Wed 100 **CARDS:**

### ★★67% *Abbey*

65-68 Lichfield Rd ST17 4LW
☎ 01785 258531 📠 01785 246875
***Dir:*** *from M6 junct 13 towards Stafford. Turn right at Esso garage continue to mini-rdbt, then follow Silkmore Lane until 2nd rdbt, hotel 0.25 on right*

Family run, this hotel has a friendly and relaxed atmosphere. The inviting public areas include a cosy bar and attractive restaurant, whilst bedrooms come in a variety of styles and sizes.

**ROOMS:** 17 en suite (3 fmly) **PARKING:** 25 **NOTES:** No dogs (ex guide dogs) No smoking in restaurant Closed 22 Dec-7 Jan **CARDS:**

### ★★60% *Vine*

Salter St ST16 2JU
☎ 01785 244112 📠 01785 246612
***Dir:*** *located in the centre of town*

This 17th-century coaching inn offers comfortable, very well-equipped bedrooms. Public areas are open plan and the exposed beams and timbers add character to the attractive dining area and bar lounges; a popular meeting place for local people.

**ROOMS:** 25 en suite (1 fmly) **PARKING:** 20 **NOTES:** No dogs (ex guide dogs) No smoking in restaurant **CARDS:**

### ⇧ Express by Holiday Inn Stafford

Stafford South, Alton Gate, Alton Court ST18 9AR
☎ 01785 212244 📠 01785 212277
e-mail: express_stafford@ingramhotels.co.uk
***Dir:*** *M6 junct13. Hotel is situated just off junct on A449 to Stafford*

A modern budget hotel offering comfortable accommodation in refreshing, spacious and comprehensively equipped bedrooms, en suite bathrooms with power showers and continental buffet breakfast included in the room rate. Suitable for business travellers or families. For further details and the Express by Holiday Inn phone number, consult the Hotel Groups page.

**ROOMS:** 103 en suite (incl. bkfst) s £58; d £58 * **CONF:** Thtr 40

> Late for dinner? Quality Standards star rating means that last orders for dinner should be no earlier than:
> ★ 6.30pm ★★ 7.00pm ★★★ 8.00pm
> ★★★★ 9.00pm ★★★★★ 10.00pm

## STAINES, Surrey Map 04 TQ07

### ★★★69% The Thames Lodge
Thames St TW18 4SF
☎ 0870 400 8121 🖷 01784 454858
e-mail: HeritageHotels_Staines.Thames_Lodge@forte-Hotels.com
**Dir:** *follow signs A30 Staines town centre, bus station on right, hotel straight ahead*
Occupying a prominent position beside the river, and close to the centre of town, this hotel offers well-equipped bedrooms, many of which have been recently refurbished. The smart and contemporary style brasserie serves modern and imaginative food. There is a choice of function rooms.
**ROOMS:** 78 en suite (16 fmly) No smoking in 48 bedrooms s £141-£206; d £153-£207 (incl. bkfst) * **LB** **FACILITIES:** STV Riverside tea garden with mooring Xmas **CONF:** Thtr 40 Class 20 Board 20 Del from £195 * **PARKING:** 40 **NOTES:** No smoking in restaurant
**CARDS:**

## STALHAM, Norfolk Map 09 TG32

### ★★70% Kingfisher
High St NR12 9AN
☎ 01692 581974 🖷 01692 582544
**Dir:** *Stalham is by-passed by A149 between Gt Yarmouth & North Walsham, hotel is located just off High St at west end*
This popular hotel is situated in the centre of this bustling market town in the heart of the Norfolk Broads. Bedrooms are spacious, pleasantly decorated and well-equipped. A wide range of food is available in the lounge bar, or guests can dine in the intimate restaurant, where they can choose from the fixed-price and carte menus.
**ROOMS:** 18 en suite (2 fmly) s £40; d £55 (incl. bkfst) * **LB** **FACILITIES:** Xmas **CONF:** Thtr 120 Class 50 Board 50 Del £60 * **PARKING:** 40 **NOTES:** No smoking in restaurant
**CARDS:**

## STALLINGBOROUGH, Lincolnshire Map 08 TA11

### ★★★64% Stallingborough Grange Hotel
Riby Rd DN41 8BU
☎ 01469 561302 🖷 01469 561338
e-mail: grange.hot@virgin.net
**Dir:** *from A180 take signs for Stallingborough Ind Est and then through the village, from rdbt take A1173 Caistor, hotel 1m on left just past windmill*
Originally an 18th-century country house, Stallingborough Grange is just outside the village. It has now developed into a popular business hotel, family-run and offering a good range of food. The Tavern provides a friendly atmosphere while bedrooms have good facilities. Service is both attentive and friendly.
**ROOMS:** 32 en suite (2 fmly) No smoking in all bedrooms s £65-£72; d £74-£80 (incl. bkfst) * **LB** **FACILITIES:** STV **CONF:** Thtr 60 Class 40 Board 28 Del from £98 * **PARKING:** 100 **NOTES:** No dogs (ex guide dogs) Civ Wed 65 **CARDS:**

## STAMFORD, Lincolnshire Map 08 TF00

### ★★★76% ⊛ The George of Stamford
71 St Martins PE9 2LB
☎ 01780 750750 & 750700 (Res) 🖷 01780 750701
e-mail: reservations@georgehotelofstamford.com
**Dir:** *turn off A1 onto B1081, 1m on left*
The George is a charming coaching inn dating back hundreds of years, the emphasis here is very much on quality and comfort. Staff are friendly, the atmosphere is relaxed and bedrooms are decorated to a high standard. Guests have a choice of eating options; the cobbled courtyard is the ideal place to dine in summer.
**ROOMS:** 47 en suite (2 fmly) No smoking in 3 bedrooms s £78-£110; d £105-£220 (incl. bkfst) * **LB** **FACILITIES:** STV Croquet lawn Xmas **CONF:** Thtr 50 Class 25 Board 25 Del from £130 * **PARKING:** 120 **NOTES:** Civ Wed 50 **CARDS:**

*continued*

### ★★★67% Garden House
St Martin's PE9 2LP
☎ 01780 763359 🖷 01780 763339
e-mail: gardenhousehotel@stamford60.freeserve.co.uk
**Dir:** *A1 to South Stamford, B1081, signposted Stamford and Burghley House, Hotel on left on entering the town*
Situated within a few minutes walk of the town centre, this sympathetically transformed 18th-century town house provides pleasant accommodation throughout. Bedrooms are well-equipped, attractively furnished and offer good levels of comfort. The public rooms include a charming lounge bar, conservatory and a smartly furnished dining room; service is both friendly and attentive.
**ROOMS:** 20 en suite (1 fmly) No smoking in 4 bedrooms s £50-£70; d £80-£95 (incl. bkfst) * **LB** **FACILITIES:** STV Xmas **CONF:** Thtr 40 Class 20 Board 20 Del from £75 * **PARKING:** 30 **NOTES:** No smoking in restaurant Civ Wed 40 **CARDS:**

### ★★67% Crown
All Saints Place PE9 2AG
☎ 01780 763136 🖷 01780 756111
e-mail: thecrownhotel@excite.com
**Dir:** *off A1 onto A43, straight through town until Red Lion Sq, hotel is behind All Saints church in the square*

CROWN

This small, privately-owned hotel is ideally situated in the town centre. Bedrooms are spacious and well equipped, some with four-poster beds. Public areas include a smart breakfast room, a lounge bar and there is also an attractive restaurant.
**ROOMS:** 17 rms (16 en suite) (2 fmly) s fr £60; d fr £75 (incl. bkfst) * **LB** **FACILITIES:** STV **CONF:** Thtr 50 Class 40 Board 35 **PARKING:** 40 **NOTES:** No dogs (ex guide dogs) **CARDS:**

## STANDISH, Greater Manchester Map 07 SD51

### *Premier Lodge*
Almond Brook Rd WN6 0SS
☎ 0870 700 1574 🖷 0870 700 1575
Premier Lodge offers modern, well-equipped, en suite accommodation suitable for both business and leisure travellers. Meals can be taken at the adjacent popular restaurant and bar, which is fully licensed. For further details, consult the Hotel Groups page.
**ROOMS:** 36 en suite

S

## STANSTEAD ABBOTS, Hertfordshire — Map 05 TL31

### ★★★★60% Briggens House

Stanstead Rd SG12 8LD
☎ 01279 829955 01279 793685
***Dir:*** *form M11 take the A414 to Hertford, after 10th rdbt look for left hand turn signposted Briggens Park, this is the hotel*

REGAL

Set in 80 acres of gentle Hertfordshire countryside, the hotel was once a stately home and boasts a marvellous arboretum, nine hole golf course, two all weather tennis courts and a heated outdoor swimming pool. There are a number of meeting rooms available for conference delegates. Lounge seating can be a little limited.

**ROOMS:** 54 en suite (3 fmly) s £68-£110; d £106-£128 (incl. bkfst) * LB **FACILITIES:** Outdoor swimming (H) Golf 9 Tennis (hard) Croquet lawn Putting green Xmas **CONF:** Thtr 120 Class 50 Board 50 **SERVICES:** Lift **PARKING:** 100 **NOTES:** No smoking in restaurant Civ Wed 100 **CARDS:**

## STANSTED AIRPORT, Essex — Map 05 TL52

### ★★★71% Whitehall

Church End CM6 2BZ
☎ 01279 850603 01279 850385
e-mail: sales@whitehallhotel.co.uk
***Dir:*** *leave M11 J8, follow signs to Stansted Airport, then hotel signs to Broxted village*

This friendly family-run hotel dates back to the Tudor period and is set in pretty gardens. The large bedrooms are comfortable and well-equipped. The character of the original building is reflected in the timber-vaulted restaurant where guests can enjoy soundly prepared dishes. This is a popular venue for conferences and weddings.

**ROOMS:** 25 en suite (3 fmly) **CONF:** Thtr 120 Class 80 Board 48 **PARKING:** 35 **NOTES:** No dogs (ex guide dogs) Closed 27-30 Dec Civ Wed 120 **CARDS:**

### Welcome Lodge

Birchanger Green, Old Dunmow Rd CM23 5QZ
☎ 01279 656477 01279 656590
e-mail: birchanger.hotel@welcomebreak.co.uk
***Dir:*** *M11 junct 8*

Welcome Break

This modern building offers accommodation in smart, spacious and well-equipped bedrooms, suitable for families and business travellers, and all with en suite bathrooms. Refreshments may be taken at the nearby family restaurant. For further details and the Welcome Break phone number, consult the Hotel Groups page.

**ROOMS:** 60 en suite s fr £69; d fr £69 *

## STANTON ST QUINTIN, Wiltshire — Map 03 ST97

### ★★★68% Stanton Manor Country House Hotel

SN14 6DQ
☎ 01666 837552 01666 837022
e-mail: reception@stantonmanor.co.uk
***Dir:*** *leave M4 junc 17 onto A429 Malmesbury/Cirencester within 200yds turn 1st left signed Stanton St Quintin entrance to hotel on left just after church*

Set in seven acres of lovely gardens, this charming Cotswold stone manor house offers all the comforts expected of a quality hotel. Every bedroom and all the delightful public areas have been totally refurbished. In the restaurant a short carte of imaginative dishes is supported by a selection of interesting wines.

**ROOMS:** 24 en suite (2 fmly) No smoking in 6 bedrooms s £75-£95; d £95-£125 (incl. bkfst) * LB **FACILITIES:** Golf 9 Croquet lawn Putting green ch fac **CONF:** Thtr 60 Class 50 Board 40 Del from £125 * **PARKING:** 40 **NOTES:** No smoking in restaurant **CARDS:**

## STAVERTON, Devon — Map 03 SX76

### ★★68% Sea Trout Inn

TQ9 6PA
☎ 01803 762274 01803 762506
***Dir:*** *turn off A38 onto A384 at Buckfastleigh, follow signs to Staverton*

Surrounded by superb countryside, this 15th-century inn is set in an elevated position in the Dart Valley. The bars are full of character and charm and offer a wide range of meals. Imaginative cuisine is served in the pretty, conservatory-style restaurant, where booking is essential. Bedrooms are comfortable and bathrooms smartly presented.

**ROOMS:** 10 en suite (1 fmly) s £43-£48; d £58-£70 (incl. bkfst) * LB **CONF:** Board 30 **PARKING:** 48 **NOTES:** No smoking in restaurant **CARDS:**

## STEEPLE ASTON, Oxfordshire — Map 04 SP42

### ★★★68% The Holt Hotel

The Holt Hotel, Nr Steeple Aston, Oxford Rd OX25 5QQ
☎ 01869 340259 01869 340865
e-mail: info@holthotel-oxford.co.uk
***Dir:*** *junct of B4030/A4260*

This attractive stone-built hotel offers well presented conference facilities and smart, spacious and comfortable public areas. Bedrooms, which are being steadily upgraded, are comfortably furnished and well-equipped for the business or leisure guest. Well-presented cooking is provided in Duvals restaurant.

**ROOMS:** 86 en suite (19 fmly) No smoking in 16 bedrooms s fr £100; d fr £116 (incl. bkfst) * LB **FACILITIES:** Spa STV Xmas **CONF:** Thtr 140 Class 70 Board 44 Del from £145 * **PARKING:** 200 **NOTES:** No smoking in restaurant Closed 24th Dec-2nd Jan Civ Wed 100 **CARDS:**

S

## STEVENAGE, Hertfordshire

Map 04 TL22

### ★★★66% Novotel Stevenage

Knebworth Park SG1 2AX
☎ 01438 346100 Fax 01438 723872
e-mail: H0992@accor-hotels.com
***Dir:*** *off junct 7 of A1(M), at entrance to Knebworth Park*

Pleasantly located in a Green Belt site, this modern red-brick building is only moments from the A1(M), which makes it a popular meeting and conference venue. The informal bar and restaurant are set up to deal with this kind of business. All the large bedrooms are well-appointed for both business guests and families and two rooms have disabled facilities..

**ROOMS:** 100 en suite (20 fmly) No smoking in 75 bedrooms s £89; d £89 * **FACILITIES:** STV Outdoor swimming (H) Special rates at local health club **CONF:** Thtr 150 Class 80 Board 70 Del from £135 * **SERVICES:** Lift **PARKING:** 100 **CARDS:**

### ★★★65% Cromwell

High St, Old Town SG1 3AZ
☎ 01438 779954 Fax 01438 742169
e-mail: cromwellhotel@corushotels.com
***Dir:*** *leave A1(M1) junct 8. Follow signs for town centre, over 2 rdbts. Join one-way system. Turn off into Old Town. Hotel is on the left after mini rdbt*

Easily accessible from the nearby A1(M), this High Street hotel has retained much of its historic charm, and offers many useful facilities for business and leisure guests alike. The attractive bedrooms are well-equipped, and some are more modern in style than others. Amongst the range of public areas, there are two bars and large meeting rooms.

**ROOMS:** 76 en suite No smoking in 33 bedrooms s £50-£99; d £50-£124 (incl. bkfst) * LB **FACILITIES:** STV Xmas **CONF:** Thtr 200 Class 60 Board 60 Del from £90 * **PARKING:** 70 **NOTES:** No smoking in restaurant RS 25-31 Dec **CARDS:**

### ★★★61% *Posthouse Stevenage*

Old London Rd, Broadwater SG2 8DS
☎ 0870 400 9076 Fax 01438 741308
***Dir:*** *off B1970*

Suitable for both the business and leisure traveller, this hotel provides spacious accommodation in well-equipped bedrooms. The older part of the building which contains the bar and restaurant has character.

**ROOMS:** 54 en suite No smoking in 27 bedrooms **CONF:** Thtr 60 Class 20 Board 30 **PARKING:** 80 **CARDS:**

> Arriving late? Four and five star hotels have night porters to assist with your luggage, and 24-hour room service.

### Ibis

Danestrete SG1 1EJ
☎ 01438 779955 Fax 01438 741880
e-mail: H2791@accor-hotels.com
***Dir:*** *in town centre adjacent to Tesco & Westgate Multi-Store*

Modern, budget hotel offering comfortable accommodation in bright and practical bedrooms. Breakfast is self-service and dinner is available in the restaurant. For further details, consult the Hotel Groups page.

**ROOMS:** 98 en suite s £29.95-£39.95; d £29.95-£39.95 *

## STEYNING, West Sussex

Map 04 TQ11

### ★★★69% The Old Tollgate

The Street BN44 3WE
☎ 01903 879494 Fax 01903 813399
e-mail: otr@fastnet.co.uk
***Dir:*** *on A283 at Steyning rdbt, turn off to Bramber, the hotel is situated approx 200yds along on the right*

A well presented hotel on the site of the old toll house. Bedrooms are spacious, smartly designed and furnished to a high standard. An extensive choice of dishes is offered in the popular carvery style restaurant. The hotel has adaptable function rooms for weddings and conferences.

**ROOMS:** 11 en suite 20 annexe en suite (5 fmly) No smoking in 16 bedrooms s £73-£120; d £73-£120 * LB **FACILITIES:** STV **CONF:** Thtr 50 Class 32 Board 26 Del from £89.95 * **SERVICES:** Lift **PARKING:** 60 **NOTES:** No dogs (ex guide dogs) Civ Wed 60
**CARDS:**

## STILTON, Cambridgeshire

Map 04 TL18

### ★★★69% Bell Inn

Great North Rd PE7 3RA
☎ 01733 241066 Fax 01733 245173
e-mail: reception@thebellstilton.co.uk
***Dir:*** *turn off A1(M) at junct 16 then follow signs for Stilton, hotel is situated on the main road in centre of village*

STILTON

A wealth of original rural features makes the Bell a charming place to stay. With its beamed ceilings and open log fires, the village bar is full of character, as is the galleried restaurant above, which offers a menu that mixes modern and traditional influences. A recent refurbishment programme to bedrooms has seen the individual styling of rooms; deluxe rooms offer four-poster beds and whirlpool baths.

**ROOMS:** 19 en suite (1 fmly) No smoking in 7 bedrooms s £56-£82; d £72-£110 (incl. bkfst) * **FACILITIES:** STV **CONF:** Thtr 100 Class 46 Board 50 Del £98.50 * **PARKING:** 30 **NOTES:** No dogs (ex guide dogs) Closed 25 Dec RS 26 Dec Civ Wed 80
**CARDS:**

S

STOCKPORT, Greater Manchester Map 07 SJ88
see also Manchester Airport

**★★★67% *Bredbury Hall Hotel & Country Club***
Goyt Valley SK6 2DH
☎ 0161 430 7421 🖹 0161 430 5079
e-mail: reservations@bredburyhallhotel.co.uk
***Dir:*** *M60 J25 signposted Bredbury, right at traffic lights, left onto Osbourne St, hotel 500mtrs on right*
With views over open countryside, this large modern hotel is near the M60. Bedrooms offer space and comfort and the restaurant serves a very wide range of freshly prepared dishes. There is a popular night-club next door to the hotel and at the last inspection a leisure centre was under construction.
**ROOMS:** 120 en suite (2 fmly) **FACILITIES:** STV Fishing Snooker Night club entertainment **CONF:** Thtr 160 Class 90 Board 70 **PARKING:** 400 **NOTES:** No dogs (ex guide dogs) Civ Wed 150
**CARDS:**

**★★★65% County Hotel Bramhall**
Bramhall Ln South SK7 2EB
☎ 0161 455 9988 🖹 0161 440 8071
(For full entry see Bramhall)

REGAL

**★★★64% Alma Lodge Hotel**
149 Buxton Rd SK2 6EL
☎ 0161 483 4431 🖹 0161 483 1983
***Dir:*** *From M60 junct 1 at rdbt take 2nd exit under railway viaduct at traffic lights opp. Debenhams turn right onto A6, hotel approx 1.5m on left*
A large hotel located on the main road close to the town and offering modern and well-equipped bedrooms. It is family owned and run and provides a good range of quality Italian cooking in Luigi's restaurant. Good function rooms are also provided.
**ROOMS:** 20 en suite 32 annexe en suite (2 fmly) No smoking in 22 bedrooms s fr £60; d fr £60 (incl. bkfst) * **LB** **CONF:** Thtr 250 Class 100 Board 60 Del from £95 * **PARKING:** 120 **NOTES:** No dogs (ex guide dogs) **CARDS:**

**★★68% *Saxon Holme***
230 Wellington Rd SK4 2QN
☎ 0161 432 2335 🖹 0161 431 8076
***Dir:*** *N, beside A6*
This well-run and comfortable hotel is situated outside the town on the A6. Bedrooms, including a number on the ground floor, have modern facilities, and reception rooms are cosy, with ornately decorated plaster ceilings. A good range of well-produced food is available.
**ROOMS:** 33 en suite (3 fmly) No smoking in 11 bedrooms **FACILITIES:** STV **CONF:** Thtr 70 Class 10 Board 20 **SERVICES:** Lift **PARKING:** 40 **NOTES:** No dogs (ex guide dogs) No smoking in restaurant **CARDS:**

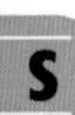
S

**★★67% Wycliffe**
74 Edgeley Rd, Edgeley SK3 9NQ
☎ 0161 477 5395 🖹 0161 476 3219
***Dir:*** *from M60 junct 2 follow A560 for Stockport, at 1st lights turn right, hotel half a mile on left*
This family run, welcoming hotel has immaculately maintained and well-equipped bedrooms. There is popular restaurant where the menu has an Italian bias, and a well stocked bar.
**ROOMS:** 20 en suite s fr £48; d fr £60 (incl. bkfst) * **FACILITIES:** STV **CONF:** Thtr 20 Class 20 Board 20 **PARKING:** 46 **NOTES:** No dogs (ex guide dogs) **CARDS:**

**⌂ Premier Lodge**
Churchgate SK1 1YG
☎ 0870 700 1484 🖹 0870 700 1485
***Dir:*** *Exit M60 junct 27 onto A626 St Marys Way, turn right at Behhams BMW garage into Spring Gardens then 2nd right into car park*
Premier Lodge offers modern, well-equipped, en suite accommodation suitable for both business and leisure travellers. Meals can be taken at the adjacent popular restaurant and bar, which is fully licensed. For further details, consult the Hotel Groups page.
**ROOMS:** 46 en suite s £46; d £46 * **CONF:** Thtr 20 Board 20

**⌂ *Travelodge***
London Rd South SK10 4NA
☎ 01625 875292 🖹 01625 875292
***Dir:*** *on A523*
Travelodge offers good quality, good value, modern accommodation. Ideal for families, the spacious, en suite bedrooms include remote-control TV, tea and coffee-making facilities, luxury beds and free morning newspaper. Meals can be taken at the nearby family restaurant. For further details and the Travelodge phone number, consult the Hotel Groups page.

**ROOMS:** 32 en suite

STOCKTON-ON-TEES, Co Durham Map 08 NZ41

**★★★★63% Swallow**
John Walker Square TS18 1AQ
☎ 01642 679721 0800 7317549
🖹 01642 601714
e-mail: stockton.swallow@whitbread.com
***Dir:*** *from A1(M) follow A177 to Town Centre cont along Riverside Road to Castlegate Car Park*
At one end of the bustling high street, nextdoor to the market, and adjacent to the new riverside commercial area, the hotel has direct access to a secure multi-storey car park. Bedrooms are smart and well-equipped, and guests have the choice of a popular brasserie or an elegant restaurant in which to dine.
**ROOMS:** 125 en suite (12 fmly) No smoking in 77 bedrooms s £95-£115; d £110-£120 (incl. bkfst) * **LB** **FACILITIES:** Spa STV Indoor swimming (H) Sauna Solarium Gym Jacuzzi Tanning booth Xmas **CONF:** Thtr 300 Class 150 Board 40 Del from £90 * **SERVICES:** Lift **PARKING:** 400 **NOTES:** No smoking in restaurant Civ Wed 250
**CARDS:**

**★★★71% ◎ Parkmore**
636 Yarm Rd, Eaglescliffe TS16 0DH
☎ 01642 786815 🖹 01642 790485
e-mail: enquiries@parkmorehotel.co.uk
***Dir:*** *turn off A19 at Crathorne, follow A67 to Yarm. Through Yarm bear right onto A135 to Stockton. Hotel approx. 1m from Yarm on left*
This hotel was originally set in a Victorian house. The bedrooms are well-equipped with the latest facilities; public rooms are comfortable and inviting. Extensive menus are available in the 'Reeds at six three six' restaurant featuring exciting combinations of flavours. A well-equipped leisure centre and good conference facilities are also features of the hotel.
**ROOMS:** 55 en suite (8 fmly) No smoking in 30 bedrooms s £60-£66; d £75-£80 * **LB** **FACILITIES:** STV Indoor swimming (H) Sauna Solarium Gym Jacuzzi Beauty salon Badminton Aerobics studio **CONF:** Thtr 140 Class 40 Board 40 Del from £94 * **PARKING:** 120 **NOTES:** No smoking in restaurant Civ Wed 90
**CARDS:**

**★★★69% *Posthouse Teeside/ Middlesbrough***

Posthouse

Low Ln, Stainton Village, Thornaby TS17 9LW
☎ 0870 400 9081 🖷 01642 594989
***Dir:*** *off A19 onto A174, then B1380 towards Stainton Village, 2nd exit at rdbt towards Stainton Village again, hotel is on right*
A large modern hotel situated in spacious open grounds on the south-east of the town. Bedrooms are of a particularly good standard and include executive and family rooms. The hotel has two bars, a lounge serving snacks all day, and the menu in "Traders" restaurant provides a good choice of dishes.
**ROOMS:** 136 en suite (10 fmly) No smoking in 87 bedrooms
**CONF:** Thtr 120 Class 60 Board 70 **PARKING:** 250
**CARDS:**

**★★67% Claireville**
519 Yarm Rd, Eaglescliffe TS16 9BG
☎ 01642 780378 🖷 01642 784109
e-mail: reception@clairev.demon.co.uk
***Dir:*** *on A135 adjacent to Eaglescliffe Golf Course, between Stockton-on-Tees and Yarm*
A family-run hotel with comfortable, pleasantly furnished bedrooms. There is a cosy bar/lounge and attractive dining room which offers a reasonably priced carte. A delightful conservatory has been added to the rear, providing extra function and lounge facilities.
**ROOMS:** 18 en suite (2 fmly) No smoking in 4 bedrooms s £48; d £60 (incl. bkfst) * **FACILITIES:** STV **CONF:** Thtr 40 Class 20 Board 25
**PARKING:** 30 **NOTES:** RS Xmas & New Year
**CARDS:**

**⌂ Express by Holiday Inn Stockton**

Express by Holiday Inn

Junction A19 & A689, Coal Ln, Wynyard Park Services, Wolviston TS22 5PZ
☎ 01740 644000 🖷 644111
***Dir:*** *A1(M) exit at J60, following signs for Hartlepool and Teeside. Continue along A689 heading straight across at small rdbts. Hotel on left on entering The Wynyard Park Services.*

A modern budget hotel offering comfortable accommodation in refreshing, spacious and comprehensively equipped bedrooms, en suite bathrooms with power showers and continental buffet breakfast included in the room rate. Suitable for business travellers or families. For further details and the Express by Holiday Inn phone number, consult the Hotel Groups page.
**ROOMS:** 49 en suite (incl. cont bkfst) s £42.50-£52.50; d £42.50-£52.50
* **CONF:** Thtr 30 Class 20 Board 18

Early start? Hotels at all star levels should provide in-room alarm clocks and/or alarm calls.

## STOKE D'ABERNON, Surrey — Map 04 TQ15

**★★★★69% Woodlands Park**

Arcadian Hotels Distinctly Different

Woodlands Ln KT11 3QB
☎ 01372 843933 🖷 01372 842704
e-mail: woodlands@arcadianhotels.co.uk
***Dir:*** *from A3 towards London, exit at Cobham. Through town centre & Stoke D'Abernon, left at garden centre into Woodlands Ln, hotel 0.5m on right*
Convenient for the motorway network, this Victorian mansion enjoys an attractive parkland setting. Bedrooms are traditionally furnished and well-equipped. There are two dining options, Quotes Bar & Brasserie and the Oak Room Restaurant.
**ROOMS:** 59 en suite (4 fmly) No smoking in 20 bedrooms s fr £130; d fr £160 * **LB** **FACILITIES:** STV Tennis (hard) Croquet lawn Xmas
**CONF:** Thtr 280 Class 100 Board 50 Del from £205 * **SERVICES:** Lift
**PARKING:** 150 **NOTES:** No dogs (ex guide dogs) Civ Wed 150
**CARDS:**

## STOKE GABRIEL, Devon — Map 03 SX85

**★★★71% Gabriel Court**
TQ9 6SF
☎ 01803 782206 🖷 01803 782333
e-mail: obeacom@aol.com
***Dir:*** *off A38 down the A384 onto the A385 towards Paignton, turn right by the Parkers Arms, follow road down until reaching Stoke Gabriel*
Set in attractive, Elizabethan terraced gardens, this charming old house is a comfortable, civilised hotel with elegant reception rooms. Owned and run by the Beacom family for over 30 years, guests are assured of friendly, attentive service. A short, fixed price menu is offered, using predominantly local produce, including vegetables from the garden. Individually designed bedrooms retain a sense of period.
**ROOMS:** 19 en suite s £55-£59; d fr £80 (incl. bkfst) *
**FACILITIES:** Outdoor swimming (H) Tennis (grass) Croquet lawn ch fac Xmas **CONF:** Thtr 20 Board 20 Del from £120 * **PARKING:** 20
**NOTES:** No smoking in restaurant **CARDS:**

## STOKENCHURCH, Buckinghamshire — Map 04 SU79

**★★★68% The Kings Arms**

Oxford Rd HP12 3TA
☎ 01494 609090 🖷 01494 484582
***Dir:*** *junct 5 of M40 turn right over motorway bridge, hotel 600yds on the left*
Located on the village green, this hotel blends traditional elegance with contemporary design. Rooms are attractively decorated and are well-equipped especially for the business guest. Public areas include a busy bar offering an extensive range of hot and cold dishes throughout the day, and a more formal restaurant. There are several smart air-conditioned conference rooms.
**ROOMS:** 43 en suite (3 fmly) No smoking in 22 bedrooms
**FACILITIES:** STV **CONF:** Thtr 200 Class 100 Board 70 Del from £140 *
**SERVICES:** Lift air con **PARKING:** 95 **NOTES:** No dogs (ex guide dogs) Civ Wed 200 **CARDS:**

## STOKE-ON-TRENT, Staffordshire — Map 07 SJ84
see also Newcastle-under-Lyme

**★★★71% Manor House**

Audley Rd ST7 2QQ
☎ 01270 884000 🖷 01270 882483
e-mail: manres@compasshotels.co.uk
(For full entry see Alsager)

S

STOKE-ON-TRENT, continued

### ★★★69% George
Swan Square, Burslem ST6 2AE
☎ 01782 577544 🖷 01782 837496
e-mail: georgestoke@btinternet.com
***Dir:*** *take A53 towards Leek, turn left at 1st set of traffic lights onto A50, follow road to Burslem centre, George hotel is on right*
This privately owned, friendly hotel stands in the centre of Burslem, close to the Royal Doulton factory. Well-equipped modern bedrooms are equally suitable for business people and tourists. A good choice of dishes is available in the elegant restaurant. In addition to the spacious lounge bar, there is a comfortable lounge for residents, and a choice of function rooms.
**ROOMS:** 39 en suite (5 fmly) s £65-£75; d £85-£95 (incl. bkfst) * LB **CONF:** Thtr 180 Class 150 Board 60 Del from £95 * **SERVICES:** Lift **PARKING:** 28 **NOTES:** No dogs (ex guide dogs) No smoking in restaurant **CARDS:**

### ★★★68% North Stafford
Station Rd, Winton Square ST4 2AE
☎ 01782 744477 🖷 01782 744580
e-mail: Reservations.NorthStafford@principalhotels.co.uk
***Dir:*** *follow signs for Railway Station and hotel is directly opposite*

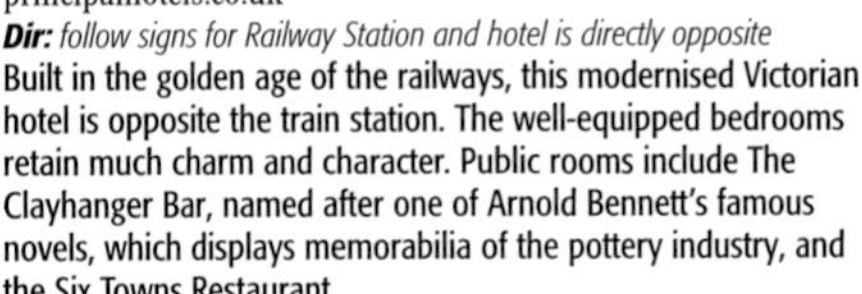

Built in the golden age of the railways, this modernised Victorian hotel is opposite the train station. The well-equipped bedrooms retain much charm and character. Public rooms include The Clayhanger Bar, named after one of Arnold Bennett's famous novels, which displays memorabilia of the pottery industry, and the Six Towns Restaurant.
**ROOMS:** 80 en suite (8 fmly) s £60-£95; d £75-£110 (incl. bkfst) * LB **FACILITIES:** STV Gym facilities at university building Xmas **CONF:** Thtr 450 Class 150 Board 85 Del from £95 * **SERVICES:** Lift **PARKING:** 120 **NOTES:** No smoking in restaurant Civ Wed 80 **CARDS:**

### ★★★66% *Haydon House*
Haydon St, Basford ST4 6JD
☎ 01782 711311 🖷 01782 717470
***Dir:*** *from M6 junct 15 A500 to Stoke-on-Trent, turn onto A53 Hanley/Newcastle, at rdbt take 1st exit, go up hill, take 2nd left at top of hill*
A Victorian property, within easy reach of Newcastle-under-Lyme town centre. The public rooms are furnished in a style befitting the age and character of the house. The bedrooms all have modern furnishings; several rooms are located in a separate house across the road. The hotel has a good reputation for its food and is popular with local diners.
**ROOMS:** 17 en suite 6 annexe en suite (4 fmly) **CONF:** Thtr 80 Class 25 Board 30 **PARKING:** 52 **NOTES:** Civ Wed 40 **CARDS:**

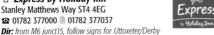

### ⇧ *Express by Holiday Inn*
Stanley Matthews Way ST4 4EG
☎ 01782 377000 🖷 01782 377037
***Dir:*** *from M6 junct15, follow signs for Uttoxeter/Derby which leads to A50. Hotel is located alongside Britannic Stadium on the A50*

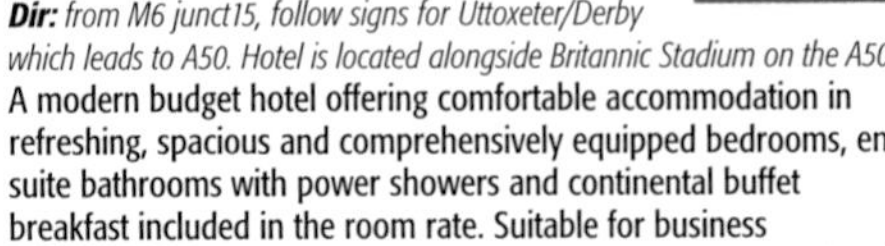

A modern budget hotel offering comfortable accommodation in refreshing, spacious and comprehensively equipped bedrooms, en suite bathrooms with power showers and continental buffet breakfast included in the room rate. Suitable for business travellers or families. For further details and the Express by Holiday Inn phone number, consult the Hotel Groups page.

**ROOMS:** 123 en suite **CONF:** Thtr 30 Class 20 Board 18

### ○ Innkeeper's Lodge Stoke on Trent
Longton Rd ST4 8BU
A new concept in the travel accommodation market. Smart rooms meet essential business requirements but also have home comforts. Dining options include all-day menus plus the added advantage of breakfast, which is included in the room price. Reservations can be made seven days a week through the room reservations number: 0870 243 0500. For further details, consult the Hotel Groups page.
**ROOMS:** 30 en suite

---

STONE, Staffordshire — Map 07 SJ93

### ★★★68% Stone House
Stafford Rd ST15 0BQ
☎ 01785 815531 🖷 01785 814764
***Dir:*** *beside A34, 0.5m S of town centre*

Set in attractively landscaped gardens and grounds, this former country house has been sympathetically extended to appeal to both leisure and business guests. Day rooms are stylish and comfortable, and the restaurant overlooks the gardens.
**ROOMS:** 50 en suite (1 fmly) No smoking in 33 bedrooms s £87; d £97 * LB **FACILITIES:** STV Indoor swimming (H) Tennis (hard) Sauna Solarium Gym **CONF:** Thtr 190 Class 60 Board 50 **PARKING:** 120 **NOTES:** No dogs (ex guide dogs) RS Sat Civ Wed 120 **CARDS:**

### ⇧ *Travelodge*
Eccleshall Rd ST15 0EU
☎ 01785 811188
***Dir:*** *between junc 14&15 M6 northbound only*
Travelodge offers good quality, good value, modern accommodation. Ideal for families, the spacious, en suite bedrooms include remote-control TV, tea and coffee-making

*continued*

facilities, luxury beds and free morning newspaper. Meals can be taken at the nearby family restaurant. For further details and the Travelodge phone number, consult the Hotel Groups page.

**ROOMS:** 49 en suite

STON EASTON, Somerset Map 03 ST65

## Premier Collection

### ★★★★ Ston Easton Park

BA3 4DF
☎ 01761 241631 01761 241377
e-mail: stoneastonpark@stoneaston.co.uk
***Dir:*** *turn off A37 onto A39, hotel is one mile from junction in village of Ston Easton*

Ston Easton Park Hotel is situated in the heart of the Mendip hills. Built in 1740, this Grade I listed Palladian mansion is surrounded by tranquil parkland and landscaped gardens. Public areas are beautifully adorned with period features, and the bedrooms have great individuality, reflecting the attention to detail which is a hallmark here. The enthusiastic staff make every effort to enhance the experience, and the cuisine shows both imagination and considered care.

**ROOMS:** 20 rms (19 en suite) 3 annexe en suite s fr £125 (incl. cont bkfst) * **LB** **FACILITIES:** Tennis (hard) Snooker Croquet lawn ch fac Xmas **CONF:** Thtr 50 Class 25 Board 26 Del from £155 * **PARKING:** 120 **NOTES:** No dogs (ex guide dogs) No children 7yrs No smoking in restaurant Civ Wed 50
**CARDS:**

STONEHOUSE, Gloucestershire Map 03 SO80

### ★★★72% Stonehouse Court

GL10 3RA
☎ 01453 825155 01453 824611
e-mail: stonehouse.court@pageant.co.uk
***Dir:*** *off M5 at J13, follow signs for Stonehouse, hotel is on right hand side approx 0.25m after 2nd rdbt*

This Grade II listed manor house dates from 1601, but has been considerably extended. Bedrooms offer modern comforts, and two of them have four-poster beds. Public rooms include a panelled

*continued*



lounge, a bar, a restaurant, a gym and extensive conference facilities.

**ROOMS:** 9 en suite 27 annexe en suite (1 fmly) No smoking in 4 bedrooms s fr £70; d fr £90 (incl. bkfst) * **LB** **FACILITIES:** STV Fishing Gym Croquet lawn Xmas **CONF:** Thtr 150 Class 75 Board 50 Del from £85 * **PARKING:** 150 **NOTES:** No smoking in restaurant Civ Wed 85
**CARDS:**

*See advert under GLOUCESTER*

## STONELEIGH, Warwickshire Map 04 SP37

### ⇧ Tulip Inn Stoneleigh Park
The NAC Stoneleigh Park CV8 2LZ
☎ 024 7669 0123 📠 024 7669 0789
e-mail: info@tulipinncoventry.com
***Dir:*** *M40 junct 15, take A46 signposted Coventry. Approx 5 m take 3rd exit A452 Leamington Spa. At next rdbt take L signed National Agricultural centre. At rdbt 1 m on, turn L onto B4113 (NAC/Stoneleigh). 1 m on L is entrance to NAC, past gatehouse to Stoneleigh Park Lodge.*
This brand new lodge is situated in the centre of the National Agricultural Centre (NAC) on Stoneleigh Estate, and is conveniently close to Coventry, Warwick and Leamington Spa. The 58 rooms are spacious, comfortable and attractively presented.
**ROOMS:** 58 en suite

## STONOR, Oxfordshire Map 04 SU78

### ★★★73% @@ Stonor Arms Hotel
RG9 6HE
☎ 01491 638866 📠 01491 638863
e-mail: stonorarms.hotel@virgin.net
***Dir:*** *off A4130 onto B480, hotel 3m on right in Stonor village*
This 18th-century coaching inn, in a quiet and picturesque village close to Henley-on-Thames, offers public rooms full of charm and pretty gardens, making this hotel a popular choice for weddings. Bedrooms are attractively furnished and come with many thoughtful extras. The quality of cooking remains high and can be enjoyed either in the conservatory or the more formal dining room.
**ROOMS:** 10 en suite No smoking in 4 bedrooms s fr £120; d fr £145 (incl. bkfst) * **FACILITIES:** Xmas **CONF:** Thtr 20 Board 12 **PARKING:** 27 **NOTES:** No smoking in restaurant Civ Wed 80 **CARDS:**

## STOURBRIDGE, West Midlands

### ○ Innkeeper's Lodge Stourbridge
Bromsgrove Rd, Hagley DY9 9LJ
A new concept in the travel accommodation market. Smart rooms meet essential business requirements but also have home comforts. Dining options include all-day menus plus the added advantage of breakfast, which is included in the room price. Reservations can be made seven days a week through the room reservations number: 0870 243 0500. For further details, consult the Hotel Groups page.
**ROOMS:** 15 en suite

## STOURPORT-ON-SEVERN, Worcestershire Map 07 SO87

### ★★★★71% Menzies Stourport Manor
Hartlebury Rd DY13 9LT
☎ 0870 6003013 📠 01332 511144
e-mail: info@menzies-hotels.co.uk
***Dir:*** *E, off B4193*
Once the home of former Prime Minister Sir Stanley Baldwin, this much extended country house is set in extensive grounds. Stourport Manor is now a busy hotel offering modern bedrooms and suites. Spacious public areas include a range of lounges, a popular brasserie, leisure and conference facilities. Service is both friendly and professional.
**ROOMS:** 68 en suite (4 fmly) No smoking in 25 bedrooms s £95; d £95 * **LB FACILITIES: Spa** STV Indoor swimming (H) Outdoor swimming (H) Tennis (hard) Squash Sauna Solarium Gym Putting green Jacuzzi Xmas **CONF:** Thtr 420 Class 120 Board 80 Del from £140 * **PARKING:** 200 **NOTES:** No dogs (ex guide dogs) No smoking in restaurant Civ Wed 350 **CARDS:**

## STOWMARKET, Suffolk Map 05 TM05

### ★★65% *Cedars*
Needham Rd IP14 2AJ
☎ 01449 612668 📠 01449 674704
e-mail: info@cedarshotel.co.uk
***Dir:*** *A1308 1m outside Stowmarket on road to Needham Market, close to junction with A1120*
Situated just off the A14 about a mile from the town centre, this friendly, privately owned hotel combines historic charm in the public areas with modern facilities in the bedrooms. The spacious restaurant offers a wide choice of interesting dishes, which may be eaten in the bar if preferred.
**ROOMS:** 25 en suite (4 fmly) **FACILITIES:** STV **CONF:** Thtr 160 Class 60 Board 60 **PARKING:** 75 **NOTES:** No smoking in restaurant Closed 25 Dec-1 Jan **CARDS:**

### ⇧ *Travelodge*
IP14 3PY
☎ 01449 615347 📠 01449 615347
***Dir:*** *on A14 westbound*
Travelodge offers good quality, good value, modern accommodation. Ideal for families, the spacious, en suite bedrooms include remote-control TV, tea and coffee-making facilities, luxury beds and free morning newspaper. Meals can be taken at the nearby family restaurant. For further details and the Travelodge phone number, consult the Hotel Groups page.

**ROOMS:** 40 en suite

## STOW-ON-THE-WOLD, Gloucestershire Map 04 SP12

### ★★★★73% @@ Wyck Hill House
Burford Rd GL54 1HY
☎ 01451 831936 📠 01451 832243
e-mail: wyckhill@wrensgroup.com
***Dir:*** *3m SE on A424 towards Burford & Swindon*
Set amidst 100 acres of woodlands and gardens, this delightful 18th-century house enjoys superb views across the Windrush Valley and is ideally positioned for a relaxing weekend exploring the Cotswolds, or for a quiet business meeting. The spacious and thoughtfully equipped bedrooms have been recently refurbished to a high standard and are divided between the main house and the original coach house. An open fire burns in the magnificent front hall and there is a cosy bar and restaurant.
**ROOMS:** 16 en suite 16 annexe en suite (1 fmly) s £110-£160; d £160-£260 (incl. bkfst) * **LB FACILITIES:** STV Croquet lawn Archery Clay pigeon shooting Ballooning Honda pilots Xmas **CONF:** Thtr 60 Class 20 Board 20 Del from £150 * **SERVICES:** Lift **PARKING:** 100 **NOTES:** No smoking in restaurant Civ Wed 80
**CARDS:**

### ★★★74% @@ The Royalist at Stow-on-the-Wold
Digbeth St GL54 1BN
☎ 01451 830670 📠 01451 870048
e-mail: info@theroyalisthotel.co.uk
***Dir:*** *M40 junct 8, follow A40 to Burford. Join A424 to Stow-on-the-Wold. Turn right onto A436, down hill, hotel on left of green*
Recorded as the 'oldest inn in England', this super hotel has a wealth of history and character. Public areas and the charming bedrooms have benefited from a very sympathetic refurbishment to ensure guest comfort at every turn. The 947 Restaurant offers a

*continued*

wealth of award winning dishes, and the Eagle and Child bar serves delicious homemade fare.

**ROOMS:** 8 en suite No smoking in all bedrooms s £90; d £130-£187 (incl. cont bkfst) * **LB** **FACILITIES:** Jacuzzi Xmas **CONF:** Thtr 25 Class 25 Board 16 Del from £80 * **PARKING:** 8 **NOTES:** No dogs (ex guide dogs) No smoking in restaurant **CARDS:**

**★★★71% The Unicorn**
Sheep St GL54 1HQ
☎ 01451 830257 01451 831090
e-mail: bookings@cotswold-inns-hotels.co.uk
***Dir:*** *situated at the junct of A429 & A436*
This friendly hotel retains much of its original 17th-century character, while offering accommodation equipped to modern standards of comfort; bedrooms are individual in style, and brightly decorated. Public areas are inviting and smartly presented.
**ROOMS:** 20 en suite No smoking in 6 bedrooms s £45-£70; d £65-£120 (incl. bkfst) * **LB** **FACILITIES:** Xmas **CONF:** Thtr 50 Class 12 Board 24 Del from £95 * **PARKING:** 60 **NOTES:** No smoking in restaurant Civ Wed 40 **CARDS:**

**★★★70% Fosse Manor**
GL54 1JX
☎ 01451 830354 01451 832486
e-mail: fossemanor@bestwestern.co.uk
***Dir:*** *1m S on A429, 300yds past junction with A424*
The hotel derives its name from its location on the historic Roman Fosse Way, now the Warwick to Cirencester road. The grey, vine clad Cotswold stone building, set in beautiful countryside, is understandably a favoured destination for leisure guests. Bedrooms are located in the recently converted coach house or in the main building, all rooms are individually furnished and decorated.
**ROOMS:** 14 en suite 6 annexe en suite (3 fmly) s £55-£80; d £98-£160 (incl. bkfst) * **LB** **FACILITIES:** Croquet lawn Beautician Golf practice net ch fac **CONF:** Thtr 40 Class 20 Board 20 Del from £110 * **PARKING:** 40 **NOTES:** No smoking in restaurant Closed 21-30 Dec Civ Wed 50 **CARDS:**

**★★★70% Grapevine**
Sheep St GL54 1AU
☎ 01451 830344 01451 832278
e-mail: aa@vines.co.uk
***Dir:*** *on A436 towards Chipping Norton. 150 yds on right, facing green*
This delightful 17th-century hotel is situated in the centre of town, and retains much of its original charm and character. The bedrooms vary in size, and are thoughtfully equipped with charming furnishings. Accomplished cooking is offered in the

*continued*

Conservatory Restaurant, with a more informal brasserie-style menu available at lunch.

**ROOMS:** 12 en suite 10 annexe en suite (2 fmly) No smoking in all bedrooms s £77-£98; d £115-£137 (incl. bkfst) * **LB** **FACILITIES:** Xmas **CONF:** Thtr 30 Class 18 Board 20 Del from £142 * **PARKING:** 23 **NOTES:** No dogs (ex guide dogs) No smoking in restaurant Civ Wed 60 **CARDS:**

**★★★66% Stow Lodge**
The Square GL54 1AB
☎ 01451 830485 01451 831671
e-mail: enquiries@stowlodge.com
***Dir:*** *in town centre*
Set in large grounds, this family-run hotel has direct access to the market square. It offers comfortable accommodation in traditionally styled bedrooms, some in a converted coach house, and good home cooking.
**ROOMS:** 11 en suite 10 annexe en suite (1 fmly) No smoking in all bedrooms s £50-£105; d £70-£125 (incl. bkfst) * **LB** **PARKING:** 30 **NOTES:** No dogs No children 5yrs No smoking in restaurant Closed Xmas-end Jan **CARDS:**

**★★71% Old Stocks**
The Square GL54 1AF
☎ 01451 830666 01451 870014
***Dir:*** *turn off A429 to town centre. Hotel is facing Village Green*
A Grade II listed hotel, built of mellow Cotswold stone, and situated in the heart of the old Market Square. Full of original charm and character, it retains stone walls and oak beams. The lounge, restaurant and bar offer attractive, comfortable areas in which to relax, and the bedrooms are well-maintained.
**ROOMS:** 15 en suite 3 annexe en suite (1 fmly) No smoking in 10 bedrooms s £40; d £80 (incl. bkfst) * **LB** **FACILITIES:** ch fac Xmas **PARKING:** 14 **NOTES:** No smoking in restaurant Closed 18-27 Dec **CARDS:**

## STRATFIELD TURGIS, Hampshire — Map 04 SU65

**★★★65% Wellington Arms**
RG27 0AS
☎ 01256 882214 01256 882934
e-mail: Wellington.Arms@virgin.net
***Dir:*** *A33 between Basingstoke & Reading*
Situated at one of the entrances to the ancestral home of the Duke of Wellington, the white Georgian façade is a familiar landmark. The bar-lounge offers seating around a log fire. The majority of bedrooms are located in the Garden Wing and offer every modern convenience. Rooms in the original building have a more period feel.
**ROOMS:** 35 en suite (2 fmly) No smoking in 3 bedrooms **CONF:** Thtr 160 Class 40 Board 50 Del from £150.50 * **PARKING:** 150 **CARDS:**

STRATFORD-UPON-AVON, Warwickshire Map 04 SP25

**★★★★74% Welcombe Hotel and Golf Course**

Warwick Rd CV37 0NR
☎ 01789 295252 01789 414666
e-mail: sales@welcombe.co.uk
***Dir:*** *1.5m NE of Stratford on A439*
This impressive Jacobean manor house is set in attractive landscaped parkland. There are bedrooms in both the modern garden wing and the original house; all are thoughtfully equipped. Public rooms are attractive, especially the lounge, with wood panelling and an ornate, black marble fireplace. The dining room offers excellent cooking from a fine menu and enjoys far reaching views of the countryside.
**ROOMS:** 64 en suite (2 fmly) s £115-£350; d £175-£750 (incl. bkfst) * LB **FACILITIES:** STV Golf 18 Tennis (hard) Fishing Snooker Solarium Gym Putting green Table tennis Xmas **CONF:** Thtr 120 Class 55 Board 26 Del from £175 * **PARKING:** 210 **NOTES:** No dogs (ex guide dogs) No smoking in restaurant Civ Wed 45
**CARDS:**

*See advert on opposite page*

**★★★★71% Billesley Manor**
Billesley, Alcester B49 6NF
☎ 01789 279955 01789 764145
e-mail: enquiries@billesleymanor.co.uk
***Dir:*** *From Stratford upon Avon, A46 in direction of Evesham. Turn R to Billesley after app 3 miles*

This 16th-century manor is set in peaceful grounds and parkland with a delightful topiary garden. The spacious bedrooms and suites, most in traditional country house style, are thoughtfully designed and well-equipped. The new cedar barns house the more contemporary designed bedrooms and conference facilities. The public areas retain many original features, such as oak panelling, exposed stone, and fireplaces.
**ROOMS:** 41 en suite 20 annexe en suite (8 fmly) s £125; d £180-£250 (incl. bkfst) * LB **FACILITIES:** Indoor swimming (H) Tennis (hard) Croquet lawn Putting green Pitch and putt Xmas **CONF:** Thtr 100 Class 60 Board 50 **PARKING:** 100 **NOTES:** No dogs (ex guide dogs) No smoking in restaurant RS Sat Civ Wed 75
**CARDS:**

*See advert on opposite page*

**★★★★71% Stratford Manor**
Warwick Rd CV37 0PY
MARSTON HOTELS
☎ 01789 731173 01789 731131
e-mail: stratfordmanor@marstonhotels.com
***Dir:*** *3m N of Stratford town centre on A439 in direction of Warwick, or leave M40 junct 15, take Stratford-upon-Avon road A439, hotel is 2m on left*
Just outside Stratford, this hotel is set against a rural backdrop, with lovely gardens. Public areas include a lounge and bar where guests may meet for coffee or an informal pre-dinner drink. There is a busy split-level restaurant, and bedrooms are spacious, with large beds and a range of useful facilities.
**ROOMS:** 104 en suite (8 fmly) No smoking in 52 bedrooms s £99-£119; d £120-£140 * LB **FACILITIES:** Spa STV Indoor swimming (H) Tennis (hard) Sauna Solarium Gym Xmas **CONF:** Thtr 360 Class 200 Board 100 Del from £136 * **SERVICES:** Lift **PARKING:** 220 **NOTES:** No dogs (ex guide dogs) No smoking in restaurant Civ Wed
**CARDS:**

**★★★★70% Stratford Victoria**
MARSTON HOTELS
Arden St CV37 6QQ
☎ 01789 271000 01789 271001
e-mail: stratfordvictoria@marstonhotels.com
***Dir:*** *A439 into Stratford, in town follow A3400 Birmingham, at traffic light junct turn left into Arden St, the hotel is 150yds on right hand side*
A new hotel with enthusiastic staff and a welcoming atmosphere. Open plan public areas include a lounge and a restaurant. Bedrooms are spacious and comfortably equipped.
**ROOMS:** 100 en suite (35 fmly) No smoking in 40 bedrooms s £89-£109; d £109-£149 * LB **FACILITIES:** STV Gym Jacuzzi Beauty Salon Xmas **CONF:** Thtr 140 Class 66 Board 54 Del from £115 * **SERVICES:** Lift **PARKING:** 96 **NOTES:** No dogs (ex guide dogs) No smoking in restaurant **CARDS:**

**★★★★67% The Shakespeare**
Chapel St CV37 6ER
☎ 0870 400 8182 01789 415411
***Dir:*** *adjoining town hall*
Right in the heart of town, this 18th-century hotel is a landmark site with its gabled timber façade. Public rooms are full of charm with exposed beams, classic staircases and open fires. Bedrooms vary in size but all provide modern comforts. The quality hotel cuisine combines traditional and modern influences.
**ROOMS:** 74 en suite No smoking in 20 bedrooms s fr £125; d fr £165 * LB **FACILITIES:** STV Xmas **CONF:** Thtr 120 Class 50 Board 40 Del from £145 * **SERVICES:** Lift **PARKING:** 34 **NOTES:** No smoking in restaurant Civ Wed 50 **CARDS:**

**★★★★66% The Alveston Manor**
Clopton Bridge CV37 7HP
☎ 0870 400 8181 01789 414095
***Dir:*** *S of Clopton Bridge*
A striking red brick and wooden façade, well-tended grounds, and a giant cedar tree all contribute to the charm of this well-established hotel. Bedrooms vary in size and character, but all provide modern comforts - the recent conversion of a coach house offers an impressive mix of comfortable full and junior suites. The Manor Grill restaurant offers menus based on popular traditional choices, and in summer months a terrace food operation offers Mediterranean-style grills.
**ROOMS:** 114 en suite No smoking in 30 bedrooms s £70-£90; d £154-£168 (incl. bkfst) * LB **FACILITIES:** STV Xmas **CONF:** Thtr 140 Class 80 Board 40 Del from £155 * **PARKING:** 200 **NOTES:** Civ Wed 36
**CARDS:**

**★★★75% Salford Hall**
WR11 5UT
Best Western
☎ 01386 871300 01386 871301
e-mail: reception@salfordhall.co.uk
(For full entry see Abbot's Salford)

Weekend away? Hotels with LB in their entry offer leisure breaks.

*continued*

## Billesley Manor HOTEL

NR. STRATFORD · UPON · AVON

This magnificent 16th century Manor House is set in 11 acres of its own private parkland and has a unique Topiary garden and sun terrace. The hotel also offers an impressive indoor heated swimming pool, tennis courts, six hole pitch and putt course, croquet lawn and rough ground - ideal for corporate events such as clay pigeon shooting, archery and quad biking. The hotel has 61 beautiful bedrooms, including Four-poster rooms and suites - all of which are ensuite and many with stunning garden views. A selection of rooms for private dining are available for family, friends or business guests - the cuisine is of the highest standards with the Stuart restaurant having been awarded 2 AA rosettes. Situated in the very heart of England, minutes away from Shakespeare's Stratford upon Avon and only 23 miles from Birmingham International Airport. An ideal location by air, rail and road set in some of England's most beautiful countryside.

*A Member of Small Luxury Hotels of the World*

**Billesley, Alcester, Nr. Stratford-upon-Avon**
**Warwickshire B49 6NF**
**Tel: (01789) 279955 Fax: (01789) 764145**

Ettington Park is a superb country house near Stratford upon Avon with 48 bedrooms, including 9 suites, each individually furnished, offering magnificent views across the surrounding countryside.

It boasts its own stables, tennis courts, indoor swimming pool, sauna, solarium, fishing, clay pigeon shooting and archery as well as being highly acclaimed for its award winning restaurant and fine wine list.

## ETTINGTON PARK

**Alderminster, Stratford upon Avon**
**Warwickshire CV37 8BU**
**Telephone: 01789-450123**

AA ★★★★

*See gazetteer under Alderminster*

## Salford Hall Hotel

**ABBOTS SALFORD, EVESHAM**
**WARWICKSHIRE WR11 5UT**
**Tel: 01386 871300 Fax: 01386 871301**

A romantic Grade I Listed Tudor building providing a perfect base for exploring the Cotswolds and Shakespeare country.
Superb food with two AA Rosettes awarded for five consecutive years. Young enthusiastic staff awarded the AA Courtesy and Care Award in 1995.
All this combines to ensure a perfect setting for a few days away.

AA ★★★★

WELCOMBE

## WELCOMBE HOTEL AND GOLF COURSE

When you arrive at the Welcombe Hotel, the sweeping driveway leads you up past the 18 hole golf course to a spectacular listed 19th century Jacobean style mansion with many original antiques which are listed at Christies. Set within 157 acres of parkland with formal gardens, lakes and a waterfall - history is inscribed in the very atmosphere!

64 bedrooms, four-posters, suites and gallery rooms. Two AA Rosetted award winning restaurant, conference facilities for up to 100 delegates theatre style. Health and beauty salon.

Just 1.5 miles from Stratford-upon-Avon, Five miles from Junction 15 on the M40 and 25 minutes from the NEC and Birmingham Airport.

**WARWICK ROAD, STRATFORD-UPON-AVON**
**WARWICKSHIRE CV37 0NR**
**TEL: 01789 295252 FAX: 01789 414666**
**Email: sales@welcombe.co.uk**

S

STRATFORD-UPON-AVON, continued

### ★★★68% The Swan's Nest

Bridgefoot CV37 7LT
☎ 0870 400 8183 🖷 01789 414547
e-mail:
heritagehotels_stratford_upon_avon.swans_nest@forte-hotels.com
***Dir:*** *from M40 junct 15, A46 to Stratford,leave at 1st island turn left onto A439 follow one way system left over river bridge hotel by river*
Partly dating back to the 17th century and with its own river frontage, this hotel has benefited from a recent refurbishment, from the compact yet stylishly designed bedrooms to the delightful riverside restaurant or the cosy lounge. The courtyard garden is ideal for weddings. Staff here are friendly and nothing is too much trouble.
**ROOMS:** 67 en suite (2 fmly) No smoking in 30 bedrooms s £115-£125; d £115-£125 * **FACILITIES:** STV Xmas **CONF:** Thtr 150 Class 80 Board 40 Del from £130 * **PARKING:** 80 **NOTES:** No smoking in restaurant Civ Wed 50 **CARDS:**

### ★★★66% Grosvenor House

Warwick Rd CV37 6YT
☎ 01789 269213 🖷 01789 266087
e-mail: sales@patenhotels.freeserve.co.uk
***Dir:*** *turn off jct 15 on M40 follow Stratford signs to A439 Warwick Rd, hotel is 7m from jct on town centre one way system*
Grosvenor House is a short distance from the town centre and many of the historic attractions. Staff are both friendly and efficient, and useful services, such as an all-day menu of refreshments in the lounge, and room service, are available. The Garden Room restaurant offers a choice of interesting modern dishes from set priced and carte menus. Bedroom styles and sizes vary; the most recent wing of new rooms are spacious and cheerfully appointed, with smart modern bathrooms.
**ROOMS:** 67 en suite (1 fmly) No smoking in 25 bedrooms s £60-£79; d £60-£90 * **LB** **FACILITIES:** Xmas **CONF:** Thtr 100 Class 50 Board 40 Del from £95 * **PARKING:** 53 **NOTES:** No dogs (ex guide dogs) No smoking in restaurant Civ Wed 80
**CARDS:**

### ★★★65% *The White Swan*

Rother St CV37 6NH
☎ 01789 297022 🖷 01789 268773
***Dir:*** *leave M40 junct15 signposted Stratford on Avon. Hotel is in the Market Square*
On the market square, this half-timbered building has retained many of its original features. Bedrooms offer a blend of tradition and comfort; some boasting beamed ceilings and larger beds. The lounge offers sofas, open fires and a warm welcome, whilst the formal restaurant and bar provides interesting dishes.
**ROOMS:** 41 en suite (3 fmly) No smoking in 16 bedrooms
**FACILITIES:** entertainment **CONF:** Thtr 30 Class 10 Board 20
**PARKING:** 10 **NOTES:** No smoking in restaurant
**CARDS:**

*See advert on opposite page*

### ★★★64% The Falcon

Chapel St CV37 6HA
☎ 01789 279953 🖷 01789 414260
e-mail: thefalcon@corushotels.com
***Dir:*** *town centre-opposite Guild Chapel and Nash House*
Situated in the heart of the town this traditional inn provides a choice of bars, a sun lounge, pretty gardens and a modern brasserie-style restaurant. Well-equipped bedrooms come in a variety of styles; the older, beamed rooms in the original section are smaller but have their own charm, and garden rooms are a newer addition and are smartly appointed.

**ROOMS:** 73 en suite 11 annexe en suite (13 fmly) No smoking in 38 bedrooms s £50-£99; d £80-£130 * **LB** **FACILITIES:** Xmas **CONF:** Thtr 200 Class 110 Board 40 Del from £99.90 * **SERVICES:** Lift
**PARKING:** 124 **NOTES:** No smoking in restaurant
**CARDS:**

### ★★★63% Charlecote Pheasant

Charlecote CV35 9EW
☎ 01789 279954 🖷 01789 470222
e-mail: charlecotepheasant@regalhotels.com
***Dir:*** *leave M40 junc15, take A429 towards Cirencester through Barford village after 2m turn right into Charlecote, hotel opp Charlecote Manor Park*

The village of Charlecote is the ideal setting for this hotel and its extensive grounds. The main building houses public rooms, restaurant and bars. Bedrooms are spacious, well-equipped and range from functional to quite luxurious.
**ROOMS:** 70 en suite (2 fmly) No smoking in 26 bedrooms s fr £99; d fr £115 * **LB** **FACILITIES:** Spa Outdoor swimming (H) Tennis (hard) Childrens Play area Xmas **CONF:** Thtr 160 Class 90 Board 50 Del from £120 * **PARKING:** 100 **NOTES:** No dogs (ex guide dogs) No smoking in restaurant RS 27-31 Dec Civ Wed 120
**CARDS:**

### ★★74% *Stratford Court*

Avenue Rd CV37 6UX
☎ 01789 297799 🖷 01789 262449
e-mail: stratfordcourt@easynet.co.uk
***Dir:*** *Stratford town centre: follow one way system taking A439, 1st left after one way system into Welcombe Rd, continue to top. Stratford Court on right*
There's a relaxed atmosphere at this delightful Edwardian property, which sits in a residential area close to the town centre. Bedrooms are furnished and equipped to a high standard with

*continued*

dramatic fabrics and furnishings. The comfortable lounge and cosy bar are available to guests.
**ROOMS:** 13 en suite (2 fmly) **PARKING:** 20 **NOTES:** No children 14yrs No smoking in restaurant **CARDS:**

### ★★65% *The New Inn Hotel & Restaurant*

Clifford Chambers CV37 8HR
☎ 01789 293402 📠 01789 292716
e-mail: thenewinn65@aol.com
***Dir:*** *Turn off A3400 onto B4632 , follow signs to shire horse centre, hotel 200yds on left*
A welcoming, family-run hotel in a pretty village. The bar has an open log fire and, together with the restaurant, offers a choice of dining options. Bedrooms are appealing, both in the new wing and the remaining six rooms which have recently been upgraded. Four-poster and disabled rooms are available.
**ROOMS:** 12 en suite (2 fmly) No smoking in all bedrooms **CONF:** Class 50 **PARKING:** 40 **NOTES:** No dogs No smoking in restaurant **CARDS:**

## STREATLEY, Berkshire — Map 04 SU58

### ★★★★68% Swan Diplomat

High St RG8 9HR
☎ 01491 878800 📠 01491 872554
e-mail: sales@swan-diplomat.co.uk
***Dir:*** *M4 junct12 towards Theale, at 2nd rdbt A340 to Pangbourne, A329 to Streatley. Right at 1st traffic lights, hotel 200yds on left, before bridge*

This stylish hotel provides the perfect riverside location for the quintessential English summer's day. Bedrooms are spacious and thoughtfully equipped, most enjoying the lovely views. Public areas include a range of comfortable lounges and the newly refurbished Racing Swan restaurant which offers an interesting range of carefully prepared dishes.
**ROOMS:** 46 en suite No smoking in 8 bedrooms s £108-£128; d £138-£155 * **LB FACILITIES:** STV Indoor swimming (H) Sauna Solarium Gym Croquet lawn Jacuzzi Boat hire, Steam room Xmas **CONF:** Thtr 100 Class 50 Board 40 Del from £165 * **PARKING:** 135 **NOTES:** Civ Wed 90 **CARDS:**

## STREET, Somerset — Map 03 ST43

### ★★★60% *Wessex*

High St BA16 0EF
☎ 01458 443383 📠 01458 446589
e-mail: Wessex@hotel-street.freeserve.co.uk
***Dir:*** *from A303 follow road B3151 to Somerton and Street*
This purpose built hotel in the centre of town has plenty of parking and is but a short walk from Clarks village. Spacious bedrooms are equipped with modern facilities. Public areas include function rooms, a cosy bar, and a comfortable restaurant offering a fixed price menu and popular carvery.
**ROOMS:** 50 en suite (2 fmly) No smoking in 24 bedrooms **FACILITIES:** STV **CONF:** Thtr 250 Class 150 Board 50 **SERVICES:** Lift **PARKING:** 90 **NOTES:** No smoking in restaurant **CARDS:**

## STRETTON, Rutland — Map 08 SK91

### ★★71% Ram Jam Inn

Great North Rd LE15 7QX
☎ 01780 410776 📠 01780 410361
e-mail: rji@rutnet.co.uk
***Dir:*** *on N bound carriageway of A1 past the B668 turn off, thru service station into hotel carpark. S bound take B668 - Oakham & follow signs under A1*
The delightful Ram Jam has an informal but stylish ambience and is very pleasant, much like a cafe bar and bistro with rooms. The English country house and continental decoration styles in the public areas complement each other well. The spacious high quality bedrooms have cheerful soft furnishings and most overlook the rear garden and orchard.
**ROOMS:** 7 en suite (1 fmly) s £46; d £56 * **CONF:** Thtr 60 Class 40 Board 40 Del £77.50 * **PARKING:** 64 **NOTES:** No smoking in restaurant Closed 25 Dec **CARDS:**

Popped the question? Hotels with Civ Wed in their entry are licensed for civil wedding ceremonies. Maximum numbers for the ceremony only are shown, e.g. Civ Wed 120

S

## STROUD, Gloucestershire Map 03 SO80

### ★★★70% *The Bear of Rodborough*

Rodborough Common GL5 5DE
☎ 01453 878522 🖷 01453 872523
e-mail: bookings@cotswold-inns-hotels.co.uk
***Dir:*** *1m S on A46, turn left to Rodborough Common*
An imposing 17th-century coaching inn, situated high above Stroud, and set in acres of National Trust Parkland. The character of the Bear speaks volumes, lounges, cocktail bar and elegant Mulberry restaurant epitomising the inherent charm of the building. Bedrooms offer comfort and style with a good selection of extra touches. There is also a traditional and popular public bar. Food is good, and based where possible on local produce.
**ROOMS:** 46 en suite (2 fmly) No smoking in 23 bedrooms
**FACILITIES:** Croquet lawn **CONF:** Thtr 60 Class 30 Board 30
**PARKING:** 122 **NOTES:** No smoking in restaurant Civ Wed 100
**CARDS:**

### ★★65% *The Bell*

Wallbridge GL5 3J5
☎ 01453 763556 🖷 01453 758611
***Dir:*** *at junct of A419/A46, outside Stroud Town Centre*
This one time public house, dating back to Victorian times, offers well-equipped and comfortable accommodation. Facilities include a meeting room, lounge bar, restaurant and convenient parking.
**ROOMS:** 12 en suite (2 fmly) **FACILITIES:** STV ch fac **CONF:** Thtr 35 Class 20 Board 16 **PARKING:** 15 **NOTES:** No smoking in restaurant
**CARDS:**

### ⇧ *Premier Lodge*

Stratford Lodge GL5 4AF
☎ 0870 700 1548 🖷 0870 700 1549
Premier Lodge offers modern, well-equipped, en suite accommodation suitable for both business and leisure travellers. Meals can be taken at the adjacent popular restaurant and bar, which is fully licensed. For further details, consult the Hotel Groups page.
**ROOMS:** 30 en suite

### ⇧ *Travelodge*

A 419 Easington, Stonehouse GL10 3SQ
☎ 01962 760779
Travelodge offers good quality, good value, modern accommodation. Ideal for families, the spacious, en suite bedrooms include remote-control TV, tea and coffee-making facilities, luxury beds and free morning newspaper. Meals can be taken at the nearby family restaurant. For further details and the Travelodge phone number, consult the Hotel Groups page.

**ROOMS:** 40 en suite

## STUDLAND, Dorset Map 04 SZ08

### ★★68% Manor House

BH19 3AU
☎ 01929 450288 🖷 01929 450288
***Dir:*** *from Bournemouth, follow signs to Sandbanks/Sandbanks ferry, over ferry, then 3m to Studland*
Views over Studland Bay are delightful at this hotel and can be enjoyed from many of the individually decorated bedrooms, some of which have four-poster beds. Downstairs, the lounge has a lovely open fire for the winter months and the panelled dining room has a baronial feel. Twenty acres of secluded gardens surround the hotel, and there is also a lovely conservatory-style dining room.
**ROOMS:** 20 en suite (9 fmly) s £83-£101; d £136-£180 (incl. bkfst & dinner) * **LB** **FACILITIES:** Tennis (hard) Croquet lawn Xmas
**CONF:** Class 25 **PARKING:** 80 **NOTES:** No children 5yrs No smoking in restaurant Closed 6-26 Jan **CARDS:**

## STURMINSTER NEWTON, Dorset Map 03 ST71

### ★★★71% ◎◎ Plumber Manor

Hazelbury Bryan Rd DT10 2AF
☎ 01258 472507 🖷 01258 473370
e-mail: book@plumbermanor.com
***Dir:*** *1.5m SW of Sturminster Newton, off A357 towards Hazelbury Bryan*

This beautiful Jacobean manor is set in extensive, lovingly tended grounds. Bedrooms in the main house retain much character, where those in the converted barns opposite tend to be more spacious and modern in style. The restaurant is very much the centre of the operation, and has an excellent reputation for good traditional cooking.
**ROOMS:** 6 en suite 10 annexe en suite s £85-£95; d £100-£150 (incl. bkfst) * **LB** **FACILITIES:** Tennis (hard) Croquet lawn **CONF:** Thtr 25 Board 12 Del from £135 * **PARKING:** 30 **NOTES:** Closed Feb
**CARDS:**

## SUDBURY, Derbyshire Map 07 SK13

### ★★★68% The Boars Head

Lichfield Rd DE6 5GX
☎ 01283 820344 🖷 01283 820075
***Dir:*** *Turn off A50 onto A515 towards Lichfield, hotel 1m on right close to railway crossing*

This roadside inn offers comfortable accommodation in well-equipped bedrooms. There is a relaxed atmosphere in the public rooms, which offer a choice of bars and dining options. The

*continued*

refurbished beamed lounge bar provides informal dining while the restaurant and cocktail bar offer a more formal environment.
**ROOMS:** 22 en suite 1 annexe en suite (1 fmly) **FACILITIES:** STV **CONF:** Thtr 25 Class 16 Board 16 **PARKING:** 85 **NOTES:** No smoking in restaurant **CARDS:**

*See advert under BURTON UPON TRENT*

## SUDBURY, Suffolk — Map 05 TL84

### ★★★69% Mill

Walnut Tree Ln CO10 1BD
☎ 01787 375544 Fax 01787 373027
***Dir:*** *from Colchester take A134 to Sudbury, follow signs for Chelmsford after town square take 2nd right*
Located on the outskirts of the town, overlooking open pastures and the River Stour, this hotel has its own mill pond and retains charming features from the building's three century history including open fires, exposed beams and a working waterwheel. Bedrooms vary in size and most enjoy a view of the river or mill pond.
**ROOMS:** 52 en suite (2 fmly) s £59; d £79-£109 * **LB**
**FACILITIES:** STV Xmas **CONF:** Thtr 70 Class 35 Board 35 Del £79 * **PARKING:** 60 **CARDS:**

## SUNDERLAND, Tyne & Wear — Map 12 NZ35

### ★★★★67% Sunderland Marriott Hotel

Marriott HOTELS · RESORTS · SUITES

Queen's Pde, Seaburn SR6 8DB
☎ 0191 529 2041 Fax 0191 529 3843
e-mail: sunderland-marriott@whitbread.com
***Dir:*** *off A19 to Sunderland N on A1231, at traffic lights follow A183 for approx 3m to seafront, where hotel is situated*

This seafront hotel offers comfortable bedrooms, those in the newer wing being particularly impressive. Public areas include a bright foyer lounge, a spacious bar and an elegant restaurant, where the gourmet menu offers bold and innovative flavour combinations. Excellent banqueting and leisure facilities are available.
**ROOMS:** 82 en suite (20 fmly) No smoking in 60 bedrooms s £99-£155; d £99-£155 * **LB** **FACILITIES:** Spa STV Indoor swimming (H) Sauna Solarium Gym Xmas **CONF:** Thtr 300 Class 150 Board 100 Del from £140 * **SERVICES:** Lift **PARKING:** 100 **NOTES:** No smoking in restaurant Civ Wed 80 **CARDS:**

### ★★★68% *Quality Friendly Hotel*

Quality Hotel

Witney Way, Boldon NE35 9PE
☎ 0191 519 1999 Fax 0191 519 0655
e-mail: admin@gb621.u-net.com
***Dir:*** *junct A19/A184*
Situated in the Business Park, this modern, purpose-built hotel is well suited to the needs of the business traveller. It offers spacious, very well-equipped bedrooms. Public areas include a leisure centre and a variety of meeting rooms.
**ROOMS:** 82 en suite (10 fmly) No smoking in 42 bedrooms
**FACILITIES:** STV Indoor swimming (H) Sauna Solarium Gym Jacuzzi ch fac **CONF:** Thtr 200 Class 100 Board 75 **PARKING:** 150
**NOTES:** Civ Wed 300 **CARDS:**

### Premier Lodge

Timber Beach Rd, Off Chessington Way, Castletown SR5 3XG
☎ 0870 700 1550 Fax 0870 700 1551
***Dir:*** *junct 64 A1 onto A1231 heading towards Sunderland, lodge on last rdbt on right*
Premier Lodge offers modern, well-equipped, en suite accommodation suitable for both business and leisure travellers. Meals can be taken at the adjacent popular restaurant and bar, which is fully licensed. For further details, consult the Hotel Groups page.
**ROOMS:** 63 en suite s fr £46; d fr £46 * **CONF:** Thtr 12 Class 12 Board 12 Del from £70.95 *

## SUTTON, Greater London — Map 04 TQ26

### ★★63% *Thatched House*

135 Cheam Rd SM1 2BN
☎ 020 8642 3131 Fax 020 8770 0684
***Dir:*** *junct 8 of M25, follow A217 to London until reaching A232, turn right onto A232, hotel is half a minute's drive on the right*
A large thatched hotel on the Epsom/Croydon road. Bedrooms, which vary in shape and size, are neatly decorated and well-equipped. Public rooms include a small lounge, a bar and a dining room overlooking the attractive garden.
**ROOMS:** 32 rms (29 en suite) 5 annexe rms **CONF:** Thtr 50 Class 30 Board 26 **PARKING:** 26 **NOTES:** No smoking in restaurant
**CARDS:**

## SUTTON COLDFIELD, West Midlands — Map 07 SP19

**Premier Collection**

### ★★★★ *New Hall*

THISTLE HOTELS

Walmley Rd B76 1QX
☎ 0121 378 2442 Fax 0121 378 4637
e-mail: new.hall@thistle.co.uk
***Dir:*** *follow A38 'Lichfield' until B4148 'Walmley'. 2.5m on B4148, at 2nd rdbt turn left and then right into Walmley Road. Hotel is on left*
Set in immaculate grounds and gardens, this 12th-century hotel is reputedly the oldest moated manor house in England. The day rooms are delightful. Divided between a purpose-built wing and the main house, the bedrooms vary in size but

*continued on p568*

S

SUTTON COLDFIELD, continued

all are furnished and decorated to a high standard. The restaurant offers imaginative dishes of a consistently high quality.
**ROOMS:** 60 en suite No smoking in 54 bedrooms **FACILITIES:** STV Golf 9 Fishing Croquet lawn Putting green Golf driving net **CONF:** Thtr 50 Class 30 Board 30 **PARKING:** 70 **NOTES:** No dogs (ex guide dogs) No smoking in restaurant RS Sat Civ Wed 70
**CARDS:**

### ★★★74% Moor Hall

Moor Hall Dr, Four Oaks B75 6LN
☎ 0121 308 3751 🖷 0121 308 8974
e-mail: mail@moorhallhotel.co.uk
***Dir:*** *at jct of A38/A453 take A453 towards Sutton Coldfield, at traffic lights turn right into Weeford Rd, Moor Hall drive is 150 yds on left*

Although only a short distance from the city centre and 15 minutes from the NEC and the motorway network, this hotel enjoys a peaceful setting, overlooking extensive grounds and an adjacent golf course. Bedrooms are well-equipped and the executive rooms particularly spacious. In the evenings, there are two choices for dinner: a formal restaurant, the Oak Room, and the informal Country Kitchen offering a carvery and blackboard specials.
**ROOMS:** 74 en suite (5 fmly) No smoking in 36 bedrooms s £105-£115; d £120-£130 (incl. bkfst) * **LB** **FACILITIES:** **Spa** STV Indoor swimming (H) Sauna Solarium Gym Jacuzzi Steam room **CONF:** Thtr 250 Class 120 Board 45 Del £140 * **SERVICES:** Lift **PARKING:** 164 **NOTES:** No dogs (ex guide dogs) Civ Wed 120 **CARDS:**

S

### ★★★67% Marston Farm

Bodymoor Heath B76 9JD
☎ 01827 872133 🖷 01827 875043
e-mail: brook@brook-hotels.demon.co.uk

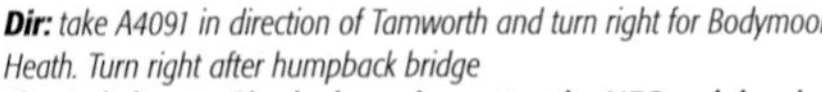

***Dir:*** *take A4091 in direction of Tamworth and turn right for Bodymoor Heath. Turn right after humpback bridge*
Situated close to Birmingham city centre, the NEC and the airport, this 17th-century farmhouse provides attractive and well-equipped accommodation to both leisure and business markets. Features of the hotel include the courtyard restaurant, permanent marquee, conference rooms and ample car parking.
**ROOMS:** 37 en suite No smoking in 5 bedrooms s £98; d £115 * **LB** **FACILITIES:** STV Tennis (hard) Fishing Croquet lawn BoulesMountain bikes Xmas **CONF:** Thtr 150 Class 80 Board 50 **PARKING:** 150 **NOTES:** No smoking in restaurant Civ Wed 120
**CARDS:**

Early start? Hotels at all star levels should provide in-room alarm clocks and/or alarm calls.

### ★★★63% Quality Hotel Sutton Court

60-66 Lichfield Rd B74 2NA
☎ 0121 354 4991 🖷 0121 355 0083
e-mail: reservations@sutton-court-hotel.co.uk
***Dir:*** *take M42 junct 9, then A446 to Lichfield. At rdbt take A453 to Sutton Coldfield. Hotel is at 2nd set of traffic lights at junct of A5127/A453*
A privately owned hotel, close to the town centre, providing modern and well-equipped bedrooms with some ladies' bedrooms available. Public rooms are comfortable and there is a good range of conference and function facilities. There is also a Deep South American-styled bar and restaurant called Savanaghs.
**ROOMS:** 54 en suite 8 annexe en suite (9 fmly) No smoking in 40 bedrooms s £55-£98; d £65-£118 (incl. bkfst) * **LB** **FACILITIES:** STV Free use of local leisure centre entertainment Xmas **CONF:** Thtr 90 Class 70 Board 50 Del from £90 * **PARKING:** 90 **NOTES:** Civ Wed 130
**CARDS:**
*See advert under BIRMINGHAM*

### ⇧ *Travelodge*

Boldmere Rd B73 5UP
☎ 0121 355 0017 🖷 0121 355 0017
***Dir:*** *2m S, on B4142*
Travelodge offers good quality, good value, modern accommodation. Ideal for families, the spacious, en suite bedrooms include remote-control TV, tea and coffee-making facilities, luxury beds and free morning newspaper. Meals can be taken at the nearby family restaurant. For further details and the Travelodge phone number, consult the Hotel Groups page.

**ROOMS:** 32 en suite

### ⇧ *Premier Lodge (Birmingham North)*

Whitehouse Common Rd B75 6HD
☎ 0870 700 1322 🖷 0870 700 1323
Premier Lodge offers modern, well-equipped, en suite accommodation suitable for both business and leisure travellers. Meals can be taken at the adjacent popular restaurant and bar, which is fully licensed. For further details, consult the Hotel Groups page.
**ROOMS:** 42 en suite

### ○ Innkeeper's Lodge Birmingham South

22225 Coventry Rd, Sheldon B26 3EH
A new concept in the travel accommodation market. Smart rooms meet essential business requirements but also have home comforts. Dining options include all-day menus plus the added advantage of breakfast, which is included in the room price. Reservations can be made seven days a week through the room reservations number: 0870 243 0500. For further details, consult the Hotel Groups page.
**ROOMS:** 85 en suite

SUTTON IN THE ELMS, Leicestershire — Map 04 SP59

### ★★66% *Mill On The Soar*

Coventry Rd LE9 6QD
☎ 01455 282419 🖷 01455 285937
***Dir:*** *SE of Leicester, on B4114*
The Mill On The Soar is a busy roadside inn which caters well for family dining. The open plan rooms include non-smoking and family areas, plus a novel over-16s area. An extensive range of snacks and bar meals is available throughout. Bedrooms are in a separate wing and are very well-equipped. The gardens to the rear lead to a falconry centre, play area, river and small lake.
**ROOMS:** 25 en suite (10 fmly) **FACILITIES:** Fishing Falconry centre **CONF:** Thtr 50 Class 20 Board 15 **PARKING:** 200 **NOTES:** No dogs (ex guide dogs) **CARDS:**

## SUTTON ON SEA, Lincolnshire
Map 09 TF58

### ★★★66% Grange & Links
Sea Ln, Sandilands LN12 2RA
☎ 01507 441334 01507 443033
e-mail: grangelinks@ic24.net
*Dir: A1111 to Sutton-on-Sea, follow signs to Sandilands*
Close to the beach in five acres of grounds, this friendly family run hotel is popular with golfers, having its own 18 hole links course. Delightful public rooms include an attractive bar together with ample lounge areas. Good home cooking is served in the traditional style dining room and most of the bedrooms are well-equipped and pleasantly furnished.
**ROOMS:** 23 en suite (10 fmly) d £78 (incl. bkfst) * **LB**
**FACILITIES:** Golf 18 Tennis (hard) Snooker Gym Croquet lawn Putting green Bowls ch fac Xmas **CONF:** Thtr 200 Board 100 Del from £75 *
**PARKING:** 60 **NOTES:** No dogs (ex guide dogs) Civ Wed 500
**CARDS:**

## SUTTON SCOTNEY, Hampshire
Map 04 SU43

### *Travelodge (North)*
SO21 3JY
☎ 01962 761016
*Dir: on A34 northbound*
Travelodge offers good quality, good value, modern accommodation. Ideal for families, the spacious, en suite bedrooms include remote-control TV, tea and coffee-making facilities, luxury beds and free morning newspaper. Meals can be taken at the nearby family restaurant. For further details and the Travelodge phone number, consult the Hotel Groups page.

**ROOMS:** 30 en suite

### *Travelodge (South)*
SO21 3JY
☎ 01962 760779
*Dir: on A34 southbound*
Travelodge offers good quality, good value, modern accommodation. Ideal for families, the spacious, en suite bedrooms include remote-control TV, tea and coffee-making facilities, luxury beds and free morning newspaper. Meals can be taken at the nearby family restaurant. For further details and the Travelodge phone number, consult the Hotel Groups page.

**ROOMS:** 40 en suite

## SUTTON UPON DERWENT, East Riding of Yorkshire
Map 08 SE74

### ★★65% Old Rectory
Sandhill Ln YO41 4BX
☎ 01904 608548 01904 608548
*Dir: off A1079 at Grimston Bar rdbt onto B1228 for Howden, through Elvington to Sutton-upon-Derwent, the hotel is situated on left opposite tennis courts*
This former country rectory stands close to the village centre and overlooks the Derwent valley. The house is large and provides spacious bedrooms together with a separate bar and lounge. Home cooking is served in the traditional-style dining room, and service is friendly and polite.
**ROOMS:** 6 rms (5 en suite) (2 fmly) s £30-£38; d fr £62 (incl. bkfst) * **LB** **FACILITIES:** STV **PARKING:** 30 **NOTES:** Closed 2 wks Xmas
**CARDS:**

## SWAFFHAM, Norfolk
Map 05 TF80

### ★★★65% George
Station Rd PE37 7LJ
☎ 01760 721238 01760 725333
*Dir: turn off A47 signposted Swaffham, hotel opposite the church of St Peter & St Paul*
This popular, family-run coaching inn is situated in the centre of town, adjacent to the market. Bedroom styles vary but all are well-equipped. There is a busy bar serving a range of snacks, and more formal meals are served in the restaurant.
**ROOMS:** 29 en suite (1 fmly) s fr £59; d fr £75 (incl. bkfst) * **LB**
**FACILITIES:** STV Xmas **CONF:** Thtr 150 Class 70 Board 70 Del from £60 * **PARKING:** 100 **NOTES:** No smoking in restaurant
**CARDS:**

## SWALLOWFIELD, Berkshire
Map 04 SU76

### ★★70% *The Mill House*
Old Basingstoke Rd, Swallowfield RG7 1PY
☎ 0118 988 3124 0118 988 5550
e-mail: info@themillhousehotel.co.uk
*Dir: M4 junct 11, S on A33, left at 1st rdbt onto B3349. Approx 1m after signpost for Three Mile Cross and Spencer's Wood, hotel is on right*
Dating back to 1823, this Georgian house originally formed part of the Stratfield Saye estate, owned by the 'Iron Duke', the 1st Duke of Wellington. Bedrooms are equipped with a comprehensive range of facilities and each is individually furnished and decorated. The popular restaurant enjoys views over an attractive back garden.
**ROOMS:** 10 en suite (2 fmly) No smoking in 2 bedrooms
**FACILITIES:** STV Croquet lawn **CONF:** Thtr 250 Class 100 Board 60
**PARKING:** 60 **NOTES:** No smoking in restaurant Closed 24 Dec-4 Jan RS Sun evenings Civ Wed 125 **CARDS:**

## SWANAGE, Dorset
Map 04 SZ07

### ★★★67% Grand
Burlington Rd BH19 1LU
☎ 01929 423353 01929 427068
e-mail: grandhotel@lineone.net
*Dir: via Sandbanks Toll Ferry from Bournemouth, follow signs to Swanage, at 2nd town centre sign take 4th left into Burlington Rd*
Spectacular views across Swanage Bay can be enjoyed from this hotel, which has access to a private beach. A sunny conservatory, a bar and well-tended gardens are available for guests' use. Bedrooms vary in size, but all are smartly decorated. Enjoyable and varied award-winning cuisine is offered in the refurbished restaurant.
**ROOMS:** 30 en suite (2 fmly) No smoking in 3 bedrooms s £59-£70; d £118-£140 (incl. bkfst & dinner) * **LB** **FACILITIES:** Spa STV Indoor swimming (H) Fishing Sauna Solarium Gym Jacuzzi Table tennis entertainment Xmas **CONF:** Thtr 120 Class 40 Board 40 Del from £83 *
**SERVICES:** Lift **PARKING:** 15 **NOTES:** No dogs No smoking in restaurant Civ Wed 120 **CARDS:**

*See advert on page 571*

### ★★★67% The Pines
Burlington Rd BH19 1LT
☎ 01929 425211 01929 422075
e-mail: reservations@pineshotel.co.uk
*Dir: follow A351 to seafront, turn left then take second right and continue to end of road*
A popular family hotel, The Pines enjoys a superb location with spectacular views across Swanage Bay to the Isle of Wight in the distance. Bedrooms offer a good level of comfort, some having the

*continued on p570*

SWANAGE, continued

added advantage of balconies. Public areas include two comfortable lounges, whilst the restaurant is the venue for good value home-cooked food or alternatively, a less formal option is available in the bar.

*The Pines, Swanage*

**ROOMS:** 49 en suite (26 fmly) s £45-£64; d £90-£128 (incl. bkfst) * LB **FACILITIES:** ch fac Xmas **CONF:** Thtr 80 Class 80 Board 30 Del from £73 * **SERVICES:** Lift **PARKING:** 60 **NOTES:** No smoking in restaurant **CARDS:**

### ★★★65% Purbeck House

91 High St BH19 2LZ
☎ 01929 422872 01929 421194
e-mail: purbeckhouse@easynet.co.uk
***Dir:*** *A351 to Swanage via Wareham, turn right into Shore Road and on into Institute Road, right into High Street*

Located close to the town centre, this former convent is set in well-tended grounds. The bedrooms are tastefully decorated and appointed with old pine furnishings. In addition to a very pleasant and spacious conservatory, the smartly presented public areas have some stunning features, such as painted ceilings, wood panelling and fine tiled floors.

**ROOMS:** 18 en suite 20 annexe en suite (5 fmly) No smoking in 3 bedrooms s £60-£72; d £88-£112 (incl. bkfst) * LB **FACILITIES:** Spa STV Croquet lawn Xmas **CONF:** Thtr 100 Class 36 Board 25 Del from £100 * **PARKING:** 42 **NOTES:** No dogs (ex guide dogs) No smoking in restaurant Civ Wed 100 **CARDS:**

See advert on opposite page

### ★★67% *Havenhurst*

Cranborne Rd BH19 1EA
☎ 01929 424224 01929 422173

This small, personally run hotel offers a friendly welcome to guests, many of whom are regular visitors. Many thoughtful facilities are provided in the neatly presented bedrooms, and there is a comfortable lounge, a conservatory and a popular bar. The freshly prepared, home-cooked meals feature an enormous range of desserts.

**ROOMS:** 17 en suite (4 fmly) **PARKING:** 20 **NOTES:** No dogs No smoking in restaurant **CARDS:**

SWANWICK See Alfreton

## SWAVESEY, Cambridgeshire — Map 05 TL36

### *Travelodge*

Travelodge

Cambridge Rd CB4 5QA
☎ 01954 789113 01954 789113
***Dir:*** *on eastbound carriageway of the A14*

Travelodge offers good quality, good value, modern accommodation. Ideal for families, the spacious, en suite bedrooms include remote-control TV, tea and coffee-making facilities, luxury beds and free morning newspaper. Meals can be taken at the nearby family restaurant. For further details and the Travelodge phone number, consult the Hotel Groups page.

**ROOMS:** 36 en suite

## SWAY, Hampshire — Map 04 SZ29

### ★★★66% String of Horses

Mead End Rd SO41 6EH
☎ 01590 682631 01590 682911
e-mail: relax@stringofhorses.co.uk
***Dir:*** *A337 Lyndhurst/Brockenhurst, right opposite Carey's Manor Hotel onto B3055 to Sway, right onto Station Rd, 2nd left,after railway station 350m on left*

A well-maintained hotel in peaceful, mature grounds, adjoining the New Forest. The majority of the well-presented bedrooms are equipped with large spa baths, and all feature thoughtful extras such as dressing gowns. There is a cosy bar, separate breakfast room and comfortable lounge overlooking the pool and garden.

**ROOMS:** 8 en suite s £73; d £104 (incl. bkfst) * LB **FACILITIES:** STV Outdoor swimming (H) Sauna Croquet lawn Jacuzzi Xmas **CONF:** Thtr 40 Board 30 Del from £115.50 * **PARKING:** 32 **NOTES:** No dogs No children 16yrs No smoking in restaurant
**CARDS:**

### ★★66% White Rose

Station Rd SO41 6BA
☎ 01590 682754 01590 682955
e-mail: whiterosesway@lineone.net
***Dir:*** *turn off B3055 Brockenhurst/New Milton road into Sway village centre*

Situated in the heart of the village, this spacious Victorian house is set in well-tended gardens complete with outdoor pool. Bedrooms are equipped and decorated to a very comfortable standard. There is also a large dining room and lounge with views over the garden.

**ROOMS:** 15 en suite (3 fmly) s fr £50; d £79-£95 (incl. bkfst) * LB **FACILITIES:** Outdoor swimming Xmas **SERVICES:** Lift **PARKING:** 50 **NOTES:** No smoking in restaurant **CARDS:**

## SWINDON, Wiltshire — Map 04 SU18

see also Wootton Bassett

### ★★★★73% Blunsdon House Hotel & Leisure Club

Best Western

Blunsdon SN26 7AS
☎ 01793 721701 01793 721056
e-mail: info@blunsdonhouse.co.uk
***Dir:*** *3m N off A419*

Set in 30 acres of well-tended grounds, Blunsdon House has a variety of public areas including three bars. The very popular Christophers restaurant offers a California grill style, while the Ridge restaurant provides an extensive selection of dishes in more formal surroundings. Bedrooms are comfortably furnished, and the smart new Pavilion rooms are especially spacious.

**ROOMS:** 120 en suite (14 fmly) No smoking in 77 bedrooms s £98-£128; d £126-£156 (incl. bkfst) * LB **FACILITIES:** STV Indoor swimming (H) Golf 9 Tennis (hard) Squash Sauna Solarium Gym Putting green Jacuzzi Beauty therapy Woodland walk Xmas **CONF:** Thtr 300 Class 200 Board 40 Del from £125 * **SERVICES:** Lift **PARKING:** 300 **NOTES:** No dogs (ex guide dogs) No smoking in restaurant Civ Wed 100
**CARDS:**

★★★★71% **De Vere**
Shaw Ridge Leisure Park, Whitehill Way
SN5 7DW
☎ 01793 878785 🖹 01793 877822
e-mail: dvs.sales@devere-hotels.com
***Dir:*** *M4 junct 16, signs for Swindon off 1st rdbt, 2nd rdbt follow signs for Link Centre over next 2 rdbts, 2nd left at 3rd rdbt, left onto slip road*
This modern, purpose built hotel is located to the west of town, adjacent to an entertainment park offering ten-pin bowling and a multiplex cinema. Bedrooms are smartly appointed and offer a good level of modern comfort. There is a range of eating options including an impressive new bar and brasserie.
**ROOMS:** 158 en suite (12 fmly) **FACILITIES:** STV Indoor swimming (H) Sauna Solarium Gym Jacuzzi Health & beauty treatment rooms Xmas **CONF:** Thtr 400 Class 168 Board 80 Del from £140 * **SERVICES:** Lift **PARKING:** 170 **NOTES:** No smoking in restaurant Civ Wed 60
**CARDS:**

★★★★65% **Swindon Marriott Hotel**
Pipers Way SN3 1SH
☎ 01793 512121 🖹 01793 513114
***Dir:*** *from junct 15 of M4 follow A419, then A4259 to Coate roundabout and B4006 signed 'Old Town'*
With convenient access to the motorway, the hotel is an easily accessible meetings venue and an ideal base from which to explore Wiltshire and the Cotswolds. The hotel offers a good range
*continued on p572*

SWINDON, continued

of public rooms, including a well-equipped leisure centre, Chats café bar and the informal, Brasserie-style Mediterrano restaurant.

*Swindon Marriott Hotel, Swindon*

**ROOMS:** 153 en suite (42 fmly) No smoking in 86 bedrooms s £120-£150; d £120-£150 * **LB** **FACILITIES:** STV Indoor swimming (H) Tennis (hard) Sauna Solarium Gym Jacuzzi Steam Room Health & Beauty Xmas **CONF:** Thtr 250 Class 100 Board 40 Del from £159 * **SERVICES:** Lift air con **PARKING:** 185 **NOTES:** No dogs (ex guide dogs) No smoking in restaurant Civ Wed 200
**CARDS:**

### ★★★78% The Pear Tree at Purton

PRIDE OF BRITAIN
MEMBER

Church End SN5 4ED
☎ 01793 772100 ▤ 01793 772369
e-mail: stay@peartreepurton.co.uk
(For full entry see Purton)

### ★★★69% *Chiseldon House*

New Rd, Chiseldon SN4 0NE
☎ 01793 741010 ▤ 01793 741059
e-mail: chiseldonhoushotel@ukonline.co.uk
***Dir:*** *M4 junct 15, A346 signposted Marlborough, at brow of hill right by Esso garage onto B4005 into New Rd, hotel 200yds on right*

Chiseldon is a traditional country house near Swindon that is ideal for a peaceful and comfortable stay. Quiet bedrooms, most of which are very spacious, are tastefully decorated with many thoughtful extras. Guests may also enjoy the Orangery Restaurant, a comfortable lounge, swimming pool and well-kept gardens.
**ROOMS:** 21 en suite (4 fmly) No smoking in 7 bedrooms
**FACILITIES:** STV Outdoor swimming (H) Croquet lawn Putting green
**CONF:** Thtr 30 Class 25 Board 16 **PARKING:** 40 **NOTES:** Civ Wed
**CARDS:**

Fancy a Singapore Sling? Bar staff in five star hotels should be skilled cocktail mixers.

### ★★★69% Landmark Hotel Swindon

Station Rd, Chiseldon SN4 9PW
☎ 01793 740149 ▤ 01793 741326
e-mail: reservations@landmarkhotel.com
***Dir:*** *M4 junct 15/A346 signposted Marlborough, at brow of hill right by Esso garage, take B4005 into New Rd. Take 2nd right signposted Station Rd. Hotel is at bottom of lane on left.*

A modern, efficient and friendly hotel set within the rural village of Chiseldon. Bedrooms and bathrooms offer high standards of space and comfort, all are equipped with many extras and have a luxurious feel. The cosy restaurant offers an excellent choice of fresh cuisine and in the summer months, dining on the pleasant rear patio is also an option.
**ROOMS:** 16 en suite No smoking in 14 bedrooms s £60-£125; d £60-£125 (incl. bkfst) * **CONF:** Thtr 30 Class 12 Board 16 Del from £110 * **SERVICES:** Lift **PARKING:** 24 **NOTES:** No smoking in restaurant Closed 23 Dec-3 Jan **CARDS:**

### ★★★67% Stanton House

The Avenue, Stanton Fitzwarren SN6 7SD
☎ 01793 861777 ▤ 01793 861857
e-mail: reception@stantonhouse.co.uk
***Dir:*** *off A419 onto A361 towards Highworth, pass Honda factory and left towards Stanton Fitzwarren about 600yds past business park, hotel on left*
Extensive grounds surround this Cotswold stone manor house. Bedrooms are smart and well-maintained. There are lovely public areas including a games room, a lounge, a bar, conference facilities and super gardens. The restaurant specialises in traditional Japanese dishes, but equally good European cuisine is also available.
**ROOMS:** 86 en suite No smoking in 3 bedrooms s £69-£95; d £109-£125 (incl. bkfst) * **LB** **FACILITIES:** STV Tennis (hard) Mah Jong **CONF:** Thtr 110 Class 70 Board 40 **SERVICES:** Lift air con **PARKING:** 110
**NOTES:** No dogs (ex guide dogs) Civ Wed 40
**CARDS:**

*See advert on opposite page*

### ★★★65% *Posthouse Swindon*

**Posthouse**

Marlborough Rd SN3 6AQ
☎ 0870 400 9079 ▤ 01793 512887
***Dir:*** *off A419 for Swindon at rdbt, onto A4259. Continue for 1m, hotel is on right opposite Coate Water Country Park*
This smart hotel provides good accommodation close to the town centre and major road networks. Bedrooms are well-decorated and have many modern, useful facilities and the small leisure complex is a plus. A good range of dishes is provided in the Restaurant and snacks can also be ordered in the lounge.
**ROOMS:** 98 en suite (30 fmly) No smoking in 65 bedrooms
**FACILITIES:** Indoor swimming (H) Sauna Solarium Gym Jacuzzi
**CONF:** Thtr 70 Class 30 Board 30 **PARKING:** 200
**CARDS:**

# Stanton House Hotel

★ ★ ★

A Cotswold stone country house hotel set in the tranquil surroundings of beautiful Wiltshire countryside.

This typically English hotel has the unusual factor of having a Japanese restaurant.

The ideal venue for a business meeting, conference, wedding or simply just to get away from it all for aweekend break with a difference.

**Stanton House Hotel**
**The Avenue, Stanton Fitzwarren**
**Swindon, Wiltshire SN6 7SD**
**Tel: 01793 861777 Fax: 01793 861857**
**www.stantonhouse.co.uk**
**reception@stantonhouse.co.uk**

This beautiful and prestigious grade 2 listed Victorian farmhouse has been tastefully restored and converted into a luxury country hotel.

Standing in its own three acres of garden and surrounded by open countryside, the hotel offers an oasis of tranquillity to business and leisure travellers.

Conference and banqueting facilities and licensed for weddings.

**MARSH FARM HOTEL**

Wootton Bassett Swindon Wiltshire SN4 8ER
(01793) 842800

# Goddard Arms Hotel

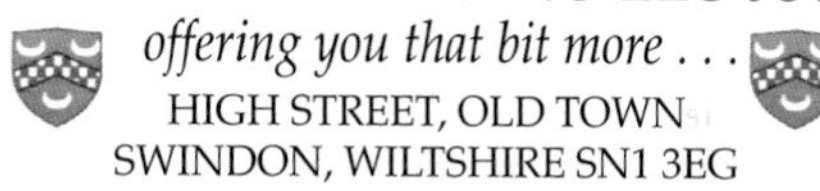

*offering you that bit more . . .*

HIGH STREET, OLD TOWN
SWINDON, WILTSHIRE SN1 3EG
AA ★ ★ ★ Tel: 01793 692313
Fax: 01793 512984 ZOFFANY
E-mail: goddardarms@zoffanyhotels.co.uk.

Situated in the heart of the Old Town and backing onto 50 acres of park land and yet close to the M4 motorway. The olde worlde ambience is combined with modern facilities to ensure a pleasant and restful stay. All 65 bedrooms including an Executive Suite are en-suite, comfortably furnished and fully equipped. Morning coffee and afternoon teas are served in our newly appointed Residents Lounge. Full a la carte restaurant. The Vaults Bar offers an extensive range of wines and real ales. Ample private parking.

AA ★★★ **Villiers Inn** ETC ★★★

• Villiers Inn is a warm-hearted, full-service hotel with personality! In the 1800s it was a farmhouse and has now been converted to include 33 first class en-suite bedrooms • Offering a choice of restaurants – *The Pig on the Wall* – a popular venue with a menu ranging from traditional fayre to contemporary dishes and the *Bo-peep Tree Room* with a slightly more formal ambience • A purpose built conference centre for up to 90 guests •

*Moormead Road, Wroughton, Swindon SN4 9BY*
*Telephone 01793 814744 Facsimile 01793 814119*
*Email: hotels@villiersinn.co.uk*
*Website: www.villiersinn.co.uk*

S

SWINDON, continued

**★★★63% Villiers Inn**
Moormead Rd, Wroughton SN4 9BY
☎ 01793 814744 📠 01793 814119
e-mail: hotels@villiersinn.co.uk
***Dir:*** *1m S of Swindon, on A4361*
An attractive period property with accommodation in a purpose built extension. Bedrooms are well-equipped while public areas include a comfortable library lounge and a spacious conservatory. The Pig on the Wall bar and bistro offers an interesting range of dishes. Conference and function facilities are also available.
**ROOMS:** 33 en suite No smoking in 10 bedrooms s £49-£79; d £69-£89 (incl. bkfst) * **LB** **FACILITIES:** STV Xmas **CONF:** Thtr 80 Class 30 Board 32 Del from £125 * **PARKING:** 60 **NOTES:** Civ Wed 120
**CARDS:**

*See advert on page 573*

**★★★62% Goddard Arms**
ZOFFANY
High St, Old Town SN1 3EG
☎ 01793 692313 📠 01793 512984
e-mail: goddardarms@zoffanyhotels.co.uk
***Dir:*** *M4 junct 15, A419 towards Cirencester, at 1st rdbt left, straight across 2nd and 3rd rdbts, hotel is on the right*
Backing onto acres of natural parkland, this historic hotel is in the heart of Old Town. Bedrooms are in the original building and two wings, all being recently refurbished. In addition to extensive conference facilities, public areas include a cellar bar and a charming restaurant.
**ROOMS:** 18 en suite 47 annexe en suite (3 fmly) No smoking in 31 bedrooms s £38-£95; d £52-£100 (incl. bkfst) * **LB** **FACILITIES:** STV **CONF:** Thtr 180 Class 100 Board 40 Del from £99 * **PARKING:** 90 **NOTES:** No dogs (ex guide dogs) No smoking in restaurant Civ Wed 180
**CARDS:**

*See advert on page 573*

**⇧ *Premier Lodge***
PREMIER LODGE
Ermin St, Blunsdon SN26 8DJ
☎ 0870 700 1554 📠 0870 700 1555
Premier Lodge offers modern, well-equipped, en suite accommodation suitable for both business and leisure travellers. Meals can be taken at the adjacent popular restaurant and bar, which is fully licensed. For further details, consult the Hotel Groups page.
**ROOMS:** 40 en suite

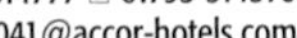

**⇧ Hotel Ibis Swindon**
ibis
Delta Business Park, Great Western Way SN5 7XG
☎ 01793 514777 📠 01793 514570
e-mail: H1041@accor-hotels.com
***Dir:*** *A3102 to Swindon, straight over rdbt, slip road onto Delta Business Park and turn left*
Modern, budget hotel offering comfortable accommodation in bright and practical bedrooms. Breakfast is self-service and dinner is available in the restaurant. For further details, consult the Hotel Groups page.
**ROOMS:** 120 en suite s £30-£42; d £30-£42 * **CONF:** Thtr 80 Class 40 Board 40

**○ Express by Holiday Inn Swindon West**

Express
by Holiday Inn
M4 Junction 16, Frankland Rd, Blagrove SN5 8UD
☎ 0870 9909690
A modern budget hotel offering comfortable accommodation in refreshing, spacious and comprehensively equipped bedrooms, en suite bathrooms with power showers and continental buffet breakfast included in the room rate. Suitable for business travellers or families. For further details and the Express by Holiday Inn phone number, consult the Hotel Groups page.

Express
Express

**ROOMS:** 118 en suite **NOTES:** Opened June 2001

SWINTON, Greater Manchester — Map 07 SD70

**⇧ *Premier Lodge (Manchester West)***
PREMIER LODGE
East Lancs Rd M27 8AA
☎ 0870 700 1472 📠 0870 700 1473
Premier Lodge offers modern, well-equipped, en suite accommodation suitable for both business and leisure travellers. Meals can be taken at the adjacent popular restaurant and bar, which is fully licensed. For further details, consult the Hotel Groups page.
**ROOMS:** 27 en suite

SYMONDS YAT (EAST), Herefordshire — Map 03 SO51

**★★66% *Saracens Head***
HR9 6JL
☎ 01600 890435 📠 01600 890034
e-mail: bookings@saracenshead.com
***Dir:*** *A40 Monmouth/Ross-on-Wye, turn off at Little Chef, signpost Goodrich & Symonds. 0.5m turn right, 1m fork right alongside River Wye to hotel*
This family-owned hostelry stands alongside the River Wye, at the heart of this renowned beauty spot. It provides traditionally furnished, well-equipped accommodation, the majority of the bedrooms have river views. In addition to the cosy residents' lounge, there is a very attractive dining room and a popular bar full of character.
**ROOMS:** 9 en suite (1 fmly) **FACILITIES:** Fishing Canoeing Mountain bike hire Walking Climbing Horse riding **PARKING:** 15 **NOTES:** No dogs (ex guide dogs) No smoking in restaurant **CARDS:**

*See advert on opposite page*

TADCASTER, North Yorkshire — Map 08 SE44

**★★★77% ❀❀ Hazlewood Castle**
Paradise Ln, Hazlewood LS24 9NJ
☎ 01937 535353 📠 01937 530630
e-mail: info@hazlewood-castle.co.uk
***Dir:*** *signposted off the A64, W of Tadcaster & before the A1/M1 link road*
Mentioned in the Domesday Book, this castle is set in 77 acres of parkland. Hospitality and service are of the highest order and staffs are only too happy to assist. Bedrooms, many of them with private sitting rooms, are split between the main house and other

*continued*

buildings in the courtyard. Dinner provides the highlight of any stay with eclectic, creative dishes.
**ROOMS:** 9 en suite 12 annexe en suite s £115-£195; d £175-£300 (incl. bkfst) * **LB** **FACILITIES:** STV Croquet lawn Clay pigeon shooting Xmas
**CONF:** Thtr 160 Class 60 Board 36 Del £170 * **PARKING:** 150
**NOTES:** No smoking in restaurant Civ Wed 120
**CARDS:**

## TADWORTH, Surrey — Map 04 TQ25

### *Premier Lodge*

PREMIER LODGE

Brighton Rd, Burgh Heath KT20 6BW
☎ 0870 700 1438 Fax 0870 700 1439
Premier Lodge offers modern, well-equipped, en suite accommodation suitable for both business and leisure travellers. Meals can be taken at the adjacent popular restaurant and bar, which is fully licensed. For further details, consult the Hotel Groups page.
**ROOMS:** 75 en suite

## TALKE, Staffordshire — Map 07 SJ85

### *Travelodge*

Newcastle Rd ST7 1UP
☎ 01782 777000 Fax 01782 777000
***Dir:*** *at junct of A34/A500*
Travelodge offers good quality, good value, modern accommodation. Ideal for families, the spacious, en suite bedrooms include remote-control TV, tea and coffee-making facilities, luxury beds and free morning newspaper. Meals can be taken at the nearby family restaurant. For further details and the Travelodge phone number, consult the Hotel Groups page.

**ROOMS:** 62 en suite **CONF:** Thtr 50 Class 25 Board 32

## TAMWORTH, Staffordshire — Map 07 SK20

### ★★72% *Drayton Court Hotel*

65 Coleshill St, Fazeley B78 3RG
☎ 01827 285805 Fax 01827 284842
***Dir:*** *M42 junct 9 then A446 to Litchfield. At next rdbt right onto A4091 after 2m Drayton Manor Park on left hotel further along on right*

Conveniently located close to the M42, this beautifully restored hotel has been lovingly refitted and upgraded. Accommodation is elegant, and thoughtfully equipped to suit both business and leisure guests. A four poster room is also available. Public areas include a panelled bar, a relaxing lounge and an attractive restaurant.
**ROOMS:** 19 en suite (3 fmly) **PARKING:** 22 **NOTES:** Closed 24-27 Dec
**CARDS:**

### ★★65% Globe Inn

Lower Gungate B79 7AW
☎ 01827 60455 Fax 01827 63575
***Dir:*** *follow signs Lower Gungate car park and shops, hotel is adjacent to car park*
Located in the centre of Tamworth, this popular inn provides well-equipped and modern accommodation. The recently refurbished public areas feature a spacious lounge bar and a relaxed dining area where a varied selection of dishes is available. There is a function room for up to 100 delegates and voucher parking adjacent to the hotel.
**ROOMS:** 18 en suite (2 fmly) No smoking in 2 bedrooms s £35-£45; d £40-£55 (incl. bkfst) * **LB** **FACILITIES:** STV entertainment Xmas
**CONF:** Class 90 Board 90 **NOTES:** No dogs (ex guide dogs) No smoking in restaurant **CARDS:**

### *Travelodge*

Green Ln B77 5PS
☎ Cen Res 0800 850950 Fax 01525 878450
***Dir:*** *A5/M42 junct 10*
Travelodge offers good quality, good value, modern accommodation. Ideal for families, the spacious, en suite bedrooms include remote-control TV, tea and coffee-making facilities, luxury beds and free morning newspaper. Meals can be taken at the nearby family restaurant. For further details and the Travelodge phone number, consult the Hotel Groups page.

**ROOMS:** 62 en suite

TANKERSLEY, South Yorkshire Map 08 SK39

**★★★69% Tankersley Manor**

MARSTON HOTELS

Church Ln S75 3DQ
☎ 01226 744700 📠 01226 745405
e-mail: info@tankersleymanor.co.uk
***Dir:*** *M1 junct 36 take A61 Sheffield road. Hotel 0.5m on left*

Dating back to the 17th century, this friendly and relaxing hotel offers formal dining, and a wide variety of bar meals in 'The Pub' with its log fires and old beams. The bedrooms, some with four-posters and one suitable for the less mobile, are modern and well-equipped. The purpose built conference centre, for up to 400 delegates, has all the latest equipment.

**ROOMS:** 70 en suite (2 fmly) No smoking in 63 bedrooms s £80-£110; d £90-£120 (incl. bkfst) * **FACILITIES:** STV special rates at local gym **CONF:** Thtr 400 Class 200 Board 50 Del from £95 * **PARKING:** 300 **NOTES:** No smoking in restaurant Civ Wed 120
**CARDS:**

*See advert under BARNSLEY*

TAPLOW, Buckinghamshire Map 04 SU98

## Premier Collection

**★★★★★ ®®® Cliveden**

SL6 0JF
☎ 01628 668561 📠 01628 661837
e-mail: reservations@clivedenhouse.co.uk

This wonderful stately home stands at the top of a gravelled boulevard. Visitors are treated as houseguests and staff recapture the tradition of fine hospitality. Bedrooms have a unique individual quality and style. Reception rooms enhance the timeless elegance of the house, and views from the Terrace Restaurant are delightful. For discreet, well-upholstered luxury, try Waldo's where menus have innovation and flair. Exceptional leisure facilities include cruises along Cliveden Reach and massages in the Pavilion.

**ROOMS:** 39 en suite No smoking in 12 bedrooms d £305-£385 * **LB FACILITIES:** Spa STV Indoor swimming (H) Outdoor swimming (H) Golf 18 Tennis (hard) Squash Snooker Sauna Solarium Gym Croquet lawn Jacuzzi Beauty treatments Boating ch fac Xmas **CONF:** Thtr 50 Board 24 Del from £325 * **SERVICES:** Lift **PARKING:** 60 **NOTES:** No smoking in restaurant Civ Wed 60
**CARDS:**

**★★★74% Taplow House Hotel**

Berry Hill SL6 0DA
☎ 01628 670056 📠 01628 773625
e-mail: taplow@wrensgroup.com
***Dir:*** *turn off A4 onto Berry Hill, hotel 0.5m on right*

Dating from 1598, this elegant Georgian manor has been beautifully restored and offers a high standard of accommodation. It boasts several air conditioned conference rooms, an elegant restaurant and a comfortable drawing room complete with an oak bar.

**ROOMS:** 34 en suite (4 fmly) No smoking in all bedrooms s £145-£300; d £175-£340 (incl. bkfst) * **LB FACILITIES:** STV Croquet lawn Putting green ch fac Xmas **CONF:** Thtr 100 Class 45 Board 40 Del from £185 * **SERVICES:** air con **PARKING:** 100 **NOTES:** No dogs (ex guide dogs) No smoking in restaurant Civ Wed 70
**CARDS:**

TARPORLEY, Cheshire Map 07 SJ56

**★★★67% The Wild Boar**

Whitchurch Rd, Beeston CW6 9NW
☎ 01829 260309 📠 01829 261081
***Dir:*** *turn off A51 Nantwich/Chester road onto A49 to Whitchurch at Red Fox pub traffic lights, hotel on left at brow of hill after about 1.5m*

Built in the 17th century as a hunting lodge, the Wild Boar is a black and white, half-timbered, Grade II listed building. Later extensions have resulted in spacious, comfortably furnished bedrooms, stylish bar and lounge areas and an intimate restaurant. There is a choice of meeting and function rooms and the hotel is popular for wedding receptions.

**ROOMS:** 37 en suite (20 fmly) No smoking in 23 bedrooms **FACILITIES:** Golf Putting green **CONF:** Thtr 100 Class 40 Board 40 Del from £100 * **NOTES:** No smoking in restaurant
**CARDS:**

*See advert under CHESTER*

TAUNTON, Somerset Map 03 ST22

## Premier Collection

**★★★ ®®® Castle**

Castle Green TA1 1NF
☎ 01823 272671 📠 01823 336066
e-mail: reception@the-castle-hotel.com
***Dir:*** *from M5 junct 25/26 follow signs to town centre and follow signs to Castle Hotel*

This hotel has been owned and run by the same family for over half a century. The wisteria covered Castle is a landmark in the centre of the town. Much thought has gone into furnishing the bedrooms and public areas, ensuring guest comfort whilst retaining the character of the original building. Renowned for their re-interpretation of many classic British

*continued*

T

dishes in the restaurant, this hotel also offers a lively, modern brasserie for less formal dining.

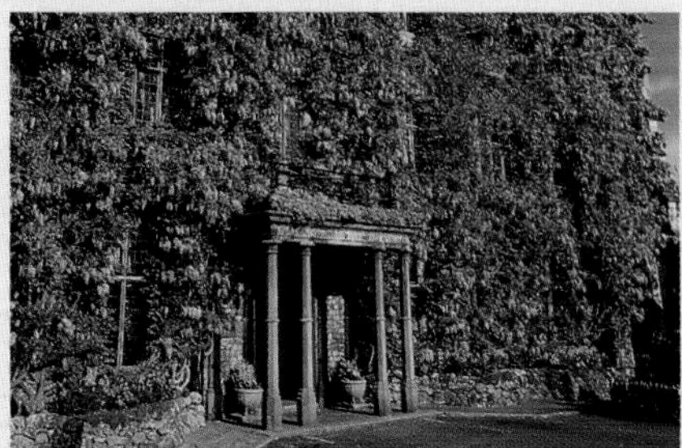

**ROOMS:** 44 en suite s £98-£120; d £150-£240 (incl. bkfst) * **FACILITIES:** STV Xmas **CONF:** Thtr 100 Class 40 Board 40 Del from £140 * **SERVICES:** Lift **PARKING:** 40 **NOTES:** No smoking in restaurant **CARDS:**

### ★★★75% The Mount Somerset

Henlade TA3 5NB
☎ 01823 442500 Fax 01823 442900
e-mail: Info@mountsomersethotel.co.uk
***Dir:*** *M5 junct 25, take A358 towards Chard/Ilminster, at Henlade right into Stoke Rd, left at T-junct at end Stoke Rd then right into drive*

Set in its own grounds this impressive Regency country house stands high on the edge of Stoke Hill with wonderful views of Taunton Vale. Bedrooms are well-appointed with wonderful beds and good facilities. The elegant public rooms have great style and intimacy. A pleasing, daily changing menu is served in the dining room.

**ROOMS:** 11 en suite No smoking in 6 bedrooms s £105; d £155 (incl. bkfst) **LB** **FACILITIES:** Arrangement with health club adjacent entertainment Xmas **CONF:** Thtr 50 Class 30 Board 20 Del from £140 * **SERVICES:** Lift **PARKING:** 100 **NOTES:** No dogs **CARDS:**

*See advert on this page*

### ★★★71% Rumwell Manor

Rumwell TA4 1EL
☎ 01823 461902 Fax 01823 254861
e-mail: reception@rumwellmanor.co.uk
***Dir:*** *leave M5 junct 26 follow signs to Wellington, turn onto A38 to Taunton, hotel is 2.5m on right*

Within easy access of the centre of Taunton and the M5, Rumwell Manor is situated in mellow Somerset countryside. An interesting selection of freshly prepared dishes is offered each evening in the candlelit restaurant. Bedrooms vary in size and style, with those in the main house offering greater space and character. In addition to the cosy bar and adjacent lounge, several meeting/conference rooms are available.

**ROOMS:** 10 en suite 10 annexe en suite (3 fmly) No smoking in 2 bedrooms s £59-£71; d £80-£95 * **LB** **FACILITIES:** ch fac Xmas **CONF:** Thtr 40 Class 24 Board 26 **PARKING:** 40 **NOTES:** No smoking in restaurant Civ Wed 50 **CARDS:**

### ★★★64% Posthouse Taunton

Posthouse

Deane Gate Av TA1 2UA
☎ 0870 400 9080 Fax 01823 332266
***Dir:*** *adjacent to junct 25 on M5*

Conveniently situated adjacent to junction 25 of the M5, this refurbished hotel is suitable for both business and leisure clientele. In addition to a range of meeting rooms, superb leisure facilities

*continued on p578*

TAUNTON, continued

are provided. The well-equipped bedrooms offer smart, modern accommodation, with a wide range of amenities.
**ROOMS:** 99 en suite (68 fmly) No smoking in 55 bedrooms s £89-£119; d £89-£119 * **LB** **FACILITIES:** STV Indoor swimming (H) Sauna Solarium Gym Jacuzzi Xmas **CONF:** Thtr 300 Class 110 Board 105 **SERVICES:** Lift **PARKING:** 300 **NOTES:** No smoking in restaurant Civ Wed **CARDS:**

**★★77% Farthings Hotel & Restaurant**
Hatch Beauchamp TA3 6SG
☎ 01823 480664 01823 481118
e-mail: farthing1@aol.com
***Dir:*** *from A358, between Taunton and Ilminster turn into Hatch Beauchamp, hotel in village centre*

In a quiet village location, this attractive Georgian hotel offers tastefully furnished and decorated bedrooms. In addition to the lounge bar, a comfortable sitting room is available for guests. A well-balanced choice of dishes is served in the dining rooms. A separate cottage is also available to rent.
**ROOMS:** 10 en suite (2 fmly) No smoking in all bedrooms s £64-£75; d £94-£104 (incl. bkfst) * **LB** **FACILITIES:** Croquet lawn Xmas **CONF:** Thtr 24 Class 18 Board 16 Del from £110 * **PARKING:** 22 **NOTES:** No dogs (ex guide dogs) No smoking in restaurant Civ Wed 61 **CARDS:**

**★★67% Corner House Hotel**
Park St TA1 4DQ
☎ 01823 284683 01823 323464
e-mail: res@corner-house.co.uk
***Dir:*** *0.3m from centre of Taunton (5 mins walk). Hotel on junct of Park Street & A38 Wellington Road*
Retaining many period features, this Victorian house is full of character and within easy walking distance of the town centre. Comfortable rooms have modern fittings and vary in size. A choice of freshly prepared dishes is offered in both the cosy bar and the more formal restaurant. The friendly staff create a relaxed atmosphere.
**ROOMS:** 33 rms (27 en suite) (4 fmly) s £38-£45; d £49 * **CONF:** Thtr 60 Class 60 Board 35 Del from £75 * **PARKING:** 42 **NOTES:** No dogs (ex guide dogs) No smoking in restaurant
**CARDS:**

*See advert on opposite page*

**★★64% Falcon**
Henlade TA3 5DH
☎ 01823 442502 01823 442670
***Dir:*** *M5 junct 25 1m E of A358 Taunton to Yeovil Road*
Minutes from the M5, this Victorian hotel is situated on the eastern side of the town and provides bedrooms of various sizes, all equipped with modern comforts. Particularly popular with business guests during the week; a convivial atmosphere prevails throughout the hotel.
**ROOMS:** 11 en suite (2 fmly) No smoking in 3 bedrooms s £50; d £65 (incl. bkfst) * **LB** **FACILITIES:** ch fac **CONF:** Thtr 50 Class 40 Board 40 Del from £83.50 * **PARKING:** 25 **CARDS:**

**⌂ *Express by Holiday Inn Taunton***

Express
by Holiday Inn

Blackbrook Park Av TA1 2RW
☎ 01823 624000 01823 624024
***Dir:*** *M5 junct25. Follow signs for Blackbrook Business Park. 100yds down on the right, just off rdbt at junct 25*

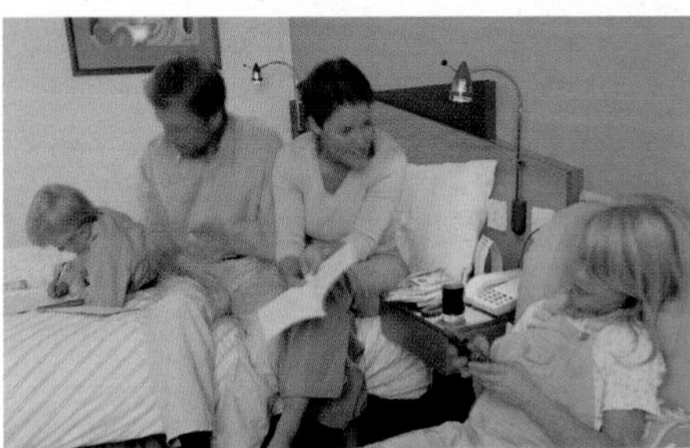

A modern budget hotel offering comfortable accommodation in refreshing, spacious and comprehensively equipped bedrooms, en suite bathrooms with power showers and continental buffet breakfast included in the room rate. Suitable for business travellers or families. For further details and the Express by Holiday Inn phone number, consult the Hotel Groups page.
**ROOMS:** 92 en suite **CONF:** Thtr 30 Class 15 Board 20

**⌂ Premier Lodge**
Ilminster Rd, Ruishton TA3 5LU
☎ 0870 700 1558 0870 700 1559
Premier Lodge offers modern, well-equipped, en suite accommodation suitable for both business and leisure travellers. Meals can be taken at the adjacent popular restaurant and bar, which is fully licensed. For further details, consult the Hotel Groups page.
**ROOMS:** 38 en suite s £42; d £42 *

**⌂ *Travelodge***

Travelodge

Herongate, Hankeridge Way, Riverside TA1 2LR
☎ 08700 850950
Travelodge offers good quality, good value, modern accommodation. Ideal for families, the spacious, en suite bedrooms include remote-control TV, tea and coffee-making facilities, luxury beds and free morning newspaper. Meals can be taken at the nearby family restaurant. For further details and the Travelodge phone number, consult the Hotel Groups page.

**ROOMS:** 50 en suite

**⌂ *Travelodge***
Riverside Retail Park, Hankridge Farm TA1 2LR
☎ 01823 444702
***Dir:*** *M5 junct 25*
Travelodge offers good quality, good value, modern accommodation. Ideal for families, the spacious, en suite bedrooms include remote-control TV, tea and coffee-making facilities, luxury beds and free morning newspaper. Meals can be taken at the nearby family restaurant. For further details and the Travelodge phone number, consult the Hotel Groups page.

**ROOMS:** 48 en suite

TAVISTOCK, Devon Map 02 SX47

**★★★71% ◎◎ *Browns Hotel & Brasserie***
80 West St PL19 8AQ
☎ 01822 618686 🖹 01822 618646
Browns has been the recent subject of an extensive renovation programme. Bedrooms are comfortable and well-equipped; the four Courtyard rooms are particularly well-presented. Guests can meet in the wine bar before enjoying a meal, brasserie style at lunchtime and a carte with a short fixed price menu during the evenings. Service is quietly relaxed, yet efficient.
**ROOMS:** 20 rms **FACILITIES:** no TV in bdrms

**★★★68% ◎◎ *Bedford***
1 Plymouth Rd PL19 8BB
☎ 01822 613221 🖹 01822 618034
***Dir:*** *M5 junct 31 - Launceston/Okehampton A30. Take A386 - Tavistock. On entering Tavistock follow signs for town centre. Hotel opposite church*

BEDFORD HOTEL

Built on the site of a Benedictine Abbey in 1820, the Bedford Hotel is an impressive, castellated building, situated in the town centre. The refurbished bedrooms are ideally equipped for both business and leisure guests, and public areas combine comfort with the hotel's abundant character. In the Woburn Restaurant, an imaginative and innovative, fixed-price menu is served, gaining a popular following locally.
**ROOMS:** 30 en suite (1 fmly) No smoking in 11 bedrooms **CONF:** Thtr 70 Class 45 Board 25 **PARKING:** 50 **NOTES:** No smoking in restaurant
**CARDS:**

TEBAY, Cumbria Map 12 NY60

**★★★71% ◎ Westmorland Hotel & Bretherdale Restaurant**
Orton CA10 3SB
☎ 015396 24351 🖹 015396 24354
e-mail: westmorlandhotel@aol.com
***Dir:*** *next to Westmorland's Tebay Services on the M6, easily reached from the southbound carriageway using the road linking the two service areas*
Convenient for Westmorland Services, this modern, friendly hotel benefits from breathtaking views over the beautiful Cumbrian countryside. Public areas are spacious and tastefully appointed, and local produce is used in the carefully prepared dishes served in the restaurant. Bedrooms are comfortable, well-equipped and include a choice of elegant executive or traditional family rooms.
**ROOMS:** 53 en suite (30 fmly) No smoking in 20 bedrooms s fr £51; d fr £61 (incl. bkfst) * **LB FACILITIES:** STV ch fac Xmas **CONF:** Thtr 80 Class 40 Board 30 Del from £90 * **SERVICES:** Lift **PARKING:** 100 **NOTES:** No smoking in restaurant Civ Wed 100
**CARDS:**

*See advert on this page*

CORNER HOUSE HOTEL

*Corner House Hotel, Taunton*

## TEES-SIDE AIRPORT, Co Durham
Map 08 NZ31

### ★★★64% *The St George*
Middleton St George, Darlington DL2 1RH
☎ 01325 332631 🖷 01325 333851
e-mail: bookings@stgeorgehotel.net.
***Dir:*** *turn off A67 bypass directly into Airport grounds*
This former wartime officers' mess is conveniently situated within walking distance of the airport terminal. Bedrooms are modern and well-equipped, and public areas are comfortable, with much flying memorabilia on display. Staff are friendly and professional and there are also versatile banqueting and conference facilities.
**ROOMS:** 59 en suite No smoking in 14 bedrooms **FACILITIES:** STV Sauna Solarium **CONF:** Thtr 160 Class 60 Board 50 **PARKING:** 100
**CARDS:**

### ○ Express by Holiday Inn Middlesbrough

Express
by Holiday Inn
Marton Rd TS4 3BS
☎ 01642 814444

A modern budget hotel offering comfortable accommodation in refreshing, spacious and comprehensively equipped bedrooms, en suite bathrooms with power showers and continental buffet breakfast included in the room rate. Suitable for business travellers or families. For further details and the Express by Holiday Inn phone number, consult the Hotel Groups page.
**ROOMS:** 74 en suite **NOTES:** Open now

## TEIGNMOUTH, Devon
Map 03 SX97

T

### ★★70% Ness House
Marine Dr, Shaldon TQ14 0HP
☎ 01626 873480 🖷 01626 873486
e-mail: nesshouse@talk21.com
***Dir:*** *from M5 take A380 turn onto A381 to Teignmouth, cross bridge to Shaldon, hotel 0.5m on left on Torquay Rd*
Overlooking the Teign Estuary, this Georgian house has kept its original character as a nobleman's summer residence. As an alternative to formal dining in the elegant restaurant, meals are also served in the bar and conservatory. Bedrooms are well-equipped, spacious and comfortable, many including a balcony and sea view.
**ROOMS:** 7 en suite 5 annexe en suite (2 fmly) No smoking in 4 bedrooms s £45-£69; d £79-£99 (incl. bkfst) * **LB** **FACILITIES:** ch fac Xmas **PARKING:** 20 **NOTES:** No smoking in restaurant Closed 24 & 25 Dec **CARDS:**

Popped the question? Hotels with Civ Wed in their entry are licensed for civil wedding ceremonies. Maximum numbers for the ceremony only are shown, e.g. Civ Wed 120

## TELFORD, Shropshire
Map 07 SJ60
see also Worfield

### ★★★★65% *Buckatree Hall*

MACDONALD
HOTELS
The Wrekin, Wellington TF6 5AL
☎ 01952 641821 🖷 01952 247540
***Dir:*** *M54 junct 7, turn left and left again for 1m*

Dating from 1820, this former hunting lodge is located in an extensive wooded estate on the slopes of the Wrekin. Bedrooms are well-equipped and have been furnished to a high standard. A suite is available, some rooms are inter-connecting, and some have balconies. Public rooms include function and conference facilities.
**ROOMS:** 60 en suite (3 fmly) No smoking in 4 bedrooms
**FACILITIES:** STV entertainment **CONF:** Thtr 200 Class 100 Board 60
**SERVICES:** Lift **PARKING:** 100 **NOTES:** No smoking in restaurant
**CARDS:**

### ★★★70% ❀❀ Valley
Best Western
TF8 7DW
☎ 01952 432247 🖷 01952 432308
e-mail: valley.hotel@ironbridge.fsnet.co.uk
***Dir:*** *M6, M54 junct 6 onto A5223 to Ironbridge*
This privately owned hotel is situated in attractive gardens, close to the famous iron bridge. It was once the home of a family who manufactured ceramic tiles, and fine examples of their craft are found throughout the house. Bedrooms vary in size and are split between the main house and a mews development. Bedrooms with four-poster beds and family bedded rooms are both available.
**ROOMS:** 35 en suite s £86-£95; d £98-£110 (incl. bkfst) * **LB**
**FACILITIES:** STV ch fac **CONF:** Thtr 200 Class 100 Board 60 Del from £100 * **PARKING:** 100 **NOTES:** No dogs (ex guide dogs) No smoking in restaurant RS 24 Dec-1 Jan Civ Wed 200
**CARDS:**

### ★★★69% Clarion Hotel Madely Court
Clarion Hotel
Castlefields Way, Madeley TF7 5DW
☎ 01952 680068 🖷 01952 684275
e-mail: admin@gb068.u-net.com
***Dir:*** *M54 junct 4, A4169 Telford, A442 at 2nd rdbt signs for Kidderminster, continue along (ignore sign to Madeley & Kidderminster) 1st left off rdbt*
This beautifully preserved 16th century manor house is set in extensive grounds and gardens, which contain a lake. Bedrooms are well-equipped and have modern comforts. Bedrooms on ground floor level and rooms with four-poster beds are both available. Facilities here include a choice of restaurants and a large self-contained banqueting suite.
**ROOMS:** 29 en suite 18 annexe en suite (1 fmly) No smoking in 6 bedrooms s £95-£120; d £110-£135 (incl. bkfst) * **LB** **FACILITIES:** STV Fishing Archery,Horse riding arranged ch fac Xmas **CONF:** Thtr 220 Class 150 Board 50 Del £149.50 * **PARKING:** 180 **NOTES:** No smoking in restaurant Civ Wed 190 **CARDS:**

### ★★★63% Telford Golf & Country Club

REGAL

Great Hay Dr, Sutton Heights TF7 4DT
☎ 01952 429977 🖷 01952 586602
**Dir:** *M54 junct 4, A442 - Kidderminster, follow signs for Telford Golf Club*

A modern and much extended former farmhouse in an elevated situation. Comfortable bedrooms are located in several different wings, some have fine views of Ironbridge Gorge and others overlook the golf course. Guests can choose to dine in the brasserie or the more informal café. Extensive facilities include the 18-hole golf course and large indoor swimming pool.
**ROOMS:** 96 en suite (16 fmly) No smoking in 36 bedrooms s £25-£100; d £40-£120 (incl. bkfst) * **LB FACILITIES: Spa** Indoor swimming (H) Golf 18 Squash Snooker Sauna Solarium Gym Putting green Jacuzzi Health & Beauty Golf driving range entertainment Xmas **CONF:** Thtr 250 Class 140 Board 60 Del from £85 * **PARKING:** 200 **NOTES:** No smoking in restaurant Civ Wed 250
**CARDS:**

### ★★68% White House

Wellington Rd, Muxton TF2 8NG
☎ 01952 604276 & 603603 🖷 01952 670336
e-mail: james@whhotel.co.uk
**Dir:** *off A518 Telford-Stafford road*
The White House is a friendly family-run hotel which provides well-equipped modern accommodation. The attractive public areas offer a choice of bars and a very pleasant restaurant, where a wide range of dishes is available. There is also a small lounge for residents, and a beer garden.
**ROOMS:** 32 en suite (3 fmly) s £50-£63; d £65-£75 (incl. bkfst) * **LB CONF:** Board 10 **PARKING:** 100 **CARDS:**

### ★★63% Arleston Inn

Arleston Ln, Wellington TF1 2LA
☎ 01952 501881 🖷 01952 506429
**Dir:** *M54 junct 6 take A5223 Ironbridge road, 4th exit at next rdbt past Lawley School right into Arleston Lane*
This small privately owned and personally run hotel is conveniently located for access to the M54 and Telford centre. The well-maintained accommodation has modern furnishings and equipment. Apart from the bar, there is a conservatory lounge, which overlooks the lovely garden, and a popular restaurant where a good choice of dishes is available.
**ROOMS:** 7 en suite s £40; d £50 (incl. bkfst) * **FACILITIES:** Xmas **PARKING:** 40 **NOTES:** No dogs (ex guide dogs) No smoking in restaurant **CARDS:**

Early start? Hotels at all star levels should provide in-room alarm clocks and/or alarm calls.

### ⇧ *Travelodge*

Travelodge

Whitchurch Dr, Shawbirch TF1 3QA
☎ 01952 251244 🖷 01952 251244
**Dir:** *1m NW, on A5223*
Travelodge offers good quality, good value, modern accommodation. Ideal for families, the spacious, en suite bedrooms include remote-control TV, tea and coffee-making facilities, luxury beds and free morning newspaper. Meals can be taken at the nearby family restaurant. For further details and the Travelodge phone number, consult the Hotel Groups page.

**ROOMS:** 40 en suite

## TEMPLE SOWERBY, Cumbria — Map 12 NY62

### ★★★71% ❀ Temple Sowerby House

CA10 1RZ
☎ 017683 61578 🖷 017683 61958
e-mail: stay@temple-sowerby.com
**Dir:** *midway between Penrith and Appleby, 7m from M6 junct 40*
Formerly the principal residence of the village, this delightful country hotel has a relaxed atmosphere. The bedrooms are individual, with both traditional and modern furnishings, many just recently upgraded. The restaurant is a particularly pleasant venue for dinner, with its low beams and candlelight, and food prepared with both care and skill. Staff are well-trained and very friendly.
**ROOMS:** 9 en suite 4 annexe en suite (2 fmly) s £68-£75; d £98-£120 (incl. bkfst) * **LB FACILITIES:** Croquet lawn ch fac **CONF:** Thtr 30 Class 20 Board 20 Del £120 * **PARKING:** 15 **NOTES:** No smoking in restaurant **CARDS:**

TENBURY WELLS, Worcestershire Map 07 SO56

### ★★66% *Cadmore Lodge*

Berrington Green, St Michaels WR15 8TQ
☎ 01584 810044 01584 810044
e-mail: info@cadmorelodge.demon.co.uk
***Dir:*** *on A4112 from Tenbury Wells to Leominster, turn right at St Michael's Church, signposted to Cadmore Lodge, hotel 0.75m on left*

This modern hotel is situated a short distance from Tenbury Wells in a secluded location on a 70-acre private estate that features a 9-hole golf course, two fishing lakes and indoor leisure facilities. The traditionally furnished bedrooms have modern facilities and a large function room, with lake views, is a popular venue for special occasions.
**ROOMS:** 14 en suite (1 fmly) No smoking in all bedrooms
**FACILITIES:** Indoor swimming (H) Golf 9 Tennis (hard) Fishing Gym Jacuzzi Bowling green Steam room **CONF:** Thtr 100 Class 40 Board 30
**PARKING:** 60 **NOTES:** No dogs No smoking in restaurant
**CARDS:**

*See advert on page 581*

TENTERDEN, Kent Map 05 TQ83

### ★★★74% London Beach Hotel & Golf Club

Ashford Rd TN30 6SP
☎ 01580 766279 01580 766681
e-mail: enquiries@londonbeach.com
***Dir:*** *M20 junct 9, follow signs to Tenterden on A28, turn right after 0.5, hotel after 1m*
Privately owned hotel situated in a rural location. The bedrooms are generous in proportion, have quality fabrics and furnishings and many useful extras. In addition they all have balconies with seating that overlook the putting green and golf course. An imaginative menu is offered in the brasserie style restaurant.
**ROOMS:** 28 en suite No smoking in 24 bedrooms s £65-£95; d £95-£130 LB **FACILITIES:** STV Golf 9 Fishing Putting green entertainment Xmas **CONF:** Thtr 200 Class 100 Board 40 Del from £125 * **SERVICES:** Lift **PARKING:** 200 **NOTES:** No dogs (ex guide dogs) No smoking in restaurant Civ Wed 200 **CARDS:**

TETBURY, Gloucestershire Map 03 ST89

## *Premier Collection*

### ★★★ Calcot Manor

Calcot GL8 8YJ
☎ 01666 890391 01666 890394
e-mail: reception@calcotmanor.co.uk
***Dir:*** *4m West of Tetbuty W at junct A4135/A46*
With a 14th-century tithe barn amongst its outbuildings, Calcot Manor retains much of its original charm. This beautiful country house offers elegant and relaxing sitting rooms where log fires burn in the winter, and a bright, stylish restaurant. The cooking is imaginative with a Mediterranean bias and good robust flavours. Children are made welcome with some specially designed family rooms and a superb playroom. The Gumstool bar offers informal dining in a country pub atmosphere.

**ROOMS:** 8 en suite 20 annexe en suite (10 fmly) s fr £120; d £135-£185 (incl. bkfst) * LB **FACILITIES:** Outdoor swimming (H) Croquet lawn Clay pigeon shooting ch fac Xmas **CONF:** Thtr 60 Class 40 Board 35 Del from £165 * **PARKING:** 150 **NOTES:** No dogs (ex guide dogs) No smoking in restaurant Civ Wed 90
**CARDS:**

### ★★★77% *Close*

8 Long St GL8 8AQ
☎ 01666 502272 01666 504401
***Dir:*** *M4 junct 17 onto A429 to Malmesbury, Tetbury signposted from here. M5 junct 14 onto B4509 follow signs to Tetbury*
With a genuine country house feel to it The Close has been a favourite with many for years. Bedrooms are decorated and furnished with an air of luxury and include many thoughtful touches. The public rooms provide a range of relaxing areas to sit and take refreshment, including the terrace in the lovely walled garden. As well as the brasserie, the main restaurant is the venue for some impressive, modern British cooking from Chef Daren Bale.
**ROOMS:** 15 en suite **FACILITIES:** STV Croquet lawn **CONF:** Thtr 50 Board 22 **PARKING:** 22 **NOTES:** No smoking in restaurant Civ Wed 50
**CARDS:**

### ★★★73% *Snooty Fox*

Market Place GL8 8DD
☎ 01666 502436 01666 503479
e-mail: res@snooty-fox.co.uk
***Dir:*** *in the centre of the town, by market place*
A popular venue for weekend breaks, this hospitable, longstanding hotel has an enviable number of regular guests. Its attractions are the historic features one expects from a 16th-century coaching inn combined with the high levels of comfort and quality. Staff are friendly.
**ROOMS:** 12 en suite **FACILITIES:** STV **CONF:** Thtr 30 Board 15
**NOTES:** No dogs (ex guide dogs) No smoking in restaurant
**CARDS:**

Packed in a hurry? Ironing facilities should be available at all star levels, either in rooms or on request.

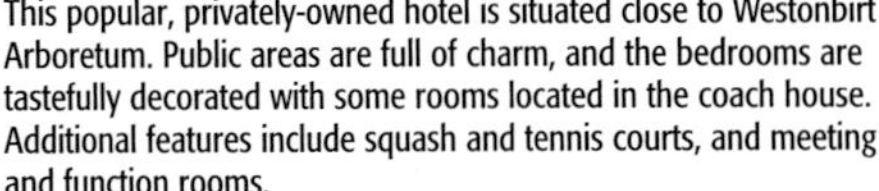

**★★★68% Hare & Hounds**
Westonbirt GL8 8QL
☎ 01666 880233 🖷 01666 880241
e-mail: hareandhoundswbt@aol.com
***Dir:*** *2.5m SW of Tetbury on A433*
This popular, privately-owned hotel is situated close to Westonbirt Arboretum. Public areas are full of charm, and the bedrooms are tastefully decorated with some rooms located in the coach house. Additional features include squash and tennis courts, and meeting and function rooms.
**ROOMS:** 24 en suite 7 annexe en suite (3 fmly) No smoking in 12 bedrooms s £68-£88; d £75-£120 * **LB** **FACILITIES:** **Spa** Tennis (hard) Squash Croquet lawn Table tennis Xmas **CONF:** Thtr 120 Class 80 Board 30 **PARKING:** 85 **CARDS:**

## TEWKESBURY, Gloucestershire — Map 03 SO83

**★★★71% Tewkesbury Park Hotel**
Lincoln Green Ln GL20 7DN
☎ 01684 295405 🖷 01684 292386
e-mail: tewkesburypark@corushotels.com
***Dir:*** *M5 junct 9 take A438 through Tewkesbury onto A38 passing Abbey on left, turn right into Lincoln Green Lane before Esso Station*
An extended 18th-century mansion with fine views over the Vale of Evesham and River Severn. There is a fully equipped leisure centre and an 18-hole golf course in the grounds. A choice of dining areas and a number of function rooms are available.
**ROOMS:** 78 en suite (12 fmly) No smoking in 35 bedrooms **FACILITIES:** STV Indoor swimming (H) Golf 18 Tennis (hard) Squash Sauna Solarium Gym Putting green Jacuzzi Activity field Xmas **CONF:** Thtr 160 Class 90 Board 60 **PARKING:** 250 **NOTES:** Civ Wed 100 **CARDS:**

**★★★65% *Bell***
57 Church St GL20 5SA
☎ 01684 293293 🖷 01684 295938
***Dir:*** *on A38 in town centre opposite Abbey*
This 14th-century former coaching house is on the edge of town, opposite the Norman Abbey. Bedrooms are comfortably furnished and feature thoughtful extras. Open plan public areas are bright and inviting and include a popular restaurant.
**ROOMS:** 25 en suite (1 fmly) No smoking in 5 bedrooms **CONF:** Thtr 40 Class 15 Board 20 **PARKING:** 35 **NOTES:** No smoking in restaurant RS 25 Dec & 1 Jan **CARDS:**

**★★★58% Royal Hop Pole**
Church St GL20 5RT
☎ 01684 293236 🖷 01684 296680
***Dir:*** *M5 junct 9 head for Tewkesbury approx 1.5m. At War Memorial rdbt straight across Hotel is on the right*
Dating back to the 14th century, this former coaching inn is located in the very heart of this picturesque town. The hotel retains many original features including sloping floors and exposed beams. Bedrooms are located either in the main house or the more modern garden wing, there is also a four-poster room.
**ROOMS:** 24 en suite 5 annexe en suite (1 fmly) No smoking in 14 bedrooms s £75-£95; d £84-£104 * **LB** **FACILITIES:** Xmas **CONF:** Thtr 50 Class 25 Board 20 Del from £99 * **PARKING:** 30 **NOTES:** No smoking in restaurant **CARDS:**

> Late for dinner? Quality Standards star rating means that last orders for dinner should be no earlier than:
> ★ 6.30pm ★★ 7.00pm ★★★ 8.00pm
> ★★★★ 9.00pm ★★★★★ 10.00pm

## THAME, Oxfordshire — Map 04 SP70

**★★★76% Spread Eagle**
Cornmarket OX9 2BW
☎ 01844 213661 🖷 01844 261380
e-mail: enquiries@spreadeaglehotel.fsnet.co.uk
***Dir:*** *town centre on A418 Oxford to Aylesbury Road, M40 junct 6 south junct 8 north*
This popular hotel is situated in the centre of the market town of Thame and is conveniently placed for the M40 and Oxford. Family run for over thirty years a warm and friendly welcome can be expected from the hosts and their staff. Accommodation varies in size and style from bedrooms in the main house to rooms in the recently built extension. A traditional restaurant offers a wide selection of interesting dishes. Extensive Banqueting facilities are available.
**ROOMS:** 33 en suite (1 fmly) s £96-£111; d £111-£131 (incl. cont bkfst) * **LB** **FACILITIES:** Xmas **CONF:** Thtr 250 Class 100 Board 50 Del from £139.95 * **PARKING:** 80 **NOTES:** No dogs (ex guide dogs) Closed 28-30 Dec Civ Wed 200 **CARDS:**

**⇧ *Travelodge***
OX9 3XD
☎ 01844 218740 🖷 01844 218740
***Dir:*** *A418/B4011*
Travelodge offers good quality, good value, modern accommodation. Ideal for families, the spacious, en suite bedrooms include remote-control TV, tea and coffee-making facilities, luxury beds and free morning newspaper. Meals can be taken at the nearby family restaurant. For further details and the Travelodge phone number, consult the Hotel Groups page.

**ROOMS:** 31 en suite

## THAXTED, Essex — Map 05 TL63

**★★72% Four Seasons**
Walden Rd CM6 2RE
☎ 01371 830129 🖷 01371 830835
e-mail: reservations@thefourseasons.fsnet.co.uk
***Dir:*** *0.5m N on the B184 at the junction with the B1051 Gt Sampford/Haverhill road*
A non-smoking, privately owned hotel set in two acres of attractive grounds within easy driving distance of Stanstead Airport. The tastefully decorated bedrooms are well laid out and feature a thoughtful range of useful extras. Public areas include the informal Grill Room as well as a more formal restaurant; guests also have the use of a quiet first floor lounge. An added advantage for guests using Stansted Airport is free parking for 14 days.
**ROOMS:** 9 en suite No smoking in all bedrooms s £55-£65; d £65-£75 * **LB** **CONF:** Thtr 70 Class 60 Board 40 **PARKING:** 60 **NOTES:** No dogs No children 12yrs No smoking in restaurant **CARDS:**

## THEALE, Berkshire — Map 04 SU67

**⇧ *Travelodge (Westbound)***
Burghfield RG30 3UQ
☎ 0118 956 6966
***Dir:*** *M4 between junc 11&12*
Travelodge offers good quality, good value, modern accommodation. Ideal for families, the spacious, en suite bedrooms include remote-control TV, tea and coffee-making facilities, luxury beds and free morning newspaper. Meals can be taken at the nearby family restaurant. For further details and the Travelodge phone number, consult the Hotel Groups page.
**ROOMS:** 40 en suite

THETFORD, Norfolk Map 05 TL88
see also Mundford & Brandon (Suffolk)

**★★65% *The Anchor Hotel***
Bridge St IP24 3AE
☎ 01842 763925 01842 766873
e-mail: anchor@norfolk-hotels.co.uk
***Dir:*** *leave A11 at Bury St Edmunds turn. Cross traffic lights, then left into Bridge Street. Hotel on right*
Close to the river, and within easy walking distance of the town centre. Built as a coaching inn in the mid-1700s, the hotel offers comfortable bedrooms with attractive pine furniture. A wide range of bar snacks is available; or dine in the High Seas Restaurant which has daily-changing and carte menus.
**ROOMS:** 16 en suite **FACILITIES:** entertainment **CONF:** Thtr 180 Class 120 Board 60 **PARKING:** 60 **NOTES:** No dogs (ex guide dogs) RS 24-25 Dec **CARDS:**

**★★65% The Thomas Paine Hotel**
White Hart St IP24 1AA
☎ 01842 755631 01842 766505
e-mail: thomaspainehotel@hotmail.com
***Dir:*** *heading N on the A11, at rdbt immediately before Thetford take A1075, the hotel is on the right hand side as you approach the town*
Close to the town centre, this popular hotel extends a friendly welcome and offers spacious public rooms and a choice of eating options in the open-plan bar and more formal restaurant. The bedrooms vary in size but all offer character and comfort.
**ROOMS:** 13 en suite (1 fmly) s £48-£53; d £60-£66 (incl. bkfst) * **LB** **FACILITIES:** Xmas **CONF:** Thtr 70 Class 35 Board 30 Del from £55 * **PARKING:** 30 **NOTES:** No smoking in restaurant
**CARDS:**

THIRSK, North Yorkshire Map 08 SE48

**★★72% Sheppard's**
Church Farm, Front St, Sowerby YO7 1JF
☎ 01845 523655 01845 524720
e-mail: sheppards@thirskny.freeserve.co.uk
***Dir:*** *take A61 Ripon road from Market Sq, at mini rdbt turn left towards Sowerby. Hotel on right 0.25m along Sowerby road*
Set in the village suburb of Sowerby, this hotel has evolved from original granary and stable buildings, grouped around a courtyard. Its restaurant and bistro offer an excellent range of dishes. The attractive bedrooms are decorated in cottage style and furnished with stripped pine.
**ROOMS:** 8 en suite No smoking in all bedrooms s fr £62; d fr £84 (incl. bkfst) **LB** **CONF:** Thtr 80 Class 40 Board 30 **PARKING:** 30 **NOTES:** No dogs No children 10yrs No smoking in restaurant Closed 1st wk Jan
**CARDS:**

**★★70% Golden Fleece**
42 Market Place YO7 1LL
☎ 01845 523108 01845 523996
e-mail: goldenfleece@bestwestern.co.uk
***Dir:*** *off A19 at Thirsk, proceed to the town centre, Hotel is situated on the southern edge of Market Place*
This delightful old coaching inn, once the haunt of Dick Turpin, lies behind a Queen Anne facade in the market square. It offers modern well equipped bedrooms, a cosy bar and a restaurant which provides a good choice of dishes. Friendly and attentive service is provided by a dedicated staff.
**ROOMS:** 18 en suite (3 fmly) s £48-£65; d £60-£105 (incl. bkfst) * **LB** **FACILITIES:** STV ch fac Xmas **CONF:** Thtr 100 Class 40 Board 40 Del from £80 * **PARKING:** 50 **NOTES:** No smoking in restaurant Civ Wed 100 **CARDS:**

**★★62% *Three Tuns Hotel***
Market Place YO7 1LH
☎ 01845 523124 01845 526126
e-mail: threetuns@talk21.com
***Dir:*** *directly on A19, A61, 6m from A1 on A168 & A61*
This imposing Georgian hotel stands in the corner of the Market Square and offers pleasantly furnished bedrooms. There is a wide variety of well-produced food available.
**ROOMS:** 10 en suite (3 fmly) No smoking in all bedrooms **CONF:** Thtr 50 Board 35 **PARKING:** 52 **NOTES:** No smoking in restaurant
**CARDS:**

THORNBURY, Gloucestershire Map 03 ST69

## *Premier Collection*

**★★★ Thornbury Castle**
Castle St BS35 1HH
☎ 01454 281182 01454 416188
e-mail: thornburycastle@compuserve.com
***Dir:*** *on A38 travelling N from Bristol take the first turning to Thornbury. At end of the High St left into Castle St, follow brown sign, entrance to Castle on left behind St Marys church*
Located in its own splendid grounds, guests at this Tudor castle have included Henry VIII, Anne Boleyn and Mary Tudor. Modern day visitors have the unrivalled opportunity to sleep in the same historic rooms. Now a fine country house hotel, its sumptuous handmade furnishings combine with modern comforts to create a truly luxurious atmosphere with history at every turn. Service is professional, and the galleried dining rooms make a memorable setting for some enjoyable meals.
**ROOMS:** 24 en suite (1 fmly) s £85-£105; d £130-£400 (incl. cont bkfst) * **LB** **FACILITIES:** **Spa** STV Croquet lawn Hot air ballooning Archery Xmas **CONF:** Thtr 90 Class 40 Board 30 **PARKING:** 40 **NOTES:** No dogs (ex guide dogs) No smoking in restaurant Closed 4 days Jan Civ Wed 50 **CARDS:**

**★★67% Thornbury Golf Lodge**
Bristol Rd BS35 3XL
☎ 01454 281144 01454 281177
***Dir:*** *from junct of M4/M5 take A38 N. At traffic lights (Berkeley Vale Motors) take left. Entrance 1m on left*
The old farmhouse exterior of Thornbury Golf Lodge disguises a completely refurbished interior with spacious and comfortable bedrooms, all well-equipped and attractively decorated. Many include pleasant views over the Centre's two golf courses or towards the Severn Estuary. Meals are taken in the adjacent golf clubhouse which features a full bar and a range of hot and cold food served all day.
**ROOMS:** 11 en suite s fr £46; d fr £46 * **LB** **FACILITIES:** STV Golf 36 Putting green **CONF:** Thtr 100 Class 40 Board 40 Del from £200 * **PARKING:** 150 **NOTES:** No dogs (ex guide dogs) No children 5yrs
**CARDS:**

## THORNE, South Yorkshire
Map 08 SE61

### ★★71% Belmont

Horsefair Green DN8 5EE
☎ 01405 812320 📠 01405 740508
e-mail: belmonthotel@cs.com

***Dir:*** *M18 exit 6 A614 signed Thorne. Hotel is on the right of the Market Place*

This pleasantly furnished town centre hotel offers well-equipped bedrooms together with newly refurbished and comfortable public rooms. A wide range of dishes are available either in the bar or restaurant.

**ROOMS:** 23 en suite (3 fmly) No smoking in 5 bedrooms s £63-£68; d £78-£99 (incl. bkfst) * **LB** **FACILITIES:** STV Putting green entertainment ch fac Xmas **CONF:** Thtr 60 Class 20 Board 25 Del from £69.95 * **PARKING:** 30 **NOTES:** Closed 24 - 28 Dec
**CARDS:**

## THORNHAM, Norfolk
Map 09 TF74

### ★★67% Lifeboat Inn

Ship Ln PE36 6LT
☎ 01485 512236 📠 01485 512323
e-mail: reception@lifeboatinn.co.uk

***Dir:*** *follow coast road from Hunstanton A149 for approx 6m and take first left after Thornham sign*

This 16th-century ale house enjoys relaxing views over open meadows to the distant horizon of Thornham Harbour and the sea beyond. The attractive bedrooms are well equipped and tastefully furnished. The popular bar and restaurant provide a wide choice of tempting meals.

**ROOMS:** 13 en suite (3 fmly) No smoking in all bedrooms s £49-£60; d £84-£90 (incl. bkfst) * **LB** **FACILITIES:** Xmas **CONF:** Thtr 50 Class 30 Board 30 **PARKING:** 120 **NOTES:** No smoking in restaurant
**CARDS:**

## THORNTON HOUGH, Merseyside
Map 07 SJ38

### ★★★70% Thornton Hall

Best Western

Neston Rd CH63 1JF
☎ 0151 336 3938 📠 0151 336 7864
e-mail: thorntonhallhotel@btinternet.com

***Dir:*** *M53 junct 4 take B5151 Neston onto B5136 to Thornton Hough*

Lying in several acres of mature grounds in a delightful village this country house was built in the 18th century by a shipping magnate. The hall still features its original stained glass windows and impressive oak panelling. Bedrooms are spacious, with good facilities. An impressive leisure centre is now part of the complex.

**ROOMS:** 63 en suite (6 fmly) No smoking in 12 bedrooms s £65-£90; d £75-£100 (incl. bkfst) * **LB** **FACILITIES:** Spa STV Indoor swimming (H) Tennis (grass) Sauna Solarium Gym Croquet lawn Putting green Jacuzzi Hot tub, Beauty Spa **CONF:** Thtr 180 Class 100 Board 60 Del from £130 * **PARKING:** 250 **NOTES:** Civ Wed
**CARDS:**

## THORNTON WATLASS, North Yorkshire
Map 08 SE28

### ★69% Buck Inn

HG4 4AH
☎ 01677 422461 📠 01677 422447
e-mail: buckwatlass@btconnect.com

***Dir:*** *A684 towards Bedale, B6268 towards Masham, after 2m turn right at crossroads to Thornton Watlass, the Hotel is situated by the Cricket Green*

This welcoming country inn is situated on the edge of the village green overlooking the cricket pitch. Old photographs are a feature of the small dining room and an open fire in the bar adds to the warm and intimate atmosphere. There is an excellent choice of dishes from an extensive menu. Bedrooms are brightly decorated, some overlook the green, others the sheltered garden at the back.

**ROOMS:** 7 rms (5 en suite) (1 fmly) s £36-£45; d £55-£60 (incl. bkfst) * **LB** **FACILITIES:** Spa Fishing Quoits Childrens play area entertainment **CONF:** Thtr 70 Class 40 Board 30 Del from £70 * **PARKING:** 10 **NOTES:** No smoking in restaurant **CARDS:**



## THORPE (DOVEDALE), Derbyshire
Map 07 SK15

### ★★★73% Izaak Walton

DE6 2AY
☎ 01335 350555 📠 01335 350539
e-mail: reception@izaakwalton-hotel.com

***Dir:*** *leave A515 on B5054, follow road to Thorpe village, continue straight through over cattle grids & 2 small bridges, take 1st right & sharp left*

This hotel is peacefully situated, with magnificent views over the valley of Dovedale to Thorpe Cloud. Many of the bedrooms have lovely views, and 'executive' rooms are particularly spacious. Meals are served in the bar area, with more formal dining in the Haddon restaurant. Staff are friendly and efficient. Fishing on the River Dove can be arranged.

**ROOMS:** 30 en suite (4 fmly) No smoking in 24 bedrooms s £85-£125; d £110-£150 (incl. bkfst) * **LB** **FACILITIES:** Fishing Fly fishing Xmas **CONF:** Thtr 50 Class 40 Board 30 Del from £118 * **PARKING:** 80 **NOTES:** No smoking in restaurant Civ Wed 70
**CARDS:**

Packed in a hurry? Ironing facilities should be available at all star levels, either in rooms or on request.

T

THORPE (DOVEDALE), continued

**★★★66% The Peveril of the Peak**
DE6 2AW
☎ 0870 400 8109 01335 350507
***Dir:*** *from M1 junct 25, A52 towards Ashbourne then A515 towards Buxton for 1m to Thorpe. From M6 junct15/16, A50 to Stoke then A515 to Ashbourne and Thorpe*
Situated in the picture book scenery of Dovedale, this hotel is named after one of Sir Walter Scott's heroic novels. Most of the bedrooms have doors opening on to the gardens, while the rest have individual patios. Some rooms have been adapted for disabled guests. There is a cosy cocktail bar, a comfortable lounge and an attractive restaurant which overlooks the gardens. Conference and meeting rooms are also available.
**ROOMS:** 46 en suite (2 fmly) No smoking in 20 bedrooms s fr £85; d fr £95 * **LB** **FACILITIES:** Tennis (hard) Xmas **CONF:** Thtr 70 Class 30 Board 36 Del from £97.50 * **PARKING:** 65 **NOTES:** No smoking in restaurant **CARDS:**

THORPE MARKET, Norfolk — Map 09 TG23

**★★74% Elderton Lodge**
Gunton Park NR11 8TZ
☎ 01263 833547 01263 834673
e-mail: enquiries@eldertonlodge.co.uk
***Dir:*** *at N Walsham take A149 towards Cromer, the hotel is approx. 3m out of North Walsham on left, just prior to entering Thorpe Market village*
Former shooting lodge situated amidst six acres of mature gardens adjacent to Gunton Hall estate. The property was once frequented by Edward VII and is an ideal place to visit when touring the Norfolk coastline. The individually decorated bedrooms are tastefully furnished and thoughtfully equipped. Public rooms include a smart lounge bar, an elegant restaurant and a sunny conservatory breakfast room.
**ROOMS:** 11 en suite No smoking in all bedrooms s £60-£70; d £95-£115 (incl. bkfst) * **LB** **FACILITIES:** Croquet lawn Xmas **CONF:** Thtr 30 Class 30 Board 16 Del from £120 * **PARKING:** 50 **NOTES:** No children 8yrs No smoking in restaurant **CARDS:**

THRAPSTON, Northamptonshire — Map 04 SP97

***Travelodge***
Thrapston Bypass NN14 4UR
☎ 01832 735199 01832 735199
***Dir:*** *on A14 link road A1/M1*
Travelodge offers good quality, good value, modern accommodation. Ideal for families, the spacious, en suite bedrooms include remote-control TV, tea and coffee-making facilities, luxury beds and free morning newspaper. Meals can be taken at the nearby family restaurant. For further details and the Travelodge phone number, consult the Hotel Groups page.

**ROOMS:** 40 en suite

THRUSSINGTON, Leicestershire — Map 08 SK61

***Travelodge***
LE7 8TF
☎ 01664 424525 01664 424525
***Dir:*** *on A46, southbound*
Travelodge offers good quality, good value, modern accommodation. Ideal for families, the spacious, en suite bedrooms include remote-control TV, tea and coffee-making facilities, luxury beds and free morning newspaper. Meals can be taken at the nearby family restaurant. For further details and the Travelodge phone number, consult the Hotel Groups page.

**ROOMS:** 32 en suite

THURLESTONE, Devon — Map 03 SX64

**★★★★72% Thurlestone**
TQ7 3NN
☎ 01548 560382 01548 561069
e-mail: enquires@thurlestone.co.uk
***Dir:*** *A38 take A384 into Totnes, A381 towards Kingsbridge, onto A379 towards Churchstow, onto B3197 turn into lane signposted to Thurlestone*
This family-owned hotel affords fabulous views of the South Devon coast from its stunning location in beautifully kept grounds. Superb leisure facilities are among the hotel's many attractions, in addition to entertainment, which is provided during the summer months. Bedrooms, all very well-equipped, now include many popular suites. The majority benefit from sea views, some have balconies. Stylish public rooms include a no smoking lounge and great outdoor bar terrace.
**ROOMS:** 64 en suite (20 fmly) s £39-£125; d £78-£250 (incl. bkfst) * **LB** **FACILITIES:** Indoor swimming (H) Outdoor swimming (H) Golf 9 Tennis (hard) Squash Snooker Sauna Solarium Gym Croquet lawn Putting green Jacuzzi Games rm Badminton Beauty fitness entertainment ch fac Xmas **CONF:** Thtr 140 Class 100 Board 40 Del from £90 * **SERVICES:** Lift **PARKING:** 121 **NOTES:** No smoking in restaurant **CARDS:**

*See advert on opposite page*

TICEHURST, East Sussex — Map 05 TQ63

**★★★★68% Dale Hill Hotel & Golf Club**
TN5 7DQ
☎ 01580 200112 01580 201249
e-mail: info@dalehill.co.uk
***Dir:*** *situated on B2087 1.25m off A21*
Ideally suited to leisure guests as well as golfers, this impressive, modern hotel offers spacious bedrooms, good leisure facilities and elegant public rooms. The conservatory brasserie serves light meals all day and the formal restaurant overlooks the 18th green. Guests can relax in the lounge bar or enjoy the clubby atmosphere of Spikes Bar.
**ROOMS:** 26 en suite (6 fmly) s £70-£100; d £80-£140 (incl. bkfst) * **LB** **FACILITIES:** Spa STV Indoor swimming (H) Golf 36 Sauna Gym Putting green ch fac Xmas **CONF:** Thtr 60 Class 40 Board 40 Del from £120 * **SERVICES:** Lift **PARKING:** 220 **NOTES:** Civ Wed 100 **CARDS:**

TINTAGEL, Cornwall & Isles of Scilly — Map 02 SX08

**★★78% Trebrea Lodge**
Trenale PL34 0HR
☎ 01840 770410 01840 770092
e-mail: trebrea-lodge@supanet.com
***Dir:*** *from A39 take Tintagel sign about 1m before Tintagel turn into Trenale*
With stunning views over Tintagel to the Cornish coastline in the distance, this charming property is decorated and furnished in keeping with the period in which it was built . Set in four acres of grounds, mainly at the rear of the property, Trebrea Lodge is personally run by the resident proprietors. Bedrooms are individually decorated with thoughtful extras. There is an elegant, first-floor drawing room and a popular snug with a log fire and

*continued*

honesty bar. Set dinners in the panelled dining room continue to prove popular with residents.
**ROOMS:** 6 en suite 1 annexe en suite No smoking in all bedrooms s £62-£68; d £86-£96 (incl. bkfst) * **LB** **PARKING:** 12 **NOTES:** No children 12yrs No smoking in restaurant Closed Jan
**CARDS:**

### ★★66% Bossiney House

Bossiney PL34 0AX
☎ 01840 770240 01840 770501
e-mail: bossineyhh@eclipse.co.uk
***Dir:*** *from A39 take B3263 into Tintagel, then Boscastle road for 0.5m to hotel on left*
This personally-run, friendly hotel is located on the outskirts of the village. Set in the grounds, an attractive, Scandinavian-style log cabin houses the majority of the leisure facilities. In addition to the set-price menu served in the dining room, a range of bar meals is also available; a comfortable lounge is provided.
**ROOMS:** 19 en suite (1 fmly) s £28-£43; d £56-£66 (incl. bkfst) * **LB**
**FACILITIES:** Indoor swimming (H) Sauna Solarium Putting green
**PARKING:** 30 **NOTES:** No smoking in restaurant Closed Nov-Jan
**CARDS:**

### ★★66% The Wootons Country Hotel

Fore St PL34 0DD
☎ 01840 770170 01840 770978
***Dir:*** *Follow A30 until sign for N Cornwall, then right onto A395. continue & then turn right onto B3314 go straight over x-rds onto B3263 to Tintagel*
This hotel offers exceptionally well-equipped bedrooms, suitable for all requirements. Located in the main street of this much visited village, the bar proves a popular venue for locals and visitors alike. An extensive range of bar meals is available, whilst in
continued
the restaurant a carte menu is offered. There are also glorious country views.
**ROOMS:** 11 en suite **FACILITIES:** **Spa** Snooker ch fac Xmas
**PARKING:** 35 **NOTES:** No dogs (ex guide dogs)
**CARDS:**

### ★★63% Atlantic View

Treknow PL34 0EJ
☎ 01840 770221 01840 770995
e-mail: atlantic-view@eclipse.co.uk
***Dir:*** *B3263 to Tregatta, turn left into Treknow, hotel situated on road to Trebarwith Strand Beach*
With coastal views, and convenient for all the attractions of Tintagel, this hotel is family run and has a relaxed atmosphere. Public areas include a bar, comfortable lounge and TV/games room. Some of the spacious bedrooms have distant sea views.
**ROOMS:** 9 en suite (1 fmly) No smoking in 3 bedrooms s £30-£34; d £60-£68 (incl. bkfst) * **LB** **FACILITIES:** **Spa** Indoor swimming (H) Indoor pool heated Apr-Oct **PARKING:** 10 **NOTES:** No smoking in restaurant Closed Nov-Jan **CARDS:**

## TITCHWELL, Norfolk

Map 09 TF74

### ★★70% *Briarfields*

Main St PE31 8BB
☎ 01485 210742 01485 210933
e-mail: briarfields@norfolk-hotels.co.uk
***Dir:*** *A149 coastal road towards Wells-next-Sea, Titchwell is the 3rd village & 7m from Hunstanton, hotel is situated on left of main road into village*
This relaxing country hotel is situated close to the Titchwell RSPB reserve. The comfortable public rooms feature two eating areas, a smart restaurant and a bar serving meals. The accommodation is
continued on p588

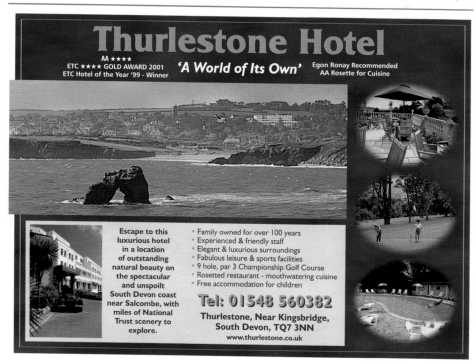

TITCHWELL, continued

attractively decorated, quite spacious and has comfortable seating. Some rooms are located out of the main building with private terrace doors.
**ROOMS:** 18 en suite (2 fmly) No smoking in 15 bedrooms **CONF:** Thtr 25 Class 12 Board 16 **PARKING:** 50 **NOTES:** No smoking in restaurant **CARDS:**

*See advert under HUNSTANTON*

## TIVERTON, Devon

Map 03 SS91

### ★★★67% Tiverton

Blundells Rd EX16 4DB
☎ 01884 256120 01884 258101
e-mail: sales@tivertonhotel.co.uk
***Dir:*** *M5 junct 27, join dual carriageway A361 Devon link road, Tiverton exit 7m W. Hotel on Blundells Rd next to business park*

Best Western

Situated on the outskirts of Tiverton and convenient for the M5, this hotel has a comfortable, relaxed atmosphere. Bedrooms are particularly spacious, well-equipped and decorated in a contemporary style. The Gallery restaurant offers a formal dining option, and lighter snacks are served in the bar area. Room service is extensive.
**ROOMS:** 74 en suite (10 fmly) No smoking in 54 bedrooms s £55-£58; d £82-£88 (incl. bkfst) * **LB** **FACILITIES:** STV ch fac Xmas **CONF:** Thtr 300 Class 140 Board 70 **PARKING:** 130 **NOTES:** No smoking in restaurant Civ Wed 170 **CARDS:**

## TIVETSHALL ST MARY, Norfolk

Map 05 TM18

### ★★74% The Old Ram Coaching Inn

Ipswich Rd NR15 2DE
☎ 01379 676794 01379 608399
e-mail: theoldram@btinternet.com
***Dir:*** *on A140 15m S of Norwich*

This popular coaching inn dates back to the 17th century and was once a staging post on the main Norwich to London road. Log fires, exposed brick and original timbers feature in the popular eating areas. Upstairs, the well-equipped bedrooms come in two types: the old split-level suites, and the modern executive rooms.
**ROOMS:** 11 en suite (1 fmly) s £45-£50; d £57-£65 * **LB**
**FACILITIES:** STV **CONF:** Thtr 20 Class 20 Board 20 Del £83.95 *
**PARKING:** 150 **NOTES:** No dogs (ex guide dogs) Closed 25 & 26 Dec
**CARDS:**

Popped the question? Hotels with Civ Wed in their entry are licensed for civil wedding ceremonies. Maximum numbers for the ceremony only are shown, e.g. Civ Wed 120

## TODDINGTON MOTORWAY SERVICE AREA (M1), Bedfordshire

Map 04 TL02

### *Travelodge*

LU5 6HR
☎ 08700 850950 01525 878452
***Dir:*** *between junct 11 & 12 M1*

Travelodge

Travelodge offers good quality, good value, modern accommodation. Ideal for families, the spacious, en suite bedrooms include remote-control TV, tea and coffee-making facilities, luxury beds and free morning newspaper. Meals can be taken at the nearby family restaurant. For further details and the Travelodge phone number, consult the Hotel Groups page.

**ROOMS:** 66 en suite

## TOLLESHUNT KNIGHTS, Essex

Map 05 TL91

### ★★★★72% Five Lakes Country House

Colchester Rd CM9 8HX
☎ 01621 868888 01621 869696
e-mail: enquiries@fivelakes.co.uk
***Dir:*** *exit A12 follow signs to Tiptree, over staggered x-rds past Wilkin's Jam Factory, fork left to Salcott, at x-rds turn right, 500 metres on right*

Magnificent hotel set amidst 300 acres of open countryside featuring two 18-hole golf courses. The spacious bedrooms are finished to a high standard and have an excellent range of facilities. The Public rooms are superb; they include five bars, an informal brasserie style restaurant and the more formal Camelot Restaurant.
**ROOMS:** 114 en suite (14 fmly) No smoking in 14 bedrooms s fr £105; d fr £148 * **LB** **FACILITIES:** **Spa** STV Indoor swimming (H) Golf 36 Tennis (hard) Squash Snooker Sauna Solarium Gym Putting green Jacuzzi Steam room Health & Beauty Spa Aerobics entertainment ch fac Xmas **CONF:** Thtr 2000 Class 700 Board 50 Del from £174.50 *
**SERVICES:** Lift **PARKING:** 500 **NOTES:** RS 24 - 27 Dec 30 Dec-3 Jan Civ Wed 350 **CARDS:**

## TONBRIDGE, Kent

Map 05 TQ54

### ★★★66% *Rose & Crown*

125 High St TN9 1DD
☎ 01732 357966 01732 357194
***Dir:*** *take A21 to Hastings. At 2nd interchange take B245 through Hildenborough. Continue to Tonbridge. At 1st t/lights right, over next set. Hotel on left*

Best Western

An attractive 15th-century coaching inn, located opposite the ruins of the old Norman castle. The hotel offers all the character of the period, combined with modern comforts. Accommodation is divided between the new extension at the rear of the hotel and

*continued*

the main building. The bar is equally popular with locals and residents and is well-known for its cricket memorabilia.
**ROOMS:** 49 en suite (1 fmly) No smoking in 23 bedrooms **CONF:** Thtr 80 Class 30 Board 35 **PARKING:** 39 **NOTES:** No dogs (ex guide dogs) **CARDS:**

### ★★66% *The Langley*

18-20 London Rd TN10 3DA
☎ 01732 353311 📠 01732 771471
e-mail: the.langley@virgin.net
***Dir:*** *turn off A21 signposted Tonbridge N on B245, hotel 500 metres on left beyond Oast Theatre*
This privately owned hotel is located just a short drive from the centre of Tonbridge and is ideally situated for business and leisure guests. Bedrooms are spacious and provide good levels of comfort. The restaurant offers a varied menu of carefully prepared fresh produce and there is a popular bar.
**ROOMS:** 34 en suite (3 fmly) No smoking in 12 bedrooms **FACILITIES:** STV **CONF:** Thtr 25 Class 15 Board 18 **SERVICES:** Lift **PARKING:** 50 **NOTES:** No dogs (ex guide dogs) No smoking in restaurant Civ Wed 80 **CARDS:**

### ⌂ Premier Lodge (Tunbridge Wells)

PREMIER LODGE

Pembury Rd TN11 0NA
☎ 0870 700 1560 📠 0870 700 1561
***Dir:*** *S off A21*
Premier Lodge offers modern, well-equipped, en suite accommodation suitable for both business and leisure travellers. Meals can be taken at the adjacent popular restaurant and bar, which is fully licensed. For further details, consult the Hotel Groups page.
**ROOMS:** 38 en suite s £49.95; d £49.95 * **CONF:** Class 16 Board 14

## TOPCLIFFE, North Yorkshire — Map 08 SE47

### ★★67% The Angel Inn

Long St YO7 3RW
☎ 01845 577237 📠 01845 578000
***Dir:*** *turn off the A168 link road (between A1(M) & A19) & the Angel Inn is situated in the centre of Topcliffe*

At the heart of Topcliffe, this attractive inn is very popular for its country-style cooking using high quality local produce. Pleasant bars lead through to a fine pub water garden. The bedrooms are well-equipped and very comfortable. Staff are friendly, and wedding ceremonies can now be carried out at the hotel.
**ROOMS:** 15 en suite (1 fmly) s £40-£45; d £54-£60 (incl. bkfst) * **LB** **FACILITIES:** **Spa** STV **CONF:** Thtr 150 Class 60 Board 50 **PARKING:** 150 **NOTES:** No dogs (ex guide dogs) Civ Wed 150 **CARDS:**

## TORBAY See under Brixham, Paignton & Torquay

## TORCROSS, Devon — Map 03 SX84

### ★71% *Greyhomes*

TQ7 2TH
☎ 01548 580220 📠 01548 580832
e-mail: howard@greyhomeshotel.co.uk
***Dir:*** *take A379 to village square, then take right fork and second left*
With spectacular views across Start Bay and Slapton Ley Nature Reserve, this delightful hotel was built in the 1920s by the present owner's grandfather. Public rooms retain much of the elegant character of the original period, and the comfortable bedrooms have modern facilities.
**ROOMS:** 6 en suite (1 fmly) **FACILITIES:** Tennis (hard) **PARKING:** 15 **NOTES:** No children 4yrs No smoking in restaurant Closed Nov-Mar **CARDS:**

## TORMARTON, Gloucestershire — Map 03 ST77

### ★★70% Compass Inn

Best Western

GL9 1JB
☎ 01454 218242 & 218577 📠 01454 218741
e-mail: info@compass-inn.co.uk
***Dir:*** *0.5m from junct 18, M4*
This friendly 18th-century coaching inn is in a tranquil setting, and features good facilities for business, leisure and conferences. Many of the bedrooms are in a modern extension, with the bars and public rooms concentrated in the main building.
**ROOMS:** 26 en suite (7 fmly) s £55-£87; d £65-£97 * **LB** **FACILITIES:** STV **CONF:** Thtr 100 Class 30 Board 34 Del from £92.50 * **PARKING:** 160 **NOTES:** Closed 24-26 Dec Civ Wed 80 **CARDS:**

## TORPOINT, Cornwall & Isles of Scilly — Map 02 SX45

### ★★70% Whitsand Bay Hotel, Golf & Country Club

Portwrinkle PL11 3BU
☎ 01503 230276 📠 01503 230329
e-mail: earlehotels@btconnect.com
***Dir:*** *5m W, off B3247. Turn off A30 at Trevlefoot rdbt on A374 to Crafthole, then take turn for Portwrinkle*
An imposing Victorian stone building with oak panelling, stained glass windows and a sweeping staircase. Bedrooms include both family rooms and a suite with a balcony. Facilities include an 18-hole cliff-top golf course and indoor swimming pool. The fixed price menu offers an interesting selection of dishes.
**ROOMS:** 39 rms (37 en suite) (15 fmly) s £44-£57; d £70-£94 (incl. bkfst) * **LB** **FACILITIES:** **Spa** Indoor swimming (H) Golf 18 Sauna Solarium Gym Putting green Beauty & hair salon Steam & Games room ch fac Xmas **CONF:** Thtr 100 Class 100 Board 40 Del from £35 * **PARKING:** 60 **NOTES:** Civ Wed 150 **CARDS:**

T

## TORQUAY, Devon — Map 03 SX96

### ★★★★★71% ❀ The Imperial

PARAMOUNT GROUP OF HOTELS

Park Hill Rd TQ1 2DG
☎ 01803 294301 📠 01803 298293
e-mail: imperialtorquay@paramount-hotels.co.uk
***Dir:*** *A380 head towards the seafront. Turn left and follow the road to the harbour, at clocktower turn right. Hotel 300yrds on right*
This well-established hotel can legitimately claim to offer some of the best views in town. Elegant public areas include the recently completed TQ1 brasserie, a large, comfortably furnished lounge and a selection of meeting rooms. The Regatta Restaurant serves a choice of menus and features superb fresh local fish. Bedrooms

*continued on p590*

TORQUAY, continued

vary in style; many have balconies and fine sea views. Service is both welcoming and professional.

*The Imperial, Torquay*

**ROOMS:** 153 en suite (7 fmly) No smoking in 26 bedrooms s £95-£125; d £170-£250 * **LB** **FACILITIES:** STV Indoor swimming (H) Outdoor swimming (H) Tennis (hard) Squash Snooker Sauna Solarium Gym Jacuzzi Beauty salon Hairdresser entertainment ch fac Xmas **CONF:** Thtr 350 Class 200 Board 30 **SERVICES:** Lift **PARKING:** 140 **NOTES:** Civ Wed 200 **CARDS:**

### ★★★★70% *Grand*

Sea Front TQ2 6NT
☎ 01803 296677 01803 213462
e-mail: grandhotel@netsite.co.uk
***Dir:*** *A380 to Torquay. At sea front turn right, then first right. Hotel is on corner, entrance is in the first turning on left*

Overlooking the bay, this Edwardian hotel offers friendly service and modern facilities. Many bedrooms and suites have sea views and balconies; all are very well-equipped. Boaters Bar also benefits from the hotel's stunning position. In the evening guests enjoy the more formal atmosphere of the Gainsborough Restaurant.

**ROOMS:** 110 en suite (30 fmly) No smoking in 30 bedrooms **FACILITIES:** STV Indoor swimming (H) Outdoor swimming (H) Tennis (hard) Snooker Sauna Solarium Gym Jacuzzi Hairdressers Beauty clinic entertainment ch fac **CONF:** Thtr 350 Class 100 Board 60 **SERVICES:** Lift **PARKING:** 55 **NOTES:** No smoking in restaurant **CARDS:**

*See advert on opposite page*

> Fancy a Singapore Sling? Bar staff in five star hotels should be skilled cocktail mixers.

### ★★★★69% Palace

Babbacombe Rd TQ1 3TG
☎ 01803 200200 01803 299899
e-mail: mail6@palacetorquay.co.uk
***Dir:*** *Head for the harbour, turn left by the clocktower into Babbacombe Rd, hotel on right after about 1m*

The hotel was formerly the summer residence of the Bishop of Exeter. Bedrooms are attractively decorated and offer many modern amenities. The extensive public areas include a choice of lounges, a cocktail bar, and leisure facilities. The large and elegant restaurant offers traditional cuisine in a formal atmosphere. There are 25 acres of grounds and gardens and a 9 hole golf course.

**ROOMS:** 141 en suite (20 fmly) No smoking in 18 bedrooms s £71-£81; d £142-£280 (incl. bkfst) * **LB** **FACILITIES:** **Spa** STV Indoor swimming (H) Outdoor swimming (H) Golf 9 Tennis (hard) Squash Snooker Sauna Gym Croquet lawn Putting green Fitness suite Table tennis entertainment ch fac Xmas **CONF:** Thtr 1000 Class 800 Board 40 Del from £115 * **SERVICES:** Lift **PARKING:** 180 **NOTES:** No dogs (ex guide dogs) No smoking in restaurant **CARDS:**

*See advert on opposite page*

### ★★★76% Orestone Manor Hotel & Restaurant

Rockhouse Ln, Maidencombe TQ1 4SX
☎ 01803 328098 01803 328336
e-mail: enquiries@orestone.co.uk
***Dir:*** *off A379 coast road, Torquay-Teignmouth. (Road was formerly B3199)*

Hidden away on the edge of the town, this attractive Georgian country house enjoys stunning views across Lyme Bay and surrounding countryside. The spacious public areas are elegantly comfortable, with a colonial theme. Individually furnished and decorated, the bedrooms vary in size and style and are priced accordingly. The restaurant offers innovative cuisine.

**ROOMS:** 12 en suite (2 fmly) s £50-£120; d £100-£160 (incl. bkfst) * **LB** **FACILITIES:** STV Outdoor swimming (H) Snooker Xmas **CONF:** Thtr 20 Class 20 Board 15 Del from £125 * **PARKING:** 35 **NOTES:** No smoking in restaurant **CARDS:**

T

T

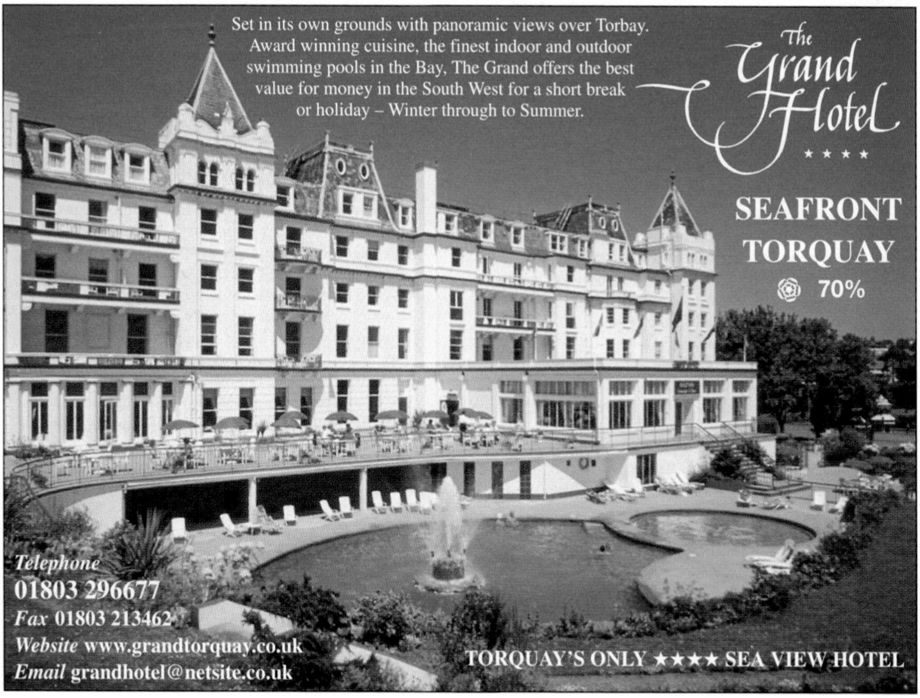

TORQUAY, continued

**★★★73% Livermead Cliff**

Best Western

Torbay Rd TQ2 6RQ
☎ 01803 299666 & 292881 01803 294496
e-mail: enquiries@livermeadcliff.co.uk
***Dir:*** *A380/A3022 to seafront, turn right, Livermead Cliff is 600yds on left*
Providing warm hospitality and attentive service, this privately-owned hotel is situated on the edge of the bay, boasting some spectacular sea views. The comfortable lounges and bar are spacious and tastefully decorated. Carefully prepared dishes are enjoyed in the elegant restaurant. Bedrooms vary in size and shape, sea facing rooms are always in heavy demand.
**ROOMS:** 64 en suite (21 fmly) s £44-£68; d £82-£133 (incl. bkfst) * LB **FACILITIES:** Outdoor swimming (H) Fishing Solarium Sun terrace Xmas **CONF:** Thtr 100 Class 40 Board 30 Del from £55 * **SERVICES:** Lift **PARKING:** 72 **NOTES:** No smoking in restaurant
**CARDS:**

**★★★73% The Osborne**
Hesketh Crescent, Meadfoot TQ1 2LL
☎ 01803 213311 01803 296788
e-mail: enq@osborne-torquay.co.uk
***Dir:*** *A380 via Newton Abbot, follow signs to seafront, follow A3022, down and turn left, turn onto B3199 and follow road to hotel*
With superb views over the beach and Torbay, the Osborne forms the centrepiece of an elegant Regency terrace. Set in five acres, its gardens lead down towards the sea, and many bedrooms benefit from fine views. The brasserie serves food all day and Langtry's Restaurant provides a more formal dining option.
**ROOMS:** 29 en suite (2 fmly) s £60-£75; d £120-£150 (incl. bkfst) * LB **FACILITIES:** STV Indoor swimming (H) Outdoor swimming (H) Tennis (hard) Snooker Sauna Solarium Gym Putting green Plunge pool ch fac Xmas **CONF:** Thtr 30 Class 28 Board 30 **SERVICES:** Lift **PARKING:** 90 **NOTES:** No dogs (ex guide dogs) No smoking in restaurant
**CARDS:**

*See advert on this page*

**★★★71% Lincombe Hall**
Meadfoot Rd TQ1 2JX
☎ 01803 213361 01803 211485
e-mail: lincombehall@lineone.net
***Dir:*** *Pass along Torquay sea front with sea on right past Princess Theatre towards harbour. At mini rdbt with clocktower, bear left & turn right at first set traffic lights. Hotel on left*
Set in five acres of grounds, close to the centre, this hotel has views over Torquay. Bedrooms are tastefully furnished and vary in size, the Sutherland rooms being the most spacious and in demand. There are comfortable lounges and Harleys restaurant offers a comprehensive choice of menu and wine.
**ROOMS:** 42 en suite (9 fmly) No smoking in 4 bedrooms s £38-£69; d £76-£127 (incl. bkfst & dinner) * LB **FACILITIES:** Spa STV Indoor swimming (H) Outdoor swimming (H) Tennis (hard) Sauna Solarium Gym Putting green Jacuzzi Play area Crazy golf Xmas **CONF:** Thtr 50 Class 30 Board 20 Del from £45 * **PARKING:** 40 **NOTES:** No smoking in restaurant **CARDS:**

**★★★70% Corbyn Head Hotel & Orchid Restaurant**
Torquay Rd, Sea Front, Livermead TQ2 6RH
☎ 01803 213611 01803 296152
e-mail: info@corbynhead.com
***Dir:*** *follow signs to Torquay seafront, turn right on seafront. Hotel situated on right hand side of seafront with green canopies*
Offering professional service and traditional hospitality, Corbyn Head overlooks Torbay, just a short walk to the town centre and harbour. The smartly uniformed team of staff provide high standards of service. Bedrooms benefit from sea views, accommodation is carefully designed and furnishings are well co-ordinated. There are two dining options, either the main restaurant or the award winning Orchid Restaurant.

**ROOMS:** 50 en suite (4 fmly) No smoking in 3 bedrooms s £55-£75; d £110-£160 (incl. bkfst & dinner) * LB **FACILITIES:** Outdoor swimming Squash Snooker Sauna Solarium entertainment Xmas **CONF:** Thtr 30 Class 20 Board 20 Del from £49.50 * **PARKING:** 50 **NOTES:** No smoking in restaurant **CARDS:**

*See advert on opposite page*

**★★★70% The Grosvenor**
Belgrave Rd TQ2 5HG
☎ 01803 294373 01803 291032
e-mail: enquiries@grosvenor-torquay.co.uk
***Dir:*** *hotel on first left, just off main beach/seafront road*
Close to the seafront and the main attractions of the bay, The

*continued on p594*



*continued*

Situated in one of Torquay's finest waterfront locations, the privately owned Corbyn Head Hotel provides a perfect setting from which you can enjoy a relaxing holiday.

The Hotel offers 49 elegantly decorated bedrooms, many with private balconies.

The Hotel also provides a tranquil bar, luxurious lounge and two restaurants, including The Orchid, awarded with two AA Rosettes for cuisine.

The Corbyn Head Hotel, where the highest standards of comfort, service and award winning cuisine combine with the warmth of West Country hospitality.

# Corbyn Head Hotel ☆☆☆

*& Orchid Restaurant*

SEA FRONT, TORQUAY, DEVON TQ2 6RH
Hotel telephone: (01803) 213611
Fax: (01803) 296152
Orchid Restaurant: (01803) 296366
*e-mail:* info@corbyhead.com
*website:* www.corbyhead.com

---

The Livermead
HOUSE

SEA FRONT, TORQUAY
DEVON TQ2 6QJ
Telephone: (01803) 294361
Fax: (01803) 200758
e-mail: RewHotels@aol.com
Website: www.Livermead.com

*Superior non-smoking sea view room*

*Built in 1820 on the edge of the Cockington Valley lies the Livermead House. This privately owned picturesque Country House Hotel is situated by the sea in 3 acres of award winning grounds and offers outstanding cuisine, luxurious surroundings and service synonomous with one of Torbay's leading hotels.*

*Please contact us for your personal copy of our new brochure.*

T

TORQUAY, continued

Grosvenor Hotel offers spacious and attractively furnished bedrooms. Guests can choose to dine in the restaurant, coffee shop or the award-winning Mima's Bistro. Many leisure facilities are available.
**ROOMS:** 46 en suite (8 fmly) s £45-£75; d £90-£150 (incl. bkfst) * LB **FACILITIES:** Spa STV Indoor swimming (H) Outdoor swimming Tennis Sauna Solarium Gym Jacuzzi mini snooker table library entertainment Xmas **CONF:** Thtr 150 Class 100 Board 40 **PARKING:** 50 **NOTES:** No dogs (ex guide dogs) No smoking in restaurant
**CARDS:**

*See advert on opposite page*

### ★★★70% Toorak

Chestnut Av TQ2 5JS
☎ 01803 291444 01803 291666
***Dir:*** *opposite Riviera Conference Centre*
Many indoor and outdoor leisure facilities are available here and in adjoining sister hotels. Conference rooms are popular and there are several relaxing lounges. Bedrooms have many modern facilities; superior 'Terrace' bedrooms are very spacious and well-decorated. The comfortable restaurant offers an interesting selection of well-prepared dishes.
**ROOMS:** 92 en suite (29 fmly) s £49-£59; d £98-£118 (incl. bkfst & dinner) * LB **FACILITIES:** Indoor swimming (H) Outdoor swimming (H) Tennis (hard) Snooker Sauna Solarium Croquet lawn Jacuzzi Childrens play area Indoor Games Arena Xmas **CONF:** Thtr 220 Class 150 Board 60 Del from £75 * **SERVICES:** Lift **PARKING:** 90 **NOTES:** No dogs (ex guide dogs) **CARDS:**

*See advert on opposite page*

### ★★★69% Livermead House

Torbay Rd TQ2 6QJ
☎ 01803 294361 01803 200758
e-mail: rewhotels@aol.com
***Dir:*** *from seafront turn right, follow A379 towards Paignton and Livermead, the hotel is opposite Institute beach*

Situated on the waterfront, Livermead House was built in the 1820s and is where Charles Kingsley wrote The Water Babies. Bedrooms have been refurbished to a high standard, and the excellent public rooms are popular for private parties, functions and meetings. A range of leisure facilities is provided and the attractive restaurant offers views of the bay.
**ROOMS:** 66 en suite (6 fmly) No smoking in 12 bedrooms s £39-£130; d £78-£132 (incl. bkfst) * LB **FACILITIES:** Outdoor swimming (H) Squash Snooker Sauna Solarium entertainment Xmas **CONF:** Thtr 320 Class 175 Board 80 Del from £48 * **SERVICES:** Lift **PARKING:** 131 **NOTES:** No smoking in restaurant **CARDS:**

### ★★★65% Belgrave

Seafront TQ2 5HE
☎ 01803 296666 01803 211308
e-mail: info@belgrave-hotel.co.uk
***Dir:*** *From Exeter take A380 to Newton Abbot & Torquay. At Torquay continue to traffic lights with Torre Station on right. Bear right into Avenue Rd continue straight to Kings Drive. Left at seafront , at traffic lights, hotel in front*

With a seafront position, this popular hotel offers a choice of two bars and spacious lounges, all taking full advantage of the hotel's prime site. There is an impressive ballroom, and a restaurant serving a daily set price menu, in addition to lunch-time snacks. The bedrooms all offer modern facilities.
**ROOMS:** 71 rms (69 en suite) (16 fmly) No smoking in 20 bedrooms s £44-£60; d £88-£120 (incl. bkfst) * LB **FACILITIES:** Spa Outdoor swimming (H) Xmas **CONF:** Thtr 200 Class 100 Board 60 Del from £58 * **SERVICES:** Lift **PARKING:** 88 **NOTES:** No smoking in restaurant
**CARDS:**

### ★★★61% Kistor Hotel

Belgrave Rd TQ2 5HF
☎ 01803 212632 01803 293219
e-mail: kistorhotel@hotmail.com
***Dir:*** *A380 to Torquay, hotel is next to Belgrave hotel at junct of Belgrave Rd and the promenade at the seafront*
Conveniently close to the promenade and within walking distance of the town centre, the hotel's bedrooms vary in size and are equipped with modern facilities. In the restaurant, a fixed price menu is offered, with straightforward cooking.
**ROOMS:** 50 en suite (14 fmly) s £30-£35; d £60-£70 (incl. bkfst) * LB **FACILITIES:** Spa Indoor swimming (H) Sauna Putting green Childrens play area entertainment Xmas **CONF:** Thtr 80 Class 30 Board 40 Del from £35 * **SERVICES:** Lift **PARKING:** 40 **NOTES:** No smoking in restaurant **CARDS:**

### ★★74% Albaston House

27 St Marychurch Rd TQ1 3JF
☎ 01803 296758 01803 211509
Albaston House is privately owned and personally run. It is situated between the town centre, historic St Marychurch and the beaches of Babbacombe. Standards of housekeeping, hospitality and service are high and the well-equipped accommodation is smartly decorated and impeccably maintained.
**ROOMS:** 13 en suite (4 fmly) s £32-£42; d £64-£64 (incl. bkfst) * LB **PARKING:** 12 **NOTES:** No smoking in restaurant Closed Jan
**CARDS:**

T

### ★★73% Oscars Hotel & Restaurant

56 Belgrave Rd TQ2 5HY
☎ 01803 293563 Fax 01803 296685
e-mail: reservations@oscars-hotel.com
**Dir:** *from A3022 into Torquay turn left, then right at next set of lights, head towards seafront, hotel is at the junction with Falkland Rd*
This attractive hotel is conveniently located for both the shops and seafront. In addition to friendly and attentive service, it offers comfortable, smartly decorated and well-furnished bedrooms. The popular bistro-style restaurant provides an extensive range of enjoyable dishes.
**ROOMS:** 14 en suite (2 fmly) s £27-£35; d £53-£70 (incl. bkfst) * LB
**PARKING:** 4 **NOTES:** No children 10yrs
**CARDS:**

### ★★72% Bute Court

Belgrave Rd TQ2 5HQ
☎ 01803 293771 Fax 01803 213429
e-mail: bute-court-hotel@talk21.com
**Dir:** *take A380 to Torquay, continue until traffic lights, bear right past police station, straight across at traffic lights, hotel 200yds on right*
In the same family ownership for over 60 years, this popular hotel is only a short walk from the seafront. Comfortably furnished with modern facilities, the recently refurbished bedrooms benefit from a few helpful extras. Spacious public rooms, night-time entertainment and leisure facilities are all added attractions.
**ROOMS:** 45 en suite (10 fmly) s £29-£35; d £58-£70 (incl. bkfst) * LB
**FACILITIES:** Outdoor swimming (H) Snooker Table tennis Darts billiards Xmas **CONF:** Class 40 **SERVICES:** Lift **PARKING:** 37
**CARDS:**

### ★★70% *Hotel Sydore*

Meadfoot Rd TQ1 2JP
☎ 01803 294758 Fax 01803 294489
e-mail: john@sydore.co.uk
**Dir:** *A380 to Harbour, left at clock tower 40 metres to traffic lights, right into Meadfoot Rd hotel 100 metres on left*
Surrounded by well tended gardens, this charming Georgian villa is within walking distance of the harbour and town centre. Full of character and individuality, the lounge and bar are comfortable and provide many talking points. Traditional cuisine is offered in the attractive restaurant, which overlooks the gardens. Bedrooms are individual in style and decor.
**ROOMS:** 13 en suite (5 fmly) No smoking in 11 bedrooms
**FACILITIES:** Croquet lawn Bar billiards Table tennis **PARKING:** 16
**NOTES:** No smoking in restaurant **CARDS:**

### ★★70% *Rawlyn House*

Rawlyn Rd, Chelston TQ2 6PL
☎ 01803 605208 Fax 01803 607040
Situated in a quiet area, this delightful hotel is surrounded by large gardens and within easy reach of the centre. With all the expected modern facilities, the bedrooms are individual in style; several rooms are located on the ground floor. Meals are freshly prepared, with a range of bar meals on offer at lunchtime.
**ROOMS:** 12 rms (11 en suite) 2 annexe en suite (1 fmly) No smoking in all bedrooms **FACILITIES:** Outdoor swimming (H) Badminton Table tennis **PARKING:** 16 **NOTES:** No dogs No smoking in restaurant Closed Nov-Apr **CARDS:**

### ★★69% *Ansteys Lea*

Babbacombe Rd, Wellswood TQ1 2QJ
☎ 01803 294843 Fax 01803 214333
e-mail: stay@ansteys-lea.com
**Dir:** *from Torquay Harbour take the Babbacombe road, hotel approx 0.75m towards Babbacombe*
This friendly hotel is a short walk from Ansteys Cove. Bedrooms

*continued on p596*



T

TORQUAY, continued

offer comfortable, well-furnished accommodation with a good range of facilities. There is an attractive lounge/TV room overlooking the garden and a heated outdoor pool. The set five-course dinner menu offers a choice of home-cooked dishes.
**ROOMS:** 24 en suite (4 fmly) **FACILITIES:** Outdoor swimming (H) Sauna Gym Putting green Table tennis **SERVICES:** air con **PARKING:** 18 **NOTES:** No smoking in restaurant Closed 3 Jan-13 Feb **CARDS:**

### ★★69% *Dunstone Hall*
Lower Warberry Rd TQ1 1QS
☎ 01803 293185 01803 201180
e-mail: info@dunstonehall.com
From its elevated position, this imposing, Victorian mansion has panoramic views over the town, to Torbay in the distance. Bedrooms are comfortable and equipped with modern facilities. Public areas include a choice of lounges, and a magnificent wooden staircase and gallery. The Edwardian conservatory has been refurbished to provide an intimate restaurant where dinner may be enjoyed.
**ROOMS:** 13 en suite (3 fmly) **FACILITIES:** Outdoor swimming (H) Arrangement with nearby Health Club **CONF:** Thtr 30 Class 30 Board 24 **PARKING:** 18 **NOTES:** No dogs (ex guide dogs) No smoking in restaurant **CARDS:**

### ★★69% Frognel Hall
Higher Woodfield Rd TQ1 2LD
☎ 01803 298339 01803 215115
e-mail: mail@frognel.co.uk
***Dir:*** *follow signs to seafront, then follow esplanade to harbour, left to Babbacombe, right at lights towards Meadfoot beach, 3rd left, Hotel on left*
In an elevated position with fine views over Torquay, the hotel has comfortable bedrooms with modern facilities. The Croppers and their friendly staff are always on hand to ensure a welcoming atmosphere and a pleasant stay. The traditional English food includes many vegetarian items.
**ROOMS:** 28 rms (27 en suite) (4 fmly) s £27-£31; d £54-£62 (incl. bkfst) * **LB** **FACILITIES:** **Spa** Sauna Croquet lawn Putting green Games room Exercise equipment entertainment Xmas **CONF:** Thtr 50 Class 30 Board 15 Del from £48 * **SERVICES:** Lift **PARKING:** 25 **NOTES:** No smoking in restaurant **CARDS:**

### ★★68% Carlton
Falkland Rd TQ2 5JJ
☎ 01803 400300 01803 400130
e-mail: dPashley@tlh.co.uk
***Dir:*** *take A380 into Torquay, follow signs to seafront, at traffic light junction on Belgrave Rd turn right into Falkland Rd hotel is 100yds on left*
Coveniently located close to the town centre, beaches and other amenities the town has to offer, this hotel remains a popular choice. The well equipped bedrooms vary in size and style, and all are smartly presented. An extensive range of leisure facilities are available, shared with the other hotels in the same group. Regular entertainment is staged in the spacious ballroom and bar.
**ROOMS:** 47 en suite (26 fmly) s £31-£48; d £62-£96 (incl. bkfst) * **FACILITIES:** Indoor swimming (H) Outdoor swimming (H) Tennis (hard) Snooker Sauna Solarium Childrens playden Adventure play ground,Ten pin Bowling entertainment ch fac Xmas **CONF:** Thtr 120 Class 60 Board 25 **SERVICES:** Lift **PARKING:** 28 **NOTES:** No dogs (ex guide dogs) No smoking in restaurant **CARDS:**

### ★★68% Gresham Court
Babbacombe Rd TQ1 1HG
☎ 01803 293007 & 293658 01803 215951
e-mail: greshamcourthotel@hotmail.com
***Dir:*** *proceed along The Strand/Harbourside & bear left into Torwood St. Cross set of lights into Babbacombe Road. Hotel is on left*
Situated close to the harbour and shops, this well run family hotel offers high levels of hospitality. In the dining room, the fixed price menu offers a varied choice of food. The bedrooms which include family rooms, are comfortable and vary in style and size.
**ROOMS:** 30 en suite (6 fmly) s £28-£38; d £56-£76 (incl. bkfst & dinner) * **LB** **FACILITIES:** **Spa** entertainment **SERVICES:** Lift **PARKING:** 14 **NOTES:** No dogs (ex guide dogs) No smoking in restaurant Closed Dec-Feb **CARDS:**

### ★★68% Red House
Rousdown Rd, Chelston TQ2 6PB
☎ 01803 607811 01803 200592
e-mail: stay@redhouse-hotel.co.uk
***Dir:*** *head for seafront/Chelston, turn into Avenue Rd, 1st set of lights turn right. Follow road past shops and church, take next left. Hotel on right*

Comfortable accommodation is provided at this relaxing hotel, situated in the quiet residential area of Chelston. In addition to the small restaurant, the hotel has an all-day informal coffee shop with an extensive menu. Varying in size and style, all the bedrooms offer modern facilities and amenities.
**ROOMS:** 10 en suite (5 fmly) s £24-£32; d £48-£64 (incl. bkfst) * **FACILITIES:** **Spa** Indoor swimming (H) Outdoor swimming (H) Sauna Solarium Gym Games room Table tennis Beauty salon pool table Xmas **CONF:** Thtr 20 Class 20 Board 16 **PARKING:** 10 **NOTES:** No smoking in restaurant **CARDS:**

*See advert on opposite page*

### ★★68% *Shelley Court*
Croft Rd TQ2 5UD
☎ 01803 295642 01803 215793
***Dir:*** *A380 from Newton Abbot, then onto A3022 to seafront, hotel is 250yds turning off Shedden Hill into Croft Rd*
This popular hotel is located close to the town and beach. Bedrooms are well appointed with modern facilities; some rooms are on the ground floor, others have the benefit of a shared balcony. The lounges enjoy attractive sea views; entertainment is regularly provided. Traditional, home cooked cuisine is offered in the dining room.
**ROOMS:** 27 en suite (3 fmly) **FACILITIES:** entertainment **PARKING:** 20 **NOTES:** No dogs No smoking in restaurant Closed 21 Dec-Jan **CARDS:**

T

### ★★68% Torcroft

Croft Rd TQ2 5UE
☎ 01803 298292 Fax 01803 291799
e-mail: torcroft@torquaydevon.fsnet.co.uk
***Dir:*** *from A390 take A3022 to Avenue Rd. Follow signs to seafront. At seafront turn left, cross lights and up Shedden Hill, first left into Croft Rd*

This elegant, Grade II listed Victorian property, is conveniently located for the town centre, shops and sea front. The quiet location also has the benefit of a large patio with seating that overlooks the well-maintained garden. Bedrooms are well-decorated and furnished.

**ROOMS:** 15 en suite (2 fmly) s £30-£40; d £60-£80 (incl. bkfst) * **LB** **FACILITIES:** Xmas **CONF:** Thtr 30 Class 20 Board 26 Del from £55 * **PARKING:** 16 **NOTES:** No dogs No children 3yrs No smoking in restaurant **CARDS:**

### ★★67% *Ansteys Cove*

327 Babbacombe Rd TQ1 3TB
☎ 0800 0284953 Fax 01803 211150
e-mail: info@ansteyscove.co.uk
***Dir:*** *A380/A3022 left onto B3199. At Babbacombe right onto Babbacombe Rd hotel 1m on right opposite Palace Hotel*

Close to the Coastal Footpath and the beaches, this family-run hotel provides comfortable, well-equipped accommodation. Imaginative, home cooked dishes are offered in the attractive restaurant, many ingredients coming from local producers; the hotel is a member of Taste of the West. A relaxing bar is also available for guests.

**ROOMS:** 11 en suite (1 fmly) No smoking in all bedrooms **FACILITIES:** STV **PARKING:** 12 **NOTES:** No dogs (ex guide dogs) No smoking in restaurant **CARDS:**

### ★★66% *Ashley Court*

107 Abbey Rd TQ2 5NP
☎ 01803 292417 & 292541 Fax 01803 215035
e-mail: reception@ashleycourt.demon.co.uk
***Dir:*** *A380 onto seafront, left to Sheddon Hill to traffic lights, hotel opposite*

Under the same family ownership for over 30 years, this hotel is located close to the seafront, amenities and attractions. Guests are assured of a comfortable, relaxing stay and the friendly staff provide a genuinely warm welcome. The outdoor pool and patio are popular during the summer months, and live entertainment is regularly provided.

**ROOMS:** 53 en suite (5 fmly) **FACILITIES:** Outdoor swimming (H) entertainment **SERVICES:** Lift **PARKING:** 28 **NOTES:** No smoking in restaurant Closed 2 Jan-13 Feb **CARDS:**

### ★★66% *Hotel Balmoral*

Meadfoot Sea Rd TQ1 2LQ
☎ 01803 293381 & 299224 Fax 01803 299224
***Dir:*** *at Torquay harbour go left at Clock Tower towards Babbacombe, after 100yds right at lghts. Follow the road to Meadfoot Beach. Hotel on right*

A friendly, well-run hotel with modern, well-equipped bedrooms and bathrooms, the Balmoral is superbly situated just two minutes' stroll from Meadfoot Beach with views to the sea. The spacious lounges and bar offer guests every comfort and pleasant views over the well-tended gardens. A good selection of traditional, home cooking is served in the bright, attractive dining room.

**ROOMS:** 24 en suite (7 fmly) **FACILITIES:** entertainment ch fac **PARKING:** 18 **NOTES:** No smoking in restaurant **CARDS:**

### ★★66% Meadfoot Bay

Meadfoot Sea Rd TQ1 2LQ
☎ 01803 294722 Fax 01803 214473
e-mail: stay@meadfoot.com

MEADFOOT BAY HOTEL, TORQUAY

Quietly situated, this Victorian villa is just a short walk from Meadfoot Beach and approximately 10 minutes from the town centre and harbour. A warm welcome is assured and every effort made to ensure a relaxed and enjoyable stay. A changing daily menu is offered with an emphasis upon honest home-cooking.

**ROOMS:** 22 en suite (1 fmly) No smoking in all bedrooms s fr £24; d fr £48 (incl. bkfst) * **LB** **FACILITIES:** Xmas **PARKING:** 15 **NOTES:** Closed Nov-Jan RS Feb-Mar **CARDS:**

TORQUAY, continued

### ★★65% Burlington

462-466 Babbacombe Rd TQ1 1HN
☎ 01803 210950 🖷 01803 200189
e-mail: burlington.hotel@virgin.net
***Dir:*** *A380 to Torquay, follow signs to seafront, left at harbour, left at clock tower, the hotel is 0.5m on right hand side*

Just a short walk from the town's harbour and shops, The Burlington provides a convenient base for guests to enjoy the many attractions of the area. In the spacious dining room, traditional dishes are served by the friendly team of staff. Public areas include a pool room, entertainment room, leisure facilities and a popular bar. Bedrooms are comfortable and available in a variety of sizes.

**ROOMS:** 55 en suite (7 fmly) **FACILITIES:** **Spa** Indoor swimming (H) Sauna Solarium Jacuzzi Games rm & machines Table tennis Pinball entertainment **PARKING:** 20 **NOTES:** No smoking in restaurant **CARDS:**

### ★★65% Coppice

Babbacombe Rd TQ1 2QJ
☎ 01803 297786 🖷 01803 211085

A friendly and comfortable hotel, The Coppice is conveniently situated just off the Babbacombe Road and within walking distance of the beaches and shops. In addition to the in/outdoor leisure facilities, evening entertainment is often provided in the spacious bar. Bedrooms are bright and airy with modern amenities.

**ROOMS:** 39 en suite (16 fmly) s £27-£39; d £53-£78 (incl. bkfst & dinner) * **LB** **FACILITIES:** **Spa** Indoor swimming (H) Outdoor swimming (H) Snooker Sauna Solarium Gym Putting green **PARKING:** 36 **NOTES:** No smoking in restaurant Closed 1 Dec-31 Jan

### ★★65% Elmington Hotel

St Agnes Ln, Chelston TQ2 6QE
☎ 01803 605192 🖷 01803 690488
e-mail: mail@elmington.co.uk
***Dir:*** *to thr rear of Torquay station*

Lovingly restored, this splendid Victorian villa has art deco additions and is set in sub-tropical gardens in a quiet residential area, close to the centre and harbour. Guest comfort here is of the utmost importance. Comfortable bedrooms are attractively decorated. There is a spacious lounge, bar and dining room with wonderful views over the bay.

**ROOMS:** 22 rms (19 en suite) (5 fmly) No smoking in all bedrooms s £30-£35; d £60-£70 (incl. bkfst) * **LB** **FACILITIES:** **Spa** Outdoor swimming (H) Croquet lawn ch fac Xmas **CONF:** Thtr 40 Class 40 Board 30 Del £50 * **PARKING:** 22 **NOTES:** No dogs (ex guide dogs) No smoking in restaurant **CARDS:**

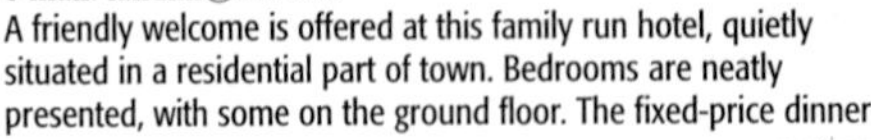

### ★★64% *Anchorage Hotel*

MINOTEL Great Britain

Cary Park, Aveland Rd TQ1 3NQ
☎ 01803 326175 🖷 01803 316439
e-mail: landlin@aol.com

A friendly welcome is offered at this family run hotel, quietly situated in a residential part of town. Bedrooms are neatly presented, with some on the ground floor. The fixed-price dinner menu offers a wide choice. Evening entertainment is provided regularly in the large comfortable lounge.

Anchorage Hotel

**ROOMS:** 53 en suite (5 fmly) No smoking in all bedrooms **FACILITIES:** Outdoor swimming (H) entertainment **CONF:** Thtr 50 Class 20 Board 24 **SERVICES:** Lift **PARKING:** 26 **NOTES:** No smoking in restaurant **CARDS:**

### ★★64% *Maycliffe*

St Lukes Rd North TQ2 5DP
☎ 01803 294964 🖷 01803 201167
***Dir:*** *left from Kings Dr, along sea front keep left lane, next lights (Belgrave Rd) proceed up Shedden Hill, 2nd right into St Lukes Rd then 1st left*

Quietly located between the town centre and the beach, The Maycliffe is a popular venue for leisure breaks. Rooms are individual in design and decor and have modern facilities; several have views over the bay. There is a comfortable lounge and an attractive bar with a cabaret on certain nights of the week.

**ROOMS:** 28 en suite (1 fmly) No smoking in 9 bedrooms **FACILITIES:** entertainment **SERVICES:** Lift **PARKING:** 10 **NOTES:** No dogs No children 10yrs No smoking in restaurant Closed 2 Jan-12 Feb **CARDS:**

### ★★63% Norcliffe

7 Babbacombe Downs Rd, Babbacombe TQ1 3LF
☎ 01803 328456 🖷 01803 328023
***Dir:*** *from M5, take A380, after Sainsbury's turn left at lights, across rdbt, left next at lights into Manor Road, from Babbacombe Rd turn left*

With marvellous views across Lyme Bay, the Norcliffe is conveniently situated on the Babbacombe Downs and ideally located for visitors to St Marychurch or nearby Oddicombe Beach. Public areas are relaxing, taking advantage of the views and include an indoor swimming pool. All bedrooms are comfortable, varying in style and size.

**ROOMS:** 27 en suite (3 fmly) s £18-£30; d £36-£72 (incl. bkfst) * **LB** **FACILITIES:** Indoor swimming (H) Sauna 3/4 size snooker table, table tennis Xmas **SERVICES:** Lift **PARKING:** 20 **NOTES:** No smoking in restaurant **CARDS:**

### ★★62% Seascape

8-10 Tor Church Rd TQ2 5UT
☎ 01803 292617 🖷 01803 299260
e-mail: enquiries@torquayseascape.co.uk
***Dir:*** *Take A380 Torquay, at Torre station turn right, left at 2nd traffic lights. Through 1 set of lights, hotel is 100yds on right after lights*

This hotel offers splendid panoramic views and is only a short stroll from the town centre. Bedrooms are comfortable and well-equipped. A selection of public rooms is available and live entertainment is provided in the bar area several times a week. Traditional English cooking is served in the bright dining room.

**ROOMS:** 60 en suite (15 fmly) s £23-£34; d £40-£62 (incl. bkfst & dinner) * **LB** **FACILITIES:** STV Sauna Solarium Darts,pool tbl,tbl tennis. entertainment Xmas **SERVICES:** Lift **PARKING:** 22 **NOTES:** No dogs (ex guide dogs) No smoking in restaurant **CARDS:**

**★★60% Roseland**
Warren Rd TQ2 5TT
☎ 01803 213829 ▤ 01803 291266
e-mail: burlington.hotel@virgin.net
***Dir:*** *at sea front turn left, up Sheddon Hill and turn right at Warren Road*
Enjoying splendid, panoramic views over Torbay, this hotel was formerly the home of Lord Lytton, Viceroy of India. The simply furnished bedrooms have modern facilities, some have the benefit of patios, others have fine sea-views. Guests enjoy regular entertainment in the bar/lounge and the small leisure complex.
**ROOMS:** 39 en suite 1 annexe en suite (8 fmly) **FACILITIES:** Indoor swimming (H) Sauna Solarium Jacuzzi Games room entertainment Xmas **SERVICES:** Lift **CARDS:**

**★★59% Regina**
Victoria Pde TQ1 2BE
☎ 01803 292904 ▤ 01803 290270

Leisureplex

***Dir:*** *on entering Torquay, follow harbour signs*
Beside the harbour and very conveniently located for the town centre, this hotel predominantly attracts leisure guests. The soundly appointed bedrooms vary in size, with front facing rooms always in popular demand. Evening entertainment is regularly provided in the bar lounge.
**ROOMS:** 68 en suite (5 fmly) s £25-£33; d £42-£58 (incl. bkfst) * **FACILITIES:** entertainment Xmas **SERVICES:** Lift **PARKING:** 6 **NOTES:** No dogs (ex guide dogs) No smoking in restaurant Closed Jan-early Feb RS Nov-Dec & late Feb-Mar (open Mon-Fri)
**CARDS:**

**★69% Westwood**
111 Abbey Rd TQ2 5NP
☎ 01803 293818 ▤ 01803 293818
e-mail: reception@westwoodhotel.co.uk
***Dir:*** *on A380 follow signs for Seafront. At lights turn left and proceed straight through next lights. Go up Sheddon Hill. At lights at top of hill, turn left into Abbey Rd, hotel is on right*
An enthusiastic and friendly welcome is offered at this small, family-run hotel within walking distance of the town centre. Regular guests enjoy the informal atmosphere, particularly in the comfortable bar. Bedrooms are tastefully decorated, offering many modern facilities.
**ROOMS:** 25 en suite (6 fmly) s £22-£27; d £44-£54 (incl. bkfst) * **LB FACILITIES:** entertainment Xmas **PARKING:** 12 **NOTES:** No dogs (ex guide dogs) No smoking in restaurant RS Oct-May
**CARDS:**

**★63% *Villa Marina***
Cockington Ln, Livermead TQ2 6QU
☎ 01803 605440 ▤ 01803 605440
e-mail: villamarina@demon.co.uk
***Dir:*** *from main seafront head towards Paignton, turn right towards Cockington Village. Hotel 70yds on left*
Just a short walk from the seafront, a warm welcome awaits guests to this family owned hotel. Wonderful views across Torbay can be enjoyed from the public rooms and the front facing bedrooms. Live entertainment is provided during the high season and a heated outdoor pool is also available.
**ROOMS:** 25 en suite (5 fmly) No smoking in all bedrooms
**FACILITIES:** Outdoor swimming (H) **PARKING:** 20 **NOTES:** No dogs (ex guide dogs) No smoking in restaurant Closed 3-30 Jan
**CARDS:**

## TOTLAND BAY See Wight, Isle of

## TOTNES, Devon — Map 03 SX86
see also Staverton

**★★65% Royal Seven Stars**
The Plains TQ9 5DD
☎ 01803 862125 & 863241 ▤ 01803 867925
***Dir:*** *A38 Devon Expressway, exit Buckfastleigh turn off onto A384, follow the signs to Totnes town centre*
Dating back to the 17th century, this centrally located hostelry remains popular with locals and residents alike. A traditional range of cuisine is served in the restaurant, with a less formal option being available. The bedrooms are comfortable and well-equipped, many retaining the original charm of the building.
**ROOMS:** 16 rms (14 en suite) (2 fmly) s £49-£59; d £62-£69 (incl. bkfst) * **LB FACILITIES:** Xmas **CONF:** Thtr 70 Class 20 Board 20
**PARKING:** 20 **CARDS:**

## TOWCESTER, Northamptonshire — Map 04 SP64

**⌂ *Travelodge***
NN12 6TQ
☎ 01327 359105 ▤ 01327 359105
***Dir:*** *A43 East Towcester by-pass*
Travelodge offers good quality, good value, modern accommodation. Ideal for families, the spacious, en suite bedrooms include remote-control TV, tea and coffee-making facilities, luxury beds and free morning newspaper. Meals can be taken at the nearby family restaurant. For further details and the Travelodge phone number, consult the Hotel Groups page.

Travelodge

**ROOMS:** 33 en suite

## TRESCO See Scilly, Isles of

## TREYARNON BAY, Cornwall & Isles of Scilly — Map 02 SW87

**★★67% Waterbeach**
PL28 8JW
☎ 01841 520292 ▤ 01841 521102
e-mail: waterbeach@aol.com
***Dir:*** *from A389 take B3276 signed Newquay, after 2.5m straight across St Merryn X-rds, 3rd turning on right signed Treyarnon then 1st right and 1st left*
Many guests return on a regular basis to this coastal hotel. Bedrooms vary in size but all are equipped to the same standard; cottage rooms are especially popular with families. Public areas are comfortable and well-proportioned. Each evening, six-course dinners are served.
**ROOMS:** 13 en suite 6 annexe en suite (9 fmly) s £43-£53; d £86-£106 (incl. bkfst & dinner) * **FACILITIES:** **Spa** Tennis (hard) Putting green ch fac **PARKING:** 20 **NOTES:** No smoking in restaurant Closed Nov-Estr
**CARDS:**

T

## TRING, Hertfordshire — Map 04 SP91

**★★★★65% ◎ Pendley Manor**
Cow Ln HP23 5QY
☎ 01442 891891 ▤ 01442 890687
e-mail: info@pendley-manor.co.uk
***Dir:*** *M25 junct 20. Take A41 leaving at Tring exit. At rdbt take exit for Berkhamsted & London. Take 1st left signposted Tring Station & Pendley Manor*
This impressive Victorian mansion is set in extensive and mature landscaped grounds. Bedrooms are located in the manor house or in the newer wing. All rooms are equipped with a useful range of extra facilities, including fax machines, and many have four-poster

*continued on p600*

TRING, continued

beds. Public areas include a traditional bar with armchairs and sofas, making this an ideal venue to relax in before dinner in the Oak Restaurant.
**ROOMS:** 74 en suite (4 fmly) No smoking in 3 bedrooms s £100; d £120-£150 (incl. bkfst) * **LB** **FACILITIES:** STV Indoor swimming (H) Tennis (hard) Snooker Sauna Gym Croquet lawn Jacuzzi Steam room Xmas **CONF:** Thtr 230 Class 100 Board 50 Del £190 * **SERVICES:** Lift **PARKING:** 250 **NOTES:** Civ Wed 200 **CARDS:**

*See advert on opposite page*

### ★★★63% The Rose & Crown

High St HP23 5AH
☎ 01442 824071 📠 01442 890735
***Dir:*** *just off the A41 between Aylesbury/Hemel Hempstead, hotel in town centre*

This Tudor style manor house offers a great deal of charm. Bedrooms vary in size, though all are comfortably equipped, with particularly smart bathrooms. The restaurant and bar form the centre of the hotel, popular with both local customers and residents.
**ROOMS:** 27 en suite (3 fmly) No smoking in 3 bedrooms s fr £85; d fr £95 * **LB** **FACILITIES:** STV Full indoor leisure facilities available at sister hotel Xmas **CONF:** Thtr 80 Class 30 Board 30 **PARKING:** 60 **NOTES:** No dogs (ex guide dogs) **CARDS:**

## TROUTBECK (NEAR WINDERMERE), Cumbria Map 07 NY40

### ★★70% Mortal Man

LA23 1PL
☎ 015394 33193 📠 015394 31261
e-mail: the-mortalman@btinternet.com
***Dir:*** *2.5m N from junct of A591/A592, turn left before church into village, right at T junction, hotel 800m on right*
Nestling in an idyllic Lakeland hamlet, the Mortal Man combines the character of a village inn with the style of a country-house hotel. Day rooms include a comfortable lounge, and a bar featuring an open fire and old beams. The dining room looks out onto the valley and the well-equipped, attractively decorated bedrooms also enjoy views of the countryside.
**ROOMS:** 12 en suite s £50-£80; d £70-£90 (incl. bkfst) * **LB** **FACILITIES:** Fishing,Hrse Riding,Sailing,Guided Walks. Xmas **CONF:** Del from £55 * **PARKING:** 20 **NOTES:** No smoking in restaurant **CARDS:**

Weekend away? Hotels with LB in their entry offer leisure breaks.

## TROWBRIDGE, Wiltshire Map 03 ST85

### ★★64% Fieldways Hotel & Health Club

Hilperton Rd BA14 7JP
☎ 01225 768336 📠 01225 753649
***Dir:*** *last property on left leaving Trowbridge on A361 towards Melksham/Chippenham/Devizes*
Fieldways Hotel and Health Club is quietly set in well-kept grounds. The hotel provides a pleasant combination of spacious, comfortably furnished bedrooms, an impressive wood panelled dining room and a considerable range of indoor leisure facilities. 'Top to Toe' days are available incorporating the wide range of beauty treatments on offer.
**ROOMS:** 8 en suite 5 annexe en suite (2 fmly) s £50-£55; d £65-£75 (incl. bkfst) * **LB** **FACILITIES:** Indoor swimming (H) Sauna Solarium Gym Jacuzzi Range of beauty treatments/massage **CONF:** Thtr 50 Class 40 Board 8 **PARKING:** 70 **NOTES:** No dogs (ex guide dogs) No smoking in restaurant **CARDS:**

## TROWELL MOTORWAY SERVICE AREA (M1), Nottinghamshire Map 08 SK44

### *Travelodge*

Travelodge

NG9 3PL
☎ 01159 320291
***Dir:*** *M1 junc 25/26 northbound*
Travelodge offers good quality, good value, modern accommodation. Ideal for families, the spacious, en suite bedrooms include remote-control TV, tea and coffee-making facilities, luxury beds and free morning newspaper. Meals can be taken at the nearby family restaurant. For further details and the Travelodge phone number, consult the Hotel Groups page.

**ROOMS:** 35 en suite

## TRURO, Cornwall & Isles of Scilly Map 02 SW84

### ★★★74% Royal

Lemon St TR1 2QB
☎ 01872 270345 📠 01872 242453
e-mail: reception@royalhotelcornwall.co.uk
***Dir:*** *follow A30 to Carland Cross then Truro. Follow brown tourists signs to hotel in city centre. Drive up to barrier to obtain a pass from reception*
Perfectly situated in the centre of Truro, The Royal Hotel has extremely impressive bedrooms. These comfortable rooms are complemented by some 'executive' rooms complete with fax machines, CD players and work stations. Mannings Brasserie offers interesting modern, ethnic and classical dishes in an informal atmosphere.
**ROOMS:** 35 en suite (4 fmly) No smoking in 22 bedrooms **FACILITIES:** STV **PARKING:** 40 **NOTES:** No dogs (ex guide dogs) Closed 25 & 26 Dec **CARDS:**

*See advert on opposite page*

### ★★★69% ® Alverton Manor

Tregolls Rd TR1 1ZQ
☎ 01872 276633 📠 01872 222989
e-mail: reception@alvertonmanor.demon.co.uk
***Dir:*** *from at Carland Cross take A39 to Truro.*
Formerly a convent, this impressive sandstone property stands in six acres of grounds, within walking distance of the city centre. Alverton Manor provides a wide range of smart bedrooms, combining comfort with character. Stylish public areas include the library and the former chapel, now a striking function room,

*continued*

T

licensed for wedding ceremonies. Both a carte and fixed price menu are offered in the elegant restaurant.
**ROOMS:** 34 en suite s £72-£84; d £109-£133 (incl. bkfst) * **LB**
**FACILITIES:** STV Golf 18 Snooker Xmas **CONF:** Thtr 370 Class 178 Board 136 Del from £95 * **SERVICES:** Lift **PARKING:** 120 **NOTES:** No smoking in restaurant Civ Wed 120 **CARDS:**

*See advert on this page*

### ★★★60% Brookdale

Tregolls Rd TR1 1JZ
☎ 01872 273513 🖹 01872 272400
e-mail: brookdale@hotelstruro.com
***Dir:*** *from A30 onto A39, at the A390 junction turn right into city centre. Hotel is 600m down hill*

In an elevated position, with easy access to the city centre, the Brookdale Hotel provides comfortable accomodation for both business and pleasure guests. The bedrooms are currently undergoing a re-furbishment programme, which should be completed ready for the spring of 2002. Service is relaxed and a range of dishes is available in the restaurant, alternatively served in the bedroom.
**ROOMS:** 22 en suite (1 fmly) No smoking in 11 bedrooms s £40-£52; d £60-£70 (incl. cont bkfst) * **LB** **PARKING:** 55 **NOTES:** No smoking in restaurant **CARDS:**

### ★★66% Carlton

Falmouth Rd TR1 2HL
☎ 01872 272450 🖹 01872 223938
e-mail: reception@carltonhotel.co.uk
***Dir:*** *On approaching Truro on A39 straight across 1st & 2nd rdbts onto bypass (Morlaix Avenue). At top of sweeping bend/hill right at mini rdbt into Falmouth Rd and the Carlton Hotel is 100m on the right*

This family owned hotel is located in a residential area, just a

*continued on p602*



T

TRURO, continued

short walk from the city centre. Caring staff offer a warm welcome to guests and make every effort to ensure a pleasant stay. Bedrooms have benefited from recent refurbishment, whilst public areas are smartly presented and comfortable. A wide selection of home cooked food is offered.
**ROOMS:** 29 en suite (4 fmly) No smoking in 12 bedrooms s £34.50-£39.50; d £47.50-£52.50 (incl. bkfst) * **LB** **FACILITIES:** Sauna Jacuzzi **CONF:** Thtr 70 Class 24 Board 36 **PARKING:** 31 **NOTES:** Closed 23 Dec-6 Jan **CARDS:**

## TUNBRIDGE WELLS (ROYAL), Kent

Map 05 TQ53

### ★★★76% The Spa

Mount Ephraim TN4 8XJ
☎ 01892 520331 01892 510575
e-mail: info@spahotel.co.uk
**Dir:** *Turn off A21 to A26,follow signposts to A264 East Grinstead, hotel is on right hand side*

An 18th-century country house, situated amidst 14 acres of beautiful grounds, overlooking the spa town of Royal Tunbridge Wells. Bedrooms, many of which overlook the attractive gardens, are smartly furnished and well-equipped. Wood-panelled public rooms include a comfortable lobby lounge, a bar, the Chandelier restaurant and smart leisure facilities.
**ROOMS:** 71 en suite (10 fmly) s £85-£52; d £105-£165 * **LB** **FACILITIES:** STV Indoor swimming (H) Tennis (hard) Riding Sauna Gym Croquet lawn Steam room Beauty Salon Jogging trail entertainment ch fac Xmas **CONF:** Thtr 300 Class 93 Board 90 Del from £120 * **SERVICES:** Lift **PARKING:** 120 **NOTES:** Civ Wed 100
**CARDS:**

*See advert on opposite page*

T

### ★★★73% Royal Wells Inn

Mount Ephraim TN4 8BE
☎ 01892 511188 01892 511908
e-mail: info@royalwells.co.uk
**Dir:** *turn off A21 onto A26 then into Tunbridge Wells avoiding town centre, at junct of A264 take right fork, Inn is 100mtrs on right*
Delightful family-run hotel situated in an elevated position with stunning views. The accommodation is being continually upgraded to provide stylish, tastefully furnished, well-equipped bedrooms. There are two eating options, The Brasserie with its extensive blackboard menu, and the refurbished Conservatory with a full carte and daily menu. The dishes are interesting and carefully prepared from fresh local produce. The wine list is well-chosen

*continued*

and offers a range of reasonably priced selections to complement the menu.

**ROOMS:** 18 en suite (2 fmly) s £65-£85; d £85-£125 (incl. bkfst) * **LB** **FACILITIES:** STV entertainment **CONF:** Thtr 100 Class 40 Board 40 Del from £97.50 * **SERVICES:** Lift **PARKING:** 28 **NOTES:** Closed 25-26 Dec Civ Wed 50 **CARDS:**

*See advert on opposite page*

### ★★65% Russell

80 London Rd TN1 1DZ
☎ 01892 544833 01892 515846
e-mail: Sales@russell-hotel.com
**Dir:** *at junct A26/A264 uphill onto A26, hotel on right*
A friendly Victorian hotel, which is close to the town centre. Bedrooms are spacious, well-equipped and include some self-contained suites in an adjacent building. Enjoyable evening meals are served in the brightly appointed restaurant.
**ROOMS:** 19 en suite 5 annexe en suite (2 fmly) No smoking in 10 bedrooms s fr £70; d fr £85 (incl. bkfst) * **LB** **FACILITIES:** STV ch fac **CONF:** Board 12 **PARKING:** 15 **NOTES:** No dogs (ex guide dogs)
**CARDS:**

## *Town House*

### ★★★★ Hotel Du Vin & Bistro

Crescent Rd TN1 2LY
☎ 01892 526455 01892 512044
e-mail: reception@tunbridgewells.hotelduvin.com
**Dir:** *follow town centre to main intersection of Mount Pleasant Rd & Crescent Rd/Church Rd. Hotel 150yds along Crescent Rd on R just past Phillips House*
Impressive Grade II listed sandstone building ideally situated for exploring this historic spa town. It was built as a private residence in 1762 and as a princess, Queen Victoria was often in residence. The spacious bedrooms are individually decorated, tastefully furnished and equipped with many thoughtful extras. The public areas feature a wonderful bistro style restaurant, two elegant lounges and a small bar.
**ROOMS:** 32 en suite d £75-£139 * **FACILITIES:** STV Snooker **CONF:** Thtr 40 Class 30 Board 25 Del from £145 * **SERVICES:** Lift **PARKING:** 40 **NOTES:** No dogs (ex guide dogs)
**CARDS:**

Read all about it! Newspapers delivered to bedrooms in four and five star hotels.

TURNERS HILL, West Sussex Map 04 TQ33

## Premier Collection

### ★★★ Alexander House Hotel

East St RH10 4QD
☎ 01342 714914 01342 717328
e-mail: info@alexanderhouse.co.uk
***Dir:*** *on B2110 between Turners Hill and East Grinstead, 6m from M23 junct 10*

Very convenient for the M23 and the airport, Alexander House nonetheless seems a million miles from the hustle and bustle. The house dates in part from the 17th century, and is set in 135 acres of lovely gardens and parkland. The stylish restaurant offers confident modern cooking, and public rooms include an oak-panelled library. Bedrooms are individually decorated and there are some full suites.

**ROOMS:** 15 en suite (5 fmly) s £135; d £165-£310 (incl. bkfst) * **LB** **FACILITIES:** STV Tennis (hard) Snooker Croquet lawn Clay shooting,Archery by arrangement. entertainment Xmas **CONF:** Thtr 70 Class 24 Board 24 **SERVICES:** Lift **PARKING:** 50 **NOTES:** No dogs (ex guide dogs) No smoking in restaurant Civ Wed 60
**CARDS:**

*See advert under GATWICK AIRPORT (LONDON)*

TUTBURY, Staffordshire Map 08 SK22

### ★★★68% Ye Olde Dog & Partridge

High St DE13 9LS
☎ 01283 813030 01283 813178
e-mail: info@dogandpartridge.net
***Dir:*** *exit A50 between Burton-on-Trent and Uttoxeter, signposted off A50 as A511*

This pleasant village hotel dates in part from the 15th century. Public rooms have recently been extended and refurbished, offering a vibrant Brasserie, complemented by a strikingly refurbished bar. Bedrooms, which vary in size and style, are individually appointed, exceptionally well-equipped and comfortably furnished.

**ROOMS:** 6 en suite 14 annexe en suite (1 fmly) No smoking in 6 bedrooms s £55-£75; d £60-£99 (incl. bkfst) * **LB** **FACILITIES:** STV Full pass to Branston G&C Club entertainment **PARKING:** 150 **NOTES:** No smoking in restaurant RS evenings 25 & 26 Dec & 1 Jan
**CARDS:**

*See advert on page 605*

Arriving late? Four and five star hotels have night porters to assist with your luggage, and 24-hour room service.

T

TWICKENHAM, Greater London
See LONDON SECTION plan 1 B2

**★★★67% Popes Grotto**
Cross Deep TW1 4RB
☎ 020 8892 3050 020 8892 2758
e-mail: popesgrotto@youngs.co.uk
***Dir:*** *A316 keep left for Twickenham, from slip road take 3rd turning at rdbt & follow signs through traffic lights & into town centre*
This hotel takes its name from the poet Alexander Pope and overlooks the River Thames. Bedrooms and public areas have been completely refurbished and offer good standards of quality and comfort throughout. Food and drink can be enjoyed in the modern bar and restaurant.
**ROOMS:** 32 en suite (9 fmly) No smoking in 25 bedrooms s £105-£120; d £115-£130 (incl. bkfst) * **LB** **FACILITIES:** STV Xmas **CONF:** Thtr 50 Class 20 Board 20 Del from £100 * **SERVICES:** Lift air con **PARKING:** 55 **NOTES:** No dogs (ex guide dogs)
**CARDS:**

**Premier Lodge**
Chertsey Rd, Whitton TW2 6LS
☎ 0870 700 1440 0870 700 1441
PREMIER LODGE
Premier Lodge offers modern, well-equipped, en suite accommodation suitable for both business and leisure travellers. Meals can be taken at the adjacent popular restaurant and bar, which is fully licensed. For further details, consult the Hotel Groups page.
**ROOMS:** 31 en suite s £50; d £50 *

TWO BRIDGES, Devon Map 02 SX67

**★★78% Prince Hall**
PL20 6SA
☎ 01822 890403 01822 890676
e-mail: bookings@princehall.co.uk
***Dir:*** *on B3357 1m E of Two Bridges road junct*
Set in the heart of Dartmoor National Park, this delightful small hotel offers spectacular views. Each of the spacious bedrooms, named after Dartmoor's tors, has been equipped with thoughtful extras. Public areas, decorated and furnished to emphasise the character and charm of the house, include a bar-lounge and a cosy sitting room.
**ROOMS:** 8 en suite (1 fmly) s £65-£100; d £68-£85 (incl. bkfst & dinner) * **LB** **FACILITIES:** Fishing Riding Croquet lawn Guided Dartmoor Walks, Fly fishing, Gardens ch fac **CONF:** Del from £90 * **PARKING:** 13 **NOTES:** No children 10yrs No smoking in restaurant Closed Jan
**CARDS:**

T

**★★72% Two Bridges Hotel**
PL20 6SW
☎ 01822 890581 01822 890575
e-mail: sales@warm-welcome-hotels.co.uk
***Dir:*** *junc of B3212 & B3357*
Surrounded by the natural splendour of Dartmoor National Park, this is an engagingly comfortable hotel for all seasons. Traditional bar food is found in the Saracen's Bar, whilst the restaurant provides more formal dining with a choice of menus featuring locally sourced produce, cooked with style and flair. Three standards of bedrooms are available.

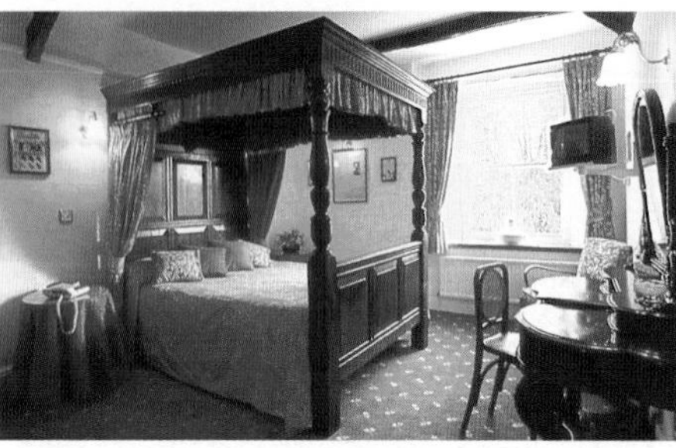

**ROOMS:** 29 en suite (2 fmly) No smoking in 21 bedrooms s £43-£70; d £85-£120 (incl. bkfst) * **LB** **FACILITIES:** STV Fishing Xmas **CONF:** Thtr 110 Class 60 Board 40 Del from £79 * **PARKING:** 100 **NOTES:** No smoking in restaurant **CARDS:**
*See advert on opposite page*

TYNEMOUTH, Tyne & Wear Map 12 NZ36

**★★★68% Grand**
Grand Pde NE30 4ER
☎ 0191 293 6666 0191 293 6665
e-mail: info@grandhotel-uk.com
***Dir:*** *A1058 for Tynemouth, when reach coastline rdbt turn right. The Grand Hotel is on right approx 0.5m along road*
Standing on the seafront and with magnificent sea views from many of its rooms, this classic Victorian resort hotel has been completely upgraded to attract the modern traveller. Public rooms retain their former elegance with an imposing reception lobby and grand staircase setting the scene. There is a choice of bars, whilst bedrooms are smartly furnished and have impressive bathrooms.
**ROOMS:** 45 annexe en suite (13 fmly) s £60-£90; d £65-£160 (incl. bkfst) * **FACILITIES:** STV entertainment Xmas **CONF:** Thtr 130 Class 40 Board 40 Del £115 * **SERVICES:** Lift **PARKING:** 18 **NOTES:** No dogs (ex guide dogs) Civ Wed 100
**CARDS:**

UCKFIELD, East Sussex Map 05 TQ42

**★★★★71% *Buxted Park Country House Hotel***
ARCADIAN HOTELS Distinctly Different
Buxted, Buxted TN22 4AY
☎ 01825 732711 01825 732770
***Dir:*** *on A272. Turn off the A22, A26, or A267 on to the A27 towards Heathfield then Buxted*
A Georgian mansion set in 300 acres of beautiful countryside, offering a grand country house atmosphere and retaining many original features. Bedrooms, mostly in the modern Garden Wing, are stylish and well-equipped. The original Victorian Orangery serves good cuisine from an interesting menu.
**ROOMS:** 44 en suite (6 fmly) No smoking in 16 bedrooms **FACILITIES:** STV Outdoor swimming (H) Fishing Snooker Sauna Solarium Gym Croquet lawn Putting green Jacuzzi Beauty salon Clay pigeon shooting Archery **CONF:** Thtr 150 Class 60 Board 40 **PARKING:** 150 **NOTES:** No dogs (ex guide dogs) No smoking in restaurant Civ Wed 80 **CARDS:**

★★★78% @@ **Horsted Place**
Little Horsted TN22 5TS
☎ 01825 750581 ▯ 01825 750459
e-mail: hotel@horstedplace.co.uk
***Dir:*** *2m S on A26 towards Lewes*
Ideally situated just on the outskirts of Uckfield and surrounded by its own estate which includes a golf club. Horsted Place is one of Britain's finest examples of Gothic revivalist architecture, inside there are many fine architectural features, including a splendid Pugin staircase. Bedrooms are notably spacious and well-appointed, many are suites.
**ROOMS:** 17 en suite 3 annexe en suite (5 fmly) s £110-£300; d £110-£330 (incl. bkfst) * **LB** **FACILITIES:** STV Indoor swimming (H) Golf 36 Tennis (hard) Croquet lawn entertainment ch fac Xmas **CONF:** Thtr 80 Class 50 Board 40 Del from £160 * **SERVICES:** Lift **PARKING:** 36 **NOTES:** No dogs (ex guide dogs) No children 7yrs No smoking in restaurant Civ Wed 90 **CARDS:**

ULLESTHORPE, Leicestershire — Map 04 SP58

★★★67% **Ullesthorpe Court Hotel & Golf Club**
Frolesworth Rd LE17 5BZ
☎ 01455 209023 ▯ 01455 202537
e-mail: bookings@ullesthorpecourt.co.uk
***Dir:*** *from junct 20 of M1 head towards Lutterworth then follow brown tourist signs*

This impressive hotel, golf and country club complex has extensive grounds and is near the motorway network, the NEC and Birmingham Airport. Public areas include a choice of restaurants and offer a good range of leisure facilities and pursuits. Bedrooms are spacious and well-equipped and there are conference facilities available.
**ROOMS:** 38 en suite (1 fmly) No smoking in 20 bedrooms s £80; d £105 (incl. bkfst) * **LB** **FACILITIES:** **Spa** STV Indoor swimming (H) Golf 18 Tennis (hard) Snooker Sauna Solarium Gym Putting green Jacuzzi Beauty room Steam room **CONF:** Thtr 100 Class 50 Board 36 Del £99.50 * **PARKING:** 500 **NOTES:** No smoking in restaurant RS 25 & 26 Dec **CARDS:**

ULLSWATER See Glenridding, Patterdale, & Watermillock

UMBERLEIGH, Devon — Map 02 SS62

★★70% **Rising Sun Inn**
EX37 9DU
☎ 01769 560447 ▯ 01769 560764
e-mail: risingsuninn@btinternet.com
***Dir:*** *situated at Umberleigh Bridge on the A377, Exeter/Barnstaple road, at the junct of the B3227*
This charming inn has long been a popular haunt for fishermen, and overlooks the river. Extensively renovated without sacrificing character, the Rising Sun provides comfortable, well-equipped

*continued on p606*

U

UMBERLEIGH, continued

bedrooms. The bar features an inglenook fireplace and fishing memorabilia. An interesting range of dishes feature on both the set price menu and blackboard specials.
**ROOMS:** 6 en suite 3 annexe en suite (1 fmly) No smoking in all bedrooms s £40; d £77 (incl. bkfst) * **LB** **FACILITIES:** STV Fishing Massage & reflexology entertainment Xmas **CONF:** Thtr 50 Board 24 Del £67 * **PARKING:** 35 **NOTES:** No smoking in restaurant
**CARDS:**

*See advert under BARNSTAPLE*

## UPHOLLAND, Lancashire — Map 07 SD50

★★★65% **Quality Hotel Skelmersdale**
Prescott Rd WN8 9PU
☎ 01695 720401 📠 01695 50953
e-mail: admin@gb656.u-net.com
***Dir:*** *exit M6 junct 26 to M58. Leave at junct 5 for 'Pimbo' & turn left at rdbt follow into Prescott Road. Hotel situated on right*
This friendly hotel has attractive grounds and a magnificent Great Hall, dating back to 1580, now used primarily for banquets and weddings. The modern bedrooms are well-equipped, and include facilities for disabled guests. Bare stone walls in the bar and restaurant give character to the public areas.
**ROOMS:** 55 en suite (3 fmly) No smoking in 35 bedrooms
**FACILITIES:** STV Xmas **CONF:** Thtr 200 Class 125 Board 70
**PARKING:** 200 **NOTES:** No smoking in restaurant Civ Wed 200
**CARDS:**

## UPPER SHERINGHAM, Norfolk — Map 09 TG14

★★★65% **Dales Country House Hotel**
Lodge Hill NR26 8TJ
☎ 01263 824555 📠 01263 822647
***Dir:*** *On B1157 1m S of Sheringham, from A148 take turning at entrance to Sheringham Park continue for 0.5m hotel on left*
This impressive hotel stands in delightful and extensive grounds on the edge of the village of Upper Sheringham. The public rooms are very comfortable with wood panelling a feature. Bedrooms are spacious and well-equipped while the service is friendly and professional. The cooking is well-presented and carefully prepared.
**ROOMS:** 17 en suite (1 fmly) No smoking in all bedrooms s £65-£77; d £90-£102 (incl. bkfst) * **LB** **FACILITIES:** Tennis (grass) Xmas **CONF:** Thtr 40 Class 20 Board 27 Del from £85 * **SERVICES:** Lift **PARKING:** 30 **NOTES:** No dogs (ex guide dogs) No children No smoking in restaurant **CARDS:**

## UPPER SLAUGHTER, Gloucestershire — Map 04 SP12

### *Premier Collection*

★★★ **Lords of the Manor**
GL54 2JD
☎ 01451 820243 📠 01451 820696
e-mail: lordsofthemanor@btinternet.com
***Dir:*** *2m W of A429. Turn off A40 onto A429, take 'The Slaughters' turning. Continue through Lower Slaughter for 1m until Upper Slaughter-hotel on right*
This 17th century manor house hotel sits in eight acres of gardens and parkland and is surrounded by Cotswold countryside. Public rooms include comfortable lounges, each with individual style, and a spacious and elegant restaurant where the dishes and kitchen brigade continue to impress for their innovation and accuracy. Bedrooms enjoy all the character and charm of the old building and offer the extra nice touches expected of an hotel operating to this high standard.

**ROOMS:** 27 en suite s £99; d £149-£299 (incl. bkfst) * **LB**
**FACILITIES:** STV Fishing Croquet lawn Xmas **CONF:** Thtr 30 Class 20 Board 20 Del £170 * **PARKING:** 40 **NOTES:** No dogs (ex guide dogs) No smoking in restaurant Civ Wed 50
**CARDS:**

## UPPINGHAM, Rutland — Map 04 SP89

★★71% **The Lake Isle**
High St East LE15 9PZ
☎ 01572 822951 📠 01572 822951
***Dir:*** *in the centre of Uppingham via Queen St*
Developed from the original restaurant, this town house hotel has bedrooms in the main house and adjacent converted cottages; all are attractively decorated and well-equipped with thoughtful extras. The ground floor public rooms are dominated by the hotel restaurant; diners choose from a small carte that offers quality cuisine. Guests can also relax in the comfortably appointed first floor lounge.
**ROOMS:** 10 en suite 2 annexe en suite s £52; d £69 (incl. bkfst) * **LB**
**CONF:** Board 10 **PARKING:** 7 **NOTES:** No smoking in restaurant
**CARDS:**

## UPTON UPON SEVERN, Worcestershire — Map 03 SO84

★★★66% **White Lion**
21 High St WR8 0HJ
☎ 01684 592551 📠 01684 593333
e-mail: reservations@whitelionhotel.demon.co.uk
***Dir:*** *from A422 take A38 towards Tewkesbury. In 8m take B4104 and after 1m cross bridge, turn left to hotel around bend on left*

Despite its Georgian façade, this town centre hostelry dates back to 1510, and is famous for being the inn depicted in Henry

*continued*

Fielding's novel Tom Jones. The public areas have a lot of character, including exposed beams. Bedrooms all have modern equipment and facilities. The hotel has a well-deserved reputation for the quality of its food.
**ROOMS:** 10 en suite s £53; d £77 (incl. bkfst) * **LB** **CONF:** Thtr 24 Class 12 Board 12 **PARKING:** 20 **NOTES:** No smoking in restaurant RS 25,26 Dec & 1 Jan **CARDS:**

## UTTOXETER, Staffordshire Map 07 SK03

### *Travelodge*

Ashbourne Rd ST14 5AA
☎ 01889 562043 01889 562043
***Dir:*** *on A50/A5030*

Travelodge

Travelodge offers good quality, good value, modern accommodation. Ideal for families, the spacious, en suite bedrooms include remote-control TV, tea and coffee-making facilities, luxury beds and free morning newspaper. Meals can be taken at the nearby family restaurant. For further details and the Travelodge phone number, consult the Hotel Groups page.

**ROOMS:** 32 en suite

## VENTNOR See Wight, Isle of

## VERYAN, Cornwall & Isles of Scilly Map 02 SW93

### ★★★★75% *Nare*

Carne Beach TR2 5PF
☎ 01872 501111 01872 501856
e-mail: office@narehotel.co.uk
***Dir:*** *from Tregony follow A3078 for approx 1.5m turn left at signpost Veryan, drive straight through village towards sea and hotel*

This delightful property offers country-house care and courtesy in a spectacular coastal setting. Many of the bedrooms have balconies, the perfect place to enjoy the invigorating sound of surf meeting sand! Fresh flowers, carefully chosen artwork and antiques, all contribute to the engaging individuality. A choice of dining options is available with a wide range of food from light snacks to superb local seafood.
**ROOMS:** 38 en suite (4 fmly) **FACILITIES:** STV Indoor swimming (H) Outdoor swimming (H) Tennis (hard) Snooker Sauna Gym Croquet lawn Jacuzzi Windsurfing Health & Beauty clinic Hotel Boat **SERVICES:** Lift **PARKING:** 80 **NOTES:** No smoking in restaurant **CARDS:**

## VIRGINIA WATER, Surrey Map 04 TQ06

### ★★70% *The Wheatsheaf*

London Rd GU25 4QF
☎ 01344 842057 01344 842932

Scottish Newcastle hotels

This property is located overlooking the lake.
Bedrooms are a good size with stylish décor and good facilities. The public area consists of a country-style bar with a substantial lunch and dinner menu. Plenty of parking is available.

## VIRGINSTOW, Devon Map 02 SX39

### ★★73% Percy's Country Hotel & Restaurant

Combeshead Estate EX21 5EA
☎ 01409 211236 01409 211275
e-mail: info@percys.co.uk

Set in 130 acres, this restored 16th-century Devon longhouse is the perfect place to take time out; friendly Labradors will happily provide an escort around the estate! Spacious bedrooms are well-

*continued*

equipped and offer high levels of comfort. The stylish restaurant is the venue for impressive cuisine, with an emphasis upon superb local organic produce.

**ROOMS:** 8 en suite (1 fmly) No smoking in all bedrooms s £59.50-£110; d £79.50-£155 (incl. bkfst) * **LB** **FACILITIES:** Fishing Riding Xmas **PARKING:** 50 **NOTES:** No smoking in restaurant
**CARDS:**

## WADEBRIDGE, Cornwall & Isles of Scilly Map 02 SW97

### ★★65% Molesworth Arms

Molesworth St PL27 7DP
☎ 01208 812055 01208 814254
e-mail: sarah@molesworth.ision.co.uk
***Dir:*** *A30 to Bodmin town centre and follow directions to Wadebridge. Over old bridge turn right and then 1st left*

Situated in a pedestrian area of the town, this 16th-century former coaching inn is an ideal base for exploring the area. The comfortable bedrooms have been decorated to retain their original character and charm. In addition to the wide range of snacks and meals served in the beamed bar, the Courtyard Restaurant offers a comprehensive carte.
**ROOMS:** 16 rms (14 en suite) (2 fmly) s fr £40; d fr £60 (incl. bkfst) * **LB** **FACILITIES:** STV **CONF:** Thtr 60 Class 50 Board 40 Del from £50 * **PARKING:** 16 **NOTES:** No smoking in restaurant
**CARDS:**

## WAKEFIELD, West Yorkshire Map 08 SE32

### ★★★73% Waterton Park

Walton Hall, The Balk, Walton WF2 6PW
☎ 01924 257911 & 249800 01924 259686
e-mail: deidrk@aol.co.uk

Best Western

***Dir:*** *3m SE off B6378 - off M1 at junct 39 towards Wakefield. At rdbt take right for Crofton. At the second set of traffic lights turn right follow signs*

Surrounded by a moat and with its own lake and extensive grounds, this impressive stone built hotel is a popular venue for weddings and conferences. There are attractive, modern

*continued on p608*

WAKEFIELD, continued

bedrooms and the public rooms include two bars and a delightful beamed restaurant. The spacious and appealing annexe bedrooms are particularly desirable.
**ROOMS:** 25 en suite 35 annexe en suite No smoking in 10 bedrooms s £90-£95; d £120-£130 (incl. bkfst) * **LB** **FACILITIES:** **Spa** STV Indoor swimming (H) Golf 18 Fishing Snooker Sauna Solarium Gym Jacuzzi Steam room Xmas **CONF:** Thtr 150 Class 80 Board 80 Del from £120 * **PARKING:** 180 **NOTES:** No dogs (ex guide dogs) No smoking in restaurant Civ Wed 80 **CARDS:**

### ★★★71% St Pierre

Barnsley Rd, Newmillerdam WF2 6QG
☎ 01924 255596 📠 01924 252746
e-mail: sales@hotelstpierre.co.uk
***Dir:*** *Exit M1 junct 39 take A636 to Wakefield, turn right at rdbt, on to Asdale Road to traffic lights. Turn right onto A61 towards Barnsley. Hotel just after lake*
This well-furnished hotel lies three miles to the south of Wakefield. The interior of the modern building has much charm, with comfortable and thoughtfully equipped bedrooms and an elegantly furnished and intimate restaurant. The public areas also include a range of conference rooms and a gymnasium. Staff are friendly and helpful.
**ROOMS:** 54 en suite (3 fmly) No smoking in 33 bedrooms s £73-£103; d £73-£103 * **LB** **FACILITIES:** STV Gym Xmas **CONF:** Thtr 130 Class 70 Board 50 Del from £65 * **SERVICES:** Lift **PARKING:** 70 **NOTES:** Civ Wed 60 **CARDS:**

### ★★★68% *Posthouse Wakefield*

Posthouse

Queen's Dr, Ossett WF5 9BE
☎ 0870 400 9082 📠 01924 276437
e-mail: gm1231@forte-hotels.com
***Dir:*** *exit M1 at junct 40 following signs for Wakefield. Hotel is on the right after 200yrds*
This modern hotel provides a good standard of accommodation. Bedrooms are smartly decorated, with many in the new 'superior' style. Traders' Restaurant offers a full menu, and refreshments are served all day in the lounge. 24-hour room service is also available and several new conference suites enhance meeting room options.
**ROOMS:** 99 en suite (27 fmly) No smoking in 71 bedrooms **CONF:** Thtr 160 Class 70 Board 100 **SERVICES:** Lift **PARKING:** 130 **CARDS:**

### ⌂ *Travelodge*

Travelodge

M1 Service Area, West Bretton WF4 4LQ
☎ 08700 850950
(For full entry see Woolley Edge)

### ⌂ Campanile

Monckton Rd WF2 7AL
☎ 01924 201054 📠 01924 201055
***Dir:*** *M1 junct 39, A636 1m towards Wakefield, left onto Monckton Road, hotel on left*
This modern building offers accommodation in smart, well-equipped bedrooms, all with en suite bathrooms. Refreshments may be taken at the informal Bistro. For further details and the Campanile phone number, consult the Hotel Groups page.

RESTAURANT

**ROOMS:** 77 annexe en suite s £30-£39; d £30-£39 * **CONF:** Thtr 35 Class 18 Board 20 Del £68 *

### ○ Express by Holiday Inn

☎ 0800 897121
A modern budget hotel offering comfortable accommodation in refreshing, spacious and comprehensively equipped bedrooms, en suite bathrooms with power showers and continental buffet breakfast included in the room rate. Suitable for business travellers or families. For further details and the Express by Holiday Inn phone number, consult the Hotel Groups page.
**ROOMS:** 74 en suite **NOTES:** Opening 2002

---

## WALLASEY, Merseyside — Map 07 SJ29

### ★★★70% *Grove House*

Grove Rd L45 3HF
☎ 0151 639 3947 & 0151 630 4558 📠 0151 639 0028
***Dir:*** *M53 junct 1, follow A544*
An immaculately maintained, family-owned hotel. Many bedrooms enjoy a view over attractive gardens to the rear; all are comfortably furnished and particularly well-equipped. The bar lounge provides a venue for drinks before dinner in the oak-panelled restaurant.
**ROOMS:** 14 en suite (3 fmly) **FACILITIES:** STV **CONF:** Thtr 60 Class 40 Board 50 **PARKING:** 28 **NOTES:** No dogs (ex guide dogs) **CARDS:**

---

## WALLINGFORD, Oxfordshire — Map 04 SU68

### ★★★72% ®® Springs

Wallingford Rd, North Stoke OX10 6BE
☎ 01491 836687 📠 01491 836877
e-mail: info@thespringshotel.co.uk
***Dir:*** *turn off the A4074 Oxford-Reading Rd onto the B4009 - Goring. The Springs is 1m on the right hand side*
The Springs Hotel is set in the heart of the Thames Valley, and has its own 18-hole golf course. The house dates back to 1874 and offers spacious and well-equipped bedrooms, many with balconies. The restaurant enjoys splendid views over the lake and

continued

grounds and other public rooms include a cosy lounge with a log fire as well as several dining rooms.

**ROOMS:** 31 en suite (3 fmly) s £90-£130; d £100-£165 (incl. bkfst) * **LB** **FACILITIES:** STV Outdoor swimming (H) Golf 18 Fishing Sauna Croquet lawn Putting green Xmas **CONF:** Thtr 60 Class 16 Board 26 Del from £160 * **PARKING:** 120 **NOTES:** No smoking in restaurant Civ Wed 50 **CARDS:**

### ★★★66% The George

PEEL HOTELS

High St OX10 0BS
☎ 01491 836665 Fax 01491 825359
e-mail: infor@george-hotel-wallingford.com
***Dir:*** *E side of A329 on N entry to town*

The main building of this hotel is believed to date back to the 16th century and it has all the delightful features to match. The majority of the well-equipped bedrooms are in a purpose-built wing; those in the main house have lots of character and comfort. Public areas include Wealh's restaurant, the popular public bar offering light snacks, and the brasserie bar serving refreshments all day.
**ROOMS:** 39 en suite (1 fmly) No smoking in 9 bedrooms s £89-£99; d £99-£120 * **LB** **FACILITIES:** STV Xmas **CONF:** Thtr 120 Class 60 Board 40 Del from £75 * **PARKING:** 60 **NOTES:** No smoking in restaurant **CARDS:**

### ★★★65% Shillingford Bridge

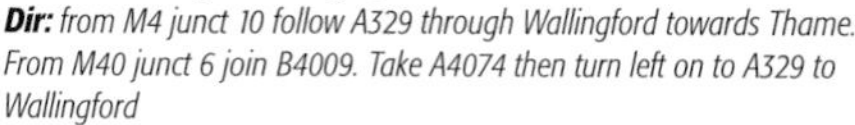
Forestdale
Hotels

Shillingford OX10 8LZ
☎ 01865 858567 Fax 01865 858636
e-mail: shillingford.bridge@forestdale.com
***Dir:*** *from M4 junct 10 follow A329 through Wallingford towards Thame. From M40 junct 6 join B4009. Take A4074 then turn left on to A329 to Wallingford*

This popular hotel, situated on the banks of the Thames, has its own moorings and a waterside open-air swimming pool. The public areas make good use of the view from the large picture windows, where guests can relax or enjoy a meal in the restaurant. Bedrooms are well-equipped and furnished with comfort in mind.
**ROOMS:** 34 en suite 8 annexe en suite (6 fmly) No smoking in 5 bedrooms s £63-£73; d £126-£146 (incl. bkfst & dinner) * **LB** **FACILITIES:** Outdoor swimming (H) Fishing Squash entertainment Xmas **CONF:** Thtr 80 Class 36 Board 26 Del £130 * **PARKING:** 100 **NOTES:** Civ Wed **CARDS:**

## WALSALL, West Midlands — Map 07 SP09

### ★★★★66% Menzies Baron's Court

MENZIES HOTELS

Walsall Rd, Walsall Wood WS9 9AH
☎ 0870 6003013 Fax 01332 511144
e-mail: info@menzies-hotels.co.uk
***Dir:*** *3m NE A461*

The Baron's Court Hotel is ideally situated for both leisure and business requirements in the heart of the Midlands. Refurbishment has seen significant improvements to bedrooms, public areas and the stylish brasserie. Additional features of the hotel include a leisure complex and conference facilities.

**ROOMS:** 95 en suite (2 fmly) No smoking in 19 bedrooms s £75; d £75 * **LB** **FACILITIES:** STV Indoor swimming (H) Sauna Solarium Gym Jacuzzi entertainment Xmas **CONF:** Thtr 200 Class 100 Board 100 Del from £110 * **SERVICES:** Lift **PARKING:** 200 **NOTES:** No smoking in restaurant Civ Wed 200 **CARDS:**

### ★★★76% The Fairlawns at Aldridge

Best
Western

178 Little Aston Rd, Aldridge WS9 0NU
☎ 01922 455122 Fax 01922 743210
e-mail: welcome@fairlawns.co.uk
***Dir:*** *off A452 towards Aldridge at crossroads with A454, Hotel 600 yards on right*

From its rural location this friendly hotel offers a wide range of facilities and modern, comfortable bedrooms. Family rooms, one room with a four-poster bed, suites and some budget rooms are available. The Fairlawns Restaurant serves a wide range of seasonal dishes. The leisure complex is predominantly for adult use and has restricted availability for young people.
**ROOMS:** 50 en suite (8 fmly) No smoking in 20 bedrooms s £63-£110; d £98-£130 (incl. bkfst) * **LB** **FACILITIES:** Spa STV Indoor swimming (H) Tennis (hard) Sauna Solarium Gym Croquet lawn Putting green Jacuzzi Dance studio Beauty Salon ch fac **CONF:** Thtr 80 Class 40 Board 30 Del from £107.50 * **PARKING:** 150 **NOTES:** No smoking in restaurant RS 23 Dec-2 Jan Civ Wed 100
**CARDS:**

### ★★★67% Quality Hotel & Suites Walsall

20 Wolverhampton Rd West, Bentley WS2 0BS
☎ 01922 724444 Fax 01922 723148
e-mail: admin@gb622.u-net.com
***Dir:*** *situated on rdbt at junct 10, M6*

All the accommodation at this conveniently located hotel is well-equipped. It includes air conditioned suites with a personal fax

continued on p610

WALSALL, continued

and kitchen with a microwave and fridge. There is an extensive all day menu, plus room service and a carvery restaurant.
**ROOMS:** 154 en suite (120 fmly) No smoking in 64 bedrooms s £50-£85; d £65-£125 * **LB** **FACILITIES:** STV Indoor swimming (H) Sauna Gym Jacuzzi **CONF:** Thtr 180 Class 70 Board 80 Del from £65 * **PARKING:** 160 **NOTES:** No dogs (ex guide dogs) No smoking in restaurant Civ Wed 120 **CARDS:**

### ★★★65% Beverley

58 Lichfield Rd WS4 2DJ
☎ 01922 614967 & 622999 01922 724187
***Dir:*** *1m N of Walsall town centre on A461 to Lichfield*
A privately owned hotel dating back to 1880. Bedrooms are pleasantly and comfortably appointed with modern fixtures and fittings and other thoughtful extras. Public areas include a separate guest lounge and a spacious lounge bar combined with a conservatory. The Gallery Restaurant provides a pleasant atmosphere in which to enjoy appetising dishes.
**ROOMS:** 40 en suite (2 fmly) No smoking in 2 bedrooms s £65-£85; d £70-£100 (incl. bkfst) * **LB** **FACILITIES:** Spa Games room ch fac **CONF:** Thtr 60 Class 30 Board 30 Del from £85 * **PARKING:** 68 **NOTES:** No dogs (ex guide dogs) No smoking in restaurant
**CARDS:**

### ★★★63% The Boundary

Birmingham Rd WS5 3AB
☎ 01922 633609 01922 635727
e-mail: boundaryhotel@talk21.com
***Dir:*** *off M6 at junct 7, A34 to Walsall. Hotel 2m on left*
Bedrooms at this modern hotel, including some on the ground floor, are soundly furnished and well-equipped. Room service is available during the evening and a limited service throughout the night. Carte and carvery meals are provided in the pleasantly appointed main restaurant or, alternatively, more informal meals are served in the public bar.
**ROOMS:** 95 en suite (3 fmly) s £55-£95; d £55-£95 * **LB** **FACILITIES:** STV Tennis (hard) entertainment **CONF:** Thtr 60 Class 30 Board 30 Del from £85 * **SERVICES:** Lift **PARKING:** 250 **NOTES:** No smoking in restaurant Civ Wed 40
**CARDS:**

### ★★63% Bescot

87 Bescot Rd WS2 9DG
☎ 01922 622447 01922 630256
e-mail: enquiries@bescothotel.com
***Dir:*** *from junct 9 M6 take Walsall road. Hotel 100mtrs on right*
The Bescot is a privately owned and business-focused hotel. Public rooms are comfortable and freshly furnished, including a large function suite and a spacious restaurant. Bedrooms have a good range of facilities and the annexe rooms are spacious, especially the two ground floor courtyard rooms. The new owners have positive plans for major refurbishment.
**ROOMS:** 22 en suite 11 annexe en suite (4 fmly) s £35-£40; d £45-£50 (incl. bkfst) * **LB** **FACILITIES:** STV Xmas **CONF:** Thtr 80 Class 50 Board 40 Del from £63.50 * **PARKING:** 55 **NOTES:** No dogs (ex guide dogs) **CARDS:**

WALTERSTONE, Herefordshire

### ★★★67% Allt-yr-Ynys Country House Hotel

HR2 0DU
☎ 01873 890307 01873 890539
e-mail: allthotel@compuserve.com
(For full entry see Abergavenny)

WALTHAM ABBEY, Essex Map 05 TL30

### ★★★★64% Waltham Abbey Marriott

Old Shire Ln EN9 3LX
☎ 01992 717170 01992 711841
e-mail: waltham.abbey@marriotthotels.co.uk
***Dir:*** *off junct 26 of M25*

Marriott HOTELS · RESORTS · SUITES

Guests have the use of a number of useful facilities, including a well-appointed leisure club, substantial car park and shuttle service to nearby transport links. Comfortable bedrooms offer a wide range of extras.
**ROOMS:** 162 en suite (14 fmly) No smoking in 132 bedrooms s fr £115; d fr £115 * **LB** **FACILITIES:** STV Indoor swimming (H) Sauna Solarium Gym Jacuzzi Steam room Beauty Salon entertainment Xmas **CONF:** Thtr 250 Class 120 Board 50 Del from £165 * **SERVICES:** air con **PARKING:** 240 **NOTES:** No dogs (ex guide dogs) No smoking in restaurant **CARDS:**

WALTON-ON-THAMES, Surrey
See also see also Weybridge

### ○ Innkeeper's Lodge Walton-on-Thames

Ashley Park Rd KT12 1JP

Innkeeper's Lodge

A new concept in the travel accommodation market. Smart rooms meet essential business requirements but also have home comforts. Dining options include all-day menus plus the added advantage of breakfast, which is included in the room price. Reservations can be made seven days a week through the room reservations number: 0870 243 0500. For further details, consult the Hotel Groups page.
**ROOMS:** 15 en suite

WANSFORD, Cambridgeshire Map 04 TL09

### ★★★74% The Haycock Hotel

PE8 6JA
☎ 01780 782223 01780 783031
***Dir:*** *at junct of A47/A1*
Situated just off the A1, this 17th-century hotel has welcomed travellers for many years. Attractive stone buildings have been restored to provide well-equipped bedrooms with thoughtful extras. Guests can dine in the main restaurant or in the Orchards conservatory brasserie. Lounges with log fires and an inviting bar form the hub of the hotel.
**ROOMS:** 50 en suite (3 fmly) No smoking in 6 bedrooms s £75-£85; d £90-£115 * **LB** **FACILITIES:** STV Fishing Petanque Xmas **CONF:** Thtr 250 Class 100 Board 40 Del from £140 * **PARKING:** 300 **NOTES:** No smoking in restaurant **CARDS:**

Fancy a Singapore Sling? Bar staff in five star hotels should be skilled cocktail mixers.

WARDLEY, Tyne & Wear Map 12 NZ36

### Travelodge

Leam Ln, Whitemare Pool NE10 8YB
☎ 0191 438 3333 📠 0191 438 3333
***Dir:*** *at junc of A194M/A184*

Travelodge offers good quality, good value, modern accommodation. Ideal for families, the spacious, en suite bedrooms include remote-control TV, tea and coffee-making facilities, luxury beds and free morning newspaper. Meals can be taken at the nearby family restaurant. For further details and the Travelodge phone number, consult the Hotel Groups page.

**ROOMS:** 71 en suite

WARE, Hertfordshire Map 05 TL31

### ★★★★★73% Marriott Hanbury Manor Hotel & Country Club

SG12 0SD
☎ 01920 487722 📠 01920 487692
e-mail: angela.thurlow@marriotthotels.co.uk
***Dir:*** *on A10 12m N of junct 25 of M25*

It is believed that the architecture of this stunning Jacobean-style mansion was inspired by nearby Hatfield House. Set in 200 acres of impressive, landscaped grounds, the hotel boasts an enviable range of leisure facilities. Bedrooms are traditionally and comfortably furnished in the country house style and have lovely marbled bathrooms. There are a number of food and drink options, including the renowned Zodiac restaurant.

**ROOMS:** 134 en suite 27 annexe en suite No smoking in 100 bedrooms s £149-£349; d £149-£349 * LB **FACILITIES:** Spa STV Indoor swimming (H) Golf 18 Tennis (hard) Snooker Sauna Solarium Gym Croquet lawn Putting green Jacuzzi Health & beauty treatments Aerobics Yoga Dance class ch fac Xmas **CONF:** Thtr 120 Class 80 Board 38 Del from £210 * **SERVICES:** Lift **PARKING:** 200 **NOTES:** No smoking in restaurant Civ Wed 120 **CARDS:**

### ★★★60% Roebuck

Baldock Street` SG12 9DR
☎ 01920 409955 📠 01920 468016
e-mail: roebuck@zoffanyhotels.co.uk
***Dir:*** *turn off A10 onto B1001 turn left at rdbt first left behind Fire Station*

Close to the town centre, this popular modern hotel offers a range of versatile conference rooms, a giant screen satellite TV and a bar with pool table. Bedrooms are spacious and well-equipped, some are suitable for disabled guests.

**ROOMS:** 50 en suite (1 fmly) No smoking in 16 bedrooms **FACILITIES:** STV **CONF:** Thtr 200 Class 100 Board 60 Del from £100 * **SERVICES:** Lift **PARKING:** 80 **NOTES:** No smoking in restaurant **CARDS:**

WAREHAM, Dorset Map 03 SY98

## Premier Collection

### ★★★ Priory

Church Green BH20 4ND
☎ 01929 551666 📠 01929 554519
e-mail: reception@theprioryhotel.co.uk
***Dir:*** *A351 at Station rdbt take North Causeway/North St, left into East St at lights, 1st right into Church St, hotel between church and river*

Set amidst four acres of well-tended gardens on the River Frome, this former priory is steeped in history and balances true professionalism with friendliness. A choice of comfortable lounges is available, enhanced by log fires during winter. Bedrooms are luxurious, especially those in the adjacent boathouse, which are particularly spacious. At dinner, both carte and set menus are offered in the vaulted, stone cellar Restaurant, whilst during the week, lunches are served in the Garden Room.

**ROOMS:** 15 en suite 4 annexe en suite s £85-£140; d £110-£215 (incl. bkfst) * LB **FACILITIES:** STV Fishing Croquet lawn Sailing Moorings for guests entertainment Xmas **CONF:** Board 20 **PARKING:** 25 **NOTES:** No dogs (ex guide dogs) No children 8yrs No smoking in restaurant **CARDS:**

### ★★★68% Springfield Country Hotel & Leisure Club

Grange Rd BH20 5AL
☎ 01929 552177 📠 01929 551862
***Dir:*** *from Wareham take Stoborough road then first right in village to join by-pass. Turn left and take first turn immediately on right for hotel*

Situated in attractive countryside, this smart hotel is notable for its extensive and popular leisure and conference facilities. Bedrooms vary in style from the main house to newer rooms, however all are smart and well-furnished.

**ROOMS:** 48 en suite (7 fmly) **FACILITIES:** Indoor swimming (H) Outdoor swimming (H) Tennis (hard) Squash Snooker Sauna Gym Jacuzzi Steam room Table tennis Beauty treatment ch fac **CONF:** Thtr 200 Class 50 Board 60 **SERVICES:** Lift **PARKING:** 150 **NOTES:** No smoking in restaurant **CARDS:**

### ★★70% Kemps Country House

East Stoke BH20 6AL
☎ 01929 462563 📠 01929 405287
e-mail: kemps.hotel@lineone.net
***Dir:*** *mid-way between Wareham/Wool on A352*

A relaxing family-owned hotel with views over the Purbeck Hills in the distance. Bedrooms are spacious, garden rooms being more modern in style. There are two comfortable lounges and an adjoining bar. An extensive choice is available from the

continued on p612

WAREHAM, continued

imaginative and innovative set menu and carte, with bar meals also being available at lunch time.
**ROOMS:** 5 rms (4 en suite) 10 annexe en suite (4 fmly) s £57-£77; d £84-£124 (incl. bkfst) **LB** **FACILITIES:** ch fac Xmas **CONF:** Thtr 50 Class 20 Board 20 Del from £79 * **PARKING:** 50 **NOTES:** No dogs (ex guide dogs) No smoking in restaurant **CARDS:**

### ★★65% *Worgret Manor*
Worgret Rd BH20 6AB
☎ 01929 552957 01929 554804
e-mail: worgretmanorhotel@btinternet.com
***Dir:*** *on A352 from Wareham to Wool-0.5m from Wareham rdbt*
On the edge of Wareham, with easy access to major routes, this privately owned, Georgian manor house offers a friendly, cheerful atmosphere. The bedrooms come in a variety of sizes. Public rooms comprise a popular bar, a quiet lounge and a restaurant where good, home cooked meals are served.
**ROOMS:** 13 rms (11 en suite) (1 fmly) No smoking in 4 bedrooms **FACILITIES:** Free use of local sports centre **CONF:** Thtr 90 **PARKING:** 25 **NOTES:** No smoking in restaurant **CARDS:**

## WARMINSTER, Wiltshire
Map 03 ST84

### ★★★★74% Bishopstrow House
BA12 9HH
☎ 01985 212312 01985 216769
e-mail: reservations@bishopstrow.co.uk
***Dir:*** *A303, A36, B3414, premises 2m on right*
Peacefully located in 27 acres of countryside, this fine example of a classical Georgian home provides the perfect location in which to relax and escape everyday concerns. In addition to comfortable lounges and log fires, enjoyable and varied cuisine is served in the pleasant restaurant. Leisure facilities include an indoor swimming pool, fitness room and a range of health and beauty treatments.
**ROOMS:** 32 en suite (3 fmly) No smoking in 1 bedroom s £99; d £195-£199 (incl. cont bkfst) * **LB** **FACILITIES:** STV Indoor swimming (H) Outdoor swimming (H) Tennis (hard) Fishing Sauna Gym Croquet lawn Clay pigeon shooting Archery Cycling entertainment ch fac Xmas **CONF:** Thtr 65 Class 32 Board 36 Del from £170 * **PARKING:** 60 **NOTES:** No smoking in restaurant Civ Wed 70
**CARDS:**

### *Travelodge*
Travelodge
A36 Bath Rd BA12 7RU
☎ 08700 850950 01525 878450
***Dir:*** *junc A350/A36*
Travelodge offers good quality, good value, modern accommodation. Ideal for families, the spacious, en suite bedrooms include remote-control TV, tea and coffee-making facilities, luxury beds and free morning newspaper. Meals can be taken at the nearby family restaurant. For further details and the Travelodge phone number, consult the Hotel Groups page.

W

**ROOMS:** 31 en suite

### ○ Angel Coaching Inn
High St, Heytesbury BA12 0ED
☎ 01985 840330
At the time of going to press, the star classification for this hotel was not confirmed. Please refer to the AA internet site www.theAA.com for current information.

## WARRINGTON, Cheshire
Map 07 SJ68

### ★★★★74% Hanover International Hotel & Club
Stretton Rd, Stretton WA4 4NS
☎ 01925 730706 01925 730740
e-mail: hotel@park-royal-int.co.uk
***Dir:*** *M56 junct 10, A49 to Warrington, at traffic lights turn right to Appleton Thorn, hotel 200 yards on right*

Ideally located close to the M56, this large, modern hotel enjoys a peaceful location. Spacious bedrooms are comfortable, attractive and thoughtfully equipped. Meals in the Harlequin Restaurant are carefully prepared. Public areas include good function facilities, an impressive leisure centre and outdoor tennis courts.
**ROOMS:** 140 en suite (15 fmly) No smoking in 54 bedrooms s £59-£102; d £69-£112 (incl. bkfst) * **LB** **FACILITIES:** Spa STV Indoor swimming (H) Tennis (hard) Sauna Solarium Gym Jacuzzi Retreat Beauty centre including hydrotherapy bath ch fac Xmas **CONF:** Thtr 400 Class 200 Board 90 Del £147 * **SERVICES:** Lift **PARKING:** 400 **NOTES:** Civ Wed 400 **CARDS:**

*See advert on opposite page*

### ★★★★73% Daresbury Park
Chester Rd, Daresbury WA4 4BB
☎ 01925 267331 01925 265615
e-mail: daresburypark.salesmanager @devere-hotels.com
***Dir:*** *entrance off M56 junct 11 rdbt*
A £10.5 million redevelopment has completely transformed this well positioned hotel. Superb public areas include a magnificent glass rotunda, two new restaurants, a wide range of meeting rooms and extensive leisure facilities. All the existing bedrooms have been refurbished to a very high standard and newly built rooms include a number of superbly appointed and equipped suites.
**ROOMS:** 181 en suite (14 fmly) No smoking in 114 bedrooms s £85-£130; d £85-£130 * **LB** **FACILITIES:** Spa STV Indoor swimming (H) Sauna Solarium Gym Jacuzzi Steam Room. Xmas **CONF:** Thtr 400 Class 250 Board 100 Del from £125 * **SERVICES:** Lift **PARKING:** 400 **NOTES:** Civ Wed 300 **CARDS:**

### ★★★72% Fir Grove
Knutsford Old Rd WA4 2LD
☎ 01925 267471 01925 601092
e-mail: firgrovehotel@bestwestern.co.uk
***Dir:*** *M6 junct 20, follow signs for A50. At Warrington, before the swing bridge over canal, turn right, and right again*
Situated in a quiet residential area, this hotel is convenient for the town centre and the M6. Comfortable, smart bedrooms are set around an attractive garden courtyard and offer some excellent extra facilities such as PlayStations and CD players. There is a

*continued*

choice of bars, a neatly appointed restaurant and excellent function and meeting facilities.
**ROOMS:** 40 en suite No smoking in 20 bedrooms s £79; d £95 (incl. bkfst) * **FACILITIES:** STV Xmas **CONF:** Thtr 200 Class 150 Board 50 Del £110 * **PARKING:** 100 **NOTES:** No smoking in restaurant Civ Wed 150 **CARDS:**

★★64% **Paddington House**
514 Old Manchester Rd WA1 3TZ
☎ 01925 816767 🖷 01925 816651
e-mail: hotel@paddingtonhouse.co.uk
***Dir:*** *located 1m from junct 21 M6 off the A57, 2 miles from Warrington town centre*
This vibrant commercial hotel is conveniently situated just over a mile from the M6. The bedrooms are attractively furnished, and include four-poster and ground-floor rooms. Diners can eat in the wood-panelled Padgate restaurant or in the cosy bar.
**ROOMS:** 37 en suite (9 fmly) No smoking in 16 bedrooms s £60-£85; d £72-£85 (incl. bkfst) * LB **FACILITIES:** ch fac **CONF:** Thtr 200 Class 100 Board 40 Del from £85 * **SERVICES:** Lift **PARKING:** 50 **NOTES:** No smoking in restaurant Civ Wed 150
**CARDS:**

MINOTEL Great Britain

⌂ **Premier Lodge (Warrington North)**
Golbourne Rd, Winwick WA2 8LF
☎ 0870 700 1562 🖷 0870 700 1563
Premier Lodge offers modern, well-equipped, en suite accommodation suitable for both business and leisure travellers. Meals can be taken at the adjacent popular restaurant and bar, which is fully licensed. For further details, consult the Hotel Groups page.
**ROOMS:** 42 en suite s £42; d £42 * **CONF:** Thtr 30 Class 20 Board 25 Del £85 *

PREMIER LODGE THE BEST. REST ASSURED.

⌂ ***Premier Lodge (Warrington South)***
Tarporley Rd, Stretton WA4 4NB
☎ 0870 700 1564 🖷 0870 700 1565
Premier Lodge offers modern, well-equipped, en suite accommodation suitable for both business and leisure travellers. Meals can be taken at the adjacent popular restaurant and bar, which is fully licensed. For further details, consult the Hotel Groups page.
**ROOMS:** 29 en suite

PREMIER LODGE THE BEST. REST ASSURED.

⌂ ***Travelodge***
Kendrick / Leigh St WA1 1UR
☎ 01925 636979
***Dir:*** *M6 junct21, follow A57 in direction of Liverpool and Widnes to Warrington town centre, through Asda roundabout, lodge next left at traffic lights*
Travelodge offers good quality, good value, modern accommodation. Ideal for families, the spacious, en suite bedrooms include remote-control TV, tea and coffee-making facilities, luxury beds and free morning newspaper. Meals can be taken at the nearby family restaurant. For further details and the Travelodge phone number, consult the Hotel Groups page.

**ROOMS:** 63 en suite

Travelodge

Popped the question? Hotels with Civ Wed in their entry are licensed for civil wedding ceremonies. Maximum numbers for the ceremony only are shown, e.g. Civ Wed 120

WARRINGTON, continued

### ○ Innkeeper's Lodge Warrington

322 Newton Rd, Lowton WA3 1HD
☎ 0870 243 0500
A new concept in the travel accommodation market. Smart rooms meet essential business requirements but also have home comforts. Dining options include all-day menus plus the added advantage of breakfast, which is included in the room price. Reservations can be made seven days a week through the room reservations number: 0870 243 0500. For further details, consult the Hotel Groups page.
**ROOMS:** 58 en suite

---

## WARWICK, Warwickshire — Map 04 SP26

see also Claverdon, Honiley & Leamington Spa (Royal)

### ★★★73% Ardencote Manor Hotel & Country Club

Lye Green Rd CV35 8LS
☎ 01926 843111 🖷 01926 842646
e-mail: hotel@ardencote.com
(For full entry see Claverdon)

### ★★★64% Lord Leycester

Jury St CV34 4EJ
☎ 01926 491481 🖷 01926 491561
e-mail: reception@lord-leycester.co.uk
***Dir:*** *M40 junc 15 onto A429. Follow road into town centre, past West Gate onto High Street and Jury Street*

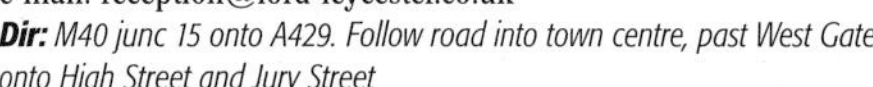

This historic Grade II property is just a short walk from the famous castle. Upgraded bedrooms and public rooms provide comfortable accommodation. A choice of eating options is available in either the informal Squires Buttery, or the carte Knights Restaurant.
**ROOMS:** 50 en suite (3 fmly) No smoking in 15 bedrooms s £55-£85; d £65-£85 (incl. bkfst) * **LB** **FACILITIES:** Xmas **CONF:** Thtr 120 Class 50 Board 40 Del from £80 * **SERVICES:** Lift **PARKING:** 40
**NOTES:** No smoking in restaurant **CARDS:**

### ★★64% Warwick Arms

17 High St CV34 4AT
☎ 01926 492759 🖷 01926 410587
***Dir:*** *off M40 junc 15, main road into Warwick, premises 100 yards past Lord Leycester Hospital*
A relaxed and friendly hotel in the heart of Warwick, close to the castle walls. Public rooms offer a cosy bar and comfortable foyer lounge area. A good choice of meals is served in the restaurant, light snacks and informal meals are available in the bar. Bedrooms vary in style and size, each has a good range of facilities.
**ROOMS:** 35 en suite (4 fmly) s £45-£55; d £55-£65 (incl. bkfst) *
**FACILITIES:** Xmas **CONF:** Thtr 100 Class 30 Board 30 Del from £75 *
**PARKING:** 21 **CARDS:**

### ⌂ Express by Holiday Inn Warwick

Express
by Holiday Inn

Stratford Rd CV34 6TW
☎ 01926 483000 🖷 01926 483033
***Dir:*** *M40 junct 15, follow signs A429 to Warwick. Take 1st turning on right*

A modern budget hotel offering comfortable accommodation in refreshing, spacious and comprehensively equipped bedrooms, en suite bathrooms with power showers and continental buffet breakfast included in the room rate. Suitable for business travellers or families. For further details and the Express by Holiday Inn phone number, consult the Hotel Groups page.
**ROOMS:** 117 en suite (incl. cont bkfst) s fr £65; d fr £65 * **CONF:** Thtr 24 Class 20 Board 18

---

## WARWICK MOTORWAY SERVICE AREA, Warwickshire — Map 04 SP35

### ⌂ Days Inn

Warwick Services, M40 Northbound, Banbury Rd CV35 0AA
☎ 01926 651681 🖷 01926 651634

e-mail: warwick.north.hotel@welcomebreak.co.uk
***Dir:*** *M40 northbound between junct 12 & 13*
This modern building offers accommodation in smart, spacious and well-equipped bedrooms, suitable for families and business travellers, and all with en suite bathrooms. Continental breakfast is available and other refreshments may be taken at the nearby family restaurant. For further details and the Days Inn phone number, consult the Hotel Groups page.
**ROOMS:** 54 en suite s £49-£54; d £49-£54 * **CONF:** Thtr 12 Class 5 Board 10

### ⌂ Welcome Lodge

Welcome
Break

Warwick Services, M40 Southbound, Banbury Rd CV35 0AA
☎ 01926 650168 🖷 01926 651601
***Dir:*** *M40 southbound between junct 13 & 12*
This modern building offers accommodation in smart, spacious and well-equipped bedrooms, suitable for families and business travellers, and all with en suite bathrooms. Refreshments may be taken at the nearby family restaurant. For further details and the Welcome Break phone number, consult the Hotel Groups page.
**ROOMS:** 40 en suite s £45; d £45 * **CONF:** Board 10

> Late for dinner? Quality Standards star rating means that last orders for dinner should be no earlier than:
> ★ 6.30pm ★★ 7.00pm ★★★ 8.00pm
> ★★★★ 9.00pm ★★★★★ 10.00pm

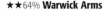

WASHINGTON, Tyne & Wear Map 12 NZ35

**★★★67% *Posthouse Newcastle/ Washington*** Posthouse
Emerson District 5 NE37 1LB
☎ 0870 400 9084 0191 415 3371
***Dir:*** *off A1 (M) exit A195-take left hand sliproad signposted district 5. Turn left at rdbt and hotel is on the left*
In its own grounds, conveniently adjacent to the A1(M), this purpose-built hotel is very popular with business travellers. Bedrooms are comfortable and well-equipped and include a number of 'superior' rooms in contemporary design. The Junction Restaurant offers a full menu and there is also a wide-ranging lounge menu and 24-hour room service.
**ROOMS:** 138 en suite (7 fmly) No smoking in 89 bedrooms
**FACILITIES:** Pitch & putt **CONF:** Thtr 100 Class 40 Board 50
**SERVICES:** Lift **PARKING:** 198 **CARDS:**

**★★★65% George Washington Golf & Country Club** REGAL
Stone Cellar Rd, District 12, High Usworth NE37 1PH
☎ 0191 402 9988 0191 415 1166
e-mail: reservations@corushotels.com
***Dir:*** *Off A1(M)junct 65 onto A194(M) take A195 signposted Washington North. Take last exit from rdbt for Washington then right at mini rdbt. Hotel 0.5 miles right*

Set in extensive grounds with two golf courses, this purpose-built hotel is popular with both business and leisure guests. Spacious, well-equipped accommodation includes some suites and family rooms. A leisure club and business centre forms part of the hotels many facilities.
**ROOMS:** 103 en suite (9 fmly) No smoking in 44 bedrooms s £79; d £89 * **LB FACILITIES:** Indoor swimming (H) Golf 18 Squash Sauna Solarium Gym Putting green Jacuzzi Golf driving range Pitch & Putt
**CONF:** Thtr 200 Class 100 Board 80 Del from £85 * **PARKING:** 200
**NOTES:** No smoking in restaurant Civ Wed 35
**CARDS:**

**⇧ Campanile** Campanile
Emerson Rd, District 5 NE37 1LE
☎ 0191 416 5010 0191 416 5023
***Dir:*** *turn off A1 at junct 64, A195 to Washington, first left at rdbt into Emerson Road, Hotel 800yds on left*
This modern building offers accommodation in smart, well-equipped bedrooms, all with en suite bathrooms. Refreshments may be taken at the informal Bistro. For further details and the Campanile phone number, consult the Hotel Groups page.

Campanile
RESTAURANT
HOTEL

**ROOMS:** 77 annexe en suite s £33-£41; d £33-£41 * **CONF:** Thtr 35 Class 18 Board 20 Del £67 *



**○ Express by Holiday Inn** Express by Holiday Inn
Emerson Rd NE38
☎ 0800 897121
A modern budget hotel offering comfortable accommodation in refreshing, spacious and comprehensively equipped bedrooms, en suite bathrooms with power showers and continental buffet breakfast included in the room rate. Suitable for

continued on p616

W

WASHINGTON, continued

business travellers or families. For further details and the Express by Holiday Inn phone number, consult the Hotel Groups page.

*Express by Holiday Inn, Washington*

**ROOMS:** 74 en suite **NOTES:** Opening November 2001

## WASHINGTON SERVICE AREA, Tyne & Wear Map 12 NZ25

### *Travelodge (North)*

Travelodge

Motorway Service Area, Portobello DH3 2SJ
☎ 01914 103436
***Dir:*** *northbound carriageway of A1(M)*
Travelodge offers good quality, good value, modern accommodation. Ideal for families, the spacious, en suite bedrooms include remote-control TV, tea and coffee-making facilities, luxury beds and free morning newspaper. Meals can be taken at the nearby family restaurant. For further details and the Travelodge phone number, consult the Hotel Groups page.

**ROOMS:** 31 en suite

### *Travelodge (South)*

Travelodge

Portobello DH3 2SJ
☎ 01914 103436
***Dir:*** *A1(M)*
Travelodge offers good quality, good value, modern accommodation. Ideal for families, the spacious, en suite bedrooms include remote-control TV, tea and coffee-making facilities, luxury beds and free morning newspaper. Meals can be taken at the nearby family restaurant. For further details and the Travelodge phone number, consult the Hotel Groups page.

**ROOMS:** 36 en suite

## WATCHET, Somerset Map 03 ST04

### ★★70% Downfield Hotel

16 St Decuman's Rd TA23 0HR
☎ 01984 631267 📠 01984 634369
***Dir:*** *from A39 1.5m out of Williton onto B3190, ignore signs to town ctr 200m past Railway St turn right at jct into St Decuman's Rd, hotel 200m on right*
Overlooking the harbour this substantial Victorian house stands in large, well kept gardens. The bedrooms range from spacious in the main house, to more compact in the Coach House. In the dining room, with its splendid chandelier, freshly prepared dinners are provided using local produce wherever possible. A comfortable sitting room is also available.
**ROOMS:** 5 en suite 2 annexe en suite (1 fmly) No smoking in all bedrooms s £34-£43; d £54-£62 (incl. bkfst) * **PARKING:** 14 **NOTES:** No smoking in restaurant **CARDS:**

## WATERGATE BAY, Cornwall & Isles of Scilly Map 02 SW86

### ★67% Tregurrian

TR8 4AB
☎ 01637 860280 📠 01637 860540
e-mail: tregurrianhotel@virgin.net
***Dir:*** *on B3276, 3m from Newquay*
Conveniently located for easy access to the famous beach, this relaxed and friendly hotel is ideal for walkers of the coastal path and families alike. The well maintained bedrooms are comfortable and vary in size. In the dining room, both breakfast and dinner are buffet style, with hearty portions served and good use of fresh ingredients.
**ROOMS:** 27 rms (22 en suite) (8 fmly) s £14-£92; d £28-£92 (incl. bkfst) * **LB** **FACILITIES:** Outdoor swimming (H) Sauna Jacuzzi Games room **PARKING:** 26 **NOTES:** No dogs (ex guide dogs) No smoking in restaurant Closed Nov-Feb **CARDS:**

## WATERHOUSES, Staffordshire Map 07 SK05

*Premier Collection*

### ★★ Old Beams Restaurant with Rooms

Leek Rd ST10 3HW
☎ 01538 308254 📠 01538 308157
***Dir:*** *on A523 Leek to Ashbourne Road*
The Old Beams Restaurant with Rooms enjoys an excellent position at the heart of this village, on the edge of the dales. The restaurant is in the main house, while the rooms are just across the road, overlooking fields and the river. All bedrooms are loosely themed around potteries, and offer considerable comfort and luxury. The Wallis family provide sophisticated yet informal service. The much-acclaimed restaurant offers a stunning range of imaginative dishes.
**ROOMS:** 5 annexe en suite s £65-£80; d £75-£120 (incl. cont bkfst) * **PARKING:** 22 **NOTES:** No dogs No smoking in restaurant Closed January RS Sun eve & Mon **CARDS:**

## WATERINGBURY, Kent Map 05 TQ65

### *Premier Lodge (Maidstone)*

PREMIER LODGE

Tonbridge Rd ME18 5NS
☎ 0870 700 1468 📠 0870 700 1469
Premier Lodge offers modern, well-equipped, en suite accommodation suitable for both business and leisure travellers. Meals can be taken at the adjacent popular restaurant and bar, which is fully licensed. For further details, consult the Hotel Groups page.
**ROOMS:** 40 en suite

WATERMILLOCK, Cumbria Map 12 NY42

**★★★77% Rampsbeck Country House**
CA11 0LP
☎ 017684 86442 & 86688 017684 86688
e-mail: enquiries@rampsbeck.fsnet.co.uk
***Dir:*** *leave M6 at junct 40, follow signs for A592 to Ullswater, at T-junct with lake in front, turn right, hotel is 1.5m along lake's edge*
This fine, country house, furnished with many period and antique pieces, lies in 18 acres of parkland on the shores of Lake Ullswater. There are three delightful lounges, an elegant restaurant and a traditional bar. Bedrooms come in three styles: the spacious rooms overlooking the lake are spectacular. Service is attentive and the cuisine a real highlight.
**ROOMS:** 20 en suite No smoking in 2 bedrooms s £60; d £100 (incl. bkfst) * **LB FACILITIES:** Fishing Croquet lawn Xmas **CONF:** Board 15 Del from £85 * **PARKING:** 30 **NOTES:** No smoking in restaurant Closed mid Jan-early Feb **CARDS:**

**★★★76% Leeming House**
CA11 0JJ
☎ 0870 400 8131 017684 86443
e-mail: HeritageHotels_Ullswater.Leeming_House@forte-hotels.com
***Dir:*** *junct 40 M6 and take A66 to Keswick. Turn left after 1m (to Ullswater). Continue for 5m until T-junct and turn right. Hotel on left (3m)*
A truly special location, the hotel has it all, the natural beauty of the Peak District national park, Ullswater as a backdrop and 20 acres of mature wooded gardens. Many rooms offer views of the lake and the rugged fells beyond, with more than half having their own balcony. Public rooms include three sumptuous lounges, a cosy bar and library.
**ROOMS:** 40 en suite No smoking in 11 bedrooms s £114-£129; d £188-£258 (incl. bkfst & dinner) * **LB FACILITIES:** STV Fishing Croquet lawn Xmas **CONF:** Thtr 35 Board 20 Del from £140 * **PARKING:** 50 **NOTES:** No smoking in restaurant Civ Wed 30
**CARDS:**

## Premier Collection

**★ Old Church**
Old Church Bay CA11 0JN
☎ 017684 86204 017684 86368
e-mail: info@oldchurch.co.uk
***Dir:*** *7m from junct 40 M6, 2.50m S of Pooley Bridge on A592*
Lake Ullswater provides the backdrop for this beautifully maintained hotel, set in its own lovely grounds. The bedrooms are well-equipped and all have smart en suite facilities. Front rooms enjoy views of Ullswater Lake and mountains. The lounge, bar and spacious lobby all with roaring fires in the winter, offer a choice of places to sit and relax. There are many board games and much reading material provided by the proprietors for guests' use.
**ROOMS:** 10 en suite s fr £65; d fr £125 (incl. bkfst) * **LB FACILITIES:** Fishing Boat hire Moorings/fishing **PARKING:** 20 **NOTES:** No dogs (ex guide dogs) No smoking in restaurant Closed Dec-Feb & Sun-Mon Mar-Nov rs Sun **CARDS:**



WATFORD, Hertfordshire Map 04 TQ19

**★★★64% The White House**
Upton Rd WD8 0JF
☎ 01923 237316 01923 233109
e-mail: info@whitehousehotel.co.uk
***Dir:*** *main Watford centre ring road goes into Exchange Rd, Upton Rd left turn off, hotel can be seen on left*

This is a well-located and popular commercial hotel. Bedrooms are practically furnished and decorated, and offer a good range of

*continued on p618*

WATFORD, continued

in-room facilities. The public areas are open plan in style and comprise a lounge/bar area and an attractive conservatory restaurant.
**ROOMS:** 60 en suite (1 fmly) No smoking in 9 bedrooms s £84-£145; d £109-£160 * **LB** **FACILITIES:** STV **CONF:** Thtr 250 Class 80 Board 50 Del from £115 * **SERVICES:** Lift **PARKING:** 40 **NOTES:** No smoking in restaurant **CARDS:**

*See advert on page 617*

## WATTON, Norfolk Map 05 TF90

### ★★67% Broom Hall Country Hotel
Richmond Rd, Saham Toney IP25 7EX
☎ 01953 882125 📠 01953 882125
e-mail: enquiries@broomhallhotel.co.uk
***Dir:*** *leave A11 at Thetford on A1075 to Watton (12m) B1108 to Swaffham, in 0.5m at rdbt take B1077 to Saham Toney, hotel 0.5m on the left*
Situated in the Norfolk village of Saham Toney amidst 15 acres of gardens and parkland, this charming Victorian country house is ideally placed for exploring East Anglia. There is a relaxing lounge with an open fire, a cosy bar and an elegant restaurant. Leisure facilities include an indoor swimming pool.
**ROOMS:** 10 en suite (3 fmly) No smoking in all bedrooms s £40-£48; d fr £68 (incl. bkfst) * **LB** **FACILITIES:** Indoor swimming (H) Snooker **CONF:** Thtr 20 Class 20 Board 20 **PARKING:** 60 **NOTES:** No dogs (ex guide dogs) No smoking in restaurant Closed 24 Dec-4 Jan Civ Wed 30 **CARDS:**

*See advert under THETFORD*

## WEEDON, Northamptonshire Map 04 SP65

### ★★62% Globe
High St NN7 4QD
☎ 01327 340336 📠 01327 349058
***Dir:*** *at crossroads of A5/A45*

GLOBE
HOTEL
THE GLOBE HOTEL

This friendly coaching inn, just three miles from the M1 is very popular with all guests. There is a charming family atmosphere throughout and service is provided in a courteous and efficient manner. Bedrooms come in a variety of styles and sizes, each is pleasantly decorated and well-equipped, and a number of rooms offer four-poster beds.
**ROOMS:** 15 en suite 3 annexe en suite (2 fmly) No smoking in 1 bedroom s £45-£50; d £55-£60 (incl. bkfst) * **FACILITIES:** STV **CONF:** Thtr 30 Class 25 Board 20 Del from £85 * **PARKING:** 30 **NOTES:** No smoking in restaurant **CARDS:**

### ⌂ Premier Lodge (Daventry)
High St NN7 4PX
☎ 0870 700 1520 📠 0870 700 1521
***Dir:*** *at A5/A45 crossroads*
Premier Lodge offers modern, well-equipped, en suite accommodation suitable for both business and leisure travellers. Meals can be taken at the adjacent popular restaurant and bar, which is fully licensed. For further details, consult the Hotel Groups page.
**ROOMS:** 45 en suite s £46; d £46 * **CONF:** Thtr 70 Class 25 Board 24 Del £90 *

PREMIER LODGE
THE BEST. REST ASSURED.

## WELLINGBOROUGH, Northamptonshire Map 04 SP86

### ★★★65% Menzies Hind
Sheep St NN8 1BY
☎ 0870 6003013 📠 01322 511144
e-mail: info@menzies-hotels.co.uk
***Dir:*** *on A509 in town centre*
Dating back to Jacobean times, this central hotel provides a good base for visiting the town. The all-day coffee shop is a smart meeting place for locals. There are extensive function and meeting rooms, bedrooms are mainly spacious and well-designed. A wide range of food is available in the restaurant.
**ROOMS:** 34 en suite (2 fmly) No smoking in 5 bedrooms s £75; d £85 * **LB** **FACILITIES:** STV Xmas **CONF:** Thtr 130 Class 60 Board 50 Del from £95 * **PARKING:** 15 **NOTES:** No smoking in restaurant Civ Wed 120 **CARDS:**

MENZIES HOTELS

### ★★63% High View
156 Midland Rd NN8 1NG
☎ 01933 278733 📠 01933 225948
e-mail: highviewhotel@supanet.com
***Dir:*** *turn off A45 onto B573, follow sign post to rail station, at Midland road T-junct turn left towards town centre, hotel approx 100yds on left*
This small hotel close to both the town centre and the railway station provides a relaxing and informal environment. The spacious, comfortable bedrooms are well-maintained, with all expected facilities. Dinner may be taken in the dining room.
**ROOMS:** 14 en suite (2 fmly) s £34-£39; d £45-£51 (incl. bkfst) * **PARKING:** 8 **NOTES:** No dogs No children 3yrs No smoking in restaurant Closed 25 Dec-1 Jan **CARDS:**

### ⌂ Hotel Ibis Wellingborough
Enstone Court NN8 2DR
☎ 01933 228333 📠 01933 228444
e-mail: H3164@accor-hotels.com
***Dir:*** *located on junct of A45 & A509 towards Kettering on the SW edge of Wellingborough*
Modern, budget hotel offering comfortable accommodation in bright and practical bedrooms. Breakfast is self-service and dinner is available in the restaurant. For further details, consult the Hotel Groups page.
**ROOMS:** 78 en suite s fr £49.95; d fr £49.95 *

ibis
ACCOR hotels

## WELLINGTON See Telford (Shropshire)

TV dinner? Room service at three stars and above.

WELLINGTON, Somerset Map 03 ST12

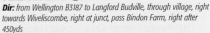

## Premier Collection

★★★ ◎◎ **_Bindon Country House Hotel & Restaurant_**

Langford Budville TA21 0RU

☎ 01823 400070 📠 01823 400071

e-mail: bindonhouse@msn.com

***Dir:*** *from Wellington B3187 to Langford Budville, through village, right towards Wiveliscombe, right at junct, pass Bindon Farm, right after 450yds*

Mentioned in the Domesday Book, this delightful country retreat is set in seven acres of formal and woodland gardens, and offers perfect peace and tranquillity. Each bedroom is named after a battle fought by the Duke of Wellington, decorated with sumptuous fabrics and is well-equipped. Public rooms are equally stunning. Dinner is prepared with flair and innovation from the best of fresh ingredients.

**ROOMS:** 12 en suite (2 fmly) No smoking in all bedrooms **FACILITIES:** Outdoor swimming (H) Tennis (hard) Croquet lawn entertainment **CONF:** Thtr 50 Class 30 Board 20 **PARKING:** 30 **NOTES:** No smoking in restaurant Civ Wed 50 **CARDS:**

*See advert under TAUNTON*

★★★62% **The Cleve Country House Hotel**

Mantle St TA21 8SN

☎ 01823 662033 📠 01823 660874

e-mail: reception@clevehotel.com

***Dir:*** *from M5 junct 26 follow signs to Wellington, then left beforeTotal Petrol Station upon leaving town*

Offering comfortable bedrooms and public areas, The Cleve Hotel is quietly located in an elevated position above the town of Wellington. The atmosphere is relaxed and guests can enjoy dining in the open plan restaurant. Two full size snooker tables are available for guest use.

**ROOMS:** 20 en suite (5 fmly) No smoking in all bedrooms s £47.50-£57.50; d £59.50-£69.50 (incl. bkfst) * **LB FACILITIES:** **Spa** Snooker Indoor swimming (H) Gym **CONF:** Thtr 150 Class 80 Board 50 Del from £68.50 * **PARKING:** 60 **NOTES:** No smoking in restaurant Civ Wed 120 **CARDS:**

★★64% **Beambridge**

Sampford Arundel TA21 0HB

☎ 01823 672223 📠 01823 673100

***Dir:*** *1.5m W on A38 between junct 26 & 27 of M5*

The Beambridge offers value for money; a relaxed and friendly hotel, ideally located at the gateway to the West Country. The dedicated team provide a smooth service, ensuring a stress free stay for all guests. A wide range of bar food is served, with the option of a more formal restaurant. The comfortable bedrooms are well-equipped and decorated, suiting all needs.

*continued*

**ROOMS:** 9 en suite (1 fmly) s £39; d £47 (incl. bkfst) * **CONF:** Thtr 100 Class 100 Board 50 **PARKING:** 100 **NOTES:** No dogs (ex guide dogs) No smoking in restaurant Closed 25-26 Dec **CARDS:**

WELLS, Somerset Map 03 ST54

★★★70% **Swan**

Best Western

Sadler St BA5 2RX

☎ 01749 836300 📠 01749 836301

e-mail: swan@bhere.co.uk

***Dir:*** *A39, A371, opp cathedral*

The Swan is a former coaching inn, and has one of the best views of the west front of Wells cathedral. The individually decorated bedrooms vary in size and style; a third of the rooms have four-poster beds, nicely complementing the 15th-century architecture. A fixed-price menu is served in the dining room, with the added bonus of a roast trolley.

**ROOMS:** 35 en suite (2 fmly) s £80-£85; d £100-£120 (incl. bkfst) * **LB FACILITIES:** Xmas **CONF:** Thtr 100 Class 30 Board 30 Del from £84.50 * **PARKING:** 30 **NOTES:** No smoking in restaurant Civ Wed 80 **CARDS:**

★★★69% ◎ **The Market Place**

One Market Place BA5 2RW

☎ 01749 836300 📠 01749 836301

e-mail: marketplace@bhere.co.uk

***Dir:*** *A39, A371 - in City Centre (Market Place) along one way system*

In the centre of the city of Wells, this unique hotel combines modern style and elegance with the character and appeal of a building dating back over 500 years. Enjoyable, bistro style dining is offered in the pleasant dining room overlooking the courtyard. All bedrooms, whether in the main house or annexe, are comfortable and well-furnished.

**ROOMS:** 24 en suite 10 annexe en suite (4 fmly) s £80-£85; d £100-£120 (incl. bkfst) * **LB FACILITIES:** Xmas **CONF:** Thtr 150 Class 75 Board 75 Del from £84.50 * **PARKING:** 30 **NOTES:** No smoking in restaurant Closed 28-31 Dec **CARDS:**

W

★★69% **White Hart**

Sadler St BA5 2RR

☎ 01749 672056 📠 01749 671074

e-mail: info@whitehart-wells.co.uk

***Dir:*** *Sadler St is the start of the one-way system. Hotel opposite the cathedral*

Situated just a short stroll from the cathedral, this former coaching inn dates back to the 15th century. The bedrooms, some of which are located in a nearby former stable block, offer comfortable, modern accommodation. Public areas include a spacious bar-lounge, a cosy landing lounge for residents and a beamed

*continued on p620*

WELLS, continued

restaurant. Guests can choose between the formal fixed-price menu or the brasserie-style menu.

WHITE HART HOTEL
AA

*White Hart, Wells*

**ROOMS:** 13 en suite (1 fmly) No smoking in 5 bedrooms s £56-£60; d £75-£80 (incl. bkfst) * **LB** **FACILITIES:** STV ch fac Xmas **CONF:** Thtr 80 Class 40 Board 35 Del from £62.50 * **PARKING:** 17 **NOTES:** No smoking in restaurant **CARDS:**

### ★69% Ancient Gate House

20 Sadler St BA5 2RR
☎ 01749 672029 🖷 01749 670319
e-mail: info@ancientgatehouse.co.uk
***Dir:*** *first hotel on left situated on the Cathedral Green, overlooking the West Front of the Cathedral*

Guests are treated to good old fashioned hospitality in a friendly informal atmosphere at this charming, family-run hotel. Bedrooms, many of which boast unrivalled cathedral views and four-poster beds, are furnished in keeping with the age of the building, but have the advantage of modern facilities. The hotel's Rugantino Restaurant remains popular, offering typically Italian specialities and some traditional English dishes.
**ROOMS:** 9 rms (7 en suite) (1 fmly) No smoking in 2 bedrooms s £50-£57.50; d fr £70 (incl. bkfst) * **LB** **FACILITIES:** ch fac **NOTES:** No smoking in restaurant Closed 25-26 Dec
**CARDS:**

### ○ Crown at Wells

Market Place BA5 2RP
☎ 01749 673457
At the time of going to press, the star classification for this hotel was not confirmed. Please refer to the AA internet site www.theAA.com for current information.

WELWYN, Hertfordshire — Map 04 TL21

### ★★★63% Quality Hotel Welwyn

The Link AL6 9XA
☎ 01438 716911 🖷 01438 714065
e-mail: admin@gb623.u-net.com
***Dir:*** *exit A1(M) junct 6 follow for A1000 Welwyn. Follow A1(M) Stevenage towards motorway again but at 3rd rdbt take first left and turn into hotel*

The hotel is well-located for access to the nearby motorway and offers a versatile range of conference and meeting rooms, making it popular with business guests. Bedrooms are suitably appointed and offer a useful range of in room facilities and amenities. Guests have the choice of two informal dining rooms and a comfortable bar in which to relax.
**ROOMS:** 96 en suite (6 fmly) No smoking in 47 bedrooms s £75; d £90 * **LB** **FACILITIES:** STV Gym Xmas **CONF:** Thtr 250 Class 60 Board 50 Del from £87.50 * **PARKING:** 150 **NOTES:** No smoking in restaurant Civ Wed 100 **CARDS:**

WELWYN GARDEN CITY, Hertfordshire — Map 04 TL21

### ★★★63% The Homestead Court Hotel

Homestead Ln AL7 4LX
☎ 01707 324336 🖷 01707 326447
***Dir:*** *turn off A1000 into Woodhall Lane and left at Pear Tree public house into Cole Green Lane. After 2 mini-rdbts turn right into Homestead Lane, hotel on left*

Less than 2 miles from the city centre, the hotel is ideally located for local businesses and tourist attractions. Bedrooms and public areas are modern and unpretentious, in keeping with the hotel's philosophy of a simple, relaxed approach to hotel keeping.
**ROOMS:** 58 en suite No smoking in 25 bedrooms s £90; d £100 * **LB** **FACILITIES:** STV Xmas **CONF:** Thtr 80 Class 35 Board 40 Del from £100 * **SERVICES:** Lift **PARKING:** 80 **NOTES:** No dogs (ex guide dogs) No smoking in restaurant **CARDS:**

WENTBRIDGE (NEAR PONTEFRACT), West Yorkshire — Map 08 SE41

### ★★★71% Wentbridge House

WF8 3JJ
☎ 01977 620444 🖷 01977 620148
e-mail: info@wentbridgehouse.co.uk
***Dir:*** *Wentbridge is 0.5m off A1 and 4m S of the M62/A1 interchange*

This well-established hotel sits in 15 acres of landscaped gardens, offering spacious, well-equipped bedrooms and a choice of bars. Service in the Fleur de Lys restaurant is polished and friendly, and a varied menu offers a good choice of interesting dishes.
**ROOMS:** 14 en suite 4 annexe en suite s £72-£98; d £88-£108 (incl. bkfst) * **CONF:** Thtr 120 Class 100 Board 60 Del from £90 * **PARKING:** 100 **NOTES:** No dogs (ex guide dogs) Closed 25 Dec-evening only Civ Wed 70 **CARDS:**

Packed in a hurry? Ironing facilities should be available at all star levels, either in rooms or on request.

## WEST AUCKLAND, Co Durham
Map 12 NZ12

**★★★70% The Manor House**
The Green DL14 9HW
☎ 01388 834834 01388 833566
e-mail: enquiries@manorhousehotel.net
***Dir:** A1(M) junct 58, then A68 to West Auckland*

MANOR HOUSE HOTEL

This historic manor house has been sympathetically extended and still retains all its original character and charm. The hotel offers a wide range and standard of facilities that meet modern expectations. Flagstone floors in the bar lead to the stylish restaurant offering artistically presented dishes. The bedrooms in the main house are particularly large.
**ROOMS:** 25 en suite 11 annexe en suite (8 fmly) **FACILITIES:** Indoor swimming (H) Sauna Solarium Gym Jacuzzi Beauty treatment Xmas
**CONF:** Thtr 100 Class 80 Board 50 **PARKING:** 200
**CARDS:**

## WEST BAY See Bridport

## WEST BEXINGTON, Dorset
Map 03 SY58

**★★70% Manor**
Beach Rd DT2 9DF
☎ 01308 897616 01308 897035
e-mail: themanorhotel@btconnect.com
This hotel stands in the scenic splendour of the tranquil village of West Bexington. The hotel itself is south facing and enjoys uninterrupted sea views. Each bedroom has its own unique charm and a number of thoughtful extras. The Cellar Bar provides a range of meals, and an imaginative selection of dishes is offered in the restaurant.
**ROOMS:** 13 rms (12 en suite) (1 fmly) **CONF:** Thtr 50 Class 60 Board 30 **PARKING:** 28 **NOTES:** No dogs Civ Wed 45
**CARDS:**

## WEST BROMWICH, West Midlands
Map 07 SP09

***Howard Johnson West Bromwich***
144 High St B70 6JJ
☎ 0121 525 8333 0800 0280 600 0121 525 8444
***Dir:** M5 junct 1 head for West Bromwich town centre, located 2 miles down road on main High Street*
**ROOMS:** 133 en suite **CONF:** Thtr 60 Class 30 Board 40

Late for dinner? Quality Standards star rating means that last orders for dinner should be no earlier than:
★ 6.30pm ★★ 7.00pm ★★★ 8.00pm
★★★★ 9.00pm ★★★★★ 10.00pm

## WESTBURY, Wiltshire
Map 03 ST85

**★★66% The Cedar**
Warminster Rd BA13 3PR
☎ 01373 822753 01373 858423
e-mail: cedarwestbury@aol.com
***Dir:** on A350, 0.5m from Westbury towards Warminster*
This 18th-century hotel offers attractive accommodation in well-equipped bedrooms that are individually decorated. The hotel provides a ideal base for exploring Bath and the surrounding area. A variety of meals is available in both the bar lounge and conservatory, while the Regency restaurant is popular for more formal dining.
**ROOMS:** 8 en suite 8 annexe en suite (4 fmly) s £55-£60; d £75-£85 (incl. bkfst) * **LB** **FACILITIES:** STV ch fac **CONF:** Thtr 40 Class 30 Board 20 **PARKING:** 35 **NOTES:** No dogs (ex guide dogs) No smoking in restaurant Closed 26 Dec-2 Jan **CARDS:**

## WEST CHILTINGTON, West Sussex
Map 04 TQ01

**★★★67% Roundabout**
Monkmead Ln RH20 2PF
☎ 01798 813838 01798 812962
e-mail: roundabouthotelltd@btinternet.com
***Dir:** A24 onto A283 turn right at mini rdbt in Storrington, left at hill top. After 1m bear left*
This well-established hotel enjoys a most peaceful setting, surrounded by gardens deep in the Sussex countryside. Mock Tudor in style, the hotel has plenty of character. Bedrooms are comfortably furnished and well-equipped. Public areas include a

continued on p622

WEST CHILTINGTON, continued

spacious lounge and bar and neatly appointed restaurant where guests are offered an extensive range of dishes.

*Roundabout, West Chiltington*

**ROOMS:** 23 en suite (4 fmly) No smoking in 2 bedrooms s £67-£72; d £98-£102 (incl. bkfst) * **LB** **FACILITIES:** STV Xmas **CONF:** Thtr 60 Class 20 Board 26 Del from £89.45 * **PARKING:** 46 **NOTES:** No children 3yrs No smoking in restaurant Civ Wed 55
**CARDS:**

*See advert on page 621*

WEST DRAYTON Hotels are listed under Heathrow Airport

## WESTLETON, Suffolk — Map 05 TM46

### ★★75% Westleton Crown

IP17 3AD
☎ 0800 328 6001 01728 648239
e-mail: reception@westletoncrown.com
***Dir:*** *turn off A12 just beyond Yoxford, northbound, and follow AA signs for 2m*

Delightful inn offering a wealth of charm and character, in a quiet village location just of the A12. Bedrooms vary in size and style but they are all smartly decorated and equipped with many thoughtful touches. The main restaurant offers an appealing daily changing menu, including vegetarian and seafood specialities. More informally, the bar has a range of real ales, blazing fires and vast array of malt whiskies.

**ROOMS:** 10 en suite 9 annexe en suite (2 fmly) No smoking in all bedrooms **CONF:** Thtr 60 Class 40 Board 30 **PARKING:** 40 **NOTES:** RS 24-26 Dec (Meals only) **CARDS:**

## WEST LULWORTH, Dorset — Map 03 SY88

### ★★71% Shirley

Main Rd BH20 5RL
☎ 01929 400358 01929 400167
e-mail: durdle@aol.com
***Dir:*** *on B3070 in centre of village*

Many guests return regularly to this attractive, family-run hotel with warm hospitality. The smart bedrooms are attractively decorated with modern facilities, and public areas include an indoor pool and two comfortable lounges. Each evening in the restaurant, guests enjoy an ample choice of good wholesome cooking.

**ROOMS:** 15 en suite (2 fmly) s £35-£36; d £70-£88 (incl. bkfst) * **LB** **FACILITIES:** Indoor swimming (H) Jacuzzi Giant chess **PARKING:** 20 **NOTES:** No smoking in restaurant Closed mid Nov-mid Feb
**CARDS:**

### ★★65% Cromwell House

Lulworth Cove BH20 5RJ
☎ 01929 400253 & 400332 01929 400566
e-mail: alastair@lds.co.uk
***Dir:*** *200 yds beyond end of West Lulworth village, turn left onto high sliproad, Cromwell House 100yds on left opposite beach car park*

With spectacular elevated views across the sea and countryside, this family-run hotel offers guests an ideal base from which to explore the area. Built in 1881 by the mayor of Weymouth, specifically as a guest house, the bedrooms are bright and attractive with co-ordinated fabrics and modern facilities. There is a traditionally furnished dining room serving home-cooked meals, and popular cream teas.

**ROOMS:** 17 en suite (3 fmly) **FACILITIES:** Outdoor swimming (H) **PARKING:** 15 **NOTES:** No smoking in restaurant Closed 22 Dec-3 Jan
**CARDS:**

## WESTON-ON-THE-GREEN, Oxfordshire — Map 04 SP51

### ★★★67% Weston Manor

OX6 8QL
☎ 01869 350621 01869 350901
e-mail: westonmanor@hotmail.com
***Dir:*** *M40 junct 9 towards Oxford (A34), leave A34 at 1st exit, turn right at rdbt (B4030), hotel is 100yds on the left*

This splendid manor house has a wealth of history. Public rooms include a foyer lounge and a magnificent vaulted restaurant with minstrels' gallery and original panelling. Bedrooms are available in the main house and a tastefully converted coach house, and though they may vary in size, each room is particularly well-equipped.

**ROOMS:** 15 en suite 20 annexe en suite (5 fmly) No smoking in 6 bedrooms s £99-£115; d £115-£199 (incl. bkfst) * **LB**
**FACILITIES:** Outdoor swimming (H) Croquet lawn Xmas **CONF:** Thtr 40 Class 20 Board 25 Del from £179 * **PARKING:** 100 **NOTES:** No dogs (ex guide dogs) No smoking in restaurant Civ Wed 60
**CARDS:**

## WESTON-SUPER-MARE, Somerset — Map 03 ST36

### ★★★66% Beachlands

17 Uphill Rd North BS23 4NG
☎ 01934 621401 01934 621966
e-mail: info@beachlandshotel.com
***Dir:*** *follow tourist signs for Tropicana from M5 junct 21, hotel overlooks golf course, it is situated 6.5m away from motorway, before reaching Tropicana*

This delightful hotel has the added bonus of a 10 metre indoor pool and sauna. It is very close to the 18-hole links course and a short walk from the seafront. Elegantly decorated public areas include a bar, a choice of lounges and a bright dining room.

continued

Bedrooms vary slightly in size and comfort but all are well-equipped.
**ROOMS:** 24 en suite (4 fmly) s £47-£60; d £85 (incl. bkfst) * **LB** **FACILITIES:** Indoor swimming (H) Sauna ch fac **CONF:** Thtr 60 Class 20 Board 30 Del from £79 * **PARKING:** 28 **NOTES:** No dogs (ex guide dogs) No smoking in restaurant Closed 23 Dec-2 Jan Civ Wed 85
**CARDS:**

### ★★74% Madeira Cove Hotel

32-34 Birnbeck Rd BS23 2BX
☎ 01934 626707 📠 01934 624882
***Dir:*** *Follow signs to western seafront, pass Grand Pier, hotel on right*
Within easy walking distance of the town centre, Madeira Cove Hotel enjoys an ideal location overlooking the sea. It has been upgraded throughout to provide comfortable and thoughtfully equipped accommodation. A good range of food is available in the well-appointed restaurant, and there is a pleasant lounge-bar.
**ROOMS:** 19 en suite 4 annexe en suite (2 fmly) No smoking in 3 bedrooms s £25-£30 (incl. bkfst) * **LB** **SERVICES:** Lift **PARKING:** 10 **NOTES:** No smoking in restaurant **CARDS:**

### ★★63% Anchorhead

Leisureplex

19 Claremont Crescent, Birnbeck Rd BS23 2EE
☎ 01934 620880 📠 01934 621767
Enjoying a very pleasant location with views across the bay, The Anchorhead offers a varied choice of comfortable lounges and a relaxing outdoor patio area. Bedrooms and bathrooms are traditionally furnished and include several ground floor rooms. Dinner and breakfast are served in the spacious dining room that also benefits from sea views.
**ROOMS:** 52 en suite (1 fmly) s £25-£33; d £42-£58 (incl. bkfst) * **LB** **FACILITIES:** entertainment Xmas **SERVICES:** Lift **NOTES:** No dogs (ex guide dogs) No smoking in restaurant Closed Dec-Feb RS Nov/March (closed Fri-Mon) **CARDS:**

### ★66% *Timbertop Aparthotel*

8 Victoria Park BS23 2HZ
☎ 01934 631178 📠 01934 414716
e-mail: francesca@timbertop.freeserve.co.uk
***Dir:*** *follow signs to pier, then 1st right (with Winter Gardens on right), 1st left Lower Church Road. Bear left then turn right to hotel*

Located in a leafy cul-de-sac, close to the seafront and Winter Gardens, this homely hotel offers a warm and personal welcome. Bedrooms are bright and fresh with pine furnishings. In addition to a small bar, there is a relaxing lounge. Substantial home-cooked dinners are provided with the emphasis on fresh ingredients.
**ROOMS:** 8 rms (7 en suite) 4 annexe en suite (2 fmly) **FACILITIES:** STV **PARKING:** 15 **NOTES:** No dogs (ex guide dogs) No smoking in restaurant **CARDS:**

## WEST THURROCK, Essex Map 05 TQ57

### Hotel Ibis Thurrock

Weston Av RM20 3JQ
☎ 01708 686000 📠 01708 680525
e-mail: H2176@accor-hotels.com
***Dir:*** *From M25 exit J31 to West Thurrock Services, turn R at 1st and 2nd rdbts then L at 3rd rdbt. The hotel is on R after 500yds alongside M25.*
Modern, budget hotel offering comfortable accommodation in bright and practical bedrooms. Breakfast is self-service and dinner is available in the restaurant. For further details, consult the Hotel Groups page.
**ROOMS:** 102 en suite s fr £45; d fr £45 *

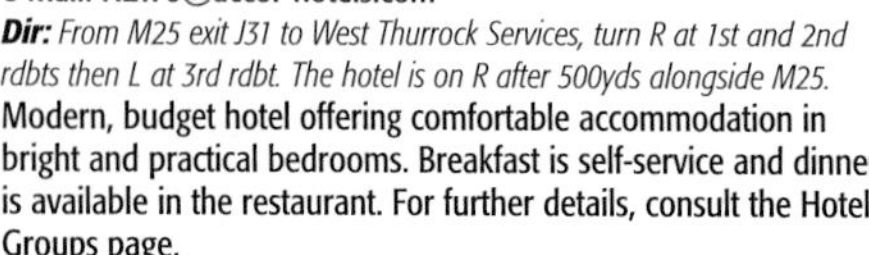

### *Travelodge*

Arterial Rd RM16 3BG
☎ 01708 891111 0800 850950 📠 01525 878450
***Dir:*** *off A1306 Arterial Rd*
Travelodge offers good quality, good value, modern accommodation. Ideal for families, the spacious, en suite bedrooms include remote-control TV, tea and coffee-making facilities, luxury beds and free morning newspaper. Meals can be taken at the nearby family restaurant. For further details and the Travelodge phone number, consult the Hotel Groups page.

**ROOMS:** 44 en suite

## WEST WITTON, North Yorkshire Map 07 SE08

### ★★69% Wensleydale Heifer Inn

DL8 4LS
☎ 01969 622322 📠 01969 624183
e-mail: heifer@daelnet.co.uk
***Dir:*** *A684, at west end of village*
This historic inn has been a landmark in the village since the 17th century; its original character still remains in the cosy lounge and atmospheric bar. It has a good reputation for comfortable accommodation, friendly service and excellent cuisine. Bedrooms are located the in inn or in a stone-built house just across the road.
**ROOMS:** 9 en suite s £60; d £80 (incl. bkfst) * **LB** **FACILITIES:** Beer garden Xmas **PARKING:** 40 **CARDS:**

## WETHERBY, West Yorkshire Map 08 SE44

### ★★★73% Wood Hall

Trip Ln, Linton LS22 4JA
☎ 01937 587271 📠 01937 584353
e-mail: events.woodhall@arcadianhotels.co.uk
***Dir:*** *from Wetherby town centre take Harrogate road N from market place and turn left to Linton, hotel is then signposted*

A striking Georgian hall in 100 acres of parkland. Conference and banqueting facilities are stylish, the leisure club has a beauty room, pool and gym. Day rooms include a smart drawing room with open fire, and an oak-panelled bar. Food is imaginative and well-prepared.
**ROOMS:** 15 en suite 27 annexe en suite (7 fmly) s £70-£90; d £70-£90 * **LB** **FACILITIES:** STV Indoor swimming (H) Fishing Snooker Solarium Gym Jacuzzi Xmas **CONF:** Thtr 140 Class 70 Board 40 Del from £139 * **SERVICES:** Lift **PARKING:** 200 **NOTES:** No smoking in restaurant Civ Wed 110 **CARDS:**

### ★★★67% Linton Springs

Sicklinghall Rd LS22 4AF
☎ 01937 585353 📠 01937 587579
e-mail: info@lintonsprings.co.uk
***Dir:*** *Turn off A661 leaving Wetherby town centre onto Linton Road. Forward into Sicklinghall Rd and Hotel situated one mile on left .*
A gracious 18th-century former shooting lodge set in 14 acres of park and woodland. Spacious oak panelled bedrooms are attractive and well-equipped. Helpful staff are an asset and the open plan reception, lounge and cocktail bar are very welcoming. The Gun Room restaurant and adjoining conservatory serves both traditional and modern British cooking.
**ROOMS:** 12 en suite (2 fmly) s £75-£95; d £95-£115 (incl. bkfst) * **FACILITIES:** STV Tennis (hard) Croquet lawn golf driving range - 250 yds. **CONF:** Thtr 80 Class 50 Board 30 Del £130 * **PARKING:** 70 **NOTES:** No dogs (ex guide dogs) Closed 1-3 Jan Civ Wed 66
**CARDS:**

### ★★★61% The Bridge Inn

Walshford LS22 5HS
☎ 01937 580115 📠 01937 580556
e-mail: bridge.walshford@virgin.net
Conveniently located adjacent to the A1, this hotel offers a choice of bars and a spacious beamed, open-plan restaurant. Bedrooms are comfortable and well-equipped. The good range of conference and banqueting suites are popular, especially with wedding parties, which have use of the Italian courtyard.
**ROOMS:** 30 en suite (1 fmly) s £55-£63; d £65-£83 (incl. bkfst) * **LB** **FACILITIES:** STV Mini Gym Xmas **CONF:** Thtr 150 Class 50 Board 50 Del from £85 * **PARKING:** 90 **NOTES:** Civ Wed 120
**CARDS:**

## WEYBRIDGE, Surrey See LONDON SECTION plan 1 A1

### ★★★★73% Oatlands Park

146 Oatlands Dr KT13 9HB
☎ 01932 847242 📠 01932 842252
e-mail: info@oatlandsparkhotel.com
***Dir:*** *through Weybridge High Street to top of Monument Hill. Hotel third of a mile on left*
This impressive building once owned by Henry VIII is situated in 10 areas of attractive grounds. The glass covered atrium and marble-pillared lounge lead into a comfortable bar and the Broadwater Restaurant is spacious and well-appointed. Bedrooms include a number of suites, and several comfortable single rooms. Leisure time may be spent playing tennis, golf or working out in the fitness centre.
**ROOMS:** 134 en suite (5 fmly) No smoking in 20 bedrooms s £120-£155; d £165-£185 * **LB** **FACILITIES:** STV Golf 9 Tennis (hard) Gym Croquet lawn Putting green Jogging course Fitness suite entertainment **CONF:** Thtr 300 Class 150 Board 70 Del from £195 * **SERVICES:** Lift **PARKING:** 140 **NOTES:** Civ Wed 200
**CARDS:**

★★★67% **The Ship**
Monument Green KT13 8BQ
☎ 01932 848364 📠 01932 857153
e-mail: info@ship-hotel.weybridge.com
PEEL HOTELS
***Dir:*** *turn off M25 junct 11, A317, at third rdbt turn left into the High Street, hotel on left*
The Ship is a spacious and comfortable hotel, which is in a great location for visitors to the town. Bedrooms have been designed with consideration for both business and leisure guests needs. The restaurant, lounge and bar are all spacious and attactively presented. Car parking is a bonus.
**ROOMS:** 39 en suite No smoking in 10 bedrooms s £121-£140; d £140-£150 * **LB** **FACILITIES:** STV **CONF:** Thtr 140 Class 70 Board 60 Del from £147 * **PARKING:** 65 **NOTES:** No dogs (ex guide dogs) No smoking in restaurant **CARDS:**

○ **Innkeeper's Lodge Weybridge**
25 Oatlands Chase KT13 9RW
Innkeeper's Lodge
A new concept in the travel accommodation market. Smart rooms meet essential business requirements but also have home comforts. Dining options include all-day menus plus the added advantage of breakfast, which is included in the room price. Reservations can be made seven days a week through the room reservations number: 0870 243 0500. For further details, consult the Hotel Groups page.
**ROOMS:** 19 en suite **NOTES:** Opening Autumn 2001

Early start? Hotels at all star levels should provide in-room alarm clocks and/or alarm calls.

WEYMOUTH, Dorset Map 03 SY67

★★★76% Moonfleet Manor
Fleet DT3 4ED
☎ 01305 786948 01305 774395
**Dir:** *A354 to Weymouth; turn right on B3157 to Bridport. At Chickerell turn left at mini rdbt to Fleet*

An enchanting hideaway peacefully located at the end of the village of Fleet, with many bedrooms overlooking Chesil Beach. The hotel is furnished with style and panache particularly the sumptuous lounges. Bedrooms are well-equipped, spacious and comfortable. Accomplished cuisine is served in the beautiful restaurant.
**ROOMS:** 33 en suite 6 annexe en suite (26 fmly) s £80-£140; d £130-£315 (incl. bkfst & dinner) * **LB** **FACILITIES:** **Spa** STV Indoor swimming (H) Tennis (hard) Squash Snooker Sauna Solarium Croquet lawn Childrens nursery ch fac Xmas **CONF:** Thtr 50 Class 18 Board 26 **SERVICES:** Lift **PARKING:** 50 **NOTES:** No smoking in restaurant
**CARDS:**

*See advert on page 625*

★★★63% **Hotel Rembrandt**
12-18 Dorchester Rd DT4 7JU
☎ 01305 764000 01305 764022
e-mail: reception@hotelrembrandt.co.uk
**Dir:** *0.75m on left after Manor rdbt on A354 from Dorchester*
Conveniently located on the edge of the town, not too far from the centre and beach, this popular hotel offers good indoor leisure amenities and bedrooms with modern facilities. The restaurant serves both carvery and carte menus. There is a choice of function and meeting rooms.
**ROOMS:** 74 en suite (5 fmly) No smoking in 30 bedrooms s £57-£75; d £79-£96 (incl. bkfst) * **LB** **FACILITIES:** STV Indoor swimming (H) Sauna Solarium Gym Jacuzzi Steam room ch fac Xmas **CONF:** Thtr 200 Class 100 Board 50 Del from £85 * **SERVICES:** Lift **PARKING:** 80 **NOTES:** No smoking in restaurant Civ Wed 100
**CARDS:**

★★★61% **Hotel Rex**
29 The Esplanade DT4 8DN
☎ 01305 760400 01305 760500
e-mail: rex@kingshotels.f9.co.uk
**Dir:** *on seafront opposite Alexandra Gardens*
With stunning views across Weymouth Bay, this hotel was originally built as a summer residence for the Duke of Clarence. Varying in outlook, bedrooms are well-equipped. The restaurant serves a wide range of popular and imaginative dishes. A well-stocked bar and comfortably furnished lounge is also provided.

HOTEL REX

**ROOMS:** 31 en suite (5 fmly) s £50-£60; d £72-£105 (incl. bkfst) * **LB** **FACILITIES:** STV entertainment **CONF:** Thtr 40 Class 30 Board 25 **SERVICES:** Lift **PARKING:** 6 **NOTES:** Closed Xmas
**CARDS:**

★★70% **Glenburn**
42 Preston Rd DT3 6PZ
☎ 01305 832353 01305 835610
**Dir:** *on A353 1.5m E of town centre*

This small friendly hotel is located within walking distance of the seafront. It offers comfortable well equipped bedrooms, and a pleasant lounge and bar. The restaurant offers a good selection of set-price and carte menus supplemented by a bar menu.
**ROOMS:** 13 en suite (2 fmly) No smoking in 8 bedrooms s £38-£45; d £57-£70 (incl. bkfst) * **FACILITIES:** Jacuzzi **CONF:** Thtr 20 Class 20 Board 15 Del £60 * **PARKING:** 15 **NOTES:** No dogs (ex guide dogs) No smoking in restaurant **CARDS:**

★★64% **Crown**
51-53 St Thomas St DT4 8EQ
☎ 01305 760800 01305 760300
e-mail: crown@kingshotels.co.uk
**Dir:** *turn off A35 at Dorchester, take A354 to Weymouth, pass over second bridge, premises on left*
Conveniently close to the harbour, beach and town's many attractions, this popular tourist hotel provides comfortable accommodation. The public areas include a brightly decorated bar, a first-floor lounge and a spacious ballroom. Meals are served in both the restaurant and bar.
**ROOMS:** 86 en suite (11 fmly) s £36; d £66 (incl. bkfst) **LB** **FACILITIES:** STV **CONF:** Class 140 Board 80 **SERVICES:** Lift **PARKING:** 14 **NOTES:** No dogs (ex guide dogs) Closed 25-26 Dec
**CARDS:**

**★★64% Hotel Prince Regent**

Best Western

139 The Esplanade DT4 7NR
☎ 01305 771313 01305 778100
***Dir:*** *from A354 follow signs for Seafront. At Jubilee Clock turn left along Seafront, for 0.25m*

Conveniently close to the town centre, harbour and opposite the beach, this welcoming resort hotel dates back to 1855 and overlooks Weymouth Bay. Bedrooms vary in styles and size, with sea-facing rooms being particularly popular. The restaurant offers a choice of menus, and entertainment is regularly provided in the ballroom during the season.

**ROOMS:** 50 en suite (20 fmly) No smoking in 10 bedrooms s £55-£67; d £79-£91 (incl. bkfst) * **LB** **FACILITIES:** STV Table tennis,Pool table **CONF:** Thtr 180 Class 150 Board 150 Del from £54 * **SERVICES:** Lift **PARKING:** 18 **NOTES:** No dogs (ex guide dogs) No smoking in restaurant Closed 24 Dec-4Jan **CARDS:**

## WHATTON, Nottinghamshire
Map 08 SK73

**★★64% *The Haven***
Grantham Rd NG13 9EU
☎ 01949 850800 01949 851454
***Dir:*** *off A52, take turning to Redmile/Belvoir Castle*

This welcoming, family-run hotel has a large public bar and dining room, in which a good range of popular dishes is available. The modern bedrooms are decorated in pleasing colour schemes and have useful facilities.

**ROOMS:** 33 en suite (5 fmly) **FACILITIES:** STV **CONF:** Thtr 100 Class 20 Board 60 **PARKING:** 70 **CARDS:**

## WHEDDON CROSS, Somerset
Map 03 SS93

**★★71% *Raleigh Manor***
TA24 7BB
☎ 01643 841484 01643 841484
***Dir:*** *at Wheddon Cross, turn right on A396 for Dunster. Private drive to Raleigh Manor on left. Raleigh Manor on right if coming from A39*

Set in Exmoor National Park, this Victorian country house enjoys stunning views over Snowdrop Valley. The individually decorated bedrooms are comfortably furnished and equipped. The relaxing lounge, snug library and conservatory all take full advantage of the lovely views. The dining room offers a choice of carefully prepared, quality dishes.

**ROOMS:** 7 en suite No smoking in all bedrooms **PARKING:** 10 **NOTES:** No dogs No children 12yrs No smoking in restaurant Closed Dec-Feb **CARDS:**

## WHICKHAM, Tyne & Wear
Map 12 NZ26

**★★★69% Gibside Arms**
Front St NE16 4JG
☎ 0191 488 9292 0191 488 8000
e-mail: reception@gibside-hotel.co.uk
***Dir:*** *turn off A1M towards Whickham on the B6317, B6317 leads onto Whickham Front Street, 2m on right*

Set a hilltop, this modern hotel in the centre of the village enjoys spectacular views over the Tyne Valley and Newcastle. The bedrooms are well equipped and smartly decorated. Public rooms include a cocktail lounge and restaurant, and a bar offering food throughout the day. There is secure garage parking.

**ROOMS:** 45 en suite (2 fmly) No smoking in 10 bedrooms s £57.50; d £69 * **LB** **FACILITIES:** STV Golf Academy at The Beamish Park entertainment Xmas **CONF:** Thtr 100 Class 50 Board 50 Del from £81.50 * **SERVICES:** Lift **PARKING:** 28 **CARDS:**

## WHITBY, North Yorkshire
Map 08 NZ81

**★★★70% Dunsley Hall**
Dunsley YO21 3TL
☎ 01947 893437 01947 893505
e-mail: reception@dunsleyhall.com
***Dir:*** *3m N of Whitby, signposted off the A171*

RECEPTION
RECEPTION

Good hospitality and good cooking is a strong feature of this country house situated just outside of town in four acres of well-tended gardens. Oak panelling, carved fireplaces and mullioned windows all add to the character of the house, which offers a well-appointed restaurant and a popular bar. Spacious bedrooms are bright, comfortable and beautifully furnished, and many have sea views.

**ROOMS:** 18 en suite (2 fmly) No smoking in 4 bedrooms **FACILITIES:** Indoor swimming (H) Tennis (hard) Sauna Solarium Gym Croquet lawn Putting green ch fac Xmas **CONF:** Thtr 60 Class 30 Board 30 **PARKING:** 20 **NOTES:** No dogs (ex guide dogs) No smoking in restaurant Civ Wed 50 **CARDS:**

## WHITBY, continued

### ★★72% Saxonville
Ladysmith Av, Argyle Rd YO21 3HX
☎ 01947 602631 📠 01947 820523
e-mail: saxonville@onyxnet.co.uk
***Dir:*** *A174 on to North Promenade. Turn inland at large four towered building visible on West Cliff into Argyle Road, then first turning on right*
This comfortable holiday hotel provides bedrooms that are nicely presented in modern style and offer all the expected amenities: refurbished bedrooms are particularly appealing. Public areas include a choice of lounges, a small bar, and an attractive restaurant; an extensive range of carefully prepared English dishes are offered here.
**ROOMS:** 22 en suite (2 fmly) No smoking in all bedrooms s £40-£45; d £80-£90 (incl. bkfst) * **LB** **CONF:** Thtr 100 Class 64 Board 56 Del from £60 * **PARKING:** 20 **NOTES:** No dogs (ex guide dogs) No smoking in restaurant Closed Nov - March RS February, March & November. **CARDS:**

*See advert on page 627*

### ★★70% Stakesby Manor
Manor Close, High Stakesby YO21 1HL
☎ 01947 602773 📠 01947 602140
e-mail: rod@stakesby-manor.co.uk
***Dir:*** *at rdbt junct of A171/B1416 take road for West Cliff. Third turning on right*

MINOTEL Great Britain

Situated in a residential area, this Georgian mansion's friendly and relaxed atmosphere attracts both business people and tourists. Inviting public areas include a comfortable bar lounge and attractive panelled dining room. Bedrooms are impressively furnished and thoughtfully equipped.
**ROOMS:** 13 en suite (2 fmly) No smoking in 6 bedrooms s £54; d £74-£80 (incl. bkfst) * **LB** **CONF:** Thtr 100 Class 46 Board 40 Del £90 * **PARKING:** 40 **NOTES:** No dogs (ex guide dogs) No smoking in restaurant Closed 24-30 Dec **CARDS:**

### ★★67% White House
Upgang Ln, West Cliff YO21 3JJ
☎ 01947 600469 📠 01947 821600
e-mail: Thomas.Campbell1@btinternet.com
***Dir:*** *on A174 beside the golf course*
This family-run hotel is on the north side of town and overlooks the golf course at Sandsend Bay. Attractively appointed bedrooms vary in size, and there is a choice of two bars where locals and visitors mingle. The bars and dining room offer a varied selection of dishes including fresh local fish.
**ROOMS:** 10 en suite (3 fmly) s £28-£35; d £56-£70 (incl. bkfst) * **LB** **FACILITIES:** Xmas **PARKING:** 50 **NOTES:** No smoking in restaurant **CARDS:**

W

### ★★64% Old West Cliff Hotel
42 Crescent Av YO21 3EQ
☎ 01947 603292 📠 01947 821716
e-mail: oldwestcliff@telinco.co.uk
***Dir:*** *leave A171, follow signs for West Cliff, approach spa complex. Hotel 100yds from centre off Crescent Gardens*
This family owned and run hotel is close to the sea and convenient for the town centre. It provides well-equipped bedrooms, a cosy lounge and separate bar. A good range of food is served in the cosy basement restaurant.
**ROOMS:** 12 en suite (6 fmly) s £33; d £54 (incl. bkfst) * **NOTES:** No dogs (ex guide dogs) No smoking in restaurant Closed 24 Dec-31 Jan **CARDS:**

## WHITLEY BAY, Tyne & Wear — Map 12 NZ37

### ★★★65% Windsor
South Pde NE26 2RF
☎ 0191 251 8888 📠 0191 297 0272
e-mail: info@windsorhotel-uk.com
***Dir:*** *from A19 Tyne Tunnel follow for A1058 to Tynemouth. At coast rdbt turn left to Whitley Bay. After 2m turn left at Rex Hotel, Windsor on left*
A popular business hotel set between the town centre and the seafront in the town's liveliest area, where fashionable bars give nights between Thursdays and Sundays a carnival atmosphere. Accommodation is smart and well-equipped, and the public areas offer a choice of bars and eating options.
**ROOMS:** 70 en suite (24 fmly) s £45-£65; d £60-£70 (incl. bkfst) * **LB** **FACILITIES:** STV **SERVICES:** Lift **PARKING:** 46 **NOTES:** No dogs (ex guide dogs) **CARDS:**

### ★★66% High Point
The Promenade NE26 2NJ
☎ 0191 251 7782 📠 0191 251 6318
e-mail: Res@highpointhotel.freeserve.co.uk
***Dir:*** *from A1058 follow signs for Tynemouth, then seafront, turn left at Sealife Centre, follow rd for 1.5m, hotel on left going into Whitley Bay*
This friendly hotel offers a good standard throughout. The smart, well-equipped bedrooms are generally spacious and many enjoy sea views. Meals are served in the attractive little restaurant or the lounge bar (arrangements for dinner on Sundays are limited).
**ROOMS:** 14 en suite (3 fmly) s £49.50; d £60 (incl. bkfst) * **LB** **FACILITIES:** Pool table, Darts, large screen TV entertainment **PARKING:** 20 **NOTES:** No dogs (ex guide dogs) **CARDS:**

## WHITNEY-ON-WYE, Herefordshire — Map 03 SO24

### ★★73% The Rhydspence Inn
HR3 6EU
☎ 01497 831262 📠 01497 831751
***Dir:*** *Hotel located 1m W of Whitney-on-Wye on A438 Hereford to Brecon road*

This former manor house dates back in part to 1380. Privately owned and personally run in a warm and friendly manner, it provides well-equipped accommodation. Public areas have a wealth of charm and character, with exposed beams, timber framed walls and welcoming log fires. A blackboard selection supplements a large bar meal choice and the elegant restaurant serves an extensive menu. The quality of the food attracts a large local following.
**ROOMS:** 7 en suite s £33-£43; d £65-£75 (incl. bkfst) * **LB** **PARKING:** 30 **NOTES:** No dogs (ex guide dogs) No smoking in restaurant Closed 2wks Jan **CARDS:**

## WICKFORD, Essex

### ○ Innkeeper's Lodge Runwell
Runwell Rd SS11 7QJ
A new concept in the travel accommodation market. Smart rooms meet essential business requirements but also have home comforts. Dining options include all-day menus plus the added advantage of breakfast, which is included in the room price. Reservations can be made seven days a week through the room reservations number: 0870 243 0500. For further details, consult the Hotel Groups page.
**ROOMS:** 24 en suite

## WICKHAM, Hampshire
Map 04 SU51

### ★★67% Old House
The Square PO17 5JG
☎ 01329 833049 01329 833672
e-mail: eng@theoldhousehotel.co.uk
***Dir:*** *2m N of Fareham off A32*
Situated in the charming Georgian village of Wickham, close to the M27, this hotel provides individually decorated, spacious bedrooms that have much character and are well-equipped with extras. There is a choice of lounges, a small bar and a popular restaurant. Off-street parking is plentiful.
**ROOMS:** 9 en suite (1 fmly) s £65-£80; d £85-£100 (incl. cont bkfst) * LB **CONF:** Board 15 **PARKING:** 12 **NOTES:** No dogs (ex guide dogs) No smoking in restaurant Closed 10 days Xmas RS Mon-Sat
**CARDS:**

## WIDNES, Cheshire
Map 07 SJ58

### ★★★65% Hill Crest
75 Cronton Ln WA8 9AR
☎ 0151 424 1616 0151 495 1348
***Dir:*** *take A5080 Cronton to traffic lights turn right and drive for 0.75m, right at T-junct, follow A5080 for 500yds. Hotel on right*

This modern hotel is situated within easy reach of the motorway to the Northwest. All bedrooms are comfortable and well-equipped, particularly the executive rooms. Suites with four-poster or canopy beds and spa baths are also available. Public areas include extensive conference facilities, Palms restaurant and bar, as well as Nelsons public bar.
**ROOMS:** 50 en suite (5 fmly) No smoking in 25 bedrooms s £46-£79; d £61-£89 (incl. bkfst) * LB **FACILITIES:** STV entertainment Xmas ch fac **CONF:** Thtr 140 Class 80 Board 40 Del from £66 * **SERVICES:** Lift **PARKING:** 150 **NOTES:** Civ Wed 160
**CARDS:**

### ★★★64% Everglades Park
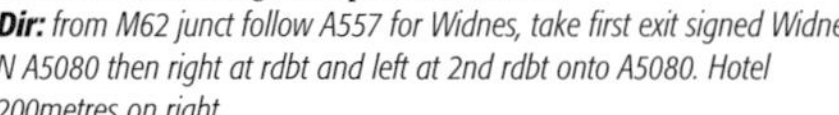
Derby Rd WA8 3UJ
☎ 0151 495 5500 0151 495 5599
e-mail: sales@everglades-park-hotel.co.uk
***Dir:*** *from M62 junct follow A557 for Widnes, take first exit signed Widnes N A5080 then right at rdbt and left at 2nd rdbt onto A5080. Hotel 200metres on right*
Bedrooms are nicely spacious at this modern hotel and offer good levels of comfort, with executive suites and family rooms also being available. A wide choice of snacks and bar meals is served in the recently refurbished Glades bar, as well as a full menu in the restaurant which overlooks the swimming pool.
**ROOMS:** 65 en suite (4 fmly) No smoking in 20 bedrooms s £55-£65; d £70-£75 (incl. bkfst) * LB **FACILITIES:** Indoor swimming (H) Croquet lawn entertainment Xmas ch fac **CONF:** Thtr 200 Class 90 Board 50 Del from £89 * **SERVICES:** air con **PARKING:** 200 **NOTES:** No dogs (ex guide dogs) Civ Wed 150 **CARDS:**

### ⌂ *Travelodge*
Fiddlers Ferry Rd WA8 2NR
☎ 08700 850950
***Dir:*** *on A562*
Travelodge offers good quality, good value, modern accommodation. Ideal for families, the spacious, en suite bedrooms include remote-control TV, tea and coffee-making facilities, luxury beds and free morning newspaper. Meals can be taken at the nearby family restaurant. For further details and the Travelodge phone number, consult the Hotel Groups page.

**ROOMS:** 32 en suite

## WIGAN, Greater Manchester
Map 07 SD50

### ★★★★64% *Kilhey Court*
Chorley Rd, Standish WN1 2XN
☎ 01257 472100 01257 422401
e-mail: reservations@kilhey.co.uk
***Dir:*** *on A5106 1.5m N of A49/A5106 junct*

This extended Victorian mansion, set in ten acres of ground overlooking Worthington lakes, offers well-appointed accommodation, including a number of magnificent suites. There are two restaurants, the casual Peligrino's and a more formal one featuring a Victorian conservatory.
**ROOMS:** 62 en suite (3 fmly) No smoking in 38 bedrooms **FACILITIES:** STV Indoor swimming (H) Fishing Sauna Solarium Gym Jacuzzi **CONF:** Thtr 180 Class 60 Board 60 **SERVICES:** Lift **PARKING:** 400 **NOTES:** No smoking in restaurant
**CARDS:**

WIGAN, continued

**★★★73% Wrightington Hotel & Country Club**
Best Western
Moss Ln, Wrightington WN6 9PB
☎ 01257 425803 01257 425830
e-mail: 100631.3514@compuserve.com
***Dir:*** *M6 junct 27, 0.25m W, hotel situated on right after church*

This privately owned, friendly modern hotel is situated in open countryside. It provides well-equipped, spacious accommodation. Public areas include an extensive leisure complex and air conditioned function and banqueting facilities.
**ROOMS:** 47 en suite (4 fmly) No smoking in 24 bedrooms s fr £72; d fr £82 (incl. bkfst) * **LB** **FACILITIES:** STV Indoor swimming (H) Squash Sauna Solarium Gym Jacuzzi Sprt Inj clinic,Hlth&Bty clinic,H'drsr **CONF:** Thtr 200 Class 120 Board 40 **PARKING:** 170 **NOTES:** Civ Wed **CARDS:**

*See advert on opposite page*

**★★★66% Quality Hotel Wigan**
Quality Hotel
Riverway WN1 3SS
☎ 01942 826888 01942 825800
e-mail: admin@gb058.u-net.com
***Dir:*** *from A49 take B5238 from rdbt, continue for 1.5m through traffic lights, through 3 more sets of lights, at 4th set turn right and take first left*
Close to the centre of the town this modern hotel offers spacious and well-equipped bedrooms. The open plan public areas include a comfortable lounge bar, adjacent to the popular restaurant which serves a good range of dishes.
**ROOMS:** 88 en suite No smoking in 35 bedrooms s £70-£76; d £80-£86 * **LB** **FACILITIES:** STV **CONF:** Thtr 200 Class 90 Board 50 Del from £70 * **SERVICES:** Lift **PARKING:** 100 **NOTES:** No smoking in restaurant Civ Wed 60 **CARDS:**

**★★★63% *Bellingham***
141-149 Wigan Ln WN1 2NB
☎ 01942 243893 01942 821027
***Dir:*** *On the A49 Wigan Lane approximately 0.5m out of town centre heading north, directly opposite Wigan Infirmary*
Situated in a leafy suburb, yet only minutes from the town centre, The Bellingham provides well-equipped, modern accommodation.

*continued*

The pleasant public areas offer a choice of bars and a selection of function rooms.

**ROOMS:** 32 en suite (4 fmly) No smoking in 2 bedrooms **FACILITIES:** STV **CONF:** Thtr 150 Class 50 Board 40 **SERVICES:** Lift **PARKING:** 40 **NOTES:** No smoking in restaurant **CARDS:**

**★★65% Bel-Air**
236 Wigan Ln WN1 2NU
☎ 01942 241410 01942 243967
e-mail: belair@hotelwigan.freeserve.co.uk
***Dir:*** *M6 junct 27, follow signs for Standish. In Standish turn right at traffic lights towards A49. Hotel is on right, 1.5m from Standish towards Wigan*
This friendly, family owned and run hotel is located just to the north of town. Accommodation is modern, bright and well-equipped. An extensive range of freshly prepared French and English dishes is offered in the restaurant.
**ROOMS:** 11 en suite (1 fmly) s £35-£39.50; d £45-£49.50 (incl. bkfst) * **CONF:** Thtr 30 Board 8 **PARKING:** 10 **NOTES:** No dogs (ex guide dogs) No smoking in restaurant **CARDS:**

**⌂ Premier Lodge**
PREMIER LODGE THE BEST, BEST ASSURED.
53 Warrington Rd, Ashton-in-Makerfield WN4 9PJ
☎ 0870 700 1572 0870 700 1573
***Dir:*** *M6 junct 23, onto A49 towards Ashton, and the Hotel is 0.5 mile on the left.*
Premier Lodge offers modern, well-equipped, en suite accommodation suitable for both business and leisure travellers. Meals can be taken at the adjacent popular restaurant and bar, which is fully licensed. For further details, consult the Hotel Groups page.
**ROOMS:** 28 en suite s £46-£46; d £46-£46 *

## WIGHT, ISLE OF — Map 04

### BEMBRIDGE — Map 04 SZ68

**★★66% Windmill Hotel**
1 Steyne Rd PO35 5UH
☎ 01983 872875 01983 874760
e-mail: info@thewindmillhotel.co.uk
***Dir:*** *0.5m from town centre, towards lifeboat station on the coast.*
This newly refurbished hotel offers spacious public rooms where a good range of food is available. Bedrooms are thoughtfully equipped while service is attentive and friendly. There are attractive gardens to front and rear.
**ROOMS:** 15 en suite (4 fmly) No smoking in all bedrooms s £40-£50; d £70-£92 (incl. bkfst) * **LB** **CONF:** Thtr 100 Class 100 Board 100 **PARKING:** 50 **NOTES:** No dogs (ex guide dogs) Civ Wed 100 **CARDS:**

BONCHURCH See Ventnor

## CHALE

Map 04 SZ47

### ★★70% Clarendon Hotel & Wight Mouse Inn

PO38 2HA
☎ 01983 730431 ▤ 01983 730431
e-mail: info@wightmouseinns.co.uk
***Dir:*** *Off A3055 onto B3399, Hotel 100 yds left next to St Andrews church.*
A charming 17th-century former coaching inn offering comfortable accommodation. Bedrooms include three suites. Guests can enjoy freshly prepared food in the smart Clarendon Restaurant or dine more informally at the very characterful Wight Mouse Inn.
**ROOMS:** 12 en suite (10 fmly) s £39; d £78 (incl. bkfst) *
**FACILITIES:** entertainment Xmas **CONF:** Class 30 Board 20
**PARKING:** 200 **CARDS:**

## COWES

Map 04 SZ49

### ★★★66% New Holmwood

Queens Rd, Egypt Point PO31 8BW
☎ 01983 292508 ▤ 01983 295020
e-mail: nholmwdh@aol.com
***Dir:*** *from A3020 at Northwood Garage traffic lights, take left hand fork & follow road until mini rdbt. 1st left then sharp right into Baring Rd and 4th left into Egypt hill. At bottom turn right, hotel on right*
Located metres from the Esplanade, the hotel enjoys excellent views. The glass-fronted restaurant is light and airy with a sun terrace, which is ideal for relaxing in the summer months. Bedrooms are comfortable and well-equipped with an on-going

*continued on p632*

COWES, continued

refurbishment programme. A small pool area and conference room are available.

*New Holmwood, Cowes*

**ROOMS:** 26 en suite (1 fmly) No smoking in 6 bedrooms s £72; d £85 (incl. bkfst) * **LB** **FACILITIES:** **Spa** STV Outdoor swimming (H) Xmas **CONF:** Thtr 150 Class 60 Board 50 Del £93 * **PARKING:** 20
**CARDS:**

*See advert on page 631*

### ★62% Duke of York

Mill Hill Rd PO31 7BT
☎ 01983 295171 🖹 01983 295047
This family-run inn is in a quiet situation close to the town centre. Bedrooms are split between the main building and a nearby annexe, and are neatly appointed. There is a well stocked bar and a pleasant restaurant offering a range of popular dishes.
**ROOMS:** 8 rms (7 en suite) 4 annexe rms (2 fmly) No smoking in 4 bedrooms s £40; d £50 (incl. bkfst) * **LB** **PARKING:** 12
**CARDS:**

## RYDE Map 04 SZ59

### ★★★64% Appley Manor

Appley Rd PO33 1PH
☎ 01983 564777 🖹 01983 564704
e-mail: appleymanor@lineone.net
***Dir:*** *on B3330*
Originally a Victorian manor house, Appley is located just five minutes from the town centre in very peaceful surroundings. The spacious bedrooms are well-furnished, with all the expected, modern facilities. There is a residents' lounge and breakfast room overlooking the gardens, and the popular Manor Inn provides a range of well-cooked meals.
**ROOMS:** 12 en suite (2 fmly) No smoking in 3 bedrooms s £36; d £46 * **PARKING:** 60 **NOTES:** No dogs (ex guide dogs)
**CARDS:**

W

### ★★70% ⚙⚙ *Biskra Beach Hotel & Restaurant*

17 Saint Thomas's St PO33 2DL
☎ 01983 567913 🖹 01983 616976
e-mail: info@biskra-hotel.com
***Dir:*** *Ryde Esplanade to West End follow St. Thomas's Street, approx. 2 mins on right*
Refurbished in a contemporary style, Biskra House has bucked the more traditional trends. The result is a light airy hotel with spacious bedrooms and well lit bathrooms. Public areas convey a stylish, light colonial feel with a spacious bar and very popular restaurant.
**ROOMS:** 14 en suite (2 fmly) **FACILITIES:** Exterior Canadian hot tub Seasonal moorings with water taxi service **CONF:** Thtr 30 Class 30 Board 25 **PARKING:** 12 **NOTES:** Civ Wed 60
**CARDS:**

### ★★63% Yelf's

Union St PO33 2LG
☎ 01983 564062 🖹 01983 563937
e-mail: manager@yelfshotel.com
***Dir:*** *from Ryde Esplanade, turn into Union St, Hotel on right*
This former coaching inn has undergone major refurbishment. Smart public areas include a busy bar, a separate lounge and an attractive dining room. Bedrooms are comfortably furnished and well-equipped.
**ROOMS:** 30 en suite (2 fmly) s fr £47; d fr £63 (incl. bkfst) *
**FACILITIES:** STV **CONF:** Thtr 70 Class 10 Board 20
**CARDS:**

## ST LAWRENCE Map 04 SZ57

### ★★69% *Rocklands*

PO38 1XH
☎ 01983 852964 🖹 01983 852964
***Dir:*** *A3055 from Ventnor to Niton, pass botanical gardens, Rare Breeds, & St Lawrence Church, hotel is 200m on right*

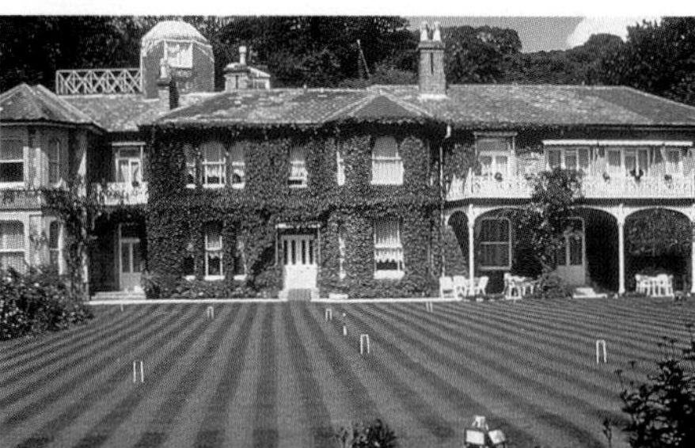

This elegant hotel is set in a peaceful location with attractive gardens. Bedrooms vary in size and décor, some with views of the gardens, but all are en suite with good facilities. Public areas are spacious with many original features, including a bar, games room and outdoor pool.
**ROOMS:** 15 en suite 4 annexe en suite (6 fmly) **FACILITIES:** Outdoor swimming (H) Snooker Sauna Solarium Croquet lawn Table tennis Games room entertainment ch fac **CONF:** Class 50 Board 40
**PARKING:** 20 **NOTES:** No dogs (ex guide dogs) No smoking in restaurant May-Oct

## SANDOWN Map 04 SZ58

### ★★67% *Cygnet Hotel*

58 Carter St PO36 8DQ
☎ 01983 402930 🖹 01983 405112
e-mail: cyghotel@aol.com
***Dir:*** *situated on the corner of Broadway - A3055 and the corner of Carter St*
Popular with tour groups, this family run hotel offers bedrooms that are mostly spacious, comfortably furnished and well-equipped. Public areas include two lounge areas and a large bar where live entertainment is regularly staged.
**ROOMS:** 45 rms (44 en suite) (9 fmly) **FACILITIES:** Indoor swimming (H) Outdoor swimming (H) Sauna Solarium Jacuzzi **SERVICES:** Lift
**PARKING:** 30 **NOTES:** No dogs (ex guide dogs) No smoking in restaurant

Packed in a hurry? Ironing facilities should be available at all star levels, either in rooms or on request.

### ★★62% Bayshore

12 - 16 Pier St PO36 8JX

Leisureplex
☎ 01983 403154 🖷 01983 406574
**Dir:** *approaching Sandown from Ryde or Newport, turn off the Broadway into Melville St, signed to Tourist Information Office. Across High St and bear right opposite pier. Hotel on right.*
This large hotel is found on the sea front opposite the pier and offers extensive public rooms where live entertainment is provided in season. The bedrooms are well-equipped and staff very friendly and helpful.
**ROOMS:** 78 en suite (19 fmly) s £25-£33; d £42-£58 (incl. bkfst) * **FACILITIES:** Sauna entertainment Xmas **SERVICES:** Lift **NOTES:** No dogs (ex guide dogs) No smoking in restaurant Closed Dec-Feb RS Nov/Mar (open Mon-Thu nights only) **CARDS:**

## SEAVIEW

Map 04 SZ69

### ★★★79% Seaview Hotel & Restaurant

High St PO34 5EX
☎ 01983 612711 🖷 01983 613729
e-mail: reception@seaviewhotel.co.uk
**Dir:** *B3330 Ryde-Seaview road, turn left via Puckpool along seafront , hotel is situated on left*
A charming family-owned and run hotel in a quiet seaside village. Bedrooms vary in size and style and all are decorated with flair. There is a quiet lounge with magazines on the first floor; as well as two bars and a separate, two-roomed restaurant. All have a nautical theme with plenty of memorabilia.
**ROOMS:** 16 en suite (1 fmly) No smoking in 2 bedrooms s £55-£80; d £70-£135 (incl. bkfst) * **LB** **FACILITIES:** Arrangement with local sports club ch fac **CONF:** Thtr 30 Class 15 Board 16 Del from £100 * **PARKING:** 12 **NOTES:** Closed 24-27 Dec
**CARDS:**

### ★★★76% *Priory Bay*

Priory Dr PO34 5BU
☎ 01983 613146 🖷 01983 616539
e-mail: reception@priorybay.co.uk
**Dir:** *B3330 towards Seaview, through Nettlestone. Do not take Seaview turning, instead continue 0.5m until sign for The Priory Bay Hotel becomes visible*

This hotel with its own stretch of beach has undergone extensive refurbishment. Public areas are comfortable as are the upgraded bedrooms. The kitchen creates interesting and imaginative dishes, using local produce as much as possible.
**ROOMS:** 19 en suite 15 annexe en suite (17 fmly) **FACILITIES:** Outdoor swimming Golf 9 Tennis (hard) Croquet lawn Private beach **CONF:** Thtr 80 Class 60 Board 30 **PARKING:** 65 **NOTES:** Civ Wed 50
**CARDS:**

### ★★67% *Springvale Hotel & Restaurant*

Springvale PO34 5AN
☎ 01983 612533
e-mail: reception@springvale-hotel.co.uk
**Dir:** *y*

A friendly hotel in a quiet beach-front location with views across the Solent. Bedrooms, varying in shape and size, are attractive and well-equipped. Public areas are traditionally furnished and include a cosy bar, dining room and small separate lounge.
**ROOMS:** 13 en suite (2 fmly) **FACILITIES:** Tennis (grass) Jacuzzi Sailing dinghy hire & tuition **CONF:** Class 30 Board 20 **PARKING:** 1
**NOTES:** No dogs (ex guide dogs) No smoking in restaurant
**CARDS:**

## SHANKLIN

Map 04 SZ58

### ★★★67% Keats Green

3 Queens Rd PO37 6AN
☎ 01983 862742 🖷 01983 868572
e-mail: keatsgreen@netguides.co.uk
**Dir:** *on A3055 follow signs Old Village/Ventnor, avoiding town centre, hotel on left past St Saviors church*

This well established hotel enjoys a super location overlooking Keats Green and Sandown Bay. Bedrooms are attractively decorated and furnished with pine. Public rooms include a comfortable bar/lounge and a smartly appointed dining room both affording lovely sea views.
**ROOMS:** 33 en suite (7 fmly) s £34-£42; d £68-£84 (incl. bkfst & dinner) * **LB** **FACILITIES:** Outdoor swimming (H) ch fac Xmas **SERVICES:** Lift **PARKING:** 34 **NOTES:** No smoking in restaurant Closed Jan-Mar **CARDS:**

SHANKLIN, continued

### ★★★64% *Luccombe Hall*

Luccombe Rd PO37 6RL
☎ 01983 862719 ⎙ 01983 863082
e-mail: reservations@luccombehall.co.uk
***Dir:*** *take A3055 to Shanklin, through old village then 1st left into Priory Rd, left into Popham Rd, 1st right into Luccombe Rd. Hotel on right*

This hotel was originally built as a summer home for the Bishop of Portsmouth in 1870. Enjoying an impressive clifftop location the property benefits from sea views and direct access to the beach. Bedrooms are comfortably furnished and well-equipped. A range of indoor and outdoor leisure facilities is available.

**ROOMS:** 30 en suite (19 fmly) **FACILITIES:** Indoor swimming (H) Outdoor swimming (H) Tennis (grass) Squash Sauna Solarium Gym Jacuzzi Games room entertainment **PARKING:** 20
**CARDS:**

### ★★★62% Holliers Hotel

5 Church Rd, Old Village PO37 6NU
☎ 01983 862764 ⎙ 01983 867134

A popular 18th-century hotel in the heart of the old village. Bedrooms are comfortably appointed and equipped with modern amenities. Public areas include a quiet first floor lounge, a smart bar with live entertainment and a spacious, brightly decorated restaurant with a comprehensive dinner menu.

**ROOMS:** 30 en suite (6 fmly) s £50-£55; d £65-£75 (incl. bkfst) * **LB** **FACILITIES:** **Spa** Indoor swimming (H) Outdoor swimming (H) Sauna Xmas **PARKING:** 50 **NOTES:** No dogs (ex guide dogs) No smoking in restaurant **CARDS:**

### ★★69% Aqua

17 The Esplanade PO37 6BN
☎ 01983 863024 ⎙ 01983 864841
e-mail: aa@aquahotel.co.uk
***Dir:*** *turn off Arthurs Hill/North Rd at fiveways junction into Hope Rd and follow through to Esplanade*

Public rooms and many of the bedrooms at this friendly, family-run hotel enjoy fine sea views. The bedrooms are well-equipped and some have the added bonus of a balcony. The sea views can also be enjoyed from the well-tended gardens and decked area to the front of the hotel.

**ROOMS:** 22 en suite (4 fmly) No smoking in all bedrooms s £30-£40; d £60-£80 (incl. bkfst) * **LB** **NOTES:** No dogs No smoking in restaurant Closed Nov-Mar **CARDS:**

### ★★69% Fernbank

Highfield Rd PO37 6PP
☎ 01983 862790 ⎙ 01983 864412
e-mail: enquiries@fernbankhotel.com
***Dir:*** *at Shanklin's old village traffic lights turn onto Victoria Ave, take 3rd left into Highfield Rd*

Set in a peaceful location, just minutes from the old village. Bedrooms are comfortably appointed and equipped with modern facilities. The smart dining room overlooks the gardens and countryside beyond. Hospitality is a strength here.

**ROOMS:** 19 en suite 5 annexe en suite (8 fmly) s £42-£48; d £86-£92.50 (incl. bkfst) * **LB** **FACILITIES:** Indoor swimming (H) Sauna Jacuzzi Petanque Xmas **CONF:** Board 14 Del from £65 * **PARKING:** 22 **NOTES:** No children 7yrs **CARDS:**

### ★★65% Hambledon

Queens Rd PO37 6AW
☎ 01983 862403 ⎙ 01983 867894
e-mail: enquiries@hambledon-hotel.co.uk
***Dir:*** *off A3055 turn left into Queens Rd at lights at the foot of Arthurs Hill*

The Hambledon specialises in walking holidays which the proprietors arrange for guests. Bedrooms are comfortable, nicely furnished and feature modern shower facilities. There is a cosy bar, adjacent lounge and a smartly appointed dining room.

**ROOMS:** 12 en suite (3 fmly) No smoking in all bedrooms s £36-£37; d £71-£74 (incl. bkfst & dinner) * **LB** **FACILITIES:** Free use of nearby indoor leisure facilities **PARKING:** 8 **NOTES:** No dogs (ex guide dogs) No smoking in restaurant Closed 1 Dec-15 Jan
**CARDS:**

### ★★64% Malton House

8 Park Rd PO37 6AY
☎ 01983 865007 ⎙ 01983 865576
e-mail: christos@excite.co.uk
***Dir:*** *from Hope Road traffic lights go straight up the hill then turn left on the third road*

A well-kept Victorian hotel in a quiet location. Recently refurbished bedrooms are brightly appointed. Public rooms include a small comfortable lounge, a bar and a dining room. The hotel is conveniently located for cliff top walks and the public lift down to the promenade.

**ROOMS:** 15 en suite (3 fmly) s £26-£28; d £44-£48 (incl. bkfst) * **FACILITIES:** Xmas **PARKING:** 12 **NOTES:** No dogs
**CARDS:**

### ★★63% Melbourne Ardenlea

Queen's Rd PO37 6AP
☎ 01983 862283 ⎙ 01983 862865
***Dir:*** *turn left at Fiveways Crossroads, off A3055, hotel on right 150yds past the tall spired church*

Conveniently located for the town centre and the lift down to the promenade, this friendly hotel continues to successfully cater for holiday makers. Spacious public areas are smartly presented, and bedrooms are traditionally furnished.

**ROOMS:** 53 en suite (9 fmly) s £37-£44; d £74-£88 (incl. bkfst & dinner) * **LB** **FACILITIES:** Indoor swimming (H) Sauna Solarium Jacuzzi Pool Table tennis entertainment ch fac **SERVICES:** Lift **PARKING:** 28 **NOTES:** Closed mid Dec-mid Feb RS Nov-mid Dec & mid Feb-Mar
**CARDS:**

○ **Bay House Hotel**
8 Chine Av PO37 6AG
☎ 01983 863180
At the time of going to press, the star classification for this hotel was not confirmed. Please refer to the AA internet site www.theAA.com for current information.

## TOTLAND BAY
Map 04 SZ38

★★★66% **Sentry Mead**
Madeira Rd PO39 0BJ
☎ 01983 753212 Fax 01983 753212
e-mail: julie@sentry-mead.co.uk
***Dir:*** *turn off A3054 at Totland war memorial rdbt, 300yds on right just before going to beach*
Just two minutes from the sea at Totland Bay, this well kept Victorian villa includes a comfortable lounge and separate bar as well as a conservatory overlooking the garden. Bedrooms feature co-ordinated soft furnishings and extras such as mineral water, biscuits and pot-pourri.
**ROOMS:** 14 en suite (4 fmly) s £30-£40; d £60-£80 * LB
**PARKING:** 10 **NOTES:** No smoking in restaurant Closed 20 Dec-4 Jan
**CARDS:**

## VENTNOR
Map 04 SZ57

★★★★71% The Royal Hotel
Belgrave Rd PO38 1JJ
☎ 01983 852186 Fax 01983 855395
e-mail: royalhotel@zetnet.co.uk
***Dir:*** *A3055 main coastal road, into Ventnor follow one way system around Town, after traffic lights turn left into Belgrave road. Hotel is on right*
The Royal Hotel provides good quality accommodation both within bedrooms and the spacious public rooms. Public areas include a sunny conservatory and restful lounge while there is also an outdoor pool. The restaurant provides an appropriate setting for good cooking from modern British menus. Staff are very caring and friendly.
**ROOMS:** 55 en suite (7 fmly) No smoking in 2 bedrooms s £60-£101; d £100-£160 (incl. bkfst) * LB **FACILITIES:** STV Outdoor swimming (H) Croquet lawn ch fac Xmas **CONF:** Thtr 100 Class 80 Board 50 Del from £100 * **SERVICES:** Lift **PARKING:** 56 **NOTES:** No dogs (ex guide dogs) No smoking in restaurant **CARDS:**
*See advert on this page*

★★★66% **Ventnor Towers**

Best Western
Madeira Rd PO38 1QT
☎ 01983 852277 Fax 01983 855536
e-mail: ventnor@inc.co.uk
***Dir:*** *first left after Trinity church, follow road for 0.25m*
This mid-Victorian hotel set in spacious grounds -from which a path leads down to the shore - is high above the bay and enjoys some splendid sea views. Lots of potted plants and fresh flowers grace day rooms which include two lounges and a roomy bar. Bedrooms include two four-posters and some with their own balconies.
**ROOMS:** 27 en suite (4 fmly) No smoking in 3 bedrooms s £55-£62; d £95 (incl. bkfst) * LB **FACILITIES:** Outdoor swimming (H) Tennis (hard) Croquet lawn Putting green Games room entertainment Xmas **CONF:** Thtr 80 Class 50 Board 35 Del from £55 * **PARKING:** 26 **NOTES:** No smoking in restaurant **CARDS:**



★★★65% **Burlington**
Bellevue Rd PO38 1DB
☎ 01983 852113 Fax 01983 853862
e-mail: patmctoldrige@burlingtonhotel.freeserve.co.uk
Eight of the attractively decorated bedrooms have balconies, and three ground floor rooms have French doors leading onto the garden. There is a cosy bar, comfortable lounge and a dining room where home-made bread rolls accompany the five-course dinners. Service is both friendly and attentive. There are plans to add a conservatory.
**ROOMS:** 24 en suite (8 fmly) **FACILITIES:** Outdoor swimming (H) **PARKING:** 20 **NOTES:** No dogs No children 3yrs No smoking in restaurant Closed Nov-Etr **CARDS:**

★★★64% **Eversley**
Park Av PO38 1LB
☎ 01983 852244 Fax 01983 853948
e-mail: eversleyhotel@fsbdial.co.uk
***Dir:*** *on A3055 west of Ventnor*
Located West of Ventnor this hotel enjoys a quiet location with some rooms offering garden and pool views. The large spacious dining room is also used for local functions. The newly decorated bar has a pool table, there is also a television room, a lounge area and a card room. Bedrooms are generally a good size.
**ROOMS:** 30 en suite (8 fmly) s £30-£45; d £58-£69 (incl. bkfst) * LB
**FACILITIES:** Outdoor swimming (H) Tennis (hard) ch fac Xmas
**CONF:** Class 40 Board 20 Del from £50 * **PARKING:** 23
**NOTES:** Closed 16 Nov-22 Dec & 2 Jan-15 Feb
**CARDS:**

W

VENTNOR, continued

**★★67% Hillside Hotel**
Mitchell Av PO38 1DR
☎ 01983 852271 📠 01983 852271
e-mail: aa@hillside-hotel.co.uk
***Dir:*** *turn off A3055 onto B3327. Hotel 0.5m on right behind tennis courts*

Hillside Hotel dates back to the 19th century and enjoys a superb location overlooking Ventnor and the sea beyond. Public areas consist of a traditional lounge, a cosy bar area with adjoining conservatory and light, airy dining room. Bedrooms are being refurbished with quality fabrics. A welcoming homely atmosphere is assured.
**ROOMS:** 12 en suite (1 fmly) No smoking in all bedrooms s £24-£26; d £48-£52 (incl. bkfst) * **LB** **FACILITIES:** Tennis (hard) **PARKING:** 12 **NOTES:** No children 5yrs No smoking in restaurant
**CARDS:**

**★★67% *St Maur Hotel***
Castle Rd PO38 1LG
☎ 01983 852570 & 853645 📠 01983 852306
***Dir:*** *W of Ventnor off main A3055 (Park Avenue)*
Guests will find a warm welcome awaits them at this hotel, where six course home cooked dinners are on offer. The well-equipped bedrooms are traditionally decorated. In addition to a spacious lounge the hotel benefits from a cosy residents' bar. The gardens here are a delight.
**ROOMS:** 14 en suite (2 fmly) **FACILITIES:** STV **PARKING:** 12 **NOTES:** No dogs No children 5yrs No smoking in restaurant Closed Dec
**CARDS:**

YARMOUTH — Map 04 SZ38

***Premier Collection***

**★★★ ◎◎◎ George Hotel**
Quay St PO41 0PE
☎ 01983 760331 📠 01983 760425
e-mail: res@thegeorge.co.uk
***Dir:*** *between the castle and the pier*
The George Hotel is set in an excellent location between the quay and the castle. This ensures that the gardens, the Brasserie and some rooms enjoy superb sea views. All of the bedrooms have been stylishly and individually decorated and there are many extra touches such as bathrobes. Fine cooking may be enjoyed in the elegant restaurant. There is also a bright brasserie, if you are looking for a less formal setting.

**ROOMS:** 16 en suite No smoking in 4 bedrooms **FACILITIES:** STV Xmas **CONF:** Thtr 30 Class 10 Board 18 Del from £175 *
**NOTES:** No children 10yrs Civ Wed
**CARDS:**

WILLERBY, East Riding of Yorkshire — Map 08 TA03

**★★★72% ◎ Willerby Manor**
Well Ln HU10 6ER
☎ 01482 652616 📠 01482 653901
e-mail: info@willerbymanor.co.uk
***Dir:*** *turn off A63, signposted Humber Bridge. Follow road, take right at rdbt by Safeway. At next rdbt hotel is signposted*
Set in a residential area, surrounded by well tended gardens, this hotel was originally the home of Sir Henry Salmon, an Edwardian shipping merchant. It has been thoughtfully extended to provide tasteful bedrooms equipped with many useful extras. The wide choice of public areas includes the Lafite Restaurant and extensive leisure facilities.
**ROOMS:** 51 en suite No smoking in 26 bedrooms s £74.50-£79.50; d £85-£99 * **LB** **FACILITIES:** STV Indoor swimming (H) Sauna Solarium Gym Croquet lawn Jacuzzi Steam room Beauty therapist Aerobic classes entertainment ch fac **CONF:** Thtr 500 Class 200 Board 100 Del from £95 * **PARKING:** 300 **NOTES:** No dogs (ex guide dogs) RS 24-26 Dec Civ Wed 300 **CARDS:**

**○ Innkeeper's Lodge Hull**
Beverley Rd HU10 6NT
A new concept in the travel accommodation market. Smart rooms meet essential business requirements but also have home comforts. Dining options include all-day menus plus the added advantage of breakfast, which is included in the room price. Reservations can be made seven days a week through the room reservations number: 0870 243 0500. For further details, consult the Hotel Groups page.
**ROOMS:** 32 en suite **NOTES:** Open Now

WILLINGTON, Co Durham — Map 12 NZ13

**★★66% Kensington Hall**
Kensington Ter DL15 0PJ
☎ 01388 745071 📠 01388 745800
e-mail: kensingtonhall@cs.com
***Dir:*** *On A690 between Durham and Crook. Hotel off the main street at the end of Kensington Terrace.*
A popular place to eat with locals, this friendly family run hotel was originally a church hall. Now converted with well-equipped en suite bedrooms, spacious and comfortable lounges and bars, and

*continued*

a restaurant offering a wide range of dishes and blackboard specials.
**ROOMS:** 10 en suite (3 fmly) No smoking in 2 bedrooms s £50; d £48-£50 (incl. bkfst) * **LB** **CONF:** Class 80 Board 50 **PARKING:** 40 **NOTES:** No dogs (ex guide dogs) No smoking in restaurant
**CARDS:**

## WILLITON, Somerset Map 03 ST04

### ★★72% *The Masons Arms Hotel*
2 North Rd TA4 4SN
☎ 01984 639200 01984 635933
e-mail: themasons@richardshotels.co.uk
***Dir:*** *M5 junct 25 onto A358 to Minehead. Turn right at Williton, after 200yds turn left into the Watchet Rd. Hotel in the middle of the road as it forks*
Lovingly restored and extended, this 16th-century thatched inn is just off the village centre, on the edge of the Quantocks. Five of the comfortable, well-equipped bedrooms are on the ground floor, and one is specifically for visitors with disabilities. An interesting range of dishes is available in both the restaurant and bar.
**ROOMS:** 2 en suite 5 annexe en suite (1 fmly) No smoking in all bedrooms **FACILITIES:** ch fac **CONF:** Thtr 16 Class 12 Board 16 **PARKING:** 20 **NOTES:** No dogs (ex guide dogs) No smoking in restaurant **CARDS:**

### ★★72% White House
Long St TA4 4QW
☎ 01984 632306 & 632777
***Dir:*** *on A39 in the centre of the village*
A relaxed and easygoing atmosphere is the hallmark of this charming little Georgian hotel. Bedrooms vary in size, those in the main building being rather more spacious, but all are well-equipped with extra touches that make this delightful hotel a home from home. Award-winning cuisine and an impressive wine list may be found in the unique dining room.
**ROOMS:** 6 rms (5 en suite) 4 annexe en suite (1 fmly) s £49-£67; d £84-£108 (incl. bkfst) * **LB** **PARKING:** 12 **NOTES:** No smoking in restaurant Closed Nov-mid May

## WILMSLOW, Cheshire Map 07 SJ88
see also Manchester Airport

### ★★★★68% Mottram Hall
Wilmslow Rd, Mottram St Andrew, Prestbury SK10 4QT
☎ 01625 828135 01625 828950
e-mail: dmh.sales@devere-hotels.com
This extremely popular hotel lies in attractive grounds in the heart of the Cheshire countyside, very conveniently located for Manchester airport and the motorway network. With extensive leisure and meeting facilities, including a magnificent golf course, and a new restaurant - Nathaniel's - this makes for a well rounded product.
**ROOMS:** 132 en suite (5 fmly) No smoking in 60 bedrooms s £120-£145; d £135-£170 (incl. bkfst) **LB** **FACILITIES:** STV Indoor swimming (H) Golf 18 Tennis (hard) Squash Snooker Sauna Solarium Gym Putting green Jacuzzi Childrens play ground entertainment ch fac **CONF:** Thtr 275 Class 140 Board 60 Del from £140 * **SERVICES:** Lift **PARKING:** 300 **NOTES:** No smoking in restaurant
**CARDS:**

### Premier Lodge
Racecourse Rd SK9 5LR
☎ 0870 700 1578 0870 700 1579
***Dir:*** *Off A538.*
Premier Lodge offers modern, well-equipped, en suite accommodation suitable for both business and leisure travellers. Meals can be taken at the adjacent popular restaurant and bar, which is fully licensed. For further details, consult the Hotel Groups page.
**ROOMS:** 37 en suite s £46; d £46 *

## WIMBORNE MINSTER, Dorset Map 04 SZ09

### ★★75% Beechleas
17 Poole Rd BH21 1QA
☎ 01202 841684 01202 849344
e-mail: beechleas@hotmail.com
***Dir:*** *on A349*

Furnished to a high standard, the spacious bedrooms at this elegant Georgian town house are well-equipped and individually styled. The lounge is very comfortable and the conservatory restaurant bright and airy. Dinner menus provide honest food; many ingredients are sourced from a local organic farm.
**ROOMS:** 5 en suite 4 annexe en suite No smoking in all bedrooms s £69-£89; d £79-£109 (incl. bkfst) * **LB** **FACILITIES:** Sailing Hotel's yacht-Poole Harbour **CONF:** Thtr 20 Class 20 Board 14 Del from £129.95 * **PARKING:** 11 **NOTES:** No smoking in restaurant Closed 25 Dec-11 Jan
**CARDS:**

## WINCANTON, Somerset Map 03 ST72

### ★★★76% Holbrook House
Holbrook BA9 8BS
☎ 01963 32377 01963 32681
e-mail: Reception@Holbrookhouse.co.uk
***Dir:*** *from A303 at Wincanton, turn left on A371 towards Castle Cary and Shepton Mallet*
This charming property, set in its own gardens, offers comfort and quality. Bedrooms have been decorated and furnished in keeping with the architecture while those in the garden wing tend to be more modern. Public rooms include a dining room where imaginative dishes and an extensive wine list are offered. There is an impressive range of leisure facilities, including tennis, swimming, a gym, beauty salons, and saunas. Holbrook House holds a licence for civil weddings.
**ROOMS:** 15 en suite 5 annexe en suite (2 fmly) s fr £80; d fr £125 (incl. cont bkfst) * **LB** **FACILITIES:** STV Indoor swimming (H) Outdoor swimming (H) Tennis (hard & grass) Sauna Gym Croquet lawn Jacuzzi Beauty treatment ch fac Xmas **CONF:** Thtr 200 Class 50 Board 55 Del from £120 * **PARKING:** 100 **NOTES:** No dogs (ex guide dogs) No smoking in restaurant Civ Wed 80
**CARDS:**

Packed in a hurry? Ironing facilities should be available at all star levels, either in rooms or on request.

W

## WINCHESTER, Hampshire
Map 04 SU42

### ★★★★73% Lainston House
Sparsholt SO21 2LT
☎ 01962 863588 01962 776672
e-mail: enquiries@lainstonhouse.com
***Dir:*** *2m NW off B3049 towards Stockbridge*

This hotel embodies the fine traditions of a quality British country house hotel. Rooms vary from spacious and well-equipped rooms in Chudleigh Court to spectacular suites in the main house. The cuisine combines fresh clear flavours with imaginative presentation.
**ROOMS:** 41 en suite (2 fmly) s £100-£200; d £150-£285 * **LB FACILITIES:** STV Tennis (hard) Fishing Gym Croquet lawn Archery Clay pigeon shooting entertainment ch fac Xmas **CONF:** Thtr 80 Class 50 Board 40 Del from £170 * **PARKING:** 150 **NOTES:** No smoking in restaurant Civ Wed 120 **CARDS:**

*See advert on opposite page*

### ★★★★65% The Wessex
Paternoster Row SO23 9LQ
☎ 0870 400 8126 01962 841503
e-mail: heritagehotels_winchester.wessex @forte-hotels.com
***Dir:*** *from M3 follow signs for town centre, at rdbt by King Alfred's statue proceed past the Guildhall and take the next left, hotel on right*
Tucked away in the centre of the city this hotel boasts fine views of the cathedral from some bedrooms and public areas. The lounge, with its large picture windows is a favourite meeting place for afternoon tea. Designed with the business and leisure guest in mind bedrooms have excellent facilities.
**ROOMS:** 94 en suite No smoking in 61 bedrooms s £138-£148; d £150-£160 (incl. bkfst) * **LB FACILITIES:** STV Solarium Free use of local leisure centre. entertainment ch fac Xmas **CONF:** Thtr 100 Class 60 Board 60 Del from £125 * **SERVICES:** Lift **PARKING:** 60 **NOTES:** No smoking in restaurant Civ Wed 100
**CARDS:**

### ★★★73% Royal
Saint Peter St SO23 8BS
☎ 01962 840840 01962 841582
e-mail: Royal@marstonhotels.com

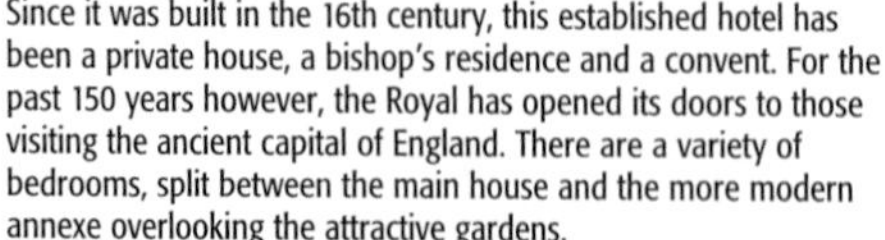

Since it was built in the 16th century, this established hotel has been a private house, a bishop's residence and a convent. For the past 150 years however, the Royal has opened its doors to those visiting the ancient capital of England. There are a variety of bedrooms, split between the main house and the more modern annexe overlooking the attractive gardens.
**ROOMS:** 75 en suite No smoking in 25 bedrooms s £87.50-£115; d £105-£145 * **LB FACILITIES:** STV Xmas **CONF:** Thtr 150 Class 50 Board 40 Del from £115 * **PARKING:** 50 **NOTES:** No smoking in restaurant Civ Wed 110 **CARDS:**

### ★★★62% Marwell
Thompson Ln, Colden Common, Marwell SO21 1JY
☎ 01962 777681 01962 777625
***Dir:*** *on B2177 opposite Marwell Zoological Park*
Guests are more likely to hear the roar of lions and tigers than traffic at this colonial-style hotel set in wooded grounds adjoining Marwell Zoological Park. The hotel combines a range of well-equipped meeting rooms, an excellent location and well appointed bedrooms, making it popular with business travellers, conference delegates and holidaymakers alike.
**ROOMS:** 68 en suite (35 fmly) No smoking in 47 bedrooms s £50-£80; d £70-£100 (incl. bkfst) * **LB FACILITIES:** STV Indoor swimming (H) Sauna Solarium Gym Jacuzzi Pool Table Xmas **CONF:** Thtr 160 Class 60 Board 60 Del from £80 * **PARKING:** 85 **NOTES:** No smoking in restaurant RS Sat Civ Wed 150 **CARDS:**

## *Town House*

### ★★★★ Hotel du Vin & Bistro
14 Southgate St SO23 9EF
☎ 01962 841414 01962 842458
e-mail: info@winchester.hotelduvin.com
***Dir:*** *M3 junct 11 towards Winchester, follow all signs. Hotel du Vin is situated approx 2m from junct 11 on left hand side just past cinema*
Relaxed, charming and unpretentious are the key words to describe this centrally located town house, which maintains a high profile amongst the locals. The individually decorated bedrooms, each sponsored by a different wine house, show considerable originality of style. The bistro serves imaginative and enjoyable food from a daily changing menu. The wine list has been selected by a master hand, offering a great choice from around the world.
**ROOMS:** 23 en suite (1 fmly) s £95-£185; d £95-£185 *
**FACILITIES:** STV Xmas **CONF:** Thtr 40 Class 30 Board 20 Del £145 * **PARKING:** 35 **NOTES:** No dogs (ex guide dogs)
**CARDS:**

## WINDERMERE, Cumbria
Map 07 SD49

## *Premier Collection*

### ★★★ Gilpin Lodge Country House Hotel & Restaurant
Crook Rd LA23 3NE
☎ 015394 88818 015394 88058
e-mail: hotel@gilpin-lodge.co.uk
***Dir:*** *M6 junct 36, take A590/A591 to rdbt North of Kendal, take B5284, hotel is 5m on the right*
Gilpin Lodge is an impeccable Victorian residence set in picturesque woodlands, moors and gardens. The sumptuous

*continued*

day rooms are furnished with fine antiques and provide deep comfort in which guests can relax and unwind. Many of the comfortable, elegant and individually styled bedrooms have four-poster beds and some have a private sun terrace. There are imaginative menus with exciting food, which is served throughout the three dining rooms.
**ROOMS:** 14 en suite s £105; d £110-£210 (incl. bkfst) * LB
**FACILITIES:** Croquet lawn Putting green Free membership at local Leisure Club Xmas **CONF:** Board 12 Del from £120 *
**PARKING:** 30 **NOTES:** No dogs No children 7yrs No smoking in restaurant **CARDS:**

## Premier Collection

★★★ Holbeck Ghyll Country House
Holbeck Ln LA23 1LU
☎ 015394 32375 015394 34743
e-mail: stay@holbeckghyll.com
*Dir: 3m North of Windermere on A591, turn right into Holbeck Lane (sign Troutbeck), hotel is 0.5m along on left*

With a peaceful setting in its own extensive grounds, this beautifully maintained hotel enjoys breathtaking views over Lake Windermere and the Langdale fells. Public rooms include luxurious, comfortable lounges and two elegant dinning rooms where memorable meals are served. A spa as well as indoor and outdoor leisure facilities also features here. Bedrooms are individually styled, beautifully furnished and

*continued*

many have either balconies or patios. Rooms in the adjacent lodge are particularly elegant and thoughtfully equipped.

**ROOMS:** 14 en suite 6 annexe en suite (1 fmly) No smoking in 6 bedrooms s £130-£220; d £180-£320 (incl. bkfst & dinner) * LB
**FACILITIES:** Spa STV Tennis (hard) Sauna Gym Croquet lawn Putting green Jacuzzi Beautician Steam room ch fac Xmas
**CONF:** Thtr 45 Class 25 Board 25 Del from £135 * **PARKING:** 30
**NOTES:** No smoking in restaurant Civ Wed 65
**CARDS:**

Late for dinner? Quality Standards star rating means that last orders for dinner should be no earlier than:
★ 6.30pm ★★ 7.00pm ★★★ 8.00pm
★★★★ 9.00pm ★★★★★ 10.00pm

WINDERMERE, continued

## Premier Collection

**★★★ ®® Linthwaite House Hotel**

Crook Rd LA23 3JA

☎ 015394 88600 015394 88601

e-mail: admin@linthwaite.com

***Dir:*** *A591 towards the lakes for 8m to large rdbt, take 1st exit (B5284), continue for 6m, hotel is on left hand side 1m past Windermere Golf Club*

Linthwaite House is set in 14 acres of hilltop grounds, including its own fishing tarn and stunning views of Lake Windermere. Inside there is a smokers' bar, comfortable lounge and conservatory. In the elegant restaurant, guests can enjoy carefully prepared meals. Bedrooms are individually decorated in both contemporary and traditional styles and are thoughtfully equipped. Service and hospitality are real strengths at this delightful hotel.

**ROOMS:** 26 en suite (1 fmly) No smoking in 19 bedrooms s £85-£115; d £90-£260 (incl. bkfst) * **LB FACILITIES:** STV Fishing Croquet lawn Putting green Free use of nearby leisure spa Xmas **CONF:** Thtr 47 Class 19 Board 22 Del from £150 * **PARKING:** 40 **NOTES:** No dogs (ex guide dogs) No smoking in restaurant Civ Wed 60 **CARDS:**

*See advert on opposite page*

**★★★76% ® Storrs Hall**

Storrs Park LA23 3LG

☎ 015394 47111 015394 47555

e-mail: reception@storrshall.co.uk

***Dir:*** *on the A592 2m S of Bowness on the Newby Bridge road*

This is a faithfully restored Georgian mansion set on a peninsula of Lake Windermere with magnificent views to three sides. Imaginatively restored bedrooms are furnished with wonderful fine arts and antiques. The public areas are comfortable with deep cushioned sofas. The atmosphere is relaxed, the hospitality is warm and the food is good.

**ROOMS:** 18 en suite s £135-£195; d £200-£310 (incl. bkfst) * **LB FACILITIES:** Fishing Sailing Water skiing Water sports Xmas **CONF:** Thtr 36 Board 24 Del from £140 * **PARKING:** 50 **NOTES:** No dogs (ex guide dogs) No children 12yrs No smoking in restaurant Closed 2 Jan-2 Feb Civ Wed 64 **CARDS:**

**★★★75% ® Beech Hill**

Best Western

Newby Bridge Rd LA23 3LR

☎ 015394 42137 015394 43745

e-mail: beechhill@richardsonhotels.co.uk

***Dir:*** *A591 towards Windermere, turn onto A590 to Newby Bridge, then take A592 toward Bowness, hotel is on left hand side 4m S from Bowness*

Situated on the banks of Lake Windermere, south of Bowness, this stylish hotel offers an impressive standard of accommodation. Elegant bedrooms, some with four-posters, have panoramic views or patio doors opening onto gardens that overlook the lake. Light lunches, drinks and afternoon tea are all served in the inviting open plan lounge

**ROOMS:** 57 en suite (4 fmly) s £69-£89; d £118-£158 (incl. bkfst & dinner) * **LB FACILITIES:** Indoor swimming (H) Fishing Sauna Solarium entertainment ch fac Xmas **CONF:** Thtr 80 Class 50 Board 40 Del from £110 * **PARKING:** 70 **NOTES:** No smoking in restaurant Civ Wed 80 **CARDS:**

**★★★75% Lindeth Howe Country House**

Lindeth Dr, Longtail Hill LA23 3JF

☎ 015394 45759 015394 46368

e-mail: hotel@lindeth-howe.co.uk

***Dir:*** *turn off A592 onto B5284 (Longtail Hill), hotel is the last driveway on the right hand side*

This delightful house, once the home of Beatrix Potter, is set in secluded woodlands and gardens, enjoying views over Lake Windermere. Bedrooms are spacious and attractively furnished, and there is a choice of comfortable lounges, as well as an indoor leisure area. The light and airy restaurant serves a good value menu featuring carefully prepared local produce.

**ROOMS:** 36 en suite (3 fmly) No smoking in 28 bedrooms s £45-£98; d £90-£160 (incl. bkfst) * **LB FACILITIES:** STV Indoor swimming (H) Sauna Solarium Gym ch fac Xmas **CONF:** Thtr 30 Class 20 Board 18 Del from £100 * **PARKING:** 50 **NOTES:** No dogs (ex guide dogs) No smoking in restaurant **CARDS:**

**★★★72% Burn How Garden House Hotel**

Back Belsfield Rd, Bowness LA23 3HH

☎ 015394 46226 015394 47000

e-mail: info@burnhow.co.uk

***Dir:*** *on entering Bowness, carry on past main lake piers on right, take first left to Hotel entrance*

Set in its own leafy grounds, this hotel is only minutes walk from both the lakeside and the town centre. Attractive, spacious rooms

*continued*

are situated in either modern chalets or in an adjacent Victorian house. Many have private patios or terraces. Superior Bay and Mews rooms are particularly well-appointed. Open plan public areas are elegant and offer splendid views.
**ROOMS:** 26 annexe en suite (10 fmly) No smoking in 2 bedrooms s £55-£75; d £76-£96 (incl. bkfst) * **LB** **FACILITIES:** ch fac Xmas **PARKING:** 30 **NOTES:** No dogs (ex guide dogs) No smoking in restaurant Closed 3-18 Jan **CARDS:**

### ★★★70% Fayrer Garden House

THE CIRCLE
Selected Individual Hotels
GREAT BRITAIN

Lyth Valley Rd, Bowness on Windermere LA23 3JP
☎ 015394 88195 Fax 015394 45986
e-mail: lakescene@fayrergarden.com
***Dir:*** *on A5074 1m from Bowness Bay*

Located high above the lake and away from the hubbub of Bowness, this turn-of-the-century residence continues to be a popular destination for discerning guests. Elegant public rooms include a panelled hall leading into a cosy sitting room and a richly furnished conservatory restaurant. The appealing bedrooms are stylishly furnished.
**ROOMS:** 18 en suite (3 fmly) No smoking in 6 bedrooms **FACILITIES:** STV Fishing Free membership of leisure club Xmas **PARKING:** 25 **NOTES:** No dogs (ex guide dogs) No smoking in restaurant Civ Wed 60 **CARDS:**

### ★★★68% Burnside

Kendal Rd, Bowness LA23 3EP
☎ 015394 42211 Fax 015394 43824
e-mail: stay@burnsidehotel.com
***Dir:*** *M6 junct 36 in direction of Windermere. Arriving at Windermere turn left for A592 to Bowness. Hotel is 300 yds past steamer pier on left*
A contemporary complex with well-tended gardens and views to the lake. At its heart is a Victorian house, extended to include comfortably furnished lounges, restaurants and spacious modern bedrooms. There is a wide range of conference and leisure facilities.
**ROOMS:** 57 en suite (15 fmly) No smoking in 18 bedrooms s £55-£80; d £100-£120 (incl. bkfst) * **LB** **FACILITIES:** STV Indoor swimming (H) Squash Snooker Sauna Solarium Gym Jacuzzi Steam rm,Badminton,Beauty salon ch fac Xmas **CONF:** Thtr 100 Class 70 Board 38 Del from £109 * **SERVICES:** Lift **PARKING:** 100 **NOTES:** No smoking in restaurant Civ Wed 120
**CARDS:**

### ★★★68% Langdale Chase

Langdale Chase LA23 1LW
☎ 015394 32201 Fax 015394 32604
e-mail: sales@langdalechase.co.uk
***Dir:*** *2m S of Ambleside and 3m N of Windermere*
This imposing country mansion has a picturesque setting amid colourful terraced gardens. Inside, the public areas feature carved

*continued*



fireplaces, oak panelling, and a unique galleried staircase. The atmospheric lounges offer lovely views of Lake Windermere, as do the restaurant and most of the spacious bedrooms. Dinner is a highlight of any visit.

**ROOMS:** 27 en suite (1 fmly) s £70-£90; d £140-£250 (incl. bkfst & dinner) * **LB** **FACILITIES:** Tennis (grass) Fishing Croquet lawn Putting green Sailing boats Xmas **CONF:** Thtr 25 Class 16 Board 20 **PARKING:** 50 **NOTES:** No smoking in restaurant Civ Wed 100
**CARDS:**

### ★★★67% *Wild Boar*

Best Western

Crook LA23 3NF
☎ 015394 45225 Fax 015394 42498
e-mail: wildboar@ehl.co.uk
***Dir:*** *2.5m S of Windermere on B5284 Crook road. From rdbt where A591, A5284 & B5284 intersect take B5284 to Crook. Continue for 3.5m, hotel is on right*
This welcoming hotel, a former coaching inn, has been

*continued on p642*

W

WINDERMERE, continued

considerably extended to provide modern comforts and facilities. Bedrooms are bright and airy and have a good range of amenities. Public areas have a more traditional feel; the rustic bar is stocked with a tempting range of refreshments. Adjacent, the heavily beamed restaurant provides an appropriate setting for enjoyable fare.
**ROOMS:** 36 en suite (3 fmly) No smoking in 6 bedrooms
**FACILITIES:** STV Use of leisure facilities at sister hotel whilst in residence.
**CONF:** Thtr 40 Class 20 Board 26 **PARKING:** 60 **NOTES:** No smoking in restaurant **CARDS:**

### ★★★66% Craig Manor

Lake Rd LA23 2JF
☎ 015394 88877 015394 88878
e-mail: info@craigmanor.co.uk
***Dir:*** *A590 to Windermere, then A591 into Windermere, turn left at Windermere hotel go through village, pass Magistrates' Court, hotel on left*
An established hotel run by an experienced and friendly team. A wide ranging menu of imaginative dishes is presented in the spacious dining room, or you can enjoy supper in the cocktail bar and the less formal Walkers Inn pub. There is a wide choice of accommodation with the most sylish rooms in the main house.
**ROOMS:** 16 en suite s £60-£72; d £90-£114 (incl. bkfst) * **LB**
**FACILITIES:** Xmas **PARKING:** 70 **NOTES:** No smoking in restaurant
**CARDS:**

### ★★★65% The Old England

Church St, Bowness LA23 3DF
☎ 0870 400 8130 015394 43432
***Dir:*** *M6 junct 36- follow signs for Windermere. Continue through Windermere town centre to Bowness. Hotel is behind St Martins Church near pier*
With arguably one of the best positions on Lake Windermere, this elegant Victorian mansion is tastefully furnished with period and antique pieces. Bedrooms are stylish and many have wonderful lake views, as do the restaurant, bar and lounge. The hotel benefits from its own outdoor heated swimming pool in the gardens, that lead down to its own private jetty.
**ROOMS:** 76 en suite (8 fmly) No smoking in 26 bedrooms s £39-£75; d £78-£150 (incl. bkfst) * **LB** **FACILITIES:** Outdoor swimming (H) Snooker entertainment Xmas **CONF:** Thtr 100 Class 40 Board 26 Del from £85 * **SERVICES:** Lift **PARKING:** 82 **NOTES:** No smoking in restaurant Civ Wed 60 **CARDS:**

### ★★★64% *Low Wood*

LA23 1LP
☎ 015394 33338 015394 34072
e-mail: lowwood@elh.co.uk
***Dir:*** *M6 junct 36, follow A590 then A591 to Windermere, continue along A591 for 3m towards Ambleside, hotel is situated on the right hand side*
Enjoying broad market appeal this hotel has a splendid outlook over Lake Windermere. Other attractions include a well-equipped leisure club, a watersports centre, and good conference facilities. Bedrooms come in mixed sizes and styles and offer the expected comforts and facilities. Public areas include a choice of contrasting bars, a relaxing lounge and a spacious dining room.
**ROOMS:** 117 en suite (13 fmly) No smoking in 18 bedrooms
**FACILITIES:** STV Indoor swimming (H) Fishing Squash Snooker Sauna Solarium Gym Croquet lawn Putting green Jacuzzi Water skiing Sub aqua diving Windsurfing Canoeing Laser clay pigeon shooting entertainment **CONF:** Thtr 340 Class 180 Board 150 **SERVICES:** Lift **PARKING:** 200 **NOTES:** No smoking in restaurant
**CARDS:**

### ★★★62% Belsfield

Kendal Rd, Bowness LA23 3EL
☎ 015394 42448 015394 46397
e-mail: belsfield@regalhotels.co.uk
***Dir:*** *from M6 junct 36 follow Windermere signs take 1st left into Windermere follow Bowness signs & the lake. In Bowness take 1st left after Royal Hotel*

This hotel stands in six acres of gardens, and many of its rooms overlook the lake. Bedrooms are comfortable and guests have a choice of lounges. Meals are served in the Chandelier Restaurant and there are good leisure facilities.
**ROOMS:** 64 en suite (6 fmly) No smoking in 17 bedrooms s £65-£70; d £90-£95 * **LB** **FACILITIES:** Indoor swimming (H) Snooker Sauna Solarium Putting green Mini golf - Pitch & Putt 9 holes Xmas **CONF:** Thtr 130 Class 60 Board 50 Del from £85 * **SERVICES:** Lift **PARKING:** 64 **NOTES:** No smoking in restaurant Civ Wed 80
**CARDS:**

## Premier Collection

### ★★ Miller Howe

Rayrigg Rd LA23 1EY
☎ 015394 42536 015394 45664
e-mail: lakeview@millerhowe.com
***Dir:*** *on A592 between Bowness & Windermere*
The elegant Miller Howe hotel is set in magnificent landscaped gardens and enjoys unrivalled stunning views of Lake Windermere. Inviting, sumptuous and spacious public areas offer the perfect setting to enjoy lunch, afternoon tea or an imaginative five-course dinner. The bedrooms are both elegant and stylish and all offer many thoughtful extras. Many of the stylish lake facing bedrooms benefit from very comfortable and well-furnished balconies.
**ROOMS:** 12 en suite **FACILITIES:** entertainment Xmas
**PARKING:** 40 **NOTES:** No children 8yrs No smoking in restaurant Closed 3 Jan-10 Feb Civ Wed 60 **CARDS:**

W

### ★★80% Lindeth Fell

Lyth Valley Rd, Bowness-on-Windermere LA23 3JP
☎ 015394 43286 & 44287 015394 47455
e-mail: kennedy@lindethfell.co.uk
***Dir:*** *1m South of Bowness on A5074*

Enjoying delightful views over the lake and fells, this smart Edwardian residence stands in glorious gardens just a short walk from the town. The comfortable bedrooms vary in style and size, while skilfully prepared dinners are served in the dining room. High levels of hospitality and service are provided by the resident owners and their attentive, friendly staff.

**ROOMS:** 14 en suite (2 fmly) s £72.50-£89; d £145-£178 (incl. bkfst & dinner) * **LB** **FACILITIES:** Fishing Riding Croquet lawn Putting green Bowling Pitch&Putt ch fac Xmas **CONF:** Board 12 Del from £96 * **PARKING:** 20 **NOTES:** No dogs No smoking in restaurant **CARDS:**

### ★★76% Cedar Manor Hotel & Restaurant

Ambleside Rd LA23 1AX
☎ 015394 43192 015394 45970
e-mail: cedarmanor@fsbdial.co.uk
***Dir:*** *0.25m N on A591 by St Marys Church*

This friendly, privately owned hotel enjoys an attractive location. Bedrooms, some in an adjacent cottage, are tastefully appointed. There is a comfortable lounge, a cosy bar and a dining room where an interesting range of dishes is offered.

**ROOMS:** 10 en suite 2 annexe en suite (4 fmly) s £32-£55; d £64-£90 (incl. bkfst) * **LB** **FACILITIES:** Private arrangements nearby free of charge to guests eg pool, sauna, solarium ch fac **PARKING:** 15 **NOTES:** No smoking in restaurant **CARDS:**

### ★★70% Glenburn

New Rd LA23 2EE
☎ 015394 42649 015394 88998
e-mail: glen.burn@virgin.net
***Dir:*** *M6 junct 36, 16m to Windermere A591, through Windermere village, go past shops and the hotel is 500yds along on the left hand side*

The
Glenburn
Hotel

Located between Windermere and Bowness, a friendly welcome

*continued*

awaits at this well-maintained hotel, set in attractive surroundings. The stylish bedrooms come in a variety of sizes and are well-equipped. There is a spacious bar lounge and an attractive restaurant, where carefully prepared meals are served.

**ROOMS:** 16 en suite (2 fmly) No smoking in all bedrooms s £35-£52.50; d £50-£85 (incl. bkfst) * **LB** **FACILITIES:** Free use of nearby country club Xmas **PARKING:** 18 **NOTES:** No children 5yrs No smoking in restaurant Closed 2 - 28 Dec **CARDS:**

### ★★68% Hideaway

Phoenix Way LA23 1DB
☎ 015394 43070 015394 48664
e-mail: enquiries@hideaway-hotel.co.uk
***Dir:*** *turn left off A591 at the Ravensworth Hotel into Phoenix Way. Hideaway Hotel is situated 100yds down the hill on the right hand side*

This welcoming family-run hotel has a secluded location just a short walk from the town centre. Bedrooms, some in a separate building across the courtyard, are individually furnished, and four-

*continued on p644*

W

WINDERMERE, continued

poster and family rooms are available. Good home-cooked meals are served in the dining room, there is a cosy bar and inviting lounge.
**ROOMS:** 10 en suite 5 annexe en suite (3 fmly) s £35-£45; d £60-£120 (incl. bkfst) * LB **FACILITIES:** Spa Free use of nearby leisure facilities Xmas **PARKING:** 16 **NOTES:** No smoking in restaurant Closed 3-31 Jan
**CARDS:**

*See advert on page 643*

### ★★67% Cranleigh
Kendal Rd, Bowness on Windermere LA23 3EW
☎ 015394 43293 📠 015394 47283
e-mail: mike@thecranleigh.com
***Dir:*** *off Lake Rd, opposite St Martin's church and along Kendal Rd for 150mtrs*
This friendly hotel is located minutes walk from the centre of town. Comfortable bedrooms vary in style and some are located in an adjacent building. Guests have a choice of lounges and freshly prepared meals are served in the attractive dining room. Free use of a nearby leisure club is also offered.
**ROOMS:** 9 en suite 6 annexe en suite (3 fmly) s £36-£57; d £48-£90 (incl. bkfst) * LB **FACILITIES:** Free membership of leisure club **PARKING:** 15 **NOTES:** No dogs (ex guide dogs) No smoking in restaurant **CARDS:**

### ★65% Willowsmere
Ambleside Rd LA23 1ES
☎ 015394 43575 & 44962 📠 015394 44962
e-mail: willowsmerehotel@hotmail.com
***Dir:*** *stay on A591, just past St Marys Church*
Guests can expect a warm welcome at this family-run hotel. Bedrooms, which vary in shape and size, are traditionally furnished. There are two comfortable lounges and an attractive dining room.
**ROOMS:** 13 en suite (7 fmly) s £22-£30; d £44-£60 (incl. bkfst) * LB **PARKING:** 20 **NOTES:** No smoking in restaurant Closed Nov - Feb RS Dec - Jan **CARDS:**

## WINDSOR, Berkshire — Map 04 SU97

### ★★★75% Sir Christopher Wren's House Hotel
Thames St SL4 1PX
☎ 01753 861354 📠 01753 860172
***Dir:*** *M4 junct 6, continue along A332, left at rdbt, left at next rdbt, 0.5m on left signposted Eton Bridge*

This historic hotel occupies an idyllic position on the banks of the Thames. Diners in the restaurant benefit from lovely views and enjoy a range of inventive dishes. The hotel offers a variety of bedrooms, from single rooms to self-contained apartments, all rooms feature fine furnishings, tasteful decor and a thoughtful range of extra facilities.
**ROOMS:** 84 en suite (11 fmly) No smoking in 22 bedrooms s fr £170; d fr £225 (incl. bkfst) * LB **FACILITIES:** STV ch fac Xmas **CONF:** Thtr 120 Class 70 Board 50 Del from £250 * **PARKING:** 30 **NOTES:** No dogs (ex guide dogs) No smoking in restaurant Civ Wed 100
**CARDS:**

### ★★★71% The Castle
18 High St SL4 1LJ
☎ 0870 400 8300 📠 01753 830244
e-mail: heritagehotels_windsor.castle@forte-hotels.com
***Dir:*** *M4 junct 6/M25 junct 15 - follow signs to Windsor town centre and castle. Hotel located at the top of hill by the castle opposite the Guildhall*
This popular hotel stands next to Windsor Castle. Smartly appointed bedrooms range from traditionally furnished to deluxe executive rooms. Public areas include an attractive lounge, a small, open-plan bar and a choice of eating options: the Castle restaurant and the more informal Freshfields.
**ROOMS:** 41 en suite 70 annexe en suite (18 fmly) No smoking in 50 bedrooms s £166; d £211 (incl. bkfst) * LB **FACILITIES:** STV ch fac Xmas **CONF:** Thtr 370 Class 155 Board 80 Del from £145 * **SERVICES:** Lift **PARKING:** 100 **NOTES:** No smoking in restaurant Civ Wed 80 **CARDS:**

*See advert on opposite page*

### ★★★66% Christopher Hotel
110 High St, Eton SL4 6AN
☎ 01753 852359 & 811677 📠 01753 830914
e-mail: sales@christopher-hotel.co.uk
***Dir:*** *M4 junct 5 signed Slough East, Colnbrook Datchet and Eton (B470) At rdbt take 2nd exit for Datchet. Right at mini rdbt for Eton, left up Eton Road (3rd rdbt). Left at junct and Hotel is halfway down the high street on the right.*
Originally dating from 1511, this old coaching inn enjoyed a racy reputation and was a major attraction for the boys of Eton College. Today, the hotel provides modern accommodation for its guests, located in the main building or in the courtyard rooms. The public areas consist of a traditional pub and a modern French-style Bistro.
**ROOMS:** 11 en suite 22 annexe en suite No smoking in 21 bedrooms s £105-£125; d £115-£145 * LB **FACILITIES:** Xmas **CONF:** Thtr 40 Class 30 Board 28 Del from £140 * **PARKING:** 23 **NOTES:** No smoking in restaurant **CARDS:**

### ★★★66% Royal Adelaide
46 Kings Rd SL4 2AG
☎ 01753 863916 📠 01753 830682
e-mail: royaladelaide@meridianleisure.com
***Dir:*** *from M4 junct 6 A322 to Windsor. Take 1st left off rdbt into Clarence Rd. At 4th set of lights right into Sheet St and forward into Kings Rd. Hotel is on right*
Conveniently located close to Windsor Castle, this attractive Georgian style hotel offers tastefully furnished, well-equipped, comfortable bedrooms. There are a range of meeting rooms, a bar

*continued*

and an elegant restaurant. The hotel is well suited to the needs of both business and leisure travellers.

**ROOMS:** 38 en suite 4 annexe en suite (5 fmly) s £89-£95; d £109-£115 (incl. bkfst) * **LB** **FACILITIES:** Xmas **CONF:** Thtr 75 Class 50 Board 40 Del from £130 * **PARKING:** 20 **NOTES:** No smoking in restaurant Civ Wed 100 **CARDS:**

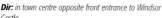

*See advert on this page*

### ★★★65% Ye Harte & Garter

High St SL4 1PH
☎ 01753 863426 🖷 01753 830527
***Dir:*** *in town centre opposite front entrance to Windsor Castle*

Situated in the heart of this historic town, the hotel has been carefully restored to combine traditional Victorian elegance with all modern comforts. Bedrooms vary in size, and offer a useful range of facilities and many have enviable views of the castle, Eton

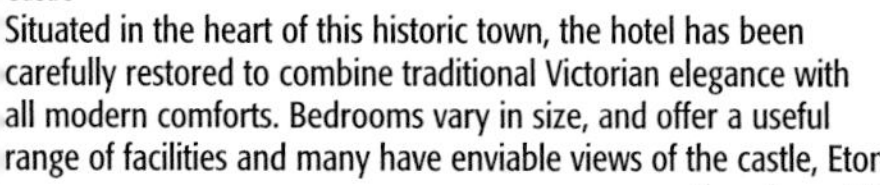

*continued on p646*

W

WINDSOR, continued

College or the Thames. There is also a café bar, two restaurants and a traditional pub.
**ROOMS:** 39 en suite (4 fmly) s £110-£180; d £120-£180 *
**FACILITIES:** STV entertainment **CONF:** Thtr 300 Class 150 Board 80 Del from £155 * **SERVICES:** Lift **NOTES:** No dogs (ex guide dogs) Civ Wed 200 **CARDS:**

### ★★72% Aurora Garden

Bolton Av SL4 3JF
☎ 01753 868686 01753 831394
e-mail: aurora@auroragarden.co.uk
***Dir:*** *junct 6 M4 onto A332 for Windsor. At first rdbt, second exit towards Staines. At third rdbt third exit for 500yds. Hotel is on right*

Located half a mile from the centre of this historic town and close to Windsor Great Park, this privately run hotel offers a relaxing environment in which to stay. The restaurant overlooks the landscaped water gardens and serves a wide choice of dishes at breakfast and dinner. Bedrooms are individually appointed with a good range of facilities.
**ROOMS:** 19 en suite (7 fmly) s £85-£95; d £100-£115 (incl. bkfst) * **LB**
**FACILITIES:** STV **CONF:** Thtr 90 Class 30 Board 25 Del from £135 *
**PARKING:** 25 **NOTES:** No smoking in restaurant Civ Wed 120
**CARDS:**

*See advert on opposite page*

### ○ Innkeeper's Lodge Old Windsor

Innkeeper's Lodge

Straight Rd, Old Windsor SL4 2RR
A new concept in the travel accommodation market. Smart rooms meet essential business requirements but also have home comforts. Dining options include all-day menus plus the added advantage of breakfast, which is included in the room price. Reservations can be made seven days a week through the room reservations number: 0870 243 0500. For further details, consult the Hotel Groups page.
**ROOMS:** 15 en suite

WINSCOMBE, Somerset — Map 03 ST45

### ⇧ *Premier Lodge*

PREMIER LODGE

Bridgwater Rd BS25 1NN
☎ 0870 700 1340 0870 700 1341
Premier Lodge offers modern, well-equipped, en suite accommodation suitable for both business and leisure travellers. Meals can be taken at the adjacent popular restaurant and bar, which is fully licensed. For further details, consult the Hotel Groups page.
**ROOMS:** 31 en suite

WINSFORD, Somerset — Map 03 SS93

### ★★★70% *Royal Oak Inn*

Exmoor National Park TA24 7JE
☎ 01643 851455 01643 851009
e-mail: enquiries@royaloak-somerset.co.uk
***Dir:*** *N from Tiverton on A396 for 15m then left to Winsford. First turning left on entering village*

Dating back to the 12th century this thatched inn is tucked away in the heart of Exmoor. There are some restored bedrooms in the main building and some in the courtyard that have more of a cottage style. In the beamed bars a selection of meals is available. A choice of comfortable lounges, including one with a log fire, is provided.
**ROOMS:** 8 en suite 6 annexe en suite (1 fmly) **FACILITIES:** Fishing Hunting Shooting **PARKING:** 23 **CARDS:**

WINTERINGHAM, Lincolnshire — Map 08 SE92

*Premier Collection*

### ★★ Winteringham Fields

DN15 9PF
☎ 01724 733096 01724 733898
e-mail: wintfields@aol.com
***Dir:*** *in the centre of the village at the X-roads*
This is a stylish 'restaurant with rooms', quietly located in the centre of Winteringham village, and is only 6 miles west of the Humber Bridge on the south bank of the River Humber. Bedrooms vary in size, and are comfortably decorated and furnished. Public areas are comfortable and inviting but it is the inspired quality of the cooking that is the main draw, combining Swiss recipes with modern ideas to provide memorable meals.
**ROOMS:** 4 en suite 6 annexe en suite No smoking in all bedrooms s £75-£125; d £95-£185 (incl. cont bkfst) * **PARKING:** 17
**NOTES:** No children 8yrs No smoking in restaurant Closed Sun, Mon & BH/2wks Xmas/Aug/late Mar **CARDS:**

## WISBECH, Cambridgeshire

Map 05 TF40

### ★★★63% White Lion

5 South Brink PE13 1JD
☎ 01945 463060 📠 01945 463069
e-mail: thewhitelionhotel@hotmail.com
***Dir:*** *From A47 proceed to city centre, turn right before traffic lights into Summers Rd, 1st left*

A former coaching overlooking the River Nene, this privately owned hotel is undergoing a major upgrade. The bedrooms are spacious and comfortably appointed; public areas include a popular bar and a pretty rear garden. There is also an air-conditioned function room.
**ROOMS:** 14 en suite (1 fmly) No smoking in 4 bedrooms s £44.95-£54.95; d £58.95-£68.95 (incl. bkfst) * **LB** **FACILITIES:** Xmas **CONF:** Thtr 80 Class 40 Board 30 Del from £89 * **PARKING:** 70 **NOTES:** No dogs (ex guide dogs) **CARDS:**

### ★★72% Crown Lodge

Downham Rd, Outwell PE14 8SE
☎ 01945 773391 & 772206 📠 01945 772668
e-mail: crownlodgehotel@hotmail.com
***Dir:*** *on A1122/A1101 approx 5m from Wisbech and 7m from Downham Market*

A popular hotel, situated on the banks of Well Creek in the village of Outwell and just a short drive from Wisbech. Bedrooms are modern and well equipped, with good levels of space and comfort. A wide selection of food is available in the popular restaurant which has a loyal following.
**ROOMS:** 10 en suite s £50; d £65 (incl. bkfst) * **LB** **FACILITIES:** Squash Snooker Solarium **CONF:** Thtr 40 Class 30 Board 20 **PARKING:** 57 **NOTES:** No smoking in restaurant **CARDS:**

### ★★66% Rose & Crown Hotel

23/24 Market Place PE13 1DG
☎ 01945 589800 📠 01945 474610
***Dir:*** *in centre of Wisbech, access from A47 & A1101*
This former hostelry has provided hospitality for adventurers and travellers for over 500 years. The wide range of spacious public rooms includes the Tidnams Tipple Inn, the coffee shop/delicatessen, the traditional Rose Restaurant and several function rooms. Accommodation is modern and comfortable.
**ROOMS:** 20 en suite (1 fmly) No smoking in 10 bedrooms s £50-£55; d £60-£65 * **LB** **FACILITIES:** Snooker **CONF:** Thtr 120 Class 70 Board 70 Del from £78.75 * **PARKING:** 20 **NOTES:** No dogs (ex guide dogs) Civ Wed 180 **CARDS:**

## WISHAW, Warwickshire

Map 07 SP19

### ★★★★75% The De Vere Belfry

B76 9PR
☎ 01675 470301 📠 01675 470256
e-mail: enquiries@thebelfry.com
***Dir:*** *take junct 9 off M42 and follow A446 towards Lichfield, the De Vere Belfry is 1m on right*
Well known as a venue for the Ryder Cup, The Belfry offers three golf courses, among other leisure facilities. Extensive public areas have been upgraded and include a stunning new health and leisure club. Guests can choose from a wide range of restaurants and bars including the fine dining French restaurant. Bedrooms vary in size, the best having fine views over the golf course.
**ROOMS:** 324 en suite (109 fmly) No smoking in 187 bedrooms s fr £160; d fr £185 (incl. bkfst) * **LB** **FACILITIES:** **Spa** STV Indoor swimming (H) Golf 54 Tennis (hard) Squash Snooker Sauna Solarium Gym Putting green Jacuzzi Night club in grounds Driving range Aquaspa entertainment ch fac Xmas **CONF:** Thtr 400 Class 220 Board 40 Del from £110 * **SERVICES:** Lift **PARKING:** 1000 **NOTES:** No dogs (ex guide dogs) No smoking in restaurant Civ Wed 200
**CARDS:**

## WITHERSLACK, Cumbria

Map 07 SD48

**★★74% Old Vicarage Country House**
Church Rd LA11 6RS
☎ 015395 52381 015395 52373
e-mail: hotel@oldvicarage.com
***Dir:*** *from A590 turn into Witherslack, take left after phone box signposted to the church, continue straight on for 0.75m*
This delightful Georgian house is peacefully situated in attractive natural gardens. Bedrooms in the main house are attractively furnished, with some fine antique pieces. The larger rooms in Orchard House have a more modern feel. Good use is made of local produce on the daily changing menu. There are two inviting lounges.
**ROOMS:** 8 en suite 5 annexe en suite (1 fmly) **FACILITIES:** Tennis (hard) Arrangement with local leisure club **PARKING:** 25 **NOTES:** No smoking in restaurant **CARDS:**

## WITHYPOOL, Somerset

Map 03 SS83

**★★74% Royal Oak Inn**
TA24 7QP
☎ 01643 831506 01643 831659
e-mail: enquiries@royaloakwithypool.co.uk
***Dir:*** *7m N of Dulverton, off B3223*

This hotel combines the character and charm of an old village inn with high standards of service and comfort. The bars retain their original atmosphere, and in addition to the range of bar meals, guests have the choice of either a set-price menu or a short carte. Bedrooms are well-equipped and comfortable.
**ROOMS:** 8 rms (7 en suite) s £70-£80; d £110-£120 (incl. bkfst) *
**FACILITIES:** Fishing Riding Shooting Safaris arranged Xmas
**PARKING:** 20 **NOTES:** No smoking in restaurant
**CARDS:**

## WITNEY, Oxfordshire

Map 04 SP30

**★★★70% Witney Four Pillars Hotel**
FOUR PILLARS HOTELS
Ducklington Ln OX8 7TJ
☎ 01993 779777 01993 703467
e-mail: enquiries@four-pillars.co.uk
***Dir:*** *M40 junct 9, A34 to A40, exit A415 Witney/Abingdon, Hotel on left, second exit for Witney*
This smart modern hotel offers well-equipped rooms. There are comfortable lounges and a popular restaurant which offers a good range of dishes. Facilities include a swimming pool, gym and sauna.
**ROOMS:** 83 en suite (16 fmly) No smoking in 30 bedrooms s £73-£89; d £83-£99 * LB **FACILITIES:** STV Indoor swimming (H) Sauna Solarium Gym Jacuzzi Whirlpool spa entertainment Xmas **CONF:** Thtr 160 Class 80 Board 46 **SERVICES:** air con **PARKING:** 170 **NOTES:** No smoking in restaurant Closed 28 - 29 Dec Civ Wed
**CARDS:**

W

## WIVELISCOMBE, Somerset

Map 03 ST02

**Premier Collection**

**★★ Langley House**
Langley Marsh TA4 2UF
☎ 01984 623318 01984 624573
e-mail: user@langley.in2home.co.uk
***Dir:*** *follow signs to Wiveliscombe town centre, turn right at town centre. Hotel 0.5m on right*
Nestling in peaceful countryside at the foot of the Brendon Hills, parts of Langley House date back to the 16th century, although it is predominantly Georgian. There are deep armchairs and comfortable sofas in the sitting room where a log fire burns on colder evenings. The bedrooms vary in size and design, but all have thoughtful extra touches. Hospitality is warm and the service is attentive. The award winning cuisine should not be missed.
**ROOMS:** 8 en suite (1 fmly) No smoking in 2 bedrooms s £85-£87.50; d £95-£127.50 (incl. bkfst) * LB **FACILITIES:** Croquet lawn ch fac Xmas **CONF:** Board 16 Del from £150 * **PARKING:** 20
**NOTES:** No smoking in restaurant **CARDS:**

## WOBURN, Bedfordshire

Map 04 SP93

**★★★70% The Bedford Arms**
George St MK17 9PX
☎ 01525 290441 01525 290432
***Dir:*** *off M1 junc 13, left to Woburn, at Woburn left at T-junc, hotel in village*
This former inn has been pleasantly refurbished and now provides a high standard of accommodation. Bedrooms are divided between the original house and a modern extension. Public rooms include an attractive restaurant, where a good choice of dishes is offered, and guests may enjoy a drink in the beamed Tavistock Bar; lounge service is readily available during the day. A good range of meeting rooms is available.
**ROOMS:** 53 en suite (4 fmly) No smoking in 10 bedrooms
**FACILITIES:** STV **CONF:** Thtr 60 Class 40 Board 40 **PARKING:** 80
**CARDS:**

## WOKINGHAM, Berkshire

Map 04 SU86

**★★★64% Edward Court Hotel**
Wellington Rd RG40 2AN
☎ 0118 977 5886 0118 977 2018
e-mail: edward-court@hotmail.com
***Dir:*** *from Wokingham follow A329 towards Reading. Left at mini-rdbt signed Railway Station/Arborfield. Next left before level crossing. Hotel on right*
Close to the town's station and with excellent parking the Edward

*continued*

Court is in an ideal location for business visitors. Bedrooms are spacious with plenty of desk space. The bar and restaurant, with comfortable seating and a friendly atmosphere, offer an excellent range of dishes that are skilfully presented.

**ROOMS:** 27 en suite No smoking in 14 bedrooms s £99-£118; d £120-£128 (incl. bkfst) * **FACILITIES:** Xmas **CONF:** Thtr 55 Class 38 Board 24 Del from £125 * **PARKING:** 45 **NOTES:** No dogs (ex guide dogs) **CARDS:**

## WOLVERHAMPTON, West Midlands Map 07 SO99

see also Himley & Worfield

### ★★★68% Park Hall Hotel

Park Dr, Goldthorn Park WV4 5AJ
☎ 01902 331121 📠 01902 344760
e-mail: enquiries@parkhallhotel.co.uk
***Dir:*** *turn off A4039 towards Penn and Wombourne, take 2nd road on left (Ednam Road) hotel is at end of road*

This 18th-century house stands in extensive grounds and gardens, a short drive from the town centre. Bedrooms vary in style, but all are well-equipped. The Terrace restaurant offers carvery buffet and conference facilities are available.
**ROOMS:** 57 en suite (4 fmly) No smoking in 4 bedrooms s £48.95-£68.95; d £68.90-£88.90 (incl. bkfst) * **LB** **FACILITIES:** STV Croquet lawn Xmas **CONF:** Thtr 450 Class 250 Board 100 Del from £95 * **PARKING:** 250 **NOTES:** No dogs (ex guide dogs) No smoking in restaurant **CARDS:**

### ★★★66% Quality Hotel Wolverhampton

Penn Rd WV3 0ER
☎ 01902 429216 📠 01902 710419
e-mail: admin@gb069.u-net.com
***Dir:*** *on A449, Wolverhampton to Kidderminster, 0.25m from ring road on right, opposite Safeway supermarket*

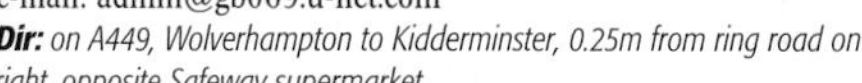

The original Victorian house has been considerably extended to create a large, busy and popular hotel. Ornately carved woodwork and ceilings still remain in the original building. All the bedrooms are well-equipped. The pleasant public areas have a lot of character and offer a choice of bars.
**ROOMS:** 66 en suite 26 annexe en suite (1 fmly) No smoking in 48 bedrooms s £81-£91; d £97-£107 (incl. bkfst) * **LB** **FACILITIES:** STV Indoor swimming (H) Sauna Gym Steam room Xmas **CONF:** Thtr 140 Class 70 Board 40 **PARKING:** 120 **NOTES:** No dogs (ex guide dogs) No smoking in restaurant Civ Wed 100
**CARDS:**

### ★★★65% Novotel Wolverhampton

Union St WV1 3JN
☎ 01902 871100 📠 01902 870054
e-mail: H1188@accor-hotels.com
***Dir:*** *6m from jct10 of M6. Following Black Country route. Take A454 to Wolverhampton. Hotel is situated on the main ring road*

This large, modern and purpose built hotel stands close to the town centre and ring road. It provides spacious, smartly presented and well-equipped accommodation, all of which contain convertible bed settees for family occupancy. In addition to the open plan lounge and bar area, there is an attractive brasserie style restaurant, which overlooks the small outdoor swimming pool.
**ROOMS:** 132 en suite (10 fmly) No smoking in 88 bedrooms s fr £72; d fr £72 * **LB** **FACILITIES:** STV Outdoor swimming (H) **CONF:** Thtr 200 Class 100 Board 80 Del from £110 * **SERVICES:** Lift **PARKING:** 120 **CARDS:**

### ★★69% Ely House

53 Tettenhall Rd WV3 9NB
☎ 01902 311311 📠 01902 421098
***Dir:*** *take A41 towards Whitchurch from town centre ring road. 200yds on left hand side after traffic lights*

This delightful property dates back to 1742 and has been tastefully converted into a charming hotel. Bedrooms are all spacious, comfortably furnished and some rooms are on the ground floor. These can be easily reached from the secure car park. There is also an attractive dining room and spacious lounge bar.
**ROOMS:** 19 en suite (2 fmly) No smoking in 2 bedrooms s £49-£59; d £59-£79 (incl. bkfst) * **FACILITIES:** Xmas **CONF:** Thtr 50 Class 30 Board 25 Del from £90 * **PARKING:** 20 **NOTES:** No dogs (ex guide dogs) No smoking in restaurant Closed 25 - 31 Dec
**CARDS:**

### ★★59% Fox Hotel International

118 School St WV3 0NR
☎ 01902 421680 📠 01902 711654
e-mail: sales@foxhotel.co.uk
***Dir:*** *in town centre on ring road junction with A449*

This privately owned, purpose-built hotel is situated on the inner ring road, close to the town centre. Its modern, well-equipped bedrooms are popular with business guests. There is a choice of bars and good meeting and function rooms.
**ROOMS:** 33 en suite (1 fmly) No smoking in 5 bedrooms s £35; d £55 (incl. bkfst) * **LB** **FACILITIES:** Spa STV Jacuzzi entertainment Xmas **CONF:** Thtr 60 Class 40 Board 40 Del from £60 * **PARKING:** 20 **NOTES:** No dogs (ex guide dogs) **CARDS:**

W

## WOOBURN COMMON, Buckinghamshire Map 04 SU98

### ★★68% Chequers Inn

Kiln Ln, Wooburn HP10 0JQ
☎ 01628 529575 📠 01628 850124
e-mail: info@chequers-inn.com
***Dir:*** *from M40 junct 2 take A40 through Beaconsfield Old Town towards High Wycombe. 2m outside town turn left into Broad Lane. Hotel is 2.5m along road*

This 17th-century inn enjoys a peaceful, rural location beside the common. Bedrooms feature stripped-pine furniture, coordinated fabrics and an excellent range of extra facilities. The bar, with its

*continued on p650*

WOOBURN COMMON, continued

massive oak post, beams and flagstone floor, is very much the focal point of the hotel and offers a wide range of freshly prepared meals. The restaurant overlooks a pretty patio, and here innovative dishes make up a choice of menus.
**ROOMS:** 17 en suite s £73-£98; d £78-£103 (incl. bkfst) * LB **FACILITIES:** STV **CONF:** Thtr 50 Class 30 Board 20 Del £140 * **PARKING:** 60 **NOTES:** No dogs (ex guide dogs) **CARDS:**

*See advert on opposite page*

WOODALL, South Yorkshire Map 08 SK48

### Days Inn

Woodall Service Area S26 7XR
☎ 0114 248 7992 Fax 0114 248 5634
e-mail: woodall.hotel@welcomebreak.co.uk
***Dir:*** *situated on the southbound side of the M1 at Woodall services between junct30/junct31*
This modern building offers accommodation in smart, spacious and well-equipped bedrooms, suitable for families and business travellers, and all with en suite bathrooms. Continental breakfast is available and other refreshments may be taken at the nearby family restaurant. For further details and the Days Inn phone number, consult the Hotel Groups page.
**ROOMS:** 38 en suite s fr £45; d fr £45 *

WOODBRIDGE, Suffolk Map 05 TM24

### ★★★76% Seckford Hall

IP13 6NU
☎ 01394 385678 Fax 01394 380610
e-mail: reception@seckford.co.uk
***Dir:*** *signposted on A12 (Woodbridge bypass). Do not follow signs for town centre*
This striking Tudor manor house, surrounded by neat well-tended grounds, is reputed to have been visited by Queen Elizabeth I and retains a great deal of original charm and character. Public rooms include a superb panelled lounge, and bedrooms are spacious, attractively decorated and equipped with many thoughtful touches. The hotel has leisure facilities that include a swimming pool and beauty salon.
**ROOMS:** 22 en suite 10 annexe en suite (4 fmly) s £79-£130; d £120-£170 (incl. bkfst) * LB **FACILITIES:** Spa Indoor swimming (H) Golf 18 Fishing Gym Putting green Beauty Salon Xmas **CONF:** Thtr 100 Class 46 Board 40 Del from £140 * **PARKING:** 200 **NOTES:** No smoking in restaurant Closed 25 Dec Civ Wed 125
**CARDS:**

### ★★★70% Ufford Park Hotel Golf & Leisure

Best Western

Yarmouth Rd, Ufford IP12 1QW
☎ 01394 383555 Fax 01394 383582
e-mail: uffordparkltd@btinternet.com
***Dir:*** *A12 N to A1152, in Melton turn left at traffic lights, premises 1m on right*
The public rooms feature an array of lounge areas as well as popular meeting and banqueting suites. The smart Vista restaurant offers a carte menu or guests can chose to dine in the carvery or informal bar area. The accommodation is modern and well-appointed, and many of the rooms overlook the golf course.
**ROOMS:** 42 en suite 8 annexe en suite (20 fmly) No smoking in 20 bedrooms s £74-£85; d £89-£129 (incl. bkfst) * LB **FACILITIES:** Spa Indoor swimming (H) Golf 18 Fishing Sauna Solarium Gym Putting green Jacuzzi Beauty Dance ch fac Xmas **CONF:** Thtr 200 Class 80 Board 80 Del from £99 * **PARKING:** 200 **NOTES:** No smoking in restaurant Civ Wed 200 **CARDS:**

WOODFORD BRIDGE, Greater London
See LONDON SECTION plan 1 H6

### ★★★★67% Menzies Prince Regent

Manor Rd IG8 8AE
☎ 0870 6003013 Fax 01332 511144
e-mail: info@menzies-hotels.co.uk
Situated on the edge of Woodford Bridge and Chingford, this hotel offers easy access to London and the M25. There are a range of well-equipped bedrooms and good conference and banqueting rooms, in addition to a smart bistro style restaurant.
**ROOMS:** 61 en suite No smoking in 10 bedrooms s £110; d £110 * LB **FACILITIES:** STV Xmas **CONF:** Thtr 500 Class 150 Board 120 Del from £140 * **SERVICES:** Lift **PARKING:** 60 **NOTES:** No smoking in restaurant Civ Wed 300 **CARDS:**

WOODFORD GREEN, Greater London
See LONDON SECTION plan 1 G6

### ★★★66% County Hotel Epping Forest

30 Oak Hill IG8 9NY
☎ 020 8787 9988 Fax 020 8506 0941
e-mail: eppingcounty@compuserve.com
***Dir:*** *from A406 take first exit left onto A104 towards Woodford. At rdbt keep right then take first left turn into Oakhill*
In a residential area on the edge of Epping Forest, this modern hotel is convenient for both the North Circular and M11. Bedrooms have been decorated and equipped to a good standard, and business guests will appreciate the business centre. Public areas include an informal brasserie.
**ROOMS:** 99 en suite (16 fmly) No smoking in 25 bedrooms **FACILITIES:** Xmas **CONF:** Thtr 150 Class 80 Board 40 **SERVICES:** Lift **PARKING:** 100 **NOTES:** No dogs (ex guide dogs) Civ Wed 200
**CARDS:**

WOODHALL SPA, Lincolnshire Map 08 TF16

### ★★★67% Petwood

Stixwould Rd LN10 6QF
☎ 01526 352411 Fax 01526 353473
e-mail: reception@petwood.co.uk
***Dir:*** *from Sleaford take A153 (signposted Skegness). At Tattershall turn left on B1192. Hotel is signposted from the village*

Standing in thirty acres of mature woodlands and gardens, this lovely Edwardian house was originally built for Lady Weignall, on a site chosen by her in the area of her favourite 'pet wood'. The hotel is furnished in the character of the period, with original features retained in the elegantly proportioned public rooms and bedrooms.
**ROOMS:** 50 en suite No smoking in 9 bedrooms s £63-£78; d £126-£166 (incl. bkfst) * LB **FACILITIES:** Snooker Croquet lawn Putting green Complimentary pass to leisure centre Xmas **CONF:** Thtr 160 Class 60 Board 50 **SERVICES:** Lift **PARKING:** 80 **NOTES:** No smoking in restaurant Civ Wed 100 **CARDS:**

★★★62% **Golf Hotel**

The Broadway LN10 6SG

☎ 01526 353535 📠 01526 353096

***Dir:*** *from A158 Lincoln-Horncastle turn onto B1191 towards Woodhall Spa. Hotel is located in the village centre just past Woodhall Spa Golf Club*

Famous for its golf course and ideally situated in the centre of the village this traditional hotel offers sound accommodation throughout. The bedrooms come in a variety of sizes and include several 'Club' style rooms. Meals are available in the Wentworth Restaurant or the Sunningdale Bar with its blackboard menu.

**ROOMS:** 50 en suite (4 fmly) s £50-£65; d £70-£85 (incl. bkfst) * LB **FACILITIES:** STV Tennis (hard) Croquet lawn Xmas **CONF:** Thtr 150 Class 45 Board 50 **PARKING:** 100 **NOTES:** No smoking in restaurant Civ Wed 120 **CARDS:**

★★63% ***Eagle Lodge***

The Broadway LN10 6ST

☎ 01526 353231 📠 01526 352797

***Dir:*** *in the centre of Woodhall Spa*

Family owned and run, this hotel is located in the town centre, providing soundly appointed accommodation together with comfortable public rooms. A good choice of food is available, including daily blackboard specials, which are served in the bar or the dining room.

**ROOMS:** 23 en suite (2 fmly) **FACILITIES:** STV entertainment **CONF:** Thtr 100 Class 50 Board 50 **PARKING:** 70 **CARDS:**

## WOODSTOCK, Oxfordshire

Map 04 SP41

★★★77% **Feathers**

Market St OX20 1SX

☎ 01993 812291 📠 01993 813158

e-mail: enquiries@feathers.co.uk

***Dir:*** *from Oxford take A44 to Woodstock, after traffic lights take first left, the hotel is on the left*

In the centre of this historic town, this small hotel provides superior quality and comfort throughout. The elegant drawing room is the place to enjoy afternoon tea, and the secluded gardens are popular in the summer. Bedrooms are individually furnished to a high standard, some with luxuries such as CD players. At our press date rosettes for food were not yet confirmed. Check the AA website for current information, www.theAA.com.

**ROOMS:** 21 en suite (4 fmly) s £89-£115; d £135-£290 (incl. bkfst) * LB **FACILITIES:** STV 1 suite has steam room Xmas **CONF:** Thtr 25 Class 10 Board 16 Del £150 * **NOTES:** No smoking in restaurant **CARDS:**

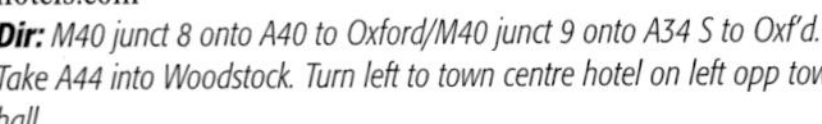

★★★67% ⊛⊛ **The Bear**

Park St OX20 1SZ

☎ 0870 400 8202 📠 01993 813380

e-mail: heritagehotels_woodstock.bear@forte-hotels.com

***Dir:*** *M40 junct 8 onto A40 to Oxford/M40 junct 9 onto A34 S to Oxf'd. Take A44 into Woodstock. Turn left to town centre hotel on left opp town hall*

This 13th-century coaching inn has exposed stone walls, heavily beamed ceilings and log fires. Bedrooms have been refurbished and provide a good standard of accommodation. The attractive restaurant offers imaginative cuisine, with a menu of traditional and contemporary dishes that changes seasonally.

**ROOMS:** 40 en suite 14 annexe en suite (2 fmly) No smoking in 20 bedrooms s £135; d £155-£225 * LB **FACILITIES:** Xmas **CONF:** Thtr 40 Class 12 Board 24 Del from £151 * **PARKING:** 30 **NOTES:** No smoking in restaurant **CARDS:**

★★70% **Kings Arms**

19 Market St OX20 1SU

☎ 01993 813636 📠 01993 813737

e-mail: enquiries@kings-woodstock.fsnet.co.uk

***Dir:*** *located on the corner of Market St and the A44 Oxford Road in the centre of Woodstock*

Situated in the centre of town just a short walk from Blenheim Palace is this appealing hotel. The spacious public areas feature an attractive bistro style restaurant and a smart bar. Bedrooms are comfortably furnished, equipped with many useful extras and have stylish decor.

**ROOMS:** 9 en suite No smoking in all bedrooms s £50-£60; d £75-£90 (incl. bkfst) * **CONF:** Thtr 50 Class 40 Board 20 Del from £95 * **NOTES:** No dogs (ex guide dogs) No smoking in restaurant **CARDS:**

## WOODY BAY, Devon

Map 03 SS64

★★64% ***Woody Bay Hotel***

EX31 4QX

☎ 01598 763264 📠 01598 763563

Popular with walkers, this hotel has commanding sweeping views over Woody Bay to the sea beyond. Bedrooms vary in style and size, with the majority benefiting from stunning views. Guests have a choice of dining options, either from the imaginative fixed price menu in the restaurant or the simple bar menu.

**ROOMS:** 10 en suite (1 fmly) **PARKING:** 10 **NOTES:** Closed Jan RS Nov, Dec & Feb **CARDS:**

Early start? Hotels at all star levels should provide in-room alarm clocks and/or alarm calls.

WOOLACOMBE, Devon  Map 02 SS44
see also Mortehoe

**★★★75% Watersmeet**
Mortehoe EX34 7EB
☎ 01271 870333 01271 870890
e-mail: watersmeethotel@compuserve.com
***Dir:*** *follow B3343 into Woolacombe, turn right onto the esplanade, hotel is situated 0.75m on left*

With magnificent views over the bay, this popular hotel provides professional and attentive service. Bedrooms vary in size, sea-facing rooms always being in demand, particularly those with private balconies. The public areas all benefit from the hotel's stunning position, especially the attractive restaurant. Each evening, an imaginative and innovative range of dishes is offered from a fixed price menu.
**ROOMS:** 22 en suite (3 fmly) s £84-£130; d £128-£240 (incl. bkfst & dinner) * LB **FACILITIES:** STV Indoor swimming (H) Outdoor swimming (H) Tennis (grass) Croquet lawn Jacuzzi entertainment ch fac Xmas **CONF:** Thtr 40 Class 25 Board 25 **PARKING:** 39 **NOTES:** No dogs (ex guide dogs) No smoking in restaurant Closed 4 Jan-10 Feb
**CARDS:**

*See advert on opposite page*

**★★★74% Woolacombe Bay**
South St EX34 7BN
☎ 01271 870388 01271 870613
e-mail: woolacombe.bayhotel@btinternet.com
***Dir:*** *from M5 junct 27 follow A361 to Mullacot Cross. Take first left onto B3343 to Woolacombe. Hotel in centre of village on the left*

This family-friendly hotel is adjacent to the beach and the village centre. The public areas are spacious and comfortable, whilst many of the well-equipped bedrooms have the benefit of balconies with splendid views over the bay. In addition to the fixed price menu served in the formal restaurant, Maxwell's bistro offers an informal alternative.
**ROOMS:** 64 en suite (27 fmly) s £84-£111; d £168-£222 (incl. bkfst & dinner) * LB **FACILITIES:** STV Indoor swimming (H) Outdoor swimming (H) Golf 9 Tennis (hard) Squash Snooker Sauna Solarium Gym Jacuzzi Beauty salon Creche Childrens club entertainment ch fac Xmas **CONF:** Thtr 200 Class 150 Board 150 Del from £65 * **SERVICES:** Lift **PARKING:** 150 **NOTES:** No dogs (ex guide dogs) No smoking in restaurant Closed 1st week Jan-mid Feb
**CARDS:**

**★★75% Little Beach**
The Esplanade EX34 7DJ
☎ 01271 870398
***Dir:*** *A361 at Barnstaple turn onto B3343 to Woolacombe*
With splendid views over Morte Bay, the Little Beach Hotel was built as a gentleman's residence in 1900. Sympathetically restored, with many of the original features retained, the hotel offers a relaxed atmosphere and friendly service. The individually furnished and decorated bedrooms are light and airy, some have their own balconies.
**ROOMS:** 9 en suite (1 fmly) No smoking in all bedrooms s £34-£48; d £48-£76 (incl. bkfst) * **PARKING:** 10 **NOTES:** No children 8 yrs No smoking in restaurant Closed Nov - Feb

**★★63% *The Royal Hotel***
Beach Rd EX34 7AB
☎ 01271 870001 01271 870701
***Dir:*** *turn off A361 at Mullacott Cross rdbt on to B3343. Follow the main road into Woolacombe, hotel on the right*
From its elevated position high above Woolacombe Bay, this family hotel offers comfortable bedrooms and an extensive range of leisure and recreational facilities. In the Lundy Restaurant, meals cater for all tastes, with the majority being on a self service basis.
**ROOMS:** 95 en suite (40 fmly) **FACILITIES:** Indoor swimming (H) Squash Snooker Sauna Solarium entertainment **SERVICES:** Lift **PARKING:** 80 **NOTES:** No dogs (ex guide dogs) No smoking in restaurant Closed 15-23 Dec & 2-15 Jan **CARDS:**

**★72% Crossways**
The Esplanade EX34 7DJ
☎ 01271 870395 01271 870395
e-mail: Via Fax Gateway
***Dir:*** *M5 junct 27 onto A361 to Barnstaple, follow signs for Ilfracombe, then Woolacombe. At sea-front turn right onto esplanade, hotel 0.5m on right*
Overlooking Combesgate Beach, Crossways Hotel offers a relaxed atmosphere and has access to National Trust moorland at the rear. Bedrooms are attractively decorated and many enjoy dramatic sea views. Public areas include a lounge, bar and spacious dining room where friendly resident proprietors provide natural hospitality.
**ROOMS:** 9 rms (7 en suite) (3 fmly) s £29-£36; d £58-£72 (incl. bkfst & dinner) * LB **PARKING:** 9 **NOTES:** No smoking in restaurant Closed last Sat in Oct-1st Sat in Mar

WOOLER, Northumberland  Map 12 NT92

**★★64% Tankerville Arms**
Cottage Rd NE71 6AD
☎ 01668 281581 01668 281387
e-mail: enquiries@tankervillehotel.co.uk
***Dir:*** *on A697*
This charming inn provides a friendly destination for those seeking peace and tranquillity in traditional surroundings. The cosy bar and restaurant boast open fires, and wide ranging menus provide

*continued*

choice to suit all. Well-equipped bedrooms come in a variety of styles with one family suite being especially popular.
**ROOMS:** 15 en suite (2 fmly) s fr £45; d fr £80 (incl. bkfst) * **LB** **CONF:** Thtr 60 Class 60 Board 30 **PARKING:** 100 **NOTES:** No smoking in restaurant Closed 22-28 Dec **CARDS:**

## WOOLLEY EDGE MOTORWAY SERVICE AREA (M1), West Yorkshire Map 08 SE31

### *Travelodge*

Travelodge

M1 Service Area, West Bretton WF4 4LQ
☎ 08700 850950
***Dir:*** *between junct 38/39, adj to service area*
Travelodge offers good quality, good value, modern accommodation. Ideal for families, the spacious, en suite bedrooms include remote-control TV, tea and coffee-making facilities, luxury beds and free morning newspaper. Meals can be taken at the nearby family restaurant. For further details and the Travelodge phone number, consult the Hotel Groups page.

**ROOMS:** 32 en suite

## WOOTTON BASSETT, Wiltshire Map 04 SU08

### ★★★70% Marsh Farm

Coped Hall SN4 8ER
☎ 01793 848044 📠 01793 851528
e-mail: marshfarmhotel@btconnect.com
***Dir:*** *take A3102 from M4, go straight on at first rdbt, at next rdbt (with garage on the left) turn right. Hotel is 200 yds on the left*
Originally a Victorian farmhouse, this hotel combines character and elegance with modern facilities. Bedrooms, including superior rooms, are decorated to a high standard; some are self contained in cottages adjacent to the main building. Formal carte and modern bistro style menus are served in Rawlings Restaurant where the atmosphere is relaxed.
**ROOMS:** 11 en suite 27 annexe en suite (1 fmly) No smoking in 11 bedrooms **FACILITIES:** STV **CONF:** Thtr 120 Class 60 Board 50 Del from £135 * **PARKING:** 150 **NOTES:** No dogs (ex guide dogs) RS 26-30 Dec Civ Wed 100 **CARDS:**

*See advert under SWINDON*

### ★★70% Noremarsh Manor Hotel

Noremarsh Rd SN4 8BW
☎ 01793 849333 📠 01793 849555
e-mail: noremarsh@aol.com
***Dir:*** *M4 junct 16 head for Wootton Bassett. Left at sign for Stoneover Rd, then right at mini-rdbt into Noremarsh Road to hotel 50yds on right*
Built in the late 17th century, this hotel is quietly set back from the road on the outskirts of town. Bedrooms are particularly well-decorated and equipped, the rooms in the main house being rather more spacious. In addition to the main restaurant, there is also a small bistro area.
**ROOMS:** 4 en suite 6 annexe en suite No smoking in 8 bedrooms s £75-£85; d £85-£111 (incl. bkfst) * **LB** **FACILITIES:** Croquet lawn Jacuzzi **CONF:** Thtr 22 Class 20 Board 20 Del from £149.22 * **PARKING:** 20 **NOTES:** No dogs (ex guide dogs) No smoking in restaurant Closed 24 Dec-2 Jan **CARDS:**

Popped the question? Hotels with Civ Wed in their entry are licensed for civil wedding ceremonies. Maximum numbers for the ceremony only are shown, e.g. Civ Wed 120

## WORCESTER, Worcestershire Map 03 SO85

### ★★★73% Pear Tree Inn & Country Hotel

Smite WR3 8SY
☎ 01905 756565 📠 01905 756777
e-mail: thepeartreeuk@aol.com
***Dir:*** *from M5 junct 6 take Droitwich road after 300yds turn 1st right into small country lane over canal bridge, up a hill, hotel on left*

This traditional English inn and country hotel has spacious bedrooms with attractive colour schemes and good facilities. Ground floor bedrooms are available, as are suites. Guests can enjoy good food and drink in warm and relaxed surroundings, with an excellent range of conference/function rooms and convenient car parking.
**ROOMS:** 24 en suite (2 fmly) No smoking in 6 bedrooms s £75; d £95 (incl. bkfst) * **LB** **FACILITIES:** STV ch fac **CONF:** Thtr 300 Class 150 Board 30 Del £120 * **PARKING:** 200 **NOTES:** No dogs (ex guide dogs) Civ Wed 100 **CARDS:**

WORCESTER, continued

### ★★★70% Bank House Hotel Golf & Country Club

Best Western

Bransford WR6 5JD
☎ 01886 833551 🖷 01886 832461
e-mail: info@bankhousehotel.co.uk
**Dir:** *M5 junct 7 follow signs to Worcester West, pick up signs for Hereford on A4440 then the A4103 Hereford Rd. Turn left, hotel approx. 2m on left*

Bank House Hotel
ENTRANCE

Partly dating back to the 17th century, Bank House is set in 123 acres overlooking the Malvern Hills, three miles west of Worcester. There is a good choice of function and conference suites, and the bedrooms are classically appointed. Facilities here include a leisure/fitness suite and an 18-hole golf course, with pro shop and clubhouse.
**ROOMS:** 68 en suite (20 fmly) No smoking in 15 bedrooms
**FACILITIES:** Outdoor swimming Golf 18 Sauna Solarium Gym Putting green Jacuzzi Xmas **CONF:** Thtr 400 Class 150 Board 70
**PARKING:** 350 **CARDS:**

### ★★★64% Star

REGAL

Foregate St WR1 1EA
☎ 01905 24308 🖷 01905 23440
**Dir:** *take A44 to city centre, right at lights into City Walls Road. Straight on at rdbt, left at lights then right at lights, follow signs for A38*

Set in the heart of Worcester stands this busy hotel. A popular bar and coffee shop are focal points and attract much local and passing trade. Bedrooms are well-equipped, comfortable. Other features include a choice of bars, function and conference rooms and a secure car park.
**ROOMS:** 45 en suite (2 fmly) No smoking in 9 bedrooms s fr £65; d fr £75 (incl. dinner) * **LB** **FACILITIES:** STV Xmas **CONF:** Thtr 125 Class 50 Board 50 **SERVICES:** Lift **PARKING:** 55 **NOTES:** No smoking in restaurant **CARDS:**

### ★★★62% *The Gifford*

High St WR1 2QR
☎ 01905 726262 🖷 01905 723458
e-mail: gm12402@forte-hotels.com
**Dir:** *leave M5 at junct 7 and follow signs for city centre. Hotel opp Worcester Cathedral*
This popular city centre hotel provides all the services today's traveller could need. Bedrooms vary, but all have modern facilities, with some of the larger rooms being suitable for families. A choice of bars and restaurants cater for a mixture of tastes.
**ROOMS:** 103 en suite (3 fmly) No smoking in 50 bedrooms **CONF:** Thtr 150 Class 100 Board 40 **SERVICES:** Lift
**CARDS:**

## WORFIELD, Shropshire — Map 07 SO79

*Premier Collection*

### ★★★ ◎◎◎ Old Vicarage

WV15 5JZ
☎ 01746 716497 & 0800 0968010
🖷 01746 716552
e-mail: admin@the-old-vicarage.demon.co.uk
**Dir:** *off A454 between Bridgnorth & Wolverhampton*
Located in a quiet and peaceful area of Shropshire, this delightful hotel is set in acres of farm and woodland and was originally an elegant Edwardian vicarage. The charming bedrooms are thoughtfully and luxuriously furnished and well-equipped, while the lounge and conservatory are the perfect places to unwind with a pot of tea or a glass of wine. The restaurant offers award winning cuisine.
**ROOMS:** 10 en suite 4 annexe en suite (1 fmly) No smoking in all bedrooms s £72.50-£110; d £130-£175 (incl. bkfst) * **LB**
**FACILITIES:** Croquet lawn Xmas **CONF:** Thtr 30 Class 30 Board 20 Del from £140 * **PARKING:** 30 **NOTES:** No smoking in restaurant
**CARDS:**

## WORKINGTON, Cumbria — Map 11 NY02

### ★★★79% Washington Central

Washington St CA14 3AY
☎ 01900 65772 🖷 01900 68770
**Dir:** *M6 junct 40 towards Keswick, follow to Workington. At traffic lights at the bottom of Ramsey Brow, turn right and follow signs for hotel*
This modern hotel enjoys a prominent town centre location. Bedrooms are smartly appointed and well-equipped. Public areas are stylish and include comfortable lounges, a spacious bar, and

*continued*

impressive leisure and function facilities. Staff are particularly friendly and attentive.
**ROOMS:** 46 en suite (4 fmly) No smoking in 37 bedrooms s £70-£90; d £105-£150 (incl. bkfst) * **LB** **FACILITIES:** STV Indoor swimming (H) Sauna Solarium Gym Jacuzzi Free bike hire Nightclub **CONF:** Thtr 300 Class 250 Board 150 Del £99.95 * **SERVICES:** Lift **PARKING:** 16 **NOTES:** No dogs (ex guide dogs) No smoking in restaurant Closed 25 Dec Civ Wed 300 **CARDS:**

### ★★★66% Hunday Manor Country House

Hunday, Winscales CA14 4JF
☎ 01900 61798 ▤ 01900 601202
e-mail: hundaymanorhotel@lineone.net
***Dir:*** *turn off A66 onto A595 towards Whitehaven, hotel is 3m along on right hand side, signposted*
Delightfully situated and enjoying distant views of the Solway Firth, this charming hotel has comfortable rooms that are well-furnished. Some of the spacious rooms have been refurbished to a high standard. The open plan bar and foyer lounge boast welcoming open fires, and the attractive restaurant is set into the lawned, woodland gardens.
**ROOMS:** 13 en suite **FACILITIES:** STV Tennis (grass) **CONF:** Thtr 25 Class 15 Board 20 **PARKING:** 50 **CARDS:**

## WORKSOP, Nottinghamshire — Map 08 SK57

### ★★★67% Clumber Park

REGAL

Clumber Park S80 3PA
☎ 01623 835333 ▤ 01623 835525
***Dir:*** *M1 junct 30/31 follow signs for Worksop. A1 Fiveways rdbt onto A614 5m NE*

This large hotel is situated in open countryside, edging on to Sherwood Forest and Clumber Park. Bedrooms are comfortably furnished and well-equipped while public areas include a choice of two restaurants. The recently refurbished Dukes Tavern is lively and informal, whilst the restaurant offers a more traditional style of service.
**ROOMS:** 48 en suite (6 fmly) No smoking in 31 bedrooms s £60; d £60 (incl. bkfst) * **LB** **FACILITIES:** STV Xmas **CONF:** Thtr 270 Class 150 Board 90 Del from £85 * **PARKING:** 200 **NOTES:** No smoking in restaurant Civ Wed 150 **CARDS:**

### ★★★66% Lion

Best Western

112 Bridge St S80 1HT
☎ 01909 477925 ▤ 01909 479038
e-mail: lionhotel@hotmail.com
***Dir:*** *A57 to town centre, turn at Walkers Garage on right and follow road to Norfolk Arms and turn left*
This former coaching inn, dating from the 16th century, has been extended to offer spacious and comfortable accommodation, including a number of suites. It is conveniently situated on the edge of the main shopping and business area of Worksop, encouraging many locals to join visitors in enjoying the wide range of dishes offered in the bar and restaurant.
**ROOMS:** 32 en suite (3 fmly) No smoking in 7 bedrooms s £62-£70; d £72-£84.50 (incl. bkfst) * **LB** **FACILITIES:** STV Xmas ch fac **SERVICES:** Lift **PARKING:** 50 **NOTES:** Civ Wed 75 **CARDS:**

### *Travelodge*

Travelodge

St Anne's Dr, Dukeries Dr S80 3QD
☎ 01909 501528 ▤ 01909 501528
***Dir:*** *on rdbt junct of A60/A57*
Travelodge offers good quality, good value, modern accommodation. Ideal for families, the spacious, en suite bedrooms include remote-control TV, tea and coffee-making facilities, luxury beds and free morning newspaper. Meals can be taken at the nearby family restaurant. For further details and the Travelodge phone number, consult the Hotel Groups page.

**ROOMS:** 40 en suite

## WORSLEY, Greater Manchester — Map 07 SD70

### ★★★66% Novotel

NOVOTEL

Worsley Brow M28 2YA
☎ 0161 799 3535 ▤ 0161 703 8207
e-mail: H0907@accor-hotels.com
***Dir:*** *adjacent to M60 junct 13*
Conveniently located adjacent to junction 13 of the M60, this modern hotel stands in its own mature grounds, complete with outdoor pool and children's play area. It provides well-equipped, comfortable accommodation and caters for both business and leisure guests as well as families. Two bedrooms have facilities for disabled guests. The open plan public areas include a pleasant restaurant, bar and lounge area.
**ROOMS:** 119 en suite (5 fmly) No smoking in 72 bedrooms s £72; d £72 * **LB** **FACILITIES:** STV Outdoor swimming (H) **CONF:** Thtr 220 Class 140 Board 50 Del £119 * **SERVICES:** Lift **PARKING:** 133 **NOTES:** Civ Wed 75 **CARDS:**

## WORTHING, West Sussex — Map 04 TQ10

### ★★★71% ⊛ Ardington

Steyne Gardens BN11 3DZ
☎ 01903 230451 ▤ 01903 526526
***Dir:*** *A27 - turn off at Lancing Grinstead Lane to seafront. Follow coast rd to right. Turn left at 1st Church into Steyne Gardens*
As popular as ever, the Ardington continues to provide excellent levels of service and hospitality. Bedrooms are modern in style, offer a comprehensive range of extra facilities and feature some very smartly appointed bathrooms. Guests can relax in the lounge-bar before going through to the restaurant.
**ROOMS:** 45 en suite (4 fmly) No smoking in 10 bedrooms s £57-£85; d £85-£105 (incl. bkfst) * **LB** **FACILITIES:** STV **CONF:** Thtr 140 Class 60 Board 35 Del from £75 * **PARKING:** 25 **NOTES:** Closed 25 Dec-4 Jan **CARDS:**

### ★★★69% Windsor House

14/20 Windsor Rd BN11 2LX
☎ 01903 239655 & 0800 9804442 ▤ 01903 210763
e-mail: reception@thewindsor.co.uk
***Dir:*** *Eastbound A259/ A27 follow Hotels east tourist signs through town centre onto seafront towards Brighton until directed to Windsor Hotel. Westbound A259, 250 metres past the speed sign change to 30, sign for Windsor Hotel*
Located on a quiet road near to the seafront, this well established hotel is popular with both business and leisure guests. Bedrooms

continued on p656

WORTHING, continued

are tastefully furnished and decorated, there is a choice of room types each with a good range of facilities. Public areas include a smart lounge/bar, appealing conservatory reception and lounge area and a popular restaurant.
**ROOMS:** 30 en suite (2 fmly) No smoking in 9 bedrooms s £70-£95; d £85-£115 (incl. bkfst) * **LB** **FACILITIES:** STV **CONF:** Thtr 120 Class 48 Board 40 Del from £65 * **PARKING:** 18 **NOTES:** No dogs (ex guide dogs) No smoking in restaurant Closed 23 - 31 Dec Civ Wed 150
**CARDS:**

★★★68% **Beach**
Marine Pde BN11 3QJ
☎ 01903 234001 📠 01903 234567
e-mail: thebeachhotel@btinternet.com
***Dir:*** *W of town centre, about 1 third of a mile from pier*
A well-established, popular hotel, with an impressive 1930s frontage. Bedrooms, some of which have sea views and balconies, are comfortably furnished and well-equipped. Public areas are spacious and comfortable, with the restaurant offering a wide choice of popular dishes. The hotel has secure parking.
**ROOMS:** 80 en suite (8 fmly) No smoking in 6 bedrooms s £60-£70; d £90-£100 (incl. bkfst) * **LB** **FACILITIES:** STV Xmas **CONF:** Thtr 200 Class 40 Board 12 Del from £72.50 * **SERVICES:** Lift **PARKING:** 55 **NOTES:** No dogs (ex guide dogs) Closed 30 Dec - 3 Jan
**CARDS:**

★★★68% **Berkeley**
86-95 Marine Pde BN11 3QD
☎ 01903 820000 📠 01903 821333
e-mail: berkeley@wakefordhotels.co.uk
***Dir:*** *follow signs to Worthing seafront, the hotel is 0.5m west from pier*
This well established hotel enjoys a central position on the seafront and is only minutes away from the high street. Bedrooms are modern in style and equipped with a good range of facilities. The public areas are tastefully decorated and include a comfortable cocktail bar and spacious restaurant.
**ROOMS:** 84 en suite (3 fmly) No smoking in 29 bedrooms s £75-£87; d £99-£110 (incl. bkfst) * **LB** **FACILITIES:** STV Xmas **CONF:** Thtr 150 Class 50 Board 50 Del from £90 * **SERVICES:** Lift **PARKING:** 35 **NOTES:** No dogs (ex guide dogs) Civ Wed 60
**CARDS:**

★★★67% **Kingsway**
Marine Pde BN11 3QQ
☎ 01903 237542 📠 01903 204173
***Dir:*** *A24 to seafront, turn West past pier and lido*
Ideally located on the seafront and close to the town centre, the Kingsway continues to provide warm hospitality to guests. Bedrooms, which are gradually being upgraded, are comfortably furnished and equipped with modern facilities. Day rooms include two comfortable lounge areas, a bar offering a good range of meals and a well-appointed restaurant.
**ROOMS:** 29 en suite 7 annexe en suite (2 fmly) No smoking in 13 bedrooms s £60-£66; d £95-£108 (incl. bkfst) * **LB** **FACILITIES:** STV Xmas **CONF:** Thtr 50 Class 20 Board 30 Del from £68 * **SERVICES:** Lift **PARKING:** 12 **NOTES:** No smoking in restaurant
**CARDS:**

★★★65% ⊛⊛ **Findon Manor**
High St, Findon BN14 0TA
☎ 01903 872733 📠 01903 877473
e-mail: findon@dircon.co.uk
***Dir:*** *500yds off A24 at the sign for Findon follow signs to Findon Manor into village*
Located in the centre of the village, Findon Manor was built as a rectory, and has a beamed lounge which doubles as the reception area. Bedrooms, several with four-posters, are attractively decorated in a traditional style. The cosy bar offers a very good range of bar food, and is popular with locals, while the restaurant overlooks a garden and offers modern and traditional dishes.
**ROOMS:** 11 en suite (2 fmly) s £53-£60; d £73-£110 (incl. bkfst) * **LB** **FACILITIES:** Xmas **CONF:** Thtr 45 Class 25 Board 26 **PARKING:** 28 **NOTES:** No dogs No smoking in restaurant Civ Wed 50
**CARDS:**

★★64% **Cavendish**
115 Marine Pde BN11 3QG
☎ 01903 236767 📠 01903 823840
e-mail: thecavendish@mistral.co.uk
***Dir:*** *on Worthing seafront 600yds west of pier*
This popular, family-run hotel enjoys a prominent seafront location. Bedrooms are well-equipped and tastefully decorated. A good range of extra facilities is also offered. Guests have an extensive choice of meal options, with a varied bar menu and both a la carte and daily menus. Limited car parking is available at the rear of the hotel.
**ROOMS:** 17 en suite (4 fmly) No smoking in 3 bedrooms s £39.50-£45; d £65-£75 (incl. bkfst) * **LB** **FACILITIES:** STV **CONF:** Thtr 30 Class 20 Board 16 **SERVICES:** air con **PARKING:** 5
**CARDS:**

WOTTON-UNDER-EDGE, Gloucestershire

○ **Tortworth Court Four Pillars**
Tortworth Court, Tortworth, Wotton-Under-Edge GL12 8HH
☎ 01993 700100 01454 263000
At the time of going to press, the star classification for this hotel was not confirmed. Please refer to the AA internet site www.theAA.com for current information.

WROTHAM, Kent Map 05 TQ65

★★★68% ***Posthouse Maidstone/ Sevenoaks***
London Rd, Wrotham Heath TN15 7RS
☎ 0870 400 9054 📠 01732 885850
Popular hotel situated just off the M26 at Wrotham Heath. Bedrooms are comfortably appointed and well-equipped. Public areas include an open plan lounge/bar, attractive restaurant and a health and fitness club.
**ROOMS:** 106 en suite (15 fmly) No smoking in 42 bedrooms **FACILITIES:** Indoor swimming (H) Sauna Solarium Gym Jacuzzi Health & fitness centre ch fac **CONF:** Thtr 60 Class 30 Board 30 **PARKING:** 110
**CARDS:**

WROXHAM, Norfolk Map 09 TG21

★★68% **Hotel Wroxham**
The Bridge NR12 8AJ
☎ 01603 782061 📠 01603 784279
e-mail: hotelwroxham@barbox.net
***Dir:*** *From Norwich take A1151 signed Wroxham and the Broads for approx 7m. Over bridge at Wroxham take the first right hand turn, a sharp right again. Hotel carpark on right.*
Popular hotel situated in the bustling town of Wroxham overlooking the Broads. Bedrooms are pleasantly decorated and well-equipped, some rooms have balconies with lovely views of the busy waterways. The open plan public rooms include the busy

*continued*

riverside bar, a lounge and a smart restaurant serving an extensive carte menu.

**ROOMS:** 18 en suite s £53-£63; d £75-£85 (incl. bkfst) * **LB** **FACILITIES:** Fishing Boating facilities (by arrangement) entertainment Xmas **CONF:** Thtr 200 Class 50 Board 20 Del from £60 * **PARKING:** 45 **NOTES:** No dogs (ex guide dogs) No smoking in restaurant **CARDS:**

### ★★59% *Kings Head*

Station Rd NR12 8UR
☎ 01603 782429 01603 784622
***Dir:*** *in centre of village*
This hotel has a large local clientele, and its situation in the heart of Wroxham makes it popular with tourists holidaying on the Norfolk Broads. Day rooms open out onto the hotel's river frontage and gardens. The carvery restaurant specialises in traditional food. Bedrooms are attractive and comfortable.
**ROOMS:** 8 en suite (2 fmly) No smoking in all bedrooms **FACILITIES:** Fishing **PARKING:** 45 **NOTES:** No dogs (ex guide dogs) No smoking in restaurant **CARDS:**

## WYMONDHAM, Norfolk — Map 05 TG10

### ★★72% Wymondham Consort Hotel

28 Market St NR18 0BB
☎ 01953 606721 01953 601361
e-mail: wymondham@bestwestern.co.uk
***Dir:*** *off A11 (M11) Thetford to Norwich road, turn left at traffic lights and left again*

Privately owned hotel situated in the centre of this bustling market town. The individually decorated bedrooms come in a variety of sizes; they are well- maintained and thoughtfully equipped. Public rooms include a cosy bar, a separate lounge, a coffee shop and an intimate restaurant, which overlooks the busy high street.
**ROOMS:** 20 en suite (1 fmly) No smoking in 10 bedrooms s £55-£60; d £68-£80 (incl. bkfst) * **LB** **CONF:** Thtr 20 Board 20 **PARKING:** 16 **NOTES:** No smoking in restaurant **CARDS:**

### ★★71% Abbey

10 Church St NR18 0PH
☎ 01953 602148 01953 606247
e-mail: paulconnor@theabbeyhotel.freeserve.co.uk
***Dir:*** *from A11 follow Wymondham sign. At traffic lights left and first left into one-way system. Continue and left into Church St*

Expect a warm welcome at this delightful hotel, close to the historic abbey. Its origins go back to the 16th century and it has kept much of its character. Bedrooms have modern comforts, and there is a pleasant ambience in the public areas, with a convivial lounge and a cosy bar in which pre-dinner drinks can be enjoyed.
**ROOMS:** 22 en suite 1 annexe en suite (3 fmly) s £60-£65; d £68-£79 (incl. bkfst) * **LB** **FACILITIES:** Xmas **SERVICES:** Lift **PARKING:** 4 **NOTES:** No smoking in restaurant **CARDS:**

*See advert under NORWICH*

## YARCOMBE, Devon — Map 03 ST20

### ★★73% The Belfry Country Hotel

EX14 9BD
☎ 01404 861234 01404 861579
***Dir:*** *on A30, 7m E of Honiton, 5m W of Chard, 10m S of M5 junct 25 at Taunton*
Built in 1872, this building was originally the village school, before conversion to an hotel in 1965. Many features have been retained, with the prettily decorated bedrooms featuring the original arched windows. Local produce is very much to the fore on a daily changing menu, offered in the attractive bar/restaurant. Please note that this is a no smoking establishment.
**ROOMS:** 6 en suite (1 fmly) No smoking in all bedrooms s £45; d £72 (incl. bkfst) **LB** **FACILITIES:** Xmas **PARKING:** 10 **NOTES:** No dogs (ex guide dogs) No children 12yrs No smoking in restaurant
**CARDS:**

## YARM, North Yorkshire — Map 08 NZ41

### ★★★75% Judges Hotel

Kirklevington TS15 9LW
☎ 01642 789000 01642 782878
e-mail: enquiries@judgeshotel.co.uk
***Dir:*** *located 1.5m from A19. At A67 junct, follow the Yarm road and hotel is clearly visible on the left hand side*
A Victorian mansion, once the lodgings for circuit judges on location in the region, set in beautiful gardens and acres of parkland. Impressive bedrooms are individually furnished and

*continued on p658*

Y

YARM, continued

equipped to a very high standard. Lounges are opulent, and excellent cuisine is served in the restaurant and conservatory.

*Judges Hotel, Yarm*

**ROOMS:** 21 en suite (3 fmly) s £132; d £169 (incl. bkfst) * **LB** **FACILITIES:** STV Croquet lawn Xmas **CONF:** Thtr 200 Class 80 Board 50 Del from £150 * **PARKING:** 102 **NOTES:** No dogs (ex guide dogs) No smoking in restaurant Civ Wed 200
**CARDS:**

YARMOUTH See Wight, Isle of

YATTENDON, Berkshire Map 04 SU57

**★★72% Royal Oak**
The Square RG18 0UG
☎ 01635 201325 01635 201926
**Dir:** *M4 junct 13, north on A34, 1st slip road right to Hermitage, left at T-junct, 2nd right signed Yattendon.*

REGAL

A restaurant with rooms would be a more accurate way of describing the Royal Oak. Although the bar remains, the main emphasis is strongly on food, good quality meals being available in both the bar and restaurant. The property only has five bedrooms but all are appointed to high standards with good bathrooms.
**ROOMS:** 5 en suite s £105; d £125 (incl. bkfst) * **LB** **FACILITIES:** STV Xmas **CONF:** Thtr 30 Class 18 Board 22 **PARKING:** 20 **NOTES:** No smoking in restaurant **CARDS:**

YELVERTON, Devon Map 02 SX56

**★★★71% Moorland Links**
PL20 6DA
☎ 01822 852245 01822 855004
e-mail: moorland.links@forestdale.com
**Dir:** *from A38 dual carriageway from Exeter to Plymouth, take A386 towards Tavistock. Continue 5m onto open moorland, hotel is 1m on left*

Forestdale Hotels

Within easy access of Plymouth but located in Dartmoor National Park, this hotel enjoys the best of both worlds. Bedrooms vary in size; larger executive rooms have balconies and most enjoy views over the nine-acre grounds and Dartmoor. Public areas include a comfortable lounge with separate bar and a restaurant with picture windows.
**ROOMS:** 45 en suite (4 fmly) No smoking in 21 bedrooms s £63-£73; d £126-£146 (incl. bkfst & dinner) * **LB** **FACILITIES:** Tennis (hard) Xmas **CONF:** Thtr 120 Class 60 Board 60 Del £115 **PARKING:** 120 **NOTES:** Civ Wed **CARDS:**

*See advert under PLYMOUTH*

YEOVIL, Somerset Map 03 ST51
see also Martock

**★★★73% Yeovil Court**
West Coker Rd BA20 2HE
☎ 01935 863746 01935 863990
e-mail: verne@yeovilcourt.freeserve.co.uk
**Dir:** *2.5m W of town centre on the A30 (Exeter)*
This comfortable, family-run hotel benefits from a very relaxed and caring atmosphere. Bedrooms are well-equipped and neatly presented; some are located in a new adjacent building. Public areas consist of a smart lounge, a popular bar and an attractive restaurant. An interesting selection from the menus combines lighter options with those more suited to special occasion dining.
**ROOMS:** 15 en suite 15 annexe en suite (4 fmly) s fr £67.50; d fr £77.50 (incl. bkfst) * **LB** **CONF:** Thtr 44 Class 20 Board 28 **PARKING:** 65 **NOTES:** No smoking in restaurant RS Sat lunch/Sun evening (restaurant)
**CARDS:**

*See advert on opposite page*

## *Premier Collection*

**★ *Little Barwick House***
Barwick Village BA22 9TD
☎ 01935 423902 01935 420908
**Dir:** *turn left off A37, Yeovil/Dorchester road, at first rdbt. Through village, take 1st left, Hotel 0.25m on left*
Situated in a quiet hamlet on the southerly side of Yeovil, this delightful listed Georgian dower house is an ideal retreat for those seeking peaceful surroundings and good food. Just one of the highlights of a stay here is a meal in the restaurant. Each bedroom has character and charm, and a range of thoughtful extras. Guests can enjoy the informal atmosphere of a private home combined with the facilities and comforts of a modern hotel.
**ROOMS:** 6 en suite **CONF:** Thtr 50 Board 26 **PARKING:** 30
**NOTES:** No smoking in restaurant Civ Wed 40
**CARDS:**

**★62% Preston**
64 Preston Rd BA20 2DL
☎ 01935 474400 📠 01935 410142
***Dir:*** *from A30 (hospital rdbt) head north on A37 Bristol road for 0.25m. At rdbt take first exit for Preston Road*
This family run hotel, situated on the outskirts of Yeovil, is popular with all types of guests. Many of the rooms have been adapted for family purposes and there is a family suite. A relaxed, friendly and informal atmosphere can be expected here.
**ROOMS:** 6 en suite 8 annexe en suite (7 fmly) **PARKING:** 19
**NOTES:** No smoking in restaurant **CARDS:**

**○ Lanes**
West Coker BA22 9AJ
☎ 01935 862555 📠 (01935) 863929
At the time of going to press, the star classification for this hotel was not confirmed. Please refer to the AA internet site www.theAA.com for current information.

## YORK, North Yorkshire
Map 08 SE65
see also Aldwark, Escrick & Pocklington

**★★★★68% Royal York**
Station Rd YO24 2AA
☎ 01904 653681 📠 01904 653271

***Dir:*** *adjacent to railway station*
This magnificent Victorian hotel, with its own private gardens, is close to the city walls. Its attractive, well-equipped bedrooms are divided between the main building and the stylish, air-conditioned garden mews. Guests have a choice of eating options - Tiles Bar, the main Rose Room restaurant or from room service. Facilities include a fully equipped leisure complex and state-of-the-art conference centre.
**ROOMS:** 166 en suite (10 fmly) s £79-£125; d £95-£145 * **LB**
**FACILITIES:** STV Indoor swimming (H) Sauna Solarium Gym Croquet lawn Jacuzzi Steam room Xmas **CONF:** Thtr 410 Class 250 Board 80 Del from £140 * **SERVICES:** Lift **PARKING:** 80 **NOTES:** No smoking in restaurant Civ Wed 100 **CARDS:**

*See advert on opposite page*

**★★★★64% York Marriott**
Tadcaster Rd YO24 1QQ
☎ 01904 701000 📠 01904 702308
e-mail: york@marriotthotels.co.uk
***Dir:*** *heading E turn off A64 at York 'West' onto A1036, hotel is on right after church and traffic lights*

Situated less than a mile from the city walls and overlooking the Knavesmire and the racecourse, the hotel offers smart modern public areas and a wide range of facilities. Bedrooms are spacious,

*continued on p660*

YORK, continued

comfortable and well-equipped. The hotel also has its own purpose built training centre and extensive parking.
**ROOMS:** 108 en suite (14 fmly) No smoking in 60 bedrooms s £89-£159; d £120-£170 * LB **FACILITIES:** STV Indoor swimming (H) Tennis (hard) Sauna Solarium Gym Croquet lawn Putting green Jacuzzi Beauty treatment Golf practice Xmas **CONF:** Thtr 170 Class 90 Board 40 Del £160 * **SERVICES:** Lift air con **PARKING:** 200 **NOTES:** No dogs (ex guide dogs) No smoking in restaurant Civ Wed 120
**CARDS:**

## Premier Collection

### ★★★ The Grange
1 Clifton YO30 6AA
☎ 01904 644744 01904 612453
e-mail: info@grangehotel.co.uk
***Dir:*** *on A19 York/Thirsk road, approx 500 yds from city centre*
This bustling Regency town house is just a few minutes' walk from York's centre. The individually designed bedrooms have been thoughtfully equipped for both business and leisure guests. Public rooms are comfortable and have been tastefully furnished for leisure guests; conference and wedding facilities are also available. There are two dining options, The Brasserie in the cellar offering an informal, relaxed atmosphere; and The Ivy with its impressive marquee trompe l'oeil and fine dining menu.
**ROOMS:** 30 en suite s £100-£165; d £118-£220 (incl. bkfst) * LB **FACILITIES:** STV Xmas **CONF:** Thtr 50 Class 20 Board 24 Del £144 * **PARKING:** 26 **NOTES:** No smoking in restaurant Civ Wed 60
**CARDS:**

## Premier Collection

### ★★★ Middlethorpe Hall
Bishopthorpe Rd, Middlethorpe YO23 2GB
☎ 01904 641241 01904 620176
e-mail: info@middlethorpe.com
***Dir:*** *from A1036 signed York (west), follow signs to Bishopthorpe and racecourse. Hotel is on right just before racecourse*

Y

This fine Georgian house, convenient for town and the racecourse, lies in acres of landscaped gardens. The bedrooms are all comfortably furnished and are split between the main house and converted stables set around an attractive courtyard. Public areas, in keeping with the style of the house, include a stately drawing room and an oak panelled dining room, where carefully prepared seasonal fare is served. A recent addition is the well-equipped spa facility.

**ROOMS:** 30 en suite s £109-£140; d £160-£325 * LB
**FACILITIES:** Spa Indoor swimming (H) Sauna Solarium Gym Croquet lawn Leisure Spa Xmas **CONF:** Thtr 56 Class 30 Board 25 Del from £164.50 * **SERVICES:** Lift **PARKING:** 70 **NOTES:** No dogs No children 8yrs No smoking in restaurant RS 25 & 31 Dec
**CARDS:**

### ★★★75% Dean Court

Best Western

Duncombe Place YO1 7EF
☎ 01904 625082 01904 620305
e-mail: info@deancourt-york.co.uk
***Dir:*** *city centre opposite York Minster*

Once housing the clergy of York Minster, this hotel provides quiet, well-equipped and comfortable bedrooms. Inviting public rooms provide a relaxing respite from the city. The restaurant has a good reputation and there is also a popular tearoom and coffee shop.
**ROOMS:** 39 en suite (2 fmly) No smoking in 11 bedrooms s £75-£82.50; d £105-£175 (incl. bkfst) * LB **FACILITIES:** STV Xmas **CONF:** Thtr 50 Class 24 Board 32 Del from £110 * **SERVICES:** Lift **PARKING:** 30 **NOTES:** No dogs (ex guide dogs) No smoking in restaurant RS 25 Dec evening Civ Wed 70 **CARDS:**

### ★★★73% *Mount Royale*
The Mount YO24 1GU
☎ 01904 628856 01904 611171
e-mail: reservations@mountroyale.co.uk
***Dir:*** *W on A1036, towards racecourse*
This friendly hotel offers comfortable bedrooms in a variety of styles, several of which lead into the delightful gardens. Public rooms include a relaxing lounge, a cosy bar, and separate cocktail lounge which overlooks the garden. A separate bistro called Oxos

*continued*

has been added this year. Freshly prepared food is presented on the daily-changing menus.
**ROOMS:** 23 en suite (2 fmly) **FACILITIES:** STV Outdoor swimming (H) Snooker Sauna Solarium Beauty treatment centre **CONF:** Thtr 25 Board 16 **PARKING:** 18 **NOTES:** No smoking in restaurant
**CARDS:**

**★★★73% Parsonage Country House**
York Rd YO19 6LF
☎ 01904 728111 ▤ 01904 728151
e-mail: reservations@parsonagehotel.co.uk
(For full entry see Escrick)

**★★★72% York Pavilion**
45 Main St, Fulford YO10 4PJ
☎ 01904 622099 ▤ 01904 626939
e-mail: help@yorkpavilionhotel.co.uk
***Dir:*** *turn off A64 York ringroad at the A19 junct towards York. Hotel 0.5m on right opposite filling station*

An attractive Georgian hotel situated in its own gardens and grounds to the south of the city. The individually designed bedrooms are well-equipped, situated in the main house or in the converted stables. There is a comfortable lounge, a conference centre and an inviting brasserie-style restaurant, where the regularly changing menu features many daily specials.
**ROOMS:** 57 en suite No smoking in 23 bedrooms s £80-£100; d £95-£120 (incl. bkfst) * **LB** **FACILITIES:** STV ch fac Xmas **CONF:** Thtr 150 Class 60 Board 45 Del from £100 * **PARKING:** 40 **NOTES:** No dogs (ex guide dogs) No smoking in restaurant Civ Wed 60
**CARDS:**

*See advert on this page*

**★★★70% Kilima Hotel**
129 Holgate Rd YO24 4AZ
☎ 01904 625787 ▤ 01904 612083
e-mail: sales@kilima.co.uk
***Dir:*** *on A59, on W outskirts*

Best Western

Completely refurbished, and with a stylish new leisure centre, the

*continued on p662*





Y

YORK, continued

Kilima is within easy walking distance of the centre. There is a relaxed and friendly atmosphere in the hotel, with professional, friendly staff providing attentive service. Bedrooms are well-equipped, and very comfortable.
**ROOMS:** 26 en suite (2 fmly) No smoking in all bedrooms s £58; d £80-£86 (incl. bkfst) * **LB** **FACILITIES:** STV Indoor swimming (H) Gym Leisure complex Steam room Xmas **CONF:** Board 14 Del from £115 * **PARKING:** 26 **NOTES:** No dogs (ex guide dogs) No smoking in restaurant **CARDS:**

### ★★★68% Ambassador
123 The Mount YO24 1DU
☎ 01904 641316 📠 01904 640259
e-mail: stay@ambassadorhotel.co.uk
***Dir:*** *A1036 York/Bishopthorpe, follow city centre signs. Hotel on right 300yds after racecourse*

Two Georgian houses which offer a quiet and relaxing haven within ten minutes walk of the centre. Bedrooms are elegant and spacious with the larger ones generally overlooking large, manicured gardens to the rear. Security cameras protect car parking, and Grays Restaurant is a comfortable setting in which to enjoy well-produced dishes.
**ROOMS:** 25 en suite (2 fmly) s £98-£118; d £118-£128 (incl. bkfst) * **LB** **FACILITIES:** entertainment Xmas **CONF:** Thtr 60 Class 24 Board 30 Del from £100 * **SERVICES:** Lift **PARKING:** 35 **NOTES:** No dogs (ex guide dogs) No smoking in restaurant Closed 24 - 28 Dec Civ Wed 50 **CARDS:**

*See advert on opposite page*

### ★★★67% Monkbar

Monkbar YO31 7JA
☎ 01904 638086 📠 01904 629195
e-mail: sales@monkbar-hotel.co.uk
***Dir:*** *300yds from York Minster fronting onto inner ring road*

Standing in a prominent position by the city walls, this large hotel provides well-equipped modern bedrooms, some in an adjoining courtyard building. There is a choice of dishes in the spacious restaurant and hospitality is a strength.
**ROOMS:** 99 en suite (3 fmly) No smoking in 45 bedrooms s £85-£95; d £125-£145 (incl. bkfst) * **LB** **FACILITIES:** Xmas **CONF:** Thtr 140 Class 80 Board 50 Del from £120 * **SERVICES:** Lift **PARKING:** 80 **NOTES:** No smoking in restaurant Civ Wed 60
**CARDS:**

### ★★★66% Posthouse York
Tadcaster Rd YO24 1QF
☎ 0870 400 9085 📠 01904 702804
e-mail: GM1244@forte-hotels.com
***Dir:*** *A1(M) take A64 towards York. After 7m, take A106 to York. Straight over at rdbt to city centre. Hotel 0.5m on right*
A modern hotel situated on the main western approach to the city centre and close to the famous racecourse, which can be seen from several of the comfortable bedrooms. Public rooms include a popular bar and the stylish Junction restaurant.
**ROOMS:** 143 en suite (37 fmly) No smoking in 83 bedrooms s £69-£89; d £69-£89 * **LB** **FACILITIES:** ch fac Xmas **CONF:** Thtr 100 Class 40 Board 40 Del from £99 * **SERVICES:** Lift **PARKING:** 137 **NOTES:** No smoking in restaurant Civ Wed **CARDS:**

### ★★★64% The Gateway to York
Hull Rd, Kexby YO41 5LD
☎ 01759 388223 📠 01759 388822
e-mail: enquiry@thegatewaytoyorkhotel.co.uk
***Dir:*** *Turn off A64 onto A1079, 3 miles towards Hull, hotel on left of main road*

This professionally run hotel backs onto eight acres of gardens, including its own fishing available to residents. Spacious bedrooms are well-equipped and the restaurant serves enjoyable food and has a pleasant bar lounge.
**ROOMS:** 30 en suite (9 fmly) No smoking in 23 bedrooms s £42.50-£49.50; d fr £49.50 * **LB** **FACILITIES:** STV Fishing Xmas **CONF:** Thtr 50 Class 30 Board 30 Del from £75 * **PARKING:** 60 **NOTES:** No smoking in restaurant Closed Jan **CARDS:**

### ★★★63% Novotel York
Fishergate YO10 4FD
☎ 01904 611660 📠 01904 610925
e-mail: H0949@accor-hotels.com
***Dir:*** *S off A19*
This smart modern hotel is just outside the city walls, and offers well-equipped accommodation. The spacious bedrooms are all identical, but are ideal for both the business guest and families. Four rooms have facilities for disabled guests. Guests can dine from the extensive room-service menu, or in the garden brasserie.
**ROOMS:** 124 en suite (124 fmly) No smoking in 93 bedrooms s £69-£79; d £79-£105 * **LB** **FACILITIES:** STV Indoor swimming (H) Internet use Childrens play area Xmas **CONF:** Thtr 210 Class 80 Board 60 Del from £108 * **SERVICES:** Lift **PARKING:** 150
**CARDS:**

**★★71% Clifton Bridge**
Water End YO30 6LL
☎ 01904 610510 ▤ 01904 640208
e-mail: enq@cliftonbridgehotel.co.uk
***Dir:** NW side of city between A19 & A59*

Clifton Bridge Hotel

Standing between Clifton Green and the River Ouse and within walking distance of the city this hotel offers good hospitality and attentive service. The house features oak panelled walls in the public rooms, and the modern bedrooms are attractively decorated. Good home cooking is served in the cosy dining room.
**ROOMS:** 14 en suite (1 fmly) No smoking in 2 bedrooms s £40-£44; d £68-£72 (incl. bkfst) * **LB** **CONF:** Thtr 20 Board 16 Del from £50 *
**PARKING:** 14 **NOTES:** No smoking in restaurant Closed 24-25 Dec
**CARDS:**

**★★70% Beechwood Close**

MINOTEL
Great Britain

19 Shipton Rd, Clifton YO30 5RE
☎ 01904 658378 ▤ 01904 647124
e-mail: bch@selcom.co.uk
***Dir:** hotel is on A19 (Thirsk Rd, between ring rd and city centre) on the right when entering 30mph zone*
This attractive, family owned hotel is situated just a mile north of the city centre. Beechwood Close Hotel offers spacious, well-equipped bedrooms. Public areas are maintained to a high standard and enjoyable food is served in the dining room.
**ROOMS:** 14 en suite (2 fmly) s £49; d £65-£80 (incl. bkfst) * **LB**
**FACILITIES:** STV **CONF:** Thtr 50 Class 40 Board 30 Del from £77.50 *
**PARKING:** 36 **NOTES:** No dogs Closed 25 Dec
**CARDS:**

**★★70% Heworth Court**
76 Heworth Green YO31 7TQ
☎ 01904 425156 ▤ 01904 415290
e-mail: hotel@heworth.co.uk
***Dir:** outer ring road towards Scarborough rdbt, exit onto A1036 Malton Rd, hotel on left*

HEWORTH COURT HOTEL

Friendly and attentive service is provided at this family-owned hotel, within walking distance of the city. Public rooms are

*continued on p664*

YORK, continued

comfortable and bedrooms are thoughtfully equipped. An extensive range of freshly prepared food is served in the Lamp Light restaurant.
**ROOMS:** 15 en suite 10 annexe en suite (5 fmly) No smoking in 15 bedrooms s £48-£81; d £56-£111 (incl. bkfst) * **LB** **FACILITIES:** STV Whisky bar Xmas **CONF:** Thtr 22 Class 12 Board 16 **PARKING:** 27 **NOTES:** No dogs (ex guide dogs) No smoking in restaurant **CARDS:**

*See advert on opposite page*

**★★70% Minster**
60 Bootham YO30 7BZ
☎ 01904 621267 01904 654719
e-mail: res@minsterhotel.co.uk
***Dir:*** *leave A1237 onto A19 towards City Centre. Hotel 2.5 miles on right*
Within easy walking distance of the Minster and the city centre, this careful conversion of two large Victorian houses, has been recently refurbished to provide comfortable, well-equipped bedrooms. There is a cosy bar and a bistro serving imaginative dishes, and meeting facilities are also available.
**ROOMS:** 31 en suite (11 fmly) No smoking in 17 bedrooms s £55-£75; d £75-£120 (incl. bkfst) * **LB** **FACILITIES:** STV Xmas **CONF:** Thtr 80 Board 30 Del from £90 * **PARKING:** 31 **NOTES:** No dogs (ex guide dogs) **CARDS:**

*See advert on page 663*

**★★69% Knavesmire Manor**
302 Tadcaster Rd YO24 1HE
☎ 01904 702941 01904 709274
e-mail: enquire@knavesmire.co.uk

THE CIRCLE
Selected Individual Hotels
GREAT BRITAIN

***Dir:*** *Follow signs for York West A1036. Ring Road/Racecourse. Follow A1036 into York city centre, Hotel on right, overlooking racecourse*

Standing opposite the racecourse this well furnished hotel offers bedrooms either in the main house or garden rooms to the rear. All are well-equipped and the public rooms offer very good comforts. Quality cooking is served in the bistro-style dining room.
**ROOMS:** 11 en suite 9 annexe en suite (2 fmly) s £49-£59; d £55-£81 (incl. bkfst) * **LB** **FACILITIES:** Indoor swimming (H) Sauna Xmas **CONF:** Thtr 40 Class 36 Board 30 **SERVICES:** Lift **PARKING:** 28 **NOTES:** No smoking in restaurant Civ Wed 60 **CARDS:**

*See advert on page 667*

**★★68% Alhambra Court**
31 St Mary's, Bootham YO30 7DD
☎ 01904 628474 01904 610690
***Dir:*** *off Bootham A19*
In a quiet side road within easy walking distance of the Minster, this attractive Georgian building is pleasantly furnished and the

*continued*

bedrooms are well-equipped. The hotel has car parking, service is cheerful and attentive, and good home cooking is a feature.

**ROOMS:** 24 en suite (4 fmly) No smoking in 14 bedrooms s £35-£48; d £50-£75 (incl. bkfst) * **LB** **SERVICES:** Lift **PARKING:** 25 **NOTES:** No dogs (ex guide dogs) No smoking in restaurant Closed 24-31 Dec & 1-7 Jan **CARDS:**

**★★65% Jacobean Lodge**
Plainville Ln, Wigginton YO32 2RG
☎ 01904 762749 01904 768403
e-mail: jaco.mk1@breathemail.net
***Dir:*** *A64-A1237-A19 signed Thirsk 0.75m take A19 to Skelton. Right at Blacksmiths Arms, 2m to hotel*

This comfortable hotel stands in open farmland. Bedrooms are modern and well-equipped, and excellent home-cooked meals are available in the pleasant bars or the restaurant. The hotel is family owned and run, and set in extensive gardens.
**ROOMS:** 8 en suite 6 annexe en suite (2 fmly) s £37.50-£40; d £60-£66 (incl. bkfst) * **LB** **FACILITIES:** Giant chess Childrens play area entertainment **CONF:** Thtr 40 Class 30 Board 30 Del from £77.50 * **PARKING:** 52 **NOTES:** No smoking in restaurant **CARDS:**

**★★65% Lady Anne Middletons Hotel**
Skeldergate YO1 6DS
☎ 01904 611570 01904 613043
e-mail: bookings@ladyannes.co.uk
***Dir:*** *A1036 towards City Centre. Right at City Walls lights, keep left, 1st left before bridge, then 1st left into Cromwell Rd. Hotel on right*
This well furnished city-centre hotel has been created from several listed buildings in the centre of York, and is very well located. Among its amenities are a bar-lounge and a dining room where a satisfying range of food is served. A leisure club is also attached.
**ROOMS:** 37 en suite 15 annexe en suite (3 fmly) No smoking in 15 bedrooms s £50-£85; d £80-£115 (incl. bkfst) * **LB** **FACILITIES:** Indoor swimming (H) Sauna Solarium Gym No leisure facilities for under 16yrs ch fac **CONF:** Thtr 100 Class 30 Board 30 Del from £90 * **PARKING:** 40 **NOTES:** No smoking in restaurant Closed 24-29 Dec **CARDS:**

*'You deserve a break'*

COMFORTABLE BEDROOMS

*A traditional English hotel only 3/4 mile from York Minster, ideally located for exploring York on foot.*

WHISKY BAR

HEWORTH COURT HOTEL

76 HEWORTH GREEN, YORK, ENGLAND

*12 minutes stroll to the Medieval Walled City of York, ample private car parking is provided at the hotel. Simply park your car and discover all the attractions "in and around" York.*

*All 28 en-suite bedrooms contain tv with 24hr news, direct dial telephone, voicemail, tea, coffee and modem point – luxury rooms have Chandeliers or 4-poster beds.*

http://www.visityork.com
**Email:** hotel@heworth.co.uk

LAMPLIGHT RESTAURANT

AA ★★

*Relax and unwind in the hotel Whisky bar before sampling the delights of the Lamplight Restaurant.*

4-POSTER ROOMS

(01904) 425156 www.visityork.com

YORK, continued

**★★65% Savages**
St Peters Grove, Clifton YO30 6AQ
☎ 01904 610818 Fax 01904 627729
***Dir:*** *off A19 at Clifton*

EXIT

Standing in a quiet side road and within easy walking distance of the city and the Minster this pleasant and well-run hotel offers a good standard of both accommodation and service. Good honest home cooking is served in the dining room and the bedrooms are well-equipped and include several large family rooms.
**ROOMS:** 21 en suite (4 fmly) No smoking in 2 bedrooms s £30-£38; d £60-£75 (incl. bkfst) * **LB** **FACILITIES:** ch fac **PARKING:** 14
**NOTES:** No dogs (ex guide dogs) No smoking in restaurant Closed 25 & 26 Dec **CARDS:**

**★★63% Abbots' Mews**
6 Marygate Ln, Bootham YO30 7DE
☎ 01904 634866 Fax 01904 612848
***Dir:*** *overlooking Marygate car park, 1st left along Bootham from York art gallery*
Well located, within minute's walk of the city and the Minster, this comfortable hotel is in a quiet cul de sac. Bedrooms are compact and include all modern facilities. The large, modern restaurant offers an extensive range of good food including some regional dishes. Good parking is a bonus.
**ROOMS:** 12 en suite 35 annexe en suite (8 fmly) **FACILITIES:** Xmas
**CONF:** Thtr 30 Class 30 Board 20 Del £75 * **PARKING:** 30
**NOTES:** No dogs (ex guide dogs) **CARDS:**
*See advert on opposite page*

**★★62% *Orchard Court Hotel***
4 St Peters Grove, Bootham YO30 6AQ
☎ 01904 653964
Situated in a quiet side road and within easy walking distance of the city, this family run hotel provides modern and comfortable accommodation. A range of home cooked dishes are available at dinner and staff are polite and friendly.

Y

**⌂ Express by Holiday Inn York**
Malton Rd YO32 9TE
☎ 01904 438660 Fax 01904 438560
***Dir:*** *A64 to Scarborough, turn L at rdbt towards York/ Harrogate. 2nd small rdbt take L to York and Huntington. Hotel on L behind Stockton on The Forrest Inn.*
A modern budget hotel offering comfortable accommodation in refreshing, spacious and comprehensively equipped bedrooms, en suite bathrooms with power showers and continental buffet breakfast included in the room rate. Suitable for business travellers or families. For further details and the Express by Holiday Inn phone number, consult the Hotel Groups page.

**ROOMS:** 49 en suite (incl. cont bkfst) d £49.90-£52.50 * **CONF:** Thtr 36 Class 25 Board 20

**⌂ Express by Holiday Inn York Clifton**
Clifton Business Park, Shipton Rd YO30 5PA
☎ 01904 659992 Fax 01904 659994
***Dir:*** *A19 from Thirsk and North - main road into York*

Express
by Holiday Inn

A modern budget hotel offering comfortable accommodation in refreshing, spacious and comprehensively equipped bedrooms, en suite bathrooms with power showers and continental buffet breakfast included in the room rate. Suitable for business travellers or families. For further details and the Express by Holiday Inn phone number, consult the Hotel Groups page.
**ROOMS:** 49 en suite (incl. cont bkfst) d £52.50 * **CONF:** Thtr 16 Class 16 Board 20

**⌂ *Travelodge***
90 Piccadilly YO1
☎ 08700 850950

Travelodge

Travelodge offers good quality, good value, modern accommodation. Ideal for families, the spacious, en suite

continued

bedrooms include remote-control TV, tea and coffee-making facilities, luxury beds and free morning newspaper. Meals can be taken at the nearby family restaurant. For further details and the Travelodge phone number, consult the Hotel Groups page.

## YOXFORD, Suffolk
Map 05 TM36

### ★★74% Satis House

IP17 3EX
☎ 01728 668418 Fax 01728 668640
e-mail: yblackmore@aol.com
***Dir:*** *set back from A12 midway between Ipswich & Lowestoft*

Charles Dickens was a friend of the family who owned the house in the mid-19th century, and the name Satis House features in *Great Expectations.* Spacious bedrooms are attractively decorated and tastefully furnished with well-chosen pieces. Public areas include an elegant lounge, smart bar and a choice of dining rooms.

**ROOMS:** 8 en suite No smoking in 1 bedroom s £65-£75; d £85-£120 (incl. bkfst) * **LB** **FACILITIES:** Tennis (hard) Sauna Jacuzzi **CONF:** Thtr 26 Class 20 Board 14 Del from £85 * **PARKING:** 30 **NOTES:** No dogs No children 7yrs No smoking in restaurant
**CARDS:**

# Channel Islands

Directory of establishments in alphabetical order of location.

Guernsey

CHANNEL ISLANDS Map 16

GUERNSEY

CATEL

**★★★75% Cobo Bay**
Cobo GY5 7HB
☎ 01481 257102 01481 254542
e-mail: reservations@cobobayhotel.com
***Dir:*** *on main West coast road*
This very popular hotel, overlooking Cobo Bay, offers modern, well-equipped and tastefully decorated accommodation. Bedrooms at the front have balconies and there is a secluded sun terrace. Guests can enjoy the candle-lit restaurant and the Chesterfield bar with its leather sofas and armchairs. The Cobo Suite is available for private parties. Hospitality is a strength here.
**ROOMS:** 36 en suite (4 fmly) s £34-£74; d £68-£108 (incl. bkfst) * LB **FACILITIES:** STV Snooker Sauna Solarium Jacuzzi **CONF:** Thtr 50 Class 30 Board 30 **SERVICES:** Lift **PARKING:** 60 **NOTES:** No dogs (ex guide dogs) Closed 2 Jan-20 Feb **CARDS:**

FERMAIN BAY

**★★★73% La Favorita**
GY4 6SD
☎ 01481 235666 01481 235413
e-mail: admin@favorita.com
***Dir:*** *at the junct of Fort Road, Sausmarez Road and Fermain Lane take the road (Fermain Lane) signposted to La Favorita Hotel and Fermain Bay*
This charming hotel is on the side of a wooded valley within walking distance of Fermain Bay. Bedrooms are smartly decorated, comfortably furnished and well-equipped. In addition to a swimming pool and sauna, other spacious public areas include a choice of lounges, bar, restaurant and a café/brasserie, open all day.
**ROOMS:** 37 en suite (6 fmly) No smoking in all bedrooms s £35-£65; d £77-£95 (incl. bkfst) * LB **FACILITIES:** Indoor swimming (H) Sauna Jacuzzi ch fac **CONF:** Thtr 70 Class 30 Board 30 **SERVICES:** Lift **PARKING:** 40 **NOTES:** No dogs No smoking in restaurant Closed 20 Dec-1 Mar **CARDS:**

**★★★68% Le Chalet**
GY4 6SD
☎ 01481 235716 01481 235718
e-mail: chalet@sarniahotels.com
***Dir:*** *from airport turn left, heading towards St Martins village. At filter turn right to Sausmarez Rd then follow sign for Fermain Bay & Le Chalet Hotel*
Nestling in the wooded valley above the bay, this family-run hotel has one of the most spectacular locations on the island. Bedrooms, all well-equipped, are tastefully furnished and decorated. There is a wood panelled lounge, bar area, restaurant and a sheltered sun terrace.
**ROOMS:** 41 en suite (5 fmly) s £40-£75; d £78-£100 (incl. bkfst) * LB **FACILITIES:** Indoor swimming (H) Sauna Solarium Jacuzzi **PARKING:** 35 **NOTES:** Closed mid Oct-mid Apr
**CARDS:**

Bad hair day? Hairdryers in all rooms three stars and above.

FOREST

**★★67% Le Chene**
Forest Rd GY8 0AH
☎ 01481 235566 01481 239456
e-mail: info@lechene.co.uk
Within easy reach of the coast, this Victorian manor house is well located for guests wishing to explore Guernsey's spectacular south coast. The building has been skilfully extended to house a range of well-equipped, modern bedrooms and most recently two popular, self catering apartments. There is a swimming pool, a cosy cellar bar and an informal restaurant.
**ROOMS:** 26 en suite (2 fmly) s £35-£50; d £50-£80 (incl. bkfst) * **FACILITIES:** Outdoor swimming (H) **PARKING:** 21 **NOTES:** No dogs No children 12yrs No smoking in restaurant Closed 11 Oct-2 May
**CARDS:**

PERELLE

**★★★73% L'Atlantique**
Perelle Bay GY7 9NA
☎ 01481 264056 01481 263800
e-mail: enquiries@perellebay.com
***Dir:*** *exit Guernsey airport, turn right and continue on this route until you reach the sea. Turn right and follow the coast road for 1.5m*
Set in its own landscaped grounds beside the bay on the west coast, the hotel is within sight, and sound, of the sea. Accommodation varies, rooms with sea view have balconies and there are suites suitable for family accommodation. There are two eating options, the restaurant and the less formal Victorian Bar.
**ROOMS:** 23 rms (21 en suite) (4 fmly) No smoking in 12 bedrooms s £42-£54; d £70-£94 (incl. bkfst) * LB **FACILITIES:** STV Outdoor swimming (H) Tariff prices include car hire ch fac **PARKING:** 80 **NOTES:** No dogs (ex guide dogs) Closed Nov-Feb
**CARDS:**

ST MARTIN

**★★★72% La Barbarie**
Saints Rd, Saints Bay GY4 6ES
☎ 01481 235217 01481 235208
e-mail: barbarie@guernsey.net
Dating from the 17th century, this former priory enjoys a peaceful setting. The character and charm of the original building has been retained and carefully combined with modern facilities. The bedrooms are tastefully decorated and the beamed restaurant offers a wide range of interesting dishes. There is also a bar menu that features fresh fish.
**ROOMS:** 23 en suite (4 fmly) s £27-£55; d £54-£85 (incl. bkfst) * LB **FACILITIES:** Outdoor swimming (H) **PARKING:** 50 **NOTES:** No dogs Closed 22-27 Dec **CARDS:**

**★★★69% Bella Luce Hotel & Restaurant**
La Fosse GY4 6EB
☎ 01481 238764 01481 239561
e-mail: info@bellalucehotel.guernsey.net
***Dir:*** *from airport, turn left to St Martins. At second set of traffic lights contiue 30yds and turn right, straight on to hotel*
This 12th-century manor house, set in pleasant and well-kept gardens, offers attractive and comfortable accommodation. The

*continued*

bar, lounge and dining room have retained much of their original character. Bar lunches are popular and the restaurant provides a more formal dining option.
**ROOMS:** 31 en suite (5 fmly) s £45-£54; d £86-£105 (incl. bkfst) * **LB**
**FACILITIES:** STV Outdoor swimming (H) Sauna Solarium ch fac Xmas
**PARKING:** 60 **NOTES:** No smoking in restaurant
**CARDS:**

*See advert on this page*

### ★★★68% Green Acres

Les Hubits GY4 6LS
☎ 01481 235711 01481 235978
e-mail: greenacres@guernsey.net
***Dir:*** *behind parish church, 2m from airport*
Within walking distance of Fermain Bay and St Peter Port which is about one mile away, Green Acres Hotel is in a peaceful, country setting. Bedrooms are neatly furnished and decorated, some of the ground floor rooms have the benefit of patio doors straight onto the terrace and pool area. Public areas include a spacious, comfortable lounge, a bar-lounge featuring an interesting menu; and a formal restaurant offering a fixed price menu.
**ROOMS:** 47 en suite (3 fmly) s £32-£55; d £64-£90 (incl. bkfst) *
**FACILITIES:** Outdoor swimming (H) ch fac **CONF:** Thtr 40 Class 25 Board 25 Del from £62 * **PARKING:** 75 **NOTES:** No dogs (ex guide dogs) No smoking in restaurant Closed Nov-Mar **CARDS:**

### ★★★68% Hotel Bon Port

Moulin Huet Bay GY4 6EW
☎ 01481 239249 01481 239596
e-mail: mail@bonport.com
***Dir:*** *exit airport turn left into St Martins village, at final traffic lights turn right, follow signs from here*
From its peaceful cliff-top location, this well-maintained hotel, boasts spectacular views over Moulin Huet Bay. The comfortable, well-equipped bedrooms vary in size, those with sea-facing balconies being the most sought-after. In addition to the spacious lounge, cosy bar and adjoining sun terraces, courteous staff serves an imaginative range of food.
**ROOMS:** 18 en suite (2 fmly) s £62-£82; d £100-£130 (incl. bkfst) * **LB**
**FACILITIES:** STV Outdoor swimming (H) Sauna Gym Croquet lawn Putting green ch fac **CONF:** Board 12 **PARKING:** 30 **NOTES:** No dogs (ex guide dogs) No smoking in restaurant
**CARDS:**

*See advert on this page*

### ★★★68% Idlerocks

Jerbourg Point GY4 6BJ
☎ 01481 237711 01481 235592
e-mail: info@idlerocks.com
This family-run hotel enjoys sea views towards the French coast in the far distance. The well-equipped, individually decorated bedrooms vary in shape and size. Delightful terraces and a cosy lounge provide ample areas for guests to relax. A choice of dining options is provided, either from the fixed price menu in Admirals Restaurant or more informally in Raffles lounge bar.
**ROOMS:** 28 en suite (4 fmly) No smoking in 11 bedrooms s £44-£90; d £68-£108 (incl. bkfst) * **LB** **FACILITIES:** STV Outdoor swimming (H) Covered swimming pool Xmas **CONF:** Thtr 100 Class 50 Board 30 Del from £75 * **PARKING:** 100 **NOTES:** No smoking in restaurant
**CARDS:**

Early start? Hotels at all star levels should provide in-room alarm clocks and/or alarm calls.





S

ST MARTIN, continued

### ★★★67% Hotel Jerbourg

Jerbourg Point GY4 6BJ
☎ 01481 238826 🖷 01481 238238
e-mail: hjerb8765@aol.com
***Dir:*** *from airport turn left and follow rd to St Martins village, then right onto filter road then straight on at lights, hotel at end of the rd on right*

A peacefully located cliff top hotel at the end of a quiet lane, with excellent sea views. Smartly appointed public areas include an extensive bar/lounge and bright conservatory-style restaurant. Bedrooms are all well-furnished, and the luxury Bay rooms are more spacious.

**ROOMS:** 32 en suite (4 fmly) No smoking in all bedrooms s £25-£50; d £40-£140 (incl. bkfst) **LB** **FACILITIES:** STV Outdoor swimming (H) Xmas **PARKING:** 50 **NOTES:** No dogs (ex guide dogs)
**CARDS:**

### ★★★64% La Trelade Country House

Forest Rd GY4 6UB
☎ 01481 235454 🖷 01481 237855
e-mail: latrelade@guernsey.net
***Dir:*** *3m out of St Peter Port, 1m from airport*

Set in attractive gardens, with a pool at the rear of the hotel, this hotel is conveniently located for easy access to the many attractions the island has to offer. Bedrooms are tastefully decorated and equipped with modern comforts. In addition to a choice of lounges, a range of light meals and snacks is offered in the popular bar; an interesting, fixed price menu being served in the hotel's restaurant.

**ROOMS:** 45 en suite (3 fmly) s £35-£58; d £70-£116 (incl. bkfst) * **LB** **FACILITIES:** STV Indoor swimming (H) Sauna Gym Xmas **CONF:** Thtr 120 Class 48 Board 40 Del from £79 * **SERVICES:** Lift **PARKING:** 120
**CARDS:**

*See advert on opposite page*

### ★★74% La Michele

Les Hubits GY4 6NB
☎ 01481 238065 🖷 01481 239492
e-mail: lamichelehotel@ukgateway.net
***Dir:*** *located in a quiet country lane, about 10 minutes walk from Fermain Bay, about 1.5m from St Peter Port*

This delightful family-run hotel enjoys a peaceful location. Bedrooms are delightfully presented, comfortably furnished and very well-equipped. Public areas include a conservatory and restaurant while hospitality and service is very attentive. There are excellent well-tended gardens for guests to enjoy.

**ROOMS:** 16 en suite (3 fmly) s £34-£46; d £68-£92 (incl. bkfst & dinner) * **LB** **FACILITIES:** Outdoor swimming (H) **PARKING:** 16 **NOTES:** No dogs (ex guide dogs) No children 9yrs No smoking in restaurant Closed Nov-Mar **CARDS:**

### ★★69% La Villette

GY4 6QG
☎ 01481 235292 🖷 01481 237699
e-mail: reservations@lavillettehotel.co.uk

Peacefully located in spacious grounds, this family-run hotel has a friendly atmosphere. Bedrooms are decorated in a modern style and are well-equipped. A range of light meals and snacks are served in the large bar, where live music is a regular feature, while in the separate restaurant a fixed price menu is provided.

**ROOMS:** 41 en suite (13 fmly) s £28-£48; d £56-£96 (incl. bkfst) * **LB** **FACILITIES:** Indoor swimming (H) Outdoor swimming (H) Solarium Gym Jacuzzi Steam room Petanque Leisure suite Beauty salon ch fac Xmas **PARKING:** 50 **NOTES:** No smoking in restaurant
**CARDS:**

### ★★66% *Carlton*

Les Caches, Forest Rd GY4 6PR
☎ 01481 235678 🖷 01481 236590
***Dir:*** *on road from airport to main town of St Peter Port*

The Carlton recently re-opened after extensive refurbishment. The public areas are smart and inviting, particularly the recently completed swimming pool and health centre. In addition to a large public bar there is a separate coffee lounge where snacks are available throughout the day.

**ROOMS:** 45 en suite 2 annexe en suite (4 fmly) **FACILITIES:** STV entertainment ch fac **NOTES:** No dogs (ex guide dogs) No smoking in restaurant **CARDS:**

*See advert on opposite page*

ST PETER PORT

### ★★★★71% Old Government House Hotel

Ann's Place GY1 4AZ
☎ 01481 724921 🖷 01481 724429
e-mail: ogh@guernsey.net
***Dir:*** *from airport hotel is located in centre of St Peter Port, overlooking harbour and neighbouring islands of Alderney, Sark and Jersey*

Furbished to a very high standard, the affectionately known OGH is one of the island's leading hotels. Bedrooms are comfortable and offer high quality accommodation. The restaurant overlooks the town and neighbouring islands, and offers fine dining while snacks are available in the Centenary bar.

**ROOMS:** 68 en suite **FACILITIES:** STV Outdoor swimming (H) Xmas **CONF:** Thtr 180 Class 150 Board 90 Del from £115 * **SERVICES:** Lift **PARKING:** 24 **NOTES:** No dogs (ex guide dogs)
**CARDS:**

### ★★★★68% St Pierre Park

Rohais GY1 1FD
☎ 01481 728282 🖷 01481 712041
e-mail: stppark@itl.net
***Dir:*** *10 minutes from airport*

Located just outside St Peter Port, this attractive, purpose built

*continued on p672*

S

ST PETER PORT, continued

hotel is set in 45 acres of parkland. The well-appointed bedrooms all have either balcony or terrace. Guests have a choice of two dining options, the casual Café Renoir, or the more formal Victor Hugo restaurant. The lounge bar with spacious terrace overlooks an elegant water feature.
**ROOMS:** 131 en suite (4 fmly) No smoking in 17 bedrooms s £135-£355; d £175-£355 (incl. bkfst) **LB** **FACILITIES:** STV Indoor swimming (H) Golf 9 Tennis (hard) Snooker Sauna Solarium Gym Croquet lawn Putting green Jacuzzi Bird watchingChild playgroundCrazy golf ch fac Xmas **CONF:** Thtr 300 Class 120 Board 30 Del from £120 **SERVICES:** Lift **PARKING:** 150 **NOTES:** No dogs (ex guide dogs) **CARDS:**

### ★★★73% La Fregate
Les Cotils GY1 1UT
☎ 01481 724624 01481 720443
e-mail: lafregate@guernsey.net

From its elevated position over St Peter Port, La Fregate enjoys many splendid views. However, it can prove difficult to locate and it is wise to ask for detailed directions. Bedrooms are comfortably furnished and well-equipped, and many have balconies. The bar and especially the restaurant are popular with both residents and locals.
**ROOMS:** 13 en suite s £65; d £80-£110 (incl. bkfst) * **FACILITIES:** STV **CONF:** Board 18 **PARKING:** 25 **NOTES:** No dogs No children 14yrs **CARDS:**

*See advert on page 671*

### ★★★73% Hotel de Havelet
Havelet GY1 1BA
☎ 01481 722199 01481 714057
e-mail: havelet@sarniahotels.com
***Dir:*** *from Guernsey airport follow signs for St Peter Port through St Martins. At bottom of 'Val de Terres' hill turn left into Havelet*
This extended Georgian hotel looks over the harbour to Castle Cornet. Many of the well-equipped bedrooms are set around a pretty colonial-style courtyard. Day rooms in the original building have period elegance; the restaurant and bar are on the other side of the car park in converted stables.
**ROOMS:** 34 en suite (4 fmly) s £45-£90; d £76-£120 (incl. bkfst) * **LB** **FACILITIES:** STV Indoor swimming (H) Sauna Jacuzzi Xmas **CONF:** Thtr 40 Class 24 Board 26 **PARKING:** 40 **NOTES:** No dogs (ex guide dogs) **CARDS:**

### ★★★70% Moore's
Pollet GY1 1WH
☎ 01481 724452 01481 714037
e-mail: moores@sarniahotels.com
***Dir:*** *left at airport, follow signs to St Peter Port, Fort Road to sea front, straight on, turn right before rdbt, continue up to hotel*
The hotel, dating in parts from the 18th century, is set just back from the harbour, but still in the heart of St Peter Port. It has kept much of its original character, combined with such modern amenities as the Sanctuary health suite. Bedrooms are comfortably appointed and well-equipped. Attractive public areas include an Austrian Patisserie, conservatory restaurant, library bar and carvery. Service is both attentive and friendly.
**ROOMS:** 46 en suite 3 annexe en suite (8 fmly) s £51-£85; d £70-£170 (incl. bkfst) * **LB** **FACILITIES:** STV Sauna Solarium Gym Jacuzzi Xmas **CONF:** Thtr 35 Class 20 Board 15 Del from £85 * **SERVICES:** Lift **NOTES:** No dogs (ex guide dogs) **CARDS:**

### ★★71% Sunnycroft
5 Constitution Steps GY1 2PN
☎ 01481 723008 01481 712225
e-mail: sunnycroft@accom.guerseycl.com

This welcoming small hotel has glorious views of the neighbouring islands of Herm, Jethou and Sark. Bedrooms are freshly decorated, many have balconies and all are equipped with modern facilities. In addition to a pleasant garden, public rooms include a bar/lounge, a sitting room, a reading room and an attractive dining room.
**ROOMS:** 12 en suite s £38-£42; d £75-£83 (incl. bkfst) * **FACILITIES:** STV **PARKING:** 3 **NOTES:** No dogs (ex guide dogs) No children 12yrs No smoking in restaurant Closed Nov-22 Mar **CARDS:**

*See advert on opposite page*

### ★★63% Duke of Normandie
Lefebvre St GY1 2JP
☎ 01481 721431 01481 711763
e-mail: dukeofnormandie@gtonline.net
***Dir:*** *From harbour rdbt St Julians Ave, 3rd left into Anns Place, continue to right up hill, then left into Lefebvre St, archway entrance on right*

Dating back to the 18th century, this modernised hotel is perfectly located if you wish to be just a stroll from the harbour of St Peter Port or adjacent to the High Street. Well-equipped accommodation is set around a courtyard, which also provides guest parking.

*continued*

Public areas include the busy bar, now restored with beams and open fireplace.
**ROOMS:** 20 en suite 17 annexe en suite (1 fmly) s £30-£42; d £60-£84 (incl. bkfst) * **LB** **FACILITIES:** STV Xmas **PARKING:** 15 **NOTES:** No dogs (ex guide dogs) No smoking in restaurant **CARDS:**

## VALE

### ★★★63% *Peninsula*

Les Dicqs GY6 8JP
☎ 01481 248400 📠 01481 248706
e-mail: peninsula@guernsey.net
Adjacent to a sandy beach and set in five acres of grounds, this modern hotel provides comfortable accommodation. Bedrooms all have additional sofa beds to suit families and good work space for the business traveller. Both fixed price and carte menus are served in the restaurant, while guests may eat more informally in the bar.
**ROOMS:** 99 en suite (99 fmly) No smoking in 18 bedrooms
**FACILITIES:** STV Outdoor swimming (H) Croquet lawn Putting green Petanque Playground **CONF:** Thtr 250 Class 140 Board 105
**SERVICES:** Lift **PARKING:** 120 **NOTES:** No smoking in restaurant
**CARDS:**

## HERM

### ★★75% White House

GY1 3HR
☎ 01481 722159 📠 01481 710066
e-mail: hotel@herm-island.com
***Dir:*** *hotel located close to harbour*
Just a twenty minute boat trip from Guernsey, this attractive island hotel enjoys a unique setting on the harbour, offering superb sea views. Set in well tended gardens, the hotel offers neatly decorated bedrooms, located in either the main house or adjacent cottages. Guests can relax in one of several comfortable lounges, enjoy a drink in one of two bars and choose from the imaginative and ambitious cuisine in the Conservatory Restaurant or more informally from the Captain's Table menu in the Ship Inn.
**ROOMS:** 16 en suite 23 annexe en suite (12 fmly) s £59-£92; d £136-£170 (incl. bkfst & dinner) * **LB** **FACILITIES:** no TV in bdrms Outdoor swimming (H) Tennis (hard) Croquet lawn ch fac **CONF:** Board 10 Del from £97 * **NOTES:** No dogs (ex guide dogs) No smoking in restaurant Closed 9 Oct-5 Apr **CARDS:**

*See advert on this page*

## JERSEY

## BEAUMONT

### ★★65% Hotel L'Hermitage

JE3 7BR
☎ 01534 733314 & 758272 📠 01534 721207
e-mail: lhermitage@jerseymail.co.uk
***Dir:*** *on N12, from airport-B36-A12 Beaumont, on left past crossroad*
A fine period house forms the heart of this large property, and public areas reflect some of the former glory of the building. The central lawned area has a large swimming pool. Bedrooms are generally spacious with bright fresh decor, some having their own balconies. St Aubins Bay is two minutes away.
**ROOMS:** 43 en suite 64 annexe en suite s £23-£40; d £43-£76 (incl. bkfst) * **FACILITIES:** Indoor swimming (H) Outdoor swimming (H) Sauna Solarium Jacuzzi entertainment **PARKING:** 100 **NOTES:** No dogs (ex guide dogs) No children 14yrs No smoking in restaurant Closed mid Oct-mid Apr **CARDS:**

TV dinner? Room service at three stars and above.



Jersey

## GOREY

### ★★★67% Old Court House
JE3 9FS
☎ 01534 854444 📠 01534 853587
e-mail: ochhotel@itl.net

A short walk from the beaches of the island's East Coast, this long-established hotel is popular with locals as well as visitors. Some bedrooms have balconies, which overlook the gardens. Spacious public areas include a restaurant, a large bar with a dance floor and a comfortable lounge.

**ROOMS:** 58 en suite (4 fmly) s £43-£62; d £85-£124 (incl. bkfst & dinner) * **FACILITIES:** STV Outdoor swimming (H) Sauna entertainment **SERVICES:** Lift **PARKING:** 40 **NOTES:** Closed Nov-Mar **CARDS:**

### ★★★66% The Moorings
Gorey Pier JE3 6EW
☎ 01534 853633 📠 01534 857618
e-mail: info@themooringshotel.com

***Dir:*** *Situated beneath Mont Orgueil Castle, Gorey Pier overlooking the sandy beach of Grouville*

The Moorings enjoys an enviable position by the harbour. The restaurant is at the heart of the public areas which include two bars and a comfortable first-floor residents' lounge. Bedrooms at the front have a fine view of the harbour and three have access to a balcony. A small sun terrace at the back of the hotel is a recent addition.

**ROOMS:** 15 en suite s £38.50-£50; d £77-£100 (incl. bkfst) * **LB** **FACILITIES:** STV Xmas **CONF:** Thtr 20 Class 20 Board 20 **CARDS:**

## ROZEL BAY

**Premier Collection**

### ★★★ Château la Chaire
Rozel Bay JE3 6AJ
☎ 01534 863354 📠 01534 865137
e-mail: res@chateau-la-chaire.co.uk

***Dir:*** *from direction of St Helier on B38 turn left in village by the Rozel Bay Inn, hotel 100yds on right*

Built as a gentleman's residence in 1843, Château La Chaire is positioned on the side of a wooded valley and surrounded by five acres of terraced gardens. Retaining much of the atmosphere of a private country house, the hotel provides a professional yet friendly style of service. Imaginative menus, which use the best of local produce, are served in the oak-panelled dining room. Individually decorated bedrooms vary in size, and feature a host of extras.

**ROOMS:** 14 en suite (1 fmly) s £90-£115; d £140-£200 (incl. bkfst) * **LB** **FACILITIES:** STV entertainment Xmas **CONF:** Board 20 **PARKING:** 30 **NOTES:** No dogs (ex guide dogs) No children 7yrs **CARDS:**

## ST AUBIN

### ★★★72% Somerville
Mont du Boulevard JE3 8AD
☎ 01534 741226 📠 01534 746621
e-mail: somerville@dolanhotels.com

***Dir:*** *from village, follow harbour then take Mont du Boulevard and second right hand bend*

This friendly hotel, enjoying spectacular views of St Aubin's Bay, is popular with the leisure traveller. Bedrooms and public areas are smart. Bedrooms vary in style and a number of superior rooms offer higher levels of luxury.

**ROOMS:** 59 en suite (7 fmly) s £88-£114; d £100-£130 (incl. bkfst) * **FACILITIES:** STV Outdoor swimming (H) entertainment Xmas **CONF:** Thtr 40 Class 25 Board 30 **SERVICES:** Lift **PARKING:** 40 **NOTES:** No dogs No children 4yrs **CARDS:**

*See advert on opposite page*

## ST BRELADE

### ★★★★78% The Atlantic
Le Mont de la Pulente JE3 8HE
☎ 01534 744101 📠 01534 744102
e-mail: info@theatlantichotel.com

SLH
Small Luxury Hotels of the World

Recently reopened after a £3.5 million refit this luxury property has 42 modern refurbished bedrooms. Quality and comfort aspects are high, heated mirrors in bathrooms, king size beds with fine cotton linen in bedrooms. First and second floor rooms have

*continued*

great views of the sea and the La Moye golf course. Cuisine remains a focus here with an interesting range of dishes.
**ROOMS:** 50 en suite s £135-£175; d £175-£255 (incl. bkfst) * LB **FACILITIES:** STV Indoor swimming (H) Outdoor swimming (H) Tennis (hard) Sauna Solarium Gym Jacuzzi Xmas **CONF:** Thtr 60 Class 40 Board 20 Del from £200 * **SERVICES:** Lift **PARKING:** 60 **NOTES:** No dogs (ex guide dogs) No smoking in restaurant Closed 1Jan-7Feb **CARDS:**

### ★★★★78% Hotel L'Horizon

ARCADIAN HOTELS Distinctly Different

St Brelade's Bay JE3 8EF
☎ 01534 743101 01534 746269
e-mail: lhorizon@hotellhorizon.com
***Dir:*** *3m from airport. 6m from harbour*

One of the most popular hotels on the island, superbly located on the golden sands of St Brelade's Bay, offering a friendly welcome and great facilities. Bedrooms are all well-equipped, many stylishly decorated with a seashore theme and some with great views.

*continued*

Public areas are bright and spacious, including a choice of three eating options. The Grill, decorated in art deco style, makes very good use of fresh seafood.
**ROOMS:** 107 en suite (7 fmly) **FACILITIES:** STV Indoor swimming (H) Sauna Gym Jacuzzi Windsurfing Water skiing entertainment **CONF:** Thtr 250 Class 58 Board 40 **SERVICES:** Lift **PARKING:** 125 **NOTES:** No dogs (ex guide dogs) **CARDS:**

### ★★★★70% Hotel La Place

Route du Coin, La Haule JE3 8BT
☎ 01534 744261 01534 745164
e-mail: hotlaplace@aol.com
***Dir:*** *turn off main St Helier/St Aubin coast rd at La Haule Manor (B25). Up hill, 2nd left (to Redhouses), 1st R. Hotel is 100mtrs on right*

Centred around a 17th-century farmhouse in a convenient rural location, the hotel offers a range of bedrooms including some designed for the business traveller and some poolside rooms with private patio. All are equipped to a good standard. Public

*continued on p676*

S

ST BRELADE, continued

areas include a cocktail bar and the restaurant, where imaginative meals are served. The sheltered pool and terrace make a great sun trap; while landscaped gardens offer a quieter alternative.
**ROOMS:** 43 en suite (1 fmly) No smoking in 25 bedrooms s £78-£110; d £112-£208 (incl. bkfst) * **LB** **FACILITIES:** STV Outdoor swimming (H) Sauna Xmas **CONF:** Thtr 120 Class 40 Board 40 Del from £115 * **PARKING:** 100 **NOTES:** No smoking in restaurant
**CARDS:**

*See advert on opposite page*

### ★★★★69% St Brelade's Bay

JE3 8EF
☎ 01534 746141 01534 747278
e-mail: info@stbreladesbayhotel.com
***Dir:*** *SW corner of the island*
Overlooking St Brelade's Bay this well-run family hotel has many regular guests and long-serving staff. Attractions include terraced gardens with a choice of pools, easy access to the beach, children's rooms and the latest new addition, a small gym and sauna. Bedrooms have now all been refurbished, most offering king size beds, many rooms have a children's room within the unit. Morning and afternoon tea are included in the tariff.
**ROOMS:** 72 en suite (50 fmly) s £101-£161; d £170-£202 (incl. bkfst) * **FACILITIES:** STV Outdoor swimming (H) Tennis (hard & grass) Snooker Sauna Gym Croquet lawn Putting green Petanque Mini-gymGames room entertainment ch fac **CONF:** Thtr 20 Board 12 Del from £125 * **SERVICES:** Lift **PARKING:** 60 **NOTES:** No dogs (ex guide dogs) No smoking in restaurant Closed 8 Oct-27 Apr
**CARDS:**

### ★★★73% Sea Crest Hotel & Restaurant

La Route Du Petit Port JE3 8HH
☎ 01534 746353 01534 747316
e-mail: seacrest@super.net.uk
***Dir:*** *from Red Houses follow 'Route Orange' A13 to hotel on right at the bottom of a dip*

The sea can not only be seen but also heard from this welcoming hotel situated on the picturesque bay of Petit Port. The restaurant has a good local reputation. All bedrooms have views of the bay, and among the hotel's amenities are a sun lounge, terrace and pool.
**ROOMS:** 7 rms (6 en suite) s £70-£80; d £120-£140 (incl. bkfst) **FACILITIES:** Outdoor swimming ch fac **PARKING:** 70 **NOTES:** No dogs (ex guide dogs) Closed Feb RS Rest closed Mon & Sun eve out of season
**CARDS:**

### ★★★70% Golden Sands

St Brelade's Bay JE3 8EF
☎ 01534 741241 01534 499366
e-mail: goldensands@dolanhotels.com
Centrally located in the popular area of St Brelade's Bay the hotel enjoys direct access to the beach. Several different styles of bedroom are offered with the majority sea-facing and equipped with balconies. All rooms are comfortable and furnished to a high standard. Public areas include a lounge, bar and restaurant which overlook the bay.

**ROOMS:** 62 en suite (5 fmly) s £44-£109; d £56-£124 (incl. bkfst) * **FACILITIES:** STV Childrens play room entertainment ch fac **SERVICES:** Lift **NOTES:** No dogs No smoking in restaurant Closed Nov-mid Apr **CARDS:**

### ★★★68% *Silver Springs*

La Route des Genets JE3 8DB
☎ 01534 746401 01534 746823
e-mail: silver@itl.net
***Dir:*** *turn right from leaving Airport onto B36 till you reach traffic lights. Turn left onto A13 & Hotel is 0.5m along this road.*
This well presented hotel set in seven acres of beautiful gardens and woodland continues to be very popular with leisure guests, in particular families. Public areas comprise a smart bar and a restaurant plus separate lounges. Bedrooms are neatly decorated and comfortably furnished, some equipped with balconies.
**ROOMS:** 88 en suite (14 fmly) **FACILITIES:** STV Outdoor swimming (H) Tennis (hard) Croquet lawn Putting green Boules Children's pool & playground Table tennis entertainment ch fac **PARKING:** 50 **NOTES:** No dogs (ex guide dogs) No smoking in restaurant Closed 25 Oct-23 Apr
**CARDS:**

*See advert on opposite page*

### ★★71% *Beau Rivage*

St Brelade's Bay JE3 8EF
☎ 01534 745983 01534 747127
e-mail: beaurivage@jerseyweb.demon.co.uk
***Dir:*** *seaward side of coast rd in centre of St Brelades Bay, 1.5m S of airport*
Almost on the beach this hotel has an enviable location. The majority of bedrooms are sea facing and nine have large, furnished balconies. The bar boasts various games machines and a juke box. There is also live music most nights during the season.
**ROOMS:** 27 en suite (9 fmly) No smoking in 1 bedroom **FACILITIES:** STV Sunbathing terrace Video games entertainment **SERVICES:** Lift **PARKING:** 16 **NOTES:** No dogs No smoking in restaurant Closed 29 Oct-6 Apr **CARDS:**

ST HELIER

### ★★★★69% The Grand

De Vere Hotels

The Esplanade JE4 8WD
☎ 01534 722301 01534 737815
e-mail: grand.jersey@devere-hotels.com
This hotel, centrally located for the town and beaches, has lovely views from front bedrooms and public areas. Bedrooms, all well-equipped, vary in size and outlook. Staff are friendly, dedicated

*continued*

S

and smartly dressed. There are two restaurants, Victoria's, and the more relaxed Regency.

**ROOMS:** 116 en suite No smoking in 22 bedrooms s £110-£130; d £150-£200 (incl. bkfst) * **LB FACILITIES:** Spa STV Indoor swimming (H) Snooker Sauna Solarium Gym Jacuzzi Beauty therapy Massage parlour,Hairdressing entertainment Xmas **CONF:** Thtr 250 Class 120 Board 80 Del from £140 * **SERVICES:** Lift **PARKING:** 27 **NOTES:** No dogs (ex guide dogs) **CARDS:**

### ★★★70% Pomme d'Or

Liberation Square JE1 3UF
☎ 01534 880110 01534 737781
e-mail: pomme@seymour-hotels-jersey.com
***Dir:*** *opposite the harbour*

Overlooking Liberation Square and the marina, this established hotel offers comfortably furnished and well-equipped bedrooms with modern amenities and 24 hour room service. Public areas include extensive conference facilities and a choice of two restaurants and coffee shop. Car parking is close at hand in the Esplanade car park.

**ROOMS:** 141 en suite (3 fmly) No smoking in 72 bedrooms s £80-£83; d £130-£136 (incl. bkfst) * **LB FACILITIES:** STV Use of Aquadome at Merton Hotel Xmas **CONF:** Thtr 220 Class 100 Board 50 Del from £82.50 * **SERVICES:** Lift **NOTES:** No dogs (ex guide dogs) **CARDS:**

### ★★★69% Royal

Best Western

David Place JE2 4TD
☎ 01534 726521 811046(Reservations)
01534 724035
e-mail: royalhot@4.net
***Dir:*** *Follow signs for ring road after passing Inn on the Park keep left and turn left at traffic lights left into Piersons Rd follow one way system to Cheapside, Rouge Bouillon A14 turn to Midvale Rd hotel on left.*

Equally suited for both the business and leisure guest, the Royal Hotel is centrally located and offers comfortable bedrooms. The elegant public areas consist of a lounge bar, No 27 bar and

continued on p678

S

ST HELIER, continued

brasserie, and a stylish restaurant. The hotel also boasts one of the largest conference rooms on the island.
**ROOMS:** 88 en suite (39 fmly) s £68-£77; d £110-£129 (incl. bkfst) * LB **FACILITIES:** entertainment Xmas ch fac **CONF:** Thtr 400 Class 150 Board 30 **SERVICES:** Lift **PARKING:** 15
**CARDS:**

*See advert on opposite page*

### ★★★69% Royal Yacht
The Weighbridge JE2 3NF
☎ 01534 720511 📠 01534 767729
e-mail: casino@itl.net
***Dir:*** *Situated in town centre, opposite the Marina and harbour, 0.5 mile from beach*
Enjoying a central location overlooking the harbour and marina, the Royal Yacht is thought to be the oldest established hotel on the island. Refurbished bedrooms are comfortably furnished, soundproofed and well-equipped. Public areas include several bars and a grillroom in addition to the main first-floor restaurant.
**ROOMS:** 45 en suite s £45-£48; d £90-£96 (incl. bkfst) * LB **FACILITIES:** STV Sauna Xmas **CONF:** Thtr 20 Class 20 Board 20 **SERVICES:** Lift **CARDS:**

### ★★★67% Apollo
St Saviours Rd JE2 4GJ
☎ 01534 725441 📠 01534 722120
e-mail: huggler@psilink.co.je
***Dir:*** *on St Saviours Road at its junct with La Motte Street. 5 mins walk from Town Centre*
Located in the centre of town, this popular hotel is equally well-suited to both the leisure and business user. Public areas have benefited from recent refurbishment including the smartly appointed front foyer and main restaurant. All bedrooms are attractively furnished. Plenty of parking and both indoor and outdoor pools are available.
**ROOMS:** 85 en suite (5 fmly) s £66-£76; d £85-£106 (incl. bkfst) * LB **FACILITIES:** STV Indoor swimming (H) Outdoor swimming (H) Sauna Solarium Gym Jacuzzi Xmas **CONF:** Thtr 150 Class 100 Board 80 **SERVICES:** Lift **PARKING:** 50 **NOTES:** No dogs (ex guide dogs) **CARDS:**

### ★★★66% Beaufort
Green St JE2 4UH
☎ 01534 732471 📠 01534 720371
e-mail: huggler@psilink.co.je
***Dir:*** *located on Green Street, 5 mins walk from main shopping centre*
Within walking distance of the main business and shopping areas, the Beaufort is ideally located for both the business and leisure traveller. All bedrooms are spacious and have excellent facilities. Public areas include a sun terrace with both indoor and outdoor pools available.
**ROOMS:** 54 en suite (4 fmly) s £69-£74; d £92-£102 (incl. bkfst) * LB **FACILITIES:** Spa STV Indoor swimming (H) Outdoor swimming (H) Jacuzzi ch fac Xmas **CONF:** Thtr 160 Class 140 Del from £75 * **SERVICES:** Lift **PARKING:** 20 **NOTES:** No dogs (ex guide dogs) **CARDS:**

### ★★★66% *Hotel Revere*
Kensington Place JE2 3PA
☎ 01534 611111 📠 01534 611116
e-mail: reservations@revere.co.uk
Located on the west side of town this 17th-century building retains many of its original features. An engagingly different hotel, bedrooms are individually decorated and have high quality bedding. Public areas include several cosy lounges, three eating options and a sun terrace with outdoor pool.
**ROOMS:** 58 en suite (4 fmly) No smoking in 14 bedrooms **FACILITIES:** STV Outdoor swimming (H) **NOTES:** No dogs (ex guide dogs) **CARDS:**

### ★★69% *Sarum Hotel*
19-21 New St Johns Rd JE2 3LD
☎ 01534 758163 📠 01534 731340
e-mail: sarum@jerseyweb.demon.co.uk
***Dir:*** *W side of St Helier, 0.5m from Town Centre*
Situated in a residential area just five minutes' walk from the town centre and beaches this friendly hotel is ideal for guests who like to have everything close by. Bedrooms are neatly decorated and comfortably furnished, most have small kitchens. Public areas include a small enclosed pool area and award winning garden.
**ROOMS:** 47 en suite **FACILITIES:** STV Outdoor swimming (H) Video games **SERVICES:** Lift **PARKING:** 11 **NOTES:** No dogs (ex guide dogs) No children No smoking in restaurant Closed 29 Oct-6 Apr
**CARDS:**

### ★★68% Uplands
St John's Rd JE2 3LE
☎ 01534 730151 📠 01534 639899
e-mail: morfarmho@itl.net
***Dir:*** *turn off main esplanade (A1) onto Pierson Rd by Grand Hotel, follow ring road for 200mtrs, third on left into St Johns Rd, hotel in 0.5m*
Uplands Hotel is set in twelve acres of farmland and yet only one mile from the centre of St Helier. Bedrooms are modern, spacious and comfortable, some overlooking the swimming pool, others have country views. Twelve self-catering cottages are also available. Plenty of parking and spacious public areas add to the attraction.
**ROOMS:** 43 en suite (3 fmly) s £36-£40; d £72-£80 (incl. bkfst) * **FACILITIES:** STV Outdoor swimming (H) Xmas **PARKING:** 44 **NOTES:** No dogs (ex guide dogs) No children 3yrs No smoking in restaurant **CARDS:**

## ST LAWRENCE

### ★★★69% Hotel Cristina
Mont Feland JE3 1JA
☎ 01534 758024 📠 01534 758028
e-mail: cristina@dolanhotels.com
***Dir:*** *turn off the A10 on to Mont Felard, hotel on the left*

In prime position above St Aubin's Bay, the Cristina has unrivalled views from most of its public areas. Another advantage is the peace and quiet of the rural location, just ten minutes' walk from

*continued*

the sea. Most bedrooms have balconies and super views. The lobby and bar have been decorated in a contemporary style.
**ROOMS:** 62 en suite (3 fmly) s £44-£90; d £56-£102 (incl. bkfst) * **FACILITIES:** STV Outdoor swimming (H) entertainment **PARKING:** 80 **NOTES:** No dogs No children 4yrs No smoking in restaurant Closed Nov-Mar **CARDS:**

### ★★67% *Hotel White Heather*

Rue de Haut, Millbrook JE3 1JZ
☎ 01534 720978 01534 720968
***Dir:*** *from A11 turn right at school, follow road, hotel on right*
Tucked away in a quiet residential area within walking distance of the beach, White Heather has many regular guests. Most bedrooms have balconies with sun beds, all are brightly decorated. Public areas are similarly comfortable and well-presented, an indoor pool is also available.
**ROOMS:** 33 en suite (3 fmly) **FACILITIES:** STV Indoor swimming (H) **PARKING:** 11 **NOTES:** No dogs (ex guide dogs) No smoking in restaurant Closed Nov-Mar **CARDS:**

## ST PETER

### ★★★69% Mermaid

JE3 7BN
☎ 01534 741255 01534 745826
e-mail: huggler@psilink.co.je
Excellent leisure facilities and a caring team of staff are just two reasons why guests regularly return to the Mermaid. Facilities include indoor and outdoor pools, putting green, driving range and tennis court. The hotel is close to the airport, making it convenient for the business visitor. Almost all of the well-equipped bedrooms have their own furnished balconies overlooking the lake in the hotel grounds.
**ROOMS:** 68 en suite s £44-£66; d £74-£102 (incl. bkfst) * **LB** **FACILITIES:** Indoor swimming (H) Outdoor swimming (H) Tennis (hard) Sauna Solarium Gym Croquet lawn Putting green Jacuzzi Xmas **CONF:** Thtr 100 Class 60 Board 50 **PARKING:** 250 **NOTES:** No dogs (ex guide dogs) **CARDS:**

Popped the question? Hotels with Civ Wed in their entry are licensed for civil wedding ceremonies. Maximum numbers for the ceremony only are shown, e.g. Civ Wed 120

## ST SAVIOUR

### Premier Collection

★★★★ ◎◎◎ **_Longueville Manor_**
JE2 7WF
☎ 01534 725501 📠 01534 731613
e-mail: longman@itl.net
***Dir:*** *take A3 E from St Helier towards Gorey. Hotel 1m on left hand side*

Relais & Châteaux

Set in 17 acres of grounds, including fine specimen trees and a lake complete with black swans; parts of Longueville Manor date back to the 13th century. The bedrooms have great style; with fresh flowers providing the personal touch along with fine embroidered bed linen and all sorts of cosseting extras. Both dining rooms are appointed to the highest standard, providing an ideal setting for the hotel's renowned cooking. Produce from the extensive kitchen garden is used where possible.

**ROOMS:** 32 en suite **FACILITIES:** STV Outdoor swimming (H) Tennis (hard) Croquet lawn **CONF:** Thtr 40 Class 30 Board 30 **SERVICES:** Lift **PARKING:** 40 **CARDS:**

Late for dinner? Quality Standards star rating means that last orders for dinner should be no earlier than:
★ 6.30pm ★★ 7.00pm ★★★ 8.00pm
★★★★ 9.00pm ★★★★★ 10.00pm

## TRINITY

★★★68% **Highfield Country**
Route d'Ebenezer JE3 5DT
☎ 01534 862194 📠 01534 865342
e-mail: reservations@highfieldjersey.com
***Dir:*** *On A8 next door to Ebenezer Chapel*

Best Western

Highfield is situated in the north east of the island, an area favoured for its walks. Bedrooms are spacious, and some have the added advantage of kitchenettes. Guests can relax in the conservatory and adjacent bar or, depending upon the weather, take a swim in either the indoor or outdoor pool. The set-price dinner menu offers good value for money.

**ROOMS:** 38 en suite (32 fmly) s £37-£53; d £64-£95 (incl. bkfst) * **FACILITIES:** Indoor swimming (H) Outdoor swimming Sauna Solarium Gym Petanque ch fac **SERVICES:** Lift **PARKING:** 41 **NOTES:** No dogs No smoking in restaurant Closed Nov-Mar
**CARDS:**

## SARK

★★69% **_Dixcart_**
Dixcart Valley GY9 0SD
☎ 01481 832015 📠 01481 832164
e-mail: dixcart@itl.net
***Dir:*** *ten minutes S of village, following signed footpath*

Dixcart offers a friendly welcome with all the comforts of home. Log fires burn, even in summer, two cosy lounges offer seclusion and the gardens beckon on a sunny day. Two eating options are available, the restaurant or the bar. Bedrooms come in a variety of shapes and sizes.

**ROOMS:** 15 en suite (5 fmly) **FACILITIES:** no TV in bdrms Horse-drawn carriage tours available ch fac **CONF:** Thtr 60 Class 20 Board 10
**CARDS:**

# Isle of Man

Directory of establishments in alphabetical order of location.

## MAN, ISLE OF — Map 06

## CASTLETOWN — Map 06 SC26

**★★★68% Castletown Golf Links**
Fort Island IM9 1UA
☎ 01624 822201 🖷 01624 824633
e-mail: fowlds@enterprise.net
***Dir:*** *A1 south of airport, turn left then left again*

Best Western

With the sea on three sides and adjoining a championship golf course, this hotel has much to offer those who look for traditional, friendly service in a relaxing environment. Bedrooms are modern and well-equipped; ground-floor rooms and suites are available. Conference facilities and proximity to the airport make it a popular business venue.

**ROOMS:** 58 en suite (3 fmly) s £68-£88; d £95-£115 (incl. bkfst) * **LB** **FACILITIES:** STV Indoor swimming (H) Golf 18 Snooker Sauna Solarium Putting green Xmas **CONF:** Thtr 200 Class 50 Board 20 Del from £87.50 * **PARKING:** 200 **CARDS:**

## DOUGLAS — Map 06 SC37

**★★★★70% Mount Murray**
Santon IM4 2HT
☎ 01624 661111 🖷 01624 611116
e-mail: hotel@enterprise.net
***Dir:*** *from Douglas head towards airport. Hotel is signposted on the road 4m from Douglas, just before Stanton*

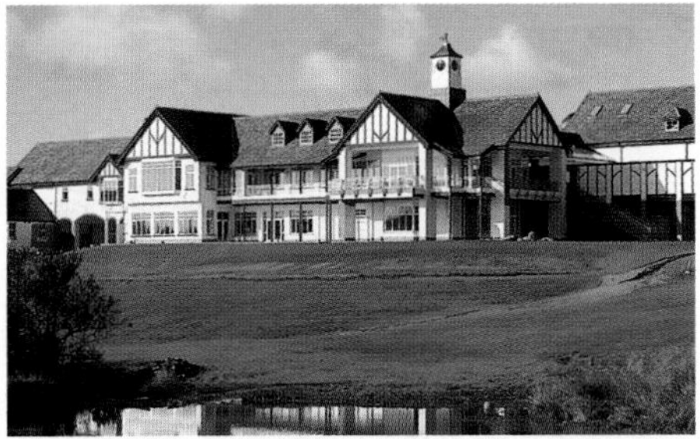

This large, modern hotel and country club offers a wide range of sporting and leisure facilities, and a health and beauty salon. The attractively appointed public areas give a choice of bars and eating options. The spacious bedrooms are well-equipped and many enjoy fine views over the 200-acre grounds and golf course. There is a very large function suite.

**ROOMS:** 90 en suite (4 fmly) No smoking in 12 bedrooms s £43-£104; d £64-£156 (incl. bkfst) * **LB** **FACILITIES:** STV Indoor swimming (H) Golf 18 Tennis (hard) Squash Sauna Solarium Gym Putting green Bowling green Driving range Sports hall Xmas **CONF:** Thtr 300 Class 260 Board 100 Del £99 * **SERVICES:** Lift **PARKING:** 400 **NOTES:** No dogs (ex guide dogs) No smoking in restaurant **CARDS:**

Bad hair day? Hairdryers in all rooms three stars and above.

**★★★★69% Sefton**
Harris Promenade IM1 2RW
☎ 01624 645500 🖷 01624 676004
e-mail: info@seftonhotel.co.im
***Dir:*** *500yds from the Ferry Dock on Douglas promenade*

This large Victorian hotel is centrally situated and dominates the promenade area. Many bedrooms have balconies overlooking the internal courtyard and water garden. The public areas offer a choice of comfortable lounges and bars as well as a range of eating options.

**ROOMS:** 104 en suite No smoking in 22 bedrooms s £68-£150; d £80-£150 * **LB** **FACILITIES:** STV Indoor swimming (H) Sauna Solarium Gym Jacuzzi Cycle hire **CONF:** Thtr 180 Class 40 Board 20 Del from £150 * **SERVICES:** Lift **PARKING:** 40 **NOTES:** No dogs (ex guide dogs) RS 26 Dec-14 Jan **CARDS:**

**★★★68% *Welbeck Hotel***
13/15 Mona Dr IM2 4LF
☎ 01624 675663 🖷 01624 661545
e-mail: welbeck@isle-of-man.com
***Dir:*** *at the crossroads of Mona & Empress Drive off Central Promenade*

Welbeck Hotel offers its guests a friendly welcome and a choice of attractive accommodation, from well-equipped bedrooms to six newly-constructed luxury apartments, each with its own lounge

*continued on p682*

DOUGLAS, continued

and small kitchen. The hotel is family-run and located within easy reach of the sea front.
**ROOMS:** 27 en suite (7 fmly) **FACILITIES:** STV **CONF:** Thtr 60 Class 36 Board 30 **SERVICES:** Lift **NOTES:** No dogs (ex guide dogs)
**CARDS:**

★★★67% **Empress**
Central Promenade IM2 4RA
☎ 01624 661155 🖹 01624 673554
e-mail: empresshotel@manx.net
The Empress Hotel is a large Victorian building on the central promenade, overlooking Douglas Bay. Well-equipped, modern bedrooms include suites, and rooms with sea views. A pianist entertains in the lounge bar most evenings. Other facilities available to guests include a lounge, a sun lounge and a brasserie-style restaurant.
**ROOMS:** 102 en suite No smoking in 6 bedrooms s £70; d £75 * **LB**
**FACILITIES:** STV Indoor swimming (H) Sauna Solarium Gym Jacuzzi entertainment Xmas **CONF:** Thtr 200 Class 150 Board 50 Del £95 *
**SERVICES:** Lift **NOTES:** No dogs (ex guide dogs)
**CARDS:**

*See advert on page 681*

PEEL Map 06 SC28

★★69% **Ballacallin House**
Dalby Village IM5 3BT
☎ 01624 841100 🖹 01624 845055
e-mail: ballacallin@advsys.co.uk

MINOTEL
Great Britain

Niarbyl

This small, private hotel in Dalby village is personally run and offers well-equipped, modern accommodation of a very good standard. Bedrooms with four-poster beds and a two bedroom suite are available. Some enjoy sea views, as do the bright restaurant and the spacious lounge bar.
**ROOMS:** 10 en suite No smoking in all bedrooms s £45; d £67.50 (incl. bkfst) * **LB** **FACILITIES:** Xmas **CONF:** Thtr 30 Class 24 Board 24 Del from £89.95 * **PARKING:** 70 **NOTES:** No smoking in restaurant
**CARDS:**

PORT ERIN Map 06 SC16

★★★67% ***Cherry Orchard***
Bridson St IM9 6AN
☎ 01624 833811 🖹 01624 833583
e-mail: enquiries@cherry-orchard.com
***Dir:*** *from Seaport/Airport take main road south past Castletown to Port Erin*
The comfortable bedrooms at this modern hotel are well equipped and attractively furnished. One room is particularly suitable for less mobile guests. The well-appointed restaurant, cosy lounge bar and leisure centre are also available to guests staying in self-catering apartments located within the same complex.
**ROOMS:** 32 en suite (12 fmly) **FACILITIES:** STV Indoor swimming (H) Sauna Solarium Gym Croquet lawn Jacuzzi Games room ch fac
**CONF:** Thtr 200 Class 120 Board 70 **SERVICES:** Lift **PARKING:** 80
**NOTES:** No dogs (ex guide dogs) No smoking in restaurant
**CARDS:**

★★★65% **Ocean Castle**
The Promenade IM9 6LH
☎ 01624 836399 🖹 01624 836537
e-mail: oceancastle@btinternet.com
This pleasant, privately owned hotel stands on the promenade, from which it overlooks the beach and bay. The modern equipped accommodation is equally suitable for both holiday makers and business people. Facilities here include a large function room.
**ROOMS:** 40 en suite (2 fmly) s £34; d £68 (incl. bkfst) * **LB**
**FACILITIES:** STV Ballroom entertainment Xmas **CONF:** Thtr 200 Class 150 Board 100 **SERVICES:** Lift **NOTES:** No smoking in restaurant
**CARDS:**

Popped the question? Hotels with Civ Wed in their entry are licensed for civil wedding ceremonies. Maximum numbers for the ceremony only are shown, e.g. Civ Wed 120

# *Hotel of the Year, Scotland*

*Pool House Hotel,*
*Poolewe*

## ABERDEEN, Aberdeen City

see also Aberdeen Airport

Map 15 NJ90

### ★★★★76% The Marcliffe at Pitfodels

North Deeside Rd AB15 9YA
☎ 01224 861000 🖷 01224 868860
e-mail: enquiries@marcliffe.com
***Dir:*** *turn off A90 onto A93 signposted Braemar. 1m on right after turn off at traffic lights*

Set in attractive landscaped grounds west of the city, this impressive hotel presents a blend of styles. A split-level conservatory restaurant, terraces and courtyards, all giving a sense of the Mediterranean, whilst the elegant and sophisticated cocktail lounge is sheer classical. Bedrooms are well-proportioned and thoughtfully equipped. Service is caring and attentive.

**ROOMS:** 42 en suite (4 fmly) No smoking in 10 bedrooms s £105-£175; d £115-£195 (incl. bkfst) * **LB** **FACILITIES:** STV Snooker Croquet lawn Putting green ch fac Xmas **CONF:** Thtr 500 Class 300 Board 24 Del from £160 * **SERVICES:** Lift **PARKING:** 160 **NOTES:** Civ Wed 360 **CARDS:**

### ★★★★73% Ardoe House

South Deeside Rd, Blairs AB12 5YP
☎ 01224 860600 🖷 01224 861283
e-mail: info@ardoe.macdonald-hotels.co.uk
***Dir:*** *4m W of city off B9077*

MACDONALD
HOTELS

Set amid extensive grounds, this impressive mansion house offers comfortable, traditional bedrooms in the main house and smart, modern accommodation in the newer wing. Many original features of the house have been retained in the delightful drawing room and the choice of contrasting bars and restaurants. The Garden Room provides an appropriate setting for a fine dining experience.

**ROOMS:** 112 en suite (3 fmly) No smoking in 81 bedrooms **FACILITIES:** STV Indoor swimming (H) Sauna Solarium Gym Croquet lawn Putting green Jacuzzi Petanque **CONF:** Thtr 500 Class 250 Board 100 **SERVICES:** Lift **PARKING:** 200 **NOTES:** No smoking in restaurant **CARDS:**

### ★★★★67% Patio

Beach Boulevard AB24 5EF
☎ 01224 633339 or 380000 🖷 01224 638833
e-mail: patioab@globalnet.co.uk
***Dir:*** *from the A90 follow signs for city centre, then for sea beach. On Beach Boulevard, turn left at traffic lights and hotel is on right*

Close to the sea front north of the city centre, this purpose-built hotel offers spacious accommodation, with a choice of smart elegant Premier Club rooms or bright contemporary standard rooms. There is an atrium with an open plan continental style café bar; there is also a restaurant.

**ROOMS:** 124 en suite (8 fmly) No smoking in 93 bedrooms **FACILITIES:** STV Indoor swimming (H) Sauna Solarium Gym Jacuzzi Steam room, Treatment Room **CONF:** Thtr 150 Class 80 Board 50 **SERVICES:** Lift **PARKING:** 196 **CARDS:**

### ★★★★65% Copthorne Hotel Aberdeen

122 Huntly St AB10 1SU
☎ 01224 630404 🖷 01224 640573
e-mail: reservations.aberdeen@mill-cop.com
***Dir:*** *W of city centre, off Union Street, up Rose Street, hotel 0.25m on right on corner with Huntly Street*

COPTHORNE

The smart bedrooms are comfortably modern in style and thoughtfully equipped. Guests will appreciate the added quality provided in the Connoisseur rooms. Mac's bar offers a relaxed atmosphere where the guest can enjoy a refreshment or dine informally. The tastefully appointed Poachers Restaurant offers a more formal dining experience.

**ROOMS:** 89 en suite (15 fmly) No smoking in 37 bedrooms s £150; d £150 * **LB** **FACILITIES:** STV **CONF:** Thtr 200 Class 100 Board 70 Del from £130 * **SERVICES:** Lift **PARKING:** 20 **NOTES:** Civ Wed 80 **CARDS:**

### ★★★74% Simpsons

59 Queens Rd AB15 4YP
☎ 01224 327777 🖷 01224 327700
e-mail: address@simpsonshotel.co.uk
***Dir:*** *turn off ring road (A90) at Earls Court rbt & drive down Queens Road. Hotel 700yds on left*

Two granite stone houses have been linked to create this exciting boutique hotel. One house contains smart modern bedrooms and luxury bathrooms, all with warm Mediterranean colour schemes. The other house contains a trendy bar leading down to a stunning brasserie where Moroccan columns support a colonnade of arches.

**ROOMS:** 38 en suite (8 fmly) No smoking in all bedrooms s £115-£125; d £125-£135 (incl. bkfst) * **FACILITIES:** STV Complimentary use of Health Club **SERVICES:** Lift air con **PARKING:** 102 **NOTES:** Closed 1 Jan **CARDS:**

### ★★★73% Atholl
54 Kings Gate AB15 4YN
☎ 01224 323505 🖷 01224 321555
e-mail: info@atholl-aberdeen.co.uk
***Dir:*** *in West End 400yds from Anderson Drive, the main ring road*
A high level of hospitality and guest care is only one feature of this popular suburban business hotel within easy reach of central amenities and the ring route. The smart modern bedrooms are comfortable and come equipped with a host of extras.
**ROOMS:** 35 en suite (1 fmly) No smoking in all bedrooms s £85; d £95 (incl. bkfst) * **LB** **FACILITIES:** STV free membership to local health club **CONF:** Thtr 60 Class 25 Board 25 Del from £115 * **PARKING:** 60 **NOTES:** No dogs (ex guide dogs) **CARDS:**

*See advert on this page*

### ★★★70% Queens Hotel
51-53 Queens Rd AB15 4YP
☎ 01224 209999 🖷 01224 209009
e-mail: enquires@vagabond-hotels.com

This business hotel is also a popular venue for local functions. Nicely presented public areas include a welcoming foyer, lounge and a bar where one can dine from the same menu as in the restaurant. Accommodation offers the elegance of the original house or the modern extension.
**ROOMS:** 27 en suite (3 fmly) No smoking in 4 bedrooms s £40-£70; d £50-£80 (incl. bkfst) * **FACILITIES:** STV **CONF:** Thtr 400 Class 150 Board 60 Del from £97.50 * **PARKING:** 80 **NOTES:** No dogs (ex guide dogs) No smoking in restaurant Closed 25-26 Dec & 1-2 Jan
**CARDS:**

### ★★★69% *Norwood Hall*
Garthdee Rd, Cults AB15 9FX
☎ 01224 868951 🖷 01224 869868
e-mail: info@norwood-hall.co.uk
***Dir:*** *off the A90, at 1st rdbt cross Bridge of Dee and turn left at the rdbt onto Garthdee Rd (B&Q and Sainsbury on the left) continue until hotel sign*

Set in wooded grounds, this Victorian mansion has many original features such as magnificent panelling, stained glass windows,

*continued*

Scottish
★★★★ HOTEL
AA ★★★
73%
Atholl
HOTEL
A TASTE of SCOTLAND member
"In a class of its own"
Set in the leafy West End overlooking Aberdeen's spectacular skyline, the privately owned Atholl Hotel is a landmark in itself. Its distinctive architecture in the sparkling granite for which the city is famous makes it instantly recognisable. At this STB 4-Star hotel nothing is ever too much trouble . . . making it truly "in a class of its own"
54 King's Gate, Aberdeen AB15 4YN
Tel: 01224 323505 Fax: 01224 321555
Email: info@atholl-aberdeen.co.uk
www-atholl-aberdeen-com

ornate plaster work and fireplaces, plus leather wall coverings have been retained. Bedrooms are smartly furbished; those in the main house mirror its character, whilst those in the newer wing are more modern.
**ROOMS:** 21 en suite (3 fmly) No smoking in 8 bedrooms **CONF:** Thtr 200 Class 80 Board 40 **PARKING:** 80 **NOTES:** No dogs (ex guide dogs) No smoking in restaurant **CARDS:**

### ★★★69% Westhill
Westhill AB32 6TT
☎ 01224 740388 🖷 01224 744354
e-mail: info@westhillhotel.co.uk
***Dir:*** *follow A944 West of the city towards Alford, Westhill is 6m out of centre on the right*
Just a short drive from the city centre and airport, this comfortable purpose-built business hotel is in the suburb of Westhill. Inviting public areas include a choice of three contrasting bars and a smart fitness centre. Meals are available in both the lounge bar and split level restaurant. Bedrooms are modern in appointment and offer a good range of amenities.
**ROOMS:** 38 en suite (2 fmly) No smoking in 8 bedrooms s £45-£68; d £60-£84 (incl. bkfst) * **LB** **FACILITIES:** STV Sauna Solarium Gym entertainment Xmas **CONF:** Thtr 300 Class 200 Board 200 Del from £74 * **SERVICES:** Lift **PARKING:** 250 **NOTES:** Civ Wed 150
**CARDS:**

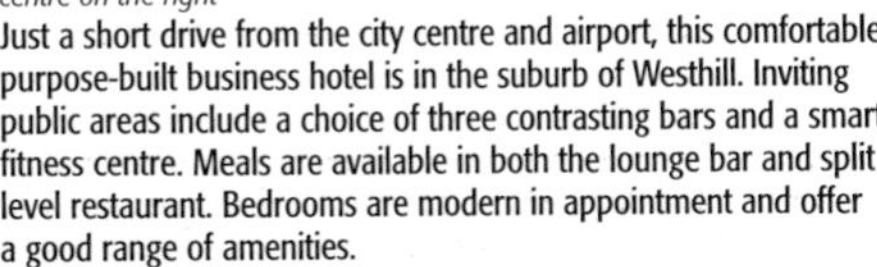
Late for dinner? Quality Standards star rating means that last orders for dinner should be no earlier than:
★ 6.30pm ★★ 7.00pm ★★★ 8.00pm
★★★★ 9.00pm ★★★★★ 10.00pm

ABERDEEN, continued

A

**★★★67% ◎ Maryculter House Hotel**
South Deeside Rd, Maryculter AB12 5GB
☎ 01224 732124 🖷 01224 733510
e-mail: info@maryculterhousehotel.co.uk
***Dir:*** *turn off A90 on S side of Aberdeen, onto B9077. Hotel located 8m along on right hand side, 0.5m beyond Templars Park*

In grounds on the banks of the River Dee, this house dates back to medieval times. It is a popular wedding and conference venue. Original stonework features in the cocktail bar and restaurant, and there is a second bar where one can eat less formally. Bedrooms are equipped with the business person in mind.
**ROOMS:** 23 en suite (1 fmly) No smoking in 17 bedrooms s £55-£75; d £70-£100 (incl. bkfst) * **LB** **FACILITIES:** STV Fishing Clay pigeon shooting Xmas **CONF:** Thtr 220 Class 100 Board 50 Del from £120 * **PARKING:** 150 **NOTES:** No smoking in restaurant
**CARDS:**

**★★★65% Grampian**
Stirling St AB11 6JU
☎ 01224 589101 🖷 01224 574288
e-mail: info@grampian.macdonald-hotels.co.uk
The Grampian Hotel is set in the heart of the city, located close to the railway station. This hotel provides modern accommodation, a library style lounge and a brasserie, which is scheduled to be changed to a steakhouse.
**ROOMS:** 49 en suite (3 fmly) s £55; d £80 (incl. bkfst) * **LB** **FACILITIES:** Xmas **CONF:** Thtr 120 Class 60 Board 40 Del from £100 * **SERVICES:** Lift **NOTES:** No smoking in restaurant
**CARDS:**

**★★★65% Posthouse Aberdeen**
Claymore Dr, Bridge of Don AB23 8BL
☎ 0870 400 9046 🖷 01224 823923
Posthouse
***Dir:*** *follow signs for Peterhead and Aberdeen Exhibition Conference Centre hotel is adjacent to AECC*
Situated in the north side of the city adjoining the Exhibition Centre, this purpose built hotel attracts oil industry personnel. Bedrooms are comfortably modern in style and offer a good range of amenities. Public areas are open-plan and one can watch TV in the bar.
**ROOMS:** 123 en suite (23 fmly) No smoking in 49 bedrooms s £38-£69; d £55-£89 * **LB** **FACILITIES:** STV Xmas **SERVICES:** Lift **PARKING:** 200 **CARDS:**

**★★★64% The Craighaar**
Waterton Rd, Bankhead AB21 9HS
☎ 01224 712275 🖷 01224 716362
e-mail: info@craighaar.co.uk
***Dir:*** *Turn off A96 (Airport/Inverness) onto A947, hotel signposted*
Convenient to the airport this welcoming hotel is a popular base

*continued*

for the visiting business person. Public areas include a spacious well-stocked panelled bar and a smart restaurant. Bedrooms range from comfortable Gallery suites to the smaller standard rooms.
**ROOMS:** 55 en suite (6 fmly) s £79-£109; d £89-£119 (incl. bkfst) * **LB** **FACILITIES:** STV **CONF:** Thtr 90 Class 33 Board 30 Del £110 * **PARKING:** 80 **NOTES:** No dogs (ex guide dogs) Closed 26 Dec & 1-2 Jan Civ Wed 40 **CARDS:**

**★★73% Craiglynn Hotel**
36 Fonthill Rd AB11 6UJ
☎ 01224 584050 🖷 01224 212225
e-mail: info@craiglynn.co.uk
THE CIRCLE Selected Individual Hotels GREAT BRITAIN
***Dir:*** *from S (A90) cross River Dee via King George VI Bridge, then Gt Southern Road to Whinhill and Bon Accord Street & hotel car park*
A fine Victorian granite stone house, Craiglynn lies in a residential area just south of the city centre. It offers a choice of lounges, where drinks are served (there is no bar). It is worth dining in, to enjoy home-cooked dinners chosen from a short selection and served at 7pm.
**ROOMS:** 9 rms (7 en suite) (1 fmly) No smoking in all bedrooms s £40-£68; d £60-£80 (incl. bkfst) * **LB** **CONF:** Class 20 **PARKING:** 9 **NOTES:** No dogs No smoking in restaurant Closed 25-26 Dec
**CARDS:**

**★★69% Dunavon House**
60 Victoria St, Dyce AB21 7EE
☎ 01224 722483 & 772496 🖷 01224 772721
e-mail: info@dunavon-hotel.com
***Dir:*** *from A96 follow A947 into Victoria St, Dyce. Hotel 500yds on right*
This Victorian villa is now a popular hotel with a good atmosphere. Well-presented throughout, it offers attractive, thoughtfully equipped bedrooms. The inviting lounge bar and restaurant offer a wide range of dishes at both lunch and dinner.
**ROOMS:** 17 en suite No smoking in 5 bedrooms s £47-£60; d £62-£70 (incl. bkfst) * **LB** **FACILITIES:** STV **PARKING:** 23 **NOTES:** No dogs (ex guide dogs) No smoking in restaurant Closed 25 Dec-4 Jan
**CARDS:**

**★★69% Mariner**
349 Great Western Rd AB10 6NW
☎ 01224 588901 🖷 01224 571621
e-mail: enquiries@vagabond-hotels.com
***Dir:*** *Turn East off Anderson Drive at Great Western Road. Hotel on right on the corner of Gray Street*
A good range of tasty meals are served in both the conservatory restaurant and lounge bar of this hotel. Smart modern bedrooms are well-equipped with trouser press and hair dryer, and there are four apartment style rooms complete with kitchen, ideal for the long-stay guest.
**ROOMS:** 14 en suite 8 annexe en suite **FACILITIES:** STV Xmas **PARKING:** 48 **NOTES:** No dogs (ex guide dogs)
**CARDS:**

**⌂ Premier Lodge (Aberdeen West)**
North Anderson Dr AB15 6DW
☎ 0870 700 1300 🖷 0870 7001301

***Dir:*** *Adjacent to Fire Station*
Premier Lodge offers modern, well-equipped, en suite accommodation suitable for both business and leisure travellers. Meals can be taken at the adjacent popular restaurant and bar, which is fully licensed. For further details, consult the Hotel Groups page.
**ROOMS:** 60 en suite s £42; d £42 *

### ⌂ *Travelodge*

Travelodge

9 Bridge St AB11 6JL
☎ 01224 584555 🖷 01224 584587
Travelodge offers good quality, good value, modern accommodation. Ideal for families, the spacious, en suite bedrooms include remote-control TV, tea and coffee-making facilities, luxury beds and free morning newspaper. Meals can be taken at the nearby family restaurant. For further details and the Travelodge phone number, consult the Hotel Groups page.

Travelodge

**ROOMS:** 95 en suite

---

ABERDEEN AIRPORT, Aberdeen City — Map 15 NJ81

### ★★★★69% Aberdeen Marriott Hotel

Marriott
HOTELS · RESORTS · SUITES

Overton Circle, Dyce AB21 7AZ
☎ 01224 770011 🖷 01224 722347
e-mail: reservations.aberdeen@marriotthotels.co.uk
***Dir:*** *follow A96 to Bucksburn village, turn right at the rdbt onto the A947. After 2m you will see the hotel at the second rdbt*

A smart and modern, purpose-built hotel in the suburb of Dyce, and set in a convenient location for access to the airport. Attractive public areas include a comfortable foyer lounge, a café bar and a split-level restaurant. Bedrooms are well-proportioned and most have work desks.

**ROOMS:** 155 en suite (68 fmly) No smoking in 88 bedrooms s £117; d £117 * **LB** **FACILITIES:** **Spa** STV Indoor swimming (H) Sauna Solarium Gym Jacuzzi Xmas **CONF:** Thtr 400 Class 200 Board 60 Del £140 * **SERVICES:** air con **PARKING:** 180 **NOTES:** No dogs (ex guide dogs) Civ Wed 320 **CARDS:**

> Popped the question? Hotels with Civ Wed in their entry are licensed for civil wedding ceremonies. Maximum numbers for the ceremony only are shown, e.g. Civ Wed 120

## ABERDOUR, Fife
Map 11 NT18

### ★★68% *Woodside*
High St KY3 0SW
☎ 01383 860328 🖹 01383 860920
e-mail: reception@woodside-hotel.demon.co.uk
***Dir:*** *E of Forth Road Bridge, across rbt into town, hotel on left after garage*

A welcoming atmosphere prevails at this long established business hotel in the centre of the village, the façade of which is adorned with colourful flowering window boxes and hanging baskets. Inviting public areas include a spacious and well-stocked bar, a comfortable foyer and an attractive restaurant. Bedrooms are varied in size and in style.
**ROOMS:** 20 en suite (1 fmly) **CONF:** Thtr 25 Class 40 Board 25
**PARKING:** 30 **CARDS:**

*See advert on page 687*

### ★★62% *The Aberdour Hotel*
38 High St KY3 0SW
☎ 01383 860325 🖹 01383 860808
e-mail: reception@aberdourhotel.co.uk

THE CIRCLE
Selected Individual Hotels
GREAT BRITAIN

***Dir:*** *take exit 1 off M90 and travel E on A291 for 5m. Hotel is located in the centre of the village opposite the post office*

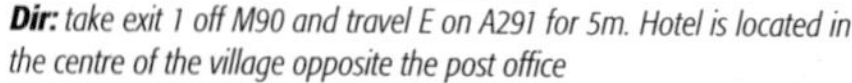

This small hotel offers a relaxed and welcoming atmosphere. Real ales feature in the cosy bar and good value home cooked fare is offered in the beamed dining room. Bedrooms, including those in the converted stable block, offer mixed styles of appointment together with a good range of amenities.
**ROOMS:** 16 en suite (4 fmly) **FACILITIES:** STV **PARKING:** 8
**CARDS:**

## ABERFELDY, Perth & Kinross
Map 14 NN84

### ★★72% Guinach House
By The Birks, Urlar Rd PH15 2ET
☎ 01887 820251 🖹 01887 829607
***Dir:*** *access off A826 Crieff road*
A warm welcome awaits guests at this family owned and run hotel, located close to the Birks on the southern edge of town. The elegant restaurant offers carefully prepared fine French-style cuisine. Bedrooms vary in size and style but all benefit from garden views and a thoughtful range of facilities.
**ROOMS:** 7 en suite No smoking in all bedrooms s fr £45.50; d fr £91 (incl. bkfst) * **PARKING:** 12 **NOTES:** No smoking in restaurant Closed 4 days Xmas **CARDS:**

> Late for dinner? Quality Standards star rating means that last orders for dinner should be no earlier than:
> ★ 6.30pm ★★ 7.00pm ★★★ 8.00pm
> ★★★★ 9.00pm ★★★★★ 10.00pm

## ABERFOYLE, Stirling
Map 11 NN50

### ★★★★64% Forest Hills
Kinlochard FK8 3TL
☎ 01877 387277 🖹 01877 387307
e-mail: forest_hills@macdonald-hotel.co.uk
***Dir:*** *3m W on B829*
Situated in the heart of the Trossachs with wonderful views of Loch Ard, this popular and comfortable hotel forms part of a resort complex. Bedrooms are mostly well-proportioned and comfortable. Public areas include a choice of inviting lounges and the Garden Restaurant. An alternative food option is offered in the relaxed and informal atmosphere of Rafters.
**ROOMS:** 56 en suite (16 fmly) No smoking in 26 bedrooms s £75-£90; d £110-£160 (incl. bkfst & dinner) * LB **FACILITIES:** Indoor swimming (H) Tennis (hard) Fishing Snooker Sauna Solarium Gym Putting green Jacuzzi entertainment ch fac Xmas **CONF:** Thtr 150 Class 60 Board 45 Del £145 * **PARKING:** 80 **NOTES:** No smoking in restaurant Civ Wed 80 **CARDS:**

## ABERLOUR See Archiestown

## ABINGTON, South Lanarkshire
Map 11 NS92

### ★★64% Abington Hotel
Abington By Biggar ML12 6SD
☎ 01864 502467 🖹 01864 502223
e-mail: info@abington-hotel.ndirect.co.uk
***Dir:*** *M74 junct 13 & follow signs into village or A702 S of Edinburgh at junct for M74 follow signs into Abington village*

This family run hotel is situated in the quiet village of Abington, and became established as a result of it position by the junction of the main road from England when heading north to Edinburgh or Glasgow. Today's travellers will find a good comfortable standard of accommodation, friendly attention and wholesome meals, all at affordable prices.
**ROOMS:** 28 en suite (6 fmly) No smoking in 19 bedrooms s £45; d £65 (incl. bkfst) * LB **CONF:** Thtr 60 Class 50 Board 50 Del from £59 * **PARKING:** 30 **NOTES:** No dogs (ex guide dogs) No smoking in restaurant **CARDS:**

### ⇧ Days Inn
ML12 6RG
☎ 01864 502782 🖹 01864 502759

DAYS INN

e-mail: abington.hotel@welcomebreak.co.uk
***Dir:*** *M74 junct 13, accessible from northbound and southbound carriageways*
This modern building offers accommodation in smart, spacious and well-equipped bedrooms, suitable for families and business travellers, and all with en suite bathrooms. Continental breakfast is available and other refreshments may be taken at the nearby

*continued*

family restaurant. For further details and the Days Inn phone number, consult the Hotel Groups page.
**ROOMS:** 54 en suite s £45-£55; d £45-£55 * **CONF:** Board 10

ACHNASHEEN, Highland Map 14 NH15

★★★65% **Ledgowan Lodge**
IV22 2EJ
☎ 01445 720252 ▤ 01445 720240
e-mail: info@ledgowanlodge.co.uk
***Dir:*** *0.25m on A890 to Kyle of Lochalsh - from Achnasheen*
This highland hotel is well-situated for exploring Western Ross. Relaxing public areas include an interesting aquarium and collection of whisky artefacts in the hall, as well as a lounge, a cosy bar and coffee shop serving meals and snacks all day. The attractive dining room offers an extensive carte. Bedrooms are comfortable and traditional.
**ROOMS:** 11 en suite (2 fmly) s £28; d £50-£75 * **PARKING:** 25
**NOTES:** No dogs No smoking in restaurant Closed Jan-Mar & Nov-Dec RS Apr & Oct **CARDS:**

ANNAN, Dumfries & Galloway Map 11 NY16

★★64% ***Queensberry Arms***
47 High St DG12 6AD
☎ 01461 202024 ▤ 01461 205998
***Dir:*** *located on left of main street, 1.5m from A75*
Formerly a coaching inn, the Queensberry Arms with its distinctive black and white façade, sits conveniently in the town centre. A variety of lounges are available hosting popular morning coffees and afternoon teas. The attractive upstairs restaurant, which has a nautical theme, serves a good range of popular dishes.
**ROOMS:** 24 en suite (3 fmly) **FACILITIES:** STV Tennis (hard & grass)
**CONF:** Thtr 70 Class 40 Board 40 **PARKING:** 30 **NOTES:** Civ Wed 70
**CARDS:**

ANSTRUTHER, Fife Map 12 NO50

★★64% **Smugglers Inn**
High St East KY10 3DQ
☎ 01333 310506 ▤ 01333 312706
e-mail: smuggs106@aol.com
***Dir:*** *on High Street East A719 after bridge*
This welcoming inn in the centre of the village is steeped in Jacobean history. In the bedrooms, attractive co-ordinated fabrics have been used to good effect to enhance the pretty colour schemes and comfortable furnishings. There is a choice of contrasting bars, a cosy lounge, and a beamed dining room.
**ROOMS:** 9 en suite (1 fmly) s £29.50-£35; d £59-£62 (incl. bkfst) * **LB**
**FACILITIES:** Darts ch fac **PARKING:** 14 **NOTES:** No dogs (ex guide dogs) **CARDS:**

ARBROATH, Angus Map 12 NO64

★★★61% **The Letham Grange Mansion House Hotel**
Colliston DD11 4RL
☎ 01241 890373 ▤ 01241 890725
e-mail: lethamgrange@sol.co.uk
***Dir:*** *leave A92 onto A933 to Brechin, Letham Grange signposted at village of Colliston*
Situated in the heart of the Angus countryside, this impressive Victorian mansion house boasts two challenging golf courses, a curling rink and attractive, comfortable bedrooms. The inviting public areas feature ornate ceilings, beautiful panelling and fine

continued



paintings, and include a relaxing drawing room, bar, conservatory and elegant dining room serving Scottish and international dishes.

**ROOMS:** 19 en suite 22 annexe en suite (1 fmly) No smoking in 4 bedrooms s £100; d £145 (incl. bkfst) * **LB** **FACILITIES:** STV Golf 36 Croquet lawn Putting green Curling rink ch fac Xmas **CONF:** Thtr 700 Class 300 Board 20 **PARKING:** 150 **NOTES:** No smoking in restaurant
**CARDS:**

*See advert on this page*

★★65% **Hotel Seaforth**
Dundee Rd DD11 1QF
☎ 01241 872232 ▤ 01241 877473
e-mail: hotelseaforth@ukonline.co.uk
***Dir:*** *on southern outskirts, on A92*
This long established commercial hotel is situated on the west side of town. The well equipped bedrooms are comfortable. Public

continued on p690

ARBROATH, continued

areas include a restaurant, a well stocked bar, as well as leisure and function facilities.

*Hotel Seaforth, Arbroath*

**ROOMS:** 19 en suite (4 fmly) s £45-£48; d £58-£60 (incl. bkfst) * **LB** **FACILITIES:** Indoor swimming (H) Snooker Sauna Gym Jacuzzi Steam room ch fac Xmas **CONF:** Thtr 120 Class 60 Board 40 Del from £51.75 * **PARKING:** 60 **NOTES:** No smoking in restaurant Civ Wed 120 **CARDS:**

## ARCHIESTOWN, Moray

Map 15 NJ24

★★76% **Archiestown**
AB38 7QL
☎ 01340 810218 01340 810239
e-mail: judith.bulger@btconnect.com
***Dir:*** *on B9102, 5m SW of Craigellachie*

Over the years anglers and holidaymakers alike have come to appreciate and enjoy the unique atmosphere of this delightful hotel. Inviting public areas include a choice of lounges and dining venues, but most favour the relaxed atmosphere of Bistro One. Bedrooms are bright and airy and come comfortably furnished.
**ROOMS:** 8 rms (7 en suite) s fr £48; d fr £96 (incl. bkfst) * **PARKING:** 20 **NOTES:** Closed Oct-9 Feb **CARDS:**

## ARDELVE, Highland

Map 14 NG82

★68% ***Loch Duich***
IV40 8DY
☎ 01599 555213 01599 555214
***Dir:*** *from Inverness A82 towards Fort William, turn right at Invermoriston on to A887 then A87 towards Kyle of Lochalsh and Ardelve*

This welcoming tourist hotel is a former drovers' inn beside the Road to the Isles. Many bedrooms have been individually refurbished. Relaxing public areas include a choice of lounges and a cosy dining room, serving the same good food as available in the popular Duich Pub.
**ROOMS:** 11 rms (9 en suite) (1 fmly) **FACILITIES:** Fishing Shooting Sailing **CONF:** Board 40 **PARKING:** 41 **NOTES:** No smoking in restaurant Closed 4 Jan-1 Mar & 19-28 Dec RS Nov-18 Dec Civ Wed 40 **CARDS:**

## ARDUAINE, Argyll & Bute

Map 10 NM71

★★★76% **Loch Melfort**
PA34 4XG
☎ 01852 200233 01852 200214
e-mail: lmhotel@aol.com
***Dir:*** *on A816, midway between Oban and Lochgilphead*

SCOTLAND'S HOTELS OF DISTINCTION

Enjoying one of the finest locations on the West Coast, this popular, family-run hotel has outstanding views across Asknish Bay towards the Islands of Jura, Scarba and Shuna. New owners have made an impact with improvements to the Cedar Wing and the Skerry Bistro. Many of the friendly staff have been here for years; and the style of the excellent cuisine is unaltered.

**ROOMS:** 7 en suite 20 annexe en suite (2 fmly) s £44-£79; d £66-£118 (incl. bkfst) * **LB** **FACILITIES:** ch fac Xmas **CONF:** Thtr 50 Class 35 Board 24 **PARKING:** 65 **NOTES:** No smoking in restaurant **CARDS:**

ARDVASAR See Skye, Isle of

## ARISAIG, Highland

Map 13 NM6

**Premier Collection**

★★★ **Arisaig House**
Beasdale PH39 4NR
☎ 01687 450622 01687 450626
e-mail: arisaighse@aol.com
***Dir:*** *3m E A830*

RELAIS & CHATEAUX.

This delightful Scottish mansion nestles peacefully amid extensive woodland and carefully tended gardens. The comfortable bedrooms provide a wealth of personal touches and classically-styled day rooms include a choice of sitting rooms, with fine furnishings, fresh floral displays, and in the cooler months, roaring log fires. The elegant panelled dining room provides an appropriate setting for the classical and modern cooking. The finest local ingredients are carefully sourced and provide a high standard of cuisine. Rates include dinner in March and November.
**ROOMS:** 12 en suite s fr £130; d £175-£295 (incl. bkfst) * **LB** **FACILITIES:** Snooker Croquet lawn **CONF:** Board 10 **PARKING:** 16 **NOTES:** No dogs (ex guide dogs) No children 8yrs No smoking in restaurant Closed Dec-Feb RS Mar&Nov(closes 2 days per week) **CARDS:**

*continued*

**★★68% Arisaig**
PH39 4NH
☎ 01687 450210 ▤ 01687 450310
e-mail: arisaighotel@dial.pipex.com
***Dir:*** *on A830 opposite the harbour*

This roadside hotel occupies an enviable position on the shores of Loch Nan Ceal with fine sea views towards the islands of Rhum, Eigg, Muck and Skye. The smartly appointed and thoughtfully equipped bedrooms are now all en suite and some enjoy the marvellous views across the bay. The comfortable public areas include a choice of lounges and bars, and a children's playroom. The atmosphere is very friendly and relaxed.
**ROOMS:** 13 en suite (2 fmly) No smoking in all bedrooms s £32-£36; d £64-£72 (incl. bkfst) * **LB** **FACILITIES:** ch fac **PARKING:** 30 **NOTES:** No smoking in restaurant Closed 24-26 Dec
**CARDS:**

## ARRAN, ISLE OF, North Ayrshire — Map 10

### BRODICK — Map 10 NS03

**★★★75% ◎◎ Auchrannie Country House**
KA27 8BZ
☎ 01770 302234 ▤ 01770 302812
e-mail: info@auchrannie.co.uk
***Dir:*** *turn right from Brodick Ferry terminal, through Brodick village, turn second left after Brodick Golf Course clubhouse, 300yds to Hotel*

Scotland's Hotels of Distinction

Genuine hospitality and extensive leisure facilities are all part of the appeal at this extended Victorian mansion, which stands in six acres of landscaped grounds. Bedrooms are well-equipped, those in the newer wing being particularly spacious. There is a choice of relaxing lounges, a bistro and the Garden Restaurant where the fixed-price menu earns two AA Rosettes.
**ROOMS:** 28 en suite (3 fmly) s £56-£71; d £92-£122 (incl. bkfst) * **LB** **FACILITIES:** STV Indoor swimming (H) Snooker Sauna Solarium Gym Jacuzzi Hair salon Aromatherapy Shiatsu ch fac Xmas **CONF:** Thtr 120 Board 30 **PARKING:** 50 **NOTES:** No dogs (ex guide dogs) No smoking in restaurant Civ Wed 100 **CARDS:**

## *Premier Collection*

**★★ ◎ Kilmichael Country House**
Glen Cloy KA27 8BY
☎ 01770 302219 ▤ 01770 302068
e-mail: enquiries@kilmichael.com
***Dir:*** *from Brodick Ferry Terminal follow northbound (Lochranza) road for 1m. At golf course turn left inland between sports field & church, follow signs*

This delightful house is rumoured to be the oldest on the island and has been lovingly restored to create a stylish,

*continued*

elegant small country house hotel. Thoughtfully equipped bedrooms, some with four-poster beds all have beautifully appointed en suites, some with spa baths. A converted barn in the well-tended grounds houses three particularly spacious, elegant rooms. There are two inviting drawing rooms and carefully prepared meals are served in the warmly decorated, smart dining room.

**ROOMS:** 4 en suite 3 annexe en suite No smoking in all bedrooms d £120-£150 (incl. bkfst) * **LB** **FACILITIES:** STV Jacuzzi **PARKING:** 12 **NOTES:** No children 12yrs No smoking in restaurant Closed Nov-Feb (ex for prior bookings) **CARDS:**

## AUCHENCAIRN, Dumfries & Galloway — Map 11 NX75

**★★★70% Balcary Bay**
DG7 1QZ
☎ 01556 640217 & 640311 ▤ 01556 640272
e-mail: reservations@balcary-bay-hotel.co.uk
***Dir:*** *on coast 2m from village*

Scotland's Hotels of Distinction

This comfortable, 17th-century hotel has a fascinating history. Overlooking Balcary Bay, it has lawns running down to the shore, and the larger bedrooms enjoy stunning views over the bay, whilst others have garden views. Dinner features imaginative dishes backed by a good wine list.
**ROOMS:** 20 en suite (2 fmly) s £61; d £108-£122 (incl. bkfst) * **LB** **FACILITIES:** ch fac **PARKING:** 50 **NOTES:** No smoking in restaurant Closed Dec-Feb **CARDS:**

## AUCHTERARDER, Perth & Kinross — Map 11 NN91

## *Premier Collection*

**★★★★★ ◎◎ The Gleneagles Hotel**
PH3 1NF
☎ 01764 662231 ▤ 01764 662134
e-mail: resort.sales@gleneagles.com
***Dir:*** *on A823*

With its international reputation for high standards, this grand hotel provides something for everyone. Set in a delightful location, Gleneagles offers a peaceful, tranquil retreat for relaxation, as well as many sporting activities, including the famous championship golf courses. Afternoon tea is a feature, and cocktails are prepared with flair and skill at the bar. The Strathearn restaurant is the fine dining option; service is

*continued on p692*

AUCHTERARDER, continued

professional, staff are friendly and nothing is too much trouble.

*The Gleneagles Hotel, Auchterarder*

**ROOMS:** 216 en suite No smoking in 118 bedrooms s £205-£430; d £305-£430 (incl. bkfst) * LB **FACILITIES:** Spa STV Indoor swimming (H) Outdoor swimming (H) Golf 18 Tennis (hard & grass) Fishing Squash Riding Snooker Sauna Solarium Gym Croquet lawn Putting green Jacuzzi Bowls, Shooting ,Falconry, Esquestrian,Off road driving,Golf driving range entertainment ch fac Xmas **CONF:** Thtr 360 Class 240 Board 70 Del from £296 * **SERVICES:** Lift **PARKING:** 200 **NOTES:** Civ Wed **CARDS:**

### ★★★81% Auchterarder House

PH3 1DZ
☎ 01764 663646 📠 01764 662939
e-mail: auchterarder@wrensgroup.com
***Dir:*** *NW off B8062 1.2m from village*

This imposing Victorian manor house is set amid 18 acres of beautiful woodland and rhododendron filled gardens. Public rooms include a conservatory breakfast room and an elegant drawing room with a log fire. The restaurant is an impressive oak-panelled room with beautiful stained glass windows and offers a high standard of cuisine using quality local produce. Bedrooms vary in size and are individually styled and furnished with antique pieces.
**ROOMS:** 15 en suite (3 fmly) s £135-£225; d £170-£295 (incl. bkfst) * LB **FACILITIES:** STV Croquet lawn Putting green Xmas **CONF:** Thtr 30 Class 30 Board 24 Del £175 * **PARKING:** 30 **NOTES:** No smoking in restaurant Civ Wed 40 **CARDS:**

### ★★★75% Duchally House Hotel

PH3 1PN
☎ 01764 663071 📠 01764 662464
***Dir:*** *leave A9 at the A823 Gleneagles exit for hotel 2m SW off A823 Dunfermline road*

Set in 27 acres and enjoying panoramic views across to far hills, this 19th century manor house has been fully refurbished. Now part of a time-share complex, the hotel offers inviting public areas that include a relaxing panelled lounge bar and elegant restaurant
**ROOMS:** 13 en suite (3 fmly) No smoking in 2 bedrooms s fr £65; d fr £110 (incl. bkfst) * LB **FACILITIES:** STV Xmas **CONF:** Thtr 40 Class 40 Board 30 Del from £99 * **PARKING:** 30 **NOTES:** No dogs (ex guide dogs) No smoking in restaurant Civ Wed 40
**CARDS:**

### ★★77% Cairn Lodge

Orchil Rd PH3 1LX
☎ 01764 662634 & 662431 📠 01764 664866
e-mail: email@cairnlodge.co.uk
***Dir:*** *from the A9 take A824 into Auchterarder then A823 signposted Crieff & Gleneagles in approx 200yds hotel on the Y junct*
This charming hotel stands in wooded grounds on the edge of the town. A clubby atmosphere prevails, with friendly staff providing good levels of service. The smart public rooms offer a choice of lounges. Bedrooms come in a variety of sizes and styles, the four new luxury rooms providing extra quality and comfort.
**ROOMS:** 11 en suite (6 fmly) No smoking in 4 bedrooms s £60-£120; d £100-£180 (incl. bkfst) * LB **FACILITIES:** Putting green ch fac Xmas **CONF:** Thtr 20 Class 20 Board 20 Del from £80 * **PARKING:** 40 **NOTES:** No dogs No smoking in restaurant Civ Wed 50
**CARDS:**

## AVIEMORE, Highland

Map 14 NH8

### ★★★66% Aviemore Highlands

Aviemore Mountain Resort PH22 1PJ
☎ 01479 810771 📠 01479 811473
e-mail: sales@aviehighlands.demon.co.uk
***Dir:*** *off A9 signed Aviemore B9152, turn left opposite railway station around Ring road Hotel is 2nd on left*
From its position in the Aviemore centre, this modern hotel enjoys lovely views of the Cairngorms, no more so than from the

*continued*

restaurant. The bedrooms are decorated with pleasing colour schemes and are all comfortably modern in appointment.

**ROOMS:** 103 en suite (37 fmly) s £55-£65; d £80-£100 * **LB** **FACILITIES:** ch fac Xmas **CONF:** Thtr 140 Class 80 Board 60 Del from £95 * **SERVICES:** Lift **PARKING:** 140 **NOTES:** No smoking in restaurant **CARDS:**

AYR, South Ayrshire Map 10 NS32

### ★★★★67% Fairfield House

12 Fairfield Rd KA7 2AR
☎ 01292 267461 01292 261456
e-mail: reservations@fairfieldhotel.co.uk
***Dir:*** *from A77 head for Ayr South (A30). Follow signs for the town centre, down Miller Road and turn left then right into Fairfield Road*

This peaceful Victorian mansion has unrestricted views across the promenade towards the Firth of Clyde. Stylish public areas include a smart restaurant and club-style lounges. Drinks and informal meals are available in the conservatory bar/brasserie. Bedrooms range from splendid spacious rooms, furnished in period style, to the attractive modern rooms in the new extension.
**ROOMS:** 40 en suite 4 annexe en suite (3 fmly) No smoking in 7 bedrooms s £95-£135; d £125-£165 (incl. cont bkfst) * **LB** **FACILITIES:** STV Indoor swimming (H) Sauna Solarium Gym Jacuzzi Xmas **CONF:** Thtr 150 Class 60 Board 60 Del £130 * **SERVICES:** Lift **PARKING:** 52 **NOTES:** No smoking in restaurant Civ Wed 110 **CARDS:**

### ★★★71% Savoy Park

16 Racecourse Rd KA7 2UT
☎ 01292 266112 01292 611488
e-mail: mail@savoypark.com
***Dir:*** *from A77 follow Holmston Road(A70)for 2m, go through Parkhouse Street and turn left into Beresford Terrace, take first right onto Bellevue Road*
This is a well-established hotel that retains many of its traditional values. Public rooms feature impressive panelled walls, ornate ceilings and open fires. The restaurant is reminiscent of a Highland

continued

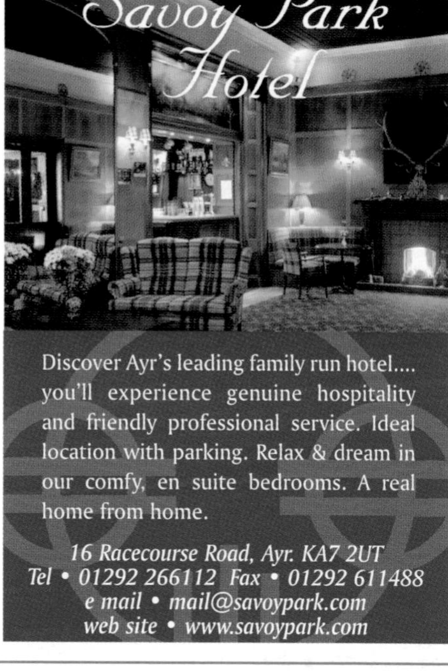
Savoy Park Hotel
Discover Ayr's leading family run hotel.... you'll experience genuine hospitality and friendly professional service. Ideal location with parking. Relax & dream in our comfy, en suite bedrooms. A real home from home.
16 Racecourse Road, Ayr. KA7 2UT
Tel • 01292 266112 Fax • 01292 611488
e mail • mail@savoypark.com
web site • www.savoypark.com

shooting lodge. Bedrooms and bathrooms are all contemporary in style with colourful decor and fabrics.

**ROOMS:** 15 en suite (3 fmly) No smoking in all bedrooms s £60-£75; d £80-£95 (incl. bkfst) * **LB** **FACILITIES:** STV ch fac Xmas **CONF:** Thtr 50 Class 40 Board 30 Del from £80 * **PARKING:** 60 **NOTES:** No smoking in restaurant Civ Wed 80 **CARDS:**

*See advert on this page*

### ★★★60% Quality Hotel Ayr

Burns Statue Square KA7 3AT
☎ 01292 263268 01292 262293
e-mail: admin@gb624.u-net.com
***Dir:*** *A70 from South/A77 from North-coming into Holmston Rd follow one way system round to front of hotel*
This Victorian railway hotel sits right by the station in the centre of town. Bedrooms are spacious, with high ceilings and large

continued on p694

AYR, continued

windows; all have modern amenities and the Premier Rooms are particularly well-equipped.
**ROOMS:** 74 en suite (18 fmly) No smoking in 31 bedrooms s £71-£83; d £83-£98 * **LB** **FACILITIES:** **Spa** STV Sauna Solarium Gym Xmas **CONF:** Thtr 250 Class 120 Board 100 Del £90 * **SERVICES:** Lift **PARKING:** 50 **NOTES:** No smoking in restaurant Civ Wed 120
**CARDS:**

### ★★ Ladyburn
KA19 7SG
☎ 01655 740585 01655 740580
e-mail: jhdh@ladyburn.freeserve.co.uk
(For full entry see Maybole)

### ★★72% Grange
37 Carrick Rd KA7 2RD
☎ 01292 265679 01292 285061
e-mail: grangehotel.ayr@btinternet.com
***Dir:*** *0.5m from rail station & city centre, turn off A77 at A713 into Ayr, straight through rdbt 0.25m to Chalmers Rd, at the end turn right hotel 100yds*
Located in a residential area, within walking distance of both the town centre and the seafront, this hotel provides friendly and attentive service. Bedrooms are individually styled, and public areas include an open-plan lounge bar and dining area. Well-presented meals regularly feature local seafood.
**ROOMS:** 8 en suite (2 fmly) s £30-£40; d £60-£80 (incl. bkfst) * **LB** **FACILITIES:** Xmas **CONF:** Thtr 100 Class 50 Board 24 **PARKING:** 25
**CARDS:**

### ★★71% Carrick Lodge
46 Carrick Rd KA7 2RE
☎ 01292 262846 01292 611101
e-mail: margaret@carricklodgehotel.co.uk
***Dir:*** *from A77, take A79 until T-junct, then right, hotel on left*
This family-run hotel on the south side of Ayr offers friendly, attentive service in a relaxed atmosphere. The bar is divided into two areas, one attractively wood-panelled, and is popular for freshly cooked meals. There is a formal dining room and a separate suite for private functions. Bedrooms are bright and cheerful.
**ROOMS:** 8 en suite (3 fmly) s £40-£48; d £60-£60 (incl. bkfst) * **FACILITIES:** Xmas **CONF:** Board 50 **PARKING:** 16 **NOTES:** No dogs (ex guide dogs) No smoking in restaurant **CARDS:**

## BALLACHULISH, Highland — Map 14 NN05

### ★★★71% Ballachulish Hotel
PH49 4JY
☎ 01855 811606 01855 821463
e-mail: reservations@freedomglen.co.uk
***Dir:*** *on A828, Fort William-Oban road 3m N of Glencoe*
A relaxed and welcoming atmosphere prevails at this long established holiday hotel which overlooks Loch Linnhe. Inviting public areas include a spacious and comfortable lounge, informal supper room, and a cocktail bar adjacent to the bold and attractive restaurant. Bedrooms vary in size and in style but all are comfortably appointed.
**ROOMS:** 54 en suite (4 fmly) s £65-£190; d £130-£190 (incl. bkfst & dinner) * **LB** **FACILITIES:** **Spa** Complimentary Membership of LeisureClub at nearby sister hotel entertainment Xmas **CONF:** Thtr 100 Class 50 Board 30 **PARKING:** 50 **NOTES:** No smoking in restaurant Closed 9-23 Dec & 5-27 Jan Civ Wed 80 **CARDS:**

*See advert on opposite page*

## BALLANTRAE, South Ayrshire — Map 10 NX08

**Premier Collection**

### ★★★ Glenapp Castle
KA26 0NZ
☎ 01465 831212 01465 831000
e-mail: enquiries@glenappcastle.com
Impressively restored over a six year period, this magnificent castle lies in well tended grounds and gardens south of the village, and provides fine views over Ailsa Craig and Arran. The all-inclusive price covers a set five-course dinner with matched wines, and afternoon tea, aperitifs and liqueurs. The delightful bedrooms are graced with antiques and period pieces and there are a number of suites. Service is both attentive and welcoming.
**ROOMS:** 17 en suite (2 fmly) No smoking in 5 bedrooms s £300-£390; d £410-£500 (incl. bkfst & dinner) * **FACILITIES:** STV Golf Tennis (hard) Croquet lawn ch fac **CONF:** Thtr 34 Class 12 Board 12 Del from £300 * **SERVICES:** Lift **PARKING:** 20 **NOTES:** No smoking in restaurant Closed Nov-Mar Civ Wed 34
**CARDS:**

*See advert on opposite page*

## BALLATER, Aberdeenshire — Map 15 NO39

### ★★★76% Darroch Learg
Braemar Rd AB35 5UX
☎ 013397 55443 013397 55252
e-mail: nigel@darrochlearg.co.uk
***Dir:*** *hotel situated on the A93, at western edge of Ballater*
This charming hotel stands in four acres of wooded grounds and enjoys a superb outlook. Public rooms are particularly comfortable and include an inviting drawing room and separate smoke room. The main focal point is the attractive conservatory restaurant where innovative modern Scottish cuisine is served. Some of the bedrooms have four-poster beds; all are comfortable and individual in style.
**ROOMS:** 13 en suite 5 annexe en suite No smoking in all bedrooms **CONF:** Thtr 25 Board 12 Del from £95 * **PARKING:** 25 **NOTES:** No smoking in restaurant Closed Xmas & Jan (ex New Year)
**CARDS:**

Popped the question? Hotels with Civ Wed in their entry are licensed for civil wedding ceremonies. Maximum numbers for the ceremony only are shown, e.g. Civ Wed 120

## Premier Collection

**★★ Balgonie Country House**

Braemar Place AB35 5NQ

☎ 013397 55482 📠 013397 55482

e-mail: balgoniech@aol.com

***Dir:** turn off A93 [Aberdeen - Perth] on western outskirts of village of Ballater, hotel is sign-posted*

This charming Edwardian style country house is a peaceful haven set in secluded gardens, with views of Glen Muick. A short walk from the village, this house is impeccably maintained and has a friendly atmosphere. Comfortable bedrooms come in two styles, period or contemporary. There is a cosy bar with an adjoining lounge. Food is foremost at Balgonie, from the excellent breakfasts to the scrumptious

*continued on p696*

BALLATER, continued

afternoon teas and daily-changing four course dinners. Service is exemplary.
**ROOMS:** 9 en suite s £70-£75; d £120-£125 (incl. bkfst) * LB **FACILITIES:** Croquet lawn Xmas **PARKING:** 12 **NOTES:** No dogs (ex guide dogs) No smoking in restaurant Closed 6 Jan-Feb
**CARDS:**

★★70% **Loch Kinord**
Ballater Rd, Dinnet AB34 5JY
☎ 013398 85229 013398 87007
e-mail: info@lochkinord.com
***Dir:*** *on A93, in the village of Dinnet*
A small family-run hotel situated between Aboyne and Ballater, well-located for leisure and sporting pursuits. It has lots of character and a friendly atmosphere. There is a cosy bar and adjoining dining room where a good range of enjoyable dishes is served.
**ROOMS:** 11 rms (9 en suite) (3 fmly) s £30-£60; d £40-£70 (incl. bkfst) * LB **FACILITIES:** Sauna Jacuzzi ch fac Xmas **CONF:** Thtr 40 Class 30 Board 30 Del from £60 * **PARKING:** 20 **NOTES:** No smoking in restaurant **CARDS:**

MINOTEL Great Britain

BALLOCH, West Dunbartonshire Map 10 NS38

★★★★★66% **Cameron House Hotel**
G83 8QZ
☎ 01389 755565 01389 759522
e-mail: devere.cameron@airtime.co.uk
***Dir:*** *from M8 (W) junct 30 for Erskine Bridge. Then A82 for Crainlarich. After 14m, at rdbt signed Luss straight on towards Luss, hotel on right*
This impressive mansion house, which has been sympathetically extended, enjoys a glorious setting beside the picturesque shore of Loch Lomond. Reception rooms are spacious and comfortable with a good choice of bar and food options available. The elegant and formal Georgian Room offers fine dining. Bedrooms range from luxury suites to the standard rooms, all tasteful in appointment and comfortably furnished.
**ROOMS:** 96 en suite (9 fmly) No smoking in all bedrooms **FACILITIES:** STV Indoor swimming (H) Golf 9 Tennis (hard) Fishing Squash Snooker Sauna Solarium Gym Croquet lawn Jacuzzi Whole range of outdoor sports entertainment ch fac Xmas **CONF:** Thtr 300 Class 80 Board 80 Del from £180 * **SERVICES:** Lift **PARKING:** 250 **NOTES:** No dogs (ex guide dogs) Civ Wed 180
**CARDS:**

De Vere Hotels

Late for dinner? Quality Standards star rating means that last orders for dinner should be no earlier than:
★ 6.30pm ★★ 7.00pm ★★★ 8.00pm
★★★★ 9.00pm ★★★★★ 10.00pm

○ **Innkeeper's Lodge Loch Lomond**
Balloch Rd G83 8LQ
A new concept in the travel accommodation market. Smart rooms meet essential business requirements but also have home comforts. Dining options include all-day menus plus the added advantage of breakfast, which is included in the room price. Reservations can be made seven days a week through the room reservations number: 0870 243 0500. For further details, consult the Hotel Groups page.
**ROOMS:** 15 en suite **NOTES:** Opening Autumn 2001

Innkeeper's Lodge

BALQUHIDDER, Stirling Map 11 NN52

★★72% **Monachyle Mhor**
FK19 8PQ
☎ 01877 384622 01877 384305
e-mail: info@monachylemhor.com
***Dir:*** *11m N of Callander on A84, turn right at Kingshouse Hotel this road takes you under the A84 towards Balquhidder, the hotel is 6m on the right*

Many guests return to this charming country hotel where a truly warm welcome and delicious food are assured. Set amid a 2000 acre estate, the hotel is in the heart of the picturesque Braes of Balquhidder. Public areas include a cosy snug bar and a relaxing sitting room, each warmed by welcoming open fires. The adjacent conservatory restaurant provides an appropriate setting for the innovative fixed-price menu. Bedrooms, including those in the rear courtyard wing, combine traditional styles with modern day amenities.
**ROOMS:** 5 en suite 5 annexe en suite No smoking in all bedrooms s £55-£75; d £75-£95 (incl. bkfst) * **FACILITIES:** Fishing Xmas **PARKING:** 20 **NOTES:** No dogs (ex guide dogs) No children 12yrs No smoking in restaurant **CARDS:**

BANCHORY, Aberdeenshire Map 15 NO69

★★★78% **Raemoir House**
Raemoir AB31 4ED
☎ 01330 824884 01330 822171
e-mail: raemoirhse@aol.com
***Dir:*** *take the A93 to Banchory turn right onto the A980, to Torphins, main drive is 2m ahead at T-junct*
A fine country mansion set in parkland which is part of a 3,500-acre estate. Gracious public rooms include a choice of sitting rooms, a cocktail bar and a Georgian dining room. These rooms have tapestry-covered walls, open fires, and fine antiques, all

Scotland's Hotels of Distinction

*continued*

reflecting the elegance of yesteryear. The bedrooms are individual in style and size.

**ROOMS:** 14 en suite 6 annexe en suite (1 fmly) s £60-£80; d £90-£120 (incl. bkfst) * **LB** **FACILITIES:** Golf 9 Tennis (hard) Croquet lawn Putting green Shooting Stalking ch fac **CONF:** Thtr 40 Class 50 Board 30 Del from £98.50 * **PARKING:** 100 **NOTES:** No smoking in restaurant Civ Wed 50 **CARDS:**

### ★★★78% Tor-na-Coille

AB31 4AB
☎ 01330 822242 🖷 01330 824012
e-mail: tornacoille@btinternet.com
***Dir:*** *on the main A93 Aberdeen/Braemar road, 0.5m west of Banchory town centre, opposite golf course*

This fine granite-stone house sits in tree-studded grounds on the west side of the town. Inviting public areas include a lovely sitting room and an elegant restaurant. Bedrooms come in a variety of styles and sizes, many mirroring the period charm of the house.
**ROOMS:** 22 en suite (4 fmly) No smoking in 17 bedrooms s £55-£75; d £110-£130 (incl. bkfst) * **LB** **FACILITIES:** Squash Croquet lawn entertainment ch fac Xmas **CONF:** Thtr 90 Class 60 Board 30 Del from £75 * **SERVICES:** Lift **PARKING:** 130 **NOTES:** No smoking in restaurant Closed 25-28 Dec Civ Wed 95 **CARDS:**

### ★★★74% Banchory Lodge

AB31 5HS
☎ 01330 822625 🖷 01330 825019
e-mail: enquiries@banchorylodge.co.uk
***Dir:*** *off A93 13m west of Aberdeen*
Long-established, this hotel enjoys a picture postcard setting in grounds by the River Dee. Inviting public areas include two lounges, a cosy bar and a restaurant giving views of the rivers Dee and Feugh. There is a choice of bedroom styles, the individual rooms in the original house, or huge rooms in a modern wing.
**ROOMS:** 22 en suite (11 fmly) s £60-£75; d £90-£110 (incl. bkfst) * **LB** **FACILITIES:** Fishing Pool room ch fac Xmas **CONF:** Thtr 30 Class 30 Board 28 Del from £95 * **PARKING:** 50 **NOTES:** No smoking in restaurant Closed 5-10 Jan Civ Wed 50 **CARDS:**

### ★★68% Burnett Arms

Best Western

25 High St AB31 5TD
☎ 01330 824944 🖷 01330 825553
e-mail: theburnett@totalise.co.uk
***Dir:*** *town centre on north side of A93, 18m from centre of Aberdeen*

KEEP

This popular, town centre hotel offers comfortably modern and well equipped bedrooms. A variety of meals can be enjoyed not only in the dining room but in the bar and foyer lounge.
**ROOMS:** 16 en suite s £56; d £78 (incl. bkfst) * **LB** **FACILITIES:** STV Xmas **CONF:** Thtr 100 Class 50 Board 50 Del from £85 * **PARKING:** 40 **NOTES:** No smoking in restaurant Civ Wed 100
**CARDS:**

*See advert under ABERDEEN*

## BANFF, Aberdeenshire — Map 15 NJ66

### ★★★67% Banff Springs

Golden Knowes Rd AB45 2JE
☎ 01261 812881 🖷 01261 815546
e-mail: info@banffspringshotel.co.uk
***Dir:*** *western outskirts of the town overlooking the beach on the A98 Banff to Inverness road*
A warm welcome is assured at this comfortable business and tourist hotel which enjoys lovely sea views. Bedrooms have pleasing colour schemes and are comfortably modern in appointment. Public areas include a smart foyer lounge and a popular bar/bistro which provides an informal dining alternative to the restaurant. A fitness room is also available.
**ROOMS:** 31 en suite **FACILITIES:** STV Gym ch fac Xmas **CONF:** Thtr 400 Class 100 Board 40 Del from £48.95 * **PARKING:** 200 **NOTES:** No smoking in restaurant **CARDS:**

## BARRA, ISLE OF, Western Isles — Map 13

## TANGASDALE — Map 13 NF60

### ★★67% Isle of Barra

Tangasdale Beach HS9 5XW
☎ 01871 810383 🖷 01871 810385
e-mail: barrahotel@aol.com
***Dir:*** *turn left after leaving ferry terminal on to the A888, hotel is 2m on the left*
Overlooking the white sands of Halaman Bay and the Atlantic Ocean beyond, this modern hotel is in a stunning location. Public areas, including a comfortable lounge and light and airy restaurant, make the most of the views, as do most of the bedrooms. The restaurant features local shellfish; and service is both friendly and attentive.
**ROOMS:** 30 en suite (2 fmly) s £62; d £112 (incl. bkfst & dinner) * **LB** **FACILITIES:** STV ch fac Xmas **CONF:** Class 70 Board 60 Del from £48 * **PARKING:** 50 **NOTES:** No smoking in restaurant Closed mid Oct-Mar exc Xmas & New Year **CARDS:**

B

## BARRHEAD, East Renfrewshire Map 11 NS45

### ★★★71% Dalmeny Park Country House
Lochlibo Rd G78 1LG
☎ 0141 881 9211 📠 0141 881 9214
e-mail: enquires@maksu-group.co.uk
***Dir:*** *on A736 towards Glasgow*
This well-established hotel stands in seven acres of delightful gardens on the outskirts of the town. The stylish bedrooms offer good comfort and quality as well as many thoughtful extras. The hotel is well-equipped for both business and leisure markets and is also popular as a wedding venue.
**ROOMS:** 20 en suite (2 fmly) No smoking in 2 bedrooms s £70-£95; d £95-£120 (incl. bkfst) * **FACILITIES:** STV Jacuzzi Xmas **CONF:** Thtr 250 Class 100 Board 60 Del from £95 * **PARKING:** 150 **NOTES:** Civ Wed 200 **CARDS:**

## BATHGATE, West Lothian Map 11 NS96

### ★★★67% Cairn Hotel
Blackburn Rd EH48 2EL
☎ 01506 633366 📠 01506 633444
***Dir:*** *M8 exit 3A (Eastbound) , at rdbt 1st left, next rdbt 2nd left, small rdbt straight on then 1st slip rd signed Blackburn, at T-junct turn right, hotel next right*
Smart, stylish public areas with ample comfortable seating, plus an attractive restaurant, are features of this modern business hotel. Bedrooms, though not large, reflect a similar standard and are well-equipped. There are also several meeting rooms.
**ROOMS:** 61 en suite (2 fmly) No smoking in 49 bedrooms s £55-£89; d £110-£178 (incl. bkfst) * LB **FACILITIES:** STV Xmas **CONF:** Thtr 250 Class 100 Board 50 Del from £95 * **SERVICES:** Lift **PARKING:** 150 **NOTES:** Civ Wed 200 **CARDS:**

### ⇧ Express by Holiday Inn Livingston
Express by Holiday Inn
Starlaw Rd EH48 1LQ
☎ 01506 650650 📠 01506 650651
***Dir:*** *M8 junct3A. Follow sliproad to 1st rdbt, take 1st exit (Bathgate). Continue on road, over bridge. At 2nd rdbt take 1st exit & hotel 200yrds on left*

A modern budget hotel offering comfortable accommodation in refreshing, spacious and comprehensively equipped bedrooms, en suite bathrooms with power showers and continental buffet breakfast included in the room rate. Suitable for business travellers or families. For further details and the Express by Holiday Inn phone number, consult the Hotel Groups page.
**ROOMS:** 74 en suite (incl. cont bkfst) s fr £52.50; d fr £52.50 * **CONF:** Thtr 25 Class 18 Board 20

Weekend away? Hotels with LB in their entry offer leisure breaks.

## BEAULY, Highland Map 14 NH54

### ★★★72% Priory
The Square IV4 7BX
☎ 01463 782309 📠 01463 782531
e-mail: reservations@priory-hotel.com
***Dir:*** *signposted from A832, into village of Beauly, hotel in village square on left*
A welcoming atmosphere prevails at this popular hotel which occupies a prime position in the village square. Bedrooms are comfortably modern in appointment and offer a good range of amenities. The tastefully appointed open plan public areas include a relaxing foyer lounge and a spacious split-level restaurant.
**ROOMS:** 34 en suite (3 fmly) No smoking in 9 bedrooms s £39.50-£47.50; d £85-£95 (incl. bkfst) * LB **FACILITIES:** STV Snooker Xmas **CONF:** Thtr 40 Class 40 Board 30 Del from £60 * **SERVICES:** Lift **PARKING:** 20 **NOTES:** No smoking in restaurant **CARDS:**

## BIGGAR, South Lanarkshire Map 11 NT03

### ★★★73% ®® Shieldhill Castle
Quothquan ML12 6NA
☎ 01899 220035 📠 01899 221092
e-mail: enquiries@shieldhill.co.uk
***Dir:*** *turn off A702 onto B7016 Biggar to Carnwath Rd in the middle of Biggar, after 2m turn left into Shieldhill rd, Hotel 1.5m on right*
Dating back in parts to 1199, with a 'new' wing built in 1826, this fortified mansion house has peaceful views of rolling countryside. Bedrooms are generally spacious and include a number of large, luxurious suites. An oak-panelled lounge leads into the Chancellor restaurant, where fresh local ingredients form the basis of award-winning cuisine.
**ROOMS:** 16 en suite No smoking in all bedrooms **FACILITIES:** Croquet lawn Jacuzzi Cycling Clay shoot Hot air ballooning ch fac Xmas **CONF:** Thtr 500 Class 200 Board 250 **PARKING:** 25 **NOTES:** No smoking in restaurant Civ Wed 250 **CARDS:**

## BLAIR ATHOLL, Perth & Kinross Map 14 NN86

### ★★70% Atholl Arms
Old North Rd PH18 5SG
☎ 01796 481205 📠 01796 481550
e-mail: hotel@athollarms.u-net.com
***Dir:*** *off main A9 to B8079, 1m into Blair Atholl, hotel is situated in the village near entrance to Blair Castle*
Set close to the railway station and Blair Castle, this long-established hotel is enjoying a renaissance under new ownership. Welcoming public rooms include a choice of bars, as well as a splendid baronial-style dining room. Bedrooms come in mixed sizes and styles, all having a good range of amenities.
**ROOMS:** 30 en suite (3 fmly) s £30-£60; d £40-£75 (incl. bkfst) * LB **FACILITIES:** Fishing Rough shooting, fishing ch fac Xmas **CONF:** Thtr 140 Class 80 Board 60 Del from £55 * **PARKING:** 130 **NOTES:** No smoking in restaurant **CARDS:**

### ★★62% Bridge of Tilt
Bridge of Tilt PH18 5SU
☎ 01796 481333 📠 01796 481335
***Dir:*** *turn off A9 onto B8079, hotel is 0.75m on left, with wishing well in front*
Focusing mainly on tour groups, this friendly hotel is situated close to Blair Castle. Bedrooms come in a variety of styles, with the chalet rooms being particularly popular. Public areas include a bar

continued

with a lounge and dining areas leading off. Live entertainment is provided three times a week in season.
**ROOMS:** 20 en suite 7 annexe en suite (7 fmly) s £25-£40; d £50-£80 (incl. bkfst) * LB **FACILITIES:** Fishing Jacuzzi Entertainment entertainment ch fac Xmas **PARKING:** 40 **NOTES:** No smoking in restaurant Closed Jan **CARDS:**

## BLAIRGOWRIE, Perth & Kinross — Map 15 NO14

see also Coupar Angus

### Premier Collection

**★★★ Kinloch House**
PH10 6SG
☎ 01250 884237 01250 884333
e-mail: info@kinlochhouse.com
***Dir:*** *3m W on A923*
This country house hotel is peacefully set in its own extensive grounds and enjoys fine country views. Public areas lead off from the beautiful oak-panelled hall and include a spacious conservatory and well-stocked bar with an endless range of malt whiskies, a relaxing lounge and an elegant restaurant. Individually styled bedrooms are thoughtfully equipped and offer high levels of quality and comfort. Smart leisure facilities are exclusive to the hotel guests.
**ROOMS:** 20 en suite s £90-£175; d £195-£280 (incl. bkfst & dinner) * LB **FACILITIES:** Spa Indoor swimming (H) Fishing Sauna Gym Croquet lawn Sailing Cycling ch fac Xmas **CONF:** Thtr 16 Class 14 Board 20 Del from £150 * **PARKING:** 40 **NOTES:** No smoking in restaurant Closed 18-29 Dec **CARDS:**

**★★★61% Angus**
46 Wellmeadow PH10 6NQ
☎ 01250 872455 01250 875615
e-mail: reservations@angushotel.com
***Dir:*** *on the main A93 Perth/Blairgowrie Rd overlooking the Wellmeadow in the town centre*
A constantly improving town centre hotel which remains popular with visiting tour groups. Bedrooms are modern and come in a variety of sizes. There is a spacious bar lounge and a restaurant offering a good value menus.
**ROOMS:** 81 en suite (4 fmly) s £45-£60; d £90-£120 (incl. bkfst) * LB **FACILITIES:** Indoor swimming (H) Sauna Solarium Jacuzzi entertainment Xmas **CONF:** Thtr 200 Class 100 Board 50 Del from £45 * **SERVICES:** Lift **PARKING:** 62 **NOTES:** No smoking in restaurant Civ Wed 150 **CARDS:**

Need to unwind? Look out for hotels with Spa in their entry.

## BOAT OF GARTEN, Highland — Map 14 NH91

**★★★70% Boat**
PH24 3BH
☎ 01479 831258 01479 831414
e-mail: holidays@boathotel.co.uk
***Dir:*** *turn off A9 N of Aviemore onto A95 & follow signposts to Boat of Garten*

A Victorian station hotel right next to what is now a preserved steam railway. It has been completely upgraded and offers smart bedrooms plus a restaurant with bold dark colour schemes and dinner that follows a similar modern route.
**ROOMS:** 32 en suite (1 fmly) No smoking in 22 bedrooms s £60; d £90 (incl. bkfst) * LB **FACILITIES:** Snooker Xmas **CONF:** Thtr 50 Class 35 Board 25 Del from £75 * **PARKING:** 36 **NOTES:** No smoking in restaurant RS Jan(3weeks) Civ Wed 60 **CARDS:**

BOTHWELL, South Lanarkshire Map 11 NS75

### ★★★67% Bothwell Bridge

89 Main St G71 8EU
☎ 01698 852246 01698 854686
**Dir:** *turn off M74 at junct 5 & follow signs to Uddingston, turn right at mini-rdbt. Hotel located just past shops on left*

HOTEL

This red sandstone mansion house is a popular business, function and conference centre. The bedrooms are mostly spacious and all are well-equipped. The conservatory drawing room provides comfortable seating and a versatile, informal, bar/meal operation. A more formal dining experience is offered in the restaurant, which has a strong Italian influence.
**ROOMS:** 90 en suite (14 fmly) No smoking in 14 bedrooms s £58-£63; d £68-£75 (incl. bkfst) * LB **FACILITIES:** STV entertainment Xmas **CONF:** Thtr 200 Class 80 Board 50 Del from £85 * **SERVICES:** Lift **PARKING:** 125 **NOTES:** No dogs (ex guide dogs)
**CARDS:**

*See advert on page 699*

BOWMORE See Islay, Isle of

BRAEMAR, Aberdeenshire Map 15 NO19

### ★★★67% The Invercauld Arms

PEEL HOTELS

AB35 5YR
☎ 013397 41605 013397 41428
e-mail: info@invercauldarms-hotel-braemar.com
**Dir:** *Follow A39 from both North(Aberdeen) & South(Perth/Dundee), hotel is situated on main road in village*

Colourful flowering baskets adorn the façade of this impressive Victorian hotel on the eastern edge of the village. Spacious public areas are comfortably traditional in style and include a choice of lounges, a tartan themed bar, and an attractive dining room. Bedrooms come in a variety of sizes, all being smart and comfortable.
**ROOMS:** 68 en suite (10 fmly) No smoking in 18 bedrooms s £85; d £110 (incl. bkfst) * **FACILITIES:** STV Xmas ch fac **CONF:** Thtr 50 Class 30 Board 26 Del from £65 * **SERVICES:** Lift **PARKING:** 60 **NOTES:** No smoking in restaurant **CARDS:**

### ★★72% *Braemar Lodge*

Glenshee Rd AB35 5YQ
☎ 013397 41627 013397 41627
**Dir:** *on the A93 south approach to Braemar*
This welcoming small hotel stands in its own well-tended garden on the north side of the village. Bedrooms are bright and airy with pleasing colour schemes and comfortable furnishings. Welcoming log fires burn on the cooler evenings in the well-stocked bar and in the adjacent lounge. Carefully prepared and substantial meals are served in the attractive restaurant.
**ROOMS:** 7 rms (6 en suite) (2 fmly) No smoking in all bedrooms
**PARKING:** 16 **NOTES:** No smoking in restaurant
**CARDS:**

BRECHIN, Angus Map 15 NO66

### ★★64% *Northern*

2/4 Clerk St DD9 6AE
☎ 01356 625505 01356 622714
e-mail: northernhotel@uku.co.uk
**Dir:** *hotel 1m from St Annes junction (north) on A90 Trunk Road, and 1.5m from Keithock junction A90 (south)*
This long-established commercial hotel is conveniently situated in the centre of town. The first floor bedrooms are comfortable and well-appointed. Public areas (alterations planned for 2001) include a choice of contrasting bars and a smart restaurant where the menus offer a varied choice at competitive prices.
**ROOMS:** 16 en suite (1 fmly) No smoking in 10 bedrooms **CONF:** Thtr 120 Class 80 Board 40 **PARKING:** 20 **NOTES:** No smoking in restaurant
**CARDS:**

BRIDGEND See Islay, Isle of

BRIDGE OF ALLAN, Stirling Map 11 NS79

### ★★★69% Royal

Best Western

Henderson St FK9 4HG
☎ 01786 832284 01786 834377
e-mail: stay@royal-stirling.co.uk
**Dir:** *M9 ,junct 11, right at rdbt for Bridge of Allan. Hotel is in the centre of Bridge of Allan on the left hand side*

This impressive Victorian hotel offers a welcoming atmosphere together with a fine dining experience. Bedrooms are comfortably modern in style and offer a good range of amenities. Public areas include a relaxing oak-panelled lounge, well stocked bar, and an elegant restaurant offering innovative Scottish fare from both the carte and fixed price menus.
**ROOMS:** 32 en suite (4 fmly) No smoking in 6 bedrooms s £70-£85; d £90-£130 (incl. bkfst) * LB **FACILITIES:** STV Xmas **CONF:** Thtr 150 Class 60 Board 50 Del from £105 * **SERVICES:** Lift **PARKING:** 40 **NOTES:** No dogs (ex guide dogs) No smoking in restaurant Civ Wed 100
**CARDS:**

## BRIDGE OF ORCHY, Argyll & Bute Map 10 NN23

**★★76% @@ Bridge of Orchy Hotel**

PA36 4AD
☎ 01838 400208 📠 01838 400313
e-mail: info@bridgeoforchy.co.uk
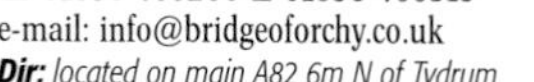
***Dir:*** *located on main A82 6m N of Tydrum*

BRIDGE OF ORCHY

Situated amid spectacular Highland scenery this completely refurbished hotel provides a welcoming atmosphere together with good food and modern comforts. The bedrooms have pretty colour schemes and are comfortably furnished in mixed modern styles. Public areas include a spacious lounge, a well-stocked bar and an elegant restaurant with Scottish fare.
**ROOMS:** 10 en suite (2 fmly) No smoking in all bedrooms s £53; d £85 (incl. bkfst) * **LB** **FACILITIES:** STV Fishing **CONF:** Thtr 40 Class 30 Board 20 **PARKING:** 50 **NOTES:** No dogs (ex guide dogs) No smoking in restaurant Closed 1 Dec-1 Jan **CARDS:**

## BRODICK See Arran, Isle of

## BRORA, Highland Map 14 NC90

**★★★72% @ Royal Marine**
Golf Rd KW9 6QS
☎ 01408 621252 📠 01408 621181
e-mail: highlandescape@btinternet.com
***Dir:*** *turn off A9 in village toward beach and golf course*
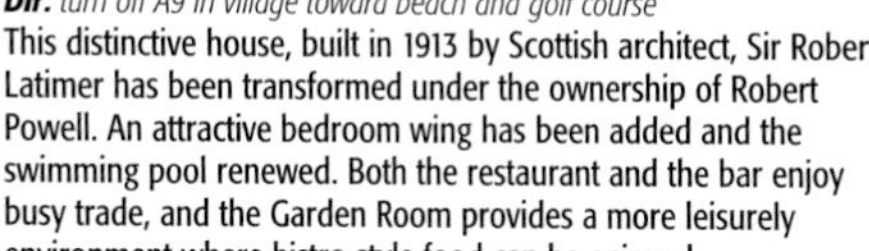
This distinctive house, built in 1913 by Scottish architect, Sir Robert Latimer has been transformed under the ownership of Robert Powell. An attractive bedroom wing has been added and the swimming pool renewed. Both the restaurant and the bar enjoy busy trade, and the Garden Room provides a more leisurely environment where bistro style food can be enjoyed.
**ROOMS:** 22 en suite (1 fmly) s £65-£85; d £98-£150 (incl. bkfst) * **LB** **FACILITIES:** STV Indoor swimming (H) Golf 18 Tennis (hard) Fishing Snooker Sauna Solarium Gym Croquet lawn Putting green Jacuzzi Ice curling rink in season Table Tennis ch fac Xmas **CONF:** Thtr 70 Class 40 Board 40 Del from £98 * **PARKING:** 40 **NOTES:** No smoking in restaurant RS Dec-Jan **CARDS:**

**★★★67% @ The Links**
Golf Rd KW9 6QS
☎ 01408 621225 📠 01408 621383
e-mail: highlandescape@btinternet.com
***Dir:*** *turn off A9 in village of Brora towards beach and golf course, hotel overlooks golf course*
This hotel occupies an enviable position overlooking the golf course towards the North Sea. The attractive bedrooms include a number of family rooms and suites. Guests can enjoy the marvellous view from the lounges and restaurant. Nearby, the

*continued*

Royal Marine Hotel, under the same ownership, offers good leisure facilities.
**ROOMS:** 23 en suite (2 fmly) s £65-£85; d £98-£150 (incl. bkfst) * **LB** **FACILITIES:** Indoor swimming (H) Fishing Snooker Sauna Solarium Gym Croquet lawn Putting green Jacuzzi Xmas **CONF:** Thtr 100 Class 40 Board 20 Del from £98 * **PARKING:** 55 **NOTES:** No smoking in restaurant Closed 31 Oct-Mar RS Apr/Oct (dinner may be in sister hotel) Civ Wed 100 **CARDS:**

## BROUGHTY FERRY, Dundee City Map 12 NO43

***Premier Lodge (Dundee East)***

PREMIER LODGE
115-117 Lawers Dr, Panmurefield DD5 3TS
☎ 0870 700 1360 📠 0870 770 1361
Premier Lodge offers modern, well-equipped, en suite accommodation suitable for both business and leisure travellers. Meals can be taken at the adjacent popular restaurant and bar, which is fully licensed. For further details, consult the Hotel Groups page.
**ROOMS:** 60 en suite

## BURNTISLAND, Fife Map 11 NT28

**★★67% Inchview Hotel**

THE CIRCLE
Selected Individual Hotels
GREAT BRITAIN
69 Kinghorn Rd KY3 9EB
☎ 01592 872239 📠 01592 874866
e-mail: inchview@msn.com
***Dir:*** *on A921 on entering Burntisland head towards town centre, hotel overlooks The Links on Kinghorn Road*
A welcoming atmosphere prevails at this family-run hotel, a listed Georgian terraced house, which looks out over the links to the Firth of Forth. Bedrooms, which vary in size and in style, offer modern comforts together with the expected amenities. The well-stocked bar offers a varied selection of meals, and in the restaurant more adventurous fare is provided.
**ROOMS:** 12 en suite (1 fmly) No smoking in 4 bedrooms s £42.50-£52.50; d £69.50-£71.50 (incl. bkfst) * **LB** **FACILITIES:** Xmas **CONF:** Thtr 60 Class 20 Board 20 Del from £70 * **PARKING:** 15 **CARDS:**

## CAIRNDOW, Argyll & Bute Map 10 NN11

**★★67% *Cairndow Stagecoach Inn***
THE CIRCLE
Selected Individual Hotels
GREAT BRITAIN
PA26 8BN
☎ 01499 600286 📠 01499 600220
e-mail: cairndinn@aol.com
***Dir:*** *from Tarbet take A83 pass Dunoon Junction to Cairndow village*

There's a relaxed atmosphere at this 18th-century inn which overlooks Loch Fyne. Characterful public areas include a comfortable beamed lounge, a well stocked bar where food is served throughout the day, and a restaurant with conservatory

*continued on p702*

CAIRNDOW, continued

extension. Bedrooms, including two superior rooms with large spa baths, are modern in style and offer expected amenities.
**ROOMS:** 13 en suite (2 fmly) No smoking in 3 bedrooms
**FACILITIES:** Sauna Solarium Gym **PARKING:** 32
**CARDS:**

C

## CALLANDER, Stirling
Map 11 NN60

### ★★★75% *Roman Camp Country House*
FK17 8BG
☎ 01877 330003 01877 331533
e-mail: mail@roman-camp-hotel.co.uk
***Dir:*** *heading north on the A84 turn left at the east end of Callander High Street, down a 300 yard driveway into the hotel grounds*

A warm welcome is assured at this comfortable country hotel, peacefully set beside the River Teith. Day rooms include charming lounges and an elegant tapestry-hung dining room. The innovative menu offers highly accomplished, modern cooking. Bedrooms are individual in style and offer many thoughtful extras.
**ROOMS:** 14 en suite (3 fmly) **FACILITIES:** Fishing **CONF:** Thtr 100 Class 40 Board 20 **PARKING:** 80 **NOTES:** No smoking in restaurant
**CARDS:**

### ★★74% Lubnaig
Leny Feus FK17 8AS
☎ 01877 330376 01877 330376
e-mail: reception@lubnaighotel.co.uk
***Dir:*** *travelling W on the A84 through main street of Callander to the W outskirts, turn right into Leny Feus, just after Poppies sign*
A welcoming and secluded hotel set in delightful gardens with an atmosphere of warmth and relaxation. The three cosy lounges and a delightful dining room all look out over the garden. The hotel's carte menu provides a good choice of dishes prepared from fine Scottish produce, complimented by a wide range of malt whiskies. Bedrooms are immaculate and very well-appointed; ground floor rooms are available.
**ROOMS:** 6 en suite 4 annexe en suite s fr £30; d £60-£78 (incl. bkfst) * **LB** **PARKING:** 10 **NOTES:** No dogs No children 7yrs No smoking in restaurant Closed Nov-Etr RS Apr (B&B only) **CARDS:**

### ★★65% Bridgend House
Bridgend FK17 8AH
☎ 01877 330130 01877 331512
e-mail: bridgendhotel@hotmail.com
***Dir:*** *proceed down Callander main street, turn onto A81 (Aberfoyle rd) over red sandstone bridge, hotel on right*
Easily recognised by its black and white façade, this is a welcoming hotel alongside the River Teith. Public areas include a popular bar, comfortable lounge, and a dining room with an attractive new extension that overlooks the garden. The bedrooms, *continued*
two with four-posters, have good quality furnishings and all the expected amenities.
**ROOMS:** 5 en suite s £35-£40; d £50-£60 (incl. bkfst) * **LB**
**FACILITIES:** STV pool tables,darts,weekly quiz entertainment Xmas
**CONF:** Thtr 100 **PARKING:** 30 **CARDS:**

### ★★64% Dalgair House
113-115 Main St FK17 8BQ
☎ 01877 330283 01877 331114
e-mail: nieto@bt.internet.com
***Dir:*** *300 metres beyond access road to golf course on main street*

THE CIRCLE
Selected Individual Hotels
GREAT BRITAIN

Dalgair House Hotel
LICENSED RESTAURANT

A relaxed atmosphere prevails at this family-run hotel in the main street. Public areas are quite informal and include a front dining area and popular bar to the rear of the house. Bedrooms, most of which have benefited from refurbishment, are brightly decorated and comfortably furnished in pine.
**ROOMS:** 8 en suite (1 fmly) s £35-£45; d £72 (incl. bkfst) * **LB**
**FACILITIES:** STV Xmas **PARKING:** 12
**CARDS:**

## CAMPBELTOWN, Argyll & Bute
Map 10 NR72

### ★★68% Seafield
Kilkerran Rd PA28 6JL
☎ 01586 554385 01586 552741
This comfortable family-run hotel enjoys lovely views of the bay. Bedrooms, some in the garden annexe, come in various sizes and offer modern appointments along with a good range of amenities. There is a bright and comfortable open-plan foyer lounge and bar, and an extensive range of home cooked dishes are available in the attractive restaurant.
**ROOMS:** 3 en suite 6 annexe en suite s £40-£60; d £60-£75 (incl. bkfst) * **LB** **PARKING:** 11 **NOTES:** No children 14yrs No smoking in restaurant
**CARDS:**

## CARNOUSTIE, Angus
Map 12 NO53

### ★★★★69% Carnoustie Golf Resort & Spa
The Links DD7 7JE
☎ 01241 411999 01241 411998
e-mail: enquiries@carnoustie-hotel.com
***Dir:*** *Right turn into Carnoustie from A92, follow golf course signs*
This imposing hotel beside the Championship Course offers guests the facility to book tee times on the three links courses. Bedrooms range from opulent suites to superior and regular rooms, while the reception areas radiate from the smart foyer and include a restaurant overlooking the course. Other facilities include a golf shop.
**ROOMS:** 85 en suite (12 fmly) s £115-£210; d £125-£220 (incl. bkfst) * **LB** **FACILITIES:** **Spa** STV Indoor swimming (H) Sauna Gym Putting green Jacuzzi Xmas **CONF:** Thtr 350 Class 150 Board 80 Del from £145 * **SERVICES:** Lift **PARKING:** 2000 **NOTES:** No smoking in restaurant RS Xmas Civ Wed 100 **CARDS:**

**★★68% Carnoustie Links**
Links Pde DD7 7JF
☎ 01241 853273 Fax 01241 853319
e-mail: enquiries@links-hotel.com
***Dir:*** *off A92, adjoining Golf Course*
This relaxed hotel is situated opposite the 18th green of the championship course, and so has particular appeal for the visiting golfer. Bedrooms have attractive colour schemes and offer comfortable modern appointments. Relaxing public areas include a golf themed bar, lounge, restaurant and a popular golf shop.
**ROOMS:** 7 en suite (4 fmly) s fr £40; d £60-£110 (incl. bkfst) * **LB** **PARKING:** 10 **NOTES:** No smoking in restaurant **CARDS:**

**★★67% Carlogie House Hotel**
Carlogie Rd DD7 6LD
☎ 01241 853185 Fax 01241 856528
e-mail: carlogie@lineone.net
***Dir:*** *A92 from Dundee to Arbroath, right at Pambride/West Haven continue to junct with A930, then sharp right. Hotel 300yds on right*
This comfortable hotel on the north side of town is popular with visiting golfers. Although variable in size, main house bedrooms are modern in style and offer a wide range of amenities. The adjacent former stable block has been converted to provide accommodation for the disabled traveller. The adventure playground in the garden is popular with children.
**ROOMS:** 12 en suite 4 annexe en suite (2 fmly) No smoking in 12 bedrooms s £45-£55; d £60-£75 (incl. bkfst) * **LB** **FACILITIES:** STV Putting green Use of facilities at local leisure centre and Fishery **CONF:** Thtr 25 Class 25 Board 16 **PARKING:** 40 **NOTES:** Closed 1-3 Jan Civ Wed 60 **CARDS:**

## CARRBRIDGE, Highland — Map 14 NH92

**★★★68% Dalrachney Lodge**
PH23 3AT
☎ 01479 841252 Fax 01479 841383
e-mail: stay@dalrachney.co.uk
***Dir:*** *follow Carrbridge signs off main A9. Located at the North end of the village on the A938*
A warm welcome is assured at this comfortable family-run Highland hotel on the edge of the village. The well-maintained bedrooms are generally spacious and are comfortably furnished in period style. The smartly presented public areas include a comfortable and relaxing sitting room, a well-stocked bar, and attractive dining room.
**ROOMS:** 11 en suite (3 fmly) No smoking in 4 bedrooms s £45-£65; d £60-£120 (incl. bkfst) * **LB** **FACILITIES:** STV Fishing Xmas **CONF:** Thtr 16 Class 16 Board 16 Del from £75 * **PARKING:** 40 **CARDS:**

## CARRUTHERSTOWN, Dumfries & Galloway — Map 11 NY17

***★★★68% Hetland Hall*** Best Western
DG1 4JX
☎ 01387 840201 Fax 01387 840211
e-mail: hetlandhallhotel@ic24.net
***Dir:*** *midway between Annan & Dumfries on A75*
This hotel is set in extensive parkland just off the A75. Appealing to a wide market, including weddings and conferences, it offers well-equipped bedrooms in variety of styles and sizes, all enhanced by attractive fabrics.

**ROOMS:** 14 en suite 15 annexe en suite (5 fmly) No smoking in 5 bedrooms **FACILITIES:** STV Indoor swimming (H) Fishing Snooker Sauna Solarium Gym Putting green Pitch & putt Toning tables/sun beds **CONF:** Thtr 200 Class 100 Board 100 **PARKING:** 45 **NOTES:** No dogs (ex guide dogs) **CARDS:**

## CASTLE DOUGLAS, Dumfries & Galloway — Map 11 NX76

***★★70% Douglas Arms***
King St DG7 1DB
☎ 01556 502231 Fax 01556 504000
e-mail: doughot@aol.com
***Dir:*** *in centre of town, adjacent to Clock Tower*
Friendly service is guaranteed at this former coaching inn situated in the centre of the town. The comfortable lounge bar is popular for meals, or guests can eat in the intimate dining room. Bedrooms are very well-equipped.
**ROOMS:** 24 en suite (1 fmly) No smoking in 8 bedrooms
**FACILITIES:** STV **CONF:** Thtr 150 Class 40 Board 40 **PARKING:** 16
**NOTES:** No smoking in restaurant Civ Wed 100
**CARDS:**

**★★68% Urr Valley**
Ernespie Rd DG7 3JG
☎ 01556 502188 Fax 01556 504055
e-mail: info@urrvalleyhotel.co.uk
***Dir:*** *off A75 towards Castle Douglas, hotel entrance approx 0.5m on left*
Reached by a long drive, this country house is set in 14 acres of woodland a mile from town. Public areas include a wood panelled foyer lounge, bar and restaurant. Bedrooms are well-equipped and in the main spacious.
**ROOMS:** 19 rms (17 en suite) (5 fmly) s £38-£45; d £70-£85 (incl. bkfst) * **LB** **FACILITIES:** STV ch fac Xmas **CONF:** Thtr 200 Class 100 Board 50 Del from £70 * **PARKING:** 100 **NOTES:** No smoking in restaurant **CARDS:**

**★★66% Imperial**
35 King St DG7 1AA
☎ 01556 502086 Fax 01556 503009
e-mail: david@thegolfhotel.co.uk
***Dir:*** *turn off A75 at sign for Castle Douglas go down main street hotel opposite the town library*
Situated in the main street, this former coaching inn, popular with golfers, offers well-equipped and cheerfully decorated bedrooms. There is a choice of bars, and good meals are served either in the foyer bar or the upstairs dining room.
**ROOMS:** 12 en suite (1 fmly) No smoking in 6 bedrooms s £36-£45; d £58-£60 (incl. bkfst) * **LB** **CONF:** Thtr 40 Class 20 Board 20 Del from £52.50 * **PARKING:** 29 **NOTES:** No smoking in restaurant Closed 23-26 Dec & 1-3 Jan **CARDS:**

C

CASTLE DOUGLAS, continued

### ★★65% King's Arms
St Andrew's St DG7 1EL
☎ 01556 502626 01556 502097
e-mail: david@galloway-golf.co.uk
**Dir:** *through main street, left at town clock, hotel situated on corner site*
This former coaching inn has a characterful interior which includes a choice of cosy bar areas and a restaurant overlooking an ivy-clad courtyard. Both the bar and the restaurant offer a good choice of menus.
**ROOMS:** 10 rms (9 en suite) (2 fmly) No smoking in 2 bedrooms s £35-£45; d £56-£60 (incl. bkfst) * **LB** **FACILITIES:** ch fac **CONF:** Thtr 35 Class 20 Board 25 Del from £45 * **PARKING:** 15 **NOTES:** No smoking in restaurant Closed 25-26 Dec & 1-2 Jan **CARDS:**

## CLACHAN-SEIL, Argyll & Bute — Map 10 NM71

### ★★74% Willowburn
PA34 4TJ
☎ 01852 300276 01852 300597
e-mail: willowburn.hotel@virgin.net
**Dir:** *0.5m from Atlantic Bridge, on left*
This welcoming holiday hotel, 12 miles south of Oban, enjoys a peaceful outlook over Clachan Sound. Friendly, attentive service and fine food are the keys to the hotel's success. There is a cosy bar, a formal dining room and a comfortable, inviting lounge. The attractive, thoughtfully equipped bedrooms have mostly pine furnishings.
**ROOMS:** 7 en suite No smoking in all bedrooms s £60-£65; d £120-£130 (incl. bkfst & dinner) * **LB** **FACILITIES:** Xmas **PARKING:** 20
**NOTES:** No smoking in restaurant Closed Jan-Feb
**CARDS:**

## CLEISH, Perth & Kinross — Map 11 NT09

### ★★★67% Nivingston House Hotel
Cleish, Kinross-shire KY13 0LS
☎ 01577 850216 01577 850238
e-mail: info@nivingstonhousehotel.co.uk
**Dir:** *From Edinburgh,cross Forth Road Bridge, take M90 north to exit 5, signed Crook of Devon(B9097). Turn left, hotel signposted 2 miles from exit*
There are fine views from this small, privately run hotel, high up in attractive grounds in the Cleish Hills. Enthusiastically managed, guests can be assured of attentive service and enjoyable meals which are served in the comfortable Blues Restaurant. There is a choice of lounges and a full-sized snooker room. Bedrooms are attractive and vary in size.
**ROOMS:** 17 en suite (1 fmly) s £70-£90; d £95-£115 (incl. bkfst) * **LB**
**FACILITIES:** Snooker Croquet lawn Putting green Jacuzzi ch fac Xmas
**CONF:** Thtr 50 Class 45 Board 25 Del from £100 * **PARKING:** 100
**NOTES:** No smoking in restaurant Closed 3 -14 Jan
**CARDS:**

## CLUANIE INN, Highland — Map 14 NH01

### ★★64% *Cluanie Inn*
Glenmoriston IV63 7YW
☎ 01320 340238 01320 340293
e-mail: claunie@ecosse.net
Set in splendid isolation at the western end of Loch Cluanie and surrounded by mountains, this roadside inn is a haven for climbers. Sympathetically extended and upgraded, it provides accommodation in smart pine-furnished bedrooms. No TV or radio reception here, but each room has a VCR and there is a video library, or bring your own.
**ROOMS:** 15 en suite **PARKING:** 10 **CARDS:**

## CLYDEBANK, West Dunbartonshire — Map 11 NS56

### ★★★★66% Beardmore
Best Western
Beardmore St G81 4SA
☎ 0141 951 6000 0141 951 6018
e-mail: beardmore.hotel@hci.co.uk
**Dir:** *M8 junct 19 follow the A814 towards Dumbarton then follow tourist signs. Turn left onto Beardsmore St and follow signs*
Beside the River Clyde, near the Erskine Bridge, this impressive modern hotel is well-placed for business guests and holiday-makers. Bedrooms are attractive and some are of 'executive' standard. Business and conference facilities are very extensive and the Citrus Restaurant serves tempting modern dishes at dinner, whilst the Café-Bar offers a more informal alternative.
**ROOMS:** 168 en suite No smoking in 112 bedrooms s fr £93; d fr £118 * **FACILITIES:** STV Indoor swimming (H) Sauna Solarium Gym Jacuzzi Beauty treatment ch fac **CONF:** Thtr 170 Class 24 Board 26 Del £135 * **SERVICES:** Lift air con **PARKING:** 150 **NOTES:** No smoking in restaurant Civ Wed **CARDS:**

### ★★★65% *Patio*
1 South Av, Clydebank Business Park G81 2RW
☎ 0141 951 1133 0141 952 3713
e-mail: patiocly@globalnet.co.uk
Situated in the local business park, this modern hotel is a popular conference and function venue. Public areas are contemporary in style and the restaurant offers a range of menus at lunch and dinner. Bedrooms have interesting lacquer and marble furniture.
**ROOMS:** 82 en suite No smoking in 16 bedrooms **FACILITIES:** STV
**CONF:** Thtr 150 Class 30 Board 30 **SERVICES:** Lift **PARKING:** 120
**CARDS:**

COLBOST See Skye, Isle of

## COLONSAY, ISLE OF, Argyll & Bute — Map 10

## SCALASAIG — Map 10 NR39

### ★★70% Isle of Colonsay Hotel
PA61 7YP
☎ 01951 200316 01951 200353
e-mail: colonsay.hotel@pipemedia.co.uk
**Dir:** *400mtrs W of Ferry Pier*
The hotel combines modern amenities with traditional comforts and offers a wonderfully relaxed atmosphere. Bedrooms are comfortably furnished and public areas include a choice of relaxing lounges, well-stocked bars, and a traditional wood-clad dining room where fresh produce features on the short daily changing fixed price menu. The coffee and craft shops are located in an adjoining building.
**ROOMS:** 11 rms (9 en suite) (2 fmly) s £69-£80; d £138-£160 (incl. bkfst & dinner) * **LB** **FACILITIES:** Xmas **PARKING:** 8 **NOTES:** No smoking in restaurant **CARDS:**

## COLVEND, Dumfries & Galloway — Map 11 NX85

### ★★68% *Clonyard House*
DG5 4QW
☎ 01556 630372 01556 630422
e-mail: nickthompson@clara.net
**Dir:** *through Dalbeattie and turn left onto A710 for about 4m*
This family run hotel is set in seven acres of grounds, which include a childrens' play area and an 'enchanted tree'. Most of the spacious, comfortable bedrooms are housed in a purpose-built extension. Meals are served in the bar lounge or in the restaurant proper.
**ROOMS:** 15 en suite (2 fmly) **CONF:** Class 35 Board 20 **PARKING:** 40
**CARDS:**

COMRIE, Perth & Kinross Map 11 NN72

**★★★73% Royal**
Melville Square PH6 2DN
☎ 01764 679200 01764 679219
e-mail: reception@royalhotel.co.uk
***Dir:*** *situated on the main square in Comrie*
A traditional façade gives little indication of the total refurbishment that has added style and elegance to this long-established hotel. Public areas blend the character of a highland lodge - bar and library - with the bright modern ambience of the restaurant and conservatory style brasserie. Bedrooms are tastefully appointed and furnished with smart reproduction antiques.
**ROOMS:** 11 en suite s £70-£90; d £110-£150 (incl. bkfst) * **LB**
**FACILITIES:** STV Fishing Pool table Fishing/shooting arranged Xmas
**PARKING:** 22 **NOTES:** No smoking in restaurant
**CARDS:**

*See advert on this page*

THE ROYAL HOTEL

*The Royal Hotel, Comrie Perthshire*

CONNEL, Argyll & Bute Map 10 NM93

**★★72% Falls of Lora**
PA37 1PB
☎ 01631 710483 01631 710694
***Dir:*** *Set back from A85, overlooking Loch Etive, 5m from Oban about 85 miles North-West of Glasgow/Edinburgh*

Personally run and welcoming, this long-established holiday hotel enjoys fine views over Loch Etive. The pleasant public areas include a comfortable, traditional lounge, a well-stocked bar with a popular bistro adjoining, and a formal dining room. Bedrooms come in a variety of styles and standards, ranging from the standard cabin rooms to the spacious luxury rooms.
**ROOMS:** 30 en suite (4 fmly) s £35-£53; d £43-£111 (incl. bkfst) * **LB**
**FACILITIES:** ch fac **CONF:** Thtr 45 Class 20 Board 15 **PARKING:** 40
**NOTES:** Closed mid Dec & Jan **CARDS:**

*See advert under OBAN*

CONTIN, Highland Map 14 NH45

**★★★74% Coul House**
IV14 9EY
☎ 01997 421487 01997 421945
e-mail: coulhouse@bestwestern.co.uk
***Dir:*** *from South by passing Inverness continue on A9 over Moray Firth bridge, after 5m take 2nd exit at rdbt on to A835 follow to Contin*
Many guests return time and time again to this Victorian country house due to its relaxed atmosphere. Bedrooms are comfortably furnished and offer individual styles of decoration. Relaxing public areas include a cosy foyer lounge with a log fire, and a lovely octagonal drawing room. Taste of Scotland specialities are featured

*continued*

in the elegant dining room while more informal meals are provided in the Bistro or Kitchen Bar.
**ROOMS:** 20 en suite (3 fmly) s £70-£85; d £110-£124 (incl. bkfst) **LB**
**FACILITIES:** STV Putting green Pitch & putt ch fac Xmas **CONF:** Thtr 50 Class 30 Board 30 Del from £58.50 * **PARKING:** 40 **NOTES:** No smoking in restaurant **CARDS:**

**★★70% Achilty**
IV14 9EG
☎ 01997 421355 01997 421923
***Dir:*** *Take A835 hotel on right through Contin*
This hotel offers a choice of comfortable lounges with plenty of reading material and some games. A good value carte menu is served in The Steading lounge bar, where rough-cut stone walls add to the character. Well-equipped bedrooms, four with external access, are bright and modern in style.
**ROOMS:** 8 en suite 4 annexe en suite (3 fmly) No smoking in 10 bedrooms s fr £55; d fr £74 (incl. bkfst) * **LB** **FACILITIES:** ch fac Xmas
**CONF:** Thtr 50 Class 50 Board 20 **PARKING:** 100
**CARDS:**

CRAIGELLACHIE, Moray Map 15 NJ24

**★★★76% Craigellachie**
AB38 9SR
☎ 01340 881204 01340 881253
e-mail: sales@craigellachie.com
***Dir:*** *on the A95 in Craigellachie, 300yds from the A95/A941 crossing*
Once the exclusive retreat of fishers, this impressive hotel now attracts a diverse market. Surrounded by distilleries, it's not surprising that over 300 malts grace the walls of the Quaich Bar, just browse, choose and sample. Imaginative well-presented

*continued on p706*

CRAIGELLACHIE, continued

dishes feature on all menus. Accommodation ranges from impressive suites and master bedrooms, to individually decorated standard rooms.

*Craigellachie, Craigellachie*

**ROOMS:** 26 en suite (1 fmly) s £95-£125; d £115-£145 (incl. bkfst) * **LB** **FACILITIES:** STV Gym Xmas **CONF:** Thtr 60 Class 36 Board 24 Del from £109.50 * **PARKING:** 50 **NOTES:** No smoking in restaurant Civ Wed 30 **CARDS:**

*See advert on opposite page*

## CRAIL, Fife — Map 12 NO60

### ★★64% Balcomie Links

Balcomie Rd KY10 3TN
☎ 01333 450237 🖷 01333 450540
e-mail: mikekadir@balcomie.fsnet.co.uk

***Dir:*** *on entering Crail follow road to village shops, at junct of High St and Market Gate turn right. This road becomes Balcomie Rd. Hotel on left*

BALCOMIE
LINKS

Especially popular with visiting golfers, this family-run hotel on the east side of the village represents good value for money in a relaxing atmosphere. Well-maintained bedrooms come in a variety of sizes and styles and offer all the expected amenities. There is a choice of well-stocked bars and a small dining room where a popular range of good value meals is served.

**ROOMS:** 15 rms (13 en suite) (2 fmly) No smoking in 3 bedrooms s £40-£45; d £64-£70 (incl. bkfst) * **LB** **FACILITIES:** STV entertainment ch fac Xmas **PARKING:** 25 **NOTES:** Civ Wed 80

**CARDS:**

## CRIEFF, Perth & Kinross — Map 11 NN82

### ★★★72% Crieff Hydro

Best Western

Ferntower Rd PH7 3LQ
☎ 01764 655555 🖷 01764 653087
e-mail: enquiries@crieffhydro.com

***Dir:*** *from Perth first right up Connaught Terrace, first right again*

The Hydro commands a panoramic position high above the town. As the focus of a 900-acre estate, the hotel offers a superb range of leisure and sporting facilities. Bedrooms range from 'standard' to 'executive', and children are well catered for. There is an all-day coffee shop and vibrant brasserie.

**ROOMS:** 203 en suite 6 annexe en suite (67 fmly) s £70-£100; d £140-£200 (incl. bkfst & dinner) * **LB** **FACILITIES:** **Spa** Indoor swimming (H) Golf 9 Tennis (hard) Fishing Squash Riding Snooker Sauna Solarium Gym Croquet lawn Putting green Jacuzzi Bowling Football Water ski-ing Cinema entertainment ch fac Xmas **CONF:** Thtr 335 Class 125 Board 68 Del from £125 * **SERVICES:** Lift **PARKING:** 205 **NOTES:** No dogs (ex guide dogs) No smoking in restaurant Civ Wed 150

**CARDS:**

### ★★65% Lockes Acre

7 Comrie Rd PH7 4BP
☎ 01764 652526 🖷 01764 652526

***Dir:*** *take A9/M9 for Perth, turn off at A822 Crieff, once in Crieff take A85 Comrie/Lochearnhead Rd, hotel on right hand side of A85 just outside Crieff*

The resident owners provide personal attention and a relaxed atmosphere at this comfortable holiday hotel, situated on the west side of town overlooking the park. Tasty good value meals are served in either the bar or dining room.

**ROOMS:** 7 rms (4 en suite) (1 fmly) s £25-£30; d £50-£56 (incl. bkfst) * **PARKING:** 35 **NOTES:** No dogs (ex guide dogs) No smoking in restaurant **CARDS:**

### ★★63% The Drummond Arms

James Square PH7 3HX
☎ 01764 652151 🖷 01764 655222
e-mail: drummondarmshotel@btinternet.com

A traditonal tourist hotel in the town square offering nicely decorated bedrooms and a choice of bars. Service is attentive and the atmosphere relaxed.

**ROOMS:** 30 rms (29 en suite) 7 annexe en suite (3 fmly) s £28-£35; d £55-£90 (incl. bkfst) * **LB** **FACILITIES:** STV Xmas **CONF:** Thtr 120 Class 60 Board 30 **SERVICES:** Lift **PARKING:** 30

**CARDS:**

## CRUDEN BAY, Aberdeenshire — Map 15 NK03

### ★★69% Red House

Aulton Rd AB42 0NJ
☎ 01779 812215 🖷 01779 812320
e-mail: ian@redhousehotel7.freeserve.co.uk

***Dir:*** *turn off A952 Aberdeen/Peterhead road at Little Chef onto the A975 towards Cruden Bay, hotel opposite golf course*

Visiting golfers have a 'soft spot' for this welcoming small hotel which overlooks the golf course to the sea beyond. Bedrooms with pleasing colour schemes are comfortably modern in style and offer a good range of amenities. Public areas are comfortable and enjoyable to use. The attractive dining room offers a wide range of competitively priced dishes from the varied menus.

**ROOMS:** 6 rms (5 en suite) (1 fmly) s £25-£50; d £50-£100 (incl. bkfst) * **LB** **FACILITIES:** 7 ball table, pool tables ch fac **CONF:** Board 180 **PARKING:** 40 **CARDS:**

## CUMBERNAULD, North Lanarkshire — Map 11 NS77

### ★★★★66% Westerwood Hotel Golf & Country Club

1 St Andrews Dr, Westerwood G68 0EW
☎ 01236 457171 🖷 01236 738478
e-mail: westerwood@morton-hotels.com

***Dir:*** *A80 exit after passing Oki factory signposted Wardpark/Castlecary then second left at Old Inns rdbt and right at mini rdbt*

Set on a hillside, with southern views and backed by an 18-hole

*continued*

golf course, this modern hotel is being dramatically improved by the new owners - Morton Hotels. With the range of leisure, conference and function facilities and 50 new bedrooms due to open later in 2001, both business and leisure guests should be fully satisfied.
**ROOMS:** 49 en suite No smoking in 3 bedrooms s £94-£110.50; d £108-£131 (incl. bkfst) * **LB** **FACILITIES:** STV Indoor swimming (H) Golf 18 Tennis (hard) Solarium Gym Putting green Jacuzzi Beauty salon Hairdresser Xmas **CONF:** Thtr 300 Class 160 Board 40 Del £124 * **SERVICES:** Lift air con **PARKING:** 204 **NOTES:** No smoking in restaurant Civ Wed 120 **CARDS:**

CUPAR, Fife — Map 11 NO31

### ★★69% Eden House
2 Pitscottie Rd KY15 4HF
☎ 01334 652510 01334 652277
e-mail: lv@eden.u-net.com
***Dir:*** *overlooking Haugh Park, Cupar on A91, 8m W of St.Andrews*

The tastefully decorated bedrooms are comfortably furnished and come with a good range of accessories. Public areas include a well-stocked bar which also provides a popular informal food option. The candle lit conservatory restaurant is a relaxed setting for the fine dining experience offered by the seasonal changing carte and fixed price menus.
**ROOMS:** 9 en suite 2 annexe en suite (3 fmly) s £48-£58; d £70-£188 (incl. bkfst) * **LB** **FACILITIES:** STV ch fac **CONF:** Thtr 40 Class 40 Board 40 **PARKING:** 18 **NOTES:** No dogs (ex guide dogs) **CARDS:**

DERVAIG See Mull, Isle of

DINGWALL, Highland — Map 14 NH55

### ★★76% *Kinkell House*
Easter Kinkell, Conon Bridge IV7 8HY
☎ 01349 861270 01349 865902
e-mail: kinkell@aol.com
***Dir:*** *10m N of Inverness turn off A9 onto B9169 for 1m*

Scotland's Hotels of Distinction

Kinkell House is a 19th-century farmhouse, restored and extended to create a delightful small country house hotel and restaurant, with splendid views over the Cromarty Firth. There are three comfortable lounges, one of which is a conservatory, and a tempting dinner menu which changes daily.
**ROOMS:** 9 en suite (1 fmly) No smoking in all bedrooms
**FACILITIES:** Croquet lawn **PARKING:** 20 **NOTES:** No smoking in restaurant Civ Wed 70 **CARDS:**

Packed in a hurry? Ironing facilities should be available at all star levels, either in rooms or on request.

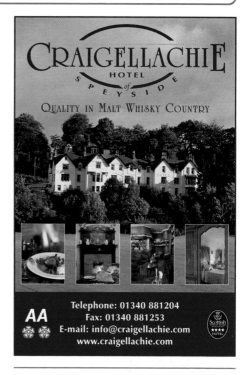



DIRLETON, East Lothian — Map 12 NT58

### ★★★71% The Open Arms
EH39 5EG
☎ 01620 850241 01620 850570
e-mail: openarms@clara.co.uk
***Dir:*** *from A1 take signs for North Berwick, pass through Gullane, 2m on left*

This long-established hotel sits by the village green and looks across to Dirleton Castle. It has the ambience of a country house, with friendly service to match. Public areas include an inviting lounge and a cosy bar, a smart brasserie and intimate restaurant. Bedrooms come in a variety of sizes.
**ROOMS:** 10 en suite (1 fmly) s £80-£90; d £100-£150 (incl. bkfst) * **LB** **FACILITIES:** Xmas **CONF:** Thtr 200 Class 150 Board 100 **PARKING:** 30 **NOTES:** No smoking in restaurant **CARDS:**

D

## DORNIE, Highland

Map 14 NG82

### ★★62% Dornie

Francis St IV40 8DT
☎ 01599 555205 🖷 01599 555429
e-mail: dornie@madasafish.com
***Dir:*** *turn off A87, signposted to the village of Dornie, hotel situated in centre of village on right*

BAR
DORNIE
HOTEL

A warm welcome awaits guests at this small hotel by the shore of Loch Duich. Bedrooms have comfortable modern appointments. Public areas include a comfortable lounge, a popular bar and an attractive restaurant.

**ROOMS:** 11 rms (6 en suite) (3 fmly) s £25-£33; d £50-£70 (incl. bkfst) * **LB** **FACILITIES:** Xmas **PARKING:** 16 **NOTES:** No smoking in restaurant **CARDS:**

## DORNOCH, Highland

Map 14 NH78

### ★★★68% Royal Golf Hotel

The 1st Tee IV25 3LG
☎ 01862 810283 🖷 01862 810923
e-mail: royalgolf@morton-hotels.com
***Dir:*** *from A9, turn right to Dornoch and continue through main street. Straight ahead at cross roads then hotel is 200yds on the right*

Beside the Royal Dornoch Golf Club and overlooking the Dornoch Firth, this well established hotel attracts international golfers. Significant refurbishment has taken place in the public areas and the bedrooms, which include two fine suites on the top floor. The split level sun lounge offers all day dining and comfortable seating from which to watch the golf.

**ROOMS:** 25 en suite (2 fmly) s £86-£98; d £108-£175 (incl. bkfst) * **LB** **FACILITIES:** ch fac Xmas **PARKING:** 20 **NOTES:** No smoking in restaurant **CARDS:**

### ★★65% *Burghfield House*

IV25 3HN
☎ 01862 810212 🖷 01862 810404
***Dir:*** *turn off A9 at Evelix junct then travel 1m into Dornoch. Just before War Memorial turn left and follow road up hill to tower in the trees*

This extended Victorian mansion stands in well-kept gardens. Bedrooms are located either in the main house or in the Garden Wing annexe, with varying styles of decor. Public areas, including a large comfortable lounge, are enhanced with antiques, fresh flowers and real fires. The bright dining room features an interesting fixed-price menu.

**ROOMS:** 13 en suite 15 annexe en suite **FACILITIES:** Sauna Putting green **CONF:** Thtr 100 Board 80 **PARKING:** 62 **CARDS:**

## DRUMNADROCHIT, Highland

Map 14 NH53

### ★★★67% Polmaily House

IV63 6XT
☎ 01456 450343 🖷 01456 450813
e-mail: polmaily@btinternet.com
***Dir:*** *in Drumnadrochit turn onto A831 signposted to Cannich, hotel is 2m on right. 1.5m from Loch Ness*

Run by a family for families, this relaxing country house is geared for children. Standing in 18 acres of lawns and woods it offers a pets' corner and well-stocked play areas (inside and out), as well as a good sized swimming pool, horse riding, tennis and lots more. All bedrooms have video TVs to keep the kids happy when mum and dad enjoy good home-cooked dinners.

**ROOMS:** 10 en suite (6 fmly) s £52-£68; d £104-£136 (incl. bkfst) * **LB** **FACILITIES:** Indoor swimming (H) Tennis (hard) Fishing Riding Croquet lawn Indoor/outdoor childs play area, Boating,Pony rides,Beauty massage ch fac Xmas **CONF:** Thtr 16 Class 8 Board 14 **PARKING:** 20 **NOTES:** No smoking in restaurant Closed 31 Oct-30 Dec & 2 Jan-Mar Civ Wed **CARDS:**

## DRYMEN, Stirling

Map 11 NS48

### ★★★68% *Buchanan Arms*

23 Main St G63 0BQ
☎ 01360 660588 🖷 01360 660943
***Dir:*** *Travelling N from Glasgow on the A81 take the turn off onto the A811, the hotel is situated at the S end of Main Street*

A former coaching inn, this long-established hotel has been extended and modernised to provide a wide range of facilities. The well-equipped bedrooms come in a variety of styles. Public areas include a small bar with a wooden floor and oak beams, a conservatory lounge and a very popular restaurant.

**ROOMS:** 52 en suite No smoking in 6 bedrooms **FACILITIES:** STV Indoor swimming (H) Fishing Squash Sauna Solarium Gym Jacuzzi entertainment **PARKING:** 100 **NOTES:** No smoking in restaurant **CARDS:**

### ★★★65% Winnock

Best Western

The Square G63 0BL
☎ 01360 660245 🖷 01360 660267
***Dir:*** *from S follow M74 onto M8 through Glasgow. Exit junct 16B, follow A809 to Aberfoyle*

The Winnock

Occupying a prominent position overlooking the village green, this is a popular hotel offering well-equipped bedrooms of various sizes and styles. The public rooms consist of a comfortable foyer lounge with open fire, a popular lounge bar, and a cosy and attractive restaurant, as well as several other versatile rooms.

**ROOMS:** 48 en suite (12 fmly) No smoking in 17 bedrooms s £49-£65; d £86-£96 (incl. bkfst) * **LB** **FACILITIES:** Petanque entertainment ch fac Xmas **CONF:** Thtr 140 Class 60 Board 70 Del from £49 * **PARKING:** 60 **NOTES:** No dogs (ex guide dogs) No smoking in restaurant Civ Wed 120 **CARDS:**

DUISDALEMORE See Skye, Isle of

## DULNAIN BRIDGE, Highland Map 14 NH92

### ★★★73% Muckrach Lodge

PH26 3LY
☎ 01479 851257 01479 851325
e-mail: muckrach.lodge@sol.co.uk
**Dir:** *from A95 Dulnain Bridge exit follow A938 towards Carrbridge. Hotel 500mtrs on right*

Muckrach is a Victorian shooting lodge, peacefully situated among attractive grounds. The friendly staff provide a high level of care and attention. Bedrooms, including some located in the Coach House, come in a variety of sizes, the larger ones being particularly well-appointed. Public rooms are very inviting, with the conservatory restaurant offering an impressive dinner menu.
**ROOMS:** 9 en suite 4 annexe en suite (2 fmly) **FACILITIES:** Beauty & aroma therapy ch fac **CONF:** Thtr 80 Class 20 Board 24 **PARKING:** 53
**NOTES:** No dogs (ex guide dogs) No smoking in restaurant
**CARDS:**

## DUMBARTON, West Dunbartonshire Map 10 NS37

### Travelodge

Milton G82 2TY
☎ 01389 765202 01389 765202
**Dir:** *1m E, on A82 westbound*
Travelodge offers good quality, good value, modern accommodation. Ideal for families, the spacious, en suite bedrooms include remote-control TV, tea and coffee-making facilities, luxury beds and free morning newspaper. Meals can be taken at the nearby family restaurant. For further details and the Travelodge phone number, consult the Hotel Groups page.

**ROOMS:** 32 en suite

## DUMFRIES, Dumfries & Galloway Map 11 NX97

see also Carrutherstown

### ★★★69% Cairndale Hotel & Leisure Club

English St DG1 2DF
☎ 01387 254111 01387 250555
e-mail: sales@cairndale.fsnet.co.uk
**Dir:** *from S turn off M6 onto A75 to Dumfries, left at first rdbt, cross railway bridge, continue to traffic lights, hotel is 1st building on left*
Within walking distance of the town centre, this hotel provides a wide range of amenities, including extensive leisure facilities and an impressive new conference and entertainment centre. Bedrooms range from stylish new suites to cosy singles.

*continued*

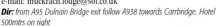

Restaurants and a coffee shop offer everything from a full dinner to a quick snack.

**ROOMS:** 91 en suite (22 fmly) No smoking in 45 bedrooms s £65-£85; d £85-£105 (incl. bkfst) * **LB** **FACILITIES:** STV Indoor swimming (H) Sauna Solarium Gym Jacuzzi Steam room entertainment ch fac Xmas
**CONF:** Thtr 300 Class 150 Board 50 Del from £99 * **SERVICES:** Lift
**PARKING:** 120 **NOTES:** Civ Wed 300 **CARDS:**

*See advert on this page*

### ★★★67% Station

49 Lovers Walk DG1 1LT
☎ 01387 254316 01387 250388
e-mail: info@stationhotel.co.uk
**Dir:** *from A75 follow signs to Dumfries town centre, hotel is opposite the railway station*
This hotel, sympathetically modernised to blend with its fine Victorian characteristics, offers well-equipped bedrooms. The Courtyard Bistro serves an extensive menu in an informal atmosphere and the Pullman dining room, which only is open at

*continued on p710*

DUMFRIES, continued

weekends, offers a carefully chosen dinner menu in more relaxed surroundings.

*Station, Dumfries*

**ROOMS:** 32 en suite (2 fmly) No smoking in 12 bedrooms s £40-£80; d £80-£110 (incl. bkfst) * **LB** **FACILITIES:** STV ch fac Xmas **CONF:** Thtr 60 Class 20 Board 30 Del £65 * **SERVICES:** Lift **PARKING:** 40 **NOTES:** Civ Wed 60 **CARDS:**

*See advert on opposite page*

### *Travelodge*

Travelodge

Annan Rd, Collin DG1 3SE
☎ 01387 750658 01387 750658
***Dir:*** *on A75*

Travelodge offers good quality, good value, modern accommodation. Ideal for families, the spacious, en suite bedrooms include remote-control TV, tea and coffee-making facilities, luxury beds and free morning newspaper. Meals can be taken at the nearby family restaurant. For further details and the Travelodge phone number, consult the Hotel Groups page.

**ROOMS:** 40 en suite

## DUNBAR, East Lothian — Map 12 NT67

### ★★67% Bayswell

Bayswell Park EH42 1AE
☎ 01368 862225 01368 862225
***Dir:*** *off A1 into Dunbar High St, turn left and follow road to left then take first right into Bayswell Park*

There is a friendly and informal atmosphere at this family-run hotel which enjoys panoramic views from its striking cliff top position. Bedroom equipment is impressive; all have videos, most have large screen TVs and three of the new bedrooms have TVs in their bathrooms.

**ROOMS:** 18 en suite (4 fmly) s fr £55; d fr £79 (incl. bkfst) * **LB** **FACILITIES:** **Spa** STV Petanque Xmas **PARKING:** 20 **CARDS:**

## DUNBLANE, Stirling — Map 11 NN70

***Premier Collection***

### ★★★ Cromlix House

Kinbuck FK15 9JT
☎ 01786 822125 01786 825450
e-mail: reservations@cromlixhousehotel.com
***Dir:*** *off the A9 N of Dunblane. Exit B8033 to Kinbuck Village cross narrow bridge drive 200yds on left*

This fine Edwardian mansion lies amidst neatly tended gardens in a 3000-acre estate. Bedrooms, many of them having a private sitting room, have the real character of a country house and are comfortably furnished. Both the drawing room and library are heated by log fires during the cooler months, whilst dinner, using local ingredients wherever possible, is served in one of two elegant dining rooms. Breakfast is taken in the conservatory overlooking the gardens.

**ROOMS:** 14 en suite s £115-£180; d £205-£245 (incl. bkfst) **LB** **FACILITIES:** Tennis (hard) Fishing Croquet lawn Clay pigeon shooting Falconry ch fac Xmas **CONF:** Thtr 40 Class 24 Board 20 Del from £150 * **PARKING:** 51 **NOTES:** No smoking in restaurant Closed 2-29 Jan RS Oct-Apr Civ Wed 55 **CARDS:**

## DUNDEE, Dundee City — Map 11 NO43

see also Auchterhouse

### ★★★70% Swallow Hotel

SWALLOW HOTELS

Kingsway West, Invergowrie DD2 5JT
☎ 01382 641122 01382 631201
e-mail: info@swallowhotels.com
***Dir:*** *turn off from A90/A929 rdbt following sign for Denhead of Gray, hotel on left*

Conveniently situated just off the Dundee bypass, this extended Victorian mansion is set amid landscaped gardens. The comfortable and well-equipped bedrooms range from attractive suites and executive rooms to smaller standard rooms. Public areas include a bright foyer lounge, well-stocked bar, an attractive restaurant and the leisure and conference centres.

**ROOMS:** 107 en suite (11 fmly) No smoking in 60 bedrooms s £98-£135; d £118-£150 (incl. bkfst) * **LB** **FACILITIES:** STV Indoor swimming (H) Sauna Solarium Gym Putting green Jacuzzi Trim trail Mountain bike hire Beauty salon Xmas **CONF:** Thtr 100 Class 36 Board 30 Del from £95 * **PARKING:** 140 **NOTES:** No smoking in restaurant Civ Wed 120 **CARDS:**

### ★★★68% Sandford Hotel

SCOTLAND'S HOTELS OF DISTINCTION

Newton Hill, Wormit DD6 8RG
☎ 01382 541802 01382 542136
e-mail: sandford.hotel@btinternet.com
***Dir:*** *Hotel located 4m S of the Tay Bridge at the junction with A914/B946*

Built around the turn of the century, Sandford Country Hotel lies in attractive gardens well off the main road. Set around a small terraced courtyard, it is a popular venue for meals, served either in the bar or restaurant. Bedrooms come in a variety of sizes, all being well-equipped.

**ROOMS:** 16 en suite (2 fmly) s £45-£70; d £60-£95 (incl. bkfst) * **LB** **FACILITIES:** STV ch fac Xmas **CONF:** Thtr 45 Class 24 Board 28 Del from £95 * **PARKING:** 30 **NOTES:** No smoking in restaurant Civ Wed 45 **CARDS:**

**★★★67% Invercarse**
371 Perth Rd DD2 1PG
☎ 01382 669231 📠 01382 644112
e-mail: invercarse@bestwestern.co.uk
***Dir:*** *from the A90 Perth to Aberdeen Road take the A85 (Taybridge) then follow signs*
This comfortable hotel, a former mansion house with its own grounds in the west end, is a popular base for visiting business people. The variable sized bedrooms are comfortable in appointment, and offer a good range of amenities. Inviting public areas include a choice of bars and a smart restaurant.
**ROOMS:** 44 en suite No smoking in 29 bedrooms s £68; d £90 (incl. bkfst) * **LB** **FACILITIES:** STV **CONF:** Thtr 300 Class 100 Board 50 Del from £69 * **PARKING:** 119 **NOTES:** No smoking in restaurant Closed 24-26 Dec & 31 Dec-2 Jan Civ Wed **CARDS:**

**★★70% *The Shaftesbury***
1 Hyndford St DD2 1HQ
☎ 01382 669216 📠 01382 641598
e-mail: reservations@shaftesbury-hotel.co.uk
***Dir:*** *from Perth follow signs to Airport, take first left at circle then turn right, follow Perth Road and turn right*
A comfortable, welcoming family-run hotel in the west end where staff are friendly and willing to please. This impressive Victorian house has been sympathetically converted. Public areas include a small relaxing lounge, a well-stocked bar and separate restaurant where the menu offers a range of light and substantial dishes prepared from quality fresh ingredients.
**ROOMS:** 12 en suite (2 fmly) **NOTES:** No smoking in restaurant
**CARDS:**

**⇧ Premier Lodge (Dundee North)**
Dayton Dr, Camberdown Leisure Park, Kingsway DD2 3SQ
☎ 0870 700 1362 📠 0870 700 1363
***Dir:*** *Turn off A90 into Coupar Angus Rd,hotel visible from dual carriage way,exit by slip road for Camperdown leisure park*
Premier Lodge offers modern, well-equipped, en suite accommodation suitable for both business and leisure travellers. Meals can be taken at the adjacent popular restaurant and bar, which is fully licensed. For further details, consult the Hotel Groups page.
**ROOMS:** 78 en suite s £42; d £42 *

**⇧ *Travelodge***
A90 Kingsway DD2 4TD
☎ 08700 850950
***Dir:*** *on A90*
Travelodge offers good quality, good value, modern accommodation. Ideal for families, the spacious, en suite bedrooms include remote-control TV, tea and coffee-making facilities, luxury beds and free morning newspaper. Meals can be taken at the nearby family restaurant. For further details and the Travelodge phone number, consult the Hotel Groups page.

**ROOMS:** 30 en suite

## DUNDONNELL, Highland — Map 14 NH08

**★★★74% ⊛⊛ Dundonnell**
Little Loch Broom IV23 2QR
☎ 01854 633204 📠 01854 633366
e-mail: selbie@dundonnellhotel.co.uk
***Dir:*** *turn off A835 at Braemore junct on to A832*
Situated by the roadside at the head of Little Loch Broom, this hospitable hotel has been extensively developed over 25 years by

*continued on p712*

DUNDONNELL, continued

the Florence family as a haven of relaxation and good food. The bedrooms are well-equipped and most enjoy fine views.
**ROOMS:** 28 en suite (2 fmly) s £60-£73; d £110-£120 (incl. bkfst) * LB **FACILITIES:** Xmas **CONF:** Thtr 70 Class 50 Board 40 Del from £75 * **PARKING:** 60 **NOTES:** No smoking in restaurant Closed 22 Nov-Feb (ex Xmas/New Year) **CARDS:**

## DUNFERMLINE, Fife

Map 11 NT08

### ★★★72% Keavil House

Crossford KY12 8QW
☎ 01383 736258 01383 621600
e-mail: keavil@queensferry-hotels.co.uk
***Dir:*** *2m W of Dunfermline on A994*

A former manor house in the village of Crossford. Public areas include a leisure centre, function facilities, a choice of bars, a comfortable lounge and a smart conservatory restaurant which specialises in carefully prepared Taste of Scotland specialities. Bedrooms, in two styles, have pleasing colour schemes and are comfortably modern in style.
**ROOMS:** 47 en suite (4 fmly) No smoking in 26 bedrooms s £60-£90; d £90-£130 * LB **FACILITIES:** STV Indoor swimming (H) Sauna Solarium Gym Jacuzzi Aerobics studio Steam room Xmas **CONF:** Thtr 200 Class 60 Board 50 Del from £90 * **PARKING:** 150 **NOTES:** No dogs (ex guide dogs) Civ Wed 150 **CARDS:**

*See advert on page 711*

### ★★★71% *Garvock House Hotel*

St John's Dr, Transy KY12 7TU
☎ 01383 621067 01383 621168
e-mail: sales@garvock.co.uk
***Dir:*** *from M90 junct 3 take A907 into Dunfermline. After football stadium turn left into Garvock Hill, then 1st right St John's Drive, hotel on right*

A welcoming atmosphere prevails at this handsome Georgian house which stands in its own grounds on the east side of town. The spacious bedrooms are modern in style and offer a good range of amenities. Two elegant lounges are serviced by a small bar and fresh produce features on the short menu in the classically styled dining room.
**ROOMS:** 11 en suite (1 fmly) No smoking in all bedrooms **CONF:** Thtr 25 Class 25 Board 25 **PARKING:** 38 **NOTES:** No smoking in restaurant **CARDS:**

### ★★★69% *Elgin*

Charlestown KY11 3EE
☎ 01383 872257 01383 873044
e-mail: Enquiries@elgin-hotel.co.uk
***Dir:*** *3m W of M90, junct 1, on loop road off A985, signposted Limekilns & Charlestown*

A comfortable, welcoming hotel overlooking the Firth of Forth to the Pentland Hills beyond. All the comfortable bedrooms offer a good range of accessories. A new extension provides a lounge and a small chapel. The Tavern bar is relaxed and informal and wide ranges of competitively priced dishes are available in the adjacent restaurant.
**ROOMS:** 12 en suite (3 fmly) No smoking in 6 bedrooms **FACILITIES:** STV **CONF:** Thtr 150 Class 80 Board 50 **PARKING:** 70 **NOTES:** No smoking in restaurant Civ Wed 160 **CARDS:**

### ★★★68% Pitbauchlie House

Aberdour Rd KY11 4PB
☎ 01383 722282 01383 620738
e-mail: info@pitbauchlie.com
***Dir:*** *leave M90 at junct 2, continue onto A823, turn onto B916. Hotel situated 0.5m on right*

A welcoming atmosphere prevails at this comfortable hotel, set amid wooded and landscaped gardens. The nicely presented public areas include a foyer lounge, an attractive restaurant overlooking the garden, and a choice of contrasting bars. Bedrooms range from tastefully appointed deluxe and executive rooms to the smaller standard rooms.
**ROOMS:** 50 en suite (2 fmly) No smoking in 19 bedrooms s £66-£82; d £83-£99 (incl. bkfst) * LB **FACILITIES:** STV Gym **CONF:** Thtr 150 Class 80 Board 60 Del from £103 * **PARKING:** 80 **NOTES:** No smoking in restaurant Civ Wed 120 **CARDS:**

### ★★★63% King Malcolm

Queensferry Rd KY11 8DS
☎ 01383 722611 01383 730865
***Dir:*** *on A823, S of town*

This popular business hotel is located on the east side of town. The top floor bedrooms have been considerably enhanced and all rooms now offer comfortable modern appointments. Public areas include a choice of bars, one with a bright conservatory extension, a foyer lounge, restaurant, and a range of banqueting facilities.
**ROOMS:** 48 en suite (2 fmly) No smoking in 24 bedrooms s £80; d £110 * **FACILITIES:** STV entertainment Xmas **CONF:** Thtr 150 Class 60 Board 50 Del £95 * **PARKING:** 60 **NOTES:** Civ Wed 70 **CARDS:**

★★★62% ***Pitfirrane Arms***
Main St, Crossford KY12 8NJ
☎ 01383 736132 ▣ 01383 621760
e-mail: info@scothotels.com
***Dir:*** *from Kincardine-follow the A985 at large rdbt take the A994 to Dunfermline, Crossford is the second village from the rdbt, hotel on right*
Situated in the village of Crossford, west of the town, this long-established business hotel offers good value accommodation. Bedrooms, which are compact and practical in appointment, have benefited from recent refurbishment. Public areas include a smart restaurant and a choice of contrasting bars.
**ROOMS:** 40 en suite (1 fmly) **FACILITIES:** STV **CONF:** Thtr 90 Class 60 Board 40 **PARKING:** 72 **NOTES:** No smoking in restaurant
**CARDS:**

★★66% **The Hideaway Lodge & Restaurant**
Kingseat Rd, Halbeath KY12 0UB
☎ 01383 725474 ▣ 01383 622428
e-mail: enquiries@thehideaway.co.uk
***Dir:*** *from M90 junct 3 follow signs for Dunfermline. At mini-rdbt turn right. Hotel 800yds on left over level crossing*
A relaxed and informal atmosphere prevails at this family-run establishment on the east side of town. The original lodge comprises a bar and restaurant where the carte menu, available in both areas, offers an extensive range of dishes. The lodge contains the smart, comfortable new bedrooms.
**ROOMS:** 8 en suite s £45; d £45 * **LB** **PARKING:** 30 **NOTES:** No dogs (ex guide dogs) **CARDS:**

## DUNKELD, Perth & Kinross — Map 11 NO04

### *Premier Collection*

★★★ ⊛⊛⊛ **Kinnaird**
Kinnaird Estate PH8 0LB
☎ 01796 482440 ▣ 01796 482289
e-mail: enquiry@kinnairdestate.com
***Dir:*** *from Perth, A9 towards Inverness until Dunkeld but do not enter, continue N for 2m then B898 on left*
This striking Edwardian mansion stands on a 9000-acre majestic Perthshire countryside estate. Public rooms are furnished with rare antique pieces and beautiful paintings. Sitting rooms are warm and inviting with their deep cushioned sofas and open fires. Individual bedrooms with rich soft furnishings are luxurious, as are the marble en suites. Stunning cooking is creative and imaginative.
**ROOMS:** 9 en suite s £320-£450; d £365-£475 (incl. bkfst & dinner) * **LB** **FACILITIES:** STV Tennis (hard) Fishing Snooker Croquet lawn Shooting **CONF:** Thtr 25 Class 10 Board 15 **SERVICES:** Lift **PARKING:** 22 **NOTES:** No dogs No children 12yrs No smoking in restaurant RS Jan-Mar (closed Mon-Wed)
**CARDS:**

★★67% **Royal Dunkeld Hotel**
Atholl St PH8 0AR
☎ 01350 727322 ▣ 01350 727989
e-mail: reservations@royaldunkeld.co.uk
***Dir:*** *Turn right off A9, follow signs A923 Blairgowrie/Coupar Angus. Hotel 200mtrs after crossing bridge*
Set in the centre of the village, this hotel offers modern bedrooms, well-equipped to include hairdryers and trouser presses. There is also a chalet annexe. Both the restaurant and dining bar feature a good range of tasty dishes.
**ROOMS:** 25 en suite 10 annexe en suite (7 fmly) s £35-£52; d £39-£75 (incl. bkfst) * **LB** **FACILITIES:** Snooker Pool tables ch fac Xmas **PARKING:** 30 **NOTES:** No smoking in restaurant
**CARDS:**

## DUNOON, Argyll & Bute — Map 10 NS17

★★76% ⊛ **Enmore**
Marine Pde, Kirn PA23 8HH
☎ 01369 702230 ▣ 01369 702148
e-mail: enmorehotel@btinternet.com
***Dir:*** *on coastal route between two ferries, 1m N of Dunoon*
This comfortable seafront hotel enjoys a wonderful outlook over the Firth of Clyde. Inviting public areas, enhanced by fresh floral displays, include a comfortable and relaxing lounge. The attractive dining room provides the setting for carefully prepared Taste of Scotland dishes. Some of the attractive bedrooms have four-poster beds, others are comfortably furnished in mixed styles.
**ROOMS:** 10 en suite (1 fmly) s £45-£75; d £70-£150 (incl. bkfst) * **LB** **FACILITIES:** Spa Squash Jacuzzi ch fac **CONF:** Thtr 25 Class 20 Board 12 Del from £65 * **PARKING:** 20 **NOTES:** No smoking in restaurant Closed 12Dec-12Feb RS Nov-Feb Civ Wed **CARDS:**

★★70% **Royal Marine**
Hunters Quay PA23 8HJ
☎ 01369 705810 ▣ 01369 702329
e-mail: rmhotel@sol.co.uk
***Dir:*** *on A815 opposite Western Ferries terminal*

This welcoming family-run hotel commands impressive views over the Firth of Clyde. The variable sized bedrooms are modern in appointment and offer a good range of amenities. Inviting public areas include a first floor lounge, well-stocked bar and the popular Ghillies café-bar. A fixed price menu is also available in the attractive dining room.
**ROOMS:** 31 en suite 10 annexe en suite (3 fmly) s £39-£47; d £58-£70 (incl. bkfst) * **LB** **FACILITIES:** Xmas **CONF:** Thtr 90 Class 40 Board 30 Del from £65 * **PARKING:** 40 **NOTES:** No dogs (ex guide dogs) No smoking in restaurant **CARDS:**

TV dinner? Room service at three stars and above.

DUNOON, continued

### ★★66% *Esplanade Hotel*

West Bay PA23 7HU
☎ 01369 704070 📠 01369 702129
e-mail: togwells@ehd.co.uk
***Dir:*** *in town centre pass main pier and continue up hill, then first left and left again at the bottom of the Avenue*

A warm welcome is assured at this family-run holiday hotel which, from its position in the West Bay, enjoys a glorious outlook over the Firth of Clyde. Relaxing public areas include a choice of comfortable lounges at ground and first floor levels and a large split-level dining room. Ranging from tastefully appointed superior and premier rooms to the smaller standard rooms, bedrooms are comfortably modern in style and offer the expected amenities.

**ROOMS:** 60 en suite 5 annexe rms (4 en suite) (4 fmly) No smoking in 3 bedrooms **FACILITIES:** Putting green entertainment **SERVICES:** Lift **PARKING:** 20 **NOTES:** No dogs (ex guide dogs) No smoking in restaurant Closed 21 Oct-20 Apr **CARDS:**

### ★★62% Selborne

Leisureplex

Clyde St, West Bay PA23 7HU
☎ 01369 702761 📠 01369 704032
***Dir:*** *proceed to town centre and turn left at roundabout adjacent to the Caledonian Macbrayne pier. Follow road past castle and turn left into Jane St and then right into Clyde St*

This holiday hotel is situated overlooking the West Bay and gives unrestricted views of the Clyde Estuary towards the Isles of Cumbrae. Tour groups are especially well catered for as good value is given and entertainment is provided most nights. Bedrooms offer the expected facilities, many having sea views.

**ROOMS:** 98 en suite s £25-£33; d £42-£58 (incl. bkfst) * **LB** **FACILITIES:** Pool table entertainment Xmas **SERVICES:** Lift **PARKING:** 30 **NOTES:** No dogs (ex guide dogs) No smoking in restaurant Closed Dec-Feb (ex Xmas) RS Nov/Mar (closed weekends) **CARDS:**

### ★70% Lyall Cliff

141 Alexandra Pde, East Bay PA23 8AW
☎ 01369 702041 📠 01369 702041
e-mail: lyallcliff@talk21.com
***Dir:*** *on A815 between Kirn and Dunoon on sea front, between the ferry terminals at Dunoon amd Hunters Quay*

This comfortable small hotel stands in its own well-tended garden on the seafront. The smartly decorated bedrooms come with mixed modern furnishings and the expected amenities. Public areas include a comfortable lounge and small library adjacent. Enjoyable home cooked fare is provided in the dining room. Musical themed weekend breaks during winter, spring and autumn are popular.

**ROOMS:** 10 en suite (3 fmly) No smoking in 8 bedrooms s £26-£30; d £44-£50 (incl. bkfst) **LB** **CONF:** Board 22 **PARKING:** 9 **NOTES:** No smoking in restaurant Closed Nov-26 Dec RS Jan-Mar **CARDS:**

## EAST KILBRIDE, South Lanarkshire — Map 11 NS65

### ★★★★71% ◎ Crutherland Country House Hotel

Strathaven Rd G75 0QZ
☎ 01355 577000 📠 01355 220855
e-mail: info@crutherland.macdonald-hotels.co.uk
***Dir:*** *off A725, in East Kilbride follow signs for Strathaven A726, approx 1.5m on A726 through Torrance rdbt and Crutherland House is on left in 150 yds*

This renovated mansion is set in 37 acres of landscaped grounds, two miles from the town centre. Behind the Georgian façade is a very spacious and comfortable hotel with extensive banqueting and leisure facilities. The bedrooms are all spacious and comfortable.

**ROOMS:** 75 en suite (26 fmly) No smoking in 62 bedrooms s £75-£89; d £90-£120 (incl. bkfst) * **LB** **FACILITIES:** STV Indoor swimming (H) Sauna Solarium Gym Steam room Technogym ch fac Xmas **CONF:** Thtr 500 Class 200 Board 100 Del from £120 * **SERVICES:** Lift **PARKING:** 150 **NOTES:** No dogs (ex guide dogs) No smoking in restaurant Civ Wed 200 **CARDS:**

### ★★★70% Bruce Hotel

Cornwall St G74 1AF
☎ 01355 229771 📠 01355 242216
e-mail: enquiries@maksu-group.co.uk
***Dir:*** *leave M74 at junct 5 on to A725 and follow to East Kilbride, follow town centre signs and turn right into Cornwall St, hotel 200yds on left*

In the centre of East Kilbride and forming part of the main shopping centre, this purpose-built hotel offers a variety of rooms. The elegant lounge bar and formal restaurant serve a range of excellent dishes. Secure car parking is available. The splendid ballroom is a major attraction.

**ROOMS:** 65 en suite No smoking in 10 bedrooms s £75-£90; d £95-£140 (incl. bkfst) * **FACILITIES:** STV entertainment Xmas **CONF:** Thtr 400 Class 120 Board 80 Del from £85 * **SERVICES:** Lift **PARKING:** 30 **CARDS:**

### ★★★65% Stuart

2 Cornwall Way, Town Centre G74 1JR
☎ 013552 21161 📠 013552 64410
***Dir:*** *6m from junct 5 off M74, head for town centre, hotel on rdbt*

This business and function hotel is convenient for the central shopping area. The split-level cocktail bar adjoins Jellowickis, which offers a varied, good value menu. In addition there is Liao's, serving a wide range of Cantonese and Pekinese dishes. Executive rooms provide the best accommodation.

**ROOMS:** 38 en suite (1 fmly) No smoking in 4 bedrooms s £65-£75; d £85-£90 (incl. bkfst) * **LB** **FACILITIES:** STV Jacuzzi entertainment **CONF:** Thtr 200 Class 80 Board 60 Del from £99.95 * **SERVICES:** Lift **NOTES:** RS Christmas & New Year's Day **CARDS:**

### ⌂ Premier Lodge

PREMIER LODGE

Eaglesham Rd G75 8LW
☎ 0870 700 1398 📠 0870 7001399
***Dir:*** *Situated 8 miles from junct 5 of M74 on the A726 at the rdbt of B764*

Premier Lodge offers modern, well-equipped, en suite accommodation suitable for both business and leisure travellers. Meals can be taken at the adjacent popular restaurant and bar, which is fully licensed. For further details, consult the Hotel Groups page.

**ROOMS:** 40 en suite s £42; d £42 *

EDINBURGH, City of Edinburgh Map 11 NT27

★★★★★69% Sheraton Grand

Sheraton HOTELS & RESORTS

1 Festival Square EH3 9SR
☎ 0131 229 9131 0131 228 4510
e-mail: grandedinburgh.sheraton@sheraton.com
***Dir:*** *follow City Centre signs(A8). Pass through Shandwick, right at lights into Lethian Rd. Right at next lights. Hotel on left at next lights*
This striking modern building forms part of an evolving development to be known as Exchange Square. Recently refurbished public rooms include a marble entrance hall with grand central staircase leading up to the popular lobby lounge. Dining options range from the informal Terrace restaurant to the fine-dining Grill Room. A stunning new six-storey health spa has been developed adjacent to the hotel.
**ROOMS:** 260 en suite (27 fmly) No smoking in 154 bedrooms **FACILITIES: Spa** STV Indoor swimming (H) Sauna Gym Jacuzzi entertainment Xmas **CONF:** Thtr 485 Class 350 Board 120 Del from £140 * **SERVICES:** Lift air con **PARKING:** 80 **NOTES:** No dogs (ex guide dogs) Civ Wed 480 **CARDS:**

★★★★★63% ***Balmoral***
1 Princes St EH2 2EQ
☎ 0131 556 2414 0131 557 8740
e-mail: reservations@balmoral-rf.demon.co.uk
***Dir:*** *the east end of Princes Street. Corner of North Bridge*
This classical Edwardian building enjoys a prime location in the heart of the city, dominating the east end of Princes Street. Tastefully decorated bedrooms are elegantly furnished and equipped with a thoughtful range of facilities. Public areas include the elegant Palm Court bar, a popular venue for afternoon teas, a smart Roman-style health spa and two contrasting restaurants; Number One for fine dining and Hadrians, a cosmopolitan brasserie.
**ROOMS:** 186 en suite No smoking in 82 bedrooms **FACILITIES: Spa** STV Indoor swimming (H) Sauna Solarium Gym Beauty salon Aromatheraphy massage Hairdressers entertainment **CONF:** Thtr 380 Class 180 Board 40 **SERVICES:** Lift air con **PARKING:** 100 **CARDS:**

★★★★78% ***Holyrood Hotel***

MACDONALD HOTELS ★★★★

Holyrood Rd EH8 6AE
☎ 0131 550 4500 0131 550 4545
e-mail: info@holyrood.macdonald-hotels.co.uk
***Dir:*** *the hotel is parallel to the Royal Mile, and near the Holyrood Palace and Dynamic Earth within Edinburgh city centre*
This impressive and immensely stylish new building sits beside the Scottish Parliament, within a stone's throw of Holyrood Palace. The air-conditioned bedrooms and suites include a special Butler's Club floor and lounge. The hotel boasts many extra services such as valet parking and evening turndown, as well as a spa and leisure facility.
**ROOMS:** 157 en suite (10 fmly) No smoking in 140 bedrooms **FACILITIES: Spa** STV Indoor swimming (H) Sauna Solarium Gym Jacuzzi Beauty treatment rooms **CONF:** Thtr 300 Class 80 Board 80 **SERVICES:** Lift air con **PARKING:** 80 **NOTES:** No smoking in restaurant **CARDS:**

Popped the question? Hotels with Civ Wed in their entry are licensed for civil wedding ceremonies. Maximum numbers for the ceremony only are shown, e.g. Civ Wed 120



★★★★74% **Marriott Dalmahoy Hotel & Country Club**

Marriott
HOTELS · RESORTS · SUITES

Kirknewton EH27 8EB
☎ 0131 333 1845 0131 333 1433
***Dir:*** *7m W of Edinburgh on the A71*

Accommodation in this impressive Adam house is comfortably traditional in appointment. Wing bedrooms are bright and modern and have particular appeal for the business guest. Nicely presented public areas include a choice of bars as well as formal and informal dining options. The hotel also boasts a well-equipped leisure centre and a choice of two testing golf courses.
**ROOMS:** 43 en suite 172 annexe en suite (59 fmly) No smoking in 136 bedrooms s £115-£175; d £115-£175 * **LB FACILITIES:** STV Indoor swimming (H) Golf 36 Tennis (hard) Sauna Solarium Gym Putting green Jacuzzi Health & beauty treatments, Steam room, Dance studio, Driving range Xmas **CONF:** Thtr 350 Class 150 Board 90 Del from £150 * **SERVICES:** Lift **PARKING:** 350 **NOTES:** No dogs (ex guide dogs) No smoking in restaurant **CARDS:**

EDINBURGH, continued

**★★★★71% ® Roxburghe**
38 Charlotte Square EH2 4HG
☎ 0131 240 5500 📠 0131 240 5555
e-mail: info@roxburghe.macdonald-hotels.co.uk
***Dir:*** *located in central Edinburgh, on corner of Charlotte St & George St*
In the heart of the city, overlooking Charlotte Square Gardens, this long-established hotel received a complete upgrade in 2000. Public areas are inviting and varied. They include relaxing lounges, a choice of bars (in the evening) and an inner concourse that looks onto a small lawn area. Smart bedrooms come in classic or contemporary style. Parking/setting down can be tricky but friendly obliging staff will assist.
**ROOMS:** 197 en suite (20 fmly) No smoking in 167 bedrooms **FACILITIES:** Indoor swimming (H) Sauna Solarium Gym Dance studio Spa treatment rooms Xmas **CONF:** Thtr 300 Class 120 Board 80 **SERVICES:** Lift **PARKING:** 20 **NOTES:** No smoking in restaurant **CARDS:**

*See advert on page 715*

**★★★★70% Carlton**
North Bridge EH1 1SD
☎ 0131 472 3000 📠 0131 556 2691
e-mail: carlton@paramount-hotels.co.uk
***Dir:*** *on North Bridge which links Princes St to the Royal Mile*
Set in the heart of the city close to the Royal Mile and railway station, the Carlton has been extensively upgraded throughout. Fully refurbished public areas include an impressive open plan reception/lobby, modern first floor bar and restaurant and basement leisure club. Air conditioned bedrooms have also received the same level of attention and are stylishly decorated with a full range of modern amenities.
**ROOMS:** 189 en suite (20 fmly) No smoking in 56 bedrooms **FACILITIES:** STV Indoor swimming (H) Tennis (hard & grass) Squash Sauna Solarium Gym Jacuzzi Table tennis Dance studio Creche entertainment Xmas **CONF:** Thtr 300 Class 160 Board 60 **SERVICES:** Lift air con **NOTES:** No dogs (ex guide dogs) No smoking in restaurant Civ Wed 150 **CARDS:**

**★★★★68% ® George Inter-Continental**
19-21 George St EH2 2PB
☎ 0131 225 1251 📠 0131 226 5644
e-mail: edinburgh@interconti.com
***Dir:*** *city centre, E side parallel to Princes Street*
This impressive hotel is situated within a short walk of Princes Street and continues to attract guests from around the world. Stylish public areas boast many fine original architectural features and include a splendid marble-floored foyer, a comfortable well-stocked bar, and a choice of contrasting eating options of which the elegant Le Chambertin Restaurant provides the fine dining experience. Bedrooms are variable in size and offer good levels of comfort along with a wide range of amenities.
**ROOMS:** 195 en suite No smoking in 73 bedrooms s £180-£205; d £199-£230 * **LB** **FACILITIES:** STV Complimentary Fitness club nearby entertainment Xmas **CONF:** Thtr 200 Class 80 Board 80 Del from £185 * **SERVICES:** Lift **PARKING:** 24 **NOTES:** No dogs (ex guide dogs) Civ Wed 100 **CARDS:**

**★★★★65% Royal Terrace**

18 Royal Ter EH7 5AQ
☎ 0131 557 3222 📠 0131 557 5334
***Dir:*** *from A1 - follow sign into city centre, turn left at the end of London Road into Bleinheim Place continuing onto Royal Terrace*
With the ambience of a town house and with friendly attentive service, this hotel forms part of a quiet Georgian terrace. Bedrooms offer a variety of styles, some lofty and spacious with four-poster beds. The upper rooms look out either over the city to the north or onto terraced gardens at the rear.
**ROOMS:** 108 en suite (19 fmly) s £90-£130; d £100-£170 * **LB** **FACILITIES:** STV Indoor swimming (H) Sauna Solarium Gym Jacuzzi Giant Chess entertainment Xmas **CONF:** Thtr 100 Class 36 Board 40 Del from £125 * **SERVICES:** Lift **NOTES:** No dogs (ex guide dogs) No smoking in restaurant Civ Wed 70 **CARDS:**

**★★★★62% Swallow Royal Scot**
111 Glasgow Rd EH12 8NF
☎ 0131 334 9191 📠 0131 316 4507
e-mail: edinburgh@marriotthotels.co.uk
***Dir:*** *From North enter on M9 and follow signs for A8 past airport. Go under Gogar rdbt sign city centre hotel on right.*

From its position on the city's western fringe, close to the bypass and convenient for the airport, showground and business park, this purpose-built hotel attracts an international clientele. Public areas radiate from the attractive marbled foyer and include two bars, and conference facilities able to accommodate large corporate groups. Significant changes to further upgrade the hotel are expected by early 2002.
**ROOMS:** 245 en suite (131 fmly) No smoking in 89 bedrooms s £90-£140; d £90-£140 * **LB** **FACILITIES:** STV Indoor swimming (H) Sauna Solarium Gym Jacuzzi Steam room entertainment Xmas **CONF:** Thtr 300 Class 120 Board 45 Del from £135 * **SERVICES:** Lift **PARKING:** 300 **NOTES:** Civ Wed 80 **CARDS:**

**★★★79% ®® Norton House**
Ingliston EH28 8LX
☎ 0131 333 1275 📠 0131 333 5305
e-mail: res.nhh@arcadianhotels.co.uk
***Dir:*** *off A8, 5m W of city centre*
Situated close to the airport on the west side of the city, this extended Victorian mansion lies in 55 acres of parkland and attracts the corporate market with its variety of meeting rooms. Bedrooms come in two styles, quietly elegant ones in the main house and modern ones in an adjoining wing. Informal dining

*continued*

options include The Gathering, and fine dining is found in the Conservatory Restaurant.

**ROOMS:** 47 en suite (2 fmly) No smoking in 27 bedrooms s £95-£170; d £115-£190 (incl. bkfst) * **LB** **FACILITIES:** STV Archery, Laser, Clay pigeon shooting, Quad biking Xmas **CONF:** Thtr 300 Class 100 Board 60 Del from £135 * **PARKING:** 200 **NOTES:** No smoking in restaurant Civ Wed 160 **CARDS:**

### ★★★75% Bruntsfield

69/74 Bruntsfield Place EH10 4HH
☎ 0131 229 1393 0131 229 5634
e-mail: bruntsfield@queensferry-hotels.co.uk
***Dir:*** *from S enter Edinburgh on A702. Hotel is located overlooking Bruntsfield Links Park. 1m S of the W end of Princes Street*

Overlooking Bruntsfield Links, this smart hotel has stylish public rooms including relaxing lounge areas; a lively pub; and a conservatory restaurant with adjoining bar. Bedrooms come in a variety of sizes and are well-equipped. Imaginative dinner menus and hearty Scottish breakfasts are served in the bright 'Potting Shed' conservatory restaurant.

**ROOMS:** 75 en suite (5 fmly) No smoking in 49 bedrooms s £69-£102; d £85-£145 * **LB** **FACILITIES:** STV Xmas **CONF:** Thtr 75 Class 30 Board 30 Del from £110 * **SERVICES:** Lift **PARKING:** 25 **NOTES:** No smoking in restaurant Civ Wed 70 **CARDS:**

*See advert on this page*

### ★★★74% Dalhousie Castle Hotel & Spa

Bonnyrigg EH19 3JB
☎ 01875 820153 01875 821936
e-mail: enquiries@dalhousiecastle.co.uk
***Dir:*** *take A7 S from Edinburgh through Lasswade & Newtongrange, turn right at Shell Garage onto B704, hotel 0.5m from junction*

This 13th century castle in beautiful parklands offers a variety of accommodation including period themed bedrooms such as Robert the Bruce and Victoria, as well as cottage style rooms situated in a lodge in the grounds. The Dungeon restaurant offers classical food at dinner whilst the conservatory style Orangerie

*continued*



opens all day. The chapel and beautiful function rooms make this a perfect wedding venue.

**ROOMS:** 27 en suite 5 annexe en suite (3 fmly) No smoking in all bedrooms s fr £110; d fr £172 (incl. bkfst) * **LB** **FACILITIES:** **Spa** STV Fishing Sauna Solarium Jacuzzi Clay pigeon shooting, Archery, Falconry Xmas **CONF:** Thtr 120 Class 60 Board 40 Del £168 * **PARKING:** 110 **NOTES:** No smoking in restaurant Closed 4-9&11-16 Jan Civ Wed 90 **CARDS:**

### ★★★73% *Posthouse Premier Edinburgh*

Corstorphine Rd EH12 6UA
☎ 0870 400 9026 0131 334 9237
***Dir:*** *adjacent to Edinburgh Zoo*

Lying next to Edinburgh zoo, this modern hotel enjoys stunning panoramic views over the city. There is an impressive business meetings complex 'The Academy', and in addition to the main restaurant and popular bar, the exciting 'Sampans' offers an

*continued on p718*

EDINBURGH, continued

authentic oriental menu. Bedrooms are well-equipped, with a choice of standard or more contemporary front-facing superior rooms.
**ROOMS:** 303 en suite (35 fmly) No smoking in 176 bedrooms
**CONF:** Thtr 110 Class 70 Board 50 **SERVICES:** Lift **PARKING:** 100
**NOTES:** No smoking in restaurant **CARDS:**

### ★★★71% Malmaison
One Tower Place EH6 7DB
☎ 0131 468 5000 0131 468 5002
e-mail: edinburgh@malmaison.com
***Dir:*** *A900 from city centre towards Leith, at end of Leith Walk continue over lights through 2 more sets of lights, left into Tower St-hotel on right*
This former Seaman's Mission stands on the waterfront overlooking the fashionable port of Leith. Bedrooms are a key feature throughout, with striking decor as well as CD players, mini bars and a number of individual, welcoming touches. In addition to the café bar, there is a brasserie serving a mix of modern and traditional dishes.
**ROOMS:** 60 en suite (6 fmly) s £115-£165; d £115-£165 * **LB**
**FACILITIES:** STV Gym **CONF:** Thtr 50 Class 16 Board 26 Del £146 *
**SERVICES:** Lift **PARKING:** 50 **CARDS:**

### ★★★70% Braid Hills

Best Western

134 Braid Rd EH10 6JD
☎ 0131 447 8888 0131 452 8477
e-mail: bookings@braidhillshotel.co.uk
***Dir:*** *2.5m S A702, opposite Braid Burn Park*

From its elevated position on the south side, this long-established hotel enjoys splendid panoramic views of the city. Bedrooms are smart, stylish and well-equipped, though varied in size. The public areas are comfortable and inviting, and guests have a dining choice of either the restaurant or bistro.
**ROOMS:** 67 en suite (6 fmly) No smoking in 8 bedrooms s £80; d £135 (incl. bkfst) * **LB** **FACILITIES:** STV Xmas **CONF:** Thtr 100 Class 50 Board 30 Del from £45 * **PARKING:** 38 **NOTES:** No dogs (ex guide dogs) No smoking in restaurant Civ Wed 170
**CARDS:**

*See advert on opposite page*

### ★★★69% Apex International
31/35 Grassmarket EH1 2HS
☎ 0131 300 3456 0131 220 5345
e-mail: international@apexhotels.co.uk
***Dir:*** *turn into Lothian Rd at the West End of Princes Street, then turn 1st left along King Stables Rd. This leads into the Grassmarket*
This modern hotel enjoys a superb city centre location, lying in an historic square in the shadow of Edinburgh Castle. It has an impressive business and conference centre, and the bedrooms are spacious and well-equipped. The restaurant boasts stunning views of the Castle whilst providing a wide ranging menu to satisfy all tastes.
**ROOMS:** 175 en suite (99 fmly) No smoking in 100 bedrooms s £90-£180; d £90-£180 * **LB** **FACILITIES:** STV Xmas **CONF:** Thtr 200 Class 120 Board 50 Del from £100 * **SERVICES:** Lift **PARKING:** 60
**NOTES:** No dogs (ex guide dogs) Civ Wed 180
**CARDS:**

### ★★★66% *Apex European*
90 Haymarket Ter EH12 5LQ
☎ 0131 474 3456 0131 474 3400
e-mail: european@apexhotels.co.uk
A smart modern hotel handy for Haymarket Station and the Conference Centre. The comfortable, well-equipped bedrooms have a bright contemporary feel, as does Tabu, the hotel's brasserie which offers reasonably priced dining.
**ROOMS:** 67 en suite No smoking in 51 bedrooms **FACILITIES:** STV
**CONF:** Thtr 100 Class 60 Board 40 **SERVICES:** Lift **PARKING:** 17
**NOTES:** No dogs (ex guide dogs) **CARDS:**

### ★★★66% Greens Hotel
24 Eglinton Crescent EH12 5BY
☎ 0131 337 1565 0131 346 2990
e-mail: Greens@british-trust-hotels.com
***Dir:*** *Hotel situated in the West End of city, directly off Corstorphine Rd*

Four Georgian houses have been converted to create this comfortable hotel in the West End. Bedrooms are well-furnished and equipped, with superior rooms being particularly spacious. Public rooms include a cosy panelled bar adjacent to the Club Room which offers an appealing alternative to the Garden Restaurant. Here, rugby buffs can savour a host of international team photographs.
**ROOMS:** 55 en suite (6 fmly) No smoking in 20 bedrooms s £55-£75; d £70-£130 (incl. bkfst) * **LB** **FACILITIES:** Xmas **CONF:** Thtr 50 Class 24 Board 30 Del from £85 * **SERVICES:** Lift **NOTES:** No smoking in restaurant Civ Wed 35 **CARDS:**

### ★★★66% Kings Manor
100 Milton Rd East EH15 2NP
☎ 0131 669 0444 0131 669 6650
e-mail: info@kingsmanor.com
***Dir:*** *follow A720 E until Old Craighall Junction then left into city until turning right at the A1/A199 intersection, hotel 200mtrs on right*
Lying on the east side of the city, convenient for the by-pass, this hotel is popular with business guests, conferences and tour

*continued*

groups. It now boasts a fine leisure complex and a bright modern bistro, which complements the more traditional restaurant.

**ROOMS:** 66 en suite (8 fmly) No smoking in 22 bedrooms s £56-£84; d £90-£145 (incl. cont bkfst) * **LB** **FACILITIES:** **Spa** STV Indoor swimming (H) Tennis (hard) Squash Sauna Solarium Gym Jacuzzi Hairdressing Health & beauty salon Xmas **CONF:** Thtr 140 Class 70 Board 50 Del from £104 * **SERVICES:** Lift **PARKING:** 100 **NOTES:** Civ Wed 120 **CARDS:**

### ★★★64% *Carlton Greens Hotel*

2 Carlton Ter EH7 5DD
☎ 0131 556 6570 Fax 0131 557 6680

CARLTON

Upgraded to provide smartly refurbished bedrooms, this hotel lies in a quiet Georgian terrace within walking distance of the city centre. **ROOMS:** 26 en suite **CONF:** Thtr 20 Class 10 Board 20 **NOTES:** No dogs (ex guide dogs) No smoking in restaurant **CARDS:**

### ★★★63% The Barnton

Queensferry Rd, Barnton EH4 6AS
☎ 0131 339 1144 Fax 0131 339 5521

PEEL HOTELS

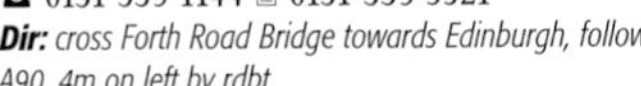

***Dir:*** *cross Forth Road Bridge towards Edinburgh, follow A90, 4m on left by rdbt*

This long-established hotel is ideally located on the A90, four miles from the city centre, the Forth Road Bridge and the airport. It offers a choice of smart executive and standard bedrooms, a restaurant and conference facilities.

**ROOMS:** 50 en suite (9 fmly) No smoking in 25 bedrooms **FACILITIES:** STV Sauna entertainment Xmas **CONF:** Thtr 150 Class 60 Board 50 **SERVICES:** Lift **PARKING:** 100 **NOTES:** No dogs (ex guide dogs) Civ Wed 100 **CARDS:**

### ★★★62% Old Waverley

43 Princes St EH2 2BY
☎ 0131 556 4648 Fax 0131 557 6316
e-mail: waverley@paramount-hotels.co.uk

PARAMOUNT GROUP OF HOTELS

***Dir:*** *in the centre of city, opposite the Scott Monument, Waverley Station and Jenners*

Positioned on Princes Street right in the heart of the city, this long-

*continued*



established hotel enjoys views of the city skyline, as well as the Scott Monument and the Castle behind. Sharing these are the front-facing bedrooms, as well as public rooms, all of which are at first floor level with a striking contemporary decor.
**ROOMS:** 66 en suite (3 fmly) No smoking in 54 bedrooms s £99; d £160 (incl. bkfst) * **LB** **FACILITIES:** STV leisure facilities at sister hotel Xmas **CONF:** Thtr 70 Class 30 Board 26 Del from £90 * **SERVICES:** Lift **NOTES:** No dogs (ex guide dogs) No smoking in restaurant **CARDS:**

### ★★★61% *Jurys Inn Edinburgh*

43 Jeffrey St EH1 1DG
☎ 0131 200 3300 Fax 0131 200 0400
e-mail: info@jurys.com

JURYS DOYLE HOTELS

***Dir:*** *A8/M8 onto Princes Street - 1m R at the Waverley Station, next L*

A modern hotel located next to Waverley Station close to the city centre. It offers large comfortable bedrooms, a smart foyer lounge, the Inn Pub and the Arches Restaurant. Breakfast is served canteen style.

**ROOMS:** 186 en suite (68 fmly) No smoking in 121 bedrooms **FACILITIES:** STV entertainment **CONF:** Thtr 50 Class 35 Board 30 **SERVICES:** Lift **NOTES:** No dogs (ex guide dogs) **CARDS:**

### ★★★60% Quality Hotel

Edinburgh Airport, Ingliston EH28 8NF
☎ 0131 333 4331 Fax 0131 333 4124

Quality Hotel

***Dir:*** *Take turning for Edinburgh Airport from M8. At rdbt before Airport terminal turn L, second L then 1st R.*

Situated beside the Royal Highland Showground at Ingliston, this modern hotel is also convenient for the airport. The spacious

*continued on p720*

EDINBURGH, continued

executive bedrooms are the pick of the accommodation, and there is a café restaurant offering a range of contemporary dishes.
**ROOMS:** 95 en suite No smoking in 64 bedrooms s £55-£65; d £55-£65 * **FACILITIES:** STV **CONF:** Thtr 70 Class 24 Board 24 **SERVICES:** Lift **PARKING:** 100 **NOTES:** No smoking in restaurant
**CARDS:**

### ★★74% *Dunstane House*
4 West Coates, Haymarket EH12 5JQ
☎ 0131 3376169 📠 0131 3376060

This small hotel offers comfortable bedrooms and is conveniently situated for the city centre. The Skerries restaurant features fish from the proprietors' native Orkney Islands, with lighter meals also offered in the Stane bar.
**ROOMS:** 16 en suite

*See advert on opposite page*

### ★★69% *Salisbury View Hotel*
64 Dalkeith Rd EH16 5AE
☎ 0131 667 1133 📠 0131 667 1133
e-mail: enquiries@salisburyviewhotel.co.uk
***Dir:*** *on the A7, approx 1m S of city centre, next to Holyrood Park*

Set on the city's south side close to the university's Pollock Halls, this intimate Georgian hotel provides a relaxed atmosphere. Potters Restaurant is the focus for fine dining and there is a cosy bar lounge (residents and diners only). Bedrooms come in a variety of sizes; all are very smart and well-equipped.
**ROOMS:** 8 en suite (1 fmly) **FACILITIES:** STV **PARKING:** 8 **NOTES:** No dogs (ex guide dogs) No smoking in restaurant Closed 23-26 Dec **CARDS:**

### ★★67% Allison House
15/17 Mayfield Gardens EH9 2AX
☎ 0131 667 8049 📠 0131 667 5001
e-mail: dh007ljh@msn.com
***Dir:*** *1m S of city centre on A701*
This family-run hotel has inviting public areas which include an attractive restaurant with a good range of dishes, and a lounge with a small residents' dispense bar. Bedrooms come in a variety of sizes, but all are well-equipped and complemented by tasteful fabrics and smart decor.
**ROOMS:** 23 rms (21 en suite) (5 fmly) s £35-£45; d £49-£90 (incl. bkfst) * **LB** **CONF:** Thtr 25 Class 12 Board 16 Del from £70 * **PARKING:** 12 **NOTES:** No smoking in restaurant
**CARDS:**

### ★★67% Murrayfield
18 Corstophine Rd EH12 6HN
☎ 0131 337 1844 📠 0131 346 8159
e-mail: reservations@murrayfieldhotel.fsbusiness.co.uk
***Dir:*** *Off main A8*
This popular hotel is situated close to the national rugby stadium and is noted for its friendly service and well-equipped bedrooms. A change of style and operation is planned by new owners Bass.
**ROOMS:** 32 en suite (3 fmly) s £40-£59; d £50-£79 (incl. bkfst) * **LB** **FACILITIES:** entertainment **CONF:** Thtr 20 Class 12 Board 20 Del from £65 * **PARKING:** 30 **CARDS:**

### ★★67% *Orwell Lodge*
29 Polwarth Ter EH11 1NH
☎ 0131 229 1044 📠 0131 228 9492
***Dir:*** *From A702 turn into Gilmore Place (opposite King's theatre) hotel 1m on the left*
Friendly staff provide attentive service at this hotel, a sympathetic conversion and extension of an elegant Victorian mansion. Bedrooms are comfortable, smartly furnished and well-equipped. The spacious bar is a focal point and tasty home-cooked meals can be enjoyed here or in the upstairs dining room.
**ROOMS:** 10 en suite No smoking in all bedrooms **FACILITIES:** entertainment **CONF:** Thtr 250 Class 120 Board 80 **PARKING:** 40 **NOTES:** No dogs (ex guide dogs) No smoking in restaurant Closed 25 Dec Civ Wed 200 **CARDS:**

### ★★65% Thrums Private Hotel
14 Minto St EH9 1RQ
☎ 0131 667 5545 & 667 8545 📠 0131 667 8707
***Dir:*** *off A701 follow city bypass - Edinburgh South - Newington/A7 - A701*
A relaxed atmosphere prevails at this personally run hotel on the south side. Public areas include a lounge with a residents' bar, whilst the dining room has a conservatory extension looking out onto the garden. The attractive bedrooms have a good range of accessories. Large family rooms are contained in a substantial mansion next door.
**ROOMS:** 6 en suite 8 annexe en suite (5 fmly) s £30-£55; d £55-£85 (incl. bkfst) * **LB** **PARKING:** 10 **NOTES:** Closed Xmas
**CARDS:**

## *Premier Collection Town House*

### ★★★★ The Howard
34 Great King St EH3 6QH
☎ 0131 315 2220 & 557 3500 📠 0131 557 6515
e-mail: reserve@thehoward.com
***Dir:*** *travelling E on Queen St, take 2nd left, Dundas St. Continue through 3 sets of lights, turn right & hotel on left*
The Howard was built in 1829 and is made up of three linked Georgian houses. Comfortable and inviting bedrooms, including some half and full suites, are features of this traditional house. Ornate chandeliers and lavish drapes characterise the drawing room, whilst the breakfast room provides an intimate, comfortable venue in which to start the

*continued*

day. Service is professional and staff throughout are genuine in their approach and keen to please.
**ROOMS:** 19 en suite s £155-£175; d £250-£450 (incl. bkfst) * **LB** **FACILITIES:** STV **CONF:** Thtr 16 Board 14 **SERVICES:** Lift **PARKING:** 10 **NOTES:** No dogs (ex guide dogs) Closed 23-28Dec &3-7Jan **CARDS:**

## *Town House*

**★★★★ The Bonham**
35 Drumsheugh Gardens EH3 7RN
☎ 0131 623 6060 & 226 6050 📠 0131 226 6080
e-mail: reserve@thebonham.com
***Dir:*** *located close to West End & Princes St*
Scotland's Hotel of the Year award winner in 2000, this imaginative conversion combines many of the terrace's Victorian features with a contemporary style. Bedrooms come in a variety of sizes and include a number of stylish suites. All have cutting edge technology offering Internet access as well as cable TV. There is a restaurant serving modern cuisine.
**ROOMS:** 48 en suite No smoking in 24 bedrooms s £135-£155; d £165-£195 (incl. cont bkfst) * **LB** **FACILITIES:** STV **CONF:** Thtr 50 Board 24 **SERVICES:** Lift **NOTES:** No dogs (ex guide dogs) Closed 3-6 Jan **CARDS:**

## *Town House*

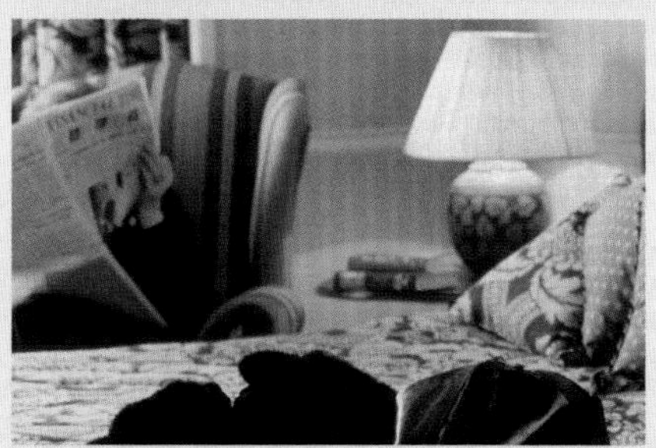

**★★★★ Channings**
South Learmonth Gardens EH4 1EZ
☎ 0131 332 3232 & 315 2226 📠 0131 332 9631
e-mail: reserve@channings.co.uk
***Dir:*** *approach Edinburgh on the A90 from Forth Road Bridge, follow signs for city centre*
Originally five Edwardian terraced houses, recent

*continued on p722*

EDINBURGH, continued

refurbishment has resulted in comfortable and attractively furnished bedrooms, equipped to meet the needs of tourists and business visitors alike. Ground floor lounges, split into a number of separate areas, have a club-like feel to them, whilst the wine bar and conservatory restaurant are definitely modern in design, providing a suitable backdrop to the carefully prepared and imaginative cuisine offered.
**ROOMS:** 46 en suite No smoking in 30 bedrooms s £130-£155; d £175-£195 (incl. bkfst) LB **FACILITIES:** STV **CONF:** Thtr 60 Board 34 Del from £140 * **SERVICES:** Lift **NOTES:** No dogs (ex guide dogs) No smoking in restaurant Closed 23-27 Dec Civ Wed 80
**CARDS:**

### ⇧ *Travelodge*
Old Craighall EH21 8RE
☎ 0131 653 6070
***Dir:*** *off A1, 2m from eastern outskirts Edinburgh*
Travelodge offers good quality, good value, modern accommodation. Ideal for families, the spacious, en suite bedrooms include remote-control TV, tea and coffee-making facilities, luxury beds and free morning newspaper. Meals can be taken at the nearby family restaurant. For further details and the Travelodge phone number, consult the Hotel Groups page.

**ROOMS:** 45 en suite

### ⇧ *Travelodge*
46 Dreghorn Link EH13 9QR
☎ 0131 441 4296 📠 0131 441 4296
***Dir:*** *6m S, A720 Ring Rd South*
Travelodge offers good quality, good value, modern accommodation. Ideal for families, the spacious, en suite bedrooms include remote-control TV, tea and coffee-making facilities, luxury beds and free morning newspaper. Meals can be taken at the nearby family restaurant. For further details and the Travelodge phone number, consult the Hotel Groups page.

**ROOMS:** 40 en suite

### ⇧ Express by Holiday Inn Edinburgh Leith
Britannia Way, Ocean Dr, Leith EH6 6LA
☎ 0131 555 4422 📠 0131 555 4646
e-mail: info@hiex-edinburgh.com
***Dir:*** *follow signs for Royal Yacht Britannia. Hotel is located just before Britannia on the right*

A modern budget hotel offering comfortable accommodation in refreshing, spacious and comprehensively equipped bedrooms, en suite bathrooms with power showers and continental buffet breakfast included in the room rate. Suitable for business travellers or families. For further details and the Express by Holiday Inn phone number, consult the Hotel Groups page.
**ROOMS:** 102 en suite (incl. cont bkfst) s £60-£85; d £60-£85 *
**CONF:** Thtr 60 Class 30 Board 30

### ⇧ *Premier Lodge (City Centre)*
Grassmarket EH1 2JF
☎ 0870 700 1370 📠 0870 700 1371
Premier Lodge offers modern, well-equipped, en suite accommodation suitable for both business and leisure travellers. Meals can be taken at the adjacent popular restaurant and bar, which is fully licensed. For further details, consult the Hotel Groups page.
**ROOMS:** 45 en suite

### ⇧ *Premier Lodge (Edinburgh East)*
City Bypass, Newcraighall EH2 8SG
☎ 0870 700 1372 📠 0870 700 1373
Premier Lodge offers modern, well-equipped, en suite accommodation suitable for both business and leisure travellers. Meals can be taken at the adjacent popular restaurant and bar, which is fully licensed. For further details, consult the Hotel Groups page.

### ⇧ *Travelodge*
33 St Marys St EH1 1TA
☎ 0131 557 6281

Travelodge

Travelodge offers good quality, good value, modern accommodation. Ideal for families, the spacious, en suite bedrooms include remote-control TV, tea and coffee-making facilities, luxury beds and free morning newspaper. Meals can be taken at the nearby family restaurant. For further details and the Travelodge phone number, consult the Hotel Groups page.

### ⇧ Hotel Ibis

ibis
Accor hotels

6 Hunter Square, (off The Royal Mile) EH1 1QW
☎ 0131 240 7000 📠 0131 240 7007
e-mail: H2039@accor-hotels.com
***Dir:*** *from Queen St (M8/M9) or Waterloo Pl (A1) crossover North Bridge (A7) & High St, take 1st right off South Bridge, this is Hunter Sq*
Modern, budget hotel offering comfortable accommodation in bright and practical bedrooms. Breakfast is self-service and dinner is available in the restaurant. For further details, consult the Hotel Groups page.
**ROOMS:** 99 en suite s £60-£70; d £60-£70 *

○ **Scotsman**
North Bridge EH1 1YT
☎ 0131 5565565
At the time of going to press, the star classification for this hotel was not confirmed. Please refer to the AA internet site www.theAA.com for current information.

○ **Menzies Belford**
69 Belford Rd EH4 3DG
☎ 0131 332 2545 🖷 0131 332 3805

***Dir:*** *second left after Haymarket Stn, hotel at bottom of Palmerston Place on left*

This hotel was acquired by Menzies as the guide went to press. Public areas are being upgraded and the company's brasserie restaurant concept is being introduced. Please refer to the AA internet site www.theAA.com for current information.
**ROOMS:** 144 rms **CONF:** Thtr 120 Class 60 Board 45

EDZELL, Angus — Map 15 NO66

★★★64% **Glenesk**
High St DD9 7TF
☎ 01356 648319 🖷 01356 647333
e-mail: glenskhotel@btconnect.com
***Dir:*** *off A90 just after Brechin Bypass*

This long established family-run hotel is at the south end of the village beside the golf course. The bedrooms vary in size and have been refurbished to offer modern appointments. Comfortable public areas include a choice of relaxing lounges, a dining room overlooking the garden, and a well-equipped leisure centre.
**ROOMS:** 24 en suite (5 fmly) s £50-£60; d £75-£98 (incl. bkfst) * **LB**
**FACILITIES:** Indoor swimming (H) Snooker Sauna Solarium Gym Croquet lawn Jacuzzi Xmas **CONF:** Thtr 120 Class 60 Board 30
**PARKING:** 81 **NOTES:** No smoking in restaurant Civ Wed 60
**CARDS:**



ELGIN, Moray — Map 15 NJ26

★★★76%  **Mansion House**
The Haugh IV30 1AW
☎ 01343 548811 🖷 01343 547916
e-mail: reception@mhelgin.co.uk
***Dir:*** *in Elgin turn off the A96 into Haugh Rd, hotel at the end of the road by the river*
A baronial-style mansion close to the River Lossie. Bedrooms are individual in size and style with a wide range of amenities and many have four-poster beds. Attractive public areas include a lounge, bar, billiard room, and a leisure club. The popular Bistro is an informal alternative to the elegant restaurant where fine cooking is offered.
**ROOMS:** 23 en suite (3 fmly) s £80-£95; d £120-£160 (incl. bkfst) * **LB**
**FACILITIES:** STV Indoor swimming (H) Snooker Sauna Solarium Gym Jacuzzi Hairdresser Beauty therapist Steam room ch fac Xmas
**CONF:** Thtr 200 Class 150 Board 50 **PARKING:** 150 **NOTES:** No dogs (ex guide dogs) No smoking in restaurant Civ Wed 180
**CARDS:**

*See advert on this page*

★★★68% **Laichmoray**
Maisondieu Rd IV30 1QR
☎ 01343 540045 🖷 01343 540055
e-mail: enquiries@laichmorayhotel.co.uk
***Dir:*** *opposite the railway station*
Convenient for the railway station, this family-run hotel has a relaxed and welcoming atmosphere. Thoughtfully equipped bedrooms vary in size and are appointed in mixed styles. The lounge and conservatory are popular for good-value bar meals,

*continued on p724*

ELGIN, continued

and high tea and carte dinners are served in the attractive restaurant. The bar features an impressive range of malt whiskies.

*Laichmoray, Elgin*

**ROOMS:** 35 rms (34 en suite) (5 fmly) No smoking in 4 bedrooms **FACILITIES:** Darts,Pool ch fac Xmas **CONF:** Thtr 200 Class 160 Board 40 **PARKING:** 60 **NOTES:** Civ Wed 120
**CARDS:**

ERISKA, Argyll & Bute — Map 10 NM94

## Premier Collection

★★★★ ◎◎◎ **Isle of Eriska**
Eriska, Ledaig PA37 1SD
☎ 01631 720371 📠 01631 720531
e-mail: office@eriska-hotel.co.uk
***Dir:*** *leave A85 at Connel and join A828 and follow for 4m, then follow signs from north of Benderloch*
This Victorian mansion house is situated on a private island approached by a small bridge. Guests are encouraged to explore the island, visiting the beaches, woodland and natural gardens; there is also an indoor swimming pool and treatment rooms. Spacious bedrooms are comfortable and boast some fine antique pieces. Public areas include a choice of different lounges as well as the part wood-panelled dining room. Local seafood and game features prominently in the carefully prepared meals.
**ROOMS:** 17 en suite s fr £175; d £220-£270 (incl. bkfst) * **LB**
**FACILITIES:** **Spa** Indoor swimming (H) Golf 6 Tennis (hard) Fishing Sauna Gym Croquet lawn Putting green Jacuzzi Steam room Skeet shooting Nature trails ch fac Xmas **CONF:** Thtr 30 Class 30 Board 30 Del from £149 * **PARKING:** 40 **NOTES:** No smoking in restaurant Closed Jan **CARDS:**

ERSKINE, Renfrewshire — Map 11 NS47

★★★66% ***The Erskine Bridge Hotel***
North Barr PA8 6AN
☎ 0141 812 0123 📠 0141 812 7642
***Dir:*** *M8 junct 30 and take A726 to Erskine. At 1st rndbt turn right 2nd straight through 3rd turn left*
Located on the banks of the River Clyde within sight of Erskine Bridge, this bright, modern hotel offers well-equipped bedrooms. Function facilities are extensive and there is a good leisure centre.
**ROOMS:** 177 en suite (26 fmly) No smoking in 88 bedrooms
**FACILITIES:** Indoor swimming (H) Sauna Solarium Gym Jacuzzi
**CONF:** Thtr 600 Class 400 Board 50 **SERVICES:** Lift **PARKING:** 350
**CARDS:**

FALKIRK, Falkirk — Map 11 NS88

★★★69% **Park Lodge Hotel**
Camelon Rd FK1 5RY
☎ 01324 628331 📠 01324 611593
e-mail: park@queensferry-hotels.co.uk
***Dir:*** *from M8 take A803 into Falkirk, hotel 1m beyond Mariner Leisure Ctr, opposite Dollar Park. From M9, A803 through Falkirk follow signs Dollar Park*
This popular corporate and banqueting hotel is located on the west side of town. Bedrooms are comfortable, modern in style and offer a good range of amenities. Public areas include a spacious lounge/bar, and the new La Bonne Auberge Brasserie where the varied menus offer something to suit everyone.
**ROOMS:** 55 en suite (3 fmly) No smoking in 32 bedrooms s £69; d £79 (incl. bkfst) * **LB** **FACILITIES:** STV **CONF:** Thtr 300 Class 180 Board 80 Del from £98 * **SERVICES:** Lift **PARKING:** 160 **NOTES:** No dogs (ex guide dogs) **CARDS:**

**Premier Lodge**
Bellsdyke Rd, Larbert FK5 4EG
☎ 0870 700 1386 📠 0870 7001387
Premier Lodge offers modern, well-equipped, en suite accommodation suitable for both business and leisure travellers. Meals can be taken at the adjacent popular restaurant and bar, which is fully licensed. For further details, consult the Hotel Groups page.
**ROOMS:** 60 en suite s £42; d £42 *

FORFAR, Angus — Map 15 NO45

★★★68% **Idvies House**
Letham DD8 2QJ
☎ 01307 818787 📠 01307 818933
e-mail: idvies@mail.com
***Dir:*** *from Forfar B9128 signed Carnoustie, 2m left at fork signed Letham & Arbroath. 1.5m to T-junct,( ignore Letham signs), left towards Arbroath, hotel on left*
Peacefully set amid quiet wooded grounds, this comfortable Victorian country house offers a relaxed and homely atmosphere. Bedrooms, with all the expected amenities, are furnished with attractive period pieces. Public areas include a well-stocked bar with a small study adjacent, and two dining rooms.
**ROOMS:** 11 en suite (1 fmly) s £47-£50; d £57-£65 (incl. bkfst) * **LB**
**FACILITIES:** STV Snooker **CONF:** Thtr 50 Class 30 Board 30
**PARKING:** 60 **NOTES:** No smoking in restaurant Closed 25 Dec-2 Jan Civ Wed 40 **CARDS:**

Fancy a Singapore Sling? Bar staff in five star hotels should be skilled cocktail mixers.

FORRES, Moray Map 14 NJ05

**★★★66% Ramnee**
Victoria Rd IV36 3BN
☎ 01309 672410 01309 673392
e-mail: ramneehotel@btconnect.com
***Dir:*** *turn off A96 at rdbt on eastern side of Forres, hotel 200yds on right*

Situated in two acres of gardens, the Ramnee Hotel was built in 1907 as a private residence and has been transformed into a country house-style hotel. Public areas are inviting and the lively lounge bar is very popular for meals.
**ROOMS:** 20 en suite (4 fmly) s £55-£95; d £95-£115 (incl. bkfst) * **LB**
**FACILITIES:** STV use of leisure facilities at sister hotel ch fac **CONF:** Thtr 100 Class 30 Board 45 Del from £97.50 * **PARKING:** 50 **NOTES:** No smoking in restaurant Closed Xmas Day/1-3Jan Civ Wed 100
**CARDS:**

*See advert on this page*



FORT WILLIAM, Highland Map 14 NN17

***Premier Collection***

**★★★★ Inverlochy Castle**
Torlundy PH33 6SN
☎ 01397 702177 01397 702953
e-mail: info@inverlochy.co.uk
RELAIS & CHATEAUX.
***Dir:*** *accessible from either A82 Glasgow-Fort William or A9 Edinburgh-Dalwhinnie. Hotel 3m N of Fort William on A82, in Torlundy*
Set amidst glorious scenery this impressive Victorian building has 500 acres of grounds. Bedrooms are lavishly appointed and spacious, some facing Ben Nevis. Private dining rooms are available, but the main dining room, adjacent to the elegant drawing room, has stunning loch and mountain views. Top quality ingredients are carefully cooked.
**ROOMS:** 17 en suite s fr £180; d fr £290 (incl. bkfst) *
**FACILITIES:** STV Tennis (hard) Fishing Snooker entertainment Xmas **PARKING:** 18 **NOTES:** No dogs (ex guide dogs) Closed 5 Jan-12 Feb Civ Wed 40 **CARDS:**

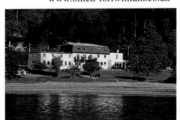

FORT WILLIAM, continued

### ★★★71% Moorings

Banavie PH33 7LY
☎ 01397 772797 ▯ 01397 772441
e-mail: reservations@moorings-fortwilliam.co.uk
***Dir:*** *3m North of Fort William off A830. Take A830 for approx 1m, cross the Caledonian canal and take first right*

This modern hotel west of Fort William is beside 'Neptune's Staircase' of the Caledonian Canal with views of Ben Nevis on clear days. Interesting meals are available as a two or four course fixed price menu in the Jacobean-style dining room, or as bar food in the Upper Deck lounge bar or popular Mariners Bar. Bedrooms have fresh decor and good facilities.
**ROOMS:** 27 en suite (1 fmly) No smoking in 6 bedrooms s £30-£60; d £60-£100 (incl. bkfst) * LB **FACILITIES:** STV ch fac Xmas **CONF:** Thtr 120 Class 40 Board 50 **PARKING:** 60 **NOTES:** No smoking in restaurant **CARDS:**

*See advert on opposite page*

### ★★71% Nevis Bank

Belford Rd PH33 6BY
☎ 01397 705721 ▯ 01397 706275
e-mail: info@nevisbankhotel.co.uk
***Dir:*** *on A82, at junct to Glen Nevis*
A relaxed and welcoming atmosphere is provided at this long-established Highland hotel which stands beside the A82 close to the access road to Glen Nevis. Public areas include a choice of contrasting bars, lounge, and attractive dining room. Bedrooms vary in size and offer modern appointments along with a good range of facilities.
**ROOMS:** 31 en suite 8 annexe en suite (3 fmly) s fr £45; d fr £80 (incl. bkfst) * LB **FACILITIES:** Sauna Solarium Gym Xmas **CONF:** Thtr 40 Class 20 Board 20 **PARKING:** 50 **NOTES:** No smoking in restaurant **CARDS:**

### ★★69% Grand

Gordon Square PH33 6DX
☎ 01397 702928 ▯ 01397 702928
e-mail: enquiries@grandhotel-scotland.co.uk
***Dir:*** *on A82 at W end of High St*
A relaxed and welcoming atmosphere is provided at this long-established family-run hotel at the south end of the High Street. Good progress is being made with the ongoing bedroom refurbishment programme, which also includes an upgrade of the bathrooms. Public areas include a choice of comfortable lounges, a well-stocked bar and attractive dining room where the carte menu offers a tempting range of freshly prepared dishes.
**ROOMS:** 33 en suite (4 fmly) s £25-£43; d £44-£65 (incl. bkfst) * LB **FACILITIES:** ch fac **CONF:** Thtr 110 Class 60 Board 20 **PARKING:** 20 **NOTES:** No smoking in restaurant Closed 31Dec-6Feb Civ Wed 80 **CARDS:**

*See advert on opposite page*

### ★★69% Imperial

Fraser's Square PH33 6DW
☎ 01397 702040 & 703921 ▯ 01397 706277
***Dir:*** *from town centre travel along Middle St approx 400mtrs from junction with A82*
This friendly, family-run hotel in the centre of town is a popular base for visiting tour groups. The modern bedrooms vary in size and offer a good range of amenities. Public areas include an attractive cocktail bar and a bright restaurant.
**ROOMS:** 32 en suite (3 fmly) s £35-£48; d £50-£70 (incl. bkfst) * LB **FACILITIES:** Xmas **CONF:** Thtr 60 Class 30 Board 30 Del from £61 * **PARKING:** 15 **NOTES:** No smoking in restaurant
**CARDS:**

### ★★68% *Milton Hotel & Leisure Club*

North Rd PH33 6TG
☎ 01397 702331 ▯ 01397 700132
e-mail: sales@miltonhotels.com
***Dir:*** *N of town, on A82*
A well-proportioned and comfortable hotel popular with tour groups and leisure guests, especially families. The leisure centre is an attraction and live entertainment features on selected evenings. Bedrooms range from smart spacious executive rooms to smaller, practical standard rooms.
**ROOMS:** 52 en suite 67 annexe en suite (14 fmly) **FACILITIES:** Indoor swimming (H) Sauna Solarium Gym Jacuzzi Beauty salon entertainment **CONF:** Thtr 220 Class 70 Board 60 **PARKING:** 140 **NOTES:** No smoking in restaurant **CARDS:**

### ★★67% *Alexandra*

The Parade PH33 6AZ
☎ 01397 702241 ▯ 01397 705554
e-mail: sales@miltonhotels.com
***Dir:*** *North end of town centre*
Located on the High Street close to the railway station, this welcoming Victorian hotel is a popular base for tour groups. Bedrooms range from modern executive and superior rooms, to the smaller and more practical standard rooms. Public areas include a choice of comfortable lounges, a restaurant and coffee shop. Leisure facilities are available to guests at the nearby sister hotel.
**ROOMS:** 97 en suite (14 fmly) **FACILITIES:** Free use of nearby leisure club entertainment **CONF:** Thtr 140 Class 40 Board 26 **SERVICES:** Lift **PARKING:** 65 **NOTES:** No smoking in restaurant
**CARDS:**

### ★★60% The Caledonian

Achintore Rd PH33 6RW
☎ 01397 703117 ▯ 01397 700550
PEEL HOTELS
***Dir:*** *on A82, just south of Fort William centre*
From its position beside the A82 on the south side of town, this modern purpose-built hotel overlooks Loch Linnhe, and is a popular base for visiting tour groups. Public areas include an open-plan foyer area with lounge and bar. Best accommodation is to be found on the lower floors where refurbishment has taken place.
**ROOMS:** 86 en suite (12 fmly) s £55-£75; d £50-£90 (incl. bkfst) * LB **FACILITIES:** Sauna entertainment ch fac Xmas **CONF:** Thtr 60 Class 40 Board 30 **SERVICES:** Lift **PARKING:** 60 **NOTES:** No smoking in restaurant **CARDS:**

Early start? Hotels at all star levels should provide in-room alarm clocks and/or alarm calls.

## FREUCHIE, Fife

Map 11 NO20

### ★★67% Lomond Hills

Parliament Square KY15 7EY
☎ 01337 857329 & 857498 🖷 01337 858180
e-mail: lomond_foresthotels@hotmail.com
***Dir:*** *in centre of village off A92 2m north of Glenrothes*

A former coaching inn has been considerably extended to create this welcoming tourist and business hotel in the centre of the village. Bedrooms come in varying sizes and styles, but all are comfortable and offer a good range of amenities. Public areas offer all the expected facilities plus a popular leisure centre.

**ROOMS:** 24 en suite (3 fmly) No smoking in 3 bedrooms s £50-£54; d £70-£75 (incl. bkfst) * **LB** **FACILITIES:** STV Indoor swimming (H) Sauna Solarium Gym Jacuzzi ch fac Xmas **CONF:** Thtr 200 Class 100 Board 80 Del from £62 * **PARKING:** 21 **NOTES:** Civ Wed 100
**CARDS:** 

## GAIRLOCH, Highland

Map 14 NG87

### ★★★67% Creag Mor Hotel

Charleston IV21 2AH
☎ 01445 712068 🖷 01445 712044
e-mail: relax@creagmorhotel.com
***Dir:*** *A9 to Inverness, then A832 following signs to Ullapool, pass through village of Garve and follow signs for Gairloch, hotel 1st on right*

Situated in the highland scenery of Wester Ross, this comfortable hotel provides pleasantly decorated bedrooms with every modern convenience. Tranquil public areas include an inviting split-level gallery bar/lounge from which views of the harbour can be

*continued on p728*

GAIRLOCH, continued

enjoyed. Local produce features strongly in the dining room and there is also an all-day menu.
**ROOMS:** 17 en suite (1 fmly) s £58-£63; d £90-£110 (incl. bkfst) * LB **FACILITIES:** Fishing Games room ch fac Xmas **CONF:** Class 40 Del from £80 * **PARKING:** 29 **NOTES:** No smoking in restaurant
**CARDS:**

*See advert on opposite page*

### ★★72% *Myrtle Bank*
Low Rd IV21 2BS
☎ 01445 712004 01445 712214
e-mail: myrtlebank@msn.com
*Dir: off B8012 Melvaig road*
A warm welcome is assured at this hotel by the shore of Loch Gairloch. The bedrooms are comfortable and several enjoy views over the loch to the Skye hills. There is a lounge, conservatory, and a bar and dining room, both serving enjoyable food.
**ROOMS:** 12 en suite (2 fmly) **PARKING:** 20 **NOTES:** No smoking in restaurant **CARDS:**

## GALASHIELS, Scottish Borders — Map 12 NT43

### ★★★66% Kingsknowes
Selkirk Rd TD1 3HY
☎ 01896 758375 01896 750377
e-mail: sylvia@kingsknowes.co.uk
*Dir: off A7 at Galashiels/ Selkirk rdbt*
A friendly, informal atmosphere pervades this family-run hotel. A Victorian turreted mansion, its public areas feature a marble entrance and imposing staircase. There is a choice of bars, one offering a good range of meals to complement the restaurant. Bedrooms are tasteful and several on the first floor are massive.
**ROOMS:** 11 en suite (3 fmly) s £54; d £80 (incl. bkfst) * LB **FACILITIES:** ch fac Xmas **CONF:** Thtr 65 Class 45 Board 30 Del from £65 * **PARKING:** 72 **NOTES:** No smoking in restaurant Civ Wed 100
**CARDS:**

### ★★★63% Woodlands House Hotel & Restaurants
Windyknowe Rd TD1 1RG
☎ 01896 754722 01896 754892
e-mail: woodlands.uk@virgin.net
*Dir: A7 into Galashiels, A72 towards Peebles, 1st L into Hall St, 2nd R*
Quietly situated in two acres of grounds, this fine Victorian Gothic mansion lies above the town, within easy walking distance of the centre. Bedrooms are generally spacious, many having views over the gardens, whilst the ground floor offers a high ceiling bar and nicely furnished restaurant, both featuring fine period architecture.
**ROOMS:** 10 en suite (1 fmly) s £50-£55; d £72-£96 (incl. bkfst) * LB **FACILITIES:** Xmas **CONF:** Thtr 50 Class 30 Board 24 **PARKING:** 35 **NOTES:** No smoking in restaurant Civ Wed 54 **CARDS:**

### ★★65% King's
56 Market St TD1 3AN
☎ 01896 755497 01896 755497
e-mail: kingshotel@talk21.com
*Dir: adjacent to southbound A7 in town centre*
A welcoming atmosphere prevails at this family-run hotel close to the town centre. Bedrooms are equipped with a good range of amenities. Freshly prepared meals are provided in the dining room and bar, while home baking accompanies the morning coffees and afternoon teas.
**ROOMS:** 7 en suite (2 fmly) No smoking in all bedrooms s £35-£46; d £50-£72 (incl. bkfst) * LB **CONF:** Thtr 80 Class 30 Board 40 Del from £65 * **PARKING:** 16 **NOTES:** No dogs (ex guide dogs) Closed 1-3 Jan Civ Wed 60 **CARDS:**

### ★★63% Abbotsford Arms
63 Stirling St TD1 1BY
☎ 01896 752517 01896 750744
*Dir: turn off A7 down Ladhope Vale, turn left opposite bus station*
A friendly and informal hotel within walking distance of the town centre. Food is served throughout the day, guests can enjoy a range of generous dishes in the bar and restaurant.
**ROOMS:** 14 en suite (2 fmly) s £38-£40; d £58-£60 (incl. bkfst) * LB **FACILITIES:** STV **CONF:** Thtr 150 Class 100 Board 100 **PARKING:** 10 **NOTES:** No dogs (ex guide dogs) Closed 24-25 & 31 Dec & 1 Jan
**CARDS:**

## GATEHOUSE OF FLEET, Dumfries & Galloway — Map 11 NX55

### ★★★★69% Cally Palace
DG7 2DL
☎ 01557 814341 01557 814522
e-mail: info@callypalace.co.uk
*Dir: From M6 and A74 follow signs for A75 Dumfries then Stranraer. At Gatehouse-of-Fleet turn right onto B727 then left at Cally.*

The grounds of this fine Victorian shooting lodge contain a vegetable garden, a croquet lawn, a small fishing loch and a maze. Antique and period furniture feature and two bedrooms have lounge areas. The large ground-floor room is suitable for guests with disabilities. A set four-course dinner is served house-party style and there is an honesty bar in the billiard room.
**ROOMS:** 55 en suite (7 fmly) s £101-£123; d £148-£172 (incl. bkfst & dinner) * LB **FACILITIES:** STV Indoor swimming (H) Golf 18 Tennis (hard) Fishing Snooker Sauna Solarium Croquet lawn Putting green Jacuzzi Table tennis Practice fairway entertainment ch fac Xmas
**CONF:** Thtr 40 Class 40 Board 25 **SERVICES:** Lift **PARKING:** 100
**NOTES:** No smoking in restaurant Closed Jan-early Feb
**CARDS:**

### ★★★64% Murray Arms
DG7 2HY
☎ 01557 814207 01557 814370
e-mail: murrayarmshotel@ukonline.co.uk
*Dir: off A75, hotel at edge of town, near clock tower*
A relaxed and welcoming atmosphere prevails at this family-run hotel, a former coaching inn at the north end of the main street. Public areas retain a comfortable, traditional feel and include a choice of lounges, a snug bar and the popular Lunky Hole restaurant where food is available all day.
**ROOMS:** 12 en suite 1 annexe en suite (3 fmly) s £45-£50; d £85-£100 (incl. bkfst) * LB **FACILITIES:** Tennis (hard) Croquet lawn Xmas
**CONF:** Thtr 120 Class 50 Board 30 Del from £70 * **PARKING:** 50
**CARDS:**

Read all about it! Newspapers delivered to bedrooms in four and five star hotels.

## GLASGOW, City of Glasgow — Map 11 NS56

see also Clydebank & Uplawmoor

### ★★★★73% Millennium Hotel Glasgow

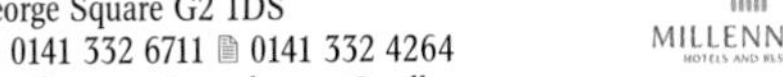

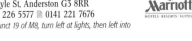

George Square G2 1DS
☎ 0141 332 6711 🖹 0141 332 4264
e-mail: reservations.glasgow@mill-cop.com

***Dir:*** *Exit M8 junct 15 follow road through 4 sets of lights, at 5th set turn left into Hanover St. George Square directly ahead, hotel right hand corner.*

Right in the heart of the city, the Millennium has pride of place overlooking George Square. Having recently undergone a massive refurbishment programme, the whole property has a contemporary air about it. Bedroom comfort has the edge with plenty of workspace for the business guest. Public areas include a glass veranda overlooking the square, a great place to unwind and people-watch.

**ROOMS:** 117 en suite No smoking in 54 bedrooms s £125-£195; d £125-£195 * **FACILITIES:** STV Gym Xmas **CONF:** Thtr 40 Class 24 Board 32 Del £140 * **SERVICES:** Lift air con **NOTES:** No dogs (ex guide dogs)
**CARDS:**

### ★★★★68% Langs Hotel

2 Port Dundas Place G2 3LD
☎ 0141 333 1500 & 352 2452 🖹 0141 333 5700

***Dir:*** *directly in front of Royal Concert Hall*

The contemporary style of this exciting new city centre hotel more than meets expectations. The spacious bedrooms, which include duplex suites, invite relaxation with Sony Playstations and CD players. They also cater well for business travellers. There is a choice of fine dining options.

**ROOMS:** 100 en suite No smoking in 60 bedrooms **FACILITIES:** STV Sauna Gym Spa & treatment rooms **CONF:** Class 12 Board 14 Del £138 * **SERVICES:** Lift **NOTES:** No dogs (ex guide dogs) No smoking in restaurant **CARDS:**

### ★★★★67% Glasgow Marriott Hotel

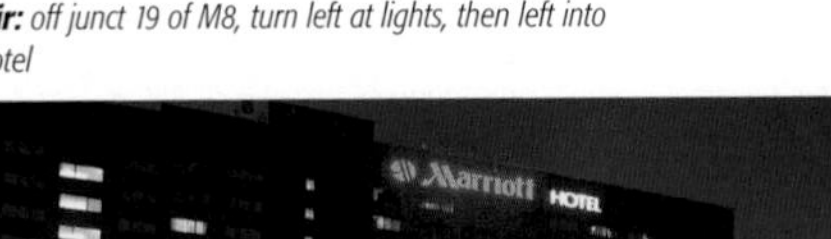
Marriott
HOTELS · RESORTS · SUITES

500 Argyle St, Anderston G3 8RR
☎ 0141 226 5577 🖹 0141 221 7676

***Dir:*** *off junct 19 of M8, turn left at lights, then left into hotel*

Marriott HOTEL

The Glasgow Marriott is a well-established and conveniently located hotel with a smart open plan lounge, informal café bar and bright fashionable restaurant. The leisure club has been upgraded and includes a gym and pool. High quality, well-equipped bedrooms benefit from air conditioning and generous beds; the suites are particularly comfortable.

**ROOMS:** 300 en suite (89 fmly) No smoking in 212 bedrooms s fr £115; d fr £115 * **LB** **FACILITIES:** STV Indoor swimming (H) Sauna Solarium Gym Heated whirlpool Beautician Xmas **CONF:** Thtr 650 Class 300 Board 50 Del from £141 * **SERVICES:** Lift air con **PARKING:** 180 **NOTES:** No dogs (ex guide dogs) Civ Wed 450
**CARDS:**

### ★★★★66% Beardmore

Best Western

Beardmore St G81 4SA
☎ 0141 951 6000 🖹 0141 951 6018
e-mail: beardmore.hotel@hci.co.uk
(For full entry see Clydebank)

### ★★★73% Carlton George Hotel

44 West George St G2 1DH
☎ 0141 353 6373 🖹 0141 353 6263
e-mail: gmgeorge@carltonhotels.co.uk

This modern centrally located hotel offers a very high standard of comfortable, mostly spacious accommodation with many thoughtful extras. The Windows rooftop restaurant is quickly gaining a good reputation for its fine dining, and staff are very attentive and pleasant. Resident guests will appreciate the comfort and facilities of their Executive Lounge.

**ROOMS:** 64 en suite No smoking in 32 bedrooms s £140-£150; d £140-£150 **LB** **FACILITIES:** STV free access to local health/fitness club Xmas **CONF:** Thtr 30 Board 30 **SERVICES:** Lift air con **NOTES:** No smoking in restaurant **CARDS:**

### ★★★73% Malmaison

Malmaison HOTELS

278 West George St G2 4LL
☎ 0141 572 1000 🖹 0141 572 1002
e-mail: glasgow@malmaison.com

***Dir:*** *from South/East-M8 Junction 18 (Charing Cross), from West/North-M8 City Centre Glasgow*

The Malmaison is built around a former church with the brasserie being situated in the crypt. Bedrooms feature a host of modern facilities such as CD players and mini bars and includes a range of split level suites. The all-day Café Mal provides lighter fare than

*continued on p730*

GLASGOW, continued

the brasserie, and there is also a small gym to work off the extra calories.
**ROOMS:** 72 en suite (4 fmly) No smoking in 20 bedrooms s £110-£165; d £110-£165 * **LB** **FACILITIES:** STV Gym Cardiovascular gym **CONF:** Thtr 35 Class 20 Board 20 Del £155 * **SERVICES:** Lift **NOTES:** No dogs (ex guide dogs) **CARDS:**

### ★★★71% Holiday Inn
161 West Nile St G1 2RL
☎ 0141 352 8300 0141 332 7447
e-mail: info@higlasgow.com
***Dir:*** *M8 jnct 16, follow signs for Royal Concert Hall, hotel is opposite*
Purpose built on a corner site close to the Theatre Royal and the Concert Hall, this contemporary hotel features the popular Bonne Auberge French restaurant, a bar area and conservatory. Bedrooms are well-equipped and comfortable with suites available. Staff are friendly and attentive.
**ROOMS:** 113 en suite (24 fmly) No smoking in 78 bedrooms s £105-£170; d £105-£170 * **FACILITIES:** **Spa** STV Mini Gym ch fac Xmas **CONF:** Thtr 120 Class 80 Board 80 Del from £125 * **SERVICES:** Lift air con **NOTES:** No dogs (ex guide dogs) Civ Wed 100
**CARDS:**

### ★★★70% Novotel Glasgow
Novotel
181 Pitt St G2 4JS
☎ 0141 222 2775 0141 204 5438
e-mail: H3136@accor-hotels.com
***Dir:*** *next to Strathclyde Police HQ*
A brand new property, the Novotel has a number of great advantages. Friendly staff, competitive rates and a limited amount of free parking have already attracted a loyal following. Bedrooms are typical of this brand, bright and functional with good working areas. There are a number of larger family rooms here. The all day Brasserie and bar menus are also available on room service.
**ROOMS:** 139 en suite (139 fmly) No smoking in 90 bedrooms s £85; d £95 * **LB** **FACILITIES:** STV Sauna Solarium Gym Steam room **CONF:** Thtr 40 Class 20 Board 20 Del from £135 * **SERVICES:** Lift air con **PARKING:** 19 **CARDS:**

### ★★★68% Jurys Glasgow
JurysDoyle Hotels
Great Western Rd G12 0XP
☎ 0141 334 8161 0141 334 3846
e-mail: glasgow_hotel@jurys.com
***Dir:*** *M8 junct 17. Take A82 signs. Continue on rd through 2 sets of lights. At 3rd set turn left, just before BP garage. Then right follow rd to hotel*
This friendly business and leisure hotel is situated in the west end beside the A82. All bedrooms have benefited from refurbishment. Inviting public areas include a choice of contrasting bars, a well-equipped leisure club, conference and banqueting facilities, and an attractive split-level restaurant offering both carte and fixed-price menus as well as the good value carvery.
**ROOMS:** 136 en suite (12 fmly) No smoking in 100 bedrooms s £69-£110; d £69-£110 * **LB** **FACILITIES:** STV Indoor swimming (H) Sauna Solarium Gym Jacuzzi entertainment Xmas **CONF:** Thtr 140 Class 80 Board 40 **SERVICES:** Lift **PARKING:** 300 **NOTES:** No smoking in restaurant Civ Wed 120 **CARDS:**

### ★★★68% *Posthouse Glasgow City*
Posthouse
Bothwell St G2 7EN
☎ 0870 400 9032 0141 221 8986
Centrally located, this modern, stylish hotel offers both a traditional carvery and an informal restaurant, with its imaginative range of international dishes. Bedroom styles vary but all accommodation is well-equipped. Extra services include a concierge and all-day room service. There is limited parking, but free parking is offered in the nearby NCP.
**ROOMS:** 247 en suite (28 fmly) No smoking in 102 bedrooms **CONF:** Thtr 850 Class 450 Board 100 **SERVICES:** Lift air con **CARDS:**

### ★★★68% Swallow Hotel

SWALLOW
HOTELS
517 Paisley Rd West G51 1RW
☎ 0141 427 3146 0141 427 4059
e-mail: info@swallowhotels.com
***Dir:*** *off M77, junct 1*

Conveniently situated for both the city centre and the airport. Bedrooms are comfortable and equipped to meet the needs of all travellers. Spacious lounges and Readers Restaurant are complemented by the popular leisure club and good meeting and function facilities.
**ROOMS:** 117 en suite (11 fmly) No smoking in 63 bedrooms **FACILITIES:** STV Indoor swimming (H) Sauna Solarium Gym Jacuzzi Steam room entertainment Xmas **CONF:** Thtr 300 Class 150 Board 30 Del from £95 * **SERVICES:** Lift **PARKING:** 150 **NOTES:** No smoking in restaurant **CARDS:**

### ★★★67% Ewington
Best Western
Balmoral Ter, 132 Queens Dr, Queens Park G42 8QW
☎ 0141 423 1152 0141 422 2030
e-mail: ewington.info@countryhotels.net
***Dir:*** *M8 junct 20 onto A77, go through 8 sets of traffic lights, left to Allison Street then right into Victoria Road to Park Gates. Turn right and hotel 500yds right.*
Part of a Victorian terrace on the south side opposite Queens Park, this is a stylish town house hotel. Dedicated staff provide friendly service. The public areas include an inviting foyer lounge, a smart restaurant and comfortable cocktail lounge. Bedrooms range in size and style and include spacious executive rooms.
**ROOMS:** 43 en suite (5 fmly) No smoking in 6 bedrooms s £79; d £99 * **LB** **FACILITIES:** STV Xmas **CONF:** Thtr 70 Class 20 Board 30 Del from £80 * **SERVICES:** Lift **PARKING:** 16 **NOTES:** Civ Wed 60
**CARDS:**

*See advert on opposite page*

### ★★★65% Sherbrooke Castle
11 Sherbrooke Av, Pollokshields G41 4PG
☎ 0141 427 4227 0141 427 5685
e-mail: mail@sherbrooke.co.uk
***Dir:*** *from M8 junct 23 left to Dumbreck Rd, then 2nd left Nithsdale Rd at lights. Hotel 0.5m on right*
Built in 1896 this impressive, turreted red-sandstone hotel is located in a residential area south of the city close to the M77. Comfortable public areas include a well-stocked bar and popular function suite with Morrisons Restaurant offering fine dining from a fixed-price menu. Bedrooms have attractive colour schemes and

*continued*

are comfortably furnished with several having superb views across the city.

**ROOMS:** 10 en suite 9 annexe en suite (2 fmly) No smoking in 6 bedrooms s £60-£110; d £80-£150 (incl. bkfst) * **LB** **FACILITIES:** STV ch fac Xmas **CONF:** Thtr 200 Class 100 Board 50 Del from £125 * **PARKING:** 80 **CARDS:**

### ★★★64% Kings Park

Mill St G73 2LX
☎ 0141 647 5491 ▤ 0141 613 3022
e-mail: enquiries@maksu-group.co.uk
***Dir:*** *on A730 East Kilbride road*

This purpose-built hotel has benefited from substantial refurbishment and is within a short drive of the city centre and East Kilbride. Bedrooms with pleasing colour schemes are comfortably modern in appointment. Public areas include a well-stocked bar and attractive restaurant. The hotel is also a popular venue for conferences and functions.

**ROOMS:** 26 en suite (4 fmly) No smoking in 4 bedrooms s £60-£85; d £80-£100 (incl. bkfst) * **FACILITIES:** STV Jacuzzi entertainment Xmas **CONF:** Thtr 250 Class 100 Board 50 Del from £85 * **PARKING:** 150 **CARDS:**

### ★★★64% Quality Hotel Glasgow

Quality Hotel

99 Gordon St G1 3SF
☎ 0141 221 9680 ▤ 0141 226 3948
e-mail: admin@gb627.u-net.com
***Dir:*** *exit 19 of M8, left into Argyle St and left into Hope St*

A splendid Victorian railway hotel, forming part of Central Station. It retains much original charm yet has modern facilities. Public rooms are impressive and continue to be upgraded and improved. Bedrooms are well-equipped and mostly spacious. Guests can eat informally in the Coffee Shop or in the main restaurant.

**ROOMS:** 222 en suite (8 fmly) No smoking in 70 bedrooms **FACILITIES:** STV Indoor swimming (H) Sauna Solarium Gym Jacuzzi Hair & beauty salon Steamroom entertainment Xmas **CONF:** Thtr 600 Class 170 Board 40 **SERVICES:** Lift **NOTES:** No smoking in restaurant **CARDS:**

### ★★★61% Carrick

REGAL

377 Argyle St G2 8LL
☎ 0141 248 2355 ▤ 0141 221 1014
***Dir:*** *junct 19 M8 bear left onto Argyle St, hotel opposite Cadogan Square 200m on right*

At the West End of one of the city's best-known streets, the hotel well suits the business guest. The compact but well-equipped bedrooms have all the essential facilities. The restaurant, lounge

continued



bar and a number of meeting rooms are on the first floor. Free overnight car parking is available nearby.

**ROOMS:** 121 en suite No smoking in 79 bedrooms s £80; d £90 * **LB** **FACILITIES:** Xmas **CONF:** Thtr 80 Class 40 Board 24 Del £85 * **SERVICES:** Lift **NOTES:** No dogs (ex guide dogs) No smoking in restaurant **CARDS:**

### ★★★60% Kelvin Park Lorne

REGAL

923 Sauchiehall St G3 7TE
☎ 0141 314 9955 ▤ 0141 337 1659
e-mail: kelvinparklorne@corushotels.com

This popular hotel is five minutes' walk from the S.E.C.C. and the Art Galleries. It offers mixed styles of smart attractive accommodation, and staff are helpful and friendly. Guests can eat informally in the bar, from the room service menu or in the smart

continued on p732

GLASGOW, continued

restaurant. There is a private car park beneath the hotel and conference facilities in a separate wing.

*Kelvin Park Lorne, Glasgow*

**ROOMS:** 100 en suite (5 fmly) No smoking in 30 bedrooms s £40-£90; d £40-£90 * LB **FACILITIES:** STV **CONF:** Thtr 300 Class 120 Board 80 Del from £85 * **SERVICES:** Lift **PARKING:** 30 **NOTES:** No smoking in restaurant Civ Wed 200 **CARDS:**

★★★60% **The Tinto Firs**
470 Kilmarnock Rd G43 2BB
☎ 0141 637 2353 📠 0141 633 1340
e-mail: Info@tintofirs-hotel-glasgow.com
***Dir:*** *4m S of Glasgow City Centre on the A77*
This modern, purpose-built hotel is four miles south of the city centre and convenient for the airport and the Burrell Collection. Comfortably furnished public areas include a choice of bars, an attractive restaurant and a smart boardroom. Bedrooms are mostly cosy studio singles which are very well-equipped.
**ROOMS:** 27 en suite (2 fmly) No smoking in 6 bedrooms s £45-£85; d £60-£95 (incl. bkfst) * **FACILITIES:** STV **CONF:** Thtr 200 Class 80 Board 50 Del from £100 * **PARKING:** 46 **NOTES:** Civ Wed 130
**CARDS:**

PEEL HOTELS

★★71% **Uplawmoor**
Neilston Rd G78 4AF
☎ 01505 850565 📠 01505 850689
e-mail: enquiries@uplawmoor.co.uk
(For full entry see Uplawmoor and advert on opposite page)

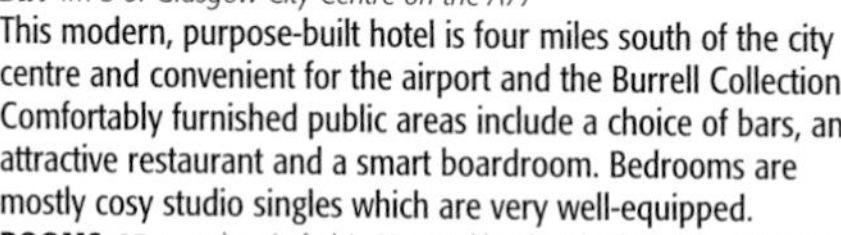

THE CIRCLE
Selected Individual Hotels
GREAT BRITAIN

## *Town House*

★★★★ **One Devonshire Gardens**
1 Devonshire Gardens G12 0UX
☎ 0141 339 2001 📠 0141 337 1663
e-mail: onedevonshire@bt.connect.com
***Dir:*** *M8 junct 17, follow signs for A82, after 1.5m turn left into Hyndland Rd, 1st right, right at mini rdbt, right at end then continue to end*
Three interconnecting town houses form this smart, elegant hotel situated in the heart of Glasgow's distinctive West End. One Devonshire Gardens is ten minutes from the city centre. Bedrooms are all individually designed and thoughtfully equipped to a high standard. Spacious suites are available, some with four-poster beds and two with their own patio. There is a stylish drawing room and a comprehensive room service menu. Imaginative, carefully prepared food is served in the adjacent Amaryllis restaurant.
**ROOMS:** 27 en suite s £165-£345; d £165-£345 * **FACILITIES:** STV ch fac **CONF:** Thtr 40 Class 20 Board 26 **NOTES:** No smoking in restaurant **CARDS:**

## *Town House*

★★★★ **The Devonshire Hotel of Glasgow**
5 Devonshire Gardens G12 0UX
☎ 0141 339 7878 📠 0141 339 3980
e-mail: devonshir5@aol.com
***Dir:*** *M8 junct 17. Right at slip road lights on to A82. Continue 1.5m. Over 1st lights, left at 2nd. 1st right, right at mini rdbt. Hotel at end of road*
Standing on the corner of an imposing tree-lined Victorian terrace, the Devonshire is one of the city's most stylish hotels. The sumptuously furnished drawing room is the focal point of the day rooms, with all the elegance and comfort expected in such a grand house. An imaginatively prepared Scottish menu is served in the small dining room and there is extensive 24-hour room service. Spacious bedrooms are richly furnished and equipped with many luxuries.
**ROOMS:** 14 en suite (3 fmly) s £100-£160; d £140-£250 * LB **FACILITIES:** STV Xmas **CONF:** Thtr 50 Class 30 Board 30 **NOTES:** No smoking in restaurant Civ Wed 50
**CARDS:**

Scotland's Hotels of Distinction

⌂ ***Travelodge***
251 Paisley Rd G5 8RA
☎ 0141 420 3882
***Dir:*** *0.5m from city centre just off junc 20 M8 from south/junc 21 M8 from north. Behind Harry Ramsden's*
Travelodge offers good quality, good value, modern accommodation. Ideal for families, the spacious, en suite bedrooms include remote-control TV, tea and coffee-making facilities, luxury beds and free morning newspaper. Meals can be taken at the nearby family restaurant. For further details and the Travelodge phone number, consult the Hotel Groups page.

**ROOMS:** 100 en suite

Travelodge

⌂ ***Express by Holiday Inn Glasgow City Centre***
112 Stockwell St G1 4LT
☎ 0141 548 5000 📠 0141 548 5048

Express
by Holiday Inn

XPRESS

A modern budget hotel offering comfortable accommodation in refreshing, spacious and comprehensively equipped bedrooms, en suite bathrooms with power showers and continental buffet breakfast included in the room rate. Suitable for business travellers or families. For further details and the Express by Holiday Inn phone number, consult the Hotel Groups page.
**ROOMS:** 128 en suite **CONF:** Thtr 30 Class 30 Board 14

## ⌂ Express by Holiday Inn Theatreland

Express
by Holiday Inn

165 West Nile St G1 2RL
☎ 0141 331 6800 ▤ 0141 331 6828
e-mail: express@higlasgow.com
***Dir:*** *follow signs to Royal Concert Hall*

A modern budget hotel offering comfortable accommodation in refreshing, spacious and comprehensively equipped bedrooms, en suite bathrooms with power showers and continental buffet breakfast included in the room rate. Suitable for business travellers or families. For further details and the Express by Holiday Inn phone number, consult the Hotel Groups page.
**ROOMS:** 88 en suite (incl. cont bkfst) s £55-£59; d £55-£59 *
**CONF:** Thtr 20 Class 4 Board 12 Del £96.45 *

## ⌂ Days Inn

DAYS INN

80 Ballater St G5 0TW
☎ 0141 429 4233 ▤ 0141 429 4244
e-mail: glasgow@daysinn.co.uk
This modern building offers accommodation in smart, spacious and well-equipped bedrooms, suitable for families and business travellers, and all with en suite bathrooms. Continental breakfast is available and other refreshments may be taken at the nearby family restaurant. For further details and the Days Inn phone number, consult the Hotel Groups page.
**ROOMS:** 114 en suite s fr £47.50; d fr £47.50 * **CONF:** Thtr 30 Class 15 Board 20

## ⌂ Premier Lodge (City Centre)

PREMIER LODGE
THE BEST. REST ASSURED.

10 Elmbank Gardens G2 4PP
☎ 0870 700 1394 ▤ 0870 700 1395
e-mail: glasgow@premierlodge.co.uk
Premier Lodge offers modern, well-equipped, en suite accommodation suitable for both business and leisure travellers. Meals can be taken at the adjacent popular restaurant and bar, which is fully licensed. For further details, consult the Hotel Groups page.
**ROOMS:** 278 en suite s £46; d £46 * **CONF:** Thtr 60 Class 25 Board 20 Del from £60 *

## ⌂ Premier Lodge (Glasgow North East)

PREMIER LODGE
THE BEST. REST ASSURED.

Cumbernauld Rd, Muirhead, Chryston G69 9BJ
☎ 0870 700 1396 ▤ 0870 700 1397
***Dir:*** *Situated off M8 junct 13 on A80 Glasgow to Stirling road.400 yds from Stepps Bypass.*
Premier Lodge offers modern, well-equipped, en suite accommodation suitable for both business and leisure travellers. Meals can be taken at the adjacent popular restaurant and bar, which is fully licensed. For further details, consult the Hotel Groups page.
**ROOMS:** 38 en suite s £42; d £42 * **CONF:** Thtr 85 Class 25 Board 30

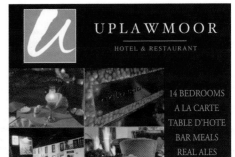



## ⌂ *Travelodge*

Travelodge

9 Hill St G3 6RP
☎ 0141 333 1515
Travelodge offers good quality, good value, modern accommodation. Ideal for families, the spacious, en suite bedrooms include remote-control TV, tea and coffee-making facilities, luxury beds and free morning newspaper. Meals can be taken at the nearby family restaurant. For further details and the Travelodge phone number, consult the Hotel Groups page.

**ROOMS:** 93 en suite

## ○ Hotel Ibis

ibis
ACCOR

220 West Regent St G2 4DQ
☎ 0141 225 6000
**ROOMS:** 141 rms **NOTES:** Open now

### GLASGOW AIRPORT, Renfrewshire — Map 11 NS46

see also Howwood

## ★★★71% Dalmeny Park Country House

Lochlibo Rd G78 1LG
☎ 0141 881 9211 ▤ 0141 881 9214
e-mail: enquiries@maksu-group.co.uk
(For full entry see Barrhead)

## ★★★70% Glynhill Hotel & Leisure Club

Paisley Rd PA4 8XB
☎ 0141 886 5555 & 885 1111 ▤ 0141 885 2838
e-mail: glynhillleisurehotel@msn.com
***Dir:*** *on M8 towards Glasgow airport,turn off at junct 27,take A741 towards Renfrew cross small rdbt approx 300yds from motorway exit Hotel on right*
A smart and welcoming hotel with bedrooms that range from

*continued on p734*

GLASGOW AIRPORT, continued

spacious executive rooms to smaller standard rooms; all are tastefully appointed with a good range of amenities. The hotel boasts a luxurious leisure complex and extensive conference facilities; the choice of contrasting bars and restaurants should suit most tastes and budgets.
**ROOMS:** 125 en suite (25 fmly) No smoking in 51 bedrooms s £76-£94; d £86-£104 (incl. bkfst) * **LB** **FACILITIES:** STV Indoor swimming (H) Snooker Sauna Solarium Gym Jacuzzi entertainment Xmas **CONF:** Thtr 450 Class 240 Del from £95 * **PARKING:** 230 **NOTES:** No dogs (ex guide dogs) Civ Wed 450 **CARDS:**

### ★★★70% *Posthouse Glasgow Airport*

Posthouse

Abbotsinch PA3 2TR
☎ 0870 400 9031 📠 0141 887 3738
e-mail: gm1791@forte-hotels.com
***Dir:*** *from E M8 junct 28 follow signs for Hotel; from W M8 junct 29 airport slip road to Hotel*

An ideal base for those about to fly, this Posthouse is situated opposite the arrivals/departure hall of the airport. It offers modern accommodation, including smartly decorated superior bedrooms, as well as good public areas and a comfortable restaurant and bar.
**ROOMS:** 298 en suite (9 fmly) No smoking in 158 bedrooms **FACILITIES:** Solarium **CONF:** Thtr 250 Class 120 Board 20 **SERVICES:** Lift air con **PARKING:** 60 **CARDS:**

### ★★★69% Lynnhurst

Park Rd PA5 8LS
☎ 01505 324331 & 324600 📠 01505 324219
e-mail: enquiries@lynnhurst.co.uk
***Dir:*** *past airport, take slip road (A737). Continue 2m & take B789. At slip rd left into Johnstone. 1st main lights right then 1st left and 2nd right*

Genuine hospitality together with high standards of guest care are the hallmarks of this family run hotel. Although variable in size, bedrooms are comfortably modern and offer a good range of amenities. Public areas present well and include a spacious bar, conservatory lounge, and an attractive panelled restaurant where fixed price and carte menus are available.
**ROOMS:** 21 en suite (2 fmly) s £50-£55; d £80 (incl. bkfst) * **LB** **FACILITIES:** STV Arrangement with local leisure centre ch fac Xmas **CONF:** Thtr 160 Class 160 Board 20 Del from £65 * **PARKING:** 100 **NOTES:** No dogs (ex guide dogs) Closed 1-3 Jan Civ Wed 175 **CARDS:**

*See advert on opposite page*

### ★★★64% *Dean Park*

91 Glasgow Rd PA4 8YB
☎ 0141 304 9955 📠 0141 885 0681
***Dir:*** *3m NE A8 - turn off M8 at junct 26 onto A8 for Renfrew, follow road for 600yds, hotel is on the left*

Situated close to the airport and with convenient access to the M8, this modern purpose-built hotel attracts both the business and leisure traveller and is also a popular venue for local functions. Although not expansive, bedrooms are comfortable and well-equipped. Public areas include a well-stocked split-level bar, an attractive restaurant offering both fixed price and carte menus, and a comfortable foyer lounge.
**ROOMS:** 118 en suite (6 fmly) **FACILITIES:** Snooker Beautician & arrangement with leisure club **CONF:** Thtr 350 Class 150 Board 100 **PARKING:** 200 **CARDS:**

### ⌂ Express by Holiday Inn

Express by Holiday Inn

St Andrews Dr PA3 2TJ
☎ 0141 842 1100 📠 0141 842 1122
e-mail: info@hiex-glasgow.com
***Dir:*** *M8 junct 28 at 1st rdbt turn right hotel on right*

A modern budget hotel offering comfortable accommodation in refreshing, spacious and comprehensively equipped bedrooms, en suite bathrooms with power showers and continental buffet breakfast included in the room rate. Suitable for business travellers or families. For further details and the Express by Holiday Inn phone number, consult the Hotel Groups page.
**ROOMS:** 143 en suite **CONF:** Thtr 75 Class 30 Board 30

## GLENCOE, Highland

Map 14 NN15

### ★★68% *Glencoe*

PA39 4HW
☎ 01855 811245 📠 01855 811687
***Dir:*** *on A82 in Glencoe village, 15m S of Fort William*

This family-run holiday hotel offers a relaxed welcoming atmosphere. The bedrooms have pleasing colour schemes and modern furnishings and all the expected amenities. Loch views can be enjoyed from the attractive restaurant, and the well-stocked bar remains popular with non-residents for its good value informal dining; the Grotto bar is also popular.
**ROOMS:** 15 en suite (4 fmly) **FACILITIES:** STV Games room **CONF:** Thtr 100 **PARKING:** 30 **NOTES:** No smoking in restaurant **CARDS:**

## GLENEAGLES See Auchterarder

## GLENFARG, Perth & Kinross

Map 11 NO11

### ★★67% Glenfarg

THE CIRCLE Selected Individual Hotels GREAT BRITAIN

Main St PH2 9NU
☎ 01577 830241 📠 01577 830665
e-mail: info@glenfarghotel.co.uk
***Dir:*** *travelling S on M90, off at junc 9, turn left, Hotel 5m; travelling N on M90, off at junc 8, second left, Hotel 2m*

This hotel, situated in the centre of the village, offers a relaxed and welcoming atmosphere. Bedrooms, whilst varying in size, are comfortable and neatly maintained. A wide ranging choice of dishes is available, served in the popular bar or in the restaurant.
**ROOMS:** 17 rms (16 en suite) (4 fmly) No smoking in all bedrooms s £40-£60; d £67 (incl. bkfst) * **LB** **FACILITIES:** STV entertainment Xmas **CONF:** Thtr 60 Class 60 Board 30 Del from £50 * **PARKING:** 20 **NOTES:** No smoking in restaurant Civ Wed 60 **CARDS:**

## GLENLUCE, Dumfries & Galloway

Map 10 NX15

**★★66% *Kelvin House Hotel***
53 Main St DG8 0PP
☎ 01581 300303 Fax 01581 300303
e-mail: kelvinhouse@lineone.net
***Dir:*** *midway between Newton Stewart & Stranraer, just off the A75.*
This small, privately run hotel is in the centre of a village in unspoilt countryside. The bedrooms are bright and spacious and there is a comfortable residents' lounge. Meals are served either in the popular bar or in the separate restaurant overlooking the garden.
**ROOMS:** 6 rms (5 en suite) (3 fmly) No smoking in 3 bedrooms
**FACILITIES:** ch fac **CONF:** Thtr 50 Class 20 Board 20
**CARDS:**

## GLENROTHES, Fife

Map 11 NO20

**★★★59% Balgeddie House**
Balgeddie Way KY6 3ET
☎ 01592 742511 Fax 01592 621702
e-mail: balgeddie@easynet.co.uk
***Dir:*** *from A911 E of Leslie follow the signs to the hotel*
This comfortable hotel, which stands in landscaped grounds, enjoys a quiet residential location. Bedrooms have attractive colour schemes and the most spacious are on the first floor. Public areas include a lounge, a cocktail bar and a restaurant.
**ROOMS:** 19 en suite (2 fmly) s £60-£69; d £70-£85 (incl. bkfst) * **LB**
**FACILITIES:** STV Riding Croquet lawn ch fac Xmas **CONF:** Thtr 300 Class 150 Board 100 Del from £90 * **PARKING:** 80 **NOTES:** No dogs (ex guide dogs) No smoking in restaurant Civ Wed 80
**CARDS:**

GLENROTHES, continued

**★★75% Rescobie**
6 Valley Dr, Leslie KY6 3BQ
☎ 01592 749555 01592 620231
e-mail: rescobiehotel@compuserve.com
***Dir:*** *turn off A92 at Glenrothes onto A911, through Leslie. End of high street follow straight ahead. Left at Zak Yule hairdressing salon. Hotel 1st left*

Any tour of Fife should include this delightful country house hotel which enjoys a peaceful setting on the fringes of the town. Victorian architecture is stylishly enhanced by modern, vibrant décor, a theme carried through to the bright and comfortable bedrooms. Creative cooking is served in the inviting dining room, and genuine hospitality is provided by the Davidson family.
**ROOMS:** 10 en suite **PARKING:** 12 **NOTES:** No dogs (ex guide dogs) No children 12yrs No smoking in restaurant
**CARDS:**

*See advert on page 735*

**Express by Holiday Inn Glenrothes**
Leslie Roundabout, Leslie Rd KY6 3EP
☎ 01592 745509 01592 743377
***Dir:*** *turn off A92 onto A911. Straight over 4 rdbts. Hotel is on the left*

Express
by Holiday Inn

A modern budget hotel offering comfortable accommodation in refreshing, spacious and comprehensively equipped bedrooms, en suite bathrooms with power showers and continental buffet breakfast included in the room rate. Suitable for business travellers or families. For further details and the Express by Holiday Inn phone number, consult the Hotel Groups page.
**ROOMS:** 49 en suite (incl. cont bkfst) s £42.50-£52.50; d £42.50-£52.50 * **CONF:** Thtr 30 Board 20

GLENSHEE (SPITTAL OF), Perth & Kinross Map 15 NO16

**★★70% Dalmunzie House**
PH10 7QG
☎ 01250 885224 01250 885225
e-mail: dalmunzie@aol.com
***Dir:*** *on the A93 at Spittal of Glenshee, follow signs to hotel*

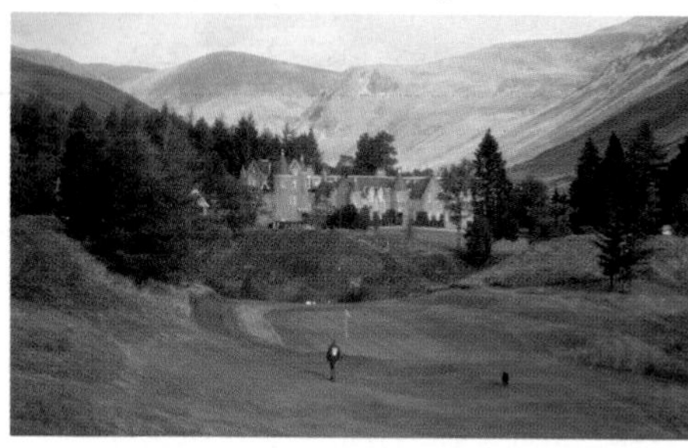

Far from the madding crowd, this turreted house is set peacefully at the head of the glen amid a 6,500-acre estate. Its beautiful location attracts walkers and golfers (to the hotel's own course) as well as skiers, being near Glenshee. Service is friendly and attentive.
**ROOMS:** 18 rms (16 en suite) s £40-£62; d £60-£112 (incl. bkfst) * **LB** **FACILITIES:** Golf 9 Tennis (hard) Fishing Croquet lawn Clay pigeon shooting Mountain bikes ch fac Xmas **CONF:** Thtr 20 Class 20 Board 20 Del from £77 * **SERVICES:** Lift **PARKING:** 32 **NOTES:** No smoking in restaurant Closed end Nov-28 Dec **CARDS:**

GRANGEMOUTH, Falkirk Map 11 NS98

**★★★72% Grange Manor**
Glensburgh FK3 8XJ
☎ 01324 474836 01324 665861
e-mail: info@grangemanor.co.uk
***Dir:*** *travelling E; off M9 at junc 6, Hotel 200m to right. Travelling W; off M9 at junc 5, A905 for 2m*
Situated south of town close to the M9 this hotel, popular with business and corporate clientele, benefits from hands-on family ownership. It offers high quality spacious accommodation with superb bathrooms. Public areas include a comfortable foyer area, lounge bar and smart restaurant. There is also a bar/bistro in the grounds.
**ROOMS:** 7 en suite 30 annexe en suite (6 fmly) No smoking in 16 bedrooms **FACILITIES:** STV Xmas **CONF:** Thtr 150 Class 68 Board 40 **PARKING:** 154 **NOTES:** No dogs (ex guide dogs)
**CARDS:**

GRANTOWN-ON-SPEY, Highland Map 14 NJ02

**★★77% Culdearn House Hotel**
THE CIRCLE Selected Individual Hotels GREAT BRITAIN
Woodlands Ter PH26 3JU
☎ 01479 872106 01479 873641
e-mail: culdearn@globalnet.co.uk
***Dir:*** *enter Grantown on the A95 from SW and turn left at 30mph sign*
Immaculately maintained both outside and in, this small hotel sits in gardens on the edge of town. Cheerful proprietors and their

*continued*

staff provide excellent hospitality and keep everyone smiling. The hotel has the atmosphere of a relaxed country house.

**ROOMS:** 9 en suite No smoking in 6 bedrooms s fr £75; d fr £150 (incl. bkfst & dinner) * **LB** **PARKING:** 12 **NOTES:** No dogs (ex guide dogs) No children 10yrs No smoking in restaurant Closed 30 Oct-28 Feb **CARDS:**

---

GREENOCK, Inverclyde Map 10 NS27

### ⌂ *Howard Johnson*

Cartsburn PA15 4RT
☎ 01475 786666 🖹 01475 786777

---

GRETNA (WITH GRETNA GREEN), Dumfries & Galloway Map 11 NY36

### ★★★67% Gretna Chase

DG16 5JB
☎ 01461 337517 🖹 01461 337766
e-mail: enquiries@gretnachase.co.uk
***Dir:*** *off A74 onto B7076, left at top of slip road, hotel 400yds on right*

A favourite venue for wedding parties, this hotel is seemingly situated in 'no man's land' between the signs for Scotland and England, surrounded by delightful gardens. The well-equipped bedrooms are comfortable and full of character, and spacious new bedrooms were due to open in mid 2001. The dining room can accommodate functions and the lounge bar is a popular retreat.

**ROOMS:** 19 en suite (9 fmly) No smoking in 6 bedrooms s £65-£75; d £79-£139 (incl. bkfst) * **LB** **FACILITIES:** Jacuzzi **CONF:** Thtr 50 Class 30 Board 20 **PARKING:** 40 **NOTES:** No dogs (ex guide dogs) **CARDS:**

### ★★★65% *Garden House*

Sarkfoot Rd DG16 5EP
☎ 01461 337621 🖹 01461 337692
***Dir:*** *just off junct 45 on the M6 at Gretna*

From its position close to the famous blacksmith's shop, this purpose-built modern hotel is especially popular for wedding receptions. Bedrooms, including several honeymoon suites, are

*continued*



spacious and modern in style. Public areas include a large open-plan foyer where you will find the lounge and restaurant with a small bar adjacent. The leisure centre and hairdressing salon are added attractions.

**ROOMS:** 21 en suite (2 fmly) **FACILITIES:** STV Indoor swimming (H) Jacuzzi **CONF:** Thtr 100 Class 80 Board 40 **PARKING:** 105 **NOTES:** No dogs (ex guide dogs) **CARDS:**

*See advert on this page*

### ★★68% Solway Lodge

MINOTEL Great Britain

Annan Rd DG16 5DN
☎ 01461 338266 🖹 01461 337791
e-mail: j.welsh@btconnect.com
***Dir:*** *A74(M), take Gretna/Longtown exit, turn left at top of road past Welcome to Scotland sign, BP petrol stn turn left for town centre 250 yds on right*

Close to the blacksmith's shop, this friendly family run hotel offers a choice of accommodation. There are two honeymoon suites in the main house, and the chalet block rooms are ideal for overnight stops. A range of home-made meals are offered in the restaurant and lounge bar.

**ROOMS:** 3 en suite 7 annexe en suite s £42-£53; d £59-£85 (incl. bkfst) * **PARKING:** 25 **NOTES:** No smoking in restaurant Closed 25 & 26 Dec RS 10 Oct-Mar **CARDS:**

### ⌂ Welcome Lodge

Welcome Break

Gretna Green, A74M Trunk Rd DG16 5HQ
☎ 01461 337566 🖹 01461 337823
e-mail: gretna.hotel@welcomebreak.co.uk
***Dir:*** *situated at the Welcome Break service area Gretna Green on A74 - Accessible from both Northbound & Southbound carriageway*

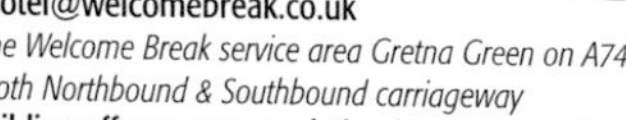

This modern building offers accommodation in smart, spacious

*continued on p738*

G

GRETNA (WITH GRETNA GREEN), continued

and well-equipped bedrooms, suitable for families and business travellers, and all with en suite bathrooms. Refreshments may be taken at the nearby family restaurant. For further details and the Welcome Break phone number, consult the Hotel Groups page.
**ROOMS:** 64 en suite s £45-£60; d £45-£60 * **CONF:** Thtr 25 Class 15 Board 12

GULLANE, East Lothian Map 12 NT48

## Premier Collection

★★★ **Greywalls**
Muirfield EH31 2EG
☎ 01620 842144 01620 842241
e-mail: hotel@greywalls.co.uk
***Dir:*** *A198, hotel is signposted at E end of village*
Designed by Lutyens, Greywalls overlooks the famous Muirfield Golf Course and guests may find themselves sleeping in the bedrooms occupied by many of the game's greats in the past. Public areas include a library with a log fire and grand piano, and a lovely sun lounge. At dinner an uncomplicated cooking style allows top quality ingredients to shine through. Bedrooms are furnished in period style and are exceptionally well-equipped and smart.
**ROOMS:** 17 en suite 5 annexe en suite s £110-£200; d £185-£220 (incl. bkfst) * **LB** **FACILITIES:** STV Tennis (hard & grass) Croquet lawn Putting green ch fac **CONF:** Thtr 30 Class 20 Board 20 Del from £190 * **PARKING:** 40 **NOTES:** No smoking in restaurant Closed Nov-Mar **CARDS:**

HALKIRK, Highland Map 15 ND15

★★63% **Ulbster Arms**
Bridge St KW12 6XY
☎ 01847 831206 & 831641 01847 831206
e-mail: ulbster-arms@ecosse.net
***Dir:*** *A9 to Thurso from Perth, 3m after village of Spittal turn Left*
Adjacent to the River Thurso, this long-established hotel is popular with the sporting clientele. Public areas include an attractive dining room, a quiet lounge and a lively lounge bar, popular for meals. Bedrooms vary in size and style and all have the expected facilities. The larger rooms are in the main house and the simpler chalet rooms at the rear have their own entrances.
**ROOMS:** 10 en suite 16 annexe en suite s £43; d £61-£76 (incl. bkfst) * **FACILITIES:** Fishing Shooting entertainment **CONF:** Thtr 30 Class 25 Board 20 **PARKING:** 36 **NOTES:** No smoking in restaurant
**CARDS:**

HAMILTON, South Lanarkshire Map 11 NS75
see also Bothwell

**Express by Holiday Inn Strathclyde**

Express
by Holiday Inn

Hamilton Rd ML1 3RB
☎ 01698 858585 01698 852375
***Dir:*** *junct 5 off M74 follow signs for Strathclyde Country park*

Express
by Holiday Inn

A modern budget hotel offering comfortable accommodation in refreshing, spacious and comprehensively equipped bedrooms, en suite bathrooms with power showers and continental buffet breakfast included in the room rate. Suitable for business travellers or families. For further details and the Express by Holiday Inn phone number, consult the Hotel Groups page.
**ROOMS:** 120 en suite (incl. cont bkfst) s £45-£61; d £45-£61 *
**CONF:** Thtr 30 Class 10 Board 15

HELENSBURGH, Argyll & Bute Map 10 NS28

★★★61% **Rosslea Hall Country House**
Ferry Rd G84 8NF
☎ 01436 439955 01436 820897
e-mail: rosslea.info@countryhotels.net
***Dir:*** *on A814, opposite church*
This early Victorian mansion stands in grounds by the shore of Gareloch. The comfortable rear bar provides an informal eating alternative to the main restaurant, an attractive, spacious and formal dining environment. The well-equipped bedrooms are gradually being upgraded.
**ROOMS:** 29 en suite 5 annexe en suite (2 fmly) No smoking in 5 bedrooms s £55-£75; d £60-£80 (incl. bkfst) * **LB** **FACILITIES:** STV Xmas **CONF:** Thtr 120 Class 120 Board 60 Del from £80 *
**PARKING:** 60 **NOTES:** No smoking in restaurant
**CARDS:**

HOWWOOD, Renfrewshire Map 10 NS3

★★★67% ***Bowfield Hotel & Country Club***
PA9 1DB
☎ 01505 705225 01505 705230
***Dir:*** *M8, A737 for 6m, left onto B787, right after 2m, follow road for 1m to hotel*
This former textile mill now houses a popular hotel which has become a convenient stop-over for travellers using Glasgow Airport. The extensive leisure facilities are being expanded and are a popular attraction. Public areas have beamed ceilings, brick and white painted walls, and welcoming open fires. Bedrooms are housed in a separate wing and offer good modern comforts and facilities.
**ROOMS:** 23 en suite (3 fmly) **FACILITIES:** Indoor swimming (H) Squash Snooker Sauna Solarium Gym Jacuzzi Health & beauty studio entertainment **CONF:** Thtr 80 Class 60 Board 20 **PARKING:** 100
**NOTES:** No dogs (ex guide dogs) No smoking in restaurant
**CARDS:**

## HUNTLY, Aberdeenshire
Map 15 NJ53

### ★★63% *Gordon Arms Hotel*
The Square AB54 8AF
☎ 01466 792288 📠 01466 794556
e-mail: reception@gordonarms.demon.co.uk

This friendly family-run hotel in the town square offers a good selection of tasty well-portioned dishes served in either the bar or restaurant. Bedrooms come in a variety of sizes.

**ROOMS:** 14 en suite (3 fmly) **FACILITIES:** entertainment **CONF:** Thtr 180 Class 120 Board 120 **CARDS:**

## INVERARAY, Argyll & Bute
Map 10 NN00

### ★★★68% The Argyll
Front St PA32 8XB
☎ 01499 302466 📠 01499 302389
e-mail: reception@the-argyll-hotel.co.uk

***Dir:*** *A82 Glasgow - Tarbet then take the A83 from Tarbet to Inveraray. The hotel is the first building facing the Loch as you enter Inveraray.*

Located beside The Arch, enjoying views of Loch Fyne, this hotel offers smart bedrooms including four executive rooms. Facilities include a choice of bars, foyer lounge and conservatory. The attractive restaurant features carefully prepared fare based on quality Scottish ingredients.

**ROOMS:** 35 en suite (7 fmly) No smoking in 4 bedrooms s £69-£79; d £98-£108 (incl. bkfst) * **LB** **FACILITIES:** Xmas ch fac **CONF:** Thtr 150 Class 80 Board 70 Del from £75 * **PARKING:** 25 **NOTES:** No dogs (ex guide dogs) No smoking in restaurant Closed 25-26 Dec Civ Wed 120 **CARDS:**

### ★★★68% Loch Fyne Hotel
PA32 8XT
☎ 01499 302148 📠 01499 302348
e-mail: lochfyne@british-trust-hotels.com

This popular holiday hotel overlooks Loch Fyne. Bedrooms are for the most part spacious and offer comfortable modern appointments. Loch views can be enjoyed from the well-stocked bar. The bistro provides an informal food alternative to the more formal restaurant. The well-equipped leisure centre is an added bonus.

**ROOMS:** 80 en suite s £35-£45; d £70-£100 (incl. bkfst) * **LB** **FACILITIES:** **Spa** Indoor swimming (H) Sauna Steam Room entertainment Xmas **CONF:** Class 30 Board 15 **SERVICES:** Lift **NOTES:** No smoking in restaurant **CARDS:**

Popped the question? Hotels with Civ Wed in their entry are licensed for civil wedding ceremonies. Maximum numbers for the ceremony only are shown, e.g. Civ Wed 120

## INVERGARRY, Highland
Map 14 NH30

### ★★★72% Glengarry Castle
PH35 4HW
☎ 01809 501254 📠 01809 501207
e-mail: castle@glengarry.net

***Dir:*** *on A82 beside Loch Oich, 0.5m from A82/A87 junction*

This charming country house stands in 50 acres close to Loch Oich. Bedrooms, including some with four-poster or half-tester beds, have pleasing colour schemes. Inviting public areas include an impressive panelled reception hall and a choice of comfortable sitting rooms. The attractive dining room provides the appropriate setting for the fine dining experience offered from the innovative fixed price menu.

**ROOMS:** 26 en suite (2 fmly) No smoking in 6 bedrooms s £55-£75; d £90-£140 (incl. bkfst) **FACILITIES:** Tennis (hard) Fishing ch fac **PARKING:** 32 **NOTES:** No smoking in restaurant Closed early Nov-mid Mar **CARDS:**

*See advert on this page*

INVERKEITHING, Fife Map 11 NT18

### ★★★63% Queensferry Lodge

St Margaret's Head, North Queensferry
KY11 1HP
☎ 01383 410000 🖹 01383 419708
e-mail: queensferry@corushotels.com

corus

***Dir:*** *from North take exit after junct 1 M90/A90, follow signs for North Queensferry. Hotel on left.*

From its position on the north side of the river this smart modern hotel enjoys fine views of famous road and rail bridges. Bright modern public areas include a comfortable foyer lounge and bar, a smart restaurant, and a good range of banqueting facilities. Bedrooms are comfortable and offer a good range of amenities.

**ROOMS:** 77 en suite (4 fmly) No smoking in 46 bedrooms s £33-£89; d £66-£105 (incl. bkfst) * LB **FACILITIES:** STV Xmas **CONF:** Thtr 150 Class 60 Board 45 Del from £95 * **SERVICES:** Lift **PARKING:** 165 **NOTES:** Civ Wed 120 **CARDS:**

INVERMORISTON, Highland Map 14 NH41

### ★★76% Glenmoriston Arms Hotel & Restaurant

IV63 7YA
☎ 01320 351206 🖹 01320 351308
e-mail: scott@lochness-glenmoriston.co.uk

***Dir:*** *at the junct of A82/A877*

A warm welcome awaits at this friendly family-run hotel close to Loch Ness. Comfortable, well-equipped bedrooms include a four-poster room with a spa bath. There is an attractive bar, and the refurbished restaurant offers a range of Taste of Scotland dishes.

**ROOMS:** 8 en suite (1 fmly) s £55-£70; d £80-£110 (incl. bkfst) * LB **FACILITIES:** Fishing Stalking Shooting Xmas **CONF:** Board 8 **PARKING:** 24 **NOTES:** No dogs No smoking in restaurant Closed early Jan-end Feb **CARDS:**

INVERNESS, Highland Map 14 NH64
see also Kirkhill

### ★★★★71% Culloden House

Culloden IV2 7BZ
☎ 01463 790461 🖹 01463 792181
e-mail: reserv@cullodenhouse.co.uk

***Dir:*** *take A96 from town and turn right for Culloden. After 1m, turn left at White Church after second traffic lights*

This imposing Georgian mansion is set in 40 acres of grounds and is where Bonnie Prince Charlie was based at the time of the Battle of Culloden. Day rooms with chandeliers and marble fireplaces include an inviting drawing room, clubby bar and the elegant Adam dining room. Bedrooms range from period suites and master rooms to comfortable contemporary rooms. No-smoking suites are in a separate mansion house in the grounds that is suitable for small seminars.

**ROOMS:** 23 en suite 5 annexe en suite (1 fmly) No smoking in 8 bedrooms s £145-£180; d £190-£270 (incl. bkfst) * LB **FACILITIES:** STV Tennis (hard) Sauna Croquet lawn Boules Badminton entertainment Xmas **CONF:** Thtr 60 Class 40 Board 30 **PARKING:** 50 **NOTES:** No smoking in restaurant Civ Wed 60 **CARDS:**

### ★★★★71% Inverness Marriott Hotel

Culcabock Rd IV2 3LP
☎ 01463 237166 🖹 01463 225208
e-mail: inverness@marriotthotels.co.uk

Marriott HOTELS · RESORTS · SUITES

***Dir:*** *from A9 S, exit Culduthel/Kingsmills 5th exit at rdbt, follow rd 0.5m, over mini-rdbt pass golf club, hotel on left after traffic lights*

Set in four acres of gardens on the south side of town, this long-established hotel provides a smart modern environment within the carefully extended original house. Well-proportioned public rooms offer a choice of relaxing lounges and a conservatory overlooking the garden. The spacious bedrooms are well-equipped and comfortable, and include impressive executive rooms, as well as two-bedroom apartment suites contained in a separate building.

**ROOMS:** 76 en suite 6 annexe en suite (11 fmly) No smoking in 29 bedrooms s £82-£118; d £95-£131 (incl. bkfst) * LB **FACILITIES:** STV Indoor swimming (H) Sauna Solarium Gym Putting green Jacuzzi Hair & beauty salon Steam room entertainment Xmas **CONF:** Thtr 100 Class 28 Board 40 Del from £123 * **SERVICES:** Lift **PARKING:** 120 **NOTES:** No smoking in restaurant **CARDS:**

### ★★★76% Craigmonie

9 Annfield Rd IV2 3HX
☎ 01463 231649 🖹 01463 233720
e-mail: info@craigmonie.com

***Dir:*** *off A9/A96 follow signs Hilton, Culcabock pass golf course second road on right*

Bedrooms at this welcoming hotel range from the attractive poolside suites, with spa bath and balcony, to standard rooms. Public areas include a lounge and bar with a conservatory extension where light meals are served. Guests can also dine in the restaurant.

**ROOMS:** 35 en suite (3 fmly) No smoking in 10 bedrooms s £75-£88; d £95-£115 (incl. bkfst) * LB **FACILITIES:** STV Indoor swimming (H) Sauna Gym Jacuzzi **CONF:** Thtr 180 Class 70 Board 50 Del from £115 * **SERVICES:** Lift **PARKING:** 60 **NOTES:** No smoking in restaurant **CARDS:**

### ★★★76% Glenmoriston Town House Hotel

20 Ness Bank IV2 4SF
☎ 01463 223777 🖹 01463 712378
e-mail: glenmoriston@cali.co.uk

***Dir:*** *located on riverside opposite theatre, 5 minutes from town centre*

Stylish contemporary designs blend well with the classical architecture of this popular hotel situated on the banks of the River Ness. Public areas include a cosy cocktail bar and a

continued

sophisticated restaurant offering a tempting range of Mediterranean influenced cuisine. The smart modern bedrooms have every facility, including CD players. Service is friendly and attentive.
**ROOMS:** 15 en suite (1 fmly) s £79-£98; d £95-£135 (incl. bkfst) * LB **FACILITIES:** STV ch fac Xmas **CONF:** Thtr 50 Class 50 Board 30 **PARKING:** 40 **NOTES:** No dogs (ex guide dogs) **CARDS:**

### ★★★74% Bunchrew House
Bunchrew IV3 8TA
☎ 01463 234917 01463 710620
e-mail: welcome@bunchrew-inverness.co.uk
***Dir:*** *leave Inverness heading W on the A862 along the shore of the Beauly Firth. Hotel on right of road 2m after crossing canal*

Genuine hospitality and good food are all part of the appeal of this delightful 17th-century mansion house, which stands in 20 acres of wooded grounds beside the shore of the Beauly Firth. Reception rooms include a relaxing drawing room, well-stocked bar, and an elegant panelled restaurant. Here the innovative menu offers a tempting range of Scottish specialities. Bedrooms are quite individual in style and offer comfortable appointments.
**ROOMS:** 11 en suite (2 fmly) s £120-£150; d £145-£195 (incl. bkfst) * LB **FACILITIES:** Fishing Xmas **CONF:** Thtr 80 Class 30 Board 30 **PARKING:** 40 **NOTES:** Civ Wed 120 **CARDS:**

### ★★★67% Lochardil House
Best Western

Stratherrick Rd IV2 4LF
☎ 01463 235995 01463 713394
e-mail: lochardil@ukonline.co.uk
***Dir:*** *follow Island Bank Road for 1m, fork left into Drummond Crescent, into Stratherrick Road, 0.5m hotel on left*
A castellated Victorian house, with attractive gardens and a friendly atmosphere. Bedrooms are comfortable and modern. There is a function suite, cocktail bar and a popular conservatory restaurant which offers a wide range of dishes at lunch and dinner.
**ROOMS:** 12 en suite s fr £78; d fr £108 (incl. bkfst) * LB **FACILITIES:** STV **CONF:** Thtr 200 Class 100 Board 60 Del from £105 * **PARKING:** 123 **NOTES:** No dogs (ex guide dogs) **CARDS:**

### ★★★66% Crown Court Hotel
The Independents

25 Southside Rd IV2 3BG
☎ 01463 234816 01463 714900
e-mail: reception@crowncourt.co.uk
***Dir:*** *from A9 at Travel Inn take right at large rdbt then cross small rdbt. Pass golf course on left then right to Annfield Rd, at lights hotel on right*
This friendly hotel is conveniently located on the southern approach to the town centre, which is just a short walk away.
*continued*

Public rooms include a smart restaurant, and the attractive bedrooms are in the main well-proportioned.
**ROOMS:** 8 en suite (2 fmly) No smoking in all bedrooms s £59-£85; d £75-£105 (incl. bkfst) * LB **FACILITIES:** STV Beauty Room Xmas **CONF:** Thtr 200 Class 60 Board 30 Del from £75 * **PARKING:** 36 **NOTES:** Civ Wed 150 **CARDS:**

### ★★★66% Loch Ness House
Best Western

Glenurquhart Rd IV3 8JL
☎ 01463 231248 01463 239327
e-mail: lnhhchris@aol.com
***Dir:*** *1.5m from town centre, overlooking Tomnahurich Bridge on canal. From A9 turn L at Longman rdbt, follow signs for A82 for 2.5miles*
This is a family-run hotel, lying close to the canal, which offers friendly and attentive service. Tasty meals can be chosen from a good range of dishes, which are available in both the restaurant and the bar.
**ROOMS:** 22 en suite (3 fmly) No smoking in 6 bedrooms s £50-£80; d £60-£115 (incl. bkfst & dinner) * LB **FACILITIES:** STV Xmas **CONF:** Thtr 150 Class 60 Board 40 Del from £70 * **PARKING:** 60 **NOTES:** No smoking in restaurant **CARDS:**

I

### ★★★63% Palace Milton
8 Ness Walk IV3 5NE
☎ 01463 223243 01463 236865
e-mail: sales@miltonhotels.com
***Dir:*** *town centre on banks of River Ness opposite Inverness castle*
Popular with tour groups, this long-established hotel enjoys views of the river and castle. Open-plan public areas include a spacious foyer with bar, lounge and separate restaurant. Wing bedrooms are comfortable and modern; styles are more varied in the original house. The well-equipped leisure centre is an added attraction.
**ROOMS:** 88 en suite (12 fmly) No smoking in 6 bedrooms s £79-£99; d £109-£129 (incl. bkfst) * LB **FACILITIES:** STV Indoor swimming (H) Sauna Solarium Gym Jacuzzi Beauty salon entertainment Xmas **CONF:** Thtr 100 Class 40 Board 40 Del from £90 * **SERVICES:** Lift **PARKING:** 20 **NOTES:** No smoking in restaurant **CARDS:**

### ★★64% *Windsor Town House*
22 Ness Bank IV2 4SF
☎ 01463 715535 01463 713262
e-mail: info@windsor-inverness.co.uk
***Dir:*** *follow signs Dores/Holm Mills-rd B862, hotel below castle along riverside*
This friendly hotel looks across the river to the Eden Court theatre and is just a short riverside walk from the town centre. Bedrooms are well-equipped and in the main offer a good level of comfort and quality. A short dinner menu is available to those wishing to dine in. Drinks are served in the cosy lounge.
**ROOMS:** 18 en suite (5 fmly) No smoking in 16 bedrooms **FACILITIES:** STV **CONF:** Class 30 **PARKING:** 14 **NOTES:** No dogs (ex guide dogs) No smoking in restaurant Closed 23 Dec-4 Jan RS 1 Nov-15 May **CARDS:**

### Express by Holiday Inn

Express
by Holiday Inn

Stoneyfield IV2 7PA
☎ 01463 732700 01463 732732
***Dir:*** *From A9 follow directions for A96 and Inverness Airport,hotel on right hand side.*
A modern budget hotel offering comfortable accommodation in refreshing, spacious and comprehensively equipped bedrooms, en suite bathrooms with power showers and continental buffet breakfast included in the room rate. Suitable for business
*continued on p742*

INVERNESS, continued

travellers or families. For further details and the Express by Holiday Inn phone number, consult the Hotel Groups page.

**ROOMS:** 94 en suite **CONF:** Thtr 35 Class 15 Board 16

INVERURIE, Aberdeenshire Map 15 NJ72

**★★★★67% ⊛⊛ Thainstone House Hotel and Country Club**

MACDONALD HOTELS ★★★★

AB51 5NT
☎ 01467 621643 🖷 01467 625084
e-mail: info@thainstone.macdonald-hotels.co.uk
***Dir:*** *A96 from Aberdeen, past Kintore, entrance to hotel at first rdbt to Thainstone, take left then immediate right to hotel*

Set in 40 acres of mature grounds, this impressive mansion house is popular for conference and banqueting events. Public areas include a choice of inviting lounges and bars, and an elegant Georgian-style restaurant is the setting for a fine dining experience. The tastefully appointed bedrooms come in a variety of sizes.
**ROOMS:** 48 en suite (3 fmly) No smoking in 32 bedrooms s £75; d £100 (incl. bkfst) * **LB** **FACILITIES:** STV Indoor swimming (H) Snooker Gym Jacuzzi Archery Shooting Grass Karts Quad Bikes Xmas **CONF:** Thtr 300 Class 100 Board 40 **SERVICES:** Lift **PARKING:** 100 **NOTES:** No dogs (ex guide dogs) No smoking in restaurant Civ Wed 130
**CARDS:**

**★★★67% *Strathburn***
Burghmuir Dr AB51 4GY
☎ 01467 624422 🖷 01467 625133
e-mail: strathburn@btconnect.com
***Dir:*** *at Blackhall rbt into Blackhall Rd for 100yds then into Burghmuir Drive*
A relaxed atmosphere prevails at this personally-run modern hotel on the west side of town. Attractive public areas include a split-level foyer lounge, a spacious bar, and a tastefully appointed restaurant. Bedrooms come in mixed sizes and offer comfortable modern styles along with a good range of amenities.
**ROOMS:** 25 en suite (2 fmly) No smoking in 18 bedrooms
**FACILITIES:** STV **CONF:** Thtr 30 Class 24 Board 16 **PARKING:** 40
**NOTES:** No dogs (ex guide dogs) No smoking in restaurant
**CARDS:**

**★★66% Ardennan House Hotel**
Old Kemnay Rd, Port Elphinstone AB51 3XD
☎ 01467 621502 🖷 01467 625818
e-mail: reception@ardennan.co.uk
Lying just off the bypass, this family-run hotel has been completely refurbished. It offers attractive well-equipped bedrooms and a relaxing lounge bar and adjoining dining area, meals being served in both.
**ROOMS:** 6 rms (5 en suite) (1 fmly) s £40; d £60 (incl. bkfst) * **LB**
**FACILITIES:** entertainment Xmas **CONF:** Thtr 80 Del from £60 *
**PARKING:** 60 **CARDS:**

IRVINE, North Ayrshire Map 10 NS33

**★★★65% *Annfield House***
6 Castle St KA12 8RJ
☎ 01294 278903 🖷 01294 278904
e-mail: annfield@tinyonline.co.uk
***Dir:*** *follow signs to Irvine. Once in the town follow signs to Bridgegate which lead to Castle Street where the hotel is located*
Set within a quiet residential area close to the town centre and harbour, this friendly, fully restored 19th-century gentleman's residence retains many of its original features and benefits from well-tended gardens. Good wholesome food is prepared from fresh ingredients. Bedrooms are mostly spacious and attractively decorated.
**ROOMS:** 9 en suite **FACILITIES:** STV ch fac **PARKING:** 28
**CARDS:**

ISLE OF Placenames incorporating the words 'Isle' or 'Isle of' will be found under the actual name, eg Isle of Arran is under Arran, Isle of.

ISLAY, ISLE OF, Argyll & Bute Map 10

BOWMORE Map 10 NR35

**★★60% *Lochside***
19 Shore St PA43 7LB
☎ 01496 810244 🖷 01496 810390
e-mail: ask@lochsidehotel.co.uk
***Dir:*** *on A846, 100yds from main village square on shore side of road*
Lovely views of Loch Indaal can be enjoyed from the rear of this relaxed and informal family-run hotel. Best use has been made of available space in the compact bedrooms, which have mixed modern appointments along with a good range of amenities. The cosy bar boasts a collection of over 400 single malt whiskies and the small dining room offers a varied range of local produce.
**ROOMS:** 8 en suite (1 fmly) **CONF:** Class 20 Board 12
**CARDS:**

Late for dinner? Quality Standards star rating means that last orders for dinner should be no earlier than:
★ 6.30pm ★★ 7.00pm ★★★ 8.00pm
★★★★ 9.00pm ★★★★★ 10.00pm

## BRIDGEND
Map 10 NR36

### ★★69% *Bridgend*
PA44 7PQ
☎ 01496 810212 📠 01496 810960
From its position in the centre of the island this welcoming hotel is an ideal base from which to explore Islay's numerous attractions. The comfortable bedrooms are furnished in mixed styles and offer a good range of amenities, though they do vary in size. There is a choice of contrasting bars and a spacious dining room.
**ROOMS:** 10 rms (9 en suite) (3 fmly) **FACILITIES:** Fishing Bowls **PARKING:** 30 **NOTES:** No smoking in restaurant
**CARDS:**

## PORT ASKAIG
Map 10 NR46

### ★★65% *Port Askaig*
PA46 7RD
☎ 01496 840245 📠 01496 840295
e-mail: hotel@portaskaig.co.uk
***Dir:*** *at Ferry Terminal*
A relaxed and informal atmosphere prevails at this long-established family-run hotel which, from its position beside the ferry terminal, enjoys a lovely outlook over the Sound of Islay to Jura. Public areas have a comfortable traditional feel and include a quiet first floor lounge, a choice of well-stocked bars and a cosy dining room. The bedrooms vary in size, are modern in style and offer the expected amenities.
**ROOMS:** 8 rms (6 en suite) (1 fmly) **PARKING:** 21 **NOTES:** No children 5yrs No smoking in restaurant **CARDS:**

## ISLE ORNSAY See Skye, Isle of

## JEDBURGH, Scottish Borders
Map 12 NT62

### ★★★74% Jedforest Hotel
Camptown TD8 6PJ
☎ 01835 840222 📠 01835 840226
e-mail: mail@jedforesthotel.freeserve.co.uk
***Dir:*** *3m S of Jedburgh off A68*

A charming country house hotel in 35 acres of grounds, Jedforest was completely refurbished in 1999. Immaculately presented throughout, it offers an attractive and stylish dining room, a bright and comfortable brasserie and a relaxing lounge with open fire. The bedrooms are very smart, with the larger ones being particularly impressive. Service is very attentive.
**ROOMS:** 8 en suite (1 fmly) No smoking in all bedrooms s £58-£75; d £85-£115 (incl. bkfst) * **LB** **FACILITIES:** Fishing Xmas **CONF:** Class 40 Board 25 **PARKING:** 20 **NOTES:** No dogs No smoking in restaurant
**CARDS:**

## JOHN O'GROATS See Lybster

## KELSO, Scottish Borders
Map 12 NT73

### ★★★74% The Roxburghe Hotel & Golf Course
Heiton TD5 8JZ
☎ 01573 450331 📠 01573 450611
e-mail: hotel@roxburghe.net
***Dir:*** *from A68 Jedburgh join A698 to Heiton, 3m SW of Kelso*
Owned by the Duke of Roxburghe, this impressive Jacobean mansion is in a peaceful parkland location close to the River Teviot. Sporting guests enjoy the shooting, fishing and golf, and all guests appreciate the individually designed, attractive bedrooms, some of which have real fires. In addition to the library bar there is also a comfortable drawing room and a dining area.
**ROOMS:** 16 en suite 6 annexe en suite (3 fmly) No smoking in 1 bedroom s £120-£230; d £120-£255 (incl. bkfst) * **LB** **FACILITIES:** STV Golf 18 Tennis (hard) Fishing Croquet lawn Putting green Clay shooting Health & Beauty Salon Mountain bike hire ch fac Xmas **CONF:** Thtr 50 Class 20 Board 20 Del from £130 * **PARKING:** 150 **NOTES:** No smoking in restaurant Closed 23-29 Dec Civ Wed 50
**CARDS:**

### ★★★70% Ednam House
Bridge St TD5 7HT
☎ 01573 224168 📠 01573 226319
e-mail: ednamhouse@excite.co.uk
***Dir:*** *50 metres from Town Square on Bridge Street leading to Abbey and Kelso Old Bridge*
This fine Georgian mansion overlooks the River Tweed and is popular with a regular sporting clientele. Accommodation styles range from standard to grand, with many benefiting from new interior designs and improved bathrooms. Public areas display the character of the house with a choice of lounges and an elegant dining room overlooking the gardens. Service is helpful and attentive.
**ROOMS:** 30 en suite (4 fmly) No smoking in 3 bedrooms s £76-£78; d £120-£157 (incl. bkfst & dinner) * **LB** **FACILITIES:** Croquet lawn Free access to Abbey Fitness Centre ch fac **CONF:** Thtr 250 Board 200 Del from £85 * **PARKING:** 60 **NOTES:** Closed 25 Dec-16 Jan Civ Wed 60
**CARDS:**

### ★★★63% *Cross Keys*
36-37 The Square TD5 7HL
☎ 01573 223303 📠 01573 225792
e-mail: cross-keys-hotel@easynet.co.uk
***Dir:*** *on approaching Kelso, follow signs for Town centre. The hotel is located in main square*
Originally a coaching inn, but now tastefully modernised, this family-run hotel overlooks Kelso's fine cobbled square. Bedrooms are either superior or standard level, and the spacious lounge bar and restaurant are supplemented by the Oak Room bar/bistro.
**ROOMS:** 27 en suite (5 fmly) No smoking in 12 bedrooms **FACILITIES:** STV **CONF:** Thtr 280 Class 220 Board 70 **SERVICES:** Lift air con **NOTES:** Civ Wed 270 **CARDS:**

### ★★65% The Queens Head Hotel
24 Bridge St TD5 7JD
☎ 01573 224636 📠 01573 224459
e-mail: info@queensheadkelso.co.uk
***Dir:*** *A1 to Coldstream, to Kelso from Berwick upon Tweed*
This town centre hotel is reputedly one of the oldest coaching inns in the country. Today's visitor can be assured that accommodation is well-equipped and comfortable and there is a wide range of wholesome meals available in the lounge bar dining area.
**ROOMS:** 11 rms (10 en suite) (3 fmly) s £37.50; d £50 (incl. bkfst) * **LB** **FACILITIES:** Pool table entertainment Xmas **CONF:** Del from £56 * **NOTES:** Civ Wed 23 **CARDS:**

K

KENMORE, Perth & Kinross Map 14 NN74

**★★★66% *Kenmore Hotel***
The Square PH15 2NU
☎ 01887 830205 📠 830262
e-mail: reception@kenmorehotel.co.uk
Dating back to 1572 and authenticated as Scotland's oldest inn, this long-established hotel has undergone sympathetic upgrading. Bedrooms have been tastefully refurbished and public rooms offer a choice of bars, one along with the restaurant above, forms an impressive riverside extension.
**ROOMS:** 27 en suite 15 annexe en suite **FACILITIES:** STV Tennis (hard) Jacuzzi entertainment **CONF:** Thtr 80 Class 60 Board 50 **SERVICES:** Lift **PARKING:** 30 **NOTES:** No smoking in restaurant
**CARDS:**

KENTALLEN, Highland Map 14 NN05

**★★73% *Holly Tree***
Kentallen Pier PA38 4BY
☎ 01631 740292 📠 01631 740345
e-mail: reception@hollytreehotel.co.uk
***Dir:*** *3m S of Ballachulish on A828*
Glorious views over Loch Linnhe are to be enjoyed from this welcoming family run hotel, created by sympathetic conversion of the old village railway station. All of the attractive bedrooms overlook the loch and two ground floor rooms are suitable for disabled guests. The restaurant has an extensive carte that offers a tempting range of delicious seafood and game specialities.
**ROOMS:** 10 en suite **FACILITIES:** Fishing **CONF:** Class 20 **PARKING:** 30 **NOTES:** No smoking in restaurant Closed Dec-Jan
**CARDS:**

KILCHRENAN, Argyll & Bute Map 10 NN02

**★★★75% Taychreggan**
PA35 1HQ
☎ 01866 833211 & 833366 📠 01866 833244
e-mail: taychreggan@btinternet.com
***Dir:*** *W from Glasgow A82 to Crianlarich, W from Crianlarich on A85 to Taynuilt, S for 7m on B845 to Kilchrenan and Taychreggan*
A friendly hotel, peacefully located on the banks of Loch Awe. Bedrooms are smartly appointed, and larger individually styled rooms, some with four-posters, are located in the original part of the house. There is a choice of lounges and a well-stocked bar offering a good selection of malts. Carefully prepared meals are served in the elegant dining room.
**ROOMS:** 19 en suite No smoking in 3 bedrooms s £95-£105; d £100-£130 (incl. bkfst) * **LB** **FACILITIES:** no TV in bdrms Fishing Snooker Xmas **CONF:** Class 15 Board 20 Del £155 * **PARKING:** 40 **NOTES:** No children 14yrs No smoking in restaurant Civ Wed 45
**CARDS:**

KILLIECRANKIE, Perth & Kinross Map 14 NN96

**★★77% Killiecrankie**
PH16 5LG
☎ 01796 473220 📠 01796 472451
e-mail: enquiries@killiecrankiehotel.co.uk
***Dir:*** *turn off A9 at Killiecrankie, hotel is 3m along B8079 on right*
A long-established hotel, set in mature grounds close to the historic Pass of Killiecrankie. Bedrooms are appealingly decorated and furnished with sensible pine units. The inviting public areas include an attractive restaurant looking onto the gardens. The cosy

continued

bar and adjacent sun lounge are popular, or residents can always repair to the quiet lounge full of books and board games.

**ROOMS:** 10 en suite (1 fmly) No smoking in 6 bedrooms s fr £89; d fr £178 (incl. bkfst & dinner) * **LB** **FACILITIES:** Croquet lawn Putting green Xmas **PARKING:** 20 **NOTES:** No smoking in restaurant Closed 3 Jan-4 Feb RS Mon-Tue Dec & Feb **CARDS:**

KILLIN, Stirling Map 11 NN53

**★★★68% Dall Lodge Country House**
Main St FK21 8TN
☎ 01567 820217 📠 01567 820726
e-mail: wilson@dalllodgehotel.co.uk
***Dir:*** *from M9 at Stirling turn left A84-Crianlarich, 3m after Lochearnhead turn right onto A827-Killin*

This fine Victorian mansion has been a local landmark for over 100 years. Smartly decorated bedrooms are comfortably modern in appointment. Public areas include an inviting conservatory lounge, and Scottish cooking is provided in the attractive restaurant, which has views of Ben Lawers, and also offers an impressive wine list.
**ROOMS:** 10 en suite (2 fmly) s £46-£53; d £70-£85 (incl. bkfst) * **LB** **FACILITIES:** Tennis (grass) **CONF:** Thtr 20 Class 16 Board 12 **PARKING:** 20 **NOTES:** No smoking in restaurant Closed Nov-Feb
**CARDS:**

*See advert on opposite page*

**★★74% The Ardeonaig Hotel & Restaurant**
South Loch Tay Side FK21 8SU
☎ 01567 820400 📠 01567 820282
e-mail: ardeonaighotel@btinternet.com
***Dir:*** *Leave A9 for Aberfeldy/Kenmore, at Kenmore turn left into South Shore Rd, hotel 9m along road on right or A84/A827 to Killin, just before Killin turn right along South Shore Rd, hotel 7m along road*
Occupying a peaceful location on the south Loch Tay road, this relaxing and informal hotel has a wonderful outlook across the Loch towards Ben Lawers. All public rooms and bedrooms have been effectively upgraded to provide good levels of comfort. The

continued

formal dining room is a fitting setting for very fine dinners. Ten acres of grounds extend down to the shores of the loch.

**ROOMS:** 12 en suite (1 fmly) No smoking in all bedrooms s £60-£80; d £90-£110 (incl. bkfst) * **LB** **FACILITIES:** Fishing Xmas **PARKING:** 20 **NOTES:** No smoking in restaurant **CARDS:**

## KILMARNOCK, East Ayrshire — Map 10 NS43

### ★★★68% Fenwick

Ayr Rd, Fenwick KA3 6AU
☎ 01560 600478 Fax 01560 600334
e-mail: fenwick@bestwestern.co.uk
***Dir:*** *hotel approx 4m N of Kilmarnock, adjacent to A77 & B751*

This modern, comfortable hotel is conveniently situated equidistant from Glasgow and the Ayrshire coast. Stylish public rooms include a cosy, fireside lounge, a bright, open plan restaurant and an informal bar area. The hotel enjoys a fine reputation for food with creative, innovative menus forming the basis for its very own dining club. Bedrooms are soundly equipped and suited to the business traveller.

**ROOMS:** 31 en suite (2 fmly) No smoking in 4 bedrooms s £55; d £75 (incl. bkfst) * **LB** **FACILITIES:** STV Clay pigeon Quad bike Xmas **CONF:** Thtr 160 Class 60 Board 18 Del £105 * **PARKING:** 80 **NOTES:** Civ Wed 100 **CARDS:**

### *Travelodge*

Kilmarnock By Pass KA1 5LQ
☎ 01563 573810 Fax 01563 573810
***Dir:*** *at Bellfield Interchange just off A77*

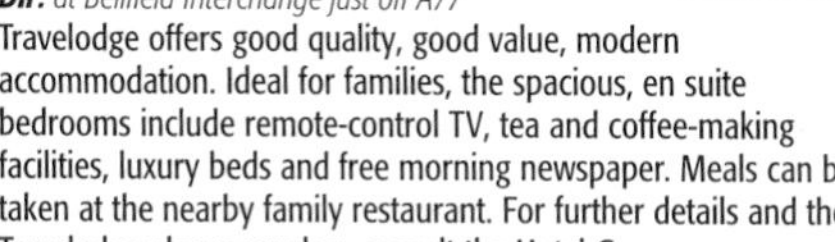

Travelodge offers good quality, good value, modern accommodation. Ideal for families, the spacious, en suite bedrooms include remote-control TV, tea and coffee-making facilities, luxury beds and free morning newspaper. Meals can be taken at the nearby family restaurant. For further details and the Travelodge phone number, consult the Hotel Groups page.

**ROOMS:** 40 en suite

## KILWINNING, North Ayrshire — Map 10 NS34

### ★★★75% Montgreenan Mansion House

Montgreenan Estate KA13 7QZ
☎ 01294 557733 Fax 01294 850397
e-mail: info@montgreenanhotel.co.uk
***Dir:*** *4m North of Irvine on A736*

Set in 48 acres of parkland and woods, this 19th-century mansion offers a peaceful atmosphere. Gracious public areas retain many original features such as ornate ceilings and marble fireplaces and include a splendid drawing room, a library, a club-style bar and a

*continued*

restaurant. Bedrooms are well-equipped and come in a variety of sizes.

**ROOMS:** 21 en suite s £70-£80; d £90-£115 (incl. bkfst) * **LB** **FACILITIES:** STV Golf 5 Tennis (hard) Snooker Croquet lawn Putting green Jacuzzi Clay pigeon shooting Quad Biking Xmas **CONF:** Thtr 110 Class 60 Board 60 Del £115 * **SERVICES:** Lift **PARKING:** 50 **NOTES:** No smoking in restaurant Civ Wed 110 **CARDS:**

## KINCLAVEN, Perth & Kinross — Map 11 NO13

### ★★★79% Ballathie House

PH1 4QN
☎ 01250 883268 Fax 01250 883396
e-mail: email@ballathiehousehotel.com
***Dir:*** *from A9 2m north of Perth, B9099 through Stanley & signposted or off A93 at Beech Hedge follow signs for Ballathie 2.5m*

Set in extensive grounds overlooking the River Tay, this splendid Scottish mansion house combines grandeur with modern comfort. The elegant restaurant overlooking the river is the perfect setting for a fine dining experience. Bedrooms range from well-proportioned Master rooms to the standard rooms. All rooms are individual in style and most feature antiques. However, for the ultimate in quality and comfort, request the Riverside Rooms set in a new development right on the banks of the river.

**ROOMS:** 27 en suite 16 annexe en suite (2 fmly) s £80-£105; d £160-£200 (incl. bkfst) * **LB** **FACILITIES:** STV Fishing Croquet lawn Putting green Xmas **CONF:** Thtr 50 Class 20 Board 30 Del from £130 * **SERVICES:** Lift **PARKING:** 50 **NOTES:** No smoking in restaurant Civ Wed 200 **CARDS:**

KINGUSSIE, Highland Map 14 NH70

## Premier Collection

**★★ ◎◎◎ The Cross**
Tweed Mill Brae, Ardbroilach Rd PH21 1TC
☎ 01540 661166 🖷 01540 661080
e-mail: relax@thecross.co.uk
***Dir:*** *from traffic lights in centre of Kingussie, travel uphill along Ardbroilach Rd for 300mtrs, turn left into Tweed Mill Brae*
This converted tweed mill, situated alongside the river, continues to offer food that is well worth a detour, alongside comfortable and individually furnished bedrooms. The lounges have a mix of rough stone walls and modern art, and hospitality is of a high order, but it is the food, above everything, that brings a steady stream of guests back to The Cross; apart, perhaps, from the wine list that exudes the proprietors' passion among its pages.
**ROOMS:** 9 en suite No smoking in all bedrooms d £190-£230 (incl. bkfst & dinner) * **LB** **PARKING:** 12 **NOTES:** No dogs (ex guide dogs) No children 12yrs No smoking in restaurant Closed Dec-Mar RS Tuesdays **CARDS:**

**★★74% ◎ The Scot House**
Newtonmore Rd PH21 1HE
☎ 01540 661351 🖷 01540 661111
e-mail: shh@sirocco.globalnet.co.uk
***Dir:*** *from A9 trunk road, take Kingussie exit, hotel is approx 0.50m at S end of village main street*
A warm welcome is assured at this friendly family-run hotel on the south side of the village. The house is meticulously maintained throughout, and one can eat well in either the cosy bar or attractive restaurant. Bedrooms are fully equipped with most being well-proportioned, which compensates for their compact bathrooms.
**ROOMS:** 9 en suite (1 fmly) s £33-£45; d £60-£70 (incl. bkfst) * **LB** **FACILITIES:** ch fac Xmas **PARKING:** 30 **NOTES:** No smoking in restaurant Closed 6-31 Jan **CARDS:**

**★★73% ◎ Osprey**
Ruthven Rd PH21 1EN
☎ 01540 661510 🖷 01540 661510
e-mail: aileen@ospreyhotel.co.uk
***Dir:*** *S end of Kingussie High St*
This delightful small hotel stands beside the Memorial Gardens. The nicely presented public areas include a choice of inviting and comfortable lounges. In the dining room, the menu offers an interesting choice of carefully prepared specialities. Attractive fabrics are used to good effect in the bright and comfortable bedrooms which are traditional in style.
**ROOMS:** 8 en suite No smoking in 6 bedrooms s £50-£55; d £90-£102 (incl. bkfst & dinner) * **LB** **PARKING:** 6 **NOTES:** No smoking in restaurant **CARDS:**

**★★67% Columba House Hotel & Garden Restaurant**
Manse Rd PH21 1JF
☎ 01540 661402 🖷 01540 661652
e-mail: reservations@columbahousehotel.co.uk
***Dir:*** *exit A9 at Kingussie/Kincraig onto A86. Turn into Manse Road and hotel is 2nd on left*

Set in secluded grounds well off the main street, this hotel offers a friendly country house atmosphere. A smart new conservatory style restaurant gives lovely views of the garden. Bedrooms - thoughtfully equipped including mini bars - are comfortably appointed, some being contained in renovated buildings adjoining the main house.
**ROOMS:** 5 en suite 5 annexe en suite (3 fmly) No smoking in 4 bedrooms s £35-£50; d £65-£75 (incl. bkfst) **LB** **FACILITIES:** ch fac **CONF:** Thtr 60 Class 30 Board 30 Del from £65 * **PARKING:** 30 **NOTES:** No smoking in restaurant **CARDS:**
See advert on opposite page

KINNESSWOOD, Perth & Kinross Map 11 NO10

**★★68% ◎ *Lomond Country Inn***
THE CIRCLE Selected Individual Hotels GREAT BRITAIN
Main St KY13 9HN
☎ 01592 840253 🖷 01592 840693
e-mail: lomondcountryinn@aol.com
***Dir:*** *M90 junct 7, follow signs for Milnthort & then Kinneswood or junct 5 follow signs for Glenrothes & Scotlandwell then Kinneswood*
Keen proprietors provide a welcoming atmosphere at this small country hotel. Bedrooms come in various sizes and offer modern amenities. There is a cosy, well-stocked bar with real ales and open fires, a small sitting room, and an elegant dining room with fine views of Loch Leven. Bar meals and restaurant dinners display innovation.
**ROOMS:** 4 en suite 8 annexe en suite (3 fmly) No smoking in 4 bedrooms **FACILITIES:** ch fac **PARKING:** 50 **NOTES:** No smoking in restaurant **CARDS:**

KINROSS, Perth & Kinross Map 11 NO10
see also Powmill

**★★★73% Green**
2 The Muirs KY13 8AS
☎ 01577 863467 🖷 01577 863180
e-mail: reservations@green-hotel.com
***Dir:*** *M90 junct 6 follow signs for Kinross, turn onto A922, the hotel is situated on this road*
Most of the comfortable bedrooms are generously proportioned, in pleasing colour schemes with smart modern furnishings. Public areas include relaxing lounges, a choice of contrasting bars, an attractive restaurant and well-stocked gift shop. Other facilities
continued

include two 18-hole golf courses, a leisure centre, squash and tennis courts, and a curling rink.

**ROOMS:** 46 en suite (4 fmly) No smoking in 12 bedrooms s £80-£100; d £140-£160 (incl. bkfst) * **LB** **FACILITIES:** STV Indoor swimming (H) Golf 36 Fishing Squash Sauna Gym Croquet lawn Putting green Curling in season ch fac **CONF:** Thtr 130 Class 75 Board 60 Del £120 * **PARKING:** 60 **CARDS:**

*See advert on this page*

**★★★69% Windlestrae Hotel Business & Leisure Centre**

REGAL

The Muirs KY13 8AS
☎ 01577 863217 📠 01577 864733
e-mail: windlestrae@corushotels.com
***Dir:*** *leave M90 junct 6 turn E into Kinross, stop at mini rdbt turn left in approx 350yds Windlestrae on right*

WINDLESTRAE HOTEL

Situated off the main road at the north end of town, this comfortable modern hotel combines a welcoming atmosphere with impressive leisure and conference facilities. Bedrooms, most of which are spacious, offer comfortable modern appointments together with a good range of amenities. Public areas include a well-stocked split-level bar, a spacious foyer lounge, and a smart restaurant.
**ROOMS:** 45 en suite (5 fmly) No smoking in 15 bedrooms s £70-£90; d £80-£100 (incl. bkfst) * **LB** **FACILITIES:** STV Indoor swimming (H) Snooker Sauna Solarium Gym Jacuzzi Beautician Steam room Toning tables Xmas **CONF:** Thtr 250 Class 100 Board 80 Del from £90 * **SERVICES:** air con **PARKING:** 80 **NOTES:** No smoking in restaurant Civ Wed 100 **CARDS:**

**⌂ *Travelodge***

Travelodge

Kincardine Rd KY13 7NQ
☎ 08700 850950 📠 01577 864108
***Dir:*** *on A977, off junct 6 of M90 Turthills Tourist Centre*
Travelodge offers good quality, good value, modern accommodation. Ideal for families, the spacious, en suite bedrooms include remote-control TV, tea and coffee-making facilities, luxury beds and free morning newspaper. Meals can be

*continued on p748*

K

KINROSS, continued

taken at the nearby family restaurant. For further details and the Travelodge phone number, consult the Hotel Groups page.

**ROOMS:** 35 en suite

KINTORE, Aberdeenshire Map 15 NJ71

### ★★66% Torryburn

School Rd AB51 0XP
☎ 01467 632269 🖷 01467 632271
***Dir:*** *travelling north from Aberdeen leave dual carriageway for the village of Kintore. Hotel on the corner of Dunecht Rd*

This welcoming family-run hotel has attractive public areas which feature a smart conservatory and supper room and a choice of comfortable bars. Bedrooms come in a variety of sizes, all being tastefully decorated and offering a good range of amenities.
**ROOMS:** 9 rms (8 en suite) (1 fmly) No smoking in all bedrooms s £35-£40; d £55-£63 (incl. bkfst) * **FACILITIES:** STV Tennis (hard) Fishing Snooker Shooting Xmas **CONF:** Class 50 Board 50 **PARKING:** 30 **NOTES:** Closed 1 Jan **CARDS:**

KIRKBEAN, Dumfries & Galloway Map 11 NX95

K

### ★★72% Cavens

DG2 8AA
☎ 01387 880234 🖷 01387 880467
e-mail: enquiries@cavens-hotel.co.uk
***Dir:*** *on entering village of Kirkbean on A710, hotel signed*

Dating back to 1752, Cavens has been home to many notable worthies. Many improvements have been made to the bedrooms and public rooms to ensure that guests will enjoy the comfort and tranquillity of this country house, set in six acres of parkland gardens. A set four-course dinner menu, using local produce, provides good value.
**ROOMS:** 8 en suite No smoking in all bedrooms s £50-£60; d £80-£100 (incl. bkfst) * **LB** **FACILITIES:** Croquet lawn Shooting, Fishing, Horse Riding Xmas **CONF:** Thtr 20 Class 20 Board 20 Del from £85 * **PARKING:** 12 **NOTES:** No smoking in restaurant
**CARDS:**

KIRKCALDY, Fife Map 11 NT29

### ★★★67% Dean Park

Chapel Level KY2 6QW
☎ 01592 261635 🖷 01592 261371
e-mail: info@deanparkhotel.co.uk
***Dir:*** *signposted from A92, Kirkcaldy West junc*

On the northern edge of town this welcoming hotel has particular appeal for the visiting business traveller and is also a popular venue for conferences and functions. Bedrooms, though varied in size and in style, are comfortably modern in appointment and offer the expected accessories. Public areas include a spacious and well-stocked bar and a smart restaurant.
**ROOMS:** 34 en suite 12 annexe en suite (2 fmly) No smoking in 3 bedrooms s £59-£69; d £89 (incl. bkfst) * **FACILITIES:** STV
**CONF:** Thtr 250 Class 125 Board 54 **SERVICES:** Lift **PARKING:** 250 **NOTES:** No dogs (ex guide dogs) Civ Wed 250
**CARDS:**

Early start? Hotels at all star levels should provide in-room alarm clocks and/or alarm calls.

### ★★★64% Dunnikier House Hotel

Dunnikier Park KY1 3LP
☎ 01592 268393 🖷 01592 642340
e-mail: recp@dunnikier-house-hotel.co.uk
***Dir:*** *turn off A92 at Kirkcaldy West, then 3rd exit on rdbt signed 'Hospital/Crematorium'. First left past school*

This privately-owned hotel is an 18th-century mansion house set in parkland beside Dunnikier Golf Course. Original features including carved fireplaces and ornate plasterwork have been retained in the public areas. Views over the parkland can be enjoyed from the lounge, and the bar offers a wide selection of whiskies. The Oswald restaurant provides an appropriate setting for fine meals which feature carefully prepared fresh local produce.
**ROOMS:** 14 en suite s £60-£75; d £90-£95 (incl. bkfst) *
**FACILITIES:** Xmas **CONF:** Thtr 70 Class 30 Board 40 Del from £105 *
**PARKING:** 100 **NOTES:** No smoking in restaurant Civ Wed 30
**CARDS:**

### ★★68% The Belvedere

THE CIRCLE
Selected Individual Hotels
GREAT BRITAIN

Coxstool, West Wemyss KY1 4SL
☎ 01592 654167 🖷 01592 655279
e-mail: info@thebelvederehotel.com
***Dir:*** *A92 from M90 junct 3, at Kirkcaldy East take A915, 1m NE turn right to Coaltown, at T-junct turn right then left, hotel 1st building in village*

Wonderful views over the Firth of Forth can be enjoyed from this welcoming hotel in the picturesque village of Coxstool. The bright, airy bedrooms are smartly decorated and offer comfortable modern furnishings. Public areas include a cosy bar and tastefully appointed restaurant.
**ROOMS:** 5 en suite 15 annexe en suite (2 fmly) s £58; d £70 (incl. bkfst) * **LB** **FACILITIES:** STV ch fac **CONF:** Thtr 40 Class 12 Board 20 Del from £57.50 * **PARKING:** 50 **NOTES:** No dogs (ex guide dogs)
**CARDS:**

KIRKCUDBRIGHT, Dumfries & Galloway Map 11 NX65

### ★★★72% Selkirk Arms

Best Western

Old High St DG6 4JG
☎ 01557 330402 🖷 01557 331639
e-mail: reception@selkirkarmshotel.co.uk
***Dir:*** *turn off A75 5m W of Castle Douglas onto A711, 5m to Kirkcudbright in centre of town*

Originally a hostelry frequented by Robert Burns (he wrote the Selkirk Grace here) the Selkirk Arms is now a smart hotel with modern, well-equipped bedrooms. Service is friendly and attentive and one can eat well in either the attractive, Rosette award-winning restaurant or in the bistro and lounge bar.
**ROOMS:** 13 en suite 3 annexe en suite (2 fmly) No smoking in 6 bedrooms **FACILITIES:** STV ch fac Xmas **CONF:** Thtr 70 Class 60 Board 40 Del from £90 * **PARKING:** 9 **NOTES:** No smoking in restaurant **CARDS:**

★★62% **Arden House Hotel**
Tongland Rd DG6 4UU
☎ 01557 330544
***Dir:*** *turn off A57 Euro route (Stranraer), 4m W of Castle Douglas onto A711. Take signs for Kirkcudbright, crossing Telford Bridge. Hotel 400m on left*
Set well back from the main road in extensive grounds on the north east side of town, this well-maintained hotel offers attractive bedrooms, a lounge bar and adjoining conservatory serving a range of popular dishes, which are also available in the dining room. It boasts an impressive function suite in its grounds.
**ROOMS:** 9 rms (8 en suite) (7 fmly) s fr £30; d fr £56 (incl. bkfst) * **CONF:** Thtr 175 Class 175 **PARKING:** 70

★★58% ***Royal***
St Cuthbert St DG6 4DY
☎ 01557 331213 01557 331513
e-mail: royal@pheasanthotel.co.uk
***Dir:*** *turn off A75 onto A711 hotel is in the centre of Kirkcudbright, on the corner at crossroads*
Refurbishment has enhanced the accommodation at this conveniently situated, town centre tourist and commercial hotel. Rooms have en suite facilities and include colour television and direct-dial telephones. There is a ground floor bar, popular with hotel guests and locals alike, and a residents lounge is located on the first floor.
**ROOMS:** 17 en suite (7 fmly) **FACILITIES:** entertainment **CONF:** Thtr 120 Class 60 Board 60 **CARDS:**

## KIRKHILL, Highland — Map 14 NH54

★★64% **Bogroy Inn**
IV5 7PX
☎ 01463 831296 01463 831296
***Dir:*** *at junct A862/B9164*
Bogroy Inn is a small and friendly roadside hotel, which in the 16th century was closely associated with whisky smuggling. Tasty meals are served in either the lounge bar or dining room. Bedrooms offer a practical standard of accommodation.
**ROOMS:** 7 en suite (3 fmly) s £28-£30; d £50-£55 (incl. bkfst) * LB **PARKING:** 40 **NOTES:** No dogs (ex guide dogs) **CARDS:**

## KYLE OF LOCHALSH, Highland — Map 13 NG72

★★★64% **Lochalsh**
Ferry Rd IV40 8AF
☎ 01599 534202 01599 534881
e-mail: mdmacrae@lochalsh-hotel.demon.co.uk
***Dir:*** *turn off A82 onto A87*
Almost next to the new Skye Bridge, this established hotel has a prominent position by the former ferry slip. The modern bedrooms vary in size and are brightly decorated. Fine views are enjoyed from public areas and the formal restaurant serves interesting modern food from a short carte.
**ROOMS:** 38 en suite (8 fmly) s £50-£75; d £90-£150 (incl. bkfst) * LB **FACILITIES:** STV Xmas **CONF:** Thtr 20 Class 20 Board 20 Del from £60 * **SERVICES:** Lift **PARKING:** 50 **NOTES:** No smoking in restaurant **CARDS:**

*See advert on this page*

Popped the question? Hotels with Civ Wed in their entry are licensed for civil wedding ceremonies. Maximum numbers for the ceremony only are shown, e.g. Civ Wed 120



## LADYBANK, Fife — Map 11 NO30

★★★65% **Fernie Castle**
Letham KY15 7RU
☎ 01337 810381 01337 810422
e-mail: mail@ferniecastle.demon.co.uk
***Dir:*** *from M90 junct 6 take A91 east (Tay Bridge/St Andrews) to Melville Lodges rdbt. Left onto A92 signed Tay Bridge. Hotel 1.2m on right*

This turreted castle is set amid 17 acres of wooded grounds in the heart of Fife. Bedrooms range from King and Queen rooms, to the more standard sized Squire and Lady rooms. Formal dining can be enjoyed in the elegant Auld Alliance Restaurant. The Keep Bar is also available, serving less formal meals, and there is a choice of relaxing lounges.
**ROOMS:** 20 en suite (2 fmly) No smoking in 12 bedrooms s £63-£85; d £125-£170 (incl. bkfst & dinner) * LB **FACILITIES:** Croquet lawn Putting green 17 acres woodland with loch entertainment ch fac Xmas **CONF:** Thtr 180 Class 120 Board 25 Del from £100 * **PARKING:** 80 **NOTES:** No smoking in restaurant Civ Wed 180
**CARDS:**

## LAIRG, Highland Map 14 NC50

**★★68% Overscaig**
Loch Shin IV27 4NY
☎ 01549 431203
***Dir:*** *on A838*
This comfortable Highland hotel stands beside the picturesque shore of Loch Shin. Bedrooms have pleasing colour schemes and are comfortably modern in style. Relaxing public areas include a well-stocked bar, a coffee lounge, and a smart dining room, which overlooks the loch. Fishing rights along with boats for the loch are also provided.
**ROOMS:** 9 en suite (2 fmly) **FACILITIES:** Fishing Xmas **PARKING:** 30
**NOTES:** No dogs (ex guide dogs)

## LANARK, South Lanarkshire Map 11 NS84

see also Biggar

**★★★63% Cartland Bridge**
Glasgow Rd ML11 9UF
☎ 01555 664426 ▤ 01555 663773
e-mail: sales@cartlandbridge.co.uk
***Dir:*** *follow A73 through Lanark towards Carluke. Hotel 1.25m on right*
Set in attractive grounds this Grade I listed mansion is popular with both business and leisure guests. Public areas feature splendid wood panelling and a gallery staircase. In addition to the restaurant, food is also available in the bar and there is a small cocktail lounge. Bedrooms vary in size and style.
**ROOMS:** 20 rms (18 en suite) (2 fmly) No smoking in 9 bedrooms s £50-£62; d £70-£85 (incl. bkfst) * **FACILITIES:** STV ch fac Xmas
**CONF:** Thtr 250 Class 180 Board 30 Del from £75 * **PARKING:** 120
**NOTES:** No smoking in restaurant Civ Wed 70
**CARDS:**

L

## LANGBANK, Renfrewshire Map 10 NS37

**★★★★67% ⊛⊛ *Gleddoch House***
PA14 6YE
☎ 01475 540711 ▤ 01475 540201
e-mail: gleddochhouse@ukonline.co.uk
***Dir:*** *signposted from B789 at Langbank rdbt*
Set above Langbank, this well established hotel enjoys spectacular views over the River Clyde. The elegant restaurant is the setting for innovative dining and attentive service. Bedrooms come in a range of styles, those in the main part of the house keep much of the original character, and the wings are more modern in style. New for 2002 will be a link between the hotel and the golf club house, which will also have some new leisure facilties.
**ROOMS:** 39 en suite (4 fmly) No smoking in 6 bedrooms
**FACILITIES:** STV Golf 18 Fishing Squash Riding Putting green Clay pigeon shooting **CONF:** Thtr 100 Class 60 Board 40 **PARKING:** 200
**CARDS:**

## LARGS, North Ayrshire Map 10 NS25

**★★★74% ⊛ Brisbane House**
14 Greenock Rd, Esplanade KA30 8NF
☎ 01475 687200 ▤ 01475 676295
e-mail: enquiries@maksu-group.co.uk
***Dir:*** *on A78 midway between Greenock and Irvine, on seafront*
Friendly staff offer a high level of hospitality and attentive service at this modernised Georgian house, looking out over the promenade to the Isle of Cumbrae. There is a choice of bars and eating options. The conservatory adjoining the lounge bar offers informal dining, and the elegant restaurant has its own

*continued*

conservatory cocktail bar. Bedrooms come in a variety of sizes and are well-equipped.
**ROOMS:** 23 en suite (2 fmly) No smoking in 5 bedrooms s £75-£100; d £95-£120 (incl. bkfst) * **LB** **FACILITIES:** STV Jacuzzi entertainment Xmas **CONF:** Thtr 120 Class 60 Board 50 Del from £90 *
**PARKING:** 60 **NOTES:** Civ Wed 120
**CARDS:**

**★★★72% Priory House**
Broomfields KA30 8DR
☎ 01475 686460 ▤ 01475 689070
e-mail: enquiries@maksu-group.co.uk
***Dir:*** *on A78 midway between Greenock and Irvine, hotel on seafront*
Standing on the seafront looking out across the Firth of Clyde, this hotel boasts a fine conservatory in which to relax and take in the views. Food is available in the restaurant, or in the bar with its own dining conservatory and extensive menu. The friendly staff provide attentive service throughout. Bedrooms vary in size, but all are thoughtfully equipped.
**ROOMS:** 21 en suite (2 fmly) No smoking in 5 bedrooms s £65-£85; d £80-£100 (incl. bkfst) * **LB** **FACILITIES:** STV Jacuzzi ch fac Xmas
**CONF:** Thtr 100 Class 50 Board 50 Del from £85 * **PARKING:** 50
**CARDS:**

**★★69% Willowbank**
96 Greenock Rd KA30 8PG
☎ 01475 672311 675435 ▤ 01475 689027
e-mail: iain@willowbankhotellargs.freeserve.co.uk
***Dir:*** *on A78*
A relaxed, friendly atmosphere prevails at this well-maintained hotel. The well-decorated bedrooms tend to be spacious and offer comfortable modern appointments, while public areas include a large, well-stocked bar, a lounge and dining room. Attractive floral baskets hanging outside are a feature during summer.
**ROOMS:** 30 en suite (4 fmly) s £54-£84; d £106-£150 (incl. bkfst) * **LB**
**FACILITIES:** entertainment ch fac Xmas **CONF:** Thtr 200 Class 100 Board 40 Del from £70 * **PARKING:** 40
**CARDS:**

## LAUDER, Scottish Borders Map 12 NT54

**★★68% Lauderdale**
1 Edinburgh Rd TD2 6TW
☎ 01578 722231 ▤ 01578 718642
e-mail: enquiries@lauderdale-hotel.co.uk
***Dir:*** *on A68 from S, drive through centre of Lauder, hotel is on right. From Edinburgh, hotel is on left at first bend after passing sign for Lauder*
Lauderdale Hotel is set on the main road on the north side of town. This friendly hotel provides good value meals in both the bar and cosy dining room. The well-equipped bedrooms are comfortable and well-kept.
**ROOMS:** 9 en suite (1 fmly) No smoking in 3 bedrooms s £29-£32; d £60-£70 (incl. bkfst) * **LB** **FACILITIES:** STV ch fac **PARKING:** 50
**NOTES:** No dogs (ex guide dogs) No smoking in restaurant
**CARDS:**

## LERWICK See Shetland

## LETTERFINLAY, Highland Map 14 NN29

**★★67% Letterfinlay Lodge**
PH34 4DZ
☎ 01397 712622
***Dir:*** *7m N of Spean Bridge, on A82 beside Loch Lochy*
This comfortable, family-run hotel stands in grounds beside the A82, overlooking Loch Lochy. There is a cosy bar, a choice of

*continued*

lounges - one of which overlooks the loch and is popular for its bar food - and an attractive dining room for a more formal dining experience. Bedrooms vary in size and are appointed in both modern and traditional styles.
**ROOMS:** 13 rms (11 en suite) (5 fmly) s £29-£40; d £57-£80 (incl. bkfst) * LB **FACILITIES:** Fishing **PARKING:** 100 **NOTES:** No smoking in restaurant Closed Nov-Feb (ex New Year)
**CARDS:**

## LEUCHARS, Fife — Map 11 NO42

### ★★★63% *Drumoig Golf Hotel*

Drumoig KY16 0BE
☎ 01382 541800 01382 542211
e-mail: drumoig@sol.co.uk
***Dir:*** *M90 to Tay Bridge turn off, then A92 Taybridge/Dundee at the Forgan rdbt turn right to Leuchars/St Andrews, hotel at bottom of the hill on the left*

Opposite the Scottish National Golf Centre, this smart hotel is especially popular with visiting golfers. Most of the modern bedrooms are contained in three separate lodges but five new luxury bedrooms have been created in the main house. Public areas include a well-stocked bar and attractive restaurant, both of which overlook the golf course.
**ROOMS:** 5 en suite 24 annexe en suite No smoking in 17 bedrooms **FACILITIES:** STV Golf 18 Fishing Gym Putting green Home of Scottish National golf centre **CONF:** Thtr 50 Class 15 Board 24 **PARKING:** 120 **NOTES:** No dogs (ex guide dogs) No smoking in restaurant
**CARDS:**

## LEWIS, ISLE OF, Western Isles — Map 13

## STORNOWAY — Map 13 NB43

### ★★★66% Cabarfeidh

HS1 2EU
☎ 01851 702604 01851 705572
e-mail: donnie@calahotels.com
***Dir:*** *1m from town centre on main road to Tarbert, turn left at rdbt and take first turn on right*
This modern hotel is situated on the edge of the town and offers spacious bedrooms, well-suited to business and leisure visitors alike. There is a choice of bars and a wide selection of dishes is served in the well-appointed restaurant, while the foyer lounge is a comfortable place to relax after dinner.
**ROOMS:** 46 en suite (36 fmly) No smoking in 12 bedrooms s £60-£75; d £95 (incl. bkfst) * LB **FACILITIES:** STV **CONF:** Thtr 350 Class 100 Board 35 Del from £65 * **SERVICES:** Lift air con **PARKING:** 100 **NOTES:** No smoking in restaurant **CARDS:**

## LOCHCARRON, Highland — Map 14 NG83

### ★★68% Lochcarron

Main St IV54 8YS
☎ 01520 722226 01520 722612
THE CIRCLE Selected Individual Hotels GREAT BRITAIN
***Dir:*** *take A9 N from Inverness, then A835 at Tore rdbt for Ullapool, then A890 Kyle of Lochalsh, hotel is in E end of village on Lochcarron*
A friendly hotel, with a touch of Irish hospitality from the Graham family. Bedrooms, two with private sitting rooms, follow a modern decorative scheme. Meals and light snacks are available all day in the bar. In the dining room the emphasis is on fresh local seafood. Both bar and restaurant look out onto the loch.
**ROOMS:** 10 rms (9 en suite) (2 fmly) No smoking in 2 bedrooms **FACILITIES:** Hunting Shooting Fishing entertainment Xmas **CONF:** Class 40 **PARKING:** 40 **NOTES:** No smoking in restaurant
**CARDS:**

*See advert on this page*

## LOCHEARNHEAD, Stirling — Map 11 NN52

### ★66% Lochearnhead

Lochside FK19 8PU
☎ 01567 830229 01567 830364
e-mail: gus@lochhot.freeserve.co.uk
***Dir:*** *from A84 follow signs Crianlarich/Callander for Lochearnhead where turn right at T-junct, hotel is 500 mtrs ahead*
This friendly hotel overlooks Loch Earn, a popular resort for visitors attracted by the extensive range of water pursuits. Lovely loch views can be enjoyed from all the public rooms. The varied

*continued on p752*

LOCHEARNHEAD, continued

menus offer a good range of home-cooked dishes in both the bar and restaurant.
**ROOMS:** 12 rms (8 en suite) s £30-£40; d £48-£62 (incl. bkfst) * LB
**FACILITIES:** STV Fishing Water, skiing. Windsurfing, Sailing,Cycling ch fac
**PARKING:** 82 **NOTES:** No smoking in restaurant Closed Dec-Mar
**CARDS:**

LOCHGILPHEAD, Argyll & Bute Map 10 NR88

**★★★68% Cairnbaan**
Crinan Canal, Cairnbaan PA31 8SJ
☎ 01546 603668 01546 606045
e-mail: cairnbaanhotel@virgin.net
***Dir:*** *2m N, A816 from Lochgilphead, hotel off B841*
This wonderfully relaxing hotel, beside lock five on the Crinan Canal, boasts comfortable lounges, a bar area and a delightful patio where many guests dine informally. The menu offered in the attractive, formal restaurant features traditional Scottish dishes carefully prepared from quality local ingredients.
**ROOMS:** 12 en suite No smoking in all bedrooms s £55-£65; d £80-£125 (incl. bkfst) * LB **CONF:** Thtr 160 Class 100 Board 80 Del £95 *
**PARKING:** 53 **NOTES:** No smoking in restaurant Civ Wed 120
**CARDS:**

**★★62% Stag Hotel & Restaurant**
Argyll St PA31 8NE
☎ 01546 602496 01546 603549
e-mail: staghotel@ukhotels.com
***Dir:*** *from central Scotland A82 then A38 to Inveraray. Turn right at mini rdbt into Main Street, hotel is large black/white turreted building at the junct of Lorne Street & Argyll Street*
This long-established hotel, which is now under new ownership, is centrally located and offers good value accommodation. The lounge bar restaurant offers a good range of popular dishes at reasonable prices. Bedrooms, although quite compact, are well-equipped.
**ROOMS:** 18 en suite (2 fmly) s £30-£45; d £40-£65 (incl. bkfst) * LB
**FACILITIES:** STV Xmas **CONF:** Thtr 50 Class 16 Board 20 Del from £49.95 * **NOTES:** No dogs (ex guide dogs)
**CARDS:**

LOCHINVER, Highland Map 14 NC02

***Courtesy & Care Award***

**★★★80% Inver Lodge**
IV27 4LU
☎ 01571 844496 01571 844395
e-mail: stay@inverlodge.com
***Dir:*** *A835 to Lochinver continue through village and turn left after village hall, follow private road for 0.5m*
This well-run, comfortable modern hotel is set on a hillside above the village with a backdrop of unspoilt wilderness and mountain scenery, and spectacular views of the harbour and bay. There is a choice of lounges and a restaurant where local ingredients are prepared with some ingenuity. Bedrooms are stylish and all with ocean views. Inver Lodge has been awarded the AA Courtesy & Care Award for Scotland 2001-2002.

**ROOMS:** 20 en suite s fr £80; d fr £130 (incl. bkfst) * LB
**FACILITIES:** STV Fishing Snooker Sauna Solarium **CONF:** Thtr 30 Board 20 **PARKING:** 30 **NOTES:** No smoking in restaurant Closed Nov-Etr **CARDS:**

LOCH LOMOND See Balloch & Luss

LOCHMADDY See North Uist, Isle of

LOCKERBIE, Dumfries & Galloway Map 11 NY18

**★★★72% Dryfesdale**
Dryfebridge DG11 2SF
☎ 01576 202427 01576 204187
e-mail: reception@dryfesdalehotel.co.uk
***Dir:*** *from A74 take 'Lockerbie North' junct, 3rd left at 1st rdbt, 1st exit left at 2nd rdbt, hotel is 200yds on left hand side*
Conveniently situated for the M74, yet suitably screened from it, this hotel features upgraded public areas and bedrooms, and there are ambitious plans for further improvements. Dinner makes good use of local produce and is served in the airy restaurant overlooking the gardens. A warm welcome is offered by the enthusiastic young staff.
**ROOMS:** 15 en suite (2 fmly) No smoking in 4 bedrooms s £55-£65; d £85-£95 (incl. bkfst) * LB **FACILITIES:** STV Golf 9 Croquet lawn Putting green Clay pigeon shooting,Fishing entertainment ch fac Xmas
**CONF:** Thtr 100 Class 80 Board 45 Del from £85 * **PARKING:** 40
**NOTES:** No smoking in restaurant Civ Wed 100
**CARDS:**

*See advert on opposite page*

**★★70% *Somerton House***
35 Carlisle Rd DG11 2DR
☎ 01576 202583/202384 01576 204218
***Dir:*** *off A74*
This fine Victorian mansion has been well-preserved and features beautiful woodwork, particularly in the restaurant. An attractive conservatory adds a new dimension and is equally popular for bar meals. Bedrooms are generally spacious and well-equipped.
**ROOMS:** 7 en suite 4 annexe en suite (2 fmly) No smoking in 4 bedrooms **CONF:** Thtr 25 Class 15 Board 15 **PARKING:** 100
**NOTES:** No smoking in restaurant **CARDS:**

**★★65% Kings Arms Hotel**
High St DG11 2JL
☎ 01576 202410 01576 202410
e-mail: reception@kingsarmshotel.co.uk
***Dir:*** *A74M, 0.5m into town centre, hotel is opposite Town Hall*
Located centrally within the town, this traditional inn provides

*continued*

extensive function facilities, an all day menu served within the cosy bars, and well-equipped accommodation. A smart restaurant sets a comfortable scene for the popular, creative dinner menus.
**ROOMS:** 14 rms (12 en suite) (1 fmly) s fr £35; d fr £60 (incl. bkfst) * **FACILITIES:** Xmas **CONF:** Thtr 80 Class 40 Board 30 Del from £50 * **PARKING:** 8 **NOTES:** No smoking in restaurant
**CARDS:**

### ★★64% Ravenshill House

12 Dumfries Rd DG11 2EF
☎ 01576 202882 📠 01576 202882
e-mail: ravenshillhouse.hotel@virgin.net
***Dir:*** *on A709 which is signed from the A74M Lockerbie junct, travel W of town centre. Hotel is 0.5m on right*
Cheerful and attentive service plus good value home cooked meals feature at this friendly family-run hotel, set in its own gardens on the edge of the town. It also boasts well-equipped bedrooms, most of which are of a good size.
**ROOMS:** 8 rms (7 en suite) (1 fmly) s £36; d £52 (incl. bkfst) * **LB** **CONF:** Thtr 30 Class 20 Board 12 **PARKING:** 35 **NOTES:** No smoking in restaurant **CARDS:**

## LUNDIN LINKS, Fife — Map 12 NO40

### ★★★75% Old Manor

Leven Rd KY8 6AJ
☎ 01333 320368 📠 01333 320911
e-mail: enquiries@oldmanorhotel.co.uk
***Dir:*** *1m E of Leven on A915 Kirkaldy-St Andrews Rd*

SCOTLAND'S HOTELS OF DISTINCTION

Situated on the western edge of the village overlooking the golf course to the Firth of Forth, this hotel provides good food with high standards of guest care. Bedrooms, with pretty colour schemes, are comfortably modern in style and offer all expected amenities.
**ROOMS:** 24 en suite (3 fmly) No smoking in 4 bedrooms s £60-£85; d £100-£180 (incl. bkfst) * **LB** **FACILITIES:** Complimentary membership of Lundin Sports Club ch fac Xmas **CONF:** Thtr 140 Class 70 Board 50 Del from £105 * **PARKING:** 100 **NOTES:** No smoking in restaurant Civ Wed 100 **CARDS:**

## LUSS, Argyll & Bute — Map 10 NS39

### ★★★71% *The Lodge on Loch Lomond*

G83 8PA
☎ 01436 860201 📠 01436 860203
e-mail: lusslomond@aol.com
***Dir:*** *turn off A82, follow sign for hotel*

Wonderful views over Loch Lomond can be enjoyed from this purpose-built hotel beside the village of Luss. Public areas include a spacious open-plan split-level bar and restaurant overlooking the loch. Bedrooms, which are fully pine finished, range from spacious executive rooms, some with balconies, to the smaller standard rooms, all with good amenities.
**ROOMS:** 29 en suite (20 fmly) **FACILITIES:** STV Sauna fishing, boating **CONF:** Thtr 35 Class 18 Board 25 **PARKING:** 82
**CARDS:**

## MALLAIG, Highland — Map 13 NM69

### ★★67% Marine

PH41 4PY
☎ 01687 462217 📠 01687 462821
e-mail: marinehotel@theinternet.com
***Dir:*** *adjacent to railway terminal, first hotel on right off A830*
A relaxed and welcoming atmosphere prevails at this family-run hotel beside the railway station and close to the ferry terminal and harbour. The bedrooms, varying in size, are comfortably modern in style and offer the expected amenities. Public areas, on the first floor, include a well-stocked bar and a small sitting area. Local seafood features strongly on the restaurant's varied menu.
**ROOMS:** 19 en suite (2 fmly) s £30-£35; d £52-£64 (incl. bkfst) * **LB** **PARKING:** 6 **NOTES:** Closed Xmas & New Year RS Nov-Mar
**CARDS:**

### ★★65% West Highland

PH41 4QZ
☎ 01687 462210 📠 01687 462130
e-mail: westhighland.hotel@virgin.net
***Dir:*** *from Fort William turn right at rdbt then 1st right up hill, from ferry left at rdbt then 1st right uphill*
This family-run holiday hotel sits on a hill above the town, and enjoys lovely views towards the Isle of Skye. Smartly refurbished public areas include a choice of comfortable lounges, bar, and

*continued on p754*

M

MALLAIG, continued

restaurant. Although variable in size and in style, all bedrooms offer comfortable modern appointments.
**ROOMS:** 34 en suite (6 fmly) No smoking in 6 bedrooms s £32-£36; d £60-£70 (incl. bkfst) * **LB** **FACILITIES:** entertainment **CONF:** Thtr 100 Class 80 Board 100 **PARKING:** 40 **NOTES:** No smoking in restaurant Closed 16 Oct-15 Mar RS 16 Mar-1 Apr **CARDS:**

## MARKINCH, Fife

Map 11 NO20

### *Premier Collection*

**★★★★ Balbirnie House**
Balbirnie Park KY7 6NE
☎ 01592 610066 01592 610529
e-mail: balbirnie@breathemail.net
***Dir:*** *turn off A92 onto B9130, entrance 0.5m on left*
Dating back to 1777, this luxury Georgian hotel has been lovingly restored to provide well-equipped, spacious accommodation. The surrounding area provides a plethora of interesting drives rewarded with quite beautiful scenery. Opulent day rooms furnished with antiques include three sitting rooms, one of which has a well-stocked bar. A stylish new conservatory restaurant provides an elegant venue in which guests can enjoy the imaginative cooking. The smart new ballroom is suited to parties of over two hundred.
**ROOMS:** 30 en suite (9 fmly) s £125-£160; d £185-£245 (incl. bkfst) * **LB** **FACILITIES:** STV Golf 18 Croquet lawn Putting green Woodland walks Jogging trails ch fac Xmas **CONF:** Thtr 220 Class 100 Board 60 Del from £156 * **PARKING:** 120 **NOTES:** No smoking in restaurant Civ Wed 200
**CARDS:**

## MAYBOLE, South Ayrshire

Map 10 NS20

### *Premier Collection*

**★★ Ladyburn**
KA19 7SG
☎ 01655 740585 01655 740580
e-mail: jhdh@ladyburn.freeserve.co.uk
***Dir:*** *Turn off A77 onto B7023, at Crosshill turn right at War Memorial onto B741 (signed Kilkerran). Ladyburn in approximately 3m.*
This charming country house is ideally situated in open countryside and surrounded by an attractive natural garden, on the edge of the magnificent Kilkerran estate. Each comfortable bedroom has distinct character and is complemented by a choice of sitting areas, the drawing room and library. Dinner comprises of a carefully cooked three

*continued*

course set menu, discussed beforehand with alternatives available. The genuine warmth of welcome is a particular feature and services are provided willingly.

**ROOMS:** 8 rms (7 en suite) No smoking in 7 bedrooms
**FACILITIES:** Croquet lawn Boules **PARKING:** 12 **NOTES:** No dogs (ex guide dogs) No children 16yrs RS Nov-Dec 2 weeks, Jan/Mar 4 weeks Civ Wed 250 **CARDS:**

## MELROSE, Scottish Borders

Map 12 NT53

**★★★66% Burt's**
The Square TD6 9PL
☎ 01896 822285 01896 822870
e-mail: burtshotel@aol.com
***Dir:*** *A6091, 2m from A68 3m S of Earlston*

BURT'S
HOTEL

Set in the Market Square, this family-run hotel continues to offer traditional hospitality in a welcoming environment. The well-stocked bar, with its open fire, is popular for informal lunches and suppers. The elegant restaurant provides formal meals artistically presented in the modern style
**ROOMS:** 20 en suite No smoking in all bedrooms s £52; d £92 (incl. bkfst) * **LB** **FACILITIES:** Shooting Salmon Fishing Xmas **CONF:** Thtr 38 Class 20 Board 20 **PARKING:** 40 **NOTES:** No smoking in restaurant Closed 24-26 Dec **CARDS:**

**★★64% George & Abbotsford**
High St TD6 9PD
☎ 01896 822308 01896 823363
e-mail: enquiries@georgeandabbotsford.co.uk
***Dir:*** *from A68 or A7 take A6091 to Melrose, hotel is in middle of High St*
Standing in the town centre, this substantial 18th-century coaching inn enjoys a mixed trade from business travellers, holidaymakers and tour groups. The lounge bar complements the dining room by serving a good range of bar meals.
**ROOMS:** 30 en suite (3 fmly) s £40-£54; d £65-£95 (incl. bkfst) * **LB** **FACILITIES:** STV Fishing **CONF:** Thtr 100 Class 50 Board 30 Del from £60 * **PARKING:** 82 **NOTES:** No smoking in restaurant
**CARDS:**

MEY, Highland Map 15 ND27

### ★★65% *Castle Arms*

KW14 8XH
☎ 01847 851244 🖹 01847 851244
***Dir:*** *on A836*

A modernised 19th-century coaching inn with uninterrupted views over the Pentland Firth to Orkney. Public areas include a well-stocked lounge bar and adjoining dining room, offering a choice of light meals. There is an interesting photographic gallery of the Royal Family. Most bedrooms are in a modern extension at the rear of the hotel, all are bright and airy.

**ROOMS:** 3 en suite 5 annexe en suite (1 fmly) **FACILITIES:** Fishing **PARKING:** 30 **NOTES:** RS Oct-Mar **CARDS:**

MOFFAT, Dumfries & Galloway Map 11 NT00

### ★★★74% Moffat House

High St DG10 9HL
☎ 01683 220039 🖹 01683 221288
e-mail: moffat@talk21.com
***Dir:*** *from M74 at Beattock (junct 15) take the A701 in 1m hotel at end of High St*

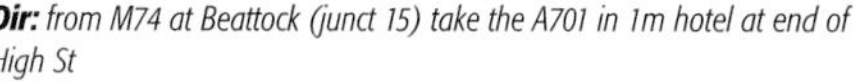

An inviting Adam style mansion, situated in the centre of town. The public rooms include a number of relaxing lounges, and the bedrooms, including some in the tastefully converted coaching house, are attractively decorated, stylish and comfortable. The ambitious menus can be sampled either in the bar or the more formal restaurant. Staff are friendly and keen to please.

**ROOMS:** 21 en suite (2 fmly) No smoking in 6 bedrooms s £50-£65; d £70-£94 (incl. bkfst) * **LB** **FACILITIES:** Xmas **CONF:** Thtr 70 Class 50 Board 40 **PARKING:** 61 **NOTES:** Civ Wed 110 **CARDS:**

### ★★★70% Auchen Castle

Beattock DG10 9SH
☎ 01683 300407 🖹 01683 300667
e-mail: reservations@auchen-castle-hotel.co.uk
***Dir:*** *M74 junct 15 at rdbt follow signs to Abington (B7076), 1m N of Moffat*

Situated close to the motorway, but separated from it by extensive grounds, terraced gardens and a lake stocked with brown trout, this impressive mansion dates back to 1849. Public rooms include a comfortable drawing room as well as a light and airy dining

*continued*

room. Bedrooms vary in size and price, and have all been attractively furnished.

**ROOMS:** 15 en suite 10 annexe en suite (12 fmly) No smoking in 10 bedrooms s £48-£75; d £55-£140 (incl. bkfst) * **LB** **FACILITIES:** STV Tennis (hard) Fishing entertainment ch fac **CONF:** Thtr 40 Board 20 Del £90 * **PARKING:** 52 **NOTES:** No smoking in restaurant **CARDS:**

### ★★76% Beechwood Country House

Harthope Place DG10 9HX
☎ 01683 220210 🖹 01683 220889
e-mail: info@beechwoodhousehotel.co.uk
***Dir:*** *at north end of town. Turn right at St Marys Church into Harthope Place and follow the 'Hotel' sign*

A delightful country house in attractive gardens, a short walk from the town. There are two comfortable lounges, one with a small

*continued on p756*

MOFFAT, continued

bar. Bedrooms are named after local rivers. The kitchen continues to delight guests with imaginative cooking.
**ROOMS:** 7 en suite (1 fmly) s £58; d £82 (incl. bkfst) * LB **FACILITIES:** ch fac Xmas **CONF:** Class 12 Board 12 Del from £85 * **PARKING:** 15 **NOTES:** No smoking in restaurant Closed 2 Jan-14 Feb Civ Wed 26 **CARDS:**

### ★★66% The Star
44 High St DG10 9EF
☎ 01683 220156 📠 01683 221524
e-mail: tim@famousstarhotel.com
***Dir:*** *M74 junct 15 signed Moffat, hotel is 2m from junct, first hotel on right in High Street*
Smart, modern and well-equipped bedrooms plus enjoyable food, served either in the bar or the restaurant, are just some of the virtues of this friendly hotel. Its claim to be the world's narrowest hotel is a novel talking point.
**ROOMS:** 8 en suite (1 fmly) s fr £40; d fr £56 (incl. bkfst) * LB **FACILITIES:** STV **NOTES:** No dogs (ex guide dogs) No smoking in restaurant **CARDS:**

## Premier Collection

### ★ Well View
Ballplay Rd DG10 9JU
☎ 01683 220184 📠 01683 220088
e-mail: info@wellview.co.uk

THE CIRCLE
Selected Individual Hotels
GREAT BRITAIN

***Dir:*** *on A708 from Moffat, pass fire station and first left*
Well View is situated on a quiet road within walking distance of the small town of Moffat. The hotel still retains many original Victorian features. Individually furnished bedrooms are comfortable and thoughtfully equipped. Dinner is certainly the highlight of a stay in this small family-run hotel; the six-course tasting menu emphasises fine ingredients which are locally sourced whenever possible.
**ROOMS:** 6 en suite No smoking in all bedrooms s £55-£65; d £75-£110 (incl. bkfst) * LB **FACILITIES:** Xmas **CONF:** Thtr 12 Board 8 Del from £80 * **PARKING:** 8 **NOTES:** No smoking in restaurant Closed 2wks Feb & 2wks Oct **CARDS:**

## MONTROSE, Angus — Map 15 NO75

### ★★★71% Links Hotel
Best Western
Mid Links DD10 8RL
☎ 01674 671000 📠 01674 672698
e-mail: reception@linkshotel.com
***Dir:*** *turn off A90 at Brechin, take A935 to Montrose, 10m turn right at Lochside junct, left at swimming pool right by tennis courts hotel 200yds*
This hotel is a former Edwardian townhouse with distinctive architecture and has been fully refurbished and restored. It is situated close to recreational facilities and central amenities. Main house bedrooms are tastefully decorated and offer comfortable pine furnishings. Wing rooms offer a variety of attractive themed styles. Public areas include a well-stocked bar, attractive restaurant, and a popular coffee shop where food is available all day.
**ROOMS:** 25 en suite No smoking in 11 bedrooms s £72-£75; d £80-£83 (incl. bkfst) * LB **FACILITIES:** STV Xmas **CONF:** Thtr 200 Class 150 Board 55 Del from £74 * **PARKING:** 30 **NOTES:** No smoking in restaurant Civ Wed 200 **CARDS:**

### ★★★65% Montrose Park
61 John St DD10 8RJ
☎ 01674 663400 📠 01674 677091
e-mail: recep@montrosepark.co.uk
***Dir:*** *from A90 turn off at A935 to A92, from A92 turn off Montrose High Street into John Street*

A welcoming hotel which, from its position on the mid links, offers convenient access to central and recreational facilities. Smart public areas include a bright foyer lounge, a popular bar and brasserie, and a tasteful, split-level restaurant.
**ROOMS:** 54 en suite 5 annexe en suite (4 fmly) No smoking in 16 bedrooms s £68-£75; d £86-£90 (incl. bkfst) * LB **FACILITIES:** Spa STV Pool table Xmas **CONF:** Thtr 200 Class 80 Board 80 **PARKING:** 50 **NOTES:** No smoking in restaurant Civ Wed 220 **CARDS:**

*See advert on opposite page*

## MORAR, Highland — Map 13 NM69

### ★★64% Morar
PH40 4PA
☎ 01687 462346 📠 01687 462212
e-mail: agmacleod@morarhotel.freeserve.co.uk
***Dir:*** *in the village of Morar on the A830 "Road to the Isle". The hotel overlooks the silver sands of Morar*
This comfortable hotel sits beside the West Highland Railway, from which lovely sea views can be enjoyed. Nicely presented public areas include an open-plan foyer which contains a bar and lounge. Good value home cooked meals are served in the adjacent restaurant overlooking the sea. Although variable in size, bedrooms are modern in appointment and offer the expected amenities.
**ROOMS:** 27 en suite No smoking in 3 bedrooms s £30-£35; d £60-£70 (incl. bkfst) * LB **FACILITIES:** Fishing entertainment Xmas **PARKING:** 50 **NOTES:** No smoking in restaurant Closed 22 Oct-Mar **CARDS:**

Early start? Hotels at all star levels should provide in-room alarm clocks and/or alarm calls.

## MUIR OF ORD, Highland  Map 14 NH55

**★★67% Ord House**

THE CIRCLE
Selected Individual Hotels
GREAT BRITAIN

IV6 7UH
☎ 01463 870492 Fax 01463 870492
e-mail: eliza@ord-house.com
***Dir:*** *turn off A9 at Tore rdbt onto A832. Follow for 5m into Muir of Ord. Turn left outside Muir of Ord, to Ullapool still on A832. Hotel 0.5m on left*

Dating back to 1637, this former laird's house lies secluded in wooded grounds. Now a country house hotel it offers simply furnished but well-proportioned accommodation. Public areas reflect the character of the house, with inviting lounges, a cosy rustic bar and a dining room serving fine country cooking.

**ROOMS:** 11 en suite s £38-£48; d £86-£96 (incl. bkfst) * **FACILITIES:** no TV in bdrms Croquet lawn Putting green Clay pigeon shooting ch fac **PARKING:** 30 **NOTES:** No smoking in restaurant Closed Nov-Feb **CARDS:**

### *Premier Collection*

**★ The Dower House**
Highfield IV6 7XN
☎ 01463 870090 Fax 01463 870090
e-mail: aa@thedowerhouse.co.uk
***Dir:*** *on Dingwall rd A862, 1m from town on left*

The Dower House is situated just north of the village. It's a delightful home where guests can feel relaxed. No need therefore for fussy pretentious service, the proprietors' restrained but no less hospitable approach being perfectly pitched. The cosy sitting room is full of books, whilst the dining room has quiet elegance and antique furniture. The charming bedrooms come in mixed sizes, one having its own sitting room.

**ROOMS:** 5 en suite 2 annexe en suite No smoking in all bedrooms s £55-£95; d £110-£150 (incl. bkfst) * **LB** **FACILITIES:** Croquet lawn Bird watching ch fac **PARKING:** 20 **NOTES:** No dogs (ex guide dogs) No smoking in restaurant Closed Xmas day & 2wks Nov **CARDS:**

## MULL, ISLE OF, Argyll & Bute  Map 10

## DERVAIG  Map 13 NM45

**★★76% Druimard Country House**
PA75 6QW
☎ 01688 400345 & 400291 Fax 01688 400345
e-mail: druimard@hotels.activebooking.com
***Dir:*** *from Craignure ferry terminal turn right towards Tobermory, go through Salen Village, after 1.5m turn left to Dervaig, hotel on right before village*

A charming Victorian country house on the edge of the village

*continued*

beside the Mull Little Theatre. Attractive colour schemes feature in the variable sized bedrooms, which are comfortably furnished and thoughtfully equipped. Two new rooms, one suitable for the less mobile, have been added this year, with external access. There is a relaxing lounge and conservatory bar, but the real focal point is the dining room, where tempting five-course dinners attract high praise.

**ROOMS:** 5 en suite 2 annexe en suite (2 fmly) s £74-£85; d £125-£153 (incl. bkfst & dinner) * **LB** **FACILITIES:** Mull Little Theatre within grounds ch fac **PARKING:** 20 **NOTES:** No smoking in restaurant Closed Nov-Mar **CARDS:**

## TOBERMORY  Map 13 NM55

**★★79% Highland Cottage**
Breadalbane St PA75 6PD
☎ 01688 302030 Fax 01688 302727
e-mail: davidandjo@highlandcottage.co.uk
***Dir:*** *A848 Craignure/Fishnish ferry terminal, pass Tobermory signs, ahead at mini rdbt across narrow bridge turn right. Hotel on right opp Fire Station*

Visitors are assured of a warm personal welcome at this charming cottage-style hotel. Bedrooms, with an island theme, are appointed to a high standard and feature antique beds and a range of thoughtful extras. Public areas include a relaxing first

*continued on p758*

M

TOBERMORY, continued

floor lounge, an honesty bar, a smart conservatory and an elegant dining room.

*Highland Cottage, Tobermory*

**ROOMS:** 6 en suite (1 fmly) No smoking in all bedrooms s £50-£73; d £87-£105 * **LB** **FACILITIES:** STV ch fac **PARKING:** 6 **NOTES:** No smoking in restaurant Closed 4wks mid Oct/mid Nov RS Oct-early Mar **CARDS:**

NAIRN, Highland Map 14 NH85

### ★★★★69% Newton

Inverness Rd IV12 4RX
☎ 01667 453144 01667 454026
e-mail: info@morton-hotels.co.uk
***Dir:*** *15m from Inverness on A96, turn left into tree lined driveway*

This impressive, welcoming hotel combines Georgian and Scottish baronial architecture. Set in 21 acres, it has views of the Moray Firth. Bedrooms are comfortable and those in the newer wing are of a particularly good standard. There is a choice of lounges, a well-stocked bar and a smart restaurant. Conference facilities are excellent.

**ROOMS:** 57 en suite (2 fmly) No smoking in 15 bedrooms s £83-£98; d £105-£150 (incl. bkfst) * **LB** **FACILITIES:** STV Tennis (hard) Fishing Use of leisure club at sister hotel ch fac Xmas **CONF:** Thtr 400 Class 150 Board 50 Del £129 * **SERVICES:** Lift **PARKING:** 80 **NOTES:** No smoking in restaurant Civ Wed 350 **CARDS:**

### ★★★★67% Golf View

Seabank Rd IV12 4HD
☎ 01667 452301 01667 455267
e-mail: golfview@morton-hotels.com
***Dir:*** *turn off A96 into Seabank Rd, follow road to end hotel on right*

The leisure centre is a major attraction at this business and tourist hotel. The conservatory provides an informal alternative to the more traditional restaurant. The bedrooms are steadily being enhanced and offer very pleasant accommodation.

**ROOMS:** 48 en suite (3 fmly) No smoking in 8 bedrooms **FACILITIES:** STV Indoor swimming (H) Tennis (hard) Sauna Solarium Gym Putting green Jacuzzi Cycle hire Xmas **CONF:** Thtr 120 Class 50 Board 40 Del from £129 * **SERVICES:** Lift **PARKING:** 40 **CARDS:**

### ★★★70% Claymore House

Seabank Rd IV12 4EY
☎ 01667 453731 01667 455290
e-mail: claymorenairnscotland@compuserve.com
***Dir:*** *turn into Seabank Rd from the A96 at the parish church. Hotel is halfway down on the right hand side*

A relaxed and welcoming atmosphere prevails at this comfortable hotel. Bedrooms have benefited from refurbishment and offer a good range of amenities. Public areas include a well-stocked bar, a conservatory lounge and an attractive restaurant. Golfing packages are available.

**ROOMS:** 13 en suite (2 fmly) No smoking in 4 bedrooms s £50-£60; d £85-£120 (incl. bkfst) * **LB** **FACILITIES:** ch fac Xmas **CONF:** Thtr 50 Class 35 Board 35 Del from £50 * **PARKING:** 30 **NOTES:** No smoking in restaurant Civ Wed 50 **CARDS:**

## Premier Collection

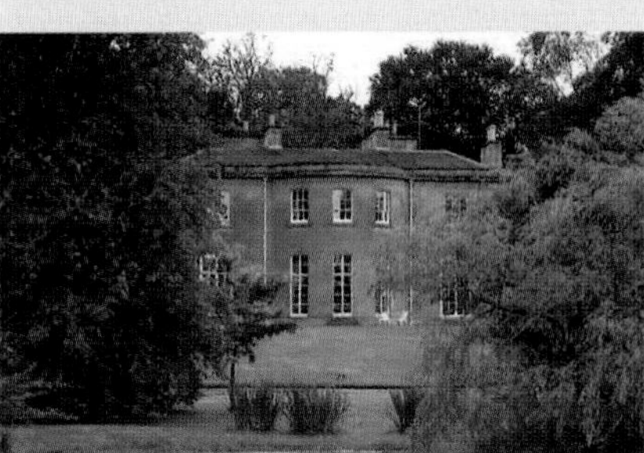

### ★★ *Boath House*

Auldearn IV12 5TE
☎ 01667 454896 01667 455469
e-mail: wendy@boath-house.demon.co.uk
***Dir:*** *2m past Nairn on A96 driving east towards Forres, signposted on main road*

Expect a warm welcome from the Matheson family at this splendid Georgian mansion, set amid twenty acres of mature wooded grounds, and lovingly restored. Excellent meals are served in the airy dining room overlooking a trout-stocked loch, while inviting lounges feature open fires. Bedrooms are striking, comfortable and include many fine antique pieces.

**ROOMS:** 6 en suite 1 annexe en suite (1 fmly) No smoking in all bedrooms **FACILITIES:** STV Fishing Sauna Gym Croquet lawn Jacuzzi Beauty & Hair salon **PARKING:** 30 **NOTES:** No smoking in restaurant Civ Wed 200 **CARDS:**

### ★★66% *Alton Burn*

Alton Burn Rd IV12 5ND
☎ 01667 452051 01667 456697
***Dir:*** *follow signs from A96 via Sandown Farm Lane*

This long-established, family-run hotel is located on the western edge of town with views over the Moray Firth. Traditional-style bedrooms vary in size and offer the expected amenities. Public

*continued*

areas include a choice of comfortable lounges, a well-stocked bar and spacious dining room.
**ROOMS:** 19 rms (17 en suite) 7 annexe en suite (6 fmly)
**FACILITIES:** Outdoor swimming (H) Tennis (hard) Putting green Games room ch fac **CONF:** Thtr 70 Class 30 Board 30 **PARKING:** 30
**NOTES:** RS Nov-Mar **CARDS:**

## NETHY BRIDGE, Highland — Map 14 NJ02

### ★★71% The Mountview Hotel
Grantown Rd PH25 3EB
☎ 01479 821248 01479 821515
e-mail: mviewhotel@aol.com
***Dir:*** *from Aviemore follow signs through Boat of Garten to Nethy Bridge, remain on main road through village. hotel on right, 100 mtrs beyond Nethy Bridge Hotel.*
Aptly named, this country house hotel enjoys stunning panoramic views from its elevated position on the edge of the village. It specialises in guided holidays and is a favoured base for birdwatching and walking groups. Public rooms include inviting lounges, whilst imaginative well-prepared dinners are served in a bright modern restaurant extension.
**ROOMS:** 12 rms (11 en suite) s fr £30; d fr £60 (incl. bkfst)
**FACILITIES:** Xmas **PARKING:** 16 **NOTES:** No dogs No smoking in restaurant **CARDS:**

## NEWBURGH, Aberdeenshire — Map 15 NJ92

### ★★72% Udny Arms
Main St AB41 6BL
☎ 01358 789444 01358 789012
e-mail: enquiry@udny.demon.co.uk
***Dir:*** *turn off A92 at Newburgh sign, hotel 2m, in centre of village on R*
This comfortable family-run hotel stands in the centre of the village overlooking the golf course on the Ythan estuary. Inviting public areas display lots of historical artefacts. There is a lovely lounge, and one can eat well in both the rustic country bars and smart split-level bistro restaurant. The bedrooms are traditionally furnished but well equipped for the modern traveller.
**ROOMS:** 26 en suite (1 fmly) No smoking in all bedrooms s £45-£68; d £60-£85 (incl. bkfst) * **LB** **FACILITIES:** Fishing Petanque **CONF:** Thtr 100 Class 30 Board 30 Del from £100 * **PARKING:** 100 **NOTES:** No smoking in restaurant **CARDS:**

## NEW LANARK, South Lanarkshire — Map 11 NS84

### ★★★71% New Lanark Mill Hotel
Scotland's Hotels of Distinction
Mill One, New Lanark Mills ML11 9DB
☎ 01555 667200 01555 667222
e-mail: hotel@newlanark.org
***Dir:*** *signposted from all major roads, M74 junct 7 also signed from M8*

This hotel occupies an impressively restored 18th-century cotton mill and is part of a heritage village nestling in the Clyde river valley. Inside, a bright modern style is balanced with features from the original mill; there is a comfortable foyer lounge with a galleried restaurant above. Views of the valley from the upper floors are wonderful.
**ROOMS:** 38 en suite (2 fmly) No smoking in 28 bedrooms s £58; d £75 (incl. bkfst) * **LB** **FACILITIES:** Fishing Access to Falls of Clyde Wildlife Reserve ch fac Xmas **CONF:** Thtr 180 Class 40 Board 50 Del from £90 * **SERVICES:** Lift **PARKING:** 75 **NOTES:** No smoking in restaurant Civ Wed 140 **CARDS:**

## NEWTON STEWART, Dumfries & Galloway — Map 10 NX46

*Premier Collection*

### ★★★ Kirroughtree House
Minnigaff DG8 6AN
☎ 01671 402141 01671 402425
e-mail: info@kirroughtreehouse.co.uk
***Dir:*** *from A75 take A712, New Galloway road, entrance to hotel 300 yds on left*
Standing in eight acres of landscaped gardens, this 17th-century mansion offers guests comfort and elegance in impressive surroundings. The splendid isolation of the huge Galloway Forest Park is right on the doorstep. Lounges have deep sofas and antique furniture. Spacious bedrooms are individually decorated with many personal touches. The hotel is justly proud of its high levels of hospitality and dinners are a highlight, served in the formal dining rooms.
**ROOMS:** 17 en suite s £80-£105; d £140-£180 (incl. bkfst) * **LB**
**FACILITIES:** STV Tennis (grass) Croquet lawn 9 hole pitch and putt Xmas **CONF:** Thtr 30 Class 20 Board 20 Del from £105 *
**PARKING:** 50 **NOTES:** No children 10yrs No smoking in restaurant Closed 4 Jan-16 Feb **CARDS:**

### ★★★64% Bruce
88 Queen St DG8 6JL
☎ 01671 402294 01671 402294
***Dir:*** *leave A75 at Newton Stewart rdbt, hotel 600mtrs on right past filling station, at junction*
Named after Robert the Bruce, this family-run hotel is just a short distance from the A75. One of the well-appointed bedrooms features a four-poster bed and the family suites contain separate bedrooms for children. Both the lounge bar and the more formal restaurant offer a choice of dishes. There is a comfortable, spacious lounge on the first floor.
**ROOMS:** 18 en suite (2 fmly) No smoking in 6 bedrooms
**FACILITIES:** ch fac Xmas **CONF:** Thtr 60 Class 70 Board 60
**PARKING:** 20 **NOTES:** No smoking in restaurant
**CARDS:**

NEWTON STEWART, continued

**★★72% Creebridge House**
DG8 6NP
☎ 01671 402121 01671 403258
e-mail: info@creebridge.co.uk
***Dir:*** *off A75*

This former shooting lodge lies secluded in attractive gardens. A comfortable drawing room and restaurant are supplemented by a lively bar/bistro offering an interesting and wide selection of dishes. The smart bedrooms come in a variety of styles and include some family suites.
**ROOMS:** 19 en suite (3 fmly) s £59; d £98 (incl. bkfst) * LB
**FACILITIES:** STV Fishing Xmas **CONF:** Thtr 70 Class 20 Board 30
**PARKING:** 50 **NOTES:** RS Nov-Mar **CARDS:**

NORTH BERWICK, East Lothian — Map 12 NT58

**★★★65% The Marine**
Cromwell Rd EH39 4LZ
☎ 0870 400 8129 01620 894480
e-mail: HeritageHotels_North_Berwick.Marine@forte-hotels.com
***Dir:*** *from A198 turn into Hamilton Rd at traffic lights then take 2nd right*
This imposing leisure and conference hotel commands stunning views across the golf course to the Firth of Forth. The well-proportioned public areas and many of the bedrooms enjoy the view. The bedrooms come in a variety of sizes, some are impressively large.
**ROOMS:** 83 en suite No smoking in 20 bedrooms s £30-£85; d £39-£125 (incl. bkfst) * LB **FACILITIES:** STV Outdoor swimming (H) Tennis (hard) Snooker Sauna Solarium Putting green Childrens playground Xmas **CONF:** Thtr 300 Class 150 Board 100 Del from £67 *
**SERVICES:** Lift **PARKING:** 202 **NOTES:** No smoking in restaurant Civ Wed 200 **CARDS:**

**★★64% Nether Abbey**
20 Dirleton Av EH39 4BQ
☎ 01620 892802 01620 895298
e-mail: bookings@netherabbey.co.uk
***Dir:*** *at junct with A198, leave A1 and continue S to rdbt, take B6371 to N Berwick, hotel is second on left when entering town*
This hotel is very popular with golfers. All of the bedrooms are stylish and very well-equipped. Downstairs the focus remains on the lively bar/bistro where tasty home cooked dishes are on offer.
**ROOMS:** 14 en suite (4 fmly) s £33-£69; d £66-£98 (incl. bkfst) * LB
**FACILITIES:** Xmas **CONF:** Thtr 80 Class 50 Board 30 **PARKING:** 40
**NOTES:** Civ Wed 50 **CARDS:**

NORTH UIST, ISLE OF, Western Isles — Map 13

LOCHMADDY — Map 13 NF96

**★★62% *Lochmaddy***
HS6 5AA
☎ 01876 500331 & 500332 01876 500210
***Dir:*** *100yds from Lochmaddy ferry terminal*
This long established hotel, situated close to the ferry terminal, is particularly popular with anglers. Bedrooms are comfortably furnished and many have fine sea views. A peat fire warms the cosy lounge, while a wide selection of bar meals offers a more informal alternative to the restaurant.
**ROOMS:** 15 en suite (1 fmly) **FACILITIES:** Fishing **PARKING:** 30
**NOTES:** No smoking in restaurant **CARDS:**

OBAN, Argyll & Bute — Map 10 NM83

**★★★66% *Alexandra***
Corran Esplanade PA34 5AA
☎ 01631 562381 01631 564497
***Dir:*** *arrive Oban on A85, descend Hill, turn right at first rdbt, hotel 200yds further on seaside*

From its position on the Esplanade this comfortable holiday hotel enjoys a wonderful panoramic view of Oban Bay. Bedrooms are brightly decorated and comfortably furnished in modern style. Spacious public areas include an inviting lounge, a well-stocked bar, an attractive dining room and leisure facilities.
**ROOMS:** 64 en suite (6 fmly) **FACILITIES:** Indoor swimming (H) Snooker Sauna Solarium Gym Steam room Games room Golf practice nets entertainment **CONF:** Class 60 Board 60 **SERVICES:** Lift
**PARKING:** 80 **NOTES:** No smoking in restaurant
**CARDS:**

**★★★62% *Columba***
North Pier PA34 5QD
☎ 01631 562183 01631 564683
***Dir:*** *A85 to Oban, first set of lights in town, turn right. The Columba Hotel is facing you*

Situated by the North Pier, many of the comfortable bedrooms at

*continued*

this popular tourist hotel overlook the bay. The public areas include a choice of contrasting bars and an attractive restaurant. Guests are welcome to use the leisure facilities at the sister hotel, The Alexandra.
**ROOMS:** 48 en suite (6 fmly) **CONF:** Thtr 70 Class 30 Board 20
**SERVICES:** Lift **PARKING:** 8 **NOTES:** No smoking in restaurant
**CARDS:**

**★★77% Manor House**
Gallanach Rd PA34 4LS
☎ 01631 562087 01631 563053
e-mail: manorhouse@aol.com
***Dir:*** *Follow signs MacBrayne Ferries and pass ferry entrance for hotel on right*

The Manor House is under new ownership, but operating very much as before, with the same attentive manager and skilled chef. The atmosphere is welcoming and the daily-changing five course dinner menu merits our Rosette Award. Many of the cosy and attractively decorated bedrooms, and some public rooms, benefit from the lovely views across the bay.
**ROOMS:** 11 en suite No smoking in all bedrooms s £90-£110; d £140-£160 (incl. bkfst & dinner) * **LB** **FACILITIES:** Xmas **PARKING:** 20 **NOTES:** No children 12yrs No smoking in restaurant RS Nov-Feb Civ Wed 20 **CARDS:**

**★★74% Willowburn**
PA34 4TJ
☎ 01852 300276 01852 300597
e-mail: willowburn.hotel@virgin.net
(For full entry see Clachan-Seil)

**★★72% Falls of Lora**
PA37 1PB
☎ 01631 710483 01631 710694
(For full entry see Connel and advert on this page)

**★★66% Dungallan House Hotel**
Gallanach Rd PA34 4PD
☎ 01631 563799 01631 566711
e-mail: welcome@dungallanhotel-oban.co.uk
***Dir:*** *at Argyll Square in town centre follow signs for Gallanch, hotel 0.5m from square*
The proprietors delight in welcoming guests to their comfortable hotel which enjoys a lovely view over Oban Bay. Public areas include a cosy lounge, comfortable bar, and an elegant dining room where careful treatment of quality fresh ingredients continues to produce good results. Bedrooms are bright and airy with comfortable furnishings.
**ROOMS:** 13 rms (11 en suite) (2 fmly) No smoking in all bedrooms s fr £57; d fr £96 (incl. bkfst) * **LB** **FACILITIES:** Xmas **CONF:** Thtr 30 Class 30 Board 40 Del from £118 * **PARKING:** 20 **NOTES:** No smoking in restaurant Closed Jan & Feb **CARDS:**

**★★61% *Caledonian***
Station Square PA34 5RT
☎ 01631 563133 01631 562998
e-mail: sales@miltonhotels.com
***Dir:*** *opposite railway station at edge of Oban Bay*
Situated opposite the railway station and ferry terminal, this large Victorian hotel, overlooking Oban Bay, has a spacious bar and choice of eating options. Bedrooms range from the comfortable modern executive and superior rooms to the smaller standards which are more practical in appointment.
**ROOMS:** 70 en suite (10 fmly) **CONF:** Thtr 120 Class 60 Board 40
**SERVICES:** Lift **PARKING:** 6 **NOTES:** No smoking in restaurant
**CARDS:**

**★★61% Lancaster**
Corran Esplanade PA34 5AD
☎ 01631 562587 01631 562587
e-mail: john@lancasterhotel.freeserve.co.uk
***Dir:*** *on seafront next to St Columba's Cathedral*
Lovely views over the bay towards the Isle of Mull can be enjoyed from this welcoming family-run hotel on the Esplanade. Bedrooms, although variable in size and in style, are comfortable and offer a good range of amenities. Public areas include a choice

*continued on p762*

OBAN, continued

of contrasting lounges and bars and the swimming pool is an added attraction.

*Lancaster, Oban*

**ROOMS:** 27 rms (24 en suite) (3 fmly) s £27-£32; d £60 (incl. bkfst) * **LB** **FACILITIES:** Spa Indoor swimming (H) Sauna Jacuzzi Steam room ch fac **CONF:** Thtr 30 Class 20 Board 12 **PARKING:** 20 **CARDS:**

OLDMELDRUM, Aberdeenshire Map 15 NJ82

### ★★64% Meldrum Arms

The Square AB51 0DS
☎ 01651 872238 ▤ 01651 872238
***Dir:*** *off the B947, in centre of village*

From its position in the centre of the village, this family-run hotel combines a welcoming atmosphere with a good range of tasty dishes served in both the bar and comfortable restaurant.

**ROOMS:** 7 en suite (1 fmly) s £38; d £58 (incl. bkfst) * **CONF:** Thtr 80 Board 40 Del from £31.25 * **PARKING:** 25 **NOTES:** No dogs (ex guide dogs) No smoking in restaurant **CARDS:**

O

ONICH, Highland Map 14 NN06

### ★★★72% Onich

PH33 6RY
☎ 01855 821214 ▤ 01855 821484
e-mail: reservations@onich-fortwilliam.co.uk
***Dir:*** *beside A82, 2m N of Ballachulish Bridge*

Best Western

Genuine hospitality together with good food are part of the appeal of this hotel. The garden extends to the shore of picturesque Loch Linnhe. Nicely presented public areas include a choice of inviting lounges and contrasting bars. Views of the loch can be enjoyed from the attractive restaurant where the menu offers a tempting range of Scottish specialities. Bedrooms, with pleasing colour schemes, are comfortably modern in appointment.

**ROOMS:** 25 en suite (6 fmly) s £30-£60; d £60-£100 (incl. bkfst) * **LB** **FACILITIES:** STV Jacuzzi Games room ch fac Xmas **CONF:** Thtr 30 Class 20 Board 20 Del from £72 * **PARKING:** 50 **NOTES:** No smoking in restaurant **CARDS:**

### ★★★70% *Lodge on the Loch*

PH33 6RY
☎ 01855 821237 ▤ 01855 821463
e-mail: reservations@freedomglen.co.uk
***Dir:*** *beside A82 - 5m N of Glencoe, 10m S of Fort William*

Scotland's Hotels of Distinction

Guests return regularly to this comfortable, holiday hotel, with its spectacular outlook over Loch Linnhe. Inviting public areas include a relaxing foyer lounge, a cosy bar with fabric draped ceiling, and a spacious restaurant offering modern Scottish cuisine. Many superior bedrooms have luxury bathrooms and loch views.

**ROOMS:** 18 rms (16 en suite) (1 fmly) **FACILITIES:** Leisure facilities at sister hotel entertainment **CONF:** Thtr 50 Class 30 Board 30 **PARKING:** 25 **NOTES:** No children 12yrs No smoking in restaurant Closed Jan-Mar & Nov-23 Dec **CARDS:**

### ★★★68% Allt-nan-Ros

PH33 6RY
☎ 01855 821210 ▤ 01855 821462
e-mail: info@allt-nan-ros.co.uk
***Dir:*** *1.5m North of Ballachulish Bridge on A82*

MINOTEL Great Britain

Highland hospitality and good food are part of the appeal of this comfortable hotel set in attractive gardens overlooking Loch Linnhe. Bedrooms are variable in size and modern in style. Inviting public areas include a pleasant lounge and bright spacious dining room, both enjoying the splendid views.

**ROOMS:** 20 en suite (2 fmly) s £75-£80; d £149-£159 (incl. bkfst & dinner) * **LB** **FACILITIES:** ch fac Xmas **PARKING:** 30 **NOTES:** No smoking in restaurant **CARDS:**

See advert under FORT WILLIAM

### ★★66% *Creag Mhor*

PH33 6RY
☎ 01855 821379 ▤ 01855 821579
***Dir:*** *beside A82*

The genial owner welcomes guests old and new to his comfortable hotel overlooking Loch Linnhe. The bar is comfortably appointed and is popular for its good value meals. There are loch views from the spacious front-facing bedrooms. Rear rooms tend to be smaller and more practical in appointment.

**ROOMS:** 14 en suite (3 fmly) **PARKING:** 35 **NOTES:** No smoking in restaurant Closed last 3 wks Nov & first 2 wks Dec RS Late Nov-17 Jan (open Xmas & New Year) **CARDS:**

PAISLEY Hotels are listed under Glasgow Airport.

PEAT INN, Fife Map 12 NO40

## *Premier Collection*

### ★★ Peat Inn

KY15 5LH
☎ 01334 840206 ▤ 01334 840530
e-mail: reception@thepeatinn.co.uk
***Dir:*** *6m SW of St Andrews at junct B940/B941*

Standing just six miles from St Andrews, The Peat Inn was once a coaching inn. It is now a long-established restaurant with rooms. The attractive restaurant has a French theme, as does the creative cooking which utilises quality, fresh local

*continued*

produce. The luxuriously appointed, split level bedroom suites offer a host of thoughtful extras and have smart Italian marble bathrooms. Although a cooked breakfast is not served, superb continental trays are served in the bedrooms.

**ROOMS:** 8 en suite (2 fmly) s £75-£95; d £145-£155 (incl. cont bkfst) * **LB** **PARKING:** 24 **NOTES:** No smoking in restaurant Closed Sun, Mon, Xmas day & New Years day
**CARDS:**

PEEBLES, Scottish Borders Map 11 NT24

### ★★★79% Cringletie House

EH45 8PL
☎ 01721 730233 01721 730244
e-mail: enquiries@cringletie.com
***Dir:*** *2m N on A703*
Set in 28 acres of grounds, this immaculately maintained baronial mansion features a superb walled garden that provides much of the kitchen's produce during the summer. Delightful public rooms include a cocktail lounge with adjoining conservatory, and a small library. The refurbished bedrooms are very comfortable and service throughout is excellent.
**ROOMS:** 14 en suite (2 fmly) s fr £75; d £150-£220 (incl. bkfst) * **LB**
**FACILITIES:** Tennis (hard) Fishing Croquet lawn Putting green Xmas
**CONF:** Thtr 60 Class 30 Board 20 Del from £130 * **PARKING:** 30
**NOTES:** No smoking in restaurant Civ Wed 50
**CARDS:**

*See advert on this page*

### ★★★72% Peebles Hydro

EH45 8LX
☎ 01721 720602 01721 722999
e-mail: reservations@peebleshotelhydro.co.uk
***Dir:*** *on A702, one third mile out of town*
Commanding panoramic views across the valley from its hillside position, this imposing Victorian hotel continues to provide well-equipped bedrooms in a variety of styles and sizes that include spacious family suites with an inter-connecting children's room. The range of leisure activities, both indoors and out, is second to none, featuring excellent facilities for children that include a sizeable indoor pool.
**ROOMS:** 133 en suite (24 fmly) s £89-£108; d £155-£190 (incl. bkfst & dinner) * **LB** **FACILITIES:** STV Indoor swimming (H) Tennis (hard) Riding Snooker Sauna Solarium Gym Croquet lawn Putting green Jacuzzi Badminton Beautician Hairdressing entertainment ch fac Xmas
**CONF:** Thtr 450 Class 200 Board 74 Del from £92.75 * **SERVICES:** Lift
**PARKING:** 200 **NOTES:** No dogs (ex guide dogs) Civ Wed 250
**CARDS:**

### ★★★68% Park

Innerleithen Rd EH45 8BA
☎ 01721 720451 01721 723510
e-mail: reserve@parkpeebles.co.uk
***Dir:*** *in centre of Peebles opposite filling station*
The Park Hotel offers pleasant, well-equipped bedrooms, which vary in size, those in the original house are particularly spacious. Public areas enjoy views of the gardens and include a tartan-clad bar, a relaxing lounge and a wood-panelled restaurant. Guests can use the extensive leisure facilities on offer at the larger sister hotel, The Hydro.
**ROOMS:** 24 en suite s £66-£76; d £120-£165 (incl. bkfst & dinner) * **LB**
**FACILITIES:** Putting green Use of facilities of Peebles Hotel Hydro Xmas
**PARKING:** 50 **CARDS:**

### ★★★67% Castle Venlaw

Edinburgh Rd EH45 8QG
☎ 01721 720384 01721 724066
e-mail: enquiries@venlaw.co.uk
***Dir:*** *off A703 Peebles/Edinburgh road, 0.75m from Peebles*
A splendid turreted mansion in four acres of grounds and gardens, set high above the town. Most of the bedrooms are very spacious and command fine views; three have an adjoining turret room. Light meals and pre-dinner drinks are served in the oak-panelled

*continued on p764*

PEEBLES, continued

Library Bar. More formal meals can be enjoyed in the attractive restaurant.

*Castle Venlaw, Peebles*

**ROOMS:** 12 en suite (3 fmly) No smoking in 5 bedrooms s £70-£85; d £120-£150 (incl. bkfst) * LB **FACILITIES:** STV Croquet lawn Xmas **CONF:** Thtr 30 Class 20 Board 20 Del from £110 * **PARKING:** 30
**CARDS:**

### ★★68% *Kingsmuir*

Springhill Rd EH45 9EP
☎ 01721 720151 📠 01721 721795
e-mail: chrisburn@kingsmuir.scotborder.co.uk
***Dir:*** *cross Tweed Bridge from High St, then straight ahead up Springhill Rd, hotel is 300 yds on right hand side*
Located in a residential area on the south side of the River Tweed, this hotel offers friendly service and well-equipped accommodation. There is a choice of lounges and good value home-cooked meals are available in the dining room and the bar.
**ROOMS:** 10 en suite (2 fmly) No smoking in 5 bedrooms **CONF:** Thtr 40 Class 20 Board 20 **PARKING:** 35 **NOTES:** No smoking in restaurant
**CARDS:**

## PERTH, Perth & Kinross — Map 11 NO12

### ★★★80% Kinfauns Castle

Kinfauns PH2 7JZ
☎ 01738 620777 📠 01738 620778
e-mail: email@kinfaunscastle.co.uk
***Dir:*** *2m beyond Perth on the A90 Perth/Dundee road*
An impressive, historic building retaining many fine architectural features, such as ornate ceilings and marble fireplaces, combined with a range of Far Eastern artefacts. Classic dishes prepared from quality produce are offered in the beautiful panelled restaurant. Bedrooms range from first class suites to master and standard rooms, all with high quality furnishings and luxurious bathrooms.
**ROOMS:** 16 en suite s £120-£180; d £180-£300 (incl. bkfst) * **FACILITIES:** STV Fishing Croquet lawn Putting green Clay pigeon shooting Archery Falconry available with prior notice Xmas **CONF:** Thtr 50 Class 40 Board 26 Del from £150 * **PARKING:** 40 **NOTES:** No children 8yrs No smoking in restaurant Closed 4-24 Jan
**CARDS:**

### ★★★76% Huntingtower

Crieff Rd PH1 3JT
☎ 01738 583771 📠 01738 583777
e-mail: reservations@huntingtowerhotel.co.uk
***Dir:*** *3m W off A85*
Set in attractive landscaped grounds, this Edwardian house has been sympathetically extended to offer smart comfortable public areas allied to a high standard of accommodation. Inviting lounges lead to a conservatory where tasty lunches are served, whilst dinners are served in the elegant restaurant. Bedrooms are generally spacious and provide a host of modern facilities.
**ROOMS:** 31 en suite 3 annexe en suite (2 fmly) s fr £89.50; d fr £110 (incl. bkfst) * LB **FACILITIES:** STV ch fac Xmas **CONF:** Thtr 200 Class 140 Board 30 Del from £103 * **SERVICES:** Lift **PARKING:** 100 **NOTES:** No smoking in restaurant Civ Wed 100
**CARDS:**

*See advert on opposite page*

### ★★★76% Murrayshall Country House Hotel & Golf Course

New Scone PH2 7PH
☎ 01738 551171 📠 01738 552595
e-mail: lin.murrayshall@virgin.net
***Dir:*** *from Perth take A94 towards Coupar Angus, 1m from Perth turn right to Murrayshall just before New Scone*
Murrayshall House is an impressive country mansion set in 300 acres of parkland incorporating two golf courses. Public rooms are inviting and stylish and offer the choice of fine dining in the Old Masters Restaurant or less formally in the attractive Clubhouse Bar. Bedrooms are all individual and provide good levels of quality and comfort, but for something really special do ask for one of the fourteen superb new suites contained in two purpose-built properties in the grounds.
**ROOMS:** 27 en suite 14 annexe en suite (17 fmly) No smoking in 1 bedroom s £80-£98; d £120-£130 (incl. bkfst) * LB **FACILITIES:** STV Golf 36 Tennis (hard) Sauna Gym Putting green Jacuzzi Driving range ch fac Xmas **CONF:** Thtr 180 Class 60 Board 30 **PARKING:** 80 **NOTES:** No smoking in restaurant Civ Wed 100
**CARDS:**

### ★★★71% Parklands

St Leonards Bank PH2 8EB
☎ 01738 622451 📠 01738 622046
e-mail: parklands.perth@virgin.net
***Dir:*** *leave M90 junct 10, after 1 mile turn left at end of park area at traffic lights, hotel on left*
Originally two separate houses, one of which was the home of the Lord Provost of Perth; the buildings have been sensitively converted to create a stylish and individual hotel. Well-equipped bedrooms are tastefully furnished with many overlooking the colourful, flower filled expanse of South Inch Park. Similar shades are reflected in The Colourist's Bistro, or for a more formal meal, the newly created Acanthus Restaurant will certainly please.
**ROOMS:** 14 en suite (1 fmly) No smoking in 4 bedrooms s £69-£89; d £79-£115 (incl. bkfst) * LB **FACILITIES:** STV **CONF:** Thtr 25 Board 16 Del from £105 * **PARKING:** 25 **NOTES:** No smoking in restaurant
**CARDS:**

### ★★★68% *Lovat*

90 Glasgow Rd PH2 0LT
☎ 01738 636555 📠 01738 643123
e-mail: e-mail@lovat.co.uk
***Dir:*** *from M90 follow signs for Stirling to rdbt, then turn right into Glasgow Rd, hotel situated 1.50m on right*
A popular business hotel on the Glasgow road. Public areas include a conservatory lounge and a well stocked bar, where the Bistro menu provides an informal eating alternative to the dining room. Bedrooms are smartly appointed and thoughtfully equipped. Service is particularly attentive.
**ROOMS:** 30 en suite (1 fmly) No smoking in 12 bedrooms **FACILITIES:** STV **CONF:** Thtr 200 Class 70 Board 70 **PARKING:** 40 **NOTES:** No dogs (ex guide dogs) No smoking in restaurant
**CARDS:**

**★★★67% Queens Hotel**
Leonard St PH2 8HB
☎ 01738 442222 🖹 01738 638496
e-mail: email@queensperth.co.uk
This popular hotel is convenient for the bus and railway stations, and provides a warm welcome and efficient levels of guest care. Superior and standard bedrooms are available, all with pleasing colour schemes and comfortable modern appointments. There is an attractive first floor restaurant and a lounge and bar. A well-equipped leisure centre is also available.
**ROOMS:** 50 en suite (6 fmly) No smoking in 16 bedrooms s £45-£79; d £70-£104 (incl. bkfst) * **LB** **FACILITIES:** STV Indoor swimming (H) Sauna Gym Jacuzzi Steam room Xmas **CONF:** Thtr 200 Class 120 Board 70 Del from £67.50 * **SERVICES:** Lift **PARKING:** 50 **NOTES:** No dogs (ex guide dogs) No smoking in restaurant Civ Wed 140
**CARDS:**

**★★★59% Quality Hotel Perth**
Leonard St PH2 8HE
☎ 01738 624141 🖹 01738 639912
e-mail: admin@gb628.u-net.com
***Dir:*** *from A9 head for city centre & pass Perth Leisure Pool on right. Turn right & continue for 300yds*
Situated beside the railway station this substantial Victorian hotel is also conveniently positioned to give easy access to central amenities. Spacious public areas with lofty ceilings include a choice of bars and lounge areas. The Premier Plus bedrooms offer more space and have extra facilities than the more varied standard rooms.
**ROOMS:** 70 en suite (4 fmly) No smoking in 25 bedrooms s £75-£87; d £87-£102 * **LB** **FACILITIES:** STV entertainment ch fac Xmas **CONF:** Thtr 300 Class 150 Board 30 Del from £75 * **SERVICES:** Lift **PARKING:** 100 **NOTES:** No smoking in restaurant Civ Wed 300
**CARDS:**

**★★70% The New County Hotel**
22-30 County Place PH2 8EE
☎ 01738 623355 🖹 01738 628969
e-mail: enquiries@newcountyhotel.com

A full upgrading programme has transformed this city centre hotel to provide a smart reception lounge and refurbished bedrooms. The restaurant offers a good selection of well-prepared dishes; food is also available throughout the day in the lounge and bar.
**ROOMS:** 23 en suite (4 fmly) s £40-£50; d £80-£100 (incl. bkfst) * **LB** **FACILITIES:** STV Xmas **CONF:** Thtr 80 Class 60 Board 50 Del from £60 * **PARKING:** 10 **NOTES:** No dogs (ex guide dogs) No smoking in restaurant **CARDS:**

**★67% Woodlea**
23 York Place PH2 8EP
☎ 01738 621744 🖹 01738 621744
***Dir:*** *take A9 into Perth city centre, hotel is on left next to church & opposite library*
A relaxed and friendly atmosphere prevails at this small family-run
*continued*

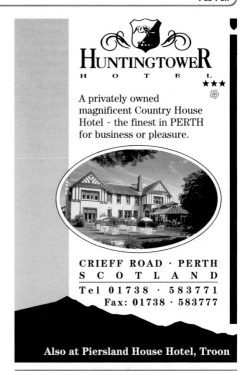



hotel close to the town centre. Well-maintained, the bright airy bedrooms make best use of available space and offer modern facilities. Public areas include a cosy lounge and the high tea menu is a popular feature in the dining room.
**ROOMS:** 13 rms (11 en suite) (2 fmly) s £30-£40; d £46-£50 (incl. bkfst) * **PARKING:** 4 **NOTES:** No dogs (ex guide dogs) No smoking in restaurant

**⇧ *Express by Holiday Inn***
200 Dunkeld Rd, Inveralmond PH1 3AQ
☎ 01738 636666 🖹 01738 633363
***Dir:*** *turn off A9 Inverness to Stirling Rd at Inveralmond rdbt onto A912 signposted Perth. Turn right at 1st rdbt & follow signs for hotel*

A modern budget hotel offering comfortable accommodation in refreshing, spacious and comprehensively equipped bedrooms, en suite bathrooms with power showers and continental buffet
*continued on p766*

PERTH, continued

breakfast included in the room rate. Suitable for business travellers or families. For further details and the Express by Holiday Inn phone number, consult the Hotel Groups page.
**ROOMS:** 81 en suite **CONF:** Thtr 60 Class 20 Board 20

## PETERHEAD, Aberdeenshire — Map 15 NK14

### ★★★★64% Waterside Inn

MACDONALD HOTELS ★★★★

Fraserburgh Rd AB42 3BN
☎ 01779 471121 🖹 01779 470670
e-mail: waterside@macdonald-hotels.co.uk
***Dir:*** *from Aberdeen A90, 1st rdbt turn left signed Fraserburgh, cross small rdbt, hotel at end of rd*

A welcoming atmosphere prevails at this popular hotel, just north of the town on the banks of the River Ugie. There is a comfortable foyer lounge, a choice of contrasting bars and an attractive split-level restaurant offering a good selection of dishes including seafood specialities. The modern bedrooms range from suites to executive and studio rooms.
**ROOMS:** 69 en suite 40 annexe en suite (15 fmly) No smoking in 55 bedrooms s £62-£80; d £72-£90 (incl. bkfst) * **LB** **FACILITIES:** STV Indoor swimming (H) Snooker Sauna Solarium Gym Jacuzzi Steam room Childrens play area Sunbeds entertainment ch fac Xmas **CONF:** Thtr 250 Class 100 Board 50 Del £125 * **PARKING:** 250 **NOTES:** No smoking in restaurant Civ Wed 250
**CARDS:**

### ★★★65% Palace

Prince St AB42 1PL
☎ 01779 474821 🖹 01779 476119
e-mail: info@palacehotel.co.uk
***Dir:*** *from Aberdeen, take the A90 and follow signs to Peterhead, on entering Peterhead, turn into Prince Street, then right into main car park*

Situated close to central amenities this comfortable business hotel is also a popular venue for local functions. Bedrooms, which range from spacious executives to the smaller standard rooms, are modern in appointment and offer the expected facilities. Public areas include a choice of contrasting bars and a split-level Brasserie Restaurant.
**ROOMS:** 66 en suite (2 fmly) No smoking in 24 bedrooms s £40-£110; d £50-£110 (incl. bkfst) * **LB** **FACILITIES:** STV Snooker entertainment Xmas **CONF:** Thtr 250 Class 120 Board 250 Del from £70 * **SERVICES:** Lift **PARKING:** 90 **NOTES:** Civ Wed 150
**CARDS:**

## PITLOCHRY, Perth & Kinross — Map 14 NN95

### ★★★76% *Pine Trees*

SCOTLAND'S HOTELS OF DISTINCTION

Strathview Ter PH16 5QR
☎ 01796 472121 🖹 01796 472460
e-mail: info@pinetrees-hotel.demon.co.uk
***Dir:*** *along main street (Atholl Road), turn into Larchwood Road, follow signs for hotel*
Set in 10 acres of secluded grounds high above the town this Victorian mansion retains many fine features including wood panelling, ornate ceilings, and a wonderful marble staircase. The atmosphere is refined and relaxing, with public rooms looking onto the lawns. Dutch furnishings grace the bedrooms.
**ROOMS:** 19 en suite No smoking in all bedrooms **FACILITIES:** Putting green entertainment **PARKING:** 20 **NOTES:** No smoking in restaurant
**CARDS:**

### ★★★72% Green Park

Clunie Bridge Rd PH16 5JY
☎ 01796 473248 🖹 01796 473520
e-mail: bookings@thegreenpark.co.uk
***Dir:*** *turn off A9 at Pitlochry, follow signs 0.25m through town, hotel on banks of Loch Faskally*

Lovely views over Loch Faskally can be enjoyed from this delightful and welcoming holiday hotel. Inviting public areas include a well stocked bar, a spacious lounge, and an attractive dining room in which to enjoy carefully prepared fare. Most of the comfortable bedrooms overlook the garden and loch. This is a non-smoking hotel.
**ROOMS:** 39 en suite No smoking in all bedrooms s £42-£65; d £84-£130 (incl. bkfst & dinner) * **LB** **FACILITIES:** Putting green Xmas **PARKING:** 45 **NOTES:** No smoking in restaurant **CARDS:**

*See advert on opposite page*

### ★★★68% Dundarach

Best Western

Perth Rd PH16 5DJ
☎ 01796 472862 🖹 01796 473024
e-mail: mail@pitlochryhotel.co.uk
***Dir:*** *S of town centre on main route*
This welcoming family run hotel stands in mature grounds at the south end of the town. Many of the original features of the inviting public areas have been retained. There is a choice of lounges, whilst the conservatory restaurant gives fine views of the Tummel

*continued*

Valley. Bedrooms are comfortable in style and a block of large purpose-built rooms will appeal to business guests.
**ROOMS:** 20 en suite 19 annexe en suite (7 fmly) No smoking in 11 bedrooms s £65; d £90 (incl. bkfst) * **LB** **FACILITIES:** **Spa** STV Sauna Xmas **CONF:** Thtr 60 Class 40 Board 40 **PARKING:** 39 **NOTES:** No dogs (ex guide dogs) No smoking in restaurant Closed Jan RS Dec-early Feb **CARDS:**

### ★★★66% Scotland's

40 Bonnethill Rd PH16 5BT
☎ 01796 472292 📠 01796 473284
e-mail: stay@scotlandshotel.co.uk

This long-established tourist hotel is located in the centre of town and boasts a well-equipped leisure centre. There is a choice of eating options, foyer lounge, and a well-stocked bar. Bedrooms vary in size and in style, all are comfortably appointed.
**ROOMS:** 75 en suite (18 fmly) No smoking in 21 bedrooms s £39-£75; d £90-£130 (incl. bkfst & dinner) * **LB** **FACILITIES:** **Spa** Indoor swimming (H) Sauna Solarium Gym Jacuzzi Therapy treatments entertainment ch fac Xmas **CONF:** Thtr 200 Class 100 Board 30 Del from £85 * **SERVICES:** Lift **PARKING:** 100 **NOTES:** No dogs (ex guide dogs) **CARDS:**

### ★★76% Knockendarroch House

Higher Oakfield PH16 5HT
☎ 01796 473473 📠 01796 474068
e-mail: info@knockendarroch.co.uk
***Dir:*** *exit A9 going N Pitlochry. After railway bridge, 1st R, 2nd L*

A friendly and relaxed atmosphere prevails at this delightful Victorian mansion, which stands in high grounds overlooking the town and Tummel Valley. There is no bar, but guests can enjoy a drink in the inviting lounges while perusing the daily fixed-price menu of freshly prepared and enjoyable dishes. Bedrooms are very comfortable and well-equipped.
**ROOMS:** 12 en suite No smoking in all bedrooms s £77-£81; d £118-£126 (incl. bkfst & dinner) * **LB** **FACILITIES:** Leisure facilities at nearby hotel **PARKING:** 30 **NOTES:** No dogs (ex guide dogs) No children 10yrs No smoking in restaurant Closed 2nd wk Nov-mid Feb
**CARDS:**

### ★★73% *Acarsaid*

8 Atholl Rd PH16 5BX
☎ 01796 472389 📠 01796 473952
e-mail: acarsaid@msn.com
***Dir:*** *take main road from A9 Perth to Inverness to Pitlochry, hotel on right hand side as you enter town*

Set in gardens by the main road on the south side of town, Acarsaid is enthusiastically managed. Inviting public areas include a choice of lounges and a bright attractive dining room comfortably set out. A courtesy coach is available to transport guests to the theatre.
**ROOMS:** 19 en suite (1 fmly) No smoking in 15 bedrooms
**PARKING:** 20 **NOTES:** No dogs (ex guide dogs) No children 10yrs No smoking in restaurant Closed 3 Jan-10 Mar **CARDS:**

Read all about it! Newspapers delivered to bedrooms in four and five star hotels.

PITLOCHRY, continued

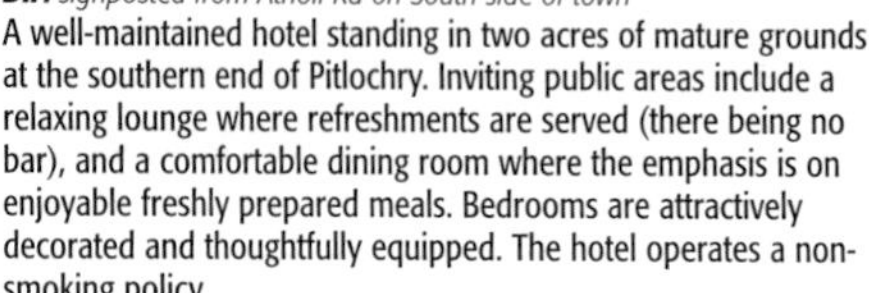
THE CIRCLE
Selected Individual Hotels
GREAT BRITAIN

### ★★71% **Birchwood**

2 East Moulin Rd PH16 5DW
☎ 01796 472477 🖷 01796 473951
e-mail: viv@birchwoodhotel.co.uk
***Dir:*** *signposted from Atholl Rd on South side of town*

A well-maintained hotel standing in two acres of mature grounds at the southern end of Pitlochry. Inviting public areas include a relaxing lounge where refreshments are served (there being no bar), and a comfortable dining room where the emphasis is on enjoyable freshly prepared meals. Bedrooms are attractively decorated and thoughtfully equipped. The hotel operates a non-smoking policy.

**ROOMS:** 12 en suite No smoking in all bedrooms s £39; d £78 (incl. bkfst) * LB **FACILITIES:** Xmas **PARKING:** 25 **NOTES:** No dogs (ex guide dogs) No smoking in restaurant Closed Jan-mid Mar
**CARDS:**

### ★★71% **Westlands of Pitlochry**

160 Atholl Rd PH16 5AR
☎ 01796 472266 🖷 01796 473994
e-mail: info@westlandshotel.co.uk
***Dir:*** *turn off A9 into centre of Pitlochry, hotel situated at N end of town*

Attractively situated in its own gardens, this hotel looks across the valley from its main road position on the north side of the town. Inviting public areas include the smart bar and spacious restaurant. The comfortable bedrooms are modern in appointment and offer a good range of amenities.

**ROOMS:** 15 en suite (2 fmly) s fr £39; d fr £78 (incl. bkfst) * LB **FACILITIES:** Fishing Xmas **CONF:** Thtr 35 Class 24 Board 20 Del £60 * **PARKING:** 28 **NOTES:** No smoking in restaurant
**CARDS:**

### ★★70% **Balrobin**

Higher Oakfield PH16 5HT
☎ 01796 472901 🖷 01796 474200
e-mail: info@balrobin.co.uk
***Dir:*** *leave A9 at Pitlochry junct, continue to town centre and follow brown tourists signs to hotel*

A welcoming atmosphere prevails at this comfortable family-run holiday hotel which, from its position above the town, enjoys views of the surrounding countryside. Public areas include a relaxing lounge, well-stocked bar, and an attractive restaurant offering traditional home cooked fare. The well-maintained bedrooms are comfortably modern in appointment.

**ROOMS:** 15 en suite (2 fmly) No smoking in all bedrooms s £38-£44; d £85-£76 (incl. bkfst) * LB **PARKING:** 15 **NOTES:** No children 5yrs No smoking in restaurant Closed Nov-Feb **CARDS:**

### ★★70% **Craigvrack**

West Moulin Rd PH16 5EQ
☎ 01796 472399 🖷 01796 473990
e-mail: irene@craigvrack-hotel.demon.co.uk
***Dir:*** *from the main street, turn into West Moulin Road, Craigvrack has three large flagpoles on the lawn and is illuminated at night*

Situated on the hill above the town, this comfortable, welcoming holiday hotel enjoys lovely views of the surrounding countryside. Well-presented public areas invite relaxation and include a choice of lounges and a well-stocked bar. The smart restaurant serves a varied menu. Bedrooms have pleasing colour schemes and modern furnishings.

CRAIGVRACK HOTEL

**ROOMS:** 16 en suite (2 fmly) s £29-£47; d £58-£70 (incl. bkfst) * LB **FACILITIES:** Xmas **CONF:** Thtr 30 Class 32 Board 16 **PARKING:** 20
**CARDS:**

### ★★69% **Moulin Hotel**

11-13 Kirkmichael Rd, Moulin PH16 5EW
☎ 01796 472196 🖷 01796 474098
e-mail: hotel@moulin.u-net.com
***Dir:*** *turn off A9 into Pitlochry in centre of town take A924 signed Braemar. Moulin village 0.75m outside Pitlochry*

The original parts of this friendly hotel date back to 1695. One of them, the Moulin bar, serves an excellent choice of bar meals as well as real ales from the hotel's own microbrewery. Alternatively, the comfortable restaurant overlooks the Moulin Burn.

**ROOMS:** 15 en suite (3 fmly) s £30-£50; d £40-£75 (incl. bkfst) * LB **CONF:** Thtr 15 Class 12 Board 10 Del from £55 * **PARKING:** 30 **NOTES:** No smoking in restaurant **CARDS:**

## PLOCKTON, Highland — Map 14 NG83

### ★★75% ❀ ***Haven***

Innes St IV52 8TW
☎ 01599 544334 & 544223 🖷 01599 544467
***Dir:*** *turn off A87 just before Kyle of Lochalsh, after Balmacara there is a signpost to Plockton, hotel on main road just before lochside*

The Dryburgh family look forward to welcoming you to their charming small hotel in the picturesque West Highland village of Plockton. Bedrooms are comfortably modern in appointment and are equipped with a good range of accessories. Two delightful suites are also available. Relaxing public areas include a choice of comfortable lounges, a snug bar, and attractive restaurant which offers a tempting range of Taste of Scotland specialities prepared from quality ingredients.

**ROOMS:** 15 en suite **PARKING:** 7 **NOTES:** No children 7yrs No smoking in restaurant Closed 20 Dec-1 Feb **CARDS:**

## POLMONT, Falkirk — Map 11 NS97

### ★★★★70% ❀ ***Inchyra Grange***

MACDONALD HOTELS ★★★★

Grange Rd FK2 0YB
☎ 01324 711911 🖷 01324 716134
***Dir:*** *just beyond BP Social Club*

This former manor house is ideally located near to the M9. Public areas are bright and modern, and include a choice of eating options. Peligrinos offers a range of Italian specialities in an informal atmosphere within the leisure club. The Priory Restaurant

continued

provides a fine, formal dining experience. Bedrooms are mostly spacious with comfortable modern appointments.

**ROOMS:** 109 en suite (5 fmly) No smoking in 57 bedrooms **FACILITIES:** STV Indoor swimming (H) Tennis (hard) Sauna Solarium Gym Jacuzzi Steam room Beauty therapy room Aerobics studio Aromatherapist **CONF:** Thtr 600 Class 250 Board 80 **SERVICES:** Lift **PARKING:** 400 **NOTES:** No smoking in restaurant
**CARDS:**

## POOLEWE, Highland
Map 14 NG88

### Hotel of the Year

**★★★75% Pool House Hotel**
IV22 2LD
☎ 01445 781272 01445 781403
e-mail: enquiries@poolhousehotel.com
***Dir:*** *6m N of Gairloch on the A832. Located in the middle of Poolewe village, next to the bridge at the edge of the sea*
Sitting on the edge of Loch Ewe, the suites and public areas at Pool House have fine views across the loch towards Inverewe gardens. Bedrooms have been re-modelled into spacious and comfortable suites, including one that is themed on the ill-fated Titanic and includes some original items from the ship. Local produce features strongly on the varied restaurant and bar menus, whilst service is friendly and attentive. Pool House has been awarded the AA Hotel of the Year Award for Scotland 2001-2002.
**ROOMS:** 5 en suite No smoking in all bedrooms s £65-£85; d £280-£350 (incl. bkfst) * Prices include dinner Oct-Apr **LB**
**FACILITIES:** Sea fishing from jetty in front of hotel Xmas
**PARKING:** 20 **NOTES:** No dogs (ex guide dogs) No children 14yrs No smoking in restaurant Closed Jan-Feb RS Nov & Dec
**CARDS:**

## PORT APPIN, Argyll & Bute
Map 14 NM94

### Premier Collection

**★★★ Airds**
PA38 4DF
☎ 01631 730236 01631 730535
e-mail: airds@airds-hotel.com
***Dir:*** *16m S of Ballachulish Bridge turn off A828 and drive for 2m*
Enjoying the most stunning outlook over Loch Linnhe with the mountains behind, this is a remote and peaceful destination away from the pressures of the modern world. The bedrooms are furnished with flair, and the lounges offer an environment for total relaxation. There is also an enclosed sun porch from which to take in the wonderful views. Meals are created in the kitchen using top quality ingredients and are prepared with a light touch.
**ROOMS:** 12 en suite s £130-£195; d £260-£310 (incl. bkfst & dinner) * **LB** **FACILITIES:** Fishing ch fac Xmas **PARKING:** 15 **NOTES:** No smoking in restaurant Closed 23-27 Dec & 6-26 Jan
**CARDS:**

RELAIS & CHATEAUX.

## PORT ASKAIG See Islay, Isle of

## PORTMAHOMACK, Highland
Map 14 NH98

**★★65% Caledonian**
Main St IV20 1YS
☎ 01862 871345 01862 871757
e-mail: info@caleyhotel.co.uk
***Dir:*** *from S A9 to Nigg rdbt then B9165 for 10m to village. From N travel through Tain, turn off for Portmahomack after 0.5m*
The Caledonian is positioned on the sea front and enjoys a lovely outlook over the Dornoch Firth to the Sutherland hills beyond. Bedrooms are comfortably modern in style and offer the expected amenities. Public areas include a well-stocked bar and smart restaurant.
**ROOMS:** 15 en suite (5 fmly) s £30-£35; d £50-£59 (incl. bkfst) * **LB**
**FACILITIES:** Spa entertainment Xmas **CONF:** Thtr 180 Class 60 Board 60 Del from £45 * **PARKING:** 16 **NOTES:** No smoking in restaurant
**CARDS:**

## PORT OF MENTEITH, Stirling
Map 11 NN50

**★★74% *Lake of Menteith***
FK8 3RA
☎ 01877 385258 01877 385671
***Dir:*** *just off A81, beside village church 200yds on right*
This is a charming holiday hotel that provides a real haven in which to relax. The inviting sitting room and conservatory enjoy stunning views over the lake. Comfortable bedrooms range from

*continued on p770*

PORT OF MENTEITH, continued

spacious superior rooms to cosy standard rooms; all are tastefully decorated and offer many thoughtful extras.
**ROOMS:** 16 en suite No smoking in all bedrooms **CONF:** Thtr 30 Board 20 **PARKING:** 35 **NOTES:** No children 8yrs No smoking in restaurant RS Nov-Feb **CARDS:**

## PORTPATRICK, Dumfries & Galloway — Map 10 NX05

### ★★★73% Fernhill
Heugh Rd DG9 8TD
☎ 01776 810220 01776 810596
e-mail: info@fernhillhotel.co.uk
***Dir:*** *from Stranraer A77 to Portpatrick, 100yds past Portpatrick village sign, turn right before war memorial. Hotel is 1st on left*
Commanding panoramic views over the harbour and the Irish Sea this friendly hotel is ideally situated for access to the many activities in the area. Bedrooms are comfortable, some with balconies overlooking the harbour. The conservatory restaurant is an ideal location for a relaxing breakfast or dinner.
**ROOMS:** 14 en suite 9 annexe en suite (3 fmly) s £45-£85; d £90-£114 (incl. bkfst) * LB **FACILITIES:** STV Leisure facilities available at sister hotel in Stranraer ch fac Xmas **CONF:** Thtr 24 Class 12 Board 12 **PARKING:** 32 **CARDS:**

## PORTREE See Skye, Isle of

## PORT WILLIAM, Dumfries & Galloway — Map 10 NX34

### ★★★66% *Corsemalzie House*
Scotland's Hotels of Distinction
DG8 9RL
☎ 01988 860254 01988 860213
e-mail: corsemalzie@ndirect.co.uk
***Dir:*** *From A75 turn left at Newton Stewart rdbt onto A714, by passing Wigtown: turn right after crossing bridge at Bladnoch onto B7005 for Corsemalzie*
Quietly situated in 40 acres of wooded grounds, this 19th-century mansion house offers a comfortable and relaxing retreat. Service is friendly and attentive. The bar is complemented by a welcoming drawing room, leading into the light and airy restaurant, where local produce features on the daily changing menu.
**ROOMS:** 14 en suite (1 fmly) No smoking in 3 bedrooms
**FACILITIES:** Fishing Croquet lawn Putting green Game shooting
**PARKING:** 31 **NOTES:** No smoking in restaurant Closed 21 Jan-5 Mar & Xmas **CARDS:**

## POWFOOT, Dumfries & Galloway — Map 11 NY16

### ★★70% *Golf*
MINOTEL Great Britain
Links Av DG12 5PN
☎ 01461 700254 01461 700288
e-mail: info@powfoothotel.co.uk
***Dir:*** *turn off M74 at Gretna onto A75 round Annan bypass, hotel sign 2m on turn left onto B724 and follow sign to Powfoot village*
Popular with golfers and providing a retreat for business people, this hotel sits next to the local golf course at the end of the village and enjoys panoramic views across the Solway Firth. Bedrooms and public areas are comfortable and service is friendly and obliging.
**ROOMS:** 18 en suite **CONF:** Thtr 150 Class 70 Board 70 **SERVICES:** air con **PARKING:** 60 **CARDS:**

Fancy a Singapore Sling? Bar staff in five star hotels should be skilled cocktail mixers.

## POWMILL, Perth & Kinross — Map 11 NT09

### ★★★66% *Gartwhinzean Hotel*
Best Western
FK14 7NW
☎ 01577 840595 01577 840779
***Dir:*** *from M90 junct 6 take A977 Kincardine Bridge Road, in approx 8m the village of Powmill, hotel at end of village*
A welcoming atmosphere prevails at this friendly country inn, which stands in its own garden. Bedrooms are contained in a modern wing and the majority are generously proportioned with attractive decor and pine furnishings. Public areas include a formal dining room, choice of contrasting bars and a bistro which are quite rustic in style. There also are good function facilities.
**ROOMS:** 23 en suite (6 fmly) No smoking in 6 bedrooms **CONF:** Thtr 250 Class 80 Board 30 **PARKING:** 150 **NOTES:** No dogs (ex guide dogs) No smoking in restaurant Civ Wed 100
**CARDS:**

## PRESTWICK, South Ayrshire — Map 10 NS32

### ★★★66% Parkstone
Esplanade KA9 1QN
☎ 01292 477286 01292 477671
e-mail: info@parkstonehotel.co.uk
***Dir:*** *from Prestwick Main St (A79) turn west to seafront - hotel 600yds*

Situated on the sea front in a quiet residential area, this family-run hotel caters for business visitors as well as golfers. There is a wing of smart new bedrooms and the original rooms are decorated to a similar standard. In addition to the enjoyable and good value restaurant meals, one can eat well from the lounge bar menu.
**ROOMS:** 22 en suite (2 fmly) s £40-£49; d £66-£70 (incl. bkfst) * LB
**CONF:** Thtr 100 **PARKING:** 34 **NOTES:** No dogs
**CARDS:**

## RENFREW For hotels see Glasgow Airport

## ROSEBANK, South Lanarkshire — Map 11 NS84

### ★★★71% Popinjay
Best Western
Lanark Rd ML8 5QB
☎ 01555 860441 01555 860204
e-mail: sales@popinjayhotel.co.uk
***Dir:*** *on A72 between Hamilton & Lanark*
This well-established hotel with Tudor style façade has grounds that extend to the banks of the River Clyde. Public areas include a panelled bar with open fireplaces and the elegant restaurant looking towards the river is a fitting venue to enjoy the fine cuisine. Functions, especially weddings, are popular (the gardens provide a lovely backdrop). The well-equipped bedrooms vary in size.
**ROOMS:** 38 en suite (2 fmly) No smoking in 19 bedrooms s £54-£75; d £75-£89 (incl. bkfst) * LB **FACILITIES:** STV Fishing ch fac Xmas
**CONF:** Thtr 250 Class 120 Board 60 Del from £84 * **PARKING:** 300
**NOTES:** Civ Wed 160 **CARDS:**

*See advert on opposite page*

## ROSLIN, Midlothian

Map 11 NT26

### ★★65% Roslin Glen

2 Penicuik Rd EH25 9LH
☎ 0131 440 2029 📠 0131 440 2229
e-mail: roslinglen@aol.com
**Dir:** *in the village of Roslin 1m from the A701 Edinburgh/Peebles Rd. 2m S of Edinburgh City bypass*

THE CIRCLE Selected Individual Hotels GREAT BRITAIN

This family-run hotel provides a relaxed, welcoming atmosphere. The bright, cheery bedrooms are thoughtfully equipped and come in a variety of sizes. A popular choice of dishes is available in the bar and cosy restaurant.
**ROOMS:** 7 en suite (2 fmly) s £54-£60; d £60-£70 (incl. bkfst) * **LB**
**FACILITIES:** STV **CONF:** Thtr 50 Class 24 Board 30 Del from £72.50 *
**PARKING:** 6 **NOTES:** No smoking in restaurant
**CARDS:**

*See advert under EDINBURGH*

## ROSYTH, Fife

Map 11 NT18

### ★★63% Gladyer Inn

Heath Rd, Ridley Dr KY11 2BT
☎ 01383 419977 📠 01383 411728
e-mail: gladyer@aol.com
**Dir:** *from junct 1 of M90 travel along Admiralty Road, past rdbt then first road on the left*

Enjoying a quiet residential location, and yet very handy for the motorway network, this hotel provides an ideal base for the business traveller. There is a choice of bars in which traditional cooking is served. At the time of going to press, the well-equipped bedrooms were being tastefully refurbished.
**ROOMS:** 21 en suite (3 fmly) s £35-£40; d £50-£55 (incl. bkfst) * **LB**
**FACILITIES:** STV entertainment **CONF:** Thtr 100 Class 70 Board 80 Del from £57.50 * **PARKING:** 81 **NOTES:** No dogs (ex guide dogs)
**CARDS:**

## ROY BRIDGE, Highland

Map 14 NN28

### ★★★72% Glenspean Lodge Hotel

PH31 4AW
☎ 01397 712223 📠 01397 712660
e-mail: wdgsl@aol.com
**Dir:** *2m E of Roy Bridge, turn right off A82 at Spean Bridge onto A86*

Best Western

This charming country house is set amid landscaped gardens in the beautiful Spean Valley. Bedrooms have attractive co-ordinated fabrics and are comfortably furnished in pine. Relaxing public areas include a spacious and well-stocked split-level bar, a

*continued*

comfortable lounge, and an elegant restaurant that features the best available local produce.

GLENSPEAN LODGE

**ROOMS:** 15 en suite No smoking in 10 bedrooms s £49-£75; d £40-£150 (incl. bkfst) * **LB** **FACILITIES:** Xmas **CONF:** Thtr 50 Class 25 Board 25 Del from £80 * **PARKING:** 50 **NOTES:** No dogs (ex guide dogs) No smoking in restaurant Closed Nov-Feb Civ Wed 65
**CARDS:**

### ★★66% The Inn at Roy Bridge

PH31 4AG
☎ 01397 712253 📠 01397 712641
e-mail: stay@stromlossit.co.uk
**Dir:** *Off A82 at Spean Bridge onto A86, signed Roy Bridge. Hotel on left at east end of village*

THE CIRCLE Selected Individual Hotels GREAT BRITAIN

A relaxed informal atmosphere prevails at this family-run holiday hotel. The spacious bar is the focal point and a favourite with both resident and non-resident diners. Alternatively one can eat in the

*continued on p772*

ROY BRIDGE, continued

attractive restaurant. Bedrooms come in a mix of sizes and styles, most being smartly modern.
**ROOMS:** 11 en suite (2 fmly) No smoking in all bedrooms s £30-£35; d £60-£80 (incl. bkfst) * **LB** **FACILITIES:** Pool table Internet Cafe ch fac Xmas **CONF:** Thtr 30 Class 18 Board 12 Del from £60 * **PARKING:** 30 **NOTES:** No smoking in restaurant Closed 10 Nov-10 Dec & 6-31 Jan Civ Wed 30 **CARDS:**

## ST ANDREWS, Fife

Map 12 NO51

see also Leuchars

### ★★★★★74% ◎◎ The Old Course Hotel

KY16 9SP
☎ 01334 474371 🖷 01334 477668
e-mail: reservations@oldcoursehotel.co.uk
***Dir:*** *close to the A91 on the outskirts of the city*
Set beside the 17th hole of the internationally renowned championship course and enjoying stunning sea views, this hotel attracts golfers from all over the world. Bedrooms come in a variety of sizes and styles, and dining options include the traditional 'Road Hole Grill' or the informal 'Sands' in which international, imaginative cuisine is served by cheerful staff. Smart public areas include cosy lounges, bright conservatory, a range of golf shops and a well-equipped spa.
**ROOMS:** 146 en suite (6 fmly) s £205-£425; d £225-£445 (incl. bkfst) * **LB** **FACILITIES:** Spa STV Indoor swimming (H) Golf 18 Sauna Solarium Gym Jacuzzi Steam room Xmas **CONF:** Thtr 300 Class 150 Board 60 **SERVICES:** Lift **PARKING:** 150 **NOTES:** Closed 24-28 Dec Civ Wed 300 **CARDS:**

### ★★★★74% ◎◎ Rusacks

Pilmour Links KY16 9JQ
☎ 0870 400 8128 🖷 01334 477896
e-mail: heritagehotel_standrews.rusacks@forte-hotels.com
***Dir:*** *from W on A91 past golf courses, through an old viaduct, hotel 200m on left before rdbt*

This longstanding and well-managed hotel continues to go from strength to strength. A number of smart new rooms with unrivalled views and balconies have been added to the already excellent and very comfortable bedrooms. In addition, stunning views, friendly staff and good food, make for an excellent hotel.
**ROOMS:** 68 en suite s £130-£160; d £210-£290 * **LB** **FACILITIES:** STV Sauna Solarium Golf Mgr to organise golf Xmas **CONF:** Thtr 90 Class 40 Board 20 Del from £90 * **SERVICES:** Lift **PARKING:** 21 **NOTES:** No smoking in restaurant Civ Wed 60
**CARDS:**

## *Premier Collection*

### ★★★ ◎◎ Rufflets Country House

Strathkinness Low Rd KY16 9TX
☎ 01334 472594 🖷 01334 478703
e-mail: reservations@rufflets.co.uk
***Dir:*** *1.5m W on B939*
The committed team at Rufflets Country House have nurtured and maintained an ethos of top class hotelkeeping and fine hospitality. The success of this approach is clear in the number of guests who return time and again. Welcoming and individually furnished lounges, overlooking the award winning gardens, are complemented by a comfortable restaurant, where imaginative Scottish cuisine is served, and a separate, popular brasserie. Thoughtfully equipped bedrooms, many with striking colour schemes, complete the package.
**ROOMS:** 19 en suite 3 annexe en suite (1 fmly) No smoking in 13 bedrooms s fr £96; d £172-£222 (incl. bkfst) * **LB**
**FACILITIES:** STV Putting green Jacuzzi Golf driving net Xmas
**CONF:** Thtr 50 Class 30 Board 25 Del from £117.50 *
**PARKING:** 52 **NOTES:** No dogs (ex guide dogs) No smoking in restaurant **CARDS:**

### ★★★77% ◎◎ St Andrews Golf

40 The Scores KY16 9AS
☎ 01334 472611 🖷 01334 472188
e-mail: reception@standrews-golf.co.uk
***Dir:*** *follow signs 'Golf Course' into Golf Place and in 200yds right into The Scores*
This stylish Victorian hotel overlooks the bay and many of the rooms have fine views over the coastline and nearby golf course. Comfortable bedrooms are attractively furnished, the lounges are relaxing and the restaurant provides carefully prepared meals, which make good use of local ingredients.
**ROOMS:** 22 en suite (9 fmly) s £102; d £155 (incl. bkfst) * **LB**
**FACILITIES:** STV Xmas ch fac **CONF:** Thtr 200 Class 80 Board 20 Del from £75 * **SERVICES:** Lift **PARKING:** 6 **NOTES:** No smoking in restaurant **CARDS:**

### ★★★66% Scores

76 The Scores KY16 9BB
☎ 01334 472451 🖷 01334 473947
e-mail: office@scoreshotel.co.uk
***Dir:*** *on entering St Andrews follow signs to West Sands and Sea Life Centre, premises facing the sea diagonally opposite the Royal & Ancient Clubhouse*
This comfortable hotel enjoys views over St Andrews Bay and is situated only a few yards from the first tee of the famous Old Course. Public areas include a choice of well-stocked bars, an all day coffee shop, and an attractive restaurant where seafood

*continued*

specials predominate. The variable sized bedrooms come with mixed appointments and a good range of amenities.
**ROOMS:** 30 en suite (1 fmly) s £59-£88; d £86-£149 (incl. bkfst) * **LB** **FACILITIES:** STV ch fac Xmas **CONF:** Thtr 150 Class 60 Board 40 Del from £97.50 * **SERVICES:** Lift **PARKING:** 10 **NOTES:** No dogs (ex guide dogs) No smoking in restaurant **CARDS:**

### ★★★63% *Drumoig Golf Hotel*
Drumoig KY16 0BE
☎ 01382 541800 🖷 01382 542211
e-mail: drumoig@sol.co.uk
(For full entry see Leuchars)

### ★★72% The Inn at Lathones
MINOTEL Great Britain
Largoward KY9 1JE
☎ 01334 840494 🖷 01334 840694
e-mail: lathones@theinn.co.uk
***Dir:*** *situated 5m S of St Andrews on A915, 0.5m before the village of Largoward on left hand side of the road, just after the hidden dip*

A lovely little country inn, parts of which date back 400 years. The friendly staff, real fires and beamed ceilings create a cosy atmosphere. The French head chef has devised a modern menu that successfully combines classic French cooking with top quality local ingredients and a few ideas from further afield. The impressive wine list includes helpful tasting notes by the proprietor.
**ROOMS:** 14 annexe en suite (2 fmly) s £65-£95; d £100-£140 (incl. bkfst) * **LB** **FACILITIES:** ch fac **CONF:** Thtr 30 Class 10 Board 20 Del from £85 * **PARKING:** 35 **NOTES:** No smoking in restaurant Closed 25-26 Dec & 3-23 Jan RS 24 Dec Civ Wed 40
**CARDS:**

### ★★69% *Russell Hotel*
26 The Scores KY16 9AS
☎ 01334 473447 🖷 01334 478279
e-mail: russellhotel@talk21.com
***Dir:*** *A91-St Andrews turn right at 2nd rdbt into Golf Place, turn right again after 200yds into The Scores, hotel in 300yds on the left*

Enjoying lovely sea views, this family-run hotel lies near to the famous Old Course. A small lounge is provided on the first floor and the bar is a popular rendezvous. An extensive range of dishes is offered here and in the adjoining Supper Room. The bedrooms are comfortably modern in style.
**ROOMS:** 10 en suite (3 fmly) **FACILITIES:** STV **NOTES:** No dogs (ex guide dogs) No smoking in restaurant **CARDS:**

### ○ St Andrews Bay Golf Resort & Spa
KY16 8PN
☎ 01334 837000
At the time of going to press, the star classification for this hotel was not confirmed. Please refer to the AA internet site www.theAA.com for current information.

## ST BOSWELLS, Scottish Borders — Map 12 NT53

### ★★★76% Dryburgh Abbey
Scotland's Hotels of Distinction
TD6 0RQ
☎ 01835 822261 🖷 01835 823945
e-mail: enquiries@dryburgh.co.uk
***Dir:*** *at St Boswells turn onto B6404 & through village. Continue 2m, then turn left B6356 Scott's View. Through Clintmains village, hotel 1.8m*
An imposing red sandstone mansion in a riverside setting next to the Abbey. The inviting public areas include a choice of lounges. Most of the thoughtfully equipped bedrooms offer good levels of comfort, with suites and spacious deluxe rooms available.
**ROOMS:** 37 en suite 1 annexe en suite (5 fmly) s £74-£119; d £148-£198 (incl. bkfst & dinner) * **FACILITIES:** Indoor swimming (H) Fishing Croquet lawn Putting green ch fac Xmas **CONF:** Thtr 150 Class 90 Board 70 Del from £80 * **SERVICES:** Lift **PARKING:** 103 **NOTES:** No smoking in restaurant **CARDS:**
*See advert under MELROSE*

### ★★69% Buccleuch Arms
The Green TD6 0EW
☎ 01835 822243 🖷 01835 823965
e-mail: bucchotel@aol.com
***Dir:*** *on A68, 8m N of Jedburgh*
Formerly a coaching inn, this charming hotel stands opposite the village green and beside the local cricket pitch. It offers a good range of meals in the hotel bar and stylish restaurant. Morning coffees and afternoon teas are served in the attractive lounge with its open fire. The well-equipped bedrooms come in a variety of sizes.
**ROOMS:** 19 en suite (2 fmly) s £40-£44; d £60-£80 (incl. bkfst) * **LB** **FACILITIES:** Putting green Xmas **CONF:** Thtr 100 Class 40 Board 30 Del from £50 * **PARKING:** 50 **NOTES:** No smoking in restaurant Closed 25 Dec **CARDS:**

## ST FILLANS, Perth & Kinross — Map 11 NN62

### ★★★67% The Four Seasons Hotel
Loch Earn PH6 2NF
☎ 01764 685333 🖷 01764 685444
e-mail: info@thefourseasonshotel.co.uk
***Dir:*** *on A85, towards W of village facing Loch*
A welcoming holiday hotel enjoying spectacular views over Loch Earn. Refurbished bedrooms are comfortable and modern. Public areas overlook the loch and include a snug bar, lounge and the Tarken Bar, an informal food option. The Meall Raemhar
*continued on p774*

ST FILLANS, continued

Restaurant offers fine dining with a tempting contemporary Scottish menu.

*The Four Seasons Hotel, St Fillans*

**ROOMS:** 12 en suite 6 annexe en suite (7 fmly) No smoking in 3 bedrooms s £35-£74; d £70-£98 (incl. bkfst) * **LB** **FACILITIES:** STV Xmas **CONF:** Thtr 95 Class 45 Board 38 **PARKING:** 40 **NOTES:** No smoking in restaurant Closed 15 Jan-15 Mar
**CARDS:**

### ★★73% Achray House

Loch Earn PH6 2NF
☎ 01764 685231 🖹 01764 685320
e-mail: achrayhotelsltd@btinternet.com
***Dir:*** *on A85 12 miles from Crieff*

A friendly holiday hotel set in gardens overlooking picturesque Loch Earn. Maintained in pristine condition, it offers smart attractive bedrooms, including a self contained lodge with fine views. A good range of hearty dishes is served in the popular conservatory and residents dining room.

**ROOMS:** 9 rms (8 en suite) 1 annexe en suite (2 fmly) s £37-£47; d £50-£69 (incl. bkfst) * **LB** **FACILITIES:** Xmas **CONF:** Class 20 Board 20 Del from £60 * **PARKING:** 30 **NOTES:** No dogs (ex guide dogs) No smoking in restaurant **CARDS:**

## SANQUHAR, Dumfries & Galloway — Map 11 NS70

### ★★67% Blackaddie House

Blackaddie Rd DG4 6JJ
☎ 01659 50270 🖹 01659 50900
***Dir:*** *turn off A76 just N of Sanquhar at Burnside Service Station. Private road to hotel 300mtrs on right*

This former rectory, which dates back to 1540, offers variable sized bedrooms which are comfortably modern in style and provide all the expected amenities. Public areas include an inviting lounge, a cosy bar with adjacent bistro, and carte restaurant.

**ROOMS:** 9 en suite (2 fmly) s fr £38; d fr £64 (incl. bkfst) * **FACILITIES:** Riding **CONF:** Thtr 50 Class 20 Board 20 **PARKING:** 25 **CARDS:**

## SCALASAIG See Colonsay, Isle of

## SCOURIE, Highland — Map 14 NC14

### ★★71% Eddrachilles

Badcall Bay IV27 4TH
☎ 01971 502080 🖹 01971 502477
e-mail: enq@eddrachilles.com
***Dir:*** *2m S on A894, 7m N of Kylesku Bridge*

An appealing holiday hotel in woodland beside the Badcall Bay, with sea views. There are inviting lounges and a popular conservatory overlooking the bay. The dining room, with its natural stone walls and flagstone floor, offers fixed-price and carte menus. The well-equipped bedrooms are smartly refurbished.

**ROOMS:** 11 en suite (1 fmly) s £49-£60; d £78-£90 (incl. bkfst) * **LB** **FACILITIES:** Fishing Boats for hire **PARKING:** 25 **NOTES:** No dogs (ex guide dogs) No children 3yrs Closed Nov-Feb **CARDS:**

### ★★68% Scourie

IV27 4SX
☎ 01971 502396 🖹 01971 502423
e-mail: patrick@scourie-hotel.co.uk
***Dir:*** *situated on A894 in the village of Scourie*

This well established hotel is an angler's paradise with extensive fishing rights available on a 25,000-acre estate. Public areas include a choice of comfortable lounges, a cosy bar and a smart dining room offering wholesome fare. The resident proprietors create a relaxed and friendly atmosphere.

**ROOMS:** 18 rms (17 en suite) 2 annexe en suite (2 fmly) s £34-£46; d £58-£80 (incl. bkfst) * **LB** **FACILITIES:** no TV in bdrms Fishing **PARKING:** 30 **NOTES:** No smoking in restaurant Closed mid Oct -end Mar **CARDS:**

## SHETLAND — Map 16

## LERWICK — Map 16 HU44

### ★★★69% Shetland

Holmsgarth Rd ZE1 0PW
☎ 01595 695515 🖹 01595 695828
e-mail: reception@shetlandhotel.co.uk
***Dir:*** *opposite P&O ferry terminal, on main route north from town centre*

This modern hotel stands directly opposite the main ferry terminal. Public areas include an open plan bar/lounge and two dining options, Oasis Bistro and the more formal Ninian Restaurant. Bedrooms are well-proportioned and comfortable.

**ROOMS:** 64 en suite (4 fmly) No smoking in 14 bedrooms s £69; d £90 (incl. bkfst) * **LB** **FACILITIES:** STV **CONF:** Thtr 300 Class 75 Board 50 **SERVICES:** Lift **PARKING:** 150 **NOTES:** No dogs (ex guide dogs) Civ Wed 200 **CARDS:**

### ★★★68% Lerwick

15 South Rd ZE1 0RB
☎ 01595 692166 🖹 01595 694419
e-mail: reception@lerwickhotel.co.uk
***Dir:*** *near town centre, on main road southwards to/from airport. 25m from main airport, located in central Lerwick*

This popular hotel has lovely views over Breiwick Bay to Bressay and Breiwick Islands. Smartly presented, it offers an attractive brasserie and a formal restaurant enjoying the sea views. Well-furnished bedrooms come in a variety of sizes.

**ROOMS:** 35 en suite (3 fmly) s £69; d £89 (incl. bkfst) * **LB** **FACILITIES:** STV **CONF:** Thtr 60 Class 40 Board 20 **PARKING:** 50 **NOTES:** No dogs (ex guide dogs) Civ Wed 100
**CARDS:**

## UNST — Map 16 HP60

### ★★64% The Baltasound

ZE2 9DS
☎ 01957 711334 🖹 01957 711358
e-mail: balta.hotel@zetnet.co.uk
***Dir:*** *from ferry from Lerwick, follow the main road north. Hotel is in Baltasound close to the pier.*

The most northerly hotel in the British Isles, this welcoming family-run hotel looks out across sea lochs. Apart from the separate breakfast room, public rooms are open plan, with comfortable

*continued*

S

lounge bar and dining room areas. Some bedrooms are in the main building, but most are in pleasant log cabins dispersed around the grounds.
**ROOMS:** 8 rms (6 en suite) 17 annexe en suite (17 fmly) No smoking in 17 bedrooms s fr £42; d fr £64 (incl. bkfst) * **FACILITIES:** Pool table **PARKING:** 20 **NOTES:** No smoking in restaurant **CARDS:**

## SHIELDAIG, Highland — Map 14 NG85

### ★74% Tigh an Eilean
IV54 8XN
☎ 01520 755251 01520 755321
e-mail: tighaneileanhotel@shieldaig.fsnet.co.uk
***Dir:*** *turn off A896 onto village road signposted Shieldaig,hotel in centre of village on loch front just along from small jetty*
Under keen new ownership this charming hotel looks out on the bay and is surrounded by whitewashed crofts and fishermen's cottages. There are three comfortable lounges and an honesty bar. The dinner menu features seafood and much local produce.
**ROOMS:** 11 en suite (1 fmly) s £49.50; d £110 (incl. bkfst) * LB **FACILITIES:** no TV in bdrms ch fac **PARKING:** 15 **NOTES:** No smoking in restaurant Closed late Oct-end Mar **CARDS:**

## SKYE, ISLE OF, Highland — Map 13

## ARDVASAR — Map 13 NG60

### ★★67% Ardvasar Hotel
Sleat IV45 8RS
☎ 01471 844223 01471 844495
e-mail: christine@ardvasar-hotel.demon.co.uk
***Dir:*** *leave ferry, drive 50yds & turn left*

Many improvements have been undertaken by the hotel's enthusiastic owners. The bedrooms in particular have benefited from refurbishment and are smartly decorated and equipped to modern standards. Public areas include an inviting lounge, a separate dining room and a bar where enjoyable food is also served.
**ROOMS:** 10 en suite (4 fmly) No smoking in 6 bedrooms s £45-£55; d £80-£90 (incl. bkfst) * LB **FACILITIES:** Spa entertainment Xmas **CONF:** Thtr 50 Board 24 **PARKING:** 30 **NOTES:** No smoking in restaurant **CARDS:**

Need to unwind? Look out for hotels with Spa in their entry.

## COLBOST — Map 13 NG24

*Premier Collection*

### ★★ Three Chimneys Restaurant & House Over-By
IV55 8ZT
☎ 01470 511258 01470 511358
e-mail: eatandstay@threechimneys.co.uk
***Dir:*** *About 4 miles west of Dunvegan village on B884 signed Glendale and Neist Point Lighthouse*
The House Over-By provides excellent accommodation in spacious split-level rooms - all of which are individually designed in harmony with the environment. Guests are served an outstanding Scottish cold breakfast, featuring fresh fruits, locally smoked meats and fish, and other regional produce, which can be taken in a bright room overlooking the sea loch. In the cottage-style Three Chimneys Restaurant visitors are enchanted by flavoursome cooking and unfussy treatment of prime Scottish ingredients.
**ROOMS:** 6 en suite (1 fmly) No smoking in all bedrooms s £130; d £160 (incl. cont bkfst) * LB **FACILITIES:** Xmas **PARKING:** 8 **NOTES:** No dogs (ex guide dogs) No smoking in restaurant Closed 7-24 Jan RS Sun **CARDS:**

## DUISDALEMORE

### ★★★70% Duisdale Country House
IV43 8QW
☎ 01471 833202 01471 833404
e-mail: marie@duisdalehotel.demon.co.uk
(For full entry see Isle Ornsay and advert on page 779)

## ISLE ORNSAY

### ★★★70% Duisdale Country House
IV43 8QW
☎ 01471 833202 01471 833404
e-mail: marie@duisdalehotel.demon.co.uk
***Dir:*** *on A851 Armadale to Broadford road, just north of the village of Isle Ornsay*
The Campbell family delight in welcoming guests to their charming country house. Standing in wooded grounds and gardens, the hotel enjoys superb views over the Sound of Sleat to the mainland hills beyond. There is a cosy library bar with a good range of

*continued on p776*

S

ISLE ORNSAY, continued

malts and well-filled bookshelves. The restaurant is the main focal point with the innovative culinary skills attracting much praise.

*Duisdale Country House, Isle Ornsay*

**ROOMS:** 17 en suite 2 annexe en suite (3 fmly) No smoking in all bedrooms s £65-£85; d £100-£140 (incl. bkfst) * **LB** **FACILITIES:** no TV in bdrms Fishing Croquet lawn Putting green Sea Fishing,Cycling **PARKING:** 20 **NOTES:** No dogs Closed Nov-Feb (Prebooking possible) Civ Wed 40 **CARDS:**

### ★★75% Kinloch Lodge

IV43 8QY
☎ 01471 833214 & 833333 01471 833277
e-mail: kinloch@dial.pipex.com
***Dir:*** *6m S of Broadford on A851, 10m N of Armadale on A851*

Set in a stunning location on the shores of Loch Na Dal, bedrooms at Kinloch Lodge are split between the main house and a newer building in the grounds. Many offer fine views of the loch and surrounding mountains. As the home of Lord and Lady MacDonald, family portraits are a feature of the two drawing rooms, warmed by roaring fires during the cooler months. Good use is made of the fine local produce available, Lady Claire overseeing dinner served in the elegant dining room. Service is both friendly and attentive.
**ROOMS:** 9 en suite 5 annexe en suite No smoking in all bedrooms s £40-£120; d £80-£190 (incl. bkfst) * **LB** **FACILITIES:** Fishing Cooking demonstrations Xmas **PARKING:** 18 **NOTES:** No smoking in restaurant Closed 22 Dec-28 Dec **CARDS:**

### ★★73% Hotel Eilean Iarmain

THE CIRCLE
Selected Individual Hotels
GREAT BRITAIN

IV43 8QR
☎ 01471 833332 01471 833275
e-mail: hotel@eilean-iarmain.co.uk
***Dir:*** *A851, A852, right to Isle Ornsay Harbour front*

This 19th-century island inn continues to provide traditional Highland hospitality and care from the friendly Gaelic staff. Bedrooms are comfortably traditional in style and four impressive new suites are now available in the converted stable block adjacent. Public areas include a wonderfully traditional timber clad pub, cosy sitting room, and a lovely candlelit restaurant which has recently been extended. The kitchen team earn much praise for their innovative modern style of cooking.

**ROOMS:** 6 en suite 10 annexe en suite (6 fmly) No smoking in 10 bedrooms s £90-£120; d £120-£200 (incl. bkfst) * **LB**
**FACILITIES:** Fishing Shooting Exibitions Whisky tasting entertainment ch fac Xmas **CONF:** Thtr 50 Class 30 Board 25 Del from £69 *
**PARKING:** 35 **NOTES:** No smoking in restaurant
**CARDS:**

*See advert on opposite page*

PORTREE — Map 13 NG44

### ★★★76% Cuillin Hills

IV51 9QU
☎ 01478 612003 01478 613092
e-mail: office@cuillinhills.demon.co.uk
***Dir:*** *turn right 0.25m N of Portree off the A855 and follow signs for hotel*

Improvements continue at this popular hotel overlooking the bay towards the Cuillin Mountains. There is a new elegant split level restaurant, where fine dining can be enjoyed; the comfortable bar offers more informal meals. The new bedrooms are most attractively finished, with plans to upgrade more bedrooms.
**ROOMS:** 21 en suite 9 annexe en suite (2 fmly) No smoking in 7 bedrooms s £35-£65; d £70-£180 (incl. bkfst) * **LB** **FACILITIES:** STV Xmas **CONF:** Thtr 100 Class 60 Board 30 Del from £80 *
**PARKING:** 56 **NOTES:** No smoking in restaurant
**CARDS:**

*See advert on opposite page*

### ★★73% Rosedale

Beaumont Crescent IV51 9DB
☎ 01478 613131 01478 612531
e-mail: michael@tianavaig.freeserve.co.uk
***Dir:*** *follow the directions to the Village Centre and Harbour, hotel is on the waterfront of Portree Harbourside*

The atmosphere is wonderfully warm at this delightful, family-run,

*continued*

waterfront hotel, which enjoys a lovely view over the bay. A labyrinth of stairs and corridors connect the comfortable lounge, well-stocked bar, coffee shop and wine bar. The charming restaurant serves a daily-changing set menu of carefully prepared specialities. Modern bedrooms offer a good range of amenities.

**ROOMS:** 20 en suite 3 annexe en suite (1 fmly) No smoking in all bedrooms s £35-£48; d £70-£102 (incl. bkfst) * **LB FACILITIES:** Xmas **PARKING:** 10 **NOTES:** No smoking in restaurant Closed Mid Nov- Mid Mar **CARDS:**

★★67% ***Royal***
IV51 9BU
☎ 01478 612525 01478 613198
e-mail: info@royal-hotel.demon.co.uk
***Dir:*** *turn off A850 on to A855, hotel is on corner overlooking the harbour*
This established hotel overlooks the picturesque harbour and has a well-equipped leisure centre. The bistro, lounge and bars are attractively decorated. In the high season, live entertainment is

*continued on p778*

PORTREE, continued

provided in the Ceilidh Room. Bedrooms offer a good standard of comfort.
**ROOMS:** 21 en suite No smoking in 14 bedrooms **FACILITIES:** Sauna Solarium Gym Jacuzzi entertainment **CONF:** Thtr 130 Board 40
**PARKING:** 14 **CARDS:**

SLEAT See Isle Ornsay Map 13 NG61

SOUTH QUEENSFERRY, City of Edinburgh

### ○ Innkeeper's Lodge South Queensferry

7 Newhalls Rd EH30 9TA
A new concept in the travel accommodation market. Smart rooms meet essential business requirements but also have home comforts. Dining options include all-day menus plus the added advantage of breakfast, which is included in the room price. Reservations can be made seven days a week through the room reservations number: 0870 243 0500. For further details, consult the Hotel Groups page.
**ROOMS:** 15 en suite **NOTES:** Open now

STIRLING, Stirling Map 11 NS79

### ★★★★66% Stirling Highland

Spittal St FK8 1DU
☎ 01786 272727 01786 272829
e-mail: stirling@paramount-hotels.co.uk
PARAMOUNT GROUP OF HOTELS
***Dir:*** *take A84 into Stirling and follow signs to Stirling Castle until you reach the Albert Hall. Turn left and left again, following signs to Castle*
Dating back to 1854 and once the town's High School, this impressive hotel is close to the famous castle. Guests can relax with a refreshment in the comfort of the Headmaster's Study before moving through to the elegant Scholars Restaurant to enjoy the innovative cuisine. The comfortably appointed bedrooms are well-equipped and maintained.
**ROOMS:** 94 en suite (4 fmly) No smoking in 56 bedrooms s £96-£110; d £122-£150 * **LB** **FACILITIES:** STV Indoor swimming (H) Squash Sauna Solarium Gym Jacuzzi Steam room Dance Studio Beauty therapist Xmas **CONF:** Thtr 100 Class 80 Board 45 Del from £120 *
**SERVICES:** Lift **PARKING:** 96 **NOTES:** No smoking in restaurant Civ Wed 100 **CARDS:**

### ★★69% Terraces

4 Melville Ter FK8 2ND
☎ 01786 472268 01786 450314
e-mail: sales@terraceshotel.com
Best Western
***Dir:*** *from A872 1st left at 2nd rdbt. At lights onto Melville Terrace (inside lane) parallel to main rd on left. Hotel at bottom*
Situated in the centre of town this popular hotel, an elegant Georgian building, provides a welcoming atmosphere to its business and leisure customers. Public areas include a well-stocked bar and a restaurant. Though of varying sizes, the bedrooms are comfortably modern in style and offer a wide range of amenities.
**ROOMS:** 17 en suite (3 fmly) No smoking in 2 bedrooms s £56-£72; d £83-£90 (incl. bkfst) * **LB** **FACILITIES:** STV Xmas **CONF:** Thtr 120 Class 60 Board 48 Del from £65 * **PARKING:** 27 **NOTES:** No smoking in restaurant Civ Wed 120 **CARDS:**

### ⌂ *Travelodge*

Pirnhall Roundabout, Snabhead FK7 8EU
☎ 08700 850950 01525 878450
Travelodge
***Dir:*** *junct M9/M80*
Travelodge offers good quality, good value, modern accommodation. Ideal for families, the spacious, en suite bedrooms include remote-control TV, tea and coffee-making facilities, luxury beds and free morning newspaper. Meals can be taken at the nearby family restaurant. For further details and the Travelodge phone number, consult the Hotel Groups page.

**ROOMS:** 37 en suite

### ⌂ Express by Holiday Inn Stirling

Springkerse Business Park FK7 7XH
☎ 01786 449922 01786 449932
e-mail: info@hiex-stirling.com
Express by Holiday Inn
***Dir:*** *M9/M80 jct 9. Take A91 Stirling/St Andrews exit. Keep on rd for 2.8m. Hotel located on 4th rdbt. Take 2nd exit to sports stadium & then 3rd to hotel*

A modern budget hotel offering comfortable accommodation in refreshing, spacious and comprehensively equipped bedrooms, en suite bathrooms with power showers and continental buffet breakfast included in the room rate. Suitable for business travellers or families. For further details and the Express by Holiday Inn phone number, consult the Hotel Groups page.
**ROOMS:** 80 en suite (incl. cont bkfst) s £55; d £55 * **CONF:** Thtr 35 Class 18 Board 16 Del £67 *

STONEHAVEN, Aberdeenshire Map 15 NO88

### ★★66% County Hotel & Leisure Club

Arduthie Rd AB39 2EH
☎ 01569 764386 01569 762214
***Dir:*** *off A90, opposite railway station*
A popular squash club is a feature of this family-run hotel on the outskirts of town, close to the railway station. Meals are served in a choice of dining rooms, one of which displays a fascinating collection of photographs and posters of old theatre, music hall and Hollywood stars.
**ROOMS:** 14 en suite (1 fmly) s £46; d £60 (incl. bkfst) * **LB**
**FACILITIES:** Squash Sauna Gym Table tennis **CONF:** Thtr 150 Class 60 Board 32 **PARKING:** 40 **NOTES:** No dogs (ex guide dogs) Civ Wed 180
**CARDS:**

Early start? Hotels at all star levels should provide in-room alarm clocks and/or alarm calls.

Popped the question? Hotels with Civ Wed in their entry are licensed for civil wedding ceremonies. Maximum numbers for the ceremony only are shown, e.g. Civ Wed 120

STORNOWAY See Lewis, Isle of

## STRACHUR, Argyll & Bute Map 10 NN00

### ★★★68% Creggans Inn

PA27 8BX
☎ 01369 860279 01369 860637
e-mail: info@creggans-inn.co.uk
***Dir:*** *follow A82/A83 Loch Lomond road to Arrochar. Continue on A83 then take A815 Strachur*

This well-established roadside hotel on the shore of Loch Fyne is now under enthusiastic new ownership for the first time in over 45 years. Many improvements have been made, including a refurbished dining room, increased lounge areas and several bedrooms and bathrooms have been enhanced. The bar continues to attract good levels of business and is popular for light meals.
**ROOMS:** 14 en suite s £105-£165; d £146-£206 (incl. bkfst & dinner) * **LB** **FACILITIES:** Fishing ch fac Xmas **CONF:** Thtr 25 Class 25 Board 25 Del from £130 * **PARKING:** 50 **NOTES:** No dogs (ex guide dogs) No smoking in restaurant **CARDS:**

## STRANRAER, Dumfries & Galloway Map 10 NX06

### ★★★★68% North West Castle

DG9 8EH
☎ 01776 704413 01776 702646
e-mail: info@northwestcastle.co.uk
***Dir:*** *on seafront, close to Stena ferry terminal*

This popular hotel overlooks the bay and ferry terminal. Public areas include an elegant dining room where a pianist plays during dinner, and an adjoining lounge with large leather armchairs and blazing fire in season. Bedrooms are well-equipped and many are very spacious.
**ROOMS:** 70 en suite 3 annexe en suite (22 fmly) s £55-£77; d £80-£109 (incl. bkfst) * **LB** **FACILITIES:** STV Indoor swimming (H) Snooker Sauna Solarium Gym Jacuzzi Curling (Oct-Apr) Games room Xmas **CONF:** Thtr 150 Class 60 Board 40 Del from £60 * **SERVICES:** Lift **PARKING:** 100 **NOTES:** No dogs (ex guide dogs) No smoking in restaurant Civ Wed 120 **CARDS:**

Arriving late? Four and five star hotels have night porters to assist with your luggage, and 24-hour room service.

Late for dinner? Quality Standards star rating means that last orders for dinner should be no earlier than:
★ 6.30pm ★★ 7.00pm ★★★ 8.00pm
★★★★ 9.00pm ★★★★★ 10.00pm

STRANRAER, continued

**★★★69% Corsewall Lighthouse Hotel**
Corsewall Point, Kirkcolm DG9 0QG
☎ 01776 853220 01776 854231
e-mail: corsewall_lighthouse@msn.com
***Dir:*** *B718 from Stranraer to Kirkcolm (approx 8m) then follow signs to Corsewall Lighthouse Hotel for a further 4m*

This listed 19th-century lighthouse is situated at the northern tip of the Rhinns of Galloway. There are a variety of styles of attractively furnished and well-equipped bedrooms, with some suites within the 20 acres of grounds. Public areas are cosy and atmospheric, and the dining room provides enjoyable locally sourced produce.
**ROOMS:** 6 en suite 3 annexe en suite (2 fmly) No smoking in 6 bedrooms s £95-£220; d £120-£260 (incl. bkfst & dinner) * **LB** **FACILITIES:** ch fac **CONF:** Thtr 20 Del from £150 * **PARKING:** 20 **NOTES:** No smoking in restaurant **CARDS:**

STRATHAVEN, South Lanarkshire Map 11 NS74

**★★★70% Strathaven**
Hamilton Rd ML10 6SZ
☎ 01357 521778 01357 520789
e-mail: info@strathavenhotel.com
This Robert Adam designed mansion house on the outskirts of town is a popular venue for functions. A wing of smart new bedrooms has been added, and all are well-equipped. Public areas include a comfortable lounge, dining room and attractive bar/lounge.
**ROOMS:** 22 en suite No smoking in 12 bedrooms s £69; d £85 (incl. bkfst) * **LB** **FACILITIES:** STV Xmas **CONF:** Thtr 180 Class 120 Board 40 Del from £84 * **PARKING:** 80 **NOTES:** No dogs (ex guide dogs) No smoking in restaurant Civ Wed 110 **CARDS:**

STRATHBLANE, Stirling

**○ The Strathblane Country House Hotel**
Milngavie Rd G63 9EH
☎ 01360 770491 01360 770345
At the time of going to press, the star classification for this hotel was not confirmed. Please refer to the AA internet site www.theAA.com for current information.

Popped the question? Hotels with Civ Wed in their entry are licensed for civil wedding ceremonies. Maximum numbers for the ceremony only are shown, e.g. Civ Wed 120

STRATHYRE, Stirling Map 11 NN51

**Premier Collection**

**★ *Creagan House***
FK18 8ND
☎ 01877 384638 01877 384319
e-mail: mail@creaganhouse.fsnet.co.uk
***Dir:*** *0.25m N of Strathyre on A84*
A cosy hotel with a friendly atmosphere. Forest walks within the Queen Elizabeth Park back this restored 17th-century farmhouse. The attractive bedrooms are thoughtfully equipped to include excellent CD/radio sets; TVs are available on request. The little lounge is inviting and refreshments are served here before and after an enjoyable meal in the impressive baronial-style dining room. Cuisine is bold, imaginative, and the two different menus are very tempting.
**ROOMS:** 5 en suite (1 fmly) No smoking in all bedrooms **CONF:** Thtr 35 Class 12 Board 35 **PARKING:** 26 **NOTES:** No smoking in restaurant Closed 28 Jan-2 Mar **CARDS:**

STRONTIAN, Highland Map 14 NM86

**★★80% Kilcamb Lodge**
PH36 4HY
☎ 01967 402257 01967 402041
e-mail: kilcamblodge@aol.com
***Dir:*** *off A861*
This sympathetically modernised former hunting lodge with loch views offers open fires, deep cushioned sofas, flowers, books and magazines in the elegant public rooms. The delightfully furnished bedrooms are thoughtfully equipped with items such as bathrobes. A short choice of well-prepared dishes is complemented by a carefully selected wine list.
**ROOMS:** 11 en suite (1 fmly) No smoking in all bedrooms s £60-£100; d £80-£130 * **LB** **FACILITIES:** Fishing Fishing rod hire Moorings ch fac Xmas **CONF:** Class 30 Board 20 **PARKING:** 20 **NOTES:** No smoking in restaurant Closed Dec-Feb (ex New Year) **CARDS:**

TAIN, Highland Map 14 NH78

**★★★75% Mansfield House**
Scotsburn Rd IV19 1PR
☎ 01862 892052 01862 892260
e-mail: mansfield@cali.co.uk
***Dir:*** *A9 from S, ignore 1st exit signed Tain and take the 2nd exit signed police station*
An impressive mansion house, in grounds opposite the Royal Academy. Inviting public areas include a comfortable bar and formal dining rooms. Innovative dishes are found on the fixed-

*continued*

priced daily dinner menu and the bar menu. Bedrooms range from tastefully appointed de luxe rooms, furnished in period style, to pleasantly redecorated rooms in the wing.

**ROOMS:** 9 en suite 10 annexe en suite (7 fmly) No smoking in 4 bedrooms s £65-£85; d £90-£170 (incl. bkfst) * LB **FACILITIES:** Croquet lawn Putting green Jacuzzi Beauty salon ch fac Xmas **CONF:** Thtr 40 Class 20 Board 20 Del from £85 * **PARKING:** 100 **NOTES:** No smoking in restaurant Civ Wed 70 **CARDS:**

### ★★★72% Morangie House

Morangie Rd IV19 1PY
☎ 01862 892281 🖹 01862 892872
e-mail: wynne@morangiehotel.com
*Dir: turn right off A9 northwards*

This welcoming family-run hotel gives fine views of the Dornoch Firth. Attractive bedrooms in the newer wing are comfortably modern whilst those in the main house are more traditional; all are well-equipped with useful accessories. An extensive range of dishes is available in the formal dining room and smart Garden Restaurant.
**ROOMS:** 26 en suite (1 fmly) No smoking in 4 bedrooms s £65-£75; d £90-£100 (incl. bkfst) * LB **FACILITIES:** STV ch fac **CONF:** Thtr 40 Class 40 Board 24 Del from £75 * **PARKING:** 40 **CARDS:**

### ★★80% Glenmorangie House

Cadboll, Fearn IV20 1XP
☎ 01862 871671 🖹 01862 871625
e-mail: relax@glenmorangieplc.co.uk
*Dir: from A9 turn onto B9175 towards Nigg and follow signs*
Owned by the famous whisky distillers, this highly individual hotel provides the very best in Highland hospitality. Peacefully located in beautiful grounds, with views over the Moray Firth, bedrooms are found both in the main house and in converted farm cottages. Prices include afternoon tea, a home-cooked four course dinner (served at a communal table) and wines chosen to complement the dishes. Don't retire without sampling a dram or two!
**ROOMS:** 6 en suite 3 annexe en suite (4 fmly) No smoking in all bedrooms s £110-£185; d £220-£370 (incl. bkfst & dinner) * LB **FACILITIES:** Fishing Croquet lawn entertainment ch fac Xmas **CONF:** Thtr 20 Class 20 Board 20 Del from £110 * **PARKING:** 20 **NOTES:** No smoking in restaurant **CARDS:**

## TANGASDALE See Barra, Isle of

## TARBERT, Argyll & Bute

### ○ Victoria

Barmore Rd PA29 6TW
☎ 01880 820236
At the time of going to press, the star classification for this hotel was not confirmed. Please refer to the AA internet site www.theAA.com for current information.

## TARBERT LOCH FYNE, Argyll & Bute Map 10 NR86

### ★★★71% Stonefield Castle

PA29 6YJ
☎ 01880 820836 🖹 01880 820929
e-mail: enquiries@stonefieldcastle.co.uk
*Dir: Off A83, 2m N of Tarbert, hotel approx 0.25 mile down driveway*
An impressive baronial mansion, set in 60 acres of splendid wooded gardens. Ornate ceilings, marble fireplaces and old family portraits add interest to the delightful day rooms, which include a choice of lounges, a bar, and a spacious restaurant, overlooking Loch Fyne. Most bedrooms are in a modern wing and are contemporary in style.
**ROOMS:** 33 en suite (1 fmly) s £82-£90; d £82-£90 (incl. bkfst & dinner) * LB **FACILITIES:** STV Fishing Snooker Xmas **CONF:** Thtr 150 Class 100 Board 60 Del £110 * **SERVICES:** Lift **PARKING:** 50 **NOTES:** No smoking in restaurant Civ Wed 50 **CARDS:**

### ★★70% The Columba Hotel

East Pier Rd PA29 6UF
☎ 01880 820808 🖹 01880 820808
e-mail: columbahotel@fsbdial.co.uk
*Dir: turn off A83 into Tarbert village. Keep loch on left, hotel in 0.5m*

This delightful Victorian hotel overlooks the harbour approach and Loch Fyne. The comfortable, traditional style bedrooms range from well-proportioned superior rooms to smaller, standard accommodation. The bar, with log fire, is full of character reflecting the heritage of the village. The elegant restaurant serves enjoyable, French-influenced, Scottish fare.
**ROOMS:** 10 en suite (3 fmly) s £37-£50; d £74-£90 (incl. bkfst) * LB **FACILITIES:** Sauna ch fac **CONF:** Thtr 30 Class 30 Board 18 Del from £70 * **PARKING:** 10 **NOTES:** No smoking in restaurant Closed 24-26 Dec **CARDS:**

TAYNUILT, Argyll & Bute Map 10 NN03

**★★60% Polfearn**
PA35 1JQ
☎ 01866 822251 01866 822251
***Dir:** turn N off A85, continue 1.5m through village down to Loch Shore*

A relaxed and friendly atmosphere prevails at this homely family-run hotel which overlooks Loch Etive. Public areas include a well-stocked bar with open fire and separate dining room. A good range of home cooked food is available in both areas. Bedrooms vary in size and in style.
**ROOMS:** 14 en suite (2 fmly) s £20-£35; d £40-£70 (incl. bkfst) * **LB**
**FACILITIES:** Fishing Boating Xmas **PARKING:** 21 **NOTES:** No smoking in restaurant RS end of January **CARDS:**

THORNHILL, Dumfries & Galloway Map 11 NX89

**★★74% Trigony House**
Closeburn DG3 5EZ
☎ 01848 331211 01848 331303
***Dir:** off A76 between Thornhill & Closeburn on the left hand side, clearly signed*

A friendly and relaxed atmosphere prevails at this Edwardian hunting lodge, set in four acres of gardens and grounds south of the village. Meals, which can be had either in the cosy bar or comfortable dining room, feature all fresh produce, organically grown when available. Bedrooms come in a variety of sizes, some are quite spacious.
**ROOMS:** 8 en suite s £40-£45; d £80 (incl. bkfst) * **LB**
**FACILITIES:** Fishing **CONF:** Thtr 30 Class 30 Board 30 **PARKING:** 20
**NOTES:** No smoking in restaurant **CARDS:**

Late for dinner? Quality Standards star rating means that last orders for dinner should be no earlier than:
★ 6.30pm ★★ 7.00pm ★★★ 8.00pm
★★★★ 9.00pm ★★★★★ 10.00pm

THURSO, Highland Map 15 ND16
see also Halkirk

**★★★63% Royal**
Traill St KW14 8EH
☎ 01847 893191 01847 895338
e-mail: royal@british-trust-hotels.com
***Dir:** Follow the A9 to Thurso, cross Thurso Bridge and at 1st set of traffic lights turn right. Hotel on right*

Set in the town centre, this traditional hotel attracts a mixed market including tours. It has been completely refurbished inside, offering comfortable lounges and a trendy bar appealing to business residents.
**ROOMS:** 102 en suite (4 fmly) s £30-£40; d £60-£70 (incl. bkfst) * **LB**
**FACILITIES:** entertainment ch fac **SERVICES:** Lift **NOTES:** No dogs (ex guide dogs) No smoking in restaurant **CARDS:**

**★★63% Ulbster Arms**
Bridge St KW12 6XY
☎ 01847 831206 & 831641 01847 831206
e-mail: ulbster-arms@ecosse.net
(For full entry see Halkirk)

TIGHNABRUAICH, Argyll & Bute Map 10 NR97

**★★73% *Royal Hotel***
Shore Rd PA21 2BE
☎ 01700 811239 01700 811300
e-mail: royalhotel@btinternet.com
***Dir:** from Stachur on A886 turn right onto the A8003 to Tighnabruaich. Hotel is located on the right at the bottom of the hill, at the 'T' junct*
Enthusiastic new owners have transformed this established hotel overlooking the Kyles of Bute. All the refurbished non smoking bedrooms have pleasing colour schemes and are comfortably furnished in traditional style. Public areas include contrasting bars, one has a popular Brasserie providing informal food. Two other dining areas feature seafood and game.
**ROOMS:** 11 en suite (1 fmly) No smoking in all bedrooms **CONF:** Class 20 Board 10 **PARKING:** 20 **NOTES:** No smoking in restaurant Closed 25-26 Dec **CARDS:**

TOBERMORY See Mull, Isle of

TOMINTOUL, Moray Map 15 NJ11

**★★★68% The Gordon Hotel & Cromdales Restaurant**
The Square AB37 9ET
☎ 01807 580206 01807 580488
e-mail: gordon@bestwestern.co.uk
***Dir:** Exit A9 at Aviemore, A95 to Grantown on Spey, A939 to Tomintoul, hotel on villiage square*
A popular base for tour groups and private holidaymakers, this

continued

friendly hotel overlooks the Village Square. Public areas are well-presented and include a choice of contrasting bars and dining rooms. Bedrooms are bright and airy with comfortable modern furnishings and a good range of accessories.

**ROOMS:** 29 en suite (2 fmly) s £30; d £60 (incl. bkfst) * **FACILITIES:** Fishing **CONF:** Thtr 100 Class 100 Board 12 Del from £75 * **PARKING:** 14 **NOTES:** No smoking in restaurant Closed 2 Nov-31 Mar **CARDS:**

## TONGUE, Highland

Map 14 NC55

### ★★71% Ben Loyal

Main St IV27 4XE
☎ 01847 611216 01847 611212
e-mail: Thebenloyalhotel@btinternet.com

***Dir:*** *Tongue lies at the intersection of the A838/A836, hotel is in the centre of village, nextdoor to The Royal Bank of Scotland*

This friendly and informal hotel enjoys a splendid view of the Kyle of Tongue and ruins of Varrich Castle. Bedrooms are smartly furnished in pine, whilst both the comfortable lounge and adjoining dining room take full advantage of the views. The latter offers a five course dinner menu featuring freshly prepared dishes using local produce, with lobsters and oysters when available.

**ROOMS:** 11 en suite s £38-£40; d £76-£80 (incl. bkfst) * **LB** **FACILITIES:** Fishing Fly fishing tuition entertainment ch fac **PARKING:** 20 **NOTES:** No smoking in restaurant Closed 25-26 Dec & 1-3 Jan RS Nov-Mar **CARDS:**

## TORRIDON, Highland

Map 14 NG95

**Premier Collection**

### ★★★ Loch Torridon Country House Hotel

IV22 2EY
☎ 01445 791242 01445 791296
e-mail: stay@lochtorridonhotel.com

***Dir:*** *from A832 at Kinlochewe, take the A896 towards Torridon, do not turn into village carry on for 1m, hotel is on right*

This fine hotel is set amidst spectacular scenery overlooking the loch. Bedrooms are generally spacious and comfortable; they are attractively furnished and have smart modern bathrooms. The welcoming lounges boast log fires, and there is a wood panelled bar with 250 malt whiskies available. The

*continued*

restaurant offers a good standard of food which makes full use of the home grown produce.

**ROOMS:** 20 en suite (1 fmly) No smoking in all bedrooms s £90-£245; d £120-£260 (incl. bkfst) * **LB** **FACILITIES:** STV Fishing Croquet lawn Pony trekking, Mountain biking, Archery,clay pigeon shooting,archery ch fac Xmas **CONF:** Board 15 Del from £110 * **SERVICES:** Lift **PARKING:** 30 **NOTES:** No smoking in restaurant Civ Wed 38 **CARDS:**

## TROON, South Ayrshire

Map 10 NS33

### ★★★★62% Marine

PARAMOUNT GROUP OF HOTELS

Crosbie Rd KA10 6HE
☎ 01292 314444 01292 316922
e-mail: marine@paramount-hotels.co.uk

***Dir:*** *from A77 to A78, then A79 onto B749. Hotel on left past the Municipal Golf Course*

In a fine location overlooking Royal Troon's 18th fairway, this hotel enjoys panoramic views of the Firth of Clyde across to the Isle of Arran. The choice of restaurants includes Rizzios and the more formal Fairways restaurant, which is open for dinner only. Bedrooms range from spacious suites to cosy standard rooms, and the well-presented staff provide a high level of service.

**ROOMS:** 74 en suite (7 fmly) No smoking in 12 bedrooms s £96-£120; d £160-£250 * **LB** **FACILITIES:** STV Indoor swimming (H) Squash Sauna Solarium Gym Putting green Jacuzzi Steam room Beauty room entertainment ch fac Xmas **CONF:** Thtr 220 Class 120 Board 60 Del from £120 * **SERVICES:** Lift **PARKING:** 200 **NOTES:** No smoking in restaurant Civ Wed 50 **CARDS:**

**Premier Collection**

### ★★★ Lochgreen House

Monktonhill Rd, Southwood KA10 7EN
☎ 01292 313343 01292 318661
e-mail: lochgreen@costley-hotels.co.uk

***Dir:*** *from A77 follow signs for Prestwick airport, 0.5m before airport take B749 to Troon. Hotel 1m on left*

Enjoying a peaceful location, this impressive hotel continues to set both regional and national standards of hospitality. The luxurious day rooms provide enough space and character to always find a corner in which to snuggle, and open fires add to the overall sense of comfort and relaxation. Well-equipped, stylish bedrooms boast a range of thoughtful extras. Local produce is handled skilfully to ensure a creative gastronomic

*continued on p784*

T

TROON, continued

experience. Staff throughout are delightful and very willing to assist.

*Lochgreen House, Troon*

**ROOMS:** 7 en suite 8 annexe en suite **FACILITIES:** Tennis (hard) Xmas **CONF:** Thtr 40 Class 16 Board 16 Del from £145 * **PARKING:** 50 **NOTES:** No dogs (ex guide dogs) No smoking in restaurant Civ Wed 40 **CARDS:**

### ★★★75% Highgrove House

Old Loans Rd KA10 7HL
☎ 01292 312511 01292 318228

This stylish hotel enjoys magnificent panoramic views over the Firth of Clyde, and a friendly and efficient team welcomes guests. The attractive split-level restaurant provides the ideal setting for impressively presented contemporary cooking. Booking is almost essential to ensure a seat in either the restaurant or the bar. Bedrooms are well equipped and smartly presented.
**ROOMS:** 9 en suite (2 fmly) **PARKING:** 50 **NOTES:** No dogs (ex guide dogs) **CARDS:**

### ★★★74% Piersland House

Craigend Rd KA10 6HD
☎ 01292 314747 01292 315613
e-mail: reservations@piersland.co.uk
***Dir:*** *just off A77 on the B749 opposite Royal Troon Golf Club*

Close to the championship golf course, this hotel has been extended over the years. Public rooms feature delightful oak panelling and large open fires. The lounge bar offers an extensive menu, while fine dinners are par for the course in the elegant restaurant. Residents can choose from three styles of bedroom, cottage suites, large superior rooms, or smaller standard rooms.
**ROOMS:** 15 en suite 13 annexe en suite (2 fmly) s £83-£90; d £119-£165 (incl. bkfst) * **LB** **FACILITIES:** STV Croquet lawn Xmas **CONF:** Thtr 100 Class 60 Board 30 Del from £90 * **PARKING:** 150 **NOTES:** No smoking in restaurant Civ Wed 75 **CARDS:**

## TURNBERRY, South Ayrshire — Map 10 NS20

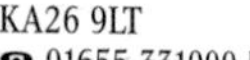

### ★★★★★74% Westin Turnberry Resort

KA26 9LT
☎ 01655 331000 01655 331706
e-mail: turnberry@westin.com
***Dir:*** *from Glasgow take the A77/M77 S towards Stranraer, 2m past Kirkoswald, follow signs for A719 Turnberry Village, hotel 500m on right*

This famous hotel enjoys magnificent views over to Arran, Ailsa Craig and the Mull of Kintyre. Facilities include a world-renowned golf course, the excellent Colin Montgomerie Golf Academy, a luxurious spa and a host of outdoor and country pursuits. Elegant bedrooms and suites are located in the main hotel, whilst the

continued

adjacent lodges provide spacious, well-equipped accommodation. Apart from the elegant, classical main restaurant, there is a Mediterranean Terrace Brasserie, or the relaxed Clubhouse.
**ROOMS:** 132 en suite 89 annexe en suite (9 fmly) No smoking in 57 bedrooms s £265-£315; d £305-£425 (incl. bkfst) * **LB** **FACILITIES:** **Spa** STV Indoor swimming (H) Golf 18 Tennis (hard) Fishing Squash Riding Snooker Sauna Solarium Gym Putting green Jacuzzi Health Spa & Leisure Club Activity Centre entertainment Xmas **CONF:** Thtr 290 Class 120 Board 90 **SERVICES:** Lift **PARKING:** 200 **CARDS:**

### ★★★77% Malin Court

KA26 9PB
☎ 01655 331457 01655 331072
e-mail: info@malincourt.co.uk
***Dir:*** *on A74 take Ayr exit. From Ayr A719 to Turnberry and Maidens*

This comfortable hotel enjoys lovely views over the Firth of Clyde and Turnberry golf courses. Public areas include a choice of lounges, plus a cocktail lounge adjoining the attractive restaurant, which serves light lunches and formal dinners. Standard and executive rooms are available, all equipped well.
**ROOMS:** 18 en suite (9 fmly) s £72-£82; d £104-£124 (incl. bkfst) * **LB** **FACILITIES:** STV Tennis (grass) Putting green Pitch & putt ch fac Xmas **CONF:** Thtr 200 Class 60 Board 30 Del from £65.50 * **SERVICES:** Lift **PARKING:** 110 **NOTES:** Civ Wed 120 **CARDS:**

*See advert on opposite page*

## TYNDRUM, Stirling — Map 10 NN33

### ★62% Invervey

FK20 8RY
☎ 01838 400219 01838 400 280
e-mail: info@inverveyhotel.co.uk
***Dir:*** *In the centre of Tyndrum beside the road, A82/85*

This wonderfully relaxing hotel, beside lock five on the Crinan Canal, boasts comfortable lounges, a bar area and a delightful patio where many guests dine informally. The menu offered in the attractive, formal restaurant features traditional Scottish dishes.
**ROOMS:** 21 rms (18 en suite) (3 fmly) s £25; d £50 (incl. bkfst) * **LB** **FACILITIES:** STV Games room Pool table entertainment Xmas **PARKING:** 50 **NOTES:** RS Nov-Apr **CARDS:**

## UNST See Shetland

## UPHALL, West Lothian — Map 11 NT07

### ★★★★67% Houstoun House

EH52 6JS
☎ 01506 853831 01506 854220
e-mail: info@houstoun.macdonaldhotels.co.uk
***Dir:*** *from M8 junct 3 follow signs for Broxburn, go straight over rdbt then at mini-rdbt turn right heading for Uphall, hotel is 1m on right*

An impressive 17th-century tower house set in 20 acres of

continued

grounds. Tastefully extended, it has a smart Country Club with stylish Italian bistro. In the original house, a stone staircase leads from the vaulted cocktail bar to three elegant dining areas. It's worth choosing one of the impressive executive bedrooms.

**ROOMS:** 25 en suite 47 annexe en suite (30 fmly) No smoking in 63 bedrooms **FACILITIES:** STV Indoor swimming (H) Sauna Solarium Gym Steam room Dance studio Beauty therapy room **CONF:** Thtr 350 Class 120 Board 70 **PARKING:** 200 **NOTES:** No dogs (ex guide dogs) No smoking in restaurant **CARDS:**

UPLAWMOOR, East Renfrewshire    Map 11 NS45

### ★★71% Uplawmoor Hotel

THE CIRCLE
Selected Individual Hotels
GREAT BRITAIN

Neilston Rd G78 4AF
☎ 01505 850565 01505 850689
e-mail: enquiries@uplawmoor.co.uk
***Dir:*** *exit at junct 2 of M77, take A736 signposted to Barrhead and Irvine. Hotel located 4m beyond Barrhead*

Set in a village off the Glasgow to Irvine road, this friendly hotel has a restaurant featuring imaginative dishes. There is a cocktail lounge adjacent, and a separate lounge bar serving food. The modern bedrooms are comfortable and well-equipped.
**ROOMS:** 14 en suite (1 fmly) No smoking in 3 bedrooms s £35-£49; d £55-£75 (incl. bkfst) * **FACILITIES:** STV **CONF:** Thtr 40 Class 12 Board 12 Del from £65 * **PARKING:** 40 **NOTES:** No dogs **CARDS:**

*See advert under GLASGOW*

WHITBURN, West Lothian    Map 11 NS96

### ★★★65% The Hilcroft

Best Western

East Main St EH47 0JU
☎ 01501 740818 01501 744013
e-mail: hilcroft@bestwestern.co.uk
***Dir:*** *M8 junct 4 follow signs for Whitburn, hotel 0.5m on left from junct*
Within easy reach of the motorway, this popular business hotel has bright cheerful public areas with food served all day in the split-level bar and Bistro restaurant. All bedrooms are well-equipped, but it is worth asking for one of the excellent executive rooms.
**ROOMS:** 31 en suite (7 fmly) No smoking in 17 bedrooms s £57-£60; d £70-£75 (incl. bkfst) * **LB** **FACILITIES:** STV Free use of Balbardie

*continued*



Sports Centre ch fac Xmas **CONF:** Thtr 200 Class 50 Board 30 Del from £58 * **PARKING:** 80 **NOTES:** No dogs (ex guide dogs) Civ Wed 200 **CARDS:**

WHITEBRIDGE, Highland    Map 14 NH41

### ★★66% Whitebridge

IV2 6UN
☎ 01456 486226 & 486272 01456 486413
e-mail: whitebridgehotel@southlochness.demon.co.uk
***Dir:*** *turn off A9 onto B851, follow signs to Fort Augustus*
A relaxed and informal atmosphere is offered at this long-established hotel. Bedrooms are varied in size and style. There is a relaxing lounge, a choice of bars, and a smart dining room serving enjoyable home-cooked fare.
**ROOMS:** 12 rms (10 en suite) (3 fmly) s £30; d £50 (incl. bkfst) * **LB** **FACILITIES:** Fishing **CONF:** Class 30 Board 25 **PARKING:** 32 **NOTES:** No smoking in restaurant Closed 21 Dec-Feb **CARDS:**

WICK, Highland    Map 15 ND35

### ★★67% Mackay's

Best Western

Union St KW1 5ED
☎ 01955 602323 01955 605930
e-mail: mackays.hotel@caithness_mm.co.uk
***Dir:*** *opposite Caithness General Hospital*
This well-established family-run hotel, standing on the south shore of the River Wick and close to the town centre, offers friendly and informal service. Many guests choose to eat in Ebenezers bar.
**ROOMS:** 27 rms (19 en suite) (4 fmly) **FACILITIES:** STV entertainment **CONF:** Thtr 100 Class 100 Board 60 **SERVICES:** Lift **NOTES:** No smoking in restaurant Closed 1-2 Jan **CARDS:**

# Hotel of the Year, Wales

## Ynyshir Hall,

Eglwysfach

ABERCRAF, Powys Map 03 SN81

**★★75% *Maes-Y-Gwernen***
School Rd SA9 1XD
☎ 01639 730218 📠 01639 730765
e-mail: maesyg@globalnet.co.uk
Situated on the edge of the Brecon Beacons, this hotel is surrounded by gardens and lawns that contain two chalet rooms and a building with gym equipment, sun bed and spa bath. Bedrooms are tastefully appointed and well-equipped. Rooms with balconies and four-poster beds are available. An extensive menu is served in the spacious restaurant, and there is an attractive conservatory and lounge.
**ROOMS:** 10 en suite No smoking in 1 bedroom **FACILITIES:** STV Sauna Solarium Gym Jacuzzi ch fac **PARKING:** 20 **NOTES:** No smoking in restaurant **CARDS:**

ABERDYFI, Gwynedd Map 06 SN69

**★★★71% Trefeddian**
LL35 0SB
☎ 01654 767213 📠 01654 767777
e-mail: tref@saqnet.co.uk
***Dir:*** *0.5m N of Aberdyfi off A493*
A holiday hotel overlooking the local golf course, surrounded by grounds and gardens. It provides sound modern accommodation with well-equipped bedrooms and bathrooms, plus some new luxury rooms with balconies and sea views. Public areas include elegantly furnished lounges, indoor swimming pool and pitch-and-putt golf green. Children are welcome and recreation areas are provided.
**ROOMS:** 59 en suite (13 fmly) No smoking in all bedrooms s £56-£72; d £116-£138 (incl. bkfst) * **LB FACILITIES:** Indoor swimming (H) Tennis (hard) Snooker Solarium Putting green Table tennis Play area,pool ch fac Xmas **CONF:** Class 25 Del from £65 * **SERVICES:** Lift

**PARKING:** 68 **NOTES:** No smoking in restaurant
**CARDS:**

*See advert on this page*

**★★74% Penhelig Arms Hotel & Restaurant**
LL35 0LT
☎ 01654 767215 📠 01654 767690
e-mail: penheligarms@saqnet.co.uk
***Dir:*** *take A493 coastal road, hotel faces Penhelig harbour*
Situated opposite the old harbour, this delightful 18th-century hotel overlooks the Dyfi Estuary and mountains beyond. The well-maintained bedrooms have very good quality furnishings and

*continued on p788*

ABERDYFI, continued

modern facilities. Four new luxurious bedrooms have recently been created in "Bodhelig", an adjacent cliff top development. The public bar retains its original character and is much loved by locals who enjoy the bar food, particularly the seafood, and real ale selections.
**ROOMS:** 10 en suite 4 annexe en suite (4 fmly) No smoking in all bedrooms s £57-£62; d £108-£122 (incl. bkfst & dinner) * LB
**FACILITIES:** ch fac **PARKING:** 12 **NOTES:** No smoking in restaurant Closed 25 & 26 Dec **CARDS:**

## ABERGAVENNY, Monmouthshire — Map 03 SO21

### ★★★67% Allt-yr-Ynys Country House Hotel
HR2 0DU
☎ 01873 890307 01873 890539
e-mail: allthotel@compuserve.com
***Dir:*** *take A465 N of Abergavenny. After 5m turn left at Old Pandy Inn in Pandy. After 300 yds turn right and hotel is 300yds on the right*

This lovely house dates back to around 1550 and Elizabeth I is reputed to have been a guest here. Most of the modern equipped bedrooms are located in separate single storey stone buildings. Public rooms, which include a comfortable lounge with an ornate ceiling, are contained within the main house.
**ROOMS:** 1 en suite 18 annexe en suite (2 fmly) No smoking in 6 bedrooms s £55-£97.50; d £95-£160 (incl. bkfst) * LB **FACILITIES:** Spa Indoor swimming (H) Fishing Sauna Jacuzzi Clay pigeon range ch fac Xmas **CONF:** Thtr 100 Class 30 Board 40 Del from £90 *
**PARKING:** 100 **NOTES:** No smoking in restaurant Civ Wed 80
**CARDS:**

### ★★★66% *Llansantffraed Court*
Llanvihangel Gobion NP7 9BA
☎ 01873 840678 01873 840674
e-mail: reception@llch.co.uk
***Dir:*** *at A465/A40 Abergavenny intersection take B4598 signposted to Usk (do not join A40). Continue towards Raglan and hotel on left after 4.5m*

In a commanding position and in its own grounds this red brick country hotel has enviable views of the Brecon Beacons. Extensive public areas are complemented by a spacious restaurant. Bedrooms are comfortably furnished with modern facilities.
**ROOMS:** 21 en suite (3 fmly) No smoking in 7 bedrooms
**FACILITIES:** STV Fishing Croquet lawn Putting green Ornamental trout lake **CONF:** Thtr 220 Class 120 Board 100 **SERVICES:** Lift
**PARKING:** 250 **NOTES:** No smoking in restaurant Civ Wed 150
**CARDS:**

### ★★70% Pantrhiwgoch Hotel & Riverside Restaurant
Brecon Rd NP8 1EP
☎ 01873 810550 01873 811880
e-mail: info@pantrhiwgoch.co.uk
***Dir:*** *on A40 midway between Abergavenny & Crickhowell beside River Usk*
Panoramic views are guaranteed at this 16th-century building, sandwiched between the River Usk and the Sugar Loaf mountain. A purpose-built wing houses the attractive, well-equipped bedrooms; all but three overlook the river and many have balconies. The riverside setting enhances the bright conservatory lounge and the traditional restaurant, where the cuisine makes extensive use of quality fresh produce. Two stretches of trout and salmon fishing are available.
**ROOMS:** 18 en suite (2 fmly) s £63-£73; d £63-£73 (incl. bkfst) * LB
**FACILITIES:** Fishing Xmas **PARKING:** 40 **NOTES:** No dogs No smoking in restaurant Civ Wed 30 **CARDS:**

## ABERGELE, Conwy — Map 06 SH97

### ★★★65% Kinmel Manor
St George's Rd LL22 9AS
☎ 01745 832014 01745 832014
e-mail: kinmelmanor@virgin.net
***Dir:*** *at Abergele exit on A55*
Set in several acres of grounds, this 16th-century manor house provides several function suites and a fully equipped leisure centre. Many original features have been retained, including superb fireplaces in the restaurant and the hall. Several family rooms are available and all bedrooms are equipped with modern amenities.
**ROOMS:** 51 en suite (3 fmly) No smoking in 12 bedrooms s £52; d £72 (incl. bkfst) * LB **FACILITIES:** Spa STV Indoor swimming (H) Sauna Solarium Gym Steam room Xmas **CONF:** Thtr 250 Class 100 Board 100 Del from £69.50 * **PARKING:** 120 **NOTES:** Civ Wed 250
**CARDS:**

## ABERPORTH, Ceredigion — Map 02 SN25

### ★★★69% Hotel Penrallt
SA43 2BS
☎ 01239 810227 01239 811375
e-mail: info@hotelpenrallt.co.uk
***Dir:*** *take B4333 signed Aberporth. Hotel 1m on the right*
This impeccably maintained Edwardian mansion is now a privately owned, personally run hotel. It stands in extensive, well-maintained grounds, while inside, original features such as carved ceiling beams and a splendid stained glass window remain. Smart public areas include an inviting restaurant and a popular bar. The bedrooms are generally spacious, with balcony and family rooms available.
**ROOMS:** 16 en suite (2 fmly) s fr £65; d fr £105 (incl. bkfst) * LB
**FACILITIES:** Indoor swimming (H) Outdoor swimming (H) Tennis (hard) Sauna Solarium Gym Putting green Jacuzzi Pool table ch fac
**CONF:** Class 60 Board 30 **PARKING:** 100 **NOTES:** No smoking in restaurant Closed 25-31 Dec **CARDS:**

★★73% Rosette **Penbontbren Farm**
Glynarthen SA44 6PE
☎ 01239 810248 Fax 01239 811129
***Dir:*** *from Cardigan, N on A487, 2nd right after Tan-y-groes, signposted. S on A487, 1st left after Sarnau, signposted Penbontbren*
This farmhouse is located in a truly rural setting. The restaurant, lounge, games room and bar are all in the main house whilst the stable blocks across the courtyard house bedrooms with high levels of comfort and lots of charm. Several rooms on the ground floor have been adapted for disabled use. The property also houses a farm museum and a nature trail.
**ROOMS:** 10 annexe en suite (10 fmly) No smoking in 2 bedrooms **FACILITIES:** Fishing Farm museum of farming tools **CONF:** Thtr 25 Class 15 Board 34 Del from £38 * **PARKING:** 50 **NOTES:** No smoking in restaurant **CARDS:**

★★61% **Highcliffe**
SA43 2DA
☎ 01239 810534 Fax 01239 810534
***Dir:*** *off B4333*
A hotel on the coast enjoying an elevated position above Cardigan Bay, with the sandy beaches close by. Hospitality is jovial and service is relaxed and informal. A wide range of meals at reasonable prices is offered in the bar and restaurant. Bedrooms are comfortable and equipped with modern facilities.
**ROOMS:** 9 rms (8 en suite) 6 annexe en suite (4 fmly) s £33.95-£39.60; d £51-£59.50 (incl. bkfst) * **LB** **FACILITIES:** Xmas **PARKING:** 18 **NOTES:** No smoking in restaurant **CARDS:**

## ABERSOCH, Gwynedd — Map 06 SH32

★★★76% Rosette **Neigwl**
Lon Sarn Bach LL53 7DY
☎ 01758 712363 Fax 01758 712544
e-mail: relax@neigwl.com
***Dir:*** *on A499, drive through Abersoch, hotel on the left overlooking the sea*
This delightful, small, family run hotel is conveniently located for access to the town, harbour and beach. It has a well-deserved reputation for its food and warm hospitality. Both the attractive restaurant and very pleasant lounge bar enjoy sea views, as do several of the tastefully appointed bedrooms.
**ROOMS:** 7 en suite 2 annexe en suite (3 fmly) s £84; d £150-£175 (incl. bkfst & dinner) **LB** **FACILITIES:** ch fac **PARKING:** 30 **NOTES:** No dogs (ex guide dogs) **CARDS:**

★★★74% Rosette Rosette **Porth Tocyn**
Bwlch Tocyn LL53 7BU
☎ 01758 713303 Fax 01758 713538
e-mail: porthtocyn.hotel@virgin.net
***Dir:*** *2.5m S follow signs 'Porth Tocyn' and Brown Highway signs marked 'Gwesty/Hotel'*
Located above Cardigan Bay with fine views over the area, Porth Tocyn is set in attractive gardens. Several elegantly furnished sitting rooms are provided and bedrooms are comfortably furnished. Children are especially welcome and have a play room. Fine food earns the restaurant a prestigious Two Rosette Award.
**ROOMS:** 17 en suite (1 fmly) No smoking in all bedrooms s £52.50-£68.50; d £70-£128 (incl. cont bkfst) * **LB** **FACILITIES:** Outdoor swimming (H) Tennis (hard) ch fac **PARKING:** 50 **NOTES:** No smoking in restaurant Closed mid Nov-wk before Etr **CARDS:**

*See advert on this page*

★★★67% **White House**
LL53 7AG
☎ 01758 713427 Fax 01758 713512
e-mail: whitehousehotel@btinternet.com
***Dir:*** *on A499 from Pwllheli hotel is on the right just before entering Abersoch village*

This well-maintained, privately owned hotel stands in an elevated position on the outskirts of Abersoch, overlooking Cardigan Bay. The modern equipped and tastefully appointed accommodation includes bedrooms for non-smokers and a two bedroom family suite. Public areas include a choice of lounges, a bright and spacious restaurant and a lounge bar with sea views.
**ROOMS:** 13 en suite (1 fmly) No smoking in 6 bedrooms s fr £65; d fr £110 (incl. bkfst) * **LB** **FACILITIES:** Xmas **CONF:** Thtr 90 Class 60 Board 40 **PARKING:** 100 **NOTES:** No smoking in restaurant
**CARDS:**

A

ABERSOCH, continued

**★★65% *Deucoch***
LL53 7LD
☎ 01758 712680 01758 712670
e-mail: deucoch@supanet.com
***Dir:*** *through Abersoch village following signs for Sarn Bach. At cross roads in Sarn Bach (approx 1m from village centre) turn right, hotel on top of hill*
This hotel sits in an elevated position above the village and enjoys lovely views. There is a choice of bars and food options. The regular carvery provides excellent value and has a large following, so booking is essential. Pretty bedrooms are equipped with satellite television and other modern amenities. The hotel specialises in golfing packages.
**ROOMS:** 10 rms (9 en suite) (2 fmly) **PARKING:** 30 **NOTES:** No smoking in restaurant **CARDS:**

ABERYSTWYTH, Ceredigion Map 06 SN58

## *Courtesy & Care Award*

**★★★75% Conrah**
Ffosrhydygaled, Chancery SY23 4DF
☎ 01970 617941 01970 624546
e-mail: enquiries@conrah.co.uk
***Dir:*** *on A487, 3.5m S of Aberystwyth*
This country house hotel stands in 22 acres of mature grounds, not far from Aberystwyth. The elegantly furnished public rooms include a choice of lounges with welcoming open fires. Conference and leisure facilities are available, while the cuisine, which is French with modern influences, continues to achieve very high standards. Rooms are in both the main house and a nearby wing. The team at Conrah have been awarded the AA Courtesy & Care Award for Wales 2001-2002.
**ROOMS:** 11 en suite 6 annexe en suite (1 fmly) s £70-£100; d £100-£135 (incl. bkfst) LB **FACILITIES:** Indoor swimming (H) Sauna Croquet lawn Table tennis **CONF:** Thtr 40 Class 20 Board 20 Del £120 * **SERVICES:** Lift **PARKING:** 50 **NOTES:** No dogs No children 5yrs No smoking in restaurant Closed 22-30 Dec Civ Wed 65 **CARDS:**

Popped the question? Hotels with Civ Wed in their entry are licensed for civil wedding ceremonies. Maximum numbers for the ceremony only are shown, e.g. Civ Wed 120

**★★★70% *Belle Vue Royal***
Marine Ter SY23 2BA
☎ 01970 617558 01970 612190
***Dir:*** *near the Pier*

Dating back more than 170 years, this family owned hotel stands on the promenade, a short walk from the shops. Family and sea-view rooms are available, all are well-equipped. Public areas include extensive function rooms and a choice of bars. Food options include bar meals and more formal restaurant dining.
**ROOMS:** 34 en suite (6 fmly) No smoking in 10 bedrooms **FACILITIES:** STV **CONF:** Thtr 70 Class 20 Board 28 **PARKING:** 15 **NOTES:** No dogs (ex guide dogs) Closed 24-26 Dec
**CARDS:**

*See advert on opposite page*

**★★68% Four Seasons**
50-54 Portland St SY23 2DX
☎ 01970 612120 01970 627458
e-mail: info@fourseasonshotel.demon.co.uk
***Dir:*** *in town centre, car park entrance in Bath Street*
Conveniently located for access to both the town centre and the seafront, this privately owned and personally run hotel is well-maintained and friendly. Bedrooms are well equipped and no smoking rooms are available. A cosy lounge is provided, plus a separate bar. There is also a room for meetings. A wide choice of food is available.
**ROOMS:** 14 rms (13 en suite) (1 fmly) No smoking in 7 bedrooms **CONF:** Thtr 25 Class 15 **PARKING:** 10 **NOTES:** No dogs (ex guide dogs) No smoking in restaurant Closed 25-31 Dec
**CARDS:**

**★★68% *Richmond***
44-45 Marine Ter SY23 2BX
☎ 01970 612201 01970 626706
***Dir:*** *on entering town follow signs for Promenade*

GWESTY
RICHMOND
HOTEL

This hotel lies in the centre of the promenade with good sea views from its day rooms and from many of the bedrooms. The public areas and bedrooms are comfortably furnished and family rooms

*continued*

are available. An attractive dining room along with a comfortable lounge and bar are provided. There is also a suite available for local functions.
**ROOMS:** 15 en suite (6 fmly) **FACILITIES:** STV **CONF:** Thtr 60 Class 22 Board 28 **PARKING:** 20 **NOTES:** No dogs (ex guide dogs) No smoking in restaurant Closed 20 Dec-3 Jan **CARDS:**

### ★★64% Groves

MINOTEL
Great Britain

44-46 North Pde SY23 2NF
☎ 01970 617623 Fax 01970 627068
e-mail: info@ghotel.force9.co.uk
***Dir:*** *N on A487, in town centre*
Conveniently located just a few minutes' walk from the shopping area and the sea front, the Groves Hotel is both a friendly and popular hotel. Functions and meetings of up to 50 people can be accommodated and the bar and cafe-style restaurant offer a good range of eating options. Bedrooms are well-equipped with modern facilities.
**ROOMS:** 9 en suite (1 fmly) No smoking in 2 bedrooms s fr £49; d fr £65 (incl. bkfst) * **LB** **CONF:** Class 24 Board 24 **PARKING:** 4 **NOTES:** No dogs (ex guide dogs) **CARDS:**

### ★★62% Marine Hotel

The Promenade SY23 2BX
☎ 01970 612444 Fax 01970 617435
e-mail: marinehotel@barbox.net
***Dir:*** *from W on A44. From north or south Wales on A487. On sea front west of pier*
The Marine Hotel is situated on the promenade overlooking Cardigan Bay. Bedrooms have been tastefully decorated, some have four-poster beds and many have sea views. The recently refurbished reception rooms are comfortable and relaxing, and meals are served in the elegant dining room or the bar.
**ROOMS:** 44 en suite (7 fmly) No smoking in 1 bedroom s £45-£55; d £70-£85 (incl. bkfst) * **LB** **FACILITIES:** **Spa** Sauna Solarium Gym Jacuzzi Xmas **CONF:** Thtr 220 Class 150 Board 60 Del from £55 * **SERVICES:** Lift **PARKING:** 15 **NOTES:** No smoking in restaurant **CARDS:**

## AMLWCH See Anglesey, Isle of

## AMMANFORD, Carmarthenshire — Map 03 SN61

### ★★68% Mill at Glynhir

Glyn-Hir, Llandybie SA18 2TE
☎ 01269 850672 Fax 01269 850672
e-mail: tgittins@aol.com
***Dir:*** *turn off A483 Llandybie signposted Golf Course*
Straddling the valley on the periphery of the Black Mountains, this former water mill is situated adjacent to the local golf course. The accommodation comprises spacious and well-equipped bedrooms around the mill. The bar/lounge and restaurant make up the public areas, which also include a heated indoor swimming pool and private golfing range.
**ROOMS:** 11 en suite s £39; d £77 * **LB** **FACILITIES:** Indoor swimming (H) Golf 18 Fishing **PARKING:** 20 **NOTES:** No children 11yrs No smoking in restaurant Closed Xmas RS 24-30 Dec
**CARDS:**

> Late for dinner? Quality Standards star rating means that last orders for dinner should be no earlier than:
> ★ 6.30pm ★★ 7.00pm ★★★ 8.00pm
> ★★★★ 9.00pm ★★★★★ 10.00pm



## ANGLESEY, ISLE OF, Isle of Anglesey — Map 06

## AMLWCH — Map 06 SH49

### ★★69% Lastra Farm

Penrhyd LL68 9TF
☎ 01407 830906 Fax 01407 832522
e-mail: booking@lastra-hotel.com
***Dir:*** *after 'Welcome to Amlwch' sign turn left. Straight across main road, left at T-junct on to Rhosgoch Rd*
This 17th-century farmhouse offers pine-furnished, colourfully decorated bedrooms. There is also a comfortable lounge and a cosy bar. A wide range of good-value food is available. The hotel can cater for functions in a separate purpose built suite.
**ROOMS:** 5 en suite 3 annexe en suite (1 fmly) s £31-£35; d £52-£60 (incl. bkfst) * **LB** **CONF:** Thtr 100 Class 80 Board 30 Del from £50 * **PARKING:** 40 **NOTES:** No smoking in restaurant Civ Wed 100
**CARDS:**

### ★★67% *Trecastell*

Bull Bay LL68 9SA
☎ 01407 830651 Fax 01407 832114
e-mail: trecastell.hotel@nol.co.uk
***Dir:*** *1m N on A5025, adjacent to Golf Club*
Near the local golf course, this traditional hotel overlooks Bull Bay. The popular bar serves a range of food, with formal dining in the attractive restaurant. Refurbished bedrooms are well-equipped. Family and sea view rooms are available
**ROOMS:** 13 rms (11 en suite) (3 fmly) **CONF:** Thtr 20 Class 10 Board 10 **PARKING:** 60 **NOTES:** No smoking in restaurant
**CARDS:**

A

## BEAUMARIS

Map 06 SH67

### ★★75% Ye Olde Bulls Head Inn

Castle St LL58 8AP
☎ 01248 810329 01248 811294
e-mail: info@bullsheadinn.co.uk
***Dir:*** *from Britannia road bridge follow A545, located in town centre*
Charles Dickens and Samuel Johnson were regular visitors to this inn. Features include exposed beams, fireplaces and antique weaponry. Richly decorated bedrooms are well-equipped. There is a spacious lounge; meetings and small functions are catered for. Food continues to attract praise in the restaurant and brasserie.
**ROOMS:** 12 en suite 1 annexe en suite No smoking in 4 bedrooms s £60-£75; d £87-£100 (incl. bkfst) * **LB CONF:** Thtr 25 Board 16 **PARKING:** 10 **NOTES:** No dogs (ex guide dogs) No smoking in restaurant Closed 25-26 Dec & 1 Jan **CARDS:**

### ★★71% Bishopsgate House

54 Castle St LL58 8BB
☎ 01248 810302 01248 810166
e-mail: hazel@johnson-ollier.freeserve.co.uk
***Dir:*** *turn off in Menai Bridge onto A545. Follow the only road into Beaumaris, hotel is on the left in the main street*
Dating back to 1760, this immaculately maintained, small hotel features fine examples of wood panelling and a Chinese Chippendale staircase. Well-equipped bedrooms are attractively decorated and two have four-poster beds.
**ROOMS:** 9 en suite s £42; d £68 (incl. bkfst) * **LB PARKING:** 8 **NOTES:** No smoking in restaurant **CARDS:**

## HOLYHEAD

Map 06 SH28

### ★★66% *Boathouse*

Newry Promenade, Newry Beach LL65 1YF
☎ 01407 762094 01407 764898
***Dir:*** *follow signs for Maring. Hotel is situated at end of Promenade*
Situated in a prominent position overlooking the harbour, the hotel makes an ideal stop for ferry travellers. Bedrooms are attractively decorated to a high standard and well equipped. Downstairs the attractive lounge bar offers a wide range of home cooked food and there is a separate dining room.
**ROOMS:** 17 en suite (1 fmly) No smoking in 15 bedrooms **CONF:** Thtr 40 Class 30 Board 30 **PARKING:** 40 **NOTES:** No smoking in restaurant **CARDS:**

### ★★63% Bull

London Rd, Valley LL65 3DP
☎ 01407 740351 01407 742328
***Dir:*** *3.5m from ferry terminal, on A5 near junct with A5025*
A busy hotel on the approach to Holyhead. Its popular bars offer good-value food and host local quizzes and other functions. Bedrooms, whether in the main building or nearby annexe, are well-equipped with modern amenities, and family rooms are available.
**ROOMS:** 9 en suite 5 annexe en suite (4 fmly) s £38; d £50 (incl. bkfst) * **LB FACILITIES:** ch fac **PARKING:** 130 **CARDS:**

## LLANFAIRPWLLGWYNGYLL

Map 06 SH57

### ★★★64% *Carreg Bran Country Hotel*

Best Western

Church Ln LL61 5YH
☎ 01248 714224 01248 715983
***Dir:*** *from Holyhead 1st junct for Llanfairpwll. Through village then 1st right before dual carriageway and bridge*
A family-run hotel close to the banks of the Menai Straits. Rooms are prettily decorated, spacious and well-equipped. The restaurant is attractive and food has a local flavour. There is a choice of bars and a large function room, popular for weddings and business meetings.
**ROOMS:** 29 en suite (3 fmly) No smoking in 7 bedrooms **CONF:** Thtr 130 Class 120 Board 100 **PARKING:** 120 **NOTES:** No smoking in restaurant Civ Wed **CARDS:**

## LLANGEFNI

Map 06 SH47

### ★★66% Bull Hotel

Bulkley Square LL77 7LR
☎ 01248 722119 01248 750488
e-mail: john@newborgh.demon.co.uk
***Dir:*** *Leave A55 at Llangefni follow signs for town centre, hotel on right on entering town through one way system*

This town centre hostelry was built in 1817. Recently refurbished, it provides well-equipped, tastefully furnished accommodation, including a room with a four-poster bed and a family bedded room. Public areas offer a choice of bars, a spacious traditionally appointed restaurant and a comfortable lounge for residents.
**ROOMS:** 13 en suite (2 fmly) No smoking in all bedrooms d £55-£85 (incl. bkfst) * **FACILITIES:** STV Pool table Xmas **PARKING:** 18 **NOTES:** No dogs (ex guide dogs) **CARDS:**

## MENAI BRIDGE

Map 06 SH57

### ★★66% *Anglesey Arms*

LL59 5EA
☎ 01248 712305 01248 712076
e-mail: bookings@theangleseyarmshotel.co.uk
***Dir:*** *on left after Menai Bridge*
This popular hotel next to the Menai Suspension Bridge sits in well-maintained, pretty gardens. The hotel provides smart, well-equipped accommodation. Bedrooms are attractively furnished in pine and equipped with thoughtful extras. There is a choice of bars and an excellent selection of meals.
**ROOMS:** 16 en suite (2 fmly) **CONF:** Thtr 60 Class 40 Board 40 **PARKING:** 60 **NOTES:** No dogs (ex guide dogs) **CARDS:**

### ★★61% Victoria Hotel

Telford Rd LL59 5DR
☎ 01248 712309 01248 716774
***Dir:*** *cross Menai Bridge, turn right at rdbt and continue 100yds to hotel*
This family run hotel is situated in Menai Bridge and with panoramic views of the Menai Straits and Britannia Bridge. Many bedrooms have their own balconies. Downstairs there are two

continued

character bars where meals are available and there is also a more formal conservatory dining room.
**ROOMS:** 14 en suite 3 annexe en suite s £30; d £46 (incl. bkfst) * **FACILITIES:** Childrens playground Xmas **CONF:** Thtr 80 Class 80 Board 50 **PARKING:** 40 **NOTES:** No smoking in restaurant Civ Wed 80
**CARDS:**

TREARDDUR BAY Map 06 SH27

**★★★71% Trearddur Bay**
LL65 2UN
☎ 01407 860301 📠 01407 861181
e-mail: mark@markdglil.demon.co.uk
***Dir:*** *Leave A55 at junct signposted for Caergeiliog.Drive through Caergeiliog and continue along A5,from A5 turn left at lights in Valley on the B4545 toward Trearddur Bay, at Power garage on right, turn left opposite garage, hotel on right*
Facilities at this fine modern hotel include extensive function and conference rooms, an indoor swimming pool and a games room. Bedrooms are well-equipped, many have sea views and suites are available. An all-day bar serves a wide range of snacks and lighter meals, supplemented by a cocktail bar and the more formal hotel restaurant.
**ROOMS:** 37 en suite (7 fmly) No smoking in 1 bedroom s £76-£108; d £114-£136 (incl. bkfst) * **LB** **FACILITIES:** STV Indoor swimming (H) Croquet lawn sailing,shooting,horse riding ,fishing entertainment ch fac Xmas **CONF:** Thtr 120 Class 60 Board 40 Del £87.50 * **PARKING:** 300 **NOTES:** No smoking in restaurant Civ Wed 120
**CARDS:**

BALA, Gwynedd Map 06 SH93

**★★★75% Pale Hall Country House**
Llandderfel LL23 7PS
☎ 01678 530285 📠 01678 530220
e-mail: palehall@fsbdial.co.uk
***Dir:*** *off the B4401 Corwen/Bala road 4m from Llandrillo*
This enchanting mansion was built in 1870 and overlooks extensive grounds and beautiful woodland. The fine entrance hall, with vaulted ceiling and galleried oak staircase, leads off to the library bar, two elegant lounges and the smart dining room. The standard of cooking remains high and is complemented by fine wines. The spacious bedrooms are furnished to the highest standards with many thoughtful extras.
**ROOMS:** 17 en suite (1 fmly) No smoking in 7 bedrooms s £69-£120; d £95-£155 (incl. bkfst) * **LB** **FACILITIES:** Fishing Clay pigeon/Game shooting Xmas **CONF:** Board 22 Del £115 * **PARKING:** 60 **NOTES:** No dogs No children No smoking in restaurant Civ Wed 40
**CARDS:**

*See advert on this page*

**★★65% Plas Coch**
High St LL23 7AB
☎ 01678 520309 📠 01678 521135
***Dir:*** *on A494, located in the center of Bala*
A focal point for the bustling town, this 18th-century coaching inn is popular with locals and guests alike. The spacious public areas include a pleasant reception lounge, separate bistro-style restaurant, and the public and lounge bars. Bedrooms are comfortable and pleasantly decorated.
**ROOMS:** 10 en suite (4 fmly) s £30-£39; d £50-£65 (incl. bkfst) * **LB** **FACILITIES:** Windsurfing Canoeing Sailing Whitewater Rafting **PARKING:** 20 **NOTES:** No dogs (ex guide dogs)
**CARDS:**



BANGOR, Gwynedd Map 06 SH57

**★★65% *Garden Hotel***
1 High St LL57 1DQ
☎ 01248 362189 📠 01248 371328
A city hotel located close to the university, hospital and railway station and a good base for touring Snowdonia and North Wales. The newly completed bedrooms are spacious and very well-equipped and the hotel also has a renowned Cantonese restaurant. A function suite is also available.
**ROOMS:** 11 rms

**⌂ *Travelodge***
Llys-y-Gwynt LL57 4BG
☎ 01248 370345 📠 01248 370345
***Dir:*** *junc A5/A55*
Travelodge offers good quality, good value, modern accommodation. Ideal for families, the spacious, en suite bedrooms include remote-control TV, tea and coffee-making facilities, luxury beds and free morning newspaper. Meals can be taken at the nearby family restaurant. For further details and the Travelodge phone number, consult the Hotel Groups page.

Travelodge

**ROOMS:** 62 en suite

Popped the question? Hotels with Civ Wed in their entry are licensed for civil wedding ceremonies. Maximum numbers for the ceremony only are shown, e.g. Civ Wed 120

BARMOUTH, Gwynedd Map 06 SH61

**★★70% Wavecrest Hotel**
8 Marine Pde LL42 1NA
☎ 01341 280330 01341 280330
e-mail: thewavecrest@talk21.com
***Dir:*** *turn left over level-crossing, then immediately right onto Marine Parade*
There are superb views over Cardigan Bay towards the Cader Idris mountains from many of the attractive rooms at this delightful hotel on the promenade. There is an open-plan bar and restaurant and a small first-floor seating area. Excellent cuisine often uses local produce and is complemented by an impressive wine list and an extensive collection of malt whiskies.
**ROOMS:** 9 en suite (4 fmly) No smoking in all bedrooms s £23-£38; d £40-£56 (incl. bkfst) * **LB** **PARKING:** 2 **NOTES:** No smoking in restaurant Closed Nov-Mar **CARDS:**

**★★69% Ty'r Graig Castle Hotel**
Llanaber Rd LL42 1YN
☎ 01341 280470 01341 281260
e-mail: tyrgraig.castle@btinternet.com
***Dir:*** *0.75m from Barmouth on the Harlech road, Seaward side*
An unusual Gothic-style hotel with impressive stained glass windows and wood-panelled walls. There is a comfortable lounge and a modern conservatory bar with sea views. Bedrooms have modern facilities and are well-equipped. Many overlook the sea. Food is of good quality, and enjoyed in a friendly and relaxed atmosphere.
**ROOMS:** 12 en suite s £42; d £65-£75 (incl. bkfst) * **LB** **CONF:** Thtr 50 Class 30 Board 20 **PARKING:** 15 **NOTES:** No smoking in restaurant Closed 25 Dec-1 Feb **CARDS:**

**★★65% Bryn Melyn**
Panorama Rd LL42 1DQ
☎ 01341 280556 01341 280342
e-mail: bryn.melyn@virgin.net
***Dir:*** *off A496, 0.25m on left - Panorama Road - leaving Barmouth for Dolgellau*
This family-run hotel has superb views over the Mawddach Estuary to the Cader Idris Mountains. Bedrooms are decorated with pretty wallpapers and fabrics and equipped with modern facilities. Public areas include a comfortable lounge and a cane-furnished conservatory. Good home cooking is on offer and vegetarians are well-looked after.
**ROOMS:** 9 rms (8 en suite) (1 fmly) s £36-£42; d £58-£84 (incl. bkfst) * **LB** **PARKING:** 10 **NOTES:** No smoking in restaurant
**CARDS:**

BARRY, Vale of Glamorgan Map 03 ST16

**★★★77% Egerton Grey Country House**
Porthkerry CF62 3BZ
☎ 01446 711666 01446 711690
e-mail: info@egertongrey.co.uk
***Dir:*** *M4 junct 33 follow signs for airport and turn left at rdbt for Porthkerry, after 500yds turn left down lane between thatched cottages*
An elegant country house that offers warm hospitality and attentive service. The charming public areas are very relaxing; period furnishings adorn the restaurant, lounge and library. Spacious bedrooms are tastefully appointed, some with wonderful original bathroom furniture. Cuisine is taken seriously at both *continued* breakfast and dinner with a menu which includes wonderful Glamorgan sausages.

**ROOMS:** 10 en suite (4 fmly) s £89.50-£110; d £95-£130 (incl. bkfst) * **LB** **FACILITIES:** STV ch fac Xmas **CONF:** Thtr 30 Class 30 Board 22 Del from £120 * **PARKING:** 41 **NOTES:** No smoking in restaurant Civ Wed 120 **CARDS:**

*See advert on opposite page*

**★★★65% Mount Sorrel**
Porthkerry Rd CF62 7XY
☎ 01446 740069 01446 746600
e-mail: reservations@mountsorrel.co.uk
Best Western
***Dir:*** *from M4 junct 33 on A4232. Follow signs for A4050 through Barry. Upon reaching mini rdbt with church opposite turn left, hotel 300mtrs on the left*
Situated in an elevated position above the town centre this is an extended Victorian property, offering comfortable accommodation. The public areas include a choice of conference rooms, restaurant and bar, together with leisure facilities.
**ROOMS:** 42 en suite (3 fmly) s £60-£80; d £95 (incl. bkfst) * **LB** **FACILITIES:** STV Indoor swimming (H) Sauna Gym Xmas **CONF:** Thtr 150 Class 100 Board 50 Del £90 * **PARKING:** 17 **NOTES:** No smoking in restaurant Civ Wed 150 **CARDS:**

BEAUMARIS See Anglesey, Isle of

BEDDGELERT, Gwynedd Map 06 SH54

**★★★66% Royal Goat**
LL55 4YE
☎ 01766 890224 01766 890422
e-mail: info@royalgoathotel.co.uk
THE CIRCLE Selected Individual Hotels GREAT BRITAIN
***Dir:*** *off A498*
At the time of our last inspection, there had just been a change of hands and the new owners were in the process of making improvements to most areas of the hotel. Privately owned and personally run, it provides well-equipped accommodation, which is equally suitable for both tourists and business people. Facilities include a choice of bars, a choice of restaurants, a lounge and function rooms.
**ROOMS:** 32 en suite (3 fmly) No smoking in 10 bedrooms s fr £45; d fr £79 (incl. bkfst) * **LB** **FACILITIES:** STV Fishing Xmas **CONF:** Thtr 80 Class 70 Board 70 **SERVICES:** Lift **PARKING:** 100
**CARDS:**

**★★71% *Tanronnen Inn***
LL55 4YB
☎ 01766 890347 01766 890606
***Dir:*** *in the centre of village*
This delightful small hotel offers comfortable, well equipped and attractively appointed accommodation, including a family room. There is also a selection of pleasant and relaxing public areas. The *continued*

wide range of bar food is popular with tourists, and more formal meals are served in the restaurant. Beddgelert has won the 'Britain in Bloom' competition for many years and the manager has an M.B.E. for his involvement with the project.
**ROOMS:** 7 en suite (3 fmly) **FACILITIES:** STV **PARKING:** 15
**NOTES:** No dogs **CARDS:**

BETWS-Y-COED, Conwy — Map 06 SH75
see also Llanrwst

### ★★★70% **Royal Oak**
Holyhead Rd LL24 0AY
☎ 01690 710219 🖷 01690 710603
e-mail: reservations@royaloakhotel.net
***Dir:*** *on main A5 in centre of town, next to St Mary's church*
This fine hotel started life as a coaching inn and now provides smart bedrooms and a wide range of public areas. There are several eating options, including a bistro, Stables Bar and the Grill Room for snacks. The main dining room serves a more formal menu.
**ROOMS:** 26 en suite (3 fmly) No smoking in 6 bedrooms s £50-£56; d £94-£96 (incl. bkfst) * **LB** **FACILITIES:** STV entertainment Xmas **CONF:** Thtr 20 Class 20 Board 20 Del from £45 * **PARKING:** 90 **NOTES:** No dogs (ex guide dogs) Closed 25-26 Dec Civ Wed 100
**CARDS:**

*See advert on this page*

Early start? Hotels at all star levels should provide in-room alarm clocks and/or alarm calls.

B

BETWS-Y-COED, continued

★★★70% **Waterloo**
LL24 0AR
☎ 01690 710411 📠 01690 710666
e-mail: reservations@waterloohotel.co.uk
***Dir:*** *A5 London-Holyhead near Waterloo Bridge*

Best
Western

This long-established hotel, named after the nearby Waterloo Bridge, is ideally located for Snowdonia. Accommodation is split between rooms in the main hotel and modern, cottage-style rooms located in buildings to the rear. The attractive Snowdonia Restaurant serves traditional Welsh specialities, and the Wellington Bar offers light meals and snacks.
**ROOMS:** 10 en suite 30 annexe en suite (2 fmly) s £59; d £99 (incl. bkfst) * LB **FACILITIES:** Indoor swimming (H) Sauna Solarium Gym Jacuzzi Steam room Xmas **CONF:** Thtr 75 Class 50 Board 25 Del from £55 * **PARKING:** 200 **NOTES:** No smoking in restaurant
**CARDS:**

★★★63% **Craig-y-Dderwen Riverside Hotel**
LL24 0AS
☎ 01690 710293 📠 01690 710362
e-mail: craig-y-dderwen@betws-y-coed.co.uk
***Dir:*** *A5 to town, cross Waterloo Bridge and take first left*

This Victorian country house hotel is set in well-maintained grounds alongside the River Conwy, at the end of a tree-lined drive. Very pleasant views can be enjoyed from many rooms, and two of the bedrooms have four-poster beds. There are comfortable lounges and the atmosphere is tranquil and relaxing.
**ROOMS:** 16 en suite (5 fmly) s £50-£80; d £60-£90 (incl. bkfst) * LB **FACILITIES:** Croquet lawn Badminton, Volleyball ch fac Xmas **CONF:** Thtr 50 Class 25 Board 12 Del from £98.40 * **PARKING:** 50 **NOTES:** No smoking in restaurant Closed 31Dec-1 Feb
**CARDS:**

Read all about it! Newspapers delivered to bedrooms in four and five star hotels.

## Premier Collection

★★ ®®® **Tan-y-Foel Country House**
Capel Garmon LL26 0RE
☎ 01690 710507 📠 01690 710681
e-mail: enquiries@tyfhotel.co.uk
***Dir:*** *off A5 at Betws-y-Coed onto A470, travel 2m North sign marked Capel Garmon on right, take this turning towards Capel Garmon for 1.5m hotel sign on left*
This 16th-century, stone-built house is perched on a wooded hillside overlooking the Conwy Valley and the town below. The interior design and colour schemes are refreshingly bold and modern - the lounge is furnished and decorated using earthy tones, and the restaurant is warmed by a wood-burning stove. Bedrooms are individually designed, those in the loft are particularly striking. The cooking is also vibrant and modern using organic produce where possible.
**ROOMS:** 5 en suite 2 annexe en suite No smoking in all bedrooms s £70-£90; d £90-£150 (incl. bkfst) * LB **PARKING:** 9 **NOTES:** No dogs (ex guide dogs) No children 7yrs No smoking in restaurant Closed mid-27 Dec RS Jan/Feb
**CARDS:**

★★68% **Fairy Glen**
LL24 0SH
☎ 01690 710269 📠 01690 710269
e-mail: fairyglenhotel@amserve.net
***Dir:*** *turn off A5 onto A470 Southbound (Dolwyddelan Road). Hotel 0.5m on left by Beaver Bridge*
This privately owned and personally run former coaching inn is over 300 years old. It is located near the Fairy Glen beauty spot, south of Betws-y-Coed. The modern accommodation is well-equipped and service is willing, friendly and attentive. Facilities include a cosy bar and a separate comfortable lounge.
**ROOMS:** 8 rms (6 en suite) (2 fmly) s £21-£36; d £42-£48 (incl. bkfst) * LB **PARKING:** 10 **NOTES:** No smoking in restaurant Closed Nov-Jan RS Feb **CARDS:**

★★67% **Park Hill**
Llanrwst Rd LL24 0HD
☎ 01690 710540 📠 01690 710540
e-mail: parkhill.hotel@virgin.net
***Dir:*** *0.5m N of Betws-y-Coed on A470 Llanrwst road*
This friendly hotel benefits from a peaceful location overlooking the village. Comfortable bedrooms come in a wide range of sizes and are well-equipped. There is a choice of lounges, seating in the covered entrance porch and a heated swimming pool is available to residents.
**ROOMS:** 9 en suite (2 fmly) s £40-£50; d £55-£72 (incl. bkfst) * LB **FACILITIES:** Indoor swimming (H) Sauna Jacuzzi Xmas **PARKING:** 11 **NOTES:** No dogs (ex guide dogs) No children 6yrs No smoking in restaurant **CARDS:**

BLACKWOOD, Caerphilly Map 03 ST19

**★★★67% Maes Manor**
NP12 0AG
☎ 01495 224551 & 220011 📠 01495 228217
***Dir:*** *A4048 to Tredega. At Pontllanfraith left at rdbt, through Blackwood High St. After 1.25m left at Rack Inn. Hotel 400yds on left*
Standing high above the town, this 19th-century manor house is set in nine acres of gardens and woodland. Bedrooms are attractively decorated with co-ordinated furnishings. The restaurant is supplemented by a choice of bars with a lounge/lobby area and a large function room, which is regularly the setting for live entertainment.
**ROOMS:** 8 en suite 14 annexe en suite (2 fmly) **PARKING:** 100
**CARDS:**

BLAENAU FFESTINIOG, Gwynedd Map 06 SH74

**★★69% Queens Hotel**
1 High St LL41 3ES
☎ 01766 830055 📠 01766 830046
e-mail: cathy@queensffestiniog.freeserve.co.uk
***Dir:*** *on A470 adjacent to Ffestiniog railway, between Betws-y-Coed & Dolgellau*
This flourishing hotel has an all-day bistro serving popular meals and snacks. A large function room is available, and bedrooms are well-equipped and attractively appointed. The hotel lies at the northern end of the famous Ffestiniog narrow gauge railway, and the bedrooms are named after locomotives which have operated on the line.
**ROOMS:** 12 en suite (4 fmly) s £40-£60; d £55-£80 (incl. bkfst) * **LB**
**FACILITIES:** STV **CONF:** Thtr 50 Class 30 Board 30 Del from £60 *
**NOTES:** No dogs (ex guide dogs) No smoking in restaurant Closed 25 Dec **CARDS:**

BONTDDU, Gwynedd Map 06 SH61

**★★★71% Bontddu Hall**
LL40 2UF
☎ 01341 430661 📠 01341 430284
e-mail: reservations@bontdduhall.fsnet.co.uk
***Dir:*** *Turn off A470 N of Dolgellau heading towards Barmouth. Halfway between Dolgellau and Barmouth on the A496*

Overlooking the beautiful Mawddach Estuary, this 19th-century house was once the country retreat of the Lord Mayor of Birmingham and is surrounded by 14 acres of landscaped gardens and wooded grounds. Bedrooms are spacious and well-equipped, some are located in purpose-built buildings in the grounds. Elegant public areas include lounges and a conservatory-style restaurant.
**ROOMS:** 15 en suite 5 annexe en suite (6 fmly) **PARKING:** 50
**NOTES:** No children 3yrs Closed Nov-Mar
**CARDS:**

*See advert under BARMOUTH*

BRECHFA, Carmarthenshire Map 02 SN53

**★★73% *Ty Mawr Country Hotel***
SA32 7RA
☎ 01267 202332 📠 01267 202437
***Dir:*** *off B4310 in centre of village*
Ty Mawr (the Big House), with the River Marlais flowing through its grounds, dates back some 450 years. The accommodation is well-maintained and public areas have both charm and character. Privately owned and personally run, the hotel is establishing a firm reputation for its friendly hospitality and good food.
**ROOMS:** 5 rms (4 en suite) (1 fmly) No smoking in all bedrooms
**PARKING:** 45 **NOTES:** No smoking in restaurant
**CARDS:**

BRECON, Powys Map 03 SO02

**★★★74% Nant Ddu Lodge**
Cwm Taf, Nant Ddu CF48 2HY
☎ 01685 379111 📠 01685 377088
e-mail: enquiries@nant-ddu-lodge.co.uk
(For full entry see Nant-Ddu and advert on this page)

**★★★73% Peterstone Court**
Llanhamlech LD3 7YB
☎ 01874 665387 📠 01874 665376
***Dir:*** *From Brecon take A40 towards Abergavenny, hotel in approximately 4m, on the right hand side*
This impressive 18th-century house is the ideal place from which to explore this remote and beautiful corner of Wales. Spacious bedrooms are furnished with antiques, comfortable armchairs and thoughtful extras such as heavy towelling robes. There is an

*continued on p798*

BRECON, continued

elegant drawing room with some fine paintings and a library. Leisure facilities include a health club and an outdoor heated pool.
**ROOMS:** 8 en suite 4 annexe en suite (1 fmly) s fr £93.75; d fr £104.75 (incl. bkfst) * **LB** **FACILITIES:** Outdoor swimming (H) Fishing Snooker Sauna Solarium Gym Croquet lawn Jacuzzi Xmas **CONF:** Thtr 180 Class 90 Board 64 Del from £104 * **PARKING:** 90 **NOTES:** No smoking in restaurant Civ Wed 60 **CARDS:**

### ★★70% Best Western Castle of Brecon

Castle Square LD3 9DB
☎ 01874 624611 01874 623737
e-mail: hotel@breconcastle.co.uk
***Dir:*** *follow signs to Town Centre. Turn opposite The Boars Head, towards Cradoc*
Standing next to the ruins of Brecon Castle, this early 19th-century coaching inn has impressive views of the Usk Valley and the Brecon Beacons National Park. Public rooms include a choice of two bars and a separate lounge, in addition to a large restaurant - the venue for some imaginative cooking. The bedrooms are modern and include a number of extra facilities. Conference and function rooms are also available.
**ROOMS:** 30 en suite 12 annexe en suite (4 fmly) s £49-£59; d £59-£79 (incl. bkfst) * **LB** **FACILITIES:** STV ch fac **CONF:** Thtr 170 Class 150 Board 80 Del from £69 * **PARKING:** 30 **NOTES:** No smoking in restaurant Closed 23-25 Dec Civ Wed 40
**CARDS:**

### ★★70% Lansdowne Hotel & Restaurant

The Watton LD3 7EG
☎ 01874 623321 01874 610438
e-mail: reception@lansdownehotel.co.uk
***Dir:*** *turn off A40/A470 onto the B4601, hotel in town centre*
A family-run hotel close to the town centre, providing good value accommodation and friendly hospitality. The bedrooms are all well-equipped, and ground floor and family rooms are available. Facilities include a traditionally furnished lounge, a split-level dining room with original stone fireplace, and a bar.
**ROOMS:** 9 en suite (2 fmly) s £28; d £48.50 (incl. bkfst) * **LB** **FACILITIES:** Xmas **NOTES:** No dogs (ex guide dogs) No children 5yrs
**CARDS:**

## BRIDGEND, Bridgend — Map 03 SS97

see also Porthcawl

### ★★★76% Coed-y-Mwstwr

Coychurch CF35 6AF
☎ 01656 860621 01656 863122
e-mail: anything@coed-y-mwstwr.com
***Dir:*** *leave A473 at Coychurch, right at petrol station. Follow signs at top of hill*
Set in 17 acres of grounds, just a few miles from the centre of Bridgend, this hotel retains many of its original features, including an impressive domed ceiling in what is now the restaurant. The spacious bedrooms, which include two full suites, offer a good range of extra facilities. A variety of meeting rooms is also available, as well as a large function suite.
**ROOMS:** 23 en suite (2 fmly) No smoking in 16 bedrooms s fr £95; d fr £135 (incl. bkfst) * **LB** **FACILITIES:** STV Outdoor swimming (H) Golf 12 Tennis (hard) Croquet lawn ch fac Xmas **CONF:** Thtr 180 Class 120 Board 50 Del from £105 * **SERVICES:** Lift **PARKING:** 100 **NOTES:** No dogs (ex guide dogs) No smoking in restaurant Civ Wed 150
**CARDS:**

### ★★★76% The Great House Restaurant & Hotel

Laleston CF32 0HP
☎ 01656 657644 01656 668892
e-mail: enquiries@great-house-laleston.co.uk
***Dir:*** *at side of A473, 400yds from its junction with A48*
A Grade II listed building, dating back to 1550. Original features such as mullioned windows, flagstone floors, oak beams and inglenook fireplaces add character, especially the great stone arch over the fireplace in the bar. Leicester's restaurant offers a wide range of seasonal and freshly prepared dishes. Bedrooms are located in the original building and a purpose built annexe, and decorated with rich colours and fabrics.
**ROOMS:** 8 en suite 8 annexe en suite No smoking in 4 bedrooms s £55-£85; d £80-£120 (incl. bkfst) * **LB** **FACILITIES:** Sauna Gym Croquet lawn Jacuzzi Health suite **CONF:** Thtr 40 Class 25 Board 20 Del £125 * **PARKING:** 40 **NOTES:** No dogs (ex guide dogs) No smoking in restaurant Closed 25 Dec-2 Jan **CARDS:**

### ★★★69% Heronston

Ewenny Rd CF35 5AW
☎ 01656 668811 01656 767391
e-mail: reservationa@heronston-hotel.demon.co.uk
***Dir:*** *M4 junct 35, follow signs for Porthcawl, at 4th rdbt turn left towards Ogmore-by-Sea (B4265) hotel 200yds on left*
Situated close to the town centre and the M4, this large modern hotel offers spacious well-equipped accommodation. Public areas which have recently been refurbished include an open plan lounge/bar, attractive restaurant, and a smart leisure club complete with a new gym. The hotel is also equipped with a variety of conference rooms.
**ROOMS:** 69 en suite 6 annexe en suite (4 fmly) No smoking in 21 bedrooms s £35-£95; d £60-£100 (incl. bkfst) * **LB** **FACILITIES:** STV Indoor swimming (H) Outdoor swimming (H) Sauna Solarium Gym Jacuzzi Steamroom ch fac **CONF:** Thtr 200 Class 80 Board 60 Del from £85 * **SERVICES:** Lift **PARKING:** 250 **NOTES:** No smoking in restaurant RS 25-26 Dec Civ Wed 250 **CARDS:**

### Welcome Lodge

Sarn Park Services CF32 9RW
☎ 01656 659218 01656 768665
e-mail: sarnpark.hotel@welcomebreak.co.uk
***Dir:*** *M4 junct 36*
This modern building offers accommodation in smart, spacious and well-equipped bedrooms, suitable for families and business travellers, and all with en suite bathrooms. Refreshments may be taken at the nearby family restaurant. For further details and the Welcome Break phone number, consult the Hotel Groups page.
**ROOMS:** 40 en suite d fr £40 * **CONF:** Thtr 30 Class 20 Board 30

### ○ Express by Holiday Inn

☎ 0800 897121
A modern budget hotel offering comfortable accommodation in refreshing, spacious and comprehensively equipped bedrooms, en suite bathrooms with power showers and continental buffet breakfast included in the

continued

room rate. Suitable for business travellers or families. For further details and the Express by Holiday Inn phone number, consult the Hotel Groups page.

**ROOMS:** 68 en suite **NOTES:** Opening October 2001

## BUILTH WELLS, Powys
Map 03 SO05

### ★★★71% Caer Beris Manor
LD2 3NP
☎ 01982 552601 01982 552586
e-mail: caerberismanor@btinternet.com
***Dir:*** *SW on A483*

There is some excellent fishing at this 19th-century country house, but you don't have to fish to appreciate the River Irfon that runs through the grounds. Many improvements have been made to the public areas and bedrooms, all benefiting from elegant decoration. Meals can be taken in the oak-panelled dining room or in the less formal conservatory.

**ROOMS:** 23 en suite (1 fmly) **FACILITIES:** STV Fishing Riding Sauna Gym Clay pigeon shooting **CONF:** Thtr 100 Class 75 Board 50 **PARKING:** 32 **NOTES:** No smoking in restaurant Civ Wed 100 **CARDS:**

## BURTON, Pembrokeshire
Map 02 SM90

### ★★66% Beggars Reach
SA73 1PD
☎ 01646 600700 01646 600560
e-mail: stay@beggars-reach.com
***Dir:*** *8m S of Haverfordwest, off A477*

This privately owned and personally run hotel was once a Georgian rectory. It stands in 4 acres of grounds and is peacefully located close to the village of Burton, to the south of Haverfordwest. Milford Haven and the ferry terminal at Pembroke Dock are both within easy reach. It provides modern equipped accommodation, which is suitable for both business people and tourists. Two of the bedrooms are located in former stables, which date back to the 14th century.

**ROOMS:** 10 en suite 2 annexe en suite (4 fmly) No smoking in 3 bedrooms s £33; d £53 (incl. bkfst) * **LB** **FACILITIES:** STV ch fac **CONF:** Thtr 40 Class 20 Board 20 Del £70 * **PARKING:** 50 **CARDS:**

## CAERNARFON, Gwynedd
Map 06 SH46

### ★★★79% Seiont Manor
Llanrug LL55 2AQ
☎ 01286 673366 01286 672840
e-mail: seiontmanor@arcadianhotels.co.uk
***Dir:*** *E on A4086, 2.5m from Caernarfon*

A splendid hotel created from authentic rural buildings in tranquil Welsh countryside near Snowdonia. Bedrooms are individually

*continued*

decorated and well-equipped, with luxurious extra touches. Public rooms are cosy and comfortable and furnished in country house fashion. Hotel cuisine often features regional specialities.

**ROOMS:** 28 en suite (7 fmly) No smoking in 8 bedrooms s £95-£120; d £95-£120 (incl. bkfst) * **LB** **FACILITIES:** **Spa** STV Indoor swimming (H) Fishing Sauna Solarium Gym ch fac Xmas **CONF:** Thtr 100 Class 40 Board 40 Del from £125 * **PARKING:** 150 **NOTES:** No smoking in restaurant Civ Wed 100 **CARDS:**

### ★★★68% Celtic Royal Hotel
Bangor St LL55 1AY
☎ 01286 674477 01286 674139
e-mail: admin@celtic-royal.co.uk
***Dir:*** *7m off A55 Expressway at Bangor*

This large, impressive, privately owned hotel is situated in the town centre. It provides attractively appointed accommodation, which includes no smoking rooms, bedrooms for disabled guests and family rooms. The spacious public areas include a bar, a

*continued on p800*

C

## CAERNARFON, continued

choice of lounges and a pleasant split level restaurant. Other facilities such as a well equipped health and leisure centre with swimming pool, a large ballroom and a choice of conference rooms are also available.
**ROOMS:** 110 en suite s £60-£70; d £90-£100 * **LB** **FACILITIES:** STV Indoor swimming (H) Sauna Solarium Gym Jacuzzi entertainment Xmas **CONF:** Thtr 300 Class 170 Board 125 Del from £69 * **SERVICES:** Lift **PARKING:** 180 **NOTES:** No dogs (ex guide dogs) No smoking in restaurant Civ Wed 120 **CARDS:**

### ★★77% Ty'n Rhos Country Hotel & Restaurant
Llanddeiniolen LL55 3AE
☎ 01248 670489 01248 670079
e-mail: enquiries@tynrhos.co.uk
***Dir:*** *situated in the hamlet of Seion between B4366 and B4547*

Ty'n Rhos is a peaceful converted farmhouse, set in lovely countryside between Snowdon and the Menai Straits. The lounge, with its slate inglenook fireplace, is elegantly furnished and there is a small bar for pre-dinner drinks. The conservatory offers a comfortable vantage point from which to admire the views and the gardens. The bedrooms, which include some in a converted former dairy, are well equipped and have modern facilities.
**ROOMS:** 11 en suite 3 annexe en suite No smoking in all bedrooms s £55; d £80-£110 (incl. bkfst) * **LB** **FACILITIES:** Croquet lawn **CONF:** Thtr 40 Class 30 Board 20 Del from £85 * **PARKING:** 14 **NOTES:** No dogs (ex guide dogs) No children 6yrs No smoking in restaurant Closed 24-30 Dec , RS Sun evening (rest closed to non-res) **CARDS:**

### ★★65% Menai Bank
North Rd LL55 1BD
☎ 01286 673297 01286 673297
e-mail: menaibankhotel@tesco.net
***Dir:*** *on A487 towards Bangor, on rdbt opposite Safeways*
Built at the turn of the last century as a private residence, this hotel provides bright, modern accommodation, some rooms overlooking views of the Menai Straits. Original features include stained glass windows and tiled fireplaces. A comfortable lounge is provided, and there is also a small bar and a games room.
**ROOMS:** 16 en suite (6 fmly) No smoking in 5 bedrooms s £30-£39; d £52-£59 (incl. bkfst) * **LB** **FACILITIES:** pool table **PARKING:** 10 **NOTES:** No smoking in restaurant **CARDS:**

### ★★65% *Stables*
Llanwnda LL54 5SD
☎ 01286 830711 & 830935 01286 830413
***Dir:*** *3m S of Caernarfon, on A499*
A pleasing rural hotel complex in North Wales. The bar and tempting restaurant reside in converted stables, with the rest of the facilities in a modern annexe, which include a breakfast room, and reception area. Bedrooms are brightly decorated and many have four poster beds.
**ROOMS:** 22 annexe en suite (8 fmly) **FACILITIES:** Outdoor swimming Guests may bring own horse to stables **CONF:** Thtr 50 Class 30 Board 30 **PARKING:** 40 **CARDS:**

## CAERPHILLY, Caerphilly — Map 03 ST18

### *Premier Lodge*
Corbetts Ln CF83 3HX
PREMIER LODGE
☎ 0870 700 1346 0870 700 1347
Premier Lodge offers modern, well-equipped, en suite accommodation suitable for both business and leisure travellers. Meals can be taken at the adjacent popular restaurant and bar, which is fully licensed. For further details, consult the Hotel Groups page.
**ROOMS:** 40 en suite

## CAPEL CURIG, Conwy — Map 06 SH75

### ★★64% Cobdens
LL24 0EE
THE CIRCLE *Selected Individual Hotels* GREAT BRITAIN
☎ 01690 720243 01690 720354
e-mail: info@cobdens.co.uk
***Dir:*** *on A5, 4m N of Betws-y-Coed*
For over 200 years this hotel in the heart of Snowdonia has been a centre for mountaineering and other outdoor pursuits. The bedrooms are modern and well-equipped, and many enjoy the lovely views. The hotel is family owned and run in a friendly manner and offers a full range of good-value meals.
**ROOMS:** 16 en suite (2 fmly) s fr £32; d fr £64 (incl. bkfst) * **FACILITIES:** Fishing Xmas **CONF:** Thtr 40 Class 30 Board 25 Del from £55 * **PARKING:** 60 **NOTES:** No smoking in restaurant RS Xmas Day **CARDS:**

## CARDIFF, Cardiff — Map 03 ST17
see also Barry

### ★★★★★71% *St David's Hotel & Spa*
Havannah St, Cardiff Bay CF10 5SD
☎ 029 2045 4045 029 2048 7056
e-mail: reservations@thestdavidshotel.com
Physically stunning, the hotel boasts unsurpassed views over Cardiff Bay, with all rooms benefiting from their own deck style balconies. All bedrooms are equipped to a high standard and are comfortably furnished. Public areas are equally impressive, with the seven-storey atrium towering above the lobby. The St David's Spa offers a comprehensive range of facilities and treatments.
**ROOMS:** 132 en suite (10 fmly) No smoking in 50 bedrooms **FACILITIES:** **Spa** STV Indoor swimming (H) Sauna Solarium Gym Jacuzzi Fitness studio entertainment **CONF:** Thtr 270 Class 110 Board 110 **SERVICES:** Lift air con **PARKING:** 80 **NOTES:** No dogs (ex guide dogs) No smoking in restaurant Civ Wed 150
**CARDS:**

### ★★★★70% Copthorne Hotel Cardiff-Caerdydd
Copthorne Way, Culverhouse Cross CF5 6DH
COPTHORNE
☎ 029 2059 9100 029 2059 9080
e-mail: sales.cardiff@mill-cop.com
***Dir:*** *M4 junct 33, A4232 for 2.5m in direction of Cardiff West and then A48*
Conveniently located for the city and airport, the Copthorne is a comfortable, popular and modern hotel with bright open-plan public areas. The well-equipped bedrooms are smartly presented

*continued*

with additional features including leisure facilities, meeting rooms and a restaurant which overlooks the lake.
**ROOMS:** 135 en suite (10 fmly) No smoking in 78 bedrooms s fr £70; d fr £75 * **LB** **FACILITIES:** STV Indoor swimming (H) Snooker Sauna Gym Jacuzzi Steam room ch fac Xmas **CONF:** Thtr 300 Class 140 Board 80 **SERVICES:** Lift **PARKING:** 225 **NOTES:** Civ Wed 180
**CARDS:**

### ★★★★67% Cardiff Marriott Hotel

Mill Ln CF10 1EZ
☎ 029 2039 9944 📠 029 2039 5578
e-mail: sara.nurse@marriotthotels.co.uk
***Dir:*** *M4 junct 29 follow signs City Centre. Turn left into High Street opposite Castle, then 2nd left, at bottom of High St into Mill Lane*

Marriott HOTELS · RESORTS · SUITES

Ideally located in the heart of the city, this large modern hotel boasts smart new public areas and a good range of services. Eating options include Chats café bar and the contemporary Mediterrano restaurant. Well-equipped bedrooms are comfortable and furnished to a high standard, with the bonus of air-conditioning. On site parking is also useful.
**ROOMS:** 182 en suite (58 fmly) No smoking in 127 bedrooms s £75-£200; d £85-£275 * **LB** **FACILITIES:** Spa STV Indoor swimming (H) Sauna Solarium Gym Jacuzzi Steam room Xmas **CONF:** Thtr 300 Class 200 Board 100 Del from £130 * **SERVICES:** Lift air con **PARKING:** 110 **NOTES:** No dogs (ex guide dogs) No smoking in restaurant Civ Wed 150
**CARDS:**

### ★★★★64% Hanover International Hotel & Club

Schooner Way, Atlantic Wharf CF10 4RT
☎ 029 2047 5000 📠 029 2048 1491

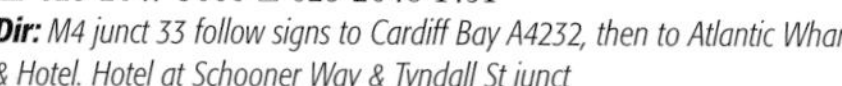

***Dir:*** *M4 junct 33 follow signs to Cardiff Bay A4232, then to Atlantic Wharf & Hotel. Hotel at Schooner Way & Tyndall St junct*

Situated in the heart of Cardiff's exciting new development area, this is a smart modern hotel. A new wing of bedrooms complements existing rooms which have been upgraded. Halyard's restaurant is the primary eating option, and lighter

*continued*

meals are available in two of the bars. Lounge areas are provided, as well as conference and leisure facilities.
**ROOMS:** 156 en suite (6 fmly) No smoking in 50 bedrooms s £100; d £120 * **LB** **FACILITIES:** STV Indoor swimming (H) Snooker Sauna Solarium Gym Jacuzzi Xmas **CONF:** Thtr 250 Class 90 Board 40 Del from £90 * **SERVICES:** Lift **PARKING:** 150 **NOTES:** No dogs (ex guide dogs) No smoking in restaurant Civ Wed 180
**CARDS:**

### ★★★★62% Angel Hotel

Castle St CF10 1SZ
☎ 029 2064 9200 📠 029 2039 6212
e-mail: angelreservations@paramount-hotels.co.uk
***Dir:*** *opposite Cardiff Castle*

PARAMOUNT GROUP OF HOTELS

This well-established hotel is ideally placed in the heart of the city overlooking the castle. Bedrooms all featuring air conditioning are decorated and furnished to a high standard. Public areas include an impressive lobby, a modern restaurant and a selection of conference rooms.
**ROOMS:** 102 en suite (4 fmly) No smoking in 32 bedrooms s £59-£130; d £70-£170 (incl. bkfst) * **LB** **FACILITIES:** STV Xmas **CONF:** Thtr 300 Class 180 Board 80 Del from £100 * **SERVICES:** Lift air con **PARKING:** 60 **NOTES:** No smoking in restaurant Civ Wed 100
**CARDS:**

### ★★★★62% Jurys Cardiff

Mary Ann St CF10 2JH
☎ 029 2034 1441 📠 029 2022 3742
e-mail: info@jurys.com
***Dir:*** *next to Ice Rink, opposite Cardiff International Arena*

JURYS DOYLE HOTELS

A stylish city centre hotel located directly opposite the Cardiff

*continued on p802*

CARDIFF, continued

International Arena. The comfortable, well-equipped bedrooms are situated around an impressive central atrium which gives access to the restaurant and Kavanagh's Irish theme bar. Extensive conference and function facilities are available in addition to a business centre.
**ROOMS:** 146 en suite (6 fmly) No smoking in 24 bedrooms **FACILITIES:** STV **CONF:** Thtr 300 Class 120 Board 50 Del from £100 * **SERVICES:** Lift **PARKING:** 55 **NOTES:** No dogs (ex guide dogs) Civ Wed 250 **CARDS:**

### ★★★74% Manor Parc Country Hotel & Restaurant

Thornhill Rd, Thornhill CF14 9UA
☎ 029 2069 3723 029 2061 4624
***Dir:*** *on A469*
This delightful country house is located on the northern edge of Cardiff. There is a warm welcome, and professional service delivered by smartly attired staff. The bedrooms are spacious and thoughtfully furnished and include a luxury suite. The public rooms offer a comfortable lounge and a restaurant with a magnificent lantern ceiling.
**ROOMS:** 12 en suite (2 fmly) s £65-£80; d £95-£130 (incl. bkfst) * **LB** **FACILITIES:** STV Tennis (hard) **CONF:** Thtr 120 Class 80 Board 50 **PARKING:** 70 **NOTES:** No dogs (ex guide dogs) Closed 24-26 Dec & 1 Jan Civ Wed 100 **CARDS:**

### ★★★72% Quality

Merthyr Rd, Tongwynlais CF15 7LD
☎ 029 2052 9988 029 2052 9977
e-mail: admin@gb629.u-net.com
***Dir:*** *M4 junct 32, exit for Tongwynlais A4054 off large rdbt, hotel on right*

In a prime location on the major interchange between Cardiff and the M4 motorway, this modern hotel provides very well-equipped, comfortable bedrooms together with bright open-plan public areas and leisure facilities. A good range of meeting rooms and extensive car parking make it a popular conference venue.
**ROOMS:** 95 en suite (12 fmly) No smoking in 47 bedrooms s £83-£105; d £83-£105 * **LB** **FACILITIES:** STV Indoor swimming (H) Sauna Solarium Gym Jacuzzi Xmas **CONF:** Thtr 180 Class 80 Board 80 Del from £70 * **SERVICES:** Lift **PARKING:** 100 **NOTES:** No smoking in restaurant Civ Wed 180 **CARDS:**

### ★★★72% St Mellons Hotel & Country Club

Castleton CF3 2XR
☎ 01633 680355 01633 680399
e-mail: stmellons@bestwestern.co.uk
***Dir:*** *M4 junct 28 follow signs into Castleton. Through village, then sharp left at brow of hill following hotel sign into driveway*
Conveniently located in its own grounds on the outskirts of Cardiff, this country house-style hotel continues to offer quality accommodation complemented by excellent leisure facilities. The bedrooms, some located in nearby wings, are spacious and well-appointed. The main house offers relaxing lounges, a bar and an elegant restaurant.
**ROOMS:** 21 en suite 20 annexe en suite (9 fmly) s £95-£125; d £105-£135 (incl. bkfst) * **LB** **FACILITIES:** STV Indoor swimming (H) Tennis (hard) Squash Sauna Solarium Gym Jacuzzi Beauty salon Xmas **CONF:** Thtr 220 Class 70 Board 40 Del from £130 * **PARKING:** 90 **NOTES:** No smoking in restaurant Civ Wed 160
**CARDS:**

### ★★★71% New House Country Hotel

Thornhill CF14 9UA
☎ 029 2052 0280 029 2052 0324
e-mail: enquiries@newhousehotel.com
***Dir:*** *on A469*
Perched amongst the Welsh hills, in tranquil rural surroundings, the New House enjoys unrivalled views of the city. The public areas comprise a lounge and bar, an elegant restaurant and various function suites. Accommodation is spacious and comfortable, in attractive, well-equipped rooms and suites, mostly located in an adjacent annexe reached by a covered walkway.
**ROOMS:** 36 en suite (3 fmly) No smoking in 3 bedrooms s £60-£87.50; d £80-£112 (incl. bkfst) * **LB** **FACILITIES:** STV Outdoor swimming (H) Xmas **CONF:** Thtr 200 Class 150 Board 200 Del from £87.50 * **PARKING:** 100 **NOTES:** No dogs (ex guide dogs) No smoking in restaurant Civ Wed 200 **CARDS:**

### ★★★70% Posthouse Cardiff

Posthouse

Pentwyn Rd, Pentwyn CF23 7XA
☎ 0870 400 8141 029 2054 9147
e-mail: gm-1047@forte-hotels.com
***Dir:*** *M4 junct 29, onto A48(M), take 2nd exit (Pentwyn) 3rd exit off the rdbt. Hotel on right, past Mercedes garage*
Convenient for Cardiff and the M4 this modern hotel is suitable for both the business and leisure traveller. Accommodation is spacious and bright with well-equipped bedrooms, all with en suite bathrooms. Extensive Conference and Leisure facilities are available on site.
**ROOMS:** 142 en suite (50 fmly) No smoking in 55 bedrooms s £39-£69; d £39-£69 * **LB** **FACILITIES:** Indoor swimming (H) Sauna Solarium Gym Jacuzzi Childrens play area ch fac **CONF:** Thtr 140 Class 70 Board 40 Del from £77 * **SERVICES:** Lift **PARKING:** 300 **NOTES:** No smoking in restaurant **CARDS:**

### ★★★66% Posthouse Cardiff City

Posthouse

Castle St CF10 1XB
☎ 0870 400 8140 029 2023 1482
***Dir:*** *M4 junct 29 east(M4) to A48(M) follow signs to city center, turn onto A470 heading to city centre follow road turn left to hotel.*
A large modern hotel with a wide range of services and amenities, designed particularly for the business traveller. Some bedrooms look out over the River Taff and the Millennium Stadium. Bedrooms are smart, comfortable and well-equipped.
**ROOMS:** 155 en suite No smoking in 102 bedrooms s £79-£99; d £79-£99 * **LB** **FACILITIES:** STV **CONF:** Thtr 150 Class 65 Board 50 Del from £119 * **SERVICES:** Lift **PARKING:** 90
**CARDS:**

### ★★65% Sandringham

21 St Mary St CF10 1PL
☎ 029 2023 2161 029 2038 3998
e-mail: hotel@sandringham21.fsnet.co.uk
***Dir:*** *M4 junct 29 follow 'City Centre' signs. Opposite the castle turn into High Street which leads to St Mary St*
Located in the heart of the city, the Sandringham offers well equipped rooms with modern facilities. A smart restaurant and bar, 'Café Jazz' complements the hotel; as the name suggests live jazz is on offer several nights a week. The hotel also has a separate bar and a breakfast room.
**ROOMS:** 28 en suite (1 fmly) No smoking in 2 bedrooms s £30-£100; d £35-£120 (incl. bkfst) * **LB** **FACILITIES:** entertainment **CONF:** Thtr 100 Class 70 Board 60 Del from £55 * **PARKING:** 10 **NOTES:** No dogs (ex guide dogs) **CARDS:**

### ⇧ Express by Holiday Inn Cardiff Bay

Express
by Holiday Inn

Schooner Way, Atlantic Wharf CF10 4EE
☎ 029 2044 9000 🖹 029 2048 8922
e-mail: sarah@cdfba.freeserve.co.uk
***Dir:*** *M4 junct 33, take A4232 & follow road to end. Left at 1st rdbt & left again past the Country Hall on right. Take 1st right & hotel is on the right*

A modern budget hotel offering comfortable accommodation in refreshing, spacious and comprehensively equipped bedrooms, en suite bathrooms with power showers and continental buffet breakfast included in the room rate. Suitable for business travellers or families. For further details and the Express by Holiday Inn phone number, consult the Hotel Groups page.
**ROOMS:** 87 en suite (incl. cont bkfst) s £62; d £62 * **CONF:** Thtr 30 Class 30 Board 20 Del £90 *

### ⇧ Hotel Ibis Cardiff

Churchill Way CF10 2HA
☎ 029 2064 9250 🖹 2920 9260
e-mail: h2936@accor-hotels.com
Modern, budget hotel offering comfortable accommodation in bright and practical bedrooms. Breakfast is self-service and dinner is available in the restaurant. For further details, consult the Hotel Groups page.
**ROOMS:** s £39.95; d £39.95 *

### ⇧ Hotel Ibis Cardiff Gate

Malthouse Av, Cardiff Gate Business Park, Pontprennau CF23 8RA
☎ 029 2073 3222 🖹 029 2073 4222
e-mail: H3159@accor-hotels.com
***Dir:*** *M4 junct 30, take slip road signed Cardiff Service Station. Hotel located on left hand side*
Modern, budget hotel offering comfortable accommodation in bright and practical bedrooms. Breakfast is self-service and dinner is available in the restaurant. For further details, consult the Hotel Groups page.
**ROOMS:** 78 en suite **CONF:** Thtr 35 Class 30 Board 20

### ⇧ *Travelodge (Cardiff Central)*

Imperial Gate, St Marys St CF10 1FA
☎ 08700 850950
Travelodge offers good quality, good value, modern accommodation. Ideal for families, the spacious, en suite bedrooms include remote-control TV, tea and coffee-making facilities, luxury beds and free morning newspaper. Meals can be taken at the nearby family restaurant. For further details and the Travelodge phone number, consult the Hotel Groups page.

Travelodge

### ⇧ *Campanile*

Campanile

Caxton Place, Pentwyn CF2 7HA
☎ 029 2054 9044 🖹 029 2054 9900
***Dir:*** *take Pentwyn exit from A48 and follow signs for Pentwyn Industrial Estate*

Hotel

This modern building offers accommodation in smart, well-equipped bedrooms, all with en suite bathrooms. Refreshments may be taken at the informal Bistro. For further details and the Campanile phone number, consult the Hotel Groups page.
**ROOMS:** 50 annexe en suite **CONF:** Thtr 35 Class 18 Board 20

### ⇧ *Travelodge (Cardiff East)*

Circle Way East, Llanedeyrn CF3 7ND
☎ 029 2054 9564 🖹 029 2054 9564
***Dir:*** *M4 junct 30, take A4232 to North Pentwyn Interchange. A48 & signs for Cardiff East & Docks. 3rd exit at Llanedeyrn Interchange, follow Circle Way East*
Travelodge offers good quality, good value, modern accommodation. Ideal for families, the spacious, en suite bedrooms include remote-control TV, tea and coffee-making facilities, luxury beds and free morning newspaper. Meals can be taken at the nearby family restaurant. For further details and the Travelodge phone number, consult the Hotel Groups page.
**ROOMS:** 32 en suite

### ⇧ *Travelodge (Cardiff West)*

Travelodge

Granada Service Area M4, Pontyclun CF72 8SA
☎ 029 2089 1141 🖹 029 2089 2497
***Dir:*** *M4, junct 33/A4232*
Travelodge offers good quality, good value, modern accommodation. Ideal for families, the spacious, en suite bedrooms include remote-control TV, tea and coffee-making facilities, luxury beds and free morning newspaper. Meals can be taken at the nearby family restaurant. For further details and the Travelodge phone number, consult the Hotel Groups page.
**ROOMS:** 50 en suite **CONF:** Thtr 45 Board 34

CARDIFF, continued

### ○ Innkeeper's Lodge Cardiff

Tyn-y-Parc Rd, Whitchurch CF14 6BG
☎ 0870 243 0500
A new concept in the travel accommodation market. Smart rooms meet essential business requirements but also have home comforts. Dining options include all-day menus plus the added advantage of breakfast, which is included in the room price. Reservations can be made seven days a week through the room reservations number: 0870 243 0500. For further details, consult the Hotel Groups page.
**ROOMS:** 52 en suite

CARDIGAN See Gwbert-on-Sea

CARMARTHEN, Carmarthenshire Map 02 SN42

### ★★63% *Falcon*

Lammas St SA31 3AP
☎ 01267 234959 & 237152 🖹 01267 221277
***Dir:*** *in town centre opposite Monument*

FALCON HOTEL
RESTAURANT
AA

A friendly private hotel, well placed in the centre of the town with good access to the shops, market and business area. Bedrooms, some with four-poster beds, are tastefully decorated and all have good facilities. The restaurant, open for lunch and dinner, has a varied selection of dishes on the carte menu and uses some of the finest local ingredients.
**ROOMS:** 14 en suite (1 fmly) **CONF:** Thtr 100 Class 50 Board 40
**PARKING:** 38 **NOTES:** Closed 25-26 Dec RS Sun
**CARDS:**

CHEPSTOW, Monmouthshire Map 03 ST59

### ★★★★71% Marriott St Pierre Hotel & Country Club

St Pierre Park NP16 6YA
☎ 01291 625261 🖹 01291 629975
***Dir:*** *M48 junct 2. At rdbt on slip road take A466 Chepstow. At next rdbt take 1st exit Caerwent A48. Hotel approx 2m on left*
Set in the rolling hills of Southern Wales, this graceful 14th-century manor house is approached through tree lined fairways. The hotel itself is a blend of the ancient and modern, with the main reception areas in the old house and the bedrooms in modern extensions or in cottages by the lakeside.

**ROOMS:** 148 en suite No smoking in 74 bedrooms s fr £77; d fr £104 (incl. bkfst) * **LB** **FACILITIES:** STV Indoor swimming (H) Golf 36 Tennis (hard) Sauna Solarium Gym Croquet lawn Putting green Jacuzzi Health spa Xmas **CONF:** Thtr 240 Class 120 Board 90 Del from £140 *
**PARKING:** 430 **NOTES:** No dogs (ex guide dogs) Civ Wed 200
**CARDS:**

### ★★★63% George

Moor St NP16 5DB
☎ 01291 625363 🖹 01291 627418
e-mail: george@drayton-manor-hotels.com
***Dir:*** *M48, junct 2, follow signs for town centre*

A former posting house, located next to the 16th-century town gate, The George retains a good deal of its historic character. A cosy, stylish bar and lounge, popular with locals, is complemented by an informal, bistro-style restaurant. Bedrooms are well-equipped, of a good size and are smartly decorated in dark wood and traditional fabrics.
**ROOMS:** 14 en suite No smoking in 7 bedrooms s fr £70; d fr £80 * **LB**
**FACILITIES:** Xmas **CONF:** Thtr 40 Class 20 Board 26 Del from £85 *
**PARKING:** 20 **NOTES:** No smoking in restaurant
**CARDS:**

### ★★★61% The Old Course

Newport Rd NP16 5PR
☎ 01291 626261 🖹 01291 626263
e-mail: bookings@oldcoursechepstow.co.uk
***Dir:*** *M48 junct 2, follow signs to Chepstow, A466 & A48 into town, hotel is on the left*
Convenient for both the M4 and the M48, this privately owned hotel lies just south of the town centre. The public areas include a spacious lounge bar, a comfortable lounge and an attractively

*continued*

appointed restaurant. There is a choice of conference rooms and a large ballroom.

**ROOMS:** 31 en suite (4 fmly) s £43-£49; d £47-£54 * **LB** **FACILITIES:** Xmas **CONF:** Thtr 240 Class 70 Board 70 Del from £82.50 * **SERVICES:** Lift **PARKING:** 180 **NOTES:** No smoking in restaurant **CARDS:**

*See advert on this page*

### ★★70% ***Castle View***

16 Bridge St NP6 5EZ
☎ 01291 620349 01291 627397
e-mail: mart@castview.demon.co.uk
***Dir:*** *opposite the castle*

Looking out on the impressive Norman castle, this 300-year old building has great charm and character. The bedrooms, a couple of which are in a separate building at the end of the garden, offer comfortable accommodation and good facilities. A recently refurbished bar and residents' lounge is supplemented by a restaurant offering a selection of fresh cooking.

**ROOMS:** 9 en suite 4 annexe en suite (7 fmly) **FACILITIES:** STV **NOTES:** No smoking in restaurant **CARDS:**

*See advert on this page*

### ★★66% ***Beaufort***

Beaufort Square NP6 5EP
☎ 01291 622497 01291 627389
e-mail: info@beauforthotelchepstow.com
***Dir:*** *off A48, at St Mary's Church turn left and left again at end of public car park into Nelson St. Hotel car park 100yds on right*

Located in the town centre, this 16th-century coaching inn is now a popular hotel. The bedrooms, including ground-floor and family rooms, are furnished and equipped in a modern style. Public areas comprise a busy bar and a restaurant offering a wide choice of dishes including steaks and pasta.

**ROOMS:** 18 en suite (2 fmly) **FACILITIES:** STV **CONF:** Thtr 40 Class 25 Board 20 **PARKING:** 14 **CARDS:**

## CHIRK, Wrexham — Map 07 SJ23

### ★★★66% **Moreton Park Lodge**

Moreton Park, Gledrid LL14 5DG
☎ 01691 776666 01691 776655
e-mail: enquiries@moretonparklodge.com
***Dir:*** *200 yds from the rdbt of the A5 and B5070*

This privately owned, purpose-built, modern hotel on the outskirts of Chirk offers well-equipped accommodation, which includes bedrooms suitable for guests with disabilities and bedrooms with separate lounge areas. Meals are available in the Lord Moreton pub/restaurant, and there is an indoor play area for children.

**ROOMS:** 46 en suite (20 fmly) No smoking in 26 bedrooms s £44.95-£54.95; d £44.95-£54.95 (incl. bkfst) * **FACILITIES:** STV Xmas **PARKING:** 100 **NOTES:** No dogs (ex guide dogs) No smoking in restaurant **CARDS:**

*See advert under OSWESTRY*

COLWYN BAY, Conwy Map 06 SH87

### ★★★65% Norfolk House

39 Princes Dr LL29 8PF
☎ 01492 531757 Fax 01492 533781
e-mail: bookings@norfolkhousehotel.fsnet.co.uk
***Dir:*** *from A55 at Colwyn Bay exit into right lane of slip road right at traffic lights pass station hotel almost opposite filling station*

Norfolk House is a privately owned and personally run hotel with a warm, friendly atmosphere. It is within easy walking distance of the seafront, town centre and railway station. The accommodation is well-equipped, comfortable and relaxing. Bedrooms are prettily decorated with family suites offered. There are several lounges, a popular bar, and conference facilities available.

**ROOMS:** 20 rms (13 en suite) 1 annexe en suite (4 fmly) No smoking in 2 bedrooms s fr £35 (incl. bkfst) * LB **FACILITIES:** STV ch fac **CONF:** Thtr 35 Class 30 Board 20 **SERVICES:** Lift **PARKING:** 30 **NOTES:** No smoking in restaurant **CARDS:**

*See advert on opposite page*

### ★★★64% Hopeside

63-67 Prince's Dr, West End LL29 8PW
☎ 01492 533244 Fax 01492 532850
e-mail: hopesidecb@aol.com
***Dir:*** *turn off A55 at Rhos-on-Sea exit, turn left at lights, hotel 50yds on right*

The promenade and town centre are within easy walking distance of this friendly hotel. The restaurant offers a good choice, and bar food and blackboard specials are also available. Bedrooms are mostly pine-furnished and all are attractively decorated. The hotel also holds a licence for civil marriage ceremonies.

**ROOMS:** 18 en suite (2 fmly) No smoking in 9 bedrooms s £39-£49; d £49-£59 (incl. bkfst) * LB **FACILITIES:** STV Sauna Gym **CONF:** Thtr 50 Class 50 Board 34 **PARKING:** 14 **NOTES:** No smoking in restaurant **CARDS:**

### ★★64% Marine

West Promenade LL28 4BP
☎ 01492 530295 Fax 0870 168 9400
e-mail: reservations@marinehotel.co.uk
***Dir:*** *turn off A55 at Old Colwyn to seafront. Turn left, and after pier turn left just before traffic lights, car park on corner*

This privately owned and personally run hotel stands on the promenade, overlooking sea views. The accommodation is soundly maintained and equipped to suit both commercial visitors and holiday makers. Facilities include a small bar and a lounge.

**ROOMS:** 14 rms (12 en suite) (4 fmly) No smoking in 9 bedrooms s fr £29; d fr £48 (incl. bkfst) * LB **PARKING:** 11 **NOTES:** No smoking in restaurant Closed mid Oct-end Apr **CARDS:**

### ★★63% Lyndale

410 Abergele Rd, Old Colwyn LL29 9AB
☎ 01492 515429 Fax 01492 518805
e-mail: lyndale@tinyworld.co.uk
***Dir:*** *exit A55 Old Colwyn, turn left. At rdbt through village continue for 1m on A547*

This family-run hotel offers a range of accommodation including family suites and a four-poster bedroom. There is a cosy bar and a comfortable foyer lounge. Weddings and other functions can be catered for and there are facilities for business meetings.

**ROOMS:** 14 en suite (3 fmly) No smoking in 3 bedrooms s £25-£38; d £45-£58 (incl. bkfst) * LB **FACILITIES:** Xmas **CONF:** Thtr 40 Class 20 Board 20 Del from £40 * **PARKING:** 20 **CARDS:**

CONWY, Conwy Map 06 SH77

### ★★★73% Groes Inn

Tyn-y-Groes LL32 8TN
☎ 01492 650545 Fax 01492 650855
***Dir:*** *leave A55 at Conwy turn off, cross Old Conwy Bridge, 1st left through Castle Walls on B5106 Trefriw road, follow road for approx 2m, hotel on right*

The original inn dates back to at least the 16th century and has charming features such as low beamed ceilings, log fires, period furniture and an abundance of bric-a-brac. It offers a choice of bars and has a beautifully appointed restaurant, with a conservatory extension opening onto the lovely rear garden. The comfortable, well equipped bedrooms are contained in a separate building; some have balconies or private terraces.

**ROOMS:** 14 en suite (1 fmly) No smoking in 6 bedrooms s £64-£95; d £81-£115 (incl. bkfst) * LB **FACILITIES:** Xmas **CONF:** Thtr 22 Class 20 Board 20 **PARKING:** 100 **CARDS:**

### ★★★66% ® Castle Hotel Conwy

High St LL32 8DB
☎ 01492 582800 Fax 01492 582300
e-mail: mail@castlewales.co.uk
***Dir:*** *A55 cross estuary towards castle turn right at mini-rdbt onto one way system into the town. Hotel is main landmark on High St*

This personally run, 16th-century hotel is one of Conwy's most distinguished buildings. Bedrooms have modern facilities, and guests will enjoy the hospitable atmosphere. Fresh flowers and paintings by a local artist feature in the traditional public rooms. A good selection of enjoyable dishes is available in the restaurant. Meals are also served in the popular bar.

**ROOMS:** 29 en suite (2 fmly) No smoking in 14 bedrooms s £50-£75; d £65-£120 (incl. bkfst) * LB **FACILITIES:** Xmas **CONF:** Thtr 30 Class 20 Board 20 Del from £75 * **PARKING:** 34 **NOTES:** No smoking in restaurant **CARDS:**

## *Premier Collection*

### ★★ ®®® The Old Rectory Country House

Llanrwst Rd, Llansanffraid Glan Conwy LL28 5LF
☎ 01492 580611 Fax 01492 584555
e-mail: info@oldrectorycountryhouse.co.uk
***Dir:*** *0.5m S from A470/A55 junct on left hand side*

A charming hotel with terraced gardens overlooking the Conwy Estuary and Snowdonia. The Old Rectory Country House Hotel has classical interior design and antique pieces, which complement the intimate public rooms. Bedrooms, most of which have sea or estuary views, are tastefully furnished in keeping with the building, and many thoughtful extra comforts are provided. The cuisine is excellent with well-

*continued*

selected ingredients carefully put together in appealing combinations. The warm and caring hospitality is also outstanding.

**ROOMS:** 4 en suite 2 annexe en suite No smoking in all bedrooms s £99-£129; d £149-£169 (incl. bkfst) * **LB** **PARKING:** 10 **NOTES:** No children 5yrs No smoking in restaurant Closed Dec-Jan RS Feb **CARDS:**

**★★71% Lodge**
LL32 8YX
☎ 01492 660766 📠 01492 660534
e-mail: bbaldon@lodgehotel.co.uk
(For full entry see Tal-y-Bont)

THE CIRCLE
Selected Individual Hotels
GREAT BRITAIN

**★★68% Tir-y-Coed Country House**
Rowen LL32 8TP
☎ 01492 650219 📠 01492 650219
e-mail: tirycoed@btinternet.com
***Dir:*** *turn off B5106 into unclassified road signposted Rowen, hotel is on fringe of village about 60mtrs N of Post Office*

This small privately owned and personally run hotel provides a haven of peace and relaxation. Standing in its own extensive and delightful garden, the house is located in the picturesque Conwy Valley. It is convenient for access to the Snowdonia and the coast. The accommodation is well-maintained and equipped, and the hospitality warm and friendly.
**ROOMS:** 7 en suite 1 annexe en suite (1 fmly) **FACILITIES:** ch fac **PARKING:** 8 **NOTES:** No smoking in restaurant Closed Xmas & New Year RS Nov-Feb **CARDS:**

**★★67% Castle Bank**
Mount Pleasant LL32 8NY
☎ 01492 593888 📠 01492 596466
e-mail: castlebank@bun.com
***Dir:*** *turn off A55 expressway at Conwy, hotel is accessed through public car park on Mount Pleasant, adjacent to the Bangor Archway in town wall*
This small, friendly hotel, near the old town walls, is well located

*continued*

for touring the surrounding countryside and attractions. Bedrooms are bright, attractively decorated and well-equipped. There is a spacious dining room with a bar and a comfortably furnished lounge.
**ROOMS:** 9 en suite (2 fmly) s £35; d £50-£55 (incl. bkfst) * **LB** **FACILITIES:** Xmas **PARKING:** 12 **NOTES:** No dogs (ex guide dogs) No smoking in restaurant **CARDS:**

## CRICCIETH, Gwynedd
Map 06 SH43

**★★★72% Bron Eifion Country House**
LL52 0SA
☎ 01766 522385 📠 01766 522003
e-mail: stay@broneifion.co.uk
***Dir:*** *0.5m outside Criccieth on A497 towards Pwllheli*

Best Western

This delightful country house is set in extensive grounds to the west of Criccieth. Most of the tasteful bedrooms have period and antique furniture, and several have four-poster beds or attractive canopies. The central hall features a minstrel's gallery, and there is

*continued on p808*

CRICCIETH, continued

a choice of comfortable lounges. The restaurant overlooks the gardens.
**ROOMS:** 19 en suite (2 fmly) s £71; d £96-£132 (incl. bkfst) * **LB** **FACILITIES:** Croquet lawn Putting green Xmas **CONF:** Thtr 30 Class 25 Board 25 **PARKING:** 80 **NOTES:** No smoking in restaurant
**CARDS:**

### ★★69% Caerwylan
LL52 0HW
☎ 01766 522547
A long established holiday hotel above the seafront; many rooms have fine views of the castle and Cardigan Bay. Comfortably furnished lounges are available for residents and the five-course menu changes daily. Bedrooms are smart, modern, and several have their own private sitting areas. The enjoyable atmosphere ensures many guests return year after year.
**ROOMS:** 25 en suite (3 fmly) s £20-£26; d £40-£52 (incl. bkfst) * **LB** **SERVICES:** Lift **PARKING:** 9 **NOTES:** No smoking in restaurant Closed Nov-Etr **CARDS:**

### ★★67% Gwyndy
Llanystumdwy LL52 0SP
☎ 01766 522720 01766 522720
***Dir:*** *turn off A497 into village of Llanystumdwy follow road for 0.25m, hotel is next to church*
A popular hotel with a 17th-century cottage and a nearby purpose-built bedroom complex. The original cottage contains the lounge, bar and restaurant, which are comfortably furnished. Exposed timbers feature and there are several stone fireplaces. Bedrooms are spacious and relaxing.
**ROOMS:** 10 annexe en suite (5 fmly) s £29-£30; d £48-£50 (incl. bkfst) * **FACILITIES:** Fishing **PARKING:** 20 **NOTES:** No smoking in restaurant Closed Nov-Mar **CARDS:**

### ★★66% Lion
Y Maes LL52 0AA
☎ 01766 522460 01766 523075
e-mail: info@lionhotelcriccieth.co.uk
***Dir:*** *turn off A497 in the centre of Criccieth on to village green north, hotel located on green*
This hotel lies just a short walk from Criccieth castle and seafront, with fine views from many rooms. The bars enjoy a good local following and staff are friendly and welcoming. Bedrooms are well-decorated and furnished, spread between the main building and nearby annexe. Regular live entertainment is held during the summer.
**ROOMS:** 34 en suite 12 annexe en suite (8 fmly) s £32-£36; d £57.50-£62.50 (incl. bkfst) * **LB** **FACILITIES:** STV entertainment Xmas **SERVICES:** Lift **PARKING:** 30 **NOTES:** No smoking in restaurant RS Nov-Mar **CARDS:**

## CRICKHOWELL, Powys — Map 03 SO21

### ★★★72% Bear
NP8 1BW
☎ 01873 810408 01873 811696
e-mail: bearhotel@aol.com
***Dir:*** *on A40 between Abergavenny and Breen*
A favourite with locals as well as visitors, the character and friendliness of this 15th-century coaching inn are renowned. The bar and restaurant areas are furnished in keeping with the building and give a comfortable area to enjoy some of the finest locally sourced ingredients prepared to a consistently high standard.
**ROOMS:** 13 en suite 13 annexe en suite (6 fmly) s £52-£98; d £68-£136 (incl. bkfst) * **CONF:** Thtr 60 Class 30 Board 20 **PARKING:** 38
**CARDS:**

*See advert on opposite page*

### ★★★71% Gliffaes Country House Hotel
NP8 1RH
☎ 01874 730371 & 0800 146719 (Freephone) 01874 730463
e-mail: calls@gliffaeshotel.com
***Dir:*** *1m from A40 - 2.5m W of Crickhowell*

This impressive country house was built in 1885. It stands in 33 acres of gardens and wooded grounds by the River Usk. Now a family owned and personally run hotel, it provides recently refurbished, good quality accommodation and has comfortable public rooms with a wealth of charm and character. The hotel has a well-deserved high reputation for its food, which is complemented by willing, friendly and attentive service.
**ROOMS:** 19 en suite 3 annexe en suite (3 fmly) s £55-£135; d £67-£145 (incl. bkfst) * **LB** **FACILITIES:** Tennis (hard) Fishing Snooker Croquet lawn Putting green Cycling Birdwatching Walking ch fac **CONF:** Thtr 40 Class 16 Board 16 Del from £135 * **PARKING:** 34 **NOTES:** No dogs (ex guide dogs) No smoking in restaurant Civ Wed 30
**CARDS:**

### ★★★65% *Manor*
Brecon Rd NP8 1SE
☎ 01873 810212 01873 811938
***Dir:*** *on A40, Crickhowell/Brecon, 0.5m from Crickhowell*

In a stunning location on a hillside high above Crickhowell, this impressive manor house was the birthplace of Sir George Everest. The bedrooms and public areas have an elegant atmosphere, and there are extensive leisure facilities. The restaurant has panoramic views and is the setting for exciting modern cooking. Guests can also dine in the informal atmosphere of the nearby Nantyffin Cider Mill, the hotel's sister operation.
**ROOMS:** 20 en suite (1 fmly) No smoking in 8 bedrooms
**FACILITIES:** Indoor swimming (H) Sauna Solarium Gym Jacuzzi Fitness assessment Sunbed **CONF:** Thtr 400 Class 300 Board 300
**PARKING:** 200 **CARDS:**

*See advert on opposite page*

C

**★★73% Ty Croeso**
The Dardy, Llangattock NP8 1PU
☎ 01873 810573 01873 810573
e-mail: tycroeso@ty-croeso-hotel.freeserve.co.uk
**Dir:** *at Shell garage on A40 take opposite road, down hill over river bridge. Turn right, after 0.5m turn left, up hill over canal, hotel signed*
Ty Croeso, meaning 'House of Welcome' lives up to its name. In the restaurant an interesting carte and a Taste of Wales set-price menu are available. Glamorgan Sausages and laverbread are available at breakfast. Public areas are comfortable and feature log fires. Bedrooms are decorated with pretty fabrics and all have good facilities.
**ROOMS:** 8 en suite (1 fmly) s £35-£45; d £60-£75 (incl. bkfst) * **LB**
**PARKING:** 20 **NOTES:** No smoking in restaurant RS 24-26 Dec
**CARDS:**

CROSS HANDS, Carmarthenshire Map 02 SN51

**Travelodge**
SA14 6NW
☎ 01269 845700 01269 845700
**Dir:** *on A48, westbound*
Travelodge offers good quality, good value, modern accommodation. Ideal for families, the spacious, en suite bedrooms include remote-control TV, tea and coffee-making facilities, luxury beds and free morning newspaper. Meals can be taken at the nearby family restaurant. For further details and the Travelodge phone number, consult the Hotel Groups page.
**ROOMS:** 32 en suite

Weekend away? Hotels with LB in their entry offer leisure breaks.

## CWMBRAN, Torfaen

Map 03 ST29

**★★★★65% Parkway**

Cwmbran Dr NP44 3UW

☎ 01633 871199 📠 01633 869160

e-mail: user@parkwayhotel.freeserve.co.uk

***Dir:*** *from M4 take A4051 for Cwmbran until you see signs for Cwmbran-Llantarnam Park. Turn right at rdbt then right for Hotel*

The hotel is purpose built and offers comfortable accommodation for a wide range of guests. For leisure guests, the sports centre provides somewhere to relax, perhaps after a meal in Ravello's restaurant. For the corporate guest the range of conference and meeting facilities should suit most needs. The coffee shop offers an informal eating option during the day.

**ROOMS:** 70 en suite (4 fmly) No smoking in 24 bedrooms s £76.50-£94; d £88.50-£106 * **LB** **FACILITIES:** STV Indoor swimming (H) Sauna Solarium Gym Jacuzzi Steam room entertainment Xmas **CONF:** Thtr 500 Class 240 Board 100 Del from £104 * **PARKING:** 300 **NOTES:** Closed 28-30 Dec Civ Wed 90 **CARDS:**

*See advert on opposite page*

## DEVIL'S BRIDGE, Ceredigion

Map 06 SN77

**★★66% *Hafod Arms***

SY23 3JL

☎ 01970 890232 📠 01970 890394

e-mail: enquiries@hafodarms.co.uk

***Dir:*** *turn off A44 at Ponterwyd. Hotel is 5m along A4120*

This stone-built former hunting lodge dates back to the 17th century and is now a family owned and run hotel providing accommodation suitable for both business people and tourists. Family bedded rooms and a four-poster room are available. In addition to the dining area and lounge, there are tea rooms, a secure car park and six acres of grounds.

**ROOMS:** 15 rms (11 en suite) (1 fmly) **CONF:** Board 25 **PARKING:** 70 **NOTES:** No children 12yrs No smoking in restaurant Closed 15 Dec-Jan **CARDS:**

## DOLGELLAU, Gwynedd

Map 06 SH71

**★★★76% Penmaenuchaf Hall**

Penmaenpool LL40 1YB

☎ 01341 422129 📠 01341 422787

e-mail: relax@penhall.co.uk

***Dir:*** *off A470 onto A493 to Tywyn. Hotel entrance is approx. 1m on the left*

Built in 1860, this impressive hall stands in 20 acres of formal gardens, grounds and woodland and enjoys magnificent views across the River Mawddach. Careful restoration by the present owners has created a comfortable and welcoming hotel. Fresh produce cooked in modern British style is served in the panelled restaurant.

*continued*

**ROOMS:** 14 en suite (2 fmly) No smoking in 5 bedrooms s £70-£110; d £110-£170 (incl. bkfst) * **LB** **FACILITIES:** Fishing Snooker Croquet lawn Xmas **CONF:** Thtr 50 Class 30 Board 22 Del from £130 * **PARKING:** 30 **NOTES:** No children 6yrs No smoking in restaurant Civ Wed 50 **CARDS:**

**★★★71% *Plas Dolmelynllyn***

Ganllwyd LL40 2HP

☎ 01341 440273 📠 01341 440640

e-mail: info@dolly-hotel.co.uk

***Dir:*** *5m N of Dolgellau on A470*

Surrounded by three acres of gardens and National Trust land, this fine house dates back to the 16th century. Spacious bedrooms are attractively furnished and offer comfortable seating as well as many thoughtful extras. Dinner is served in the comfortable dining room, adjacent to the conservatory bar.

**ROOMS:** 10 en suite No smoking in all bedrooms **FACILITIES:** STV Fishing Mountain walking Mountain Bike riding **CONF:** Thtr 20 Class 20 Board 20 **PARKING:** 20 **NOTES:** No smoking in restaurant Closed Nov-Feb **CARDS:**

**★★★70% Dolserau Hall**

LL40 2AG

☎ 01341 422522 📠 01341 422400

e-mail: aa@dhh.co.uk

***Dir:*** *1.5m outside town between A494 to Bala and A470 to Dinas Mawddwy*

This privately owned, personally run and friendly hotel lies in attractive grounds extending to the river and is surrounded by green fields. Several comfortable lounges are provided and welcoming log fires are lit during cold weather. The smart bedrooms are well-equipped and have comfortable seating. A varied menu offers very competently prepared dishes.

**ROOMS:** 15 en suite (3 fmly) s £45-£52.50; d £85-£120 (incl. bkfst & dinner) * **LB** **FACILITIES:** STV Xmas **SERVICES:** Lift **PARKING:** 70 **NOTES:** No children 6yrs No smoking in restaurant Closed mid Nov-mid Feb (ex Xmas & New Year) **CARDS:**

*See advert on opposite page*

**★★72% George III Hotel**

Penmaenpool LL40 1YD

☎ 01341 422525 📠 01341 423565

e-mail: reception@george-3rd.co.uk

***Dir:*** *turn left off A470 towards Tywyn, approx. 2m, turn right for toll bridge then 1st left for hotel*

On the banks of the Mawddach Estuary, this delightful small hotel started life as an inn and a chandlers to the local boatyard. A nearby building, now housing several bedrooms, was the local railway station. Bedrooms are well-equipped and many enjoy river views. There is a choice of bars, all providing a wide range of food. More formal dining is available in the restaurant.

**ROOMS:** 6 en suite 5 annexe en suite s £45-£58; d £80-£98 (incl. bkfst) * **LB** **FACILITIES:** Fishing Free fishing permits, Mountain bike hire **PARKING:** 60 **NOTES:** No smoking in restaurant **CARDS:**

**★★66% *Fronoleu Farm***

Tabor LL40 2PS

☎ 01341 422361 & 422197 📠 01341 422023

***Dir:*** *From Machynlleth, at junct of the A487 with A470, take road signed Tabor opposite Cross Foxes and continue for 1.25m*

This 16th-century farmhouse lies in the shadow of Cader Idris. Carefully extended over recent years, it retains many original features. The bar and lounge are both located in the old building where there are exposed timbers and open fires. Most of the

*continued on p812*

Dolserau Hall
Country House Hotel
Dolgellau LL40 2AG
Dolserau Hall with Cader Idris towering above

With magnificent scenery, wonderful views, great walking country, superb traditional cuisine, comfort and a warm welcome, it is no surprise that so many of our guests keep on coming back. Special breaks all year and Christmas and New Year programme. Call us now for our comprehensive colour brochure pack.

Tel: (01341) 422522
email: welcome@dhh.co.uk
Website www.dhh.co.uk

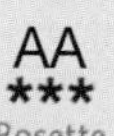
AA
★★★
Rosette

# ROYAL SHIP HOTEL★

**Queens Square, Dolgellau, Gwynedd**
**Telephone Dolgellau 01341 422209**

• Situated in the Cader Idris mountain range • Ideally situated in the centre of town • Family Rooms • Colour TV in all En-suite Rooms • Ideally situated for touring North and Mid Wales • Great Little Trains of Wales • Slate Mines at Blaenau • Mountain Walking • Cyclists Trek • Golf • Robinson's Traditional Draught Beer • Access and Barclaycard accepted • Colour Brochure on request •

AA ★★★★

# The Parkway Hotel

WTB ★★★★

Cwmbran Drive, Cwmbran, Gwent NP44 3UW
Telephone: (01633) 871199 Facsimile: (01633) 869160

The Parkway is a 4 star luxury hotel designed and developed on a Mediterranean theme. Facilities include 70 en suite bedrooms, Ravellos Restaurant, Lounge Area with open log fire and the exclusive 'Colonial Club' health and leisure complex with 15 metre level deck swimming pool, spa bath, sauna, steam room, solariums and gymnasium. It is ideally located between Newport and Cwmbran with some of the most beautiful Welsh countryside on its doorstep. Nearby attractions include — Brecon Beacons National Park, Wye Valley, City of Cardiff and the Big Pit Mining Museum.

at The Parkway

DOLGELLAU, continued

bedrooms are in a modern extension and these are spacious and well-equipped. The restaurant attracts a large local following.
**ROOMS:** 11 rms (7 en suite) (3 fmly) No smoking in 6 bedrooms **FACILITIES:** Fishing **CONF:** Thtr 150 Class 80 Board 80 **PARKING:** 60 **CARDS:**

★67% **Royal Ship**
Queens Square LL40 1AR
☎ 01341 422209 01341 421027
***Dir:*** *located in the centre of the town*
The Royal Ship dates from 1813 when it was a coaching inn. There are three bars and several lounges, all most comfortably furnished and appointed. It is very much the centre of local activities and a wide range of food is available. Bedrooms are tastefully decorated and fitted with modern amenities.
**ROOMS:** 24 rms (18 en suite) (4 fmly) s £28-£38; d £45-£65 (incl. bkfst) * LB **FACILITIES:** STV Xmas **CONF:** Thtr 80 Class 60 Board 60 Del from £51.75 * **PARKING:** 12 **NOTES:** No dogs (ex guide dogs) No smoking in restaurant **CARDS:**

*See advert on page 811*

DOLWYDDELAN, Conwy — Map 06 SH75

★★65% **Elen's Castle**
LL25 0EJ
☎ 01690 750207 01690 750207
e-mail: elens98@aol.com
***Dir:*** *on A470, 5m S of Betws-y-Coed*
This small hotel is very friendly and was operated as a beer house in the 18th century. The original bar, complete with a slab floor and pot-belly stove, remains, and there are two cosy sitting rooms with open fires and exposed timbers. Two of the bedrooms have four-poster beds and families can be accommodated. A good range of bar and restaurant food is provided.
**ROOMS:** 9 rms (8 en suite) (2 fmly) No smoking in 2 bedrooms s £20-£40; d £34-£70 (incl. bkfst) * LB **FACILITIES:** Xmas **PARKING:** 40 **NOTES:** No dogs (ex guide dogs) No smoking in restaurant **CARDS:**

EGLWYSFACH, Ceredigion — Map 06 SN69

*Hotel of the Year*

★★★ ®®® **Ynyshir Hall**
SY20 8TA
☎ 01654 781209 01654 781366
e-mail: info@ynyshir-hall.co.uk
***Dir:*** *off A487, 5.5m S of Machynlleth, signposted from the main road*
This fine country house hotel, awarded Hotel of the Year for Wales 2001-2002, is set in 12 acres of scenic gardens. Since the 16th century the house has been cherished by a succession of eminent owners. The bedrooms vary in size and all are individually designed, furnished with antiques, and equipped with a range of thoughtful extras. Both the bar and the drawing room are adorned with striking paintings of local scenes, and excellent cuisine is served in the smart dining room.
**ROOMS:** 8 en suite 2 annexe en suite No smoking in all bedrooms s £110-£150; d £125-£205 (incl. bkfst) * LB **FACILITIES:** Croquet lawn Xmas **CONF:** Thtr 25 Class 20 Board 18 Del from £120 * **PARKING:** 20 **NOTES:** No children 9yrs No smoking in restaurant Closed 5-23 Jan Civ Wed 40 **CARDS:**

EWLOE, Flintshire — Map 07 SJ36

★★★★72% ® **De Vere St David's Park**
St Davids Park CH5 3YB
☎ 01244 520800 01244 520930
e-mail: reservations.st.davids@devere-hotels.com
***Dir:*** *take A494 Queensferry to Mold for 4m, then take left slip road B5127 signposted Buckley, hotel can be seen at rdbt*
This fine modern hotel conveniently located for both Chester and North Wales provides well-equipped, attractive accommodation including four-poster suites and family rooms. Public areas include leisure and spa facilities, an all day café, the popular Fountains Restaurant and, nearby, the hotel's own golf course.
**ROOMS:** 145 en suite (27 fmly) No smoking in 54 bedrooms s £114; d £124 * LB **FACILITIES:** Indoor swimming (H) Golf 18 Tennis (hard) Snooker Sauna Solarium Gym Putting green Jacuzzi Steam bath Beauty Therapist Playroom Xmas **CONF:** Thtr 300 Class 150 Board 40 Del £142 * **SERVICES:** Lift **PARKING:** 240 **NOTES:** No smoking in restaurant Civ Wed 100 **CARDS:**

FISHGUARD, Pembrokeshire — Map 02 SM93

★★69% **Cartref**
15-19 High St SA65 9AW
☎ 01348 872430 01348 873664
e-mail: cartref@themail.co.uk
***Dir:*** *on A40 in town centre*
This personally run and friendly hotel is close to the town centre and is convenient for access to the ferry terminal. The well-maintained and modern equipped accommodation includes family bedded rooms. A limited number of secure garage spaces are available.
**ROOMS:** 10 en suite (2 fmly) s £32-£38; d £48-£54 (incl. bkfst) * LB **PARKING:** 4 **NOTES:** No smoking in restaurant **CARDS:**

★★61% ***Abergwaun***
The Market Square SA65 9HA
☎ 01348 872077 01348 875412
***Dir:*** *on A40 in the centre of town*
Originally a coaching inn, this privately owned and run hotel stands in the main square of the town, with the ferry terminal in easy reach. It has been considerably modernised over recent years and now provides smart pine-furnished bedrooms. A comfortable bar serves a good range of bar food and the restaurant offers a selection of more substantial meals.
**ROOMS:** 10 en suite (2 fmly) **CONF:** Thtr 50 Class 20 Board 24 **PARKING:** 3 **NOTES:** No dogs **CARDS:**

## GLYN CEIRIOG, Wrexham
Map 07 SJ23

### ★★★64% Golden Pheasant
LL20 7BB
☎ 01691 718281 🖷 01691 718479
**Dir:** *take B4500 at Chirk, continue along this road for 5m, follow hotel signs*
This 18th-century hostelry is on the edge of the village surrounded by hills and countryside. There is a choice of bars, as well as a lounge and a restaurant. To the rear is a courtyard with shrub and flower beds. There is also an aviary with exotic birds. Bedrooms include four-posters and family rooms.
**ROOMS:** 19 en suite (5 fmly) **FACILITIES:** ch fac **CONF:** Thtr 60 Board 10 Del from £65 * **PARKING:** 45 **NOTES:** No smoking in restaurant
**CARDS:**

## GWBERT-ON-SEA, Ceredigion
Map 02 SN15

### ★★★67% *Cliff*
SA43 1PP
☎ 01239 613241 🖷 01239 615391

This privately owned hotel sits on the cliff top at Gwbert on Sea, just north of Cardigan. Most of the spacious and comfortable public rooms have superb sea views, as do many of the bedrooms. Apart from conference and function facilities, the hotel has a wide range of leisure activities, including an outdoor swimming pool and 9 hole golf course, in its 30 acres of grounds.
**ROOMS:** 70 en suite (4 fmly) No smoking in 10 bedrooms
**FACILITIES:** Outdoor swimming (H) Golf 9 Fishing Squash Snooker Sauna Solarium Gym Putting green Sea fishing **CONF:** Thtr 200 Class 100 Board 64 **SERVICES:** Lift **PARKING:** 100 **NOTES:** Closed 25-26 Dec
**CARDS:**

## HALKYN, Flintshire
Map 07 SJ27

### ⌂ *Travelodge*
Travelodge

CH8 8RF
☎ 01352 780952 🖷 01352 780952
**Dir:** *on A55, westbound*
Travelodge offers good quality, good value, modern accommodation. Ideal for families, the spacious, en suite bedrooms include remote-control TV, tea and coffee-making facilities, luxury beds and free morning newspaper. Meals can be taken at the nearby family restaurant. For further details and the Travelodge phone number, consult the Hotel Groups page.

**ROOMS:** 31 en suite

## HARLECH See Talsarnau

## HAVERFORDWEST, Pembrokeshire
Map 02 SM91
see also Burton

### ★★67% Hotel Mariners
MINOTEL Great Britain

Mariners Square SA61 2DU
☎ 01437 763353 🖷 01437 764258
**Dir:** *follow signs to town centre, over bridge, up High St, take 1st turning on the right Dark St hotel at the end*
Located just out of the town centre, this privately owned, friendly hotel dates back to 1625. The bedrooms are equipped with modern facilities and are well-maintained. Family bedded rooms are available. The popular bar is a focus for the town and offers a good range of food in addition to that available in the more formal restaurant.
**ROOMS:** 28 en suite (5 fmly) No smoking in 3 bedrooms s £52.50-£60.75; d £72.50-£78.50 (incl. bkfst) * **LB** **FACILITIES:** STV Short mat bowls **CONF:** Thtr 50 Class 20 Board 20 **PARKING:** 50 **NOTES:** Closed 26-27 Dec & 1 Jan **CARDS:**

### ★★66% *Wilton House*
6 Quay St SA61 1BG
☎ 01437 760033 🖷 01437 760297
e-mail: phil@wiltonhousehotel.fsbdial.co.uk
A friendly family-run hotel just a short walk form the town centre and next to the River Cleddau. Public areas include a lounge, a bar/bistro style restaurant serving home-made dishes, a solarium and a heated outdoor swimming pool. Bedrooms are attractively decorated; family rooms are also available.
**ROOMS:** 10 en suite (3 fmly) **FACILITIES:** Outdoor swimming (H) Solarium **PARKING:** 6 **NOTES:** No dogs (ex guide dogs) No smoking in restaurant **CARDS:**

## HAY-ON-WYE, Powys
Map 03 SO24

### ★★★66% The Swan-at-Hay
Church St HR3 5DQ
☎ 01497 821188 🖷 01497 821424
**Dir:** *enter Hay-on-Wye on B4350 from Brecon, hotel on left. From any other route follow signs for Brecon & just before leaving town hotel on right*
A coaching inn built in 1821, close to the town centre. Well-equipped accommodation includes rooms in converted cottages across the courtyard car park. Facilities include a large function room, a room for smaller meetings, a choice of bars, a comfortable lounge and a bright and pleasant restaurant.
**ROOMS:** 16 en suite 3 annexe en suite (1 fmly) s £50; d £70-£90 (incl. bkfst) * **LB** **FACILITIES:** Fishing ch fac Xmas **CONF:** Thtr 140 Class 60 Board 50 Del from £85 * **PARKING:** 18 **NOTES:** No smoking in restaurant Civ Wed 90 **CARDS:**

### ★★67% Baskerville Arms
Clyro HR3 5RZ
☎ 01497 820670 🖷 01497 821609
e-mail: arms@baskerville.com
**Dir:** *from Hereford follow Brecon A438 into Clyro. Hotel signposted*
This large, Georgian coaching inn is located in the village of Clyro, near Hay-on-Wye. It was originally called The Swan and features as such in Kilvert's Diaries. Now a privately owned and personally run hotel, it is popular for its food. The carte restaurant menu and bar meals provide a good choice of dishes.
**ROOMS:** 12 rms (10 en suite) (1 fmly) No smoking in 3 bedrooms s £27.50-£35; d £60 (incl. bkfst) * **LB** **FACILITIES:** Fishing Games room ch fac **CONF:** Thtr 65 Class 40 Board 36 **PARKING:** 12
**NOTES:** No dogs (ex guide dogs) No smoking in restaurant
**CARDS:**

HAY-ON-WYE, continued

**★★66% Old Black Lion**
26 Lion St HR3 5AD
☎ 01497 820841
***Dir:*** *from TIC car park turn right along Oxford Rd, pass Nat West bank, next left (Lion St), hotel 20yds on right*
This fine old coaching inn, with a history stretching back several centuries, has a wealth of charm and character. It was occupied by Oliver Cromwell during the siege of Hay Castle. Privately-owned, it provides cosy and well-equipped bedrooms, some of which are located in an adjacent building. A wide range of food is provided and service is friendly.
**ROOMS:** 6 rms (5 en suite) 4 annexe en suite (1 fmly) No smoking in all bedrooms s £32.50-£45; d £70 (incl. bkfst) * **LB** **FACILITIES:** Xmas **PARKING:** 16 **NOTES:** No dogs (ex guide dogs) No children 5yrs No smoking in restaurant **CARDS:**

HIRWAUN, Rhondda Cynon Taff — Map 03 SN90

**★★★62% *Ty Newydd Country Hotel***
Penderyn Rd CF44 9SX
☎ 01685 813433 📠 01685 813139
***Dir:*** *off A4059, close to A465*
This country mansion set in 2.3 acres of woodland has been carefully restored and extended. The older bedrooms have antique furnishings and most rooms are spacious, well equipped and comfortable. All are non-smoking. There is a pleasant panelled bar, an attractive restaurant and comfortable lounges, where welcoming log fires are lit in cold weather.
**ROOMS:** 27 en suite (2 fmly) **CONF:** Thtr 300 Class 100 Board 40 **PARKING:** 100 **NOTES:** No dogs No smoking in restaurant Civ Wed 160 **CARDS:**

HOLYHEAD See Anglesey, Isle of

HOLYWELL, Flintshire — Map 07 SJ17

**★★67% Stamford Gate**
Halkyn Rd CH8 7SJ
☎ 01352 712942 📠 01352 713309
***Dir:*** *take Holywell turn off A55 on to A5026, hotel 1m on right*
This busy, friendly hotel is conveniently situated just off the A55 and provides comfortable, well-equipped accommodation. Public areas include extensive conference and banqueting suites, a popular restaurant and a spacious bar offering carefully prepared meals at lunch and in the evening.
**ROOMS:** 12 en suite **FACILITIES:** STV entertainment **PARKING:** 100 **NOTES:** No dogs (ex guide dogs) **CARDS:**

ISLE OF Placenames incorporating the words 'Isle' or 'Isle of' will be found under the actual name, eg Isle of Anglesey is under Anglesey, Isle of.

KNIGHTON, Powys — Map 07 SO27

**★★★63% *The Knighton Hotel***
Broad St LD7 1BL
☎ 01547 520530 📠 01547 520529
e-mail: knightonhotel@freeserve.co.uk
The impressive free-standing staircase at the centre of this market town hotel is reputedly the only example in Europe. The hotel is an amalgamation of a 16th-century coaching inn and a 19th-century manor house. The public areas comprise a bar, an attractive and spacious restaurant and a coffee shop.
**ROOMS:** 15 en suite **CONF:** Thtr 150 Class 75 Board 90 **SERVICES:** Lift **PARKING:** 15 **NOTES:** No children 12yrs No smoking in restaurant Civ Wed 120 **CARDS:**

**★★78% Milebrook House**
Milebrook LD7 1LT
☎ 01547 528632 📠 01547 520509
e-mail: hotel@milebrook.kc3ltd.co.uk
***Dir:*** *2m E, on A4113*
Set in 3 acres of grounds in the Teme Valley, this charming house dates back to 1760. Since it was converted into a hotel in 1987 it has acquired a well-deserved reputation for its warm hospitality, the comfort and quality of the accommodation and the quality of its food. The bedrooms, which include rooms on ground floor level, are well-equipped.
**ROOMS:** 10 en suite (2 fmly) No smoking in all bedrooms s £52.50-£56.60; d £77.80-£86 (incl. bkfst) * **LB** **FACILITIES:** Fishing Croquet lawn Badminton,Trout Fly Fishing Xmas **CONF:** Class 30 **PARKING:** 21 **NOTES:** No dogs No children 8yrs No smoking in restaurant RS Mon **CARDS:**

LAMPETER, Ceredigion — Map 02 SN54
see also Crugybar

**★★★66% Falcondale Mansion**
SA48 7RX
☎ 01570 422910 📠 01570 423559
***Dir:*** *800yds W of Lampeter High Street A475 or 1.5m NW of Lampeter A482*

This charming Victorian property is set in extensive grounds and beautiful parkland. Bedrooms are generally spacious, well-equipped and smartly presented. Bars and lounges are comfortable with additional facilities including conservatory and function rooms.
**ROOMS:** 19 en suite (8 fmly) s £50-£65; d £80-£110 (incl. bkfst) * **LB** **FACILITIES:** Tennis (hard) Fishing Putting green **CONF:** Thtr 60 Class 30 Board 25 Del £85 * **SERVICES:** Lift **PARKING:** 80 **NOTES:** No dogs No smoking in restaurant **CARDS:**
*See advert on opposite page*

LAMPHEY See Pembroke

LANGLAND BAY, Swansea — Map 02 SS68

**★★★70% *Langland Court***
Langland Court Rd SA3 4TD
☎ 01792 361545 📠 01792 362302
***Dir:*** *take B4593 towards Langland and turn left at St Peter's church*
Langland Court is a large, friendly Victorian property with lots of original character. Particularly impressive are the oak panelled public areas and the imposing stairway. Bedrooms are generally spacious and include some family rooms and an annexe with
*continued*

ground floor access. There is a formal restaurant supplemented by the more relaxed surroundings of Polly's wine bar.

**ROOMS:** 14 en suite 5 annexe en suite (5 fmly) No smoking in 2 bedrooms **FACILITIES:** STV **CONF:** Thtr 150 Class 60 Board 40 **PARKING:** 45 **NOTES:** No dogs (ex guide dogs) No smoking in restaurant Civ Wed 100 **CARDS:**

### ★★67% Wittemberg

MINOTEL Great Britain

Rotherslade Rd SA3 4QN
☎ 01792 369696 📠 01792 366995
e-mail: enquiries@wittemberghotel.co.uk
***Dir:*** *from Swansea follow bay to Mumbles. 1m from Mumbles turn right at White Rose Pub. Take 3rd left next to chapel then left into Rotherslade Rd*
Just a short walk from the beaches of Langland Bay, this friendly small hotel is close to Mumbles, Swansea and the Gower Peninsula. The public areas include a bar, a lounge and a restaurant which is the venue for good wholesome cooking. Bedrooms are well-maintained, comfortable and have modern facilities.
**ROOMS:** 11 en suite (2 fmly) s £38-£50; d £58-£80 (incl. bkfst) * **LB** **FACILITIES:** Jacuzzi **PARKING:** 12 **NOTES:** Closed Jan RS Nov **CARDS:**

## LLANARMON DYFFRYN CEIRIOG, Wrexham — Map 07 SJ13

### ★★70% West Arms

LL20 7LD
☎ 01691 600665 600612 📠 01691 600622
e-mail: gowestarms@aol.com
***Dir:*** *turn off A483/A5 at Chirk, in Chirk take B4500 to Ceiriog Valley, Llanarmon is 11m at the end of B4500*

Set in the beautiful Ceiriog Valley, this delightful hotel has a wealth of charm and character. There is a comfortable lounge, a room for private dining and two bars, as well as a pleasant restaurant offering a fixed-price menu of freshly cooked dishes. The attractive bedrooms have a mixture of modern and period furnishings.
**ROOMS:** 12 en suite 4 annexe en suite (1 fmly) s £49.50-£61.50; d £89-£109 (incl. bkfst) * **LB** **FACILITIES:** Fishing ch fac Xmas **CONF:** Thtr 60 Class 50 Board 50 Del from £99 * **PARKING:** 22 **NOTES:** No smoking in restaurant Civ Wed 80 **CARDS:**

*See advert on this page*





L

LLANBEDR, Gwynedd Map 06 SH52

**★★68% Cae Nest Hall Country House**
LL45 2NL
☎ 01341 241349 ▯ 01341 241349
e-mail: cae-nest@uk2.so-net.com
***Dir:*** *turn off A496 at Victoria Pub, turn left at the War Memorial (100yds from pub) then straight ahead to hotel approx 300yds*

A delightful small country house that dates back to the 15th century and lies in pleasant grounds. Original features include flagstone floors in the bar and an old black stove in the dining room. Pretty wallpapers and fabrics are used to good effect in the bedrooms and other modern facilities are provided.
**ROOMS:** 10 en suite (3 fmly) No smoking in all bedrooms s £42-£59.50; d £64-£79 (incl. bkfst) * **LB** **PARKING:** 10 **NOTES:** No dogs No smoking in restaurant

**★★62% Ty Mawr**
LL45 2NH
☎ 01341 241440 ▯ 01341 241440
e-mail: tymawrhotel@netscapeonline.co.uk
***Dir:*** *travelling from Barmouth, turn right after the bridge in the village, hotel 50yds on left, look for brown tourist signs*

Located in a picturesque village, this family-run hotel has a relaxed, friendly atmosphere. Its pleasant grounds opposite the River Artro are a popular beer garden during fine weather. The attractive, cane-furnished bar offers a blackboard selection and a good choice of real ales. A more formal menu is available in the restaurant. Bedrooms are smart and brightly decorated.
**ROOMS:** 10 en suite (2 fmly) No smoking in 5 bedrooms s £30-£37; d £50-£60 (incl. bkfst) * **LB** **FACILITIES:** STV ch fac **CONF:** Class 25 **PARKING:** 30 **NOTES:** No smoking in restaurant Closed 24-26 Dec
**CARDS:**

LLANBERIS, Gwynedd Map 06 SH56

**★★★68% Royal Victoria**
LL55 4TY
☎ 01286 870253 ▯ 01286 870149
e-mail: info@royalvictoria.fsnet.co.uk
***Dir:*** *on A4086 Caernarfon to Llanberis road, directly opposite Snowdon Mountain railway*
A well-established hotel, near the foot of Snowdon, between the Peris and Padarn lakes. Pretty gardens and grounds are an attractive backdrop for the many weddings held here. Bedrooms have been refurbished and are well-equipped. There are spacious lounges and bars, and also a large dining room with conservatory, overlooking the lakes.
**ROOMS:** 106 en suite (9 fmly) s £25-£49.50; d £50-£99 (incl. bkfst) * **LB** **FACILITIES:** STV Mountaineering,Cycling,Walking entertainment Xmas **CONF:** Thtr 100 Class 60 Board 50 Del from £75 * **SERVICES:** Lift **PARKING:** 300 **NOTES:** No smoking in restaurant Civ Wed 100 **CARDS:**

*See advert on opposite page*

**★★66% *Lake View***
Tan-y-Pant LL55 4EL
☎ 01286 870422 ▯ 01286 872591
***Dir:*** *1m from Llanberis on A4086 towards Caernarfon*
The lake itself is impossible to miss, as the vast expanse of water is just across the road from the hotel. Dramatic landscapes are all around, with Snowdon itself only a short distance away. The bar, restaurant and comfortable lounge have an appealing, country inn character. The bedrooms have modern facilities and are well-maintained.
**ROOMS:** 10 rms (9 en suite) (3 fmly) **PARKING:** 20
**CARDS:**

LLANDEGLA, Denbighshire Map 07 SJ25

**★★★72% ®® Bodidris Hall**
LL11 3AL
☎ 01978 790434 ▯ 01978 790335
***Dir:*** *in village take A5104 at Crown pub towards Chester. Hotel 1m on left*
This impressive manor house is quietly located, surrounded by ornamental gardens and mature woodlands. It has an interesting history and wealth of charm and character, with original features such as oak beams and inglenook fireplaces. Bedrooms are furnished with antique pieces and some have four-poster beds. Dining here is an enjoyable experience; the food is cooked with flair and stylishly presented.
**ROOMS:** 9 en suite No smoking in 3 bedrooms s £85-£99; d £105-£155 (incl. bkfst) * **LB** **FACILITIES:** Fishing Clay pigeon & Driven shooting Falconry Xmas **CONF:** Thtr 50 Class 25 Board 20 Del from £99 * **PARKING:** 80 **NOTES:** No dogs (ex guide dogs) No smoking in restaurant Civ Wed 65 **CARDS:**

LLANDEILO, Carmarthenshire Map 03 SN62

**★★★72% The Plough Inn**
Rhosmaen SA19 6NP
☎ 01558 823431 ▯ 01558 823969
e-mail: enquiries@ploughrhosmaen.co.uk
***Dir:*** *1m N, on A40*
This friendly inn, run by the Rocca family for over thirty years has stunning views over the Towy Valley and Black Mountains. Bedrooms, some on the ground floor, have modern facilities and are complemented by a gym and sauna. Public areas include an

*continued*

attractively appointed restaurant, a cosy bar and conference facilities.

**ROOMS:** 12 en suite s £50; d £65-£70 (incl. cont bkfst) * **FACILITIES:** STV Sauna Gym ch fac **CONF:** Thtr 45 Class 24 Board 24 **PARKING:** 70 **NOTES:** No dogs Closed 25 Dec RS Sun (restaurant closed) **CARDS:**

*See advert on this page*

### ★★★71% Cawdor Arms

Rhosmaen St SA19 6EN
☎ 01558 823500 01558 822399
e-mail: cawdor.arms@btinternet.com
***Dir:*** *centre of Llandeilo town, 20 mins from M4 junct 49. Follow signs to Llandeilo*

A warm welcome is offered to guests at this impressive Georgian hotel in the centre of Llandeilo. The hotel has elegantly furnished public rooms and bedrooms, some with four-poster beds. An impressive and locally popular menu is offered.

**ROOMS:** 17 en suite (2 fmly) No smoking in 11 bedrooms s £45-£60; d £60-£80 (incl. bkfst) * **LB** **FACILITIES:** entertainment Xmas **CONF:** Thtr 70 Class 50 Board 26 **PARKING:** 7 **NOTES:** No smoking in restaurant **CARDS:**

### ★62% White Hart Inn

36 Carmarthen Rd SA19 6RS
☎ 01558 823419 01558 823089
e-mail: therese@whitehartinn.fsnet.co.uk
***Dir:*** *Turn off A40 onto A483, hotel 200yds on left*

This privately owned roadside hostelry is situated on the outskirts of Llandeilo. It provides accommodation equipped with all modern comforts. Facilities include a meetings room and a large function room.

**ROOMS:** 11 rms (8 en suite) (2 fmly) s £26-£40; d £40-£60 (incl. bkfst) * **FACILITIES:** STV **PARKING:** 50 **NOTES:** No dogs (ex guide dogs) Civ Wed 80 **CARDS:**

## LLANDRILLO, Denbighshire — Map 06 SJ03

### Premier Collection

### ★★ Tyddyn Llan Country Hotel & Restaurant

LL21 0ST
☎ 01490 440264 01490 440414
e-mail: tyddynllanhotel@compuserve.com
***Dir:*** *on B4401, Corwen-Bala road*

Set in landscaped gardens amongst fine scenery, this small elegant Georgian house has been carefully restored to provide an idyllic, comfortable country retreat. The hotel is well placed to explore the magnificence of Snowdonia and its many castles and monuments. Individually styled bedrooms

*continued on p818*

L

LLANDRILLO, continued

are tastefully furnished and roaring log fires during the winter months warm the delightful lounges. The elegant restaurant serves an imaginative selection of excellent dishes, created from quality local produce.

*Tyddyn Llan Country Hotel, Ambleside*

**ROOMS:** 10 en suite (2 fmly) s £67.50-£85; d £105-£140 (incl. bkfst) * LB **FACILITIES:** Fishing Croquet lawn ch fac Xmas **CONF:** Thtr 30 Class 30 Board 20 Del from £120 * **PARKING:** 30 **NOTES:** No smoking in restaurant Civ Wed 30 **CARDS:**

L

## LLANDRINDOD WELLS, Powys — Map 03 SO06

see also Penybont

### ★★★68% Hotel Metropole

Temple St LD1 5DY
☎ 01597 823700 🖷 01597 824828
e-mail: info@metropole.co.uk
***Dir:*** *on A483 in centre of town*

The centre of this famous spa town is dominated by this Victorian hotel, which has been personally run by the same family for over 100 years. The lobby leads to a choice of bars and an elegant lounge. Bedrooms vary in style, all are quite spacious and well-equipped.

**ROOMS:** 121 en suite (2 fmly) No smoking in 57 bedrooms s £59-£71; d £79-£94 (incl. bkfst) **LB** **FACILITIES:** Indoor swimming (H) Sauna Solarium Jacuzzi Beauty salon Rowing & Cycling machines Xmas **CONF:** Thtr 300 Class 200 Board 80 Del from £77 * **SERVICES:** Lift **PARKING:** 150 **NOTES:** No smoking in restaurant Civ Wed 250 **CARDS:**

*See advert on opposite page*

Fancy a Singapore Sling? Bar staff in five star hotels should be skilled cocktail mixers.

### ★★66% *Greenway Manor Hotel*

Crossgates LD1 6RF
☎ 01597 851230 🖷 01597 851912
***Dir:*** *0.25m from Crossgate village island, on A44 towards Rhayader*

This Edwardian, mock-Tudor property is close to the Elan Valley. A friendly, family-run hotel, its 12 acres of grounds include a mile of private fishing. The well-equipped bedrooms are tastefully decorated, and two have four-poster beds. There is a pleasant restaurant, a spacious lounge bar and a choice of comfortable lounges.

**ROOMS:** 12 en suite (1 fmly) No smoking in 4 bedrooms **FACILITIES:** STV Fishing **CONF:** Thtr 40 Class 36 Board 26 **PARKING:** 30 **NOTES:** No dogs (ex guide dogs) No smoking in restaurant Closed 24 Dec-1 Jan Civ Wed 60 **CARDS:**

## LLANDUDNO, Conwy — Map 06 SH78

*Premier Collection*

### ★★★★ 🏵🏵 Bodysgallen Hall

RELAIS & CHATEAUX.

LL30 1RS
☎ 01492 584466 🖷 01492 582519
e-mail: info@bodysgallen.com
***Dir:*** *take A55 to intersection with A470, then follow A470 towards Llandudno. Hotel 1m on right*

Set in 200 acres of parkland and formal gardens, this 17th century house is in an elevated position allowing views towards Snowdonia and across to Conwy castle. Bedrooms, some of which are converted cottages in the grounds, are comfortably furnished, whilst public areas include a choice of lounges displaying fine antiques and great character. Friendly and attentive service is discreetly offered, whilst the restaurant features fine local produce, carefully prepared.

**ROOMS:** 19 en suite 16 annexe en suite (2 fmly) No smoking in 5 bedrooms s £109-£115; d £145-£250 * **LB** **FACILITIES:** Spa Indoor swimming (H) Tennis (hard) Sauna Solarium Gym Croquet lawn Jacuzzi Beauty salons Steam room Club room entertainment Xmas **CONF:** Thtr 50 Class 30 Board 24 Del from £140 * **PARKING:** 50 **NOTES:** No dogs (ex guide dogs) No children 8yrs No smoking in restaurant **CARDS:**

### ★★★74% 🏵 Empire

Church Walks LL30 2HE
☎ 01492 860555 🖷 01492 860791
e-mail: reservations@empirehotel.co.uk
***Dir:*** *A55 from Chester - Leave at intersection for Llandudno (A470). Follow signs for town centre - Hotel is at end & facing main street*

Run by the same family for over 50 years, the Empire offers luxuriously appointed bedrooms with every modern facility. The 'Number 72' rooms are particularly sumptuous. The indoor pool is overlooked by an all-day restaurant, and there is also an outdoor

*continued*

pool and roof garden. The Watkins restaurant offers an interesting fixed-price menu.

**ROOMS:** 50 en suite 8 annexe en suite (3 fmly) s £57.50-£72.50; d £85-£110 (incl. bkfst) * **LB** **FACILITIES:** **Spa** STV Indoor swimming (H) Outdoor swimming (H) Sauna Beauty treatments entertainment Xmas **CONF:** Thtr 36 Class 20 Board 20 Del from £85 * **SERVICES:** Lift **PARKING:** 40 **NOTES:** No dogs (ex guide dogs) Closed 16-27 Dec **CARDS:**

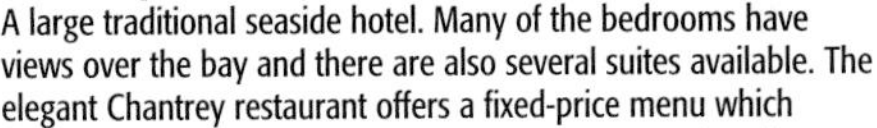

*See advert on this page*

**★★★68% Imperial**

The Promenade LL30 1AP
☎ 01492 877466 01492 878043
e-mail: imphotel@btinternet.com

A large traditional seaside hotel. Many of the bedrooms have views over the bay and there are also several suites available. The elegant Chantrey restaurant offers a fixed-price menu which

*continued on p820*

LLANDUDNO, continued

changes monthly and uses local produce. There is a fully equipped leisure club and extensive conference and banqueting facilities.

*Imperial, Llandudno*

**ROOMS:** 100 en suite (10 fmly) **FACILITIES:** STV Indoor swimming (H) Sauna Solarium Gym Jacuzzi Beauty therapist Hairdressing **CONF:** Thtr 150 Class 50 Board 50 **SERVICES:** Lift **PARKING:** 40
**CARDS:**

*See advert on page 819*

### ★★★65% St George's

The Promenade LL30 2LG
☎ 01492 877544 01492 877788
e-mail: stgeorges@ccsmm.co.uk
***Dir:*** *A55-A470, follow the road to the promenade, 0.25m, the hotel is on the corner, overlooking the sweep of Llandudno Bay*

This popular and friendly seafront hotel was the first to be built in the town. Its many Victorian features include the splendid, ornate Wedgwood Room. The main lounges overlook the bay and incorporate a coffee shop serving hot and cold snacks. A variety of room sizes is available; several have views over the sea and some have balconies.

**ROOMS:** 84 en suite (6 fmly) No smoking in 12 bedrooms s £60-£100; d £90-£130 (incl. bkfst) * **LB** **FACILITIES:** **Spa** STV Sauna Solarium Jacuzzi Hairdressing Health & beauty salon Xmas **CONF:** Thtr 250 Class 200 Board 45 Del from £75 * **SERVICES:** Lift **PARKING:** 36
**NOTES:** No dogs (ex guide dogs) No smoking in restaurant Civ Wed 100
**CARDS:**

### ★★★61% *Chatsworth House*

Central Promenade LL30 2XS
☎ 01492 860788 01492 871417

This traditional family-run Victorian hotel occupies a central position on the promenade and caters for many families and groups. There is an indoor swimming pool, a sauna and a solarium. Well-maintained public areas complement modern bedrooms, some of them quite spacious.

**ROOMS:** 72 en suite (19 fmly) **FACILITIES:** Indoor swimming (H) Sauna Jacuzzi **SERVICES:** Lift **PARKING:** 9 **CARDS:**

### ★★★60% Risboro

Clement Av LL30 2ED
☎ 01492 876343 01492 879881
e-mail: risborohotel@ukonline.co.uk
***Dir:*** *A55 to Llandudno, follow A470 into town centre, at large roundabout turn left then take 3rd right*

Situated close to the foot of the Great Orme and convenient for the seafront and town centre, this popular family hotel provides agreeable bedrooms. Amongst the extensive public areas there is a comfortable lounge with a small terrace and a large restaurant overlooking the pool.

**ROOMS:** 65 en suite (7 fmly) s £40-£50; d £80-£100 (incl. bkfst) * **LB**
**FACILITIES:** Indoor swimming (H) Sauna Solarium Gym Jacuzzi Xmas
**CONF:** Thtr 150 Class 100 Board 80 Del from £75 * **SERVICES:** Lift
**PARKING:** 40 **NOTES:** No smoking in restaurant
**CARDS:**

## *Premier Collection*

### ★★ St Tudno Hotel and Restaurant

The Promenade LL30 2LP
☎ 01492 874411 01492 860407
e-mail: sttudnohotel@btinternet.com
***Dir:*** *on reaching Promenade drive towards the pier, hotel is opposite pier entrance & gardens*

A high quality resort hotel, which although not the place for buckets and spades, will receive toddlers as warmly as adults. The bedrooms, some with sea views, offer a wide choice of sizes and individual styles, so discuss exact requirements at the time of booking. Public rooms include a no-smoking lounge, a convivial bar-lounge, and a small indoor pool. The air-conditioned Garden Room Restaurant is the focal point for enjoyable cuisine using good local produce.

**ROOMS:** 19 en suite (4 fmly) No smoking in 3 bedrooms s £78-£150; d £95-£270 (incl. bkfst) * **LB** **FACILITIES:** STV Indoor swimming (H) entertainment Xmas **CONF:** Thtr 40 Class 25 Board 20 Del from £135 * **SERVICES:** Lift **PARKING:** 12 **NOTES:** No smoking in restaurant **CARDS:**

### ★★73% Epperstone

15 Abbey Rd LL30 2EE
☎ 01492 878746 01492 871223
***Dir:*** *A55-A470 to Mostyn Street. At rdbt turn left, take 4th right into York Road. Hotel on junction of York road and Abbey Road*

This delightful hotel with wonderful gardens, is privately owned and personally run. It is located in a residential part of town,

continued

within easy walking distance of the seafront and shopping area. Bedrooms are attractively decorated and thoughtfully equipped. They include a room on ground floor level and a two bedroomed family unit. Two lounges are available, a comfortable no-smoking room and a Victorian-style conservatory. A daily changing menu is offered in the bright dining room.
**ROOMS:** 8 en suite (5 fmly) No smoking in all bedrooms s fr £25; d fr £50 (incl. bkfst) * **LB** **FACILITIES:** STV Xmas **PARKING:** 8 **NOTES:** No smoking in restaurant **CARDS:**

### ★★72% Dunoon

Gloddaeth St LL30 2DW
☎ 01492 860787 01492 860031
e-mail: reservations@dunoonhotel.demon.co.uk

THE CIRCLE Selected Individual Hotels GREAT BRITAIN

Run by the same family for over 40 years, this welcoming hotel is near the promenade and shopping area. Bedrooms are attractively furnished and well-equipped; there is a choice of lounges and a separate bar in addition to the restaurant. There is also a pool table.
**ROOMS:** 51 en suite 3 annexe en suite (10 fmly) s fr £45; d £76-£88 (incl. bkfst) * **LB** **FACILITIES:** STV Solarium **SERVICES:** Lift **PARKING:** 24 **NOTES:** Closed mid Nov-mid Mar
**CARDS:**

### ★★72% Tan-Lan

Great Orme's Rd, West Shore LL30 2AR
☎ 01492 860221 01492 870219
e-mail: info@tanlanhotel.co.uk
***Dir:*** *turn off A55 onto A546 signposted Deganwy. Straight over 2 rdbts, approx 3m from A55, hotel on left just over mini rdbt*

Warm and friendly hospitality is one of the many strengths at this well-maintained, small, privately owned and personally run hotel. It is located on Llandudno's West Shore, close to the Great Orme. The recently refurbished bedrooms are modern and well-equipped. No smoking rooms and bedrooms on ground floor level are both available. Facilities here include a pleasant dining room, lounge and bar.
**ROOMS:** 17 en suite (3 fmly) No smoking in 3 bedrooms s £25-£37; d £50-£54 (incl. bkfst) * **LB** **FACILITIES:** Xmas **PARKING:** 12 **NOTES:** No smoking in restaurant Closed 2 Jan-10 Feb & 4 Nov-24 Dec
**CARDS:**

### ★★71% Belle Vue

26 North Pde LL30 2LP
☎ 01492 879547 01492 870001
***Dir:*** *follow the promenade towards the pier, as the road bends the Belle Vue Hotel is on the left*

This privately owned and personally run hotel stands in an elevated position on the eastern side of the Great Orme, from where it overlooks panoramic views of the promenade, beach and bay. It has many attributes, not least the warm and friendly hospitality of owners Richard and David, who go to great lengths to ensure their guests are properly cared for. The recently refurbished bedrooms are well-equipped and tastefully appointed. In addition to the attractive dining room, there is a bar and a separate, comfortable lounge.
**ROOMS:** 13 en suite (4 fmly) No smoking in all bedrooms s £33-£42; d £54-£73 (incl. bkfst) * **LB** **FACILITIES:** Xmas **SERVICES:** Lift **PARKING:** 12 **NOTES:** No smoking in restaurant
**CARDS:**

### ★★71% Sunnymede

West Pde LL30 2BD
☎ 01492 877130 01492 871824
***Dir:*** *from A55 follow signs for Llandudno & Deganwy. At 1st rdbt after Deganwy take 1st exit towards the sea. At corner turn left & follow rd for 400yds*

Sunnymede is a friendly family-run hotel located on Llandudno's

continued

West Shore. Many rooms have views over the Conwy Estuary and Snowdonia. Modern bedrooms are attractively decorated and well-equipped. Bar and lounge areas are particularly comfortable and attractive. All areas of the hotel have benefited from recently completed refurbishment work.
**ROOMS:** 15 en suite (3 fmly) s £39; d £78-£82 (incl. bkfst & dinner) * **LB** **FACILITIES:** Xmas **PARKING:** 18 **NOTES:** No children 3yrs No smoking in restaurant Closed Jan-Feb **CARDS:**

### ★★70% Sandringham

West Pde LL30 2BD
☎ 01492 876513 & 876447 01492 872753
e-mail: sandringham@which.net
***Dir:*** *enter Llandudno on A470 follow signs for West Shore, hotel is located in centre of West Shore Promenade*

The same owners have personally run this well-maintained hotel for over 20 years. Situated on the West Shore, it has superb views over the Conwy Estuary towards Snowdonia. There are two restaurants and a full range of bar food. Bedrooms are tastefully decorated and well-appointed. Some are located on ground floor level. Family rooms are also available.
**ROOMS:** 18 en suite (3 fmly) s £29.50-£36; d £59-£64 (incl. bkfst) * **LB** **FACILITIES:** STV Xmas **CONF:** Thtr 70 Class 60 Board 30 Del from £55 * **PARKING:** 6 **NOTES:** No dogs No smoking in restaurant RS 25 & 26 Dec Civ Wed **CARDS:**

### ★★70% Tynedale

Central Promenade LL30 2XS
☎ 01492 877426 01492 871213
e-mail: enquiries@tynedalehotel.co.uk
***Dir:*** *on promenade opposite bandstand*

Tour groups are well catered for at this privately owned and personally run hotel, and regular live entertainment is a feature. Public areas include good lounge facilities and an attractive patio overlooking the bay. The well-maintained bedrooms are fresh and well-equipped. Many have good views over the sea front and the Great Orme.
**ROOMS:** 54 en suite (4 fmly) No smoking in all bedrooms s £42-£47; d £68-£94 (incl. bkfst) * **LB** **FACILITIES:** entertainment Xmas **SERVICES:** Lift **PARKING:** 30 **NOTES:** No dogs (ex guide dogs) No smoking in restaurant **CARDS:**

L

### ★★70% *Wilton*

South Pde LL30 2LN
☎ 01492 878343 01492 876086
e-mail: info@wiltonhotel.com
***Dir:*** *from A470 head towards promenade, Pier & Great Orme. At Pier turn left before cenotaph - Prince Edwards Sq. Hotel last on left before rdbt*

This well maintained hotel is situated just off the promenade and is close to the main shopping centre. Privately owned and personally run in a very friendly manner, it has very pretty, well-equipped bedrooms. There is a comfortable lounge bar for residents and good value meals are available.
**ROOMS:** 14 en suite (7 fmly) No smoking in 4 bedrooms **FACILITIES:** STV **PARKING:** 3 **NOTES:** No smoking in restaurant Closed 28 Nov-6 Feb RS early & late season **CARDS:**

### ★★67% Somerset

St Georges Crescent, Promenade LL30 2LF
☎ 01492 876540 01492 863700
***Dir:*** *on the Promenade*

With its sister hotel, The Wavecrest, this cheerful holiday hotel occupies an ideal location on the central promenade and there are superb views over the bay from many rooms. Regular entertainment is provided as well as a range of bar and lounge

continued on p822

LLANDUDNO, continued

areas. Bedrooms are well-decorated and modern facilities are provided.
**ROOMS:** 37 en suite (4 fmly) s £30-£43 (incl. bkfst) * **LB**
**FACILITIES:** Games room entertainment Xmas **CONF:** Thtr 70 Class 70 Board 30 **SERVICES:** Lift **PARKING:** 20 **NOTES:** No smoking in restaurant Closed Dec-Feb **CARDS:**

**★★66% Bedford**
Promenade LL30 1BN
☎ 01492 876647 🖹 01492 860185
e-mail: enquiries@thebedford.com
***Dir:*** *at intersection of A55/A470, take exit for Llandudno (A470) and continue until 4th rdbt. Take exit for Craig-y-Don (B115) and turn right*
This hotel is located on the eastern approach to Llandudno at Craig-y-Don. Many of the well-equipped bedrooms are suitable for families and enjoy fine views over the bay towards both the Great Orme and Little Orme. The hotel's Italian restaurant and pizzeria is popular with locals. Facilities include a choice of lounges and a function/meeting room.
**ROOMS:** 27 en suite (2 fmly) No smoking in 3 bedrooms s £32-£36; d £46-£55 (incl. bkfst) * **LB** **FACILITIES:** STV Xmas **CONF:** Thtr 30 Class 20 Board 20 Del from £40 * **SERVICES:** Lift **PARKING:** 21
**CARDS:**

**★★66% Esplanade**
Glan-y-Mor Pde, Promenade LL30 2LL
☎ 0800 318688 (freephone) & 01492 860300 🖹 01492 860418
e-mail: info@esplanadehotel.co.uk
***Dir:*** *turn off A55 at Llandudno junct & proceed on A470, follow signs to promenade, left towards Great Orme. Hotel 500 yds left*
This family owned and run hotel stands on the promenade, overlooking views of the bay. It is conveniently close to the town centre and other amenities. Bedrooms vary in size and style, but all have modern equipment and facilities. Family bedded rooms are available. Public areas are bright and attractively appointed. Facilities include a room for functions and conferences.
**ROOMS:** 59 en suite (17 fmly) s £18-£39; d £36-£78 (incl. bkfst) * **LB**
**FACILITIES:** entertainment Xmas **CONF:** Thtr 80 Class 40 Board 40 Del from £37.50 * **SERVICES:** Lift **PARKING:** 30 **NOTES:** Closed 3 Jan-1Feb
**CARDS:**

**★★66% Hydro Hotel**
Neville Crescent LL30 1AT
☎ 01492 870101 🖹 01492 870992

Leisureplex

***Dir:*** *follow signs for theatre to seafront, then proceed towards pier. Hotel short distance after theatre on left facing North Bay*
This large hotel is situated on the promenade, overlooking sea views. The modern equipped accommodation represents very good value for money. Public areas are quite extensive and include a choice of lounges, a games/snooker room and a ballroom, where entertainment is provided every night. The hotel is a popular venue for coach tour parties.
**ROOMS:** 112 en suite (4 fmly) s £25-£33; d £42-£58 (incl. bkfst) * **LB**
**FACILITIES:** Snooker Sauna Gym entertainment Xmas **CONF:** Thtr 260 Class 40 Del from £65 * **SERVICES:** Lift **PARKING:** 10 **NOTES:** No dogs (ex guide dogs) No smoking in restaurant Closed Jan-mid Feb RS Nov & mid Feb-Mar (open Mon-Fri) **CARDS:**

**★★66% *Leamore***
40 Lloyd St LL30 2YG
☎ 01492 875552 🖹 01492 879386
***Dir:*** *300 mtrs on seafront, opposite life boat station*
This hotel is conveniently located for access to the town centre, the promenade and other amenities. It provides warm and friendly hospitality and well-equipped accommodation. Nadege James is a talented singer who frequently entertains her guests.
**ROOMS:** 12 rms (8 en suite) (4 fmly) No smoking in all bedrooms
**FACILITIES:** entertainment **PARKING:** 6 **NOTES:** No dogs (ex guide dogs) No smoking in restaurant Closed Dec

**★★66% Ravenhurst**
West Pde LL30 2BB
☎ 01492 875525 🖹 01248 681143
***Dir:*** *on West Shore, opposite boating pool*
This privately owned, comfortable hotel lies on Llandudno's West Shore with lovely views over the Conwy Estuary towards Snowdonia. The modern equipped accommodation includes family suites and bedrooms on ground floor level. There is a choice of lounges and a bar, and a daily changed fixed-price menu is provided in the dining room.
**ROOMS:** 25 en suite (3 fmly) s £25-£29; d £50-£58 (incl. bkfst) * **LB**
**FACILITIES:** Xmas **PARKING:** 15 **NOTES:** Closed Dec-Feb
**CARDS:**

**★★66% Stratford**
8 Craig-y-Don Pde, Promenade LL30 1BG
☎ 01492 877962 🖹 01492 877962
e-mail: stratfordhotel@aol.com
***Dir:*** *from A55 take A470 to Llandudno at 4th rdbt take Craig-y-Don sign to Promenade*
A pleasant holiday hotel on the Craig-y-Don promenade. The Conference Centre and theatre are nearby, with the local shops only a short walk away. The comfortable bedrooms include many canopied beds. A daily changing menu provides generously priced home cooking. Guests have a comfortable lounge, separate bar and an inviting patio overlooking the sea.
**ROOMS:** 10 en suite (4 fmly) s £21-£27; d £38-£50 (incl. bkfst) * **LB**
**FACILITIES:** STV **NOTES:** No smoking in restaurant Closed Dec-Feb
**CARDS:**

**★★65% Ormescliffe**
East Pde LL30 1BE
☎ 01492 877191 🖹 01492 860311
e-mail: ormescliffe@clara.net
This family-run hotel lies at the eastern end of the promenade and is convenient for the theatre and conference centre. Bedrooms are modern and well-equipped, several are suitable for families and most have superb views over the seafront and Great Orme. Comfortable bars and lounges are provided and there is a ballroom with regular live entertainment. The atmosphere is warm and relaxing.
**ROOMS:** 61 en suite (7 fmly) No smoking in 6 bedrooms s £42-£44; d £84-£88 (incl. bkfst) * **LB** **FACILITIES:** Snooker Table tennis Xmas
**CONF:** Thtr 120 Class 120 Board 80 **SERVICES:** Lift **PARKING:** 15
**NOTES:** No smoking in restaurant Closed 2 Jan-2 Feb
**CARDS:**

**★★65% Wavecrest**
St Georges Crescent, Central Promenade LL30 2LF
☎ 01492 860615 🖹 01492 863700
***Dir:*** *on promenade behind Marks & Spencer*
The Wavecrest is the sister hotel of the adjoining Somerset, and public areas are shared. It lies on the central promenade and most bedrooms have lovely sea views. Lounge and bar areas are comfortably furnished and a games room is available. Staff are friendly and regular entertainment is staged.
**ROOMS:** 41 en suite (7 fmly) s £30-£39 (incl. bkfst) * **LB**
**FACILITIES:** entertainment Xmas **CONF:** Class 70 **SERVICES:** Lift
**PARKING:** 12 **NOTES:** No smoking in restaurant Closed Dec-Feb
**CARDS:**

★★64% **Ambassador Hotel**
Grand Promenade LL30 2NR
☎ 01492 876886 Fax 01492 876347
***Dir:*** *turn off A55 onto A470. Take turn to Promenade, then left towards pier*
This friendly, family owned and run hotel is situated on the sea front, close to the town centre. Bedrooms are tastefully decorated and many have sea views. Public areas include a choice of lounges, a patisserie, bar and restaurant.
**ROOMS:** 57 en suite (8 fmly) s £27-£45; d £50-£95 (incl. bkfst) * LB **FACILITIES:** entertainment Xmas **CONF:** Thtr 45 Class 14 Board 20 Del from £43 * **SERVICES:** Lift **PARKING:** 11 **NOTES:** No dogs (ex guide dogs) No smoking in restaurant **CARDS:**

★★64% ***Evans***
Charlton St LL30 2AA
☎ 01492 860784 Fax 01492 860784
This friendly, privately owned hotel provides comfortable, well-appointed bedrooms including some family rooms. Spacious public areas include a well-equipped games room and comfortable lounge bar, where regular live evening entertainment is held. Dinner is served until 7pm and a non-cooked supper can be provided for later arrivals.
**ROOMS:** 50 en suite (4 fmly) **FACILITIES:** STV Snooker Solarium entertainment **SERVICES:** Lift **NOTES:** No dogs (ex guide dogs) No smoking in restaurant Closed Jan

★★64% **Headlands**
Hill Ter LL30 1NT
☎ 01492 877485
This privately owned and personally run hotel changed hands in January 2001 and at the time of our last inspection the new owners had made several improvements. It stands high on the side of the Great Orme from where it overlooks panoramic views of the seafront, beach and bay. Bedrooms are well-equipped and equally suitable for both business people and holidaymakers.
**ROOMS:** 15 en suite (3 fmly) No smoking in all bedrooms s £39; d £78 (incl. bkfst & dinner) * LB **FACILITIES:** Xmas **PARKING:** 7 **NOTES:** No children 5yrs No smoking in restaurant Closed 4 Jan-15 Mar
**CARDS:**

★★64% **Oak Alyn**
2 Deganwy Av LL30 2YB
☎ 01492 860320 Fax 01492 860320
***Dir:*** *situated in the centre of Llandudno, 200 yards from the Town Hall, opposite the Catholic Church*
This privately owned and personally run hotel has been much improved by the present owners since they took over in 1998. It is close to the town centre and within a few minutes walk of the promenade. Bedrooms have modern equipment and facilities. There is a bright and pleasant dining room with a conservatory extension, and a lounge bar.
**ROOMS:** 12 en suite (2 fmly) s £20-£22; d £40-£44 (incl. bkfst) * LB **FACILITIES:** Xmas **CONF:** Thtr 26 Class 30 Del from £35 * **PARKING:** 16 **NOTES:** No dogs (ex guide dogs) No smoking in restaurant Closed 22-31 Dec **CARDS:**

★★60% **Royal**
Church Walks LL30 2HW
☎ 01492 876476 Fax 01492 870210
e-mail: royalllandudno@aol.com
***Dir:*** *exit A55 for A470 to Llandudno. Follow through town to T-jct, then left into Church Walks. Hotel 200yds on left, almost opp. Great Orme tram station*
This privately owned hotel is reputed to be the first hotel in Llandudno. It is located on the eastern side of the Great Orme and is conveniently close to the town centre and sea front. The well-equipped accommodation is particularly popular with golfers and coach tour groups.
**ROOMS:** 38 rms (36 en suite) (7 fmly) s fr £35; d £70-£80 (incl. bkfst) * LB **FACILITIES:** Putting green Xmas **CONF:** Del from £47.50 * **SERVICES:** Lift **PARKING:** 20 **NOTES:** No dogs (ex guide dogs) No smoking in restaurant **CARDS:**

★63% **Min-y-Don**
North Pde LL30 2LP
☎ 01492 876511 Fax 01492 878169
***Dir:*** *leave A55 Expressway Llandudno junct taking A470. Through Martyn St, turn right at rdbt then left North Parade*
This cheerful family-run hotel is located under the Great Orme, opposite the pier. Bedrooms include several suitable for families and many have lovely views over the bay. Regular entertainment is held and there are comfortable lounge and bar areas.
**ROOMS:** 28 rms (19 en suite) (12 fmly) **FACILITIES:** Xmas **SERVICES:** air con **PARKING:** 7 **NOTES:** No dogs No smoking in restaurant Closed Jan-Feb **CARDS:**

## LLANELLI, Carmarthenshire — Map 02 SN50

★★★66% **Diplomat Hotel**
Felinfoel SA15 3PJ
☎ 01554 756156 Fax 01554 751649
***Dir:*** *from M4 exit junct 48 onto A4138 then B4303 hotel in 0.75m on the right*
Best Western
A Victorian mansion in several acres of mature grounds. Public rooms include good lounge and bar areas, a large function suite and fully equipped leisure centre. Bedrooms are well-appointed and available in the mansion and the nearby coach house.
**ROOMS:** 23 en suite 8 annexe en suite (2 fmly) No smoking in 6 bedrooms s £65; d £85 (incl. bkfst) * LB **FACILITIES:** Indoor swimming (H) Sauna Solarium Gym Jacuzzi entertainment Xmas **CONF:** Thtr 450 Class 150 Board 100 Del £88 * **SERVICES:** Lift **PARKING:** 250 **NOTES:** Civ Wed 400
**CARDS:**

★★69% **Ashburnham**
Ashburnham Rd, Pembrey SA16 0TH
☎ 01554 834343 & 834455 Fax 01554 834483
e-mail: post@epco.demon.co.uk
***Dir:*** *M4 junct 48, A4138 to Llanelli, A484 West to Pembrey, look out for road sign as entering village*
Amelia Earhart stayed at this friendly hotel after finishing her historic trans-Atlantic flight of 1928. Public areas include a bright bar and restaurant offering a good choice of menus, extensive function facilities and a children's outdoor play area. Bedrooms have modern furnishings and facilities with family rooms also available.
**ROOMS:** 12 en suite (2 fmly) s £50; d £68 (incl. bkfst) * LB **FACILITIES:** various within 1 mile of hotel ch fac **CONF:** Thtr 150 Class 150 Board 80 Del from £65 * **PARKING:** 100 **NOTES:** No smoking in restaurant RS 25 Dec Civ Wed 120 **CARDS:**

★★67% **Miramar**
158 Station Rd SA15 1YU
☎ 01554 754726 & 773607 Fax 01554 772454
e-mail: hotelmiramar@aol.com
***Dir:*** *take junct 48 on M4. Follow road to Llanelli then follow railway station signs. Hotel is adjacent to the station*
This friendly, family-run hotel is conveniently located opposite the railway station close to the town centre. Accommodation is well-maintained and comfortable with modern facilities. There is a

*continued on p824*

LLANELLI, continued

cheerful bar, offering a good range of bar meals and the restaurant menu provides an extensive choice of dishes, including a number of Portuguese specialities.
**ROOMS:** 12 en suite (2 fmly) s £25-£28; d £40-£45 (incl. bkfst) * **PARKING:** 10 **NOTES:** No dogs (ex guide dogs) No smoking in restaurant **CARDS:**

LLANFAIRPWLLGWYNGYLL See Anglesey, Isle of

LLANFYLLIN, Powys Map 06 SJ11

### ★★67% Cain Valley

High St SY22 5AQ
☎ 01691 648366 ▯ 01691 648307
***Dir:*** *at the end of A490 - Llanfyllin, 12m from Welshpool. Hotel is situated in the centre of town on the square, car park at the rear*
A family run, Grade II listed coaching inn with exposed beams and a Jacobean staircase. The comfortable accommodation includes family rooms. Public areas include a choice of bars where a range of food is available. Alternatively, diners can choose from the extensive restaurant carte.
**ROOMS:** 13 en suite (3 fmly) s £37-£41; d £61-£68 (incl. bkfst) * **LB** **PARKING:** 12 **NOTES:** No smoking in restaurant
**CARDS:**

LLANGAMMARCH WELLS, Powys Map 03 SN94

**Premier Collection**

### ★★★ ⊛⊛ Lake Country House

LD4 4BS
☎ 01591 620202 & 620474
▯ 01591 620457
e-mail: info@lakecountryhouse.co.uk
***Dir:*** *from Builth Wells head W on A483 to Garth (6m approx) turn left for Llangammarch Wells follow signs for hotel*
This Victorian country house hotel comes complete with a nine hole par three golf course, lake, fifty acres of wooded grounds and a river. Bedrooms are individually decorated and furnished with designer fabrics and with many extra comforts as standard. Traditional afternoon teas are served in the lounge in front of a log fire. In addition to the elegant restaurant there is a separate bar and billiard room. The kitchen produces award-winning cuisine.
**ROOMS:** 19 en suite (1 fmly) No smoking in 6 bedrooms s £90-£130; d £130-£210 (incl. bkfst) * **LB** **FACILITIES:** Golf 9 Tennis (hard) Fishing Snooker Croquet lawn Putting green Clay pigeon shooting ch fac Xmas **CONF:** Thtr 80 Class 30 Board 25 Del from £90 * **PARKING:** 72 **NOTES:** No smoking in restaurant Civ Wed 90
**CARDS:**

LLANGEFNI See Anglesey, Isle of

LLANGOLLEN, Denbighshire Map 07 SJ24
see also Glyn Ceiriog

### ★★★70% The Wild Pheasant Hotel & Restaurant

Berwyn Rd LL20 8AD
☎ 01978 860629 ▯ 01978 861837
e-mail: wild.pheasant@talk21.com
***Dir:*** *hotel situated 0.5m from town centre on the left hand side of the main A5 towards Betws-y-Coed/Holyhead*

A professionally run hotel providing smart, modern accommodation. Bedrooms, some with four-poster beds, are well equipped. The reception area, resembling an old village square, has comfortable seating. There is a choice of bars and a range of eating options including a formal restaurant. A self-contained function suite is available.
**ROOMS:** 34 en suite (2 fmly) No smoking in 6 bedrooms s £60; d £94 (incl. bkfst) * **LB** **FACILITIES:** Laser pigeon shooting,Canoeing Xmas **CONF:** Thtr 140 Class 70 Board 50 Del £95 * **PARKING:** 100 **NOTES:** No smoking in restaurant Civ Wed 140
**CARDS:**

### ★★★69% ⊛ Bryn Howel

LL20 7UW
☎ 01978 860331 ▯ 01978 860119
e-mail: hotel@brynhowel.demon.co.uk
***Dir:*** *follow signs for Llangollen on A539. Pass through Acrefair & Trevor, continue for 2m & hotel is on left*
Set in its own well tended gardens with magnificent views across the Vale of Llangollen, this carefully extended hotel dates back to 1896. Accommodation is thoughtfully equipped and includes several spacious junior suites. Public areas include conference and function facilities, a spacious restaurant, an attractively furnished bar and comfortable lounges.
**ROOMS:** 36 en suite s £45-£88; d £99-£114 (incl. bkfst) * **LB** **FACILITIES:** STV Fishing Sauna Solarium Croquet lawn ch fac Xmas **CONF:** Thtr 250 Class 60 Board 50 Del £99.70 * **SERVICES:** Lift **PARKING:** 200 **NOTES:** No dogs (ex guide dogs) No smoking in restaurant Civ Wed 300 **CARDS:**

### ★★★61% Hand

Peel Hotels

Bridge St LL20 8PL
☎ 01978 860303 ▯ 01978 861277
e-mail: info@hand-hotel-llangollen.com
***Dir:*** *from A539, turn right over bridge, drive up Castle St, at lights turn left onto A5 towards Oswestry, hotel car park is 2nd turning on left hand side*
Situated close to the town centre, this 18th-century coaching inn has gardens leading down to the River Dee, for which the hotel has fishing rights. The bedrooms are well-appointed, several to a

continued

very high standard. Good cuisine is served in the restaurant, which has river views. Lighter meals are available in the hotel bar.
**ROOMS:** 58 en suite (3 fmly) No smoking in 11 bedrooms s £25-£65; d £45-£80 (incl. bkfst) * **LB** **FACILITIES:** Fishing entertainment Xmas **CONF:** Thtr 100 Class 50 Board 50 Del from £47 * **PARKING:** 40 **NOTES:** No smoking in restaurant **CARDS:**

### ★★66% Chain Bridge Hotel

Berwyn LL20 8BS
☎ 01978 860215 🖹 01978 861841
e-mail: chainbridge@hotmail.com
***Dir:*** *1.5m A539 W of Llangollen(signed Horsehoe Pass) left to B5103, 500 yds signed entrance left.(over narrow bridge, along towpath to hotel)*
The hotel is situated in an idyllic location on the banks of the river Dee and takes its name from the bridge which spans the river. The historic town of Llangollen is about two miles away and the Shropshire Union canal runs nearby. Rooms are comfortably furnished and some are suitable for families. Downstairs the restaurant overlooks the river and meals are also available in the Tudor bar. Function facilities are also available.
**ROOMS:** 29 en suite 4 annexe en suite (2 fmly) No smoking in 5 bedrooms s fr £45; d fr £80 (incl. bkfst) * **LB** **FACILITIES:** STV Fishing entertainment Xmas **CONF:** Thtr 80 Class 80 Board 50 **PARKING:** 40 **NOTES:** No smoking in restaurant Civ Wed 120
**CARDS:**

### ★★63% *Abbey Grange Hotel*

LL20 8DD
☎ 01978 860753 🖹 01978 869070
e-mail: enquiries@abbey-grange-hotel.co.uk

The hotel is situated close to Llangollen and is a good base for exploring Offa's Dyke and the surrounding countryside. Rooms are spacious and well-equipped, and some are suitable for families. Guests can dine in the restaurant or the bar, and outside there is a sun patio and large children's play area.
**ROOMS:** 8 en suite (3 fmly) **PARKING:** 40
**CARDS:**

## LLANGYBI, Monmouthshire — Map 03 ST39

### ★★★★63% *Cwrt Bleddyn Hotel & Country Club*

Arcadian Hotels Distinctly Different

NP15 1PG
☎ 01633 450521 🖹 01633 450220
***Dir:*** *M4 junct 25 follow signs Caerleon and around 1-way system, straight over mini-rdbt, follow country road for 4m, hotel on left*
Cwrt Bleddyn is an attractive Victorian building set in parkland in the Welsh Borders. Most of the bedrooms are smartly modernised; some have four-posters and carved oak furniture. Four are located in a separate cottage. All have many little extras to cosset guests.

*continued*

The hotel is a popular venue for conferences, functions and weddings.
**ROOMS:** 29 en suite 4 annexe en suite No smoking in 9 bedrooms **FACILITIES:** STV Indoor swimming (H) Tennis (hard) Squash Sauna Solarium Gym Jacuzzi Beauty salon **CONF:** Thtr 200 Class 60 Board 40 **PARKING:** 100 **NOTES:** No dogs (ex guide dogs) No smoking in restaurant **CARDS:**

## LLANRHIDIAN, Swansea

### ○ North Gower

SA3 1EE
☎ 01792 390042
At the time of going to press, the star classification for this hotel was not confirmed. Please refer to the AA internet site www.theAA.com for current information.

## LLANRWST, Conwy — Map 06 SH76

see also Betws-y-Coed

### ★★★65% Maenan Abbey

Maenan LL26 0UL
☎ 01492 660247 🖹 01492 660734
e-mail: reservations@manab.co.uk
***Dir:*** *3m N on A470*
This personally run private hotel was built as an abbey in 1850 on the site of a 13th-century monastery. It is now a popular venue for weddings; the grounds and magnificent galleried staircase make an ideal backdrop for photographs. Bedrooms include a large suite and are equipped with modern facilities. A wide range of food is served in the bars and restaurant.
**ROOMS:** 14 en suite (2 fmly) s £35-£45; d £49-£79 (incl. bkfst) * **LB** **FACILITIES:** Fishing guided mountain walks Xmas **CONF:** Thtr 50 Class 30 Board 30 Del from £15 * **PARKING:** 60 **NOTES:** No smoking in restaurant Civ Wed 90 **CARDS:**

## LLANWDDYN, Powys — Map 06 SJ01

### ★★★73% ®® Lake Vyrnwy

Lake Vyrnwy SY10 0LY
☎ 01691 870692 🖹 01691 870259
e-mail: res@lakevyrnwy.com
***Dir:*** *on A4393, 200yds past dam*

This fine country house hotel lies in 26,000 acres of woodland above Lake Vyrnwy. It provides a wide range of bedrooms, most with superb views and many with four-poster beds and balconies. The extensive public rooms are elegantly furnished and include a choice of bars. The Tavern bar serves meals while the main restaurant offers more formal dining.
**ROOMS:** 35 en suite (4 fmly) s £80-£125; d £110-£182 (incl. bkfst) * **LB** **FACILITIES:** STV Tennis (hard) Fishing Riding Game/Clay shooting, Sailing, Cycling,Archery,Quad trekking,Fly fishing Xmas **CONF:** Thtr 120 Class 60 Board 45 Del from £150 * **PARKING:** 70 **NOTES:** No smoking in restaurant Civ Wed 120 **CARDS:**

## LLANWRTYD WELLS, Powys Map 03 SN84

**★★73% Carlton House**
Dolycoed Rd LD5 4RA
☎ 01591 610248 01591 610242
e-mail: info@carltonrestaurant.co.uk
***Dir:*** *centre of town*
Carlton House stands in this beautiful and unspoilt area of Wales, reputed to be the smallest rural town in Britain. The bedrooms are striking, each being decorated with a different theme with high levels of comfort. The communal areas are pleasing with warm, fresh colours and period furniture. The hotel cuisine is rated very highly, and is perfectly complimented by a very well chosen wine list.
**ROOMS:** 7 rms (5 en suite) (2 fmly) s £30-£45; d £60-£75 (incl. bkfst) * **LB FACILITIES:** Pony trekking Mountain biking **NOTES:** No smoking in restaurant RS 15-30 Dec **CARDS:**

## LLYSWEN, Powys Map 03 SO13

### Premier Collection

**★★★★ Llangoed Hall**
LD3 0YP
☎ 01874 754525 01874 754545
e-mail: office@llangoedhall.com
***Dir:*** *follow A470 through village of Llyswen for 2m. Hotel drive on right hand side*
Set amidst beautiful countryside this imposing country house offers an exterior remodelled by Clough Williams-Ellis (of Portmeirion fame). Inside there is a splendid balance between comfort, grandeur and interest with wood-burning open fires, deep-cushioned sofas, and a range of artwork and artefacts. Bedrooms are furnished with a pleasing mix of antiques and Laura Ashley designs together with smart bathrooms. The hotel cuisine complements the opulent surroundings with accomplished, imaginative cooking.
**ROOMS:** 23 en suite s £130-£280; d £165-£320 (incl. bkfst) * **LB FACILITIES:** STV Tennis (hard) Fishing Croquet lawn Mazes Clay pigeon shooting snooker ch fac Xmas **CONF:** Thtr 80 Class 40 Board 32 Del from £150 * **PARKING:** 85 **NOTES:** No dogs (ex guide dogs) No children 8yrs No smoking in restaurant Civ Wed 60 **CARDS:**

## MACHYNLLETH, Powys Map 06 SH70
see also Eglwysfach

**★★63% Wynnstay**
Maengwyn St SY20 8AE
☎ 01654 702941 01654 703884
e-mail: info@wynnstay-hotel.com
***Dir:*** *at junct of A487/A489*
Long established, this former posting house lies in the centre of historic Machynlleth. Bedrooms, which include no smoking rooms and family bedded rooms, have modern facilities. The bars are popular with locals and a good range of food is available. The restaurant offers more formal dining and guests can choose from a fixed price menu.
**ROOMS:** 23 en suite (3 fmly) No smoking in 7 bedrooms s £45-£55; d £70-£100 (incl. bkfst) * **LB FACILITIES:** Xmas **CONF:** Thtr 40 Class 20 Board 24 Del from £60 * **PARKING:** 30 **NOTES:** No smoking in restaurant **CARDS:**

*See advert on opposite page*

## MANORBIER, Pembrokeshire Map 02 SS09

**★★65% *Castle Mead***
SA70 7TA
☎ 01834 871358 01834 871358
THE CIRCLE Selected Individual Hotels GREAT BRITAIN
***Dir:*** *A4139 towards Pembroke from Tenby, turn onto B4585 into village and follow signs to beach and castle. Hotel on left above beach*
Benefiting from a superb location with spectacular views of the bay, the Norman church and Manorbier Castle, this family-run establishment has a friendly and welcoming style. Public areas that include a sea view restaurant, bar and residents' lounge are complemented by an extensive garden. Bedrooms are generally quite spacious and offer modern facilities throughout.
**ROOMS:** 5 en suite 3 annexe en suite (2 fmly) No smoking in 2 bedrooms **PARKING:** 20 **NOTES:** Closed Nov-Feb
**CARDS:**

## MENAI BRIDGE See Anglesey, Isle of

## MERTHYR TYDFIL, Merthyr Tydfil Map 03 SO00
see also Nant-Ddu

**★★★69% Tregenna**
Park Ter CF47 8RF
☎ 01685 723627 & 382055 01685 721951
e-mail: reception@tregenna.co.uk
Quiet surroundings and a warm welcome give guests a relaxing start to their stay at this family-run hotel, just north of the town centre. Bedrooms are well-equipped; half of them are housed in a purpose-built wing. The traditionally furnished restaurant and bar serves a good selection of meals.
**ROOMS:** 29 en suite (9 fmly) No smoking in 4 bedrooms s £45-£48; d £55-£60 (incl. bkfst) * **LB FACILITIES:** STV Xmas **CONF:** Thtr 70 Class 70 Board 30 **PARKING:** 60 **NOTES:** No dogs (ex guide dogs)
**CARDS:**

## MISKIN, Rhondda Cynon Taff Map 03 ST08

**★★★★69% *Miskin Manor***
Groes Faen, Pontyclun CF72 8ND
☎ 01443 224204 01443 237606
e-mail: info@miskin-manor.co.uk
***Dir:*** *M4 junct 34 & follow hotel signs - 300yds on left*
This manor house is set in 20 acres of grounds, only minutes away from the M4. Public areas are spacious and comfortable and include a variety of function rooms. Bedrooms are furnished to a high standard and include some located in converted stables and cottages. Frederick's health club has leisure facilities and a bar/bistro.
**ROOMS:** 35 en suite 11 annexe en suite **FACILITIES:** STV Indoor swimming (H) Squash Sauna Solarium Gym Croquet lawn Jacuzzi **CONF:** Thtr 160 Class 80 Board 65 **PARKING:** 200 **NOTES:** No smoking in restaurant Civ Wed 200 **CARDS:**

*See advert under CARDIFF*

*continued*

## MOLD, Flintshire Map 07 SJ26

see also Northop Hall

### ★★★65% Beaufort Park Hotel

Alltami Rd, New Brighton CH7 6RQ
☎ 01352 758646 🖹 01352 757132
e-mail: bph@beaufortparkhotel.co.uk

***Dir:*** *A55 - take Mold slip road, A494. Through Alltami traffic lights. Over mini rdbt by petrol station towards Mold, A5119. Hotel 100yds on right*

This large, modern hotel is conveniently located a short drive from the North Wales Expressway and offers various styles of spacious accommodation. There are extensive public areas, which include several meeting and function rooms. There is a formal restaurant and the popular Arches bar where a wide range of meals is available.

**ROOMS:** 106 en suite (4 fmly) No smoking in 25 bedrooms s £95; d £110 (incl. bkfst) * **LB** **FACILITIES:** Squash Jacuzzi Darts Games Room entertainment ch fac Xmas **CONF:** Thtr 250 Class 120 Board 50 Del from £95 * **PARKING:** 200 **NOTES:** Civ Wed 80
**CARDS:**

### ★★65% Bryn Awel

Denbigh Rd CH7 1BL
☎ 01352 758622 🖹 01352 758625
e-mail: bryn@awel.fsbusiness.co.uk

***Dir:*** *NW edge of town, on A541*

Situated on the edge of the town centre, this privately run hotel offers well-equipped modern accommodation, some of it located in a purpose built annexe. Public areas include a small but well-equipped function room, a lounge bar offering an extensive selection of bar meals and an attractive bistro style restaurant.

**ROOMS:** 8 en suite 10 annexe en suite No smoking in 11 bedrooms s £40-£45; d £55-£60 (incl. bkfst) * **LB** **CONF:** Thtr 30 Class 15 Board 20 Del £69 * **PARKING:** 45 **NOTES:** No smoking in restaurant
**CARDS:**

## MONMOUTH, Monmouthshire Map 03 SO51

see also Whitebrook

### ★★66% Riverside

MINOTEL Great Britain

Cinderhill St NP25 5EY
☎ 01600 715577 & 713236 🖹 01600 712668

***Dir:*** *leave A40 signposted Rockfield & Monmouth hotel on left beyond garage & before rdbt*

Just a short walk from the famous 13th-century bridge, this privately owned hotel offers comfortable accommodation and a relaxed and informal atmosphere. Bedrooms are well-equipped and comfortably decorated. Public areas include an attractive restaurant, a pleasant bar and a conservatory lounge at the rear of the property.

**ROOMS:** 17 en suite (2 fmly) No smoking in 2 bedrooms s £49; d £68 (incl. bkfst) * **LB** **FACILITIES:** Xmas **CONF:** Thtr 150 Class 60 Board 40 Del £57.50 * **PARKING:** 30 **NOTES:** No smoking in restaurant
**CARDS:**

## MONTGOMERY, Powys Map 07 SO29

### ★★70% ® Dragon

MINOTEL Great Britain

SY15 6PA
☎ 01686 668359 🖹 01686 668287
e-mail: reception@dragonhotel.com

***Dir:*** *behind the Town Hall*

This fine 17th-century coaching inn stands in the centre of Montgomery. Beams and timbers from the nearby castle, which was destroyed by Cromwell, are visible in the lounge and bar. A wide choice of soundly prepared, wholesome food is available in

*continued*

both the restaurant and bar. Bedrooms are well-equipped and family rooms are available.

**ROOMS:** 20 en suite (6 fmly) No smoking in 5 bedrooms s £45-£55; d £75 (incl. bkfst) * **LB** **FACILITIES:** Indoor swimming (H) Sauna entertainment Xmas **CONF:** Thtr 40 Class 30 Board 25 Del from £56 * **PARKING:** 21 **NOTES:** No smoking in restaurant
**CARDS:**

## MUMBLES (NEAR SWANSEA), Swansea Map 02 SS68

### ★★★64% St Anne's

Western Ln SA3 4EY
☎ 01792 369147 🖹 01792 360537
e-mail: info@stanneshotel-mumbles.com

***Dir:*** *follow A483/A4067 to Mumbles, on reaching village drive straight over mini rdbt and cont along road, Western Lane is 3rd right*

St.ANNE'S
HOTEL

Standing on a hillside above Swansea, this former convent school enjoys some superb views over Swansea Bay. The accommodation

*continued on p828*

M

MUMBLES (NEAR SWANSEA), continued

is modern and bedrooms are well-maintained with good facilities. Many rooms overlook the sea, as do the public areas that include a spacious lounge with a large picture window.
**ROOMS:** 33 en suite (3 fmly) No smoking in 7 bedrooms s £52-£60; d £58-£69.50 (incl. bkfst) * **LB** **FACILITIES:** STV **CONF:** Thtr 100 Class 50 Board 50 Del £65 * **PARKING:** 50 **NOTES:** No smoking in restaurant **CARDS:**

*See advert under SWANSEA*

NANT-DDU (NEAR MERTHYR TYDFIL), Powys Map 03 SO01

### ★★★74% Nant Ddu Lodge

Cwm Taf, Nant Ddu CF48 2HY
☎ 01685 379111 01685 377088
e-mail: enquiries@nant-ddu-lodge.co.uk
***Dir:*** *6m N of Merthyr Tydfil & 12m S of Brecon on main A470 between Merthyr and Brecon*

This 19th-century Georgian hotel is situated in the picturesque Brecon Beacons, a stone's throw from Nant Ddu (Black Stream). Bedrooms are attractively furnished and offer a good range of facilities. The charming bar and bistro areas are the focal point, serving good, imaginative food.
**ROOMS:** 12 en suite 10 annexe en suite (3 fmly) s £55-£69.50; d £69.50-£95 (incl. cont bkfst) * **LB** **FACILITIES:** STV **CONF:** Thtr 30 Class 15 Board 20 Del from £80 * **PARKING:** 60 **NOTES:** No smoking in restaurant RS 24-26 Dec **CARDS:**

*See advert under BRECON*

NEATH, Neath Port Talbot Map 03 SS79

### ★★65% Castle Hotel

The Parade SA11 1RB
☎ 01639 641119 & 643581 01639 641624
***Dir:*** *M4 junct43, follow signs for Neath town centre, 500yds past railway station hotel is situated on right hand side*
The Castle is an old coaching inn in the heart of Neath. Reputedly frequented by Lord Nelson; it is also where the Welsh Rugby Union was founded over a century ago. The bars and restaurant are popular local venues and there are function and conference rooms available. The bedrooms are well-equipped and generally spacious.
**ROOMS:** 29 en suite (3 fmly) No smoking in 4 bedrooms s £55-£65; d £65-£75 (incl. bkfst) * **LB** **FACILITIES:** STV entertainment **CONF:** Thtr 160 Class 75 Board 50 **PARKING:** 26 **NOTES:** No dogs (ex guide dogs) **CARDS:**

Arriving late? Four and five star hotels have night porters to assist with your luggage, and 24-hour room service.

NEVERN, Pembrokeshire Map 02 SN03

### ★★68% Trewern Arms

SA42 0NB
☎ 01239 820395 01239 820173
***Dir:*** *off A487 coast road - midway between Cardigan and Fishguard*
This ivy clad 16th-century inn has a wealth of charm and character. Original features include stone flagged floors, exposed stone walls and beamed ceilings in the two bars and the attractively appointed restaurant. The modern bedrooms are spacious and comfortable and include family bedded rooms.
**ROOMS:** 10 en suite (4 fmly) s £35; d £50 (incl. bkfst) * **FACILITIES:** Fishing Riding Xmas **PARKING:** 100 **NOTES:** No dogs **CARDS:**

NEWPORT, Newport Map 03 ST38

### ★★★★★77% The Celtic Manor Resort

Coldra Woods NP18 1HQ
☎ 01633 413000 01633 412910
e-mail: postbox@celtic-manor.com
***Dir:*** *M4 junct 24, A48 Newport centre. Hotel is 1st R past Alcatel*
At the gateway to Wales, this luxurious resort boasts some of the most far-ranging facilities to be found anywhere in the UK. Its sheer scale must be seen to be believed. There are three challenging golf courses and the international convention centre is capable of accommodating 1500 delegates. In addition there are 40 other banqueting and meeting rooms. The huge atrium makes a striking first impression and leads onto smart lounges, restaurants and luxurious guest bedrooms and suites.
**ROOMS:** 400 en suite (28 fmly) No smoking in 167 bedrooms s £165-£1293; d £178-£1293 * **LB** **FACILITIES:** Spa STV Indoor swimming (H) Golf 54 Tennis (hard) Snooker Sauna Solarium Gym Putting green Jacuzzi Golf school entertainment ch fac Xmas **CONF:** Thtr 1500 Class 300 Board 50 Del from £175 * **SERVICES:** Lift air con **PARKING:** 1300 **NOTES:** No dogs (ex guide dogs) Civ Wed 100
**CARDS:**

### ★★★67% Newport Lodge

Bryn Bevan, Brynglas Rd NP20 5QN
☎ 01633 821818 01633 856360
e-mail: info@newportlodgehotel.co.uk
***Dir:*** *M4 junct 26 follow signs Newport Town centre. Turn left after 0.5m onto Malpal Road, up hill for 0.5m to hotel*
On the edge of the town centre, and convenient for the M4, this is a purpose-built, friendly hotel. The bistro-style restaurant, offers a wide range of freshly prepared dishes. The bedrooms are well-maintained with modern facilities.
**ROOMS:** 27 en suite No smoking in 8 bedrooms s £70-£80; d £90-£115 (incl. bkfst) * **LB** **CONF:** Thtr 25 Class 20 Board 20 **PARKING:** 63 **NOTES:** No children 14yrs **CARDS:**

### ★★★66% Kings

High St NP20 1QU
☎ 01633 842020 01633 244667
e-mail: kingshotels.wales@netscapeonline.co.uk
***Dir:*** *from town centre, take left hand road (not flyover) right hand lane to next rdbt, 3rd exit off across front of hotel then left for carpark*
Situated right in the town centre, this privately owned hotel offers comfortable bedrooms and bright spacious public areas. Facilities include a choice of function rooms and a large ballroom.
**ROOMS:** 61 en suite (15 fmly) No smoking in 20 bedrooms s £59-£64; d £74-£101 * **LB** **FACILITIES:** STV entertainment Xmas **CONF:** Thtr 150 Class 70 Board 50 Del from £95 * **SERVICES:** Lift **PARKING:** 50 **NOTES:** No dogs (ex guide dogs) Closed 26 Dec-4 Jan Civ Wed
**CARDS:**

*See advert on opposite page*

M

NORTHOP, Flintshire Map 07 SJ26

**★★★77% Soughton Hall**
CH7 6AB
☎ 01352 840811 01352 840382
e-mail: info@soughtonhall.co.uk
***Dir:*** *A55-B5126, after 500mtrs turn left for Northop, left at traffic lights (A5119-Mold). After 0.5m look for signs on left for the hall*
Built as a Bishop's Palace in 1714, this is a truly elegant country house with its own magnificent grounds. Bedrooms are individually decorated and furnished with fine antiques and rich fabrics. There are several spacious day rooms furnished in keeping with the style of the house. Adjacent, the bustling, trendy Stables bar and restaurant offers a contrast to fine dining in the main hotel.
**ROOMS:** 14 en suite (2 fmly) s fr £98; d fr £130 (incl. bkfst) * **LB**
**FACILITIES:** Golf 18 Tennis (hard) Riding Croquet lawn ch fac Xmas
**CONF:** Thtr 40 Class 40 Board 20 Del from £128 * **PARKING:** 100
**NOTES:** No dogs (ex guide dogs) No smoking in restaurant Civ Wed 120
**CARDS:**

NORTHOP HALL, Flintshire Map 07 SJ26

***Travelodge***
CH7 6HB
☎ 01244 816473 01244 816473
***Dir:*** *on A55, eastbound*
Travelodge offers good quality, good value, modern accommodation. Ideal for families, the spacious, en suite bedrooms include remote-control TV, tea and coffee-making facilities, luxury beds and free morning newspaper. Meals can be taken at the nearby family restaurant. For further details and the Travelodge phone number, consult the Hotel Groups page.

**ROOMS:** 40 en suite

PEMBROKE, Pembrokeshire Map 02 SM90

**★★★74% Lamphey Court**
Lamphey SA71 5NT
☎ 01646 672273 01646 672480
e-mail: info@lampheycourt.co.uk
***Dir:*** *take A477 to Pembroke. Turn left at Village Milton. In Lamphey village hotel on right*
This fine Georgian mansion lies in several acres of mature grounds and landscaped gardens. Bedrooms are tastefully furnished and appointed and well-equipped. Some are located in a nearby converted coach house and some are on ground floor level. Public areas are elegantly appointed and offer a choice of formal or informal dining.
**ROOMS:** 26 en suite 11 annexe en suite (15 fmly) s £69-£81; d £100-£130 (incl. bkfst) * **LB** **FACILITIES:** STV Indoor swimming (H) Tennis (hard) Sauna Solarium Gym Jacuzzi Yacht charter ch fac Xmas
**CONF:** Thtr 80 Class 60 Board 40 Del from £99 * **PARKING:** 50
**NOTES:** No dogs (ex guide dogs) Civ Wed 80
**CARDS:**

*See advert on this page*

**★★70% Lamphey Hall**
Lamphey SA71 5NR
☎ 01646 672394 01646 672369
e-mail: lamphey@globalnet.co.uk
***Dir:*** *on A4139 Pembroke/Tenby Road in centre of village, opposite parish church*
The pretty village of Lamphey is the setting for this welcoming, family-run hotel. The two restaurants, one of which is an informal

*continued on p830*

PEMBROKE, continued

bistro, are at the hub of the operation and are popular with locals as well as visitors. Bedrooms are smart and modern; ground floor and family bedded rooms are available. Residents have use of a central lounge and a bar.
**ROOMS:** 10 en suite (1 fmly) No smoking in 1 bedroom s £40-£50; d £60-£65 (incl. bkfst) * **FACILITIES:** Jacuzzi **PARKING:** 26
**NOTES:** No dogs No smoking in restaurant RS 26 Dec-mid Jan
**CARDS:**

### ★★61% Old Kings Arms
Main St SA71 4JS
☎ 01646 683611 01646 682335
***Dir:*** *situated in Main Street. Approach from Carmarthen, Tenby or Pembroke Dock*
At the centre of the bustling town this former coaching inn is very much at the heart of local activities and a favourite with locals. The restaurant and bar with traditional stone walls, flagged floors and roaring log fires, offers good, wholesome food.
**ROOMS:** 21 en suite s £33-£40; d £45-£48 (incl. bkfst) * **PARKING:** 21
**NOTES:** Closed 25-26 Dec & 1 Jan **CARDS:**

## PEMBROKE DOCK, Pembrokeshire — Map 02 SM90

### ★★★67% *Cleddau Bridge*
Essex Rd SA72 6EG
☎ 01646 685961 & 0800 279 4055 01646 685746
e-mail: information@cleddaubridgehotel.co.uk
***Dir:*** *M4 to Camarthen A40 to St Clears A477 to Pembroke Dock at rdbt 2nd exit for Haverfordwest via the toll bridge take left before the toll bridge*
This purpose built hotel is situated at the Pembroke Dock end of the Cleddau Bridge, from where it overlooks impressive views of the river. It provides modern well-equipped accommodation including suites, all located on ground level. The hotel is a very popular venue for weddings and other functions. Facilities include an outdoor heated swimming pool.
**ROOMS:** 24 en suite (2 fmly) No smoking in 12 bedrooms
**FACILITIES:** STV Outdoor swimming (H) **CONF:** Thtr 160 Class 60 Board 60 **PARKING:** 140 **CARDS:**

## PENCOED, Bridgend — Map 03 SS98

### ★★★73% St Mary's Hotel & Country Club
Best Western
St Marys Golf Club CF35 5EA
☎ 01656 861100 & 860280 01656 863400
e-mail: stmaryshotel@hotmail.com
***Dir:*** *M4 junct 35, on A473*

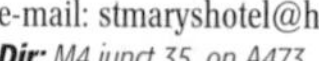

The stone buildings that comprise this modern hotel and golf course were formerly a 16th-century farmhouse. The two golf courses, 9 and 18 hole, surround the hotel buildings and form a pleasant backdrop to the public areas and bedrooms, many of which look out over the fairways. Inside, there is a choice of bars and Rafters Restaurant with its stone walls and exposed beams. The bedrooms are generous in size and benefit from good quality furnishings.
**ROOMS:** 24 en suite (19 fmly) s £50-£75; d £60-£99 (incl. bkfst) * **LB**
**FACILITIES:** STV Golf 27 Tennis (hard) Putting green Floodlit driving range Xmas **CONF:** Thtr 120 Class 60 Board 40 Del from £99.50 *
**PARKING:** 140 **NOTES:** No dogs (ex guide dogs)
**CARDS:**

*See advert on opposite page*

### ⌂ *Travelodge*
Travelodge
Old Mill, Felindre Rd CF35 5HU
☎ 01656 864404 01656 864404
***Dir:*** *on A473*
Travelodge offers good quality, good value, modern accommodation. Ideal for families, the spacious, en suite bedrooms include remote-control TV, tea and coffee-making facilities, luxury beds and free morning newspaper. Meals can be taken at the nearby family restaurant. For further details and the Travelodge phone number, consult the Hotel Groups page.

**ROOMS:** 40 en suite

## PONTERWYD, Ceredigion — Map 06 SN78

### ★★65% The George Borrow Hotel
THE CIRCLE
Selected Individual Hotels
GREAT BRITAIN
SY23 3AD
☎ 01970 890230 01970 890587
e-mail: georgeborrow@clara.net
***Dir:*** *on A44 Aberystwyth-Llangurig road. Aberystwyth side of village*

The George Borrow Hotel

This friendly family hotel nestles in the foothills of the Cambrian Mountains about 12 miles from the university town of Aberystwyth. The hotel provides an ideal base for walking, fishing and bird watching (the red kite abounds) and is an excellent base for touring mid Wales. Rooms are comfortable with their own facilities and downstairs there are two character bars and a restaurant where a good range of meals is available.
**ROOMS:** 9 en suite (2 fmly) s £25; d £50 (incl. bkfst) * **LB**
**CONF:** Thtr 40 Class 30 Board 30 Del from £35 * **PARKING:** 54
**NOTES:** No smoking in restaurant **CARDS:**

## PONTYCLUN, Rhondda Cynon Taff — Map 03 ST08

### ★★★★71% Vale Hotel Golf & Country Club
Hensol Park CF72 8JY
☎ 01443 667800 01443 667801
e-mail: reservations@vale-hotel.com
***Dir:*** *M4 junct 34, follow signs to Pontyclun, hotel 3 mins drive from junct. & signposted*
This large, privately owned hotel, golf and leisure complex is

*continued*

P

surrounded by extensive landscaped grounds which contain two golf courses. Other facilities include a large and extremely well-equipped health Spa and Racquet club, as well as a selection of function and conference suites. There are bright, spacious and airy public areas. The bedrooms, over half, with private balconies, are spacious, comfortable and very well equipped.

**ROOMS:** 30 en suite 113 annexe en suite (17 fmly) No smoking in 71 bedrooms s £75-£125; d £85-£135 (incl. bkfst) * **LB** **FACILITIES:** **Spa** STV Indoor swimming (H) Golf 18 Tennis (hard) Fishing Squash Riding Sauna Solarium Gym Putting green Jacuzzi Beauty treatments Hydrotherapy treatments Childrens club ch fac **CONF:** Thtr 250 Class 180 Board 60 Del from £135 * **SERVICES:** Lift air con **PARKING:** 400 **NOTES:** Civ Wed 100 **CARDS:**

PONTYPOOL, Torfaen Map 03 SO20

**Express by Holiday Inn**
New Mill Roundabout NP4 0RH
☎ 01495 755266 🖷 01495 755331
***Dir:*** *At junct of A4042 and A472, adjacent to the Harvester Restaurant*

A modern budget hotel offering comfortable accommodation in refreshing, spacious and comprehensively equipped bedrooms, en suite bathrooms with power showers and continental buffet breakfast included in the room rate. Suitable for business travellers or families. For further details and the Express by Holiday Inn phone number, consult the Hotel Groups page.

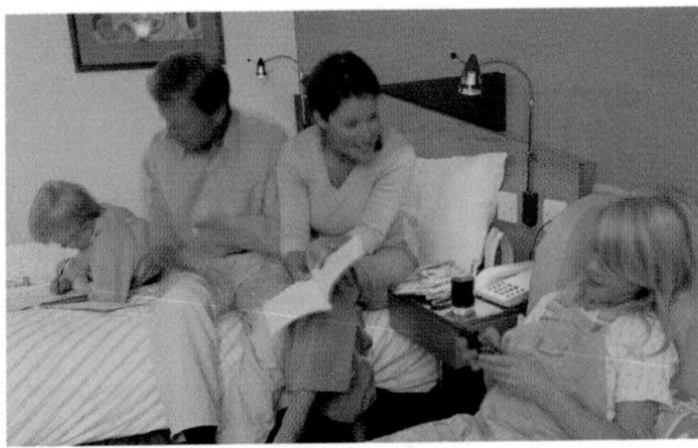

**ROOMS:** 49 en suite **CONF:** Thtr 30 Class 25 Board 18

PONTYPRIDD, Rhondda Cynon Taff Map 03 ST08

★★★69% **Llechwen Hall**
Llanfabon CF37 4HP
☎ 01443 742050 & 743020 🖷 01443 742189
e-mail: llechwen@aol.com
***Dir:*** *A470 N towards Merthyr Tydfil, then A472, then onto A4054 for Cilfynydd. After 0.25m turn left at hotel sign and follow to top of hill*

Dating back to the 17th century, this country house hotel enjoys a stunning mountain-top location. Bedrooms are divided between

continued on p832

PONTYPRIDD, continued

the main house and a smart new coach house. There is a choice of two restaurants, both offer a range of popular dishes.

LECHWEN
HALL

*Llechwen Hall, Pontypridd*

**ROOMS:** 12 en suite 8 annexe en suite (6 fmly) No smoking in 8 bedrooms **FACILITIES:** STV ch fac **CONF:** Thtr 50 Class 30 Board 30 Del from £75 * **PARKING:** 100 **CARDS:**

**★★★67% Heritage Park**
Coed Cae Rd, Trehafod CF37 2NP
☎ 01443 687057 📠 01443 687060
e-mail: heritageparkhotel@talk21.com
***Dir:*** *off A4058, follow signs to the Rhondda Heritage Park*
Adjacent to the Rhondda Heritage Park, this privately owned, modern hotel is suitable for all types of guest. The spacious bedrooms include ground floor and interconnecting rooms, and a room equipped for less able guests. Meals can be taken in the attractive, wood-beamed, "Loft Restaurant".
**ROOMS:** 44 en suite (4 fmly) No smoking in 19 bedrooms s £61-£75; d fr £76 (incl. bkfst) * **LB FACILITIES:** STV Indoor swimming (H) Sauna Solarium Gym Jacuzzi Xmas **CONF:** Thtr 150 Class 40 Board 30 Del from £90 * **PARKING:** 150 **NOTES:** No smoking in restaurant Civ Wed 90 **CARDS:**

P

PORT EINON, Swansea Map 02 SS48

**★★63% *Culver House***
SA3 1NN
☎ 01792 390755
***Dir:*** *in village continue past church turn right at post office, 50yds on turn left, hotel a further 100yds on left*
This privately owned and personally run small hotel is just a few hundred yards from the shoreline, and is ideal for those visiting the Gower Peninsula. Many of modern bedrooms have sea views. The restaurant serves home cooking meals and is supplemented by a bar and lounge.
**ROOMS:** 10 rms (8 en suite) (3 fmly) No smoking in all bedrooms **PARKING:** 8 **NOTES:** No smoking in restaurant Closed 1-30 Nov **CARDS:**

PORTHCAWL, Bridgend Map 03 SS87

**★★★68% Atlantic**
West Dr CF36 3LT
☎ 01656 785011 📠 01656 771877
e-mail: enquiries@atlantichotelporthcawl.co.uk
***Dir:*** *M4 junct 35 or 37, follow signs for Porthcawl, on entering Porthcawl follow signs for Seafront/Promenade, hotel on seafront*
This privately owned and personally run, friendly hotel is located on the seafront, a short walk from the town centre. Guests can enjoy sea views from the sun terrace, bright conservatory and

*continued*

some of the bedrooms. Bedrooms are well-maintained and decorated, and feature good levels of equipment.
**ROOMS:** 18 en suite (2 fmly) s £40-£65; d £60-£90 (incl. bkfst) * **LB FACILITIES:** STV Xmas **CONF:** Thtr 50 Class 50 Board 25 **SERVICES:** Lift **PARKING:** 20 **NOTES:** No dogs (ex guide dogs) **CARDS:**

**★★★64% Seabank**
The Promenade CF36 3LU
☎ 01656 782261 📠 01656 785363
e-mail: info@seabankhotel.co.uk
***Dir:*** *M4 junct 37, follow A4229 to seafront, hotel is located on the promenade*

This large privately owned hotel stands on the promenade and overlooks the sea. The well-equipped accommodation includes rooms with four-poster beds, and most enjoy sea views. There is a spacious restaurant, a lounge bar and a choice of lounges.
**ROOMS:** 67 en suite (2 fmly) No smoking in 15 bedrooms s £59.50; d £80 (incl. bkfst) * **LB FACILITIES:** Spa STV Sauna Gym Jacuzzi entertainment Xmas **CONF:** Thtr 250 Class 150 Board 70 Del £85 * **SERVICES:** Lift **PARKING:** 140 **NOTES:** No dogs (ex guide dogs) Civ Wed 100 **CARDS:**

*See advert under BRIDGEND and on opposite page*

**★★61% *Glenaub***
50 Mary St CF36 3YA
☎ 01656 788242 & 788846 📠 01656 773649
***Dir:*** *M4 junct 37 follow signs for Porthcawl town centre, turn left before Somerfield supermarket, 1st right into carpark*
Located just a short walk from the town centre and the seafront, this personally run hotel offers comfortable accommodation and a warm welcome. The lounge bar has an attractive conservatory extension and there is a traditionally furnished dining room.
**ROOMS:** 18 en suite **FACILITIES:** STV **PARKING:** 12 **NOTES:** No dogs (ex guide dogs) **CARDS:**

PORTMEIRION, Gwynedd Map 06 SH53

**★★★78% ®® The Hotel Portmeirion & Castell Deudraeth**
LL48 6ET
☎ 01766 770000 📠 01766 771331
e-mail: hotel@portmeirion-village.com
***Dir:*** *2m W, Portmeirion village is S off A487*
Nestling under the wooded slopes of the famous Italianate village, (as featured in the cult 1960s TV series,'The Prisoner') and looking out over the sandy estuary towards Snowdonia, this hotel has one of the finest settings in Wales. Many rooms have balconies and private sitting rooms and most are located within the village and

*continued*

command spectacular views. Public areas are elegantly furnished and mostly Welsh-speaking staff offer warm hospitality.

**ROOMS:** 25 en suite 26 annexe en suite (4 fmly) **FACILITIES:** STV Outdoor swimming (H) Tennis (hard) Beauty Salon Xmas **CONF:** Thtr 100 **PARKING:** 40 **NOTES:** No dogs No smoking in restaurant Civ Wed 100 **CARDS:**

*See advert on this page*

## PORT TALBOT, Neath Port Talbot — Map 03 SS79

### ★★★68% Aberavon Beach

SA12 6QP
☎ 01639 884949 01639 897885
e-mail: sales@aberavonbeach.com
***Dir:*** *M4 junct 41 (A48) signs for Aberavon Beach & Hollywood Park*

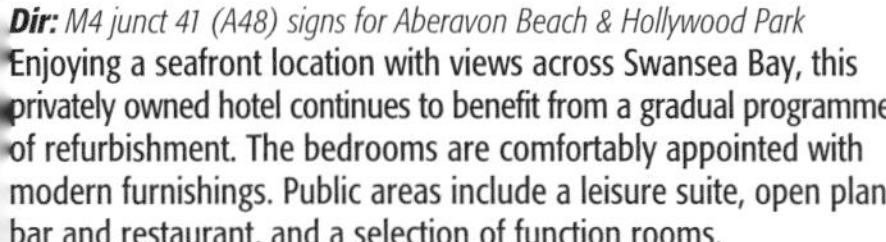

Enjoying a seafront location with views across Swansea Bay, this privately owned hotel continues to benefit from a gradual programme of refurbishment. The bedrooms are comfortably appointed with modern furnishings. Public areas include a leisure suite, open plan bar and restaurant, and a selection of function rooms.

**ROOMS:** 52 en suite (6 fmly) s £69-£72; d £79-£82 (incl. bkfst) * **LB** **FACILITIES:** Indoor swimming (H) Sauna Jacuzzi All weather leisure centre entertainment Xmas **CONF:** Thtr 300 Class 200 Board 50 Del from £100 * **SERVICES:** Lift **PARKING:** 150 **NOTES:** No smoking in restaurant Civ Wed 300 **CARDS:**

*See advert under SWANSEA*

## PRESTATYN, Denbighshire — Map 06 SJ08

### ★★67% Traeth Ganol Hotel

41 Beach Rd West LL19 7LL
☎ 01745 853594 01745 886687
e-mail: info@hotel-prestatyn.co.uk
***Dir:*** *from A55 follow brown tourist signs to Nova Centre & beaches. Hotel beyond Nova, fourth property from end of cul-de-sac*

This small, friendly, family-run hotel is close to the seafront, the championship golf course and the Nova leisure complex. The bedrooms are spacious, freshly decorated and well equipped. Downstairs there is a comfortable lounge and a cosy bar and restaurant.

**ROOMS:** 9 en suite (6 fmly) No smoking in all bedrooms s £39-£54; d £56-£62 (incl. bkfst) * **LB** **PARKING:** 12 **NOTES:** No dogs (ex guide dogs) No smoking in restaurant **CARDS:**

## PRESTEIGNE, Powys — Map 03 SO36

### ★★★65% Radnorshire Arms

High St LD8 2BE
☎ 01544 267406 01544 260418
e-mail: radnorshire@drayton-manor-hotels.com
***Dir:*** *A456 through Kidderminster, Bewdley and Tenbury Wells, through to Wooferton near Ludlow then B4362 to Presteigne*

This delightful 17th-century timbered coaching inn features

*continued on p834*

P

PRESTEIGNE, continued

original panelling and real fires in the public rooms. Bedrooms are split between the main building and an annexe across the pretty garden; most are spacious with a full range of facilities.
**ROOMS:** 8 en suite 8 annexe en suite (6 fmly) No smoking in 5 bedrooms s £50-£75; d £50-£104 (incl. bkfst) * **LB** **FACILITIES:** ch fac Xmas **CONF:** Thtr 60 Class 40 Board 30 Del from £75 * **PARKING:** 54
**NOTES:** No smoking in restaurant Civ Wed 60
**CARDS:**

RAGLAN, Monmouthshire — Map 03 SO40

### ⌂ *Travelodge*

Travelodge

Granada Services A40, Nr Monmouth NP5 4BB
☎ 01600 740444
***Dir:*** *on A40 near junct with A449*
Travelodge offers good quality, good value, modern accommodation. Ideal for families, the spacious, en suite bedrooms include remote-control TV, tea and coffee-making facilities, luxury beds and free morning newspaper. Meals can be taken at the nearby family restaurant. For further details and the Travelodge phone number, consult the Hotel Groups page.

**ROOMS:** 42 en suite

REYNOLDSTON, Swansea — Map 02 SS48

*Premier Collection*

### ★★ ⊛⊛⊛ Fairyhill

SA3 1BS
☎ 01792 390139 🖷 01792 391358
e-mail: postbox@fairyhill.net
***Dir:*** *just outside Reynoldston off the A4118 from Swansea in the middle of the Gower Peninsula*
Fairyhill is an impressive stone-built 18th century mansion which is set in 24 acres of grounds. The hotel benefits from a tranquil location in the heart of the Gower Peninsula. The bedrooms are all individually decorated and are furnished with style. There is a choice of comfortable seating areas, with log fires contributing to the warm and relaxed atmosphere. The cuisine is imaginative and accomplished, and features many local specialities.
**ROOMS:** 8 en suite s £110-£210; d £125-£225 (incl. bkfst) * **LB**
**FACILITIES:** Croquet lawn mountain bikes available **CONF:** Thtr 40 Class 20 Board 26 **PARKING:** 50 **NOTES:** No dogs (ex guide dogs) No children 8yrs No smoking in restaurant Closed 24-26Dec&1-17Jan
**CARDS:**

RHAYADER, Powys — Map 03 SN96

### ★★67% Brynafon Country House

South St LD6 5BL
☎ 01597 810735 🖷 01597 810111
e-mail: info@brynafon.co.uk
***Dir:*** *0.5m from Rhayader on the main A470 road to Builth Wells*

This imposing stone built building dates back to 1878 and stands in its own pleasant garden, half a mile south of the town. It served as a workhouse until 1932. Now a privately owned and personally run hotel, it provides well-equipped accommodation and has public areas with lots of charm and character. Facilities include rooms for meetings or small conferences.
**ROOMS:** 16 en suite 2 annexe en suite No smoking in 2 bedrooms s £35-£50; d £50-£80 (incl. bkfst) * **LB** **FACILITIES:** Toning beds
**CONF:** Thtr 30 Class 30 Board 20 Del from £75 * **PARKING:** 40
**NOTES:** No smoking in restaurant Closed 18-27 Dec
**CARDS:**

RHOSSILI, Swansea — Map 02 SS48

### ★★56% *Worms Head*

SA3 1PP
☎ 01792 390512 🖷 01792 391115
***Dir:*** *from Swansea take A4118 to Scurlage. Turn right onto B4247 to Rhossili. Drive through village until car park on left, and hotel is opposite*

Set in a commanding position overlooking Rhosili beach and Worms Head, this hotel is perfectly placed to explore the Gower Peninsula. Most bedrooms and public areas have superb cliff top views. Bedrooms are comfortably furnished with convenient extras. The hotel has two bars and a restaurant.
**ROOMS:** 19 rms (17 en suite) (5 fmly) No smoking in 10 bedrooms
**FACILITIES:** STV ch fac **CONF:** Thtr 80 Class 40 Board 20 **NOTES:** No smoking in restaurant **CARDS:**

P

RHYL, Denbighshire Map 06 SJ08

**★★60% Marina**
Marine Dr LL18 3AU
☎ 01745 342371 📠 01745 342371
This old established holiday hotel is located on the seafront, and the town centre is just a short walk away. Several function suites are provided and there is a choice of bars. Live entertainment is regularly held. Bedrooms include several suitable for families and many have fine sea views.
**ROOMS:** 29 en suite (6 fmly) **FACILITIES:** entertainment Xmas **CONF:** Thtr 300 Class 250 Board 200 **SERVICES:** Lift **PARKING:** 75 **NOTES:** No dogs (ex guide dogs) **CARDS:**

ROSSETT, Wrexham Map 07 SJ35

**★★★71% Llyndir Hall**
Llyndir Ln LL12 0AY
☎ 01244 571648 📠 01244 571258
e-mail: llyndir.hall@pageant.co.uk
***Dir:*** *5m S of Chester follow signs for Pulford on B5445. On entering Rossett hotel is set back off road*

Located on the English/Welsh border within easy reach of both Chester and Wrexham, this charming old former manor house lies in several acres of mature grounds. The well-equipped accommodation is popular with leisure guests as well as business people, including delegates using the Business Training Centre and conference rooms. Other facilities here include an impressive leisure centre, a choice of comfortable lounges and a brasserie style restaurant.
**ROOMS:** 38 en suite (3 fmly) No smoking in 12 bedrooms s £50-£75; d £90-£120 (incl. bkfst) * **LB FACILITIES:** STV Indoor swimming (H) Solarium Gym Croquet lawn Jacuzzi Steam room ch fac Xmas **CONF:** Thtr 140 Class 60 Board 40 Del from £90 * **PARKING:** 80 **NOTES:** No smoking in restaurant Civ Wed 120 **CARDS:**

**★★★71% Rossett Hall Hotel**
Chester Rd LL12 0DE
☎ 01244 571000 📠 01244 571505
***Dir:*** *from M56 take M53 which becomes A55. Take Wrexham/Chester exit & head to Wrexham. Onto B5445 & Hotel entrance in Rossett village*
This hotel, which in places dates back to 1750, lies in several acres of mature gardens in the lovely Welsh border country. Pretty bedrooms are generally spacious and are well equipped and furnished. Bedrooms on ground floor level, rooms suitable for disabled guests and a full suite are all available. A comfortable foyer lounge is provided and Oscar's bistro serves a wide range of skilfully prepared dishes. Function and conference facilities are available.

**ROOMS:** 30 en suite (2 fmly) No smoking in 15 bedrooms s £70; d £90 (incl. bkfst) * **LB FACILITIES:** STV ch fac Xmas **CONF:** Thtr 120 Class 50 Board 50 Del from £80 * **PARKING:** 120 **NOTES:** No dogs (ex guide dogs) Civ Wed 120 **CARDS:**
*See advert under CHESTER*

RUTHIN, Denbighshire Map 06 SJ15

**★★★68% Ruthin Castle**
LL15 2NU
☎ 01824 702664 📠 01824 705978
e-mail: reservations@ruthincastle.co.uk
***Dir:*** *A550 to Mold, A494 to Ruthin, castle at end of Castle St just off town square*
The main part of this impressive castle was built in the early 19th century but there are many ruins in the impressive grounds that date back much further. The elegantly panelled public areas include a restaurant and bar along with a medieval banqueting hall. There is also a coffee shop. Many of the modern equipped bedrooms are spacious and furnished with fine period pieces.
**ROOMS:** 58 en suite (6 fmly) s £69-£83; d £91-£105 (incl. bkfst) * **LB FACILITIES:** Fishing Snooker entertainment **CONF:** Thtr 150 Class 100 Board 80 Del from £95.75 * **SERVICES:** Lift **PARKING:** 200 **NOTES:** No dogs (ex guide dogs) Civ Wed 150 **CARDS:**

ST ASAPH, Denbighshire Map 06 SJ07

**★★★67% *Oriel House***
Upper Denbigh Rd LL17 0LW
☎ 01745 582716 📠 01745 585208
***Dir:*** *turn off A55 on to A525, left at cathedral 1m along A525 on right hand side*
Set in several acres of mature grounds south of St Asaph, bedrooms are generally spacious with many having been refurbished. Staff are friendly and hospitable and the new Terrace restaurant offers imaginative food specialising in local produce. Extensive function facilities are provided, catering for business meetings and weddings.
**ROOMS:** 19 en suite (1 fmly) **FACILITIES:** STV Fishing Snooker **CONF:** Thtr 250 Class 150 Board 50 **PARKING:** 200 **NOTES:** Closed 26 Dec **CARDS:**

**★★65% Plas Elwy Hotel & Restaurant**
The Roe LL17 0LT
☎ 01745 582263 & 582089 📠 01745 583864
e-mail: plaselwy@gtleisure.co.uk
***Dir:*** *turn left off A55 at junct A525 signposted Rhyl/St Asaph. On left opposite petrol station*
This hotel, which dates back to 1850, has retained much of its
*continued on p836*

S

ST ASAPH, continued

original character. Bedrooms in the purpose-built extension are spacious - one has a four-poster bed - and those in the main building are equally well-equipped. Public rooms are smart and comfortably furnished. A range of food options is provided in the attractive restaurant.
**ROOMS:** 7 en suite 6 annexe en suite (2 fmly) No smoking in 2 bedrooms s £40-£46; d £58-£68 (incl. bkfst) * **PARKING:** 25 **NOTES:** No dogs (ex guide dogs) No smoking in restaurant **CARDS:**

## ST CLEARS, Carmarthenshire — Map 02 SN21

### ★★68% Forge Restaurant & Lodge
SA33 4NA
☎ 01994 230300 🖷 01994 231577
***Dir:*** *1m E, beside A40*
This family owned business has developed over the last 50 years into a modern motel complex with an adjoining leisure centre. The bedrooms are in modern buildings that are spacious and furnished to high standards. Another building houses an all-day restaurant and bar, and also includes a function suite.
**ROOMS:** 18 annexe en suite (8 fmly) **FACILITIES:** Indoor swimming (H) Sauna Gym **CONF:** Thtr 80 Class 80 Board 80 **PARKING:** 80 **NOTES:** Closed 25 & 26 Dec **CARDS:**

### ⌂ *Travelodge*
Travelodge
Tenby Rd SA32 4JN
☎ 01994 231153
Travelodge offers good quality, good value, modern accommodation. Ideal for families, the spacious, en suite bedrooms include remote-control TV, tea and coffee-making facilities, luxury beds and free morning newspaper. Meals can be taken at the nearby family restaurant. For further details and the Travelodge phone number, consult the Hotel Groups page.

## ST DAVID'S, Pembrokeshire — Map 02 SM72

### ★★★77% ֍֍ Warpool Court
SA62 6BN
☎ 01437 720300 🖷 01437 720676
e-mail: warpool@enterprise.net
***Dir:*** *from Cross Square bear left beside Cartref Restaurant to go down Goat St. Pass Farmers Arms pub and after 400mtrs bear left following hotel sign entrance on right*

Originally the cathedral choir school, Warpool Court Hotel is set in landscaped gardens looking out to sea. The lounges are spacious and comfortable. Bedrooms are well-furnished and equipped with modern facilities. Gastronomic delights feature in the restaurant.
**ROOMS:** 25 en suite (3 fmly) s £73-£88; d £122-£206 (incl. bkfst) * LB **FACILITIES:** Indoor swimming (H) Tennis (hard) Sauna Gym Croquet lawn ch fac Xmas **CONF:** Thtr 40 Class 25 Board 25 **PARKING:** 100 **NOTES:** No smoking in restaurant Closed Jan Civ Wed 100 **CARDS:**

### ★★71% ֍ St Non's Hotel
Catherine St SA62 6RJ
☎ 01437 720239 🖷 01437 721839
e-mail: stnons@enterprise.net
***Dir:*** *from Cross Square in St Davids bear left between Midland Bank and Cartref Restaurant, follow road for 700yds, hotel on the left*
The hotel is situated close to the cathedral and the 14th-century Bishops' Palace. Well-equipped modern accommodation includes ground floor rooms. The spacious restaurant offers a range of tempting dishes.
**ROOMS:** 21 en suite (4 fmly) s £49-£59; d £74-£94 (incl. bkfst) * LB **CONF:** Thtr 32 Class 32 Board 32 **PARKING:** 40 **NOTES:** No smoking in restaurant Closed Dec & Nov **CARDS:**

### ★★70% Old Cross
Cross Square SA62 6SP
☎ 01437 720387 🖷 01437 720394
e-mail: enquiries@oldcrosshotel.co.uk
***Dir:*** *right in centre of St David's facing Cross Square*
This privately owned and friendly hotel is located in the centre of historic St David's. Parts of the property date back to the 18th century. The famous cathedral is just a short walk away. The bedrooms are generally spacious with good facilities and some are suitable for families. There is a choice of comfortable lounges along with a bar and a restaurant.
**ROOMS:** 16 en suite (1 fmly) No smoking in 5 bedrooms s £33-£52; d £56-£88 (incl. bkfst) * LB **FACILITIES:** ch fac **PARKING:** 18 **NOTES:** Closed Xmas-1 Feb **CARDS:**

### ★★61% Grove Hotel
High St SA62 6SB
☎ 01437 720341 🖷 01437 720770
e-mail: ggpengelly@aol.com
***Dir:*** *A487 from Haverfordwest to St Davids, hotel on right opposite new Tourist Information Centre, at top of High St*
This small personally run hotel is a good base for exploring St David's and the West Wales coast. A lively bar is supplemented by a restaurant with some good home cooking. Bedrooms vary in size and style.
**ROOMS:** 10 rms (9 en suite) No smoking in all bedrooms s £31; d £62 (incl. bkfst) * LB **FACILITIES:** Spa ch fac **PARKING:** 30 **NOTES:** No smoking in restaurant RS 25 Dec **CARDS:**

## SAUNDERSFOOT, Pembrokeshire — Map 02 SN10

### ★★★67% St Brides
St Brides Hill SA69 9NH
☎ 01834 812304 🖷 01834 811766
e-mail: reservations@stbrideshotel.com
***Dir:*** *on Tenby road, overlooking the harbour*
Standing high above the town, this hotel boasts superb views of the coastline and harbour. Bedrooms vary in size and style, with

*continued*

S

some family rooms available. Spacious public areas include a comfortable bar in addition to the restaurant.

**ROOMS:** 43 en suite (2 fmly) No smoking in 6 bedrooms s £63-£68; d £96-£108 (incl. bkfst) * **LB** **FACILITIES:** Xmas **CONF:** Thtr 150 Class 80 Board 60 Del from £75 * **PARKING:** 70 **NOTES:** Civ Wed 175 **CARDS:**

**★★66% Jalna**
Stammers Rd SA69 9HH
☎ 01834 812282 ▯ 01834 812166
e-mail: jalnahotel@aol.com
***Dir:*** *turn off A478 at Pentlepoir onto B4316 into Saundersfoot, take 1st junction on the right leaving the village for Tenby, hotel is on the right*
This small and friendly hotel lies just 200 yards from the harbour. Bedrooms are well-equipped, with modern amenities. A cosy lounge is available as well as a bar, and a daily fixed-price menu that offers good value food.
**ROOMS:** 13 en suite (7 fmly) No smoking in 6 bedrooms s £30-£40; d £50-£70 (incl. bkfst) * **LB** **PARKING:** 14 **NOTES:** No dogs (ex guide dogs) No smoking in restaurant **CARDS:**

**★★65% Rhodewood House**
St Brides Hill SA69 9NU
☎ 01834 812200 ▯ 01834 815005
e-mail: relax@rhodewood.co.uk
***Dir:*** *from St Clears, take A477 to Kilgetty, then A478 to Tenby, turn left onto B4316 signposted Saundersfoot*
This well established, privately owned and personally run hotel is just a short walk from the town centre and the harbour and is popular with coach tour groups. Live entertainment is regularly provided for guests. Bedrooms are equipped with modern amenities and many useful extras, and ground floor rooms are available.
**ROOMS:** 45 en suite (13 fmly) No smoking in 6 bedrooms s £30-£40; d £50-£70 (incl. bkfst) * **LB** **FACILITIES:** STV entertainment ch fac Xmas **CONF:** Thtr 100 Board 100 **PARKING:** 70 **NOTES:** No dogs (ex guide dogs) Closed 3 Jan-1Feb **CARDS:**

**★★64% Merlewood**
St Brides Hill SA69 9NP
☎ 01834 812421 & 813295 ▯ 01834 814886
e-mail: merlewood@saundersfoot.freeserve.co.uk
***Dir:*** *turn off A477 onto A4316, hotel on other side of village on St Brides Hill*
A purpose-built resort-style hotel, Merlewood is popular with more mature guests, as it offers ground floor and family rooms among its modern equipped accommodation. Public areas include a bright dining room, a large lounge bar and a mini-launderette; outside is a lovely garden.
**ROOMS:** 29 en suite (8 fmly) s £28-£30; d £50-£54 (incl. bkfst) * **LB** **FACILITIES:** Outdoor swimming (H) Putting green Children's swings & slide, Table tennis entertainment ch fac Xmas **CONF:** Thtr 60 Class 100 Board 40 **PARKING:** 34 **NOTES:** No dogs (ex guide dogs) No smoking in restaurant Closed Nov-Mar RS Xmas & New Year
**CARDS:**

SWANSEA, Swansea Map 03 SS69
see also Port Talbot

**★★★★68% Swansea Marriott Hotel**

Marriott
HOTELS · RESORTS · SUITES
The Maritime Quarter SA1 3SS
☎ 01792 642020 ▯ 01792 650345
***Dir:*** *M4 junct 42, follow A483 to the City Centre past Leisure Centre, then follow signs to Maritime Quarter*

Enjoying glorious views over the bay, this smart property is well-situated on the marina. A large and bustling hotel, it offers spacious, well-equipped bedrooms, which benefit from large beds and extra facilities such as satellite TV and trouser presses. There are several meeting rooms and a popular leisure club.
**ROOMS:** 117 en suite (49 fmly) No smoking in 85 bedrooms s £79-£99; d £79-£99 * **LB** **FACILITIES:** STV Indoor swimming (H) Sauna Gym Jacuzzi **CONF:** Thtr 250 Class 120 Board 30 Del from £100 * **SERVICES:** Lift air con **PARKING:** 122 **NOTES:** No dogs (ex guide dogs) No smoking in restaurant Civ Wed 250
**CARDS:**

S

SWANSEA, continued

**★★★65% Posthouse Swansea**
The Kingsway Circle SA1 5LS
☎ 0870 400 9078 🖷 01792 456044
e-mail: gm1212@forte-hotels.com
**Dir:** *M4 junct 42, A483 Swansea exit. Signs for city centre W. At lights after Sainsbury's, right along Wind St then left at lights, hotel ahead at rdbt*
In the centre of town, this Posthouse offers comfortable accommodation and useful amenities, including a good Spa leisure club. Dining options include the lounge, The Junction restaurant or the more informal Mongolian Barbecue. Rooms are comfortably furnished.
**ROOMS:** 106 en suite (12 fmly) No smoking in 66 bedrooms s £65-£89; d £65-£89 * LB **FACILITIES:** Indoor swimming (H) Sauna Solarium Gym Xmas **CONF:** Thtr 230 Class 120 Board 60 Del £70 *
**SERVICES:** Lift **PARKING:** 42 **CARDS:**

Posthouse

**★★ ®®® Fairyhill**
SA3 1BS
☎ 01792 390139 🖷 01792 391358
e-mail: postbox@fairyhill.net
(For full entry see Reynoldston)

**★★74% Beaumont**
72-73 Walter Rd SA1 4QA
☎ 01792 643956 🖷 01792 643044
e-mail: info@beaumonthotel.co.uk
**Dir:** *From M4 head for city centre. Follow signs for Uplands and Sketty. 0.5m from centre along Walter Rd, hotel is on the left opposite St James church*

This family run hotel within easy reach of the city centre and the Gower has recently refurbished public areas and bedrooms where care has been taken in the co-ordination and quality of the decor. A spacious and airy conservatory gives a relaxing and comfortable area to enjoy a home cooked meal.
**ROOMS:** 16 en suite (3 fmly) s £50-£60; d £70-£90 (incl. bkfst) * LB
**CONF:** Class 50 Board 30 Del from £80 * **PARKING:** 12 **NOTES:** No smoking in restaurant Closed 25 & 26 Dec
**CARDS:**

*See advert on opposite page*

**★★74% ® Windsor Lodge**
Mount Pleasant SA1 6EG
☎ 01792 642158 & 652744 🖷 01792 648996
**Dir:** *M4 exit 42 onto A483, turn right at lights past Sainsburys, turn left at station, turn right immediately after 2nd set of lights*
Just a short walk from the city centre, this is a welcoming family-run hotel. Both bedrooms and public areas are attractively decorated; there is a choice of lounge areas and a deservedly popular restaurant.
**ROOMS:** 18 en suite (2 fmly) s £50-£55; d £60-£65 (incl. bkfst) * LB
**CONF:** Thtr 30 Class 15 Board 24 **PARKING:** 26 **NOTES:** No smoking in restaurant Closed 25-26 Dec **CARDS:**

**★★56% *Worms Head***
SA3 1PP
☎ 01792 390512 🖷 01792 391115
(For full entry see Rhossili)

**⌂ *Travelodge***
Penllergaer SA4 1GT
☎ 01792 896222 🖷 01792 898806
**Dir:** *M4 junct 47*
Travelodge offers good quality, good value, modern accommodation. Ideal for families, the spacious, en suite bedrooms include remote-control TV, tea and coffee-making facilities, luxury beds and free morning newspaper. Meals can be taken at the nearby family restaurant. For further details and the Travelodge phone number, consult the Hotel Groups page.
**ROOMS:** 50 en suite **CONF:** Thtr 25 Class 32 Board 20

Travelodge

TALSARNAU, Gwynedd — Map 06 SH63

*Premier Collection*

**★★ ®®® Maes y Neuadd**
LL47 6YA
☎ 01766 780200 🖷 01766 780211
e-mail: maes@neuadd.com
**Dir:** *3m NE of Harlech, signposted on an unclassed road off B4573*
This personally run hotel dates back to the 14th century, various additions over the centuries have resulted in a substantial stone-built house enjoying fine views over the mountains and across the bay to the Llyn Peninsula. Bedrooms, some in an adjacent coach house, are individually furnished and many have fine antique pieces. Public areas display a similar welcoming character, including the restaurant where the team makes good use of locally sourced ingredients to produce fine meals.
**ROOMS:** 12 en suite 4 annexe en suite s £142-£178; d £187-£223 (incl. bkfst & dinner) * LB **FACILITIES:** Croquet lawn clay pigeon,cooking tuition ch fac Xmas **CONF:** Thtr 20 Class 10 Board 16 Del £150 * **PARKING:** 50 **NOTES:** No smoking in restaurant Civ Wed 65 **CARDS:**

Pride of Britain Member

**★★66% Estuary Motel**
LL47 6TA
☎ 01766 771155 🖷 01766 771697
**Dir:** *4m N of Harlech, on the A496*
At the edge of the village, set amid wooded slopes, this family-run hotel provides modern accommodation. Bedrooms are spacious and well-equipped and there is a small lounge. The restaurant serves a popular carte menu and offers good value for money.
**ROOMS:** 10 en suite (2 fmly) No smoking in 6 bedrooms s £38; d £55 (incl. bkfst) * LB **PARKING:** 30 **NOTES:** No smoking in restaurant
**CARDS:**

**★★** 64% ***Tregwylan***
LL47 6YG
☎ 01766 770424 🖷 01766 771317
***Dir:*** *off A496, 0.5m N of Talsarnau and 4m N of Harlech*
Located above the bay and enjoying superb views, this family-run hotel offers genuine Welsh hospitality. The bedrooms are prettily decorated and there is an attractive restaurant and a cosy bar. Pretty grounds surround the hotel.
**ROOMS:** 10 en suite (3 fmly) **PARKING:** 20 **NOTES:** No dogs (ex guide dogs) No smoking in restaurant Closed Jan-mid Feb
**CARDS:**

## TAL-Y-BONT (NEAR CONWY), Gwynedd Map 06 SH76

**★★** 71% **Lodge**
LL32 8YX
☎ 01492 660766 🖷 01492 660534
e-mail: bbaldon@lodgehotel.co.uk

THE CIRCLE
*Selected Individual Hotels*
GREAT BRITAIN

***Dir:*** *on B5106, hotel on right hand side of the road when entering village*
Situated in a beautiful part of the Conwy Valleys, the Lodge Hotel has modern bedrooms, some of which are suitable for families. A welcoming log fire burns in the bar lounge during the winter months while diners peruse the daily changing menu. Much of the produce comes from the hotel's gardens and home-cooked meals are served in generous portions.
**ROOMS:** 14 annexe en suite No smoking in 6 bedrooms s £57.50-£77; d £85-£123 (incl. bkfst) * **LB** **FACILITIES:** Xmas **PARKING:** 50
**NOTES:** No smoking in restaurant RS Winter
**CARDS:**

## TAL-Y-LLYN, Gwynedd Map 06 SH70

**★★** 73% **Minffordd**
LL36 9AJ
☎ 01654 761665 🖷 01654 761517
e-mail: hotel@minffordd.com
***Dir:*** *at junct of A487/B4405 midway between Dolgellau and Machynlleth*
Located in spectacular countryside below Cader Idris, this delightful former drovers' inn is a haven of peace and relaxation. Warm and friendly hospitality from the owners is one of the major strengths here. Original features such as exposed timbers and thick stone walls remain but bedrooms are modern and well-equipped. Guests have a choice of comfortable lounges and there is also a cosy bar. The hotel is non-smoking throughout.
**ROOMS:** 7 en suite No smoking in all bedrooms s £39-£47; d £78 (incl. bkfst) * **LB** **FACILITIES:** no TV in bdrms Xmas **PARKING:** 14
**NOTES:** No children 13yrs No smoking in restaurant
**CARDS:**

## TENBY, Pembrokeshire Map 02 SN10

**★★★** 77% ◎ **Penally Abbey Country House**
Penally SA70 7PY
☎ 01834 843033 🖷 01834 844714
e-mail: penally.abbey@btinternet.com
***Dir:*** *1.5m from Tenby, off A4139, overlooking golf course, close to Penally village green & Carmarthen Bay*
This fine old country house has a wealth of charm and character. Standing in 5 acres of gardens and woodland, it overlooks Tenby golf course to Carmarthen Bay. All the bedrooms are spacious, comfortable and have thoughtful decoration and superior furnishings. On the ground floor the drawing room, bar, elegant restaurant and conservatory are all stylishly appointed.
**ROOMS:** 8 en suite 4 annexe en suite (3 fmly) s £98; d £110-£138 (incl. bkfst) * **LB** **FACILITIES:** Indoor swimming (H) Snooker Xmas
**CONF:** Board 14 Del from £114 * **PARKING:** 14 **NOTES:** No dogs (ex guide dogs) No smoking in restaurant Civ Wed 50
**CARDS:**

TENBY, continued

**★★★74% Atlantic**
The Esplanade SA70 7DU
☎ 01834 842881 & 844176 01834 842881 ex 256
e-mail: enquiries@atlantic-hotel.uk.com
***Dir:*** *take A478 into Tenby & follow signs to town centre, keep town walls on left then turn right at Esplanade, hotel half way along on right*
The Atlantic Hotel is set on the promenade and overlooks the South Beach and Caldy Island. Bedrooms are tastefully decorated and well-equipped with modern facilities. Public rooms include a cocktail bar, two restaurants and a comfortable residents' lounge, with the added facilities of swimming pool and solarium.
**ROOMS:** 42 en suite (11 fmly) No smoking in 2 bedrooms s £62-£68; d £86-£136 (incl. bkfst) * **FACILITIES:** STV Indoor swimming (H) Solarium Jacuzzi Steam room **SERVICES:** Lift **PARKING:** 28 **NOTES:** Closed 20-27 Dec **CARDS:**

**★★★68% Heywood Mount**
Heywood Ln SA70 8DA
☎ 01834 842087 01834 842087
e-mail: reception@heywoodmount.co.uk
***Dir:*** *follow signs for Wild Life Park when entering Tenby this will lead into Heywood Lane, Heywood Mount is the third hotel on the left*
This privately owned and personally run hotel is situated in a peaceful residential area, but within easy reach of Tenby's beaches and town centre. The well maintained 18th-century house is surrounded by extensive, mature and attractive gardens. The ground floor public areas include a comfortable lounge, bar and restaurant. Several of the nicely appointed bedrooms are on ground floor level. Service is willing, friendly and attentive.
**ROOMS:** 21 en suite (4 fmly) No smoking in 11 bedrooms s £30-£50; d £60-£100 (incl. bkfst) * **LB** **FACILITIES:** Indoor swimming (H) Sauna Solarium Gym Jacuzzi Xmas **CONF:** Class 50 Board 30 **PARKING:** 25 **NOTES:** No dogs No smoking in restaurant
**CARDS:**

*See advert on opposite page*

**★★★66% Fourcroft**
North Beach SA70 8AP
☎ 01834 842886 01834 842888
e-mail: hospitality@fourcroft-hotel.co.uk
***Dir:*** *from A478, after "Welcome to Tenby" sign bear left towards North Beach & walled town. On reaching sea front turn sharp left. Hotel on left*
This friendly, family-run hotel offers a beach-front location, together with a number of extra facilities that make it particularly suitable for families with children. Guests have direct access to the beach through the hotel's cliff-top gardens. Bedrooms are of a good size, with modern facilities. Besides the bar, lounge and restaurant, the public areas include an outdoor pool, jacuzzi, games room and play area.
**ROOMS:** 43 en suite (11 fmly) No smoking in 10 bedrooms s £31-£49; d £62-£98 (incl. bkfst) * **LB** **FACILITIES:** Outdoor swimming (H) Sauna Jacuzzi Table tennis Giant chess Human Gyroscope ch fac Xmas **CONF:** Thtr 90 Class 40 Board 50 Del from £80 * **SERVICES:** Lift **PARKING:** 6 **NOTES:** No smoking in restaurant Civ Wed 100
**CARDS:**

**★★72% *Panorama Hotel & Restaurant***
The Esplanade SA70 7DU
☎ 01834 844976 01834 844976
e-mail: mail@panoramahotel.f9.co.uk
***Dir:*** *from A478 follow 'South Beach' & 'Town Centre' signs. Sharp left under railway arches, up Greenhill Road, onto South Parade then Esplanade*
This charming little hotel is part of a Victorian terrace, overlooking the South Beach and Caldy Island. It provides a variety of sizes and styles of non-smoking bedrooms, all of which are well-equipped. Facilities include a cosy bar and an elegantly appointed restaurant, where a good choice of skilfully prepared dishes is available.
**ROOMS:** 7 en suite (2 fmly) No smoking in all bedrooms **NOTES:** No dogs (ex guide dogs) No smoking in restaurant
**CARDS:**

**★★69% Hammonds Park**
Narberth Rd SA70 8HT
☎ 01834 842696 01834 844295
e-mail: reservations@hoteltenby.com
***Dir:*** *take left turn off A478 into Narberth Rd leading to North Beach & Bus Park, look for white sign with hotel name in red*
This cosy, family-run hotel is situated 500 yards from North Beach and the town centre. The non-smoking bedrooms are all well-equipped and have modern facilities; four-poster and ground-floor rooms are available. Many of the dining tables are situated in the bright conservatory, which leads into a cosy bar.
**ROOMS:** 12 en suite (5 fmly) No smoking in all bedrooms s £36-£44; d £42-£55 (incl. bkfst) * **LB** **FACILITIES:** Gym Jacuzzi Natural Therapy clinic **PARKING:** 14 **NOTES:** No dogs (ex guide dogs) No smoking in restaurant **CARDS:**

**★★67% *Tenby House Hotel***
Tudor Square SA70 7AJ
☎ 01834 842000 01834 844647
e-mail: tenbyhouse@virgin.net
***Dir:*** *in town centre pass St Mary's Church on right into Tudor Square. Hotel on right at end of Square*
This privately owned and personally run hotel is conveniently located in the town centre, just a few minutes' walk from the harbour, beach and other amenities. The accommodation has been recently upgraded to a good standard and is well-equipped. Facilities include a pleasant bar which has tremendous character and a separate bistro style restaurant. Garage parking is available nearby.
**ROOMS:** 18 en suite No smoking in all bedrooms **FACILITIES:** Games room entertainment **PARKING:** 14 **NOTES:** No dogs (ex guide dogs)
**CARDS:**

**★★60% Albany Hotel**
22/23 The Norton SA70 8AB
☎ 01834 842698 01834 844770
***Dir:*** *follow signs for North Beach, past sign for coach/carpark first hotel on right - opposite Tourist Info Office.*
This family run holiday hotel lies near the resort's North Beach and is a short walk from the town centre. Bedrooms are functional and all are equipped with modern facilities. The hotel is popular with tour groups and live entertainment is regularly held.
**ROOMS:** 24 rms s £20-£25; d £40-£50 (incl. bkfst) * **LB** **NOTES:** No dogs (ex guide dogs) No smoking in restaurant
**CARDS:**

THREE COCKS, Powys — Map 03 SO13

**★★73% Three Cocks**
LD3 0SL
☎ 01497 847215 01497 847339
***Dir:*** *on A438, between Brecon & Hereford*
A unique 15th-century inn surrounded by the rugged countryside of the Brecon Beacons National Park. Stone and timber abound in the public rooms, which include the restaurant, bar and separate lounge. The bedrooms are modestly decorated and do not have televisions. The cuisine is tempting, with some influences from Belgium.
**ROOMS:** 7 rms (6 en suite) (2 fmly) s £45-£67; d fr £67 (incl. bkfst) * **LB** **FACILITIES:** no TV in bdrms **PARKING:** 40 **NOTES:** No dogs (ex guide dogs) Closed Dec & Jan RS Tue **CARDS:**

T

## TINTERN, Monmouthshire

Map 03 SO50

### ★★73% Parva Farmhouse Hotel & Restaurant

THE CIRCLE
Selected Individual Hotels
GREAT BRITAIN

NP16 6SQ
☎ 01291 689411 & 689511 01291 689557
e-mail: parva-hotelintern@hotmail.com
***Dir:*** *From S leave M48 junct 2, N edge of village on A466. From N 10m S of Monmouth town & M50*

On the banks of the River Wye, this 17th-century farmhouse retains many original features and a wealth of character. The lounge is comfortable and the bedrooms are tastefully furnished. Wholesome and delicious home cooking is served in the dining room.
**ROOMS:** 9 en suite (3 fmly) s fr £50; d fr £74 (incl. bkfst) * **LB**
**FACILITIES:** Cycle hire ch fac **CONF:** Thtr 12 Board 12 Del from £65 *
**PARKING:** 10 **NOTES:** No smoking in restaurant
**CARDS:**

### ★★70% Royal George

Best Western

NP16 6SF
☎ 01291 689205 01291 689448
e-mail: royalgeorgetintern@hotmail.com
***Dir:*** *turn off M48 on to A466, 4m along this road into Tintern 2nd on left*
This delightful hotel provides comfortably equipped and spacious accommodation, including bedrooms with balconies overlooking the well tended garden. Family bedded rooms and rooms on the ground floor level are available. The public areas include a choice of bars, and a large function room.
**ROOMS:** 2 en suite 14 annexe en suite (13 fmly) No smoking in 9 bedrooms s £62-£72; d £88-£98 (incl. bkfst) * **LB**
**FACILITIES:** entertainment **CONF:** Thtr 120 Class 40 Board 50 Del from £74 * **PARKING:** 50 **NOTES:** No smoking in restaurant Civ Wed 60
**CARDS:**

## TREARDDUR BAY See Anglesey, Isle of

## TREFRIW, Conwy

Map 06 SH76

### ★★70% Hafod Country Hotel

LL27 0RQ
☎ 01492 640029 01492 641351
e-mail: hafod@breathemail.net
***Dir:*** *on B5106 - between A5 at Betws-y-Coed and A55 at Conwy, on the southern edge of the village of Trefriw*
This former farmhouse in the picturesque Conwy Valley is now a fine modern hotel. The tasteful bedrooms feature period furnishings and thoughtful extras such as baskets of fresh fruit; many rooms have private balconies. There is a character sitting

*continued*

room and a cosy bar. The fixed-price menu is imaginative and makes good use of fresh, local produce.

**ROOMS:** 6 en suite No smoking in all bedrooms s £40-£60; d £65-£85 (incl. bkfst) * **LB** **FACILITIES:** Xmas **PARKING:** 14 **NOTES:** No children 11yrs No smoking in restaurant Closed early Jan-mid Feb
**CARDS:**

### ★★69% Princes Arms

LL27 0JP
☎ 01492 640592 01492 640559
e-mail: enquiries@princes-arms.co.uk
***Dir:*** *take A470 to Llanrwst left onto B5106 over bridge & follow to Trefriw, hotel just through village on left*
Located in the Conwy Valley, this privately owned and personally run hotel offers superb views from many bedrooms. Apartments with two bedrooms are available and ideal for families. The main restaurant is attractive and provides excellent food. There is also a

*continued on p842*

T

TREFRIW, continued

brasserie which offers comfortable surroundings and log fires.

Princes Arms, Trefriw

**ROOMS:** 14 en suite (5 fmly) s £36-£40; d £68-£76 (incl. bkfst) * **LB** **FACILITIES:** STV ch fac Xmas **CONF:** Thtr 80 Class 40 Board 20 Del from £60 * **PARKING:** 40 **NOTES:** No dogs (ex guide dogs) No smoking in restaurant **CARDS:**

## TYWYN, Gwynedd

Map 06 SH50

### ★61% Greenfield

High St LL36 9AD
☎ 01654 710354 🖷 01654 710354
e-mail: greentywyn@aol.com
***Dir:*** *on A493, opposite leisure centre*

In the middle of a small seaside town, this family-run hotel also operates a busy restaurant offering a good range of inexpensive meals. Bedrooms are plainly furnished but all are fresh and bright. Each has modern facilities and several are suitable for families.
**ROOMS:** 8 rms (6 en suite) (2 fmly) s £17-£20; d £35-£37 (incl. bkfst) * **NOTES:** No dogs (ex guide dogs) No smoking in restaurant Closed Jan-Feb RS Nov-Mar **CARDS:**

## USK, Monmouthshire

Map 03 SO30

### ★★★72% Three Salmons

Porthycarne St NP15 1RY
☎ 01291 672133 🖷 01291 673979
e-mail: threesalmons.hotel@talk21.com
***Dir:*** *turn off A449, 1m to Usk, hotel on corner of Porthycarne St, B4598*

This 17th-century coaching inn offers spacious bedrooms that are comfortably furnished and well-maintained. Ostlers restaurant offers carefully prepared dishes. The bar serves an extensive range of meals and there is a pleasant rear garden.
**ROOMS:** 10 en suite 14 annexe en suite (1 fmly) s £75-£80; d £75-£95 (incl. bkfst) * **LB** **FACILITIES:** STV Xmas **CONF:** Thtr 100 Class 40 Board 50 Del £99 * **PARKING:** 38 **NOTES:** No dogs (ex guide dogs) No smoking in restaurant Civ Wed 100 **CARDS:**

*See advert on opposite page*

### ★★★69% *Glen-yr-Afon House*

Pontypool Rd NP15 1SY
☎ 01291 672302 & 673202 🖷 01291 672597
e-mail: enquiries@glen-yr-afon.co.uk
***Dir:*** *A472 through Usk High St, over river follow rd around to R hotel on L*

This large Victorian property stands in well maintained gardens. The young staff provide friendly service. Bedrooms are in the original house and a new wing. Public areas consist of a comfortable lounge, a bar and a traditionally furnished restaurant.
**ROOMS:** 28 en suite (2 fmly) No smoking in 14 bedrooms **FACILITIES:** STV Croquet lawn **CONF:** Thtr 100 Class 200 Board 30 **SERVICES:** Lift **PARKING:** 101 **NOTES:** No smoking in restaurant Civ Wed 200 **CARDS:**

## WELSHPOOL, Powys

Map 07 SJ20

### ★★★68% Royal Oak

The Cross SY21 7DG
☎ 01938 552217 🖷 01938 556652
e-mail: oakwpool@aol.com
***Dir:*** *by traffic lights at junct of A483/A458*

A traditional market town hotel that dates back over 350 years. It provides well-equipped bedrooms, a choice of bars and extensive function facilities. The 'cafe bar' style restaurant provides a good choice of popular dishes throughout the day and evening.
**ROOMS:** 24 en suite (2 fmly) No smoking in 10 bedrooms s £58.50; d £85 (incl. bkfst) * **LB** **FACILITIES:** STV **CONF:** Thtr 120 Class 60 Board 80 Del from £36 * **PARKING:** 40 **NOTES:** Civ Wed 100 **CARDS:**

### ★★64% Golfa Hall

Llanfair Rd SY21 9AF
☎ 01938 553399 🖷 01938 554777
e-mail: golfahall@welshpool.sagehost.co.uk
***Dir:*** *1.5m W of Welshpool on the A458 to Dolgellau*

Set on the Powys Castle estate, this privately owned and personally run hotel was originally a Georgian farmhouse. Some of the well-equipped bedrooms are contained in a separate stone built cottage. Elegant public rooms include a meeting room and a comfortable non-smoking lounge. The hotel also has a large self contained function suite.
**ROOMS:** 10 en suite 4 annexe en suite (4 fmly) s £45-£65; d £65-£95 (incl. bkfst) * **LB** **FACILITIES:** Xmas **CONF:** Thtr 120 Class 16 Board 16 Del from £80 * **PARKING:** 26 **NOTES:** No dogs (ex guide dogs) No smoking in restaurant Civ Wed 50 **CARDS:**

## WHITEBROOK, Monmouthshire

Map 03 SO50

### ★★70% Crown at Whitebrook

NP25 4TX
☎ 01600 860254 🖷 01600 860607
e-mail: crown@whitebrook.demon.co.uk
***Dir:*** *turn W off A466, 50yds S of Bigsweir Bridge*

This private hotel is quietly located in a wooded valley. Most of the

*continued*

well-equipped bedrooms enjoy views of the valley or the country garden. Cuisine makes good use of quality local ingredients in a seasonal fixed-price menu, which is complemented by a well-chosen wine list.
**ROOMS:** 10 en suite s £52.50; d £85 (incl. bkfst) * **LB**
**FACILITIES:** Jacuzzi **CONF:** Board 10 **PARKING:** 40 **NOTES:** No children 12yrs No smoking in restaurant Closed 2 wks Xmas/New Year
**CARDS:**

WOLF'S CASTLE, Pembrokeshire Map 02 SM92

### ★★73% *Wolfscastle Country Hotel*

SA62 5LZ
☎ 01437 741688 & 741225 01437 741383
e-mail: andy741225@aol.com
***Dir:*** *on the A40 in the village of Wolf's Castle, at top of hill on left*
This large, stone-built house dates back to the mid-19th century and has stunning views of the village. Accommodation is well-maintained and includes a room with a four-poster bed and a family room. There is a pleasant bar, and an attractive restaurant where a good range of carefully prepared dishes is available.
**ROOMS:** 20 en suite 4 annexe en suite (2 fmly) **FACILITIES:** STV entertainment **CONF:** Thtr 100 Class 100 Board 30 **PARKING:** 60 **NOTES:** No smoking in restaurant Closed 24-26 Dec RS Sun nights Civ Wed 60 **CARDS:**

WREXHAM, Wrexham Map 07 SJ35

### ★★★67% Cross Lanes Hotel & Restaurant

Best Western

Cross Lanes, Bangor Rd, Marchwiel LL13 0TF
☎ 01978 780555 01978 780568
e-mail: guestservices@crosslanes.co.uk
***Dir:*** *3m SE of Wrexham, on A525*

This privately owned and personally run hotel was built as a private house in 1890. It stands in over six acres of beautiful grounds. Bedrooms, which include two with four-poster beds, are well-equipped and meet the needs of today's traveller. "Kagan's Brasserie" restaurant offers a fine selection of well-produced food.
**ROOMS:** 16 en suite (1 fmly) s £68-£74; d fr £88 (incl. cont bkfst) * **LB FACILITIES:** Croquet lawn Putting green Fishing rights Xmas **CONF:** Thtr 120 Class 60 Board 40 **PARKING:** 80 **NOTES:** No dogs (ex guide dogs) No smoking in restaurant Closed 25 Dec (night) & 26 Dec Civ Wed 120 **CARDS:**

*See advert under CHESTER*

### ★★★66% Llwyn Onn Hall

Cefn Rd LL13 0NY
☎ 01978 261225 01978 363233
e-mail: llwynonnhallhotel@breathemail.net
***Dir:*** *between A525 Wrexham-Whitchurch road & A534 Wrexham-Nantwich road. Easy access Wrexham Ind Estate, 2m off main Wrexham-Chester A483*
Surrounded by open countryside this fine, 17th-century manor

*continued*

house is set in several acres of mature grounds. Exposed timbers remain and the original oak staircase is still in use. Bedrooms are equipped with modern facilities and one room has a four-poster bed which Bonnie Prince Charlie is reputed to have slept in.

**ROOMS:** 13 en suite (1 fmly) No smoking in 4 bedrooms s £64-£72; d £84 (incl. bkfst) * **LB CONF:** Thtr 60 Class 40 Board 12 Del £105.75 * **PARKING:** 40 **NOTES:** No dogs (ex guide dogs) No smoking in restaurant **CARDS:**

### *Travelodge*

Travelodge

Wrexham By Pass, Rhostyllen LL14 4EJ
☎ 01978 365705 01978 365705
***Dir:*** *2m S, A483/A5152 roundabout*
Travelodge offers good quality, good value, modern accommodation. Ideal for families, the spacious, en suite bedrooms include remote-control TV, tea and coffee-making facilities, luxury beds and free morning newspaper. Meals can be taken at the nearby family restaurant. For further details and the Travelodge phone number, consult the Hotel Groups page.
**ROOMS:** 32 en suite

Ireland

# Hotel of the Year, Ireland

## Aghadoe Heights Hotel,

Killarney

A

## ABBEYLEIX, Co Laois Map 01 C3

### ★★★64% *Abbeyleix Manor Hotel*

☎ 0502 30111 Fax 0502 30220
e-mail: info@abbeyleixmanorhotel.com
***Dir:*** *hotel situated on N8 (main Dublin-Cork road) just S of Abbeyleix Town*

This attractive hotel, on the outskirts of Abbeyleix heritage town, is ideal for those travelling on the National Route. Relaxing areas include a themed bar which serves snacks all day, an inviting foyer lounge and a conservatory. Fine dining is avaliable in Knaptons restaurant. Spacious and comfortable bedrooms are furnished with locally crafted wood.

**ROOMS:** 23 en suite (2 fmly) **SERVICES:** air con **PARKING:** 270 **NOTES:** No dogs (ex guide dogs) No smoking in restaurant Closed 25-26 Dec **CARDS:**

## ADARE, Co Limerick Map 01 B3

### ★★★77% ®®® *Dunraven Arms*

MANOR HOUSE

☎ 061 396633 Fax 061 396541
e-mail: dunraven@iol.ie
***Dir:*** *first building as you enter the village*

Located in one of Ireland's prettiest villages, the Dunraven Arms dates from 1792. It is a traditional country inn in style and atmosphere. Comfortable lounges and bedrooms, attractive gardens and good food all add to the experience of a stay here.

**ROOMS:** 75 en suite (1 fmly) **FACILITIES:** STV Indoor swimming (H) Fishing Riding Sauna Gym Jacuzzi **CONF:** Thtr 300 Class 200 Board 50 **SERVICES:** Lift **PARKING:** 90 **NOTES:** No smoking in restaurant **CARDS:**

### ★★★59% *Fitzgeralds Woodlands House Hotel*

village inn HOTELS

Knockanes
☎ 061 605100 Fax 061 396073
e-mail: reception@woodlands-hotel.ie
***Dir:*** *turn left at Lantern Lodge on N21 S of Limerick. Hotel 0.5m on right*

Set in 44 acres of woodland on the outskirts of Adare, this family-run hotel is friendly and welcoming. Comfortable bedrooms are all well-appointed and are available in three styles, the newest featuring extras such as jacuzzis. The hotel specialises in golf break holidays.

**ROOMS:** 92 en suite (36 fmly) **FACILITIES:** STV Indoor swimming (H) Sauna Solarium Gym Jacuzzi Health & beauty salon Thermal spa entertainment **CONF:** Thtr 400 Class 200 Board 50 **PARKING:** 290 **NOTES:** No dogs (ex guide dogs) No children 6wks Closed 24-25 Dec **CARDS:**

> € The Euro will be phased in during 2002 (R.O.I. only). Make sure you check prices and currency when booking.

## AGHADOWEY, Co Londonderry Map 01 C6

### ★★71% Brown Trout Golf & Country Inn

209 Agivey Rd BT51 4AD
☎ 028 7086 8209 Fax 028 7086 8878
e-mail: bill@browntroutinn.com
***Dir:*** *on intersection of A54/B66 on main road to Coleraine*

This friendly inn, with its own golf course, is set on the banks of the Agivey River. A courtyard area houses cheerfully decorated and spacious bedrooms, and there are also four splendid cottage suites. The restaurant serves wholesome home-cooked fare and food is also available in the lounge bar.

**ROOMS:** 15 en suite (11 fmly) s £50-£60; d £65-£85 (incl. bkfst) * **LB** **FACILITIES:** Golf 9 Fishing Gym Putting green Game fishing river entertainment Xmas **CONF:** Thtr 40 Class 24 Board 28 Del from £50 * **PARKING:** 80 **CARDS:**

## AHERLOW, Co Tipperary Map 01 B3

### ★★★62% Aherlow House

☎ 062 56153 Fax 062 56212
e-mail: aherlow@iol.ie
***Dir:*** *6km from Tipperary, coming from Limerick turn right at the traffic lights, follow sign posts for hotel*

Located in a coniferous forest with superb views of the Galtee Mountains, this Tudor-style house offers comfortable public rooms, including a relaxing drawing room, a spacious lounge bar and a restaurant. Accommodation is well-equipped and an additional wing has been added. The attentive staff create a warm and friendly atmosphere.

**ROOMS:** 29 en suite (23 fmly) **FACILITIES:** STV Guided Walks entertainment ch fac **CONF:** Thtr 400 Class 200 Board 50 **PARKING:** 200 **NOTES:** No dogs (ex guide dogs) Closed 6 Jan-30 Mar(excl weekends) Civ Wed 300 **CARDS:**

## ARDARA, Co Donegal Map 01 B5

### ★★★56% *Nesbitt Arms*

☎ 075 41103 Fax 075 41895
e-mail: nesbitta@indigo.ie
***Dir:*** *from Donegal town, take N56, turning N for Ardara as signposted*

This hotel, built in 1838, is situated in the centre of Ardara heritage town. Bedrooms, contemporary in style, vary in size. There is a comfortable, spacious foyer lounge featuring an open fire and a traditional style bar and bistro serves food all day. Breakfast and dinner are served in Weavers restaurant.

**ROOMS:** 19 en suite (4 fmly) **FACILITIES:** entertainment **CONF:** Thtr 200 Class 100 **NOTES:** No dogs No smoking in restaurant **CARDS:**

## ARDMORE, Co Waterford Map 01 C2

### ★62% *Round Tower*

☎ 024 94494 & 94382 Fax 024 94254
e-mail: rth@eircom.net
***Dir:*** *Ardmore is located off the main N25 Rosslare-Cork route. Turn off onto Route R673. Hotel is situated in centre of village*

A large country house set in its own grounds in a pretty fishing village, boasting a blue flag beach, lovely marked cliff walks and much of early monastic interest. The atmosphere is friendly and there is a comfortable lounge, panelled bar and a conservatory, where bar food is served. A carte menu is available in the restaurant, featuring 'catch of the day' seafood.

**ROOMS:** 12 en suite (4 fmly) **CONF:** Thtr 50 Class 25 Board 30 **SERVICES:** air con **PARKING:** 40 **NOTES:** RS Oct-Apr **CARDS:**

ARKLOW, Co Wicklow Map 01 D3

**★★★65% Arklow Bay**
Ferrybank
☎ 0402 32309 Fax 0402 32300
e-mail: arklowbay@eircom.net
***Dir:*** *turn off N11 at By-Pass for Arklow. After 1 mile turn left 200 yds on left hand side.*
This hotel enjoys panoramic views of Arklow Bay and fishing port. There are comfortable lounges and the bar serves meals all day. There is also a fine dining restaurant. Most bedrooms have sea views and are well appointed. There are conference and leisure facilities.
**ROOMS:** 55 en suite (5 fmly) s IEP50-IEP90; d IEP100-IEP120 (incl. bkfst) * **LB** **FACILITIES:** **Spa** STV Indoor swimming (H) Sauna Solarium Gym Jacuzzi entertainment ch fac Xmas **CONF:** Thtr 500 Class 300 Board 50 Del from IEP79.50 * **PARKING:** 100 **NOTES:** No dogs (ex guide dogs) **CARDS:**

ARTHURSTOWN, Co Wexford Map 01 C2

*Premier Collection*

**★★★ *Dunbrody Country House Hotel & Restaurant***
☎ 051 389600 Fax 051 389601
e-mail: dunbrody@indigo.ie
***Dir:*** *From N11 follow signs for Duncannon & Ballyhack (R733). Hotel is 20m on from turn off. Turn left at gate lodge on approaching Arthurstown*
Surrounded by peaceful parkland, this elegant Georgian manor house lies near the coast. The priorities here are tranquillity, generous hospitality and award-winning cuisine. The attractive bedrooms are all individually styled with marbled bathrooms. Activities nearby include walking, golf and horse riding.
**ROOMS:** 20 en suite (4 fmly) No smoking in 2 bedrooms **FACILITIES:** Riding Croquet lawn clay pigeon shooting **CONF:** Thtr 200 Class 100 Board 100 **PARKING:** 40 **NOTES:** No dogs (ex guide dogs) Closed 24-26 Dec **CARDS:**

ASHFORD, Co Wicklow Map 01 D3

**★★63% *Cullenmore Hotel***
☎ 0404 40187 Fax 0404 40471
e-mail: cullenmore@eircom.net
***Dir:*** *located N of Ashford on the N11 main Dublin/Wexford Rosslaire Road, 32km S of Dublin*
This hotel is in a very convenient location for golfers, with numerous courses nearby and it is only a 45 minute drive from Dublin. It offers a smart lounge, adjoining the bar, where good value bar food is available, in addition to the fixed price menu served in the restaurant. There is also a conference/ banqueting suite.
**ROOMS:** 17 en suite (4 fmly) **FACILITIES:** STV **CONF:** Board 30 **PARKING:** 100 **NOTES:** No dogs (ex guide dogs) Closed 24-27 Dec **CARDS:**

Popped the question? Hotels with Civ Wed in their entry are licensed for civil wedding ceremonies. Maximum numbers for the ceremony only are shown, e.g. Civ Wed 120



ATHLONE, Co Westmeath Map 01 C4

**★★★70% *Hodson Bay***
Hodson Bay
☎ 0902 92444 Fax 0902 80520
e-mail: info@hodsonbayhotel.com
***Dir:*** *from N6 take N61 to Roscommon. Take right turn - hotel situated 1km on Lough Ree*

Close to the River Shannon and right on the shore of Lough Ree, this historic hotel has been reconstructed and extended to provide comfortable accommodation. With a golf course to the rear and a marina to the front, most of the rooms have excellent views.
**ROOMS:** 133 en suite (23 fmly) No smoking in 3 bedrooms **FACILITIES:** STV Indoor swimming (H) Golf 18 Fishing Sauna Solarium Gym Steam room entertainment **CONF:** Thtr 1000 Class 300 Board 300 **SERVICES:** Lift **PARKING:** 300 **NOTES:** No dogs (ex guide dogs) **CARDS:**

*See advert on this page*

ATHLONE, continued

### ★★★59% *Prince of Wales*
☎ 0902 72626 📠 0902 75658
***Dir:*** *in centre of town, opposite Bank of Ireland*
Situated in the centre of Athlone, this modern hotel offers comfortable, well-equipped bedrooms. Its spacious restaurant and lounge bar are comfortable and pleasantly furnished.
**ROOMS:** 73 en suite (15 fmly) No smoking in 10 bedrooms
**FACILITIES:** STV entertainment **CONF:** Thtr 270 Class 140 Board 50
**PARKING:** 35 **NOTES:** No dogs (ex guide dogs) RS 24-25 Dec
**CARDS:**

### ★★68% Royal Hoey
Mardyke St
☎ 0902 72924 & 75395 📠 0902 75194

ROYAL HOEY HOTEL

Upholding a tradition of warm hospitality is the priority at this family-run hotel. Located in the centre of town, it has a comfortable foyer lounge bar and restaurant and the coffee shop serves snacks all day. Bedrooms are carefully maintained and well-appointed.
**ROOMS:** 38 en suite (8 fmly) No smoking in 10 bedrooms s IEP38-IEP44; d IEP75-IEP90 (incl. bkfst) * **LB** **FACILITIES:** STV entertainment
**CONF:** Thtr 250 Class 130 Board 40 **SERVICES:** Lift air con
**PARKING:** 50 **NOTES:** No dogs (ex guide dogs) Closed 25-27 Dec
**CARDS:**

## BALLINASLOE, Co Galway — Map 01 B4

### ★★★64% Haydens Gateway Hotel
☎ 065 68 23000 📠 065 68 23759
e-mail: reservations@lynchotels.com
***Dir:*** *located on the main Dublin/Galway road N6*
Built around 1803, this fine hotel offers excellent service and can offer family rooms and newly refurbished executive rooms. Meals are served throughout the day, either in the Garbally Restaurant, with its extensive carte menu or the award-winning coffee shop which serves full meals, snacks and home-baking.
**ROOMS:** 47 en suite (8 fmly) s IEP63-IEP80; d IEP86-IEP118 (incl. bkfst & dinner) * **LB** **FACILITIES:** STV entertainment Xmas **CONF:** Thtr 300 Class 160 Board 50 Del from IEP40 * **SERVICES:** Lift **PARKING:** 100
**NOTES:** No dogs (ex guide dogs) Civ Wed 300
**CARDS:**

> Late for dinner? Quality Standards star rating means that last orders for dinner should be no earlier than:
> ★ 6.30pm ★★ 7.00pm ★★★ 8.00pm
> ★★★★ 9.00pm ★★★★★ 10.00pm

## BALLINLOUGH, Co Roscommon — Map 01 B4

### ★★★70% *Whitehouse Hotel*
☎ 0907 40112 📠 0907 40993
e-mail: thewhitehousehotel@eircom.net
***Dir:*** *Between Castlerea & Ballyhaunis*
The staff are friendly at this comfortable hotel with appealing decor and spacious bedrooms. Facilities include a TV lounge, restaurant, comfortable bars and a well-equipped conference/banqueting suite. The hotel is convenient for Lake O'Flynn and Knock Airport.
**ROOMS:** 19 en suite (5 fmly) No smoking in all bedrooms
**FACILITIES:** STV entertainment **CONF:** Thtr 250 Class 200 Board 50
**SERVICES:** Lift air con **NOTES:** No dogs (ex guide dogs) Closed 25 Dec
**CARDS:**

## BALLYBOFEY, Co Donegal — Map 01 C5

### ★★★70% *Kee's*
Stranorlar
☎ 074 31018 📠 074 31917
***Dir:*** *2km NE on N15, in Stranorlar village*
The Kee family have extensively refurbished and extended this former coaching inn. Facilities include an elegant conservatory lounge, bar, award-winning restaurant and a bistro. Bedrooms are attractively furnished and well-equipped.
**ROOMS:** 53 en suite (10 fmly) **FACILITIES:** STV Indoor swimming (H) Sauna Solarium Gym Jacuzzi Mountain bikes for hire entertainment
**CONF:** Thtr 250 Class 100 Board 30 **SERVICES:** Lift **PARKING:** 90
**CARDS:**

## BALLYCONNELL, Co Cavan — Map 01 C4

### ★★★★67% Slieve Russell Hotel Golf & Country Club
☎ 049 9526 444 📠 049 9526 474
e-mail: slieve-russell@quinn-hotels.com
***Dir:*** *From Dublin take N3 towards Cavan. At rdbt before Cavan follow Enniskillen Sign and go to Belturbet. From Belturbet go towards Ballyconnell. Hotel approx 6 miles from Belturbet on left.*
This imposing hotel stands in 300 acres, which also accommodate a championship golf course. Public areas include a range of lounges, a restaurant and brasserie and a leisure centre. Bedrooms are tastefully furnished and equipped to a high standard.
**ROOMS:** 159 en suite (79 fmly) s IEP95-IEP135; d IEP160-IEP220 (incl. bkfst) * **LB** **FACILITIES:** **Spa** STV Indoor swimming (H) Golf 18 Tennis (hard) Squash Snooker Sauna Solarium Gym Jacuzzi Steam Room, Hair & Beauty Salon,Driving range entertainment Xmas **CONF:** Thtr 800 Class 450 Board 40 Del from IEP126 * **SERVICES:** Lift **PARKING:** 600
**NOTES:** No dogs (ex guide dogs) **CARDS:**

## BALLYCOTTON, Co Cork — Map 01 C2

### ★★★73% Bay View
MANOR HOUSE
☎ 021 4646746 📠 021 4646075
e-mail: bayhotel@iol.ie
***Dir:*** *turn off N25 at Castlemartyr and follow signs to Ballycotton*
Situated in a fishing village overlooking Ballycotton Bay, the Bay View has a particularly pleasant atmosphere. The comfortable public areas and bedrooms all benefit from the beautiful location. Sit on the patio or terraced gardens, or dine in the award-winning restaurant.
**ROOMS:** 35 en suite s IEP80-IEP95; d IEP120-IEP150 (incl. bkfst) * **LB**
**FACILITIES:** STV Horse riding Fishing Golf(nearby) entertainment ch fac
**CONF:** Thtr 60 Class 30 Board 24 **SERVICES:** Lift air con
**PARKING:** 40 **NOTES:** No dogs (ex guide dogs) Closed Nov-Apr
**CARDS:**

BALLYHEIGE, Co Kerry Map 01 A2

**★★★65% The White Sands**
☎ 066 7133 102 Fax 066 7133 357
e-mail: culv@indigo.ie
***Dir:*** *18km from Tralee town on coast road in North Kerry, the hotel is situated on left on main street*
Friendly staff welcome guests to this family run hotel, situated beside the beach and close to golf clubs. Attractively decorated throughout, facilities include a lounge bar, traditional pub, good restaurant and comfortable bedrooms.
**ROOMS:** 81 en suite **FACILITIES:** STV entertainment **SERVICES:** Lift air con **PARKING:** 40 **NOTES:** Closed Nov-Feb **CARDS:**

BALLYLICKEY, Co Cork Map 01 B2

**★★★76% *Sea View***
☎ 027 50073 & 50462 Fax 027 51555
e-mail: seaviewhousehotel@eircom.net
***Dir:*** *5km from Bantry, 11km from Glengarriff on N71*
Lovely gardens surround this delightful country house, personally run by the owner, Kathleen O'Sullivan whose team of staff are exceptionally pleasant. Comfort and good cuisine are the priorities. Bedrooms are individually styled, and some are on the ground floor.
**ROOMS:** 17 en suite (3 fmly) **FACILITIES:** STV **PARKING:** 32
**NOTES:** No smoking in restaurant Closed mid Nov-mid Mar
**CARDS:**

IEP refers to Irish Punts – see page 13 for more information.

BALLYMENA, Co Antrim Map 01 D5

**★★★★69% Galgorm Manor**
BT42 1EA
☎ 028 2588 1001 ⎙ 028 2588 0080
e-mail: mail@galgorm.com
***Dir:*** *1m outside Ballymena on A42, between Galgorm & Cullybackey*
Set in 85 acres of private grounds, beside the River Maine, this 19th-century mansion offers spacious comfortable bedrooms. Public areas include a welcoming cocktail bar and elegant restaurant, as well as Gillies, a lively and atmospheric locals' bar. Also on the estate are an equestrian centre and a grand conference hall.
**ROOMS:** 24 en suite (6 fmly) s fr £99; d fr £119 (incl. bkfst) * **LB** **FACILITIES:** STV Fishing Riding Clay pigeon shooting,Archery,Waterskiing entertainment ch fac Xmas **CONF:** Thtr 500 Class 200 Board 12 Del from £90 * **PARKING:** 170 **NOTES:** No dogs (ex guide dogs) RS 25-26 Dec Civ Wed 200 **CARDS:**

*See advert on page 849*

**★★★66% *Adair Arms***
1 Ballymoney Rd BT43 5BS
☎ 028 2565 3674 ⎙ 028 2564 0436
e-mail: reservations@adairarms.com
Conveniently situated close to the centre of the town, this hotel offers spacious bedrooms suitably equipped to meet the needs of business and leisure visitors alike. A large comfortable lounge bar leads into the brightly furnished restaurant and there is also a Grill offering lighter meals.
**ROOMS:** 44 en suite (3 fmly) **FACILITIES:** STV entertainment **CONF:** Thtr 250 Class 150 Board 60 **SERVICES:** air con **PARKING:** 50 **NOTES:** No dogs (ex guide dogs) Closed 25 Dec
**CARDS:**

*See advert on page 849*

BALLYNAHINCH, Co Galway Map 01 A4

**★★★★74% *Ballynahinch Castle***
☎ 095 31006 & 31086 ⎙ 095 31085
e-mail: bhinch@iol.ie
***Dir:*** *W from Galway on N59 direction Clifden. After village of Recess take Roundstone turn, 4km from turn off*
At the foot of Ben Lettery, this hotel stands on the banks of the famous salmon river, the Ballynahinch. Bedrooms are spacious, individually designed and comfortably equipped. There is a marvellous atmosphere in the Castle Bar. Game and fresh local produce are a treat in the charming restaurant.
**ROOMS:** 40 en suite No smoking in 4 bedrooms **FACILITIES:** STV Tennis (hard) Fishing Croquet lawn River & Lakeside walks entertainment **CONF:** Thtr 30 Class 20 Board 20 **PARKING:** 55 **NOTES:** No dogs (ex guide dogs) Closed Feb & 20-26 Dec **CARDS:**

BALLYVAUGHAN, Co Clare Map 01 B3

## *Premier Collection*

**★★★ Gregans Castle**
☎ 065 7077 005 ⎙ 065 7077 111
e-mail: res@gregans.ie
***Dir:*** *3.5miles S of the village of Ballyvaughan on the road N67*
Standing at the foot of Corkscrew Hill, with dramatic views over Galway Bay, this 15/16th-century tower house is situated in an area which is rich in archaeological, geological and botanical interest. A high level of personal service and hospitality has earned the hotel special commendations in recent years and the welcoming staff fulfil their reputation. The cuisine is also excellent with the emphasis placed on good food, using fresh local produce.

**ROOMS:** 22 en suite **FACILITIES:** no TV in bdrms Croquet lawn **PARKING:** 25 **NOTES:** No dogs No smoking in restaurant Closed 31 Oct-30 Mar **CARDS:**

**★★★62% Hyland's Hotel**
☎ 065 7077037 ⎙ 065 7077131
e-mail: hylands@tinet.ie
***Dir:*** *From Dublin take N6 to Craughwell, then follow N67 to village*

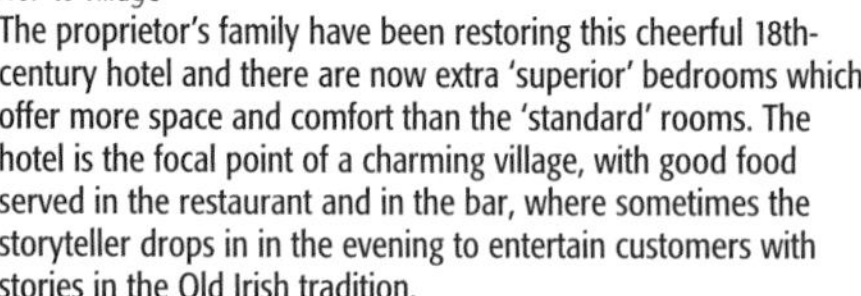

The proprietor's family have been restoring this cheerful 18th-century hotel and there are now extra 'superior' bedrooms which offer more space and comfort than the 'standard' rooms. The hotel is the focal point of a charming village, with good food served in the restaurant and in the bar, where sometimes the storyteller drops in in the evening to entertain customers with stories in the Old Irish tradition.
**ROOMS:** 30 en suite (2 fmly) No smoking in 10 bedrooms s IEP57-IEP65; d IEP78-IEP94 (incl. bkfst) * **LB** **FACILITIES:** Riding entertainment **PARKING:** 50 **NOTES:** No dogs Closed Dec-Jan RS Oct-Dec & Feb-May **CARDS:**

BALTIMORE, Co Cork Map 01 B1

**★★★64% Baltimore Harbour Resort Hotel & Leisure Centre**
☎ 028 20361 ⎙ 028 20466
e-mail: info@bhrhotel.ie
***Dir:*** *S from Cork city N71 to Skibbereen, continue on R595 13km to Baltimore*
This smart, friendly, hotel is set in a delightful position, overlooking the harbour. It has spacious, linked public areas, the restful lounge has deep sofas and a turf fire, and the bar and garden room open out onto the patio and gardens. Fresh local ingredients are served in the dining room. Bedrooms are well-appointed, all have sea views.
**ROOMS:** 64 en suite (30 fmly) s IEP75; d IEP110 (incl. bkfst) * **LB** **FACILITIES:** Indoor swimming (H) Sauna Gym Croquet lawn Jacuzzi Table Tennis, In-house video channel entertainment Xmas **CONF:** Thtr 120 Class 100 Board 30 Del from IEP65 * **SERVICES:** Lift **PARKING:** 80 **NOTES:** No dogs (ex guide dogs) No smoking in restaurant Closed Jan-mid Feb RS mid Nov-Dec
**CARDS:**

€ The Euro will be phased in during 2002 (R.O.I. only). Make sure you check prices and currency when booking.

B

**★★★59% Casey's of Baltimore**
☎ 028 20197 Fax 028 20509
e-mail: caseys@eircom.net
***Dir:*** *Take the N71 from Cork to Skibbereen, follow R595 from Skibbereen*
Set in an elevated position, overlooking the harbour, this warm and friendly hotel offers attractive, comfortable bedrooms. Both the lounge and the restaurant enjoy superb views. The restaurant features seafood dishes and there is a traditional pub. Ferry trips to nearby islands are popular.
**ROOMS:** 14 en suite (1 fmly) **FACILITIES:** STV entertainment **PARKING:** 50 **NOTES:** No dogs Closed 19-26 Feb,5-18 Nov & 21-27 Dec **CARDS:**

## BANGOR, Co Down — Map 01 D5

**★★★70% Clandeboye Lodge**
10 Estate Rd, Clandeboye BT19 1UR
☎ 028 9185 2500 Fax 028 9185 2772
e-mail: info@clandeboyelodge.com
***Dir:*** *from Belfast on A2 turn right at signpost. 500yds down Ballysallagh Road turn left and take Crawfords Burn road. Hotel is 200yds on left.*
Located three miles west of Bangor, Clandeboye Lodge nestles in landscaped and wooded grounds. The hotel provides high quality accommodation as well as extensive conferencing facilities. Public areas also include a bright open-plan foyer bar and attractive lounge.
**ROOMS:** 43 en suite (2 fmly) No smoking in 13 bedrooms s £63-£80; d £70-£90 (incl. bkfst) * **LB** **FACILITIES:** STV **CONF:** Thtr 350 Class 110 Board 50 Del from £84.50 * **SERVICES:** Lift **PARKING:** 250 **NOTES:** No dogs (ex guide dogs) Closed 24-26 Dec
**CARDS:**

**★★★67% Marine Court**
The Marina BT20 5ED
☎ 028 9145 1100 Fax 028 9145 1200
e-mail: admin@marinecourt.fsnet.co.uk
***Dir:*** *Passing Belfast city airport follow A2 through Holywood to Bangor, down main street follow road to left for seafront*
Enjoying a seafront location, the Marine Court offers a good range of conference and leisure facilities suited to both the business and leisure guest. Extensive public areas include the first floor restaurant and cocktail bar. Alternatively, the popular Lord Nelson's Bistro/Bar is more relaxed and there is also a lively bar called Callico Jack's.
**ROOMS:** 52 en suite (11 fmly) No smoking in 16 bedrooms s £50-£80; d £60-£90 (incl. bkfst) * **LB** **FACILITIES:** STV Indoor swimming (H) Solarium Gym Steam room entertainment Xmas **CONF:** Thtr 350 Class 150 Del from £100 * **SERVICES:** Lift **PARKING:** 30 **NOTES:** No dogs (ex guide dogs) RS 25 Dec Civ Wed 200 **CARDS:**

**★★★60% Royal**
Seafront BT20 5ED
☎ 028 9127 1866 Fax 028 9146 7810/028 9145 6283
e-mail: royalhotelbangor@cs.com
***Dir:*** *take A2 from Belfast. Proceed through Bangor town centre to seafront. Turn right-Hotel 300 yards overlooking Marina*
This substantial Victorian hotel enjoys a seafront position and overlooks the marina. Bedrooms are comfortable and modern in style. Public areas are traditional and include a choice of contrasting bars and a popular brasserie. The Quays restaurant provides a more formal dining experience.
**ROOMS:** 50 en suite s £63-£73; d £75-£85 (incl. bkfst) * **LB** **FACILITIES:** STV entertainment **CONF:** Thtr 80 Class 60 Board 40 Del from £90 * **SERVICES:** Lift **NOTES:** No dogs (ex guide dogs) Closed 25 Dec **CARDS:**

## BANTRY, Co Cork — Map 01 B2

**★★★61% Westlodge**
☎ 027 50360 Fax 027 50438
This modern, busy hotel has a popular leisure centre. It is set in its own grounds, on the outskirts of the town, overlooking the bay.
**ROOMS:** 90 en suite (20 fmly) **FACILITIES:** Indoor swimming (H) Tennis (hard) Squash Snooker Sauna Solarium Gym Putting green Jacuzzi Pitch & Putt,wooded walks entertainment **CONF:** Thtr 400 Class 200 Board 24 **SERVICES:** air con **PARKING:** 400 **NOTES:** No dogs (ex guide dogs) Closed 23-27 Dec **CARDS:**

## BARNA, Co Galway — Map 01 B3

**★★63% The Twelve Pins Hotel**
☎ 091 592368 Fax 091 592485
e-mail: the12pinshotel@eircom.net
***Dir:*** *5m W of Galway on R336. Follow signs for Spiddal*
A cheerful yellow building on the Connemara coast road. The comfortable bar is well-known for its convivial atmosphere, and the restaurant offers popular dishes including lobster. New bedrooms are well equipped, and two are suitable for wheelchair users. Close to golf courses.
**ROOMS:** 18 rms (16 en suite) (9 fmly) No smoking in all bedrooms **FACILITIES:** STV entertainment **PARKING:** 80 **NOTES:** No dogs (ex guide dogs) 24-25 Dec **CARDS:**

## BELFAST — Map 01 D5

**★★★70% Malone Lodge**
60 Eglantine Av BT9 6DY
☎ 028 9038 8000 Fax 028 9038 8088
e-mail: info@malonelodgehotel.com
***Dir:*** *At hospital rdbt exit towards Bouchar Rd, left at 1st rdbt, right at lights at top, 1st left is Eglantine Ave*
This smart modern hotel close to the university and city centre has been completely refurbished and extended to a most pleasant standard. Comfortable public areas include an open plan foyer lounge, a tastefully appointed split-level restaurant and a well stocked bar. Bedrooms, though varied in size, are comfortably modern in appointment and offer a good range of facilities.
**ROOMS:** 51 en suite (5 fmly) s £60-£120; d £80-£140 (incl. bkfst) * **LB** **FACILITIES:** STV Sauna Gym **CONF:** Thtr 150 Class 90 Board 40 Del from £120 * **SERVICES:** Lift **PARKING:** 35 **NOTES:** No dogs (ex guide dogs) Closed part of Jul RS 25-30 Dec
**CARDS:**

**★★★70% Posthouse Premier Belfast**
22 Ormeau Av BT2 8HS
☎ 0870 400 9005 Fax 028 9062 6546
e-mail: reservations-belfastcity@posthouse-hotel.com
***Dir:*** *From M1/M2 onto West Link at Grosvenor Rd rdbt follow signpost for city centre. Take 1st right then 2nd left into Hope St, at 2nd lights trun left into Bedford St at next lights turn right into Ormeau Ave, hotel on right*
This new, contemporary hotel is located in the heart of the city centre's 'golden mile' which makes it ideal for business, shopping, exploring the city's tourist attractions and entertainment hot spots. The air-conditioned bedrooms are modern in style and offer a comprehensive range of facilities. Public rooms include a staffed business centre and state of the art health club.
**ROOMS:** 170 en suite (73 fmly) No smoking in 108 bedrooms s £109; d £109 * **LB** **FACILITIES:** STV Indoor swimming (H) Sauna Solarium Gym Jacuzzi Beauty treatments Steam room Workout studio entertainment **CONF:** Thtr 120 Class 58 Board 30 Del from £138 * **SERVICES:** Lift air con **PARKING:** 40 **NOTES:** No dogs (ex guide dogs) RS 24 Dec-3 Jan **CARDS:**

BELFAST, continued

### ★★★69% The Crescent Townhouse

13 Lower Crescent BT7 1NR
☎ 028 9032 3349 📠 028 9032 0646
e-mail: info@crescenttownhouse.com
**Dir:** *S towards Queens University, hotel is on Botanic Avenue opposite Botanic Train Station*

A stylish, smartly presented Regency town house situated next to the botanic gardens station. The popular Bar Twelve and Metro Brasserie are on the ground floor and the reception and bedrooms are situated on the upper floors. Bedrooms are smartly furnished in a country house style.

**ROOMS:** 11 en suite No smoking in 2 bedrooms s £65-£80; d £90-£100 (incl. bkfst) * **FACILITIES:** Spa entertainment **NOTES:** No dogs (ex guide dogs) Closed 25-27 Dec & part of Jul **CARDS:**

### ★★★64% Jurys Belfast Inn

JURYS DOYLE HOTELS

Fisherwick Place, Great Victoria St BT2 7AP
☎ 028 9053 3500 📠 028 9053 3511
e-mail: info@jurys.com
**Dir:** *at the intersection of Grosvenor Road and Great Victoria St, beside the Opera House*

In the heart of Belfast, this smart hotel is well-equipped for business guests. Public areas are contemporary in style and include a foyer lounge, a bar and a smart restaurant. Bedrooms are spacious with pretty fabrics and offer a good range of amenities.

**ROOMS:** 190 en suite No smoking in 76 bedrooms s £68; d £68 * **FACILITIES:** STV entertainment **CONF:** Thtr 30 Class 16 Board 16 **SERVICES:** Lift **NOTES:** No dogs (ex guide dogs) Closed 24-26 Dec **CARDS:**

### ⌂ Holiday Inn Express Belfast

Express by Holiday Inn

106a University St BT7 1HP
☎ 028 9031 1909 📠 028 9031 1910
e-mail: express@holidayinn-ireland.com
**Dir:** *behind Queens University. Turn left at lights on Botanic Ave onto University St. Holiday Inn on left, 500yds down street*

A modern budget hotel offering comfortable accommodation in refreshing, spacious and comprehensively equipped bedrooms, en suite bathrooms with power showers and continental buffet breakfast included in the room rate. Suitable for business travellers or families. For further details and the Express by Holiday Inn phone number, consult the Hotel Groups page.

**ROOMS:** 114 en suite (incl. cont bkfst) s £50-£65; d £50-£65 * **CONF:** Thtr 200 Class 100 Board 70 Del from £125 *

### ⌂ *Travelodge*

Travelodge

15 Brunswick St BT2 7GE
☎ 028 9033 3555 📠 028 9023 2999
**Dir:** *from M2 follow city centre signs to Oxford St turn right to May St, Brunswick St is 4th on left*

Travelodge

Travelodge offers good quality, good value, modern accommodation. Ideal for families, the spacious, en suite bedrooms include remote-control TV, tea and coffee-making facilities, luxury beds and free morning newspaper. Meals can be taken at the nearby family restaurant. For further details and the Travelodge phone number, consult the Hotel Groups page.

**ROOMS:** 76 en suite **CONF:** Thtr 65 Class 50 Board 34

BETTYSTOWN, Co Meath — Map 01 D4

### ★★★★63% *Neptune Beach Hotel & Leisure Club*

☎ 041 9827107 📠 041 9827412
e-mail: info@neptunebeach.ie
**Dir:** *Bettystown is located just off the main Dublin/Belfast road N1*

This hotel, overlooking the sea, has access to a sandy beach. Public areas include an inviting lounge and an attractive Winter Garden. Many bedrooms enjoy sea views and there is a leisure club with pool, gym and jacuzzi.

**ROOMS:** 38 en suite No smoking in 14 bedrooms **FACILITIES:** STV Indoor swimming (H) Sauna Solarium Gym Jacuzzi Steam room Kiddies pool entertainment **CONF:** Thtr 250 Class 150 **SERVICES:** Lift **PARKING:** 60 **NOTES:** No dogs (ex guide dogs) No smoking in restaurant **CARDS:**

BIRR, Co Offaly — Map 01 C3

### ★★★60% *County Arms*

☎ 0509 20791 📠 0509 21234
e-mail: countyarmshotel@tinet.ie
**Dir:** *take N7 from Dublin to Roscrea, N62 to Birr, hotel on right before the church*

This fine Georgian house has comfortable bedrooms, all furnished and decorated to a very high standard. The rooms overlook the meticulously kept Victorian walled gardens which supply the fruit, vegetables and herbs to the hotel kitchens. There is a choice of two restaurants, a bar and a comfortable lounge.

**ROOMS:** 24 en suite (4 fmly) No smoking in 2 bedrooms **FACILITIES:** STV entertainment **CONF:** Thtr 250 Class 250 Board 150 **PARKING:** 150 **NOTES:** No dogs (ex guide dogs) RS 25 Dec **CARDS:**

BLARNEY, Co Cork — Map 01 B2

### ★★★68% Christy's

☎ 021 4385011 📠 021 4385350
e-mail: christys@blarney.ie
**Dir:** *N20, exit at the Blarney sign, at the R617 5km from Cork city*

Part of the famous Blarney Woollen Mills and skilfully converted into a hotel, Christy's stands within sight of the historic castle. Staff are pleasantly attentive and the restaurant and library have a relaxing atmosphere. Adjacent to the hotel is an interesting shopping complex including Christy's Pub and self-service restaurant.

**ROOMS:** 49 en suite (2 fmly) No smoking in 10 bedrooms s IEP65; d IEP104 (incl. bkfst) * **LB** **FACILITIES:** Squash Sauna Solarium Gym Fitness classes **CONF:** Thtr 300 Class 100 Board 20 **SERVICES:** Lift **PARKING:** 200 **NOTES:** No dogs (ex guide dogs) **CARDS:**

BLESSINGTON, Co Wicklow — Map 01 D3

### ★★★66% *Downshire House*

☎ 045 865199 📠 045 865335
e-mail: info@downshirehouse.com
**Dir:** *on N81*

This family-run Georgian house is renowned for its friendly atmosphere. Bedrooms are comfortable and come in a variety of sizes, while the public areas are relaxing and inviting. Cooking is in

*continued*

traditional country house style. The hotel is located in the main street in the village, near to the Wicklow hills, amid some lovely scenery.
**ROOMS:** 14 en suite 11 annexe en suite **FACILITIES:** Tennis (hard) Croquet lawn Table tennis **CONF:** Thtr 40 Class 20 Board 20 **PARKING:** 30 **NOTES:** No dogs (ex guide dogs) Closed 22 Dec-6 Jan **CARDS:**

## BRAY, Co Wicklow — Map 01 D4

### ★★★60% *Woodland Court*
Southern Cross
☎ 01 2760258 📠 01 2760298
e-mail: info@woodlandscourthotel.ie
Situated opposite Kilruddery House, this new hotel is comfortable and attractively appointed throughout. Most bedrooms are spacious and all have modern facilities. The large lobby lounge has a bar and access to the grounds. There are conference facilities and a large car park.
**ROOMS:** 65 en suite (4 fmly) **CONF:** Thtr 60 Class 30 Board 20 **SERVICES:** Lift **PARKING:** 70 **NOTES:** No dogs (ex guide dogs) No smoking in restaurant Closed 24-26 Dec **CARDS:**

### ★★★59% Royal
Main St
☎ 01 2862935 📠 01 2867373
***Dir:*** *from N11, First exit for Bray, 2nd exit from rdbt, through 2 sets traffic lights across bridge, hotel on the left side*
The Royal Hotel stands on the main street, near to the seafront, just a few miles from the Dun Laoghaire ferryport. The hotel has a well-equipped leisure centre.
**ROOMS:** 91 en suite (10 fmly) s IEP68-IEP90; d IEP110-IEP140 (incl. bkfst) * **LB** **FACILITIES:** Indoor swimming (H) Sauna Solarium Gym Jacuzzi Massage and beauty clinic Therapy room Whirlpool spa entertainment ch fac Xmas **CONF:** Thtr 300 Class 200 Board 100 Del from IEP105 * **SERVICES:** Lift **PARKING:** 100 **NOTES:** No dogs (ex guide dogs) Civ Wed **CARDS:**

## BUNBEG, Co Donegal — Map 01 B6

### ★★★68% ®® *Ostan Gweedore*
☎ 075 31177 & 31188 📠 075 31726
e-mail: ostangweedore@ireland.com
***Dir:*** *1km up coast from Bunbeg crossroads - first road left down to sea*
This hotel offers spacious and well-equipped bedrooms. Day rooms are designed to take full advantage of the ever-changing seascape and run the length of the hotel. Fresh seafood features daily on the carefully prepared menus.
**ROOMS:** 39 en suite (6 fmly) **FACILITIES:** STV Indoor swimming (H) Sauna Solarium Gym Jacuzzi entertainment **CONF:** Thtr 250 Class 150 **PARKING:** 80 **NOTES:** No dogs (ex guide dogs) Closed Dec-Jan RS Oct, Nov, Dec, Feb & Mar **CARDS:**

## BUNRATTY, Co Clare — Map 01 B3

### ★★★69% ® *Fitzpatrick Bunratty*
☎ 061 361177 📠 061 471252
e-mail: info@fitzpatrick.com
***Dir:*** *take Bunratty by-pass, exit off Limerick/Shannon dual carriageway*
Situated in the picturesque village of Bunratty, famous for its medieval castle, this modern ranch-style building is surrounded by lawns and flower beds. Bedrooms and public rooms are richly timbered, and there is a helipad in the grounds.
**ROOMS:** 115 en suite (7 fmly) No smoking in 7 bedrooms **FACILITIES:** STV Indoor swimming (H) Sauna Gym Jacuzzi Steam room entertainment **CONF:** Thtr 1000 Class 550 Board 100 **PARKING:** 150 **NOTES:** No dogs (ex guide dogs) RS 24-25 Dec **CARDS:**

## CAHERCIVEEN, Co Kerry — Map 01 A2

### ★★60% *Caherciveen Park Hotel*
Valentia Rd
☎ 066 9472543 📠 066 9472893
e-mail: chp@cahedaniel.net
***Dir:*** *hotel located on the main ring road in Caherciveen Town (Waterville end of town)*
In one of the villages on the Ring of Kerry, this pleasant hotel is near to the coast and many places of interest. There is an inviting bar and restaurant. The hotel is well-located for trips to the nearby islands, which are well worth a visit.
**ROOMS:** 24 en suite (4 fmly) No smoking in 12 bedrooms **FACILITIES:** STV dancing room Games room entertainment **CONF:** Class 25 Board 60 **PARKING:** 100 **NOTES:** No dogs (ex guide dogs) Closed 25 Dec Civ Wed 700 **CARDS:**

## CAHERDANIEL, Co Kerry — Map 01 A2

### ★★★63% Derrynane
☎ 066 9475136 📠 066 9475160
e-mail: info@derrynane.com
***Dir:*** *hotel is just off the main road. 2 mins walking distance*
Halfway around the famous Ring of Kerry, this modern hotel, overlooking the sea, offers a relaxed and friendly atmosphere. The gardens and some of the bedrooms take advantage of the spectacular sea views. The area is ideal for touring and enjoying the scenery and there are plenty of quiet beaches.
**ROOMS:** 74 en suite (30 fmly) s IEP54-IEP65; d IEP78-IEP100 (incl. bkfst) * **LB** **FACILITIES:** STV Outdoor swimming (H) Tennis (hard) Sauna Solarium Gym Steam room entertainment ch fac **PARKING:** 60 **NOTES:** No smoking in restaurant Closed 4 Oct-15 Apr **CARDS:**

## CAHIR, Co Tipperary — Map 01 C3

### ★★★67% ® *Cahir House*
The Square
☎ 52 42727 📠 52 42727
e-mail: cahirhousehotel@tinet.ie
***Dir:*** *travelling S on N8 turn off at Cahir by-pass follow N24 to town, hotel on square in centre of town, car park at rear*
In the centre of Cahir, this hotel has been extending hospitality to visitors since the days of the famous Bianconi horse-drawn coaches. It offers modern comforts in well-equipped and tastefully furnished rooms and maintains traditional standards of welcome and cuisine. The hotel is an ideal base from which to explore.
**ROOMS:** 31 en suite (3 fmly) No smoking in 17 bedrooms **FACILITIES:** STV entertainment **CONF:** Thtr 500 Class 300 Board 80 **PARKING:** 80 **NOTES:** No dogs (ex guide dogs) Closed 25 Dec RS 24-26 Dec & Good Fri **CARDS:**

## CARLOW, Co Carlow — Map 01 C3

### ★★★72% ® *Dolmen*
Kilkenny Rd
☎ 0503 42002 📠 0503 42375
e-mail: reservations@dolmenhotel.ie
***Dir:*** *approx 1m outside Corlow town on the main Kilkenny-Waterford road. Approx 0.5m on right past The Institute of Technology*
In 20 acres of landscaped grounds, this hotel nestles in a peaceful riverside location. Guests can relax in the grounds or take advantage of the free coarse fishing. There is a spacious reception and foyer, a large bar and restaurant, and a luxurious boardroom,

*continued on p854*

CARLOW, continued

which doubles as an additional lounge, overlooking the river. Bedrooms are all well-equipped and comfortable.
**ROOMS:** 40 en suite 12 annexe en suite (1 fmly) **FACILITIES:** STV Fishing **CONF:** Thtr 1000 Class 300 Board 50 **SERVICES:** air con **PARKING:** 300 **NOTES:** No dogs (ex guide dogs) **CARDS:**

*See advert on opposite page*

★★★68% ***Seven Oaks***
Athy Rd
☎ 0503 31308 0503 32155
e-mail: sevenoak@tinet.ie
Staff are friendly and helpful at this hotel, where extensive refurbishment has considerably enhanced facilities. These include a spacious lounge, comfortable new bedrooms and a leisure club. The popular restaurant is also being extended and there is a relaxing bar.
**ROOMS:** 32 en suite (3 fmly) **FACILITIES:** STV Fishing entertainment **CONF:** Thtr 400 Class 150 Board 80 **SERVICES:** Lift air con **PARKING:** 165 **NOTES:** No dogs (ex guide dogs) Closed 25 Dec & Good Friday **CARDS:**

CARNA, Co Galway — Map 01 A4

★★★61% ***Carna Bay Hotel***
☎ 095 32255 095 32530
e-mail: carnaby@iol.ie
***Dir:*** *from Galway take N59 to Recess, then left onto R340 for 8/10m*
This family-run hotel overlooks Carna Bay on the Connemara coast and has a relaxed and friendly atmosphere. Public areas are comfortable and spacious. Food is available all day in the bar, where traditional music and dancing take place on weekend nights. Most of the comfortable bedrooms enjoy sea views.
**ROOMS:** 26 en suite (1 fmly) No smoking in 10 bedrooms **FACILITIES:** STV ch fac **PARKING:** 60 **NOTES:** No smoking in restaurant Closed 23-26 Dec **CARDS:**

CARNLOUGH, Co Antrim — Map 01 D6

★★★69% ***Londonderry Arms***
20 Harbour Rd BT44 0EU
☎ 028 2888 5255 028 2888 5263
***Dir:*** *14m N from Larne on the coast road*
Originally built in the mid-19th century as a coaching inn by Lady Londonderry, the building was owned at one time by her grandson, Winston Churchill. Today the hotel's Georgian architecture and rooms are still evident. The hotel enjoys a prime location in this pretty fishing village overlooking the Antrim coast.
**ROOMS:** 35 en suite (5 fmly) **FACILITIES:** STV Fishing Cycles available **CONF:** Thtr 100 Class 50 Board 50 **SERVICES:** Lift **PARKING:** 50 **NOTES:** No dogs **CARDS:**

CARRICKFERGUS, Co Antrim — Map 01 D5

★★66% **Dobbins Inn**
6-8 High St BT38 7AP
☎ 028 9335 1905 028 9335 1905
e-mail: info@dobbinsinnhotel.co.uk
***Dir:*** *from Belfast take M2, keep right at rdbt follow A2 to Carrickfergus, turn left opp castle*
Colourful window boxes adorn the front of this popular inn, near the ancient castle and sea front. Public areas are furnished to a modern standard without compromising the inn's interesting, historical character. Bedrooms vary in size and style but all provide modern comforts.
**ROOMS:** 15 en suite (2 fmly) s £44; d £64 (incl. bkfst) * **LB FACILITIES:** entertainment **CONF:** Del £60 * **NOTES:** Closed 25-26 Dec & 1 Jan RS Good Friday **CARDS:**

CARRICKMACROSS, Co Monaghan — Map 01 C4

★★★★75% **Nuremore**
☎ 042 9661438 042 9661853
e-mail: nuremore@eircom.net
***Dir:*** *3km S of Carrickmacross, on main Dublin/Derry road*
Overlooking a lake and 18-hole golf course, this hotel is a quiet retreat with excellent facilities. This Victorian mansion has spacious public areas and a wide variety of indoor and outdoor leisure and sporting facilities for the energetic. A very good restaurant serves imaginative dishes. A dedicated team ensures a pleasant visit to this friendly hotel.
**ROOMS:** 72 en suite No smoking in 11 bedrooms s IEP110-IEP140; d IEP160-IEP210 (incl. bkfst) * **LB FACILITIES:** STV Indoor swimming (H) Golf 18 Tennis (grass) Fishing Squash Snooker Sauna Solarium Gym Putting green Jacuzzi Beauty treatments Aromatherapy Xmas **CONF:** Thtr 250 Class 55 Board 30 **SERVICES:** Lift air con **PARKING:** 200 **NOTES:** No dogs (ex guide dogs) **CARDS:**

CARRICK-ON-SHANNON, Co Leitrim — Map 01 B2

★★★★60% ***The Landmark***
☎ 078 22222 078 22233
e-mail: landmarkhotel@eircom.net
Overlooking the River Shannon, close to the Marina, this new hotel offers luxurious public areas including a choice of bars and restaurants, lounges, a leisure club and ballroom. Pleasant staff will be pleased to arrange cruising, horse riding, golf and angling.

CASHEL, Co Galway — Map 01 A4

***Premier Collection***

★★★ **Cashel House**
☎ 095 31001 095 31077
e-mail: info@cashel-house-hotel.com
***Dir:*** *turn S off N59, hotel 1.5km W of Recess*
Cashel House is a mid-19th century house, which stands at the head of Cashel Bay in the heart of Connemara on the West Coast of Ireland. Fifty acres of award-winning gardens and woodland walks are the setting for this gracious country house hotel. The comfortable lounges have turf fires and antique furnishings. The restaurant offers local produce such

*continued*

as Connemara lamb. Bedrooms are appealing and luxury suites are available.
**ROOMS:** 32 en suite (4 fmly) s IEP96-IEP225; d IEP192-IEP237 (incl. bkfst) * **LB** **FACILITIES:** STV Outdoor swimming Tennis (hard) Fishing Riding Xmas **PARKING:** 40 **NOTES:** No children 5yrs No smoking in restaurant Closed 4 Jan-4 Feb
**CARDS:**

### ★★★77% Zetland Country House

Cashel Bay
☎ 095 31111 095 31117
e-mail: zetland@iol.ie
***Dir:*** *N59 from Galway towards Clifden, turn right after Recess onto R340, after approx 4m turn left onto R341, hotel is 1m ahead on right*

Set in very attractive gardens featuring unusual rock formations, flowers, shrubs and woodland, this peaceful country house overlooks Cashel Bay. Public areas include a fine lounge and reading room as well as a smart cocktail bar. Many of the bedrooms have sea or garden views. Warm hospitality is matched by good food and service.
**ROOMS:** 19 en suite (10 fmly) s IEP89-IEP100; d IEP124-IEP146 (incl. bkfst) * **LB** **FACILITIES:** STV Tennis (hard) Fishing Snooker Croquet lawn **CONF:** Board 20 **PARKING:** 32 **NOTES:** No smoking in restaurant Closed Nov-9 Apr **CARDS:**

## CASHEL, Co Tipperary — Map 01 C3

### ★★★★64% *Cashel Palace Hotel*

☎ 062 62707 062 61521
e-mail: reception@cashel-palace.ie
***Dir:*** *in centre of Cashel town*
The Rock of Cashel, floodlit at night, forms a dramatic backdrop to this 18th-century former bishop's palace. An elegant drawing room has garden access and luxurious bedrooms in the main house are most comfortable. Those in the adjacent mews are ideal for families/groups.
**ROOMS:** 13 en suite 10 annexe en suite (8 fmly) No smoking in 5 bedrooms **FACILITIES:** STV Fishing Private path walk to the Rock of Cashel ch fac **CONF:** Thtr 80 Class 45 Board 40 **SERVICES:** Lift **PARKING:** 35 **NOTES:** No dogs (ex guide dogs)
**CARDS:**

## CASTLEBAR, Co Mayo — Map 01 B4

### ★★★67% *Breaffy House*

☎ 094 22033 094 22276
e-mail: breaffyhotel@anu.ie
***Dir:*** *on N60 in direction of Tuam and Galway*
This 19th-century manor house stands in 100 acres of leafy woodlands. Inside there are several lounges and a wing of luxuriously appointed bedrooms, which are an equal match for the attractively decorated rooms in the original house. Other facilities include a restaurant, a choice of bars and conference suites.
**ROOMS:** 59 en suite (3 fmly) **FACILITIES:** STV Gym Croquet lawn Crazy golf **CONF:** Thtr 250 Class 150 Board 50 **SERVICES:** Lift **PARKING:** 300 **NOTES:** No dogs (ex guide dogs) Closed 23-26 Dec Civ Wed 250 **CARDS:**

### ★★67% *Welcome Inn*

☎ 094 22288 & 22054 094 21766
e-mail: cb.welcome@mayo-ireland.ie
***Dir:*** *take N5 to Castlebar situated near the town centre via ring road & rdbts passed the Church of the Holy Rosary*
This town centre hotel offers a range of modern facilities behind its Tudor frontage, including a banqueting/conference centre.
*continued*

Bedrooms are well-equipped and there is a night club with disco on some evenings, as well as traditional music nights in the summer.
**ROOMS:** 40 en suite (5 fmly) **FACILITIES:** STV entertainment **CONF:** Thtr 500 Class 350 **SERVICES:** Lift **PARKING:** 100 **NOTES:** No dogs (ex guide dogs) Closed 23-25 Dec **CARDS:**

## CASTLECONNELL, Co Limerick — Map 01 B3

### ★★★66% *Castle Oaks House*

☎ 061 377666 061 377717
e-mail: info@castle-oaks.com
***Dir:*** *turn off N7 8km outside Limerick City. Hotel is 3km on left*
A fine old Georgian house with grounds reaching down to the River Shannon, set in the tiny village of Castleconnell. The hotel has been upgraded and guests can enjoy first class comfort in well-equipped modern bedrooms. Facilities include river walks, good fishing and free use of a leisure centre.
**ROOMS:** 20 en suite (9 fmly) No smoking in 1 bedroom **FACILITIES:** STV Indoor swimming (H) Golf 9 Tennis (hard) Fishing Snooker Sauna Solarium Gym Jacuzzi Angling centre entertainment **CONF:** Thtr 350 Class 95 Board 40 **PARKING:** 200 **NOTES:** No dogs (ex guide dogs) Closed 24-26 Dec **CARDS:**

## CAVAN, Co Cavan — Map 01 C4

### ★★★65% Kilmore

Dublin Rd
☎ 049 4332288 049 4332458
e-mail: kilmore@quinn-hotels.com
***Dir:*** *approx 3km from Cavan on N3*
Set on a hillside on the outskirts of Cavan, easily accessible from
*continued on p856*

CAVAN, continued

the main N3 route, this comfortable hotel features spacious public areas. Good food is served in the Annalee Restaurant, which is always appreciated by guests returning from fishing, golf, windsurfing or boating, all available nearby.
**ROOMS:** 39 en suite (17 fmly) s fr IEP52; d fr IEP82 (incl. bkfst) * **LB** **FACILITIES:** STV entertainment Xmas **CONF:** Thtr 300 Class 200 Board 60 **SERVICES:** air con **PARKING:** 450 **NOTES:** No dogs (ex guide dogs) **CARDS:**

## CLIFDEN, Co Galway — Map 01 A4

### ★★★78% Rock Glen Country House Hotel

MANOR HOUSE

☎ 095 21035 & 21393 095 21737
e-mail: rockglen@iol.ie
***Dir:** N6 from Dublin to Galway, N57 from Galway to Clifden*
A comfortable converted 18th-century shooting lodge set in lovely grounds and gardens. Elegance abounds throughout the gracious drawing room, cocktail bar and restaurant. The admirable hosts and attentive staff, and the experience of good company and food, make this peaceful retreat beguiling.
**ROOMS:** 26 en suite (2 fmly) s IEP92-IEP109; d IEP116-IEP140 (incl. bkfst) * **LB** **FACILITIES:** STV Tennis (hard) Snooker Croquet lawn Putting green entertainment Xmas **PARKING:** 50 **NOTES:** No smoking in restaurant Closed mid Nov-mid Feb except New Year
**CARDS:**

### *Courtesy & Care Award*

### ★★★76% Abbeyglen Castle

MANOR HOUSE

Sky Rd
☎ 095 21201 095 21797
e-mail: info@abbeyglen.ie
***Dir:** take N59 from Galway to Clifden. Hotel is 1km from Clifden on the Sky Road*
In a tranquil setting overlooking Clifden, the charming atmosphere at Abbeyglen owes much to the dedication of father and son team, Paul and Brian Hughes, and their attentive staff. Some fine new bedrooms have recently been added, and there is a lovely restaurant, and a bar where musical evenings often develop. Golf tours can be arranged. The team at Abbeyglen Castle have been awarded the AA Courtesy & Care Award for Ireland 2001-2002.
**ROOMS:** 36 en suite No smoking in 10 bedrooms s IEP82-IEP95; d IEP115-IEP140 (incl. bkfst) * **LB** **FACILITIES:** STV Outdoor swimming (H) Tennis (hard) Snooker Sauna Putting green Jacuzzi entertainment Xmas **CONF:** Thtr 100 Class 50 Board 40 Del from IEP145 * **SERVICES:** Lift **PARKING:** 40 **NOTES:** No children Closed 11 Jan-1 Feb **CARDS:**

### ★★★69% Ardagh

Ballyconneely Rd
☎ 095 21384 095 21314
e-mail: ardaghhotel@eircom.net
***Dir:** N59 Galway to Clifden, signposted for Ballyconneely*
A family-run hotel in a quiet location, the Ardagh is just over a mile from Clifden. The restaurant overlooks the bay and serves impressive food. Fine lounges take full advantage of the views of Ardbear Bay.
**ROOMS:** 21 en suite (2 fmly) s IEP70-IEP83; d IEP99-IEP125 (incl. bkfst) * **LB** **PARKING:** 35 **NOTES:** No dogs Closed Nov-Mar
**CARDS:**

### ★★★62% Alcock & Brown Hotel

☎ 095 21206 & 21086 095 21842
e-mail: alcockandbrown@eircom.net
***Dir:** Take N59 from Galway via Oughterard, hotel in centre of town*
A comfortable town centre hotel. The bar and restaurant are inviting with particularly pleasant decor. The menu offers a wide range of good food with many fish specialities. The friendly, attentive staff offer good service.
**ROOMS:** 19 annexe en suite s IEP49-IEP58; d IEP68-IEP85 (incl. bkfst) * **LB** **FACILITIES:** STV entertainment Xmas **NOTES:** No dogs (ex guide dogs) Closed 23-25 Dec **CARDS:**

## CLONAKILTY, Co Cork — Map 01 B2

### ★★★★75% *The Lodge & Spa at Inchydoney Island*

☎ 023 33143 023 35229
e-mail: reservations@inchydoneyisland.com
***Dir:** follow N71 West Cork road to Clonakilty, at entry rdbt in Clonakilty take 2nd exit and follow signs to Lodge and Spa*
A former winner of Hotel of the Year for Ireland this luxurious hotel enjoys a stunning location on the coastline, with steps down to a sandy beach. Bedrooms are furnished in a warm, contemporary style, most have sea views. The lounge is superb and there is a cocktail bar with a patio and also a library. The restaurant serves an imaginative menu.
**ROOMS:** 67 en suite (24 fmly) No smoking in 17 bedrooms **FACILITIES:** **Spa** STV Indoor swimming (H) Fishing Riding Snooker Sauna Gym Jacuzzi Thalassotherapy spa **CONF:** Thtr 300 Class 150 Board 100 **SERVICES:** Lift **PARKING:** 200 **NOTES:** No dogs
**CARDS:**

## CLONMEL, Co Tipperary — Map 01 C2

### ★★★74% Minella

☎ 052 22388 052 24381
e-mail: hotelminella@eircom.net
This family-run hotel, set in nine acres of well kept grounds on the banks of the river Suir, offers comfort and courteous service. Facilities include a cocktail bar and lounge overlooking the gardens and a leisure centre and putting greens. Bedrooms are all tastefully decorated and well-equipped, some have jacuzzis.
**ROOMS:** 70 en suite (8 fmly) No smoking in 16 bedrooms s IEP70-IEP85; d IEP110-IEP130 (incl. bkfst) * **LB** **FACILITIES:** STV Indoor swimming (H) Tennis (hard) Fishing Sauna Gym Croquet lawn Jacuzzi Aerobics room **CONF:** Thtr 500 Class 300 Board 20 Del from IEP105 * **PARKING:** 100 **NOTES:** No dogs No smoking in restaurant Closed 24-28 Dec **CARDS:**

IEP refers to Irish Punts – see page 13 for more information.

## COBH, Co Cork
Map 01 B2

### ★★★67% Watersedge
Yacht Club Quay
☎ 021 4815566 📠 021 4812011
e-mail: watersedge@eircom.net
***Dir:*** *follow road signs for Cobh Heritage Centre & Fota Golf Club*

This delightful property is situated on the waterfront beside the Heritage Centre and railway station. Guests can enjoy spectacular views of the harbour from the restaurant. Spacious bedrooms are furnished to a high standard and four ground floor rooms have their own balconies.

**ROOMS:** 19 en suite (5 fmly) No smoking in 6 bedrooms s IEP50-IEP70; d IEP70-IEP130 (incl. bkfst) * **LB** **PARKING:** 25 **NOTES:** No dogs (ex guide dogs) **CARDS:**

## COLLOONEY, Co Sligo
Map 01 B5

### ★★★56% *Markree Castle*
☎ 071 67800 📠 071 67840
e-mail: markree@iol.ie
***Dir:*** *turn off N4 at Collooney rdbt, take R290 towards Dromahaire. Just north of junct with N17, 11km S of Sligo, hotel gates on right hand side after 1km*

This magnificent castle dates back to 1640 and has all the grandeur expected in such a great building. Considerable restoration work has taken place to transform this historic building into a hotel and the imposing Knockmuldowney Restaurant gives a taste of the style.

**ROOMS:** 30 en suite (2 fmly) **FACILITIES:** Riding Croquet lawn **CONF:** Thtr 50 Class 30 Board 20 **SERVICES:** Lift **PARKING:** 60 **NOTES:** No smoking in restaurant Closed 24-26 Dec **CARDS:**

## CORK, Co Cork
Map 01 B2

**Premier Collection**

### ★★★★ *Hayfield Manor*
Perrott Av, College Rd
☎ 021 315600 📠 021 316839
e-mail: enquiries@hayfieldmanor.ie
***Dir:*** *1m W of Cork city centre-head for N22 to Killarney, turn left at University Gates off Western Rd. Turn right into College Rd, left into Perrott Ave*

Hayfield Manor offers privacy and seclusion. This fine hotel is part of a grand two-acre estate and gardens and has every modern comfort. It maintains an atmosphere of tranquillity and the bedrooms are spacious, containing many thoughtful extras. Guests also have access to the exclusive health club. Public rooms feature elegant architecture, carefully combined

*continued*



with fine furnishings and real fires to create an atmosphere of intimacy. The Manor Room restaurant serves dishes from the interesting carte.

**ROOMS:** 87 en suite No smoking in 25 bedrooms **FACILITIES:** STV Indoor swimming (H) Gym Jacuzzi Steam room entertainment **CONF:** Thtr 100 Class 60 Board 40 **SERVICES:** Lift air con **PARKING:** 100 **NOTES:** No dogs (ex guide dogs) **CARDS:**

*See advert on this page*

### ★★★★76% *The Kingsley Hotel*
Victoria Cross
☎ 021 4800500 📠 021 4800527
e-mail: resv@kingsleyhotel.com

Situated on the banks of the river Lee, the Kingsley is a luxurious hotel with good facilities. Bedrooms are excellent and feature several thoughtful extra touches. Guests have use of a comfortable lounge and library. Contemporary and informal trends are evident in the bar and restaurant.

**ROOMS:** 69 en suite No smoking in 36 bedrooms **FACILITIES:** STV Indoor swimming (H) Fishing Sauna Solarium Gym Jacuzzi **CONF:** Thtr 80 Class 50 Board 32 **SERVICES:** Lift air con **PARKING:** 250 **CARDS:**

### ★★★★70% *Rochestown Park Hotel*
Rochestown Rd, Douglas
☎ 021 892233 📠 021 892178
e-mail: info@rochestownpark.com
***Dir:*** *from Lee Tunnel, 2nd exit left off dual carriageway. Continue for 400mtrs, then first left and right at small rdbt. Hotel 600mtrs on right*

Set amongst chestnut trees in mature gardens, this hotel has much

*continued on p858*

CORK, continued

to offer, including an excellent Conference & Exhibition Centre. Staff are pleasant and professional and a variety of room styles is available including suites. Peacefully set in lovely gardens on the south side of the city, yet also convenient for the airport and ferries.
**ROOMS:** 115 en suite (17 fmly) **FACILITIES:** STV Indoor swimming (H) Sauna Solarium Gym Jacuzzi Thalasso therapy & beauty centre **CONF:** Thtr 800 Class 360 Board 100 **SERVICES:** Lift **PARKING:** 600 **NOTES:** No dogs Closed 25-26 Dec **CARDS:**

### ★★★★69% Jurys

JURYS DOYLE HOTELS

Western Rd
☎ 021 276622 021 274477
e-mail: info@jurysdoyle.com
***Dir:*** *close to city centre, on main Killarney road as you exit Cork, past the court-house on the right hand side, situated 500yrds on the left*
This hotel enjoys a riverside setting near to the university and within walking distance of the city centre. The public areas have a fresh outlook, with a comfortable library lounge, in addition to leisure and conference facilities. Bedrooms are well-equipped.
**ROOMS:** 185 en suite (23 fmly) No smoking in 48 bedrooms s IEP130-IEP152; d IEP150-IEP172 (incl. bkfst) * **LB** **FACILITIES:** STV Indoor swimming (H) Outdoor swimming (H) Squash Sauna Gym Jacuzzi entertainment Xmas **CONF:** Thtr 700 Class 400 Board 150 Del from IEP135 * **SERVICES:** Lift **PARKING:** 231 **NOTES:** No dogs (ex guide dogs) Closed 25-27 Dec **CARDS:**

### ★★★★65% Silver Springs Moran

Tivoli
☎ 021 507533 021 507641
e-mail: silverspringshotel@hotmail.com
***Dir:*** *from N8 south-bound take Silver Springs exit. Turn right across overpass - hotel is on right*

SILVERSPRINGS
MORAN HOTEL

Under new ownership, this hotel offers a choice of bedrooms including the refurbished Tower Rooms and the larger Club Rooms. There is a spacious lounge, a bar and restaurant, excellent conference facilities and a helipad. Guests have use of a nearby leisure centre and there is a nine-hole golf course within the grounds.
**ROOMS:** 109 en suite (50 fmly) No smoking in 4 bedrooms s IEP95-IEP115; d IEP115-IEP136 * **LB** **FACILITIES:** STV Indoor swimming (H) Tennis (hard) Squash Snooker Sauna Gym Jacuzzi Aerobics classes entertainment Xmas **CONF:** Thtr 800 Class 500 Board 50 Del from IEP102 * **SERVICES:** Lift **PARKING:** 450 **NOTES:** No dogs (ex guide dogs) Closed 24-25 Dec Civ Wed 450 **CARDS:**

### ★★★69% *Imperial Hotel*

South Mall
☎ 021 274040 021 275375
This fine hotel has a hospitable and welcoming atmosphere. The reception rooms are on a grand scale, particularly the foyer, with its beautiful crystal chandelier and paintings. Bedrooms are of a high standard and Clouds Restaurant is earning a reputation for good food.
**ROOMS:** 98 en suite (12 fmly) **FACILITIES:** STV entertainment **CONF:** Thtr 400 Class 200 Board 150 **SERVICES:** Lift **PARKING:** 40 **NOTES:** No dogs (ex guide dogs) Closed 24 Dec-2 Jan **CARDS:**

### ★★★67% *Ambassador*

Military Hill, St Lukes
☎ 021 4551996 021 4551997
e-mail: reservations@ambassadorhotel.ie
***Dir:*** *city centre, just off Wellington Road*
Many pleasing features distinguish this sandstone and granite building which dates from the 19th century. Today it is a fine hotel with commanding views of the city and a feeling of space throughout. Some bedrooms have balconies, all are well-equipped. Public areas include a cocktail lounge, bar and restaurant.
**ROOMS:** 60 en suite (8 fmly) No smoking in 8 bedrooms **FACILITIES:** STV entertainment **CONF:** Thtr 80 Class 40 Board 35 **SERVICES:** Lift **PARKING:** 60 **NOTES:** No dogs (ex guide dogs) Closed 24-25 Dec Civ Wed 60 **CARDS:**

### ★★★67% Gresham Metropole Hotel & Leisure Centre

GRESHAM HOTELS

MacCurtain St
☎ 021 4508122 021 4506450
e-mail: ryan@indigo.ie
***Dir:*** *hotel is in the city centre located on MacCurtain St - leading to N25 main Dublin Rd*

This city centre hotel has recently been refurbished, and some fine new conference facilities have been added. Bedrooms vary in size and are well-equipped and comfortable. There is a leisure centre, waterside restaurant, and a café. Ask at reception for car park information.
**ROOMS:** 113 en suite (3 fmly) No smoking in 6 bedrooms s IEP110-IEP190; d IEP120-IEP190 (incl. bkfst) * **LB** **FACILITIES:** STV Indoor swimming (H) Snooker Sauna Solarium Gym Jacuzzi entertainment Xmas **CONF:** Thtr 500 Class 180 Board 60 Del from IEP125 * **SERVICES:** Lift **PARKING:** 240 **NOTES:** No dogs (ex guide dogs) **CARDS:**

*See advert on page 845*

### ★★★65% Arbutus Lodge

Middle Glanmire Rd, Montenotte
☎ 021 501237 021 502893
e-mail: info@arbutuslodge.net
This family-run period house, set above terraced gardens, overlooks the city. Facilities include comfortable lounges, a bar, an elegant restaurant, a pub and a banqueting suite. Guests can also enjoy the patio terrace and tennis courts.
**ROOMS:** 16 en suite s fr IEP60; d fr IEP95 (incl. bkfst) * **LB** **FACILITIES:** STV Tennis (hard) Xmas **CONF:** Thtr 100 Class 60 Board 30 **PARKING:** 35 **NOTES:** No dogs (ex guide dogs) Closed 24-28 Dec **CARDS:**

**★★★59% Jurys Inn**
Anderson's Quay
☎ 021 4276444 🖹 021 4276144
e-mail: enquiry@jurys.com
***Dir:*** *Located in the city centre, on river beside eastern approach to the city from Dublin and South link road to airport*
Attractively decorated in a modern style, this hotel overlooks the River Lee and is just a short walk from the main street. Rooms can accommodate three adults or two adults and two children. The restaurant is informal in style and there is also a lively pub.
**ROOMS:** 133 en suite No smoking in 32 bedrooms d IEP56-IEP96 **FACILITIES:** STV entertainment **CONF:** Thtr 35 Class 20 Board 20 **SERVICES:** Lift **PARKING:** 22 **NOTES:** No dogs (ex guide dogs) Closed 24-26 Dec **CARDS:**

JURYS DOYLE HOTELS

***Travelodge***
Blackash
☎ 01 21310722 🖹 01 21310707
***Dir:*** *at rdbt junc of South Ring Road/Kinsale Rd R600*
Travelodge offers good quality, good value, modern accommodation. Ideal for families, the spacious, en suite bedrooms include remote-control TV, tea and coffee-making facilities, luxury beds and free morning newspaper. Meals can be taken at the nearby family restaurant. For further details and the Travelodge phone number, consult the Hotel Groups page.

Travelodge

**ROOMS:** 40 en suite

## COURTMACSHERRY, Co Cork — Map 01 B2

***★60% Courtmacsherry***
☎ 023 46198 🖹 023 46137
e-mail: cmv@indigo.ie
***Dir:*** *take M71 to Bandon, R602 to Timoleague. From Timoleague head for Courtmacsherry, hotel is by the beach at the far end of the town*
This Georgian house is set in attractive grounds near the beach. The hotel is family-run, and its main selling points are the good quality meals served in the kitchen and a riding school available to all ages. Fishing and tennis are also available.
**ROOMS:** 12 rms (10 en suite) (1 fmly) **FACILITIES:** STV Tennis (hard & grass) Riding Shore fishing from hotel beach **PARKING:** 60 **NOTES:** Closed Oct-Mar **CARDS:**

## COURTOWN HARBOUR, Co Wexford — Map 01 D3

**★★68% Courtown**
☎ 055 25210 & 25108 🖹 055 25304
e-mail: courtown@indigo.ie
***Dir:*** *8km off N11*
Situated in the town centre, near to the beach and an 18-hole golf course, this refurbished hotel offers relaxing public areas including a comfortable lounge and spacious bar on two levels. Facilities include a restaurant and an indoor swimming pool.
**ROOMS:** 21 en suite (4 fmly) s fr IEP60; d fr IEP90 (incl. bkfst) * **LB** **FACILITIES:** STV Indoor swimming (H) Golf 18 Tennis (hard & grass) Fishing Squash Riding Sauna Solarium Gym Jacuzzi Steam room Massage Crazy golf entertainment **PARKING:** 10 **NOTES:** No dogs (ex guide dogs) Closed Nov-16 Mar **CARDS:**

**★★66% Bay View**
☎ 055 25307 🖹 055 25576
e-mail: bayview@iol.ie
***Dir:*** *Clearly signposted to Courtown,turn left before Gorey off N11,hotel situated in main square over looking harbour*
Recently refurbished public areas are very comfortable and include a bar, lounge and restaurant overlooking the marina and shoreline. A tennis court adjoins the hotel and there is an 18-hole golf course nearby. Some bedrooms have sea views and there are four self-catering apartments, which have full use of hotel facilities.
**ROOMS:** 17 en suite (12 fmly) s IEP50; d IEP80 (incl. bkfst) * **LB** **FACILITIES:** Tennis (hard) Squash **PARKING:** 30 **NOTES:** No dogs (ex guide dogs) No smoking in restaurant Closed 30 Nov-14 Mar
**CARDS:**

## CRAWFORDSBURN, Co Down — Map 01 D5

**★★★72% Old Inn**
15 Main St BT19 1JH
☎ 028 9185 3255 🖹 028 9185 2775
e-mail: info@theoldinn.com
***Dir:*** *A2, passing Belfast Airport and Holywood, 3m past Holywood sign for The Old Inn, 100yds turn L at lights, follow rd into village, hotel is on left*
Enjoying a peaceful rural setting not far from Belfast, the Old Inn is reputed to date back to 1614. Much original character has been retained in the public rooms, which include cosy bars, a stylish bistro and a fine dining restaurant. Bedrooms vary in size and in style, and all are well-equipped.
**ROOMS:** 32 en suite (4 fmly) No smoking in 6 bedrooms s £45-£65; d fr £85 (incl. bkfst) * **LB** **FACILITIES:** STV ch fac Xmas **CONF:** Thtr 120 Class 27 Board 40 Del from £90 * **PARKING:** 65 **NOTES:** No dogs (ex guide dogs) No smoking in restaurant
**CARDS:**

## CROSSHAVEN, Co Cork — Map 01 B2

***★★65% Whispering Pines Hotel***
☎ 021 831843 & 831448 🖹 021 831679
There is something inviting about this comfortable hotel with its sun lounge and bar overlooking the river. The hospitality is warming and the kitchen caters well for all its guests, particularly anglers, for whom fishing boats and equipment are available for hire. Transfers from Cork Airport can be arranged if required.
**ROOMS:** 15 en suite (6 fmly) **FACILITIES:** STV Own angling boats fish daily **PARKING:** 40 **NOTES:** No dogs (ex guide dogs)
**CARDS:**

## DELGANY, Co Wicklow — Map 01 D3

**★★★★61% Glenview**
Glen O' the Downs
☎ 01287 3399 🖹 01287 7511
e-mail: glenview@iol.ie
***Dir:*** *From Dublin city centre follow signs for N11 past Bray on southbound side of N11*
In a lovely hillside location overlooking terraced gardens, extensive refurbishment has resulted in luxurious lounges, a restaurant with delightful views and a conservatory bar. Excellent conference facilities. Bedrooms are well-equipped, and golf, horse riding and other tourist amenities are available nearby.
**ROOMS:** 74 en suite (11 fmly) No smoking in 11 bedrooms s IEP115-IEP135; d IEP170-IEP190 (incl. bkfst) * **LB** **FACILITIES:** **Spa** STV Indoor swimming (H) Sauna Solarium Gym Croquet lawn Jacuzzi entertainment Xmas **CONF:** Thtr 220 Class 120 **SERVICES:** Lift **PARKING:** 200 **NOTES:** No dogs (ex guide dogs)
**CARDS:**

> Popped the question? Hotels with Civ Wed in their entry are licensed for civil wedding ceremonies. Maximum numbers for the ceremony only are shown, e.g. Civ Wed 120

## DINGLE, Co Kerry
Map 01 A2

### ★★★72% Dingle Skellig Hotel
☎ 066 9150200 066 9151501
e-mail: dsk@iol.ie
**Dir:** *On shores of Dingle Harbour on entering Dingle from Killarney/Tralee-Dingle road N86*
On the outskirts of the town, overlooking the bay, this modern hotel has bright, airy bedrooms and pleasant public areas, making it an excellent base for holidaymakers.
**ROOMS:** 116 en suite s IEP65-IEP120; d IEP100-IEP200 (incl. bkfst) * **LB** **FACILITIES:** STV Indoor swimming (H) Solarium Gym Jacuzzi Massage/aromatherapy/reflexology entertainment ch fac Xmas **CONF:** Thtr 250 Class 140 Board 80 Del IEP115 * **SERVICES:** Lift **PARKING:** 150 **NOTES:** No dogs (ex guide dogs)
**CARDS:**

## DONEGAL, Co Donegal
Map 01 B5

### ★★★74% Harvey's Point Country
Lough Eske
☎ 073 22208 073 22352
e-mail: reservations@harveyspoint.com
**Dir:** *from Donegal, take N56 then 1st right signposted Loch Eske/Harvey's Point. Hotel is approx 10 mins drive*
This modern hotel is in a superb lakeside location on Lough Eske, and was built with guests' peace and comfort in mind. There are spacious public rooms, excellent cuisine and a wide range of facilities.
**ROOMS:** 20 en suite 12 annexe en suite No smoking in all bedrooms s IEP70-IEP75; d IEP110-IEP120 (incl. bkfst) * **LB** **FACILITIES:** STV Tennis (hard) entertainment Xmas **CONF:** Thtr 200 Class 200 Board 50 Del from IEP80 * **PARKING:** 300 **NOTES:** No children 10yrs No smoking in restaurant **CARDS:**

### ★★★63% Abbey
The Diamond
☎ 073 21014 073 23660
e-mail: whitegrp@iol.ie
**Dir:** *located in centre of Donegal Town - N15 from Sligo*
This friendly hotel is situated in the centre of the town overlooking the square. The Abbey Restaurant is an inviting place to eat lunch and dinner and hot food is available all day in the coffee shop. The lounge bar has an adjoining patio and there is nightly entertainment. Bedrooms are comfortable and well-appointed.
**ROOMS:** 95 en suite (12 fmly) No smoking in 4 bedrooms s IEP50-IEP60; d IEP90-IEP100 (incl. bkfst) * **LB** **FACILITIES:** STV Leisure facilities available at sister hotel entertainment **CONF:** Thtr 400 Class 300 Board 300 **SERVICES:** Lift air con **PARKING:** 20 **NOTES:** Closed 25-26 Dec **CARDS:**

## DOOLIN, Co Clare
Map 01 B3

### ★★★64% *Aran View House*
Coast Rd
☎ 065 7074061 & 7074420 065 7074540
e-mail: booking@aranview.com
Situated in 100 acres of rolling farmland and commanding panoramic views of the Aran Islands, this hotel offers attractive and comfortably furnished accommodation. Staff are welcoming, the atmosphere is convivial, and there is traditional music and song in the bar three times a week.
**ROOMS:** 13 en suite 6 annexe en suite (1 fmly)
**FACILITIES:** entertainment **PARKING:** 40 **NOTES:** Closed 1 Nov-1 Apr
**CARDS:**

*See advert on opposite page*

## DROGHEDA, Co Louth
Map 01 D4

### ★★★61% *Boyne Valley Hotel & Country Club*
Stameen, Dublin Rd
☎ 041 9837737 041 9839188
**Dir:** *N1 towards Belfast, north of Dublin Airport on right - up Avenue before town of Droghedah*
This historic mansion stands in 16 acres of gardens and woodlands on the outskirts of Drogheda. Much emphasis is placed here on good food and attentive service and all the accommodation is well-furnished and provides high standards of comfort. There are extensive ammenities including a leisure centre.
**ROOMS:** 35 en suite (4 fmly) **FACILITIES:** STV Indoor swimming (H) Tennis (hard) Sauna Solarium Gym Putting green Jacuzzi Pitch & putt entertainment **CONF:** Thtr 150 Class 100 Board 25 **PARKING:** 200 **NOTES:** No dogs (ex guide dogs) **CARDS:**

## DUBLIN, Co Dublin
Map 01 D4
see also Portmarnock

### ★★★★★79% *The Merrion Hotel*
Upper Merrion St
☎ 01 6030600 01 6030700
e-mail: info@merrionhotel.com
**Dir:** *situated at the top of Upper Merrion Street on the left hand side, beyond Government buildings which are on the right hand side*
The understated façade of four Grade I listed Georgian town houses belies the splendid interiors of this gracious city centre hotel. The garden suite bedrooms encircle the 18th-century style gardens. Luxurious surroundings, fine attention to detail, good cuisine and service, and friendly, efficient staff contribute to The Merrion's special ambience.
**ROOMS:** 145 en suite No smoking in 65 bedrooms **FACILITIES:** Spa STV Indoor swimming (H) Sauna Gym **CONF:** Thtr 60 Class 25 Board 25 **SERVICES:** Lift air con **PARKING:** 60 **NOTES:** No dogs (ex guide dogs) **CARDS:**

### ★★★★★66% *Radisson SAS St Helen's Hotel*
Stillorgan Rd, Blackrock
☎ 01 2186000 01 2186030
**Dir:** *from city centre take N11 due S, Hotel 4km on left hand side of dual carriageway*
A fine 18th-century mansion, with many period features, including a magnificent Italian marble fireplace in the lounge. The Orangerie is popular for drinks and there are two restaurants. Many bedrooms have views of the lovely terraced gardens and suites and penthouse suites are available, as well as rooms for disabled guests.
**ROOMS:** 151 en suite No smoking in 75 bedrooms **FACILITIES:** STV Snooker Gym Croquet lawn Beauty salon entertainment **CONF:** Thtr 350 Class 150 Board 70 Del from IEP185 * **SERVICES:** Lift air con **PARKING:** 230 **NOTES:** No dogs (ex guide dogs)
**CARDS:**

### ★★★★★64% Berkeley Court
Lansdowne Rd
☎ 01 6601711 01 6617238
e-mail: berkeley-court@jurysdoyle.com
**Dir:** *from N11 turn right at Donnybrook Church, 1st left brings you over bridge, turn right immediately then take 1st left, hotel is first on the left*
The Berkeley Court Hotel offers luxurious and comfortable public areas, all of which have been refurbished in recent months. Two restaurants, a particularly inviting lounge and bar and good facilities for both corporate and leisure guests are available.

*continued*

Ongoing refurbishment of the bedrooms includes the addition of air conditioning. Friendly staff are very helpful.
**ROOMS:** 188 en suite No smoking in 50 bedrooms s IEP230; d IEP260 * LB **FACILITIES:** STV Hair & Beauty salon entertainment Xmas **CONF:** Thtr 450 Class 210 Board 60 Del IEP190 * **SERVICES:** Lift **PARKING:** 120 **NOTES:** No dogs (ex guide dogs)
**CARDS:**

## *Premier Collection*

★★★★ ◎◎ ***The Clarence***
6-8 Wellington Quay
☎ 01 4070800 ▤ 01 4070820
e-mail: reservations@theclarence.ie
***Dir:*** *from O'Connell Bridge, drive westwards along quays, through the 1st set of traffic lights (at the Ha'penny Bridge) the hotel is 500mtrs further on*
The Clarence Hotel is situated in the heart of Dublin city centre within walking distance of many restaurants and theatres, galleries and museums, shopping areas and Temple Bar. The Clarence is the perfect location for business and pleasure. This is an individual and very tasteful hotel offering richly furnished bedrooms. For sheer luxury, the two-bedroom penthouse suite is outstanding. Public areas include a long gallery with luxurious sofas. The bar is smart and the restaurant serves fine cuisine.
**ROOMS:** 50 en suite **FACILITIES:** STV **CONF:** Thtr 50 Class 24 Board 30 **SERVICES:** Lift **NOTES:** No dogs (ex guide dogs)
**CARDS:**

★★★★75% ◎◎ ***The Herbert Park Hotel***
Ballsbridge
☎ 01 6672200 ▤ 01 6672595
e-mail: reservations@herbertparkhotel.ie
***Dir:*** *2m from city centre Dublin*
Contemporary style bedrooms have extras such as air-conditioning, mini-bars and safes. The marble tiled foyer leads to the Terrace Lounge, restaurant and bar. The Mezzanine lounge is for residents only and the Pavilion restaurant has views of the park. Executive suites and rooms, conference facilities and a fitness suite are also available.
**ROOMS:** 153 en suite (4 fmly) No smoking in 30 bedrooms **FACILITIES:** STV Gym Located off Herbert Park entertainment **CONF:** Thtr 100 Class 55 Board 50 **SERVICES:** Lift air con **PARKING:** 80 **NOTES:** No dogs (ex guide dogs)
**CARDS:**

Early start? Hotels at all star levels should provide in-room alarm clocks and/or alarm calls.

DUBLIN, continued

### ★★★★73% Jurys Hotel Dublin

JURYS DOYLE HOTELS

Pembroke Rd, Ballsbridge
☎ 01 6605000 🖷 01 6605540
e-mail: ballsbridge_hotel@jurysdoyle.com
***Dir:*** *from Dun Laoghaire, follow signs for city to Merrion Rd, Ballsbridge & Pembroke Rd, hotel is at intersection of Pembroke Rd and Northumberland Rd*

This establishment has two identities: Jurys Hotel and The Towers at Jurys. The first is large and popular, boasting several restaurants and bars, as well as good conference and leisure facilities. The Towers specialises in discreet luxury, with spacious bedrooms and private suites. The complex is the flagship of the Jurys chain.
**ROOMS:** 294 en suite (27 fmly) No smoking in 150 bedrooms s fr IEP135; d fr IEP135 * **LB** **FACILITIES:** STV Indoor swimming (H) Outdoor swimming (H) Sauna Gym Jacuzzi Hairdresser, Beauty Salon with Masseuse Xmas **CONF:** Thtr 850 Class 450 Board 100 **SERVICES:** Lift **PARKING:** 280 **NOTES:** No dogs (ex guide dogs) **CARDS:**

### ★★★★73% *Shelbourne Meridien Hotel*

St Stephen's Green
☎ 01 6634500 🖷 01 6616006
***Dir:*** *in city centre*

A Dublin landmark since 1824, with strong literary and historical links, this elegant Georgian hotel boasts gracious reception rooms, a choice of restaurants, a leisure centre and popular bars. Bedrooms are smart, well-appointed and comfortable.
**ROOMS:** 164 en suite (3 fmly) No smoking in 9 bedrooms **FACILITIES:** Indoor swimming (H) Sauna Gym Jacuzzi **CONF:** Thtr 400 Class 180 Board 60 **SERVICES:** Lift **PARKING:** 36 **CARDS:**

### ★★★★72% *The Fitzwilliam*

St Stephen's Green
☎ 01 4787000 🖷 01 4787878
e-mail: enq@fitzwilliamh.com
***Dir:*** *located in city centre on St Stephen's Green, adjacent to the top of Grafton Street*

Contemporary, elegant, Conran designed luxury hotel, overlooking St Stephen's Green. The hotel features a distinctive foyer lounge, bar and award-winning restaurant. Stylish bedrooms, with excellent bathrooms, are equipped with modern facilities and some have park views and balconies. Staff are friendly, professional and helpful.
**ROOMS:** 130 en suite No smoking in 31 bedrooms **FACILITIES:** STV **CONF:** Thtr 80 Class 50 Board 35 **SERVICES:** Lift **PARKING:** 85 **NOTES:** No dogs (ex guide dogs) **CARDS:**

### ★★★★70% Clarion Hotel I.F.S.C

I.F.S.C
☎ 01 4338800 🖷 01 4338801
e-mail: info@clarionhotelifsc.com

Excellent design and appointments give the edge to this impressive hotel where the themes of work, dining, and rest are brought to life with well-managed clarity of purpose, attentive staff, restful, air-conditioned bedrooms and an Asian-influenced restaurant. More casual dining is available in the bar.

### ★★★★69% *Gresham*

GRESHAM HOTELS

O'Connel St
☎ 01 8746881 🖷 01 8787175
e-mail: ryan@indigo.ie
***Dir:*** *on O'Connel St, just off M1 close to the GPO*

A commitment to traditional standards of hotel keeping is evident at the Gresham Hotel. Bedrooms are well-equipped and there is a foyer lounge serving snacks and afternoon teas. There is also the Aberdeen restaurant and 24-hour room service.
**ROOMS:** 288 en suite (4 fmly) No smoking in 26 bedrooms **FACILITIES:** STV Gym **CONF:** Thtr 350 Class 200 Board 100 **SERVICES:** Lift air con **PARKING:** 150 **NOTES:** No dogs (ex guide dogs) **CARDS:**

*See advert on page 845*

### ★★★★68% *Burlington*

Upper Leeson St
☎ 01 6605222 🖷 01 6603172

Close to the city, this comfortable hotel features well-appointed bedrooms, with some superior executive rooms available. Public areas include the smart Diplomat restaurant and a residents' bar, in addition to the popular Buck Mulligan's Dublin pub.
**ROOMS:** 526 en suite (6 fmly) No smoking in 95 bedrooms **FACILITIES:** STV Use of facilities at fitness club **CONF:** Thtr 1500 Class 650 Board 40 **SERVICES:** Lift **PARKING:** 400 **NOTES:** No dogs (ex guide dogs) **CARDS:**

### ★★★★66% *The Plaza Hotel*

Belgard Rd, Tallaght
☎ 01 4624200 🖷 01 4624600
e-mail: reservations@plazahotel.ie
***Dir:*** *6m from city centre, at S end of M50 motorway*

A Contemporary hotel beside the Tallaght complex, with spacious public areas, good corporate facilities, a secure car park and a choice of bars. The formal Mezzanine restaurant enjoys views of

*continued*

the distant mountains. Comfortable bedrooms are well-equipped and include modem points.

**ROOMS:** 122 en suite (2 fmly) No smoking in 61 bedrooms **FACILITIES:** STV entertainment **CONF:** Thtr 200 Class 150 Board 50 **SERVICES:** Lift air con **PARKING:** 520 **NOTES:** No dogs (ex guide dogs) Closed 24-29 Dec **CARDS:**

### ★★★★ 64% Clontarf Castle Hotel

Castle Av, Clontarf
☎ 01 8332321 01 8330418
e-mail: info@clontarfcastle.ie
***Dir:*** *M1 towards town centre, right at Whitehall Church, left at T-junct, straight on at lights, right onto Castle Ave, hotel entrance on right at rdbt*

Dating back to the 12th century, this castle has been refurbished, and many of the features of previous eras have been combined with contemporary styled bedrooms, all well-equipped and comfortable. Extensive banquet and conference facilities are available and a popular caberet runs from May to October. Modern cuisine is served in Templars Bistro.

**ROOMS:** 110 en suite (4 fmly) No smoking in 30 bedrooms **FACILITIES:** STV Gym **CONF:** Thtr 600 Class 250 Board 60 **SERVICES:** Lift **PARKING:** 130 **NOTES:** No dogs (ex guide dogs) Closed 24-25 Dec **CARDS:**

### ★★★★ 64% Red Cow Morans

Red Cow Complex, Naas Rd
☎ 01 4593650 01 4591588
e-mail: reservations@morangroup.ie
***Dir:*** *at junction of M50 & N7 Naas road on the city side of the motorway*

This smart hotel complex centres on the original Red Cow Inn, and its purpose-built extensions provide excellent conference facilities. Public areas are well-furnished and strikingly decorated. Bedrooms are spacious, smartly presented and well-equipped.

**ROOMS:** 123 en suite (5 fmly) No smoking in 44 bedrooms **FACILITIES:** STV entertainment **CONF:** Thtr 700 Class 520 Board 150 **SERVICES:** Lift air con **PARKING:** 700 **NOTES:** No dogs (ex guide dogs) **CARDS:**

### ★★★★ 60% Stillorgan Park

Stillorgan Rd
☎ 01 2881621 01 2831610
e-mail: sales@stillorganpark.com

Attractive decor and strong design are features of this recently rebuilt hotel. Comfortable public areas include a contemporary restaurant and inviting bar. A new air-conditioned banqueting and conference centre has all the latest communication technology. Bedrooms are well-equipped and the attentive staff are helpful.

**ROOMS:** 100 en suite (12 fmly) No smoking in 16 bedrooms **FACILITIES:** STV Special rates for residents at Westwood Leisure Centre entertainment **CONF:** Thtr 180 Class 110 Board 50 **SERVICES:** Lift air con **PARKING:** 350 **NOTES:** No dogs (ex guide dogs) **CARDS:**

### ★★★ 76% The Hibernian

Eastmoreland Place, Ballsbridge
☎ 01 6687666 01 6602655
e-mail: info@hibernianhotel.com
***Dir:*** *turn right from Mespil Rd into Baggot St Upper, then take 1st left into Eastmoreland Place/St Mary's Rd, the hotel is at the end on the left*

A previous winner of the AA Courtesy and Care Award, this hotel, an imposing building of magnificent architectural style, prides itself on the warmth of service it offers to guests. Real comfort and extra touches feature in the bedrooms. The Patrick Kavanagh Restaurant serves high quality food and there is also a conservatory, a library and a cocktail lounge.

**ROOMS:** 40 en suite No smoking in 13 bedrooms s IEP150-IEP190; d IEP150-IEP190 * **LB** **FACILITIES:** STV **CONF:** Thtr 20 Board 20 Del IEP160 * **SERVICES:** Lift **PARKING:** 18 **NOTES:** No dogs (ex guide dogs) Closed 24-27 Dec **CARDS:**

DUBLIN, continued

### ★★★70% Marine
Sutton Cross
☎ 01 8390000 01 8390442
e-mail: sales@marinehotel.ie
***Dir:*** *take rd from M1 towards Dublin City Centre, take second exit for Coolock, continue until T-junct and turn left, after 1m hotel on right*
On the north shore of Dublin Bay, this hotel is situated in attractive gardens. The restaurant specialises in seafood. Bedrooms are attractively decorated and well-equipped, and there is also a business centre. Public areas are comfortable and the hotel is only a 25 minute drive from Dublin airport.
**ROOMS:** 48 en suite (5 fmly) No smoking in 7 bedrooms s IEP110-IEP125; d IEP165-IEP180 (incl. bkfst) * **LB** **FACILITIES:** STV Indoor swimming (H) Sauna Steam Room **CONF:** Thtr 220 Class 140 Board 40 Del from IEP140 * **SERVICES:** Lift **PARKING:** 150 **NOTES:** No dogs (ex guide dogs) Closed 25-27 Dec **CARDS:**

### ★★★70% *The Schoolhouse Hotel*
2-8 Northumberland Rd
☎ 01 6675014 01 6675015
e-mail: school@schoolhousehotel.iol.ie
***Dir:*** *from N11 turn right at Lesson St Bridge, Avis on right. Through 2 sets of lights, pass Mespil Hotel, & turn left. Hotel 100yds on right*
A period red-brick building, dating from 1861, this hotel retains many original features. Satchels Restaurant and the Inkwell Bar continue the school theme. Bedrooms are inviting and feature custom-made oak furniture, which is very comfortable.
**ROOMS:** 31 en suite No smoking in 10 bedrooms **FACILITIES:** STV **CONF:** Class 15 Board 20 **SERVICES:** Lift air con **PARKING:** 21 **NOTES:** No dogs Closed 24-28 Dec **CARDS:**

### ★★★69% *Longfield's Hotel*
Fitzwilliam St
☎ 01 6761367 01 6761542
e-mail: info@longfields.ie
***Dir:*** *take Shelbourne Hotel exit from St Stephens Green, continue down Baggot St for 400m, turn left at Fitzwilliam St junct and Longfields is on the left*
This intimate town house hotel lies close to the city centre. Here, guests can enjoy good food and a relaxed atmosphere. An emphasis is placed on good service and hospitality.
**ROOMS:** 24 en suite **FACILITIES:** STV **SERVICES:** Lift **NOTES:** No dogs (ex guide dogs) RS 23-27 Dec **CARDS:**

*See advert on opposite page*

### ★★★69% Posthouse Dublin
Dublin Airport
☎ 01 8080500 01 8446002
e-mail: gm1767@forte-hotels.com
***Dir:*** *Hotel entrance is 1000yds from main road entrance to Dublin airport, on the right hand side*
A large, modern hotel with a wide range of services and amenities, designed particularly for the business traveller. Bedrooms are smart, comfortable and well-equipped.
**ROOMS:** 249 en suite (3 fmly) No smoking in 100 bedrooms s IEP149; d IEP149 * **FACILITIES:** STV Free swim gym use at ALSAA club other facilities at small suppl charge entertainment **CONF:** Thtr 130 Class 130 Board 50 Del from IEP135 * **PARKING:** 250 **NOTES:** No dogs (ex guide dogs) Closed 24-25 Dec RS 31 Dec **CARDS:**

### ★★★68% Clarion Stephen's Hall All-Suite Hotel
The Earlsfort Centre, Lower Leeson St
☎ 01 6381111 01 6381122
e-mail: stephens@premgroup.com
***Dir:*** *from N11 into Dublin, hotel is on left after Hatch St junction, before St Stephens Green*
Adjacent to St Stephen's Green, this hotel offers a wide range of accommodation including penthouses, town houses, suites and studios, all with comfortable lounges and fully fitted kitchens. Some rooms include PCs with ISDN connections. There are also office facilities, room service and an inviting bistro.
**ROOMS:** 31 en suite (9 fmly) s IEP110-IEP155; d IEP135-IEP190 * **LB** **FACILITIES:** STV **CONF:** Thtr 10 Class 15 Board 10 **SERVICES:** Lift **PARKING:** 40 **NOTES:** No dogs (ex guide dogs) RS 24 Dec-4 Jan **CARDS:**

*See advert on opposite page*

### ★★★68% *Jurys Green Isle*
Naas Rd
☎ 01 4593406 01 4592178
***Dir:*** *on N7, 10km SW of the city centre*
The Green Isle Hotel lies on the southern outskirts of Dublin. Bedrooms, both standard and executive, are generously proportioned and stylishly furnished. Public areas include the Tower Restaurant, a spacious lobby, and Rosie O'Gradys Bar.
**ROOMS:** 90 en suite **FACILITIES:** STV **CONF:** Thtr 300 Class 100 Board 100 **SERVICES:** Lift **PARKING:** 250 **NOTES:** No dogs (ex guide dogs) **CARDS:**

### ★★★68% *Jurys Montrose*
Stillorgan Rd
☎ 01 2693311 01 2691164
Close to the campus of University College, this hotel offers smartly decorated, comfortable bedrooms. The public areas include good lounge space, a carvery bar and a more formal restaurant. The hotel is situated in a quiet suburb, a short distance from the city centre.
**ROOMS:** 179 en suite (6 fmly) No smoking in 12 bedrooms **FACILITIES:** STV entertainment **CONF:** Thtr 80 Class 40 Board 40 **SERVICES:** Lift **PARKING:** 150 **NOTES:** No dogs (ex guide dogs) **CARDS:**

### ★★★68% Jurys Tara Hotel
Merrion Rd
☎ 01 2694666 01 2691027
e-mail: tara-hotel@jurysdoyle.com
***Dir:*** *After RTE Studios on N11 turn right, turn right at St Vincents hospital, after St Marys home the hotel is on the right.*
The well-equipped bedrooms of this hotel enjoy spectacular views of Dublin Bay and Howth Head. Attractively decorated public areas include a comfortable and relaxing foyer lounge, PJ Branagans Pub and a split-level conservatory restaurant.
**ROOMS:** 113 en suite (2 fmly) s IEP89-IEP109; d IEP89-IEP109 * **FACILITIES:** STV **CONF:** Thtr 300 Class 100 Board 40 Del from IEP145 * **SERVICES:** Lift **PARKING:** 140 **NOTES:** No dogs (ex guide dogs) **CARDS:**

### ★★★67% *Bewley's Hotel Ballsbridge*
Merrion Rd, Ballsbridge
☎ 01 6681111 01 6681999
e-mail: res@bewleyshotels.com
Very conveniently located beside the RDS Showgrounds, this friendly hotel offers comfortable and good value accommodation. The informal restaurant is relaxed and serves interesting dishes, and there is a patio for summer dining.
**ROOMS:** 220 en suite (25 fmly) No smoking in 140 bedrooms **FACILITIES:** STV **SERVICES:** Lift **PARKING:** 240 **NOTES:** No dogs Closed 24-26 Dec **CARDS:**

*See advert on opposite page*

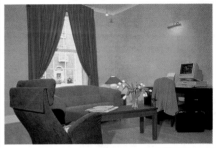

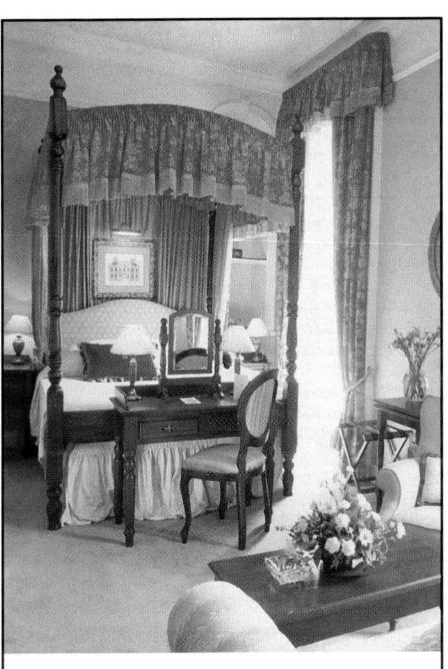

Longfield's Hotel, Dublin

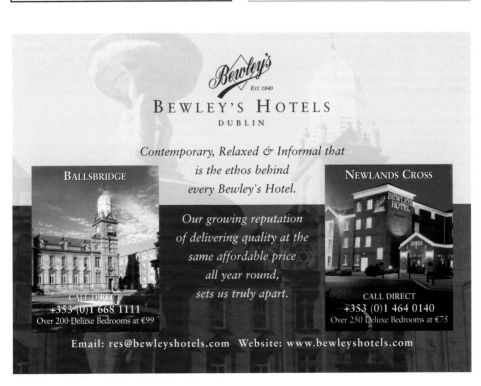

DUBLIN, continued

★★★67% ***Jurys Skylon***
Drumcondra Rd
☎ 01 8379121 📠 01 8372778
In a convenient location, with easy access to the city centre, this hotel offers very well-appointed bedrooms. There is a spacious lobby lounge and a comfortable bar. Good value dishes are served in the restaurant.
**ROOMS:** 92 en suite (10 fmly) **CONF:** Thtr 35 Class 20 Board 20 **SERVICES:** Lift **NOTES:** No dogs **CARDS:**

D

★★★66% ***Camden Court***
Camden St
☎ 01 4759666 📠 01 4759677
e-mail: sales@camdencourthotel.com
This hotel has a number of fine features in addition to its convenient location. These include spacious public areas, a leisure centre, well-equipped bedrooms, a summer beer garden and the bonus of a car park in the city centre. The restaurant opens for lunch and dinner.
**ROOMS:** 246 en suite (33 fmly) No smoking in 13 bedrooms **FACILITIES:** Indoor swimming (H) Sauna Solarium Gym Jacuzzi **CONF:** Thtr 40 Class 40 Board 20 **SERVICES:** Lift **PARKING:** 96 **NOTES:** No dogs Closed Xmas/New Year **CARDS:**

★★★65% ***Bewley's Hotel Newlands Cross***
Newlands Cross, Naas Rd
☎ 01 464 0140 📠 01 464 0900
e-mail: res@bewleyshotels.com
***Dir:*** *from M50 junct 9 take N7 Naas road, hotel is short distance from junct of N7 with Belgard Rd at Newlands Cross*
This hotel, on the outskirts of Dublin, has a bright and airy atmosphere. A spacious lobby and a residents' lounge are provided and there is a restaurant serving snacks during the day and more formal evening meals. Bedrooms are competitively priced and are furnished to a high standard.
**ROOMS:** 260 en suite (260 fmly) No smoking in 165 bedrooms **FACILITIES:** STV **CONF:** Board 20 **SERVICES:** Lift **PARKING:** 200 **NOTES:** No dogs (ex guide dogs) Closed 24-26 Dec
**CARDS:**

*See advert on page 865*

★★★65% ***Buswells***
23-27 Molesworth St
☎ 01 6146500 📠 01 6762090
e-mail: buswells@quinn-hotels.com
***Dir:*** *located on the corner of Molesworth St & Kildare St opposite Dail Eireann (Government Buildings)*
A popular rendezvous, Buswells is convenient for Dublin's main shopping and cultural attractions. Bedrooms are well-equipped and attractively decorated. The club-style bar is the focal point and there are two restaurants.
**ROOMS:** 69 en suite (17 fmly) No smoking in 6 bedrooms **FACILITIES:** Consession at nearby fitness club Complementary overnight parking **CONF:** Thtr 84 Class 30 Board 24 **SERVICES:** Lift **NOTES:** No dogs (ex guide dogs) Closed 25 & 26 Dec RS 24 Dec
**CARDS:**

★★★65% **Temple Bar**
Fleet St, Temple Bar
☎ 01 6773333 📠 01 6773088
e-mail: templeb@iol.ie
***Dir:*** *from Trinity College, head for O'Connell Bridge & take the 1st left onto Fleet St & the hotel is on the right hand side*
This stylish hotel lies in the heart of old Dublin and is ideally situated for experiencing the cultural life of the city. Comfortable, well-equipped bedrooms are competitively priced, and good food is served throughout the day.
**ROOMS:** 129 en suite (6 fmly) No smoking in 10 bedrooms **FACILITIES:** STV **CONF:** Thtr 80 Class 40 Board 40 **SERVICES:** Lift **NOTES:** No dogs (ex guide dogs) Closed 24 & 25 Dec
**CARDS:**

★★★63% ***Mount Herbert Hotel***
Herbert Rd, Lansdowne Rd
☎ 01 6684321 📠 01 6607077
e-mail: info@mountherberthotel.ie
***Dir:*** *close Lansdowne Road Rugby Stadium, 220mtrs from Dart Rail Station*
Located near to local places of interest, this hotel offers comfortable public rooms, well equipped bedrooms and a friendly atmosphere. There is a spacious lounge, a TV room, a cocktail bar and a lovely restaurant, overlooking the floodit gardens, which serves good value cuisine. There are also a children's playground and conference rooms.
**ROOMS:** 175 en suite 10 annexe en suite (15 fmly) **FACILITIES:** STV Sauna Solarium Childrens playground Badminton court **CONF:** Thtr 80 Class 60 Board 40 **SERVICES:** Lift **PARKING:** 90 **NOTES:** No dogs (ex guide dogs) **CARDS:**

★★★62% ***Abberley Court***
Belgard Rd, Tallaght
☎ 01 4596000 📠 01 4621000
e-mail: abberley@iol.ie
***Dir:*** *opposite The Square town centre at the junct of Belgard Rd and Tallaght by-pass (N81)*
Located beside an excellent complex of shops, restaurants and a cinema, this hotel is very smartly furnished. Public areas include a lounge bar that serves food all day and the first floor Court Restaurant. There are sports facilities available nearby.
**ROOMS:** 40 en suite (34 fmly) No smoking in 2 bedrooms **CONF:** Thtr 200 Class 70 Board 70 **SERVICES:** Lift **PARKING:** 450 **NOTES:** No dogs (ex guide dogs) Closed 25 Dec **CARDS:**

★★★62% ***The Mercer Hotel***
Mercer St Lower
☎ 01 4782179 📠 01 4780328
e-mail: stay@mercerhotel.ie
***Dir:*** *St Stephens Green at the shopping centre turn left down King St, then left at end of road, hotel on left*

A team of friendly staff create a pleasant atmosphere at this city centre hotel. Bedrooms are attractively decorated and well equipped, with fridges and CD players, as well as the usual amenities. Public areas include an inviting lounge with cocktail bar and a restaurant.
**ROOMS:** 21 en suite (1 fmly) No smoking in 4 bedrooms **FACILITIES:** STV **CONF:** Thtr 100 Class 80 Board 60 **SERVICES:** Lift air con **PARKING:** 21 **NOTES:** No dogs Civ Wed 60 **CARDS:**

### ★★★61% *Quality Charville Hotel & Suites*
Lower Rathmines Rd
☎ 01 4066100 📠 01 4066200
e-mail: info@charvillehotel.ie
***Dir:*** *From M50 turn left to town centre, continue 3m through Terenure, Lathgar and into Rathmines village, hotel on left side of village*
This modern style hotel is within walking distance of the town centre and offers comfortable and well-appointed, mainly suite, accommodation. There is a cocktail bar attached to the bistro style Carmines restaurant on the first floor. The TramCo theme bar is next door and serves snacks all day.
**ROOMS:** 51 en suite (2 fmly) No smoking in 9 bedrooms **FACILITIES:** STV **CONF:** Thtr 20 Class 12 Board 10 **SERVICES:** Lift **PARKING:** 35 **NOTES:** No dogs (ex guide dogs) Closed 24-27 Dec **CARDS:**

### ★★★59% Jurys Christchurch Inn
Christchurch Place
☎ 01 4540000 📠 01 4540012
e-mail: info@jurys.com
***Dir:*** *N7 onto Naas Rd, follow signs for city centre upto O'Connell St, continue past Trinity College turn right onto Dame St up to Lord Edward St, hotel is on left*
Centrally located opposite the 12th-century Cathedral, this hotel is close to the Temple Bar and all the city amenities. The foyer lounge and pub are popular meeting places and there is also an informal restaurant. The bedrooms are well-appointed and can accommodate families.
**ROOMS:** 182 en suite No smoking in 37 bedrooms s IEP71-IEP75; d IEP71-IEP75 * **SERVICES:** Lift **NOTES:** No dogs (ex guide dogs) Closed 24-26 Dec **CARDS:**

### ★★★59% *Jurys Custom House Inn*
Custom House Quay
☎ 01 6075000 📠 01 8290400
Overlooking the River Liffey, this hotel is situated less than ten minutes' walk away from the city's main shopping and tourist areas. Family rooms offer good value for money and facilities for business guests are excellent.
**ROOMS:** 239 en suite No smoking in 140 bedrooms **FACILITIES:** STV **CONF:** Thtr 90 Class 52 Board 40 **SERVICES:** Lift **NOTES:** No dogs (ex guide dogs) Closed 25-26 Dec **CARDS:**

### ★★★56% *The Parliament Hotel*
Lord Edward St
☎ 01 6708777 📠 01 6708787
e-mail: info@regencyhotels.com
***Dir:*** *adjacent to Dublin Castle in the Temple Bar area*
An attractive hotel, near to the Temple Bar area and Dublin Castle, offering a friendly welcome to all its guests. It provides well-furnished bedrooms, decorated in a modern style. There is also a popular bar and a separate restaurant.
**ROOMS:** 63 en suite (8 fmly) No smoking in 22 bedrooms **FACILITIES:** STV **CONF:** Thtr 20 Board 10 **SERVICES:** Lift **NOTES:** No dogs (ex guide dogs) No smoking in restaurant
**CARDS:**

### ★★64% *Harding*
Copper Alley, Fishamble St, Christchurch
☎ 01 6796500 📠 01 6796504
e-mail: harding.hotel@usitworld.com
***Dir:*** *located at the top of Dame St beside Christchurch cathedral, on the edge of Dublin's Temple Bar area*
At the heart of the fascinating Temple Bar area of Dublin, this purpose-built hotel has a friendly atmosphere and offers good-value accommodation. Its Peruvian-style bar and Fitzers Restaurant are popular meeting places. There are plenty of shops, bars and restaurants in the area.
**ROOMS:** 53 en suite (14 fmly) **FACILITIES:** STV entertainment **SERVICES:** Lift **NOTES:** No dogs (ex guide dogs) Closed 23-26 Dec **CARDS:**

### ⌂ *Travelodge*
Swords By Pass
☎ 01 8409233 📠 01 8409257
***Dir:*** *on N1 Dublin/Belfast road*
Travelodge offers good quality, good value, modern accommodation. Ideal for families, the spacious, en suite bedrooms include remote-control TV, tea and coffee-making facilities, luxury beds and free morning newspaper. Meals can be taken at the nearby family restaurant. For further details and the Travelodge phone number, consult the Hotel Groups page.

**ROOMS:** 40 en suite

### ⌂ *Travelodge Castleknock*
Auburn Av Roundabout, Navan Rd
☎ 01 8202626
Travelodge offers good quality, good value, modern accommodation. Ideal for families, the spacious, en suite bedrooms include remote-control TV, tea and coffee-making facilities, luxury beds and free morning newspaper. Meals can be taken at the nearby family restaurant. For further details and the Travelodge phone number, consult the Hotel Groups page.

## DUNDALK, Co Louth
Map 01 D4

### ★★★71% Ballymascanlon House
☎ 042 9371124 📠 042 9371598
e-mail: info@ballymascanlon.com
***Dir:*** *N of Dundalk take T62 to Carlingford. Hotel is approx 1km*
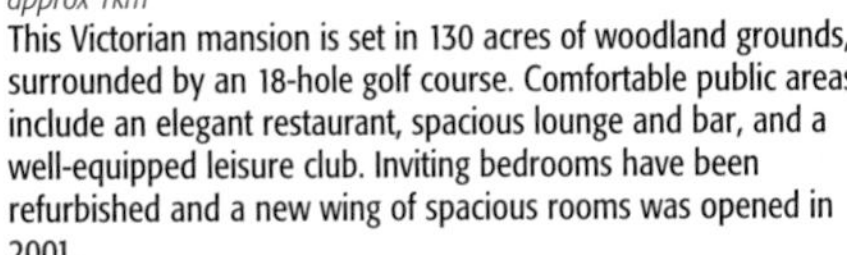
This Victorian mansion is set in 130 acres of woodland grounds, surrounded by an 18-hole golf course. Comfortable public areas include an elegant restaurant, spacious lounge and bar, and a well-equipped leisure club. Inviting bedrooms have been refurbished and a new wing of spacious rooms was opened in 2001.
**ROOMS:** 90 en suite (11 fmly) No smoking in 28 bedrooms s IEP74-IEP78; d IEP104-IEP110 (incl. bkfst) * **LB** **FACILITIES:** STV Indoor swimming (H) Golf 18 Tennis (hard) Sauna Gym Putting green Jacuzzi entertainment **CONF:** Thtr 300 Class 160 Board 75 Del IEP125 * **SERVICES:** Lift **PARKING:** 250 **NOTES:** No dogs (ex guide dogs) Closed 24-26 Dec **CARDS:**

### ★★★59% Fairways Hotel
Dublin Rd
☎ 042 9321500 📠 042 9321511
e-mail: info@fairways.ie
***Dir:*** *on N1 3km S of Dundalk*
Situated south of Dundalk, on the main Dublin/Belfast route, this modern family-run hotel offers well-decorated, comfortable bedrooms. A wide range of food is available all day and golf can be organised, by the hotel, on a choice of nearby local golf courses.
**ROOMS:** 102 en suite (2 fmly) No smoking in 20 bedrooms s IEP65-IEP70; d IEP95-IEP100 (incl. bkfst) * **LB** **FACILITIES:** STV Tennis (hard) entertainment **CONF:** Thtr 1000 Class 500 **PARKING:** 300 **NOTES:** No dogs (ex guide dogs) Closed 25 Dec **CARDS:**

DUNDALK, continued

**★★58% Imperial**
Park St
☎ 042 9332241 🖹 042 9337909
e-mail: info@imperialhoteldundalk.com
Bedrooms at this town centre hotel are being refurbished, and the upgraded rooms are worth requesting. Facilities include a restaurant, coffee shop and a bar, where there is music until midnight. Discos are held on Thursdays to Sundays in Club Tivoli.
**ROOMS:** 47 en suite (47 fmly) s IEP50-IEP65; d IEP70-IEP85 (incl. bkfst) * **LB** **FACILITIES:** STV **CONF:** Thtr 400 Class 125 Board 50 Del from IEP55 * **SERVICES:** Lift **PARKING:** 25 **NOTES:** Closed 25 Dec
**CARDS:**

DUNFANAGHY, Co Donegal Map 01 C6

**★★★65% *Arnold's***
☎ 074 36208 🖹 074 36352
e-mail: arnoldshotel@eircom.net
***Dir:*** *on N56 from Letterkenny hotel is on left entering the village*
On the coast, with miles of sandy beaches close at hand. Public areas offer comfortable seating, and facilities include two restaurants and two bars. There is a choice of bedrooms, from well-equipped standard rooms to larger ones with sofas.
**ROOMS:** 30 en suite (10 fmly) **FACILITIES:** STV Tennis (hard) Fishing Riding Croquet lawn Putting green entertainment **PARKING:** 60 **NOTES:** No dogs (ex guide dogs) Closed Nov-mid Mar RS wknds Nov-mid Mar **CARDS:**

DUNGANNON, Co Tyrone Map 01 C5

**⇧ *Cohannon Inn***
212 Ballynakilly Rd BT71 6HJ
☎ 028 8772 4488 🖹 028 8775 2217
e-mail: enquiries@cohannon-inn.com
***Dir:*** *400yds from junct 14 on M1*
The Cohannon Inn offers competitive prices and well-maintained accommodation. Rooms are located behind the Inn complex in a smart purpose-built wing. Public areas are smartly furnished and wide-ranging menus are served throughout the day.
**ROOMS:** 50 en suite **CONF:** Thtr 150 Class 150 Board 100

DUNGARVAN, Co Waterford Map 01 C2

**★★★58% Lawlors**
☎ 058 41122 & 41056 🖹 058 41000
e-mail: info@lawlors-hotel.ie
***Dir:*** *off N25*
An ideal base for touring the local area, this friendly family-run hotel caters for both business and leisure guests.
**ROOMS:** 89 en suite (8 fmly) **LB** **FACILITIES:** entertainment Xmas **CONF:** Thtr 420 Class 215 Board 420 **SERVICES:** Lift **NOTES:** Closed 25 Dec **CARDS:**

DUN LAOGHAIRE, Co Dublin Map 01 D4

**★★★68% Gresham Royal Marine**
Marine Rd
☎ 01 2801911 🖹 01 2801089
GRESHAM HOTELS
e-mail: royalmarine@eircom.net
***Dir:*** *follow signs for 'Car Ferry'*
Set in four acres, overlooking Dun Laoghaire harbour, the Victorian Royal Marine is a local landmark. The hotel has a range of contemporary facilities including a restaurant, bars, the popular Bay Lounge and attractive gardens. The hotel has easy access to the city centre.

*continued*

**ROOMS:** 103 en suite No smoking in 10 bedrooms s IEP150; d IEP180 (incl. bkfst) * **LB** **FACILITIES:** STV entertainment Xmas **CONF:** Thtr 450 Class 300 Del from IEP147 * **SERVICES:** Lift **PARKING:** 300 **NOTES:** No dogs (ex guide dogs) **CARDS:**

*See advert on page 845*

ENNIS, Co Clare Map 01 B3

**★★★★70% *Woodstock***
Shannaway Rd
☎ 065 684 6600 🖹 065 684 6611
e-mail: info@woodstockhotel.com
Set in mature woodland, this newly built luxurious hotel overlooks Woodstock Championship Golf Course. The impressive lobby has comfortable lounge areas and leads into the drawing room and library. Spikes Brasserie serves contemporary dishes and enjoys spectacular views. Spacious bedrooms offer comfort and individuality, and the Spa offers a full range of leisure facilities including jacuzzi and sauna.
**ROOMS:** 67 en suite No smoking in 47 bedrooms **FACILITIES:** **Spa** STV Indoor swimming (H) Golf 18 Sauna Solarium Gym Jacuzzi steam room entertainment ch fac **CONF:** Thtr 200 Class 160 Board 50 Del IEP120 * **SERVICES:** Lift air con **NOTES:** No dogs (ex guide dogs) Closed 25-26 Dec **CARDS:**

**★★★65% *Temple Gate***
The Square
☎ 065 6823300 🖹 065 6823322
e-mail: templegh@iol.ie
***Dir:*** *from Ennis follow signs for Temple Gate*
A smart hotel in the centre of Ennis. Incorporating a 19th-century gothic style building, public areas are carefully planned and include a comfortable lounge library, Preachers Pub and Le Bistro Restaurant. Bedrooms are well-equipped and attractively decorated.
**ROOMS:** 73 en suite (3 fmly) No smoking in 11 bedrooms **FACILITIES:** STV entertainment **CONF:** Thtr 90 Class 50 Board 35 **SERVICES:** Lift **PARKING:** 52 **NOTES:** No dogs (ex guide dogs) Closed 25 Dec **CARDS:**

**★★65% *Magowna House***
Inch, Kilmaley
☎ 065 6839009 🖹 065 6839258
e-mail: Magowna@iol.ie
***Dir:*** *on R474 off N18 pass golf course, and after approx 5km, hotel is signposted off to right, 300mtrs from junction*
This small family-run hotel, stands in 14 acres of grounds just off the R474 road to Ennis Golf Club and Kilmaley at Inch. The hotel provides a good standard of comfort and enjoyable meals. Good local fishing, boats for hire and a golf practice area are among the activities in the neighbourhood.
**ROOMS:** 10 en suite (3 fmly) No smoking in 4 bedrooms **FACILITIES:** 3 Boats for hire **CONF:** Thtr 350 Class 200 Board 20 **PARKING:** 60 **NOTES:** Closed 24-26 Dec **CARDS:**

## ENNISCORTHY, Co Wexford

Map 01 D3

### ★★★69% *Riverside Park Hotel*

The Promenade
☎ 054 37800 📠 054 37900
***Dir:*** *0.5km from New Bridge, centre of Enniscorthy town, N11 Dublin/Rosslare Road*

Situated in a picturesque position beside the River Slaney, this hotel is easily distinguished by its terracotta and blue colour scheme. The foyer is equally dramatic and the public areas all take full advantage of the riverside views, including the Mill House pub. The spacious, attractively decorated bedrooms have every modern comfort.

**ROOMS:** 60 en suite (50 fmly) No smoking in 6 bedrooms
**FACILITIES:** STV entertainment **CONF:** Thtr 800 Class 500 Board 100
**SERVICES:** Lift **NOTES:** No dogs (ex guide dogs)
**CARDS:**

### ★60% *Murphy-Flood's*

Market Square
☎ 054 33413 📠 054 33413
***Dir:*** *follow signs to hotel in the town centre*

A family-run hotel in the centre of a lively market town, Murphy-Flood's has a comfortable bar where carvery lunches, grills and snacks are served throughout the day. Accommodation is pleasing and comfortable.

**ROOMS:** 21 rms (18 en suite) (2 fmly) No smoking in 2 bedrooms
**FACILITIES:** entertainment **CONF:** Thtr 200 Class 100 Board 60
**NOTES:** No dogs (ex guide dogs) Closed 25 Dec
**CARDS:**

## ENNISKILLEN, Co Fermanagh

Map 01 C5

### ★★★★68% Killyhevlin

BT74 6RW
☎ 028 6632 3481 📠 028 6632 4726
e-mail: info@killyhevlin.com
***Dir:*** *2m S, off A4*

A modern, stylish hotel in a delightful location on the shores of Lough Erne, just south of the town. Bedrooms are particularly spacious, well-equipped, and many enjoy panoramic views. An open-plan restaurant and informal bar complement the comfortable lounges. Staff throughout are friendly and nothing is too much trouble.

**ROOMS:** 43 en suite (32 fmly) s £63-£73; d £85-£105 (incl. bkfst) * **LB**
**FACILITIES:** STV Fishing entertainment Xmas **CONF:** Thtr 600 Class 160 Board 140 Del from £87.50 * **PARKING:** 500 **NOTES:** No dogs (ex guide dogs) Closed 25 Dec **CARDS:**

## FERMOY, Co Cork

Map 01 B2

### ★★★69% *Castlehyde Hotel*

Castlehyde
☎ 025 31865 📠 025 31485
e-mail: cashyde@iol.ie
***Dir:*** *turn off N8 just outside Fermoy onto N72 Fermoy-Mallow. Hotel in 2m*

Carefully restored 18th-century courtyard buildings, where old meets new sympathetically and comfortably. Individually styled bedrooms are attractively decorated and include five cottage suites. The welcoming lobby lounge features an open fire and there is a stylish restaurant overlooking the gardens and woodland.

**ROOMS:** 24 en suite (5 fmly) No smoking in 10 bedrooms
**FACILITIES:** STV Outdoor swimming (H) entertainment **CONF:** Thtr 30 Class 18 Board 14 **PARKING:** 35 **NOTES:** No dogs (ex guide dogs) No smoking in restaurant RS Feb **CARDS:**

## GALWAY, Co Galway

Map 01 B3

*Premier Collection*

### ★★★★ Glenlo Abbey

Bushypark
☎ 091 526666 📠 091 527800
e-mail: glenlo@iol.ie
***Dir:*** *4km from Galway City Centre on the N59*

Glenlo Abbey is a glorious building, which is over 260 years old. This restored abbey stands in a landscaped 134-acre estate, which overlooks a beautiful loch. The original building houses a boardroom, business centre, conference and banqueting facilities. The bedrooms are in a modern wing and the hotel boasts superb views. Glenlo Abbey offers guests the use of a library, the restaurants, a cocktail bar and a cellar bar.

**ROOMS:** 46 en suite No smoking in 10 bedrooms **FACILITIES:** STV Golf 18 Fishing Putting green Boating Clay pigeon shooting entertainment ch fac **CONF:** Thtr 220 Class 100 Board 50 Del IEP170 * **SERVICES:** Lift **PARKING:** 150 **NOTES:** No dogs (ex guide dogs) No smoking in restaurant **CARDS:**

### ★★★★71% Radisson SAS Hotel

Lough Atalia Rd
☎ 091 539300 📠 091 539380
e-mail: Info.Galway@RadissonSAS.com
***Dir:*** *take N6 into Galway City. At "Hunstman Inn" roundabout turn 1st left. At next trafiic lights take left side of fork. Continue for 0.5m, hotel at next right hand junction.*

A prime position on the waterfront at Lough Atalia, striking interior design and excellent levels of comfort and quality are the keynotes of this new hotel. Bedrooms are well-equipped, there are spacious lounges, a bar, and a restaurant which features local seafood specialities, and the corporate and leisure facilities are very good.

**ROOMS:** 202 en suite (10 fmly) No smoking in 132 bedrooms s IEP115-IEP305; d IEP150-IEP305 * **FACILITIES:** STV Indoor swimming (H) Sauna Gym Jacuzzi Xmas **CONF:** Thtr 660 Class 480 Board 12 Del from IEP142 * **SERVICES:** Lift air con **PARKING:** 260 **NOTES:** No dogs (ex guide dogs) **CARDS:**

### ★★★★68% Ardilaun Conference & Leisure Centre

Taylor's Hill
☎ 091 521433 📠 091 521546
e-mail: ardilaun@iol.ie
***Dir:*** *take 4th left after 4th rdbt leading from main Dublin road*

Formerly a country mansion this hotel has comfortable lounges and the dining room overlooks beautiful gardens. Bedrooms are

*continued on p870*

GALWAY, continued

spacious, well-furnished and individually decorated. Guests can enjoy extensive leisure facilities.
**ROOMS:** 90 en suite (16 fmly) No smoking in 6 bedrooms s IEP85-IEP95; d IEP120-IEP150 (incl. bkfst) * **LB** **FACILITIES:** STV Indoor swimming (H) Snooker Sauna Solarium Gym Jacuzzi Treatment & Analysis Rooms Xmas **CONF:** Thtr 450 Class 200 Board 40 **SERVICES:** Lift **PARKING:** 220 **NOTES:** No smoking in restaurant Closed 23-28 Dec **CARDS:**

### ★★★★65% *Galway Bay Hotel Conference & Leisure Centre*

The Promenade, Salthill
☎ 091 520520 091 520530
e-mail: info@galwaybayhotel.net
***Dir:*** *on the promenade in Salthill on the coast road to Connemara. Follow signs to Salthill from all major routes*

Commanding lovely views from its seafront setting, the Galway Bay is a plush and peaceful hotel. The conservatory lounge and patio are the perfect setting in which to relax and enjoy the scenery. Dining options include the Lobster Pot restaurant, the Cafe Lido or a traditional Irish pub. Bedrooms are attractive and comfortable.
**ROOMS:** 153 en suite (10 fmly) No smoking in 24 bedrooms **FACILITIES:** STV Indoor swimming (H) Sauna Gym Steam room entertainment **CONF:** Thtr 1100 Class 325 **SERVICES:** Lift **PARKING:** 300 **NOTES:** No dogs (ex guide dogs)
**CARDS:**

*See advert on opposite page*

### ★★★★65% Westwood House Hotel

Dangan, Upper Newcastle
☎ 091 521442 091 521400
e-mail: westwoodreservations@eircom.net
***Dir:*** *from N6 enter Galway, continue on N6 following signs for Clifden (N59) once on Clifden Rd the Westwood House Hotel is on left*
Close to the university on the edge of the city, this hotel is luxuriously appointed. The public rooms include a themed bar, a restaurant and lounges. Bedrooms are comfortable and well-equipped.
**ROOMS:** 58 en suite (44 fmly) No smoking in 17 bedrooms s IEP50-IEP99; d IEP70-IEP149 (incl. bkfst) * **LB** **FACILITIES:** STV Kingfisher Health and Leisure club Xmas **CONF:** Thtr 350 Class 200 Board 70 Del from IEP89.95 * **SERVICES:** Lift air con **PARKING:** 130 **NOTES:** No dogs (ex guide dogs) Closed 24-25 Dec Civ Wed 275
**CARDS:**

> € The Euro will be phased in during 2002 (R.O.I. only). Make sure you check prices and currency when booking.

### ★★★★60% *Park House Hotel & Eyre House Restaurants*

Forster St, Eyre Square
☎ 091 564924 091 569219
e-mail: parkhousehotel@eircom.net
***Dir:*** *in view of Eyre Square, city centre, Galway*
Easily accessible, this hotel offers bedrooms, all well-decorated and furnished, which vary in size. Public rooms include comfortable lounges, a spacious dining room and a carvery bar.
**ROOMS:** 57 en suite **FACILITIES:** STV entertainment **CONF:** Thtr 50 Class 30 Board 30 **SERVICES:** Lift **PARKING:** 26 **NOTES:** No dogs (ex guide dogs) Closed 24-26 Dec **CARDS:**

### ★★★65% *Galway Ryan*

Dublin Rd
☎ 091 753181 091 753187
e-mail: ryan@indigo.ie
***Dir:*** *follow signs to Galway City West off N7*

A modern hotel with comfortable, well equipped accommodation boasting extensive leisure facilities.
**ROOMS:** 96 en suite (96 fmly) No smoking in 6 bedrooms **FACILITIES:** STV Indoor swimming (H) Tennis (hard) Sauna Gym Sports hall Steam rooms entertainment **CONF:** Thtr 80 Class 110 Board 30 **SERVICES:** Lift **PARKING:** 100 **NOTES:** No dogs Closed 25 Dec
**CARDS:**

*See advert on page 845*

### ★★★64% Galway Harbour Hotel

The Harbour
☎ 091 569466 091 569455
e-mail: info@galwayharbourhotel.com
***Dir:*** *Follow signs for Galway City East, at rdbt take 1st exit to Galway City, follow signs to docks, hotel approx 1m from rdbt on left*
This hotel is part of the newly developed Galway Harbour, in the heart of the city. Contemporary in style, it has a large lobby lounge with open fires. Bedrooms are smart, comfortable and very well-equipped. There is a café bar and restaurant, and secure parking is a bonus.
**ROOMS:** 90 en suite No smoking in 34 bedrooms s IEP59-IEP120; d IEP59-IEP120 * **FACILITIES:** STV **CONF:** Thtr 90 Class 50 Board 16 **SERVICES:** Lift **PARKING:** 64 **NOTES:** No dogs (ex guide dogs)
**CARDS:**

### ★★★63% *Menlo Park Hotel*

Terryland
☎ 091 761122 091 761222
e-mail: menlopkh@iol.ie
***Dir:*** *located at Terryland rdbt off N6 and N84 (Castlebar Rd)*
Major routes are within easy reach, and the town's commercial area is close by. Bedrooms are comfortable and offer a choice of standard and executive rooms, the latter having sofas and fax

*continued*

machines. There is a contemporary restaurant and bar and a residents' lounge.
**ROOMS:** 44 en suite (6 fmly) No smoking in 10 bedrooms
**FACILITIES:** STV **CONF:** Thtr 200 Class 100 Board 40 **SERVICES:** Lift air con **PARKING:** 100 **NOTES:** No dogs (ex guide dogs) Closed 24-25 Dec **CARDS:**

### ★★★60% Lochlurgain

22 Monksfield, Upper Salthill
☎ 091 529595 Fax 091 522399
e-mail: lochlurgain@eircom.net
***Dir:*** *off R336 behind Bank of Ireland beside RC church*
This small family-run hotel stands in a quiet street, at Salthill, beside the Roman Catholic church. Service is of a very good standard and the bedrooms are comfortable, extras include electric blankets in season. Public rooms are attractively decorated.
**ROOMS:** 13 en suite (3 fmly) s IEP39-IEP65; d IEP65-IEP125 (incl. bkfst) * **LB** **FACILITIES:** STV **PARKING:** 8 **NOTES:** No dogs (ex guide dogs) No smoking in restaurant Closed 26 Oct-13 Mar **CARDS:**

### ★★★59% *Jurys Galway Inn*

JURYS DOYLE HOTELS

Quay St
☎ 091 566444 Fax 091 568415
e-mail: enquiry@jurys.com
***Dir:*** *N6 follow signs for Docks. On arrival at Docks take Salthill Rd for 2-3 minutes*
This modern hotel stands at the heart of the city opposite the famous Spanish Arch. The hotel has an attractive patio and a garden bounded by the river. The 'one price' room rate and comfortable bedrooms ensure its popularity and this is an ideal base to tour the area.
**ROOMS:** 128 en suite (6 fmly) No smoking in 39 bedrooms
**FACILITIES:** STV entertainment **CONF:** Thtr 40 Class 40 Board 40
**SERVICES:** Lift **NOTES:** No dogs (ex guide dogs) Closed 24-26 Dec
**CARDS:**

### ★★★58% *Victoria*

Victoria Place, Eyre Square
☎ 091 567433 Fax 091 565880
e-mail: bookings@victoriahotel.ie
***Dir:*** *off Eyre Sq on Victoria Place, Beside the rail station*
This city-centre hotel lies off Eyre Square. Bedrooms are well-equipped and other facilities include 24-hour room service, a good bar and a pleasant restaurant. The atmosphere is relaxing and staff are friendly and attentive.
**ROOMS:** 57 en suite (20 fmly) No smoking in 1 bedroom
**FACILITIES:** STV **CONF:** Thtr 50 Class 30 Board 25 **SERVICES:** Lift
**NOTES:** No dogs (ex guide dogs) Closed 25 Dec
**CARDS:**

## GARRYVOE, Co Cork — Map 01 C2

### ★★67% Garryvoe

☎ 021 4646718 Fax 021 4646824
e-mail: garryvoehotel@eircom.net
***Dir:*** *turn off N25 onto L72 at Castlemartyr between Midleton and Youghal and continue for 6km*
A comfortable, family-run hotel with caring staff, the Garryvoe has been upgraded. It stands in a delightful position facing a sandy beach and the first floor lounge overlooks the sea. There is a hotel bar and also a public bar.
**ROOMS:** 19 en suite (2 fmly) s IEP55-IEP60; d IEP70-IEP80 (incl. bkfst) * **LB** **FACILITIES:** Tennis (hard) Putting green ch fac **CONF:** Thtr 400 Class 250 Del from IEP80 * **PARKING:** 25 **NOTES:** No dogs (ex guide dogs) Closed 25 Dec **CARDS:**



## GLENDALOUGH, Co Wicklow — Map 01 D3

### ★★★58% *The Glendalough*

☎ 0404 45135 Fax 0404 45142
Forest and mountains provide the setting for this long-established hotel, beside the famous monastic site. The hotel has been refurbished and additional bedrooms, many with lovely views, are now available. Bar food is available and the charming restaurant overlooks the river and forest. The whole area is ideal for walking, golf and trout fishing.
**ROOMS:** 44 en suite (3 fmly) **FACILITIES:** STV Fishing entertainment
**CONF:** Thtr 200 Class 150 Board 50 **SERVICES:** Lift **PARKING:** 100
**NOTES:** No dogs (ex guide dogs) Closed 1 Dec-Jan
**CARDS:**

## GOREY, Co Wexford — Map 01 D3

**Premier Collection**

### ★★★ *Marlfield House*

RELAIS & CHATEAUX

☎ 055 21124 Fax 055 21572
e-mail: info@marlfieldhouse.ie
***Dir:*** *1.5km outside Gorey on the Courtown Harbour road*
This distinctive Regency house was once the residence of the Earl of Courtown. The current hotel retains an atmosphere of elegance and luxury throughout. Public areas include a library, drawing room and dining room leading into a conservatory which overlooks the grounds and a wildlife reserve. Bedrooms are in keeping with the style of the

*continued on p872*

GOREY, continued

downstairs rooms and there are some superb suites. Druids Glen and several other golf courses are nearby.

*Marlfield House, Gorey*

**ROOMS:** 19 en suite (3 fmly) **FACILITIES:** STV Tennis (hard) Sauna Croquet lawn **CONF:** Thtr 60 Board 20 **PARKING:** 50 **NOTES:** No smoking in restaurant Closed 15 Dec-30 Jan **CARDS:**

○ ***Ashdown Park Hotel***
The Coach Rd
☎ 055 80500 📠 055 80777
e-mail: info@ashdownparkhotel.com
At the time of going to press, the star classification for this hotel was not confirmed. Please refer to the AA internet site www.theAA.com for current information.
**ROOMS:** 60 en suite **NOTES:** Due to open September 2001

GOUGANE BARRA, Co Cork — Map 01 B2

★★64% ***Gougane Barra***
☎ 026 47069 📠 026 47226
e-mail: gouganbarrahotel@tinet.ie
***Dir:*** *off N22*
Right on the shore of the lake, the Gougane Barra Hotel is very popular. Refurbishments have improved the restaurant, bedrooms and bathrooms, all of which have lovely views. Guests can be met from their train, boat or plane by prior arrangement.
**ROOMS:** 27 en suite **FACILITIES:** STV Fishing **PARKING:** 25 **NOTES:** No dogs (ex guide dogs) No smoking in restaurant Closed 13 Oct-13 Apr **CARDS:**

HILLSBOROUGH, Co Down — Map 01 D5

★★★66% ***White Gables***
14 Dromore Rd BT26 6HS
☎ 028 9268 2755 📠 028 9268 9532
***Dir:*** *join M2 (Belfast) then M1 west, join A1 at junct 7 to Dublin. Take Hillsborough turn, go through village, hotel is on right hand side*
A comfortable, modern hotel appealing to business guests. Bedrooms range in size and style but all rooms are comfortable and well-equipped. Smart public areas include a bright, marble floored foyer lounge, attractive split-level restaurant and a popular all-day coffee shop.
**ROOMS:** 31 en suite No smoking in 8 bedrooms **FACILITIES:** STV **CONF:** Thtr 120 Class 40 Board 25 **PARKING:** 120 **NOTES:** No dogs (ex guide dogs) Closed 24-25 Dec RS Sun ( residents only before 7pm) **CARDS:**

INISHANNON, Co Cork — Map 01 B2

★★★66% **Inishannon House**
MANOR HOUSE
☎ 021 4775121 📠 021 4775609
***Dir:*** *off N71 at eastern end of village*
A charming hotel, the River Bandon flows by this eye-catching country house, complemented by attractive walks and gardens. Good food is prepared from the freshest ingredients, with seafood dishes a speciality.
**ROOMS:** 12 en suite 1 annexe en suite (4 fmly) s IEP85-IEP120; d IEP140-IEP185 (incl. bkfst) * **LB** **FACILITIES:** STV Fishing Xmas **CONF:** Thtr 200 Class 80 Board 50 Del from IEP115 * **PARKING:** 150 **CARDS:**

IRVINESTOWN, Co Fermanagh — Map 01 C5

★★66% ***Mahons***
Mill St BT74 1GS
☎ 028 6862 1656 📠 028 6862 8344
e-mail: mahonshotel@lakeland.net
***Dir:*** *on A32 midway between Enniskillen and Omagh - beside town clock in centre of Irvinestown*
A family-run hotel which has offered warm hospitality for over 100 years. Public areas, especially the bar, are filled with a collection of curiosities. In the restaurant, the extensive carte offers a wide range of dishes. The prettily decorated bedrooms come in a variety of sizes.
**ROOMS:** 18 en suite (4 fmly) **FACILITIES:** STV Tennis (hard) Riding Solarium entertainment **CONF:** Thtr 450 Class 200 **PARKING:** 40 **NOTES:** Closed 25 Dec **CARDS:**

KENMARE, Co Kerry — Map 01 B2

## *Premier Collection*

★★★★ **Park Hotel Kenmare**
☎ 064 41200 📠 064 41402
e-mail: info@parkkenmare.com
***Dir:*** *on R569 beside golf course*
The Park is a luxurious country house hotel on the famous Ring of Kerry. This limestone building, which is over 100 years old, stands above terraced gardens, that overlook the estuary of the Kenmare River, and borders the town of Kenmare. The backdrop to this hotel is Ireland's highest mountain range, and many walks can be taken here. Warm hospitality and professional excellence are provided. There are spacious suites and the restaurant offers very good food and fine wines.
**ROOMS:** 49 en suite (2 fmly) No smoking in 5 bedrooms s IEP149-IEP168; d IEP264-IEP378 (incl. bkfst) * **LB** **FACILITIES:** STV Golf 18 Tennis (hard) Snooker Gym Croquet lawn Putting green entertainment Xmas **CONF:** Thtr 60 Class 40 Board 28 **SERVICES:** Lift **PARKING:** 60 **NOTES:** No dogs (ex guide dogs) No smoking in restaurant Closed 3 Jan-13 Apr & 29 Oct-23 Dec Civ Wed 120 **CARDS:**

## Premier Collection

**★★★★ Sheen Falls Lodge**

☎ 064 41600 📠 064 41386

e-mail: info@sheenfallslodge.ie

RELAIS & CHATEAUX.

***Dir:*** *from Kenmare take N71 to Glengarriff over the suspension bridge, take the first turn left*

This beautiful hotel, once a former fishing lodge, stands beside the Sheen River, and is surrounded by a lovely salt water bay and the mountains in the distance. The cascading Sheen Falls are floodlit at night, creating a magical atmosphere, which can be enjoyed from the restaurant. A luxurious lounge, library, billiards room and cocktail bar complete the public rooms and there are three grades of comfortable bedrooms. The town is just a five minute drive away.

**ROOMS:** 61 en suite (14 fmly) No smoking in 10 bedrooms **FACILITIES:** STV Indoor swimming (H) Tennis (hard) Fishing Riding Snooker Sauna Solarium Gym Croquet lawn Jacuzzi Table tennis Steam room,clay pigeon shooting,cycling,vintage car rides, entertainment ch fac **CONF:** Thtr 120 Class 65 Board 50 **SERVICES:** Lift **PARKING:** 76 **NOTES:** No dogs (ex guide dogs) Closed 2 Jan-2 Feb RS Closed Mon Tue Wed in Dec **CARDS:**

**★★★68% Dromquinna Manor**

Blackwater Bridge

☎ 064 41657 📠 064 41791

e-mail: info@dromquinna.com

***Dir:*** *take road to Kenmare, take the N70 towards Sneem (ring of Kerry Rd). Hotel 3m down on the left*

A lovely hotel, standing on the Ring of Kerry, in 42 acres of grounds on the banks of the river Kenmare. Public areas include a Great Hall, pleasant sitting rooms, and a welcoming bar. Bedrooms vary in size and there is a unique and much sought-after treehouse suite. On the riverside are the bistro, play areas for children and a marina with facilities for sailing, fishing and watersports.

**ROOMS:** 28 en suite 18 annexe en suite (6 fmly) s IEP55-IEP110; d IEP110-IEP180 (incl. bkfst) * **LB FACILITIES:** Tennis (hard) Fishing Riding Croquet lawn Table tennis **PARKING:** 80 **NOTES:** No dogs (ex guide dogs) Closed Nov-Feb **CARDS:**

*See advert on this page*

KENMARE, continued

★★★65% ***Riversdale House***
☎ 064 41299 🖹 064 41075
This hotel has wonderful views and nestles on the shores of Kenmare Bay, close to the town centre. In the bedrooms, floor-length window alcoves take advantage of the clarity of light for which Kenmare is famous, and on the top floor are four recommended mini-suites with balconies.
**ROOMS:** 64 en suite **FACILITIES:** STV entertainment **CONF:** Thtr 300 Class 250 Board 50 **SERVICES:** Lift **PARKING:** 200 **NOTES:** Closed Nov-Mar **CARDS:**

KILDARE, Co Kildare Map 01 C3

★★63% ***Curragh Lodge***
Dublin Rd
☎ 045 522144 521136 🖹 045 521274
e-mail: clhotel@iol.ie
***Dir:*** *travelling from Dublin City Centre, follow signs for S or N7 motorway. Hotel 28m from City Centre, on left when entering Kildare town*
Curragh Lodge is located in Kildare town and within walking distance of the Irish National Stud and Japanese Gardens. There is a cosy lounge and a modern open-plan bar and restaurant. Bedrooms are comfortable and well-equipped.
**ROOMS:** 21 en suite (3 fmly) No smoking in 4 bedrooms
**FACILITIES:** STV entertainment **PARKING:** 30
**CARDS:**

KILKEE, Co Clare Map 01 B3

★★64% **Halpin's**
Erin St
☎ 065 9056032 🖹 065 9056317
e-mail: halpins@iol.ie
***Dir:*** *Centre of Kilkee town.*

Halpin's Hotel

The finest tradition of hotel service is offered at this family-run hotel which has a commanding view over the old Victorian town. The attractive bedrooms are comfortable.
**ROOMS:** 12 en suite (6 fmly) No smoking in 4 bedrooms s IEP45-IEP60; d IEP70-IEP90 (incl. bkfst) * **LB** **FACILITIES:** STV Tennis (hard) **CONF:** Thtr 60 Class 36 Board 30 Del from IEP50 * **SERVICES:** air con **NOTES:** No dogs 15 Mar-15 Nov **CARDS:**

KILKENNY, Co Kilkenny Map 01 C3

★★★★65% ***Kilkenny Ormonde***
Ormonde St
☎ 056 23900 🖹 056 23977
e-mail: info@kilkennyormonde.com
***Dir:*** *located in Kilkenny Town Centre off Patricks St. Hotel opposite multi-story car park*
This new contemporary styled hotel has a large lounge and reception area, a bar and a choice of two restaurants. Comfortable bedrooms are attractive, and facilities include data ports. There are conference and banqueting facilities, and a leisure club.
**ROOMS:** 118 en suite (6 fmly) No smoking in 70 bedrooms
**FACILITIES:** STV Indoor swimming (H) Sauna Solarium Gym Jacuzzi entertainment ch fac **CONF:** Thtr 420 Class 200 Board 36
**SERVICES:** Lift air con **NOTES:** No dogs (ex guide dogs)
**CARDS:**

★★★★65% ***Kilkenny River Court Hotel***
The Bridge, John St
☎ 056 23388 🖹 056 23389
e-mail: krch@iol.ie
***Dir:*** *at the bridge in the town centre, just opposite Kilkenny Castle*
Once into the private courtyard, the superb location is a revelation. The Riverside restaurant and bar enjoy lovely views, with Kilkenny Castle in the background and attentive staff ensure good service. Friendliness, good corporate and leisure facilities and comfortable bedrooms all contribute to the experience of staying here.
**ROOMS:** 90 en suite (4 fmly) No smoking in 20 bedrooms
**FACILITIES:** STV Indoor swimming (H) Sauna Gym Jacuzzi **CONF:** Thtr 240 Class 180 Board 4 **SERVICES:** Lift **PARKING:** 84 **NOTES:** No dogs (ex guide dogs) **CARDS:**

★★★71% **Newpark**
☎ 056 22122 🖹 056 61111
e-mail: info@newparkhotel.com
A friendly hotel with an impressive foyer lounge, a bar/bistro and conference suites. A purpose-built bedroom wing offers a choice of rooms, decorated and equipped to a high standard.
**ROOMS:** 111 en suite (42 fmly) No smoking in 8 bedrooms s IEP79-IEP99; d IEP106-IEP126 * **LB** **FACILITIES:** STV Indoor swimming (H) Sauna Solarium Gym Jacuzzi Plunge pool Xmas **CONF:** Thtr 600 Class 300 Board 50 Del from IEP99 * **PARKING:** 350 **NOTES:** No dogs (ex guide dogs) No smoking in restaurant **CARDS:**

★★★64% ***Langton House***
69 John St
☎ 056 65133 🖹 056 63693
***Dir:*** *take N9 & N10 from Dublin follow signs for city centre at outskirts of Kilkenny turn to left Langtons 500 metres on left after 1st set of lights*
The exterior of this period town house hotel belies its internal size, which is large enough to include a ballroom. No expense has been spared in refurbishing the hotel. Lovely fabrics enhance the richness of specially designed mahogany furniture in the comfortable bedrooms, where marble tiled bathrooms also gleam. The well-known restaurant and pub are both very popular.
**ROOMS:** 10 en suite 16 annexe en suite No smoking in 4 bedrooms
**FACILITIES:** STV entertainment **PARKING:** 60 **NOTES:** No dogs (ex guide dogs) Closed 25 Dec **CARDS:**

KILL, Co Kildare Map 01 D4

★★★63% ***Ambassador***
☎ 045 886700 🖹 045 886777
e-mail: quinn-hotels@sqgroup.com
***Dir:*** *Close to Dublin centre on the N7 to the south and south west*
Set beside the N7, 16 miles from Dublin the Ambassador offers comfortable and well-appointed accommodation. The Ambassador Lounge carvery and the Diplomat Restaurant both offer tempting dishes, and there is also a bar.
**ROOMS:** 36 en suite (36 fmly) **FACILITIES:** STV entertainment
**CONF:** Thtr 260 Class 140 Board 60 **PARKING:** 150 **NOTES:** No dogs (ex guide dogs) **CARDS:**

KILLARNEY, Co Kerry Map 01 B2

## Premier Collection

### ★★★★ Killarney Park

Kenmare Place
☎ 064 35555 064 35266
e-mail: info@killarneyparkhotel.ie
**Dir:** *N22 from Cork to Killarney. At 1st rdbt take 1st exit to Town Centre and at 2nd rdbt take 1st exit. Hotel is 2nd entrance on the left*

On the edge of town, this charming purpose-built hotel combines elegance with comfort. The hotel has a warm atmosphere with rich colours and fabrics, open fires, and welcoming staff. Public rooms and bedrooms are very comfortable indeed.

**ROOMS:** 75 en suite (4 fmly) No smoking in 35 bedrooms s IEP170-IEP250; d IEP240-IEP500 (incl. bkfst) * LB **FACILITIES:** STV Indoor swimming (H) Snooker Sauna Gym Jacuzzi Outdoor Canadian hot-tub Plunge pool Xmas **CONF:** Thtr 150 Class 70 Board 35 Del from IEP250 * **SERVICES:** Lift air con **PARKING:** 70 **NOTES:** No dogs (ex guide dogs) Closed 24-26 Dec
**CARDS:**

## Hotel of the Year

### ★★★★79% Aghadoe Heights

☎ 064 31766 064 31345
e-mail: info@aghadoeheights.com
**Dir:** *16km S of Kerry Airport and 5km N of Killarney. Signposted off the N22 Tralee road*

Superbly located overlooking Loch Lein, this hotel has been extensively refurbished to a very high standard. On the first floor the award-winning restaurant enjoys panoramic views of mountains and lakes, also shared by the stylish, air conditioned bedrooms, some of which have their own sun decks. There is a spacious lounge, a cocktail bar and a banqueting/conference suite. The staff are extremely friendly and welcoming, and nothing is too much trouble. Aghadoe Heights has been chosen as Hotel of the Year for Ireland 2001-2002.

**ROOMS:** 69 en suite No smoking in 6 bedrooms **FACILITIES:** STV Indoor swimming (H) Tennis (hard) Fishing Sauna Solarium Gym Jacuzzi Plunge pool,Beauty Treatment entertainment **CONF:** Thtr 120 Class 60 Board 40 Del from IEP265 **SERVICES:** Lift **PARKING:** 120 **NOTES:** No dogs No smoking in restaurant
**CARDS:**

### ★★★★67% *Muckross Park Hotel*

Muckross Village
☎ 064 31938 064 31965
e-mail: muckrossparkhotel@tinet.ie
**Dir:** *from Killarney take road to Kenmare, hotel 4km on left, adjacent to National Park, Muckross House & Gardens*

An 18th century hotel set in the heart of the Killarney National Park. Relaxing lounge areas feature comfortable furniture, warm colour schemes and chandeliers. Bedrooms are attractively decorated and well-equipped. Good food is served in the Bluepool restaurant, as well as the adjacent thatched pub, Molly Darcys, which offers live entertainment.

**ROOMS:** 27 en suite (2 fmly) No smoking in 2 bedrooms **FACILITIES:** STV **CONF:** Thtr 200 Class 80 Board 40 **PARKING:** 250 **NOTES:** No dogs (ex guide dogs) No smoking in restaurant Closed Dec-Feb **CARDS:**

### ★★★69% Cahernane

MANOR HOUSE

Muckross Rd
☎ 064 31895 064 34340
e-mail: cahernane@tinet.ie

This fine old country mansion with a magnificent mountain backdrop enjoys panoramic views from its setting beside the lake. Elegant period furnishings, fresh flowers and the glow of silver combine to create a welcoming atmosphere. Service is attentive but unobtrusive, and cuisine is of a high standard.

**ROOMS:** 12 en suite 26 annexe en suite s IEP95-IEP115; d IEP145-IEP180 (incl. bkfst) * LB **FACILITIES:** Tennis (hard) Fishing Croquet lawn entertainment **SERVICES:** Lift air con **PARKING:** 50 **NOTES:** No dogs (ex guide dogs) No smoking in restaurant Closed 2 Nov-Mar
**CARDS:**

### ★★★69% Gleneagle

☎ 064 36000 064 32646
e-mail: gleneagl@iol.ie
**Dir:** *1m outside Killarney town on the Kenmare Road - N71*

Excellent facilities for both leisure and corporate guests are offered in this family run hotel. The impressive new Events Centre is one of the largest in the country with a 2000 delegate capacity. Public areas are spacious, and the dedicated owners personally oversee the day to day running of the hotel.

**ROOMS:** 250 en suite (57 fmly) No smoking in 20 bedrooms **FACILITIES:** STV Indoor swimming (H) Tennis (hard) Fishing Squash Snooker Sauna Solarium Gym Jacuzzi Pitch & Putt Table tennis Steam room entertainment Xmas **CONF:** Thtr 2500 Class 1000 Board 50 **SERVICES:** Lift **PARKING:** 500 **CARDS:**

KILLARNEY, continued

### ★★★68% Castlerosse

☎ 064 31144 ▯ 064 31031
e-mail: castler@iol.ie
***Dir:*** *from Killarney town take R562 for Killorglin and The Ring of Kerry, hotel is 1.5km from town on the left hand side*

Set in 6,000 acres of land overlooking Lough Leane, this beautiful hotel offers warm hospitality and good food, as well as special facilities on the adjoining championship golf courses. Boating and fishing trips are available on nearby lakes.

**ROOMS:** 121 en suite (27 fmly) No smoking in 4 bedrooms s IEP60-IEP80; d IEP96-IEP124 (incl. bkfst) * **LB** **FACILITIES:** Indoor swimming (H) Golf 9 Tennis (hard) Snooker Sauna Gym Jacuzzi Golfing & riding arranged entertainment **CONF:** Thtr 200 Class 100 Board 40 **SERVICES:** Lift **PARKING:** 100 **NOTES:** No dogs (ex guide dogs) Closed Dec-Feb **CARDS:**

### ★★★67% Lake

Muckross Rd
☎ 064 31035 ▯ 064 31902
e-mail: lakehotel@eircom.net
***Dir:*** *Kenmare road out of Killarney*

Approached by a wooded drive, this former mansion stands in lovely countryside with lake and mountain views, and woodland walks. Bedrooms are well-equipped and some have balconies and four-poster beds. Public rooms are spacious and the lounge has kept an atmosphere of traditional comfort.

**ROOMS:** 65 en suite (10 fmly) s IEP50-IEP300; d IEP70-IEP300 (incl. bkfst) * **LB** **FACILITIES:** **Spa** STV Tennis (hard) Fishing Sauna Gym Putting green out door hot tub entertainment **CONF:** Thtr 80 Class 60 Board 40 **SERVICES:** Lift air con **PARKING:** 140 **NOTES:** No dogs (ex guide dogs) No smoking in restaurant Closed 18 Dec-10 Feb **CARDS:**

*See advert on opposite page*

### ★★★66% *Killarney Ryan*

Cork Rd
☎ 064 31555 ▯ 064 32438
e-mail: ryan@indigo.ie
***Dir:*** *on N22 route*

On the outskirts of Killarney, this hotel offers good standards of comfort. Public rooms include a large lounge, a restaurant and lounge bar opening on to the gardens. Many of the bedrooms can accommodate families, and the Ryan Group offer an all-inclusive summer holiday rate which can be good value.

**ROOMS:** 168 en suite (168 fmly) No smoking in 20 bedrooms **FACILITIES:** STV Indoor swimming (H) Tennis (hard) Sauna Jacuzzi Steam room Crazy golf entertainment ch fac **SERVICES:** Lift **PARKING:** 180 **NOTES:** No dogs Closed Dec & Jan **CARDS:**

*See advert on page 845*

### ★★★65% International

Best Western

Kenmare Pl
☎ 064 31816 ▯ 064 31837
e-mail: inter@iol.ie
***Dir:*** *Take N21 from Limerick to Farranfore N22 from Farranfore to Killarney turn right at 1st rdbt entering Killarney follow town bypass rd exits hotel*

This hotel offers quality bedrooms with modern comforts. Hannigan's Bar and the lounge are popular and bar snacks are available. There is a more intimate dining room, where soft candlelight glows against mahogany panelling. There is a library, snooker room and a keen interest is taken in golfing guests - tee times can be arranged at any of the many courses in the area.

**ROOMS:** 80 en suite (6 fmly) s IEP40-IEP65; d IEP65-IEP100 (incl. bkfst) * **LB** **FACILITIES:** **Spa** STV Billards entertainment **CONF:** Thtr 200 Class 100 Board 25 **SERVICES:** Lift **NOTES:** No dogs (ex guide dogs) No smoking in restaurant Closed 23-27 Dec **CARDS:**

### ★★★64% ® *Arbutus*

College St
☎ 064 31037 ▯ 064 34033
e-mail: arbutushotel@tinet.ie

This attractive hotel has been completely renovated and its entrance now features a fine foyer lounge and a second lounge adjoining the bar. There is a good restaurant, serving freshly prepared dishes based on local Irish produce. Bedrooms are comfortable with modern facilities.

**ROOMS:** 39 en suite (4 fmly) **FACILITIES:** STV **NOTES:** No dogs (ex guide dogs) Closed 19-30 Dec **CARDS:**

*See advert on opposite page*

### ★★★63% *Killarney Court Hotel*
Tralee Rd
☎ 064 37070 Fax 064 37060
e-mail: stay@irishcourthotels.com
***Dir:*** *Travelling from Tralee on the main Tralee Rd, the 1st rdbt towards Killarney, hotel on left*
Purpose built to a high standard, this new stone-fronted hotel has spacious public areas, an inviting pub and a contemporary restaurant offering a mix of transatlantic influences and traditional cuisine. The large bedrooms are attractively furnished and very comfortable. Bar food is served all day, as well as a carvery lunch.
**ROOMS:** 96 en suite (8 fmly) No smoking in 6 bedrooms
**FACILITIES:** STV Sauna Gym Jacuzzi Steam room **CONF:** Thtr 120 Class 70 Board 60 **SERVICES:** Lift **PARKING:** 130 **NOTES:** Closed 25 Dec **CARDS:**

### ★★★63% *White Gates*
Muckross Rd
☎ 064 31164 Fax 064 34850
***Dir:*** *1km from Killarney town on Muckross road on left*

village inn HOTELS

Distinctive blue and ochre paintwork draws the eye to this hotel. The same flair for colour combinations is evident throughout the interior and bedrooms are particularly attractive. The natural harmony of wood and stone is a feature of the well-designed lounge bar and the restaurant, with its conservatory front, is filled with light. There is also a very comfortable lounge.
**ROOMS:** 27 en suite **FACILITIES:** STV entertainment **CONF:** Class 50 **PARKING:** 50 **NOTES:** No dogs (ex guide dogs) Closed 21-29 Dec **CARDS:**

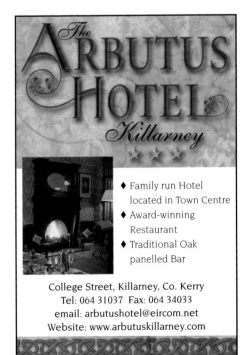

### ★★★59% Scotts Garden Hotel
College St
☎ 064 31060 Fax 064 36656
e-mail: scottskill@eircom.net
***Dir:*** *N20/N22 to town, at Friary go left. 500mtrs along on East Avenue Rd entrance to car park*
Located in the town centre, this hotel offers pleasant bedrooms, a bar and a patio garden. Special concessions are available at the sister Gleneagles Hotel's leisure facilities.
**ROOMS:** 52 en suite (4 fmly) s IEP51-IEP66; d IEP70-IEP100 (incl. bkfst & dinner) * **FACILITIES:** entertainment Xmas **SERVICES:** Lift **PARKING:** 60 **NOTES:** No dogs (ex guide dogs) No smoking in restaurant Closed 24-25 Dec **CARDS:**

### ★★63% *Darby O'Gills*
Lissivigeen, Mallow Rd
☎ 064 34168 & 34919 Fax 064 36794
A modern country house, offering smart, spacious and well-equipped bedrooms. Dinner is served in the restaurant, and bar food in the comfortable lounge bar. There is also a traditional Irish pub.
**ROOMS:** 13 en suite (3 fmly) **FACILITIES:** STV entertainment **CONF:** Thtr 250 Class 150 Board 60 **SERVICES:** air con **PARKING:** 150 **NOTES:** No dogs (ex guide dogs) Closed 25 Dec **CARDS:**

## KILLASHEE, Co Kildare — Map 01 D3

### ○ *Killashee House*
☎ 045 879277 Fax 045 879266
At the time of going to press, the star classification for this hotel was not confirmed. Please refer to the AA internet site www.theAA.com for current information.
**ROOMS:** 84 en suite **NOTES:** Open

## KILLINEY, Co Dublin
Map 01 D4

### ★★★★65% Fitzpatrick Castle
☎ 01 2305400 📠 01 2305430
e-mail: reservations@fitzpatricks.com
**Dir:** *Leaving Dun Laoghaire port turn left, continue on coast road, turn right at lights left at next lights. Follow road to Dalkey village, right at McDonaghs pub, immediate left, continue up hill hotel at the top*
Situated in large grounds, this converted castle has been extensively refurbished. Facilities include a comfortable lounge, restaurant and bar. A new floor of executive rooms has its own lounge with express check-in/out facility. There is a helipad, and a courtesy coach available for transfers to and from the airport.
**ROOMS:** 113 en suite (42 fmly) No smoking in 38 bedrooms s IEP120-IEP160; d IEP147-IEP187 * **LB** **FACILITIES:** STV Indoor swimming (H) Sauna Solarium Gym Beauty/hairdressing salon Steam room entertainment ch fac Xmas **CONF:** Thtr 400 Class 250 Board 80 Del from IEP160 * **SERVICES:** Lift **PARKING:** 300 **NOTES:** No dogs (ex guide dogs) RS 24-26Dec **CARDS:**

### ★★★65% Court
☎ 01 2851622 📠 01 2852085
e-mail: book@killineycourt.ie
Quality Hotel
**Dir:** *from Dublin-N11 via Donnybrook and Stillorgan, turn left off dual carriageway at traffic lights 1.6km after Cabinteely, right at next traffic lights*
Overlooking the breathtaking Killiney Bay, this Victorian mansion with pleasing grounds is only 12 miles from Dublin with excellent train links. There is a choice of bars and restaurants, and bedrooms are spacious, most have sea views. The international conference facilities include translating equipment.
**ROOMS:** 86 en suite (29 fmly) No smoking in 20 bedrooms s IEP104-IEP114; d IEP115-IEP153 (incl. bkfst) * **LB** **FACILITIES:** Beach in front of hotel Xmas **CONF:** Thtr 300 Class 180 Board 60 Del from IEP129 * **SERVICES:** Lift **PARKING:** 200 **NOTES:** No dogs (ex guide dogs) **CARDS:**

## KILTIMAGH, Co Mayo
Map 01 B4

### ★★65% *Cill Aod-in Hotel*
Main St
☎ 094 81761 📠 094 81838
e-mail: cillaodain@tinet.com
village inn HOTELS
**Dir:** *located in Kiltimagh Town Centre*
Situated in the heart of historic Kiltimagh, this hotel offers comfortable public areas, including a lounge, bar and bistro and an appealing restaurant, where enjoyable cuisine is served. There is also a rooftop garden. Guests are made to feel very welcome at this home from home. Easy on-and off-street parking is available opposite the hotel.
**ROOMS:** 19 en suite (4 fmly) No smoking in 4 bedrooms **FACILITIES:** STV Riding **NOTES:** No dogs (ex guide dogs) **CARDS:**

## KINGSCOURT, Co Cavan
Map 01 C4

### ★★★66% *Cabra Castle*
☎ 042 9667030 📠 042 9667039
e-mail: cabrach@iol.ie
MANOR HOUSE
Rebuilt in 1808, the Castle stands in 100 acres of parkland and is part of a national park. The staff are friendly and welcoming. The main reception rooms are elegant and invite relaxation and there are some courtyard bedrooms. The pleasant bar leads out onto a patio garden. There is free golf to residents and fishing and archery nearby.
**ROOMS:** 20 en suite 46 annexe en suite (5 fmly) **FACILITIES:** Golf 9 Riding entertainment **CONF:** Thtr 300 Class 100 Board 50 **PARKING:** 200 **NOTES:** Closed 25-27 Dec **CARDS:**

## KINSALE, Co Cork
Map 01 B2

### ★★★73% *Actons*
Pier Rd
☎ 021 4772135 📠 021 4772231
e-mail: actonsh@indigo.ie
**Dir:** *hotel is located in the Town Centre area facing Kinsale Harbour, 500 yards from Yacht Club Marina*
The location of this hotel, set in gardens overlooking the waterfront and marina, is ideal. The hotel has a bar and bistro and the Captain's Table restaurant, which continues to offer enjoyable food. The luxurious lounge is comfortable and bedrooms are all of a good standard. Friendly and attentive staff contribute greatly towards the enjoyment of a visit.
**ROOMS:** 76 en suite (20 fmly) **FACILITIES:** STV Indoor swimming (H) Sauna Solarium Gym entertainment **CONF:** Thtr 350 Class 200 Board 100 **SERVICES:** Lift **PARKING:** 70 **NOTES:** No dogs (ex guide dogs) Closed 7 Jan-8 Feb **CARDS:**

### ★★★69% Trident
Worlds End
☎ 021 4772301 📠 021 4774173
e-mail: info@tridenthotel.com
**Dir:** *take R600 from Cork city to Kinsale, drive along the Kinsale waterfront, the hotel is located just beyond the pier, on the waterfront*
Located at the harbour's edge, the Trident Hotel has its own marina with boats for hire. Many of the bedrooms have superb views and two have balconies. The restaurant and lounge both overlook the harbour and pleasant staff provide hospitable service.
**ROOMS:** 58 en suite (2 fmly) s IEP72-IEP95; d IEP94-IEP138 (incl. bkfst) * **LB** **FACILITIES:** Sauna Gym Jacuzzi Steam room Xmas **CONF:** Thtr 2 Class 170 Board 60 Del from IEP105 * **SERVICES:** Lift **PARKING:** 60 **NOTES:** No dogs (ex guide dogs) Closed 25-26 Dec **CARDS:**

## KNOCK, Co Mayo
Map 01 B4

### ★★★65% *Knock House*
Ballyhaunis Rd
☎ 094 88088 📠 094 88044
e-mail: hotel@knock-shrive.ie
**Dir:** *The hotel is located on the Ballyhaunis Road,1/2km from Knock village*
Adjacent to the Marian shrine and basilica, set in landscaped gardens, this creatively designed hotel features extensive use of limestone and natural wood finishes. Facilities include two spacious lounges, restaurant, dispense bar and conference centre. Contemporary bedrooms are decorated in soft colours, six rooms are suitable for disabled guests. There is a medical assessment centre for guests who require special care.
**ROOMS:** 68 en suite (12 fmly) **FACILITIES:** ch fac **CONF:** Thtr 150 Class 90 Board 45 **SERVICES:** Lift **PARKING:** 150 **NOTES:** No dogs (ex guide dogs) **CARDS:**

### ★★★61% *Belmont*
☎ 094 88122 📠 094 88532
e-mail: belmonthotel@tinet.ie
**Dir:** *on the N17, Galway side of Knock Village. Turn right at Burke's supermarket & Pub. Hotel 150yards on right*
**ROOMS:** 64 en suite (6 fmly) No smoking in 3 bedrooms **FACILITIES:** Solarium Gym Jacuzzi Steamroom Natural health therapies entertainment **CONF:** Thtr 500 Class 100 Board 20 **SERVICES:** Lift air con **PARKING:** 110 **NOTES:** No dogs (ex guide dogs) No smoking in restaurant Closed 25 & 26 Dec **CARDS:**

## LAHINCH, Co Clare
Map 01 B3

### ★★★59% *Aberdeen Arms*
☎ 065 81100 🖹 065 81228
e-mail: aberdeen@websters.ie
***Dir:*** *56km from Shannon airport, N18 to Ennis, N85 to Ennistymon, turn left, approx 3km to Lahinch, turn left at top of Main St*
A popular and recently modernised hotel offering very comfortable day rooms where guests can expect to mingle with the golfing fraternity playing the famous Lahinch Links Course. Bedrooms are furnished in a popular style and well-equipped.
**ROOMS:** 55 en suite **FACILITIES:** STV Snooker Sauna Jacuzzi **CONF:** Thtr 200 Class 100 Board 50 **PARKING:** 85 **NOTES:** No dogs (ex guide dogs) **CARDS:**

## LEIGHLINBRIDGE, Co Carlow
Map 01 C3

### ★★64% *Lord Begenal Inn*
☎ 0503 21668 🖹 0503 22629
e-mail: info@lordbagenal.com
Set on the banks of the River Barrow in this picturesque village, this attractive inn has its own private marina. The new bedrooms are comfortable and well-equipped and the traditional bar is a cluster of small cosy rooms with log fires. Fine dining is available in the restaurant.
**FACILITIES:** no TV in bdrms

## LEIXLIP, Co Kildare
Map 01 D4

### ★★★76% *Leixlip House*
Captains Hill
☎ 01 6242268 🖹 01 6244177
e-mail: manager@leixliphouse.com
***Dir:*** *from Leixlip motorway junct continue into village. Turn right at lights and continue up hill*
This lovely stone-built country house dates from the 18th century and retains many of its original features. Accommodation is of high quality, as is the service, and the restaurant serves enjoyable meals.
**ROOMS:** 19 en suite (2 fmly) **FACILITIES:** STV **CONF:** Thtr 130 Class 60 Board 40 **PARKING:** 64 **NOTES:** No dogs
**CARDS:**

## LIMAVADY, Co Londonderry
Map 01 C6

### ★★★★69% Radisson Roe Park Hotel & Golf Resort
BT49 9LB
☎ 028 7772 2222 🖹 028 7772 2313
e-mail: reservations@radissonroepark.com
***Dir:*** *on the A2 Londonderry/Limavady road, 16m from Londonderry, 1m from Limavady*
This impressive hotel with its own golf course enjoys a secluded countryside location. The spacious, modern bedrooms are well-equipped and many have excellent views of the fairways. The Courtyard restaurant provides a fine dining experience and the Coach House brasserie offers a lighter menu. Leisure facilities are extensive.
**ROOMS:** 64 en suite (15 fmly) No smoking in 16 bedrooms **FACILITIES:** STV Indoor swimming (H) Golf 18 Fishing Sauna Solarium Gym Croquet lawn Putting green Jacuzzi Floodlit driving range practice area,outside tees,golf training academy. ch fac Xmas **CONF:** Thtr 450 Class 190 Del from £85 * **SERVICES:** Lift **PARKING:** 300 **NOTES:** No dogs (ex guide dogs) **CARDS:**

## LIMERICK, Co Limerick
Map 01 B3

### ★★★★67% Castletroy Park
Dublin Rd
☎ 061 335566 🖹 061 331117
e-mail: sales@castletroy-park.ie
***Dir:*** *on N7(main Dublin road),3 miles from Limerick city,25 mins from Shannon international airport*
Encircled by gardens close to the University of Limerick, this hotel feels light and airy, and combines modern comforts with attractive decor. Fax and computer points in the bedrooms are popular with business guests while McLaughlin's Restaurant serves good food and is a popular meeting place.
**ROOMS:** 107 en suite (78 fmly) No smoking in 70 bedrooms s IEP105-IEP145; d IEP125-IEP165 (incl. bkfst) * **LB** **FACILITIES:** STV Indoor swimming (H) Sauna Gym Jacuzzi Running track Steam room entertainment **CONF:** Thtr 450 Class 270 Board 100 **SERVICES:** Lift **PARKING:** 160 **NOTES:** No dogs (ex guide dogs) Closed 24-26 Dec
**CARDS:**

### ★★★73% *Jurys*
Ennis Rd
JURYS DOYLE HOTELS
☎ 061 327777 🖹 061 326400
e-mail: bookings@jurys.com
***Dir:*** *located at junction of Ennis Rd, O'Callaghan Strand and Sarsfield Bridge*
This hotel, standing in four acres of riverside grounds, offers excellent corporate and leisure facilities, including an indoor swimming pool. Bedrooms come in two styles, executive or standard and there is also a bar and restaurant.
**ROOMS:** 95 en suite (22 fmly) No smoking in 16 bedrooms **FACILITIES:** STV Indoor swimming (H) Tennis (hard) Sauna Gym Jacuzzi Steam room Plunge pool **CONF:** Thtr 200 Class 90 Board 45 **PARKING:** 200 **NOTES:** No dogs (ex guide dogs) Closed 24-27 Dec
**CARDS:**

### ★★★70% *Gresham Ardhu*
Ennis Rd
☎ 061 453922 🖹 061 326333
e-mail: ryan@indigo.ie
***Dir:*** *on N18, Ennis road*

GRESHAM HOTELS

Close to the city, in its own grounds, the Gresham Ardhu has smart public areas located in the original part of this classic house including, lounges and restaurants, a cocktail bar with a fire, sofas and a pianist. The well-equipped bedrooms are located in a modern extension with 24-hour room service. Other facilities include conference suites, a business centre and patio gardens.
**ROOMS:** 181 en suite (181 fmly) No smoking in 19 bedrooms **FACILITIES:** STV Gym Gym nearby available free to guests entertainment **CONF:** Thtr 130 Class 60 Board 40 **SERVICES:** Lift **PARKING:** 180 **NOTES:** No dogs **CARDS:**

*See advert on page 845*

LIMERICK, continued

**★★★64% *Two Mile Inn***
Ennis Rd
☎ 061 326255 061 453783
***Dir:*** *on N22, near Bunratty Castle & airport*
On the outskirts of Limerick city near Bunratty Castle and Shannon Airport, the Two Mile Inn has a new pub and restaurant, as well as a spacious lounge and comfortable bedrooms.
**ROOMS:** 123 en suite (30 fmly) No smoking in 67 bedrooms
**FACILITIES:** STV **CONF:** Thtr 350 Class 200 Board 40 **PARKING:** 300
**NOTES:** No dogs (ex guide dogs) **CARDS:**

**★★★62% *Greenhills***
Caherdavin
☎ 061 453033 061 453307
***Dir:*** *situated on the N18, approx 2m from City Centre*
Set in 3.5 acres of lovely landscaped gardens, the hotel has a fine leisure centre and good conference facilities. Bedrooms have been refurbished and are attractive and comfortable. Food is served all day in the Carvery bar, and there is a large car park.
**ROOMS:** 58 en suite (4 fmly) **FACILITIES:** STV Indoor swimming (H) Tennis (hard) Sauna Solarium Gym Jacuzzi Beauty parlour Massage
**CONF:** Thtr 500 Class 200 Board 50 **PARKING:** 150 **NOTES:** No dogs
**CARDS:**

**★★★62% Woodfield House**
Ennis Rd
☎ 061 453022 061 326755
e-mail: woodfieldhousehotel@eircom.net
***Dir:*** *on outskirts of city on main Shannon road*
This intimate hotel stands on the N18, a short distance from the city centre. The smart bedrooms are comfortable and well-appointed. There is a dining room, and the bar serves food all day.
**ROOMS:** 26 en suite (3 fmly) s IEP50-IEP59; d IEP79-IEP99 (incl. bkfst) * **LB** **FACILITIES:** STV Tennis (hard) **CONF:** Thtr 130 Class 60 Board 60 Del from IEP60 * **SERVICES:** air con **PARKING:** 80 **NOTES:** No dogs (ex guide dogs) Closed 24-25 Dec Civ Wed 100
**CARDS:**

**★★★60% *Jurys Inn Limerick***
Lower Mallow St
☎ 061 207000 061 400966
e-mail: info@jurys.com
***Dir:*** *from N7 follow signs for City Centre into O'Connell St, turn off at N18 (Shannon/Galway), hotel is off O'Connell St*
A smartly decorated new hotel on the city side of the river, convenient for the shopping and business areas. Facilities include a spacious foyer, bar and restaurant, a boardroom for meetings and an elevator to all floors. Bedrooms are well-equipped and offer good value, especially the family rooms. Staff are friendly and enthusiastic.
**ROOMS:** 151 en suite (108 fmly) No smoking in 56 bedrooms
**FACILITIES:** STV entertainment **CONF:** Thtr 50 Class 25 Board 18
**SERVICES:** Lift **NOTES:** No dogs (ex guide dogs) Closed 24-26 Dec
**CARDS:**

**○ *Travelodge***
Ennis Rd, Clondrinagh
☎ 0800 850950

Arriving late? Four and five star hotels have night porters to assist with your luggage, and 24-hour room service.

LISDOONVARNA, Co Clare — Map 01 B3

**★★★60% Sheedy's Restaurant & Hotel**
☎ 065 7074026 065 7074555
e-mail: enquiries@sheedyscountryhouse.com
Situated in attractive gardens, Sheedy's has a new image, with new, very comfortable bedrooms and bathrooms. Family-run, the hotel provides warm hospitality, comfort, and good food from its award-winning restaurant.
**ROOMS:** 11 en suite (1 fmly) s IEP55-IEP75; d IEP80-IEP130 (incl. bkfst) * **LB** **PARKING:** 40 **NOTES:** No dogs (ex guide dogs) No smoking in restaurant Closed mid Oct-Etr **CARDS:**

LISMORE, Co Waterford — Map 01 C2

**★★66% *Ballyrafter House***
☎ 058 54002 058 53050
***Dir:*** *1km from Lismore opposite Lismore Castle*
A welcoming country house, set in its own grounds opposite Lismore Castle. Inside, most of the bedrooms are pleasantly furnished in pine. The bar and conservatory are where guests, anglers and locals meet to discuss the day's events. The hotel has its own salmon fishing on the River Blackwater.
**ROOMS:** 10 en suite (1 fmly) **FACILITIES:** Fishing Riding Putting green
**PARKING:** 20 **NOTES:** No dogs (ex guide dogs) Closed Nov-Feb
**CARDS:**

LONDONDERRY, Co Londonderry — Map 01 C5

**★★★72% Beech Hill Country House Hotel**
32 Ardmore Rd BT47 3QP
☎ 028 7134 9279 028 7134 5366
e-mail: info@beech-hill.com
***Dir:*** *From A6 Londonderry-Belfast take Faughan Bridge turning and continue 1m to hotel opposite Ardmore Chapel*
Dating back to 1729, Beech Hill is an impressive mansion, standing in 32 acres of woodlands and gardens with waterfalls. Public areas are comfortable with fine dining provided in the attractively extended formal dining room. The splendid bedroom wing provides spacious well-equipped rooms, in addition to those in the main house.
**ROOMS:** 17 en suite 10 annexe en suite (4 fmly) s £75-£85; d £100-£130 (incl. bkfst) * **LB** **FACILITIES:** Tennis (hard) Sauna Gym Jacuzzi ch fac **CONF:** Thtr 100 Class 50 Board 30 Del from £85 *
**SERVICES:** Lift **PARKING:** 75 **NOTES:** No dogs (ex guide dogs) No smoking in restaurant Closed 24-25 Dec **CARDS:**

**★★★68% Trinity Hotel**
22-24 Strand Rd BT48 7AB
☎ 028 7127 1271 028 7127 1277
e-mail: ifo@thetrinityhotel.com
***Dir:*** *to get to Derry City Centre cross River Foyle, follow signs for city centre, hotel is approx 0.5m from Guildhall adjecent to shopping centre/cinema*
In the middle of the city centre, this modern hotel is proving popular with both business and leisure guests. The design is decidedly contemporary and has created a good deal of interest. Public areas include a continental-style café bar and a bistro. The bedrooms are very modern in design.
**ROOMS:** 40 en suite (17 fmly) s £65-£75; d £80-£90 (incl. bkfst) * **LB**
**FACILITIES:** STV Conservatory entertainment **CONF:** Thtr 70 Class 30 Board 25 **SERVICES:** Lift **PARKING:** 30 **NOTES:** No dogs (ex guide dogs) **CARDS:**

## LUCAN, Co Dublin
Map 01 D4

### ★★★70% Finnstown Country House Hotel & Golf Course
Newcastle Rd
☎ 01 6010700 🖹 01 6281088
e-mail: manager@finnstown-hotel.ie
***Dir:*** *from M1 take 1st exit onto M50 S/bound. 1st exit after Toll Bridge. At rdbt take 3rd left (N4 W). Left at t/lights. Over next 2 rdbt. Hotel on right*
Set in 45 acres of wooded grounds, Finnstown is a calm and peaceful country house. There is a wide choice of bedroom styles and the garden suites are particularly good. Reception rooms are inviting and furnished in period style.
**ROOMS:** 25 en suite 26 annexe en suite No smoking in 27 bedrooms s IEP95-IEP140; d IEP90-IEP180 (incl. bkfst) * **LB FACILITIES:** STV Indoor swimming (H) Tennis (hard & grass) Solarium Gym Croquet lawn Putting green Turkish bath, Table tennis, Massage, Pool Table, Games Room ch fac Xmas **CONF:** Thtr 100 Class 60 Board 30 Del from IEP142 * **PARKING:** 90 **CARDS:**
*See advert under DUBLIN*

### ★★★64% *Lucan Spa*
☎ 01 6280495 & 6280497 🖹 01 6280841
***Dir:*** *hotel is located on N4, approx 11km from city centre, approx 20 mins from Dublin airport*
Set in its own grounds, the Lucan Spa is a fine Georgian house. Guests have complimentary use of Lucan Golf Course, adjacent to the hotel. A conference centre with facilities for 600 delegates is also available.
**ROOMS:** 71 rms (61 en suite) (15 fmly) No smoking in 21 bedrooms **FACILITIES:** STV Golf 18 entertainment **CONF:** Thtr 600 Class 250 Board 80 **SERVICES:** Lift air con **PARKING:** 90 **NOTES:** No dogs (ex guide dogs) Closed 25 Dec **CARDS:**

## MACREDDIN, Co Wicklow
Map 01 D3

### ★★★★71% ®® *Brooklodge at MacCreddin*
Macreddin Village
☎ 0402 36444 🖹 0402 36580
e-mail: brooklodge@macreddin.ie

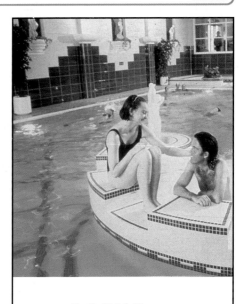

## MACROOM, Co Cork
Map 01 B2

### ★★72% ® Castle
village inn HOTELS
Main St
☎ 026 41074 🖹 026 41505
e-mail: castlehotel@eircom.net
***Dir:*** *on N22 midway between Cork & Killarney*
The Castle Hotel contains a new leisure centre and some fine bedrooms. The hotel service is excellent and guests feel very much at home. There is a pleasant lounge and a function room, while the food in the restaurant and the bar, is well-cooked and imaginatively presented.
**ROOMS:** 42 en suite (5 fmly) s IEP58-IEP65; d IEP78-IEP93 (incl. bkfst) * **LB FACILITIES: Spa** STV Indoor swimming (H) Solarium Gym Jacuzzi Steam Room entertainment **CONF:** Board 20 **SERVICES:** air con **PARKING:** 30 **NOTES:** No dogs No smoking in restaurant Closed 24-28 Dec **CARDS:**
*See advert on this page*

€ The Euro will be phased in during 2002 (R.O.I. only). Make sure you check prices and currency when booking.



## MALLOW, Co Cork
Map 01 B2

**Premier Collection**

### ★★★ ®®® Longueville House
RELAIS & CHATEAUX.
☎ 022 47156 & 47306 🖹 022 47459
e-mail: info@longuevillehouse.ie
***Dir:*** *3 miles west of Mallow via N72 Road to Killarney, right turn at Ballyclough junct,hotel entrance 200yds left*
This 18th-century Georgian mansion is set in a wooded estate and has many fine features. There are comfortable bedrooms, which overlook the river valley and the courtyard maze. The two elegant sitting rooms both have fine examples of Italian plasterwork and an Adams mantelpiece graces the Presidents Restaurant. Cuisine in the hotel restaurant is very exciting and
*continued on p882*

MALLOW, continued

inventive, and makes good use of produce, which is fresh, and of excellent quality.
**ROOMS:** 22 en suite (5 fmly) No smoking in 5 bedrooms s IEP65; d IEP125-IEP135 (incl. bkfst) * **LB** **FACILITIES:** STV Fishing Croquet lawn Country Walks on estate **CONF:** Thtr 50 Class 30 Board 30 Del from IEP170 * **PARKING:** 30 **NOTES:** No dogs (ex guide dogs) No smoking in restaurant Closed Mid Nov-Mid Mar
**CARDS:**

★★★63% ***Springfort Hall Hotel***
☎ 022 21278 022 21557
e-mail: stay@springfort-hall.com
***Dir:*** *on Mallow/Limerick road N20, right turn off at 2 Pot House R581, hotel 500mtrs on right sign over gate*
This 18th century country manor is tucked away amid tranquil woodlands. There is an attractive oval dining room, as well as a drawing room and lounge bar. The comfortable bedrooms are mainly in the new wing and are spacious and well-appointed, with superb country views.
**ROOMS:** 50 en suite (4 fmly) **FACILITIES:** STV entertainment **CONF:** Thtr 300 Class 200 Board 50 **PARKING:** 200 **NOTES:** No dogs (ex guide dogs) Closed 23 Dec-2 Jan Civ Wed 250
**CARDS:**

MAYNOOTH, Co Kildare Map 01 C4

★★★74% ***Moyglare Manor***
Moyglare
☎ 01 6286351 01 6285405
e-mail: moyglare@iol.ie
***Dir:*** *turn off N4 at Maynooth/Naas, then right to Maynooth town. Keep right at St Marys Church and continue 2m then left at X-roads*
This elegant 18th-century house is a haven of calm, set in its own grounds in rich pasture land. Guests arrive along an imposing avenue and are greeted with genuine hospitality. Bedrooms are beautifully furnished in keeping with the Georgian style of the house, and there are several peaceful lounges and a convivial bar. The hotel cuisine has a justified high reputation.
**ROOMS:** 17 en suite (1 fmly) No smoking in 5 bedrooms **FACILITIES:** STV Tennis **CONF:** Thtr 30 Board 20 **PARKING:** 120 **NOTES:** No dogs (ex guide dogs) No children 12yrs No smoking in restaurant Closed 24-26 Dec **CARDS:**

MIDLETON, Co Cork Map 01 C2

★★★66% ***Midleton Park***
☎ 021 631767 021 631605
e-mail: info@midletonparkhotel.ie
***Dir:*** *from Cork, turn off N25 hotel on right hand side. From Waterford, turn off N25, over bridge until T-junct, turn right, hotel on right*
This purpose-built hotel, situated in an area of great interest, is just off the N25 Cork/Rosslare route, ten miles from Cork. The hotel features fine, spacious and well appointed bedrooms and the comfortable restaurant offers good food and attentive service. Conference and banqueting facilities are available.
**ROOMS:** 40 en suite (12 fmly) No smoking in 6 bedrooms **FACILITIES:** STV **CONF:** Thtr 400 Class 200 Board 40 **SERVICES:** air con **PARKING:** 500 **NOTES:** No dogs (ex guide dogs) Closed 25 Dec
**CARDS:**

MONAGHAN, Co Monaghan Map 01 C5

★★★★60% **Hillgrove**
Old Armagh Rd
☎ 047 81288 047 84951
e-mail: hillgrovegm@quinn-hotels.com
***Dir:*** *turn off N2 at Cathedral, cont for 400mtrs, on left just beyond Cathedral*
**ROOMS:** 44 en suite (2 fmly) s IEP58-IEP60; d IEP92-IEP96 (incl. bkfst) * **LB** **FACILITIES:** STV Jacuzzi entertainment Xmas **CONF:** Thtr 1200 Class 600 Board 200 Del from IEP84 * **SERVICES:** Lift air con **PARKING:** 430 **NOTES:** No dogs (ex guide dogs)
**CARDS:**

NAVAN, Co Meath Map 01 C4

★★★62% ***Ardboyne Hotel***
Dublin Rd
☎ 046 23119 046 22355
e-mail: ardboyne@quinn-hotels.com
***Dir:*** *From Dublin-N3 north through Blanchards Town to Navan, hotel is on left hand side on N3*
This welcoming hotel is situated on the edge of Navan. Bedrooms are comfortably furnished and freshly decorated, and overlook pretty gardens. Public areas are smartly furnished and include an inviting lounge warmed by an open fire, a well-appointed dining room and a saloon style bar. Conference suites are available.
**ROOMS:** 29 en suite (25 fmly) No smoking in 10 bedrooms **FACILITIES:** STV entertainment **CONF:** Thtr 400 Class 200 Board 150 **PARKING:** 186 **NOTES:** No dogs Closed 24-26 Dec
**CARDS:**

NENAGH, Co Tipperary Map 01 B3

★★★68% ***Abbey Court***
Dublin Rd
☎ 067 41111 067 41022
e-mail: abycourt@indigo.ie
***Dir:*** *Hotel 2 mins from O'Connor's Shopping Centre on Dublin side of Nenagh*
**ROOMS:** 46 en suite (3 fmly) No smoking in 10 bedrooms **FACILITIES:** STV entertainment **CONF:** Thtr 600 Class 150 Board 60 **SERVICES:** Lift air con **PARKING:** 200 **NOTES:** No dogs (ex guide dogs) Closed 25 Dec **CARDS:**

NEWBRIDGE, Co Kildare Map 01 C3

★★★73% **Keadeen**
☎ 045 431666 045 434402
e-mail: keadeen@iol.ie
***Dir:*** *M7 junct 10, (Newbridge, Curragh) at rdbt follow round to right and go in direction of Newbridge, hotel is on left 1km from rdbt*
This family-owned hotel is set in eight acres of landscaped gardens, and has good leisure facilities. Comfortable public areas include a spacious drawing room, reception foyer and two bars. The hotel is well-placed for Dublin Airport and the Mondello racing circuit.
**ROOMS:** 55 en suite (4 fmly) No smoking in 5 bedrooms s IEP95-IEP200; d IEP140-IEP200 (incl. bkfst) * **LB** **FACILITIES:** STV Indoor swimming (H) Sauna Solarium Gym Jacuzzi Aerobics studio Treatment room Massage entertainment Xmas **CONF:** Thtr 800 Class 300 Board 40 Del from IEP112 * **PARKING:** 200 **NOTES:** No dogs (ex guide dogs) Closed 24 Dec-3 Jan RS low season **CARDS:**

NEWCASTLE, Co Down Map 01 D5

**★★64% *Enniskeen House***
98 Bryansford Rd BT33 0LF
☎ 028 4372 2392 🖷 028 4372 4084
e-mail: enniskeen-hotel@demon.co.uk
***Dir:*** *from Newcastle town centre follow signs for Tollymore Forest Park, hotel 1m on left*
Set in delightful gardens in a residential area, this hotel's relaxing ambience is enhanced by its thoughtful staff. Bedrooms vary but all are well equipped; many enjoy super views of the surrounding mountains and countryside. The formal dining room serves traditional cuisine and the first-floor lounge makes the best of the coastal views.
**ROOMS:** 12 en suite (1 fmly) No smoking in 3 bedrooms **CONF:** Thtr 60 Class 24 **SERVICES:** Lift **PARKING:** 45 **NOTES:** No dogs No smoking in restaurant Closed 12 Nov-14 Mar
**CARDS:**

NEWMARKET-ON-FERGUS, Co Clare Map 01 B3

**★★★★★73% *Dromoland Castle***
☎ 061 368144 🖷 061 363355
e-mail: sales@dromoland.ie
Described as a "very large, early 18th-century, gothic revival, castellated, irregular, multi-towered ashlar castle" Dromoland offers superbly appointed accommodation and facilities. The spacious, thoughtfully equipped and richly decorated bedrooms offer excellent levels of comfort. The magnificent public areas, warmed by log fires, are no less impressive. The hotel has two restaurants including the more formal Earl of Thomond. There are also immaculately maintained grounds and excellent leisure and meeting facilities.
**ROOMS:** 75 en suite (20 fmly) **FACILITIES:** STV Golf 18 Tennis (hard) Fishing Snooker Sauna Solarium Gym Putting green entertainment **CONF:** Thtr 450 Class 320 Board 80 **PARKING:** 120 **NOTES:** No dogs No smoking in restaurant **CARDS:**

NEW ROSS, Co Wexford Map 01 C3

**★★★64% *Clarion Brandon House Hotel***
Wexford Rd
☎ 051 421703 🖷 051 421567
e-mail: brandonhouse@eircom.net
***Dir:*** *Drive down the quays on Rosslake Road N25, hotel gates on the left 1.5km from the quays*
Set in its own grounds, this Victorian manor house has been refurbished, with the addition of a new bedroom wing and extensive leisure centre. Large period rooms include an inviting foyer and library with log fires, a comfortable lounge bar and attractive restaurant. Bedrooms are spacious and well-appointed and the front rooms enjoy lovely views.
**ROOMS:** 61 en suite **FACILITIES:** STV Indoor swimming (H) Sauna Solarium Gym Jacuzzi Beauty treatment rooms entertainment **CONF:** Thtr 300 Class 200 Board 100 **PARKING:** 250 **NOTES:** No dogs (ex guide dogs) **CARDS:**

ORANMORE, Co Galway Map 01 B3

**★★★65% *Galway Bay Golf & Country Club Hotel***
☎ 091 790500 🖷 091 790510
e-mail: gbay.golf@iol.ie
***Dir:*** *follow signs from Oranmore for 3km entrance beside the Galway Bay Sailing Club*
A stylish and friendly hotel, overlooking the golf course on the Penville Peninsula. Christie O'Connor Jnr designed this championship course and there is a grandstand view of the first fairway from the smart lounge. The bedrooms, all well-equipped, range from executive suites, with their own sitting rooms, to standard rooms. The hotel cuisine is of a consistently high standard.
**ROOMS:** 90 en suite **FACILITIES:** STV Golf 18 Putting green Golf practice range Parkland walks **CONF:** Thtr 160 Class 100 Board 30 **SERVICES:** Lift **PARKING:** 200 **NOTES:** No dogs (ex guide dogs) Closed 24-26 Dec **CARDS:**



OUGHTERARD, Co Galway Map 01 B4

**★★★67% *Ross Lake House***
Rosscahill
☎ 091 550109 & 550154 🖷 091 550184
e-mail: rosslake@iol.ie
***Dir:*** *22km from Galway City on N59, Galway - Clifden road. Turn left after village of Rosscahill*
Set in a peaceful woodland estate, this personally-run Georgian house offers a warm welcome. Good food is a feature, and carefully chosen produce includes Connemara lamb and fresh fish. Golf, lake fishing and boating are all near by.
**ROOMS:** 13 en suite **FACILITIES:** STV Tennis (hard) **PARKING:** 150 **NOTES:** No smoking in restaurant Closed Nov-mid Mar
**CARDS:**

PARKNASILLA, Co Kerry Map 01 A2

**★★★★79% *Great Southern***
☎ 064 45122 🖷 064 45323
e-mail: res@parknasilla.gsh.ie
***Dir:*** *on Kenmare road 3km from Sneem village*
The Great Southern on Kenmare Bay has fine sea views from many of its bedrooms. There are spacious, comfortable lounges,

continued on p884

P

PARKNASILLA, continued

the excellent Pygmalion Retaurant and an impressive range of leisure facilities. Service is delightfully warm and welcoming.

Great Southern, Parknasilla

**ROOMS:** 26 en suite 59 annexe en suite (6 fmly) No smoking in 11 bedrooms **FACILITIES:** STV Indoor swimming (H) Golf 9 Tennis (hard) Fishing Riding Snooker Sauna Croquet lawn Jacuzzi Bike hire Windsurfing Clay pigeon shooting Archery entertainment **CONF:** Thtr 100 Class 80 Board 20 **SERVICES:** Lift **PARKING:** 60 **NOTES:** No dogs (ex guide dogs) **CARDS:**

See advert on page 883

## PORTAFERRY, Co Down — Map 01 D5

### ★★★67% Portaferry

10 The Strand BT22 1PE
☎ 028 4272 8231 028 4272 8999
e-mail: portaferry@iol.ie
***Dir:*** *situated on Lough Shore opposite ferry terminal*

There are many reasons for visitors to come to the area, whether it be golfing, walking, bird watching or an interest in culture and history. The picturesque town is a centre for yachting and sea angling. The hotel itself is situated on the shores of the beautiful Strangford Lough and many of its bedrooms have superb waterside views.

**ROOMS:** 14 en suite **FACILITIES:** STV **PARKING:** 6 **NOTES:** No dogs (ex guide dogs) Closed 24-25 Dec **CARDS:**

## PORTMARNOCK, Co Dublin — Map 01 D4

### ★★★★77% Portmarnock Hotel & Golf Links

Strand Rd
☎ 01 8460611 01 8462442
e-mail: marketing@portmarnock.com
***Dir:*** *Dublin Airport-N1, rdbt 1st exit, 2nd rdbt 2nd exit, next rdbt 3rd exit, T-junct turn left, over crossrds and cont, hotel is left past the Strand*

Enjoying a superb location overlooking the sea and the PGA Championship Golf Links, this 19th century former home of the Jameson whiskey family is now a smart hotel. Bedrooms are modern, while the public areas are furnished with period style. The Osborne Restaurant comes highly recommended.

**ROOMS:** 103 en suite No smoking in 6 bedrooms **FACILITIES:** STV Golf 18 Putting green **CONF:** Thtr 300 Class 110 Board 80 **SERVICES:** Lift **PARKING:** 200 **NOTES:** No dogs (ex guide dogs) **CARDS:**

See advert under DUBLIN

> Packed in a hurry? Ironing facilities should be available at all star levels, either in rooms or on request.

## PORTRUSH, Co Antrim — Map 01 C6

### ★★★71% The Royal Court

233 Ballybogey Rd BT56 8NF
☎ 028 7082 2236 028 7082 3176
e-mail: royalcourthotel@aol.com
***Dir:*** *from Ballymena head N on M2 which joins Ballymoney rdbt. Take 3rd exit to Portrush on B62. Hotel situated at end of road*

Situated east of the town, this comfortable hotel enjoys panoramic, coastal views to the East Strand beach, Donegal, and the Scottish Islands. Bedrooms are spacious, and some have balconies giving superb views. Extensive menus served in the restaurant and informal bar make good use of creative, wholesome cooking.

**ROOMS:** 18 en suite (10 fmly) **FACILITIES:** STV **CONF:** Thtr 100 Class 70 Board 50 **PARKING:** 200 **NOTES:** No dogs (ex guide dogs) Closed 26 Dec **CARDS:**

### ★★★56% Causeway Coast

36 Ballyreagh Rd BT56 8LR
☎ 028 7082 2435 028 70824495
e-mail: info@causewaycoast.com
***Dir:*** *on A2 Antrim Coast Road, between Portrush & Portstewart, opposite Ballyreagh Golf Course*

A purpose-built hotel and conference centre overlooking Ballyreagh golf course to the sea. Improvements include the addition of 20 more bedrooms and the creation of a leisure centre. Public areas are pleasing and decorated in a modern style.

**ROOMS:** 21 en suite (2 fmly) **FACILITIES:** entertainment **CONF:** Thtr 500 Class 170 **PARKING:** 172 **NOTES:** No dogs (ex guide dogs) Closed 25 Dec **CARDS:**

## PORTUMNA, Co Galway — Map 01 B3

### ★★★65% Shannon Oaks Hotel & Country Club

☎ 0509 41777 0509 41357
e-mail: sales@shannonoaks.ie

Situated in eight acres of grounds on the edge of Portumna National Forest, this recently rebuilt hotel has a comfortable lounge, restaurant and bar where live entertainment takes place regularly. Spacious bedrooms are air-conditioned and well-equipped. There is an indoor pool, fitness centre, and conference and banqueting facilities, as well as extensive car parking.

**ROOMS:** 63 en suite **FACILITIES:** STV Indoor swimming (H) Tennis (hard) Sauna Solarium Gym Jacuzzi entertainment **CONF:** Thtr 600 Class 380 Board 15 **SERVICES:** Lift air con **PARKING:** 360 **NOTES:** No dogs (ex guide dogs) **CARDS:**

## RATHMULLAN, Co Donegal — Map 01 C6

### ★★★73% Fort Royal

MANOR HOUSE

Fort Royal
☎ 074 58100 074 58103www
e-mail: fortroyal@eircom.net
***Dir:*** *take R245 from Letterkenny, through Rathmullan village, hotel is signposted*

On the shores of Lough Swilly, this period house stands in 18 acres of grounds and has private access to a secluded beach. The sitting room is a restful place overlooking the sea. Enjoyable meals

continued

P

are served in the restaurant, and the bar is inviting. Bedrooms are attractively decorated.

**ROOMS:** 11 en suite 4 annexe en suite (3 fmly) s IEP75-IEP90; d IEP130-IEP140 (incl. bkfst) * LB **FACILITIES:** Golf 9 Tennis (hard) Squash Croquet lawn **PARKING:** 40 **NOTES:** No smoking in restaurant Closed Nov-Etr **CARDS:**

★59% ***Pier***

☎ 074 58178 & 58115 📠 074 58115

***Dir:*** *on sea front, near harbour*

This pleasant hotel stands directly opposite a sandy beach on the western shores of Lough Swilly. There is a comfortable lounge, a dining room and a bar. A good angling centre and golf course are available nearby.

**ROOMS:** 10 en suite (2 fmly) **FACILITIES:** no TV in bdrms entertainment **NOTES:** No dogs (ex guide dogs) Closed Nov-May RS Apr-May & Oct **CARDS:**

## RATHNEW, Co Wicklow — Map 01 D3

### *Premier Collection*

★★★ **Tinakilly Country House & Restaurant**

☎ 0404 69274 📠 0404 67806

e-mail: reservations@tinakilly.ie

***Dir:*** *follow the N11/M11 to Rathnew village, cont on R750 towards Wicklow. Entrance to hotel is approx 500mtrs from the village on left*

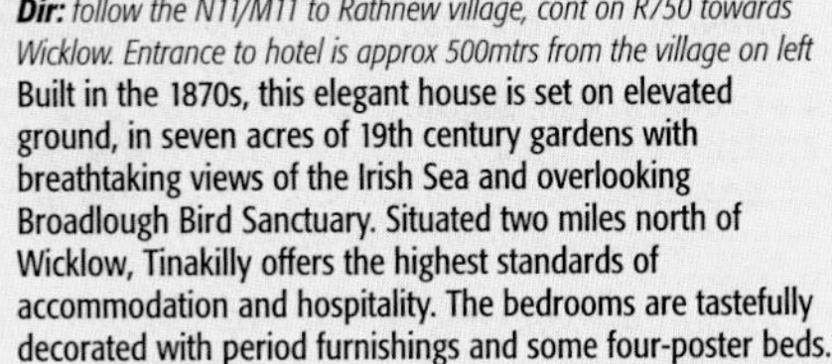

Built in the 1870s, this elegant house is set on elevated ground, in seven acres of 19th century gardens with breathtaking views of the Irish Sea and overlooking Broadlough Bird Sanctuary. Situated two miles north of Wicklow, Tinakilly offers the highest standards of accommodation and hospitality. The bedrooms are tastefully decorated with period furnishings and some four-poster beds.

*continued*

Country house cuisine is served, including fresh fish, game and home-grown vegetables.

**ROOMS:** 51 en suite s IEP122-IEP130; d IEP148-IEP164 (incl. bkfst) * LB **FACILITIES:** STV Tennis (hard) Gym Croquet lawn 7 acres of gardens mapped for walking entertainment ch fac Xmas **CONF:** Thtr 65 Class 48 Board 41 **SERVICES:** Lift **PARKING:** 60 **NOTES:** No dogs (ex guide dogs) RS 24-26 Dec & 31 Dec-2 Jan **CARDS:**

★★★67% ***Hunter's***

☎ 0404 40106 📠 0404 40338

***Dir:*** *1.5km from village off N11*

A delightful hotel which is one of Ireland's oldest coaching inns. Noted for its prize-winning gardens bordering the River Vartry, the introduction of modern facilities has not detracted from the character of the original hotel. The restaurant has a good reputation for carefully prepared dishes which make the best use of high quality local produce. An ideal centre for touring, golf, and also commercial trade.

**ROOMS:** 16 en suite (2 fmly) **CONF:** Class 40 Board 16 **PARKING:** 50 **NOTES:** No dogs (ex guide dogs) Closed 24-26 Dec **CARDS:**

## RECESS, Co Galway — Map 01 A4

★★★77% **Lough Inagh Lodge**

Inagh Valley

☎ 095 34706 & 34694 📠 095 34708

e-mail: inagh@iol.ie

***Dir:*** *after Recess take R344 towards Kylemore through Inagh valley, hotel is in middle of valley*

A luxurious hotel, formerly a 19th century hunting lodge. Its setting, fronted by a good fishing lake, includes lovely mountain views. Large lounges and an oak-lined bar provide warmth and comfort, and the spacious bedrooms are beautifully furnished. The food is a highlight of any stay here.

**ROOMS:** 12 en suite s IEP77-IEP88; d IEP121-IEP143 (incl. bkfst) * LB **FACILITIES:** STV Fishing Hill walking, **CONF:** Thtr 20 Class 20 Board 20 **SERVICES:** air con **PARKING:** 16 **NOTES:** No smoking in restaurant Closed 15 Dec-15 Mar **CARDS:**

## RENVYLE, Co Galway — Map 01 A4

★★★66% ***Renvyle House Hotel***

☎ 095 43511 📠 095 43515

e-mail: renvyle@iol.ie

***Dir:*** *N59 west of Galway towards Clifden Pass through Oughterard & Maam Cross, at Recess turn right, Keymore turn left, Letterfrack turn right, hotel 5m*

This historic country house nestles between the mountains and the ocean on the unspoilt coast of Connemara. Spacious

*continued on p886*

RENVYLE, continued

comfortable lounges and turf fires combined with friendly staff make a stay here relaxing and memorable. Bedrooms vary in size and are well equipped with spectacular views. Good leisure facilities include hard tennis courts, snooker room, outdoor pool, and a 9-hole golf course.
**ROOMS:** 65 en suite (8 fmly) **FACILITIES:** STV Outdoor swimming (H) Golf 9 Tennis (hard) Fishing Riding Snooker Croquet lawn ch fac **CONF:** Thtr 200 Class 80 Board 80 Del from IEP60 * **PARKING:** 60 **NOTES:** Closed 2 Jan-28 Feb **CARDS:**

## ROSCOMMON, Co Roscommon — Map 01 B4

### ★★★65% Abbey

Galway Rd
☎ 0903 26240 & 26505 📠 0903 26021
e-mail: cmv@indigo.ie
***Dir:*** *on N63 opposite railway station*
Set in its own grounds just outside Roscommon, this fine manor house dates back over 100 years. The bedrooms are well-decorated, with a choice of period style rooms in the original part of the house, while those in the newer wing are more contemporary. Service is attentive and the hotel has a friendly atmosphere.
**ROOMS:** 25 en suite No smoking in 2 bedrooms **FACILITIES:** STV ch fac **CONF:** Thtr 300 Class 200 Board 25 **PARKING:** 100 **NOTES:** No dogs Closed 25-26 Dec **CARDS:**

## ROSSCARBERY, Co Cork — Map 01 B2

### ★★★69% *Celtic Ross*

☎ 023 48722 📠 023 48723
e-mail: info@celticrosshotel.com
***Dir:*** *on N71*

Overlooking a lagoon, on the edge of a peaceful village this hotel is a striking landmark on the West Cork coastline. The spacious public areas are luxuriously appointed with rich fabrics and polished Irish elm, yew bog oakwood and cherrywood. There is a cocktail bar and an Irish pub where a lunchtime carvery is on offer.
**ROOMS:** 67 en suite (30 fmly) No smoking in 10 bedrooms **FACILITIES:** STV Indoor swimming (H) Sauna Gym Jacuzzi Steam room entertainment **CONF:** Thtr 250 Class 80 Board 80 **SERVICES:** Lift air con **PARKING:** 200 **NOTES:** No dogs (ex guide dogs) **CARDS:**

## ROSSLARE, Co Wexford — Map 01 D2

### ★★★★78% ◎◎ *Kelly's Resort*

☎ 053 32114 📠 053 32222
e-mail: kellyhot@iol.ie
***Dir:*** *10 miles from Wexford town,turn off N25 on the Rosslare/Wexford road*
The range of facilities on offer is extensive at this popular seafront hotel, and include a leisure centre, health treatments, indoor and outdoor tennis courts, a children's crèche and spacious gardens. La Marine Bistro is the setting for good modern cuisine, while the main restaurant continues to produce award-winning food. Public rooms are adorned with contemporary Irish art.

**ROOMS:** 99 annexe en suite (15 fmly) **FACILITIES:** STV Indoor swimming (H) Tennis (hard) Squash Snooker Sauna Solarium Gym Croquet lawn Jacuzzi Bowls Plunge pool Badminton Crazy golf Outdoor Canadian hot tub entertainment ch fac **CONF:** Thtr 30 Class 30 Board 20 **SERVICES:** Lift **PARKING:** 99 **NOTES:** No dogs Closed mid Dec-late Feb **CARDS:**

### ★★★64% Crosbie Cedars

☎ 053 32124 📠 053 32243
e-mail: info@crosbiecedars.iol.ie
***Dir:*** *turn off N25 at Ashfield crossroads. Follow brown signs at cross for Rosslare village. Take 1st left, hotel is situated on right.*
This hotel is within walking distance of miles of safe, sandy beach, championship golf links and many other activities. The attractive foyer features a white baby grand piano, and there is a choice of bars - the relaxing Tavern Bar and Library, and Bunkers which provides entertainment at weekends. Bedrooms are well equipped, bright and spacious.
**ROOMS:** 34 en suite (28 fmly) s IEP44.50-IEP59.50; d IEP64-IEP94 (incl. bkfst) * **LB FACILITIES:** STV entertainment ch fac **CONF:** Thtr 250 Class 70 Board 70 **SERVICES:** Lift **PARKING:** 157 **NOTES:** No dogs (ex guide dogs) **CARDS:**

## ROSSLARE HARBOUR, Co Wexford — Map 01 D2

### ★★65% ◎ *Danby Lodge Hotel*

Killinick
☎ 053 58191
This hotel is attached to the house of 18th-century landscape painter Francis Danby. Conveniently situated for the ferry terminal at Rosslare, it offers well equipped, stylish accommodation, including three rooms in the restored stone built coach house. The cosy bar and dining room look out over a pretty garden.
**ROOMS:** 14 en suite

## ROSSNOWLAGH, Co Donegal — Map 01 B5

### ★★★77% ◎◎ Sand House

MANOR HOUSE

☎ 072 51777 📠 072 52100
e-mail: info@sandhouse-hotel.ie
***Dir:*** *on coast road from Ballyshannon in the centre of Donegal Bay*
Set in a crescent of golden sands five miles north of Ballyshannon, this hotel is well-known for its hospitality, good cuisine and

*continued*

service. Many rooms have sea views and a conservatory lounge provides a relaxing retreat.

**ROOMS:** 46 en suite (6 fmly) s IEP60-IEP90; d IEP100-IEP150 (incl. bkfst) * **LB** **FACILITIES:** STV Tennis (hard) Croquet lawn Putting green Mini-golf Surfing Canoeing Sailing entertainment **CONF:** Thtr 60 Class 40 Board 30 Del from IEP75 * **PARKING:** 42 **NOTES:** No smoking in restaurant Closed mid Oct-Etr **CARDS:**

## ROUNDSTONE, Co Galway — Map 01 A4

### ★★70% *Eldons*

☎ 095 35933 & 35942 ⎙ 095 35871

***Dir:*** *off N59 through Toombedla then lt to village*

This distinctive building stands on the main street of a picturesque fishing village. Guests are assured a warm welcome at this hotel along with good service. The seafood restaurant, Bedla, serves a good choice of dishes.

**ROOMS:** 13 en suite 6 annexe en suite (2 fmly) **FACILITIES:** entertainment **SERVICES:** Lift **NOTES:** No dogs Closed 4 Nov-16 Mar **CARDS:**

## SALTHILL See Galway

## SHANNON, Co Clare — Map 01 B3

### ★★★60% *Quality Shannon Hotel*

Ballycasey

☎ 061 364588 ⎙ 061 364045

e-mail: sales@qualityshannon.com

***Dir:*** *3m from Shannon International Airport*

This friendly hotel, conveniently situated just three miles from Shannon Airport, is close to Bunnatty Castle and multinational companies in the Shannon Free Zone. It offers contemporary styled bedrooms, the Old Lodge bar, an all day carvery, a steak house restaurant and meeting rooms.

**ROOMS:** 54 en suite (3 fmly) No smoking in 10 bedrooms **FACILITIES:** STV entertainment **CONF:** Thtr 20 Class 12 Board 12 **SERVICES:** Lift **PARKING:** 130 **NOTES:** No dogs (ex guide dogs) Closed 24-25 Dec **CARDS:**

## SKIBBEREEN, Co Cork — Map 01 B2

### ★★65% *Eldon*

Bridge St

☎ 028 22000 ⎙ 028 22191

e-mail: welcome@eldon-hotel.ie

***Dir:*** *On the N71 west*

Good food, good drink and good company can all be found here. The atmosphere at this family run hotel is friendly, there is a comfortable bar with patio gardens, and car parking to the rear of the hotel.

**ROOMS:** 19 en suite No smoking in 4 bedrooms **FACILITIES:** Fishing use of local leisure centre entertainment **PARKING:** 40 **NOTES:** Closed 24-27 Dec **CARDS:**

## SLANE, Co Meath — Map 01 D4

### ★★★61% Conyngham Arms

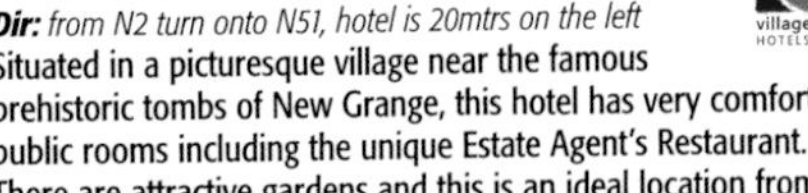
village inn
HOTELS

☎ 041 9884444 ⎙ 041 9824205

***Dir:*** *from N2 turn onto N51, hotel is 20mtrs on the left*

Situated in a picturesque village near the famous prehistoric tombs of New Grange, this hotel has very comfortable public rooms including the unique Estate Agent's Restaurant. There are attractive gardens and this is an ideal location from which to explore the historic area including Tara and the Boyne Valley. Bedrooms are well-presented.

**ROOMS:** 16 en suite (4 fmly) s fr IEP40; d fr IEP75 (incl. bkfst) * **LB** **FACILITIES:** STV **CONF:** Thtr 150 Class 120 **PARKING:** 12 **NOTES:** No dogs (ex guide dogs) **CARDS:**

## SLIGO, Co Sligo — Map 01 B5

### ★★★71% Sligo Park

Pearse Rd

☎ 071 60291 ⎙ 071 69556

e-mail: sligopk@leehotels.ie

***Dir:*** *on N4 1 mile from Sligo on Dublin Road also on Galway Road*

Set in seven acres of parkland on the southern edge of Sligo, this hotel is an ideal touring centre for the many attractions of Yeats country. The bedrooms offer good modern facilities, in particular the excellent 'executive' rooms. The restaurant is particularly attractive and inviting. A comprehensive leisure centre is an added attraction, and there are good beaches close at hand.

**ROOMS:** 110 en suite No smoking in 4 bedrooms s IEP69-IEP75; d IEP105-IEP115 (incl. bkfst) * **LB** **FACILITIES:** Indoor swimming (H) Tennis (hard) Snooker Sauna Solarium Gym Jacuzzi Steam room Plunge pool entertainment Xmas **CONF:** Thtr 520 Class 350 Board 50 **PARKING:** 200 **NOTES:** No dogs (ex guide dogs) RS 24-26 & 31 Dec **CARDS:**

### ★★★65% Tower

Quay St

☎ 071 44000 ⎙ 071 46888

e-mail: towersl@iol.ie

***Dir:*** *in the centre of Sligo*

Pleasantly located beside the quay, this attractively furnished hotel is right in the town centre. There is a smart foyer lounge, a pleasant restaurant and bar; the bedrooms are comfortable and well equipped. Guests have access to the local leisure and fitness centre at reduced rates.

**ROOMS:** 58 en suite No smoking in 12 bedrooms s IEP49-IEP65; d IEP69-IEP100 (incl. bkfst) * **LB** **CONF:** Thtr 200 Class 60 Board 50 Del from IEP80 * **SERVICES:** Lift air con **PARKING:** 20 **NOTES:** No dogs (ex guide dogs) No smoking in restaurant Closed 24-28 Dec **CARDS:**

### ★★63% *Ocean View Hotel*

Strandhill

☎ 071 68115

This family-run hotel, situated in a seaside village to the west of Sligo town, is close to a sandy beach, golf courses and an equestrian centre. Bedrooms are attractively decorated and facilities include a comfortable bar, a restaurant and a residents' lounge.

### ★★61% *Silver Swan*

☎ 071 43231 ⎙ 071 42232

***Dir:*** *situated on the banks of the Garavogue River in the town centre beside G.P.O. and on the junction of N4, N15, N16*

Family-owned, this hotel stands beside the Garavogue River in the

*continued on p888*

S

SLIGO, continued

heart of Sligo. The bedrooms are well-furnished and comfortable with good bathrooms, some with aero-spa baths. The Horseshoe Bar is a popular spot for snacks and drinks.
**ROOMS:** 29 en suite **FACILITIES:** entertainment **CONF:** Thtr 100 Class 60 Board 30 **PARKING:** 40 **NOTES:** No dogs (ex guide dogs) No smoking in restaurant Closed 25 & 26 Dec **CARDS:**

STRAFFAN, Co Kildare Map 01 D4

## Premier Collection

★★★★★ ⓇⓇⓇ **The Kildare Hotel & Golf Club**
☎ 01 6017200 📠 01 6017299
e-mail: resontsales@kclub.ie
***Dir:*** *from Dublin take N4, take exit for R406 hotel entrance is on right in Straffan*
The luxurious Kildare Hotel and Country Club is set in 330 acres of park and woodland. The hotel boasts a golf course designed by Arnold Palmer - the venue for the 2005 Ryder Cup. Opulent reception rooms include the Chinese Drawing Room, which overlooks the gardens and the River Liffey. Richly furnished bedrooms are most comfortable and extremely well-equipped. Staff are very attentive, and there are extensive leisure and conference facilities.
**ROOMS:** 69 en suite 10 annexe en suite (10 fmly) d fr IEP350 * **LB** **FACILITIES:** STV Indoor swimming (H) Golf 18 Tennis (hard) Fishing Squash Snooker Sauna Solarium Gym Croquet lawn Putting green Jacuzzi Beauty salon Driving range Golf tuition Fishing tuition entertainment ch fac Xmas **CONF:** Thtr 160 Class 60 Board 40 Del from IEP249 * **SERVICES:** Lift **PARKING:** 205 **NOTES:** No dogs **CARDS:**

★★★76% ⓇⓇ **Barberstown Castle**
☎ 01 6288157 📠 01 6277027
e-mail: castleir@iol.ie

Dating from the 13th century, this castle houses a hotel which provides the highest standards of comfort. Inviting public rooms range from the original castle keep, now housing one of the two restaurants, to the soft warmth of the drawing room and cocktail bar. Bedrooms are well-equipped and appointed.
**ROOMS:** 22 en suite s IEP94-IEP110; d IEP150-IEP172 (incl. bkfst) * **LB** **FACILITIES:** STV entertainment **CONF:** Thtr 50 Class 40 Board 30 Del from IEP150 * **PARKING:** 200 **NOTES:** No dogs No children 12yrs No smoking in restaurant Closed 24-26 Dec & 5-27 Jan
**CARDS:**

*See advert under DUBLIN*

TEMPLEGLANTINE, Co Limerick Map 01 B2

★★★59% ***The Devon Inn***
☎ 069 84122 📠 069 84255
***Dir:*** *midway between Limerick City and Killarney on N21*
A hotel with a smart reception area, comfortable foyer lounge, and all-day bar and restaurant. Bedrooms offer spacious accommodation with good quality wood finishes and thoughtful extras. Salmon and trout fishing are available, along with golf.
**ROOMS:** 59 en suite (20 fmly) **FACILITIES:** STV **CONF:** Thtr 400 Class 200 Board 30 **PARKING:** 200 **NOTES:** Closed 24-25 Dec
**CARDS:**

THOMASTOWN, Co Kilkenny Map 01 C3

## Premier Collection

★★★★ ⓇⓇ **Mount Juliet**
☎ 056 73000 📠 056 73019
e-mail: info@mountjuliet.ie
***Dir:*** *take M7 from Dublin, N9 towards Waterford then to the Mount Juliet on the N9 via Carlow and Gowran*
Mount Juliet is set in 1500 acres of parkland and includes a Jack Nicklaus designed golf course. The Irish Opens were played at this golf course in 1993 and 1994, and this beautiful Palladian mansion has now become a very special hotel. The elegant and spacious public rooms retain much of the original architectural features. Ornate plasterwork and fine Adam fireplaces now feature in the cocktail bar, the restaurant and the drawing room.
**ROOMS:** 32 en suite 27 annexe en suite No smoking in 1 bedroom s IEP140-IEP310; d IEP140-IEP400 * **LB** **FACILITIES:** Spa STV Indoor swimming (H) Golf 18 Tennis (hard) Fishing Riding Snooker Sauna Gym Croquet lawn Putting green Beauty salon, Archery, Cycling, Clay pigeon shooting, Golf tuition, Xmas **CONF:** Thtr 200 Class 70 Board 50 Del from IEP130 * **PARKING:** 200 **NOTES:** No dogs (ex guide dogs) No smoking in restaurant
**CARDS:**

S

*continued*

## TRALEE, Co Kerry — Map 01 A2

### ★★★69% *Meadowlands Hotel*
Oakpark
☎ 066 7180444 🖹 066 7180964
e-mail: medlands@iol.ie
***Dir:*** *1km from Tralee town centre on N69*
This smart new hotel has been built to a high standard and is within walking distance of the town centre. There is stylish use of colour, tile and timber throughout, and the tastefully decorated bedrooms are comfortable and fitted with locally crafted pine furniture.
**ROOMS:** 27 en suite (3 fmly) **FACILITIES:** STV entertainment **CONF:** Thtr 40 Class 40 Board 20 **SERVICES:** Lift air con **PARKING:** 120 **NOTES:** No dogs (ex guide dogs) Closed 24-26 Dec **CARDS:**

### ★★★64% Abbey Gate
Maine St
☎ 066 7129888 🖹 066 7129821
e-mail: abbeygat@iol.ie
***Dir:*** *in town centre*
The Abbey Gate is a smartly appointed town centre hotel. The well-equipped bedrooms include some suitable for those with mobility problems. Public areas include a spacious foyer and lounge area with attractive decor, a traditional pub, 'The Old Market Place' where carvery lunches are served, a cocktail bar, the Vineyard Restaurant and banqueting and conference suites.
**ROOMS:** 100 en suite (4 fmly) s IEP58-IEP98; d IEP60-IEP110 (incl. bkfst) * **LB** **FACILITIES:** STV entertainment Xmas **CONF:** Thtr 450 Class 250 Board 40 Del from IEP75 * **SERVICES:** Lift **PARKING:** 40 **NOTES:** No dogs (ex guide dogs) RS 24-26 Dec **CARDS:**

## TRAMORE, Co Waterford — Map 01 C2

### ★★★63% *Majestic*
☎ 051 381761 🖹 051 381766
***Dir:*** *turn off N25 through Waterford onto R675 to Tramore*
A warm welcome awaits at this hotel, overlooking Tramore Bay and 10km from Waterford City. All bedrooms are well-equipped. The restaurant specialises in local fresh seafood and steak dishes. Full leisure facilities are available to residents at Splashworld Health & Fitness Club across the road from the hotel.
**ROOMS:** 57 en suite (4 fmly) No smoking in 5 bedrooms **FACILITIES:** STV Outdoor swimming (H) **SERVICES:** Lift **PARKING:** 10 **NOTES:** No dogs (ex guide dogs) **CARDS:**

## VIRGINIA, Co Cavan — Map 01 C4

### ★★67% ❀ *The Park*
Virginia Park
☎ 049 8547235 🖹 049 8547203
e-mail: virginiapark@eircom.net
***Dir:*** *Turn off N3 in Virginia onto R194.Hotel 500yds on left*
A charming hotel built in 1750 as the summer retreat of the Marquis of Headford. Situated at the end of a beech avenue on a 100-acre estate, it has a 9-hole golf course and lovely mature gardens. Dinner is served in the Marquis dining room, overlooking Lough Ramor.
**ROOMS:** 18 en suite (1 fmly) **FACILITIES:** Golf 9 **CONF:** Thtr 70 Class 40 Board 40 **PARKING:** 50 **NOTES:** No dogs No smoking in restaurant **CARDS:**

## WATERFORD, Co Waterford — Map 01 C2

### ★★★★74% ❀❀ Waterford Castle
The Island
☎ 051 878203 🖹 051 879316
e-mail: info@waterfordcastle.com
***Dir:*** *from city centre, turn onto Dunmore East Rd, continue for 1.5m, pass hospital, 0.5m left after lights, ferry at bottom of road*
Picturesque and enchanting, this historic castle which dates back to Norman times, is a former home of the Fitzgerald clan. Reached by a chain link ferry, just a short distance from the mainland, the castle has a grand entrance hall boasting Elizabethan panelling and a cavernous fireplace. Enjoyable cuisine is served in the Munster Room, where fixed-price and carte menus are complemented by a good wine list. Bedrooms, all comfortable, include The Presidential Suite.
**ROOMS:** 19 en suite (2 fmly) **FACILITIES:** STV Golf 18 Tennis (hard) Croquet lawn Putting green Clay pigeon shooting,archery(group) entertainment **CONF:** Thtr 30 Board 15 **SERVICES:** Lift **PARKING:** 50 **NOTES:** No dogs (ex guide dogs) No smoking in restaurant **CARDS:**

### ★★★71% ❀ Granville
Best Western
The Quay
☎ 051 305555 🖹 051 305566
e-mail: stay@granville-hotel.ie
***Dir:*** *take the N25 to the waterfront, city centre , opposite the Clock Tower*

Situated on the quayside, this charming old hotel has been extensively refurbished to a high standard, while still retaining its original character. Bedrooms, in a choice of standard or executive rooms, are comfortable. The public areas and the restaurant are all appointed to a very high standard.
**ROOMS:** 100 en suite (5 fmly) No smoking in 20 bedrooms s IEP80-IEP85; d IEP140-IEP150 (incl. bkfst) * **LB** **FACILITIES:** STV entertainment Xmas **CONF:** Thtr 200 Class 150 Board 30 Del IEP90 * **SERVICES:** Lift **PARKING:** 300 **NOTES:** No dogs (ex guide dogs) Closed 25-26 Dec **CARDS:**

### ★★★68% Tower
The Mall
☎ 051 875801 🖹 051 870129
e-mail: towerw@iol.ie
***Dir:*** *opposite Reginald's Tower in the centre of town hotel located at end of quay in Waterford on N25 the Cork Road*
Extensive refurbishment has given the hotel a new look including two smart new restaurants, a carvery and a bistro, a new conference venue and upgraded bedrooms. A comfortable riverside lounge bar, a leisure centre and rear car park are also provided.
**ROOMS:** 139 en suite (10 fmly) s IEP56-IEP95; d IEP89-IEP140 (incl. bkfst) * **LB** **FACILITIES:** Indoor swimming (H) Sauna Solarium Gym Jacuzzi entertainment ch fac Xmas **CONF:** Thtr 500 Class 250 Board 100 **SERVICES:** Lift **PARKING:** 90 **NOTES:** No dogs (ex guide dogs) Closed 24-28 Dec **CARDS:**

W

WATERFORD, continued

### ★★★66% Dooley's

30 The Quay
☎ 051 873531 051 870262
e-mail: hotel@dooleys-hotel.ie
***Dir:*** *on N25*
Situated in the heart of Waterford overlooking the quayside, Dooley's is a comfortable family-run hotel. The smart public areas and bedrooms offer comfortable and stylish accommodation, and there is an elevator to all floors. Guests are very well cared for in a warm and friendly atmosphere.
**ROOMS:** 113 en suite (3 fmly) No smoking in 17 bedrooms
**FACILITIES:** STV Land & Water based Activities entertainment
**CONF:** Thtr 240 Class 150 Board 100 **SERVICES:** Lift **NOTES:** No dogs (ex guide dogs) Closed 25-27 Dec **CARDS:**

### ★★★65% *Waterford Manor*

Killotteran, Butlerstown
☎ 051 377814 051 354545
***Dir:*** *N25 from Waterford to Cork, right 2m after Waterford Crystal, left at end of road, hotel 3yds on right*
Set in 20 acres of mature grounds, this period residence is situated on the outskirts of Waterford. Refurbishment has taken place here, and facilities now include lounges, restaurant, and a new bar bistro which overlooks the gardens. There is also a new business centre and exhibition hall.
**ROOMS:** 10 en suite (3 fmly) No smoking in 6 bedrooms
**FACILITIES:** STV Tennis (hard) ch fac **CONF:** Thtr 600 Class 300 Board 40 **PARKING:** 400 **NOTES:** No dogs (ex guide dogs) No smoking in restaurant RS 25 Dec **CARDS:**

### ★★★63% Bridge Hotel

1 The Quay
☎ 051 877222 051 877229
e-mail: bridgehotel@treacyhotelsgroup.com
***Dir:*** *the Hotel is located opposite the Waterford City Bridge when following the N25*
This busy hotel stands near the City Bridge, convenient for the shops and local amenities. The bedrooms are well-furnished and really comfortable. Public areas include a country-style bistro, a restaurant, a traditional Irish pub and a relaxing lounge bar.
**ROOMS:** 100 en suite (20 fmly) No smoking in 4 bedrooms
**FACILITIES:** STV entertainment **CONF:** Thtr 400 Class 300 Board 70
**SERVICES:** Lift air con **PARKING:** 200 **NOTES:** No dogs Closed 25 Dec
**CARDS:**

### ★★★61% *Jurys*

Ferrybank
JURYS DOYLE HOTELS
☎ 051 832111 051 832863
e-mail: michaelwalsh@jurys.com
***Dir:*** *on N25 1km from City Centre*
In an elevated setting in 38 acres of parkland, this modern hotel enjoys spectacular views overlooking the city and harbour. Public areas are comfortable and bedrooms are spacious and well-equipped. Guests can enjoy the many activities available in the extensive leisure centre.
**ROOMS:** 98 en suite (20 fmly) No smoking in 4 bedrooms
**FACILITIES:** Indoor swimming (H) Tennis (hard) Sauna Solarium Gym Jacuzzi Steam room Plunge pool Jacuzzi entertainment **CONF:** Thtr 700 Class 400 Board 100 **SERVICES:** Lift **PARKING:** 300 **NOTES:** No dogs (ex guide dogs) Closed 24-27 Dec **CARDS:**

W

### ★★★58% *Ivory's Hotel*

Tramore Rd
☎ 051 358888 051 358899
e-mail: ivoryhotel@voyager.ie
***Dir:*** *N25 to Cork. After 600yds exit Tramore R675. Hotel on R*
This modern, family-run hotel is near the Waterford Glass factory. Bedrooms are comfortable and well-appointed, offering family and standard rooms. There is a choice of dining options, a patio with garden seating, and a children's play area, as well as secure parking. Close to a number of golf courses and fishing.
**ROOMS:** 40 en suite (20 fmly) No smoking in 20 bedrooms
**FACILITIES:** STV ch fac **PARKING:** 120 **CARDS:**

### Travelodge

Travelodge

Cork Rd
☎ 051 358885 051 358890
***Dir:*** *On N25, 1km from Waterford Glass Visitors Centre*
Travelodge offers good quality, good value, modern accommodation. Ideal for families, the spacious, en suite bedrooms include remote-control TV, tea and coffee-making facilities, luxury beds and free morning newspaper. Meals can be taken at the nearby family restaurant. For further details and the Travelodge phone number, consult the Hotel Groups page.

**ROOMS:** 32 en suite s IEP40-IEP50; d IEP40-IEP50 *

WATERVILLE, Co Kerry — Map 01 A2

### ★★★72% Butler Arms

MANOR HOUSE

☎ 066 9474144 066 9474520
e-mail: butarms@iol.ie
***Dir:*** *centre of Waterville on seafront. N70 Ring of Kerry*

Standing on the Ring of Kerry overlooking the ocean, the Butler Arms offers traditional high standards of service. Most of the bedrooms have marble bathrooms and enjoy sea views, whilst public areas include spacious lounges and a billiards room. An 18-hole championship golf course is situated opposite.
**ROOMS:** 42 en suite (1 fmly) No smoking in 9 bedrooms s IEP95-IEP135; d IEP140-IEP180 (incl. bkfst) * **LB** **FACILITIES:** STV Tennis (hard) Fishing Snooker **SERVICES:** Lift **PARKING:** 50 **NOTES:** No dogs (ex guide dogs) Closed Jan-Apr & Oct-Dec **CARDS:**

WESTPORT, Co Mayo — Map 01 B4

### ★★★73% *Hotel Westport*

The Demesne, Newport Rd
☎ 098 25122 098 26739
e-mail: sales@hotelwestport.co.uk
***Dir:*** *N5 to Westport, at end of Castlebar St turn right, first right, first left, follow road to end*
Opposite the grounds of Westport House, this hotel offers welcoming accommodation comprising a new reception foyer,

*continued*

lounge, spacious restaurant and comfortable bedrooms including six suites. The hotel has much to offer the leisure and business guest, with a swimming pool, sauna and gym, and conference and syndicate rooms.
**ROOMS:** 129 en suite (36 fmly) **FACILITIES:** STV Indoor swimming (H) Sauna Solarium Gym Jacuzzi Steam room Lounger pool & childrens pool Jet stream entertainment ch fac **CONF:** Thtr 500 Class 150 Board 60 **SERVICES:** Lift **PARKING:** 220 **NOTES:** No dogs (ex guide dogs) No smoking in restaurant **CARDS:**

### ★★★70% *Ardmore Country House*

The Quay
☎ 098 25994 098 27795
A charming country house hotel, elevated over the quay, within walking distance of the town centre. The attractive restaurant and relaxing lounges overlook Clew Bay, with Croagh Patrick in the background. Individually styled bedrooms are spacious and comfortable, most have spectacular sea views.

### ★★★65% *The Atlantic Coast Hotel*

The Quay
☎ 098 29000 098 29111
e-mail: achotel@iol.ie
***Dir:*** *N5 follow signs into Westport then Louisburgh on R335 1m from Westport*
In an appealing location, overlooking the harbour, this former mill is now a distinctive hotel. Bedrooms are contemporary in style and offer all modern facilities, and there is a spacious lounge and bar. The candlelit Blue Wave Restaurant on the fourth floor serves good food in a very pleasant ambience.
**ROOMS:** 85 en suite (3 fmly) **FACILITIES:** STV Indoor swimming (H) Sauna Solarium Gym Treatment rooms entertainment ch fac **CONF:** Thtr 180 Class 140 Board 70 **SERVICES:** Lift **PARKING:** 60 **NOTES:** No dogs (ex guide dogs) Closed 23-27 Dec **CARDS:**

### ★★★62% The Olde Railway

The Mall
☎ 098 25166 & 25605 098 25090
e-mail: railway@anu.ie
***Dir:*** *overlooking the Carrowbeg River in the town centre*
Set on a tree-lined mall overlooking the river, this classic coaching inn offers a welcoming atmosphere with blazing turf fires. There is a variety of bedroom sizes, including some very spacious rooms, all are well-equipped. Communal areas include an attractively furnished bar, a comfortable lounge and a Conservatory Restaurant with access to the patio and barbecue area.
**ROOMS:** 24 en suite (2 fmly) s IEP45-IEP85; d IEP60-IEP140 (incl. bkfst) * **LB FACILITIES:** STV Fishing & Shooting arranged entertainment **PARKING:** 34 **NOTES:** No dogs (ex guide dogs) No smoking in restaurant **CARDS:**

*See advert on this page*

### ★★★59% The Central Hotel

The Octagon
☎ 098 25027 098 26316
e-mail: thecentralhotel@anu.ie
***Dir:*** *Leave N5 at Castlebar to Westport, hotel located at the top of the town*
Situated in the Octagon in the town centre, this friendly hotel marries old-fashioned charm with modern comforts very successfully. There is a choice of dining options, both formal and

*continued*

informal, public areas have a relaxed atmosphere, and the well-equipped bedrooms are comfortable.
**ROOMS:** 36 en suite (4 fmly) s IEP35-IEP55; d IEP80-IEP90 (incl. bkfst) * **LB FACILITIES:** Leisure facilities for hotel guest close nearby entertainment **CONF:** Thtr 250 Class 150 Board 30 Del from IEP90 * **SERVICES:** Lift **PARKING:** 40 **NOTES:** No dogs (ex guide dogs) Closed 24-25 Dec **CARDS:**

### ★★66% *Clew Bay Hotel*

village inn HOTELS

James St
☎ 098 28088 098 25783
e-mail: clewbay@anu.ie
***Dir:*** *At the bottom of James St, which is parallel to the main street. Two doors away from the tourist office*
A warm and friendly family-run hotel in the town centre. Recently refurbished bedrooms are well-equipped and attractive. Guests can enjoy traditional Irish music in the Tubber Bar. The restaurant overlooks the Carrowbeg River at the rear.
**ROOMS:** 35 en suite (3 fmly) No smoking in 5 bedrooms **FACILITIES:** STV entertainment **NOTES:** Closed Xmas & New Year **CARDS:**

## WEXFORD, Co Wexford — Map 01 D3

### ★★★★68% Ferrycarrig

Ferrycarrig Bridge
☎ 053 20999 053 20982
e-mail: ferrycarrig@griffingroup.ie
***Dir:*** *on N11 by Slaney Estuary, beside Ferrycarrig Castle*
Set in one of the most inspiring locations in Ireland, this lovely hotel has sweeping views across the estuary. The public rooms curve round the waterfront and include a fine leisure centre. The

*continued on p892*

W

WEXFORD, continued

bedrooms are freshly furbished with particularly good rooms available in the new extension. Both restaurants are at the water's edge; the lively bistro offers a wide menu, while Tides restaurant offers gourmet cuisine.

*Ferrycarrig, Wexford*

**ROOMS:** 103 en suite (3 fmly) No smoking in 45 bedrooms s IEP75-IEP450; d IEP130-IEP450 (incl. bkfst) * **LB** **FACILITIES:** STV Indoor swimming (H) Sauna Solarium Gym Jacuzzi Aerobics Beauty treatments on request Hairdresser entertainment Xmas **CONF:** Thtr 400 Class 250 Board 60 Del from IEP198 * **SERVICES:** Lift **PARKING:** 235 **NOTES:** No dogs (ex guide dogs) **CARDS:**

### ★★★72% Talbot

Trinity St
☎ 053 22566 053 23377
e-mail: talbotwx@eircom.net
***Dir:*** *from Rosslare, take N11 & follow the signs for Wexford, hotel on the right hand side of the Quays - 12miles*

Centrally situated on the quayside, this hotel has been extensively refurbished. All the well-equipped bedrooms offer custom-made oak furniture and attractive decor. Day rooms include a spacious foyer, comfortable lounge, and a bar with an open fireplace. The attractive restaurant serves interesting food, and there are good leisure facilities.

**ROOMS:** 100 en suite (12 fmly) No smoking in 10 bedrooms s IEP70-IEP80; d IEP110-IEP130 (incl. bkfst) * **LB** **FACILITIES:** STV Indoor swimming (H) Sauna Solarium Gym Jacuzzi Childrens room Beauty Salon entertainment Xmas **CONF:** Thtr 450 Class 250 Board 110 **SERVICES:** Lift **PARKING:** 160 **NOTES:** No dogs (ex guide dogs) Closed 24-25 Dec **CARDS:**

*See advert on opposite page*

### ★★★70% Whitford House

New Line Rd
☎ 053 43444 & 43845 053 46399
e-mail: whitford@indigo.ie
***Dir:*** *located left off second rdbt on main Dublin to Rosslare road, (N11)*

A family run hotel on the edge of Wexford with a choice of lounges, a spacious bar and a restaurant offering a good value menu with a variety of seafood dishes. The comfortable bedrooms are equipped with modern facilities, and de-luxe patio rooms are available. Additional guest facilities include an indoor swimming pool, tennis courts and a children's playground.

**ROOMS:** 36 en suite (28 fmly) s IEP46-IEP65; d IEP72-IEP100 (incl. bkfst) * **LB** **FACILITIES:** STV Indoor swimming (H) Tennis (hard) Childrens playground entertainment **CONF:** Board 50 **PARKING:** 140 **NOTES:** No dogs Closed 23 Dec-13 Jan RS 24 Dec-Jan **CARDS:**

### ★★★63% River Bank House Hotel

☎ 053 23611 053 23342
e-mail: river@indigo.ie
***Dir:*** *beside Wexford Bridge on R741*

As its name suggests, this hotel overlooks the River Slaney. Public areas include a very smart foyer, attractively decorated dining room and a Victorian style bar where food is served all day. Bedrooms are comfortable and well-equipped.

**ROOMS:** 24 en suite s IEP63-IEP73; d IEP100-IEP120 (incl. bkfst) * **LB** **FACILITIES:** STV **PARKING:** 40 **NOTES:** No dogs (ex guide dogs) Closed 24-25 Dec **CARDS:**

### ★★★60% *White's Hotel*

George St
☎ 053 22311 053 45000
e-mail: info@whiteshotel.iol.ie

Best Western

***Dir:*** *on entering Wexford Town from the N11 or N25 follow directional signs for White's Hotel*

This historic former coaching inn provides comfortable modern facilities while retaining much of its charm. The entrance is through a modern extension, and entertainment is provided in the converted saddlery and forge.

**ROOMS:** 76 en suite 6 annexe en suite (1 fmly) **FACILITIES:** STV Sauna Gym Jacuzzi Disco Bar entertainment **CONF:** Thtr 400 Class 250 Board 100 **SERVICES:** Lift **PARKING:** 100 **NOTES:** No dogs (ex guide dogs) **CARDS:**

WICKLOW See Rathnew

WOODENBRIDGE, Co Wicklow Map 01 D3

### ★★★64% Woodenbridge

☎ 0402 35146 0402 35573
e-mail: wbhotel@iol.ie
***Dir:*** *between Avoca & Arklow*

This comfortable hotel in the Vale of Avoca, under an hour's drive from the ferry ports of Dun Laoghaire and Rosslare, and close to the N11, continues to thrive. With new bedrooms and a modern conference and banqueting suite the hotel facilities are excellent. Hospitality and good food is assured, golf and fishing are on the doorstep.

**ROOMS:** 23 en suite (13 fmly) s IEP50-IEP65; d IEP80-IEP110 (incl. bkfst) * **LB** **FACILITIES:** STV Xmas **CONF:** Thtr 200 Class 200 Board 200 **PARKING:** 100 **NOTES:** No dogs **CARDS:**

## YOUGHAL, Co Cork Map 01 C2

★★66% Devonshire Arms

Pearse Square

☎ 024 92827 & 92018 📠 024 92900

This 19th-century hotel has been restored with considerable care and attention to detail. It offers good food in both the restaurant and the bar.

**ROOMS:** 10 en suite (3 fmly) **CONF:** Class 150 **PARKING:** 20

**NOTES:** No dogs (ex guide dogs) Closed Xmas

**CARDS:**

€ The Euro will be phased in during 2002 (R.O.I. only).
Make sure you check prices and currency when booking.





Y

# KEY TO ATLAS

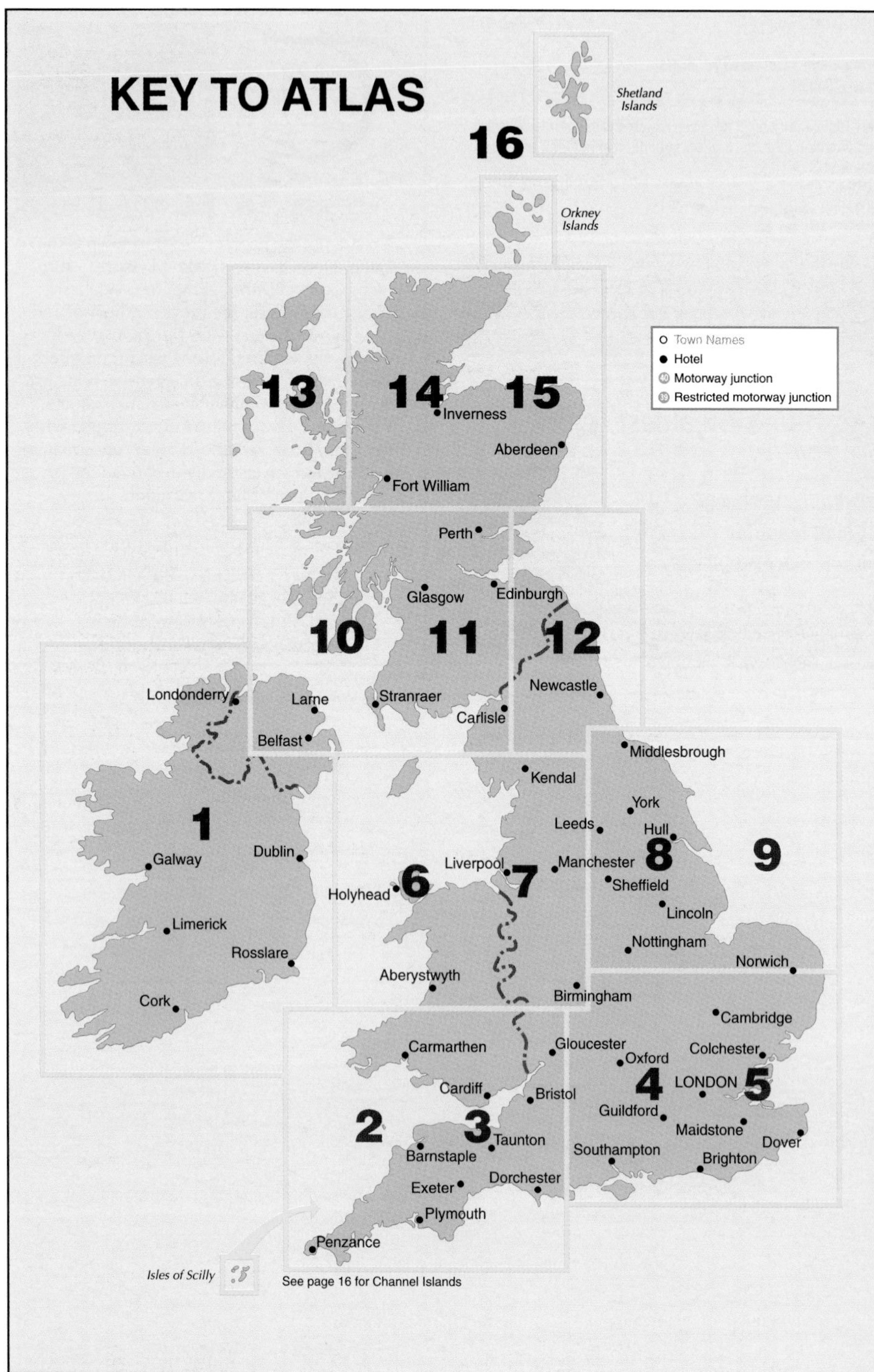
Shetland Islands
16
Orkney Islands
Town Names
Hotel
Motorway junction
Restricted motorway junction
13
14
15
Inverness
Aberdeen
Fort William
Perth
Glasgow
Edinburgh
10
11
12
Londonderry
Larne
Stranraer
Newcastle
Belfast
Carlisle
Middlesbrough
Kendal
York
1
Leeds
Hull
Galway
Dublin
Liverpool
Manchester
8
9
Holyhead
6
7
Sheffield
Limerick
Lincoln
Rosslare
Nottingham
Norwich
Aberystwyth
Cork
Birmingham
Cambridge
Carmarthen
Gloucester
Colchester
Oxford
Cardiff
4
LONDON
5
Bristol
Guildford
2
3
Maidstone
Taunton
Dover
Barnstaple
Southampton
Brighton
Exeter
Dorchester
Plymouth
Penzance
Isles of Scilly

See page 16 for Channel Islands

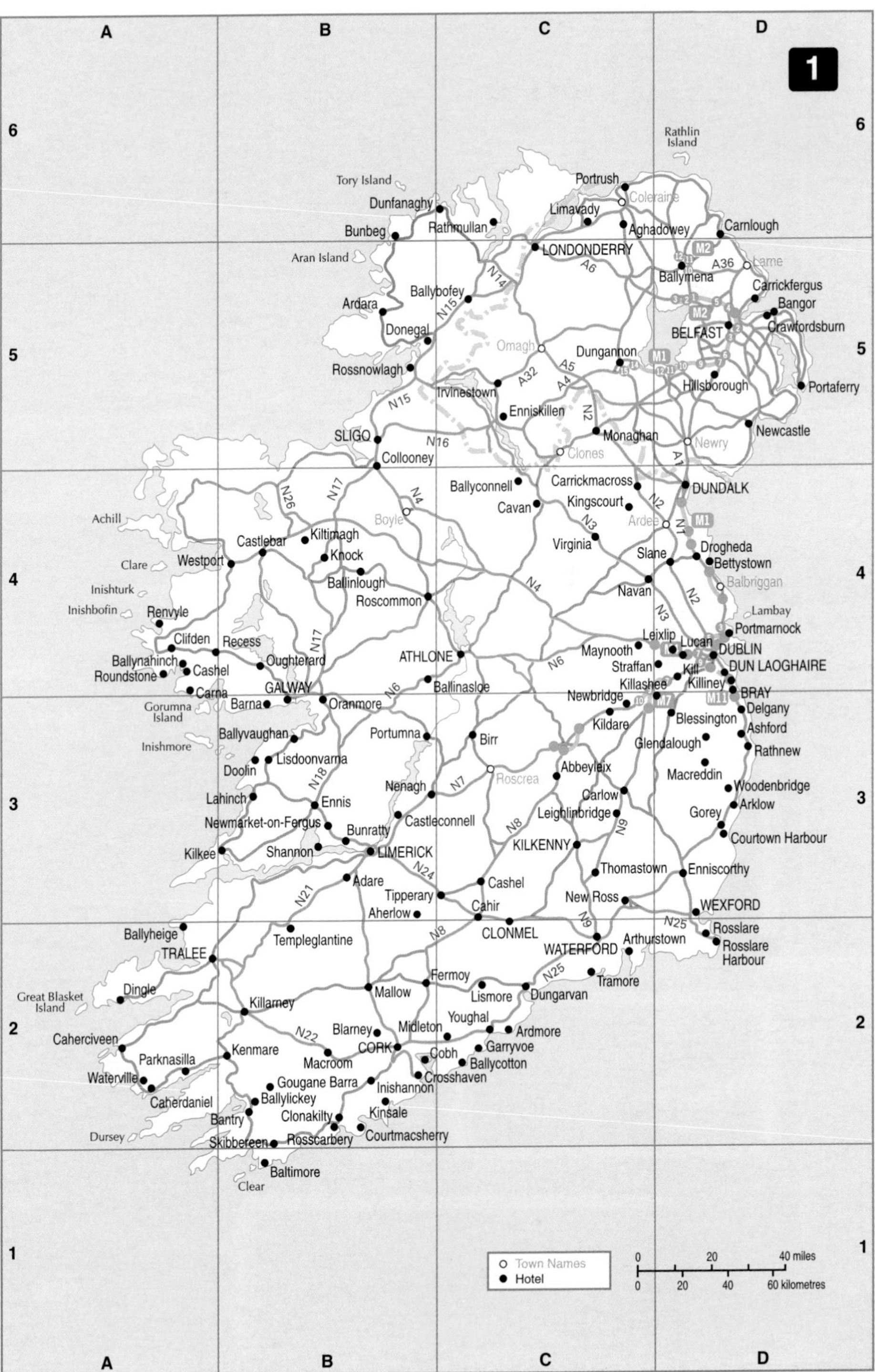

1
A
B
C
D
6
5
4
3
2
1
Rathlin Island
Tory Island
Portrush
Coleraine
Dunfanaghy
Limavady
Aghadowey
Carnlough
Bunbeg
Rathmullan
Aran Island
LONDONDERRY
M2
A36
Larne
A6
Ballymena
N14
Ballybofey
Carrickfergus
Ardara
N15
Bangor
M2
Crawfordsburn
BELFAST
Donegal
Omagh
Dungannon
M1
Rossnowlagh
A5
Hillsborough
Portaferry
A32
A4
Irvinestown
N15
Enniskillen
N2
Newcastle
SLIGO
N16
Monaghan
Newry
Clones
A1
Collooney
Carrickmacross
DUNDALK
N26
N17
Ballyconnell
N4
Cavan
Kingscourt
N2
Achill
Boyle
Ardee
M1
N3
N1
Kiltimagh
Castlebar
Virginia
Drogheda
Clare
Westport
Knock
Slane
Bettystown
Ballinlough
N4
Navan
Balbriggan
Inishturk
Roscommon
N2
Inishbofin
Renvyle
N3
Lambay
N17
Leixlip
Portmarnock
Clifden
Recess
Maynooth
Lucan
DUBLIN
Ballynahinch
Oughterard
ATHLONE
N6
Straffan
Kill
DUN LAOGHAIRE
Roundstone
Cashel
Ballinasloe
Killashee
Killiney
Carna
GALWAY
N6
Newbridge
M7
M11
BRAY
Gorumna Island
Barna
Oranmore
Delgany
Blessington
Kildare
Ashford
Ballyvaughan
Portumna
Birr
Inishmore
Glendalough
Rathnew
Lisdoonvarna
Doolin
Roscrea
Abbeyleix
Macreddin
N18
N7
Nenagh
Woodenbridge
Lahinch
Carlow
Arklow
Ennis
Gorey
Castleconnell
N8
Leighlinbridge
Newmarket-on-Fergus
N9
Bunratty
Courtown Harbour
KILKENNY
Kilkee
Shannon
LIMERICK
N24
Thomastown
Enniscorthy
Adare
N21
Cashel
Tipperary
New Ross
WEXFORD
Aherlow
Cahir
N9
N25
CLONMEL
Rosslare
Ballyheige
N8
Templeglantine
WATERFORD
Arthurstown
Rosslare Harbour
TRALEE
N25
Tramore
Fermoy
Dingle
Mallow
Lismore
Dungarvan
Great Blasket Island
Killarney
Youghal
Ardmore
Caherciveen
Blarney
Midleton
N22
CORK
Garryvoe
Kenmare
Macroom
Cobh
Parknasilla
Ballycotton
Waterville
Crosshaven
Gougane Barra
Inishannon
Caherdaniel
Ballylickey
Kinsale
Clonakilty
Bantry
Courtmacsherry
Dursey
Rosscarbery
Skibbereen
Baltimore
Clear
Town Names
Hotel
0
20
40 miles
0
20
40
60 kilometres

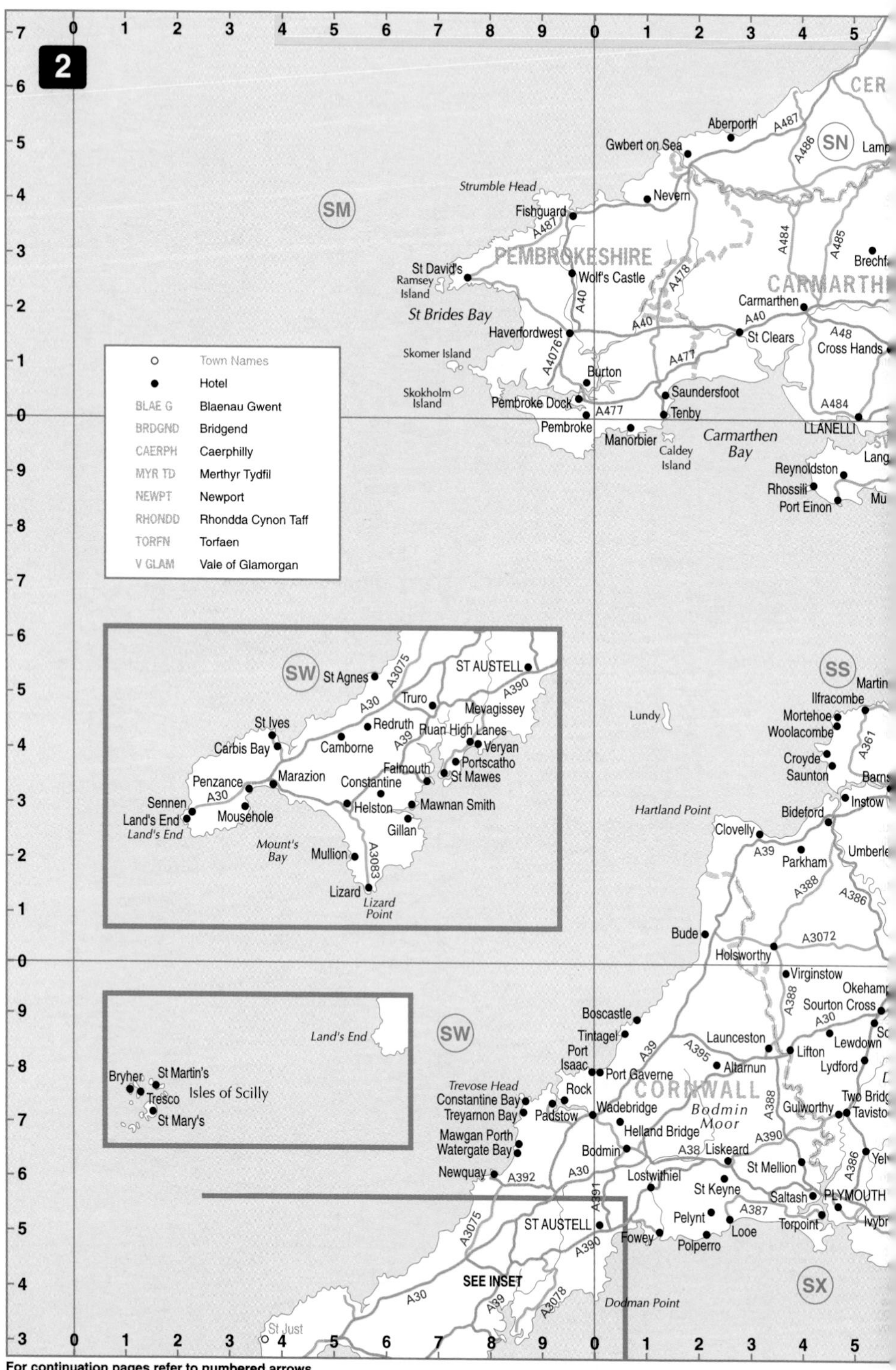

SM
SN
SW
SS
SX
Town Names
Hotel
BLAE G
Blaenau Gwent
BRDGND
Bridgend
CAERPH
Caerphilly
MYR TD
Merthyr Tydfil
NEWPT
Newport
RHONDD
Rhondda Cynon Taff
TORFN
Torfaen
V GLAM
Vale of Glamorgan
PEMBROKESHIRE
CORNWALL
Aberporth
Gwbert on Sea
Strumble Head
Nevern
Fishguard
St David's
Ramsey Island
Wolf's Castle
St Brides Bay
Carmarthen
Haverfordwest
St Clears
Cross Hands
Skomer Island
Burton
Skokholm Island
Saundersfoot
Pembroke Dock
Tenby
Pembroke
Manorbier
Caldey Island
Carmarthen Bay
LLANELLI
Reynoldston
Rhossili
Port Einon
A487
A486
A484
A485
A478
A40
A4076
A477
A48
ST AUSTELL
St Agnes
Truro
Mevagissey
St Ives
Redruth
Ruan High Lanes
Carbis Bay
Camborne
Veryan
Portscatho
Falmouth
St Mawes
Penzance
Marazion
Constantine
Sennen
Helston
Mawnan Smith
Land's End
Mousehole
Gillan
Mount's Bay
Mullion
Lizard
Lizard Point
A30
A39
A3075
A390
A3083
Lundy
Martin
Ilfracombe
Mortehoe
Woolacombe
Croyde
Saunton
Instow
Hartland Point
Bideford
Clovelly
Parkham
Bude
Holsworthy
Virginstow
Sourton Cross
Lewdown
Boscastle
Tintagel
Launceston
Lifton
Port Isaac
Altarnun
Lydford
Port Gaverne
Trevose Head
Rock
Constantine Bay
Treyarnon Bay
Padstow
Wadebridge
Bodmin Moor
Gulworthy
Two Bridges
Helland Bridge
Mawgan Porth
Watergate Bay
Bodmin
Liskeard
St Mellion
Newquay
Lostwithiel
St Keyne
Saltash
PLYMOUTH
Pelynt
Torpoint
Fowey
Looe
Polperro
Isles of Scilly
Bryher
St Martin's
Tresco
St Mary's
SEE INSET
Dodman Point
St Just
A361
A388
A386
A3072
A395
A392
A391
A387
A3078


For continuation pages refer to numbered arrows

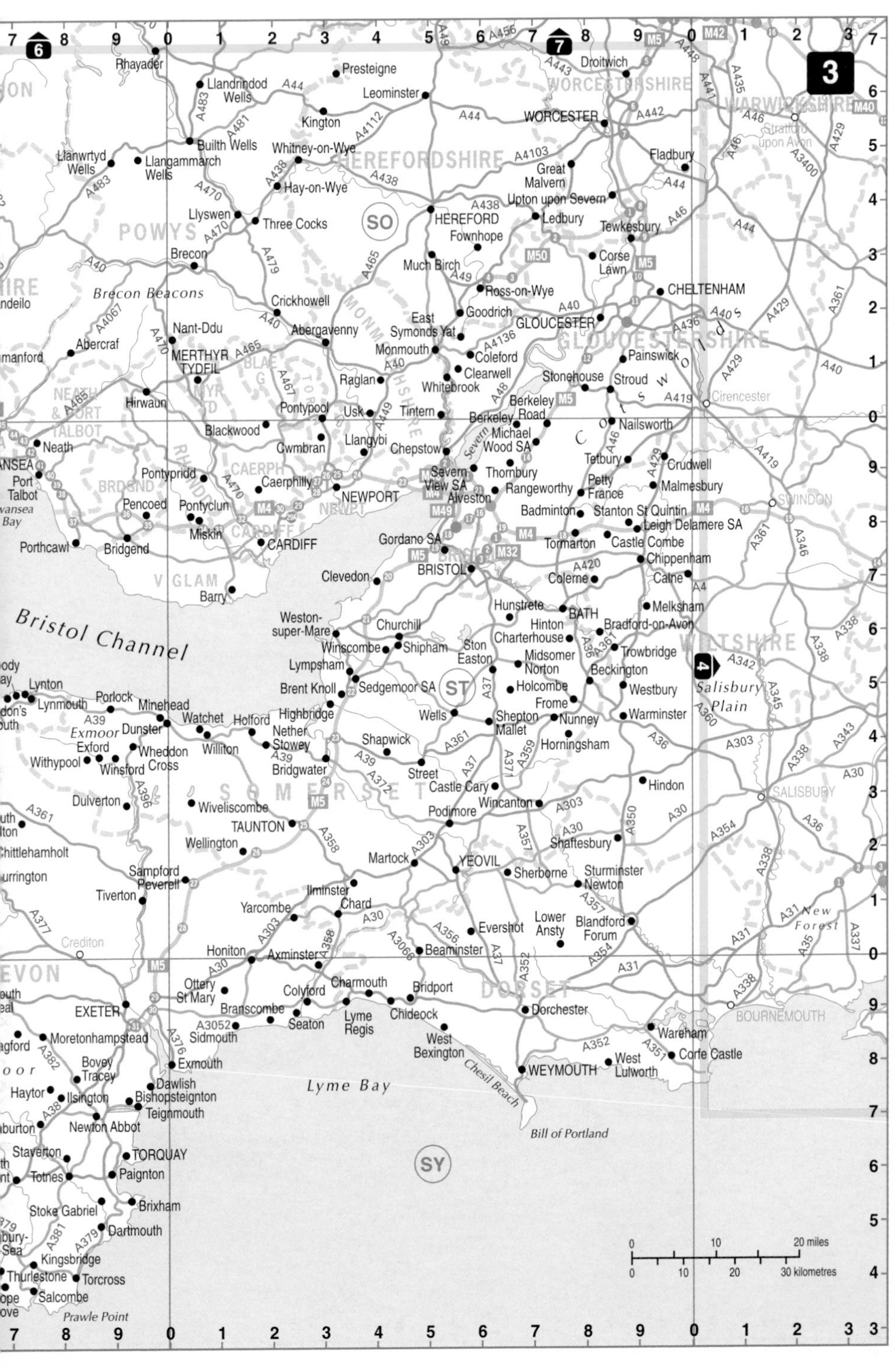

3
6
7
4
Rhayader
Presteigne
Llandrindod Wells
Leominster
Droitwich
WORCESTERSHIRE
WARWICKSHIRE
Kington
WORCESTER
Stratford upon Avon
Builth Wells
Llanwrtyd Wells
Llangammarch Wells
Whitney-on-Wye
HEREFORDSHIRE
Fladbury
Great Malvern
Hay-on-Wye
Upton upon Severn
Llyswen
Three Cocks
HEREFORD
Ledbury
Tewkesbury
POWYS
SO
Fownhope
Brecon
Much Birch
Corse Lawn
CHELTENHAM
Brecon Beacons
Ross-on-Wye
Crickhowell
Goodrich
GLOUCESTER
East Symonds Yat
GLOUCESTERSHIRE
Nant-Ddu
Abergavenny
Monmouth
Coleford
Painswick
Abercraf
MERTHYR TYDFIL
Clearwell
Stonehouse
Stroud
Raglan
Whitebrook
Cirencester
Cotswold
Hirwaun
Pontypool
Usk
Tintern
Berkeley
Berkeley Road
Nailsworth
Blackwood
Llangybi
Michael Wood SA
Neath
Cwmbran
Chepstow
Tetbury
Crudwell
Severn
Port Talbot
Pontypridd
Caerphilly
Severn View SA
Thornbury
Petty France
Malmesbury
NEWPORT
Alveston
Rangeworthy
SWINDON
Pencoed
Pontyclun
Badminton
Stanton St Quintin
Leigh Delamere SA
Miskin
Bridgend
CARDIFF
Gordano SA
Tormarton
Castle Combe
Porthcawl
Chippenham
BRISTOL
Clevedon
Colerne
Calne
V GLAM
Barry
Hunstrete
Melksham
Bristol Channel
Weston-super-Mare
Churchill
BATH
Bradford-on-Avon
Hinton Charterhouse
Winscombe
Shipham
Ston Easton
Midsomer Norton
Trowbridge
WILTSHIRE
Lympsham
Beckington
Lynton
Brent Knoll
Sedgemoor SA
ST
Holcombe
Westbury
Salisbury Plain
Lynmouth
Porlock
Minehead
Frome
Watchet
Holford
Highbridge
Wells
Shepton Mallet
Nunney
Warminster
Exmoor
Dunster
Nether Stowey
Exford
Williton
Shapwick
Horningsham
Withypool
Wheddon Cross
Winsford
Bridgwater
Street
Hindon
SOMERSET
Castle Cary
SALISBURY
Dulverton
Wiveliscombe
Wincanton
Podimore
TAUNTON
Shaftesbury
Wellington
Martock
YEOVIL
Sherborne
Sturminster Newton
Sampford Peverell
Ilminster
Tiverton
Chard
Yarcombe
New Forest
Lower Ansty
Blandford Forum
Evershot
Crediton
Honiton
Axminster
Beaminster
DEVON
Ottery St Mary
Charmouth
Colyford
Bridport
DORSET
EXETER
Branscombe
Seaton
Lyme Regis
Chideock
Dorchester
BOURNEMOUTH
Sidmouth
West Bexington
Wareham
Moretonhampstead
Corfe Castle
Bovey Tracey
Exmouth
West Lulworth
WEYMOUTH
Chesil Beach
Dawlish
Lyme Bay
Haytor
Ilsington
Bishopsteignton
Teignmouth
Newton Abbot
Bill of Portland
Staverton
TORQUAY
SY
Totnes
Paignton
Brixham
Stoke Gabriel
Dartmouth
Kingsbridge
Thurlestone
Torcross
Salcombe
Prawle Point
0 10 20 miles
0 10 20 30 kilometres

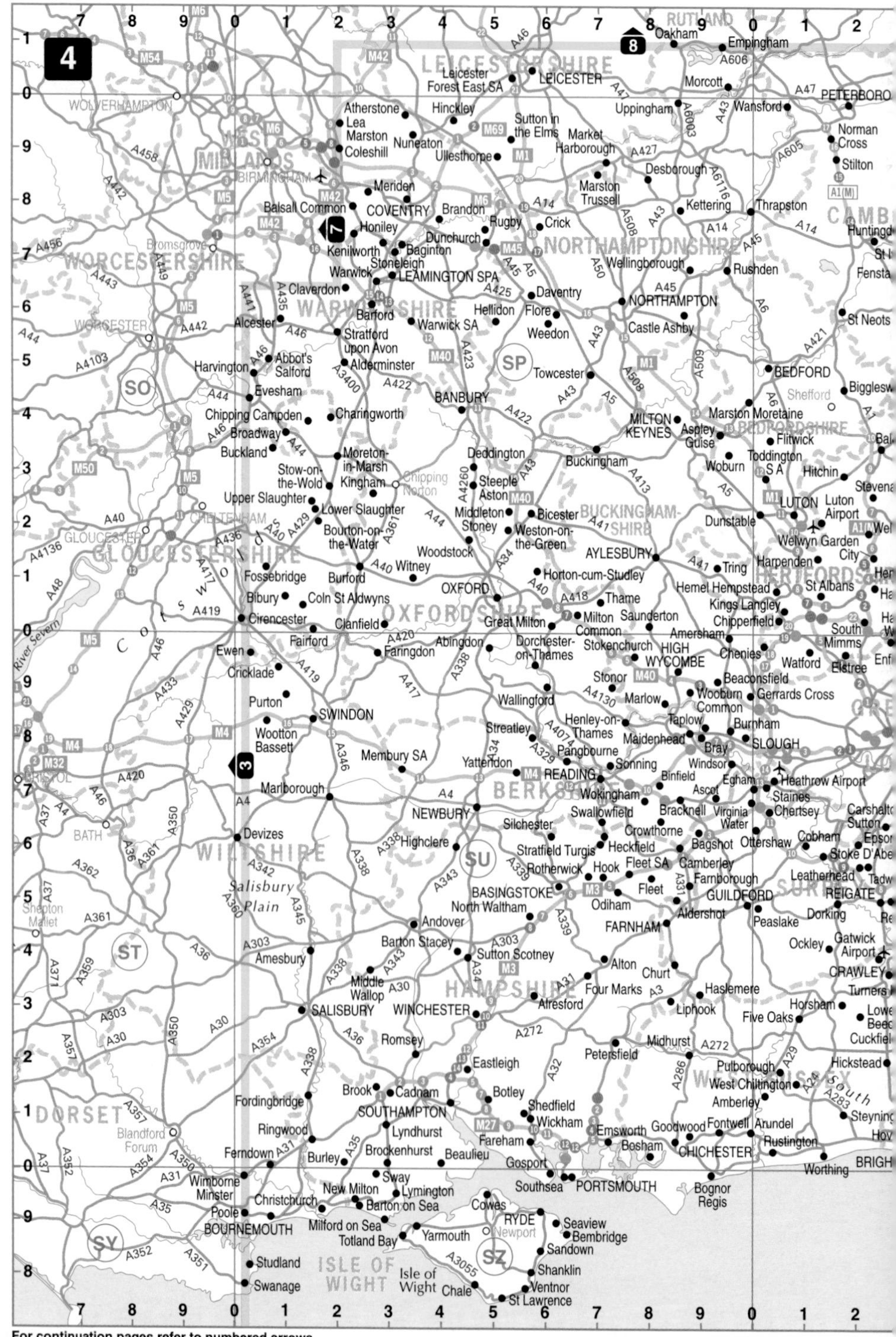

4
8
RUTLAND
Oakham
Empingham
A606
LEICESTERSHIRE
Leicester Forest East SA
LEICESTER
Morcott
A47
PETERBOROUGH
WOLVERHAMPTON
Atherstone
Lea Marston
Coleshill
Hinckley
Nuneaton
Sutton in the Elms
Market Harborough
Uppingham
Wansford
Norman Cross
Stilton
WEST MIDLANDS
BIRMINGHAM
Ullesthorpe
A427
Desborough
Meriden
Balsall Common
COVENTRY
Brandon
Marston Trussell
Kettering
Thrapston
A14
Honiley
Rugby
Crick
Bromsgrove
WORCESTERSHIRE
Kenilworth
Baginton
Dunchurch
NORTHAMPTONSHIRE
Huntingdon
Stoneleigh
Wellingborough
Rushden
Warwick
LEAMINGTON SPA
Claverdon
A425
Daventry
A45
NORTHAMPTON
Fenstanton
WARWICKSHIRE
Hellidon
Flore
Weedon
Castle Ashby
St Neots
Alcester
WORCESTER
Barford
Warwick SA
Stratford upon Avon
Alderminster
Abbot's Salford
Harvington
Evesham
SO
SP
Towcester
BEDFORD
Biggleswade
Shefford
BANBURY
A422
MILTON KEYNES
Marston Moretaine
Aspley Guise
BEDFORDSHIRE
Flitwick
Chipping Campden
Charingworth
Broadway
Buckland
Moreton-in-Marsh
Deddington
Buckingham
Woburn
Toddington S A
Hitchin
Stow-on-the-Wold
Kingham
Chipping Norton
Steeple Aston
Upper Slaughter
Lower Slaughter
Middleton Stoney
Bicester
BUCKINGHAMSHIRE
LUTON
Luton Airport
Dunstable
CHELTENHAM
GLOUCESTER
Bourton-on-the-Water
Weston-on-the-Green
Welwyn Garden City
GLOUCESTERSHIRE
Woodstock
AYLESBURY
Tring
Harpenden
HERTFORDSHIRE
Fossebridge
Burford
Witney
Horton-cum-Studley
OXFORD
Hemel Hempstead
St Albans
Bibury
Coln St Aldwyns
Thame
Kings Langley
Cotswold
Cirencester
OXFORDSHIRE
Great Milton
Milton Common
Saunderton
Chipperfield
A419
Clanfield
River Severn
Fairford
Abingdon
Dorchester-on-Thames
Amersham
South Mimms
Ewen
Faringdon
Stokenchurch
HIGH WYCOMBE
Chenies
Watford
Elstree
Cricklade
Stonor
Beaconsfield
Purton
Wallingford
Marlow
Wooburn Common
Gerrards Cross
SWINDON
Henley-on-Thames
Taplow
Burnham
Wootton Bassett
Streatley
Maidenhead
Bray
SLOUGH
Membury SA
Pangbourne
Sonning
Windsor
BRISTOL
Yattendon
READING
Binfield
Egham
Heathrow Airport
Marlborough
BERKSHIRE
Wokingham
Ascot
Staines
NEWBURY
Swallowfield
Bracknell
Virginia Water
Chertsey
Carshalton
Sutton
BATH
Devizes
Silchester
Crowthorne
Cobham
Epsom
Highclere
Heckfield
Bagshot
Ottershaw
Stoke D'Abernon
WILTSHIRE
SU
Stratfield Turgis
Rotherwick
Hook
Fleet SA
Camberley
Leatherhead
Salisbury Plain
BASINGSTOKE
Fleet
Farnborough
GUILDFORD
SURREY
REIGATE
Shepton Mallet
North Waltham
Odiham
Aldershot
Dorking
Andover
FARNHAM
Peaslake
Barton Stacey
Sutton Scotney
Ockley
Gatwick Airport
ST
Amesbury
Alton
Churt
CRAWLEY
HAMPSHIRE
Middle Wallop
Four Marks
Haslemere
Alresford
Liphook
Horsham
SALISBURY
WINCHESTER
Five Oaks
Romsey
Petersfield
Midhurst
Eastleigh
Pulborough
Hickstead
WEST SUSSEX
Brook
Cadnam
Botley
West Chiltington
Fordingbridge
SOUTHAMPTON
Shedfield
Amberley
South Downs
DORSET
Blandford Forum
Ringwood
Lyndhurst
Wickham
Emsworth
Goodwood
Fontwell
Arundel
Steyning
Fareham
Bosham
CHICHESTER
Rustington
Ferndown
Burley
Brockenhurst
Beaulieu
Gosport
Worthing
BRIGHTON
Wimborne Minster
Sway
Southsea
PORTSMOUTH
Bognor Regis
New Milton
Lymington
Christchurch
Barton on Sea
Cowes
Poole
RYDE
Newport
Seaview
Bembridge
BOURNEMOUTH
Milford on Sea
Totland Bay
Yarmouth
Sandown
SY
SZ
Studland
ISLE OF WIGHT
Isle of Wight
Shanklin
Swanage
Chale
Ventnor
St Lawrence
M6
M54
M42
M69
M1
M6
M5
M45
M40
M50
M4
M32
M3
M27
M25
A1(M)
A46
A458
A442
A456
A449
A443
A44
A4103
A441
A435
A3400
A423
A5
A43
A50
A508
A509
A6
A421
A6003
A43
A605
A6116
A413
A41
A361
A4260
A34
A40
A436
A429
A417
A4136
A48
A420
A417
A338
A4130
A4074
A329
A4
A346
A433
A37
A350
A36
A362
A342
A345
A360
A303
A339
A343
A371
A359
A357
A30
A354
A36
A31
A272
A32
A286
A29
A24
A283
A3
A35
A352
A351
A3055
A338
A303
A27
7 8 9 0 1 2 3 4 5 6 7 8 9 0 1 2


For continuation pages refer to numbered arrows

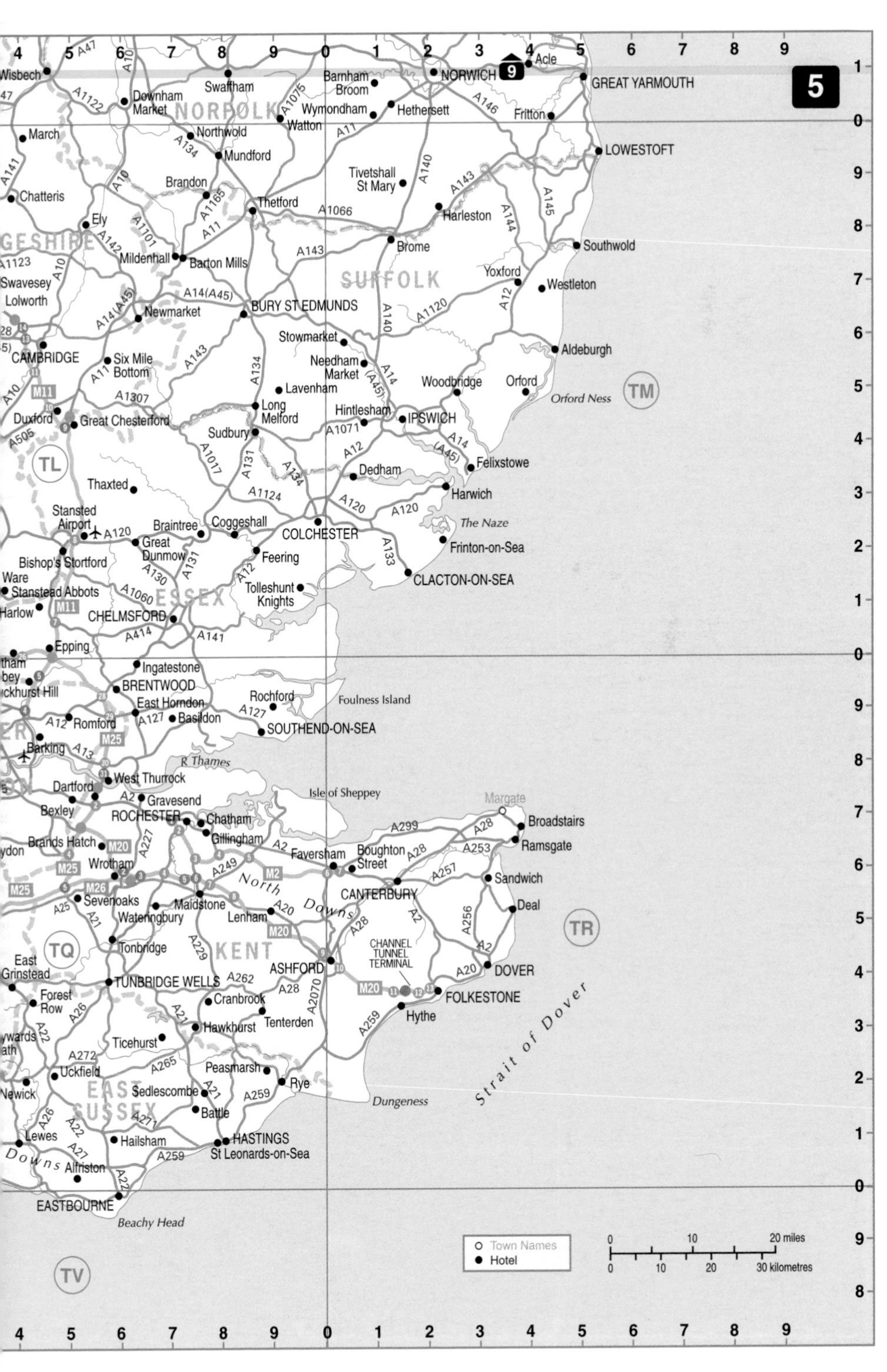

5
NORFOLK
SUFFOLK
ESSEX
KENT
EAST SUSSEX
Wisbech
Downham Market
Swaffham
Barnham Broom
NORWICH
Acle
GREAT YARMOUTH
Wymondham
Hethersett
Fritton
Watton
March
Northwold
Mundford
LOWESTOFT
Tivetshall St Mary
Chatteris
Brandon
Thetford
Harleston
Ely
Brome
Southwold
Mildenhall
Barton Mills
Yoxford
Westleton
Swavesey
Lolworth
Newmarket
BURY ST EDMUNDS
Stowmarket
Aldeburgh
CAMBRIDGE
Six Mile Bottom
Needham Market
Woodbridge
Orford
Lavenham
Orford Ness
Duxford
Great Chesterford
Long Melford
Hintlesham
IPSWICH
Sudbury
Felixstowe
Dedham
Thaxted
Harwich
Stansted Airport
Braintree
Coggeshall
The Naze
Great Dunmow
COLCHESTER
Frinton-on-Sea
Bishop's Stortford
Feering
Ware
CLACTON-ON-SEA
Stanstead Abbots
Tolleshunt Knights
Harlow
CHELMSFORD
Epping
Ingatestone
BRENTWOOD
Rochford
Foulness Island
East Horndon
Romford
Basildon
SOUTHEND-ON-SEA
Barking
R Thames
West Thurrock
Dartford
Gravesend
Isle of Sheppey
Margate
Bexley
ROCHESTER
Chatham
Broadstairs
Gillingham
Ramsgate
Brands Hatch
Faversham
Boughton Street
Wrotham
Sandwich
North Downs
CANTERBURY
Sevenoaks
Maidstone
Deal
Wateringbury
Lenham
Tonbridge
CHANNEL TUNNEL TERMINAL
East Grinstead
ASHFORD
DOVER
TUNBRIDGE WELLS
Forest Row
Cranbrook
FOLKESTONE
Tenterden
Hythe
Hawkhurst
Strait of Dover
Ticehurst
Peasmarsh
Uckfield
Rye
Sedlescombe
Newick
Battle
Dungeness
Lewes
Hailsham
HASTINGS
St Leonards-on-Sea
Downs
Alfriston
EASTBOURNE
Beachy Head
TL
TM
TQ
TR
TV
Town Names
Hotel
0 10 20 miles
0 10 20 30 kilometres

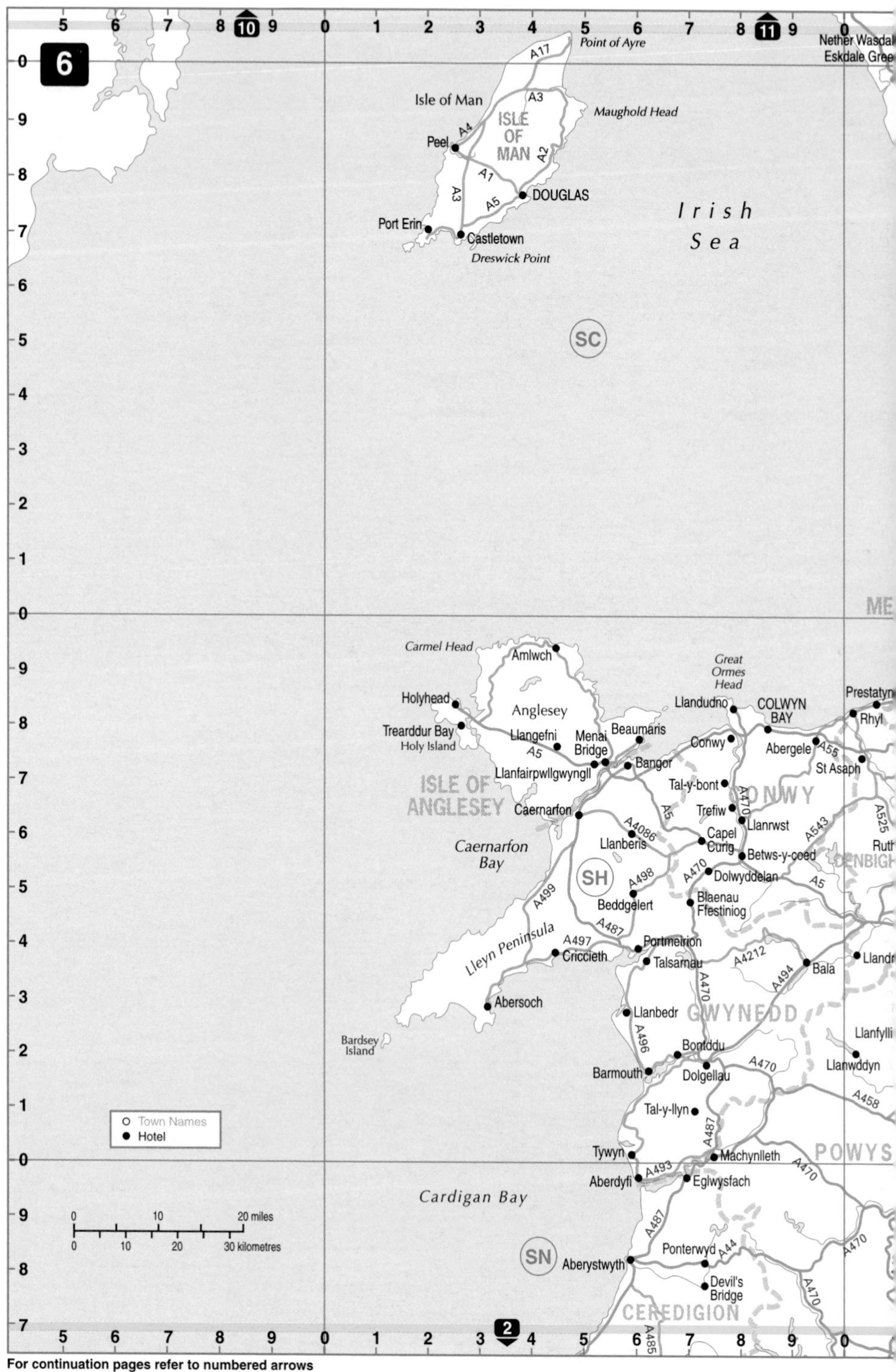
6
Isle of Man
ISLE OF MAN
Point of Ayre
Maughold Head
Peel
DOUGLAS
Port Erin
Castletown
Dreswick Point
Irish Sea
SC
Carmel Head
Amlwch
Holyhead
Trearddur Bay
Holy Island
Anglesey
Llangefni
Menai Bridge
Beaumaris
Bangor
Llanfairpwllgwyngll
ISLE OF ANGLESEY
Caernarfon
Caernarfon Bay
Great Ormes Head
Llandudno
COLWYN BAY
Conwy
Abergele
Prestatyn
Rhyl
St Asaph
Tal-y-bont
Trefiw
Llanrwst
CONWY
Capel Curig
Llanberis
Betws-y-coed
Dolwyddelan
SH
Beddgelert
Blaenau Ffestiniog
Lleyn Peninsula
Portmeirion
Criccieth
Talsarnau
Bala
Abersoch
Llanbedr
GWYNEDD
Bardsey Island
Bontddu
Barmouth
Dolgellau
Llanfylli
Llanwddyn
Tal-y-llyn
Tywyn
Machynlleth
POWYS
Aberdyfi
Eglwysfach
Cardigan Bay
SN
Aberystwyth
Ponterwyd
Devil's Bridge
CEREDIGION
Nether Wasdal
Eskdale Gree
Town Names
Hotel
0 10 20 miles
0 10 20 30 kilometres

For continuation pages refer to numbered arrows

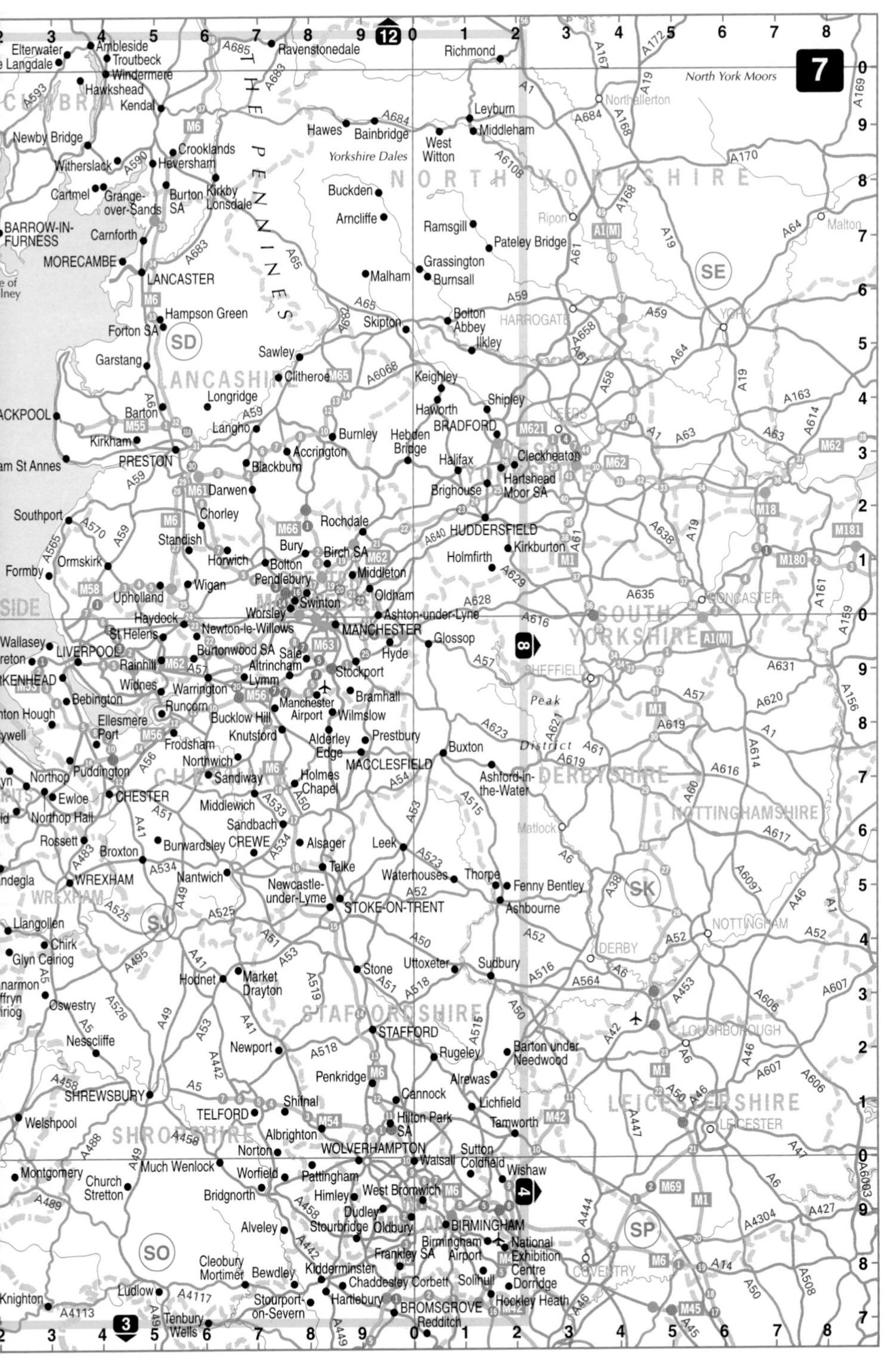
7
North York Moors
NORTH YORKSHIRE
Yorkshire Dales
THE PENNINES
LANCASHIRE
WEST YORKSHIRE
SOUTH YORKSHIRE
DERBYSHIRE
NOTTINGHAMSHIRE
STAFFORDSHIRE
LEICESTERSHIRE
SHROPSHIRE
CHESHIRE
CUMBRIA
Peak District
Richmond
Leyburn
Middleham
Hawes
Bainbridge
West Witton
Northallerton
Ripon
Malton
Harrogate
York
Leeds
Bradford
Keighley
Haworth
Ilkley
Skipton
Halifax
Huddersfield
Doncaster
Sheffield
Manchester
Liverpool
Preston
Blackpool
Lancaster
Kendal
Windermere
Chester
Wrexham
Crewe
Stoke-on-Trent
Stafford
Derby
Nottingham
Leicester
Loughborough
Birmingham
Wolverhampton
Coventry
Shrewsbury
Telford
Ludlow
Kidderminster
Bromsgrove
Redditch
Lichfield
Tamworth
Buxton
Macclesfield
Matlock
Ashbourne
SD
SE
SK
SJ
SO
SP
12
8
4
3

8
DURHAM
NORTH YORKSHIRE
WEST YORKSHIRE
SOUTH YORKSHIRE
EAST RIDING OF YORKSHIRE
LANCASHIRE
GREATER MANCHESTER
CHESHIRE
DERBYSHIRE
NOTTINGHAMSHIRE
LINCOLNSHIRE
STAFFORDSHIRE
LEICESTERSHIRE
RUTLAND
THE PENNINES
Yorkshire Dales
North York Moors
Peak District
The Wolds
R Humber
NY
NZ
SD
SE
SJ
SK
Spennymoor
Peterlee
HARTLEPOOL
Rushyford
Sedgefield
Redworth
Stockton-on-Tees
Saltburn-by-the-Sea
MIDDLESBROUGH
Easington
DARLINGTON
Tees-side Airport
Guisborough
Yarm
Whitby
Crathorne
Scotch Corner
Goathland
Ravenscar
Catterick Bridge
Northallerton
Rosedale Abbey
Lastingham
Hackness
SCARBOROUGH
Hawes
Thornton Watlass
Kirkbymoorside
Appleton-le-Moors
Helmsley
Pickhill
Thirsk
East Ayton
Pickering
Masham
Filey
Topcliffe
Hunmanby
Flamborough Head
Ripon
Hovingham
Malton
Flamborough
Boroughbridge
Easingwold
Langtoft
BRIDLINGTON
Markington
Settle
Aldwark
Knaresborough
Great Driffield
Harrogate
Skipton
YORK
Pocklington
Wetherby
Bilbrough
Sutton upon Derwent
Brandesburton
Bramhope
Escrick
Tadcaster
Beverley
LEEDS
Garforth
Selby
South Cave
Little Weighton
BRADFORD
Hambleton
Willerby
HULL
Halifax
Morley
Castleford
Monk Fryston
North Ferriby
Gomersal
Batley
Ferrybridge S A
Goole
Pontefract
Darrington
Winteringham
Barton-upon-Humber
Dewsbury
Wakefield
Wentbridge
HUDDERSFIELD
Woolley Edge S A
Barnsdale Bar S A
Thorne
SCUNTHORPE
Immingham
Stallingborough
Barnsley
Carcroft
Epworth
Brigg
CLEETHORPES
DONCASTER
MANCHESTER
Tankersley
Rossington
Rotherham
Bawtry
SHEFFIELD
Blyth
Bamford
Woodall
Hathersage
Dronfield
Worksop
East Retford
Renishaw
Barlborough
Grindleford
MACCLESFIELD
Markham Moor
Baslow
Chesterfield
LINCOLN
Horncastle
Bakewell
Branston
Woodhall Spa
Rowsley
MANSFIELD
Matlock
North Muskham
South Normanton
Alfreton
NEWARK-ON-TRENT
Belper
STOKE-ON-TRENT
Hucknall
Gunthorpe
Sleaford
BOSTON
Breadsall
Trowell SA
NOTTINGHAM
Whatton
Belton
DERBY
Risley
Sandiacre
Long Eaton
Langar
GRANTHAM
Tutbury
Shardlow
Colsterworth
Spalding
STAFFORD
East Midlands Airport
Burton upon Trent
LOUGHBOROUGH
Melton Mowbray
South Witham
Quorn
Rothley
Thrussington
Stretton
Coalville
Markfield
Stamford
12
7
4
A1(M)
M1
M62
M18
M180
M181
M621
M65
M66
M63
M67
M56
M6
M42
M54
A1
A19
A66
A64
A65
A61
A63
A614
A165
A170
A171
A174
A172
A167
A168
A684
A689
A688
A685
A683
A6108
A59
A58
A62
A616
A628
A629
A635
A646
A650
A6068
A682
A163
A166
A1079
A1035
A1033
A160
A18
A46
A631
A57
A619
A623
A621
A624
A6
A537
A556
A533
A50
A54
A53
A523
A52
A500
A51
A519
A518
A34
A41
A516
A564
A444
A38
A42
A453
A606
A607
A6097
A17
A15
A16
A6121
A1
A153
A157
A158
A159
A156
A161
A164
A169
A447
A515
A520
A670
For continuation pages refer to numbered arrows

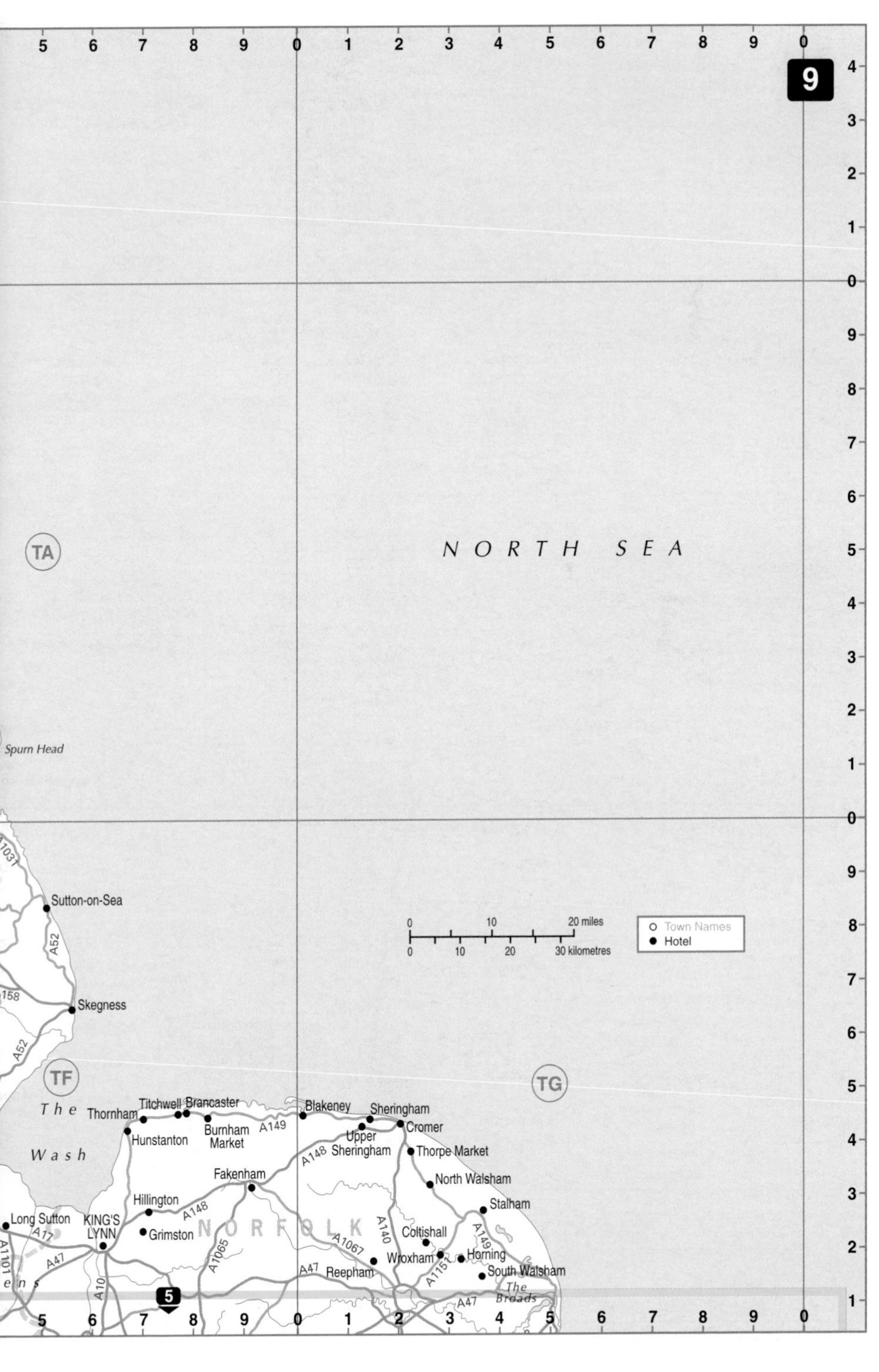
9
NORTH SEA
TA
TF
TG
Spurn Head
Sutton-on-Sea
Skegness
The Wash
Thornham
Titchwell
Brancaster
Hunstanton
Burnham Market
Blakeney
Sheringham
Upper Sheringham
Cromer
Thorpe Market
North Walsham
Stalham
Fakenham
Hillington
Grimston
Long Sutton
KING'S LYNN
NORFOLK
Coltishall
Wroxham
Horning
South Walsham
Reepham
The Broads
A149
A148
A140
A1067
A1065
A47
A17
A10
A52
A1151
0 10 20 miles
0 10 20 30 kilometres
Town Names
Hotel
5

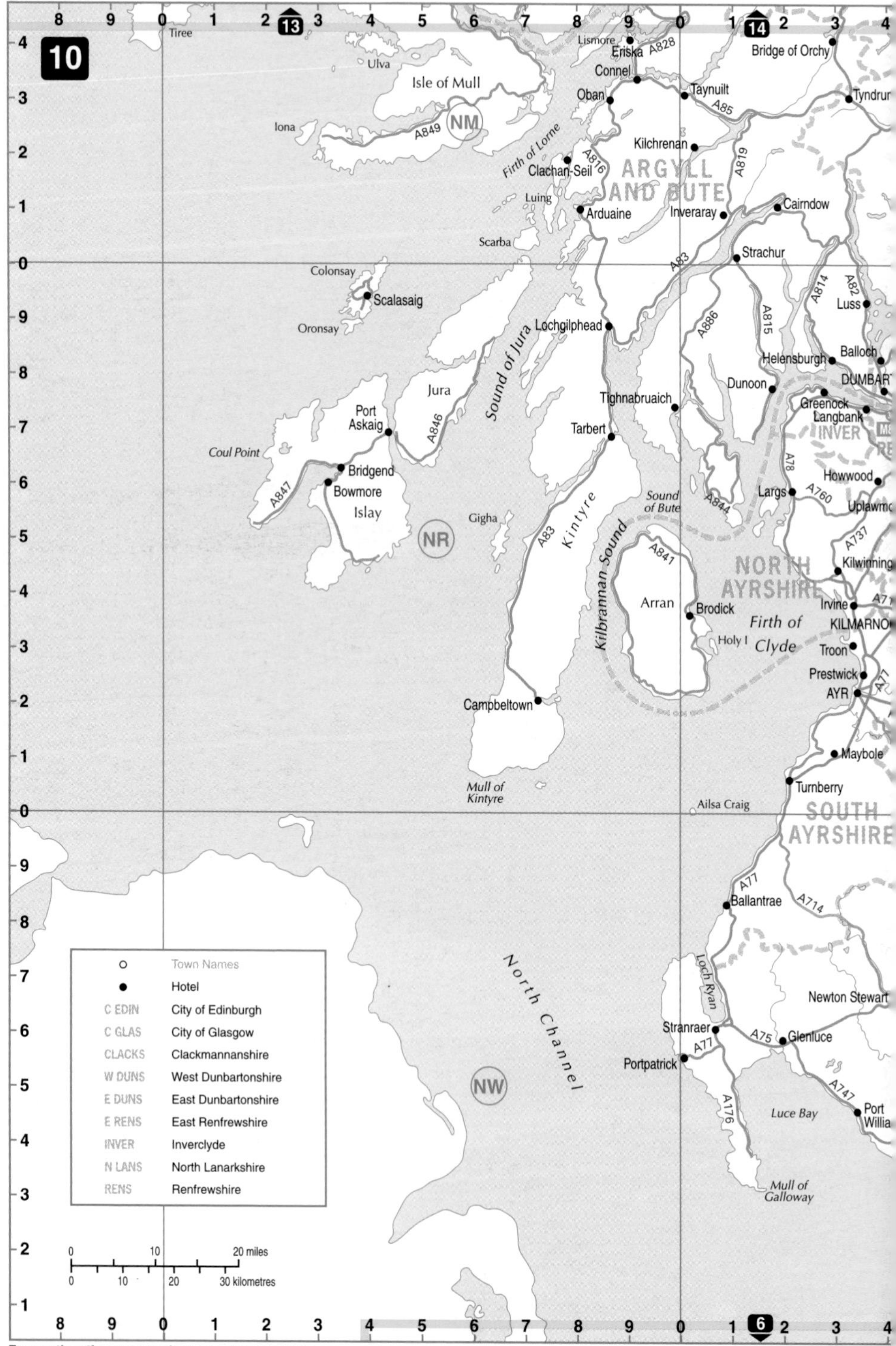
10
Tiree
Ulva
Isle of Mull
Iona
A849
NM
Lismore
Eriska
A828
Connel
Oban
Taynuilt
A85
Bridge of Orchy
Firth of Lorne
Clachan-Seil
A816
Kilchrenan
ARGYLL
AND BUTE
A819
Luing
Arduaine
Inveraray
Cairndow
Scarba
Strachur
A83
Colonsay
Scalasaig
Oronsay
A814
A82
Luss
Sound of Jura
Lochgilphead
A886
A815
Balloch
Helensburgh
Dunoon
Jura
Tighnabruaich
Greenock
Langbank
INVER
Port
Askaig
A846
Tarbert
Coul Point
Bridgend
Bowmore
A847
Islay
Howwood
A78
Largs
A760
Sound
of Bute
A844
Kintyre
NR
Gigha
A83
Kilbrannan Sound
A841
A737
NORTH
AYRSHIRE
Arran
Brodick
Irvine
Firth of
Clyde
Holy I
Troon
Prestwick
AYR
Campbeltown
Maybole
Turnberry
Mull of
Kintyre
Ailsa Craig
SOUTH
AYRSHIRE
A77
Ballantrae
A714
Town Names
Hotel
C EDIN City of Edinburgh
C GLAS City of Glasgow
CLACKS Clackmannanshire
W DUNS West Dunbartonshire
E DUNS East Dunbartonshire
E RENS East Renfrewshire
INVER Inverclyde
N LANS North Lanarkshire
RENS Renfrewshire
North Channel
Loch Ryan
Newton Stewart
Stranraer
A75
Glenluce
A77
Portpatrick
NW
A747
A716
Luce Bay
Mull of
Galloway
0 10 20 miles
0 10 20 30 kilometres
13
14
6

For continuation pages refer to numbered arrows

11
NORTH SEA
PERTH AND KINROSS
DUNDEE CITY
DUNDEE
PERTH
Firth of Tay
Leuchars
St Andrews Bay
St Andrews
Fife Ness
Cupar
Glenrothes
KIRKCALDY
Firth of Forth
Isle of May
Dunbar
EDINBURGH
EAST LOTHIAN
St Abb's Head
Lammermuir Hills
Berwick-upon-Tweed
Holy Island
STIRLING
Dunblane
Bridge of Allan
Falkirk
Grangemouth
Dunfermline
Rosyth
Bathgate
GLASGOW
Clydebank
East Kilbride
Hamilton
Lanark
New Lanark
Biggar
Peebles
Southern Uplands
Galashiels
BORDERS (SCOTTISH)
Kelso
Jedburgh
Hawick
The Cheviot Hills
Abington
Sanquhar
Moffat
Thornhill
DUMFRIES AND GALLOWAY
NORTHUMBERLAND
Otterburn
DUMFRIES
Lockerbie
Annan
Gretna
CARLISLE
Hexham
Castle Douglas
Kirkcudbright
Gatehouse of Fleet
Solway Firth
Silloth
WORKINGTON
Cockermouth
Keswick
Penrith
DURHAM
CUMBRIA
Lake District
Grasmere
Gosforth

12
15
11
7
8
Arbroath
Carnoustie
Broughty Ferry
DUNDEE CITY
PERTH
Firth of Tay
NO
St Andrews Bay
St Andrews
FIFE
Peat Inn
Fife Ness
Crail
GLENROTHES
Lundin Links
Anstruther
Isle of May
NORTH SEA
Firth of Forth
Dirleton
North Berwick
Gullane
Dunbar
Dunfermline
EDINBURGH
WEST LOTHIAN
C EDIN
EAST LOTHIAN
MIDLOTHIAN
St Abb's Head
Lammermuir Hills
Town Names
Hotel
C EDIN City of Edinburgh
0 10 20 miles
0 10 20 30 kilometres
Berwick-upon-Tweed
NT
NU
Lauder
Holy Island
Peebles
Galashiels
Cornhill-on-Tweed
Bamburgh
Melrose
Kelso
Belford
Seahouses
BORDERS (SCOTTISH)
St Boswells
Wooler
Embleton
Jedburgh
The Cheviot Hills
Hawick
Alnwick
Moffat
Otterburn
Longhorsley
DUMFRIES AND GALLOWAY
NORTHUMBERLAND
Morpeth
Bellingham
Seaton Burn
Whitley Bay
Chollerford
Matfen
Newcastle Airport
NEWCASTLE UPON TYNE
Tynemouth
South Shields
Corbridge
Wardley
Brampton
Hexham
Whickham
Gateshead
CARLISLE
SUNDERLAND
Washington
Blanchland
Washington S A
Beamish
NY
Consett
NZ
Houghton le Spring
Alston
Seaham
Southwaite SA
DURHAM
CUMBRIA
Willington
Fir Tree
DURHAM
HARTLEPOOL
Penrith
Temple Sowerby
West Auckland
Keswick
Watermillock
Appleby-in-Westmorland
Romaldkirk
MIDDLESBROUGH
Howtown
Barnard Castle
Shap
DARLINGTON
Lake District
Tebay

For continuation pages refer to numbered arrows

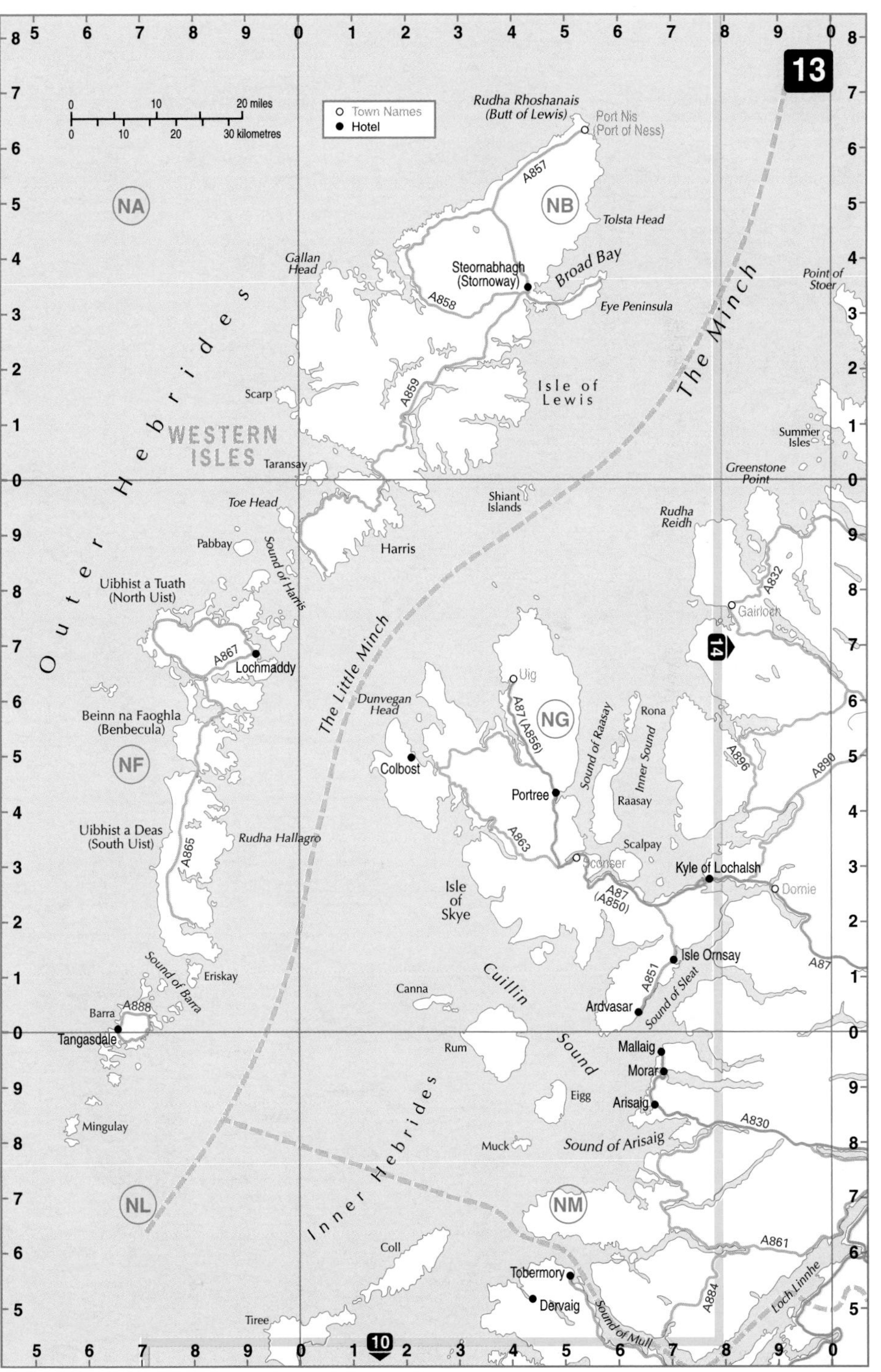
13
Town Names
Hotel
20 miles
30 kilometres
Rudha Rhoshanais
(Butt of Lewis)
Port Nis
(Port of Ness)
NA
NB
Tolsta Head
Gallan Head
Steornabhagh
(Stornoway)
Broad Bay
Eye Peninsula
Point of Stoer
The Minch
Outer Hebrides
Isle of Lewis
Scarp
WESTERN ISLES
Taransay
Summer Isles
Greenstone Point
Shiant Islands
Toe Head
Rudha Reidh
Pabbay
Sound of Harris
Harris
Uibhist a Tuath
(North Uist)
Gairloch
Lochmaddy
The Little Minch
Uig
Dunvegan Head
Beinn na Faoghla
(Benbecula)
NG
Sound of Raasay
Rona
Inner Sound
NF
Colbost
Portree
Raasay
Uibhist a Deas
(South Uist)
Rudha Hallagro
Scalpay
Sconser
Kyle of Lochalsh
Dornie
Isle of Skye
Isle Ornsay
Sound of Barra
Eriskay
Cuillin Sound
Canna
Ardvasar
Sound of Sleat
Barra
Tangasdale
Rum
Mallaig
Morar
Eigg
Arisaig
Inner Hebrides
Mingulay
Muck
Sound of Arisaig
NL
NM
Coll
Tobermory
Dervaig
Sound of Mull
Loch Linnhe
Tiree
10
14

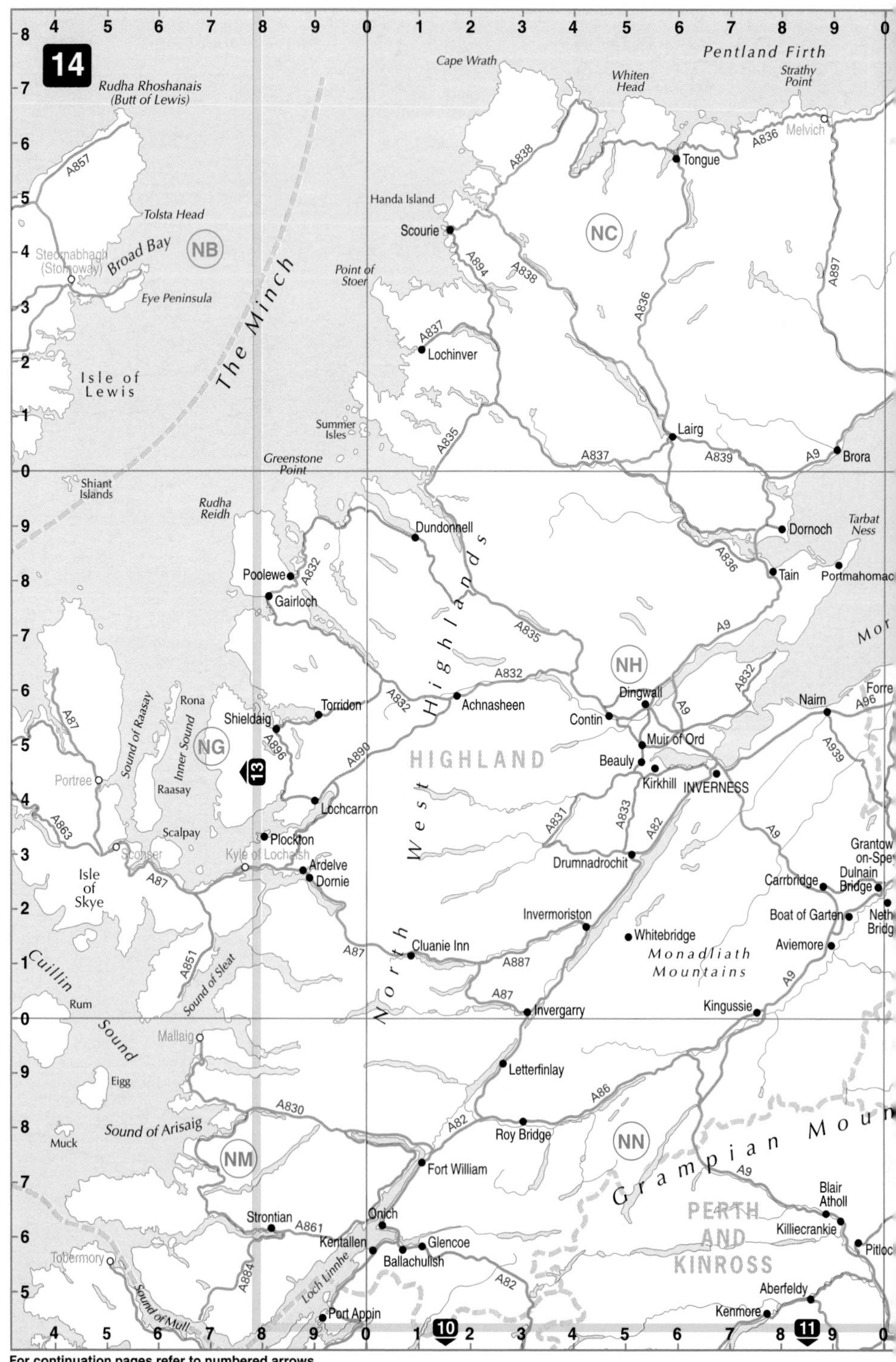

14
Pentland Firth
Cape Wrath
Whiten Head
Strathy Point
Rudha Rhoshanais (Butt of Lewis)
Melvich
A836
Tongue
A838
A857
Handa Island
Scourie
NC
Tolsta Head
Steornabhagh (Stornoway)
Broad Bay
NB
A894
A838
A836
A897
Point of Stoer
Eye Peninsula
The Minch
A837
Lochinver
Isle of Lewis
Summer Isles
A835
Lairg
A837
A839
A9
Brora
Greenstone Point
Shiant Islands
Rudha Reidh
Dundonnell
Dornoch
Tarbat Ness
A836
Poolewe
A832
Tain
Portmahomack
Gairloch
A835
A9
NH
A832
A832
A832
Rona
Dingwall
Torridon
Achnasheen
Contin
A9
Nairn
A96
Shieldaig
Muir of Ord
A896
A890
HIGHLAND
Beauly
A939
NG
13
Inner Sound
Sound of Raasay
Kirkhill
INVERNESS
Portree
Raasay
Lochcarron
A831
A833
A82
A87
A863
Scalpay
Plockton
A9
Sconser
Kyle of Lochalsh
Ardelve
Dornie
Drumnadrochit
Grantown-on-Spey
Isle of Skye
A87
Carrbridge
Dulnain Bridge
Boat of Garten
Nethy Bridge
Invermoriston
Whitebridge
Cluanie Inn
A87
A887
Aviemore
Monadliath Mountains
A851
Cuillin
Sound of Sleat
A87
A9
Rum
Invergarry
Kingussie
North West Highlands
Sound
Mallaig
Letterfinlay
Eigg
A86
A830
A82
Roy Bridge
NN
Muck
Sound of Arisaig
NM
Fort William
Grampian Mountains
A9
Blair Atholl
Strontian
Onich
A861
PERTH AND KINROSS
Killiecrankie
Kentallen
Glencoe
Ballachulish
Pitlochry
Tobermory
A884
Loch Linnhe
A82
Sound of Mull
Aberfeldy
Port Appin
Kenmore
10
11


For continuation pages refer to numbered arrows

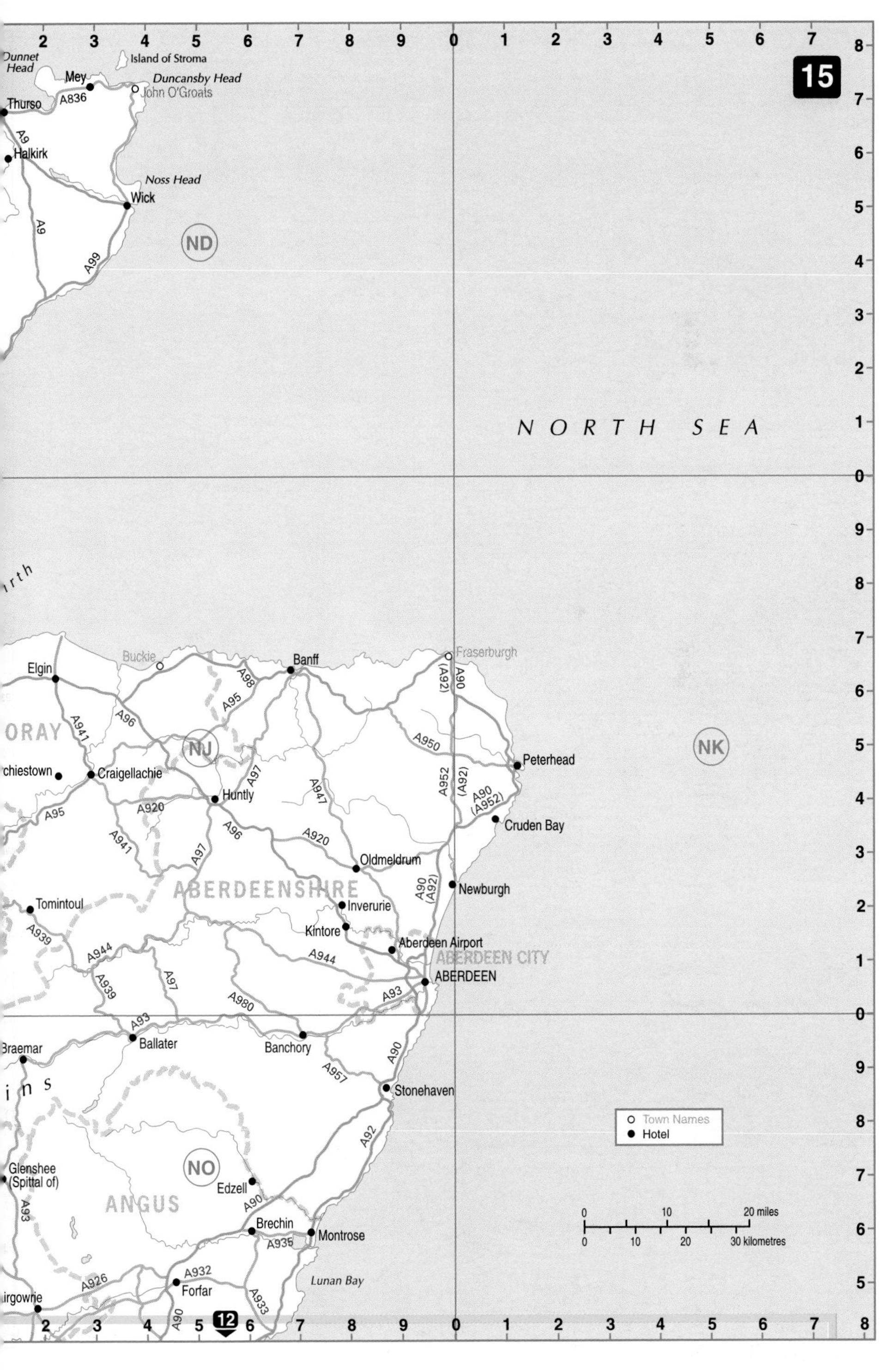
15
Dunnet Head
Island of Stroma
Mey
Duncansby Head
John O'Groats
Thurso
A836
A9
Halkirk
Noss Head
Wick
ND
A99
NORTH SEA
Elgin
Buckie
Banff
Fraserburgh
A98
A95
A96
A941
ORAY
NJ
A950
A90
(A92)
Peterhead
NK
Craigellachie
A97
A952
Huntly
A947
A90 (A952)
Cruden Bay
A920
A95
A941
A96
A920
A97
Oldmeldrum
ABERDEENSHIRE
A90 (A92)
Newburgh
Tomintoul
Inverurie
Kintore
A939
Aberdeen Airport
A944
A944
ABERDEEN CITY
ABERDEEN
A939
A97
A980
A93
A93
Ballater
Banchory
Braemar
A90
A957
Stonehaven
Town Names
Hotel
A92
NO
Glenshee (Spittal of)
Edzell
A93
ANGUS
A90
Brechin
Montrose
A935
0 10 20 miles
0 10 20 30 kilometres
A932
A926
Forfar
Lunan Bay
A933
A90
12

**16**

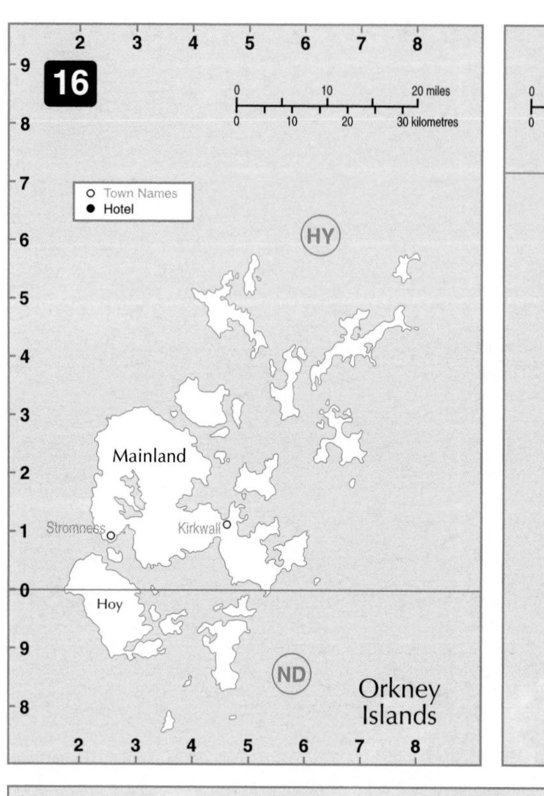

0 10 20 miles
0 10 20 30 kilometres
Town Names
Hotel
HY
Mainland
Stromness
Kirkwall
Hoy
ND
Orkney Islands


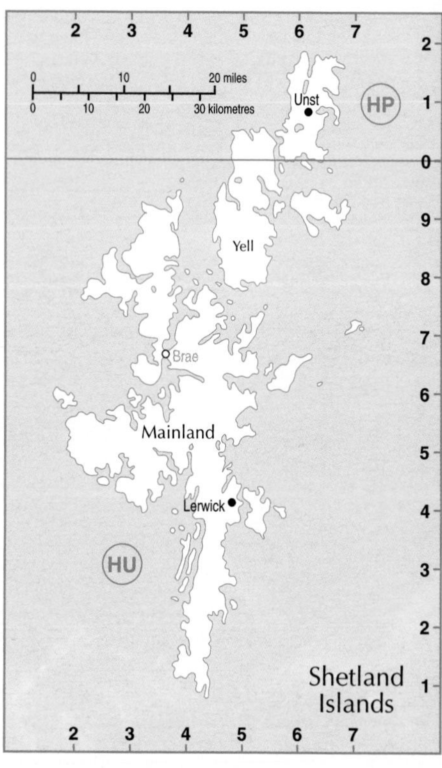

0 10 20 miles
0 10 20 30 kilometres
Unst
HP
Yell
Brae
Mainland
Lerwick
HU
Shetland Islands

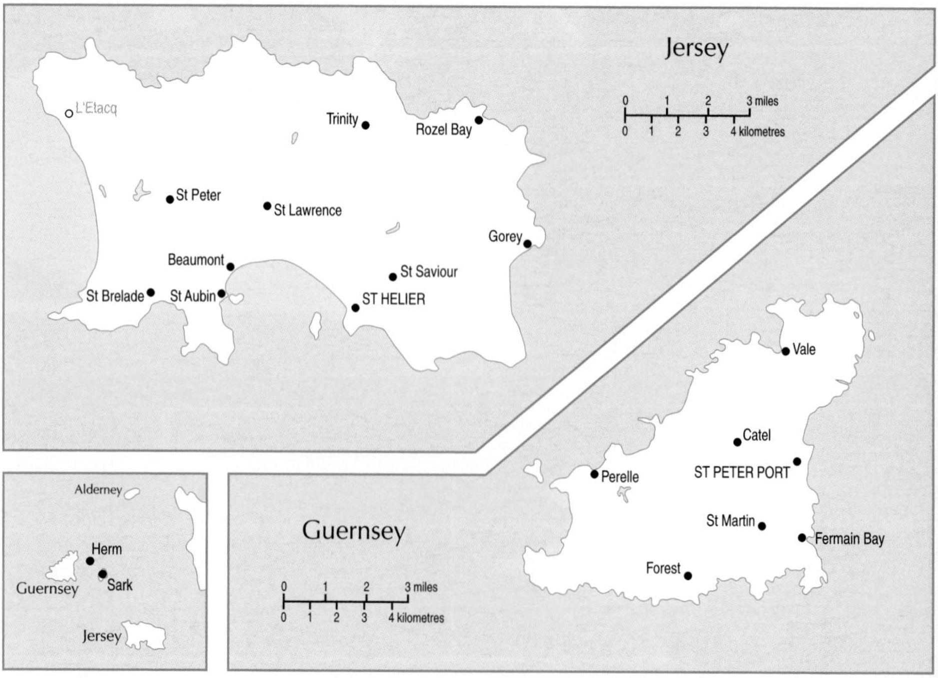

Jersey

0 1 2 3 miles
0 1 2 3 4 kilometres

L'Etacq
Trinity
Rozel Bay
St Peter
St Lawrence
Gorey
Beaumont
St Saviour
St Brelade
St Aubin
ST HELIER

Guernsey

0 1 2 3 miles
0 1 2 3 4 kilometres

Vale
Catel
Perelle
ST PETER PORT
St Martin
Fermain Bay
Forest

Alderney
Herm
Guernsey
Sark
Jersey

# Index of Hotels with Spas

# Hotels with Spas

The following index lists AA-rated hotels with spas, alphabetically by town. Facilities at these hotels range from purpose-built health spas offering a full range of beauty treatments and alternative therapies, to smaller health clubs with saunas and jacuzzis. Many hotels not listed here also have leisure facilities; see the FACILITIES section of individual entries in the gazetteer section of the guide. This index was believed correct at our press date; please contact the hotels directly for further information on the facilities and treatments available.

## ENGLAND

ALDWARK
Aldwark Manor Hotel, Golf & Country Club
☎ 01347 838146

AMBLESIDE
Skelwith Bridge Hotel
☎ 015394 32115

ASHFORD
Eastwell Manor
☎ 01233 213000

BARNHAM BROOM
Barnham Broom Hotel & Country Club
☎ 01603 759393

BARNSLEY
Ardsley House Hotel & Health Club
☎ 01226 309955

BARNSTAPLE
Barnstaple Hotel
☎ 01271 376221

BASINGSTOKE
Apollo Hotel
☎ 01256 796700

BASINGSTOKE
Hanover International Hotel & Club
☎ 01256 764161

BATH
The Bath Spa
☎ 0870 4008222

BERKELEY
Prince Of Wales Hotel
☎ 01453 810474

BEXLEYHEATH
Bexleyheath Marriott Hotel
☎ 020 8298 1000

BIRMINGHAM
Crowne Plaza Birmingham
☎ 0121 631 2000

BLACKPOOL
De Vere Hotel
☎ 01253 838866

BOURNEMOUTH
Bay View Court Hotel
☎ 01202 294449

BOURNEMOUTH
Chinehurst Hotel
☎ 01202 764583

BOURNEMOUTH
East Anglia Hotel
☎ 01202 765163

BOURNEMOUTH
Elstead Hotel
☎ 01202 293071

BOURNEMOUTH
Fircroft Hotel
☎ 01202 309771

BOURNEMOUTH
Hotel Courtlands
☎ 01202 302442

BOURNEMOUTH
Queens Hotel
☎ 01202 554415

BOURNEMOUTH
Suncliff Hotel
☎ 01202 291711

BOVEY TRACEY
Coombe Cross Hotel
☎ 01626 832476

*Chewton Glen, New Milton*

BRACKNELL
Coppid Beech
☎ 01344 303333

BRADFORD
Cedar Court Hotel
☎ 01274 406606

BRANDS HATCH
Brandshatch Place
☎ 01474 872239

BRIGHTON
The Grand
☎ 01273 224300

BRISTOL
Aztec Hotel
☎ 01454 201090

BRISTOL
Bristol Marriott Royal Hotel
☎ 0117 925 5100

BROADWAY
The Lygon Arms
☎ 01386 852255

BROXTON
De Vere Carden Park Hotel
☎ 01829 731000

BUDE
Falcon Hotel
☎ 01288 352005

CHELTENHAM
Cheltenham Park Hotel
☎ 01242 222021

CHELTENHAM
The Prestbury House Hotel & Restaurant
☎ 01242 529533

CHORLEY
Park Hall Hotel
☎ 01257 452090

CHORLEY
Premier Lodge
☎ 0870 700 1354

CHORLEY
Shaw Hill Hotel Golf & Country Club
☎ 01257 269221

COLCHESTER
The Stoke by Nayland Club Hotel
☎ 01206 262836

COLERNE
Lucknam Park
☎ 01225 742777

COPTHORNE
Copthorne Hotel London Gatwick
☎ 01342 348800

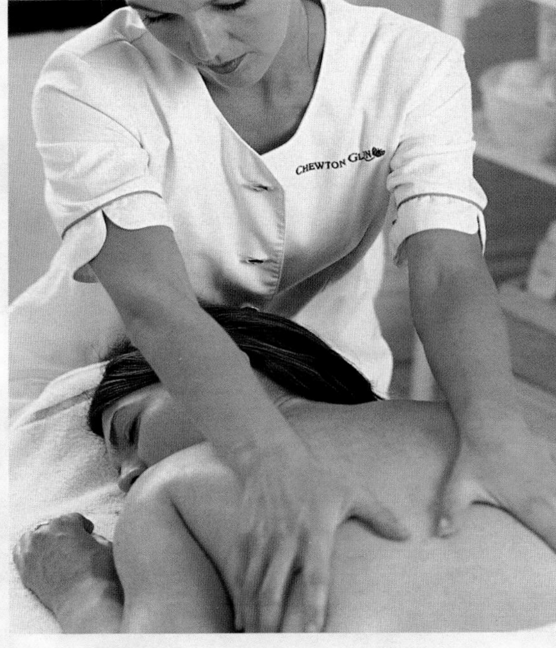
CHEWTON GLEN

*Chewton Glen, New Milton*

COWES
New Holmwood Hotel
☎ 01983 292508

CREWE
Hunters Lodge Hotel
☎ 01270 583440

DARTFORD
Rowhill Grange Hotel & Spa
☎ 01322 615136

DARTMOUTH
Stoke Lodge Hotel
☎ 01803 770523

DARWEN
Whitehall Hotel
☎ 01254 701595

DOVER
Wallett's Court Country House Hotel
☎ 01304 852424

EASTBOURNE
Grand Hotel
☎ 01323 412345

FALMOUTH
Falmouth Beach Resort Hotel
☎ 01326 312999

FALMOUTH
Royal Duchy Hotel
☎ 01326 313042

FERNDOWN
The Dormy
☎ 01202 872121

FOREST ROW
Ashdown Park Hotel
☎ 01342 824988

FOWEY
Fowey Hotel
☎ 01726 832551

FOWNHOPE
Green Man Inn
☎ 01432 860243

GRASMERE
Red Lion Hotel
☎ 015394 35456

HADLEY WOOD
West Lodge Park Hotel
☎ 020 8216 3900

HANDFORTH
Belfry House Hotel
☎ 0161 437 0511

*The Celtic Manor Resort, Newport*

HARLOW
Swallow Churchgate Hotel
☎ 01279 420246

HARROGATE
Swallow St George Hotel
☎ 01423 561431

HAYDOCK
Posthouse Haydock
☎ 0870 400 9039

HEATHROW AIRPORT
London Marriott Hotel, Heathrow
☎ 020 8990 1100

HEMEL HEMPSTEAD
The Bobsleigh Inn
☎ 01442 833276

HEXHAM
De Vere Slaley Hall
☎ 01434 673350

HINCKLEY
Sketchley Grange Hotel
☎ 01455 251133

HINTLESHAM
Hintlesham Hall Hotel
☎ 01473 652334

HORWICH
De Vere White's Hotel
☎ 01204 667788

HULL
Quality Hotel Hull
☎ 01482 325087

ILSINGTON
The Ilsington Country House Hotel
☎ 01364 661452

KIDDERMINSTER
Stone Manor Hotel
☎ 01562 777555

KNARESBOROUGH
Dower House Hotel
☎ 01423 863302

LEICESTER
Time Out Hotel & Leisure
☎ 0116 278 7898

LEWES
White Hart Hotel
☎ 01273 476694

LIVERPOOL
Liverpool Marriott Hotel South
☎ 0151 4945000

LONDON NW1
Landmark Hotel
☎ 020 7631 8000

LONDON SE1
London Marriott Hotel, County Hall
☎ 020 7928 5200

LONDON SW1
The Berkeley
☎ 020 7235 6000

LONDON SW1
Mandarin Oriental Hyde Park
☎ 020 7235 2000

LONDON SW7
Rembrandt Hotel
☎ 020 7589 8100

LONDON W1
Athenaeum Hotel & Apartments
☎ 020 7499 3464

LONDON W1
The Dorchester
☎ 020 7629 8888

LOUTH
Kenwick Park Hotel
☎ 01507 608806

LYMINGTON
Passford House Hotel
☎ 01590 682398

MAIDENHEAD
Elva Lodge Hotel
☎ 01628 622948

MALHAM
The Buck Inn Hotel
☎ 01729 830317

MANCHESTER
Malmaison
☎ 0161 278 1000

MAWNAN SMITH
Budock Vean - The Hotel on the River
☎ 01326 252100

MAWNAN SMITH
Meudon Hotel
☎ 01326 250541

MELTON MOWBRAY
Stapleford Park
☎ 01572 787522

MILDENHALL
Riverside Hotel
☎ 01638 717274

MILTON KEYNES
Quality Hotel & Suites Milton Keynes
☎ 01908 561666

NEW MILTON
Chewton Glen Hotel
☎ 01425 275341

NEWBURY
Regency Park Hotel
☎ 01635 871555

NEWBURY
The Vineyard at Stockcross
☎ 01635 528770

NEWBY BRIDGE
Lakeside Hotel
☎ 015395 30001

NEWBY BRIDGE
Whitewater Hotel
☎ 015395 31133

NEWCASTLE UPON TYNE
Copthorne Hotel Newcastle
☎ 0191 222 0333

NEWQUAY
Esplanade Hotel
☎ 01637 873333

NEWQUAY
Headland Hotel
☎ 01637 872211

NEWTON ABBOT
Passage House Hotel
☎ 01626 355515

NORWICH
De Vere Dunston Hall
☎ 01508 470444

NORWICH
Marriott Sprowston Manor Hotel & Country Club
☎ 01603 410871

OAKHAM
Barnsdale Lodge Hotel
☎ 01572 724678

OKEHAMPTON
Manor House Hotel
☎ 01837 53053

OSWESTRY
Pen-y-Dyffryn Country Hotel
☎ 01691 653700

OSWESTRY
Wynnstay Hotel
☎ 01691 655261

OXFORD
Oxford Spires Four Pillars Hotel
☎ 01865 324324

OXFORD
Oxford Thames Four Pillars Hotel
☎ 01865 334444

PEASMARSH
Flackley Ash Hotel
☎ 01797 230651

PENKRIDGE
Quality Hotel Stafford
☎ 01785 712459

PETERBOROUGH
Peterborough Marriott Hotel
☎ 01733 371111

PLYMOUTH
Posthouse Plymouth
☎ 0870 400 9064

POOLE
Haven Hotel
☎ 01202 707333

POOLE
Sandbanks Hotel
☎ 01202 707377

PORTSMOUTH
Innlodge Hotel
☎ 023 9265 0510

PORTSMOUTH
Portsmouth Marriott Hotel
☎ 023 9238 3151

PRESTON
Preston Marriott Hotel
☎ 01772 864087

PUDDINGTON
Craxton Wood
☎ 0151 347 4040

READING
Millennium Madejski Hotel Reading
☎ 0118 925 3500

REDRUTH
Penventon Hotel
☎ 01209 203000

RICHMOND UPON THAMES
The Richmond Hill Hotel
☎ 020 8940 2247

RISLEY
Risley Hall Hotel
☎ 0115 939 9000

ROTHERHAM
Courtyard by Marriott Rotherham
☎ 01709 830630

ROTHERHAM
Hellaby Hall Hotel
☎ 01709 702701

RUNCORN
Posthouse Warrington/Runcorn
☎ 0870 400 9070

RUSHYFORD
Swallow Eden Arms Hotel
☎ 01388 720541

SAUNTON
Saunton Sands Hotel
☎ 01271 890212

SCARBOROUGH
Ambassador Hotel
☎ 01723 362841

SCOTCH CORNER
Quality Hotel Scotch Corner
☎ 01748 850900

SHAFTESBURY
Royal Chase Hotel
☎ 01747 853355

SHANKLIN
Holliers Hotel
☎ 01983 862764

SHEDFIELD
Marriott Meon Valley Hotel & Country Club
☎ 01329 833455

*Chewton Glen, New Milton*

SHEFFIELD
Sheffield Marriott Hotel
☎ 0114 258 3811

SHIPLEY
Marriott Hollins Hall
Hotel & Country Club
☎ 01274 530053

SHREWSBURY
Albright Hussey Hotel
☎ 01939 290571

SHREWSBURY
Albrighton Hall Hotel
☎ 01939 291000

SIDMOUTH
The Royal York &
Faulkner Hotel
☎ 01395 513043 &
0800 220714

SIDMOUTH
Victoria Hotel
☎ 01395 512651

SILLOTH
The Skinburness Hotel
☎ 016973 32332

SOLIHULL
Renaissance Solihull Hotel
☎ 0121 711 3000

ST ALBANS
Sopwell House Hotel,
Country Club & Spa
☎ 01727 864477

ST AUSTELL
Carlyon Bay Hotel
☎ 01726 812304

ST IVES
Carbis Bay Hotel
☎ 01736 795311

ST IVES
Tregenna Castle Hotel
☎ 01736 795254

ST MELLION
St Mellion International
☎ 01579 351351

ST NEOTS
Abbotsley Golf Hotel
& Country Club
☎ 01480 474000

STEEPLE ASTON
The Holt Hotel
☎ 01869 340259

STOCKTON-ON-TEES
Swallow Hotel
☎ 01642 679721

STOURPORT-ON-SEVERN
Menzies Stourport Manor
☎ 0870 6003013

STRATFORD-UPON-AVON
Charlecote Pheasant
☎ 01789 279954

STRATFORD-UPON-AVON
Stratford Manor
☎ 01789 731173

STRETTON
Hanover International
Hotel & Club
☎ 01925 730706

SUNDERLAND
Sunderland Marriott Hotel
☎ 0191 529 2041

SUTTON COLDFIELD
Moor Hall Hotel
☎ 0121 308 3751

SWANAGE
Grand Hotel
☎ 01929 423353

SWANAGE
Purbeck House Hotel
☎ 01929 422872

TALLAND BAY
Talland Bay Hotel
☎ 01503 272667

TELFORD
Telford Golf & Country Club
☎ 01952 429977

TETBURY
Hare & Hounds Hotel
☎ 01666 880233

THORNBURY
Thornbury Castle
☎ 01454 281182

THORNTON HOUGH
Thornton Hall Hotel
☎ 0151 336 3938

THORNTON WATLASS
Buck Inn
☎ 01677 422461

TICEHURST
Dale Hill Hotel & Golf Club
☎ 01580 200112

TINTAGEL
Atlantic View Hotel
☎ 01840 770221

*The Celtic Manor Resort, Newport*

Chewton Glen, New Milton

TINTAGEL
The Wootons Country Hotel
☎ 01840 770170
TOLLESHUNT KNIGHTS
Five Lakes Hotel, Golf, Country Club & Spa
☎ 01621 868888
TOPCLIFFE
The Angel Inn
☎ 01845 577237
TORPOINT
Whitsand Bay Hotel, Golf & Country Club
☎ 01503 230276
TORQUAY
Belgrave Hotel
☎ 01803 296666
TORQUAY
Burlington Hotel
☎ 01803 210950
TORQUAY
Coppice Hotel
☎ 01803 297786
TORQUAY
Elmington Hotel
☎ 01803 605192
TORQUAY
Frognel Hall Hotel
☎ 01803 298339
TORQUAY
Gresham Court
☎ 01803 293007
TORQUAY
Kistor Hotel
☎ 01803 212632
TORQUAY
Lincombe Hall Hotel
☎ 01803 213361
TORQUAY
Palace Hotel
☎ 01803 200200
TORQUAY
Red House Hotel
☎ 01803 607811
TORQUAY
The Grosvenor Hotel
☎ 01803 294373
TRESCO
New Inn
☎ 01720 422844
TREYARNON BAY
Waterbeach Hotel
☎ 01841 520292
ULLESTHORPE
Ullesthorpe Court Country Hotel & Golf Club
☎ 01455 209023
WAKEFIELD
Waterton Park Hotel
☎ 01924 257911
WALSALL
Beverley Hotel
☎ 01922 614967
WALSALL
The Fairlawns at Aldridge
☎ 01922 455122
WALTERSTONE
Allt-yr-Ynys Country House Hotel
☎ 01873 890307
WARE
Marriott Hanbury Manor Hotel & Country Club
☎ 01920 487722
WARRINGTON
Daresbury Park Hotel
☎ 01925 267331
WELLINGTON
The Cleve Country House Hotel
☎ 01823 662033
WEYMOUTH
Moonfleet Manor
☎ 01305 786948
WINDERMERE
Hideaway Hotel
☎ 015394 43070
WINDERMERE
Holbeck Ghyll Country House Hotel
☎ 015394 32375
WISHAW
The De Vere Belfry
☎ 01675 470301
WOLVERHAMPTON
Fox Hotel International
☎ 01902 421680
WOODBRIDGE
Seckford Hall Hotel
☎ 01394 385678
WOODBRIDGE
Ufford Park Hotel Golf & Leisure
☎ 01394 383555
YORK Middlethorpe Hall Hotel
☎ 01904 641241

## CHANNEL ISLANDS

ST HELIER
Beaufort Hotel
☎ 01534 732471
ST HELIER
The Grand Hotel
☎ 01534 722301

## SCOTLAND

ABERDEEN
Aberdeen Marriott Hotel
☎ 01224 770011

ARDVASAR
Ardvasar Hotel
☎ 01471 844223

AUCHTERARDER
The Gleneagles Hotel
☎ 01764 662231

AYR
Quality Hotel Ayr
☎ 01292 263268

BALLACHULISH
Ballachulish Hotel
☎ 01855 811606

BLAIRGOWRIE
Kinloch House Hotel
☎ 01250 884237

CARNOUSTIE
Carnoustie Hotel
Golf Resort & Spa
☎ 01241 411999

CRIEFF
Crieff Hydro
☎ 01764 655555

DUNBAR
Bayswell Hotel
☎ 01368 862225

DUNOON
Enmore Hotel
☎ 01369 702230

EDINBURGH
Balmoral
☎ 0131 556 2414

EDINBURGH
Dalhousie Castle
Hotel & Spa
☎ 01875 820153

EDINBURGH
Holyrood Hotel
☎ 0131 550 4500

EDINBURGH
Kings Manor
☎ 0131 669 0444

EDINBURGH
The Sheraton Grand Hotel
☎ 0131 229 9131

ERISKA
Isle of Eriska
☎ 01631 720371

GLASGOW
Holiday Inn
☎ 0141 352 8300

INVERARAY
Loch Fyne Hotel
☎ 01499 302148

MONTROSE
Montrose Park Hotel
☎ 01674 663400

OBAN
Lancaster Hotel
☎ 01631 562587

PITLOCHRY
Dundarach Hotel
☎ 01796 472862

PITLOCHRY
Scotland's Hotel
☎ 01796 472292

PORTMAHOMACK
Caledonian Hotel
☎ 01862 871345

TURNBERRY
The Westin Turnberry
Resort Hotel
☎ 01655 331000

## WALES

ABERGELE
Kinmel Manor Hotel
☎ 01745 832014

ABERYSTWYTH
Marine Hotel
☎ 01970 612444

CAERNARFON
Seiont Manor Hotel
☎ 01286 673366

CARDIFF
Cardiff Marriott Hotel
☎ 029 2039 9944

CARDIFF
St David's Hotel & Spa
☎ 029 2045 4045

LLANDUDNO
Bodysgallen Hall Hotel
☎ 01492 584466

LLANDUDNO
Empire Hotel
☎ 01492 860555

LLANDUDNO
St George's Hotel
☎ 01492 877544

NEWPORT
The Celtic Manor Resort
☎ 01633 413000

PONTYCLUN
Vale Hotel Golf &
Country Club
☎ 01443 667800

PORTHCAWL
Seabank Hotel
☎ 01656 782261

ST DAVID'S
Grove Hotel
☎ 01437 720341

## IRELAND

ARKLOW
Arklow Bay Hotel
☎ 0402 32309

BALLYCONNELL
Slieve Russell Hotel Golf
and Country Club
☎ 049 9526 444

BELFAST
The Crescent Townhouse
☎ 028 9032 3349

CLONAKILTY
The Lodge & Spa
at Inchydoney Island
☎ 023 33143

DELGANY
Glenview Hotel
☎ 01287 3399

DUBLIN
The Merrion Hotel
☎ 01 6030600

KILLARNEY
International Hotel
☎ 064 31816

KILLARNEY
Lake Hotel
☎ 064 31035

MACROOM
Castle Hotel
☎ 026 41074

THOMASTOWN
Mount Juliet Hotel
☎ 056 73000

## Photograph Credits

Permission for the use of the main photographs in the preliminary pages of this guide was kindly given by the Radisson Edwardian Picture Library

Other photographs were used with the permission of the following:

English Rose Hotels
The Celtic Manor Resort, Newport
Chewton Glen, New Milton
Cliveden, Taplow
The St David's Hotel & Spa, Cardiff
The Lodge & Spa at Inchydoney Island, Clonakilty
The Merrion Hotel, Dublin

Readers'
Report form

Please send this form to:
Editor, The Hotel Guide,
Lifestyle Guides,
The Automobile Association,
Fanum House,
Basingstoke RG21 4EA

or fax: 01256 491647
or e-mail: lifestyleguides@theAA.com

Please use this form to recommend any hotel you have visited, whether it is in the guide or not currently listed. Feedback from readers helps us to keep our guide accurate and up to date. Please note, however, that if you have a complaint to make during a visit, we strongly recommend that you discuss the matter with the hotel management there and then so that they have a chance to put things right before your visit is spoilt. The AA does not undertake to arbitrate between you and the hotel management, or to obtain compensation or engage in correspondence.

Date:

Your name (block capitals)

Your address (block capitals)

..................................................................................................................

..................................................................................................................

..................................................................................................................

.............................................................. e-mail address:

Comments

..................................................................................................................

..................................................................................................................

..................................................................................................................

..................................................................................................................

..................................................................................................................

..................................................................................................................

..................................................................................................................

..................................................................................................................

(please attach a separate sheet if necessary)

Please tick here if you DO NOT wish to receive details of AA offers or products ☐

**PTO**

| | YES | NO |
|---|---|---|
| **Have you bought this guide before?** | ☐ | ☐ |

**Have you bought any other accommodation, restaurant, pub, or food guides recently? If yes, which ones?**

...........................................................................................................................

...........................................................................................................................

**Why did you buy this guide? (circle all that apply)**

holiday short break business travel special occasion
find a civil wedding venue find a venue for another event e.g. conference
other.......................................................................................

**How often do you stay in hotels? (circle one choice)**

more than once a month once a month once in 2-3 months
once in six months once a year less than once a year

**Please answer these questions to help us make improvements to the guide:**

**Which of these factors are most important when choosing a hotel?**

Price Location Awards/ratings Service

Decor/surroundings Previous experience Recommendation

Other (please state):.........................................................................................

**Do you read the editorial features in the guide?** ..................................................

**Do you use the location atlas?**..........................................................................

**Which elements of the guide do you find the most useful when choosing a hotel?**

Description Photo Advertisement Star rating

**Can you suggest any improvements to the guide?**

...........................................................................................................................

...........................................................................................................................

...........................................................................................................................

...........................................................................................................................

Please send this form to:
Editor, The Hotel Guide,
Lifestyle Guides,
The Automobile Association,
Fanum House,
Basingstoke RG21 4EA

or fax: 01256 491647
or e-mail: lifestyleguides@theAA.com

# Readers' Report form

Please use this form to recommend any hotel you have visited, whether it is in the guide or not currently listed. Feedback from readers helps us to keep our guide accurate and up to date. Please note, however, that if you have a complaint to make during a visit, we strongly recommend that you discuss the matter with the hotel management there and then so that they have a chance to put things right before your visit is spoilt. The AA does not undertake to arbitrate between you and the hotel management, or to obtain compensation or engage in correspondence.

Date:

Your name (block capitals)

Your address (block capitals)

..........................................................................................................................

..........................................................................................................................

..........................................................................................................................

................................................................ e-mail address:

Comments

..........................................................................................................................

..........................................................................................................................

..........................................................................................................................

..........................................................................................................................

..........................................................................................................................

..........................................................................................................................

..........................................................................................................................

..........................................................................................................................

(please attach a separate sheet if necessary)

Please tick here if you DO NOT wish to receive details of AA offers or products ☐

**PTO**

| | YES | NO |
|---|---|---|
| **Have you bought this guide before?** | ☐ | ☐ |

**Have you bought any other accommodation, restaurant, pub, or food guides recently? If yes, which ones?**

......................................................................................................................................

......................................................................................................................................

**Why did you buy this guide? (circle all that apply)**

holiday short break business travel special occasion

find a civil wedding venue find a venue for another event e.g. conference

other.........................................................................................

**How often do you stay in hotels? (circle one choice)**

more than once a month once a month once in 2-3 months

once in six months once a year less than once a year

**Please answer these questions to help us make improvements to the guide:**

**Which of these factors are most important when choosing a hotel?**

Price Location Awards/ratings Service

Decor/surroundings Previous experience Recommendation

Other (please state):..........................................................................................

**Do you read the editorial features in the guide?** ...............................................

**Do you use the location atlas?**.....................................................................

**Which elements of the guide do you find the most useful when choosing a hotel?**

Description Photo Advertisement Star rating

**Can you suggest any improvements to the guide?**

......................................................................................................................................

......................................................................................................................................

......................................................................................................................................

......................................................................................................................................

# Readers' Report form

Please send this form to:
Editor, The Hotel Guide,
Lifestyle Guides,
The Automobile Association,
Fanum House,
Basingstoke RG21 4EA

or fax: 01256 491647
or e-mail: lifestyleguides@theAA.com

Please use this form to recommend any hotel you have visited, whether it is in the guide or not currently listed. Feedback from readers helps us to keep our guide accurate and up to date. Please note, however, that if you have a complaint to make during a visit, we strongly recommend that you discuss the matter with the hotel management there and then so that they have a chance to put things right before your visit is spoilt. The AA does not undertake to arbitrate between you and the hotel management, or to obtain compensation or engage in correspondence.

Date:

Your name (block capitals)

Your address (block capitals)

........................................................................................................................

........................................................................................................................

........................................................................................................................

.............................................................. e-mail address:

Comments

........................................................................................................................

........................................................................................................................

........................................................................................................................

........................................................................................................................

........................................................................................................................

........................................................................................................................

........................................................................................................................

........................................................................................................................

(please attach a separate sheet if necessary)

Please tick here if you DO NOT wish to receive details of AA offers or products ☐

**PTO**

| | YES | NO |
|---|---|---|
| **Have you bought this guide before?** | ☐ | ☐ |

**Have you bought any other accommodation, restaurant, pub, or food guides recently? If yes, which ones?**

.......................................................................................................................

.......................................................................................................................

**Why did you buy this guide? (circle all that apply)**

holiday short break business travel special occasion

find a civil wedding venue find a venue for another event e.g. conference

other...........................................................................................

**How often do you stay in hotels? (circle one choice)**

more than once a month once a month once in 2-3 months

once in six months once a year less than once a year

**Please answer these questions to help us make improvements to the guide:**

**Which of these factors are most important when choosing a hotel?**

Price Location Awards/ratings Service

Decor/surroundings Previous experience Recommendation

Other (please state):.......................................................................................

**Do you read the editorial features in the guide?** ...................................................

**Do you use the location atlas?**.........................................................................

**Which elements of the guide do you find the most useful when choosing a hotel?**

Description Photo Advertisement Star rating

**Can you suggest any improvements to the guide?**

.......................................................................................................................

.......................................................................................................................

.......................................................................................................................

.......................................................................................................................